YELLOWBOOK

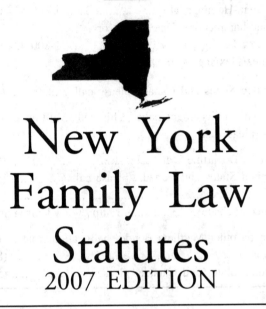

New York Family Law Statutes

2007 EDITION

Domestic Relations Law

Family Court Act and Related Court Rules

Social Services Law

Court Directory

As amended by the 2006 Regular Legislative Session through June 22, 2006.
(Current through Laws of 2006, Chapters 1 through 510, except 277, 291, 423 and 435)

REVISED INDEX

QUESTIONS ABOUT THIS PUBLICATION?

For questions about the **Editorial Content** appearing in these volumes or reprint permission, please call:

Juan M. Flugelman-Hammer, at .... 1-800-424-0651 ext. 3266
juan.m.flugelman-hammer@lexisnexis.com or
Reggie Rodriguez, Jr., J.D., at .... 1-800-424-0651 ext. 3384
reginald.rodriguez@lexisnexis.com

Outside the United States and Canada please call .... (415) 908-3200

For assistance with replacement pages, shipments, billing or other customer service matters, please call:

Customer Services Department at .... (800) 833-9844
Outside the United States and Canada, please call .... (518) 487-3000
Fax number .... (518) 487-3584
Customer Service Website .... http://www.lexisnexis.com/custserv/

For information on other Matthew Bender publications, please call:
Your account manager .... (800) 223-1940
Outside the United States and Canada, please call .... (518) 487-3000

ISBN 1-4224-0626-1

Editorial Offices
744 Broad Street, Newark, NJ 07102 (973) 820-2000
201 Mission St., San Francisco, CA 94105-1831 (415) 908-3200
www.lexis.com

MATTHEW◆BENDER

TABLE OF CONTENTS

TABLE OF 2006 FAMILY LAW AMENDMENTS

Section	Action	Chapter

Domestic Relations Law

Section	Action	Chapter
75-g	Amended	184
75-i	Amended	184
75-j	Amended	184
75-h	Amended	184
112-b	Amended	437
113	Amended	185

Family Court Act

Section	Action	Chapter
115	Amended	185
262	Amended	437
343.1	Amended	320
352.3	Amended	253
412	Amended	320
446	Amended	253
551	Amended	253
633	Amended	437
656	Amended	253
759	Amended	253
842	Added	253
845	Amended	331
1012	Amended	320
1027	Amended	12
1028-a	Amended	12
1052	Amended	12
1052-c	Amended	12
1055	Amended	12
1055	Amended	437
1056	Amended	253
1071	Amended	437
1072	Amended	437
1089	Amended	437
1112	Amended	437
1118	Amended	437
1121	Amended	437

Social Services Law

Section	Action	Chapter
20	Amended	485
131-o	Amended	57

Section	Action	Chapter
131-aa	Amended	58
145-b	Amended	442
153	Repealed	58
153	Added	58
159	Amended	58
168	Amended	179
209	Amended	57
335-b	Amended	58, 136
335-c	Added	109
336	Amended	136
336-c	Amended	136
341	Amended	61
358-a	Amended	12, 437
363-c	Added	57
363-c	Amended	109
363-d	Added	442
364-f	Amended	57
364-i	Amended	124, 176
364-j	Amended	57
364-j-2	Amended	57, 109
365-a	Amended	57, 109
365-i	Amended	57
365-j	Added	442
366	Amended	57, 58, 95, 109, 176
366-a	Added	57, 109
367-a	Amended	57, 61, 109, 220
367-b	Amended	442
367-c	Amended	57
367-q	Amended	57, 109
367-r	Amended	57, 109
367-s	Amended	57
367-s	Repealed	109
367-s	Amended	109
367-t	Added	57
367-t	Repealed	109
367-t	Added	109
368-a	Amended	57, 176
369-dd	Amended	57
369-ee	Amended	57
374	Amended	372
383-c	Amended	185
384	Amended	185
384-a	Amended	12
384-b	Amended	185, 460
390	Amended	319
390-e	Added	459
409-e	Amended	437

Amendments

Section	Action	Chapter
413	Amended	130
418	Amended	485
421	Amended	525
422	Amended	494
422-b	Amended	485
424	Added	494
453	Amended	518
460-a	Amended	58
461-d	Amended	317

DOMESTIC RELATIONS LAW

LAWS 1909, EFF. FEB. 17, 1909, AS AMENDED BY THE 2006 REGULAR LEGISLATIVE SESSION THROUGH JUNE 22, 2006.

(Sections effective February 17, 1909 except as otherwise indicated.)

———

Table of Contents

ARTICLE 1

SHORT TITLE; DEFINITIONS

SUMMARY OF ARTICLE

Section   1.   **Short title.**
         2.   **Definitions.**

§ 1.   Short title.

This chapter shall be known as the "Domestic Relations Law."

§ 2.   Definitions.

A "minor" or "infant," as used in this chapter, is a person under the age of eighteen years.

Amended by Laws 1974, Ch. 920, eff. Sept. 1, 1974, but is not to be construed to alter, change, affect, impair or defeat any rights, obligations, or interests heretofore accrued, incurred or conferred prior to the effective date.

ARTICLE 2

MARRIAGES

———

SUMMARY OF ARTICLE

(Repealed and transferred sections noted under appropriate section number of text.)

§ 5.　Incestuous and void marriages.

A marriage is incestuous and void whether the relatives are legitimate or illegitimate between either:

1.　An ancestor and a descendant;

2.　A brother and sister of either the whole or the half blood;

3.　An uncle and niece or an aunt and nephew.

If a marriage prohibited by the foregoing provisions of this section be solemnized it shall be void, and the parties thereto shall each be fined not less than fifty nor more than one hundred dollars and may, in the discretion of the court in addition to said fine, be imprisoned for a term not exceeding six months. Any person who shall knowingly and wilfully solemnize such marriage, or procure or aid in the solemnization of the same, shall be deemed guilty of a misdemeanor and shall be fined or imprisoned in like manner.

§ 6.　Void marriages.

A marriage is absolutely void if contracted by a person whose husband or wife by a former marriage is living, unless either:

1.　Such former marriage has been annulled or has been dissolved for a cause other than the adultery of such person; provided, that if such former marriage has been dissolved for the cause of the adultery of such person, he or she may marry again in the cases provided for in section eight of this chapter and such subsequent marriage shall be valid;

3.　Such former marriage has been dissolved pursuant to section seven-a* of this chapter.

Amended by Laws 1915, Ch. 266; Laws 1922, Ch. 279; Laws 1950, Ch. 144; Laws 1967, Ch. 680, eff. Sept. 1, 1967.

* Section 7-a repealed and transferred to Dom. Rel. Law §§ 220, 221 by Laws 1962, Ch. 313, eff. Sept. 1, 1963.

Subd. 2 **repealed** by Laws 1981, Ch. 118, eff. July 17, 1981; refer to civil rights law § 79-a(1).

§ 7.   Voidable marriages.

A marriage is void from the time its nullity is declared by a court of competent jurisdiction if either party thereto:

1.   Is under the age of legal consent, which is eighteen years, provided that such nonage shall not of itself constitute an absolute right to the annulment of such marriage, but such annulment shall be in the discretion of the court which shall take into consideration all the facts and circumstances surrounding such marriage;

2.   Is incapable of consenting to a marriage for want of understanding;

3.   Is incapable of entering into the married state for physical cause;

4.   Consent to such marriage by reason of force, duress or fraud;

5.   Has been incurably mentally ill for a period of five years or more.

Amended by Laws 1922, Chs. 279, 313; Laws 1924, Ch. 165; Laws 1928, Ch. 589; Laws 1929, Ch. 537; Laws 1945, Ch. 686; Laws 1948, Ch. 362, Laws 1958, Ch. 804; Laws 1962, Ch. 313, eff. Sept. 1. 1963; Laws 1978, Ch. 550, § 14, eff. July 24, 1978.

§ 7-a.   Dissolution of marriage on ground of absence.

Repealed by Laws 1962, Ch. 313, § 2, eff. Sept. 1, 1963, and transferred to Dom. Rel. Law §§ 220, 221.

§ 8.   Marriage after divorce.

Whenever, and whether prior or subsequent to September first, nineteen hundred sixty-seven, a marriage has been dissolved by divorce, either party may marry again.

Amended by Laws 1915, Ch. 266; Laws 1919, Ch. 265; Laws 1966, Ch. 254; Laws 1968, Ch. 584, eff. June 16, 1968.

DRL

ARTICLE 3

SOLEMNIZATION, PROOF AND EFFECT OF MARRIAGE

_____

SUMMARY OF ARTICLE

(Repealed and transferred sections noted under appropriate section number of text.)

§ 10. Marriage a civil contract.

Marriage, so far as its validity in law is concerned, continues to be a civil contract, to which the consent of parties capable in law of making a contract is essential.

§ 11. By whom a marriage must be solemnized.

No marriage shall be valid unless solemnized by either:

1. A clergyman or minister of any religion, or by the senior leader, or any of the other leaders, of The Society for Ethical Culture in the city of New York, having its principal office in the borough of Manhattan, or by the leader of the Brooklyn Society for Ethical Culture, having its principal office in the borough of Brooklyn of the city of New York, or of the Westchester Ethical Society, having its principal office in Westchester County, or of the Ethical Culture Society of Long Island, having its principal office in Nassau County, or of the Riverdale-Yonkers Ethical Society having its principal office in Bronx County, or by the leader of any other ethical culture society affiliated with the American Ethical Union.

2. A mayor of a village, a county executive of a county, or a mayor, recorder, city magistrate, police justice or police magistrate of a city, a former mayor or the city clerk of a city of the first class of over one million inhabitants or any of his or her deputies or not more than four regular clerks, designated by him or her for such purpose as provided in section eleven-a of this chapter, except that in cities which contain more than one hundred thousand and less than one million inhabitants, a marriage shall be solemnized by the mayor, or police justice, and by no other officer of such city, except as provided in subdivisions one and three of this section.

3. A judge of the federal circuit court of appeals for the second circuit, a judge of a federal district court for the northern, southern, eastern or western district of New York, a judge of the United States Court of International Trade, a federal administrative law judge presiding in this state, a justice or judge of a court of the unified court system, a housing judge of the Civil Court of the city of New York, a retired justice or judge of the unified court system or a retired housing judge of the Civil Court of the city of New York certified pursuant to paragraph (k) of subdivision two of section two hundred twelve of the judiciary law, the clerk of the appellate division of the supreme court in each judicial department or a county clerk of a county wholly within cities having a population of one million or more; or,

4. A written contract of marriage signed by both parties and at least two witnesses, all of whom shall subscribe the same within this state, stating the place of residence of each of the parties and witnesses and the date and place of marriage, and acknowledged before a judge of a court of record of this state by

the parties and witnesses in the manner required for the acknowledgment of a conveyance of real estate to entitle the same to be recorded.

5. Notwithstanding any other provision of this article, where either or both of the parties is under the age of eighteen years a marriage shall be solemnized only by those authorized in subdivision one of this section or by (1) the mayor of a city or village, or county executive of a county, or by (2) a judge of the federal circuit court of appeals for the second circuit, a judge of a federal district court for the northern, southern, eastern or western district of New York, a judge of the United States court of international trade, or a justice or a judge of a court of the unified court system, or by (3) a housing judge of the civil court of the city of New York, or by (4) a former mayor or the clerk of a city of the first class of over one million inhabitants or any of his or her deputies designated by him or her for such purposes as provided in section eleven-a of this chapter.

6. Notwithstanding any other provisions of this article to the contrary no marriage shall be solemnized by a public officer specified in this section, other than a judge of a federal district court for the northern, southern, eastern or western district of New York, a judge of the United States court of international trade, a federal administrative law judge presiding in this state, a judge or justice of the unified court system of this state, a housing judge of the civil court of the city of New York, or a retired judge or justice of the unified court system or a retired housing judge of the civil court certified pursuant to paragraph (k) of subdivision two of section two hundred twelve of the judiciary law, outside the territorial jurisdiction in which he or she was elected or appointed. Such a public officer, however, elected or appointed within the city of New York may solemnize a marriage anywhere within such city.

7. The term "clergyman" or "minister" when used in this article, shall include those defined in section two of the religious corporations law. The word "magistrate," when so used, includes any person referred to in the second or third subdivision.

Amended by Laws 1911, Ch. 610; Laws 1912, Ch. 166; Laws 1913, Ch. 490; Laws 1916, Ch. 524; Laws 1918, Ch. 620; Laws 1920, Ch. 231; Laws 1922, Ch. 326; Laws 1926, Chs. 144, 590, 635; Laws 1927, Ch. 547; Laws 1929, Ch. 606; Laws 1930, Ch. 423; Laws 1933, Chs. 244, 606; Laws 1935, Ch. 535; Laws 1939, Ch. 304; Laws 1940, Ch. 142; Laws 1942, Ch. 579; Laws 1945, Ch. 12; Laws 1947, Ch. 674; Laws 1952, Ch. 647; Laws 1954, Ch. 765; Laws 1957, Ch. 721; Laws 1959, Ch. 319; Laws 1962, Chs. 63, 689; Laws 1963, Ch. 765; Laws 1964, Chs. 509, 559; Laws 1968, Chs. 221, 625, 723; Laws 1970, Ch. 378; Laws 1971, Ch. 321, Ch. 730; (5) and (6); Laws 1972, Ch. 720; Laws 1973, Ch. 196; Laws 1974, Chs. 764, 920; Laws 1975, Ch. 256; Laws 1977, Ch. 239; Laws 1978, Ch. 88, eff. Apr. 25, 1978; Laws 1978, Ch. 615, eff. July 24, 1978; Laws 1981, Ch. 149, eff. May 29, 1981; Laws 1983, Ch. 484, eff. Jan. 1, 1984; Laws 1985, Ch. 321, eff. July 11, 1985; Laws 1987, Ch. 95, eff. June 5, 1987; Laws 1987, Ch. 147, eff. June 21, 1987; Laws 1987, Ch. 277, eff. July 20, 1987; Laws 1987, Ch. 283, eff. July 20, 1987; Laws 1987, Ch. 313, eff. July 20, 1987; Laws 1988, Ch. 92, § 1, eff. May 23, 1988; Laws 1990, Ch. 153, §§ 1, 2, eff. May 16, 1990; Laws 1991, Ch. 39, eff. Apr. 6,

1991; Laws 1992, Ch. 404, §§ 1, 2, eff. July 17, 1992; Laws 1996, Ch. 264, §§ 1 and 2, eff. July 2, 1996.

§ 11-a. Duty of city clerk in certain cities of the first class; facsimile signature of said clerk authorized.

1. a. The city clerk of a city of the first class of over one million inhabitants may designate in writing any of his deputies or not more than four from among the permanent members of his staff to perform marriage ceremonies, which designation shall be in writing and be filed in the office of such city clerk. The day of such filing shall be endorsed on the designation. Any such designation shall be and remain in effect for six months from the filing thereof.

b. Whenever persons to whom the city clerk of any such city of the first class shall have issued a marriage license shall request him to solemnize the rites of matrimony between them and present to him such license it shall be the duty of such clerk, either in person or by one of his deputies or the permanent members of his staff so designated by him to solemnize such marriage; provided, however, that nothing contained either in this section or in subdivision two of section eleven of this chapter shall be construed as empowering or requiring either the said city clerk or any of his designated deputies or the permanent members of his staff so designated to solemnize marriages at any place other than at the office of such city clerk.

c. Notwithstanding any other provision of this article upon presentation to said city clerk in person or to any of his deputies of such license by one or both of such persons under the age of eighteen years with a request to solemnize the rites of matrimony between them, it shall be the duty of such city clerk either in person or by one of his deputies to solemnize such marriage provided there is submitted to said city clerk, in addition, the written request therefor by the parents of any such persons under the age of eighteen years and provided further that said parents shall be personally present at such requested solemnization.

d. In all cases in which the city clerk of such city or one of his deputies or the permanent members of his staff so designated shall perform a marriage ceremony such official shall demand and be entitled to collect therefor a fee to be fixed by the council of the City of New York not exceeding twenty–five dollars, which sum shall be paid by the contracting parties before or immediately upon the solemnization of the marriage; and all such fees so received shall be paid over to the commissioner of finance of the city.

2. The signature and seal of said clerk of cities of the first class of over one million inhabitants upon the marriage license, certificate of marriage, registration, and marriage search provided by this article may be a facsimile imprinted, stamped, or engraved thereon.

3. The said clerk of cities of the first class of one million inhabitants or more may designate among the permanent members of his staff one or more individuals who shall be permitted to sign his name and affix his official seal upon the

marriage license, certificate of marriage registration, and marriage search provided by this article requiring the signature and seal of the city clerk.

Added by Laws 1916, Ch. 524; **amended** by Laws 1918, Ch. 620; Laws 1922, Ch. 326; Laws 1945, Ch. 12; Laws 1959, Ch. 116; Laws 1963, Ch. 335; Laws 1964, Ch. 576; Laws 1969, Ch. 407; Laws 1971, Ch. 321; Laws 1974, Ch. 920, eff. Sept. 1, 1974; Laws 1978, Ch. 655, § 41, eff. July 24, 1978; Laws 1990, Ch. 424, § 1, eff. Sept. 8, 1990; Laws 1990, Ch. 424, § 2, eff. Sept. 8, 1990.

§ 11-b. Registration of persons performing marriage ceremonies in the city of New York.

Every person authorized by law to perform the marriage ceremony, before performing any such ceremonies in the city of New York, shall register his or her name and address in the office of the city clerk of the city of New York. Every such person, before performing any marriage ceremonies subsequent to a change in his or her address, shall likewise register such change of address. Such city clerk is hereby empowered to cancel the registration of any person so registered upon satisfactory proof that the registration was fraudulent, or upon satisfactory proof that such person is no longer entitled to perform such ceremony.

Added by Laws 1938, Ch. 608, eff. July 1, 1938.

§ 11-c. Marriage officers.

1. Notwithstanding the provisions of section eleven of this article or any other law, the governing body of any village, town, or city may appoint one or more marriage officers who shall have the authority to solemnize a marriage which marriage shall be valid if performed in accordance with other provisions of law. Nothing herein contained shall nullify the authority of other persons authorized to solemnize marriages.

2. The number of such marriage officers appointed for a municipality shall be determined by the governing body of the municipality. Such marriage officers shall be eighteen years of age or over, and they shall reside in the municipality by which they are appointed. A marriage officer shall have the authority to solemnize a marriage within the territory of the municipality which makes the appointment.

3. A marriage officer may receive a salary or wage in an amount to be determined by the governing body of the municipality which appoints him or her. In the event that a marriage officer receives a salary or wage, he or she shall not receive any remuneration or consideration from any other source for performing his or her duties. In the event that a marriage officer does not receive a salary or wage, he or she may accept and keep up to seventy-five dollars for each marriage at which he or she officiates, paid by or on behalf of the persons married.

4. The term of office of a marriage officer shall be as determined by the governing body which makes the appointment but shall not exceed four years.

A marriage officer shall serve at the pleasure of the appointing authority and may be removed from office with or without cause on ten days written notice filed with the clerk of the municipality and sent by registered mail return receipt requested to the marriage officer.

Added by Laws 1988, Ch. 49, § 1, eff. Jan. 1, 1989.

§ 12. Marriage, how solemnized.

No particular form or ceremony is required when a marriage is solemnized as herein provided by a clergyman or magistrate, but the parties must solemnly declare in the presence of a clergyman or magistrate and the attending witness or witnesses that they take each other as husband and wife. In every case, at least one witness besides the clergyman or magistrate must be present at the ceremony.

The preceding provisions of this chapter, so far as they relate to the manner of solemnizing marriages, shall not affect marriages among the people called friends or quakers; nor marriages among the people of any other denominations having as such any particular mode of solemnizing marriages; but such marriages must be solemnized in the manner heretofore used and practiced in their respective societies or denominations, and marriages so solemnized shall be as valid as if this article had not been enacted.

§ 13. Marriage licenses.

It shall be necessary for all persons intended to be married in New York state to obtain a marriage license from a town or city clerk in New York state and to deliver said license, within sixty days, to the clergyman or magistrate who is to officiate before the marriage ceremony may be performed. In case of a marriage contracted pursuant to subdivision four of section eleven of this chapter, such license shall be delivered to the judge of the court of record before whom the acknowledgment is to be taken. If either party to the marriage resides upon an island located not less than twenty-five miles from the office or residence of the town clerk of the town of which such island is a part, and if such office or residence is not on such island such license may be obtained from any justice of the peace residing on such island, and such justice, in respect to powers and duties relating to marriage licenses, shall be subject to the provisions of this article governing town clerks and shall file all statements or affidavits received by him while acting under the provisions of this section with the town clerk of such town.

Amended by Laws 1914, Ch. 230; Laws 1918, Ch. 236; Laws 1929, Ch. 125; Laws 1935, Ch. 535; Laws 1938, Ch. 640; Laws 1939, Ch. 110; Laws 1943, Ch. 414; Laws 1957, Ch. 720, eff. Apr. 19, 1957.

§ 13-a. Physician's examination and serological test of applicant for marriage license.

Repealed by Laws 1985, Ch. 674, eff. Aug. 1, 1985.

§ 13-aa. Test to determine the presence of sickle cell anemia.

1. On and after the effective date of this act, such test as may be necessary shall be given to each applicant for a marriage license who is not of the Caucasian, Indian or Oriental race for the purposes of discovering the existence of sickle cell anemia and notifying the applicant of the results of such test.

2. No application for a marriage license shall be denied solely on the ground that such test proves positive, nor shall the absence of such test invalidate a marriage.

3. The provisions of this section shall not apply to any person who refuses to take such test because of his religious beliefs.

Added by Laws 1972, Ch. 994, eff. Sept. 1, 1972.

§ 13-b. Time within which marriage may be solemnized.

A marriage shall not be solemnized within twenty-four hours after the issuance of the marriage license, unless authorized by an order of a court of record as hereinafter provided, nor shall it be solemnized after sixty days from the date of the issuance of the marriage license unless authorized pursuant to section three hundred fifty-four-c of the executive law. Every license to marry hereafter issued by a town or city clerk, in addition to other requirements specified by this chapter, must contain a statement of the day and the hour the license is issued and the period during which the marriage may be solemnized. It shall be the duty of the clergyman or magistrate performing the marriage ceremony, or if the marriage is solemnized by written contract, of the judge before whom the contract is acknowledged, to annex to or endorse upon the marriage license the date and hour the marriage is solemnized. A judge or justice of the supreme court of this state or the county judge of the county in which either party to be married resides, or if such party is under sixteen years of age, the judge of the family court of such county, if it shall appear from an examination of the license and any other proofs submitted by the parties that one of the parties is in danger of imminent death, or by reason of other emergency public interest will be promoted thereby, or that such delay will work irreparable injury or great hardship upon the contracting parties, or one of them, may make an order authorizing the immediate solemnization of the marriage and upon filing such order with the clergyman or magistrate performing the marriage ceremony, or if the marriage is to be solemnized by written contract, with the judge before whom the contract is acknowledged, such clergyman or magistrate may solemnize such marriage, or such judge may take such acknowledgment as the case may be, without waiting for such three day period and twenty-four hour period to elapse. The clergyman, magistrate or judge must file such order with the town or city clerk who issued the license within five days after the marriage is solemnized. Such town or city clerk must record and index the order in the book required to be kept by him for recording affidavits, statements, consents and licenses, and when so recorded the order shall become a public record and available in any prosecution under this section. A person who shall solemnize a marriage in violation of this section shall be guilty of a misdemeanor and upon conviction thereof shall be punished by a fine of fifty dollars for each offense, and in addition thereto, his right to solemnize a marriage shall be suspended for ninety days.

Added by Laws 1937, Ch. 294 as § 13-a; **renumbered** as § 13-b and **amended** by Laws 1938, Ch. 640; Laws 1939, Ch. 110; Laws 1962, Ch. 689; Laws 1970, Ch. 835; Laws 1974, Ch. 1025, eff. July 1, 1975, adding reference to serological tests under DRL § 13-a; effective date postponed by Laws 1975, Ch. 174; Laws 1976, Ch. 449; Laws 1977, Ch. 104; Laws 1978, Ch. 272; Laws 1979, Ch. 320 to July 1, 1980; Laws 1981, Ch. 26, changing time from ten to three days, eff. Sept. 1, 1981; Laws 1984, Ch. 126, eff. Sept. 1, 1984; by Laws 1985, Ch. 674, eff. Aug. 1, 1985; Laws 2005, ch. 723, §2, eff. Oct. 11, 2005.

§ 13-c.   Twenty-four hour provision waived in certain cases.

This section expired on July 1, 1973.

§ 13-d.   Duty of clerk issuing marriage license.

1. It shall be the duty of each town and each city clerk or duly authorized deputy acting in the clerk's stead, upon the issuance of a marriage license to display to the parties a typed or printed statement containing substantially the same following information:

"Rubella, also known as 'German measles,' is a common childhood disease. It is usually not serious to children who contract it themselves, but can be a tragic crippler of unborn babies if transmitted to pregnant women.

Rubella infection poses a grave threat to the unborn child, especially during the first four months of pregnancy. It can lead to miscarriage, stillbirth, or one or all of the tragic defects such as deafness, blindness, crippling congenital heart disease, mental retardation and muscular and bone defects.

In order to be immune to rubella, one must either receive the rubella vaccine or actually have had the disease. To see whether you are susceptible to rubella, you can get a blood test from your doctor. Even more important is the availability of a rubella vaccine which will prevent you from ever contracting the disease.

In order to protect yourself, your family, and your friends, please take steps to prevent the tragic effects of rubella. Please contact your family doctor, health care provider, public health facility or clinic for further information."

2. It shall also be the duty of each town and city clerk or duly authorized deputy acting in the clerk's stead to provide to each applicant for a marriage license information regarding the Thalassemia Trait. The department of health shall prepare information including but not limited to, the blood disorder Thalassemia Trait and other inherited conditions affecting the population of New York state.

3. No cause of action for damages shall arise in favor of any person or person yet to be born by reason of any failure to comply with the provisions of this section.

Added by Laws 1986, Ch. 371, eff. Oct. 19, 1986; **amended** by Laws 1996, Ch. 428, eff. Jan. 1, 1997, renumbering former subd. (2) as (3) and adding new subd. (2); Laws 1996, Ch. 429, eff. Jan. 1, 1997.

§ 14. Town and city clerks to issue marriage licenses; form.

The town or city clerk of each and every town or city in this state is hereby empowered to issue marriage licenses to any parties applying for the same who may be entitled under the laws of this state to apply therefor and to contract matrimony, authorizing the marriage of such parties, which license shall be substantially in the following form:

State of New York County of . . . . . . .City or town of . . . .

Know all men by this certificate that any person authorized by law to perform marriage ceremonies within the state of New York to whom this may come, he not knowing any lawful impediment thereto, is hereby authorized and empowered to solemnize the rites of matrimony between . . . . of . . . . in the county of . . . . and state of New York and . . . . of . . . . in the county of . . . . and state of New York and to certify the same to the said parties or either of them under his hand and seal in his ministerial or official capacity and thereupon he is required to return his certificate in the form hereto annexed. The statements endorsed hereon or annexed hereto, by me subscribed, contain a full and true abstract of all of the facts concerning such parties disclosed by their affidavits or verified statements presented to me upon the application for this license. This certificate is to be returned addressed to the undersigned at, street, city, town, village, state.

In testimony whereof, I have hereunto set my hand and affixed the seal of said town or city at . . . . this . . . . .day of . . . . .20 . . . ., at . . . . m. Seal.

The form of the certificate annexed to said license and therein referred to shall be as follows:

I, ... a . . . ., residing at . . . . in the county of . . . . and state of New York do hereby certify that I did on this

. . . . day of . . . . in the year, 20 . . . . at . . . . m, at . . . . in the county of . . . . and the state of New York, solemnize the rites of matrimony between . . . . of . . . . in the county of . . . . and state of New York, and . . . . of . . . . in the county of . . . . and state of New York in the presence of . . . . and . . . . as witness, and the license therefor is hereto annexed.

Witness my hand . . . . in the county of . . . . this . . . . day of . . . ., 20 . . . .

In the presence of

. . . .

. . . .

. . . .

There shall be endorsed upon the license or annexed thereto at the end thereof, subscribed by the clerk, an abstract of the facts concerning the parties as disclosed in their affidavits or verified statements at the time of the application for the license made in conformity to the provisions of section fifteen of this chapter.

There shall also be stated upon the license the exact period during which the marriage may be solemnized.

The license issued, including the abstract of facts, and the certificate duly signed by the person who shall have solemnized the marriage therein authorized, shall be returned by him, and where the marriage is solemnized by a written contract, the judge before whom acknowledgment is made shall forward such contract and marriage license to the office of the town or city clerk who issued the license within five days succeeding the date of the solemnizing of the marriage therein authorized and any person or persons who shall wilfully neglect to make such return within the time above required shall be deemed guilty of a misdemeanor and upon conviction thereof shall be punished by a fine of not less than twenty-five dollars or more than fifty dollars for each and every offense.

When a marriage is solemnized by a city, town or village justice outside of the territorial jurisdiction in which such justice was elected or appointed, as provided in subdivision six of section eleven of this chapter, there shall be affixed to such license prior to filing, the official or common seal of the court or of the municipality in which such justice was elected or appointed.

Amended by Laws 1912, Ch. 216; Laws 1926, Ch. 635; Laws 1929, Ch. 247; Laws 1935, Ch. 535; Laws 1937, Ch. 294; Laws 1938, Ch. 640; Laws 1939, Ch. 110; Laws 1957, Ch. 719; Laws 1969, Ch. 261; Laws 1977, Ch. 239; Laws 1977, Ch. 690, eff. July 1, 1978; Laws 1978, Ch. 615, eff. July 24, 1978; Laws 1983, Ch. 484, eff. Jan. 1, 1984; Laws 1985, Ch. 674, eff. Aug, 1, 1985.

§ 14-a. Town and city clerks to issue certificates of marriage registration; form.

1. Upon receipt of the return of the marriage license, properly endorsed and completed by the person who shall have solemnized a marriage as provided in this article, the town and city clerks of each and every town or city in the state shall, after abstracting, recording and indexing the statement of performance of solemnization, issue to the couple within fifteen days after such receipt or return of the completed marriage license a certificate of marriage, which certificate shall be substantially in the following form and contain the following facts:

Record No. . . . . of Year . . . .

THIS IS TO CERTIFY

that . . . ., first name, premarriage surname, new surname (if applicable), residing at . . . .,

who was born on . . . ., at . . . .,

date

and . . . ., first name, premarriage surname, new surname (if applicable) residing at . . . .,

who was born . . . ., at . . . .,

date

were married on . . . . at . . . .,

date

as shown by the duly registered license and certificate of marriage of said persons on file in this office.

(SEAL)

. . . .
Town or City Clerk

Dated at . . . ., N.Y.

. . . .

No other facts contained in the affidavits, statements, consents or licenses shall be certified by such town and city clerks, unless expressly requested in writing by the man or woman named in such affidavit, license, statement or record.

2. a. Such town and city clerks shall be entitled to a fee for such certificate, payable at the time of issuance of the marriage license, in a sum not exceeding ten dollars, to be fixed in the case of town clerks by the town board, and in the case of city clerks by the common council or governing body of such cities. The town and city clerks shall, upon request of any applicant whose name appears thereon, issue a similar certificate of marriage, as set forth above, and similarly

expanded with additional facts upon the express additional request, for all marriages heretofore indexed and recorded in the office of the town or city clerks. For such certificate of marriage, the town and city clerks shall be entitled to a fee not exceeding ten dollars, to be fixed in the case of town clerks by the town board, and in the case of city clerks by the common council or governing body of such city.

b.   In addition to the foregoing, upon request of any applicant whose name appears thereon for a certificate of marriage, the town or city clerk may issue a photograph, micro-photograph or photocopy of the original marriage record on file in the office of such clerk. Such photograph, micro-photograph or photocopy, when certified by the town or city clerk, shall be deemed an original record for all purposes, including introduction in evidence in all courts or administrative agencies. For such certificate of marriage and the certification thereof, the town or city clerk shall be entitled to a fee not exceeding ten dollars, to be fixed in the case of town clerks by the town board, and in the case of city clerks by the common council or governing body of such city.

3.   No fee shall be charged for any certificate when required by the veterans administration or by the division of veterans' affairs of the state of New York to be used in determining the eligibility of any person to participate in the benefits made available by the veterans administration or by the state of New York.

4.   A copy of the record of marriage registration when properly certified by the city and town clerks or their duly authorized deputies, as herein provided, shall be prima facie evidence of the facts therein stated and in all actions, proceedings or applications, judicial, administrative or otherwise, and any such certificate of registration of marriage shall be accepted with the same force and effect with respect to the facts therein stated as the original certificate of marriage or certified copy thereof.

Added by Laws 1962, Ch. 588; **amended** by Laws 1963, Ch. 297; Laws 1968, Ch. 545; Laws 1980, Ch. 355, eff. June 23, 1980; Laws 1981, Ch. 103, eff. June 1, 1981; Laws 1981, Ch. 1043, eff. Nov. 11, 1981; Laws 1983, Ch. 484, eff. Jan. 1, 1984; Laws 1985, Ch. 583, eff. Sept. 1, 1985; Laws 1991, Ch. 413, § 52, eff. Oct. 17, 1991.

§ 15.   Duty of town and city clerks.

1.   (a) It shall be the duty of the town or city clerk when an application for a marriage license is made to him or her to require each of the contracting parties to sign and verify a statement or affidavit before such clerk or one of his or her deputies, containing the following information. From the groom: Full name of husband, place of residence, social security number, age, occupation, place of birth, name of father, country of birth, maiden name of mother, country of birth, number of marriage. From the bride: Full name of bride, place of residence, social security number, age, occupation, place of birth, name of father, country of birth, maiden name of mother, country of birth, number of marriage. The said clerk shall also embody in the statement if either or both of the applicants have been

previously married, a statement as to whether the former husband or husbands or the former wife or wives of the respective applicants are living or dead and as to whether either or both of said applicants are divorced persons, if so, when and where and against whom the divorce or divorces were granted and shall also embody therein a statement that no legal impediment exists as to the right of each of the applicants to enter into the marriage state. The town or city clerk is hereby given full power and authority to administer oaths and may require the applicants to produce witnesses to identify them or either of them and may examine under oath or otherwise other witnesses as to any material inquiry pertaining to the issuing of the license, and if the applicant is a divorced person the clerk may also require the production of a certified copy of the decree of the divorce, or proof of an existing marriage of parties who apply for a license to be used for a second or subsequent ceremony; provided, however, that in cities of the first class the verified statements and affidavits may be made before any regular clerk of the city clerk's office designated for that purpose by the city clerk.

(b)   Every application for a marriage license shall contain a statement to the following effect:

NOTICE TO APPLICANTS

(1)   Every person has the right to adopt any name by which he or she wishes to be known simply by using that name consistently and without intent to defraud.

(2)   A person's last name (surname) does not automatically change upon marriage, and neither party to the marriage must change his or her last name. Parties to a marriage need not have the same last name.

(3)   One or both parties to a marriage may elect to change the surname by which he or she wishes to be known after the solemnization of the marriage by entering the new name in the space below. Such entry shall consist of one of the following surnames:

(i)   the surname of the other spouse; or

(ii)   any former surname of either spouse; or

(iii)   a name combining into a single surname all or a segment of the premarriage surname or any former surname of each spouse; or

(iv)   a combination name separated by a hyphen, provided that each part of such combination surname is the premarriage surname, or any former surname, of each of the spouses.

(4)   The use of this option will have the effect of providing a record of the change of name. The marriage certificate, containing the new name, if any, constitutes proof that the use of the new name, of the retention of the former name, is lawful.

(5)   Neither the use of, nor the failure to use, this option of selecting a new surname by means of this application abrogates the right of each person to adopt a different name through usage at some future date.

. . . .

(Optional — Enter new surname above)

2. If it appears from the affidavits and statements so taken, that the persons for whose marriage the license in question is demanded are legally competent to marry, the said clerk shall issue such license except in the following cases. If it shall appear upon an application that the applicant is under eighteen years of age, before the town or city clerk shall issue a license, he shall require documentary proof of age in the form of an original or certified copy of a birth record, a certification of birth issued by the state department of health, a local registrar of vital statistics or other public officer charged with similar duties by the laws of any other state, territory or country, a baptismal record, passport, automobile driver's license, life insurance policy, employment certificate, school record, immigration record, naturalization record or court record, showing the date of birth of such minor. If the town or city clerk shall be in doubt as to whether an applicant claiming to be over eighteen years of age is actually over eighteen years of age, he shall, before issuing such license, require documentary proof as above defined. If it shall appear upon an application of the applicants as provided in this section or upon information required by the clerk that either party is at least sixteen years of age but under eighteen years of age, then the town or city clerk before he shall issue a license shall require the written consent to the marriage from both parents of the minor or minors or such as shall then be living, or if the parents of both are dead, then the written consent of the guardian or guardians of such minor or minors. If one of the parents has been missing and has not been seen or heard from for a period of one year preceding the time of the application for the license, although diligent inquiry has been made to learn the whereabouts of such parent, the town or city clerk may issue a license to such minor upon the sworn statement and consent of the other parent. If the marriage of the parents of such minor has been dissolved by decree of divorce or annulment, the consent of the parent to whom the court which granted the decree has awarded the custody of such minor shall be sufficient. If there is no parent or guardian of the minor or minors living to their knowledge then the town or city clerk shall require the written consent to the marriage of the person under whose care or government the minor or minors may be before a license shall be issued. If a parent of such minor has been adjudicated an incompetent, the town or city clerk may issue a license to such minor upon the production of a certified copy of such judgment so determining and upon the written consent of the other parent. If there is no other parent whose consent is required by this section, then and in such event the town or city clerk shall require the written consent of the guardian of such minor or of the person under whose care or government the minor may be before a license shall be issued. The parents, guardians, or other persons whose consent it shall be necessary to obtain and file with the town or city clerk before the license shall issue, shall personally appear and acknowledge or execute the same before the town or city clerk, or some other officer authorized to administer oaths and take acknowledgments provided that where such affidavit or acknowledgment is made before an official other than an officer designated in section two

hundred ninety-eight of the real property law as authorized to take such affidavit or acknowledgment if a conveyance of real property were being acknowledged or proved, or if a certificate of authentication would be required by section three hundred ten of the real property law to entitle the instrument to be recorded if it were a conveyance of real property, the consent when filed must have attached thereto a certificate of authentication.

3. If it shall appear upon an application for a marriage license that either party is under the age of sixteen years, the town or city clerk shall require, in addition to any consents provided for in this section, the written approval and consent of a justice of the supreme court or of a judge of the family court, having jurisdiction over the town or city in which the application is made, to be attached to or endorsed upon the application, before the license is issued. The application for such approval and consent shall be heard by the judge at chambers. All papers and records pertaining to any such application shall be sealed by him and withheld from inspection, except by order of a court of competent jurisdiction. Before issuing any licenses herein provided for, the town or city clerk shall be entitled to a fee of thirty dollars, which sum shall be paid by the applicants before or at the time the license is issued. Any town or city clerk who shall issue a license to marry any persons one or both of whom shall not be at the time of the marriage under such license legally competent to marry without first requiring the parties to such marriage to make such affidavits and statements or who shall not require the production of documentary proof of age or the procuring of the approval and consents provided for by this article, which shall show that the parties authorized by said license to be married are legally competent to marry, shall be guilty of a misdemeanor and on conviction thereof shall be fined in the sum of one hundred dollars for each and every offense. On or before the fifteenth day of each month, each town and city clerk, except in the city of New York, shall transmit to the state commissioner of health twenty-two dollars and fifty cents of the amount received for each fee collected, which shall be paid into the vital records management account as provided by section ninety-seven-cccc of the state finance law. In any city the balance of all fees collected for the issuing of a marriage license, or for solemnizing a marriage, so far as collected for services rendered by any officer or employee of such city, shall be paid monthly into the city treasury and may by ordinance be credited to any fund therein designated, and said ordinance, when duly enacted, shall have the force of law in such city. Notwithstanding any other provisions of this article, the clerk of any city with the approval of the governing body of such city is hereby authorized to designate, in writing filed in the city clerk's office, a deputy clerk, if any, and/or other city employees in such office to receive applications for, examine applications, investigate and issue marriage licenses in the absence or inability of the clerk of said city to act, and said deputy and/or employees so designated are hereby vested with all the powers and duties of said city clerk relative thereto. Such deputy and/or employees shall perform said duties without additional compensation.

DRL

4. Notwithstanding any other provision of this section, the city clerk of the city of New York, before issuing any licenses herein provided for, shall be entitled to a fee of twenty–five dollars, which sum shall be paid by the applicants before or at the time the license is issued and all such fees so received shall be paid monthly into the city treasury.

Amended by Laws 1912, Ch. 241; Laws 1917, Ch. 503; Laws 1921, Ch. 317; Laws 1926, Ch. 635; Laws 1927, Ch. 547; Laws 1929, Ch. 633; Laws 1931, Ch. 511; Laws 1932, Ch. 285; Laws 1935, Ch. 535; Laws 1937, Ch. 706; Laws 1938, Ch. 640; Laws 1939, Ch. 110; Laws 1960, Ch. 1026; Laws 1962, Ch. 689; Laws 1964, Ch. 168; Laws 1965, Chs. 102, 142; Laws 1972, Ch. 561; Laws 1974, Ch. 920; Laws 1980, Ch. 356; Laws 1981, Ch. 103, eff. June 1, 1981; Laws 1984, Ch. 126, eff. Sept. 1, 1984; Laws 1985, Ch. 583, eff. Sept. 1, 1985; Laws 1989, Ch. 61, § 265, eff. Apr. 19, 1989; Laws 1990, Ch. 424, § 1, eff. Sept. 8, 1990, Laws 1997, Ch. 398, § 30, eff. Nov. 11, 1997; Laws 2003, Ch. 62, Part W2, § 5, eff. May 15, 2003, amending subd. 3.

§ 15-a.   Marriages of minors under fourteen years of age.

Any marriage in which either party is under the age of fourteen years is hereby prohibited. Any town or city clerk who shall knowingly issue a marriage license to any persons, one or both of whom shall be at the time of their contemplated marriage actually under the age of fourteen years, shall be guilty of a misdemeanor and on conviction thereof shall be fined in the sum of one hundred dollars.

Added by Laws 1926, Ch. 590; **amended** by Laws 1927, Ch. 547; Laws 1928, Ch. 43, eff. Feb. 15, 1928; Laws 1984, Ch. 126, eff. Sept. 1, 1984.

§ 15-b.   Temporary provisions authorizing issuance of license, upon court order, without consent of a parent in armed forces of the United States, merchant marine and allied forces, and absent from the United States.

This section expired on July 1, 1947.

§ 16.   False statements and affidavits.

Any person who shall in any affidavit or statement required or provided for in this article wilfully and falsely swear in regard to any material fact as to the competency of any person for whose marriage the license in question or concerning the procuring or issuing of which such affidavit or statement may be made shall be deemed guilty of perjury and on conviction thereof shall be punished as provided by the statutes of this state.

§ 17.   Clergyman or officer violating article; penalty.

If any clergyman or other person authorized by the laws of this state to perform marriage ceremonies shall solemnize or presume to solemnize any marriage between any parties without a license being presented to him or them as herein provided or with knowledge that either party is legally incompetent to contract matrimony as is provided for in this article he shall be guilty of a misdemeanor and on conviction thereof shall be punished by a fine not less than fifty dollars nor more than five hundred dollars or by imprisonment for a term not exceeding one year.

§ 18. Clergyman or officer, when protected.

Any such clergymen or officer as aforesaid to whom any such license duly issued may come and not having personal knowledge of the incompetency of either party therein named to contract matrimony, may lawfully solemnize matrimony between them.

§ 19. Records to be kept by town and city clerks.

1.   Each town and city clerk hereby empowered to issue marriage licenses shall keep a book supplied by the state department of health in which such clerk shall record and index such information as is required therein, which book shall be kept and preserved as a part of the public records of his office. Whenever an application is made for a search of such records the city or town clerk, excepting the city clerk of the city of New York, may make such search and furnish certificate of the result to the applicant upon the payment of a fee of five dollars for a search of one year and a further fee of one dollar for the second year for which such search is requested and fifty cents for each additional year thereafter, which fees shall be paid in advance of such search. Whenever an application is made for a search of such records in the city of New York, the city clerk of the city of New York may make such search and furnish a certificate of the result to the applicant upon the payment of a fee of five dollars for a search of one year and a further fee of one dollar for the second year for which search is requested and fifty cents each additional year thereafter. Notwithstanding any other provision of this article, no fee shall be charged for any search or certificate when required by the veterans administration or by the division of veterans' affairs of the state of New York to be used in determining the eligibility of any person to participate in the benefits made available by the veterans administration or by the state of New York. All such affidavits, statements and consents, immediately upon the taking or receiving of the same by the town or city clerk, shall be recorded and indexed as provided herein and shall be public records and open to public inspection whenever the same may be necessary or required for judicial or other proper purposes. At such times as the commissioner shall direct, the said town or city clerk, excepting the city clerk of the city New York, shall file in the office of the state department of health the original of each affidavit, statement, consent, order of a justice or judge authorizing immediate solemnization of marriage license and certificate, filed with or made before such clerk during the preceding month. Such clerk shall not be required to file any of said documents with the state department of health until the license is returned with the certificate showing that the marriage to which they refer has been actually performed.

DRL

The county clerks of the counties comprising the city of New York shall cause all original applications and original licenses with the marriage solemnization statements thereon heretofore filed with each, and all papers and records and binders relating to such original documents pertaining to marriage licenses issued by said city clerk, in their custody and possession to be removed, transferred, and delivered to the borough offices of the city clerk in each of said counties.

2.   (a) In lieu of the requirement of maintaining a book supplied by the state department of health pursuant to subdivision one hereof, each town or city clerk may cause all information as is required by law or rule or regulation of the department to be kept in such books to be photocopied, photographed, microphotographed or reproduced on film which shall be kept and preserved as part of the public records of his office together with an index thereto. Such photographic film shall be of durable material and the device used to reproduce such records on such film shall be one which accurately reproduces the original record in all details.

(b)   Such photocopy or photographic film shall be deemed to be an original record for all purposes, including introduction in evidence in all courts or administrative agencies. A transcript, exemplification or certified copy thereof shall, for all purposes, be deemed to be a transcript, exemplification or certified copy of the original.

Amended by Laws 1912, Ch. 241; Laws 1916, Ch. 381; Laws 1920, Ch. 213; Laws 1921, Ch. 32; Laws 1926, Ch. 635; Laws 1927, Ch. 231; Laws 1935, Ch. 535; Laws 1936, Ch. 163; Laws 1937, Ch. 294; Laws 1938, Ch. 640; Laws 1951, Ch. 550; Laws 1954, Ch. 607; Laws 1959, Ch. 117; Laws 1962, Ch. 72; Laws 1967, Ch. 141; Laws 1968, Chs. 545, 764; Laws 1970, Ch. 695; Laws 1981, Ch. 103, eff. June 1, 1981; Laws 1983, Ch. 484, eff. Jan. 1, 1984; Laws 1985, Ch. 674, eff. Aug. 1, 1985.

§ 19-a.   Marriages on vessels; reports and records.

The master, chief officer, ship's surgeon, or the company, corporation, charterer, or person having the management and control of any vessel which shall arrive at the port of New York, shall report, in writing, to the city clerk of the city of New York within three days after the arrival of such vessel the marriage of any resident of such city occurring thereon at sea, and shall file with such clerk a transcript of the entry made in the log book of such vessel in respect to any such marriage.

Added by Laws 1939, Ch. 661; **amended** by Laws 1968, Ch. 764, eff. Sept. 15, 1968.

§ 20.   Records to be kept by the state department of health and the city clerk of the city of New York.

All original affidavits, statements, consents and licenses with certificates attached, and also all written contracts of marriages outside of the city of New York shall be kept on file and properly indexed by the state department of health, and such similar evidences of marriage in the city of New York shall be kept on file and properly indexed by the city clerk of the city of New York. They shall be carefully examined, and if any such are incomplete or unsatisfactory the state commissioner of health and in the city of New York the city clerk shall require such further information to be supplied as may be necessary to make the record complete and satisfactory. Whenever it is claimed that a mistake has been made through inadvertence in any of the statements, affidavits or other papers required by this section to be filed with the state department of health, and in the city of New York with the city clerk's office, the state commissioner of health and in the city of New York the city clerk may file with the same, affidavits upon the part of the person claiming to be aggrieved by such mistake, showing the true facts and the reason for the mistake and may make a note upon such original paper, statement or affidavit showing that a mistake is claimed to have been made and the nature thereof.

DRL

　　Amended by Laws 1915, Ch. 422; Laws 1917, Ch. 245; Laws 1921, Ch. 317; Laws 1926, Ch. 635; Laws 1968, Ch. 764, eff. Sept. 15, 1968.

§ 20-a.　Certified transcripts of records; state commissioner of health may furnish.

　　The state commissioner of health or person authorized by him shall, upon request, supply to any applicant a certified transcript of any marriage registered under the provisions of this article, unless he is satisfied that the same does not appear to be necessary or required for judicial or other proper purposes. Any transcript of the record of a marriage, when properly certified by the state commissioner of health or person authorized to act for him, shall be prima facie evidence in all courts and places of the facts therein stated. For any search of the files and records conducted for authorized research purposes, the state commissioner of health shall be entitled to a fee of twenty dollars for each hour or fractional part of an hour of time of search, together with a fee of two dollars for each uncertified copy or abstract of such marriage record requested by the applicant, said fees to be paid by the applicant. Each applicant for a certified transcript of a marriage record shall remit to the state commissioner of health a fee of thirty dollars in payment for the search of the files and records and the furnishing of a certified copy if such record is found or for a certification that a search discloses no record of a marriage.

　　Added by Laws 1926, Ch. 635; **amended** by Laws 1935, Ch. 535; Laws 1952, Ch. 250; Laws 1968, Ch. 545; Laws 1981, Ch. 103, eff. June 1, 1981; Laws 2003, Ch. 62, Part W2, § 6, eff. May 15, 2003.

§ 20-b.　Certification of marriage; state commissioner of health may furnish.

　　1.　The state commissioner of health or person authorized by him shall, upon request, issue to any applicant a certification of any marriage registered under the provisions of this article, unless he is satisfied that the same does not appear to be necessary or required for judicial or other proper purposes. Any such certification of marriage made by such commissioner or person authorized to act for him shall be prima facie evidence in all courts and places of the facts therein stated.

2. Such certification shall contain a statement of the respective names, dates and places of birth and places of the then residence of each of the parties to such marriage and the date and the place thereof.

3. Each applicant for a certification of marriage shall remit to the commissioner with such application a fee of thirty dollars in payment for the search of the files and records and the furnishing of such certification if a record thereof is found or for a certification that a search discloses no record of a marriage.

4. The federal agency in charge of vital statistics may obtain, at a fee acceptable to the commissioner, information from marriage records for use solely as statistical data.

Added by Laws 1968, Ch. 545, eff. Sept. 1, 1968; amended by Laws 1981, Ch. 103, eff. June 1, 1981, adding subd. 4; Laws 2003, Ch. 62, Part W2, § 7, eff. May 15, 2003, amending sub. 3.

§ 21. Forms and books to be furnished.

The proper books for registration, blank forms for marriage licenses, certificates, statements and affidavits and such other blanks as shall be necessary to comply with the provisions of this article, shall be prepared by the state department of health and shall be furnished by said department at the expense of the state to the town and city clerks filing records with the state department of health in such quantities as their necessities shall require.

Amended by Laws 1926, Ch. 635; Laws 1936, Ch. 163, eff. Mar. 24, 1936.

§ 22. Penalty for violation.

Any town or city clerk who shall violate any of the provisions of this article or shall fail to comply therewith shall be deemed guilty of a misdemeanor and shall pay a fine not exceeding the sum of one hundred dollars on conviction thereof.

Amended by Laws 1926, Ch. 635, eff. Apr. 29, 1926.

§ 23. Supervision of and inspection of town and city clerks' records by state commissioner of health.

The registration and recording of all marriages outside the city of New York shall be under the supervision of the state commissioner of health. The commissioner, either personally or by an accredited representative, may at any time inspect the record and index of marriage licenses issued by any town or city clerk and promulgate rules and regulations for insuring complete registration. When he shall deem it necessary, he shall report cases of violation of any of the provisions of this article to the district attorney of the county, with a statement of the facts and circumstances; and when any such case is reported to him by the state commissioner of health, the prosecuting attorney shall forthwith initiate and promptly follow up the necessary court proceedings against the person or persons responsible for the alleged violation of law. Upon request of the state commissioner of health, the attorney-general shall assist in the enforcement of the provisions of this article.

Added by Laws 1926, Ch. 635, eff. Apr. 29, 1926.

§ 24. Effect of marriage on legitimacy of children.

1.   A child heretofore or hereafter born of parents who prior or subsequent to the birth of such child shall have entered into a civil or religious marriage, or shall have consummated a common-law marriage where such marriage is recognized as valid, in the manner authorized by the law of the place where such marriage takes place, is the legitimate child of both natural parents notwithstanding that such marriage is void or voidable or has been or shall hereafter be annulled or judicially declared void.

2.   Nothing herein contained shall be deemed to affect the construction of any will or other instrument executed before the time this act shall take effect or any right or interest in property or right of action vested or accrued before the time this act shall take effect, or to limit the operation of any judicial determination heretofore made containing express provision with respect to the legitimacy, maintenance or custody of any child, or to affect any adoption proceeding heretofore commenced, or limit the effect of any order or orders entered in such adoption proceeding.

Added and former § 24 **repealed** by Laws 1969, Ch. 325, eff. Apr. 30, 1969.

§ 25. License, when to be obtained.

The provisions of this article pertaining to the granting of the licenses before a marriage can be lawfully celebrated apply to all persons who assume the marriage relation in accordance with subdivision four of section eleven of this chapter. Nothing in this article contained shall be construed to render void by reason of a failure to procure a marriage license any marriage solemnized between persons of full age nor to render void any marriage between minors or with a minor under the legal age of consent where the consent of parent or guardian has been given and such marriage shall be for such cause voidable only as to minors or a minor upon complaint of such minors or minor or of the parent or guardian thereof.

ARTICLE 3–A

UNIFORM SUPPORT OF DEPENDENTS LAW
(*Repealed*)

————

(Article 3–A was repealed by Laws 1997, Ch. 398, § 36, eff. Dec. 31, 1997, except as to those cases pending which were maintainable under subdivision 1 of section 35 of the domestic relations law; provided, however, no new petition may be commenced under Article 3–A. Exception enacted by Laws 1998, Ch. 214, § 38-a, eff. July 7, 1998 and deemed in full force and effect Dec. 31, 1997)

Editor's Note: The establishment and enforcement of interstate child and spousal support is now covered by the newly added Article 5-B, the Uniform Interstate Family Support Act, of the Family Court Act. (L. 1997, ch. 398 § § 36 and 37).

SUMMARY OF ARTICLE

§ 30.　Short title; purpose [*Repealed*].

This article may be cited and referred to as the uniform support of dependents law. The purpose of this article is to secure support in civil proceedings for dependent spouses and children from persons legally responsible for their support.

Added by Laws 1958, Ch. 146; Laws 1980, Ch. 281, eff. July 19, 1980; **repealed** by Laws 1997, Ch. 398, § 36, eff. Dec. 31, 1997.

§ 31. Definitions [*Repealed*].

As used in this article, unless the context shall require otherwise, the following terms shall have the meanings ascribed to them by this section:

1. "State" shall mean and include any state, territory or possession of the United States, the District of Columbia, any province or territory of the Dominion of Canada, or any foreign country.

2. "Court" shall mean the family court of the state of New York; when the context requires, it shall mean and include a court of another state defined in and upon which appropriate jurisdiction has been conferred by a substantially similar reciprocal law.

3. "Child" includes a step child, foster child, child born out of wedlock or legally adopted child and means a child under twenty-one years of age.

4. "Dependent" shall mean and include any person who is entitled to support pursuant to this article.

5. "Petitioner" shall mean and include each dependent person for whom support is sought in a proceeding instituted pursuant to this article.

6. "Respondent" shall mean and include each person against whom a proceeding is instituted pursuant to this article.

7. "Petitioner's representative" shall mean and include a corporation counsel, county attorney, state's attorney, commonwealth attorney and any other public officer, by whatever title his public office may be known, charged by law with the duty of instituting, maintaining or prosecuting a proceeding under this article or under the laws of the state or states wherein the petitioner and the respondent reside.

8. "Summons" shall mean and include a subpoena, warrant, citation, order or other notice, by whatever name known, provided for by the laws of the state or states wherein the petitioner and the respondent reside as the means for requiring the appearance and attendance in court of the respondent in a proceeding instituted pursuant to this article.

9. "Initiating state" shall mean the state of domicile or residence of the petitioner.

10. "Responding state" shall mean the state wherein the respondent resides or is domiciled or found.

Added by Laws 1958, Ch. 146, eff. July 1, 1958; **amended** by Laws 1962, Ch. 689; Laws 1967, Ch. 184; Laws 1968, Ch. 46; Laws 1973, Ch. 75, eff. Mar. 13, 1973; **repealed** by Laws 1997, Ch. 398, § 36, eff. Dec. 31, 1997.

DRL

§ 32. Persons legally liable for support of dependents [*Repealed*].

For the purpose of this article, the following persons in one state are declared to be liable for the support of dependents residing or found in the same state or in another state having substantially similar or reciprocal laws, and, if possessed of sufficient means or able to earn such means, may be required to pay for such support a fair and reasonable sum, as may be determined by the court having jurisdiction of the respondent in a proceeding instituted under this article:

1. Husband liable for support of his wife or former wife;

2. Wife liable for support of her husband or former husband;

3. Parents liable for support of their child or children under twenty-one years of age. If possessed of sufficient means or able to earn such means, either or both parents shall be required to pay for child support a fair and reasonable sum as the court may determine. The court shall make its award for child support pursuant to section two hundred forty of this chapter.

Added by Laws 1958, Ch. 146, eff. July 1, 1958; **amended** by Laws 1966, Ch. 131, repealing subd. (7); Laws 1967, Ch. 184, repealing subds. (4) and (6) and renumbering subd. (5) as (4); Laws 1980, Ch. 281, eff. July 19, 1980; Laws 1981, Ch. 763, eff. July 27, 1981; Laws 1983, Ch. 362, eff. June 26, 1983; Laws 1989, Ch. 567, § 3, eff. Sept. 15, 1989; **repealed** by Laws 1997, Ch. 398, § 36, eff. Dec. 31, 1997.

§ 33. Additional provisions regarding liability for support [*Repealed*].

For the purposes of this article:

1. A child or children born of parents who, at any time prior or subsequent to the birth of such child, have entered into a civil or religious marriage ceremony, shall be deemed the legitimate child or children of both parents, regardless of the validity of such marriage.

2. A child or children born of parents who held or hold themselves out as husband and wife by virtue of a common law marriage recognized as valid by the laws of the initiating state and of the responding state shall be deemed the legitimate child or children of both parents.

3. A person who was or is held out as a spouse by another person by virtue of a common law marriage recognized as valid by the laws of the initiating state and of the responding state shall be deemed the legitimate spouse of such other person.

4. Notwithstanding the fact that the respondent has obtained in any state or country a final decree of divorce or separation from his or her spouse or a decree dissolving his or her marriage, the respondent shall be deemed legally liable for the support of any dependent child of such marriage and for support of the former spouse.

5. The natural parents of a child born out of wedlock shall be severally liable for the support of such child, but the liability of the natural father shall not be

enforceable unless he has been adjudicated to be the child's father by a court of competent jurisdiction, or he has acknowledged or shall acknowledge paternity of the child in open court or by a verified written statement.

6. No person shall be liable for the support of a child who has been adopted by his or her spouse, if such child was adopted after the adopting spouse is living separate and apart from the non-adopting spouse pursuant to a legally recognizable separation agreement or decree under this chapter. Such liability shall not be imposed for so long as the spouses remain separate and apart after the adoption.

Added by Laws 1958, Ch. 146; **amended** by Laws 1980, Ch. 281, eff. July 19, 1980; Laws 1981, Ch. 763, eff. July 27, 1981; Laws 1984, Ch. 745, eff. Dec. 3, 1984; **repealed** by Laws 1997, Ch. 398, § 36, eff. Dec. 31, 1997.

§ 34. Jurisdiction and powers of court [*Repealed*].

For the purposes of this article:

1. The court shall have jurisdiction regardless of the state of last residence or domicile of the petitioner and the respondent and whether or not the respondent has ever been a resident of the initiating state or the dependent person has ever been a resident of the responding state.

2. The court of the responding state shall have the power to order the respondent to pay sums sufficient to provide necessary food, shelter, clothing, care, medical or hospital expenses, expenses of confinement, expenses of education of a child, funeral expenses and such other reasonable and proper expenses of the petitioner as justice requires, having due regard to the circumstances of the respective parties. Where the petitioner's needs are so urgent as to require it, the court may make a temporary order for support pending a final determination.

3. The court of the responding state shall have the power to make an order determining whether the respondent is the biological father of a child for whom support is sought pursuant to the provisions of this article, in accordance with the requirements of subdivision nineteen of section thirty-seven of this article.

4. The courts of both the initiating state and the responding state shall have the power to order testimony to be taken in either or both of such states by deposition or written interrogatories, and to limit the nature of and the extent to which the right so to take testimony shall be exercised, provided that the respondent is given a full and fair opportunity to answer the allegations of the petitioner.

Added by Laws 1958, Ch. 146, eff. July 1, 1958; **amended** by Laws 1959, Ch. 149, eff. Mar. 24, 1959; Laws 1987, Ch. 815, eff. Dec. 5, 1987; **repealed** by Laws 1997, Ch. 398, § 36, eff. Dec. 31, 1997.

§ 34-a. Powers of court; visitation [*Repealed*].

In any proceeding to compel support of a dependent pursuant to the applicable provisions of this article, where the petitioner and respondent are residents of or domiciled or found in different counties within the state of New York, the courts of either the initiating county or responding county shall have the power, in addition to the powers granted by section thirty-four of this article, to make reasonable provisions for visitation of a child or children of the petitioner or respondent or for the visitation of a child or children otherwise in the care or custody of the petitioner and for whom support is the obligation of the respondent.

Added by Laws 1977, Ch. 379, eff. July 6, 1977; **repealed** by Laws 1997, Ch. 398, § 36, eff. Dec. 31, 1997.

§ 35. Cases in which proceedings are maintainable [*Repealed*].

A proceeding to compel support of a dependent may be maintained under this article in any of the following cases:

1. Where the petitioner and the respondent are residents of or domiciled or found in different counties of the same state. Whenever a proceeding hereunder is so maintained, the terms "initiating state" and "responding state" as used in this article shall be read and construed to mean and include respectively "initiating county" and "responding county" in relation to any such proceeding within the same state.

2. Where the petitioner resides in one state and the respondent is a resident of or is domiciled or found in another state having substantially similar or reciprocal laws.

3. Where the respondent is not and never was a resident of or domiciled in the initiating state and the petitioner resides or is domiciled in such state and the respondent is believed to be a resident of or domiciled in another state having substantially similar or reciprocal laws.

4. Where the respondent was or is a resident of or domiciled in the initiating state and has departed or departs from such state leaving therein a dependent in need of and entitled to support under this article and is believed to be a resident of or domiciled in another state having substantially similar or reciprocal laws.

Added by Laws 1958, Ch. 146, eff. July 1, 1958; **repealed** by Laws 1997, Ch. 398, § 36, eff. Dec. 31, 1997.

§ 36. Remedies of a public agency [*Repealed*].

Whenever the state or a political subdivision, or any official agency thereof, is furnishing support or is likely to furnish support to a dependent it shall have the same right to invoke the provisions of this article as the dependent to whom the duty of support is owed.

Added by Laws 1958, Ch. 146, eff. July 1, 1958; **repealed** by Laws 1997, Ch. 398, § 36, eff. Dec. 31, 1997.

§ 37. Procedure [*Repealed*].

1. A proceeding under this article shall be commenced by a petitioner by filing a verified petition in the court in the county of the state wherein he resides or is domiciled, showing the name, age, residence and circumstances of the petitioner, alleging that he is in need of and is entitled to support from the respondent, giving his name, age, residence and circumstances, and praying that the respondent be compelled to furnish such support. If, after the filing of such petition, the petitioner shall become a resident of or domiciled in a county of the state other than the county wherein the initiating court is located, such petitioner may, by filing a verified application with the court in the county of the state wherein he then resides or is domiciled, pray that the proceeding be removed to the court in the county of the state wherein he then resides or is domiciled. Any judge of the court in which such verified application for removal has been filed may thereafter issue an order directed to the initiating court directing that the entire file be forwarded to the court wherein such verified application for removal has been filed and a copy of such order be sent to the responding state court, if any. Upon receipt of said entire file by the court wherein said verified application for removal has been filed, said court shall acknowledge receipt of such file to both the original initiating court and the responding state court, if any, take full jurisdiction over the proceeding in place of the original initiating court, and exercise such jurisdiction with all the same powers and to the same extent as if the proceeding had originally been commenced in said court.

2. If the respondent be a resident of or domiciled in such state and the court has or can acquire jurisdiction of the person of the respondent under existing laws in effect in such state, such laws shall govern and control the procedure to be followed in such proceeding.

3. If the respondent be not a resident of or domiciled in or cannot be found in the initiating state, a judge of such court shall certify that a verified petition has been filed in his court in a proceeding against the respondent under this article to compel the support of the petitioner, that a summons, duly issued out of his court for service upon the respondent has been returned with an affidavit to the effect that the respondent cannot with due diligence be located or served with such process in the initiating state, that the respondent is believed to be residing or domiciled in the responding state and that, in his opinion, the respondent should be compelled to answer such petition and should be dealt with according to law, and he shall transmit such certificate and certified copies of such petition and summons, and a copy of this uniform support of dependents law, as amended, to the appropriate court in the responding state. If the responding state is a province or territory of the Dominion of Canada, the judge of the initiating state shall also set forth in his certificate the weekly or monthly amount in United States money which, in his opinion, the respondent should be required to pay for

support of the petitioner, but that such recommendation is provisional only and subject to confirmation or modification by the court of the responding state. In the event that the court of the initiating state shall have before it satisfactory evidence that the respondent is not within the initiating state or cannot be served with process there, the summons and affidavit required herein may be omitted and the certificate shall contain a statement of the reasons for said omissions and the pertinent evidence supporting the same.

4. Any judge of a court in the county of the responding state in which the respondent resides or is domiciled or found, upon presentation to him of such certificate and certified copies of such petition and summons, and of a copy of this uniform support of dependents law, as amended, shall fix a time and place for a hearing on such petition and shall issue a summons out of his court, directed to the respondent, duly requiring him to appear at such time and place. If the judge discovers that the respondent cannot be found in that county, but that he resides or is domiciled or found in another county of the responding state, the papers received from the court of the initiating state may be forwarded to the court in such other county, and the initiating state court shall thereupon be notified of such transfer. Upon receipt of the papers by the court of the county where the respondent is found, it shall acknowledge receipt of such papers to both the initiating state court and the original responding state court, take full jurisdiction over the proceeding in place of the original responding state court, and exercise such jurisdiction with all the same powers and to the same extent as if it had received the papers in the first instance direct from the initiating state court.

5. It shall not be necessary for the petitioner or the petitioner's witnesses to appear personally at such hearing, but it shall be the duty of the petitioner's representative of the responding state to appear on behalf of and represent the petitioner at all stages of the proceeding. If the petitioner does not reside, work, or is not domiciled in the county in which the petition has been filed, or within fifty miles of said county, all pre-trial discovery upon the petitioner shall be by written interrogatories, deposition upon written questions, requests for production of documents, and/or requests for admission; provided, however, that if the respondent asserts as a defense that he is not the father of the child for whom support is sought and it appears to the court that the defense is not frivolous, the court may adjudicate the paternity issue if both of the parties are present at the hearing or the proof required in the case indicates that the presence of either or both of the parties is not necessary. Otherwise the court may adjourn the hearing until the paternity issue has been adjudicated.

6. If at such hearing the respondent controverts the petition and enters a verified denial of any of the material allegations thereof, the judge presiding at such hearing shall stay the proceedings and transmit to the judge of the court in the initiating state a transcript of the clerk's minutes showing the denials entered by the respondent.

7. Upon receipt by the judge of the court in the initiating state of such transcript, such court shall take such proof, including the testimony of the

petitioner and the petitioner's witnesses and such other evidence as the court may deem proper, and, after due deliberation, the court shall make its recommendation, based on all of such proof and evidence, and shall transmit to the court in the responding state a certified transcript of such proof and evidence and of its proceedings and recommendation in connection therewith.

8. Upon the receipt of such transcript, the court in the responding state shall resume its hearing in the proceeding and shall give the respondent a reasonable opportunity to appear and reply.

9. Upon the resumption of such hearing, the respondent shall have the right to examine or cross-examine the petitioner and the petitioner's witnesses by means of depositions or written interrogatories, and the petitioner shall have the right to examine or cross-examine the respondent and the respondent's witnesses by means of depositions or written interrogatories.

10. If a respondent, duly summoned by a court in the responding state, wilfully fails without good cause to appear as directed in the summons, he shall be punished in the same manner and to the same extent as is provided by law for the punishment of a defendant or witness who wilfully disobeys a summons or subpoena duly issued out of such court in any other action or proceeding cognizable by said court.

11. If, on the return day of the summons, the respondent appears at the time and place specified therein and fails to answer the petition or admits the allegations thereof or, if, after a hearing has been duly held by the court in the responding state in accordance with the provisions of this section, such court has found and determined that the prayer of the petitioner, or any part thereof, is supported by the evidence adduced in the proceeding, and that the petitioner is in need of and entitled to support from the respondent, the court shall make and enter an order directing the respondent to furnish support to the petitioner and to pay therefor such sum as the court shall determine, having due regard to the parties' means and circumstances. A certified copy of such order shall be transmitted by the court to the court in the initiating state and such copy shall be filed with and made a part of the records of such court in such proceeding. The court may place the respondent on probation on such terms and conditions as the court may deem proper or necessary to assure faithful compliance by the respondent with such order. The court shall also have power to require the respondent to furnish recognizance in the form of a cash deposit or surety bond in such amount as the court may deem proper and just to assure the payment of the amount required to be paid by the respondent for the support of the petitioner.

12. The court making such order shall have the power to direct the respondent to make the payments required thereby at specified intervals to the support collection units as designated by the appropriate social services district and to report personally to such unit or bureau at such times as may be deemed necessary and the respondent shall at all times be under the supervision of such unit.

13. A respondent who shall wilfully fail to comply with or violate the terms or conditions of the support order or of his probation shall be punished by the

DRL

court in the same manner and to the same extent as is provided by law for a contempt of such court or a violation of probation ordered by such court in any other suit or proceeding cognizable by such court.

14. Upon the receipt of a payment made by the respondent pursuant to the order of the court of the responding state in any proceeding under this article, the support collection unit as designated by the appropriate social services district shall forthwith transmit the same to the court of the initiating state.

15. The support collection unit as designated by the appropriate social services district in the responding state, upon request, shall, not later than thirty days following the end of each fiscal year, furnish to the court of the initiating state an itemized statement under oath of all payments made by the respondent during such fiscal year for the support of the petitioner in such proceeding.

16. The court of the initiating state shall receive and accept all payments made by the respondent to the support collection unit as designated by the appropriate social services district of the responding state and transmitted by the latter on behalf of the respondent. Upon receipt of any such payment, and under such rules as the court of the initiating state may prescribe, the court, or support collection unit as designated by the appropriate social services district, as the court may direct, shall deliver such payment to the dependent person entitled thereto, take a proper receipt and acquittance therefor, and keep a permanent record thereof.

17. The court of the responding state may use any power to enforce a duty of support against a respondent under this article which is otherwise available to it under the laws of the responding state.

18. Any court of the responding state having jurisdiction under this article, upon receipt of the entire file from the original responding state court, may acquire jurisdiction over the respondent in the same manner and same extent as that of the original responding state court.

19. In any case in which a respondent asserts as a defense that he is not the father of the child and in which a determination that he is the father of the child is a necessary prerequisite to a determination of the obligation to support, the court of the responding state shall notify the court of the initiating state that the action can be maintained only if the mother and child submit to a blood test as described in section five hundred thirty-two of the family court act. If the mother and child agree to, or are ordered to submit to the blood test, the court shall order the respondent to submit to such test and the results of such test shall be admitted into evidence in accordance with such section of the family court act. If any test results in the exclusion of the respondent as the father of the child, the court shall so find and shall dismiss the support proceeding. If the test does not exclude the respondent as father the proceeding shall continue and the court shall determine the issue of paternity based on all available evidence, in accordance with article five of the family court act, including such blood test result, utilizing the procedures set forth in this article. If the court determines that the respondent

is not the father of the child and is not otherwise responsible for the support of the child, it shall so find and shall dismiss the support proceeding or any part thereof in which support for the child is sought. If the court determines that the respondent is the father or is otherwise legally responsible for the support of the child, it shall enter an order of filiation, where appropriate, pursuant to article five of the family court act and an order of support pursuant to article four of the family court act.

Added by Laws 1958, Ch. 146, eff. July 1, 1958; **amended** by Laws 1960, Ch. 354; Laws 1966, Ch. 299; Laws 1968, Ch. 46, eff. Mar. 19, 1968; Laws 1977, Ch. 516, § 24, eff. Jan. 1, 1978; Laws 1987, Ch. 815, eff. Dec. 5, 1987; **repealed** by Laws 1997, Ch. 398, § 36, eff. Dec. 31, 1997.

§ 37-a. Registration of foreign support orders [*Repealed*].

1. If the duty of support for any child or spouse or former spouse is based on a foreign support order of a state which has a reciprocal enforcement of support act, the petitioner shall have the additional remedies provided in this section.

2. The petitioner, or support collection unit on petitioner's behalf, may register the foreign support order in a court of this state in the manner, with the effect, and for the purposes herein provided.

3. The clerk of the court shall maintain a Registry of Foreign Support Orders in which he shall file foreign support orders.

4. If this state is acting either as a responding or an initiating state the support collection unit as designated by the appropriate social services district, upon the request of the court, shall represent the petitioner in proceedings under this section.

5. (a) A petitioner seeking to register a foreign support order in a court of this state shall transmit to the clerk of the court (1) three certified copies of the order with all modifications thereof, (2) one copy of the reciprocal enforcement of support act of the state in which the order was made, and (3) a verified statement showing the post office address of the respondent, the amount of support remaining unpaid, a description and to the best of the petitioner's knowledge the location of any property of the respondent available upon execution, the name and address of any employer or income payor as defined in section fifty-two hundred forty-one of the civil practice law and rules, and a list of the states in which the order is registered. Upon receipt of these documents the clerk of the court, without payment of a filing fee or other cost to the petitioner, shall file them in the Registry of Foreign Support Orders. The filing constitutes registration under this section.

(b) Promptly upon registration the clerk of the court shall send by certified or registered mail to the respondent at the address given a notice of the registration with a copy of the registered support order and the post office address of the petitioner. The clerk shall also docket the case with the court. If the support order has been registered pursuant to a request made through the title IV-D program of the federal social security act, the clerk shall also notify the respondent that payments pursuant to the order are to be made payable to the support collection unit and shall provide to the respondent the address of the support collection unit as designated by the appropriate social services district. The clerk shall notify the support collection unit of this action and the support collection unit shall proceed diligently to enforce the order.

6.   (a) Upon registration the registered foreign support order shall be enforced and satisfied in the same manner as a support order issued by a court of this state. If the court applies New York law, the order shall be subject to the same procedures, defenses, and proceedings for reopening, vacating, or staying as a support order of this state. Registration under this section shall not confer jurisdiction over the parties for purposes other than enforcement of the registered order.

(b)   The respondent shall have twenty days after the mailing of notice of the registration in which to petition the court to vacate the registration. If no such petition is filed, the registered support order is confirmed. At the hearing the respondent may present only matters that would be available as defenses in an action to enforce a foreign money judgement. If the respondent shows to the court that an appeal from the order is pending or will be taken or that a stay of execution has been granted the court shall stay enforcement of the order until the appeal is concluded, the time for appeal has expired, or the order is vacated, upon satisfactory proof that the respondent has furnished security for payment of the support ordered as required by the rendering state. If the respondent shows to the court any ground upon which the support order is likely to be vacated, the court shall stay enforcement of the order pending a decision on the motion if the respondent furnishes the same security for payment of the support ordered that is required for a support order of this state.

7.   Enforcement of a foreign support order registered pursuant to this section shall include collection of any arrears which may have accrued under such order prior to registration hereunder, in addition to any amounts becoming due and owing following such registration.

8.   Notwithstanding any other provision of this section, no support collection unit shall be required to register, enforce or represent a petitioner with respect to a foreign support order that is for the support of a spouse or former spouse unless such collection unit has undertaken to simultaneously register, enforce or represent a petitioner with respect to an order for the support of a child residing with such spouse or former spouse pursuant to title IV-D of the federal social security act.

Added by Laws 1980, Ch. 227, eff. Aug. 9, 1980; amended by Laws 1985, Ch. 809, eff. Nov. 1, 1985, adding subd. (7); Laws 1987, Ch. 815, eff. Dec. 5, 1987; Laws 1992, Ch. 199, § 1, eff. June 23, 1992; repealed by Laws 1997, Ch. 398, § 36, eff. Dec. 31, 1997.

§ 38. Appeals; effectiveness of orders [*Repealed*].

Any respondent in a proceeding brought under the provisions of this article shall have the same right of appeal as in civil proceedings or actions brought in the same court. Any order for support made by the court shall not be affected by an appeal but shall continue in effect until the appeal is decided and thereafter, if the order is affirmed, until changed by further order of the court.

Added by Laws 1958, Ch. 146, eff. July 1, 1958; repealed by Laws 1997, Ch. 398, § 36, eff. Dec. 31, 1997.

§ 38-a. Evidence and presumptions [*Repealed*].*

In any hearing under this act in either an initiating state court or a responding state court, there shall be applicable the same presumptions and other rules of evidence, whether statutory, decisional, or under court rules, as are available to the parties in other civil proceedings or actions brought in that same court.

Added by Laws 1958, Ch. 234, eff. Mar. 18, 1958, as § 6-b of Ch. 807, Laws 1949, Uniform Support of Dependent's Law. Laws 1949, Ch. 807 was repealed by Laws 1958, Ch. 146 and incorporated into the Domestic Relations Law; repealed by Laws 1997, Ch. 398, § 36, eff. Dec. 31, 1997.

* Section number assigned by McKinney's Consolidated Laws of New York, Domestic Relations Law, Book 14, adopted for this publication; *see* Rinner v. Cannon, 33 A.D.2d 923, 307 N.Y.S.2d 272 (2d Dept. 1970).

§ 39. Duty of petitioners' representatives [*Repealed*].

It shall be the duty of all petitioners' representatives of this state to appear in this state on behalf of and represent the petitioner in every proceeding pursuant to this article, at the time the petition is filed and at all stages of the proceeding thereafter, and to obtain and present such evidence or proof as may be required by the court in the initiating state or the responding state.

Added by Laws 1958, Ch. 146, eff. July 1, 1958; repealed by Laws 1997, Ch. 398, § 36, eff. Dec. 31, 1997.

§ 40. Expenses of proceedings [*Repealed*].

Expenses of stenographic records of court proceedings and of certification of court records shall be a county charge and shall be paid out of the county treasury.

Added by Laws 1958, Ch. 146, eff. July 1, 1958; repealed by Laws 1997, Ch. 398, § 36, eff. Dec. 31, 1997.

§ 41. Construction of article [*Repealed*].

1. This article shall be construed to furnish an additional or alternative civil remedy and shall in no way affect or impair any other remedy, civil or criminal,

provided in any other statute and available to the petitioner in relation to the same subject matter.

2. This article shall not be construed to confer jurisdiction on the court of the initiating or responding state in any pending or future action for divorce, legal separation or annulment.

> **Added** by Laws 1958, Ch. 146, eff. July 1, 1958; **repealed** by Laws 1997, Ch. 398, § 36, eff. Dec. 31, 1997.

§ 41-a.   Proceedings not to be stayed [*Repealed*].*

No pending and undetermined action for divorce, separation, annulment, or dissolution or habeas corpus custody proceeding instituted by the respondent shall operate to stay any proceeding under this act against such respondent for support of a dependent.

> **Added** by Laws 1958, Ch. 538, eff. Apr. 10, 1958, as § 8-a, of Ch. 807, Laws of 1949, uniform support of dependents law. Ch. 807 was repealed by Laws 1958, Ch. 146, § 2. § 8-a was saved from repeal by Laws 1958, Ch. 146, § 5, set forth under § 38-a *supra*. **Repealed** by Laws 1997, Ch. 398, § 36, eff. Dec. 31, 1997.

> * Section number assigned by McKinney's Consolidated Laws of New York, Domestic Relations Law, Book 14, adopted for this publication.

§ 42.   Uniformity of interpretation [*Repealed*].

This article shall be so interpreted and construed as to effectuate its general purpose to make uniform the law of the states which enact it.

> **Added** by Laws 1958, Ch. 146, eff. July 1, 1958; **repealed** by Laws 1997, Ch. 398, § 36, eff. Dec. 31, 1997.

§ 43.   Separability [*Repealed*].

If any part of this article or the application thereof to any person or circumstances is adjudged invalid by a court of competent jurisdiction, such judgment shall not affect or impair the validity of the remainder of such article or the application thereof to other persons and circumstances.

> **Added** by Laws 1958, Ch. 146, eff. July 1, 1958; **repealed** by Laws 1997, Ch. 398, § 36, eff. Dec. 31, 1997.

ARTICLE 4

CERTAIN RIGHTS AND LIABILITIES OF HUSBAND AND WIFE

DRL

SUMMARY OF ARTICLE

(Repealed and transferred sections noted under appropriate section number of text.)

§ 50. Property of married woman.

Property, real or personal, now owned by a married woman, or hereafter owned by a woman at the time of her marriage, or acquired by her as prescribed in this chapter, and the rents, issues, proceeds and profits thereof, shall continue to be her sole and separate property as if she were unmarried, and shall not be subject to her husband's control or disposal nor liable for his debts.

§ 51. Powers of married woman.

Repealed by Laws 1963, Ch. 576, § 19-101, and transferred to General Obligations Law §§ 3-301, 5-311, eff. Sept. 27, 1964.

§ 52. Insurance of married person's life.

The right of a married person to cause the life of his or her spouse or any other person to be insured and to dispose of any interest such married person may have in a policy of insurance on the life of the other spouse or of any other person shall be governed by the insurance law and by statutes and rules of law governing rights of a married person in respect to property and the acquisition, use, enjoyment and disposition thereof.

Amended by Laws 1957, Ch. 821; Laws 1980, Ch. 281, eff. July 19, 1980.

§ 53. Contracts in contemplation of marriage.

Repealed by Laws 1963, Ch. 576, § 19-101, and transferred to General Obligations Law § 3-303, eff. Sept. 27, 1964.

§ 54. Liability of husband for ante-nuptial debts.

Repealed by Laws 1963, Ch. 576, § 19-101, and transferred to the General Obligations Law § 3-307, eff. Sept. 27, 1964.

§ 55. Contract of married woman not to bind husband.

Repealed by Laws 1963, Ch. 576, § 19-101, and transferred to General Obligations Law § 3-305, eff. Sept. 27, 1964.

§ 56. Husband and wife may convey to each other or make partition.

Repealed by Laws 1963, Ch. 576, § 19-101, and transferred to General Obligations Law § 3-309, eff. Sept. 27, 1964.

§ 56-a. Marital relationship not to affect construction of instruments and transactions involving personal property.

Repealed by Laws 1963, Ch. 576, § 19-101, and transferred to General Obligations Law § 3-311, eff. Sept. 27, 1964.

§ 57. Right of action by or against married woman, and by husband or wife against the other, for torts.

Repealed by Laws 1963, Ch. 576, § 19-101, and transferred to General Obligations Law § 3-313, eff. Sept. 27, 1964.

§ 58. Pardon not to restore marital rights.

A pardon granted to a person sentenced to imprisonment for life within this state does not restore that person to the rights of a previous marriage or to the guardianship of a child, the issue of such a marriage.

§ 59. Compelling transfer of trust property.

Repealed by Laws 1976, Ch. 62, eff. Sept. 1, 1976.

§ 60. Married woman's right of action for wages.

Repealed by Laws 1963, Ch. 576, § 19-101, and transferred to General Obligations Law, § 3-315, eff. Sept. 27, 1964.

§ 61. Married woman's domicile.

The domicile of a married man or woman shall be established for all purposes without regard to sex.

Added by Laws 1929, Ch. 456; **amended** by Laws 1976, Ch. 62, eff. Sept. 1, 1976.

ARTICLE 5

THE CUSTODY AND WAGES OF CHILDREN

SUMMARY OF ARTICLE

(Repealed and transferred sections noted under appropriate section number of text.)

§ 70. Habeas corpus for child detained by parent.

(a) Where a minor child is residing within this state, either parent may apply to the supreme court for a writ of habeas corpus to have such minor child brought before such court; and on the return thereof, the court, on due consideration, may award the natural guardianship, charge and custody of such child to either parent for such time, under such regulations and restrictions, and with such provisions and directions, as the case may require, and may at any time thereafter vacate or modify such order. In all cases there shall be no prima facie right to the custody of the child in either parent, but the court shall determine solely what is for the best interest of the child, and what will best promote its welfare and happiness, and make award accordingly.

(b) Any order under this section which applies to rights of visitation with a child remanded or placed in the care of a person, official, agency or institution pursuant to article ten of the family court act or pursuant to an instrument approved under section three hundred fifty eight-a of the social services law, shall be enforceable pursuant to the provisions of part eight of article ten of such act, sections three hundred fifty-eight-a and three hundred eighty-four-a of the social services law and other applicable provisions of law against any person or official having care and custody, or temporary care and custody, of such child.

Amended by Laws 1923, Ch. 235; Laws 1964, Ch. 564, eff. Apr. 16, 1964; Laws 1988, Ch. 457, § 7, eff. Nov. 1, 1988.

§ 71. Special proceeding or habeas corpus to obtain visitation rights in respect to certain infant siblings.

Where circumstances show that conditions exist which equity would see fit to intervene, a brother or sister or, if he or she be a minor, a proper person on his or her behalf of a child, whether by half or whole blood, may apply to the supreme court by commencing a special proceeding or for a writ of habeas corpus to have such child brought before such court, or may apply to the family court pursuant to subdivision (b) of section six hundred fifty-one of the family court act; and on the return thereof, the court, by order, after due notice to the parent or any other person or party having the care, custody, and control of such child, to be given in such manner as the court shall prescribe, may make such directions as the best interest of the child may require, for visitation rights for such brother or sister in respect to such child.

Added by Laws 1989, Ch. 318, eff. July 10, 1989.

§ 72. Special proceeding or habeas corpus to obtain visitation rights or custody in respect to certain infant grandchildren.

1.   Where either or both of the parents of a minor child, residing within this state, is or are deceased, or where circumstances show that conditions exist which equity would see fit to intervene, a grandparent or the grandparents of such child may apply to the supreme court by commencing a special proceeding or for a writ of habeas corpus to have such child brought before such court, or may apply to the family court pursuant to subdivision (b) of section six hundred fifty-one of the family court act; and on the return thereof, the court, by order, after due notice to the parent or any other person or party having the care, custody, and control of such child, to be given in such manner as the court shall prescribe, may make such directions as the best interest of the child may require, for visitation rights for such grandparent or grandparents in respect to such child.

2.   (a) Where a grandparent or the grandparents of a minor child, residing within this state, can demonstrate to the satisfaction of the court the existence of extraordinary circumstances, such grandparent or grandparents of such child may apply to the supreme court by commencing a special proceeding or for a writ of habeas corpus to have such child brought before such court, or may apply to family court pursuant to subdivision (b) of section six hundred fifty-one of the family court act; and on the return thereof, the court, by order, after due notice to the parent or any other person or party having the care, custody, and control of such child, to be given in such manner as the court shall prescribe, may make such directions as the best interests of the child may require, for custody rights for such grandparent or grandparents in respect to such child. An extended disruption of custody, as such term is defined in this section, shall constitute an extraordinary circumstance.

(b)   For the purposes of this section "extended disruption of custody" shall include, but not be limited to, a prolonged separation of the respondent parent and the child for at least twenty-four continuous months during which the parent voluntarily relinquished care and control of the child and the child resided in the household of the petitioner grandparent or grandparents, provided, however, that the court may find that extraordinary circumstances exist should the prolonged separation have lasted for less than twenty-four months.

(c)   Nothing in this section shall limit the ability of parties to enter into consensual custody agreements absent the existence of extraordinary circumstances.

Added by Laws 1966, Ch. 631, eff. Sept. 1, 1966; **amended** by Laws 1975, Ch. 431, eff. July 1, 1975; Laws 1986, Ch. 252, eff. July 1, 1986; Laws 1988, Ch. 457, § 8, eff. Aug. 1, 1988; Laws 2003, Ch. 657, § 2, amending section title, renumbering opening paragraph to sub. 1 and adding sub. 2, par. (a), (b) and (c), eff. Jan. 5, 2004.

§ 72.   Payment of wages to minor; when valid.

Repealed by Laws 1963, Ch. 576, § 19-101, and transferred to General Obligations Law, § 3-109, eff. Sept. 27, 1964.

§ 73.   Legitimacy of children born by artificial insemination.

1.   Any child born to a married woman by means of artificial insemination performed by persons duly authorized to practice medicine and with the consent in writing of the woman and her husband, shall be deemed the legitimate, natural child of the husband and his wife for all purposes.

2.   The aforesaid written consent shall be executed and acknowledged by both the husband and wife and the physician who performs the technique shall certify that he had rendered the service.

Added by Laws 1974, Ch. 303, eff. May 7, 1974.

§ 74.   Judicial approval of certain contracts for services of infants; effect of approval; guardianship of savings.

Repealed by Laws 1963, Ch. 576, § 19-101, and transferred to General Obligations Law, § 3-105, eff. Sept. 27, 1964.

§ 74-a.   Certain contracts of parents or guardians respecting employment of infants not enforceable unless approved.

Repealed by Laws 1963, Ch. 576, § 19-101, and transferred to General Obligations Law, §§ 3-107, 1-203, eff. Sept. 27, 1964.

ARTICLE 5-A
UNIFORM CHILD CUSTODY JURISDICTION ACT

———

[Article 5-A was added by Laws 1977, Ch. 493, eff. Sept. 1, 1978, and is repealed by Laws 2001, Ch. 386, effective April 28, 2002.]

ARTICLE 5–A

UNIFORM CHILD CUSTODY JURISDICTION AND ENFORCEMENT ACT

———

[L. 2001, Ch. 386 repealed the former Article 5-A of the Domestic Relations Law and added the following new Article 5-A, which became effective April 28, 2002.]

SUMMARY OF ARTICLE

TITLE I: GENERAL PROVISIONS

§ 75.   Short title and statement of legislative intent.

1. This article may be cited as the "uniform child custody jurisdiction and enforcement act".

2. It is the intent of the legislature in enacting this article to provide an effective mechanism to obtain and enforce orders of custody and visitation across state lines and to do so in a manner that ensures that the safety of the children is paramount and that victims of domestic violence and child abuse are protected. It is further the intent of the legislature that this article be construed so as to ensure that custody and visitation by perpetrators of domestic violence or homicide of a parent, legal custodian, legal guardian, sibling, half-sibling or step-sibling of

a child is restricted pursuant to subdivision one-c of section two hundred forty of this chapter and section one thousand eighty-five of the family court act.

§ 75-a.   Definitions.

In this article:

1.   "Abandoned" means left without provision for reasonable and necessary care or supervision.

2.   "Child" means an individual who has not attained eighteen years of age.

3.   "Child custody determination" means a judgment, decree, or other order of a court providing for the legal custody, physical custody, or visitation with respect to a child. The term includes a permanent, temporary, initial, and modification order. The term does not include an order relating to child support or other monetary obligation of an individual.

4.   "Child custody proceeding" means a proceeding in which legal custody, physical custody, or visitation with respect to a child is an issue. The term includes a proceeding for divorce, separation, neglect, abuse, dependency, guardianship, paternity, termination of parental rights, and protection from domestic violence, in which the issue may appear. The term does not include a proceeding involving juvenile delinquency, person in need of supervision, contractual emancipation, or enforcement under title three of this article.

5.   "Commencement" means the filing of the first pleading in a proceeding.

6.   "Court" means an entity authorized under the law of a state to establish, enforce, or modify a child custody determination.

7.   "Home state" means the state in which a child lived with a parent or a person acting as a parent for at least six consecutive months immediately before the commencement of a child custody proceeding. In the case of a child less than six months of age, the term means the state in which the child lived from birth with any of the persons mentioned. A period of temporary absence of any of the mentioned persons is part of the period.

8.   "Initial determination" means the first child custody determination concerning a particular child.

9.   "Issuing court" means the court that makes a child custody determination for which enforcement is sought under this article.

10.   "Issuing state" means the state in which a child custody determination is made.

11.   "Modification" means a child custody determination that changes, replaces, supersedes, or is otherwise made after a previous determination concerning the same child, whether or not it is made by the court that made the previous determination.

12.   "Person" means an individual, corporation, business trust, estate, trust, partnership, limited liability company, association, joint venture, government,

governmental subdivision, agency or instrumentality, public corporation or any other legal or commercial entity.

13. "Person acting as a parent" means a person, other than a parent, who:

(a) has physical custody of the child or has had physical custody for a period of six consecutive months, including any temporary absence, within one year immediately before the commencement of a child custody proceeding; and

(b) has been awarded legal custody by a court or claims a right to legal custody under the law of this state.

14. "Physical custody" means the physical care and supervision of a child.

15. "State" means a state of the United States, the District of Columbia, Puerto Rico, the United States Virgin Islands, or any territory or insular possession subject to the jurisdiction of the United States.

16. "Tribe" means an Indian tribe or band, or Alaskan Native village, which is recognized by federal law or formally acknowledged by a state.

17. "Warrant" means an order issued by a court authorizing law enforcement officers to take physical custody of a child.

18. "Law enforcement officer" means a police officer as defined in subdivision thirty-four of section 1.20 of the criminal procedure law.

§ 75-b. Proceedings governed by other laws.

This article does not govern an adoption proceeding or a proceeding pertaining to the authorization of emergency medical care for a child.

§ 75-c. Application to Indian tribes.

1. A child custody proceeding that pertains to an Indian child as defined in the Indian Child Welfare Act, 25 U.S.C. § 1901 et seq., is not subject to this article to the extent that it is governed by the Indian Child Welfare Act.

2. A court of this state shall treat a tribe as if it were a state of the United States for the purpose of applying this title and title two of this article.

3. A child custody determination made by a tribe under factual circumstances in substantial conformity with the jurisdictional standards of this article must be recognized and enforced under title three of this article.

§ 75-d. International application of article.

1. A court of this state shall treat a foreign country as if it were a state of the United States for the purpose of applying this title and title two of this article.

2. Except as otherwise provided in subdivision three of this section, a child custody determination made in a foreign country under factual circumstances in substantial conformity with the jurisdictional standards of this article must be recognized and enforced under title three of this article.

3. A court of this state need not apply this article if the child custody law of a foreign country as written or as applied violates fundamental principles of human rights.

§ 75-e. Effect of child custody determination.

A child custody determination made by a court of this state that had jurisdiction under this article binds all persons who have been served in accordance with the laws of this state or notified in accordance with section seventy-five-g of this title or who have submitted to the jurisdiction of the court, and who have been given an opportunity to be heard. As to those persons, the determination is conclusive as to all decided issues of law and fact except to the extent the determination is modified or except to the extent that enforcement of an order would violate subdivision one-c of section two hundred forty of this chapter or section one thousand eighty-five of the family court act.

§ 75-f. Priority.

If a question of existence or exercise of jurisdiction under this article is raised in a child custody proceeding, the question, upon request of a party, child or law guardian must be given priority on the calendar and handled expeditiously.

§ 75-g Notice to persons outside state.

1. Notice required for the exercise of jurisdiction when a person is outside this state shall be given in a manner prescribed by the law of this state for service of process, as provided in paragraph (a), (b) or (c) of this subdivision, or by the law of the state in which the service is made, as provided in paragraph (d) of this subdivision. Notice must be given in a manner reasonably calculated to give actual notice. If a person cannot be served with notice within the state, the court shall require that such person be served in a manner reasonably calculated to give actual notice, as follows:

(a) by personal delivery outside the state in the manner prescribed by section three hundred thirteen of the civil practice law and rules; or

(b) by any form of mail requesting a receipt; or

(c) in such manner as the court, upon motion, directs, including publication, if service is impracticable under paragraph (a) or (b) of this subdivision; or

(d) in such manner as prescribed by the law of the state in which service is made.

2. Proof of service outside the state shall be by affidavit of the individual who made the service, or in the manner prescribed by the order pursuant to which service is made. If service is made by mail, proof may be by a receipt signed by the addressee or other evidence of delivery to the addressee. Proof of service may also be in the manner prescribed by the law of the state in which the service is made.

3. Notice is not required for the exercise of jurisdiction with respect to a person who submits to the jurisdiction of the court.

Added by Laws 1974, Ch. 303, eff. May 7, 1974; Laws 2006, ch. 184, §1, eff. July 26, 2006.

§ 75-h. Appearance and limited immunity.

1. A party to a child custody proceeding, including a modification proceeding, or a petitioner or respondent in a proceeding to enforce or register a child custody determination, is not subject to personal jurisdiction in this state for another proceeding or purpose solely by reason of having participated, or of having been physically present for the purpose of participating, in the proceeding.

2. A person who is subject to personal jurisdiction in this state on a basis other than physical presence is not immune from service of process in this state. A party present in this state who is subject to the jurisdiction of another state is not immune from service of process allowable under the laws of that state.

3. The immunity granted by subdivision one of this section does not extend to civil litigation based on acts unrelated to the participation in a proceeding under this article committed by an individual while present in this state.

Added by Laws 2001, Ch. 386, §1, eff. April 28, 2002.

§ 75-i. Communication between courts.

1. A court of this state may communicate and, pursuant to subdivision four of section seventy-six-c, subdivision two of section seventy-six-e and section seventy-seven-f of this article, must communicate, with a court in another state concerning a proceeding arising under this article.

2. The court may allow the parties to participate in the communication. If the parties are not able to participate in the communication, they must be given the opportunity to present facts and legal arguments before a decision on jurisdiction is made.

3. Communication between courts on schedules, calendars, court records, and similar matters may occur without informing the parties. A record need not be made of the communication.

4. Except as otherwise provided in subdivision three of this section, a record must be made of a communication under this section. The parties must be informed promptly of the communication and granted access to the record.

5. For the purposes of this section, "record" means information that is inscribed on a tangible medium or that is stored in an electronic or other medium and is retrievable in perceivable form.

Amended by Laws 2006, ch. 184, §2, eff. July 26, 2006.

§ 75-j   Taking testimony in another state.

1. In addition to other procedures available to a party, a party to a child custody proceeding may offer testimony of witnesses who are located in another state, including testimony of the parties and the child, by deposition or other means allowable in this state for testimony taken in another state. The court on its own motion may order that the testimony of a person be taken in another state and may prescribe the manner in which and the terms upon which the testimony is taken.

2. A court of this state may permit an individual residing in another state to be deposed or to testify by telephone, audiovisual means, or other electronic means before a designated court or at another location in that state. A court of this state shall cooperate with courts of other states in designating an appropriate location for the deposition or testimony and the procedures to be followed by the persons taking such deposition or testimony. Any such testimony or deposition shall be recorded and preserved for transcription.

3. Documentary evidence transmitted from another state to a court of this state by technological means that do not produce an original writing may not be excluded from evidence on an objection based on the means of transmission.

Amended by Laws 2006, ch. 184, §3, eff. July 26, 2006.

§ 75-k.   Cooperation between courts; preservation of records.

1. A court of this state may request the appropriate court of another state to:

(a)   hold an evidentiary hearing;

(b).   order a person to produce or give evidence pursuant to procedures of that state;

(c)   order that an evaluation be made with respect to the custody of a child involved in a pending proceeding;

(d)   forward to the court of this state a certified copy of the transcript of the record of the hearing, the evidence otherwise presented, and any evaluation prepared in compliance with the request; and

(e)   order a party to a child custody proceeding or any person having physical custody of the child to appear in the proceeding with or without the child.

2. Upon the request of a court of another state, a court of this state may hold a hearing or enter an order described in subdivision one of this section.

3. Travel and other necessary and reasonable expenses incurred under subdivisions one and two of this section may be assessed against the parties according to the law of this state.

4. A court of this state shall preserve the pleadings, orders, decrees, records of hearings, evaluations, and other pertinent records with respect to a child custody proceeding at least until the child attains eighteen years of age. Upon

appropriate request by a court or law enforcement official of another state, the court shall forward a certified copy of those records.

TITLE II: JURISDICTION

JURISDICTION

§ 76. Initial child custody jurisdiction.

1. Except as otherwise provided in section seventy-six-c of this title, a court of this state has jurisdiction to make an initial child custody determination only if:

(a) this state is the home state of the child on the date of the commencement of the proceeding, or was the home state of the child within six months before the commencement of the proceeding and the child is absent from this state but a parent or person acting as a parent continues to live in this state;

(b) a court of another state does not have jurisdiction under paragraph (a) of this subdivision, or a court of the home state of the child has declined to exercise jurisdiction on the ground that this state is the more appropriate forum under section seventy-six-f or seventy-six-g of this title, and:

(i) the child and the child's parents, or the child and at least one parent or a person acting as a parent, have a significant connection with this state other than mere physical presence; and

(ii) substantial evidence is available in this state concerning the child's care, protection, training, and personal relationships;

(c) all courts having jurisdiction under paragraph (a) or (b) of this subdivision have declined to exercise jurisdiction on the ground that a court of this state is the more appropriate forum to determine the custody of the child under section seventy-six-f or seventy-six-g of this title; or

(d) no court of any other state would have jurisdiction under the criteria specified in paragraph (a), (b) or (c) of this subdivision.

2. Subdivision one of this section is the exclusive jurisdictional basis for making a child custody determination by a court of this state.

3. Physical presence of, or personal jurisdiction over, a party or a child is not necessary or sufficient to make a child custody determination.

§ 76-a.   Exclusive, continuing jurisdiction.

1.   Except as otherwise provided in section seventy-six-c of this title, a court of this state which has made a child custody determination consistent with section seventy-six or seventy-six-b of this title has exclusive, continuing jurisdiction over the determination until:

(a)   a court of this state determines that neither the child, the child and one parent, nor the child and a person acting as a parent have a significant connection with this state and that substantial evidence is no longer available in this state concerning the child's care, protection, training, and personal relationships; or

(b)   a court of this state or a court of another state determines that the child, the child's parents, and any person acting as a parent do not presently reside in this state.

2.   A court of this state which has made a child custody determination and does not have exclusive, continuing jurisdiction under this section may modify that determination only if it has jurisdiction to make an initial determination under section seventy-six of this title.

§ 76-b.   Jurisdiction to modify determination.

Except as otherwise provided in section seventy-six-c of this title, a court of this state may not modify a child custody determination made by a court of another state unless a court of this state has jurisdiction to make an initial determination under paragraph (a) or (b) of subdivision one of section seventy-six of this title and:

1.   The court of the other state determines it no longer has exclusive, continuing jurisdiction under section seventy-six-a of this title or that a court of this state would be a more convenient forum under section seventy-six-f of this title; or

2.   A court of this state or a court of the other state determines that the child, the child's parents, and any person acting as a parent do not presently reside in the other state.

§ 76-c.   Temporary emergency jurisdiction.

1.   A court of this state has temporary emergency jurisdiction if the child is present in this state and the child has been abandoned or it is necessary in an emergency to protect the child, a sibling or parent of the child.

2.   If there is no previous child custody determination that is entitled to be enforced under this article and a child custody proceeding has not been commenced in a court of a state having jurisdiction under sections seventy-six through seventy-six-b of this title, a child custody determination made under this section remains in effect until an order is obtained from a court of a state having jurisdiction under sections seventy-six through seventy-six-b of this title. Where the child who is the subject of a child custody determination under this section

is in imminent risk of harm, any order issued under this section shall remain in effect until a court of a state having jurisdiction under sections seventy-six through seventy-six-b of this title has taken steps to assure the protection of the child. If a child custody proceeding has not been or is not commenced in a court of a state having jurisdiction under sections seventy-six through seventy-six-b of this title, a child custody determination made under this section becomes a final determination, if it so provides and this state becomes the home state of the child.

3. If there is a previous child custody determination that is entitled to be enforced under this article, or a child custody proceeding has been commenced in a court of a state having jurisdiction under sections seventy-six through seventy-six-b of this title, any order issued by a court of this state under this section must specify in the order a period that the court considers adequate to allow the person seeking an order to obtain an order from the state having jurisdiction under sections seventy-six through seventy-six-b of this title. The order issued in this state remains in effect until an order is obtained from the other state within the period specified or the period expires, provided, however, that where the child who is the subject of a child custody determination under this section is in imminent risk of harm, any order issued under this section shall remain in effect until a court of a state having jurisdiction under sections seventy-six through seventy-six-b of this title has taken steps to assure the protection of the child.

4. A court of this state which has been asked to make a child custody determination under this section, upon being informed that a child custody proceeding has been commenced in, or a child custody determination has been made by, a court of a state having jurisdiction under sections seventy-six through seventy-six-b of this title, shall immediately communicate with the other court. A court of this state which is exercising jurisdiction pursuant to sections seventy-six through seventy-six-b of this title, upon being informed that a child custody proceeding has been commenced in, or a child custody determination has been made by, a court of another state under a statute similar to this section shall immediately communicate with the court of that state to resolve the emergency, protect the safety of the parties and the child, and determine a period for the duration of the temporary order.

§ 76-d. Notice; opportunity to be heard; joinder.

1. Before a child custody determination is made under this article, notice and an opportunity to be heard in accordance with the standards of section seventy-five-g of this article must be given to all persons entitled to notice under the law of this state as in child custody proceedings between residents of this state, any parent whose parental rights have not been previously terminated, and any person having physical custody of the child.

2. This article does not govern the enforceability of a child custody determination made without notice or an opportunity to be heard.

3. The obligation to join a party and the right to intervene as a party in a child custody proceeding under this article are governed by the laws of this state as in child custody proceedings between residents of this state.

§ 76-e. Simultaneous proceedings.

1. Except as otherwise provided in section seventy-six-c of this title, a court of this state may not exercise its jurisdiction under this title if, at the time of the commencement of the proceeding, a proceeding concerning the custody of the child has been commenced in a court of another state having jurisdiction substantially in conformity with this article, unless the proceeding has been terminated or is stayed by the court of the other state because a court of this state is a more convenient forum under section seventy-six-f of this title.

2. Except as otherwise provided in section seventy-six-c of this title, a court of this state, before hearing a child custody proceeding, shall examine the court documents and other information supplied by the parties pursuant to section seventy-six-h of this title. If the court determines that a child custody proceeding has been commenced in a court in another state having jurisdiction substantially in accordance with this article, the court of this state shall stay its proceeding and communicate with the court of the other state. If the court of the state having jurisdiction substantially in accordance with this article does not determine that the court of this state is a more appropriate forum, the court of this state shall dismiss the proceeding.

3. In a proceeding to modify a child custody determination, a court of this state shall determine whether a proceeding to enforce the determination has been commenced in another state. If a proceeding to enforce a child custody determination has been commenced in another state, the court may:

(a) stay the proceeding for modification pending the entry of an order of a court of the other state enforcing, staying, denying, or dismissing the proceeding for enforcement:

(b) enjoin the parties from continuing with the proceeding for enforcement; or

(c) proceed with the modification under conditions it considers appropriate.

§ 76-f. Inconvenient forum.

1. A court of this state which has jurisdiction under this article to make a child custody determination may decline to exercise its jurisdiction at any time if it determines that it is an inconvenient forum under the circumstances and that a court of another state is a more appropriate forum. The issue of inconvenient forum may be raised upon motion of a party, the child or the law guardian, or upon the court's own motion, or request of another court.

2. Before determining whether it is an inconvenient forum, a court of this state shall consider whether it is appropriate for a court of another state to exercise

jurisdiction. For this purpose, the court shall allow the parties to submit information and shall consider all relevant factors, including:

(a) whether domestic violence or mistreatment or abuse of a child or sibling has occurred and is likely to continue in the future and which state could best protect the parties and the child;

(b) the length of time the child has resided outside this state;

(c) the distance between the court in this state and the court in the state that would assume jurisdiction;

(d) the relative financial circumstances of the parties;

(e) any agreement of the parties as to which state should assume jurisdiction;

(f) the nature and location of the evidence required to resolve the pending litigation, including testimony of the child;

(g) the ability of the court of each state to decide the issue expeditiously and the procedures necessary to present the evidence; and

(h) the familiarity of the court of each state with the facts and issues in the pending litigation.

3. If a court of this state determines that it is an inconvenient forum and that a court of another state is a more appropriate forum, it shall stay the proceedings upon condition that a child custody proceeding be promptly commenced in another designated state and may impose any other condition the court considers just and proper.

4. A court of this state may decline to exercise its jurisdiction under this article if a child custody determination is incidental to an action for divorce or another proceeding while still retaining jurisdiction over the divorce or other proceeding.

§ 76-g. Jurisdiction declined by reason of conduct.

1. Except as otherwise provided in section seventy-six-c of this title or by other law of this state, if a court of this state has jurisdiction under this article because a person seeking to invoke its jurisdiction has engaged in unjustifiable conduct, the court shall decline to exercise its jurisdiction unless:

(a) the parents and all persons acting as parents have acquiesced in the exercise of jurisdiction;

(b) a court of the state otherwise having jurisdiction under sections seventy-six through seventy-six-b of this title determines that this state is a more appropriate forum under section seventy-six-f of this title; or

(c) no court of any other state would have jurisdiction under the criteria specified in sections seventy-six through seventy-six-b of this title.

2. If a court of this state declines to exercise its jurisdiction pursuant to subdivision one of this section, it may fashion an appropriate remedy to ensure

4. If a party to a child custody proceeding who is outside this state is directed to appear under subdivision two of this section or desires to appear personally before the court with or without the child, the court may require another party to pay reasonable and necessary travel and other expenses of the party so appearing and of the child.

TITLE III: ENFORCEMENT

§ 77. Definitions.

As used in this title:

1. "Petitioner" means a person who seeks enforcement of an order for return of a child under the Hague Convention on the Civil Aspects of International Child Abduction or enforcement of a child custody determination.

2. "Respondent" means a person against whom a proceeding has been commenced for enforcement of an order for return of a child under the Hague Convention on the Civil Aspects of International Child Abduction or enforcement of a child custody determination.

§ 77-a. Enforcement under Hague Convention.

Under this act, a court of this state may enforce an order for the return of the child made under the Hague Convention on the Civil Aspects of International Child Abduction as if it were a child custody determination.

§ 77-b. Duty to enforce.

1. A court of this state shall recognize and enforce a child custody determination of a court of another state if the latter court exercised jurisdiction in substantial conformity with this article or the determination was made under

factual circumstances meeting the jurisdictional standards of this article and the determination has not been modified in accordance with this article; provided, however, that recognition and enforcement of the determination would not violate subdivision one-c of section two hundred forty of this chapter or section one thousand eighty-five of the family court act.

2.   A court of this state may utilize any remedy available under other law of this state to enforce a child custody determination made by a court of another state. The remedies provided in this title are cumulative and do not affect the availability of other remedies to enforce a child custody determination.

DRL

§ 77-c.   Temporary visitation.

1.   A court of this state which does not have jurisdiction to modify a child custody determination, may, if consistent with subdivision one-c of section two hundred forty of this chapter or section one thousand eighty-five of the family court act, issue a temporary order enforcing:

(a)   a visitation schedule made by a court of another state; or

(b).   the visitation provisions of a child custody determination of another state that does not provide for a specific visitation schedule.

2.   If a court of this state makes an order under paragraph (b) of subdivision one of this section, it shall specify in the order a period that it considers adequate to allow the petitioner to obtain an order from a court having jurisdiction under the criteria specified in title two of this article. The order remains in effect until an order is obtained from the other court or the period expires.

§ 77-d.   Registration of child custody determination.

1.   A child custody determination issued by a court of another state may be registered in this state, with or without a simultaneous request for enforcement, by sending to the appropriate court in this state;

(a)   a letter or other document requesting registration;

(b)   two copies, including one certified copy, of the determination sought to be registered, and a statement under penalty of perjury that to the best of the knowledge and belief of the person seeking registration the order has not been modified; and

(c)   except as otherwise provided in section seventy-six-h of this article, the name and address of the person seeking registration and any parent or person acting as a parent who has been awarded custody or visitation in the child custody determination sought to be registered.

2.   On receipt of the documents required by subdivision one of this section, the registering court shall:

(a)   cause the determination to be filed as a foreign judgment, together with one copy of any accompanying documents and information, regardless of their form; and

(b)   serve notice upon the persons named pursuant to subdivision one of this section and provide them with an opportunity to contest the registration in accordance with this section.

3.   The notice required by paragraph (b) of subdivision two of this section must state that:

(a)   a registered determination is enforceable as of the date of the registration in the same manner as a determination issued by a court of this state;

(b)   a hearing to contest the validity of the registered determination must be requested within twenty days after service of notice; and

(c)   failure to contest the registration will result in confirmation of the child custody determination and preclude further contest of that determination with respect to any matter that could have been asserted.

4.   A person seeking to contest the validity of a registered order must request a hearing within twenty days after service of the notice. At that hearing, the court shall confirm the registered order unless the person contesting registration establishes that:

(a)   the issuing court did not have jurisdiction under title two of this article;

(b)   the child custody determination sought to be registered has been vacated, stayed, or modified by a court having jurisdiction to do so under title two of this article; or

(c)   the person contesting registration was entitled to notice, but notice was not given in accordance with the standards of section seventy-five-g of this article, in the proceedings before the court that issued the order for which registration is sought.

5.   If a timely request for a hearing to contest the validity of the registration is not made, the registration is confirmed as a matter of law and the person requesting registration and all persons served must be notified of the confirmation.

6.   Confirmation of a registered order, whether by operation of law or after notice and hearing, precludes further contest of the order with respect to any matter that could have been asserted at the time of registration.

§ 77-e.   Enforcement of registered determination.

1.   A court of this state may grant any relief normally available under the laws of this state to enforce a registered child custody determination made by a court of another state.

2.   A court of this state shall recognize and enforce, but may not modify, except in accordance with title two of this article, a registered child custody determination of a court of another state; provided, however, that recognition and enforcement of the determination would not violate subdivision one-c of section two hundred forty of this chapter or section one thousand eighty-five of the family court act.

§ 77-f. Simultaneous proceedings.

If a proceeding for enforcement under this title is commenced in a court of this state and the court determines that a proceeding to modify the determination is pending in a court of another state having jurisdiction to modify the determination under title two of this article, the enforcing court shall immediately communicate with the modifying court. The proceeding for enforcement continues unless the enforcing court, after consultation with the modifying court, stays or dismisses the proceeding.

§ 77-g. Expedited enforcement of child custody determination.

1.   A petition under this title must be verified. Certified copies of all orders sought to be enforced and of any order confirming registration must be attached to the petition. A copy of a certified copy of an order may be attached instead of the original.

2.   A petition for enforcement of a child custody determination must state:

(a).   whether the court that issued the determination identified the jurisdictional basis it relied upon in exercising jurisdiction and, if so, what the basis was;

(b)   whether the determination for which enforcement is sought has been vacated, stayed, or modified by a court whose decision must be enforced under this article and, if so, identify the court, the case number, and the nature of the proceeding;

(c)   whether any proceeding has been commenced that could affect the current proceeding, including proceedings relating to domestic violence, child abuse or neglect, protective orders, termination of parental rights, and adoptions and, if so, identify the court, the case number, and the nature of the proceeding;

(d)   the present physical address of the child and the respondent, if known;

(e)   whether relief in addition to the immediate physical custody of the child and attorney's fees is sought, including a request for assistance from law enforcement officials and, if so, the relief sought; and

(f)   if the child custody determination has been registered and confirmed under section seventy-seven-d of this title, the date and place of registration.

3.   Upon the filing of a petition, the court shall issue an order directing the respondent to appear in person with or without the child at a hearing within three court days and may enter any order necessary to ensure the safety of the parties and the child. The hearing must be held not more than three court days after the filing of the petition, provided that the petition has been served not less than twenty-four hours prior to the hearing. Service may be by any means directed by the court pursuant to section three hundred eight of the civil practice law and rules. The court may extend the date of the hearing briefly for good cause shown or upon the request of the petitioner.

4.   An order issued under subdivision three of this section must state the time and place of the hearing and advise the respondent that at the hearing the court

will order that the petitioner may take immediate physical custody of the child and the payment of fees, costs, and expenses under section seventy-seven-k of this title, and may schedule a hearing to determine whether further relief is appropriate, unless the respondent appears and establishes that:

(a)   the child custody determination has not been registered and confirmed under section seventy-seven-d of this title and that:

(1)   the issuing court did not have jurisdiction under title two of this article;

(2)   the child custody determination for which enforcement is sought has been vacated, stayed, or modified by a court having jurisdiction to do so under title two of this article or that enforcement would violate subdivision one-c of section two hundred forty of this chapter or section one thousand eighty-five of the family court act;

(3)   the respondent was entitled to notice, but notice was not given in accordance with the standards of section seventy-five-g of this article, in the proceedings before the court that issued the order for which enforcement is sought; or

(b)   the child custody determination for which enforcement is sought was registered and confirmed under section seventy-seven-c of this title, but has been vacated, stayed, or modified by a court of a state having jurisdiction to do so under title two of this article.

§ 77-h.   Service of petition and order.

Except as otherwise provided in section seventy-seven-j of this title, the petition and order must be served, by any method authorized by the law of this state, upon respondent and any person who has physical custody of the child. Service may be made outside the state in the manner prescribed by section seventy-five-g of this article.

Amended by Laws 2006, ch. 184, §4, eff. July 26, 2006.

§ 77-i.   Hearing and order.

1.   Unless the court issues a temporary emergency order pursuant to section seventy-six-c of this article, upon a finding that a petitioner is entitled to immediate physical custody of the child, the court shall order that the petitioner may take immediate physical custody of the child unless the respondent establishes that:

(a)   the child custody determination has not been registered and confirmed under section seventy-seven-d of this title and that:

(i)   the issuing court did not have jurisdiction under title two of this article;

(ii)   the child custody determination for which enforcement is sought has been vacated, stayed, or modified by a court of a state having jurisdiction to do so under title two of this article or enforcement of the determination would violate subdivision one-c of section two hundred forty of this chapter or section one thousand eighty-five of the family court act; or

(iii) the respondent was entitled to notice, but notice was not given in accordance with the standards of section seventy-five-g of this article, in the proceedings before the court that issued the order for which enforcement is sought; or

(b) the child custody determination for which enforcement is sought was registered and confirmed under section seventy-seven-d of this title but has been vacated, stayed, or modified by a court of a state having jurisdiction to do so under title two of this article.

2. The court shall award the fees, costs, and expenses authorized under section seventy-seven-k of this title and may grant additional relief, including a request for the assistance of law enforcement officials, and set a further hearing to determine whether additional relief is appropriate.

3. If a party called to testify refuses to answer on the ground that the testimony may be self-incriminating, the court may draw an adverse inference from the refusal.

4. A privilege against disclosure of communications between spouses and a defense of immunity based on the relationship of husband and wife or parent and child may not be invoked in a proceeding under this act.

§ 77-j. Warrant to take physical custody of child.

1. Upon the filing of a petition seeking enforcement of a child custody determination, the petitioner may file a verified application for the issuance of a warrant to take physical custody of the child if the child is at imminent risk of suffering serious physical harm or of removal from this state.

2. If the court, upon the testimony of the petitioner or other witness, finds that the child is likely to suffer imminent serious physical harm or to be removed from this state, it may issue a warrant to take physical custody of the child. Except in extraordinary circumstances, the petition must be heard on the next court day after the warrant is executed. Any adjournment for extraordinary circumstances shall be for not more than three court days. The application for the warrant must include the statements required by subdivision two of section seventy-seven-g of this title.

3. A warrant to take physical custody of a child must:

(a) recite the facts upon which a conclusion of imminent serious physical harm or removal from the jurisdiction is based;

(b) direct law enforcement officers to take physical custody of the child immediately and deliver the child to the petitioner or, where necessary, to act jointly with the local child protective service to take immediate steps to protect the child; and

(c) provide for the placement of the child pending final relief.

4.   The respondent must be served with the petition, warrant, and order immediately after the child is taken into physical custody.

5.   A warrant to take physical custody of a child is enforceable throughout this state. If the court finds on the basis of the testimony of the petitioner or other witness that a less intrusive remedy is not effective, it may authorize law enforcement officers to enter private property in order to execute the warrant and take physical custody of the child. If required by exigent circumstances of the case and necessary to the protection of the child, the court may authorize law enforcement officers to make a forcible entry at any hour.

6.   The court may impose conditions upon placement of a child to ensure the appearance of the child and the child's custodian.

§ 77-k.   Costs, fees and expenses.

1.   The court shall award the prevailing party, including a state, necessary and reasonable expenses incurred by or on behalf of the party, including costs, communication expenses, attorney's fees, investigative fees, expenses for witnesses, travel expenses, and child care during the course of the proceedings, unless the party from whom fees or expenses are sought establishes that the award would be inappropriate. No fees, costs or expenses shall be assessed against a party who is fleeing an incident of domestic violence or mistreatment or abuse of a child or sibling, unless the court is convinced by a preponderance of evidence that such assessment would be clearly appropriate.

2.   The court may not assess fees, costs, or expenses against a state unless authorized by law other than this article.

§ 77-l.   Recognition and enforcement.

A court of this state shall accord full faith and credit to an order issued by another state and consistent with this article which enforces a child custody determination by a court of another state unless the order has been vacated, stayed, or modified by a court having jurisdiction to do so under title two of this article, unless recognition and enforcement would violate subdivision one-c of section two hundred forty of this chapter or section one thousand eighty-five of the family court act.

§ 77-m.   Appeals.

An appeal may be taken from a final order in a proceeding under this title in accordance with article fifty-five of the civil practice law and rules and article eleven of the family court act and may be granted a preference in the discretion of the court to which the appeal is taken. Unless the court enters a temporary emergency order under section seventy-six-c of this article, the enforcing court may not stay an order enforcing a child custody determination pending appeal.

§ 77-n.　Role of prosecutor or public official.

1.　In a case arising under this article or involving the Hague Convention on the Civil Aspects of International Child Abduction, the prosecutor or other appropriate public official may take any lawful action, including resort to a proceeding under this title or any other available civil proceeding to locate a child, obtain the return of a child, or enforce a child custody determination if there is:

　(a)　an existing child custody determination;

　(b)　a request to do so from a court in a pending child custody proceeding;

　(c)　a reasonable belief that a criminal statute has been violated; or

　(d)　a reasonable belief that the child has been wrongfully removed or retained in violation of the Hague Convention on the Civil Aspects of International Child Abduction.

2.　A prosecutor or appropriate public official acting under this section acts on behalf of the state or local government entity and may not represent any private party.

§ 77-o.　Role of law enforcement.

At the request of a prosecutor or other appropriate public official acting under section seventy-seven-n of this title, a law enforcement officer, as defined in subdivision thirty-four of section 1.20 of the criminal procedure law, may take any lawful action reasonably necessary to locate a child or a party and assist a prosecutor or appropriate public official with responsibilities under section seventy-seven-n of this title.

§ 77-p.　Costs and expenses.

If the respondent is not the prevailing party, the court may assess against the respondent all direct expenses and costs incurred by the prosecutor or other appropriate public official and law enforcement officers under section seventy-seven-n or seventy-seven-o of this title.

TITLE IV: MISCELLANEOUS PROVISIONS

§ 78.　Application and construction.

In applying and construing this article, consideration must be given to the need to promote uniformity of the law with respect to its subject matter among states that enact it.

§ 78-a.　Severability clause.

If any provision of this article or its application to any person or circumstance is held invalid, the invalidity does not affect other provisions or applications of this article which can be given effect without the invalid provision or application, and to this end the provisions of this article are severable.

ARTICLE 6

GUARDIANS

SUMMARY OF ARTICLE

(Repealed and transferred sections noted under appropriate section number of text.)

§ 80. Guardians in socage.

Where a minor for whom a general guardian of the property has not been appointed shall acquire real property, the guardianship of his property with the rights, powers and duties of a guardian in socage belongs: (1) to the parents jointly, or, if they be separated, or divorced, to the parent who has been given the custody of the minor by a decree of court, or in the absence of such a decree, to the parent having the actual custody of the minor; (2) if one of the parents be dead, to the sole surviving parent; (3) if there be no father or mother, to the nearest and eldest relative of full age, not under any legal incapacity.

The rights and authority of every such guardian shall be superseded by a testamentary or other guardian appointed in pursuance of this article or in pursuance of article ten of the surrogates court act [SCPA Art. 17].

Amended by Laws 1924, Ch. 439; Laws 1925, Ch. 44, eff. Feb. 24, 1925.

§ 81. Appointment of guardians by parent.

A married woman is a joint guardian of her children with her husband, with equal powers, rights and duties in regard to them. Upon the death of either father or mother, the surviving parent, whether of full age or a minor, of a child likely to be born, or of any living child under the age of eighteen years and unmarried, may, by deed or last will, duly executed, dispose of the custody and tuition of such child during its minority or for any less time, to any person or persons. Such surviving parent may appoint a guardian or guardians of the person and of the property of the infant and in making such appointment shall not be limited to the appointment of the same person or persons in both capacities. Either the father or mother may in the lifetime of them both, by last will duly executed, appoint the other the guardian of the person and property of such child, during its minority. Either the father or mother may in the lifetime of them both by last will duly executed, and with the written consent of the other duly acknowledged, appoint the other and a third person to be the guardians of the person and property of such child during its minority, and in making such appointment shall not be limited to the appointment of the same person or persons in both capacities. Such consent must have as part thereof a sworn statement that the consenting parent in so consenting, is motivated solely by the welfare of the child or children, the guardianship of whom is the subject of such consent, and that such consenting parent has not received and will not receive any consideration for such consent, and such consent may be revoked by such consenting parent at any time prior to the death of the other, by filing in the office of the county clerk of the county in which said other then resides, a written revocation of such consent, subscribed and acknowledged by the person so revoking, with proof of service of a copy thereof on such other parent in the manner provided for service of a summons. An appointment of a guardian of the person and property of an infant made duly executed last will of his father or mother shall be valid and effective if at the time the will is admitted to probate the other parent shall have died or the surviving parent be an adjudicated incompetent. If both parents die under circumstances which render it difficult or impossible to determine which of them died first and both of them left last wills appointing the same person as guardian, the appointment shall be valid and effective. If both parents die under circumstances which render it difficult or impossible to determine which of them died first, leaving last wills appointing different persons as guardians, the surrogate's court shall determine which of the appointments will best serve the welfare of the child and issue letters of guardianship accordingly. If at any time during the minority of the infant the surviving parent becomes competent to serve as guardian, he may apply to the court which issued letters of guardianship to the guardian appointed by will for a decree revoking such letters and the court shall on such application make such order or decree as justice requires. A person appointed guardian in pursuance of this section shall not exercise the power of authority thereof unless such will is admitted to probate, or such deed executed and recorded as provided by SCPA 1710.

Amended by Laws 1925, Ch. 67; Laws 1935, Ch. 597; Laws 1940, Ch. 825; Laws 1949, Ch. 251; Laws 1959, Ch. 31; Laws 1962, Ch. 313; Laws 1966, Ch. 961; Laws 1974, Ch. 920, eff. Sept. 1, 1974.

§ 82. Powers and duties of such guardians.

Every such disposition, from the time it takes effect, shall vest in the person to whom made, if he accepts the appointment, all the rights and powers, and subject him to all the duties and obligations of a guardian of such minor, and shall be valid and effectual against every other person claiming the custody and tuition of such minor, as guardian in socage or otherwise. He may take the custody and charge of the tuition of such minor, and may maintain all proper actions for the wrongful taking or detention of the minor, and shall recover damages in such actions for the benefit of his ward. He shall also take the custody and management of the personal estate of such minor and the profits of his real estate, during the time for which such disposition shall have been made, and may bring such actions in relation thereto as a guardian in socage might by law.

§ 83. Duties and liabilities of all general guardians.

A general guardian or guardian in socage shall safely keep the property of his ward that shall come into his custody, and shall not make or suffer any waste, sale or destruction of such property or inheritance, but shall keep in repair and maintain the houses, gardens and other appurtenances to the lands of his ward, by and with the issues and profits thereof, or with such other moneys belonging to his ward as shall be in his possession; and shall deliver the same to his ward, when he comes to full age, in at least as good condition as such guardian received the same, inevitable decay and injury only excepted; and shall answer to his ward for the issues and profits of the real estate, received by him, by a lawful account, to be settled before any court, judge or surrogate having authority to settle the accounts of general and testamentary guardians; and any order, judgment or decree in any action or proceeding to settle such accounts may be enforced to the same extent, and in like manner as in the case of general and testamentary guardians. If any guardian shall make or suffer any waste, sale or destruction of the inheritance of his ward, he shall lose the custody of the same, and of such ward, and shall be liable to the ward for any damage caused thereby.

Amended by Laws 1944, Ch. 287, eff. Mar. 23, 1944.

§ 84. Guardianship of married minor.

The lawful marriage of a person before he or she attains majority terminates a general guardianship with respect to his or her person, but not with respect to his or her property.

Amended by Laws 1976, Ch. 62, eff. Sept. 1, 1976.

§ 85. Investment of trust funds by guardian.

A guardian holding funds for investment has the powers provided by section twenty-one of the personal property law and must not invest the funds in any other securities or manner.

Amended by Laws 1936, Ch. 848; Laws 1950, Ch. 464, eff. July 1, 1950.

§§ 86-88. Guardianship, records and care and custody of children in orphan asylums and other institutions.

Repealed by Laws 1923, Ch. 706 and subject matter now covered by Social Services Law.

ARTICLE 7

ADOPTION

SUMMARY OF ARTICLE

(Repealed and transferred sections noted under appropriate section number of text.)

TITLE 1: ADOPTIONS GENERALLY

§ 109. Definitions.

When used in this article, unless the context or subject matter manifestly requires a different interpretation:

1. "Adoptive parent" or "adoptor" shall mean a person adopting and "adoptive child" or "adoptee" shall mean a person adopted.

2. "Judge" shall mean a judge of the family court of any county in the state.

3. "Surrogate" shall mean the surrogate of any county in the state and any other judicial officer while acting in the capacity of surrogate.

4. "Authorized agency" shall mean an authorized agency as defined in the social services law and, for the purpose of this article, shall include such corporations incorporated or organized under the laws of this state as may be specifically authorized by their certificates of incorporation to receive children for purposes of adoption.

5. "Private-placement adoption" shall mean any adoption other than that of a minor who has been placed for adoption by an authorized agency.

6. "Lawful custody" shall mean a custody (a) specifically authorized by statute or (b) pursuant to judgment, decree or order of a court or (c) otherwise authorized by law.

7. "A child who has been surrendered to an authorized agency for the purpose of adoption" shall mean a child who has been surrendered to such an agency pursuant to the provisions of section three hundred eighty-three-c or three hundred eighty-four of the social services law.

Added by Laws 1938, Ch. 606; amended by Laws 1941, Ch. 13; Laws 1960, Ch. 717; Laws 1961, Ch. 147; Laws 1962, Chs. 689, 947; Laws 1970, Ch. 570, eff. Sept. 1, 1970, which substituted "adoptive" for "foster" and inserted new terms "adoptor" and "adoptee"; Laws 1976, Ch. 666, eff. Jan. 1, 1977; Laws 1989, Ch. 751, § 1, eff. Jan. 1, 1990; Laws 1991, Ch. 48, eff. Apr. 12, 1991.

§ 110. Who may adopt; effect of article.

An adult unmarried person or an adult husband and his adult wife together may adopt another person. An adult married person who is living separate and apart from his or her spouse pursuant to a decree or judgment of separation or pursuant to a written agreement of separation subscribed by the parties thereto and acknowledged or proved in the form required to entitle a deed to be recorded or an adult married person who has been living separate and apart from his or her spouse for at least three years prior to the commencement of the adoption proceeding may adopt another person; provided, however, that the person so adopted shall not be deemed the child or stepchild of the non-adopting spouse for the purposes of inheritance or support rights or obligations or for any other purposes. An adult or minor husband and his adult or minor wife together may adopt a child of either of them born in or out of wedlock and an adult or minor husband or an adult or minor wife may adopt such a child of the other spouse. No person shall hereafter be adopted except in pursuance of this article, and in conformity with section three hundred seventy-three of the social services law.

An adult married person who has executed a legally enforceable separation agreement or is a party to a marriage in which a valid decree of separation has been entered or has been living separate and apart from his or her spouse for at least three years prior to commencing an adoption proceeding and who becomes or has been the custodian of a child placed in their care as a result of court ordered foster care may apply to such authorized agency for placement of said child with them for the purpose of adoption. Final determination of the propriety of said adoption of such foster child, however, shall be within the sole discretion of the court, as otherwise provided herein.

Adoption is the legal proceeding whereby a person takes another person into the relation of child and thereby acquires the rights and incurs the responsibilities of parent in respect of such other person.

A proceeding conducted in pursuance of this article shall constitute a judicial proceeding. An order of adoption or abrogation made therein by a surrogate or by a judge shall have the force and effect of and shall be entitled to all the presumptions attaching to a judgment rendered by a court of general jurisdiction in a common law action.

No adoption heretofore lawfully made shall be abrogated by the enactment of this article. All such adoptions shall have the effect of lawful adoptions hereunder.

Nothing in this article in regard to a minor adopted pursuant hereto inheriting from the adoptive parent applies to any will, devise or trust made or created before June twenty-fifth, eighteen hundred seventy-three, nor alters, changes or interferes with such will, devise or trust. As to any such will, devise or trust a minor adopted before that date is not an heir so as to alter estates or trusts or devises in wills so made or created. Nothing in this article in regard to an adult adopted pursuant hereto inheriting from the adoptive parent applies to any will, devise or trust made or created before April twenty-second, nineteen hundred fifteen, nor alters, changes or interferes with such will, devise or trust. As to any such will, devise or trust an adult so adopted is not an heir so as to alter estates or trusts or devises in wills so made or created.

It shall be unlawful to preclude a prospective adoptive parent or parents solely on the basis that the adoptor or adopters has had, or has cancer, or any other disease. Nothing herein shall prevent the rejection of a prospective applicant based upon his or her poor health or limited life expectancy.

Added by Laws 1938, Ch. 606; **amended** by Laws 1943, Ch. 186; Laws 1951, Ch. 211; Laws 1961, Ch. 147; Laws 1970, Ch. 570, eff. Sept. 1, 1970, which substituted "adoptive" for "foster" in the last unnumbered paragraph; Laws 1984, Ch. 218, eff. June 19, 1984; Laws 1984, Ch. 745, eff. Dec. 3, 1984; Laws 1991, Ch. 254, eff. July 1, 1991; Laws 1999, Ch. 522, eff. Sept. 28, 1999.

Note—Laws 1980, Ch. 688, eff. June 26, 1980, provides:

§ 1. If there is a child whose natural mother was married after the birth of such child to an individual, who, although not the child's natural father resided with such child and her natural mother and treated such child in all respects as his own child and although never formally adopting such child during her childhood, gave such child the use of his family name, it having been the husband's intention to adopt the child of his then wife, which adoption was never consummated; and, if such husband, having subsequently been divorced from the child's natural mother, continues to desire to adopt such child and the child, having attained the age of twenty-one years, also desires that the former husband of her natural mother should become the adoptive parent of such child without detriment to the status of and with the express consent and approval of the natural mother of such child; and, if the present wife of the adoptive parent is in accord with the wishes of all of the parties, it is the finding of the legislature that notwithstanding any provision of law to the contrary, that under such circumstances the former husband should be allowed to adopt such child.

§ 2. Notwithstanding any other provision of law to the contrary, upon the filing, within six months of the enactment of this act, of a petition and all other required papers and documents pursuant to article seven of the domestic relations law with the surrogate or family court wherein either the adoptive child or the adoptive parent resides, together with a duly authenticated consent to such adoption executed by the present spouse of the adoptive parent and by the natural mother of such adoptive child, either of such courts may within thirty days thereafter, upon such investigation and notice as the court may direct, grant an order of adoption approving the adoption by the adoptive parent pursuant to section one hundred fourteen of the domestic relations law and provide for the filing of the order in the manner prescribed by law.

    Editor's Note: Laws 1974, Ch. 410 contains substantially the same provisions as set forth in the above note, the only difference being that the former law provides that the child must have reached the "age of majority" and not "twenty-one years." Although Ch. 688 of Laws 1980 does not explicitly repeal the 1974 provision it may impliedly repeal the 1974 provision.

§ 111.   Whose consent required.

    1.   Subject to the limitations hereinafter set forth consent to adoption shall be required as follows:

    (a)   Of the adoptive child, if over fourteen years of age, unless the judge or surrogate in his discretion dispenses with such consent;

    (b)   Of the parents or surviving parent, whether adult or infant, of a child conceived or born in wedlock;

    (c)   Of the mother, whether adult or infant, of a child born out of wedlock;

    (d)   Of the father, whether adult or infant, of a child born out-of-wedlock and placed with the adoptive parents more than six months after birth, but only if such father shall have maintained substantial and continuous or repeated contact with the child as manifested by: (i) the payment by the father toward the support of the child of a fair and reasonable sum, according to the father's means, and either (ii) the father's visiting the child at least monthly when physically and financially able to do so and not prevented from doing so by the person or authorized agency having lawful custody of the child, or (iii) the father's regular communication with the child or with the person or agency having the care or custody of the child, when physically and financially unable to visit the child or prevented from doing so by the person or authorized agency having lawful custody of the child. The subjective intent of the father, whether expressed or otherwise, unsupported by evidence of acts specified in this paragraph manifesting such intent, shall not preclude a determination that the father failed to maintain substantial and continuous or repeated contact with the child. In making such a determination, the court shall not require a showing of diligent efforts by any person or agency to encourage the father to perform the acts specified in this paragraph. A father, whether adult or infant, of a child born out-of-wedlock, who openly lived with the child for a period of six months within the one year period immediately preceding the placement of the child for adoption and who during such period openly held himself out to be the father of such child shall be deemed to have maintained substantial and continuous contact with the child for the purpose of this subdivision.

(e)   Of the father, whether adult or infant, of a child born out-of-wedlock who is under the age of six months at the time he is placed for adoption, but only if: (i) such father openly lived with the child or the child's mother for a continuous period of six months immediately preceding the placement of the child for adoption; and (ii) such father openly held himself out to be the father of such child during such period; and (iii) such father paid a fair and reasonable sum, in accordance with his means, for the medical, hospital and nursing expenses incurred in connection with the mother's pregnancy or with the birth of the child.

(f)   Of any person or authorized agency having lawful custody of the adoptive child.

2.   The consent shall not be required of a parent or of any other person having custody of the child:

(a)   who evinces an intent to forego his or her parental or custodial rights and obligations as manifested by his or her failure for a period of six months to visit the child and communicate with the child or person having legal custody of the child, although able to do so; or

(b)   who has surrendered the child to an authorized agency under the provisions of section three hundred eighty-three-c or three hundred eighty-four of the social services law; or

(c)   for whose child a guardian has been appointed under the provisions of section three hundred eighty-four-b of the social services law; or

(d)   who, by reason of mental illness or mental retardation, as defined in subdivision six of section three hundred eighty-four-b of the social services law, is presently and for the foreseeable future unable to provide proper care for the child. The determination as to whether a parent is mentally ill or mentally retarded shall be made in accordance with the criteria and procedures set forth in subdivision six of section three hundred eighty-four-b of the social services law; or

(e)   who has executed an instrument, which shall be irrevocable, denying the paternity of the child, such instrument having been executed after conception and acknowledged or proved in the manner required to permit the recording of a deed.

3.   (a) Notice of the proposed adoption shall be given as the judge or surrogate may direct and an opportunity to be heard to a person whose consent to adoption is required pursuant to subdivision one and who has not already provided such consent.

(b)   Notice and an opportunity to be heard upon the proposed adoption may be afforded to a parent whose consent to adoption may not be required pursuant to subdivision two, if the judge or surrogate so orders.

(c)   Notice under this subdivision shall be given in such manner as the judge or surrogate may direct.

(d)   Notwithstanding any other provision of law, neither the notice of a proposed adoption nor any process in such proceeding shall be required to contain the name of the person or persons seeking to adopt the child.

4. Where the adoptive child is over the age of eighteen years the consents specified in paragraphs (b), (c) and (d) of subdivision one of this section shall not be required, and the judge or surrogate in his discretion may direct that the consent specified in paragraph (f) of subdivision one of this section shall not be required if in his opinion the best interests of the adoptive child will be promoted by the adoption and such consent cannot for any reason be obtained.

5. An adoptive child who has once been lawfully adopted may be readopted directly from such child's adoptive parents in the same manner as from its natural parents. In such case the consent of such natural parents shall not be required but the judge or surrogate in his discretion may require that notice be given to the natural parents in such manner as he may prescribe.

6. For the purposes of paragraph (a) of subdivision two:

(a) In the absence of evidence to the contrary, the ability to visit and communicate with a child or person having custody of the child shall be presumed.

(b) Evidence of insubstantial or infrequent visits or communication by the parent or other person having custody of the child shall not, of itself, be sufficient as a matter of law to preclude a finding that the consent of such parent or person to the child's adoption shall not be required.

(c) The subjective intent of the parent or other person having custody of the child, whether expressed or otherwise, unsupported by evidence of acts specified in paragraph (a) of subdivision two manifesting such intent, shall not preclude a determination that the consent of such parent or other person to the child's adoption shall not be required.

(d) Payment by a parent toward the support of the child of a fair and reasonable sum, according to the parent's means, shall be deemed a substantial communication by such parent with the child or person having legal custody of the child.

Added by Laws 1938, Ch. 606; **amended** by Laws 1941, Ch. 13; Laws 1942, Ch. 118; Laws 1945, Ch. 531; Laws 1959, Chs. 168, 448; Laws 1961, Ch. 147; Laws 1962, Ch. 689; Laws 1970, Ch. 570, which substituted "adoptive" for "foster" and "social services law" for "social welfare law"; Laws 1973, Ch. 195; Laws 1974, Chs. 842, 843, requiring consent to adoption of parent divorced on account of adultery, eff. Aug. 6, 1974 but shall not apply to any adoption where a child has been placed for adoption by an authorized agency prior to such date or to an adoption proceeding commenced prior to such date; Ch. 920 Laws 1975, Ch. 246 Laws 1975, Ch. 704; Laws 1976, Ch. 666; Laws 1980, Ch. 575, eff. July 26, 1980; Laws 1983, Ch. 152, eff. May 31, 1983; Laws 1983, Ch. 911, eff. Jan. 1, 1983, provided, however, that nothing herein contained shall be construed so as to alter, affect, impair, defeat or restore any right, obligations, duties or interests accrued, incurred, conferred or terminated prior to the effective date; Laws 1985, Ch. 918, eff. Dec. 20, 1985; Laws 1991, Ch. 48, eff. Apr. 12, 1991; Laws 1997, Ch. 375, eff. Aug. 5, 1997.

Editor's Note: In *Matter of Raquel Marie X.,* 76 N.Y.2d 387, 559 N.Y.S.2d 855 (1990), the Court of Appeals declared DRL § 111(1)(e) to be unconstitutional. The New York State Legislature has not amended this provision.

§ 111-a. Notice in certain proceedings to fathers of children born out-of-wedlock.

1. Notwithstanding any inconsistent provisions of this or any other law, and in addition to the notice requirements of any law pertaining to persons other than those specified in subdivision two of this section, notice as provided herein shall be given to the persons specified in subdivision two of this section of any adoption proceeding initiated pursuant to this article or of any proceeding initiated pursuant to section one hundred fifteen-b relating to the revocation of an adoption consent, when such proceeding involves a child born out-of-wedlock provided, however, that such notice shall not be required to be given to any person who previously has been given notice of any proceeding involving the child, pursuant to section three hundred eighty-four-c of the social services law, and provided further that notice in an adoption proceeding, pursuant to this section shall not be required to be given to any person who has previously received notice of any proceeding pursuant to section one hundred fifteen-b.

In addition to such other requirements as may be applicable to the petition in any proceeding in which notice must be given pursuant to this section, the petition shall set forth the names and last known addresses of all persons required to be given notice of the proceeding, pursuant to this section, and there shall be shown by the petition or by affidavit or other proof satisfactory to the court that there are no persons other than those set forth in the petition who are entitled to notice. For the purpose of determining persons entitled to notice of adoption proceedings initiated pursuant to this article, persons specified in subdivision two of this section shall not include any person who has been convicted of rape in the first degree involving forcible compulsion, under subdivision one of section 130.35 of the penal law, when the child who is the subject of the proceeding was conceived as a result of such rape.

2. Persons entitled to notice, pursuant to subdivision one of this section, shall include:

(a) any person adjudicated by a court in this state to be the father of the child;

(b) any person adjudicated by a court of another state or territory of the United States to be the father of the child, when a certified copy of the court order has been filed with the putative father registry, pursuant to section three hundred seventy-two-c of the social services law;

(c) any person who has timely filed an unrevoked notice of intent to claim paternity of the child, pursuant to section three hundred seventy-two-c of the social services law;

(d) any person who is recorded on the child's birth certificate as the child's father;

(e) any person who is openly living with the child and the child's mother at the time the proceeding is initiated and who is holding himself out to be the child's father;

(f) any person who has been identified as the child's father by the mother in written, sworn statement;

(g) any person who was married to the child's mother within six months subsequent to the birth of the child and prior to the execution of a surrender instrument or the initiation of a proceeding pursuant to section three hundred eighty-four-b of the social services law; and

(h) any person who has filed with the putative father registry an instrument acknowledging paternity of the child, pursuant to section 4–1.2 of the estates, powers and trusts law.

3. The provisions of this section shall not apply to persons entitled to notice pursuant to section one hundred eleven. The sole purpose of notice under this section shall be to enable the person served pursuant to subdivision two to present evidence to the court relevant to the best interests of the child.

4. Notice under this section shall be given at least twenty days prior to the proceeding by delivery of a copy of the petition and notice to the person. Upon showing to the court, by affidavit or otherwise, on or before the date of the proceeding or within such further time as the court may allow, that personal service cannot be effected at the person's last known address with reasonable effort, notice may be given, without prior court order therefor, at least twenty days prior to the proceeding by registered or certified mail directed to the person's last known address or, where the person has filed a notice of intent to claim paternity pursuant to section three hundred seventy-two-c of the social services law, to the address last entered therein. Notice by publication shall not be required to be given to a person entitled to notice pursuant to the provisions of this section.

5. A person may waive his right to notice under this section by written instrument subscribed by him and acknowledged or proved in the manner required for the execution of a surrender instrument pursuant to section three hundred eighty-four of the social services law.

6. The notice given to persons pursuant to this section shall inform them of the time, date, place and purpose of the proceeding and shall also apprise such persons that their failure to appear shall constitute a denial of their interest in the child which denial may result, without further notice, in the adoption or other disposition of the custody of the child.

7. No order of adoption and no order of the court pursuant to section one hundred fifteen-b shall be vacated, annulled or reversed upon the application of any person who was properly served with notice in accordance with this section but failed to appear, or who waived notice pursuant to subdivision five. Nor shall any order of adoption be vacated, annulled or reversed upon the application of any person who was properly served with notice in accordance with this section

in any previous proceeding pursuant to section one hundred fifteen-b in which the court determined that the best interests of the child would be served by adoption of the child by the adoptive parents.

Added by Laws 1976, Ch. 665, eff. Jan. 1, 1977; **amended** by Laws 1977, Ch. 862; Laws 1980, Ch. 575, eff. July 26, 1980; Laws 1993, Ch. 353, § 1, eff. July 21, 1993.

§ 111-b. Determination of issue of paternity by surrogate; limitations.

1. In the course of an adoption proceeding conducted pursuant to this article the surrogate shall have jurisdiction to determine any issue of paternity arising in the course of the same proceeding and to make findings and issue an order thereon.

2. Such determination shall be made substantially in accordance with the relevant and otherwise consistent provisions of the family court act except that the surrogate shall have no power to grant any relief relating to support of the child as an incident thereto.

3. A judge of the family court shall continue to exercise all of the powers relating to adoption and declaration of paternity conferred upon the family court by law.

Added by Laws 1980, Ch. 575, eff. July 26, 1980, until Sept. 1, 1986; Laws 1984, Ch. 469, eff. July 20, 1984, until Sept. 1, 1986; Laws 1986, Ch. 484, eff. July 21, 1986.

TITLE 2: ADOPTION FROM AN AUTHORIZED AGENCY

§ 112. General provisions relating to adoption from authorized agencies.

In an adoption from an authorized agency the following requirements shall be observed:

1. The adoptive parents or parent and the adoptive child must appear for examination before a judge or surrogate of the county specified in section one hundred thirteen of this title. The judge or surrogate, however, may in his discretion dispense with the personal appearance of the adoptive child or of an adoptive parent who is on active duty in the armed forces of the United States.

2. The adoptive parents or parent and the adoptive child if over eighteen years of age must present to such judge or surrogate (a) a petition stating the

names and place of residence of the petitioners; whether they are of full age; whether they are married or unmarried and, if married, whether they are living together as husband and wife; the first name, date and place of birth of the adoptive child as nearly as the same can be ascertained; a statement on information and belief that there will be annexed to the petition a schedule verified by a duly constituted official of the authorized agency as required by this section; the religious faith of the petitioners; the religious faith of the adoptive child and his or her parents as nearly as the same can be ascertained; the manner in which the adoptive parents obtained the adoptive child; whether the child was placed or brought into the state of New York from out of state for the purpose of adoption, whether the placement was subject to the provisions of section three hundred seventy-four-a of the social services law and if the placement was subject to the provisions of such section, whether the provisions of such section were complied with; the period of time during which the adoptive child has resided with the adoptive parents; the occupation and approximate income of the petitioners, including support and maintenance, if any, to be received on behalf of the adoptive child from a commissioner of social services, pursuant to the social services law, and the new name, if any, by which the adoptive child is to be known; whether the adoptive parent or parents has or have knowledge that an adoptive parent is the subject of an indicated report, as such terms are defined in section four hundred twelve of the social services law, filed with the statewide central register of child abuse and maltreatment pursuant to title six of article six of the social services law, or has been the subject of or the respondent in a child protective proceeding commenced under article en of the family court act, which proceeding resulted in an order finding that the child is an abused or neglected child; that no previous application has been made to any court or judge for the relief sought or if so made, the disposition of it and a statement as to whether the adoptive child had been previously adopted, all of which statements shall be taken prima facie as true; (b) an agreement on the part of the adoptive parents or parent to adopt and treat the adoptive child as their or his or her own lawful child; (c) the consents required by section one hundred eleven of this article.

2-a. In the petition provided for in subdivision two of this section, the adoptive parents or parent and the adoptive child if over eighteen years of age shall present to the judge or surrogate as nearly as can be ascertained the heritage of the parents, which shall include nationality, ethnic background and race; education, which shall be the number of years of school completed by the parents at the time of the birth of the adoptive child; general physical appearance of the parents at the time of the birth of the adoptive child, which shall include height, weight, color of hair, eyes, skin; occupation of the parents at the time of the birth of the adoptive child; health and medical history of the parents at the time of the birth of the adoptive child, including all available information setting forth conditions or diseases believed to be hereditary, any drugs or medication taken during the pregnancy by the child's mother; and any other information which may be a factor influencing the child's present or future health, talents, hobbies and special interests of parents. The petition shall also include the names and current addresses of the biological parents, if known.

3.　The authorized agency must present to such judge or surrogate a schedule to be annexed to the petition which shall be verified by a duly constituted official of the authorized agency having custody of the adoptive child or actually placing the child for adoption and shall contain (1) the full name of the child, (2) the manner in which the authorized agency obtained custody of the adoptive child, (3) the facts, if any, which render unnecessary the consent of either or both of the parents of the adoptive child, (4) a statement whether either parent had ever requested the agency to return the child to the parent, within thirty days of the execution and delivery of an instrument of surrender to an authorized agency and, if so, all facts relating thereto. If a request for return of the child to a parent be made after the presentation to the court of the petition and schedule, the authorized agency shall promptly report to the court in writing the facts relating thereto and (5) all available information comprising the child's medical history. If the child was placed into the state of New York for the purpose of adoption and such placement was subject to the provisions of section three hundred seventy-four-a of the social services law, the authorized agency shall attach to the petition a copy of the document, signed by New York's administrator of the interstate compact for the placement of children or his designee, which informs the agency or person who placed the child into the state that such placement complied with the provisions of the compact.

4.　None of the papers in the proceeding shall state the surname of the child in the title and no petition, agreement, consent, affidavit, nor any other document which is required to be signed by the adoptive parents shall contain the surname of the adoptive child.

5.　The petition must be verified, the agreement and consents executed and acknowledged and the proof given by the respective persons before such judge or surrogate; but where the verification, agreement or necessary consent is duly acknowledged or proved and certified in form sufficient to entitle a conveyance to be recorded in this state (except that when executed and acknowledged within the state of New York, no certificate of the county clerk shall be required), such judge or surrogate may grant the order of adoption without the personal appearance of such persons or parties or any of them for good cause shown, which reason shall be recited in the order of adoption.

6.　Where the adoptive child is less than eighteen years of age, no order of adoption shall be made until such child has resided with the adoptive parents for at least three months unless the judge or surrogate in his discretion shall dispense with such period of residence and shall recite in the order the reason for such action. When the adoptive parents are the foster parents in whose home the adoptive child has been placed out or boarded out for a period in excess of three months, such period shall be deemed to constitute the required period of residence.

7.   Before making an order of adoption the judge or surrogate shall inquire of the department of social services and the department shall inform the court whether an adoptive parent is the subject of an indicated report, as such terms are defined in section four hundred twelve of the social services law, filed with the statewide central register of child abuse and maltreatment pursuant to title six of article six of the social services law and shall cause to be made an investigation by a disinterested person or by an authorized agency specifically designated by the judge or surrogate to examine into the allegations set forth in the petition and to ascertain such other facts relating to the adoptive child and adoptive parents as will give such judge or surrogate adequate basis for determining the propriety of approving the adoption. A written report of such investigation shall be submitted before the order of adoption is made. As used in this subdivision, "disinterested person" includes the probation service of the family court. Such an inquiry shall not be required if the findings of such an inquiry made within the past twelve months is available to the judge or surrogate.

8.   Rules of court shall permit the filing of a petition for adoption of a child whose custody and guardianship has not yet been committed to an authorized agency where a proceeding to terminate parental rights is pending. Such adoption petition shall be filed in the court where the termination of parental rights proceeding is pending. The clerk of such court shall accept the adoption petition for filing and processing and shall request such inquiries of the department of social services as are required by subdivision seven of this section, provided, however, that the petition, supporting documents and the fact of their filing shall not be provided to the judge before whom the petition for termination of parental rights is pending until such time as fact-finding is concluded under such petition.

Added by Laws 1938, Ch. 606; **amended** by Laws 1943, Ch. 610; Laws 1945, Chs. 98, 231; Laws 1946, Ch. 187; Laws 1961, Ch. 147; Laws 1962, Chs. 689, 690; Laws 1967, Ch. 740; Laws 1968, Chs. 320, 1038; Laws 1970, Ch. 570, which substituted "adoptive" for "foster" throughout the section; Laws 1973, Ch. 613; Laws 1974, Ch. 1011, eff. Sept. 1, 1974; Laws 1975, Ch. 424, eff. July 8, 1975; Laws 1976, Ch. 666, eff. Jan. 1, 1977; Laws 1985, Ch. 531, eff. Oct. 22, 1985; Laws 1989, Ch. 707, eff. July 24, 1989; Laws 1989, Ch. 751, eff. Jan. 1, 1990; Laws 1991, Ch. 164, §§ 3, 4, eff. Jan. 1, 1992; Laws 1991, Ch. 588, § 7, eff. Sept. 30, 1991; Laws 1996, Ch. 309, § 275, eff. July 13, 1996.

§ 112-a.   Expedited calendaring of adoption proceedings.

1.   The adoption proceeding shall be deemed filed upon receipt by the clerk of the court of all the documents required in subdivisions two, two-a, three, five and seven of section one hundred twelve of this title, and by rules of the court, together with an affidavit of readiness from the petitioner's attorney. The affidavit of readiness shall attest that the petitioner has prepared a petition for the adoption of the child and has collected documentation as required by such rules and subdivisions two, two-a, three and five of section one hundred twelve of this title.

2.   Upon the filing of the documents required by subdivision one of this section, the court, pursuant to rules promulgated by the chief administrator of

the court, shall schedule the proceeding for a review, to take place within time frames established by such rules, to determine if there is adequate basis for approving the adoption.

(a) If such basis is found, the appearance of the adoptive parents and child before the court for approval of the adoption shall be calendared pursuant to such rules.

(b) If, upon the court's review, the court finds that there is not an adequate basis for approval of the adoption, the court shall direct such further hearings, submissions or appearances as may be required, and the proceedings shall be adjourned as required for such purposes.

3. [*Until November 14, 2005.*] The chief administrator of the court shall establish by rule time frames for the calendaring and disposition of adoption proceedings and shall report by the thirty-first day of December of each year to the governor and the legislature on the implementation of such rules and their impact upon adoptions from authorized agencies.

3. [*Eff. November 14, 2005.*] The chief administrator of the court shall establish by rule time frames for the calendaring and disposition of adoption proceedings and shall report by the thirty-first day of December of each year to the governor and the temporary president of the senate, speaker of the assembly, and chairpersons of the judiciary and children and families committees on the implementation of such rules and their impact upon adoptions from authorized agencies.

Added by Laws 1993, Ch. 294, § 3, eff. Sept. 19, 1993; **amended** by Laws 2005, Ch. 524, § 14, amending sub. 3, eff. November 14, 2005.

§ 112-b   Post-adoption contact agreements; judicial approval; enforcement.

1. Nothing in this section shall be construed to prohibit the parties to a proceeding under this chapter from entering into an agreement regarding communication with or contact between an adoptive child, adoptive parent or parents and a birth parent or parents and/or the adoptive child's biological siblings or half-siblings.

2. Agreements regarding communication or contact between an adoptive child, adoptive parent or parents, and a birth parent or parents and/or biological siblings or half-siblings of an adoptive child shall not be legally enforceable unless the terms of the agreement are incorporated into a written court order entered in accordance with the provisions of this section. The court shall not incorporate an agreement regarding communication or contact into an order un-less the terms and conditions of the agreement have been set forth in writing and consented to in writing by the parties to the agreement, including the law guardian representing the adoptive child. The court shall not enter a proposed order unless the court that approved the surrender of the child determined and stated in its

order that the communication with or contact between the adoptive child, the prospective adoptive parent or parents and a birth parent or parents and/or biological siblings or half-siblings, as agreed upon and as set forth in the agreement, would be in the adoptive child's best interests. Notwithstanding any other provision of law, a copy of the order entered pursuant to this section incorporating the post-adoption contact agreement shall be given to all parties who have agreed to the terms and conditions of such order.

3. Failure to comply with the terms and conditions of an approved order regarding communication or contact that has been entered by the court pursuant to this section shall not be grounds for setting aside an adoption decree or revocation of written consent to an adoption after that consent has been approved by the court as provided in this section.

4. An order incorporating an agreement regarding communication or contact entered under this section may be enforced by any party to the agreement or the law guardian by filing a petition in the family court in the county where the adoption was approved. Such petition shall have annexed to it a copy of the order approving the agreement regarding communication or contact. The court shall not enforce an order under this section unless it finds that the enforcement is in the child's best interests.

5. If a birth parent has surrendered a child to an authorized agency pursuant to the provisions of section three hundred eighty-three-c or section three hundred eighty-four of the social services law, and if the court before whom the surrender instrument was presented for approval approved an agreement providing for communication or contact pursuant to paragraph (a) of subdivision two of section three hundred eighty-three-c or paragraph (a) of subdivision two of section three hundred eighty-four of the social services law, a copy of the surrender instrument and of the approved agreement shall be annexed to the petition of adoption. The court shall issue an order incorporating the terms and conditions of the approved agreement into the order of adoption. Notwithstanding any other provision of law, a copy of any order entered pursuant to this subdivision shall be given to the parties who approved such agreement.

6. If a surrender instrument executed by a birth parent pursuant to section three hundred eighty-three-c or three hundred eighty-four of the social services law contains terms and conditions that provide for communication with or contact between a child and a birth parent or parents, such terms and conditions shall not be legally enforceable after any adoption approved by a court pursuant to this article unless the court has entered an order pursuant to this section incorporating those terms and conditions into a court ordered adoption agreement.

Added by Laws 2005, ch. 3, §63 (Part A), eff. Dec. 21, 2005; **Amended** by Laws 2006, ch. 437, §17, eff. July 26, 2006.

§ 113. Special provisions relating to adoption from authorized agencies.

1. An authorized agency may consent to the adoption of a minor whose custody and guardianship has been transferred to such agency. An authorized

agency may also consent to the adoption of a minor whose care and custody has been transferred to such agency pursuant to section one thousand fifty-five of the family court act or section three hundred eighty-four-a of the social services law, where such child's parents are both deceased, or where one parent is deceased and the other parent is not a person entitled to notice pursuant to sections one hundred eleven and one hundred eleven-a of this chapter.

2. In accordance with subparagraph three of paragraph (g) of subdivision six of section three hundred ninety-eight of the social services law, an authorized agency may submit a written request to a social services district with a population of more than two million for approval to consent to the adoption of a child whose custody and guardianship, or of a child where such child's parents are both deceased, or where one parent is deceased and the other parent is not entitled to notice pursuant to sections one hundred eleven and one hundred eleven-a of this chapter, and whose care and custody, has been transferred to a social services official and who has been placed by the social services official with the authorized agency. If the request is not disapproved by the social services district within sixty days after its submission, it shall be deemed approved, and the authorized agency may give all necessary consent to the adoption of the child. Nothing herein shall result in the transfer of care and custody or custody and guardianship of the child from the social services official to the authorized agency.

3. [Until Oct 24, 2006] The agreement of adoption shall be executed by such authorized agency. If the adoption petition is filed pursuant to subdivision eight of section one hundred twelve of this article or subdivision ten of section three hundred eighty-three-c or subdivision eleven of section three hundred eighty-four-b of the social services law, the petition shall be filed in the county where the termination ofparental rights proceeding or judicial surrender proceeding, as applicable, is pending. In any other agency adoption proceeding the petition shall be filed in the county in which parental rights had been terminated or a judicial surrender had been approved or in the county where the adoptive parents reside or, if such adoptive parents do not reside in this state, in the county where such authorized agency has its principal office. Neither such authorized agency nor any officer or agent thereof need appear before the judge or surrogate. The judge or surrogate in his or her discretion may accept the report of an authorized agency verified by one of its officers or agents as the report of investigation hereinbefore required. In making orders of adoption the judge or surrogate when practicable must give custody only to persons of the same religious faith as that of the adoptive child in accordance with article six of the social services law.

3. [Eff. Oct 24, 2006]

(a) The agreement of adoption shall be executed by such authorized agency.

(b) (i) If the adoption petition is filed pursuant to subdivision eight of section one hundred twelve of this article or subdivision ten of section three hundred eighty-three-c or subdivision eleven of section three hundred eighty-four-b of the social services law, the petition shall be filed in the county where the termination of parental rights proceeding or judicial surrender proceeding, as applicable, is pending and shall be assigned, wherever practicable, to the same judge.

(ii) In any other agency adoption proceeding, the petition shall be filed in the same court and, wherever practicable, shall be assigned to the same judge of the county in which parental rights had been terminated, a judicial surrender had been approved or the most recent proceeding under article ten or ten-A of the family court act or section three hundred fifty-eight-a of the social services law had been heard, whichever occurred last, or in the county where the adoptive parents reside or, if such adoptive parents do not reside in this state, in the county where such authorized agency has its principal office. The following procedures shall be applicable in cases where the child is under the jurisdiction of a family court, but where the adoption petition has been filed in a court other than the court that presided over the termination of parental rights, surrender or most recent proceeding under article ten or ten-A of the family court act or section three hundred fifty-eight-a of the social services law, whichever occurred last:

(A) Before hearing such an adoption proceeding, the court in which the adoption petition was filed shall ascertain whether the child is under the jurisdiction of a family court as a result of a placement under article ten or ten-A of the family court act or section three hundred fifty-eight-a of the social services law, a surrender under section three hundred eighty-three-c or three hundred eighty-four of the social services law or an order committing guardianship and custody under article six of the family court act or section three hundred eighty-four-b of the social services law, and, if so, which court exercised jurisdiction over the most recent permanency or other proceeding involving the child.

(B) If the court determines that the child is under the jurisdiction of a different family court, the court in which the adoption petition was filed shall stay its proceeding for not more than thirty days and shall communicate with the family court judge who exercised jurisdiction over the most recent permanency or other proceeding involving the child. The communication shall be recorded or summarized on the record by the court in which the adoption petition was filed. Both courts shall notify the parties and law guardian, if any, in their respective proceedings and shall give them an opportunity to present facts and legal argument or to participate in the communication prior to the issuance of a decision on jurisdiction.

(C) The family court judge who exercised jurisdiction over the most recent permanency or other proceeding involving the child shall determine whether he or she should assume or decline jurisdiction over the adoption proceeding. In making its determination, the family court judge shall consider, among other factors: the relative familiarity of each court with the facts and circumstances regarding permanency planning for, and the needs and best interests of, the child; the ability of the law guardian to continue to represent the child in the adoption proceeding, if appropriate; the convenience of each court to the residence of the prospective adoptive parent or parents; and the relative ability of each court to hear and determine the adoption petition expeditiously. The court in which the adoption petition was filed shall issue an order incorporating this determination of jurisdiction within thirty days of the filing of the adoption petition.

(D)   If the family court that exercised jurisdiction over the most recent permanency or other proceeding determines that it should exercise jurisdiction over the adoption petition, the order of the court in which the adoption petition was filed shall direct the transfer of the proceeding forthwith but in no event more than thirty-five days after the filing of the petition. The petition shall be assigned, wherever practicable, to the family court judge who heard the most recent permanency or other proceeding involving the child.

(E)   If the family court that exercised jurisdiction over the permanency or other proceeding involving the child declines to exercise jurisdiction over the adoption petition, the court in which the adoption petition was filed shall issue an order incorporating that determination and shall proceed forthwith.

(iii)   Neither such authorized agency nor any officer or agent thereof need appear before the judge or surrogate. The judge or surrogate in his or her discretion may accept the report of an authorized agency verified by one of its officers or agents as the report of investigation hereinbefore required. In making orders of adoption the judge or surrogate when practicable must give custody only to persons of the same religious faith as that of the adoptive child in accordance with article six of the social services law.

Added by Laws 1938, Ch. 606; **amended** by Laws 1941, Ch. 13; Laws 1961, Ch. 147; Laws 1970, Ch. 570, eff. Sept. 1, 1970, which substituted "adoptive" for "foster" and "social services law" for "social welfare law"; Laws 1993, Ch. 108, § 1, eff. Oct. 12, 1993; Laws 1995, Ch. 83, § 251, eff. July 1, 1995; Laws 1996, Ch. 607, § 2, eff. Sept. 4, 1996; Laws 1997, Ch. 375, § 2, eff. Aug. 5, 1997; Laws 1998, Ch. 531, § 1, eff. Oct. 27, 1998; Laws 2006, ch. 185, §7, eff. Oct. 24, 2006.

§ 114.   Order of adoption.

1.   If satisfied that the best interests of the adoptive child will be promoted thereby the judge or surrogate shall make an order approving the adoption and directing that the adoptive child shall thenceforth be regarded and treated in all respects as the child of the adoptive parents or parent. In determining whether the best interests of the adoptive child will be promoted by the adoption, the judge or surrogate shall give due consideration to any assurance by a commissioner of social services that he will provide necessary support and maintenance for the adoptive child pursuant to the social services law. Such order shall contain the full name, date and place of birth and reference to the schedule annexed to the petition containing the medical history of the child in the body thereof and shall direct that the child's medical history, heritage of the parents, which shall include nationality, ethnic background and race; education, which shall be the number of years of school completed by the parents at the time of the birth of the adoptive child; general physical appearance of the parents at the time of the birth of the adoptive child, which shall include height, weight, color of hair, eyes, skin;

occupation of the parents at the time of the birth of the adoptive child; health and medical history of the parents at the time of the birth of the adoptive child, including all available information setting forth conditions or diseases believed to be hereditary, any drugs or medication taken during the pregnancy by the child's mother; and any other information which may be a factor influencing the child's present or future health, talents, hobbies and special interests of parents as contained in the petition be furnished to the adoptive parents. If the judge or surrogate is also satisfied that there is no reasonable objection to the change of name proposed, the order shall direct that the name of the adoptive child be changed to the name stated in the agreement of adoption and that henceforth he shall be known by that name. All such orders made by a family court judge of Westchester county since September first, nineteen hundred sixty-two, and on file in the office of the county clerk of such county shall be transferred to the clerk of the family court of such county. Such order and all the papers in the proceeding shall be filed in the office of the court granting the adoption and the order shall be entered in books which shall be kept under seal and which shall be indexed by the name of the adoptive parents and by the full original name of the child. Such order, including orders heretofore entered, shall be subject to inspection and examination only as hereinafter provided. Notwithstanding the fact that adoption records shall be sealed and secret, they may be microfilmed and processed pursuant to an order of the court, provided that such order provides that the confidentiality of such records be maintained. If the confidentiality is violated, the person or company violating it can be found guilty of contempt of court. The fact that the adoptive child was born out of wedlock shall in no case appear in such order. The written report of the investigation together with all other papers pertaining to the adoption shall be kept by the judge or surrogate as a permanent record of his court and such papers must be sealed by him and with-held from inspection. No certified copy of the order of adoption shall issue unless authorized by court order, except that certified copies may issue to the agency or agencies in the proceeding prior to the sealing of the papers. Before the record is sealed, such order may be granted upon written ex parte application on good cause shown and upon such conditions as the court may impose. After the record is sealed, such order may be granted only upon notice as hereinafter provided for disclosure or access and inspection of records. The clerk upon request of a person or agency entitled thereto shall issue certificates of adoption which shall contain only the new name of the child and the date and place of birth of the child, the name of the adoptive parents and the date when and court where the adoption was granted, which certificate as to the facts recited therein shall have the same force and effect as a certified copy of an order of adoption.

2. No person, including the attorney for the adoptive parents shall disclose the surname of the child directly or indirectly to the adoptive parents except upon order of the court. No person shall be allowed access to such sealed records and order and any index thereof except upon an order of a judge or surrogate of the court in which the order was made or of a justice of the supreme court. No order for disclosure or access and inspection shall be granted except on good cause

shown and on due notice to the adoptive parents and to such additional persons as the court may direct. Nothing contained herein shall be deemed to require the state commissioner of health or his designee to secure a court order authorizing disclosure of information contained in adoption or birth records requested pursuant to the authority of section forty-one hundred thirty-eight-c or section forty-one hundred thirty-eight-d of the public health law; upon the receipt of such request for information, the court shall transmit the information authorized to be released thereunder to the state commissioner of health or his designee.

3.   In like manner as a court of general jurisdiction exercises such powers, a judge or surrogate of the court in which the order of adoption was made may open, vacate or set aside such order of adoption for fraud, newly discovered evidence or other sufficient cause.

4.   Good cause for disclosure or access to and inspection of sealed adoption records and orders and any index thereof, hereinafter the "adoption records", under this section may be established on medical grounds as provided herein. Certification from a physician licensed to practice medicine in the state of New York that relief under this subdivision is required to address a serious physical or mental illness shall be prima facie evidence of good cause. Such certification shall identify the information required to address such illness. Except where there is an immediate medical need for the information sought, in which case the court may grant access to the adoption records directly to the petitioner, the court hearing petition under the subdivision shall appoint a guardian ad litem or other disinterested person, who shall have access to the adoption records for the purpose of obtaining the medical information sought from those records or, where the records are insufficient for such purpose, through contacting the biological parents. The guardian or other disinterested person shall offer a biological parent the option of disclosing the medical information sought by the petitioner pursuant to this subdivision, as well as the option of granting consent to examine the parent's medical records. If the guardian or other disinterested person appointed does not obtain the medical information sought by the petitioner, such guardian or disinterested person shall make a report of his or her efforts to obtain such information to the court. Where further efforts to obtain such information are appropriate, the court may in its discretion authorize direct disclosure or access to and inspection of the adoption records by the petitioner.

Added by Laws 1938, Ch. 606; **amended** by Laws 1943, Ch. 591; Laws 1944, Chs. 29, 255; Laws 1945, Ch. 220; Laws 1950, Ch. 559; Laws 1951, Ch. 256; Laws 1954, Ch. 633; Laws 1959, Ch. 499; Laws 1960, Ch. 218; Laws 1961, Ch. 147; Laws 1962, Ch. 689; Laws 1968, Chs. 320, 365, 1038; Laws 1970, Ch. 570, eff. Sept. 1, 1970, which substituted "adoptive" for "foster" and "social services" for "social welfare"; Laws 1974, Chs. 261, 1011, both eff. Sept. 1, 1974; amended by Laws 1976, Ch. 666, eff. Jan. 1, 1977; Laws 1985, Ch. 37, eff. Apr. 16, 1985; Laws 1989, Ch. 751, § 4, eff. Jan. 1, 1990; Laws 1992, Ch. 559, § 11, eff. July 24, 1992; Laws 1994, Ch. 601, § 1, eff. Oct. 24, 1994.

TITLE 3: PRIVATE-PLACEMENT ADOPTION

§ 115. General provisions relating to private-placement adoptions.

1.   (a) Except as otherwise provided in this title, private-placement adoptions shall be effected in the same manner as provided in sections one hundred twelve and one hundred fourteen of title two of this article.

(b)   A person or persons seeking to commence a private-placement adoption shall, prior to the submission of a petition for such adoption and prior to any transfer of physical custody of an adoptive child, be certified as a qualified adoptive parent or parents by a court of competent jurisdiction pursuant to section one hundred fifteen-d of this title. The provisions of such section may be waived upon the court's own motion or upon the application of any party for good cause shown.

(c)   A nonresident person or persons seeking to commence a private place-ment adoption of a child present within the state at the time of placement shall, prior to any transfer of physical custody of an adoptive child, make application for certification as a qualified adoptive parent or parents by a court of competent jurisdiction pursuant to section one hundred fifteen-d of this title. Upon applica-tion of such person or persons, the court of the county to which the certification petition is properly filed may take or retain jurisdiction of the adoption proceed-ing. The provisions of this paragraph may be waived upon the court's own motion or upon the application of any party for good cause shown.

2.   The proceeding shall be instituted in the county where the adoptive parents reside or, if such adoptive parents do not reside in this state, in the county where the adoptive child resides.

3.   The adoptive parents or parent, the adoptive child and all persons whose consent is required by section one hundred eleven of this article must appear for examination before the judge or surrogate of the court where the adoption proceedings are instituted. The judge or surrogate may dispense with the personal appearance of the adoptive child or of an adoptive parent who is on active duty in the armed forces of the United States.

4.   The agreement of adoption shall be executed by the adoptive parents or parent.

5.   Where the petition alleges that either or both of the natural parents of the child have been deprived of civil rights or are mentally ill or mentally retarded,

proof shall be submitted that such disability exists at the time of the proposed adoption.

6. The adoptive parent or parents shall also present in an affidavit a description of any change of circumstances since their certification as a qualified adoptive parent or parents, pursuant to section one hundred fifteen-d of this title, which may be relevant and material to such certification.

7. Where the adoptive child is to be adopted upon the consent of some person other than his father or mother, there shall also be presented the affidavit of such person showing how he or she obtained lawful custody of the child.

8. The adoptive parent or parents shall also present an affidavit describing all fees, compensation and other remunerations paid by such parent or parents on account of or incidental to the birth or care of the adoptive child, the pregnancy or care of the adoptive child's mother or the placement or adoption of the child and on account of or incidental to assistance in arrangements for such placement or adoption. The attorney representing the adoptive parents shall also present an affidavit describing all fees, compensation and other remuneration received by him on account of or incidental to the placement or adoption of the child or assistance in arrangements for such placement or adoption.

9. The petition must be verified, the agreement and consents executed and acknowledged the proof given and the affidavit sworn to by the respective persons before such judge or surrogate; but where the verification, agreement or consent of an adoptive parent, parent or person whose consent is necessary to the adoption is duly acknowledged or proved and certified in form sufficient to entitle a conveyance to be recorded in this state, (except that when executed and acknowledge within the state of New York, no certificate of the county clerk shall be required), such judge or surrogate may grant the order of adoption without the personal appearance of such adoptive parent, parent or person. The judge or surrogate may, in his discretion, dispense with the requirement that the adoptive child appear for examination or join in the petition, where otherwise required. In any adoption proceeding where the judge or surrogate shall dispense with the personal appearance of such adoptive parent, parent, person whose consent is necessary to the adoption, or adoptive child, the reason therefor must be for good cause shown, and shall be recited in the order of adoption.

10. In all cases where the consents of the persons mentioned in subdivision two, three and four of section one hundred eleven of this article are not required or where the adoptive child is an adult notice of such application shall be served upon such persons as the judge or surrogate may direct.

11. The provisions of title two prohibiting the surname of the child from appearing in the papers, prohibiting disclosure of the surname of the child to the adoptive parents, and requiring a separate application for issuance of a certified copy of an order of adoption prior to the sealing of the papers, requiring the filing of a verified schedule, shall not apply to private-placement adoptions; provided, however, that the facts required to be stated in the verified schedule in an agency adoption shall be set forth in the petition.

DRL

12.   (a) If the child who is being adopted was placed or brought into New York for the purpose of adoption from a state which is a party to the interstate compact on the placement of children and the provisions of the compact applied to such placements, the petition must contain a statement that the provisions of section three hundred seventy-four-a of the social services law were complied with and where applicable, that the provisions of section three hundred eighty-two of such law were also complied with.

(b)   If the child who is being adopted was placed or brought into New York for the purpose of adoption from a state which is not a party to the interstate compact on the placement of children, the petition, where applicable, must contain a statement that the provisions of section three hundred eighty-two of the social services law were complied with.

13.   If the placement of a child into the state of New York is subject to the provisions of sections three hundred seventy-four-a and/or three hundred eighty-two of the social services law, there shall be attached to the petition a copy of the document signed by New York's administrator of the interstate compact on the placement of children or his designee which informs the agency or person who placed the child into the state that such placement complied with the provisions of the compact and/or a copy of the license which is issued pursuant to the provisions of section three hundred eighty-two of the social services law to the person, institution, corporation or agency which placed or brought the child into this state.

Added by Laws 1961, Ch. 147, and former § 115 renumbered as § 117; Laws 1968, Ch. 1038; Laws 1970, Ch. 570, eff. Sept. 1, 1970, which substituted "adoptive" for "foster" throughout the section; Laws 1976, Ch. 666, eff. Jan. 1, 1977; **amended** by Laws 1981, Ch. 283, eff. Sept. 1, 1981; Laws 1985, Ch. 531, eff. Oct. 22, 1985; Laws 1989, Ch. 700, eff. Nov. 1, 1989; Laws 1992, Ch. 704, § 3, eff. July 31, 1992.

§ 115-a.   Special provisions relating to children to be brought into the state for private-placement adoption.

1.   In the case of a child whose admission to the United States as an eligible orphan with non-quota immigrant status pursuant to the federal immigration and nationality act is sought for the purpose of adoption in the state of New York, the following pre-adoption requirements shall be observed:

(a)   The adoptive parents or parent must present to a judge or surrogate having jurisdiction of adoption proceedings, in the county of residence of such adoptive parents or parent, a verified written application containing the information set forth in subdivision two of this section, in such form as the judge or surrogate may prescribe for an order of pre-adoption investigation, to determine whether the adoption may be in the best interests of the child.

(b)   The adoptive parents or parent must appear for examination before the judge or surrogate of the court where the pre-adoption proceedings are instituted.

(c) The application must be accompanied by duly authenticated documentary evidence: (1) that the child is an alien under the age of sixteen and (2) that he is an orphan because of the death or disappearance of both parents, or because of abandonment, or desertion by, or separation or loss from, both parents, or who has only one parent due to the death or disappearance of, abandonment, or desertion by, or separation or loss from the other parent, and the remaining parent is incapable of providing care for such orphan and has in writing irrevocably released him for emigration and adoption, and has consented to the proposed adoption. In all cases where the orphan has no remaining parent under the circumstances set forth above, documentary evidence must be presented that the person, public authority or duly constituted agency having lawful custody of the orphan at the time of the making of the application, hereunder, has in writing irrevocably released him for immigration and adoption and has consented to the proposed adoption and (3) that the adoptive parents agree to adopt and treat the adoptive child as their or his or her own lawful child.

(d) In addition thereto such additional releases and consents as the court may in its sound discretion require.

2. The verified written application shall contain the following information: the names and place of residence of the adoptive parent or parents; whether they are of full age; whether they are married or unmarried and, if married, whether they are living together as husband and wife; the name, date and place of birth of the adoptive child as nearly as the same can be ascertained; the religious faith of the adoptive parent or parents; the religious faith of the adoptive child and his parents as nearly as the same can be ascertained; the medical history of the adoptive child as nearly as the same can be ascertained; the occupation and approximate income of the adoptive parent or parents, and the name by which the adoptive child is to be known; that no previous application has been made to any court or judge for the relief sought or if so made, the disposition of it and a statement as to whether the adoptive child has been previously adopted, if such fact is known to the adoptive parent or parents; the facts which establish that the child is an eligible orphan who would be entitled to enter the United States with non-quota immigrant status for the purpose of adoption in New York state, pursuant to the provisions in the federal immigration and nationality act, in such case made; the circumstances whereby, and names and addresses of the intermediaries, if any, through whom the adoptive parent or parents learned of the existence and eligibility of the child and the names and addresses of the person or persons, public authority or duly constituted agency in the land of the child's residence executing the written release of the child for emigration and adoption, and the consent to such adoption, the circumstances under which the release and consent were obtained, insofar as they are known to the adoptive parent or parents.

2-a. The verified written application shall contain the following information: the heritage of the parents as nearly as the same can be ascertained, which shall include nationality, ethnic background and race; education, which shall be the number of years of school completed by the parents at the time of the birth of the adoptive child; general physical appearance of the parents at the time of the birth of the adoptive child, which shall include height, weight, color of hair, eyes, skin; occupation of the parents at the time of the birth of the adoptive child; health and medical history of the parents at the time of the birth of the adoptive child, including all available information setting forth conditions or diseases believed to be hereditary, any drugs or medication taken during the pregnancy by the child's mother; and any other information which may be a factor influencing the child's present or future health, talents, hobbies and special interests of parents.

3. Upon receiving the verified written application, required documentary evidence, agreement and consents, the judge or surrogate, upon finding that the applicable provisions of section one hundred fifteen-a have been complied with and that it appears that the proposed adoption may be in the best interests of the child, shall issue an order of pre-adoption investigation hereunder. The order of pre-adoption investigation shall require that the report of such investigation be made by a disinterested person who in the opinion of the judge or surrogate is qualified by training and experience, or by an authorized agency specifically designated by him to examine into the statements set forth in the application. The investigator shall make a written report of his investigation into the truth and accuracy of the statements in the application and where applicable, into the validity of the documentary evidence, submitted with the application, and he shall ascertain as fully as possible, and incorporate in his report the various factors which may bear upon the determination of the application for adoption including, but not limited to, the following information:

(a) the marital and family status, and history, of adoptive parents;

(b) the physical and mental health of the adoptive parents;

(c) the property owned by and the income of the adoptive parents;

(d) the compensation paid or agreed upon with respect to the placement of the child for adoption;

(e) whether either adoptive parent has ever been respondent in any proceeding concerning allegedly neglected, abandoned or delinquent children;

(f) the desirability of bringing the child into New York state for private-placement adoption;

(g) any other facts relating the familial, social, religious, emotional and financial circumstances of the adoptive parents which may be relevant to a determination of suitability of the adoption.

The written report of pre-adoption investigation shall be submitted to the judge or surrogate within thirty days after the same is directed to be made, unless for good cause shown the judge or surrogate shall grant a reasonable extension of such period. The report shall be filed with the judge or surrogate, in any event, before the court shall issue its pre-adoption certificate that it appears that the adoption is in the best interests of the child.

4. On the return of the pre-adoption investigation order the judge or surrogate shall examine the written report of the pre-adoption investigation, and shall determine upon the basis of such written report and such further proof, if any, as he may deem necessary, whether to issue a pre-adoption certificate as provided for in this subdivision.

If the court is satisfied that the adoption may be in the best interests of the child, and that there has been compliance with all requirements hereof and is satisfied that the moral and temporal interests of the child will be promoted by the adoption, the judge or surrogate shall issue an original certificate under seal of the court and two certified copies thereof, setting forth the fact that a pre-adoption investigation has been conducted, and reciting the documents and papers submitted therewith and stating that in the opinion of the court there is compliance with all applicable laws and that it appears from such investigation that the moral and temporal interests of the child will be promoted by the proposed adoption.

The original certificate shall be filed with the clerk of the court, one certified copy with the state commissioner of social services, and the adoptive parents shall receive the second certified copy. The fact that the adoptive child was born out of wedlock shall in no case appear in such certificate. The written report of pre-adoption investigation together with all other papers pertaining to the pre-adoption investigation and the original certificate shall be kept by the court as a permanent record and such papers must be sealed by the judge and withheld from inspection. No person shall be allowed access to such sealed records and original certificate and any index thereof except upon an order of the court in which the pre-adoption certificate was made or an order of a justice of the supreme court. No order for access and inspection shall be granted except on due notice to the adoptive parents and on good cause shown. In like manner as a court of general jurisdiction exercises such powers, the court in which the pre-adoption certificate was made may open, vacate or set aside such certificate for fraud, newly discovered evidence or other sufficient cause.

5. The private-placement adoption of children who have been brought into the United States and the state for such purpose and placed with the adoptive parent or parents, shall be effected after issuance of the pre-adoption certificate, in the manner provided by this title, excepting that (a) the petition shall also recite the pre-adoption proceedings, and (b) the court may in its discretion for good cause shown, waive a subsequent investigation. In such case the order of adoption shall recite the reason for such action.

6. In any case where there has been a failure to comply with the requirements of this section, if applicable, no order of adoption shall be made until one year after the court shall have received the petition to adopt. The court may shorten such waiting period for good cause shown, and, in such case the order of adoption shall recite the reason for such action.

7. The provisions of this section, shall not be applicable to the adoption of children placed out or to be placed out for adoption by an authorized agency as defined in section three hundred seventy-one of the social services law.

8.   Notwithstanding any provision of law to the contrary, where a child is placed with a couple or individual in New York for the purpose of adoption, and where said adoption has theretofore been finalized in the country of birth, outside of the United States, the couple or person may petition the court in their county of residence in New York state, for the readoption of said child in accordance with the provisions of this chapter, providing for adoptions originally commenced in this state. In any proceeding for readoption, proof of finalization of an adoption outside the United States shall be prima facie evidence of the consent of those parties required to give consent to an adoption pursuant to section one hundred eleven of this article.

Added by Laws 1962, Ch. 527; amended by Laws 1965, Ch. 251; Laws 1970, Ch. 570, eff. Sept. 1, 1970, which substituted "adoptive" for "foster" throughout the section and "social services" for "social welfare"; Laws 1974, Ch. 1011; Laws 1975, Ch. 605; Laws 1979, Ch. 368, eff. Nov. 1, 1979; Laws 1983, Ch. 79, eff. May 10, 1983; Laws 1989, Ch. 148, § 1, eff. July 17, 1989; Laws 1989, Ch. 751, § 5, eff. Jan. 1, 1990; Laws 1990, Ch. 547, § 1, eff. July. 18, 1990.

§ 115-b.   Special provisions relating to consents in private-placement adoptions.

1.   A duly executed and acknowledged consent to a private-placement adoption shall state that no action or proceeding may be maintained by the consenting parent for the custody of the child to be adopted except as provided in this section. Notwithstanding any other section of law, a consent to adoption executed by a person who is in foster care shall only be executed before a judge of the family court.

2.   Judicial consents. (a) A consent to a private placement adoption may be executed or acknowledged before any judge or surrogate in this state having jurisdiction over adoption proceedings. Such consent shall state that it is irrevocable upon such execution or acknowledgment. A consent executed or acknowledged before a court in another state shall satisfy the requirements of this section if it is executed by a resident of the other state before a court of record which has jurisdiction over adoption proceedings in that state, and a certified copy of the transcript of that proceeding, showing compliance with paragraph (b) of this subdivision, is filed as part of the adoption proceeding in this state.

(b)   At the time that a parent appears before a judge or surrogate to execute or acknowledge a consent to adoption, the judge or surrogate shall inform such parent of the consequences of such act pursuant to the provisions of this section, including informing such parent of the right to be represented by legal counsel of the parent's own choosing; of the right to obtain supportive counseling and of any rights the parent may have pursuant to section two hundred sixty-two of the family court act, section four hundred seven of the surrogate's court procedure act, or section thirty-five of the judiciary law. The judge or surrogate shall give such parent a copy of such consent upon the execution thereof.

3. Extrajudicial consents. (a) Whenever a consent is not executed or acknowledged before a judge or surrogate pursuant to subdivision two of this section such consent shall become irrevocable forty-five days after the execution of the consent unless written notice of revocation thereof is received by the court in which the adoption proceeding is to be commenced within said forty-five days.

(b) Notwithstanding that such written notice is received within said forty-five days, the notice of revocation shall be given effect only if the adoptive parents fail to oppose such revocation, as provided in subdivision six of this section, or, if they oppose such revocation and the court as provided in subdivision six of this section has determined that the best interests of the child will be served by giving force and effect to such revocation.

4. (a) In any case where a consent is not executed or acknowledged before a judge or surrogate pursuant to subdivision two of this section, the consent shall state, in conspicuous print of at least eighteen point type:

(i) the name and address of the court in which the adoption proceeding has been or is to be commenced; and

(ii) that the consent may be revoked within forty-five days of the execution of the document and where the consent is not revoked within said forty-five days no proceeding may be maintained by the parent for the return of the custody of the child; and

(iii) that such revocation must be in writing and received by the court where the adoption proceeding is to be commenced within forty-five days of the execution of said consent; and

(iv) that, if the adoptive parents contest the revocation, timely notice of the revocation will not necessarily result in the return of the child to the parent's custody, and that the rights of the parent to custody of the child shall not be superior to those of the adoptive parents but that a hearing will be required before a judge pursuant to the provisions of this section to determine: (1) whether the notice of revocation was timely and properly given; and if necessary, (2) whether the best interests of the child will be served by: (A) returning custody of the child to the parent; or (B) by continuing the adoption proceeding commenced by the adoptive parents; or (C) by disposition other than adoption by the adoptive parents; or (D) by placement of the child with an authorized agency, and if any such determination is made, the court shall make such disposition of the custody of the child as will best serve the interests of the child; and

(v) that the parent has the right to legal representation of the parent's own choosing; the right to obtain supportive counseling and may have the right to have the court appoint an attorney pursuant to section two hundred sixty-two of the family court act, section four hundred seven of the surrogate's court procedure act, or section thirty-five of the judiciary law.

(b) Such consent shall be executed or acknowledged before a notary public or other officer authorized to take proof of deeds.

(c)   A copy of such consent shall be given to such parent upon the execution thereof.

(d)   The adoptive parent may commence the adoption proceeding in a court of competent jurisdiction other than the court named in the consent provided that such commencement is initiated more than forty-five days after the consent is executed. Such commencement shall not revive, extend or toll the period for revocation of a consent pursuant to this section.

5.   For the purposes of commencing an adoption proceeding, the clerk of a court of competent jurisdiction shall accept an adoption petition for filing which is complete on its face and shall not require any supplementary documentation as a condition of filing. Nothing in this section shall compel a court to hear an adoption petition until all documents necessary to the adoption proceeding have been filed to the satisfaction of the court.

6.   (a) A parent may revoke his consent to adoption only by giving notice, in writing, of such revocation, no later than forty-five days after the execution of the consent, or twenty days after the receipt of a notice of denial, withdrawal or removal pursuant to paragraph (a) of subdivision four of section seventeen hundred twenty-five of surrogate's court procedure act, whichever is later, to the court in which the adoption proceeding has been or is to be commenced. Such notice shall set forth the name and address of the court in which the adoption proceeding is to be commenced, the address of the parent and may, in addition, set forth the name and address of the attorney for the parent.

(b)   If, within forty-five days of the execution of the consent, the court has received such notice of revocation, the court shall promptly notify the adoptive parents and their attorney, by certified mail, of the receipt by the court of such notice of revocation.

(i)   Such notice to the adoptive parents shall set forth that if within fifteen days from the date of such notice the court has not received from the adoptive parents or their attorneys notice, in writing, of their intention to oppose such revocation by the parents, the adoption proceeding will be dismissed and that, in case of such dismissal, the court will send to the parents, the adoptive parents and their respective attorneys the notice of dismissal, as provided in paragraph (c) of this subdivision.

(ii)   Such notice to the adoptive parents shall further set forth that if, within fifteen days from the date of such notice, the court shall receive from the adoptive parents notice, in writing, of their intention to oppose such revocation by the parents, the court will, upon notice to the parents, the adoptive parents and their respective attorneys, proceed, as provided in paragraph (d) of this subdivision, to a determination of whether such notice of revocation by the parents shall be given force and effect and to a determination of what disposition shall be made of the custody of the child.

(c)   If the adoption proceeding is dismissed pursuant to the provisions of paragraph (b) of this subdivision,

(i)　Written notice of such dismissal shall forthwith be sent to the parent, the adoptive parents and their respective attorneys.

(ii)　Such notice of dismissal shall set forth the name and address of the parent, the name and address of the attorney for the parent, if any, the name and address of the attorney for the adoptive parents.

(iii)　Such notice of dismissal shall further set forth that if the child is not returned to the custody of the parent within ten days from the date of such notice of dismissal, the court will forthwith upon request, in writing, by the parent or by the attorney for the parent, furnish to said parent or attorney so requesting, the names and address of the adoptive parents.

(iv)　such notice of dismissal shall further state that, in the event the custody of the child is not returned to the parent by the adoptive parents upon request therefor, a proceeding to obtain custody may be instituted by the parent in the Supreme Court or the Family Court.

(d)　If, pursuant to the provisions of paragraph (b) of this subdivision, the adoptive parents give timely and proper notice of their intention to oppose the revocation of the parent's consent:

(i)　The court shall promptly notify, in writing, the parent, the adoptive parents, their respective attorneys, and the law guardian appointed pursuant to section two hundred forty-nine of the family court act or a guardian ad litem appointed pursuant to section four hundred three-a of the surrogate's court procedure act, that the court will, upon the date specified in such notice by the court, or as soon thereafter as the parties may be heard pursuant to this paragraph, hear and determine whether revocation of the consent of the parent was timely and properly given and whether the adoptive parent's notice of intent to oppose such revocation was timely and properly given and if necessary, hear and determine what disposition should be made with respect to the custody of the child.

(ii)　The court shall, upon the date specified, take proof as to whether the best interests of the child will be served by returning custody of the child to the parents, or by the adoption of the child by the adoptive parents, or by placement of the child with an authorized agency for foster care with or without authority to consent to the adoption of the child, or by other disposition of the custody of the child.

(iii)　If the court determines that the best interests of the child will be served by returning custody of the child to the parent or by placement of the child with an authorized agency or by disposition other than adoption by the adoptive parents, the revocation of consent shall be given force and effect and the court shall make such disposition of the custody of the child as will best serve the interests of the child.

(iv)　If the court determines that the best interests of the child will be served by adoption of the child by the adoptive parents, the court shall enter an order

denying any force or effect to the notice of revocation of consent and shall dispose of the custody of the child as if no such notice of revocation had given by the parent.

(v)   In such proceeding the parent or parents who consented to such adoption shall have no right to the custody of the child superior to that of the adoptive parents, notwithstanding that the parent or parents who consented to the adoption are fit, competent and able to duly maintain, support and educate the child. The custody of such child shall be awarded solely on the basis of the best interests of the child, and there shall be no presumption that such interests will be promoted by any particular custodial disposition.

7.   Nothing contained in this section shall limit or affect the power and authority of the court in an adoption proceeding, pursuant to the provisions of section one hundred sixteen of this title, to remove the child from the home of the adoptive parents, upon the ground that the welfare of the child requires such action, and thereupon to return the child to a birth parent or place the child with an authorized agency, or, in the case of a surrogate, transfer the child to the family court; nor shall this section bar actions or proceedings brought on the ground of fraud, duress or coercion in the execution or inducement of an adoption consent.

8.   The provisions of this section shall not apply to petitions brought by a step-parent for the adoption of a step-child where the step-child has resided with the birth parent and the step-parent for a continuous period of at least one year.

Added by Laws 1972, Ch. 639, eff. Aug. 28, 1972, but shall not apply to adoption consents executed prior thereto; amended by Laws 1973, Ch. 1035, eff. Sept. 22, 1973; Laws 1983, Ch. 218, eff. June 3, 1983; Laws 1986, Ch. 817, eff. Sept. 1, 1986; Laws 1988, Ch. 557, § 1, eff. Oct. 1, 1988; Laws 1989, Ch. 722, § 1, eff. Oct. 1, 1989; Laws 1994, Ch. 371, § 1, eff. July 20, 1994; Laws 1994, Ch. 601, § 2, eff. Oct. 24, 1994; Laws 2002, Ch. 312, § 1, eff. Aug. 6, 2002.

§ 115-c.   Temporary guardianship by adoptive parent.

In any case where physical custody of a child is transferred from the child's parent or guardian to another person or persons for the purposes of adoption and a consent to the adoption of such child has been executed pursuant to section one hundred fifteen-b of this title, the adoptive parent or parents shall, within ten court days of taking physical custody, either file a petition for adoption with a court of competent jurisdiction or file an application for temporary guardianship of the person of the child pursuant to this section with the court in which the adoption will be filed, pursuant to section seventeen hundred twenty-five of the surrogate's court procedure act or section six hundred sixty-one of the family court act except as otherwise provided herein. Such application shall include an affidavit by the adoptive parent or parents describing any change of circumstances since their certification as a qualified adoptive parent or parents, pursuant to section one hundred fifteen-d of this title, which may be material to such certification. Such a petition for adoption shall also be deemed an application for temporary

guardianship, where no prior application for an order for temporary guardianship has been filed.

In any case where the adoptive parent or parents take physical custody of an adoptive child and requirements for certification as a qualified adoptive parent or parents have been waived, pursuant to section one hundred fifteen-d of this title, an application for temporary guardianship or petition for adoption for such child shall be filed with the court not later than five court days from obtaining physical custody of such child. Such time period may be extended upon motion of any person or upon the court's own motion for good cause shown.

Added by Laws 1988, Ch. 557, § 2, eff. Oct. 1, 1988; **amended** by Laws 1989, Ch. 700, § 3, eff. Nov. 1, 1989.

§ 115-d. Petition for certification.

1. Except as provided for in subdivision eight of this section, a person or persons petitioning for certification as a qualified adoptive parent or parents shall upon a form, promulgated by the chief administrator of the courts, provide to the court:

(a) the applicant's name or applicants' names, residential address and telephone number;

(b) a statement by the applicant or applicants that they are seeking certification by the court as a person or persons qualified to take physical custody of an infant prior to or contemporaneous with the filing of a private-placement adoption petition;

(c) a statement by the applicant or applicants as to whether such applicant or applicants have been the subject of an indicated report of child abuse or maltreatment, pursuant to title six of article six of the social services law; and

(d) a statement that a pre-placement investigation will be undertaken by a disinterested person, as such term is defined in subdivision four of this section, and that a written report of such investigation will be furnished directly to the court by such disinterested person with a copy of such report to be delivered simultaneously to the applicant or applicants. Such disinterested person shall certify to the court that he or she is a disinterested person and has no interest in the outcome of the party's or parties' application. Such disinterested person shall further disclose to the court any fee paid or to be paid to such person for services rendered in connection with the pre-placement investigation.

Such petition shall also require information regarding:

(i) the marital and family status and history of the adoptive parent or parents;

(ii) the physical and mental health of the adoptive parent or parents;

(iii) the property owned by and the income of adoptive parent or parents;

(iv) whether the adoptive parent or either of the adoptive parents has ever been a respondent in any proceeding concerning allegedly abused, neglected, abandoned or delinquent children; and

(v)   whether the applicant or applicants have made any prior application for certification as a qualified adoptive parent or parents and, if so, the disposition of such application for certification.

2.   In any case where the applicant or applicants do not intend to cause a pre-placement investigation to be undertaken pursuant to the provisions of paragraph (d) of subdivision one of this section, such applicant or applicants shall request the court to appoint a disinterested person to conduct such pre-placement investigation. The investigative written report shall be submitted to the judge or surrogate within thirty days, unless for good cause shown the judge or surrogate shall grant a reasonable extension of such period.

3.   Such applicant or applicants shall be financially responsible for the costs of any pre-placement investigation conducted pursuant to subdivision one or two of this section.

3-a.   (a) The court shall submit fingerprint cards and order a report from the division of criminal justice services setting forth any existing criminal history record of the applicant for certification as a qualified adoptive parent.

(b)   Notwithstanding any other provision of law to the contrary, a petition for certification as a qualified adoptive parent shall be denied where a criminal history record of the applicant reveals a conviction for (i) a felony conviction at any time involving: (1) child abuse or neglect; (2) spousal abuse; (3) a crime against a child, including child pornography; or (4) a crime involving violence, including rape, sexual assault, or homicide, other than a crime involving physical assault or battery; or (ii) a felony conviction within the past five years for physical assault, battery, or a drug-related offense; unless the applicant demonstrates that: (A) such denial will create an unreasonable risk of harm to the physical or mental health of the child; and (B) certification of the applicant will not place the child's safety in jeopardy and will be in the best interests of the child.

(c)   For the purposes of this subdivision, "spousal abuse" is an offense defined in section 120.05 or 120.10 of the penal law where the victim of such offense was the defendant's spouse; provided, however, spousal abuse shall not include a crime in which the applicant was the defendant, and the court finds in accordance with this subdivision that he or she was the victim of physical, sexual or psychological abuse by the victim of such offense and such abuse was a factor in causing the applicant to commit such offense.

4.   A pre-placement investigation conducted pursuant to the provisions of this section shall be made by a disinterested person who in the opinion of the judge or surrogate is qualified by training and experience to examine into the allegations set forth in the application and any other factors which may be relevant to the suitability of the applicant or applicants as a qualified adoptive parent or parents. For the purposes of this section, a disinterested person shall also include a licensed master social worker, licensed clinical social worker, the probation service of the family court or an authorized agency specifically designated by the court to conduct pre-placement investigations.

5. Such disinterested person shall file with the court a written report of his or her investigation into the truth and accuracy of the allegations set forth in the application and his or her investigation of the various factors which may be relevant to the suitability of the applicant or applicants as qualified adoptive parents. Such investigation shall include, but not be limited to, a personal interview and visit at the applicant's or applicants' home and an investigation of any other facts relating to the familial, social, religious, emotional and financial circumstances of the adoptive parent or parents which may be relevant to certification as a qualified adoptive parent or parents.

6. Certification and provisional certification. If after consideration of the report submitted by the disinterested person, and all other relevant and material factors, the court grants the application, the applicant or applicants may accept physical custody of a child for the purposes of adoption, either prior to or contemporaneous with the filing of an adoption petition. The order granting the petition shall be valid for a period not to exceed eighteen months and shall be accepted as proof of certification by any court of competent jurisdiction within the state. The court may in its discretion grant a conditional order of certification upon satisfactory completion and submission of a petition wherein the prospective adoptive parent or parents indicate no prior criminal convictions or founded findings of child abuse or neglect, and after completion of a disinterested person investigation provided for in this section, pending completion of any further reports, investigations or inquiries ordered by the court or required by any other statute or court rule. A conditional order of certification shall be valid and remain in force and effect until replaced by an order of certification or by an order denying the petition, whichever shall first occur, but in no event shall such provisional certification continue beyond one hundred eighty days from the date of original issuance. If the court denies the petition, the reasons for such denial shall be stated on the record or in the order.

7. Nothing in this section shall be deemed to waive, limit or restrict the provisions of any other law requiring any inquiry, disinterested person investigation or court review of any persons seeking to adopt a child under any provision of law.

8. The provisions of this section shall not apply to any petitions brought by a step-parent for the adoption of a step-child where the step-child has resided with the birth parent and the stepparent for a continuous period of at least one year.

9. Extension of certification. When a petition for adoption is filed by a qualified parent or parents previously certified and the balance of the time period remaining under such certification in accordance with subdivision six of this section is less than one year, the court may on its own motion or on the motion of the petitioners extend the time period of the original certification to a date eighteen months from the date of filing of the adoption petition. When a petition for adoption is filed by a qualified parent or parents who have previously been certified by an order which has expired within a year preceding the date of the adoption petition, the court may extend the termination date of the earlier

certification until eighteen months from the filing of such petition, provided the petitioner apply for such extension and set forth any change of circumstances of the qualified parent or parents since issuance and expiration of the last certification which may be relevant and material to the extension of such certification and affix thereto written verification of any such changed circumstance or lack thereof by a disinterested person as defined in subdivision four of this section. Except as is provided for by this subdivision, the court shall not extend a previously expired order of certification. Any further certification shall require the filing of a new petition for certification in accordance with subdivision six of this section.

In any instance when the court determines whether to extend a certification under this subdivision, the court, in its discretion, may order each or any of (a) a report from the statewide central registry of child abuse and maltreatment to determine whether the child or the petitioner is or has been the subject of or another person named in an indicated report, as such terms are defined in section four hundred twelve of the social services law, filed with such register, (b) a report from the division of criminal justice services setting forth any criminal record of such petitioner or petitioners, and (c) an additional pre-placement investigation to be undertaken by a disinterested person. Nothing herein shall be deemed to require that the court enter such an order.

Added by Laws 1989, Ch. 700, § 4, eff. Nov. 1, 1989; **amended** by Laws 1990, Ch. 508, eff. July 19, 1990; Laws 1992, Ch. 704, §§ 1, 2, eff. July 31, 1992; Laws 1994, Ch. 601, § 10, eff. Oct. 24, 1994; Laws 1999, Ch. 7, § 54, eff. Feb. 11, 1999; Laws 2000, Ch. 145, § 18, eff. July 1, 2000; Laws 2002, Ch. 312, § 2, eff. Aug. 6, 2002; Laws 2004, Ch. 230, § 3, eff. July 27, 2004.

§ 116. Orders of investigation and order of adoption.

1. When the adoptive child is less than eighteen years of age, no order of adoption shall be made until three months after the court shall have received the petition to adopt, except where the spouse of the adoptive parent is the birth parent of the child and the child has resided with the birth parent and adoptive parent for more than three months, such waiting period shall not be required. The judge or surrogate may shorten such waiting period for good cause shown, and, in such case the order of adoption shall recite the reason for such action. The three months residence period specified in section one hundred twelve of title two of this article and the three months waiting period provided in this subdivision may run concurrently in whole or in part.

2. Stage one of private-placement adoption. At the time of receiving the petition, agreement and consents, the judge or surrogate, upon finding that the applicable provisions of this title have been complied with and that it appears that the adoption may be in the best interests of the child, shall issue an order of investigation hereunder. The order of investigation shall require that the report of such investigation be made in accordance with subdivision three of this section,

and may require or authorize further investigations from time to time until the granting of the order of adoption. Such order shall direct that such investigation shall not unnecessarily duplicate any previous investigations which have been made of the petitioner or petitioners pursuant to section one hundred fifteen-d of this title. Should such investigation give apparent cause, the judge or surrogate shall require the petitioner or petitioners to show cause why the child should not be removed from the home, upon due notice to all persons whose consent is required for the adoption, and in any case where the consent of the birth mother would not otherwise be required, the judge or surrogate may in his discretion require that she be given due notice. On the return date the judge or surrogate shall take proof of the facts shown by any such investigation. If the court is satisfied that the welfare of the child requires that it be removed from the home, the judge or surrogate shall by order remove the child from the home of the petitioner or petitioners and return the child to a birth parent or place the child with an appropriate authorized agency, or, in the case of a surrogate, transfer the child to the family court.The judge or surrogate may also require that notice be given to an appropriate authorized agency.

3.   The judge or surrogate shall cause to be made an investigation by a disinterested person who in the opinion of the judge or surrogate is qualified by training and experience, or by an authorized agency specifically designated by him to examine into the allegations set forth in the petition. A post-placement investigation conducted pursuant to the provisions of this section shall be made by a disinterested person who in the opinion of the judge or surrogate is qualified by training and experience to perform post-placement investigations. Such disinterested person shall certify to the court that he or she is a disinterested person and has no interest in the outcome of petitioner's or petitioners' application. Such disinterested person shall further disclose to the court any fee paid or to be paid to such person for services rendered in connection with the post-placement investigation. The investigator shall make a written report of his investigation into the truth and accuracy of the allegations of the petition, and, where applicable, into the statements contained in the affidavit required by section one hundred fifteen of this title, and he shall ascertain as fully as possible, and incorporate in his report the various factors which may bear upon the determination of the application for adoption including, but not limited to, the following information:

(a)   the marital and family status, and history, of the adoptive parents and adoptive child;

(b)   the physical and mental health of the adoptive parents and adoptive child;

(c)   the property owned by and the income of the adoptive parents;

(d)   the compensation paid or agreed upon with respect to the placement of the child for adoption;

(e)   whether either adoptive parent has ever been respondent in any proceeding concerning allegedly abused, neglected, abandoned or delinquent children;

DRL

(f) any other facts relating to the familial, social, religious, emotional and financial circumstances of the adoptive parents which may be relevant to a determination of adoption.

The written report of investigation shall be submitted to the judge or surrogate within thirty days after the same is directed to be made, unless for good cause shown the judge or surrogate shall grant a reasonable extension of such period. The report shall be filed with the judge or surrogate, in any event, before the final order of adoption is granted.

4. Stage two of private-placement adoption. If the judge or surrogate has found that there has been compliance with all the requirements hereof and is satisfied that the best interests of the child will be promoted by granting an order of adoption, the provisions of section one hundred fourteen of title two of this article shall apply.

5. As used in this section, "disinterested person" includes the probation service of the family court, a licensed master social worker, licensed clinical social worker, or an authorized agency specifically designated by the court to conduct pre-placement investigations.

Added by Laws 1961, Ch. 147; **amended** by Laws 1962, Ch. 690; Laws 1964, Ch. 569; Laws 1970, Ch. 570, eff. Sept. 1, 1970, which substituted "adoptive" for "foster" in subds. (1), (3); Laws 1976, Ch. 666, eff. Jan. 1, 1977; Laws 1989, Ch. 700, § 5, eff. Nov. 1, 1989; Laws 1997, Ch. 375, § 3, eff. Aug. 5, 1997; Laws 1999, Ch. 81, § 1, eff. June 22, 1999; Laws 2000, Ch. 423, § 1, eff. Sept. 20, 2000; Laws 2002, Ch. 312, § 3, eff. Aug. 6, 2002; Laws 2004, Ch. 230, § 4, amending sub. 5, eff. July 7, 2004.

TITLE 4: EFFECT OF ADOPTION FROM AN AUTHORIZED AGENCY, OF PRIVATE-PLACEMENT ADOPTION, AND ABROGATIONS THEREOF.

Section   117.   Effect of adoption.

§ 117. Effect of adoption.

1.   (a) After the making of an order of adoption the birth parents of the adoptive child shall be relieved of all parental duties toward and of all responsibilities for and shall have no rights over such adoptive child or to his property by descent or succession, except as hereinafter stated.

(b) The rights of an adoptive child to inheritance and succession from and through his birth parents shall terminate upon the making of the order of adoption except as hereinafter provided.

(c) The adoptive parents or parent and the adoptive child shall sustain toward each other the legal relation of parent and child and shall have all the rights and be subject to all the duties of that relation including the rights of inheritance from and through each other and the birth and adopted kindred of the adoptive parents or parent.

(d)   When a birth or adoptive parent, having lawful custody of a child, marries or remarries and consents that the stepparent may adopt such child, such consent shall not relieve the parent so consenting of any parental duty toward such child nor shall such consent or the order of adoption affect the rights of such consenting spouse and such adoptive child to inherit from and through each other and the birth and adopted kindred of such consenting spouse.

(e)   Notwithstanding the provisions of paragraphs (a), (b) and (d) of this subdivision, as to estates of persons dying after the thirty-first day of August, nineteen hundred eighty-seven, if:

(1)   the decedent is the adoptive child's birth grandparent or is a descendant of such grandparent, and

(2)   an adoptive parent (i) is married to the child's birth parent, (ii) is the child's birth grandparent, or (iii) is descended from such grandparent, the rights of an adoptive child to inheritance and succession from and through either birth parent shall not terminate upon the making of the order of adoption.

However, an adoptive child who is related to the decedent both by birth relationship and by adoption shall be entitled to inherit only under the birth relationship unless the decedent is also the adoptive parent, in which case the adoptive child shall then be entitled to inherit pursuant to the adoptive relationship only.

(f)   The right of inheritance of an adoptive child extends to the distributees of such child and such distributees shall be the same as if he were the birth child of the adoptive parent.

(g)   Adoptive children and birth children shall have all the rights of fraternal relationship including the right of inheritance from each other. Such right of inheritance extends to the distributees of such adoptive children and birth children and such distributees shall be the same as if each such child were the birth child of the adoptive parents.

(h)   The consent of the parent of a child to the adoption of such child by his or her spouse shall operate to vest in the adopting spouse only the rights as distributee of a birth parent and shall leave otherwise unaffected the rights as distributee of the consenting spouse.

(i)   This subdivision shall apply only to the intestate descent and distribution of real and personal property.

2.   (a) Except as hereinafter stated, after the making of an order of adoption, adopted children and their issue thereafter are strangers to any birth relatives for the purpose of the interpretation or construction of a disposition in any instrument, whether executed before or after the order of adoption, which does not express a contrary intention or does not expressly include the individual by name or by some classification not based on a parent-child or family relationship.

(b)   As to the wills of persons executed after the thirty-first day of August, nineteen hundred eighty-six, or to lifetime instruments executed after such date

DRL

whether executed before or after the order of adoption, a designation of a class of persons described in section 2-1.3 of the estates, powers and trusts law shall, unless the will or instrument expresses a contrary intention, be deemed to include an adoptive child who was a member of such class in his or her birth relationship prior to adoption, and the issue of such child, only if:

(1)　an adoptive parent (i) is married to the child's birth parent, (ii) is the child's birth grandparent, or (iii) is a descendant of such grandparent, and

(2)　the testator or creator is the child's birth grandparent or a descendant of such grandparent.

(c)　A person who, by reason of this subdivision, would be a member of the designated class, or a member of two or more designated classes pursuant to a single instrument, both by birth relationship and by adoption shall be entitled to benefit only under the birth relationship, unless the testator or creator is the adoptive parent, in which case the person shall then be entitled to benefit only under the adoptive relationship.

(d)　The provisions of this subdivision shall not impair or defeat any rights which have vested on or before the thirty-first day of August, nineteen hundred eighty-six, or which have vested prior to the adoption regardless of when the adoption occurred.

3.　The provisions of law affected by the provisions of this section in force prior to March first, nineteen hundred sixty-four shall apply to the estates or wills of persons dying prior thereto and to lifetime instruments theretofore executed which on said date were not subject to grantor's power to revoke or amend.

Added by Laws 1938, Ch. 606 as § 115; **amended** by Laws 1940, Ch. 442; **renumbered** as § 117 by Laws 1961, Ch. 147; **amended** by Laws 1963, Ch. 406; Laws 1966, Ch. 14; Laws 1970, Ch. 570, eff. Sept. 1, 1970, which substituted "adoptive" for "foster" in subd. (1); Laws 1986, Ch. 408 Sept. 1, 1986; Laws 1987, Ch. 499, eff. Sept. 1, 1987; Laws 2002, Ch. 312, § 4, eff. Aug. 6, 2002.

§ 118.　Abrogation by consent.

Repealed by Laws 1974, Ch. 1035, eff. June 15, 1974.

§ 118-a.　Abrogation by or on behalf of an adoptive child.

Repealed by Laws 1974, Ch. 1035, eff. June 15, 1974.

§ 118-b.　Abrogation by adoptive parent.

Repealed by Laws 1974, Ch. 1035, eff. June 5, 1974.

§ 118-c.　Jurisdiction to abrogate adoption.

Repealed by Laws 1974, Ch. 1035, eff. June 5, 1974.

ARTICLE 8

SURROGATE PARENTING CONTRACTS

§ 121. Definitions.

When used in this article, unless the context or subject matter manifestly requires a different interpretation:

1. "Birth mother" shall mean a woman who gives birth to a child pursuant to a surrogate parenting contract.

2. "Genetic father" shall mean a man who provides sperm for the birth of a child born pursuant to a surrogate parenting contract.

3. "Genetic mother" shall mean a woman who provides an ovum for the birth of a child born pursuant to a surrogate parenting contract.

4. "Surrogate parenting contract" shall mean any agreement, oral or written, in which:

(a) A woman agrees either to be inseminated with the sperm of a man who is not her husband or to be impregnated with an embryo that is the product of an ovum fertilized with the sperm of a man who is not her husband; and

(b) The woman agrees to, or intends to, surrender or consent to the adoption of the child born as a result of such insemination or impregnation.

Added by Laws 1992, Ch. 308, § 1, eff. July 17, 1993.

§ 122. Public policy.

Surrogate parenting contracts are hereby declared contrary to the public policy of this state, and are void and unenforceable.

Added by Laws 1992, Ch. 308, § 1, eff. July 17, 1993.

§ 123. Prohibitions and penalties.

1. No person or other entity shall knowingly request, accept, receive, pay or give any fee, compensation or other remuneration, directly or indirectly, in

connection with any surrogate parenting contract, or induce, arrange or otherwise assist in arranging a surrogate parenting contract for a fee, compensation or other remuneration, except for:

(a)   Payments in connection with the adoption of a child permitted by subdivision six of section three hundred seventy-four of the social services law and disclosed pursuant to subdivision eight of section one hundred fifteen of this chapter; or

(b)   Payments for reasonable and actual medical fees and hospital expenses for artificial insemination or in vitro fertilization services incurred by the mother in connection with the birth of the child.

2.   (a) A birth mother or her husband, a genetic father and his wife, and, if the genetic mother is not the birth mother, the genetic mother and her husband who violate this section shall be subject to a civil penalty not to exceed five hundred dollars.

(b)   Any other person or entity who or which induces, arranges or otherwise assists in the formation of a surrogate parenting contract for a fee, compensation or other remuneration or otherwise violates this section shall be subject to a civil penalty not to exceed ten thousand dollars and forfeiture to the state of any such fee, compensation or remuneration in accordance with the provisions of subdivision (a) of section seven thousand two hundred one of the civil practice law and rules, for the first such offense. Any person or entity who or which induces, arranges or otherwise assists in the formation of a surrogate parenting contract for a fee, compensation or other remuneration or otherwise violates this section, after having been once subject to a civil penalty for violating this section, shall be guilty of a felony.

Added by Laws 1992, Ch. 308, § 1, eff. July 17, 1993.

§ 124.   Proceedings regarding parental rights, status or obligations.

In any action or proceeding involving a dispute between the birth mother and (i) the genetic father, (ii) the genetic mother, (iii) both the genetic father and genetic mother, or (iv) the parent or parents of the genetic father or genetic mother, regarding parental rights, status or obligations with respect to a child born pursuant to a surrogate parenting contract:

1.   The court shall not consider the birth mother's participation in a surrogate parenting contract as adverse to her parental rights, status, or obligations; and

2.   The court, having regard to the circumstances of the case and of the respective parties including the parties' relative ability to pay such fees and expenses, in its discretion and in the interests of justice, may award to either party reasonable and actual counsel fees and legal expenses incurred in connection with such action or proceeding. Such award may be made in the order or judgment by which the particular action or proceeding is finally determined, or by one or more orders from time to time before the final order or judgment, or by both such

order or orders and the final order or judgment; provided, however, that in any dispute involving a birth mother who has executed a valid surrender or consent to the adoption, nothing in this section shall empower a court to make any award that it would not otherwise be empowered to direct.

Added by Laws 1992, Ch. 308, § 1, eff. July 17, 1993.

DRL

ARTICLE 9

ACTION TO ANNUL A MARRIAGE OR DECLARE IT VOID

———

SUMMARY OF ARTICLE

(Repealed and transferred sections noted under appropriate section number of text.)

§ 140. Action for judgment declaring nullity of void marriages or annulling voidable marriage.

(a) Former husband or wife living. An action to declare the nullity of a void marriage upon the ground that the former husband or wife of one of the parties was living, the former marriage being in force, may be maintained by either of the parties during the lifetime of the other, or by the former husband or wife.

(b) Party under age of consent. An action to annul a marriage on the ground that one or both of the parties had not attained the age of legal consent may be maintained by the infant, or by either parent of the infant, or by the guardian of the infant's person; or the court may allow the action to be maintained by any person as the next friend of the infant. But a marriage shall not be annulled under this subdivision at the suit of a party who was of the age of legal consent when it was contracted, or by a party who for any time after he or she attained that age freely cohabited with the other party as husband or wife.

(c) Party a mentally retarded person or mentally ill person. An action to annul a marriage on the ground that one of the parties thereto was a mentally retarded person may be maintained at any time during the lifetime of either party by any relative of the mentally retarded person who has an interest to avoid the marriage. An action to annul a marriage on the ground that one of the parties thereto was a mentally ill person may be maintained at any time during the continuance of the mental illness, or, after the death of the mentally ill person in that condition, and during the life of the other party to the marriage, by any relative of the mentally ill person who has an interest to avoid the marriage. Such an action may also be maintained by the mentally ill person at any time after restoration to a sound mind; but in that case, the marriage should not be annulled if it appears that the parties freely cohabited as husband and wife after the mentally ill person was restored to a sound mind. Where one of the parties to a marriage was a mentally ill person at the time of the marriage, an action may also be maintained by the other party at any time during the continuance of the mental illness, provided the plaintiff did not know of the mental illness at the time of the marriage. Where no relative of the mentally retarded person or mentally ill person brings an action to annul the marriage and the mentally ill person is not restored to sound mind, the court may allow an action for that purpose to be maintained at any time during the lifetime of both the parties to the marriage, by any person as the next friend of the mentally retarded person or mentally ill person.

(d) Physical incapacity. An action to annul a marriage on the ground that one of the parties was physically incapable of entering into the marriage state may be maintained by the injured party against the party whose incapacity is alleged; or such an action may be maintained by the party who was incapable against the other party, provided the incapable party was unaware of the incapacity at the time of marriage, or if aware of such incapacity, did not know it was incurable. Such an action can be maintained only where an incapacity continues and is incurable, and must be commenced before five years have expired since the marriage.

(e) Consent by force, duress or fraud. An action to annul a marriage on the ground that the consent of one of the parties thereto was obtained by force or duress may be maintained at any time by the party whose consent was so obtained. An action to annul a marriage on the ground that the consent of one of the parties thereto was obtained by fraud may be maintained by the party whose consent was so obtained within the limitations of time for enforcing a civil remedy of the civil practice law and rules. Any such action may also be maintained during the lifetime of the other party by the parent, or the guardian of the person of the party whose consent was so obtained, or by any relative of that party who has an interest to avoid the marriage, provided that in an action to annul a marriage on the ground of fraud the limitation prescribed in the civil practice law and rules has not run. But a marriage shall not be annulled on the ground of force or duress if it appears that, at any time before the commencement of the action, the parties thereto voluntarily cohabited as husband and wife; or on the ground of fraud, if it appears that, at any time before the commencement thereof, the parties voluntarily cohabited as husband and wife with a full knowledge of the facts constituting the fraud.

(f) Incurable mental illness for five years. An action to annul a marriage upon the ground that one of the parties has been incurably mentally ill for a period of five years or more may be maintained by or on behalf of either of the parties to such marriage.

Added by Laws 1962, Ch. 313, eff. Sept. 1, 1963, from former CPA §§ 1132-1141; **amended** by Laws 1963, Ch. 458; Laws 1978, Ch. 550, § 15, eff. July 24, 1978.

§ 141. Action to annul marriage on ground of incurable mental illness for five years; procedure; support.

1. If the marriage be annulled on the ground of the mental illness of a spouse, the court may include in the judgment an order providing for his or her suitable support, care and maintenance during life from the property or income of the other spouse. The court shall specify the amount of such support, care and maintenance and, before rendering judgment, may exact security for such support, care and maintenance during life and shall order the filing and recording of the instrument creating such security in the office of the clerk of the county in which the action is brought and the filing of two certified copies thereof with the office of mental health at its Albany office. The provisions of the judgment relating to support, care and maintenance of the mentally ill spouse during his or her life and to security therefor may be modified or amended at any time by the court upon due notice to the other party and other interested parties as the court may direct and in proper case the value of the suitable support, care and maintenance to such spouse during the balance of his or her life based upon appropriate mortality tables may be adjudged and determined by the court in which the estate of a deceased spouse is being administered and the same may be recovered on behalf of the mentally ill spouse from the estate of the deceased spouse. If the mentally ill spouse is maintained in an institution or otherwise under the jurisdiction of the office of mental health the suitable support, care and maintenance as required in the judgment, unless otherwise directed by the court, shall be the charge established by the commissioner of mental health and such charge may be recovered in the manner provided by law. Such amount shall continue to be so required for the support of the mentally ill spouse in the event of his or her removal from the custody of the office of mental health unless thereafter otherwise directed by the court. Any security exacted for the suitable support, care and maintenance during life of the mentally ill spouse shall be available to that spouse or any person on his or her behalf or to any person or agency providing support, care and maintenance for such spouse in the event that the required payments for such support, care and maintenance have not been made and upon application to the court the other spouse shall be ordered and directed to provide additional or further security.

2. Judgment annulling a marriage on such ground shall not be rendered until, in addition to any other proofs in the case, a thorough examination of the alleged mentally ill party shall have been made by three physicians who are recognized authorities on mental disease, to be appointed by the court, all of whom shall have agreed that such party is incurably mentally ill and shall have so reported to the court. In such action, the testimony of a physician attached to a state hospital in the department of mental hygiene as to information which he acquired in attending a patient in a professional capacity at such hospital, shall be taken before a

referee appointed by a judge of the court in which such action is pending if the court in its discretion shall determine that the distance such physician must travel to attend the trial would be a great inconvenience to him or the hospital, or that other sufficient reason exists for the appointment of a referee for such purpose; provided, however, that any judge of such court at any time in his discretion, notwithstanding such deposition, may order that a subpoena issue for the attendance and examination of such physician upon the trial of the action. In such case a copy of the order shall be served together with the subpoena.

3. Except as provided in paragraph five, when the person alleged to be incurably mentally ill is confined in a state hospital for the mentally ill of this state, one, and one only, of the physicians so appointed shall be a member of the resident medical staff of such hospital designated by the director thereof. If the alleged incurably mentally ill person is not confined in a state hospital for the mentally ill of this state, one of the examining physicians named in pursuance of this section shall be the director of a state hospital for the mentally ill if the alleged mentally ill person is within this state, or the superintendent or comparable officer of a state hospital for the mentally ill of the state or country where the alleged mentally ill person is present if the alleged mentally ill person is outside of this state. The report of such superintendent or comparable officer of a state hospital for the mentally ill of such other state or country shall not be received in evidence or considered by the court unless he shall be a well educated physician with at least five years of training and experience in the care and treatment of persons suffering from mental disorders.

4. When the plaintiff has been permitted to bring such action or prosecute the same as a poor person and the alleged incurably mentally ill defendant is present within this state, the court shall appoint three physicians who are examining physicians, as defined by section 1.05 of the mental hygiene law, in the employment of the department of mental hygiene. If the alleged mentally ill person be outside of this state, the court may, upon proof thereof, appoint three examining physicians who are qualified under the laws or regulations of the foreign state or country where the alleged mentally ill person is present and who have qualifications comparable to those specified in section 1.05 of the mental hygiene law of the state, provided, however, that one of such examining physicians shall be the superintendent or comparable officer of a state hospital for the mentally ill of such foreign state or country with qualifications as specified in paragraph four. Such examiners shall make the examination of the alleged mentally ill party present in this state and file with the court a verified report of their findings and conclusions without costs to such plaintiff when the plaintiff is a poor person. Examination of an alleged mentally ill party present outside of this state shall be made at the expense of the plaintiff. Such report shall be received in evidence upon the trial of the action without the personal appearance or testimony of such examiners. If the court shall deem it necessary that the testimony of any such examiners be taken, the court may order the taking of such testimony by deposition only. The examiners so appointed by the court may be

members of the resident medical staff of any state hospital, whether or not the alleged mentally ill person is being confined there.

Added by Laws 1962, Ch. 313, eff. Sept. 1, 1963; **amended** by Laws 1966, Ch. 572; Laws 1973, Ch. 195; Laws 1978, Ch. 550; Laws 1980, Ch. 281, eff. July 19, 1980.

Editor's Note: Laws 1980, Ch. 281 repealed § 141(2) and renumbered former subdivisions (3) (4) and (5) to be (2) (3) and (4). However, references to paragraphs within these subdivisions were never modified by the Legislature to reflect these changes.

§ 142. Dismissal of complaint in action by next friend to annul a marriage.

Where the next friend of an infant, mentally retarded person or mentally ill person maintains an action annulling a marriage, the court may dismiss the complaint if justice so requires, although, in a like case, the party to the marriage, if plaintiff, would be entitled to judgment.

Added by Laws 1962, Ch. 313, eff. Sept. 1, 1963, from former CPA § 1145; **amended** by Laws 1978, Ch. 550, § 17, eff. July 24, 1978.

§ 143. Jury trial.

In an action to annul a marriage, except where it is founded upon an allegation of the physical incapacity of one of the parties thereto, there is a right to trial by a jury of all the issues of fact.

Added by Laws 1962, Ch. 313, eff. Sept. 1, 1963, from former CPA § 1142; **amended** by Laws 1963, Ch. 685, eff. Sept. 1, 1963.

§ 144. Proof required.

1.   In an action to annul a marriage, a final judgment annulling the marriage shall not be rendered by default for want of an appearance or pleading, or by consent, or upon a trial of an issue, without proof of the facts upon which the allegation of nullity is founded. Plaintiff shall prove that there has been no such cohabitation between the parties as would bar a judgment except that in an action under subdivision (c) of section one hundred forty the plaintiff may prove instead that the mental illness still continues.

2.   In an action, whether or not contested, brought to annul a marriage, the declaration or confession of either party to the marriage is not alone sufficient as proof, but other satisfactory evidence of the facts must be produced.

Added by Laws 1962, Ch. 313, eff. Sept. 1, 1963, from former CPA § 1143; **amended** by Laws 1978, Ch. 550, § 18, eff. July 24, 1978.

§ 145. Legitimacy of children.

Repealed by Laws 1969, Ch. 325, § 2, eff. April 30, 1969 and transferred to Dom. Rel. Law § 24.

§ 146. Judgment, how far conclusive.

A final judgment, annulling a marriage rendered during the lifetime of both the parties is conclusive evidence of the invalidity of the marriage in every court of record or not of record, in any action or special proceeding, civil or criminal. Such a judgment rendered after the death of either party to the marriage is conclusive only as against the parties to the action and those claiming under them.

Added by Laws 1962, Ch. 313, eff. Sept. 1, 1963, from former CPA § 1146.

DRL

ARTICLE 10

ACTION FOR DIVORCE

SUMMARY OF ARTICLE

(Repealed and transferred sections noted under appropriate section number of text.)

§ 170.   Action for divorce.

An action for divorce may be maintained by a husband or wife to procure a judgment divorcing the parties and dissolving the marriage on any of the following grounds:

(1)   The cruel and inhuman treatment of the plaintiff by the defendant such that the conduct of the defendant so endangers the physical or mental well being of the plaintiff as renders it unsafe or improper for the plaintiff to cohabit with the defendant.

(2)   The abandonment of the plaintiff by the defendant for a period of one or more years.

(3)   The confinement of the defendant in prison for a period of three or more consecutive years after the marriage of plaintiff and defendant.

(4)   The commission of an act of adultery, provided that adultery for the purposes of articles ten, eleven, and eleven-A of this chapter, is hereby defined as the commission of an act of sexual intercourse, oral sexual conduct or anal sexual conduct, voluntarily performed by the defendant, with a person other than the plaintiff after the marriage of plaintiff and defendant. Oral sexual conduct and anal sexual conduct include, but are not limited to, sexual conduct as defined in subdivision two of section 130.00 and subdivision three of section 130.20 of the penal law.

(5)   The husband and wife have lived apart pursuant to a decree or judgment of separation for a period of one or more years after the granting of such decree or judgment, and satisfactory proof has been submitted by the plaintiff that he

or she has substantially performed all the terms and conditions of such decree or judgment.

(6) The husband and wife have lived separate and apart pursuant to a written agreement of separation, subscribed by the parties thereto and acknowledged or proved in the form required to entitle a deed to be recorded, for a period of one or more years after the execution of such agreement and satisfactory proof has been submitted by the plaintiff that he or she has substantially performed all the terms and conditions of such agreement. Such agreement shall be filed in the office of the clerk of the county wherein either party resides. In lieu of filing such agreement, either party to such agreement may file a memorandum of such agreement, which memorandum shall be similarly subscribed and acknowledged or proved as was the agreement of separation and shall contain the following information: (a) the names and addresses of each of the parties, (b) the date of marriage of the parties, (c) the date of the agreement of separation and (d) the date of this subscription and acknowledgement or proof of such agreement of separation.

Added by Laws 1966, Ch. 254, eff. Sept. 1, 1967; **amended** by Laws 1967, Ch. 648; Laws 1968, Ch. 700; Laws 1969, Ch. 964; Laws 1970, Chs. 867, 835; Laws 1971, Ch. 801; Laws 1972, Ch. 719; Laws 1974, Ch. 920, eff. Sept. 1, 1974, Ch. 1047, eff. June 15, 1974; Laws 1975, Ch. 415, eff. July 8, 1975; Laws 2003, Ch. 264, § 53, amending sub. 4, eff. Nov. 1, 2003.

1967-1975 Amendments

Subd. (1) added by Laws 1966, Ch. 254, eff. Sept. 1, 1967.

Subd. (2) added by Laws 1966, Ch. 254, eff. Sept. 1, 1967, provided a qualifying abandonment period of two years, reduced to one year by Laws 1970, Ch. 835, eff. Sept. 1, 1972. See Ch. 835 § 4 *infra*. Subd. (3) amended by Laws 1968, Ch. 700, eff. June 16, 1968, by substituting "in" for "to" prison.

Subd. (4) amended by Laws 1968, Ch. 700, eff. June 16, 1968, which added the second sentence relating to deviate sexual intercourse. Subd. (5) amended by Laws 1968, Ch. 700, eff. June 16, 1968, which added "or judgment" following "decree" and substituted "substantially" for "duly"; Laws 1970, Ch. 835, eff. Sept. 1, 1972, which substituted "one or more" for "two" years. See Ch. 835 § 4 set forth *infra*. Subd. (6) amended by Laws 1967, Ch. 648, eff. Sept. 1, 1967, by providing for filing a memorandum of agreement in lieu of the separation agreement; Laws 1968, Ch. 700, eff. June 16, 1968, adding a requirement that the separation agreement be subscribed and acknowledged "on or after August first, nineteen hundred sixty-six," substituting "substantially" for "duly" performed and deleting the last provision requiring exhibition of the original separation agreement to the county clerk upon filing a memorandum of agreement; Laws 1969, Ch. 964, eff. May 26, 1969, which substituted "April twenty-seventh" for "August first"; Laws 1970, Ch. 867, eff. May 18, 1970, which deleted "on or after April twenty-seventh, nineteen hundred sixty-six," and substituted "by either party to such agreement, prior to commencement of an action as authorized herein" for "within thirty days after the execution thereof"; Laws 1970, Ch. 835, eff. Sept. 1, 1972 (see Ch. 835 § 4 set forth *infra*) which amended subd. (6) in the form in which it was amended by Laws 1968, Ch. 700, by substituting "one or more" for "two" years. Laws 1971, Ch. 801, § 1, amended Laws 1970, Ch. 835 (2nd subd. (6) *supra*) to conform to Laws 1970, Ch. 867 (1st subd. (6)) by deleting the cutoff date of April 27, 1966 and the thirty-day filing period in divorce actions commenced on or after Sept. 1, 1972, based upon a separation agreement. Laws 1971, Ch. 801, §§ 1 and 2, amended both subds. (6) *supra,* to provide that a separation agreement may be proved as well as acknowledged.

Laws 1970, Ch. 835 § 4 provides:

§ 4. This act shall take effect September first, nineteen hundred seventy-two and apply to all actions or proceedings undertaken on or after that date, provided that the one year period specified in section one hundred seventy of the domestic relations law shall not be computed to include any period prior to September first, nineteen hundred seventy-one.

Subd. (6-a) added by Laws 1972, Ch. 719, provided that parties between the ages of eighteen and twenty-one were allowed to enter into a binding separation agreement with the consent and approval of the supreme court, repealed by Laws 1974, Ch. 920, which also provided that the age of majority commences at eighteen.

Subd. (7) added by Laws 1974, Ch. 1047, eff. June 15, 1974; repealed, amended, and re-enacted as new § 170–a *infra* by Laws 1975, Ch. 415, eff. July 8, 1975.

§ 170-a.   Special action.

a.   A spouse against whom a decree of divorce has been obtained under the provisions of subdivision five or six of section one hundred seventy of this chapter, where the decree, judgment or agreement of separation was obtained or entered into prior to January twenty-first, nineteen hundred seventy, may institute an action in which there shall be recoverable, in addition to any rights under this or any other provisions of law, an amount equivalent to the value of any economic and property rights of which the spouse was deprived by virtue of such decree, except where the grounds for the separation judgment would have excluded recovery of economic and property rights.

b.   In determining the value of the economic and property rights described in subdivision a hereof, the plaintiff's interest shall be calculated as though the defendant died intestate as if the death of the defendant had immediately antedated the divorce.

c.   If the defendant shall establish that intervening circumstances have rendered an award described in subdivision a hereof inequitable, the court may award to the plaintiff such portion of such economic and property rights as justice may require.

d.   If the defendant shall establish that the plaintiff has expressly or impliedly waived all or some portion of the aforesaid economic or property rights, the court shall deny recovery of all such rights, or deny recovery of the portion of such rights as justice may require.

e.   Actions under this subdivision may be brought:

(i)   Within two years of the enactment of this section, or

(ii)   Within two years of the obtainment of the subject divorce, whichever is later.

Added by Laws 1975, Ch. 415, eff. July 8, 1975.

§ 171.   When divorce denied, although adultery proved.

In either of the following cases, the plaintiff is not entitled to a divorce, although the adultery is established:

1.   Where the offense was committed by the procurement or with the connivance of the plaintiff.

2.   Where the offense charged has been forgiven by the plaintiff. The forgiveness may be proven, either affirmatively, or by the voluntary cohabitation of the parties with the knowledge of the fact.

3.   Where there has been no express forgiveness, and no voluntary cohabitation of the parties, but the action was not commenced within five years after the discovery by the plaintiff of the offense charged.

4.   Where the plaintiff has also been guilty of adultery under such circumstances that the defendant would have been entitled, if innocent, to a divorce.

Added by Laws 1962, Ch. 313, eff. Sept. 1, 1963, from former CPA § 1153.

§ 172.   Co-respondent as party.

1.   In an action brought to obtain a divorce on the ground of adultery the plaintiff or defendant may serve a copy of his pleading on a co-respondent named therein. At any time within twenty days after such service, the co-respondent may appear to defend such action so far as the issues affect him. If no such service be made, then at any time before the entry of judgment a co-respondent named in any of the pleadings may make a written demand on any party for a copy of a summons and a pleading served by such party, which must be served within ten days thereafter, and he may appear to defend such action so far as the issues affect him.

2.   In an action for divorce where a co-respondent has appeared and defended, in case no one of the allegations of adultery controverted by such co-respondent shall be proven, such co-respondent shall be entitled to a bill of costs against the person naming him as such co-respondent, which bill of costs shall consist only of the sum now allowed by law as a trial fee, and disbursements.

Added by Laws 1962, Ch. 313, eff. Sept. 1, 1963, from former CPA §§ 1151, 1152.

DRL

§ 173.　Jury trial.

In an action for divorce there is a right to trial by jury of the issues of the grounds for granting the divorce.

Added by Laws 1962, Ch. 313, eff. Sept. 1, 1963, from former CPA § 1149; **amended** by Laws 1966, Ch. 254, eff. Sept. 1, 1967.

§ 174.　Pleading and proof.

Repealed by Laws 1966, Ch. 254, § 4, eff. Sept. 1, 1967, and subject matter transferred to Dom. Rel. Law § 211.

§ 175.　Legitimacy of children.

1.　Where the action for divorce is brought by the wife, the legitimacy of any child of the parties, born or begotten before the commencement of the action, is not affected by the judgment dissolving the marriage.

2.　Where the action for divorce is brought by the husband, the legitimacy of a child born or begotten before the commission of the offense charged is not affected by a judgment dissolving the marriage; but the legitimacy of any other child of the wife may be determined as one of the issues in the action. In the absence of proof to the contrary, the legitimacy of all the children begotten before the commencement of the action must be presumed.

Added by Laws 1962, Ch. 313, eff. Sept. 1, 1963, from former CPA §§ 1154, 1157.

§ 176.　Property rights in action by wife.

Repealed by Laws 1981, Ch. 147, eff. May 29, 1981.

ARTICLE 11

ACTION FOR SEPARATION

———

SUMMARY OF ARTICLE

(Repealed and transferred sections noted under appropriate section number of text.)

§ 200. Action for separation.

An action may be maintained by a husband or wife against the other party to the marriage to procure a judgment separating the parties from bed and board, forever, or for a limited time, for any of the following causes:

1. The cruel and inhuman treatment of the plaintiff by the defendant such that the conduct of the defendant so endangers the physical or mental well being of the plaintiff as renders it unsafe or improper for the plaintiff to cohabit with the defendant.

2. The abandonment of the plaintiff by the defendant.

3. The neglect or refusal of the defendant-spouse to provide for the support of the plaintiff-spouse where the defendant-spouse is chargeable with such support under the provisions of section thirty-two of this chapter or of section four hundred twelve of the family court act.

4. The commission of an act of adultery by the defendant; except where such offense is committed by the procurement or with the connivance of the plaintiff or where there is voluntary cohabitation of the parties with the knowledge of the offense or where action was not commenced within five years after the discovery by the plaintiff of the offense charged or where the plaintiff has also been guilty of adultery under such circumstances that the defendant would have been entitled, if innocent, to a divorce, provided that adultery for the purposes of this subdivision is hereby defined as the commission of an act of sexual intercourse, oral sexual conduct or anal sexual conduct, voluntarily performed by the defendant, with a person other than the plaintiff after the marriage of plaintiff and defendant. Oral sexual conduct and anal sexual conduct include, but are not limited to, sexual conduct as defined in subdivision two of section 130.00 and subdivision three of section 130.20 of the penal law.

5.   The confinement of the defendant in prison for a period of three or more consecutive years after the marriage of plaintiff and defendant.

Added by Laws 1962, Ch. 313, eff. Sept. 1, 1963, from former CPA § 1161; **amended** by Laws 1966, Ch. 254; Laws 1968, Ch. 702, eff. June 16, 1968; Laws 1981, Ch. 300, eff. Sept. 1, 1981, to render subd. 3 gender-neutral; Laws 2003, Ch. 264, § 54, amending sub. 4, eff. Nov. 1, 2003.

§ 201.   Proof.

Repealed by Laws 1966, Ch. 254, eff. Sept. 1, 1967 and subject matter transferred to Dom. Rel. Law § 211.

§ 202.   Defense of justification.

The defendant in an action for separation from bed and board may set up, in justification, the misconduct of the plaintiff; and if that defense is established to the satisfaction of the court, the defendant is entitled to judgment.

Added by Laws 1962, Ch. 313, eff. Sept. 1, 1963, from former CPA § 1163.

§ 203.   Judgment for separation revocable.

Upon the joint application of the parties, accompanied with satisfactory evidence of their reconciliation, a judgment for a separation, forever, or for a limited period, rendered as prescribed in this article, may be revoked at any time by the court which rendered it, subject to such regulations and restrictions as the court thinks fit to impose.

Added by Laws 1962, Ch. 313, eff. Sept. 1, 1963, from former CPA § 1165.

ARTICLE 11–A

SPECIAL PROVISIONS RELATING TO DIVORCE AND SEPARATION

SUMMARY OF ARTICLE

§ 210.　Limitations on actions for divorce and separation.

No action for divorce or separation may be maintained on a ground which arose more than five years before the date of the commencement of that action for divorce or separation except where:

(a)　In an action for divorce, the grounds therefor are one of those specified in subdivision (2), (4), (5) or (6) of section one hundred seventy of this chapter, or

(b)　In an action for separation, the grounds therefor are one of those specified in subdivision 2 or 4 of section two hundred of this chapter.

Added by Laws 1966, Ch. 254; **amended** by Laws 1967, Ch. 648; Laws 1968, Ch. 799, eff. Sept. 1, 1968; Laws 1985, Ch. 641, eff. July 28, 1985.

§ 211.　Pleadings, proof and motions.

A matrimonial action shall be commenced by the filing of a summons with the notice designated in section two hundred thirty-two of this chapter, or a summons and verified complaint as provided in section three hundred four of the civil practice law and rules. A final judgment shall be entered by default for want of appearance or pleading, or by consent, only upon competent oral proof or upon written proof that may be considered on a motion for summary judgment. Where a complaint or counterclaim in an action for divorce or separation charges adultery, the answer or reply thereto may be made without verifying it, except that an answer containing a counterclaim must be verified as to that counterclaim. All other pleadings in a matrimonial action shall be verified.

Added by Laws 1966, Ch. 254; **amended** by Laws 1968, Ch. 701; Laws 1970, Ch. 483; Laws 1973, Ch. 1034, eff. July 1, 1973; Laws 1978, Ch. 528, 532, eff. Jan. 1, 1979; Laws 1992, Ch. 216, § 21, eff. July 1, 1992.

DRL

ARTICLE 11–B
CONCILIATION BUREAU

§§ 215-215-g. Repealed by Laws 1973, Ch. 1034, eff. July 1, 1973.

ARTICLE 12

DISSOLUTION OF MARRIAGE ON GROUND OF ABSENCE

SUMMARY OF ARTICLE

Section 220. Special proceeding to dissolve marriage on the ground of absence.

221. Procedure.

§ 220. Special proceeding to dissolve marriage on the ground of absence.

A special proceeding to dissolve a marriage on the ground of absence may be maintained in either of the following cases:

1. Where the petitioner is a resident of this state and has been a resident thereof for one year immediately preceding the commencement of the special proceeding.

2. Where the matrimonial domicile at the time of the disappearance of the absent spouse was within the state.

Added by Laws 1962, Ch. 313, eff. Sept. 1, 1963.

§ 221. Procedure.

The petition shall allege that the husband or wife of such party has absented himself or herself for five successive years then last past without being known to such party to be living during that time; that such party believes such husband or wife to be dead; and that a diligent search has been made to discover evidence showing that such husband or wife is living, and no such evidence has been found. The court shall thereupon by order require notice of the presentation and object of such petition to be published in a newspaper in the English language designated in the order as most likely to give notice to such absent husband or wife once each week for three successive weeks; such notice shall be directed to the husband or wife who has so absented himself or herself and shall state the time and place of the hearing upon such petition, which time shall be not less than forty days after the completion of the publication of such notice; said notice must be subscribed with the name of the petitioner and with the name of the petitioner's attorney and with his office address, specifying a place within the state where there is a post-office. If in a city, said notice must also set forth the street and street number, if any, of such attorney's office address or other suitable designation of the particular locality in which said office address is located. In addition to the foregoing requirements said notice must be in substantially the following form, the blanks being properly filled: "Supreme court, ... county. In the matter of the application of . . . . for dissolution of his or her marriage with . . . . To . . . .: Take notice that a petition has been presented to this court by . . . ., your husband or wife, for the dissolution of your marriage on the ground that you have absented yourself for five successive years last past without being known to him or her to be living and that he or she believes you to be dead, and that pursuant to an order of said court, entered the . . . . day of . . . ., 20 . ., a hearing will be hd upon said petition at the said supreme court, ... term part . . . ., in the . . . . county court house, in the . . . ., state of New York, on the . . . . day of . . . ., 20 . ., at . . . . o'clock in the . . . . noon. Dated . . . ."; and if the court, after the filing of proof of the proper publication of said notice and after a hearing and proof taken, is satisfied of the truth of all the allegations contained in the petition, it may make a final order dissolving such marriage.

Added by Laws 1962, Ch. 313; **amended** by Laws 1971, Ch. 161, eff. Apr. 21, 1971.

ARTICLE 13

PROVISIONS APPLICABLE TO MORE THAN ONE TYPE OF MATRIMONIAL ACTION

SUMMARY OF ARTICLE

(Repealed and transferred sections noted under appropriate section number of text.)

DRL

§ 230. Required residence of parties.

An action to annul a marriage, or to declare the nullity of a void marriage, or for divorce or separation may be maintained only when:

1. The parties were married in the state and either party is a resident thereof when the action is commenced and has been a resident for a continuous period of one year immediately preceding, or

2. The parties have resided in this state as husband and wife and either party is a resident thereof when the action is commenced and has been a resident for a continuous period of one year immediately preceding, or

3. The cause occurred in the state and either party has been a resident thereof for a continuous period of at least one year immediately preceding the commencement of the action, or

4. The cause occurred in the state and both parties are residents thereof at the time of the commencement of the action, or

5. Either party has been a resident of the state for a continuous period of at least two years immediately preceding the commencement of the action.

Added by Laws 1962, Ch. 313, from former CPA § 1165-a; **amended** by Laws 1963, Ch. 685; Laws 1966, Ch. 254, eff. Sept. 1, 1967.

§ 231. Residence of married persons.

If a married person dwells within the state when he or she commences an action against his or her spouse for divorce, annulment or separation, such person is deemed a resident thereof, although his or her spouse resides elsewhere.

Added by Laws 1962, Ch. 313, eff. Sept. 1, 1963, from former CPA § 1166; **amended** by Laws 1976, Ch. 62, eff. Sept. 1, 1976.

§ 232. Notice of nature of matrimonial action; proof of service.

a.   In an action to annul a marriage or for divorce or separation, if the complaint is not personally served with the summons, the summons shall have legibly written or printed upon the face thereof: "Action to annul a marriage," "Action to declare the nullity of a void marriage," "Action for a divorce," or "Action for a separation," as the case may be, and shall specify the nature of any ancillary relief demanded. A judgment shall not be rendered in favor of the plaintiff upon the defendant's default in appearing or pleading, unless either (1) the summons and a copy of the complaint were personally delivered to the defendant; or (2) the copy of the summons (a) personally delivered to the defendant, or (b) served on the defendant pursuant to an order directing the method of service of the summons in accordance with the provisions of section three hundred eight or three hundred fifteen of the civil practice law and rules, shall contain such notice.

b.   An affidavit or certificate proving service shall state affirmatively in the body thereof that the required notice was written or printed on the face of the copy of the summons delivered to the defendant and what knowledge the affiant or officer who executed the certificate had that he was the defendant named and how he acquired such knowledge. The court may require the affiant or officer who executed the affidavit or certificate to appear in court and be examined in respect thereto.

Added by Laws 1962, Ch. 313 from former CPA § 1167; **amended** by Laws 1963, Ch. 685; Laws 1969, Ch. 712; Laws 1974, Ch. 765, eff. July 7, 1974; Laws 1978, Ch. 528, eff. Jan. 1, 1979.

§ 233. Sequestration of defendant's property in action for divorce, separation or annulment where defendant cannot be personally served.

Where in an action for divorce, separation, annulment or declaration of nullity of a void marriage it appears to the court that the defendant is not within the state, or cannot be found therein, or is concealing himself or herself therein, so that process cannot be personally served upon the defendant, the court may at any time and from time to time make any order or orders without notice directing the sequestration of his or her property, both real and personal and whether tangible or intangible, within the state, and may appoint a receiver thereof, or by injunction or otherwise take the same into its possession and control. The property thus sequestered and the income therefrom may be applied in whole or in part and from time to time, under the direction of the court and as justice may require, to the payment of such sum or sums as the court may deem it proper to award, by order or judgment as the case may be, and during the pendency of the action or at the termination thereof, for the education or maintenance of any of the children of a marriage, or for the support of a spouse, or for his or her expenses in bringing and carrying on said action and the proceedings incidental thereto or connected therewith; and if the rents and profits of the real estate, together with the other property so sequestered, be insufficient to pay the sums of money required, the court, upon such terms and conditions as it may prescribe, may direct the mortgage or sale of sufficient of said real estate to pay such sums. The court may appoint the plaintiff spouse receiver or sequestrator in such cases. The court may authorize such spouse to use and occupy, free of any liability for rent or use and occupation or otherwise, any house or other suitable property of the defendant spouse as a dwelling for himself or herself with or without the children of the marriage, and may likewise turn over to the plaintiff spouse for the use of such spouse with or without the children of the marriage any chattel or chattels of the defendant spouse. The relief herein provided for is in addition to any and every other remedy to which a spouse may be entitled under the law.

Added by Laws 1962, Ch. 313, eff. Sept. 1, 1963 from former CPA § 1171-a; **amended** by Laws 1980, Ch. 281, eff. July 19, 1980.

§ 234.   Title to or occupancy and possession of property.

In any action for divorce, for a separation, for an annulment or to declare the nullity of a void marriage, the court may (1) determine any question as to the title to property arising between the parties, and (2) make such direction, between the parties, concerning the possession of property, as in the court's discretion justice requires having regard to the circumstances of the case and of the respective parties. Such direction may be made in the final judgment, or by one or more orders from time to time before or subsequent to final judgment, or by both such order or orders and final judgment. Where the title to real property is affected, a copy of such judgment, order or decree, duly certified by the clerk of the court wherein said judgment was rendered, shall be recorded in the office of the recording officer of the county in which such property is situated, as provided by section two hundred ninety-seven-b of the real property law.

Added by Laws 1962, Ch. 313, from former CPA § 1164-a; **amended** by Laws 1963, Ch. 685, eff. Sept. 1, 1963.

§ 235.   Information as to details of matrimonial actions or proceedings.

1.   An officer of the court with whom the proceedings in a matrimonial action or a written agreement of separation or an action or proceeding for custody, visitation or maintenance of a child are filed, or before whom the testimony is taken, or his clerk, either before or after the termination of the suit, shall not permit a copy of any of the pleadings, affidavits, findings of fact, conclusions of law, judgment of dissolution, written agreement of separation or memorandum thereof, or testimony, or any examination or perusal thereof, to be taken by any other person than a party, or the attorney or counsel of a party, except by order of the court.

2.   If the evidence on the trial of such an action or proceeding be such that public interest requires that the examination of the witnesses should not be public,

the court or referee may exclude all persons from the room except the parties to the action and their counsel, and in such case may order the evidence, when filed with the clerk, sealed up, to be exhibited only to the parties to the action or proceeding or someone interested, on order of the court.

3. Upon the application of any person to the county clerk or other officer in charge of public records within a county for evidence of the disposition, judgment or order with respect to a matrimonial action, the clerk or other such officer shall issue a "certificate of disposition," duly certifying the nature and effect of such disposition, judgment, order and shall in no manner evidence the subject matter of the pleadings or testimony, findings of fact, conclusions of law or judgment of dissolution derived in any such action.

4. Any county, city, town or village clerk or other municipal official issuing marriage licenses shall be required to accept, as evidence of dissolution of marriage, such "certificate of disposition" in lieu of a complete copy of the findings of fact, conclusions of law and judgment of dissolution.

5. The limitations of subdivisions one, two and three of this section in relation to confidentiality shall cease to apply one hundred years after date of filing, and such records shall thereupon be public records available to public inspection.

Added by Laws 1962, Ch. 313, from former RCP Rule 278; **amended** by Laws 1966, Ch. 254; Laws 1968, Ch. 445; Laws 1974, Ch. 1027; Laws 1978, Ch. 438, eff. July 19, 1978; Laws 1979, Ch. 122, eff. May 22, 1979; Laws 1979, Ch. 121, eff. Jan. 1, 1980.

§ 236. Special controlling provisions; prior actions or proceedings; new actions or proceedings.

Except as otherwise expressly provided in this section, the provisions of part A shall be controlling with respect to any action or proceeding commenced prior to the date on which the provisions of this section as amended become effective and the provisions of part B shall be controlling with respect to any action or proceeding commenced on or after such effective date. Any reference to this section or the provisions hereof in any action, proceeding, judgment, order, rule or agreement shall be deemed and construed to refer to either the provisions of part A or part B respectively and exclusively, determined as provided in this paragraph any inconsistent provision of law notwithstanding.

PART A   PRIOR ACTIONS OR PROCEEDINGS

Alimony, temporary and permanent.

1. Alimony. In any action or proceeding brought (1) during the lifetime of both parties to the marriage to annul a marriage or declare the nullity of a void marriage, or (2) for a separation, or (3) for a divorce, the court may direct either spouse to provide suitably for the support of the other as, in the court's discretion,

justice requires, having regard to the length of time of the marriage, the ability of each spouse to be self supporting, the circumstances of the case and of the respective parties. Such direction may require the payment of a sum or sums of money either directly to either spouse or to third persons for real and personal property and services furnished to either spouse, or for the rental of or mortgage amortization or interest payments, insurance, taxes, repairs or other carrying charges on premises occupied by either spouse, or for both payments to either spouse and to such third persons. Such direction shall be effective as of the date of the application therefor, and any retroactive amount of alimony due shall be paid in one sum or periodic sums, as the court shall direct, taking into account any amount of temporary alimony which has been paid. Such direction may be made in the final judgment in such action or proceeding, or by one or more orders from time to time before or subsequent to final judgment, or by both such order or orders and the final judgment. Such direction may be made notwithstanding that the parties continue to reside in the same abode and notwithstanding that the court refuses to grant the relief requested by either spouse (1) by reason of a finding by the court that a divorce, annulment or judgment declaring the marriage a nullity had previously been granted to either spouse in an action in which jurisdiction over the person of the other spouse was not obtained, or (2) by reason of the misconduct of the other spouse, unless such misconduct would itself constitute grounds for separation or divorce, or (3) by reason of a failure of proof of the grounds of either spouse's action or counterclaim. Any order or judgment made as in this section provided may combine in one lump sum any amount payable to either spouse under this section with any amount payable to either spouse under section two hundred forty of this chapter. Upon the application of either spouse, upon such notice to the other party and given in such manner as the court shall direct, the court may annul or modify any such direction, whether made by order or by final judgment, or in case no such direction shall have been made in the final judgment may, with respect to any judgment of annulment or declaring the nullity of a void marriage rendered on or after September first, nineteen hundred forty or any judgment of separation or divorce whenever rendered, amend the judgment by inserting such direction. Subject to the provisions of section two hundred forty-four of this chapter, no such modification or annulment shall reduce or annul arrears accrued prior to the making of such application unless the defaulting party shows good cause for failure to make application for relief from the judgment or order directing such payment prior to the accrual of such arrears. Such modification may increase such support nunc pro tunc based on newly discovered evidence.

2. Compulsory financial disclosure. In all matrimonial actions and proceedings commenced on or after September first, nineteen hundred seventy-five in supreme court in which alimony, maintenance or support is in issue and all support proceedings in family court, there shall be compulsory disclosure by both parties of their respective financial states. No showing of special circumstances shall be required before such disclosure is ordered. A sworn statement of net worth shall be provided upon receipt of a notice in writing demanding the same,

within twenty days after the receipt thereof. In the event said statement is not demanded, it shall be filed by each party, within ten days after joinder of issue, in the court in which the procedure is pending. As used in this section, the term net worth shall mean the amount by which total assets including income exceed total liabilities including fixed financial obligations. It shall include all income and assets of whatsoever kind and nature and wherever situated and shall include a list of all assets transferred in any manner during the preceding three years, or the length of the marriage, whichever is shorter; provided, however that transfers in the routine course of business which resulted in an exchange of assets of substantially equivalent value need not be specifically disclosed where such assets are otherwise identified in the statement of net worth. Noncompliance shall be punishable by any or all of the penalties prescribed in section thirty-one hundred twenty-six of the civil practice law and rules, in examination before or during trial.

DRL

PART B   NEW ACTIONS OR PROCEEDINGS

Maintenance and distributive award.

1. Definitions. Whenever used in this part, the following terms shall have the respective meanings hereinafter set forth or indicated:

a. The term "maintenance" shall mean payments provided for in a valid agreement between the parties or awarded by the court in accordance with the provisions of subdivision six of this part, to be paid at fixed intervals for a definite or indefinite period of time, but an award of maintenance shall terminate upon the death of either party or upon the recipient's valid or invalid marriage, or upon modification pursuant to paragraph (b) of subdivision nine of section two hundred thirty-six of this part or section two hundred forty-eight of this chapter.

b. The term "distributive award" shall mean payments provided for in a valid agreement between the parties or awarded by the court, in lieu of or to supplement, facilitate or effectuate the division or distribution of property where authorized in a matrimonial action, and payable either in a lump sum or over a period of time in fixed amounts. Distributive awards shall not include payments which are treated as ordinary income to the recipient under the provisions of the United States Internal Revenue Code.

c. The term "marital property" shall mean all property acquired by either or both spouses during the marriage and before the execution of a separation agreement or the commencement of a matrimonial action, regardless of the form in which title is held, except as otherwise provided in agreement pursuant to subdivision three of this part. Marital property shall not include separate property as hereinafter defined.

d. The term "separate property" shall mean:

(1)   property acquired before marriage or property acquired by bequest, devise, or descent, or gift from a party other than the spouse;

(2)   compensation for personal injuries;

(3)   property acquired in exchange for or the increase in value of separate property, except to the extent that such appreciation is due in part to the contributions or efforts of the other spouse;

(4)   property described as separate property by written agreement of the parties pursuant to subdivision three of this part.

    e.   The term "custodial parent" shall mean a parent to whom custody of a child or children is granted by a valid agreement between the parties or by an order or decree of a court.

    f.   The term "child support" shall mean a sum paid pursuant to court order or decree by either or both parents or pursuant to a valid agreement between the parties for care, maintenance and education of any unemancipated child under the age of twenty-one years.

    2.   Matrimonial actions. Except as provided in subdivision five of this part, the provisions of this part shall be applicable to actions for an annulment or dissolution of a marriage, for a divorce, for a separation, for a declaration of the nullity of a void marriage, for a declaration of the validity or nullity of a foreign judgment of divorce, for a declaration of the validity or nullity of a marriage, and to proceedings to obtain maintenance or a distribution of marital property following a foreign judgment of divorce, commenced on and after the effective date of this part. Any application which seeks a modification of a judgment, order or decree made in an action commenced prior to the effective date of this part shall be heard and determined in accordance with the provisions of part a of this section.

    3.   Agreement of the parties. An agreement by the parties, made before or during the marriage, shall be valid and enforceable in a matrimonial action if such agreement is in writing, subscribed by the parties, and acknowledged or proven in the manner required to entitle a deed to be recorded. Notwithstanding any other provision of law, an acknowledgment of an agreement made before marriage may be executed before any person authorized to solemnize a marriage pursuant to subdivisions one, two and three of section eleven of this chapter. Such an agreement may include (1) a contract to make a testamentary provision of any kind, or a waiver of any right to elect against the provisions of a will; (2) provision for the ownership, division or distribution of separate and marital property; (3) provision for the amount and duration of maintenance or other terms and conditions of the marriage relationship, subject to the provisions of section 5-311 of the general obligations law, and provided that such terms were fair and reasonable at the time of the making of the agreement and are not unconscionable at the time of entry of final judgment; and (4) provision for the custody, care, education and maintenance of any child of the parties, subject to the provisions of section two

hundred forty of this article. Nothing in this subdivision shall be deemed to affect the validity of any agreement made prior to the effective date of this subdivision.

4. Compulsory financial disclosure.

a. In all matrimonial actions and proceedings in which alimony, maintenance or support is in issue, there shall be compulsory disclosure by both parties of their respective financial states. No showing of special circumstances shall be required before such disclosure is ordered. A sworn statement of net worth shall be provided upon receipt of a notice in writing demanding the same, within twenty days after the receipt thereof. In the event said statement is not demanded, it shall be filed with the clerk of the court by each party, within ten days after joinder of issue, in the court in which the proceeding is pending. As used in this part, the term "net worth" shall mean the amount by which total assets including income exceed total liabilities including fixed financial obligations. It shall include all income and assets of whatsoever kind and nature and wherever situated and shall include a list of all assets transferred in any manner during the preceding three years, or the length of the marriage, whichever is shorter; provided, however that transfers in the routine course of business which resulted in an exchange of assets of substantially equivalent value need not be specifically disclosed where such assets are otherwise identified in the statement of net worth. All such sworn statements of net worth shall be accompanied by a current and representative paycheck stub and the most recently filed state and federal income tax returns including a copy of the W-2(s) wage and tax statement(s) submitted with the returns. In addition, both parties shall provide information relating to any and all group health plans available to them for the provision of care or other medical benefits by insurance or otherwise for the benefit of the child or children for whom support is sought, including all such information as may be required to be included in a qualified medical child support order as defined in section six hundred nine of the Employee Retirement Income Security Act of 1974 (29 USC 1169) including, but not limited to: (i) the name and last known mailing address of each party and of each dependent to be covered by the order; (ii) the identification and a description of each group health plan available for the benefit or coverage of the disclosing party and the child or children for whom support is sought; (iii) a detailed description of the type of coverage available from each group health plan for the potential benefit of each such dependent; (iv) the identification of the plan administrator for each such group health plan and the address of such administrator; (v) the identification numbers for each such group health plan; and (vi) such other information as may be required by the court. Noncompliance shall be punishable by any or all of the penalties prescribed in section thirty-one hundred twenty-six of the civil practice law and rules, in examination before or during trial.

b. As soon as practicable after a matrimonial action has been commenced, the court shall set the date or dates the parties shall use for the valuation of each asset. The valuation date or dates may be anytime from the date of commencement of the action to the date of trial.

5. Disposition of property in certain matrimonial actions. a. Except where the parties have provided in an agreement for the disposition of their property pursuant to subdivision three of this part, the court, in an action wherein all or part of the relief granted is divorce, or the dissolution, annulment or declaration of the nullity of a marriage, and in proceedings to obtain a distribution of marital property following a foreign judgment of divorce, shall determine the respective rights of the parties in their separate or marital property, and shall provide for the disposition thereof in the final judgment.

b. Separate property shall remain such.

c. Marital property shall be distributed equitably between the parties, considering the circumstances of the case and of the respective parties.

d. In determining an equitable disposition of property under paragraph c, the court shall consider:

(1) the income and property of each party at the time of marriage, and at the time of the commencement of the action;

(2) the duration of the marriage and the age and health of both parties;

(3) the need of a custodial parent to occupy or own the marital residence and to use or own its household effects;

(4) the loss of inheritance and pension rights upon dissolution of the marriage as of the date of dissolution;

(5) any award of maintenance under subdivision six of this part;

(6) any equitable claim to, interest in, or direct or indirect contribution made to the acquisition of such marital property by the party not having title, including joint efforts or expenditures and contributions and services as a spouse, parent, wage earner and homemaker, and to the career or career potential of the other party;

(7) the liquid or non-liquid character of all marital property;

(8) the probable future financial circumstances of each party;

(9) the impossibility or difficulty of evaluating any component asset or any interest in a business, corporation or profession, and the economic desirability of retaining such asset or interest intact and free from any claim or interference by the other party;

(10) the tax consequences to each party;

(11) the wasteful dissipation of assets by either spouse;

(12) any transfer or encumbrance made in contemplation of a matrimonial action without fair consideration;

(13) any other factor which the court shall expressly find to be just and proper.

e. In any action in which the court shall determine that an equitable distribution is appropriate but would be impractical or burdensome or where the distribution of an interest in a business, corporation or profession would be contrary to law, the court in lieu of such equitable distribution shall make a distributive award in order to achieve equity between the parties. The court, in its discretion, also may make a distributive award to supplement, facilitate or effectuate a distribution of marital property.

f.   In addition to the disposition of property as set forth above, the court may make such order regarding the use and occupancy of the marital home and its household effects as provided in section two hundred thirty-four of this chapter, without regard to the form of ownership of such property.

g.   In any decision made pursuant to this subdivision, the court shall set forth the factors it considered and the reasons for its decision and such may not be waived by either party or counsel.

h.   In any decision made pursuant to this subdivision the court shall, where appropriate, consider the effect of a barrier to remarriage, as defined in subdivision six of section two hundred fifty-three of this article, on the factors enumerated in paragraph d of this subdivision.

6.   Maintenance. a. Except where the parties have entered into an agreement pursuant to subdivision three of this part providing for maintenance, in any matrimonial action the court may order temporary maintenance or maintenance in such amount as justice requires, having regard for the standard of living of the parties established during the marriage, whether the party in whose favor maintenance is granted lacks sufficient property and income to provide for his or her reasonable needs and whether the other party has sufficient property or income to provide for the reasonable needs of the other and the circumstances of the case and of the respective parties. Such order shall be effective as of the date of the application therefor, and any retroactive amount of maintenance due shall be paid in one sum or periodic sums, as the court shall direct, taking into account any amount of temporary maintenance which has been paid. In determining the amount and duration of maintenance the court shall consider:

(1)   the income and property of the respective parties including marital property distributed pursuant to subdivision five of this part;

(2)   the duration of the marriage and the age and health of both parties;

(3)   the present and future earning capacity of both parties;

(4)   the ability of the party seeking maintenance to become self-supporting and, if applicable, the period of time and training necessary therefor;

(5)   reduced or lost lifetime earning capacity of the party seeking maintenance as a result of having foregone or delayed education, training, employment, or career opportunities during the marriage;

(6)   the presence of children of the marriage in the respective homes of the parties;

(7)   the tax consequences to each party;

(8) contributions and services of the party seeking maintenance as a spouse, parent, wage earner and homemaker, and to the career or career potential of the other party;

(9) the wasteful dissipation of marital property by either spouse;

(10) any transfer or encumbrance made in contemplation of a matrimonial action without fair consideration; and

(11) any other factor which the court shall expressly find to be just and proper.

b. In any decision made pursuant to this subdivision, the court shall set forth the factors it considered and the reasons for its decision and such may not be waived by either party or counsel.

c. The court may award permanent maintenance, but an award of maintenance shall terminate upon the death of either party or upon the recipient's valid or invalid marriage, or upon modification pursuant to paragraph (b) of subdivision nine of section two hundred thirty-six of this part or section two hundred forty-eight of this chapter.

d. In any decision made pursuant to this subdivision the court shall, where appropriate, consider the effect of a barrier to remarriage, as defined in subdivision six of section two hundred fifty-three of this article, on the factors enumerated in paragraph a of this subdivision.

7. Child support.

a. In any matrimonial action, or in an independent action for child support, the court as provided in section two hundred forty of this chapter shall order either or both parents to pay temporary child support or child support without requiring a showing of immediate or emergency need. The court shall make an order for temporary child support notwithstanding that information with respect to income and assets of either or both parents may be unavailable. Where such information is available, the court may make an order for temporary child support pursuant to section two hundred forty of this article. Such order shall, except as provided for herein, be effective as of the date of the application therefor, and any retroactive amount of child support due shall be support arrears/past due support and shall be paid in one sum or periodic sums, as the court shall direct, taking into account any amount of temporary child support which has been paid. In addition, such retroactive child support shall be enforceable in any manner provided by law including, but not limited to, an execution for support enforcement pursuant to subdivision (b) of section fifty-two hundred forty-one of the civil practice law and rules. When a child receiving support is a public assistance recipient, or the order of support is being enforced or is to be enforced pursuant to section one hundred eleven-g of the social services law, the court shall establish the amount of retroactive child support and notify the parties that such amount shall be enforced by the support collection unit pursuant to an execution for support enforcement as provided for in subdivision (b) of section fifty-two hundred forty-one of the civil practice law and rules, or in such periodic payments as would have been authorized had such an execution been issued. In such case, the court shall not direct the schedule of repayment of retroactive support. The court shall not consider the misconduct of either party but shall make its award for child support pursuant to section two hundred forty of this article.

b. Notwithstanding any other provision of law, any written application or motion to the court for the establishment of a child support obligation for persons not in receipt of family assistance must contain either a request for child support enforcement services which would authorize the collection of the support obligation by the immediate issuance of an income execution for support enforcement as provided for by this chapter, completed in the manner specified in section one hundred eleven-g of the social services law; or a statement that the applicant has applied for or is in receipt of such services; or a statement that the applicant knows of the availability of such services, has declined them at this time and where support enforcement services pursuant to section one hundred eleven-g of the social services law have been declined that the applicant understands that an income deduction order may be issued pursuant to subdivision (c) of section five thousand two hundred forty-two of the civil practice law and rules without other child support enforcement services and that payment of an administrative fee may be required. The court shall provide a copy of any such request for child support enforcement services to the support collection unit of the appropriate social services district any time it directs payments to be made to such support collection unit. Additionally, the copy of any such request shall be accompanied by the name, address and social security number of the parties; the date and place of the parties' marriage; the name and date of birth of the child or children; and the name and address of the employers and income payors of the party from whom child support is sought. Unless the party receiving child support has applied for or is receiving such services, the court shall not direct such payments to be made to the support collection unit, as established in section one hundred eleven-h of the social services law.

c. The court shall direct that a copy of any child support or combined child and spousal support order issued by the court on or after the first day of October, nineteen hundred ninety-eight, in any proceeding under this section be provided promptly to the state case registry established pursuant to subdivision four-a of section one hundred eleven-b of the social services law.

8. Special relief in matrimonial actions.

a. In any matrimonial action the court may order a party to purchase, maintain or assign a policy of insurance providing benefits for health and hospital care and related services for either spouse or children of the marriage not to exceed such period of time as such party shall be obligated to provide maintenance, child support or make payments of a distributive award. The court may also order a party to purchase, maintain or assign a policy of accident insurance or insurance on the life of either spouse, and to designate in the case of life insurance, either spouse or children of the marriage, or in the case of accident insurance, the insured spouse as irrevocable beneficiaries during a period of time fixed by the court. The obligation to provide such insurance shall cease upon the termination of the spouse's duty to provide maintenance, child support or a distributive award. A copy of such order shall be served, by registered mail, on the home office of the insurer specifying the name and mailing address of the spouse or children, provided that failure to so serve the insurer shall not affect the validity of the order.

b.   In any action where the court has ordered temporary maintenance, maintenance, distributive award or child support, the court may direct that a payment be made directly to the other spouse or a third person for real and personal property and services furnished to the other spouse, or for the rental or mortgage amortization or interest payments, insurances, taxes, repairs or other carrying charges on premises occupied by the other spouse, or for both payments to the other spouse and to such third persons. Such direction may be made notwithstanding that the parties continue to reside in the same abode and notwithstanding that the court refuses to grant the relief requested by the other spouse.

c.   Any order or judgment made as in this section provided may combine any amount payable to either spouse under this section with any amount payable to such spouse as child support or under section two hundred forty of this chapter.

9.   Enforcement and modification of orders and judgments in matrimonial actions. a. All orders or judgments entered in matrimonial actions shall be enforceable pursuant to section fifty-two hundred forty-one or fifty-two hundred forty-two of the civil practice law and rules, or in any other manner provided by law. Orders or judgments for child support, alimony and maintenance shall also be enforceable pursuant to article fifty-two of the civil practice law and rules upon a debtor's default as such term is defined in paragraph seven of subdivision (a) of section fifty-two hundred forty-one of the civil practice law and rules. The establishment of a default shall be subject to the procedures established for the determination of a mistake of fact for income executions pursuant to subdivision (e) of section fifty-two hundred forty-one of the civil practice law and rules. For the purposes of enforcement of child support orders or combined spousal and child support orders pursuant to section five thousand two hundred forty-one of the civil practice law and rules, a "default" shall be deemed to include amounts arising from retroactive support. The court may, and if a party shall fail or refuse to pay maintenance, distributive award or child support the court shall, upon notice and an opportunity to the defaulting party to be heard, require the party to furnish a surety, or the sequestering and sale of assets for the purpose of enforcing any award for maintenance, distributive award or child support and for the payment of reasonable and necessary attorney's fees and disbursements.

b.   Upon application by either party, the court may annul or modify any prior order or judgment as to maintenance or child support, upon a showing of the recipient's inability to be self-supporting or a substantial change in circumstance or termination of child support awarded pursuant to section two hundred forty of this article, including financial hardship. Where, after the effective date of this part, a separation agreement remains in force no modification of a prior order or judgment incorporating the terms of said agreement shall be made as to maintenance without a showing of extreme hardship on either party, in which event the judgment or order as modified shall supersede the terms of the prior agreement and judgment for such period of time and under such circumstances as the court determines. Provided, however, that no modification or annulment shall reduce or annul any arrears of child support which have accrued prior to the date of application to annul or modify any prior order or judgment as to child support. The court shall not reduce or annul any arrears of maintenance which have been reduced to final judgment pursuant to section two hundred forty-four of this chapter. No other arrears of maintenance which have accrued prior to the making of such application shall be subject to modification or annulment unless the defaulting party shows good cause for failure to make application for relief from the judgment or order directing such payment prior to the accrual of such arrears and the facts and circumstances constituting good cause are set forth in a written memorandum of decision. Such modification may increase maintenance or child support nunc pro tunc as of the date of application based on newly discovered evidence. Any retroactive amount of maintenance, or child support due shall, except as provided for herein, be paid in one sum or periodic sums, as the court directs, taking into account any temporary or partial payments which have been made. Any retroactive amount of child support due shall be support arrears/past due support. In addition, such retroactive child support shall be enforceable in any manner provided by law including, but not limited to, an execution for support enforcement pursuant to subdivision (b) of section fifty-two hundred forty-one of the civil practice law and rules. When a child receiving support is a public assistance recipient, or the order of support is being enforced or is to be enforced pursuant to section one hundred eleven-g of the social services law, the court shall establish the amount of retroactive child support and notify the parties that such amount shall be enforced by the support collection unit pursuant to an execution for support enforcement as provided for in subdivision (b) of section fifty-two hundred forty-one of the civil practice law and rules, or in such periodic payments as would have been authorized had such an execution been issued. In such case, the court shall not direct the schedule of repayment of retroactive support. The provisions of this subdivision shall not apply to a separation agreement made prior to the effective date of this part.

c. Notwithstanding any other provision of law, any written application or motion to the court for the modification or enforcement of a child support or combined maintenance and child support order for persons not in receipt of family assistance must contain either a request for child support enforcement services which would authorize the collection of the support obligation by the immediate issuance of an income execution for support enforcement as provided for by this chapter, completed in the manner specified in section one hundred eleven-g of the social services law; or a statement that the applicant has applied for or is in receipt of such services; or a statement that the applicant knows of the availability of such services, has declined them at this time and where support enforcement

DRL

services pursuant to section one hundred eleven-g of the social services law have been declined that the applicant understands that an income deduction order may be issued pursuant to subdivision (c) of section five thousand two hundred forty-two of the civil practice law and rules without other child support enforcement services and that payment of an administrative fee may be required. The court shall provide a copy of any such request for child support enforcement services to the support collection unit of the appropriate social services district any time it directs payments to be made to such support collection unit. Additionally, the copy of such request shall be accompanied by the name, address and social security number of the parties; the date and place of the parties' marriage; the name and date of birth of the child or children; and the name and address of the employers and income payors of the party ordered to pay child support to the other party. Unless the party receiving child support or combined maintenance and child support has applied for or is receiving such services, the court shall not direct such payments to be made to the support collection unit, as established in section one hundred eleven-h of the social services law.

d. The court shall direct that a copy of any child support or combined child and spousal support order issued by the court on or after the first day of October, nineteen hundred ninety-eight, in any proceeding under this section be provided promptly to the state case registry established pursuant to subdivision four-a of section one hundred eleven-b of the social services law.

Added by Laws 1962, Ch. 313, from former CPA §§ 1140-a, 1155, 1164, 1170, 1170-b; **amended** by Laws 1963, Ch. 685; Laws 1968, Ch. 699; Laws 1980, Ch. 281, Ch. 645, eff. July 19, 1980; Laws 1981, Ch. 695, eff. Oct. 19, 1981, Part A, subd. 1, Part B, subds. 6, 7 and 9; Laws 1984, Ch. 790, eff. Aug. 5, 1984, Part B, Subd. 9; Laws 1985, Ch. 809, eff. Nov. 1, 1985; Laws 1986, Ch. 884, eff. Aug. 2, 1986, except for the amendments to Part B, subd. 4 and Part B, subd. 5 which are eff. Sept. 1, 1986; Laws 1986, Ch. 892, eff. Aug. 2, 1986; Laws 1987, Ch. 815, eff. Dec. 5, 1987; Laws 1987, Ch. 815, eff. Aug. 7, 1987; Laws 1989, Ch. 567, eff. Sept. 15, 1989; Laws 1990, Ch. 818, §§ 4, 5, eff. Sept. 30, 1990; Laws 1992, Ch. 41, §§ 139, 140, eff. Apr. 2, 1992; Laws 1992, Ch. 415, §§ 1, 2, eff. Aug. 16, 1992; Laws 1993, Ch. 59, § 9, eff. July 1, 1993; Laws 1993, Ch. 354, § 2, eff. July 1, 1993; Laws 1994, Ch. 170, §§ 359-360, eff. June 15, 1994; Laws 1997, Ch. 398, §§ 4, 5 and 141, eff. Jan. 1, 1998; Laws 1997, Ch. 436, § 1, Part B, §§ 105 and 106, eff. Aug. 20, 1997, amending subds. B(7)(b) and B(9)(c); Laws 1998, Ch. 214, § 56, eff. Nov. 4, 1998, § 61, eff. July 7, 1998, deemed in full force and effect Jan. 1, 1998 and Ch. 393, § 2, eff. July 22, 1998; Laws 1999, Ch. 275, § 2, eff. Sept. 18, 1999; Laws 2003, Ch. 595, § 1, eff. Sept. 22, 2003.

§ 237. Counsel fees and expenses.

(a) In any action or proceeding brought (1) to annul a marriage or to declare the nullity of a void marriage, or (2) for a separation, or (3) for a divorce, or (4) to declare the validity or nullity of a judgment of divorce rendered against a spouse who was the defendant in any action outside the State of New York and did not appear therein where such spouse asserts the nullity of such foreign judgment, or (5) to enjoin the prosecution in any other jurisdiction of an action for a divorce, the court may direct either spouse or, where an action for annulment is maintained after the death of a spouse may direct the person or persons maintaining the action, to pay such sum or sums of money directly to the attorney of the other spouse to enable that spouse to carry on or defend the action or proceeding as, in the court's discretion, justice requires, having regard to the circumstances of the case and of the respective parties. Such direction must be made in the final judgment in such action or proceeding, or by one or more orders from time to time before final judgment, or by both such order or orders and the final judgment; provided, however, such direction shall be made prior to final judgment where it is shown that such order is required to enable the petitioning party to properly proceed. Any applications for counsel fees and expenses may be maintained by the attorney for either spouse in his own name in the same proceeding.

(b) Upon any application to annul or modify an order or judgment for alimony or for custody, visitation, or maintenance of a child, made as in section two hundred thirty-six or section two hundred forty provided, or upon any application by writ of habeas corpus or by petition and order to show cause concerning custody, visitation or maintenance of a child, the court may direct a spouse or parent to pay such sum or sums of money for the prosecution or the defense of the application or proceeding by the other spouse or parent as, in the court's discretion, justice requires, having regard to the circumstances of the case and of the respective parties. With respect to any such application or proceeding, such direction may be made in the order or judgment by which the particular application or proceeding is finally determined, or by one or more orders from time to time before the final order or judgment, or by both such order or orders and the final order or judgment. Any applications for counsel fees and expenses may be maintained by the attorney for either spouse in counsel's own name in the same proceeding. Representation by an attorney pursuant to paragraph (b) of subdivision nine of section one hundred eleven-b of the social services law shall not preclude an award of counsel fees to an applicant which would otherwise be allowed under this section.

(c) In any action or proceeding for failure to obey any lawful order compelling payment of support or maintenance, or distributive award the court shall, upon a finding that such failure was willful, order respondent to pay counsel fees to the attorney representing the petitioner.

(d) The term "expenses" as used in subdivisions (a) and (b) of this section shall include, but shall not be limited to, accountant fees, appraisal fees, actuarial fees, investigative fees and other fees and expenses that the court may determine to be necessary to enable a spouse to carry on or defend an action or proceeding under this section. In determining the appropriateness and necessity of fees, the court shall consider:

　　1. The nature of the marital property involved;

　　2. The difficulties involved, if any, in identifying and evaluating the marital property;

3. The services rendered and an estimate of the time involved; and

4. The applicant's financial status.

Added by Laws 1962, Ch. 313, from former CPA §§ 1169, 1169-a; **amended** by Laws 1963, Chs. 341, 685; Laws 1978, Ch. 444; Laws 1980, Ch. 281, eff. July 19, 1980; Laws 1983, Ch. 86, eff. June 9, 1983; Laws 1983, Ch. 287, eff. Sept. 1, 1983; Laws 1986, Ch. 149, eff. June 16, 1986; Laws 1986, Ch. 892, eff. Aug. 2, 1986; Laws 1987, Ch. 482, eff. July 30, 1987; Laws 1992, Ch. 422, § 1, eff. July 17, 1992.

§ 238. Expenses in enforcement proceedings.

In any action or proceeding to compel the payment of any sum of money required to be paid by a judgment or order entered in an action for divorce, separation, annulment or declaration of nullity of a void marriage, or in any proceeding pursuant to section two hundred forty-three, two hundred forty-four, two hundred forty-five, or two hundred forty-six, the court may in its discretion require either party to pay the expenses of the other in bringing, carrying on, or defending such action or proceeding. In any such action or proceeding, applications for counsel fees and expenses may be maintained by the attorney for the respective parties in counsel's own name and in counsel's own behalf.

Added by Laws 1962, Ch. 313, eff. Sept. 1, 1963, from former CPA § 1172-d; **amended** by Laws 1963, Ch. 685; Laws 1978, Ch. 529, eff. July 24, 1978.

§ 239. Stay in divorce or separation action on default of payment.

In an action for divorce or separation the court or the judge thereof may refuse to grant an order to stay proceedings, where the only default is the failure of a spouse to pay alimony, maintenance or counsel fees due to his or her inability to make such payments. In no event shall a spouse who has been imprisoned for contempt of court for failure to pay alimony, maintenance or counsel fees or by virtue of an order of arrest as a provisional remedy under the civil practice law and rules be stayed from proceeding with the prosecution or defense of an action where the only default is the failure of such spouse to pay alimony, maintenance or counsel fees.

Added by Laws 1962, Ch. 313, eff. Sept. 1, 1963, from former CPA § 167-a; **amended** by Laws 1980, Ch. 281, eff. July 19, 1980.

§ 240. Custody and child support; orders of protection.

1. (a) In any action or proceeding brought (1) to annul a marriage or to declare the nullity of a void marriage, or (2) for a separation, or (3) for a divorce, or (4) to obtain, by a writ of habeas corpus or by petition and order to show cause, the custody of or right to visitation with any child of a marriage, the court shall require verification of the status of any child of the marriage with respect to such child's custody and support, including any prior orders, and shall enter orders

for custody and support as, in the court's discretion, justice requires, having regard to the circumstances of the case and of the respective parties and to the best interests of the child and subject to the provisions of subdivision one-c of this section. Where either party to an action concerning custody of or a right to visitation with a child alleges in a sworn petition or complaint or sworn answer, cross-petition, counterclaim or other sworn responsive pleading that the other party has committed an act of domestic violence against the party making the allegation or a family or household member of either party, as such family or household member is defined in article eight of the family court act, and such allegations are proven by a preponderance of the evidence, the court must consider the effect of such domestic violence upon the best interests of the child, together with such other facts and circumstances as the court deems relevant in making a direction pursuant to this section. An order directing the payment of child support shall contain the social security numbers of the named parties. In all cases there shall be no prima facie right to the custody of the child in either parent. Such direction shall make provision for child support out of the property of either or both parents. The court shall make its award for child support pursuant to subdivision one-b of this section. Such direction may provide for reasonable visitation rights to the maternal and/or paternal grandparents of any child of the parties. Such direction as it applies to rights of visitation with a child remanded or placed in the care of a person, official, agency or institution pursuant to article ten of the family court act, or pursuant to an instrument approved under section three hundred fifty-eight-a of the social services law, shall be enforceable pursuant to part eight of article ten of the family court act and sections three hundred fifty-eight-a and three hundred eighty-four-a of the social services law and other applicable provisions of law against any person having care and custody, or temporary care and custody, of the child. Notwithstanding any other provision of law, any written application or motion to the court for the establishment, modification or enforcement of a child support obligation for persons not in receipt of public assistance and care must contain either a request for child support enforcement services which would authorize the collection of the support obligation by the immediate issuance of an income execution for support enforcement as provided for by this chapter, completed in the manner specified in section one hundred eleven-g of the social services law; or a statement that the applicant has applied for or is in receipt of such services; or a statement that the applicant knows of the availability of such services, has declined them at this time and where support enforcement services pursuant to section one hundred eleven-g of the social services law have been declined that the applicant understands that an income deduction order may be issued pursuant to subdivision (c) of section fifty-two hundred forty-two of the civil practice law and rules without other child support enforcement services and that payment of an administrative fee may be required. The court shall provide a copy of any such request for child support enforcement services to the support collection unit of the appropriate social services district any time it directs payments to be made to such support collection unit. Additionally, the copy of any such request shall be accompanied by the name, address and social security number of the parties; the date and place of the parties' marriage; the name and date of birth of the child or children; and the name and address of the employers and income payors of the party from whom child support is sought or from the party ordered to pay child support to the other party. Such direction may require the payment of a sum or sums of money either directly to the custodial parent or to third persons for goods or services furnished for such child, or for both payments to the custodial parent and to such third persons; provided, however, that unless the party seeking or receiving child support has applied for or is receiving such services, the court shall not direct such payments to be made to the support collection unit, as established in section one hundred eleven-h of the social services law. Every order directing the payment of support shall require that if either parent currently, or at any time in the future, has health insurance benefits available that may be extended or obtained to cover the child, such parent is required to exercise the option of additional coverage in favor of such child and execute and deliver to such person any forms, notices, documents or instruments necessary to assure timely payment of any health insurance claims for such child.

(b)　As used in this section, the following terms shall have the following meanings:

(1)　"Health insurance benefits" means any medical, dental, optical and prescription drugs and health care services or other health care benefits that may be provided for a dependent through an employer or organization, including such employers or organizations which are self insured, or through other available health insurance or health care coverage plans.

(2)　"Available health insurance benefits" means any health insurance benefits that are reasonable in cost and that are reasonably accessible to the person on whose behalf the petition is brought. Health insurance benefits that are not reasonable in cost or whose services are not reasonably accessible to such person, shall be considered unavailable.

(c)　When the person on whose behalf the petition is brought is a child, the court shall consider the availability of health insurance benefits to all parties and shall take the following action to ensure that health insurance benefits are provided for the benefit of the child:

(1)　Where the child is presently covered by health insurance benefits, the court shall direct in the order of support that such coverage be maintained, unless either parent requests the court to make a direction for health insurance benefits coverage pursuant to paragraph two of this subdivision.

(2)　Where the child is not presently covered by health insurance benefits, the court shall make a determination as follows:

(i)　If only one parent has available health insurance benefits, the court shall direct in the order of support that such parent provide health insurance benefits.

(ii)　If both parents have available health insurance benefits the court shall direct in the order of support that either parent or both parents provide such health insurance. The court shall make such determination based on the circumstances of the case, including, but not limited to, the cost and comprehensiveness of the respective health insurance benefits and the best interests of the child.

(iii)   If neither parent has available health insurance benefits, the court shall direct in the order of support that the custodial parent apply for the state's child health insurance plan pursuant to title one-A of article twenty-five of the public health law and the medical assistance program established pursuant to title eleven of article five of the social services law. If eligible for such coverage, the court shall prorate the cost of any premium or family contribution in accordance with paragraph (d) of this subdivision. A direction issued under this subdivision shall not limit or alter either parent's obligation to obtain health insurance benefits at such time as they become available, as required pursuant to paragraph (a) of this subdivision.

(d)   The cost of providing health insurance benefits pursuant to paragraph (c) of this subdivision shall be prorated between the parties in the same proportion as each parent's income is to the combined parental income. If the custodial parent is ordered to provide such benefits, the non-custodial parent's pro rata share of such costs shall be added to the basic support obligation. If the non-custodial parent is ordered to provide such benefits, the custodial parent's pro rata share of such costs shall be deducted from the basic support obligation. Where the court finds that such proration is unjust or inappropriate, the court shall:

(1)   order the parties to pay such amount of the cost of health insurance benefits as the court finds just and appropriate;

(2)   add or subtract such amount in the manner set forth in this subdivision; and

(3)   set forth in the order the factors it considered, the amount of each party's share of the cost and the reason or reasons the court did not order such pro rata apportionment.

(e)   The court shall provide in the order of support that the legally responsible relative immediately notify the other party, or the other party and the support collection unit when the order is issued on behalf of a child in receipt of public assistance and care or in receipt of services pursuant to section one hundred eleven-g of the social services law, of any change in health insurance benefits, including any termination of benefits, change in the health insurance benefit carrier, premium, or extent and availability of existing or new benefits.

(f)   Where the court determines that health insurance benefits are available, the court shall provide in the order of support that the legally responsible relative immediately enroll the eligible dependents named in the order who are otherwise eligible for such benefits without regard to any seasonal enrollment restrictions. Such order shall further direct the legally responsible relative to maintain such benefits as long as they remain available to such relative. Such order shall further direct the legally responsible relative to assign all insurance reimbursement payments for health care expenses incurred for his or her eligible dependents to the provider of such services or the party actually having incurred and satisfied such expenses, as appropriate.

(g) When the court issues an order of child support or combined child and spousal support on behalf of persons in receipt of public assistance and care or in receipt of services pursuant to section one hundred eleven-g of the social services law, such order shall further direct that the provision of health care benefits shall be immediately enforced pursuant to section fifty-two hundred forty-one of the civil practice law and rules.

(h) When the court issues an order of child support or combined child and spousal support on behalf of persons other than those in receipt of public assistance and care or in receipt of services pursuant to section one hundred eleven-g of the social services law, the court shall also issue a separate order which shall include the necessary direction to ensure the order's characterization as a qualified medical child support order as defined by section six hundred nine of the employee retirement income security act of 1974 (29 USC 1169). Such order shall: (i) clearly state that it creates or recognizes the existence of the right of the named dependent to be enrolled and to receive benefits for which the legally responsible relative is eligible under the available group health plans, and shall clearly specify the name, social security number and mailing address of the legally responsible relative, and of each dependent to be covered by the order; (ii) provide a clear description of the type of coverage to be provided by the group health plan to each such dependent or the manner in which the type of coverage is to be determined; and (iii) specify the period of time to which the order applies. The court shall not require the group health plan to provide any type or form of benefit or option not otherwise provided under the group health plan except to the extent necessary to meet the requirements of a law relating to medical child support described in section one thousand three hundred and ninety-six g of title forty-two of the United States code.

(i) Upon a finding that a legally responsible relative wilfully failed to obtain health insurance benefits in violation of a court order, such relative will be presumptively liable for all health care expenses incurred on behalf of such dependents from the first date such dependents were eligible to be enrolled to receive health insurance benefits after the issuance of the order of support directing the acquisition of such coverage.

(j) The order shall be effective as of the date of the application therefor, and any retroactive amount of child support due shall be support arrears/past due support and shall, except as provided for herein, be paid in one lump sum or periodic sums, as the court shall direct, taking into account any amount of tempo-rary support which has been paid. In addition, such retroactive child support shall be enforceable in any manner provided by law including, but not limited to, an execution for support enforcement pursuant to subdivision (b) of section fifty-two hundred forty-one of the civil practice law and rules. When a child receiving support is a public assistance recipient, or the order of support is being enforced or is to be enforced pursuant to section one hundred eleven-g of the social services law, the court shall establish the amount of retroactive child support and notify the parties that such amount shall be enforced by the support collection unit pursuant to an execution for support enforcement as provided for in subdivision (b) of section fifty-two hundred forty-one of the civil practice law and rules, or in such periodic payments as would have been authorized had such an execution been issued. In such case, the courts shall not direct the schedule of repayment of retroactive support. Where such direction is for child support and paternity has been established by a voluntary acknowledgement of paternity as defined in section forty-one hundred thirty-five-b of the public health law, the court shall inquire of the parties whether the acknowledgement has been duly filed, and unless satisfied that it has been so filed shall require the clerk of the court to file such acknowledgement with the appropriate registrar within five business days. Such direction may be made in the final judgment in such action or proceeding, or by one or more orders from time to time before or subsequent to final judgment, or by both such order or orders and the final judgment. Such direction may be made notwithstanding that the court for any reason whatsoever, other than lack of jurisdiction, refuses to grant the relief requested in the action or proceeding. Any order or judgment made as in this section provided may combine in one lump sum any amount payable to the custodial parent under this section with any amount payable to such parent under section two hundred thirty-six of this article. Upon the application of either parent, or of any other person or party having the care, custody and control of such child pursuant to such judgment or order, after such notice to the other party, parties or persons having such care, custody and control and given in such manner as the court shall direct, the court may annul or modify any such direction, whether made by order or final judgment, or in case no such direction shall have been made in the final judgment may, with respect to any judgment of annulment or declaring the nullity of a void marriage rendered on or after September first, nineteen hundred forty, or any judgment of separation or divorce whenever rendered, amend the judgment by inserting such direction. Subject to the provisions of section two hundred forty-four of this article, no such modification or annulment shall reduce or annul arrears accrued prior to the making of such application unless the defaulting party shows good cause for failure to make application for relief from the judgment or order directing such payment prior to the accrual of such arrears. Such modification may increase such child support nunc pro tunc as of the date of application based on newly discovered evidence. Any retroactive amount of child support due shall be support arrears/past due support and shall be paid in one lump sum or periodic sums, as the court shall direct, taking into account any amount of temporary child support which has been paid. In addition, such retroactive child support shall be enforceable in any manner provided by law including, but not limited to, an execution for support enforcement pursuant to subdivision (b) of section fifty-two hundred forty-one of the civil practice law and rules.

1-a.   In any proceeding brought pursuant to this section to determine the custody or visitation of minors, a report made to the statewide central register of child abuse and maltreatment, pursuant to title six of article six of the social services law, or a portion thereof, which is otherwise admissible as a business record pursuant to rule forty-five hundred eighteen of the civil practice law and rules shall not be admissible in evidence, notwithstanding such rule, unless an investigation of such report conducted pursuant to title six of article six of the social services law has determined that there is some credible evidence of the alleged abuse or maltreatment and that the subject of the report has been notified that the report is indicated. In addition, of such report has been reviewed by the state commissioner of social services or his designee and has been determined to be unfounded, it shall not be admissible in evidence. If such report has been so reviewed and has been amended to delete any finding, each such deleted finding shall not be admissible. If the state commissioner of social services or his designee has amended the report to add any new finding, each such new finding, together with any portion of the original report not deleted by the commissioner or his designee, shall be admissible if it meets the other requirements of this subdivision and is otherwise admissible as a business record. If such a report, or portion thereof, is admissible in evidence but is uncorroborated, it shall not be sufficient to make a fact finding of abuse or maltreatment in such proceeding. Any other evidence tending to support the reliability of such report shall be sufficient corroboration.

1-b.   (a) The court shall make its award for child support pursuant to the provisions of this subdivision. The court may vary from the amount of the basic child support obligation determined pursuant to paragraph (c) of this subdivision only in accordance with paragraph (f) of this subdivision.

(b)   For purposes of this subdivision, the following definitions shall be used:

(1)   "Basic child support obligation" shall mean the sum derived by adding the amounts determined by the application of subparagraphs two and three of paragraph (c) of this subdivision except as increased pursuant to subparagraphs four, five, six and seven of such paragraph.

(2)   "Child support" shall mean a sum to be paid pursuant to court order or decree by either or both parents or pursuant to a valid agreement between the parties for care, maintenance and education of any unemancipated child under the age of twenty-one years.

(3)   "Child support percentage" shall mean:

(i)   seventeen percent of the combined parental income for one child;

(ii)   twenty-five percent of the combined parental income for two children;

(iii)   twenty-nine percent of the combined parental income for three children;

(iv)   thirty-one percent of the combined parental income for four children; and

(v)   no less than thirty-five percent of the combined parental income for five or more children.

(4)   "Combined parental income" shall mean the sum of the income of both parents.

(5)   "Income" shall mean, but shall not be limited to, the sum of the amounts determined by the application of clauses (i), (ii), (iii), (iv), (v) and (vi) of this subparagraph reduced by the amount determined by the application of clause (vii) of this subparagraph:

(i)   gross (total) income as should have been or should be reported in the most recent federal income tax return. If an individual files his/her federal income tax return as a married person filing jointly, such person shall be required to prepare a form, sworn to under penalty of law, disclosing his/her gross income individually;

(ii)   to the extent not already included in gross income in clause (i) of this subparagraph, investment income reduced by sums expended in connection with such investment;

(iii)   to the extent not already included in gross income in clauses (i) and (ii) of this subparagraph, the amount of income or compensation voluntarily deferred and income received, if any, from the following sources:

(A)   workers' compensation,

(B)   disability benefits,

(C)   unemployment insurance benefits,

(D)   social security benefits,

(E)   veterans benefits,

(F)   pensions and retirement benefits,

(G)   fellowships and stipends, and

(H)   annuity payments;

(iv)   at the discretion of the court, the court may attribute, or impute income from, such other resources as may be available to the parent, including, but not limited to:

(A)   non-income producing assets,

(B)   meals, lodging, memberships, automobiles or other perquisites that are provided as part of compensation for employment to the extent that such perquisites constitute expenditures for personal use, or which expenditures directly or indirectly confer personal economic benefits,

(C)   fringe benefits provided as part of compensation for employment, and

(D)   money, goods, or services provided by relatives and friends;

(v)   an amount imputed as income based upon the parent's former resources or income, if the court determines that a parent has reduced resources or income in order to reduce or avoid the parent's obligation for child support;

(vi) to the extent not already included in gross income in clauses (i) and (ii) of this subparagraph, the following self-employment deductions attributable to self-employment carried on by the taxpayer:

(A) any depreciation deduction greater than depreciation calculated on a straight-line basis for the purpose of determining business income or investment credits, and

(B) entertainment and travel allowances deducted from business income to the extent said allowances reduce personal expenditures;

(vii) the following shall be deducted from income prior to applying the provisions of paragraph (c) of this subdivision:

(A) unreimbursed employee business expenses except to the extent said expenses reduce personal expenditures,

(B) alimony or maintenance actually paid to a spouse not a party to the instant action pursuant to court order or validly executed written agreement,

(C) alimony or maintenance actually paid or to be paid to a spouse that is a party to the instant action pursuant to an existing court order or contained in the order to be entered by the court, or pursuant to a validly executed written agreement, provided the order or agreement provides for a specific adjustment, in accordance with this subdivision, in the amount of child support payable upon the termination of alimony or maintenance to such spouse,

(D) child support actually paid pursuant to court order or written agreement on behalf of any child for whom the parent has a legal duty of support and who is not subject to the instant action,

(E) public assistance,

(F) supplemental security income,

(G) New York City or Yonkers income or earnings taxes actually paid, and

(H) Federal Insurance Contributions Act (FICA) taxes actually paid.

(6) "Self-support reserve" shall mean one hundred thirty-five percent of the poverty income guidelines amount for a single person as reported by the federal Department of Health and Human Services. For the calendar year nineteen hundred eighty-nine, the self-support reserve shall be eight thousand sixty-five dollars. On March first of each year, the self-support reserve shall be revised to reflect the annual updating of the poverty income guidelines as reported by the federal Department of Health and Human Services for a single person household.

(c) The amount of the basic child support obligation shall be determined in accordance with the provision of this paragraph:

(1) The court shall determine the combined parental income.

(2) The court shall multiply the combined parental income up to eighty thousand dollars by the appropriate child support percentage and such amount shall be prorated in the same proportion as each parent's income is to the combined parental income.

(3)   Where the combined parental income exceeds the dollar amount set forth in subparagraph two of this paragraph, the court shall determine the amount of child support for the amount of the combined parental income in excess of such dollar amount through consideration of the factors set forth in paragraph (f) of this subdivision and/or the child support percentage.

(4)   Where the custodial parent is working, or receiving elementary or secondary education, or higher education or vocational training which the court determines will lead to employment, and incurs child care expenses as a result thereof, the court shall determine reasonable child care expenses and such child care expenses, where incurred, shall be prorated in the same proportion as each parent's income is to the combined parental income. Each parent's pro rata share of the child care expenses shall be separately stated and added to the sum of subparagraphs two and three of this paragraph.

(5)   The court shall prorate each parent's share of future reasonable health care expenses of the child not covered by insurance in the same proportion as each parent's income is to the combined parental income. The noncustodial parent's pro rata share of such health care expenses shall be paid in a manner determined by the court, including direct payment to the health care provider.

(6)   Where the court determines that the custodial parent is seeking work and incurs child care expenses as a result thereof, the court may determine reasonable child care expenses and may apportion the same between the custodial and noncustodial parent. The noncustodial parent's share of such expenses shall be separately stated and paid in a manner determined by the court.

(7)   Where the court determines, having regard for the circumstances of the case and of the respective parties and in the best interests of the child, and as justice requires, that the present or future provision of post-secondary, private, special, or enriched education for the child is appropriate, the court may award educational expenses. The noncustodial parent shall pay educational expenses, as awarded, in a manner determined by the court, including direct payment to the educational provider.

(d)   Notwithstanding the provisions of paragraph (c) of this subdivision, where the annual amount of the basic child support obligation would reduce the noncustodial parent's income below the poverty income guidelines amount for a single person as reported by the federal department of health and human services, the basic child support obligation shall be twenty-five dollars per month or the difference between the noncustodial parent's income and the self-support reserve, whichever is greater. Notwithstanding the provisions of paragraph (c) of this subdivision, where the annual amount of the basic child support obligation would reduce the noncustodial parent's income below the self-support reserve but not below the poverty income guidelines amount for a single person as reported by the federal department of health and human services, the basic child support obligation shall be fifty dollars per month or the difference between the noncustodial parent's income and the self-support reserve, whichever is greater.

(e) Where a parent is or may be entitled to receive nonrecurring payments from extraordinary sources not otherwise considered as income pursuant to this section, including but not limited to:

(1) Life insurance policies;

(2) Discharges of indebtedness;

(3) Recovery of bad debts and delinquency amounts;

(4) Gifts and inheritances; and

(5) Lottery winnings, the court, in accordance with paragraphs (c), (d) and (f) of this subdivision may allocate a proportion of the same to child support, and such amount shall be paid in a manner determined by the court.

(f) The court shall calculate the basic child support obligation, and the noncustodial parent's pro rata share of the basic child support obligation. Unless the court finds that the noncustodial parents's pro-rata share of the basic child support obligation is unjust or inappropriate, which finding shall be based upon consideration of the following factors:

(1) The financial resources of the custodial and noncustodial parent, and those of the child;

(2) The physical and emotional health of the child and his/her special needs and aptitudes;

(3) The standard of living the child would have enjoyed had the marriage or household not been dissolved;

(4) The tax consequences to the parties;

(5) The nonmonetary contributions that the parents will make toward the care and well-being of the child;

(6) The educational needs of either parent;

(7) A determination that the gross income of one parent is substantially less than the other parent's gross income;

(8) The needs of the children of the noncustodial parent for whom the noncustodial parent is providing support who are not subject to the instant action and whose support has not been deducted from income pursuant to subclause (d) of clause (vii) of subparagraph five of paragraph (b) of this subdivision, and the financial resources of any person obligated to support such children, provided, however, that this factor may apply only if the resources available to support such children are less than the resources available to support the children who are subject to the instant action;

(9) Provided that the child is not on public assistance (i) extraordinary expenses incurred by the noncustodial parent in exercising visitation, or (ii) expenses incurred by the noncustodial parent in extended visitation provided that the custodial parent's expenses are substantially reduced as a result thereof; and

(10) Any other factors the court determines are relevant in each case, the court shall order the noncustodial parent to pay his or her pro rata share of the basic child support obligation, and may order the noncustodial parent to pay an amount pursuant to paragraph (e) of this subdivision.

(g) Where the court finds that the noncustodial parent's pro rata share of the basic child support obligation is unjust or inappropriate, the court shall order the noncustodial parent to pay such amount of child support as the court finds just and appropriate, and the court shall set forth, in a written order, the factors it considered; the amount of each party's pro rata share of the basic child support obligation; and the reasons that the court did not order the basic child support obligation. Such written order may not be waived by either party or counsel; provided, however, and notwithstanding any other provision of law, the court shall not find that the noncustodial parent's pro rata share of such obligation is unjust or inappropriate on the basis that such share exceeds the portion of a public assistance grant which is attributable to a child or children. In no instance shall the court order child support below twenty-five dollars per month. Where the noncustodial parent's income is less than or equal to the poverty income guidelines amount for a single person as reported by the federal department of health and human services, unpaid child support arrears in excess of five hundred dollars shall not accrue.

(h) A validly executed agreement or stipulation voluntarily entered into between the parties after the effective date of this subdivision presented to the court for incorporation in an order or judgment shall include a provision stating that the parties have been advised of the provisions of this subdivision, and that the basic child support obligation provided for therein would presumptively result in the correct amount of child support to be awarded. In the event that such agreement or stipulation deviates from the basic child support obligation, the agreement or stipulation must specify the amount that such basic child support obligation would have been and the reason or reasons that such agreement or stipulation does not provide for payment of that amount. Such provision may not be waived by either party or counsel. Nothing contained in this subdivision shall be construed to alter the rights of the parties to voluntarily enter into validly executed agreements or stipulations which deviate from the basic child support obligation provided such agreements or stipulations comply with the provisions of this paragraph. The court shall, however, retain discretion with respect to child support pursuant to this section. Any court order or judgment incorporating a validly executed agreement or stipulation which deviates from the basic child support obligation shall set forth the court's reasons for such deviation.

(i) Where either or both parties are unrepresented, the court shall not enter an order or judgment other than a temporary order pursuant to section two hundred thirty-seven of this article, that includes a provision for child support unless the unrepresented party or parties have received a copy of the child support standards chart promulgated by the commissioner of social services pursuant to subdivision two of section one hundred eleven-i of the social services law. Where either party is in receipt of child support enforcement services through the local social services district, the local social services district child support enforcement unit shall advise such party of the amount derived from application of the child support percentage and that such amount serves as a starting point for the determination of the child support award, and shall provide such party with a copy of the child support standards chart. In no instance shall the court approve any voluntary support agreement or compromise that includes an amount for child support less than twenty-five dollars per month.

(j)   In addition to financial disclosure required in section two hundred thirty-six of this article, the court may require that the income and/or expenses of either party be verified with documentation including, but not limited to, past and present income tax returns, employer statements, pay stubs, corporate, business, or partnership books and records, corporate and business tax returns, and receipts for expenses or such other means of verification as the court determines appropriate. Nothing herein shall affect any party's right to pursue discovery pursuant to this chapter, the civil practice law and rules, or the family court act.

(k)   When a party has defaulted and/or the court is otherwise presented with insufficient evidence to determine gross income, the court shall order child support based upon the needs or standard of living of the child, whichever is greater. Such order may be retroactively modified upward, without a showing of change in circumstances.

(l)   In any action or proceeding for modification of an order of child support existing prior to the effective date of this paragraph, brought pursuant to this article, the child support standards set forth in this subdivision shall not constitute a change of circumstances warranting modification of such support order; provided, however, that (1) where the circumstances warrant modification of such order, or (2) where any party objects to an adjusted child support order made or proposed at the direction of the support collection unit pursuant to section one hundred eleven-h or one hundred eleven-n of the social services law, and the court is reviewing the current order of child support, such standards shall be applied by the court in its determination with regard to the request for modification, or disposition of an objection to an adjusted child support order made or proposed by a support collection unit. In applying such standards, when the order to be modified incorporates by reference or merges with a validly executed separation agreement or stipulation of settlement, the court may consider, in addition to the factors set forth in paragraph (f) of this subdivision, the provisions of such agreement or stipulation concerning property distribution, distributive award and/or maintenance in determining whether the amount calculated by using the standards would be unjust or inappropriate.

1-c.   (a) Notwithstanding any other provision of this chapter to the contrary, no court shall make an order providing for visitation or custody to a person who has been convicted of murder in the first or second degree in this state, or convicted of an offense in another jurisdiction which, if committed in this state, would constitute either murder in the first or second degree, of a parent, legal custodian legal guardian, sibling, half-sibling or step-sibling of any child who is the subject of the proceeding. Pending determination of a petition for visitation or custody, such child shall not visit and no person shall visit with such child present, such person who has been convicted of murder in the first or second degree in this state, or convicted of and offense in another jurisdiction which, if committed in this state, would constitute either murder in the first or second degree, of a parent, legal custodian legal guardian, sibling, half-sibling or step-sibling of a child who is the subject of the proceeding without the consent of such child's custodian or legal guardian.

(b) Notwithstanding paragraph (a) of this subdivision a court may order visitation or custody where:

(i) (A) Such child is of suitable age to signify assent and such child assents to such visitation or custody; or

(B) if such child is not of suitable age to signify assent, the child's custodian or legal guardian assents to such order; or

(C) the person who has been convicted of murder in the first or second degree, or an offense in another jurisdiction which if committed in this state, would constitute either murder in the first or second degree, can prove by a preponderance of the evidence that:

(1) He or she, or a family or household member of either party, was a victim of domestic violence by the victim of such murder; and

(2) the domestic violence was causally related to the commission of such murder; and

(ii) the court finds that such visitation or custody is in the best interests of the child.

(c) For the purpose of making a determination pursuant to clause (c) of subparagraph (i) of paragraph (b) of this subdivision, the court shall not be bound by the findings of fact, conclusions of law or ultimate conclusion as determined by the proceedings leading to the conviction of murder in the first or second degree in this state or of an offense in another jurisdiction which, if committed in this state, would constitute murder in either the first or second degree, of a parent, legal guardian, legal custodian, sibling, half-sibling or step-sibling of a child who is the subject of the proceeding. In all proceedings under this section, a law guardian shall be appointed for the child.

2. a. An order directing payment of money for child support shall be enforceable pursuant to section fifty-two hundred forty-one or fifty-two hundred forty-two of the civil practice law and rules or in any other manner provided by law. Such orders or judgments for child support and maintenance shall also be enforceable pursuant to article fifty-two of the civil practice law and rules upon a debtor's default as such term is defined in paragraph seven of subdivision (a) of section fifty-two hundred forty-one of the civil practice law and rules. The establishment of a default shall be subject to the procedures established for the

DRL

determination of a mistake of fact for income executions pursuant to subdivision (e) of section fifty-two hundred forty-one of the civil practice law and rules. For the purposes of enforcement of child support orders or combined spousal and child support orders pursuant to section five thousand two hundred forty-one of the civil practice law and rules, a "default" shall be deemed to include amounts arising from retroactive support.

b.   (1) When a child receiving support is a public assistance recipient, or the order of support is being enforced or is to be enforced pursuant to section one hundred eleven-g of the social services law, the court shall direct that the child support payments be made to the support collection unit. Unless (i) the court finds and sets forth in writing the reasons that there is good cause not to require immediate income withholding; or (ii) when the child is not in receipt of public assistance, a written agreement providing for an alternative arrangement has been reached between the parties, the support collection unit shall issue an income execution immediately for child support or combined maintenance and child support, and may issue an execution for medical support enforcement in accordance with the provisions of the order of support. Such written agreement may include an oral stipulation made on the record resulting in a written order. For purposes of this paragraph, good cause shall mean substantial harm to the debtor. The absence of an arrearage or the mere issuance of an income execution shall not constitute good cause. When an immediate income execution or an execution for medical support enforcement is issued by the support collection unit, such income execution shall be issued pursuant to section five thousand two hundred forty-one of the civil practice law and rules, except that the provisions thereof relating to mistake of fact, default and any other provisions which are not relevant to the issuance of an income execution pursuant to this paragraph shall not apply; provided, however, that if the support collection unit makes an error in the issuance of an income execution pursuant to this paragraph, and such error is to the detriment of the debtor, the support collection unit shall have thirty days after notification by the debtor to correct the error. Where permitted under federal law and where the record of the proceedings contains such information, such order shall include on its face the social security number and the name and address of the employer, if any, of the person chargeable with support; provided, however, that failure to comply with this requirement shall not invalidate such order. When the court determines that there is good cause not to immediately issue an income execution or when the parties agree to an alternative arrangement as provided in this paragraph, the court shall provide expressly in the order of support that the support collection unit shall not issue an immediate income execution. Notwithstanding any such order, the support collection unit shall issue an income execution for support enforcement when the debtor defaults on the support obligation, as defined in section five thousand two hundred forty-one of the civil practice law and rules.

(2)   When the court issues an order of child support or combined child and spousal support on behalf of persons other than those in receipt of public

assistance or in receipt of services pursuant to section one hundred eleven-g of the social services law, the court shall issue an income deduction order pursuant to subdivision (c) of section five thousand two hundred forty-two of the civil practice law and rules at the same time it issues the order of support. The court shall enter the income deduction order unless the court finds and sets forth in writing (i) the reasons that there is good cause not to require immediate income withholding; or (ii) that an agreement providing for an alternative arrangement has been reached between the parties. Such agreement may include a written agreement or an oral stipulation, made on the record, that results in a written order. For purposes of this paragraph, good cause shall mean substantial harm to the debtor. The absence of an arrearage or the mere issuance of an income deduction order shall not constitute good cause. Where permitted under federal law and where the record of the proceedings contains such information, such order shall include on its face the social security number and the name and address of the employer, if any, of the person chargeable with support; provided, however, that failure to comply with this requirement shall not invalidate the order. When the court determines that there is good cause not to issue an income deduction order immediately or when the parties agree to an alternative arrangement as provided in this paragraph, the court shall provide expressly in the order of support the basis for its decision and shall not issue an income deduction order.

c. Any order of support issued on behalf of a child in receipt of family assistance or child support enforcement services pursuant to section one hundred eleven-g of the social services law shall be subject to review and adjustment by the support collection unit pursuant to section one hundred eleven-n of the social services law. Such review and adjustment shall be in addition to any other activities undertaken by the support collection unit relating to the establishment, modification, and enforcement of support orders payable to such unit.

3. Order of protection. a. The court may make an order of protection in assistance or as a condition of any other order made under this section. The order of protection may set forth reasonable conditions of behavior to be observed for a specified time by any party. Such an order may require any party:

(1) to stay away from the home, school, business or place of employment of the child, other parent or any other party, and to stay away from any other specific location designated by the court;

(2) to permit a parent, or a person entitled to visitation by a court order or a separation agreement, to visit the child at stated periods;

(3) to refrain from committing a family offense, as defined in subdivision one of section 530.11 of the criminal procedure law, or any criminal offense against the child or against the other parent or against any person to whom custody of the child is awarded or from harassing, intimidating or threatening such persons;

(4) to permit a designated party to enter the residence during a specified period of time in order to remove personal belongings not in issue in a proceeding or action under this chapter or the family court act; or

(5) to refrain from acts of commission or omission that create an unreasonable risk to the health, safety or welfare of a child.

(6) to pay the reasonable counsel fees and disbursements involved in obtaining or enforcing the order of the person who is protected by such order if such order is issued or enforced.

(7) to observe such other conditions as are necessary to further the purposes of protection.

b. An order of protection entered pursuant to this subdivision shall bear in a conspicuous manner, on the front page of said order, the language "Order of protection issued pursuant to section two hundred forty of the domestic relations law". The absence of such language shall not affect the validity of such order. The presentation of a copy of such an order to any peace officer acting pursuant to his or her special duties, or police officer, shall constitute authority, for that officer to arrest a person when that person has violated the terms of such an order, and bring such person before the court and, otherwise, so far as lies within the officer's power, to aid in securing the protection such order was intended to afford.

c. An order of protection entered pursuant to this subdivision may be made in the final judgment in any matrimonial action or in a proceeding to obtain custody of or visitation with any child under this section, or by one or more orders from time to time before or subsequent to final judgment, or by both such order or orders and the final judgment. The order of protection may remain in effect after entry of a final matrimonial judgment and during the minority of any child whose custody or visitation is the subject of a provision of a final judgment or any order. An order of protection may be entered notwithstanding that the court for any reason whatsoever, other than lack of jurisdiction, refuses to grant the relief requested in the action or proceeding.

d. The chief administrator of the courts shall promulgate appropriate uniform temporary orders of protection and orders of protection forms, applicable to proceedings under this article, to be used throughout the state. Such forms shall be promulgated and developed in a manner to ensure the compatibility of such forms with the statewide computerized registry established pursuant to section two hundred twenty-one-a of the executive law.

e. No order of protection may direct any party to observe conditions of behavior unless: (i) the party requesting the order of protection has served and filed an action, proceeding, counter-claim or written motion and, (ii) the court has made a finding on the record that such party is entitled to issuance of the order of protection which may result from a judicial finding of fact, judicial acceptance of an admission by the party against whom the order was issued or judicial finding that the party against whom the order is issued has given knowing, intelligent and voluntary consent to its issuance. The provisions of this subdivision shall not preclude the court from issuing a temporary order of protection upon the court's own motion or where a motion for such relief is made to the court, for good cause shown.

Any party moving for a temporary order of protection pursuant to this subdivision during hours when the court is open shall be entitled to file such motion or pleading containing such prayer for emergency relief on the same day that such person first appears at such court, and a hearing on the motion or portion of the pleading requesting such emergency relief shall be held on the same day or the next day that the court is in session following the filing of such motion or pleading.

Upon issuance of an order of protection or temporary order of protection or upon a violation of such order, the court may make an order in accordance with section eight hundred forty-two-a of the family court act directing the surrender of firearms, revoking or suspending a party's firearms license, and/or directing that such party be ineligible to receive a firearms license. Upon issuance of an order of protection pursuant to this section or upon a finding of a violation thereof, the court also may direct payment of restitution in an amount not to exceed ten thousand dollars in accordance with subdivision (e) of section eight hundred forty-one of such act; provided, however, that in no case shall an order of restitution be issued where the court determines that the party against whom the order would be issued has already compensated the injured party or where such compensation is incorporated in a final judgment or settlement of the action.

3-a. Service of order of protection. If a temporary order of protection has been issued upon a default, unless the party requesting the order states on the record that she or he will arrange for other means for service or deliver the order to a peace or police officer directly for service, the court shall immediately deliver a copy of the temporary order of protection or order of protection to a peace officer, acting pursuant to his or her special duties and designated by the court, or to a police officer as defined in paragraph (b) or (d) of subdivision thirty-four of section 1.20 of the criminal procedure law, or, in the city of New York, to a designated representative of the police department of the city of New York. Any peace or police officer or designated person receiving a temporary order of protection or an order of protection as provided hereunder shall serve or provide for the service thereof together with any associated papers that may be served simultaneously, at any address designated therewith, including the summons and petition or complaint if not previously served. Service of such temporary order of protection or order of protection and associated papers shall, insofar as practicable, be achieved promptly. An officer or designated person obliged to perform service pursuant to this subdivision, and his or her employer, shall not be liable for damages resulting from failure to achieve service where, having made a reasonable effort, such officer or designated person is unable to locate and serve the temporary order of protection or order of protection at any address provided by the party requesting the order. A statement subscribed by the officer or designated person, and affirmed by him or her to be true under the penalties of perjury, stating the papers served, the date, time, address or in the event there is no address, place, and manner of service, the name and a brief physical description of the party served, shall be proof of service of the summons, petition and temporary order of protection or order of protection. When the temporary order of protection or order of protection and other papers, if any, have been served, such officer or designated person shall provide the court with an affirmation, certificate or affidavit of service and shall provide notification of the date and time of such service to the statewide computer registry established pursuant to section two hundred twenty-one-a of the executive law.

3-b. Emergency powers; local criminal court. If the court that issued an order of protection or temporary order of protection under this section or warrant in connection thereto is not in session when an arrest is made for an alleged violation of the order or upon a warrant issued in connection with such violation, the arrested person shall be brought before a local criminal court in the county of arrest or in the county in which such warrant is returnable pursuant to article one hundred twenty of the criminal procedure law and arraigned by such court. Such local criminal court shall order the commitment of the arrested person to the custody of the sheriff, admit to, fix or accept bail, or release the arrested person on his or her recognizance pending appearance in the court that issued the order of protection, temporary order of protection or warrant. In making such order, such local criminal court shall consider the bail recommendation, if any, made by the supreme or family court as indicated on the warrant or certificate of warrant. Unless the petitioner or complainant requests otherwise, the court, in addition to scheduling further criminal proceedings, if any, regarding such alleged family offense or violation allegation, shall make such matter returnable in the supreme or family court, as applicable, on the next day such court is in session.

3-c. Orders of protection; filing and enforcement of out-of-state orders. A valid order of protection or temporary order of protection issued by a court of competent jurisdiction in another state, territorial or tribal jurisdiction shall be accorded full faith and credit and enforced as if it were issued by a court within the state for as long as the order remains in effect in the issuing jurisdiction in accordance with sections two thousand two hundred sixty-five and two thousand two hundred sixty-six of title eighteen of the United States Code.

a. An order issued by a court of competent jurisdiction in another state, territorial or tribal jurisdiction shall be deemed valid if:

(1) the issuing court had personal jurisdiction over the parties and over the subject matter under the law of the issuing jurisdiction;

(2) the person against whom the order was issued had reasonable notice and an opportunity to be heard prior to issuance of the order; provided, however, that if the order was a temporary order of protection issued in the absence of such person, that notice had been given and that an opportunity to be heard had been provided within a reasonable period of time after the issuance of the order; and

(3) in the case of orders of protection or temporary orders of protection issued against both a petitioner and respondent, the order or portion thereof sought to be enforced was supported by: (i) a pleading requesting such order, including, but not limited to, a petition, cross-petition or counterclaim; and (ii)

a judicial finding that the requesting party is entitled to the issuance of the order, which may result from a judicial finding of fact, judicial acceptance of an admission by the party against whom the order was issued or judicial finding that the party against whom the order was issued had give knowing, intelligent and voluntary consent to its issuance.

b. Notwithstanding the provisions of article fifty-four of the civil practice law and rules, an order of protection or temporary order of protection issued by a court of competent jurisdiction in another state, territorial or tribal jurisdiction, accompanied by a sworn affidavit that upon information and belief such order is in effect as written and has not been vacated or modified, may be filed without fee with the clerk of the court, who shall transmit information regarding such order to the statewide registry of orders of protection and warrants established pursuant to section two hundred twenty-one-a of the executive law; provided, however, that such filing and registry entry shall not be required for enforcement of the order.

4. * One-time adjustment of child support orders issued prior to September fifteenth, nineteen hundred eighty-nine. Any party to a child support order issued prior to September fifteenth, nineteen hundred eighty-nine on the behalf of a child in receipt of public assistance or child support services pursuant to section one hundred eleven-g of the social services law may request that the support collection unit undertake one review of the order for adjustment purposes pursuant to section one hundred eleven-h of the social services law. A hearing on the adjustment of such order shall be granted upon the objection of either party pursuant to the provisions of this section. An order shall be adjusted if as of the date of the support collection unit's review of the correct amount of child support as calculated pursuant to the provisions of this section would deviate by at least ten percent from the child support ordered in the current order of support. Additionally, a new order shall be issued upon a showing that the current order of support does not provide for the health care needs of the child through insurance or otherwise. Eligibility of the child for medical assistance shall not relieve any obligation the parties otherwise have to provide for the health care needs of the child. The support collection unit's review of a child support order shall be made on notice to all parties to the current support order. Nothing herein shall be deemed in any way to limit, restrict, expand or impair the rights of any party to file for a modification of a child support order as is otherwise provided by law.

(1) Upon mailing of an adjustment finding and where appropriate a proposed order in conformity with such finding filed by either party or by the support collection unit, a party shall have thirty-five days from the date of mailing to submit to the court identified thereon specific written objections to such finding and proposed order.

(a) If specific written objections are submitted by either party or by the support collection unit, a hearing shall be scheduled by the court on notice to the parties and the support collection unit, who then shall have the right to be heard by the court and to offer evidence in support of or in opposition to adjustment of the support order.

(b) The party filing the specific written objections shall bear the burden of going forward and the burden of proof; provided, however, that if the support collection unit has failed to provide the documentation and information required by subdivision fourteen of section one hundred eleven-h of the social services law, the court shall first require the support collection unit to furnish such documents and information to the parties and the court.

(c) If the court finds by a preponderance of the evidence that the specific written objections have been proven, the court shall recalculate or readjust the proposed adjusted order accordingly or, for good cause, shall remand the order to the support collection unit for submission of a new proposed adjusted order. Any readjusted order so issued by the court or resubmitted by the support collection unit after a remand by the court shall be effective as of the date the proposed adjusted order would have been effective had no specific written objections been filed.

(d) If the court finds that the specific written objections have not been proven by a preponderance of the evidence, the court shall immediately issue the adjusted order as submitted by the support collection unit, which shall be effective as of the date the order would have been effective had no specific written exceptions been filed.

(e) If the court receives no specific written objections to the support order within thirty-five days of the mailing of the proposed order the clerk of the court shall immediately enter the order without further review, modification, or other prior action by the court or any judge or support magistrate thereof, and the clerk shall immediately transmit copies of the order of support to the parties and to the support collection unit.

(2) A motion to vacate an order of support adjusted pursuant to this section may be made no later than forty-five days after an adjusted support order is executed by the court where no specific written objections to the proposed order have been timely received by the court. Such motion shall be granted only upon a determination by the court issuing such order that personal jurisdiction was not timely obtained over the moving party.

5. ** Provision of child support orders to the state case registry. The court shall direct that a copy of any child support or combined child and spousal support order issued by the court on or after the first day of October, nineteen hundred ninety-eight, in any proceeding under this section be provided promptly to the state case registry established pursuant to subdivision four-a of section one hundred eleven-b of the social services law.

5. ** On-going cost of living adjustment of child support orders issued prior to September fifteenth, nineteen hundred eighty-nine. Any party to a child support order issued prior to September fifteenth, nineteen hundred eighty-nine on the behalf of a child in receipt of public assistance or child support services pursuant

to section one hundred eleven-g of the social services law may request that the support collection unit review the order for a cost of living adjustment in accordance with the provisions of section two hundred forty-c of this article.

* **Editor's Note:** The amendments made to subdivision 4 by Laws 1997, Ch. 398 § 4 shall not apply to review and adjustment requests, actions, proceedings, objections, or issuance of adjusted orders pending on or before December 31, 1997. Such requests, actions, proceedings, objections, or issuance of adjusted orders may proceed as if such provisions were not amended by Laws 1997, Ch. 398 § 4. *See* Laws 1998, Ch. 214 § 64.

** **Editor's Note:** Two versions of Subd. 5. are provided. The first version was added by Laws 1997, Ch. 398, § 6, eff. Oct. 1, 1998. The second was added by Laws 1997, Ch. 398, § 103, eff. Jan. 1, 1998, with no reference to the prior version.

Added by Laws 1962, Ch. 313, from former CPA §§ 1140, 1155, 1164, 1170, 1170-b; **amended** by Laws 1963, Ch. 685; Laws 1976, Ch. 133; Laws 1980, Ch. 281, 645, eff. July 19, 1980, Ch. 530, eff. Aug. 23, 1980; Laws 1981, Ch. 695, eff. Oct. 19, 1981; Laws 1981, Ch. 416, eff. Aug. 6, 1981, added subd. 2(6); Laws 1983, Ch. 347, eff. Aug. 22, 1983; Laws 1985, Ch. 809, eff. Nov. 1, 1985; Laws 1986, Ch. 849, eff. Aug. 2, 1986; Laws 1986, Ch. 892, eff. Aug. 2, 1986; Laws 1988, Ch. 452, § 1, eff. Aug. 1, 1988; Laws 1988, Ch. 457, § 9, eff. Aug. 1, 1988; Laws 1989, Ch. 164, eff. Oct. 15, 1989; Laws 1989, Ch. 567, § 6, eff. Sept. 15, 1989; Laws 1990, Ch. 818, §§ 7, 8, eff. July 25, 1990, and applicable to all pending petitions, motions and applications for child support; Laws 1990, Ch. 818, § 6, eff. Sept. 30, 1990; Laws 1990, Ch. 818, § 9, eff. Nov. 1, 1990, and applicable to all pending petitions, motions and applications for child support; Laws 1992, Ch. 41, §§ 141, 145, 146, eff. Apr. 2, 1992; Laws 1993, Ch. 59, §§ 3, 4, 10, 23, eff. July 1, 1993; § 17, adding subd. (4) to DRL § 240; § 24, adding para. (c) to DRL § 240(2); Laws 1993, Ch. 354, § 1, eff. July 1, 1993; Laws 1994, Ch. 170, §§ 361-362, eff. June 15, 1994, and § 363, eff. June 9, 1994; Laws 1995, Ch. 81, §§ 237-239, eff. July 1, 1995; Laws 1995, Ch. 349, § 3, eff. Nov. 30, 1995; Laws 1995, Ch. 389, § 1, eff. Nov. 30, 1995; Laws 1995, Ch. 429, § 2, eff. Oct. 1, 1995; Laws 1995, h. 483, §§ 1 -2, eff. Nov. 1, 1995; Laws 1995, Ch. 538, § 2, eff. Oct. 31, 1995; Laws 1996, Ch. 12, § 17, eff. Feb. 15, 1996 and is applicable to reports of suspected child abuse or maltreatment registered on or after the effective date; Laws 1996, Ch. 85, § 2, eff. May 21, 1996, and applicable to all actions or proceedings concerning custody of or a right to visitation with a child whether such action or proceeding was commenced pursuant to this section or any other provision of law; Laws 1997, Ch. 398, §§ 142, 94, 95, 102, 103 eff. Jan. 1, 1998, § 6 eff. Oct. 1, 1998, and Ch. 186, § 13, eff. July 8, 1997; Laws 1998, Ch. 150, §§ 1 and 2, eff. July. 7, 1998, Ch. 214, § 57, eff. Nov. 4, 1998, and § 64, eff. July 7, 1998, deemed in full force and effect Jan. 1, 1998, and Ch. 597, §§ 1 and 2, eff. Dec. 22, 1998; Laws 1999, Ch. 378, § 1, eff. July. 27, 1999; Laws 1999, Ch. 606, § 1, eff. Nov. 1, 2000; Laws 2000, Ch. 483, § 1, eff. Oct. 20, 2000, reverting effective dates for the closing paragraphs of subd. 3 to Nov. 9, 1999; Laws 2002, Ch. 624, § 4, eff. Oct. 2, 2002; provided, however, that sections six through sixteen of this act shall take effect on the thirtieth day after it shall have become a law; provided, further, that the amendments to subdivisions 12 and 15 of section 111-b of the social services law made by sections six and seven of this act shall not affect the repeal of such subdivisions and shall be deemed to be repealed therewith; Laws 2003, Ch. 81, § 11, eff. June 18, 2003, amending sub. 4, par. 1, subpar. (e).

§ 240-a. Judgment or decree; additional provision.

In any action or proceeding brought under the provisions of this chapter wherein all or part of the relief granted is divorce or annulment of a marriage any interlocutory or final judgment or decree shall contain, as a part thereof, the social security numbers of the named parties in the action or proceeding, as well as a provision that each party may resume the use of his or her premarriage surname or any other former surname.

Added by Laws 1973 Ch. 642, eff. July 11, 1973; **amended** by Laws 1982, Ch. 668, eff. July 22, 1982; Laws 1985, Ch. 583, eff. Sept. 1, 1985; Laws 1997, Ch. 398, § 31, eff. Nov. 11, 1997.

§ 240-b. Order of support by parent.

When the court makes an order of support pursuant to section two hundred forty of this article, and where permitted under federal law and where the record of the proceedings contains such information, the court shall require the social security number of such parent to be affixed to such order; provided, however, that no such order shall be invalid because of the omission of such number. Where the record of the proceedings contains such information, such order shall also include on its face the name and address of the employer, if any, of the person chargeable with support provided, however, that failure to comply with this requirement shall not invalidate such order. Where the order of child support or combined child and spouse support is made on behalf of persons in receipt of public assistance or in receipt of services pursuant to section one hundred eleven-g of the social services law, the court shall require each party to provide, and update upon any change, the following information to the court by reporting such change to the support collection unit designated by the appropriate social services district: social security number, residential and mailing addresses, telephone number, driver's license number; and name, address and telephone number of the parties' employers. Due process requirements for notice and service of process for subsequent hearings are met, with respect to such party, upon sending written notice by first class mail to the most recent residential address on record with the support collection unit; or by sending by first class mail written notice to the most recent employer address on record with the support collection unit, if a true copy thereof also is sent by first class mail to the most recent residential address on record with the support collection unit. Any such order issued on or after the first day of October, nineteen hundred ninety-nine shall also include, where available, the social security number of each child on whose behalf support has been ordered.

Added by Laws 1997, Ch. 398, § 65, eff. Jan. 1, 1998; **amended** by Laws 1998, Ch. 214, § 42, eff. July 7, 1998, deemed in full force and effect Jan. 1, 1998.

§ 240-c. Review and cost of living adjustment of child support orders.

1. Request. Any party to a child support order issued on behalf of a child in receipt of public assistance, or child support enforcement services pursuant

to section one hundred eleven-g of the social services law may request that the support collection unit review the order for cost of living adjustment purposes pursuant to section one hundred eleven-n of the social services law.

2.   Adjustment process.

(a)   A cost of living adjustment shall be made by the support collection unit with respect to an order of support under review if the sum of the annual average changes of the consumer price index for all urban consumers (CPI-U), as published annually by the United States Department of Labor Bureau of Labor Statistics, is ten percent or greater.

(b)   The cost of living adjustment and adjusted child support obligation amount as calculated by the review shall be reflected on the adjusted order issued by the support collection unit and mailed to the parties by first class mail. The child support obligation amount contained in the adjusted order shall be due and owing on the date the first payment is due under the terms of the order of support which was reviewed and adjusted occurring on or after the effective date of the adjusted order.

(c)   The support collection unit shall provide a copy of the adjusted order to the court which issued the most recent order of support, which shall append it to the order.

3.   Objection process. (a) An objection to a cost of living adjustment, as reflected in an adjusted order issued by a support collection unit, may be made to the court by either party to the order, or by the support collection unit, and shall be submitted to the court in writing within thirty-five days from the date of mailing of the adjusted order. A copy of the written objection shall be provided by the objecting party to the other party and to the support collection unit.

(b)   Where such objections are timely filed, the cost of living adjustment shall not take effect, and a hearing on the adjustment of such order shall be granted pursuant to the provisions of this section, which shall result in either:

(1)   The issuance by the court of a new order of support in accordance with the child support standards as set forth in section two hundred forty of this article; or

(2)   Where application of the child support standards as set forth in section two hundred forty of this article results in a determination that no adjustment is appropriate, an order of no adjustment.

(c)   Any order of support made by the court under this section shall occur without the requirement for proof or showing of a change in circumstances.

(d)   The court shall conduct the hearing and make its determination no later than forty-five days from the date it receives an objection. If the order under review does not provide for health insurance benefits for the child, the court shall make a determination regarding such benefits pursuant to section two hundred forty of this article. The clerk of the court shall immediately transmit copies of the order of support or order of no adjustment issued by the court pursuant to this subdivision to the parties and the support collection unit. Where a hearing results in the issuance of a new order of support, the effective date of the court order shall be the earlier of the date of the court determination or the date the cost of living adjustment would have been effective had it not been challenged.

(e)   Where no objection has been timely raised to a cost of living adjustment as reflected in an adjusted order, such adjustment shall become final without further review by the court or any judge or support magistrate thereof.

4.   Modification of orders. Nothing herein shall be deemed in any way to limit, restrict, expand or impair the rights of any party to file for a modification of a child support order as is otherwise provided by law.

5.   Notice. Parties eligible for adjustment of child support orders shall receive notice of the right to review such orders as follows:

(a)   All applications or motions by the support collection unit or by persons seeking support enforcement services through the support collection unit for the establishment, modification, enforcement, violation or adjustment of child support orders shall on their face in conspicuous type state:

NOTE: (1) A COURT ORDER OF SUPPORT RESULTING FROM A PRO-CEEDING COMMENCED BY THIS APPLICATION (MOTION) SHALL BE ADJUSTED BY THE APPLICATION OF A COST OF LIVING ADJUST-MENT AT THE DIRECTION OF THE SUPPORT COLLECTION UNIT NO EARLIER THAN TWENTY-FOUR MONTHS AFTER SUCH ORDER IS ISSUED, LAST MODIFIED OR LAST ADJUSTED, UPON THE REQUEST OF ANY PARTY TO THE ORDER OR PURSUANT TO PARAGRAPH (2) BELOW. SUCH COST OF LIVING ADJUSTMENT SHALL BE ON NOTICE TO BOTH PARTIES WHO, IF THEY OBJECT TO THE COST OF LIVING ADJUSTMENT, SHALL HAVE THE RIGHT TO BE HEARD BY THE COURT AND TO PRESENT EVIDENCE WHICH THE COURT WILL CON-SIDER IN ADJUSTING THE CHILD SUPPORT ORDER IN ACCORDANCE WITH SUBDIVISION 1-B OF SECTION TWO HUNDRED FORTY OF THE DOMESTIC RELATIONS LAW, KNOWN AS THE CHILD SUPPORT STAN-DARDS ACT.

(2) A PARTY SEEKING SUPPORT FOR ANY CHILD(REN) RECEIVING FAMILY ASSISTANCE SHALL HAVE A CHILD SUPPORT ORDER RE-VIEWED AND ADJUSTED AT THE DIRECTION OF THE SUPPORT COL-LECTION UNIT NO EARLIER THAN TWENTY-FOUR MONTHS AFTER SUCH ORDER IS ISSUED, LAST MODIFIED OR LAST ADJUSTED BY THE SUPPORT COLLECTION UNIT, WITHOUT FURTHER APPLICATION BY ANY PARTY. ALL PARTIES WILL RECEIVE A COPY OF THE ADJUSTED ORDER.

(3) WHERE ANY PARTY FAILS TO PROVIDE, AND UPDATE UPON ANY CHANGE, THE SUPPORT COLLECTION UNIT WITH A CURRENT ADDRESS, AS REQUIRED BY SECTION TWO HUNDRED FORTY-B OF THE DOMESTIC RELATIONS LAW, TO WHICH AN ADJUSTED ORDER

CAN BE SENT, THE SUPPORT OBLIGATION AMOUNT CONTAINED THEREIN SHALL BECOME DUE AND OWING ON THE DATE THE FIRST PAYMENT IS DUE UNDER THE TERMS OF THE ORDER OF SUPPORT WHICH WAS REVIEWED AND ADJUSTED OCCURRING ON OR AFTER THE EFFECTIVE DATE OF THE ADJUSTED ORDER, REGARDLESS OF WHETHER OR NOT THE PARTY HAS RECEIVED A COPY OF THE ADJUSTED ORDER.

(b)   All court orders of support payable through a support collection unit shall on their face in conspicuous type state:

NOTE: (1) THIS ORDER OF CHILD SUPPORT SHALL BE ADJUSTED BY THE APPLICATION OF A COST OF LIVING ADJUSTMENT AT THE DIRECTION OF THE SUPPORT COLLECTION UNIT NO EARLIER THAN TWENTY-FOUR MONTHS AFTER THIS ORDER IS ISSUED, LAST MODIFIED OR LAST ADJUSTED, UPON THE REQUEST OF ANY PARTY TO THE ORDER OR PURSUANT TO PARAGRAPH (2) BELOW. UPON APPLICATION OF A COST OF LIVING ADJUSTMENT AT THE DIRECTION OF THE SUPPORT COLLECTION UNIT, AN ADJUSTED ORDER SHALL BE SENT TO THE PARTIES WHO, IF THEY OBJECT TO THE COST OF LIVING ADJUSTMENT, SHALL HAVE THIRTY-FIVE (35) DAYS FROM THE DATE OF MAILING TO SUBMIT A WRITTEN OBJECTION TO THE COURT INDICATED ON SUCH ADJUSTED ORDER. UPON RECEIPT OF SUCH WRITTEN OBJECTION, THE COURT SHALL SCHEDULE A HEARING AT WHICH THE PARTIES MAY BE PRESENT TO OFFER EVIDENCE WHICH THE COURT WILL CONSIDER IN ADJUSTING THE CHILD SUPPORT ORDER IN ACCORDANCE WITH THE CHILD SUPPORT STANDARDS ACT.

(2) A RECIPIENT OF FAMILY ASSISTANCE SHALL HAVE THE CHILD SUPPORT ORDER REVIEWED AND ADJUSTED AT THE DIRECTION OF THE SUPPORT COLLECTION UNIT NO EARLIER THAN TWENTY-FOUR MONTHS AFTER SUCH ORDER IS ISSUED, LAST MODIFIED OR LAST ADJUSTED WITHOUT FURTHER APPLICATION BY ANY PARTY. ALL PARTIES WILL RECEIVE A COPY OF THE ADJUSTED ORDER.

(3) WHERE ANY PARTY FAILS TO PROVIDE, AND UPDATE UPON ANY CHANGE, THE SUPPORT COLLECTION UNIT WITH A CURRENT ADDRESS, AS REQUIRED BY SECTION TWO HUNDRED FORTY-B OF THE DOMESTIC RELATIONS LAW, TO WHICH AN ADJUSTED ORDER CAN BE SENT, THE SUPPORT OBLIGATION AMOUNT CONTAINED THEREIN SHALL BECOME DUE AND OWING ON THE DATE THE FIRST PAYMENT IS DUE UNDER THE TERMS OF THE ORDER OF SUPPORT WHICH WAS REVIEWED AND ADJUSTED OCCURRING ON OR AFTER THE EFFECTIVE DATE OF THE ADJUSTED ORDER, REGARDLESS OF WHETHER OR NOT THE PARTY HAS RECEIVED A COPY OF THE ADJUSTED ORDER.

DRL

Added by Laws 1997, Ch. 398, § 65, eff. Jan. 1, 1998; **amended** by Laws 2002, Ch. 624, § 5, eff. Oct. 2, 2002; provided, however, that sections six through sixteen of this act shall take effect on the thirtieth day after it shall have become a law; provided, further, that the amendments to subdivisions 12 and 15 of section 111-b of the social services law made by sections six and seven of this act shall not affect the repeal of such subdivisions and shall be deemed to be repealed therewith; Laws 2003, Ch. 81, § 12, eff. June 18, 2003, amending sub. 3, par (e).

§ 241. Interference with or withholding of visitation rights; alimony or maintenance suspension.

When it appears to the satisfaction of the court that a custodial parent receiving alimony or maintenance pursuant to an order, judgment or decree of a court of competent jurisdiction has wrongfully interfered with or withheld visitation rights provided by such order, judgment or decree, the court in its discretion, may suspend such payments or cancel any arrears that may have accrued during the time that visitation rights have been or are being interfered with or withheld. Nothing in this section shall constitute a defense in any court to an application to enforce payment of child support or grounds for the cancellation of arrears for child support.

Added by Laws 1978, Ch. 232, eff. June 5, 1978; **amended** by Laws 1980, Ch. 281, eff. July 19, 1980; Laws 1986, Ch. 892, eff. Aug. 5, 1986.

§ 242. Final judgment in action to annul a voidable marriage or for divorce.

Repealed by Laws 1968, Ch. 645, eff. June 16, 1968.

§ 243. Security for payments by defendant in action for divorce, separation or annulment; sequestration.

Where a judgment rendered or an order made in an action in this state for divorce, separation or annulment, or for a declaration of nullity of a void marriage, or a judgment rendered in another state for divorce upon any of the grounds provided in section one hundred seventy of this chapter, or for separation or separate support and maintenance for any of the causes specified in section two hundred, or for relief, however designated, granted upon grounds which in this state would be grounds for annulment of marriage or for a declaration of nullity of a void marriage, upon which an action has been brought in this state and judgment rendered therein, requires a spouse to provide for the education or maintenance of any of the children of a marriage, or for the support of his or her spouse, the court, in its discretion, also may direct the spouse from whom maintenance or support is sought to give reasonable security, in such a manner and within such a time as it thinks proper, for the payment, from time to time, of the sums of money required for that purpose. If he or she fails to give the security, or to make any payment required by the terms of such a judgment or order, whether or not security has been given therefor, or to pay any sum of money for the support and maintenance of the children or the support and maintenance of the spouse during the pendency of the action, or for counsel fees and expenses which he or she is required to pay by a judgment or order, the court may cause his or her personal property and the rents and profits of his or her real property to be sequestered, and may appoint a receiver thereof. The rents and profits and other property so sequestered may be applied, from time to time, under the direction of the court, to the payment of any of the sums of money specified in this section, as justice requires; and if the same shall be insufficient to pay the sums of money required, the court, on application of the receiver, may direct the mortgage or sale of such real property by the receiver, under such terms and conditions as it may prescribe, sufficient to pay such sums.

DRL

Added by Laws 1962, Ch. 313, from former CPA 1171; amended by Laws 1963, Ch. 685; Laws 1980, Ch. 281, eff. July 19, 1980.

§ 244.　Enforcement by execution of judgment or order in action for divorce, separation or annulment.

Where a spouse in an action for divorce, separation or annulment, or declaration of nullity of a void marriage, or a person other than a spouse when an action for an annulment is maintained after the death of a spouse, defaults in paying any sum of money as required by the judgment or order directing the payment thereof, or as required by the terms of an agreement or stipulation incorporated by reference in a judgment, such direction shall be enforceable pursuant to section fifty-two hundred forty-one or fifty-two hundred forty-two of the civil practice law and rules. Upon application the court shall make an order directing the entry of judgment for the amount of arrears of child support together with costs and disbursements. The court shall make an order directing the entry of judgment for the amount of arrears of any other payments so directed, together with costs and disbursements, unless the defaulting party shows good cause for failure to make application for relief from the judgment or order directing such payment prior to the accrual of such arrears. The court shall not make an order reducing or cancelling arrears unless the facts and circumstances constituting good cause are set forth in a written memorandum of decision. The application for such order shall be upon such notice to the spouse or other person as the court may direct. Such judgment may be enforced by execution or in any other manner provided by law for the collection of money judgments. The relief herein provided for is in addition to any and every other remedy to which a spouse may be entitled under the law; provided that when a judgment for such arrears or any part thereof shall have been entered pursuant to this section, such judgment shall thereafter not be subject to modification under the discretionary power granted by this section; and after the entry of such judgment the judgment creditor shall not hereafter be entitled to collect by any form of remedy any greater portion of such arrears than that represented by the judgment so entered. Such judgment shall provide for the payment of interest on the amount of any arrears if the default was willful, in that the obligated spouse knowingly, consciously and voluntarily disregarded the obligation under a lawful court order. Such interest shall be computed from the date on which the payment was due, at the prevailing rate of interest on judgments as provided in the civil practice law and rules.

Added by Laws 1962, Ch. 313, from former CPA § 1171-b; **amended** by Laws 1963, Chs. 667, 685; Laws 1980, Ch. 241, eff. July 15, 1980, Ch. 281, Ch. 645, eff. July 19, 1980; Laws 1981, Ch. 695, eff. Oct. 19, 1981; Laws 1983, Ch. 111, eff. May 17, 1983; Laws 1985, Ch. 809, eff. Nov. 1, 1985; Laws 1986, Ch. 892, eff. Aug. 5, 1986; Laws 1988, Ch. 327, § 1, eff. July 25, 1988.

§ 244-a. Enforcement of arrears which accrue during pendency of an enforcement proceeding.

In any proceeding for enforcement of payment of any sum of money as required by judgment or order the party seeking enforcement may amend the papers in support of the application for enforcement to include any additional arrears which have accrued since the commencement of such enforcement proceeding at the time of a hearing upon or submission of the matter, provided that written notice of the intention to so amend has been given eight days previously.

Added by Laws 1980, Ch. 646, eff. June 30, 1980; **amended** by Laws 1981, Ch. 239, eff. June 15, 1981.

§ 244-b. Child support proceedings and enforcement of arrears; suspension of driving privileges.

(a) In any proceeding for the enforcement of a direction or agreement, incorporated in a judgment or order, to pay any sum of money as child support or combined child and spousal support, if the court is satisfied by competent proof that the respondent has accumulated support arrears equivalent to or greater than the amount of support due pursuant to such judgment or order for a period of four months, the court may order the department of motor vehicles to suspend the respondent's driving privileges, and if such order issues, the respondent may apply to the department of motor vehicles for a restricted use license pursuant to section five hundred thirty of the vehicle and traffic law. The court may at any time upon payment of arrears or partial payment of arrears by the respondent order the department of motor vehicles to terminate the suspension of respondent's driving privileges. For purposes of determining whether a support obligor has accumulated support arrears equivalent to or greater than the amount of support due for a period of four months, the amount of any retroactive support, other than periodic payments of retroactive support which are past due, shall not be included in the calculation of support arrears pursuant to this section.

(b) If the respondent, after receiving appropriate notice, fails to comply with a summons, subpoena or warrant relating to a paternity or child support proceeding, the court may order the department of motor vehicles to suspend the respondent's driving privileges. The court may subsequently order the department of motor vehicles to terminate the suspension of the respondent's driving privileges; however, the court shall order the termination of such suspension when the court is satisfied that the respondent has fully complied with all summonses, subpoenas and warrants relating to a paternity or child support proceeding.

(c)   The provisions of subdivision (a) of this section shall not apply to:

(i)   respondents who are receiving public assistance or supplemental security income; or

(ii)   respondents whose income as defined by subparagraph five of paragraph (b) of subdivision one-b of section two hundred forty of this chapter falls below the self-support reserve as defined by subparagraph six of paragraph (b) of subdivision one-b of section two hundred forty of this chapter; or

(iii)   respondents whose income as defined by subparagraph five of paragraph (b) of subdivision one-b of section two hundred forty of this chapter remaining after the payment of the current support obligation would fall below the self-support reserve as defined by subparagraph six of paragraph (b) of subdivision one-b of section two hundred forty of this chapter.

(d)   The court's discretionary decision not to suspend driving privileges shall not have any res judicata effect or preclude any other agency with statutory authority to direct the department of motor vehicles to suspend driving privileges.

Added by Laws 1995, Ch. 81, § 233, eff. July 1, 1995; **amended** by Laws 1997, Ch. 398, §§ 116 and 117, eff. Jan. 1, 1998; Laws 2002, Ch. 624, § 14, eff. Oct. 2, 2002; provided, however, that sections six through sixteen of this act shall take effect on the thirtieth day after it shall have become a law; provided, further, that the amendments to subdivisions 12 and 15 of section 111-b of the social services law made by sections six and seven of this act shall not affect the repeal of such subdivisions and shall be deemed to be repealed therewith.

§ 244-c.   Child support proceedings and enforcement of arrears; suspensions of state professional, occupational and business licenses.

(a)   In any proceeding for enforcement of a direction or agreement, incorporated in a judgement or order, to pay any sum of money as child support or combined child and spousal support, if the court is satisfied by competent proof that the respondent has accumulated support arrears equivalent to or greater than the amount of support due pursuant to such judgment or order for a period of four months and that the respondent is licensed, permitted or registered by or with a board, department, authority or office of this state to conduct a trade, business, profession or occupation, the court may order such board, department, authority or office to commence proceedings as required by law regarding the suspension of such license, permit, registration, or authority to practice and to inform the court of the actions it has taken pursuant to such proceedings. For purposes of determining whether a respondent has accumulated support arrears equivalent to or greater than the amount of support due for a period of four months, the amount of any retroactive support, other than periodic payments of retroactive support which are past due, shall not be included in the calculation of support arrears pursuant to this section.

(b) If the respondent, after receiving appropriate notice, fails to comply with a summons, subpoena or warrant relating to a paternity or child support proceeding, and the court has determined that the respondent is licensed, permitted or registered by or with a board, department, authority or office of this state or one of its political subdivisions or instrumentalities to conduct a trade, business, profession or occupation, the court may order such board, department, authority or office to commence proceedings as required by law regarding the suspension of such license, permit, registration or authority to practice and to inform the court of the actions it has taken pursuant to such proceeding. The court may subsequently order such board, department, authority or office to terminate the suspension of the respondent's license, permit, registration or authority to practice; however, the court shall order the termination of such suspension when the court is satisfied that the respondent has fully complied with all summons, subpoenas and warrants relating to a paternity or child support proceeding.

(c) If the court determines that the suspension of the license, permit or registration of the respondent would create an extreme hardship to either the licensee, permittee or registrant or to persons whom he or she serves, the court may, in lieu of suspension, suspend the order described in subdivision (a) of this section to the licensing entity for a period not to exceed one year. If, on or before the expiration of this period, the court has not received competent proof presented at hearing that the respondent is in full compliance with his or her support obligation, the court shall cause the suspension of the order to be rescinded and shall further cause such order to be served upon the licensing entity.

(d) The provisions of subdivision (a) of this section shall not apply to:

(i) respondents who are receiving public assistance or supplemental security income; or

(ii) respondents whose income as defined by subparagraph five of paragraph (b) of subdivision one-b of section two hundred forty of the domestic relations law falls below the self-support reserve as defined by subparagraph six of paragraph (b) of subdivision one-b of section two hundred forty of the domestic relations law, or

(iii) respondents whose income as defined by subparagraph five of paragraph (b) of subdivision one-b of section two hundred forty of the domestic relations law remaining after the payment of the current support obligation would fall below the self-support reserve as defined by subparagraph six of paragraph (b) of subdivision one-b of section two hundred forty of the domestic relations law.

(e) The court shall inform the respondent that competent proof for purposes of proving payment to a licensing entity shall be a certified check, notice issued by the court, or notice from a support collection unit where the order is for payment to the support collection unit.

Added by Laws 1995, Ch. 81, § 218, eff. July 1, 1995; **amended** by Laws 1997, Ch. 398, §§ 118 and 119, eff. Jan. 1, 1998; Laws 2002, Ch. 624, § 15, eff. Nov. 1, 2002; provided, however, that sections six through sixteen of this act shall take effect on the thirtieth day after it shall have become a law; provided, further, that the amendments to subdivisions 12 and 15 of section 111-b of the social services law made by sections six and seven of this act shall not affect the repeal of such subdivisions and shall be deemed to be repealed therewith.

§ 244-d. Child support proceedings and enforcement of arrears; suspension of recreational license.

(a)   In any proceeding for enforcement of a direction or agreement, incorporated in a judgement or order, to pay any sum of money as child support or combined child and spousal support, if the court is satisfied by competent proof that the respondent has accumulated support arrears equivalent to or greater than the amount of support due pursuant to such judgment or order for a period of four months, the court may order any agency responsible for the issuance of a recreational license to suspend or refuse to reissue a license to the respondent, or deny application for such license by the respondent. For purposes of determining whether a respondent has accumulated support arrears equivalent to or greater than the amount of support due for a period of four months, the amount of any retroactive support, other than periodic payments of retroactive support which are past due, shall not be included in the calculation of support arrears pursuant to this section.

(b)   If the respondent, after receiving appropriate notice, fails to comply with a summons, subpoena, or warrant relating to a paternity or child support proceeding, the court may order any agency responsible for the issuance of a recreational license to suspend or to refuse to reissue a license to the respondent or to deny application for such license by the respondent. The court may subsequently order such agency to terminate the adverse action regarding the respondent's license; however, the court shall order the termination of such suspension or other adverse action when the court is satisfied that the respondent has fully complied with the requirements of all summons, subpoenas, and warrants relating to a paternity or child support proceeding.

(c)   The provisions of subdivision (a) of this section shall not apply to:

(i)   respondents who are receiving public assistance or supplemental security income; or

(ii)   respondents whose income as defined by subparagraph five of paragraph (b) of subdivision one-b of section two hundred forty of the domestic relations law falls below the self-support reserve as defined by subparagraph six of paragraph (b) of subdivision one-b of section two hundred forty of this article; or

(iii) respondents whose income as defined by subparagraph five of paragraph (b) of subdivision one-b of section two hundred forty of this article remaining after the payment of the current support obligation would fall below the self-support reserve as defined by subparagraph six of paragraph (b) of subdivision one-b of section two hundred forty of this article.

Added by Laws 1997, Ch. 398, § 131, eff. Jan. 1, 1998; **amended** by Laws 2002, Ch. 624, § 16, eff. Oct 2, 2002; provided, however, that sections six through sixteen of this act shall take effect on the thirtieth day after it shall have become a law; provided, further, that the amendments to subdivisions 12 and 15 of section 111-b of the social services law made by sections six and seven of this act shall not affect the repeal of such subdivisions and shall be deemed to be repealed therewith.

§ 245. Enforcement by contempt proceedings of judgment or order in action for divorce, separation or annulment.

Where a spouse, in an action for divorce, separation, annulment or declaration of nullity of a void marriage, or for the enforcement in this state of a judgment for divorce, separation, annulment or declaration of nullity of a void marriage rendered in another state, makes default in paying any sum of money as required by the judgment or order directing the payment thereof, and it appears presumptively, to the satisfaction of the court, that payment cannot be enforced pursuant to section two hundred forty-three or two hundred forty-four of this chapter or section fifty-two hundred forty-one or fifty-two hundred forty-two of the civil practice law and rules, the aggrieved spouse may make application pursuant to the provisions of seven hundred fifty-six of the judiciary law to punish the defaulting spouse for contempt, and where the judgment or order directs the payment to be made in installments, or at stated intervals, failure to make such single payment or installment may be punished as therein provided, and such punishment, either by fine or commitment, shall not be a bar to a subsequent proceeding to punish the defaulting spouse as for a contempt for failure to pay subsequent installments, but for such purpose such spouse may be proceeded against under the said order in the same manner and with the same effect as though such installment payment was directed to be paid by a separate and distinct order, and the provisions of the civil rights law are hereby superseded so far as they are in conflict therewith. Such application may also be made without any previous sequestration or direction to give security where the court is satisfied that they would be ineffectual. No demand of any kind upon the defaulting spouse shall be necessary in order that he or she be proceeded against and punished for failure to make any such payment or to pay any such installment; personal service upon the defaulting spouse of an uncertified copy of the judgment or order under which the default has occurred shall be sufficient.

Added by Laws 1962, Ch. 313, eff. Sept. 1, 1963, from former CPA § 1172; **amended** by Laws 1975, Ch. 497; Laws 1977, Ch. 437; Laws 1980, Ch. 281, eff. July 19, 1980; Laws 1985, Ch. 809, eff. Nov. 1, 1985.

§ 246. Persons financially unable to comply with orders or judgments directing the payment of alimony.

1. Any person who, by an order or judgment made or entered in an action for divorce, separation, annulment or declaration of the nullity of a void marriage or an action for the enforcement in this state of a judgment for divorce, separation or annulment or declaring the nullity of a void marriage rendered in another state, is directed to make payment of any sum or sums of money and against whom an order to punish for a contempt of court has been made pursuant to the provisions of section two hundred forty-five of this chapter or the judiciary law may, if financially unable to comply with the order or judgment to make such payment, upon such notice to such parties as the court may direct, make application to the court for an order relieving him from such payment and such contempt order. The court, upon the hearing of such application, if satisfied from the proofs and evidence offered and submitted that the applicant is financially unable to make such payment may, upon a showing of good cause until further order of the court, modify the order or judgment to make such payment and relieve him from such contempt order. No such modification shall reduce or annul unpaid sums or installments accrued prior to the making of such application unless the defaulting party shows good cause for failure to make application for relief from the judgement or order directing such payment prior to the accrual of such arrears. Such modification may increase such support nunc pro tunc based on newly discovered evidence.

2. Whenever, upon application to the court by an interested party, it appears to the satisfaction of the court that any person, who has been relieved totally or partially from making any such payment pursuant to the provisions of this section, is no longer financially unable to comply with the order or judgment to make such payment, then the court may, upon a showing of good cause modify or revoke its order relieving him totally or partially from making such payment.

3. Any person may assert his financial inability to comply with the directions contained in an order or judgment made or entered in an action for divorce, separation, annulment or declaration of the nullity of a void marriage or an action for the enforcement in this state of a judgment for divorce, separation or annulment or declaring the nullity of a void marriage rendered in another state, as a defense in a proceeding instituted against him under section two hundred forty-five or under the judiciary law to punish him for his failure to comply with such directions and, if the court, upon the hearing of such contempt proceeding, is satisfied from the proofs and evidence offered and submitted that the defendant is financially unable to comply with such order or judgment, it may, in its discretion, until further order of the court, make an order modifying such order or judgment and denying the application to punish the defendant for contempt. No such modification shall reduce or annul arrears accrued prior to the making of such application unless the defaulting party shows good cause for failure to make application for relief from the judgment or order directing such payment prior to the accrual of such arrears. Such modification may increase such support

nunc pro tunc as of the date of the application based on newly discovered evidence. Any retroactive amount of support due shall be paid in one sum or periodic sums, as the court shall direct, taking into account any amount of temporary support which has been paid.

     Added by Laws 1962, Ch. 313, from former CPA § 1172-a; **amended** by Laws 1963, Ch. 685; Laws 1977, Ch. 516; Laws 1980, Ch. 645, eff. July 19, 1980; Laws 1981, Ch. 695, eff. Oct. 19, 1981, subd. 3.

§ 247.   Alimony or maintenance payments suspended during confinement in prison.

    Notwithstanding any inconsistent provision of this article, the provision of any judgment or order rendered or made in an action for divorce, separation, annulment or declaration of nullity of a void marriage, requiring the payment of moneys by one spouse for the support of the other shall be suspended and inoperative so far as punishment for contempt is concerned during the period in which the defaulting spouse shall be imprisoned pursuant to any order adjudging him or her in contempt for failure to comply with any provision in such order.

     Added by Laws 1962, Ch. 313, eff. Sept. 1, 1963, from former CPA § 1172-b; **amended** by Laws 1980, Ch. 281, eff. July 19, 1980.

§ 248.   Modification of judgment or order in action for divorce or annulment.

    Where an action for divorce or for annulment or for a declaration of the nullity of a void marriage is brought by a husband or wife, and a final judgment of divorce or a final judgment annulling the marriage or declaring its nullity has been rendered, the court, by order upon the application of the husband on notice, and on proof of the marriage of the wife after such final judgment, must modify such final judgment and any orders made with respect thereto by annulling the provisions of such final judgment or orders, or of both, directing payments of money for the support of the wife. The court in its discretion upon application of the husband on notice, upon proof that the wife is habitually living with another man and holding herself out as his wife, although not married to such man, may modify such final judgment and any orders made with respect thereto by annulling the provisions of such final judgment or orders or of both, directing payment of money for the support of such wife.

     Added by Laws 1962, Ch. 313, eff. Sept. 1, 1963, from former CPA § 1172-c; **amended** by Laws 1975, Ch. 604, eff. Aug. 31, 1975.

§ 249.   Trial preferences in matrimonial actions.

    Upon motion of either party or upon its own motion, the court may direct that any action or proceeding brought (1) to annul a marriage or to declare the nullity of a void marriage, or (2) for a separation, or (3) for a divorce, or (4) to enjoin the prosecution in any other jurisdiction of an action for divorce, be placed forthwith by the clerk on the supreme court calendar and be entitled to preference in the trial thereof, in accordance with Rule 3403 of the civil practice law and rules, provided that in the courts' discretion, justice so requires. Such direction may be made by separate order or in any order granted in any such action or proceeding upon any application made pursuant to sections two hundred thirty-six, two hundred thirty-seven or two hundred forty of this article.

Such direction, in the event no note of issue has been previously filed with the clerk, may also require either party to file with the clerk proof of service of the summons, two copies of the note of issue and such other data as may be required.

Added by Laws 1965, Ch. 296, eff. May 28, 1965.

§ 250.   Divorces obtained outside the state of New York.

Repealed by Laws 1973, Ch. 67, eff. Sept. 1, 1973.

§ 250.   Compulsory financial disclosure.

Repealed by Laws 1980, Ch. 281, eff. July 19, 1980.

§ 251.   Filing of order in family court.

When, in a matrimonial action, the supreme court refers the issues of support, custody or visitation to the family court, the order or judgment shall provide that a copy thereof shall be filed by the plaintiff's attorney, within ten days, with the clerk of the family court therein specified.

Added by Laws 1973, Ch. 164, eff. Sept. 1, 1973.

§ 252.   Effect of pendency of action for divorce, separation or annulment on petition for order of protection.

1.   In an action for divorce, separation or annulment or in an action to declare the nullity of a void marriage in the supreme court, the supreme court or the family court shall entertain an application for an order of protection or temporary order of protection by either party. Such an order may require any party:

(a)   to stay away from the home, school, business or place of employment of the child, other parent or any other party, and to stay away from any other specific location designated by the court;

(b)   to permit a parent, or a person entitled to visitation by a court order or a separation agreement, to visit the child at stated periods;

(c)   to refrain from committing a family offense, as defined in subdivision one of section 530.11 of the criminal procedure law, or any criminal offense against such child or against the other parent or against any person to whom custody of the child is awarded or from harassing, intimidating or threatening such persons;

(d) to permit a designated party to enter the residence during a specified period of time in order to remove personal belongings not in issue in a proceeding or action under this chapter or the family court act;

(e) to refrain from acts of commission or omission that create an unreasonable risk to the health, safety or welfare of a child;

(f) to pay the reasonable counsel fees and disbursements involved in obtaining or enforcing the order of the person who is protected by such order if such order is issued or enforced; or

(g) to observe such other conditions as are necessary to further the purposes of protection.

2. An order of protection entered pursuant to this subdivision shall bear in a conspicuous manner, on the front page of said order, the language "order of protection issued pursuant to section two hundred fifty-two of the domestic relations law." The absence of such language shall not affect the validity of such order. The presentation of a copy of such an order to any peace officer acting pursuant to his or her special duties, or police officer, shall constitute authority, for that officer to arrest a person when that person has violated the terms of such an order, and bring such person before the court and, otherwise, so far as lies within the officer's power, to aid in securing the protection such order was intended to afford.

2-a. If the court that issued an order of protection or temporary order of protection under this section or warrant in connection thereto is not in session when an arrest is made for an alleged violation of the order or upon a warrant issued in connection with such violation, the arrested person shall be brought before a local criminal court in the county of arrest or in the county in which such warrant is returnable pursuant to article one hundred twenty of the criminal procedure law and arraigned by such court. Such local criminal court shall order the commitment of the arrested person to the custody of the sheriff, admit to, fix or accept bail, or release the arrested person on his or her recognizance pending appearance in the court that issued the order of protection, temporary order of protection or warrant. In making such order, such local criminal court shall consider the bail recommendations, if any, made by the supreme or family court as indicated on the warrant or certificate of warrant. Unless the petitioner or complainant requests otherwise, the court, in addition to scheduling further criminal proceedings, if any, regarding such alleged family offense or violation allegation, shall make such matter returnable in the supreme or family court, as applicable, on the next day such court is in session.

3. An order of protection entered pursuant to this subdivision may be made in the final judgment in any matrimonial action, or by one or more orders from time to time before or subsequent to final judgment, or by both such order or orders and the final judgment. The order of protection may remain in effect after

entry of a final matrimonial judgment and during the minority of any child whose custody or visitation is the subject of a provision of a final judgment or any order. An order of protection may be entered notwithstanding that the court for any reason whatsoever, other than lack of jurisdiction, refuses to grant the relief requested in the action or proceeding.

4. No order of protection may direct any party to observe conditions of behavior unless: (i) the party requesting the order of protection has served and filed an action, proceeding, counterclaim or written motion and, (ii) the court has made a finding on the record that such party is entitled to issuance of the order of protection which may result from a judicial finding of fact, judicial acceptance of an admission by the party against whom the order was issued or judicial finding that the party against whom the order is issued has given knowing, intelligent and voluntary consent to its issuance. The provisions of this subdivision shall not preclude the court from issuing a temporary order of protection upon the court's own motion or where a motion for such relief is made to the court, for good cause shown.

5. Except with respect to enforcement pursuant to a criminal prosecution under article two hundred fifteen of the penal law, the supreme court may provide in an order made pursuant to this section that the order may be enforced or modified only in the supreme court. If the supreme court so provides, the family court may not entertain an application to enforce or modify such an order of the supreme court.

6. In any such matrimonial action however, the court may not sua sponte consolidate actions or make, vacate or modify orders of protection issued in family court involving the same parties except upon motion and with notice to the non-moving party. Such non-moving party shall be given an opportunity to be heard.

7. A valid order of protection or temporary order of protection issued by a court of competent jurisdiction in another state, territorial or tribal jurisdiction shall be accorded full faith and credit and enforced as if it were issued by a court within the state for as long as the order remains in effect in the issuing jurisdiction in accordance with sections two thousand two hundred sixty-five and two thousand two hundred sixty-six of title eighteen of the United States Code.

(a) An order issued by a court of competent jurisdiction in another state, territorial or tribal jurisdiction shall be deemed valid if:

(i) The issuing court had personal jurisdiction over the parties and over the subject matter under the law of the issuing jurisdiction;

(ii) the person against whom the order was issued had reasonable notice and an opportunity to be heard prior to issuance of the order; provided, however, that if the order was a temporary order of protection issued in the absence of such person, that notice had been given and that an opportunity to be heard had been provided within a reasonable period of time after the issuance of the order; and

(iii) in the case of orders of protection or temporary orders of protection issued against both a petitioner and respondent, the order or portion thereof sought to be enforced was supported by: (a) a pleading requesting such order, including, but not limited to, a petition, cross-petition or counterclaim; and (b) a judicial finding that the requesting party is entitled to the issuance of the order, which may result from a judicial finding of fact, judicial acceptance of an admission by the party against whom the order was issued or judicial finding that the party against whom the order was issued had given knowing, intelligent and voluntary consent to its issuance.

(b) Notwithstanding the provisions of article fifty-four of the civil practice law and rules, an order of protection or temporary order of protection issued by a court of competent jurisdiction in another state, territorial or tribal jurisdiction, accompanied by a sworn affidavit that upon information and belief such order is in effect as written and has not been vacated or modified, may be filed without fee with the clerk of the court, who shall transmit information regarding such order to the statewide registry of orders of protection and warrants established pursuant to section two hundred twenty-one-a of the executive law; provided, however, that such filing and registry entry shall not be required for enforcement of the order.

8. Any party moving for a temporary order of protection pursuant to this subdivision during hours when the court is open shall be entitled to file such motion or pleading containing such prayer for emergency relief on the same day that such person first appears at such court, and a hearing on the motion or portion of the pleading requesting such emergency relief shall be held on the same day or the next day that the court is in session following the filing of such motion or pleading.

9. Upon issuance of an order of protection or temporary order of protection or upon a violation of such order, the court may take an order in accordance with section eight hundred forty-two-a of the family court act directing the surrender of firearms, revoking or suspending a party's firearms license, and/or directing that such party be ineligible to receive a firearms license. Upon issuance of an order of protection pursuant to this section or upon a finding of a violation thereof, the court also may direct payment of restitution in an amount not to exceed ten thousand dollars in accordance with subdivision (e) of section eight hundred forty-one of such act; provided, however, that in no case shall an order of restitution be issued where the court determines that the party against whom the order would be issued has already compensated the injured party or where such compensation is incorporated in a final judgment or settlement of the action.

Added by Laws of 1977, Ch. 449, eff. Sept. 1, 1977; **amended** by Laws 1994, Ch. 222, § 52, eff. Jan. 1, 1995; Laws 1995, Ch. 349, § 6, eff. July 28, 1995; Laws 1997, Ch. 186, § 14, eff. July 8, 1997; Laws 1998, Ch. 597, §§ 3 and 4, eff. Dec. 22, 1998; Laws 1999, Ch. 606, § 2, eff. Nov. 1, 2000; Laws 2000, Ch. 483, § 1, eff. Oct. 20, 2000, reverting effective dates for subds. 8 and 9 to Nov. 9, 1999.

§ 253. Removal of barriers to remarriage.

1. This section applies only to a marriage solemnized in this state or in any other jurisdiction by a person specified in subdivision one of section eleven of this chapter.

2. Any party to a marriage defined in subdivision one of this section who commences a proceeding to annul the marriage or for a divorce must allege, in his or her verified complaint (i) that, to the best of his or her knowledge, that he or she has taken or that he or she will take, prior to the entry of final judgment, all steps solely within his or her power to remove any barrier to the defendant's remarriage following the annulment or divorce; or (ii) that the defendant has waived in writing the requirements of this subdivision.

3. No final judgment of annulment or divorce shall thereafter be entered unless the plaintiff shall have filed and served a sworn statement: (i) that, to the best of his or her knowledge, he or she has, prior to the entry of such final judgment, taken all steps solely within his or her power to remove all barriers to the defendant's remarriage following the annulment or divorce; or (ii) that the defendant has waived in writing the requirements of this subdivision.

4. In any action for divorce based on subdivisions five and six of section one hundred seventy of this chapter in which the defendant enters a general appearance and does not contest the requested relief, no final judgment of annulment or divorce shall be entered unless both parties shall have filed and served sworn statements: (i) that he or she has, to the best of his or her knowledge, taken all steps solely within his or her power to remove all barriers to the other party's remarriage following the annulment or divorce; or (ii) that the other party has waived in writing the requirements of this subdivision.

5. The writing attesting to any waiver of the requirements of subdivision two, three or four of this section shall be filed with the court prior to the entry of a final judgment of annulment or divorce.

6. As used in the sworn statements prescribed by this section "barrier to remarriage" includes, without limitation, any religious or conscientious restraint or inhibition, of which the party required to make the verified statement is aware, that is imposed on a party to a marriage, under the principles held by the clergyman or minister who has solemnized the marriage, by reason of the other party's commission or withholding of any voluntary act. Nothing in this section shall be construed to require any party to consult with any clergyman or minister to determine whether there exists any such religious or conscientious restraint or inhibition. It shall not be deemed a "barrier to remarriage" within the meaning of this section if the restraint or inhibition cannot be removed by the party's voluntary act. Nor shall it be deemed a "barrier to remarriage" if the party must incur expenses in connection with removal of the restraint or inhibition and the other party refuses to provide reasonable reimbursement for such expenses. "All steps solely within his or her power" shall not be construed to include application to a marriage tribunal or other similar organization or agency of a religious

denomination which has authority to annul or dissolve a marriage under the rules of such denomination.

7.   No final judgment of annulment or divorce shall be entered, notwithstanding the filing of the plaintiff's sworn statement prescribed by this section, if the clergyman or minister who has solemnized the marriage certifies, in a sworn statement, that he or she has solemnized the marriage and that, to his or her knowledge, the plaintiff has failed to take all steps solely within his or her power to remove all barriers to the defendant's remarriage following the annulment or divorce, provided that the said clergyman or minister is alive and available and competent to testify at the time when final judgment would be entered.

8.   Any person who knowingly submits a false sworn statement under this section shall be guilty of making an apparently sworn false statement in the first degree and shall be punished in accordance with section 210.40 of the penal law.

9.   Nothing in this section shall be construed to authorize any court to inquire into or determine any ecclesiastical or religious issue. The truth of any statement submitted pursuant to this section shall not be the subject of any judicial inquiry, except as provided in subdivision eight of this section.

Added by Laws 1983, Ch. 979, eff. Aug. 8, 1983; **amended** by Laws 1984, Ch. 945, eff. Aug. 6, 1984.

§ 254.   Confidentiality.

1.   Notwithstanding any other provision of law, in any proceeding for custody, divorce, separation or annulment, whether or not an order of protection or temporary order of protection is sought or has been sought in the past, the court may, upon its own motion or upon the motion of any party or the law guardian, authorize any party or the child to keep his or her address confidential from any adverse party or the child, as appropriate, in any pleadings or other papers submitted to the court, where the court finds that the disclosure of the address or other identifying information would pose an unreasonable risk to the health or safety of a party or the child. Pending such a finding, any address or other identifying information of the child or party seeking confidentiality shall be safeguarded and sealed in order to prevent its inadvertent or unauthorized use or disclosure.

2.   Notwithstanding any other provision of law, if a party or a child has resided or resides in a residential program for victims of domestic violence as defined in section four hundred fifty-nine-a of the social services law, the present address of the party and the child and the address of the residential program for victims of domestic violence shall not be revealed.

3.   Upon authorization as provided in subdivision one of this section, the identifying information shall be sealed and shall not be disclosed in any pleading or other document filed in a proceeding under this article. The court shall designate the clerk of the court or such other disinterested person as it deems appropriate, with consent of such disinterested person, as the agent for service

of process for the party whose address is to remain confidential and shall notify the adverse party of such designation in writing. The clerk or disinterested person designated by the court shall, when served with process or other papers on behalf of the party whose address is to remain confidential, promptly notify such party whose address is to remain confidential and forward such process or papers to him or her.

4. In any case in which such a confidentiality authorization is made, the party whose address is to remain confidential shall inform the clerk of the court or disinterested person designated by the court of any change in address for purposes of receipt of service or process or any papers.

Added by Laws 2001, Ch. 236, eff. Sept. 4, 2001.

ARTICLE 15

LAWS REPEALED: WHEN TO TAKE EFFECT

SUMMARY OF ARTICLE

(Added by Laws 1909, Ch. 9, 240, 241, renumbered Art. 15, §§ 270, 271, and § 272 added by Laws 1962, Ch. 313, eff. Sept. 1, 1963.)

Section   270.   **Laws repealed.**
            271.   **When to take effect.**
            272.   **References in this chapter.**

§ 270.   Laws repealed.

Of the laws enumerated in the schedule hereto annexed, that portion specified in the last column is hereby repealed.

§ 271.   When to take effect.

This chapter shall take effect immediately.

§ 272.   References in this chapter.

Whenever in this chapter any reference is made to the children's court act of the state of New York, the children's court or a judge thereof, or to the domestic relations court act of the city of New York, the domestic relations court of the city of New York or a justice thereof, such reference shall, on and after the effective date of legislation implementing the establishment of the family court, the officers thereof, and prescribing its powers and duties, be deemed to refer, respectively, to such legislation, the family court or a judge thereof, as the case may be, to the extent that such references may be made applicable.

Amended by Laws 1963, Ch. 685, § 14, eff. Sept. 1, 1963.

Schedule of Laws Repealed

Revised Statutes . . . . Part 2, chapter 1, title 1, section 5–7

Revised Statutes . . . . Part 2, chapter 8 . . All

Laws of	Chapter	Section
1788	. . 15	 1–8
1796	. . 20	. . . . All
1801	. . 11	. . . . 6, 7, 8, 14
1815	. . 221	. . . . All
1816	. . 75	. . . .
1818	. . 47	 2
1822	. . 206	. . . . All
1826	. . 254	. . . .
1828	. . 20	. . . . 18 (2d Meet.)
1828	. . 21	. . . . 1, 43, 201, 208, 231, 247, 358, 481 (2d Meet.)
1830	. . 320	 24–29
1840	. . 80	. . . . All
1845	. . 11	. . . .
1848	. . 200	. . . . All
1849	. . 375	. . . .
1850	. . 266	. . . . All
1851	. . 321	. . . .
1853	. . 576	. . . . All
1855	. . 159	. . . .
1858	. . 187	. . . . All
1860	. . 90	. . . .
1862	. . 70	. . . . All
1862	. . 172	. . . .
1866	. . 656	. . . . All
1870	. . 277	. . . .
1870	. . 431	. . . . All
1871	. . 32	. . . .
1871	. . 934	. . . . All
1873	. . 25	. . . .
1873	. . 821	. . . . All
1873	. . 830	. . . .
1875	. . 522	. . . . All
1877	. . 430	. . . .
1878	. . 112	. . . . 1, 2
1878	. . 300	. . . . All
1879	. . 164	. . . .
1879	. . 248	. . . . All
1879	. . 321	. . . .
1880	. . 472	. . . . All
1881	. . 442	. . . . 939, 940
1884	. . 381	. . . . All
1884	. . 438	. . . . All, except § 2 and first sentence of § 4.

DRL

1886	340	All
1887	24	
1887	77	All
1887	537	
1887	703	All
1888	78	
1888	437	All
1888	454	
1888	485	All
1889	58	
1889	415	All
1890	51	
1892	594	All
1893	175	
1893	242	All
1893	601	
1894	54	All
1895	531	
1896	272	All
1897	408	
1897	417	9, pt. relating to guardians.
1897	452	All
1899	159	
1899	448	All
1899	498	
1899	725	All
1901	339	
1902	289	All
1902	295	1, pt. amending Laws 1897, Ch. 417 § 9, as to guardians.
1902	522	All
1903	369	
1905	495	All
1905	499	All
1907	480	
1907	669	1, pt. amending Laws 1897, Ch. 417, § 9, as to guardians.
1907	742	All
1908	73	
Code Civil Procedure		450, from words "and all sums" to "of the wife"; 1206; 1273, last sentence; 1761.

FAMILY COURT ACT OF THE STATE OF NEW YORK

LAWS 1962, CH. 686, EFF. SEPT. 1, 1962, AS AMENDED BY THE 2006 REGULAR LEGISLATIVE SESSION THROUGH JUNE 22, 2006.

(Sections effective Sept. 1, 1962 except as otherwise indicated.)

———

Table of Contents

FCA

ARTICLE 1

FAMILY COURT ESTABLISHED

SUMMARY OF ARTICLE

Part 1.   Applicability of act and creation of court.

§ 111.   Title of act.

The title of this act is "the family court act of the state of New York." It may be cited as "The Family Court Act."

§ 112.   Applicability.

The family court act applies in all counties of the state of New York.

§ 113.   Establishment of court.

The family court of the state of New York is established in each county of the state as part of the unified court system for the state.

§ 114. "Exclusive original jurisdiction."

When used in this act "exclusive original jurisdiction" means that the proceedings over which the family court is given such jurisdiction must be originated in the family court in the manner prescribed by this act. The provisions of this act shall in no way limit or impair the jurisdiction of the supreme court as set forth in section seven of article six of the constitution of the state of New York.

§ 115   Jurisdiction of family court.

(a)   The family court has exclusive original jurisdiction over

(i)   abuse and neglect proceedings, as set forth in article ten;

(ii)   support proceedings, as set forth in article four;

(iii)   proceedings to determine paternity and for the support of children born out-of-wedlock, as set forth in article five;

(iv)   [Until Oct 24, 2006] proceedings to permanently terminate parental rights to guardianship and custody of a child by reason of permanent neglect, as set forth in part one of article six of this act and paragraph (d) of subdivision four of section three hundred eighty-four-b of the social services law, and by reason of mental illness, mental retardation and severe or repeated child abuse, as set forth in paragraphs (c) and (e) of subdivision four of section three hundred eighty-four-b of the social services law;

(iv)   [Eff Oct 24, 2006] proceedings to permanently terminate parental rights to guardianship and custody of a child: (A) by reason of permanent neglect, as set forth in part one of article six of this act and paragraph (d) of subdivision four of section three hundred eighty-four-b of the social services law, (B) by reason of mental illness, mental retardation and severe or repeated child abuse, as set forth in paragraphs (c) and (e) of subdivision four of section three hundred eighty-four-b of the social services law, and (C) by reason of the death of one or both parents, where no guardian of the person of the child has been lawfully appointed, or by reason of abandonment of the child for a period of six months immediately prior to the filing of the petition, where a child is under the jurisdiction of the family court as a result of a placement in foster care by the family court pursuant to article ten or ten-A of this act or section three hundred fifty-eight-a of the social services law, unless the court declines jurisdiction pursuant to section three hundred eighty-four-b of the social services law;

(v)   proceedings concerning whether a person is in need of supervision, as set forth in article seven; and

(vi)   proceedings concerning juvenile delinquency as set forth in article three.

(b)   The family court has such other jurisdiction as is set forth in this act, including jurisdiction over habeas corpus proceedings and over applications for support, maintenance, a distribution of marital property and custody in matrimonial actions when referred to the family court by the supreme court, conciliation proceedings, and proceedings concerning physically handicapped and mentally defective or retarded children.

(c) The family court has such other jurisdiction as is provided by law, including but not limited to: proceedings concerning adoption and custody of children, as set forth in parts two and three of article six of this act; proceedings concerning the uniform interstate family support act, as set forth in article five-B of this act; proceedings concerning children in foster care and care and custody of children, as set forth in sections three hundred fifty-eight-a and three hundred eighty-four-a of the social services law and article ten-A of this act; proceedings concerning guardianship and custody of children by reason of the death of, or abandonment or surrender by, the parent or parents, as set forth in sections three hundred eighty-three-c, three hundred eighty-four and paragraphs (a) and (b) of subdivision four of section three hundred eighty-four-b of the social services law; proceedings concerning standby guardianship and guardianship of the person as set forth in part four of article six of this act and article seventeen of the surrogate's court procedure act; and proceedings concerning the interstate compact on juveniles as set forth in chapter one hundred fifty-five of the laws of nineteen hundred fifty-five, as amended, the interstate compact on the placement of children, as set forth in section three hundred seventy-four-a of the social services law, and the uniform child custody jurisdiction and enforcement act, as set forth in article five-A of the domestic relations law.

(d) Notwithstanding subdivisions (a) through (c) of this section, jurisdiction of the family court and tribal courts of Indian tribes designated by the Secretary of the Interior over those child custody proceedings provided for in articles three, seven, ten and ten-A of this act and sections three hundred fifty-eight-a and three hundred eighty-four-b of the social services law involving Indian children as defined in subdivision thirty-six of section two of the social services law shall be subject to the terms and conditions set forth in applicable sections of title twenty-five of the United States code; provided that tribal courts of Indian tribes designated as such by the state of New York shall have jurisdiction over such child custody proceedings involving Indian children to the same extent as federally designated Indian tribes upon the approval of the state office of children and family services pursuant to section thirty-nine of the social services law.

(e) The family court has concurrent jurisdiction with the criminal court over all family offenses as defined in article eight of this act.

(f) The family court has jurisdiction to direct the commencement of proceedings to suspend the driving privileges, recreational licenses and permits, and license, permit, registration or authority to practice of persons who are delinquent in their child or combined child and spousal support obligations or persons who have failed, after receiving appropriate notice, to comply with summonses, subpoenas or warrants relating to paternity and child support proceedings as set forth in sections four hundred fifty-eight-a, four hundred fifty-eight-b, four hundred fifty-eight-c, five hundred forty-eight-a, five hundred forty-eight-b, and five hundred.

Such jurisdiction shall include jurisdiction over all boards, departments, authorities or offices of the state for the purposes of implementing such section. Jurisdiction of family court.

Amended by Laws 1964, Ch. 383; Laws 1970, Ch. 962; Laws 1973, Ch. 907; Laws 1974, Ch. 239; Laws 1980, Ch. 281, eff. July 19, 1980, Ch. 471, eff. July 23, 1980; Laws 1982, Ch. 920, eff. July 1, 1983; Laws 1983, Ch. 398, eff. July 1, 1983; Laws 1987, Ch. 462, eff. July 27, 1987; Laws 1994, Ch. 384, § 2, eff. July 20, 1994; Laws 1994, Ch. 222, §§ 3-4, eff. Jan. 1, 1995; Laws 1995, Ch. 81, § 200, eff. July 1, 1995; Laws 1997, Ch. 398, § 108, eff. Jan. 1, 1998; Laws 2002, Ch. 409, §§ 1, 2, eff. Aug. 13, 2002; L. 2005, Ch. 3, §§ 1, amending sub.(c), (d), eff. Aug. 23, 2005; Laws 2006, Ch. 185, § 1, eff. Oct. 26, 2006.

§ 116. Religion of custodial persons and agencies.

(a) Whenever a child is remanded or committed by the court to any duly authorized association, agency, society or institution, other than an institution supported and controlled by the state or a subdivision thereof, such commitment must be made, when practicable, to a duly authorized association, agency, society or institution under the control of persons of the same religious faith or persuasion as that of the child.

(b) Whenever any child thus committed is placed by any such association, agency, society or institution in a family, or in the home, or in the custody, of any person other than that of its natural or adopted parent or parents, or when so placed or paroled directly by the court, such placement or parole must, when practicable, be with or in the custody of a person or persons of the same religious faith or persuasion as that of the child.

(c) In appointing guardians of children, except guardians ad litem, and in granting orders of adoption of children, the court must, when practicable, appoint only as such guardians, and only give custody through adoption to, persons of the same religious faith or persuasion as that of the child.

(d) The provisions of paragraphs (a), (b) and (c) of this section shall be interpreted literally, so as to assure that in the care, protection, guardianship, discipline or control of any child his religious faith shall be preserved and protected by the court. But this section shall not be construed so as to prevent the remanding of a child, during the pendency of a proceeding, to a place of detention designated by rules of court nor to the placing of a child in a hospital or similar institution for necessary treatment.

(e) The words "when practicable" as used in this section shall be interpreted as being without force or effect if there is a proper or suitable person of the same religious faith or persuasion as that of the child available for appointment as guardian, or to be designated as custodian, or to whom control may be given, or to whom orders of adoption may be granted; or if there is a duly authorized association, agency, society or institution under the control of persons of the same religious faith or persuasion as that of the child, at the time available and willing to assume the responsibility for the custody of or control over any such child.

FCA

(f)   If a child is placed in the custody, or under the supervision or control, of a person or of persons of a religious faith or persuasion different from that of the child, or if a guardian of a child is appointed whose religious faith or persuasion is different from that of the child, or if orders of adoption are granted to a person or persons whose religious faith is different from that of the child adopted, or if a child is remanded or committed to a duly authorized association, agency, society or institution, or to any other place, which is under the control of persons of a religious faith or persuasion different from that of the child, the court shall state or recite the facts which impel it to make such disposition and such statement shall be made a part of the minutes of the proceeding.

(g)   The provisions of subdivisions (a), (b), (c), (d), (e) and (f) of this section shall, so far as consistent with the best interests of the child, and where practicable, be applied so as to give effect to the religious wishes of the natural mother, if the child is born out-of-wedlock, or if born in-wedlock, the religious wishes of the parents of the child, or if only one of the parents of an in-wedlock child is then living, the religious wishes of the parent then living. Religious wishes of a parent shall include wishes that the child be placed in the same religion as the parent or in a different religion from the parent or with indifference to religion or with religion a subordinate consideration. Expressed religious wishes of a parent shall mean those which have been set forth in a writing signed by the parent, except that, in a non-agency adoption, such writing shall be an affidavit of the parent. In the absence of expressed religious wishes, as defined in this subdivision, determination of the religious wishes, if any, of the parent, shall be made upon the other facts of the particular case, and, if there is no evidence to the contrary, it shall be presumed that the parent wishes the child to be reared in the religion of the parent.

Amended by Laws 1970, Ch. 494, eff. May 8, 1970.

§ 117.   Parts of court.

(a)   There is hereby established in the family court a "child abuse part." Such part shall be held separate from all other proceedings of the court, and shall have jurisdiction over all proceedings in the family court involving abused children, and shall be charged with the immediate protection of these children. All cases involving abuse shall be originated in or be transferred to this part from other parts as they are made known to the court unless there is or was before the court a proceeding involving any members of the same family or household, in which event the judge who heard said proceeding may hear the case involving abuse. Consistent with its primary purpose, nothing in this section is intended to prevent the child abuse part from hearing other cases.

(b)   For every juvenile delinquency proceeding under article three involving an allegation of an act committed by a person which, if done by an adult, would be a crime (i) defined in sections 125.27 (murder in the first degree); 125.25 (murder in the second degree); 135.25 (kidnapping in the first degree); or 150.20

(arson in the first degree) of the penal law committed by a person thirteen, fourteen or fifteen years of age; (ii) defined in sections 120.10 (assault in the first degree); 125.20 (manslaughter in the first degree); 130.35 (rape in the first degree); 130.50 (criminal sexual act in the first degree); 135.20 (kidnapping in the second degree), but only where the abduction involved the use or threat of use of deadly physical force; 150.15 (arson in the second degree); or 160.15 (robbery in the first degree) of the penal law committed by a person thirteen, fourteen or fifteen years of age; (iii) defined in the penal law as an attempt to commit murder in the first or second degree or kidnapping in the first degree committed by a person thirteen, fourteen or fifteen years of age; (iv) defined in section 140.30 (burglary in the first degree); subdivision one of section 140.25 (burglary in the second degree); subdivision two of section 160.10 (robbery in the second degree) of the penal law; subdivision four of section 265.02 of the penal law, where such firearm is possessed on school grounds, as that phrase is defined in subdivision fourteen of section 220.00 of the penal law; or section 265.03 of the penal law, where such machine gun or such firearm is possessed on school grounds, as that phrase is defined in subdivision fourteen of section 220.00 of the penal law committed by a person fourteen or fifteen years of age; (v) defined in section 120.05 (assault in the second degree) or 160.10 (robbery in the second degree) of the penal law committed by a person fourteen or fifteen years of age but only where there has been a prior finding by a court that such person has previously committed an act which, if committed by an adult, would be the crime of assault in the second degree, robbery in the second degree or any designated felony act specified in clause (i), (ii) or (iii) of this subdivision regardless of the age of such person at the time of the commission of the prior act; or (vi) other than a misdemeanor, committed by a person at least seven but less than sixteen years of age, but only where there has been two prior findings by the court that such person has committed a prior act which, if committed by an adult would be a felony:

(i)   There is hereby established in the family court in the city of New York at least one "designated felony act part." Such part or parts shall be held separate from all other proceedings of the court, and shall have jurisdiction over all proceedings involving such an allegation. All such proceedings shall be originated in or be transferred to this part from other parts as they are made known to the court.

(ii)   Outside the city of New York, all proceedings involving such an allegation shall have a hearing preference over every other proceeding in the court, except proceedings under article ten.

(c)   The chief administrator of the courts may establish one or more separate support parts in each family court for the purpose of expediting support proceedings instituted pursuant to articles four, five and five-A of this act. Where such separate support parts are established, all such proceedings shall be originated in or be transferred to this part or parts as they are made known to the court and shall be heard by support magistrates in accordance with section four hundred thirty-nine of this act.

(d) The appellate division of the supreme court in each department may provide, in accordance with the standards and policies established by the administrative board of the judicial conference, that the family court in counties within its department shall or may be organized into such other parts, if any, as may be appropriate.

Amended by Laws 1970, Ch. 962; Laws 1976, Ch. 608, eff. Oct. 19, 1976, adding new subd. (b) and relettering former subd. (b) as subd. (c); Laws 1982, Ch. 920, eff. July 1, 1983; Laws 1985, Ch. 809, eff. Nov. 1, 1985; Laws 1998, Ch. 435, § 7, eff. Nov. 1, 1998; Laws 2003, Ch. 81, § 1, eff. June 18, 2003, amending sub. (c), and Ch. 264, § 58, amending sub. (b), eff. Nov. 1, 2003.

§ 118. Seal.

The seal of the family court consists of an engraving of the arms of the state of New York and the words "Family Court of the State of New York" followed by the name of the county in which the family court using the seal is located.

§ 119. Definitions.

When used in this act and unless the specific context indicates otherwise:

(a) "Duly authorized association, agency, society or institution" means a society for the prevention of cruelty to children duly incorporated under the laws of this state; any institution supported or controlled by the state or by a subdivision thereof; any public welfare official of this state; or an association, agency, society, or institution, duly empowered to care for children, which

(i) is incorporated under the laws of this state;

(ii) actually has its place of business or home within the state; and

(iii) is approved, visited, inspected and supervised by the state department of social services or which shall submit and consent to the approval, visitation, inspection and supervision of the department.

(b) "Person legally responsible for the child's care" includes the child's custodian, guardian, or any other person responsible for the child's care at the relevant time.

(c) The term "infant" or "minor" means a person who has not attained the age of eighteen years.

Amended by Laws 1963, Ch. 691; Laws 1974, Ch. 937, adding subd. (c), eff. Sept. 1, 1974, but is not construed to alter, change, affect, impair or defeat any rights, obligations or interests heretofore accrued, incurred, or conferred prior to the effective date; Laws 1978, Ch. 555, eff. July 24, 1978.

§ 120. Expenses of the court.

(a) All salaries of the judicial and non-judicial personnel of the court and all other expenses of the court whatsoever, except as provided in subdivision (b), shall within the city of New York, be a city charge and in the counties outside the city of New York, a county charge; provided however, that the final determination of the itemized estimates of the annual financial needs of the court shall be made by the appropriate governing bodies of such counties and the city of New York in the manner provided in article seven-a of the judiciary law, and section twenty-nine of article six of the constitution.

(b)   Salaries of support magistrates appointed in proceedings to compel support pursuant to section four hundred thirty-nine of this act shall be a state charge payable out of funds appropriated to the office of court administration for that purpose.

Added by Laws 1962, Ch. 687, eff. Sept. 1, 1968; **amended** by Laws 1977, Ch. 388, eff. Sept. 1, 1977; Laws 2003, Ch. 81, § 2, eff. June 18, 2003, amending sub. (b).

Part 2.   Number, appointment, term and compensation of judges within the city of New York.

(Repealed and transferred sections noted under appropriate section number of text.)

Section   121.   **Number of judges.**
           122.   **Continuance in office.**
           123.   **Appointment by mayor.**
           124.   **Eligibility for appointment.**
           126.   **Vacancies.**

§ 121.   Number of judges in the city of New York.

Repealed by Laws 1962 Ch. 687 effective Sept. 1, 1962. See new § 121 added by Laws 1962 Ch. 687, eff. Sept. 1, 1962.

§ 121.   Number of judges.

The family court within the city of New York shall consist of forty-four judges and, as of July first, nineteen hundred ninety, shall consist of forty-five judges and, as of April first, nineteen hundred ninety-one, shall consist of forty-seven judges. At least one of the persons appointed to the office of judge of the family court created by this section, shall be a resident of the county of Richmond and hereafter there shall be at least one family court judge resident in each county of the city of New York. The amount of compensation for such new family court judges shall be equal to the compensation payable to existing family court judges in the city of New York.

Added by Laws 1962, Ch. 687; **amended** by Laws 1965, Ch. 864; Laws 1968, Ch. 987, eff. June 1, 1968; Laws 1982, Ch. 500, eff. July 13, 1982; Laws 1990, Ch. 209, § 4, eff. June 2, 1990.

§ 122. Continuance in office.

The justices of the domestic relations court of the city of New York in office on the effective date of this act, shall for the remainder of the term of their appointment continue in office as judges of the family court in the county within the city of New York in which they reside.

§ 123. Appointment by mayor.

The mayor of the city of New York shall appoint the judges of the family court in counties within the city of New York for a term of ten years.

§ 124. Eligibility for appointment.

No person, other than one who holds such office at the effective date of this act, may assume the office of judge of the family court within the city of New York unless he has been admitted to practice law in this state at least ten years prior to the date of such appointment. In making such appointments, the mayor of the city of New York shall select persons who are especially qualified for the court's work by reason of their character, personality, tact, patience and common sense.

§ 125. Compensation.

Repealed by Laws 1975, Ch. 150, eff. June 3, 1975, and subject matter transferred to new § 183 of the Judiciary Law.

§ 126. Vacancies.

When a vacancy occurs, otherwise than by expiration of term on the last day of any year, in the office of judge of the family court in a county within the city of New York, the vacancy shall be filled by appointment of the mayor of the city of New York for the unexpired term.

§ 127. Compensation.

Repealed by Laws 1962 Ch. 687, eff. Sept. 1, 1962.

Part 3. Number, election, term and compensation of judges not within the city of New York.

(Repealed and transferred sections noted under appropriate section number of text.)

138. **Additional compensation for designated judge.**

§ 131. Number of judges.

Repealed by Laws 1962 Ch. 687, § 5. see new § 131, eff. Sept. 1, 1962, infra.

§ 131. Number of judges.

The number of judges of the family court for each county outside the city of New York shall be as follows:

(a)   In each county in which there was a separate office or offices of judge of the children's court authorized by law on the thirty-first day of August nineteen hundred sixty-two, the number of judges of the family court for such county shall be equal to the number of offices so authorized except those authorized by certificate filed pursuant to subdivision two of section four of the children's court act of the state of New York subsequent to March first, nineteen hundred sixty-two; and, effective May fifteenth, nineteen hundred sixty-three, there shall be a separate office of judge of the family court for the county of Niagara; and, effective May fifteenth, nineteen hundred sixty-three, there shall be a separate office of judge of the family court for the county of Ulster; and, effective January first, nineteen hundred sixty-four, there shall be a separate office of judge of the family court for the county of St. Lawrence; and, effective January first, nineteen hundred sixty-five, there shall be a separate office of judge of the family court for the county of Chautauqua; and, effective January first, nineteen hundred sixty-seven, there shall be a separate office of judge of the family court for the county of Oneida; and, effective January first, nineteen hundred sixty-five, there shall be a separate office of judge of the family court for the county of Jefferson; and, effective January first, nineteen hundred sixty-six, there shall be a separate office of judge of the family court for the county of Rockland.

(b)   In the other counties except the counties of Chautauqua, Jefferson and Oneida, a judge of the county court shall act as and discharge the duties of judge of the family court.

(c)   In the counties of Chautauqua, Jefferson and Oneida, upon the expiration of the term of office of the special county judge who was continued as a judge of the family court pursuant to section one hundred thirty-two of this act, or if there was no special county judge in office on the effective date of this act, a judge of the county court of each such county shall act as and discharge the duties of judge of the family court.

(d)   In the county of Nassau there shall be eight family court judges and the number of such judges now existing in said county is hereby increased accordingly.

(e)   In the county of Monroe there shall be six family court judges and the number of such judges now existing in said county is hereby increased accordingly; in the county of Erie there shall be six family court judges and the number

FCA

of such judges now existing in said county is hereby increased accordingly. In the county of Albany there shall be a total of three family court judges and the number of such judges now existing in such county is hereby increased accordingly.

(f)   In the county of Onondaga there shall be three additional family court judges and the number of such judges now existing in such county is hereby increased accordingly. The compensation of each such additional family court judge shall be the same as the compensation of existing family court judges in such county.

(g)   There shall be a separate office of judge of the family court for the counties of Oswego and Sullivan and the compensation payable for each such separate office of judge of the family court shall be twenty-five thousand dollars per annum. In the county of Saratoga there shall be an additional family court judge and the number of such judges now existing in such county is hereby increased accordingly. The compensation of such additional family court judge shall be the same as the compensation of the existing family court judge in such county.

(h)   In the county of Westchester there shall be three additional family court judges and the number of such judges now existing is hereby increased accordingly. The compensation of each additional family court judge shall be the same as the existing family court judge in such county.

(i)   In the county of Schenectady there shall be one additional family court judge and the number of such judges now existing is hereby increased accordingly. The compensation of the additional family court judge shall be the same as the existing family court judge in such county.

(j)   In the county of Genesee there shall be one additional family court judge and the number of such judges now existing is hereby increased accordingly. The compensation of the additional family court judge shall be the same as the existing family court judge in such county.

(k)   In the county of Rockland there shall be one additional family court judge and the number of such judges now existing is hereby increased accordingly. The compensation of the additional family court judge shall be the same as the existing family court judge in such county.

(l)   In the county of Dutchess there shall be two additional family court judges and the number of such judges now existing is hereby increased accordingly. The compensation of the additional family court judges shall be the same as the compensation paid to each of the existing family court judges in such county pursuant to section two hundred twenty-one-e of the judiciary law.

(m)   In the county of Niagara there shall be one additional family court judge and the number of such judges now existing is hereby increased accordingly. The compensation of the additional family court judge shall be the same as the existing family court judge in such county.

(n)   In the county of Ulster there shall be one additional family court judge and the number of such judges now existing is hereby increased accordingly. The compensation of the additional family court judge shall be the same as the existing family court judge in such county.

(o)   In the county of Oneida there shall be two additional family court judges making a total of three family court judges in such county. The number of such judges now existing in such county is hereby increased accordingly. The compensation of the additional family court judges shall be the same as the compensation of the existing family court judge in such county.

(p)   In the county of Suffolk there shall be four additional family court judges making a total of ten family court judges in such county. The number of such judges now existing in such county is hereby increased accordingly. The compensation of each such family court judge shall be the same as the compensation of existing family court judges in such county.

(q)   In the county of Rensselaer, there shall be one additional family court judge and the number of judges now existing is hereby increased accordingly. The compensation of the additional family court judge shall be the same as the existing family court judge in such county.

(r)   In the county of Orange there shall be three additional family court judges, making a total of four family court judges, and the number of such judges now existing is hereby increased accordingly. The compensation of each such additional family court judge shall be the same as the compensation paid to each of the existing family court judges in such county.

(s)   In the county of Broome there shall be a total of three family court judges and the number of such judges now existing is hereby increased accordingly. The compensation of such additional family court judge shall be the same as the compensation paid to each of the existing family court judges in such county.

(t)   There shall be a separate office of judge of the family court for the county of Clinton and the compensation payable for such separate office of judge of the family court shall be the same as the compensation payable to the judge of the county court of Clinton county.

Added by Laws 1962, Ch. 687, § 6, eff. Sept. 1, 1962; **amended** by Laws 1962, Ch. 702; Laws 1963, Chs. 776, 778, 832, 949; Laws 1964, Chs. 89, 655, 670, 671 678, 680, 686; Laws 1968, Ch. 987; Laws 1970, Chs. 125, 1015; Laws 1971, Chs. 158, 215, 392; Laws 1972, Chs. 133, 548; Laws 1973, Chs. 295, 603; Laws 1974, Ch. 353, Laws 1974, Ch. 567, increasing the number of additional Family Court judges in Westchester County from one to two, provides that the additional judge shall first be elected at the general election to be held in Nov., 1974, and shall take office on Jan. 1, 1975; Laws 1975, Ch. 205; Laws 1975, Ch. 555, increasing the number of Family Court judges in Nassau County from seven to eight, provides that the additional judge shall first be elected at the general election to be held in Nov. 1975 and shall take office on Jan. 1, 1976; Laws 1977, Ch. 489, eff. Aug. 1, 1977; Laws 1977, Ch. 490, eff. Aug. 1, 1977, adding subd. (q); Laws 1978, Ch. 699, eff. July 24, 1978; Laws 1982, Ch. 500, eff. July 13, 1982, provided, however, that the additional judges authorized in subds. (f), (h) and (p) shall be elected at the general election to be held in Nov. 1983, and shall take office on Jan. 1, 1984; Laws 1984, Ch. 572, eff. July 27, 1984 and the office of family court judge of the county of Saratoga authorized by this act shall be filled for a full term at the next general election held not less than three months after such effective date; Laws 1985, Ch. 547, eff. July 24, 1985, which amended first subd. (j) and relettered it subd. (r), and the office of family court judge of the county of Orange authorized by the act is to be filled for a full term at the next general election to be held in Nov. 1985; Laws 1987, Ch. 318, eff. July 20, 1987, provided that the additional family court judge in the county of Dutchess provided for in this act shall first be elected at the general election to be held in Nov. 1988 and shall take office Jan. 1, 1989; Laws 1990, Ch. 209, § 5, eff. June 2, 1990; Laws 1992, Ch. 588, § 1, eff. July 24, 1992; Laws 1998, Ch. 117, § 1, eff. June 26, 1998, amending subsection (o), and Ch. 232, § 1, eff. July 7, 1998, adding subsection (t). The additional family court judges provided for by these 1998 amendments shall first be elected at the general election to be held in November 1998 and shall first take office January 1, 1999; Laws 2000, Ch. 178, § 1, eff. July 19, 2000, amending subsection (e); Laws 2005, Ch. 240, § 4, eff. August 1, 2005, amending subsection (r).

§ 132. Continuance in office.

The special county judges of the counties of Broome, Chautauqua, Jefferson, Oneida and Rockland and the judges of the children's courts in all counties outside the city of New York in office at midnight on August thirty-first, nineteen hundred sixty-two, shall be judges of the family court in and for the county in which they hold office for the remainder of the terms for which they were elected or appointed.

§ 133. Vacancies.

When a vacancy occurs, otherwise than by expiration of term, in the office of judge of the family court in a county not within the city of New York, the vacancy shall be filled for a full term at the next general election held not less than three months after such vacancy occurs and, until the vacancy shall be so filled, the governor by and with the advice and consent of the senate, if the senate shall be in session, or, if the senate not be in session, the governor may fill such vacancy by an appointment which shall continue until and including the last day of December next after the election at which the vacancy shall be filled.

§ 134. Eligibility for office.

No person, other than one who holds such office on the effective date of this act may serve in the office of judge of the family court unless he or she has been admitted to practice law in the state of New York for at least ten years as of the date he or she commences the duties of office.

Amended by Laws 1993, Ch. 511, § 1, eff. July 26, 1993.

§ 135. Term of office.

The term of office of a judge elected to the family court in a county outside the city of New York is ten years.

§ 136. Compensation of judge elected to family court.

Repealed by Laws 1962, Ch. 687. See Laws 1962 Ch. 687 enacted eff. Sept. 1, 1962, infra.

§ 136. Compensation.

Repealed by Laws 1975, Ch. 150, eff. June 3, 1975, and subject matter transferred to new § 183 of the Judiciary Law.

§ 137. County judge or surrogate designated as family court judge.

Repealed by Laws 1962 Ch. 687. See new § 137 Laws 1962 Ch. 687, effective Sept. 1, 1962 infra.

§ 137. County judge designated as family court judge.

In each county referred to in subdivisions (b) and (c) of section one hundred thirty-one of this act in which there is more than one county judge, the appellate division of the supreme court of the judicial department in which such county is located shall designate and may revoke any designation of, one or more of the county judges within the county to act as and discharge the duties of family court judge.

FCA

     Added by Laws 1962, Ch. 687; Laws 1971, Ch. 1064, eff. Sept. 1, 1971.

§ 138. Additional compensation for designated judge.

Any additional compensation for a judge designated under section one hundred thirty-seven to act and discharge the duties of family court judge shall be as provided by law.

Part 4. Family court judges.

Section	141.	Findings.
	142.	Authority to visit school or institution.
	143.	Authority to attend meetings of association.
	144.	Activity in community organizations.
	145.	Liability of judge.
	146.	Temporary assignment of judges.

§ 141. Findings.

This act defines the conditions on which the family court may intervene in the life of a child, parent and spouse. Once these conditions are satisfied, the court is given a wide range of powers for dealing with the complexities of family life so that its action may fit the particular needs of those before it. The judges of the court are thus given a wide discretion and grave responsibilities.

The people of the state of New York have concluded that legal training and experience should be required before any person may assume the office of family court judge and so provided in section twenty, paragraph a, of the judiciary article of the constitution of the state of New York. Judges of the family court should also be familiar with areas of learning and practice that often are not supplied by the practice of law.

§ 142. Authority to visit school or institution.

Judges of the family court may officially visit any school or institution to which any person within the jurisdiction of the court of which he is an officer may be remanded or committed, and the authorities responsible for paying their respective salaries are authorized and required to approve and pay the necessary traveling expenses incurred by such judges in making such visits.

§ 143. Authority to attend meetings of association.

Judges discharging the duties of family court judge may attend conferences and meetings of the association of judges of the family court, and the fiscal authorities responsible for paying their respective salaries are authorized and required to approve and pay the necessary traveling expenses incurred by such judges in attending such conferences and meetings, if within the authorized appropriation.

§ 144. Activity in community organizations.

Any judge discharging the duties of family court judge is authorized to serve as an officer or member of the governing body of any corporation or association organized and maintained exclusively for religious, charitable, benevolent, or educational purposes.

Amended by Laws 1962, Ch. 687, eff. Sept. 1, 1962.

§ 145. Liability of judge.

Any family court judge who in good faith issues process in any proceeding under this act shall not be liable therefor unless it is shown that his action in so doing was malicious or a deliberate abuse of his discretion.

§ 146. Temporary assignment of judges.

Nothing in this act is intended to prevent the temporary assignment of family court judges by the appropriate administrative judge to counties other than the one to which they were elected or appointed for the purpose of meeting a temporary need for judicial personnel or for greater contact between courts.

Added Laws 1972, Ch. 1016, eff. June 8, 1972.

Part 5. General powers.

FCA

§ 151. Judges as magistrates.

Judges of the family court are magistrates.

§ 152. Power to administer oaths.

(a) Each family court judge may administer oaths and take acknowledgments, and may designate an official of his court so to do.

(b) In conducting a hearing under this act, a judge may dispense with the formality of placing a minor under oath before taking his testimony.

§ 153. Subpoena, warrant and other process to compel attendance.

The family court may issue a subpoena or in a proper case a warrant or other process to secure or compel the attendance of an adult respondent or child or any other person whose testimony or presence at a hearing or proceeding is deemed by the court to be necessary, and to admit to, fix or accept bail, or parole him pending the completion of the hearing or proceeding. The court is also authorized to issue a subpoena duces tecum in accordance with the applicable provisions of the civil practice act and, upon its effective date, in accordance with the applicable provisions of the CPLR. A judge of the family court is also authorized to hear and decide motions relating to child support subpoenas issued pursuant to section one hundred eleven-p of the social services law.

Amended by Laws 1963, Ch. 809, eff. Apr. 26, 1963; Laws 1997, Ch. 398, § 60, eff. Jan. 1, 1998.

§ 153-a.   Warrant of arrest; when and how executed.

(a)   A warrant of arrest may be executed on any day of the week, and at any hour of the day or night.

(b)   Unless encountering physical resistance, flight of other factors rendering normal procedure impractical, the arresting police officer must inform the subject named therein that a warrant for his arrest for attendance at the proceeding designated therein has been issued. Upon request of such subject, the police officer must show him the warrant if he has it in his possession. The officer need not have the warrant in his possession, and if he has not, he must show it to the subject upon request as soon after the arrest as possible.

(c)   In order to effect the arrest, the police officer may use such physical force as is justifiable pursuant to section 35.30 of the penal law.

(d)   In order to effect the arrest, the police officer may enter any premises in which he reasonably believes the subject named therein to be present. Before such entry, he must give, or make reasonable effort to give, notice of his authority and purpose to an occupant thereof.

(e)   If the officer, after giving such notice, is not admitted, he may enter such premises, and by a breaking if necessary.

Added by Laws 1975, Ch. 416, eff. July 8, 1975.

§ 153-b.   Service of process request for order of protection.

Whenever a petitioner requests an order of protection or temporary order of protection under any article of this act:

(a)   the summons and the petition and, if one has been issued, the temporary order of protection, or a copy or copies thereof, may be served on any day of the week, and at any hour of the day or night;

(b)   a peace officer, acting pursuant to his or her special duties, or a police officer may serve the summons and the petition and, if one has been issued, the temporary order of protection;

(c)   if a temporary order of protection has been issued, or an order of protection has been issued upon a default, unless the party requesting the order states on the record that she or he will arrange for other means for service or deliver the order to a peace or police officer directly for service, the court shall immediately deliver a copy of the temporary order of protection or order of protection to a peace officer, acting pursuant to his or her special duties and designated by the court, or to a police officer as defined in paragraph of section 1.20 of the criminal procedure law, or to any other county or municipal officer who may be directed to effect service under section two hundred fifty-five of the family court act, or, in the city of New York, to a designated representative of the police department of the city of New York. Any peace or police officer or designated person receiving a temporary order of protection or an order of protection as provided hereunder shall serve or provide for the service thereof together with any associated papers that may be served simultaneously, at any address designated therewith, including the summons and petition if not previously served. Service of such temporary order of protection, or order of protection, and associated papers, shall insofar as practicable, be achieved promptly. An officer or designated person obliged to perform service pursuant to this subdivision, and his or her employer, shall not be liable for damages resulting from failure to achieve service where, having made a reasonable effort, such officer is unable to locate and serve the temporary order of protection or order of protection at any address provided by the party requesting the order;

(d) a statement subscribed by the officer or designated person, and affirmed by him or her to be true under the penalties of perjury, stating the papers served, the date, time, address or in the event there is no address, place, and manner of service, the name and a brief physical description of the party served, shall be proof of the service of the summons, petition and temporary order of protection or order of protection. When the temporary order of protection or order of protection and other papers, if any, have been served, such officer or designated person shall provide the court with an affirmation, certificate or affidavit of service when the temporary order of protection has been served and shall provide notification of the date and time of such service to the statewide computer registry established pursuant to section two hundred twenty-one-a of the executive law.

Added by Laws 1981, Ch. 416, eff. Aug. 6, 1981; **amended** by Laws 1987, Ch. 821, eff. Aug. 7, 1987; Laws 1988, Ch. 200, § 1, eff. Nov. 1, 1988; Laws 1994, Ch. 46, eff. June 10, 1994; Laws 1995, Ch. 429, § 1, Oct. 1, 1995.

§ 153-c. Temporary order of protection.

Any person appearing at family court when the court is open requesting a temporary order of protection under any article of this act shall be entitled to file a petition without delay on the same day such person first appears at the family court, and a hearing on that request shall be held on the same day or the next day that the family court is open following the filing of such petition.

Added by Laws 1981, Ch. 416, eff. Aug. 6, 1981.

§ 154. State-wide process.

(a) The family court may send process or other mandates in any matter in which it has jurisdiction into any county of the state for service or execution in like manner and with the same force and effect as similar process or mandates of county courts as provided by law.

(b) In a proceeding to establish paternity or to establish, modify or enforce support, the court may send process without the state in the same manner and with the same effect as process sent within the state in the exercise of personal jurisdiction over any person subject to the jurisdiction of the court under section three hundred one or three hundred two of the civil practice law and rules or under section 580-201 of article five-b of the family court act, notwithstanding that such person is not a resident or domiciliary of the state.

(c) In a proceeding arising under article four, five, six, eight or ten of this act in which an order of protection is sought or in which a violation of an order of protection is alleged, the court may send process without the state in the same manner and with the same effect as process sent within the state in the exercise of personal jurisdiction over any person, subject to the jurisdiction of the court under section three hundred one or three hundred two of the civil practice law and rules, notwithstanding that such person is not a resident or domiciliary of the state, so long as: (1) the act or acts giving rise to the application for issuance or enforcement of the order of protection occurred within the state; and (2) the applicant for the order of protection resides or is domiciled in the state or has substantial contacts in the state, including but not limited to, presence on a regular basis in the state. Upon good cause shown, the court may issue a temporary order of protection in accordance with article four, five, six, eight or ten of this act. Where personal jurisdiction over a non-resident or non-domiciliary respondent would not be obtainable but for this subdivision, the papers to be served shall include a conspicuous notice that the exercise of such jurisdiction is limited to the issue of the order of protection. Where service of a petition and summons upon a non-resident or non-domiciliary respondent is required, such service shall be made at least twenty days before the return date. Where service is effected on an out-of-state respondent and the respondent defaults by failing to appear, the court may on its own motion, or upon application of any party or the law guardian, proceed to a hearing with respect to issuance or enforcement of the order of protection. Nothing in this section shall be construed to affect or alter the exercise of personal jurisdiction with respect to issues other than the order of protection.

Amended by Laws 1983, Ch. 291, eff. Mar. 13, 1984; Laws 1995, Ch. 441, § 1, eff. Oct. 31, 1995; Laws 1997, Ch. 398 § 37 (§ 580-905), eff. Dec. 31, 1997; Laws 1998, Ch. 214 § 38, eff. July 7, 1998, and deemed in full force and effect Dec. 31, 1997.

§ 154-a. Service of petition.

In every proceeding in family court, a copy of the petition filed therein shall be served upon the respondent at the time of service of process or, if that is not practicable, at the first court appearance by respondent.

Added by Laws 1983, Ch. 119, eff. May 23, 1983.

§ 154-b. Order of protection; answer and counter-claims; confidentiality of address.

1. In every proceeding under articles four, five, six and eight of this act in which an order of protection is requested, the respondent may file with the court

an answer to the petition and a counter-claim. A counter-claim shall be heard in the same manner as a petition and may be heard on the return date of the petition, provided that the counter-claim is served on the petitioner no later than five days prior to the return date and said counter-claim and proof of service is filed with the court. The petitioner may file and serve a reply to the counter-claim. A denial of the allegations of the counter-claim shall be presumed if the petitioner does not file and serve a reply.

2.　　(a) Notwithstanding any other provision of law, in any proceeding under article four, five, five-b, six, eight or ten of this act, whether or not an order of protection or temporary order of protection is sought or has been sought in the past, the court may, upon its own motion or upon the motion of any party or the law guardian, authorize any party or the child to keep his or her address confidential from any adverse party or the child, as appropriate, in any pleadings or other papers submitted to the court, where the court finds that disclosure of such address or other identifying information would pose an unreasonable risk to the health or safety of a party or the child. Pending such a finding, any address or other identifying information of the child or party seeking confidentiality shall be safeguarded and sealed in order to prevent its inadvertent or unauthorized use or disclosure.

(b)　Notwithstanding any other provision of law, if a party and a child has resided or resides in a residential program for victims of domestic violence as defined in section four hundred fifty-nine-a of the social services law, the present address of such party and of the child and the address of the residential program for victims of domestic violence shall not be revealed.

(c)　Upon such authorization, the court shall designate the clerk of the court or such other disinterested person as it deems appropriate, with consent of such disinterested person, as the agent for service of process for the party whose address is to remain confidential and shall notify the adverse party of such designation in writing. The clerk or disinterested person designated by the court shall, when served with process on behalf of the party whose address is to remain confidential, promptly notify such party whose address is to remain confidential and forward such process to him or her.

(d)　In any case in which such confidentiality authorization is made, the party whose address is to remain confidential shall inform the clerk of the court or disinterested person designated by the court of any change in address for purposes of receipt of service of process or any papers.

Added by Laws 1988, Ch. 706, eff. Sept. 2, 1988; **amended** by Laws 1994, Ch. 222, § 5, eff. Jan. 1, 1995; Laws 1995, Ch. 388, § 1, eff. Oct. 31, 1995; Laws 1995, Ch. 538, § 1, eff. Oct. 31, 1995; Laws 1997, Ch. 186, § 1, eff. July 8, 1997; Laws 2001, Ch. 236, § 1, eff. Sept. 4, 2001.

§ 154-c. Orders of protection; procedural requirements.

1.   Expiration dates. Any order of protection or temporary order of protection issued under articles four, five, six and eight of this act shall plainly state the date that such order expires.

2.   Modifications of orders of protection. Except as provided in subdivision two of section one hundred fifty-four-d of this act, any motion to vacate or modify any order of protection or temporary order of protection issued under this act shall be on notice to the non-moving party and the law guardian, if any.

3.   Pleadings and requisite findings. No order of protection may direct any party to observe conditions of behavior unless: (i) the party requesting the order of protection has served and filed a petition or counter-claim in accordance with article four, five, six or eight of this act and, (ii) the court has made a finding on the record that such party is entitled to issuance of the order of protection which may result from a judicial finding of fact, judicial acceptance of an admission by the party against whom the order was issued or judicial finding that the party against whom the order is issued has given knowing, intelligent and voluntary consent to its issuance. Nothing herein shall be deemed to limit or restrict the authority of the court to issue a temporary order of protection on an ex parte basis.

Added by Laws 1997, Ch. 186, § 2, eff. July 8, 1997; **amended** by Laws 1998, Ch. 597, § 5, eff. Dec. 22, 1998.

§ 154-d. Emergency powers; local criminal courts.

1.   Issuance of temporary orders of protection. Upon the request of the petitioner, a local criminal court may on an ex parte basis issue a temporary order of protection pending a hearing in family court, provided that a sworn affidavit, certified in accordance with subdivision one of section 100.30 of the criminal procedure law is submitted: (i) alleging that the family court is not in session; (ii) alleging that a family offense, as defined in subdivision one of section eight hundred twelve of this act or subdivision one of section 530.11 of the criminal procedure law, has been committed; (iii) alleging that a family offense petition has been filed or will be filed in family court on the next day the court is in session; and (iv) showing good cause. Upon appearance in a local criminal court, the petitioner shall be advised that he or she may continue with the proceeding either in family court or, upon the filing of a local criminal court accusatory instrument, in criminal court or both. Upon issuance of a temporary order of protection where petitioner requests that it be returnable in family court, the local criminal court shall transfer the matter forthwith to the family court and shall make the matter returnable in family court on the next day the family court is in session, or as soon thereafter as practicable, but in no event more than four calendar days after issuance of the order. The local criminal court, upon issuing a temporary order of protection returnable in family court pursuant to this subdivision shall immediately forward in a manner designed to ensure arrival

before the return date set in the order, a copy of the temporary order of protection and sworn affidavit to the family court and shall provide a copy of such temporary order of protection to the petitioner; provided, however, that if the temporary order of protection and affidavit are transmitted by facsimile or other electronic means, the original order and affidavit shall be forwarded to the family court immediately thereafter. Any temporary order of protection issued pursuant to this subdivision shall be issued to the respondent and copies shall be filed as required in subdivisions six and eight of section 530.12 of the criminal procedure law for orders of protection issued pursuant to such section. Any temporary order of protection issued pursuant to this subdivision shall plainly state the date that such order expires which, in the case of an order returnable in family court, shall be not more than four calendar days after its issuance, unless sooner vacated or modified by the family court. A petitioner requesting a temporary order of protection returnable in family court pursuant to this subdivision in a case in which a family court petition has not been filed shall be informed that such temporary order of protection shall expire as provided for herein, unless the petitioner files a petition pursuant to subdivision one of section eight hundred twenty-one of this act on or before the return date in family court and the family court issues a temporary order of protection as authorized under article eight of this act. Nothing in this subdivision shall limit or restrict the petitioner's right to proceed directly and without court referral in either a criminal or family court, or both, as provided for in section one hundred fifteen of this act and section 100.07 of the criminal procedure law.

2. Modifications of orders of protection or temporary orders of protection. Upon the request of the petitioner, a local criminal court may on an ex parte basis modify a temporary order of protection or order of protection which has been issued under article four, five, six or eight of this act pending a hearing in family court, provided that a sworn affidavit, verified in accordance with subdivision one of section 100.30 of the criminal procedure law, is submitted: (i) alleging that the family court is not in session and (ii) showing good cause, including a showing that the existing order is insufficient for the purposes of protection of the petitioner, the petitioner's child or children or other members of the petitioner's family or household. The local criminal court shall make the matter regarding the modification of the order returnable in family court on the next day the family court is in session, or as soon thereafter as practicable, but in no event more than four calendar days after issuance of the modified order. The local criminal court shall immediately forward, in a manner designed to ensure arrival before the return date set in the order, a copy of the modified order if any and sworn affidavit to the family court and shall provide a copy of such modified order, if any, and affidavit to the petitioner; provided, however, that if the modified order and affidavit are transmitted to the family court by facsimile or other electronic means, the original copy of such modified order and affidavit shall be forwarded to the family court immediately thereafter. Any modified temporary order of protection or order of protection issued pursuant to this subdivision shall be issued to the respondent, and copies shall be filed as provided in

FCA

subdivisions six and eight of section 530.12 of the criminal procedure law for orders of protection issued pursuant to such section.

Added by Laws 1997, Ch. 186, § 3, eff. July 8, 1997.

§ 154-e.   Orders of protection; filing and enforcement of out-of-state orders.

A valid order of protection or temporary order of protection issued by a court of competent jurisdiction in another state, territorial or tribal jurisdiction shall be accorded full faith and credit and enforced under article eight of this act as if it were issued by a court within the state for as long as the order remains in effect in the issuing jurisdiction in accordance with sections two thousand two hundred sixty-five and two thousand two hundred sixty-six of title eighteen of the United States Code.

1.   An order issued by a court of competent jurisdiction in another state, territorial or tribal jurisdiction shall be deemed valid if:

a.   The issuing court had personal jurisdiction over the parties and over the subject matter under the law of the issuing jurisdiction;

b.   The person against whom the order was issued had reasonable notice and an opportunity to be heard prior to issuance of the order; provided, however, that if the order was a temporary order of protection issued in the absence of such person, that notice had been given and that an opportunity to be heard had been provided within a reasonable period of time after the issuance of the order; and

c.   In the case of orders of protection or temporary orders of protection issued against both a petitioner and respondent, the order or portion thereof sought to be enforced was supported by: (i) a pleading requesting such order, including, but not limited to, a petition, cross-petition or counterclaim; and (ii) a judicial finding that the requesting party is entitled to the issuance of the order which may result from a judicial finding of fact, judicial acceptance of an admission by the party against whom the order was issued or judicial finding that the party against whom the order was issued had given knowing, intelligent and voluntary consent to its issuance.

2.   Notwithstanding the provisions of article fifty-four of the civil practice law and rules, an order of protection or temporary order of protection issued by a court of competent jurisdiction in another state, territorial or tribal jurisdiction, accompanied by a sworn affidavit that upon information and belief such order is in effect as written and has not been vacated or modified, may be filed without fee with the clerk of the family court, who shall transmit information regarding such order to the statewide registry of orders of protection and warrants established pursuant to section two hundred twenty-one-a of the executive law; provided, however, that such filing and registry entry shall not be required for enforcement of the order.

Added by Laws 1998, Ch. 597, § 6, eff. Dec. 22, 1998.

§ 155. Arrested adult.

1. If an adult respondent is arrested under this act when the family court is not in session, he or she shall be taken to the most accessible magistrate and arraigned. The production of a warrant issued by the family court, a certificate of warrant, a copy or a certificate of the order of protection or temporary order of protection, an order of protection or temporary order of protection, or a record of such warrant or order from the statewide computer registry established pursuant to section two hundred twenty-one-a of the executive law shall be evidence of the filing of an information, petition or sworn affidavit, as provided in section one hundred fifty-four-d of this article. Upon consideration of the bail recommendation, if any, made by the family court and indicated on the warrant or certificate of warrant, the magistrate shall thereupon commit such respondent to the custody of the sheriff, as defined in subdivision thirty-five of section 1.20 of the criminal procedure law, admit to, fix or accept bail, or parole him or her for hearing before the family court, subject to the provisions of subdivision four of section 530.11 of the criminal procedure law concerning arrests upon a violation of an order of protection.

2. If no warrant, order of protection or temporary order of protection has been issued by the family court, whether or not an information or petition has been filed, and an act alleged to be a family offense as defined in section eight hundred twelve of this act is the basis of an arrest, the magistrate shall permit the filing of an information, accusatory instrument or sworn affidavit as provided for in section one hundred fifty-four-d of this article, verified in accordance with subdivision one of section 100.30 of the criminal procedure law, alleging facts in support of a petition pursuant to article eight of this act. The magistrate shall thereupon commit such respondent to the custody of the sheriff, as defined in subdivision thirty-five of section 1.20 of the criminal procedure law, admit to, fix or accept bail, or parole such respondent for hearing before the family court and/or appropriate criminal court.

Amended by Laws 1963, Ch. 809; Laws 1978, Ch. 628; Laws 1980, Ch. 530, eff. Aug. 23, 1980; Laws 1983, Ch. 376, eff. Sept. 1, 1983; Laws 1994, Ch. 222, § 55, eff. Jan. 1, 1995; Laws 1997, Ch. 186, § 4, eff. July 8, 1997.

§ 155-a. Admission to bail.

A desk officer in charge at a police station, county jail or police headquarters, or any of his or her superior officers, may, in such place, take cash bail for his or her appearance before the appropriate court the next morning from any person arrested pursuant to a warrant issued by the family court; provided that such arrest occurs between eleven o'clock in the morning and eight o'clock the next morning, except that in the city of New York bail shall be taken between two o'clock in the afternoon and eight o'clock the next morning. The amount of such cash bail shall be the amount fixed in the warrant of arrest.

FCA

Added by Laws 1971, Ch. 545, § 13, eff. Sept. 1, 1971; **amended** by Laws 1997, Ch. 186, § 5, eff. July 8, 1997.

§ 156. Contempts.

The provisions of the judiciary law relating to civil and criminal contempts shall apply to the family court in any proceeding in which it has jurisdiction under this act or any other law, and a violation of an order of the family court in any such proceeding which directs a party, person, association, agency, institution, partnership or corporation to do an act or refrain from doing an act shall be punishable under such provisions of the judiciary law, unless a specific punishment or other remedy for such violation is provided in this act or any other law.

Repealed former § 156 and new section **added** by Laws 1975, Ch. 496, eff. July 29, 1975.

§ 157. Interpretation of this part.

If there is any conflict between the application of any provision of this part to any proceeding under this act and any provision of the article of this act governing the proceeding, the article governing the proceeding controls.

§ 158. Protective custody of material witness; duration.

(a) The family court may place in protective custody a person under sixteen years of age who is a material witness, as provided by law.

(b) No order of protective custody under paragraph (a) may extend for a period of more than fourteen days. For good cause shown, the court may renew the order for additional periods of fourteen days, but the total period of protective custody under this part may not exceed forty-two days.

Part 6. General provisions concerning hearings.

§ 161. Days and hours court open; availability of judge.

(a) The days and hours the court is open shall be as provided by rule of court.

(b) For purposes of sections seven hundred twenty-eight and one thousand twenty-two of this act, rules of court may authorize a judge other than a judge of the family court to perform the functions of a family court judge under those sections.

(c) For purposes of subdivision (a) of section four hundred thirty, subdivision (a) of section five hundred fifty, subdivision (a) of section six hundred fifty-five, subdivision (a) of section seven hundred forty, subdivision one of section eight hundred twenty-eight and subdivision (a) of section one thousand twenty-nine of this act, any magistrate is authorized to perform the functions of a family court judge as prescribed in such sections.

Amended by Laws 1981, Ch. 416, eff. Aug. 6, 1981; Laws 1982, Ch. 516, eff. July 13, 1982.

§ 162. Waiting room for children.

So far as possible a waiting room with a competent person in charge shall be provided for the care of children brought to the family court under this act.

§ 163. Separate hearing when child appears.

Any case under this act in which children are directly involved or appear shall be heard separately and apart from the hearing of cases against adults, and, where practicable, room separate and apart from a regular court room shall be provided for the use of the family court, together with suitable quarters for the use of the judge, probation officers and other employees of the court.

Amended by Laws 1962, Ch. 700, eff. Sept. 1, 1962.

§ 164. Judicial notice of matters of law; proof of statutes, decrees and decisions of another state or county.

The provisions of the civil practice law and rules and any rules regulating judicial notice and authentication and proof of records shall, unless otherwise prescribed by this act, apply to proceedings under this act to the extent that they are appropriate to the proceedings involved.

Amended by 1970 Laws, Ch. 962, eff. May 1, 1970.

§ 165. Procedure.

(a) Where the method of procedure in any proceeding in which the family court has jurisdiction is not prescribed by this act, the procedure shall be in accord with rules adopted by the administrative board of the judicial conference or, if none has been adopted, with the provisions of the civil practice act to the extent they are suitable to the proceeding involved. Upon the effective date of the CPLR, where the method of procedure in any proceeding in which the family court has jurisdiction is not prescribed, the provisions of the civil practice law and rules shall apply to the extent that they are appropriate to the proceedings involved.

FCA

(b) In any proceeding commenced pursuant to the provisions of the social services law in which the family court has exercised jurisdiction, the provisions of article one, two and eleven of the family court act shall apply to the extent that they do not conflict with the specific provisions of the social services law.

Amended by Laws 1963, Ch. 809, eff. Apr. 26, 1963; Laws 1976, Ch. 308, eff. July 8, 1976, adding subd. (b).

§ 166. Privacy of records.

The records of any proceeding in the family court shall not be open to indiscriminate public inspection. However, the court in its discretion in any case may permit the inspection of any papers or records. Any duly authorized agency, association, society or institution to which a child is committed may cause an inspection of the record of investigation to be had and may in the discretion of the court obtain a copy of the whole or part of such record.

§ 167. Effect of personal appearance.

Whenever a person, whether adult or child, to whom a summons shall have been directed shall physically appear before the court on the return day of such summons, it shall be conclusively presumed that the summons was duly served upon such person in accordance with the provisions of this act unless such person or some one in his behalf shall on such return day make objection to the manner of service.

§ 168. Notice of order of protection.

1. In any case in which an order of protection or temporary order of protection has been made by the family court, the clerk of the court shall issue a copy of such order to the petitioner and respondent and to any other person affected by the order. The presentation of a copy of an order of protection or temporary order of protection or a warrant or a certificate of warrant to any peace officer, acting pursuant to his special duties, or police officer shall constitute authority for him to arrest a person charged with violating the terms of such order of protection or temporary order of protection and bring such person before the court and, otherwise, so far as lies within his power, to aid in securing the protection such order was intended to afford, provided, however, that any outstanding, unexpired certificate of order of protection or temporary order of protection shall have the same force and effect as a copy of such order or temporary order.

2. A copy of an order of protection or temporary order of protection shall be filed by the clerk of the court with the sheriff's office or police department in the county in which the petitioner resides, or, if the petitioner resides within a city, with the police department of such city. A copy of such order of protection or temporary order of protection may from time to time be filed by the clerk of the court with any other police department or sheriff's office having jurisdiction of the residence, work place and school of anyone intended to be protected by

such order. A copy of the order of protection or temporary order of protection may also be filed by the petitioner with any appropriate police department or sheriff's office having jurisdiction. Any subsequent amendment or revocation of such order shall be filed in the same manner as herein provided. Any outstanding, unexpired certificate or order of protection or temporary order of protection shall be filed in the same manner as a copy of an order of protection or temporary order of protection.

3. Any order of protection or temporary order of protection issued by the family court shall bear, in a conspicuous manner, the language, as the case may be, "this order constitutes an order of protection" or "this order constitutes a temporary order of protection," on the front page of said order. The absence of such language shall not affect the validity of such order.

Amended by Laws 1978, Ch. 628, Ch. 629; Laws 1980, Ch. 530, eff. Aug. 23, 1980, Ch. 843, eff. Sept. 1, 1980; Laws 1981, Ch. 416, eff. Aug. 6, 1981; Laws 1989, Ch. 164, § 1, eff. Oct. 15, 1989.

Part 7. Proceeding in counties other than original county.

Editor's Note: Domestic Relations Law § 37(1), amended by Laws, 1966, Ch. 299, eff. May 3, 1966, permits a proceeding commenced pursuant to the uniform support of dependents law to be removed from the initiating court to a court in the county within the state to which the petitioner's residence or domicile has been changed.

§ 171. Enforcement or modification of orders in other county.

A lawful order of the family court in any county may be enforced or modified in that county or in the family court in any other county in which the party affected by the order resides or is found.

§171-a.

Repealed Laws 1999, ch. 533, § 1, eff. Sept. 28, 1999.

§ 172. Commencement of enforcement and modification proceedings in other county.

An enforcement or modification proceeding commenced in the family court in a county other than that in which the order was made is commenced by a petition alleging that fact in addition to the facts required under this act for enforcement or modification orders. An original or certified copy of the order sought to be enforced or modified shall be attached to the petition.

§ 173. Transfer of papers to other county.

If the family court in which an enforcement or modification proceeding is brought under this article does not transfer it under section one hundred seventy-four, it shall advise the family court that issued the order sought to be enforced or modified of the commencement of such proceedings and shall request that court to forward to it a copy of all or any of the papers on which the order was based. The requested court shall forthwith comply with the request.

§ 174. Transfer of proceedings to another county.

The family court in a county may for good cause transfer a proceeding to a family court in any other county where the proceeding might have been originated and shall transfer a proceeding laying venue in the wrong county to a family court in any county where the proceeding might have been originated.

§ 175. Violation of probation in other county.

If an act or omission which constitutes a violation of the terms of probation allegedly occurs in a county other than the one in which the order of probation was made, the family court in either county may hear the allegation of a violation of the terms of probation and proceed in accordance with the provisions of this act.

§ 176. Inter-county probation.

If a person placed under probation by the family court resides in or moves to a county other than the county in which he was placed on probation, the family court which placed him on probation may transfer the proceedings to the county in which the probationer resides or to which he has moved or may place him under the supervision of the probation service attached to the family court in which the probationer resides or to which he has moved.

ARTICLE 2

ADMINISTRATION, MEDICAL EXAMINATIONS, LAW GUARDIANS, AUXILIARY SERVICES

———

SUMMARY OF ARTICLE

FCA

Part 1. Administration.

§ 211. Administration and operation of family court.

The administration and operation of the family court shall be in accord with article seven-a of the judiciary law.

§ 212. Rules of court.

(a) The administrative board of the judicial conference shall prepare rules of court when required by this act and may prepare rules of court when authorized by this act. To the extent practicable, any rule of court prepared under this act shall apply uniformly throughout the state of New York.

(b) In exercising its responsibilities under paragraph (a), the administrative board may designate a committee of judges of the family court and of such consultants as it deems appropriate to draft rules for approval by the administrative board.

§ 213. Reports to administrative board, legislature and governor.

(a)   In addition to any reports required by the administrative board of the judicial conference under article seven-a of the judiciary law, the administrative board shall, as soon as practicable, require the family court in each county to include in its reports to the administrative board and the administrative board shall include in its annual report to the legislature information, by county, showing:

(i)   the number of children temporarily removed under section one thousand twenty-two before the filing of a petition, the number of children temporarily removed without court order under section ten hundred twenty-four of this act, and the period of time between such removal and the filing of a petition;

(ii)   the number of children temporarily removed under section one thousand twenty-seven after the filing of a petition and the period of time that passed after such removal until its termination;

(iii)   the number of placements under section one thousand fifty-two by person, agency or institution in which the placement is made and the number of orders extending the period of placement;

(iv)   the number of children released and the number detained under sections seven hundred twenty-eight and 307.4;

(v)   the number of alleged juvenile delinquents released and the number detained under section 320.5 and the number of alleged persons in need of supervision released and detained under section seven hundred thirty-nine, and the duration of the detention in both groups;

(vi)   the number of adjudicated juvenile delinquents placed under section 353.3 and the number of adjudicated persons in need of supervision placed under section seven hundred fifty-six by person, agency or institution in which the placement is made, and the number of orders extending the period of placement;

(vii)   the number of adjudicated juvenile delinquents put on probation under section 353.2 and the number of adjudicated persons in need of supervision put on probation under section seven hundred fifty-seven and the duration of such probation;

(viii)   the number, nature and disposition of cases involving child abuse under article ten of this act, including total number of new cases, their nature, whether heard by the child abuse part, the age and sex of the children involved, the type of petitioner, the number of children temporarily removed both before and after the filing of a petition, the length of time and number of adjournments between the filing of a petition and the fact-finding hearing, the number of cases that are dismissed, withdrawn, sustained and admitted to, the length of time and number of adjournments between the fact-finding hearing and the dispositional hearing, and the final disposition of such cases.

(b)   Rules of court shall as soon as practicable implement this section by prescribing appropriate forms for reports and may require such additional information as may be appropriate. The administrative board of the judicial conference may request the state department of correction and the state department of social welfare to assist it in the preparation and processing of reports under this section, and those departments, when so requested, shall render such assistance as is possible.

Para. (ix) **added** by Laws 1972, Ch. 1016, eff. June 8, 1972; **amended** by Laws 1982, Ch. 920, eff. July 1, 1983; Laws 1989, Ch. 727, § 1, eff. Oct. 1, 1989.

§ 214. State administrator to prescribe forms.

The state administrator shall promulgate a uniform, statewide petition for adoption and may prescribe such other forms as may be proper for the efficient and just administration of this act, including forms for petitions, summons, warrants, subpoenas, undertakings, and orders authorized by this act.

Amended by Laws 1977, Ch. 229, eff. June 7, 1977; Laws 1989, Ch. 751, eff. Jan. 1, 1990.

§ 215. Continuance in office of non-judicial personnel.

(a)   Officers and employees of the domestic relations court of the city of New York shall, to the extent practicable, be transferred to the family court in counties within the city of New York in accord with article seven-a of the judiciary law. To the extent practicable, those assigned to a division of the domestic relations court located in a particular county shall be assigned to the family court in that county.

(b)   Officers and employees of the children's court in each county outside the city of New York shall, to the extent practicable, be transferred to the family court in their respective counties in accord with article seven-a of the judiciary law.

§ 216-a. Clerk of court.

There shall be a clerk of court for the family court in each county. The clerk of court shall keep the court records and seal and have such other responsibilities as may be provided in accord with article seven-a of the judiciary law.

§ 216-b. Petition forms.

The clerk of the court shall give petition forms to any person requesting them.

Added by Laws 1981, Ch. 416, eff. Aug. 6, 1981.

§ 216-c. Preparation of petitions.

(a)   Whenever a petitioner is not represented by counsel, any person who assists in the preparation of a petition shall include all allegations presented by the petitioner.

(b)   No clerk of the court or probation officer may prevent any person who wishes to file a petition from having such petition filed with the court immediately.

(c)   If there is a question regarding whether or not the family court has jurisdiction of the matter, the petition shall be prepared and the clerk shall file the petition and refer the petition to the court for determination of all issues including the jurisdictional question.

(d)   This section shall not be applicable to juvenile delinquency proceedings.

Added by Laws 1981, Ch. 416, eff. Aug. 6, 1981.

§ 217.   Orders; filing and service.

1.   An order shall be in writing and signed with the judge's signature or initials by the judge who made it. The form of such order shall be promulgated by the chief administrator of the courts pursuant to section two hundred fourteen of this article.

2.   The original of an order of the family court shall be filed with the clerk of the family court in the county in which the family court making the order is located.

3.   The court shall file or direct the filing of an order within twenty days of the decision of the court. If the court directs that such order be settled on notice, such twenty day period shall commence on the date on which such order is settled.

4.   The court shall direct service of a copy of an order in whatever manner it deems appropriate. If the court makes no direction, the applicable provisions of the civil practice law and rules shall apply. Where the clerk of the court is directed to serve such order, the clerk shall note in the court record the manner and date of service and the person to whom such order was served.

Added by Laws 1991, Ch. 582, § 1, eff. Jan. 1, 1992; **amended** by Laws 1998, Ch. 186, § 1, eff. July 7, 1998.

Former FCA § 217 repealed by Laws 1991, Ch. 582, § 1, eff. Jan. 1, 1992.

Part 2.   Support bureau; Duties to cooperate.

(Repealed and transferred sections noted under appropriate section number of text.)

§ 221.   Support bureau.

Repealed by Laws 1977, Ch. 516, § 11, eff. Jan. 1, 1978. See new § 221 added by Laws 1977, Ch. 615, eff. Jan. 1, 1978.

§ 221. Support collection unit; local probation department.

1. When referred to in this chapter, the support collection unit designated by the appropriate social services district, shall be deemed to refer to any support collection unit established by a social services district pursuant to the provisions of section one hundred eleven-h of the social services law, or to a local public agency, where such agency is responsible for the performance of all the functions of the support collection unit pursuant to an agreement under the provisions of section one hundred eleven-h of the social services law.

2. The local probation department shall be responsible for providing services to the family court, in accordance with the provisions of subdivision six of section two hundred fifty-six of the executive law.

Added by Laws 1977, Ch. 516, eff. Jan. 1, 1978.

§ 222. Functions of support bureau.

Repealed by Laws 1977, Ch. 516, eff. Jan. 1, 1978.

§ 223. Transmittal of information to probation service.

Repealed by Laws 1977, Ch. 516, eff. Jan. 1, 1978.

§ 224. Property interest in money paid to support bureau.

Repealed by Laws 1977, Ch. 516, eff. Jan. 1, 1978.

§ 225. Unclaimed funds.

Repealed by Laws 1977, Ch. 516, eff. Jan. 1, 1978.

§ 226. Claim after deposit.

Repealed by Laws 1977, Ch. 516, eff. Jan. 1, 1978.

§ 227. Payment to comptroller after ten years.

Repealed by Laws 1977, Ch. 516, eff. Jan. 1, 1978.

§ 228. Cooperation by banks and other fiduciary institutions.

Banks and other fiduciary institutions are authorized and required to report to the court, when so requested, full information relative to any fund therein deposited by a petitioner or respondent in a proceeding under articles four or five of this act.

FCA

§ 229. Cooperation by employer.

Employers are authorized and required to report to the court, when so requested, full information as to the earnings of a petitioner or respondent in a proceeding under articles four or five of this act.

Part 3. Medical examinations and treatment.

(Repealed and transferred sections noted under appropriate section number of text.)

§ 231. Jurisdiction over children with retarded mental development.

Repealed by Laws 1976, Ch. 853, eff. July 1, 1976.

§ 231. Jurisdiction over mentally retarded children.

If it shall appear to the court that any child within its jurisdiction is mentally retarded, the court may cause such child to be examined as provided in the mental hygiene law and if found to be mentally retarded as therein defined, may commit such child in accordance with the provisions of such law.

Added by Laws 1976, Ch. 853, eff. July 1, 1976.

§ 232. Educational and medical service.

Repealed by Laws 1976, Ch. 853, eff. July 1, 1976.

§ 232. Jurisdiction over children with physical disabilities.

(a) The family court has jurisdiction over children with physical disabilities.

(b) "Physically handicapped child" means a person under twenty-one years of age who, by reason of a physical disability, whether congenital or acquired by accident, injury or disease, is or may be expected to be totally or partially incapacitated for education or for remunerative occupation, as provided in the education law, or has a physical disability, as provided in section two thousand five hundred eighty-one of the public health law.

(c) (1) Whenever a parent or other person who has been ordered to contribute to the cost of medical service authorized pursuant to section two thousand five hundred eighty-two of the public health law refuses to or fails to make such contribution, the health commissioner or the medical director of the program for children with physical disabilities, as the case may be, may institute a proceeding in the family court to compel such contribution. In any case where an order has been granted pursuant to section 556-18.0 or section 17-121 of the administrative code of the city of New York the department of health services administration, under the conditions specified in such section, may institute a proceeding in the family court to compel the parents of a child for whom care, treatment, appliances or devices have been ordered pursuant to such section, or other persons legally chargeable with the support of such child, to contribute such portion of the expense of such care, treatment, appliances, or devices as may be just, by payments in installments or otherwise.

(2) A parent or other person who has been ordered by the commissioner of health of a county or part-county health district, the medical director of a county program for children with physical disabilities, or the department of health of the city of New York, to contribute to the cost of medical services authorized under section two thousand five hundred eighty-two of the public health law, may petition the family court to review such order and determine the extent, if any, of his financial liability. In any such proceeding, the court may by order require such parent or other person to pay part or all of the expense of such service in a lump sum or in such weekly or monthly installments as the court may decide.

Added by Laws 1976, Ch. 853, eff. July 1, 1976; **amended** by Laws 1978, Ch. 655, § 128, eff. July 24, 1978; Laws 1986, Ch. 654, eff. July 26, 1986.

§ 233. Compensation and liability for support and care in counties outside the city of New York.

Repealed by Laws 1976, Ch. 853, eff. July 1, 1976.

§ 233. Medical services.

Whenever a child within the jurisdiction of the court appears to the court to be in need of medical, surgical, therapeutic, or hospital care or treatment, a suitable order may be made therefor.

Added by Laws 1976, Ch. 853, eff. July 1, 1976.

§ 234. Educational service in counties within the city of New York.

Repealed by Laws 1976, Ch. 853, eff. July 1, 1976.

§ 234. Compensation and liability for support and care in counties outside the city of New York.

(a) Whenever a child is detained, placed or committed under the provisions of this act to an authorized agency, or to any person other than his parent and is retained in accordance with the rules of the state board of social welfare, compensation for his care and maintenance shall be a charge on the county. The compensation paid by the county for care and maintenance of the child may be charged back to a city or town in the county in accordance with and to the extent permitted by the provisions of the social services law. All bills for such care and maintenance to be paid from public funds shall be paid by the county treasurer from moneys appropriated for public assistance and care in the county social services district by warrant of the commissioner of social services.

(b)   The court may, after issuance and service of an order to show cause upon the parent or other person having the duty under the law to support such child, adjudge that such parent or other person shall pay to the court such sum as will cover in whole or in part the support of such child, and willful failure to pay such sum may, in the discretion of the court, be punished as for a criminal contempt of court. When a person liable to such payment on order, as herein provided, is before the court in the proceeding relating to the commitment or placement, a formal order to show cause may be dispensed with in the discretion of the court.

(c)   (i) The social services district from which the detention, placement or commitment is made shall be entitled to be reimbursed by another social services district for its expenditures for care and maintenance of the child, if, and to the extent that, it would have been entitled to be reimbursed therefor by such other district had the care been provided under and pursuant to the provisions of the social services law. The commissioner of social services of the social services district from which the commitment was made may enforce repayment from the other social services district in accordance with the provisions of the social services law.

(ii)   In accordance with the provisions of the social services law and the rules and regulations of the state department of social services relating to state charges, and from funds available to the state department of social services therefor, the state shall reimburse the social services district for the full cost of care and maintenance of the child, in the event the child is a state charge as defined by the social services law.

Added by Laws 1976, Ch. 853, eff. July 1, 1976.

§ 235.   Compensation and liability for support and care in counties within the city of New York.

(a)   Upon the detention, placement or commitment of a child by the family court in a county within the city of New York to a public or private institution other than a shelter maintained and conducted by a society for the prevention of cruelty to children, the department of social services of the city of New York shall investigate the ability of the parent of the child, or other person legally chargeable, to contribute in whole or in part to the expense incurred by the city of New York on account of the maintenance of such child.

(b)   If in the opinion of the department of social services such parent or legal custodian is able to contribute in whole or in part the commissioner of social services shall thereupon institute a proceeding in the family court to compel such parent or person legally chargeable to contribute such portion of such expense on account of maintenance of such child as shall be proper and just.

Amended by Laws 1969, Ch. 407; Laws 1976, Ch. 853, eff. July 1, 1976.

§ 236.   Powers of the family court with regard to certain handicapped children.

1.   * This section shall apply for: (a) services provided to children with handicapping conditions as defined in subdivision one of section forty-four hundred one of the education law who were not eligible, prior to September first, nineteen hundred eighty-six, for educational services during July and August pursuant to article seventy-three, eighty-five, eighty-seven, eighty-eight or eighty-nine of the education law; (b) for services provided to children with handicapping conditions who meet all the criteria of subdivision one of section forty-four hundred one of the education law except that such children are under the age of five and are not entitled to attend public schools without the payment of tuition pursuant to section thirty-two hundred two of the education law and that such children are also not eligible for educational services pursuant to article seventy-three, eighty-five, eighty-seven, eighty-eight or eighty-nine of the education law; (c) for services provided to children with handicapping conditions who meet all the criteria of subdivision one of section forty-four hundred one of the education law except that such children are five years of age or under and: (i) are first eligible to attend public school in the nineteen hundred eighty-seven—eighty-eight or the nineteen hundred eighty-eight—eighty-nine school year but are not eligible for educational services pursuant to the education law during the months of July and August, nineteen hundred eighty-seven or nineteen hundred eighty-eight, or (ii) are not eligible to commence a state appointment pursuant to article eighty-five, eighty-seven or eighty-eight of the education law during the months of July and August; (d) for services provided during the nineteen hundred eighty-nine—ninety school year, pursuant to the provisions of subdivision six of section forty-four hundred ten of the education law; (e) for services provided on or after July first, nineteen hundred eighty-nine to children with handicapping conditions who meet the criteria f subdivision one of section forty-four hundred one of the education law except that such children are three years of age or under and (i) are not eligible for services pursuant to section forty-four hundred ten of such law, or (ii) are not eligible for services through a state appointment pursuant to article eighty-five, eighty-seven or eighty-eight of such law; and (f) for services provided to children with handicapping conditions who meet the criteria of subdivision one of section forty-four hundred one of the education law and who, on or before June thirtieth, nineteen hundred ninety-three, are receiving services or who, as of July first, nineteen hundred ninety-three, have petitioned for services pursuant to this section prior to such date and which

complete petition has not been denied prior to October first, nineteen hundred ninety-three and whose parent has elected to continue the provision of such services until the child is no longer an eligible child under title II-a of article twenty-five of the public health law or is eligible for services pursuant to section forty-four hundred ten of the education law.

(g)   Notwithstanding any other provision of this section, this section shall not apply for services to children who were not receiving services prior to July first, nineteen hundred ninety-three, or who, as of July first, nineteen hundred ninety-three, have petitioned for services prior to July first, nineteen hundred ninety-three and whose complete petition has been denied prior to October first, nineteen hundred ninety-three.

1.   * This section shall apply for: (a) services provided to children with handicapping conditions as defined in subdivision one of section forty-four hundred one of the education law who were not eligible, prior to September first, nineteen hundred eighty-six, for educational services during July and August pursuant to article seventy-three, eighty-five, eighty-seven, eighty-eight or eighty-nine of the education law; (b) for services provided to children with handicapping conditions who meet all the criteria of subdivision one of section forty-four hundred one of the education law except that such children are under the age of five and are not entitled to attend public schools without the payment of tuition pursuant to section thirty-two hundred two of the education law and that such children are also not eligible for educational services pursuant to article seventy-three, eighty-five, eighty-seven, eighty-eight or eighty-nine of the education law; (c) for services provided to children with handicapping conditions who meet all the criteria of subdivision one of section forty-four hundred one of the education law except that such children are five years of age or under and: (i) are first eligible to attend public school in the nineteen hundred eighty-seven— eighty-eight or the nineteen hundred eighty-eight—eighty-nine school year but are not eligible for educational services pursuant to the education law during the months of July and August, nineteen hundred eighty-seven or nineteen hundred eighty-eight, or (ii) are not eligible to commence a state appointment pursuant to article eighty-five, eighty-seven or eighty-eight of the education law during the months of July and August; (d) for services provided during the nineteen hundred eighty-nine—ninety school year, pursuant to the provisions of subdivision six of section forty-four hundred ten of the education law; (e) for services provided prior to July first, nineteen hundred ninety-one to children with handicapping conditions who met the criteria of subdivision one of section forty-four hundred one of the education law except that such children were three years of age or under and (i) were not eligible for services pursuant to section forty-four hundred ten of such law, or (ii) were not eligible for services through a state appointment pursuant to article eighty-five, eighty-seven or eighty-eight of such law; and (f) for services provided on or after July first, nineteen hundred ninety-one to children with handicapping conditions who meet the criteria of subdivision one of section forty-four hundred one of the education law except that such

children are three years of age or under and (i) are not eligible for services pursuant to section forty-four hundred ten of such law, or who are first eligible for services pursuant to such section whose parents or persons in parental relationship elect to have them continue to be eligible to receive services pursuant to this section through August thirty-first of the calendar year in which the child turns three or (ii) are not eligible for services through a state appointment pursuant to article eighty-five, eighty-seven or eighty-eight of such law.

2. Whenever such a child within the jurisdiction of the court pursuant to this section appears to the court to be in need of special educational services as provided in section forty-four hundred six of the education law, including transportation, tuition or maintenance, a suitable order may be made for the education of such child in its home, a hospital, or other suitable institution, and the expenses thereof, when approved by the court and duly audited, shall be a charge upon the county or the city of New York thereof wherein the child is domiciled at the time application is made to the court for such order.

3. (a) Every such order for services to be provided after September first, nineteen hundred eighty-six which provides for the transportation of a child shall further require that such transportation shall be provided by the county or the city of New York, as the case may be, and, that the city of New York may delegate the authority to provide such transportation to the board of education of such city.

(b) Such order shall further require that such transportation shall be provided within thirty days of the issuance of such order, and shall be provided as part of a municipal cooperation agreement or as part of a contract awarded to the lowest responsible bidder in accordance with the provisions of section one hundred three of the general municipal law and that buses and vehicles utilized in the performance of such contract shall meet the minimum requirements for school age children as established by the commissioner of transportation.

Added by Laws 1976, Ch. 853, eff. July 1, 1976; **amended** by Laws 1986, Ch. 683, eff. July 30, 1986; Laws 1987, Ch. 53, eff. Apr. 1, 1987; Laws 1988, Ch. 53, § 57, eff. Mar. 2,1988; Laws 1989, Ch. 53 § 58, eff. Apr. 14, 1989, and deemed to be in full force and effect as of Apr. 1, 1989; Laws 1989, Ch. 243 § 4, eff. July 5, 1989, and deemed to be in full force and effect as of July 1, 1989; Laws 1989, Ch. 391 § 25, eff. July 13, 1989, and deemed to be in full force and effect as of Apr. 1, 1989; Laws 1992, Ch. 130, § 2, eff. Apr. 1, 1992; Laws 1992, Ch. 428, § 8, eff. July 1, 1993; Laws 1992, Ch. 705, §§ 13, 14, eff. July 31, 1992, July 1, 1992.

* **Editor's note:** Two versions of FCA § 236(1) are provided. Laws 1992, Ch. 705 amended FCA § 236(1) without reference to the amendments made to that provision by Laws 1992, Ch. 428. The first version of FCA § 236(1) reflects amendments made by Laws 1992, Chs. 130 and 428 and by Laws 1993, Ch. 231, § 15, eff. July 1, 1993. The second version reflects amendments made by Laws 1992, Chs. 130 and 705.

Part 4. Law guardians.

(Repealed and transferred sections noted under appropriate section number of text.)

§ 241. Findings and purpose.

This act declares that minors who are the subject of family court proceedings or appeals in proceedings originating in the family court should be represented by counsel of their own choosing or by law guardians. This declaration is based on a finding that counsel is often indispensable [sic] to a practical realization of due process of law and may be helpful in making reasoned determinations of fact and proper orders of disposition. This part establishes a system of law guardians for minors who often require the assistance of counsel to help protect their interests and to help them express their wishes to the court. Nothing in this act is intended to preclude any other interested person from appearing by counsel.

Amended by Laws 1970, Ch. 962, eff. May 1, 1970; Laws 1988, Ch. 476, § 3, eff. Jan. 1, 1989.

§ 242. Law guardian.

As used in this act, "law guardian" refers to an attorney admitted to practice law in the state of New York and designated under this part to represent minors pursuant to section two hundred and forty-nine of this act.

Amended by Laws 1970, Ch. 962, eff. May 1, 1970.

§ 243. Designation.

(a) The office of court administration may enter into an agreement with a legal aid society for the society to provide law guardians for the family court or appeals in proceedings originating in the family court in a county having a legal aid society.

(b) The appellate division of the supreme court for the judicial department in which a county is located may, upon determining that a county panel designated pursuant to subdivision (c) of this section is not sufficient to afford appropriate law guardian services, enter into an agreement, subject to regulations as may be promulgated by the administrative board of the courts, with any qualified attorney or attorneys to serve as law guardian or as law guardians for the family court or appeals in proceedings originating in the family court in that county.

(c) The appellate division of the supreme court for the judicial department in which a county is located may designate a panel of law guardians for the family court and appeals in proceedings originating in the family court in that county, subject to the approval of the administrative board of the courts. For this purpose, it may invite a bar association to recommend qualified persons for consideration by the said appellate division in making its designation, subject to standards as may be promulgated by such administrative board.

Repealed and new § 243 **added** by Laws 1974, Ch. 833, eff. July 1, 1974; **amended** by Laws 1988, Ch. 476, § 4, eff. Jan. 1, 1989; Laws 1995, Ch. 443, § 1, eff. Aug. 2, 1995.

§ 244. Duration of designation.

(a) An agreement pursuant to subdivision (a) of section two hundred forty-three of this chapter may be terminated by the office of court administration by serving notice on the society sixty days prior to the effective date of the termination.

(b) No designations pursuant to subdivision (c) of such section two hundred forty-three may be for a term of more than one year, but successive designations may be made. The appellate division proceeding pursuant to such subdivision (c) may at any time increase or decrease the number of law guardians designated in any county and may rescind any designation at any time, subject to the approval of the office of court administration.

Repealed and new § 244 **added** by Laws 1974, Ch. 833, eff. July 1, 1974.

§ 245. Compensation.

(a) If the office of court administration proceeds pursuant to subdivision (a) of section two hundred forty-three of this chapter, the agreement shall provide that the society shall be reimbursed on a cost basis for services rendered under the agreement. The agreement shall contain a general plan for the organization and operation of the providing of law guardians by the respective legal aid society, approved by the said administrative board, and the office of court administration may require such reports as it deems necessary from the society.

(b) If an appellate division proceeds pursuant to subdivision (b) of such section two hundred forty-three, the agreement may provide that the attorney or attorneys shall be reimbursed on a cost basis for services rendered under the agreement. The agreement shall contain a general plan for the organization and operation of the providing of law guardians by the respective attorney or attorneys, and the appellate division may require such reports as it deems necessary from the attorney or attorneys.

(c) If an appellate division proceeds pursuant to subdivision (c) of such section two hundred forty-three, law guardians shall be compensated and allowed expenses and disbursements in the same amounts established by subdivision three of section thirty-five of the judiciary law.

Repealed and new § 245 **added** by Laws 1974, Ch. 833, eff. July 1, 1974; **amended** by Laws 1978, Ch. 700, eff. Jan. 1, 1979; Laws 1986, Ch. 25, eff. Apr. 3, 1986; Laws 1995, Ch. 443, § 2, eff. Aug. 2, 1995.

§ 246. Supervision by administrative board.

The administrative board of the judicial conference may prescribe standards for the exercise of the powers granted to the appellate divisions under this part and may require such reports as it deems desirable.

§ 247. Reports by administrative board.

Repealed by Laws 1974, Ch. 833, eff. July 1, 1974.

§ 248. Appropriations.

The costs of law guardians under section two hundred forty-five shall be payable by the state of New York within the amounts appropriated therefor.

Amended by Laws 1962, Ch. 687; Laws 1974, Ch. 833, eff. July 1, 1974.

§ 249. Appointment of law guardian.

(a) In a proceeding under article three, seven, ten or ten-A of this act or where a revocation of an adoption consent is opposed under section one hundred fifteen-b of the domestic relations law or in any proceeding under section three hundred fifty-eight-a, three hundred eighty-three-c, three hundred eighty-four or three hundred eighty-four-b of the social services law or when a minor is sought to be placed in protective custody under section one hundred fifty-eight of this act, the family court shall appoint a law guardian to represent a minor who is the subject of the proceeding or who is sought to be placed in protective custody, if independent legal representation is not available to such minor. In any proceeding to extend or continue the placement of a juvenile delinquent or person in need of supervision pursuant to section seven hundred fifty-six or 353.3 of this act or any proceeding to extend or continue a commitment to the custody of the commissioner of mental health or the commissioner of mental retardation and developmental disabilities pursuant to section 322.2 of this act, the court shall not permit the respondent to waive the right to be represented by counsel chosen by the respondent, respondent's parent, or other person legally responsible for the respondent's care, or by a law guardian. In any other proceeding in which the court has jurisdiction, the court may appoint a law guardian to represent the child, when, in the opinion of the family court judge, such representation will serve the purposes of this act, if independent legal counsel is not available to the child. The family court on its own motion may make such appointment.

(b) In making an appointment of a law guardian pursuant to this section, the court shall, to the extent practicable and appropriate, appoint the same law guardian who has previously represented the child. Notwithstanding any other provision of law, in a proceeding under article three following an order of removal made pursuant to article seven hundred twenty-five of the criminal procedure law, the court shall, wherever practicable, appoint the counsel representing the juvenile offender in the criminal proceedings as law guardian.

Amended by Laws 1970, Ch. 962; Laws 1975, Ch. 682, Ch. 709; Laws 1976,Ch. 656; Laws 1977, Ch. 859; Laws 1978, Ch. 481; Laws 1979, Ch. 531, eff. Sept. 10, 1979; Laws 1982, Ch. 920, eff. July 1, 1983; Laws 1986, Ch. 817, eff. Sept. 1, 1986; Laws 1986, 902, eff. Aug. 5, 1986; Laws 1986, Ch. 817, eff. Sept. 1, 1986; Laws 1986, Ch. 902, eff. Aug. 5, 1986; Laws 1989, Ch. 321, eff. July 10, 1989; Laws 1999, Ch. 506, eff. Sept. 28, 1999; Laws 2002, Ch. 76, § 1, eff. Aug. 19, 2002; L. 2005, Ch. 3, § 2, amending sub.(a), eff. Aug. 23, 2005.

§ 249-a.   Waiver of counsel.

A minor who is a subject of a juvenile delinquency or person in need of supervision proceeding shall be presumed to lack the requisite knowledge and maturity to waive the appointment of a law guardian. This presumption may be rebutted only after a law guardian has been appointed and the court determines after a hearing at which the law guardian appears and participates and upon clear and convincing evidence that (a) the minor understands the nature of the charges, the possible dispositional alternatives and the possible defenses to the charges, (b) the minor possesses the maturity, knowledge and intelligence necessary to conduct his own defense, and (c) waiver is in the best interest of the minor.

Added by Laws 1978, Ch. 513, eff. July 20, 1978.

Part 5.   Auxiliary services.

§ 251.   Medical examinations.

(a) After the filing of a petition under this act over which the family court appears to have jurisdiction, the court may order any person within its jurisdiction and the parent or other person legally responsible for the care of any child within its jurisdiction to be examined by a physician, psychiatrist or psychologist appointed or designated for that purpose by the court when such an examination will serve the purposes of this act, the court may remand any such person for physical or psychiatric examination to, or direct such person to appear for such examination at:

(1) the department of health of the city of New York, if the court is located in a county within the city of New York, or

(2) a hospital maintained by the county in which the court is located, if the court is in a county outside the city of New York, or

(3) a hospital maintained by the state of New York, or

(4) a qualified private institution approved for such purpose by the local social services department.

Provided, however, that, outside of the city of New York, if the court shall order a psychiatric examination of any such person, the court may direct the director of an institution in the department of mental hygiene serving the institutional district in which the court is located to cause such examination to be made. Such director shall be afforded an opportunity to be heard before the court makes any such direction. The director may designate a member of the staff of the institution or any psychiatrist in the state to make the examination. The psychiatrist shall forthwith examine such person. The examination may be made in the place where the person may be or the court may remand such person to, or otherwise direct that such person appear at, such institution or to a hospital or other place for such examination. During the time such person is at such institution for examination, the director may administer or cause to be administered to such person such psychiatric, medical or other therapeutic treatment as in the director's discretion should be administered. The chief administrator of the courts shall prescribe the form of an order for examination. Upon completion of the examination, the director shall transmit to the court the report of the psychiatrist who conducted the examination.

(b) Except for examinations conducted pursuant to section 322.1 of this act where the family court determines that an inpatient examination is necessary, or those ordered after a fact-finding hearing has been completed under article three or seven of this act and the court determines according to the criteria in subdivision three of section 320.5 or subdivision (a) of section seven hundred thirty-nine of this act that the child should be detained pending disposition, or unless otherwise consented to by the adult to be examined or by the law guardian representing the respondent, all examinations pursuant to this section shall be conducted on an outpatient basis. An order for remand after a fact-finding hearing under article three or seven of this act shall include findings on the record supporting the need for examination in a residential facility and a determination that it is the most appropriate facility. Remands for examinations shall be for a period determined by the facility, which shall not exceed thirty days, except that, upon motion by the person detained on its own motion, the court may, for good cause shown, terminate the remand at any time.

(c)   Nothing in this section shall preclude the issuance of an order by the family court pursuant to section 9.43 of the mental hygiene law for emergency admission for immediate care, observation and treatment of a person before the court or pursuant to section twenty-one hundred twenty of the public health law for commitment for care and maintenance of a person before the court.

Amended by Laws 1962, Ch. 700; Laws 1965, Ch. 767; Laws 1969, Ch. 407; Laws 1974, Ch. 1037; Laws 1976, Ch. 880; Laws 1978, Ch. 442, eff. Sept. 17, 1978; Ch. 655, § 129, eff. July 25, 1978; Laws 1993, Ch. 296, § 1, eff. July 21, 1993.

§ 252.   Probation service.

(a)   The family court in each county shall have a probation service. This service may include volunteer probation officers when necessary, provided they have the qualifications required of salaried officers, but no such volunteer probation officer shall be a chief probation officer or receive pay from public funds for his services.

(b)   The methods, organization, and responsibilities of the probation service shall be defined by rule of court, which shall not be inconsistent with any provision of law.

(c)   When there is a sufficient number of probation officers of the same religious faith as that of a child to be placed on probation, the child shall be placed on probation with a probation officer of the same religious faith as that of the child.

(d)   The probation service shall be available to assist the court and participate in all proceedings under this act, including supervision of the family or individual family members pending final disposition of a child protection proceeding under article ten.

Amended by Laws 1973, Ch. 1039, eff. Sept. 1, 1973.

§ 252-a.   Fees. [*Expires September 1, 2005.*]

(a)   Notwithstanding any other provision of law, every county, including the city of New York, may adopt a local law authorizing its probation department which is ordered to conduct an investigation pursuant to section six hundred fifty-three of this chapter, to be entitled to a fee of not less than fifty dollars and not more than five hundred dollars from the parties in such proceeding for performing such investigation. Such fee shall be based on the party's ability to pay the fee and the schedule for payment shall be fixed by the court issuing the order for investigation, pursuant to the guidelines issued by the director of the division of probation and correctional alternatives, and may in the discretion of the court be waived when the parties lack sufficient means to pay the fee. The court shall apportion the fee between the parties based upon the respective financial circumstances of the parties and the equities of the case.

FCA

(b) Fees pursuant to this section shall be paid directly to the local probation department to be retained and utilized for local probation services, and shall not be considered by the division of probation when determining state aid reimbursement pursuant to section two hundred forty-six of the executive law.

Amended by L. 2001, Ch. 95, § 14, eff. July 13, 2001, extending repeal date from Sept. 1, 2001 to Sept. 1, 2003; Laws 2003, Ch. 16, § 12, eff. March 31, 2003, extending the expiration until Sept. 1, 2005.

§ 253. Auxiliary services.

The family court in any county shall have such other auxiliary services as will serve the purposes of this act and as are within its authorized appropriation.

§ 254. Presentation by corporation counsel, county attorney or district attorney.

(a) The family court or the appropriate appellate division of the supreme court may request the corporation counsel of the city of New York or the appropriate county attorney to present the case in support of the petition when, in the opinion of the family court or appellate division such presentation will serve the purposes of the act. When so requested, the corporation counsel or county attorney shall present the case in support of the petition and assist in all stages of the proceedings, including appeals in connection therewith. Nothing herein shall be deemed to affect the provisions of section five hundred thirty-five of this chapter.

(b) In all cases involving abuse, the corporation counsel of the city of New York and outside the city of New York, the appropriate district attorney shall be a necessary party to the proceeding.

Amended by Laws 1963, Ch. 979; Laws 1970, Ch. 962; Laws 1976, Ch. 878, eff. Feb. 1, 1977, adding subd. (c); Laws 1978, Ch. 512, eff. Sept. 1, 1978; Laws 1984, Ch. 392, eff. July 18, 1984.

Editor's Note: See 1964 amendment to FCA § 438.

§ 254-a. Procedure for district attorney presentation.

1. The county attorney and the district attorney of a county, and the corporation counsel of the city of New York and the district attorney of any county in such city,may enter into an agreement whereby the district attorney shall present the case in support of the petition in which a designated felony act has been alleged.

2. Where such agreement has been entered into, in the case of a respondent who is alleged to have done two or more acts which, if done by an adult, would constitute joinable offenses pursuant to subdivision two of section 200.20 of the criminal procedure law, the district attorney shall present the juvenile

delinquency petition with respect to all such acts, notwithstanding less than all of such acts constitute designated felony acts.

3. Where such agreement has been entered into, the district attorney shall also present petitions which have been filed against all respondents who are accused of participating, in concert, in the commission of a designated felony act, notwithstanding less than all of such respondents are charged with having committed a designated felony act. Such petition shall be adjudicated in a single fact-finding hearing, unless the court orders separate fact-finding hearings for good cause shown.

4. When presenting cases the district attorney shall have the same powers under this act as the corporation counsel or county attorney and shall assist in all stages of the proceedings including appeals in connection therewith.

5. Such agreement shall be subject to the approval in the city of New York of its mayor, and outside the city of the respective county executive, if there be one, otherwise, the board of supervisors.

6. The district attorney may elect to present the petition against a respondent, who was the defendant in a criminal proceeding removed to the family court pursuant to article seven hundred twenty-five of the criminal procedure law, when a proceeding under article three is commenced as a result of the order of removal.

Laws 1978, Ch. 512, eff. Sept. 1, 1978, **added** subd. 1-5 subd. 6 by Laws 1978, Ch. 481, eff. Sept. 1, 1978; **amended** by Laws 1982, Ch. 920, eff. July 1, 1983.

§ 255. Cooperation of officials and organizations.

It is hereby made the duty of, and the family court or a judge thereof may order, any state, county, municipal and school district officer and employee to render such assistance and cooperation as shall be within his legal authority, as may be required, to further the objects of this act provided, however, that with respect to a school district an order made pursuant to this section shall be limited to requiring the performance of the duties imposed upon the school district and board of education or trustees thereof pursuant to sections four thousand five, forty four hundred two and forty four hundred four of the education law, to review, evaluate, recommend, and determine the appropriate special services or programs necessary to meet the needs of a handicapped child, but shall not require the provisions of a specific service or program, and such order shall be made only where it appears to the court or judge that adequate administrative procedure to require the performance of such duties is not available. It is hereby made the duty of and the family court or judge thereof may order, any agency or other institution to render such information, assistance and cooperation as shall be within its legal authority concerning a child who is or shall be under its care, treatment, supervision or custody as may be required to further the objects of this act. The court is authorized to seek the cooperation of, and may use, within its authorized appropriation therefor, the services of all societies or organizations, public or private, having for their object the protection or aid of children or families,

FCA

including family counseling services, to the end that the court may be assisted in every reasonable way to give the children and families within its jurisdiction such care, protection and assistance as will best enhance their welfare.

    Amended by Laws 1963, Chs. 811, 979; Laws 1972, Ch. 1016; Laws 1977, Ch. 470; Laws 1980, Ch. 563, eff. July 1, 1981.

§ 256.   Visitation, inspection and supervision by state department of social services or board of social welfare.

Any child placed or committed under order of the court shall be subject to such visitation, inspection and supervision as the state board of social welfare or department of social services shall provide for or require.

    Amended by Laws 1978, Ch. 555, eff. July 24, 1978.

Part 6.   Counsel for indigent adults in family court proceedings.

    Section   261.   **Legislative findings and purpose.**
                 262.   **Assignment of counsel for indigent persons.**

§ 261.   Legislative findings and purpose.

Persons involved in certain family court proceedings may face the infringements of fundamental interests and rights, including the loss of a child's society and the possibility of criminal charges, and therefore have a constitutional right to counsel in such proceedings. Counsel is often indispensable to a practical realization of due process of law and may be helpful to the court in making reasoned determinations of fact and proper orders of disposition. The purpose of this part is to provide a means of implementing the right to assigned counsel for indigent persons in proceedings under this act.

    Added by Laws 1975, Ch. 682, eff. Jan. 1, 1976.

§ 262.   Assignment of counsel for indigent persons.

    (a)   Each of the persons described below in this subdivision has the right to the assistance of counsel. When such person first appears in court, the judge shall advise such person before proceeding that he or she has the right to be represented by counsel of his or her own choosing, of the right to have an adjournment to confer with counsel, and of the right to have counsel assigned by the court in any case where he or she is financially unable to obtain the same:

    (i)   the respondent in any proceeding under article ten or article ten-A of this act and the petitioner in any proceeding under part eight of article ten of this act;

    (ii)   the petitioner and the respondent in any proceeding under article eight of this act;

    (iii)   the respondent in any proceeding under part three of article six of this act;

(iv)   the parent, foster parent, or other person having physical or legal custody of the child in any proceeding under article ten or ten-A of this act or section three hundred fifty-eight-a, three hundred eighty-four or three hundred eighty-four-b of the social services law, and a non-custodial parent or grandparent served with notice pursuant to paragraph (e) of subdivision two of section three hundred eighty-four-a of the social services law;

(v)   the parent of any child seeking custody or contesting the substantial infringement of his or her right to custody of such child, in any proceeding before the court in which the court has jurisdiction to determine such custody;

(vi)   any person in any proceeding before the court in which an order or other determination is being sought to hold such person in contempt of the court or in willful violation of a previous order of the court, except for a contempt which may be punished summarily under section seven hundred fifty-five of the judiciary law;

(vii)   the parent of a child in any adoption proceeding who opposes the adoption of such child.

(viii)   the respondent in any proceeding under article five of this act in relation to the establishment of paternity.

(b)   Assignment of counsel in other cases. In addition to the cases listed in subdivision (a) of this section, a judge may assign counsel to represent any adult in a proceeding under this act if he determines that such assignment of counsel is mandated by the constitution of the state of New York or of the United States, and includes such determination in the order assigning counsel;

(c)   Implementation. Any order for the assignment of counsel issued under this part shall be implemented as provided in article eighteen-B of the county law.

Added by Laws 1975, Ch. 682, eff. Jan. 1, 1976; **amended** by Laws 1976, Ch. 666; Laws 1978, Ch. 456, eff. July 1, 1978; Laws 1981, Ch. 693, eff. July 21, 1981; Laws 1988, Ch. 457, § 1, eff. Nov. 1, 1988; L. 2005, Ch. 3, § 3, amending sub.(a), eff. Aug. 23, 2005; Laws 2006, Ch. 437, § 1, eff. July 26, 2006.

FCA

ARTICLE 3
NEGLECT PROCEEDINGS
___

(Repealed by Laws 1970, Ch. 962, eff. May 1, 1970.)

ARTICLE 3

JUVENILE DELINQUENCY

———

(Added by Laws 1982, Ch. 920, eff. July 1, 1983.)

SUMMARY OF ARTICLE

Part 1.   Jurisdiction and preliminary procedures.

FCA

§ 301.1. Purpose.

The purpose of this article is to establish procedures in accordance with due process of law (a) to determine whether a person is a juvenile delinquent and (b) to issue an appropriate order of disposition for any person who is adjudged a juvenile delinquent. In any proceeding under this article, the court shall consider the needs and best interests of the respondent as well as the need for protection of the community.

§ 301.2. Definitions

As used in this article, the following terms shall have the following meanings:

1. "Juvenile delinquent" means a person over seven and less than sixteen years of age, who, having committed an act that would constitute a crime if committed by an adult, (a) is not criminally responsible for such conduct by reason of infancy, or (b) is the defendant in an action ordered removed from a criminal court to the family court pursuant to article seven hundred twenty-five of the criminal procedure law.

2. "Respondent" means the person against whom a juvenile delinquency petition is filed pursuant to section 310.1. Provided, however, that any act of the respondent required or authorized under this article may be performed by his attorney or law guardian unless expressly provided otherwise.

3. "Detention" means the temporary care and maintenance of children away from their own homes, as defined in section five hundred two of the executive law. Detention of a person alleged to be or adjudicated as a juvenile delinquent shall be authorized only in a facility certified by the division for youth as a detention facility pursuant to section five hundred three of the executive law.

4. "Secure detention facility" means a facility characterized by physically restricting construction, hardware and procedures.

5. "Non-secure detention facility" means a facility characterized by the absence of physically restricting construction, hardware and procedures.

6. "Fact-finding hearing" means a hearing to determine whether the respondent or respondents committed the crime or crimes alleged in the petition or petitions.

7. "Dispositional hearing" means a hearing to determine whether the respondent requires supervision, treatment or confinement.

8. "Designated felony act" means an act which, if done by an adult, would be a crime: (i) defined in sections 125.27 (murder in the first degree); 125.25 (murder in the second degree); 135.25 (kidnapping in the first degree); or 150.20 (arson in the first degree) of the penal law committed by a person thirteen, fourteen or fifteen years of age; (ii) defined in sections 120.10 (assault in the first degree); 125.20 (manslaughter in the first degree); 130.35 (rape in the first degree); 130.50 (criminal sexual act in the first degree); 130.70 (aggravated sexual abuse in the first degree); 135.20 (kidnapping in the second degree) but only where the abduction involved the use or threat of use of deadly physical force; 150.15 (arson in the second degree) or 160.15 (robbery in the first degree) of the penal law committed by a person thirteen, fourteen or fifteen years of age; (iii) defined in the penal law as an attempt to commit murder in the first or second degree or kidnapping in the first degree committed by a person thirteen, fourteen or fifteen years of age; (iv) defined in section 140.30 (burglary in the first degree); subdivision one of section 140.25 (burglary in the second degree); subdivision two of section 160.10 (robbery in the second degree) of the penal law; subdivision four of section 265.02 of the penal law, where such firearm is possessed on school grounds, as that phrase is defined in subdivision fourteen of section 220.00 of the penal law; or section 265.03 of the penal law, where such machine gun or such firearm is possessed on school grounds, as that phrase is defined in subdivision fourteen of section 220.00 of the penal law committed by a person fourteen or fifteen years of age; (v) defined in section 120.05 (assault in the second degree) or 160.10 (robbery in the second degree) of the penal law committed by a person fourteen or fifteen years of age but only where there has been a prior finding by a court that such person has previously committed an act which, if committed by an adult, would be the crime of assault in the second degree, robbery in the second degree or any designated felony act specified in paragraph (i), (ii), or (iii) of this subdivision regardless of the age of such person at the time of the commission of the prior act; or (vi) other than a misdemeanor committed by a person at least seven but less than sixteen years of age, but only where there has been two prior findings by the court that such person has committed a prior felony.

9. "Designated class A felony act" means a designated felony act defined in paragraph (i) of subdivision eight.

10. "Secure facility" means a residential facility in which the respondent may be placed under this article, which is characterized by physically restricting construction, hardware and procedures, and is designated as a secure facility by the division for youth.

11. "Restrictive placement" means a placement pursuant to section 353.5.

FCA

12. "Presentment agency" means the agency or authority which pursuant to section two hundred fifty-four or two hundred fifty-four-a is responsible for presenting a juvenile delinquency petition.

13. "Incapacitated person" means a respondent who, as a result of mental illness, mental retardation or developmental disability as defined in subdivisions twenty, twenty-one and twenty-two of section 1.03 of the mental hygiene law, lacks capacity to understand the proceedings against him or to assist in his own defense.

14. Any reference in this article to the commission of a crime includes any act which, if done by an adult, would constitute a crime.

15. "Aggravated circumstances" shall have the same meaning as the definition of such term in subdivision (j) of section one thousand twelve of this act.

16. "Permanency hearing" means an initial hearing or subsequent hearing held in accordance with the provisions of this article for the purpose of reviewing the foster care status of the respondent and the appropriateness of the permanency plan developed by the commissioner of social services or the office of children and family services.

17. "Designated educational official" shall mean (a) an employee or representative of a school district who is designated by the school district or (b) an employee or representative of a charter school or private elementary or secondary school who is designated by such school to receive records pursuant to this article and to coordinate the student's participation in programs which may exist in the school district or community, including: non-violent conflict resolution programs, peer mediation programs and youth courts, extended day programs and other school violence prevention and intervention programs which may exist in the school district or community. Such notification shall be kept separate and apart from such student's school records and shall be accessible only by the designated educational official. Such notification shall not be part of such student's permanent school record and shall not be appended to or included in any documentation regarding such student and shall be destroyed at such time as such student is no longer enrolled in the school district. At no time shall such notification be used for any purpose other than those specified in this subdivision.

Amended by Laws 1983, Ch. 398, eff. July 1, 1983; Laws 1985, Ch. 663, eff. Aug. 27, 1985; Laws 1987, Ch. 419, eff. Sept. 1, 1987; Laws 1992, Ch. 465, § 32, eff. Jan. 13, 1993; Laws 1998, Ch. 435, § 8, eff. Nov. 1, 1998; Laws 1999, Ch. 7, § 28, eff. Feb. 11, 1999; Laws 2000, Ch. 181, § 17, eff. Nov. 1, 2000, adding subsection (17); L. 2001, Ch. 380, § 8, amending subd. 17, deemed in full force and effect on and after Nov. 1, 2000; Laws 2003, Ch. 264, § 59, amending sub. 8, par. (ii), eff. Nov. 1, 2003; L. 2005, Ch. 3, § 1, amending sub. 15, eff. Aug. 23, 2005.

§ 301.3. Applicability of article to actions and matters occurring before and after effective date.

1. The provisions of this article apply exclusively to:

(a) all juvenile delinquency actions and proceedings commenced upon or after the effective date thereof and all appeals and other post-judgment proceedings relating or attaching thereto; and

(b) all matters of juvenile delinquency procedure prescribed in this article which do not constitute a part of any particular action or case occurring upon or after such effective date.

2. The provisions of this article apply to:

(a) all juvenile delinquency actions and proceedings commenced prior to the effective date thereof but still pending on such date; and

(b) all appeals and other post-judgment proceedings commenced upon or after such effective date which relate or attach to juvenile delinquency actions and proceedings commenced or concluded prior to such effective date provided that, if application of such provisions in any particular case would not be feasible or would work injustice, the provisions of article seven pertaining to juvenile delinquency actions apply thereto, as such article seven read immediately prior to the effective date of this article.

3. The provisions of this article do not impair or render ineffectual any proceedings or procedural matters which occurred prior to the effective date thereof.

Amended by Laws 1983, Ch. 398, eff. July 1, 1983.

§ 301.4. Application of certain amendments, repeals or additions to article seven as it pertained to juvenile delinquency actions.

Repealed by Laws 1983, Ch. 398, eff. July 1, 1983.

§ 301.4. Separability clause.

If any clause, sentence, paragraph, section or part of this article shall be adjudged by any court of competent jurisdiction to be invalid, such judgment shall not affect, impair, or invalidate the remainder thereof, but shall be confined in its operation to the clause, sentence, paragraph, section or part thereof directly involved in the controversy in which such judgment shall have been rendered.

§ 302.1. Jurisdiction.

1. The family court has exclusive original jurisdiction over any proceeding to determine whether a person is a juvenile delinquent.

2. In determining the jurisdiction of the court the age of such person at the time the delinquent act allegedly was committed is controlling.

§ 302.2. Statute of limitations.

A juvenile delinquency proceeding must be commenced within the period of limitation prescribed in section 30.10 of the criminal procedure law or, unless the alleged act is a designated felony as defined in subdivision eight of section 301.2, commenced before the respondent's eighteenth birthday, whichever occurs earlier. When the alleged act constitutes a designated felony as defined in subdivision eight of section 301.2 such proceeding must be commenced within such period of limitation or before the respondent's twentieth birthday, whichever occurs earlier.

§ 302.3. Venue.

1.   Juvenile delinquency proceedings shall be originated in the county in which the act or acts referred to in the petition allegedly occurred. For purposes of determining venue, article twenty of the criminal procedure law shall apply.

2.   Upon motion of the respondent or the appropriate presentment agency the family court in which the proceedings have been originated may order, for good cause shown, that the proceeding be transferred to another county. If the order is issued after motion by the presentment agency, the court may impose such conditions as it deems equitable and appropriate to ensure that the transfer does not subject the respondent to an unreasonable burden in making his defense.

3.   Any motion made pursuant to subdivision two by the respondent shall be made within the time prescribed by section 332.2. Any such motion by a presentment agency must be based upon papers stating the ground therefor and must be made within thirty days from the date that the action was originated unless such time is extended for good cause shown.

4.   Except for designated felony act petitions, after entering a finding pursuant to subdivision one of section 345.1, and prior to the commencement of the dispositional hearing the court may, in its discretion and for good cause shown, order that the proceeding be transferred to the county in which the respondent resides. The court shall not order such a transfer, however, unless it grants the respondent and the presentment agency an opportunity to state on the record whether each approves or disapproves of such a transfer and the reasons therefor. The court shall take into consideration the provisions of subdivisions two and three of section 340.2 in determining such transfer.

Amended by Laws 1982, Ch. 926, eff. July 1, 1983; Laws 1983, Ch. 398, eff. July 1, 1983; Laws 1999, Ch. 173, § 1, eff. July 6, 1999.

§ 303.1. Criminal procedure law.

1.   The provisions of the criminal procedure law shall not apply to proceedings under this article unless the applicability of such provisions are specifically prescribed by this act.

2.   A court may, however, consider judicial interpretations of appropriate provisions of the criminal procedure law to the extent that such interpretations may assist the court in interpreting similar provisions of this article.

§ 303.2. Double jeopardy.

The provisions of article forty of the criminal procedure law concerning double jeopardy shall apply to juvenile delinquency proceedings.

§ 303.3. Defenses.

The provisions of articles twenty-five, thirty-five and forty and section 30.05 of the penal law shall be applicable to juvenile delinquency proceedings.

§ 304.1. Detention.

1. A facility certified by the state division for youth as a juvenile facility must be operated in conformity with the regulations of the state division for youth and shall be subject to the visitation and inspection of the state board of social welfare.

2. No child to whom the provisions of this article may apply shall be detained in any prison, jail, lockup, or other place used for adults convicted of crime or under arrest and charged with crime without the approval of the state division for youth in the case of each child and the statement of its reasons therefor. The state division for youth shall promulgate and publish the rules which it shall apply in determining whether approval should be granted pursuant to this subdivision.

3. The detention of a child under ten years of age in a secure detention facility shall not be directed under any of the provisions of this article.

4. A detention facility which receives a child under subdivision four of section 305.2. shall immediately notify the child's parent or other person legally responsible for his care or, if such legally responsible person is unavailable the person with whom the child resides, that he has been placed in detention.

Amended by Laws 1987, Ch. 419, eff. Sept. 1, 1987.

§ 304.2. Temporary order of protection.

(1) Upon application by the presentment agency, the court may issue a temporary order of protection against a respondent for good cause shown, ex parte or upon notice, at any time after a juvenile is taken into custody, pursuant to section 305.1 or 305.2 or upon the issuance of an appearance ticket pursuant to section 307.1 or upon the filing of a petition pursuant to section 310.1.

(2) A temporary order of protection may contain any of the provisions authorized on the making of an order of protection under section 352.3.

(3) A temporary order of protection is not a finding of wrongdoing.

(4) A temporary order of protection may remain in effect until an order of disposition is entered.

Added by Laws 1984, ch. 683, eff. Aug. 31, 1984.

§ 305.1.　Custody by a private person.

1.　A private person may take a child under the age of sixteen into custody in cases in which he may arrest an adult for a crime under section 140.30 of the criminal procedure law.

2.　Before taking such child under the age of sixteen into custody, a private person must inform the child of the cause thereof and require him to submit, except when he is taken into custody on pursuit immediately after the commission of a crime.

3.　After taking such child into custody, a private person must take the child, without unnecessary delay, to the child's home, to a family court, or to a police officer or peace officer.

Amended by Laws 1983, Ch. 398, eff. July 1, 1983.

§ 305.2.　Custody by a peace officer or a police officer without a warrant.

1.　For purposes of this section, the word "officer" means a peace officer or a police officer.

2.　An officer may take a child under the age of sixteen into custody without a warrant in cases in which he may arrest a person for a crime under article one hundred forty of the criminal procedure law.

3.　If an officer takes such child into custody or if a child is delivered to him under section 305.1, he shall immediately notify the parent or other person legally responsible for the child's care, or if such legally responsible person is unavailable the person with whom the child resides, that the child has been taken into custody.

4.　After making every reasonable effort to give notice under subdivision three, the officer shall:

(a)　release the child to the custody of his parents or other person legally responsible for his care upon the issuance in accordance with section 307.1 of a family court appearance ticket to the child and the person to whose custody the child is released; or

(b)　forthwith and with all reasonable speed take the child directly, and without his first being taken to the police station house, to the family court located in the county in which the act occasioning the taking into custody allegedly was committed, unless the officer determines that it is necessary to question the child, in which case he may take the child to a facility designated by the chief administrator of the courts as a suitable place for the questioning of children or, upon the consent of a parent or other person legally responsible for the care of the child, to the child's residence and there question him for a reasonable period of time; or

(c) take the child to a place certified by the state division for youth as a juvenile detention facility for the reception of children.

5. If such child has allegedly committed a designated felony act as defined in subdivision eight of section 301.2, and the family court in the county is in session, the officer shall forthwith take the child directly to such family court unless the officer takes the child to a facility for questioning in accordance with paragraph (b) of subdivision four. If such child has not allegedly committed a designated felony act and such family court is in session, the officer shall either forthwith take the child directly to such family court unless the officer takes the child to a facility for questioning in accordance with paragraph (b) of subdivision four or release the child in accordance with paragraph (a) of subdivision four.

6. In all other cases, and in the absence of special circumstances, the officer shall release the child in accordance with paragraph (a) of subdivision four.

7. A child shall not be questioned pursuant to this section unless he and a person required to be notified pursuant to subdivision three if present, have been advised:

(a) of the child's right to remain silent;

(b) that the statements made by the child may be used in a court of law;

(c) of the child's right to have an attorney present at such questioning; and

(d) of the child's right to have an attorney provided for him without charge if he is indigent.

8. In determining the suitability of questioning and determining the reasonable period of time for questioning such a child, the child's age, the presence or absence of his parents or other persons legally responsible for his care and notification pursuant to subdivision three shall be included among relevant considerations.

Amended by Laws 1983, Ch. 398, eff. July 1, 1983; Laws 1985, Ch. 663, eff. Aug. 27, 1985; Laws 1987, Ch. 492, eff. July 30, 1987.

§ 306.1. Fingerprinting of certain alleged juvenile delinquents.

1. Following the arrest of a child alleged to be a juvenile delinquent, or the filing of a delinquency petition involving a child who has not been arrested, the arresting officer or other appropriate police officer or agency shall take or cause to be taken fingerprints of such child if:

(a) the child is eleven years of age or older and the crime which is the subject of the arrest or which is charged in the petition constitutes a class A or B felony; or

(b) the child is thirteen years of age or older and the crime which is the subject of the arrest or which is charged in the petition constitutes a class C, D or E felony.

2. Whenever fingerprints are required to be taken pursuant to subdivision one, the photograph and palmprints of the arrested child may also be taken.

3. The taking of fingerprints, palmprints, photographs, and related information concerning the child and the facts and circumstances of the acts charged in the juvenile delinquency proceeding shall be in accordance with standards established by the commissioner of the division of criminal justice services and by applicable provisions of this article.

4. Upon the taking of fingerprints pursuant to subdivision one the appropriate officer or agency shall, without unnecessary delay, forward such fingerprints to the division of criminal justice services and shall not retain such fingerprints or any copy thereof. Copies of photographs and palmprints taken pursuant to this section shall be kept confidential and only in the exclusive possession of such law enforcement agency, separate and apart from files of adults.

Amended by Laws 1996, Ch. 645, eff. Nov. 1, 1996.

§ 306.2. Fingerprinting; duties of the division of criminal justice services.

1. Upon receipt of fingerprints taken pursuant to section 306.1. the division of criminal justice services shall retain such fingerprints distinctly identifiable from adult criminal records except as provided in section 354.1 and shall not release such fingerprints to a federal depository or to any person except as authorized by this act. The division shall promulgate regulations to protect the confidentiality of such fingerprints and related information and to prevent access thereto, by, and the distribution thereof to, persons not authorized by law.

2. Upon receipt of such fingerprints, the division of criminal justice services shall classify them and search its records for information concerning an adjudication or pending matter involving the person arrested. The division shall promptly transmit to such forwarding officer or agency a report containing any information on file with respect to such person's previous adjudications and pending matters or a report stating that the person arrested has no previous record according to its files. Notwithstanding the foregoing, where the division has not received disposition information within two years of an arrest, the division shall, until such information or up-to-date status information is received, withhold the record of that arrest and any related activity in disseminating criminal history information.

3. Upon receipt of a report of the division of criminal justice services pursuant to this section, the recipient office or agency must promptly transmit two copies of such report to the family court in which the proceeding may be originated and two copies thereof to the presentment agency who shall furnish a copy thereof to counsel for the respondent or to the respondent's law guardian.

Amended by Laws 1983, Ch. 398, eff. July 1, 1983; Laws 1996, Ch. 645, §2, eff. Sept. 13, 1996, and applicable retroactively to a person whose fingerprints were taken pursuant to section 306.1 of the family court act or who was initially fingerprinted as a juvenile offender on or after January 1, 1986 and whose fingerprints are on file with the division of criminal justice services, provided that in the case of a juvenile offender action the case was subsequently removed to family court.

§ 307.1. Family court appearance ticket.

1. A family court appearance ticket is a written notice issued and subscribed by a peace officer or police officer, a probation service director or his designee or the administrator responsible for operating a detention facility or his designee, directing a child and his parent or other person legally responsible for his care to appear, without security, at a designated probation service on a specified return date in connection with the child's alleged commission of the crime or crimes specified on such appearance ticket. The form of a family court appearance ticket shall be prescribed by rules of the chief administrator of the courts.

2. If the crime alleged to have been committed by the child is a designated felony as defined by subdivision eight of section 301.2. the return date shall be no later than seventy-two hours excluding Saturdays, Sundays and public holidays after issuance of such family court appearance ticket. If the crime alleged to have been committed by such child is not a designated felony, the return date shall be no later than fourteen days after the issuance of such appearance ticket.

3. A copy of the family court appearance ticket shall be forwarded by the issuing person or agency to the complainant, respondent, respondent's parent, and appropriate probation service within twenty-four hours after its issuance.

Amended by Laws 1983, Ch. 398, eff. July 1, 1983.

§ 307.2. Appearance ticket procedures.

1. If a child fails to appear on the return date specified on a family court appearance ticket, the probation service may refer the matter forthwith to the appropriate presentment agency or may, in its discretion, attempt to secure the attendance of the child. Upon exercise of its discretion, probation services shall take appropriate action under law including, but not limited to, written notification to the child and parent or other person legally responsible for his care or telephone communications with the child and parent or other person legally responsible for his care. Efforts to secure the attendance of the child shall not extend beyond seven days subsequent to such return date and the probation service must refer the matter to the appropriate presentment agency within such period. Upon referral, the presentment agency may take whatever action it deems appropriate, including the filing of a petition pursuant to section 311.1.

2. If the complainant fails to appear on the return date specified on such appearance ticket, the probation service may in its discretion, attempt to secure his voluntary attendance. Upon exercise of its discretion, probation services may take appropriate action under law including, but not limited to, written notification to the complainant or telephone communications with the complainant. Efforts to secure the voluntary attendance of such person shall not extend beyond

FCA

seven days subsequent to such return date and the probation service shall refer the matter to the appropriate presentment agency within such period. Upon referral, the presentment agency may take whatever action it deems appropriate, including the issuance of a subpoena or the filing of a petition pursuant to section 311.1.

3. If a petition is filed subsequent to the issuance of an appearance ticket the appearance ticket shall be made part of the probation service file.

Amended by Laws 1983, Ch. 398, eff. July 1, 1983; Laws 1985, Ch. 586, eff. July 28, 1985.

§ 307.3. Rules of court authorizing release before filing of petition.

1. The agency responsible for operating a detention facility pursuant to section two hundred eighteen-a of the county law, five hundred ten-a of the executive law or other applicable provisions of law, shall release a child in custody before the filing of a petition to the custody of his parents or other person legally responsible for his care, or if such legally responsible person is unavailable, to a person with whom he resides, when the events occasioning the taking into custody do not appear to involve allegations that the child committed a delinquent act.

2. When practicable such agency may release a child before the filing of a petition to the custody of his parents or other person legally responsible for his care, or if such legally responsible person is unavailable, to a person with whom he resides, when the events occasioning the taking into custody appear to involve allegations that the child committed a delinquent act.

3. If a child is released under this section, the child and the person legally responsible for his care shall be issued a family court appearance ticket in accordance with section 307.1.

4. If the agency for any reason does not release a child under this section, such child shall be brought before the appropriate family court within seventy-two hours or the next day the court is in session, whichever is sooner. Such agency shall thereupon file an application for an order pursuant to section 307.4 and shall forthwith serve a copy of the application upon the appropriate presentment agency. Nothing in this subdivision shall preclude the adjustment of suitable cases pursuant to section 308.1.

Amended by Laws 1987, Ch. 419, eff. Sept. 1, 1987.

§ 307.4. Hearing following detention.

1. If a child in custody is brought before a judge of the family court before a petition is filed upon a written application pursuant to subdivision four of section 307.3, the judge shall hold a hearing for the purpose of making a preliminary determination of whether the court appears to have jurisdiction over the child.

2. At such hearing the court must appoint a law guardian to represent the child pursuant to the provisions of section two hundred forty-nine if independent legal representation is not available to such child.

3. The provisions of sections 320.3 and 341.2 shall apply at such hearing.

4. After such hearing, the judge shall order the release of the child to the custody of his parent or other person legally responsible for his care if:

(a) the court does not appear to have jurisdiction, or

(b) the events occasioning the taking into custody do not appear to involve allegations that the child committed a delinquent act, or

(c) the events occasioning the taking into custody appear to involve acts which constitute juvenile delinquency, unless the court finds and states facts and reasons which would support a detention order pursuant to section 320.5.

5. Such hearing shall be held within seventy-two hours of the time detention commenced or the next day the court is in session, whichever is sooner.

6. The appropriate presentment agency shall present the application at a hearing pursuant to this section.

7. A petition shall be filed and a probable-cause hearing held under section 325.1 within four days of the conclusion of a hearing under this section. If a petition is not filed within four days the child shall be released.

8. Upon a finding of facts and reasons which support a detention order pursuant to section 320.5 of this chapter, the court shall also determine and state in any order directing detention:

(a) whether the continuation of the child in the child's home would be contrary to the best interests of the child based upon, and limited to, the facts and circumstances available to the court at the time of the hearing held in accordance with this section; and

(b) where appropriate and consistent with the need for protection of the community, whether reasonable efforts were made prior to the date of the court hearing that resulted in the detention order issued in accordance with this section to prevent or eliminate the need for removal of the child from his or her home or, if the child had been removed from his or her home prior to the initial appearance, where appropriate and consistent with the need for protection of the community, whether reasonable efforts were made to make it possible for the child to safely return home.

Amended by Laws 1987, Ch. 419, eff. Sept. 1, 1987; Laws 2000, Ch. 145 § 18, eff. July 1, 2000, adding subsection (8).

§ 308.1. Rules of court for preliminary procedure.

1. Rules of court shall authorize and determine the circumstances under which the probation service may confer with any person seeking to have a

juvenile delinquency petition filed, the potential respondent and other interested persons concerning the advisability of requesting that a petition be filed.

2. Except as provided in subdivisions three and four, the probation service may, in accordance with rules of court, adjust suitable cases before a petition is filed. The inability of the respondent or his or her family to make restitution shall not be a factor in a decision to adjust a case or in a recommendation to the presentment agency pursuant to subdivision six of this section. Nothing in this section shall prohibit the probation service or the court from directing a respondent to obtain employment and to make restitution from the earnings from such employment.

3. The probation service shall not adjust a case in which the child has allegedly committed a designated felony act unless it has received the written approval of the court.

4. The probation service shall not adjust a case in which the child has allegedly committed a delinquent act which would be a crime defined in section 120.25, (reckless endangerment in the first degree), subdivision one of section 125.15, (manslaughter in the second degree), subdivision one of section 130.25, (rape in the third degree), subdivision one of section 130.40, (criminal sexual act in the third degree), subdivision one or two of section 130.65, (sexual abuse in the first degree), section 135.65, (coercion in the first degree), section 140.20, (burglary in the third degree), section 150.10, (arson in the third degree), section 160.05, (robbery in the third degree), subdivision two, three or four of section 265.02, (criminal possession of a weapon in the third degree), section 265.03, (criminal possession of a weapon in the second degree), or section 265.04, (criminal possession of a dangerous weapon in the first degree) of the penal law where the child has previously had one or more adjustments of a case in which such child allegedly committed an act which would be a crime specified in this subdivision unless it has received written approval from the court and the appropriate presentment agency.

5. The fact that a child is detained prior to the filing of a petition shall not preclude the probation service from adjusting a case; upon adjusting such a case the probation service shall notify the detention facility to release the child.

6. The probation service shall not transmit or otherwise communicate to the presentment agency any statement made by the child to a probation officer. However, the probation service may make a recommendation regarding adjustment of the case to the presentment agency and provide such information, including any report made by the arresting officer and record of previous adjustments and arrests, as it shall deem relevant.

7. No statement made to the probation service prior to the filing of a petition may be admitted into evidence at a fact-finding hearing or, if the proceeding is transferred to a criminal court, at any time prior to a conviction.

8. The probation service may not prevent any person who wishes to request that a petition be filed from having access to the appropriate presentment agency for that purpose.

9. Efforts at adjustment pursuant to rules of court under this section may not extend for a period of more than two months without leave of the court, which may extend the period for an additional two months.

10. If a case is not adjusted by the probation service, such service shall notify the appropriate presentment agency of that fact within forty-eight hours or the next court day, whichever occurs later.

11. The probation service may not be authorized under this section to compel any person to appear at any conference, produce any papers, or visit any place.

12. The probation service shall certify to the division of criminal justice services and to the appropriate police department or law enforcement agency whenever it adjusts a case in which the potential respondent's fingerprints were taken pursuant to section 306.1 in any manner other than the filing of a petition for juvenile delinquency for an act which, if committed by an adult, would constitute a felony, provided, however, in the case of a child eleven or twelve years of age, such certification shall be made only if the act would constitute a class A or B felony.

13. The provisions of this section shall not apply where the petition is an order of removal to the family court pursuant to article seven hundred twenty-five of the criminal procedure law.

FCA

Amended by Laws 1982, Ch. 926, eff. July 1, 1983; Laws 1983, Ch. 398, eff. July 1, 1983; Laws 1985 Ch. 663, eff. Aug. 27, 1985; Laws 1988, Ch. 252, § 1, eff. July 11, 1988; Laws 2003, Ch. 264, § 60, amending sub. 4, eff. Nov. 1, 2003.

§ 310.1. Originating a juvenile delinquency proceeding.

1. A proceeding to adjudicate a person a juvenile delinquent is originated by the filing of a petition.

2. Only a presentment agency may originate a juvenile delinquency proceeding.

3. If the appropriate agency does not originate a proceeding within thirty days of receipt of notice from the probation service pursuant to subdivision ten of section 308.1, it shall notify in writing the complainant of that fact.

Amended by Laws 1982, Ch. 926, eff. July 1, 1983; Laws 1983, Ch. 398. eff. July 1, 1983.

§ 310.2. Speedy trial.

After a petition has been filed, or upon the signing of an order of removal pursuant to section 725.05 of the criminal procedure law, the respondent is entitled to a speedy fact-finding hearing.

Amended by Laws 1990, Ch. 223, § 1, eff. June 13, 1990.

§ 311.1.   The petition; definition and contents.

1.   A petition originating a juvenile delinquency proceeding is a written accusation by an authorized presentment agency.

2.   A petition shall charge at least one crime and may, in addition, charge in separate counts one or more other crimes, provided that all such crimes are joinable in accord with section 311.6.

3.   A petition must contain:

(a)   the name of the family court in which it is filed;

(b)   the title of the action;

(c)   the fact that the respondent is a person under sixteen years of age at the time of the alleged act or acts;

(d)   a separate accusation or count addressed to each crime charged, if there be more than one;

(e)   the precise crime or crimes charged;

(f)   a statement in each count that the crime charged was committed in a designated county;

(g)   a statement in each count that the crime charged therein was committed on, or on or about, a designated date, or during a designated period of time;

(h)   a plain and concise factual statement in each count which, without allegations of an evidentiary nature, asserts facts supporting every element of the crime charged and the respondent's commission thereof with sufficient precision to clearly apprise the respondent of the conduct which is the subject of the accusation;

(i)   the name or names, if known, of other persons who are charged as co-respondents in the family court or as adults in a criminal court proceeding in the commission of the crime or crimes charged;

(j)   a statement that the respondent requires supervision, treatment or confinement; and

(k)   the signature of the appropriate presentment attorney.

4.   A petition shall be verified in accordance with the civil practice law and rules and shall conform to the provisions of section 311.2.

5.   If the petition alleges that the respondent committed a designated felony act, if shall so state, and the term "designated felony act petition" shall be prominently marked thereon. Certified copies of prior delinquency findings shall constitute sufficient proof of such findings for the purpose of filing a designated felony petition. If all the allegations of a designated felony act are dismissed or withdrawn or the respondent is found to have committed crimes which are not designated felony acts, the term "designated felony act petition" shall be stricken from the petition.

6. The form of petition shall be prescribed by the chief administrator of the courts. A petition shall be entitled "In the Matter of," followed by the name of the respondent.

7. When an order of removal pursuant to article seven hundred twenty-five of the criminal procedure law is filed with the clerk of the court, such order and those pleadings and proceedings, other than the minutes of any hearing inquiry or trial, grand jury proceeding, or of any plea accepted or entered, held in this action that has not yet been transcribed shall be transferred with it and shall be deemed to be a petition filed pursuant to subdivision one of section 310.1 containing all of the allegations required by this section notwithstanding that such allegations may not be set forth in the manner therein prescribed. Where the order or the grand jury request annexed to the order specified an act that is a designated felony act, the clerk shall annex to the order a sufficient statement and marking to make it a designated felony act petition. The date such order is filed with the clerk of the court shall be deemed the date a petition was filed under this article. For purposes of service in accord with section 312.1, however, only the order of removal shall be deemed the petition. All minutes of any hearing inquiry or trial held in this action, the minutes of any grand jury proceeding and the minutes of any plea accepted and entered shall be transferred to the family court within thirty days.

Amended by Laws 1982, Ch. 926, eff. July 1, 1983; Laws 1983, Ch. 398, eff. July 1, 1983.

§ 311.2. Sufficiency of petition.

A petition, or a count thereof, is sufficient on its face when:

1. it substantially conforms to the requirements prescribed in section 311.1; and

2. the allegations of the factual part of the petition, together with those of any supporting depositions which may accompany it, provide reasonable cause to believe that the respondent committed the crime or crimes charged; and

3. non-hearsay allegations of the factual part of the petition or of any supporting depositions establish, if true, every element of each crime charged and the respondent's commission thereof.

§ 311.3. Petition; fact-finding hearings.

1. When two or more respondents are charged in separate petitions with the same crime or crimes the court shall conduct a single or consolidated fact-finding hearing. The court, however, upon motion of a respondent or the presentment agency, may, in its discretion and for good cause shown, order that any respondent be granted a fact-finding hearing separate from the other respondents. Such motion must be made within the period prescribed in section 332.2.

2. If such petitions, in addition to charging the same crime or crimes against the different respondents, charge other crimes not common to all, the court may

nevertheless conduct a single fact-finding hearing for the crime or crimes common to all.

§ 311.4. Substitution of petition or finding.

1. At any time in the proceedings the court, upon motion or a respondent or its own motion, may, with the consent of the presentment agency and with the consent of the respondent, substitute a petition alleging that the respondent is in need of supervision for a petition alleging that the respondent is a juvenile delinquent.

2. At the conclusion of the dispositional hearing the court, upon motion of the respondent or its own motion, may in its discretion and with the consent of the respondent, substitute a finding that the respondent is a person in need of supervision for a finding that the respondent is a juvenile delinquent.

Amended by Laws 1983, Ch. 398, eff. July 1, 1983.

§ 311.5. Amendment of the petition.

1. At any time before or during the fact-finding hearing, the court may, upon application of the presentment agency and with notice to the respondent and an opportunity to be heard, order the amendment of a petition with respect to defects, errors or variances from the proof relating to matters of form, time, place, names of persons and the like, when such amendment does not tend to prejudice the respondent on the merits. Upon permitting such an amendment, the court must, upon application of the respondent, order any adjournment which may be necessary to accord the respondent an adequate opportunity to prepare his defense.

2. A petition may not be amended for the purpose of curing:

(a) a failure to charge or state a crime; or

(b) legal insufficiency of the factual allegations; or

(c) a misjoinder of crimes.

§ 311.6. Joinder, severance and consolidation.

1. Two crimes are joinable and may be included as separate counts in the same petition when:

(a) they are based upon the same act or upon the same criminal transaction, as that term is defined in subdivision two; or

(b) even though based upon different criminal transactions, such crimes, or the criminal transactions underlying them, are of such nature that either proof of the first crime would be material and admissible as evidence in chief upon a fact-finding hearing of the second, or proof of the second would be material and admissible as evidence in chief upon a fact-finding hearing of the first; or

(c) even though based upon different criminal transactions, and even though not joinable pursuant to paragraph (b), such crimes are defined by the same or similar statutory provisions and consequently are the same or similar in law.

2. "Criminal transaction" means conduct which establishes at least one crime, and which is comprised of two or more or a group of acts either:

(a) so closely related and connected in point of time and circumstance of commission as to constitute a single criminal incident; or

(b) so closely related in criminal purpose or objective as to constitute elements or integral parts of a single criminal venture.

3. In any case where two or more crimes or groups of crimes charged in a petition are based upon different criminal transactions, and where their joinability rests solely upon the fact that such crimes, or as the case may be at least one offense of each group, are the same or similar in law, as prescribed in paragraph (c) of subdivision one, the court, in the interest of justice and for good cause shown, may upon application of either the respondent or the presentment agency order that any one of such crimes or groups of crimes be tried separately from the other or others, or that two or more thereof be tried together but separately from two or more others thereof. Such application must be made within the period prescribed in section 332.2.

4. When two or more petitions against the same respondent charge different crimes of a kind that are joinable in a single petition pursuant to subdivision one, the court may, upon application of either the presentment agency or respondent order that such petitions be consolidated and treated as a single petition for trial purposes. Such application must be made within the period prescribed in section 332.2. If the respondent requests consolidation with respect to crimes which are, pursuant to paragraph (a) of subdivision one, of a kind that are joinable in a single petition by reason of being based upon the same act or criminal transaction, the court must order such consolidation unless good cause to the contrary be shown.

Amended by Laws 1983, Ch. 398, eff. July 1, 1983.

§ 312.1. Issuance and service of summons.

1. After a petition has been filed, the court may cause a copy thereof and a summons to be issued, requiring the respondent personally and his parent or other person legally responsible for his care, or, if such legally responsible person is not available, a person with whom he resides, to appear for the initial appearance as defined by section 320.1 at a time and place named. The summons shall be signed by a judge or by the clerk of the court.

2. Service of a summons and petition shall be made by delivery of a true copy thereof to the person summoned at least twenty-four hours before the time stated therein for appearance.

3. If after reasonable effort, personal service as provided in subdivision two is not made, the court may at any stage in the proceedings make an order providing for service in any manner the court directs.

FCA

§ 312.2. Issuance of a warrant.

1. The court may issue a warrant, directing that the respondent personally or other person legally responsible for his or her care or, if such legally responsible person is not available, a person with whom he or she resides, be brought before the court, when a petition has been filed and it appears that:

(a) a summons cannot be served; or

(b) such person has refused to obey a summons or family court appearance ticket; or

(c) the respondent or other person is likely to leave the jurisdiction; or

(d) a summons, in the court's opinion, would be ineffectual; or

(e) a respondent has failed to appear.

2. Upon issuance of a warrant due to the respondent's failure to appear for a scheduled court date, the court shall adjourn the matter to a date certain within thirty days for a report on the efforts made to secure the respondent's appearance in court. The court may order that the person legally responsible for the respondent's care or, if such legally responsible person is not available, a person with whom the respondent resides, appear on the adjourned date. Upon receiving the report, for good cause, the court may order further reports and may require further appearances of the person legally responsible for the respondent's care or, if such person legally responsible is not available, a person with whom the respondent resides. Upon receiving the initial or any subsequent report, the court shall set forth in writing its findings of fact as to the efforts, if any, made up to that date to secure the respondent's appearance in court.

Amended by Laws 1994, Ch. 501, § 1, eff. July 26, 1994.

§ 315.1. Motion to dismiss; defective petition.

1. A petition or a count thereof is defective when:

(a) it does not substantially conform to the requirements stated in sections 311.1 and 311.2; provided that a petition may not be dismissed as defective, but must instead be amended when the defect or irregularity is of a kind that may be cured by amendment pursuant to section 311.5, and where the presentment agency moves to so amend; or

(b) the allegations demonstrate that the court does not have jurisdiction of the crime charged; or

(c) the statute defining the crime charged is unconstitutional or otherwise invalid.

2. An order dismissing a petition as defective may be issued upon motion of the respondent or of the court itself.

3. A motion to dismiss under this section must be made within the time provided for in section 332.2.

Amended by Laws 1985, Ch. 663, eff. Aug. 27, 1985.

§ 315.2. Motion to dismiss in furtherance of justice.

1.   A petition or any part or count thereof may at any time be dismissed in furtherance of justice when, even though there may be no basis for dismissal as a matter of law, such dismissal is required as a matter of judicial discretion by the existence of some compelling further consideration or circumstances clearly demonstrating that a finding of delinquency or continued proceedings would constitute or result in injustice. In determining whether such compelling further consideration or circumstances exist, the court shall, to the extent applicable, examine and consider, individually and collectively, the following:

(a)   the seriousness and circumstances of the crime;

(b)   the extent of harm caused by the crime;

(c)   any exceptionally serious misconduct of law enforcement personnel in the investigation and arrest of the respondent or in the presentment of the petition;

(d)   the history, character and condition of the respondent;

(e)   the needs and best interest of the respondent;

(f)   the need for protection of the community; and

(g)   any other relevant fact indicating that a finding would serve no useful purpose.

2.   An order dismissing a petition in the interest of justice may be issued upon motion of the presentment agency, the court itself or of the respondent. Upon issuing such an order, the court must set forth its reasons therefor upon the record.

3.   Such a motion brought by the presentment agency or the respondent must be in writing and may be filed at any time subsequent to the filing of the petition. Notice of the motion shall be served upon the opposing party not less than eight days prior to the return date of the motion. Answering affidavits shall be served at least two days prior to the return date of such motion.

Amended by Laws 1982, Ch. 926, eff. July 1, 1983.

§ 315.3. Adjournment in contemplation of dismissal.

1.   Except where the petition alleges that the respondent has committed a designated felony act, the court may at any time prior to the entering of a finding under section 352.1 and with the consent of the respondent order that the proceeding be "adjourned in contemplation of dismissal." An adjournment in contemplation of dismissal is an adjournment of the proceeding, for a period not to exceed six months, with a view to ultimate dismissal of the petition in furtherance of justice. Upon issuing such an order, providing such terms and conditions as the court deems appropriate, the court must release the respondent. The court may, as a condition of an adjournment in contemplation of dismissal

order, in cases where the record indicates that the consumption of alcohol may have been a contributing factor, require the respondent to attend and complete an alcohol awareness program established pursuant to paragraph six-a of subdivision (a) of section 19.07 of the mental hygiene law. Upon *ex parte* motion by the presentment agency, or upon the court's own motion, made at the time the order is issued or at any time during its duration, the court may restore the matter to the calendar. If the proceeding is not restored, the petition is, at the expiration of the order, deemed to have been dismissed by the court in furtherance of justice.

2. Rules of court shall define the permissible terms and conditions which may be included in an order that the proceeding be adjourned in contemplation of dismissal; such permissible terms and conditions may include supervision by the probation service, a requirement that the respondent cooperate with a mental health, social services or other appropriate community facility or agency to which the respondent may be referred and a requirement that the respondent comply with such other reasonable conditions as the court shall determine to be necessary or appropriate to ameliorate the conduct which gave rise to the filing of the petition or to prevent placement with the commissioner of social services or the division for youth.

3. An order adjourning a petition in contemplation of dismissal may be issued upon motion of the presentment agency, the court itself, or the respondent. Upon issuing such an order, the court must set forth its reasons therefor upon the record.

Amended by Laws 1985, Ch. 880; Laws 1987, Ch. 101; Laws 1989, Ch. 161, Laws 1991, Ch. 168, § 14, eff. June 28, 1991 to eliminate the expiration date of 1985 amendment; Laws 1991, Ch. 237, § 1, eff. July 31, 1991.

Part 2.   Initial appearance and probable cause hearing.

325.3.   **The probable-cause hearing; determination.**

§ 320.1.   The initial appearance; definition.

When used in this article "initial appearance" means the proceeding on the date the respondent first appears before the court after a petition has been filed and any adjournments thereof, for the purposes specified in section 320.4.

§ 320.2.   The initial appearance; timing; adjournment and appointment of counsel.

1.   If the respondent is detained, the initial appearance shall be held no later than seventy-two hours after a petition is filed or the next day the court is in session, whichever is sooner. If the respondent is not detained, the initial appearance shall be held as soon as practicable and, absent good cause shown, within ten days after a petition is filed. If a warrant for the respondent's arrest has been issued pursuant to section 312.2 of this article due to the respondent's failure to appear for an initial appearance of which he or she had notice, computation of the time within which the initial appearance must be held shall exclude the period extending from the date the court issues the warrant to the date the respondent is returned pursuant to the warrant or appears voluntarily; provided, however, no period of time may be excluded hereunder unless the respondent's location cannot be determined by the exercise of due diligence or, if the respondent's location is known, his or her presence in court cannot be obtained by the exercise of due diligence. In determining whether due diligence has been exercised, the court shall consider, among other factors, the report presented to the court pursuant to subdivision two of section 312.2 of this article.

2.   At the initial appearance the court must appoint a law guardian to represent the respondent pursuant to the provisions of section two hundred forty-nine if independent legal representation is not available to such respondent.

3.   The initial appearance may be adjourned for no longer than seventy-two hours or until the next court day, whichever is sooner, to enable an appointed law guardian or other counsel to appear before the court.

4.   The clerk of the court shall notify the presentment agency and any appointed law guardian of the initial appearance date.

    Amended by Laws 1985, Ch. 663, eff. Aug. 27, 1985; Laws 1994, Ch. 501, § 2, eff. July 26, 1994.

§ 320.3.   Notice of rights.

At the time the respondent first appears before the court, the respondent and his parent or other person legally responsible for his care shall be advised of the respondent's right to remain silent and of his right to be represented by counsel chosen by him or by a law guardian assigned by the court. Provided, however, that in the event of the failure of the respondent's parent or other person legally responsible for his care to appear, after reasonable and substantial effort has been made to notify such parent or responsible person of the commencement of the proceeding and such initial appearance, the court shall appoint a law guardian.

§ 320.4.   The initial appearance; procedures.

1.   At the initial appearance the court must inform the respondent, or cause him to be informed in its presence, of the charge or charges contained in the petition, and the presentment agency must cause the respondent and his counsel or law guardian to be furnished with a copy of the petition.

2.   At the initial appearance the court shall determine:

(a)   whether detention is necessary pursuant to section 320.5; and

(b)   whether the case should be referred to the probation service pursuant to section 320.6; and

(c)   if the child is detained, the date of the probable-cause hearing pursuant to section 325.1 unless such hearing has already been held; and

(d)   the date of the fact-finding hearing; and

(e)   such other issues as may be properly before it.

§ 320.5.   The initial appearance; release or detention.

1.   At the initial appearance, the court in its discretion may release the respondent or direct his detention.

2.   Rules of court shall define permissible terms and conditions of release. The court may in its discretion release the respondent upon such terms and conditions as it deems appropriate. The respondent shall be given a written copy of any such terms and conditions. The court may modify or enlarge such terms and conditions at any time prior to the expiration of the respondent's release.

3.   The court shall not direct detention unless it finds and states the facts and reasons for so finding that unless the respondent is detained:

(a)   there is a substantial probability that he will not appear in court on the return date; or

(b)   there is a serious risk that he may before the return date commit an act which if committed by an adult would constitute a crime.

4.   At the initial appearance the presentment agency may introduce the respondent's previous delinquency findings entered by a family court. If the respondent has been fingerprinted for the current charge pursuant to section 306.1, the presentment agency may also introduce the fingerprint records maintained by the division of criminal justice services. The clerk of court and the probation service shall cooperate with the presentment agency in making available the appropriate records. At the conclusion of the initial appearance such fingerprint records shall be returned to the presentment agency and shall not be made a part of the court record.

5. Upon a finding of facts and reasons which support a detention order pursuant to subdivision three of this section, the court shall also determine and state in any order directing detention:

(a) whether the continuation of the respondent in the respondent's home would be contrary to the best interests of the respondent based upon, and limited to, the facts and circumstances available to the court at the time of the initial appearance; and

(b) where appropriate and consistent with the need for protection of the community, whether reasonable efforts were made prior to the date of the court appearance that resulted in the detention order issued in accordance with this section to prevent or eliminate the need for removal of the respondent from his or her home or, if the respondent had been removed from his or her home prior to the initial appearance, where appropriate and consistent with the need for protection of the community, whether reasonable efforts were made to make it possible for the respondent to safely return home.

Amended by Laws 1982, Ch. 926, eff. July 1, 1983; Laws 1985, Ch. 319, eff. July 11, 1985; Laws 2000, Ch. 145 § 8, eff. July 1, 2000, adding subsection (5).

FCA

§ 320.6. The initial appearance; referral to the probation service.

1. If the petition alleges the commission of the designated felony act or the commission of a crime enumerated in subdivision four of section 308.1. the probation service shall make a recommendation to the court at the initial appearance regarding the suitability of adjusting the case pursuant to section 308.1.

2. At the initial appearance the court may, with the consent of the victim or complainant and the respondent, refer a case to the probation service for adjustment services. In the case of a designated felony petition the consent of the presentment agency shall also be required to refer a case to probation services for adjustment services.

3. If the court refers a case to the probation service pursuant to this section and the probation service adjusts the case, the petition shall be dismissed.

4. If such case is referred to the probation service, the provisions of section 308.1, except subdivision thirteen thereof, shall apply.

Amended by Laws 1982, Ch. 926, eff. July 1, 1983; Laws 1983, Ch. 398, eff. July 1, 1983.

§ 321.1. Entry of an admission or a denial.

1. At the initial appearance the respondent shall admit or deny each charge contained in the petition unless the petition is dismissed or the proceeding otherwise terminated.

2.   If the respondent refuses to admit or deny each such charge or remains mute, the court must enter a denial in his behalf as to any charge neither admitted nor denied.

§ 321.2.   Admissions to part of a petition; admissions concerning other petitions.

1.   A respondent may as a matter of right enter an admission to those allegations in the petition which are determinable at the fact-finding hearing.

2.   Where the petition charges but one crime, a respondent may, with the consent of the court and the appropriate presentment agency, enter an admission of a lesser included crime as defined in section 1.20 of the criminal procedure law.

3.   Where the petition charges more than one crime in separate counts a respondent may, with the consent of the court and the appropriate presentment agency, enter an admission to part of the petition or a lesser included crime upon the condition that such admission constitutes a complete disposition of these allegations in the petition which are determinable at the fact-finding hearing.

Amended by Laws 1982, Ch. 926, eff. July 1, 1983; Laws 1983, Ch. 980, eff. Aug. 8, 1983.

§ 321.3.   Acceptance of an admission.

1.   The court shall not consent to the entry of an admission unless it has advised the respondent of his right to a fact-finding hearing. The court shall also ascertain through allocation of the respondent and his parent or other person legally responsible for his care, if present, that

(a)   he committed the act or acts to which he is entering an admission,

(b)   he is voluntarily waiving his right to a fact-finding hearing, and

(c)   he is aware of the possible specific dispositional orders. The provisions of this subdivision shall not be waived.

2.   Upon consenting to the entry of an admission pursuant to this section, the court must state the reasons for granting such consent.

3.   Upon the entry of an admission pursuant to this section the court shall enter an appropriate order pursuant to section 345.1 and schedule a dispositional hearing pursuant to section 350.1.

Amended by Laws 1982, Ch. 926, eff. July 1, 1983; Laws 1983, Ch. 398, eff. July 1, 1983; Laws 1983, Ch. 980, eff. Aug. 8, 1983.

§ 321.4.   Withdrawal of an admission or denial.

1.   A respondent who has entered a denial of a petition may as a matter of right withdraw such denial at any time before the conclusion of the fact-finding hearing and enter an admission to the entire petition.

2. At any time prior to the entry of a finding under section 352.1 the court in its discretion may permit a respondent who has entered an admission to the entire petition or to part of the petition to withdraw such admission, and in such event the entire petition as it existed at the time of the admission shall be restored.

Amended by Laws 1983, Ch. 398, eff. July 1, 1983.

§ 322.1. Incapacitated person; examination reports.

1. At any proceeding under this article, the court must issue an order that the respondent be examined as provided herein when it is of the opinion that the respondent may be an incapacitated person. Notwithstanding the provisions of this or any other law, the court may direct that the examination be conducted on an outpatient basis when the respondent is not in custody at the time the court issues an order of examination. The court shall order that two qualified psychiatric examiners as defined in subdivision seven of section 730.10 of the criminal procedure law examine the respondent to determine if he is mentally ill, mentally retarded or developmentally disabled.

2. If an order of examination has been issued pursuant to subdivision one, the proceedings shall be adjourned until the examination reports have been filed with the court. Every such report shall be filed within ten days after entry of such order. Upon a showing of special circumstances and a finding that a longer period is necessary to complete the examination and report, the court may extend the time for filing the examination report.

3. Each report shall state the examiner's opinion as to whether the respondent is or is not an incapacitated person, the nature and extent of his examination and, if he finds the respondent is an incapacitated person, his diagnosis and prognosis and a detailed statement of the reasons for his opinion by making particular reference to those aspects of the proceedings wherein the respondent lacks capacity to understand or to assist in his own defense. The chief administrator of the courts shall prescribe the form for the examination report.

Amended by Laws 1994, Ch. 566, § 2, eff. July 26, 1994.

§ 322.2. Proceedings to determine capacity.

1. Upon the receipt of examination reports ordered under section 322.1, the court shall conduct a hearing to determine whether the respondent is an incapacitated person. The respondent, the counsel or law guardian for the respondent, the presentment agency and the commissioner of mental health or the commissioner of mental retardation and developmental disabilities, as appropriate, shall be notified of such hearing at least five days prior to the date thereof and afforded an opportunity to be heard.

2. If the court finds that the respondent is not an incapacitated person, it shall continue the delinquency proceedings.

FCA

3. If the court finds that the respondent is an incapacitated person, the court shall schedule a hearing to determine whether there is probable cause to believe that the respondent committed a crime. The order of proceeding at such hearing shall conform to section 325.2.

4. If the court finds that there is probable cause to believe that the respondent committed a misdemeanor, the respondent shall be committed to the custody of the appropriate commissioner for a reasonable period not to exceed ninety days. The court shall dismiss the petition on the issuance of the order of commitment.

5. (a) If the court finds that there is probable cause to believe that the respondent committed a felony, it shall order the respondent committed to the custody of the commissioner of mental health or the commissioner of mental retardation and developmental disabilities for an initial period not to exceed one year from the date of such order. Such period may be extended annually upon further application to the court by the commissioner having custody or his designee. Such application must be made not more than sixty days prior to the expiration of such period of forms that have been prescribed by the chief administrator of the courts. At that time, the commissioner must give written notice of the application to the respondent, the counsel or law guardian representing the respondent and the mental hygiene legal service if the respondent is at a residential facility. Upon receipt of such application, the court must conduct a hearing to determine the issue of capacity. If, at the conclusion of a hearing conducted pursuant to this subdivision, the court finds that the respondent is no longer incapacitated, he shall be returned to the family court for further proceedings pursuant to this article. If the court is satisfied that the respondent continues to be incapacitated, the court shall authorize continued custody of the respondent by the commissioner for a period not to exceed one year. Such extensions shall not continue beyond a reasonable period of time necessary to determine whether the respondent will attain the capacity to proceed to a fact finding hearing in the foreseeable future but in no event shall continue beyond the respondent's eighteenth birthday.

(b) If a respondent is in the custody of the commissioner upon the respondent's eighteenth birthday, the commissioner shall notify the clerk of the court that the respondent was in his custody on such date and the court shall dismiss the petition.

(c) If the court finds that there is probable cause to believe that the respondent has committed a designated felony act, the court shall require that treatment be provided in a residential facility within the appropriate office of the department of mental hygiene.

(d) The commissioner shall review the condition of the respondent within forty-five days after the respondent is committed to the custody of the commissioner. He shall make a second review within ninety days after the respondent is committed to his custody. Thereafter, he shall review the condition of the respondent every ninety days. The respondent and the counsel or law guardian for the respondent, shall be notified of any such review and afforded an opportunity to be heard. The commissioner having custody shall apply to the court for an order dismissing the petition whenever he determines that there is a substantial probability that the respondent will continue to be incapacitated for the foreseeable future. At the time of such application the commissioner must give written notice of application to the respondent, the presentment agency and the mental hygiene legal service if the respondent is at a residential facility. Upon receipt of such application, the court may on its own motion conduct a hearing to determine whether there is substantial probability that the respondent will continue to be incapacitated for the foreseeable future and it must conduct such hearing if a demand therefor is made by the respondent or the mental hygiene legal service within ten days from the date that notice of application was given to them. The respondent may apply to the court for an order of dismissal on the same ground.

6. Any order pursuant to this section dismissing a petition shall not preclude an application for voluntary or involuntary care and treatment in a facility of the appropriate office of the department of mental hygiene pursuant to the provisions of the mental hygiene law. Unless the respondent is admitted pursuant to such an application he shall be released.

7. If the commissioner having custody of a child committed to a residential facility determines at any time that such child may be more appropriately treated in a non-residential facility, he may petition the family court for a hearing. If the court finds after a hearing that treatment in a non-residential facility would be more appropriate for such child, the court shall modify its order of commitment to authorize transfer of such child to a non-residential facility. Application for such a hearing may be made by the respondent.

8. If the commissioner having custody of the child determines at any time that such child is not an incapacitated person, he shall petition the court for a hearing. The respondent and the presentment agency shall be notified of such hearing within twenty-four hours of the scheduling of such hearing and afforded an opportunity to be heard. Application for such a hearing may be made by the respondent. If the court finds after the hearing that the child is no longer incapacitated, he shall be returned to the family court for further proceedings pursuant to this article.

9. Time spent by the respondent in the custody of a commissioner of an office within the department of mental hygiene or in a local hospital or detention facility pending transfer to the custody of the commissioner after a finding of incapacity, shall be credited and applied towards the period of placement specified in a disposition order on the original petition.

Amended by Laws 1985, Ch. 789, eff. Apr. 1, 1986.

§ 325.1.   The probable-cause hearing; time.

1. At the initial appearance, if the respondent denies a charge contained in the petition and the court determines that he shall be detained for more than three

days pending a fact-finding hearing, the court shall schedule a probable-cause hearing to determine the issues specified in section 325.3.

2.   Such probable-cause hearing shall be held within three days following the initial appearance or within four days following the filing of a petition, whichever occurs sooner.

3.   For good cause shown, the court may adjourn the hearing for no more than an additional three court days.

4.   The respondent may waive the probable-cause hearing, but the fact that the respondent is not ready for a fact-finding hearing shall not be deemed such a waiver.

5.   Where the petition consists of an order of removal pursuant to article seven hundred twenty-five of the criminal procedure law, unless the removal was pursuant to subdivision three of section 725.05 of such law and the respondent was not afforded a probable cause hearing pursuant to subdivision three of section 180.75 of such law for a reason other than his waiver thereof pursuant to subdivision two of section 180.75 of such law, the petition shall be deemed to be based upon a determination that probable cause exists to believe the respondent is a juvenile delinquent and the respondent shall not be entitled to any further inquiry on the subject of whether probable cause exists. After the filing of any such petition the court must, however, exercise independent, de novo discretion with respect to release or detention as set forth in section 320.5.

Amended by Laws 1983, Ch. 398, eff. July 1, 1983.

§ 325.2.   The probable-cause hearing; order of proceeding.

1.   The order of a probable-cause hearing held pursuant to section 325.1 or 322.2 shall be as follows:

(a)   the presentment agency must call and examine witnesses and offer evidence in support of the charge;

(b)   the respondent may, as a matter of right, testify in his own behalf; if the respondent so testifies, his testimony may not be introduced against him in any future proceeding, except to impeach his testimony at such future proceeding as inconsistent prior testimony;

(c)   upon request of the respondent, the court shall, except for good cause shown, permit him to call and examine other witnesses or to produce other evidence in his behalf.

2.   Each witness, whether called by the presentment agency or by the respondent, must, unless he would be authorized to give unsworn evidence at a fact-finding hearing, testify under oath. Each witness, including any respondent testifying in his own behalf, may be cross-examined.

3.   Only non-hearsay evidence shall be admissible to demonstrate reasonable cause to believe that the respondent committed a crime; except that reports of

experts and technicians in professional and scientific fields and sworn statements of the kinds admissible at a hearing upon a felony complaint in a criminal court may be admitted, unless the court determines, upon application of the respondent, that such hearsay evidence is, under the particular circumstances of the case, not sufficiently reliable, in which case the court shall require that the witness testify in person and be subject to cross-examination.

4.   Such hearing should be completed at one session. In the interest of justice however, it may be adjourned by the court, but no such adjournment may be for more than one court day.

§ 325.3.   The probable-cause hearing; determination.

1.   At the conclusion of a probable-cause hearing held pursuant to section 325.1 the court shall determine in accordance with the evidentiary standards applicable to a hearing on a felony complaint in a criminal court:

(a)   whether it is reasonable to believe that a crime was committed; and

(b)   whether it is reasonable to believe that the respondent committed such crime.

2.   The court shall state on the record the section or sections of the penal law or other law which it is reasonable to believe the respondent violated.

3.   If the court finds that there is reasonable cause pursuant to subdivision one, it shall further determine whether continued detention is necessary pursuant to section 320.5.

4.   If the court does not find that there is reasonable cause to believe that a crime was committed and that the respondent committed it, the case shall be adjourned and the respondent released from detention. If the court or the presentment agency cannot hold a probable cause hearing within the limits of subdivision two of section 325.1, the court may dismiss the petition without prejudice or for good cause shown adjourn the hearing and release the respondent pursuant to section 320.5.

Amended by Laws 1982, Ch. 926, eff. July 1, 1983.

Part 3.   Discovery.

§ 330.1.   Bill of particulars.

Repealed by Laws 1983, Ch. 398, eff. July 1, 1983.

§ 330.1.   Bill of particulars.

1.   Definitions.

(a)   "Bill of particulars" is a written statement by the presentment agency specifying, as required by this section, items of factual information which are not recited in the petition and which pertain to the offense charged and including the substance of each respondent's conduct encompassed by the charge which the presentment agency intends to prove at a fact-finding hearing on its direct case, and whether the presentment agency intends to prove that the respondent acted as principal or accomplice or both. However, the presentment agency shall not be required to include in the bill of particulars matters of evidence relating to how the presentment agency intends to prove the elements of the offense charged or how the presentment agency intends to prove any item of factual information included in the bill of particulars.

(b)   "Request for a bill of particulars" is a written request served by respondent upon the presentment agency, without leave of the court, requesting a bill of particulars, specifying the items of factual information desired, and alleging that respondent cannot adequately prepare or conduct his defense without the information requested.

2.   Bill of particulars upon request. Upon a timely request for a bill of particulars by a respondent against whom a petition is pending, the presentment agency shall within fifteen days of the service of the request or as soon thereafter as is practicable, serve upon the respondent or his attorney or law guardian and file with the court, the bill of particulars, except to the extent the presentment agency shall have refused to comply with the request pursuant to subdivision four of this section. If the respondent is detained, the court shall direct the filing of the bill of particulars on an expedited basis and prior to the commencement of the fact-finding hearing.

3.   Timeliness of request. A request for a bill of particulars shall be timely if made within thirty days after the conclusion of the initial appearance and before commencement of the fact-finding hearing. If the respondent is not represented by counsel or a law guardian, and has requested an adjournment to retain counsel or to have a law guardian appointed, the thirty-day period shall commence, for the purposes of a request for a bill or particulars by the respondent, on the date counsel or a law guardian initially appeared on respondent's behalf. However, the court may direct compliance with a request for a bill of particulars that, for good cause shown, could not have been made within the time specified.

4. Request refused. The presentment agency may refuse to comply with the request for a bill of particulars or any portion of the request for a bill of particulars to the extent it reasonably believes that the item of factual information requested is not authorized to be included in a bill of particulars, or that such information is not necessary to enable the respondent adequately to prepare or conduct his defense, or that a protective order would be warranted or that the demand is untimely. Such refusal shall be made in writing, which shall set forth the grounds of such belief as fully as possible, consistent with the reason for the refusal. Within fifteen days of the request or as soon thereafter as practicable, the refusal shall be served upon the respondent and a copy shall be filed with the court.

5. Court ordered bill of particulars. Where a presentment agency has timely served a written refusal pursuant to subdivision four of this section and upon motion, made in writing, of a respondent, who has made a request for a bill of particulars and whose request has not been complied with in whole or in part, the court must, to the extent a protective order is not warranted, order the presentment agency to comply with the request if it is satisfied that the items of factual information requested are authorized to be included in a bill of particulars, and that such information is necessary to enable the respondent adequately to prepare or conduct his defense and, if the request was untimely, a finding of good cause for the delay. Where a presentment agency has not timely served a written refusal pursuant to subdivision four of this section the court must, unless it is satisfied that the presentment agency has shown good cause why such an order should not be issued, issue an order requiring the presentment agency to comply or providing for any other order authorized by subdivision one of section 331.6.

6. Motion procedure. A motion for a bill of particulars shall be made as prescribed in section 332.1. Upon an order granting a motion pursuant to this section, the presentment agency must file with the court a bill of particulars, reciting every item of information designated in the order, and serve a copy thereof upon the respondent. Pending such filing and service, the fact-finding hearing is stayed.

7. Protective order.

(a) The court may, upon motion of the presentment agency, or of any affected person, or upon determination of a motion of respondent for a court-ordered bill of particulars, or upon its own initiative, issue a protective order denying, limiting, conditioning, delaying or regulating the bill of particulars for good cause, including constitutional limitations, danger to the integrity of physical evidence or a substantial risk of physical harm, intimidation, economic reprisal, bribery or unjustified annoyance or embarrassment to any person or an adverse effect upon the legitimate needs of law enforcement, including the protection of the confidentiality of informants, or any other factor or set of factors which outweighs the need for the bill of particulars.

(b) An order limiting, conditioning, delaying or regulating the bill of particulars may, among other things, require that any material copied or derived therefrom be maintained in the exclusive possession of the attorney or law guardian for the respondent and be used for the exclusive purpose of preparing for the defense of the juvenile delinquency proceeding.

8. Amendment. At any time before commencement of the fact-finding hearing, the presentment agency may, without leave of the court, serve upon respondent and file with the court an amended bill of particulars. At any time during the fact-finding hearing, upon application of the presentment agency and with notice to the respondent and an opportunity for him to be heard, the court must, upon finding that no undue prejudice will accrue to respondent and that the presentment agency has acted in good faith, permit the presentment agency to amend the bill of particulars. Upon any amendment of the bill of particulars, the court must, upon application of respondent, order an adjournment of the fact-finding hearing or any other action it deems appropriate which may, by reason of the amendment, be necessary to accord the respondent an adequate opportunity to defend.

Added by Laws 1983, Ch. 398, eff. July 1, 1983.

§ 330.2. Suppression of evidence.

1. A respondent in a juvenile delinquency proceeding may make a motion to suppress evidence in accordance with sections 710.20 and 710.60 of the criminal procedure law.

2. Whenever the presentment agency intends to offer at a fact-finding hearing evidence described in section 710.20 or subdivision one of section 710.30 of the criminal procedure law, such agency must serve upon respondent notice of such intention. Such notice must be served within fifteen days after the conclusion of the initial appearance or before the fact-finding hearing, whichever occurs first, unless the court, for good cause shown, permits later service and accords the respondent a reasonable opportunity to make a suppression motion thereafter. If the respondent is detained, the court shall direct that such notice be served on an expedited basis.

3. When a motion to suppress evidence is made before the commencement of the fact-finding hearing, the fact-finding hearing shall not be held until the determination of the motion.

4. After the pre-trial determination and denial of the motion, if the court is satisfied, upon a showing by the respondent, that additional pertinent facts have been discovered by the respondent which could not have been discovered by the respondent with reasonable diligence before determination of the motion, it may permit him to renew. Such motion to renew shall be made prior to the commencement of the fact-finding hearing, unless the additional pertinent facts were discovered during the fact-finding hearing.

5. Upon granting a motion to suppress evidence, the court must order that the evidence in question be excluded. When the order excludes tangible property

unlawfully taken from the respondent's possession, and when such property is not otherwise subject to lawful retention, the court may, upon request of the respondent, further order that such property be restored to him.

6. An order finally denying a motion to suppress evidence may be reviewed upon an appeal from an ensuing finding of delinquency, notwithstanding the fact that such finding is entered upon an admission made by the respondent, unless the respondent, upon an admission, expressly waives his right to appeal.

7. A motion to suppress evidence is the exclusive method of challenging the admissibility of evidence upon the grounds specified in this section, and a respondent who does not make such a motion waives his right to judicial determination of any such contention.

8. In the absence of service of notice upon a respondent as prescribed in this section, no evidence of a kind specified in subdivision two may be received against him at the fact-finding hearing unless he has, despite the lack of such notice, moved to suppress such evidence and such motion has been denied.

9. An order granting a motion to suppress evidence shall be deemed an order of disposition appealable under section eleven hundred twelve. In taking such an appeal the presentment agency must file, in addition to a notice of appeal, a statement alleging that the deprivation of the use of the evidence ordered suppressed has rendered the sum of the proof available to the presentment agency either:

(a) insufficient as a matter of law, or

(b) so weak in its entirety that any reasonable possibility of proving the allegations contained in the petition has been effectively destroyed. If the respondent is in detention he shall be released pending such appeal unless the court, upon conducting a hearing, enters an order continuing detention. An order continuing detention under this subdivision may be stayed by the appropriate appellate division.

10. The taking of an appeal by the presentment agency pursuant to subdivision nine constitutes a bar to the presentment of the petition involving the evidence ordered suppressed, unless and until such suppression is reversed upon appeal and vacated.

Amended by Laws 1985, Ch. 663, eff. Aug. 27, 1985.

§ 331.1. Discovery; definition of terms.

The following definitions are applicable to this section and sections 331.2 through 331.7.

1. "Demand to produce" means a written notice served by and on a party, without leave of the court, demanding to inspect property pursuant to section 331.2 or 331.3 and giving reasonable notice of the time at which the demanding party wishes to inspect the property designated.

2. "Attorneys' work product" means property to the extent that it contains the opinions, theories or conclusions of the presentment agency, law guardian, counsel for the respondent or members of their staffs.

3. "Property" means any existing tangible personal or real property, including but not limited to, books, records, reports, memoranda, papers, photographs, tapes or other electronic recordings, articles of clothing, fingerprints, blood samples, fingernail scrapings or handwriting specimens, but excluding attorneys' work product.

4. "Co-respondent" means a person whose name appears in the petition pursuant to paragraph (1) of subdivision three of section 311.1.

§ 331.2. Discovery; upon demand of a party.

1. Except to the extent protected by court order, upon a demand to produce by a respondent, the presentment agency shall disclose to the respondent and make available for inspection, photography, copying or testing, the following property:

(a) any written, recorded or oral statement of the respondent, or by a co-respondent, made, other than in the course of the criminal transaction, to a public servant engaged in law enforcement activity or to a person then acting under his direction or in cooperation with him;

(b) any transcript of testimony relating to the proceeding pending against the respondent, given by the respondent, or by a co-respondent, before any grand jury;

(c) any written report or document, or portion thereof, concerning a physical or mental examination, or scientific test or experiment, relating to the proceeding which was made by, or at the request or direction of a public servant engaged in law enforcement activity or which was made by a person whom the presentment agency intends to call as a witness at a hearing, or which the presentment agency intends to introduce at a hearing;

(d) any photograph or drawing relating to the proceeding which was made or completed by a public servant engaged in law enforcement activity, or which was made by a person whom the presentment agency intends to call as a witness at a hearing, or which the presentment agency intends to introduce at a hearing;

(e) any other property obtained from the respondent or a co-respondent;

(f) any tapes or other electronic recordings which the presentment agency intends to introduce at the fact-finding hearing, irrespective of whether such recording was made during the course of the criminal transaction;

(g) anything required to be disclosed, prior to the fact-finding hearing, to the respondent by the presentment agency, pursuant to the constitution of this state or of the United States; and

(h) the approximate date, time and place of the offense charged and of respondent's arrest.

2. (a) The presentment agency shall make a diligent, good faith effort to ascertain the existence of property demanded pursuant to subdivision one and to cause such property to be made available for discovery where it exists but is not within the presentment agency's possession, custody or control; provided, that the presentment agency shall not be required to obtain by subpoena duces tecum demanded material which the respondent may thereby obtain.

(b) In any case in which the property includes grand jury testimony, the presentment agency shall forthwith request that the district attorney provide a transcript of such testimony; upon receiving such a request, the district attorney shall promptly apply to the appropriate criminal court, with written notice to the presentment agency and the respondent, for a written order pursuant to section three hundred-twenty-five of the judiciary law releasing a transcript of testimony to the presentment agency.

3. Except to the extent protected by court order, upon demand to produce by the presentment agency, the respondent shall disclose and make available for inspection, photography, copying or testing, subject to constitutional limitations:

(a) any written report or document, or portion thereof, concerning a physical examination, or scientific test, experiment, or comparison, made by or at the request or direction of, the respondent, if the respondent intends to introduce such report or document at a hearing or if the respondent has filed a notice of defense of mental disease or defect pursuant to section 335.1 and such report or document relates thereto, or if such report or document was made by a person, other than respondent, whom respondent intends to call as a witness at a hearing; and

(b) any photograph, drawing, tape or other electronic recording which the respondent intends to introduce at a hearing.

4. Except to the extent protected by court order, upon demand to produce by the presentment agency, a respondent who has served a written notice, under section 335.1 of intention to rely upon the defense of mental disease or defect shall disclose and make available for inspection, photography, copying or testing, subject to constitutional limitations, any written report or document, or portion thereof, concerning a mental examination made by or at the request or direction of the respondent.

5. The respondent shall make a diligent good faith effort to make such property available for discovery pursuant to subdivisions three and four where it exists but the property is not within his possession, custody or control, provided that the respondent shall not be required to obtain by subpoena duces tecum demanded material that the presentment agency may thereby obtain.

6. Notwithstanding the provisions of subdivisions one through five, the presentment agency or the respondent, as the case may be, may refuse to disclose any information which he reasonably believes is not discoverable by a demand to produce, or for which he reasonably believes protective order pursuant to section 331.5 would be warranted. Such refusal shall be made in writing, which shall set forth the grounds of such belief as fully as possible, consistent with the

objective of the refusal. The writing shall be served upon the demanding party and a copy shall be filed with the court.

   Amended by Laws 1983, Ch. 398, eff. July 1, 1983.

§ 331.3. Discovery; upon court order.

   1.   Upon motion of respondent the court, (a) must order discovery as to any material not disclosed upon a demand pursuant to section 331.2, if it finds that the presentment agency's refusal to disclose such material is not justified; (b) must, unless it is satisfied that the presentment agency has shown good cause why such an order should not be issued, order discovery or any other order authorized by subdivision one of section 331.6 as to any material not disclosed upon demand pursuant to section 331.2 where the presentment agency has failed to serve a timely written refusal pursuant to subdivision six of section 331.2; and (c) may order discovery with respect to any other property which the presentment agency intends to introduce at the fact-finding hearing, upon a showing by the respondent that discovery with respect to such property is material to the preparation of his defense, and that the request is reasonable. Upon granting the motion pursuant to paragraph (c) hereof, the court shall, upon motion of the presentment agency showing such to be material to the preparation of its case and that the request is reasonable, condition its order of discovery by further directing discovery by the presentment agency of property, of the same kind or character as that authorized to be inspected by the respondent which he intends to introduce at the fact-finding hearing.

   2.   Upon motion of the presentment agency, and subject to constitutional limitation, the court;

   (a)   must order discovery as to any property not disclosed upon a demand pursuant to section 331.2, if it finds that the respondent's refusal to disclose such material is not justified; and

   (b)   may order the respondent to provide non-testimonial evidence. Such order may, among other things, require the respondent to:

   (i)   appear in a line-up;

   (ii)   speak for identification by witness or potential witness;

   (iii)   be fingerprinted, provided that the respondent is subject to fingerprinting pursuant to this article;

   (iv)   pose for photographs not involving reenactment of an event, provided the respondent is subject to fingerprinting pursuant to this article;

   (v)   permit the taking of samples of blood, hair or other materials from his body in a manner not involving an unreasonable intrusion thereof or a risk of serious physical injury thereto;

   (vi)   provide specimens of his handwriting; and

   (vii)   submit to a reasonable physical or medical inspection of his body.

This subdivision shall not be construed to limit, expand or otherwise affect the issuance of a similar court order, as may be authorized by law, before the filing of a petition consistent with such rights as the respondent may derive from this article, the constitution of this state or of the United States.

3.   An order pursuant to this section may be denied, limited or conditioned as provided in section 331.5.

Amended by Laws 1983, Ch. 398, eff. July 1, 1983.

§ 331.4.   Discovery; of prior statements and history of witnesses.

1.   At the commencement of the fact-finding hearing, the presentment agency shall, subject to a protective order, make available to the respondent:

(a)   any written or recorded statement, including any testimony before a grand jury and any examination videotaped pursuant to section 190.32 of the criminal procedure law, made by a person whom the presentment agency intends to call as a witness at the fact-finding hearing, and which relates to the subject matter of the witness's testimony. When such a statement includes grand jury testimony, the presentment agency shall request that the district attorney provide a transcript of testimony prior to the commencement of the fact-finding hearing; upon receiving such a request, the district attorney shall promptly apply to the appropriate criminal court, with written notice to the presentment agency and the respondent, for a written order pursuant to section three hundred twenty-five of the judiciary law releasing a transcript of testimony to the presentment agency;

(b)   a record of judgment of conviction of a witness the presentment agency intends to call at the fact-finding hearing if such record is known by the presentment agency to exist;

(c)   the existence of any pending criminal action against a witness the presentment agency intends to call at the fact-finding hearing, if the pending criminal action is known by the presentment agency to exist.

The provisions of paragraphs (b) and (c) shall not be construed to require the presentment agency to fingerprint a witness or otherwise cause the division of criminal justice services or other law enforcement agency or court to issue a report concerning a witness.

2.   At the conclusion of the presentment agency's direct case and before the commencement of the respondent's direct case, the respondent shall, subject to a protective order, make available to the presentment agency

(a)   any written or recorded statement made by a person other than the respondent whom the respondent intends to call as a witness at the fact-finding hearing and which relates to the subject matter of the witness's testimony;

(b)   a record of judgment of conviction of a witness, other than the respondent,the respondent intends to call at a hearing if the record of conviction is known by the respondent to exist; and

FCA

(c) the existence of any pending criminal action against a witness other than the respondent, the respondent intends to call at a hearing, if the pending criminal action is known by the respondent to exist.

3. Subject to a protective order, at a pre-fact-finding hearing held upon a motion pursuant to section 330.2, at which a witness is called to testify, each party at the conclusion of the direct examination of each of its witnesses, shall, upon request of the other party, make available to that party to the extent not previously disclosed:

(a) any written or recorded statement, including any testimony before a grand jury, made by such witness other than the respondent, which relates to the subject-matter of the witness's testimony. When such a statement includes grand jury testimony, the presentment agency shall request that the district attorney provide a transcript of testimony prior to the commencement of the pre-fact-finding hearing; upon receiving such a request, the district attorney shall promptly apply to the appropriate criminal court, with written notice to the presentment agency and the respondent, for a written order pursuant to section three hundred twenty-five of the judiciary law releasing a transcript of testimony to the presentment agency;

(b) a record of a judgment of conviction of such witness other than the respondent if the record of conviction is known by the presentment agency or respondent, as the case may be, to exist; and

(c) the existence of any pending criminal action against such witness other than the respondent, if the pending criminal action is known by the presentment agency or respondent, as the case may be, to exist.

Amended by Laws 1983, Ch. 398, eff. July 1, 1983; Laws 1985, Ch. 584, eff. July 28, 1985.

§ 331.5. Discovery; protective orders, continuing duty to disclose.

1. The court may, upon motion of either party, or of any affected person, or upon determination of a motion of either party for an order of discovery, or upon its own initiative, issue a protective order denying, limiting, conditioning, delaying or regulating discovery for good cause, including constitutional limitations, danger to the integrity of physical evidence or a substantial risk or physical harm, intimidation, economic reprisal, bribery or unjustified annoyance or embarrassment to any person or an adverse effect upon the legitimate needs of law enforcement, including the protection of the confidentiality of informants, or any other factor or set of factors which outweighs the usefulness of the discovery.

2. An order limiting, conditioning, delaying or regulating discovery may, among other things, require that any material copied or derived therefrom be maintained in the exclusive possession of the attorney for the discovering party and be used for the exclusive purpose of preparing for the defense or presentment of the action.

3. A motion for a protective order shall suspend discovery of the particular matter in dispute.

4. If, after complying with the provisions of sections 331.2 through 331.7 or an order pursuant thereto, a party finds, either before or during the fact-finding hearing, additional material subject to discovery or covered by such order, he shall promptly comply with the demand or order, refuse to comply with the demand where refusal is authorized, or apply for a protective order pursuant to this section.

§ 331.6. Discovery; sanctions.

1. If, during the course of discovery proceedings, the court finds that a party has failed to comply with any of the provisions of sections 331.2 through 331.7, the court may order such party to permit discovery of the property not previously disclosed, grant a continuance, issue a protective order, prohibit the introduction of certain evidence or the calling of certain witnesses or take any other appropriate action.

2. The failure of the presentment agency to call as a witness a person specified in subdivision one of section 331.2 or any party to introduce disclosed material at the fact-finding hearing shall not, by itself constitute grounds for any sanction or for adverse comment thereupon by any party.

§ 331.7. Discovery; demand and motion procedure.

1. If the respondent is in detention:

(a) a demand to produce shall be made within seven days after the conclusion of the initial appearance or prior to the commencement of the fact-finding hearing, whichever occurs sooner, unless the court grants an extension for good cause shown;

(b) a refusal to comply with a demand to produce shall be made within five days of the service of the demand to produce, but for good cause may be made thereafter;

(c) absent a refusal to comply with a demand to produce, compliance with such demand shall be made within seven days of the service of the demand or as soon thereafter as practicable. The court, however, may order compliance within a shorter period of time.

2. If the respondent is not in detention:

(a) a demand to produce shall be made within fifteen days after the conclusion of the initial appearance unless extended for good cause shown, but in no event later than the commencement of the fact-finding hearing;

(b) a refusal to comply with a demand to produce shall be made within fifteen days of the service of the demand to produce, but for good cause may be made thereafter;

FCA

(c)   absent a refusal to comply with a demand to produce, compliance with such demand shall be made within fifteen days of the service of the demand or as soon thereafter as practicable.

3.   If the respondent is not in detention, a motion by the presentment agency for discovery shall be made within thirty days after the conclusion of the initial appearance, but for good cause shown may be made at any time before commencement of the fact-finding hearing. If the respondent is in detention such motion shall be made within fourteen days after the conclusion of the initial appearance or prior to the commencement of the fact-finding hearing, whichever occurs sooner.

4.   A motion by a respondent for discovery shall be made as prescribed in section 332.2.

5.   Where the interests of justice so require, the court may permit a party to a motion for an order of discovery or a protective order, or other affected person, to submit papers or to testify ex parte or in camera. Any such papers and transcripts of such testimony shall be sealed, but shall constitute a part of the record on appeal. If practical, a judge who receives papers or testimony in camera shall refer the case to a different judge of the same court to preside at the fact-finding hearing.

Amended by Laws 1983, Ch. 398, eff. July 1, 1983.

§ 332.1.   Pre-trial motions; definition.

"Pre-trial motion" as used in this article means any motion by a respondent which seeks an order of the court:

1.   transferring a proceeding pursuant to section 302.3; or

2.   granting a separate fact-finding hearing pursuant to section 311.3; or

3.   granting separate fact-finding hearings or consolidating petitions pursuant to section 311.6; or

4.   dismissing a petition pursuant to section 315.1; or

5.   granting a bill of particulars pursuant to section 330.1; or

6.   granting discovery pursuant to section 331.3; or

7.   suppressing the use at the fact-finding hearing of any evidence pursuant to section 330.2; or

8.   dismissing a petition, or any count thereof, on the ground that the respondent has been denied a speedy fact-finding hearing contrary to section 310.2; or

9.   dismissing a petition, or any count thereof, on the ground that the proceeding is untimely, pursuant to section 302.2; or

10.   dismissing a petition, or any count thereof, on the ground that the proceeding is barred in accordance with the laws applicable pursuant to section 303.2.

Amended by Laws 1983, Ch. 398, eff. July 1, 1983.

§ 332.2. Pre-trial motions; procedure.

1. Except as otherwise expressly provided in this article, all pretrial motions shall be filed within thirty days after the conclusion of the initial appearance and before commencement of the fact-finding hearing, or within such additional times as the court may fix upon application of the respondent made prior to entering a finding pursuant to section 345.1. If the respondent is not represented by counsel or a law guardian and has requested an adjournment to retain counsel or to have a law guardian appointed, such thirty-day period shall commence on the date counsel or a law guardian initially appears on the respondent's behalf. A motion made pursuant to subdivision eight of section 332.1 must be made prior to the commencement of a fact-finding hearing or the entry of an admission.

2. All pre-trial motions with supporting affidavits, exhibits and memoranda of law, if any, shall be included within the same set of motion papers wherever practicable, and shall be made returnable on the same date, unless the respondent shows that it would be prejudicial to the defense were a single judge to consider all such motions. Where one motion seeks to provide the basis for making another motion, it shall be deemed impracticable to include both motions in the same set of motion papers.

3. Notwithstanding the provisions of subdivisions one and two, the court must entertain and decide on its merits, at any time before the conclusion of the fact-finding hearing, any appropriate motion based upon grounds of which the respondent could not, with due diligence, have been previously aware, or which, for other good cause, could not reasonably have raised within the period specified in subdivision one. Any other pre-trial motions made after such thirty day period may be summarily denied, but the court, in the interest of justice and for good cause shown may, in its discretion, at any time before a finding is entered, entertain and dispose of the motion on the merits.

4. If the respondent is detained, the court shall hear and determine pre-trial motions on an expedited basis.

Amended by Laws 1983, Ch. 398, eff. July 1, 1983.

§ 335.1. Notice of defense of mental disease or defect.

Evidence of mental disease or defect of the respondent excluding his responsibility under this article is not admissible at the fact-finding hearing unless the respondent serves upon the presentment agency and files with the court a written notice of intention to rely upon such defense. Such notice must be served and filed before the fact-finding hearing and not more than thirty days after the conclusion of the initial appearance, whichever is sooner. In the interest of justice and for good cause shown, however, the court may permit such service and filing to be made at any later time prior to the conclusion of the fact-finding hearing.

FCA

§ 335.2.　Notice of alibi.

1.　At any time not more than fifteen days after the conclusion of the initial appearance and before the fact-finding hearing the presentment agency may serve upon the respondent and file a copy thereof with the court, a demand that if the respondent intends to offer a defense that at the time of the commission of the crime charged he was at some place or places other than the scene of the crime, and to call witnesses in support of such defense, he must within ten days of service of such demand, serve upon such agency, and file a copy thereof with the court, a "notice of alibi," reciting; (a) the place or places where the respondent claims to have been at the time in question, and (b) the names, the residential addresses, the places of employment and the addresses thereof of every such alibi witness upon whom he intends to rely. For good cause shown, the court may extend the period for service of the notice.

2.　Within a reasonable time after receipt of the respondent's witness list but not later than ten days before the fact-finding hearing, the presentment agency must serve upon the respondent and file a copy thereof with the court, a list of witnesses such agency proposes to offer in rebuttal to discredit the respondent's alibi at the trial together with the residential addresses, the places of employment and the addresses thereof of any such rebuttal witnesses. A witness who will testify that the respondent was at the scene of the crime is not such an alibi rebuttal witness. For good cause shown, the court may extend the period for service.

3.　If at the trial the respondent calls such an alibi witness without having served the demanded notice of alibi, or if having served such a notice he calls a witness not specified therein, the court may exclude any testimony of such witness relating to the alibi defense. The court may in its discretion receive such testimony, but before doing so, it must, upon application of the presentment agency, grant a reasonable adjournment.

4.　Similarly, if the presentment agency fails to serve and file a list of any rebuttal witnesses, the provisions of subdivision three shall reciprocally apply.

5.　Both the respondent and the presentment agency shall be under a continuing duty to promptly disclose the names and addresses of additional witnesses which come to the attention of either party subsequent to filing his witness list as provided in this section.

Part 4.　The fact-finding hearing.

§ 340.1.   Time of fact-finding hearing.

1.   If the respondent is in detention and the highest count in the petition charges the commission of a class A, B, or C felony, the fact-finding hearing shall commence not more than fourteen days after the conclusion of the initial appearance except as provided in subdivision four. If the respondent is in detention and the highest count in such petition is less than a class C felony the fact-finding hearing shall commence no more than three days after the conclusion of the initial appearance except as provided in subdivision four.

2.   If the respondent is not in detention the fact-finding hearing shall commence not more than sixty days after the conclusion of the initial appearance except as provided in subdivision four.

3.   For the purposes of this section, in any case where a proceeding has been removed to the family court pursuant to an order issued pursuant to section 725.05 of the criminal procedure law, the date specified in such order for the defendant's appearance in the family court shall constitute the date of initial appearance.

4.   The court may adjourn a fact-finding hearing:

(a)   on its own motion or on motion of the presentment agency for good cause shown for not more than three days if the respondent is in detention and not more than thirty days if the respondent is not in detention; provided, however, that if there is probable cause to believe the respondent committed a homicide or a crime which resulted in a person being incapacitated from attending court, the court may adjourn the hearing for a reasonable length of time; or

(b)   on motion by the respondent for good cause shown for not more than thirty days; or

(c)   on its own motion for not more than six months if the proceeding has been adjourned in contemplation of dismissal pursuant to section 315.3.

5. The court shall state on the record the reason for any adjournment of the fact-finding hearing.

6. Successive motions to adjourn a fact-finding hearing shall not be granted in the absence of showing, on the record, of special circumstances; such circumstances shall not include calendar congestion or the status of the court's docket or backlog.

7. For purposes of this section, if a warrant for the respondent's arrest has been issued pursuant to section 312.2 of this article due to the respondent's failure to appear for a scheduled fact-finding hearing, computation of the time within which such hearing must take place shall exclude the period extending from the date of issuance of the bench warrant for respondent's arrest because of his or her failure to appear to the date the respondent subsequently appears in court pursuant to a bench warrant or appears voluntarily; provided, however, no period of time may be excluded hereunder unless the respondent's location cannot be determined by the exercise of due diligence or, if the respondent's location is known, his or her presence in court cannot be obtained by the exercise of due diligence. In determining whether due diligence has been exercised, the court shall consider, among other factors, the report presented to the court pursuant to subdivision two of section 312.2 of this article.

Amended by Laws 1985, Ch. 663, eff. Aug. 27, 1985; Laws 1990, Ch. 223, eff. June 13, 1990; Laws 1994, Ch. 501, § 3, eff. July 26, 1994.

§ 340.2. Presiding judge.

1. The judge who presides at the commencement of the fact-finding hearing shall continue to preside until such hearing is concluded and an order entered pursuant to section 345.1 unless a mistrial is declared.

2. The judge who presides at the fact-finding hearing or accepts an admission pursuant to section 321.3 shall preside at any other subsequent hearing in the proceeding, including but not limited to the dispositional hearing.

3. Notwithstanding the provisions of subdivision two, the rules of the family court shall provide for the assignment of the proceeding to another judge of the court when the appropriate judge cannot preside:

(a) by reason of illness, disability, vacation or no longer being a judge of the court in that county; or

(b) by reason of removal from the proceeding due to bias, prejudice or similar grounds; or

(c) because it is not practicable for the judge to preside.

4. The provisions of this section shall not be waived.

Amended by Laws 1999, Ch. 173, § 2, eff. July 6, 1999.

§ 341.1. Exclusion of general public.

The general public may be excluded from any proceeding under this article and only such persons and the representatives of authorized agencies as have a direct interest in the case shall be admitted thereto.

§ 341.2. Presence of respondent and his parent.

1. The respondent and his counsel or law guardian shall be personally present at any hearing under this article and at the initial appearance.

2. If a respondent conducts himself in so disorderly and disruptive a manner that the hearing cannot be carried on with him in the courtroom, the court may order a recess for the purpose of enabling his parent or other person responsible for his care and his law guardian or counsel to exercise full efforts to assist the respondent to conduct himself so as to permit the proceedings to resume in an orderly manner. If such efforts fail, the respondent may be removed from the courtroom if, after he is warned by the court that he will be removed, he continues such disorderly and disruptive conduct. Such time shall not extend beyond the minimum period necessary to restore order.

3. The respondent's parent or other person responsible for his care shall be present at any hearing under this article and at the initial appearance. However, the court shall not be prevented from proceeding by the absence of such parent or person if reasonable and substantial effort has been made to notify such parent or other person and if the respondent and his law guardian or counsel are present.

§ 342.1. The fact-finding hearing; order of procedure.

The order of the fact-finding hearing shall be as follows:

1. The court shall permit the parties to deliver opening addresses. If both parties deliver opening addresses, the presentment agency's address shall be delivered first.

2. The presentment agency must offer evidence in support of the petition.

3. The respondent may offer evidence in his defense.

4. The presentment agency may offer evidence in rebuttal of the respondent's evidence, and the respondent may then offer evidence in rebuttal of the presentment agency's evidence. The court may in its discretion permit the parties to offer further rebuttal or surrebuttal evidence in this pattern. In the interest of justice, the court may permit either party to offer evidence upon rebuttal which is not technically of a rebuttal nature but more properly a part of the offering party's original case.

5. At the conclusion of the evidence, the respondent shall have the right to deliver a summation.

6. The presentment agency shall then have the right to deliver a summation.

7. The court must then consider the case and enter a finding.

§ 342.2. Evidence in fact-finding hearings; required quantum.

1. Only evidence that is competent, material and relevant may be admitted at a fact-finding hearing.

2. Any determination at the conclusion of a fact-finding hearing that a respondent committed an act or acts which if committed by an adult would be a crime must be based on proof beyond a reasonable doubt.

3. An order of removal pursuant to a direction authorized by sections 220.10, 310.85 and 330.25 of the criminal procedure law constitutes proof beyond a reasonable doubt and a determination that the respondent did the act or acts specified therein in accordance with section 725.05 of the criminal procedure law.

§ 343.1. Rules of evidence; testimony given by children.

1. Any person may be a witness in a delinquency proceeding unless the court finds that, by reason of infancy or mental disease or defect, he does not possess sufficient intelligence or capacity to justify reception of his evidence.

2. Every witness more than nine years old may testify only under oath unless the court is satisfied that such witness cannot, as a result of mental disease or defect, understand the nature of an oath. A witness less than nine years old may not testify under oath unless the court is satisfied that he or she understands the nature of an oath. If under either of the above provisions, a witness is deemed to be ineligible to testify under oath, the witness may nevertheless be permitted to give unsworn evidence if the court is satisfied that the witness possesses sufficient intelligence and capacity to justify the reception thereof.

3. A respondent may not be found to be delinquent solely upon the unsworn evidence given pursuant to subdivision two.

4. A child witness may give testimony in accordance with the provisions of article sixty-five of the criminal procedure law, provided such child is declared vulnerable in accordance with subdivision one of section 65.10 of such law. A child witness means a person fourteen years old or less who is or will be called to testify in any proceeding concerning an act defined in article one hundred thirty of the penal law or section 255.25, 255.26 or 255.27 of such law, which act would constitute a crime if committed by an adult. The provisions of this subdivision shall expire and be deemed repealed on the same date as article sixty-five of the criminal procedure law expires and is deemed repealed pursuant to section five of chapter five hundred five of the laws of nineteen hundred eighty-five, as from time to time, amended.

Amended by Laws 1988, Ch. 331, § 1, eff. Nov. 1, 1988; Laws 2003, Ch. 264, § 61, amending sub. 2, eff. Nov. 1, 2003; Laws 2004, Ch. 362, § 1, amending sub. 4, eff. Nov. 1, 2004; Laws 2006, Ch. 320, §27, eff. Nov 1, 2006.

§ 343.2.   Rules of evidence; corroboration of accomplice testimony.

1.   A respondent may not be found to be delinquent upon the testimony of an accomplice unsupported by corroborative evidence tending to connect the respondent with the commission of the crime or crimes charged in the petition.

2.   An "accomplice" means a witness in a juvenile delinquency proceeding who, according to evidence adduced in such proceeding, may reasonably be considered to have participated in:

(a)   the crime charged; or

(b)   a crime based on the same or some of the same facts or conduct which constitutes the crime charged in the petition.

3.   A witness who is an accomplice as defined in subdivision two is no less such because a proceeding, conviction or finding of delinquency against him would be barred or precluded by some defense or exemption such as infancy, immunity or previous prosecution amounting to a collateral impediment to such proceeding, conviction or finding, not affecting the conclusion that such witness engaged in the conduct constituting the crime with the mental state required for the commission thereof.

§ 343.3.   Rules of evidence; identification by means of previous recognition in absence of present identification.

1.   In any juvenile delinquency proceeding in which the respondent's commission of a crime is in issue, testimony as provided in subdivision two may be given by a witness when:

(a)   such witness testifies that:

(i)   he observed the person claimed by the presentment agency to be the respondent either at the time and place of the commission of the crime or upon some other occasion relevant to the case; and

(ii)   on a subsequent occasion he observed, under circumstances consistent with such rights as an accused person may derive under the constitution of this state or of the United States, a person whom he recognized as the same person whom he had observed on the first incriminating occasion; and

(iii)   he is unable at the proceeding to state, on the basis of present recollection, whether or not the respondent is the person in question; and

(b)   it is established that the respondent is in fact the person whom the witness observed and recognized on the second occasion. Such fact may be established by testimony of another person or persons to whom the witness promptly declared his recognition on such occasion.

2.   Under circumstances prescribed in subdivision one, such witness may testify at the proceeding that the person whom he observed and recognized on the second occasion is the same person whom he observed on the first or incriminating occasion. Such testimony, together with the evidence that the

respondent is in fact the person whom the witness observed and recognized on the second occasion, constitutes evidence in chief.

§ 343.4. Rules of evidence; identification by means of previous recognition, in addition to present identification.

In any juvenile delinquency proceeding in which the respondent's commission of a crime is in issue, a witness who testifies that:

(a) he observed the person claimed by the presentment agency to be the respondent either at the time and place of the commission of the crime or upon some other occasion relevant to the case, and

(b) on the basis of present recollection, the respondent is the person in question, and

(c) on a subsequent occasion he observed the respondent, under circumstances consistent with such rights as an accused person may derive under the constitution of this state or of the United States, and then also recognized him as the same person whom he had observed on the first or incriminating occasion, may, in addition to making an identification of the respondent at the delinquency proceeding on the basis of present recollection as the person whom he observed on the first or incriminating occasion, also describe his previous recognition of the respondent and testify that the person whom he observed on such second occasion is the same person whom he had observed on the first or incriminating occasion. Such testimony constitutes evidence in chief.

§ 343.5. Rules of evidence; impeachment of own witness by proof of prior contradictory statement.

1. When, upon examination by the party who called him, a witness in a delinquency proceeding gives testimony upon a material issue of the case which tends to disprove the position of such party, such party may introduce evidence that such witness has previously made either a written statement signed by him or an oral statement under oath contradictory to such testimony.

2. Evidence concerning a prior contradictory statement introduced pursuant to subdivision one may be received only for the purpose of impeaching the credibility of the witness with respect to his testimony upon the subject, and does not constitute evidence in chief.

3. When a witness has made a prior signed or sworn statement contradictory to his testimony in a delinquency proceeding upon a material issue of the case, but his testimony does not tend to disprove the position of the party who called him and elicited such testimony, evidence that the witness made such prior statement is not admissible, and such party may not use such prior statement for the purpose of refreshing the recollection of the witness in a manner that discloses its contents to the court.

§ 344.1. Rules of evidence; proof of previous conviction or delinquency finding.

1. If in the course of a juvenile delinquency proceeding, any witness, including a respondent, is properly asked whether he was previously convicted of a specified offense and answers in the negative or in an equivocal manner, the party adverse to the one who called him may independently prove such conviction. If in response to proper inquiry whether he has ever been convicted of any offense the witness answers in the negative or in an equivocal manner, the adverse party may independently prove any previous conviction.

2. If a respondent in a juvenile delinquency proceeding, through the testimony of a witness other than respondent called by him, offers evidence of his good character, the presentment agency may independently prove any previous finding of delinquency of the respondent for a crime the commission of which would tend to negate any character trait or quality attributed to the respondent in such witness' testimony.

§ 344.2. Rules of evidence; statements of respondent; corroboration.

1. Evidence of a written or oral confession, admission, or other statement made by a respondent with respect to his participation or lack of participation in the crime charged, may not be received in evidence against him in a juvenile delinquency proceeding if such statement was involuntarily made.

2. A confession, admission or other statement is "involuntarily made" by a respondent when it is obtained from him:

(a) by any person by the use or threatened use of physical force upon the respondent or another person, or by means of any other improper conduct or undue pressure which impaired the respondent's physical or mental condition to the extent of undermining his ability to make a choice whether or not to make a statement; or

(b) by a public servant engaged in law enforcement activity or by a person then acting under his direction or in cooperation with him;

(i) by means of any promise or statement of fact, which promise or statement creates a substantial risk that the respondent might falsely incriminate himself; or

(ii) in violation of such rights as the respondent may derive from the constitution of this state or of the United States; or

(iii) in violation of section 305.2.

3. A child may not be found to be delinquent based on the commission of any crime solely upon evidence of a confession or admission made by him without additional proof that the crime charged has been committed.

§ 344.3. Rules of evidence; psychiatric testimony in certain cases.

When, in connection with a defense of mental disease or defect, a psychiatrist or licensed psychologist who has examined the respondent testifies at the fact-finding hearing concerning the respondent's mental condition at the time of the conduct charged to constitute a crime, he must be permitted to make a statement as to the nature of the examination, the diagnosis of the mental condition of the respondent and his opinion as to the extent, if any, to which the capacity of the respondent to know or appreciate the nature and consequences of such conduct, or its wrongfulness, was impaired as a result of mental disease or defect at that time. The psychiatrist must be permitted to make any explanation reasonably serving to clarify his diagnosis and opinion, and may be cross-examined as to any matter bearing on his competency or credibility or the validity of his diagnosis or opinion.

§ 344.4. Rules of evidence; admissibility of evidence of victim's sexual conduct in sex offense cases.

Evidence of a victim's sexual conduct shall not be admissible in a juvenile delinquency proceeding for a crime or an attempt to commit a crime defined in article one hundred thirty of the penal law unless such evidence:

1. proves or tends to prove specific instances of the victim's prior sexual conduct with the accused; or

2. proves or tends to prove that the victim has been convicted of an offense under section 230.00 of the penal law within three years prior to the sex offense which is the subject of the juvenile delinquency proceeding; or

3. rebuts evidence introduced by the presentment agency of the victim's failure to engage in sexual intercourse, oral sexual conduct, anal sexual conduct or sexual contact during a given period of time; or

4. rebuts evidence introduced by the presentment agency which proves or tends to prove that the accused is the cause of pregnancy or disease of the victim, or the source of semen found in the victim; or

5. is determined by the court after an offer of proof by the accused, or such hearing as the court may require, and a statement by the court of its findings of fact essential to its determination, to be relevant and admissible in the interests of justice.

Added by Laws 1987, Ch. 761, eff. Nov. 1, 1987; **amended** by Laws 2003, Ch. 264, § 62, amending sub. 3, eff. Nov. 1, 2003.

§ 345.1. Orders.

1. If the allegations of a petition or specific counts of a petition concerning the commission of a crime or crimes are established, the court shall enter an appropriate order and schedule a dispositional hearing pursuant to section 350.1.

The order shall specify the count or counts of the petition upon which such order is based and the section or sections of the penal law or other law under which the act or acts so stated would constitute a crime if committed by an adult. If the respondent or respondents are found to have committed a designated felony act, the order shall so state.

2. If the allegations of a petition or specific counts of a petition under this article are not established, the court shall enter an order dismissing the petition or specific counts therein.

§ 346.1. Fact-finding hearing; removal.

Where the proceeding was commenced by the filing of an order of removal pursuant to a direction authorized by section 220.10, 310.85 or 330.25 of the criminal procedure law, the requirements of a fact-finding hearing shall be deemed to have been satisfied upon the filing of the order and no further fact-finding hearing need be held; provided, however, that where any specification required by subdivision five of section 725.05 of the criminal procedure law is not clear, the court may examine such records or hold such hearing as it deems necessary to clarify said specification.

§ 347.1. Required testing of the respondent in certain proceedings.

1. (a) In any proceeding where the respondent is found pursuant to section 345.1 or 346.1 of this article, to have committed a felony offense enumerated in any section of article one hundred thirty of the penal law, or any subdivision of section 130.20 of such law, for which an act of "sexual intercourse", "oral sexual conduct", or "anal sexual conduct", as those terms are defined in section 130.00 of the penal law, is required as an essential element for the commission thereof, the court must, upon a request of the victim, order that the respondent submit to human immunodeficiency (HIV) related testing. The testing is to be conducted by a state, county, or local public health officer designated by the order. Test results, which shall not be disclosed to the court, shall be communicated to the respondent and the victim named in the order in accordance with the provisions of section twenty-seven hundred eighty-five-a of the public health law.

(b) For the purposes of this section, the term "victim" means the person with whom the respondent engaged in an act of "sexual intercourse", "oral sexual conduct", or "anal sexual conduct", as those terms are defined in section 130.00 of the penal law, where such conduct with such victim was the basis for the court's finding that the respondent committed acts constituting one or more of the offenses specified in paragraph (a) of this subdivision.

2. Any request made by the victim pursuant to this section must be in writing, filed with the court and provided by the court to the defendant and his or her counsel. The request must be filed with the court prior to or within ten days after the filing of an order in accordance with section 345.1 or 346.1 of this article,

provided that, for good cause shown, the court may permit such request to be filed at any time prior to the entry of an order of disposition.

3.   Any requests, related papers and orders made or filed pursuant to this section, together with any papers or proceedings related thereto, shall be sealed by the court and not made available for any purpose, except as may be necessary for the conduct of judicial proceedings directly related to the provisions of this section. All proceedings on such requests shall be held in camera.

4.   The application for an order to compel a respondent to undergo an HIV related test may be made by the victim but, if the victim is an infant or incompetent person, the application may also be made by a representative as defined in section twelve hundred one of the civil practice law and rules. The application must state that (a) the applicant was the victim of the offense, enumerated in paragraph (a) of subdivision one of this section, which the court found the defendant to have committed; and (b) the applicant has been offered counseling by a public health officer and been advised of (i) the limitations on the information to be obtained through an HIV test on the proposed subject; (ii) current scientific assessments of the risk of transmission of HIV from the exposure he or she may have experienced; and (iii) the need for the applicant to undergo HIV related testing to definitively determine his or her HIV status.

5.   The court shall conduct a hearing only if necessary to determine if the applicant is the victim of the offense the respondent was found to have committed. The court ordered test must be performed within fifteen days of the date on which the court ordered the test, provided however that whenever the respondent is not tested within the period prescribed by the court, the court must again order that the respondent undergo an HIV related test.

6.   (a) Test results shall be disclosed subject to the following limitations, which shall be specified in any order issued pursuant to this section:

(i)   disclosure of confidential HIV related information shall be limited to that information which is necessary to fulfill the purpose for which the order is granted;

(ii)   disclosure of confidential HIV related information shall be limited to the person making the application; redisclosure shall be permitted only to the victim, the victim's immediate family, guardian, physicians, attorneys, medical or mental health providers and to his or her past and future contacts to whom there was or is a reasonable risk of HIV transmission and shall not be permitted to any other person or the court.

(b)   Unless inconsistent with this section, the court's order shall direct compliance with and conform to the provisions of article twenty seven-f of the public health law. Such order shall include measures to protect against disclosure to others of the identity and HIV status of the applicant and of the person tested and may include such other measures as the court deems necessary to protect confidential information.

7. Any failure to comply with the provisions of this section or section twenty-seven hundred eighty-five-a of the public health law shall not impair the validity of any order of disposition entered by the court.

8. No information obtained as a result of a consent, hearing or court order for testing issued pursuant to this section nor any information derived therefrom may be used as evidence in any criminal or civil proceeding against the respondent which relates to events that were the basis for the respondent's conviction, provided however that nothing herein shall prevent prosecution of a witness testifying in any court hearing held pursuant to this section for perjury pursuant to article two hundred ten of the penal law.

Added by Laws 1995, Ch. 76, § 2, eff. Aug. 1, 1995; **amended** by Laws 2003, Ch. 264, § 63, amending sub. 1, eff. Nov. 1, 2003.

Part 5. The dispositional hearing.

(Repealed and transferred sections noted under appropriate section number of text.)

---

§ 350.1. Time of dispositional hearing.

1. If the respondent is detained and has not been found to have committed a designated felony act the dispositional hearing shall commence not more than

ten days after the entry of an order pursuant to subdivision one of section 345.1. except as provided in subdivision three.

2.   In all other cases, the dispositional hearing shall commence not more than fifty days after entry of an order pursuant to subdivision one of section 345.1, except as provided in subdivision three.

3.   The court may adjourn the dispositional hearing:

(a)   on its own motion or on motion of the presentment agency for good cause shown for not more than ten days; or

(b)   on motion by the respondent for good cause shown for not more than thirty days.

4.   The court shall state on the record the reason for any adjournment of the dispositional hearing.

5.   Successive motions to adjourn a dispositional hearing beyond the limits enumerated in subdivision one or two shall not be granted in the absence of a showing, on the record, of special circumstances; special circumstances shall not include calendar congestion or the status of the court's docket or backlog.

Amended by Laws 1982, Ch. 926, eff. July 1, 1983; Laws 1983, Ch. 398, eff. July 1, 1983.

§ 350.2.   Order of removal.

1.   Where the proceeding has been commenced by the filing of an order of removal pursuant to a direction authorized by sections 220.10, 310.85 and 330.25 of the criminal procedure law, the date of filing in the family court shall be deemed for purposes of section 350.1 to be the date of the entry of an order pursuant to subdivision one of section 345.1.

2.   The clerk of court shall calendar an appearance to be held within seven days from the date the order of removal was filed. At such appearance the court shall schedule a dispositional hearing in accordance with section 350.1 and determine such other issues as may properly be before it.

§ 350.3.   Dispositional hearings; evidence and required quantum of proof—appearance of presentment agency.

1.   Only evidence that is material and relevant may be admitted during a dispositional hearing.

2.   An adjudication at the conclusion of a dispositional hearing must be based on a preponderance of the evidence.

3.   The presentment agency shall appear at the dispositional hearing.

§ 350.4.   Order of procedure.

The order of the dispositional hearing shall be as follows:

1. The court, with the consent of the parties, may direct the probation service to summarize its investigation report if one has been prepared and, in its discretion, deliver any further statement concerning the advisability of specific dispositional alternatives.

2. The court may in its discretion call witnesses, including the preparer of probation reports or diagnostic studies, to offer evidence concerning the advisability of specific dispositional alternatives. Such witnesses may be cross-examined by the presentment agency and the respondent.

3. The presentment agency may call witnesses to offer such evidence including the preparer of a probation report or a diagnostic study.

4. The respondent may call witnesses, to offer such evidence, including the preparer of a probation report or a diagnostic study.

5. The court may permit the presentment agency or respondent to offer such rebuttal or surrebuttal evidence as it may deem appropriate.

6. The presentment agency may deliver a statement concerning the advisability of specific dispositional alternatives.

7. The respondent may deliver such a statement.

8. The court shall then permit rebuttal statements by both the presentment agency and the respondent.

9. The court shall then consider the case and enter a dispositional order.

   Amended by Laws 1982, Ch. 926, eff. July 1, 1983; Laws 1983, Ch. 398, eff. July 1, 1983.

§ 351.1. Probation, investigation and diagnostic assessment.

1. Following a determination that a respondent has committed a designated felony act and prior to the dispositional hearing, the judge shall order a probation investigation and a diagnostic assessment. For the purposes of this article, the probation investigation shall include, but not be limited to, the history of the juvenile including previous conduct, the family situation, any previous psychological and psychiatric reports, school adjustment, previous social assistance provided by voluntary or public agencies and the response of the juvenile to such assistance. For the purposes of this article, the diagnostic assessment shall include, but not be limited to, psychological tests and psychiatric interviews to determine mental capacity and achievement, emotional stability and mental disabilities. It shall include a clinical assessment of the situational factors that may have contributed to the act or acts. When feasible, expert opinion shall be rendered as to the risk presented by the juvenile to others or himself, with a recommendation as to the need for a restrictive placement.

2. Following a determination that a respondent committed a crime and prior to the dispositional hearing, the court shall order a probation investigation and may order a diagnostic assessment.

3. A child shall not be placed in accord with section 353.3 unless the court has ordered a probation investigation prior to the dispositional hearing; a child shall not be placed in accord with section 353.4 unless the court has ordered a diagnostic assessment prior to such hearing.

4. When it appears that such information would be relevant to the findings of the court or the order of disposition, each investigation report prepared pursuant to this section shall contain a victim impact statement which shall include an analysis of the victim's version of the offense, the extent of injury or economic loss or damage to the victim, including the amount of unreimbursed medical expenses, if any, and the views of the victim relating to disposition including the amount of restitution sought by the victim, subject to availability of such information. In the case of a homicide or where the victim is unable to assist in the preparation of the victim impact statement, the information may be acquired from the victim's family. Nothing contained in this section shall be interpreted to require that a victim or his or her family supply information for the preparation of an investigation report or that the dispositional hearing should be delayed in order to obtain such information.

5. (a) All diagnostic assessments and probation investigation reports shall be submitted to the court and made available by the court for inspection and copying by the presentment agency and the respondent at least five court days prior to the commencement of the dispositional hearing. All such reports shall be made available by the court for inspection and copying by the presentment agency and the respondent in connection with any appeal in the case.

(b) The victim impact statement shall be made available to the victim or the victim's family by the presentment agency prior to sentencing.

6. All reports or memoranda prepared or obtained by the probation service for the purpose of a dispositional hearing shall be deemed confidential information furnished to the court and shall be subject to disclosure solely in accordance with this section or as otherwise provided for by law. Except as provided under section 320.5 such reports or memoranda shall not be furnished to the court prior to the entry of an order pursuant to section 345.1.

7. The probation services which prepare the investigation reports shall be responsible for the collection and transmission to the state division of probation and correctional alternatives, of data on the number of victim impact statements prepared, pursuant to regulations of the division. Such information shall be transmitted to the crime victims board and included in the board's annual report pursuant to subdivision twenty of section six hundred twenty-three of the executive law.

Amended by Laws 1983, Ch. 398, eff. July 1, 1983; Laws 1985, Ch. 585, eff. July 28, 1985; Laws 1985, Ch. 880, Laws 1987, Ch. 101; Laws 1989, Ch. 161; Laws 1991, Ch. 168, § 14, eff. June 28, 1991, which eliminated the expiration date of the 1985 amendment; Laws 1986, Ch. 418, eff. Nov. 1, 1986; Laws 2004, Ch. 317, § 1, amending sub. 4, eff. Nov. 8, 2004.

§ 352.1.　Findings.

1.　If, upon the conclusion of the dispositional hearing, the court determines that the respondent requires supervision, treatment or confinement, the court shall enter a finding that such respondent is a juvenile delinquent and order an appropriate disposition pursuant to section 352.2.

2.　If, upon the conclusion of the dispositional hearing, the court determines that the respondent does not require supervision, treatment or confinement, the petition shall be dismissed.

§ 352.2.　Order of disposition.

1.　Upon the conclusion of the dispositional hearing, the court shall enter an order of disposition:

(a)　conditionally discharging the respondent in accord with section 353.1; or

(b)　putting the respondent on probation in accord with section 353.2; or

(c)　continuing the proceeding and placing the respondent in accord with section 353.3; or

(d)　placing the respondent in accord with section 353.4; or

(e)　continuing the proceeding and placing the respondent under a restrictive placement in accord with section 353.5.

2.　(a) In determining an appropriate order the court shall consider the needs and best interests of the respondent as well as the need for protection of the community. If the respondent has committed a designated felony act the court shall determine the appropriate disposition in accord with section 353.5. In all other cases the court shall order the least restrictive available alternative enumerated in subdivision one which is consistent with the needs and best interests of the respondent and the need for protection of the community.

(b)　In an order of disposition entered pursuant to section 353.3 or 353.4 of this chapter, or where the court has determined pursuant to section 353.5 of this chapter that restrictive placement is not required, which order places the respondent with the commissioner of social services or with the office of children and family services for placement with an authorized agency or class of authorized agencies or in such facilities designated by the office of children and family services as are eligible for federal reimbursement pursuant to title IV-E of the social security act, the court in its order shall determine (i) that continuation in the respondent's home would be contrary to the best interests of the respondent; or in the case of a respondent for whom the court has determined that continuation in his or her home would not be contrary to the best interests of the respondent, that continuation in the respondent's home would be contrary to the need for protection of the community; (ii) that where appropriate, and where consistent with the need for protection of the community, reasonable efforts were made prior

FCA

to the date of the dispositional hearing to prevent or eliminate the need for removal of the respondent from his or her home, or if the child was removed from his or her home prior to the dispositional hearing where appropriate and where consistent with the need for safety of the community whether reasonable efforts were made to make it possible for the child to return safely home. If the court determines that reasonable efforts to prevent or eliminate the need for removal of the child from the home were not made but that the lack of such efforts was appropriate under the circumstances, or consistent with the need for protection of the community, or both, the court order shall include such a finding; and (iii) in the case of a child who has attained the age of sixteen, the services needed, if any, to assist the child to make the transition from foster care to independent living.

(c) For the purpose of this section, when an order is entered pursuant to section 353.3 or 353.4 of this article, reasonable efforts to prevent or eliminate the need for removing the respondent from the home of the respondent or to make it possible for the respondent to return safely to the home of the respondent shall not be required where the court determines that:

(1) the parent of such respondent has subjected the respondent to aggravated circumstances, as defined in subdivision fifteen of section 301.2 of this article;

(2) the parent of such child has been convicted of (i) murder in the first degree as defined in section 125.27 or murder in the second degree as defined in section 125.25 of the penal law and the victim was another child of the parent; or (ii) manslaughter in the first degree as defined in section 125.20 or manslaughter in the second degree as defined in section 125.15 of the penal law and the victim was another child of the parent, provided, however, that the parent must have acted voluntarily in committing such crime;

(3) the parent of such child has been convicted of an attempt to commit any of the foregoing crimes, and the victim or intended victim was the child or another child of the parent; or has been convicted of criminal solicitation as defined in article one hundred, conspiracy as defined in article one hundred five or criminal facilitation as defined in article one hundred fifteen of the penal law for conspiring, soliciting or facilitating any of the foregoing crimes, and the victim or intended victim was the child or another child of the parent;

(4) the parent of such respondent has been convicted of assault in the second degree as defined in section 120.05, assault in the first degree as defined in section 120.10 or aggravated assault upon a person less than eleven years old as defined in section 120.12 of the penal law, and the commission of one of the foregoing crimes resulted in serious physical injury to the respondent or another child of the parent;

(5) the parent of such respondent has been convicted in any other jurisdiction of an offense which includes all of the essential elements of any crime specified in subparagraph two, three or four of this paragraph, and the victim of such offense was the respondent or another child of the parent; or

(6) the parental rights of the parent to a sibling of such respondent have been involuntarily terminated; unless the court determines that providing reasonable efforts would be in the best interests of the child, not contrary to the health and safety of the child, and would likely result in the reunification of the parent and the child in the foreseeable future. The court shall state such findings in its order.

If the court determines that reasonable efforts are not required because of one of the grounds set forth above, a permanency hearing shall be held pursuant to section 355.5 of this article within thirty days of the finding of the court that such efforts are not required. The social services official or the office of children and family services, where the respondent was placed with such office, shall subsequent to the permanency hearing make reasonable efforts to place the respondent in a timely manner and to complete whatever steps are necessary to finalize the permanent placement of the respondent as set forth in the permanency plan approved by the court. If reasonable efforts are determined by the court not to be required because of one of the grounds set forth in this paragraph, the social services official may file a petition for termination of parental rights in accordance with section three hundred eighty-four-b of the social services law.

(d) For the purposes of this section, in determining reasonable efforts to be made with respect to the respondent, and in making such reasonable efforts, the respondent's health and safety shall be the paramount concern.

(e) For the purpose of this section, a sibling shall include a half-sibling.

3. The order shall state the court's reasons for the particular disposition, including, in the case of a restrictive placement pursuant to section 353.5, the specific findings of fact required in such section.

Amended by Laws 1985, Ch. 880; Laws 1987, Ch. 101; Laws 1989, Ch. 161; Ch. 198, eff. June 28, 1991; Laws 1988, Ch. 478, § 1, eff. Nov. 1, 1988; Laws 1991, Ch. 198, § 1, eff. June 28, 1991; Laws 1992, Ch. 465, § 33, eff. Jan. 13, 1993; Laws 1999, Ch. 7, § 29, eff. Feb. 11, 1999; Laws 2000, Ch. 145, §§ 9 and 10, eff. July 1, 2000.

§ 352.3. Order of protection.

(1) Upon the issuance of an order pursuant to section 315.3 or the entry of an order of disposition pursuant to section 352.2, a court may enter an order of protection against any respondent for good cause shown. The order may require that the respondent: (a) stay away from the home, school, business or place of employment of the victims of the alleged offense; or (b) refrain from harassing, intimidating, threatening or otherwise interfering with the victim or victims of the alleged offense and such members of the family or household of such victim or victims as shall be specifically named by the court in such order; or (c) refrain from intentionally injuring or killing, without justification, any companion animal the respondent knows to be owned, possessed, leased, kept or held by the petitioner or a minor child residing in the household. "Companion animal", as used in this subdivision, shall have the same meaning as in subdivision five of section three hundred fifty of the agriculture and markets law.

(2)   An order of protection shall remain in effect for the period specified by the court, but shall not exceed the period of time specified in any order of disposition or order adjourning a proceeding in contemplation of dismissal.

Added by Laws 1984, ch. 683, eff. Aug. 31, 1984; Laws 2006, Ch. 253, §1, eff. July 26, 2006.

§ 353.1.   Conditional discharge.

1.   The court may conditionally discharge the respondent if the court, having regard for the nature and circumstances of the crime and for the history, character and condition of the respondent, is of the opinion that consistent with subdivision two of section 352.2, neither the public interest nor the ends of justice would be served by a placement and that probation supervision is not appropriate.

2.   When the court orders a conditional discharge the respondent shall be released with respect to the finding upon which such order is based without placement or probation supervision but subject, during the period of conditional discharge, to such conditions enumerated in subdivision two of section 353.2, as the court may determine. The court shall order the period of conditional discharge authorized by subdivision three and shall specify the conditions to be complied with. The court may modify or enlarge the conditions at any time prior to the expiration or termination of the period of conditional discharge. Such action may not, however, be taken unless the respondent is personally present, except that the respondent need not be present if the modification consists solely of the elimination or relaxation of one or more conditions.

3.   The maximum period of a conditional discharge shall not exceed one year.

4.   The respondent must be given a written copy of the conditions at the time a conditional discharge is ordered or modified, provided, however, that whenever the respondent has not been personally present at the time of a modification, the court shall notify the respondent in writing within twenty days after such modification, specifying the nature of the elimination or relaxation of any condition and the effective date thereof. A copy of such conditions must be filed with and become part of the record of the case.

5.   A finding that the respondent committed an additional crime after the conditional discharge has been ordered and prior to expiration and termination of the period of such order constitutes a ground for revocation of such order irrespective of whether such fact is specified as a condition of the order.

Amended by Laws 1983, Ch. 398, eff. July 1, 1983.

§ 353.2.   Probation.

1.   The court may order a period of probation if the court, having regard for the nature and circumstances of the crime and the history, character and condition of the respondent, is of the opinion that:

(a)   placement of respondent is not or may not be necessary;

(b)   the respondent is in need of guidance, training or other assistance which can be effectively administered through probation; and

(c)   such disposition is consistent with the provisions of subdivision two of section 352.2.

2.   When ordering a period of probation or a conditional discharge pursuant to section 353.1, the court may, as a condition of such order require that the respondent:

(a)   attend school regularly and obey all rules and regulations of the school;

(b)   obey all reasonable commands of the parent or other person legally responsible for the respondent's care;

(c)   abstain from visiting designated places or associating with named individuals;

(d)   avoid injurious or vicious activities;

(e)   co-operate with a mental health, social services or other appropriate community facility or agency to which the respondent is referred;

(f)   make restitution or perform services for the public good pursuant to section 353.6 provided the respondent is over ten years of age;

(g)   except when the respondent has been assigned to a facility in accordance with subdivision four of section five hundred four of the executive law, in cases wherein the record indicates that the consumption of alcohol by the respondent may have been a contributing factor, attend and complete an alcohol awareness program established pursuant to section 19.25 of the mental hygiene law; and

(h)   comply with such other reasonable conditions as the court shall determine to be necessary or appropriate to ameliorate the conduct which gave rise to the filing of the petition or to prevent placement with the commissioner of social services or the division for youth.

3.   When ordering a period of probation, the court may, as a condition of such order, further require that the respondent:

(a)   meet with a probation officer when directed to do so by that officer and permit the officer to visit the respondent at home or elsewhere;

(b)   permit the probation officer to obtain information from any person or agency from whom respondent is receiving or was directed to receive diagnosis, treatment or counseling;

(c)   permit the probation officer to obtain information from the respondent's school;

(d)   co-operate with the probation officer in seeking to obtain and in accepting employment, and supply records and reports of earnings to the officer when requested to do so;

(e) obtain permission from the probation officer for any absence from respondent's residence in excess of two weeks; and

(f) with the consent of the division for youth, spend a specified portion of the probation period, not exceeding one year, in a nonsecure facility provided by the division for youth pursuant to article nineteen-g of the executive law.

4. A finding that the respondent committed an additional crime after probation supervision has been ordered and prior to expiration or termination of the period of such order constitutes a ground for revocation of such order irrespective of whether such fact is specified as a condition of such order.

5. The respondent must be given a written copy of the conditions at the time probation supervision is ordered. A copy of such conditions must be filed with and become part of the record of the case.

6. The maximum period of probation shall not exceed two years. If the court finds at the conclusion of the original period and after a hearing that exceptional circumstances require an additional year of probation, the court may continue the probation for an additional year.

Amended by Laws 1983, Ch. 398, eff. July 1, 1983; Laws 1985 Ch. 880; Laws 1987, Ch. 101; Laws 1989, Ch. 161; Laws 1991, Ch. 168, § 14, eff. June 28, 1991, which eliminated the expiration date of the 1985 amendment; Laws 1992, Ch. 465, § 34, eff. Jan. 13, 1993; Laws 1993, Ch. 124, § 2, eff. June 21, 1993.

§ 353.3. Placement.

1. In accordance with section 352.2, the court may place the respondent in his own home or in the custody of a suitable relative or other suitable private person or the commissioner of social services or the division for youth pursuant to article nineteen-G of the executive law, subject to the orders of the court.

2. Where the respondent is placed with the commissioner of social services, the court may direct the commissioner to place him with an authorized agency or class of authorized agencies. Unless the dispositional order provides otherwise, the court so directing shall include one of the following alternatives to apply in the event that the commissioner is unable to so place the respondent:

(a) the commissioner shall apply to the court for an order to stay, modify, set aside, or vacate such directive pursuant to the provisions of section 355.1; or

(b) the commissioner shall return the respondent to the family court for a new dispositional hearing and order.

3. Where the respondent is placed with the division for youth, the court shall, unless it directs the division to place him with an authorized agency or class of authorized agencies pursuant to subdivision four authorize the division to do one of the following:

(a) place the respondent in a secure facility without a further hearing at any time or from time to time during the first sixty days of residency in division for youth facilities. Notwithstanding the discretion of the division to place the respondent in a secure facility at any time during the first sixty days of residency in a division for youth facility, the respondent may be placed in a nonsecure facility. In the event that the division desires to transfer a respondent to a secure facility at any time after the first sixty days of residency in division facilities, a hearing shall be held pursuant to subdivision three of section five hundred four-a of the executive law; or

(b)　place the respondent in a limited secure facility. The respondent may be transferred by the division to a secure facility after a hearing is held pursuant to section five hundred four-a of the executive law; provided, however, that during the first twenty days of residency in division facilities, the respondent shall not be transferred to a secure facility unless the respondent has committed an act or acts which are exceptionally dangerous to the respondent or to others; or

(c)　place the respondent in a nonsecure facility. No respondent placed pursuant to this paragraph may be transferred by the division for youth to a secure facility.

4.　Where the respondent is placed with the division for youth, the court may direct the division to place the respondent with an authorized agency or class of authorized agencies and in the event the division is unable to so place the respondent or, discontinues the placement with the authorized agency, the respondent shall be deemed to have been placed with the division pursuant to paragraph (b) or (c) of subdivision three of this section. In such cases, the division shall notify the court, presentment agency, law guardian and parent or other person responsible for the respondent's care, of the reason for discontinuing the placement with the authorized agency and the level and location of the youth's placement.

5.　If the respondent has committed a felony the initial period of placement shall not exceed eighteen months. If the respondent has committed a misdemeanor such initial period of placement shall not exceed twelve months. If the respondent has been in detention pending disposition, the initial period of placement ordered under this section shall be credited with and diminished by the amount of time spent by the respondent in detention prior to the commencement of the placement unless the court finds that all or part of such credit would not serve the needs and best interests of the respondent or the need for protection of the community.

6.　The court may at any time conduct a hearing in accordance with section 355.1 concerning the need for continuing a placement.

7.　The place in which or the person with whom the respondent has been placed under this section shall submit a report to the court, law guardian or attorney of record, and presentment agency at the conclusion of the placement period, except as provided in paragraphs (a) and (b) of this subdivision. Such report shall include recommendations and such supporting data as is appropriate. The court may extend a placement pursuant to section 355.3 of this article.

FCA

(a) Where the respondent is placed pursuant to subdivision two or three of this section and where the agency is not seeking an extension of the placement pursuant to section 355.3 of this article, such report shall be submitted not later than thirty days prior to the conclusion of the placement.

(b) Where the respondent is placed pursuant to subdivision two or three of this section and where the agency is seeking an extension of the placement pursuant to section 355.3 of this article and a permanency hearing pursuant to section 355.5 of this article, such report shall be submitted not later than sixty days prior to the date on which the permanency hearing must be held and shall be annexed to the petition for a permanency hearing and extension of placement.

(c) Where the respondent is placed pursuant to subdivision two or three of this section, such report shall contain a plan for the release, or conditional release (pursuant to section five hundred ten-a of the executive law), of the respondent to the custody of his or her parent or other person legally responsible, to independent living or to another permanency alternative as provided in paragraph (d) of subdivision seven of section 355.5 of this article. If the respondent is subject to article sixty-five of the education law or elects to participate in an educational program leading to a high school diploma, such plan shall include, but not be limited to, the steps that the agency with which the respondent is placed has taken and will be taking to facilitate the enrollment of the respondent in a school or educational program leading to a high school diploma following release, or, if such release occurs during the summer recess, upon the commencement of the next school term. If the respondent is not subject to article sixty-five of the education law and does not elect to participate in an educational program leading to a high school diploma, such plan shall include, but not be limited to, the steps that the agency with which the respondent is placed has taken and will be taking to assist the respondent to become gainfully employed or enrolled in a vocational program following release.

8. In its discretion, the court may recommend restitution or require services for the public good pursuant to section 353.6 in conjunction with an order of placement.

9. If the court places a respondent with the division for youth pursuant to this section after finding that such child committed a felony the court may, in its discretion, further order that such respondent shall be confined in a residential facility for a minimum period set by the order, not to exceed six months.

10. A placement pursuant to this section with the commissioner of social services shall not be directed in any detention facility, but the court may direct detention pending transfer to a placement authorized and ordered under this section for no more than thirty days after the order of placement is made or in a city of one million or more, for no more than fifteen days after such order of placement is made. Such direction shall be subject to extension pursuant to subdivision three of section three hundred ninety-eight of the social services law.

Amended by Laws 1987, Ch. 419, eff. Sept. 1, 1987; Laws 1992, Ch. 465, § 35, eff. Jan. 13, 1993; Laws 2000, Ch. 181, § 19, eff. Jan. 1, 2001, amending subsection (7).

§ 353.4.   Transfer of certain juvenile delinquents.

1.   If at the conclusion of the dispositional hearing and in accordance with section 352.2 the court finds that the respondent has a mental illness, mental retardation or developmental disability, as defined in section 1.03 of the mental hygiene law, which is likely to result in serious harm to himself or others, the court may issue an order placing such respondent with the division for youth or, with the consent of the local commissioner, with a local commissioner of social services. Any such order shall direct the temporary transfer for admission of the respondent to the custody of either the commissioner of mental health or the commissioner of mental retardation and developmental disabilities who shall arrange the admission of the respondent to the appropriate facility of the department of mental hygiene. The director of a hospital operated by the office of mental health may, subject to the provisions of section 9.51 of the mental hygiene law, transfer a person admitted to the hospital pursuant to this subdivision to a residential treatment facility for children and youth, as that term is defined in section 1.03 of the mental hygiene law, if care and treatment in such a facility would more appropriately meet the needs of the respondent. Persons temporarily transferred to such custody under this provision may be retained for care and treatment for a period of up to one year and whenever appropriate shall be transferred back to the division for youth pursuant to the provisions of section five hundred nine of the executive law or transferred back to the local commissioner of social services. Within thirty days of such transfer back, application shall be made by the division for youth or the local commissioner of social services to the placing court to conduct a further dispositional hearing at which the court may make any order authorized under section 352.2, except that the period of any further order of disposition shall take into account the period of placement hereunder. Likelihood to result in serious arm shall mean (a) substantial risk of physical harm to himself as manifested by threats or attempts at suicide or serious bodily harm or other conduct demonstrating he is dangerous to himself or (b) a substantial risk of physical harm to other persons as manifested by homicidal or other violent behavior by which others are placed in reasonable fear of serious bodily harm.

2.   (a) Where the order of disposition is for a restrictive placement under section 353.5 if the court at the dispositional hearing finds that the respondent has a mental illness, mental retardation or developmental disability, as defined in section 1.03 of the mental hygiene law, which is likely to result in serious harm to himself or others, the court may, as part of the order of disposition, direct the temporary transfer, for a period of up to one year, of the respondent to the custody of the commissioner of mental health or of mental retardation and developmental disabilities who shall arrange for the admission of the respondent to an appropriate facility under his jurisdiction within thirty days of such order. The director

FCA

of the facility so designated by the commissioner shall accept such respondent for admission.

(b) Persons transferred to the office of mental health or of mental retardation and developmental disabilities, pursuant to this subdivision, shall be retained by such office for care and treatment for the period designated by the court. At any time prior to the expiration of such period, if the director of the facility determines that the child is no longer mentally ill or no longer in need of active treatment, the responsible office shall make application to the family court for an order transferring the child back to the division for youth. Not more than thirty days before the expiration of such period, there shall be a hearing, at which time the court may:

(i) extend the temporary transfer of the respondent for an additional period of up to one year to the custody of the commissioner of mental health or the commissioner of mental retardation and developmental disabilities pursuant to this subdivision; or

(ii) continue the restrictive placement of the respondent in the custody of the division for youth.

(c) During such temporary transfer, the respondent shall continue to be under restrictive placement with the division for youth. Whenever the respondent is transferred back to the division the conditions of the placement as set forth in section 353.5 shall apply. Time spent by the respondent in the custody of the commissioner of mental health or the commissioner of mental retardation and developmental disabilities shall be credited and applied towards the period of placement.

3. No dispositional hearing at which proof of a mental disability as defined in section 1.03 of the mental hygiene law is to be offered shall be completed until the commissioner of mental health or commissioner of mental retardation and developmental disabilities, as appropriate, have been notified and afforded an opportunity to be heard at such dispositional hearing.

4. No order of disposition placing the respondent in accordance with this section shall be entered except upon clear and convincing evidence which shall include the testimony of two examining physicians as provided in section two hundred fifty one.

5. If the respondent has been in detention pending disposition, the initial period of placement ordered under this section shall be credited with and diminished by the amount of time spent by the respondent in detention prior to the commencement of the placement unless the court finds that all or part of such credit would not serve the needs and best interests of the respondent or the need for protection of the community.

Amended by Laws 1987, Ch. 419, eff. Sept. 1, 1987; Laws 1992, Ch. 465, §§ 36, 37, eff. Jan. 13, 1993.

§ 353.5. Designated felony acts; restrictive placement.

1. Where the respondent is found to have committed a designated felony act, the order of disposition shall be made within twenty days of the conclusion of the dispositional hearing and shall include a finding based on a preponderance of the evidence as to whether, for the purposes of this article, the respondent does or does not require a restrictive placement under this section, in connection with which the court shall make specific written findings of fact as to each of the elements set forth in paragraphs (a) through (e) in subdivision two as related to the particular respondent. If the court finds that a restrictive placement under this section is not required, the court shall enter any other order of disposition provided in section 352.2. If the court finds that a restrictive placement is required, it shall continue the proceeding and enter an order of disposition for a restrictive placement. Every order under this section shall be a dispositional order, shall be made after a dispositional hearing and shall state the grounds for the order.

2. In determining whether a restrictive placement is required, the court shall consider:

(a) the needs and best interests of the respondent;

(b) the record and background of the respondent, including but not limited to information disclosed in the probation investigation and diagnostic assessment;

(c) the nature and circumstances of the offense, including whether any injury was inflicted by the respondent or another participant;

(d) the need for protection of the community; and

(e) the age and physical condition of the victim.

3. Notwithstanding the provisions of subdivision two, the court shall order a restrictive placement in any case where the respondent is found to have committed a designated felony act in which the respondent inflicted serious physical injury, as that term is defined in subdivision ten of section 10.00 of the penal law, upon another person who is sixty two years of age or more.

4. When the order is for a restrictive placement in the case of a youth found to have committed a designated class A felony act.

(a) the order shall provide that:

(i) the respondent shall be placed with the division for youth for an initial period of five years. If the respondent has been in detention pending disposition, the initial period of placement ordered under this section shall be credited with and diminished by the amount of time spent by the respondent in detention prior to the commencement of the placement unless the court finds that all or part of such credit would not serve the needs and best interests of the respondent or the need for protection of the community.

(ii) the respondent shall initially be confined in a secure facility for a period set by the order, to be not less than twelve nor more than eighteen months provided however, where the order of the court is made in compliance with subdivision five the respondent shall initially be confined in a secure facility for eighteen months.

(iii)   after the period set under clause (ii), the respondent shall be placed in a residential facility for a period of twelve months.

(iv)   the respondent may not be released from a secure facility or transferred to a facility other than a secure facility during the period provided in clause (ii) of this paragraph, nor may the respondent be released from a residential facility during the period provided in clause (iii). No home visits shall be permitted during the period of secure confinement set by the court order or one year, whichever is less, except for emergency visits for medical treatment or severe illness or death in the family. All home visits must be accompanied home visits: (A) while a youth is confined in a secure facility, whether such confinement is pursuant to a court order or otherwise; (B) while a youth is confined in a residential facility other than a secure facility within six months after confinement in a secure facility; and (C) while a youth is confined in a residential facility other than a secure facility in excess of six months after confinement in a secure facility unless two accompanied home visits have already occurred. An "accompanied home visit" shall mean a home visit during which the youth shall be accompanied at all times while outside the secure or residential facility by appropriate personnel of the division for youth designated pursuant to regulations of the director of the division.

(b)   notwithstanding any other provision of law, during the first twelve months of the respondent's placement, no motion, hearing or order may be made, held or granted pursuant to section 355.1 provided however, that during such period a motion to vacate the order may be made pursuant to 355.1, but only upon grounds set forth in section 440.10 of the criminal procedure law.

(c)   during the placement or any extension thereof:

(i)   after the expiration of the period provided in clause (iii) of paragraph (a), the respondent shall not be released from a residential facility without the written approval of the director of the division for youth or his designated deputy director.

(ii)   the respondent shall be subject to intensive supervision whenever not in a secure or residential facility.

(iii)   the respondent shall not be discharged from the custody of the division for youth, unless a motion therefor under section 355.1 is granted by the court, which motion shall not be made prior to the expiration of three years of the placement.

(iv)   unless otherwise specified in the order, the division shall report in writing to the court not less than once every six months during the placement on the status, adjustment and progress of the respondent.

(d)   upon the expiration of the initial period of placement, or any extension thereof, the placement may be extended in accordance with section 355.3 on a petition of any party or the division for youth after a dispositional hearing, for an additional period not to exceed twelve months, but no initial placement or extension of placement under this section may continue beyond the respondent's twenty first birthday.

(e) the court may also make an order pursuant to subdivision two of section 353.4.

5. When the order is for a restrictive placement in the case of a youth found to have committed a designated felony act, other than a designated class A felony act.

(a) the order shall provide that:

(i) the respondent shall be placed with the division for youth for an initial period of three years. If the respondent has been in detention pending disposition, the initial period of placement ordered under this section shall be credited with and diminished by the amount of time spent by the respondent in detention prior to the commencement of the placement unless the court finds that all or part of such credit would not serve the needs and best interests of the respondent or the need for protection of the community.

(ii) the respondent shall initially be confined in a secure facility for a period set by the order, to be not less than six nor more than twelve months.

(iii) after the period set under clause (ii), the respondent shall be placed in a residential facility for a period set by the order, to be not less than six nor more than twelve months.

(iv) the respondent may not be released from a secure facility or transferred to a facility other than a secure facility during the period provided by the court pursuant to clause (ii), nor may the respondent be released from a residential facility during the period provided by the court pursuant to clause (iii). No home visits shall be permitted during the period of secure confinement set by the court order or one year, whichever is less, except for emergency visits for medical treatment or severe illness or death in the family. All home visits must be accompanied home visits: (A) while a youth is confined in a secure facility, whether such confinement is pursuant to a court order or otherwise; (B) while a youth is confined in a residential facility other than a secure facility within six months after confinement in a secure facility; and (C) while a youth is confined in a residential facility other than a secure facility in excess of six months after confinement in a secure facility unless two accompanied home visits have already occurred. An "accompanied home visit" shall mean a home visit during which the youth shall be accompanied at all times while outside the secure or residential facility by appropriate personnel of the division for youth designated pursuant to regulations of the director of the division.

(b) notwithstanding any other provisions of law, during the first six months of the respondent's placement, no motion, hearing or order may be made, held or granted pursuant to section 355.1; provided, however, that during such period

FCA

a motion to vacate the order may be made pursuant to such section, but only upon grounds set forth in section 440.10 of the criminal procedure law.

(c)　during the placement or any extension thereof:

(i)　after the expiration of the period provided in clause (iii) of paragraph (a), the respondent shall not be released from a residential facility without the written approval of the director of the division for youth or his designated deputy director.

(ii)　the respondent shall be subject to intensive supervision whenever not in a secure or residential facility.

(iii)　the respondent shall not be discharged from the custody of his division for youth.

(iv)　unless otherwise specified in the order, the division shall report in writing to the court not less than once every six months during the placement on the status, adjustment and progress of the respondent.

(d)　upon the expiration of the initial period of placement or any extension thereof, the placement may be extended in accordance with section 355.3 upon petition of any party or the division for youth, after a dispositional hearing, for an additional period not to exceed twelve months, but no initial placement or extension of placement under this section may continue beyond the respondent's twenty-first birthday.

(e)　the court may also make an order pursuant to subdivision two of section 353.4.

6.　When the order is for a restrictive placement in the case of a youth found to have committed any designated felony act and such youth has been found by a court to have committed a designated felony act on a prior occasion, regardless of the age of such youth at the time of commission of such prior act, the order of the court shall be made pursuant to subdivision four.

7.　If the dispositional hearing has been adjourned on a finding of specific circumstances pursuant to subdivision six of section 350.1 while the respondent is in detention, where a restrictive placement is subsequently ordered, time spent by the respondent in detention during such additional adjournment shall be credited and applied against any term of secure confinement ordered by the court pursuant to subdivision four or five.

8.　The division for youth shall retain the power to continue the confinement of the youth in a secure or other residential facility beyond the periods specified by the court, within the term of the placement.

Amended by Laws 1983, Ch. 398, eff. July 1, 1983; Laws 1987, Ch. 419, eff. Sept. 1, 1987; Laws 1993, Ch. 687, §§ 10, 11, eff. Dec. 2, 1993.

§ 353.6.　Restitution.

1.　At the conclusion of the dispositional hearing in cases involving respondents over ten years of age the court may: (a) recommend as a condition of placement, or order as a condition of probation or conditional discharge, restitution in an amount representing a fair and reasonable cost to replace the property, repair the damage caused by the respondent or provide the victim with compensation for unreimbursed medical expenses, not, however, to exceed one thousand five hundred dollars. In the case of a placement, the court may recommend that the respondent pay out of his or her own funds or earnings the amount of replacement, damage or unreimbursed medical expenses, either in a lump sum or in periodic payments in amounts set by the agency with which he or she is placed, and in the case of probation or conditional discharge, the court may require that the respondent pay out of his or her own funds or earnings the amount of replacement, damage or unreimbursed medical expenses, either in a lump sum or in periodic payments in amounts set by the court; and/or

(b) order as a condition of placement, probation or conditional discharge, services for the public good, taking into consideration the age and physical condition of the respondent.

2. If the court recommends restitution or requires services for the public good in conjunction with an order of placement pursuant to section 353.3 or 353.5 the placement shall be made only to an authorized agency, including the division for youth, which has adopted rules and regulations for the supervision of such a program, which rules and regulations, except in the case of the division for youth, shall be subject to the approval of the state department of social services. Such rules and regulations shall include, but not be limited to provisions: (i) assuring that the conditions of work, including wages, meet the standards therefor prescribed pursuant to the labor law; (ii) affording coverage to the respondent under the workers' compensation law as an employee of such agency, department, division or institution; (iii) assuring that the entity receiving such services shall not utilize the same to replace its regular employees; and (iv) providing for reports to the court not less frequently then every six months.

3. If the court requires restitutions or services for the public good as a condition of probation or conditional discharge, it shall provide that an agency or person supervise the restitution or services and that such agency or person report to the court not less frequently than every six months. Upon the written notice submitted by a school district to the court and the appropriate probation department or agency which submits probation recommendations or reports to the court, the court may provide that such school district shall supervise the performance of services for the public good.

4. The court, upon receipt of the reports provided for in subdivisions two and three may, on its own motion or the motion of the agency, probation service or the presentment agency, hold a hearing pursuant to section 355.1 to determine whether the dispositional order should be modified.

Amended by Laws 1983, Ch. 877, eff. Aug. 8, 1983; Laws 2004, Ch. 317, § 2, amending sub. 1, par (a), eff. Nov. 8, 2004.

§ 353.7.   Alcohol awareness program.

Repealed by Laws 1993, Ch. 124, § 1, eff. June 21, 1993.

§ 354.1.   **Retention and destruction of fingerprints of persons alleged to be juvenile delinquents.**

1.   If a person whose fingerprints, palmprints or photographs were taken pursuant to section 306.1 or was initially fingerprinted as a juvenile offender and the action is subsequently removed to family court pursuant to article seven hundred twenty five of the criminal procedure law is adjudicated to be a juvenile delinquent for a felony, the family court shall forward or cause to be forwarded to the division of criminal justice services notification of such adjudication and such related information as may be required by such division, provided, however, in the case of a person eleven or twelve years of age such notification shall be provided only if the act upon which the adjudication is based would constitute a class A or B felony.

2.   If a person whose fingerprints, palmprints or photographs were taken pursuant to section 306.1 or was initially fingerprinted as a juvenile offender and the action is subsequently removed to family court pursuant to article seven hundred twenty-five of the criminal procedure law has had all petitions disposed of by the family court in any manner other than an adjudication of juvenile delinquency for a felony, but in the case of acts committed when such person was eleven or twelve years of age which would constitute a class A or B felony only, all such fingerprints, palmprints, photographs, and copies thereof, and all information relating to such allegations obtained by the division of criminal justice services pursuant to section 306.1 shall be destroyed forthwith. The clerk of the court shall notify the commissioner of the division of criminal justice services and the heads of all police departments and law enforcement agencies having copies of such records, who shall destroy such records without unnecessary delay.

3.   If the appropriate presentment agency does not originate a proceeding under section 310.1 for a case in which the potential respondent's fingerprints were taken pursuant to section 306.1, the presentment agency shall serve a certification of such action upon the division of criminal justice services, and upon the appropriate police department or law enforcement agency.

4.   If, following the taking into custody of a person alleged to be a juvenile delinquent and the taking and forwarding to the division of criminal justice services of such person's fingerprints but prior to referral to the probation department or to the family court, an officer or agency, elects not to proceed further, such officer or agency shall serve a certification of such election upon the division of criminal justice services.

5.   Upon certification pursuant to subdivision twelve of section 308.1 or subdivision three or four of this section, the department or agency shall destroy

forthwith all fingerprints, palmprints, photographs, and copies thereof, and all other information obtained in the case pursuant to section 306.1. Upon receipt of such certification, the division of criminal justice services and all police departments and law enforcement agencies having copies of such records shall destroy them.

6. If a person fingerprinted pursuant to section 306.1 and subsequently adjudicated a juvenile delinquent for a felony, but in the case of acts committed when such a person was eleven or twelve years of age which would constitute a class A or B felony only, is subsequently convicted of a crime, all fingerprints and related information obtained by the division of criminal justice services pursuant to such section and not destroyed pursuant to subdivisions two, five and seven or subdivision twelve of section 308.1 shall become part of such division's permanent adult criminal record for that person, notwithstanding section 381.2 or 381.3.

7. When a person fingerprinted pursuant to section 306.1 and subsequently adjudicated a juvenile delinquent for a felony, but in the case of acts committed when such person was eleven or twelve years of age which would constitute a class A or B felony only, reaches the age of twenty-one, or has been discharged from placement under this act for at least three years, whichever occurs later, and has no criminal convictions or pending criminal actions which ultimately terminate in a criminal conviction, all fingerprints, palmprints, photographs, and related information and copies thereof obtained pursuant to section 306.1 in the possession of the division of criminal justice services, any police department, law enforcement agency or any other agency shall be destroyed forthwith. The division of criminal justice services shall notify the agency or agencies which forwarded fingerprints to such division pursuant to section 306.1 of their obligation to destroy those records in their possession. In the case of a pending criminal action which does not terminate in a criminal conviction, such records shall be destroyed forthwith upon such determination.

Amended by Laws 1983, Ch. 398, eff. July 1, 1983; Laws 1996, Ch. 645,§ 3, eff. Sept. 13, 1996, and applicable retroactively to a person whose fingerprints were taken pursuant to section 306.1 of the family court act or who was initially fingerprinted as a juvenile offender on or after January 1, 1986 and whose fingerprints are on file with the division of criminal justice services, provided that in the case of a juvenile offender action the case was subsequently removed to family court.

§ 354.2. Duties of counsel or law guardian.

1. If the court has entered a dispositional order pursuant to section 352.2, it shall be the duty of the respondent's counsel or law guardian to promptly advise such respondent and his parent or other person responsible for his care in writing of his right to appeal to the appropriate appellate division of the supreme court, the time limitations involved, the manner of instituting an appeal and obtaining a transcript of the testimony and the right to apply for leave to appeal as a poor person if he is unable to pay the cost of an appeal. It shall be the further duty

of such counsel or law guardian to explain to the respondent and his parent or person responsible for his care the procedures for instituting an appeal, the possible reasons upon which an appeal may be based and the nature and possible consequences of the appellate process.

2.   It shall also be the duty of such counsel or law guardian to ascertain whether the respondent wishes to appeal and, if so, to serve and file the necessary notice of appeal.

3.   If the respondent has been permitted to waive the appointment of a law guardian pursuant to section two hundred forty-nine-a, it shall be the duty of the court to provide the notice and explanation pursuant to subdivision one and, if the respondent indicates that he wishes to appeal, the clerk of the court shall file and serve the notice of appeal.

§ 355.1.   New hearing; staying, modifying or terminating an order.

1.   Upon a showing of a substantial change of circumstances, the court may on its own motion or on motion of the respondent or his parent or person responsible for his care:

(a)   grant a new fact finding or dispositional hearing; or

(b)   stay execution of, set aside, modify, terminate or vacate any order issued in the course of a proceeding under this article.

2.   An order issued under section 353.3, may, upon a showing of a substantial change of circumstances, be set aside, modified, vacated or terminated upon motion of the commissioner of social services or the division for youth with whom the respondent has been placed.

3.   If the court issues a new order of disposition under this section the date such order expires shall not be later than the expiration date of the original order.

    Amended by Laws 1983, Ch. 398, eff. July 1, 1983.

§ 355.2.   Motion procedures.

1.   A motion for relief pursuant to section 355.1 must be in writing and must state the specific relief requested. If the motion is based upon the existence or occurrence of facts the motion papers must contain sworn allegations thereof; such sworn allegations may be based upon personal knowledge of the affiant or upon information and belief provided that in the latter event the affidavit must state the sources of such information and the grounds of such belief.

2.   Notice of such motion, including the court's own motion, shall be served upon the respondent, the presentment agency and the commissioner of social services or the division for youth having custody of the respondent. Motions shall be noticed in accordance with the civil practice law and rules.

3.   Each party to the motion shall have the right to oral argument and the court shall conduct a hearing to resolve any material question of fact.

4.   Regardless of whether a hearing is conducted, the court, upon determining the motion, must set forth on the record its findings of fact, its conclusions of law and the reasons for its determination.

5.   If the motion is denied, a motion requesting the same or similar relief cannot be filed for a period of ninety days after such denial, unless the order of denial permits renewal at an earlier time.

§ 355.3.   Extension of placement.

1.   In any case in which the respondent has been placed pursuant to section 353.3 the respondent, the person with whom the respondent has been placed, the commissioner of social services, or the division for youth may petition the court to extend such placement. Such petition shall be filed at least sixty days prior to the expiration of the period of placement, except for good cause shown but in no event shall such petition be filed after the original expiration date.

2.   The court shall conduct a hearing concerning the need for continuing the placement. The respondent, the presentment agency and the agency with whom the respondent has been placed shall be notified of such hearing and shall have the opportunity to be heard thereat. If the petition is filed within sixty days prior to the expiration of the period of placement, the court shall first determine at such hearing whether good cause has been shown. If good cause is not shown, the court shall dismiss the petition.

3.   The provisions of sections 350.3 and 350.4 shall apply at such hearing.

4.   At the conclusion of the hearing the court may, in its discretion, order an extension of the placement for not more than one year. The court must consider and determine in its order:

(i)   that where appropriate, and where consistent with the need for the protection of the community, reasonable efforts were made to make it possible for the respondent to safely return to his or her home;

(ii)   in the case of a respondent who has attained the age of sixteen, the services needed, if any, to assist the child to make the transition from foster care to independent living; and

(iii)   in the case of a child placed outside New York State, whether the out-of-state placement continues to be appropriate and in the best interests of the child.

5.   Pending final determination of a petition to extend such placement filed in accordance with the provisions of this section, the court may, on its own motion or at the request of the petitioner or respondent, enter one or more temporary orders extending a period of placement for a period not to exceed thirty days upon satisfactory proof showing probable cause for continuing such placement and that each temporary order is necessary. The court may order additional temporary extensions, not to exceed a total of fifteen days, if the court is unable to conclude the hearing within the thirty day temporary extension period. In no event shall the aggregate number of days in extensions granted or ordered under this

FCA

subdivision total more than forty-five days. The petition shall be dismissed if a decision is not rendered within the period of placement or any temporary extension thereof.

6. Successive extensions of placement under this section may be granted, but no placement may be made or continued beyond the respondent's eighteenth birthday without the child's consent and in no event past the child's twenty first birthday.

Amended by Laws 1983, Ch. 398, eff. July 1, 1983; Laws 1985, Ch. 663, eff. Aug. 27, 1985; Laws 1991, Ch. 198, § 2, eff. June 28, 1991; Laws 1992, Ch. 363, § 1, eff. July 17, 1992; Laws 1993, Ch. 687, § 12, eff. Dec. 2, 1993; Laws 1995, Ch. 454, § 1, eff. Oct. 1, 1995; Laws 2000, Ch. 145, § 11, eff. July 1, 2000.

§ 355.4.   Provisions for routine medical, dental and mental health services and treatment.

1. At the conclusion of the dispositional hearing pursuant to this article, where the respondent is to be placed with the division for youth, the court shall inquire as to whether the parents or legal guardian of the youth, if present, will consent for the division to provide routine medical, dental and mental health services and treatment.

2. Notwithstanding subdivision one of this section, where the court places a youth with the division pursuant to this article and no medical consent has been obtained prior to an order of disposition, the placement order shall be deemed to grant consent for the division for youth to provide for routine medical, dental and mental health services and treatment to such youth so placed.

3. Subject to regulations of the department of health, routine medical, dental and mental health services and treatment is defined for the purposes of this section to mean any routine diagnosis or treatment, including without limitation the administration of medications or nutrition, the extraction of bodily fluids for analysis, and dental care performed with a local anesthetic. Routine mental health treatment shall not include psychiatric administration of medication unless it is part of an ongoing mental health plan or unless it is otherwise authorized by law.

4. (a) At any time during placement or at an extension of placement hearing, a parent or legal guardian may make a motion objecting to routine medical, dental or mental health services and treatment being provided to such youth as authorized under the provisions of subdivision one of this section.

(b) Such notice of motion shall be served on the youth, the presentment agency and the division not less than seven days prior to the return date of the motion. The persons on whom the notice of motion is served shall answer the motion not less than two days before the return date. On examining the motion and answer and, in its discretion, after hearing argument, the court shall enter an order, granting or denying the motion.

5. Nothing in this section shall preclude a youth from consenting on his or her own behalf to any medical, dental or mental health service and treatment

where otherwise authorized by law to do so, or the division for youth from petitioning the court pursuant to section two hundred thirty-three of this act, as appropriate.

Added by Laws 1992, Ch. 479, § 1, eff. July 17, 1992.

§ 355.5. Permanency hearing.

1. For the purposes of this section the term "non-secure facility" means a facility operated by an authorized agency in accordance with an operating certificate issued pursuant to the social services law or a facility, not including a secure or limited secure facility, with a capacity of twenty-five beds or less operated by the office of children and family services in accordance with section five hundred four of the executive law.

2. Where a respondent is placed with a commissioner of social services or the office of children and family services pursuant to section 353.3 of this article for a period of twelve or fewer months and resides in a foster home or non-secure facility;

(a) the initial permanency hearing shall be held no later than twelve months after the respondent who was placed with a commissioner of social services or the office of children and family services entered foster care and such permanency hearing shall be held in conjunction with an extension of placement hearing held pursuant to section 355.3 of this article.

(b) Subsequent permanency hearings shall be held no later than every twelve months following the respondent's initial permanency hearing and shall be held in conjunction with an extension of placement hearing held pursuant to section 355.3 of this article.

3. Where a respondent is placed with a commissioner of social services or the office of children and family services pursuant to section 353.3 of this article for a period in excess of twelve months and resides in a foster home or in a non-secure facility;

(a) the initial permanency hearing shall be held no later than twelve months after the respondent who was placed with a commissioner of social services or the office of children and family services entered foster care.

(b) Subsequent permanency hearings shall be held no later than every twelve months following the respondent's initial twelve months in placement; provided, however, that they shall be held in conjunction with an extension of placement hearing held pursuant to section 355.3 of this article.

4. For the purposes of this section, the respondent shall be considered to have entered foster care sixty days after the respondent was removed from his or her home pursuant to this article.

5. A petition for an initial or subsequent permanency hearing shall be filed by the office of children and family services or by the commissioner of social

FCA

services with whom the respondent was placed. Such petition shall be filed no later than sixty days prior to the end of the month in which an initial or subsequent permanency hearing must be held, as directed in subdivision two of this section.

6.   The foster parent caring for the respondent or any pre-adoptive parent or relative providing care for the respondent shall be provided with notice of any permanency hearing held pursuant to this section by the office of children and family services or the commissioner of social services with whom the respondent was placed. Such foster parent, pre-adoptive parent and relative shall be afforded an opportunity to be heard at any such hearing; provided, however, no such foster parent, pre-adoptive parent or relative shall be construed to be a party to the hearing solely on the basis of such notice and opportunity to be heard. The failure of the foster parent, pre-adoptive parent, or relative caring for the child to appear at a permanency hearing shall constitute a waiver of the opportunity to be heard and such failure to appear shall not cause a delay of the permanency hearing nor shall such failure to appear be a ground for the invalidation of any order issued by the court pursuant to this section.

7.   At the permanency hearing, the court must consider and determine in its order:

(a)   Where appropriate, that reasonable efforts were made to make it possible for the respondent to return safely to his or her home, or if the permanency plan for the respondent is adoption, guardianship or some other permanent living arrangement other than reunification with the parent or parents of the respondent, that reasonable efforts were made to make and finalize such alternate permanent placement;

(b)   In the case of a respondent who has attained the age of sixteen, The services needed, if any, to assist the respondent to make the transition from foster care to independent living;

(c)   in the case of a respondent placed outside of this state, whether the out-of-state placement continues to be appropriate and in the best interests of the respondent;

(d)   with regard to the completion of placement ordered by the court pursuant to section 353.3 or 355.3 of this article: whether and when the respondent: (i) will be returned to the parent; (ii) should be placed for adoption with the local commissioner of social services filing a petition for termination of parental rights; (iii) should be referred for legal guardianship; (iv) should be placed permanently with a fit and willing relative; or (v) should be placed in another planned permanent living arrangement if the office of children and family services or the local commissioner of social services has documented to the court a compelling reason for determining that it would not be in the best interest of the respondent to return home, be referred for termination of parental rights and placed for adoption, placed with a fit and willing relative, or placed with a legal guardian; and

(e)   with regard to the completion or extension of placement ordered by the court pursuant to section 353.3 or 355.3 of this article, the steps that must be taken by the agency with which the respondent is placed to implement the plan for release or conditional release submitted pursuant to paragraph (c) of subdivision seven of section 353.3 of this article, the adequacy of such plan and any modifications that should be made to such plan.

8.   The court shall not reduce or terminate the placement of the respondent prior to the completion of the period of placement ordered by the court pursuant to section 353.3 or 355.3 of this article.

Added by Laws 1999, Ch. 7, § 30, eff. Feb. 11, 1999; **amended** by Laws 2000, Ch. 145, § 11, effective July 1, 2000, amending subsections (2) and (3), and Ch. 181, § 20, eff. Jan. 1, 2001, amending subsection (7).

Part 6.   Post-dispositional procedures.

§ 360.1.   Jurisdiction and supervision of respondent placed on probation.

1.   A respondent who is placed on probation shall remain under the legal jurisdiction of the court pending expiration or termination of the period of the order of probation.

2.   The probation service shall supervise the respondent during the period of such legal jurisdiction.

3.   If at any time during the period of probation the court has reasonable cause to believe that the respondent has violated a condition of the probation order, it may issue a search order. A search order is an order directed to a probation officer authorizing such officer to search the person of the respondent or any personal property which he owns or which is in his possession.

4.   In executing a search order pursuant to this section, a probation officer may be assisted by a police officer.

§ 360.2.   Petition of violation.

1.   If at any time during the period of an order of probation or conditional discharge the probation service has reasonable cause to believe that the respondent has violated a condition thereof, it may file a petition of violation.

2.   The petition must be verified and subscribed by the probation service or the appropriate presentment agency. Such petition must stipulate the condition

or conditions of the order violated and a reasonable description of the time, place, and manner in which the violation occurred. Non-hearsay allegations of the factual part of the petition or of any supporting depositions must establish, if true, every violation charged.

3.   The court must promptly take reasonable and appropriate action to cause the respondent to appear before it for the purpose of enabling the court to make a determination with respect to the alleged violation. Such action may include the issuance of a summons under section 312.1 or the issuance of a warrant under section 312.2

4.   If a petition is filed under subdivision one, the period of probation as prescribed by section 353.2 shall be interrupted as of the date of the filing of the petition. Such interruption shall continue until a final determination as to the petition has been made by the court pursuant to a hearing held in accordance with section 360.3 or until such time as the respondent reaches the maximum age of acceptance into a division for youth facility.

5.   If the court determines there was no violation of probation by the respondent the period of interruption shall be credited to the period of probation.

§ 360.3.   Hearing on violation.

1.   The court may not revoke an order of probation or conditional discharge unless: (a) the court has found that the respondent has violated a condition of such order; and (b) the respondent has had an opportunity to be heard. The respondent is entitled to a hearing in accordance with this section promptly after a petition of violation has been filed.

2.   At the time of his first appearance following the filing of a petition of violation the court must: (a) advise the respondent of the contents of the petition and furnish him with a copy thereof; (b) determine whether the respondent should be released or detained pursuant to section 320.5; and (c) ask the respondent whether he wishes to make any statement with respect to the violation. If the respondent makes a statement, the court may accept it and base its decision thereon; the provisions of subdivision two of section 321.3 shall apply in determining whether a statement should be accepted. If the court does not accept such statement or if the respondent does not make a statement, the court shall proceed with the hearing. Upon request, the court shall grant a reasonable adjournment to the respondent to enable him to prepare for the hearing.

3.   At such hearing, the court may receive any relevant, competent and material evidence. The respondent may cross-examine witnesses and may present evidence on his own behalf.

4.   The respondent is entitled to counsel at all stages of a proceeding under this section and the court shall advise him of such right at the outset of the proceeding.

5.   The presentment agency shall present the petition in all stages of this part.

6.   At the conclusion of the hearing the court may revoke, continue or modify the order of probation or conditional discharge. If the court revokes the order, it shall order a different disposition pursuant to section 352.2. If the court continues the order of probation or conditional discharge, it shall dismiss the petition of violation.

Amended by Laws 1982, Ch. 926, eff. July 1, 1983.

§ 365.1.   Appeal; authorized as of right.

1.   An appeal to the appropriate appellate division may be taken as of right by the respondent from any order of disposition under this article in accordance with article eleven.

2.   An appeal to the appropriate appellate division may be taken as of right by the presentment agency from the following orders of the family court:

(a)   an order dismissing a petition prior to the commencement of a fact finding hearing; or

(b)   an order of disposition, but only upon the ground that such order was invalid as a matter of law; or

(c)   an order suppressing evidence entered before the commencement of the fact finding hearing pursuant to section 330.2, provided that such presentment agency files a statement pursuant to subdivision nine of section 330.2.

Amended by Laws 1985, Ch. 663, eff. Aug. 27, 1985.

§ 365.2.   Appeal by permission.

An Appeal may be taken by the respondent in the discretion of the appropriate appellate division, from any other order under this article.

§ 365.3.   Notice of appeal.

1.   An appeal shall be taken by filing a written notice of appeal, in duplicate, with the clerk of the family court in which the order was entered.

2.   If the respondent is the appellant, he must also serve a copy of such notice of appeal upon the appropriate presentment agency.

3.   If the presentment agency is the appellant, it must serve a copy of such notice of appeal upon the respondent and upon the attorney or law guardian who last appeared for him in the family court.

4.   Following the filing with him of the notice of appeal in duplicate, the clerk of the family court must endorse upon such instruments the filing date and must transmit the duplicate notice of appeal to the clerk of the appropriate appellate division of the supreme court.

FCA

Part 7. Securing testimony and records

---

§ 370.1. Securing the attendance of witnesses: securing certain testimony.

1. The provisions of article six hundred twenty of the criminal procedure law concerning the securing of attendance of witnesses by material witness order shall apply to proceedings under this article.

2. Article six hundred sixty, six hundred seventy and six hundred eighty of the criminal procedure law concerning the securing of testimony for use in a subsequent proceeding, the use of testimony given in a previous proceeding and the examination of witness by commission shall apply to proceedings under this article.

3. The provisions of the uniform act to secure attendance of witnesses from without the state in criminal cases, as incorporated in article six hundred forty of the criminal procedure law, shall apply to proceedings under this article.

§ 375.1. Order upon termination of a delinquency action in favor of the respondent.

1. Upon termination of a delinquency proceeding against a respondent in favor of such respondent, unless the presentment agency upon written motion with not less than eight days notice to such respondent demonstrates to the satisfaction of the court that the interests of justice require otherwise or the court on its own motion with not less than eight days notice to such respondent determines that the interest of justice require otherwise and states the reason for such determination on the record, the clerk of the court shall immediately notify the law guardian or counsel for the child, the director of the appropriate presentment agency, and the heads of the appropriate probation department and police department or other law enforcement agency, that the proceeding has terminated in favor of the respondent and, unless the court has directed otherwise, that the records of such action or proceeding, other than those destroyed pursuant to section 354.1 of this act, shall be sealed. Upon receipt of such notification all official records and papers, including judgments and orders of the court, but not including public court decisions or opinions or records and briefs on appeal, relating to the arrest, the prosecution and the probation service proceedings, including all duplicates or copies thereof, on file with the court, police agency,

probation service and presentment agency shall be sealed and not made available to any person or public or private agency. Such records shall remain sealed during the pendency of any motion made pursuant to this subdivision.

2. For the purposes of subdivision one, a delinquency proceeding shall be considered terminated in favor of a respondent where:

(a) the petition is withdrawn; or

(b) the petition is dismissed under section 315.1 or 315.2 and the presentment agency has not appealed from such order or the determination of an appeal or appeals from such order has been against the presentment agency; or

(c) the petition has been deemed to have been dismissed under section 315.3 and the presentment agency has not appealed from such order or the determination of an appeal or appeals from such order has been against the presentment agency; or

(d) the petition is dismissed without prejudice under subdivision four of section 325.3 and the presentment agency has not appealed from such order or the determination of an appeal or appeals from such order has been against the presentment agency; or

FCA

(e) the entire petition has been dismissed under subdivision two of section 345.1; or

(f) the petition is dismissed under subdivision two of section 352.1; or

(g) prior to the filing of a petition the probation department has adjusted the case or terminated the case without adjustment; or

(h) prior to the filing of a petition the presentment agency chooses not to proceed to petition; or

(i) the petition is dismissed pursuant to a motion made in accordance with subdivision eight, nine or ten of section 332.1.

3. Records sealed pursuant to subdivision one shall be made available to the respondent or his designated agent and the records and papers of a probation service shall be available to any probation service for the purpose of complying with subdivision four of section 308.1.

4. If prior to the filing of a petition the presentment agency elects not to commence a delinquency action it shall serve a certification of such disposition upon the appropriate probation service and the appropriate police department or law enforcement agency, which, upon receipt thereto, shall comply with the provision of subdivision one in the same manner as is required with respect to an order of the court.

5. If the probation service adjusts a delinquency case it shall serve a certification of such disposition upon the appropriate police department or law enforcement agency which, upon receipt thereof, shall comply with the provisions of subdivision one in the same manner as is required thereunder with respect to an order of a court.

6.   A respondent in whose favor a delinquency proceeding was terminated prior to the effective date of this section may upon motion apply to the court, upon not less than twenty days notice to the presentment agency, for an order granting him the relief set forth in subdivision one, and such order shall be granted unless the presentment agency demonstrates to the satisfaction of the court that the interests of justice require otherwise. A respondent in whose favor a delinquency action or proceeding was terminated as defined by subdivisions four and five prior to the effective date of this section, may apply to the appropriate presentment agency or probation service for a certification as described in such subdivisions granting him the relief set forth therein and such certification shall be granted by such presentment agency or probation service.

Amended by Laws 1983, Ch. 398, eff. July 1, 1983; Laws 1987, Ch. 105, eff. June 8, 1987; Laws 1987, Ch. 423, eff. Aug. 27, 1987; Laws 1996, Ch. 645, § 4, eff. Sept. 13, 1996, and applicable retroactively to a person whose fingerprints were taken pursuant to section 306.1 of the family court act or who was initially fingerprinted as a juvenile offender on or after January 1, 1986 and whose fingerprints are on file with the division of criminal justice services, provided that in the case of a juvenile offender action the case was subsequently removed to family court.

§ 375.2.   Motion to seal after a finding.

1.   If an action has resulted in a finding of delinquency pursuant to subdivision one of section 352.1 other than a finding that the respondent committed a designated felony act, the court may, in the interest of justice and upon motion of the respondent, order the sealing of appropriate records pursuant to subdivision one of section 375.1.

2.   Such motion must be in writing and may be filed at any time subsequent to the entering of such finding. Notice of such motion shall be served upon the presentment agency not less than eight days prior to the return date of the motion. Answering affidavits shall be served at least two days before such time.

3.   The court shall state on the record its reasons for granting or denying the motion.

4.   If such motion is denied, it may not be renewed for a period of one year, unless the order of denial permits renewal at an earlier time.

5.   The court shall not order the sealing of any record except as prescribed by this section or section 375.1.

6.   Such a motion cannot be filed until the respondent's sixteenth birthday.

Amended by Laws 1982, Ch. 926, eff. July 1, 1983; Laws 1983, Ch. 398, eff. July 1, 1983.

§ 375.3.   Expungement of court records.

Nothing contained in this article shall preclude the court's use of its inherent power to order the expungement of court records.

Added by Laws 1983, Ch. 398, eff. July 1, 1983.

Part 8.　General provisions.

---

§ 380.1.　Nature and effect of adjudication.

1.　No adjudication under this article may be denominated a conviction and no person adjudicated a juvenile delinquent shall be denominated a criminal by reason of such adjudication.

2.　No adjudication under this article shall operate as a forfeiture of any right or privilege or disqualify any person from holding any public office or receiving any license granted by public authority. Such adjudication shall not operate as a disqualification of any person to pursue or engage in any lawful activity, occupation, profession, or calling.

3.　Except where specifically required by statute, no person shall be required to divulge information pertaining to the arrest of the respondent or any subsequent proceeding under this article; provided, however, whenever a person adjudicated a juvenile delinquent has been placed with the office of children and family services pursuant to section 353.3 of this article, and is thereafter enrolled as a student in a public or private elementary or secondary school, the court that has adjudicated such person shall provide notification of such adjudication to the designated educational official of the school in which such person is enrolled as a student. Such notification shall be used by the designated educational official only for purposes related to the execution of the student's educational plan, where applicable, successful school adjustment and reentry into the community. Such notification shall be kept separate and apart from such student's school records and shall be accessible only by the designated educational official. Such notification shall not be part of such student's permanent school record and shall not be appended to or included in any documentation regarding such student and shall be destroyed at such time as such student is no longer enrolled in the school district. At no time shall such notification be used for any purpose other than those specified in this subdivision.

Amended by Laws 2000, Ch. 181 § 18, eff. Nov. 1, 2000.

§ 381.1.   Transfer of records and information to institutions and agencies.

Whenever a person is placed in an institution suitable for placement of a person adjudicated a juvenile delinquent maintained by the state or any subdivision thereof or to an authorized agency including the division for youth, the family court placing such person shall forthwith transmit a copy of the orders of the family court pursuant to sections 352.1 and 352.2 and of the probation report and all other relevant evaluative records in the possession of the family court and probation department related to such person, including but not limited to any diagnostic, educational, medical, psychological, and psychiatric records with respect to such person to such institution or agency notwithstanding any contrary provision of law.

§ 381.2.   Use of records in other courts.

1.   Neither the fact that a person was before the family court under this article for a hearing nor any confession, admission, or statement made by him to the court or to any officer thereof in any stage of the proceeding is admissible as evidence against him or his interests in any other court.

2.   Notwithstanding the provisions of subdivision one, another court, in imposing sentence upon an adult after conviction may receive and consider the records and information on file with the family court unless such records and information have been sealed pursuant to section 375.1

     Amended by Laws 1982, Ch. 926, eff. July 1, 1983.

§ 381.3.   Use of police records.

1.   All police records relating to the arrest and disposition of any person under this article shall be kept in files separate and apart from the arrests of adults and shall be withheld from public inspection.

2.   Notwithstanding the provisions of subdivision one, the family court in the county in which the petition was adjudicated may, upon motion and for good cause shown, order such records open:

   (a)   to the respondent or his parent or person responsible for his care; or

   (b)   if the respondent is subsequently convicted of a crime, to a judge of the court in which he was convicted, unless such record has been sealed pursuant to section 375.1.

3.   An order issued under subdivision two must be in writing.

     Amended by Laws 1982, Ch. 926, eff. July 1, 1983.

§ 385.1.   Reports.

1.   In addition to reports filed pursuant to section two hundred thirteen, the chief administrator of the courts shall include in its annual report to the legislature

and the governor information, by county, showing the total number of delinquency cases filed under this article, the precise crime or crimes charged in such petitions by penal law section, the number of respondents included in such petitions, the number of cases heard in the designated felony parts, the age of the alleged victim by crime, the length of time and number of adjournments between the filing of a petition and the conclusion of the fact finding process, the number of cases dismissed by the court, the number withdrawn, the number admitted to in whole or in part, the number of contested fact finding hearings and their result, the precise crime, if any, found to have been committed, the length of time and number of adjournments between the fact finding hearing and the conclusion of the dispositional hearing and the final precise disposition of such cases. Designated felony cases shall be separately reported by each event or fact enumerated in this section. Cases removed from criminal courts shall also be separately reported by each event and fact enumerated in this section.

2. The division of probation and correctional alternatives shall include in its annual report to the legislature and the governor information, by county, showing the total number of delinquency cases adjusted prior to filing.

Amended by Laws 1985, Ch. 134, eff. Apr. 1, 1985.

§ 385.2. Consolidation of records within a city having a population of one million or more.

Notwithstanding any other provision of law, in a city having a population of one million or more, an index of the records of the local probation departments located in the counties comprising such city for proceedings under article three shall be consolidated and filed in a central office for use by the family court and local probation service in each such county. After consultation with the state administrative judge, the state director of probation and correctional alternatives shall specify the information to be contained in such index and the organization of such consolidated file.

Amended by Laws 1985, Ch. 134, eff. Apr. 1, 1985.

ARTICLE 4

SUPPORT PROCEEDINGS

———

SUMMARY OF ARTICLE

Part 1.   Jurisdiction and duties of support.

(Repealed and transferred sections noted under appropriate section number of text.)

diction.

has exclusive original jurisdiction over proceedings for
under this article and in proceedings under article five-B
form interstate family support act. On its own motion,
he proceedings also direct the filing of a neglect
of this act.

July 19, 1980; Laws 1983, Ch. 112, eff. May
1, 1998.

§ 412. Married person's duty to support spouse.

A married person is chargeable with the support of his or her spouse and, if possessed of sufficient means or able to earn such means, may be required to pay for his or her support a fair and reasonable sum, as the court may determine, having due regard to the circumstances of the respective parties.

Amended by Laws 1980, Ch. 281, eff. July 19, 1980.

§ 413. Parents' duty to support child.

1.   (a) Except as provided in subdivision two of this section, the parents of a child under the age of twenty-one years are chargeable with the support of such child and, if possessed of sufficient means or able to earn such means, shall be required to pay for child support a fair and reasonable sum as the court may determine. The court shall make its award for child support pursuant to the provisions of this subdivision. The court may vary from the amount of the basic child support obligation determined pursuant to paragraph (c) of this subdivision only in accordance with paragraph (f) of this subdivision.

(b)   For purposes of this subdivision, the following definitions shall be used:

(1)   "basic child support obligation" shall mean the sum derived by adding the amounts determined by the application of subparagraphs two and three of paragraph (c) of this subdivision except as increased pursuant to subparagraphs four, five, six and seven of such paragraph.

(2)   "child support" shall mean a sum to be paid pursuant to court order or decree by either or both parents or pursuant to a valid agreement between the parties for care, maintenance and education of any unemancipated child under the age of twenty-one years.

(3)   "child support percentage" shall mean:

(i)   seventeen percent of the combined parental income for one child;

(ii)   twenty-five percent of the combined parental income for two children;

(iii)   twenty-nine percent of the combined parental income for three children;

(iv)   thirty-one percent of the combined parental income for four children; and

(v)   no less than thirty-five percent of the combined parental income for five or more children.

(4)   "combined parental income" shall mean the sum of the income of both parents.

(5)   "income" shall mean, but shall not be limited to, the sum of the amounts determined by the application of clauses (i), (ii), (iii), (iv), (v) and (vi) of this subparagraph reduced by the amount determined by the application of clause (vii) of this subparagraph:

(i)   gross (total) income as should have been or should be reported in the most recent federal income tax return. If an individual files his/her federal income tax return as a married person filing jointly, such person shall be required to prepare a form, sworn to under penalty of law, disclosing his/her gross income individually;

(ii)   to the extent not already included in gross income in clause (i) of this subparagraph, investment income reduced by sums expended in connection with such investment;

(iii)   to the extent not already included in gross income in clauses (i) and (ii) of this subparagraph, the amount of income or compensation voluntarily deferred and income received, if any, from the following sources:

(A)   workers' compensation,

(B)   disability benefits,

(C)   unemployment insurance benefits,

(D)   social security benefits,

(E)   veterans benefits,

(F)   pensions and retirement benefits,

(G)   fellowships and stipends, and

(H)   annuity payments;

(iv)   at the discretion of the court, the court may attribute or impute income from, such other resources as may be available to the parent, including, but not limited to:

(A)   non-income producing assets,

(B)   meals, lodging, memberships, automobiles or other perquisites that are provided as part of compensation for employment to the extent that such perquisites constitute expenditures for personal use, or which expenditures directly or indirectly confer personal economic benefits,

(C)   fringe benefits provided as part of compensation for employment, and

(D)   money, goods, or services provided by relatives and friends;

(v)   an amount imputed as income based upon the parent's former resources or income, if the court determines that a parent has reduced resources or income in order to reduce or avoid the parent's obligation for child support;

(vi)   to the extent not already included in gross income in clauses (i) and (ii) of this subparagraph, the following self-employment deductions attributable to self-employment carried on by the taxpayer:

(A)   any depreciation deduction greater than depreciation calculated on a straight-line basis for the purpose of determining business income or investment credits, and

(B)   entertainment and travel allowances deducted from business income to the extent said allowances reduce personal expenditures;

(vii)   the following shall be deducted from income prior to applying the provisions of paragraph (c) of this subdivision:

(A)   unreimbursed employee business expenses except to the extent said expenses reduce personal expenditures,

(B)   alimony or maintenance actually paid to a spouse not a party to the instant action pursuant to court order or validly executed written agreement,

(C)   alimony or maintenance actually paid or to be paid to a spouse that is a party to the instant action pursuant to an existing court order or contained in the order to be entered by the court, or pursuant to a validly executed written agreement, provided the order or agreement provides for a specific adjustment, in accordance with this subdivision, in the amount of child support payable upon the termination of alimony or maintenance to such spouse,

(D)   child support actually paid pursuant to court order or written agreement on behalf of any child for whom the parent has a legal duty of support and who is not subject to the instant action,

(E)   public assistance,

(F)   supplemental security income,

(G)   New York city or Yonkers income or earnings taxes actually paid, and

(H)   Federal Insurance Contributions Act (FICA) taxes actually paid.

(6)   "self-support reserve" shall mean one hundred thirty-five percent of the poverty income guidelines amount for a single person as reported by the federal Department of Health and Human Services. For the calendar year nineteen hundred eighty-nine, the self-support reserve shall be eight thousand sixty-five dollars. On March first of each year, the self-support reserve shall be revised to reflect the annual updating of the poverty income guidelines as reported by the federal department of health and human services for a single person household.

(c)   amount of the basic child support obligation shall be determined in accordance with the provision of this paragraph:

(1)   the court shall determine the combined parental income.

(2)   the Court shall multiply the combined parental income up to eighty thousand dollars by the appropriate child support percentage and such amount shall be prorated in the same proportion as each parent's income is to the combined parental income.

(3)   where the combined parental income exceeds the dollar amount set forth in subparagraph two of this paragraph, the court shall determine the amount of child support for the amount of the combined parental income in excess of such dollar amount through consideration of the factors set forth in paragraph (f) of this subdivision and/or the child support percentage.

FCA

(4)   where the custodial parent is working, or receiving elementary or secondary education, or higher education or vocational training which the court determines will lead to employment, and incurs child care expenses as a result thereof, the court shall determine reasonable child care expenses and such child care expenses, where incurred, shall be prorated in the same proportion as each parent's income is to the combined parental income. Each parent's pro rata share of the child care expenses shall be separately stated and added to the sum of subparagraphs two and three of this paragraph.

(5)   the court shall prorate each parent's share of future reasonable health care expenses of the child not covered by insurance in the same proportion as each parent's income is to the combined parental income. The non-custodial parent's pro rata share of such health care expenses shall be paid in a manner determined by the court, including direct payment to the health care provider.

(6)   where the court determines that the custodial parent is seeking work and incurs child care expenses as a result thereof, the court may determine reasonable child care expenses and may apportion the same between the custodial and non-custodial parent. The non-custodial parent's share of such expenses shall be separately stated and paid in a manner determined by the court.

(7)   where the court determines, having regard for the circumstances of the case and of the respective parties and in the best interests of the child, and as justice requires, that the present or future provision of post-secondary, private, special, or enriched education for the child is appropriate, the court may award educational expenses. The non-custodial parent shall pay educational expenses, as awarded, in a manner determined by the court, including direct payment to the educational provider.

(d)   Notwithstanding the provisions of paragraph (c) of this subdivision, where the annual amount of the basic child support obligation would reduce the non-custodial parent's income below the poverty income guidelines amount for a single person as reported by the federal department of health and human services, the basic child support obligation shall be twenty-five dollars per month or the difference between the non-custodial parent's income and the self-support reserve, whichever is greater. Notwithstanding the provisions of paragraph (c) of this subdivision, where the annual amount of the basic child support obligation would reduce the non-custodial parent's income below the self-support reserve but not below the poverty income guidelines amount for a single person as reported by the federal Department of Health and Human Services, the basic child support obligation shall be fifty dollars per month or the difference between the non-custodial parent's income and the self-support reserve, whichever is greater.

(e)   Where a parent is or may be entitled to receive non-recurring payments from extraordinary sources not otherwise considered as income pursuant to this section, including but not limited to:

(1)   life insurance policies;

(2)   discharges of indebtedness;

(3)   recovery of bad debts and delinquency amounts;

(4)   gifts and inheritances; and

(5)   lottery winnings, the court, in accordance with paragraphs (c), (d) and (f) of this subdivision may allocate a proportion of the same to child support, and such amount shall be paid in a manner determined by the court.

(f)   The court shall calculate the basic child support obligation, and the non-custodial parent's pro rata share of the basic child support obligation. Unless the court finds that the non-custodial parents's pro rata share of the basic child support obligation is unjust or inappropriate, which finding shall be based upon consideration of the following factors:

(1)   the financial resources of the custodial and non-custodial parent, and those of the child;

(2)   the physical and emotional health of the child and his/her special needs and aptitudes;

(3)   the standard of living the child would have enjoyed had the marriage or household not been dissolved;

(4)   the tax consequences to the parties;

(5)   the non-monetary contributions that the parents will make toward the care and well-being of the child;

(6)   the educational needs of either parent;

(7)   a determination that the gross income of one parent is substantially less than the other parent's gross income;

(8)   the needs of the children of the non-custodial parent for whom the non-custodial parent is providing support who are not subject to the instant action and whose support has not been deducted from income pursuant to subclause (d) of clause (vii) of subparagraph five of paragraph (b) of this subdivision, and the financial resources of any person obligated to support such children, provided, however, that this factor may apply only if the resources available to support such children are less than the resources available to support the children who are subject to the instant action;

(9)   provided that the child is not on public assistance (i) extraordinary expenses incurred by the non-custodial parent in exercising visitation, or (ii) expenses incurred by the non-custodial parent in extended visitation provided that the custodial parent's expenses are substantially reduced as a result thereof; and

(10)   any other factors the court determines are relevant in each case, the court shall order the non-custodial parent to pay his or her pro rata share of the basic child support obligation, and may order the noncustodial parent to pay an amount pursuant to paragraph (e) of this subdivision.

(g)   Where the court finds that the noncustodial parent's pro rata share of the basic child support obligation is unjust or inappropriate, the court shall order the noncustodial parent to pay such amount of child support as the court finds just and appropriate, and the court shall set forth, in a written order: the factors it considered; the amount of each party's pro rata share of the basic child support obligation; and the reasons that the court did not order the basic child support obligation. Such written order may not be waived by either party or counsel; provided however, and notwithstanding any other provision of law, including but not limited to section four hundred fifteen of this act, the court shall not find that the noncustodial parent's pro rata share of such obligation is unjust or inappropriate on the basis that such share exceeds the portion of a public assistance grant which is attributable to a child or children. In no instance shall the court order child support below twenty-five dollars per month. Where the noncustodial parent's income is less than or equal to the poverty income guidelines amount for a single person as reported by the federal department of health and human services, unpaid child support arrears in excess of five hundred dollars shall not accrue.

(h) A validly executed agreement or stipulation voluntarily entered into between the parties after the effective date of this subdivision presented to the court for incorporation in an order or judgment shall include a provision stating that the parties have been advised of the provisions of this subdivision and that the basic child support obligation provided for therein would presumptively result in the correct amount of child support to be awarded. In the event that such agreement or stipulation deviates from the basic child support obligation, the agreement or stipulation must specify the amount that such basic child support obligation would have been and the reason or reasons that such agreement or stipulation does not provide for payment of that amount. Such provision may not be waived by either party or counsel. Nothing contained in this subdivision shall be construed to alter the rights of the parties to voluntarily enter into validly executed agreements or stipulations which deviate from the basic child support obligation provided such agreements or stipulations comply with the provisions of this paragraph. The court shall, however, retain discretion with respect to child support pursuant to this section. Any court order or judgment incorporating a validly executed agreement or stipulation which deviates from the basic child support obligation shall set forth the court's reasons for such deviation.

(i) Where either or both parties are unrepresented, the court shall not enter an order or judgment other than a temporary order pursuant to section two hundred thirty-seven of this article, that includes a provision for child support unless the unrepresented party or parties have received a copy of the child support standards chart promulgated by the commissioner of social services pursuant to subdivision two of section one hundred eleven-i of the social services law. Where either party is in receipt of child support enforcement services through the local social services district, the local social services district child support enforcement unit shall advise such party of the amount derived from application of the child support percentage and that such amount serves as a starting point for the determination of the child support award, and shall provide such party with a copy of the child support standards chart. In no instance shall the court approve any voluntary support agreement or compromise that includes an amount for child support less than twenty-five dollars per month.

(j)   In addition to financial disclosure required in section four hundred twenty-four-a of this article, the court may require that the income and/or expenses of either party be verified with documentation including, but not limited to, past and present income tax returns, employer statements, pay stubs, corporate, business, or partnership books and records, corporate and business tax returns, and receipts for expenses or such other means of verification as the court determines appropriate. Nothing herein shall affect any party's right to pursue discovery pursuant to this chapter, the civil practice law and rules, or the family court act.

(k)   When a party has defaulted and/or the court is otherwise presented with insufficient evidence to determine gross income, the court shall order child support based upon the needs or standard of living of the child, whichever is greater. Such order may be retroactively modified upward, without a showing of change in circumstances.

(l)   In any action or proceeding for modification of an order of child support existing prior to the effective date of this paragraph, brought pursuant to this article, the child support standards set forth in paragraphs (a) through (k) of this subdivision shall not constitute grounds for modification of such support order; provided, however, that (1) where the circumstances warrant modification of such order, or (2) where any party objects to an adjusted child support order made or proposed at the direction of the support collection unit pursuant to section one hundred eleven-h or one hundred eleven-n of the social services law, and the court is reviewing the current order of child support, such standards shall be applied by the court in its determination with regard to the request for modification or disposition of an objection to an adjusted child support order made or proposed by a support collection unit. In applying such standards, when the order to be modified incorporates by reference or merges with a validly executed separation agreement or stipulation of settlement, the court may consider, in addition to the factors set forth in paragraph (f) of this subdivision, the provisions of such agreement or stipulation concerning property distribution, distributive award and/or maintenance in determining whether the amount calculated by using the standards would be unjust or inappropriate.

2.   Nothing in this article shall impose any liability upon a person to support the adopted child of his or her spouse, if such child was adopted after the adopting spouse is living separate and apart from the non-adopting spouse pursuant to a legally recognizable separation agreement or decree under the domestic relations law. Such liability shall not be imposed for so long as the spouses remain separate and apart after the adoption.

3.   a. One-time adjustment of child support orders issued prior to September fifteenth, nineteen hundred eighty-nine. Any party to a child support order issued

prior to September fifteenth, nineteen hundred eighty-nine on the behalf of a child in receipt of public assistance or child support services pursuant to section one hundred eleven-g of the social services law may request that the support collection unit undertake one review of the order for adjustment purposes pursuant to section one hundred eleven-h of the social services law. A hearing on the adjustment of such order shall be granted upon the objection of either party pursuant to the provisions of this section. An order shall be adjusted if as of the date of the support collection unit's review of the correct amount of child support as calculated pursuant to the provisions of this section would deviate by at least ten percent from the child support ordered in the last permanent support order of the court. Additionally, a new support order shall be issued upon a showing that the current order of support does not provide for the health care needs of the child through insurance or otherwise. Eligibility of the child for medical assistance shall not relieve any obligation the parties otherwise have to provide for the health care needs of the child. The support collection unit's review of a child support order shall be made on notice to all parties to the current support order and shall be subject to the provisions of section four hundred twenty-four-a of this article. Nothing herein shall be deemed in any way to limit, restrict, expand or impair the rights of any party to file for a modification of a child support order as is otherwise provided by law.

b. Upon receipt of an adjustment finding and where appropriate a proposed order in conformity with such finding filed by either party or by the support collection unit, a party shall have thirty-five days from the date of mailing of the adjustment finding and proposed adjusted order, if any, to submit to the court identified thereon specific written objections to such finding and proposed order.

(1) If specific written objections are submitted by either party or by the support collection unit, a hearing shall be scheduled by the court on notice to the parties and the support collection unit, who shall have the right to be heard by the court and to offer evidence in support of or in opposition to adjustment of the support order.

(2) The party filing the specific written objections shall bear the burden of going forward and the burden of proof; provided, however, that if the support collection unit has failed to provide the documentation and information required by subdivision fourteen of section one hundred eleven-h of the social services law, the court shall first require the support collection unit to furnish such documents and information to the parties and the court.

(3) If the court finds by a preponderance of the evidence that the specific written objections have been proven, the court shall recalculate or readjust the proposed adjusted order accordingly or, for good cause, shall remand the order to the support collection unit for submission of a new proposed adjusted order. Any readjusted order so issued by the court or resubmitted by the support collection unit following remand by the court shall be effective as of the date the proposed adjusted order would have been effective had no written objections been filed.

(4)   If the court finds that the specific written objections have not been proven by a preponderance of the evidence, the court shall immediately issue the adjusted order, which shall be effective as of the date the order would have been effective had no written objections been filed.

(5)   If the determination of the specific written objections has been made by a family court support magistrate, the parties shall be permitted to obtain judicial review of such determination by filing timely written objections pursuant to subdivision (e) of section four hundred thirty-nine of this act.

(6)   If the court receives no specific written objections to the support order within thirty-five days of the mailing of the proposed order, the clerk of the court shall immediately issue the order without any further review, modification, or other prior action by the court or any judge or support magistrate thereof, and the clerk shall immediately transmit copies of the order of support to the parties and to the support collection unit.

c.   A motion to vacate an order of support adjusted pursuant to this section may be made no later than forty-five days after an adjusted support order is executed by the court where no specific written objections to the proposed order have been timely received by the court. Such motion shall be granted only upon a determination by the court issuing such order that personal jurisdiction was not timely obtained over the moving party.

4.   On-going cost of living adjustment of child support orders issued prior to September fifteenth, nineteen hundred eighty-nine. Any party to a child support order issued prior to September fifteenth, nineteen hundred eighty-nine on the behalf of a child in receipt of public assistance or child support services pursuant to section one hundred eleven-g of the social services law may request that the support collection unit review the order for a cost of living adjustment in accordance with the provisions of section four hundred thirteen-a of this article.

* Note: The amendments made to subdivision 3 by Laws 1997, Ch. 398 § 4 shall not apply to review and adjustment requests, actions, proceedings, objections, or issuance of adjusted orders pending on or before Dec. 31, 1997. Such requests, actions, proceedings, objections, or issuance of adjusted orders may proceed as if such provisions were not amended by Laws 1997, Ch. 398 § 4. *See* Laws 1998, Ch. 214 § 64.

Amended by Laws 1966, Ch. 256; Laws 1974, Ch. 937; Laws 1980, Ch. 281, eff. July 19, 1980; Laws 1983, Ch. 362, eff. June 26, 1983; Laws 1984, ch. 745, eff. Dec. 3, 1984; Laws 1989, Ch. 567, § 8, eff. Sept. 15, 1989; Laws 1990, Ch. 818, §§ 10, 11, eff. July 25, 1990, and applicable to all pending petitions, motions and applications for child support; Laws 1992, Ch. 41, §§ 147, 148, eff. Apr. 2, 1992; Laws 1993, Ch. 59, § 21, eff. July 1, 1993; Laws 1993, Ch. 59, § 18, adding new subd. (3); Laws 1994, Ch. 170, § 367, eff. June 9, 1994; Laws 1995, Ch. 81, §§ 240-241, eff. July 1, 1995; Laws 1997, Ch. 398, §§ 97, 100, and 101, eff. Jan. 1, 1998; Laws 1998, Ch. 214, § 64, eff. July 7, 1998, deemed in full force and effect Jan. 1, 1998; Laws 2003, Ch. 81, § 3, eff. June 18, 2003, amending sub. 3, par. b, subpar. 5 and 6.

FCA

§ 413-a. Review and cost of living adjustment of child support orders.

1. Request. Any party to a child support order issued on behalf of a child in receipt of public assistance, or child support enforcement services pursuant to section one hundred eleven-g of the social services law, may request that the support collection unit review the order for cost of living adjustment purposes pursuant to section one hundred eleven-n of the social services law.

2. Adjustment process. (a) A cost of living adjustment shall be made by the support collection unit with respect to an order of support under review if the sum of the annual average changes of the consumer price index for all urban consumers (CPI-U), as published annually by the United States Department of Labor Bureau of Labor Statistics, is ten percent or greater.

(b) The cost of living adjustment and adjusted child support obligation amount as calculated by the review shall be reflected on the adjusted order issued by the support collection unit and mailed to the parties by first class mail. The child support obligation amount contained in the adjusted order shall be due and owing on the date the first payment is due under the terms of the order of support which was reviewed and adjusted occurring on or after the effective date of the adjusted order.

(c) The support collection unit shall provide a copy of the adjusted order to the court which issued the most recent order of support, which shall append it to the order.

3. Objection process. (a) An objection to a cost of living adjustment, as reflected in an adjusted order issued by a support collection unit, may be made to the court by either party to the order, or by the support collection unit, and shall be submitted to the court in writing within thirty-five days from the date of mailing of the adjusted order. A copy of the written objection shall be provided by the objecting party to the other party and to the support collection unit.

(b) Where such objections are timely filed, the cost of living adjustment shall not take effect, and a hearing on the adjustment of such order shall be granted pursuant to the provisions of this section, which shall result in either:

(1) the issuance by the court of a new order of support in accordance with the child support standards as set forth in section four hundred thirteen of this article; or

(2) where application of the child support standards as set forth in section four hundred thirteen of this article results in a determination that no adjustment is appropriate, an order of no adjustment.

(c) Any order of support made by the court under this section shall occur without the requirement for proof or showing of a change in circumstances.

(d) The court shall conduct the hearing and make its determination no later than forty-five days from the date it receives an objection. If the order under review does not provide for health insurance benefits for the child, the court shall make a determination regarding such benefits pursuant to section four hundred sixteen of this part. The clerk of the court shall immediately transmit copies of the order of support or order of no adjustment issued by the court pursuant to this subdivision to the parties and the support collection unit. Where a hearing results in the issuance of a new order of support, the effective date of the court order shall be the earlier of the date of the court determination or the date the cost of living adjustment would have been effective had it not been challenged.

(e) Where no objection has been timely raised to a cost of living adjustment as reflected in an adjusted order, such adjustment shall become final without further review by the court or any judge or support magistrate thereof.

4. Modification of orders. Nothing herein shall be deemed in any way to limit, restrict, expand or impair the rights of any party to file for a modification of a child support order as is otherwise provided by law.

5. Notice. Parties eligible for adjustment of child support orders shall receive notice of the right to review such orders as follows:

(a) all applications or motions by the support collection unit or by persons seeking support enforcement services through the support collection unit for the establishment, modification, enforcement, violation or adjustment of child support orders shall on their face in conspicuous type state:

NOTE: (1) A COURT ORDER OF SUPPORT RESULTING FROM A PRO-CEEDING COMMENCED BY THIS APPLICATION (PETITION) SHALL BE ADJUSTED BY THE APPLICATION OF A COST OF LIVING ADJUST-MENT AT THE DIRECTION OF THE SUPPORT COLLECTION UNIT NO EARLIER THAN TWENTY-FOUR MONTHS AFTER SUCH ORDER IS ISSUED, LAST MODIFIED OR LAST ADJUSTED, UPON THE REQUEST OF ANY PARTY TO THE ORDER OR PURSUANT TO PARAGRAPH (2) BELOW. SUCH COST OF LIVING ADJUSTMENT SHALL BE ON NOTICE TO BOTH PARTIES WHO, IF THEY OBJECT TO THE COST OF LIVING ADJUSTMENT, SHALL HAVE THE RIGHT TO BE HEARD BY THE COURT AND TO PRESENT EVIDENCE WHICH THE COURT WILL CON-SIDER IN ADJUSTING THE CHILD SUPPORT ORDER IN ACCORDANCE WITH SECTION FOUR HUNDRED THIRTEEN OF THE FAMILY COURT ACT, KNOWN AS THE CHILD SUPPORT STANDARDS ACT.

(2) A PARTY SEEKING SUPPORT FOR ANY CHILD(REN) RECEIVING FAMILY ASSISTANCE SHALL HAVE A CHILD SUPPORT ORDER RE-VIEWED AND ADJUSTED AT THE DIRECTION OF THE SUPPORT COL-LECTION UNIT NO EARLIER THAN TWENTY-FOUR MONTHS AFTER SUCH ORDER IS ISSUED, LAST MODIFIED OR LAST ADJUSTED BY THE SUPPORT COLLECTION UNIT, WITHOUT FURTHER APPLICATION BY ANY PARTY. ALL PARTIES WILL RECEIVE A COPY OF THE ADJUSTED ORDER.

(3) WHERE ANY PARTY FAILS TO PROVIDE, AND UPDATE UPON ANY CHANGE, THE SUPPORT COLLECTION UNIT WITH A CURRENT

ADDRESS, AS REQUIRED BY SECTION FOUR HUNDRED FORTY-THREE OF THE FAMILY COURT ACT, TO WHICH AN ADJUSTED ORDER CAN BE SENT, THE SUPPORT OBLIGATION AMOUNT CONTAINED THEREIN SHALL BECOME DUE AND OWING ON THE DATE THE FIRST PAYMENT IS DUE UNDER THE TERMS OF THE ORDER OF SUPPORT WHICH WAS REVIEWED AND ADJUSTED OCCURRING ON OR AFTER THE EFFECTIVE DATE OF THE ADJUSTED ORDER, REGARDLESS OF WHETHER OR NOT THE PARTY HAS RECEIVED A COPY OF THE ADJUSTED ORDER.

(b)   all court orders of support payable through a support collection unit shall on their face in conspicuous type state:

NOTE: (1) THIS ORDER OF CHILD SUPPORT SHALL BE ADJUSTED BY THE APPLICATION OF A COST OF LIVING ADJUSTMENT AT THE DIRECTION OF THE SUPPORT COLLECTION UNIT NO EARLIER THAN TWENTY-FOUR MONTHS AFTER THIS ORDER IS ISSUED, LAST MODIFIED OR LAST ADJUSTED, UPON THE REQUEST OF ANY PARTY TO THE ORDER OR PURSUANT TO PARAGRAPH (2) BELOW. UPON APPLICATION OF A COST OF LIVING ADJUSTMENT AT THE DIRECTION OF THE SUPPORT COLLECTION UNIT, AN ADJUSTED ORDER SHALL BE SENT TO THE PARTIES WHO, IF THEY OBJECT TO THE COST OF LIVING ADJUSTMENT, SHALL HAVE THIRTY-FIVE (35) DAYS FROM THE DATE OF MAILING TO SUBMIT A WRITTEN OBJECTION TO THE COURT INDICATED ON SUCH ADJUSTED ORDER. UPON RECEIPT OF SUCH WRITTEN OBJECTION, THE COURT SHALL SCHEDULE A HEARING AT WHICH THE PARTIES MAY BE PRESENT TO OFFER EVIDENCE WHICH THE COURT WILL CONSIDER IN ADJUSTING THE CHILD SUPPORT ORDER IN ACCORDANCE WITH THE CHILD SUPPORT STANDARDS ACT.

(2) A RECIPIENT OF FAMILY ASSISTANCE SHALL HAVE THE CHILD SUPPORT ORDER REVIEWED AND ADJUSTED AT THE DIRECTION OF THE SUPPORT COLLECTION UNIT NO EARLIER THAN TWENTY-FOUR MONTHS AFTER SUCH ORDER IS ISSUED, LAST MODIFIED OR LAST ADJUSTED WITHOUT FURTHER APPLICATION OF ANY PARTY. ALL PARTIES WILL RECEIVE NOTICE OF ADJUSTMENT FINDINGS.

(3) WHERE ANY PARTY FAILS TO PROVIDE, AND UPDATE UPON ANY CHANGE, THE SUPPORT COLLECTION UNIT WITH A CURRENT ADDRESS, AS REQUIRED BY SECTION FOUR HUNDRED FORTY-THREE OF THE FAMILY COURT ACT, TO WHICH AN ADJUSTED ORDER CAN BE SENT, THE SUPPORT OBLIGATION AMOUNT CONTAINED THEREIN SHALL BECOME DUE AND OWING ON THE DATE THE FIRST PAYMENT IS DUE UNDER THE TERMS OF THE ORDER OF SUPPORT WHICH WAS REVIEWED AND ADJUSTED OCCURRING ON OR AFTER THE EFFECTIVE DATE OF THE ORDER, REGARDLESS OF

WHETHER OR NOT THE PARTY HAS RECEIVED A COPY OF THE ADJUSTED ORDER.

Added by Laws 1997, Ch. 398, § 99, eff. Jan. 1, 1998; **amended** by Laws 2002, Ch. 624, § 1, eff. Oct. 2, 2002; provided, however, that sections six through sixteen of this act shall take effect on the thirtieth day after it shall have become a law; provided, further, that the amendments to subdivisions 12 and 15 of section 111-b of the social services law made by sections six and seven of this act shall not affect the repeal of such subdivisions and shall be deemed to be repealed therewith; Laws 2003, Ch. 81, § 4, eff. June 18, 2003, amending sub 3, par. (e).

§ 414. Mother's duty to support child; apportionment.

Repealed by Laws 1980, Ch. 281, eff. July 19, 1980.

§ 415. Duties to support recipient of public assistance or welfare and patients in institutions in the department of mental hygiene.

Except as otherwise provided by law, the spouse or parent of a recipient of public assistance or care or of a person liable to become in need thereof or of a patient in an institution in the department of mental hygiene, if of sufficient ability, is responsible for the support of such person or patient, provided that a parent shall be responsible only for the support of his child or children who have not attained the age of twenty-one years. In its discretion, the court may require any such person to contribute a fair and reasonable sum for the support of such relative and may apportion the costs of such support among such persons as may be just and appropriate in view of the needs of the petitioner and the other circumstances of the case and their respective means. Stepparents shall in like manner be responsible for the support of children under the age of twenty-one years.

Amended by Laws 1965, Ch. 674; Laws 1966, Ch. 256; Laws 1974, Ch. 937; Laws 1977, Ch. 777, eff. Aug. 5, 1977.

§ 416. Elements of support; provisions for accident, life and health insurance benefits.

(a) The court may include in the requirements for an order for support the providing of necessary shelter, food, clothing, care, medical attention, expenses of confinement, the expense of education, payment of funeral expenses, and other proper and reasonable expenses.

(b) The court may also order a party to purchase, maintain, or assign a policy of accident insurance or insurance on the life of either party and designate in the case of life insurance, the person or persons on whose behalf the petition is brought or in the case of accident insurance, the insured party as irrevocable beneficiaries during a period of time fixed by the court. The obligation to provide such insurance shall cease upon the termination of such party's duty to provide support.

(c)   Every support order shall provide that if any legally responsible relative currently, or at any time in the future, has health insurance benefits available that may be extended or obtained to cover any person on whose behalf the petition is brought, such responsible relative is required to exercise the option of additional coverage in favor of such person whom he or she is legally responsible to support and to execute and deliver to such person any forms, notices, documents, or instruments to assure timely payment of any health insurance claims for such person.

(d)   As used in this section, the following terms shall have the following meanings: (1) "Health insurance benefits" means any medical, dental, optical and prescription drugs and health care services or other health care benefits that may be provided for a dependent through an employer or organization, including such employers or organizations which are self insured, or through other available health insurance or health care coverage plans.

(2)   "Available health insurance benefits" means any health insurance benefits that are reasonable in cost and that are reasonably accessible to the person on whose behalf the petition is brought. Health insurance benefits that are not reasonable in cost or whose services are not reasonably accessible to such person shall be considered unavailable.

(e)   When the person on whose behalf the petition is brought is a child, the court shall consider the availability of health insurance benefits to all parties and shall take the following action to insure that health insurance benefits are provided for the benefit of the child:

(1)   Where the child is presently covered by health insurance benefits, the court shall direct in the order of support that such coverage be maintained, unless either parent requests the court to make a direction for health insurance benefits coverage pursuant to paragraph two of this subdivision.

(2)   Where the child is not presently covered by health insurance benefits, the court shall make its determination as follows:

(i)   If only one parent has available health insurance benefits, the court shall direct in the order of support that such parent provide health insurance benefits.

(ii)   If both parents have available health insurance benefits the court shall direct in the order of support that either parent or both parents provide such health insurance. The court shall make such determination based on the circumstances of the case, including, but not limited to, the cost and comprehensiveness of the respective health insurance benefits and the best interests of the child.

(iii)   If neither parent has available health insurance benefits, the court shall direct in the order of support that the custodial parent apply for the state's child health insurance plan pursuant to title one-A of article twenty-five of the public health law and the medical assistance program established pursuant to title eleven of article five of the social services law. If eligible for such coverage, the court shall prorate the cost of any premium or family contribution in accordance with subdivision (f) of this section. A direction issued under this subdivision shall not limit or alter either parent's obligation to obtain health insurance benefits at such time as they become available as required pursuant to subdivision (c) of this section.

(f)   The cost of providing health insurance benefits pursuant to subdivision (e) of this section shall be prorated between the parties in the same proportion as each parent's income is to the combined parental income. If the custodial parent is ordered to provide such benefits, the non-custodial parent's pro rata share of such costs shall be added to the basic support obligation. If the non-custodial parent is ordered to provide such benefits, the custodial parent's pro rata share of such costs shall be deducted from the basic support obligation. Where the court finds that such proration is unjust or inappropriate, the court shall:

(1)   order the parties to pay such amount of the cost of health insurance benefits as the court finds just and appropriate;

(2)   add or subtract such amount in the manner set forth herein; and

(3)   set forth in the order the factors it considered, the amount of each party's share of the cost and the reason or reasons the court did not order such pro rata apportionment.

FCA

(g)   The court shall provide in the order of support that the legally responsible relative immediately notify the other party, or the other party and the support collection unit when the order is issued on behalf of a child in receipt of public assistance and care or in receipt of services pursuant to section one hundred eleven-g of the social services law, of any change in health insurance benefits, including any termination of benefits, change in the health insurance benefit carrier, premium, or extent and availability of existing or new benefits.

(h)   Where the court determines that health insurance benefits are available, the court shall provide in the order of support that the legally responsible relative immediately enroll the eligible dependents named in the order who are otherwise eligible for such benefits without regard to any seasonal enrollment restrictions. The support order shall further direct the legally responsible relative to maintain such benefits as long as they remain available to such relative. Such order shall further direct the legally responsible relative to assign all insurance reimbursement payments for health care expenses incurred for his or her eligible dependents to the provider of such services or the party actually having incurred and satisfied such expenses, as appropriate.

(i)   When the court issues an order of child support or combined child and spousal support on behalf of persons in receipt of public assistance and care or in receipt of services pursuant to section one hundred eleven-g of the social services law, such order shall further direct that the provision of health care benefits shall be immediately enforced pursuant to section fifty-two hundred forty-one of the civil practice law and rules.

(j) When the court issues an order of child support or combined child and spousal support on behalf of persons other than those in receipt of public assistance and care or in receipt of services pursuant to section one hundred eleven-g of the social services law, the court shall also issue a separate order which shall include the necessary direction to ensure the order's characterization as a qualified medical child support order as defined by section six hundred nine of the employee retirement income security act of 1974 (29 USC 1169). Such order shall: (i) clearly state that it creates or recognizes the existence of the right of the named dependent to be enrolled and to receive benefits for which the legally responsible relative is eligible under the available group health plans, and shall clearly specify the name, social security number and mailing address of the legally responsible relative, and of each dependent to be covered by the order; (ii) provide a clear description of the type of coverage to be provided by the group health plan to each such dependent or the manner in which the type of coverage is to be determined; and (iii) specify the period of time to which the order applies. The court shall not require the group health plan to provide any type or form of benefit or option not otherwise provided under the group health plan except to the extent necessary to meet the requirements of a law relating to medical child support described in section one thousand three hundred and ninety-six g-1of title forty-two of the United States code.

(k) Upon a finding that a legally responsible relative wilfully failed to obtain health insurance benefits in violation of a court order, such relative will be presumptively liable for all health care expenses incurred on behalf of such dependents from the first date such dependents were eligible to be enrolled to receive health insurance benefits after the issuance of the order of support directing the acquisition of such coverage.

Amended by Laws 1974, Ch. 937, eff. Sept. 1, 1974; Laws 1978, Ch. 456, eff. July 1, 1978; Laws 1984, Ch. 794, eff. Sept. 1, 1984; Laws 1986, Ch. 849, eff. Aug. 2, 1986; amended by Laws 1993, Ch. 59 § 7, eff. July 1, 1993; Laws 1994, Ch. 170, § 368, eff. June 9, 1994; Laws 1997, Ch. 398, § 143, eff. Jan. 1, 1998; Laws 1998, Ch. 214, § 58, eff. Nov. 4, 1998, and Ch. 393, § 1, eff. July 22, 1998; Laws 2002, Ch. 624, § 2, eff. Oct. 2, 2002, **redesignated** former subd. (a) to become new subds. (a), (b), and (c), former subd. (b) to become new subd. (d), (e), (f), (g), and (h), former subds. (e), (f), and (g) to become new subds. (i), (j), and (k).

§ 417. Child of ceremonial marriage.

A child born of parents who at any time prior or subsequent to the birth of said child shall have entered into a ceremonial marriage shall be deemed the legitimate child of both parents for all purposes of this article regardless of the validity of such marriage.

§ 418. Genetic marker and DNA tests; admissibility of records or reports of test results; costs of tests.

(a) The court, on its own motion or motion of any party, when paternity is contested, shall order the mother, the child and the alleged father to submit to one or more genetic marker or DNA marker tests of a type generally acknowledged as reliable by an accreditation body designated by the secretary of the federal department of health and human services and performed by a laboratory approved by such an accreditation body and by the commissioner of health or by a duly qualified physician to aid in the determination of whether the alleged father is or is not the father of the child. No such test shall be ordered, however, upon a written finding by the court that it is not in the best interests of the child on the basis of res judicata, equitable estoppel or the presumption of legitimacy of a child born to a married woman. The record or report of the results of any such genetic marker or DNA test shall be received in evidence, pursuant to subdivision (e) of rule forty-five hundred eighteen of the civil practice law and rules where no timely objection in writing has been made thereto. Any order pursuant to this section shall state in plain language that the results of such test shall be admitted into evidence, pursuant to rule forty-five hundred eighteen of the civil practice law and rules absent timely objections thereto and that if such timely objections are not made, they shall be deemed waived and shall not be heard by the court. If the record or report of results of any such genetic marker or DNA test or tests indicate at least a ninety-five percent probability of paternity, the admission of such record or report shall create a rebuttable presumption of paternity, and, if unrebutted, shall establish the paternity of and liability for the support of a child pursuant to this article and article five of this act.

FCA

(b)   Whenever the court directs a genetic marker or DNA test pursuant to this section, a report made as provided in subdivision (a) of this section may be received in evidence pursuant to rule forty-five hundred eighteen of the civil practice law and rules if offered by any party.

(c)   The cost of any test ordered pursuant to subdivision (a) of this section shall be, in the first instance, paid by the moving party. If the moving party is financially unable to pay such cost, the court may direct any qualified public health officer to conduct such test, if practicable; otherwise, the court may direct payment from the funds of the appropriate local social service district. In its order of disposition, however, the court may direct that the cost of any such test be apportioned between the parties according to their respective abilities to pay or be assessed against the party who does not prevail on the issue of paternity, unless such party is financially unable to pay.

Amended by Laws 1981, Ch. 9, eff. Mar. 2, 1981; Laws 1982, Ch. 773, eff. Sept. 27, 1982; Laws 1982, Ch. 695, eff. July 22, 1982; Laws 1983, Ch. 311, eff. June 21, 1983; Laws 1984, Ch. 792, eff. Aug. 5, 1984 and applicable to any action or proceeding pending on or commenced after the effective date; Laws 1990, Ch. 818, § 12, eff. July 25, 1990, and applicable to all pending petitions, motions and applications for child support; Laws 1994, Ch. 170, § 352, eff. June 15, 1994; Laws 1997, Ch. 398, § 79, eff. Nov. 11, 1997; Laws 1998, Ch. 214, § 44, eff. July 7, 1998.

Part 2. Venue and preliminary procedure.

Editor's Note: Domestic Relations Law § 37(1), amended by Laws 1966, Ch. 299 eff. May 3, 1966, permits a proceeding commenced pursuant to the uniform support of dependents law to be removed from the initiating court to a court in the county within the state to which the petitioner's residence or domicile has been changed.

§ 421. Venue.

Proceedings to compel support under this article may be originated in the county in which one of the parties resides or is domiciled at the time of the filing of the petition. Upon application, the family court may change the place of trial of a proceeding in accordance with article five of the civil practice law and rules.

Amended by Laws 1965, Ch. 305, eff. Sept. 1, 1965; Laws 1980, Ch. 281, eff. July 19, 1980; Laws 1986, Ch. 892, eff. Aug. 2, 1986.

§ 422. Persons who may originate proceedings.

(a) A husband, wife, child, or relative in need of public assistance or care may originate a proceeding under this article to compel a person chargeable with the support to support the petitioner as required by law. A social services official may originate a proceeding under this article if so authorized by section one hundred and two of the social services law. The commissioner of mental health may originate a proceeding under this article when authorized by article forty-three of the mental hygiene law. A parent or guardian, of a child, or other person in loco parentis, or a representative of an incorporated charitable or philanthropic society having a legitimate interest in the petitioner, or, when the petitioner is unable because of his physical or mental condition to file a petition, a guardian ad litem, or a committee, conservator, next friend or other person appointed by the court, may file a petition in behalf of a dependent relative.

(b) Any party to a decree of divorce, separation, or annulment may originate a proceeding to enforce or modify a decree of the supreme court or a court of competent jurisdiction, not of the state of New York, as is provided in part six of this article.

Amended by Laws, 1966, Ch. 256; Laws 1968, Ch. 331; Laws 1973, Ch. 195; Laws 1980, Ch. 281, eff. July 19, 1980; Laws 1981, Ch. 115, eff. May 18, 1981.

§ 423.　Petition; prior demand not required.

Proceedings under this article are commenced by the filing of a petition, which may be made on information and belief. The petitioner need not make a demand upon the respondent for support as a condition precedent to the filing of a petition for support. Any such petition for the establishment, modification and/or enforcement of a child support obligation for persons not in receipt of family assistance, which contains a request for child support enforcement services completed in a manner as specified in section one hundred eleven-g of the social services law, shall constitute an application for such services.

Amended by Laws 1981, Ch. 622, eff. July 21, 1981, but deemed effective as of Aug. 1, 1976; Laws 1990, Ch. 818, § 13, eff. Sept. 30, 1990; Laws 1997, Ch. 436, § 1 Part B, § 110, eff. Aug. 20, 1997.

§ 424.　Probation services.

1.　A local probation service may provide services to a party seeking to establish, modify or enforce a support obligation where there is a contract with the appropriate social services district for the performance of support collection services under section one hundred eleven-h of the social services law.

2.　A local probation service may provide services to persons ordered to pay support seeking to modify such orders.

3.　The probation service may not prevent any person who wishes to file a petition under this article from having access to the court for that purpose nor may the probation service compel any person to appear at any conference, produce any papers or visit any place.

Added by Laws 1986, Ch. 892, eff. Aug. 2, 1986; former § 424 **repealed** by Laws 1986, Ch. 892, eff. Aug. 2, 1986.

§ 424-a.　Compulsory financial disclosure.

Except as provided herein:

(a)　In all support proceedings in family court, there shall be compulsory disclosure by both parties of their respective financial states, provided, however, that this requirement shall not apply to a social services official who is a party in any support proceeding under this act. No showing of special circumstances shall be required before such disclosure is ordered and such disclosure may not be waived by either party or by the court. A sworn statement of net worth shall be filed with the clerk of the court on a date to be fixed by the court, no later than ten days after the return date of the petition. As used in this part, the term "net worth" shall mean the amount by which total assets including income exceed total liabilities including fixed financial obligations. It shall include all income and assets of whatsoever kind and nature and wherever situated and shall include a list of all assets transferred in any manner during the preceding three years, or the length of the marriage, whichever is shorter, provided, however, that transfers in the routine course of business which resulted in an exchange of assets of substantially equivalent value need not be specifically disclosed where such assets are otherwise identified in the statement of net worth. All such sworn statements of net worth shall be accompanied by a current and representative paycheck stub and the most recently filed state and federal income tax returns including a copy of the W-2(s) wage and tax statement(s) submitted with the returns. In addition, both parties shall provide information relating to any and all group health plans available to them for the provision of care or other medical benefits by insurance or otherwise for the benefit of the child or children for whom support is sought, including all such information as may be required to be included in a qualified medical child support order as defined in section six hundred nine of the Employee Retirement Income Security act of 1974 (29 USC 1169) including, but not limited to: (i) the name and last known mailing address of each party and of each dependent to be covered by the order; (ii) the identification and a description of each group health plan available for the benefit or coverage of the disclosing party and the child or children for whom support is sought; (iii) a detailed description of the type of coverage available from each group health plan for the potential benefit of each such dependent; (iv) the identification of the plan administrator for each such group health plan and the address of such administrator; (v) the identification numbers for each such group health plan; and (vi) such other information as may be required by the court;

(b) When a respondent fails, without good cause, to file a sworn statement of net worth, a current and representative paycheck stub and the most recently filed state and federal income tax returns, including a copy of the W-2(s) wage and tax statement submitted with the returns, or to provide information relating to all group health plans available for the provision of care or other medical benefits by insurance or otherwise for the benefit of the disclosing party and the child or children for whom support is sought, as provided in subdivision (a) of this section, the court on its own motion or on application shall grant the relief demanded in the petition or shall order that, for purposes of the support proceeding, the respondent shall be precluded from offering evidence as to respondent's financial ability to pay support;

(c) When a petitioner other than a social services official fails, without good cause to file a sworn statement of net worth, a current and representative paycheck stub and the most recently filed state and federal income tax returns, as provided in subdivision (a) of this section, the court may on its own motion or upon application of any party adjourn such proceeding until such time as the petitioner files with the court such statements and tax returns. The provisions of this subdivision shall not apply to proceedings establishing temporary support or proceedings for the enforcement of a support order or support provision of a separation agreement or stipulation.

Added by Laws 1977, Ch. 516, eff. July 1, 1977; **amended** by Laws, 1980, Ch. 281, eff. July 19, 1980; Laws 1986, Ch. 892, eff. Aug. 2, 1986; Laws 1987, Ch. 815, eff. Dec. 5, 1987; Laws 1989, Ch. 715, eff. Aug. 23, 1989; Laws 1997, Ch. 398, § 144, eff. Jan. 1, 1998; Laws 1998, Ch. 214, § 59, eff. Nov. 4, 1998.

§ 425. Agreement to support.

If an agreement for the support of the petitioner is brought about, it must be reduced to writing and submitted to the family court or a support magistrate appointed pursuant to section four hundred thirty-nine of this act for approval. If the court or support magistrate approves it, the court without further hearing may thereupon enter an order for the support of the petitioner by the respondent in accordance with the agreement, which shall be binding upon the respondent and shall in all respects be a valid order as though made after process had been issued out of the court. The court record shall show that such order was made upon agreement.

Added by Laws 1986, Ch. 892, eff. Aug. 2, 1986; Laws 2003, Ch. 81, § 5, eff. June 18, 2003.

§ 426. Issuance of summons.

(a) On the filing of a petition under this article, the court may cause a copy of the petition and a summons to be issued, requiring the respondent to show cause why the order of support and other and further relief prayed for by the petition should not be made.

(b) The summons shall contain or have attached thereto a notice stating: (i) that a respondent's failure to appear shall result in entry of an order of default; (ii) that the respondent must provide the court with proof of his or her income and assets; (iii) that a temporary or permanent order of support will be made on the return date of the summons; and (iv) that a respondent's failure to appear may result in the suspension of his or her driving privileges; state professional, occupational and business licenses; and recreational licenses and permits.

Added by Laws 1986, Ch. 892, eff. Aug. 2, 1986; **amended** by Laws 1997, Ch. 398, § 109, eff. Jan. 1, 1998.

§ 427. Service of summons.

(a) Personal service of a summons and petition may be made by delivery of a true copy thereof to the person summoned at least eight days before the time stated therein for appearance; or by delivery of a true copy thereof to a person of suitable age and discretion at the actual place of business, dwelling place or usual place of abode of the person to be served and by mailing a true copy thereof to the person to be served at his last known residence at least eight days before the time stated in the summons for appearance; proof of service shall identify such person of suitable age and discretion and state the date, time and place of service.

(b)   If after reasonable effort, personal service is not made, the court may at any stage in the proceedings make an order providing for substituted service in the manner provided for substituted service in the civil practice law and rules.

(c)   In any case, whether or not service is attempted under subdivision (a) or (b) of this section, service of a summons and petition under this section may be effected by mail alone to the last known address of the person to be served. Service by mail alone shall be made at least eight days before the time stated in the summons for appearance. If service is by mail alone, the court will enter an order of support by default if there is proof satisfactory to the court that the respondent had actual notice of the commencement of the proceeding which may be established upon sufficient proof that the summons and petition were in fact mailed by certified mail and signed for at the respondent's correct street address or signed for at the post office. If service by certified mail at the respondent's correct street address cannot be accomplished, service pursuant to subdivisions one, two, three or four of section three hundred eight of the civil practice law and rules shall be deemed good and sufficient service. Upon failure of the respondent to obey a summons served in accordance with the provisions of this section by means other than mail alone, the court will enter an order of support by default. Such order of support shall be made pursuant to the provisions set forth in section four hundred thirteen of this article. The respondent shall have the right to make a motion for relief from such default order within one year from the date such order was entered.

Amended by Laws 1975, Ch. 41; Laws 1978, Ch. 170, eff. May 23, 1978; Ch. 439, eff. Sept. 1, 1978 Ch. 456, eff. July 1, 1978; Laws 1979, Ch. 106, eff. May 21, 1979; Laws 1984, Ch. 791, eff. Aug. 5, 1984; Laws 1993, Ch. 59, § 26, eff. July 1, 1993.

§ 428.   Issuance of warrant; certificate of warrant.

(a)   The court may issue a warrant, directing that the respondent be arrested, brought before the court, when a petition is presented to the court under section four hundred twenty-three and it appears that

(i)   the summons cannot be served; or

(ii)   the respondent has failed to obey the summons; or

(iii)   the respondent is likely to leave the jurisdiction; or

(iv)   a summons, in the court's opinion, would be ineffectual; or

(v)   the safety of the petitioner is endangered; or

(vi)   a respondent on bail or on parole has failed to appear.

(b)   The petitioner may not serve a warrant upon the respondent, unless the court itself grants such permission upon the application of the petitioner. The clerk of the court may issue to the petitioner or to the representative of an incorporated charitable or philanthropic society having a legitimate interest in the family a certificate stating that a warrant for the respondent has been issued by the court. The presentation of such certificate by said petitioner or representative to any peace officer, acting pursuant to his special duties, or police officer authorizes him to arrest the respondent and take him to court.

(c)   A certificate of warrant expires ninety days from the date of issue but may be renewed from time to time by the clerk of the court.

(d)   Rules of court shall provide that a record of all unserved warrants be kept and that periodic reports concerning unserved warrants be made.

Amended by Laws 1980, Ch. 843, eff. Sept. 1, 1980.

§ 429.   Sequestration of respondent's property.

Where in a proceeding under this article it appears to the court that the respondent is not within the state, or cannot be found therein, or is concealing himself or herself therein, so that process cannot be personally served upon the respondent, the court may at any time and from time to time make any order or orders without notice directing the sequestration of his or her property, both real and personal and whether tangible or intangible, within the state, and may appoint a receiver thereof, or by injunction or otherwise take the same into its possession and control. The property thus sequestered and the income therefrom may be applied in whole or in part and from time to time, under the direction of the court and as justice may require, to the payment of such sum or sums as the court may deem it proper to award, by order, and during the pendency of the proceeding or at the termination thereof, for the education or maintenance of any of the children of a marriage, or for the support of a spouse, or for his or her expenses in bringing and carrying on said proceeding; and if the rents and profits of the real estate, together with the other property so sequestered, be insufficient to pay the sums of money required, the court, upon such terms and conditions as it may prescribe, may direct the mortgage or sale of sufficient of said real estate to pay such sums. The court may appoint petitioning spouse receiver or sequestrator in such cases. The court may authorize such spouse to use and occupy, free of any liability for rent or use and occupation or otherwise, any house or other suitable property of the respondent spouse as a dwelling for himself or herself with or without the children of the marriage,, and may likewise turn over to the petitioning spouse for the use of such spouse with or without the children of the marriage any chattel or chattels of the respondent spouse. The relief herein provided for is in addition to any and every other remedy to which a spouse may be entitled under the law.

Added by Laws 1966, Ch. 721, eff. Sept. 1, 1966 and former § 429 repealed; **amended** by Laws 1980, Ch. 281, eff. July 19, 1980.

§ 430.   Temporary order of protection.

(a)   Upon the filing of a petition under this article, the court for good cause shown may issue a temporary order of protection which may contain any of the provisions authorized on the making of an order of protection under section four hundred forty-six.

(b) A temporary order of protection is not a finding of wrongdoing.

(c) The court may issue or extend a temporary order of protection ex parte or on notice simultaneously with the issuance of a warrant, directing that the respondent be arrested and brought before the court pursuant to section four hundred twenty-eight of this article.

Added by Laws 1964, Ch. 566, eff. Apr. 16, 1964; **amended** by Laws 1981, Ch. 416, eff. Aug. 6, 1981.

Part 3. Hearing

§ 431. Preliminary procedure on warrant.

(a) When a respondent is taken into custody pursuant to a warrant issued by a family court in New York City under section four hundred twenty-eight, he shall be taken before the court issuing the warrant if the respondent is taken into custody in New York City. If the respondent is taken into custody in a county not within New York City, he shall be taken before a family judge in that county.

(b) When a respondent is taken into custody pursuant to a warrant issued by a family court in a county not within the city of New York, he shall be taken before the court issuing the warrant if the respondent is taken into custody in the county in which the court sits. If the respondent is taken into custody in a different county, he shall be brought before a family court judge in that county.

§ 432. Procedure before court.

The court before whom the respondent is taken under section four hundred thirty-one may require an undertaking to appear or in default thereof may place the respondent in custody until the hearing commences.

§ 433. Hearing.

(a) Upon the return of the summons or when a respondent is brought before the court pursuant to a warrant, the court shall proceed to hear and determine the case. The respondent shall be informed of the contents of the petition, advised of his right to counsel, and shall be given opportunity to be heard and to present witnesses. The court may exclude the public from the court room in a proper case.

(b)   If the initial return of a summons or warrant is before a judge of the court, when support is an issue, the judge must make an immediate order, either temporary or permanent with regard to support. If a temporary order is made, the court shall refer the issue of support to a support magistrate for final determination pursuant to sections four hundred thirty-nine and four hundred thirty-nine-a of this act. Procedures shall be established by the chief administrator of the courts which shall provide for the disposition of all support matters or a referral to a support magistrate prior to the conclusion of a respondent's first appearance before the court. Such procedures shall provide for referral of support issues by appropriate clerical staff of the family court at any time after a petition has been presented to the court.

(c)   In any proceeding under this article, the court may permit a party or a witness to be deposed or to testify by telephone, audio-visual means, or other electronic means at a designated family court or other location:

(i)   where such party or witness resides in a county other than that of the family court where the case is pending and that of any contiguous county; pro-vided, however, that for the purposes of this section, the five counties of New York city shall be treated as one county;

(ii)   where such party or witness is presently incarcerated and will be incarcerated on the date on which the hearing or deposition is scheduled and is not expected to be released within a reasonable period of time after the date on which the hearing or deposition is scheduled; or

(iii)   where the court determines that it would be an undue hardship for such party or witness to testify or to be deposed at the family court where the case is pending.

(d)   Any such deposition or testimony taken by telephone, audio-visual means or other electronic means in accordance with subdivision (c) of this section shall be recorded and preserved for transcription. Where a party or witness is deposed or testifies by telephone, audio-visual or other electronic means pursuant to this section, documentary evidence referred to by a party or witness or the court may be transmitted by facsimile, telecopier, or other electronic means and may not be excluded from evidence by reason of an objection based on the means of transmission. The chief administrator of the courts shall promulgate rules to facilitate the taking of testimony by telephone, audio-visual means or other elec-tronic means.

Amended by Laws 1985, Ch. 809, eff. Nov. 1, 1985; Laws 2000, Ch. 475, eff. Dec. 19, 2000, adding subsections (c) and (d); Laws 2003, Ch. 81, § 6, eff. June 18, 2003, amending sub. (b).

§ 434. Order for temporary child support.

The court shall make an order for temporary child support pending a final determination, in an amount sufficient to meet the needs of the child, without a showing of immediate or emergency need. The court shall make an order for temporary child support notwithstanding that information with respect to income and assets of the respondent may be unavailable. Where such information is available, the court may make an award for temporary child support pursuant to the formula set forth in subdivision one of section four hundred thirteen of this article.

Amended by Laws 1986, Ch. 892, eff. Aug. 2, 1986; Laws 1989, Ch. 567, § 9, eff. Sept. 15, 1989.

§ 434-a. Order for temporary spousal support.

The court may make an order for temporary spousal support pending a final determination, notwithstanding that information with respect to income and assets of the respondent may be unavailable.

Added by Laws 1990, Ch. 601, § 1, eff. July 18, 1990.

§ 435. Procedure; adjournment; confidentiality of requests.

(a) Hearings are conducted by the court without a jury. The court may adjourn the hearing to enable it to make inquiry into the surroundings, conditions and capacities of the child, into the financial abilities and responsibilities of both parents and for other proper cause. If the court so adjourns the hearing, it may require the respondent to give an undertaking to appear or in default thereof may commit him until the hearing resumes.

(b) Hearings are conducted without a jury. The support magistrate may adjourn the hearing in order to make inquiry into the surroundings, conditions and capacities of the child and into the financial abilities and responsibilities of both parents and for other proper cause including a referral of issues required to be determined by a judge. If the support magistrate so adjourns the hearing, the support magistrate shall make a temporary order of support, pending a final determination, and may require the respondent to give an undertaking to appear or in default thereof may, subject to the provisions in section four hundred thirty-nine of this act and confirmation by a judge, commit him or her until the hearing resumes. The support magistrate shall enter an order of support on default if the respondent fails to answer or appear after having been properly served.

(c) Reports prepared by the probation service for use by the court at any time prior to the making of an order of disposition shall be deemed confidential information furnished to the court which the court in a proper case may, in its discretion, withhold from or disclose in whole or in part to the support magistrate, law guardian, counsel, party in interest, or other appropriate person. Such reports may not be made available to the court prior to a determination that the respondent is liable under this article for the support of the petitioner.

Amended by Laws 1977, Ch. 388, eff. Sept. 1, 1977; Laws 1985, Ch. 809, eff. Nov. 1, 1985; Laws 2003, Ch. 81, § 7, eff. June 18, 2003, amending sub. (b) and (c).

§ 436. Competence of spouse.

Wives and husbands are competent witnesses against each other in a hearing under section four hundred thirty-three and may testify to non-access in such a hearing.

§ 437. Presumption of sufficient means.

A respondent is prima facie presumed in a hearing under section four hundred thirty-three and section four hundred fifty-four to have sufficient means to support his or her spouse and children under the age of twenty-one years.

Amended by Laws 1974, Ch. 810; Ch. 937; Laws 1980, Ch. 281, eff. July 19, 1980.

§ 438. Counsel fees.

(a) In any proceeding under this article, including proceedings for support of a spouse and children, or for support of children only, or at any hearing to modify or enforce an order entered in that proceeding or a proceeding to modify a decree of divorce, separation, or annulment, including an appeal under article eleven the court may allow counsel fees at any stage of the proceeding, to the attorney representing the spouse, former spouse or person on behalf of children.

(b) In any proceeding for failure to obey any lawful order compelling payment of support of a spouse or former spouse and children, or of children only, the court shall, upon a finding that such failure was willful, order respondent to pay counsel fees to the attorney representing the petitioner or person on behalf of the children. Representation by an attorney pursuant to paragraph (b) of subdivision nine of section one hundred eleven-b of the social services law shall not preclude an award of counsel fees to an applicant which would otherwise be allowed under this section.

Amended by Laws 1963, Ch. 809; Laws 1964, Ch. 52; Laws 1968, Ch. 331; Laws 1980, Ch. 281, eff. July 19, 1980; Laws 1986, Ch. 149, eff. June 16, 1986; Laws 1986, Ch. 892, eff. Aug. 2, 1986.

§ 439. Support magistrates.

(a) [Expires and deemed repealed June 30, 2007], as amended by L 1995, ch 81, L 1997, ch 398, L 2003, ch 81, §8, L 2004, ch 336, §1, L 2005, ch 576, §1 The chief administrator of the courts shall provide, in accordance with subdivision (f) of this section, for the appointment of a sufficient number of support magistrates to hear and determine support proceedings. Except as hereinafter provided, support magistrates shall be empowered to hear, determine and grant any relief within the powers of the court in any proceeding under this article, articles five, five-A, and five-B and sections two hundred thirty-four and two hundred thirty-five of this act, and objections raised pursuant to section five thousand two hundred forty-one of the civil practice law and rules. Support magistrates shall not be empowered to hear, determine and grant any relief with respect to issues specified in subdivision five of section four hundred fifty-four or section four hundred fifty-five of this act, issues of contested paternity involving claims of equitable estoppel, custody, visitation including visitation as a defense, and orders of protection or exclusive possession of the home, which shall be referred to a judge as provided in subdivision (b) or (c) of this section. Where an order of filiation is issued by a judge in a paternity proceeding and child support is in issue, the judge, or support magistrate upon referral from the judge, shall be authorized to immediately make a temporary or final order of support, as applicable. A support magistrate shall have the authority to hear and decide motions and issue summonses and subpoenas to produce persons pursuant to section one hundred fifty-three of this act, hear and decide proceedings and issue any order authorized by subdivision (g) of section five thousand two hundred forty-one of the civil practice law and rules, issue subpoenas to produce prisoners pursuant to section two thousand three hundred two of the civil practice law and rules and make a determination that any person before the support magistrate is in violation of an order of the court as authorized by section one hundred fifty-six of this act subject to confirmation by a judge of the court who shall impose any punishment for such violation as provided by law. A determination by a support magistrate that a person is in willful violation of an order under subdivision three of section four hundred fifty-four of this article and that recommends commitment shall be transmitted to the parties, accompanied by findings of fact, but the determination shall have no force and effect until confirmed by a judge of the court.

(a)   [Eff June 30, 2007], as amended by L 1994, ch 463, L 1997, ch 398, L 2003, ch 81, §9, L 2004, ch 336, §2, L 2005, ch 576, §2 The chief administrator of the courts shall provide, in accordance with subdivision (f) of this section, for the appointment of a sufficient number of support magistrates to hear and determine support proceedings. Except as hereinafter provided, support magistrates shall be empowered to hear, determine and grant any relief within the powers of the court in any proceeding under this article, articles five, five-A, and five-B and sections two hundred thirty-four and two hundred thirty-five of this act, and objections raised pursuant to section five thousand two hundred forty-one of the civil practice law and rules. Support magistrates shall not be empowered to hear, determine and grant any relief with respect to issues specified in section four hundred fifty-five of this act, issues of contested paternity involving claims of equitable estoppel, custody, visitation including visitation as a defense, and orders of protection or exclusive possession of the home, which shall be referred to a judge as provided in subdivision (b) or (c) of this section. Where an order of filiation is issued by a judge in a paternity proceeding and child support is in issue, the judge, or support magistrate upon referral from the judge, shall be authorized to immediately make a temporary or final order of support, as applicable. A support magistrate shall have the authority to hear and decide motions and issue summonses and subpoenas to produce persons pursuant to section one hundred fifty-three of this act, hear and decide proceedings and issue any order authorized by subdivision (g) of section five thousand two hundred forty-one of the civil practice law and rules, issue subpoenas to produce prisoners pursuant to section two thousand three hundred two of the civil practice law and rules and make a determination that any person before the support magistrate is in violation of an order of the court as authorized by section one hundred fifty-six of this act subject to confirmation by a judge of the court who shall impose any punishment for such violation as provided by law. A determination by a support magistrate that a person is in willful violation of an order under subdivision three of section four hundred fifty-four of this article and that recommends commitment shall be transmitted to the parties, accompanied by findings of fact, but the determination shall have no force and effect until confirmed by a judge of the court.

(b) In any proceeding to establish paternity which is heard by a support magistrate, the support magistrate shall advise the mother and putative father of the right to be represented by counsel and shall advise the mother and putative father of their right to blood grouping or other genetic marker or DNA tests in accordance with section five hundred thirty-two of this act. The support magistrate shall order that such tests be conducted in accordance with section five hundred thirty-two of this act. The support magistrate shall be empowered to hear and determine all matters related to the proceeding including the making of an order of filiation pursuant to section five hundred forty-two of this act, provided, however, that where the respondent denies paternity and paternity is contested on the grounds of equitable estoppel, the support magistrate shall not be empowered to determine the issue of paternity, but shall transfer the proceeding to a judge of the court for a determination of the issue of paternity. Where an order of filiation is issued by a judge in a paternity proceeding and child support is in issue, the judge, or support magistrate upon referral from the judge, shall be authorized to immediately make a temporary or final order of support, as applicable. Whenever an order of filiation is made by a support magistrate, the support magistrate also shall make a final or temporary order of support.

(c) The support magistrate, in any proceeding in which issues specified in section four hundred fifty-five of this act, or issues of custody, visitation, including visitation as a defense, orders of protection or exclusive possession of the home are present or in which paternity is contested on the grounds of equitable estoppel, shall make a temporary order of support and refer the proceeding to a judge. Upon determination of such issue by a judge, the judge may make a final determination of the issue of support, or immediately refer the proceeding to a support magistrate for further proceedings regarding child support or other matters within the authority of the support magistrate.

FCA

(d) Rules of evidence shall be applicable in proceedings before a support magistrate. A support magistrate shall have the power to issue subpoenas, to administer oaths and to direct the parties to engage in and permit such disclosure as will expedite the disposition of issues. The assignment of proceedings and matters to support magistrates, the conduct of the trial before a support magistrate, the contents and filing of a support magistrate's findings of fact and decision and all matters incidental to proceedings before support magistrates shall be in accordance with rules provided for by the chief administrator of the courts. Proceedings held before a support magistrate may be recorded mechanically as provided by the chief administrator of the courts. A transcript of such proceeding may be made available in accordance with the rules of the chief administrator of the courts.

(e) The determination of a support magistrate shall include findings of fact and, except with respect to a determination of a willful violation of an order under subdivision three of section four hundred fifty-four of this article where commitment is recommended as provided in subdivision (a) of this section, a final order which shall be entered and transmitted to the parties. Specific written objections to a final order of a support magistrate may be filed by either party with the court within thirty days after receipt of the order in court or by personal service, or, if the objecting party or parties did not receive the order in court or by personal service, thirty-five days after mailing of the order to such party or parties. A party filing objections shall serve a copy of such objections upon the opposing party, who shall have thirteen days from such service to serve and file a written rebuttal to such objections. Proof of service upon the opposing party shall be filed with the court at the time of filing of objections and any rebuttal. Within fifteen days after the rebuttal is filed, or the time to file such rebuttal has expired, whichever is applicable, the judge, based upon a review of the objections and the rebuttal, if any, shall (i) remand one or more issues of fact to the support magistrate, (ii) make, with or without holding a new hearing, his or her own findings of fact and order, or (iii) deny the objections. Pending review of the objections and the rebuttal, if any, the order of the support magistrate shall be in full force and effect and no stay of such order shall be granted. In the event a new order is issued, payments made by the respondent in excess of the new order shall be applied as a credit to future support obligations. The final order of a support magistrate, after objections and the rebuttal, if any, have been reviewed by a judge, may be appealed pursuant to article eleven of this act.

(f) The chief administrator shall promulgate written rules for the selection, appointment, reappointment, compensation and training of support magistrates who shall be attorneys admitted to the practice of law in this state for at least three years and who shall be knowledgeable with respect to the family court and federal and state support law and programs. Support magistrates shall be appointed on a full-time basis for a term of three years and may be reappointed for subsequent terms which shall be five years in length, except that the rules promulgated hereunder may permit the appointment of an acting support magistrate to serve during a support magistrate's authorized leave of absence. Where it is determined that the employment of a full-time support magistrate is not required, one or more counties may agree to share the services of a full-time support magistrate or a support magistrate may be appointed to serve within one or more counties on a part-time basis.

Added by Laws 1985, Ch. 809, eff. Nov. 1, 1985; **amended** by Laws 1986, Ch. 892, eff. Aug. 2, 1986; Laws 1987, Ch. 856, eff. Dec. 23, 1987; Laws 1988, Ch. 461, eff. Aug. 1, 1988; Laws 1990, Ch. 409, § 1, eff. July 10, 1990; Laws 1994, Ch. 463, § 1, eff. Oct. 18, 1994; Laws 1995, Ch. 81, § 215, eff. July 1, 1995; Laws 1996, Ch. 242, eff. June 26, 1996; Laws 1997, Ch. 398, § 44, eff. Jan. 1, 1998; Laws 1998, Ch. 214, § 83-a, eff. July 7, 1998, extending expiration date of subsection (a) to June 30, 1999; Laws 1999, Ch. 140, § 1, eff. June 29, 1999, deemed eff. June 30, 1999, extending expiration date of subsection (a) to June 30, 2001; Laws 2001, Ch. 72, § 1, eff. June 29, 2001, extending expiration date of subsection (a) to June 30, 2003; Laws 2003, Ch. 75, §§ 1, 2, eff. June 18, 2003, amending sub. (f), and shall apply to hearing examiners appointed on or after such date, Ch. 81, §§ 8, 9, 14 eff. June 30, 2003; Laws 2004, Ch. 336, sect;§ 1–3, 5, amending subs. (a), (b), (c), and (e), eff. Nov. 8, 2004; Laws 2005, Ch. 576, § 3, amending subs. (a), eff. Aug. 23, 2005; L. 2005, Ch. 576, §§ 1, amending sub. (a), (b), (c), eff. Aug. 23, 2005.

§ 439-a. Expedited process.

(a)   When used in this section, expedited process means a process in effect in the family court which reduces the processing time of support order establishment and enforcement efforts from the date of successful service of process on the respondent to the date on which a support obligation or enforcement order is entered, the petition is voluntarily withdrawn or the petition is dismissed on the merits or for lack of jurisdiction of the respondent, by the referral of proceedings to hearing examiners appointed and qualified under section four hundred thirty-nine of this article and exercising the powers set forth in such section.

(b)   The chief administrator shall assign a sufficient number of support magistrates to ensure that such expedited process shall conform to the requirements of such case processing as set forth in federal statutes and regulations promulgated by the federal secretary of health and human services.

(c)   The use of an expedited process shall be required (i) in any county which has a population of four hundred thousand or more or which is wholly within a city and (ii) in any county which has a population of less than four hundred thousand and for which the state has not been granted an exemption from the federal expedited process required by federal statutes and regulations of the federal secretary of health and human services.

(d)   The chief administrator of the courts may request of the state commissioner of social services that an exemption from use of an expedited process as required by this section and section four hundred thirty-nine of this article in counties which are not wholly within a city and which have a population of less than four hundred thousand be applied for from the federal secretary of health and human services pursuant to federal statutes and regulations providing for waivers from the federal expedited process requirements. The chief administrator of the courts shall, upon making such a request, provide such information in the possession of the office of court administrator which supports an exemption from use of an expedited process to the state commissioner of social services. Upon receipt of such a request from the chief administrator of the courts, the state commissioner of social services with the approval of the local commissioner of social services may apply to the federal secretary of health and human services for exemption from use of an expedited process. If application for such exemption is made, the state commissioner of social services shall, promptly upon receiving notification from the federal department of health and human services, inform the chief administrator of the courts and the local commissioners of social services of the granting or denial of any such application.

Added by Laws 1985, Ch. 809, eff. Nov. 1, 1985; **amended** by Laws 1990, Ch. 818, § 14, eff. Sept. 30, 1990; Laws 2003, Ch. 81, § 10, eff. June 18, 2003, amending sub. (b).

Part 4.   Orders.

(Repealed and transferred sections noted under appropriate section number of text.)

§ 440.   Order of support.

1.   (a) Any support order made by the court in any proceeding under the provisions of article five-B of this act, pursuant to a reference from the supreme court under section two hundred fifty-one of the domestic relations law or under the provisions of article four, five or five-A of this act (i) shall direct that payments of child support or combined child and spousal support collected on behalf of persons in receipt of services pursuant to section one hundred eleven-g of the social services law, or on behalf of persons in receipt of public assistance be made to the support collection unit designated by the appropriate social services district, which shall receive and disburse funds so paid; or (ii) shall be enforced pursuant to subdivision (c) of section five thousand two hundred forty-two of the civil practice law and rules at the same time that the court issues an order of support; and (iii) shall in either case, except as provided for herein, be

effective as of the earlier of the date of the filing of the petition therefor, or, if the children for whom support is sought are in receipt of public assistance, the date for which their eligibility for public assistance was effective. Any retroactive amount of support due shall be support arrears/past due support and shall be paid in one sum or periodic sums, as the court directs, and any amount of temporary support which has been paid to be taken into account in calculating any amount of such retroactive support due. In addition, such retroactive child support shall be enforceable in any manner provided by law including, but not limited to, an execution for support enforcement pursuant to subdivision (b) of section fifty-two hundred forty-one of the civil practice law and rules. When a child receiving support is a public assistance recipient, or the order of support is being enforced or is to be enforced pursuant to section one hundred eleven-g of the social services law, the court shall establish the amount of retroactive child support and notify the parties that such amount shall be enforced by the support collection unit pursuant to an execution for support enforcement as provided for in subdivision (b) of section fifty-two hundred forty-one of the civil practice law and rules, or in such periodic payments as would have been authorized had such an execution been issued. In such case, the court shall not direct the schedule of repayment of retroactive support. Where such direction is for child support and paternity has been established by a voluntary acknowledgment of paternity as defined in section forty-one hundred thirty-five-b of the public health law, the court shall inquire of the parties whether the acknowledgment has been duly filed, and unless satisfied that it has been so filed shall require the clerk of the court to file such acknowledgment with the appropriate registrar within five business days. The court shall not direct that support payments be made to the support collection unit unless the child, who is the subject of the order, is in receipt of public assistance or child support services pursuant to section one hundred eleven-g of the social services law. Any such order shall be enforceable pursuant to section fifty-two hundred forty-one or fifty-two hundred forty-two of the civil practice law and rules, or in any other manner provided by law. Such orders or judgments for child support and maintenance shall also be enforceable pursuant to article fifty-two of the civil practice law and rules upon a debtor's default as such term is defined in paragraph seven of subdivision (a) of section fifty-two hundred forty-one of the civil practice law and rules. The establishment of a default shall be subject to the procedures established for the determination of a mistake of fact for income executions pursuant to subdivision (e) of section fifty-two hundred forty-one of the civil practice law and rules. For the purposes of enforcement of child support orders or combined spousal and child support orders pursuant to section five thousand two hundred forty-one of the civil practice law and rules, a "default" shall be deemed to include amounts arising from retroactive support. Where permitted under federal law and where the record of the proceedings contains such information, such order shall include on its face the social security number and the name and address of the employer, if any, of the person chargeable with support provided, however, that failure to comply with this requirement shall not invalidate such order.

FCA

(b)   (1) When the court issues an order of child support or combined child and spousal support on behalf of persons in receipt of public assistance or in receipt of services pursuant to section one hundred eleven-g of the social services law, the support collection unit shall issue an income execution immediately for child support or combined spousal and child support, and shall issue an execution for medical support enforcement in accordance with the provisions of the order of support unless: (i) the court finds and sets forth in writing the reasons that there is good cause not to require immediate income withholding; or (ii) when the child is not in receipt of public assistance, a written agreement providing for an alternative arrangement has been reached between the parties. Such written agreement may include an oral stipulation made on the record resulting in a written order. For purposes of this paragraph, good cause shall mean substantial harm to the debtor. The absence of an arrearage or the mere issuance of an income execution shall not constitute good cause. When an immediate income execution or an execution for medical support enforcement is issued by the support collection unit, such execution shall be issued pursuant to section five thousand two hundred forty-one of the civil practice law and rules, except that the provisions thereof relating to mistake of fact, default and any other provisions which are not relevant to the issuance of an execution pursuant to this paragraph shall not apply; provided, however, that if the support collection unit makes an error in the issuance of an execution pursuant to this paragraph, and such error is to the detriment of the debtor, the support collection unit shall have thirty days after notification by the debtor to correct the error. Where permitted under federal law and where the record of the proceedings contains such information, such order shall include on its face the social security number and the name and address of the employer, if any, of the person chargeable with support; provided, however, that failure to comply with this requirement shall not invalidate such order. When the court determines that there is good cause not to immediately issue an income execution or when the parties agree to an alternative arrangement as provided in this paragraph, the court shall provide expressly in the order of support that the support collection unit shall not issue an immediate income execution. Notwithstanding any such order, the support collection unit shall issue an income execution for support enforcement when the debtor defaults on the support obligation, as defined in section five thousand two hundred forty-one of the civil practice law and rules. When an income execution for support enforcement is issued pursuant to this paragraph, such income execution shall supersede any income deduction order previously issued for enforcement of the same support order pursuant to subdivision (c) of section five thousand two hundred forty-two of the civil practice law and rules, whereupon such income deduction order shall cease to have further effect.

(2)   When the court issues an order of child support or combined child and spousal support on behalf of persons other than those in receipt of public assistance or in receipt of services pursuant to section one hundred eleven-g of the social services law, the court shall issue an income deduction order pursuant to subdivision (c) of section five thousand two hundred forty-two of the civil

practice law and rules at the same time at which it issues the order of support. The court shall enter the income deduction order unless the court finds and sets forth in writing: (i) the reasons that there is good cause not to require immediate income withholding; or (ii) that an agreement providing for an alternative arrangement has been reached between the parties. Such agreement may include a written agreement or an oral stipulation, made on the record, that results in a written order. For purposes of this paragraph, good cause shall mean substantial harm to the debtor. The absence of an arrearage or the mere issuance of an income deduction order shall not constitute good cause. Where permitted under federal law and where the record of the proceedings contains such information, the order shall include on its face the social security number and the name and address of the employer, if any, of the person chargeable with support; provided, however, that failure to comply with this requirement shall not invalidate the order. When the court determines that there is good cause not to immediately issue an income deduction order or when the parties agree to an alternative arrangement as provided in this paragraph, the court shall not issue an income deduction order. In addition, the court shall make provisions for health insurance benefits in accordance with the requirements of section four hundred sixteen of this article.

(c)   Any order of support issued on behalf of a child in receipt of family assistance or child support enforcement services pursuant to section one hundred eleven-g of the social services law shall be subject to review and adjustment by the support collection unit pursuant to section one hundred eleven-n of the social services law, section two hundred forty-c of the domestic relations law and section four hundred thirteen-a of this article. Such review and adjustment shall be in addition to any other activities undertaken by the support collection unit relating to the establishment, modification, and enforcement of support orders payable to such unit.

2.   The court shall require any person chargeable with support under the provisions of article five-B of this act or under any support order made pursuant to a reference from the supreme court under section two hundred fifty-one of the domestic relations law or in any proceeding under the provisions of article four, five or five-A of this act to provide his or her social security number, the name and address of his or her employer and to report any changes of employer or change in employment status affecting compensation received, including rate of compensation or loss of employment, to the support collection unit designated by the appropriate social services district and to keep such support collection unit advised of his or her current employer and current employment status; provided, however, that a social security number may be required only where permitted under federal law.

3.   The amount of support determined in accordance with the statewide child support standards, as set forth in section four hundred thirteen of this act, shall constitute prima facie evidence of the ability of any person chargeable with support in accordance with the provisions of article three-a of the domestic relations law or under any support order made pursuant to a reference from the

supreme court under section two hundred fifty-one of the domestic relations law or in any proceeding under the provisions of article four, five or five-a of this chapter to support or contribute such amount towards the support of his or her children.

4. Any support order made by the court in any proceeding under the provisions of article five-B of this act, pursuant to a reference from the supreme court under section two hundred fifty-one of the domestic relations law or under the provisions of article four, five or five-A of this act shall include, on its face, a notice printed or typewritten in a size equal to at least eight point bold type informing the respondent that a willful failure to obey the order may, after court hearing, result in commitment to jail for a term not to exceed six months for contempt of court.

5. The court shall direct that a copy of any child support or combined child and spousal support order issued by the court on or after the first day of October, nineteen hundred ninety-eight, in any proceeding pursuant to a reference from the supreme court under section two hundred fifty-one of the domestic relations law or under the provisions of article four, five, five-a or five-b of this act be provided promptly to the state case registry established pursuant to subdivision four-a of section one hundred eleven-b of the social services law.

6. Any order of support made by the court shall provide for health insurance benefits pursuant to section four hundred sixteen of this article.

Added by Laws 1977, Ch. 516; **amended** by Laws 1978, Ch. 456, eff. July 1, 1978; Laws 1983, Ch. 274, eff. July 11, 1983; Laws 1984, ch. 632, eff. July 27, 1984; Laws 1985, Ch. 809, eff. Nov. 1, 1985; Laws 1986, Ch. 892, eff. Aug. 5, 1986; Laws 1989, Ch. 567, § 10, eff. Sept. 15, 1989; Laws 1990, Ch. 818, § 15, eff. Nov. 1, 1990, and applicable to all pending petitions, motions and applications for child support; Laws 1992, Ch. 41, § 142, eff. Apr. 2, 1992; Laws 1993, Ch. 59, §§ 2, 11, eff. July 1, 1993; Laws 1993, Ch. 59, § 22, adding new para. (c) to FCA § 440(1); Laws 1993, Ch. 354, § 3, eff. July 1, 1993; Laws 1994, Ch. 170, §§ 364-365, eff. June 15, 1994; Laws 1997, Ch. 398, §§ 45, 46, and 98, eff. Jan. 1, 1998, and § 7, eff. Oct. 1, 1998, adding new para. (5) to FCA § 440; Laws 1998, Ch. 214, § 59-a, eff. Nov. 4, 1998; Laws 2002, Ch. 624, § 3, eff. Oct. 2, 2002, adding subd. 6.

§ 441. Order dismissing petition.

If the allegations of a petition under this article are not established by competent proof, the court shall dismiss the petition. If a neglect petition was filed in the support proceeding, the court retains jurisdiction over the neglect petition whether or not it dismisses the support petition.

§ 442. Order of support by a spouse.

If the court finds after a hearing that a husband or wife is chargeable under section four hundred twelve with the support of his or her spouse and is possessed of sufficient means or able to earn such means, the court shall make an order requiring the husband or wife to pay weekly or at other fixed periods a fair and reasonable sum for or towards the support of the other spouse. The court shall require the spouse chargeable with support to make his or her residence known at all times should he or she move from the address last known to the court by reporting such change to the support collection unit designated by the appropriate social services district. Failure to report such change shall subject him or her to the provisions of section four hundred fifty-four of this act.

   Amended by Laws 1966, Ch. 559; Laws 1977, Ch. 516; Laws 1980, Ch. 281, eff. July 19, 1980.

§ 443.   Order of support by parent; duration.

   If the court finds after a hearing that a parent is chargeable under section four hundred thirteen of this act with the support of his or her child and is possessed of sufficient means or able to earn such means, the court shall make an order requiring the parent to pay weekly or at other fixed periods a fair and reasonable sum for or towards the support of such child. Where permitted under federal law and where the record of the proceedings contains such information, the court shall also require the social security number of such parent to be affixed to such order; provided, however, that no such order shall be invalid because of the omission of such number. Where the record of the proceedings contains such information, such order shall also include on its face the name and address of the employer, if any, of the person chargeable with support provided, however, that failure to comply with this requirement shall not invalidate such order. Where the order of child support or combined child and spouse support is made on behalf of persons in receipt of public assistance or in receipt of services pursuant to section one hundred eleven-g of the social services law, the court shall require each party to provide, and update upon any change, the following information to the court by reporting such change to the support collection unit designated by the appropriate social services district: social security number, residential and mailing addresses, telephone number, driver's license number; and name, address and telephone number of the parties' employers. Due process requirements for notice and service of process for subsequent hearings are met, with respect to such party, upon sending written notice by first class mail to the most recent residential address on record with the support collection unit; or by sending by first class mail written notice to the most recent employer address on record with the support collection unit, if a true copy thereof also is sent by first class mail to the most recent residential address on record with the support collection unit. Any such order issued on or after the first day of October, nineteen hundred ninety-nine shall also include, where available, the social security number of each child on whose behalf support has been ordered. Failure to report such changes shall subject the parent to the provisions of section four hundred fifty-four of this act.

   Amended by Laws 1966, Chs. 256, 559; Laws 1974, Ch. 937; Laws 1977, Ch. 516; Laws 1980, Ch. 281, eff. July 19, 1980; Laws 1988, Ch. 115, § 1, eff. July 13, 1988; Laws

FCA

1994, Ch. 544, § 1, eff. Aug. 25, 1994; Laws 1997, Ch. 398, § 66, eff. Jan. 1, 1998; Laws 1998, Ch. 214, § 43, eff. July 7, 1998, deemed in full force and effect Jan. 1, 1998.

§ 444. Order of support by mother; duration.

Repealed by Laws 1980, Ch. 281, eff. July 19, 1980.

§ 445. Order of support by relative; duration.

(a) If the court finds after a hearing that a relative, including a stepparent, should be held responsible under section four hundred fifteen for support, the court in its discretion may make an order requiring such person to contribute a fair and reasonable sum for the support of such person.

(b) For good cause shown, the court may at any time terminate or modify an order made under this section.

§ 446. Order of protection.

The court may make an order of protection in assistance or as a condition of any other order made under this part. The order of protection may set forth reasonable conditions of behavior to be observed for a specified time by the petitioner or respondent or both. No order of protection may direct any party to observe conditions of behavior unless the party requesting the order of protection has served and filed a petition or counter-claim in accordance with section one hundred fifty-four-b of this act. Such an order may require the petitioner or the respondent:

(a) to stay away from the home, school, business or place of employment of any other party, the other spouse, the other parent or the child, and to stay away from any other specific location designated by the court;

(b) to permit a parent, or a person entitled to visitation by a court order or a separation agreement, to visit the child at stated periods;

(c) to refrain from committing a family offense, as defined in subdivision one of section eight hundred twelve of this act, or any criminal offense against the child or against the other parent or against any person to whom custody of the child is awarded, or from harassing, intimidating or threatening such persons;

(d) to permit a designated party to enter the residence during a specified period of time in order to remove personal belongings not in issue in this proceeding or in any other proceeding or action under this act or the domestic relations law;

(e) to refrain from acts of commission or omission that create an unreasonable risk to the health, safety or welfare of a child;

(f) to participate in an educational program and to pay the costs thereof if the person has the means to do so, provided however that nothing contained herein shall be deemed to require payment of the costs of any such program by the state or any political subdivision thereof;

(g)   to provide, either directly or by means of medical and health insurance, for expenses incurred for medical care and treatment arising from the incident or incidents forming the basis for the issuance of the order;

(h)   to observe such other conditions as are necessary to further the purposes of protection.

The court may also award custody of the child, during the term of the order of protection to either parent, or to an appropriate relative within the second degree. Nothing in this section gives the court power to place or board out any child or to commit a child to an institution or agency. In making orders of protection, the court shall so act as to insure that in the care, protection, discipline and guardianship of the child his religious faith shall be preserved and protected.

Notwithstanding the foregoing provisions, an order of protection, or temporary order of protection where applicable, may be entered against a former spouse and persons who have a child in common, regardless whether such persons have been married or have lived together at any time.

(h)   1. to refrain from intentionally injuring or killing, without justification, any companion animal the respondent knows to be owned, possessed, leased, kept or held by the petitioner or a minor child residing in the household.

2.   "Companion animal", as used in this section, shall have the same meaning as in subdivision five of section three hundred fifty of the agriculture and markets law.

(i)   to observe such other conditions as are necessary to further the purposes of protection.

The court may also award custody of the child, during the term of the order of protection to either parent, or to an appropriate relative within the second degree. Nothing in this section gives the court power to place or board out any child or to commit a child to an institution or agency. In making orders of protection, the court shall so act as to insure that in the care, protection, discipline and guardianship of the child his religious faith shall be preserved and protected.

Notwithstanding the foregoing provisions, an order of protection, or temporary order of protection where applicable, may be entered against a former spouse and persons who have a child in common, regardless whether such persons have been married or have lived together at any time.

Amended by Laws 1981, Ch. 416, eff. Aug. 6, 1981; Laws 1981, Ch. 965, eff. Aug. 6, 1981; Laws 1984, Ch. 948, eff. Nov. 1, 1984; Laws 1988, Ch. 706, eff. Sept. 2, 1988; Laws 1995, Ch. 483, §§ 3 and 4, eff. Nov. 1, 1995; Laws 2006, ch. 253, §2, eff. July 26, 2006.

§ 447.   Order of visitation.

(a)   In the absence of an order of custody or of visitation entered by the supreme court, the court may make an order of custody or of visitation, in accordance with subdivision one of section two hundred forty of the domestic relations law, requiring one parent to permit the other to visit the children at stated periods without an order of protection, even where the parents are divorced and the support order is for a child only.

(b) Any order of the family court under this section shall terminate when the supreme court makes an order of custody or of visitation concerning the children, unless the supreme court continues the order of the family court.

Amended by Laws 1996, Ch. 85, § 3, eff. May 21, 1996, and applicable to all actions or proceedings concerning custody of or a right to visitation with a child whether such action or proceeding was commenced pursuant to section 240 of the domestic relations law or any other provision of law.

§ 448. Enforcement by income deduction.

Orders of support shall be enforceable pursuant to section fifty-two hundred forty-one or fifty-two hundred forty-two of the civil practice law and rules, or in any other manner provided by law. The family court is hereby authorized to enter an order with respect to an income deduction, in accordance with the provisions of section fifty-two hundred forty-two of the civil practice law and rules, in any support proceeding under the provisions of article five-B of this act under any support order made pursuant to a reference from the supreme court under section two hundred fifty-one of the domestic relations law or in any support proceeding under the provisions of article four, five or five-A of this act.

Added by Laws 1977, Ch. 516, § 19, eff. Jan. 1, 1978; amended by Laws 1985, Ch. 809, eff. Nov. 1, 1985; Laws 1986, Ch. 892, eff. Aug. 2, 1986; Laws 1997, Ch. 398, § 47, eff. Jan. 1, 1998.

§ 449. Effective date of order of support.

1. Any order of spousal support made under this article shall be effective as of the date of the filing of the petition therefor, and any retroactive amount of support due shall be paid in one sum or periodic sums, as the court shall direct, to the petitioner, to the custodial parent or to third persons. Any amount of temporary support which has been paid shall be taken into account in calculating any amount of retroactive support due.

2. Any order of child support made under this article shall be effective as of the earlier of the date of the filing of the petition therefor, or, if the children for whom support is sought are in receipt of public assistance, the date for which their eligibility for public assistance was effective. Any retroactive amount of support due shall be support arrears/past-due support and shall be paid in one sum or periodic sums, as the court shall direct, to the petitioner, to the custodial parent or to third persons. Any amount of temporary support which has been paid shall be taken into account in calculating any amount of retroactive support due. In addition, such retroactive child support shall be enforceable in any manner

provided by law including, but not limited to, an execution for support enforcement pursuant to subdivision (b) of section fifty-two hundred forty-one of the civil practice law and rules.

Added by Laws 1981, Ch. 695, eff. Oct. 19, 1981; **amended** by Laws 1992, Ch. 41, § 143, eff. Apr. 2, 1992.

Part 5. Compliance with orders.

(Repealed and transferred sections noted under appropriate section number of text.)

§ 451. Continuing jurisdiction.

Except as provided in article five-b of this act, the court has continuing jurisdiction over any support proceeding brought under this article until its judgment is completely satisfied and may modify, set aside or vacate any order issued in the course of the proceeding, provided, however, that the modification, set aside or vacatur shall not reduce or annul child support arrears accrued prior to the making of an application pursuant to this section. The court shall not reduce or annul any other arrears unless the defaulting party shows good cause for failure to make application for relief from the judgment or order directing payment prior to the accrual of the arrears, in which case the facts and circumstances constituting such good cause shall be set forth in a written memorandum of decision. A modification may increase support payments nunc pro tunc as of the date of the initial application for support based on newly discovered evidence. Any retroactive amount of support due shall be paid in one lump sum or periodic sums, as the court directs, taking into account any amount of support which has been paid. Upon an application to modify, set aside or vacate an order of support, no hearing shall be required unless such application shall be supported by affidavit and other evidentiary material sufficient to establish a prima facie case for the relief requested.

Amended by Laws 1984, Ch. 631, eff. Sept. 1, 1984; Laws 1985, Ch. 809, eff. Nov. 1, 1985; Laws 1986, Ch. 892, eff. Aug. 2, 1986; Laws 1999, Ch. 533, § 2, eff. Sept. 28, 1999.

§ 452. Rules of court.

Repealed by Laws 1986, Ch. 892, eff. Aug. 5, 1986.

§ 453. Petition; violation of court order.

Proceedings under this part shall be originated by the filing of a petition containing an allegation that the respondent has failed to obey a lawful order of this court.

(a) Persons who may originate proceedings. The original petitioner, the support collection unit, or any person to whom the order is payable expressly or who may originate proceedings under section four hundred twenty-two of this article may originate a proceeding under this part.

(b) Issuance of summons. Upon the filing of a petition under this part, the court may cause a copy of the petition and a summons to be issued, requiring the respondent to show cause why he should not be dealt with in accordance with section four hundred fifty-four of this part. The summons shall include on its face, printed or typewritten in a size equal to at least eight point bold type, a notice, warning the respondent that a failure to appear in court may result in immediate arrest, and that, after an appearance in court, a finding that the respondent willfully failed to obey the order may result in commitment to jail for a term not to exceed six months, for contempt of court. The notice shall also advise the respondent of the right to counsel, and the right to assigned counsel, if indigent.

(c) Service of summons. Upon the issuance of a summons, the provisions of section four hundred twenty-seven of this article shall apply, except that no order of commitment may be entered upon the default in appearance by the respondent if service has been made by mail alone notwithstanding proof of actual notice of the commencement of the proceeding.

(d) Issuance of warrant. The court may issue a warrant, directing that the respondent be arrested and brought before the court, pursuant to section four hundred twenty-eight of this article.

Added by Laws 1978, Ch. 456, eff. July 1, 1978.

§ 454. Powers of the court on violation of a support order.

1. If a respondent is brought before the court for failure to obey any lawful order of support and if, after hearing, the court is satisfied by competent proof that the respondent has failed to obey any such order, the court may use any or all of the powers conferred upon it by this part. The court has the power to use any or all enforcement powers in every proceeding brought for violation of a court order under this part regardless of the relief requested in the petition.

2. Upon a finding that a respondent has failed to comply with any lawful order of support:

(a) the court shall enter a money judgment under section four hundred sixty of this article; and

(b) the court may make an income deduction order for support enforcement under section fifty-two hundred forty-two of the civil practice law and rules;

(c) the court may require the respondent to post an undertaking under section four hundred seventy-one of this article;

(d) the court may make an order of sequestration under section four hundred fifty-seven of this article;

(e) the court may suspend the respondent's driving privileges pursuant to section four hundred fifty-eight-a of this article;

(f) the court may suspend the respondent's state professional or business license pursuant to section four hundred fifty-eight-b of this article;

(g) the court may suspend the recreational license or licenses of the respondent pursuant to section four hundred fifty-eight-c of this article.

(h) The court may require the respondent, if the persons for whom the respondent has failed to pay support are applicants for or recipients of public assistance, to participate in work activities as defined in title nine-b of article five of the social services law. Those respondents ordered to participate in work activities need not be applicants for or recipients of public assistance.

3. Upon a finding by the court that a respondent has willfully failed to obey any lawful order to support, the court shall order respondent to pay counsel fees to the attorney representing petitioner pursuant to section four hundred thirty-eight of this act and may in addition to or in lieu of any or all of the powers conferred in subdivision two of this section or any other section of law:

(a) commit the respondent to jail for a term not to exceed six months. Such commitment may be served upon certain specified days or parts of days as the court may direct, and the court may, at any time within the term of such sentence, revoke such suspension and commit the respondent for the remainder of the original sentence, or suspend the remainder of such sentence. For purposes of this subdivision, failure to pay support, as ordered, shall constitute prima facie evidence of a willful violation. Such commitment does not prevent the court from subsequently committing the respondent for failure thereafter to comply with any such order; or

(b) require the respondent to participate in a rehabilitative program if the court determines that such participation would assist the respondent in complying with such order of support and access to such a program is available. Such rehabilitative programs shall include, but not be limited to, work preparation and skill programs, non-residential alcohol and substance abuse programs and educational programs; or

(c) place the respondent on probation under such conditions as the court may determine and in accordance with the provisions of the criminal procedure law; or

4. The court shall not deny any request for relief pursuant to this section unless the facts and circumstances constituting the reasons for its determination are set forth in a written memorandum of decision.

5. [*Expires June 30, 2005.*] The court may review a support collection unit's denial of a challenge made by a support obligor pursuant to paragraph (d) of subdivision twelve of section one hundred eleven-b of the social services law if objections thereto are filed by a support obligor who has received notice that the department of social services intends to notify the department of motor vehicles that the support obligor's driving privileges are to be suspended. Specific written objections to a support collection unit's denial may be filed by the support obligor within thirty-five days of the mailing of the notice of the support collection unit's denial. A support obligor who files such objections shall serve a copy of the objections upon the support collection unit, which shall have ten days from such service to file a written rebuttal to such objections and a copy of the record upon which the support collection unit's denial was made, including all documentation submitted by the support obligor. Proof of service shall be filed with the court at the time of filing of objections and any rebuttal. The court's review shall be based upon the record and submissions of the support obligor and the support collection unit upon which the support collection unit's denial was made. Within forty-five days after the rebuttal, if any, is filed, the family court judge shall (i) deny the objections and remand to the support collection unit or (ii) affirm the objections if the court finds the determination of the support collection unit is based upon a clearly erroneous determination of fact or error of law, whereupon the court shall direct the support collection unit not to notify the department of motor vehicles to suspend the support obligor's driving privileges. Provisions set forth herein relating to procedures for appeal to the family court by individuals subject to suspension of driving privileges for failure to pay child support shall apply solely to such cases and not affect or modify any other procedure for review or appeal of administrative enforcement of child support requirements.

Amended by Laws 1965, Ch. 522; Laws 1966, Ch. 721; Laws 1968, Ch. 804, eff. June 16, 1968; Laws 1971, Ch. 1097; Laws 1977, Ch. 437, Ch. 516; Laws 1978, Ch. 456; Laws 1980, Ch. 241, eff. July 15, 1980; Laws 1982, Ch. 654, eff. July 22, 1982; Laws 1983, Ch. 746, eff. Sept. 26, 1983; Laws 1986, Ch. 892, eff. Aug. 2, 1986; Laws 1995, Ch. 81, § 230, eff. July 1, 1995; Laws 1995, Ch. 81, § 216, eff. July 1, 1995, and deemed repealed on June 30, 1998; Laws 1996, Ch. 309, § 466, eff. July 13, 1996; Laws 1996, Ch. 699, eff. Oct. 9, 1996; Laws 1997, Ch. 398, § 132, eff. Jan. 1, 1998, adding new para. (g) to FCA § 454(2); Laws 1998, Ch. 214, § 63, eff. July 7, 1998, deemed in full force and effect Jan. 1, 1998, and § 83-a, eff. July 7, 1998, extending the expiration date of subsection (5) to June 30, 1999; Laws 1999, Ch. 140, § 1, eff. June 29, 1999, deemed in full force and effect June 30, 1999, extending the expiration date of subsection (5) to June 30, 2001; Laws 2001, Ch. 72, § 1, eff. June 29, 2001, extending the expiration date of subsection (5) to June 30, 2003; Laws 2003, Ch. 87, § 1, eff. July 1, 2003 and shall be deemed to have been in full force and effect on and after June 30, 2003, extending the expiration date until June 30, 2005.

§ 455.   Commitment.

1.   The court may at any time suspend an order of commitment upon such reasonable conditions, if any, as the court deems appropriate to carry out the purposes of this article without placing the respondent on probation or may place him on probation under such conditions as the court may determine and in accordance with the provisions of the criminal procedure law. For good cause shown, the court may at any time revoke the suspension of the order of commitment.

2.   Except as provided in article five-b of this act, any respondent against whom an order of commitment has been issued, if financially unable to comply with any lawful order issued under this article, upon such notice to such parties as the court may direct, may make application to the court for an order relieving him or her of payments directed in such order and the commitment order. The court, upon the hearing on such application, if satisfied by competent proof that the respondent is financially unable to comply with such order may, upon a showing of good cause until further order of the court, modify such order and relieve the respondent from the commitment order. No such modification shall reduce or annul unpaid sums or installments accrued prior to the making of such application unless the defaulting party shows good cause for failure to make application for relief from the order directing payment prior to the accrual of such arrears. Such modification may increase the amount to be paid pursuant to a lawful order issued under this article nunc pro tunc based on newly discovered evidence.

3.   Whenever, upon application to the court by an interested party, it appears to the satisfaction of the court that any person, who has been relieved totally or partially from making any payment pursuant to the provisions of this section, is no longer financially unable to comply with the order to make such payment, then the court may, upon a showing of good cause modify or revoke its order relieving such person totally or partially from making such payment.

4.   Notwithstanding any inconsistent provision of this article, the provision of any order issued under this article requiring the payment of money by one spouse for the support of the other shall be suspended and inoperative so far as punishment for contempt is concerned during the period in which the defaulting spouse is imprisoned pursuant to any order adjudging him or her in contempt for failure to comply with any provision in such order.

5.   Any respondent may assert his or her financial inability to comply with the directions contained in an order issued under this article or an order or judgment entered in a matrimonial action or in an action for the enforcement in this state of a judgment in a matrimonial action rendered in another state, as a defense in a proceeding instituted against him or her under subdivision one of

FCA

section four hundred fifty-four of this article or under the judiciary law to punish him or her for failure to comply with such directions. If the court, upon the hearing of such contempt proceeding, is satisfied by competent proof that the respondent is financially unable to comply with such order or judgment, it may, in its discretion, until further order of the court, make an order modifying such order or judgment and denying the application to punish the respondent for contempt; provided, however, that if an order or judgement for child support issued by another state is before the court solely for enforcement, the court may only modify the order in accordance with article five-b of this act. No such modification shall reduce or annul arrears accrued prior to the making of such application for modification unless the defaulting party shows good cause for failure to make application for relief from the order or judgment directing such payment prior to the accrual of such arrears. Such modification may increase such support nunc pro tunc as of the date of the application based on newly discovered evidence. Any retroactive amount of support due shall be paid in one sum or periodic sums, as the court shall direct, taking into account any amount of temporary support which has been paid.

Amended by Laws 1971, Ch. 1097, § 41, eff. Sept. 1, 1971; Laws 1983, Ch. 746, eff. Sept. 26, 1983; Laws 1999, Ch. 533, § 3, eff. Sept. 28, 1999.

§ 456. Probation.

(a) No person may be placed on probation under this article unless the court makes an order to that effect, either at the time of the making of an order of support or under section four hundred fifty-four. The period of probation may continue so long as an order of support, order of protection or order of visitation applies to such person.

(b) The court may at any time, where circumstances warrant it, revoke an order of probation. Upon such revocation, the probationer shall be brought to court, which may, without further hearing, make any order that might have been made at the time the order of probation was made.

Amended by Laws 1963, Ch. 809, eff. Apr. 26, 1963.

§ 457. Order of sequestration on failure to obey support order.

If an order of support is made under this article and the respondent has failed to obey it and either leaves or threatens to leave the state, the court on application may issue an order of sequestration of his property within the state, providing that such property may be taken, sequestered and applied in like manner as is provided in section four hundred twenty-nine.

Amended by Laws 1963, Ch. 809; Laws 1966, Ch. 721, eff. Sept. 1, 1966.

§ 458. Cancellation of arrears.

Repealed by Laws 1983, Ch. 746, eff. Sept. 26, 1983.

§ 458-a. Enforcement of arrears; suspension of driving privileges.

(a)   If the respondent has accumulated support arrears equivalent to or greater than the amount of support due pursuant to court order for a period of four months, the court may order the department of motor vehicles to suspend the respondent's driving privileges, and if such order issues, the respondent may apply to the department of motor vehicles for a restricted use license pursuant to section five hundred thirty of the vehicle and traffic law. The court may at any time upon payment of arrears or partial payment of arrears by the respondent order the department of motor vehicles to terminate the suspension of respondent's driving privileges. For purposes of determining whether a support obligor has accumulated support arrears equivalent to or greater than the amount of support due for a period of four months, the amount of any retroactive support, other than periodic payments of retroactive support which are past due, shall not be included in the calculation of support arrears pursuant to this section.

(b)   If the respondent, after receiving appropriate notice, fails to comply with a summons, subpoena or warrant relating to a paternity or child support proceeding, the court may order the department of motor vehicles to suspend the respondent's driving privileges. The court may subsequently order the department of motor vehicles to terminate the suspension of the respondent's driving privileges; however, the court shall order the termination of such suspension when the court is satisfied that the respondent has fully complied with the requirements of all summonses, subpoenas and warrants relating to a paternity or child support proceeding. Nothing in this subdivision shall authorize the court to terminate the respondent's suspension of driving privileges except as provided in this subdivision.

(c)   The provisions of subdivision (a) of this section shall not apply to:

(i)   respondents who are receiving public assistance or supplemental security income; or

(ii)   respondents whose income as defined by subparagraph five of paragraph (b) of subdivision one of section four hundred thirteen of this act falls below the self-support reserve as defined by subparagraph six of paragraph (b) of subdivision one of section four hundred thirteen of this act; or

(iii)   respondents whose income as defined by subparagraph five of paragraph (b) of subdivision one of section four hundred thirteen of this act remaining after the payment of the current support obligation would fall below the self-support reserve as defined by subparagraph six of paragraph (b) of subdivision one of section four hundred thirteen of this act.

(d)   The court's discretionary decision not to suspend driving privileges shall not have any res judicata effect or preclude any other agency with statutory authority to direct the department of motor vehicles to suspend driving privileges.

FCA

Added by Laws 1995, Ch. 81, § 231, eff. July 1, 1995; **amended** by Laws 1997, Ch. 398, § 110, eff. Jan. 1, 1998; Laws 2002, Ch. 624, § 11, eff. Nov. 1, 2002, amending subd. (a).

§ 458-b.   Child support proceedings and enforcement of arrears; suspension of state professional, occupational and business licenses.

(a)   If the respondent has accumulated support arrears equivalent to or greater than the amount of support due pursuant to court order for a period of four months and the court has determined that the respondent is licensed, permitted or registered by or with a board, department, authority or office of this state to conduct a trade, business, profession or occupation, the court may order such board, department, authority or office to commence proceedings as required by law regarding the suspension of such license, permit, registration or authority to practice and to inform the court of the actions it has taken pursuant to such proceedings. For purposes of determining whether a respondent has accumulated support arrears equivalent to or greater than the amount of support due for a period of four months, the amount of any retroactive support, other than periodic payments of retroactive support which are past due, shall not be included in the calculation of support arrears pursuant to this section.

(b)   If the respondent after receiving appropriate notice, fails to comply with a summons, subpoena or warrant relating to a paternity or child support proceeding, and the court has determined that the respondent is licensed, permitted or registered by or with a board, department, authority or office of this state or one of its political subdivisions or instrumentalities to conduct a trade, business, profession or occupation, the court may order such board, department, authority or office to commence proceedings as required by law regarding the suspension of such license, permit, registration or authority to practice and to inform the court of the actions it has taken pursuant to such proceeding. The court may subsequently order such board, department, authority or office to terminate the suspension of the respondent's license, permit, registration or authority to practice; however, the court shall order the termination of such suspension when the court is satisfied that the respondent has fully complied with the requirements of all summonses, subpoenas and warrants relating to a paternity or child support proceeding.

(c)   If the court determines that the suspension of the license, permit or registration of the respondent would create an extreme hardship to either the licensee, permittee or registrant or to persons whom he or she serves, the court may, in lieu of suspension, suspend the order described in subdivision (a) of this section to the licensing entity for a period not to exceed one year. If on or before the expiration of this period the court has not received competent proof presented at hearing that the respondent is in full compliance with his or her support obligation and has fully complied with all summons, subpoenas and warrants relating to a paternity or child support proceeding, the court shall cause the suspension of the order to be removed and shall further cause such order to be served upon the licensing entity.

(d)   The provisions of subdivision (a) of this section shall not apply to:

(i)   respondents who are receiving public assistance or supplemental security income; or

(ii)   respondents whose income as defined by subparagraph five of paragraph (b) of subdivision one of section four hundred thirteen of this act falls below the self-support reserve as defined by subparagraph six of paragraph (b) of subdivision one of section four hundred thirteen of this act; or

(iii)   respondents whose income as defined by subparagraph five of paragraph (b) of subdivision one of section four hundred thirteen of this act remaining after the payment of the current support obligation would fall below the self-support reserve as defined by subparagraph six of paragraph (b) of subdivision one of section four hundred thirteen of this act.

(e)   The court shall inform the respondent that competent proof for purposes of proving payment to a licensing entity shall be a certified check, notice issued by the court, or notice from a support collection unit where the order is for payment to the support collection unit.

Added by Laws 1995, Ch. 81, § 232, eff. July 1, 1995; **amended** by Laws 1997, Ch. 398, §§ 111 and 112, eff. Jan. 1, 1998; § 112 relettered subdivisions (b), (c) and (d) of FCA § 458-b as subdivisions (c), (d) and (e), and a new subdivision (b) was added; **amended** by Laws 2002, Ch. 624, § 12, eff. Nov. 1, 2002, amending subd. (a).

§ 458-c.   Child support proceedings and enforcement of arrears; suspension of recreational licenses.

(a)   If the respondent has accumulated support arrears equivalent to or greater than the amount of current support for four months, the court may order any agency responsible for the issuance of a recreational license to suspend or refuse to reissue a license to the respondent, or deny application for such license by the respondent. For purposes of determining whether a respondent has accumulated support arrears equivalent to or greater than the amount of current support due for a period of four months, the existence of any retroactive support shall not be included in the calculation of support arrears pursuant to this section.

(b)   If the respondent has accumulated support arrears equivalent to or greater than the amount of support due pursuant to court order for a period of four months, the court may order any agency responsible for the issuance of a recreational license to suspend or refuse to reissue a license to the respondent, or deny application for such license by the respondent. For purposes of determining whether a respondent has accumulated support arrears equivalent to or greater than the amount of support due for a period of four months, the amount of any retroactive support, other than periodic payments of retroactive support which are past due, shall not be included in the calculation of support arrears pursuant to this section.

(c)   The provisions of subdivision (a) of this section shall not apply to:

(i)   respondents who are receiving public assistance or supplemental security income; or

(ii)   respondents whose income as defined by subparagraph five of paragraph (b) of subdivision one of section four hundred thirteen of this act falls below the self-support reserve as defined by subparagraph six of paragraph (b) of subdivision one of section four hundred thirteen of this article; or

(iii)   respondents whose income as defined by subparagraph five of paragraph (b) of subdivision one of section four hundred thirteen of this article remaining after the payment of the current support obligation would fall below the self-support reserve as defined by subparagraph six of paragraph (b) of subdivision one of section four hundred thirteen of this article.

Added by Laws 1997, Ch. 398, § 130, eff. Jan. 1, 1998; amended by Laws 2002, Ch. 624, § 13, eff. Nov. 1, 2002, amending subd. (a).

§ 459.   Order with respect to public employee.

Repealed by Laws 1977, Ch. 516, eff. January 1, 1978.

§ 459.   Additional arrears.

If a respondent has failed to obey a lawful order under this article the party seeking enforcement may amend the petition to include any additional arrears which have accrued from the commencement of such enforcement proceeding up to the date of the hearing, provided that written notice of the intention to so amend has been given eight days previously.

Added by Laws 1980, Ch. 646, eff. June 30, 1980; amended by Laws 1981, Ch. 239, eff. June 15, 1981.

§ 460.   Entry and docketing of a money judgment.

1.   Where the family court enters an order:

(a)   requiring any party to provide for the support of another party, or child, or both; or

(b)   providing for the support or maintenance of a spouse or former spouse, or child, or both, on a referral from the supreme court in an action for divorce, separation, annulment or a proceeding for the determination of the custody of a minor by writ of habeas corpus or by petition and order to show cause; or

(c)   enforcing or modifying an order or decree of a court of competent jurisdiction not of the state of New York providing for the support of the petitioner and/or child support; or

(d)   awarding support under article five-B of this act; or

(e) awarding counsel fees under this act; and the party defaults in paying any sum of money due as required by the order directing the payment thereof, the court, without regard to the amount due, shall make [sic] an order directing the entry of judgment for the amount of child support arrears, together with costs and disbursements. The court shall make an order directing the entry of judgment for the amount of arrears of any other payments so directed, together with costs and disbursements, unless the defaulting party shows good cause for failure to make application for relief from the judgment or order directing such payment prior to the accrual of such arrears. The court shall not make an order reducing or cancelling such arrears unless the facts and circumstances constituting good cause are set forth in a written memorandum of decision. The application for such order shall be made upon such notice to the party or other person as the court may direct. Such judgment shall provide for the payment of interest on the amount of any arrears if the default was willful, in that the defaulting party knowingly, consciously and voluntarily disregarded the obligation under a lawful court order. Such interest shall be computed from the date on which the payment was due, at the prevailing rate of interest on judgments as provided in the civil practice law and rules.

FCA

2. A certified copy of the order directing the entry of a money judgment shall be entered in the office of the clerk of the county in which the proceeding was commenced. Said clerk shall docket the same in the book kept by him for the docketing of judgments as if said order were a transcript of a judgment directed for the amount designated in the order. An order docketed under this subdivision shall have the same effect as a docketed judgment entered in the supreme court within the county where it is docketed and may be enforced by execution or in any other manner provided by law for the collection of a money judgment.

3. The relief provided for herein shall be in addition to any and every other remedy which may be provided under the law including, but not limited to, the remedies provided under the provisions of section four hundred fifty-four of this act and sections fifty-two hundred forty-one and fifty-two hundred forty-two of the civil practice law and rules; provided that when a judgment for such arrears has been entered pursuant to this section, such judgment shall not thereafter be subject to modification or be affected by the provisions of section four hundred sixty-two of this act. After the entry of any order hereunder, the judgment creditor shall not thereafter be entitled to collect, by any form of remedy, any greater portion of such arrears than that represented by the order so entered.

Added by Laws 1968, ch. 927, eff. June 22, 1968, and applying to all pending proceedings in the family court; **amended** by Laws 1980, Chs. 281, 645, eff. July 19, 1980; Laws 1982, Ch. 654, eff. July 25, 1980; Laws 1983, Ch. 746, eff. Sept. 26, 1983; Laws 1985, Ch. 809, eff. Nov. 1, 1985; Laws 1986, Ch. 892, eff. Aug. 2, 1986; Laws 1987, Ch. 815, eff. Aug. 7, 1987; Laws 1997, Ch. 398, § 48, eff. Jan. 1, 1998.

Part 6.   Effect of action for separation, divorce or annulment.

(Repealed and transferred sections noted under appropriate section number of text.)

§ 461.   Duty to support child after separation agreement, separation, or termination of marriage.

(a)   A separation agreement, a decree of separation, and a final decree or judgment terminating a marriage relationship does not eliminate or diminish either parent's duty to support a child of the marriage under section four hundred thirteen of this article. In the absence of an order of the supreme court or of another court of competent jurisdiction requiring support of the child, the family court may entertain a petition and make an order for its support.

(b)   If an order of the supreme court or of another court of competent jurisdiction requires support of the child, the family court may

(i)   entertain an application to enforce the order requiring support; or

(ii)   entertain an application to modify such order on the ground that changed circumstances requires such modification, unless the order of the supreme court provides that the supreme court retains exclusive jurisdiction to enforce or modify the order.

(c)   In an action for divorce, separation or annulment in the supreme court, the supreme court on its own motion or on motion of one of the parties may refer an application for temporary or permanent support or both of a child of the marriage to the family court. If the supreme court so refers the application, the family court shall have jurisdiction to determine the application with the same powers possessed by the supreme court and the family court's disposition of the application shall be an order of the family court appealable only under article eleven of this act.

Amended by Laws 1970, Ch. 28; Laws 1980, Ch. 281, eff. July 19, 1980.

§ 462. Effect of support order in matrimonial action on duration of family court support order for child.

Any order of the family court requiring support of a child terminates when the supreme court makes an order in an action for divorce, separation or annulment providing for the support of the child, unless the supreme court continues the order of the family court.

§ 463. Effect of separation agreement on duty to support a spouse.

A separation agreement does not preclude the filing of a petition and the making of an order under section four hundred forty-five of this article for support of a spouse who is likely to become in need of public assistance or care.

    Amended by Laws 1980, Ch. 281, eff. July 19, 1980.

§ 464. Effect of pendency of action for divorce, separation or annulment on petition for support of a spouse.

(a)   In a matrimonial action in the supreme court, the supreme court on its own motion or on motion of either spouse may refer to the family court an application for temporary or permanent support, or for maintenance or a distribution of marital property. If the supreme court so refers an application, the family court has jurisdiction to determine the application with the same powers possessed by the supreme court and the family court's disposition of the application is an order of the family court appealable only under article eleven of this act.

(b)   In the absence of an order of referral under paragraph (a) of this section and in the absence of an order by the supreme court granting temporary or permanent support or maintenance, the family court during the pendency of such action may entertain a petition and may make an order under section four hundred forty-five of this article for a spouse who is likely to become in need of public assistance or care.

    Amended by Laws 1963, Ch. 809; Laws 1980, Ch. 281, eff. July 19, 1980.

§ 465. Effect of denial of support in action for separation.

After final adjudication of an action for separation in which the supreme court denies support to a spouse, the family court may entertain a petition and make an order for support of such spouse

(a)   under section four hundred forty-two of this article if in the opinion of the family court the circumstances of the parties have changed, or

(b)   under section four hundred forty-five of this article if it is shown to the satisfaction of the family court that the petitioner is likely to become in need of public assistance or care.

Amended by Laws 1980, Ch. 281, eff. July 19, 1980.

§ 466. Effect of granting of support in action for divorce, separation or annulment.

(a) The supreme court may provide in an order or decree granting temporary or permanent support or maintenance in an action for divorce, separation or annulment that only the family court may entertain an application to enforce or, upon a showing to the family court that there has been a subsequent change of circumstance and that modification is required, to modify such order or decree. If the supreme court so provides, the family court shall entertain such an application and any disposition by the family court of the application is an order of the family court appealable only under article eleven of this act.

(b) The supreme court may provide in an order or decree granting alimony, maintenance or support in an action for divorce, separation or annulment that the order or decree may be enforced or modified only in the supreme court. If the supreme court so provides, the family court may not entertain an application to enforce or modify an order or decree of the supreme court involving the parties to the action.

(c) If the supreme court enters an order or decree granting alimony, maintenance or support in an action for divorce, separation or annulment and if the supreme court does not exercise the authority given under subdivision (a) or (b) of this section; or if a court of competent jurisdiction not of the state of New York shall enter an order or decree granting alimony, maintenance or support in any such action, the family court may

(i) entertain an application to enforce the order or decree granting alimony or maintenance, or

(ii) entertain an application to modify the order or decree granting alimony or maintenance on the ground that there has been a subsequent change of circumstances and that modification is required.

Amended by Laws 1965, Ch. 355; Laws 1970, Ch. 28; Laws 1972, Ch. 721; Laws 1980, Ch. 281, eff. July 19, 1980.

§ 467. Referral by supreme court of applications to fix custody in action for divorce, separation or annulment.

(a) In an action for divorce, separation or annulment, the supreme court may refer to the family court the determination of applications to fix temporary or permanent custody or visitation, applications to enforce judgments and orders of custody or visitation, and applications to modify judgments and orders of custody which modification may be granted only upon a showing to the family court that there has been a subsequent change of circumstances and that modification is required.

(b)   In the event no such referral has been made and unless the supreme court provides in the order or judgment awarding custody or visitation in an action for divorce, separation or annulment, that it may be enforced or modified only in the supreme court, the family court may: (i) determine an application to enforce the order or judgment awarding custody or visitation, or (ii) determine an application to modify the order or judgment awarding custody or visitation upon a showing that there has been a subsequent change of circumstances and modification is required.

(c)   In any determination of an application pursuant to this section, the family court shall have jurisdiction to determine such applications, in accordance with subdivision one of section two hundred forty of the domestic relations law, with the same powers possessed by the supreme court, and the family court's disposition of any such application is an order of the family court appealable only under article eleven of this act.

Amended by Laws 1963, Ch. 809, eff. Apr. 26, 1963; Laws 1981, Ch. 40, eff. Sept. 1, 1981; Laws 1996, Ch. 85, § 4, eff. May 21, 1996 and applicable to all actions or proceedings concerning custody of or a right to visitation with a child whether such action or proceeding was commenced pursuant to section 240 of the domestic relations law or any other provision of law.

§ 468.   Application to modify out-of-state order or judgment fixing custody.

Laws 1966, Ch. 580, eff. September 1, 1966, § 468 renumbered as § 654.

§ 469.   Rules of court; venue.

(a)   Rules of court under section four hundred twenty-four of this article may be made applicable with such modifications, if any, as may be appropriate to the determination of applications referred to the family court by the supreme court under part six of this article.

(b)   The supreme court referring an application to the family court under part six may designate a county within the judicial district as the county in which the application is to be determined. If the supreme court does not designate the county, section four hundred twenty-one of this article applies.

(c)   Section four hundred twenty-one of this article applies in determining the county in which an application under section four hundred sixty-one, section four hundred sixty-six or section six hundred fifty-four may be heard.

Amended by Laws 1967, Ch. 346; Laws 1980, Ch. 178, eff. Sept. 1, 1980.

Part 7.   Undertaking.

Section   471.   **Undertaking for support and cash deposits.**
          472.   **Undertaking to be filed.**

§ 471. Undertaking for support and cash deposits.

The court may in its discretion require either a written undertaking with sufficient surety approved by the court or may require that cash be posted to secure compliance by the respondent with the order for support for such period. Such undertaking shall be for a definite period, not to exceed three years, and the required amount of the principal of such undertaking shall not exceed the total payments for support required for three years and shall be so stated in the order for support. After hearing and for good cause shown, the court may extend an undertaking requirement by requiring a new undertaking similar to the original undertaking. The respondent may deposit cash with the clerk, or when the court so orders, with the support collection unit designated by the appropriate social services district, when the order for support directs payments to such unit. When such cash has been deposited with the support collection unit and the respondent fails to make any payment, when due, within such period, payment shall be made by the support collection unit to the petitioner out of such cash. When cash is posted as security, as herein provided, the person or persons so posting such cash shall at the expiration of the period for which such security shall have been ordered be entitled to the return of such cash less any amount which shall have been paid therefrom to the petitioner by reason of any default or defaults in payments on the part of the respondent. The form of the undertaking and the form and manner of justification of the surety shall conform to the rules of court.

Amended by Laws 1987, Ch. 815, eff. Aug. 7, 1987.

§ 472. Undertaking to be filed.

If the property securing the undertaking consists of real estate, the undertaking shall be filed with the county clerk of the county in which the real estate is located and the same shall constitute a lien upon the real estate specified in the undertaking. The county clerk of each county is hereby directed to accept such undertakings for filing and to provide proper and sufficient books and indexes wherein the same shall be entered.

§ 473. Substitution of surety.

The court may at any time thereafter, before or after there has been a default, if all arrears have been paid in case there shall have been a default on such undertaking, accept a new undertaking in lieu of the original undertaking, and the court shall enter an order discharging such undertaking.

§ 474. Default.

A default in the terms of the order shall constitute a breach of the undertaking. When there has been a default the court shall cause an affidavit to be drawn, verified and filed by any person familiar with the facts. The surety shall thereupon be personally served, or served by registered mail at the address given in the undertaking or subsequent address furnished by said surety in writing, with notice of such default and shall be required to attend at the court on a day certain and show cause why judgment should not be entered on the undertaking and the amount thereof applied to the relief of the petitioner for the amount in default. If the surety appears and pays the amount in arrears the court may remit the forfeiture. Inability to serve the surety shall not be prejudicial to the renewal of proceedings against the respondent.

§ 475. Procedure as to defaults.

If the surety contests the default the court shall hear and determine the issue. In the event that the court finds that a default has been suffered, it shall make an order specifying the amount in default and forfeiting the undertaking or cash deposit to the extent of such default. A certified copy of such order shall be filed in the county clerk's office with a certified copy of the undertaking and thereupon the said clerk shall docket the same in the book kept by the clerk for the docketing of judgments, as if the same was a transcript of a judgment directed for the amount of such sum in default. The certified copy of the undertaking and of the order shall be the judgment record. Such judgment shall be a lien on all of the real estate and collectible out of the real and personal property of the surety. An execution may be issued to collect the amount thereof in the same manner as upon a judgment recovered in any court of record.

FCA

Amended by Laws 1987, Ch. 815, eff. Aug. 7, 1987.

§ 476. Forfeitures applied to support of petitioner.

(a) All sums collected from the surety by judgment as well as forfeited cash deposits shall be applied by the clerk of court to the support of the petitioners for whose benefit the order for support was made. Subsequent defaults shall be proceeded upon in the same manner until the amount of the principal of the undertaking or the cash deposited has been recovered in full.

(b) Where the respondent, or any one in his behalf, shall have deposited with the court monies as surety for compliance with the terms of the order of support and the respondent shall have died, the court may make an order directing the payment to the petitioner of all monies still in possession of the court in conformance with the order of support.

§ 477. Surrender of respondent by surety.

A surety may at any time surrender a respondent to the court. The respondent shall thereupon be dealt with as provided in the order for support. If the arrears on the order for support with interest thereon are paid in full, the court may make an order discharging the surety of any further liability and directing the return of the balance of the cash on deposit to the person entitled thereto.

§ 478. Termination of surety's liability.

Whenever the liability on an undertaking has ceased, the court shall make an order to that effect. Upon receipt of a certified copy of the order, the county clerk shall discharge of record the lien of the undertaking.

§ 479. When new security required.

After an undertaking has been given or cash has been deposited and it shall appear upon proof by affidavit either

(a) that a judgment entered upon default cannot be collected; or

(b) that the liability of the surety has ceased; or

(c) that the money deposited has been applied in full; or

(d) that personal service cannot be effected upon the surety or the person depositing the cash; or

(e) if for any reason the court shall find that there is not sufficient security, the court may issue a summons requiring the respondent to appear or a warrant for the arrest of the respondent, and require him to give new or additional security. In default thereof the court may commit him under the original order in the manner hereinabove provided.

ARTICLE 5

PATERNITY PROCEEDINGS

SUMMARY OF ARTICLE

Part 1. Jurisdiction and duties to support.

§ 511. Jurisdiction.

Except as otherwise provided, the family court has exclusive original jurisdiction in proceedings to establish paternity and, in any such proceedings in which it makes a finding of paternity, to order support and to make orders of custody or of visitation, as set forth in this article. On its own motion, the court may at any time in the proceedings also direct the filing of a neglect petition in accord with the provisions of article ten of this act. In accordance with the provisions of section one hundred eleven-b of the domestic relations law, the surrogate's court has original jurisdiction concurrent with the family court to determine the issues relating to the establishment of paternity.

Amended by Laws 1971, Ch. 952; Laws 1980, Ch. 575, eff. July 26, 1980; Laws 1984, Ch. 469, eff. July 20, 1984; Laws 1986, Ch. 484, eff. July 21, 1986, which eliminated the expiration date of the 1980 amendment; Laws 1999, Ch. 533, § 4, eff. Sept. 28, 1999.

§ 512. Definitions.

When used in this article, (a) The phrase "child born out of wedlock" refers to a child who is begotten and born out of lawful matrimony.

(b) The word "child" refers to a child born out of wedlock.

(c) The word "mother" refers to the mother of a child born out of wedlock.

(d) The word "father" refers to the father of a child born out-of-wedlock.

Amended by Laws 1976, Ch. 665, eff. Jan. 1, 1977.

§ 513. Obligation of parents.

Subject to the provisions of paragraph (F) of subdivision six of section three hundred ninety-eight of the social services law, each parent of a child born out of wedlock is chargeable with the support of such child including the child's funeral expenses and, if possessed of sufficient means or able to earn such means, shall be required to pay child support. A court shall make an award for child support pursuant to subdivision one of section four hundred thirteen of this act.

Amended by Laws 1986, Ch. 892, eff. Aug. 2, 1986; Laws 1989, Ch. 567, § 11, eff. Sept. 15, 1989.

§ 514. Liability of father to mother.

The father is liable to pay the reasonable expenses of the mother's confinement and recovery and such reasonable expenses in connection with her pregnancy as the court in its discretion may deem proper; provided, however, where the mother's confinement, recovery and expenses in connection with her pregnancy were paid under the medical assistance program on the mother's behalf, the father may be liable to the social services district furnishing such medical assistance and to the state department of social services for the full amount of medical assistance so expended, as the court in its discretion may deem proper.

Amended by Laws 1995, Ch. 81, § 102, eff. June 20, 1995.

§ 515. Governmental obligation to child.

In case of the neglect or inability of the parents to provide for the support and education of the child, it shall be supported by the county, city or town chargeable therewith under the provisions of the social welfare law.

§ 516. Agreement or compromise.

(a) An agreement or compromise made by the mother or by some authorized person on behalf of either the mother or child concerning the support of either is binding upon the mother and child only when the court determines that adequate provision has been made and is fully secured and approves said agreement or compromise.

(b) No agreement or compromise under this section shall be approved until notice and opportunity to be heard are given to the public welfare official of the county, city or town where the mother resides or the child is found.

(c) The complete performance of the agreement or compromise, when so approved, bars other remedies of the mother or child for the support and education of the child.

§ 516-a. Acknowledgment of paternity.

(a) An acknowledgment of paternity executed pursuant to section one hundred eleven-k of the social services law or section four thousand one hundred thirty-five-b of the public health law shall establish the paternity of and liability for the support of a child pursuant to this act. Such acknowledgment must be reduced to writing and filed pursuant to section four thousand one hundred thirty-five-b of the public health law with the registrar of the district in which the birth occurred and in which the birth certificate has been filed. No further judicial or administrative proceedings are required to ratify an unchallenged acknowledgment of paternity.

(b) An acknowledgment of paternity executed pursuant to section one hundred eleven-k of the social services law or section four thousand one hundred thirty-five-b of the public health law may be rescinded by either signator's filing of a petition with the court to vacate the acknowledgment within the earlier of sixty days of the date of signing the acknowledgment or the date of an administrative or a judicial proceeding (including a proceeding to establish a support order) relating to the child in which either signator is a party. For purposes of this section, the "date of an administrative or a judicial proceeding" shall be the date by which the respondent is required to answer the petition. After the expiration of sixty days of the execution of the acknowledgment, either signator may challenge the acknowledgment of paternity in court only on the basis of fraud, duress, or material mistake of fact, with the burden of proof on the party challenging the voluntary acknowledgment. Upon receiving a party's challenge to an acknowledgment, the court shall order genetic marker tests or DNA tests for the determination of the child's paternity and shall make a finding of paternity, if appropriate, in accordance with this article. Neither signator's legal obligations, including the obligation for child support arising from the acknowledgment, may be suspended during the challenge to the acknowledgment except for good cause as the court may find. If a party petitions to rescind an acknowledgment and if the court determines that the alleged father is not the father of the child, or if the court finds that an acknowledgment is invalid because it was executed on the basis of fraud, duress, or material mistake of fact, the court shall vacate the acknowledgment of paternity and shall immediately provide a copy of the order to the registrar of the district in which the child's birth certificate is filed and also to the putative father registry operated by the department of social services pursuant to section three hundred seventy-two-c of the social services law. In addition, if the mother of the child who is the subject of the acknowledgment is in receipt of child support services pursuant to title six-a of article three of the social services law, the court shall immediately provide a copy of the order to the child support enforcement unit of the social services district that provides the mother with such services.

(c) A determination of paternity made by any other state, whether established through the parents' acknowledgment of paternity or through an administrative or judicial process, must be accorded full faith and credit, if and only if such acknowledgment meets the requirements set forth in section 452(a)(7) of the social security act.

Added by Laws 1985, Ch. 809, eff. Nov. 1, 1985; **amended** by Laws 1993, Ch. 59, § 27, eff. July 1, 1993; Laws 1994, Ch. 170, § 353, eff. June 15, 1994; Laws 1997, Ch. 398, § 81, eff. Nov. 11, 1997.

§ 517. Time for instituting proceedings.

Proceedings to establish the paternity of a child may be instituted during the pregnancy of the mother or after the birth of the child, but shall not be brought after the child reaches the age of twenty-one years, unless paternity has been acknowledged by the father in writing or by furnishing support.

Amended by Laws 1976, Ch. 665, eff. Jan. 1, 1977, adding subd. (c); Laws 1979, Ch. 452, eff. Aug. 4, 1979; Laws 1983, Ch. 305, eff. June 21, 1983; Laws 1985, Ch. 809, eff. Nov. 1, 1985, and applicable to all persons under the age of twenty-one on such eff. date. Section 38 of Ch. 809 provides that no person shall be barred from commencing proceedings to establish paternity solely because such person may have been barred from commencing such proceedings prior thereto.

§ 518. Effect of death, absence, or mental illness of mother.

If, at any time before or after a petition is filed, the mother dies or becomes mentally ill or cannot be found within the state, neither the proceeding nor the right to commence the proceeding shall abate but may be commenced or continued by any of the persons authorized by this article to commence a paternity proceeding.

Amended by Laws 1978, Ch. 550, § 26, eff. July 24, 1978; Laws 1983, Ch. 310, eff. June 21, 1983.

§ 519. Effect of death, absence or mental illness of putative father.

If, at any time before or after a petition is filed, the putative father dies, or becomes mentally ill or cannot be found within the state, neither the proceeding nor the right to commence the proceeding shall necessarily abate but may be commenced or continued by any of the persons authorized by this article to commence a paternity proceeding where:

(a) the putative father was the petitioner in the paternity proceeding; or,

(b)   the putative father acknowledged paternity of the child in open court; or,

(c)   a genetic marker or DNA test had been administered to the putative father prior to his death; or,

(d)   the putative father has openly and notoriously acknowledged the child as his own.

Added by Laws 1987, Ch. 434, eff. July 27, 1987; **amended** by Laws 1999, Ch. 533, § 5, eff. Sept. 28, 1999.

Part 2.   Venue and preliminary procedure.

FCA

§ 521.   Venue.

Proceedings to establish paternity may be originated in the county where the mother or child resides or is found or in the county where the putative father resides or is found. The fact that the child was born outside of the state of New York does not bar a proceeding to establish paternity in the county where the putative father resides or is found or in the county where the mother resides or the child is found.

§ 522.   Persons who may originate proceedings.

Proceedings to establish the paternity of the child and to compel support under this article may be commenced by the mother, whether a minor or not, by a person alleging to be the father, whether a minor or not, by the child or child's guardian or other person standing in a parental relation or being the next of kin of the child, or by any authorized representative of an incorporated society doing charitable or philanthropic work, or if the mother or child is or is likely to become a public charge on a county, city or town, by a public welfare official of the county, city or town where the mother resides or the child is found. If a proceeding is originated by a public welfare official and thereafter withdrawn or dismissed without consideration on the merits, such withdrawal or dismissal shall be without prejudice to other persons.

Amended by Laws 1976, Ch. 665, eff. Jan. 1, 1977; Laws 1985, Ch. 809, eff. Nov. 1, 1985; Laws 1986, Ch. 892, eff. Aug. 2, 1986.

§ 523. Petition.

Proceedings are commenced by the filing of a verified petition, alleging that the person named as respondent, or the petitioner if the petitioner is a person alleging to be the child's father, is the father of the child and petitioning the court to issue a summons or a warrant, requiring the respondent to show cause why the court should not enter a declaration of paternity, an order of support, and such other and further relief as may be appropriate under the circumstances. The petition shall be in writing and verified by the petitioner. Any such petition for the establishment of paternity or the establishment, modification and/or enforcement of a child support obligation for persons not in receipt of family assistance, which contains a request for child support enforcement services completed in a manner as specified in section one hundred eleven-g of the social services law, shall constitute an application for such services.

Amended by Laws 1976, Ch. 665, eff. Jan. 1, 1977; Laws 1981, Ch. 622, eff. July 21, 1981, but deemed eff. as of Aug. 1, 1976; Laws 1990, Ch. 818, § 16, eff. Sept. 30, 1990; Laws 1997, Ch. 398, § 32, eff. Jan. 1, 1998.

§ 524. Issuance of summons.

(a) On receiving a petition sufficient in law commencing a paternity proceeding, the court shall cause a summons to be issued, requiring the respondent to show cause why the declaration of paternity, order of filiation, order of support and other and further relief prayed for by the petition should not be made.

(b) The summons shall contain or have attached thereto a notice stating:

(i) that the respondent's failure to appear shall result in the default entry of an order of filiation by the court upon proof of respondent's actual notice of the commencement of the proceeding; and

(ii) That a respondent's failure to appear may result in the suspension of his or her driving privileges; state professional, occupational and business licenses; and sporting licenses and permits.

Amended by Laws 1993, Ch. 59, § 28, eff. July 1, 1993; Laws 1997, Ch. 398, § 113, eff. Jan. 1, 1998.

§ 525. Service of summons.

(a) Personal service of a summons and petition shall be made by delivery of a true copy thereof to the person summoned at least eight days before the time stated therein for appearance; or by delivery of a true copy thereof to a person of suitable age and discretion at the actual place of business, dwelling place or usual place of abode of the person to be served and by mailing a true copy thereof to the person to be served at his last known residence at least eight days before the time stated in the summons for appearance; proof of service shall identify such person of suitable age and discretion and state the date, time and place of service. If so requested by one acting on behalf of the respondent or by a parent or other person legally responsible for his care, the court shall not proceed with the hearing or proceeding earlier than eight days after such service.

(b) If after reasonable effort, personal service is not made, the court may at any stage in the proceedings make an order providing for substituted service in the manner provided for substituted service in the civil practice law and rules.

(c) In any case, whether or not service is attempted under subdivision (a) or (b) of this section, service of a summons and petition under this section may be effected by mail alone to the last known address of the person to be served. Service by mail alone shall be made at least eight days before the time stated in the summons for appearance. If service is by mail alone, the court will enter an order of filiation by default if there is proof satisfactory to the court that the respondent had actual notice of the commencement of the proceeding, which may be established upon sufficient proof that the summons and petition were in fact mailed by certified mail and signed for at the respondent's correct street address or signed for at the post office. If service by certified mail at the respondent's correct street address cannot be accomplished, service pursuant to subdivision one, two, three or four of section three hundred eight of the civil practice law and rules shall be deemed good and sufficient service. Upon failure of the respondent to obey a summons served in accordance with the provisions of this section by means other than mail alone, the court will enter an order of filiation by default. The respondent shall have the right to make a motion for relief from such default order within one year from the date such order was entered.

FCA

Added by Laws 1978, Ch. 456, eff. Sept. 1, 1978; **amended** by Laws 1979, Ch. 106, eff. May 21, 1979; Laws 1984, Ch. 791, eff. Aug. 5, 1984; Laws 1993, Ch. 59, § 29, eff. July 1, 1993.

§ 526. Issuance of warrant.

The court may issue a warrant, directing that the respondent be arrested and brought before the court, when a petition is presented to the court under section five hundred twenty-three and it appears that

(a) the summons cannot be served; or

(b) the respondent has failed to obey the summons; or

(c) the respondent is likely to leave the jurisdiction; or

(d) a summons, in the court's opinion, would be ineffectual; or

(e) the safety of the petitioner is endangered; or

(f) a respondent on bail or on parole has failed to appear.

§ 527. Preliminary procedure on warrant.

(a) When a respondent is taken into custody pursuant to a warrant issued by a family court in a county in New York City under section five hundred twenty-six, he or she shall be taken before the court issuing the warrant if the respondent is taken into custody in New York city. If the respondent is taken into custody in a county not within New York City, he or she shall be taken before a family court judge in that county.

(b)   When a respondent is taken into custody pursuant to a warrant issued by a family court in a county not within the city of New York, he or she shall be taken before the court issuing the warrant if the respondent is taken into custody in the county in which the court sits. If the respondent is taken into custody in a different county, he or she shall be brought before a family court judge in that county.

Amended by Laws 1976, Ch. 665, eff. Jan. 1, 1977; Laws 1999, Ch. 533, § 6, eff. Sept. 28, 1999.

§ 528.   Procedure before court.

The court before whom the respondent is taken under section five hundred twenty-seven may require an undertaking to appear or in default thereof may place the respondent in custody.

Amended by Laws 1999, Ch. 533, § 7, eff. Sept. 28, 1999.

Part 3.   Hearings.

§ 531.   Hearing.

The trial shall be by the court without a jury. The mother or the alleged father shall be competent to testify but the respondent shall not be compelled to testify. If the mother is married both she and her husband may testify to nonaccess. If the respondent shall offer testimony of access by others at or about the time charged in the complaint, such testimony shall not be competent or admissible in evidence except when corroborated by other facts and circumstances tending to prove such access. The court may exclude the general public from the room where the proceedings are heard and may admit only persons directly interested in the case, including officers of the court and witnesses.

Amended by Laws 1976, Ch. 665, eff. Jan. 1, 1977.

§ 531-a. **Testimony by telephone, audio-visual means or other electronic means.**

(a)   In any proceeding under this article, the court may permit a party or a witness to be deposed or to testify by telephone, audio-visual means, or other electronic means at a designated family court or other location:

(i)   where such party or witness resides in a county other than that of the family court where the case is pending and that of any contiguous county; provided, however, that for the purposes of this section, the five counties of New York city shall be treated as one county;

(ii)   where such party or witness is presently incarcerated and will be incarcerated on the date on which the hearing or deposition is scheduled and is not expected to be released within a reasonable period of time after the date on which the hearing is scheduled; or

(iii)   where the court determines that it would be an undue hardship for such party or witness to testify or to be deposed at the family court where the case is pending.

(b)   Any such deposition or testimony taken by telephone, audio-visual means or other electronic means in accordance with subdivision (a) of this section shall be recorded and preserved for transcription. Where a party or witness is deposed or testifies by telephone, audio-visual or other electronic means pursuant to this section, documentary evidence referred to by a party or witness or the court may be transmitted by facsimile, telecopier, or other electronic means and may not be excluded from evidence by reason of an objection based on the means of transmission. The chief administrator of the courts shall promulgate rules to facilitate the taking of testimony by telephone, audio-visual means or other electronic means.

Added by Laws 2000, Ch. 475 § 2, eff. Dec. 19, 2000.

§ 532. **Genetic marker and DNA tests; admissibility of records or reports of test results; costs of tests.**

(a)   The court shall advise the parties of their right to one or more genetic marker tests or DNA tests and, on the court's own motion or the motion of any party, shall order the mother, her child and the alleged father to submit to one or more genetic marker or DNA tests of a type generally acknowledged as reliable by an accreditation body designated by the secretary of the federal department of health and human services and performed by a laboratory approved by such an accreditation body and by the commissioner of health or by a duly qualified physician to aid in the determination of whether the alleged father is or is not the father of the child. No such test shall be ordered, however, upon a written finding by the court that it is not in the best interests of the child on the basis of res judicata, equitable estoppel, or the presumption of legitimacy of a child born to a married woman. The record or report of the results of any such genetic marker or DNA test ordered pursuant to this section or pursuant to section one hundred eleven-k of the social services law shall be received in evidence by the court pursuant to subdivision (e) of rule forty-five hundred eighteen of the civil practice law and rules where no timely objection in writing has been made thereto and that if such timely objections are not made, they shall be deemed waived and shall not be heard by the court. If the record or report of the results of any such genetic marker or DNA test or tests indicate at least a ninety-five percent probability of paternity, the admission of such record or report shall create a rebuttable presumption of paternity, and shall establish, if unrebutted, the paternity of and liability for the support of a child pursuant to this article and article four of this act.

(b) Whenever the court directs a genetic marker or DNA test pursuant to this section, a report made as provided in subdivision (a) of this section may be received in evidence pursuant to rule forty-five hundred eighteen of the civil practice law and rules if offered by any party.

(c) The cost of any test ordered pursuant to subdivision (a) of this section shall be, in the first instance, paid by the moving party. If the moving party is financially unable to pay such cost, the court may direct any qualified public health officer to conduct such test, if practicable; otherwise, the court may direct payment from the funds of the appropriate social services district. In its order of disposition, however, the court may direct that the cost of any such test be apportioned between the parties according to their respective abilities to pay or be assessed against the party who does not prevail on the issue of paternity, unless such party is financially unable to pay.

Amended by Laws 1976, Ch. 665, eff. Jan. 1, 1977; Laws 1981, Ch. 9, eff. Mar. 2, 1981; Laws 1982, Ch. 773, eff. Sept. 27, 1982; Laws 1982, Ch. 695, eff. July 22, 1982; Laws 1983, Ch. 311, eff. June 21, 1983; Laws 1984, Ch. 792, eff. Aug. 5, 1984 and applicable to any action or proceeding pending on or commenced after its effective date; Laws 1994, Ch. 170, § 354, eff. June 15, 1994; Laws 1997, Ch. 398, § 80, eff. Nov. 11, 1997; Laws 1998, Ch. 214, § 45, eff. July 7, 1998.

§ 533. Adjournment on application of party.

The court, on application of either party, may for good cause shown grant such adjournments as may be necessary. If an adjournment is granted upon the request of either party, the court may require the respondent to give an undertaking for appearance.

Amended by Laws 1976, Ch. 665, eff. Jan. 1, 1977.

§ 534. Adjournment on motion of court.

On its own motion, the court may adjourn the hearing after it has made a finding of paternity to enable it to make inquiry into the surroundings, conditions and capacities of the child, into the financial abilities and responsibilities of both parents or for other proper cause. If the court so adjourns the hearing, it may require the respondent to give an undertaking to appear.

Amended by Laws 1976, Ch. 665, eff. Jan. 1, 1977.

§ 535. Counsel for social services commissioner.

(a) The corporation counsel of the city of New York shall represent the social services commissioner of such city in all proceedings under this article in which the commissioner is the petitioner.

(b) In any county outside the city of New York in which attorneys have been appointed pursuant to section sixty-six of the social services law, such attorneys may represent the social services commissioner of such county in all proceedings under this article in which the commissioner is the petitioner.

(c) Except as provided in subdivision (b) of this section, in any county outside the city of New York, the county attorney, or an attorney designated by the county executive, if there be one, otherwise by the board of supervisors, shall represent the social services commissioner of the county in all proceedings under this article in which the commissioner is the petitioner.

Amended by Laws 1984, Ch. 206, eff. Jan. 1, 1985.

FCA

§ 536. Counsel fees.

Once an order of filiation is made, the court in its discretion may allow counsel fees to the attorney for the prevailing party, if he or she is unable to pay such counsel fees. Representation by an attorney pursuant to paragraph (b) of subdivision nine of section one hundred eleven-b of the social services law shall not preclude an award of counsel fees to an applicant which would otherwise be allowed under this section.

Amended by Laws 1981, Ch. 300, eff. Sept. 1, 1981; Laws 1986, Ch. 892, eff. Aug. 2, 1986.

Part 4. Orders.

§ 541.   Order dismissing petition.

If the court finds the male party is not the father of the child, it shall dismiss the petition. If a neglect petition was filed in the paternity proceeding, the court retains jurisdiction over the neglect petition whether or not it dismisses the paternity petition.

Amended by Laws 1976, Ch. 665, eff. Jan. 1, 1977.

§ 542.   Order of filiation.

(a)   If the court finds the male party is the father of the child, it shall make an order of filiation, declaring paternity. Such order shall contain the social security number of the declared father.

(b)   If the respondent willfully fails to appear before the court subsequent to the administration and analysis of a genetic marker test or DNA test administered pursuant to sections four hundred eighteen and five hundred thirty-two of this act or section one hundred eleven-k of the social services law, and if such test does not exclude the respondent as being the father of the child or the court determines that there exists clear and convincing evidence of paternity, the court shall enter an order of temporary support notwithstanding that paternity of such child has not been established nor an order of filiation entered against the respondent. The respondent shall be prospectively relieved from liability for support under such order of temporary support upon the respondent's appearance before the court.

(c)   If the respondent willfully fails to comply with an order made by either the court pursuant to sections four hundred eighteen and five hundred thirty-two of this act or by a social services official or designee pursuant to section one hundred eleven-k of the social services law, and willfully fails to appear before the court when otherwise required, the court shall enter an order of temporary support notwithstanding that paternity of the subject child has not been established nor an order of filiation entered against the respondent. The respondent shall be prospectively relieved from liability for support under such order of temporary support upon the respondent's compliance with such order and subsequent appearance before the court.

Amended by Laws 1976, Ch. 665, eff. Jan. 1, 1977; Laws 1993, Ch. 354, § 4, eff. July 1, 1993; Laws 1997, Ch. 398, §§ 33 and 78, eff. Nov. 11, 1997.

§ 543. Transmission of order of filiation.

When an order of filiation is made, the clerk of the court shall forthwith transmit to the state commissioner of health on a form prescribed by him a written notification as to such order, together with such other facts as may assist in identifying the birth record of the person whose paternity was in issue. When it appears to the clerk that the person whose paternity was established was born in New York city, he shall forthwith transmit the written notification aforesaid to the commissioner of health of the city of New York instead of to the state commissioner of health.

§ 544. Transmission of abrogation of filiation order.

If an order of filiation is abrogated by a later judgment or order of the court that originally made the order or by another court on appeal, that fact shall be immediately communicated in writing by the clerk of the court that originally made the order of filiation to the state commissioner of health on a form prescribed by him. If notice of the order was given to the commissioner of health of New York city, notice of abrogation shall be transmitted to him.

§ 545. Order of support by parents.

1. In a proceeding in which the court has made an order of filiation, the court shall direct the parent or parents possessed of sufficient means or able to earn such means to pay weekly or at other fixed periods a fair and reasonable sum according to their respective means as the court may determine and apportion for such child's support and education, until the child is twenty-one. The order shall be effective as of the earlier of the date of the application for an order of filiation, or, if the children for whom support is sought are in receipt of public assistance, the date for which their eligibility for public assistance was effective. Any retroactive amount of child support shall be support arrears/past-due support and shall be paid in one sum or periodic sums as the court shall direct, taking into account any amount of temporary support which has been paid. In addition, such retroactive child support shall be enforceable in any manner provided by law including, but not limited to, an execution for support enforcement pursuant to subdivision (b) of section fifty-two hundred forty-one of the civil practice law and rules. The court shall direct such parent to make his or her residence known at all times should he or she move from the address last known to the court by reporting such change to the support collection unit designated by the appropriate social services district. The order shall contain the social security numbers of the named parents. The order may also direct each parent to pay an amount as the court may determine and apportion for the support of the child prior to the making of the order of filiation, and may direct each parent to pay an amount as the court may determine and apportion for (i) the funeral expenses if the child has died; (ii) the necessary expenses incurred by or for the mother in connection with her confinement and recovery; and (iii) such expenses in connection with the pregnancy of the mother as the court may deem proper. In addition, The court

shall make provisions for health insurance benefits in accordance with the requirements of section four hundred sixteen of this act.

2. The court, in its discretion, taking into consideration the means of the father and his ability to pay and the needs of the child, may direct the payment of a reasonable sum or periodic sums to the mother as reimbursement for the needs of the child accruing from the date of the birth of the child to the date of the application for an order of filiation.

Added by Laws 1981, Ch. 68, eff. Jan. 1, 1982; former § 545 **amended** by Laws 1981, Ch. 300, eff. Sept. 1, 1981 to render statute gender-neutral; Laws 1981, Ch. 68, eff. Jan. 1, 1982; Laws 1981, Ch. 695, eff. Oct. 19, 1981 to provide as follows: "The order shall be effective as of the date of the application for an order of filiation, and any retroactive amount of support shall be paid in one sum or periodic sums as the court shall direct, taking into account any amount of temporary support which has been paid."; Laws 1982, Ch. 26, eff. June 28, 1982; Laws 1984, Ch. 794, eff. Sept. 1, 1984; Laws 1986, Ch. 849, 892, eff. Aug. 2, 1986; Laws 1992, Ch. 41, § 144, eff. Apr. 2, 1992; Laws 1997, Ch. 398, § 145, eff. Jan. 1, 1998; Laws 1998, Ch. 214, § 60, eff. Nov. 4, 1998.

§ 546. Payment to parent or support collection unit.

(a) The court may require the payment to be made to the parent having custody of the child or to the support collection unit as designated by the appropriate social services district.

(b) The support collection unit as designated by the appropriate social services district shall report to the court as the court may direct, the amounts received and paid over.

Amended by Laws 1977, Ch. 516, eff. Jan. 1, 1978; Laws 1981, Ch. 300, eff. Sept. 1, 1981.

§ 547. Substitution of trustee.

The court, on motion of a party or otherwise, may at any time for good cause shown substitute another trustee for the one designated and acting.

Amended by Laws 1976, Ch. 665, eff. Jan. 1, 1977.

§ 548. Compliance with orders.

The provisions of part five and part seven of article four of this act apply when an order is issued under this article.

Amended by Laws 1967, Ch. 459; Laws 1972, Ch. 970, eff. June 8, 1972.

§ 548-a. Paternity or child support proceedings; suspension of driving privileges.

(a) If the respondent, after receiving appropriate notice, fails to comply with a summons, subpoena or warrant relating to a paternity or child support proceeding, the court may order the department of motor vehicles to suspend the respondent's driving privileges.

(b) The court may subsequently order the department of motor vehicles to terminate the suspension of the respondent's driving privileges; however, the court shall order the termination of such suspension when the court is satisfied that the respondent has fully complied with the requirements of all summonses, subpoenas and warrants relating to a paternity or child support proceeding.

Added by Laws 1997, Ch. 398, § 114, eff. Jan. 1, 1998

§ 548-b. Paternity or child support proceedings; suspension of state professional, occupational and business licenses.

(a) If the respondent, after receiving appropriate notice, fails to comply with a summons, subpoena or warrant relating to a paternity or child support proceeding, and the court has determined that the respondent is licensed, permitted or registered by or with a board, department, authority or office of this state or one of its political subdivisions or instrumentalities to conduct a trade, business, profession or occupation, the court may order such board, department, authority or office to commence proceedings as required by law regarding the suspension of such license, permit, registration or authority to practice and to inform the court of the actions it has taken pursuant to such proceeding.

(b) The court may subsequently order such board, department, authority or office to terminate the suspension of the respondent's license, permit, registration or authority to practice; however, the court shall order the termination of such suspension when the court is satisfied that the respondent has fully complied with all summons, subpoenas and warrants relating to a paternity or child support proceeding.

Added by Laws 1997, Ch. 398, § 115, eff. Jan. 1, 1998

§ 548-c. Paternity or child support proceedings; suspension of recreational licenses.

If the respondent, after receiving appropriate notice, fails to comply with a summons, subpoena, or warrant relating to a paternity or child support proceeding, the court may order any agency responsible for the issuance of a recreational license to suspend or to refuse to reissue a license to the respondent or to deny application for such license by the respondent. The court may subsequently order such agency to terminate the adverse action regarding the respondent's license; however, the court shall order the termination of such suspension or other adverse action when the court is satisfied that the respondent has fully complied with the requirements of all summons, subpoenas, and warrants relating to a paternity or child support proceeding.

Added by Laws 1997, Ch. 398, § 129, eff. Jan. 1, 1998

§ 549. Order of visitation.

(a)   If an order of filiation is made or if a paternity agreement or compromise is approved by the court, in the absence of an order of custody or of visitation entered by the supreme court the family court may make an order of custody or of visitation, in accordance with subdivision one of section two hundred forty of the domestic relations law, requiring one parent to permit the other to visit the child or children at stated periods.

(b)   Any order of the family court under this section shall terminate when the supreme court makes an order of custody or of visitation concerning the child or children, unless the supreme court continues the order of the family court.

Added by Laws 1971, Ch. 952, eff. June 25, 1971; amended by Laws 1996, Ch. 85, § 5, eff. May 21, 1996 and applicable to all actions or proceedings concerning custody of or a right to visitation with a child whether such action or proceeding was commenced pursuant to section 240 of the domestic relations law or any other provision of law.

§ 550. Temporary order of protection.

(a)   Upon the filing of a petition or counter-claim under this article, the court for good cause shown may issue a temporary order of protection which may contain any of the provisions authorized on the making of an order of protection under section five hundred fifty-one.

(b)   A temporary order of protection is not a finding of wrongdoing.

(c)   The court may issue or extend a temporary order of protection ex parte or on notice simultaneously with the issuance of a warrant directing that the respondent be arrested and brought before the court pursuant to section five hundred twenty-six of this article.

Notwithstanding the foregoing provisions, an order of protection, or temporary order of protection where applicable, may be entered against a former spouse and persons who have a child in common, regardless whether such persons have been married or have lived together at any time.

Added by Laws 1972, Ch. 970, eff. June 8, 1972; amended by Laws 1981, Ch. 416, eff. Aug. 6, 1981, added subds. (b) and (c); Laws 1984, Ch. 948, eff. Nov. 1, 1984; Laws 1988, Ch. 706, eff. Sept. 2, 1988.

§ 551. Order of protection.

The court may make an order of protection in assistance or as a condition of any other order made under this article. The order of protection may set forth reasonable conditions of behavior to be observed for a specified time by the petitioner or respondent or both. No order of protection may direct any party to observe conditions of behavior unless the party requesting the order of protection has served and filed a petition or counter-claim in accordance with section one hundred fifty-four-b of this act. Such an order may require the petitioner or the respondent:

(a) to stay away from the home, school, business or place of employment of any other party, the other parent, or the child, and to stay away from any other specific location designated by the court;

(b) to permit a parent, or a person entitled to visitation by a court order or a separation agreement to visit the child at stated periods;

(c) to refrain from committing a family offense, as defined in subdivision one of section eight hundred twelve of this act, or any criminal offense against the child or against the other parent or against any person to whom custody of the child is awarded, or from harassing, intimidating or threatening such persons;

(d) to permit a designated party to enter the residence during a specified period of time in order to remove personal belongings not in issue in this proceeding or in any other proceeding or action under this act or the domestic relations law;

(e) to refrain from acts of commission or omission that create an unreasonable risk to the health, safety or welfare of a child;

(f) to participate in an educational program and to pay the costs thereof if the person has the means to do so, provided, however, that nothing contained herein shall be deemed to require payment of the costs of any such program by the state or any political subdivision thereof;

(g) to provide, either directly or by means of medical and health insurance, for expenses incurred for medical care and treatment arising from the incident or incidents forming the basis for the issuance of the order;

(h) to pay the reasonable counsel fees and disbursements involved in obtaining or enforcing the order of the person who is protected by such order if such order is issued or enforced, whether or not an order of filiation is made.

(i) 1. to refrain from intentionally injuring or killing, without justification, any companion animal the respondent knows to be owned, possessed, leased, kept or held by the petitioner or a minor child residing in the household.

2. [Companion animal], as used in this section, shall have the same meaning as in subdivision five of section three hundred fifty of the agriculture and markets law.

(j) to observe such other conditions as are necessary to further the purposes of protection.

The court may also award custody of the child, during the term of the order of protection to either parent, or to an appropriate relative within the second degree. Nothing in this section gives the court power to place or board out any child or to commit a child to an institution or agency. In making orders of protection, the court shall so act as to insure that in the care, protection, discipline and guardianship of the child his religious faith shall be preserved and protected.

Notwithstanding the foregoing provisions, an order of protection, or temporary order of protection where applicable, may be entered against a former spouse and persons who have a child in common, regardless whether such persons have been married or have lived together at any time.

Added by Laws 1972, Ch. 970, eff. June 8, 1972; **amended** by Laws 1981, Ch. 416, eff. Aug. 6, 1981; Laws 1981, Ch. 965, eff. Aug. 6, 1981, adding subds. (f), (g) and (h); Laws 1984, Ch. 948, eff. Nov. 1, 1984; Laws 1988, Ch. 706, eff. Sept. 2, 1988; Laws 1995, Ch. 483, §§ 5 and 6, eff. Nov. 1, 1995; Laws 2006, ch. 253, §3, eff. July 26, 2006.

Part 5.   Related proceedings.

Section   561.   **Proceedings to compel support by mother.**
           562.   **Proceedings to compel support by mother and father.**
           563.   **Paternity and support proceedings combined; apportionment.**
           564.   **Order of filiation in other proceedings.**
           565.   **A proceeding to challenge testing directive.**

§ 561.   Proceedings to compel support by mother.

Proceedings may be initiated under article four of this act to compel a mother who fails to support her child to do so in accord with the provisions of article four of this act.

§ 562.   Proceedings to compel support by mother and father.

Proceedings to compel a father who does not deny paternity of a child and the mother of the child to support the child may be instituted in accord with the provisions of article four of this act, unless an agreement or compromise is made in accord with section five hundred seventeen.

§ 563.   Paternity and support proceedings combined; apportionment.

When a proceeding to establish paternity is initiated under this article, the court on its own motion or on motion of any person qualified under article four of this act to file a support petition may direct the filing of a petition under article four to compel the mother to support her child. If the court enters an order of filiation, it may apportion the costs of the support and education of the child between the parents according to their respective means and responsibilities.

§ 564.   Order of filiation in other proceedings.

(a)   In any proceeding in the family court, whether under this act or under any other law, if there is an allegation or statement in a petition that a person is the father of a child who is a party to the proceeding or also is a subject of the proceeding and if it shall appear that the child is a child born out-of-wedlock, the court may make an order of filiation declaring the paternity of the child in accordance with the provisions of this section.

(b) The court may make such an order of filiation if (1) both parents are before the court, (2) the father waives both the filing of a petition under section five hundred twenty-three of this act and the right to a hearing under section five hundred thirty-three of this act, and (3) the court is satisfied as to the paternity of the child from the testimony or sworn statements of the parents.

(c) The court may in any such proceeding in its discretion direct either the mother or any other person empowered under section five hundred twenty-two of this act to file a verified petition under section five hundred twenty-three of this act.

(d) The provisions of part four of this article five shall apply to any order of filiation made under this section. The court may in its discretion direct a severance of proceedings upon such order of filiation from the proceeding upon the petition referred to in subdivision (a) of this section.

(e) For the purposes of this section the term "petition" shall include a complaint in a civil action, an accusatory instrument under the criminal procedure law, a writ of habeas corpus, a petition for supplemental relief, and any amendment in writing of any of the foregoing.

Added by Laws 1978, Ch. 440, eff. June 19, 1978 and applies to pending petitions and proceedings.

§ 565. A proceeding to challenge testing directive.

The court is authorized to hear and decide motions to challenge a directive by the department of social services requiring a party to submit to genetic testing, pursuant to section one hundred eleven-k of the social services law. Nothing contained in this section shall be deemed to preclude the authority of a local social services district from filing a petition pursuant to this article.

Added by Laws 1997, Ch. 398, § 77, eff. Nov. 11, 1997.

ARTICLE 5–A

SPECIAL PROVISIONS RELATING TO ENFORCEMENT OF SUPPORT AND ESTABLISHMENT OF PATERNITY

SUMMARY OF ARTICLE

(Repealed and transfered sections are noted under appropriate section number of text.)

§ 571.   Enforcement of support and establishment of paternity.

1.   Any inconsistent provision of this law or any other law notwithstanding, in cases where a social services official has accepted, on behalf of the state and a social services district, an assignment of support rights from a person applying for or receiving family assistance in accordance with the provisions of the social services law, the social services official or an authorized representative of the state is authorized to bring a proceeding or proceedings in the family court pursuant to article four of this act to enforce such support rights and, when appropriate or necessary, to establish the paternity of a child pursuant to article five of this act.

2.   The official who brings such a proceeding and the attorney representing him shall be deemed to represent the interests of all persons, officials and agencies having an interest in the assignment. The court shall determine, in accordance with applicable provisions of law, whether such person is a necessary party to the proceeding and whether independent counsel need be appointed to represent any party to the assignment or any other person having an interest in the support right.

3.   (a) Any support order made by the court in such a proceeding shall direct that payments be made directly to the support collection unit, as designated by the appropriate social services district, so long as there is in effect an assignment of support rights to such district. Further, the order shall provide that when the person or family no longer receives public assistance, payments shall continue to be made to the support collection unit, unless the person or family requests otherwise. When the person or family is no longer receiving public assistance, the social services district shall notify the parties to the order that the person or family upon request to the social services official and without further judicial intervention may receive support payments directly. If such a request is made,

the person paying support shall be so notified and shall be informed that unless such person applies for an order pursuant to section four hundred forty of this act within thirty days, the person or family may receive such payments directly.

(b)   The entry of an order of support under this section shall not preclude an assignor who is no longer receiving public assistance from instituting a support proceeding and receiving a hearing de novo on the amount of support to which the assignor is entitled at that time.

4.   Any order for support made by the court in such a proceeding shall specify the amount of support to be paid on behalf of the spouse, if any, and the amount to be paid on behalf of each child.

5.   In cases where a support agreement or compromise is entered into between a social services official and the absent parent, the social services official may petition the court for approval of such agreement or compromise in accordance with the provisions of section four hundred twenty-five of this chapter which provisions shall apply thereto.

6.   In cases where an order for support has been made by a family court and upon notification to the court that an assignment of support rights has thereafter been made to the social services official responsible for furnishing family assistance, payments pursuant to such order shall be made to such official until he or she notifies the court of the termination of the assignment.

7.   Any inconsistent provision of the law notwithstanding, the provision of this section shall also apply to cases brought in accordance with title six-A of article three of the social services law involving persons who are not applicants for or recipients of family assistance.

8.   Any other inconsistent provision of law notwithstanding, if an applicant for or recipient of family assistance is pregnant, and a proceeding to establish paternity has been filed, and the allegation of paternity is denied by the respondent there shall be a stay of all paternity proceedings until sixty days after the birth of the child.

9.   Any order of support made pursuant to this section shall be effective as of the date of the application therefor, and any retroactive amount of support shall be paid in one sum or periodic sums as the court shall direct, taking into account any amount of temporary support which has been paid.

10.   (a) When a person has applied for and is receiving public assistance and care and an assignment of support rights has been made or has applied for and is receiving child support enforcement services pursuant to section one hundred eleven-g of the social services law, or is receiving such services in another state, and such person has an existing order of support which does not direct that support payments be made to the support collection unit, the social services district shall, upon notice to the parties and without further judicial intervention, direct that support payments be made directly to the appropriate support collection unit.

(b)   When a child is in foster care, in this state or in another state, and where there is an existing order for the support of such child which does not direct that support payments be made to the support collection unit, the social services district shall, upon notice to the parties and without further judicial intervention, direct that support payments be made directly to the appropriate support collection unit.

11.   A support order of another state payable to a support collection unit as a result of a notice pursuant to this section or through a court order shall be deemed to be an order on behalf of persons receiving services under title six-A of article three of the social services law and shall be enforceable in the same manner as such orders.

Added by Laws 1975, Ch. 685; **amended** by Laws 1977, Ch. 516; Laws 1978, Ch. 456; Laws 1979, Ch. 520, eff. July 10, 1979, adding subd. 8; Laws 1981, Ch. 695, eff. Oct. 19, 1981, adding subd. 9; Laws 1986, Ch. 892, eff. Aug. 2, 1986; Laws 1997, Ch. 398, § 64, eff. Jan. 1, 1998, adding new para. (10) to FCA § 571; and Ch. 436, § 1 Part B, § 111, eff. Aug. 20, 1997; Laws 1998, Ch. 214, §§ 41 and 83, eff. July 7, 1998, deemed in full force and effect Jan. 1, 1998.

§ 572.   Petitioner's representative.

Repealed by Laws 1998, Ch. 214, eff. July 7, 1998.

§ 573.   Pleadings and documents.

Repealed by Laws 1998, Ch. 214, eff. July 7, 1998, deemed in full force and effect Dec. 31, 1997.

§ 574.   Definition of "state".

Repealed by Laws 1998, Ch. 214, eff. July 7, 1998, deemed in full force and effect Dec. 31, 1997.

ARTICLE 5–B

UNIFORM INTERSTATE FAMILY SUPPORT ACT

SUMMARY OF ARTICLE

Part 1. GENERAL PROVISIONS.

§ 580-101. Definitions.

In this article:

(1) "Child" means an individual, whether over or under the age of majority, who is or is alleged to be owed a duty of support by the individual's parent or who is or is alleged to be the beneficiary of a support order directed to the parent.

(2) "Child support order" means a support order for a child, including a child who has attained the age of majority under the law of the issuing state.

(3) "Duty of support" means an obligation imposed or imposable by law to provide support for a child, spouse, or former spouse, including an unsatisfied obligation to provide support.

(4) "Home state" means the state in which a child lived with a parent or a person acting as parent for at least six consecutive months immediately preceding

the time of filing of a petition or comparable pleading for support and, if a child is less than six months old, the state in which the child lived from birth with any of them. A period of temporary absence of any of them is counted as part of the six-month or other period.

(5) "Income" includes earnings or other periodic entitlements to money from any source and any other property subject to withholding for support as defined by section five thousand two hundred forty-one of the civil practice law and rules.

(6) "Income withholding order" means an order or other legal process directed to an obligor's employer or other income payor, as defined by section five thousand two hundred forty-one or five thousand two hundred forty-two of the civil practice law and rules to withhold support from the income of the obligor.

(7) "Initiating state" means a state from which a proceeding is forwarded or in which a proceeding is filed for forwarding to a responding state under this article or a law or procedure substantially similar to this article, the uniform reciprocal enforcement of support act, or the revised uniform reciprocal enforcement of support act.

(8) "Initiating tribunal" means the authorized tribunal in an initiating state.

(9) "Issuing state" means the state in which a tribunal issues a support order or renders a judgment determining parentage.

(10) "Issuing tribunal" means the tribunal that issues a support order or renders a judgment determining parentage.

(11) "Law" includes decisional and statutory law and rules and regulations having the force of law.

(12) "Obligee" means:

(i) an individual to whom a duty of support is or is alleged to be owed or in whose favor a support order has been issued or a judgment determining parentage has been rendered;

(ii) a state or political subdivision to which the rights under a duty of support or support order have been assigned or which has independent claims based on financial assistance provided to an individual obligee; or

(iii) an individual seeking a judgment determining parentage of the individual's child.

(13) "Obligor" means an individual, or the estate of a decedent:

(i) who owes or is alleged to owe a duty of support;

(ii) who is alleged but has not been adjudicated to be a parent of a child; or

(iii) who is liable under a support order.

(14) "Register" means to file a support order or judgment determining parentage in the tribunal.

(15) "Registering tribunal" means a tribunal in which a support order is registered.

(16) "Responding state" means a state in which a proceeding is filed or to which a proceeding is forwarded for filing from an initiating state under this article, or a law or procedure substantially similar to this article, the uniform reciprocal enforcement of support act, or the revised uniform reciprocal enforcement of support act.

(17) "Responding tribunal" means the authorized tribunal in a responding state.

(18) "Spousal support order" means a support order for a spouse or former spouse of the obligor.

(19) "State" means a state of the United States, the District of Columbia, Puerto Rico, the United States Virgin Islands or any territory or insular possession subject to the jurisdiction of the United States. The term includes: (i) an Indian tribe; and (ii) a foreign jurisdiction that has enacted a law or established procedures for issuance and enforcement of support orders which are substantially similar to the procedures under this article, the uniform reciprocal enforcement of support act, or the revised uniform reciprocal enforcement of support act.

(20) "Support enforcement agency" means a public official or agency authorized to seek:

(i) enforcement of support orders or laws relating to the duty of support;

(ii) establishment or modification of child support;

(iii) determination of parentage; or

(iv) to locate obligors or their assets.

(21) "Support order" means a judgment, decree, or order, whether temporary, final, or subject to modification, for the benefit of a child, a spouse, or a former spouse, which provides for monetary support, health care, arrearages, or reimbursement, and may include related costs and fees, interest, income withholding, attorney's fees, and other relief.

(22) "Tribunal" means a court, administrative agency, or quasi-judicial entity authorized to establish, enforce, or modify support orders or to determine parentage.

§ 580-102. Tribunal of state.

The family court is the tribunal of this state.

§ 580-103. Remedies cumulative.

Remedies provided by this article are cumulative and do not affect the availability of remedies under other law.

Part 2. JURISDICTION.

Part 2.A. EXTENDED PERSONAL JURISDICTION.

§ 580-201. Bases for jurisdiction over nonresident.

In a proceeding to establish, enforce, or modify a support order or to determine parentage, the tribunal of this state may exercise personal jurisdiction over a nonresident individual or the individual's guardian or conservator if:

(1) the individual is personally served with a summons and petition within this state;

(2) the individual submits to the jurisdiction of this state by consent, by entering a general appearance, or by filing a responsive document having the effect of waiving any contest to personal jurisdiction;

(3) the individual resided with the child in this state;

(4) the individual resided in this state and provided prenatal expenses or support for the child;

(5) the child resides in this state as a result of the acts or directives of the individual;

(6) the individual engaged in sexual intercourse in this state and the child may have been conceived by that act of intercourse;

(7) the individual asserted parentage in the putative father registry maintained in this state by the department of social services; or

(8) there is any other basis consistent with the constitutions of this state and the united states for the exercise of personal jurisdiction.

§ 580-202. Procedure when exercising jurisdiction over nonresident.

A tribunal of this state exercising personal jurisdiction over a nonresident under section 580-201 may apply section 580-316 (special rules of evidence and procedure) to receive evidence from another state, and section 580-318 (assistance with discovery) to obtain discovery through a tribunal of another state. In all other respects, parts three through seven do not apply and the tribunal shall apply the procedural and substantive law of this state, including the rules on choice of law other than those established by this article.

Part 2.B. PROCEEDINGS INVOLVING TWO OR MORE STATES.

§ 580-203. Initiating and responding tribunal of state.

Under this article, a tribunal of this state may serve as an initiating tribunal to forward proceedings to another state and as a responding tribunal for proceedings initiated in another state.

§ 580-204. Simultaneous proceedings in another state.

(a)   A tribunal of this state may exercise jurisdiction to establish a support order if the petition or comparable pleading is filed after a pleading is filed in another state only if:

(1)   the petition or comparable pleading in this state is filed before the expiration of the time allowed in the other state for filing a responsive pleading challenging the exercise of jurisdiction by the other state;

(2)   the contesting party timely challenges the exercise of jurisdiction in the other state; and

(3)   if relevant, this state is the home state of the child.

(b)   A tribunal of this state may not exercise jurisdiction to establish a support order if the petition or comparable pleading is filed before a petition or comparable pleading is filed in another state if:

(1)   the petition or comparable pleading in the other state is filed before the expiration of the time allowed in this state for filing a responsive pleading challenging the exercise of jurisdiction by this state;

(2)   the contesting party timely challenges the exercise of jurisdiction in this state; and

(3)   if relevant, the other state is the home state of the child.

Amended by Laws 1998, Ch. 214, § 32, eff. July 7, 1998, deemed in full force and effect Dec. 31, 1997.

§ 580-205. Continuing, exclusive jurisdiction.

(a)   A tribunal of this state issuing a support order consistent with the law of this state has continuing, exclusive jurisdiction over a child support order:

(1)   as long as this state remains the residence of the obligor, the individual obligee, or the child for whose benefit the support order is issued; or

(2)   until all of the parties who are individuals have filed written consents with the tribunal of this state for a tribunal of another state to modify the order and assume continuing, exclusive jurisdiction.

(b)   A tribunal of this state issuing a child-support order consistent with the law of this state may not exercise its continuing jurisdiction to modify the order if the order has been modified by a tribunal of another state pursuant to the uniform interstate family support act (UIFSA) or a law substantially similar to UIFSA.

(c) If a child-support order of this state is modified by a tribunal of another state pursuant to UIFSA or a law substantially similar to UIFSA, a tribunal of this state loses its continuing, exclusive jurisdiction with regard to prospective enforcement of the order issued in this state, and may only:

(1) enforce the order that was modified as to amounts accruing before the modification;

(2) enforce nonmodifiable aspects of that order; and

(3) provide other appropriate relief for violations of that order which occurred before the effective date of the modification.

(d) A tribunal of this state shall recognize the continuing, exclusive jurisdiction of a tribunal of another state which has issued a child support order pursuant to UIFSA or a law substantially similar to UIFSA.

(e) A temporary support order issued ex parte or pending resolution of a jurisdictional conflict does not create continuing, exclusive jurisdiction in the issuing tribunal.

(f) A tribunal of this state issuing a support order consistent with the law of this state has continuing, exclusive jurisdiction over a spousal support order throughout the existence of the support obligation. A tribunal of this state may not modify a spousal support order issued by a tribunal of another state having continuing, exclusive jurisdiction over that order under the law of that state.

§ 580-206. Enforcement and modification of support order by tribunal having continuing jurisdiction.

(a) A tribunal of this state may serve as an initiating tribunal to request a tribunal of another state to enforce or modify a support order issued in that state.

(b) A tribunal of this state having continuing, exclusive jurisdiction over a support order may act as a responding tribunal to enforce or modify the order. If a party subject to the continuing, exclusive jurisdiction of the tribunal no longer resides in the issuing state, in subsequent proceedings the tribunal may apply section 580-316 (Special Rules of Evidence and Procedure) to receive evidence from another state and section 580-318 (Assistance with Discovery) to obtain discovery through a tribunal of another state.

(c) A tribunal of this state which lacks continuing, exclusive jurisdiction over a spousal support order may not serve as a responding tribunal to modify a spousal support order of another state.

Part 2.C. RECONCILIATION OF MULTIPLE ORDERS.

§ 580-207. Recognition of controlling child support order.

(a) If a proceeding is brought under this article and only one tribunal has issued a child support order, the order of that tribunal controls and must be so recognized.

(b) If a proceeding is brought under this article, and two or more child support orders have been issued by tribunals of this state or another state with regard to the same obligor and child, a tribunal of this state shall apply the following rules in determining which order to recognize for purposes of continuing, exclusive jurisdiction:

(1) if only one of the tribunals would have continuing, exclusive jurisdiction under this article, the order of that tribunal controls and must be so recognized.

(2) if more than one of the tribunals would have continuing, exclusive jurisdiction under this article, an order issued by a tribunal in the current home state of the child controls and must be so recognized, but if an order has not been issued in the current home state of the child, the order most recently issued controls and must be so recognized.

(3) if none of the tribunals would have continuing, exclusive jurisdiction under this article, the tribunal of this state having jurisdiction over the parties shall issue a child-support order which controls and must be so recognized.

(c) If two or more child support orders have been issued for the same obligor and child and if the obligor or the individual obligee resides in this state, a party may request a tribunal of this state to determine which order controls and must be so recognized under subdivision (b). The request must be accompanied by a certified copy of every support order in effect. The requesting party shall give notice of the request to each party whose rights may be affected by the determination.

(d) The tribunal that issued the controlling order under subdivision (a), (b) or (c) is the tribunal that has continuing, exclusive jurisdiction under section 580-205.

(e) A tribunal of this state which determines by order the identity of the controlling order under paragraphs one and two of subdivision (b) of this section or which issues a new controlling order under paragraph three of subdivision (b) of this section shall state in that order the basis upon which the tribunal made its determination.

(f) Within thirty days after issuance of an order determining the identity of the controlling order, the party obtaining the order shall file a certified copy of it with each tribunal that issued or registered an earlier order of child support. A party who obtains the order and fails to file a certified copy is subject to appropriate sanctions by a tribunal in which the issue of failure to file arises. The failure to file does not affect the validity or enforceability of the controlling order.

§ 580-208. Multiple child support orders for two or more obligees.

In responding to multiple registrations or petitions for enforcement of two or more child support orders in effect at the same time with regard to the same obligor and different individual obligees, at least one of which was issued by a tribunal of another state, a tribunal of this state shall enforce those orders in the same manner as if the multiple orders had been issued by a tribunal of this state.

§ 580-209. Credit for payments.

Amounts collected and credited for a particular period pursuant to a support order issued by a tribunal of another state must be credited against the amounts accruing or accrued for the same period under a support order issued by the tribunal of this state.

Part 3. CIVIL PROVISIONS OF GENERAL APPLICATION.

§ 580-301. Proceedings under article.

(a) Except as otherwise provided in this article, this part applies to all proceedings under this article.

(b) This article provides for the following proceedings:

(1) establishment of an order for spousal support or child support pursuant to part four;

(2) enforcement of a support order and income-withholding order of another state without registration pursuant to part five;

(3) registration of an order for spousal support or child support of another state for enforcement pursuant to part six;

(4)   modification of an order for child support or spousal support issued by a tribunal of this state pursuant to part two.B.;

(5)   registration of an order for child support of another state for modification pursuant to part six;

(6)   determination of parentage pursuant to part seven; and

(7)   assertion of jurisdiction over nonresidents pursuant to part two.A.

(c)   An individual petitioner or a support enforcement agency may commence a proceeding authorized under this article by filing a petition in an initiating tribunal for forwarding to a responding tribunal or by filing a petition or a comparable pleading directly in a tribunal of another state which has or can obtain personal jurisdiction over the respondent.

§ 580-302.   Action by minor parent.

A Minor parent, or a guardian or other legal representative of a minor parent, may maintain a proceeding on behalf of or for the benefit of the minor's child.

§ 580-303.   Application of law of state.

Except as otherwise provided by this article, a responding tribunal of this state:

(1)   shall apply the procedural and substantive law, including the rules on choice of law, generally applicable to similar proceedings originating in this state and may exercise all powers and provide all remedies available in those proceedings; and

(2)   shall determine the duty of support and the amount payable in accordance with the law and support guidelines of this state.

§ 580-304.   Duties of initiating tribunal.

(a)   Upon the filing of a petition authorized by this article, an initiating tribunal of this state shall forward three copies of the petition and its accompanying documents:

(1)   to the responding tribunal or appropriate support enforcement agency in the responding state; or

(2)   if the identity of the responding tribunal is unknown, to the state information agency of the responding state with a request that they be forwarded to the appropriate tribunal and that receipt be acknowledged.

(b)   if a responding state has not enacted this article or a law or procedure substantially similar to this article, a tribunal of this state may issue a certificate or other document and make findings required by the law of the responding state. If the responding state is a foreign jurisdiction, the tribunal may specify the amount of support sought and provide other documents necessary to satisfy the requirements of the responding state.

§ 580-305. Duties and powers of responding tribunal.

(a) When a responding tribunal of this state receives a petition or comparable pleading from an initiating tribunal or directly pursuant to subdivision (c) of section 580-301 of this part (proceedings under this article), it shall cause the petition or pleading to be filed and notify the petitioner where and when it was filed.

(b) A responding tribunal of this state, to the extent otherwise authorized by law, may do one or more of the following:

(1) issue or enforce a support order, modify a child support order, or render a judgment to determine parentage;

(2) order an obligor to comply with a support order, specifying the amount and the manner of compliance;

(3) order income-withholding;

(4) determine the amount of any arrearages, and specify a method of payment;

(5) enforce orders by civil or criminal contempt, or both;

(6) set aside property for satisfaction of the support order;

(7) place liens and order execution on the obligor's property;

(8) order an obligor to keep the tribunal informed of the obligor's current residential address, telephone number, employer, address of employment, and telephone number at the place of employment;

(9) issue a warrant for an obligor who has failed after proper notice to appear at a hearing ordered by the tribunal and enter the warrant in any local and state computer systems for criminal warrants;

(10) order the obligor to seek appropriate employment by specified methods;

(11) award reasonable attorney's fees and other fees and costs; and

(12) grant any other available remedy.

(c) A responding tribunal of this state shall include in a support order issued under this article, or in the documents accompanying the order, the calculations on which the support order is based.

(d) A responding tribunal of this state may not condition the payment of a support order issued under this article upon compliance by a party with provisions for visitation.

(e) If a responding tribunal of this state issues an order under this article, the tribunal shall send a copy of the order to the petitioner and the respondent and to the initiating tribunal, if any.

§ 580-306. Inappropriate tribunal.

If a petition or comparable pleading is received by an inappropriate tribunal of this state, it shall forward the pleading and accompanying documents to an appropriate tribunal in this state or another state and notify the petitioner where and when the pleading was sent.

§ 580-307.　Duties of support enforcement agency.

(a)　A support enforcement agency of this state, upon request, shall provide services to a petitioner which shall, for the purposes of this section, be defined as a petitioner in receipt of services under article six-A of the social services law, in a proceeding under this article.

(b)　A support enforcement agency that is providing services to the petitioner as appropriate shall:

(1)　take all steps necessary to enable an appropriate tribunal in this state or another state to obtain jurisdiction over the respondent;

(2)　request an appropriate tribunal to set a date, time, and place for a hearing;

(3)　make a reasonable effort to obtain all relevant information, including information as to income and property of the parties;

(4)　within ten days, exclusive of Saturdays, Sundays, and legal holidays, after receipt of a written notice from an initiating, responding, or registering tribunal, send a copy of the notice to the petitioner;

(5)　within ten days, exclusive of Saturdays, Sundays, and legal holidays, after receipt of a written communication from the respondent or the respondent's attorney, send a copy of the communication to the petitioner; and

(6)　notify the petitioner if jurisdiction over the respondent cannot be obtained.

(c)　This article does not create or negate a relationship of attorney and client or other fiduciary relationship between a support enforcement agency or the attorney for the agency and the individual being assisted by the agency.

Amended by Laws 1998, Ch. 214, § 31-a, eff. July 7, 1998, deemed in full force and effect Dec. 31, 1997.

§ 580-308.　Duty of attorney general.

If the attorney general determines that the support enforcement agency is neglecting or refusing to provide services to an individual, the attorney general may order the agency to perform its duties under this article or may provide those services directly to the individual.

§ 580-309.　Private counsel.

An individual may employ private counsel to represent the individual in proceedings authorized by this article.

§ 580-310.　Duties of state information agency.

(a)　The state department of social services pursuant to section one hundred eleven of the social services law is the state information agency under this article.

(b) The state information agency shall:

(1) compile and maintain a current list, including addresses, of the tribunals in this state which have jurisdiction under this article and any support enforcement agencies in this state and transmit a copy to the state information agency of every other state;

(2) maintain a register of tribunals and support enforcement agencies received from other states;

(3) forward to the appropriate tribunal in the place in this state in which the individual obligee or the obligor resides, or in which the obligor's property is believed to be located, all documents concerning a proceeding under this article received from an initiating tribunal or the state information agency of the initiating state; and

(4) obtain information concerning the location of the obligor and the obligor's property within this state not exempt from execution, by such means as postal verification and federal or state locator services, examination of telephone directories, requests for the obligor's address from employers, and examination of governmental records, including, to the extent not prohibited by other law, those relating to real property, vital statistics, law enforcement, taxation, motor vehicles, driver's licenses, and social security.

§ 580-311. Pleadings and accompanying documents.

(a) A petitioner seeking to establish or modify a support order or to determine parentage in a proceeding under this article must verify the petition. Unless otherwise ordered under section 580-312 (nondisclosure of information in exceptional circumstances), the petition or accompanying documents must provide, so far as known, the name, residential address, and social security numbers of the obligor and the obligee, and the name, sex, residential address, social security number, and date of birth of each child for whom support is sought. The petition must be accompanied by a certified copy of any support order in effect. The petition may include any other information that may assist in locating or identifying the respondent.

(b) The petition must specify the relief sought. The petition and accompanying documents must conform substantially with the requirements imposed by the forms mandated by federal law for use in cases filed by a support enforcement agency.

§ 580-312. Nondisclosure of information in exceptional circumstances.

Upon a finding, which may be made ex parte, that the health, safety, or liberty of a party or child would be unreasonably put at risk by the disclosure of identifying information, or if an existing order so provides, a tribunal shall order that the address of the child or party or other identifying information not be disclosed in a pleading or other document filed in a proceeding under this article.

§ 580-313.   Costs and fees.

(a)   The petitioner may not be required to pay a filing fee or other costs.

(b)   If an obligee prevails, a responding tribunal may assess against an obligor filing fees, reasonable attorney's fees, other costs, and necessary travel and other reasonable expenses incurred by the obligee and the obligee's witnesses. The tribunal may not assess fees, costs, or expenses against the obligee or the support enforcement agency of either the initiating or the responding state, except as provided by other law. Attorney's fees may be taxed as costs, and may be ordered paid directly to the attorney, who may enforce the order in the attorney's own name. Payment of support owed to the obligee has priority over fees, costs and expenses.

(c)   The tribunal shall order the payment of costs and reasonable attorney's fees if it determines that a hearing was requested primarily for delay. In a proceeding under part six of this article (Enforcement and modification of support order after registration), a hearing is presumed to have been requested primarily for delay if a registered support order is confirmed or enforced without change.

§ 580-314.   Limited immunity of petitioner.

(a)   Participation by a petitioner in a proceeding before a responding tribunal, whether in person, by private attorney, or through services provided by the support enforcement agency, does not confer personal jurisdiction over the petitioner in another proceeding.

(b)   A petitioner is not amenable to service of civil process while physically present in this state to participate in a proceeding under this article.

(c)   The immunity granted by this section does not extend to civil litigation based on acts unrelated to a proceeding under this article committed by a party while present in this state to participate in the proceeding.

§ 580-315.   Nonparentage as defense.

A party whose parentage of a child has been previously determined by or pursuant to law may not plead nonparentage as a defense to a proceeding under this article.

§ 580-316.   Special rules of evidence and procedure.

(a)   The physical presence of the petitioner in a responding tribunal of this state is not required for the establishment, enforcement, or modification of a support order or the rendition of a judgment determining parentage.

(b)   A verified petition, affidavit, document substantially complying with federally mandated forms, and a document incorporated by reference in any of them, not excluded under the hearsay rule if given in person, is admissible in evidence if given under oath by a party or witness residing in another state.

(c)   A copy of the record of child support payments certified as a true copy of the original by the custodian of the record may be forwarded to a responding tribunal. The copy is evidence of facts asserted in it, and is admissible to show whether payments were made.

(d)   Copies of bills for testing for parentage, and for prenatal and postnatal health care of the mother and child, furnished to the adverse party at least ten days before trial, are admissible in evidence to prove the amount of the charges billed and that the charges were reasonable, necessary, and customary.

(e)   Documentary evidence transmitted from another state to a tribunal of this state by telephone, telecopier, or other means that do not provide an original writing may not be excluded from evidence on an objection based on the means of transmission.

(f)   In a proceeding under this article, a tribunal of this state may permit a party or witness residing in another state to be deposed or to testify by telephone, audiovisual means, or other electronic means at a designated tribunal or other location in that state. A tribunal of this state shall cooperate with tribunals of other states in designating an appropriate location for the deposition or testimony.

(g)   If a party called to testify at a civil hearing refuses to answer on the ground that the testimony may be self-incriminating, the trier of fact may draw an adverse inference from the refusal.

(h)   A privilege against disclosure of communications between spouses does not apply in a proceeding under this article.

(i)   The defense of immunity based on the relationship of husband and wife or parent and child does not apply in a proceeding under this article.

§ 580-317.   Communications between tribunals.

A tribunal of this state may communicate with a tribunal of another state in writing, or by telephone or other means, to obtain information concerning the laws of that state, the legal effect of a judgment, decree, or order of that tribunal, and the status of a proceeding in the other state. A tribunal of this state may furnish similar information by similar means to a tribunal of another state.

§ 580-318.   Assistance with discovery.

A tribunal of this state may:

(1)   request a tribunal of another state to assist in obtaining discovery; and

(2)   upon request, compel a person over whom it has jurisdiction to respond to a discovery order issued by a tribunal of another state.

§ 580-319.   Receipt and disbursement of payments.

A support enforcement agency or tribunal of this state shall disburse promptly any amounts received pursuant to a support order, as directed by the order. The agency or tribunal shall furnish to a requesting party or tribunal of another state a certified statement by the custodian of the record of the amounts and dates of all payments received.

Part 4.　ESTABLISHMENT OF SUPPORT ORDER.

Section 580-401.　Petition to establish support order.

§ 580-401.　Petition to establish support order.

(a)　If a support order entitled to recognition under this article has not been issued, a responding tribunal of this state may issue a support order if:

(1)　the individual seeking the order resides in another state; or

(2)　the support enforcement agency seeking the order is located in another state.

(b)　The tribunal may issue a temporary child support order if:

(1)　the respondent has signed a verified statement acknowledging parentage;

(2)　the respondent has been determined by or pursuant to law to be the parent; or

(3)　there is other clear and convincing evidence that the respondent is the child's parent.

(c)　Upon finding, after notice and opportunity to be heard, that an obligor owes a duty of support, the tribunal shall issue a support order directed to the obligor and may issue other orders pursuant to section 580-305 (duties and powers of responding tribunal).

Part 5.　ENFORCEMENT OF ORDER OF ANOTHER STATE WITHOUT REGISTRATION.

§ 580-501.　Employer's receipt of income-withholding order of another state.

An income-withholding order issued in another state may be sent to the person or entity defined as the obligor's employer or income payor under section five thousand two hundred forty-one of the civil practice law and rules (for purposes of this part and section 580-605 of this article employer shall also include income payor) without first filing a petition or comparable pleading or registering the order with a tribunal of this state.

Amended by Laws 1998, Ch. 214, § 31-b, eff. July 7, 1998, deemed in full force and effect Dec. 31, 1997.

§ 580-502. Employer's compliance with income-withholding order of another state.

(a)   Upon receipt of an income-withholding order, the obligor's employer shall immediately provide a copy of the order to the obligor.

(b)   The employer shall treat an income-withholding order issued in another state which appears regular on its face as if it had been issued by a tribunal of this state.

(c)   Except as otherwise provided in subdivision (d) and section 580-503, the employer shall withhold and distribute the funds as directed in the withholding order by complying with terms of the order which specify:

(1)   the duration and amount of periodic payments of current child support, stated as a sum certain;

(2)   the person or agency designated to receive payments and the address to which the payments are to be forwarded;

(3)   medical support, whether in the form of periodic cash payment, stated as a sum certain, or ordering the obligor to provide health insurance coverage for the child under a policy available through the obligor's employment;

(4)   the amount of periodic payments of fees and costs for a support enforcement agency, the issuing tribunal, and the obligee's attorney, stated as sums certain; and

(5)   the amount of periodic payments of arrearages and interest on arrearages, stated as sums certain.

(d)   An employer shall comply with the law of the state of the obligor's principal place of employment for withholding from income with respect to:

(1)   the employer's fee for processing an income-withholding order;

(2)   the maximum amount permitted to be withheld from the obligor's income; and

(3)   the times within which the employer must implement the withholding order and forward the child support payment.

§ 580-503. Employer's compliance with multiple income-withholding orders.

If an obligor's employer receives multiple income-withholding orders with respect to the earnings of the same obligor, the employer satisfies the terms of the multiple orders if the employer complies with the law of the state of the obligor's principal place of employment to establish the priorities for withholding and allocating income withheld for multiple child support obligees.

§ 580-504. Immunity from civil liability.

An employer who complies with an income-withholding order issued in another state in accordance with this article is not subject to civil liability to an individual or agency with regard to the employer's withholding of child support from the obligor's income.

§ 580-505. Penalties for noncompliance.

An employer who willfully fails to comply with an income-withholding order issued by another state and received for enforcement is subject to the same penalties that may be imposed for noncompliance with an order issued by a tribunal of this state.

§ 580-506. Contest by obligor.

(a)   An obligor may contest the validity or enforcement of an income-withholding order issued in another state and received directly by an employer in this state in the same manner as if the order had been issued by a tribunal of this state. Section 580-604 (Choice of law) applies to the contest.

(b)   The obligor shall give notice of the contest to:

(1)   a support enforcement agency providing services to the obligee;

(2)   each employer that has directly received an income-withholding order; and

(3)   the person or agency designated to receive payments in the income-withholding order or if no person or agency is designated, to the obligee.

§ 580-507. Administrative enforcement of orders.

(a)   A party seeking to enforce a support order or an income-withholding order, or both, issued by a tribunal of another state may send the documents required for registering the order to a support enforcement agency of this state.

(b)   Upon receipt of the documents, the support enforcement agency, without initially seeking to register the order, shall consider and, if appropriate, use any administrative procedure authorized by the law of this state to enforce a support order or an income-withholding order, or both. If the obligor does not contest administrative enforcement, the order need not be registered. If the obligor contests the validity or administrative enforcement of the order, the support enforcement agency shall register the order pursuant to this article.

FCA

Part 6. ENFORCEMENT AND MODIFICATION OF SUPPORT ORDER AFTER REGISTRATION.

Part 6.A. REGISTRATION AND ENFORCEMENT OF SUPPORT ORDER.

§ 580-601. Registration of order for enforcement.

A support order or an income-withholding order issued by a tribunal of another state may be registered in this state for enforcement.

§ 580-602. Procedure to register order for enforcement.

(a) A support order or income-withholding order of another state may be registered in this state by sending the following documents and information to the appropriate tribunal in this state:

(1) a letter of transmittal to the tribunal requesting registration and enforcement;

(2) two copies, including one certified copy, of all orders to be registered, including any modification of an order;

(3) a sworn statement by the party seeking registration or a certified statement by the custodian of the records showing the amount of any arrearage;

(4) the name of the obligor and, if known:

(i) the obligor's address and social security number;

(ii) the name and address of the obligor's employer and any other source of income of the obligor; and

(iii) a description and the location of property of the obligor in this state not exempt from execution; and

(5) the name and address of the obligee and, if applicable, the agency or person to whom support payments are to be remitted.

(b) On receipt of a request for registration, the registering tribunal shall cause the order to be filed as a foreign judgment, together with one copy of the documents and information, regardless of their form.

(c) A petition or comparable pleading seeking a remedy that must be affirmatively sought under other laws of this state may be filed at the same time as the request for registration or later. The pleading must specify the grounds for the remedy sought.

§ 580-603.　Effect of registration for enforcement.

(a)　A support order or income-withholding order issued in another state is registered when the order is filed in the registering tribunal of this state.

(b)　A registered order issued in another state is enforceable in the same manner and is subject to the same procedures as an order issued by a tribunal of this state.

(c)　Except as otherwise provided in this article, a tribunal of this state shall recognize and enforce, but may not modify, a registered order if the issuing tribunal had jurisdiction.

§ 580-604.　Choice of law.

(a)　The law of the issuing state governs the nature, extent, amount, and duration of current payments and other obligations of support and the payment of arrearages under the order.

(b)　In a proceeding for arrearages, the statute of limitation under the laws of this state or of the issuing state, whichever is longer, applies.

Part 6.B.　CONTEST OF VALIDITY OR ENFORCEMENT.

§ 580-605.　Notice of registration of order.

(a)　When a support order or income-withholding order issued in another state is registered, the registering tribunal shall notify the nonregistering party. The notice must be accompanied by a copy of the registered order and the documents and relevant information accompanying the order.

(b)　The notice must inform the nonregistering party:

(1)　that a registered order is enforceable as of the date of registration in the same manner as an order issued by a tribunal of this state;

(2)　that a hearing to contest the validity or enforcement of the registered order must be requested within twenty days after notice;

(3)　that failure to contest the validity or enforcement of the registered order in a timely manner will result in confirmation of the order and enforcement of the order and the alleged arrearages and precludes further contest of that order with respect to any matter that could have been asserted; and

(4)　of the amount of any alleged arrearages.

(c)　Upon registration of an income-withholding order for enforcement, the registering tribunal shall notify the obligor's employer pursuant to section five

FCA

thousand two hundred forty-one or section five thousand two hundred forty-two of the civil practice law and rules.

Amended by Laws 1998, Ch. 214, § 33, eff. July 7, 1998, deemed in full force and effect Dec. 31, 1997.

§ 580-606.   Procedure to contest validity or enforcement of registered order.

(a)   A nonregistering party seeking to contest the validity or enforcement of a registered order in this state shall request a hearing within twenty days after notice of the registration. The nonregistering party may seek to vacate the registration, to assert any defense to an allegation of noncompliance with the registered order, or to contest the remedies being sought or the amount of any alleged arrearages pursuant to section 580-607 (Contest of registration or enforcement).

(b)   If the nonregistering party fails to contest the validity or enforcement of the registered order in a timely manner, the order is confirmed by operation of law.

(c)   If a nonregistering party requests a hearing to contest the validity or enforcement of the registered order, the registering tribunal shall schedule the matter for hearing and give notice to the parties of the date, time, and place of the hearing.

§ 580-607.   Contest of registration or enforcement.

(a)   A party contesting the validity or enforcement of a registered order or seeking to vacate the registration has the burden of proving one or more of the following defenses:

(1)   the issuing tribunal lacked personal jurisdiction over the contesting party;

(2)   the order was obtained by fraud;

(3)   the order has been vacated, suspended, or modified by a later order;

(4)   the issuing tribunal has stayed the order pending appeal;

(5)   there is a defense under the law of this state to the remedy sought;

(6)   full or partial payment has been made; or

(7)   the statute of limitation under section 580-604 (Choice of law) precludes enforcement of some or all of the arrearages.

(b)   If a party presents evidence establishing a full or partial defense under subdivision (a), a tribunal may stay enforcement of the registered order, continue the proceeding to permit production of additional relevant evidence, and issue other appropriate orders. An uncontested portion of the registered order may be enforced by all remedies available under the law of this state.

(c)   If the contesting party does not establish a defense under subdivision (a) of this section to the validity or enforcement of the order, the registering tribunal shall issue an order confirming the order.

§ 580-608.　Confirmed order.

Confirmation of a registered order, whether by operation of law or after notice and hearing, precludes further contest of the order with respect to any matter that could have been asserted at the time of registration.

Part 6.C.　REGISTRATION AND MODIFICATION OF CHILD SUPPORT ORDER.

§ 580-609.　Procedure to register child support order of another state for modification.

A party or support enforcement agency seeking to modify, or to modify and enforce, a child support order issued in another state shall register that order in this state in the same manner provided in part six-A if the order has not been registered. A petition for modification may be filed at the same time as a request for registration, or later. The pleading must specify the grounds for modification.

§ 580-610.　Effect of registration for modification.

A tribunal of this state may enforce a child support order of another state registered for purposes of modification, in the same manner as if the order had been issued by a tribunal of this state, but the registered order may be modified only if the requirements of section 580-611 (modification of child support order of another state) have been met.

§ 580-611.　Modification of child support order of another state.

(a)   After a child support order issued in another state has been registered in this state, the responding tribunal of this state may modify that order only if section 580-613 does not apply and after notice and hearing it finds that:

(1)   the following requirements are met:

(i)   the child, the individual obligee, and the obligor do not reside in the issuing state;

(ii)   a petitioner who is a nonresident of this state seeks modification; and

(iii)   the respondent is subject to the personal jurisdiction of the tribunal of this state; or

(2)   the child, or a party who is an individual, is subject to the personal jurisdiction of the tribunal of this state and all of the parties who are individuals have filed written consents in the issuing tribunal for a tribunal of this state to modify the support order and assume continuing, exclusive jurisdiction over the order. However, if the issuing state is a foreign jurisdiction that has not enacted a law or established procedures substantially similar to the procedures under this article, the consent otherwise required of an individual residing in this state is not required for the tribunal to assume jurisdiction to modify the child support order.

(b)   Modification of a registered child support order is subject to the same requirements, procedures, and defenses that apply to the modification of an order issued by a tribunal of this state and the order may be enforced and satisfied in the same manner.

(c)   A tribunal of this state may not modify any aspect of a child support order that may not be modified under the law of the issuing state. If two or more tribunals have issued child support orders for the same obligor and child, the order that controls and must be so recognized under section 580-207 establishes the aspects of the support order which are nonmodifiable.

(d)   On issuance of an order modifying a child support order issued in another state, a tribunal of this state becomes the tribunal having continuing, exclusive jurisdiction.

§ 580-612.   Recognition of order modified in another state.

A tribunal of this state shall recognize a modification of its earlier child-support order by a tribunal of another state which assumed jurisdiction pursuant to UIFSA or a law substantially similar to UIFSA, and, upon request, except as otherwise provided in this article, shall:

(1)   enforce the order that was modified only as to amounts accruing before the modification;

(2)   enforce only nonmodifiable aspects of that order;

(3)   provide other appropriate relief only for violations of that order which occurred before the effective date of the modification; and

(4)   recognize the modifying order of the other state, upon registration, for the purpose of enforcement.

§ 580-613.   Jurisdiction to modify child-support order of another state when individual parties reside in this state.

(a)   If all of the parties who are individuals reside in this state and the child does not reside in the issuing state, a tribunal of this state has jurisdiction to enforce and to modify the issuing state's child support order in a proceeding to register that order.

(b) A tribunal of this state exercising jurisdiction under this section shall apply the provisions of parts one and two, this part, and the procedural and substantive law of this state to the proceeding for enforcement or modification. Parts three, four, five, seven and eight of this article do not apply.

Amended by Laws 1998, Ch. 214, § 31, eff. July 7, 1998, deemed in full force and effect Dec. 31, 1997.

§ 580-614. Notice to issuing tribunal of modification.

Within thirty days after issuance of a modified child support order, the party obtaining the modification shall file a certified copy of the order with the issuing tribunal that had continuing, exclusive jurisdiction over the earlier order, and in each tribunal in which the party knows the earlier order has been registered. A party who obtains the order and fails to file a certified copy is subject to appropriate sanctions by a tribunal in which the issue of failure to file arises. The failure to file does not affect the validity or enforceability of the modified order of the new tribunal having continuing, exclusive jurisdiction.

Part 7. DETERMINATION OF PARENTAGE.

Section 580-701. Proceeding to determine parentage.

§ 580-701. Proceeding to determine parentage.

(a) A tribunal of this state may serve as an initiating or responding tribunal in a proceeding brought under this article or a law or procedure substantially similar to this article, the uniform reciprocal enforcement of support act, or the revised uniform reciprocal enforcement of support act to determine that the petitioner is a parent of a particular child or to determine that a respondent is a parent of that child.

(b) In a proceeding to determine parentage, a responding tribunal of this state shall apply the procedural and substantive law of this state, and the rules of this state on choice of law.

Amended by Laws 1998, Ch. 214, § 34, eff. July 7, 1998, deemed in full force and effect Dec. 31, 1997.

Part 8. INTERSTATE RENDITION.

Section 580-801. Grounds for rendition.
580-802. Conditions of rendition.

§ 580-801.   Grounds for rendition.

(a)   For purposes of this article, "governor" includes an individual performing the functions of governor or the executive authority of a state covered by this article.

(b)   The governor of this state may:

(1)   demand that the governor of another state surrender an individual found in the other state who is charged criminally in this state with having failed to provide for the support of an obligee; or

(2)   on the demand by the governor of another state, surrender an individual found in this state who is charged criminally in the other state with having failed to provide for the support of an obligee.

(c)   A provision for extradition of individuals not inconsistent with this article applies to the demand even if the individual whose surrender is demanded was not in the demanding state when the crime was allegedly committed and has not fled therefrom.

§ 580-802.   Conditions of rendition.

(a)   Before making demand that the governor of another state surrender an individual charged criminally in this state with having failed to provide for the support of an obligee, the governor of this state may require a prosecutor of this state to demonstrate that at least sixty days previously the obligee had initiated proceedings for support pursuant to this article or that the proceeding would be of no avail.

(b)   If, under this article or a law substantially similar to this article, the Uniform Reciprocal Enforcement of Support Act, or the Revised Uniform Reciprocal Enforcement of Support Act, the governor of another state makes a demand that the governor of this state surrender an individual charged criminally in that state with having failed to provide for the support of a child or other individual to whom a duty of support is owed, the governor may require a prosecutor to investigate the demand and report whether a proceeding for support has been initiated or would be effective. If it appears that a proceeding would be effective but has not been initiated, the governor may delay honoring the demand for a reasonable time to permit the initiation of a proceeding.

(c)   If a proceeding for support has been initiated and the individual whose rendition is demanded prevails, the governor may decline to honor the demand. If the petitioner prevails and the individual whose rendition is demanded is subject to a support order, the governor may decline to honor the demand if the individual is complying with the support order.

Amended by Laws 1998, Ch. 214, § 35, eff. July 7, 1998, deemed in full force and effect Dec. 31, 1997.

Part 9.   MISCELLANEOUS PROVISIONS.

§ 580-901.   Uniformity of application and construction.

This article shall be applied and construed to effectuate its general purpose to make uniform the law with respect to the subject of this article among states enacting it.

§ 580-902.   Short title.

This article may be cited as the uniform interstate family support act.

§ 580-903.   Severability clause.

If any provision of this article or its application to any person or circumstance is held invalid, the invalidity does not affect other provisions or applications of this article which can be given effect without the invalid provision or application, and to this end the provisions of this article are severable.

     Amended by Laws 1998, Ch. 214, § 37, eff. July 7, 1998, deemed in full force and effect Dec. 31, 1997.

§ 580-904.   Effective date.

This article takes effect on the thirty first day of December, nineteen hundred ninety-seven, and shall apply to actions, proceedings, and accompanying documents filed and orders issued on or before the thirtieth day of December, nineteen hundred ninety-seven which substantially comply with the requirements of article three-A of the domestic relations law and shall apply to all actions or proceedings on or after such effective date.

     Added by Laws 1997, Ch. 398, § 37, eff. Jan. 1, 1998; Laws 1998, Ch. 214, § 36, eff. July 7, 1998, deemed in full force and effect Dec. 31, 1997.

§ 580-905.   Repeals.

Article three-A of the domestic relations law is repealed except as to pending cases maintainable under subdivision one of section thirty-five of the domestic relations law; provided, however, no new petition may be commenced under such article three-A.

Amendments.

Section four hundred eleven, subdivision (a) of section four hundred thirty-nine, paragraph (a) of subdivision one and subdivisions two and four of section four hundred forty, section four hundred forty-eight, and paragraph (d) of subdivision one of section four hundred sixty of the family court act; subdivision four and subdivision fourteen of section one hundred eleven-b, paragraph f of subdivision two of section one hundred eleven-c, subdivisions one, five, eight and ten of section one hundred eleven-h, subdivision one of section one hundred eleven-k, subdivision one of section one hundred eleven-m, and subdivision one of section one hundred eleven-n of the social services law; paragraph one of subdivision (a) of section five thousand two hundred forty-one, and paragraph one of subdivision (c) of section five thousand two hundred forty-two of the civil practice law and rules are amended to conform to section 466(f) of the social security act, as amended by section 321 of title III of the personal responsibility and work opportunity reconciliation act of 1996 (P.L. 104-193).

Amended by Laws 1998, Ch. 214, § 37, eff. July 7, 1998, deemed in full force and effect Dec. 31, 1997.

ARTICLE 6

PERMANENT TERMINATION OF PARENTAL RIGHTS, ADOPTION, GUARDIANSHIP AND CUSTODY

SUMMARY OF ARTICLE

Part 1. Permanent termination of parental custody by reason of permanent neglect.

(Repealed and transferred sections noted under appropriate section number of text.)

§ 611. Permanently neglected child; purpose of part.

The purpose of this part is to provide the procedures for proceedings initiated in family court, pursuant to section three hundred eighty-four-b of the social services law, for the commitment of the guardianship and custody of a child upon the ground that the child is a permanently neglected child. As used in this part "permanently neglected child" shall mean permanently neglected child as defined in subdivision seven of section three hundred eighty-four-b of the social services law, and unless the context requires otherwise, the provisions of such section three hundred eighty-four-b shall be deemed applicable requirements in addition to the procedures contained in this part. All references in this part to petitions and proceedings initiated "under this part": shall be deemed references to petitions and proceedings initiated under section three hundred eighty-four-b of the social services law upon the ground that the child is a permanently neglected child.

Amended by Laws 1971, Ch. 901; Laws 1973, Ch. 870, eff. June 22, 1973; Laws 1975, Ch. 700, eff. Sept. 8, 1975; Laws 1975, Ch. 704; Laws 1976, Ch. 666, eff. Jan. 1, 1977.

§ 612. Jurisdiction.

Repealed by Laws 1976, Ch. 666, eff. Jan. 1, 1977.

§ 613. Venue.

Repealed by Laws 1976, Ch. 666, eff. Jan. 1, 1977.

§ 614. Originating proceeding for the commitment of the guardianship and custody of a permanently neglected child

1.   A proceeding for the commitment of the guardianship and custody of a child on the ground of permanent neglect is originated by a petition, alleging:

(a)   the child is a person under eighteen years of age;

(b)   the child is in the care of an authorized agency;

(c)   the authorized agency has made diligent efforts to encourage and strengthen the parental relationship and specifying the efforts made or that such efforts would be detrimental to the best interests of the child and specifying the reasons therefor;

(d)   the parent or custodian, notwithstanding the agency's efforts, has failed for a period of either at least one year or fifteen out of the most recent twenty-two months following the date such child came into the care of an authorized agency substantially and continuously or repeatedly to maintain contact with or plan for the future of the child, although physically and financially able to do so; and

(e)   the best interests of the child require that the guardianship and custody of the child be committed to an authorized agency or to a foster parent authorized to originate this proceeding under section one thousand eighty-nine of this act.

2.   Where the petitioner is not the authorized agency, allegations relating to the efforts of the authorized agency may be made upon information and belief.

Amended by Laws 1971, Ch. 901; Laws 1973, Ch. 804, eff. Sept. 1, 1973 and Ch. 870; Laws 1975, Ch. 700, eff. Sept. 8, 1975; Laws 1975, Ch. 701; Laws 1976, Ch. 666, eff. Jan. 1, 1977; L. 2005, Ch. 3, § 4, amending sub. 1, eff. Aug. 23, 2005.

§ 615. Person who may originate proceedings.

Repealed by Laws 1976, Ch. 666, eff. Jan. 1, 1977.

§ 616. Issuance of summons.

On the filing of a petition under this part, the court may cause a copy of the petition and a summons to be issued, requiring the parent to show cause why the court should not enter an order committing the guardianship and custody of the child to the petitioner for the reason that the child is permanently neglected.

Amended by Laws 1976, Ch. 666, eff. Jan. 1, 1977.

§ 617. Service of summons.

(a) Service of a summons and petition under this part shall be made by delivery of a true copy thereof to the person summoned at least twenty days before the time stated therein for appearance. If so requested by the parent or other person legally responsible for the child's care, the court may extend the time for appearance and answer.

(b) If after reasonable effort, personal service is not made, such substituted service or service by publication as may be ordered by the judge shall be sufficient.

(c) Personal service within or without the state or in a foreign country shall be made in accordance with the provisions of section three hundred seven of the surrogate's court procedure act, as the same may be amended from time to time, with respect to service of a citation.

(d) Service of the summons and other process with a notice as specified herein by publication shall be made in accordance with the provisions of CPLR 316, provided, however, that a single publication of the summons or other process with a notice as specified herein in only one newspaper designated in the order shall be sufficient. In no event shall the whole petition be published. The petition shall be delivered to the person summoned at the first court appearance pursuant to section one hundred fifty-four-a of this chapter. The notice to be published with the summons or other process shall state:

1. the date, time, place and purpose of the proceeding,

2. that upon failure of the person summoned to appear, all of his or her parental rights in the child may be terminated, and

3. that his or her failure to appear shall constitute a denial of his or her interest in the child, which denial may result, without further notice, in the transfer or commitment of the child's care, custody or guardianship or in the child's adoption in this or any subsequent proceeding in which such care, custody or guardianship or adoption may be at issue.

Amended by Laws 1969, ch. 769, eff. Sept. 1, 1969; Laws 1976, Ch. 666, eff. Jan. 1, 1977; Laws 1986, Ch. 811, eff. Aug. 2, 1986.

§ 621.   Notice of rights; assignment of counsel.

Repealed by Laws 1975, Ch. 682, eff. Jan. 1, 1976.

§ 622.   Definition of "fact-finding hearing."

When used in this part, "fact-finding hearing" means in the case of a petition for the commitment of the guardianship and custody of a child, a hearing to determine whether the allegations required by paragraphs (a), (b), (c), and (d) of subdivision one of section six hundred fourteen are supported by clear and convincing proof.

Amended by Laws 1963, Ch. 529; Laws 1976, Ch. 666, eff. Jan. 1, 1977; Laws 1982, Ch. 123, eff. May 24, 1982.

§ 623.   Definition of "dispositional hearing."

When used in this part, "dispositional hearing" means a hearing to determine what order of disposition should be made in accordance with the best interests of the child. Where the disposition ordered is the commitment of guardianship and custody in accordance with section six hundred thirty-four of this part, an initial freed child permanency hearing and all subsequent permanency hearings shall be held in accordance with article ten-A of this act.

Amended by Laws 1976, Ch. 666, eff. Jan. 1, 1977; **amended** by Laws 2002, Ch. 663, § 1, eff. Dec. 3, 2002; L. 2005, Ch. 3, § 5, amending 623, eff. Aug. 23, 2005.

§ 624.   Evidence.

Only competent, material and relevant evidence may be admitted in a fact-finding hearing; only material and relevant evidence may be admitted in a dispositional hearing. Evidence of parental contact or of failure to maintain contact with a child subsequent to the date of the filing of a petition under this part shall be inadmissible in the fact-finding hearing. Such evidence may be admitted in the dispositional hearing but shall not, of itself, be sufficient as a matter of law to preclude or require an order committing the guardianship and custody of the child.

Amended by Laws 1963, Ch. 529; Laws 1976, Ch. 666, eff. Jan. 1, 1977.

§ 625.   Sequence of hearings.

(a)   Upon completion of the fact-finding hearing, the dispositional hearing may commence immediately after the required findings are made; provided, however, that if all parties consent the court may, upon motion of any party or upon its own motion, dispense with the dispositional hearing and make an order of disposition on the basis of competent evidence admitted at the fact-finding hearing. Where the disposition ordered is the commitment of guardianship and custody in accordance with section six hundred thirty-four of this part, an initial freed child permanency hearing and all subsequent permanency hearings shall be held in accordance with article ten-A of this act.

(b)　Reports prepared by the probation service or a duly authorized agency for use by the court prior to the making of an order of disposition shall be deemed confidential information furnished to the court which the court in a proper case may, in its discretion, withhold from or disclose in whole or in part to the law guardian, counsel, party in interest, or other appropriate person. Such reports may not be furnished to the court prior to the completion of a fact-finding hearing, but may be used in a dispositional hearing or in the making of an order of disposition without a dispositional hearing pursuant to subdivision (a) of this section.

Amended by Laws 1963, Ch. 529; Laws 1976, Ch. 666, eff. Jan. 1, 1977; **amended** by Laws 2002, Ch. 663, § 2, eff. Oct. 2, 2002; L. 2005, Ch. 3, § 6, amending sub. (a), eff. Aug. 23, 2005.

§ 626.　Adjournments.

(a)　The court may adjourn a fact-finding hearing or a dispositional hearing for good cause shown on its own motion or on motion made on behalf of the child, or on motion of the parent or other person responsible for the care of the child.

(b)　At the conclusion of a fact-finding hearing and after it has made findings required before a dispositional hearing may commence, the court may adjourn the proceedings to enable it to make inquiry into the surroundings, conditions, and capacities of the persons involved in the proceedings.

Amended by Laws 1963, Ch. 529, eff. Apr. 23, 1963.

§ 631.　Disposition on adjudication of permanent neglect.

At the conclusion of a dispositional hearing on a petition for the commitment of the guardianship and custody of a child, the court shall enter an order of disposition:

(a)　dismissing the petition in accord with section six hundred thirty-two; or

(b)　suspending judgment in accord with section six hundred thirty-three; or

(c)　committing the guardianship and custody of the child in accord with section six hundred thirty-four.

An order of disposition shall be made, pursuant to this section, solely on the basis of the best interests of the child, and there shall be no presumption that such interests will be promoted by any particular disposition.

Amended by Laws 1975, Ch. 701; Laws 1976, Ch. 666, eff. Jan. 1, 1977.

§ 632. Order dismissing petition.

(a) If the allegations of a petition under this part are not established, the court shall dismiss the petition.

(b) If a motion or application has been made in the course of a proceeding under this part to reconsider an underlying order of placement or commitment, or upon the court's own motion on notice to all parties, the court retains jurisdiction to dispose of that motion or application regardless of whether it dismisses the petition.

Amended by Laws 1991, Ch. 588, § 7, eff. Sept. 30, 1991.

§ 633. Suspended judgment.

(a) Rules of court shall define permissible terms and conditions of a suspended judgment. These terms and conditions shall relate to the acts or omissions of the parent or other person responsible for the care of the child.

(b) The maximum duration of a suspended judgment under this section is one year, unless the court finds at the conclusion of that period that exceptional circumstances require an extension of that period for one additional period of up to one year. Successive extensions may not be granted.

(c) The order of suspended judgment must set forth the duration, terms and conditions of the suspended judgment, and must contain a date certain for a court review not later than thirty days prior to the expiration of the period of suspended judgment. The order of suspended judgment must also state in conspicuous print that a failure to obey the order may lead to its revocation and to the issuance of an order terminating parental rights and committing the guardianship and custody of the child to an authorized agency for the purposes of adoption. A copy of the order of suspended judgment, along with the current permanency plan, must be furnished to the respondent.

(d) Not later than sixty days before the expiration of the period of suspended judgment, the petitioner shall file a report with the family court and all parties, including the respondent and his or her attorney, the law guardian and intervenors, if any, regarding the respondent's compliance with the terms of suspended judgment. The report shall be reviewed by the court on the scheduled court date. Unless a motion or order to show cause has been filed prior to the expiration of the period of suspended judgment alleging a violation or seeking an extension of the period of the suspended judgment, the terms of the disposition of suspended judgment shall be deemed satisfied and an order committing the guardianship and custody of the child shall not be entered.

(e) If, prior to the expiration of the period of the suspended judgment, a motion or order to show cause is filed that alleges a violation of the terms and conditions of the suspended judgment, or that seeks to extend the period of the suspended judgment for an additional period of up to one year, then the period of the suspended judgment is tolled until entry of the order that disposes of the motion or order to show cause.

(f)   Upon finding that the respondent has violated the terms and conditions of the order of suspended judgment, the court may enter an order revoking the order of suspended judgment and terminating the parental rights of the respondent or, where such extension is in the best interests of the child, extend the period of suspended judgment for an additional period of up to one year, if no prior extension has been granted.

(g)   If an order of suspended judgment has been satisfied or has been extended, but the child nonetheless remains in foster care pursuant to a placement under article ten of this act or section three hundred fifty-eight-a of the social services law, a permanency hearing shall be completed as previously scheduled pursuant to section one thousand eighty-nine of this act, but no later than six months after the completion of the last permanency hearing. If guardianship and custody of the child have been transferred to the authorized agency upon an order revoking the order of suspended judgment, a permanency hearing shall be completed pursuant to paragraph one of subdivision (a) of section one thousand eighty-nine of this act immediately following, but in no event later than sixty days after, the earlier of the court's statement of its order on the record or issuance of its written order.

Amended by Laws 2005, Ch. 3, §7 (Part A), eff. Dec 21, 2005; Laws 2006, Ch. 437, §2, eff. July 26, 2006.

§ 634.   Commitment of guardianship and custody; further orders.

The court may enter an order under section six hundred thirty-one committing the guardianship and custody of the child to the petitioner on such conditions, if any, as it deems proper.

Amended by Laws 1976, Ch. 666, eff. Jan. 1, 1977.

Part 2.   Adoption.

Section   641.   Jurisdiction over adoption proceedings.
       642.   Rules of court.

§ 641.   Jurisdiction over adoption proceedings.

The family court has original jurisdiction concurrent with the surrogate's courts over adoption proceedings under article seven of the domestic relations law.

Amended by Laws 1964, Ch. 383; Laws 1965, Ch. 339, § 1; Laws 1966, Ch. 479, § 1; Laws 1967, Ch. 146 § 1; Laws 1968, Ch. 258, § 1; Laws 1970, Ch. 484; Laws 1972, Ch. 423; Laws 1974, Ch. 416; Laws 1976, Ch. 153; Laws 1978, Ch. 160; Laws 1980, Ch. 188, eff. June 2, 1980; Laws 1982, Ch. 232, eff. June 15, 1982; Laws 1984, Ch. 267, eff. Sept. 1, 1984; Laws 1985, Ch. 331, eff. July 16, 1985.

§ 642. Rules of court.

Rules of court, not inconsistent with any provision of article seven of the domestic relations law, may authorize the probation service to interview such persons and obtain such data as will aid the court in determining a petition under that article.

Part 3. Custody.

Editor's note: Domestic Relations Law § 72, added by Laws 1966, Ch. 631, eff. Sept. 1, 1966, permits grandparents to apply to the supreme court for a writ of habeas corpus to obtain visitation rights with respect to certain infant grandchildren.

§ 651. Jurisdiction over habeas corpus proceedings and petitions for custody and visitation of minors.

(a)   When referred from the supreme court or county court to the family court, the family court has jurisdiction to determine, in accordance with subdivision one of section two hundred forty of the domestic relations law and with the same powers possessed by the supreme court in addition to its own powers, habeas corpus proceedings and proceedings brought by petition and order to show cause, for the determination of the custody or visitation of minors.

(b)   When initiated in the family court, the family court has jurisdiction to determine, in accordance with subdivision one of section two hundred forty of the domestic relations law and with the same powers possessed by the supreme court in addition to its own powers, habeas corpus proceedings and proceedings brought by petition and order to show cause, for the determination of the custody or visitation of minors, including applications by a grandparent or grandparents for visitation or custody rights pursuant to section seventy-two or two hundred forty of the domestic relations law.

(c)   When initiated in the family court pursuant to a petition under part eight of article ten of this act or section three hundred fifty-eight-a of the social services law, the family court has jurisdiction to enforce or modify orders or judgments of the supreme court relating to the visitation of minors in foster care, notwithstanding any limitation contained in subdivision (b) of section four hundred sixty-seven of this act.

(d)   With respect to applications by a grandparent or grandparents for visitation or custody rights, made pursuant to section seventy-two or two hundred forty of the domestic relations law, with a child remanded or placed in the care of a person, official, agency or institution pursuant to the provisions of article ten of this act, the applicant, in such manner as the court shall prescribe, shall serve a copy of the application upon the social services official having care and custody of such child, and the child's law guardian, who shall be afforded an opportunity to be heard thereon.

Amended by Laws 1966, Ch. 686; Laws 1970, Ch. 913; Laws 1972, Ch. 535; Laws 1973, Ch. 916; Laws 1978, Ch. 443, eff. June 19, 1978; Laws 1983, Ch. 250, eff. June 3, 1983; Laws 1988, Ch. 457, § 2, eff. Nov. 1, 1988; Laws 1988, Ch. 457, § 3, eff. Nov 1, 1988; Laws 1996, Ch. 85, § 6, eff. May 21, 1996 and applicable to all actions or proceedings concerning custody of or a right to visitation with a child whether such action or proceeding was commenced pursuant to section 240 of the domestic relations law or any other provision of law; Laws 2003, Ch. 657, § 3, amending sub. (b) and (d), eff. Jan. 5, 2004.

§ 651-a. Reports of child abuse and maltreatment; admissibility.

In any proceeding brought pursuant to this section to determine the custody or visitation of minors, a report made to the statewide central register of child abuse and maltreatment, pursuant to title six of article six of the social services law, or a portion thereof, which is otherwise admissible as a business record pursuant to rule forty-five hundred eighteen of the civil practice law and rules shall not be admissible in evidence, notwithstanding such rule, unless an investigation of such report conducted pursuant to title six of article six of the social services law has determined that there is some credible evidence of the alleged abuse or maltreatment, that the subject of the report has been notified that the report is indicated. In addition, if such report has been reviewed by the state commissioner of social services or his designee and has been determined to be unfounded, it shall not be admissible in evidence. If such report has been so reviewed and has been amended to delete any finding, each such deleted finding shall not be admissible. If the state commissioner of social services or his designee has amended the report to add any new finding, each such new finding, together with any portion of the original report not deleted by the commissioner or his designee, shall be admissible if it meets the other requirements of this section and is otherwise admissible as a business record. If such a report, or portion thereof, is admissible in evidence but is uncorroborated, it shall not be sufficient to make a fact finding of abuse or maltreatment in such proceeding. Any other evidence tending to support the reliability of such report shall be sufficient corroboration.

Added by Laws 1988, Ch. 452, § 2, eff. Aug. 1, 1988; **amended** by Laws 1996, Ch. 12, § 18, eff. Feb. 15, 1996, and applicable to reports of suspected child abuse or maltreatment registered on or after the effective date.

§ 652. Jurisdiction over applications to fix custody in matrimonial actions on referral from supreme court.

(a) When referred from the supreme court to the family court, the family court has jurisdiction to determine, with the same powers possessed by the supreme court, applications to fix temporary or permanent custody and applications to modify judgments and orders of custody or visitation in actions and proceedings for marital separation, divorce, annulment of marriage and dissolution of marriage. Applications to modify judgments and orders of custody may be granted by the family court under this section only upon the showing to the family court that there has been a subsequent change of circumstances and that modification is required.

(b) In the event no such referral has been made and unless the supreme court provides in the order or judgment awarding custody or visitation in an action for divorce, separation or annulment, that it may be enforced or modified only in the supreme court, the family court may:

(i) determine an application to enforce the order or judgment awarding custody or visitation, or

(ii) determine an application to modify the order or judgment awarding custody or visitation upon a showing that there has been a subsequent change of circumstances and modification is required.

(c) In any determination of an application pursuant to this section, the family court shall have jurisdiction to determine such applications, in accordance with subdivision one of section two hundred forty of the domestic relations law, with the same powers possessed by the supreme court, and the family court's disposition of any such application is an order of the family court appealable only under article eleven of this act.

Amended by Laws 1981, Ch. 40, eff. Sept. 1, 1981; Laws 1996, Ch. 85,§ 7, eff. May 21, 1996 and applicable to all actions or proceedings concerning custody of or a right to visitation with a child whether such action or proceeding was commenced pursuant to section 240 of the domestic relations law or any other provision of law.

§ 653. Rules of court.

Rules of court, not inconsistent with any law, may authorize the probation service to interview such persons and obtain such data as will aid the court in determining a habeas corpus or custody proceeding under section six hundred fifty-one.

Amended by Laws 1966, Ch. 580, eff. Sept. 1, 1966.

§ 654. Application to modify out-of-state order or judgment fixing custody.

Repealed by Laws 2002, Ch. 409, § 3, eff. Aug. 13, 2002.

§ 655. Temporary order of protection.

(a)   Upon the filing of a petition or counter-claim under this article, the court for good cause shown may issue a temporary order of protection which may contain any of the provisions authorized on the making of an order of protection under section six hundred fifty-six of this article.

(b)   A temporary order of protection is not a finding of wrongdoing.

(c)   The court may issue or extend a temporary order of protection ex parte or on notice simultaneously with the issuance of a warrant directing that the respondent be arrested and brought before the court pursuant to section six hundred seventy-one of this article.

(d)   The court shall not require anyone seeking a temporary order of protection under this section to first request that child protective services investigate the allegations or to first request permission to file a petition under article ten of this act.

Notwithstanding the foregoing provisions, an order of protection, or temporary order of protection where applicable, may be entered against a former spouse and persons who have a child in common, regardless whether such persons have been married or have lived together at any time.

Added by Laws 1981, Ch. 416, eff. Aug. 6, 1981; **amended** by Laws 1982, Ch. 516, eff. July 13, 1982; Laws 1983, Ch. 347, eff. Aug. 22, 1983; Laws 1984, Ch. 948, eff. Nov. 1, 1984; Laws 1988, Ch. 706, eff. Sept. 2, 1988.

§ 656. Order of protection.

The court may make an order of protection and an order of probation in assistance or as a condition of any other order made under this part. The order of protection may set forth reasonable conditions of behavior to be observed for a specific time by any petitioner or any respondent, and shall specify if an order of probation is in effect. No order of protection may direct any party to observe conditions of behavior unless the party requesting the order of protection has served and filed a petition or counter-claim in accordance with section one hundred fifty-four-b of this act. Such an order may require the petitioner or the respondent:

(a)   to stay away from the home, school, business or place of employment of any other party, the other spouse or parent, or the child, and to stay away from any other specific location designated by the court;

(b)   to permit a parent, or a person entitled to visitation by a court order or a separation agreement, to visit the child at stated periods;

(c) to refrain from committing a family offense, as defined in subdivision one of section eight hundred twelve of this act, or any criminal offense against the child or against the other parent or against any person to whom custody of the child is awarded, or from harassing, intimidating or threatening such persons;

(d) to permit a designated party to enter the residence during a specified period of time in order to remove personal belongings not in issue in this proceeding or in any other proceeding or action under this act or the domestic relations law;

(e) to refrain from acts of commission or omission that create an unreasonable risk to the health, safety or welfare of a child;

(f) to participate in an educational program and to pay the costs thereof if the person has the means to do so, provided however that nothing contained herein shall be deemed to require payment of the costs of any such program by the state or any political subdivision thereof;

(g) to provide, either directly or by means of medical and health insurance, for expenses incurred for medical care and treatment arising from the incident or incidents forming the basis for the issuance of the order;

(h) to pay the reasonable counsel fees and disbursements involved in obtaining or enforcing the order of the person who is protected by such order if such order is issued or enforced;

(i) 1. to refrain from intentionally injuring or killing, without justification, any companion animal the respondent knows to be owned, possessed, leased, kept or held by the petitioner or a minor child residing in the household.

2. "Companion animal", as used in this section, shall have the same meaning as in subdivision five of section three hundred fifty of the agriculture and markets law.

(j) to observe such other conditions as are necessary to further the purposes of protection.

1. The court shall not require anyone seeking an order of protection under this section to first request that child protective services investigate the allegations or to first request permission to file a petition under article ten of this act.

2. Notwithstanding the foregoing provisions, an order of protection, or temporary order of protection where applicable, may be entered against a former spouse and persons who have a child in common, regardless whether such persons have been married or have lived together at any time.

Added by Laws 1980, Ch. 530, eff. Aug. 23, 1980; **amended** by Laws 1981, Ch. 416, eff. Aug. 6, 1981, renumbering as § 655 to § 656, and adding subds. (f) and (g); Laws 1981, Ch. 965, eff. Aug. 6, 1981; Laws 1983, Ch. 347, eff. Aug. 22, 1983; Laws 1984, Ch. 948, eff. Nov. 1, 1984; Laws 1988, Ch. 706 § 6, eff. Sept. 2, 1988; Laws 1995, Ch. 483, §§ 7 and 8, eff. Nov. 1, 1995; Laws 2006, ch. 253, §4, eff. July 26, 2006.

Part 4. Guardianship.

§ 661. Jurisdiction.

The family court has like jurisdiction and authority as is now conferred on county and surrogates courts as concerns the guardianship of the person of a minor. The provisions of the surrogate's court procedure act shall apply to the extent they are applicable to guardianship of the person of a minor and do not conflict with the specific provisions of this act.

    Amended by Laws 1987, Ch. 180, eff. June 29, 1987; Laws 1988, Ch. 232, § 1, eff. July 8, 1988.

§ 662. Rules of court.

Rules of court, not inconsistent with any law, may authorize the probation service to interview such persons and obtain such data as will aid the court in exercising its power under section six hundred sixty-one.

§ 663. Guardian of person to file copy of order of appointment.

Upon the appointment and qualification of guardian of the person of a minor as provided in section six hundred sixty-one of this act, letters of guardianship shall thereupon issue from this court.

    Added by Laws 1966, Ch. 961, eff. Sept. 1, 1967; **amended** by Laws 1988, Ch. 232, § 2, eff. July 8, 1988.

§ 664. Recording in camera interviews of infants.

(a) The court shall not conduct an in camera interview of an infant in any action or proceeding to fix temporary or permanent custody or to modify judgments and orders of custody concerning marital separation, divorce, annulment of marriage and dissolution of marriage unless a stenographic record of such interview is made.

(b) If an appeal is taken to the appellate division from a judgment or order of the court on any such action or proceeding, the stenographic record of any such interview shall be made a part of the record and forwarded under seal to the appellate division.

    Added by Laws 1985, Ch. 785, eff. Aug. 1, 1985.

Part 5. Warrant.

Section 671. Issuance of warrant; certificate of warrant.

§ 671. Issuance of warrant; certificate of warrant.

(a) The court may issue a warrant, directing that the respondent be arrested, brought before the court, when a petition is presented to the court under sections six hundred fourteen, six hundred fifty-one, six hundred fifty-four, six hundred fifty-five and six hundred fifty-six of this article or section three hundred eighty-four-b of the social services law and it appears that:

(i) the summons cannot be served; or

(ii) the respondent has failed to obey the summons; or

(iii) the respondent is likely to leave the jurisdiction; or

(iv) a summons, in the court's opinion, would be ineffectual; or

(v) the safety of the petitioner or child is endangered; or

(vi) a respondent on bail or on parole has failed to appear.

(b) The petitioner may not serve a warrant upon the respondent unless the court itself grants such permission upon the application of the petitioner. The clerk of the court may issue to the petitioner or to the representative of an incorporated charitable or philanthropic society having a legitimate interest in the family a certificate stating that a warrant for the respondent has been issued by the court. The presentation of such certificate by said petitioner or representative to any peace officer, acting pursuant to his special duties, or police officer authorizes him to arrest the respondent and take him to court.

(c) A certificate of warrant expires ninety days from the date of issue but may be renewed from time to time by the clerk of the court.

(d) Rules of court shall provide that a record of all unserved warrants be kept and that periodic reports concerning unserved warrants be made.

Added by Laws 1981, Ch. 416, eff. Aug. 6, 1981.

ARTICLE 7

PROCEEDINGS CONCERNING WHETHER A PERSON IS IN NEED OF SUPERVISION

SUMMARY OF ARTICLE

Part 1.　Jurisdiction

(Repealed and transferred sections noted under appropriate section number of text.)

§ 711.　Purpose.

The purpose of this article is to provide a due process of law (a) for considering a claim that a person is in need of supervision and (b) for devising an appropriate order of disposition for any person adjudged in need of supervision.

Amended by Laws 1976, Ch. 878, eff. July 26, 1976; Laws 1982, Ch. 920, eff. July 1, 1983.

§ 712.　Definitions.

As used in this article, the following terms shall have the following meanings:

(a)　"Person in need of supervision". A person less than eighteen years of age who does not attend school in accordance with the provisions of part one of article sixty-five of the education law or who is incorrigible, ungovernable or habitually disobedient and beyond the lawful control of a parent or other person legally responsible for such child's care, or other lawful authority, or who violates the provisions of section 221.05 of the penal law.

(b) "Detention." The temporary care and maintenance of children away from their own homes as defined in section five hundred two of the executive law.

(c) "Secure detention facility." A facility characterized by physically restricting construction, hardware and procedures.

(d) "Non-secure detention facility." A facility characterized by the absence of physically restricting construction, hardware and procedures.

(e) "Fact-finding hearing." A hearing to determine whether the respondent did the acts alleged to show that he violated a law or is incorrigible, ungovernable or habitually disobedient and beyond the control of his parents, guardian or legal custodian.

(f) "Dispositional hearing." A hearing to determine whether the respondent requires supervision or treatment.

(g) "Aggravated circumstances." Aggravated circumstances shall have the same meaning as the definition of such term in subdivision (j) of section one thousand twelve of this act.

(h) "Permanency hearing." A hearing held in accordance with paragraph (b) of subdivision two of section seven hundred fifty-four or section seven hundred fifty-six-a of this article for the purpose of reviewing the foster care status of the respondent and the appropriateness of the permanency plan developed by the social services official on behalf of such respondent.

(i) "Diversion services." Services provided to children and families pursuant to section seven hundred thirty-five of this article for the purpose of avoiding the need to file a petition or direct the detention of the child. Diversion services shall include: efforts to adjust cases pursuant to this article before a petition is filed, or by order of the court, after the petition is filed but before fact-finding is commenced; and preventive services provided in accordance with section four hundred nine-a of the social services law to avert the placement of the child into foster care, including crisis intervention and respite services.

Amended by Laws 1970, Ch. 906; Laws 1976, Ch. 878, eff. Feb. 1, 1977; Laws 1977, Ch. 283; Ch. 360; Laws 1978, Ch. 478, Ch. 481; Laws 1979, Ch. 411, eff. Aug. 5, 1979, Ch. 531, eff. Sept. 10, 1979; Laws 1981, Ch. 335; Laws 1982, Ch. 920, eff. July 1, 1983; Laws 1987, Ch. 419, eff. Sept. 1, 1987; Laws 1992, Ch. 465, § 38, eff. Jan. 13, 1993; Laws 1999, Ch. 7, § 31, eff. Feb. 11, 1999; Laws 2000, Ch. 596, eff. Nov. 1, 2001; Laws 2005, Ch. 57, § 1 (Part E), deemed eff. on and after April 1, 2005; L. 2005, Ch. 3, § 2, amending sub. (g), eff. Aug. 23, 2005.

§ 713. Jurisdiction.

The family court has exclusive original jurisdiction over any proceeding involving a person alleged to be a person in need of supervision.

Amended by Laws 1982, Ch. 920, eff. July 1, 1983.

§ 714. Determination of age.

(a) In determining the jurisdiction of the court under section seven hundred thirteen the age of the respondent at the time the need for supervision allegedly arose is controlling.

(b) If the respondent is within the jurisdiction of the court, but the proceedings were initiated after the respondent's eighteenth birthday, the family court shall dismiss a petition to determine whether a person is in need of supervision.

Amended by Laws 1982, Ch. 920, eff. July 1, 1983.

§ 715. Crime punishable by death or life imprisonment when fifteen.

Repealed by Laws 1967, Ch. 680, eff. Sept. 1, 1967.

§ 716. Substitution of petition.

On its own motion and at any time in the proceedings, the court may substitute a neglect petition under article ten for a petition to determine whether a person is in need of supervision.

Amended by Laws 1982, Ch. 920, eff. July 1, 1983; Laws 1983, Ch. 398, eff. July 1, 1983.

§ 717. Venue.

Proceedings under this article are originated in the county in which the act or acts referred to in the petition allegedly occurred. On motion made on behalf of the respondent or by his parent or other person legally responsible for his care or on the court's motion and for good cause shown, the court may transfer the proceedings to another county.

Amended by Laws 1963, Ch. 409, eff. Apr. 16, 1963.

§ 718. Return of runaway.

(a) A peace officer, acting pursuant to such peace officer's special duties, or a police officer may return to a parent or other person legally responsible for such child's care any child under the age of eighteen who has run away from home without just cause or who, in the reasonable conclusion of the officer, appears to have run away from home without just cause. For purposes of this action, a police officer or peace officer may reasonably conclude that a child has run away from home when the child refuses to give his or her name or the name and address of a parent or other person legally responsible for such child's care or when the officer has reason to doubt that the name or address given are the actual name and address of the parent or other person legally responsible for the child's care.

(b)   A peace officer, acting pursuant to the peace officer's special duties, or a police officer is authorized to take a youth who has run away from home or who, in the reasonable opinion of the officer, appears to have run away from home, to a facility certified or approved for such purpose by the office of children and family services, if the peace officer or police officer is unable, or if it is unsafe, to return the youth to his or her home or to the custody of his or her parent or other person legally responsible for his or her care. Any such facility receiving a youth shall inform a parent or other person responsible for such youth's care.

(c)   If a child placed pursuant to this article in the custody of a commissioner of social services or an authorized agency shall run away from the custody of such commissioner or authorized agency, any peace officer, acting pursuant to his special duties, or police officer may apprehend, restrain, and return such child to such location as such commissioner shall direct or to such authorized agency and it shall be the duty of any such officer to assist any representative of the commissioner or agency to take into custody any such child upon the request of such representative.

Amended by Laws 1963, Chs. 809, 811; Laws 1971, Ch. 888; Laws 1976, Ch. 607, Ch. 880; Laws 1980, Ch. 843, eff. Sept. 1, 1980; Laws 1987, Ch. 419, § 17, eff. Sept. 1, 1987; Laws 2000, Ch. 596, eff. Nov. 1, 2001; Laws 2005, Ch. 57, § 2 (Part E), eff. April 12, 2005, deemed eff. on and after April 1, 2005.

Part 2.   Custody and detention.

(Repealed and transferred sections noted under appropriate section number of text.)

§ 720.   Detention.

1.   No child to whom the provisions of this article may apply, shall be detained in any prison, jail, lockup, or other place used for adults convicted of crime or under arrest and charged with a crime.

2.   The detention of a child in a secure detention facility shall not be directed under any of the provisions of this article.

3. Detention of a person alleged to be or adjudicated as a person in need of supervision shall be authorized only in a detention facility certified by the division for youth except as provided in subdivision four of this section.

4. Whenever detention is authorized and ordered pursuant to this article, for a person alleged to be or adjudicated as a person in need of supervision, a family court in a city having a population of one million or more shall, notwithstanding any other provision of law, direct detention in a foster care facility established and maintained pursuant to the social services law. In all other respects, the detention of such a person in a foster care facility shall be subject to the identical terms and conditions for detention as are set forth in this article and in section two hundred thirty-five of this act.

5. (a) The court shall not order or direct detention under this article, unless the court determines that there is no substantial likelihood that the youth and his or her family will continue to benefit from diversion services and that all available alternatives to detention have been exhausted; and

    (b) Where the youth is sixteen years of age or older, the court shall not order or direct detention under this article, unless the court determines and states in its order that special circumstances exist to warrant such detention.

FCA

    Added by Laws 1973, Ch. 1037; Laws 1976, Ch. 880, eff. Nov. 29, 1976, Ch. 878, eff. Feb. 1, 1977; **amended** by Laws 1978, Ch. 548, eff. Jan. 1, 1979; Laws 1978, Ch. 555, eff. July 24, 1978; Laws 1987, Ch. 419, eff. Sept. 1, 1987; L. 2001, Ch. 383, § 3, adding subd. 5, eff. July 1, 2002; L. 2005, Ch. 57, § 3 (Part E), amending subd. 5, eff. April 12, 2005, deemed eff. on and after April 1, 2005.

§ 721. Custody by police officer or peace officer without a warrant.

Repealed by Laws 1982, Ch. 920, eff. July 1, 1983.

§ 722. Custody by private person without a warrant.

Repealed by Laws 1982, Ch. 920, eff. July 1, 1983.

§ 723. Duties of private person before and after taking into custody.

    (a) Before taking into custody, a private person must inform the person to be taken into custody of the cause thereof and require him to submit.

    (b) After taking into custody, a private person must take the person, without unnecessary delay, to his home, to a family court judge or deliver him to a peace officer, who is acting pursuant to his special duties, or a police officer.

    Amended by Laws 1980, Ch. 843, eff. Sept. 1, 1980; Laws 1982, Ch. 920, eff. July 1, 1983.

§ 724.　Duties of police officer or peace officer after taking into custody or on delivery by private person.

(a)　If a peace officer or a police officer takes into custody or if a person is delivered to him under section seven hundred twenty-three, the officer shall immediately notify the parent or other person legally responsible for his care, or the person with whom he is domiciled, that he has been taken into custody.

(b)　After making every reasonable effort to give notice under paragraph (a), the officer shall

(i)　release the youth to the custody of his or her parent or other person legally responsible for his or her care upon the written promise, without security, of the person to whose custody the youth is released that he or she will produce the youth before the lead agency designated pursuant to section seven hundred thirty-five of this article in that county at a time and place specified in writing; or

(ii)　forthwith and with all reasonable speed take the youth directly, and without first being taken to the police station house, to the designated lead agency located in the county in which the act occasioning the taking into custody allegedly was done, unless the officer determines that it is necessary to question the youth, in which case he or she may take the youth to a facility designated by the chief administrator of the courts as a suitable place for the questioning of youth or, upon the consent of a parent or other person legally responsible for the care of the youth, to the youth's residence and there question him or her for a reasonable period of time; or

(iii)　take a youth in need of crisis intervention or respite services to an approved runaway program or other approved respite or crisis program; or

(iv)　take the youth directly to the family court located in the county in which the act occasioning the taking into custody was allegedly done, provided that the officer affirms on the record that he or she attempted to exercise the options identified in paragraphs (i), (ii) and (iii) of this subdivision, was unable to exercise these options, and the reasons therefor.

(c)　In the absence of special circumstances, the officer shall release the child in accord with paragraph (b) (i).

(d)　In determining what is a "reasonable period of time" for questioning a child, the child's age and the presence or absence of his parents or other person legally responsible for his care shall be included among the relevant considerations.

Amended by Laws 1963, Ch. 809; Laws 1970, Ch. 669; Laws of 1972, Ch. 166; Laws 1973, Ch. 1037; Laws 1976, Ch. 880; Laws 1980, Ch. 843, eff. Sept. 1, 1980; Laws 1982, Ch. 920, eff. July 1, 1983; Laws 1984, Ch. 629, eff. July 27, 1984; Laws 1987, Ch. 492, eff. July 30, 1987; Laws 2005, Ch. 57, § 4 (Part E), eff. April 12, 2005, deemed eff. on and after April 1, 2005.

§ 724-a. Fingerprinting of certain alleged juvenile delinquents.

Repealed by Laws 1982, Ch. 920, eff. July 1, 1983.

§ 724-b. Fingerprinting; duties of the division of criminal justice services.

Repealed by Laws 1982, Ch. 920, eff. July 1, 1983.

§ 725. Summons or warrant on failure to appear.

The family court before which a person failed to produce a child pursuant to a written promise given under section seven hundred twenty-four may issue a summons requiring the child and the person who failed to produce him to appear at the court at a time and place specified in the summons or may issue a warrant for either or both of them, directing that either or both be brought to the court at a time and place specified in the warrant.

§ 726. Duty of facility receiving custody.

Repealed by Laws 1982, Ch. 920, eff. July 1, 1983.

§ 727. Rules of court authorizing release before filing of petition.

(a)   The agency responsible for operating a detention facility or in a city of one million or more, the agency responsible for operating a foster care facility, may release a child in custody before the filing of a petition to the custody of his parents or other relative, guardian or legal custodian when the events occasioning the taking into custody appear to involve a petition to determine whether a person is in need of supervision rather than a petition to determine whether a person is a juvenile delinquent.

(b)   When a release is made under this section such release may, but need not, be conditioned upon the giving of a recognizance in accord with section seven hundred twenty-four (b)(i).

(c)   If the probation service for any reason does not release a child under this section, the child shall promptly be brought before a judge of the court, if practicable, and section seven hundred twenty-eight shall apply.

Amended by Laws 1970, Ch. 978, eff. May 19, 1970; Laws 1982, Ch. 920, eff. July 1, 1983; Laws 1987, Ch. 419, eff. Sept. 1, 1987.

§ 728. Discharge, release or detention by judge after hearing and before filing of petition in custody cases.

(a)   If a child in custody is brought before a judge of the family court before a petition is filed, the judge shall hold a hearing for the purpose of making a preliminary determination of whether the court appears to have jurisdiction over the child. At the commencement of the hearing, the judge shall advise the child of his right to remain silent, his right to be represented by counsel of his own choosing, and of his right to have a law guardian assigned in accord with part four of article two of this act. He must also allow the child a reasonable time to send for his parents or other person legally responsible for his care, and for counsel, and adjourn the hearing for that purpose.

(b) After hearing, the judge shall order the release of the child to the custody of his parent or other person legally responsible for his care if the court does not appear to have jurisdiction.

(c) An order of release under this section may, but need not, be conditioned upon the giving of a recognizance in accord with sections seven hundred twenty-four (b) (i).

(d) Upon a finding of facts and reasons which support a detention order pursuant to this section, the court shall also determine and state in any order directing detention:

(i) that there is no substantial likelihood that the youth and his or her family will continue to benefit from diversion services and that all available alternatives to detention have been exhausted; and

(ii) whether continuation of the child in the child's home would be contrary to the best interests of the child based upon, and limited to, the facts and circumstances available to the court at the time of the hearing held in accordance with this section; and

(iii) where appropriate, whether reasonable efforts were made prior to the date of the court hearing that resulted in the detention order, to prevent or eliminate the need for removal of the child from his or her home or, if the child had been removed from his or her home prior to the court appearance pursuant to this section, where appropriate, whether reasonable efforts were made to make it possible for the child to safely return home.

Amended by Laws 1982, Ch. 920, eff. July 1, 1983; Laws 1987, Ch. 419, eff. Sept. 1, 1987; Laws 2000, Ch. 145 § 13, eff. July 1, 2000, adding subsection (d); Laws 2005, Ch. 57 § 5 (Part E), eff. April 12, 2005, deemed eff. on and after April 1, 2005, amending subsection (d).

§ 729. Duration of detention before filing of petition or hearing.

No person may be detained under this article for more than seventy-two hours or the next day the court is in session, whichever is sooner, without a hearing under section seven hundred twenty-eight.

Amended by Laws 1964, Ch. 96, eff. Mar. 16, 1964.

Part 3.   Preliminary procedure.

(Repealed and transferred sections noted under appropriate section number of text.)

§ 731.   Originating juvenile delinquency proceeding.

Repealed by Laws 1982, Ch. 920, eff. July 1, 1983.

§ 732.   Originating proceeding to adjudicate need for supervision.

A proceeding to adjudicate a person to be in need of supervision is originated by the filing of a petition, alleging:

(a)   the respondent is an habitual truant or is incorrigible, ungovernable, or habitually disobedient and beyond the lawful control of his or her parents, guardian or lawful custodian, and specifying the acts on which the allegations are based and the time and place they allegedly occurred. Where habitual truancy is alleged or the petitioner is a school district or local educational agency, the petition shall also include the steps taken by the responsible school district or local educational agency to improve the school attendance and/or conduct of the respondent;

(b)   the respondent was under eighteen years of age at the time of the specified acts;

(c)   the respondent requires supervision or treatment; and

(d)   the petitioner has complied with the provisions of section seven hundred thirty-five of this article.

Amended by Laws 2000, Ch. 596, eff. Nov. 1, 2001; Laws 2005, Ch. 57, § 6 (Part E), eff. April 12, 2005, deemed eff. on and after April 1, 2005.

§ 733.   Persons who may originate proceedings.

The following persons may originate a proceeding under this article:

(a)   a peace officer, acting pursuant to his special duties, or a police officer;

(b)   the parent or other person legally responsible for his care;

(c) any person who has suffered injury as a result of the alleged activity of a person alleged to be in need of supervision, or a witness to such activity;

(d) the recognized agents of any duly authorized agency, association, society or institution; or

(e) the presentment agency that consented to substitute a petition alleging the person is in need of supervision for a petition alleging that the person is a juvenile delinquent pursuant to section 311.4.

Amended by Laws 1978, Ch. 481; Laws 1980, Ch. 843, eff. Sept. 1, 1980; Laws 1982, Ch. 920, eff. July 1, 1983; Laws 1983, Ch. 398, eff. July 1, 1983.

§ 734. Rules of court for preliminary procedure.

Repealed by Laws 2005, Ch. 57, eff. April 12, 2005.

§ 734-a. Approving a petition in a juvenile delinquency proceeding.

Repealed by Laws 1982, Ch. 920, eff. July 1, 1983.

§ 735. Admissibility of statements made during preliminary conference.

Repealed by Laws 1985, Ch. 813, eff. Aug. 2, 1985, and reenacted as § 734(e).

§ 735. Preliminary procedure; diversion services.

(a) Each county and any city having a population of one million or more shall offer diversion services as defined in section seven hundred twelve of this article to youth who are at risk of being the subject of a person in need of supervision petition. Such services shall be designed to provide an immediate response to families in crisis, to identify and utilize appropriate alternatives to detention and to divert youth from being the subject of a petition in family court. Each county and such city shall designate either the local social services district or the probation department as lead agency for the purposes of providing diversion services.

(b) The designated lead agency shall:

(i) confer with any person seeking to file a petition, the youth who may be a potential respondent, his or her family, and other interested persons, concerning the provision of diversion services before any petition may be filed; and

(ii) diligently attempt to prevent the filing of a petition under this article or, after the petition is filed, to prevent the placement of the youth into foster care; and

(iii) assess whether the youth would benefit from residential respite services; and

(iv)   determine whether alternatives to detention are appropriate to avoid remand of the youth to detention.

(c)   Any person or agency seeking to file a petition pursuant to this article which does not have attached thereto the documentation required by subdivision (g) of this section shall be referred by the clerk of the court to the designated lead agency which shall schedule and hold, on reasonable notice to the potential petitioner, the youth and his or her parent or other person legally responsible for his or her care, at least one conference in order to determine the factual circumstances and determine whether the youth and his or her family should receive diversion services pursuant to this section. Diversion services shall include clearly documented diligent attempts to provide appropriate services to the youth and his or her family unless it is determined that there is no substantial likelihood that the youth and his or her family will benefit from further diversion attempts. Notwithstanding the provisions of section two hundred sixteen-c of this act, the clerk shall not accept for filing under this part any petition that does not have attached thereto the documentation required by subdivision (g) of this section.

(d)   Diversion services shall include documented diligent attempts to engage the youth and his or her family in appropriately targeted community-based services, but shall not be limited to:

(i)   providing, at the first contact, information on the availability of or a referral to services in the geographic area where the youth and his or her family are located that may be of benefit in avoiding the need to file a petition under this article; including the availability, for up to twenty-one days, of a residential respite program, if the youth and his or her parent or other person legally responsible for his or her care agree, and the availability of other non-residential crisis intervention programs such as family crisis counseling or alternative dispute resolution programs.

(ii)   scheduling and holding at least one conference with the youth and his or her family and the person or representatives of the entity seeking to file a petition under this article concerning alternatives to filing a petition and services that are available. Diversion services shall include clearly documented diligent attempts to provide appropriate services to the youth and his or her family before it may be determined that there is no substantial likelihood that the youth and his or her family will benefit from further attempts.

(iii)   where the entity seeking to file a petition is a school district or local educational agency, the designated lead agency shall review the steps taken by the school district or local educational agency to improve the youth's attendance and/or conduct in school and attempt to engage the school district or local educational agency in further diversion attempts, if it appears from review that such attempts will be beneficial to the youth.

(e)   The designated lead agency shall maintain a written record with respect to each youth and his or her family for whom it considers providing or provides

FCA

diversion services pursuant to this section. The record shall be made available to the court at or prior to the initial appearance of the youth in any proceeding initiated pursuant to this article.

(f) Efforts to prevent the filing of a petition pursuant to this section may extend until the designated lead agency determines that there is no substantial likelihood that the youth and his or her family will benefit from further attempts. Efforts at diversion pursuant to this section may continue after the filing of a petition where the designated lead agency determines that the youth and his or her family will benefit from further attempts to prevent the youth from entering foster care.

(g) (i) The designated lead agency shall promptly give written notice to the potential petitioner whenever attempts to prevent the filing of a petition have terminated, and shall indicate in such notice whether efforts were successful. The notice shall also detail the diligent attempts made to divert the case if a determination has made that there is no substantial likelihood that the youth will benefit from further attempts. No persons in need of supervision petition may be filed pursuant to this article during the period the designated lead agency is providing diversion services. A finding by the designated lead agency that the case has been successfully diverted shall constitute presumptive evidence that the underlying allegations have been successfully resolved in any petition based upon the same factual allegations. No petition may be filed pursuant to this article by the parent or other person legally responsible for the youth where diversion services have been terminated because of the failure of the parent or other person legally responsible for the youth to consent to or actively participate.

(ii) The clerk of the court shall accept a petition for filing only if it has attached thereto the following:

(A) if the potential petitioner is the parent or other person legally responsible for the youth, a notice from the designated lead agency indicating there is no bar to the filing of the petition as the potential petitioner consented to and actively participated in diversion services; and

(B) a notice from the designated lead agency stating that it has terminated diversion services because it has determined that there is no substantial likelihood that the youth and his or her family will benefit from further attempts, and that the case has not been successfully diverted.

(h) No statement made to the designated lead agency or to any agency or organization to which the potential respondent, prior to the filing of the petition, or if the petition has been filed, prior to the time the respondent has been notified that attempts at diversion will not be made or have been terminated, or prior to the commencement of a fact-finding hearing if attempts at diversion have not terminated previously, may be admitted into evidence at a fact-finding hearing or, if the proceeding is transferred to a criminal court, at any time prior to a conviction.

Added by Laws 1985, Ch. 813, eff. Aug. 2, 1985; **amended** by Laws 1988, Ch. 290, § 1, eff. July 25, 1988; **Repealed and reenacted** as § 735 by Laws 2005, Ch. 57, § 7, (Part E), eff. April 12, 2005, deemed eff. on and after April 1, 2005.

§ 736. Issuance of summons.

(1) On the filing of a petition under this article, the court may cause a copy of the petition and a summons to be issued, requiring the respondent and his parent or other person legally responsible for his care, or with whom he is domiciled, to appear at the court at a time and place named to answer the petition. The summons shall be signed by the court or by the clerk or deputy clerk of the court. If those on whom a summons must be served are before the court at the time of the filing of a petition, the provisions of part four of this article shall be followed.

(2) In proceedings originated pursuant to subdivision (b) of section seven hundred thirty-three of this article, the court shall cause a copy of the petition and notice of the time and place to be heard to be served upon any parent of the respondent or other person legally responsible for the respondent's care who has not signed the petition, provided that the address of such parent or other person legally responsible is known to the court or is ascertainable by the court. Such petition shall include a notice that, upon placement of the child in the care and custody of the department of social services or any other agency, said parent may be named as a respondent in a child support proceeding brought pursuant to article four of this act. Service shall be made by the clerk of the court by mailing such notice and petition by ordinary first class mail to such parent or other person legally responsible at such person's last known residence.

(3) In proceedings originated pursuant to subdivision (a), (c), (d) or (e) of section seven hundred thirty-three of this article, the court shall cause a copy of the petition and notice of the time and place to be heard to be served upon each parent of the respondent or other person legally responsible for the respondent's care, provided that the address of such parent or other person legally responsible is known to the court or is ascertainable by the court. Service shall be made by the clerk of the court by mailing such notice and petition by ordinary first class mail to such parent or other person legally responsible at such person's last known residence.

Amended by Laws 1989, Ch. 474, eff. Aug. 15, 1989; Laws 1995, Ch. 652, § 1, eff. Aug. 8, 1995.

§ 737. Service of summons.

(a) Service of a summons and petition shall be made by delivery of a true copy thereof to the person summoned at least twenty-four hours before the time stated therein for appearance. If so requested by one acting on behalf of the respondent or by a parent or other person legally responsible for his care, the court shall not proceed with the hearing or proceeding earlier than three days after such service.

(b) If after reasonable effort, personal service is not made, the court may at any stage in the proceedings make an order providing for substituted service in the manner provided for substituted service in civil process in courts of record.

§ 738. Issuance of warrant for respondent or other person legally responsible for care.

The court may issue a warrant, directing that the respondent or other person legally responsible for his care or with whom he is domiciled be brought before the court, when a petition is filed with the court under this article and it appears that

(a) the summons cannot be served; or

(b) the respondent or other person has refused to obey the summons; or

(c) the respondent or other person is likely to leave the jurisdiction; or

(d) a summons, in the court's opinion, would be ineffectual; or

(e) a respondent on bail or on parole has failed to appear.

A warrant issued for a respondent under this section shall expire at the end of six months from the date of its issuance, unless extended for an additional period of not more than six months upon application by the petitioner for good cause shown.

Amended by Laws 1986, Ch. 459, eff. Aug. 20, 1986, and shall not apply to warrants issued prior to Aug. 20, 1986.

§ 739. Release or detention after filing of petition and prior to order of disposition.

(a) After the filing of a petition under section seven hundred thirty-two of this article, the court in its discretion may release the respondent or direct his or her detention. However, the court shall not direct detention unless it finds and states the facts and reasons for so finding that unless the respondent is detained there is a substantial probability that the respondent will not appear in court on the return dateand all available alternatives to detention have been exhausted.

(b) Unless the respondent waives a determination that probable cause exists to believe that he is a person in need of supervision, no detention under this section may last more than three days (i) unless the court finds, pursuant to the evidentiary standards applicable to a hearing on a felony complaint in a criminal court, that such probable cause exists, or (ii) unless special circumstances exist, in which cases such detention may be extended not more than an additional three days exclusive of Saturdays, Sundays and public holidays.

(c) Upon a finding of facts and reasons which support a detention order pursuant to subdivision (a) of this section, the court shall also determine and state in any order directing detention:

(i)   whether continuation of the respondent in the respondent's home would be contrary to the best interests of the respondent based upon, and limited to, the facts and circumstance available to the court at the time of the court's determination in accordance with this section; and

(ii)   where appropriate, whether reasonable efforts were made prior to the date of the court order directing detention in accordance with this section, to prevent or eliminate the need for removal of the respondent from his or her home or, if the respondent had been removed from his other home prior to the court appearance pursuant to this section, where appropriate, whether reasonable efforts were made to make it possible for the respondent to safely return home.

Amended by Laws 1975, Ch. 837; Laws 1976, Ch. 880; Laws 1978, Ch. 481, eff. Sept. 1, 1978; Laws 1979, Ch. 411, eff. Aug. 5, 1979; Laws 1982, Ch. 920, eff. July 1, 1983; Laws 2000, Ch. 145, eff. July 1, 2000, adding subsection (c); Laws 2005, Ch. 57, eff. April 12, 2005, deemed eff. on and after April 1, 2005, amending subsection (a).

§ 740.   Temporary order of protection.

(a)   Upon the filing of a petition under this article, the court for good cause shown may issue a temporary order of protection which may contain any of the provisions authorized on the making of an order of protection under section seven hundred fifty-nine.

(b)   A temporary order of protection is not a finding of wrongdoing.

(c)   The court may issue or extend a temporary order of protection ex parte or on notice simultaneously with the issuance of a warrant directing that the respondent be arrested and brought before the court pursuant to section seven hundred thirty-eight of this part.

Added by Laws 1964, Ch. 566, eff. Apr. 16, 1964; **amended** by Laws 1981, Ch. 416, eff. Aug. 6, 1981.

Part 4.   Hearings

(Repealed and transferred sections noted under appropriate section number of text.)

750.   **Probation reports; probation investigation and diagnostic assessment.**

§ 741.   Notice of rights; general provision.

(a)   At the initial appearance of a respondent in a proceeding and at the commencement of any hearing under this article, the respondent and his parent or other person legally responsible for his care shall be advised of the respondent's right to remain silent and of his right to be represented by counsel chosen by him or his parent or other person legally responsible for his care, or by a law guardian assigned by the court under part four of article two. Provided, however, that in the event of the failure of the respondent's parent or other person legally responsible for his care to appear, after reasonable and substantial effort has been made to notify such parent or responsible person of the commencement of the proceeding and such initial appearance, the court shall appoint a law guardian and shall, unless inappropriate also appoint a guardian ad litem for such respondent, and in such event, shall inform the respondent of such rights in the presence of such law guardian and any guardian ad litem.

(b)   The general public may be excluded from any hearing under this article and only such persons and the representatives of authorized agencies admitted thereto as have a direct interest in the case.

(c)   At any hearing under this article, the court shall not be prevented from proceeding by the absence of the respondent's parent or other person responsible for his care if reasonable and substantial effort has been made to notify such parent or responsible person of the occurrence of the hearing and if the respondent and his law guardian are present. The court shall, unless inappropriate, also appoint a guardian ad litem who shall be present at such hearing and any subsequent hearing.

Amended by Laws 1975, Ch. 837; Laws 1979, Ch. 531, eff. Sept. 10, 1979; Laws 1981, Ch. 331, eff. Aug. 28, 1981; Laws 1982, Ch. 920, eff. July 1, 1983.

§ 741-a.   Notice and opportunity to be heard.

The foster parent caring for the child or any pre-adoptive parent or relative providing care for the respondent shall be provided with notice of any permanency hearing held pursuant to this article by the social services official. Such foster parent, pre-adoptive parent or relative shall be afforded an opportunity to be heard at any such hearing; provided, however, no such foster parent, pre-adoptive parent or relative shall be construed to be a party to the hearing solely on the basis of such notice and opportunity to be heard. The failure of the foster parent, pre-adoptive parent, or relative caring for the child to appear at a permanency hearing shall constitute a waiver of the opportunity to be heard and such failure to appear shall not cause a delay of the permanency hearing nor shall such failure to appear be a ground for the invalidation of any order issued by the court pursuant to this section.

Added by Laws 1999, Ch. 7, § 32, eff. Feb. 11, 1999.

§ 742. Definition of "fact-finding hearing."

Repealed by Laws 1976, Ch. 878, eff. Feb. 1, 1977.

§ 742. Judge to preside in juvenile delinquency proceedings.

Repealed by Laws 1982, Ch. 920, eff. July 1, 1983.

§ 742. Diversion attempts.

(a) Whenever a petition is filed pursuant to this article, the lead agency designated pursuant to section seven hundred thirty-five of this article shall file a written report with the court indicating any previous actions it has taken with respect to the case.

(b) At the initial appearance of the respondent, the court shall review any termination of diversion services pursuant to such section, and the documentation of diligent attempts to provide appropriate services and determine whether such efforts or services provided are sufficient and may, subject to the provisions of section seven hundred forty-eight of this article, order that additional diversion attempts be undertaken by the designated lead agency. The court may order the youth and the parent or other person legally responsible for the youth to participate in diversion services. If the designated lead agency thereafter determines that the case has been successfully resolved, it shall so notify the court, and the court shall dismiss the petition.

Added by Laws 1985, Ch. 813, eff. Aug. 2, 1985; **Amended** by Laws 2005, Ch. 57, eff. April 12, 2005, deemed eff. on and after April 1, 2005.

§ 743. Definition of "dispositional hearing."

Repealed by Laws 1976, Ch. 878, eff. Feb. 1, 1977.

§ 743. Appearances at juvenile delinquency dispositional hearings.

Repealed by Laws 1982, Ch. 920, eff. July 1, 1983.

§ 744. Evidence in fact-finding hearings; required quantum.

(a) Only evidence that is competent, material and relevant may be admitted in a fact-finding hearing.

(b) Any determination at the conclusion of a fact-finding hearing that a respondent did an act or acts must be based on proof beyond a reasonable doubt. For this purpose, an uncorroborated confession made out of court by a respondent is not sufficient.

Amended by Laws 1963, Ch. 529; Laws 1976, Ch. 191, eff. May 25, 1976; Laws 1978, Ch. 481, eff. Sept. 1, 1978; Laws 1982, Ch. 920, eff. July 1, 1983.

§ 745. Evidence in dispositional hearings; required quantum of proof.

(a) Only evidence that is material and relevant may be admitted during a dispositional hearing.

(b) An adjudication at the conclusion of a dispositional hearing must be based on a preponderance of the evidence.

§ 746. Sequence of hearings.

Upon completion of the fact-finding hearing the dispositional hearing may commence immediately after the required findings are made.

Amended by Laws 1963, Ch. 529; Law 1976, Ch. 878, repealing former subd. (b); Laws 1978, Ch. 481, eff. Sept. 1, 1978, adding new subd. (b); Laws 1982, Ch. 920, eff. July 1, 1983.

§ 747. Time of fact-finding hearing.

A fact-finding hearing shall commence not more than three days after the filing of a petition under this article if the respondent is in detention.

Amended by Laws 1963, Ch. 529, eff. Apr. 23, 1963; Laws 1975, Ch. 837, eff. Sept. 1, 1975; Laws 1982, Ch. 920, eff. July 1, 1983.

§ 748. Adjournment of fact-finding hearing.

(a) If the respondent is in detention, the court may adjourn a fact-finding hearing

(i) on its own motion or on motion of the petitioner for good cause shown for not more than three days;

(ii) on motion on behalf of the respondent or by his parent or other person legally responsible for his care for good cause shown, for a reasonable period of time.

(b) Successive motions to adjourn a fact-finding hearing may be granted only under special circumstances.

(c) The court shall state on the record the reason for any adjournment of the fact-finding hearing.

Amended by Laws 1963, Ch. 529; Laws 1965, Ch. 284; Laws 1976, Ch. 878, eff. Feb. 1, 1977; Laws 1977, Ch. 283, eff. Aug. 20, 1977; Laws 1982, Ch. 920, eff. July 1, 1983.

§ 748-a.   Proceedings to determine capacity.

Repealed by Laws 1982, Ch. 920, eff. July 1, 1983.

§ 749.   Adjournment after fact-finding hearing or during dispositional hearing.

(a)   Upon or after a fact-finding hearing, the court may, upon its own motion or upon a motion of a party to the proceeding, order that the proceeding be "adjourned in contemplation of dismissal." An adjournment in contemplation of dismissal is an adjournment of the proceeding, for a period not to exceed six months with a view to ultimate dismissal of the petition in furtherance of justice. Upon issuing such an order, upon such permissible terms and conditions as the rules of court shall define, the court must release the individual. The court may, as a condition of an adjournment in contemplation of dismissal order, in cases where the record indicates that the consumption of alcohol may have been a contributing factor, require the respondent to attend and complete an alcohol awareness program established pursuant to paragraph six-a of subdivision (a) of section 19.07 of the mental hygiene law. Upon application of the petitioner, or upon the court's own motion, made at any time during the duration of the order, the court may restore the matter to the calendar. If the proceeding is not so restored, the petition is at the expiration of the order, deemed to have been dismissed by the court in furtherance of justice.

(b)   On its own motion, the court may adjourn the proceedings on conclusion of a fact finding hearing or during a dispositional hearing to enable it to make inquiry into the surroundings, conditions and capacities of the respondent. An adjournment on the court's motion may not be for a period of more than ten days if the respondent is detained, in which case not more than a total of two such adjournments may be granted in the absence of special circumstances. If the respondent is not detained, an adjournment may be for a reasonable time, but the total number of adjourned days may not exceed two months.

(c)   On motion on behalf of the respondent or by his parent or other person legally responsible for his care, the court may adjourn the proceedings on conclusion of a fact-finding hearing or during a dispositional hearing for a reasonable period of time.

Amended by Laws 1973, Ch. 806; Laws 1976, Ch. 878, eff. Feb. 1, 1977; Laws 1977, Ch. 283, eff. Aug. 20, 1977; Laws 1982, Ch. 920, eff. July 1, 1983; Laws 1991, Ch. 237, § 3, eff. July 31, 1991.

§ 750.   Probation reports; probation investigation and diagnostic assessment.

1.   All reports or memoranda prepared or obtained by the probation service shall be deemed confidential information furnished to the court and shall be subject to disclosure solely in accordance with this section or as otherwise

provided for by law. Except as provided in section seven hundred thirty-five of this article, such reports or memoranda shall not be furnished to the court prior to the completion of the fact-finding hearing and the making of the required findings.

2.　After the completion of the fact-finding hearing and the making of the required findings and prior to the dispositional hearing, the reports or memoranda prepared or obtained by the probation service and furnished to the court shall be made available by the court for examination and copying by the child's law guardian or counsel or by the respondent if he is not represented by a law guardian or other counsel. All diagnostic assessments and probation investigation reports shall be submitted to the court at least five court days prior to the commencement of the dispositional hearing. In its discretion the court may except from disclosure a part or parts of the reports or memoranda which are not relevant to a proper disposition, or sources of information which have been obtained on a promise of confidentiality, or any other portion thereof, disclosure of which would not be in the interest of justice. In all cases where a part or parts of the reports or memoranda are not disclosed, the court shall state for the record that a part or parts of the reports or memoranda have been excepted and the reasons for its action. The action of the court excepting information from disclosure shall be subject to review on any appeal from the order of disposition. If such reports or memoranda are made available to respondent or his law guardian or counsel, they shall also be made available to the counsel presenting the petition pursuant to section two hundred fifty-four and, in the court's discretion, to any other attorney representing the petitioner.

Added by Laws 1976, Ch. 878, eff. Feb. 1, 1977; **amended** by Laws 1977, Ch. 204, eff. June 1, 1977; Laws 1978, Ch. 478, § 5, eff. Sept. 1, 1978; Laws 1982, Ch. 920, eff. July 1, 1983; Laws 1985, Ch. 813, eff. Aug. 2, 1985; Laws 1986, Ch. 121, eff. July 2, 1986; Laws 1987, Ch. 106, eff. July 8, 1987.

Part 5.　Orders.

(Repealed and transferred sections noted under appropriate section number of text.)

§ 751. Order dismissing petition.

If the allegations of a petition under this article are not established, the court shall dismiss the petition. The court may in its discretion dismiss a petition under this article, in the interests of justice where attempts have been made to adjust the case as provided for in sections seven hundred thirty-five and seven hundred forty-two of this article and the probation service has exhausted its efforts to successfully adjust such case as a result of the petition's failure to provide reasonable assistance to the probation service.

>   **Amended** by Laws 1993, Ch. 100, § 1, eff. Sept. 12, 1993.

§ 752. Finding.

If the allegations of a petition under this article are established in accord with part three, the court shall enter an order finding that the respondent is a person in need of supervision. The order shall state the grounds for the finding and the facts upon which it is based.

>   **Amended** by Laws 1976, Ch. 878, eff. Feb. 1, 1977; Laws 1982, Ch. 920, eff. July 1, 1983.

§ 753. Disposition on adjudication of juvenile delinquency.

Repealed by Laws 1982, Ch. 920, eff. July 1, 1983.

§ 753-a. Designated felony acts; restrictive placement.

Repealed by Laws 1982, Ch. 920, eff. July 1, 1983.

§ 753-b. Fingerprinting of juveniles.

Repealed by Laws 1977, Ch. 447, eff. Sept. 1, 1977.

§ 753-b. Retention and destruction of fingerprints of persons alleged to be juvenile delinquents.

Repealed by Laws 1982, Ch. 920, eff. July 1, 1983.

§ 754. Disposition on adjudication of person in need of supervision.

1.   Upon an adjudication of person in need of supervision, the court shall enter an order of disposition:

(a)   Discharging the respondent with warning;

(b)   Suspending judgment in accord with section seven hundred fifty-five;

(c)   Continuing the proceeding and placing the respondent in accord with section seven hundred fifty-six; provided, however, that the court shall not place the respondent in accord with section seven hundred fifty-six where the respondent is sixteen years of age or older, unless the court determines and states in its order that special circumstances exist to warrant such placement; or

(d)   Putting the respondent on probation in accord with section seven hundred fifty-seven.

2.   (a) The order shall state the court's reasons for the particular disposition. If the court places the child in accordance with section seven hundred fifty-six of this part, the court in its order shall determine: (i) whether continuation in the child's home would be contrary to the best interest of the child and where appropriate, that reasonable efforts were made prior to the date of the dispositional hearing held pursuant to this article to prevent or eliminate the need for removal of the child from his or her home and, if the child was removed from his or her home prior to the date of such hearing, that such removal was in the child's best interest and, where appropriate, reasonable efforts were made to make it possible for the child to return safely home. If the court determines that reasonable efforts to prevent or eliminate the need for removal of the child from the home were not made but that the lack of such efforts was appropriate under the circumstances, the court order shall include such a finding; and (ii) in the case of a child who has attained the age of sixteen, the services needed, if any, to assist the child to make the transition from foster care to independent living. Nothing in this subdivision shall be construed to modify the standards for directing detention set forth in section seven hundred thirty-nine of this article.

(b)   For the purpose of this section, reasonable efforts to prevent or eliminate the need for removing the child from the home of the child or to make it possible for the child to return safely to the home of the child shall not be required where the court determines that:

(i)   the parent of such child has subjected the child to aggravated circumstances, as defined in subdivision (g) of section seven hundred twelve of this article;

(ii)   the parent of such child has been convicted of (a) murder in the first degree as defined in section 125.27 or murder in the second degree as defined in section 125.25 of the penal law and the victim was another child of the parent; or (b) manslaughter in the first degree as defined in section 125.20 or manslaughter in the second degree as defined in section 125.15 of the penal law and the victim was another child of the parent, provided, however, that the parent must have acted voluntarily in committing such crime;

(iii)   the parent of such child has been convicted of an attempt to commit any of the crimes set forth in subparagraphs (i) and (ii) of this paragraph, and the victim or intended victim was the child or another child of the parent; or has been convicted of criminal solicitation as defined in article one hundred, conspiracy as defined in article one hundred five or criminal facilitation as defined in article one hundred fifteen of the penal law for conspiring, soliciting or facilitating any of the foregoing crimes, and the victim or intended victim was the child or another child of the parent;

(iv)   the parent of such child has been convicted of assault in the second degree as defined in section 120.05, assault in the first degree as defined in section 120.10 or aggravated assault upon a person less than eleven years old as defined in section 120.12 of the penal law, and the commission of one of the foregoing crimes resulted in serious physical injury to the child or another child of the parent;

(v)   the parent of such child has been convicted in any other jurisdiction of an offense which includes all of the essential elements of any crime specified in subparagraph (ii), (iii) or (iv) of this paragraph, and the victim of such offense was the child or another child of the parent; or

(vi)   the parental rights of the parent to a sibling of such child have been involuntarily terminated; unless the court determines that providing reasonable efforts would be in the best interests of the child, not contrary to the health and safety of the child, and would likely result in the reunification of the parent and the child in the foreseeable future. The court shall state such findings in its order. If the court determines that reasonable efforts are not required because of one of the grounds set forth above, a permanency hearing shall be held within thirty days of the finding of the court that such efforts are not required. At the permanency hearing, the court shall determine the appropriateness of the permanency plan prepared by the social services official which shall include whether and when the child: (a) will be returned to the parent; (b) should be placed for adoption with the social services official filing a petition for termination of parental rights; (c) should be referred for legal guardianship; (d) should be placed permanently with a fit and willing relative; or (e) should be placed in another planned permanent living arrangement if the social services official has documented to the court a compelling reason for determining that it would not be in the best interest of the child to return home, be referred for termination of parental rights and placed for adoption, placed with a fit and willing relative, or placed with a legal guardian. The social services official shall thereafter make reasonable efforts to place the child in a timely manner and to complete whatever steps are necessary to finalize the permanent placement of the child as set forth in the permanency plan approved by the court. If reasonable efforts are determined by the court not to be required because of one of the grounds set forth in this paragraph, the social services official may file a petition for termination of parental rights in accordance with section three hundred eighty-four-b of the social services law.

(c)   For the purpose of this section, in determining reasonable efforts to be made with respect to a child, and in making such reasonable efforts, the child's health and safety shall be the paramount concern.

(d)   For the purpose of this section, a sibling shall include a half-sibling.

Amended by Laws 1976, Ch. 878, eff. Feb. 1, 1977; Laws 1985, Ch. 813, eff. Aug. 2, 1985; Laws 1987, Ch. 419, eff. Sept. 1, 1987; Laws 1988, Ch. 478, § 2, eff. Nov. 1, 1988; Laws 1991, Ch. 198, § 3, eff. June 28, 1991; Laws 1999, Ch. 7, § 33, eff. Feb. 11, 1999; L. 2001, Ch. 383, § 4, amending subd. 1(c), eff. July 1, 2002.

§ 755. Suspended judgment.

(a)   Rules of court shall define permissible terms and conditions of a suspended judgment. The court may order as a condition of a suspended judgment restitution or services for public good pursuant to section seven hundred fifty-eight-a, and, except when the respondent has been assigned to a facility in accordance with subdivision four of section five hundred four of the executive law, in cases wherein the record indicates that the consumption of alcohol by the respondent may have been a contributing factor, the court may order attendance at and completion of an alcohol awareness program established pursuant to section 19.25 of the mental hygiene law.

(b)   The maximum duration of any term or condition of a suspended judgment is one year, unless the court finds at the conclusion of that period that exceptional circumstances require an additional period of one year.

     Amended by Laws 1976, Ch. 882, eff. Apr. 1, 1977; Laws 1993, Ch. 124, § 4, eff. June 21, 1993.

§ 756. Placement.

(a)   (i) For purposes of section seven hundred fifty-four, the court may place the child in its own home or in the custody of a suitable relative or other suitable private person or a commissioner of social services, subject to the orders of the court.

(ii)   Where the child is placed with the commissioner of social services, the court may direct the commissioner to place the child with an authorized agency or class of authorized agencies. Unless the dispositional order provides otherwise, the court so directing shall include one of the following alternatives to apply in the event that the commissioner is unable to so place the child:

(1)   the commissioner shall apply to the court for an order to stay, modify, set aside, or vacate such directive pursuant to the provisions of section seven hundred sixty-two or seven hundred sixty-three; or

(2)   the commissioner shall return the child to the family court for a new dispositional hearing and order.

(iii)   [Repealed]

(iv)   [Repealed]

(b)   Placements under this section may be for an initial period of twelve months. The court may extend a placement pursuant to section seven hundred fifty-six-a. In its discretion, the court may recommend restitution or require services for public good pursuant to section seven hundred fifty-eight-a in conjunction with an order of placement. For the purposes of calculating the initial period of placement, such placement shall be deemed to have commenced sixty days after the date the child was removed from his or her home in accordance with the provisions of this article. If the respondent has been in detention pending disposition, the initial period of placement ordered under this section shall be credited with and diminished by the amount of time spent by the respondent in detention prior to the commencement of the placement unless the court finds that all or part of such credit would not serve the best interests of the respondent.

(c) A placement pursuant to this section with the commissioner of social services shall not be directed in any detention facility, but the court may direct detention pending transfer to a placement authorized and ordered under this section for no more than than fifteen days after such order of placement is made. Such direction shall be subject to extension pursuant to subdivision three of section three hundred ninety-eight of the social services law, upon written documentation to the office of children and family services that the youth is in need of specialized treatment or placement and the diligent efforts by the commissioner of social services to locate an appropriate placement.

Added by Laws 1962, Ch. 700, eff. Sept. 1, 1962; **amended** by Laws 1963, Chs. 477, 809, 811, 831; Laws 1964, Ch. 333; Laws 1965, Ch. 126; Laws 1966, Ch. 705; Laws 1968, Ch. 874, eff. July 1, 1968; Laws 1971, Ch. 947; Laws 1974, Ch. 937; Laws 1976, Ch. 514, eff. Aug. 1, 1976, repealing subd. (a), as amended by Laws 1963, Ch. 831, by Laws 1976, Ch. 112, eff. Apr. 6, 1976, thereby retaining subd. (a), as amended by Laws 1971, Ch. 947; Laws 1976, Ch. 882, eff. Apr. 1, 1977; Laws 1978, Ch. 478, §§ 9, 10 and 11, eff. Sept. 1, 1978; Laws 1982, Ch. 920, eff. July 1, 1983; Laws 1986, Ch. 604, eff. Sept. 22, 1986; Laws 1987, Ch. 419, eff. Sept. 1, 1987; Laws 1992, Ch. 465, §§ 39, 40, eff. Jan. 13, 1993; Laws 1996, Ch. 309, §§ 28, 29, eff. July 13, 1996, except that persons in need of supervision in the custody of the division for youth prior to the effective date shall be governed by the provisions of law in effect at the time of their placement; Laws 1999, Ch. 7, § 34, eff. Feb. 11, 1999; Laws 2005, Ch. 57, § 10 (Part E), eff. April 12, 2005, deemed eff. on and after April 1, 2005.

§ 756-a. Extension of placement.

(a)   In any case in which the child has been placed pursuant to section seven hundred fifty-six, the child, the person with whom the child has been placed or the commissioner of social services may petition the court to extend such placement. Such petition shall be filed at least sixty days prior to the expiration of the period of placement, except for good cause shown, but in no event shall such petition be filed after the original expiration date.

(b)   The court shall conduct a permanency hearing concerning the need for continuing the placement. The child, the person with whom the child has been placed and the commissioner of social services shall be notified of such hearing and shall have the opportunity to be heard thereat.

(c)   The provisions of section seven hundred forty-five shall apply at such permanency hearing. If the petition is filed within sixty days prior to the expiration of the period of placement, the court shall first determine at such permanency hearing whether good cause has been shown. If good cause is not shown, the court shall dismiss the petition.

FCA

(d)   At the conclusion of the permanency hearing the court may, in its discretion, order an extension of the placement for not more than one year. The court must consider and determine in its order:

(i)   where appropriate, that reasonable efforts were made to make it possible for the child to safely return to his or her home, or if the permanency plan for the child is adoption, guardianship or some other permanent living arrangement other than reunification with the parent or parents of the child, reasonable efforts are being made to make and finalize such alternate permanent placement;

(ii)   in the case of a child who has attained the age of sixteen, the services needed, if any, to assist the child to make the transition from foster care to independent living;

(iii)   in the case of a child placed outside New York state, whether the out-of-state placement continues to be appropriate and in the best interests of the child; and

(iv)   whether and when the child: (A) will be returned to the parent; (B) should be placed for adoption with the social services official filing a petition for termination of parental rights; (C) should be referred for legal guardianship; (D) should be placed permanently with a fit and willing relative; or (E) should be placed in another planned permanent living arrangement if the social services official has documented to the court a compelling reason for determining that it would not be in the best interest of the child to return home, be referred for termination of parental rights and placed for adoption, placed with a fit and willing relative, or placed with a legal guardian.

(e)   Pending final determination of a petition to extend such placement filed in accordance with the provisions of this section, the court may, on its own motion or at the request of the petitioner or respondent, enter one or more temporary orders extending a period of placement not to exceed thirty days upon satisfactory proof showing probable cause for continuing such placement and that each temporary order is necessary. The court may order additional temporary extensions, not to exceed a total of fifteen days, if the court is unable to conclude the hearing within the thirty day temporary extension period. In no event shall the aggregate number of days in extensions granted or ordered under this subdivision total more than forty-five days. The petition shall be dismissed if a decision is not rendered within the period of placement or any temporary extension thereof. Notwithstanding any provision of law to the contrary, the initial permanency hearing shall be held within twelve months of the date the child was placed into care pursuant to section seven hundred fifty-six of this article and no later than every twelve months thereafter. For the purposes of this section, the date the child was placed into care shall be sixty days after the child was removed from his or her home in accordance with the provisions of this section.

(f)   Successive extensions of placement under this section may be granted, but no placement may be made or continued beyond the child's eighteenth birthday without his or her consent and in no event past his or her twenty-first birthday.

Added by Laws 1986, Ch. 604, eff. Sept. 22, 1986; **amended** by Laws 1991, Ch. 198, § 4, eff. June 28, 1991; Laws 1992, Ch. 363, § 2, eff. July 17, 1992; Laws 1993, Ch. 687, § 13, eff. Dec. 2, 1993; Laws 1995, Ch. 454, § 2, eff. Oct. 1, 1995; Laws 1996, Ch. 309, § 30, eff. July 13, 1996, except that persons in need of supervision in the custody of the division for youth prior to the effective date shall be governed by the provisions of law in effect at the time of their placement; Laws 1999, Ch. 7, §§ 35–38, eff. Feb. 11, 1999.

§ 756-b. Provisions for routine medical, dental and mental health services and treatment.

Repealed by Laws 1996, Ch. 309, § 31, eff. July 13, 1996, except that persons in need of supervision in the custody of the division for youth prior to the effective date shall be governed by the provisions of law in effect at the time of their placement.

§ 757. Probation.

(a)   Rules of court shall define permissible terms and conditions of probation.

(b)   The maximum period of probation shall not exceed one year. If the court finds at the conclusion of the original period that exceptional circumstances require an additional year of probation, the court may continue probation for an additional year.

(c)   The court may order as a condition of probation restitution or services for public good pursuant to section seven hundred fifty-eight-a.

(d)   In cases wherein the record indicates that the consumption of alcohol by the respondent may have been a contributing factor, the court may order as a condition of probation attendance at and completion of an alcohol awareness program established pursuant to section 19.25 of the mental hygiene law.

Amended by Laws 1970, Ch. 993; Laws 1976, Ch. 882, eff. Apr. 1, 1977; Laws 1982, Ch. 920, eff. July 1, 1983; Laws 1993, Ch. 124, § 5, adding new para. (d) to FCA § 757, eff. June 21, 1993; Laws 1996, Ch. 309, § 32, eff. July 13, 1996, except that persons in need of supervision in the custody of the division for youth prior to the effective date shall be governed by the provisions of law in effect at the time of their placement.

§ 758. Commitment.

Repealed by Laws 1976, Ch. 878, eff. Feb. 1, 1977.

§ 758-a. Restitution.

1.   In cases involving acts of infants over ten and less than sixteen years of age, the court may

(a)   recommend as a condition of placement, or order as a condition of probation or suspended judgment, restitution in an amount representing a fair and reasonable cost to replace the property or repair the damage caused by the infant, not, however, to exceed one thousand dollars. In the case of a placement, the court may recommend that the infant pay out of his or her own funds or earnings the amount of replacement or damage, either in a lump sum or in periodic payments in amounts set by the agency with which he is placed, and in the case of probation or suspended judgment, the court may require that the infant pay out of his or her own funds or earnings the amount of replacement or damage, either in a lump sum or in periodic payments in amounts set by the court; and/or

(b)   Order as a condition of placement, probation or suspended judgment, services for the public good, taking into consideration the age and physical condition of the infant.

2.   If the court recommends restitution or requires services for the public good in conjunction with an order of placement pursuant to section seven hundred fifty-six, the placement shall be made only to an authorized agency which has adopted rules and regulations for the supervision of such a program, which rules and regulations shall be subject to the approval of the state department of social services. Such rules and regulations shall include, but not be limited to provisions (i) assuring that the conditions of work, including wages, meet the standards therefor prescribed pursuant to the labor law; (ii) affording coverage to the child under the workers' compensation law as an employee of such agency, department or institution; (iii) assuring that the entity receiving such services shall not utilize the same to replace its regular employees; and (iv) providing for reports to the court not less frequently than every six months, unless the order provides otherwise.

3.   If the court requires restitution or services for the public good as a condition of probation or suspended judgment, it shall provide that an agency or person supervise the restitution or services and that such agency or person report to the court not less frequently than every six months, unless the order provides otherwise. Upon the written notice sent by a school district to the court and the appropriate probation department or agency which submits probation recommendations or reports to the court, the court may provide that such school district shall supervise the performance of services for the public good.

4.   The court, upon receipt of the reports provided for in subdivision two or three of this section may, on its own motion or the motion of any party or the agency, hold a hearing to determine whether the placement should be altered or modified.

Added by Laws 1976, Ch. 882, eff. Apr. 1, 1977; **amended** by Laws 1977, Ch. 283, eff. Apr. 1, 1977; Laws 1979, Ch. 568, eff. July 10, 1979; Laws Ch. 73, eff. July 30, 1979; Laws 1982, Ch. 920, eff. July 1, 1983; Laws 1987, Ch. 4, 31, eff. Mar. 24, 1987; Laws 1996, Ch. 309, § 33, eff. July 13, 1996, except that persons in need of supervision in the custody of the division for youth prior to the effective date shall be governed by the provisions of law in effect at the time of their placement.

§ 758-b.   Alcohol awareness program.

Repealed by Laws 1993, Ch. 124, § 3, eff. June 21, 1993.

§ 759. Order of protection.

The court may make an order of protection in assistance or as a condition of any order issued under this article. The order of protection may set forth reasonable conditions of behavior to be observed for a specified time by a person who is before the court and is a parent or other person legally responsible for the child's care or the spouse of the parent or other person legally responsible for the child's care, or respondent or both. Such an order may require any such person

(a)   to stay away from the home, school, business or place of employment of any other party, the other spouse, the other parent or the child, and to stay away from any other specific location designated by the court;

(b)   to permit a parent, or a person entitled to visitation by a court order or a separation agreement, to visit the child at stated periods;

(c)   to refrain from committing a family offense, as defined in subdivision one of section eight hundred twelve of this act, or any criminal offense against the child or against the other parent or against any person to whom custody of the child is awarded, or from harassing, intimidating or threatening such persons;

(d)   to permit a designated party to enter the residence during a specified period of time in order to remove personal belongings not in issue in this proceeding or in any other proceeding or action under this act or the domestic relations law;

(e)   to refrain from acts of commission or omission that create an unreasonable risk to the health, safety or welfare of a child;

(f)   to participate in family counseling or other professional counseling activities, or other services, including alternative dispute resolution services conducted by an authorized person or an authorized agency to which the youth has been referred or placed, deemed necessary for the rehabilitation of the youth, provided that such family counseling, other counseling activity or other necessary services are not contrary to such person's religious beliefs;

(g)   to provide, either directly or by means of medical and health insurance, for expenses incurred for medical care and treatment arising from the incident or incidents forming the basis for the issuance of the order;

(h)   1. to refrain from intentionally injuring or killing, without justification, any companion animal the respondent knows to be owned, possessed, leased, kept or held by the petitioner or a minor child residing in the household.

2.   [Companion animal], as used in this section, shall have the same meaning as in subdivision five of section three hundred fifty of the agriculture and markets law.

(i)   to observe such other conditions as are necessary to further the purposes of protection.

The court may also award custody of the child, during the term of the order of protection to either parent, or to an appropriate relative within the second degree. Nothing in this section gives the court power to place or board out any child to an institution or agency. In making orders of protection, the court shall so act as to insure that in the care, protection, discipline and guardianship of the child his religious faith shall be preserved and protected.

Notwithstanding the foregoing provisions, an order of protection, or temporary order of protection where applicable, may be entered against a former spouse and persons who have a child in common, regardless whether such persons have been married or have lived together at any time.

Amended by Laws 1976, Ch. 606, eff. Sept. 1, 1976; Laws 1977, Ch. 283, eff. June 21, 1977; Laws 1981, Ch. 965, eff. Aug. 6, 1981; Laws 1984, Ch. 948, eff. Nov. 1, 1984; Laws 1995, Ch. 483, § 9 and 10, eff. Nov. 1, 1995; Laws 1996, Ch. 309, § 34, eff. July 13, 1996, except that persons in need of supervision in the custody of the division for youth prior to the effective date shall be governed by the provisions of law in effect at the time of their placement; Laws 2005, Ch. 57, § 11 (Part E), eff. April 12, 2005, deemed eff. on and after April 1, 2005, amending sub. (f); Laws 2006, ch. 253, §5, eff. July 26, 2006.

§ 760.   Transfer of juvenile delinquents.

Repealed by Laws 1982, Ch. 920, eff. July 1, 1983.

§ 760.   Duties of counsel or law guardian.

1. If the court has entered a dispositional order pursuant to section seven hundred fifty-four it shall be the duty of the respondent's counsel or law guardian to promptly advise such respondent and if his parent or other person responsible for his care is not the petitioner, such parent or other person responsible for his care, in writing of his right to appeal to the appropriate appellate division of the supreme court, the time limitations involved, the manner of instituting an appeal and obtaining a transcript of the testimony and the right to apply for leave to appeal as a poor person if he is unable to pay the cost of an appeal. It shall be the further duty of such counsel or law guardian to explain to the respondent and if his parent or other person responsible for his care is not the petitioner, such parent or person responsible for his care, the procedures for instituting an appeal, the possible reasons upon which an appeal may be based and the nature and possible consequences of the appellate process.

2. It shall also be the duty of such counsel or law guardian to ascertain whether the respondent wishes to appeal and, if so, to serve and file the necessary notice of appeal.

3. If the respondent has been permitted to waive the appointment of a law guardian pursuant to section two hundred forty-nine-a, it shall be the duty of the court to provide the notice and explanation pursuant to subdivision one and, if the respondent indicates that he wishes to appeal, the clerk of the court shall file and serve the notice of appeal.

Added by Laws 1989, Ch. 9, eff. Nov. 1, 1989.

Part 6. New hearing and reconsideration of orders.

§ 761. New hearing.

On its own motion or on motion of any interested person acting on behalf of the respondent, the court may for good cause grant a new fact-finding or dispositional hearing under this article.

Amended by Laws 1963, by Ch. 529, eff. Apr. 23, 1963; Laws 1972, Ch. 721, eff. May 30, 1972.

§ 762. Staying, modifying, setting aside or vacating order.

For good cause, the court on its own motion or on motion of any interested person acting on behalf of the respondent may stay execution of, arrest, set aside, modify or vacate any order issued in the course of a proceeding under this article.

§ 763. Notice of motion.

Notice of motion under section seven hundred sixty-one of seven hundred sixty-two, including the court's own motion, shall be served upon parties and any agency or institution having custody of the child not less than seven days prior to the return date of the motion. The persons on whom the notice of motions is served shall answer the motion not less than two days before the return date. On examining the motion and answer and, in its discretion, after hearing argument, the court shall enter an order, granting or denying the motion.

Amended by Laws 1963, Ch. 409, eff. Apr. 16, 1963.

§ 764. Petition to terminate placement.

Any parent or guardian or duly authorized agency or next friend of a person placed under section seven hundred fifty-six may petition to the court for an order terminating the placement. The petition must be verified and must show:

(a)   that an application for release of the respondent was made to the duly authorized agency with which the child was placed;

(b)   that the application was denied or was not granted within thirty days from the day application was made; and

(c)   the grounds for the petition.

Amended by Laws 1976, Ch. 878, eff. Feb. 1, 1977; Laws 1977, Ch. 283, eff. June 21, 1977; Laws 1982, Ch. 920, eff. July 1, 1983.

§ 765.   Service of petition; answer.

A copy of a petition under section seven hundred sixty-four shall be served promptly upon the duly authorized agency or the institution having custody of the person, whose duty it is to file an answer to the petition within five days from the day of service.

§ 766.   Examination of petition and answer; hearing.

The court shall promptly examine the petition and answer. If the court concludes that a hearing should be had, it may proceed upon due notice to all concerned to hear the facts and determine whether continued placement serves the purposes of this article. If the court concludes that a hearing need not be had, it shall enter an order granting or denying the petition.

Amended by Laws 1977, Ch. 283, eff. June 21, 1977.

§ 767.   Orders on hearing.

(a)   If the court determines after hearing that continued placement serves the purposes of this article, it shall deny the petition. The court may, on its own motion, reduce the duration of the placement, change the agency in which the child is placed, or direct the agency to make such other arrangements for the person's care and welfare as the facts of the case may require.

(b)   If the court determines after hearing that continued placement does not serve the purposes of this article, the court shall discharge the person from the custody of the agency and may place the person on probation or under the supervision of the court.

Amended by Laws 1977, Ch. 283, eff. June 21, 1977.

§ 768.   Successive petitions.

If a petition under section seven hundred sixty-four is denied, it may not be renewed for a period of ninety days after the denial, unless the order of denial permits renewal at an earlier time.

Part 7.   Compliance with orders.

§ 771. Discontinuation of treatment by agency or institution.

If an authorized agency in which a person is placed under section seven hundred fifty-six

(a) discontinues or suspends its work; or

(b) is unwilling to continue to care for the person for the reason that support by the state of New York or one of its political subdivisions has been discontinued; or

(c) so fundamentally alters its program that the person can no longer benefit from it, the person shall be returned by the agency to the court which entered the order of placement.

Amended by Laws 1977, Ch. 283, eff. June 21, 1977.

§ 772. Action on return from agency or institution.

If a person is returned to the court under section seven hundred seventy-one, the court may make any order that might have been made at the time the order of placement was made, except that the maximum duration authorized for any such order shall be decreased by the time spent in placement.

Amended by Laws 1977, Ch. 283, eff. June 21, 1977.

§ 773. Petition for transfer for incorrigibility.

Any institution, society or agency in which a person was placed under section seven hundred fifty-six may petition to the court which made the order of placement for transfer of that person to a society or agency, governed or controlled by persons of the same religious faith or persuasion as that of the child, where practicable, or, if not practicable, to some other suitable institution, or to some other suitable institution on the ground that such person

(a) is incorrigible and that his or her presence is seriously detrimental to the welfare of the applicant institution, society, agency or other person in its care, or

(b) after placement by the court was released on parole or probation from such institution, society or agency and a term or condition of the release was

FCA

willfully violated. The petition shall be verified by an officer of the applicant institution, society or agency and shall specify the act or acts bringing the person within this section.

Amended by Laws 1977, Ch. 283, eff. June 21, 1977; Laws 1982, Ch. 920, eff. July 1, 1983.

§ 774. Action on petition for transfer.

On receiving a petition under section seven hundred seventy-three, the court may proceed under sections seven hundred thirty-seven, seven hundred thirty-eight or seven hundred thirty-nine with respect to the issuance of a summons or warrant and sections seven hundred twenty-seven and seven hundred twenty-nine govern questions of detention and failure to comply with a promise to appear. Due notice of the petition and a copy of the petition shall also be served personally or by mail upon the office of the locality chargeable for the support of the person involved and upon the person involved and his parents and other persons.

§ 775. Order on hearing.

(a) After hearing a petition under section seven hundred seventy-three, the court may:

(i) dismiss the petition;

(ii) grant the petition, making such placement, if the court was authorized to make such placement upon the original adjudication; or

(iii) terminate the prior order of placement and either discharge the respondent or place him on probation.

(b) If the court grants the petition and orders commitment or placement, the respondent shall thereupon be transferred to the custody of the person, agency or institution provided by the court's order.

Amended by Laws 1977, Ch. 283, eff. June 21, 1977.

§ 776. Failure to comply with terms and conditions of suspended judgment.

If a respondent is brought before the court for failure to comply with reasonable terms and conditions of a suspended judgment issued under this article and if, after hearing, the court is satisfied by competent proof that the respondent failed to comply with such terms and conditions, the court may revoke the suspension of judgment and proceed to make any order that might have been made at the time judgment was suspended.

§ 777. Failure to comply with terms of placement at home.

If a person placed in his own home subject to orders of the court leaves home without the court's permission, he may be brought before the court and if, after hearing, the court is satisfied by competent proof that the respondent left home without just cause, the court may revoke the order of placement and proceed to make any order that might have been made at the time the order of placement was made. It may also continue the order of placement and, on due notice and after hearing, enter an order of protection for the duration of the placement.

§ 778. Failure to comply with terms of placement in authorized agency.

If a person is placed in the custody of a suitable institution in accord with section seven hundred fifty-six and leaves the institution without permission of the superintendent or person in charge and without permission of the court, and if, after hearing, the court is satisfied by competent proof that the respondent left the institution without just cause, the court may revoke the order of placement and proceed to make any order that might have been made at the time the order of placement was made or any order authorized under section seven hundred fifty-six.

Amended by Laws 1963, Ch. 809, eff. Apr. 26, 1963; Laws 1982, Ch. 920, eff. July 1, 1983.

§ 779. Failure to comply with terms of probation.

If a respondent is brought before the court for failure to comply with reasonable terms and conditions of an order of probation issued under this article and if, after hearing, the court is satisfied by competent proof that the respondent without just cause failed to comply with such terms and conditions, the court may revoke the order of probation and proceed to make any order that might have been made at the time the order of probation was entered.

§ 779-a. Declaration of delinquency concerning juvenile delinquents and persons in need of supervision.

If, at any time during the period of a disposition of probation, the court has reasonable cause to believe the respondent has violated a condition of the disposition, it may declare the respondent delinquent and file a written declaration of delinquency. Upon such filing, the respondent shall be declared delinquent of his disposition of probation and such disposition shall be tolled. The court then must promptly take reason-able and appropriate action to cause the respondent to appear before it for the purpose of enabling the court to make a final determination with respect to the alleged delinquency. The time for prompt court action shall not be construed against the probation service when the respondent has absconded from probation supervision and the respondent's whereabouts are unknown. The court must be notified promptly of the circumstances of any such probationers.

Added by Laws 1981, Ch. 775, eff. Aug. 26, 1981; amended by Laws 1996, Ch. 309, § 35, eff. July 13, 1996, except that persons in need of supervision in the custody of the division for youth prior to the effective date shall be governed by the provisions of law in effect at the time of their placement.

§ 780.   Failure to comply with order of protection.

If any person is brought before the court for failure to comply with the terms and conditions of an order of protection properly issued under this article and applicable to him and if, after hearing, the court is satisfied by competent proof that that person without just cause failed to comply with such terms and conditions, the court may modify or revoke the order of protection, or commit said person, if he willfully violated the order, to jail for a term not to exceed six months, or both. The court may suspend an order of commitment under this section on condition that the said person comply with the order of protection.

Added by Laws 1963, Ch. 809, eff. Apr. 26, 1963.

Part 8.   Effect of proceedings.

§ 781.   Nature of adjudication.

No adjudication under this article may be denominated a conviction, and no person adjudicated a person in need of supervision under this article shall be denominated a criminal by reason of such adjudication.

Amended by Laws 1982, Ch. 920, eff. July 1, 1983.

§ 782.   Effect of adjudication.

No adjudication under this article shall operate as a forfeiture of any right or privilege or disqualify any person from subsequently holding public office or receiving any license granted by public authority.

§ 782-a.   Transfer of records and information to institutions and agencies.

Whenever a person is placed with an institution suitable for the placement of a person adjudicated in need of supervision maintained by the state or any subdivision thereof or to an authorized agency, the family court so placing such person shall forthwith transmit a copy of the orders of the family court pursuant to sections seven hundred fifty-two and seven hundred fifty-four, and of the probation report and all other relevant evaluative records in the possession of the family court and probation department related to such child, including but not limited to any diagnostic, educational, medical, psychological and psychiatric records with respect to such person to such institution or agency, notwithstanding any contrary provision of law.

Added by Laws 1976, Ch. 878, eff. Feb. 1, 1977; amended by Laws 1977, Ch. 283, eff. June 21, 1977; Laws 1982, Ch. 920, eff. July 1, 1983; Laws 1996, Ch. 309, § 36, eff. July 13, 1996, except that persons in need of supervision in the custody of the division for youth prior to the effective date shall be governed by the provisions of law in effect at the time of their placement.

§ 783. Use of record in other court.

Neither the fact that a person was before the family court under this article for a hearing nor any confession, admission or statement made by him to the court or to any officer thereof in any stage of the proceeding is admissible as evidence against him or his interests in any other court. Another court, in imposing sentence upon an adult after conviction, may receive and consider the records and information on file with the family court concerning such person when he was a child.

§ 783-a. Consolidation of records within a city having a population of one million or more.

Notwithstanding any other provision of law, in a city having a population of one million or more, an index of the records of the local probation departments located in the counties comprising such city for proceedings under article seven shall be consolidated and filed in a central office for use by the family court and local probation service in each such county. After consultation with the state administrative judge, the state director of probation and correctional alternatives shall specify the information to be contained in such index and the organization of such consolidated file.

Added by Laws 1976, Ch. 587, eff. July 1, 1977; amended by Laws 1985, Ch. 134, eff. Apr. 1, 1985.

§ 784. Use of police records.

All police records relating to the arrest and disposition of any person under this article shall be kept in files separate and apart from the arrests of adults and shall be withheld from public inspection, but such records shall be open to inspection upon good cause shown by the parent, guardian, next friend or attorney of that person upon the written order of a judge of the family court in the county in which the order was made or, if the person is subsequently convicted of a crime, of a judge of the court in which he was convicted.

FCA

ARTICLE 8

FAMILY OFFENSES PROCEEDINGS

SUMMARY OF ARTICLE

Part 1. Jurisdiction.

(Repealed and transferred sections noted under appropriate section number of text.)

§ 811. Finding and purpose.

Repealed by Laws 1981, Ch. 416, eff. Aug. 6, 1981.

§ 812. Procedures for family offense proceedings.

1. Jurisdiction. The family court and the criminal courts shall have concurrent jurisdiction over any proceeding concerning acts which would constitute disorderly conduct, harassment in the first degree, harassment in the second degree, aggravated harassment in the second degree, stalking in the first degree, stalking in the second degree, stalking in the third degree, stalking in the fourth degree, menacing in the second degree, menacing in the third degree, reckless endangerment, assault in the second degree, assault in the third degree or an attempted assault between spouses or former spouses, or between parent and child or between members of the same family or household except that if the respondent would not be criminally responsible by reason of age pursuant to section 30.00 of the penal law, then the family court shall have exclusive jurisdiction over such proceeding. Notwithstanding a complainant's election to

proceed in family court, the criminal court shall not be divested of jurisdiction to hear a family offense proceeding pursuant to this section. For purposes of this article, "disorderly conduct" includes disorderly conduct not in a public place. For purposes of this article, "members of the same family or household" shall mean the following:

(a)   persons related by consanguinity or affinity;

(b)   persons legally married to one another;

(c)   persons formerly married to one another; and

(d)   persons who have a child in common regardless whether such persons have been married or have lived together at any time.

2.   Information to petitioner or complainant. The chief administrator of the courts shall designate the appropriate probation officers, warrant officers, sheriffs, police officers or any other law enforcement officials, to inform any petitioner or complainant bringing a proceeding under this article, before such proceeding is commenced, of the procedures available for the institution of family offense proceedings, including but not limited to the following:

(a)   That there is concurrent jurisdiction with respect to family offenses in both family court and the criminal courts;

(b)   That a family court proceeding is a civil proceeding and is for the purpose of attempting to stop the violence, end the family disruption and obtain protection. Referrals for counseling, or counseling services, are available through probation for this purpose;

(c)   That a proceeding in the criminal courts is for the purpose of prosecution of the offender and can result in a criminal conviction of the offender;

(d)   That a proceeding or action subject to the provisions of this section is initiated at the time of the filing of an accusatory instrument or family court petition, not at the time of arrest, or request for arrest, if any;

(e)   [*Repealed.*]

(f)   that an arrest may precede the commencement of a family court or a criminal court proceeding, but an arrest is not a requirement for commencing either proceeding; provided, however, that the arrest of an alleged offender shall be made under the circumstances described in subdivision four of section 140.10 of the criminal procedure law;

(g)   that notwithstanding a complainant's election to proceed in family court, the criminal court shall not be divested of jurisdiction to hear a family offense proceeding pursuant to this section.

3.   Official responsibility. No official or other person designated pursuant to subdivision two of this section shall discourage or prevent any person who wishes to file a petition or sign a complaint from having access to any court for that purpose.

FCA

4. Official forms. The chief administrator of the court shall prescribe an appropriate form to implement subdivision two of this section.

5. Notice. Every police officer, peace officer or district attorney investigating a family offense under this article shall advise the victim of the availability of a shelter or other services in the community, and shall immediately give the victim written notice of the legal rights and remedies available to a victim of a family offense under the relevant provisions of the criminal procedure law, the family court act and the domestic relations law. Such notice shall be available in English and Spanish and, if necessary, shall be delivered orally and shall include but not be limited to the following statement:

"If you are the victim of domestic violence, you may request that the officer assist in providing for your safety and that of your children, including providing information on how to obtain a temporary order of protection. You may also request that the officer assist you in obtaining your essential personal effects and locating and taking you, or assist in making arrangement to take you, and your children to a safe place within such officer's jurisdiction, including but not limited to a domestic violence program, a family member's or a friend's residence, or a similar place of safety. When the officer's jurisdiction is more than a single county, you may ask the officer to take you or make arrangements to take you and your children to a place of safety in the county where the incident occurred. If you or your children are in need of medical treatment, you have the right to request that the officer assist you in obtaining such medical treatment. You may request a copy of any incident reports at no cost from the law enforcement agency. You have the right to seek legal counsel of your own choosing and if you proceed in family court and if it is determined that you cannot afford an attorney, one must be appointed to represent you without cost to you.

You may ask the district attorney or a law enforcement officer to file a criminal complaint. You also have the right to file a petition in the family court when a family offense has been committed against you. You have the right to have your petition and request for an order of protection filed on the same day you appear in court, and such request must be heard that same day or the next day court is in session. Either court may issue an order of protection from conduct constituting a family offense which could include, among other provisions, an order for the respondent or defendant to stay away from you and your children. The family court may also order the payment of temporary child support and award temporary custody of your children. If the family court is not in session, you may seek immediate assistance from the criminal court in obtaining an order of protection.

The forms you need to obtain an order of protection are available from the family court and the local criminal court (the addresses and telephone numbers shall be listed). The resources available in this community for information relating to domestic violence, treatment of injuries, and places of safety and shelters can be accessed by calling the following 800 numbers (the statewide

English and Spanish language 800 numbers shall be listed and space shall be provided for local domestic violence hotline telephone numbers).

Filing a criminal complaint or a family court petition containing allegations that are knowingly false is a crime."

The division of criminal justice services in consultation with the state office for the prevention of domestic violence shall prepare the form of such written notice consistent with the provisions of this section and distribute copies thereof to the appropriate law enforcement officials pursuant to subdivision nine of section eight hundred forty-one of the executive law. Additionally, copies of such notice shall be provided to the chief administrator of the courts to be distributed to victims of family offenses through the family court at such time as such persons first come before the court and to the state department of health for distribution to all hospitals defined under article twenty-eight of the public health law. No cause of action for damages shall arise in favor of any person by reason of any failure to comply with the provisions of this subdivision except upon a showing of gross negligence or willful misconduct.

Amended by Laws 1964, Ch. 156; Laws 1969, Ch. 736; Laws 1977, Ch. 449; Laws 1978, Ch. 628, 629; Laws 1980, Ch. 530, eff. June 24, 1980; Laws 1981, Ch. 416, eff. Aug. 6, 1981; Laws 1983, Ch. 925, eff. Aug. 8, 1983; Laws 1984, Ch. 948, eff. Nov. 1, 1984; Laws 1986, Ch. 847, eff. Nov. 1, 1986; Laws 1990, Ch. 577, § 1, eff. Nov. 1, 1990; Laws 1990, Ch. 667, § 2, eff. Nov. 1, 1990; Laws 1992, Ch. 345, § 7, eff. Nov. 1, 1992; Laws 1994, Ch. 222, §§ 6-9, eff. Jan. 1, 1995; Laws 1994, Ch. 224, § 1, eff. Jan. 1, 1995; Laws 1995, Ch. 440, § 1, eff. Nov. 1, 1995; Laws 1999, Ch. 125, §§ 3 and 4, eff. June 29, 1999; Laws 1999, Ch. 635, § 7, eff. Dec. 1, 1999.

§ 813. Transfer to family court.

Repealed by Laws 1977, Ch. 449, eff. Sept. 1, 1977.

§ 813. Transfer to criminal court.

1. At any time prior to a finding on the petition the court may, with the consent of the petitioner and upon reasonable notice to the district attorney, who shall have an opportunity to be heard, order that any matter which is the subject of a proceeding commenced pursuant to this article be prosecuted as a criminal action in an appropriate criminal court if the court determines that the interests of justice so require.

2. The court may simultaneously with the transfer of any matter to the appropriate criminal court, issue or continue a temporary order of protection which, notwithstanding any other provision of law, shall continue in effect, absent action by the appropriate criminal court pursuant to subdivision three of section 530.12 of the criminal procedure law, until the defendant is arraigned upon an accusatory instrument filed pursuant to this section in such criminal court.

3. Nothing herein shall be deemed to limit or restrict a petitioner's rights to proceed directly and without court referral in either criminal or family court, or

both, as provided for in section one hundred fifteen of this act and section 100.07 of the criminal procedure law.

    Added by Laws 1978, Ch. 628; **amended** by Laws 1980, Ch. 530, eff. Aug. 23, 1980; Laws 1994, Ch. 222, § 10, eff. Jan. 1, 1995.

§ 814. Rules of court regarding concurrent jurisdiction.

    The chief administrator of the courts pursuant to paragraph (e) of subdivision two of section two hundred twelve of the judiciary law shall promulgate rules to facilitate record sharing and other communication between the criminal and family courts, subject to applicable provisions of the criminal procedure law and the family court act pertaining to the confidentiality, expungement and sealing of records, where such courts exercise concurrent jurisdiction over family offense proceedings.

    Added by Laws 1994, Ch. 222, § 11, eff. Jan. 1, 1995.

§ 814-a. Uniform forms.

    The chief administrator of the courts, shall promulgate appropriate uniform temporary orders of protection and orders of protection forms, applicable to proceedings under this article, to be used throughout the state. Such forms shall be promulgated and developed in a manner to ensure the compatibility of such forms with the statewide computerized registry established pursuant to section two hundred twenty-one-a of the executive law.

    Added by Laws 1994, Ch. 224, § 15, eff. Jan. 1, 1995.

§ 815. Transcript of family offense proceedings; request by district attorney.

    The court shall, upon the written request of a district attorney stating that such transcript is necessary in order to conduct a criminal investigation or prosecution involving the petitioner or respondent, provide a copy of the transcript of any proceedings under this article, to such district attorney. Such transcript shall not be redisclosed except as necessary for such investigation or prosecution.

    Added by Laws 1994, Ch. 222, § 12, eff. Jan. 1, 1995; **amended** by Laws 1994, Ch. 224, § 2, eff. Jan. 1, 1995.

§ 816. Transfer from family court in discretion of family court.

Repealed by Laws 1977, Ch. 449, eff. Sept. 1, 1977.

§ 817. Support, paternity and child protection.

    On its own motion and at any time in proceedings under this article, the court may direct the filing of a child protective petition under article ten of this chapter, a support petition under article four, or a paternity petition under article five of this act and consolidate the proceedings.

Amended by Laws 1964, Ch. 156, eff. Mar. 23, 1964; Laws 1978, Ch. 391, eff. July 24, 1978.

§ 818. Venue.

Proceedings under this article may be originated in the county in which the act or acts referred to in the petition allegedly occurred or in which the family or household resides or in which any party resides. For the purposes of this section, residence shall include any residential program for victims of domestic violence, as defined in subdivision four of section four hundred fifty-nine-a of the social services law, or facility which provides shelter to homeless persons or families on an emergency or temporary basis.

Amended by Laws 1964, Ch. 156, eff. Mar. 23, 1964; Laws 1981, Ch. 416, eff. Aug. 6, 1981; **added** by Laws 1986, Ch. 39, eff. Nov. 1, 1986; Laws 1996, Ch. 539, § 3, eff. Aug. 8, 1996; Laws 2004, Ch. 391, § 1, eff. Aug. 17, 2004.

FCA

Part 2. Preliminary procedure.

§ 821. Originating proceedings.

1. A proceeding under this article is originated by the filing of a petition containing the following:

(a) An allegation that the respondent assaulted or attempted to assault his or her spouse, or former spouse, parent, child or other member of the same family or household or engaged in disorderly conduct, harassment, stalking, menacing or reckless endangerment toward any such person; and

(b) The relationship of the alleged offender to the petitioner;

(c) The name of each and every child in the family or household and the relationship of the child, if any, to the petitioner and to the respondent;

(d) A request for an order of protection or the use of the court's conciliation procedures; and

(e) An allegation as to whether any accusatory instrument alleging an act specified in paragraph (a) of this subdivision has been verified with respect to the same act alleged in the petition. Appended to the copy of the petition provided to the petitioner shall be a copy of the notice described in subdivision five of section eight hundred twelve of this article.

2. When family court is not in session, an arrest and initial appearance by the defendant or respondent may be in a criminal court, as provided in sections one hundred fifty-four-d and one hundred fifty-five of this act.

Amended by Laws 1969, Ch. 736, eff. Sept. 1, 1969; **repealed** and new § 821 **added** by Laws 1977, Ch. 449, eff. Sept. 1, 1977; **amended** by Laws 1978, Ch. 628, 629, eff. July 24, 1978; Laws 1984, Ch. 948, eff. Nov. 1, 1984; Laws 1988, Ch. 271, § 2, eff. July 19, 1988; Laws 1990, Ch. 577, § 2, eff. Nov. 1, 1990; Laws 1994, Ch. 222, §§ 6, 13 and 14, eff. Jan. 1, 1995; Laws 1997, Ch. 186, § 6, eff. July 8, 1997; Laws 1999, Ch. 635, § 8, eff. Dec. 1, 1999.

§ 821-a. Preliminary procedure.

1. Upon the filing of a petition under this article, the court shall advise the petitioner of the right to retain legal representation or if indigent, the right to have counsel appointed pursuant to section two hundred sixty-two of this act.

2. Upon the filing of a petition under this article, the court may:

(a) issue a summons pursuant to section eight hundred twenty-six of this part or issue a warrant pursuant to section eight hundred twenty-seven of this part;

(b) issue a temporary order of protection in favor of the petitioner and, where appropriate, the petitioner's children or any other children residing in the petitioner's household, pursuant to section eight hundred twenty-eight of this part.

3. Where the respondent is brought before the court pursuant to a summons under section eight hundred twenty-six of this part or a warrant issued under section eight hundred twenty-seven of this part, or where a respondent voluntarily appears before the court after such summons or warrant has been issued, the court shall:

(a) advise the parties of the right to retain legal representation or, if indigent, the right to have counsel appointed pursuant to section two hundred sixty-two of this act;

(b) advise the respondent of the allegations contained in the petition before the court; and

(c) provide the respondent with a copy of such petition; and the court may:

(i) order the release of the respondent on his or her own recognizance pending further appearances as required by the court;

(ii) direct that the respondent post bail in a manner authorized pursuant to section one hundred fifty-five-a of this act in an amount set by the court; or

(iii) issue a commitment order directing that the respondent be remanded to the custody of the county sheriff or other appropriate law enforcement official until such time as bail is posted as required by the court.

4. Where the court directs that the respondent post bail or that the respondent be committed to the custody of a law enforcement official as provided for herein, and the respondent fails to post bail or otherwise remains in custody, a hearing shall be held without unreasonable delay but in no event later than one hundred twenty hours after the arrest of the respondent or in the event that a Saturday, Sunday, or legal holiday occurs during such custody, one hundred forty-four hours after the arrest of the respondent, to determine upon material and relevant evidence whether sufficient cause exists to keep the respondent in custody. If the court determines that sufficient cause does not exist or if no hearing is timely held, the respondent shall immediately be released on the respondent's own recognizance.

5. (a) At such time as the petitioner first appears before the court, the court shall advise the petitioner that the petitioner may: continue with the hearing and disposition of such petition in the family court; or have the allegations contained therein heard in an appropriate criminal court; or proceed concurrently in both family and criminal court.

(b) Where the petitioner seeks to have the petition heard and determined in the family court, the court shall set the matter down for further proceedings pursuant to the provisions of this article. Nothing herein shall be deemed to limit or restrict petitioner's rights to seek to proceed directly in either criminal or family court, or both, as provided for in section one hundred fifteen of this act and section 100.07 of the criminal procedure law.

6. When both parties first appear before the court, the court shall inquire as to the existence of any other orders of protection involving the parties.

Added by Laws 1994, Ch. 222, § 15, eff. Jan. 1, 1995.

§ 822. Person who may originate proceedings.

(a) Any person in the relation to the respondent of spouse, or former spouse, parent, child, or member of the same family or household:

(b) A duly authorized agency, association, society, or institution;

(c) A peace officer, acting pursuant to his special duties, or a police officer;

(d) A person on the court's own motion.

Amended by Laws 1980, Ch. 843, eff. Sept. 1, 1980; Laws 1984, eff. Nov. 1, 1984.

§ 823. Rules of court for preliminary procedure.

(a) Rules of court may authorize the probation service

(i) to confer with any person seeking to file a petition, the potential petitioner and other interested persons concerning the advisability of filing a petition under this article, and

(ii) to attempt through conciliation and agreement informally to adjust suitable cases before a petition is filed over which the court apparently would have jurisdiction.

(b) The probation service may not prevent any person who wishes to file a petition under this article from having access to the court for that purpose.

(c) Efforts at adjustment pursuant to rules of court under this section may not extend for a period of more than two months without leave of a judge of the court, who may extend the period for an additional sixty days. Two successive extensions may be granted under this section.

(d) The probation service may not be authorized under this section to compel any person to appear at any conference, produce any papers, or visit any place.

(e) If agreement to cease offensive conduct is reached, it must be reduced to writing and submitted to the family court for approval. If the court approves it, the court without further hearing may thereupon enter an order of protection in accordance with the agreement, which shall be binding upon the respondent and shall in all respects be a valid order. The court record shall show that such order was made upon agreement.

Added by Laws 1977, Ch., 449, eff. Sept. 1, 1977.

§ 824. Admissibility of statements made during preliminary conference.

No statement made during a preliminary conference may be admitted into evidence at a fact-finding hearing under this act or in a criminal court at any time prior to conviction.

Amended by Laws 1963, Ch. 529, eff. Apr. 23, 1963.

§ 825. Issuance of summons.

On the filing of a petition under this article, the court may cause a copy of the petition and a summons to be issued, requiring the respondent to appear at the court at a time and place to answer the petition.

§ 826. Service of summons.

(a) Unless the court issues a warrant pursuant to section eight hundred twenty-seven of this part, service of a summons and petition shall be made by delivery of a true copy thereof to the person summoned at least twenty-four hours before the time stated therein for appearance. If so requested by the respondent, the court shall not proceed with the hearing or proceeding earlier than three days after such service.

(b) If after reasonable effort, personal service is not made, the court may at any stage in the proceedings make an order providing for substituted service in the manner provided for substituted service in civil process in courts of record.

Amended by Laws 1994, Ch. 222, § 16, eff. Jan. 1, 1995.

§ 827. Issuance of warrant; certificate of warrant.

(a) The court may issue a warrant, directing that the respondent be brought before the court, when a petition is presented to the court under section eight hundred twenty-one and it appears that

(i)   the summons cannot be served; or

(ii)   the respondent has failed to obey the summons; or

(iii)   the respondent is likely to leave the jurisdiction; or

(iv)   a summons, in the court's opinion, would be ineffectual; or

(v)   the safety of the petitioner is endangered; or

(vi)   the safety of a child is endangered; or

(vii)   aggravating circumstances exist which require the immediate arrest of the respondent. For the purposes of this section aggravating circumstances shall mean physical injury or serious physical injury to the petitioner caused by the respondent, the use of a dangerous instrument against the petitioner by the respondent, a history of repeated violations of prior orders of protection by the respondent, prior convictions for crimes against the petitioner by the respondent or the exposure of any family or household member to physical injury by the respondent and like incidents, behaviors and occurrences which to the court constitute an immediate and ongoing danger to the petitioner, or any member of the petitioner's family or household.

(b) The petitioner may not serve a warrant upon the respondent, unless the court itself grants such permission upon the application of the petitioner. The clerk of the court may issue to the petitioner or to the representative of an incorporated charitable or philanthropic society having a legitimate interest in the family a certificate stating that a warrant for the respondent has been issued by the court. The presentation of such certificate by said petitioner or representative to any peace officer, acting pursuant to his special duties, or a police officer authorizes him to arrest the respondent and take him to court.

(c) A certificate of warrant expires ninety days from the date of issue but may be renewed from time to time by the clerk of the court.

(d) Rules of court shall provide that a record of all unserved warrants be kept and that periodic reports concerning unserved warrants be made.

Amended by Laws 1980, Ch. 843, eff. Sept. 1, 1980; Laws 1988, Ch. 271, § 1, eff. July 19, 1988; Laws 1994, Ch. 222, § 17, eff. Jan. 1, 1995.

FCA

§ 828.　Temporary order of protection; temporary order for child support.

1.　(a) Upon the filing of a petition or counter-claim under this article, the court for good cause shown may issue a temporary order of protection, which may contain any of the provisions authorized on the making of an order of protection under section eight hundred forty-two, provided that the court shall make a determination, and the court shall state such determination in a written decision or on the record, whether to impose a condition pursuant to this subdivision, provided further, however, that failure to make such a determination shall not affect the validity of such order of protection. In making such determination, the court shall consider, but shall not be limited to consideration of, whether the temporary order of protection is likely to achieve its purpose in the absence of such a condition, conduct subject to prior orders of protection, prior incidents of abuse, extent of past or present injury, threats, drug or alcohol abuse, and access of weapons.

(b)　Upon the filing of a petition under this article, or as soon thereafter as the petitioner appears before the court, the court shall advise the petitioner of the right to proceed in both the family and criminal courts, pursuant to the provisions of section one hundred fifteen of this act.

2.　A temporary order of protection is not a finding of wrongdoing.

3.　The court may issue or extend a temporary order of protection ex parte or on notice simultaneously with the issuance of a warrant, directing that the respondent be arrested and brought before the court, pursuant to section eight hundred twenty-seven of this article.

4.　Notwithstanding the provisions of section eight hundred seventeen of this article the court may, together with a temporary order of protection issued pursuant to this section, issue an order for temporary child support, in an amount sufficient to meet the needs of the child, without a showing of immediate or emergency need. The court shall make an order for temporary child support notwithstanding that information with respect to income and assets of the respondent may be unavailable. Where such information is available, the court may make an award for temporary child support pursuant to the formula set forth in subdivision one of section four hundred thirteen of this act. An order making such award shall be deemed to have been issued pursuant to article four of this act. Upon making an order for temporary child support pursuant to this subdivision, the court shall advise the petitioner of the availability of child support enforcement services by the support collection unit of the local department of social services, to enforce the temporary order and to assist in securing continued child support, and shall set the support matter down for further proceedings in accordance with article four of this act.

Where the court determines that the respondent has employer-provided medical insurance, the court may further direct, as part of an order of temporary support under this subdivision, that a medical support execution be issued and served upon the respondent's employer as provided for in section fifty-two hundred forty-one of the civil practice law and rules.

Added by Laws 1964, Ch. 156, eff. Mar. 23, 1964; amended by Laws 1977, Ch. 449; Laws 1980, Ch. 530, eff. June 24, 1980; Laws 1988, Ch. 702, § 2, eff. Sept. 2, 1988; Laws 1988, Ch. 706, § 7, eff. Sept. 2, 1988; Laws 1994, Ch. 222, §§ 17-a to 19, eff. Jan. 1, 1995.

Part 3. Hearing.

(Repealed and transferred sections noted under appropriate section number of text.)

§ 831. Notice of rights; assignment of counsel.

Repealed by Laws 1975, Ch. 682, eff. Jan. 1, 1976.

§ 832. Definition of "fact-finding hearing."

When used in this article, fact-finding hearing means a hearing to determine whether the allegations of a petition under section eight hundred twenty-one are supported by a fair preponderance of the evidence.

Amended by Laws 1963, Ch. 529, eff. Apr. 23, 1963.

§ 833. Definition of "dispositional hearing."

When used in this article, dispositional hearing means in the case of a petition under this article a hearing to determine what order of disposition should be made.

§ 834. Evidence.

Only competent, material and relevant evidence may be admitted in a fact-finding hearing; only material and relevant evidence may be admitted in a dispositional hearing.

Amended by Laws 1963, Ch. 529, eff. Apr. 23, 1963.

§ 835. Sequence of hearings.

(a) Upon completion of the fact-finding hearing, the dispositional hearing may commence immediately after the required findings are made.

(b) Reports prepared by the probation service for use by the court at any time prior to the making of an order of disposition shall be deemed confidential information furnished to the court which the court in a proper case may, in its discretion, withhold from or disclose in whole or in part to the law guardian, counsel, party in interest, or other appropriate person. Such reports may not be furnished to the court prior to the completion of a fact-finding hearing, but may be used in a dispositional hearing.

Amended by Laws 1963, Ch. 529, eff. Apr. 23, 1963.

§ 836. Adjournments.

(a) The court may adjourn a fact-finding hearing or a dispositional hearing for good cause shown on its own motion or on motion of either party.

(b) At the conclusion of a fact-finding hearing and after it has made findings required before a dispositional hearing may commence, the court may adjourn the proceedings to enable it to make inquiry into the surroundings, conditions, and capacities of the persons involved in the proceedings.

Amended by Laws 1963, Ch. 529, eff. Apr. 23, 1963.

§ 838. Petitioner and respondent may have friend or relative present.

Unless the court shall find it undesirable, the petitioner shall be entitled to a non-witness friend, relative, counselor or social worker present in the court room. This section does not authorize any such person to take part in the proceedings. However, at any time during the proceeding, the court may call such person as a witness and take his or her testimony. Unless the court shall find it undesirable, the respondent shall be entitled to a non-witness friend, relative, counselor or social worker present in the court room in the event such respondent is not represented by legal counsel. This section does not authorize any such person to take part in the proceedings. However, at any time during the proceeding, the court may call such person as a witness and take his or her testimony.

Added by Laws 1977, Ch. 449, eff. Sept. 1, 1977.

Part 4. Orders.

(Repealed and transferred sections noted under appropriate section number of text.)

§ 841. Orders of disposition.

At the conclusion of a dispositional hearing under this article, the court may enter an order:

(a) dismissing the petition, if the allegations of the petition are not established; or

(b) suspending judgment for a period not in excess of six months; or

(c) placing the respondent on probation for a period not exceeding one year, and requiring respondent to participate in a batterer's education program designed to help end violent behavior, which may include referral to drug and alcohol counseling, and to pay the costs thereof if respondent has the means to do so, provided however that nothing contained herein shall be deemed to require payment of the costs of any such program by the petitioner, the state or any political subdivision thereof; or

(d) making an order of protection in accord with section eight hundred forty-two of this part; or

(e) directing payment of restitution in an amount not to exceed ten thousand dollars. An order of restitution may be made in conjunction with any order of disposition authorized under subdivisions (b), (c), or (d) of this section. In no case shall an order of restitution be issued where the court determines that the respondent has already paid such restitution as part of the disposition or settlement of another proceeding arising from the same act or acts alleged in the petition before the court.

No order of protection may direct any party to observe conditions of behavior unless the party requesting the order of protection has served and filed a petition or counter-claim in accordance with section one hundred fifty-four-b of this act. Nothing in this section shall preclude the issuance of a temporary order of protection ex parte, pursuant to section eight hundred twenty-eight of this article.

Nothing in this section shall preclude the issuance of both an order of probation and an order of protection as part of the order of disposition.

Notwithstanding the foregoing provisions, an order of protection, or temporary order of protection where applicable, may be entered against a former spouse and persons who have a child in common, regardless whether such persons have been married or have lived together at any time.

Amended by Laws 1977, Ch., 449; Laws 1980, Ch. 531, eff. June 24, 1980; Laws 1981, Ch. 416, eff. Aug. 6, 1981; Laws 1984, Ch. 948, eff. Nov. 1, 1984; Laws 1988, Ch. 706, § 8, eff. Sept. 2, 1988; Laws 1994, Ch. 222, §§ 20-21, eff. Jan. 1, 1995.

FCA

§ 842. Order of protection.

An order of protection under section eight hundred forty-one of this part shall set forth reasonable conditions of behavior to be observed for a period not in excess of two years by the petitioner or respondent or for a period not in excess of five years upon (i) a finding by the court on the record of the existence of aggravating circumstances as defined in paragraph (vii) of subdivision (a) of section eight hundred twenty-seven of this article; or (ii) a finding by the court on the record that the conduct alleged in the petition is in violation of a valid order of protection. Any finding of aggravating circumstances pursuant to this section shall be stated on the record and upon the order of protection. Any order of protection issued pursuant to this section shall specify if an order of probation is in effect. Any order of protection issued pursuant to this section may require the petitioner or the respondent:

(a) to stay away from the home, school, business or place of employment of any other party, the other spouse, the other parent, or the child, and to stay away from any other specific location designated by the court, provided that the court shall make a determination, and shall state such determination in a written decision or on the record, whether to impose a condition pursuant to this subdivision, provided further, however, that failure to make such a determination shall not affect the validity of such order of protection. In making such determination, the court shall consider, but shall not be limited to consideration of, whether the order of protection is likely to achieve its purpose in the absence of such a condition, conduct subject to prior orders of protection, prior incidents of abuse, extent of past or present injury, threats, drug or alcohol abuse, and access to weapons;

(b) to permit a parent, or a person entitled to visitation by a court order or a separation agreement, to visit the child at stated periods;

(c) to refrain from committing a family offense, as defined in subdivision one of section eight hundred twelve of this act, or any criminal offense against the child or against the other parent or against any person to whom custody of the child is awarded, or from harassing, intimidating or threatening such persons;

(d) to permit a designated party to enter the residence during a specified period of time in order to remove personal belongings not in issue in this proceeding or in any other proceeding or action under this act or the domestic relations law;

(e) to refrain from acts of commission or omission that create an unreasonable risk to the health, safety or welfare of a child;

(f) to pay the reasonable counsel fees and disbursements involved in obtaining or enforcing the order of the person who is protected by such order if such order is issued or enforced;

(g) to require the respondent to participate in a batterer's education program designed to help end violent behavior, which may include referral to drug and alcohol counselling, and to pay the costs thereof if the person has the means to do so, provided however that nothing contained herein shall be deemed to require payment of the costs of any such program by the petitioner, the state or any political subdivision thereof; and

(h) to provide, either directly or by means of medical and health insurance, for expenses incurred for medical care and treatment arising from the incident or incidents forming the basis for the issuance of the order;

(i) 1. to refrain from intentionally injuring or killing, without justification, any companion animal the respondent knows to be owned, possessed, leased, kept or held by the petitioner or a minor child residing in the household.

2. "Companion animal", as used in this section, shall have the same meaning as in subdivision five of section three hundred fifty of the agriculture and markets law.

(j) to observe such other conditions as are necessary to further the purposes of protection.

The court may also award custody of the child, during the term of the order of protection to either parent, or to an appropriate relative within the second degree. Nothing in this section gives the court power to place or board out any child or to commit a child to an institution or agency. The court may also upon the showing of special circumstances extend the order of protection for a reasonable period of time.

Notwithstanding the provisions of section eight hundred seventeen of this article, where a temporary order of child support has not already been issued, the court may in addition to the issuance of an order of protection pursuant to this section, issue an order for temporary child support in an amount sufficient to meet the needs of the child, without a showing of immediate or emergency need. The court shall make an order for temporary child support notwithstanding that information with respect to income and assets of the respondent may be unavailable. Where such information is available, the court may make an award for temporary child support pursuant to the formula set forth in subdivision one of section four hundred thirteen of this act. Temporary orders of support issued pursuant to this article shall be deemed to have been issued pursuant to section four hundred thirteen of this act.

Upon making an order for temporary child support pursuant to this subdivision, the court shall advise the petitioner of the availability of child support enforcement services by the support collection unit of the local department of social services, to enforce the temporary order and to assist in securing continued child support, and shall set the support matter down for further proceedings in accordance with article four of this act.

Where the court determines that the respondent has employer-provided medical insurance, the court may further direct, as part of an order of temporary support under this subdivision, that a medical support execution be issued and served upon the respondent's employer as provided for in section fifty-two hundred forty-one of the civil practice law and rules.

Notwithstanding the foregoing provisions, an order of protection, or temporary order of protection where applicable, may be entered against a former spouse and persons who have a child in common, regardless whether such persons have been married or have lived together at any time.

Amended by Laws 1972, Ch. 761; Laws 1980, Ch. 532, eff. June 24, 1980; Laws 1981, Ch. 416, eff. Aug. 6, 1981; Laws 1981, Ch. 965, eff. Aug. 6, 1981; Laws 1984, Ch. 948, eff. Nov. 1, 1984; Laws 1988, Ch. 702, eff. Sept. 2, 1988; Laws 1988, Ch. 706, eff. Sept. 2, 1988; Laws 1994, Ch. 222, § 22, eff. Jan. 1, 1995; Laws 1994, Ch. 224, § 3, eff. Jan. 1, 1995; Laws 1995, Ch. 483, §§ 11–12, eff. Nov. 1, 1995; Laws 2003, Ch. 579, § 1, eff. Oct. 22, 2003; Laws 2006, ch. 253, §6, eff. July 26, 2006.

§ 842-a.   Notice of order of protection.

Repealed by Laws 1980, Ch. 530, eff. Aug. 23, 1980.

§ 842-a.   Suspension and revocation of a license to carry, possess, repair or dispose of a firearm or firearms pursuant to section 400.00 of the penal law and ineligibility for such a license; order to surrender firearms.

1.   Mandatory and permissive suspension of firearms license and ineligibility for such a license upon the issuance of a temporary order of protection. Whenever a temporary order of protection is issued pursuant to section eight hundred twenty-eight of this article:

(a)   the court shall suspend any such existing license possessed by the respondent, order the respondent ineligible for such a license, and order the immediate surrender of any or all firearms owned or possessed where the court receives information that gives the court good cause to believe that: (i) the respondent has a prior conviction of any violent felony offense as defined in section 70.02 of the penal law; (ii) the respondent has previously been found to have willfully failed to obey a prior order of protection and such willful failure involved (A) the infliction of serious physical injury, as defined in subdivision ten of section 10.00 of the penal law, (B) the use or threatened use of a deadly weapon or dangerous instrument as those terms are defined in subdivisions twelve and thirteen of section 10.00 of the penal law, or (C) behavior constituting any violent felony offense as defined in section 70.02 of the penal law; or (iii) the respondent has a prior conviction for stalking in the first degree as defined in section 120.60 of the penal law, stalking in the second degree as defined in section 120.55 of the penal law, stalking in the third degree as defined in section 120.50 of the penal law or stalking in the fourth degree as defined in section 120.45 of such law; and

(b)   the court may where the court finds a substantial risk that the respondent may use or threaten to use a firearm unlawfully against the person or persons for whose protection the temporary order of protection is issued, suspend any such existing license possessed by the respondent, order the respondent ineligible for such a license, and order the immediate surrender of any or all firearms owned or possessed.

2. Mandatory and permissive revocation or suspension of firearms license and ineligibility for such a license upon the issuance of an order of protection. Whenever an order of protection is issued pursuant to section eight hundred forty-one of this part:

(a) the court shall revoke any such existing license possessed by the respondent, order the respondent ineligible for such a license, and order the immediate surrender of any or all firearms owned or possessed where the court finds that the conduct which resulted in the issuance of the order of protection involved (i) the infliction of serious physical injury, as defined in subdivision ten of section 10.00 of the penal law, (ii) the use or threatened use of a deadly weapon or dangerous instrument as those terms are defined in subdivisions twelve and thirteen of section 10.00 of the penal law, or (iii) behavior constituting any violent felony offense as defined in section 70.02 of the penal law; and

(b) the court may, where the court finds a substantial risk that the respondent may use or threaten to use a firearm unlawfully against the person or persons for whose protection the order of protection is issued, (i) revoke any such existing license possessed by the respondent, order the respondent ineligible for such a license and order the immediate surrender of any or all firearms owned or possessed or (ii) suspend or continue to suspend any such existing license possessed by the respondent, order the respondent ineligible for such a license, and order the immediate surrender of any or all firearms owned or possessed.

3. Mandatory and permissive revocation or suspension of firearms license and ineligibility for such a license upon a finding of a willful failure to obey an order of protection. Whenever a respondent has been found, pursuant to section eight hundred forty-six-a of this part to have willfully failed to obey an order of protection issued by this court or an order of protection issued by a court of competent jurisdiction in another state, territorial or tribal jurisdiction, in addition to any other remedies available pursuant to section eight hundred forty-six-a of this part:

(a) the court shall revoke any such existing license possessed by the respondent, order the respondent ineligible for such a license, and order the immediate surrender of any or all firearms owned or possessed where the willful failure to obey such order involves (i) the infliction of serious physical injury, as defined in subdivision ten of section 10.00 of the penal law, (ii) the use or threatened use of a deadly weapon or dangerous instrument as those terms are defined in subdivisions twelve and thirteen of section 10.00 of the penal law, or (iii) behavior constituting any violent felony offense as defined in section 70.02 of the penal law; or (iv) behavior constituting stalking in the first degree as defined in section 120.60 of the penal law, stalking in the second degree as defined in section 120.55 of the penal law, stalking in the third degree as defined in section 120.50 of the penal law or stalking in the fourth degree as defined in section 120.45 of such law; and

(b) the court may where the court finds a substantial risk that the respondent may use or threaten to use a firearm unlawfully against the person or persons for whose protection the order of protection was issued, (i) revoke any such existing license possessed by the respondent, order the respondent ineligible for such a license, whether or not the respondent possesses such a license, and order the immediate surrender of any or all firearms owned or possessed or (ii) suspend any such existing license possessed by the respondent, order the respondent ineligible for such a license, and order the immediate surrender of any or all firearms owned or possessed.

4. Suspension. Any suspension order issued pursuant to this section shall remain in effect for the duration of the temporary order of protection or order of protection, unless modified or vacated by the court.

5. Surrender. (a) Where an order to surrender one or more firearms has been issued, the temporary order of protection or order of protection shall specify the place where such firearms shall be surrendered, shall specify a date and time by which the surrender shall be completed and, to the extent possible, shall describe such firearms to be surrendered and shall direct the authority receiving such surrendered firearms to immediately notify the court of such surrender.

(b) The prompt surrender of one or more firearms pursuant to a court order issued pursuant this section shall be considered a voluntary surrender for purposes of subparagraph (f) of paragraph one of subdivision a of section 265.20 of the penal law. The disposition of any such firearms shall be in accordance with the provisions of subdivision six of section 400.05 of the penal law.

(c) The provisions of this section shall not be deemed to limit, restrict or otherwise impair the authority of the court to order and direct the surrender of any or all pistols, revolvers, rifles, shotguns or other firearms owned or possessed by a respondent pursuant to this act.

6. Notice. (a) Where an order of revocation, suspension or ineligibility has been issued pursuant to this section, any temporary order of protection or order of protection issued shall state that such firearm license has been suspended or revoked or that the respondent is ineligible for such license, as the case may be.

(b) The court revoking or suspending the license, ordering the respondent ineligible for such license, or ordering the surrender of any firearm shall immediately notify the statewide registry of orders of protection and the duly constituted police authorities of the locality of such action.

(c) The court revoking or suspending the license or ordering the defendant ineligible for such license shall give written notice thereof without unnecessary delay to the division of state police at its office in the city of Albany.

(d) Where an order of revocation, suspension, ineligibility, or surrender is modified or vacated, the court shall immediately notify the statewide registry of orders of protection and the duly constituted police authorities of the locality concerning such action and shall give written notice thereof without unnecessary delay to the division of state police at its office in the city of Albany.

7. Hearing. The respondent shall have the right to a hearing before the court regarding any revocation, suspension, ineligibility or surrender order issued pursuant to this section, provided that nothing in this subdivision shall preclude the court from issuing any such order prior to a hearing. Where the court has issued such an order prior to a hearing, it shall commence such hearing within fourteen days of the date such order was issued. 8. Nothing in this section shall delay or otherwise interfere with the issuance of a temporary order of protection.

Added by Laws 1996, Ch. 644, § 4, eff. Nov. 1, 1996; **amended** by Laws 1998, Ch. 597, § 7, eff. Dec. 22, 1998; Laws 1999, Ch. 635, §§ 8 & 9, eff. Dec. 1, 1999; Laws 2000, Ch. 434, § 3, eff. Oct. 20, 2000.

§ 843. Rules of court.

Rules of court shall define permissible terms and conditions of any order issued under section eight hundred forty-one, paragraphs (b), (c) and (d).

§ 844. Reconsideration and modification.

For good cause shown, the family court may after hearing reconsider and modify any order issued under paragraphs (b), (c) and (d) of section eight hundred forty-one.

§ 845. Effect of order of disposition.

Repealed by Laws 1994, Ch. 222, § 53, eff. January 1, 1995.

§ 846. Petition; violation of court order.

Proceedings under this part shall be originated by the filing of a petition containing an allegation that the respondent has failed to obey a lawful order of this court or an order of protection issued by a court of competent jurisdiction of another state, territorial or tribal jurisdiction.

(a) Persons who may originate proceedings. The original petitioner, or any person who may originate proceedings under section eight hundred twenty-two of this article, may originate a proceeding under this part.

(b) Issuance of summons. (i) Upon the filing of a petition under this part, the court may cause a copy of the petition and summons to be issued requiring the respondent to show cause why respondent should not be dealt with in accordance with section eight hundred forty-six-a of this part. The summons shall include on its face, printed or typewritten in a size equal to at least eight point bold type, a notice warning the respondent that a failure to appear in court may result in immediate arrest, and that, after an appearance in court, a finding that the respondent willfully failed to obey the order may result in commitment to jail for a term not to exceed six months, for contempt of court. The notice shall also advise the respondent of the right to counsel, and the right to assigned counsel, if indigent.

(ii) Upon the filing of a petition under this part alleging a violation of a lawful order of this or any other court, as provided in this section, the court may, on its own motion, or on motion of the petitioner:

(A) hear the violation petition and take such action as is authorized under this article; or

(B) retain jurisdiction to hear and determine whether such violation constitutes contempt of court, and transfer the allegations of criminal conduct constituting such violation to the district attorney for prosecution pursuant to section eight hundred thirteen of this article; or

(C) transfer the entire proceeding to the criminal court pursuant to section eight hundred thirteen of this article.

(c) Service of summons. Upon issuance of a summons, the provisions of section eight hundred twenty-six of this article shall apply, except that no order of commitment may be entered upon default in appearance by the respondent if service has been made pursuant to subdivision (b) of such section.

(d) Issuance of warrant. The court may issue a warrant, directing that the respondent be arrested and brought before the court, pursuant to section eight hundred twenty-seven of this article.

Added by Laws 1980, Ch. 530, eff. June 24, 1980; **amended** by Laws 1994, Ch. 222, § 23, eff. Jan. 1, 1995; Laws 1998, Ch. 597, § 8, eff. Dec. 22, 1998.

§ 846-a.   Powers on failure to obey order.

If a respondent is brought before the court for failure to obey any lawful order issued under this article or an order of protection issued by a court of competent jurisdiction of another state, territorial or tribal jurisdiction in a proceeding and if, after hearing, the court is satisfied by competent proof that the respondent has willfully failed to obey any such order, the court may modify an existing order to add reasonable conditions of behavior to the existing order of protection, make a new order of protection in accordance with section eight hundred forty-two, may order the forfeiture of bail in a manner consistent with article five hundred forty of the criminal procedure law if bail has been ordered pursuant to this act, may order the respondent to pay the petitioner's reasonable and necessary counsel fees in connection with the violation petition where the court finds that the violation of its order was willful, and may commit the respondent to jail for a term not to exceed six months. Such commitment may be served upon certain specified days or parts of days as the court may direct, and the court may, at any time within the term of such sentence, revoke such suspension and commit the respondent for the remainder of the original sentence, or suspend the remainder of such sentence. If the court determines that the willful failure to obey such order involves violent behavior constituting the crimes of menacing, reckless endangerment, assault or attempted assault and if such a respondent is licensed to carry, possess, repair and dispose of firearms pursuant to section 400.00 of the penal law, the court may also immediately revoke such license and may arrange for the immediate surrender and disposal of any firearm such respondent owns or possesses. If the willful failure to obey such order involves the infliction of serious physical injury as defined in subdivision ten of section 10.00 of the penal law or the use or threatened use of a deadly weapon or dangerous instrument, as those terms are defined in subdivisions twelve and thirteen of section 10.00 of the penal law, such revocation and immediate surrender and disposal of any firearm owned or possessed by respondent shall be mandatory, pursuant to subdivision eleven of section 400.00 of the penal law.

Amended by Laws 1965, Ch. 522; Laws 1980, Ch. 530, eff. Aug 23, 1980; **renumbered** from § 846 to 846-a and new § 846 **added**; **amended** by Laws 1981, Ch. 416, eff. Aug. 6, 1981; Laws 1993, Ch. 498, § 1, eff. Nov. 1, 1993; Laws 1994, Ch. 222, § 24, eff. Jan. 1, 1995; Laws 1998, Ch. 597, § 9, eff. Dec. 22, 1998.

§ 847. Procedures for violation of orders of protection; certain cases.

An assault, attempted assault or other family offense as defined in section eight hundred twelve of this article which occurs subsequent to the issuance of an order of protection under this article shall be deemed a new offense for which the petitioner may file a petition alleging a violation of an order of protection or file a new petition alleging a new family offense and may seek to have an accusatory instrument filed in a criminal court, as authorized by section one hundred fifteen of this act.

Amended by Laws 1994, Ch. 222, § 25, eff. Jan. 1, 1995.

FCA

ARTICLE 9

CONCILIATION PROCEEDINGS

SUMMARY OF ARTICLE

§ 911.   Purpose.

This article is designed to implement section thirteen-c, subdivision six, of article six of the constitution by making available an informal conciliation procedure to those whose marriage is in trouble.

§ 912.   Jurisdiction.

The family court has original jurisdiction over conciliation proceedings under this article.

§ 913.   Support and family offense proceedings.

On its own motion and at any time in a proceeding under this article, the court may direct the filing of a support petition under article four or a family offense petition under article eight of this act.

§ 914.   No effect on marital status.

The family court in a proceeding under this article may not issue any order affecting the marital status of the petitioner or of the petitioner's spouse or relieving either of any marital obligation.

§ 915.   Confidentiality of statements.

All statements made in proceedings under this article are confidential and shall not be admissible in evidence in any subsequent proceeding or action.

Part 2. Procedure.

§ 921. Originating proceeding.

A spouse may originate a conciliation proceeding under this article by filing a petition stating that his or her marriage is in difficulty and that the conciliation services of the family court are needed.

§ 922. Preliminary procedure.

The probation service is authorized to confer with a potential petitioner and may invite the potential petitioner's spouse and any other interested person to attend such conferences as appear to be advisable in conciliating the spouses. The probation service is also authorized after the filing of a petition to confer with the petitioner and to invite the petitioner's spouse to attend such conferences as appear to be advisable in conciliating the spouses.

Amended by Laws 1963, Ch. 979, eff. Apr. 30, 1963.

§ 923. Referral to voluntary agency.

(a) The probation service may recommend to the petitioner and to the petitioner's spouse that they consult with interested voluntary social or religious agencies in the community. If they consent, the service may thereupon refer them to any such interested voluntary agency.

(b) The probation service may not prevent any person from having access to the court for the purpose of having conciliation proceedings under this article.

§ 924. Attendance at conference.

If the petitioner's spouse does not attend a conference to which he or she has been invited after the filing of a petition under section nine hundred twenty-one, the petitioner may apply to the court for an order directing the petitioner's spouse to attend a conciliation conference. The court may enter an order directing the petitioner's spouse to appear in court on not less than five days' notice and, if the court concludes after hearing that it will serve the purposes of this article to require attendance at a conference, may direct the petitioner's spouse to attend a conference.

Amended by Laws 1963, Ch. 979, eff. Apr. 30, 1963.

FCA

§ 925. Continuation of proceeding.

If the petitioner's spouse attends a conference to which he or she has been invited under section nine hundred twenty-two or has been directed to attend under section nine hundred twenty-four and thereafter does not attend any conciliation conference, the court, on due notice to both spouses, may hold a hearing to determine whether the proceeding should be continued. If it concludes that conciliation under the auspices of the family court is not feasible, it may refer the parties to interested voluntary social or religious agencies in the community and shall terminate the proceeding under this article. If it concludes that further efforts at conciliation under this article should be undertaken, it may direct the spouses to attend another conciliation conference.

Amended by Laws 1963, Ch. 979, eff. Apr. 30, 1963.

§ 926. Duration of proceeding.

Unless both spouses consent to the continuation of a conciliation proceeding under this article, it terminates ninety days after the filing of the petition.

ARTICLE 10

CHILD PROTECTIVE PROCEEDINGS

———

(Former Article 10 of the Family Court Act was repealed by Laws 1970, Ch. 962 and new Article 10 of the Family Court Act was enacted by Laws 1970, Ch. 962, eff. May 1, 1970. New Article 10 was derived from former Article 3 of the Family Court Act regarding procedures relating to neglected children which was repealed by Laws 1970, Ch. 962, and former Article 10 relating to proceedings of abused children in, addition to other measures designed to further protect children.)

FCA

SUMMARY OF ARTICLE

Part 1. Jurisdiction.

(Repealed and transferred sections noted under appropriate section number of text.)

§ 1011. Purpose.

This article is designed to establish procedures to help protect children from injury or mistreatment and to help safeguard their physical, mental, and emotional well-being. It is designed to provide a due process of law for determining when the state, through its family court, may intervene against the wishes of a parent on behalf of a child so that his needs are properly met.

§ 1012.   Definitions and presumptions.

When used in this article and unless the specific context indicates otherwise:

(a) "Respondent" includes any parent or other person legally responsible for a child's care who is alleged to have abused or neglected such child;

(b) "Child" means any person or persons alleged to have been abused or neglected, whichever the case may be;

(c) "A case involving abuse" means any proceeding under this article in which there are allegations that one or more of the children of, or the legal responsibility of, the respondent are abused children;

(d) "Drug" means any substance defined as a controlled substance in section thirty-three hundred six of the public health law;

(e) "Abused child" means a child less than eighteen years of age whose parent or other person legally responsible for his care

(i) inflicts or allows to be inflicted upon such child physical injury by other than accidental means which causes or creates a substantial risk of death, or serious or protracted disfigurement, or protracted impairment of physical or emotional health or protracted loss or impairment of the function of any bodily organ, or

(ii) creates or allows to be created a substantial risk of physical injury to such child by other than accidental means which would be likely to cause death or serious or protracted disfigurement, or protracted impairment of physical or emotional health or protracted loss or impairment of the function of any bodily organ, or

(iii) [Until Nov 1, 2006] commits, or allows to be committed an offense against such child defined in article one hundred thirty of the penal law; allows, permits or encourages such child to engage in any act described in sections 230.25, 230.30 and 230.32 of the penal law; commits any of the acts described in section 255.25 of the penal law; or allows such child to engage in acts or conduct described in article two hundred sixty-three of the penal law provided, however, that (a) the corroboration requirements contained in the penal law and (b) the age requirement for the application of article two hundred sixty-three of such law shall not apply to proceedings under this article.

(iii) [Eff. Nov 1, 2006] commits, or allows to be committed an offense against such child defined in article one hundred thirty of the penal law; allows, permits or encourages such child to engage in any act described in sections 230.25, 230.30 and 230.32 of the penal law; commits any of the acts described in sections 255.25, 255.26 and 255.27 of the penal law; or allows such child to engage in acts or conduct described in article two hundred sixty-three of the penal law provided, however, that (a) the corroboration requirements contained in the penal law and (b) the age requirement for the application of article two hundred sixty-three of such law shall not apply to proceedings under this article.

(f)   "Neglected child" means a child less than eighteen years of age

(i)   whose physical, mental or emotional condition has been impaired or is in imminent danger of becoming impaired as a result of the failure of his parent or other person legally responsible for his care to exercise a minimum degree of care

(A)   in supplying the child with adequate food, clothing, shelter or education in accordance with the provisions of part one of article sixty-five of the education law, or medical, dental, optometrical or surgical care, though financially able to do so or offered financial or other reasonable means to do so; or

(B)   in providing the child with proper supervision or guardianship, by unreasonably inflicting or allowing to be inflicted harm, or a substantial risk thereof, including the infliction of excessive corporal punishment; or by misusing a drug or drugs; or by misusing alcoholic beverages to the extent that he loses self-control of his actions; or by any other acts of a similarly serious nature requiring the aid of the court; provided, however, that where the respondent is voluntarily and regularly participating in a rehabilitative program, evidence that the respondent has repeatedly misused a drug or drugs or alcoholic beverages to the extent that he loses self-control of his actions shall not establish that the child is a neglected child in the absenceof evidence establishing that the child's physical, mental or emotional condition has been impaired or is in imminent danger of becoming impaired as set forth in paragraph (i) of this subdivision; or

(ii)   who has been abandoned, in accordance with the definition and other criteria set forth in subdivision five of section three hundred eighty-four-b of the social services law, by his parents or other person legally responsible for his care.

(g)   "Person legally responsible" includes the child's custodian, guardian, or any other person responsible for the child's care at the relevant time. Custodian may include any person continually or at regular intervals found in the same household as the child when the conduct of such person causes or contributes to the abuse or neglect of the child.

(h)   "Impairment of emotional health" and "impairment of mental or emotional condition" includes a state of substantially diminished psychological or intellectual functioning in relation to, but not limited to, such factors as failure to thrive, control of aggressive or self-destructive impulses, ability to think and reason, or acting out or misbehavior, including incorrigibility, ungovernability or habitual truancy; provided, however, that such impairment must be clearly attributable to the unwillingness or inability of the respondent to exercise a minimum degree of care toward the child.

(i)   "Child protective agency" means any duly authorized society for the prevention of cruelty to children or the child protective service of the appropriate local department of social services or such other agencies with whom the local department has arranged for the provision of child protective services under the local plan for child protective services or an Indian tribe that has entered into an agreement with the state department of social services pursuant to section thirty-nine of the social services law to provide child protective services.

(j) "Aggravated circumstances" means where a child has been either severely or repeatedly abused, as defined in subdivision eight of section three hundred eighty-four-b of the social services law; or where a child has subsequently been found to be an abused child, as defined in paragraph (i) or (iii) of subdivision (e) of this section, within five years after return home following placement in foster care as a result of being found to be a neglected child, as defined in subdivision (f) of this section, provided that the respondent or respondents in each of the foregoing proceedings was the same; or where the court finds by clear and convincing evidence that the parent of a child in foster care has refused and has failed completely, over a period of at least six months from the date of removal, to engage in services necessary to eliminate the risk of abuse or neglect if returned to the parent, and has failed to secure services on his or her own or otherwise adequately prepare for the return home and, after being informed by the court that such an admission could eliminate the requirement that the local department of social services provide reunification services to the parent, the parent has stated in court under oath that he or she intends to continue to refuse such necessary services and is unwilling to secure such services independently or otherwise prepare for the child's return home; provided, however, that if the court finds that adequate justification exists for the failure to engage in or secure such services, including but not limited to a lack of child care, a lack of transportation, and an inability to attend services that conflict with the parent's work schedule, such failure shall not constitute an aggravated circumstance; or where a court has determined a child five days old or younger was abandoned by a parent with an intent to wholly abandon such child and with the intent that the child be safe from physical injury and cared for in an appropriate manner.

(k) "Permanency hearing" means a hearing held in accordance with section one thousand eighty-nine of this act for the purpose of reviewing the foster care status of the child and the appropriateness of the permanency plan developed by the social services district or agency.

Amended by Laws 1971, Ch. 469; Laws 1972, Ch. 1015; Laws 1973, Chs. 276, 1039; Laws 1976, Ch. 666, eff. Jan. 1, 1977; Laws 1977, Ch. 518, eff. Aug. 1, 1977, "and shall apply to any act of abuse of any child under the age of eighteen which act shall take place on or after the date on which this act shall have become a law"; Laws 1981, Ch. 984, eff. July 31, 1981; Laws 1984, Ch. 191, eff. Sept. 1, 1984; Laws 1985, Ch. 676, eff. Aug. 1, 1985; Laws 1996, Ch. 309, § 276, eff. July 13, 1996; Laws 1999, Ch. 7, §§ 39 & 40, eff. Feb. 11, 1999; Laws 2005, ch. 3, §8 (Part A), eff. Dec 21, 2005; Laws 2005, ch. 3, §3 (Part B), eff. Nov 21, 2005; Laws 2006, ch. 320, §28, eff. Nov 1, 2006.

§ 1013. Jurisdiction.

(a) The family court has exclusive original jurisdiction over proceedings under this article alleging the abuse or neglect of a child.

(b)   For the protection of children, the family court has jurisdiction over proceedings under this article notwithstanding the fact that a criminal court also has or may be exercising jurisdiction over the facts alleged in the petition or complaint.

(c)   In determining the jurisdiction of the court under this article, the age of the child at the time the proceedings are initiated is controlling.

(d)   In determining the jurisdiction of the court under this article, the child need not be currently in the care or custody of the respondent of the court otherwise has jurisdiction over the matter.

§ 1014.   Transfer to and from family court; concurrent proceedings.

(a)   The family court may transfer upon a hearing any proceedings originated under this article to an appropriate criminal court or may refer such proceeding to the appropriate district attorney if it concludes, that the processes of the family court are inappropriate or insufficient. The family court may continue the proceeding under this article after such transfer or referral and if the proceeding is continued, the family court may enter any preliminary order, as authorized by section one thousand twenty-seven, in order to protect the interests of the child pending a final order of disposition.

(b)   Any criminal complaint charging facts amounting to abuse or neglect under this article may be transferred by the criminal court in which the complaint was made to the family court in the county in which the criminal court is located, unless the family court has transferred the proceeding to the criminal court. The family court shall then, upon a hearing, determine what further action is appropriate. After the family court makes this determination, any criminal complaint may be transferred back to the criminal court, with or without retention of the proceeding in the family court, or may be retained solely in the family court, or if there appears to be no basis for the complaint, it may be dismissed by the family court. If the family court determines a petition should be filed, proceedings under this act shall be commenced as soon as practicable.

(c)   Nothing in this article shall be interpreted to preclude concurrent proceedings in the family court and a criminal court.

(d)   In any hearing conducted by the family court under this section, the court may grant the respondent or potential respondent testimonial immunity in any subsequent criminal court proceeding.

Amended by Laws 1972, Ch. 1016, eff. June 8, 1972.

§ 1015.   Venue.

(a)   Proceedings under this article may be originated in the county in which the child resides or is domiciled at the time of the filing of the petition or in the county in which the person having custody of the child resides or is domiciled. For the purposes of this section, residence shall include a dwelling unit or facility which provides shelter to homeless persons or families on an emergency or temporary basis.

(b) If in another proceeding under this act the court directs the filing of an abuse or neglect petition, the venue provision of the article under which the other proceeding is brought and the provisions of part seven of article one shall apply.

Amended by Laws 1987, Ch. 97, eff. June 8, 1987.

§ 1015-a. Court-ordered services.

In any proceeding under this article, the court may order a social services official to provide or arrange for the provision of services or assistance to the child and his or her family to facilitate the protection of the child, the rehabilitation of the family and, as appropriate, the discharge of the child from foster care. Such order shall not include the provision of any service or assistance to the child and his or her family which is not authorized or required to be made available pursuant to the comprehensive annual services program plan then in effect. In any order issued pursuant to this section the court may require a social service official to make periodic progress reports to the court on the implementation of such order. Nothing in such order shall preclude any party from exercising its rights under this article or any other provision of law relating to the return of the care and custody of the child by a social services official to the parent, parents or guardian. Violation of such order shall be subject to punishment pursuant to section seven hundred fifty-three of the judiciary law.

Added by Laws 1987, Ch. 760, eff. Aug. 7, 1987.

§ 1016. Appointment of law guardian.

The court shall appoint a law guardian to represent a child who has been allegedly abused or neglected upon the earliest occurrence of any of the following: (i) the court receiving notice, pursuant to paragraph (iv) of subdivision (b) of section ten hundred twenty-four of this act, of the emergency removal of the child; (ii) an application for an order for removal of the child prior to the filing of a petition, pursuant to section one thousand twenty-two of this act; or (iii) the filing of a petition alleging abuse or neglect pursuant to this article.

Whenever a law guardian has been appointed by the family court pursuant to section two hundred forty-nine of this act to represent a child in a proceeding under this article, such appointment shall continue without further court order or appointment during (i) an order of disposition issued by the court pursuant to section one thousand fifty-two of this article directing supervision, protection or suspending judgment, or any extension thereof; (ii) an adjournment in contemplation of dismissal as provided for in section one thousand thirty-nine of this article or any extension thereof; or (iii) the pendency of the foster care placement ordered pursuant to section one thousand fifty-two of this article. All notices and reports required by law shall be provided to such law guardian. Such appointment shall terminate upon the expiration of such order, unless another appointment of a law guardian has been made by the court or unless such law guardian makes application to the court to be relieved of his or her appointment. Upon approval of such application to be relieved, the court shall immediately appoint another law guardian to whom all notices and reports required by law shall be provided.

A law guardian shall be entitled to compensation pursuant to applicable provisions of law for services rendered up to and including disposition of the petition. The law guardian shall, by separate application, be entitled to compensation for services rendered subsequent to the disposition of the petition.

Nothing in this section shall be construed to limit the authority of the court to remove a law guardian from his or her assignment.

Added by Laws 1990, Ch. 319, § 1, eff. Jan. 1, 1991; **amended** by Laws 1990, Ch. 560, § 1, eff. Jan. 1, 1991; Laws 1997, Ch. 353, § 1, eff. Nov. 3, 1997; L. 2005, Ch. 3, § 9, amending para 2, eff. Aug. 23, 2005.

§ 1017. Placement of children.

1. [As amended, L 2005, chs 3, §10 (Part A) and 671, §1] In any proceeding under this article, when the court determines that a child must be removed from his or her home, pursuant to part two of this article, or placed, pursuant to section one thousand fifty-five of this article, the court shall direct the local commissioner of social services to conduct an immediate investigation to locate any non-respondent parent of the child and any relatives of the child, including all of the child's grandparents, all suitable relatives identified by any respondent parent or any non-respondent parent and any relative identified by a child over the age of five as a relative who plays or has played a significant positive role in his or her life, and inform them of the pendency of the proceeding and of the opportunity for becoming foster parents or for seeking custody or care of the child, and that the child may be adopted by foster parents if attempts at reunification with the birth parent are not required or are unsuccessful. The local commissioner of social services shall record the results of such investigation, including, but not limited to, the name, last known address, social security number, employer's address and any other identifying information to the extent known regarding any non-respondent parent, in the uniform case record maintained pursuant to section four hundred nine-f of the social services law. For the purpose of this section, "non-respondent parent"; shall include a person entitled to notice of the pendency of the proceeding and of the right to intervene as an interested party pursuant to subdivision (d) of section one thousand thirty-five of this article, and a non-custodial parent entitled to notice and the right to enforce visitation rights pursuant to subdivision (e) of section one thousand thirty-five of this article. The court shall determine:

(a) whether there is a suitable non-respondent parent or other person related to the child with whom such child may appropriately reside; and

(b) in the case of a relative, whether such relative seeks approval as a foster parent pursuant to the social services law for the purposes of providing care for such child, or wishes to provide free care and custody for the child during the pendency of any orders pursuant to this article.

2. The court shall, upon receipt of the report of the investigation ordered pursuant to subdivision one of this section:

(a) where the court determines that the child may reside with a suitable non-respondent parent or other relative or other suitable person, either:

(i) place the child in the custody of such non-respondent parent, other relative or other suitable person pursuant to article six of this act and conduct such other and further investigations as the court deems necessary; or

(ii) place the child in the custody of such non-respondent parent, other relative or other suitable person pursuant to this article during the pendency of the proceeding or until further order of the court, whichever is earlier and conduct such other and further investigations as the court deems necessary; or

(iii) remand or place the child, as applicable, with the local commissioner of social services and direct such commissioner to have the child reside with such relative or other suitable person and further direct such commissioner pursuant to regulations of the office of children and family services, to commence an investigation of the home of such relative or other suitable person within twenty-four hours and thereafter approve such relative or other suitable person, if qualified, as a foster parent. If such home is found to be unqualified for approval, the local commissioner shall report such fact to the court forthwith.

(b) where the court determines that a suitable non-respondent parent or other person related to the child cannot be located, remand or place the child with a suitable person, pursuant to subdivision (b) of section one thousand twenty-seven or subdivision (a) of section one thousand fifty-five of this article, or remand or place the child in the custody of the local commissioner of social services pursuant to subdivision (b) of section one thousand twenty-seven or subdivision (a) of section one thousand fifty-five of this article. The court in its discretion may direct that such commissioner have the child reside in a specific certified foster home where the court determines that such placement is in furtherance of the child's best interests.

3. Nothing in this section shall be deemed to limit, impair or restrict the ability of the court to remove a child from his or her home as authorized by law, or the right of a party to a hearing pursuant to section ten hundred twenty-eight of this article.

Added by Laws 1989, Ch. 744, § 1, eff. July 24, 1989; Laws 2003, Ch. 657, § 4, amending sub. 1, eff. Jan. 1, 2004; L. 2005, Ch. 3, §§ 10, amending sub. 1, 2, eff. Aug. 23, 2005.

§ 1018.　Conferencing and mediation.

In any proceeding initiated pursuant to this article, the court may, at its discretion, authorize the use of conferencing or mediation at any point in the proceedings to further a plan for the child that fosters the child's health, safety, and wellbeing. Such conferencing or mediation may involve interested relatives or other adults who are significant in the life of the child.

　　Add, L 2005, ch 3, §11 (Part A), eff Dec 21, 2005 (see 2005 note below); Former §1018, add, L 1969, ch 264, §2; repealed, L 1970, ch 962, §9, eff May 1, 1970; Prior §1018, add, L 1962, ch 686; renumbered §1118, L 1969, ch 264, §2, eff June 1, 1969; L. 2005, Ch. 3, § 11, eff. Aug. 23, 2005.

§ 1019.　Repealed

　　Add, L 1969, ch 264, §2; repealed, L 1970, ch 962, §9, eff May 1, 1970; Former §1019, add, L 1962, ch 686; amd, L 1962, ch 687, §13; renumbered §1119, L 1969, ch 264, §2, eff June 1, 1969.

§ 1020.　Repealed

　　Add, L 1969, ch 264, §2; repealed, L 1970, ch 962, §9, eff May 1, 1970; Former §1020, add. 1969, ch 264, §2; repealed, L 1970, ch 962, §9, eff May 1, 1970.

Part 2.　Temporary removal and preliminary orders.

§ 1021.　Temporary removal with consent

A peace officer, acting pursuant to his or her special duties, or a police officer or an agent of a duly authorized agency, association, society or institution may temporarily remove a child from the place where he or she is residing with the written consent of his or her parent or other person legally responsible for his or her care, if the child is suspected to be an abused or neglected child under this article. The officer or agent shall, coincident with consent or removal, give written notice to the parent or other person legally responsible for the child's care of the right to apply to the family court for the return of the child pursuant to section one thousand twenty-eight of this article, and of the right to be represented by counsel and the procedures for those who are indigent to obtain counsel in proceedings brought pursuant to this article. Such notice shall also include the name, title, organization, address and telephone number of the person removing the child; the name, address and telephone number of the authorized agency to which the child will be taken, if available; and the telephone number of the person to be contacted for visits with the child. A copy of the instrument whereby the parent or legally responsible person has given such consent to such removal shall be appended to the petition alleging abuse or neglect of the removed child and made a part of the permanent court record of the proceeding. A copy of such instrument and notice of the telephone number of the child protective agency to contact to ascertain the date, time and place of the filing of the petition and of the hearing that will be held pursuant to section one thousand twenty-seven of this article shall be given to the parent or legally responsible person. Unless the child is returned sooner, a petition shall be filed within three court days from the date of removal. In such a case, a hearing shall be held no later than the next court day after the petition is filed and findings shall be made as required pursuant to section one thousand twenty-seven of this article.

Amended by Laws 1980, Ch. 843, eff. Sept. 1, 1980; Laws 1990, Ch. 205, § 1, eff. Sept. 1, 1990; L. 2005, Ch. 3, § 12, eff. Aug. 23, 2005.

§ 1022. Preliminary orders of court before petition filed.

(a)   (i) The family court may enter an order directing the temporary removal of a child from the place where he or she is residing before the filing of a petition under this article, if

(A)   the parent or other person legally responsible for the child's care is absent or, though present, was asked and refused to consent to the temporary removal of the child and was informed of an intent to apply for an order under this section and of the information required by section one thousand twenty-three of this part; and

(B)   the child appears so to suffer from the abuse or neglect of his or her parent or other person legally responsible for his or her care that his or her immediate removal is necessary to avoid imminent danger to the child's life or health; and

(C)   there is not enough time to file a petition and hold a preliminary hearing under section one thousand twenty-seven of this part.

(ii)   When a child protective agency applies to a court for the immediate removal of a child pursuant to this subdivision, the court shall calendar the matter for that day and shall continue the matter on successive subsequent court days, if necessary, until a decision is made by the court.

(iii)   In determining whether temporary removal of the child is necessary to avoid imminent risk to the child's life or health, the court shall consider and determine in its order whether continuation in the child's home would be contrary to the best interests of the child and where appropriate, whether reasonable efforts were made prior to the date of application for the order directing such temporary removal to prevent or eliminate the need for removal of the child from the home. If the court determines that reasonable efforts to prevent or eliminate the need for removal of the child from the home were not made but that the lack of such efforts was appropriate under the circumstances, the court order shall include such a finding.

(iv)   If the court determines that reasonable efforts to prevent or eliminate the need for removal of the child from the home were not made but that such efforts were appropriate under the circumstances, the court shall order the child protective agency to provide or arrange for the provision of appropriate services or assistance to the child and the child's family pursuant to section one thousand fifteen-a of this article or subdivision (c) of this section.

(v)   The court shall also consider and determine whether imminent risk to the child would be eliminated by the issuance of a temporary order of protection, pursuant to section one thousand twenty-nine of this part, directing the removal of a person or persons from the child's residence.

(vi)   Any order directing the temporary removal of a child pursuant to this section shall state the court's findings with respect to the necessity of such removal, whether the respondent was present at the hearing and, if not, what notice the respondent was given of the hearing, whether the respondent was represented by counsel, and, if not, whether the respondent waived his or her right to counsel.

(vii)   At the conclusion of a hearing where it has been determined that a child should be removed from his or her parent or other person legally responsible, the court shall set the date certain for an initial permanency hearing pursuant to paragraph two of subdivision (a) of section one thousand eighty-nine of this act. The date certain shall be included in the written order issued pursuant to subdivision (b) of this section and shall set forth the date certain scheduled for the permanency hearing.

(b)   Any written order pursuant to this section shall be issued immediately, but in no event later than the next court day following the removal of the child. The order shall specify the facility to which the child is to be brought. Except for good cause shown or unless the child is sooner returned to the place where he or she was residing, a petition shall be filed under this article within three court days of the issuance of the order. The court shall hold a hearing pursuant to section one thousand twenty-seven of this part no later than the next court day following the filing of the petition if the respondent was not present, or was present and unrepresented by counsel, and has not waived his or her right to counsel, for the hearing pursuant to this section.

(c)   The family court, before the filing of a petition under this article, may enter an order authorizing the provision of services or assistance, including authorizing a physician or hospital to provide emergency medical or surgical procedures, if

(i)   such procedures are necessary to safeguard the life or health of the child; and

(ii)   there is not enough time to file a petition and hold a preliminary hearing under section one thousand twenty-seven. Where the court orders a social services official to provide or contract for services or assistance pursuant to this section, such order shall be limited to services or assistance authorized or required to be made available pursuant to the comprehensive annual services program plan then in effect.

(d)   The person removing the child shall, coincident with removal, give written notice to the parent or other person legally responsible for the child's care of the right to apply to the family court for the return of the child pursuant to section one thousand twenty-eight of this act, the name, title, organization, address and telephone number of the person removing the child, the name and telephone number of the child care agency to which the child will be taken, if available, the telephone number of the person to be contacted for visits with the child, and the information required by section one thousand twenty-three of this act. Such notice shall be personally served upon the parent or other person at the residence of the child provided, that if such person is not present at the child's residence at the time of removal, a copy of the notice shall be affixed to the door of such residence and a copy shall be mailed to such person at his or her last known place of residence within twenty-four hours after the removal of the child. If the place of removal is not the child's residence, a copy of the notice shall be personally served upon the parent or person legally responsible for the child's care forthwith, or affixed to the door of the child's residence and mailed to the parent or other person legally responsible for the child's care at his or her last known place of residence within twenty-four hours after the removal. The form of the notice shall be prescribed by the chief administrator of the courts.

(e)   Nothing in this section shall be deemed to require that the court order the temporary removal of a child as a condition of ordering services or assistance, including emergency medical or surgical procedures pursuant to subdivision (c) of this section.

(f)   The court may issue a temporary order of protection pursuant to section ten hundred twenty-nine of this article as an alternative to or in conjunction with any other order or disposition authorized under this section.

Amended by Laws 1982, Ch. 379, eff. Sept. 1, 1982; Laws 1987, Ch. 776, eff. Aug. 7, 1987; Laws 1988, Ch. 478, § 3, eff. Nov. 1, 1988; Laws 1988, Ch. 527, § 1, eff. Aug. 11, 1988; Laws 1988, Ch. 673, § 1, eff. Sept. 1, 1988; Laws 1989, Ch. 727, § 2, eff. Oct. 1, 1989; Laws 1990, Ch. 171, § 1, eff. Sept. 1, 1990; L. 2005, Ch. 3, § 13, eff. Aug. 23, 2005.

§ 1022-a.   Preliminary orders; notice and appointment of counsel.

At a hearing held pursuant to section ten hundred twenty-two of this act at which the respondent is present, the court shall advise the respondent of the allegations in the application and shall appoint counsel for the respondent pursuant to section two hundred sixty-two of this act where the respondent is indigent.

    Added by Laws 1990, Ch. 336, § 2, eff. Sept. 1, 1990.

§ 1023.   Procedure for issuance of temporary order.

Any person who may originate a proceeding under this article may apply for, or the court on its own motion may issue, an order of temporary removal under section one thousand twenty-two or one thousand twenty-seven or an order for the provision of services or assistance, including emergency medical or surgical procedures pursuant to subdivision (c) of section one thousand twenty-two, or a temporary order of protection pursuant to section ten hundred twenty-nine. The applicant or, where designated by the court, any other appropriate person, shall make every reasonable effort, with due regard for any necessity for immediate protective action, to inform the parent or other person legally responsible for the child's care of the intent to apply for the order, of the date and the time that the application will be made, the address of the court where the application will be made, of the right of the parent or other person legally responsible for the child's care to be present at the application and at any hearing held thereon and, of the right to be represented by counsel, including procedures for obtaining counsel, if indigent.

FCA

    Amended by Laws 1973, Ch. 1029, eff. Sept. 1, 1973; Laws 1987, Ch. 776, eff. Aug. 7, 1987; Laws 1988, Ch. 527, eff. Aug. 11, 1988; Laws 1988, Ch. 673, § 2, eff. Sept. 1, 1988; Laws 1990, Ch. 170, § 1, eff. Sept. 1, 1990.

§ 1024.   Emergency removal without court order.

   (a)   A peace officer, acting pursuant to his special duties, police officer, or a law enforcement official, or an agent of a duly incorporated society for the prevention of cruelty to children or a designated employee of a city or county department of social services shall take all necessary measures to protect a child's life or health including, when appropriate, taking or keeping a child in protective custody, and any physician shall notify the local department of social services or appropriate police authorities to take custody of any child such physician is treating, without an order under section one thousand twenty-two and without the consent of the parent or other person legally responsible for the child's care, regardless of whether the parent or other person legally responsible for the child's care is absent, if (i) such person has reasonable cause to believe that the child is in such circumstance or condition that his continuing in said place of residence or in the care and custody of the parent or person legally responsible for the child's care presents an imminent danger to the child's life or health; and

(ii)   there is not time enough to apply for an order under section one thousand twenty-two.

(b)   If a person authorized by this section removes or keeps custody of a child, he shall (i) bring the child immediately to a place approved for such purpose by the local social services department, unless the person is a physician treating the child and the child is or will be presently admitted to a hospital, and

(ii)   make every reasonable effort to inform the parent or other person legally responsible for the child's care of the facility to which he has brought the child, and

(iii)   give, coincident with removal, written notice to the parent or other person legally responsible for the child's care of the right to apply to the family court for the return of the child pursuant to section one thousand twenty-eight of this act, and of the right to be represented by counsel in proceedings brought pursuant to this article and procedures for obtaining counsel, if indigent. Such notice shall also include the name, title, organization, address and telephone number of the person removing the child, the name, address, and telephone number of the authorized agency to which the child will be taken, if available, the telephone number of the person to be contacted for visits with the child, and the information required by section one thousand twenty-three of this act. Such notice shall be personally served upon the parent or other person at the residence of the child provided, that if such person is not present at the child's residence at the time of removal, a copy of the notice shall be affixed to the door of such residence and a copy shall be mailed to such person at his or her last known place of residence within twenty-four hours after the removal of the child. If the place of removal is not the child's residence, a copy of the notice shall be personally served upon the parent or person legally responsible for the child's care forthwith, or affixed to the door of the child's residence and mailed to the parent or other person legally responsible for the child's care at his or her last known place of residence within twenty-four hours after the removal. An affidavit of such service shall be filed with the clerk of the court within twenty-four hours of serving such notice exclusive of weekends and holidays pursuant to the provisions of this section. The form of the notice shall be prescribed by the chief administrator of the courts. Failure to file an affidavit of service as required by this subdivision shall not constitute grounds for return of the child.

(iv)   inform the court and make a report pursuant to title six of the social services law, as soon as possible.

(c)   Any person or institution acting in good faith in the removal or keeping of a child pursuant to this section shall have immunity from any liability, civil or criminal, that might otherwise be incurred or imposed as a result of such removal or keeping.

(d)   Where the physician keeping a child in his custody pending action by the local department of social services or appropriate police authorities does so in his capacity as a member of the staff of a hospital or similar institution, he shall notify the person in charge of the institution, or his designated agent, who shall then become responsible for the further care of such child.

(e)   Any physician keeping a child in his custody pursuant to this section shall have the right to keep such child in his custody until such time as the custody of the child has been transferred to the appropriate police authorities or the social services official of the city or county in which the physician maintains his place of business. If the social services official receives custody of a child pursuant to the provisions of this section, he shall promptly inform the parent or other person responsible for such child's care and the family court of his action.

Amended by Laws 1973, Ch. 1039; Laws 1976, Ch. 880; Laws 1980, Ch. 843, eff. Sept. 1, 1980; Laws 1982, Ch. 379, eff. Sept. 1, 1982; Laws 1985, Ch. 677, eff. Aug. 1, 1985; Laws 1987, Ch. 162, eff. Oct. 27, 1987; Laws 1989, Ch. 727, § 3, eff. Oct. 1, 1989; Laws 1990, Ch. 170, § 2, eff. Sept. 1, 1990.

§ 1026.   Action by the appropriate person designated by the court and child protective agency upon emergency removal

(a)   The appropriate person designated by the court or a child protective agency when informed that there has been an emergency removal of a child from his or her home without court order shall

(i)   make every reasonable effort to communicate immediately with the child's parent or other person legally responsible for his or her care, and

(ii)   except in cases involving abuse, cause a child thus removed to be returned, if it concludes there is not an imminent risk to the child's health in so doing. In cases involving abuse, the child protective agency may recommend to the court that the child be returned or that no petition be filed.

(b)   The child protective agency may, but need not, condition the return of a child under this section upon the giving of a written promise, without security, of the parent or other person legally responsible for the child's care that he or she will appear at the family court at a time and place specified in the recognizance and may also require him or her to bring the child with him or her.

(c)   If the child protective agency for any reason does not return the child under this section after an emergency removal pursuant to section one thousand twenty-four of this part on the same day that the child is removed, or if the child protective agency concludes it appropriate after an emergency removal pursuant to section one thousand twenty-four of this part, it shall cause a petition to be filed under this part no later than the next court day after the child was removed. The court may order an extension, only upon good cause shown, of up to three court days from the date of such child's removal. A hearing shall be held no later than the next court day after the petition is filed and findings shall be made as required pursuant to section one thousand twenty-seven of this part.

Amended by Laws 1973, Ch. 1039, eff. Sept. 1, 1973; Laws 1987, Ch. 478, eff. Nov. 27, 1987; Laws 1988, Ch. 233, § 1, eff. July 8, 1988.

§ 1027. Hearing and preliminary orders after filing of petition.

(a)   (i) In any case where the child has been removed without court order or where there has been a hearing pursuant to section one thousand twenty-two of this part at which the respondent was not present, or was not represented by counsel and did not waive his or her right to counsel, the family court shall hold a hearing. Such hearing shall be held no later than the next court day after the filing of a petition to determine whether the child's interests require protection, including whether the child should be returned to the parent or other person legally responsible, pending a final order of disposition and shall continue on successive court days, if necessary, until a decision is made by the court.

(ii)   In any such case where the child has been removed, any person originating a proceeding under this article shall, or the law guardian may apply for, or the court on its own motion may order, a hearing at any time after the petition is filed to determine whether the child's interests require protection pending a final order of disposition. Such hearing must be scheduled for no later than the next court day after the application for such hearing has been made.

(iii)   In any case under this article in which a child has not been removed from his or her parent or other person legally responsible, any person originating a proceeding under this article or the law guardian may apply for, or the court on its own motion may order, a hearing at any time after the petition is filed to determine whether the child's interests require protection, including whether the child should be removed from his or her parent or other person legally responsible, pending a final order of disposition. Such hearing must be scheduled for no later than the next court day after the application for such hearing has been made.

(iv)   Notice of a hearing shall be provided pursuant to section one thousand twenty-three of this part.

(b)   (i) Upon such hearing, if the court finds that removal is necessary to avoid imminent risk to the child's life or health, it shall remove or continue the removal of the child. If the court makes such a determination that removal is necessary, the court shall immediately inquire as to the status of any efforts made by the local social services district to locate relatives of the child, including any non-respondent parent and all of the child's grandparents, as required pursuant to section one thousand seventeen of this article. The court shall also inquire as to whether the child, if over the age of five, has identified any relatives who play or have played a significant positive role in his or her life and whether any respondent parent or any non-respondent parent has identified any suitable relatives. Such inquiry shall include whether any relative who has been located has expressed an interest in becoming a foster parent for the child or in seeking custody or care of the child. Upon completion of such inquiry, the court shall remand or place the child:

(A)   with the local commissioner of social services and the court may direct such commissioner to have the child reside with a relative or other suitable person who has indicated a desire to become a foster parent for the child and further direct such commissioner, pursuant to regulations of the office of children and family services, to commence an investigation of the home of such relative or other suitable person within twenty-four hours and thereafter expedite approval or certification of such relative or other suitable person, if qualified, as a foster parent. If such home is found to be unqualified for approval or certification, the local commissioner shall report such fact to the court forthwith so that the court may make a placement determination that is in the best interests of the child;

(B) to a place approved for such purpose by the social services district; or

(C) in the custody of a relative or suitable person other than the respondent.

(ii) Such order shall state the court's findings which support the necessity of such removal, whether the respondent was present at the hearing and, if not, what notice the respondent was given of the hearing, and, where a pre-petition removal has occurred, whether such removal took place pursuant to section one thousand twenty-one, one thousand twenty-two or one thousand twenty-four of this part. If the parent or other person legally responsible for the child's care is physically present at the time the child is removed, and has not previously been served with the summons and petition, the summons and petition shall be served upon such parent or person coincident with such removal. If such parent or person is not physically present at the time the child is removed, service of the summons and petition shall be governed by section one thousand thirty-six of this article. In determining whether removal or continuing the removal of a child is necessary to avoid imminent risk to the child's life or health, the court shall consider and determine in its order whether continuation in the child's home would be contrary to the best interests of the child and where appropriate, whether reasonable efforts were made prior to the date of the hearing held under subdivision (a) of this section to prevent or eliminate the need for removal of the child from the home and, if the child was removed from his or her home prior to the date of the hearing held under subdivision (a) of this section, where appropriate, that reasonable efforts were made to make it possible for the child to safely return home.

(iii) If the court determines that reasonable efforts to prevent or eliminate the need for removal of the child from the home were not made but that the lack of such efforts was appropriate under the circumstances, the court order shall include such a finding.

(iv) If the court determines that reasonable efforts to prevent or eliminate the need for removal of the child from the home were not made but that such efforts were appropriate under the circumstances, the court shall order the child protective agency to provide or arrange for the provision of appropriate services or assistance to the child and the child's family pursuant to section one thousand fifteen-a or as enumerated in subdivision (c) of section one thousand twenty-two of this article, notwithstanding the fact that a petition has been filed.

(v) The court shall also consider and determine whether imminent risk to the child would be eliminated by the issuance of a temporary order of protection, pursuant to section one thousand twenty-nine of this part, directing the removal of a person or persons from the child's residence.

(c) Upon such hearing, the court may, for good cause shown, issue a preliminary order of protection which may contain any of the provisions authorized on the making of an order of protection under section one thousand fifty-six of this act.

(d) Upon such hearing, the court may, for good cause shown, release the child to the custody of his parent or other person legally responsible for his care, pending a final order of disposition, in accord with section one thousand fifty-four.

(e) Upon such hearing, the court may authorize a physician or hospital to provide medical or surgical procedures if such procedures are necessary to safeguard the child's life or health.

(f) If the court grants or denies a preliminary order requested pursuant to this section, it shall state the grounds for such decision.

(g) In all cases involving abuse the court shall order, and in all cases involving neglect the court may order, an examination of the child pursuant to section two hundred fifty-one of this act or by a physician appointed or designated for the purpose by the court. As part of such examination, the physician shall arrange to have colored photographs taken as soon as practical of the areas of trauma visible on such child and may, if indicated, arrange to have a radiological examination performed on the child. The physician, on the completion of such examination, shall forward the results thereof together with the color photographs to the court ordering such examination. The court may dispense with such examination in those cases which were commenced on the basis of a physical examination by a physician. Unless colored photographs have already been taken or unless there are no areas of visible trauma, the court shall arrange to have colored photographs taken even if the examination is dispensed with.

(h) At the conclusion of a hearing where it has been determined that a child should be removed from his or her parent or other person legally responsible, the court shall set a date certain for an initial permanency hearing pursuant to paragraph two of subdivision (a) of section one thousand eighty-nine of this act. The date certain shall be included in the written order issued pursuant to subdivision (b) of this section and shall set forth the date certain scheduled for the permanency hearing. A copy of such order shall be provided to the parent or other person legally responsible for the child's care.

Amended by Laws 1976, Ch. 880, eff. Nov. 29, 1976; Laws 1987, Ch. 469, eff. July 27, 1987; Laws 1988, Ch. 478, §§ 4, 5, eff. Nov. 1, 1988; Laws 1988, Ch. 527, § 4, eff. Aug. 11, 1988; Laws 1989, Ch. 727, § 4, eff. Oct. 1, 1989; Laws 1990, Ch. 171, § 2, eff. Sept. 1, 1990; Laws 1991, Ch. 198, eff. June 28, 1991; Laws 1994, Ch. 36, eff. Apr. 4, 1994; Laws 2000, Ch. 145, § 15, eff. July 1, 2000; Laws 2005, ch. 3, §15 (Part A), eff. Dec 21, 2005; Laws 2005, ch. 671, §2, eff. March 15, 2006. Laws 2006, ch. 12, §1, eff. March 15, 2006.

§ **1027-a. Placement of siblings.**

When a social services official removes a child pursuant to this part, such official shall place such child with his or her minor siblings or half-siblings who have been or are being remanded to or placed in the care and custody of such official unless, in the judgment of such official, such placement is contrary to the best interests of the children. Placement with siblings or half-siblings shall be presumptively in the child's best interests unless such placement would be contrary to the child's health, safety, or welfare. If such placement is not immediately available at the time of the removal of the child, such official shall provide or arrange for the provision of such placement within thirty days.

Added by Laws 1990, Ch. 854, § 3, eff. Sept. 1, 1990.

§ **1028. Application to return child temporarily removed.**

(a) Upon the application of the parent or other person legally responsible for the care of a child temporarily removed under this part or upon the application of the law guardian for an order returning the child, the court shall hold a hearing to determine whether the child should be returned (i) unless there has been a hearing pursuant to section ten hundred twenty-seven of this article on the removal of the child at which the parent or other person legally responsible was present and had the opportunity to be represented by counsel, or (ii) upon good cause shown. Except for good cause shown, such hearing shall be held within three court days of the application and shall not be adjourned. Upon such hearing, the court shall grant the application, unless it finds that the return presents an imminent risk to the child's life or health. If a parent or other person legally responsible for the care of a child waives his or her right to a hearing under this section, the court shall advise such person at that time that, notwithstanding such waiver, an application under this section may be made at any time during the pendency of the proceedings.

(b) In determining whether temporary removal of the child is necessary to avoid imminent risk to the child's life or health, the court shall consider and determine in its order whether continuation in the child's home would be contrary to the best interests of the child and where appropriate, whether reasonable efforts were made prior to the date of the hearing to prevent or eliminate the need for removal of the child from the home and where appropriate, whether reasonable efforts were made after removal of the child to make it possible for the child to safely return home.

(c) If the court determines that reasonable efforts to prevent or eliminate the need for removal of the child from the home were not made but that the lack of such efforts was appropriate under the circumstances, the court order shall include such a finding.

(d) If the court determines that reasonable efforts to prevent or eliminate the need for removal of the child from the home were not made but that such efforts were appropriate under the circumstances, the court shall order the child protective agency to provide or arrange for the provision of appropriate services or assistance to the child and the child's family pursuant to section one thousand fifteen-a or as enumerated in subdivision (c) of section one thousand twenty-two of this article, notwithstanding the fact that a petition has been filed.

(e) The court may issue a temporary order of protection pursuant to section ten hundred twenty-nine of this article as an alternative to or in conjunction with any other order or disposition authorized under this section.

(f) The court shall also consider and determine whether imminent risk to the child would be eliminated by the issuance of a temporary order of protection, pursuant to section ten hundred twenty-nine of this article, directing the removal of a person or persons from the child's residence.

Amended by Laws 1987, Ch. 469, eff. July 27, 1987; Laws 1988, Ch. 478, § 6, eff. Nov. 1, 1988; Laws 1988, Ch. 527, eff. Aug. 11, 1988; Laws 1988, Ch. 673, § 3, eff. Sept. 1, 1988; Laws 1989, Ch. 727, § 5, eff. Oct. 1, 1989; Laws 1990, Ch. 140, § 1, eff. Sept. 1, 1990; Laws 1991, Ch. 198, § 6, eff. June 28, 1991; Laws 1992, Ch. 697, § 1, eff. July 31, 1992; Laws 1994, Ch. 36, eff. Apr. 4, 1994; Laws 2000, Ch. 145, § 16, eff. July 1, 2000.

§ 1028-a. Application of a relative to become a foster parent.

(a) Upon the application of a relative to become a foster parent of a child in foster care, the court shall, subject to the provisions of this subdivision, hold a hearing to determine whether the child should be placed with a relative in foster care. Such hearing shall only be held if:

(i) the relative is related within the third degree of consanguinity to either parent;

(ii) the child has been temporarily removed under this part, or placed pursuant to section one thousand fifty-five of this article, and placed in non-relative foster care;

(iii) the relative indicates a willingness to become the foster parent for such child and has not refused previously to be considered as a foster parent or custodian of the child, provided, however, that an inability to provide immediate care for the child due to a lack of resources or inadequate housing, educational or other arrangements necessary to care appropriately for the child shall not constitute a previous refusal;

(iv) the local social services district has refused to place the child with the relative for reasons other than the relative's failure to qualify as a foster parent pursuant to the regulations of the office of children and family services; and

(v) the application is brought within six months from the date the relative received notice that the child was being removed or had been removed from his or her home and no later than twelve months from the date that the child was removed.

(b)   The court shall give due consideration to such application and shall make the determination as to whether the child should be placed in foster care with the relative based on the best interests of the child.

(c)   After such hearing, if the court determines that placement in foster care with the relative is in the best interests of the child, the court shall direct the local commissioner of social services, pursuant to regulations of the office of children and family services, to commence an investigation of the home of the relative within twenty-four hours and thereafter expedite approval or certification of such relative, if qualified, as a foster parent. No child, however, shall be placed with a relative prior to final approval or certification of such relative as a foster parent.

Added by Laws 2005, Ch. 671, §3, eff. March 15, 2006; **Amended** by Laws 2006, ch. 12, §2, eff. March 15, 2006.

§ 1029.   Temporary order of protection.

(a)   The family court, upon the application of any person who may originate a proceeding under this article, for good cause shown, may issue a temporary order of protection, before or after the filing of such petition, which may contain any of the provisions authorized on the making of an order of protection under section ten hundred fifty-six. If such order is granted before the filing of a petition and a petition is not filed under this article within ten days from the granting of such order, the order shall be vacated. In any case where a petition has been filed and a law guardian appointed, such law guardian may make application for a temporary order of protection pursuant to the provisions of this section.

(b)   A temporary order of protection is not a finding of wrongdoing.

(c)   The court may issue or extend a temporary order of protection ex parte or on notice simultaneously with the issuance of a warrant directing that the respondent be arrested and brought before the court pursuant to section ten hundred thirty-seven of this article.

(d)   Nothing in this section shall: (i) limit the power of the court to order removal of a child pursuant to this article where the court finds that there is imminent danger to a child's life or health; or (ii) limit the authority of authorized persons to remove a child without a court order pursuant to section one thousand twenty-four of this article; or (iii) be construed to authorize the court to award permanent custody of a child to a parent or relative pursuant to a temporary order of protection.

Added by Laws 1975, Ch. 495, eff. July 29, 1975; **amended** by Laws 1981, Ch. 416, eff. Aug. 6, 1981; Laws 1987, Ch. 67, § 1, eff. May 16, 1987; Laws 1988, Ch. 673, § 4, eff. Sept. 1, 1988.

§ 1030.   Order of visitation by a respondent.

(a)   A respondent shall have the right to reasonable and regularly scheduled visitation with a child in the temporary custody of a social services official pursuant to this part or pursuant to subdivision (d) of section one thousand fifty-one of this article, unless limited by an order of the family court.

(b)　A respondent who has not been afforded such visitation may apply to the court for an order requiring the local social services official having temporary custody of the child pursuant to this part or pursuant to subdivision (d) of section one thousand fifty-one of this article, to permit the respondent to visit the child at stated periods. Such application shall be made upon notice to the local social services official and to any law guardian appointed to represent the child, who shall be afforded an opportunity to be heard thereon.

(c)　A respondent shall be granted reasonable and regularly scheduled visitation unless the court finds that the child's life or health would be endangered thereby, but the court may order visitation under the supervision of an employee of a local social services department upon a finding that such supervised visitation is in the best interest of the child.

(d)　An order made under this section may be modified by the court for good cause shown, upon application by any party or the child's law guardian, and upon notice of such application to all other parties and the child's law guardian, who shall be afforded an opportunity to be heard thereon.

(e)　An order made under this section shall terminate upon the entry of an order of disposition pursuant to part five of this article.

　　Added by Laws 1988, Ch. 457, § 4, eff. Nov. 1, 1988.

Part 3.　Preliminary procedure

§ 1031.　Originating proceeding to determine abuse or neglect.

(a)　A proceeding under this article is originated by the filing of a petition in which facts sufficient to establish that a child is an abused or neglected child under this article are alleged.

(b)   Allegations of abuse and neglect may be contained in the same petition. Where more than one child is the legal responsibility of the respondent, it may be alleged in the same petition that one or more children are abused children, or that one or more children are neglected children, or both.

(c)   On its own motion and at any time in the proceedings, the court may substitute for a petition to determine abuse a petition to determine neglect if the facts established are not sufficient to make a finding of abuse, as defined by this article.

(d)   A proceeding under this article may be originated by a child protective agency pursuant to section one thousand thirty-two, notwithstanding that the child is in the care and custody of such agency. In such event, the petition shall allege facts sufficient to establish that the return of the child to the care and custody of his parent or other person legally responsible for his care would place the child in imminent danger of becoming an abused or neglected child.

(e)   In any case where a child has been removed prior to the filing of a petition, the petition alleging abuse or neglect of said child shall state the date and time of the removal, the circumstances necessitating such removal, whether the removal occurred pursuant to section ten hundred twenty-one, ten hundred twenty-two or ten hundred twenty-four of this act, and if the removal occurred without court order, the reason there was not sufficient time to obtain a court order pursuant to section ten hundred twenty-two of this act.

(f)   A petition alleging abuse shall contain a notice in conspicuous print that a fact-finding that a child is severely or repeatedly abused as defined in subdivision eight of section three hundred eighty-four-b of the social services law, by clear and convincing evidence, could constitute a basis to terminate parental rights in a proceeding pursuant to section three hundred eighty-four-b of the social services law.

Amended by Laws 1976, Ch. 666, eff. Jan. 1, 1977; Laws 1990, Ch. 171, § 3, eff. Sept. 1, 1990; Laws 1999, Ch. 7, § 41, eff. Feb. 11, 1999.

§ 1032.   Persons who may originate proceedings.

The following may originate a proceeding under this article:

(a)   a child protective agency, or

(b)   a person on the court's direction.

Former § 1032 **repealed** and new § 1032 **added** by Laws 1973, Ch. 1039, eff. Sept. 1, 1973.

§ 1033.   Access to the court for the purpose of filing a petition.

Any person seeking to file a petition at the court's direction, pursuant to subdivision (b) of section one thousand thirty-two shall have access to the court for the purpose of making an ex parte application therefor. Nothing in this section, however, is intended to prevent a family court judge from requiring such person to first report to an appropriate child protective agency.

Former § 1033 **repealed** and new § 1033 **added** by Laws 1973, Ch. 1039, eff. Sept. 1, 1973.

§ 1033-a.   Initial appearance.

For the purposes of this section, "initial appearance" means the proceeding on the date the respondent first appears before the court after the petition has been filed and any adjournments thereof.

Added by Laws 1990, Ch. 336, § 1, eff. Sept. 1, 1990.

§ 1033-b.   Initial appearance; procedures.

1.   (a) At the initial appearance, the court shall appoint a law guardian to represent the interests of any child named in a petition who is alleged to be abused or neglected, unless a law guardian has already been appointed for such child pursuant to section ten hundred sixteen of this act.

(b)   At the initial appearance, the court shall advise the respondent of the allegations in the petition and further advise the respondent of the right to an adjournment of the proceeding in order to obtain counsel. The recitation of such rights shall not be waived except that the recitation of the allegations in the petition may be waived upon the consent of the counsel for the respondent and such counsel's representation on the record that he or she has explained such allegations to the respondent and has provided the respondent with a copy of the petition and the respondent's acknowledgment of receipt of the petition and such explanation.

(c)   At the initial appearance, the court shall appoint counsel for indigent respondents pursuant to section two hundred sixty-two of this act.

(d)   In any case where a child has been removed, the court shall advise the respondent of the right to a hearing, pursuant to section ten hundred twenty-eight of this act, for the return of the child and that such hearing may be requested at any time during the proceeding. The recitation of such rights shall not be waived.

(e)   At the initial appearance, the court shall inquire of the child protective agency whether such agency intends to prove that the child is a severely or repeatedly abused child as defined in subdivision eight of section three hundred eighty-four-b of the social services law, by clear and convincing evidence. Where the agency advises the court that it intends to submit such proof, the court shall so advise the respondent.

2.   * Notice of the initial appearance shall be given to the respondent or the respondent's attorney if known, the petitioner and the child's law guardian, if already appointed.

[*FCA § 1033–b(2) was repealed by Laws 1991, Ch. 69, § 2, eff. April 22, 1991.*]

Added by Laws 1990, Ch. 336, § 1, eff. Sept. 1, 1990; **amended** by Laws 1991, Ch. 69, § 2, eff. Apr. 22, 1991; Laws 1991, Ch. 75, § 1, eff. Apr. 26, 1991; Laws 1992, Ch. 111, § 1, eff. May 21, 1992; Laws 1999, Ch. 7, § 42, eff. Feb. 11, 1999.

* **Editor's Note:** FCA § 1033–b(2) was repealed by Laws 1991, Ch. 69, § 2, eff. Apr. 22, 1991. However, FCA § 1033–b was subsequently amended by Laws 1991, Ch. 75, § 1, eff. Apr. 26, 1991, which left FCA § 1033–b(2) unaltered and made no reference to its repeal by Laws 1991, Ch. 69, § 2.

§ 1034.   Power to order investigations.

1.   A family court judge may order the child protective service of the appropriate department of social services or request any other appropriate child protective agency to conduct a child protective investigation as described by the social services law and report its findings to the court:

(a)   in any proceedings under this article, or

(b)   in order to determine whether a proceeding under this article should be initiated.

2.   Where there is probable cause to believe that an abused or neglected child may be found on premises, an order under this section may authorize a person conducting the child protective investigation, accompanied by a police officer, to enter the premises to determine whether such a child is present. The standard of proof and procedure for such an authorization shall be the same as for a search warrant under the criminal procedure law.

Former § 1034 **repealed** and new § 1034 **added** by Laws 1973, Ch. 1039, eff. Sept. 1, 1973; **amended** by Laws 1978, Ch. 627, eff. Sept. 1, 1978.

§ 1035.   Issuance of summons; notice to certain interested persons and intervention.

(a)   On the filing of a petition under this article where the child has been removed from his or her home, unless a warrant is issued pursuant to section one thousand thirty-seven of this part, the court shall cause a copy of the petition and a summons to be issued the same day the petition is filed, clearly marked on the face thereof "Child Abuse Case", as applicable, requiring the parent or other person legally responsible for the child's care or with whom he or she had been residing to appear at the court within three court days to answer the petition, unless a shorter time for a hearing to occur is prescribed in part two of this article.

(b)   In a proceeding to determine abuse or neglect, the summons shall contain a statement in conspicuous print informing the respondent that:

(i)   the proceeding may lead to the filing of a petition under the social services law for the termination of respondent's parental rights and commitment of guardianship and custody of the child for the purpose of adoption; and

(ii) if the child is placed and remains in foster care for fifteen of the most recent twenty-two months, the agency may be required by law to file a petition for termination of respondent's parental rights and commitment of guardianship and custody of the child for the purposes of adoption.

(c) On the filing of a petition under this article where the child has not been removed from his or her home, the court shall forthwith cause a copy of the petition and a summons to be issued, clearly marked on the face thereof "Child Abuse Case", as applicable, requiring the parent or other person legally responsible for the child's care or with whom the child is residing to appear at the court to answer the petition within seven court days. The court may also require the person thus summoned to produce the child at the time and place named.

(d) Where the respondent is not the child's parent, service of the summons and petition shall also be ordered on both of the child's parents; where only one of the child's parents is the respondent, service of the summons and petition shall also be ordered on the child's other parent. The summons and petition shall be accompanied by a notice of pendency of the child protective proceeding advising the parents or parent of the right to appear and participate in the proceeding as an interested party intervenor for the purpose of seeking temporary and permanent custody of the child, and to participate thereby in all arguments and hearings insofar as they affect the temporary custody of the child during fact-finding proceedings, and in all phases of dispositional proceedings. The notice shall also indicate that:

(i) upon good cause, the court may order an investigation pursuant to section one thousand thirty-four of this part to determine whether a petition should be filed naming such parent or parents as respondents;

(ii) if the court determines that the child must be removed from his or her home, the court may order an investigation to determine whether the non-respondent parent or parents would be suitable custodians for the child; and

(iii) if the child is placed and remains in foster care for fifteen of the most recent twenty-two months, the agency may be required by law to file a petition for termination of the parental rights of the parent or parents and commitment of guardianship and custody of the child for the purposes of adoption, even if the parent or parents were not named as a respondent or as respondents in the child abuse or neglect proceeding.

(e) The summons, petition and notice of pendency of a child protective proceeding served on the child's non-custodial parent in accordance with subdivision (d) of this section shall, if applicable, be served together with a notice that the child was removed from his or her home by a social services official. Such notice shall also include the name and address of the official to whom temporary custody of the child has been transferred, the name and address of the agency or official with whom the child has been temporarily placed, if different, and shall advise such parent of the right to request temporary and permanent custody and to seek enforcement of visitation rights with the child as provided for in part eight of this article.

(f) The child's adult sibling, grandparent, aunt or uncle not named as respondent in the petition, may, upon consent of the child's parent appearing in the proceeding, or where such parent has not appeared then without such consent, move to intervene in the proceeding as an interested party intervenor for the purpose of seeking temporary or permanent custody of the child, and upon the granting of such motion shall be permitted to participate in all arguments and hearings insofar as they affect the temporary custody of the child during fact-finding proceedings, and in all phases of dispositional proceedings. Such motions for intervention shall be liberally granted.

Amended by Laws 1981, Ch. 739, eff. Oct. 26, 1981; the Laws 1986, Ch. 699, eff. Aug. 29, 1986; Laws 1987, Ch. 443, eff. July 27, 1987; Laws 1988, Ch. 457, § 5, eff. Nov. 1, 1988; Laws 2003, Ch. 526, §§ 1, 2 & 3, eff. Dec. 16, 2003, amending sub. (b), (d), and (e); L. 2005, Ch. 3, § 16, eff. Aug. 23, 2005.

§ 1036. Service of summons.

(a) Except as provided in subdivision (c) of this section, in cases involving abuse, the petition and summons shall be served within two court days after their issuance. If they cannot be served within that time, such fact shall be reported to the court with the reasons thereof within three court days after their issuance and the court shall thereafter issue a warrant in accordance with the provisions of section one thousand thirty-seven. The court shall also, unless dispensed with for good cause shown, direct that the child be brought before the court. Issuance of a warrant shall not be required where process is sent without the state as provided for in subdivision (c) of this section.

(b) Service of a summons and petition shall be made by delivery of a true copy thereof to the person summoned at least twenty-four hours before the time stated therein for appearance.

(c) In cases involving either abuse or neglect, the court may send process without the state in the same manner and with the same effect as process sent within the state in the exercise of personal jurisdiction over any person subject to the jurisdiction of the court under section three hundred one or three hundred two of the civil practice law and rules, notwithstanding that such person is not a resident or domiciliary of the state, where the allegedly abused or neglected child resides or is domiciled within the state and the alleged abuse or neglect occurred within the state. In cases involving abuse where service of a petition and summons upon a non-resident or non-domiciliary respondent is required, such service shall be made within ten days after its issuance. if service can not be effected in ten days, an extension of the period to effect service may be granted by the court for good cause shown upon application of any party or the law guardian. Where service is effected on an out of state respondent and the respondent defaults by failing to appear to answer the petition, the court may on its own motion, or upon application of any party or the law guardian proceed to a fact finding hearing thereon.

FCA

(d)   If after reasonable effort, personal service is not made, the court may at any stage in the proceedings make an order providing for substituted service in the manner provided for substituted service in civil process in courts of record.

Amended by Laws 1990, Ch. 268, § 1, eff. Sept. 1, 1990; Laws 1991, Ch. 69, § 1, eff. Apr. 22, 1991.

§ 1037.   Issuance of warrant and reports to court.

(a)   The court may issue a warrant directing the parent, or other person legally responsible for the child's care or with whom he is residing to be brought before the court, when a petition is filed with the court under this article and it appears that (i) the summons cannot be served; or

(ii)   the summoned person has refused to obey the summons; or

(iii)   the parent or other person legally responsible for the child's care is likely to leave the jurisdiction; or

(iv)   a summons, in the court's opinion, would be ineffectual; or

(v)   the safety of the child is endangered; or

(vi)   the safety of a parent, person legally responsible for the child's care or with whom he is residing, foster parent or temporary custodian is endangered.

(b)   When issuing a warrant under this section, the court may also direct that the child be brought before the court.

(c)   In any case involving abuse, the warrant shall be clearly marked on the face thereof Child Abuse Case. If a warrant is not executed within two court days of its issuance, such fact shall be reported to the court within three court days of its issuance. Rules of court shall provide that reports of unexecuted warrants issued under this article shall be periodically made to the court.

(d)   In a proceeding to determine abuse, the warrant shall contain a statement clearly marked on the face thereof, that the proceeding could lead to a proceeding under the social services law for the commitment of guardianship and custody of the child and that the rights of the respondent with respect to said child may be terminated in such proceeding under such law.

Amended by Laws 1981, Ch. 739, eff. Oct. 26, 1981; Laws 1988, Ch. 271, § 3, eff. July 19, 1988.

§ 1038.   Records and discovery involving abuse and neglect.

(a)   Each hospital and any other public or private agency having custody of any records, photographs or other evidence relating to abuse or neglect, upon the subpoena of the court, the corporation counsel, county attorney, district attorney, counsel for the child, or one of the parties to the proceeding, shall be required to send such records, photographs or evidence to the court for use in any proceeding relating to abuse or neglect under this article. Notwithstanding any other provision of law to the contrary, service of any such subpoena on a hospital may be made by certified mail, return receipt requested, to the director of the hospital. The court shall establish procedures for the receipt and safeguarding of such records.

(b) Pursuant to a demand pursuant to section thirty-one hundred twenty of the civil practice law and rules, a petitioner or social services official shall provide to a respondent or the law guardian any records, photographs or other evidence demanded relevant to the proceeding, for inspection and photocopying. The petitioner or social services official may delete the identity of the persons who filed reports pursuant to section four hundred fifteen of the social services law, unless such petitioner or official intends to offer such reports into evidence at a hearing held pursuant to this article. The petitioner or social services official may move for a protective order to withhold records, photographs or evidence which will not be offered into evidence and the disclosure of which is likely to endanger the life or health of the child.

(c) A respondent or the law guardian may move for an order directing that any child who is the subject of a proceeding under this article be made available for examination by a physician, psychologist or social worker selected by such party or law guardian. In determining the motion, the court shall consider the need of the respondent or law guardian for such examination to assist in the preparation of the case and the potential harm to the child from the examination. Nothing in this section shall preclude the parties from agreeing upon a person to conduct such examination without court order.

Any examination or interview, other than a physical examination, of a child who is the subject of a proceeding under this article, for the purposes of offering expert testimony to a court regarding the sexual abuse of the child, as such term is defined by section one thousand twelve of this article, may, in the discretion of the court, be videotaped in its entirety with access to be provided to the court, the law guardian and all parties. In determining whether such examination or interview should be videotaped, the court shall consider the effect of the videotaping on the reliability of the examination, the effect of the videotaping on the child and the needs of the parties, including the law guardian, for the videotape. Prior to admitting a videotape of an examination or interview into evidence, the person conducting such examination or the person operating the video camera shall submit to the court a verified statement confirming that such videotape is a complete and unaltered videographic record of such examination of the child. The proponent of entry of the videotape into evidence must establish that the potential prejudicial effect is substantially outweighed by the probative value of the videotape in assessing the reliability of the validator in court. Nothing in this section shall in any way affect the admissibility of such evidence in any other court proceeding. The chief administrator of the courts shall promulgate regulations protecting the confidentiality and security of such tapes, and regulating the access thereto, consistent with the provisions of this section.

(d)   Unless otherwise proscribed by this article, the provisions and limitations of article thirty-one of the civil practice law and rules shall apply to proceedings under this article. In determining any motion for a protective order, the court shall consider the need of the party for the discovery to assist in the preparation of the case and any potential harm to the child from the discovery. The court shall set a schedule for discovery to avoid unnecessary delay.

> **Amended** by Laws 1989, Ch. 272, eff. July 7, 1989; Laws 1989, Ch. 724, eff. July 24, 1989; Laws 1990, Ch. 867, § 1, eff. Sept. 1, 1990; Laws 1991, Ch. 694, § 1, eff. Oct. 31, 1991; Laws 1992, Ch. 65, § 1, eff. July 13, 1992.

§ 1038-a.   Discovery: upon court order.

Upon motion of a petitioner or law guardian, the court may order a respondent to provide nontestimonial evidence, only if the court finds probable cause that the evidence is reasonably related to establishing the allegations in a petition filed pursuant to this article. Such order may include, but not be limited to, provision for the taking of samples of blood, urine, hair or other materials from the respondent's body in a manner not involving an unreasonable intrusion or risk of serious physical injury to the respondent.

> **Added** by Laws 1987, Ch. 793, eff. Aug. 7, 1987; **amended** by Laws 1991, Ch. 162, eff. June 10, 1991.

§ 1039.   Adjournment in contemplation of dismissal.

(a)   Prior to or upon a fact-finding hearing, the court may upon a motion by the petitioner with the consent of the respondent and the child's attorney or law guardian or upon its own motion with the consent of the petitioner, the respondent and the child's attorney or law guardian, order that the proceeding be "adjourned in contemplation of dismissal." Under no circumstances shall the court order any party to consent to an order under this section. The court may make such order only after it has apprised the respondent of the provisions of this section and it is satisfied that the respondent understands the effect of such provisions.

(b)   An adjournment in contemplation of dismissal is an adjournment of the proceeding for a period not to exceed one year with a view to ultimate dismissal of the petition in furtherance of justice. Upon the consent of the petitioner, the respondent and the child's attorney or law guardian, the court may issue an order extending such period for such time and upon such conditions as may be agreeable to the parties.

(c)   Such order may include terms and conditions agreeable to the parties and to the court, provided that such terms and conditions shall include a requirement that the child and the respondent be under the supervision of a child protective agency during the adjournment period. In any order issued pursuant to this section, such agency shall be directed to make a progress report to the court, the parties and the child's law guardian on the implementation of such order, no later than ninety days after the issuance of such order, unless the court determines that the facts and circumstances of the case do not require such reports to be made. The child protective agency shall make further reports to the court, the parties and the law guardian in such manner and at such times as the court may direct.

(d) Upon application of the respondent, the petitioner, the child's attorney or law guardian or upon the court's own motion, made at any time during the duration of the order, if the child protective agency has failed substantially to provide the respondent with adequate supervision or to observe the terms and conditions of the order, the court may direct the child protective agency to observe such terms and conditions and provide adequate supervision or may make any order authorized pursuant to section two hundred fifty-five of this act.

(e) Upon application of the petitioner or the child's attorney or law guardian, or upon the court's own motion, made at any time during the duration of the order, the court may restore the matter to the calendar, if the court finds after a hearing that the respondent has failed substantially to observe the terms and conditions of the order or to cooperate with the supervising child protective agency. In such event, unless the parties consent to an order pursuant to section one thousand fifty-one of this act or unless the petition is dismissed upon the consent of the petitioner, the court shall thereupon proceed to a fact finding hearing under this article no later than sixty days after such application unless such period is extended by the court for good cause shown.

(f) If the proceeding is not so restored to the calendar, the petition is, at the expiration of the adjournment period, deemed to have been dismissed by the court in furtherance of justice unless an application is pending pursuant to subdivision (e) of this section. If such application is granted the petition shall not be dismissed and shall proceed in accordance with the provisions of such subdivision (e).

(g) Notwithstanding the provisions of this section, the court, may, at any time prior to dismissal of the petition pursuant to subdivision (f), issue an order authorized pursuant to section one thousand twenty-seven.

     Added by Laws 1975, Ch. 707, eff. Aug. 9, 1975; **amended** by Laws 1985, Ch. 601, eff. Nov. 25, 1985; Laws 1990, Ch. 167, § 1, eff. May 21, 1990; Laws 1990, Ch. 194, § 1, eff. Sept. 1, 1990; Laws 1990, Ch. 323, § 1, eff. Sept. 1, 1990.

§ 1039-a. Procedures following adjournment in contemplation of dismissal.

The local child protective service shall notify the child's law guardian of an indicated report of child abuse or maltreatment in which the respondent is a subject of the report or another person named in the report, as such terms are defined in section four hundred twelve of the social services law, while any order issued pursuant to section ten hundred thirty-nine or extension thereof remains in effect.

Added by Laws 1990, Ch. 317, § 2, eff. Sept. 1, 1990; amended by Laws 1991, Ch. 69, § 3, eff. Apr. 22, 1991.

§ 1039-b.   Termination of reasonable efforts.

(a)   In conjunction with, or at any time subsequent to, the filing of a petition under section ten hundred thirty-one of this chapter, the social services official may file a motion upon notice requesting a finding that reasonable efforts to return the child to his or her home are no longer required.

(b)   For the purpose of this section, reasonable efforts to make it possible for the child to return safely to his or her home shall not be required where the court determines that:

(1)   the parent of such child has subjected the child to aggravated circumstances, as defined in subdivision (j) of section ten hundred twelve of this article;

(2)   the parent of such child has been convicted of (i) murder in the first degree as defined in section 125.27 or murder in the second degree as defined in section 125.25 of the penal law and the victim was another child of the parent; or (ii) manslaughter in the first degree as defined in section 125.20 or manslaughter in the second degree as defined in section 125.15 of the penal law and the victim was another child of the parent, provided, however, that the parent must have acted voluntarily in committing such crime;

(3)   the parent of such child has been convicted of an attempt to commit any of the foregoing crimes, and the victim or intended victim was the child or another child of the parent; or has been convicted of criminal solicitation as defined in article one hundred, conspiracy as defined in article one hundred five or criminal facilitation as defined in article one hundred fifteen of the penal law for conspiring, soliciting or facilitating any of the foregoing crimes, and the victim or intended victim was the child or another child of the parent;

(4)   the parent of such child has been convicted of assault in the second degree as defined in section 120.05, assault in the first degree as defined in section 120.10 or aggravated assault upon a person less than eleven years old as defined in section 120.12 of the penal law, and the commission of one of the foregoing crimes resulted in serious physical injury to the child or another child of the parent;

(5)   the parent of such child has been convicted in any other jurisdiction of an offense which includes all of the essential elements of any crime specified in paragraph two, three or four of this subdivision, and the victim of such offense was the child or another child of the parent; or

(6)   the parental rights of the parent to a sibling of such child have been involuntarily terminated; unless the court determines that providing reasonable efforts would be in the best interests of the child, not contrary to the health and safety of the child, and would likely result in the reunification of the parent and the child in the foreseeable future. The court shall state such findings in its order.

If the court determines that reasonable efforts are not required because of one of the grounds set forth above, a permanency hearing shall be held within thirty days of the finding of the court that such efforts are not required. At the permanency hearing, the court shall determine the appropriateness of the permanency plan prepared by the social services official which shall include whether or when the child: (i) will be returned to the parent; (ii) should be placed for adoption with the social services official filing a petition for termination of parental rights; (iii) should be referred for legal guardianship; (iv) should be placed permanently with a fit and willing relative; or (v) should be placed in another planned permanent living arrangement if the social services official has documented to the court a compelling reason for determining that it would not be in the best interest of the child to return home, be referred for termination of parental rights and placed for adoption, placed with a fit and willing relative, or placed with a legal guardian. The social services official shall thereafter make reasonable efforts to place the child in a timely manner and to complete whatever steps are necessary to finalize the permanent placement of the child as set forth in the permanency plan approved by the court. If reasonable efforts are determined by the court not to be required because of one of the grounds set forth in this paragraph, the social services official may file a petition for termination of parental rights in accordance with section three hundred eighty-four-b of the social services law.

(c)   For the purpose of this section, in determining reasonable effort to be made with respect to a child, and in making such reasonable efforts, the child's health and safety shall be the paramount concern; and

(d)   For the purpose of this section, a sibling shall include a half-sibling.

   Added by Laws 1999, Ch. 7, § 43, eff. Feb. 11, 1999.

Part 4. Hearings.

§ 1040.   Notice and opportunity to be heard.

   The foster parent caring for the child or any pre-adoptive parent or relative providing care for the child shall be provided with notice of any permanency hearing held pursuant to this article by the social services official. Such foster parent, pre-adoptive parent or relative shall be afforded an opportunity to be heard at any such hearing; provided, however, no such foster parent, pre-adoptive parent or relative shall be construed to be a party to the hearing solely on the basis of such notice and opportunity to be heard. The failure of the foster parent, pre-adoptive parent, or relative caring for the child to appear at a permanency hearing shall constitute a waiver of the opportunity to be heard and such failure to appear shall not cause a delay of the permanency hearing nor shall such failure to appear be a ground for the invalidation of any order issued by the court pursuant to this section.

Added by Laws 1999, Ch. 7, § 44, eff. Feb. 11, 1999.

§ 1041.   Required findings concerning notice.

No fact finding hearing may commence under this article unless the court enters a finding:

(a)   that the parent or other person legally responsible for the child's care is present at the hearing and has been served with a copy of the petition; or

(b)   if the parent or other person legally responsible for the care of the child is not present, that every reasonable effort has been made to effect service under section ten hundred thirty-six or ten hundred thirty-seven.

Amended by Laws 1972, Ch. 1015, eff. Aug. 7, 1972.

§ 1042.   Effect of absence of parent or other person responsible for care.

If the parent or other person legally responsible for the child's care is not present, the court may proceed to hear a petition under this article only if the child is represented by counsel, a law guardian, or a guardian ad litem. The parent or other person legally responsible for the child's care shall be served with a copy of the order of disposition with written notice of its entry pursuant to section one thousand thirty-six of this article. Within one year of such service or substituted service pursuant to section one thousand thirty-six of this article, the parent or other person legally responsible for the child's care may move to vacate the order of disposition and schedule a rehearing. Such motion shall be granted on an affidavit showing such relationship or responsibility and a meritorious defense to the petition, unless the court finds that the parent or other person willfully refused to appear at the hearing, in which case the court may deny the motion.

Add, L 1970, ch 962, §9, eff May 1, 1970, with substance transferred from former §342; also, derived in part from former §1016; Amd, L 2005, ch 3, §4 (Part B), eff Nov 21, 2005; L. 2005, Ch. 3, §   4, eff. Aug. 23, 2005.

§ 1043. Hearings not open to the public.

The general public may be excluded from any hearing under this article and only such persons and the representatives of authorized agencies admitted thereto as have an interest in the case.

    Amended by Laws 1973, Ch. 615, eff. July 1, 1973; Laws 1975, Ch. 682, eff. Jan. 1, 1976.

§ 1044. Definition of "fact-finding hearing."

When used in this article, "fact-finding hearing" means a hearing to determine whether the child is an abused or neglected child as defined by this article.

§ 1045. Definition of "dispositional hearing."

When used in this article, "dispositional hearing" means a hearing to determine what order of disposition should be made.

§ 1046. Evidence.

   (a)   In any hearing under this article

   (i)   proof of the abuse or neglect of one child shall be admissible evidence on the issue of the abuse or neglect of any other child of, or the legal responsibility of, the respondent; and

   (ii)   proof of injuries sustained by a child or of the condition of a child of such a nature as would ordinarily not be sustained or exist except by reason of the acts or omissions of the parent or other person responsible for the care of such child shall be prima facie evidence of child abuse or neglect, as the case may be, of the parent or other person legally responsible; and

   (iii)   proof that a person repeatedly misuses a drug or drugs or alcoholic beverages, to the extent that it has or would ordinarily have the effect of producing in the user thereof a substantial state of stupor, unconsciousness, intoxication, hallucination, disorientation, or incompetence, or a substantial impairment of judgment, or a substantial manifestation of irrationality, shall be prima facie evidence that a child of or who is the legal responsibility of such person is a neglected child except that such drug or alcoholic beverage misuse shall not be prima facie evidence of neglect when such person is voluntarily and regularly participating in a recognized rehabilitative program; and

   (iv)   any writing, record or photograph, whether in the form of an entry in a book or otherwise, made as a memorandum or record of any condition, act, transaction, occurrence or event relating to a child in an abuse or neglect proceeding of any hospital or any other public or private agency shall be admissible in evidence in proof of that condition, act, transaction, occurrence or event, if the judge finds that it was made in the regular course of the business of any hospital, or any other public or private agency and that it was in the regular course of such business to make it, at the time of the act, transaction, occurrence or event, or within a reasonable time thereafter. A certification by the head of or by a responsible employee of the hospital or agency that the writing, record or photograph is the full and complete record of said condition, act, transaction, occurrence or event and that it was made in the regular course of the business of the hospital or agency and that it was in the regular course of such business to make it, at the time of the condition, act, transaction, occurrence or event, or within a reasonable time thereafter, shall be prima facie evidence of the facts contained in such certification. A certification by someone other than the head of the hospital or agency shall be accompanied by a photocopy of a delegation of authority signed by both the head of the hospital or agency and by such other employee. All other circumstances of the making of the memorandum, record or photograph, including lack of personal knowledge of the maker, may be proved to affect its weight, but they shall not affect its admissibility; and

(v) any report filed with the statewide central register of child abuse and maltreatment by a person or official required to do so pursuant to section four hundred thirteen of the social services law shall be admissible in evidence; and

(vi) previous statements made by the child relating to any allegations of abuse or neglect shall be admissible in evidence, but if uncorroborated, such statements shall not be sufficient to make a fact-finding of abuse or neglect. Any other evidence tending to support the reliability of the previous statements, including, but not limited to the types of evidence defined in this subdivision shall be sufficient corroboration. The testimony of the child shall not be necessary to make a fact-finding of abuse or neglect; and

(vii) neither the privilege attaching to confidential communications between husband and wife, as set forth in section forty-five hundred two of the civil practice law and rules, nor the physician-patient and related privileges, as set forth in section forty-five hundred four of the civil practice law and rules, nor the psychologist-client privilege, as set forth in section forty-five hundred seven of the civil practice law and rules, nor the social worker-client privilege, as set forth in section forty-five hundred eight of the civil practice law and rules, nor the rape crisis counselor-client privilege, as set forth in section forty-five hundred ten of the civil practice law and rules, shall be a ground for excluding evidence which otherwise would be admissible.

(viii) proof of the "impairment of emotional health" or "impairment of mental or emotional condition" as a result of the unwillingness or inability of the respondent to exercise a minimum degree of care toward a child may include competent opinion or expert testimony and may include proof that such impairment lessened during a period when the child was in the care, custody or supervision of a person or agency other than the respondent.

(b) In a fact-finding hearing:

(i) any determination that the child is an abused or neglected child must be based on a preponderance of evidence;

(ii) whenever a determination of severe or repeated abuse is based upon clear and convincing evidence, the fact-finding order shall state that such determination is based on clear and convincing evidence; and

(iii) except as otherwise provided by this article, only competent, material and relevant evidence may be admitted.

(c) In a dispositional hearing and during all other stages of a proceeding under this article, except a fact-finding hearing, only material and relevant evidence may be admitted.

Amended by Laws 1972, Ch. 1015, eff. Aug. 7, 1972; Laws 1979, Ch. 81, eff. Aug. 8, 1979; Laws 1981, Ch. 64, eff. Apr. 8, 1981; Laws 1981, Ch. 984, eff. July 31, 1981; Laws 1985, Ch. 724, eff. Aug. 1, 1985; Laws 1993, Ch. 432, § 3, eff. Jan. 22, 1994; Laws 1999, Ch. 7, § 45, eff. Feb. 11, 1999.

§ 1047. Sequence of hearings.

(a) Upon completion of the fact-finding hearing, the dispositional hearing may commence immediately after the required findings are made.

(b) Reports prepared by the probation service or a duly authorized association, agency, society or institution for use by the court at any time for the making of an order of disposition shall be deemed confidential information furnished to the court which the court shall make available for inspection and copying by all counsel. The court may, in its discretion, withhold from disclosure a part or parts of the reports which are not relevant to a proper disposition, or sources of information which have been obtained on a promise of confidentiality, or any other portion thereof, disclosure of which would not be in the interests of justice or in the best interests of the child. In all cases where a part or parts of the reports are not disclosed, the court shall state for the record that a part or parts of the reports have been excepted and the reasons for its action. The action of the court excepting information from disclosure shall be subject to review on appeal from the order of disposition. Such reports may not be furnished to the court prior to the completion of a fact-finding hearing, but may be used in a dispositional hearing.

Amended by Laws 1988, Ch. 102, § 1, eff. Jun. 3, 1988.

§ 1048. Adjournments.

(a) The court may adjourn a fact-finding hearing or a dispositional hearing for good cause shown on its own motion, or on motion of the corporation counsel, county attorney or district attorney, or on motion of the petitioner or on motion of the child or on his behalf or of the parent or other person legally responsible for the care of the child. If so requested by the parent or other person legally responsible for the care of the child, the court shall not proceed with a fact-finding hearing earlier than three days after service of summons and petition, unless

FCA

emergency medical or surgical procedures are necessary to safeguard the life or health of the child.

(b) At the conclusion of a fact-finding hearing and after the court has made findings required before a dispositional hearing may commence, the court on its own motion or motion of the respondent, the petitioner or the law guardian order a reasonable adjournment of the proceedings, to enable the court to make inquiry into the surroundings, conditions, and capacities of the persons involved in the proceedings.

(c) Whenever a child has been remanded to the care of an agency or institution under section ten hundred fifty-one of this article, notice of any dispositional hearing shall be served upon the agency or institution with whom the child was placed and upon the agency supervising the care of the child on behalf of the agency with whom the child was placed. Service of notice of the adjourned hearing shall be made in such manner and on such notice as the court may, in its discretion, prescribe. Any such agency or institution served with notice pursuant to this subdivision may apply to the court for leave to be heard.

Amended by Laws 1978, Ch. 103, eff. Oct. 1, 1978; Laws 1990, Ch. 141, § 1, eff. Sept. 1, 1990.

§ 1049. Special consideration in certain cases.

In scheduling hearings and investigations, the court shall give priority to proceedings under this article involving abuse or in which a child has been removed from home before a final order of disposition. Any adjournment granted in the course of such a proceeding should be for as short a time as is practicable.

Part 5. Orders.

§ 1051. Sustaining or dismissing petition.

(a) If facts sufficient to sustain the petition are established in accord with part four of this article, or if all parties and the law guardian consent, the court shall, subject to the provisions of subdivision (c) of this section, enter an order finding that the child is an abused child or a neglected child and shall state the grounds for the finding.

(b) If the proof does not conform to the specific allegations of the petition, the court may amend the allegations to conform to the proof; provided, however, that in such case the respondent shall be given reasonable time to prepare to answer the amended allegations.

(c) If facts sufficient to sustain the petition under this article are not established, or if, in a case of alleged neglect, the court concludes that its aid is not required on the record before it, the court shall dismiss the petition and shall state on the record the grounds for the dismissal.

(d) If the court makes a finding of abuse or neglect, it shall determine, based upon the facts adduced during the fact-finding hearing and any other additional facts presented to it, whether a preliminary order pursuant to section one thousand twenty-seven is required to protect the child's interests pending a final order of disposition. The court shall state the grounds for its determination. In addition, a child found to be abused or neglected may be removed and remanded to a place approved for such purpose by the local social services department or be placed in the custody of a suitable person, pending a final order of disposition, if the court finds that there is a substantial probability that the final order of disposition will be an order of placement under section one thousand fifty-five. In determining whether substantial probability exists, the court shall consider the requirements of subdivision (b) of section one thousand fifty-two.

(e) If the court makes a finding of abuse, it shall specify the paragraph or paragraphs of subdivision (e) of section one thousand twelve of this act which it finds have been established. If the court makes a finding of abuse as defined in paragraph (iii) of subdivision (e) of section one thousand twelve of this act, it shall make a further finding of the specific sex offense as defined in article one hundred thirty of the penal law. In addition to a finding of abuse, the court may enter a finding of severe abuse or repeated abuse, as defined in paragraphs (a) and (b) of subdivision eight of section three hundred eighty-four-b of the social services law, which shall be admissible in a proceeding to terminate parental rights pursuant to paragraph (e) of subdivision four of section three hundred eighty-four-b of the social services law. If the court makes such additional finding of severe abuse or repeated abuse, the court shall state the grounds for its determination, which shall be based upon clear and convincing evidence.

(f) Prior to accepting an admission to an allegation or permitting a respondent to consent to a finding of neglect or abuse, the court shall inform the respondent that such an admission or consent will result in the court making a fact-finding order of neglect or abuse, as the case may be, and shall further inform the respondent of the potential consequences of such order, including but not limited to the following:

(i) that the court will have the power to make an order of disposition, which may include an order placing the subject child or children in foster care until completion of the initial permanency hearing scheduled pursuant to section one thousand eighty-nine of this act and subject to successive extensions of placement at any subsequent permanency hearings;

(ii)   that the placement of the children in foster care may, if the parent fails to maintain contact with or plan for the future of the child, lead to proceedings for the termination of parental rights and to the possibility of adoption of the child if the child remains in foster care for fifteen of the most recent twenty-two months, the agency may be required by law to file a petition to terminate parental rights;

(iii)   that the report made to the state central register of child abuse and maltreatment upon which the petition is based will remain on file until ten years after the eighteenth birthday of the youngest child named in such report, that the respondent will be unable to obtain expungement of such report, and that the existence of such report may be made known to employers seeking to screen employee applicants in the field of child care, and to child care agencies if the respondent applies to become a foster parent or adoptive parent.

Any finding upon such an admission or consent made without such notice being given by the court shall be vacated upon motion of any party. In no event shall a person other than the respondent, either in person or in writing, make an admission or consent to a finding of neglect or abuse.

Amended by Laws 1970, Ch. 1015; Laws 1976, Ch. 880, eff. Nov. 29, 1976; Laws 1981, Ch. 739, eff. Oct. 26, 1981; Laws 1987, Ch. 160, eff. June 29, 1987; Laws 1988, Ch. 478, § 7, eff. Nov. 1, 1988; Laws 1990, Ch. 187, § 1, eff. Sept. 1, 1990; Laws 1994, Ch. 430, § 1, eff. Oct. 18, 1994; Laws 1999, Ch. 7, §§ 46 & 47, eff. Feb. 11, 1999; L. 2005, Ch. 3, § 17, eff. Aug. 23, 2005.

§ 1052.   Disposition on adjudication.

(a)   At the conclusion of a dispositional hearing under this article, the court shall enter an order of disposition;

(i)   suspending judgment in accord with section one thousand fifty-three; or

(ii)   releasing the child to the custody of his parents or other person legally responsible in accord with section one thousand fifty-four; or

(iii)   placing the child in accord with section one thousand fifty-five; or

(iv)   making an order of protection in accord with one thousand fifty-six; or

(v)   placing the respondent under supervision in accord with section one thousand fifty-seven.

(b)   (i) The order of the court shall state the grounds for any disposition made under this section. If the court places the child in accord with section one thousand fifty-five of this part, the court in its order shall determine:

(A)   whether continuation in the child's home would be contrary to the best interests of the child and where appropriate, that reasonable efforts were made prior to the date of the dispositional hearing held pursuant to this article to prevent or eliminate the need for removal of the child from his or her home and if the child was removed from the home prior to the date of such hearing, that such removal was in the child's best interests and, where appropriate, reasonable efforts were made to make it possible for the child to safely return home. If the court determines that reasonable efforts to prevent or eliminate the need for removal of the child from the home were not made but that the lack of such efforts was appropriate under the circumstances, the court order shall include such a finding, or if the permanency plan for the child is adoption, guardianship or some other permanent living arrangement other than reunification with the parent or parents of the child, the court order shall include a finding that reasonable efforts are being made to make and finalize such alternate permanent placement.

For the purpose of this section, reasonable efforts to prevent or eliminate the need for removing the child from the home of the child or to make it possible for the child to return safely to the home of the child shall not be required where, upon motion with notice by the social services official, the court determines that:

(1) the parent of such child has subjected the child to aggravated circumstances, as defined in subdivision (j) of section one thousand twelve of this article;

(2) the parent of such child has been convicted of (i) murder in the first degree as defined in section 125.27 or murder in the second degree as defined in section 125.25 of the penal law and the victim was another child of the parent; or (ii) manslaughter in the first degree as defined in section 125.20 or manslaughter in the second degree as defined in section 125.15 of the penal law and the victim was another child of the parent, provided, however, that the parent must have acted voluntarily in committing such crime;

(3) the parent of such child has been convicted of an attempt to commit any of the foregoing crimes, and the victim or intended victim was the child or another child of the parent; or has been convicted of criminal solicitation as defined in article one hundred, conspiracy as defined in article one hundred five or criminal facilitation as defined in article one hundred fifteen of the penal law for conspiring, soliciting or facilitating any of the foregoing crimes, and the victim or intended victim was the child or another child of the parent;

(4) the parent of such child has been convicted of assault in the second degree as defined in section 120.05, assault in the first degree as defined in section 120.10 or aggravated assault upon a person less than eleven years old as defined in section 120.12 of the penal law, and the commission of one of the foregoing crimes resulted in serious physical injury to the child or another child of the parent;

(5) the parent of such child has been convicted in any other jurisdiction of an offense which includes all of the essential elements of any crime specified in clause two, three or four of this subparagraph, and the victim of such offense was the child or another child of the parent; or

(6) the parental rights of the parent to a sibling of such child have been involuntarily terminated;

unless the court determines that providing reasonable efforts would be in the best interests of the child, not contrary to the health and safety of the child, and would likely result in the reunification of the parent and the child in the foreseeable future. The court shall state such findings in its order.

If the court determines that reasonable efforts are not to be required because of one of the grounds set forth above, a permanency hearing shall be held within thirty days of the finding of the court that such efforts are not required. At the permanency hearing, the court shall determine the appropriateness of the permanency plan prepared by the social services official which shall include whether or when the child: (i) will be returned to the parent; (ii) should be placed for adoption with the social services official filing a petition for termination of parental rights; (iii) should be referred for legal guardianship; (iv) should be placed permanently with a fit and willing relative; or (v) should be placed in another planned permanent living arrangement if the social services official has documented to the court a compelling reason for determining that it would not be in the best interest of the child to return home, be referred for termination of parental rights and placed for adoption, placed with a fit and willing relative, or placed with a legal guardian. The social services official shall thereafter make reasonable efforts to place the child in a timely manner and to complete whatever steps are necessary to finalize the permanent placement of the child as set forth in the permanency plan approved by the court. If reasonable efforts are determined by the court not to be required because of one of the grounds set forth in this paragraph, the social services official may file a petition for termination of parental rights in accordance with section three hundred eighty-four-b of the social services law.

For the purpose of this section, in determining reasonable effort to be made with respect to a child, and in making such reasonable efforts, the child's health and safety shall be the paramount concern.

For the purpose of this section, a sibling shall include a half-sibling;

(B) if the child has attained the age of sixteen, the services needed, if any, to assist the child to make the transition from foster care to independent living. Where the court finds that the local department of social services has not made reasonable efforts to prevent or eliminate the need for placement, and that such efforts would be appropriate, it shall direct the local department of social services to make such efforts pursuant to section one thousand fifteen-a of this article, and shall adjourn the hearing for a reasonable period of time for such purpose when the court determines that additional time is necessary and appropriate to make such efforts; and

(C) whether the local social services district made a reasonable search to locate relatives of the child as required pursuant to section one thousand seventeen of this article. In making such determination, the court shall consider whether the local social services district engaged in a search to locate any non-respondent parent and whether the local social services district attempted to locate all of the child's grandparents, all suitable relatives identified by any respondent parent and any non-respondent parent and all relatives identified by a child over the age of five as relatives who play or have played a significant positive role in the child's life.

(ii) The court shall also consider and determine whether the need for placement of the child would be eliminated by the issuance of an order of protection, as provided for in paragraph (iv) of subdivision (a) of this section, directing the removal of a person or persons from the child's residence. Such determination shall consider the occurrence, if any, of domestic violence in the child's residence.

(c) Prior to granting an order of disposition pursuant to subdivision (a) of this section following an adjudication of child abuse, as defined in paragraph (i) of subdivision (e) of section ten hundred twelve of this act or a finding of a felony sex offense as defined in sections 130.25, 130.30, 130.35, 130.40, 130.45, 130.50, 130.65 and 130.70 of the penal law, the court shall advise the respondent that any subsequent adjudication of child abuse, as defined in paragraph (i) of subdivision (e) of section one thousand twelve of this act or any subsequent finding of a felony sex offense as defined in those sections of the penal law herein enumerated, arising out of acts of the respondent may result in the commitment of the guardianship and custody of the child or another child pursuant to section three hundred eighty-four-b of the social services law. The order in such cases shall contain a statement that any subsequent adjudication of child abuse or finding of a felony sex offense as described herein may result in the commitment of the guardianship and custody of the child, or another child pursuant to section three hundred eighty-four-b of the social services law.

Amended by Laws 1973, Ch. 1039, eff. Sept. 1, 1973; Laws 1981, Ch. 739, eff. Oct. 26, 1981; Laws 1984, Ch. 872, eff. Oct. 4, 1984; Laws 1986, Ch. 161, eff. June 16, 1986; Laws 1988, Ch. 478, § 8, eff. Nov. 1, 1988; Laws 1989, Ch. 727, § 6, eff. Oct. 1, 1989; Laws 1991, Ch. 198, § 7, eff. June 28, 1991; Laws 1992, Ch. 538, § 1, eff. Sept. 1, 1992; Laws 1999, Ch. 7, §§ 48 & 49, eff. Feb. 11, 1999; Laws 2005, ch. 671, §4, eff. March 15, 2006; Laws 2006, ch. 12, §3, eff. March 15, 2006.

§ 1052-a. Post-dispositional procedures.

The local child protective service shall notify the child's law guardian of an indicated report of child abuse or maltreatment in which the respondent is a subject of the report or another person named in the report, as such terms are defined in section four hundred twelve of the social services law, while any order issued pursuant to paragraph (i), (iii), (iv) or (v) of subdivision (a) of section ten hundred fifty-two remains in effect against the respondent.

Added by Laws 1990, Ch. 317, § 1, eff. Sept. 1, 1990; **amended** by Laws 1991, Ch. 69, § 4, eff. Apr. 22, 1991.

§ 1052-b. Duties of counsel.

1. If the court has entered a dispositional order pursuant to section one thousand fifty-two it shall be the duty of the respondent's counsel promptly to advise such respondent in writing of his or her right to appeal to the appropriate appellate division of the supreme court, the time limitations involved, the manner of instituting an appeal and obtaining a transcript of the testimony and the right to apply for leave to appeal as a poor person if the respondent is unable to pay the cost of an appeal. It shall be the further duty of such counsel to explain to the respondent the procedures for instituting an appeal, the possible reasons upon which an appeal may be based and the nature and possible consequences of the appellate process.

2. It also shall be the duty of such counsel to ascertain whether the respondent wishes to appeal and, if so, to serve and file the necessary notice of appeal.

Amended by Laws 1991, Ch. 113, § 1, eff. Sept. 1, 1991.

§ 1052-c. Duty to report investigations to locate non-respondent parents or relatives.

Upon a determination by the court to enter an order of disposition placing the child in accordance with section one thousand fifty-five of this part, the court shall immediately require the local social services district to report to the court the results of any investigation to locate any non-respondent parent or relatives of the child, including all of the child's grandparents, all suitable relatives identified by any respondent parent and any non-respondent parent and all relatives identified by a child over the age of five as relatives who play or have played a significant positive role in the child's life, as required pursuant to section one thousand seventeen of the article. Such report shall include whether any non-respondent parent has expressed an interest in seeking custody of the child or whether any relative who has been located has expressed an interest in becoming a foster parent for the child or in seeking custody or care of the child.

Added by Laws 2005, ch. 671, §5, eff. March 15, 2006; **Amended** by Laws 2006, ch. 12, §4, eff. March 15, 2006.

§ 1053. Suspended judgment.

(a) Rules of court shall define permissible terms and conditions of a suspended judgment. These terms and conditions shall relate to the acts or omissions of the parent or other person legally responsible for the care of the child.

(b) The maximum duration of any term or condition of a suspended judgment is one year, unless the court finds at the conclusion of that period, upon a hearing, that exceptional circumstances require an extension thereof for an additional year.

(c) Except as provided for herein, in any order issued pursuant to this section, the court may require the child protective agency to make progress reports to the court, the parties, and the child's law guardian on the implementation of such order. Where the order of disposition is issued upon the consent of the parties and the child's law guardian, such agency shall report to the court, the parties and the child's law guardian no later than ninety days after the issuance of the order, unless the court determines that the facts and circumstances of the case do not require such report to be made.

Amended by Laws 1990, Ch. 323, § 2, eff. Sept. 1, 1990.

§ 1054. Release to custody of parent or other person responsible for care; supervision or order of protection.

(a) If the order of disposition releases the child to the custody of his parent or other person legally responsible for his care at the time of the filing of the petition, the court may place the person to whose custody the child is released under supervision of a child protective agency or of a social services official or duly authorized agency, or may enter an order of protection under section ten hundred fifty-six, or both. An order of supervision entered under this section shall set forth the terms and conditions of such supervision that the respondent must meet and the actions that the child protective agency, social services official or duly authorized agency must take to exercise such supervision. Except as provided for herein, in any order issued pursuant to this section, the court may require the child protective agency to make progress reports to the court, the parties, and the child's law guardian on the implementation of such order. Where the order of disposition is issued upon the consent of the parties and the child's law guardian, such agency shall report to the court, the parties and the child's law guardian no later than ninety days after the issuance of the order, unless the court determines that the facts and circumstances of the case do not require such report to be made.

(b) Rules of court shall define permissible terms and conditions of supervision under this section. The duration of any period of supervision shall be for an initial period of no more than one year and the court may at the expiration of that period, upon a hearing and for good cause shown, make successive extensions of such supervision of up to one year each.

Amended by Laws 1973, Ch. 1039, eff. Sept. 1, 1973; Laws 1989, Ch. 458, § 1, eff. Nov. 1, 1989; Laws 1990, Ch. 206, § 1, eff. Sept. 1, 1990; Laws 1990, Ch. 323, § 3, eff. Sept. 1, 1990.

§ 1055. Placement.

(a) For purposes of section one thousand fifty-two of this part the court may place the child in the custody of a relative or other suitable person, or of the local commissioner of social services or of such other officer, board or department as may be authorized to receive children as public charges, or a duly authorized association, agency, society or in an institution suitable for the placement of a child. The court may also place the child in the custody of the local commissioner of social services and may direct such commissioner to have the child reside with a relative or other suitable person who has indicated a desire to become a foster parent for the child and further direct such commissioner, pursuant to regulations of the office of children and family services, to commence an investigation of the home of such relative or other suitable person within twenty-four hours and thereafter expedite approval or certification of such relative or other suitable person, if qualified, as a foster parent. If such home is found to be unqualified for approval or certification, the local commissioner shall report such fact to the court forthwith so that the court may make a placement determination that is in the best interests of the child.

(b)   (i) The court shall state on the record its findings supporting the placement in any order of placement made under this section. The order of placement shall include, but not be limited to:

(A)   a description of the visitation plan;

(B)   a direction that the respondent or respondents shall be notified of the planning conference or conferences to be held pursuant to subdivision three of section four hundred nine-e of the social services law, of their right to attend the conference, and of their right to have counsel or another representative or companion with them;

(C)   a date certain for the permanency hearing, which may be the previously-scheduled date certain, but in no event more than eight months from the date of removal of the child from his or her home. Provided, however, that if there is a sibling or half-sibling of the child who was previously removed from the home pursuant to this article, the date certain for the permanency hearing shall be the date certain previously scheduled for the sibling or half-sibling of the child who was the first child removed from the home, where such sibling or half-sibling has a permanency hearing date certain scheduled within the next eight months, but in no event later than eight months from the date of removal of the child from his or her home;

(D)   a notice that if the child remains in foster care for fifteen of the most recent twenty-two months, the agency may be required by law to file a petition to terminate parental rights. A copy of the court's order and the service plan shall be given to the respondent; and

(E)   where the permanency goal is return to the parent and it is anticipated that the child may be finally discharged to his or her parent before the next scheduled permanency hearing, the court may provide the local social services district with authority to finally discharge the child to the parent without further court hearing, provided that ten days prior written notice is served upon the court and law guardian. If the court on its own motion or the law guardian on motion to the court does not request the matter to be brought for review before final discharge, no further permanency hearings will be required. The local social services district may also discharge the child on a trial basis to the parent unless the court has prohibited such trial discharge or unless the court has conditioned such trial discharge on another event. For the purposes of this section, trial discharge shall mean that the child is physically returned to the parent while the child remains in the care and custody of the local social services district. Permanency hearings shall continue to be held for any child who has returned to his or her parents on a trial discharge. Where the permanency goal for a child aging out of foster care is another planned permanent living arrangement that includes a significant connection to an adult willing to be a permanency resource for the child, the local social services district may also discharge the child on a trial basis to the planned permanent living arrangements, unless the court has prohibited or otherwise conditioned such a trial discharge. Trial discharge for a child aging out of foster care shall mean that a child is physically discharged but the local social services district retains care and custody or custody and guardianship of the child and there remains a date certain for the scheduled permanency hearing. Children placed under this section shall be placed until the court completes the initial permanency hearing scheduled pursuant to article ten-A of this act. Should the court determine pursuant to article ten-A of this act that placement shall be extended beyond completion of the scheduled permanency hearing, such extended placement and any such successive extensions of placement shall expire at the completion of the next scheduled permanency hearing, unless the court shall determine, pursuant to article ten-A of this act, to continue to extend such placement.

(ii)   Upon placing a child under the age of one, who has been abandoned, with a local commissioner of social services, the court shall, where either of the parents do not appear after due notice, include in its order of disposition pursuant to section one thousand fifty-two of this part, a direction that such commissioner shall promptly commence a diligent search to locate the child's non-appearing parent or parents or other known relatives who are legally responsible for the child, and to commence a proceeding to commit the guardianship and custody of such child to an authorized agency pursuant to section three hundred eighty-four-b of the social services law, six months from the date that care and custody of the child was transferred to the commissioner, unless there has been communication and visitation between such child and such parent or parents or other known relatives or persons legally responsible for the child. In addition to such diligent search the local commissioner of social services shall provide written notice to the child's parent or parents or other known relatives or persons legally responsible as provided for in this paragraph. Such notice shall be served upon such parent or parents or other known relatives or persons legally responsible in the manner required for service of process pursuant to section six hundred seventeen of this act. Information regarding such diligent search, including, but not limited to, the name, last known address, social security number, employer's address and any other identifying information to the extent known regarding the non-appearing parent, shall be recorded in the uniform case record maintained pursuant to section four hundred nine-f of the social services law.

(iii)   Notice as required by paragraph (ii) of this subdivision shall state:

FCA

(A) that the local commissioner of social services shall initiate a proceeding to commit the guardianship and custody of the subject child to an authorized agency and that such proceeding shall be commenced six months from the date the child was placed in the care and custody of such commissioner with such date to be specified in the notice;

(B) that there has been no visitation and communication between the parent and the child since the child has been placed with the local commissioner of social services and that if no such visitation and communication with the child occurs within six months of the date the child was placed with such commissioner the child will be deemed an abandoned child as defined in section three hundred eighty-four-b of the social services law and a proceeding will be commenced to commit the guardianship and custody of the subject child to an authorized agency;

(C) that it is the legal responsibility of the local commissioner of social services to reunite and reconcile families whenever possible and to offer services and assistance for that purpose;

(D) the name, address and telephone number of the caseworker assigned to the subject child who can provide information, services and assistance with respect to reuniting the family;

(E) that it is the responsibility of the parent, relative or other person legally responsible for the child to visit and communicate with the child and that such visitation and communication may avoid the necessity of initiating a petition for the transfer of custody and guardianship of the child.

Such notice shall be printed in both Spanish and English and contain in conspicuous print and in plain language the information set forth in this paragraph.

(c) In addition to or in lieu of an order of placement made pursuant to subdivision (b) of this section, the court may make an order directing a child protective agency, social services official or other duly authorized agency to undertake diligent efforts to encourage and strengthen the parental relationship when it finds such efforts will not be detrimental to the best interests of the child. Such efforts shall include encouraging and facilitating visitation with the child by the parent or other person legally responsible for the child's care. Such order may include a specific plan of action for such agency or official including, but not limited to, requirements that such agency or official assist the parent or other person responsible for the child's care in obtaining adequate housing, employment, counseling, medical care or psychiatric treatment. Such order shall also include encouraging and facilitating visitation with the child by the non-custodial parent and grandparents who have obtained orders pursuant to part eight of this article, and may include encouraging and facilitating visitation with the child by the child's siblings. Nothing in this subdivision shall be deemed to limit the authority of the court to make an order pursuant to section two hundred fifty-five of this act.

(d)   In addition to or in lieu of an order of placement made pursuant to subdivision (b) of this section, the court may make an order directing a social services official or other duly authorized agency to institute a proceeding to legally free the child for adoption, if the court finds reasonable cause to believe that grounds therefor exist. Upon a failure by such official or agency to institute such a proceeding within ninety days after entry of such order, the court shall permit the foster parent or parents in whose home the child resides to institute such a proceeding unless the social services official or other duly authorized agency caring for the child, for good cause shown and upon due notice to all parties to the proceeding, has obtained a modification or extension of such order, or unless the court has reasonable cause to believe that such foster parent or parents would not obtain approval of their petition to adopt the children in a subsequent adoption proceeding.

(e)   No placement may be made or continued under this section beyond the child's eighteenth birthday without his or her consent and in no event past his or her twenty-first birthday.

(f)   If a child is placed in the custody of the local commissioner of social services or other officer, board or department authorized to receive children as public charges, such person shall provide for such child as in the case of a destitute child or as otherwise authorized by law.

(g)   If the parent or person legally responsible for the care of any such child or with whom such child resides receives public assistance and care, any portion of which is attributable to such child, a copy of the order of the court providing for the placement of such child from his or her home shall be furnished to the appropriate social services official, who shall reduce the public assistance and care furnished such parent or other person by the amount attributable to such child, provided, however, that when the child service plan prepared pursuant to section four hundred nine-e of the social services law includes a goal of discharge of the child to the parent or person legally responsible for the care of the child or other member of the household, such social services official shall not, to the extent that federal reimbursement is available therefor, reduce the portion attributable to such child which is intended to meet the cost of shelter and fuel for heating.

(h)   Any order made under this section shall be suspended upon the entry of an order of disposition with respect to a child whose custody and guardianship have been committed pursuant to section three hundred eighty-four-b of the social services law, and shall expire upon the expiration of the time for appeal of such order or upon the final determination of any such appeal and any subsequent appeals authorized by law; provided, however, that where custody and guardianship have been committed pursuant to section three hundred eighty-four-b of the social services law or where the child has been surrendered pursuant to section three hundred eighty-three-c or three hundred eighty-four of the social services law, the child shall nonetheless be deemed to continue in foster care until such time as an adoption or other alternative living arrangement is finalized. A permanency hearing or hearings regarding such child shall be conducted in accordance with article ten-A of this act. Nothing in this subdivision shall cause such order of placement to be suspended or to expire with respect to any parent or other person whose consent is required for an adoption against whom an order of disposition committing guardianship and custody of the child has not been made.

(i) In making an order under this section, the court may direct a local commissioner of social services to place the subject child together with minor siblings or half-siblings who have been placed in the custody of the commissioner, or to provide or arrange for regular visitation and other forms of communication between such child and siblings where the court finds that such placement or visitation and communication is in the child's best interests. Placement or regular visitation and communication with siblings or half-siblings shall be presumptively in the child's best interests unless such placement or visitation and communication would be contrary to the child's health, safety or welfare, or the lack of geographic proximity precludes or prevents visitation.

Amended by Laws 1974, Ch. 937, eff. Sept. 1, 1974; Laws 1975, Ch. 220, eff. Aug. 16, 1975; Laws 1976, Ch. 666, eff. Jan. 1, 1977; Laws 1982, Ch. 117, eff. Sept. 1, 1982; Laws 1987, Ch. 75, eff. Sept. 19, 1987; Laws 1987 Ch. 129, eff. July 15, 1987; Laws 1988, Ch. 638, eff. Jan. 1, 1989; Laws 1989, Ch. 458, § 2, eff. Nov. 1, 1989; Laws 1989, Ch. 747, § 1, eff. July 24, 1989; Laws 1990, Ch. 283, § 1, eff. Sept. 1, 1990; Laws 1990, Ch. 323, § 4, eff. Sept. 1, 1990; Laws 1990, Ch. 605, § 1, eff. Oct. 1, 1990; Laws 1990, Ch. 854, § 4, eff. Sept. 1, 1990; Laws 1992, Ch. 538, §§ 2 and 3, eff. Sept. 1, 1992; Laws 1997, Ch. 353, § 2, eff. Nov. 3, 1997; Laws 1998, Ch. 164, § 1, eff. July 7, 1998; Laws 1999, Ch. 7, §§ 49 and 50, eff. Feb. 11, 1999; **amended** by L. 2002, Ch. 663, § 3, eff. Dec. 3, 2002; Laws 2005, ch. 3, §18 (Part A), eff. Dec 21, 2005, Laws 2005, ch. 671, §6, eff. March 15, 2006, Laws 2006, ch. 12, §5, eff. March 15, 2006; Laws 2006, ch. 437, §3, eff. July 26, 2006.

§ 1055-a. Repealed.

Add, L 1988, ch 638, §3, eff Jan 1, 1989; Sub 1, par (c), amd, L 1991, ch 48, §3, eff April 12, 1991; Sub 3, par (c), amd, L 1999, ch 7, §51, eff Feb 11, 1999; Sub 4, amd, L 1999, ch 7, §52, eff Feb 11, 1999; Sub 4, opening par, amd, L 1999, ch 7, §52, eff Feb 11, 1999; Sub 4, par (c), amd, L 1999, ch 7, §52, eff Feb 11, 1999; Sub 4, par (d), amd, L 1997, ch 353, §3, L 1999, ch 7, §52, eff Feb 11, 1999; Sub 4, par (e), add, L 1997, ch 353, §3, eff Nov 3, 1997; Former sub 4, par (e), redesignated sub 4, par (f), L 1997, ch 353, §3, eff Nov 3, 1997; Sub 4, par (f), formerly sub 4, par (e), so designated, L 1997, ch 353, §3, eff Nov 3, 1997; Sub 6, par (a), amd, L 1999, ch 7, §53, eff Feb 11, 1999; Sub 7, par (a), amd, L 1995, ch 454, §3, eff Oct 1, 1995; Sub 8, amd, L 1991, ch 198, §8, L 1995, ch 454, §4, eff Oct 1, 1995; Sub 12, amd, L 1997, ch 353, §4, eff Nov 3, 1997; Amd, L 1999, ch 534, §§1, 2, eff Dec 27, 1999, L 2000, ch 145, §17, eff July 1, 2000; L 2002, ch 76, §2, eff Aug 19, 2002, L 2002, ch 83, §24 (Part C), eff May 29, 2002, deemed eff April 1, 2002, expires and repealed June 30, 2007; L 2002, ch 663, §§4–8, eff Dec 3, 2002, L 2003, ch 588, §1, eff Sept 22, 2003; repealed, L 2005, ch 3, §19 (Part A), eff Dec 21, 2005.

§ 1055-a. Substantial failure of a material condition of surrender; enforcement of a contact agreement.

(a) In case of a substantial failure of a material condition in a surrender executed pursuant to section three hundred eighty-three-c of the social services law prior to finalization of the adoption of the child, the court shall possess continuing jurisdiction in accordance with subdivision six of such section to rehear the matter upon the filing of a petition by the authorized agency, the parent or the law guardian for the child or whenever the court deems necessary. In such case, the authorized agency shall notify the parent, unless such notice is expressly waived by a statement written by the parent and appended to or included in such instrument, the law guardian for the child and the court that approved the surrender within twenty days of any substantial failure to comply with a material condition of the surrender prior to the finalization of the adoption of the child. In such case, the authorized agency shall file a petition on notice to the parent unless notice is expressly waived by a statement written by the parent and appended to or included in such instrument and the law guardian in accordance with this section within thirty days of such failure, except for good cause shown, in order for the court to review such failure and, where necessary, to hold a hearing; provided, however, that in the absence of such filing, the parent and/or law guardian for the child may file such a petition at any time up to sixty days after notification of the failure. Such petition filed by a parent or law guardian must be filed prior to the adoption of the child.

(b) If an agreement for continuing contact and communication pursuant to paragraph (b) of subdivision two of section three hundred eighty-three-c of the social services law is approved by the court, and the child who is the subject of the approved agreement has not yet been adopted, any party to the approved agreement may file a petition with the family court in the county where the agreement was approved to enforce such agreement. A copy of the approved agreement shall be annexed to such petition. The court shall enter an order enforcing communication or contact pursuant to the terms and conditions of the agreement unless the court finds that enforcement would not be in the best interests of the child.

(c) Nothing in this section shall limit the rights and remedies available to the parties and the law guardian pursuant to section one hundred twelve-b of the domestic relations law with respect to a failure to comply with a material condition of a surrender subsequent to the finalization of the adoption of the child.

Add, L 2005, ch 3, §19 (Part A), eff Dec 21, 2005; Former §1055-a, repealed, L 2005, ch 3, §19 (Part A), eff Dec 21, 2005; L. 2005, Ch. 3, § 19, eff. Aug. 23, 2005.

§ 1056. Order of protection.

1. The court may make an order of protection in assistance or as a condition of any other order made under this part. Such order of protection shall remain in effect concurrently with, shall expire no later than the expiration date of, and

may be extended concurrently with, such other order made under this part, except as provided in subdivision four of this section. The order of protection may set forth reasonable conditions of behavior to be observed for a specified time by a person who is before the court and is a parent or a person legally responsible for the child's care or the spouse of the parent or other person legally responsible for the child's care, or both. Such an order may require any such person

(a) to stay away from the home, school, business or place of employment of the other spouse, parent or person legally responsible for the child's care or the child, and to stay away from any other specific location designated by the court;

(b) to permit a parent, or a person entitled to visitation by a court order or a separation agreement, to visit the child at stated periods;

(c) to refrain from committing a family offense, as defined in subdivision one of section eight hundred twelve of this act, or any criminal offense against the child or against the other parent or against any person to whom custody of the child is awarded, or from harassing, intimidating or threatening such persons;

(d) to permit a designated party to enter the residence during a specified period of time in order to remove personal belongings not in issue in this proceeding or in any other proceeding or action under this act or the domestic relations law;

(e) to refrain from acts of commission or omission that create an unreasonable risk to the health, safety and welfare of a child;

(f) to provide, either directly or by means of medical and health insurance, for expenses incurred for medical care and treatment arising from the incident or incidents forming the basis for the issuance of the order.

(g)

1. to refrain from intentionally injuring or killing, without justification, any companion animal the respondent knows to be owned, possessed, leased, kept or held by the petitioner or a minor child residing in the household.

2. "Companion animal", as used in this section, shall have the same meaning as in subdivision five of section three hundred fifty of the agriculture and markets law.

(h) to observe such other conditions as are necessary to further the purposes of protection.

2. The court may also award custody of the child, during the term of the order of protection to either parent, or to an appropriate relative within the second degree. Nothing in this section gives the court power to place or board out any child or to commit a child to an institution or agency. In making orders of protection, the court shall so act as to insure that in the care, protection, discipline and guardianship of the child his religious faith shall be preserved and protected.

3. Notwithstanding the foregoing provisions, an order of protection, or temporary order of protection where applicable, may be entered against a former

spouse and persons who have a child in common, regardless whether such persons have been married or have lived together at any time.

4. The court may enter an order of protection independently of any other order made under this part, against a person who was a member of the child's household or a person legally responsible as defined in section one thousand twelve of this chapter, and who is no longer a member of such household at the time of the disposition and who is not related by blood or marriage to the child or a member of the child's household. An order of protection entered pursuant to this subdivision may be for any period of time up to the child's eighteenth birthday and upon such conditions as the court deems necessary and proper to protect the health and safety of the child and the child's caretaker.

Amended by Laws 1981, Ch. 965, eff. Aug. 6, 1981; Laws 1984, Ch. 948, eff. Nov. 1, 1984; Laws 1989, Ch. 220, eff. Oct. 1, 1989; Laws 1990, Ch. 622, eff. Sept. 1, 1990; Laws 1995, Ch. 483, §§ 13–14, eff. Nov. 1, 1995; Laws 2006, ch. 253, §7, eff. July 26, 2006.

§ 1057. Supervision.

The court may place the respondent under supervision of a child protective agency or of a social services official or duly authorized agency. An order of supervision entered under this section shall set forth the terms and conditions of such supervision that the respondent must meet and the actions that the child protective agency, social services official or duly authorized agency must take to exercise such supervision. Except as provided for herein, in any order issued pursuant to this section, the court may require the child protective agency to make progress reports to the court, the parties, and the child's law guardian on the implementation of such order. Where the order of disposition is issued upon the consent of the parties and the child's law guardian, such agency shall report to the court, the parties and the child's law guardian no later than ninety days after the issuance of the order, unless the court determines that the facts and circumstances of the case do not require such report to be made. Rules of court shall define permissible terms and conditions of supervision under this section. The duration of any period of supervision shall be for an initial period of no more than one year and the court may at the expiration of that period, upon a hearing and for good cause shown, make successive extensions of such supervision of up to one year each.

Amended by Laws 1973, Ch. 1039, eff. Sept. 1, 1973; Laws 1989, Ch. 458, § 3, eff. Nov. 1, 1989; Laws 1990, Ch. 206, § 2, eff. Sept. 1, 1990; Laws 1990, Ch. 323, § 5, eff. Sept. 1, 1990.

§ 1058. Expiration of orders.

No later than sixty days prior to the expiration of an order issued pursuant to paragraph (i), (ii), (iv), or (v) of subdivision (a) of section one thousand fifty-two of this part or prior to the conclusion of the period of an adjournment in contemplation of dismissal pursuant to section one thousand thirty-nine of this article, where no application has been made seeking extension of such orders or adjournments and, with respect to an adjournment in contemplation of dismissal, no violations of the court's order are before the court, the child protective agency shall, whether or not the child has been or will be returned to the family, report to the court, the parties, including any non-respondent parent and the child's law guardian on the status and circumstances of the child and family and any actions taken or contemplated by such agency with respect to such child and family.

Added by Laws 1990, Ch. 318, § 1, eff. Sept. 1, 1990; amended by Laws 1991, Ch. 75, § 3, eff. Apr. 26, 1991; L. 2005, Ch. 3, § 20, eff. Aug. 23, 2005.

§ 1059. Abandoned child.

If the court finds that a child was abandoned by his parents or by the other person lawfully charged with his care, it may make an order so finding and may discharge the child to the custody of the commissioner of social services who shall provide for such child as in the case of a destitute child or as otherwise authorized by law. In such case the court shall direct the commissioner to institute a proceeding pursuant to section three hundred eighty-four-b of the social services law to legally free such child for adoption.

Amended by Laws 1976, Ch. 666, eff. Jan. 1, 1977, renumbering former section 1058 as 1059.

Part 6. New hearing and reconsideration of orders.

§ 1061. Staying, modifying, setting aside or vacating order.

For good cause shown and after due notice, the court on its own motion, on motion of the corporation counsel, county attorney or district attorney or on motion of the petitioner, or on motion of the child or on his behalf, or on motion of the parent or other person responsible for the child's care may stay execution, of arrest, set aside, modify or vacate any order issued in the course of a proceeding under this article.

§ 1062. Motion to terminate placement.

Any interested person acting on behalf of a child placed under section one thousand fifty-five of this article, the child's parent, or the person legally responsible for the child may make a motion to the court for an order terminating the placement. The motion must:

(a)   show that an application for the child's return to his or her home was made to an appropriate person in the place in which the child was placed;

(b)   show that the application was denied or was not granted within thirty days from the day application was made; and

(c)   be accompanied by a sworn affidavit stating the grounds for the motion.

Add, L 1970, ch 962, §9, eff May 1, 1970, with substance transferred from former §362; Amd, L 2005, ch 3, §21 (Part A), eff Dec 21, 2005; Section heading, amd, L 2005, ch 3, §21 (Part A), eff Dec 21, 2005; Opening par, amd, L 2005, ch 3, §21 (Part A), eff Dec 21, 2005; Sub (a), amd, L 2005, ch 3, §21 (Part A), eff Dec 21, 2005; Sub (b), amd, L 2005, ch 3, §21 (Part A), eff Dec 21, 2005; Sub (c), amd, L 2005, ch 3, §21 (Part A), eff Dec 21, 2005; L. 2005, Ch. 3, § 21, eff. Aug. 23, 2005.

§ 1063.   Service of motion; answer.

A copy of a motion under section one thousand sixty-two of this part shall promptly be served by regular mail upon the duly authorized agency or the institution having custody of the child and upon the law guardian, each of whose duty it is to file an answer to the motion within five days of the receipt of the motion.

Add, L 1970, ch 962, §9, eff May 1, 1970, with substance transferred from former §363; Amd, L 2005, ch 3, §22 (Part A), eff Dec 21, 2005; L. 2005, Ch. 3, § 22, eff. Aug. 23, 2005; Section heading, amd, L 2005, ch 3, §22 (Part A), eff Dec 21, 2005.

§ 1064.   Examination of motion and answers; hearing.

The court shall promptly examine the motion and answers. If the court concludes that a hearing should be had, it may proceed upon due notice to all concerned to hear the facts and determine whether continued placement serves the purposes of this article. If the court concludes that a hearing need not be had, it shall enter an order granting or denying the motion.

Add, L 1970, ch 962, §9, eff May 1, 1970, with substance transferred from former §364; Amd, L 2005, ch 3, §23 (Part A), eff Dec 21, 2005; L. 2005, Ch. 3, § 23, eff. Aug. 23, 2005; Section heading, amd, L 2005, ch 3, §23 (Part A), eff Dec 21, 2005.

§ 1065.   Orders on hearing.

(a)   If the court determines after hearing that continued placement serves the purposes of this article, it shall deny the motion. The court may, on its own motion, determine a schedule for the return of the child, change the agency or institution in which the child is placed, or direct the agency or institution to make such other arrangements for the child's care and welfare as the facts of the case may require.

(b)   If the court determines after hearing that continued placement does not serve the purposes of this article, the court shall discharge the child from the custody of the agency or the institution in accord with section one thousand fifty-four of this article.

Add, L 1970, ch 962, §9, eff May 1, 1970, with substance transferred from former §365; L. 2005, Ch. 3, § 24, eff. Aug. 23, 2005.; Amd, L 2005, ch 3, §24 (Part A), eff Dec 21, 2005; Sub (a), amd, L 2005, ch 3, §24 (Part A), eff Dec 21, 2005; Sub (b), amd, L 2005, ch 3, §24 (Part A), eff Dec 21, 2005.

§ 1066.   Successive motions.

If a motion under section one thousand sixty-two of this part is denied, it may not be renewed for a period of ninety days after the denial, unless the order of denial permits renewal at an earlier time.

Add, L 1970, ch 962, §9, eff May 1, 1970, with substance transferred from former §366; L. 2005, Ch. 3, § 25, eff. Aug. 23, 2005; Amd, L 2005, ch 3, §25 (Part A), eff Dec 21, 2005; Section heading, amd, L 2005, ch 3, §25 (Part A), eff Dec 21, 2005.

§ 1067.   Discontinuation of treatment by agency or institution.

A child placed with an authorized agency under section one thousand fifty-five shall be returned to the court which entered the order of placement, if the agency

(a)   discontinues or suspends its work; or

(b)   is unwilling to continue to care for the child for the reason that support by the state of New York or one of its political subdivisions has been discontinued; or

(c)   so fundamentally alters its program that the child can no longer benefit from it.

§ 1068.   Action on return from agency or institution.

[Until Dec 21, 2005], §1068 reads as set out below: If a person is returned to the court under section three hundred sixty-seven,

the court may make any order that might have been made at the time of the order of placement.

[Eff Dec 21, 2005], §1068 reads as set out below: If a person is returned to the court under section one thousand sixty-seven of this part, the court may make any order that might have been made at the time of the order of placement.

Add, L 1970, ch 962, §9, eff May 1, 1970. Substance transferred from former §368; L. 2005, Ch. 3, § 26, eff. Aug. 23, 2005; Amd, L 2005, ch 3, §26 (Part A), eff Dec 21, 2005.

§ 1069. Rules of court.

Rules of court may authorize an agency with which a child is placed pursuant to section three hundred fifty-five to arrange for the child's care by another person or authorized agency. In the event such an arrangement is made, the agency making the arrangement shall, within one week of the making of the arrangement, advise the court of the change and reason therefor.

Part 7. Compliance with orders.

§ 1071. Failure to comply with terms and conditions of suspended judgment.

FCA

If, prior to the expiration of the period of the suspended judgment, a motion or order to show cause is filed that alleges that a parent or other person legally responsible for a child's care violated the terms and conditions of a suspended judgment issued under section one thousand fifty-three of this article, the period of the suspended judgment shall be tolled pending disposition of the motion or order to show cause. If, after hearing, the court is satisfied by competent proof that the parent or other person violated the order of suspended judgment, the court may revoke the suspension of judgment and enter any order that might have been made at the time judgment was suspended.

Amended by Laws 2006, ch. 347, §5, eff. July 26, 2006.

§ 1072. Failure to comply with terms and conditions of supervision.

If, prior to the expiration of the period of an order of supervision pursuant to section one thousand fifty-four or one thousand fifty-seven of this article, a motion or order to show cause is filed that alleges that a parent or other person legally responsible for a child's care violated the terms and conditions of an order of supervision issued under section one thousand fifty-four or one thousand fifty-seven of this article, the period of the order of supervision shall be tolled pending disposition of the motion or order to show cause. If, after hearing, the court is satisfied by competent proof that the parent or other person violated the order of supervision willfully and without just cause, the court may:

(a) revoke the order of supervision or of protection and enter any order that might have been made at the time the order of supervision was made, or

(b) commit the parent or other person who willfully and without just cause violated the order to jail for a term not to exceed six months.

Amended by Laws 1973, Ch. 1039, eff. Sept. 1, 1973; Laws 2006, ch. 437, §6, eff. July 26, 2006.

§ 1073. Effect of running away from place of placement.

If a child placed under section one thousand fifty-five runs away from the place of placement the court may, after hearing, revoke the order of placement and make any order, including an order of placement, that might have been made at the time the order of placement was made. The court may require that the child be present at such hearing and shall appoint a law guardian to represent him.

§ 1074. Release from responsibility under order of placement.

Those responsible for the operation of a place where a child has been placed under section one thousand fifty-five may petition the court for leave to return the child to the court and for good cause shown be released from responsibility under the order of placement. After hearing, the court may grant the petition and make any order, including an order of placement, that might have been made at the time the order of placement was made.

§ 1075. Special duties of law guardian.

In addition to all other duties and responsibilities necessary to the representation of a child who is the subject of a proceeding under this article, a law guardian shall upon receipt of a report from a child protective agency pursuant to sections ten hundred thirty-nine, ten hundred thirty-nine-a, ten hundred fifty-two-a, ten hundred fifty-three, ten hundred fifty-four, ten hundred fifty-five, ten hundred fifty-seven and ten hundred fifty-eight, review the information contained therein and make a determination as to whether there is reasonable cause to suspect that the child is at risk of further abuse or neglect or that there has been a substantive violation of a court order. Where the law guardian makes such a determination, the law guardian shall apply to the court for appropriate relief pursuant to section ten hundred sixty-one. Nothing contained in this section shall relieve a child protective agency or social services official of its duties pursuant to this act or the social services law.

Added by Laws 1990, Ch. 316, § 1, eff. Sept. 1, 1990.

Part 8. Visitation of minors in foster care.

§ 1081. Visitation rights.

1. A non-custodial parent or grandparent shall have the visitation rights with a child remanded or placed in the care of a social services official pursuant to this article as conferred by order of the family court or by any order or judgment of the supreme court, or by written agreement between the parents as described in section two hundred thirty-six of the domestic relations law, subject to the provisions of section one thousand eighty-two of this part.

2. A non-custodial parent or any grandparent or grandparents who have not been afforded the visitation rights described in subdivision one of this section, shall have the right to petition the court for enforcement of visitation rights with a child remanded or placed in the care of a social services official pursuant to this article, as such visitation rights have been conferred by order of the family court or by any order or judgment of the supreme court, or by written agreement between the parents as described in section two hundred thirty-six of the domestic relations law.

3. (a) The petition by a non-custodial parent shall allege that such parent has visitation rights conferred by order of the family court or by any order or judgment of the supreme court or by written agreement between the parents as described in section two hundred thirty-six of the domestic relations law, shall have a copy of such order, judgment or agreement attached thereto, shall request enforcement of such rights pursuant to this part, and shall state, when known by the petitioner, that visitation rights with the child by any grandparent or grandparents have been conferred by order of the supreme court or family court pursuant to section seventy-two or two hundred forty of the domestic relations law, and shall provide the name and address of such grandparent or grandparents.

(b) A petition by a grandparent or grandparents shall allege that such grandparent or grandparents have been granted visitation rights with the child pursuant to section seventy-two or two hundred forty of the domestic relations law, or subdivision (b) of section six hundred fifty-one of this act, shall have a copy of such order or judgment attached thereto, and shall request enforcement of such rights pursuant to this part.

4. The petition shall be served upon the respondent in a proceeding under this article, the local social services official having the care of the child, any grandparent or grandparents named in the petition as having visitation rights conferred by court order pursuant to section seventy-two or two hundred forty of the domestic relations law, and upon the child's law guardian. The petition shall be served in such manner as the court may direct.

5. Upon receipt of such petition the court shall, subject to the provisions of section one thousand eighty-two of this part, require that any order of a family court or order or judgment of the supreme court, or any agreement between the parents as described in subdivision one of this section, granting visitation rights to the non-custodial parent, grandparent or grandparents, be incorporated in any preliminary order or order of placement made under this article to the extent that

such order, judgment or agreement confers visitation rights. In any case where a dispositional hearing has not been held or will not be held within thirty days of the filing of such petition the court shall order the person, official, agency or institution caring for the child pursuant to this article to comply with such part of the order, judgment or agreement granting visitation rights. Violation of such order shall be punishable pursuant to section seven hundred fifty-three of the judiciary law.

Added by Laws 1988, Ch. 457, eff. Nov. 1, 1988.

§ 1082. Approval, modification or denial of visitation rights.

1.   (a) Upon receipt of a petition pursuant to subdivision four of section one thousand eighty-one of this part, the local department of social services shall make inquiry of the state central register of child abuse and maltreatment to determine whether or not the petitioner is a subject of an indicated report of child abuse or maltreatment, as such terms are defined in section four hundred twelve of the social services law, and shall further ascertain whether or not the petitioner is a respondent in a proceeding under this article whereby the child with whom visitation is sought has been allegedly abused or neglected or has been adjudicated as an abused or neglected child.

(b)   The department, the law guardian and the respondent in a proceeding under this article, shall have the right to be heard in respect to a petition for an order to enforce visitation rights under this part.

2.   Where the local department of social services or the law guardian opposes a petition described in section one thousand eighty-one of this part, the department or the law guardian as appropriate shall serve and file an answer to the petition. The court shall, upon the filing of such answer, set a date for a hearing on such petition and shall notify the parents, grandparent or grandparents, the department and the law guardian of such hearing date.

3.   Whenever a hearing described in subdivision two of this section is to be held within ten court days of a dispositional hearing authorized under this article, the court may in its discretion hear such petition as part of such dispositional hearing.

4.   In any hearing under this section, the court shall approve such petition unless the court finds upon competent, relevant and material evidence that enforcement of visitation rights as described in the order, judgment or agreement would endanger the child's life or health. Upon such a finding, the court shall make an order denying such petition or make such other order affecting enforcement of visitation rights as the court deems to be in the best interests of the child.

5.   (a) Where a petition is approved pursuant to this section the parties may agree in writing to an alternative schedule of visitation equivalent to and consistent with the original or modified visitation order or agreement where such

alternative schedule reflects changed circumstances of the parties and is consistent with the best interests of the child.

(b) In the absence of such an agreement between the parties, the court may, in its discretion, order an alternative schedule of visitation as defined herein, where it determines that such schedule is necessary to facilitate visitation and to protect the best interests of the child.

Added by Laws 1988, Ch. 457, eff. Nov. 1, 1988.

§ 1083. Duration of orders affecting visitation rights.

1. Where an order of the court has been made incorporating an order, judgment or agreement conferring visitation rights with a child on a non-custodial parent or grandparent into a dispositional order under this article, or where the court otherwise orders compliance by a person, official, agency or institution caring for the child, with an order, judgment or agreement granting visitation rights, such order shall remain in effect for the length of time the child remains in such care pursuant to this article, unless such order is subsequently modified by the court for good cause shown.

2. Where the court makes an order denying a petition seeking enforcement of visitation rights or makes an order modifying visitation rights, pursuant to the provisions of section one thousand eighty-two of this part, such order shall remain in effect for the length of time the child is placed with a person, official, agency or institution caring for the child pursuant to this article, unless such order is subsequently modified by the court for good cause shown.

Added by Laws 1988, Ch. 457, eff. Nov. 1, 1988.

§ 1084. Out of wedlock children; paternity.

No visitation right shall be enforceable under this part concerning any person claiming to be a parent of an out of wedlock child without an adjudication of the paternity of such person by a court of competent jurisdiction, or without an acknowledgment of the paternity of such person executed pursuant to applicable provisions of law.

Added by Laws 1988, Ch. 457, eff. Nov. 1, 1988.

§ 1085. Visitation and custody rights unenforceable; murder of parent, custodian, guardian, or child.

1. No visitation or custody order shall be enforceable under this part by a person who has been convicted of murder in the first or second degree in this state, or convicted of an offense in another jurisdiction which, if committed in this state, would constitute either murder in the first or second degree, of a parent, legal custodian, legal guardian, sibling, half-sibling or step-sibling of the child unless:

(i)   (A) such child is of suitable age to signify assent and such child assents to such visitation or custody; or

(B)   if such child is not of suitable age to signify assent the child's custodian or legal guardian assents to such order; or

(C)   the person who has been convicted of murder in the first or second degree, or an offense in another jurisdiction which if committed in this state, would constitute either murder in the first or second degree, can prove by a preponderance of the evidence that:

(1)   he or she, or a family or household member of either party, was a victim of domestic violence by the victim of such murder; and

(2)   the domestic violence was causally related to the commission of such murder; and

(ii)   the court finds that such visitation or custody is in the best interest of the child.

2.   Pending determination of a petition for visitation or custody such child shall not visit and no person shall visit, with such child present, such person, legal guardian or legal custodian who has been convicted of murder in the first or second degree in this state, or an offense in another jurisdiction which, if committed in this state, would constitute either murder in the first or second degree, of the other parent, legal guardian, legal custodian, sibling, half-sibling or step-sibling of such child, without the consent of such child's custodian or legal guardian.

3.   Nothing contained in this section shall be construed to require a court, without petition from any of the interested parties, to review a previously issued order of visitation or custody or denial of such petition.

4.   For the purposes of making a determination pursuant to subparagraph (c) of paragraph (i) of subdivision one of this section, the court shall not be bound by the findings of fact, conclusions of law or ultimate conclusion as determined by the proceedings leading to the conviction of murder in the first or second degree in this state or of an offense in another jurisdiction which, if committed in this state, would constitute murder in either the first or second degree, of a parent, legal guardian, legal custodian, sibling, half-sibling or step-sibling of a child who is the subject of the proceeding. In all proceedings under this section, a law guardian shall be appointed for the child.

Added by Laws 1998, Ch. 150, § 3, eff. July 7, 1998; **amended** by Laws 1999, Ch. 378, § 2, eff. July 27, 1999.

10-A

Permanency Hearings for Children Placed Out of Their Homes.

―――

Add, L. 2005, Ch. 3, §27 eff. Dec. 21, 2005.

FCA

§ 1086. Purpose.

The purpose of this article is to establish uniform procedures for permanency hearings for all children who are placed in foster care pursuant to section three hundred fifty-eight-a, three hundred eighty-four or three hundred eighty-four-a of the social services law or pursuant to section one thousand twenty-two, one thousand twenty-seven, or one thousand fifty-two of this act; children who are directly placed with a relative pursuant to section one thousand seventeen or one thousand fifty-five of this act; and children who are freed for adoption. It is meant to provide children placed out of their homes timely and effective judicial review that promotes permanency, safety and well-being in their lives.

Add, L. 2005, Ch. 3, § 27, eff. Aug. 23, 2005; L 2005, ch 3, §27 (Part A), eff Dec 21, 2005.

§ 1087. Definitions.

When used in this article, the following terms shall have the following meanings:

(a) "Child" shall mean a person under the age of eighteen who is placed in foster care pursuant to section three hundred fifty-eight-a, three hundred eighty-four or three hundred eighty-four-a of the social services law or pursuant to section one thousand twenty-two, one thousand twenty-seven, or one thousand fifty-two of this act; or directly placed with a relative pursuant to section one thousand seventeen or one thousand fifty-five of this act; or who has been freed for adoption or a person between the ages of eighteen and twenty-one who has consented to continuation in foster care.

(b) "Child freed for adoption" shall mean a person whose custody and guardianship has been committed to an authorized agency pursuant to section three hundred eighty-three-c, three hundred eighty-four, or three hundred eighty-four-b of the social services law. Such category shall include a person whose parent or parents have died during the period in which the child was in foster care and for whom there is no surviving parent who would be entitled to notice or consent pursuant to section one hundred eleven or one hundred eleven-a of the domestic relations law. Such category shall not include a child who has been freed for adoption with respect to one parent but who has another parent whose consent to an adoption is required pursuant to section one hundred eleven of the domestic relations law.

(c) "Foster care" shall mean care provided by an authorized agency to a child in a foster family, free or boarding home; agency boarding home; group home; child care institution, health care facility or any combination thereof.

(d) "Agency" means an authorized agency as defined in paragraphs (a) and (b) of subdivision ten of section three hundred seventy-one of the social services law, to which the care and custody or custody and guardianship of a child has been transferred or committed.

(e) "Permanency hearing report" shall mean a sworn report submitted by the social services district to the court and the parties prior to each permanency hearing regarding the health and well-being of the child, the reasonable efforts that have been made since the last hearing to promote permanency for the child, and the recommended permanency plan for the child.

Add, L. 2005, Ch. 3, § 27, eff. Aug. 23, 2005; L 2005, ch 3, §27 (Part A), eff Dec 21, 2005.

§ 1088.　Continuing court jurisdiction.

If a child is placed pursuant to section three hundred fifty-eight-a, three hundred eighty-four, or three hundred eighty-four-a of the social services law, or pursuant to section one thousand seventeen, one thousand twenty-two, one thousand twenty-seven or one thousand fifty-two of this act, or directly placed with a relative pursuant to section one thousand seventeen or one thousand fifty-five of this act; or if the child is freed for adoption pursuant to section three hundred eighty-three-c, three hundred eighty-four or three hundred eighty-four-b of the social services law, the case shall remain on the court's calendar and the court shall maintain jurisdiction over the case until the child is discharged from placement and all orders regarding supervision, protection or services have expired. The court shall rehear the matter whenever it deems necessary or desirable, or upon motion by any party entitled to notice in proceedings under this article, or by the law guardian for the child, and whenever a permanency hearing is required by this article. While the court maintains jurisdiction over the case, the provisions of section one thousand thirty-eight of this act shall continue to apply.

Add, L. 2005, Ch. 3, § 27, eff. Aug. 23, 2005; L 2005, ch 3, §27 (Part A), eff Dec 21, 2005.

§ 1089. Permanency hearings.

(a) Scheduling, commencement and completion of permanency hearings.

(1) Children freed for adoption. At the conclusion of the dispositional hearing at which the child was freed for adoption in a proceeding pursuant to section three hundred eighty-three-c, three hundred eighty-four or three hundred eighty-four-b of the social services law, the court shall set a date certain for the initial freed child permanency hearing and advise all parties in court of the date set, except for the respondent or respondents. The permanency hearing shall be commenced no later than thirty days after the hearing at which the child was freed and shall be completed within thirty days, unless the court determines to hold the permanency hearing immediately upon completion of the hearing at which the child was freed, provided adequate notice has been given.

(2) All other permanency hearings. At the conclusion of the hearing pursuant to section one thousand twenty-two, one thousand twenty-seven, or one thousand fifty-two of this act at which the child was remanded or placed and upon the court's approval of a voluntary placement instrument pursuant to section three hundred fifty-eight-a of the social services law, the court shall set a date certain for an initial permanency hearing, advise all parties in court of the date set and include the date in the order. Orders issued in subsequent court hearings prior to the permanency hearing, including, but not limited to, the order of placement issued pursuant to section one thousand fifty-five of this act, shall include the date certain for the permanency hearing. The initial permanency hearing shall be commenced no later than six months from the date which is sixty days after the child was removed from his or her home; provided, however, that if a sibling or half-sibling of the child has previously been removed from the home and has a permanency hearing date certain scheduled within the next eight months, the permanency hearing for each child subsequently removed from the home shall be scheduled on the same date certain that has been set for the first child removed from the home, unless such sibling or half-sibling has been removed from the home pursuant to article three or seven of this act. The permanency hearing shall be completed within thirty days of the scheduled date certain.

(3) Subsequent permanency hearings for a child who continues in out-of-home placement or who is freed for adoption shall be scheduled for a date certain which shall be no later than six months from the completion of the previous permanency hearing and such subsequent permanency hearings shall be completed within thirty days of the date certain set for such hearings.

(b) Notice of permanency hearings.

(1) No later than fourteen days before the date certain for a permanency hearing scheduled pursuant to this section, the local social services district shall serve the notice of the permanency hearing and the permanency hearing report by regular mail upon:

(i)   the child's parent, including any non-respondent parent, unless the parental rights of the parent have been terminated or surrendered and any other person legally responsible for the child's care at the most recent address or addresses known to the local social services district or agency, and the foster parent in whose home the child currently resides, each of whom shall be a party to the proceeding; and

(ii)   the agency supervising the care of the child on behalf of the social services district with whom the child was placed, the child's law guardian, and the attorney for the respondent parent.

(2)   The notice and the permanency hearing report shall also be provided to any pre-adoptive parent or relative providing care for the child and shall be submitted to the court. The notice of the permanency hearing only shall be provided to a former foster parent in whose home the child previously had resided for a continuous period of twelve months in foster care, if any, unless the court, on motion of any party or on its own motion, dispenses with such notice on the basis that such notice would not be in the child's best interests. However, such pre-adoptive parent, relative, or former foster parent, on the basis of such notice, shall have an opportunity to be heard but shall not be a party to the permanency hearing. The failure of such pre-adoptive parent, relative or former foster parent to appear at a permanency hearing shall constitute a waiver of the opportunity to be heard. Such failure to appear shall not cause a delay of the permanency hearing nor be a ground for the invalidation of any order issued by the court pursuant to this section.

(c)   Content of the permanency hearing report. The permanency hearing report shall include, but need not be limited to, up-to-date and accurate information regarding:

(1)   the child's current permanency goal, which may be:

(i)   return to the parent or parents;

(ii)   placement for adoption with the local social services official filing a petition for termination of parental rights;

(iii)   referral for legal guardianship;

(iv)   permanent placement with a fit and willing relative; or

(v)   placement in another planned permanent living arrangement that includes a significant connection to an adult who is willing to be a permanency resource for the child, including documentation of the compelling reason for determining that it would not be in the best interests of the child to be returned home, placed for adoption, placed with a legal guardian, or placed with a fit and willing relative;

(2)   the health, well-being, and status of the child since the last hearing including:

(i)   a description of the child's health and well-being;

(ii)   information regarding the child's current placement;

(iii)   an update on the educational and other progress the child has made since the last hearing including a description of the steps that have been taken by the local social services district or agency to enable prompt delivery of appropriate educational and vocational services to the child, including, but not be limited to:

(A)   where the child is subject to article sixty-five of the education law or elects to participate in an educational program leading to a high school diploma, the steps that the local social services district or agency has taken to promptly enable the child to be enrolled or to continue enrollment in an appropriate school or educational program leading to a high school diploma;

(B)   where the child is eligible to be enrolled in a pre-kindergarten program pursuant to section thirty-six hundred two-e of the education law, the steps that the local social services district or agency has taken to promptly enable the child to be enrolled in an appropriate pre-kindergarten program, if available;

(C)   where the child is under three years of age and is involved in an indicated case of child abuse or neglect, or where the local social services district suspects that the child may have a disability as defined in subdivision five of section twenty-five hundred forty-one of the public health law or if the child has been found eligible to receive early intervention or special educational services prior to or during the foster care placement, in accordance with title two-A of article twenty-five of the public health law or article eighty-nine of the education law, the steps that the local social services district or agency has taken to make any necessary referrals of the child for early intervention, pre-school special educational or special educational evaluations or services, as appropriate, and any available information regarding any evaluations and services which are being provided or are scheduled to be provided in accordance with applicable law; and

(D)   where the child is at least sixteen and not subject to article sixty-five of the education law and elects not to participate in an educational program leading to a high school diploma, the steps that the local social services district has taken to assist the child to become gainfully employed or enrolled in a vocational program;

(iv)   a description of the visitation plan or plans describing the persons with whom the child visits, including any siblings, and the frequency, duration and quality of the visits;

(v)   where a child has attained the age of fourteen, a description of the services and assistance that are being provided to enable the child to learn independent living skills; and

(vi)   a description of any other services being provided to the child;

(3)   the status of the parent, including:

(i)   the services that have been offered to the parent to enable the child to safely return home;

(ii)   the steps the parent has taken to use the services;

(iii)   any barriers encountered to the delivery of such services;

(iv) the progress the parent has made toward reunification; and

(v) a description of any other steps the parent has taken to comply with and achieve the permanency plan, if applicable.

(4) a description of the reasonable efforts to achieve the child's permanency plan that have been taken by the local social services district or agency since the last hearing. The description shall include:

(i) unless the child is freed for adoption or there has been a determination by a court that such efforts are not required pursuant to section one thousand thirty-nine-b of this act, the reasonable efforts that have been made by the local social services district or agency to eliminate the need for placement of the child and to enable the child to safely return home, including a description of any services that have been provided;

(ii) where the permanency plan is adoption, guardianship, placement with a fit and willing relative or another planned permanent living arrangement other than return to parent, the reasonable efforts that have been made by the local social services district or agency to make and finalize such alternate permanent placement, including a description of any services that have been provided;

(iii) where return home of the child is not likely, the reasonable efforts that have been made by the local social services district or agency to evaluate and plan for another permanent plan and any steps taken to further a permanent plan other than return to the child's parent; or

(iv) where a child has been freed for adoption, a description of the reasonable efforts that will be taken to facilitate the adoption of the child; and

(5) the recommended permanency plan including:

(i) a recommendation regarding whether the child's current permanency goal should be continued or modified, the reasons therefor, and the anticipated date for meeting the goal;

(ii) a recommendation regarding whether the child's placement should be extended and the reasons for the recommendation;

(iii) any proposed changes in the child's current placement, trial discharge or discharge that may occur before the next permanency hearing;

(iv) a description of the steps that will be taken by the local social services district or agency to continue to enable prompt delivery of appropriate educational and vocational services to the child in his or her current placement and during any potential change in the child's foster care placement, during any trial discharge, and after discharge of the child in accordance with the plans for the child's placement until the next permanency hearing;

(v) whether any modification to the visitation plan or plans is recommended and the reasons therefor;

(vi) where a child has attained the age of fourteen or will attain the age of fourteen before the next permanency hearing, a description of the services and assistance that will be provided to enable the child to learn independent living skills;

(vii)   where a child has been placed outside this state, whether the out-of-state placement continues to be appropriate, necessary and in the best interests of the child;

(viii)   where return home of the child is not likely, the efforts that will be made to evaluate or plan for another permanent plan; and

(ix)   in the case of a child who has been freed for adoption:

(A)   a description of services and assistance that will be provided to the child and the prospective adoptive parent to expedite the adoption of the child;

(B)   information regarding the child's eligibility for adoption subsidy pursuant to title nine of article six of the social services law; and

(C)   if the child is over age fourteen and has voluntarily withheld his or her consent to an adoption, the facts and circumstances regarding the child's decision to withhold consent and the reasons therefor.

(d)   Court findings and order. At the conclusion of each permanency hearing, the court shall, upon the proof adduced, in accordance with the best interests and safety of the child, including whether the child would be at risk of abuse or neglect if returned to the parent or other person legally responsible, determine and issue its findings, and enter an order of disposition in writing:

(1)   directing that the placement of the child be terminated and the child returned to the parent or other person legally responsible for the child's care with such further orders as the court deems appropriate; or

(2)   where the child is not returned to the parent or other person legally responsible:

(i)   whether the permanency goal for the child should be approved or modified and the anticipated date for achieving the goal. The permanency goal may be determined to be:

(A)   return to parent;

(B)   placement for adoption with the local social services official filing a petition for termination of parental rights;

(C)   referral for legal guardianship;

(D)   permanent placement with a fit and willing relative; or

(E)   placement in another planned permanent living arrangement that includes a significant connection to an adult willing to be a permanency resource for the child if the local social services official has documented to the court a compelling reason for determining that it would not be in the best interests of the child to return home, be referred for termination of parental rights and placed for adoption, placed with a fit and willing relative, or placed with a legal guardian;

(ii)   placing the child in the custody of a fit and willing relative or other suitable person, or continuing the placement of the child until the completion of the next permanency hearing, provided, however, that no placement may be continued under this section beyond the child's eighteenth birthday without his or her consent and in no event past the child's twenty-first birthday;

(iii)   determining whether reasonable efforts have been made to effectuate the child's permanency plan as follows:

(A)   unless the child is freed for adoption or there has been a determination by a court that such efforts are not required pursuant to section one thousand thirty-nine-b of this act, whether reasonable efforts have been made to eliminate the need for placement of the child and to enable the child to safely return home;

(B)   where the permanency plan is adoption, guardianship, placement with a fit and willing relative or another planned permanent living arrangement other than return to parent, whether reasonable efforts have been made to make and finalize such alternate permanent placement;

(iv)   where return home of the child is not likely, what efforts should be made to evaluate or plan for another permanent plan;

(v)   the steps that must be taken by the local social services official or agency to implement the educational and vocational program components of the permanency hearing report submitted pursuant to subdivision (c) of this section, and any modifications that should be made to such plan;

(vi)   specifying the date certain for the next scheduled permanency hearing;

(vii)   where placement of the child is extended, such order shall also include:

(A)   a description of the visitation plan or plans;

(B)   where the child is not freed for adoption, a direction that the child's parent or parents, including any non-respondent parent or other person legally responsible for the child's care shall be notified of the planning conference or conferences to be held pursuant to subdivision three of section four hundred nine-e of the social services law and notification of their right to attend such conference or conferences and their right to have counsel or another representative with them;

(C)   where the child is not freed for adoption, a direction that the parent or other person legally responsible for the child's care keep the local social services district or agency apprised of his or her current whereabouts and a current mailing address;

(D)   where the child is not freed for adoption, a notice that if the child remains in foster care for fifteen of the most recent twenty-two months, the local social services district or agency may be required by law to file a petition to terminate parental rights;

(E)   where a child has been freed for adoption and is over age fourteen and has voluntarily withheld his or her consent to an adoption, the facts and circumstances with regard to the child's decision to withhold consent and the reasons therefor;

(F)   where a child has been placed outside of this state, whether the out-of-state placement continues to be appropriate, necessary and in the best interests of the child;

(G)   where a child has or will before the next permanency hearing reach the age of fourteen, the services and assistance necessary to assist the child in learning independent living skills; and

(viii)   any other findings or orders that the court deems appropriate, which may include:

(A)   Whether the court should issue any orders for services in the manner specified in section one thousand fifteen-a of this act in order to achieve the permanency plan and, if so, what services should be ordered.

(B)   Where a child has been freed for adoption, the order may also:

(I)   direct that such child be placed for adoption in the foster family home where he or she resides or has resided or with any other suitable person or persons;

(II)   direct the local social services district to provide services or assistance to the child and the prospective adoptive parent authorized or required to be made available pursuant to the comprehensive annual services program plan then in effect. Such order shall include, where appropriate, the evaluation of eligibility for adoption subsidy pursuant to title nine of article six of the social services law, but shall not require the provision of such subsidy. Violation of such an order shall be subject to punishment pursuant to section seven hundred fifty-three of the judiciary law; and

(III)   recommend that the office of children and family services investigate the facts and circumstances concerning the discharge of responsibilities for the care and welfare of such child by a local social services district pursuant to section three hundred ninety-five of the social services law.

(C)   Where the permanency goal is return to parent and it is anticipated that the child may be returned home before the next scheduled permanency hearing, the court may provide the local social services district with authority to finally discharge the child to the parent without further court hearing, provided that ten days prior written notice is served upon the court and law guardian. If the court on its own motion or the law guardian on motion to the court does not request the matter to be brought for review before final discharge, no further permanency hearings will be required. The local social services district may also discharge the child on a trial basis to the parent unless the court has prohibited such trial discharge or unless the court has conditioned such trial discharge on another event. For the purposes of this section, trial discharge shall mean that the child is physically returned to the parent while the child remains in the care and custody of the local social services district. Permanency hearings shall continue to be held for any child who has returned to his or her parents on a trial discharge. Where the permanency goal for a child aging out of foster care is another planned permanent living arrangement that includes a significant connection to an adult willing to be a permanency resource for the child, the local social services district may also discharge the child on a trial basis to the planned permanent living arrangements, unless the court has prohibited or otherwise conditioned such a trial discharge. Trial discharge for a child aging out of foster care shall mean that a child is physically discharged but the local social services district retains care and custody or custody and guardianship of the child and there remains a date certain for the scheduled permanency hearing.

(D)　The court may make an order of protection in the manner specified by section one thousand fifty-six of this act in assistance or as a condition of any other order made under this section. The order of protection may set forth reasonable conditions of behavior to be observed for a specified period of time by a person before the court.

(E)　Where the court finds reasonable cause to believe that grounds for termination of parental rights exist, the court may direct the local social services district or other agency to institute a proceeding to legally free the child for adoption pursuant to section three hundred eighty-four-b of the social services law. Upon a failure by such agency to institute such proceeding within ninety days after entry of such order, the court shall permit the foster parent or parents in whose home the child resides to institute such a proceeding unless the local social services district or other agency, for good cause shown and upon due notice to all the parties to the proceeding, has obtained a modification or extension of such order, or unless the court has reasonable cause to believe that such foster parent or parents would not obtain approval of their petition to adopt the child in a subsequent adoption proceeding.

(F)　The court may make an order directing a local social services district or agency to undertake diligent efforts to encourage and strengthen the parental relationship when it finds such efforts will not be detrimental to the best interests of the child and there has been no prior court finding that such efforts are not required. Such efforts shall include encouraging and facilitating visitation with the child by the parent or other person legally responsible for the child's care. Such order may include a specific plan of action for the local social services district or agency including, but not limited to, requirements that such agency assist the parent or other person legally responsible for the child's care in obtaining adequate housing, employment, counseling, medical care or psychiatric treatment. Such order shall also include encouraging and facilitating visitation with the child by the noncustodial parent and grandparents who have the right to visitation pursuant to section one thousand eighty-one of this act, and may include encouraging and facilitating visitation with the child by the child's siblings. Nothing in this subdivision shall be deemed to limit the authority of the court to make an order pursuant to section two hundred fifty-five of this act.

(G) Except as provided for herein, in any order issued pursuant to this section, the court may require the local social services district or agency to make progress reports to the court, the parties, and the child's law guardian on the implementation of such order.

(H) Where a child freed for adoption has not been placed in a prospective adoptive home and the court has entered an order of disposition directing that the child be placed for adoption or directing the provision of services or assistance to the child and the agency charged with the guardianship and custody of the child fails, prior to the next scheduled permanency hearing, to comply with such order, the court at the time of such hearing may, in the best interests of the child, enter an order committing the guardianship and custody of the child to another authorized agency or may make any other order authorized pursuant to section two hundred fifty-five of this act.

(e) Service of court order and permanency hearing report. A copy of the court order which includes the date certain for the next permanency hearing and the permanency hearing report as approved, adjusted, or modified by the court, shall be given to the parent or other person legally responsible for the child.

FCA

Add, L. 2005, Ch. 3, § 27, eff. Aug. 23, 2005; L 2005, ch 3, §27 (Part A), eff Dec 21, 2005; Sub (a), par (2), amd, L 2006, ch 437, §7, eff July 26, 2006; Sub (a), par (3), amd, L 2006, ch 437, §7, eff July 26, 2006; Sub (b), par (1), subpar (i), amd, L 2006, ch 437, §8, eff July 26, 2006; Sub (b), par (2), amd, L 2006, ch 437, §9, eff July 26, 2006; Sub (d), par (2), subpar (viii), cl (C), amd, L 2006, ch 437, §10, eff July 26, 2006.

§ 1090. Representation of parties.

(a) If a law guardian for the child has been appointed by the family court in a proceeding pursuant to section three hundred fifty-eight-a, three hundred eighty-three-c, three hundred eighty-four, or three hundred eighty-four-b of the social services law, or article ten of this act, the appointment of the law guardian shall continue without further court order or appointment, unless another appointment of a law guardian has been made by the court, until the child is discharged from placement and all orders regarding supervision, protection or services have expired. All notices, reports and motions required by law shall be provided to such law guardian. The law guardian may be relieved of his or her representation upon application to the court for termination of the appointment. Upon approval of the application, the court shall immediately appoint another law guardian to whom all notices, reports, and motions required by law shall be provided.

(b) The appointment of an attorney for the respondent parent or parents pursuant to section two hundred sixty-two of this act shall continue without further order of the court. The appointment shall expire upon the expiration of the time for appeal of an order of disposition against the respondent parent committing custody and guardianship of the child pursuant to section three hundred eighty-four-b of the social services law or upon final determination of any appeal or subsequent appeals authorized by law, or upon entry of an order approving a surrender pursuant to the provisions of section three hundred eighty-three-c of the social services law. All notices, reports and motions required by law shall be served upon the attorney for the respondent parent or parents. The attorney may be relieved of his or her representation upon application to the court for termination of the appointment. If the application is approved, the court shall immediately appoint another attorney for the respondent parent or parents pursuant to section two hundred sixty-two of this act upon whom all notices, reports, and motions required by law shall be provided.

Add, L. 2005, Ch. 3, § 27, eff. Aug. 23, 2005; L 2005, ch 3, §27 (Part A), eff Dec 21, 2005.

ARTICLE 11

APPEALS

SUMMARY OF ARTICLE

§ 1111. Appeals to appellate division.

An appeal may be taken to the appellate division of the supreme court of the judicial department in which the family court whose order is appealed from is located.

Amended by Laws 1969, Ch. 264, eff. June 1, 1969.

§ 1112. Appealable orders.

a. An appeal may be taken as of right from any order of disposition and, in the discretion of the appropriate appellate division, from any other order under this act. An appeal from an intermediate or final order in a case involving abuse or neglect may be taken as of right to the appellate division of the supreme court. Pending the determination of such appeal, such order shall be stayed where the effect of such orderwould be to discharge the child, if the family court or the court before which such appeal is pending finds that such a stay is necessary to avoid imminent risk to the child's life or health. A preference in accordance with rule five thousand five hundred twenty-one of the civil practice law and rules shall be afforded, without the necessity of a motion, for appeals under article three; parts one and two of article six; articles seven, ten, and ten-A of this act; and sections three hundred fifty-eight-a, three hundred eighty-three-c, three hundred eighty-four, and three hundred eighty-four-b of the social services law.

b.   In any proceeding pursuant to article ten of this act or in any proceeding pursuant to article ten-A of this act that originated as a proceeding under article ten of this act where the family court issues an order which will result in the return of a child previously remanded or placed by the family court in the custody of someone other than the respondent, such order shall be stayed until five p.m. of the next business day after the day on which such order is issued unless such stay is waived by all parties to the proceeding by written stipulation or upon the record in family court. Nothing herein shall be deemed to affect the discretion of a judge of the family court to stay an order returning a child to the custody of a respondent for a longer period of time than set forth in this subdivision.

Amended by Laws 1969, Ch. 264; Laws 1970, Ch. 962, eff. May 1, 1970; Laws 1983, Ch. 232, eff. June 3, 1983; Laws 1991, Ch. 34, § 1, eff. Apr. 6, 1991; Laws 2005, ch. 3 §28 (Part A), eff. Dec 21, 2005; Laws 2006, ch. 437, §11, eff. July 26, 2006.

§ 1113.   Time of appeal.

An appeal under this article must be taken no later than thirty days after the service by a party or the law guardian upon the appellant of any order from which the appeal is taken, thirty days from receipt of the order by the appellant in court or thirty-five days from the mailing of the order to the appellant by the clerk of the court, whichever is earliest.

All such orders shall contain the following statement in conspicuous print: "pursuant to section 1113 of the family court act, an appeal must be taken within thirty days of receipt of the order by appellant in court, thirty-five days from the mailing of the order to the appellant by the clerk of the court, or thirty days after service by a party or law guardian upon the appellant, whichever is earliest." When service of the order is made by the court, the time to take an appeal shall not commence unless the order contains such statement and there is an official notation in the court record as to the date and the manner of service of the order.

Amended by Laws 1991, Ch. 582, § 2, eff. Jan. 1, 1992; Laws 1997, Ch. 461, § 1, eff. Jan. 1, 1998 and applicable to all orders issued on or after Jan. 1, 1998.

§ 1114.   Effect of appeal; stay.

(a)   The timely filing of a notice of appeal under this article does not stay the order from which the appeal is taken.

(b)   Except as provided in subdivision (d) of this section, a justice of the appellate division to which an appeal is taken may stay execution of the order from which the appeal is taken on such conditions, if any, as may be appropriate.

(c)   If the order appealed from is an order of support under articles four or five, the stay may be conditioned upon the giving of sufficient surety by a written undertaking approved by such judge of the appellate division, that during the pendency of the appeal, the appellant will pay the amount specified in the order to the family court from whose order the appeal is taken. The stay may further provide that the family court (i) shall hold such payments in escrow, pending determination of the appeal or (ii) shall disburse such payments or any part of them for the support of the petitioner or other person for whose benefit the order was made.

(d) Any party to a child protective proceeding, or the law guardian, may apply to a justice of the appellate division for a stay of an order issued pursuant to part two of article ten of this chapter returning a child to the custody of a respondent. The party applying for the stay shall notify the attorneys for all parties and the law guardian of the time and place of such application. If requested by any party present, oral argument shall be had on the application, except for good cause stated upon the record. The party applying for the stay shall state in the application the errors of fact or law allegedly committed by the family court. A party applying to the court for the granting or continuation of such stay shall make every reasonable effort to obtain a complete transcript of the proceeding before the family court.

If a stay is granted, a schedule shall be set for an expedited appeal.

FCA

Amended by Laws 1991, Ch. 417, §§ 1, 2, eff. Sept. 1, 1991.

§ 1115. Notices of appeal

An appeal as of right shall be taken by filing the original notice of appeal with the clerk of the family court in which the order was made and from which the appeal is taken.

A notice of appeal shall be served on any adverse party as provided for in subdivision one of section five thousand five hundred fifteen of the civil practice law and rules and upon the law guardian, if any. The appellant shall file two copies of such notice, together with proof of service, with the clerk of the family court who shall forthwith transmit one copy of such notice to the clerk of the appropriate appellate division or as otherwise required by such appellate division.

Formerly §1015, add, L 1962, ch 686; renumbered §1115, L 1969, ch 264, §1; amd, L 1974, ch 393, §1, eff Aug 15, 1974; Sub (a), formerly entire section, so designated sub (a), L 1991, ch 582, §3, eff Jan 1, 1992; Sub (b), add, L 1991, ch 582, §3, eff Jan 1, 1992; L. 2005, Ch. 3, § 29, eff. Aug. 23, 2005; First undesignated par, formerly sub (a), so designated and amd, L 2005, ch 3, §29 (Part A), eff Dec 21, 2005; Second undesignated par, formerly sub (b), so designated and amd, L 2005, ch 3, §29 (Part A), eff Dec 21, 2005; Sub (a), redesignated first undesignated par, L 2005, ch 3, §29 (Part A), eff Dec 21, 2005; Sub (b), redesignated second undesignated par, L 2005, ch 3, §29 (Part A), eff Dec 21, 2005.

§ 1116. Printed case and brief not required.

In appeals under this article, a printed case on appeal or a printed brief shall not be required.

§ 1117. Costs.

When costs and disbursements on an appeal in a proceeding instituted by a social services official are awarded to the respondent, they shall be a county charge and be paid by the county.

Amended by Laws 1988, Ch. 476, eff. Jan. 1, 1989.

§ 1118. Applicability of civil practice act and rules of civil procedure.

Repealed by Laws 1990, Ch. 324, § 1, eff. June 30, 1990.

§ 1118. Applicability of civil practice law and rules.

The provisions of the civil practice law and rules apply where appropriate to appeals under this article, provided, however, that the fees required by section eight thousand twenty-two of the civil practice law and rules shall not be required where the attorney for the appellant or attorney for the movant, as applicable, certifies that such appellant or movant has been assigned counsel or a law guardian pursuant to section two hundred forty-nine, two hundred sixty-two or eleven hundred twenty of this act or section seven hundred twenty-two of the county law, or is represented by a legal aid society or a legal services program or other nonprofit organization, which has as its primary purpose the furnishing of legal services to indigent persons, or by private counsel working on behalf of or under the auspices of such society or organization. Where the attorney for the appellant or the attorney for the movant certifies in accordance with procedures established by the appropriate appellate division that the appellant or movant has been represented in family court by assigned counsel or a law guardian, pursuant to section two hundred forty-nine, two hundred sixty-two or eleven hundred twenty of this act or section seven hundred twenty-two of the county law, or is represented by a legal aid society or legal services program or some other nonprofit organization, which has as its primary purpose the furnishing of legal services to indigent persons, or by private counsel working on behalf or under the auspices of such society or organization, and that the appellant, who has indicated an intention to appeal, or movant, continues to be eligible for assignment of counsel and, in the case of counsel assigned to represent an adult party, continues to be indigent, the appellant or movant shall be presumed eligible for poor person relief pursuant to section eleven hundred one of the civil practice law and rules and for assignment of counsel on appeal without further motion. The appointment of counsel and granting of poor person relief by the appellate division shall continue for the purpose of filing a notice of appeal or motion for leave to appeal to the court of appeals.

Added by Laws 1990, Ch. 324, § 1, eff. June 30, 1990; Laws 2005, ch. 3, §30 (Part A), eff. Dec 21, 2000, Laws 2006, ch. 437, §12, eff. July 26, 2006.

§ **1119.   Effective date.**

This act shall take effect September first, nineteen hundred sixty-two.

Amended by Laws 1962, Ch. 687, eff. Sept. 1. 1962.

§ **1120.   Counsel or law guardian on appeal.**

(a)   Upon an appeal in a proceeding under this act, the appellate division to which such appeal is taken, or is sought to be taken, shall assign counsel to any person upon a showing that such person is one of the persons described in section two hundred sixty-two of this act and is financially unable to obtain independent counsel or upon certification by an attorney in accordance with section eleven hundred eighteen of this article. The appellate division to which such appeal is taken, or is sought to be taken, may in its discretion assign counsel to any party to the appeal. Counsel assigned under this section shall be compensated and shall receive reimbursement for expenses reasonably incurred in the same manner provided by section seven hundred twenty-two-b of the county law. The appointment of counsel by the appellate division shall continue for the purpose of filing a notice of appeal or motion for leave to appeal to the court of appeals. Counsel may be relieved of his or her representation upon application to the court to which the appeal is taken for termination of the appointment, by the court on its own motion or, in the case of a motion for leave to appeal to the court of appeals, upon application to the appellate division. Upon termination of the appointment of counsel for an indigent party the court shall promptly appoint another attorney.

(b)   Whenever a law guardian has been appointed by the family court pursuant to section two hundred forty-nine of this act to represent a child in a proceeding described therein, the appointment shall continue without further court order or appointment where (i) the law guardian on behalf of the child files a notice of appeal, or (ii) where a party to the original proceeding files a notice of appeal. The law guardian may be relieved of his representation upon application to the court to which the appeal is taken for termination of the appointment. Upon approval of such application the court shall appoint another law guardian.

(c)   An appellate court may appoint a law guardian to represent a child in an appeal in a proceeding originating in the family court where a law guardian was not representing the child at the time of the entry of the order appealed from or at the time of the filing of the motion for permission to appeal and when independent legal representation is not available to such child.

(d)   Nothing in this section shall be deemed to relieve law guardians of their duties pursuant to subdivision one of sections 354.2 and seven hundred sixty of this act.

(e)   Law guardians appointed or continuing to represent a person under this section shall be compensated and shall receive reimbursement for expenses

FCA

reasonably incurred in the same manner provided by section thirty-five of the judiciary law.

(f)   In any case where a law guardian is or shall be representing a child in an appellate proceeding pursuant to subdivision (b) or (c) of this section, such law guardian shall be served with a copy of the notice of appeal.

Added by Laws 1975, Ch. 682, eff. Jan. 1, 1976; amended by Laws 1988, Ch. 476, § 2, eff. Jan. 1, 1989; Laws 1991, Ch. 75, § 2, eff. Apr. 26, 1991; Laws 1991, Ch. 582, § 4, eff. Jan. 1, 1992; L. 2005, Ch. 3, § 31, eff. Aug. 23, 2005.

§ 1121.   Special procedures.

1.   Consistent with the provisions of sections 354.2, seven hundred sixty and one thousand fifty-two-b of this act the provisions of this section shall apply to appeals taken from orders issued pursuant to articles three, seven, ten and ten-A and parts one and two of article six of this act, and pursuant to sections three hundred fifty-eight-a, three hundred eighty-three-c, three hundred eighty-four, and three hundred eighty-four-b of the social services law.

2.   Upon the filing of such order, it shall be the duty of counsel to the parties and the law guardian to promptly advise the parties in writing of the right to appeal to the appropriate appellate division of the supreme court, the time limitations involved, the manner of instituting an appeal and obtaining a transcript of the testimony and the right to apply for leave to appeal as a poor person if the party is unable to pay the cost of an appeal. It shall be the further duty of such counsel or law guardian to explain to the client the procedures for instituting an appeal, the possible reasons upon which an appeal may be based and the nature and possible consequences of the appellate process.

3.   It shall also be the duty of such counsel or law guardian to ascertain whether the party represented by such attorney wishes to appeal and, if so, to serve and file the necessary notice of appeal and, as applicable, to apply for leave to appeal as a poor person, to file a certification of continued eligibility for appointment of counsel pursuant to section eleven hundred eighteen of this article, and to submit such other documents as may be required by the appropriate appellate division.

4.   If the party has been permitted to waive the appointment of a law guardian or counsel appointed pursuant to section two hundred forty-nine-a or two hundred sixty-two of this act, it shall be the duty of the court to advise the party of the right to the appointment of a law guardian or counsel for the purpose of filing an appeal.

5.   Where a party wishes to appeal, it shall also be the duty of such counsel or law guardian, where appropriate, to apply for assignment of counsel for such party pursuant to applicable provisions of this act, the judiciary law and the civil practice law and rules, and to file a certification of continued eligibility for appointment of counsel and, in the case of counsel assigned to represent an adult

party, continued indigency, pursuant to section eleven hundred eighteen of this article and to submit such other documents as may be required by the appropriate appellate division.

6.   (a) Except as provided for herein, counsel for the appellant shall, no later than ten days after filing the notice of appeal, request preparation of the transcript of the proceeding appealed therefrom.

(b)   Counsel assigned or appointed pursuant to article eleven of the civil practice law and rules or section eleven hundred twenty of this act shall, no later than ten days after receipt of notice of such appointment, request preparation of the transcript of the proceeding appealed from.

(c)   In any case where counsel is assigned or appointed pursuant to paragraph (b) of this subdivision subsequent to the filing of the notice of appeal, such counsel shall, within ten days of such assignment or appointment, request preparation of the transcript of the proceeding appealed from.

(d)   Where the appellant is seeking relief to proceed as a poor person pursuant to article eleven of the civil practice law and rules, the transcript of the proceeding appealed from shall be requested within ten days of the order determining the motion.

7.   Such transcript shall be completed within thirty days from the receipt of the request of the appellant. Where such transcript is not completed within such time period, the court reporter or director of the transcription service responsible for the preparation of the transcript shall notify the administrative judge of the appropriate judicial district. Such administrative judge shall establish procedures to effectuate the timely preparation of such transcript. The appellate divisions may establish additional procedures to effectuate the timely preparation of transcripts.

The appellate division shall establish procedures to ensure the expeditious filing and service of the appellant's brief, the answering brief and any reply brief, which may include scheduling orders. The appellant shall perfect the appeal within sixty days of receipt of the transcript of the proceeding appealed from or within any different time that the appellate division has by rule prescribed for perfecting such appeals under subdivision (c) of rule five thousand five hundred thirty of the civil practice law and rules or as otherwise specified by the appellate division. Such sixty day or other prescribed period may be extended by the appellate division for good cause shown upon written application to the appellate division showing merit to the appeal and a reasonable ground for an extension of time. Upon the granting of such an extension of time the appellate division shall issue new specific deadlines by which the appellant's brief, the answering brief and any reply brief must be filed and served.

Added by Laws 1991, Ch. 582, § 5, eff. Jan. 1, 1992; Laws 2005, ch. 3, §32 (Part A), eff. Dec 21, 2005; Laws 2006, ch. 437, §13, eff. July 26, 2006.

ARTICLE 12

SEPARABILITY

SUMMARY OF ARTICLE

Section 1211. Separability.

§ 1211. Separability.

If any provision of this act or the application thereof to any person or circumstances is held to be invalid, the remainder of the act and the application of such provision to other persons or circumstances shall not be affected thereby.

Added by Laws 1970, Ch. 962, eff. May 1, 1970.

UNIFORM RULES FOR THE FAMILY COURT

(22 N.Y.C.R.R. Part 205)

SYNOPSIS

§ 205.1. Application of Part; waiver; additional rules; definitions.

(a)   Application. This Part shall be applicable to all proceedings in the Family Court.

(b)   Waiver. For good cause shown, and in the interests of justice, the court in a proceeding may waive compliance with any of these rules in this Part, other than sections 205.2 and 205.3, unless prohibited from doing so by statute or by a rule of the Chief Judge.

(c)   Additional rules. Local court rules, not inconsistent with law or with these rules, shall comply with Part 9 of the Rules of the Chief Judge (22 NYCRR Part 9).

Ct. Rules

(d)   Statutory applicability. The provisions of this Part shall be construed consistent with the Family Court Act, the Domestic Relations Law and, where applicable, the Social Services Law. Matters not covered by these rules or the foregoing statutes are governed by the Civil Practice Law and Rules.

(e)   Definitions. (1) Chief Administrator of the Courts in this Part also includes a designee of the Administrator.

(2)   Unless otherwise defined in this Part, or the context otherwise requires, all terms used in this Part shall have the same meaning as they have in the Family Court Act, the Domestic Relations Law, the Social Services Law and the Civil Practice Law and Rules, as applicable.

§ 205.2.   Terms and parts of court.

(a)   Terms of court. A term of court is a four-week session of court, and there shall be 13 terms of court in a year, unless otherwise provided in the annual schedule of terms established by the Chief Administrator of the Courts, which also shall specify the dates of such terms.

(b)   Parts of court. A part of court is a designated unit of the court in which specified business of the court is to be conducted by a judge or quasi-judicial officer. There shall be such parts of court, including those mandated by statute, as may be authorized from time to time by the Chief Administrator of the Courts.

§ 205.3.   Individual assignment system; structure.

(a)   General. There shall be established for all proceedings heard in the Family Court an individual assignment system which provides for the continuous supervision of each proceeding by a single judge or, where appropriate, a single support magistrate. For the purposes of this Part, the word "judge" shall include a "support magistrate," where appropriate. Except as otherwise may be authorized by the Chief Administrator or by these rules, every proceeding shall be assigned and heard pursuant to the individual assignment system.

(b)   Assignments. Proceedings shall be assigned to a judge of the court upon the filing with the court of the first document in the case. Assignments shall be made by the clerk of the court pursuant to a method of random selection authorized by the Chief Administrator. The judge thereby assigned shall be known as the "assigned judge" with respect to that matter and, except as otherwise provided in subdivision (c) or by law, shall conduct all further proceedings therein.

(c)   Exceptions. (1) Where the requirements of matters already assigned to a judge are such as to limit the ability of the judge to handle additional cases, the Chief Administrator may authorize that new assignments to the judge be suspended until the judge is able to handle additional cases.

(2)   The Chief Administrator may authorize the establishment in any court of special categories of proceedings for assignment to judges specially assigned

to hear such proceedings. Where more than one judge is specially assigned to hear a particular category of proceeding, the assignment of such proceedings to the judges so assigned shall be at random.

(3) Matters requiring immediate disposition may be assigned to a judge designated to hear such matters when the assigned judge is not available.

(4) The Chief Administrator may authorize the transfer of any proceeding and any matter relating to a proceeding from one judge to another in accordance with the needs of the court.

(5) Assignment of cases to judges pursuant to this section shall be consistent with section 205.27 of this Part.

(6) Multiple proceedings involving members of the same family shall be assigned to be heard by a single judge to the extent feasible and appropriate including, but not limited to, child protective, foster care placement, family offense and custody proceedings.

§ 205.4. Access to Family Court proceedings.

(a) The Family Court is open to the public. Members of the public, including the news media, shall have access to all courtrooms, lobbies, public waiting areas and other common areas of the Family Court otherwise open to individuals having business before the court.

(b) The general public or any person may be excluded from a courtroom only if the judge presiding in the courtroom determines, on a case-by-case basis based upon supporting evidence, that such exclusion is warranted in that case. In exercising this inherent and statutory discretion, the judge may consider, among other factors, whether:

(1) the person is causing or is likely to cause a disruption in the proceedings;

(2) the presence of the person is objected to by one of the parties, including the law guardian, for a compelling reason;

(3) the orderly and sound administration of justice, including the nature of the proceeding, the privacy interests of individuals before the court, and the need for protection of the litigants, in particular, children, from harm requires that some or all observers be excluded from the courtroom;

(4) less restrictive alternatives to exclusion are unavailable or inappropriate to the circumstances of the particular case.

Whenever the judge exercises discretion to exclude any person or the general public from a proceeding or part of a proceeding in Family Court, the judge shall make findings prior to ordering exclusion.

(c) When necessary to preserve the decorum of the proceedings, the judge shall instruct representatives of the news media and others regarding the permissible use of the courtroom and other facilities of the court, the assignment of seats to representatives of the news media on an equitable basis, and any other

Ct. Rules

matters that may affect the conduct of the proceedings and the well-being and safety of the litigants therein.

(d) Audio-visual coverage of Family Court facilities and proceedings shall be governed by Part 29 of the Rules of the Chief Judge and Part 131 of the Rules of the Chief Administrator.

(e) Nothing in this section shall limit the responsibility and authority of the Chief Administrator of the Courts, or the administrative judges with the approval of the Chief Administrator of the Courts, to formulate and effectuate such reasonable rules and procedures consistent with this section as may be necessary and proper to ensure that the access by the public, including the press, to proceedings in the Family Court shall comport with the security needs of the courthouse, the safety of persons having business before the court and the proper conduct of court business.

§ 205.5. Privacy of Family Court records.

Subject to limitations and procedures set by statute and case law, the following shall be permitted access to the pleadings, legal papers formally filed in a proceeding, findings, decisions and orders and, subject to the provisions of CPLR 8002, transcribed minutes of any hearing held in the proceeding:

(a) the petitioner, presentment agency and adult respondent in the Family Court proceeding and their attorneys;

(b) when a child is either a party to, or the child's custody may be affected by, the proceedings:

(1) the parents or persons legally responsible for the care of that child and their attorneys;

(2) the guardian, guardian *ad litem* and law guardian or attorney for that child;

(3) an authorized representative of the child protective agency involved in the proceeding or the probation service;

(4) an agency to which custody has been granted by an order of the Family Court and its attorney; and

(c) a representative of the State Commission on Judicial Conduct, upon application to the appropriate Deputy Chief Administrator, or his or her designee, containing an affirmation that the commission is inquiring into a complaint under article 2-A of the Judiciary Law, and that the inquiry is subject to the confidentiality provisions of said article;

(d) in proceedings under Articles 4, 5, 6 and 8 of the Family Court Act in which temporary or final orders of protection have been issued:

(1) where a related criminal action may, but has not yet been commenced, a prosecutor upon affirmation that such records are necessary to conduct an investigation or prosecution; and

(2)　where a related criminal action has been commenced, a prosecutor or defense attorney in accordance with procedures set forth in the Criminal Procedure Law provided, however, that prosecutors may request transcripts of Family Court proceedings in accordance with § 815 of the Family Court Act, and provided further that any records or information disclosed pursuant to this subdivision must be retained as confidential and may not be redisclosed except as necessary for such investigation or use in the criminal action.

(e)　another court when necessary for a pending proceeding involving one or more parties or children who are or were the parties in, or subjects of, a proceeding in the Family Court pursuant to Article 4, 5, 6, 8 or 10 of the Family Court Act. Only certified copies of pleadings and orders in, as well as information regarding the status of, such Family Court proceeding may be transmitted without court order pursuant to this section. Any information or records disclosed pursuant to this paragraph may not be re-disclosed except as necessary to the pending proceeding.

Where the Family Court has authorized that the address of a party or child be kept confidential in accordance with Family Court Act § 154-b(2), any record or document disclosed pursuant to this section shall have such address redacted or otherwise safeguarded.

§ 205.6.　Periodic reports.

Reports on forms to be furnished by the Office of Court Administration shall be filed with that office by the Family Court in each county, as follows:

(a)　On or before the 20th day of each term, a report shall be filed in the Office of Court Administration for each of the following instances in which an order of disposition was entered in the preceding month:

(1)　every proceeding instituted under article 10 of the Family Court Act; and

(2)　every proceeding instituted under article 7 of the Family Court Act.

(b)　No later than five calendar days thereafter, a separate weekly account for the preceding week ending Sunday shall be filed in the Office of Court Administration concerning:

(1)　new cases;

(2)　assignment of judges;

(3)　appearances of counsel; and

(4)　judicial activity;

unless the requirement therefor is otherwise specifically suspended, in whole or in part, by the Office of Court Administration.

(c)　On or before the 20th day of the first term of each year, an inventory of the cases pending as of the first day of the first term of that year shall be filed in the Office of Court Administration, and an inventory of pending cases shall also be filed at such other times as may be specified by the Office of Court Administration.

§ 205.7. Papers filed in court; docket number; prefix; forms.

(a) The forms set forth in Chapter IV of Subtitle D of this Title, designated "Forms of the Family Court of the State of New York" and "Adoption Forms of the Family Court and Surrogate's Court of the State of New York," respectively, shall be the official forms of the court and shall, in substantially the same form as set forth, be uniformly used throughout the State. Examples of these forms shall be available at the clerk's office of any Family Court.

(b) The prefixes for the docket numbers assigned to Family Court proceedings shall be:

A—Adoption

AS—Adoption Surrender

B—Commitment of guardianship and custody (§§ 384, 384-b, Social Services Law)

C—Conciliation

D—Delinquency (including transfers from criminal courts)

E—Designated felony delinquency (including transfers from criminal courts)

F—Support

G—Guardianship (§ 661, Family Court Act)

K—Foster care review

L—Approval of foster care placement

M—Consent to marry

N—Neglect or child abuse (child protective proceeding)

O—Family offenses

P—Paternity

R—Referred from Supreme Court (except delinquency)

S—Person in need of supervision

U—Uniform Interstate Family Support Law

V—Custody of minors (§ 651, Family Court Act)

W—Material witness

Z—Miscellaneous

(c) Proceedings for extensions of placement shall bear the prefix of the original proceeding in which the placement was made.

(d) The case docket number shall appear on the outside cover and first page to the right of the caption of every paper tendered for filing in the proceeding.

Each such cover and first page also shall contain an indication of the county of venue and a brief description of the nature of the paper and, where the case has been assigned to an individual judge, shall contain the name of the assigned judge to the right of the caption. In addition to complying with the provisions of CPLR 2101, every paper filed in court shall have annexed thereto appropriate proof of service on all parties where required, and every paper, other than an exhibit or a printed official form promulgated in accordance with section 214 of the Family Court Act, shall contain writing on one side only and, if typewritten, shall have at least double space between each line, except for quotations and the names and addresses of attorneys appearing in the action, and shall have at least one-inch margins.

§ 205.8.   Submission of papers to judge.

All papers for signature or consideration of the court shall be presented to the clerk of the court in the appropriate courtroom or clerk's office, except that when the clerk is unavailable or the judge so directs, papers may be submitted to the judge and a copy filed with the clerk at the first available opportunity. All papers for any judge which are filed in the clerk's office shall be promptly delivered to the judge by the clerk. The papers shall be clearly addressed to the judge for whom they are intended and prominently show the nature of the papers, the title and docket number of the proceeding in which they are filed, the judge's name and the name of the attorney or party submitting them.

§ 205.9.   Miscellaneous proceedings.

All proceedings for which the procedure has not been prescribed by provisions of the Family Court Act, the Domestic Relations Law or the Social Services Law, including but not limited to proceedings involving consent to marry, Interstate Compact on Juveniles and material witnesses, shall be commenced by the filing of a petition and shall require the entry of a written order.

§ 205.10.   Notice of appearance.

Each attorney appearing in a proceeding is required to file a written notice of appearance on or before the time of the attorney's first appearance in court or no later than 10 days after appointment or retainer, whichever is sooner. The notice shall contain the attorney's name, office address and telephone number, and the name of the person on whose behalf he or she is appearing.

§ 205.11.   Service and filing of motion papers.

Where motions are required to be on notice:

(a)   The motion shall be made returnable at such hour as the assigned judge directs.

(b)   At the time of service of the notice of motion, the moving party shall serve copies of all affidavits and briefs upon all the of the attorneys for the parties

Ct. Rules

or upon the parties appearing *pro se*. The answering party shall serve copies of all affidavits and briefs as required by CPLR 2214. Affidavits shall be for a statement of the relevant facts, and briefs shall be for a statement of the relevant law. Unless otherwise directed by the court, answering and reply affidavits and all papers required to be furnished to the court by the Family Court Act or CPLR 2214(c) must be filed no later than the time of argument or submission of the motion.

(c) The assigned judge may determine that any or all motions in that proceeding shall be orally argued and may direct that moving and responding papers shall be filed with the court prior to the time of argument.

(d) Unless oral argument has been requested by a party and permitted by the court, or directed by the court, motion papers received by the clerk of the court on or before the return date shall be deemed submitted as of the return date. A party requesting oral argument shall set forth such request in its notice of motion or on the first page of the answering papers, as the case may be. A party requesting oral argument on a motion brought on by an order to show cause shall do so as soon as practicable before the time the motion is to be heard.

(e) Hearings on motions shall be held when required by statute or ordered by the assigned judge in the judge's discretion.

§ 205.12. Conference.

(a) In any proceeding, a conference or conferences shall be ordered by the court as required as soon as practicable after the proceeding has been assigned.

(b) The matters which may be considered at such conference may include, among other things:

(1) completion of discovery;

(2) filing of motions;

(3) argument or hearing of motions;

(4) fixing of a date for fact-finding hearing;

(5) simplification and limitation of issues;

(6) amendment of pleadings or bills of particulars;

(7) admissions of fact;

(8) stipulations as to admissibility of documents;

(9) completion or modification of financial disclosure;

(10) possibilities for settlement; and

(11) limitation of number of expert witnesses.

(c) Where parties are represented by counsel, an attorney thoroughly familiar with the action and authorized to act on behalf of the party or accompanied by a person empowered to act on behalf of the party represented shall appear at such conference.

(d)   At the conclusion of a conference, the court shall make a written order including its directions to the parties as well as stipulations of counsel. Alternatively, in the court's discretion, all directions of the court and stipulations of counsel shall be formally placed on the record.

§ 205.13.   Engagement of counsel.

No adjournment shall be granted on the ground of engagement of counsel except in accordance with Part 125 of the Rules of the Chief Administrator of the Courts (22 NYCRR Part 125).

§ 205.14   Time limitations for proceedings involving custody or visitation.

In any proceeding brought pursuant to sections 467, 651 or 652 of the Family Court Act to determine temporary or permanent custody or visitation, once a hearing or trial is commenced, it shall proceed to conclusion within 90 days.

§ 205.15.   Submission of orders for signature.

(a)   Proposed orders, with proof of service on all parties, must be submitted for signature unless otherwise directed by the court within 30 days after the signing and filing of the decision directing that the order be settled or submitted.

(b)   When settlement of an order is directed by the court:

(1)   a copy of the proposed order or judgment with notice of settlement, returnable at the office of the clerk of the part in which the order or judgment was granted, or before the judge of the court if the court has so directed or if the clerk is unavailable, shall be served on all parties either:

(i)   by personal service not less than five days before the date of settlement; or

(ii)   by mail not less than ten days before the date of settlement;

(2)   proposed counter-orders or judgments shall be made returnable on the same date and at the same place, and shall be served on all parties by personal service, not less than two days, or by mail, not less than seven days, before the date of settlement.

§ 205.16.   Motion for judicial determination that reasonable efforts are not required for child in foster care.

(a)   This section shall govern any motion for a judicial determination, pursuant to section 352.2(2)(c), 754(2)(b), 1039-b or 1052(b) of the Family Court Act or section 358-a(3)(b) or 392(6-a) of the Social Services Law, that reasonable efforts to prevent or eliminate the need for removal of the child from the home or to make it possible to reunify the child with his or her parents are not required.

(b)   A motion for such a determination shall be filed in writing on notice to the parties, including the law guardian, on the form officially promulgated by

Ct. Rules

the Chief Administrator of the Courts and set forth in Chapter IV of Subtitle D of this Title and shall contain all information required therein.

§ 205.17. Permanency hearings for child in foster care.

(a) This section shall govern all permanency hearings conducted pursuant to Articles 3, 7 and 10 of the Family Court Act and sections 358-a and 392 of the Social Services Law.

(b) Filing deadlines.

(1) A petition for the initial permanency hearing in a case brought pursuant to Article 3 or 7 of the Family Court Act or section 358-a or 392 of the Social Services Law shall be filed at least 60 days prior to the expiration of one year following the entry of the child into foster care.

(2) A petition for the initial permanency hearing in a case arising under Article 10 of the Family Court Act shall be filed at least 60 days prior to the expiration of one year following the entry of the child into foster care. For purposes of this paragraph, the child shall be deemed to have entered foster care on the earlier of the date of the fact finding of abuse or neglect of the child pursuant to section 1051 of the Family Court Act or 60 days after the date the child was removed from his or her home.

(3) In a case brought pursuant to section 1055-a of the Family Court Act with respect to a child who has been freed for adoption but not placed in an adoptive home, or who has been freed for adoption and placed in an adoptive home but for whom a petition for adoption has not been filed, a petition for a permanency hearing shall be filed 60 days prior to the earlier of the expiration of one year following the last permanency hearing or six months after the child has been freed for adoption. With respect to a child freed for adoption for whom an adoption petition is pending, a petition for a permanency hearing shall be filed 60 days prior to the expiration of one year following the last permanency hearing.

(4) In any case in which the court has made a determination, pursuant to section 352.2(2)(c), 754(2)(b), 1039-b or 1052(b) of the Family Court Act or section 358-a(3)(b) or 392(6-a) of the Social Services Law, that reasonable efforts to prevent or eliminate the need for removal of the child from the home or make it possible to reunify the child with his or her parents are not required, a permanency hearing must be held within 30 days of such finding. In such a case, a petition for a permanency hearing shall be filed and served on an expedited basis as directed by the court.

(5) Following the initial permanency hearing in a case in which a child remains in foster care, a petition for a subsequent permanency hearing shall be filed at least 60 days prior to the expiration of one year following the date of the preceding permanency hearing, except as provided in paragraph (3) or (4).

(c) Required notice and service. In addition to serving the petition and accompanying papers upon the parties, including the law guardian, the petitioner shall provide notice of the permanency hearing to the foster parent caring for the child and any pre-adoptive parent or relative providing care for the child in accordance with sections 355.5(6), 741-a, 1040 and 1055-a(4) of the Family Court Act and sections 358-a(4)(c) and 392(4)(i) of the Social Services Law. The petitioner shall submit on or before the return date appropriate proof of service upon the parties and documentation of the notice or notices given to any foster parent, pre-adoptive parent or relative.

(d) Required papers to be filed.

(1) A permanency petition shall be filed on the form officially promulgated by the Chief Administrator of the Courts and set forth in Chapter IV of Subtitle D of this Title, and shall contain all information required therein. The petition shall include, but not be limited to, the following: the date by which the permanency hearing must be held; the date by which any subsequent permanency petition be filed; the proposed permanency goal for the child; the reasonable efforts, if any, undertaken to achieve the child's return to his or her parents and other permanency goal; the visitation plan for the child and his or her sibling or siblings and, if parental rights have not been terminated, for his or her parent or parents; and current information regarding the status of services ordered by the court to be provided, as well as other services that have been provided, to the child and his or her parent or parents.

(2) In all cases, the permanency petition shall be accompanied by the most recent Uniform Case Review containing, at minimum: the child's permanency goal and projected timeframe for its achievement; the reasonable efforts that have been undertaken and are planned to achieve the goal; impediments, if any, that have been encountered in achieving the goal; and the service plan for the child and (where parental rights have not been terminated) the child's parent or parents. The permanency petition shall be accompanied by additional reports as directed by the court. A permanency petition filed pursuant to Article 3 of the Family Court Act shall contain or have annexed to it a plan for the release or conditional release of the child, as required by section 353.3(7) of the Family Court Act.

(3) Not later than five days prior to the date of the permanency hearing, the petitioner shall file a report containing updated information with the court and shall provide copies to the parties, the law guardian, the foster parent caring for the child and any pre-adoptive parent or relative providing care for the child. The report shall provide information, including, but not limited to: the current status of the child; changes, if any, in the child's foster care placement, permanency goal or service plan; updated information regarding allegations in the petition and accompanying documents and any further reports directed by the court.

205.18 to 205.19   [Reserved]

§ 205.20. Designation of a facility for the questioning of children in custody (juvenile delinquency).

(a) The district administrative judge in each judicial district outside the City of New York and the administrative judge for the Family Court within the City of New York, or a designee, shall arrange for the inspection of any facility within the judicial district proposed for designation as suitable for the questioning of children pursuant to section 305.2 of the Family Court Act, and if found suitable, the district administrative judge or the administrative judge for the Family Court within the City of New York, as appropriate, shall recommend its designation to the Chief Administrator of the Courts.

(b)   Every recommendation to the Chief Administrator of the Courts shall include:

(1)   the room number or identification, the type of facility in which the room is located, the address and the hours of access;

(2)   the name of the police or other law enforcement agency, department of probation, Family Court judge or other interested person or agency which proposed the designation of the particular facility;

(3)   a signed and dated copy of the report of inspection of the proposed facility, made at the direction of the district administrative judge or the administrative judge for the Family Court within the City of New York; and

(4)   the factors upon which the recommendation is based.

(c)   Any facility recommended for designation as suitable for the questioning of children shall be separate from areas accessible to the general public and adult detainees.

(d)   Insofar as possible, the district administrative judge or the administrative judge for the Family Court within the City of New York, in making a recommendation for designation, shall seek to assure an adequate number and reasonable geographic distribution of designated questioning facilities, and that:

(1)   the room is located in a police facility or in a governmental facility not regularly or exclusively used for the education or care of children;

(2)   the room presents an office-like, rather than a jail-like, setting;

(3)   the room is clean and well maintained;

(4)   the room is well-lit and heated;

(5)   there are separate toilet facilities for children or, in the alternative, procedures insuring the privacy and safety of the children when in use;

(6)   there is a separate entrance for children, or, in the alternative, there are procedures which minimize public exposure and avoid mingling with the adult detainees;

(7)   a person will be in attendance with the child whenever the room is in use as a questioning facility, such person to be a policewoman or other qualified female person when the child is a female; and

(8)   any other factors relevant to suitability for designation are considered.

(e)   The appropriate district administrative judge or the administrative judge for the Family Court within the City of New York, or a designee, when notified of any material physical change in a facility designated for the questioning of children, shall arrange for the reinspection of such facility concerning its continued suitability for designation.

(f) A current list of facilities designated for the questioning of children within each judicial district and within the City of New York shall be maintained by the district administrative judge and the administrative judge for the Family Court within the City of New York, and shall be kept for easy public inspection in each Family Court in that judicial district and within the City of New York. A current statewide list shall be maintained in the office of the Chief Administrator of the Courts. These lists shall be kept available for public inspection.

§ 205.21. Authorization to detention agency for release of a child taken into custody before the filing of a petition (juvenile delinquency).

(a) When a child is brought to a detention facility prior to the filing of a petition, pursuant to section 305.2 of the Family Court Act, the agency responsible for operating the detention facility is authorized to release the child before the filing of a petition when the events that occasioned the taking into custody do not appear to involve allegations that the child committed a delinquent act.

(b) If the events occasioning the taking into custody do appear to involve allegations that the child committed a delinquent act, the agency is authorized to release the child where practicable and issue an appearance ticket in accordance with section 307.1 of the Family Court Act, unless special circumstances exist which require the detention of the child, including whether:

(1) there is a substantial probability that the child will not appear or be produced at the appropriate probation service at a specified time and place; or

(2) there is a serious risk that, before the petition is filed, the child may commit an act which, if committed by an adult, would constitute a crime; or

(3) the alleged conduct by the child involved the use or threatened use of violence; or

(4) there is reason to believe that a proceeding to determine whether the child is a juvenile delinquent or juvenile offender is currently pending.

(c) Any child released pursuant to this rule shall be released to the custody of his or her parent or other person legally responsible for his or her care, or if such legally responsible person is unavailable, to a person with whom he or she resides.

§ 205.22. Preliminary probation conferences and procedures (juvenile delinquency).

(a) The probation service shall conduct preliminary conferences with any person seeking to have a juvenile delinquency petition filed, the potential respondent and other interested persons, including the complainant or victim, on the

Ct. Rules

same day that such persons appear at a probation service pursuant to section 305.2(4)(a), 307.1 or 320.6 of the Family Court Act, concerning the advisability of requesting that a juvenile delinquency petition be filed and in order to gather information needed for a determination of the suitability of the case for adjustment. The probation service shall permit any participant who is represented by a lawyer to be accompanied by the lawyer at any preliminary conference.

(b) During the preliminary probation conferences, the probation service shall ascertain, from the person seeking to have a juvenile delinquency petition filed, a brief statement of the underlying events and, if known to that person, a brief statement of factors that would be of assistance to the court in determining whether the potential respondent should be detained or released in the event that a petition is filed.

(c) In order to determine whether the case is suitable for the adjustment process, the probation service shall consider the following circumstances, among others:

(1) the age of the potential respondent; and

(2) whether the conduct of the potential respondent allegedly involved:

(i) an act or acts causing or threatening to cause death, substantial pain or serious physical injury to another;

(ii) the use or knowing possession of a dangerous instrument or deadly weapon;

(iii) the use or threatened use of violence to compel a person to engage in sexual intercourse, deviant sexual intercourse or sexual contact;

(iv) the use or threatened use of violence to obtain property;

(v) the use or threatened use of deadly physical force with the intent to restrain the liberty of another;

(vi) the intentional starting of a fire or the causing of an explosion which resulted in damage to a building;

(vii) a serious risk to the welfare and safety of the community; or

(viii) an act which seriously endangered the safety of the potential respondent or another person;

(3) whether there is a substantial likelihood that a potential respondent will not appear at scheduled conferences with the probation service or with an agency to which he or she may be referred;

(4) whether there is a substantial likelihood that the potential respondent will not participate in or cooperate with the adjustment process;

(5) whether there is a substantial likelihood that, in order to adjust the case successfully, the potential respondent would require services that could not be administered effectively in less than four months;

(6) whether there is a substantial likelihood that the potential respondent will, during the adjustment process:

(i) commit an act which, if committed by an adult, would be a crime; or

(ii) engage in conduct that endangers the physical or emotional health of the potential respondent or a member of the potential respondent's family or household; or

(iii) harass or menace the complainant, victim or person seeking to have a juvenile delinquency petition filed, or a member of that person's family or household, where demonstrated by prior conduct or threats;

(7) whether there is pending another proceeding to determine whether the potential respondent is a person in need of supervision, a juvenile delinquent or a juvenile offender;

(8) whether there have been prior adjustments or adjournments in contemplation of dismissal in other juvenile delinquency proceedings;

(9) whether there has been a prior adjudication of the potential respondent as a juvenile delinquent or juvenile offender;

(10) whether there is a substantial likelihood that the adjustment process would not be successful unless the potential respondent is temporarily removed from his or her home and that such removal could not be accomplished without invoking the court process; and

(11) whether a proceeding has been or will be instituted against another person for acting jointly with the potential respondent.

(d) At the first appearance at a conference by each of the persons listed in subdivision (a) of this section, the probation service shall inform such person concerning the function and limitations of, and the alternatives to, the adjustment process, and that:

(1) he or she has the right to participate in the adjustment process;

(2) the probation service is not authorized to and cannot compel any person to appear at any conference, produce any papers or visit any place;

(3) the person seeking to have a juvenile delinquency petition filed is entitled to have access to the appropriate presentment agency at any time for the purpose of requesting that a petition be filed under article 3 of the Family Court Act;

(4) the adjustment process may continue for a period of two months and may be extended for an additional two months upon written application to the court and approval thereof;

(5) statements made to the probation service are subject to the confidentiality provisions contained in sections 308.1(6) and (7) of the Family Court Act; and

(6) if the adjustment process is commenced but is not successfully concluded, the person participating therein may be notified orally or in writing of that fact and that the case will be referred to the appropriate presentment agency; oral notification will be confirmed in writing.

Ct. Rules

(e) If the adjustment process is not commenced:

(1) the record of the probation service shall contain a statement of the grounds therefor; and

(2) the probation service shall give written notice to the persons listed in subdivision (a) of this section who have appeared that:

(i) the adjustment process will not be commenced;

(ii) the case will be referred to the appropriate presentment agency; and

(iii) they are entitled to have access to the presentment agency for the purpose of requesting that a petition be filed under article 3 of the Family Court Act.

§ 205.23. Duties of the probation service and procedure relating to the adjustment process (juvenile delinquency).

(a) Upon a determination by the probation service that a case is suitable for the adjustment process, it shall include in the process the potential respondent and any other persons listed in section 205.22(a) of this part who wish to participate therein. The probation service shall permit any participant who is represented by a lawyer to be accompanied by the lawyer at any conference.

(b) If an extension of the period of the adjustment process is sought, the probation service shall apply in writing to the court and shall set forth the services rendered to the potential respondent, the date of commencement of those services, the degree of success achieved, the services proposed to be rendered and a statement by the assigned probation officer that, in the judgment of such person, the matter will not be successfully adjusted unless an extension is granted.

(c) The probation service may discontinue the adjustment process if, at any time:

(1) the potential respondent or the person seeking to have a juvenile delinquency petition filed requests that it do so; or

(2) the potential respondent refuses to cooperate with the probation service or any agency to which the potential respondent or a member of his or her family has been referred.

(d) If the adjustment process is not successfully concluded, the probation service shall notify all the persons who participated therein in writing:

(1) that the adjustment process has not been successfully concluded;

(2) that the appropriate presentment agency will be notified within 48 hours or the next court day, whichever occurs later; and

(3) that access may be had to the presentment agency to request that a petition be filed;

and, in addition to the above, shall notify the potential respondent in writing of the reasons therefor.

(e)   The case record of the probation service required to be kept pursuant to section 243 of the Executive Law and the regulations promulgated thereunder shall contain a statement of the grounds upon which:

(1)   the adjustment process was commenced but was not successfully concluded; or

(2)   the adjustment process was commenced and successfully concluded.

§ 205.24.   Terms and conditions of order adjourning a proceeding in contemplation of dismissal in accordance with section 315.3 of the Family Court Act.

(a)   An order adjourning a proceeding in contemplation of dismissal pursuant to section 315.3 of the Family Court Act shall be related to the alleged or adjudicated acts or omissions of respondent and shall contain at least one of the following terms and conditions directing the respondent to:

(1)   attend school regularly and obey all rules and regulations of the school;

(2)   obey all reasonable commands of the parent or other person legally responsible for respondent's care;

(3)   avoid injurious or vicious activities;

(4)   abstain from associating with named individuals;

(5)   abstain from visiting designated places;

(6)   abstain from the use of alcoholic beverages, hallucinogenic drugs, habit-forming drugs not lawfully prescribed for the respondent's use, or any other harmful or dangerous substance;

(7)   cooperate with a mental health, social services or other appropriate community facility or agency to which the respondent is referred;

(8)   restore property taken from the complainant or victim, or replace property taken from the complainant or victim, the cost of said replacement not to exceed $1,500;

(9)   repair any damage to, or defacement of, the property of the complainant or victim, the cost of said repair not to exceed $1,500;

(10)   cooperate in accepting medical or psychiatric diagnosis and treatment, alcoholism or drug abuse treatment or counseling services and permit an agency delivering that service to furnish the court with information concerning the diagnosis, treatment or counseling;

(11)   attend and complete an alcohol awareness program established pursuant to section 19.25 of the Mental Hygiene Law;

(12)   abstain from disruptive behavior in the home and in the community;

(13)   abstain from any act which, if done by an adult, would be an offense; and

Ct. Rules

(14)   comply with such other reasonable terms and conditions as may be permitted by law and as the court shall determine to be necessary or appropriate to ameliorate the conduct which gave rise to the filing of the petition or to prevent placement with the Commissioner of Social Services or the Office of Children and Family Services.

(b)   An order adjourning a proceeding in contemplation of dismissal pursuant to section 315.3 of the Family Court Act may direct that the probation service supervise respondent's compliance with the terms and conditions of said order, and may set a time or times at which the probation service shall report to the court, orally or in writing, concerning compliance with the terms and conditions of said order.

(c)   A copy of the order setting forth the terms and conditions imposed, and the duration thereof, shall be furnished to the respondent and to the parent or other person legally responsible for the respondent.

§ 205.25.   Terms and conditions of order releasing respondent in accordance with section 320.5 of the Family Court Act.

(a)   An order releasing a respondent at the initial appearance in accordance with section 320.5 of the Family Court Act may contain one or more of the following terms and conditions, directing the respondent to:

(1)   attend school regularly;

(2)   abstain from any act which, if done by an adult, would be an offense;

(3)   observe a specified curfew which must be reasonable in relation to the ends sought to be achieved and narrowly drawn;

(4)   participate in a program duly authorized as an alternative to detention; or

(5)   comply with such other reasonable terms and conditions as the court shall determine to be necessary or appropriate.

(b)   A copy of the order setting forth terms and conditions imposed, and the duration thereof, shall be furnished at the time of issuance to the respondent and, if present, to the parent or other person legally responsible for the respondent.

§ 205.26.   Procedure when remanded child absconds.

(a)   When a child absconds from a facility to which he or she was duly remanded, written notice of that fact shall be given within 48 hours, by an authorized representative of the facility, to the clerk of the court from which the remand was made. The notice shall state the name of the child, the docket number of the pending proceeding in which the child was remanded, the date on which the child absconded and the efforts made to locate and secure the return of the child. Every order of remand shall include a direction embodying the requirements of this subdivision.

(b) Upon receipt of the written notice of absconding, the clerk shall cause the proceeding to be placed on the court calendar no later than the next court day for such action as the court may deem appropriate, and shall give notice of such court date to the presentment agency and law guardian or privately retained counsel of the child.

§ 205.27. Procedure for assignment, in accordance with section 340.2(3) of the Family Court Act, of a proceeding to another judge when the appropriate judge cannot preside.

Except for proceedings transferred in accordance with section 302.3(4) of the Family Court Act, when a judge who has presided at the fact-finding hearing, or accepted an admission pursuant to section 321.3 of such act, in a juvenile delinquency proceeding, cannot preside at another subsequent hearing, including the dispositional hearing, for the reasons set forth in section 340.2(3), the assignment of the proceeding to another judge of the court shall be made as authorized by the Chief Administrator of the Courts.

§ 205.28. Procedures for compliance with Adoption and Safe Families Act.

(a) Pre-petition and pretrial detention; required findings. In any case in which detention is ordered by the court pursuant to sections 307.4 or 320.5 of the Family Court Act, the court shall make additional, specific written findings regarding the following issues:

(1) whether the continuation of the respondent in his or her home would be contrary to his or her best interests; and

(2) where appropriate and consistent with the need for protection of the community, whether reasonable efforts were made, prior to the date of the court hearing that resulted in the detention order, to prevent or eliminate the need for removal of the respondent from his or her home, or, if the respondent had been removed from his or her home prior to the initial appearance, where appropriate and consistent with the need for protection of the community, whether reasonable efforts were made to make it possible for the respondent to safely return home. The court may request the presentment agency and the local probation department to provide information to the court to aid in its determinations and may also consider information provided by the law guardian.

(b) Motion for an order that reasonable efforts are not required. A motion for a judicial determination, pursuant to section 352.2(2)(c) of the Family Court Act, that reasonable efforts to prevent or eliminate the need for removal of the respondent from his or her home or to make it possible to reunify the respondent with his or her parents are not required, shall be governed by section 205.16 of this Part.

(c) Placement; required findings. In any case in which the court is considering ordering placement pursuant to section 353.3 or 353.4 of the Family Court

Act, the presentment agency, local probation department, local commissioner of social services and New York State Office of Children and Family Services shall provide information to the court to aid in its required determination of the following issues:

(1)   whether continuation in the respondent's home would be contrary to the best interests of the respondent, and, in the case of a respondent for whom the court has determined that continuation in his or her home would not be contrary to the best interests of the respondent, whether continuation in the respondent's home would be contrary to the need for protection of the community;

(2)   whether, where appropriate and where consistent with the need for protection of the community, reasonable efforts were made, prior to the date of the dispositional hearing, to prevent or eliminate the need for removal of the respondent from his or her home, and, if the respondent was removed from his or her home prior to the dispositional hearing, where appropriate and where consistent with the need for protection of the community, whether reasonable efforts were made to make it possible for the respondent to return home safely. If the court determines that reasonable efforts to prevent or eliminate the need for removal of the respondent from the home were not made, but that the lack of such efforts was appropriate under the circumstances, or consistent with the need for protection of the community, or both, the court order shall include such a finding;

(3)   in the case of a respondent who has attained the age of 16, the services needed, if any, to assist the respondent to make the transition from foster care to independent living; and

(4)   in the case of an order of placement specifying a particular authorized agency or foster care provider, the position of the New York State Office of Children and Family Services or local department of social services, as applicable, regarding such placement.

(d)   Permanency hearing; extension of placement. A petition for a permanency hearing and, if applicable, an extension of placement, pursuant to sections 355.3 and 355.5 of the Family Court Act, shall be filed at least 60 days prior to the expiration of one year following the respondent's entry into foster care; provided, however, that if the Family Court makes a determination, pursuant to section 352.2(2)(c) of the Family Court Act, that reasonable efforts are not required to prevent or eliminate the need for removal of the respondent from his or her home or to make it possible to reunify the respondent with his or her parents, the permanency hearing shall be held within 30 days of such finding and the petition for the permanency hearing shall be filed and served on an expedited basis as directed by the court. Following the initial permanency hearing in a case in which the respondent remains in placement, a petition for a subsequent permanency hearing and, if applicable, extension of placement, shall be filed at least 60 days prior to the expiration of one year following the date of the preceding permanency hearing. All petitions for permanency hearings shall be governed by section 205.17 of this Part.

205.29   **[Reserved]**

§ 205.30.   Preliminary probation conferences and procedures (support).

(a)   Any person except a commissioner of social services, a social services official or a person who is receiving paternity and support services pursuant to section 111-g of the Social Services Law, seeking to file a petition for support under article 4 of the Family Court Act, may first be referred to the probation service concerning the advisability of filing a petition.

(b)   The probation service shall be available to meet and confer concerning the advisability of filing a petition with the person seeking to file a petition for support, the potential respondent and any other interested person no later than the next regularly scheduled court day. The probation service shall permit any participant who is represented by a lawyer to be accompanied at any preliminary conference by the lawyer, who shall be identified by the probation officer to the other party, and shall not discourage any person from seeking to file a petition.

(c)   At the first appearance at a conference by each of the persons listed in subdivision (b) of this section, the probation service shall inform such person concerning the function and limitations of, and the alternative to, the adjustment process, and that:

(1)   the purpose of the adjustment process is to discover whether it will be possible to arrive at a voluntary agreement for support without filing a petition;

(2)   the person seeking to file a petition for support is entitled to request that the probation service confer with him or her, the potential respondent and any other interested person concerning the advisability of filing a petition for support under article 4 of the Family Court Act;

(3)   if the assistance of the probation service is not requested or, if requested, is subsequently declined, the person seeking to file a petition for support is entitled to have access to the court at any time for that purpose and may proceed to file a petition for support;

(4)   the probation service is not authorized to, and shall not, compel any person, including the person seeking support, to appear at any conference, produce any papers or visit any place;

(5)   the adjustment process must commence within 15 days from the date of the request for a conference, may continue for a period of two months from the date of that request, and may be extended for an additional 60 days upon written application to the court containing the consent of the person seeking to file a petition;

(6)   if the adjustment process is not successful, the persons participating therein shall be notified in writing of that fact and that the person seeking to file a petition for support is entitled to access to the court for that purpose; and

(7)   if the adjustment of the matter results in a voluntary agreement for support of the petitioner and any dependents:

(i)   it shall be reduced to writing by the probation service, signed by both parties to it, and submitted to the Family Court for approval;

(ii)   if the court approves it, the court may, without further hearing, enter an order for support pursuant to section 425 of the Family Court Act in accordance with the agreement;

(iii)   the order when entered shall be binding upon the parties and shall in all respects be a valid order, and the Family Court may entertain a proceeding for enforcement of the order should there not be compliance with the order; and

(iv)   unless the agreement is submitted to the Family Court and an order is issued, the Family Court will not entertain a proceeding for the enforcement of the agreement should the agreement not be complied with.

(d)   If the adjustment process is not commenced, the probation service shall give written notice to the persons listed in subdivision (b) of this section that:

(1)   the adjustment process will not be commenced, and the reasons therefor;

(2)   the person seeking to file a petition for support is entitled to access to the court for that purpose; and

(3)   if applicable, the adjustment process was not commenced on the ground that the court would not have jurisdiction over the case, and the question of the court's jurisdiction may be tested by filing a petition.

§ 205.31.   Duties of the probation service and procedures relating to the adjustment process (support).

(a)   If the assistance of the probation service is requested by the person seeking to file a petition for support, and it appears that it may be possible to arrive at a voluntary agreement for support, the adjustment process shall commence within 15 days from the date of request, and shall include the person seeking to file a petition for support, the potential respondent and any other person listed in subdivision (b) of section 205.30 of this Part who wishes to participate therein. The probation service shall permit any participant who is represented by a lawyer to be accompanied at any conference by the lawyer, who shall be identified by the probation officer to the other party, and shall not discourage any person from seeking to file a petition.

(b)   If an extension of the period of the adjustment process is sought, the probation service shall apply in writing to the court and shall set forth the services rendered, the date of commencement of those services, the degree of success achieved and the services proposed to be rendered. The application shall set forth the reasons why, in the opinion of the assigned probation officer, additional time is needed to adjust the matter, and shall contain the signed consent of the person seeking to file a petition for support.

(c)   The probation service shall discontinue its efforts at adjustment if, at any time:

(1) the person seeking to file a petition for support or the potential respondent requests that it do so; or

(2) it appears to the probation service that there is no reasonable likelihood that a voluntary agreement for support will result.

(d) If the adjustment process is not successfully concluded, the probation service shall notify all the persons who participated therein, in writing:

(1) that the adjustment process has not been successfully concluded and the reasons therefor; and

(2) that the person seeking to file a petition for support is entitled to access to the court for that purpose.

(e) If the adjustment process results in an agreement for the support of the petitioner and any dependents:

(1) it shall be reduced to writing by the probation service, shall be signed by both parties to it, and shall be submitted to the court, together with a petition for approval of the agreement and a proposed order incorporating the agreement; and

(2) if the agreement is approved by the court, a copy of the order shall be furnished by the probation service to the person seeking to file a petition for support and the potential respondent, in person if they are present, and by mail if their presence has been dispensed with by the court.

§ 205.32. Support magistrates.

(a) Support magistrates shall be appointed by the Chief Administrator of the Courts to hear and determine support proceedings in Family Court pursuant to section 439 of the Family Court Act. They shall be attorneys admitted to the practice of law in New York for at least five years and shall be knowledgeable with respect to Family Court procedure, family law and Federal and State support law and programs.

(b) Term.

(1) Support magistrates shall be appointed as nonjudicial employees of the Unified Court System on a full-time basis for a term of three years, and in the discretion of the Chief Administrator, may be reappointed for subsequent five-year terms, provided that if the Chief Administrator determines that the employment of a full-time support magistrate is not required in a particular court, the services of a full-time support magistrate may be shared by one or more counties or a support magistrate may be appointed to serve within one or more counties on a part-time basis.

(2) In the discretion of the Chief Administrator, an acting support magistrate may be appointed to serve during a support magistrate's authorized leave of absence. In making such appointment, the provisions for selection of support magistrates set forth in subdivision (c) of this section may be modified by the Chief Administrator as appropriate to the particular circumstances.

Ct. Rules

(3) A support magistrate shall be subject to removal or other disciplinary action pursuant to the procedure set forth in section 25.29(b) of the Rules of the Chief Judge (22 NYCRR 25.29[b]).

(c) Selection of support magistrates.

(1) The district administrative judge for the judicial district in which the county or counties where the support magistrate is authorized to serve is located, or the administrative judge for the courts in Nassau County or the administrative judge for the courts in Suffolk County, if the support magistrate is authorized to serve in either of those counties, or the administrative judge for the Family Court within the City of New York, if the support magistrate is to serve in New York City, shall:

(i) publish an announcement in the law journal serving the affected county or counties inviting applications from the bar or, if there is no law journal serving such area, in a newspaper of general circulation; and

(ii) communicate directly with bar associations in the affected county or counties to invite applicants to apply.

(2) The announcements and communications shall set forth the qualifications for selection as contained in subdivision (a) of this section, the compensation, the term of appointment and requirements concerning restrictions on the private practice of law.

(3) A committee consisting of an administrative judge, a judge of the Family Court and a designee of the Chief Administrator shall screen each applicant for qualifications, character and ability to handle the support magistrate responsibilities, and shall forward the names of recommended nominees, with a summary of their qualifications, to the Chief Administrator, who shall make the appointment. The appointment order shall indicate the court or courts in which the support magistrate shall serve. The Chief Administrator further may authorize temporary assignments to additional courts.

(d) Training. The Chief Administrator shall authorize such training for support magistrates as appropriate to ensure the effective performance of their duties.

(e) Compensation and expenses. Compensation for support magistrates shall be fixed by the Chief Administrator. Support magistrates shall be entitled to reimbursement of actual and necessary travel expenses in accordance with the rules governing the reimbursement of the travel expenses of nonjudicial court employees of the State of New York.

§ 205.33. Assignment of support magistrates.

The supervising judge of the Family Court in the county in which the support magistrate will serve, or the deputy administrative judge for the Family Court within the City of New York, if the support magistrate is to serve in New York City, shall assign support magistrates as required by the needs of the courts, in conformance with law and in conformance with section 205.3 of this Part.

§ 205.34. Referrals to support magistrates.

(a) A summons or warrant in support proceedings shall be made returnable by the clerk of the court before a support magistrate in the first instance, unless otherwise provided by the court. A net worth statement form prescribed by the Chief Administrator shall be appended by the clerk to the summons to be served upon the respondent and shall be given to the petitioner upon the filing of the petition.

(b) Whenever the parties are before a judge of the court when support is an issue, the judge shall make an immediate order, either temporary or permanent, with respect to support. If a temporary order is made, the court shall refer the issues of support to a support magistrate.

(c) The above provisions shall apply to initial determinations of support, subsequent modification or violation proceedings, and support proceedings referred to Family Court by the Supreme Court pursuant to part 6 of article 4 of the Family Court Act.

§ 205.35. Conduct of hearing.

(a) Unless otherwise specified in the order of reference, the support magistrate shall conduct the hearing in the same manner as a court trying an issue without a jury in conformance with the procedures set forth in the Civil Practice Law and Rules and with section 205.3 of this Part.

(b) If a full or partial agreement is reached between the parties during the hearing, it shall be placed on the record and, if approved, shall be incorporated into an order, which shall be duly entered.

(c) The support magistrate shall require the exchange and filing of affidavits of financial disclosure.

§ 205.36. Findings of fact; transmission of findings of fact and other information; quarterly reports.

(a) Findings of fact shall be in writing and shall include, where applicable, the income and expenses of each party, the basis for liability for support and an assessment of the needs of the children. The findings of fact shall be set forth on a form prescribed by the Chief Administrator. A copy of the findings of fact shall accompany the order of support.

(b) At the time of the entry of the order of support, the clerk of the court shall cause a copy of the findings of fact and order of support to be served either in person or by mail upon the parties to the proceeding or their attorneys. When the findings and order are transmitted to a party appearing *pro se,* they shall be accompanied by information about the objection process, including the requirements for a transcript, the time limitations governing the filing of objections and rebuttals, and the necessity for affidavits of service on the opposing party of all papers filed with the court.

Ct. Rules

(c)   Each support magistrate shall file with the Chief Administrator, in such form as may be required, a quarterly report indicating the matters that have been pending undecided before such hearing examiner [support magistrate]* for a period of 30 days after final submission, and the reasons therefor.

* Bracketed words added by publisher.

§ 205.37.   Recording of hearings; objections.

(a)   Hearings may be recorded mechanically. Any equipment used for such mechanical recording or for the production of such recording shall have the prior approval of the Chief Administrator of the Courts.

(b)   Mechanical recordings shall be appropriately and clearly identified with the name of the case, docket number and date of hearing for storage and retrieval with proper precautions taken for security and preservation of confidentiality. Where hearings are recorded mechanically, the clerk of the court shall provide a means for the making of a duplicate recording or for an alternative method for preparation of a transcript where required by a judge reviewing objections to an order of a support magistrate or when requested by a party.

(c)   A transcript of the proceeding before the support magistrate shall be prepared where required by the judge to whom objections have been submitted for review, in which event costs of duplication and of transcript preparation shall be borne by the objecting party. Either party may request a duplicate recording or transcript, in which event costs of duplication of the recording or preparation of the transcript shall be borne by the requesting party. A transcript shall bear the certification of the transcriber that the transcript is a true and accurate transcription of the proceeding. A party who is financially unable to pay the cost of the duplicate recording or the preparation of a transcript may seek leave of the court to proceed as a poor person pursuant to article 11 of the Civil Practice Law and Rules.

(d)   Objections to the order of the support magistrate and rebuttals thereto shall be accompanied by an affidavit of service on the opposing party.

§ 205.38.   Record and report of unexecuted warrants issued pursuant to section 428 of the Family Court Act.

(a)   The clerk of court for the Family Court in each county shall obtain and keep a record of executed warrants issued pursuant to section 428 of the Family Court Act.

(b)   At the end of each six-month period, on the first of January and on the first of July in each year, a report concerning all unexecuted warrants issued pursuant to section 428 of the Family Court Act shall be made and filed with the Office of Court Administration, on a form to be supplied by the Office of Court Administration.

§ 205.39. Authority of probation when there is a failure to obey a lawful order of the court (support).

(a) The probation service, at the request of the petitioner, is authorized to confer with the respondent and the petitioner whenever any respondent fails to obey a lawful order of the court made under article 4 of the Family Court Act or an order of support made under article 5 of the Family Court Act concerning the existence of the violation, the reason for it and the likelihood that there will be compliance in the future. The probation service shall permit any participant who is represented by a lawyer to be accompanied at any conference by the lawyer, who shall be identified by the probation officer to the other party, and shall not discourage any person from seeking to file a petition to enforce compliance.

(b) Before holding any conference pursuant to subdivision (a) of this section:

(1) The probation service shall notify the respondent in writing that:

(i) the probation service is willing to confer with the respondent and must hear from the respondent within seven days if a conference is to be held; and

(ii) the petitioner is entitled to petition the court to enforce compliance with the order;

(2) a copy of this notice shall be furnished to the petitioner; and

(3) if the respondent does not communicate with the probation service within seven days, the probation service shall advise the petitioner that he or she may petition the court to enforce compliance with the order.

(c) If, at a conference held pursuant to subdivision (a) of this section, it shall appear to the probation service that the failure to comply with the order was not willful and that there is a substantial likelihood that compliance with the order will result, the probation service is authorized to adjust the matter informally. An existing order may not be modified by informal adjustment without the filing of a petition for such modification and the approval of the court thereof. Efforts at adjustment pursuant to this subdivision shall not extend beyond the conference held pursuant to subdivision (a) of this section.

(d) The probation service is not authorized to, and shall not, discuss with the petitioner or the respondent:

(1) the advisability or likely outcome of filing a petition to enforce compliance with the order; or

(2) the amount of arrears that would be awarded or cancelled by the court if a petition to enforce the order were filed.

§ 205.40. Preliminary probation conferences and procedures upon a referral from Supreme Court (support).

(a) When an application is referred to the Family Court by the Supreme Court pursuant to part 6 of article 4 of the Family Court Act, the parties may first be

Ct. Rules

referred to the probation service, which shall inform them at the first conference concerning the function and limitations of and the alternatives to the adjustment process in accordance with section 205.30(c) of this Part.

(b) The probation service, at the request of either party to the proceeding, shall be available to meet with the parties and other interested persons no later than the next regularly-scheduled court day concerning the willingness of the parties to resolve those issues by voluntary agreement. The probation service shall permit any participant who is represented by a lawyer to be accompanied at any preliminary conference by the lawyer, who shall be identified by the probation officer to the other party, and shall not discourage any person from seeking to file a petition.

§ 205.41. Duties of the probation service and procedures relating to the adjustment process upon referral from Supreme Court (support).

(a) If the assistance of the probation service is requested by either party to the proceeding, efforts at adjustment shall commence within 15 days from the date of the request and may continue for a period of two months from the date of request. The court may extend the adjustment process for an additional 60 days upon written application containing the consent of the person seeking to file a petition.

(b) The probation service shall permit any participant who is represented by a lawyer to be accompanied at any conference by the lawyer, who shall be identified by the probation officer to the other party.

(c) If an extension of the period of the adjustment process is sought, the probation service shall apply in writing to the court and shall set forth the services rendered, the date of commencement of those services, the degree of success achieved and the services proposed to be rendered. The application shall set forth the reasons why, in the opinion of the assigned probation officer, additional time is needed to adjust the matter, and shall contain the signed consent of the parties and a statement by the probation officer that there is a substantial likelihood that a voluntary agreement would be reached if an extension were granted.

(d) The probation service shall discontinue the adjustment process if, at any time:

(1) either party requests that it do so; or

(2) it appears to the probation service that there is no substantial likelihood that a voluntary agreement will result.

(e) If the adjustment process is not successfully concluded, the probation service shall notify the persons who participated therein in writing:

(1) that the adjustment process has not been successfully concluded, and the reasons therefor;

(2)   that either party is entitled to access to the court to have the issues which have been referred determined at a fact-finding hearing.

(f)   If the adjustment process results in a voluntary agreement on the issues referred:

(1)   it shall be reduced to writing by the probation service, shall be signed by both parties to it, and shall be submitted to the court, together with a petition for approval of the agreement and a proposed order incorporating the agreement;

(2)   if the agreement is approved by the court, a copy of the order made by the court shall be furnished by the probation service to the parties, in person if they are present, and by mail if their presence has been dispensed with by the court.

§ 205.42. Submission by support collection units of proposed adjusted orders of support.

(a)   A submission by a support collection unit pursuant to section 413 of the Family Court Act for adjustment of a child support order shall include the following, which shall be submitted on forms promulgated by the Chief Administrator of the Courts:

(1)   an affidavit from the support collection unit, with findings in support of adjustment;

(2)   a proposed adjusted order of support; and

(3)   a notice to the parties of the proposed adjusted order and of the rights of the parties, including the addresses of the court and the support collection unit.

The documents set forth in this subdivision shall be filed with the clerk of the court within 10 days of mailing to the parties, together with an affidavit of service of these documents upon the parties.

(b)   Where a written objection is received by the clerk of the court within 35 days of mailing to the parties of the documents set forth in subdivision (a) of this section, the court shall schedule a hearing upon notice to the support collection unit and the parties.

(c)   Where no timely objection is received by the court, the court shall sign the order upon the court's being satisfied that the requirements of sections 111-h of the Social Services Law and 413 of the Family Court Act have been met, and shall transmit copies of the order to the support collection unit for service on the parties. Absent unusual circumstances, the court shall sign the order or dismiss the application within 10 business days after the conclusion of the 35-day objection period.

§ 205.43. Hearings to determine willful non-payment of child support.

(a)   A petition that alleges a willful violation or seeks enforcement of an order of support shall be scheduled as soon as possible for a first appearance date in

Family Court but in no event more than 30 days of the filing of the violation or enforcement petition.

(b)   After service is made, the judge or support magistrate must commence a hearing to determine a willful violation within 30 days of the date noticed in the summons. The hearing must be concluded within 60 days of its commencement.

(c)   Neither party shall be permitted more than one adjournment to secure counsel, except for good cause shown.

(d)   On the scheduled hearing date on the issue of willfulness, the hearing may not be adjourned except for the following reasons:

(1)   actual engagement of counsel pursuant to Part 125 of the Rules of the Chief Administrator;

(2)   illness of a party; or

(3)   other good cause shown.

No adjournment shall be in excess of 14 days.

(e)   If a willfulness hearing has commenced and must be continued, the adjourned date shall be within seven court days.

(f)   Upon the conclusion of a willfulness hearing in a case heard by a support magistrate, the support magistrate shall issue written findings of fact within five court days.

(g)   In a case heard by a support magistrate, if the support magistrate makes a finding of willfulness, the written findings shall include the following;

(1)   the specific facts upon which the finding of willfulness is based;

(2)   the specific amount of arrears established and a money judgment for such amount. An award of attorney's fees may be issued with the findings or at a later date after the case is heard by the Family Court judge;

(3)   a recommendation regarding the sanctions that should be imposed, including a recommendation whether the sanction of incarceration is recommended;

(4)   a recommendation, as appropriate, regarding a specific dollar amount to be paid or a specific plan to repay the arrears.

(h)   In a case heard by a support magistrate, if counsel is assigned, the assignment shall continue through the confirmation proceeding before the Family Court judge without further order of the court.

(i)   In a case heard by a support magistrate, a Family Court judge may confirm the findings of the support magistrate by adopting his or her findings and recommendations in whole or in part. Alternatively, the Family Court judge may modify or refuse to confirm the findings and recommendations and may refer the matter back to the support magistrate for further proceedings. The court may, if necessary, conduct an evidentiary hearing.

§ 205.44. Testimony by telephone, audio-visual or other electronic means in child support and paternity cases.

(a) This section shall govern applications for testimony to be taken by telephone, audio-visual means or other electronic means in accordance with sections 433, 531-a and 580-316 of the Family Court Act.

(b) A party or witness seeking to testify by telephone, audio-visual means or other electronic means must complete an application on the form officially promulgated by the Chief Administrator of the Courts and set forth in Chapter IV of Subtitle D of this Title and, except for good cause shown, must file such application with the court not less than three days in advance of the hearing date. The applicant shall attempt to arrange to provide such testimony at a designated tribunal or the child support enforcement agency, as defined in the federal Social Security Act (42 U.S.C. Title IV-D) in that party's state, or county if within the state. The court may permit the testimony to be taken at any suitable location acceptable to the court, including but not limited to, the party's or witness' counsel's office, personal residence or place of business.

(c) The applicant must provide all financial documentation ordered to be disclosed by the court pursuant to section 424 or 580-316 of the Family Court Act, as applicable, before he or she will be permitted to testify by telephone, audio-visual means or other electronic means. The financial documentation may be provided by personal delivery, mailing, facsimile, telecopier or any other electronic means that is acceptable to the court.

(d) The court shall transmit a copy of its decision by mail, facsimile, telecopier, or electronic means to the applicant and the parties.

The court shall state its reasons in writing for denying any request to appear by telephone, audio-visual means or other electronic means.

205.45 to 205.49   **[Reserved]**

§ 205.50. Terms and conditions of order suspending judgment in accordance with section 633 of the Family Court Act or section 384-b(8)(c) of the Social Services Law.

(a) An order suspending judgment entered pursuant to section 631 of the Family Court Act or section 384-b(8)(c) of the Social Services Law shall be related to the adjudicated acts or omissions of respondent and shall contain at least one of the following terms and conditions requiring respondent to:

(1) sustain communication of a substantial nature with the child by letter or telephone at stated intervals;

(2) maintain consistent contact with the child, including visits or outings at stated intervals;

(3) participate with the authorized agency in developing and effectuating a plan for the future of the child;

(4) cooperate with the authorized agency's court-approved plan for encouraging and strengthening the parental relationship;

(5) contribute toward the cost of maintaining the child if possessed of sufficient means or able to earn such means;

(6) seek to obtain and provide proper housing for the child;

(7) cooperate in seeking to obtain and in accepting medical or psychiatric diagnosis or treatment, alcoholism or drug abuse treatment, employment or family counselling or child guidance, and permit information to be obtained by the court from any person or agency from whom the respondent is receiving or was directed to receive such services; and

(8) satisfy such other reasonable terms and conditions as the court shall determine to be necessary or appropriate to ameliorate the acts or omissions which gave rise to the filing of the petition.

(b) The order shall set forth the duration, terms and conditions of the suspended judgment. A copy of the order, along with a current service plan, shall be furnished to the respondent. The order shall contain a written statement informing the respondent that a failure to obey the order may lead to its revocation and to the issuance of an order for the commitment of the guardianship and custody of a child. Where the child is in foster care, the order shall set forth the visitation plan for the child and the respondent, as well as for the child and his or her sibling or siblings, if any, and shall require the agency to notify the respondent of case conferences. The order shall further contain a determination in accordance with subdivision 12 of section 384-b of the Social Services Law of the existence of any person or persons to whom notice of an adoption would be required pursuant to section 111-b of the Domestic Relations Law and, if so, whether such person or persons were given notice of the termination of parental rights proceeding and whether such person or persons appeared.

(c) The court may set a time or times at which the respondent or the authorized agency caring the child shall report to the court as to whether there is compliance with the terms and conditions of the suspended judgment.

(d) If a respondent fails to comply with the terms and conditions of an order suspending judgment made pursuant to section 631 of the Family Court Act or section 384-b(8)(c) of the Social Services Law:

(1) a petition for the revocation of the order may be filed;

(2) the petition shall contain a concise statement of the acts or omissions alleged to constitute noncompliance with the order;

(3) service of a summons and a copy of the petition shall be made as provided for by section 617 of the Family Court Act; and

(4) if, after a hearing, the court is satisfied that the allegations of the petition have been established, the court may modify, revise or revoke the order of suspended judgment.

(e)   The court may at any time, upon notice and opportunity to be heard to the parties, their attorneys and the law guardian, revise, modify or enlarge the terms and conditions of a suspended judgment previously imposed.

§ 205.51.   Proceedings involving custody of a Native American child.

In any proceeding in which the custody of a child is to be determined, the petition shall set forth whether the child is a Native American child subject to the Indian Child Welfare Act of 1978 (25 U.S.C. §§ 1901-1963), and the Court shall proceed further, as appropriate, in accordance with the provisions of that act.

§ 205.52.   Adoption rules; application.

(a)   Sections 205.53 through 205.55 of this Part shall be applicable to all agency and private-placement adoption proceedings in Family Court.

(b)   In any agency adoption, a petition may be filed to adopt a child who is the subject of a termination of parental rights proceeding and whose custody and guardianship has not yet been committed to an authorized agency, provided that:

(i)   the adoption petition is filed in the same court where the termination of parental rights proceeding is pending; and

(ii)   the adoption petition, supporting documents and the fact of their filing shall not be provided to the judge before whom the petition for termination of parental rights is pending until such time as fact-finding is concluded under that petition.

§ 205.53.   Papers required in an adoption proceeding.

(a)   All papers submitted in an adoption proceeding shall comply with section 205.7 of this part.

(b)   In addition to those papers required by the Domestic Relations Law, the following papers, unless otherwise dispensed with by the court, shall be submitted and filed prior to the placement of any adoption proceeding on the calendar:

(1)   a certified copy of the birth certificate of the adoptive child;

(2)   an affidavit or affidavits by an attorney admitted to practice in the State of New York or, in the discretion of the court, by a person other than an attorney who is known to the court, identifying each of the parties;

(3)   a certified marriage certificate, where the adoptive parents are husband and wife or where an individual adoptive parent is the spouse of the natural parent;

(4)   a certified copy of a decree or judgment, where an adoptive parent's marriage has been terminated by decree or judgment;

(5)   a certified death certificate, where an adoptive or natural parent's marriage has been terminated by death or where it is alleged that consent or notice is not required because of death;

(6)   a proposed order of adoption;

(7)   a copy of the attorney's affidavit of financial disclosure filed with the Office of Court Administration pursuant to 22 N.Y.C.R.R. 603.23, 691.23, 806.14 or 1022.33; and either an attorney's affirmation that the affidavit has been personally delivered or mailed in accordance with such rules or the dated receipt from the Office of Court Administration; and

(8)   an affidavit of financial disclosure from the adoptive parent or parents, and from any person whose consent to the adoption is required by law, setting forth the following information:

(i)   name, address and telephone number of the affiant;

(ii)   status of the affiant in the proceeding and relationship, if any, to the adoptive child;

(iii)   docket number of the adoption proceeding;

(iv)   the date and terms of every agreement, written or otherwise, between the affiant and any attorney pertaining to any fees, compensation or other remuneration paid or to be paid by or on behalf of the adoptive parents or the natural parents, directly or indirectly, including but not limited to retainer fees on account of or incidental to the placement or adoption of the child or assistance in arrangements for such placement or adoption;

(v)   the total amount of fees, compensation or other remuneration to be paid to such attorney by the affiant, directly or indirectly, including the date and amounts of each payment already made, if any, on account of or incidental to the placement or adoption of the child or assistance in arrangements for such placement or adoption;

(vi)   the name and address of any other person, agency, association, corporation, institution, society or organization who received or will receive any fees, compensation or other remuneration from the affiant, directly or indirectly, on account of or incidental to the birth or care of the adoptive child, the pregnancy or care of the adoptive child's mother or the placement or adoption of the child and on account of or incidental to assistance in arrangements for such placement or proposed adoption; the amount of each such fee, compensation or other remuneration; and the reason for or services rendered, if any, in connection with each such fee, compensation or other remuneration; and

(vii)   the name and address of any person, agency, association, corporation, society or organization who has or will pay the affiant any fee, compensation or other remuneration, directly or indirectly, on account of or incidental to the birth or care of the adoptive child, the pregnancy or care of the adoptive child's mother, or the placement or adoption of the child and on account of or incidental to assistance in arrangements for such placement or adoption; the amount of each such fee, compensation or other remuneration; and the reason for or services rendered, if any, in connection with each such fee, compensation or other remuneration.

(9)   in the case of an adoption from an authorized agency in accordance with Title 2 of Article 7 of the Domestic Relations Law, a copy of the criminal history summary report made by the New York State Office of Children and Family Services to the authorized agency pursuant to section 378-a of the Social Services Law regarding the criminal record or records of the prospective adoptive parent or parents and any adult over the age of 18 currently residing in the home.

(c)   Prior to the signing of an order of adoption, the court may in its discretion require the filing of a supplemental affidavit by the adoptive parent or parents, any person whose consent to the adoption is required, the authorized agency and the attorney for any of the aforementioned, setting forth any additional information pertaining to allegations in the petition or in any affidavit filed in the proceeding.

§ 205.54.   Investigation by disinterested person; adoption.

(a)   The probation service or an authorized agency or disinterested person is authorized to, and at the request of the court, shall, interview such persons and obtain such data as will aid the court in determining the truth and accuracy of an adoption petition under article 7 of the Domestic Relations Law, including the allegations set forth in the schedule annexed to the petition pursuant to section 112(3) of that law and such other facts as are necessary to a determination of the petition.

(b)   The adoptive parent or parents and other persons concerned with the proceeding shall be notified of the date, time and place of any interview by a disinterested person or authorized agency designated by the court in accordance with sections 112 and 116 of the Domestic Relations Law.

(c)   The written report of the investigation conducted pursuant to subdivision (a) of this section shall be submitted to the court within 30 days from the date on which it was ordered, or earlier as the court may direct, unless, for good cause the court shall grant an extension for a reasonable period of time not to exc an additional 30 days.

§ 205.55.   Special applications.

All applications, including applications to dispense with all personal appearances, the period of residence of a child, after filing of the adoption petition, shall be made accompanied by affidavits setting forth the reaso facts relevant thereto.

§ 205.56.   Investigation by disintere

(a)   The probation service or an a authorized to, and at the request of th obtain such data as will aid the court i

(1) determining custody in a proceeding under section 467 or 651 of the Family Court Act;

(2) exercising its power under section 661 of the Family Court Act to appoint a guardian of the person of a minor under the jurisdiction of the court.

(b) The written report of the investigation conducted pursuant to subdivision (a) of this section shall be submitted to the court within 30 days from the date on which it was ordered, or earlier as the court may direct, unless, for good cause, the court shall grant an extension for a reasonable period of time not to exceed an additional 30 days.

§ 205.57. Petition for guardianship by adoptive parent.

(a) When a petition for temporary guardianship has been filed by an adoptive parent or parents pursuant to section 115-c of the Domestic Relations Law, the clerk of the court in which the petition has been filed shall distribute a written notice to the adoptive parents and lawyers who have appeared, and to the Commissioner of Social Services or the Director of the Probation Service, as appropriate, indicating that:

(1) a petition for adoption must be filed in the court in which the application for temporary guardianship has been brought within 45 days from the date of the signing of the consent to the adoption;

(2) any order or decree of temporary guardianship will expire no later than nine months following its issuance or upon the entry of a final order of adoption whichever is sooner, unless, upon application to the court, it is extended for good cause; and

(3) any order or decree of temporary guardianship will terminate upon withdrawal or denial of a petition to adopt the child, unless the court orders a continuation of such order or decree.

(b) In addition to and without regard to the date set for the hearing of the petition, the clerk of the court shall calendar the case for the 45th day from the date of the signing of the consent to the adoption. If no petition for adoption has ~~en filed by the 45th day, the court shall schedule a hearing and shall order the~~ ~~opriate agency to conduct an investigation forthwith, if one had not been~~ ~~previously.~~

Proceedings for certification as a qualified adoptive parent or parents.

~~e petition in a proceeding for certification as a qualified adoptive~~
~~lleges that petitioner or petitioners will cause a preplacement~~
~~ndertaken, the petition shall include the name and address~~
~~son by whom such investigation will be conducted.~~

~~disinterested person conducting the preplacement~~
~~y such person directly with the court, with a copy~~
~~taneously to the applicant or applicants.~~

(c) The court shall order a report (1) from the statewide central register of child abuse and maltreatment setting forth whether the child or the petitioner is, or petitioners are, the subject of or another person named in an indicated report, as such terms are defined in section 412 of the Social Services Law, filed with such register; and (2) from the New York State Division of Criminal Justice Services setting forth any existing criminal record of such petitioner or petitioners, in accordance with section 115-d(3-a) of the Domestic Relations Law; provided, however, that were the petitioner(s) have been fingerprinted pursuant to section 378-a of the Social Services Law, the authorized agency in possession of a current criminal history summary report from the New York State Office of Children and Family Services may be requested to provide such report to the court in lieu of a report from the New York State Division of Criminal Justice Services.

§ 205.59. Calendaring of proceedings for adoption from an authorized agency.

Proceedings for adoption from an authorized agency shall be calendared as follows:

(a) Within 60 days of the filing of the petition and documents specified in section 112-a of the Domestic Relations Law, the court shall schedule a review of said petition and documents to take place to determine if there is adequate basis for approving the adoption.

(b) If such basis is found, the court shall schedule the appearance of the adoptive parent(s) and child before the court, for approval of the adoption, within 30 days of the date of the review.

(c) If, upon the court's review, the court finds that there is not an adequate basis for approval of the adoption, the court shall direct such further hearings, submissions or appearances as may be required, and the proceeding shall be adjourned as required for such purposes.

§ 205.60. Designation of a facility for the questioning of children in custody (PINS).

Designation of facilities for the questioning of children pursuant to section 724(b)(ii) of the Family Court Act shall be in accordance with section 205.20 of this Part.

§ 205.61. Authorization to release a child taken into custody before the filing of a petition (PINS).

When a child is brought to a detention facility pursuant to section 724(b)(iii) of the Family Court Act, the administrator responsible for operating the detention facility is authorized, before the filing of a petition, to release the child to the custody of a parent or other relative, guardian or legal custodian when the events that occasioned the taking into custody appear to involve a petition to determine whether the child is a person in need of supervision rather than a petition to determine whether the child is a juvenile delinquent.

§ 205.62. Preliminary probation conferences and procedures (PINS).

(Not applicable in jurisdictions that have designated an assessment service pursuant to an approved assessment and services plan as described in section 243-a of the Executive Law; reference should be made to the procedures set forth in section 735 of the Family Court Act.)

(a)   Any person seeking to originate a proceeding under article 7 of the Family Court Act to determine whether a child is a person in need of supervision shall first be referred to the probation service.

(b)   The probation service shall begin to conduct preliminary conferences with the person seeking to originate the proceeding, the potential respondent and any other interested person, on the same day that such persons are referred to the probation service, concerning the advisability of filing a petition and in order to gather information needed for a determination of the suitability of the case for adjustment. The probation service shall permit any participant who is represented by a lawyer to be accompanied by the lawyer at any preliminary conference.

(c)   During the preliminary probation conferences, the probation service shall ascertain, from the person seeking to originate the proceeding, a brief statement of the underlying events and, if known to that person, a brief statement of factors that would be of assistance to the court in determining whether the potential respondent should be detained or released in the event that a petition is filed.

(d)   In order to determine whether the case is suitable for the adjustment process, the probation service shall consider the following circumstances, among others:

(1)   the age of the potential respondent;

(2)   whether the conduct of the potential respondent allegedly involved:

(i)   a serious risk to the welfare and safety of the community; or

(ii)   an act which seriously endangered the safety of the potential respondent or another person;

(3)   whether there is a substantial likelihood that the potential respondent would not appear at scheduled conferences with the probation service or with an agency to which he or she may be referred;

(4)   whether there is a substantial likelihood that the potential respondent will not participate in or cooperate with the adjustment process;

(5)   whether there is a substantial likelihood that, in order to adjust the case successfully, the potential respondent would require services that could not be administered effectively in less than four months;

(6)   whether there is a substantial likelihood that the potential respondent will, during the adjustment process:

(i) engage in conduct that endangers the physical or emotional health of the potential respondent or a member of the potential respondent's family or household; or

(ii) harass or menace the person seeking to originate the proceeding or the complainant or a member of that person's family or household, where demonstrated by prior conduct or threats;

(7) whether there is pending another proceeding to determine whether the potential respondent is a person in need of supervision, a juvenile delinquent or a juvenile offender;

(8) whether there have been prior adjustments or adjournments in contemplation of dismissal under article 3 or 7 of the Family Court Act;

(9) whether there has been a prior adjudication of the potential respondent as a person in need of supervision, a juvenile delinquent or a juvenile offender;

(10) whether there is a substantial likelihood that the adjustment process would not be successful unless the potential respondent is temporarily removed from his or her home and that such removal could not be accomplished without invoking court process; and

(11) whether the potential respondent refuses to return home or refuses to remain at home and the reasons therefor do not justify the filing of a proceeding under article 10 of the Family Court Act.

(e) At the first appearance at a conference by each of the persons listed in subdivision (b) of this section, the probation service shall inform such person concerning the function and limitations of, and the alternatives to, the adjustment process and that:

(1) he or she has the right to participate in the adjustment process;

(2) the probation service is not authorized to and cannot compel any person to appear at any conference, produce any papers or visit any place;

(3) the person seeking to originate the proceeding is entitled to have access to the court at any time for the purpose of filing a petition under article 7 of the Family Court Act;

(4) the adjustment process may continue for a period of two months and may be extended for an additional 60 days upon written application to the court;

(5) statements made to the probation service are subject to the confidentiality provisions contained in section 735 of the Family Court Act; and

(6) if the adjustment process is commenced but is not successfully concluded, the persons participating therein may be notified orally or in writing of that fact and that the person seeking to originate the proceeding is entitled to access to the court for the purpose of filing a petition; oral notification will be confirmed in writing.

(f) If the adjustment process is not commenced:

(1)   the record of the probation service shall contain a statement of the grounds therefor; and

(2)   the probation service shall give written notice to the persons listed in subdivision (b) of this section who have appeared:

(i)   that the adjustment process will not be commenced;

(ii)   that the person seeking to originate the proceeding is entitled to access to the court for the purpose of filing a petition; and

(iii)   that, where applicable, the adjustment process was not commenced on the ground that the court would not have jurisdiction over the case and that the person seeking to originate the proceeding may test the question of the court's jurisdiction by filing a petition.

§ 205.63.   Duties of the probation service and procedures relating to the adjustment process (PINS).

(Not applicable in jurisdictions that have designated an assessment service pursuant to an approved assessment and services plan as described in section 243-a of the Executive Law; reference should be made to the procedures set forth in section 735 of the Family Court Act.)

(a)   Upon a determination by the probation service that a case is suitable for the adjustment process, it shall include in the process the potential respondent and any other persons listed in section 205.62(b) of this Part who wish to participate therein. The probation service shall permit any participant who is represented by a lawyer to be accompanied by the lawyer at any conference.

(b)   If an extension of the period of the adjustment process is sought, the probation service shall apply in writing to the court and shall set forth the services rendered to the potential respondent, the date of commencement of those services, the degree of success achieved, the services proposed to be rendered and a statement by the assigned probation officer that, in the judgment of such person, the matter will not be successfully adjusted unless an extension is granted.

(c)   The probation service may discontinue the adjustment process if, at any time:

(1)   the potential respondent or the person seeking to originate the proceeding requests that it do so;

(2)   the potential respondent refuses to cooperate with the probation service or any agency to which the potential respondent or a member of his or her family has been referred.

(d)   If the adjustment process is not successfully concluded, the probation service shall notify all the persons who participated therein, in writing:

(1)   that the adjustment process has not been successfully concluded; and

(2)   that the person seeking to originate the proceeding is entitled to access to the court for the purposes of filing a petition;

and, in addition to the above, shall notify the potential respondent in writing of the reasons therefor.

(e)   The case record of the probation service required to be kept pursuant to section 243 of the Executive Law and the regulations promulgated thereunder shall contain a statement of the grounds upon which:

(1)   the adjustment process was commenced but was not successfully concluded; or

(2)   the adjustment process was commenced and successfully concluded.

§ 205.64.   Procedure when remanded child absconds (PINS).

(a)   When a child absconds from a facility to which he or she was remanded pursuant to section 739 of the Family Court Act, written notice of that fact shall be given within 48 hours by an authorized representative of the facility to the clerk of the court from which the remand was made. The notice shall state the name of the child, the docket number of the pending proceeding in which the child was remanded, the date on which the child absconded, and the efforts made to secure the return of the child. Every order of remand pursuant to section 739 shall include a direction embodying the requirements of this subdivision.

(b)   Upon receipt of the written notice of absconding, the clerk shall cause the proceeding to be placed on the court calendar no later than the next court day for such action as the court may deem appropriate and shall give notice of such court date to the petitioner, presentment agency and law guardian or privately retained counsel of the child.

§ 205.65.   Terms and conditions of order adjourning a proceeding in contemplation of dismissal entered in accordance with section 749(a) of the Family Court Act (PINS).

(a)   An order adjourning a proceeding in contemplation of dismissal pursuant to section 749(a) of the Family Court Act shall contain at least one of the following terms and conditions directing the respondent to:

(1)   attend school regularly and obey all rules and regulations of the school;

(2)   obey all reasonable commands of the parent or other person legally responsible for the respondent's care;

(3)   avoid injurious or vicious activities;

(4)   abstain from associating with named individuals;

(5)   abstain from visiting designated places;

(6)   abstain from the use of alcoholic beverages, hallucinogenic drugs, habit-forming drugs not lawfully prescribed for the respondent's use, or any other harmful or dangerous substance;

(7)   cooperate with a mental health or other appropriate community facility to which the respondent is referred;

Ct. Rules

(8) restore property taken from the petitioner, complainant or victim, or replace property taken from the petitioner, complainant or victim, the cost of said replacement not to exceed $1,500;

(9) repair any damage to, or defacement of, the property of the petitioner, complainant or victim, the cost of said repair not to exceed $1,500;

(10) cooperate in accepting medical or psychiatric diagnosis and treatment, alcoholism or drug abuse treatment or counseling services, and permit an agency delivering that service to furnish the court with information concerning the diagnosis, treatment or counseling;

(11) attend and complete an alcohol awareness program established pursuant to section 19.25 of the Mental Hygiene Law;

(12) abstain from disruptive behavior in the home and in the community; or

(13) comply with such other reasonable terms and conditions as may be permitted by law and as the court shall determine to be necessary or appropriate to ameliorate the conduct which gave rise to the filing of the petition.

(b) An order adjourning a proceeding in contemplation of dismissal pursuant to section 749(b) of the Family Court Act may set a time or times at which the probation service shall report to the court, orally or in writing, concerning compliance with the terms and conditions of said order.

(c) A copy of the order setting forth the terms and conditions imposed and the duration thereof shall be furnished to the respondent and to the parent or other person legally responsible for the respondent.

§ 205.66. Terms and conditions of order in accordance with section 755 or 757 of the Family Court Act (PINS).

(a) An order suspending judgment entered pursuant to section 754 of the Family Court Act shall be reasonably related to the adjudicated acts or omissions of the respondent and shall contain at least one of the following terms and conditions directing the respondent to:

(1) attend school regularly and obey all rules and regulations of the school;

(2) obey all reasonable commands of the parent or other person legally responsible for the respondent's care;

(3) avoid injurious or vicious activities;

(4) abstain from associating with named individuals;

(5) abstain from visiting designated places;

(6) abstain from the use of alcoholic beverages, hallucinogenic drugs, habit-forming drugs not lawfully prescribed for the respondent's use, or any other harmful or dangerous substance;

(7) cooperate with a mental health or other appropriate community facility to which the respondent is referred;

(8)   make restitution or perform services for the public good;

(9)   restore property taken from the petitioner, complainant or victim, or replace property taken from the petitioner, complainant or victim, the cost of said replacement not to exceed $1,000;

(10)   repair any damage to, or defacement of, the property of the petitioner, complainant or victim, the cost of said repair not to exceed $1,000;

(11)   abstain from disruptive behavior in the home and in the community;

(12)   cooperate in accepting medical or psychiatric diagnosis and treatment, alcoholism or drug abuse treatment or counseling services, and permit an agency delivering that service to furnish the court with information concerning the diagnosis, treatment or counseling;

(13)   attend and complete an alcohol awareness program established pursuant to 19.25 of the Mental Hygiene Law;

(14)   comply with such other reasonable terms and conditions as the court shall determine to be necessary or appropriate to ameliorate the conduct which gave rise to the filing of the petition.

(b)   An order placing the respondent on probation in accordance with section 757 of the Family Court Act shall contain at least one of the following terms and conditions, in addition to any of the terms and conditions set forth in subdivision (a) of this section, directing the respondent to:

(1)   meet with the assigned probation officer when directed to do so by that officer;

(2)   permit the assigned probation officer to visit the respondent at home or at school;

(3)   permit the assigned probation officer to obtain information from any person or agency from whom the respondent is receiving or was directed to receive diagnosis, treatment or counseling;

(4)   permit the assigned probation officer to obtain information from the respondent's school;

(5)   cooperate with the assigned probation officer in seeking to obtain and in accepting employment and employment counseling services;

(6)   submit records and reports of earnings to the assigned probation officer when requested to do so by that officer;

(7)   obtain permission from the assigned probation officer for any absence from the county or residence in excess of two weeks;

(8)   attend and complete an alcohol awareness program established pursuant to section 19.25 of the Mental Hygiene Law; or

(9)   do or refrain from doing any other specified act of omission or commission that, in the opinion of the court, is necessary and appropriate to implement or facilitate the order placing the respondent on probation.

Ct. Rules

(c)   An order entered pursuant to section 754 of the Family Court Act may set a time or times at which the probation service shall report to the court, orally or in writing, concerning compliance with the terms and conditions of said order.

(d)   A copy of the order setting forth the terms and conditions imposed and the duration thereof shall be furnished to the respondent and to the parent or other person legally responsible for the respondent.

§ 205.67.   Procedures for compliance with Adoption and Safe Families Act.

(a)   Pretrial detention; required findings. In any case in which detention is ordered by the court pursuant to section 728 or 739 of the Family Court Act, the court shall make additional, specific written findings regarding the following issues:

(1)   whether the continuation of the respondent in his or her home would be contrary to his or her best interests; and

(2)   whether reasonable efforts, where appropriate, were made, prior to the date of the court hearing that resulted in the detention order, to prevent or eliminate the need for removal of the respondent from his or her home, or, if the respondent had been removed from his or her home prior to such court hearing, whether reasonable efforts, where appropriate, were made to make it possible for the respondent to safely return home.

The court may request the petitioner, presentment agency, if any, and the local probation department to provide information to the court to aid in its determinations and may also consider information provided by the law guardian.

(b)   Motion for an order that reasonable efforts are not required. A motion for a judicial determination, pursuant to section 754(2)(b) of the Family Court Act, that reasonable efforts to prevent or eliminate the need for removal of the respondent from his or her home or to make it possible to reunify the respondent with his or her parents are not required shall be governed by section 205.16 of this Part.

(c)   Placement; required findings. In any case in which the court is considering ordering placement pursuant to section 756 of the Family Court Act, the petitioner, presentment agency, if any, local probation department and local commissioner of social services shall provide information to the court to aid in its required determination of the following issues:

(1)   whether continuation in the respondent's home would be contrary to his or her best interests, and, if the respondent was removed from his or her home prior to the date of such hearing, whether such removal was in his or her best interests;

(2)   whether reasonable efforts, where appropriate, were made, prior to the date of the dispositional hearing, to prevent or eliminate the need for removal of the respondent from his or her home, and, if the respondent was removed from

his or her home prior to the date of such hearing, whether reasonable efforts, where appropriate, were made to make it possible for the respondent to return safely home. If the court determines that reasonable efforts to prevent or eliminate the need for removal of the respondent from his or her home were not made, but that the lack of such efforts was appropriate under the circumstances, the court order shall include such a finding;

(3) in the case of a respondent who has attained the age of 16, the services needed, if any, to assist the respondent to make the transition from foster care to independent living; and

(4) in the case of an order of placement specifying a particular authorized agency or foster care provider, the position of the local commissioner of social services regarding such placement.

(d) Permanency hearing; extension of placement. A petition for a permanency hearing and, if applicable, an extension of placement, pursuant to section 756-a of the Family Court Act, shall be filed at least 60 days prior to the expiration of one year following the respondent's entry into foster care; provided, however, that if the Family Court makes a determination, pursuant to section 754(2)(b) of the Family Court Act, that reasonable efforts are not required to prevent or eliminate the need for removal of the respondent from his or her home or to make it possible to reunify the respondent with his or her parents, the permanency hearing shall be held within 30 days of such finding and the petition for the permanency hearing shall be filed and served on an expedited basis as directed by the court. Following the initial permanency hearing in a case in which the respondent remains in placement, a petition for a subsequent permanency hearing and, if applicable, extension of placement shall be filed a least 60 days prior to the expiration of one year following the date of the preceding permanency hearing. All petitions for permanency hearings shall be governed by section 205.17 of this Part.

205.68 to 205.69   [Reserved]

§ 205.70. Designation of persons to inform complainant of procedures available for the institution of family offense proceedings.

Pursuant to section 812 of the Family Court Act, the following persons are hereby designated to inform any petitioner or complainant seeking to bring a proceeding under article 8 of the Family Court Act of the procedures available for the institution of these proceedings, before such proceeding or action is commenced:

(a) within the City of New York:

(1) the commanding officer of the police precinct wherein the offense is alleged to have occurred; or

(2) any police officer attached to such precinct who is designated by such commanding officer;

(b)　outside the City of New York:

(1)　the commanding officer of any law enforcement agency providing police service in the county wherein the offense is alleged to have occurred; or

(2)　any police officer attached to such law enforcement agency who is designated by such commanding officer;

(c)　the district attorney, corporation counsel or county attorney in the county wherein the offense is alleged to have occurred, or any assistant district attorney, assistant corporation counsel or assistant county attorney who is designated by such district attorney, corporation counsel or county attorney;

(d)　any probation officer in the employ of the State of New York, or any political subdivision thereof, providing probation service in the criminal court or in the intake unit of the Family Court in the county in which a proceeding may be instituted;

(e)　the clerk of the Family Court and the clerk of the criminal court located in the county in which the proceeding may be instituted, or any clerk in that court designated by such clerk of the family or criminal court; and

(f)　judges of all local criminal courts outside the City of New York having jurisdiction over the alleged offense.

§ 205.71.　Preliminary probation conferences and procedures (family offenses).

(a)　Any person seeking to file a family offense petition under article 8 of the Family Court Act may first be referred to the probation service concerning the advisability of filing a petition.

(b)　Upon such referral, the probation service shall inform such person:

(1)　concerning the procedures available for the institution of family offense proceedings, including the information set forth in subdivision 2 of section 812 of the Family Court Act; and

(2)　that the person seeking to file a family offense petition is entitled to request that the probation service confer with him or her, the potential respondent and any other interested person concerning the advisability of filing a petition requesting:

(i)　an order of protection;

(ii)　a temporary order of protection; or

(iii)　the use of the court's conciliation procedure.

(c)　The probation service, at the request of the person seeking to file a family offense petition, shall commence conducting preliminary conferences concerning the advisability of filing a petition with that person, the potential respondent and any other interested person no later than the next regularly scheduled court day. The probation service shall permit any participant who is represented by a lawyer to be accompanied at any preliminary conference by the lawyer, who shall be identified by the probation officer to the other party, and shall not discourage any person from seeking to file a petition.

(d) At the first appearance at a conference by each of the persons listed in subdivision (c) of this section, the probation service shall inform such person concerning the function and limitations of, and the alternatives to, the adjustment process, and that:

(1) the purpose of the adjustment process is to attempt through conciliation and agreement to arrive at a cessation of the conduct forming the basis of the family offense complaint without filing a petition in court;

(2) the probation service may confer with the persons listed in subdivision (c) of this section if it shall appear to the probation service that:

(i) there is a reasonable likelihood that the adjustment process will result in a cessation of the conduct forming the basis of the family offense complaint; and

(ii) there is no reasonable likelihood that the potential respondent will, during the period of the adjustment, inflict or threaten to inflict physical injury on the person seeking to obtain relief, or any other member of the same family or household, if the filing of a petition is delayed;

(3) the probation service is not authorized to, and shall not, compel any person, including the person seeking to file a family offense petition, to appear at any conference, produce any papers or visit any place;

(4) the person seeking to file a family offense petition is entitled to request that the probation service confer with him or her, the potential respondent and any other interested person concerning the advisability of filing a family offense petition under article 8 of the Family Court Act;

(5) if the assistance of the probation service is not requested or, if requested, is subsequently declined, the person seeking to file a family offense petition is entitled to have access to the court at any time, even after having consented to an extension of the adjustment period, and may proceed to file a family offense petition;

(6) no statements made during any preliminary conference with the probation service may be admitted into evidence at a fact-finding hearing held in the Family Court or at any proceeding conducted in a criminal court at any time prior to conviction;

(7) the adjustment process must commence within seven days from the date of the request for a conference, may continue for a period of two months from the date of that request and may be twice extended by the court for two periods of up to 60 days each upon written application to the court containing the consent and signature of the person seeking to file a family offense petition;

(8) if a petition is filed, a temporary order of protection may be issued for good cause shown, and unless a petition is filed, the court may not issue any order of protection;

(9)   if the adjustment process is not successful, the persons participating therein shall be notified in writing of that fact, and that the person seeking to file a family offense petition is entitled to access to the court for that purpose;

(10)   if the matter has been successfully adjusted, the persons participating therein shall be notified in writing of that fact; and

(11)   if the adjustment of the matter results in a voluntary agreement concerning the cessation of the offensive conduct forming the basis of the family offense complaint:

(i)   it shall be reduced to writing by the probation service, signed by both parties to it and submitted to the Family Court for approval;

(ii)   if the court approves it, the court may, without further hearing, enter an order of protection pursuant to section 823 of the Family Court in accordance with the agreement; and

(iii)   the order when entered shall be binding on the respondent and shall in all respects be a valid order.

(e)   If the adjustment process is not commenced, the probation service shall give written notice to the persons listed in subdivision (c) of this section that:

(1)   the adjustment process was not commenced and the reasons therefor;

(2)   the person seeking to file a family offense petition is entitled to access to the court for that purpose; and

(3)   if applicable, the adjustment process was not commenced on the ground that the court would not have jurisdiction over the case, and the person seeking to file a family offense petition may test the question of the court's jurisdiction by filing a petition.

§ 205.72.   Duties of the probation service and procedures relating to the adjustment process (family offenses).

(a)   If the assistance of the probation service is requested by the person seeking to file a family offense petition, the adjustment process shall commence within seven days from the request. The probation service shall permit any participant who is represented by a lawyer to be accompanied at any conference by the lawyer, who shall be identified by the probation officer to the other party, and shall not discourage any person from seeking to file a petition.

(b)   If an extension of the period of the adjustment process is sought, the probation service shall, with the written consent of the person seeking to file a family offense petition, apply in writing to the court and shall set forth the services rendered, the date of commencement of those services, the degree of success achieved, the services proposed to be rendered and a statement by the assigned probation officer: that there is no imminent risk that if an extension of the period is granted the potential respondent will, during the extended period of adjustment, endanger the health or safety of the person seeking to file a family offense petition or any other member of the same family or household, and the facts upon which the opinion is based; and that the matter will not be successfully adjusted unless an extension is granted.

(c) The probation service shall discontinue its efforts at adjustment if, at any time:

(1) the person seeking to file a family offense petition or the potential respondent requests that it do so; or

(2) it appears to the probation service that:

(i) there is no reasonable likelihood that a cessation of the conduct forming the basis of the family offense complaint will result; or

(ii) there is an imminent risk that the potential respondent will inflict or threaten to inflict physical injury upon the person seeking to file a family offense petition or upon any other member of the same family or household; or

(iii) the potential respondent has inflicted or threatened to inflict physical injury on the person seeking to file a family offense petition or any other member of the same family or household since efforts at adjustment began.

(d) If the adjustment process is not successfully concluded, the probation service shall notify in writing all the persons who participated therein:

(1) that the adjustment process has not been successfully concluded and the reasons therefor; and

(2) that the person seeking to file a family offense petition is entitled to access to the court for that purpose.

(e) If the adjustment process results in an agreement for the cessation of the conduct forming the basis of the family offense complaint:

(1) it shall be reduced to writing by the probation service, shall be signed by both parties to it, and shall be submitted to the court, together with a petition for approval of the agreement and a proposed order incorporating the agreement; and

(2) if the agreement is approved by the court, a copy of the order shall be furnished by the probation service to the person seeking to file a family offense petition and the potential respondent, in person if they are present, and by mail if their presence has been dispensed with by the court.

§ 205.73. Record and report of unexecuted warrants issued pursuant to section 827 of the Family Court Act (family offenses).

(a) The clerk of court for the Family Court in each county shall obtain and keep a record of unexecuted warrants issued pursuant to section 827 of the Family Court Act.

(b) At the end of each six-month period, on the first of January and on the first of July in each year, a report concerning all unexecuted warrants issued pursuant to section 827 of the Family Court Act shall be made and filed with the Office of Court Administration on a form to be supplied by the Office of Court Administration.

§ 205.74. Terms and conditions of order in accordance with sections 841(b)–(e), 842 and 843 of the Family Court Act (family offenses).

(a) An order suspending judgment entered pursuant to section 841(b) of the Family Court Act shall contain at least one of the following terms and conditions directing the respondent to:

(1) stay away from the residence of the person against whom the family offense was committed;

(2) stay away from the place of employment or place of education attended by the person against whom the family offense was committed;

(3) abstain from communicating by any means, including, but not limited to, telephone, letter, e-mail or other electronic means with the person against whom the family offense was committed;

(4) abstain from repeating the conduct adjudicated a family offense at the fact-finding hearing;

(5) cooperate in seeking to obtain and in accepting medical or psychiatric diagnosis and treatment, alcoholism or drug abuse treatment, or employment or counseling or child guidance services, or participate in a batterer's educational program designed to help end violent behavior, and permit information to be obtained by the court from any person or agency from whom the respondent is receiving or was directed to receive such services or participate in such program;

(6) allow medical or psychiatric treatment to be furnished to the person against whom the family offense was committed, or any other named family member or household member who is a dependent of the respondent and whose need for medical or psychiatric treatment was occasioned, in whole or in part, by the conduct adjudicated a family offense;

(7) cooperate with the person against whom the family offense was committed, the head of the household or parent, in maintaining the home or household;

(8) pay restitution in an amount not to exceed $10,000; or

(9) comply with such other reasonable terms and conditions as the court shall deem necessary or appropriate to ameliorate the acts or omissions which gave rise to the filing of the petition.

(b) An order placing the respondent on probation in accordance with section 841(c) of the Family Court Act shall contain at least one of the following terms and conditions, directing the respondent to:

(1) observe one or more of the terms and conditions set forth in subdivision (a) of this section;

(2) meet with the assigned probation officer when directed to do so by that officer;

(3) cooperate with the assigned probation officer in arranging for and allowing visitation in the family residence or household;

(4) cooperate in seeking to obtain and in accepting medical treatment, psychiatric diagnosis and treatment, alcoholism or drug abuse treatment, or employment or counseling services, or participate in a batterer's educational program designed to help end violent behavior, and permit the assigned probation officer to obtain information from any person or agency from whom the respondent is receiving or was directed to receive such services or participate in such program.

(c) An order of protection entered in accordance with section 841(d) of the Family Court Act may, in addition to the terms and conditions enumerated in sections 842 and 842-a of the Family Court Act, require the petitioner, respondent or both, or, if before the court, any other member of the household, to:

(1) abstain from communicating by any means, including, but not limited to, telephone, letter, e-mail or other electronic means with the person against whom the family offense was committed;

(2) stay away from the place of employment or place of education attended by the person against whom the family offense was committed, of a child or a parent, or of another member of the same family or household;

(3) refrain from engaging in any conduct which interferes with the custody of a child as set forth in the order;

(4) cooperate in seeking to obtain and in accepting medical treatment, psychiatric diagnosis and treatment, alcoholism or drug abuse treatment, or employment or counseling services, or participate in a batterer's educational program designated to help end violent behavior, and permit information to be obtained by the court from any person or agency from whom the respondent is receiving or was directed to receive such services or participate in such program;

(5) pay restitution in an amount not to exceed $10,000; or

(6) comply with such other reasonable terms and conditions as the court may deem necessary and appropriate to ameliorate the acts or omissions which gave rise to the filing of the petition.

(d) A copy of the order setting forth its duration and the terms and conditions imposed shall be furnished to the respondent and to the person or persons against whom the family offense was committed.

(e) Each order issued pursuant to section 828 or 841(b), (c), (d) or (e) of the Family Court Act shall contain a written statement informing the respondent that a failure to obey the order may result in commitment to jail for a term not to exceed six months. Each order issued pursuant to section 828 or 841(d) shall contain a written statement informing the respondent that a failure to obey the order may result in incarceration up to seven years.

Ct. Rules

205.75 to 205.79   [Reserved]

§ 205.80. Procedure when remanded child absconds (child protective proceeding).

(a) When a child absconds from a shelter or holding facility to which the child was remanded pursuant to section 1027(b) or 1051(d) of the Family Court Act, written notice of that fact, signed by an authorized representative of the facility, shall be sent within 48 hours to the clerk of the court from which the remand was made. The notice shall state the name of the child, the docket number of the pending proceeding in which the child was remanded, the date on which the child absconded, and the efforts made to secure the return of the child. Every order of remand pursuant to sections 1027(b) or 1051(d) shall include a direction embodying the requirement of this subdivision.

(b) Upon receipt of a written notice of absconding, the clerk of the court shall cause the proceeding to be placed on the calendar for the next court day for such action as the court shall deem appropriate, and shall give notice of such court date to the petitioner and law guardian or privately retained counsel of the child.

§ 205.81. Procedures for compliance with Adoption and Safe Families Act.

(a) Temporary removal; required findings. In any case in which removal of the child is ordered by the court pursuant to Part 2 of Article 10 of the Family Court Act, the court shall make additional, specific written findings regarding the following issues:

(1) whether the continuation of the child in his or her home would be contrary to his or her best interests; and

(2) whether reasonable efforts, where appropriate, were made, prior to the date of the court hearing that resulted in the removal order, to prevent or eliminate the need for removal of the child from his or her home, and, if the child had been removed from his or her home prior to such court hearing, whether reasonably efforts, where appropriate, were made to make it possible for the child to safely return home. The petitioner shall provide information to the court to aid in its determinations. The court may also consider information provided by respondents and the law guardian.

(b) Motion for an order that reasonable efforts are not required. A motion for a judicial determination, pursuant to section 1039-b of the Family Court Act, that reasonable efforts to prevent or eliminate the need for removal of the child from his or her home or to make it possible to reunify the child with his or her parents are not required shall be governed by section 205.16 of this Part.

(c) Placement; required findings. In any care in which the court is considering ordering placement pursuant to section 1055 of the Family Court Act, the petitioner shall provide information to the court to aid in its required determination of the following issues:

(1) whether continuation in the child's home would be contrary to his or her best interests and, if the child was removed from his or her home prior to the date of such hearing, whether such removal was in his or her best interests;

(2) whether reasonably efforts, where appropriate, were made, prior to the date of the dispositional hearing, to prevent or eliminate the need for removal of the child from his or her home and, if the child was removed from his or her home prior to the date of such hearing, whether reasonably efforts, where appropriate, were made to make it possible for the child to return safely home. If the court determines that reasonable efforts to prevent or eliminate the need for removal of the child from his or her home were not made, but that the lack of such efforts was appropriate under the circumstances, the court order shall include such a finding;

(3) in the case of a child for whom the permanency plan is adoption, guardianship or some other permanent living arrangement other than reunification with the parent or parents of the child, whether reasonable efforts have been made to make and finalize such other permanency plan;

(4) in the case of a respondent who has attained the age of 16, the services needed, if any, to assist the respondent to make the transition from foster care to independent living; and

(5) in the case of an order of placement specifying a particular authorized agency or foster care provider, the position of the local commissioner of social services regarding such placement.

(d) *Permanency hearing; extension of placement.* A petition for a permanency hearing and, if applicable, an extension of placement, pursuant to section 1055 of the Family Court Act, shall be filed at least 60 days prior to the expiration of one year following the child's entry into foster care. For purposes of this section, the child's entry into foster care shall be deemed to have commenced the earlier of the date of the fact finding of abuse or neglect of the child pursuant to section 1051 of the Family Court Act or 60 days after the date the child was removed from his or her home; provided, however, that if the court makes a determination, pursuant to section 1039-b of the Family Court Act, that reasonable efforts are not required to prevent or eliminate the need for removal of the child from his or her home or to make it possible to reunify the child with his or her parents, the permanency hearing shall be held within 30 days of such determination and the petition for the permanency hearing shall be filed and served on an expedited basis as directed by the court. Following the initial permanency hearing in a case in which the child remains in placement, a petition for a subsequent permanency hearing and, if applicable, extension of placement shall be filed at least 60 days prior to the expiration of one year following the date of the preceding permanency hearing. All petitions for permanency hearings shall be governed by section 205.17 of this Part.

Ct. Rules

§ 205.82. Record and report of unexecuted warrants issued pursuant to article 10 of the Family Court Act (child protective proceeding).

(a)   The clerk of court for the Family Court in each county shall obtain and keep a record of unexecuted warrants issued pursuant to article 10 of the Family Court Act.

(b)   At the end of each six-month period, on the first of January and on the first of July in each year, a report concerning all unexecuted warrants issued pursuant to article ten of the Family Court Act shall be made and filed with the Office of Court Administration on a form to be supplied by the Office of Court Administration.

§ 205.83. Terms and conditions of order in accordance with sections 1053, 1054 and 1057 of the Family Court Act (child protective proceeding).

(a)   An order suspending judgment entered pursuant to section 1052 of the Family Court Act shall, where the child is in foster care, set forth the visitation plan between respondent and the child and between the child and his or her sibling or siblings, if any, and shall require the agency to notify the respondent of case conferences. A copy of the order, along with a current service plan, shall be furnished to the respondent. Any order suspending judgment entered pursuant to section 1052 of the Family Court Act shall contain at least one of the following terms and conditions that relate to the adjudicated acts or omissions of the respondent, directing the respondent to:

(1)   refrain from or eliminate specified acts or conditions found at the fact-finding hearing to constitute or to have caused neglect or abuse;

(2)   provide adequate and proper food, housing, clothing, medical care, and for the other needs of the child;

(3)   provide proper care and supervision to the child and cooperate in obtaining, accepting or allowing medical or psychiatric diagnosis or treatment, alcoholism or drug abuse treatment, counseling or child guidance services for the child;

(4)   take proper steps to insure the child's regular attendance at school; and

(5)   cooperate in obtaining and accepting medical treatment, psychiatric diagnosis and treatment, alcoholism or drug abuse treatment, employment or counseling services, or child guidance, and permit a child protective agency to obtain information from any person or agency from whom the respondent or the child is receiving or was directed to receive treatment or counseling.

(b)   An order pursuant to section 1054 of the Family Court Act placing the person to whose custody the child is released under the supervision of a child protective agency, social services officer or duly authorized agency, or an order pursuant to section 1057 placing the respondent under the supervision of a child protective agency, social services official or authorized agency, shall contain at least one of the following terms and conditions requiring the respondent to:

(1)   observe any of the terms and conditions set forth in subdivision (a) of this section;

(2)   cooperate with the supervising agency in remedying specified acts or omissions found at the fact-finding hearing to constitute or to have caused the neglect or abuse;

(3)   meet with the supervising agency alone and with the child when directed to do so by that agency;

(4)   report to the supervising agency when directed to do so by that agency;

(5)   cooperate with the supervising agency in arranging for and allowing visitation in the home or other place;

(6)   notify the supervising agency immediately of any change of residence or employment of the respondent or of the child;

(7)   do or refrain from doing any other specified act of omission or commission that, in the judgment of the court, is necessary to protect the child from injury or mistreatment and to help safeguard the physical, mental and emotional well-being of the child.

(c)   When an order is made pursuant to section 1054 or 1057 of the Family Court Act:

(1)   the court shall notify the supervising agency in writing of its designation to act and shall furnish to that agency a copy of the order setting forth the terms and conditions imposed;

(2)   the order shall be accompanied by a written statement informing the respondent that a willful failure to obey the terms and conditions imposed may result in commitment to jail for a term not to exceed six months; and

(3)   the court may, if it concludes that it is necessary for the protection of the child, direct the supervising agency to furnish a written report to the court at stated intervals not to exceed six months setting forth whether, and to what extent:

(i)   there has been any alteration in the respondent's maintenance of the child that is adversely affecting the child' s health or well-being;

(ii)   there is compliance with the terms and conditions of the order of supervision; and

(iii)   the supervising agency has furnished supporting services to the respondent.

(d)   A copy of the order, setting forth its duration and the terms and conditions imposed, shall be furnished to the respondent.

Ct. Rules

205.84   [Reserved]

§ 205.85.   Procedure when a child who has been placed absconds (child protective proceeding).

(a)   When a child placed pursuant to section 1055 of the Family Court Act absconds, written notice of that fact shall be sent within 48 hours to the clerk of the court from which the placement was made. The notice shall be signed by the custodial person or by an authorized representative of the place of placement and shall state the name of the child, the docket number of the proceeding in which the child was placed, the date on which the child absconded, and the efforts made to secure the return of the child. Every order of placement pursuant to section 1055 shall include a direction embodying the requirement of this subdivision.

(b)   Upon receipt of the written notice of absconding, the clerk of the court shall cause the proceeding to be placed on the calendar no later than the next court day for such action as the court may deem appropriate.

§ 205.86.   Videotapes of interviews of children alleged to have been sexually abused.

(a)   In any case in which, pursuant to section 1038(c) of the Family Court Act, a videotape is made of an expert's interview with a child alleged to have been sexually abused, the attorney for the party requesting the videotaping, or the party, if unrepresented, shall promptly after the videotaping has been completed:

(1)   cause to be prepared a duplicate videotape, certified by the preparer as a complete and unaltered copy of the original videotape;

(2)   deposit the original videotape, certified by the preparer as the original, with the Clerk of the Family Court; and

(3)   submit for signature to the judge before whom the case is pending a proposed order authorizing the retention of the duplicate videotape by the attorney, (or the party, if unrepresented) and directing that retention be in conformance with this section.

Both the original videotape and the duplicate thereof shall be labelled with the name of the case, the Family Court docket number, the name of the child, the name of the interviewer, the name and address of the technician who prepared the videotape, the date of the interview, and the total elapsed time of the videotape.

(b)   Upon receipt, the clerk shall hold the original videotape in a secure place limited to access only by authorized court personnel.

(c)   (1) Except as provided in paragraph (2) of this subdivision, the duplicate videotape shall remain in the custody of the attorney for the party who requested it, or the party, if not represented (the "custodian").

(2) The duplicate videotape shall be available for pretrial disclosure pursuant to article 10 of the Family Court Act and any other applicable law. Consistent therewith, the custodian shall permit an attorney for a party, or the party, if not represented by counsel, to borrow the duplicate videotape for a reasonable period of time so that it may be viewed, provided the person to whom it is loaned first certifies, by affidavit filed with the court, that he or she will comply with this subdivision.

(3) A person borrowing the duplicate videotape as provided in paragraph (2) of this subdivision shall not lend it or otherwise surrender custody thereof to any person other than the custodian, and upon returning such videotape to the custodian, such person shall certify, by affidavit filed with the court, that he or she has complied with the provisions of this subdivision.

(4) Subject to court order otherwise, the duplicate videotape may not be viewed by any person other than a party or his or her counsel or prospective expert witnesses. No copy of the duplicate videotape may be made.

(d) Failure to comply with the provisions of this rule shall be punishable by contempt of court.

Ct. Rules

RULES OF THE CHIEF JUDGE

Part 7   LAW GUARDIANS

(Statutory authority: Constitution, art. VI, § 28[c])

SYNOPSIS

Section 7.1.   **Standards to regulate designation of lawyers who may be appointed law guardians to represent minors in Family Court proceedings.**

§ 7.1.   Standards to regulate designation of lawyers who may be appointed law guardians to represent minors in Family Court proceedings.

(a)   Each of the Appellate Divisions shall by January 1, 1980 promulgate rules pertaining to the establishment and operation of a panel of lawyers qualified for assignment as law guardians to represent minors in proceedings in Family Court.

(b)   The panel plan, which consists of the rules so promulgated, may provide for the creation of a departmental advisory committee, whose membership may be representative of the bar associations, law school faculties and the lay public, among others.

(c)   The panel plan shall contain standards and administrative procedures for continuing evaluation of the panel plan and panel lawyers.

(d)   The panel plan shall set forth standards for appointment to the panel, which may include litigation experience in matters within the jurisdiction of the Family Court, participation in a panel plan training program, or other qualifying criteria.

(e)   The panel plan shall set forth standards for removal from the panel and provide a removal process or mechanism.

(f)   The panel plan shall provide for a continuing program of training and education for members of the panel.

(g)   Annual reports on the operation of the panels, for each calendar year shall be filed by the Appellate Divisions with the Chief Administrator of the Courts, no later than July 1st of the next succeeding calendar year.

Ct. Rules

UNIFORM CIVIL RULES FOR THE SUPREME COURT AND COUNTY COURT

(22 N.Y.C.R.R. Part 202 — Selected Rules)

SYNOPSIS

§ 202.16.   Matrimonial actions; calendar control of financial disclosure in actions and proceedings involving alimony, maintenance, child support and equitable distribution; motions for alimony, counsel fees *pendente lite*, and child support; special rules.

  (a)   *Applicability.* This section shall be applicable to all contested actions and proceedings in the Supreme Court in which statements of net worth are required by section 236 of the Domestic Relations Law to be filed and in which a judicial determination may be made with respect to alimony, counsel fees, *pendente lite,* maintenance, custody and visitation, child support, or the equitable distribution of property, including those referred to Family Court by the Supreme Court pursuant to section 464 of the Family Court Act.

  (b)   *Form of statements of net worth.* Sworn statements of net worth, except as provided in subdivision (k) hereof, exchanged and filed with the court pursuant to section 236 of the Domestic Relations Law, shall be in substantial compliance with the Statement of Net Worth form contained in appendix A of this Part.

  (c)   *Retainer agreements.* (1) A signed copy of the attorney's retainer agreement with the client shall accompany the statement of net worth filed with the court, and the court shall examine the agreement to assure that it conforms to Appellate Division attorney conduct and disciplinary rules. Where substitution of counsel occurs after the filing with the court of the net worth statement, a signed copy of the attorney's retainer agreement shall be filed with the court within 10 days of its execution. An attorney seeking to obtain an interest in any property of his or her client to secure payment of the attorney's fee shall make application to the court for approval of said interest on notice to the client and to his or her adversary. The application may be granted only after the court reviews the finances of the parties and an application for attorney's fees.

(2)   An attorney seeking to obtain an interest in any property of his or her client to secure payment of the attorney's fee shall make application to the court for approval of said interest on notice to the client and to his or her adversary. The application may be granted only after the court reviews the finances of the parties and an application for attorney's fees.

(d)   *Request for judicial intervention.* A request for judicial intervention shall be filed with the court by the plaintiff no later than 45 days from the date of service of the summons and complaint or summons with notice upon the defendant, unless both parties file a notice of no necessity with the court, in which event the request for judicial intervention may be filed no later than 120 days from the date of service of the summons and complaint or summons with notice upon the defendant. Notwithstanding section 202.6(a) of this Part, the court shall accept a request for judicial intervention that is not accompanied by other papers to be filed in court.

(e)   *Certification.* Every paper served on another party or filed or submitted to the court in a matrimonial action shall be signed as provided in section 130-1.1-a of this title.

(f)   *Preliminary conference.* (1) In all actions or proceedings to which this section of the rules is applicable, a preliminary conference shall be ordered by the court to be held within 45 days after the action has been assigned. Such order shall set the time and date for the conference and shall specify the papers that shall be exchanged between the parties and filed with the court. These papers must be exchanged and filed no later than 10 days prior to the preliminary conference, unless the court directs otherwise. These papers shall include:

(i)   statements of net worth;

(ii)   all paycheck stubs for the current calendar year and the last paycheck stub for the immediately preceding calendar year;

(iii)   all filed state and federal income tax returns for the previous three years, including both personal returns and returns filed on behalf of any partnership or closely held corporation of which the party is a partner or shareholder;

(iv)   all W-2 wage and tax statements, 1099 forms, and K-1 forms for any year in the past three years in which the party did not file state and federal income tax returns;

(v)   all statements of accounts received during the past three years from each financial institution in which the party has maintained any account in which cash or securities are held;

(vi)   the statements immediately preceding and following the date of commencement of the matrimonial action pertaining to: (A) any policy of life insurance having a cash or dividend surrender value; and (B) any deferred compensation plan of any type or nature in which the party has an interest including, but not limited to, Individual Retirement Accounts, pensions, profit-sharing plans, Keogh plans, 401(k) plans and other retirement plans.

Both parties personally must be present in court at the time of the conference, and the judge personally shall address the parties at some time during the conference.

(2) The matters to be considered at the conference may include, among other things:

(i) applications for *pendente lite* relief, including interim counsel fees;

(ii) compliance with the requirement of compulsory financial disclosure, including the exchange and filing of a supplemental statement of net worth indicating material changes in any previously exchanged and filed statement of net worth;

(iii) simplification and limitation of the issues;

(iv) the establishment of a timetable for the completion of all disclosure proceedings, provided that all such procedures must be completed and the note of issue filed within six months from the commencement of the conference, unless otherwise shortened or extended by the court depending upon the circumstances of the case; and

(v) any other matters which the court shall deem appropriate.

(3) At the close of the conference, the court shall direct the parties to stipulate, in writing or on the record, as to all resolved issues, which the court then shall "so order," and as to all issues with respect to fault, custody and finance that remain unresolved. Any issues with respect to fault, custody and finance that are not specifically described in writing or on the record at that time may not be raised in the action unless good cause is shown. The court shall fix a schedule for discovery as to all unresolved issues and, in a noncomplex case, shall schedule a date for trial not later than six months from the date of the conference. The court may appoint a law guardian for the infant children, or may direct the parties to file with the court, within 30 days of the conference, a list of suitable law guardians for selection by the court. The court also may direct that a list of expert witnesses be filed with the court within 30 days of the conference from which the court may select a neutral expert to assist the court. The court shall schedule a compliance conference unless the court dispenses with the conference based upon a stipulation of compliance filed by the parties. Unless the court excuses their presence, the parties personally must be present in court at the time of the compliance conference. If the parties are present in court, the judge personally shall address them at some time during the conference.

(g) *Expert witnesses.* (1) Responses to demands for expert information pursuant to CPLR 3101(d) shall be served within 20 days following service of such demands.

(2) Each expert witness whom a party expects to call at the trial shall file with the court a written report, which shall be exchanged and filed with the court

no later than 60 days before the date set for trial, and reply reports, if any, shall be exchanged and filed no later than 30 days before such date. Failure to file with the court a report in conformance with these requirements may, in the court's discretion, preclude the use of the expert. Except for good cause shown, the reports exchanged between the parties shall be the only reports admissible at trial. Late retention of experts and consequent late submission of reports shall be permitted only upon a showing of good cause as authorized by CPLR 3101(d)(1)(i). In the discretion of the court, written reports may be used to substitute for direct testimony at the trial, but the reports shall be submitted by the expert under oath, and the expert shall be present and available for cross-examination. In the discretion of the court, in a proper case, parties may be bound by the expert's report in their direct case.

(h) *Statement of proposed disposition.* (1) Each party shall exchange a statement setting forth the following:

(i)   the assets claimed to be marital property;

(ii)   the assets claimed to be separate property;

(iii)   an allocation of debts or liabilities to specific marital or separate assets, where appropriate;

(iv)   the amount requested for maintenance, indicating and elaborating upon the statutory factors forming the basis for the maintenance requests;

(v)   the proposal for equitable distribution, where appropriate, indicating and elaborating upon the statutory factors forming the basis for the proposed distribution;

(vi)   the proposal for a distributive award, if requested, including a showing of the need for a distributive award;

(vii)   the proposed plan for child support, indicating and elaborating upon the statutory factors upon which the proposal is based; and

(viii)   the proposed plan for custody and visitation of any children involved in the proceeding, setting forth the reasons therefor.

(2)   A copy of any written agreement entered into by the parties relating to financial arrangements or custody or visitation shall be annexed to the statement referred to in paragraph (1) of this subdivision.

(3)   The statement referred to in paragraph (1) of this subdivision, with proof of service upon the other party, shall, with the note of issue, be filed with the court. The other party, if he or she has not already done so, shall file with the court a statement complying with paragraph (1) of this subdivision within 20 days of such service.

(i) *Filing of note of issue.* No action or proceeding to which this section is applicable shall be deemed ready for trial unless there is compliance with this section by the party filing the note of issue and certificate of readiness.

(j) *Referral to Family Court.* In all actions or proceedings to which this section is applicable referred to the Family Court by the Supreme Court pursuant to section 464 of the Family Court Act, all statements, including supplemental statements, exchanged and filed by the parties pursuant to this section shall be transmitted to the Family Court with the order of referral.

(k) *Motions for alimony, maintenance, counsel fees pendente lite and child support (other than under section 237(c) or 238 of the Domestic Relations Law).* Unless, on application made to the court, the requirements of this subdivision be waived for good cause shown, or unless otherwise expressly provided by any provision of the CPLR or other statute, the following requirements shall govern motions for alimony, maintenance, counsel fees (other than a motion made Pursuant to section 237(c) or 238 of the Domestic Relations Law for counsel fees for services rendered by an attorney to secure the enforcement of a previously granted order or decree) or child support or any modification of an award thereof:

(1) Such motion shall be made before or at the preliminary conference, if practicable.

(2) No motion shall be heard unless the moving papers include a statement of net worth in the official form prescribed by subdivision (b) of this section.

(3) No motion for counsel fees shall be heard unless the moving papers also include the affidavit of the movant's attorney stating the moneys, if any, received on account of such attorney's fee from the movant or any other person on behalf of the movant, and the moneys such attorney has been promised by, or the agreement made with, the movant or other persons on behalf of the movant, concerning or in payment of the fee.

(4) The party opposing any motion shall be deemed to have admitted, for the purpose of the motion but not otherwise, such facts set forth in the moving party's statement of net worth as are not controverted in:

(i) a statement of net worth, in the official form prescribed by this section, completed and sworn to by the opposing party, and made a part of the answering papers; or

(ii) other sworn statements or affidavits with respect to any fact which is not feasible to controvert in the opposing party's statement of net worth.

(5) The failure to comply with the provisions of this subdivision shall be good cause, in the discretion of the judge presiding, either:

(i) to draw an inference favorable to the adverse party with respect to any disputed fact or issue affected by such failure; or

(ii) to deny the motion without prejudice to renewal upon compliance with the provisions of this section.

(6) The notice of motion submitted with any motion for or related to interim maintenance or child support shall contain a notation indicating the nature of the motion. Any such motion shall be determined within 30 days after the motion is submitted for decision.

(7) Upon any application for an award of counsel fees or appraisal/accounting fees made prior to the conclusion of the trial of the action, the court shall set forth in specific detail, in writing or on the record, the factors it considered and the reasons for its decision.

(l) Hearings or trials pertaining to temporary or permanent custody or visitation shall proceed from day to day to conclusion. With respect to other issues before the court, to the extent feasible, trial should proceed from day to day to conclusion.

. . . . COURT OF THE STATE OF NEW YORK
COUNTY OF . . . .

. . . .,

                     Plaintiff,

   –against–

. . . .,

                     Defendant.

STATEMENT OF
NET WORTH
(D.R.L. § 236)

Index No. . . . .

Date of commencement of action

. . . .

(Complete all items, marking "NONE," "INAPPLICABLE" and "UN-KNOWN," if appropriate)

STATE OF . . . .
COUNTY OF. . . . . . .

    ss.:

. . . ., the (Petitioner) (Respondent) (Plaintiff) (Defendant) herein, being duly sworn, deposes and says that the following is an accurate statement as of . . . ., of my net worth (assets of whatsoever kind and nature and wherever situated minus liabilities), statement of income from all sources and statement of assets transferred of whatsoever kind and nature and wherever situated:

I. FAMILY DATA:

    (a)   Husband's age _____

    (b)   Wife's age _____

    (c)   Date married _____

    (d)   Date (separated) (divorced) _____

    (e)   Number of dependent children under 21 years _____

    (f)   Names and ages of children

    (g)   Custody of Children _____Husband _____Wife

    (h)   Minor children of prior marriage: _____Husband _____Wife

Ct. Rules

(i)   (Husband) (Wife) (paying) (receiving) \$_____ as alimony (maintenance) and/or \$_____ child support in connection with prior marriage:

(j)   Custody of children of prior marriage:
Name _____
Address _____

(k)   Is marital residence occupied by Husband _____
Wife_____ Both _____

(l)   Husband's present address
_____

Wife's present address
_____

(m)   Occupation of Husband _____ Occupation of Wife
_____

(n)   Husband's employer
_____

(o)   Wife's employer
_____

(p)   Education, training and skills [Include dates of attainment of degrees, etc.]
        Husband _____
        Wife _____

(q)   Husband's health _____

(r)   Wife's health _____

(s)   Children's health _____

II.   EXPENSES: (You may elect to list all expenses on a weekly basis or all expenses on a monthly basis, however, you must be consistent. If any items are paid on a monthly basis, divide by 4.3 to obtain weekly payments; if any items are paid on a weekly basis, multiply by 4.3 to obtain monthly payment. Attach additional sheet, if needed. Items included under "Other" should be listed separately with separate dollar amounts.)

        Expenses listed [ ] weekly   [ ] monthly

(a) Housing
  1. Rent   _____   4. Condominium charges   _____
  2. Mortgage and   _____   5. Cooperative apartment   _____
      amortization   maintenance
  3. Real estate taxes   _____
                                Total: Housing   \$_____

(b) Utilities
  1. Fuel oil   _____   4. Telephone   _____
  2. Gas   _____   5. Water   _____
  3. Electricity   _____
                                Total: Utilities   \$_____

(c) Food
1. Groceries _____   5. Liquor/alcohol _____
2. School lunches _____   6. Home entertainment _____
3. Lunches at work _____   7. Other _____ _____
4. Dining Out _____

         Total: Food $_____

(d) Clothing
1. Husband _____   3. Children _____
2. Wife _____   4. Other _____ _____

         Total: Clothing $_____

(e) Laundry
1. Laundry at home _____   3. Other _____ _____
2. Dry cleaning _____

         Total: Laundry $_____

(f) Insurance
1. Life _____   6. Medical plan _____
2. Homeowner's/tenant's _____   7. Dental plan _____
3. Fire, theft and liability _____   8. Optical plan _____
4. Automotive _____   9. Disability _____
5. Umbrella policy _____   10. Worker's compensation _____
         11. Other _____ _____

         Total: Insurance $_____

(g) Unreimbursed medical
1. Medical _____   5. Surgical, nursing,
2. Dental _____   hospital _____
3. Optical _____   6. Other _____
4. Pharmaceutical _____

         Total:
         Unreimbursed medical $_____

(h) Household maintenance
1. Repairs _____   5. Painting _____
2. Furniture, furnishings,   6. Sanitation/carting _____
   housewares _____   7. Gardening/landscaping _____
3. Cleaning Supplies _____   8. Snow removal _____
4. Appliances, including   9. Extermination _____
   maintenance _____   10. Other _____ _____
         Total:
         Household maintenance $_____

(i) Household help
1. Babysitter _____   3. Other _____ _____
2. Domestic (housekeeper, _____
   maid, etc.)

         Total: Household help $_____

(j) Automotive
Year: _____ Make: _____ Personal: _____ Business: _____
Year: _____ Make: _____ Personal: _____ Business: _____
Year: _____ Make: _____ Personal: _____ Business: _____
1. Payments _____   4. Car wash _____
2. Gas and oil _____   5. Registration and license _____
3. Repairs _____   6. Parking and tolls _____
         7. Other _____ _____

Ct. Rules

Total: Automotive $_____

(k) Educational
1. Nursery and pre-school _____
2. Primary and secondary _____
3. College _____
4. Post-graduate _____
5. Religious instruction _____
6. School transportation _____
7. School supplies/books _____
8. Tutoring _____
9. School events _____
10. Other _____ _____
Total: Educational $_____

(l) Recreational
1. Summer camp _____
2. Vacations _____
3. Movies _____
4. Theatre, ballet, etc. _____
5. Video rentals _____
6. Tapes, CD's, etc. _____
7. Cable television _____
8. Team sports _____
9. Country club/pool club _____
10. Health club _____
11. Sporting goods _____
12. Hobbies _____
13. Music/dance lessons _____
14. Sports lessons _____
15. Birthday parties _____
16. Other _____ _____
Total: Recreational $_____

(m) Income taxes
1. Federal _____
2. State _____
3. City _____
4. Social Security and
   Medicare _____
Total: Income taxes $_____

(n) Miscellaneous
1. Beauty parlor/barber _____
2. Beauty aids/cosmetics,
   drug items _____
3. Cigarettes/tobacco _____
4. Books, magazines,
   newspapers _____
5. Children's allowances _____
6. Gifts _____
7. Charitable contributions _____
8. Religious organization
   dues _____
9. Union and
   organization dues _____
10. Commutation and
    transportation _____
11. Veterinarian/pet
    expenses _____
12. Child support payments
    (prior marriage) _____
13. Alimony and maintenance payments
    (prior marriage) _____
14. Loan payments _____
15. Unreimbursed business
    expenses _____
Total: Miscellaneous $_____

(o) Other
1. _____ _____
3. _____ _____
3. _____ _____
4. _____ _____
Total: Other $_____
TOTAL EXPENSES: $_____

III. GROSS INCOME: (State source of income and annual amount. Attach additional sheet, if needed).

(a) Salary or wages: (State whether income has changed during the year preceding date of this affidavit _____. If so, set forth name and address of all employers during preceding year and average weekly wage paid by each. Indicate overtime earnings separately. Attach previous year's W-2 or income tax return.)

     _____   _____

     _____   _____

(b) Weekly deductions:
1. Federal tax . . . . _____
2. New York State tax . . . . . _____
3. Local tax . . . . _____
4. Social security . . . . _____
5. Medicare . . . . _____
6. Other payroll deductions   _____
   (specify) . . . .

(c) Social Security number _____

(d) Number and names of dependents claimed: _____

(e) Bonus, commissions, fringe   _____
benefits (use of auto, memberships,
etc.) . . . .

(f) Partnership, royalties, sale of assets   _____
(income and installment payments)

  . . . .

(g) Dividends and interest (state   _____
whether taxable or not) . . . . . .

(h) Real estate (income only) . . . . .   _____

(i) Trust, profit sharing and annuities   _____
(principal distribution and income)

  . . . .

(j) Pension (income only) . . . . . .   _____

(k) Awards, prizes, grants (state   _____
whether taxable)

(l) Bequests, legacies and gifts . . . .   _____

(m) Income from all other sources   _____

  . . . .
   (including alimony, maintenance
or child support from prior
marriage)

(n) Tax preference items:
1. Long term capital gain   _____
   deduction . . . .
2. Depreciation, amortization or   _____
   depletion . . . .
3. Stock options — excess of fair   _____
   market value over amount
   paid . . . .

(o) If any child or other member of   _____
     your household is employed, set
     forth name and that person's
     annual income

(p) social Security . . . .   _____

(q) Disability benefits . . . .   _____

(r) Public assistance   . . . .   _____

(s) Other . . . .   _____

                       TOTAL INCOME:_____

IV.   ASSETS: (If any asset is held jointly with spouse or another, so state, and set forth your respective shares. Attach additional sheets, if needed.)

A.   Cash Accounts

     Cash

         1.1   a.   Location_____

              b.   Source of funds_____

              c.   Amount _____ $_____

                                 Total: Cash $_____

     Checking Accounts

         2.1   a.   Financial institution_____

              b.   Account number_____

              c.   Title holder_____

              d.   Date opened_____

              e.   Source of Funds_____

              f.   Balance _____ $_____

         2.2   a.   Financial institution_____

              b.   Account number_____

              c.   Title Holder_____

              d.   Date opened_____

              e.   Source of Funds_____

              f.   Balance_____ $_____

                          Total: Checking $_____

     Savings accounts (including individual, joint, totten trust, certificates of deposit, treasury notes)

         3.1   a.   Financial institution_____

              b.   Account number_____

              c.   Title holder_____

              d.   Type of account_____

              e.   Date opened_____

              f.   Source of funds_____

              g.   Balance_____ $_____

         3.2   a.   Financial institution_____

              b.   Account number_____

              c.   Title holder_____

              d.   Type of account_____

              e.   Date opened_____

              f.   Source of funds_____

              g.   Balance_____ $_____

                          Total: Savings $_____

Security deposits, earnest money, etc.

    4.1 a. Location_____

           b. Title owner_____

           c. Type of deposit_____

           e. Source of funds_____

           f. Date of deposit_____

           g. Amount_____ $_____

                            Total: Security Deposits, etc.

                                         $_____

Other

    5.1 a. Location_____

           b. Title owner_____

           c. Type of account_____

           d. Source of funds_____

           e. Date of deposit_____

           f. Amount_____ $_____

                                  Total: Other $_____

                                  Total: Cash Accounts $_____

B.   Securities

    Bonds, notes, mortgages

      1.1 a. Description of security_____

           b. Title holder_____

           c. Location_____

           d. Date of acquisition_____

           e. Original price or value_____

           f. Source of funds to acquire_____

           g. Current value_____ $_____

                                Total: Bonds, notes, etc.

                                         $_____

    Stocks, options and commodity contracts

      2.1 a. Description of security_____

           b. Title holder_____

           c. Location_____

           d. Date of acquisition_____

           e. Original price or value_____

           f. Source of funds to acquire_____

           g. Current value_____ $_____

      2.2 a. Description of security_____

           b. Title holder_____

           c. Location_____

           d. Date of acquisition_____

           e. Original price or value_____

           f. Source of funds to acquire_____

           g. Current value_____ $_____

      2.3 a. Description of security_____

           b. Title holder_____

           c. Location_____

           d. Date of acquisition_____

           e. Original price or value_____

           f. Source of funds to acquire_____

           g. Current value_____ $_____

Ct. Rules

$ Total: Stocks, options, etc.

$_____

Broker margin accounts
3.1　a.　　Name and address of broker_____
　　　b.　　Title holder_____
　　　c.　　Date account opened_____
　　　d.　　Original value of account_____
　　　e.　　Source of funds_____
　　　f.　　Current value_____　　　$_____

Total: Margin accounts

$_____

Total value of securities:

$_____

C.　Loans to others and accounts receivable
　　　1.1　a.　　Debtor's name and address_____
　　　　　b.　　Original amount of loan or debt_____
　　　　　c.　　Source of funds from which loan made
　　　　　　　　or origin of debt_____
　　　　　d.　　Date payment(s) due_____
　　　　　e.　　Current amount due _____　　$_____

　　　1.2　a.　　Debtor's name and address_____
　　　　　b.　　Original amount of loan or debt_____
　　　　　c.　　Source of funds from which loan made
　　　　　　　　or Origin of debt_____
　　　　　d.　　Date payment(s) due_____
　　　　　e.　　Current amount due_____　　$_____

Total: Loans and accounts
receivable

$_____

D.　Value of interest in any business
　　　1.1　a.　　Name and address of business_____
　　　　　b.　　Type of business (corporate, partnership,
　　　　　　　　sole proprietorship or other)_____
　　　　　c.　　Your capital contribution_____
　　　　　d.　　Your percentage of interest_____
　　　　　e.　　Date of acquisition_____
　　　　　f.　　Original price or value_____
　　　　　g.　　Source of funds to acquire_____
　　　　　h.　　Method of valuation_____
　　　　　i.　　Other relevant information_____
　　　　　j.　　Current net worth of business _____　　$_____

Total: Value of business interest

$_____

E.　Cash surrender value of life insurance
　　　1.1　a.　　Insurer's name and address_____
　　　　　b.　　Name of insured_____
　　　　　c.　　Policy number_____
　　　　　d.　　Face amount of policy_____
　　　　　e.　　Policy owner_____
　　　　　f.　　Date of acquisition_____
　　　　　g.　　Source of funding to acquire_____

   h.   Current cash surrender value _____ $_____
                   Total: Value of life insurance
                                         $_____

F.   Vehicles (automobile, boat, plane, truck, camper, etc.)

      1.1   a.   Description_____
            b.   Title owner_____
            c.   Date of acquisition_____
            d.   Original price_____
            e.   Source of funds to acquire_____
            f.   Amount of current lien unpaid_____
            g.   Current fair market value _____ $_____

      1.2   a.   Description_____
            b.   Title owner_____
            c.   Date of acquisition_____
            d.   Original price_____
            e.   Source of funds to acquire_____
            f.   Amount of current lien unpaid_____
            g.   Current fair market value _____ $_____
                          Total: Value of Vehicles
                                     $_____

G.   Real estate (including real property, leaseholds, life estates, etc. at market value — do not deduct any mortgage)

      1.1   a.   Description_____
            b.   Title owner_____
            c.   Date of acquisition_____
            d.   Original price_____
            e.   Source of funds to acquire_____
            f.   Amount of mortgage or lien unpaid_____
            g.   Estimated current market value _____ $_____

      1.2   a.   Description_____
            b.   Title owner_____
            c.   Date of acquisition_____
            d.   Original price_____
            e.   Source of funds to acquire_____
            f.   Amount of mortgage or lien unpaid_____
            g.   Estimated current market value _____ $_____

      1.3   a.   Description_____
            b.   Title owner_____
            c.   Date of acquisition_____
            d.   Original price_____
            e.   Source of funds to acquire_____
            f.   Amount of mortgage or lien unpaid_____
            g.   Estimated current market value _____ $_____
                          Total: Value of real estate
                                     $_____

H.   Vested interests in trusts (pension, profit sharing, legacies, deferred compensation and others)

      1.1   a.   Description of trust_____
            b.   Location of assets_____
            c.   Title owner_____
            d.   Date of acquisition_____

Ct. Rules

    e.   Original investment_____

    f.   Source of funds_____

    g.   Amount of unpaid liens_____

    h.   Current value_____ $_____

1.2 a.   Description of trust_____

    b.   Location of assets_____

    c.   Title owner_____

    d.   Date of acquisition_____

    e.   Original investment_____

    f.   Source of funds_____

    g.   Amount of unpaid liens_____

    h.   Current value _____ $_____

Total: Vested interest in trusts $_____

I.   Contingent interests (stock options, interests subject to life estates, prospective inheritances, etc.)

1.1 a.   Description_____

    b.   Location_____

    c.   Date of vesting_____

    d.   Title owner_____

    e.   Date of acquisition_____

    f.   Original price or value_____

    g.   Source of funds to acquire_____

    h.   Method of valuation_____

    i.   Current value _____ $_____

Total: Contingent interests $_____

J.   Household furnishings

1.1 a.   Description_____

    b.   Location_____

    c.   Title owner_____

    d.   Original price_____

    e.   Source of funds to acquire_____

    f.   Amount of lien unpaid_____

    g.   Current value_____ $_____

Total: Household furnishings $_____

K.   Jewelry, art, antiques, precious objects, gold and precious metals (only if valued at more than $500)

1.1 a.   Description_____

    b.   Title owner_____

    c.   Location_____

    d.   Original price or value_____

    e.   Source of funds to acquire_____

    f.   Amount of lien unpaid_____

    g.   Current value _____ $_____

1.2 a.   Description_____

    b.   Title owner_____

    c.   Location_____

    d.   Original price or value_____

    e.   Source of funds to acquire_____

    f.   Amount of lien unpaid_____

         g.   Current value _____ $_____

                              Total: Jewelry, art, etc.:

                                         $_____

L.   Other (e.g., tax shelter investments, collections, judgments, causes of action, patents, trademarks, copyrights, and any other asset not hereinabove itemized)

         1.1   a.   Description_____
                b.   Title owner_____
                c.   Location_____
                d.   Original price or value_____
                e.   Source of funds to acquire_____
                f.   Amount of lien unpaid_____
                g.   Current value _____ $_____

         1.2   a.   Description_____
                b.   Title owner_____
                c.   Location_____
                d.   Original price or value_____
                e.   Source of funds to acquire_____
                f.   Amount of lien unpaid_____
                g.   current value _____ $_____

                               Total: Other $_____

                               TOTAL: ASSETS $_____

V.   LIABILITIES

A.   Accounts payable

         1.1   a.   Name and address of creditor_____
                b.   Debtor_____
                c.   Amount of original debt_____
                d.   Date of incurring debt_____
                e.   Purpose_____
                f.   Monthly or other periodic payment_____
                g.   Amount of current debt_____ $_____

         1.2   a.   Name and address of creditor_____
                b.   Debtor_____
                c.   Amount of original debt_____
                d.   Date of incurring debt_____
                e.   Purpose_____
                f.   Monthly or other periodic payment_____
                g.   Amount of current debt_____ $_____

         1.3   a.   Name and address of creditor_____
                b.   Debtor_____
                c.   Amount of original debt_____
                d.   Date of incurring debt_____
                e.   Purpose_____
                f.   Monthly or other periodic payment_____
                g.   Amount of current debt_____ $_____

         1.4   a.   Name and address of creditor_____
                b.   Debtor_____
                c.   Amount of original debt_____
                d.   Date of incurring debt_____
                e.   Purpose_____
                f.   Monthly or other periodic payment_____

      g.   Amount of current debt_____ $_____

   1.5 a.   Name and address of creditor_____
      b.   Debtor_____
      c.   Amount of original debt_____
      d.   Date of incurring debt_____
      e.   Purpose_____
      f.   Monthly or other periodic payment_____
      g.   Amount of current debt_____ $_____

                 Total: Accounts payable $_____

B.   Notes payable
   1.1 a.   Name and address of note holder_____
      b.   Debtor_____
      c.   Amount of original debt_____
      d.   Date of incurring debt_____
      e.   Purpose_____
      f.   Monthly or other periodic payment_____
      g.   Amount of current debt_____ $_____

   1.2 a.   Name and address of note holder_____
      b.   Debtor_____
      c.   Amount of original debt_____
      d.   Date of incurring debt_____
      e.   Purpose_____
      f.   Monthly or other periodic payment_____
      g.   Amount of current debt_____ $_____

                 Total: Notes payable$_____

C.   Installment accounts payable (security agreements, chattel mortgages)
   1.1 a.   Name and address of creditor_____
      b.   Debtor_____
      c.   Amount of original debt_____
      d.   Date of incurring debt_____
      e.   Purpose_____
      f.   Monthly or other periodic payment_____
      g.   Amount of current debt_____ $_____

   1.2 a.   Name and address of creditor_____
      b.   Debtor_____
      c.   Amount of original debt_____
      d.   Date of incurring debt_____
      e.   Purpose_____
      f.   Monthly or other periodic payment_____
      g.   Amount of current debt_____ $_____

                 Total: Installment accounts $_____

D.   Brokers' margin accounts
   1.1 a.   Name and address of broker_____
      b.   Amount of original debt_____
      c.   Date of incurring debt_____
      d.   Purpose_____
      e.   Monthly or other periodic payment_____
      f.   Amount of current debt_____ $_____

                 Total: Brokers' margin accounts $_____

E.   Mortgages payable on real estate
       1.1   a.   Name and address of mortgagee_____
             b.   Address of property mortgaged_____
             c.   Mortgagor(s)_____
             d.   Original debt_____
             e.   Date of incurring debt_____
             f.   Monthly or other periodic payment_____
             g.   Maturity Date_____
             h.   Amount of current debt_____ $_____

       1.2   a.   Name and address of mortgagee_____
             b.   Address of property mortgaged_____
             c.   Mortgagor(s)_____
             d.   original debt_____
             e.   Date of incurring debt_____
             f.   Monthly or other periodic payment_____
             g.   Maturity date_____
             h.   Amount of current debt_____ $_____
                               Total: Mortgages payable
                                    $_____

F.   Taxes payable
       1.1   a.   Description of tax_____
             b.   Amount of tax_____
             c.   Date due_____
                             Total: Taxes payable $_____

G.   Loans on life insurance policies
       1.1   a.   Name and address of insurer_____
             b.   Amount of loan_____
             c.   Date incurred_____
             d.   Purpose_____
             e.   Name of borrower_____
             f.   Monthly or other periodic payment $____
             g.   Amount of current debt _____ $_____
                             Total: Life insurance loans
                                    $_____

H.   Other liabilities
       1.1   a.   Description_____
             b.   Name and address of creditor_____
             c.   Debtor_____
             d.   Original amount of debt_____
             e.   Date incurred_____
             f.   Purpose_____
             g.   Monthly or other periodic payment_____
             h.   Amount of current debt _____ $_____

       1.2   a.   Description_____
             b.   Name and address of creditor_____
             c.   Debtor_____
             d.   Original amount of debt_____
             e.   Date incurred_____
             f.   Purpose_____
             g.   Monthly or other periodic payment_____
             h.   Amount of current debt _____ $_____
                             Total: Other liabilities $_____

Ct. Rules

TOTAL LIABILITIES:

$_____

NET WORTH

TOTAL ASSETS: $_____

TOTAL LIABILITIES: (minus)   ($_____)

NET WORTH: $_____

VI. ASSETS TRANSFERRED: (List all assets transferred in any manner during the preceding three years, or length of the marriage, whichever is shorter [transfers in the routine course of business which resulted in an exchange of assets of substantially equivalent value need not be specifically disclosed where such assets are otherwise identified in the statement of net worth]).

Description of Property	To Whom Transferred and Relationship to Transferee	Date of Transfer	Value
_____	_____	_____	_____
_____	_____	_____	_____
_____	_____	_____	_____
_____	_____	_____	_____

VII. SUPPORT REQUIREMENTS:

(a) Deponent is at present (paying) (receiving) $_____ per (week) (month), and prior to separation (paid) (received) $_____ per (week) (month) to cover expenses for _____

These payments are being made (voluntarily) (pursuant to court order or judgment) (pursuant to separation agreement), and there are (no) arrears outstanding (in the sum of $_____ to date).

(b) Deponent requests for support of each child $_____ per (week) (month). Total for children $_____

(c) Deponent requests for support of self $_____ per (week) (month).

(d) The day of the (week) (month) on which payment should be made is _____

VIII. COUNSEL FEE REQUIREMENTS:

(a) Deponent requests for counsel fee and disbursements the sum of _____

(b) Deponent has paid counsel the sum of $_____ and has agreed with counsel concerning fees as follows:

_____

(c) There is (not) a retainer agreement or written agreement relating to payment of legal fees. (A copy of any such agreement must be annexed.)

IX. ACCOUNTANT AND APPRAISAL FEES REQUIREMENTS:

(a) Deponent requests for accountants' fees and disbursements the sum of $_____ (Include basis for fee, e.g., hourly rate, flat rate)

(b) Deponent requests for appraisal fees and disbursements the sum of $_____ (Include basis for fee, e.g., hourly rate, flat rate)

(c)   Deponent requires the services of an accountant for the following reasons:

_____

_____

(d)   Deponent requires the services of an appraiser for the following reasons:

_____

_____

X.   Other data concerning the financial circumstances of the parties that should be brought to the attention of the Court are:

_____

_____

_____

_____

_____

    The foregoing statements and a rider consisting of _____ page(s) annexed hereto and made part hereof, have been carefully read by the undersigned who states that they are true and correct.

                       _____

                           (Petitioner)   (Respondent)
                           (Plaintiff)   (Defendant)

Sworn to before me this
. . . . .day of, 20. . . . .

                 . . . .
                 Signature of Attorney

                 . . . .
                 Attorney's Name (Print or Type)

                 . . . .

                 . . . .

                 . . . .
                 Attorney's Address & Telephone Number

Ct. Rules

§ 202.18.   Testimony of court-appointed expert witness in matrimonial action or proceeding.

    In any action or proceeding tried without a jury to which section 237 of the Domestic Relations Law applies, the court may appoint a psychiatrist, psychologist, social worker or other appropriate expert to give testimony with respect to custody or visitation, and may appoint an accountant, appraiser, actuary or other appropriate expert to give testimony with respect to equitable distribution or a distributive award. The cost of such expert witness shall be paid by a party or parties as the court shall direct.

§ 202.68.   Proceedings involving custody of an Indian child.

    In any proceeding in which the custody of a child is to be determined, the court, when it has reason to believe that the child is an Indian child within the meaning of the Indian Child Welfare Act of 1948 (92 Stat. 3069), shall require the verification of the child's status in accordance with that act and proceed further, as appropriate, in accordance with the provisions of that act.

APPELLATE DIVISION RULES

(Selected Rules)

SUBCHAPTER A

RULES OF THE FIRST JUDICIAL DEPARTMENT APPELLATE DIVISION

SYNOPSIS

Part 600. Appeals

§ 600.6. Appeals from Family Court.

An appeal from the Family Court may be prosecuted in accordance with any of the procedures specified in section 600.5 of this part. Any party to such an appeal may elect to file eight reproduced copies of the brief and appendix, if any, with proof of service of one copy, in lieu of a printed or otherwise reproduced brief and appendix as required by section 600.10 of the rules. The appeal may also be perfected upon the original record (transcript of hearing, if any, to be ordered by appellant and filed with the clerk of the Family Court) and eight reproduced copies of the brief. There shall be prefixed to the record the statement required by CPLR 5531; an additional copy of the statement shall be filed with the clerk of this court.

Part 603.   Conduct of Attorneys

§ 603.23.   Attorney's affidavit in agency and private adoptions.

(a)   Every attorney appearing for an adoptive parent, a natural parent, or an adoption agency in an adoption proceeding in the courts within this judicial department, shall, prior to the entry of an adoption decree, file with the Office of Court Administration of the State of New York, and with the court in which the adoption proceeding has been initiated, a signed statement under oath setting forth the following information:

(1)   name of attorney;

(2)   association with firm (if any);

(3)   business address;

(4)   telephone number;

(5)   docket number of adoption proceeding;

(6)   court where adoption has been filed;

(7)   the date and terms of every agreement, written or otherwise, between the attorney and the adoptive parents, the natural parents, or anyone else on their behalf, pertaining to any compensation or thing of value paid or given or to be paid, or given by or on behalf of the adoptive parents or the natural parents, including but not limited to retainer fees;

(8)   the date and amount of any compensation paid or thing of value given, and the amount of total compensation to be paid, or thing of value to be given to the attorney by the adoptive parents, the natural parents, or by anyone else on account of or incidental to any assistance or service in connection with the proposed adoption;

(9)   a brief statement of the nature of the services rendered;

(10)   the name and address of any other attorney or attorneys who shared in the fees received in connection with the services, or to whom any compensation or thing of value was paid or is to be paid, directly or indirectly, by the attorney; the amount of such compensation or thing of value;

(11)   the name and address of any other attorney or attorneys, if known, who received or will receive any compensation or thing of value, directly or indirectly,

from the adoptive parents, natural parents, agency, or other source, on account of or incidental to any assistance or service in connection with the proposed adoption; the amount of such compensation or thing of value, if known;

(12)   the name and address of any other person, agency, association, corporation, institution, society or organization who received or will receive any compensation or thing of value from the attorney, directly or indirectly, on account of or incidental to any assistance or service in connection with the proposed adoption; the amount of such compensation or thing of value;

(13)   the name and address, if known, of any person, agency, association, corporation, institution, society, or organization to whom compensation or thing of value has been paid or given, or is to be paid or given by any source for the placing out of, or on account of, or incidental to assistance in arrangements for the placement or adoption of the adoptive child; the amount of such compensation or thing of value and the services performed or the purposes for which the payment was made; and

(14)   a brief statement as to the date and manner in which the initial contact occurred between the attorney and the adoptive parents or natural parents with respect to the proposed adoption.

(b)   Names or other information likely to identify the natural or adoptive parents or the adoptive child are to be omitted from the information to be supplied in the attorney's statement.

(c)   Such statement may be filed personally by the attorney, or his representative, at the main office of the Office of Court Administration in the City of New York, and upon such filing he shall receive a date-stamped receipt containing the code number assigned to the original so filed. Such statement may also be filed by ordinary mail, addressed to:

Office of Court Administration—Adoption Affidavits

Post Office Box No. 2016

New York, N.Y. 10008

(d)   All statements filed by attorneys shall be deemed to be confidential, and the information therein contained shall not be divulged or made available for inspection or examination to any person, other than the client of the attorney in the adoption proceeding, except upon written order of the presiding justice of the Appellate Division.

Part 611.   Law Guardian Plan

§ 611.1.   Introduction.

(a)   (1) The Family Court panels now established in the First Judicial Department pursuant to article 18-B of the County Law and pertinent provisions of the Family Court Act, shall continue in effect and shall constitute the Family Court Panel Plan in the First Judicial Department.

(2) The law guardian roster of attorneys certified pursuant to the Rules of the Chief Administrator Part 36 and the former Rules of the Court Part 614, to accept appointment as a law guardian for an infant child or children pursuant to Family Court § 249(a), Civil Practice Law and Rules § 1202, or Uniform Rules of the Trial Court § 202.16(f)(3), shall continue in effect in this department as part of the Law Guardian Plan.

(3) The Family Court Panel Plan and the law guardian roster are merged to form the Law Guardian Plan. An attorney certified for appointment in one capacity shall be deemed certified for appointment in the other capacity and by virtue of the certification agrees to accept assignments and appointments in Supreme Court or Family Court.

(b) The Law Guardian Director, appointed by the Presiding Justice of the Appellate Division, First Department, shall administer the Law Guardian Plan.

§ 611.2. Assignment of counsel in Family Court.

Counsel to be assigned pursuant to the Family Court Act, section 262, shall be selected from such panels as have been established by the Assigned Counsel Plan in the First Judicial Department.

§ 611.3. Appointment of law guardians in Family Court.

Where for sufficient reason law guardians to be appointed pursuant to section 249 of the Family Court Act cannot otherwise by designated as provided in section 243(a) of such act, the court may draw upon such panels as have been established by the Assigned Counsel Plan for the First Judicial Department as if such panels had been separately established pursuant to section 243(c) of such act.

§ 611.4. Certification of attorneys.

Certificaton of an attorney as a member of any panel of the Law Guardian Plan shall be for a one year term subject to: (a) annual redesignation pursuant to Family Court Act, section 244(b); and, (b) recertification as directed by the justices of the Appellate Division, First Department.

§ 611.5. Departmental Advisory Committee.

Commencing January 1, 1980 the justices of the Appellate Division, First Department established a Departmental Advisory Committee to the Family Court. This Committee shall remain in operation and have the authority and responsibility to oversee the operation of the Law Guardian Plan and to consider all matters that pertain to the qualifications, performance and professional conduct of individual plan attorneys in their assignments and appointments as plan attorneys, and the representation of indigent parties in Family Court proceedings.

§ 611.6.　Composition of the Department Advisory Committee.

(a)　The Committee shall be composed of no fewer than fifteen attorneys who shall be experienced in Family Court and domestic relations proceedings, three Family Court judges, one mental health expert, one representative from each of the three bar associations designated in the Rules of the Court § 612.3, one faculty member of an accredited law school in the First Judicial Department, the Law Guardian Director and the Assigned Counsel Plan Administrator.

(b)　The Justices of the Appellate Division, First Department shall nominate all Committee members, except the representatives of the three bar associations, who shall be nominated by the respective presidents of those associations. The presiding Justice may appoint such additional members to the Committee as will facilitate its operation. The term of appointment for each Committee member, except the Law Guardian Director and Assigned Counsel Plan Administrator, shall be staggered and for a period of three years subject to renomination by the justices of the Appellate Division. The term of appointment for the Law Guardian Director and the Assigned Counsel Plan Administrator shall be co-extensive with the term of their respective positions.

(c)　The Presiding Justice shall designate a chair and vice-chair of the Committee.

§ 611.7.　Duties of the Departmental Advisory Committee.

The Departmental Advisory Committee shall conduct its activities and carry out the duties enumerated in this Part pursuant to the Bylaws of the Assigned Counsel Plan Central Screening Committee, set forth in Part 612 Appendix A of the Rules of the Court. The Law Guardian Director shall be substituted where reference in the Bylaws is made to the Administrator.

§ 611.8.　Screening process.

(a)　All applicants for plan membership shall be screened by the Departmental Advisory Committee.

(b)　The Committee, in accordance with standards for admission to the panels, entitled *General Requirements for All Applicants to the Family Court Panels* and *General Requirements for Law Guardian to Qualify for Appointment in Domestic Relations Matters*, shall make a determination as to whether an attorney is qualified for membership on any of the panels.

§ 611.9.　Continuing legal education.

(a)　The Departmental Advisory Committee, in cooperation with the Assigned Counsel Plan, the Continuing Legal Education Office and the three bar associations designated in the Rules of the Court § 612.3, shall: (1) on a continuing basis, develop and conduct training and education programs that focus on domestic relations law and practice before the Family Court; (2) annually

Ct. Rules

promulgate a list of recommended training and education programs pertaining to domestic relations law and family law sponsored by independent providers of legal education; and (3) organize and operate a co-counsel program.

(b) Members of the Law Guardian Plan biennially must complete at least eight hours of training and education programs that are either sponsored by the Departmental Advisory Committee or included on the list of recommended programs referred to in subsection (a).

§ 611.10. Annual report.

(a) No later than September 30 of each calendar year the Departmental Advisory Committee shall file with the Appellate Division a written evaluation of the panels and the panel attorneys, setting forth information regarding the performance of plan attorneys, efficiency of the panels as a means of representing indigent parties, the training and education programs sponsored and recommended by the Committee, and proposals for improving the operation of the Law Guardian Plan. In preparing the written evaluation, the Committee may consult with Family Court judges and bar associations. Plan attorneys shall cooperate with the Committee in preparing the evaluation.

(b) An annual report of the operation of the Family Court panels shall be filed by the Appellate Division with the Chief Administrator of the Unified Court System no later than January 31, of each calendar year.

§ 611.11. Continuity of powers.

Nothing contained in this Part shall be construed to limit the powers of the Appellate Division or the Presiding Justice thereof or the Administrator of the Assigned Counsel Plan otherwise granted pursuant to law.

§ 611.12. Members of the Departmental Advisory Committee as volunteers.

The members of the Departmental Advisory Committee, as volunteers, are expressly authorized to participate in a State-sponsored volunteer program within the meaning of Public Officers Law section 17 (a).

§ 611.13. Complaints.

The Departmental Advisory Committee may receive and investigate complaints against individual plan members appointed pursuant to this part according to the procedures set forth in Part 612 Appendix A of the Rules of the Court.

§ 611.14. Use of records.

All papers, records and documents involving a complaint relating to the discharge of a panel attorney's duties shall be sealed and deemed private and confidential. However, upon good cause being shown, the justices of the Appellate Division or the presiding justice thereof may, by written order, permit to be divulged all or any part of such papers, records and documents. In the discretion of the presiding justice, such order may be made either with notice to the persons or attorneys to be affected thereby, or upon such notice to them as the presiding justice may direct. Records of the Departmental Advisory Committee shall be made available, upon request, without the necessity for such order, to the Departmental Disciplinary Committee for the Appellate Division, First Judicial Department.

Ct. Rules

SUBCHAPTER B

RULES OF THE SECOND JUDICIAL DEPARTMENT
APPELLATE DIVISION

____

SYNOPSIS

Part 671. Additional Duties of Counsel and the Court Clerk in Criminal Actions, in Habeas Corpus and CPLR Article 78 Proceedings, and in Proceedings Instituted by Motion Made Pursuant to CPL 440.10 or 440.20

§ 671.10. Duties of assigned counsel in the Surrogate's Court and the Family Court.

(a) Upon the entry of an order in the Surrogate's Court and Family Court from which an appeal may be taken, it shall be the duty of assigned counsel for the unsuccessful party, immediately after the entry of the order, to give either by mail or personally, written notice to the client advising of the right to appeal, and request written instructions as to whether he or she desires to take an appeal or to make such application. Thereafter, if the client gives to counsel timely written notice of his or her desire to appeal or to make such application, counsel shall promptly serve and file the necessary formal notice of appeal, or make application to this court for permission to appeal. Unless counsel shall have been retained to prosecute the appeal, the notice of appeal may contain the additional statement that it is being served and filed on appellant's behalf pursuant to this rule and that it shall not be deemed to be counsel's appearance as appellant's attorney on the appeal.

(b) In counsel's written notice to the client advising of the right to appeal or to make application for permission to appeal, counsel shall also set forth:

(1) the applicable time limitations with respect to the taking of the appeal or the making of the application for permission to appeal;

(2) the manner of instituting the appeal and, if a trial or hearing was held and stenographic minutes taken, the manner of obtaining a typewritten transcript of such minutes; and

(3) the client's right, upon proof of his or her financial inability to retain counsel and to pay the costs and expenses of the appeal, to make application to this court for the assignment of counsel to prosecute the appeal; and, if stenographic minutes were taken, for a direction to the clerk and the stenographer of the trial court that a typewritten transcript of such minutes be furnished without charge to assigned counsel or, if the client prosecutes the appeal *pro se*, to the client; and

(4) in such notice counsel shall also request the written instructions of his client, and if the client thereafter gives counsel timely written notice of his or her desire to make application for permission to appeal or to apply for the relief provided in paragraph (3) of this section, or to make any one or all of these applications, counsel shall proceed promptly to do so.

(c) Counsel shall also advise the client that in those cases where permission to appeal is required, applications for the foregoing relief will be considered only if such permission is granted.

(d)   If the assigned counsel represented the successful party in the court in which the order being appealed was entered, such assignment shall remain in effect and counsel shall continue to represent the successful party as the respondent on the appeal until entry of the order determining the appeal and until counsel shall have performed any additional applicable duties imposed upon him or her by these rules, or until counsel shall have been otherwise relieved of his assignment.

Part 678.   Assigned Counsel Plan, Second and Eleventh Judicial Districts

§ 678.11.   Assignment of counsel.

Assignment of counsel by the Family Court, Supreme Court or Surrogate's Court to represent indigent adults in proceedings pursuant to section 262 of the Family Court Act, shall be made from law guardian panels designated pursuant to Part 679 of this Title (the rules of the Appellate Division, Second Department). Attorneys so assigned shall be subject to those court rules including the rules relating to evaluation and removal.

Part 679.   Family Court Law Guardian Plan

§ 679.1.   Family Court law guardian plan established.

There is hereby established in the counties of the Second Judicial Department a plan for the operation of the Family Court law guardian panels designated pursuant to Family Court Act § 243(c).

§ 679.2.   Law guardian director.

The law guardian plan for the Second Judicial Department shall be administered by the director of the law guardian program who shall be appointed by the Appellate Division of the Supreme Court, Second Judicial Department, and supervised by the Presiding Justice.

§ 679.3.   Law guardian director.

The director of the law guardian program shall administer the plan in accordance with the law, these rules, and with the procedures promulgated by the law guardian advisory committees.

§ 679.4.   Advisory committees.

The following Family Court law guardian advisory committees shall be established:

(a)   There shall be a single committee for the counties of Kings, Queens and Richmond, which shall be composed of the Deputy New York City

Administrative Judge-Family Division or his or her designee, a representative of each of the county bar associations, a member of the faculty of an accredited law school, and three additional members at least one of whom shall be a non-attorney.

(b) In Nassau County, the committee shall be composed of the Deputy Administrative Judge of the Family Court, a representative of the county bar association, a member of the faculty of an accredited law school, and three additional members at least one of whom shall be a non-attorney.

(c) In Suffolk County, the committee shall be composed of the Deputy Administrative Judge of the Family Court, a representative of the county bar association, a member of the faculty of an accredited law school, and three additional members at least one of whom shall be a non-attorney.

(d) There shall be a single committee for the counties of Dutchess, Orange, Putnam, Rockland and Westchester, which shall be composed of the Deputy Administrative Judge of the Family Court, Ninth Judicial District, a representative from each county bar association, a member of the faculty of an accredited law school, and nine additional members at least three of whom shall be non-attorneys.

(e) On each advisory committee the family Court Judge member shall serve as chairperson. All the members shall be designated by the Appellate Division, Second Judicial Department, for three-year terms, and may be reappointed for additional terms. The bar association representative members shall be appointed upon recommendation of the respective bar associations. Committee members may not serve on the law guardian panels.

(f) The director of the law guardian program shall sit as an *officio* member of each advisory committee.

(g) The members of the law guardian advisory committees as volunteers are expressly authorized to participate in a State-sponsored volunteer program within the meaning of the Public Officers Law § 17.

§ 679.5. Duties of the advisory committees.

Subject to the supervision of the Appellate Division, the advisory committees shall establish procedures for appointment and reappointment of attorneys to serve on the law guardian panels, for periodic evaluation of attorneys who serve on the law guardian panels, for training of attorneys on the law guardian panels, for investigating complaints made against members of the law guardian panels, and for removal of attorneys from the law guardian panels.

§ 679.6. Eligibility requirements.

(a) To be eligible for recommendation for appointment to a panel designated pursuant to Family Court Act § 243 or to a panel established for attorneys assigned to the bar of the State of New York, in good standing, and shall have served as counsel or co-counsel in the Family Court in a minimum of three proceedings under Family Court Act article 3, article 6 and article 10.

(b) The advisory committees shall establish co-counsel or mentoring programs to provide experience to admitted attorneys who wish to serve on the panel but lack the qualifications required by paragraph (a).

(c) The minimum requirements may be waived if, in the opinion of the advisory committees, the applicant is otherwise qualified by reason of education, training or substantial trial experience.

(d) The advisory committees may set forth such additional requirements and procedures as they see fit, subject to approval by the Appellate Division.

§ 679.7. Designation of panels.

The Appellate Division shall designate the law guardian panel for each county from attorneys recommended by the advisory committees. Appointments to the panel shall not exceed one year, but any panel member may be reappointed.

§ 679.8. Periodic evaluation of law guardians.

The advisory committees shall establish procedures to periodically evaluate the representation provided to juveniles by each member of the law guardian panel. In conducting the periodic evaluation the advisory committees shall seek information from Family Court judges and other appropriate and knowledgeable persons. The advisory committees shall not recommend for reappointment any attorney whose representation the committees determine to be unsatisfactory.

§ 679.9. Training and education.

The advisory committees, in cooperation with the director of the law guardian program shall establish a training and education program for members of the law guardian panels. Such a program may be established in conjunction with bar associations, local law schools or other competent organizations. The advisory committees shall make attendance at training programs a requirement for continued membership on the law guardian panels.

§ 679.10. Recommendation for removal.

An advisory committee may, at any time, recommend to the Presiding Justice that an attorney be removed from the panel. Such recommendation shall be submitted in writing, together with a report of the basis for such recommendation. Such recommendation shall not be required where an attorney is not reappointed at the expiration of his or her term. The Presiding Justice shall have the power to remove members of the Family Court law guardian panels and members of panels established for attorneys assigned pursuant to Family Court Act § 262.

§ 679.11. Assignments of counsel.

Assignments of counsel by the Family Court, Supreme Court or Surrogate's Court to represent children in proceedings wherein compensation is paid privately by one or more of the parties or is authorized pursuant to Judiciary Law 35 shall be made from law guardian panels designated pursuant to these rules. This section shall not apply to institutional providers appointed pursuant to Family Court Act § 243(a).

§ 679.12. Annual evaluations.

On June 30th of each year, commencing with June 30, 1991, each advisory committee shall submit to the Appellate Division an evaluation of the operation of the plan and the training programs, and recommendations as to procedures, if any, which should be adopted to improve the performance of the plan and the training programs.

§ 679.13. Annual reports.

A report of the operation of the law guardian panels shall be filed by the Appellate Division with the Chief Administrator of the Courts on August 1st of each year, commencing August 1, 1991.

§ 679.14. Compensation of law guardians.

(a) Claims by law guardians for services rendered pursuant to Family Court Act § 245 shall be submitted for approval to the Family Court Judge on forms authorized by the Chief Administrator of the Courts. After approval or modification, the Family Court shall forward the claim to the Appellate Division for review by the Presiding Justice or his or her designee. If approved, the Presiding Justice or designee shall certify the claim to the Comptroller for payment.

(b) Claims for compensation by law guardians in excess of the statutory limits set by Family Court Act § 245 and Judiciary Law § 35 shall be accompanied by a sworn statement by the law guardian describing the the nature of the proceeding, specifying the time and services rendered and expenses incurred, and detailing the circumstances deemed to be extraordinary that justify a fee in excess of the statutory limits. In the absence of the law guardian's supporting affidavit, excess compensation shall not be allowed. The Family Court, in granting an excess compensation claim, shall make a written finding setting forth the extrordinary circumstances justifying a fee in excess of statutory limits.

§ 679.15. Construction.

Nothing contained in this Part shall be construed to limit the powers of the Appellate Division, the Presiding Justice, or the administrator of the assigned counsel plan, otherwise granted pursuant to law.

Ct. Rules

Part 691. Conduct of Attorneys

§ 691.23. Attorney's affidavit in agency and private placement adoptions.

(a)   Every attorney appearing for an adoptive parent, a natural parent, or an adoption agency in an adoption proceeding in the courts within this judicial department, shall, prior to the entry of an adoption decree, file with the Office of Court Administration of the State of New York and with the court in which the adoption proceeding has been initiated, a signed statement under oath setting forth the following information:

(1)   name of attorney;

(2)   association with firm (if any);

(3)   business address;

(4)   telephone number;

(5)   docket number of adoption proceeding;

(6)   court where adoption has been filed;

(7)   the date and terms of every agreement, written or otherwise, between the attorney and the adoptive parents, the natural parents, or anyone else on their behalf, pertaining to any compensation or thing of value paid or given or to be paid, or given by or on behalf of the adoptive parents or the natural parents, including but not limited to retainer fees;

(8)   the date and amount of any compensation paid or thing of value given, and the amount of total compensation to be paid, or thing of value to be given to the attorney by the adoptive parents, the natural parents, or by anyone else on account of or incidental to any assistance or service in connection with the proposed adoption;

(9)   a brief statement of the nature of the services rendered;

(10)   the name and address of any other attorney or attorneys who shared in the fees received in connection with the services, or to whom any compensation or thing of value was paid or is to be paid, directly or indirectly, by the attorney; the amount of such compensation or thing of value;

(11)   the name and address of any other attorney or attorneys, if known, who received or will receive any compensation or thing of value, directly or indirectly, from the adoptive parents, natural parents, agency, or other source, on account of or incidental to any assistance or service in connection with the proposed adoption; the amount of such compensation or thing of value, if known;

(12)   the name and address of any other person, agency, association, corporation, institution, society or organization who received or will receive any compensation or thing of value from the attorney, directly or indirectly, on

account of or incidental to any assistance or service in connection with the proposed adoption; the amount of such compensation or thing of value;

(13)   the name and address, if known, of any person, agency, association, corporation, institution, society, or organization to whom compensation or thing of value has been paid or given, or is to be paid or given by any source for the placing out of, or on account of, or incidental to assistance in arrangements for the placement or adoption of the adoptive child; the amount of such compensation or thing of value and the services performed or the purposes for which the payment was made; and

(14)   a brief statement as to the date and manner in which the initial contact occurred between the attorney and the adoptive parents or natural parents with respect to the proposed adoption.

(b)   Names or other information likely to identify the natural or adoptive parents or the adoptive child are to be omitted from the information to be supplied in the attorney's statement.

(c)   Such statement may be filed personally by the attorney, or his representative, at the main office of the Office of Court Administration in the City of New York, and upon such filing he shall receive a date-stamped receipt containing the code number assigned to the original so filed. Such statement may also be filed by ordinary mail, addressed to:

Office of Court Administration—Adoption Affidavits

Post Office Box No. 2016

New York, N.Y. 10008

(d)   All statements filed by attorneys shall be deemed to be confidential, and the information therein contained shall not be divulged or made available for inspection or examination to any person, other than the client of the attorney in the adoption proceeding, except upon written order of the presiding justice of the Appellate Division.

Ct. Rules

SUBCHAPTER C

RULES OF THE THIRD JUDICIAL DEPARTMENT APPELLATE DIVISION

—

SYNOPSIS

Part 806.   Conduct of Attorneys

§ 806.14.   Attorney's affidavit in agency and private placement adoptions.

(a)   Every attorney appearing for an adoptive parent, a natural parent, or an adoption agency in an adoption proceeding in the courts within this judicial department, shall, prior to the entry of an adoption decree, file with the Office of Court Administration of the State of New York, and with the court in which the adoption proceeding has been initiated, a signed statement under oath setting forth the following information:

(1)   name of attorney;

(2)   association with firm (if any);

(3)   business address;

(4)   telephone number;

(5)   docket number of adoption proceeding;

(6)   court where adoption has been filed;

(7)   the date and terms of every agreement, written or otherwise, between the attorney and the adoptive parents, the natural parents, or anyone else on their behalf, pertaining to any compensation or thing of value paid or given or to be

paid, or given by or on behalf of the adoptive parents or the natural parents, including but not limited to retainer fees;

(8)   the date and amount of any compensation paid or thing of value given, and the amount of total compensation to be paid, or thing of value to be given to the attorney by the adoptive parents, the natural parents, or by anyone else on account of or incidental to any assistance or service in connection with the proposed adoption;

(9)   a brief statement of the nature of the services rendered;

(10)   the name and address of any other attorney or attorneys who shared in the fees received in connection with the services, or to whom any compensation or thing of value was paid or is to be paid, directly or indirectly, by the attorney; the amount of such compensation or thing of value;

(11)   the name and address of any other attorney or attorneys, if known, who received or will receive any compensation or thing of value, directly or indirectly, from the adoptive parents, natural parents, agency, or other source, on account of or incidental to any assistance or service in connection with the proposed adoption; the amount of such compensation or thing of value, if known;

(12)   the name and address of any other person, agency, association, corporation, institution, society or organization who received or will receive any compensation or thing of value from the attorney, directly or indirectly, on account of or incidental to any assistance or service in connection with the proposed adoption; the amount of such compensation or thing of value;

(13)   the name and address, if known, of any person, agency, association, corporation, institution, society, or organization to whom compensation or thing of value has been paid or given, or is to be paid or given by any source for the placing out of, or on account of, or incidental to assistance in arrangements for the placement or adoption of the adoptive child; the amount of such compensation or thing of value and the services performed or the purposes for which the payment was made; and

(14)   a brief statement as to the date and manner in which the initial contact occurred between the attorney and the adoptive parents or natural parents with respect to the proposed adoption.

(b)   Names or other information likely to identify the natural or adoptive parents or the adoptive child are to be omitted from the information to be supplied in the attorney's statement.

(c)   Such statement may be filed personally by the attorney, or his representative, at the main office of the Office of Court Administration in the City of New York, and upon such filing he shall receive a date-stamped receipt containing the code number assigned to the original so filed. Such statement may also be filed by ordinary mail, addressed to:

Office of Court Administration—Adoption Affidavits

Post Office Box No. 2016

New York, N.Y. 10008

(d) All statements filed by attorneys shall be deemed to be confidential, and the information therein contained shall not be divulged or made available for inspection or examination to any person, other than the client of the attorney in the adoption proceeding, except upon written order of the presiding justice of the Appellate Division.

Part 835.   Family Court Law Guardian Panels

§ 835.1.   Departmental Advisory Committee.

The presiding justice shall appoint a departmental advisory committee consisting of at least one Supreme Court Justice, one Family Court judge, one law guardian panel member, one representative of a family and child welfare agency, one law school professor, one county attorney, and such additional persons as the presiding justice deems necessary to perform the functions of the advisory committee. The clerk of the Appellate Division, Third Judicial Department, shall be a member of the committee *ex officio*. The term of appointment shall be for two years. The departmental advisory committee shall oversee the operation of the law guardian program in this department and shall annually make recommendations to the presiding justice with respect to promulgation of standards and administrative procedures for improvement of the quality of law guardian representation in the department.

§ 835.2.   Law Guardian Panel.

(a)   Initial designation to law guardian panel.

(1) *Eligibility.* An attorney is eligible for designation as a member of the law guardian panel of a county of this department when the attorney:

(A) Is a member in good standing of the Bar of the State of New York;

(B) Has attended two days of introductory law guardian training conducted by the Appellate Division; and

(C) Has attained experience in law guardian representation by:

(i) Substantial participation, either as counsel of record or as co-counsel with a law guardian mentor, in:

(1) A juvenile delinquency or person in need of supervision proceeding;

(2) A child abuse, child neglect, or termination of parental rights proceeding; and

(3) A custody or visitation proceeding; and

(ii) Participation as counsel or co-counsel in, or observation of, two hearings in Family Court at which testimony is taken.

(2) *Application.* An attorney may, at any time, apply for membership on a law guardian panel designated for a county in this department. Such an

application shall be in the form prescribed by the Appellate Division, and shall be submitted to a Family Court judge of the county.

(3) *Action by the Family Court Judge.* The Family Court judge shall review the application, and take one of the following actions:

(A) When the judge determines that the attorney has met the eligibility requirement of paragraph (1) above, and is otherwise qualified to provide appropriate representation for children, the judge shall approve the application and forward it to the Appellate Division with the recommendation that the attorney be added to the county law guardian panel;

(B) Except as provided in (C) below, when the judge determines that the attorney has not met the eligibility requirements of paragraph (1) above, the judge shall defer action on the application, forward a copy of the application to the Appellate Division, and refer the attorney to a law guardian mentor;

(C) When the judge determines for good cause that an attorney should not be designated as a law guardian panel member, the judge shall deny the application in writing, stating the basis for the denial, regardless of whether or not the attorney has met the eligibility requirements of paragraph (1) above. The attorney may request review of such denial by the Appellate Division.

(4) *Waiver of eligibility requirements.* The Appellate Division may waive the eligibility requirements set forth in paragraphs (1)(B) and (C) above when:

(A) An attorney requests such waiver in writing, endorsed by a judge of Family Court; and

(B) The attorney has sufficient relevant experience in the practice of law to demonstrate clearly his ability to represent children effectively; provided, however, that an attorney added to a law guardian panel based on a waiver granted pursuant to this paragraph must attend two days of introductory training conducted by the Appellate Division within one year of designation.

(5) *Law guardian mentors.* When a judge of Family Court has deferred action on the application of an attorney for membership on a law guardian panel pursuant to paragraph (3)(B) above, the judge shall designate an experience law guardian as a mentor to assist the attorney in meeting the eligibility requirements of paragraph (1)(C) above, and to familiarize the attorney with the representation of children and the operation of the Law Guardian Program. With the agreement of the mentor, the attorney may act as co-counsel in a proceeding specified in paragraph (1)(C)(i) above to which the mentor has been assigned as a law guardian, provided, however, that the mentor shall be the attorney of record in the proceeding and shall be responsible for all aspects of the representation provided. When the attorney has met the eligibility requirements, he or she shall so inform the Family Court judge, who shall then take action as provided in paragraph (3) above.

(b) Redesignation of panels.

(1) The Appellate Division shall, on or before January first of each year, designate an annual law guardian panel for each county in the department from

Ct. Rules

lists of attorneys approved with respect to their competency by the Family Court judges of such counties upon consideration of the following factors:

(A) Rapport with clients;

(B) Case preparation;

(C) Legal knowledge;

(D) Vigor of advocacy; and

(E) Punctuality.

(2) All current members of an annual law guardian panel for a county shall be redesignated to the annual law guardian panel, provided the law guardian has complied with the appropriate training and education requirement set forth in section 835.4(b) or this Part, and provided further that the law guardian has been found qualified for redesignation upon consideration of the factors of law guardian competency in paragraph (b)(1)(A–E) above.

(3) When a Family Court judge determines that a current law guardian should not be redesignated to the annual county law guardian panel, the judge shall submit to the Appellate Division a written recommendation to the effect, setting for the basis of the recommendation with specific reference to the factors of law guardian competency. The Appellate Division shall provide written notice of the recommendation and a copy of the written recommendation to the law guardian concerned, who may submit to the Appellate Division a written response and such additional documentation as the law guardian believes may assist the Appellate Division in considering the judge's recommendation.

(c) **Limitations on annual law guardian panel membership.** When adequate numbers of attorneys are available in a county:

(1) Only the names of attorneys who reside or maintain an office in the county should appear on the panel list for that county; and

(2) The Family Court judge or judges of the county may decline to designate additional attorneys to the panel.

(d) **Removal from annual law guardian panel.** An attorney may, at any time, apply to a Family Court judge of the county in which he or she serves on a law guardian panel to have his or her name removed from the panel list. Upon receipt of such request, the Family Court judge may make a written recommendation to the Appellate Division that the attorney's name be removed; upon receipt of such recommendation, the Appellate Division shall remove the attorney's name from the panel list, if appropriate. If the Family Court judge denies such request, such denial shall be in writing and state the reasons for the denial. The attorney may request review of such denial by the Appellate Division.

Notwithstanding the provisions of subdivision (b) above, a Family Court judge may, at any time, recommend to the Appellate Division the removal of an attorney's name from an annual law guardian panel for good cause, including, but not limited to, misconduct of lack of diligence in performing law guardian assignments.

The Appellate Division may, on its own motion at any time, remove an attorney's name from an annual law guardian panel.

§ 835.3. Assignment of law guardians.

(a) Any attorney designated to an annual law guardian panel in a county may also be assigned as a law guardian in any other county in the third department, provided the assigning Family Court judge has obtained the prior approval of a Family Court judge of the county in which the attorney has been designated to an annual law guardian panel and of the Appellate Division.

(b) The following factors, among others, should be considered when law guardian assignments are made:

(1) the experience and qualifications of the law guardian;

(2) the nature and difficulty of the case;

(3) continuity of representation of the minor in successive proceedings; and

(4) that assignments among law guardians on a panel are made in a fair and impartial manner.

(c) No law guardian shall be assigned to represent a minor when such assignment may involve a legal or ethical conflict of interest. Law guardians serving in the following positions or employed by any of the following offices shall not be assigned to serve as a law guardian in those types of proceedings in which, by virtue of such position or employment, they have either similar or equivalent subject matter jurisdiction or responsibilities or, in the county in which they are employed, the office by which they are employed participates as a party: judge or justice of a city, town or village court; law clerk to a judge or justice; district attorney; county attorney, or municipal corporation counsel. Whenever an attorney designated to an annual law guardian panel accepts employment in any of the above positions or offices, the attorney shall inform a Family Court judge of the county in which he or she serves on an annual law guardian panel of such employment; the attorney may complete any matter previously assigned to him, provided the Family Court judge approves of the completion of such assignment and provided completion of such assignment involves no legal or ethical conflict of interest.

§ 835.4. Training and education.

(a) Law guardians shall be expected to be thoroughly familiar with:

(1) provisions of the Family Court Act and relevant provisions of the Domestic Relations Law, Social Services Law, Penal Law and Criminal Procedure Law;

(2) the basic principles of child development and behavior;

(3) the existence and availability of community-based treatment resources and residential facilities; and

(4) recent case law and legislation relating to the foregoing.

(b) To be eligible for redesignation to a law guardian panel in this department pursuant to section 835.2(b) of this Part, a law guardian shall have completed within the preceding two years at least one day of training and education for law guardians sponsored or co-sponsored by the Appellate Division, Third Department. If prior approval is obtained from the Appellate Division, Third Department, by the law guardian or the sponsoring organization, attendance at an appropriate educational and training program sponsored or co-sponsored by one or more of the following or similar organizations may be substituted: the Appellate Divisions of the First, Second or Fourth Departments; the American Bar Association; the New York State Bar Association; a Family Court; a local or regional bar association or law guardian association; a law school; or a legal aid society. This biennial continuing education and training requirement for law guardians may also be fulfilled by (a) viewing videotapes approved for such purpose by the Appellate Division, Third Department, and filing with the Appellate Division, Third Department an affidavit attesting to such a viewing or (b) attendance at one day of training and education for newly-designated law guardians as described in section 835.2(a)(1)(B) of this Part.

For good cause shown and upon the written recommendation of a Family Court Judge, the may waive or defer the training and education requirement set forth herein.

§ 835.5. Compensation.

(a) Claims by law guardians for services rendered pursuant to Family Court Act, section 245, shall be submitted for approval to the Family Court judge on forms authorized by the Chief Administrator of the Courts; after approval or modification, the Family Court shall forward the claim to the Appellate Division for approval and certification to the Comptroller for payment. If a claim is received by the Appellate Division more than 90 days after the date of completion of services, the law guardian may be requested to provide an affidavit (i) stating that counsel has not previously applied for payment or been paid for the services in question, and (ii) explaining the reasons for the delay in submitting the claim for payment. The Appellate Division reserves the right to disapprove any claim for compensation by a law guardian received more than 90 days after the date of completion of services.

(b) Claims for compensation by law guardians in excess of the statutory limits set by Family Court Act § 245 and Judiciary Law § 35 shall be accompanied by a sworn statement by the law guardian describing the nature of the proceeding, specifying the time and services rendered and expenses incurred, and detailing the circumstances deemed to be extraordinary justifying a fee in excess of the statutory limits. In the absence of the attorney's affidavit in support of the excess fee, compensation in excess of statutory limits shall not be allowed.

(1)   The following are among the factors which may be considered in determining whether extraordinary circumstances exist justifying a fee in excess of statutory limits:

(i)   unusually complex factual or legal issues;

(ii)   novel issues of law requiring extensive legal research;

(iii)   lengthy and necessary trial or other in-court proceedings which alone raise the compensation claim above statutory limits; and

(iv)   other unique or unusual circumstances which required the law guardian to spend time on a case raising the compensation claim above statutory limits.

(2)   The expenditure of time alone will not ordinarily be considered an extraordinary circumstance warranting additional compensation.

(c)   When a law guardian expects the reasonable expenses, allowable pursuant to Family Court Act § 245 and Judiciary Law § 35 to exceed the sum of $1,000, for investigative, expert or other services, the law guardian, before incurring such expenses, shall obtain the approval of the judge presiding in the proceeding and of the Appellate Division.

Ct. Rules

SUBCHAPTER D

RULES OF THE FOURTH JUDICIAL DEPARTMENT APPELLATE DIVISION

SYNOPSIS

Part 1022.   Attorneys

§ 1022.12.   Compensation of attorneys assigned as defense counsel.

(a)   No attorney assigned as defense counsel in a criminal case shall demand, accept, receive or agree to accept any payment, gratuity or reward, or any promise of payment, gratuity, reward, thing of value or personal advantage from the defendant or other person, except as expressly authorized by statute or by written order of a court.

(b)   All vouchers submitted by attorneys, psychiatrists or physicians, pursuant to section 35 of the Judiciary Law and section 722(b) of the County Law in which the compensation sought exceeds the statutory limits shall be submitted to the judge or justice before whom the matter was heard for approval or modification. The attorney, psychiatrist or physician shall attach thereto an affidavit describing the unusual or extraordinary circumstances which warrant the additional fee. Time itself does not necessarily constitute an extraordinary circumstance.

(c)   A judge or justice approving such a fee, shall certify that the circumstances are unusual or extraordinary and that therefore a fee in excess of the statutory limit has been earned and the amount thereof. A magistrate, judge or justice of the assigning court, if he approves of such a fee, shall certify that the circumstances are unusual or extraordinary and that therefore a fee in excess of the statutory limit has been earned and the amount thereof. Such certification shall state circumstances, other than additional time, which justify the fee recommended. In the absence of either the attorney's affidavit of the court's certification, additional compensation shall not be allowed.

(d)   All vouchers regarding fees of attorneys, psychiatrists or physicians appointed pursuant to Judiciary Law section 35 shall be submitted within 90 days after the date on which the proceeding is completed. Expenditures other than compensation shall be submitted in itemized form.

§ 1022.33.   Attorney's affidavit in agency and private placement adoptions.

(a)   Every attorney appearing for an adoptive parent, a natural parent, or an adoption agency in an adoption proceeding in the courts within this judicial department, shall, prior to the entry of an adoption decree, file with the Office of Court Administration of the State of New York, and with the court in which the adoption proceeding has been initiated, a signed statement under oath setting forth the following information:

(1)   name of attorney;

(2)   association with firm (if any);

(3)   business address;

(4)   telephone number;

(5)   docket number of adoption proceeding;

(6)   court where adoption has been filed;

(7)   the date and terms of every agreement, written or otherwise, between the attorney and the adoptive parents, the natural parents, or anyone else on their behalf, pertaining to any compensation or thing of value paid or given or to be paid, or given by or on behalf of the adoptive parents or the natural parents, including but not limited to retainer fees;

(8)   the date and amount of any compensation paid or thing of value given, and the amount of total compensation to be paid, or thing of value to be given to the attorney by the adoptive parents, the natural parents, or by anyone else on account of or incidental to any assistance or service in connection with the proposed adoption;

(9)   a brief statement of the nature of the services rendered;

(10)   the name and address of any other attorney or attorneys who shared in the fees received in connection with the services, or to whom any compensation or thing of value was paid or is to be paid, directly or indirectly, by the attorney; the amount of such compensation or thing of value;

(11)   the name and address of any other attorney or attorneys, if known, who received or will receive any compensation or thing of value, directly or indirectly,

Ct. Rules

from the adoptive parents, natural parents, agency, or other source, on account of or incidental to any assistance or service in connection with the proposed adoption; the amount of such compensation or thing of value, if known;

(12) the name and address of any other person, agency, association, corporation, institution, society or organization who received or will receive any compensation or thing of value from the attorney, directly or indirectly, on account of or incidental to any assistance or service in connection with the proposed adoption; the amount of such compensation or thing of value;

(13) the name and address, if known, of any person, agency, association, corporation, institution, society, or organization to whom compensation or thing of value has been paid or given, or is to be paid or given by any source for the placing out of, or on account of, or incidental to assistance in arrangements for the placement or adoption of the adoptive child; the amount of such compensation or thing of value and the services performed or the purposes for which the payment was made; and

(14) a brief statement as to the date and manner in which the initial contact occurred between the attorney and the adoptive parents or natural parents with respect to the proposed adoption.

(b) Names or other information likely to identify the natural or adoptive parents or the adoptive child are to be omitted from the information to be supplied in the attorney's statement.

(c) Such statement may be filed personally by the attorney, or his representative, at the main office of the Office of Court Administration in the City of New York, and upon such filing he shall receive a date-stamped receipt containing the code number assigned to the original so filed. Such statement may also be filed by ordinary mail, addressed to:

Office of Court Administration—Adoption Affidavits

Post Office Box No. 2016

New York, N.Y. 10008

(d) All statements filed by attorneys shall be deemed to be confidential, and the information therein contained shall not be divulged or made available for inspection or examination to any person, other than the client of the attorney in the adoption proceeding, except upon written order of the presiding justice of the Appellate Division.

Part 1032. Operation of Law Guardian Program

§ 1032.1. Law guardian office; law guardian director.

(a) A law guardian office for the Fourth Judicial Department is established to ensure the provision of the highest quality of representation for children and to administer the law guardian program in a manner sensitive to local needs.

(b) The function of the law guardian office shall be to provide continuing administrative direction to the law guardian program in the Fourth Judicial Department and to secure the cooperation of local bar associations, law schools and governmental agencies in order to achieve the goal specified in subdivision (a) of this section.

(c) The law guardian office shall be administered by a law guardian director who shall be appointed by the Appellate Division and supervised by the presiding justice. The duties of the law guardian director shall include but not be limited to the following:

(1) to administer the law guardian program office in accordance with the law and these rules;

(2) with the approval of the presiding justice and in consultation with the departmental advisory committee, to implement standards, guidelines and procedures for the improvement of the law guardian program in the Fourth Judicial Department;

(3) in conjunction with local family courts, local bar associations, law schools or any other competent organization and in consultation with the departmental advisory committee, to provide a continuing program of law guardian training and education that will allow applicant attorneys to satisfy requirements for designation to the panel, and to improve and maintain the professional competence of attorneys serving as law guardians;

(4) to consult with the law guardian directors in the First, Second and Third Judicial Departments and with the Office of Court Administration to coordinate the operation of the programs in each department; and

(5) to prepare the annual report on the operation of the law guardian program in the Fourth Department.

§ 1032.2. Departmental advisory committee.

(a) The presiding justice shall appoint a chairperson and the members of the departmental advisory committee, which shall consist of at least one Supreme Court judge, one Family Court judge, one law guardian engaged in private practice, one representative of a family and child care agency, one law school professor, one county attorney, one person who is not an attorney and who is not an employee of any branch of government, a member of the staff of the Appellate Division who shall be a nonvoting member and such other members as the presiding justice deems necessary to enable the committee to perform the functions specified in this section. The term of appointment shall be staggered and for a period of two years subject to reappointment by the presiding justice.

(b) The departmental advisory committee may make recommendations to the presiding justice and the law guardian director with respect to:

(1) training of law guardians;

Ct. Rules

(2) the promulgation of rules, standards and administrative procedures for effective law guardian representation in the department;

(3) procedures necessary to insure that panel members are designated and assigned in a fair and impartial manner, having regard to the nature and difficulty of each case and the special qualifications of panel members; and

(4) procedures necessary to improve the operation thereof throughout the department.

§ 1032.3. Members of departmental advisory committee are volunteers.

Each member of the departmental advisory committee is a volunteer expressly authorized to participate in a State-sponsored volunteer program as provided in section 17(1) of the Public Officers Law.

§ 1032.4. Law guardian panel.

(a) Initial designation to law guardian panel.

(1) Eligibility. An attorney is eligible for designation as a member of the law guardian panel of a county of this department when the attorney:

(i) is a member in good standing of the Bar of the State of New York and in any other jurisdiction in which the attorney is admitted to the practice of law;

(ii) has attended 12 hours of law guardian introductory training conducted by the law guardian program; and

(iii) has obtained experience in law guardian representation by appearing either as attorney of record, associate counsel or co-counsel for a party in a minimum of three proceedings under article 3, article 6, article 7, or article 10 of the Family Court Act; or has been found by a Family Court judge to be well qualified by reason of education, training or substantial trial experience.

(2) Application. An attorney may, at any time, apply for membership on a county law guardian panel in this department. Such application shall be in the form prescribed by the Appellate Division and shall be submitted for consideration to the supervising judge of Family Court in those counties where the supervising judge sits and in other counties to the senior Family Court judge.

(3) Action by the Family Court judge. The supervising or senior Family Court judge shall review the application and take one of the following actions:

(i) When the judge determines that the attorney has met the eligibility requirements of paragraph (1) of this subdivision and is otherwise qualified to provide appropriate representation for children, the judge shall approve the application and forward it for consideration by the Appellate Division. If the judge finds the attorney to be well qualified under subparagraph (1) (iii) of this subdivision, the judge shall submit the basis of the finding in writing to the Appellate Division.

(ii) When the judge determines for good cause that an attorney should not be designated as a law guardian panel member, the judge shall deny the application and state the reason for the denial in writing. The attorney may request reconsideration of such denial by the Appellate Division.

(4)   Waiver of eligibility requirements. The Appellate Division may waive the eligibility requirements set forth in subparagraphs (1) (ii) and (iii) of this subdivision when an attorney requests such waiver in writing, endorsed by the supervising or senior Family Court judge; and

(i)   the attorney has sufficient relevant experience in the practice of law to demonstrate clearly the ability to represent children effectively; provided, however, that an attorney added to a law guardian panel based upon a waiver granted pursuant to this paragraph must attend 12 hours of introductory training conducted by the law guardian program within one year of designation.

(5)   Action by the Appellate Division. Upon receipt of the application and the recommendation of the supervising or senior Family Court judge that an attorney be placed on the law guardian panel, the Appellate Division shall:

(i)   designate the attorney to a county panel; or

(ii)   request further information from the applicant, which may include an interview; or

(iii)   decline to designate the attorney to a county panel. If not designated to a county panel, the attorney shall be informed of the basis of the decision and may request reconsideration.

(b)   Redesignation of panels.

(1)   The Appellate Division shall, on or before April 1 of each year, designate an annual law guardian panel for each county in the department from lists of attorneys who have been found competent by the supervising judge of Family Court in those counties where the supervising Family Court judge sits and in other counties by the senior Family Court judge upon consideration of the following factors:

(i)   legal knowledge;

(ii)   rapport with clients;

(iii)   vigorous advocacy;

(iv)   case preparation; and

(v)   courtroom demeanor.

(2)   To be eligible for redesignation to a panel a law guardian shall:

(i)   have completed within the preceding two years at least one training program conducted by the law guardian program. If prior approval is obtained from the Appellate Division, attendance at an appropriate educational and training program sponsored or cosponsored by another New York State Judicial Department, bar association, law school or legal aid society, may be substituted for training conducted by the law guardian program; and

(ii) have been found competent by the supervising or senior Family Court judge of the county upon consideration of the factors of law guardian competency set forth in subparagraph (1)(i) -(v) of this subdivision.

§ 1032.5. Assignment of law guardians.

(a) Any attorney designated to a law guardian panel in the Fourth Department may be assigned as a law guardian in any adjoining county in the Fourth Department and in any other county not adjoining may be assigned upon prior approval of the Appellate Division.

(b) No law guardian shall be assigned to represent a minor when such assignment involves an ethical conflict of interest. Attorneys serving in the following positions or employed by the following offices, if otherwise eligible for designation, shall disclose such employment to the court: judge or justice of a city, town or village court; law clerk to a judge or justice; district attorney; county attorney; and municipal corporation counsel. Attorneys serving in any of the above positions or employed by any of the above offices, shall not be appointed as a law guardian in proceedings in which, by virtue of such position or employment, they have similar or equal subject matter jurisdiction or, in the county in which they are employed, the office in which they are employed participates as a party.

(c) Removal from law guardian panel. An attorney may request that his or her name be removed from a law guardian panel. Upon receipt of such request, the Appellate Division shall remove the attorney's name from the panel. A Family Court judge, Supreme Court justice or surrogate may, at any time, recommend to the Appellate Division the removal of an attorney's name from a law guardian panel for good cause, including, but not limited to, misconduct, lack of diligence in performing law guardian assignments, or unwillingness to serve. An attorney whose name appears on a law guardian panel for two consecutive years and who has not served as a law guardian shall be removed from the list by the Appellate Division. The Appellate Division may, on its own motion at any time, remove an attorney's name from an annual law guardian panel. Regardless of the basis for removal from the law guardian panel, an attorney may request reconsideration of such removal.

(d) Assignment of counsel by the Supreme or a Surrogate's Court to represent children in proceedings wherein compensation is authorized pursuant to Judiciary Law § 35(7) shall be made from the panel designated pursuant to subdivision 1032.4.

§ 1032.6. Compensation

(a) A law guardian seeking compensation for services rendered pursuant to Family Court Act § 245 shall submit a claim for approval to the Family Court on forms authorized by the Chief Administrator of the Courts. The Family Court shall certify the claim, subject to appropriate modifications, and shall forward the claim to the Appellate Division for approval and certification to the Comptroller for payment. When a claim is received by the Appellate Division more than 90 days after the law guardian has completed the assignment, the law guardian shall provide an affidavit stating that the law guardian has not been paid for the services rendered, that a claim has not been submitted previously, and the reasons why the claim was not received within the 90-day period. The Appellate Division may, in the exercise of its discretion, disapprove any claim not received with the 90-day period.

(b)   Compensation in excess of the limits established by Family Court Act § 245 and Judiciary Law § 35 shall not be approved absent a showing of extraordinary circumstances. A law guardian submitting a claim for compensation in excess of the statutory limits shall submit, with the claim, an affidavit detailing the nature of the proceeding in which the services were rendered, the services rendered, the time expended, the expenses incurred and the facts that would support a finding of extraordinary circumstances. Absent such an affidavit, a fee in excess of the statutory limits shall not be approved.

(c)   In determining whether there are extraordinary circumstances warranting compensation in excess of the statutory limits, the Family Court and the Appellate Division shall consider:

(1)   Whether the matter involved unusually complex factual or legal issues;

(2)   Whether a novel issue of law, which required extensive legal research was involved;

(3)   Whether a lengthy trial or other in-court proceedings were necessary; and

(4)   Any other unique or unusual circumstances.

The expenditure of time alone, however, shall not constitute an extraordinary circumstance.

(d)   When a law guardian anticipates that expenses, as authorized pursuant to Family Court Act § 245 and Judiciary Law § 35, will exceed $300, the law guardian shall, before incurring such expenses, obtain approval of the Family Court and the Appellate Division.

Ct. Rules

STANDARDS AND ADMINISTRATIVE POLICIES

(Selected Rules)

SUBCHAPTER A

RULES OF THE CHIEF JUDGE

Part 41. INTEGRATED DOMESTIC VIOLENCE PARTS

§ **141.1   Definitions. (a)** *IDV part* shall refer to an integrated domestic violence part established by the Chief Administrator of the Courts pursuant to section 141.2 of this Part.

(b)   For purposes of this rule and its application to an IDV Part established in a county, an *IDV-eligible case* shall refer to both of the following when they are simultaneously pending in the county: a domestic violence case commenced in a criminal court and a case commenced in Supreme or Family Court that involves a party or witness in the domestic violence case. If so provided by the administrative order promulgated pursuant to section 141.2 of this Part for such county:

(1)   an *IDV-eligible case* shall also refer to each of the following: any case in criminal court, Family Court or Supreme Court where there is simultaneously pending in the county another case in any other of these courts having a common party or in which a disposition may affect the interests of a party in the first case; and

(2)   where cases are IDV-eligible and are disposed of in an IDV Part, subsequent cases that would have been IDV-eligible were they to have been pending simultaneously with the cases already disposed of shall be IDV-eligible; and

Ct. Rules

(3) in Monroe County, any domestic violence case pending in a criminal court in the county if necessary to best utilize available court and community resources for domestic violence cases.

§ 141.2 Establishment of IDV parts. Following consultation with and agreement of the presiding judge of the Judicial Department in which a county is located, the Chief Administrator, by administrative order, may establish an IDV part in Supreme Court in such county and assign one or more justices to preside therein.

§ 141.3 Identification of IDV-eligible cases. Procedures shall be established in each court so as to insure that cases pending before it are identified as IDV-eligible at the earliest possible time.

§ 141.4 Transfer of IDV-eligible cases. Unless the administrative order establishing an IDV Part in a county shall otherwise provide:

(a) Where an IDV-eligible case is pending in a court other than Supreme Court in such county:

(1) Originals or copies of papers and other documents filed in such court in connection with the case shall, directly following its identification as IDV-eligible, be sent by the court to the IDV Part.

(2) Not later than five days following receipt of the original papers and other documents in an IDV-eligible case in an IDV Part, the justice presiding in such Part shall determine whether or not a transfer of the case to the Supreme Court would promote the administration of justice. If the justice determines that it would, he or she may order such transfer, in which event the case shall be referred for disposition to the IDV Part, all original papers, if not already sent, shall be sent from the originating court to the IDV Part, and all further proceedings shall be conducted therein. If the justice determines that such a transfer would not promote the administration of justice, he or she shall cause all papers and other documents in the case to be returned to the court from which they were received, where all further proceedings in such case shall be conducted in accordance with law.

(3) Notwithstanding the provisions of paragraph (1) and (2) of this subdivision, where the case is a criminal case and the defendant is held by the local criminal court for the action of a grand jury empaneled by a County Court, only copies of the papers and other documents filed with such court shall be delivered to the IDV Part; and the justice presiding therein may at any time order a transfer of the case to the Supreme Court provided he or she determines that such a transfer would promote the administration of justice. The original papers and other documents filed with the local criminal court shall be delivered to the County Court as required by section 180.30(1) of the Criminal Procedure Law.

(b) Where the IDV-eligible case is a case pending in Supreme Court, it shall be referred for disposition to the IDV Part of such court and all further proceedings shall be conducted therein.

§ 141.5 Procedure in an IDV part. (a) Unless otherwise authorized or required by law, no case transferred from another court to the Supreme Court and referred for disposition to an IDV Part thereof may be consolidated with any other case pending before such IDV Part.

(b) Each case transferred from another court to the Supreme Court and referred for disposition to an IDV Part thereof shall be subject to the same substantive and procedural law as would have applied to it had it not been transferred, and no party thereto shall be required to pay any fee for the assignment of an index number thereto upon such transfer.

Ct. Rules

SOCIAL SERVICES LAW

**ADDED BY LAWS 1940, CH. 619, EFF. MARCH 1, 1941, AS
AMENDED BY THE 2006 REGULAR LEGISLATIVE SESSION
THROUGH JUNE 22, 2006.**

(Sections effective March 1, 1941 except as otherwise indicated.)

———

Table of Contents

SSL

ARTICLE 1

SHORT TITLE; DEFINITIONS

SUMMARY OF ARTICLE

Section 1. Short title.
2. Definitions.

§ 1. Short title.

This chapter shall be known as the social services law.

Amended by Laws 1967, Ch. 728, eff. July 1, 1967.

§ 2. Definitions.

When used in this chapter unless otherwise expressly stated or unless the context or subject matter requires a different interpretation.

1. Department means the state department of social services, provided however that for purposes of titles eleven, eleven-A and eleven-B of article five of this chapter, department means the state department of health, except that in subdivisions two and three of section three hundred sixty-four-i, clause (d) of subparagraph three of paragraph (b) of subdivision two of section three hundred sixty-six, paragraph (b) of subdivision four of section three hundred sixty-six, subdivisions one through five of section three hundred sixty-six-a, subdivision seven of section three hundred sixty-six-a, and section three hundred sixty-eight-c of this chapter and where the context thereof clearly requires otherwise, department means the state department of social services.

2. Board means the state board of social welfare as continued by the executive law.

3. [Repealed.]

4. [Repealed.]

5. [Repealed.]

6. Commissioner means the state commissioner of social services, provided however that for purposes of titles eleven, eleven-A and eleven-B of article five of this chapter, commissioner means the state commissioner of health, except that in clause (c) of subparagraph three of paragraph (b) of subdivision two of section three hundred sixty-six of this chapter and where the context thereof clearly

requires otherwise, commissioner means the state commissioner of social services.

7. Social services district means a city or county social services district as constituted by section sixty-one.

8. County commissioner of social services shall mean the county officer, board or commission, by whatever title known, having authority to give the public assistance and care for the administration of which a county social services district is responsible.

9. City commissioner of social services shall mean the city officer, board or commission, by whatever title known, having authority to give the public assistance and care for the administration of which a city social services district is responsible.

10. Commissioner of social services shall mean a city or county commissioner of social services.

11. [*Repealed.*]

12. [*Repealed.*]

13. [*Repealed.*]

14. Social services official shall mean a county commissioner of social services, a city commissioner of social services, a town social services officer or city social services officer to whom the power or duty referred to is assigned under the provisions of this chapter. In any law where reference is made by any title to an official charged with the duty of caring for the poor in a town, city or county, it shall be understood as referring to the one of the above mentioned social services officials on whom the power or duty referred to is conferred under the provisions of this chapter.

15. Public home means an adult care facility or a residential health care facility operated by a social services district. In any law where reference is made by any name to an almshouse maintained at public expense, it shall be construed as referring to a public home.

16. Legislative body means the board or boards empowered to make appropriations for public assistance and care in a county, town or city.

17. Social services department means the division or officer of city government or the office or official or board charged with the authority to administer public assistance or care in the county social services district.

18. Public assistance and care includes family assistance, safety net assistance, veteran assistance, medical assistance for needy persons, institutional care for adults and child care granted at public expense pursuant to this chapter.

19. Public assistance refers to family assistance, safety net assistance and veteran assistance.

20. [*Repealed*]

21. Adult care facility shall mean a family type home for adults, a shelter for adults, a residence for adults, an enriched housing program or an adult home, which provides temporary or long-term residential care and services to adults who, though not requiring continual medical or nursing care as provided by facilities licensed pursuant to article twenty-eight of the public health law or articles nineteen, twenty-three, thirty-one and thirty-two of the mental hygiene law, are by reason of physical or other limitations associated with age, physical or mental disabilities or other factors, unable or substantially unable to live independently.

22. A family type home for adults shall mean an adult care facility established and operated for the purpose of providing long-term residential care and personal care and/or supervision to four or fewer adult persons unrelated to the operator.

23. A shelter for adults shall mean an adult care facility established and operated for the purpose of providing temporary residential care, room, board, supervision, information and referral, and where required by the department or otherwise deemed necessary by the operator, social rehabilitation services, for adults in need of temporary accommodations, supervision and services. Such definition shall not include facilities providing such temporary residential services to fewer than twenty persons, unless such facility is operated by a social services district.

24. A residence for adults shall mean an adult care facility established and operated for the purposes of providing long-term residential care, room, board, housekeeping and supervision to five or more adults, unrelated to the operator. The provisions of this subdivision shall not apply to any housing projects established pursuant to the private housing finance law, the public housing law, the membership corporations law or the not-for-profit corporation law except for those distinct programs operated by such projects which provide supervision and/or personal care and which are approved or certified by the department.

25. An adult home shall mean an adult care facility established and operated for the purpose of providing long-term residential care, room, board, housekeeping, personal care, (either directly or indirectly), and supervision to five or more adults unrelated to the operator. The provisions of this subdivision shall not apply to any housing projects established pursuant to the private housing finance law, the public housing law, the membership corporations law or the not-for-profit corporation law except for those distinct programs operated by such projects which provide supervision and/or personal care and which are approved or certified by the department.

26. A private proprietary residence for adults shall mean a residence for adults, as defined by subdivision twenty-four of this section, which is operated for compensation and profit.

27. A private proprietary adult home shall mean an adult home, as defined by subdivision twenty-five of this section, which is operated for compensation and profit.

28. An enriched housing program shall mean an adult care facility established and operated for the purpose of providing long-term residential care to five or more adults, primarily persons sixty-five years of age or older, in community-integrated settings resembling independent housing units. Such program shall provide or arrange the provision of room, and provide board, housekeeping, personal care and supervision.

29. For purposes of title two, and, where applicable, title one of article seven of this chapter, an operator shall include any natural person or entity which provides or purports to provide residential care and services in an adult care facility.

30. An intermediate care facility shall mean a facility or part thereof approved by the state department of health to provide therein health-related care and services to persons who because of their physical or mental condition, or both, require institutional care and services, in addition to board and lodging, but who do not have such an illness, disease, injury, or other condition as to require the institutional care and services provided only by a hospital or nursing home, providing such facility meets standards of safety and sanitation in accordance with state and federal requirements in addition to those applicable to nursing homes under state law.

31. The term "infant" or "minor" shall mean a person who has not attained the age of eighteen years except with respect to article six of this chapter.

32. "Residential treatment facility for children and youth" shall have the meaning defined in section 1.03 of the mental hygiene law.

33. "Residential care center for adults" shall have the meaning defined in section 1.03 of the mental hygiene law.

[No subdivision 34 has been enacted.]

35. "Indian tribe" shall mean those tribes designated as Indian tribes by the bureau of Indian affairs of the federal department of the interior or by the state of New York.

36. "Indian child" shall mean any unmarried person who:

(a) is under the age of eighteen; or

(b) is under the age of twenty-one, entered foster care prior to his/her eighteenth birthday and remains in care, and who:

    (i) is a member of an Indian tribe, or

    (ii) is eligible for membership in an Indian tribe, or

    (iii) is the biological child of a member of an Indian tribe and is residing on or is domiciled within an Indian reservation.

SSL

37. [*Expires July 1, 2008.*] "Comprehensive psychiatric emergency program" shall have the meaning defined in section 1.03 of the mental hygiene law.

Amended by Laws 1946, Ch. 200; Laws 1948, Ch. 798; Laws 1951, Chs. 77, 455; Laws 1956, Ch. 589; Laws 1961, Ch. 195; Laws 1964, Ch. 555; Laws 1965, Ch. 121; Laws 1966, Ch. 256; Laws 1967, Ch. 728; Laws 1968, Chs. 424, 994; Laws 1969, Ch. 348; Laws 1974, Ch. 909; Ch. 1080, deemed to have been in full force and effect on and after Jan. 1, 1974; subd. 4 repealed by Laws 1971, Ch. 110; Laws 1971, Ch. 807, **renumbering** former subd. 27 to 28 and **adding** subd. 29; subds. 3 and 5 **repealed** by Laws 1971, Ch. 947; Laws 1972, Ch. 694; subd. 30 **added** by Laws 1974, Ch. 909; Laws 1977, Ch. 450, eff. July 19, 1977 which **added** subd. 31; Ch. 863, eff. Aug. 11, 1977, **repealing** subds. 11, 12, 13, 21(d); **amended** by Laws 1981, Ch. 601, eff. Oct. 1, 1981, **repealing** subds. 15, 16, 17, 24, 25, 26, 27, 29, **renumbering** subds. 18, 19, 20, 21, 22 as subds. 16, 17, 18, 19, 20, **added** new subds. 21, 22, 23, 24, 25, 26, 27, 28, **amending** and **renumbering** subd. 28 to 29; **amended** by Laws 1981, Ch. 947, eff. July 1, 1981, **added** subd. 32; **amended** by Laws 1984, Ch. 626, eff. Nov. 26, 1984; **amended** by Laws 1985, Ch. 351, eff. July 18, 1985, **added** subd. 34; **amended** by Laws 1986, Ch. 779, eff. Nov. 30, 1986; Laws 1989, Ch. 19; Laws 1991, Ch. 268, eff. July 5, 1991, extends the effective date until July 1, 1993; **amended** by Laws 1987, Ch. 462, eff. July 27, 1987, **added** new subds. 35 and 36; **amended** by Laws 1987, Ch. 838, eff. Aug. 7, 1987, subd. 32 **repealed,** subds. 33 and 34 **renumbered** 32 and 33; **amended** by Laws 1989, Ch. 723, § 15, eff. July 24, 1989 through July 24, 1994, at which time subd. (37) **added** by this act shall be deemed to be **repealed** and Social Services Law § 2 **amended** by this act shall revert to its text as it existed prior to the effective date of this act; **amended** by Laws 1994, Ch. 598, § 8, eff. July 24, 1994, extending the period that subd. (37) remains effective to July 1, 2000; **amended** by Laws 1995, Ch. 81, § 195, eff. Apr. 1, 1995, repealing subds. 19 and 20; **amended** by Laws 1996, Ch. 218, eff. June 25, 1996; **amended** by Laws 1996, Ch. 474, §§ 236, 237, eff. Oct. 1, 1996; **amended** by Laws 1997, Ch. 436, § 1 Part B, §§ 2 and 3, **adding** new para. (19) to SSL § 2, eff. Aug. 20, 1997; **amended** by Laws 1999, Ch. 124, § 1, eff. June 29, 1999, extending the effective date of subd. (21) to July 1, 2002; **amended** by Laws 1999, Ch. 558, § 44, eff. Oct. 5, 1999; **amended** by Laws 2000, Ch. 93, eff. June 23, 2000, extending the expiration date of subd. (37) to July 1, 2004; **amended** by Laws 2004, Ch. 2, § 3, amending subd. 25, eff. Feb. 23, 2005, Ch. 131, § 1, eff. June 29, 2004, extending the expiration date of subd. (37) to July 1, 2008.

ARTICLE 2

DEPARTMENT AND STATE BOARD OF SOCIAL WELFARE

SUMMARY OF ARTICLE

(Repealed and transferred sections noted under appropriate section number of text.)

SSL

§ 5.   Department of social welfare.

The state department of social welfare, provided for in the constitution, is hereby continued.

§ 6.   State board of social welfare.

Repealed by Laws 1971, Ch. 110, eff. July 1, 1971.

§ 7.   Qualifications of members.

Repealed by Laws 1971, Ch. 110, eff. July 1, 1971.

§ 8.   Organization of the board.

Repealed by Laws 1971, Ch. 110, eff. July 1, 1971.

§ 9.   Removal and vacancies.

Repealed by Laws 1971, Ch. 110, eff. July 1, 1971.

§ 10.   Compensation and expenses.

Repealed by Laws 1971, Ch. 110, eff. July 1, 1971.

§ 11.   Commissioner of social services.

The chief executive and administrative officer of the department shall be the commissioner of social services, who shall be appointed by the governor with the advice and consent of the senate.

    Amended by Laws 1964, Ch. 281; Laws 1971, Ch. 111, eff. Apr. 7, 1971.

§ 12.   Deputy commissioners.

The commissioner shall appoint and remove at pleasure a first deputy commissioner, and such other deputy commissioners as he shall deem necessary for the proper organization and general classification of the work of the department, each of whom shall be in the exempt class of the civil service.

    Amended by Laws 1963, Ch. 935; Laws 1964, Ch. 281; Laws 1971, Ch. 110, eff. July 1, 1971.

§ 13.   Organization of the department.

The commissioner shall determine the structure of departmental organization.

Amended by Laws 1964, Ch. 281; Laws 1971, Ch. 110, eff. July 1, 1971.

§ 14. Employees; compensation.

In addition to his deputies, the commissioner may appoint and remove from time to time, in accordance with law and any applicable rules of the state civil service commission, such employees as he may deem necessary for the efficient administration of the department. The compensation of employees appointed by the commissioner pursuant to this section shall be determined by him in accordance with law.

§ 15. Administrative areas; state social services officers.

Repealed by Laws 1972, Ch. 804, eff. Apr. 1, 1972.

§ 16. Offices of the department.

The department shall be provided with suitably furnished rooms for its offices. The principal office of the department shall be in the county of Albany.

Amended by Laws 1969, Ch. 55; Laws 1971, Ch. 110, eff. July 1, 1971.

§ 17. Powers and duties of the commissioner.

The commissioner shall

(a) determine the policies and principles upon which public assistance, services and care shall be provided within the state both by the state itself and by the local governmental units within the limits hereinafter prescribed in this chapter;

(b) make known his policies and principles to local social services officials and to public and private institutions and welfare agencies subject to his regulatory and advisory powers;

(c) in consultation with the civil service commission, establish minimum qualifications for positions in local social services departments and classify such positions according to differing capabilities, skills, responsibilities and education suitable to the various phases of welfare administration, not inconsistent with the standards and guidelines of a duly authorized federal agency, having due regard for recruitment of personnel and the requirements and varying types of communities within the state. Notwithstanding any inconsistent provision of law, rule or regulation, when (i) a position is vacant and not filled for a continuous period of three months, and (ii) provided that no person meeting all the prescribed minimum qualifications is available therefore, the local social services commissioner may, if in accordance with federal standards, waive those qualifications which he deems least essential for such position and make a provisional appointment of a person otherwise qualified therefor;

(d) submit an annual report to the governor and the legislature prior to the fifteenth day of December of each year. Such annual report shall include the

SSL

following: the affairs of the department and the status of welfare programs in the state with recommendations for the improvement and development of welfare programs; a report on the department's fair hearing system, as required by section twenty-two of this article; a written evaluation report on the delivery of child welfare services in the state, as required by subdivision five of section four hundred seven of this chapter; a report of the operations of the state central register of child abuse and maltreatment and the various local child protective services, as required by section four hundred twenty-six of this chapter; a report on the number and status and the findings of investigations of deaths of children pursuant to subdivision five of section twenty of this chapter; a report on the progress of the development and operation of the child care review system, as required by subdivision nine of section four hundred forty-two of this chapter; commencing before December fifteenth, nineteen hundred eighty-four and terminating on December fifteenth, nineteen hundred eighty-nine, a progress report on the planning and implementation of the teenage services act as required by the provisions of section four hundred nine-m of title four-B of this chapter; an analysis of the information contained in the registry of community facilities, as required by paragraph (b) of subdivision two of section four hundred sixty-three-a of this chapter; and a report on the operation of the child support enforcement program, as required by chapter six hundred eighty-five of the laws of nineteen hundred seventy-five;

(e)   work cooperatively with the commissioner of the office of mental health and the commissioner of the office of mental retardation and developmental disabilities to assist the commissioner of education in furnishing integrated employment services to individuals with severe disabilities, including the development of an integrated employment implementation plan pursuant to article twenty-one of the education law;

(f)   in conjunction with the commissioner of education, develop and annually review a plan to ensure coordination and access to education for homeless children, in accordance with the provisions of section thirty two hundred nine of the education law, and monitor compliance of local social services districts with such plan;

(g)   require participation of all employees of a child protective service in a training course which has been developed by the office for the prevention of domestic violence in conjunction with the office of children and family services whose purpose is to develop an understanding of the dynamics of domestic violence and its connection to child abuse and neglect. Such course shall:

(i)   pay special attention to the need to screen for domestic violence;

(ii)   place emphasis on the psychological harm experienced by children whose environment is impacted by familial violence and accordingly explore avenues to keep such children with the non-abusive parent rather than placing them in foster care further traumatizing both the victim and the children;

(iii)   provide instruction regarding the scope of legal remedies for the abused parent;

(iv) identify obstacles that prevent individuals from leaving their batterers and examine safety options and services available for the victim;

(v) provide information pertaining to the unique barriers facing certain immigrant women and the options available under the federal Violence Against Women Act;

(vi) analyze procedures available to sanction and educate the abusing partner; and

(vii) emphasize the need for the system to hold the abusing partner responsible by appropriate referrals to law enforcement.

(h) exercise such other powers and perform such other duties as may be imposed by law.

Amended by Laws 1950, Ch. 364; Laws 1960, Ch. 834; Laws 1964, Ch. 281; Laws 1965, Ch. 122; Laws 1971, Ch. 108; Laws 1971, Ch. 110, eff. July 1, 1971; and Ch. 1067, eff. July 2, 1971; **amended** by Laws 1982, Ch. 384, eff. Apr. 1, 1983; **amended** by Laws 1984, Ch. 975, eff. July 1, 1984; Laws 1990, Ch. 49, which eliminated the expiration date of the 1984 amendment; **amended** by Laws 1989, Ch. 749, § 1, eff. July 25, 1989; **amended** by Laws 1992, Ch. 515, § 11, eff. July 1, 1992; **amended** by Laws 1994, Ch. 569, § 1, eff. Aug. 25, 1994; **amended** by Laws 2002, Ch. 280, § 1, eff. Dec. 4, 2002, **added** new subd. (g) and **relettered** old subd. (g) to (h).

Laws 2002, Ch. 182, § 13 provides:

Nothing in this act shall be construed to amend or repeal any provision of chapter 436 of the laws of 1997 or to limit the scope of any legislative proposals that may be developed pursuant to section 125 of part B of such chapter. Notwithstanding any other provision of this act or of section 123 of part B of such chapter, the office of children and family services, as the transferee of all functions, powers, duties and obligations of the former division for youth pursuant to chapter 436 of the laws of 1997, shall also hold and be responsible for all functions, powers, duties and obligations of the former state youth commission, as transferred and assigned to, assumed by and devolved upon the former division for youth pursuant to chapter 881 of the laws of 1960, except that those powers that could be exercised only with the approval of the council on youth shall hereafter not be so limited.

§ 18. Rules of the board.

Repealed by Laws 1971, Ch. 110, eff. July 1, 1971.

§ 19. Record of proceedings of the board; certificates and subpoenas.

Repealed by Laws 1971, Ch. 110, eff. July 1, 1971.

§ 20. Powers and duties of the department.

1. [*Repealed.*]

2. The department shall, as provided in this chapter:

(a) administer all the forms of public welfare work for which the state is responsible;

(b)   supervise all social services work, as the same may be administered by any local unit of government and the social services officials thereof within the state, advise them in the performance of their official duties and regulate the financial assistance granted by the state in connection with said work;

(c)   distribute, reimburse and grant as herein provided the funds appropriated by the legislature for such participation and also such funds as may be received from the federal government for such purpose or purposes.

3.   The department is authorized:

(a)   to supervise local social services departments and in exercising such supervision the department shall approve or disapprove rules, regulations and procedures made by local social services officials within thirty days after filing of same with the commissioner; such rules, regulations and procedures shall become operative immediately upon approval or on the thirtieth day after such submission to the commissioner unless the commissioner shall specifically disapprove said rule, regulation or procedure as being inconsistent with law or regulations of the department;

(b)   in accordance with the provisions of this chapter to make reimbursements of local welfare costs on a participating basis established by law, to advance grants of money for local welfare purposes and to administer a discretionary fund for such purposes within the limit of available appropriations;

(c)   to pay such per centum as the legislature shall determine, of the salaries of local administrative personnel as it shall determine to be qualified to perform the duties assigned;

(d)   to establish rules, regulations and policies to carry out its powers and duties under this chapter;

(e)   to withhold or deny state reimbursement, in whole or in part, from or to any social services district or any city or town thereof, in the event of the failure of either of them to comply with law, rules or regulations of the department relating to public assistance and care or the administration thereof;

(f)   to promulgate any regulations the commissioner determines are necessary, in accordance with the provisions of section one hundred eleven-b of this chapter, and to withhold or deny state reimbursement, in whole or in part, from or to any social services district, in the event of the failure of any such district to comply with such regulations relating to such district's organization, administration, management or program. Upon withholding or denying state reimbursement, the commissioner shall notify the temporary president of the senate, the speaker of the assembly and the chairman of the senate finance committee and assembly ways and means committee;

(g)   to formulate plans for the recruitment, utilization and training of volunteers to assist in performing services and other duties in social services districts for the purpose of improving participation in public welfare programs;

(h) for the purpose of the proper administration of programs of public assistance and care, to enter into agreements not inconsistent with federal law, with public agencies responsible for the administration of public assistance and care in any geographically contiguous state, to receive information from such public agencies which is substantially similar to information obtained by the department from the wage reporting system operated by the state department of taxation and finance pursuant to section one hundred seventy-one-a of the tax law and, subject to the approval of the state department of taxation and finance, to provide such public agencies with information obtained from such wage reporting system; provided, however, that no such agreement shall be entered into with a public agency of any geographically contiguous state unless such state has by law established standards of confidentiality which are substantially similar to those contained in this chapter prohibiting the disclosure of such information. Upon receipt of wage information from such public agencies, the department shall furnish such information to the local social services districts;

(i) to assure conformance with federal law, by entering into agreements with the federal social security administration and public agencies in other states responsible for administering the food stamp program or programs under title I, II, IV-A, IV-D, X, XIV, XVI, or XIX of the social security act under which the department will provide such agencies, when required by federal law and only to the extent so required, with data which may be of use in establishing or verifying eligibility for or benefit amounts in such programs or ability to pay support for a person receiving support collection services including data obtained from the wage reporting system operated by the state department of taxation and finance pursuant to section one hundred seventy-one-a of the tax law.

4. The Department shall not withhold state reimbursement from or deny state reimbursement to a social services district, until written notice is given to the commissioner of the social services district affected, except when the reason for the proposed withholding or denying is that such commissioner does not meet the minimum qualifications required for such position, to the body or officer that appointed or purported to appoint such commissioner:

(a) entirely for any period; or

(b) in whole or in part, on ten per centum or more of all the cases in receipt of public assistance in such district in any period; or

(c) in whole or in part, on ten per centum or more of the cases in receipt of a specific category of assistance in such district in any period; or

(d) for any period, in an amount equal to or greater than ten per centum of the state reimbursement otherwise due the district for such period.

5. (a) In the case of the death of a child whose care and custody or custody and guardianship has been transferred to an authorized agency, or the death of a child for whom any local department of social services has an open child protective services or preventive services case, or in the case of a report made to the central register involving the death of a child, the office of children and

SSL

family services shall (i) investigate or provide for an investigation of the cause of and circumstances surrounding such death, (ii) review such investigation, and (iii) prepare and issue a report on such death, except where a report is issued by an approved local or regional fatality review team in accordance with section four hundred twenty-two-b of this chapter.

(b)   Such report shall include (i) the cause of death, whether from natural or other causes, (ii) identification of child protective or other services provided or actions taken regarding such child and his or her family, (iii) any extraordinary or pertinent information concerning the circumstances of the child's death, (iv) whether the child or the child's family had received assistance, care or services from the social services district prior to such child's death, (v) any action or further investigation undertaken by the department or by the local social services district since the death of the child, and (vi) as appropriate, recommendations for local or state administrative or policy changes.

Such report shall contain no information that would identify the name of the deceased child, his or her siblings, the parent or other person legally responsible for the child or any other members of the child's household, but shall refer instead to the case, which may be denoted in any fashion determined appropriate by the department or a local social services district. In making a fatality report available to the public pursuant to paragraph (c) of this subdivision, the department may respond to a child specific request for such report if the commissioner determines that such disclosure is not contrary to the best interests of the deceased child's siblings or other children in the household, pursuant to subdivision five of section four hundred twenty-two-a of this chapter. Except as it may apply directly to the cause of the death of the child, nothing herein shall be deemed to authorize the release or disclosure to the public of the substance or content of any psychological, psychiatric, therapeutic, clinical or medical reports, evaluations or like materials or information pertaining to such child or the child's family.

(c)   No later than six months from the date of the death of such child, the department shall forward its report to the social services district, chief county executive officer, chairperson of the local legislative body of the county where the child's death occurred and the social services district which had care and custody or custody and guardianship of the child, if different. The department shall notify the temporary president of the senate and the speaker of the assembly as to the issuance of such reports and, in addition to the requirements of section seventeen of this chapter, shall submit an annual cumulative report to the governor and the legislature incorporating the data in the above reports and including appropriate findings and recommendations. Such reports concerning the death of a child and such cumulative reports shall immediately thereafter be made available to the public after such forwarding or submittal.

(d)   To enable the office of children and family services or a local or regional fatality review team to prepare such report, the office of children and family services or a local or regional fatality review team may request and shall timely receive from departments, boards, bureaus or other agencies of the state, or any of its political subdivisions, or any duly authorized agency, or any other agency which provided assistance, care or services to the deceased child such information as they are authorized to provide.

6. The department is directed to seek appropriate approvals from federal officials to permit commissioners of jurors in each social services district to obtain the names and addresses of persons applying for or receiving aid to dependent children, Medicaid, or home relief authorized by this chapter for purposes of identifying prospective jurors. Upon receiving such approval or upon determining that no approval is necessary, notwithstanding sections one hundred thirty-six and three hundred sixty-nine of this chapter, the department shall provide lists of such persons to the chief administrator of the courts, appointed pursuant to section two hundred ten of the judiciary law. The lists shall be provided for the sole purpose of integration into lists of prospective jurors as provided by section five hundred six of the judiciary law. The chief administrator of the courts shall upon request provide information from the lists to the commissioner of jurors in each county or, in a county within a city having a population of one million or more, the county clerk of said county, solely for the purpose of compiling lists of prospective jurors for the appropriate county. The lists shall be provided only pursuant to a cooperative agreement between the chief administrator of the courts and the commissioner that guarantees that all necessary steps shall be taken by the chief administrator of the courts, the commissioners of jurors and the county clerks to ensure that the lists are kept confidential and that there is no unauthorized use or disclosure of such lists. Furthermore, the lists will be provided only if the chief administrator of the courts determines that the lists are needed for integration into lists of prospective jurors in one or more counties. Commissioners of jurors and county clerks receiving such lists shall not use any information derived from such list for any purpose other than for the selection of jurors and shall take appropriate steps to see that the confidentiality of such information is maintained.

Amended by Laws 1946, Ch. 200; Laws 1950, Ch. 466; Laws 1955, Ch. 143; Laws 1964, Ch. 488; Laws 1969, Ch. 643; Laws 1971, Ch.110; Laws 1972, Ch. 971; Laws 1977, Ch. 516,Ch. 863; amended by Laws 1978, Ch. 456, eff. July, 1978; amended by Ch. 473, eff. July 11, 1978; amended by the Laws 1986, Ch. 882, eff. Aug. 2, 1986; amended by Laws 1989, Ch. 749, § 2, eff. July 25, 1989; amended by Laws 1990, Ch. 304, § 1, eff. Dec. 27, 1990; amended by Laws 1994, Ch. 442, § 1, eff. July 20, 1994; amended by Laws 1996, Ch. 12, § 3, eff. Feb. 15, 1996, and applicable to fatality reports issued by the department on or after Dec. 1, 1995; amended by Laws 1999, Ch. 136, §§ 1 & 2, eff. June 30, 1999; Laws 2006, ch. 485, §3, eff. Dec 14, 2006.

Laws 2002, Ch. 182, § 13 provides:

Nothing in this act shall be construed to amend or repeal any provision of chapter 436 of the laws of 1997 or to limit the scope of any legislative proposals that may be developed pursuant to section 125 of part B of such chapter. Notwithstanding any other provision of this act or of section 123 of part B of such chapter, the office of children and family services, as the transferee of all functions, powers, duties and obligations of the former division for youth pursuant to chapter 436 of the laws of 1997, shall also hold and be responsible for all functions, powers, duties and obligations of the former state youth commission, as transferred and assigned to, assumed by and devolved upon the former division for youth pursuant to chapter 881 of the laws of 1960, except that those powers that could be exercised only with the approval of the council on youth shall hereafter not be so limited.

§ 20-a.   Local personnel; limitations on department's power.

Notwithstanding any inconsistent provision of this chapter, the board, the commissioner or the department, acting singly or in unison, shall not have the power, directly or indirectly to prescribe the number of persons to be employed in any social services district providing the district complies with the minimum federal standards relating thereto.

Added by Laws 1971, Ch. 107, eff. Apr. 7, 1971.

§ 20-b.   Plan for in-home care of senior citizens.

On or before the first day of April, nineteen hundred eighty-two the New York state council for home care services, in consultation with the commissioner of social services and the office for the aging, shall prepare a plan designed to ease the burden of families providing care for elderly parents in the home of the parents or the homes of their families. Recommendations are to be made concerning, but not limited to, tax exemptions and increased availability of supportive services.

Added by Laws 1981, Ch. 979, eff. July 31, 1981.

§ 20-c.   Privatization.

1. Except as otherwise specified in the appropriation for system support and information services program in the office of temporary disability assistance within the department of family assistance, the department shall not enter into any contract with a private entity under which that entity would perform any of the public assistance and care eligibility determination functions, duties or obligations of the department as set forth in this chapter.

(b) * Social services districts may enter into a contract or agreement for the performance of functions, duties or obligations required to be performed pursuant to this chapter, however, the collective bargaining representative of employees who normally perform such functions or provide such services for such social services district shall be permitted the opportunity to competitively bid for any contract let pursuant to this section with the overall cost and quality of the proposal being major criteria in the selection.

2. No contract with a contractor for services pursuant to this section shall be entered into by the office or district unless the office or district contracting for such service has:

(a)   Provided the certified collective bargaining organization representing the permanent employees affected by the district's exercise of its right to contract out with sixty days advance notice of its intent to contract out for services pursuant to this section;

(b) Considered whether the proposed contract will result in actual cost savings to the office; and

(c) Evaluated and made a favorable determination based upon a required disclosure of information from the potential contractor regarding any final actions relating to (a) the responsibility taken by any contracting agency, law enforcement authority or the department of labor against bidders, contractors or subcontractors and (b) debarments pursuant to express statutory authorization.

3. A contract shall not be approved unless it contains a description of the service quality expectations pursuant to the contract and a description of the method by which the quality of services shall be monitored and evaluated by the district based upon specific performance measures contained in the contract. The proposed contract must include specific provisions pertaining to the qualifications of the staff that will perform the work under the contract. The proposed contract shall contain specific information regarding the actual number of employees to be retained, hours of work, wage rates and associated benefit levels, titles, and job descriptions.

4. Existing rights. Nothing in this section shall be deemed to diminish the rights, privileges, or remedies of any employee under any other local law or under the applicable collective bargaining agreement.

5. The provisions of this section shall not impair, restrict or otherwise modify applicable restrictions contained in federal law and regulations promulgated thereto.

* As enacted.

Added by Laws 1997, Ch. 436, § 1 Part B, § 151, eff. Aug. 20, 1997.

§ 21. Welfare management system.

1. The department shall design and implement a welfare management system which shall be capable of receiving, maintaining and processing information relating to persons who have applied for or been determined eligible for benefits under any program for which the department has supervisory responsibilities under this chapter, for the purpose of providing individual and aggregate data to such districts to assist them in making eligibility determinations and basic management decisions, to the department to assist it in supervising the local administration of such programs, and to the governor and the legislature as may be necessary to assist in making major administrative and policy decisions affecting such programs. Such system shall be designed so as to assist local districts and the state in achieving the following goals:

a. reducing mismanagement in the administration of such program, detecting fraudulent practices, and helping identify policies or conditions that will reduce or deter fraud;

b.　promoting efficiency in local district determinations of eligibility for public assistance and care and other programs supervised by the department, to expedite such determinations and to reduce unauthorized or excessive payments;

c.　achieving compliance with federal laws and regulations and maximizing utilization of federal funds;

d.　improving data collection and retention techniques and developing uniform reporting forms and procedures;

e.　initiating implementation of such a system for districts other than the district comprising the city of New York, in a manner compatible with expansion of such system to the district comprising the city of New York;

f.　being developed and implemented in each social services district, to the extent possible consistent with statewide uniformity, in a manner compatible with maximum utilization of existing data processing systems and capabilities of such district and with minimum local participation by such district in administrative expenditures directly attributable to the design and implementation of such system; and

g.　achieving such other goals consistent with this chapter and other laws as are desirable for improving the administration of such programs.

2.　The department shall promulgate regulations, specifying the types of information to be collected and transmitted by each social services district to the department, the methods for collection and transmittal of such information, and the procedures for utilization by social services districts of the data maintained by the welfare management system. Any such regulations shall be published for comment at least thirty days in advance of their promulgation and shall be filed with the secretary of state at least sixty days in advance of the effective date of any such requirement.

3.　Information relating to persons applying for or receiving benefits under programs pursuant to this chapter shall be considered confidential and shall not be disclosed to persons or agencies other than those considered entitled to such information in accordance with section one hundred thirty-six of this chapter, when such disclosure is necessary for the proper administration of such programs.

4.　The commissioner of labor and his or her designees shall be entitled to access to the welfare management system and the information contained therein for the purpose of administration of the programs for public assistance recipients set forth in title nine-B of article five of this chapter. Use of the information relating to persons applying for or receiving benefits under such programs by the department of labor will be in accordance with the provisions of this chapter.

5.　The commissioner of health and his or her designees shall be entitled to access to the welfare management system and the information contained therein for the purpose of administration of the program of medical assistance for needy persons set forth in title eleven of article five of this chapter. Use of the information relating to persons applying for or receiving benefits under such program by the department of health will be in accordance with the provisions of section one hundred thirty-six of this chapter.

6.   By no later than forty-five days following the end of each calendar quarter after the second quarter of calendar year nineteen hundred seventy-six, the department shall, until full implementation has been achieved in all social services districts, report to the governor and the legislature regarding the current status of the welfare management system, summarizing the progress achieved during the previous quarter and the anticipated major achievements of the succeeding two calendar quarters. The report shall include the current and anticipated overall expenditure and staffing levels for functions relating to the system, and shall specify each district affected or anticipated to be affected during the succeeding two calendar quarters and summarize the manner in which each such district is, or is anticipated to be, affected.

7.   (a) The full cost of expenditures by the state for the design, development and implementation of the welfare management system shall be borne by the state, utilizing any federal funds made available for such purposes. Social services districts shall not be responsible for participating in state expenditures for any of the following: acquisition, installation, maintenance and operation of a state computer; acquisition, installation and maintenance of the telecommunications network and equipment; development and provision of state mandated forms; modification of existing data processing operations determined by the department to be necessary to assure systems compatibility; and development and provision of training materials and equipment, and costs of staff for training provided by the state.

(b)   Expenditures by a social services district for data entry operators determined necessary by the department during the period of conversion to full operation of the welfare management system for such district shall be subject to reimbursement by the state in accordance with section one hundred fifty-three of this chapter to the extent of one hundred per centum of such expenditures after first deducting therefrom any federal funds properly received or to be received on account of such expenditures.

(c)   Expenditures by a social services district other than those set forth in this section shall be subject to state reimbursement as administrative costs in accordance with section one hundred fifty-three of this chapter to the extent of fifty per centum thereof, after first deducting therefrom any federal funds properly received or to be received on account of such expenditures.

(d)   The department is hereby authorized to enter into written agreements, subject to the approval of the director of the budget, with not more than three social services districts by which such districts agree to undertake additional administrative functions relating to design, development and testing of the welfare management system, subject to one hundred percent state reimbursement for administrative costs attributable to such functions, after first deducting therefrom any federal funds properly received or to be received on account of such expenditures.

SSL

8.　The department may enter into the case file of each applicant for or recipient of benefits under the programs of food stamps, aid to dependent children, home relief, veteran assistance, emergency assistance to adults, or medical assistance for whom a case file has been established on the welfare management system information it receives from the appropriate governmental agency concerning a client who has applied for or has been determined to be eligible for workers' compensation benefits, unemployment insurance benefits, and benefits being paid pursuant to titles two and sixteen of the federal social security act (including supplemental state payments). The department may rebudget any case for which it makes an entry where the information received indicates that rebudgeting is appropriate. The department shall immediately notify the appropriate social services district that an applicant or recipient's case has been rebudgeted or of any other direct entry of information into a case file. A social services district shall not be held responsible for any costs incurred as a result of data erroneously entered by the department into the welfare management system.

Added by Laws 1976, Ch. 638, eff. July 21, 1976; **amended** and **adding** new subdivisions (4) and (5) and **renumbering** subdivisions (4), (5) and (6) as (6), (7) and (8) by Laws 1995, Ch. 664, §1, eff. Aug. 8, 1995; Laws 1997, Ch. 436, § 1, Part B, § 144, eff. Aug. 20, 1997,

§ 21-a.　Electronic benefit transfer system.

Any electronic benefit transfer system shall be implemented by the department on a statewide basis and shall be administered pursuant to the provisions of this section.

1.　Any contract entered into on behalf of local social services districts for electronic benefit transfer services shall ensure that there are a sufficient number of access points in each local social services district to ensure an adequate distribution of such services. Upon implementation of an electronic benefit transfer system in a local social services district or in any political or other geographic subdivision of such district, the department shall publish a list identifying the number and location of access points within such district or subdivision, and shall seek and accept public comment on the adequacy of recipient access to electronic benefit transfer services within such district or subdivision. The department shall seek to maximize recipient access to electronic benefit transfer services by working with the contractor to establish access points at a broad range of businesses and community facilities including, but not limited to, community centers, senior citizen centers, educational and job skills training sites, and local housing authorities.

2.　The department or the designated agent thereof shall utilize appropriate materials and training to provide each recipient with adequate instruction on the use of the electronic benefit transfer system, which shall include, but not be limited to, the following:

(a)　the types of transactions and services provided by means of an electronic benefit transfer system, and any limitations thereon;

(b)　the rights, responsibilities and liabilities applicable to recipients that receive benefits by means of an electronic benefit transfer system;

(c)　the procedure for reporting the loss or theft of a system access device, or any unauthorized transaction;

(d)　the process for the replacement of a lost or stolen system access device, and the procedure to access benefits, if needed, until such time as such device can be replaced; and

(e)　the procedure by which participants can access information about their benefit account or accounts including, but not limited to, a toll-free telephone number which would provide recipients with account balances and transaction history.

Added by Laws 1997, Ch. 436, § 1, Part B, § 144-a, eff. Aug. 20, 1997.

§ 22.　Appeals and fair hearings; judicial review

1.　Any person described in subdivision three of this section, or any individual authorized to act on behalf of any such person, may appeal to the department from decisions of social services officials or failures to make decisions upon grounds specified in subdivision five of this section. The department shall review the case and give such person an opportunity for a fair hearing thereon. The department may also, on its own motion, review any decision made or any case in which a decision has not been made by a social services official within the time specified by law or regulations of the department. The department may make such additional investigation as it may deem necessary, and the commissioner shall make such decision as is justified and is in conformity with the provisions of this chapter, the regulations of the department, a comprehensive annual services program plan then in effect pursuant to title twenty of the federal social security act and any other applicable provisions of law.

2.　In connection with any appeal pursuant to this section, with or without a fair hearing, the commissioner may designate and authorize one or more appropriate members of his staff to consider and decide such appeals. Any staff member so designated and authorized shall have authority to decide such appeals on behalf of the commissioner with the same force and effect as if the commissioner had made the decisions. Fair hearings held in connection with such appeals shall be held on behalf of the commissioner by members of his staff who are employed for such purposes or who have been designated and authorized by him therefor. The provisions of this subdivision shall apply to fair hearings conducted pursuant to subdivision eight of section four hundred twenty-two of this chapter, and to any hearing required pursuant to this chapter concerning the denial, suspension or revocation of any permit, certificate or license, and to any hearing held pursuant to section four hundred fifty-five of this chapter.

SSL

3.   Persons entitled to appeal to the department pursuant to this section shall include:

(a)   Applicants for or recipients of aid to dependent children, emergency assistance for families with dependent children, home relief, veteran assistance, medical assistance for needy persons and any service authorized or required to be made available in the geographic area in which such person resides, pursuant to the provisions of this chapter;

(b)   Applicants for or participants in the food stamp program, pursuant to section ninety-five of this chapter and regulations of the department;

(c)   Applicants for or recipients of emergency assistance for aged, blind and disabled persons, pursuant to title eight of article five of this chapter, so long as such emergency assistance is available pursuant to such law;

(d)   Aggrieved persons described in section four hundred of this chapter;

(e)   [Expires and repealed June 30, 2007] Aggrieved persons, agencies or social services districts described in section three hundred seventy-two-e of this chapter;

(f)   Other persons entitled to an opportunity for fair hearings pursuant to regulations of the department.

4.   (a) Except as provided in paragraph (c) of subdivision two of section four hundred twenty-four-a of this chapter and in paragraph (b) of this subdivision, any appeal pursuant to this section must be requested within sixty days after the date of the action or failure to act complained of.

(b)   Unless a different period is mandated by federal law or regulations, a person is allowed to request a fair hearing on any action of a social services district relating to food stamp benefits or loss of food stamp benefits which occurred in the ninety days preceding the request for a hearing. For purposes of this paragraph, such action includes a denial of a request for restoration of any benefits lost more than ninety days but less than a year prior to the request. In addition, at any time within the period for which a person is certified to receive food stamp benefits, such person may request a fair hearing to dispute the current level of benefits.

5.   Grounds for such appeals shall be specified in regulations of the department, but shall include at least the following:

(a)   Denial of any application.

(b)   Failure to act upon any application within thirty days after filing, except applications for home relief, or failure to comply with laws and regulations requiring that priority be given to certain applications for assistance, or failure to act on any application for home relief within forty-five days after filing.

(c)   Inadequacy in amount or manner of payment of assistance.

(d)   Discontinuance in whole or in part of assistance, or termination of a service authorized or required to be made available pursuant to the comprehensive annual services program plan then in effect.

(e) Failure to permit a parent or guardian to visit the child or failure to provide supportive services, which shall include preventive and other supportive services authorized to be provided pursuant to the state consolidated services plan, to the child and to the parent or guardian, pursuant to an instrument executed under section three hundred eighty-four-a of this chapter.

(f) Failure to provide adoption services or assistance to a prospective adoptive parent on behalf of a child freed for adoption as defined in subdivision (b) of section one thousand eighty-seven of the family court act pursuant to section three hundred seventy-two-b of this chapter and the local social services district's consolidated services plan.

6. In scheduling fair hearings on appeals concerning applications for emergency assistance pursuant to section three hundred fifty-j or title eight of article five of this chapter, the department shall give priority to the hearing and determination of such appeals.

7. For the purposes of this section, except subdivision nine, social services officials shall include the persons described in subdivision fourteen of section two of this chapter and also the head of any bureau of the department which exercises responsibility pursuant to this chapter for determining eligibility for and furnishing public assistance and care to persons in family care pursuant to section one hundred thirty-eight-a of this chapter, or for determining eligibility for and furnishing medical assistance pursuant to subdivision two, three or four of section three hundred sixty-five of this chapter, or for determining eligibility for and furnishing services pursuant to section two hundred fifty-three of this chapter.

8. The department shall promulgate such regulations, not inconsistent with federal or state law, as may be necessary to implement the provisions of this section. Such regulations shall require that a copy of all decisions made concerning appeals pursuant to this section shall be sent to each party to such appeals and their representatives, if any.

9. (a) All decisions of the commissioner pursuant to this section shall be binding upon the social services districts involved and shall be complied with by the social services officials thereof.

(b) Any aggrieved party to an appeal, including a social services official provided an application by any such social services official has not been determined by any federal agency to be in violation of federal law, may apply for review as provided in article seventy-eight of the civil practice law and rules.

(c) The provisions of paragraph (a) shall be applicable to a social services official after the decision of the commissioner becomes final and binding unless a court stays such decision. No such stay shall be issued by any court unless the social services official establishes that irreputable harm will result if a stay is not granted, and the probability that he will succeed on the merits. In an action or proceeding to review a decision of the commissioner, the applicant or recipient and his representative, if any, shall be served with copies of all pleadings and shall be allowed to intervene in such action or proceeding as a matter of right.

SSL

Notwithstanding any provision of the civil practice law and rules or any other law to the contrary, any application by a social services official for a stay in a proceeding commenced by such official pursuant to this section shall be determined by the appropriate appellate division, and not by a justice of the supreme court. Whenever the commissioner has sustained an appeal by a recipient of public assistance or care with respect to benefits which were continued pending the fair hearing decision, the appellate division shall not stay the fair hearing decision prior to the initial determination of the proceeding initiated pursuant to this section for the review of such fair hearing decision.

(d)   Every person entitled to a benefit pursuant to a decision of the commissioner under this section, shall be advised to contact the department in a manner specified by department regulations, in the event that a local social services district does not comply with such decision.

10.   In connection with every determination of an appeal pursuant to this section, the department shall inform every party thereto, and his representative, if any, of the availability of judicial review and the time limitation thereon.

11.   The provisions of subdivisions three and four of section twenty of this chapter shall be applicable to state reimbursement otherwise payable to any social services district in the event of the failure of a social services official to comply with a commissioner's determination upon an appeal within the time required by regulations of the department or such additional time as the commissioner may allow. In the event that the court stays any such determination in a proceeding pursuant to article seventy-eight of the civil practice law and rules, state reimbursement shall not be withheld or denied pursuant to this subdivision for non-compliance during such stay. Nothing in this subdivision shall limit the power of a court in a proceeding pursuant to article seventy-eight of the civil practice law and rules to order a social services official to comply with a commissioner's determination upon an appeal.

12.   Every applicant or recipient of public assistance and care shall be informed in writing, through the distribution of an informational pamphlet, at the time of application and at the time of any action affecting his receipt of assistance or care:

(a)   of his right to an appeal or fair hearing;

(b)   of the method by which he may obtain an appeal or fair hearing;

(c)   of his right to representation by legal counsel, or by a relative, friend, or other spokesmen, or that he may represent himself;

(d)   of the availability of community legal services to assist him in the appeal or fair hearings process;

(e)   of the nature of the precedures procedures to be followed throughout an appeal or fair hearing;

(f)   of the types of information he may wish to submit at an appeal or fair hearing;

(g) of any additional information which would clarify the appeals and fair hearings procedure for applicants and recipients of public assistance and care, and would assist such persons in more adequate preparation for such hearings.

13. Whenever under other provisions of this chapter an applicant or recipient of public assistance or care may appeal to the department a decision of a social services official, or the failure of such official to act on his application within the required period, and may request a fair hearing thereon, if such applicant or recipient requires legal services in connection with such an appeal and fair hearing and such services are not otherwise available to him, the social services official shall, upon request, make provision for payment for such legal services if required by federal law or regulations.

14. To provide an analysis of the outcome of the fair hearings process within the office of temporary and disability assistance to identify inadequacies and potential improvements in the functioning of the fair hearings system, such office shall prepare for inclusion in the annual report required by subdivision (d) of section seventeen of this article to be filed with the governor and the legislature prior to the fifteenth day of December of each year, a report containing with respect to income maintenance programs, including the family assistance program, the safety net assistance program, the medical assistance program and any other program, the number of affirmations and reversals by local districts and by program including a breakdown by local districts of the number of fair hearings requested by program and the number of fair hearings held by program, formal requests by local districts and recipients for reconsideration or rehearing of appeals, and a summary of court actions on hearing decisions.

Added by Laws 1978, Ch. 473, § 2, eff. July 11, 1978; **amended** by Laws 1979, Ch. 611, eff. Apr. 1, 1980, adding a new subd. (e) and relettering the present (e) to (f). "The provisions of paragraph (b) of subdivision nine, shall be applicable only to appeals decided by the state commissioner of social services or his designee after the effective date"; **amended** by Laws 1982, Ch. 384, eff. Apr. 1, 1983; **amended** by Laws 1985, Ch. 808, eff. Oct. 31, 1985; **amended** by Laws 1986, Ch. 902, eff. Aug. 5, 1986; **amended** by Laws 1988, Ch. 341, § 1, eff. July 25, 1988; **amended** by Laws 1992, Ch. 41, § 121, eff. Apr. 2, 1992; **amended** by Laws 2002, Ch. 83, Part C, §§ 9, 28, eff. May 29, 2002, amending subd. (e), deemed eff. April 1, 2002, expires and repealed June 30, 2007. **amended** by Laws 2005, Ch. 524, § 44, eff. November 14, 2005; L. 2005, Ch. 3, sect; 33, eff. Aug. 23, 2005.

* So in original. Probably should read "irreparable harm."

§ 23. Wage reporting system.

1. The department is authorized to provide information obtained from the wage reporting system as operated by the state department of taxation and finance:

(a) to social services districts with respect to applicants for and recipients of public assistance and care or other benefits pursuant to this chapter for which such districts are responsible, with respect to any person legally responsible for the support of such applicants and recipients and with respect to any person legally responsible for the support of a recipient of services under section one hundred eleven-g of this chapter or to any agent of any entity that is under contract with the child support program pursuant to title six-a of article three of this chapter,

(b)   to a public agency responsible for the administration of public assistance and care in any geographically contiguous state with which the department has an agreement with respect to wage information pursuant to paragraph (h) of subdivision three of section twenty of this article,

(c)   * to the federal parent locator service, maintained by the federal department of health and human services, as required by section one hundred twenty-four of the federal family support act of nineteen hundred eighty-eight, for the purpose of enabling the department to fulfill obligations and responsibilities otherwise incumbent upon the state department of labor.

(c)   * to social services districts with respect to participants in employment or training programs authorized pursuant to this chapter who are current recipients of public assistance and care or who are former recipients of public assistance and care (except that with regard to former recipients, information which relates to a particular former recipient shall be provided with client identifying data deleted), for the purpose of evaluating the effect of participation in such programs on such current and former recipients, and

(e)   to the federal social security administration or public agency of another state with which the department has an agreement with respect to wage information pursuant to paragraph (i) of subdivision three of section twenty of this article.

2.   Notwithstanding any law to the contrary, the department, upon request by the office of welfare inspector general, shall provide said office with such information it receives from the wage reporting system operated by the department of taxation and finance that the office of welfare inspector general deems necessary to carry out its functions and duties under article four of the executive law.

3.   Information obtained by the department from the wage reporting system operated by the state department of taxation and finance shall be considered confidential and shall not be disclosed to persons or agencies other than those considered entitled to such information when such disclosure is necessary for the proper administration of programs of public assistance and care or for the proper administration of the child support program pursuant to title six-a of article three of this chapter. For the purpose of this subdivision, any disclosure made pursuant to subdivision one of this section shall be considered necessary for the proper administration of programs of public assistance and care and the federal parent locator service shall be considered an agency entitled to such information as is necessary for the proper administration of the child support program pursuant to title six-a of article three of this chapter.

Added by Laws 1978, Ch. 545, eff. July 24, 1978; Laws 1981, Ch. 45; Laws 1984, Ch. 37; Laws 1987, Ch. 9; Laws 1989, Ch. 2; Laws 1990, Ch. 304, which eliminated the expiration date of the section; **Amended** by Laws 1986, Ch. 791, eff. Aug. 2, 1986; **amended** by Laws 1986, Ch. 882, eff. Aug. 2, 1986; **amended** by Laws 1987, Ch. 792, eff. Nov. 1, 1987; **amended** by Laws 1990, Ch. 304, § 2, eff. Dec. 27, 1990; **amended** by Laws 1990, Ch. 818, §§ 17, 18, eff. July 25, 1990; **amended** by Laws 1997, Ch. 398, § 14, eff. Jan. 1, 1998.

* **Editor's Note:** Two versions of Social Services Law § 23(1)(c) are provided. The first version reflects amendments made by Laws 1990, Ch. 818, eff. July 25, 1990. The second version reflects amendments made by Laws 1990, Ch. 304, eff. Dec. 27, 1990. These 1990 amendments made no reference to each other.

§ 24. Orders of board directed to institutions.

Repealed by Laws 1971, Ch. 110, eff. July 1, 1971.

§ 25. Correction of evils in administration of institutions.

Repealed by Laws 1971, Ch. 110, eff. July 1, 1971.

§ 26. Delegation of visitation, inspection and supervision power.

Repealed by Laws 1971, Ch. 110, eff. July 1, 1971.

§ 27. Duties of the attorney-general and district attorneys.

Repealed by Laws 1971, Ch. 110, eff. July 1, 1971.

§ 28. Gifts and bequests.

The department may receive and retain any money or other personal property given or bequeathed to the department or a division or bureau thereof and shall expend the same in accordance with the general powers and duties of the department for the purposes for which it is given or, if unaccompanied by conditions or limitations, for such purposes as it may determine.

SSL

Amended by Laws 1964, Ch. 281; Laws 1971, Ch. 110, eff. July 1, 1971.

§ 29. Federal agency.

The department, with the approval of the governor, may accept a designation from, and act as, the agent of the federal security agency or other duly authorized federal agency in the administration of relief and related activities, activities affecting the welfare of individuals and communities, and the disbursement or expenditure of federal funds or commodities in relation thereto within the state of New York.

Added by Laws 1951, Ch. 5; **amended** by Laws 1964, Ch. 281, eff. Apr. 3, 1964.

§ 29-a. Special provisions regarding maintenance of needy families; federal waivers required.

Repealed by Laws 1997, Ch. 436, § 1, Part B, § 40, eff. Aug. 20, 1997.

§ 30. Continuation of salaries of local and state welfare employees receiving training for the better performance of their duties.

Subject to the approval of the department, the board of supervisors of a county and the appropriating body of a city or town may include in its appropriations moneys for the continuation of the salaries of their local welfare employees who are on leave receiving additional training for the better performance of their duties, provided that no such salaries shall be so continued to a greater extent than will reimburse such employee for the loss of earnings while on such leave. Salaries of the employees of the department may be continued in a similar fashion.

§ 31. Fellowships and scholarships for local and state public welfare employees.

The department, under regulations which it shall prescribe, and from moneys received or appropriated for such purpose, is authorized to grant fellowships and scholarships to local and state public welfare employees to enable them to receive additional training for the better performance of their duties.

§ 32. Reciprocal agreements.

The department is authorized to enter into reciprocal agreements with corresponding state agencies of other states regarding interstate transportation of dependent and indigent persons, and to arrange with the propert* officials in this state for the acceptance, transfer and support of person receiving public assistance and care in other states in accordance with the terms of such reciprocal agreements, but this state shall not nor shall any county or other political subdivision of this state be committed to the support of persons who are not, in the opinion of the department, entitled to public support by the laws of this state. No agreement made pursuant to the provisions of this section shall become effective until the attorney-general has approved its form and sufficiency and determined its legal effect.

* Should probably be "proper."

§ 33. Contracts for supplies and commodities needed in the administration of assistance.

The department may

(a) make agreements for supplies and commodities needed in the administration of assistance and care, under which local welfare units may, subject to the approval of the department, purchase such supplies and commodities; and

(b) in accordance with requisitions duly approved by the commissioner of general services, purchase as the agent of local welfare units and on their request, supplies or commodities needed in the administration of assistance and care and make payments therefor after making proper deductions from state reimbursements due the local units which avail themselves of the provisions of this subdivision.

Amended by Laws 1962, Ch. 399, eff. Apr. 9, 1962.

§ 34. General powers and duties of the commissioner.

1. The commissioner of social services shall be the chief administrative officer of the department.

2. All the administrative and executive powers and duties of the department shall be vested in the commissioner.

3. The commissioner shall

(a) continue to have, exercise, and perform the functions, powers and duties conferred by law upon the commissioner of social services;

(b) execute and issue the determinations, decisions, orders, notices, licenses and certificates of the department as may be required in the exercise and performance of the functions, powers and duties conferred upon or vested in the department;

(c) take cognizance of the interests of health and welfare of the inhabitants of the state who lack or are threatened with the deprivation of the necessaries of life and of all matters pertaining thereto;

(d) exercise general supervision over the work of all local welfare authorities;

(e) enforce this chapter and the regulations of the department within the state and in the local governmental units;

(f) establish regulations for administration of public assistance and care within the state both by the state itself and by the local governmental units, in accordance with law;

(g) provide technical assistance, advisory and consultative services to business, industry and labor to encourage their sponsorship of day care centers.

(h) in consultation with the department of education, the department of health, the division for youth, the office of mental retardation and developmental disabilities and the office of mental health, establish guidelines for the acceptance by social services officials of notices that children in foster care are at risk of educational placements, as provided for in subparagraph four of paragraph b of subdivision one of section forty-four hundred two of the education law. Such guidelines shall be designed to assure that the social services district receiving such a notice inquire into the educational needs of the child and the circumstances of the foster care placement, and to assure that the social services district responds as appropriate to any request by a committee on special education to participate in the proceedings of the committee;

(i)   exercise such other powers and perform such other duties as may be required by law.

4.   Notwithstanding any inconsistent provision of the civil service law, the commissioner may, if he finds that the chief executive officer of any county or city social services department has failed properly to perform his duties as required by law or rules and regulations of the department, present charges and specifications thereof to the appointing officer or authority of such county or city social services district. Such appointing officer or authority shall, upon receipt of such charges or specifications give notice thereof to the chief executive officer of the social services department and shall make inquiry into the merits of such specifications at a hearing thereon. The commissioner may present his evidence at such hearing and recommend removal or other appropriate sanctions. In the event the appointing authority finds the charges and specifications made by the commissioner are substantiated, the appointing officer or authority shall forthwith remove such chief executive officer or apply other sanctions. Any deputy or other employee of any such officer may also be removed or sanctioned upon the recommendation of the commissioner, in the same manner. Such removal or other sanction may not be appealed to a civil service commission, but may be subject to review pursuant to article seventy-eight of the civil practice law and rules. The provisions of this section shall not be deemed to preclude the exercise of the power of removal or sanction by the officer or authority having the power of appointment.

5.   The commissioner or any official by him authorized so to do

(a)   may conduct any inquiry pertinent or material to the discharge of the duties imposed upon him by law;

(b)   is empowered to subpoena witnesses, administer oaths, take testimony and compel the production of such books, papers, records and documents as may be relevant to any such investigation.

6.   The commissioner may exercise such additional powers and duties as may be required for the effective administration of the department and of the state system of public aid and assistance.

Amended by Laws 1964, Ch. 281; Laws 1970, Ch. 278; Laws 1971, Ch. 110; Laws 1971, Ch. 735, eff. Sept. 1, 1971; **amended** by Laws 1994, Ch. 600, § 2, eff. Jan. 1, 1995.

§ 34-a.   Services planning requirements.

1.   (a) Each social services district shall prepare a multi-year consolidated services plan encompassing adult services and family and children's services, which shall include diversion services provided pursuant to section seven hundred thirty-five of the family court act.

(b) Commencing with the years following preparation of the multi-year consolidated services plan, each local district shall also be required to prepare an annual implementation report.

2. (a) The commissioner shall have authority to promulgate regulations specifying the contents of both the multi-year services plan and the annual implementation reports, provided however that such regulations shall not be inconsistent with the standards of review by the commissioner of such plan and reports specified in subdivision four of this section.

(b) The regulations promulgated pursuant to paragraph (a) of this subdivision shall require the multi-year services plan and where appropriate the annual implementation reports, to include a summary of the understanding between the local social services district and the district attorney's office, which outlines the cooperative procedures to be followed by both parties in investigating incidents of child abuse and maltreatment, consistent with their respective obligations for the investigation or prosecution of such incidents, as otherwise required by law.

3. (a) There shall be a public hearing on the multi-year services plan or each annual implementation report. Commencing in nineteen hundred eighty-two, such public hearing shall be held only after fifteen days notice is provided in a newspaper of general circulation within the county. Such notice shall specifically identify the times of the public hearing in which the child protective services and other services components of the multi-year services plan or annual implementation reports are to be considered.

(b) Commencing in nineteen hundred eighty-two, after such hearing, the multi-year services plan or the annual implementation reports shall be submitted for approval to the chief executive officer of the county or to the legislative body in those counties without a chief executive officer. Full approval of the multi-year services plan or of the annual implementation report by the chief executive officer or legislative body shall be required before submission of such plan or report to the commissioner.

(c) Commencing in nineteen hundred eighty-two, the multi-year services plan or the annual implementation reports shall not be forwarded to the commissioner until at least fifteen days have passed from the date of the public hearing thereon.

4. (a) Except as provided in paragraph (b) of this subdivision, the commissioner shall review both the multi-year services plan and the annual implementation reports submitted by the social services district, using standards consistent with the provisions of sections one hundred thirty-one-l, four hundred nine-d and four hundred twenty-three of this chapter, and shall notify such district, in writing, of approval of such plan or reports in whole or in part; provided, however, that for any portions not approved, the commissioner shall in writing to the district specify the portions not approved, the reasons for such determination, the actions required for resubmittal of such portions, and the time period of resubmittal; and provided further, that disapproval of a portion of such plan or report shall not

render the entire plan or report invalid. No portion of the multi-year services plan or of the annual implementation reports shall be finally disapproved until the district has had at least one opportunity for resubmittal. Upon resubmittal, or if no resubmittal is made within the time specified, the commissioner may grant further extensions to the district to allow it to resubmit any unapproved portions, or may finally disapprove such portions. Any social services district aggrieved by a final disapproval of the commissioner under this section shall have the right to a fair hearing in accordance with the appropriate provisions of this chapter. An adverse fair hearing decision shall be reviewable pursuant to article seventy-eight of the civil practice law and rules. State reimbursement may be withheld for all or a portion of a local district's activities, if the multi-year services plan, annual implementation report, or portions of either are disapproved.

(b)   The commissioner of the office of children and family services shall review and approve or disapprove the diversion services portion of the plan jointly with the director of probation and correctional alternatives or any other successor agency or entity. The requirements for the portion of the plan and report regarding the provision of diversion services shall be jointly established by the commissioner of the office of children and family services and the director of probation and correctional alternatives or any other successor agency or entity. The multi-year services plan and where appropriate the annual implementation reports shall be based upon a written understanding between the local social services district and the probation department which outlines the cooperative procedures to be followed by both parties regarding diversion services pursuant to section seven hundred thirty-five of the family court act, consistent with their respective obligations as otherwise required by law.

5.   The commissioner shall promulgate regulations concerning the time by which:

(a)   each local social services district shall submit its multi-year services plan and annual implementation report;

(b)   the commissioner shall, in writing, notify a local district of approval or disapproval of all or parts of such district's multi-year services plan or annual implementation reports; and

(c)   each local social services district shall submit a revised version of its multi-year services plan or annual implementation report, or parts thereof.

6.   (a) Notwithstanding any other provision of law, the office of children and family services shall plan for the statewide implementation, by the thirty-first day of December, two thousand eight, of the use by counties of a child and family services plan that combines the multiyear consolidated services plan required by this section and the county comprehensive plan required by section four hundred twenty of the executive law into a single plan.

(b)   All counties shall implement a county child and family services plan prior to or by the two thousand eight plan year in accordance with a schedule developed by the office of children and family services and shall continue to implement such a plan thereafter. With the approval of such office, a county may implement such a plan before the date required by such schedule.

(c)   The office of children and family services may waive any regulatory requirements relating to the content and timing of multi-year consolidated services plans and annual implementation reports that may impede the ability of a county to implement a county child and family services plan.

(d)   Nothing in this subdivision shall be deemed to affect county planning requirements under the mental hygiene law.

Added by Laws 1981, Ch. 681, eff. July 21, 1981; Laws 1983, Ch. 539; Laws 1987, Ch. 231, eff. July 7, 1987, which eliminated the expiration date of the section; **amended** by Laws 1985, Ch. 677, eff. Jan. 1, 1986; **amended** by Laws 1987, Ch. 231, eff. July 7, 1987; **amended** by Laws 1988, Ch. 707, § 6, eff. Sept. 2, 1988; **amended** by Laws 1995, Ch. 83, § 222, eff. July 1, 1995; **amended** by Laws 2004, Ch. 160, § 1, eff. July 20, 2004; **amended** by Laws 2005, Ch. 57, § 17 (Part E), eff. April 12, 2004, deemed eff. on and after April 1, 2005.

§ 35.   Legal representation of individuals whose federal disability benefits have been denied or may be discontinued; advisory committee.

1.   a. There is hereby established within the department an advisory committee on legal advocacy (hereinafter to be referred to as the "advisory committee") which shall consist of nine members or their designated representatives. The advisory committee shall consist of the following nine members: the commissioner of mental health, the commissioner of mental retardation and developmental disabilities, the advocate for the disabled and six members appointed by the governor. The six members appointed by the governor shall include three representatives of interested public and private groups, and shall include three representatives of county government and the city of New York to be appointed from a list of six names submitted by the New York state association of counties. The commissioner shall coordinate the functions and activities of the department with those of the advisory committee.

b.   The advisory committee shall make recommendations regarding criteria for selection of grant applications, review applications awarded pursuant to the provisions of this section, make recommendations thereon to the commissioner and exercise and perform such other advisory functions as are related to the purposes of this section; provided however that the committee shall meet at least once every six months.

2.   The commissioner, after consultation with the advisory committee, shall make grants, within the amounts appropriated for that purpose, to not-for-profit legal services corporations and not-for-profit agencies serving the disabled and local social services districts, to provide for representation of persons whose federal disability benefits including supplemental security income and social security disability insurance have been denied or may be discontinued for the

SSL

purpose of representing these persons in appropriate proceedings. When the commissioner has contracted with a local social services district to provide such representation, the legislative body of such district may authorize and make provision for the commissioner of social services of the district to obtain necessary legal services on a fee for services basis or other appropriate basis which the department may approve. Such legal services may be provided by not-for-profit legal services corporations, not-for-profit agencies serving the disabled or private attorneys.

3.　The commissioner shall submit a report to the chairman of the senate finance committee and the chairman of the assembly ways and means committee on or before the first day of October, nineteen hundred ninety-eight and biannually thereafter. Such a report shall include but not be limited to a review of the basis for selection of participating entities; the administrative method used to carry out the program; the number of cases appealed by district; the disposition of such appeals; an identification of the savings and costs of the program to the state and localities by district; an evaluation of the continuing need for legal representation provided by the program and recommendations for possible federal and state legislative and regulatory actions relating thereto.

4.　Responsibility for local financial participation shall be determined by the commissioner based on either costs of and the number of district residents served by each local entity or the alternative cost allocation procedure deemed appropriate by the commissioner in consultation with the advisory committee.

Added by Laws 1983, Ch. 627, eff. July 25, 1983, and in effect until July 1, 1995; **amended** by Laws 1990, Ch. 770, § 1, eff. July 25, 1990; **amended** by Laws 1992, Ch. 300, § 1, eff. July 1, 1992, until July 1, 1995; **amended** by Laws 1995, Ch. 81, § 129, eff. June 20, 1995; **amended** by Laws 1995, Ch. 81, § 130, eff. June 20, 1995, extending the period the section remains effective to July 1, 1997; **amended** and repeal date deleted by Laws 1997, Ch. 114, §§ 1 and 2, eff. June 17, 1997,

§ 35-a.　Private proprietary convalescent homes and homes for adults; special provisions.

Repealed by Laws 1971, Ch. 110, eff. July 1, 1971.

§ 35-b.　Establishment of private hospitals for profit.

Repealed by Laws 1970, Ch. 617, eff. June 1, 1970.

§ 35-b.　Residences for adults.

Repealed by Laws 1971, Ch. 110, eff. July 1, 1971.

§ 35-c.　Dispensaries, clinics.

Repealed by Laws 1970, Ch. 617, eff. June 1, 1970.

§ 35-c. Prohibition against advertising as facility for the aging.

Repealed by Laws 1971, Ch. 110, eff. July 1, 1971.

§ 36. Studies.

The department shall, in so far as available appropriations will permit, study and collect information in relation to

(a) the number and conditions of persons who lack or are threatened with the deprivation of the necessaries of life, or seek, or are receiving public assistance or care and all matters pertaining thereto, including the causes thereof and advise measures for their relief, and also for the relief of those in receipt of aid from private charity;

(b) unemployment, poverty, economic distress and other problems of social welfare generally as may be useful in the discharge of its duties or contribute to the promotion of social and economic security;

(c) the number of recipients of aid in, and the receipts and expenditures of, each public welfare district;

(d) dependency and local conditions relative thereto;

(e) such other matters in respect to public and private charities as it may deem advisable; and shall publish such information as it deems of public concern and which may be of value in the performance of its duties.

Amended by Laws 1941, Ch. 82; Laws 1966, Ch. 100; Laws 1971, Ch. 110, 947, both eff. July 1, 1971.

§ 36-a. Department research and demonstration projects.

1. The department is authorized to sponsor, conduct and participate in research and demonstration projects designed to ascertain and eliminate the causes of dependency and to rehabilitate recipients of public assistance and care or to demonstrate the utilization of research in the administration of public assistance and care.

2. Except where a specific appropriation has been made therefor, no such research or demonstration project requiring the expenditure of state funds shall be instituted without prior approval of the director of the budget.

3. The department may request the cooperation of any county or city social services district in connection with any such research or demonstration project sponsored or conducted by the department.

Added by Laws 1969, Ch. 481, eff. May 10, 1969, from former § 36-a **added** by Laws 1963, Ch. 40 and **repealed** by Laws 1969, Ch. 481.

SSL

§ 36-b.   Local flexibility incentive pilot program.

1.   The department, in cooperation with the Department of Labor, is authorized to establish the local flexibility incentive pilot program to enable social services districts or groups of social services districts, at local option, to demonstrate innovations and efficiencies to aid public assistance recipients in attaining self-sufficiency.

2.   Upon application of a social services district, the department, in cooperation with the department of labor, is authorized to approve funding for pilot programs subject to the approval of the director of the budget, separate from state aid that said social services district or social services districts would otherwise be eligible to receive, and to waive state regulations that would impede the successful completion of a project, provided that the demonstration project is consistent with applicable state and federal statutes and will not impair the general health or welfare of the people receiving services under such project or others receiving services in the applying social services district. The department is authorized, in consultation with the department of labor where appropriate to impose appropriate alternative standards in place of any waived requirements.

3.   Applications for pilot project approval shall include, but not be limited to, the name of the applying social services district or group of social services districts, the population, size of its welfare-related programs including medical assistance, family assistance, safety net assistance, emergency assistance to families or its successor programs; size of the population to be subject to the pilot project, the project proposed, with quantified cost savings and an explanation of how such project, if approved, would result in cost containment of the amounts described in the application or improvements in the delivery of services and benefits; the start date and completion date of the project; whether, if successful, the project would require funding in future years; and identification, as necessary, of any rules, regulations or statutory requirements that could impede the successful completion of the project.

4.   If a project is approved, then, notwithstanding any inconsistent provision of law, the department shall provide funding of the project within amounts available by appropriation therefor, provided that no social services district or group of social services districts shall receive more than twenty-five percent of the funds available in any single year. No payment will be made until thirty days after the agreement has been executed. An approved applicant that shall achieve its cost-savings goal shall receive full reimbursement for the costs of such project as such amount shall have been approved by the department in cooperation with the department of labor. In no case shall the state or any of its agencies require remission or repayment of funds saved by any applicant. Reimbursement for successful applicants pursuant to the provisions of this section shall not take place until the department shall have been satisfied as to the savings levels actually achieved.

5.   Each social services district or group of social services districts implementing a pilot project under this section shall establish an on-going program

evaluation and assessment program employing objective measurements and systematic analysis to determine the manner and extent to which the project is achieving the intended primary objective of the project. Each evaluation and assessment program shall include an annual performance plan with goals which establish target levels of performance expressed as tangible, measurable objectives against which actual achievement can be compared, including a goal expressed as a qualitative standard, value or rate. Each participating social services district or group of social services districts shall submit an annual program performance report for the prior fiscal year to the department, the department of labor and to the governor, the speaker of the assembly and the majority leader of the senate documenting the performance achieved compared with the performance goals established for the pilot project, improvements in the quality of services provided and any cost savings; an explanation if a performance goal was not met and an assessment of the effectiveness in achieving performance goals.

6.   Notwithstanding any provision of law to the contrary, state reimbursement for expenditures made by a social services district for administration of any project, including expenditures made in connection with the development, if performed by a county employee or employees, implementation and operation thereof, shall not be subject to any limitations on administrative expenditures, ceilings or caps which otherwise would apply to the reimbursement of such administrative expenditures.

Added by Laws 1997, Ch. 436, § 1 Part B, § 4, eff. Aug. 20, 1997.

§ 37.   Reports of and to department.

The department may collect and, so far as it shall deem advantageous, embody in its annual reports information relating to the best manner of dealing with those who require assistance from public funds, or who receive aid from private charity and represent its views as to the best methods of caring for dependent children and such other matters as the commissioner may deem advisable.

Amended by Laws 1963, Ch. 114; Laws 1964, Chs. 281, 324; Laws 1965, Ch. 795; Laws 1971, Ch. 110, eff. July 1, 1971.

§ 38.   Commission for the blind and visually handicapped.

The New York state commission for the blind an visually handicapped shall continue to exercise and perform its duties, as prescribed by law, and the regulations of the department subject to the supervision and control of the commissioner; and such commission shall be a bureau of the department.

Amended by Laws 1964, Ch. 281; Laws 1966, Ch. 309; Laws 1971, Ch. 110, eff. July 1, 1971 and Ch. 1052, eff. July 2, 1971; Laws 1977, Ch. 520, eff. Aug. 1, 1977.

§ 39   Indian affairs.

1. Powers and duties, if any, conferred or imposed, in terms, by laws now in force, on the governor, commissioners of the land office and the superintendent of purchase or fiscal supervisor of state charities, so far only as they relate to affairs of Indians, or on the commissioner of education, so far only as they relate to affairs of Indians other than the education of children upon the Indian reservations, except such powers and duties, if any, as may have been conferred or imposed, in terms, on either of such officers, in relation to such affairs, by laws enacted and in effect since July first, nineteen hundred and twenty-four, shall continue to be exercised and performed by the department, instead of by the officers named.

2. The office of children and family services may enter into an agreement with an Indian tribe for the provision of foster care, preventive and adoptive services to Indian children as defined in subdivision thirty-six of section two of this chapter and for the provision of adult and child protective services to Indians residing upon the tribe's reservation in the state, after the Indian tribe has submitted to the office of children and family services a plan that satisfactorily demonstrates that such tribe is able to meet the applicable standards for foster care services, preventive services, adoptive services, and adult and child protective services set forth in the applicable federal and state law and regulations. The office of children and family services is authorized to reimburse such tribe for the full cost of foster care, preventive services, adult and child protective services, and adoptive services and care, after deducting any federal funds properly received on account thereof.

3. Any Indian tribe designated as such by the Secretary of the Interior which became subject to the jurisdiction of courts of the state of New York pursuant to sections two hundred thirty-two and two hundred thirty-three of title twenty-five of the United States code or any other federal law, may reassume jurisdiction over those child custody proceedings provided for in articles three, seven, ten, and ten-A of the family court act and sections three hundred fifty-eight-a and three hundred eighty-four-b of this chapter involving Indian children provided that the Secretary of the Interior has granted approval pursuant to and in accordance with the applicable sections of title twenty-five of the United States code.

4. Any Indian tribe designated as such by the state of New York which is subject to the jurisdiction of the courts of the state of New York, may reassume jurisdiction over those child custody proceedings provided for in articles three, seven, ten, and ten-A of the family court act, and sections three hundred fifty-eight-a and three hundred eighty-four-b of this chapter involving Indian children provided that the local commissioner has granted approval in accordance with rules and regulations established by the department.

5. (a) An Indian tribe approved to assume jurisdiction shall have exclusive jurisdiction over any child custody proceeding involving an Indian child who resides or is domiciled within the reservation of such tribe, except where such

jurisdiction is otherwise vested in the courts of the state of New York by existing federal law. Where an Indian child is a ward of a tribal court, the Indian tribe shall retain exclusive jurisdiction, notwithstanding the residence or domicile of the child.

(b) Notwithstanding the provisions of paragraph (a) of this subdivision, nothing herein shall be construed to prevent the emergency removal of an Indian child who is a resident of or is domiciled on a reservation, but temporarily located off the reservation, from his parents or Indian custodian or the emergency placement of such child in a foster home or institution, under applicable state law in order to prevent imminent physical damage or harm to the child. The state authority, official or agency shall insure that the emergency removal or placement terminates immediately when such removal or placement is no longer necessary to prevent imminent physical damage or harm to the child and shall expeditiously initiate a child custody proceeding subject to the provisions of this section, transfer the child to the jurisdiction of the appropriate Indian tribe, or restore the child to the parent or Indian custodian as may be appropriate.

6. In any state court child custody proceeding involving the foster care placement of, or termination of parental rights to an Indian child not domiciled or residing within the reservation of the Indian child's tribe, the court, in the absence of good cause to the contrary, shall transfer such proceeding to the jurisdiction of the tribe, absent objection by either parent, upon the petition of either parent or the Indian custodian or the Indian child's tribe; provided, however, that such transfer shall be subject to declination by the tribal court of such tribe.

7. In any state court proceeding involving the foster care placement of or the termination of parental rights to an Indian child, the Indian custodian of the child and the Indian tribe shall have a right to intervene at any point in the proceeding.

8. The department may enter into an agreement, contract or compact with an Indian tribe or intertribal consortium for the provision of welfare related services by social services districts or by any tribe or tribes in connection with a tribal plan for direct tribal funding and administration of federal temporary assistance to needy families block grant monies.

SSL

Amended by Laws 1987, Ch. 462, eff. July 27, 1987; **amended** by Laws 1995, Ch. 83, § 223, eff. July 1, 1995; **amended** by Laws 1996, Ch. 309, § 277, eff. July 13, 1996; **amended** by Laws 1997, Ch. 436, § 1 Part B, § 5, eff. Aug. 20, 1997 **adding** new subdivision (8) to SSL § 39; **amended** by Laws 2004, Ch. 322, § 1, eff. Aug. 10, 2004, amending subd. (2); L. 2005, Ch. 3, sect; 34 (Part A), eff. Aug. 23, 2005..

§ 40. Real property; acquisition by purchase or appropriation.

Repealed by Laws 1977, Ch. 840 eff. Jan. 1, 1978.

§ 40. Real property; purchase or acquisition.

1. The commissioner, when an appropriation therefor has been made by the legislature, may acquire any real property which he may deem necessary for any departmental purpose by purchase or, in the manner provided in the eminent domain procedure law. Title to any such real property shall be taken in the name of and be vested in the people of the state of New York; provided, however, that no real property shall be so acquired by purchase unless the title thereto shall be approved by the attorney general.

2. Whenever real property is to be acquired pursuant to the eminent domain procedure law, the commissioner shall cause to be made by the state department of transportation an accurate acquisition map as so provided in such law.

3. On the approval of such map by the commissioner, the original tracing of such map shall be filed in the main office of the department pursuant to the eminent domain procedure law.

4. If the commissioner shall determine, prior to the filing of such map in the office of the clerk or register of the county, that changes, alterations or modifications of such map as filed in the office of the department should be made, he or she shall, subject to the provisions of article two of the eminent domain procedure law, if applicable, direct the preparation by the department of transportation of an amended map. On the approval of such amended map by the commissioner, it shall be filed in the main office of the department and the amended map shall thereupon in all respects and for all purposes supersede the map previously filed.

5. If the commissioner shall determine, prior to the filing of a copy of such acquisition map in the office of the county clerk or register as provided in paragraph three of subdivision (A) of section four hundred two of the eminent domain procedure law, that such map should be withdrawn, he or she may file a certificate of withdrawal in the offices of the department and of the department of law. Upon the filing of such certificate of withdrawal, the map to which it refers shall be cancelled, and all rights thereunder shall cease and determine.

6. The commissioner shall deliver to the attorney general a copy of such acquisition map, whereupon it shall be the duty of the attorney general to advise and certify to the commissioner the names of the owners of the property, easements, interests or rights described in the said acquisition map, including the owners of any right, title or interest therein, pursuant to the requirements of section four hundred three of the eminent domain procedure law.

7. If, at or after the vesting of title to such property in the people of the state of New York as provided for in the eminent domain procedure law, the commissioner shall deem it necessary to cause the removal of an owner or occupancy from any real property so acquired, he may cause such owner or occupant to be removed therefrom by proceeding in accordance with section four hundred five of the eminent domain procedure law. The proceeding shall be

brought in the name of the commissioner as agent of the state and the attorney general shall represent the petitioner in the proceedings. No execution shall issue for costs, if any, awarded against the state or the commissioner, but they shall be part of the costs of the acquisition of the real property and be paid in like manner. Proceedings may be brought separately against one or more of the owners or occupants of any such property, or one proceeding may be brought against all or several of the owners or occupants of any or all such property within the territorial jurisdiction of the same court, justice or judge; judgment shall be made for immediate removal of persons defaulting in appearance or in answering, or withdrawing their answers, if any, without awaiting the trial or decision of issues raised by contestants, if any.

8. Upon making any agreement provided for in section three hundred four of the eminent domain procedure law, the commissioner shall deliver to the comptroller such agreement and a certificate stating the amount due such owner or owners thereunder on account of such acquisition of his or their property and the amounts so fixed shall be paid out of the state treasury after audit by the comptroller from moneys appropriated for the acquisition of such real property, but not until there shall have appropriated for the acquisition of such real property, but not until there shall have been filed with the comptroller a certificate of the attorney general showing the person or persons claiming the amount so agreed upon to be legally entitled thereto.

9. Application for reimbursement of incidental expenses as provided in section seven hundred two of the eminent domain procedure law shall be made to the commissioner upon forms prescribed by him and shall be accompanied by such information and evidence as the commissioner may require. Upon approval of such application, the commissioner shall deliver a copy thereof to the comptroller together with a certificate stating the amount due thereof, and the amount so fixed shall be paid out of the state treasury after audit by the comptroller from monies appropriated for the acquisition of property under this section.

10. The commissioner, with the approval of the director of the budget, shall establish and may from time to time amend rules and regulations authorizing the payment of actual reasonable and necessary moving expenses of occupants of property acquired pursuant to this section; of actual direct losses of tangible personal property as a result of moving or discontinuing a business or farm operation, but not exceeding an amount equal to the reasonable expenses that would have been required to relocate such property, as determined by the commissioner; and actual reasonable expenses in searching for a replacement business or farm; or in hardship cases for the advance payment of such expenses and losses. For the purpose of making payment of such expenses and losses only the term "business" means any lawful activity conducted primarily for assisting in the purchase, sale, resale, manufacture, processing or marketing of products, commodities, personal property or services by the erection and maintenance of an outdoor advertising display or displays, whether or not such display or displays

are located on the premises on which any of the above activities are conducted. Such rules and regulations may further define the terms used in this subdivision. In lieu of such actual reasonable and necessary moving expenses, any such displaced owner or tenant of residential property may elect to accept a moving expense allowance, plus a dislocation allowance, determined in accordance with a schedule prepared by the commissioner and made a part of such rules and regulations. In lieu of such actual reasonable and necessary moving expenses, any such displaced owner or tenant of commercial property who relocates or discontinues his business or farm operation may elect to accept a fixed relocation payment in an amount equal to the average annual net earnings of the business or farm operation, except that such payment shall be not less than two thousand five hundred dollars nor more than ten thousand dollars. In the case of a business, no such fixed relocation payment shall be made unless the commissioner finds and determines that the business cannot be relocated without a substantial loss of its existing patronage, and that the business is not part of a commercial enterprise having at least one other establishment, which is not being acquired by the state or the United States, which is engaged in the same or similar business. In the case of a business which is to be discontinued but for which the findings and determinations set forth above cannot be made, the commissioner may prepare an estimate of what the actual reasonable and necessary moving expenses, exclusive of any storage charges, would be if the business were to be relocated and enter into an agreed settlement with the owner of such business for an amount not to exceed such estimate in lieu of such actual reasonable and necessary moving expenses. Application for payment under this subdivision shall be made to the commissioner upon forms prescribed by him and shall be accompanied by such information and evidence as the commissioner may require. Upon approval of such application, the commissioner shall deliver a copy thereof to the comptroller together with a certificate stating the amount due thereunder, and the amount so fixed shall be paid out of the state treasury after audit by the comptroller from moneys appropriated for the acquisition of property under this section. As used in this subdivision the term "commercial property" shall include property owned by an individual, family, partnership, corporation, association or a nonprofit organization and includes a farm operation. As used in this subdivision the term "business" means any lawful activity, except a farm operation, conducted primarily for the purchase, sale, lease and rental of personal and real property, and for the manufacture, processing, or marketing of products, commodities, or any other personal property; for the sale of services to the public; or by a nonprofit organization.

11.   Authorization is hereby given to the commissioner to make supplemental relocation payments, separately computed and stated, to displaced owners and tenants of residential property acquired pursuant to this section who are entitled thereto, as determined by him. The commissioner, with the approval of the director of the budget, may establish and from time to time amend rules and regulations providing for such supplemental relocation payments. Such rules and regulations may further define the terms used in this subdivision. In the case of

property acquired pursuant to this section which is improved by a dwelling actually owned and occupied by the displaced owner for not less than one hundred eighty days immediately prior to initiation of negotiations for the acquisition of such property, such payment to such owner shall not exceed fifteen thousand dollars. Such payment shall be the amount, if any, which, when added to the acquisition payment equals the average price, established by the commissioner on a class, group or individual basis, required to obtain a comparable replacement dwelling that is decent, safe and sanitary to accommodate the displaced owner, reasonably accessible to public services and places of employment and available on the private market, but in no event shall such payment exceed the difference between acquisition payment and the actual purchase price of the replacement dwelling. Such payment shall include an amount which will compensate such displaced owner for any increased interest costs which such person is required to pay for financing the acquisition of any such comparable replacement dwelling. Such amount shall be paid only if the dwelling acquired pursuant to this section was encumbered by a bona fide mortgage which was a valid lien on such dwelling for not less than one hundred eighty days prior to the initiation of negotiations for the acquisition of such dwelling. Such amount shall be equal to the excess in the aggregate interest and other debt service costs of that amount f the principal of the mortgage on the replacement dwelling which is equal to the unpaid balance of the mortgage on the acquired dwelling, over the remainder term of the mortgage on the acquired dwelling, reduced to discounted present value. The discount rate shall be the prevailing interest rate paid on savings deposits by commercial banks in the general area in which the replacement dwelling is located. Any such mortgage interest differential payment shall, notwithstanding the provisions of section twenty-six-b of the general construction law, be in lieu of and in full satisfaction of the requirements of such section. Such payment shall include reasonable expenses incurred by such displaced owner for evidence of title, recording fees and other closing costs incident to the purchase of the replacement dwelling, but not including prepaid expenses. Such payment shall be made only to a displaced owner who purchases and occupies a replacement dwelling which is decent, safe and sanitary within one year subsequent to the date on which he is required to move from the dwelling acquired pursuant to this section or the date on which he receives from the state final payment of all costs of the acquired dwelling, whichever occurs later, except advance payment of such amount may be made in hardship cases. In the case of property acquired pursuant to this section from which an individual or family, not otherwise eligible to receive a payment pursuant to the above provisions of this subdivision, is displaced from any dwelling thereon which has been actually and lawfully occupied by such individual or family for not less than ninety days immediately prior to the initiation of negotiations for the acquisition of such property, such payment to such individual or family shall not exceed four thousand dollars. Such payment shall be the amount which is necessary to enable such individual or family to lease or rent for a period not to exceed four years, a decent, safe, and sanitary dwelling of standards adequate to accommodate such individual or family in areas not generally less desirable in regard to public utilities and public and commercial facilities and reasonably accessible to his place of employment, but shall not exceed four thousand dollars, or to make the down payment, including reasonable expenses incurred by such individual or family for evidence of title, recording fees, and other closing costs incident to the purchase of the replacement dwelling, but not including prepaid expenses, on the purchase of a decent, safe and sanitary dwelling of standards adequate to accommodate such individual or family in areas not generally less desirable in regard to public utilities and public and commercial facilities, but shall not exceed four thousand dollars, except if such amount exceeds two thousand dollars, such person must equally match any such amount in excess of two thousand dollars, in making the down payment. Such payments may be made in installments as determined by the commissioner. Application for payment under this subdivision shall be made to the commissioner upon forms prescribed by him and shall be accompanied by such information and evidence as the commissioner may require. Upon approval of such application, the commissioner shall deliver a copy thereof to the comptroller, together with a certificate stating the amount due thereunder, and the amount so fixed shall be paid out of the state treasury after audit by the comptroller from moneys appropriated for acquisition of property under this section.

12.   The owner of any real property so acquired may present to the court of claims, pursuant to subdivision (A) of section five hundred three of the eminent domain procedure law, a claim for the value of such property and for other legal damages as provided by law for the filing of claims with the court of claims. Awards and judgments of the court of claims shall be paid in the same manner as awards and judgments of that court for the acquisition of lands generally and shall be paid out of the state treasury after audit by the comptroller from moneys appropriated for the acquisition of such real property.

13.   Expenses incurred in the acquisition of the property, including the cost of title searches, service and publication of notices, and expenses incurred in proceedings for the removal of owners or occupants, shall be deemed to be part of the cost of the acquisition of such real property and shall be paid accordingly out of any moneys appropriated for the acquisition of such property.

14.   If the commissioner shall determine subsequent to the acquisition of a temporary easement in any real property that the purposes for which such easement right was acquired have been accomplished and that the exercise of such easement is no longer necessary, he shall make his certificate that the exercise of such easement is no longer necessary and that such easement right is therefore terminated, released and extinguished. The commissioner shall cause such certificate to be filed in the office of the department of state and upon such filing all rights acquired by the state in such property shall cease and determine. The commissioner shall cause a certified copy of such certificate as so filed in the office of the department of state to be mailed to the owner of the property affected, as certified by the attorney general, if the place of residence of such

owner is known or can be ascertained by a reasonable effort and such commissioner shall cause a further certified copy of such certificate to be filed in the office of the recording officer of each county in which the property affected or any part thereof is situated. On the filing of such certified copy of such certificate with such recording officer, it shall be his duty to record the same in his office in the books used for recording deeds and to index the same against the name of the people of the state of New York as grantor.

Added by Laws 1977, Ch. 840, eff. Jan. 1, 1978; **amended** by Laws 1996, Ch. 394, § 19, eff. July 30, 1996, and applicable to all appropriation maps filed after the effective date.

§ 41. Civil actions against officers and employees of the department; indemnification.

Added by Laws 1973, Ch. 701. Expired Mar. 31, 1974.

SSL

ARTICLE 2–A
DIVISION OF LOCAL INCOME MAINTENANCE AND MEDICAL ASSISTANCE ADMINISTRATION

———

Article 2-A, which created the division of local income maintenance and medical assistance administration, expired by its own terms March 31, 1974, pursuant to Laws 1973, Ch. 703, § 3.

ARTICLE 2-A

SHELTER AND SUPPORTED HOUSING PROGRAMS

——

SUMMARY OF ARTICLE

TITLE 1—HOMELESS HOUSING AND ASSISTANCE PROGRAM

§ 41. Legislative findings and purpose.

The legislature hereby finds that large numbers of people in communities across our state are unable to secure housing for themselves and are living in the streets or in emergency shelters, despite current efforts by public and private agencies to provide adequate housing for those in need; that the present condition is contrary to the public interest and threatens the health, safety, welfare, comfort and security of the people of the state; that communities across the state must each do their share to assist the homeless; and that the public interest requires that state financial assistance be provided to construct or rehabilitate housing units for the homeless in communities throughout New York state and to explore alternative means of meeting their long-term housing needs, consistent with the fiscal constraints faced by New York state. The legislature, therefore, finds that a special fund should be established, to fund capital programs sponsored by not-for-profit corporations, charitable organizations, wholly owned subsidiaries of not-for-profit corporations or of charitable organizations, public corporations and municipalities that will expand and improve the supply of shelter and other housing arrangements for homeless persons.

Amended by Laws 1986, Ch. 458, eff. July 21, 1986.

§ 42.   Definitions.

As used in this article, the following terms shall have the following meanings unless the context clearly requires otherwise:

1.   "Homeless project" shall mean a specific facility, including lands, buildings and improvements acquired, constructed, renovated or rehabilitated and operated by a not-for-profit corporation, charitable organization, wholly owned subsidiary of a not-for-profit corporation or of a charitable organization, public corporation or a municipality to increase the availability of housing for homeless persons, which may include other non-housing services such as but not limited to dining, recreational, sanitary, social, medical and mental health services as may be deemed by the commissioner to be essential to such a project.

2.   "Homeless person" shall mean an undomiciled person who is unable to secure permanent and stable housing without special assistance, as determined by the commissioner.

3.   "Project cost" shall mean the cost of any or all undertakings necessary for planning, financing, land acquisition, demolition, construction, rehabilitation, equipment and site development.

4.   "Not-for-profit corporation" and "charitable organization" shall mean entities established pursuant to the not-for-profit corporation law or otherwise established pursuant to law.

5.   "Public corporation" shall mean a municipal corporation, a district corporation, or a public benefit corporation.

Amended by Laws 1986, Ch. 458, eff. July 21, 1986.

§ 43.   Homeless housing and assistance contracts.

1.   Within the limits of funds available in the homeless housing and assistance fund, the commissioner is hereby authorized to enter into contracts with municipalities to provide state financial assistance for the project costs attributable to the establishment of homeless housing projects. The municipalities that enter into contracts with the commissioner shall undertake the establishment of the homeless housing project or shall contract with a not-for-profit corporation or charitable organization to undertake the project, pursuant to this article.

2.   Subject to the approval of the director of the budget, the commissioner is hereby authorized to enter into contracts with not-for-profit corporations or subsidiaries thereof, public corporations or charitable organizations or subsidiaries thereof to provide state financial assistance for the project costs attributable to the establishment of homeless projects.

3.   The state financial assistance shall be in the form of grants, loans or loan guarantees, as the commissioner may determine provided, however, that financial assistance to a for-profit subsidiary of a not-for-profit corporation or of a charitable organization must be in the form of a loan or loan guarantee. Any loan

SSL

to a for-profit subsidiary shall be repaid under such terms as will protect the financial viability of the project. Subject to the approval of the division of the budget, the commissioner may contract with other state agencies, public benefit corporation's or private institutions to administer a loan or loan guarantee program pursuant to regulations to be promulgated by the commissioner.

4.   The commissioner shall require that, in order to receive funds pursuant to this article, the municipality, not-for-profit corporation or subsidiary thereof, public corporation or charitable organization or subsidiary thereof must submit an operating plan. Such plan shall include:

(a)   the manner in which the operating expenses of the project shall be met;

(b)   the services that will be provided to homeless persons, including procedures for intake, referral and outreach;

(c)   the responsibilities of the municipality and social services district for the operation of the project;

(d)   the specific population that will be served by the project and how the project will address the population's special needs;

(e)   the category of facility proposed to be established; and

(f)   evidence demonstrating that such project complies or will comply with existing local, state and federal laws and regulations.

5.   The commissioner may use up to one percent of the appropriation for any fiscal year to pay for technical assistance in support of project development and operation. Technical assistance may include assistance with general project development and operation, support services development, architecture and engineering, legal services and financial services and may be provided by individuals and not-for-profit or business corporations. The providers of technical assistance shall be chosen by the department based on such information as the department shall require in a request for proposals or in any other competitive process which satisfies the provisions of the state finance law.

6.   Prior to entering into a contract for the establishment and operation of a homeless project pursuant to this section, the commissioner shall determine that the not-for-profit corporation or subsidiary thereof, public corporation or charitable organization or subsidiary thereof that proposes to undertake the homeless project is a bona fide organization which shall have demonstrated by its past and current activities that it has the ability to maintain, manage or operate homeless projects, that the organization is financially responsible, that the proposed project is financially viable and that the project plan has been determined to be appropriate for the needs of the homeless in the relevant community.

7.   Every contract entered into for the establishment and operation of a homeless project pursuant to this article shall contain a provision that in the event the property which is the subject of such contract ceases to be used as a homeless

project during a seven-year period commencing with the date of the commissioner's written approval of occupancy of the homeless project, or such longer period of time as may be established in the contract, or in case of any other substantial violation, the commissioner may terminate the contract and may require the repayment of any moneys previously advanced to the municipality, not-for-profit corporation or subsidiary thereof, public corporation or charitable organization or subsidiary thereof pursuant to the terms of such contract. Where the municipality has entered into a contract with a not-for-profit corporation or subsidiary thereof, public corporation or charitable organization or subsidiary thereof, the commissioner may, pursuant to this subdivision, require that the municipality terminate the contract with such corporation. Any money repaid pursuant to this subdivision shall be returned to the homeless housing and assistance fund.

8. Each contract entered into for the establishment and operation of a homeless project pursuant to this article shall be subject to the approval of the director of the budget and shall provide for payment to the municipality, not-for-profit corporation or subsidiary thereof, public corporation or charitable organization or subsidiary thereof for the project costs related to the homeless project to be established by it, pursuant to a payment schedule. The full amount of the contract, or any appropriate portion thereof, as determined by the commissioner and subject to the approval of the director of the budget, shall be available for payment at any time on or after the effective date of the contract.

9. Notwithstanding any other provision of this article, the commissioner may, subject to the approval of the director of the budget, enter into contracts to provide financial assistance for other than project costs where such financial assistance can be demonstrated to be necessary; provided, however, that no more than twenty-five per centum of the total amount appropriated for the purposes of this article in any fiscal year shall be allocated in contracts for other than project costs. In determining whether financial assistance for other than project costs is necessary, the commissioner shall consider the proposed project's plan for meeting operating expenses, the efforts made by the contracting organizations to secure alternative sources of funding for other than project costs, and such other factors as the commissioner shall deem appropriate.

10. Notwithstanding any other provision of this article, the state shall not, in the exercise of its responsibilities pursuant to this article, assume the legal title to projects developed pursuant to this article.

11. The municipality, not-for-profit corporation or subsidiary thereof, public corporation or charitable organization or subsidiary thereof seeking financial assistance pursuant to this article shall, within thirty days of its application for such assistance, notify the local planning board, as defined by section twenty-seven of the general city law, section two hundred seventy-one of the town law, section 7–718 of the village law, or section eighty-four of the charter of the city of New York, appropriate for the geographic area in which the proposed homeless project would be located, and shall provide such board with information regarding the proposed homeless project.

SSL

Amended by Laws 1986, Ch. 458, eff. July 21, 1986.

§ 44. General and administrative provisions.

1. The department, in consultation with the division of housing and community renewal, the office of mental health and other appropriate agencies, shall issue and promulgate rules and regulations for the administration of this article. The rules and regulations shall provide that state financial assistance pursuant to this article will not be available unless an application has been filed by the municipality, not-for-profit corporation or subsidiary thereof, public corporation or charitable organization or subsidiary thereof with the department pursuant to a request for proposals issued by the commissioner. The rules and regulations shall include provisions concerning eligibility of municipalities and contracting not-for-profit corporations or subsidiaries thereof, public corporations and charitable organizations or subsidiaries thereof for state financial assistance; the form of the applications for contracts; funding criteria and the funding determination process; the form of the contracts; supervision and evaluation of the contracting municipalities or corporations; reporting, budgeting and record-keeping requirements; provisions for modification, termination, extension and renewal of contracts; and such other matters not inconsistent with the purposes and provisions of this article as the commissioner shall deem necessary, proper or appropriate.

2. The commissioner may provide that preference be given to contract applications that (a) involve other sources of funds (municipal, federal or any source other than the state), in-kind contributions made by such sources, or involve projects receiving state financial assistance pursuant to chapters three hundred thirty-eight, three hundred thirty-nine and five hundred forty-nine of the laws of nineteen hundred eighty-two, in order to maximize the effect of state financial assistance or (b) involve innovative and cost-effective homeless projects that may help resolve the long-term problems of the homeless or (c) involve the rehabilitation of existing structures.

3. The commissioner shall, in consultation with the commissioner of housing and community renewal, the commissioner of mental health and the commissioners of other appropriate agencies, evaluate the need for homeless projects in various areas of the state and among various populations, including, but not limited to, homeless men, women, families and runaway youth, and shall allocate funds, to the extent practicable, to meet these needs; provided, however, that no more than fifty per centum of the total amount appropriated pursuant to this article in any fiscal year shall be allocated to contracts with any single municipality.

4. The department shall provide for the review, at periodic intervals, of the performance of the municipalities, not-for-profit corporations or subsidiaries thereof, public corporations and charitable organizations or subsidiaries thereof receiving financial assistance pursuant to this article. Such review shall, among other things, be for the purposes of ascertaining conformity to contractual provisions, the financial integrity and efficiency of the organizations and the

evaluation of the project. Contracts entered into pursuant to this article may be terminated by the commissioner upon a finding of substantial nonperformance or other breach by the organization of its obligations under its contract with the municipality.

5.   The commissioner shall require that all homeless projects that received financial assistance pursuant to this article shall comply with all regulations applicable to projects of this type promulgated by the department, by the division of housing and community renewal and other municipal, state and federal regulations and laws. The commissioner may terminate any contract upon a finding that a substantial violation of such regulations or laws has remained uncorrected for a substantial period of time.

6.   In order to further the purposes of this article, social services districts shall, in accordance with regulations promulgated by the department, undertake such efforts as may be necessary and practicable to assist homeless persons apply for and obtain appropriate governmental assistance.

7.   On or before February first, nineteen hundred eighty-four and on or before February first of each year thereafter in which contracts under this section are in force, the commissioner shall submit to the governor, the temporary president of the senate and the speaker of the assembly a report detailing progress and evaluating results, to date, of the program.

8.   Notwithstanding the provisions of any general or special law, the director of the budget is authorized to transfer to the homeless housing and assistance account funds otherwise appropriated or reappropriated to the department of social services for the fiscal years beginning on and after April one, nineteen hundred ninety, in an amount or amounts the director of the budget determines to be necessary to carry out the provisions of the homeless housing and assistance program.

Amended by Laws 1986, Ch. 458, eff. July 21, 1986; **amended** by Laws 1990, Ch. 215, § 7, eff. June 8, 1990.

TITLE 2—SINGLE ROOM OCCUPANCY SUPPORT SERVICES PROGRAM

SSL

§ 45.   Definitions.

As used in this title, the following terms shall have the following meanings unless the context clearly requires otherwise:

1. "Eligible cost" shall mean the cost to deliver one or more services to eligible residents to assist such residents to live independently, including information and referral, resident services coordination, crisis intervention, and other like services. Eligible cost shall not include: those costs associated with maintenance and operation of physical plant; those costs associated with support services or maintenance provided or financially assisted by other state or municipal programs; or those costs associated with support services provided in residential care programs licensed by a state department or agency. When two or more eligible projects exist in the same geographic area, services shall be provided in common among such projects whenever feasible.

2. "Eligible applicant" shall mean a not-for-profit corporation or charitable organization which operates single room occupancy units qualifying as an eligible project.

3. "Eligible resident" shall mean a person residing in a single room occupancy unit who is in need of services to live independently. In the event that the income of such resident exceeds one hundred fifty percent of the poverty level, the eligible project may charge a service fee to the eligible resident not to exceed fifty percent of the total cost of services provided pursuant to this title in such project divided by the number of eligible residents in the project.

4. "Eligible project" shall mean those single room occupancy units occupied by eligible residents, within a building or portion thereof which is operated by an eligible applicant.

5. "Single room occupancy unit" shall mean a private room providing living and sleeping space for no more than two persons with access to bathing and toilet facilities, within a building or portion thereof which is operated by an eligible applicant; provided, however, that in no event shall such unit be located in:

(a) hotels, motels or other dwellings occupied transiently;

(b) shelters for families or adults, as defined by the commissioner;

(c) residential facilities or institutions which are required to be licensed by any state agency;

(d) college or school dormitories;

(e) clubhouses;

(f) housing intended for use primarily or exclusively by the employees of a single company or institution; or

(g) convents or monasteries.

The unit itself may contain a kitchen and/or a bathroom.

6. "In-kind expenditures" shall mean the cash value of eligible costs that are not reimbursed under this title and may include but not be limited to materials, equipment, space or paid or volunteer staff.

Added by Laws 1987, Ch. 765, eff. Aug. 7, 1987; **amended** by Laws 1994, Ch. 349, § 1, eff. July 20, 1994.

§ 45-a.　Single room occupancy support services program.

There is hereby established under the administration of the commissioner a single room occupancy support services program, to provide financial assistance, subject to limitations stated in appropriations therefor, in the form of grants, to eligible applicants for eligible costs of services to assist eligible residents of single room occupancy units to live independently. The commissioner, subject to the approval of the director of the budget and within amounts appropriated therefor, shall request proposals from local social services districts for funds to support grants made pursuant to this title. Copies of such requests for proposals shall be simultaneously distributed to eligible applicants known to the commissioner and the availability of such proposals shall be publicized by the department. Local social services districts will be chosen competitively based upon such proposals for funding. Criteria to be used by the commissioner in awarding funding among local social services districts shall include but not be limited to the anticipated need for single room occupancy units within each district; the ability of the local social services district to properly supervise the single room occupancy support services program; and the appropriateness of the support services for the population to be served.

Added by Laws 1987, Ch. 765, eff. Aug. 7, 1987.

§ 45-b.　Notice of funding availability; contracts.

A local social services district that receives funding pursuant to this title shall issue notices of funding availability together with application forms for financial assistance under this title, provided that such notices, application forms and competitive award procedures are approved in advance by the department. When such applications are approved, the local social services official is authorized to enter into contracts with eligible applicants to provide financial assistance in the form of grants for eligible costs.

Added by Laws 1987, Ch. 765, eff. Aug. 7, 1987.

§ 45-c.　Direct application by eligible applicants.

Upon receipt of a copy of the request for proposals issued pursuant to section forty-five-a of this title, an eligible applicant may notify the local social services district in which its eligible project is located of its desire to participate in the single room occupancy support services program. In the event that the local social services district does not submit a proposal pursuant to section forty-five-a of this title, such eligible applicant that has notified the local social services district of its desire to participate may submit an application directly to the commissioner for financial assistance under this title. Criteria to be used by the commissioner

SSL

in awarding funding directly to such eligible applicants shall include but not be limited to the anticipated need for single room occupancy units within the district where the eligible project is located, and the appropriateness of the support services for the population to be served. Before directly awarding any funding to eligible applicants, the commissioner shall consult with the local social services district where the eligible project is located regarding the need for single room occupancy units within such district, the ability of the eligible project to provide single room occupancy services and any other factors which are necessary to effectively evaluate direct application by eligible projects. When such applications are approved, the commissioner, within the amounts appropriated under this title, and subject to the limitations set forth in this section and section forty-five-d of this title, is authorized to enter into contracts with eligible applicants, to provide financial assistance in the form of grants for eligible costs.

　　　Added by Laws 1987, Ch. 765, eff. Aug. 7, 1987.

§ 45-d.　Operating plans.

　　1.　Contracts with not-for-profit corporations and charitable organizations shall be approved by the social services district, or the commissioner in the case of direct applications, in accordance with an operational plan submitted pursuant to the provisions of subdivision two of this section.

　　2.　The social services district, or the commissioner in the case of direct applications, shall require that, in order to receive funds pursuant to this title, the not-for-profit corporation or charitable organization must submit an operating plan. Preference shall be given to plans which demonstrate that existing state, federal, local and private dollars will be utilized to the fullest extent possible to fund the service costs of the project. Such plans shall include but not be limited to:

　　(a)　the manner in which the capital expenses of the project shall be met;

　　(b)　the services that will be provided to the residents of the project;

　　(c)　the specific population that will be served by the project and how the project will address the population's special needs;

　　(d)　a description of the manner in which coordination with other federal, state, local and private funding sources shall be achieved;

　　(e)　the cost per month per eligible resident of the services to be provided; and

　　(f)　evidence demonstrating that such project complies or will comply with existing local, state and federal laws and regulations.

　　3.　Prior to entering into a contract pursuant to this title, the social services district, or the commissioner in the case of direct applications, shall determine that the not-for-profit corporation or charitable organization submitting such plan is a bona fide organization which shall have demonstrated by its past and current activities that it has the ability to maintain, manage or operate such project, that the organization is financially responsible, that the proposed project is financially viable and that the project has been determined to be appropriate for the needs of the homeless in the relevant community.

Added by Laws 1987, Ch. 765, eff. Aug. 7, 1987.

§ 45-e. Reimbursement.

Expenditures made by a social services district for grants made pursuant to this title shall be reimbursed by the state at the rate of fifty per centum, after first deducting therefrom any federal funds properly received or to be received on account thereof; provided, however, that in lieu of local financial participation required by this section, the commissioner may permit a social services district to substitute actual or in-kind expenditures incurred by eligible applicants in the operation of eligible projects if the commissioner determines that:

(a)   local social services district financial participation is unavailable in all or a portion of such expenditures although such district financial participation in the single room occupancy support services program equals or exceeds such financial participation in the previous program year; and

(b)   such eligible projects require financial assistance under this title to ensure the financial viability of supportive services programs.

Actual or in-kind expenditures made by an eligible applicant receiving assistance pursuant to section forty-five-c of this title shall be reimbursed by the state at the rate of fifty per centum after first deducting therefrom any federal funds properly received or to be received on account thereof.

Added by Laws 1987, Ch. 765, eff. Aug. 7, 1987.

§ 45-f. Administration.

1.   The commissioner shall promulgate rules and regulations for the administration of this title. Such rules and regulations shall include but not be limited to provisions concerning eligibility of not-for-profit corporations and charitable organizations for single room occupancy support project assistance, funding criteria and the funding determination process, supervision and evaluation of the contracting corporations and organizations and any other matters consistent with the purposes of this title.

2.   The social services district, or the commissioner in the case of direct applications, shall provide for the review, at periodic intervals, of the performance of the not-for-profit corporations and charitable organizations receiving financial assistance pursuant to this title. Such review shall, among other things, be for the purpose of ascertaining conformity to contractual provisions, the financial integrity and efficiency of the organizations and the evaluation of the project. Contracts entered into pursuant to this title may be terminated by the social

services district, or the commissioner in the case of direct applications, upon a finding of substantial nonperformance or other breach by the corporation or organization of its obligations under its contract.

3.   In order to further the purposes of this article, social services districts shall, in accordance with regulations promulgated by the department, undertake such efforts as may be necessary and practicable to assist eligible residents to apply for and obtain appropriate governmental assistance.

4.   The department, subject to the approval of the director of the budget, may retain up to five percent of the total amount appropriated pursuant to this title in any fiscal year for administrative purposes.

Added by Laws 1987, Ch. 765, eff. Aug. 7, 1987.

§ 45-g.   Annual report.

Beginning October first, nineteen hundred eighty-eight, and each year thereafter, the commissioner shall report to the governor and legislature on the success of the single room occupancy support services program in assisting eligible residents to live independently.

Added by Laws 1987, Ch. 765, eff. Aug. 7, 1987.

TITLE 3—HOUSING DEMONSTRATION PROGRAM

[*Repealed, eff. June 30, 1990, by Laws 1987, Ch. 796, § 6, eff. Aug. 7, 1987.*]

TITLE 4—HOMELESSNESS INTERVENTION PROGRAM

§ 48.   Legislative intent.

The legislature finds that there are a significant number of homeless and at-risk households living in temporary and unstable conditions which would benefit from the provision of a comprehensive assistance program. The legislature further finds that the current system of providing services to such households would be improved by ensuring that a broad range of flexible, individualized assistance is available to stabilize households and to better meet divergent local needs. The legislature, therefore, finds that state financial assistance should be made available for the purpose of providing supportive services designed to stabilize households by attempting to avoid homelessness and, for those who are currently homeless, by facilitating the transition form homelessness to permanent housing.

Added by Laws 1987, Ch. 777, eff. Jan. 1, 1988; **amended** by Laws 1998, Ch. 204, § 1, eff. July 7, 1998.

§ 49. Definitions.

For the purposes of this title, the following terms shall have the following meanings:

1. "Homeless" shall mean an undomiciled household which is unable to secure permanent and habitable housing without special assistance, as determined by the commissioner, including but not limited to households temporarily residing in emergency shelters, transitional facilities, hotels/motels, or substandard conditions.

2. "Household" shall mean a single individual or family, including couples without dependent children who, or which, are eligible to receive public assistance.

3. "Eligible applicant" shall mean local social services districts or not-for-profit corporations serving homeless and at-risk households.

4. "At-risk" shall mean a household threatened with homelessness and those with a history of frequent moves.

5. "Homelessness intervention services" shall mean services which are designed to stabilize at-risk and homeless households by avoiding homelessness or assisting households to secure permanent and habitable housing. Such services may include, but need not be limited to the following:

(a) services to resolve conflicts between landlords and tenants and to facilitate fair and workable solutions;

(b) legal services to households threatened with the loss of their homes through eviction, harassment or other means;

(c) tenant activities to educate households in the areas of tenant Rights and responsibilities, and to organize tenants to remedy housing problems such as code violations, landlord abandonment and harassment;

(d) benefits/entitlements advocacy to ensure that households are receiving all federal, state and local benefits to which they are entitled, such as temporary assistance to needy families, safety net assistance, food stamps, supplemental security income, rent security deposits, furniture and household moving expenses;

(e) relocation assistance which provides for the identification of and referral to permanent and habitable housing, transportation services, landlord/tenant lease negotiation services and assistance in establishing utility services; and

(f) the provision of or referral to support services designed to stabilize households in permanent and habitable housing including services related to substance abuse, domestic violence, housekeeping, budgeting, education, day care, employment, parenting, mental health, physical health, and such other services deemed necessary by the office of temporary and disability assistance.

SSL

Service provided to homeless households pursuant to this paragraph must be provided for a period of at least six months beginning the first day of the month following the month in which such household secured permanent housing.

    Added by Laws 1987, Ch. 777, eff. Jan. 1, 1988; **amended** by Laws 1997, Ch. 436, § 1 Part B, § 62, eff. Aug. 20, 1997; **amended** by Laws 1998, Ch. 204, § 1, eff. July 7, 1998.

§ 50.   Homeless intervention contracts. *

1.   The commissioner shall, within the amounts appropriated therefor, select through a competitive request-for-proposal process, local social services districts and not-for-profit corporations serving homeless and at-risk households to provide homelessness intervention services to homeless and at-risk households. In order to ensure that contracts are awarded and services provided in geographic areas of the state to homeless and at risk households in greatest need, and to maximize the effect of state funds, the commissioner shall, prior to entering into a contract with an eligible applicant pursuant to this section, consider the extent to which existing homelessness intervention services are available in the local social services district and the extent to which these services should be expanded.

2.   The commissioner shall require eligible applicants to submit operating plans in order to receive funding pursuant to this article. Such plans shall include:

(a)   a description of the homeless intervention services to be provided, including procedures for intake, referral, outreach, the provision of services, follow-up and anticipated outcomes;

(b)   the specific population that will be served and how the services provided will address the population's special needs;

(c)   a description of the manner in which coordination with other federal, state, local and privately funded services will be achieved; and

(d)   a description of how the services will be designed to assist households transition from a reliance on outside interventions and move toward housing stability and economic self reliance.

3.   Prior to entering into a contract pursuant to this section, the commissioner shall determine that the eligible applicant is a bona fide organization which shall have demonstrated by its past and current activities that it has the ability to provide such services, that the organization is financially responsible and that the operating plan is appropriate for the needs of households to be served.

   * **Editor's Note**: So in original. Should probably be "Homelessness intervention contracts."

    Added by Laws 1987, Ch. 777, eff. Jan. 1, 1988; **amended** by Laws 1998, Ch. 204, § 1, eff. July 7, 1998.

§ 51.   Regulations.

The office of temporary and disability assistance shall, in consultation with other agencies deemed appropriate by the commissioner, promulgate such rules and regulations as are necessary to carry out the provisions of this article.

Added by Laws 1987, Ch. 777, eff. Jan. 1, 1988; **amended** by Laws 1998, Ch. 204, § 1, eff. July 7, 1998.

§ 52.   Reports.

On or before February first, nineteen hundred eighty-nine and on or before February first of each year thereafter in which contracts under this article are in force, the commissioner shall submit to the governor, the temporary president of the senate and the speaker of the assembly a report detailing progress and evaluating results, to date, of the program. Such report shall include, but not be limited to a review of the basis for selection of eligible applicants; the number of persons served; a review of the efforts made to prevent homelessness and to provide permanent housing for homeless households, including a list of the number of persons and families, by project, who received services; an identification of the estimated savings and costs of the program to the state and localities; and an evaluation of continuing needs for homelessness intervention services.

Added by Laws 1987, Ch. 777, eff. Jan. 1, 1988; **amended** by Laws 1998, Ch. 204, § 1, eff. July 7, 1998.

ARTICLE 3

LOCAL PUBLIC WELFARE ORGANIZATION; POWERS AND DUTIES

———

SUMMARY OF ARTICLE

* Dissolution of city and town social services districts, other than a city social services district containing one or more counties.

** There is no Title 7-A.

§ 1. Any inconsistent provision of law, general, special, or local, notwithstanding, each city and town which is a social services district, except any city social services district containing one or more countries, shall be dissolved as a social services district at midnight on the thirty-first day of December, nineteen hundred seventy-two, and from and after the first day of January, nineteen hundred seventy-three each such city and town shall form and be part of the social services district of the county in which it is located.

§ 2. From and after the first day of January, nineteen hundred seventy-three, all responsiblity for all categories of public assistance and care, including administration thereof, theretofore borne by the social services district or districts dissolved by section one of this act shall devolve upon the appropriate county social services district which shall continue to have responsiblity for public assistance and care in the territory included in such county social services district prior to such date; provided, however, that in each of the five years next succeeding dissolution, there shall be paid to the appropriate county social services district in equal quarterly installments commencing on March thirty-first, nineteen hundred seventy-three by a city or town dissolved as a social services district by this act, and there shall be allocated to and charged against and county taxes levied therefor in the territory formerly comprising the county district, a percentage of an amount representing the total cost, including attributable administrative costs but exclusive of state or federal reimbursement, of the public assistance and care which shall have been furnished, respectively, to local charges in the city or town district or in the territory then comprising the county district in the year nineteen hundred seventy-two, as follows: eighty percent of such amount in nineteen hundred seventy-three, sixty percent in nineteen hundred seventy-four, forty percent in nineteen hundred seventy-five, twenty-five percent in nineteen hundred seventy-six and ten percent in nineteen hundred seventy-seven. In each of the five years next succeeding dissolution, the balance of the cost, including attributable administrative costs but exclusive of state or federal reimbursement, of public assistance and care furnished by the county social services district to local charges found in the city or town and in the territory formerly comprising the county district, which is not offset by the payments or charges required by this section, shall be allocated to and county taxes levied therefor in the entire county social services district, including the territory of the dissolved district or districts. In the year nineteen seventy-eight and thereafter all the costs attributable to the former city or town district and the territory formerly comprising the county district shall be charged to and all the taxes therefor shall be levied in the entire county social services district. If the rate of federal or state reimbursement to social services districts should increase in any of the five years next succeeding dissolution, the cost applicable in calculating the city's or town's obligation to the county and the amount allocated to and charged against the territory formerly comprising the county district for any such year shall be proportionately reduced.

§ 3. All indebtedness and any contractual or other liabilities, and interest thereon, including all costs of public assistance and care and attributable administrative costs, incurred by any city social services district and any town social services district prior to the dissolution date of such district, as specified in section one of this act, shall be a charge upon and shall be paid by the city or town in which such dissolved district is located, likewise all indebtedness and any contractual or other liabilities, and interest thereon, including all costs of public assistance and care and attributable administrative costs, incurred by the county social district prior to December thirty-first, nineteen hundred seventy-two, shall be a charge upon and county taxes shall be levied therefor, in the territory formerly comprising the county social services district, provided, however, that the rights and obligations of an executory contract necessary for the implementation of a city or town district's duties shall be assumed by the county district from and after the date of such dissolution. The governing legislative body of the municipality responsible for a dissolved district shall have the authority, in the manner provided by law, to adopt and amend local laws, ordinances or resolutions imposing in such city or town taxes which shall be used to pay any and all obligation specified in this section.

Notwithstanding the preceding paragraph of this section or any inconsistent provisions of any general, special or local law, on or after the effective date of this act, no city or town social services district affected by this act shall make any executory contract, necessary for the implementation of such district's duties, which terms of performance cannot be fully executed prior to midnight on the thirty-first day of December, nineteen hundred seventy-two.

§ 4. For the purposes of enabling the county social services district to fulfill its obligations under section two of this act, the district or districts to be dissolved shall furnish the county social services district, on or before September first, nineteen hundred seventy-two with estimates of the cost of public assistance and care and administration thereof which such district will incur in that year, or the county social services districts may make such estimates, provided, however, that the actual amount of such costs, as verified by the state department of social services, shall serve as the basis for determining the amounts to be paid by the city or town in which such district was located or charged against the county social services district pursuant to the formula in said section two.

§ 5. Notwithstanding any inconsistent provisions of any general, special or local law, any city or town dissolved as a social services district by this act, and all departments, boards, agencies, and other instrumentalities thereof, may lease or grant, transfer and convey to the country in which it is located, with or without consideration or for such consideration mutually agreed upon, and such county may lease or accept and receive any real or personal property or assigned asset, or any interest therein owned by such city or town or such departments, boards, agencies, or other instrumentalities thereof, and utilized or held in connection with the administration of public assistance and care in such city or town, and all such leases, grants, transfers, and conveyances heretofore made are hereby legalized, validated, ratified, and confirmed. The personnel of a dissolved city or town social services district may be transferred by the governing body of the appropriate county to the county district.

Nothing contained herein shall prevent such city or town, through its governing body, and such county social services district from agreeing upon compensation, if any, to be paid by such city or town to such county social services district for capital projects financed by such county directly relating to social services programs, and toward which such city or town had not contributed. In the event of failure to agree thereupon, the matter may be arbitrated in accordance with section six hereof.

§ 6. 1. Upon the dissolution of a city or town social services district and in the event mutual agreement of a value for real property to be leased or transferred as provided in section five of this act cannot be had, such city or town or the county in which it is located may, at its option, notify the chief executive officer of such city, town or county, as the case may be, of its intent to require an appraisal of the market value or value of a lease of real property owned by it and utilized or held in connection with the administration of public assistance and care in such municipality. Such notification shall also designate the name of a competent, disinterested appraiser.

2. Within twenty days of receipt of such notice, the municipality receiving such notice also designate the name of a second competent, disinterested appraiser.

3. The two appraisers so designated shall within fifteen days of the service of the notice provided in subdivision two, designate a competent and disinterested umpire and failing to do so upon the request of either appraiser theretofore designated, such umpire shall be selected by a judge of the supreme court in the county in which the property is located.

4. The appraisers shall then appraise the market value of the property to be transferred or a reasonable value of the lease thereof in the case of property to be leased to a county.

5. Failing to agree on a value, the appraisers shall each submit to the umpire their respective appraisals and the reasons therefor. Such umpire shall then determine the reasonable value based upon the report of the appraisers as well as other facts and circumstances which he deems relevant and such determination shall be binding on the respective parties.

§ 7. Any inconsistent provision of law, general, special or local, notwithstanding, any contractual obligation heretofore entered into by a city social service district under a lease and sublease with the New York state housing finance agency for the construction, reconstruction, rehabilitation or improvement of a health facility pursuant to section forty-seven-d of article three of the private housing finance law and the health and mental hygiene facilities improvement act shall be deemed to be assumed by the appropriate county social services district from and after the date of the dissolution of such city social services district, and the provisions of paragraph b of subdivision four of section forty-seven-d of article three of the private housing finance law shall apply with respect to the payment of state aid payable thereafter to such county social services district pursuant to section three hundred sixty-eight-a of the social services law.

Added by Laws 1972, Ch. 28, eff. Feb. 29, 1972.

TITLE 1—APPLICATION

(Repealed and transferred sections noted under appropriate section number of text.)

Section 56. City social services districts.

§ 51. Albany county.

Repealed by Laws 1977, Ch. 863, eff. Aug. 11, 1977.

§ 52. Erie county.

Repealed by Laws 1977, Ch. 863, eff. Aug. 11, 1977.

§ 53. Onondaga county.

Repealed by Laws 1977, Ch. 863, eff. Aug. 11, 1977.

§ 54. Westchester county.

Repealed by Laws 1977, Ch. 863. eff. Aug. 11, 1977.

§ 55. Certain towns in Broome county.

Repealed by Laws 1977, ch. 863, eff. Apr. 1, 1978.

§ 56. City social services districts.

The city of New York shall have all the powers and duties of a social services district insofar as consistent with the provisions of the special and local laws relating to such city. The officers thereof charged with the administration of public assistance and care shall have additional powers and duties of a commissioner of social services not inconsistent with the laws relating to said city.

Amended by Laws 1941, Ch. 499; Laws 1947, Ch. 2; Laws 1966, Ch. 23; Laws 1977, Ch. 863, eff. Apr. 1, 1978.

§ 57. Cities in county social services districts.

Each city, other than the city of New York shall form part of the county social services district of the county in which it is situated and shall not assume any powers and responsibilities for the administration or expense of public assistance and care, in addition to those specified in subdivision two of section sixty-nine, except pursuant to the provisions of sections seventy-four and seventy-four-a of this chapter.

Added by Laws 1946, Ch. 200; amended by Laws 1977, Ch. 863, eff. Apr. 1, 1978.

§ 58. Application.

Nothing in this chapter shall be deemed to take away the jurisdiction or any power or duty of the family court, the department, the state department of education or the state department of health.

SSL

Amended by Laws 1946, Ch. 200; Laws 1962, Ch. 690, eff. Sept. 1, 1962.

TITLE 2—PUBLIC WELFARE DISTRICTS AND THEIR RESPONSIBILITY FOR PUBLIC ASSISTANCE AND CARE

———

(Repealed and transferred sections noted under appropriate section number of text.)

§ 61. Social services districts.

For the purpose of administration of public assistance and care the state shall be divided into county and city social services districts as follows:

1. The city of New York is hereby constituted a city social services district.

2. Each of the counties of the state not included in subdivision one of this section is hereby constituted a county social services district.

Amended by Laws 1941, Ch. 499; Laws 1947, Ch. 2; Laws 1966, Ch. 23; Laws 1977, Ch. 863, eff. Apr. 1, 1978.

§ 62. Responsibility for public assistance and care.

1. Subject to reimbursement in the cases hereinafter provided for, each public welfare district shall be responsible for the assistance and care of any person who resides or is found in its territory and who is in need of public assistance and care which he is unable to provide for himself.

2. [*Repealed.*]

3. [*Repealed.*]

4. [*Repealed.*]

5. This section is subject to the following exceptions:

(a) Notwithstanding any other provisions of this chapter, in the event a recipient removes from one to another social services district in the state, a social services official administering safety net assistance or family assistance to such recipient shall continue such assistance and shall provide medical assistance for such recipient for a period ending on the last day of the calendar month next succeeding the calendar month in which such removal occurred, provided such recipient is otherwise eligible for such assistance; and in the event an eligible person removes from one to another social services district in the state, a social services official shall continue to administer medical assistance to such person for a period not to extend beyond the last day of the calendar month next succeeding the calendar month in which such removal occurred, provided such person is otherwise eligible for such assistance and has not become a recipient of public assistance or care in the district to which he has removed.

(b) If a public welfare district, town or city provides care for a person in a family home, boarding home, nursing home, convalescent home, hospital or institution outside of its territory and pays for such care directly or through a grant made to the recipient, the public welfare district, town or city making such provision shall continue to be responsible for payment for such care as long as the recipient is in need thereof. In the event any other type of public assistance and care is needed by a person receiving such care, it shall be furnished and paid for by the public welfare district, town or city which would be responsible for such required assistance and care if such person had remained in the territory of the district, town or city making such provision; the public welfare district, town or city making such provision shall likewise be responsible for the care, removal and burial of the body of any such person who shall die, and the expense thereof.

The public welfare district, town or city which, pursuant to the provisions of this paragraph, is providing public assistance and care for the mother of an infant, on the date of birth of such infant, shall be responsible for providing public assistance or care required by such infant on and after the date of his birth; and such public welfare district, town or city shall be deemed to have made provision for the care of such infant outside of its territory.

When a child who has been cared for away from his own home by or on behalf of a public welfare district, pursuant to title two of article six or other provisions of this chapter, the family court act of the state of New York, or other provisions of law, is discharged, pursuant to law, to his parents or parent, brother, sister, uncle, aunt or legal guardian, who are or is then residing outside the territory of such public welfare district, such discharge shall terminate the responsibility of such public welfare district to furnish public assistance and care for such child pursuant to this paragraph; and upon such discharge it shall become the responsibility of the public welfare district wherein such child is thereafter to reside with his relative or legal guardian to provide necessary public assistance and care for him as in the case of any other child residing therein.

The provisions of this paragraph shall not be deemed to authorize or empower towns or cities of a county public welfare district to exercise responsibilities with relation to public assistance and care inconsistent with the responsibilities imposed or conferred on them by other provisions of this chapter.

(c) When a mentally ill, mentally retarded or epileptic person is in need of public assistance or care while on convalescent status or community status from a state hospital or institution under the provision of section 29.15 of the mental hygiene law, the public welfare district, town or city from which he was admitted to such hospital or institution shall be responsible for providing and paying for such assistance or care as in the case of other persons requiring public assistance or care as in the case of other persons requiring public assistance and care, except that such responsibility shall continue during any period such person is on convalescent status or community status outside the territory of such public welfare district, town or city and shall continue thereafter in accordance with the provisions of this paragraph and paragraph (b) if such person was receiving or should have been receiving public assistance or care from such public welfare district, town or city outside its territory at the time he was discharged from such convalescent status or community status.

(d)   When a person, either upon admission to a hospital, nursing home, intermediate care facility, adult home, enriched housing program or residence for adults located in a social services district other than the district in which he was then residing, or while in such hospital, nursing home, intermediate care facility, adult home, enriched housing program or residence for adults, is or becomes in need of medical assistance, the social services district from which he was admitted to such hospital, nursing home, intermediate care facility, adult home, enriched housing program or residence for adults shall be responsible for providing such medical assistance for so long as such person is eligible therefor. If while such person is receiving care in such hospital, nursing home, intermediate care facility, adult home, enriched housing program or residence for adults or when discharged therefrom, is in need of any other type of public assistance or care, the social services district, town or city from which the person was admitted to such hospital, nursing home, intermediate care facility, adult home, enriched housing program or residence for adults shall be responsible for providing and paying for such public assistance or care as in the case of other persons requiring public assistance and care in its territory, and such responsibility shall continue thereafter in accordance with the provisions of this paragraph and paragraph (b) of this subdivision if such person was receiving or should have been receiving public assistance or care from such social services district, town or city; such social services district, town or city shall likewise be responsible for the care, removal or burial of the body of any such person who shall die, and for the expense thereof. The provisions of this paragraph shall likewise be applicable to the care of an eligible person who, while temporarily absent from the social services district in which he then resided, was admitted to a hospital or nursing home in another social services district prior to the effective date hereof.

(e)   A public welfare district which provides medical assistance for needy persons pursuant to the provisions of title eleven of article five of this chapter, shall not charge back any part of the cost of such assistance to another public welfare district.

(f)   (1) The social services district in which a victim of domestic violence, as defined in article six-A of this chapter, was residing at the time of the alleged domestic violence shall be responsible, in accordance with section one hundred thirty-one-u of this chapter, for the cost of emergency shelter and care provided to such victim and his or her minor children at a residential program for victims of domestic violence, as defined in article six-A of this chapter, whether or not such program is located in the social services district or in another social services district if such victim:

a. was receiving public assistance at the time of entry to the program or

b. applies for public assistance and care during the time the victim was residing in such program.

(2) The social services district to which such application is submitted shall forward the completed application to the district in which the victim resided at the time of the alleged domestic violence.

(3) Responsibility for the cost of shelter and care pursuant to this paragraph shall be limited to the period during which the victim and his or her children, if any, reside in such program. Responsibility for public assistance and care for any period after termination of such residency shall be determined pursuant to other provisions of this section.

(g) [*Expires September 1, 2005, pursuant to Laws 2003, Ch. 16, § 17.*] (1) When a person applies for medical parole, and is in need of public assistance, including medical assistance, the department of correctional services shall cause an application for such assistance to be forwarded to the department of social services.

(2) Upon receipt of an application for public assistance, including medical assistance, forwarded by the state department of correctional services for persons meeting the conditions of medical parole, financial eligibility for such assistance and care shall be determined by the New York state department of social services prior to the person's parole.

(3) Determination of continuing eligibility for public assistance, including medical assistance, and care will be the responsibility of the social services district into which such person is released.

(4) Any inconsistent provision of this chapter or other law notwithstanding, when a person is released on medical parole pursuant to section two hundred fifty-nine-r of the executive law and is in need of public assistance, including medical assistance, the social services district in which such person was convicted and from which he or she was committed to the custody of the state department of correctional services shall be responsible for the administrative costs of the initial and any subsequent eligibility determination and the costs of any public assistance, including medical assistance, following such person's release on medical parole for so long as such person is eligible therefor.

6. Homeless children. (a) Notwithstanding any other provision of law to the contrary, the social services district which provides assistance or services to a homeless child in temporary housing located outside the school district of origin shall notify the commissioner of education, the school district of origin and the school district designated by the child, parent or person in parental relation pursuant to subdivision two of section thirty-two hundred nine of the education law within five days of such designation as the school district which such child

shall attend upon instruction. Such notice shall include the name of the child, the name of the parent or person in parental relation to the child, if any, the name and location of the temporary housing arrangement, the name of the school district of origin and any other information required by the commissioner of education.

(b)   For the purposes of this subdivision the terms "homeless child", and "school district of origin" shall be as defined in section thirty-two hundred nine of the education law.

(c)   A social services district shall provide for the transportation of each homeless child who is eligible for benefits pursuant to section three hundred fifty-j of this chapter to and from a temporary housing location in which the child was placed by the social services district and the school attended by such child pursuant to section thirty-two hundred nine of the education law, if such temporary housing facility is located outside of the designated school district pursuant to paragraph a of subdivision two of section thirty-two hundred nine of the education law. A social services district shall be authorized to contract with a board of education or a board of cooperative educational services for the provision of such transportation. This paragraph shall apply to placements made by a social services district without regard to whether a payment is made by the district to the operator of the temporary housing facility.

Added by Laws 1946, Ch. 200; **amended** by Laws 1947, Ch. 808; Laws 1949, Ch. 827; Laws 1951, Ch. 77; Laws 1956, Ch. 27; Laws 1959, Ch. 577; Laws 1960, Ch. 712; Laws 1961, Ch. 195; Laws 1962, Chs. 482, 689; Laws 1963, Ch. 522; Laws 1964, Ch. 436; Laws 1966, Chs. 100, 256; Laws 1967, Chs. 150, 490; Laws 1970, Ch. 258; Laws 1973, Chs. 178, 195, 344; Laws 1974, Ch. 621, Ch. 1080; Laws 1975, Ch. 513; Laws 1977, Ch. 660, eff. Apr. 1, 1978; Ch. 863, eff. Aug. 11, 1977, repealing subd. (2); Laws 1979, Ch. 277, eff. June 2, 1979. See Leg. His. for Soc. Serv. L. § 365 *infra*. **Amended** by Laws 1987, Ch. 838, eff. Aug. 7, 1987; **amended** by Laws 1988, Ch. 348, § 2, eff. July 27, 1988; **amended** by Laws 1992, Ch. 55, § 290, eff. Apr. 10, 1992 until Apr. 10, 1994; **amended** by Laws 1992, Ch. 293, § 16, eff. June 30, 1992; **amended** by Laws 1994, Ch. 169, § 95, eff. Apr. 1, 1994; **amended** by Laws 1994, Ch. 569, § 2, eff. Aug. 25, 1994; **amended** by Laws 1995, Ch. 81, § 196, eff. Apr. 1, 1995; **amended** by Laws 1996, Ch. 48, eff. Apr. 12, 1996 until Apr. 10, 1998; **amended** by Laws 1997, Ch. 436, § 1 Part B, § 63, eff. Aug. 20, 1997; **amended** by Laws 1998, Ch. 38, § 1, eff. Apr. 8, 1998, extending expiration and applicability of subd. (5)(g) to Apr. 10, 2000; **amended** by Laws 2000, Ch. 16, § 1, eff. Mar. 30, 2000, extending expiration and applicability of subd. (5)(g) to Sept. 1, 2001; **amended** by Laws 2001, Ch. 95, § 18, eff. July 13, 2001, extending expiration and applicability of subd. (5)(g) to Sept. 1, 2003, Ch. 150, § 3 Part B, eff. Aug. 14, 2001, Ch. 433, § 1, amending subd. 5(d), eff. Nov. 13, 2001; Laws 2003, Ch. 16, § 17, extending the expiration date of subd. (g) until Sept. 1, 2005, eff. March 31, 2003.

Editor's Note: L. 2001, Ch. 433, § 2, provides:

Persons residing in a hospital, nursing home, intermediate care facility, adult home, enriched housing program or residence for adults on the date this act takes effect and who is receiving public assistanceand/or medical assistance shall continue to be the responsibility of the social services district paying for such residents on such date.

§ 63. Chargeback between districts prohibited; exception.

Repealed by Laws 1977, Ch. 863, eff. Aug. 11, 1977.

§ 64. Separation of social services from eligibility and assistance payments functions.

Notwithstanding any provision of law, rule or regulation every social services district shall be organized to effect a separation of social services from eligibility and assistance payments functions as follows:

1.   The commissioner shall issue within ten days of the effective date hereof, guidelines to the social services districts of the state outlining the principles and purposes to be attained in the separation of social services from the functions of eligibility and assistance payments, and defining the content of services which may be included under the term "social services" and of the functions associated with eligibility and assistance payments.

2.   Each social services district shall submit to the commissioner by July first, nineteen hundred seventy-one, its own plan for separation, together with its timetable for implementation of the plan.

3.   Upon finding that the plan conforms to the applicable minimum federal requirements, the commissioner shall approve such plan.

4.   Each social services district shall submit to the commissioner, in accordance with applicable federal law and regulations, modifications of its approved plan for separation of social services from eligibility and assistance payments functions. Each social services district shall prepare, in accordance with applicable federal law and regulations, for the effective operation of such approved plan as so modified.

Added by Laws 1971, Ch. 109, eff. Apr. 7, 1971; **amended** Laws 1972, Ch. 942, eff. June 8, 1972.

SSL

TITLE 3—COUNTY PUBLIC WELFARE DISTRICTS

(Repealed and transferred sections noted under appropriate section number of text.)

———

§ 65.   County commissioners of public welfare.

1.   There shall be a county commissioner of public welfare in each county public welfare district who shall administer the public assistance and care for which the county public welfare district is responsible and shall have general supervision and care of persons in need in the territory over which he has jurisdiction.

2.   The county commissioner shall be responsible for the administration of all the assistance and care for which the county is responsible

3.   The county commissioner shall act as the agent of the department in all matters relating to assistance and care administered or authorized by the town public welfare officers.

4.   The county commissioner shall be appointed in accordance with the provisions of section one hundred sixteen of this chapter or other provisions of law relating to the appointment of such commissioner.

5.   [*Repealed.*]

6.   (a) A county commissioner is authorized and required to provide safety net assistance for persons residing or found in a city or town of the county when in his judgment they are eligible for and in immediate need of such assistance and either: the city or town public welfare officer, as the case may be, is absent from his city or town under circumstances indicating his absence may extend beyond two days and such officer has no deputy or assistant authorized to grant such assistance or his or her deputy or assistant is also absent from such city or town under circumstances indicating his or her absence may also be for a period of more than two days; or, such county commissioner shall have appealed to the department, pursuant to section seventy-four-h, the decision of the social services official of such city or town not to grant the safety net assistance recommended by such commissioner after his or her staff shall have investigated the application for assistance pursuant to the provisions of section one hundred thirty-two. Such county commissioner may continue to grant safety net assistance in the former case until the city or town public welfare officer or his or her deputy or assistant returns to such city or town, and in the latter case until the department shall have decided the appeal of the county commissioner.

(b)   Expenditures of a county for safety net assistance pursuant to this section may be made from county social services funds appropriated or otherwise made available therefor and shall be subject to reimbursement by the state in accordance with and to the extent authorized by section one hundred fifty-three; and the local share of such expenditures shall become a charge on, and shall be reimbursed to the county by the city or town which was otherwise responsible for furnishing the safety net assistance for which the expenditure was made, provided the county commissioner shall give appropriate written notice thereof to the appropriate city or town public welfare officer within thirty days of the date the expenditure was made by the county and provided further that in the case of an appeal to the department that such appeal shall be decided in favor of the county.

7. (a) In the event of a vacancy in the office of county commissioner of social services the appointing authority may, subject to the provisions of paragraph (b) of this subdivision, appoint as acting commissioner of social services any employee of the county social services agency. Such appointment shall be for no longer than one year.

(b) Prior to filing a vacancy in the office of county commissioner of social services the appointing authority shall certify to the state commissioner of social services: (i) that there is an unavailability of qualified candidates; (ii) that the district is making continued efforts to recruit qualified candidates; (iii) that the appointment shall be effective only until a qualified person becomes available; and (iv) that a waiver by the appointing authority of any specific qualification required by section one hundred sixteen of this chapter shall not be effective without the consent of the state commissioner of social services.

(c) The acting commissioner may be paid compensation in addition to his normal salary during the period of time that he serves as acting commissioner.

(d) The acting commissioner shall have the same power as a commissioner during the period of time that he serves as acting commissioner.

(e) Service as an acting commissioner shall in no way affect the permanent civil service status, or any other employment rights of the appointee.

Amended by Laws 1946, Ch. 200; Laws 1948, Ch. 795; Laws 1955, Ch. 143; Laws 1960, Ch. 24; Laws 1965, Ch. 1071; Laws 1974, Ch. 819; **amended** by Laws 1977, Ch. 863, eff. Aug. 11, 1977, subd. (5) repealed, subds. (6) and (7) are not renumbered; **amended** by Laws 1997, Ch. 436, § 1 Part B, § 64, eff. Aug. 20, 1997.

§ 66. County appointments and bonds.

1. The legislative body of the county may authorize the appointment of any number of deputy commissioners of social services, physicians to care for sick persons in their homes, other assistants and employees, including attorneys to perform duties it considers necessary to carry out the provisions of this chapter. However, such legislative body may also authorize that such attorneys, in addition to performing the duties assigned to them by the county commissioner, may be deputized by the county attorney to perform duties on his behalf in connection with the work of the social services department.

2. The county commissioner shall appoint deputy commissioners, physicians, assistants and employees so authorized and direct their work.

3. Each county commissioner and deputy commissioner shall be required to give bond before entering upon his duties. The board of supervisors shall fix the

SSL

amount of such bond and may require and fix the amount of bond to be given by any other assistant or employee whose appointment is authorized. The expense of any bond required in connection with the work of a county public welfare official or employee shall be paid from county public welfare funds.

4. In accordance with federal and state regulations each county social services commissioner shall appoint a citizens advisory committee or committees to exercise and perform such functions, powers, and duties as the regulations of the department may require.

Amended by Laws 1955, Ch. 208; Laws 1961, Ch. 467; Laws 1966, Ch. 256; Laws 1976, Ch. 326, eff. June 8, 1976; amended by Laws 1973 Ch. 288, eff. May 8, 1973.

§ 67. Town public welfare officers; appointment of staff.

1. The town board of each town responsible for the expense of providing safety net assistance for persons residing or found in such town shall appoint a social services official or authorize a supervisor of the town to act as such official. It may in its discretion appoint an assistant town social services official and other employees to assist the town social services official in carrying out his or her duties. The town social services official, his or her assistant and other employees shall hold office during the pleasure of the town board. The town board shall fix the salary to be paid a town social services official, his or her assistant or other employees or fix the amount per hour to be paid them when they are performing any duty connected with their office.

2. The town public welfare officer shall be responsible for the authorization of the assistance and care for which the town is responsible and shall assist the county commissioner in the administration of assistance and care to persons residing or found in his town for whose care the county public welfare district is responsible. Except as otherwise agreed and arranged by and between the county commissioner and the town public welfare officer, the town public welfare officer shall receive all applications for public assistance and care made in his town by residents of such town, and he shall forward each such application to the county commissioner immediately after the receipt of the same. He shall have all the powers and perform all the duties of a public welfare official applicable to the work hereby assigned.

3. In case of emergency and until it is possible for the county commissioner either to take charge of the case or to make a complete investigation, the town public welfare officer may grant such temporary assistance and care as may be necessary. All such grants made by the town public welfare officer shall be made in accordance with the rules and regulations of the department and the regulations established by the county commissioner of public welfare.

Amended by Laws 1946, Ch. 200; Laws 1948, Ch. 817; Laws 1966, Ch. 256, eff. Apr. 30, 1966; amended by Laws 1997, Ch. 436, § 1 Part B, § 65, eff. Aug. 20, 1997.

§ 68.　City public welfare officers; appointment of staff.

Repealed by Laws 1977, Ch. 863, eff. Aug. 11, 1977.

§ 69.　Responsibility for public assistance and care in a county social services district.

The responsibility for the administration of public assistance and care in a county social services district and the expense thereof may either be borne by the county social services district or be divided between such district and the towns and cities therein as hereinafter provided.

1.　Unless otherwise determined by the board of supervisors as hereinafter provided, each town shall be responsible for the expense of providing safety net assistance for persons residing or found in such town.

2.　Unless otherwise determined by the board of supervisors as hereinafter provided, a city forming a part of a county social services district shall be responsible for the expense of providing safety net assistance for any person residing or found in its territory.

3.　A county social services district shall be responsible for the expense of providing all assistance and care for persons residing or found in a town or city in its territory for which such town or city is not responsible under the provisions of subdivisions one and two of this section. The expense of such assistance and care granted by a county social services district shall be subject to reimbursement by the state in the cases provided for by section sixty-two or by any other provision of this chapter.

Amended by Laws 1946, Ch. 200; Laws 1966, Ch. 256; **amended** by Laws 1977, Ch. 863, eff. Aug. 11, 1977; **amended** by Laws 1997, Ch. 436, § 1 Part B, § 66, eff. Aug. 20, 1997.

§ 70.　Chargeback of the cost of assistance and care.

Repealed by Laws 1977, Ch. 863, eff. Aug. 11, 1977.

§ 71.　Commitments.

Commitments to a county home may be made by such town and city public welfare officers as are authorized by the county commissioner. All other commitments to hospitals or other institutions at the expense of the county public welfare district shall be made by the county commissioner, or by such other official as may be authorized pursuant to the provisions of this chapter.

Amended by Laws 1946, Ch. 200, eff. Apr. 1, 1946.

§ 72. Power of the board of supervisors to assume responsibility for assistance and care.

1. The board of supervisors of the county may, by resolution adopted by a majority vote, direct that the cost of all or any part of the assistance and care for which the towns and cities are made responsible under the provisions of subdivisions one and two of section sixty-nine shall be a charge on the county social services district and administered under the direction of the county commissioner.

2. Copies of any such resolution shall be sent to each town clerk and to the mayor and clerk of each city in the county social services district within ten days after the adoption of the resolution. However, no resolution adopted by the board of supervisors pursuant to subdivision one of this section shall take effect in a city in the county social services district until confirmed by the legislative body of the city.

Added by Laws 1946, Ch. 200; amended by Laws 1977, Ch. 863, eff. Aug. 11, 1977.

§ 73. Power of the board of supervisors to change the administrative system of the county social services district.

When pursuant to section seventy-two, the board of supervisors has adopted a resolution directing that the cost of all public assistance and care shall be a charge on the county social services district:

1. The county social services district shall, after the date fixed by such resolution, be responsible for administration of public assistance and care in all of the towns of its district and thereafter all provisions of this chapter as to the powers and duties of towns and of town social services officers shall be inoperative in such county social services district. The appointment of all town social services officers and employees shall terminate on the date when such resolution takes effect.

2. (a) Such resolution shall not take effect in a city in a county social services district unless it is confirmed by act of the legislative body of the city in accordance with the provisions of this paragraph. The legislative body of such a city may confirm the resolution of the board of supervisors (1) on or before the first day of October in the year in which such resolution was adopted by the board of supervisors, and make such confirmation effective on the first day of January next succeeding such confirmation, provided the resolution of the board of supervisors takes effect in the towns of the county on or before such first day of January, or (2) at any other time or date, and make such confirmation effective on any date not earlier than the date the resolution of the board of supervisors takes effect in the towns of the county, provided the board of supervisors shall by resolution specifically approve such confirmation.

(b) On the day after a city confirms a resolution of the board of supervisors pursuant to paragraph (a), the mayor or the city clerk shall send a written notice of such confirmation to the clerk of the board of supervisors of the county. He shall also send a copy of such notice to the county commissioner of social services and the county commissioner shall thereupon notify the department.

(c) If a city in the county social services district shall confirm the resolution of the board of supervisors in accordance with the provisions of paragraph (a), the county social services district shall, on and after the effective date of such confirmation be responsible for administration of public assistance and care in such city, and thereafter all provisions of this chapter as to the powers and duties of a city in a county social services district and of city social services officers shall be inoperative in such city.

(d) Unless and until a city in the county social services district shall confirm the resolution of the board of supervisors in accordance with the provisions of paragraph (a), the responsibility of such city for assistance and care in its territory shall not be affected by such resolution, and the city shall be governed by the provisions of this chapter and other laws relating to cities which form part of a county social services district and to city social services officers; and the city shall continue to be responsible for the cost of public assistance and care under the provisions of subdivision two of section sixty-nine, except as otherwise provided in title three-a of this article. The cost of any assistance and care given to local charges residing or found in such city, paid by the county social services district under the provisions of subdivision three of section sixty-nine, shall be a charge on the county social services district.

3. The board of supervisors shall make such additional appropriations and authorize the appointment of such number of deputy commissioners, other assistants and employees as it may deem necessary to provide adequate administration of the public assistance and care for which the county social services district is made responsible under the provisions of this section.

Added by Laws 1946, Ch. 200; **amended** by Laws 1948, Chs. 796, 818, 871; Laws 1949, Ch. 392; Laws 1950, Ch. 200; Laws 1966, Ch. 256; **amended** by Laws 1977, Ch. 863, eff. Aug. 11, 1977.

TITLE 3-A—INTEGRATION OF LOCAL PUBLIC WELFARE ADMINISTRATION

(Repealed and transferred sections noted under appropriate section number of text.)

SSL

§ 74. Initial election of options by cities in county public welfare districts.

Repealed by Laws 1977, Ch. 863, eff. Aug. 11, 1977.

§ 74. Administration of assistance by or on behalf of certain cities.

1.   Each city, other than the city of New York, which is responsible for one or more types of public assistance and care on the date this section becomes effective shall function under section seventy-four-a of this chapter.

2.   Any city subject to the provisions of subdivision one of this section may confirm and make effective therein, pursuant to subdivision two of section seventy-three of this chapter, a resolution of the county legislative body adopted pursuant to section seventy-two of this chapter directing that the cost of all public assistance and care shall be a charge on the county social services district.

Added by Laws 1977, Ch. 863, eff. Aug. 11, 1977.

§ 74-a. Election of options by cities in county public welfare districts subsequent to initial election of options.

Repealed by Laws 1977, Ch. 863, eff. Aug. 11, 1977, which renumbered Former Soc. Serv. L. § 74-d as § 74-a.

§ 74-a. Administration of assistance by county for city; reimbursements and advances; cost to county to be raised by tax on taxable property of city and to be included in county tax levy.*

1.   The county shall administer in and for the city the public assistance and care for the administration of which the city is responsible and shall be entitled to all reimbursements and advances against reimbursements on account of the assistance and care so administered to which the city would otherwise be entitled and which would otherwise be payable to the city in accordance with the provisions of this chapter.

2.   The cost to the county of all assistance and care thus administered by the county in and for the city shall be a charge against and be levied as a tax upon the taxable property of the city and the amount to be so raised by tax shall be included by the county in its next ensuing tax levy.

Added by Laws 1946, Ch. 200; amended by Laws 1948, Ch. 871; amended by Laws 1966, Ch. 256; amended by Laws 1977, Ch. 863, eff. Aug. 11, 1977, Soc. Serv. L. § 74–d renumbered as § 74–a and subd. (3) deleted.

* Formerly § 74-d.

§ 74-b. Option I: Administration of assistance by county for city; contract; revolving fund.

Repealed by Laws 1977, Ch. 863, eff. Aug. 11, 1977.

§ 74-c. Option II: Administration of assistance by county for city; contract; revolving fund; city service office and officer.

Repealed by Laws 1977, Ch. 863, eff. Aug. 11, 1977.

§ 74-e. Option IV: Administration of assistance by city, and as agent for county; contract; revolving fund.

Repealed by Laws 1977, Ch. 863, eff. Aug. 11, 1977.

§ 74-f. Option V: City administration of home relief.

Repealed by Laws 1977, Ch. 863, eff. Aug. 11, 1977.

§ 74-g. Approval of certain county public welfare district plans including provisions for completely integrated public welfare services in the cities of such district.

Repealed by Laws 1955, Ch. 143, eff. Apr. 1, 1956.

§ 74-h. Appeals and reviews.

1. A social services official responsible in an individual case for either the authorization of assistance or the investigation of the application for assistance and the making of a recommendation relative to such application shall have the right to appeal to the department from a decision made in such case by another social services official.

Upon receiving such an appeal, the department shall issue a written determination which shall be binding on all the social services officials involved in such appeal.

2. The department on its own motion may review any case for the purpose of determining whether assistance and care has been adequately or properly provided. After making such a review, the department may issue such written determination as it may deem proper, and such determination shall be binding on all the social services officials concerned.

Added by Laws 1946, Ch. 200; **amended** by Laws 1977, Ch. 863, eff. Aug. 11, 1977.

§ 74-i. Transfer of personnel; county, city and town.

1. When, pursuant to the provisions of this chapter or of any other law, the functions, powers and duties exercised by a city or town in the administration

SSL

of public assistance and care, are transferred or assigned, in whole or in part, to a county, provision shall be made for the county to employ so much of the staff employed by such city or town in the administration and execution of the functions, powers and duties so transferred or assigned as may be practicable and necessary. Officers and employees shall be transferred without further examination or qualification and they shall retain their respective civil service classification and status provided that, in determining the officers and employees to be transferred to a county, such officers and employees shall be selected within each grade of each class of positions in the order of their original appointment in the service of the city or town, as the case may be. Officers and employees in the competitive class of the civil service of the city or town who are not transferred to the county shall have their names entered upon appropriate city or town preferred lists, as the case may be, pursuant to section thirty-one of the civil service law. Temporary and provisional employees may be transferred and shall, thereafter, be subject to such examinations as are required by law. If the functions transferred are retransferred in accordance with the provisions of this chapter, upon such retransfer, the officers or employees who were transferred and who are employed by the county on the date of such retransfer shall likewise be retransferred; and, thereafter, they shall be deemed officers and employees of the city or town from which they were originally transferred, and they shall retain their civil service status, rights and privileges.

2.   When, pursuant to the provisions of this chapter, the functions, powers and duties exercised by a county in the administration of public assistance and care are transferred or assigned, in whole or in part, to a city, or are assumed in part by a city or town which elects, pursuant to this chapter or any other law, to constitute itself a public welfare district, provision shall be made for the city or town to employ so much of the staff employed by such county in the administration and execution of the functions, powers and duties so transferred, assigned or assumed as may be practicable and necessary. Officers and employees shall be transferred without further examination or qualification and they shall retain their respective civil service classification and status provided that, in determining the officers and employees to be transferred to the city or town, such officers and employees shall be selected within each grade of each class of positions in the order of their original appointment in the service of the county. Officers and employees in the competitive class of the civil service of the county who are not transferred to the city or town shall have their names entered upon appropriate county preferred lists, pursuant to section thirty-one of the civil service law. Temporary and provisional employees may be transferred and shall, thereafter, be subject to such examinations as are required by law. If the functions transferred are retransferred in accordance with the provisions of this chapter, upon such retransfer, the officers and employees who are transferred and who are employed by the city on the date of such retransfer shall likewise be retransferred; and, thereafter, they shall be deemed officers and employees of the county, and they shall retain their civil service status, rights and privileges.

Added by Laws 1946, Ch. 200; **amended** by Laws 1946, Ch. 201, eff. Apr. 1, 1946.

§ 74-j. Special provision for the election of options by certain towns having the powers of a city in a county public welfare district.

Repealed by Laws 1977, Ch. 863, eff. Aug. 11, 1977.

§ 75. Right of election of certain cities to become city public welfare districts.

Repealed by Laws 1977, Ch. 863, eff. Apr. 1, 1978.

§ 75-a. Right of election of certain towns having the powers of a city in a county public welfare district.

Repealed by Laws 1977, Ch. 863, eff. Apr. 1, 1978.

TITLE 4—CITY PUBLIC WELFARE DISTRICTS

(Repealed and transferred sections noted under appropriate section number of text.)

——

§ 76. Powers and duties of city public welfare districts.

Repealed by Laws 1977, Ch. 863, eff. Apr. 1, 1978.

§ 77. City commissioners of public welfare; appointment of staff.

1.   There shall be a city commissioner of public welfare in each city public welfare district, who shall administer the public assistance and care for which the city public welfare district is responsible.

2.   The officer appointed, in accordance with section one hundred sixteen of this chapter, to administer public assistance and care in a city which is constituted a city public welfare district, shall have the powers and perform the duties of the city commissioner of public welfare.

3.   When the duties of a city commissioner are by the provisions of special or local law relating to the city assigned to more than one department of the city government, the administrative officer of each such department shall have such of the powers and perform such of the duties of a city commissioner as may be applicable to the work assigned to such department, and all the provisions of this chapter shall be so interpreted.

SSL

4. The city commissioner of public welfare shall appoint deputy commissioners, assistants and employees authorized by the legislative body of the city and shall direct their work. When authorized by such legislative body such city commissioner may appoint attorneys to perform duties other than those assigned to the corporation counsel or city attorney. However, if such city commissioner shall approve and if authorized by such legislative body, such attorneys may, in addition to performing the duties assigned to them by such city commissioner, be deputized by the corporation counsel or city attorney to perform duties on his behalf in connection with the work of the welfare department. The city commissioner shall appoint physicians to visit sick persons in their homes when authorized by the legislative body of such city.

Amended by Laws 1946, Ch. 200; Laws 1955, Chs. 143, 208; Laws 1965, Ch. 1071; Laws 1966, Ch. 256, eff. Apr. 30, 1966.

§ 78. Citizens advisory committees.

In accordance with federal and state regulations, each city social services commissioner shall appoint a citizens advisory committee or committees to exercise and perform such functions, powers, and duties as the regulations of the department may require.

Added by Laws 1961, Ch. 467; former § 78 **repealed** and new § 78 **added** by Laws 1973 Ch. 288 eff. May 8, 1973.

§ 79. Plan for the homeless.

The mayor of New York City shall submit to the legislature and the governor a copy of the revised and updated five-year plan for housing the homeless in New York City which is required under section 21-121 of the administrative code of the city of New York, no later than February fourteenth of each year.

Added by Laws 1990, Ch. 374, § 1, eff. July 10, 1990.

TITLE 4-A—SALARIES OF LOCAL CASE WORKERS

(Repealed and transferred sections noted under appropriate section number of text.)

§ 79. Minimum salaries of local case workers.

Repealed by Laws 1971, Ch. 123, eff. Apr. 12, 1971.

§ 79-a. Higher salaries for case workers and other social service personnel having graduate training.

Repealed by Laws 1971, Ch. 123, eff. Apr. 12, 1971.

§ 79-b.   Use of subprofessional staff.

Repealed by Laws 1971, Ch. 123, eff. Apr. 12, 1971.

TITLE 5—RECORDS, REPORTS, FUNDS AND APPROPRIATIONS

——

§ 80.   Records.

All social services officials shall keep the records required by this chapter and the department.

Amended by Laws 1946, Ch. 200; **amended** by Laws 1977, Ch. 863, eff. Aug. 11, 1977.

§ 81.   Reports.

1.   The county commissioner shall make: (a) Such reports and furnish such information to the department with respect to the work of the county social services district as is required by this chapter and the department.

(b)   An annual report to the board of supervisors concerning the work of the county social services district and additional reports at such times and covering such facts as the board of supervisors may require.

(c)   If any of the cost of assistance and care paid for by the county social services district is charged back to the towns and cities thereof, a report to the county treasurer at the end of the fiscal year, stating the per capita maintenance cost per day in the county home and an itemized statement of the amount to be charged each town and city for the assistance and care given either in the county home or elsewhere to persons residing or found in each town or city and a statement of all expenditures and receipts in behalf of such persons.

(d) Current reports to the city and town social services officers of persons residing in their cities and towns who are in receipt of public assistance and care from the county.

2. A town social services officer shall make:

(a) An annual report to the town board concerning his work and additional reports at such times and covering such facts as the town board may require.

(b) An annual report to the county commissioner and any additional reports at such time and covering such facts as may be required by the county commissioner or the department.

3. A city commissioner of social services shall make:

(a) Such reports to the department with respect to his work as are required by this chapter and the department.

(b) An annual report to the mayor of the city or to any other official or board authorized to receive such report and additional reports at such times and covering such facts as may be required.

4. Such annual reports shall include an itemized statement of all money received by the social services official and all money expended by him, and a detailed statement in regard to the recipients of public assistance and care. Town and city social services shall furnish the county commissioner with all data, relating to their work and persons in receipt of public assistance and care, necessary to enable the county commissioner to make the reports required by the department.

Amended by Laws 1946, Ch. 200; **amended** by Laws 1977, Ch. 863, eff. Aug. 11, 1977.

§ 82. Accounts.

All social services officials shall keep such accounts regarding the receipt and disbursements of the social services funds, and of any trust funds, as may be required by law or directed by the department.

Amended by Laws 1946, Ch. 200; **amended** by Laws 1977, Ch. 863, eff. Aug. 11, 1977.

§ 83. County social services funds.

1. The county treasurer shall be the treasurer of the county social services district.

2. Except as hereinafter provided, disbursements for administration and public assistance and care from county social services funds shall be made only on warrants drawn by the county commissioner for the payment of bills and claims, in accordance with the provisions of law relating to such county and after audit by such county commissioner, except that in counties having a county comptroller or a county auditor such claims shall be audited by the county comptroller or county auditor after approval by the county commissioner.

3. Payments for board and incidental expenses of children cared for in boarding homes or in the homes of relatives or in institutions maintained by an authorized agency provided under title two of article six or on order of the family court of the county, may be made upon schedules showing the names of the persons or institutions with whom such children are boarded, the names of children boarded with each of them, the monthly rate of board to be paid for each such child, the period covered by each such schedule, the amount due for the board of each child during such period, an itemized account of the amount allowed for incidentals, if any, in the case of each child, and the total amount due to each such person or institution, verified by the commissioner and audited as hereinbefore provided and without the presentation of verified bills or claims by such persons or institutions.

Amended by Laws 1941, Ch. 84; Laws 1946, Ch. 200; **amended** by Laws 1955, Ch. 387; Laws 1962, Ch. 689; Laws 1977, Ch. 863, eff. Aug. 11, 1977.

§ 84. County commissioner's revolving fund.

A board of supervisors may authorize the county treasurer to furnish the county commissioner with an emergency revolving fund. Moneys from this fund shall be used only where it would be a hardship on the applicant or recipient to wait for the issuance of a grant in accordance with regularly established disbursement procedures. Reimbursement of expenditures from this fund shall be made at least monthly upon the presentation of itemized statements or vouchers chargeable to the appropriate programs of assistance in accordance with established procedures.

Amended by Laws 1946, Ch. 200; **amended** by Laws 1961, Ch. 262, eff. Apr. 3, 1961.

§ 85. Monthly reports of county commissioner to county treasurer.

The county commissioner shall pay over to the county treasurer on or before the tenth day of each month all money received by him in connection with the work of his public welfare district and make a report giving the source of all such receipts during the preceding calendar month.

Amended by Laws 1960, Ch. 546; **amended** by Laws 1962, Ch. 153, eff. Mar. 13, 1962.

SSL

§ 86.   Town public welfare funds.

1.   The taxes levied for public assistance and care in a town shall be paid to the town supervisor, who, without prior audit, shall disburse them on written order of the town public welfare officer for the payment of bills and claims submitted in accordance with the provisions of law relating to such town. All such bills and claims shall be filed annually with the town clerk.

2.   The town supervisor shall, without prior audit, issue individual checks to persons as authorized by the town welfare officer on forms as either prescribed or approved by the state department of social welfare, or such supervisor shall pay over to the town welfare officer for use as a revolving fund such amount as the town board authorizes. When a revolving fund has been established, the town welfare officer shall furnish to the town a bond in such penal sum and with such sureties as the town board may approve, conditioned upon the faithful discharge of his duties. Whenever a revolving fund has been established the welfare officer shall pay all welfare claims for which the town is legally responsible excepting salaries and other compensations from such revolving fund. Upon receiving such revolving fund the town welfare officer shall deposit such sum of money received in an official bank account, in the bank or trust company designated for such purpose by the town board, and he shall also enter in a suitable book or books kept by him for that purpose a record of the receipts and payments of such revolving fund. From appropriations for town welfare purposes the town supervisor shall, each month, on presentation by the town welfare officer of bills and claims, submitted in accordance with the provisions of law relating to such town, and statements of other disbursements on forms as either prescribed or approved by the state department of social welfare, reimburse such revolving fund for the amount of disbursements therefrom during the preceding month.

Added by Laws 1946, Ch. 200; **amended** by Laws 1947, Ch. 681; Laws 1955, Ch. 387; Laws 1959, Ch. 92; **amended** by Laws 1962, Ch. 136, eff. Jan. 1, 1963.

§ 86-a.   City public welfare funds.

The taxes levied for public assistance and care in a city, or in a city public welfare district, shall be paid to the city treasurer, or the commissioner of finance in the city of New York, and disbursed in accordance with the provisions of law relating to such city for the payment of bills and claims, provided such provisions of law are not inconsistent with the provisions of this chapter.

Added by Laws 1946, Ch. 200; **amended** by Laws 1955, Ch. 387; Laws 1964, Ch. 576; **amended** by Laws 1969, Ch. 407, eff. May 9, 1969; **amended** by Laws 1978, Ch. 655, § 115, eff. July 24, 1978.

§ 87.   Special funds.

1.   When a county commissioner shall receive any money as guardian of a minor or to be used for some particular person or purpose, he shall deposit it with

the county treasurer, who shall keep such money in a special account to be drawn on by the county commissioner for the person or purpose designated.

2. When a town social services officer shall receive such money he shall deposit it in a bank approved by the town supervisor to be drawn on by the town social services officer and the town supervisor jointly for the person or purpose designated.

3. When a city commissioner of social services shall receive such money, he shall deposit it with the official having charge of the funds of such city, who shall keep it either in a separate account to be requisitioned by the city commissioner or in one or more common trust funds established and maintained pursuant to the charter of such city.

Amended by Laws 1977, Ch. 863; **amended** by Laws 1980, Ch. 408, eff. June 23, 1980.

§ 88. Responsibility for adequate appropriations.

It shall be the duty of the board of supervisors of a county, the town board of a town and the appropriating body of a city to make adequate appropriations and to take such action as may be necessary to provide the public assistance and care required by this chapter.

§ 89. Estimates in county public welfare districts.

1. The county commissioner shall submit annually, in the manner prescribed by, and on or before the date fixed by or pursuant to law, an itemized estimate of revenues and the amount of money needed for the ensuing fiscal year for the public assistance and care for which the county is responsible, and for the administration thereof.

2. A town social services officer shall prepare and file annually with the town budget officer and the county commissioner of social services, at the time specified in section one hundred four of the town law, an itemized estimate of the amount needed for the ensuing year for administration and for public assistance and care. The town board shall include the amount necessary to be raised by tax in the annual estimate submitted to the board of supervisors as provided by the town law.

3. (a) A city public welfare officer shall submit an itemized estimate of the amount needed for the ensuing year for administration and public assistance and care to the mayor or other authority provided by law and to the county commissioner of public welfare.

(b) When, pursuant to the provisions of title three-a of this article, the county commissioner is administering the public assistance and care for which a city is responsible, and there is no city public welfare officer, the county commissioner shall make and submit an estimate for the city in the place and stead of a city public welfare officer.

SSL

Amended by Laws 1941, Ch. 601; Laws 1946, Ch. 200; Laws 1951, Ch. 247; **amended** by Laws 1969, Ch. 1049, eff. Jan. 1, 1971.

§ 90.   Appropriations in county public welfare districts.

1.   (a) The board of supervisors shall appoint a committee of its members to consider the estimates presented by the town boards in the county public welfare district. If any town shall fail to submit an estimate as provided by the previous section, the county commissioner shall prepare and submit to such committee an estimate of the amount needed for administration and public assistance and care in such town. The committee shall recommend to the board of supervisors the amount it considers necessary for the ensuing fiscal year for the various forms of public assistance and care and administrative expenses in each of the towns in the county public welfare district.

(b)   The board of supervisors shall approve an estimate for each town in the county public welfare district and shall levy taxes in each such town for the amount of the approved estimate for such town.

2.   The legislative body of a city forming part of a county public welfare district shall appropriate the amount it considers necessary for administration and public assistance and care in such city and shall cause taxes to be levied for the amount of such appropriation.

Nothing contained in this section shall be construed to prevent the financing of any such expenditure, in whole or in part, pursuant to the local finance law.

3.   The board of supervisors shall appropriate, in the manner provided by law, the amount it considers necessary for the ensuing fiscal year for the various forms of public assistance and care and administrative expenses in the county public welfare district and shall cause the necessary taxes to be levied therefor in the territory of the county public welfare district.

Amended by Laws 1943, Ch. 710; Laws 1946, Ch. 200; **amended** by Laws 1951, Ch. 247, eff. Mar. 24, 1951.

§ 90-a.   Taxes for county public welfare districts.

Taxes for each form of assistance or care administered by the county public welfare district shall be levied only in the territory in which the county public welfare district is responsible for the administration of such form thereof.

Added by Laws 1951, Ch. 247, eff. Mar. 24, 1951.

§ 91.   Estimates and appropriations in city public welfare districts.

The city commissioner of public welfare shall present to the mayor or other authority provided by law in such city an itemized estimate of the amount of money needed for the ensuing year for the administration of the city public welfare district and for public assistance and care. The legislative body of the city public welfare district shall appropriate the amount necessary for such purpose and shall cause taxes to be levied for the amount of such appropriation.

Nothing contained in this section shall be construed to prevent the financing of any such expenditure, in whole or in part, pursuant to the local finance law.

Amended by Laws 1943, Ch. 710, eff. Sept. 2, 1945.

§ 92. Deficiency appropriations.

1.   (a) Should the sums appropriated for medical assistance for needy persons, family assistance, or care and protection of children pursuant to article six of this chapter and their administration be expended or contracted or become exhausted during the year for the purposes for which they were appropriated, or should no appropriation have been made, additional sums shall be appropriated by the proper appropriating bodies, as occasion demands, to carry out the provisions of this chapter.

(b)   In cities such additional sums if appropriated shall be paid from unexpended balances not required by law to be expended for a specific purpose, or from contingent funds when such exist.

(c)   In counties, such additional appropriations shall be paid from funds in the county treasury available therefor, provided that such funds were raised by taxes levied in a territory identical with that in which such sums may be expended, and then only to the extent of any excess thereof not needed for other purposes under other provisions of this chapter.

(d)   Nothing contained in this section, however, shall be construed to prevent the financing of such deficiency appropriations pursuant to the local finance law.

2.   All the provisions of subdivision one in regard to cities shall be applicable to towns in Dutchess county, and, in every city or town thereof, except in the city of Poughkeepsie, the amount of such additional sums must first be approved by the county commissioner of public welfare by writing filed with the city or town clerk.

Amended by Laws 1943, Ch. 710; Laws 1951, Ch. 77; Laws 1952, Ch. 328; Laws 1963, Ch. 426; Laws 1966, Ch. 256; **amended** by Laws 1974, Ch. 1080, eff. Jan. 1, 1974; **amended** by Laws 1997, Ch. 436, § 1 Part B, § 67, eff. Aug. 20, 1997.

§ 93. Provisions for financing home relief.

1.   Definitions. When used in this section:

(a)   Home relief means home relief as defined in section one hundred fifty-seven and also includes all administrative expenses of home relief.

(b)   Local share of home relief means the total cost or estimated cost of home relief after deducting the amount or the estimated amount of state aid received or to be received therefor under the then existing law and rules.

(c) [*Repealed by Laws 1943, Ch. 712, § 3, eff. July 2, 1944.*]

(d) City means any city responsible for the administration of home relief.

2. Estimates and appropriations. Each county, city and town shall make an annual estimate and appropriation of the total amount required for the fiscal year for home relief in accordance with this article. Such estimates shall show not only the total amount so required, but the estimated state aid to be received, and the estimated local share of home relief.

3. Additional appropriations to supply deficiencies in the annual appropriations. Should the sum or the aggregate of the sums appropriated or amounts available and authorized to be expended in any county, city or town be less than the amount required in any year for home relief, supplemental appropriations may be made from time to time, and that case not less than the same percentage of the local share of home relief included in such supplemental appropriations may be raised by taxes levied for the next fiscal year as would have been raised by taxes for the current fiscal year if the amount of supplemental appropriation had been contained in the annual appropriation for the current fiscal year.

4. [*Repealed by Laws 1943, Ch. 712, § 3, eff. July 2, 1944.*]

5. [*Repealed by Laws 1943, Ch. 712, § 3, eff. July 2, 1944.*]

6. County taxes. County taxes for the payment of obligations and interest thereon, issued for home relief shall be a charge upon the entire county but shall be levied in the first instance against all the taxable property in the territory in which the county public welfare district is responsible for the administration of such home relief.

7. [*Repealed by Laws 1943, Ch. 712, § 3, eff. July 2, 1944.*]

8. Notwithstanding any inconsistent provision of this section, until the commencement of the fiscal year in any county, city or town next following December first, nineteen hundred forty-six, the local share of the cost of home relief in any year, in lieu of being raised by tax, may be paid from any other funds available, provided, however, no monies shall be borrowed to pay the cost of home relief.

Amended by Laws 1941, Chs. 82, 499, 564, 633; Laws 1943, Chs. 674, 710, 712; Laws 1945, Chs. 324, 838; **amended** by Laws 1949, Ch. 99, eff. Mar. 9, 1949.

§ 94. Federal donated commodities.

1. (a) Until his social services district has been included in the food stamp distribution program or programs under section ninety-five, each commissioner of social services is authorized and required, in accordance with regulations of the department, to assist needy families and individuals of his social services district to obtain federal donated commodities for their use, by certifying, when such is the case, that they are eligible to receive such commodities, and by distributing such commodities to eligible families and individuals. However, only

those who are receiving or are eligible for public assistance or care and such others as may qualify in accordance with federal requirements and standards promulgated by the department shall be certified as eligible to receive such commodities.

(b) Each commissioner of social services shall develop and submit to the department for its approval a plan describing his district's operations under this section, which plan shall accord with federal and state requirements.

2. Federal donated commodities shall not be deemed or construed to be public assistance and care or a substitute, in whole or in part, therefor; and the receipt of such commodities by eligible families and individuals shall not subject them, their legally responsible relatives, their property or their estates to any demand, claim or liability on account thereof.

3. A person's need or eligibility for public assistance or care shall not be affected by his receipt of federal donated commodities.

4. Any inconsistent provisions of law notwithstanding, expenditures made by social services districts for the purpose of certifying eligibility of needy families and individuals for federal donated commodities and for distributing such commodities to them shall be deemed to be expenditures for the administration of public assistance and care and shall be subject to reimbursement by the state in accordance with the provisions of section one hundred fifty-three to the extent of one hundred per centum thereof.

Added by Laws 1956, Ch. 240; **amended** by Laws 1960, Ch. 275; **amended** by Laws 1969, Ch. 1015; **amended** by Laws 1970, Ch. 115, eff. Mar. 24, 1970

Laws 1969, Ch. 1015, §§ 3, 4, 5, **amended** by Laws 1970, Ch. 115, provide:

§ 3. Notwithstanding any inconsistent provision of law, each social services district shall make appropriate provision for the additional cost of meals for public assistance recipients who live alone in accommodations without cooking facilities, in accordance with regulations of the state department of social services approved by the director of the budget. Expenditures made by social services districts pursuant to the provisions of this section shall be deemed to be expenditures for public assistance and care and shall be subject to reimbursement by the state in accordance with the provisions of section one hundred fifty-three of the social services law.

§ 4. Each social services district shall make provision for nutrition education for recipients of public assistance and other needy persons receiving federal donated food commodities or food stamps under the provisions of sections ninety-four or ninety-five of the social services law, in accordance with regulations of the state department of social services. Expenditures made by social services districts for the purposes of this section, provided they are approved by the state department of social services, shall be subject to reimbursement by the state at the rate of one hundred per centum thereof, in accordance with the provisions of section one hundred fifty-three of the social services law.

§ 5. In the event that the appropriate federal law would allow both donated commodities and food stamps to be received by needy persons for the same period, the

SSL

social services districts of the state may be required by the state department of social services, with the approval of the director of the budget, to make provision for both pursuant to sections ninety-four and ninety-five of the social services law, any inconsistent provisions thereof notwithstanding.

§ 95. Food stamp program.

1. (a) The department is authorized to submit the plan required by the federal food stamp act of nineteen hundred sixty-four, to the secretary of the federal department of agriculture for approval, and to act for the state in any negotiations relative to the submission and approval of such plan, and may make such arrangements and take such action, not inconsistent with law, as may be required to obtain and retain such approval, to implement such plan, and to secure for the state the benefits available under such act.

(b) The department is authorized to accept a designation, in accordance with the provisions of section twenty-nine, under any other federal law which may make food stamps available for needy families and individuals, and to perform such functions as may be appropriate, permitted or required by or pursuant to such law.

2. The department is empowered, with the consent and approval of the governor, to delegate or assign to any other department or agency of the state the performance of such function or functions under the plan or designation as may be appropriate and permitted or required by the appropriate federal law or regulations. Any state department or agency is hereby empowered and required to perform the function or functions so delegated or assigned to it.

3. (a) Each commissioner of social services is authorized and required, in accordance with regulations of the department, to make application for inclusion of his social services district in the federal food stamp plan or plans and to assist needy families and individuals of his social services district to obtain nutritionally adequate diets through participation in such federal food stamp plan or plans. However, only those persons who qualify for food stamps in accordance with federal and state requirements, and standards promulgated by the department, shall be certified as eligible to receive such stamps.

(b) Each commissioner of social services is authorized and required, subject to state and federal requirements therefor, to act on behalf of the department and receive, store, and issue food stamps, either directly, or with the approval of the department, through a banking institution and/or other appropriate public or private agency.

(c) Each commissioner of social services shall develop and submit to the department for its approval a plan describing his district's operations under this section, which plan shall accord with federal and state requirements.

4. A person's need or eligibility for public assistance and care shall not be affected by his receipt of food stamps.

5. Any inconsistent provision of law notwithstanding, the value of any free food stamps provided an eligible person shall not be considered income or resources for any purpose, including taxation.

6. (a) Any inconsistent provision of law notwithstanding, expenditures made by a social services district for the purpose of certifying eligibility of needy families and individuals, including those who are not in receipt of public assistance and care, for food stamps, and for distributing and redeeming such stamps shall be deemed to be expenditures for the administration of public assistance care, and shall be subject to reimbursement by the state in accordance with the provisions of section one hundred fifty-three of this chapter to the extent of one hundred percent in accordance with paragraph (b) of this subdivision.

(b) Such expenditures for food stamp administrative costs shall be subject to reimbursement by the state in accordance with regulations to be promulgated by the department, which regulations shall be subject to the approval of the director of the budget, shall be consistent with federal law and regulations, and shall be based on:

(i) an allocation of administrative costs attributable to both food stamps and home relief to permit maximum use of federal funds; and

(ii) an allocation of administrative costs attributable to both food stamps and aid to dependent children such that only those administrative costs that cannot be allocated to aid to dependent children are allocated to the food stamp program, provided, however, that if federal law, regulations, or cost allocation procedures require those administrative costs that may be allocated to be allocated between aid to dependent children and food stamps, then the administrative costs so allocated to food stamps shall be reimbursed as costs of public assistance and care in accordance with the provisions of paragraphs a and d of subdivision one of section one hundred fifty-three of this chapter.

7. When an eligible recipient under this section is issued an authorization to participate in the food stamp program by written or electronic means, such authorization to participate may be redeemed for food stamp program coupons at designated redemption centers by the recipient or by an authorized representative. When an eligible recipient under this section is issued food stamp program coupons, such food stamp program coupons may be used to purchase food items from a food distributor by the recipient or by an authorized representative. Any other transfer or sale of authorizations to participate or food stamp program coupons shall constitute an unauthorized use of said authorizations or coupons. For the purposes of this subdivision, "authorized representative" shall be defined in regulations promulgated by the commissioner.

8. Except as part of a transaction pursuant to subdivision seven of this section or as necessary for a food distributor to redeem food stamp program coupons subsequent to such a transaction, any acquisition, acceptance, purchase, possession, sale, transfer, alteration or manufacture of authorizations to participate or food stamp program coupons, real or counterfeit, by any person shall constitute

an unauthorized use of said authorizations or coupons. For purposes of this subdivision, the term "person" shall mean any individual, corporation, partnership, association, agency, or other legal entity, or any part thereof.

9.   (a) The parent or other individual who is living with and exercising parental control over a child under the age of eighteen who has an absent parent is not eligible to participate in the food stamp program if such person refuses to cooperate with the department in establishing the paternity of the child (if the child is born out of wedlock) and in obtaining support for the child or the parent (or other individual) and the child. This paragraph does not apply to the parent (or other individual) if the department determines that there is good cause for the refusal to cooperate.

(b)   A putative or identified noncustodial parent of a child under the age of eighteen is not eligible to participate in the food stamp program if such individual refuses to cooperate with the department in establishing the paternity of the child (if the child is born out of wedlock) and in providing support for the child. The use of the information collected pursuant to this paragraph shall be limited to the purposes for which the information is collected and is subject to the confidentiality provisions set forth in section one hundred thirty-six of this chapter.

(c)   To the extent not inconsistent with federal law and regulations, an individual is not eligible to participate in the food stamp program as a member of any household if the individual is under court order to pay child or combined child and spousal support and has accumulated support arrears equivalent to or greater than the amount of current support due for a period of four months.

10.   (a) Social services districts are authorized to operate a food assistance program in accordance with regulations promulgated by the office of temporary and disability assistance within the department of family assistance. Social services district participation in the food assistance program is optional. Districts opting to participate in the food assistance program shall provide written notification to the office. Such written notification shall include, but not be limited to, a statement whereby the district agrees to operate a food assistance program in accordance with federal and state statutory, regulatory and policy requirements.

(b)   In order to be eligible to receive benefits in the food assistance program, a person must:

(i)   be otherwise fully eligible to receive federal food stamp benefits except for the provisions of section four hundred two of the Personal Responsibility And Work Opportunity Reconciliation Act of 1996 (P.L. 104-193) as amended by the Farm Security and Rural Investment Act of 2002 (P.L. 107-171); and

(ii)   on August twenty-second, nineteen hundred ninety-six, have been living in the United States; and

(iii)   (1) be identified as a victim of domestic violence through procedures outlined in section three hundred forty-nine-a of this chapter or classified as a qualified alien through application of the provisions contained in subsection (c) of 8 USC § 1641; or

(2)   be elderly as defined by 7 USC 2012; and

(iv)   not have been absent from the United States for more than ninety days within the twelve month period immediately preceding the date of application for the food assistance program; and

(v)   apply to the United States department of justice, immigration and naturalization services for United States citizenship. If the applicant for the food assistance program is eligible to apply for United States citizenship, such application shall be made no later than thirty days from the date of application for the food assistance program. If the applicant for the food assistance program is not eligible to apply for United States citizenship on the date of application for the food assistance program, such application for citizenship must be made no later than thirty days after the person becomes eligible to apply for United States citizenship in accordance with the requirements of the United States immigration and naturalization services.

(c)   Social services districts shall be financially responsible for fifty percent of the non-federal share of the necessary costs of operating the food assistance program, including the cost of purchasing the food stamps and any other payments to the federal government required for participating in the program. To the extent that the office of temporary and disability assistance makes expenditures to operate the food assistance program on behalf of a social services district, the participating social services district shall reimburse the office for fifty percent of the non-federal share of such costs.

(d)   Any provision of federal or state law or regulations imposing a sanction, fine, disqualification or other penalty, including criminal penalties, for any violation of such law or regulation with respect to the food stamp program shall apply to the food assistance program.

(e)   The office of temporary and disability assistance is authorized to submit a plan to the federal government in accordance with federal law (P.L. 105-18) in order to secure federal approval to operate the food assistance program in accordance with that law. Such plan shall describe the conditions and procedures under which the benefits will be issued including eligibility standards, benefit levels, and the methodology the office will use to determine the payments due to the federal government.

(f)   The office of temporary and disability assistance is authorized to purchase food stamps from the federal government for use in the food assistance program and to make such other expenditures as are necessary to operate the program. The office of temporary and disability assistance may operate the food assistance program using food stamp coupons or other access devices including an electronic benefit transfer card, personal identification number or debit card. To the extent that such means of benefit issuance is being used by participants in the federal food stamp program in New York state.

SSL

(g)   At the time of application for the food assistance program, an applicant shall, as a condition of receiving such assistance, present proof of identity to the social services official as the office of temporary and disability assistance may require by regulation and the applicant shall provide such proof thereafter whenever required by such official. The commissioner of the social services district shall require that a recipient of food assistance benefits comply with the requirements of an automated fraud prevention system as established for recipients of public assistance and care in accordance with the provisions of this chapter. Such system shall be used to establish personally unique identification factors to prevent fraud and multiple enrollments. The social services district shall be responsible for fifty percent of the costs of establishing and operating such system in accordance with paragraph (c) of this subdivision. Personally identifying information about applicants for and recipients of the food assistance program obtained through the establishment or operation of the system by the office, social services districts or by a contractor shall be kept confidential in accordance with section one hundred thirty-six of this chapter and the regulations of the office.

(h)   Any inconsistent provision of law notwithstanding, in the event the federal government assesses a penalty, sanction, or fine because of a social services district's incorrect issuance of food stamp benefits in cases where the household consists of both federally participating food stamp program recipients and recipients under the food assistance program, social services districts shall be responsible for one hundred percent of the penalty, sanction, or fine assessed by the federal government.

(i)   The commissioner of the office of temporary and disability assistance is authorized to file regulations on an emergency basis that are deemed by the commissioner to be necessary to implement the food assistance program.

(j)   If any clause, sentence, paragraph or subdivision of this section shall be adjudged by any court of competent jurisdiction to be invalid, such judgement shall not affect, impair or invalidate the remainder thereof, but shall be confined in its operation to the clause, sentence, paragraph or subdivision thereof directly involved in the controversy in which such judgement shall have been rendered.

(k)   This subdivision shall be effective only when and for so long as that federal approval, as set forth in paragraph (e) of this subdivision, has been obtained. This subdivision shall terminate and cease to be in force and effect on and after September thirtieth, two thousand five.

11.   Notwithstanding any other provision of law to the contrary, the office of temporary and disability assistance within the department of family assistance shall develop a brief, simplified application form for the food stamp program only. The office of temporary and disability assistance shall develop the form in consultation with food stamp outreach organizations and consider how the form may be used to reach as many potential applicants as possible, especially those over sixty years of age and those who are employed.

* As enacted.

Added by Laws 1965, Ch. 225; **amended** by Laws 1966, Ch. 268; Laws 1969, Ch. 1015; Laws 1979, Ch. 313, eff. Jan. 1, 1979; **amended** by Laws 1983, Ch. 22, eff. Jan. 1, 1979; **amended** by Laws 1986, Ch. 452, eff. Nov. 1, 1986; **amended** by Laws 1997, Ch. 436, § 1 Part B, § 53 and 148-b, eff. Aug. 20, 1997; **amended** by Laws 2001, Ch. 362, §§ 1, 2, eff. Oct. 3, 2001; **amended** by Laws 2002, Ch. 333, § 1, eff. Aug. 6, 2002; **amended** by Laws 2003, Ch. 360, §§ 1, 2, eff. Apr. 1, 2003.

§ 95-a.   State food stamp outreach program.

1. In accordance with federal requirements and to the extent that federal matching funds are available, the department shall develop and implement an outreach plan to inform low-income households potentially eligible to receive food stamps of the availability and benefits of the program and to encourage the participation of eligible households that wish to participate.

2. In developing and implementing such a plan the department and/or its local districts are authorized and empowered, subject to the approval of the director of the budget and provided that federal aid is available therefor, to enter into contractual agreements with public and/or private organizations to develop and implement local regional, and statewide outreach programs.

3. Each commissioner of social services shall develop and submit to the department on an annual basis for its approval, a local outreach plan governing the use of local social services personnel and services provided by federally funded and other agencies and organizations to inform potentially eligible households of the availability and benefits of the program and to encourage and facilitate the participation of eligible households. The department shall provide commissioners of social services with technical assistance as needed to carry out the provisions of this subdivision.

4. As part of each local outreach plan, social services officials shall take all steps necessary to maintain a supply of information leaflets in public buildings, including but not limited to local unemployment insurance and employment services offices of the department of labor, institutions and facilities under the supervision or control of the department of health, food stores, union halls, community centers and local agencies providing services to the elderly to help insure that eligible persons are informed of the food stamp program.

5. The department shall periodically distribute to all newspapers, and to television and radio stations throughout the state, public service announcements describing the food stamp program, including the toll-free telephone numbers for food stamp information, and shall promptly inform such media of significant changes in the program affecting eligibility requirements and/or the amount of the food stamp bonus.

6. The department shall establish procedures in cooperation with the industrial commissioner of the department of labor to ensure that informational leaflets about the food stamp program are sent to each local employment services office for distribution pursuant to section five hundred and forty of the labor law. Each

SSL

leaflet shall include but not be limited to: the phone number for the New York State food stamp hotline, estimated maximum income eligibility levels by household size for participation in the food stamp program and the availability of local social services departments to provide additional information about the program.

7. In accordance with applicable federal laws rules and regulations the department shall make available appropriate bilingual materials so that potentially eligible non-English speaking individuals may be informed about the food stamp program.

8. The department shall promulgate rules and regulations and take all other actions necessary for the effective implementation of this section.

Added by Laws 1978, Ch. 546, eff. Oct. 22, 1978.

§ 96. Use of subprofessional staff.

Any inconsistent provision of law, general, special or local notwithstanding, a local social services district shall provide for the training and use of subprofessional staff, with particular emphasis on the use of public assistance recipients in accordance with state and federal requirements.

Added by Laws 1971, Ch. 298, eff. May 24, 1971.

§ 97. Low-income home energy assistance program.

1. The department is authorized to develop and submit to the governor the application and plan required by title twenty-six of the federal omnibus budget reconciliation act of nineteen hundred eighty-one, and to amend and to take whatever other action may be necessary with respect to such plan, including, but not limited to, acting for the state in any negotiations relative to the submission of such plan, and making such arrangements and taking such action, not inconsistent with law, as may be required to submit, implement, administer and operate such plan, and to secure for the state the benefits available under such act.

2. Each social services district shall be required, in accordance with the state plan and federal regulations, to participate in the federal low-income home energy assistance program and to assist eligible households found in such districts to obtain low-income home energy assistance. However, only those persons who qualify for low-income home energy assistance in accordance with federal and state requirements, and standards promulgated by the department, shall be certified as eligible for and entitled to receive said home energy assistance. No person, however, shall be certified as eligible for and entitled to receive said home energy assistance if no federal funds are available for such purpose.

3. Any inconsistent provision of law notwithstanding, the amount of any home energy assistance payments or allowances provided to an eligible household under said plan shall not be considered income or resources of such

households, or of any member thereof, for any purpose under any federal or state law, including any law relating to taxation, food stamps, public assistance or other benefits available pursuant to this chapter.

4. Expenditures made by a social services district pursuant to the federal low-income home energy assistance program, including the costs of administration, shall be subject to one hundred percent reimbursement by the state, if and for so long as federal funds are available for the full amount of such expenditures.

5. No less than fifteen percent of the funds available to New York state under the federal low-income home energy assistance program shall be used for low-cost residential weatherization or other energy-related home repair for low-income households, as follows:

a. No less than ten percent of the funds available to New York state under the federal low-income home energy assistance program shall be allocated to the division of housing and community renewal for its weatherization assistance program and shall be expended as provided in the annual New York state weatherization plan.

b. Administrative funds to implement the program described in this subdivision at the state and local levels shall be set at ten percent of the total amount allocated to the division of housing and community renewal. Administrative monies shall be derived from funds identified by the division of the budget as that portion of the home energy assistance program grant reported to the federal department of health and human services for state administration of such program.

Added by Laws 1983, Ch. 785, eff. July 30, 1983; **amended** by Laws 1992, Ch. 774, § 2, eff. Aug. 7, 1992; **amended** by Laws 1996, Ch. 309, § 154, eff. July 13, 1996.

TITLE 6—POWERS TO ENFORCE SUPPORT

———

(Repealed and transferred sections noted under appropriate section number of text).

SSL

§ 101. Liability of relatives to support.

1. Except as otherwise provided by law, the spouse or parent of a recipient of public assistance or care or of a person liable to become in need thereof shall, if of sufficient ability, be responsible for the support of such person, provided that a parent shall be responsible only for the support of a child under the age of twenty-one years. Stepparents shall in like manner be responsible for the support of stepchildren under the age of twenty-one years. Nothing herein shall impose any liability upon a person to support the adopted child of his or her spouse if such child was adopted after the adopting spouse is living separate and apart from the non-adopting spouse pursuant to a legally recognizable separation agreement or decree under the domestic relations law. Such liability shall not be imposed for so long as the spouses remain separate and apart after the adoption.

2. The liability imposed by this section shall be for the benefit of the public welfare district concerned or any legally incorporated non-profit institution which receives payments from any governmental agency for the care of medically indigent persons, and such liability may be enforced by appropriate proceedings and actions in a court of competent jurisdiction. Such proceedings and actions may be brought by such an institution in any court wherein a similar proceeding or action could be brought by a public welfare official.

3. The expiration of any period of time for the payment of maintenance by a court in a matrimonial action shall not be a bar to the enforcement of the liability imposed by this section.

Amended by Laws 1945, Ch. 656; Laws 1960, Ch. 1088; Laws 1965, Ch. 52; Laws 1966, Ch. 256; Laws 1974, Ch. 909; Laws 1977, Ch. 777; **amended** by Laws 1980, Ch. 281, eff. July 19, 1980; **amended** by Laws 1984, Ch. 745, eff. Dec. 3, 1984.

§ 101-a. Proceedings to compel support by persons in need thereof.

A recipient of public assistance or care or a person liable to become in need thereof may bring proceedings in a court of competent jurisdictions against any person responsible for his or her support as provided in section one hundred one of this chapter to compel any such person so responsible to provide for or contribute to such support.

Added by Laws 1960, Ch. 943; **amended** by Laws 1972, Ch. 687; **amended** by Laws 1976, Ch. 326, eff. June 8, 1976.

Note.—Laws 1972, Ch. 687 § 4 provides:

The provisions of this act shall be ineffective to the extent that they are determined to be not in compliance with federal law regulations pertaining to public assistance and care.

§ 102. Powers of public welfare officials to bring and defend suits.

A public welfare official responsible, by or pursuant to any provision of this chapter, for the administration of the public assistance or care granted or applied for is empowered to bring proceedings in a court of competent jurisdiction:

1. to compel any person liable by law for support to contribute to the support of any person cared for at public expense, or person liable to become so dependent. A bond may be required of such person liable for support to indemnify the public welfare district against the cost of the support of such person;

2. to recover penalties, forfeitures and prosecute any bonds, undertakings and recognizances; and

3. to defend in any court all matters relating to the support of persons at public expense.

Amended by Laws 1946, Ch. 200, eff. Apr. 1, 1946.

§ 103. Seizure of property of persons liable for support.

The responsible public welfare official may apply to a court having jurisdiction in actions involving an amount equal to the value of property to be seized for a warrant to seize the real or personal estate of a person who absents himself, leaving any one for whose support he is liable dependent upon public support or liable to become so dependent. If such a warrant be issued, the public welfare official may seize the property and apply the proceeds as directed by the court.

§ 104. Recovery from a person discovered to have property.

1. A public welfare official may bring action or proceeding against a person discovered to have real or personal property, or against the estate or the executors, administrators and successors in interest of a person who dies leaving real or personal property, if such person, or any one for whose support he is or was liable, received assistance and care during the preceding ten years, and shall be entitled to recover up to the value of such property the cost of such assistance or care. Any public assistance or care received by such person shall constitute an implied contract. No claim of a public welfare official against the estate or the executors,

SSL

administrators and successors in interest of a person who dies leaving real or personal property, shall be barred or defeated, in whole or in part, by any lack of sufficiency of ability on the part of such person during the period assistance and care were received.

Nor shall the claim asserted by a public welfare official against any person under this section be impaired, impeded, barred or defeated, in whole or in part, on the grounds that another person or persons may also have been liable to contribute.

In all claims of the public welfare official made under this section the public welfare official shall be deemed a preferred creditor.

2.   No right of action shall accrue against a person under twenty-one years of age by reason of the assistance or care granted to him unless at the time it was granted the person was possessed of money and property in excess of his reasonable requirements, taking into account his maintenance, education, medical care and any other factors applicable to his condition.

3.   To the extent described in section 7-1.12 of the estates, powers and trusts law, the trustee of a supplemental needs trust which conforms to the provisions of such section 7-1.12 shall not be deemed to be holding assets for the benefit of a beneficiary who may otherwise be the subject of a claim under this section and no action may be brought against either the trust or the trustee to recover the cost of assistance or care provided to such person, or anyone for whose support such person is or was liable.

4.   Any inconsistent provision of this chapter or of any other law notwithstanding, a social services official may not assert any claim under any provision of this chapter to recover payments of public assistance if such payments were reimbursed by child support collections.

Amended by Laws 1941, Ch. 82; Laws 1953, Ch. 838; Laws 1961, Ch. 55; Laws 1963, Ch. 509; Laws 1964, Ch. 573; Laws 1968, Ch. 448; **amended** by Laws 1974, Ch. 909, eff. Sept. 1, 1974; **amended** by Laws 1993, Ch. 433, § 3, **adding** new subd. (3) eff. July 26, 1993; **amended** by Laws 2003, Ch.340, § 1, adding subd. (4) eff. Jan 1, 2004.

§ 104-a.   Transfer of property for the purpose of qualifying for assistance; presumption.

For the purposes of the provisions of this chapter disqualifying a person from eligibility for a category of public assistance or care by reason of his voluntary transfer of property, a transfer of property made within one year from the date of the person's application for such assistance shall be presumed to have been made for the purpose of qualifying for such assistance.

Added by Laws 1971, Ch. 550, eff. June 17, 1971.

§ 104-b.   Liens for public assistance and care on claims and suits for personal injuries.

1.   If a recipient of public assistance and care shall have a right of action, suit, claim, counterclaim or demand against another on account of any personal injuries suffered by such recipient, then the public welfare official for the public welfare district providing such assistance and care shall have a lien for such amount as may be fixed by the public welfare official not exceeding, however, the total amount of such assistance and care furnished by such public welfare official on and after the date when such injuries were incurred.

The welfare commissioner shall endeavor to ascertain whether such person, firm or corporation alleged to be responsible for such injuries is insured with a liability insurance company, as the case may be, and the name thereof.

2.   No such lien shall be effective, however, unless a written notice containing the name and address of the injured recipient, the date and place of the accident, and the name of the person, firm or corporation alleged to be liable to the injured party for such injuries, together with a brief statement of the nature of the lien, the amount claimed and that a lien is claimed upon the said right of action, suit, claim, counterclaim or demand by the public welfare official be served prior to the payment of any moneys to such injured party, by certified with returnreceipt or registered mail upon such person, firm or corporation, and his or her, its or their attorney, if known, and upon any insurance carrier which has insured such person, firm or corporation against such liability. A copy of the notice of lien shall be mailed to such carrier at least twenty days prior to the date on which such carrier makes a payment to the injured party. Except as against such carrier, the effectiveness of the lien against any other party shall not be impaired by the failure to mail the required notice to such carrier. In addition, a true copy of such notice shall be served by regular mail to the welfare recipient and to his or her attorney, if known. Such mailing shall be deemed to be effective, notwithstanding any inaccuracy or omission, if the information contained therein shall be sufficient to enable those to whom the notice is given to identify the injured recipient and the occurrence upon which his or her claim for damages is based.

3.   Upon the service of the notice, as aforesaid, the local public welfare official shall file a true copy thereof in the office of the clerk of the county in which his office is located, and, thereupon the lien of the public welfare official in the amount therein stated shall attach to any verdict, decision, decree, judgment, award or final order in any suit, action or proceeding in any court or administrative tribunal of this state respecting such injuries, as well as the proceeds of any settlement thereof, and the proceeds of any settlement of any claim or demand respecting such injuries prior to suit or action.

4.   An amended notice of lien may be served and filed by such public welfare official in the same manner and subject to the provisions of this section governing the notice of lien originally served and filed pursuant to this section.

SSL

5.   (a) The person, firm, corporation or insurance carrier, having notice that a social services official has served and filed a notice of lien, and intending to make payment on the personal injury claim upon which the lien was filed, shall notify the social services official by certified or registered mail, at least ten days prior to the date such payment is proposed to be made, of the amount and date thereof.

(b)   Notwithstanding any inconsistent provision of this section, the social services official shall have the right to serve and file by certified or registered mail, within five days after receipt of such notice, excluding Saturdays, Sundays, and holidays, an amended notice of lien to include the amount of public assistance and care furnished to the recipient after the date such official served and filed the notice of lien or the last previous amendment thereof.

(c)   A person, firm, corporation or insurance carrier that fails to give the notice required by paragraph (a) of this subdivision shall be liable to the social services official to the same extent that it would have been liable had such notice been given and the social services official had filed the amended notice of lien provided for in paragraph (b) of this subdivision.

6.   Such lien may be enforced by action against those alleged to be liable for such injuries, as aforesaid, by the local public welfare official in any court of appropriate jurisdiction.

7.   The aforesaid lien shall be valid and effective, when the notice thereof and the statement are served and filed as aforesaid, and shall continue until released and discharged by the local public welfare official by an instrument in writing and filed in the said county clerk's office, and no release, payment, discharge or satisfaction of any such claim, demand, right of action, suit or counterclaim shall be valid or effective against such lien.

8.   The county clerk shall, at the expense of the county, provide a suitable book with proper index, to be called the public welfare lien docket, in which he shall enter the names of the public welfare official and the recipient, the date and place of the accident and the name or names of those alleged to be liable for such injuries, as aforesaid.

9.   The provisions of this section to the contrary notwithstanding, the lien herein created shall be subject and subordinate to the lien on the amount recovered by verdict, report, decision, judgment, award or decree, settlement or compromise, of any attorney or attorneys retained by any such injured person to prosecute his claim for damages for personal injuries, having or acquiring by virtue of such retainer a lien on the cause of action of any such injured person, or on the verdict, report, decision, judgment, decree made in, or any settlement or compromise of, any such action or claim for damages for personal injuries.

10.   The provisions of this section to the contrary notwithstanding, the lien herein created shall be subordinate to the lien of any hospital claimed under and to the extent recognized by section one hundred eighty-nine of the lien law, but

only for treatment, care and maintenance given, prior to or in excess of the public assistance and care granted by the public welfare official.

11.   The provisions of this section shall not be deemed to adversely affect the right of a public welfare official who has taken an assignment of the proceeds of any such right of action, suit, claim, counterclaim or demand, to recover under such assignment the total amount of assistance and care for which such assignment was made.

12.   The provisions of this section to the contrary notwithstanding, the lien herein created shall not apply with respect to any claim or benefits payable to the recipients of any form of public assistance or care, part of which is paid for by the government of the United States or any agency thereof when, in the opinion of the commissioner, such lien would jeopardize the continuation of such federal contribution.

13.   The provisions of this section to the contrary notwithstanding, the public welfare official may in his discretion release to the injured person an amount not to exceed the cost of two years' maintenance from the lien herein created.

This section shall not apply to any claim or award which is or may be allowed pursuant to the provisions of the workmen's compensation law or the volunteer firemen's benefit law.

14.   Any inconsistent provision of this chapter or of any other law notwithstanding, a social services official may not assert any claim under any provision of this chapter to recover payments of public assistance if such payments were reimbursed by child support collections.

Added by Laws 1964, Ch. 382; **amended** by Laws 1965, Ch. 271; Laws 1969, Ch. 560, eff. Sept. 1, 1969; formerly § 104-a **renumbered** 104-b by Laws 1971, Ch. 550, eff. June 17, 1971; **amended** by Laws 2003, Ch.340, § 2, **adding** new subd. (14) eff. Jan 1, 2004; **amended** by Laws 2005, Ch. 281, § 1, eff. July 19, 2005.

§ 105.   Claim on insurance.

If a person, who has received public assistance or care, shall die leaving insurance, and the estate of the assured is named as beneficiary, or no beneficiary is named, the social services official shall be entitled to a preferred claim to be paid out of such insurance to the amount of the cost of such assistance and care, and for funeral expenses not to exceed two hundred fifty dollars. If the insured leaves a surviving spouse or children under the age of twenty-one years who are, or are liable to become, public charges, the social services official may, in his discretion, waive his claim to such insurance or any part thereof to which he would otherwise be entitled.

Amended by Laws 1944, Ch. 688; Laws 1958, Ch. 772; Laws 1974, Ch. 909; Laws 1976, Ch. 152, eff. Sept. 1, 1976.

§ 106.　Powers of social services official to receive and dispose of a deed, mortgage, or lien.

1.　A social services official responsible, by or pursuant to any provision of this chapter, for the administration of assistance or care granted or applied for may accept a deed of real property and/or a mortgage thereon on behalf of the public welfare district for the assistance and care of a person at public expense but such property shall not be considered as public property and shall remain on the tax rolls and such deed or mortgage shall be subject to redemption as provided in paragraph (a) of subdivision two hereof.

2.　(a) (1) Until such property or mortgage is sold, assigned or foreclosed pursuant to law by the social services official, the person giving such deed or mortgage, or his estate or those entitled thereto, may redeem the same by the payment of all expenses incurred for the support of the person, and for repairs and taxes paid on such property; provided, however, that a social services official may enter into a contract for such redemption, subject to the provisions of this paragraph, and containing such terms and conditions, including provisions for periodic payments, with or without interest, as the social services official shall deem appropriate, for an amount less than the full expenses incurred for the support of the person and for repairs and taxes paid on such property (hereinafter called a "lesser sum"), which lesser sum shall in no event be less than the difference between the appraised value of such property and the total of the then unpaid principal balance of any recorded mortgages and the unpaid balance of sums secured by other liens against such property.

(2)　In the case of a redemption for a lesser sum, the social services official shall obtain (i) an appraisal of the current market value of such property, by an appraiser acceptable to both parties, and (ii) a statement of the principal balance of any recorded mortgages or other liens against such property (excluding the debt secured by the deed, mortgage or lien of the social services official). Any expenses incurred pursuant to this paragraph shall be audited and allowed in the same manner as other official expenses.

(3)　Every redemption contract for any lesser sum shall be approved by the department upon an application by the social services official containing the appraisal and statement required by subparagraph two, a statement by the social services official of his reasons for entering into the contract for such lesser sum and any other information required by regulations of the department.

(4)　So long s the terms of the approved redemption contract are performed, no public sale of such property shall be held.

(5)　So long as the terms of the approved redemption contract are performed, no public sale of such property shall be held.

(6)　The redemption for a lesser sum shall reduce the claim of the social services official against the recipient on the implied contract under section one hundred four of this chapter or under any other law, to the extent of all sums paid in redemption.

(b)   In order to allow a minimum period for redemption, the public welfare official shall not sell the property or mortgage until after the expiration of one year from the date he received the deed or mortgage, but if unoccupied property has not been redeemed within six months from the date of death of the person who conveyed it to him by deed the public welfare official may thereafter, and before the expiration of such year, sell the property.

(c)   Except as otherwise provided in this chapter, upon the death of the person or his receiving institutional care, if the mortgage has not been redeemed, sold or assigned, the public welfare official may enforce collection of the mortgage debt in the manner provided for the foreclosure of mortgages by action.

(d)   Provided the department shall have given its approval in writing, the public welfare official may, when in his judgment it is advisable and in the public interest, release a part of the property from the lien of the mortgage to permit, and in consideration of, the sale of such part by the owner and the application of the proceeds to reduce said mortgage or to satisfy and discharge or reduce a prior or superior mortgage.

(e)   While real property covered by a deed or mortgage is occupied, in whole or in part, by an aged, blind or disabled person who executed such deed or mortgage to the social services official for old age assistance, assistance to the blind or aid to the disabled granted to such person before January first, nineteen hundred seventy-four, the social services official shall not sell the property or assign or enforce the mortgage unless it appears reasonably certain that the sale or other disposition of the property will not materially adversely affect the welfare of such person. After the death of such person no claim for assistance granted him shall be enforced against any real property while it is occupied by the surviving spouse.

(f)   Except as otherwise provided, upon the death of a person who executed a lien to the social services official in return for old age assistance, assistance to the blind or aid to the disabled granted prior to January first, nineteen hundred seventy-four, or before the death of such person if it appears reasonably certain that the sale or other disposition of the property will not materially adversely affect the welfare of such person, the social services official may enforce such lien in the manner provided by article three of the lien law. After the death of such person the lien may not be enforced against real property while it is occupied by the surviving spouse.

3.   The sale of any parcel of real property or mortgage on real property by the public welfare official, under the provisions of this section, shall be made at a public sale, held at least two weeks after notice thereof shall have been published in a newspaper having a general circulation in that section of the county in which the real property is located. Such notice shall specify the time and place of such public sale and shall contain a brief description of the premises to be sold, or upon which the mortgage is a lien, as the case may be. Unless in the judgment of the public welfare official, it shall be in the public interest to reject all bids, such parcel or mortgage shall be sold to the highest responsible bidder.

4.   Any inconsistent provision of this chapter or of any other law notwithstanding, a social services official may not assert any claim under any provision of this chapter to recover payments of public assistance if such payments were reimbursed by child support collections.

Amended by Laws 1942, Ch. 921; Laws 1946, Ch. 200; Laws 1947, Ch. 673; Laws 1948, Ch. 271; Laws 1952, Ch. 43; Laws 1955, Ch. 150; Laws 1962, Ch. 310; Laws 1972, Ch. 764; **amended** by Laws 1974, Ch. 1080, eff. Jan. 1, 1974; by Laws 2003, Ch.340, § 3, **amended** by Laws 340, § 3, eff. Jan 1, 2004.

§ 106-a.   Exemption from payment of fees for instruments affecting real or personal property; exemption of mortgages from mortgage recording tax.

Any inconsistent provision of law notwithstanding, a social services official shall not be required to pay any fee to any clerk, register or other public officer for entering, filing, registering or recording any instrument affecting real or personal property or to the surrogate court when such official in taking any proceeding with respect to the estate of a person who was a recipient of benefits from social services pertaining to the exercise by the social services official of any of the powers conferred or duties imposed upon him by any of the provisions of this chapter. Mortgages on real property taken by social services officials pursuant to this chapter for assistance and care of persons at public expense shall be exempt from the mortgage recording taxes imposed by article eleven of the tax law. The exemption from mortgage recording taxes herein provided shall also apply to all mortgages heretofore taken by social services officials and recorded without payment of mortgage taxes, retroactively to the date of recording of such mortgages.

Added by Laws 1952, Ch. 142; **amended** by Laws 1953, Ch. 254; **amended** by Laws 1955, Ch. 474; **amended** by Laws 1972, Ch. 438, eff. May 22, 1972.

§ 106-b.   Adjustment for incorrect payments.

Any inconsistent provision of law notwithstanding, a social services official shall, in accordance with the regulations of the department and consistent with federal law and regulations, take all necessary steps to correct any overpayment or underpayment to a public assistance recipient; provided, however, that a social services official may waive recovery of a past overpayment, in the case of an individual who is not currently a recipient of public assistance, where the cost of recovery is greater than the cost of collections as determined in accordance with department regulations consistent with federal law and regulations. For purposes of this section, overpayment shall include payments made to an eligible person in excess of his needs as defined in this chapter and payments made to ineligible persons (including payments made to such persons pending a fair hearings decision). The commissioner shall promulgate regulations to implement procedures for correcting overpayments and underpayments. The procedures for correcting overpayments shall be designed to minimize adverse impact on the recipient, and to the extent possible avoid undue hardship. Notwithstanding any other provision of law to the contrary, no underpayment shall be corrected with respect to a person who is currently not eligible for or in receipt of home relief or aid to dependent children, except that corrective payments may be made with respect to persons formerly eligible for or in receipt of aid to dependent children to the extent that federal law and regulations require.

Added by Laws 1974, Ch. 979, eff. June 13, 1974 provided, however, that the provisions of the act are effective with respect to overpayments made prior to the effective date; the act also ratified acts to recoup overpayments taken by social services officials pursuant to department regulations prior to the effective date; **amended** by Laws 1981, Ch. 1053, eff. Jan. 1, 1982; **amended** by Laws 1985, Ch. 42, eff. Oct. 1, 1984; **amended** by Laws 1995, Ch. 81, § 185, eff. July 1, 1995.

§ 106-c.   Crediting of overpayment of tax to obligation of public assistance recipients.

1.   The commissioner shall enter into an agreement with the commissioner of taxation and finance which shall set forth the procedures for the crediting of overpayments of tax owed to an individual taxpayer, estate or trust to the repayment of overpayments of grants and allowances owed to the department or a social services district by such person pursuant to the provisions of section one hundred seventy-one-f of the tax law and is authorized to furnish to the commissioner of taxation and finance such information and to take such other actions as may be necessary to carry out the agreement provided for in such section, for the crediting of overpayments of tax to repayment of overpayments of public assistance. The department shall by regulation establish procedures by which any individual, estate or trust which is the subject of a certification to the department of taxation and finance in accordance with such agreement may contest such certification. Such regulations and the notice required by subdivision three of section one hundred seventy-one-f of the tax law shall set forth defenses which may be available to the individual, estate or trust to contest such certification and the manner in which a review of the certification based on such defenses may be obtained.

2.   In accordance with such agreement and the provisions of section one hundred seventy-one-f of the tax law, the department shall be entitled to receive payments to satisfy the payment obligation of a person receiving or who has received grants and allowances pursuant to section one hundred thirty-one-a, section one hundred thirty-one-s, section three hundred one, and section three hundred fifty-j of this chapter, in accordance with a written final determination of the department or a social services district, provided that no proceeding for administrative or judicial review shall then be pending and the time for initiation of such proceeding shall have expired.

Added by Laws 1995, Ch. 81, § 174, eff. Sept. 1, 1995.

§ 107.   Disposal of seized property and penalties collected.

All properties seized and penalties collected shall be administered in accordance with the direction of the court having jurisdiction. After the expenses approved by the court have been paid the balance shall be used for the maintenance of such person, or to reimburse the public welfare fund for expenditures previously made for his assistance or care.

§ 108.   Appointment of guardians for minors; notice of accounting.

If the beneficiary of such seized property or penalty which is collected shall be a minor who is not in the custody of a parent and for whom no guardian has been appointed, the court having jurisdiction over the matter shall appoint a guardian of the property for such minor. Notice of the accounting shall be given to the person, or the executors, administrators or successors in interest of the person, for whose support the property has been seized or the penalty collected, and to the guardian of any minor affected thereby.

§ 109.   Trust funds to be established.

A public welfare official shall deposit any funds received from the seizure of property or collection of penalties for the support of a living person. Such fund shall, as provided in section eighty-seven, be held and used upon such terms as the court shall direct for the benefit of such person. If the beneficiary of the fund is a minor, the court may require the public welfare official to give security and to report.

§ 110.   Support of children in schools for juvenile delinquents.

Repealed by Laws 1971, Ch. 947, eff. July 1, 1971 and subject matter transferred to Executive Law, Art. 19-g.

§ 110-a.   Special provisions for legal services to enforce support to recover costs of public assistance and care to establish paternity.

1.   Any inconsistent provision of law notwithstanding, the appropriating body of a social services district may authorize and make provision for the social services commissioner of such district to obtain: (a)necessary legal services on a fee for service basis or other appropriate basis which the department may approve, to obtain support from spouses and parents, to recover costs of public assistance and care granted, to establish paternity, and to initiate and prosecute proceedings for the commitment of the guardianship and custody of destitute or dependent children to authorized agencies, pursuant to the provisions of this chapter and the domestic relations law, the family court act and other laws, and (b) necessary services of private investigators, licensed pursuant to section seventy of the general business law, on a fee for service or other appropriate basis

which the department may approve, to provide investigative assistance in efforts of the district to locate absent parents and fathers of children born out of wedlock.

2.   Expenditures made by a social services district for the costs of such services shall be subject to reimbursement by the state pursuant to the provisions of section one hundred fifty-three or other appropriate provisions of this chapter.

Added by Laws 1974, Ch. 773; **amended** by Laws 1977, Ch. 756; **amended** by Laws 1978, Ch. 456, eff. July 1, 1978.

§ 111.   Functions of the department.

To assist welfare departments to carry out their responsibilities, powers and duties to enforce the liability of persons for the support of certain of their dependents who are applicants for or recipients of public assistance or care or who are in receipt of child support services pursuant to section one hundred eleven-g of this chapter, the department shall:

1.   Continue to act as, and perform the functions of, state information agent for the purposes of the uniform interstate family support act of this state (Article 5-B of the Family Court Act) and reciprocal laws of other states.

2.   As required by section three hundred seventy-two-a, aid in the location of deserting parents and, for such purpose, operate a central registry of deserting parents, obtain and transmit pertinent information and data from public officials and agencies and assist in the training of local personnel employed to locate such parents.

3.   Stimulate and encourage cooperation, through the holding of meetings and the exchange of information, between and among public officials, law enforcement agencies and courts having powers and duties relating to the enforcement of the liability of persons for the support of indigent members of their families, including cooperation with public officials, agencies and courts of other states.

4.   Upon request, or when required to do so by other provisions of law, advise such officials in the performance of their duties hereinabove referred to.

5.   Develop or assist in the development of appropriate forms, guides, manuals, handbooks and other material which may be necessary or useful effectively to accomplish the foregoing and the purposes therefor.

Added by Laws 1962, Ch. 245, eff. Mar. 27, 1962; **amended** by Laws 1997, Ch. 398, § 41, eff. Jan. 1, 1998.

TITLE 6-A—ESTABLISHMENT OF PATERNITY AND ENFORCEMENT OF SUPPORT

§ 111-a. Federal aid; state plan.

1. The department is hereby designated as the single state agency to supervise the administration of the state's child support program provided for by this title, and a single organizational unit shall be established within the department for such purposes.

2. The department shall develop and submit a state child support program plan as required by part D of title IV of the federal social security act to the federal department of health, education and welfare for approval pursuant to such part in order to qualify the state for federal aid under such part. The department shall act for the state in any negotiations relative to the submission and approval of such plan and shall make such arrangements as may be necessary to obtain and retain such approval and to secure for the state the benefits of the provisions of such federal act relating to child support programs. The department shall promulgate regulations not inconsistent with law as may be necessary to assure that such plan conforms to the provisions of such part and any federal regulations adopted pursuant thereto. The department shall make all reports required by law to be made to such federal department in the form and manner required by federal regulations.

Added by Laws 1975, Ch. 685. Laws 1975, Ch. 685, § 10 provides:

"In order for the state to maximize federal aid under parts IV–A [42 U.S.C. §§ 601 *et seq.,* 'Aid to Families with Dependent Children'] and IV–D [42 U.S.C. §§ 651 *et seq.,* 'Child Support and Establishment of Paternity'] of the federal social security act, and to obtain maximum benefits from collection of support with respect to persons applying for or receiving aid to dependent children, all officials having responsibilities with relation to establishing paternity, enforcing support obligations and collecting support payments shall at all times fully cooperate with all other such officials, and are authorized to enter into cooperative arrangements, including written agreements, for such purposes."

Amended by Laws 1976, Ch. 326; Laws 1977, Ch. 516; Laws 1978, Ch. 456, § 19, eff. July 1, 1978, which provides:

"This act shall take effect on the first day of July, nineteen hundred seventy-five, provided, however, that by no later than January fifteenth of each year the commissioner shall prepare and submit to the governor and the legislature a detailed report setting forth: (a) the problems that have been encountered in implementing an effective child support enforcement program; (b) the effectiveness of local social services districts in operating such programs; (c) his recommendations as to modifying any administrative or judicial powers, duties, functions or procedures, including any recommendations for statutory changes that may be necessary, to improve the operation and administration of the child support program."

Amended by Laws 1982, Ch. 384, eff. Apr. 1, 1983.

§ 111-b. Functions, powers and duties of the department.

1. The single organizational unit within the department shall be responsible for the supervision of the activities of state and local officials relating to establishment of paternity of children born out of wedlock, location of absent parents and enforcement of support obligations of legally responsible relatives to contribute for the support of their dependents.

2. The department is hereby authorized to accept, on behalf of the state and the social services districts concerned, assignments of support rights owed to persons receiving (i) aid to dependent children pursuant to title ten of article five of this chapter or, (ii) where appropriate, foster care maintenance payments made pursuant to title IV-E of the federal social security act; provided however, that it will not be appropriate where such requirement will have a negative impact upon the health, safety or welfare of such child or other individuals in the household or impair the likelihood of the child returning to his or her family when discharged from foster care, or (iii) home relief pursuant to title three of article five of this chapter. Notwithstanding any inconsistent provisions of title six of this article or any other provisions of law, the department may enforce such assigned support rights either directly, through social services officials or, if there is in effect an approved agreement between the social services official and another governmental agency, through such other agency. In any proceeding to enforce such assignment, the official bringing such proceeding shall have the same rights as if the proceeding were being brought to enforce section four hundred fifteen of the family court act.

2-a. The department shall prepare a notice which shall be distributed by social services officials to persons who may be required to assign support rights which notice shall explain the rights and obligations that may result from the establishment of paternity and the right of the assignor to be kept informed, upon request, of the time, date and place of any proceedings involving the assignor and such other information as the department believes is pertinent. The notice shall state that the attorney initiating the proceeding represents the department.

3. In appropriate cases, the department is authorized to utilize support enforcement and collection and location services made available through the secretary of health and human services including the services of federal courts, the federal parent locator service, the federal case registry of child support orders,

the national directory of new hires, and the treasury department, if and so long as authorized and required by federal law.

4.   The department shall maintain and operate a parent locator service with respect to cases being provided services pursuant to this title. To effectuate the purposes of this subdivision, the commissioner shall request and receive from the departments, authorities, boards, bureaus, commissions, corporations, councils, funds, offices, or other agencies of the state, or any of its political subdivisions, and all such organizational entities of the state and social services districts are hereby directed, to provide and the political subdivisions are hereby authorized to provide, such assistance and data as will enable the department and social services districts to properly carry out their powers and duties to locate such parents and to enforce their liability for the support of their children. Any records established pursuant to the provisions of this section shall be available only to the secretary of health and human services, office of the inspector general, social services districts, district attorneys, county attorneys, corporation counsels, and courts having jurisdiction in any proceeding under article four, five, five-A, or five-B of the family court act; provided, however, no organizational entity of the state need make available any data or information which is otherwise required by statute to be maintained in a confidential manner.

4-a.   (a) The department shall maintain and operate a state case registry that contains records with respect to:

(1)   each case receiving services pursuant to this title; and

(2)   each support order established or modified in the state on or after the first day of October, nineteen hundred ninety-eight.

(b)   For the purpose of subparagraph two of paragraph (a) of this subdivision, the term support order means a judgment, decree, or order, whether temporary, final, or subject to modification, issued by a court or an administrative agency of competent jurisdiction, including any adjusted order issued by a support collection unit, for the support and maintenance of a child, including a child who has attained the age of majority under the law of the issuing state, or a child and the parent with whom the child is living, which provides for monetary support, health care, arrearages, or reimbursement, and which may include related costs and fees, interest and penalties, income withholding, attorney's fees, and other relief.

(c)   Each case record in the state case registry with respect to cases described in subparagraph one of paragraph (a) of this subdivision for which a support order has been established shall include a record of:

(1)   the amount of monthly (or other periodic) support owed under the order, and other amounts (including arrearages, interest or late payment penalties, and fees) due or overdue under the order;

(2)   any amount described in subparagraph one of this paragraph that has been collected;

(3)   the distribution of such collected amounts;

(4)   the birth date of any child for whom the order requires the provision of support; and

(5)   the amount of any lien imposed with respect to the order pursuant to section one hundred eleven-u of this article.

(d)   The department shall update and monitor each case record in the state registry described in subparagraph one of paragraph (a) of this subdivision on the basis of:

(1)   information on administrative actions and administrative and judicial proceedings and orders relating to paternity and support;

(2)   information obtained from comparison with federal, state or local sources of information;

(3)   information on support collections and distributions; and

(4)   any other relevant information.

(e)   Information maintained as part of the state case registry shall be made available to other state and federal agencies as provided for in federal statutes and regulations promulgated by the federal secretary of health and human services.

5.   (a) There shall be established for each state fiscal year a statewide child support collections goal for amounts of collections of support obligations pursuant to this title, which goal shall be set forth in that portion of the state's local assistance budget intended for the appropriation of reimbursement to social services districts pursuant to this chapter. The commissioner shall, subject to the approval of the director of the budget, annually allocate a portion of the statewide goal to each social services district, which portion shall be based upon the district's portion of the statewide aid to dependent children program and other relevant factors.

(b)   Notwithstanding any inconsistent provision of section one hundred fifty-three of this chapter, for each social services district which fails to meet its portion of the collection goal established by this section, the commissioner shall deny state reimbursement for such district's expenditures for aid to dependent children, in an amount equal to the difference between the amount of nonfederal funds such district is required to repay to the state out of collections actually made and the amount of nonfederal funds such district would have been required to repay to the state had it met its collection goal.

(c)   Any social services district which has been determined to have failed to meet its portion of the collection goal may request a redetermination by the commissioner or his designee in a manner to be established by department regulations. Upon a showing by such district that such failure was due in whole or in part to factors other than those administrative and processing functions or organizations which are subject to the jurisdiction of such district's local legislative body, the commissioner shall waive such failure in whole or in part and shall restore all or a corresponding portion of any state reimbursement previously denied pursuant to this section.

(d) For purposes of determining the amount of child support collections which are attributable toward meeting a district's portion of the statewide collections goal, any amounts collected by one social services district on behalf of another shall be credited to the district to which support payments have been assigned. Support payments collected on behalf of another state or on behalf of persons not in receipt of aid to dependent children shall not be taken into consideration in determining whether such district has met its goal.

(e) The department may for purposes of administrative convenience set monthly or quarterly goals based upon each district's annual goal and may deny reimbursement on a monthly or quarterly basis, subject to a final adjustment at the end of each year reflecting the extent to which each such district has met its portion of the statewide annual goal.

6. When the commissioner has determined that a social services district has failed to meet its portion of the statewide child support collections goal, as determined in accordance with the provisions of subdivision five of this section, or has failed to comply with the applicable provisions of federal law and regulations, he shall notify such district and the appropriate local legislative body of such determination and may promulgate any regulations he determines are necessary to improve such district's organization, administration, management or program. Such regulations shall be fully complied with by the effective date of such regulations.

7. The department, through the commissioner, shall enter into the agreement provided for in section one hundred seventy-one-c of the tax law and is authorized to furnish to the commissioner of taxation and finance and the state tax commission such information and to take such other actions as may be necessary to carry out the agreement provided for in such section, for the crediting of overpayments of tax to past-due support which is owed to persons receiving services pursuant to this title and title six-B of this article. A person receiving services under this title shall receive a pro rata share of the overpayment of tax, based on the amount of past-due support owed to such person as certified to the tax commission by the department pursuant to section one hundred seventy-one-c of the tax law, in cases where the individual, estate or trust owing past-due support to such person owes past-due support to other persons or entities so certified to the tax commission by the department. Amounts certified to the state tax commission under such agreement may include amounts specified in subdivision eight of this section. The amount paid by the state comptroller to the department pursuant to subdivision one of section one hundred seventy-one-c of the tax law shall be distributed in accordance with applicable provisions of this chapter and the department's regulations. To the extent permitted by federal law, the department may also certify amounts to the federal department of health and

human services for tax interception to the same extent as it certifies amounts pursuant to such section of the tax law.

The department shall by regulation establish procedures by which any individual, estate or trust which is the subject of a certification to the state tax commission in accordance with such agreement may contest such certification based on defenses that are not subject to family court jurisdiction. Such regulations and the notice required by subdivision four of section one hundred seventy-one-c of the tax law shall set forth defenses which may be available to the individual, estate or trust to contest such certification, and the manner in which a review of the certification based on such defenses may be obtained.

8.   (a) Amounts certified to the state tax commission under the agreement described in subdivision seven of this section for persons who are receiving services pursuant to this title may include:

(i)   amounts representing delinquencies which have accrued under a court order of support;

(ii)   with respect to any court order of support made before September first, nineteen hundred eighty-four which provided for periodic payments toward an established arrears amount, the entire amount of such arrears where the respondent is, at any time after September first, nineteen hundred eighty-four, delinquent in making such periodic payments; and

(iii)   with respect to any court order of support made on or after September first, nineteen hundred eighty-four which establishes an arrears amount, the entire amount of such arrears, unless such order includes a finding that anticipated tax refunds pursuant to the most recently filed state and federal tax returns have been considered by the court and taken into account in determining the amount of periodic payments to be made toward the arrears amount, or in determining the amount of the current support order, and expressly provides that such arrears are not to be so certified.

(b)   For the purpose of the state child support program any payment made by a respondent which is insufficient to fully satisfy both a current court order of support and a periodic payment toward the balance of any arrears amount established by court order shall be first applied toward the current order of support or any delinquency thereon and then toward the periodic payment on any arrears amount established by court order unless otherwise required by federal regulation.

10.   (a) * The department, through the commissioner, shall enter into the agreement provided for in section sixteen hundred thirteen-a of the tax law and is authorized to furnish to the director of the lottery and the division of the lottery such information and to take such other actions as may be necessary to carry out the provisions of the agreement provided for in such section, for the crediting of lottery prizes of six hundred dollars or more to past-due support which is owed to persons receiving services pursuant to this title. A person receiving services under this title shall receive a pro rata share of the prize winning based on the

SSL

amount of past-due support owed to such person as provided to the division of the lottery by the department pursuant to section sixteen hundred thirteen-a of the tax law, in cases where the individual, estate or trust owing past-due support to such person owes past-due support to other persons or entities so provided to the division of the lottery by the department. Amounts provided to the division of the lottery under such agreement may include amounts specified in this subdivision. The amount paid by the state comptroller to the department pursuant to subdivision one of section sixteen hundred thirteen-a of the tax law shall be distributed in accordance with applicable provisions of this chapter and the department's regulations.

(b)   The department shall by regulation establish procedures by which any individual, estate or trust which is the subject of crediting of any lottery prize of six hundred dollars or more to the state division of the lottery in accordance with such agreement may contest such crediting based on defenses that are not subject to family court jurisdiction. Such regulations shall require that notice be given to the individual, estate or trust which shall set forth:

(i)   defenses which may be available to the individual, estate or trust to contest such crediting;

(ii)   the manner in which a review of the crediting of lottery prizes of six hundred dollars or more based on such defenses may be obtained;

(iii)   the address and telephone number of the local department of social services' support collection unit which may be contacted with respect to correction of any error in such crediting concerning such individual's, estate's or trust's liability for past-due support or with respect to payment of such liability; and

(iv)   the time frame by which such a defense must be made.

10.   * The commissioner must review the child support standards act at least once every four years to ensure that its application results in the determination of appropriate child support amounts. As part of such review, the commissioner must consider economic data on the cost of raising children and analyze case data, gathered through sampling or other methods, on the application of, and deviations from the basic child support obligation. The analysis of the data must be used to ensure that such deviations are limited and, if appropriate, necessary revisions to the child support standards act must be submitted to the legislature to accomplish such purpose.

* **Editor's Note:** Two versions of Subd. (10) are provided. The first version was added by Laws 1989, Ch. 392, § 2, eff. Jan. 1, 1990. The second was added by Laws 1992, Ch. 41, § 150, eff. Apr. 2, 1992, with no reference to the prior version.

11.   (a) Amounts certified to the division of the lottery under the agreement described in subdivision ten of this section for persons who are receiving services pursuant to this title may include:

(i)   amounts representing delinquencies which have accrued under a court order of support;

(ii)   with respect to any court order of support made which establishes an arrears amount, the entire amount of such arrears.

(b)   For the purpose of the state child support program any payment made by a respondent which is insufficient to fully satisfy both a current court order of support and a periodic payment toward the balance of any arrears amount established by court order shall be first applied toward the current order of support or any delinquency thereon and then toward the periodic payment on any arrears amount established by court order unless otherwise required by federal regulation.

12.   [*Expires and repealed June 30, 2005.*] (a) The department, through the commissioner, shall enter into the agreement provided for in section five hundred ten of the vehicle and traffic law and is authorized to furnish to the commissioner of motor vehicles such information and to take such actions as may be necessary to carry out the agreement provided for in such section, for the enforcement of child support orders through the suspension of delinquent obligors' driving privileges.

(b)   (1) When a support obligor who is or was under a court order to pay child support or combined child and spousal support to a support collection unit on behalf of persons receiving services under this title has accumulated support arrears equivalent to or greater than the amount of support due pursuant to such order for a period of four months, the office of temporary and disability assistance shall notify the support obligor in writing that his or her continued failure to pay the support arrears shall result in notification to the department of motor vehicles to suspend the support obligor's driving privileges unless the support obligor complies with the requirements set forth in paragraph (e) of this subdivision. For purposes of determining whether a support obligor has accumulated support arrears equivalent to or greater than the amount of support due for a period of four months, the amount of any retroactive support, other than periodic payments of retroactive support which are past due, shall not be included in the calculation of support arrears pursuant to this section; however, if at least four months of support arrears have accumulated subsequent to the date of the court order, the entire amount of any retroactive support may be collected pursuant to the provisions of this subdivision or as otherwise authorized by law.

(2)   The department shall provide the notice required by subparagraph one of this paragraph by first class mail to the support obligor's last known address or such other place where the support obligor is likely to receive notice, or in the same manner as a summons may be served. Forty-five days after the date of such notice, if the support obligor has not challenged the determination of the support collection unit pursuant to subparagraph one of paragraph (d) of this subdivision or if the support obligor has failed to satisfy the arrears/past due support or to otherwise comply with the requirements set forth in paragraph (e) of this subdivision, the department shall notify the department of motor vehicles that the support obligor's driving privileges are to be suspended pursuant to section five hundred ten of the vehicle and traffic law. Upon the support obligor's

SSL

compliance with the provisions of paragraph (e) of this subdivision, the department shall advise the department of motor vehicles within five business days that the suspension of the support obligor's driving privileges shall be terminated. If the support obligor appears in person at the support collection unit to satisfy the requirements of paragraph (e) of this subdivision, the support collection unit shall immediately provide a notice of compliance to the support obligor, in addition to the notice sent directly to the department of motor vehicles.

(3) Notwithstanding the requirements of this subdivision, no notice shall be issued by the department pursuant to subparagraph one of this paragraph to a support obligor from whom support payments are being received by the support collection unit as a result of an income execution or an income deduction order issued pursuant to section five thousand two hundred forty-one or five thousand two hundred forty-two of the civil practice law and rules.

(c) The notice provided to a support obligor by the department pursuant to paragraph (b) of this subdivision shall contain the caption of the order of support, the date the order of support was entered, the court in which it was entered, the amount of the periodic payments directed, and the amount of arrears/past due support. In addition, the notice shall include:

(1) an explanation of the action required pursuant to paragraph (e) of this subdivision to be taken by the support obligor to avoid the suspension of his or her driving privileges;

(2) a statement that forty-five days after the date of the notice, the department of motor vehicles will be notified to suspend the support obligor's driving privileges unless the support obligor may challenge the support collection unit's determination as set forth in paragraph (d) of this subdivision within forty-five days of the date of such notice; a statement of the manner in which the support obligor may challenge the determination, and a statement that if the support obligor challenges the determination, a review will be completed by the support collection unit within seventy-five days of the date of the notice;

(3) a statement that if the support obligor does not challenge the support collection unit's determination then the department of motor vehicles shall be notified to suspend the support obligor's driving privileges unless the support obligor contacts the support collection unit to arrange for full payment or commencement of satisfactory payment arrangements on the arrears/past due support, or to comply otherwise with the requirements set forth in paragraph (e) of this subdivision, within forty-five days of the date of the notice;

(4) the address and telephone number of the support collection unit that the support obligor may contact to request information about a challenge or to comply with the requirements set forth in paragraph (e) of this subdivision;

(5) a statement that the suspension of driving privileges will continue until the support obligor pays the support arrears or complies otherwise with the requirements set forth in paragraph (e) of this subdivision; and

(6) a statement printed in boldface type that the support obligor's intentional submission of false written statements to the support collection unit for the purpose of frustrating or defeating the lawful enforcement of support obligations is punishable pursuant to section 175.35 of the penal law.

(d) (1) A support obligor may challenge in writing the correctness of the determination of the support collection unit that the obligor's driving privileges should be suspended, and in support of the challenge may submit documentation demonstrating mistaken identity, error in calculation of arrears, financial exemption from license suspension pursuant to the conditions enumerated in paragraph (e) of this subdivision, the absence of an underlying court order to support such determination, or other reason that the person is not subject to such determination. Such documents may include but are not limited to a copy of the order of support pursuant to which the obligor claims to have made payment, other relevant court orders, copies of cancelled checks, receipts for support payments, pay stubs or other documents identifying wage withholding, and proof of identity. The support collection unit shall review the documentation submitted by the support obligor, shall adjust the support obligor's account if appropriate, and shall notify the support obligor of the results of the review initiated in response to the challenge within seventy-five days from the date of the notice required by paragraph (b) of this subdivision. If the support collection unit's review indicates that the determination to suspend driving privileges was correct, the support collection unit shall notify the support obligor of the results of the review and that the support obligor has thirty-five days from the date of mailing of such notice to satisfy the full amount of the arrears or commence payment of the arrears/past due support as specified in paragraph (e) of this subdivision and if the support obligor fails to do so, the support collection unit shall notify the department of motor vehicles to suspend the support obligor's driving privileges pursuant to section five hundred ten of the vehicle and traffic law. The support obligor shall be further notified that if the support obligor files objections with the family court and serves these objections on the support collection unit within thirty-five days from the date of mailing of the notice denying the challenge pursuant to subdivision five of section four hundred fifty-four of the family court act, the support collection unit shall not notify the department of motor vehicles to suspend the support obligor's driving privileges until fifteen days after entry of judgement by the family court denying the objections.

(2) A support obligor may within thirty-five days of mailing of the notice denying his or her challenge by the support collection unit request that the family court review the support collection unit's determination pursuant to subdivision five of section four hundred fifty-four of the family court act. If the support obligor requests the family court to review the determination of the support collection unit, the support collection unit shall not notify the department of motor vehicles to suspend the support obligor's driving privileges until fifteen days after mailing of a copy of the judgment by the family court to the support obligor denying the objections.

SSL

(e)   A support obligor who has received a notice that his or her driving privileges shall be suspended may avoid the suspension by:

(1)   making full payment of all arrears/past due support to the support collection unit; or

(2)   making satisfactory payment arrangements with the support collection unit for payment of the arrears/past due support and the current support obligation." Satisfactory payment arrangements" shall mean:

(i)   execution of a confession of judgment for the total balance of the arrears/past due support; and

(ii)   execution of a verified statement of net worth on a form prescribed by the commissioner setting forth the obligor's income from all sources, liquid assets and holdings, copies of the obligor's drivers license, most recent federal and state tax return, and a representative pay stub, and an eighteen month employment history; and

(iii)   execution and verification of a stipulation that the obligor will notify the support collection unit of all future changes of address until such time as the obligation to pay support is terminated; and

(iv)   payment of support to the support collection unit by income execution pursuant to section five thousand two hundred forty-one of the civil practice law and rules, which shall include deductions sufficient to ensure compliance with the direction in the order of support and shall include an additional amount to be applied to the reduction of arrears as required by subdivision (b) of such section, or by execution of an agreement for payment of the arrears/past due support and any current support directly to the support collection unit in an amount which is consistent with that which would have been made under such an income execution; provided however, that where the support obligor fails to comply with the agreement, he/she may avoid or terminate the suspension of driving privileges only by making at least fifty percent payment of all arrears/past due support to the support collection unit and in addition, entering into a payment plan pursuant to this subdivision with the support collection unit within fifteen days. However, in any case when the support obligor fails to comply with a payment plan as described herein more than once within twelve months, the obligor must pay the balance of all arrears/past due support to avoid or terminate license suspension. "Failure to comply" for these purposes shall mean missing payments in an amount equivalent to four months of support under the payment plan, unless the support obligor demonstrates that he or she has filed a petition for modification that is pending; or

(3)   providing documentation that shows the support obligor is receiving public assistance or supplemental security income; or

(4)   providing to the support collection unit the documentation required by clauses (i) through (iii) of subparagraph two of this paragraph, where such documentation is sufficient for the support collection unit to determine:

(i) that the support obligor's income, as defined by subparagraph five of paragraph (b) of subdivision one of section four hundred thirteen of the family court act, falls below the self-support reserve as defined by subparagraph six of paragraph (b) of subdivision one of section four hundred thirteen of the family court act; or

(ii) that the amount of the support obligor's income, as defined by subparagraph five of paragraph (b) of subdivision one of section four hundred thirteen of the family court act, remaining after the payment of the current support obligation would fall below the self-support reserve as defined by subparagraph six of paragraph (b) of subdivision one of section four hundred thirteen of the family court act.

(f)   A support obligor who alleges that he or she has not received actual notice pursuant to paragraph one of subdivision (b) of this section and whose driving privileges were suspended may at any time request a review pursuant to subdivision (d) of this section or comply with the requirements of subdivision (e) of this section, and upon a determination that he or she has not accumulated support arrears equivalent to or greater than the amount of support due for a period of four months or that he or she meets the requirements of subdivision (e) of this section, the department shall notify the department of motor vehicles that the suspension of driving privileges shall be terminated.

13.   (a) The commissioner shall enter into the agreement provided for in section one hundred seventy-one-g of the tax law and is authorized to furnish to the commissioner of taxation and finance any information, and to take such other actions, as may be necessary to carry out the agreement provided for in such section, for the purpose of reviewing support orders pursuant to subdivision twelve of section one hundred eleven-h of this title.

(b)   Information obtained under paragraph (a) of this subdivision shall be confidential and shall not be disclosed to persons or agencies other than those entitled to such information when such disclosure is necessary for the proper administration of the child support enforcement program pursuant to this title.

14.   The department is authorized to receive and transmit funds paid pursuant to any order of child support or child and spousal support issued on or after the first day of January, nineteen hundred ninety-four under the provisions of section two hundred thirty-six or two hundred forty of the domestic relations law, or article four, five, five-A or five-B of the family court act, and which the court has ordered to be paid pursuant to an income deduction order issued by the court pursuant to subdivision (c) of section five thousand two hundred forty-two of the civil practice law and rules. Such funds received shall be transmitted within five business days of their receipt. The department shall maintain records of its receipt and transmission of funds and furnish such records to the parties to the order upon request. The department shall be entitled to collect an annual service fee not to exceed the maximum fee permitted pursuant to federal law for its provision of such services. Funds received in satisfaction of such fee shall be deposited in an

SSL

account and shall be made available to the department for costs incurred in the implementation of this section. The department shall not furnish any additional services to the parties to enforce the support obligation; however, a party seeking enforcement of a support obligation may apply for enforcement services pursuant to section one hundred eleven-g of this title. The department shall not be responsible for the receipt and transmission of any funds until after it has received a copy of the income deduction order and the person entitled to the payment of support pursuant to the order of support has submitted payment of the annual service fee, and unless its records show that it has received such funds on behalf of the parties to the order, and that the party to whom the funds are to be transmitted has provided the department with his or her correct address.

15. [*Expires and repealed June 30, 2005.*] (a) The department, through the commissioner, shall enter into the agreement provided for in section one hundred seventy-one-i of the tax law and is authorized to furnish to the commissioner of taxation and finance such information and to take such other actions as may be necessary to carry out such agreement.

(b)   (1) When a support obligor who is or was under a court order to pay child support or combined child and spousal support to a support collection unit on behalf of persons receiving services under this title has accumulated support arrears equivalent to or greater than the amount of support due pursuant to such order for a period of four months, the office of temporary and disability assistance shall notify the support obligor in writing that his or her continued failure to fully pay the support arrears shall result in notification to the department of taxation and finance that they are authorized to collect such arrearage. For purposes of determining whether a support obligor has accumulated support arrears equivalent to or greater than the amount of support due for a period of four months, the amount of any retroactive support, other than periodic payments of retroactive support which are past due, shall not be included in the calculation of support arrears pursuant to this section; however, if at least four months of support arrears have accumulated subsequent to the date of the court order, the entire amount of any retroactive support may be collected pursuant to the provisions of this subdivision or as otherwise authorized by law.

(2)   The department shall provide the notice required by subparagraph one of this paragraph by first class mail to the support obligor's last known address or such other place where the support obligor is likely to receive notice by first class mail. Forty-five days after the date of such notice, if the support obligor has not challenged the determination of the support collection unit pursuant to subparagraph one of paragraph (d) of this subdivision or if the support obligor has failed to satisfy the arrears, the department shall notify the department of taxation and finance that the support obligor's support arrearage are authorized to be collected as prescribed in subparagraph one of this paragraph.

(3)   Notwithstanding the requirements of this subdivision, no notice shall be issued by the department pursuant to subparagraph one of this paragraph to a support obligor from whom support payments are being received by the support

collection unit as a result of an income execution or an income deduction order issued pursuant to section five thousand two hundred forty-one or five thousand two hundred forty-two of the civil practice law and rules.

(c)   The notice provided to a support obligor by the department pursuant to paragraph (b) of this subdivision shall contain the caption of the order of support, the date the order of support was entered, the court in which it was entered, the amount of the periodic payments directed, and the amount of arrears. In addition, the notice shall include:

(1)   a statement that unless the support arrears are satisfied within forty-five days after the date of the notice, the department of taxation and finance will be notified that they are authorized to commence collection action unless the support obligor challenges the support collection unit's determination as set forth in paragraph (d) of this subdivision within forty-five days of the date of such notice; a statement of the manner in which the support obligor may challenge the determination, and a statement that if the support obligor challenges the determination, a review will be completed by the support collection unit within seventy-five days of the date of the notice;

(2)   a statement that if the support obligor does not challenge the support collection unit's determination then the department of taxation and finance shall be notified that they are authorized to commence collection action unless the support obligor contacts the support collection unit to arrange for full payment of the arrears;

(3)   the address and telephone number of the support collection unit that the support obligor may contact to request information about a challenge to the determination of the support collection unit;

(4)   a statement that the collection actions by the department of taxation and finance is authorized to continue until the support obligor pays the support arrears; and

(5)   a statement printed in boldface type that the support obligor's intentional submission of false written statements to the support collection unit for the purpose of frustrating or defeating the lawful enforcement of support obligations is punishable pursuant to section 175.35 of the penal law.

(d)   A support obligor who has received a notice that his or her support arrearage shall be referred to the department of taxation and finance for collection action may avoid such action by making payment of all arrears to the support collection unit; providing documentation that shows the support obligor is receiving public assistance, medical assistance, food stamps or supplemental security income; or providing to the support collection unit the documentation sufficient for the support collection unit to determine:

(1)   an error in the calculation of the obligor's support arrears which would render the obligor ineligible for collection by the department of taxation and finance; or

(2)   a mistake in the identity of the obligor showing that the individual making the challenge is not the obligor identified by the department; or

(3)   the absence of an underlying court order for support pursuant to which the obligor's arrears gave rise to eligibility for collection action on such arrears by the department of taxation and finance.

16.   [*Expires and repealed June 30, 2005.*] Bureaus of special hearings; child support unit. (a) The department is authorized to establish a bureau of special hearings; child support unit solely for the purposes of providing administrative law judges to decide objections to the determination of a support collection unit to refer an obligor's arrears to the department of taxation and finance for collection pursuant to subdivision nineteen of section one hundred eleven-h of this title. The administrative law judges employed by the unit shall serve exclusively within the unit and shall not be utilized for any purpose other than those described in this subdivision and shall be salaried employees of the department and shall not be removed from such unit except for cause.

(b)   The unit shall review a support collection unit's denial of a challenge made by a support obligor pursuant to paragraph two of subdivision nineteen of section one hundred eleven-h of this title if objections thereto are filed by a support obligor who has received notice that the department intends to notify the department of taxation and finance to collect such support obligor's support arrears. Specific written objections to a support collection unit's denial must be submitted by the support obligor to the unit within thirty days of the date of the notice of the support collection unit's denial. A support obligor who files such objections shall serve a copy of the objections upon the support collection unit, which shall have ten days from such service to file a written rebuttal to such objections and a copy of the record upon which the support collection unit's denial was made, including all documentation submitted by the support obligor. Proof of service shall be filed with the unit at the time of filing of objections and any rebuttal. The unit's review shall be based solely upon the record and submissions of the support obligor and the support collection unit upon which the support collection unit's denial was made. Within fifteen days after the rebuttal, if any, is filed, an administrative law judge of the unit shall (i) deny the objections and remand to the support collection unit or (ii) affirm the objections if the administrative law judge finds the determination of the support collection unit is based upon an erroneous determination of fact by the support collection unit. Such decision shall pertain solely to the mistaken identity of the obligor, a prejudicial error in the calculation of the obligor's arrears, the obligor's financial exemption from collection of support arrears by the department of taxation and finance or the absence of an underlying court order establishing arrears to support eligibility for such enforcement. Upon an affirmation of the objections the administrative law judge shall direct the support collection unit not to notify the department of taxation and finance of their authority to collect the support obligor's arrears. Provisions set forth in this subdivision relating to procedures for hearing objections by the unit shall apply solely to such cases and not affect or modify any other procedure for review or appeal of administrative enforcement of child support requirements. The decision of the administrative law judge pursuant to this section shall be final and not reviewable by the commissioner, and shall be reviewable only pursuant to article seventy-eight of the civil practice law and rules.

17. Special services for review and adjustment. The department shall develop procedures for and require local social services districts to dedicate special staff to the review and adjustment of child support orders entered prior to September fifteenth, nineteen hundred eighty-nine on behalf of children in receipt of public assistance or child support services pursuant to section one hundred eleven-g of this title. Such review and adjustment shall be performed pursuant to subdivisions twelve, thirteen, fourteen, fifteen and sixteen of section one hundred eleven-h of this title. All such cases shall be reviewed and if necessary adjusted no later than December thirty-first, two thousand.

Added by Laws 1975, Ch. 685. See legislative history of § 111-a, *supra;* amended by Laws 1976, Ch. 326; Laws 1977, Ch. 77, Ch. 516; amended by Laws 1978, Ch. 456, § 4 eff. July 1, 1978; amended by Laws 1982, Ch. 545, eff. July 20, 1982, adding subd. (7), however, subd. (7) shall only apply to overpayments for taxable years beginning after Dec. 31, 1981; amended by Laws 1984, Ch. 793, eff. Sept. 1, 1984; amended by Laws 1985, Ch. 809, eff. Nov. 1, 1985; amended by Laws 1986, Ch. 892, adding subd. 2-a, eff. Aug. 2, 1986, and adding subd. 9, eff. Apr. 1, 1987; amended by Laws 1987, Ch. 815, eff. Aug. 7, 1987; amended by Laws 1987, Ch. 815, eff. June 30, 1987; amended by Laws 1989, Ch. 392, § 2, eff. Jan. 1, 1990; amended by Laws 1989, Ch. 567, § 12, eff. Sept. 15, 1989; amended by Laws 1992, Ch. 41, §§ 122, 123, 150, eff. Apr. 2, 1992; amended by Laws 1993, Ch. 59, § 19, eff. July 1, 1993; amended by Laws 1994, Ch. 170, § 366, eff. June 15, 1994; amended by Laws 1994, Ch. 170, § 378, eff. Apr. 1, 1994, extending the period that subd. (9) remains effective until Sept. 3, 1996; amended by Laws 1995, Ch. 81, § 208, eff. July 1, 1995, adding subd. 12, which expires June 30, 1998; amended by Laws 1996, Ch. 309, § 467, eff. July 13, 1996; amended by Laws 1996, Ch. 586, eff. Aug. 8, 1996, extending the period that subd. (9) remains effective until Sept. 3, 1998; amended by Laws 1996, Ch. 706, § 1, eff. Dec. 1, 1996, added new subdivisions 15 and 16, which expire on June 30, 1999; amended by Laws 1997, Ch. 398, § 8, eff. Oct. 1, 1997, and §§ 9, 10, 49; and § 107 adding new subdivision (17) to SSL § 111-b, eff. Jan. 1, 1998; amended by Laws 1998, Ch. 214, § 83-a, eff. July 7, 1998, extending the expiration date of subd. (12) to June 30, 1999; amended by Laws 1999, Ch. 139, §§ 1 & 2, eff. June 29, 1999, deemed eff. June 30, 1999, amending subd. (16)(b) and extending the effective date of subds. (15) & (16) to June 30, 2001, and Ch. 140, § 1, extending the effective date of subd. (12) to June 30, 2001; amended by Laws 2001, Chs. 68, 72, § 1, eff. June 29, 2001, extending the effective date to June 30, 2003; amended by Laws 2002, Ch. 624, eff. Nov. 2, 2002; provided, however, that sections six through sixteen of this act shall take effect on the thirtieth day after it shall have become a law; provided, further, that the amendments to subdivisions 12 and 15 of section 111-b of the social services law made by sections six and seven of this act shall not affect the repeal of such subdivisions and shall be deemed to be repealed therewith; Laws 2003, Ch. 87, § 1, extending the expiration date until Sept. 1, 2005, eff. July 1, 2003 and shall be deemed in full force and effect on and after June 30, 2003; Ch. 88 § 1, extending expiration date until Sept. 1, 2005, eff. July 1, 2003 and shall be deemed in full force and effect on and after June 30, 2003.

This act shall take effect December 1, 1996 and shall expire and be deemed repealed on June 30, [2003] 2005; provided, however, that the department of taxation and finance may continue to collect child support and combined child and spousal support arrears for cases referred to such department prior to June 30, [2003] 2005; and provided, further, that the commissioners of social services and taxation and finance are authorized to promulgate regulations on an emergency basis to ensure the implementation of the provisions of this act and may take any steps necessary to implement the provisions of this act on or after the date it shall have become a law.

§ 111-c.   Functions, powers and duties of social services officials.

1. Each social services district shall establish a single organizational unit which shall be responsible for such district's activities in assisting the state in the location of absent parents, establishment of paternity and enforcement and collection of support in accordance with the regulations of the department.

2. Each social services district shall:

a. obtain assignments to the state and to such district of support rights of each applicant for or recipient of aid to dependent children or home relief required to execute such an assignment as a condition of receiving assistance;

b. report to the state all recipients of aid to dependent children or home relief with respect to whom a parent has been reported absent from the household;

c. obtain information regarding the income and resources of absent parents whose whereabouts are known, and shall have access to the statement of net worth filed pursuant to section four hundred twenty-four-a of the family court act and supporting documentation in any case where support collection services are being provided as may be necessary to ascertain their ability to support or contribute to the support of their dependents;

d. enforce support obligations owed to the state and to the social services district pursuant to subdivision two of section one hundred eleven-b of this chapter; and disburse amounts collected as support payments in accordance with the provisions of this chapter and the regulations of the department, including the disbursement to the aid to dependent children family of up to the first fifty dollars collected as current support;

e. make periodic reports and perform such other functions in accordance with the regulations of the department as may be necessary to assure compliance with federal child support program requirements.

f. confer with a potential respondent, respondent or other interested person in a proceeding under article four, five, five-A or five-B of the family court act in an attempt to obtain support payments from such potential respondent or respondent;

g. obtain from respondent, when appropriate and in accordance with the procedures established by section one hundred eleven-k of this chapter, an acknowledgement of paternity or an agreement to make support payments, or both;

h. report periodically to consumer reporting agencies (as defined in section 603(f) of the Fair Credit Reporting Act (15 U.S.C. 1681a(f)) information regarding past-due support owed by the parent owing support. Such information must be made available whenever a parent who owes past-due support, and shall indicate the name of the parent and the amount of the delinquency. However, such information shall not be made available to (i) a consumer reporting agency that the office determines does not have sufficient capability to systematically and timely make accurate use of such information, or (ii) an entity that has not furnished evidence satisfactory to the office that the entity is a consumer reporting agency. In determining whether a consumer reporting agency lacks sufficient capability to systematically and timely make accurate use of such information, the office may require such agency to demonstrate its ability to comply with the provisions of section three hundred eighty-j of the general business law and any other requirements the office may prescribe by regulation. A social services official, at least ten days prior to making the information available to a consumer reporting agency, must provide notice to the parent who owes the support informing such parent of the proposed release of the information to the consumer reporting agency and informing such parent of the opportunity to be heard and the methods available for contesting the accuracy of the information.

3. Notwithstanding the foregoing, the social services official shall not be required to establish the paternity of any child born out-of-wedlock, or to secure support for any child, with respect to whom such official has determined that such actions would be detrimental to the best interests of the child, in accordance with procedures and criteria established by regulations of the department consistent with federal law.

Added by Laws 1975, Ch. 685. See legislative history of § 111-a *supra;* **amended** by Laws 1976, Ch. 326; Laws 1977, Ch. 516; Laws 1978, Ch. 456, eff. July 1, 1978; **amended** by Laws 1985, Ch. 42, eff. Oct. 1, 1984, and Ch. 809, eff. Aug. 15, 1985; **amended** by Laws 1986, Ch. 892, eff. Aug. 2, 1986; **amended** by Laws 1992, Ch. 41, § 124, eff. Apr. 2, 1992; **amended** by Laws 1995, Ch. 81, § 217, eff. July 1, 1995; **amended** by Laws 1997, Ch. 398, § 90, eff. Nov. 11, 1997, and § 50, eff. Jan. 1, 1998; **amended** by Laws 1998, Ch. 214, § 4, eff. July 7, 1998, deemed in full force and effect Jan. 1, 1998.

§ 111-d. State reimbursement.

1. The provisions of section one hundred fifty-three of this chapter shall be applicable to expenditures by social services districts for activities related to the establishment of paternity of children born out of wedlock, the location of deserting parents and the enforcement and collection of support obligations owed to recipients of aid to dependent children and persons receiving services pursuant to section one hundred eleven-g of this title.

SSL

2.   The local share of expenditures incurred by the department for the provision of centralized collection and disbursement services pursuant to section one hundred eleven-h of this title shall be charged back to the social services districts. The local share shall be fifty percentum of the amount expended by the department after deducting therefrom any federal funds properly received or to be received on account thereof; provided, however, that a social services district's share of the costs related to the centralized collection and disbursement functions shall not exceed those incurred for the year immediately preceding implementation of such functions, except to the extent to which those costs would have increased had centralization of collection and disbursement functions not occurred.

Added by Laws 1975, Ch. 685. See legislative history of § 111–a, *supra;* Laws 1976, Ch. 326; Laws 1977, Ch. 516; Laws 1978, Ch. 456, eff. July 1, 1978; **amended** by Laws 1990, Ch. 502, § 1, eff. July 18, 1990, through Sept. 30, 1995, at which time the section shall expire and be deemed repealed; **amended** by Laws 1995, Ch. 81, § 234, eff. July 1, 1995, removing the section's expiration date.

§ 111-e.   Reimbursement to the state.

1.   A share of any support payments collected by the social services official, less any amount disbursed to the family receiving family assistance, shall, subject to section one hundred eleven-f, be paid to the state as reimbursement toward the amount contributed by the state and federal governments to assistance furnished to such family. Such share shall bear the same ratio to the amounts collected as the state and federal funds bear to assistance granted.

2.   Whenever one social services district makes collections on behalf of a person or family for whom another social services district or another state is responsible for providing assistance, the amount collected shall be paid to the district or such other state responsible for providing such assistance, in accordance with the regulations of the department.

Added by Laws 1975, Ch. 685. See legislative history of § 111–a, *supra;* **amended**by Laws 1976, Ch. 326; Laws 1977, Ch. 516; Laws 1978, Ch. 456, eff. July 1, 1978; **amended** by Laws 1997, Ch. 436, § 1 Part B, § 68, eff. Aug. 20, 1997.

§ 111-f.   Federal incentives.

The department is authorized to distribute to local districts the full amount of federal incentive payments received under title IV-D of the federal social security act.

Added by Laws 1986, Ch. 892, eff. Aug 2, 1986, former § 111-f **repealed.**

§ 111-g.   Availability of paternity and support services.

The department and the social services districts, in accordance with the regulations of the department, shall make services relating to the establishment of paternity and the establishment and enforcement of support obligations available to persons not receiving family assistance upon application by such persons. Such persons must apply by (i) completing and signing a form as prescribed by the department, or (ii) filing a petition with the court or applying to the court in a proceeding for the establishment of paternity and/or establishment and/or enforcement of a support obligation, which includes a statement signed by the person requesting services clearly indicating that such person is applying for child support enforcement services pursuant to this title. The department may, by regulation, require payment of an application fee for such services and the deduction of costs in excess of such fee from amounts collected on behalf of such persons.

Added by Laws 1975, Ch. 685. See legislative history of § 111–a, *supra;* **amended** by Laws 1977, Ch. 516; **amended** by Laws 1981, Ch. 622, eff. July 21, 1981 but deemed in effect as of Aug. 1, 1976; **amended** by Laws 1987, Ch. 815, eff. Aug. 7, 1987; **amended** by Laws 1990, Ch. 818, § 19, eff. Sept. 30, 1990; **amended** by Laws 1997, Ch. 436, § 1 Part B, § 69, eff. Aug. 20, 1997.

§ 111-h. Support collection unit.

1. Each social services district shall establish a support collection unit in accordance with regulations of the department to collect, account for and disburse funds paid pursuant to any order of child support or child and spousal support issued under the provisions of section two hundred thirty-six or two hundred forty of the domestic relations law, or article four, five, five-A or five-B of the family court act; provided however, that the department, subject to availability of funds, shall furnish centralized collection and disbursement services for and on behalf of each social services district. Until such time as the department performs collection and disbursement functions for a particular social services district, that social services district shall continue to perform those functions.

2. The support collection unit shall inform the petitioner and respondent of any case in which a required payment has not been made within two weeks after it was due and shall assist in securing voluntary compliance with such orders or in preparation and submission of a petition for a violation of a support order. Upon the written request of the debtor, the support collection unit shall issue an income execution as provided in section fifty-two hundred forty-one of the civil practice law and rules, except that the provisions of subdivisions (d) and (e) thereof shall not apply. Upon receipt of written revocation of such request, the support collection unit shall notify the employer or income payor that the levy is no longer effective, and the execution shall be returned.

3. The support collection unit shall require that a person applying for child support enforcement services provide his or her name, address and social security number and disclose whether he or she is in receipt of safety net assistance or family assistance; provided, however, that a social security number may be required only where permitted under federal law.

SSL

4.   Any and all moneys paid into the support collection unit pursuant to an order of support made under the family court act or the domestic relations law, where the petitioner is not a recipient of public assistance, shall upon payment into such support collection unit be deemed for all purposes to be the property of the person for whom such money is to be paid.

5.   With respect to any funds paid to the support collection unit established by a social services district pursuant to an order of support under the provisions of article four, five, five-A or five-B of the family court act and which have remained unclaimed for not less than two years after diligent effort to locate the person entitled to such funds, the family court may enter an order decreeing

(a)   that the funds be returned to the person who paid the funds pursuant to the order of support, or

(b)   that the funds be deposited with the county treasurer or commissioner of finance of the city of New York, whose duty it shall be to receive such funds and invest them for a period of five years in such securities as are specified by law for investment by savings banks, the interest on such securities to accrue and become part of such funds.

6.   If a claimant proves to the satisfaction of the family court within five years after the deposit of funds under paragraph (b) of subdivision five of this section his just and legal claim to any part of the funds, the court may require that repayment shall be made to the claimant as provided by order of the court. The clerk of the court shall issue a certificate under the official seal of the court embodying the terms and provisions of the order and transmit the certificate to the office of the county treasurer or commissioner of finance of the city of New York with whom the funds were deposited. The certificate shall constitute the authority of the county treasurer or commissioner of finance of the city of New York for making such repayment.

7.   Upon the expiration of five years from the date of deposit with the county treasurer or commissioner of finance of the city of New York under paragraph (b) of subdivision five of this section, all such funds remaining in the custody of the county treasurer or commissioner of finance of the city of New York shall be paid to the state comptroller pursuant to the provisions of section six hundred two of the abandoned property law and such payment shall be accomplished by the report required by section six hundred three of the abandoned property law.

8.   Banks and other fiduciary institutions are authorized and required to report to the support collection unit, when so requested, full information relative to any fund therein deposited by a petitioner or respondent in a proceeding under section two hundred thirty-six or two hundred forty of the domestic relations law or article five-B of the family court act, where there is an order of support payable through the support collection unit or article four, five or five-A of the family court act.

9.   Employers are authorized and required to report to the support collection unit, when so requested, full information as to the earnings of a petitioner or

respondent in a proceeding under section two hundred thirty-six or two hundred forty of the domestic relations law or article five-B of the family court act, where there is an order of support payable through the support collection unit or article four, five, five-A or five-B of the family court act. Employers also are authorized and required to report to the support collection unit, when so requested, information relating to any group health plans available for the provision of care or other medical benefits by insurance or otherwise for the benefit of the employee and/or the child or children for whom such parties are legally responsible for support.

10. The support collection unit is authorized and required to report to the family court, when so requested, full information relative to amounts paid or any arrearages by a respondent in a proceeding under articles four, five, five-A or article five-B of the family court act.

11. The department may provide for the performance of the collection and disbursement functions of the support collection units by contract with a fiscal agent. For purposes of any reference to support collection unit in this chapter or any other law, the fiscal agent under contract with a the department shall be deemed to be part of all support collection units for which the fiscal agent performs collection and disbursement functions.

12. * In any case where the child support order was issued prior to September fifteenth, nineteen hundred eighty-nine in which there is an assignment of support rights or in which a request for an adjustment review is made, the support collection unit shall initiate a one-time review of the order for adjustment purposes unless: (i) the child is in receipt of public assistance, and the support collection unit determines that such review would not be in the best interest of the child or the custodial parent, and neither parent has requested review; or (ii) the child is not in receipt of public assistance and neither parent has requested such review. The support collection unit shall conduct such review in a manner consistent with section four hundred thirteen of the family court act and subdivision one-b of section two hundred forty of the domestic relations law, commonly referred to as the child support guidelines, and the definition of adjustment as set forth in subdivision three of section four hundred thirteen of the family court act and paragraph b of subdivision one of section two hundred forty of the domestic relations law.

13. Upon the conclusion of the adjustment review, the support collection unit shall send the findings of such review by first class mail to the parties, together with a notice describing the rights of the parties to seek adjustment pursuant to applicable provisions of law.

14. Where the support collection unit determines that there is a basis for an upward adjustment, it shall also file a proposed order together with an affidavit in support thereof with the clerk of the appropriate court, and send a copy of such proposed order and affidavit by first class mail to the parties.

15. Where the support collection unit has determined that an adjustment review is appropriate, and the child or children are in receipt of public assistance,

the unit shall, at least thirty days before the commencement of such review, notify the parties that the support collection unit will commence review, and provide notice of their obligations pursuant to subdivision sixteen of this section. Such notice shall also be provided, whether or not a child is in receipt of public assistance, upon a request by any party for adjustment review.

16.　* Such notice shall include a statement that the party must, within thirty-five days of the date of mailing of the notice, send to the support collection unit:

(i)　a current and representative paycheck stub with respect to each source of employment income;

(ii)　copies of the most recently filed state and federal income tax returns; and

(iii)　a sworn statement of net worth which shall also identify the carrier and policy number of all health insurance currently in place, for the benefit of the obligor and eligible dependents, and whether such coverage has been in place for the previous year.

The notice shall also include a statement that the party may schedule a conference with the support collection unit and submit a written explanation of his or her present tax and financial information to determine the appropriate modification, and thereby may avoid further administrative and judicial proceedings.

The notice shall also state that in the event the party fails to provide such information within thirty-five days of the date of the mailing of the notice, the department of social services shall be entitled to make use of certain tax data from the commissioner of taxation and finance pursuant to section one hundred seventy-one-g of the tax law and section one hundred eleven-c of the social services law to initiate proceedings to adjust the child support order.

17.　The department shall develop and disseminate a notice informing both parties to child support orders issued prior to September fifteenth, nineteen hundred eighty-nine, of the availability of the one-time adjustment of child support orders pursuant to the provisions of subdivision three of section four hundred thirteen of the family court act and subdivision four of section two hundred forty of the domestic relations law. The department shall also develop a notice that shall set out the options for adjustment of child support orders issued prior to September fifteenth, nineteen hundred eighty-nine, and the methods for exercising those options. Said notice shall be sent by first class mail to persons in receipt of services pursuant to this title, and shall contain a reply form and envelope with postage pre-paid.

18.　The support collection unit shall undertake a public service campaign as soon as practicable to inform citizens of the possibility of driver, business and professional license suspension for support enforcement.

19.　[*Expires and repealed June 30, 2005.*] (1) A support obligor may challenge in writing the correctness of the determination of the support collection unit pursuant to this section and section one hundred seventy-one-i of the tax law that the obligor's arrearage should be collected through the department of taxation and finance, and in support of the challenge may submit documentation demonstrating mistaken identity, error in calculation of arrears, financial exemption from such collection, the absence of an underlying court order establishing arrears to support such determination. Such documents may include a copy of the order of support pursuant to which the obligor claims to have made payment, other relevant court orders, copies of cancelled checks, receipts for support payments, pay stubs or other documents identifying wage withholding, proof of identity, and like documents. The support collection unit shall review the documentation submitted by the support obligor, shall adjust the support obligor's account if appropriate, and shall notify the support obligor of the results of the review initiated in response to the challenge within seventy-five days from the date of the notice required. If the support collection unit's review indicates that the determination to refer to the department of taxation and finance for collection was correct, the support collection unit shall notify the support obligor of the results of the review and that the support obligor has thirty days from the date of such notice to satisfy the full amount of the arrears. If the support obligor fails to do so, the support collection unit shall notify the department of taxation and finance that they are authorized to commence collection of the arrears. The support obligor shall be further notified that if the support obligor files objections to the review determination of the support collection unit with the bureau of special hearings; child support unit of the department pursuant to subdivision sixteen of section one hundred eleven-b of this title, and serves these objections on the support collection unit within thirty days from the date of notice denying the challenge, the support collection unit shall not notify the department of taxation and finance of their authority to collect the arrearages until fifteen days after receipt of a decision by the administrative law judge pursuant to such section.

(2)   A support obligor may within thirty days of the date of notice denying his or her challenge by the support collection unit file objections to such denial with the bureau of special hearings; child support unit of the department which shall review the support collection unit's determination to refer the obligor's case to the department of taxation and finance for collection pursuant to subdivision sixteen of section one hundred eleven-b of this title. If the support obligor timely files such objections with such bureau the support collection unit shall not notify the department of taxation and finance of their authority to collect the arrearages until fifteen days after entry of an order by the administrative law judge denying the objections.

* Note: The amendments made to subdivisions 12 and 16 by Laws 1997, Ch. 398 § 4 shall not apply to review and adjustment requests, actions, proceedings, objections, or issuance of adjusted orders pending on or before December 31, 1997. Such requests, actions, proceedings, objections, or issuance of adjusted orders may proceed as if such provisions were not amended by Laws 1997, Ch. 398 § 4. *See* Laws 1998, Ch. 214 § 64.

SSL

Added by Laws 1977, Ch. 516, § 5, eff. Jan. 1, 1978; **amended** by Laws 1977, Ch. 517, eff. Jan. 1, 1978; **amended** by Laws 1978, Ch. 655, eff. July 24, 1978; **amended** by Laws 1986, Ch. 892, eff. Aug. 2, 1986; **amended** by Laws 1987, Ch. 815, eff. Aug. 7, 1987; **amended** by Laws 1990, Ch. 502, § 2, eff. July 18, 1990, through Sept. 30, 1995, at which time it shall expire and be deemed repealed; **amended** by Laws 1993, Ch. 59, § 20, **adding** new subds. (12) -(17), eff. July 1, 1993; **amended** by Laws 1995, Ch. 81, §§ 235, 242, eff. July 1, 1995; **amended** by Laws 1995, Ch. 81, § 234, eff. July 1, 1995, removing the expiration date of Subd. 1 and Subd. 11; **amended** by Laws 1996, Ch. 706, eff. Dec. 1, 1996 added new subd. 19, which expires June 30, 1999; **amended** by Laws 1997, Ch. 398, §§ 51, 146, 104–106, eff. Jan. 1, 1998; **amended** by Laws 1997, Ch. 436, § 1 Part B, § 70, eff. Aug. 20, 1997; **amended** by Laws 1998, Ch. 214 § 64; **amended** by Laws 1999, Ch. 139, § 1, extending the effective date of subd. (19) to June 30, 2001; **amended** by Laws 2001, Ch. 68, § 1, eff. June 27, 2001, extending the effective date of subd. (19) to June 30, 2003; Laws 2003, Ch. 88, § 1, extending the expiration of subd. 19 until Sept. 1, 2005, eff. July 1, 2003 and shall be deemed in full force and effect on and after June 30, 2003.

This act shall take effect December 1, 1996 and shall expire and be deemed repealed on June 30, [2003] 2005; provided, however, that the department of taxation and finance may continue to collect child support and combined child and spousal support arrears for cases referred to such department prior to June 30, [2003] 2005; and provided, further, that the commissioners of social services and taxation and finance are authorized to promulgate regulations on an emergency basis to ensure the implementation of the provisions of this act and may take any steps necessary to implement the provisions of this act on or after the date it shall have become a law.

§ 111-i.   Child support standards.

1.   Each social services district shall ascertain the ability of an absent parent to support or contribute to the support of his or her children, in accordance with the statewide child support standards as set forth in subdivision one of section four hundred thirteen of the family court act.

2.   (a) The commissioner shall publish annually in department regulations the revised self-support reserve as defined in section two hundred forty of the domestic relations law to reflect the annual updating of the poverty income guidelines amount for a single person as reported by the federal department of health and human services.

(b)   The commissioner shall publish in department regulations a child support standards chart to reflect the dollar amounts yielded through application of the child support percentage as defined in section two hundred forty of the domestic relations law.

Added by Laws 1977, Ch. 516, § 6, eff. July 1, 1977; **amended** by Laws 1978, Ch. 456, eff. Jan. 1, 1978; **amended** by Laws 1989, Ch. 567, § 13, eff. Sept. 15, 1989.

§ 111-j.   Interception of unemployment insurance benefits.

1.   (a) The department shall determine on a periodic basis whether any individual receiving unemployment insurance benefits pursuant to article

eighteen of the state's labor law owes child support obligations which are being enforced by the department or the child support enforcement unit of a social services district and shall enforce any child support obligations which are owed by such individual but are not being met through an agreement with such individual to have specific amounts withheld from such benefits otherwise payable to such individual and by submitting a copy of such agreement to the New York state department of labor.

(b) In the absence of such an agreement, the department shall enforce any such child support obligations as authorized by the court in any order establishing such obligations and as otherwise provided by law.

2. Any amounts of unemployment insurance benefits deducted, withheld and paid over by the department of labor pursuant to section five hundred ninety-six of the labor law shall be treated as if it were paid to the person entitled to such compensation and paid by such person to the department or appropriate child support collection unit toward satisfaction of such person's child support obligations. Each agency or district receiving payments deducted by the department of labor shall reimburse that department for the administrative costs attributable thereto.

Added by laws 1982, Ch. 204, eff. Sept. 27, 1982.

§ 111-k. Procedures relating to acknowledgments of paternity, agreements to support, and genetic tests.

1. A social services official or his or her designated representative who confers with a potential respondent or respondent, hereinafter referred to in this section as the "respondent", the mother of a child born out of wedlock and any other interested persons, pursuant to section one hundred eleven-c of this title, may obtain:

(a) An acknowledgment of paternity of a child, as provided for in article five-B or section five hundred sixteen-a of the family court act, by a written statement, witnessed by two people not related to the signator or as provided for in section four thousand one hundred thirty-five-b of the public health law. Prior to the execution of such acknowledgment by the child's mother and the respondent, they shall be advised, orally, which may be through the use of audio or video equipment, and in writing, of the consequences of making such an acknowledgment. Upon the signing of an acknowledgment of paternity pursuant to this section, the social services official or his or her representative shall file the original acknowledgment with the registrar.

(b) An agreement to make support payments as provided in section four hundred twenty-five of the family court act. Prior to the execution of such agreement, the respondent shall be advised, orally, which may be through the use of audio or video equipment, and in writing, of the consequences of such agreement, that the respondent can be held liable for support only if the family court, after a hearing, makes an order of support; that respondent has a right to consult with an attorney and that the agreement will be submitted to the family court for approval pursuant to section four hundred twenty-five of the family court act; and that by executing the agreement, the respondent waives any right to a hearing regarding any matter contained in such agreement.

2.   (a) When the paternity of a child is contested, a social services official or designated representative may order the mother, the child, and the alleged father to submit to one or more genetic marker or DNA tests of a type generally acknowledged as reliable by an accreditation body designated by the secretary of the federal department of health and human services and performed by a laboratory approved by such an accreditation body and by the commissioner of health or by a duly qualified physician to aid in the determination of whether or not the alleged father is the father of the child. The order may be issued prior or subsequent to the filing of a petition with the court to establish paternity, shall be served on the parties by certified mail, and shall include a sworn statement which either (i) alleges paternity and sets forth facts establishing a reasonable possibility of the requisite sexual contact between the parties, or (ii) denies paternity and sets forth facts establishing a reasonable possibility that the party is not the father. The parties shall not be required to submit to the administration and analysis of such tests if they sign a voluntary acknowledgment of paternity in accordance with paragraph (a) of subdivision one of this section, or if there has been a written finding by the court that it is not in the best interests of the child on the basis of res judicata, equitable estoppel or the presumption of legiti-macy of a child born to a married woman.

(b)   The record or report of the results of any such genetic marker or DNA test may be submitted to the family court as evidence pursuant to subdivision (e) of rule forty-five hundred eighteen of the civil practice law and rules where no timely objection in writing has been made thereto.

(c)   The cost of any test ordered pursuant to this section shall be paid by the social services district provided however, that the alleged father shall reimburse the district for the cost of such test at such time as the alleged father's paternity is established by a voluntary acknowledgment of paternity or an order of filiation. If either party contests the results of genetic marker or DNA tests, an additional test may be ordered upon written request to the social services district and ad-vance payment by the requesting party.

(d)   The parties shall be required to submit to such tests and appear at any conference scheduled by the social services official or designee to discuss the notice of the allegation of paternity or to discuss the results of such tests. If the alleged father fails to appear at any such conference or fails to submit to such genetic marker or DNA tests, the social services official or designee shall petition the court to establish paternity, provide the court with a copy of the records or reports of such tests if any, and request the court to issue an order for temporary support pursuant to section five hundred forty-two of the family court act.

Added by Laws 1985, Ch. 809, eff. Nov. 1, 1985; **amended** by Laws 1993, Ch. 59, § 25, eff. July 1, 1993; **amended** by Laws 1994, Ch. 170, § 357, eff. June 15, 1994; **amended** by Laws 1997, Ch. 398, § 76, eff. Nov. 11, 1997; **amended** by Laws 1998, Ch. 214, § 2, eff. July 7, 1998, deemed in full force and effect Nov. 11, 1997.

§ 111-l. Authorization of demonstration program.

Repealed by Laws 1997, Ch. 436, § 1 Part B, § 111, eff. Aug. 20, 1997

TITLE 6-B—SERVICES FOR ENFORCEMENT OF SUPPORT PROVIDED BY THE DEPARTMENT OF SOCIAL SERVICES

———

§ 111-m. Agreement relating to information obtained by the state directory of new hires.

The department, through the commissioner, shall enter into the agreement provided for in section one hundred seventy-one-h of the tax law, and shall take such other actions as may be necessary to carry out the agreement provided for in such section for matching recipient records of public assistance and of the child support enforcement program with information provided by employers to the state directory of new hires for the purposes of verifying eligibility for such public assistance programs and for the administration of the child support enforcement program.

Added by Laws 1997, Ch. 398, § 16, eff. Oct. 1, 1997.

L. 1997, Ch. 398, § 16 **relettered** SSL § 111-m to SSL § 111-y.

SSL

§ 111-n. Review and cost of living adjustment of support orders.

1. Orders subject to review. In accordance with the timeframes set forth in subdivision three of this section, the support collection unit shall conduct a review for adjustment purposes of:

(a) all orders of support being enforced pursuant to this title on behalf of persons in receipt of family assistance; and

(b) those orders of support being enforced pursuant to this title on behalf of persons not in receipt of family assistance, for which a request for a cost of living adjustment review has been received from either party to the order.

2. Definitions. For purposes of this section, the following definitions shall be used:

(a) "Adjusted child support obligation amount" shall mean the sum of the cost of living adjustment and the support obligation amount contained in the order under review.

(b) "Adjusted order" shall mean an order issued by the support collection unit reflecting a change to the obligation amount of the most recently issued order of support made on behalf of a child in receipt of family assistance or child support enforcement services pursuant to section one hundred eleven-g of this title.

(c) "Cost of living adjustment" shall mean the amount by which the support obligation is changed as the result of a review, and shall be determined based upon annual average changes to the consumer price index for all urban consumers (CPI-U), as published by the United States department of labor bureau of labor statistics, for the years preceding the year of the review, as follows:

(1) Identify the CPI-U "percent change from the previous annual average" for each year preceding the year of the review, beginning with and including the later of the year in which the most recent order was issued or nineteen hundred ninety-four, and calculate the sum of the percentages for those years.

(2) Where the sum as calculated pursuant to subparagraph one of this paragraph equals or exceeds ten percent, multiply the support obligation in the order under review by such percentage. The product is the cost of living adjustment.

(d) "Order" shall mean an original, modified, or adjusted order of support; or, after a hearing in response to objections to a cost of living adjustment as set forth in an adjusted order of support, the order of support reflecting the application of the child support standards pursuant to section two hundred forty of the domestic relations law or section four hundred thirteen of the family court act, or an order of no adjustment.

(e) "Review" shall mean the calculation of the cost of living adjustment and the adjusted child support obligation amount by the support collection unit for the most recently issued order of support made on behalf of a child in receipt of family assistance, or child support enforcement services pursuant to section one hundred eleven-g of this title.

3.   Timeframes. The review of support orders for cost of living adjustment purposes shall be conducted by the support collection unit in accordance with the following timeframes:

(a)   For all orders of support on behalf of persons in receipt of family assistance, a review shall be conducted during the second calendar year following the year in which the order was issued, or the current year, whichever is later. Any cost of living adjustment resulting from a review shall be effective sixty days following the date of the adjusted order, or twenty-four months after the date of the order under review, whichever is later.

(b)   For all orders of support on behalf of persons not in receipt of family assistance, a review shall be conducted during the second calendar year following the year in which the order was issued, or the current year, whichever is later; provided, however, that no such review shall occur unless a request for such review has been received from a party to the order. Any cost of living adjustment resulting from a review shall be effective sixty days following the date of the adjusted order, or twenty-four months after the date of the order under review, whichever is later.

4.   Adjustment process. (a) A cost of living adjustment shall be made by the support collection unit with respect to each order of support under review, if the sum of the annual average changes of the consumer price index for all urban consumers (CPI-U), as published by the United States department of labor bureau of labor statistics, is ten percent or greater. The child support obligation amount, as increased by the cost of living adjustment calculated during the review, shall be rounded to the nearest dollar. In the event that the sum of the annual average changes of the CPI-U is less than ten percent, no cost of living adjustment shall occur.

(b)   Upon the conclusion of the adjustment review, the support collection unit shall issue and send an adjusted order by first class mail to the parties. The cost of living adjustment and the adjusted child support obligation amount as calculated by the review shall be reflected in the adjusted order. The child support obligation amount contained in the adjusted order shall be due and owing on the date the first payment is due under the terms of the order of support which was reviewed and adjusted occurring on or after the effective date of the adjusted order.

(c)   the support collection unit shall provide a copy of the adjusted order to the court which issued the most recent order of support, which shall append it to the order.

5.   Objections. (a) Where there is an objection to a cost of living adjustment, either party or the support collection unit shall have thirty-five days from the date of mailing of the adjusted order by the support collection unit to submit to the

SSL

court identified thereon written objections, requesting a hearing on the adjustment of the order of support.

(b)   If objections are submitted timely to the court, the cost of living adjustment shall not take effect, and a hearing shall be scheduled by the court. The hearing shall be conducted and a determination made by the court pursuant to section two hundred forty-c of the domestic relations law or section four hundred thirteen-a of the family court act.

(c)   Where no objection has been timely raised to a cost of living adjustment as reflected in an adjusted order, such adjusted order shall become final without further review by the court or any judge or support magistrate thereof.

6.   Adjusted order–form. The adjusted order shall contain the following information:

(a)   the caption of the order of support subject to the review, the date of such order, and the court in which it was entered;

(b)   the identification, telephone number, and address of the support collection unit which conducted the review;

(c)   the cost of living adjustment and the adjusted child support obligation amount as calculated during the review of the order, and a statement that such amount shall be due and owing on the date the first payment is due under the term of the order of support which was reviewed and adjusted, occurring on or after the effective date of the adjusted order;

(d)   the definition of cost of living adjustment;

(e)   a statement that the child support obligation amount, as increased by the cost of living adjustment, has been rounded to the nearest dollar;

(f)   a statement that all other provisions of the order of support which was reviewed and adjusted remain in full force and effect;

(g)   a statement that the application of a cost of living adjustment in no way limits, restricts, expands, or impairs the rights of any party to file for a modification of a child support order as otherwise provided by law;

(h)   a statement that where either party objects to the cost of living adjustment, the party has the right to be heard by the court and to present evidence to the court which the court will consider in adjusting the child support order in compliance with section four hundred thirteen of the family court act or section two hundred forty of the domestic relations law, known as the child support standards act; provided, however, that written objections are filed with the court within thirty-five days from the date the adjusted order was mailed by the support collection unit; that when filing objections the objecting party should attach a copy of the adjusted order, if available; and

(i)   a statement that where any party fails to provide, and update upon any change, the support collection unit with a current address to which an adjusted order can be sent, the support obligation amount contained therein shall become due and owing on the date the first payment is due under the order of support which was reviewed and adjusted occurring on or after the effective date of the adjusted order, regardless of whether or not the party has received a copy of the adjusted order.

7. Notice of right to review. On or after the first day of January, nineteen hundred ninety-eight, any order of support twenty-four or more months old which was issued on behalf of a child in receipt of family assistance or child support enforcement services pursuant to section one hundred eleven-g of this title, is eligible for a cost of living adjustment every two years. The support collection unit shall notify the parties to the order of their right to make a written request to the support collection unit for a cost of living adjustment of such support order. Such notice shall contain the amount of the cost of living adjustment, the amount of the adjusted child support obligation, the applicable CPI-U used in the calculation of that amount, the address and telephone number of the support collection unit where assistance can be obtained in commencing an adjustment review, and other information deemed necessary and relevant by the department, and shall be sent to the parties by first class mail at their last known address, and shall contain a reply form and envelope with postage pre-paid. The support collection unit shall provide the notice described herein not less than once every two years.

Added by Laws 1997, Ch. 398, § 93, eff. Jan. 1, 1998; **amended** by Laws 1998, Ch. 214, § 3, eff. July 7, 1998, deemed in full force and effect Jan. 1, 1998; Laws 2003, Ch. 81, § 13, eff. June 18, 2003, amending subd. 5(c).

L. 1997, Ch. 398, § 16 **relettered** SSL § 111-n to SSL § 111-z.

§ 111-o. Data matches with financial institutions.

The department or a social services district, through the commissioner, is authorized to enter into agreements with financial institutions as provided for in subdivision two of section four of the banking law and subsection (e) of section three hundred twenty of the insurance law, and is authorized to furnish to and receive from those and any other financial institutions, as defined in paragraph one of subdivision (d) of section four hundred sixty-nine a of the federal social security act, such information as may be necessary to carry out the agreements provided for in section four of the banking law and section three hundred twenty of the insurance law, for the enforcement of child support orders.

Added by Laws 1997, Ch. 398, § 136, eff. Jan. 1, 1998.

§ 111-p. Authority to issue subpoenas.

The department or the child support enforcement unit coordinator or support collection unit supervisor of a social services district, or his or her designee, or another state's child support enforcement agency governed by title IV-D of the social security act, shall be authorized, whether or not a proceeding is currently

SSL

pending, to subpoena from any person, public or private entity or governmental agency, and such person, entity or agency shall provide any financial or other information needed to establish paternity and to establish, modify or enforce any support order. If a subpoena is served when a petition is not currently pending, the supreme court or a judge of the family court may hear and decide all motions relating to the subpoena. If the subpoena is served after a petition has been served, the court in which the petition is returnable shall hear and decide all motions relating to the subpoena. Any such person, entity, or agency shall provide the subpoenaed information by the date as specified in the subpoena. Such subpoena shall be subject to the provisions of article twenty-three of the civil practice law and rules. The department or district may impose a penalty for failure to respond to such information subpoenas pursuant to section twenty-three hundred eight of the civil practice law and rules.

Added by Laws 1997, Ch. 398, § 54, eff. Jan. 1, 1998.

§ 111-q.   Voiding of fraudulent transfers of income or property.

The department or a social services district, or its authorized representative, after obtaining information that a debtor has transferred income, property or other assets to avoid payment to a child support creditor shall, pursuant to article ten of the debtor and creditor law (1) commence a proceeding to void such transfer; or (2) obtain a settlement that is in the best interests of the child support creditor. Provided, however, that no settlement shall reduce or annul any arrears of child support which have accrued prior to the date of settlement.

Added by Laws 1997, Ch. 398, § 54, eff. Jan. 1, 1998.

§ 111-r.   Requirement to respond to requests for information.

All employers, as defined in section one hundred eleven-m of this article (including for-profit, not-for-profit and governmental employers), are required to provide information promptly on the employment, compensation and benefits of any individual employed by such employer as an employee or contractor, when the department or a social services district or its authorized representative, or another state's child support enforcement agency governed by title IV-D of the social security act, requests such information for the purpose of establishing paternity, or establishing, modifying or enforcing an order of support. To the extent feasible, such information shall be requested and provided using automated systems, and shall include, but is not limited to, information regarding the individual's last known address, date of birth, social security number, plans providing health care or other medical benefits by insurance or otherwise, wages, salaries, earnings or other income of such individual. Notwithstanding any other provision of law to the contrary, such officials are not required to obtain an order from any judicial or administrative tribunal in order to request or receive such information. The department shall be authorized to impose a penalty for failure to respond to such requests of five hundred dollars for an initial failure and seven hundred dollars for the second and subsequent failure.

Added by Laws 1997, Ch. 398, § 54, eff. Jan. 1, 1998.

§ 111-s.   Access to information contained in government and private records.

1.   For the purpose of establishing paternity, or establishing, modifying or enforcing an order of support, the department or a social services district or its authorized representative, and child support enforcement agencies of other states established pursuant to title IV-D of the social security act, without the necessity of obtaining an order from any other judicial or administrative tribunal and subject to safeguards on privacy and information security, shall have access to information contained in the following records:

(a)   records of other state and local government agencies including:

(i)   vital statistics (including records of marriage, birth and divorce);

(ii)   state and local tax and revenue records (including information on residence address, employer, income and assets);

(iii)   records concerning real and titled personal property;

(iv)   records of occupational and professional licenses, and records concerning the ownership and control of corporations, partnerships and other business entities;

(v)   employment security records;

(vi)   records of agencies administering public assistance programs;

(vii)   records of the department of motor vehicles; and

(viii)   corrections records; and

(b)   certain records held by private corporations, companies, or other entities with respect to individuals who owe or are owed support (or against or with respect to whom a support obligation is being sought), consisting of:

(i)   pursuant to an administrative subpoena authorized by section one hundred eleven-p of this title, the names, addresses, telephone numbers and dates of birth of such individuals, and the names and addresses of the employers of such individuals, as appearing in customer records of public utilities companies and corporations, including, but not limited to, cable television, gas, electric, steam, and telephone companies and corporations, as defined in section two of the public service law, doing business within the state of New York; and

(ii)   information on such individuals held by financial institutions, including information regarding assets and liabilities.

2.   Notwithstanding any other provision of law to the contrary, any government or private entity to which a request for access to information is directed

pursuant to subdivision one of this section, is authorized and required to comply with such request. To the extent feasible, access to such information shall be requested and provided using automated systems. Any government or private entity which discloses information pursuant to this section shall not be liable under any federal or state law to any person for such disclosure, or for any other action taken in good faith to comply with this subdivision.

Added by Laws 1997, Ch. 398, § 54, eff. Jan. 1, 1998.

§ 111-t. Authority to secure assets.

The department or a social services district or its authorized representative, or another state's child support enforcement agency governed by title IV-D of the social security act, for the purpose of collecting overdue support, shall be authorized in accordance with all applicable provisions of law, to secure assets otherwise due a support obligor by:

1. Intercepting or seizing periodic or lump sum payments due such obligor from:

(a) a state or local agency, including unemployment compensation, workers' compensation, and other benefits; and

(b) judgments, settlements and lottery winnings;

2. Attaching and seizing assets of such obligors which are held in financial institutions;

3. Attaching public and private retirement funds of such obligors; and

4. Imposing liens against real and personal property owned by such obligors; and where appropriate, forcing the sale of property owned by such obligors and distributing proceeds from the sale of such properties.

Added by Laws 1997, Ch. 398, § 54, eff. Jan. 1, 1998.

§ 111-u. Liens.

1. The office of temporary and disability assistance, or a social services district, or its authorized representative shall have a lien against real and personal property owned by a support obligor when such support obligor is or was under a court order to pay child support or combined child and spousal support to a support collection unit on behalf of persons receiving services under this title, and such obligor has accumulated support arrears/past due in an amount equal to or greater than the amount of support due pursuant to such order for a period of four months. Such lien shall incorporate unpaid support which accrues in the future.

2. For the purposes of determining whether a support obligor has accumulated support arrears/past due support for a period of four months, the amount of any retroactive support, other than periodic payments of retroactive support

which are past due, shall not be included in the calculation of arrears/past due support pursuant to this section; however, if at least four months of support arrears/past due support have accumulated subsequent to the date of the court order, the entire amount of any retroactive support may be collected pursuant to the provisions of this subdivision or as otherwise authorized by law.

3. When the office of temporary and disability assistance, or a social services district, or its authorized representative on behalf of a person receiving services pursuant to this title determines that the requisite amount of child support is past due, it shall send, by first class mail, a notice of intent to file a lien to the support obligor. The obligor may assert a mistake of fact and shall have an opportunity to make a submission in support of the assertion. The assertion and any supporting papers shall be submitted within thirty-five days from the date a notice was mailed. Thereafter, the social services district shall determine the merits of the assertion, and shall notify the obligor of its determination within ninety days after notice to the obligor was mailed.

4. If the social services district finds no mistake of fact exists or, the obligor fails to assert a mistake of fact within the thirty-five days, the social services district may file a notice of lien, which shall contain the caption of the support order and a statement of arrears and which shall constitute a lien on the property. The social services district shall not enforce its lien until after expiration of any applicable period for review of an administrative action or, if the obligor has initiated a proceeding pursuant to article seventy-eight of the civil practice law and rules, until completion of such review.

5. Filing of the notice of the lien shall be as provided in sections sixty-five and two hundred eleven of the lien law, article forty-six of the vehicle and traffic law, or as otherwise authorized by law.

6. Within five days before or thirty days after filing the notice of the lien, the social services district shall send by first class mail a copy of such notice upon the owner of the property.

Added by Laws 1997, Ch. 398, § 67, eff. Jan. 1, 1998; **amended** by Laws 1998, Ch. 214, § 5, eff. July 7, 1998, deemed in full force and effect Jan. 1, 1998; **amended** by Laws 2002, Ch. 624, § 10, eff. Nov. 1, 2002.

§ 111-v. Confidentiality, integrity, and security of information.

1. The department, in consultation with appropriate agencies including but not limited to the New York state office for the prevention of domestic violence, shall by regulation prescribe and implement safeguards on the confidentiality, integrity, accuracy, access, and the use of all confidential information and other data handled or maintained, including data obtained pursuant to section one hundred eleven-o of this article and including such information and data maintained in the automated child support enforcement system. Such information and data shall be maintained in a confidential manner designed to protect the privacy rights of the parties and shall not be disclosed except for the purpose of,

and to the extent necessary to, establish paternity, or establish, modify or enforce an order of support.

2. These safeguards shall include provisions for the following:

(a) policies restricting access to and sharing of information and data, including:

(1) safeguards against unauthorized use or disclosure of information relating to procedures or actions to establish paternity or to establish or enforce support;

(2) prohibitions against the release of information on the whereabouts of one party to another party against whom an order of protection with respect to the former party has been entered; and

(3) prohibitions against the release of information on the whereabouts of one party to another party if the department has reason to believe that the release of the information may result in the physical or emotional harm to the former party.

(b) systems controls to ensure strict adherence to policies.

(c) monitoring of access to and use of the automated system to prevent unauthorized access or use.

(d) training in security procedures for all staff with access, and provisions of information regarding these requirements and penalties.

(e) administrative penalties for unauthorized access, disclosure, or use of confidential data.

3. If any person discloses confidential information in violation of this section, any individual who incurs damages due to the disclosure may recover such damages in a civil action.

4. Any person who willfully releases or permits the release of any confidential information obtained pursuant to this title to persons or agencies not authorized by this title or regulations promulgated thereunder to receive it shall be guilty of a class A misdemeanor.

5. The safeguards established pursuant to this section shall apply to staff of the department, local social services districts, and any contractor.

Added by Laws 1997, Ch. 398, § 54, eff. Jan. 1, 1998.

§ 111-y. Spousal support; crediting of overpayments of tax to past-due support.

1. The department shall provide services for the crediting of overpayments of tax to past-due support, pursuant to section one hundred seventy-one-c of the tax law, which is owed to any current or former spouse entitled to enforce an order of support, who applies to the department for such services, if such spouse is not eligible to receive services pursuant to title six-A of this article. For purposes of this section, "order of support" means any final order, decree or judgment in a matrimonial action or family court proceeding, or any foreign

support order, decree or judgment which is registered pursuant to article five-B of the family court act which requires the payment of alimony, maintenance or support.

2.   (a) An applicant for services under this section shall provide the department with the following:

(i)   a certified transcript of a money judgment for a sum certain for arrears accrued under an order of support;

(ii)   a sworn statement that the order of support is no longer subject to appellate judicial review and that the sum set forth as uncollected on the judgment is accurate;

(iii)   the name and address of the applicant; and

(iv)   the name, last known address and social security number of the person or entity owing past-due support against whom a judgment has been obtained.

(b)   If an application for services is rejected by the department, the department shall inform the applicant in writing of the reason for such rejection.

3.   An applicant for services under this section shall receive a pro rata share of the overpayment of tax, based on the amount of past-due support owed to such applicant as certified to the tax commission by the department pursuant to section one hundred seventy-one-c of the tax law, in cases where the individual, estate or trust owing past-due support to such applicant owes past-due support to other persons or entities so certified to the tax commission by the department.

4.   The department shall promulgate such regulations as are necessary to carry out the provisions of this section, including regulations as to the date by which an applicant for services under this section shall provide the department with the information and documentation required in subdivision two of this section.

Added by Laws 1985, Ch. 809, eff. Aug. 15, 1985; **relettered** from (m) eff. Oct. 1, 1997, and **amended** by Laws 1997, Ch. 398, §§ 16 and 52, eff. Jan. 1, 1998.

§ 111-z.   Spousal and child support; crediting of overpayments of tax to past-due support.

1.   The department shall provide services for the crediting of overpayments of tax to past-due support, pursuant to section one hundred seventy-one-c of the tax law, which is owed to persons entitled to enforce an order of support, for persons not receiving public assistance who are eligible to receive services pursuant to title six-A of this article, but who do not receive such services. For purposes of this section, "order of support" shall mean any final order, decree or judgment in a matrimonial action or family court proceeding, or any foreign support order, decree or judgment which is registered pursuant to article five-B of the family court act which requires the payment of alimony, maintenance, support or child support.

2.   (a) An applicant for services under this section shall provide the department with the following:

SSL

(i)   a certified transcript of a money judgment for a sum certain for arrears accrued under an order of support;

(ii)   a sworn statement that the order of support is no longer subject to appellate judicial review and that the sum set forth as uncollected on the judgment is accurate;

(iii)   the name and address of the applicant; and

(iv)   the name, last known address and social security number of the person or entity owing past-due support against whom a judgment has been obtained.

(b)   If an application for services is rejected by the department, the department shall inform the applicant in writing of the reason for such rejection.

(c)   The department shall inform applicants for services under this section of the support collection and enforcement services available through the support collection units pursuant to title six-A of this article.

3.   An applicant for services under this section shall receive a pro rata share of the overpayment of tax, based on the amount of past-due support owed to such applicant as certified to the tax commission by the department pursuant to section one hundred seventy-one-c of the tax law, in cases where the individual, estate or trust owing past-due support to such applicant owes past-due support to other persons or entities so certified to the tax commission by the department.

4.   The department may charge an applicant for services under this section a fee based on cost, but not to exceed the lesser of twenty-five dollars or the amount of overpayment of tax received by the department. The department shall recover such fee from such overpayment and pay any balance to the applicant. The fee provided for herein shall not be a charge against the individual, estate or trust owing past-due support.

5.   The department shall promulgate such regulations as are necessary to carry out the provisions of this section, including regulations as to the date by which an applicant for services under this section shall provide the department with the information and documentation required in subdivision two of this section.

Added by Law 1985, Ch. 809, eff. Aug. 15, 1985; **relettered** from (n) eff. Jan. 1, 1998, and **amended** eff. Jan. 1, 1998. by Laws 1997, Ch. 398, §§ 93 and 53.

TITLE 7—LOCAL PERSONNEL TRAINING; RESEARCH AND DEMONSTRATION PROJECTS; SPECIAL STATE REIMBURSEMENT

———

§ 112. Local personnel training.

Each public welfare district shall make provision, with the assistance and cooperation of the department, for suitable training of employees of its welfare department. Such provision shall include such of the following as the department may approve or require for such district: employment of qualified training directors and/or teachers; the granting of scholarships and fellowships continuing salaries of employees while undergoing training, pursuant to section thirty; contracting with approved schools, colleges and universities for courses of instruction and/or classes or special classes; sponsoring, conducting and participating in seminars, workshops and meetings and allowing or requiring attendance of selected employees; payment of stipends and expenses, within prescribed limits, of employees undergoing training.

Added by Laws 1963, Ch. 503, eff. Apr. 1, 1963.

§ 113. Participation in research and demonstration projects.

Public welfare districts are authorized to sponsor, conduct and participate in the operation of such research and demonstration projects as the department may approve, for the purpose of reducing dependency and eliminating the causes thereof. Public welfare districts shall cooperate with the department in the conduct of such projects whenever the department shall request or require such participation and cooperation.

Added by Laws 1963, Ch. 503, eff. Apr. 1, 1963.

§ 114. Special state reimbursement.

Any inconsistent provision of sections one hundred fifty-three, two hundred fifty-seven or other provisions of this chapter notwithstanding, expenditures made by public welfare districts for salaries of qualified training directors pursuant to section one hundred twelve and for salaries of employees while on educational leave pursuant to section thirty and one hundred twelve shall, if approved by the department, be subject to reimbursement by the state in accordance with the regulations of the department as follows:

there shall be paid to each such district

(a) the amount of federal funds, if any, properly received or to be received on account of such expenditures;

(b) the full amount expended for such purposes, after first deducting therefrom any federal funds properly received or to be received on account thereof.

Added by Laws 1963, Ch. 503; **amended** by Laws 1971, Ch. 110, eff. July 1, 1971.

SSL

§ 115. Training and utilization of volunteers.

Subject to the approval of the department, public welfare districts are authorized to sponsor and conduct programs for the recruitment, training and utilization of volunteers to assist welfare district employees in the performance of office duties and to aid in performing services in welfare districts including but not limited to the following:

(a)   friendly visiting of the indigent aged;

(b)   finding homes for foster children;

(c)   escorting and transporting recipients to clinics and other destinations;

(d)   aiding in location of improved housing;

(e)   teaching homemaking skills and aiding in budgeting and care of the household;

(f)   providing tutoring and other educational aid; and

(g)   giving information, screening requests and performing other services in waiting rooms of welfare centers.

Added by Laws 1964, Ch. 455, eff. Apr. 10, 1964.

TITLE 7-B—CHIEF EXECUTIVE OFFICERS OF LOCAL WELFARE DEPARTMENTS: APPOINTMENT

————

Section 116.   Chief executive officers of local welfare departments; qualifications; appointment and removal; term.

§ 116. Chief executive officers of local welfare departments; qualifications; appointment and removal; term.

1.   Any inconsistent provision of law, notwithstanding, the position of the chief executive officer of a county or city social services department, whether referred to as commissioner or by other title, shall be in the non-competitive class of the civil service, except any which is or may hereafter be in the competitive class. Appointments to such positions in the non-competitive class shall be for terms of five years and shall be made by the appropriate county or city body or officer. However, no person may be appointed to or serve in any such position who does not meet the minimum qualifications required therefor by the state commissioner of social services pursuant to section seventeen.

2.   Any inconsistent provision of law, general, special or local, notwithstanding, the chief executive officer of a county or city social services department shall also be subject to removal or sanction in accordance with the provisions of section thirty-four of this chapter.

3. As used in subdivision one "the appropriate county or city body or officer" shall mean and refer:

(a) in the case of a county, to the board of supervisors thereof, except when the county has a county executive, county president, county manager or other officer or board authorized to appoint heads of administrative departments or the chief executive officer of the social services department, in which case it shall mean such executive, president, manager, other officer or board;

(b) in the case of a city, to the mayor, manager, other officer, or the board having authority to appoint department heads or the chief executive officer of the social services department.

Added by Laws 1965, Ch. 1071; **amended** by Laws 1971, Ch. 110; **amended** by Laws 1971, Ch. 735; **amended** by Laws 1977, Ch. 863, eff. Apr. 1, 1978.

SSL

ARTICLE 4

RESIDENCE AND REMOVAL

SUMMARY OF ARTICLE

(Repealed and transferred sections noted under appropriate section number of text.)

[*Article 4 added, and former Art. 4, §§ 117–127 repealed, by Laws 1946, Ch. 200, eff. Apr. 1, 1946.*]

§ 117.　State residence.

1.　Any person who shall reside in the state continuously for one year under the conditions hereinafter specified shall be deemed to have state residence. State residence so acquired shall continue until such person shall have removed from the state and remained therefrom for one year; provided, however, that no person shall lose state residence by absence from the state while serving in the armed forces of the United States or in the United States merchant marine, or while attached to and serving with the armed forces of the United States and, provided further, that no member of the family of any such person shall lose state residence by absence from the state while living with or near such person during the period of such service and on account thereof.

2.　An infant shall, at the time of birth, whether within or without the state, be deemed to have state residence if he is in the custody of both parents and either of them has state residence or if the parent having his custody has state residence. State residence so acquired by a child born within the state shall continue until the child shall have removed from the state and remained therefrom for one year. State residence so acquired by a child born without the state shall terminate when he becomes one year of age if he remains without the state during such year. For the purpose of this subdivision and section, a child born out of wedlock whose natural parents were living together on the date of his birth shall be deemed to have been in the custody of both his parents on such date if his natural father has acknowledged or been adjudicated to be such.

3.   (a) Notwithstanding any other provision of law, no public assistance benefits shall be paid to or for any person who is not a resident of the state as provided in this article, except that assistance shall be provided to a person who is otherwise eligible during the first twelve months in the state at a rate not exceeding the higher of fifty percent of the amount otherwise payable or the standard of need applicable to the person under the laws of the state, if any, in which he or she resided immediately prior to arrival in this state, but under no circumstances may such allowances exceed the amounts payable to a resident under this chapter; and no assistance shall be provided for any alien during the first twelve months such person resides in the United States, except as set forth in paragraph (b) of this subdivision and except persons domiciled in the state on the effective date of this section, and except as otherwise required by federal law. For purposes of this section, the standard of payment applicable in another state shall refer to a schedule of comparative grants to be promulgated biennially, setting forth the amount of that state's maximum standard of payment with respect to each such program, if any, for each household size for any state which financially participates in or mandates a program under title IV-A of the federal social security act or a general assistance or disability assistance program.

(b)   This subdivision shall not apply to any person entitled to federally funded refugee cash assistance under title IV of the Immigration and Nationality Act or to any person participating in a project authorized under section 412(e) of the immigration and nationality act.

Added by Laws 1946, Ch. 200; **amended** by Laws 1950, Ch. 259; Laws 1959, Ch. 472, eff. Apr. 16, 1959; **amended** by Laws 1997, Ch. 436, § 1 Part B, § 6, eff. Aug. 20, 1997; **amended** by Laws 1998, Ch. 214, § 6, eff. July 7, 1998, deemed in full force and effect Aug. 20, 1997.

§ 118.   Qualification on residence.

The continuous residence required to acquire state residence or to establish liability for payment for hospital or other institutional care shall not include any period during which the person was (a) a patient in a hospital, or

(b)   an inmate of any public institution or any incorporated private institution, or

(c)   if a child under the age of twenty-one years, in a boarding home under the care of an authorized agency, or

(d)   residing on any military reservation.

If, however, the periods of residence immediately prior and subsequent to the period specified in a, b, c, or d, shall together equal the required period of residence, such person shall be deemed to have had the required continuous residence.

Added by Laws 1946, Ch. 200; **amended** by Laws 1974, Ch. 909, eff. Sept. 1, 1974.

§ 118-a.   Newborn infants; liability of public welfare districts for hospital or other institutional care.

Repealed by Laws 1977, Ch. 863, eff. Aug. 11, 1977.

§ 118-b.   Newborn infants; liability of a city or town in a county public welfare district for hospital care.

Repealed by Laws 1977, Ch. 863, eff. Aug. 11, 1977.

§ 118-c.   Family court cases; state charges.

In the event a child who is residing on any Native American reservation within the state is committed or placed by a court of competent jurisdiction as a delinquent, abused, neglected, or abandoned child, or person in need of supervision, or upon any ground specified in section three hundred eighty-four-b of this chapter, the state shall reimburse the social services district from which the child was committed for the full cost of care and maintenance of the child.

Added by Laws 1949, Ch. 827; **amended** by Laws 1962, Ch. 689, eff. Sept. 1, 1962; Laws 1977, Ch. 863, eff. Aug. 11, 1977; **amended** by Laws 1995, Ch. 81, § 158, eff. Apr. 1, 1995.

§ 119.   Procedure to establish liability between districts for hospital, other institutional and nursing home care.

Repealed by Laws 1977, Ch. 863, eff. Aug. 11, 1977.

§ 120.   Actions between districts for cost of care subject to chargeback.

Repealed by Laws 1977, Ch. 863, eff. Aug 11, 1977.

§ 121.   Removal of persons to another state or country.

1.   When any person who is cared for at the expense of the state or of any public welfare district has settlement or residence or otherwise belongs to or has legally responsible relatives able or friends willing to undertake the obligations to support him or to aid in supporting him in any other state or country, the department may furnish him with transportation to such state or country, provided, in its judgment the interest of the state and the welfare of such person will be thereby promoted.

2.   The expense of such removal shall be paid from the state treasury on the audit and warrant of the comptroller pursuant to a verified account submitted by the department and in accordance with the provisions of paragraph d of subdivision one of section one hundred fifty-three of this chapter.

Added by Laws 1946, Ch. 200, eff. Apr. 1, 1946. **Amended** by Laws 1995, Ch. 81, § 156, eff. Apr. 1, 1995.

§ 122. Aliens.

1.   Notwithstanding any law to the contrary, no person except a citizen or an alien who has been duly naturalized as a citizen shall be eligible for additional state payments for aged, blind and disabled persons, family assistance, safety net assistance, services funded under title XX of the federal social security act, or medical assistance, subject to the following exceptions:

(a)   The following persons shall, if otherwise eligible, receive benefits under such programs:

(i)   a refugee who entered the United States within the previous five years with respect to benefits under the temporary assistance to needy families block grant program and the safety net assistance program and within the previous seven years with respect to medical assistance;

(ii)   an asylee who was granted asylum within the previous five years with respect to benefits under the temporary assistance to needy families block grant program and the safety net assistance program and within the previous seven years with respect to medical assistance;

(iii)   a person for whom deportation was withheld within the previous five years with respect to benefits under the temporary assistance to needy families block grant program and the safety net assistance program and within the previous seven years with respect to medical assistance;

(iv)   except as otherwise required by federal law, a person lawfully admitted for permanent residence who has worked for or can be credited with forty qualifying quarters as defined under title II of the federal Social Security Act, exclusive of any quarter after the thirty-first day of December, nineteen hundred ninety-six in which such person or such person's parent or spouse received any federal means tested assistance;

(v)   any alien lawfully residing in the state who is on active duty in the armed forces (other than active duty for training) or who has received an honorable discharge (and not on account of alienage) from the armed forces or the spouse, unremarried surviving spouse or unmarried dependent child of any such alien, if such alien, spouse or dependent child is a qualified alien as defined in section 431 of the federal personal responsibility and work opportunity reconciliation act of 1996 (8 U.S. Code 1641), as amended;

(vi)   an alien granted status as a Cuban and Haitian entrant as defined in section 501(e) of the federal Refugee Education Act of 1980 within the previous five years with respect to benefits under the temporary assistance to needy families block grant program, and safety net assistance and within the previous seven years with respect to medical assistance; and

(vii)   an alien admitted to the United States as an Amerasian immigrant as described in section 402(a)(2)(a) of the federal personal responsibility and work opportunity reconciliation act of 1996 within the previous five years with respect to benefits under the temporary assistance to needy families block grant program,

SSL

and safety net assistance and within the previous seven years with respect to medical assistance.

(b)   the following persons, not described in paragraph (a) of this subdivision, shall, if otherwise eligible, be eligible for family assistance, medical assistance, and safety net assistance:

(i)   an alien who is a qualified alien as defined in section 431 of the federal personal responsibility and work opportunity reconciliation act of 1996 (8 U.S. Code 1641), as amended, who entered the United States before the twenty-second day of August, nineteen hundred ninety-six and continuously resided in the United States until attaining qualified status; and

(ii)   a qualified alien who entered the United States five years or more earlier with a status within the meaning of the term "qualified alien" as defined in section 431 of the federal personal responsibility and work opportunity reconciliation act of 1996 (8 U.S. Code 1641), as amended, if such entry occurred on or after the twenty-second day of August, nineteen hundred ninety-six.

(c)   The following persons, not described in paragraph (a) or (b) of this subdivision, shall, if otherwise eligible, be eligible for safety net assistance and medical assistance, except that medical assistance shall be limited to care and services (not including care and services related to an organ transplant procedure) necessary for the treatment of an emergency medical condition as that term is defined in section 1903 of the federal social security act unless and until federal financial participation is available for the costs of providing medical assistance provided, however, that any such person who, on the fourth day of August, nineteen hundred ninety-seven was residing in a residential health care facility licensed by the department of health or in a residential facility licensed, operated or funded by the office of mental health or the office of mental retardation and developmental disabilities, and was in receipt of a medical assistance authorization based on a finding that he or she was a person permanently residing in the United States under color of law shall, if otherwise eligible, be eligible for medical assistance and provided, further, that any such person who, on the fourth day of August, nineteen hundred ninety-seven, was diagnosed as having AIDS, as defined in subdivision one of section two thousand seven hundred eighty of the public health law, and was in receipt of medical assistance authorization pursuant to title eleven of article five of this chapter based on a finding that he or she was a person permanently residing in the United States under color of law shall, if otherwise eligible, be eligible for medical assistance and provided, further, that any such person who, on the fourth day of August, nineteen hundred ninety-seven, was diagnosed as having aids, as defined in subdivision one of section two thousand seven hundred eighty of the public health law, and was in receipt of medical assistance authorization pursuant to title eleven of article five of this chapter based on a finding that he or she was a person permanently residing in the United States under color of law shall, if otherwise eligible, be eligible for medical assistance:

(i)   a qualified alien who entered the United States less than five years earlier or for less than five years has had a status within the meaning of the term "qualified alien" as defined in section 431 of the federal personal responsibility and work opportunity reconciliation act of 1996 (8 U.S. Code 1641), as amended, if such entry occurred on or after the twenty-second day of August, nineteen hundred ninety-six; and

(ii)   an alien whose status is not within the meaning of the term "qualified alien" as defined in section 431 of the federal personal responsibility and work opportunity reconciliation act of 1996 (8 U.S. Code 1641), as amended, but who is otherwise permanently residing in the United States under color of law.

(d)   A person paroled into the United States for a period of less than one year shall, if otherwise eligible, be eligible to receive any state or local non-federal assistance provided under this chapter on the same terms as such programs are available to persons who are qualified aliens as defined in section 431 of the federal personal responsibility and work opportunity reconciliation act of 1996 (8 U.S. Code 1641), as amended.

(e)   Nothing herein shall preclude the receipt by any alien of community based non-cash assistance in accordance with the directions of the United States attorney general or the receipt of medical assistance for care and services (not including care and services related to an organ transplant procedure) necessary to treat an emergency medical condition as that term is defined in section 1903 of the federal social security act.

(f)   An alien who is not ineligible for federal supplemental security income benefits by reason of alien status shall, if otherwise eligible, be eligible to receive additional state payments for aged, blind or disabled persons under section two hundred nine of this chapter.

(g)   Aliens receiving supplemental security income benefits or additional state payments for aged, blind and disabled persons under section two hundred nine of this chapter shall be eligible for medical assistance if otherwise eligible.

(h)   Qualified aliens as defined in section 431 of the federal personal responsibility and work opportunity reconciliation act of 1996 (8 U.S. Code 1641), as amended, if otherwise eligible and except as otherwise provided by federal law, shall be eligible for services pursuant to title XX of the federal social security act.

2.   Any alien, including an alien who is not a qualified alien as defined in section 431 of the federal personal responsibility and work opportunity reconciliation act of 1996 (8 U.S. Code 1641), as amended, is eligible for adult protective services and services and assistance relating to child protection to the extent that such person is otherwise eligible pursuant to this chapter and the regulations of the department.

3.   Each social services district shall report to the department, in accordance with regulations of the department, the name and address and other identifying

SSL

information known to it with respect to any alien known to be unlawfully in the United States.

4. To the extent permitted by federal law and regulation, the income and resources of a sponsor of an alien, who has signed an affidavit of support pursuant to section 213A of the immigration and naturalization act, and the income and resources of such sponsor's spouse, shall be deemed available to such alien for purposes of determining the eligibility of such alien for assistance funded under the temporary assistance to needy families block grant and medical assistance.

5. If and to the extent that the family assistance, safety net assistance, state additional payments in the supplemental security income program, emergency assistance to aged, blind or disabled adults or medical assistance is paid to or on behalf of an alien for whom an affidavit of support pursuant to section 213a of the immigration and naturalization act has been signed, the social services district shall request reimbursement by the sponsor in the amount of such assistance, and, if the sponsor does not within forty-five days of such request indicate a willingness to commence payments, such social services district may commence an action against the sponsor pursuant to the affidavit. Remedies available to enforce an affidavit of support include all of the remedies described in sections 3201, 3202, 3204 and 3205 of title 28 of the United States code, as well as an order for specific performance and payment of legal fees and other costs of collection, and include corresponding remedies available under state law; provided, however, that no action shall be brought more than ten years after assistance was last given.

6. Nothing in this section shall be interpreted as affecting the eligibility for pre-natal care benefits for persons otherwise eligible for such benefits.

Added by Laws 1997, Ch. 436, § 1 Part B, § 7, eff. Aug. 20, 1997, and shall be deemed to have been in full force and effect on and after Aug. 22, 1996 except that provisions relating to medical assistance benefits shall take effect immediately and provided, further, that the food stamps provisions shall take effect Aug. 31, 1997 or such other date as may be consistent with federal laws governing eligibility for such program; **amended** by Laws 1998, Ch. 214, §§ 7 and 28, eff. July 7, 1998, and deemed in full force and effect Aug. 20, 1997, and Ch. 58, Part E § 5, eff. Apr. 28, 1998, deemed in full force and effect Apr. 1, 1998; **amended** by Laws 2002, Ch. 16, § 1, eff. Feb. 1, 2002.

ARTICLE 5

ASSISTANCE AND CARE

SUMMARY OF ARTICLE

TITLE 1—GENERAL PROVISIONS

(Repealed and transferred sections noted under appropriate section number of text.)

SSL

§ 131. Assistance, care and services to be given.

1. It shall be the duty of social services officials, insofar as funds are available for that purpose, to provide adequately for those unable to maintain themselves, in accordance with the requirements of this article and other provisions of this chapter. They shall, whenever possible, administer such care, treatment and service as may restore such persons to a condition of self-support or self-care, and shall further give such service to those liable to become destitute as may prevent the necessity of their becoming public charges.

2. It shall be the duty of social services officials, insofar as funds are available for that purpose, to cooperate with the directors of state department of mental hygiene facilities in order to assist patients discharged or about to be discharged from mental hygiene institutions in their transition to a condition of self-support and self-care in the community.

3. As far as possible families shall be kept together, they shall not be separated for reasons of poverty alone, and they shall be provided services to maintain and strengthen family life. In providing such services, the public welfare official may utilize appropriate community resources, including non-profit private agencies. Whenever practicable, assistance and service shall be given a needy person in his own home. The commissioner of public welfare may,

however, in his discretion, provide assistance and care in a boarding home, a home of a relative, a public or private home or institution, or in a hospital.

4. For needy persons who are members of a family household, the standard of need for determining their eligibility for public assistance shall be as prescribed by section one hundred thirty-one-a of this chapter and applicable federal requirements. For needy persons who are not members of a family household, the department shall continue to determine the standard of need for determining their eligibility for public assistance pursuant to the provisions of this chapter and applicable federal requirements.

5. No public assistance shall be given to an applicant for or recipient of public assistance who has failed to comply with the requirements of this chapter, or has refused to accept employment in which he or she is able to engage.

5-a. The state commissioner of labor, in cooperation with the commissioner and with individual local social services officials, is hereby authorized to locate jobs services personnel wherever appropriate, in order to achieve the employment objectives of this chapter. Local social services officials, in cooperation with the commissioner and the commissioner of labor, are authorized to locate social services personnel wherever appropriate, in order to achieve the employment objectives of this chapter.

6. No individual who is under the age of eighteen and is not married, who resides with and provides care for his or her dependent child or is pregnant and otherwise entitled to family assistance shall receive family assistance for himself or herself unless the individual, individual and child or pregnant woman resides in a place of residence maintained as a home by the individual's parent, legal guardian or other adult relative or in an adult-supervised supportive living arrangement. Where possible, any such benefits to be paid on behalf of such individual, individual and child or pregnant woman shall be provided by the social services district to the parent, legal guardian or other adult relative with whom such individual, individual and child or pregnant woman resides.

The requirement to reside with a parent, guardian or adult relative shall not apply if (a) the individual has no living parent, legal guardian or other appropriate adult relative who is living or whose whereabouts are known or (b) no living parent or legal guardian of such individual allows the individual to live in his or her home or (c) the individual or minor child is being or has been subjected to serious physical or emotional harm, sexual abuse or exploitation in the residence of the parent or guardian or (d) substantial evidence exists of imminent or serious harm if such individual or dependent child were to live in the same residence with the individual's parent or legal guardian or (e) it is in the minor child's best interests to waive such requirement with respect to the individual or minor child, as determined in accordance with department regulations, consistent with federal law and regulations. Unless the individual's current living arrangement is appropriate, an individual and his or her minor child who are not required hereunder to reside with a parent, guardian or adult relative shall be required as a condition of assistance to reside in an adult supervised supportive living arrangement approved by the district in accordance with standards set by the department and taking into account the needs and concerns of the individual, including but not limited to a second chance home or maternity home. A "second chance home" is a facility which provides teen parents with a supportive and supervised living arrangement in which they are required to learn parenting skills, including child development, family budgeting, health and nutrition and other skills to promote long-term economic independence and the well-being of their children. Social services districts shall provide adult supervised supportive living arrangements or assist individuals in locating them. If a child subject to the requirements of this subdivision alleges facts which, if true, would render the requirement to live with a parent, guardian or other adult relative inapplicable by reason of paragraph (c) or (d) of this subdivision, a social services district shall take no action to deny assistance under the authority of this subdivision unless it has duly investigated in accordance with section four hundred twenty-four of this chapter and made a contrary finding. If a social services district denies assistance after a child alleges facts which, if true, would render this subdivision inapplicable by reason of paragraph (c) or (d) of this subdivision, the applicant shall be entitled to a fair hearing pursuant to section twenty-two of this chapter held within thirty days of the request, if the request is timely made.

7. a. Care, treatment and service as provided in subdivision one of this section may include, in accordance with applicable federal and state requirements, if any, medical care, instruction and work training to restore health, aptitudes and capabilities or develop new aptitudes and skills for the purpose of preparing individuals for gainful employment.

b. A public welfare official responsible for the assistance and care of a person who, in the judgment of such official, is employable or potentially employable, may require such person to receive suitable medical care and/or undergo suitable instruction and/or work training. Any such person who wilfully refuses to accept such medical care, refuses or fails to report for or cooperate in a program of instruction and/or work training as required by the public welfare official, shall be ineligible to receive public assistance and care. However, the requirements of this provision relating to instruction and work training shall not apply in the case of a person who is not available for employment by reason of age, health or other disability.

c. The provisions of this section shall not confer authority on a social services official to provide instruction which is available through the public school system, but regulations of the department may make provision for such authority when special need therefor is demonstrated.

7-a. [*Repealed.*]

8. This section shall be construed to require the employment of such employees as may be necessary and qualified to perform or provide the specialized services indicated by federal or state requirements.

9. Upon determining that a person is eligible for any form or category of public assistance, the social services official shall issue to any such person to whom payment is to be made, an appropriate identification card, with a photograph affixed, in a form approved by the department, which shall be used as the department, by regulation, may prescribe for improved administration. Any person, including the drawee bank, may require the presentation of such identification card as a condition for the acceptance and payment of a public assistance check.

10. Any applicant who voluntarily terminated his or her employment or voluntarily reduced his or her earning capacity for the purpose of qualifying for public assistance or a larger amount thereof shall be disqualified from receiving such assistance for ninety days from such termination or reduction, unless otherwise required by federal law or regulation. Any applicant who applies for public assistance within ninety days after voluntarily terminating his or her employment or reducing his or her earning capacity shall, unless otherwise required by federal law or regulation, be deemed to have voluntarily terminated his or her employment or reduced his or her earning capacity for the purpose of qualifying for such assistance or a larger amount thereof, in the absence of evidence to the contrary supplied by such person.

11. Social services officials are hereby authorized to furnish assistance which duplicates assistance already granted, but, unless otherwise specifically required by the provisions of title eight of article five of this chapter, (i) in no event shall such officials be required to furnish such assistance and (ii) in no event shall state reimbursement be available for such expenditures, provided, however, that any payment required by a court of competent jurisdiction shall be subject to state reimbursement.

12. Notwithstanding any provision of this chapter or other law to the contrary, no public assistance or food stamps shall be given to any individual during the ten-year period that begins on the date the individual is convicted in federal or state court of having made a fraudulent statement or representation with respect to his or her place of residence in order to receive public assistance, medical assistance or food stamps simultaneously from two or more states or supplemental security income in two or more states. The preceding sentence shall not apply with respect to a conviction of an individual in any month beginning after the president of the united states grants a pardon with respect to the conduct which was the subject of the conviction.

13. Social services districts shall provide all applicants and recipients of public assistance with children five years of age or less with information and a schedule regarding age-appropriate immunizations for children in accordance with the recommendations of the department of health and the immunization practices advisory committee of the United States department of health and human services. The telephone number of the local county health department shall be included on the immunization schedule.

14.　(a) Notwithstanding any provision of this chapter or other law to the contrary, no public assistance shall be given to any individual who is (i) fleeing to avoid prosecution or custody or conviction under the laws of the place from which the individual flees for a crime, or an attempt to commit a crime, which is a felony under the laws of the place from which the individual flees or which, in the case of the state of New Jersey, is a high misdemeanor under the laws of such state or (ii) violating a condition of probation or parole imposed under federal or state law.

(b)　For purposes of this section, if and to the extent permitted by federal law, a person shall be considered to be violating a condition of probation or parole only if:

(i)　he or she is currently an absconder from probation or parole supervision and a warrant alleging such a violation is outstanding; or

(ii)　he or she has been found by judicial determination to have violated probation or by administrative adjudication by the division of parole to have violated parole.

Such person shall be considered to be violating a condition of probation or parole only until he or she is restored to probation or parole supervision or released from custody, or until the expiration of the person's maximum period of imprisonment or supervision, whichever occurs first.

(c)　A person considered to be violating a condition of probation or parole under this section shall include a person who is violating a condition of probation or parole imposed under federal law.

(d)　For purposes of this section, probation or parole shall include conditional release, wherever applicable.

15.　Notwithstanding any provision of this chapter or other law to the contrary, no public assistance shall be given to or for any minor child who has been or is expected to be absent from the home of his or her parent or other caretaker relative for a consecutive period of forty-five days or more without good cause as set forth in regulations of the department, nor shall any assistance be given to any parent or other caretaker relative who fails to notify the social services district of the absence of the minor child within five days after it becomes clear to the parent (or relative) that the child will be absent for a consecutive period of forty-five days or more. Good cause shall include absence for placement in foster care if the goal set forth in the child service plan under section four hundred nine-e of this chapter is the return of the child to a member of the household, or attendance at school or hospitalization, if it is in the best interests of the child to return home and return is expected within a reasonable time.

16.　If, in accordance with section one hundred fifty-eight, three hundred forty-nine-b or other provisions of this chapter, the social services official determines that an individual is not cooperating in establishing paternity or in establishing, modifying, or enforcing a support order with respect to a child of the individual, and the individual does not have good cause for such failure or is not otherwise excepted from so cooperating in accordance with regulations of the department, the assistance given to the household shall be reduced by twenty-five percent.

17. [*Subd. (17) not enacted.*]

18.   Notwithstanding any provision of this chapter or other law to the contrary, no public assistance shall be given to any parent under the age of eighteen, who is not married and has a minor child twelve weeks of age or more in his or her care and who has not successfully completed a high school education or its equivalent if such individual does not participate in educational activities directed toward the attainment of a high school diploma or its equivalent or an alternative educational or training program directly related to employment and approved by the social services district. No person shall be denied assistance under this subdivision during any period of time in which enrollment in required educational activities is not available. Nothing herein shall prohibit a social services district from requiring any person to work toward attaining a secondary school diploma or its equivalent unless such person has been determined by a medical, psychiatric or other appropriate professional to lack the requisite capacity to complete successfully such a course of study.

19.   When a recipient claims that his or her system access device has been lost, stolen, or destroyed, or that the security features of the card have been compromised, the local social services district, subject to reasonable terms and conditions set forth in department regulations and policies, shall provide the recipient with a replacement card within forty-eight hours exclusive of weekends and holidays.

Amended by Laws 1950, Ch. 364; Laws 1959, Chs. 593, 715; Laws 1962, Ch. 593 Laws 1963, Chs. 186, 1014; Laws 1969, Chs. 184, 587; Laws 1970, Chs. 517, 568; Laws 1971, Chs. 102, 103, 110, 946, 298; Laws 1972, Chs. 683, 685, 941; Laws 1974, Chs. 621, 909; Laws 1977, Ch. 77, Ch. 759; Laws 1978, Ch. 473; Laws 1978, Ch. 556; **amended** by Laws 1980, Ch. 743, eff. June 30, 1980 until June 30, 1982; Ch. 744, eff. July 1, 1980 except new subd. (5) which becomes effective on July 1, 1982 and new subd. (6) which becomes effective on June 30, 1982; **amended** by Laws 1981, Ch. 300, eff. Sept. 1, 1981; **amended** by Laws 1982, Ch. 388, eff. July 1, 1982; **amended** by Laws 1982, Ch. 399, eff. June 28, 1982; **amended** by Laws 1982, Ch. 400, eff. June 28, 1982; **amended** by Laws 1983, Ch. 422, eff. July 8, 1983; **amended** by Laws 1984, Ch. 321, eff. July 1, 1984, provided that employment services plans submitted by local social services districts for approval, pursuant to § 131 of the Social Services Law, shall in the calendar year 1984 be submitted to the commissioner of social services by Sept. 1, 1984, and the commissioner's approval or comment and/or changes shall be completed by Sept. 31, 1984; **amended** by Laws 1984, Ch. 352, eff. July 1, 1984; **amended** by Laws 1985, Ch. 42, eff. Oct. 1, 1984; **amended** by Laws 1990, Ch. 453, §§ 6, 7, eff. Oct. 1, 1990; **amended** by Laws 1995, Ch. 81, §§ 147, 148, 187, eff. July 1, 1995; **amended** by Laws 1996, Ch. 61, eff. Oct. 20, 1996, **added** subd. 13; **amended** by Laws 1997, Ch. 436, § 1 Part B, §§ 10, 11, 42, and 144-b, eff. Aug. 20, 1997; **amended** by Laws 1998, Ch. 214, § 9 eff. July 7, 1998.

§ 131-a.   Monthly grants and allowances of public assistance.

1.   Any inconsistent provision of this chapter or other law notwithstanding, social services officials shall, in accordance with the provisions of this section and regulations of the department, provide public assistance to needy persons who constitute or are members of a family household, who are determined to be eligible in accordance with standards of need established in subdivision two. Provision for such persons, for all items of need, less any available income or resources which are not required to be disregarded by other provisions of this chapter, shall be made in accordance with this section. Such provision shall be made in monthly or semi-monthly allowances and grants within the limits of the schedules included in subdivision three of this section except for additional amounts which shall be included therein for shelter, fuel for heating, additional cost of meals for persons who are unable to prepare meals at home and for other items for which specific provision is otherwise made in article five. As used in this section the term "shelter" may include a grant not to exceed two thousand five hundred dollars toward the purchase of an interest in a cooperative. A social services official shall require assignment of recipient's equity in such cooperative housing in accordance with the rules of the board and regulations of the department.

2.   (a) the following schedule shall be the standard of monthly need for determining eligibility for all categories of assistance in and by all social services districts:

Number of Persons in Household

One	Two	Three	Four	Five	Six
$112	$179	$238	$307	$379	$438

For each additional person in the household there shall be added an additional amount of sixty dollars monthly.

(b)   In addition to the above, the standard of need shall include amounts for shelter and fuel for heating, amounts for home energy payments (including amounts for supplemental home energy grants), amounts for additional cost of meals for persons who are unable to prepare meals at home and amounts for other items when required by individual case circumstances for which specific provision is otherwise made in article five of this chapter. For purposes of determining the amount to be included in the standard of need for shelter and fuel for heating, to the extent that federal reimbursement is available therefor, social services officials shall include in the household any child who has entered foster care pursuant to section three hundred eighty-four-a of this chapter who was eligible for and in receipt of assistance and care as a member of the household in and for the month of entry into foster care and for whom the family service plan, as defined in section four hundred nine-e of this chapter, includes a goal of discharge to a member of the household.

SSL

(c)   If by the application of the standard of need as provided for in this subdivision the monthly need of an individual or household is less than ten dollars, such individual or household shall not be considered in need of cash assistance but shall be deemed to be a recipient of assistance for all other purposes including determining eligibility for medical assistance and social rehabilitative services.

(d)   The standard of monthly need, when not a whole dollar amount, shall be rounded to the next lower whole dollar amount.

3.   (a) Persons and families determined to be eligible by the application of the standard of need prescribed by the provisions of subdivision two less any available income or resources which are not required to be disregarded by other provisions of this chapter, shall receive maximum monthly grants and allowances in all social services districts in accordance with the following schedule, for public assistance:

Number of Persons in Household

One	Two	Three	Four	Five	Six
$112	$179	$238	$307	$379	$438

For each additional eligible needy person in the household there shall be an additional allowance of sixty dollars monthly.

(b)   Notwithstanding the provisions of this section or any other law to the contrary, no payment of public assistance shall be made for any month if the amount of such payment would be less than ten dollars per month.

(c)   The amount of the monthly grant and allowance, when not a whole dollar amount, shall be rounded to the next lower whole dollar amount.

3-a, 3-b.   [*Repealed.*]

3-c.   Commencing July first, nineteen hundred eighty-one, persons and families determined to be eligible by the application of the standard of need prescribed by the provision of subdivision two of this section, shall receive a home energy grant equal to the following monthly amounts:

Number of Persons in Household

One	Two	Three	Four	Five	Six
$14.10	$22.50	$30.00	$38.70	$47.70	$55.20

For each additional needy person in the household, there shall be added an additional amount of seven dollars and fifty cents.

3-d.   Commencing January first, nineteen hundred eighty-six, for persons and families determined to be eligible by the application of the standard of need prescribed by the provisions of subdivision two of this section, the amounts set forth in paragraph (a) of subdivision three of this section, after application of subdivision three-c of this section, shall be increased by the following amounts as a monthly supplemental home energy grant:

Number of Persons in Household

One	Two	Three	Four	Five	Six
$11	$17	$23	$30	$37	$42

For each additional needy person in the household, there shall be added an additional amount of five dollars monthly.

4. If federal requirements make it necessary to adjust any schedule of grants and allowances, or part thereof, the department shall make such adjustments but the adjusted schedule of grants and allowances shall not exceed the schedule of monthly amounts in subdivision two above.

5. Notwithstanding any other provisions of this chapter or other law, a social services official may make provisions for the following items and services: (a) replacement of necessary furniture and clothing for persons in need of public assistance who have suffered the loss of such items as the result of fire, flood or other like catastrophe, provided provisions therefor cannot otherwise be made;

(b) purchase of necessary and essential furniture required for the establishment of a home for persons in need of public assistance, provided provision therefor cannot otherwise be made;

(c) essential repair of heating equipment, cooking stoves, and refrigerators used by persons in need of public assistance in their homes, provided provision therefor cannot otherwise be made except that replacement may be authorized when less expensive than repair;

(d) camp fees when funds cannot be obtained from other sources for children receiving aid to dependent children assistance not in excess of maximum fees as established by regulations of the department; life insurance premiums provided the policy is assigned to the department, or in cases where the recipient is aged, his or her life expectancy is short, or he or she is deemed uninsurable;

(e) provision of allowances as prescribed by regulations of the department to meet the needs of a pregnant woman, beginning with the fourth month of pregnancy which has been medically verified;

6. [*Repealed.*]

7. Whenever a social services official finds that a recipient of public assistance has failed to fully apply the amount allowed in his grant for shelter to the payment of rent for his housing accommodations, unless rent is being withheld pursuant to law or court order, the social services official shall furnish such recipient's shelter allowance in the form of direct payments to the owner of such housing accommodations or his or her designated agent.

SSL

8.   (a) In determining the need for aid provided pursuant to the public assistance programs, the following income earned during a month by applicants for or recipients of such aid shall be exempt and disregarded:

(i)   all of the earned income of a dependent child receiving such aid or for whom an application for such aid has been made, who is a fulltime student or part-time student attending a school, college, or university, or a course of vocational or technical training designed to fit him for gainful employment;

(ii)   from the earned income of any child or relative applying for or receiving aid pursuant to such program, or of any other individual living in the same household as such relative and child whose needs are taken into account in making such determination, the first ninety dollars of the total of such earned income for such month;

(iii)   forty-two percent of the earned income for such month of any recipient in a household containing a dependent child which remains after application of all other subparagraphs of this paragraph; provided, however, that such percentage amount shall be adjusted in June of each year, commencing in nineteen hundred ninety-eight, to reflect changes in the most recently issued poverty guidelines of the United States Bureau of the Census, such that a household of three without special needs, living in a heated apartment in New York city and without unearned income would become ineligible for assistance with gross earnings equal to the poverty level in such guidelines; provided, however, that no assistance shall be given to any household with gross earned and unearned income, exclusive of income described in subparagraphs (i) and (vi) of this paragraph, in excess of such poverty level;

(iv)   [Deleted by Laws 1997, Ch. 436, § 1, Part B, § 12 and not replaced.]

(v)   the first fifty dollars received in such month which represent support payments timely paid in and for such month and the first fifty dollars received in such month which represent support payments timely paid in and for each of any prior months, in any household applying for or receiving public assistance, including support payments collected and paid to the public assistance household by the social services district;

(vi)   in any calendar year, all of the earned income of a dependent child receiving such aid who is a full-time student;

(vii)   all of the income of a dependent child living with a parent or other caretaker relative, who is receiving such aid or for whom an application for such aid has been made, which is derived from participation in a program carried out under the federal job training partnership act (P.L. 97-300) provided, however, that in the case of earned income such disregard must be applied for at least, but no longer than, six months per calendar year for each such child.

(viii)   any federal income taxes refunded by reason of section thirty-two of the Internal Revenue Code of nineteen hundred eighty-six relating to the earned income tax credit or any payment by an employer under section three thousand five hundred seven of such code relating to advance payment of the earned income tax credit.

(b)   Notwithstanding the provisions of paragraph (a) of this subdivision, there shall not be disregarded under subparagraphs (ii) and (iii) of such paragraph any earned income of any of the persons to which subparagraph (ii) of such paragraph applies if such person:

(i)   terminated his employment or reduced his earned income without good cause, within a period of not less than seventy-five days, or such other period of time as required by federal law or regulation, prior to a determination of need for public assistance;

(ii)   refused without good cause, within such seventy-five day period, to accept employment in which he is able to engage, which is offered through the public employment office of the New York state department of labor or refused to accept employment otherwise offered by an employer if the offer of such employer is determined by an appropriate social services official to be a bona fide offer of employment; or

(iii)   failed without good cause to make a timely report to the appropriate social services district of earned income received in the month a determination of need is made.

(c)   There shall not be disregarded under subparagraph (iii) of paragraph (a) of this subdivision any earned income of any of the persons specified in subparagraph (ii) of such paragraph, if the income of such person was in excess of his or her need, unless such person received public assistance in one or more of the four months preceding the month of need determination.

9.   In determining the eligibility of a child for public assistance and the amount of such assistance for any month there shall be taken into consideration so much of the income of such dependent child's stepparent living in the same household as such child as exceeds the sum of:

(a)   the first seventy-five dollars of the total of the stepparent's earned income for such month, or such lesser amount as the department may prescribe in the case of a stepparent not engaged in full-time employment or not employed throughout such month consistent with federal law and regulations;

(b)   the standard of need as contained in this section for a family of the same composition as the stepparent and those other individuals living in the same household as the child who are not applying for or receiving benefits and are claimed by such stepparent as dependents for purposes of determining such stepparent's federal income tax liability;

(c)   amounts paid by the stepparent to individuals not living in such household and claimed by such stepparent as dependents for purposes of determining such stepparent's federal personal income tax liability; and

(d)   payments of alimony or child support made by such stepparent with respect to individuals not living in such household.

10.   (a) Notwithstanding the provisions of this section or any other law to the contrary, no person or family shall be eligible for public assistance for any month in which the total income of the family, excluding benefits received under such programs and without application of the income exemptions and disregards provided in subparagraphs (ii) and (iii) of paragraph (a) of subdivision eight of this section, exceeds one hundred eighty-five percent of the standard of need for a family of the same composition. Provided, however, that the income disregards provided in subparagraphs (v), (vi) and (vii) of paragraph (a) of subdivision eight of this section shall be applied in making the eligibility determination required by this paragraph.

(b)   For purposes of this subdivision, the term standard of need shall include the amounts in the schedule set forth in paragraph (a) of subdivision two of this section plus amounts for shelter, and fuel for heating as prescribed by regulations of the department, amounts for home energy payments provided pursuant to subdivision three-c of this section and amounts for other items when required by individual case circumstances for which specific provision is otherwise made in this article.

11.   [*Repealed.*]

12.   (a) No public assistance household having income which, after application of applicable disregards, exceeds the household standard of need, because of the receipt in any month of a nonrecurring lump sum of earned or unearned income, shall be eligible for public assistance for a period equal to the full number of months derived by dividing (i) the sum of the lump sum income and all other income received in such month which is not excluded under subdivision eight of this section; by (ii) the standard of need for a family size which consists of the public assistance household plus any other individuals whose lump sum income is considered available to such household. Any income remaining from this calculation is income in the first month following such period of ineligibility.

(b)   At any time after determining the period of ineligibility as required in paragraph (a) of this subdivision, the social services official shall recalculate the remaining period of ineligibility in such circumstances and under such conditions as the department shall prescribe by regulation, subject to paragraph (c) of this subdivision and consistent with federal law and regulations.

(c)   The social services official shall exclude from any lump sum income any amounts which are exempt and disregarded as cash and liquid or nonliquid resources pursuant to section one hundred thirty-one-n of this title and shall recalculate the period of ineligibility caused by receipt of a nonrecurring lump sum of income subject to this subdivision to the extent that such income is applied to any or all of the following within ninety days of receipt: an automobile needed for the applicant or recipient to seek or retain employment or for travel to and from work activities as defined in section three hundred thirty-six of this chapter, a bank account or accounts, or a burial plot or plots, or a funeral agreement or agreements, the values of which are exempt and disregarded as a resource pursuant to section one hundred thirty-one-n of this title.

13. Pursuant to regulations of the office of temporary and disability assistance, public assistance eligibility shall, to the extent permitted by federal law, not lapse solely by reason of the death of the adult relative caretaker of a minor child, until arrangements are completed for the addition of the child to another public assistance household, reclassification of the case, foster care or other appropriate financial support. For purposes of subdivision eight of section one hundred fifty-three of this article, safety net assistance given to such a child during the first forty-five days after application therefor shall be regarded as being given to meet emergency circumstances.

Added by Laws 1970, Ch. 517; **amended** by Laws 1971, Chs. 133, 110, 298, 737; **amended** by Laws 1972, Ch. 523, eff. May 24, 1972; Laws 1973, Ch. 150; Laws 1974, Ch. 189, eff. July 1, 1974; Ch. 1080, deemed to have been in full force and effect on and after Jan. 1, 1974; Laws 1976, Ch. 953, eff. Aug. 27, 1976; former subd. (5) **repealed** Laws 1972, Ch. 523; subd. (7) **added** by Laws 1972, Ch. 943; former subds. (8)-(11) **added** by Laws 1973, Ch. 516, eff. Jan. 1, 1974, **expired** Apr. 1, 1974; subs. 3-a, 3-b **added** by Laws 1977, Ch. 77, eff. Apr. 1, 1977 until Mar. 31, 1978; **amended** by Laws 1981, Ch. 102, eff. July 1, 1981; **amended** by Laws 1981, Ch. 1053, eff. Jan. 1, 1982; **amended** by Laws 1983, Ch. 548, eff. Sept. 1, 1983; **amended** by Laws 1983, Ch. 742, eff. July 27, 1983; **amended** by Laws 1985 (see 1985 Amendments note *infra*); **amended** by Laws 1987, Ch. 467, eff. July 27, 1987, Ch. 521, eff. July 30, 1987; **amended** by Laws 1989, Ch. 77, §§ 4, 5, 6, eff. Jan. 1, 1990; **amended** by Laws 1989, Ch. 734, eff. Oct. 1, 1989; **amended** by Laws 1989, Ch. 747, § 2, eff. July 24, 1989; **amended** by Laws 1990, Ch. 453, § 2, eff. Oct. 1, 1990; **amended** by Laws 1990, Ch. 453, § 3, eff. Oct. 1, 1990, deemed in full force and effect as of Apr. 1, 1990; **amended** by Laws 1990, Ch. 818, § 20, eff. Sept. 30, 1990; **amended** by Laws 1991, Ch. 413, § 69, eff. July 19, 1991; **amended** by Laws 1993, Ch. 87, § 1, eff. June 1, 1993; **amended** by Laws 1995, Ch. 81, §§ 153-154, eff. July 1, 1995; **amended** by Laws 1997, Ch. 436, § 1 Part B, §§ 6 and 12, eff. Aug. 20, 1997; **amended** by Laws 1998, Ch. 214, § 10, deemed in full force and effect Aug. 20, 1997; **amended** by Laws 2000, Ch. 477, § 3, eff. Nov. 19, 2000, adding subsection (13); **amended** by Laws 2002, Ch. 246, §§ 1, 2, eff. July 30, 2002; **amended** by Laws 2003, Ch. 373, § 1, eff. Dec. 16, 2003.

1985 Amendments

Amended by Laws 1985, Ch. 42, eff. as follows: **amended** § 8(a)(ii), (iii), (iv), eff. Oct. 1, 1984; **added** § 8(a)(v), eff. Oct. 1, 1984; **added** § 8(a)(vi), eff. June 1, 1984; **amended** § 10(a), eff. June 1, 1984; **amended** § 10(a), eff. Oct. 1, 1984; **added** § 11, eff. for months beginning after Sept. 30, 1984 and ending before Oct. 1, 1987; **added** § 12, eff. Oct. 1, 1984; **amended** by Laws 1985, Ch. 60, eff. Jan. 1, 1986; **amended** by Laws 1985, Ch. 568, eff. July 26, 1985.

§ 131-b. Fees for services.

If and only to the extent the imposition of a fee is required by federal law and regulation to insure continued full federal financial participation in the state's plan for services under applicable federal law and regulations, the department shall, by regulation, require a local social services district to impose a fee for any service made available by that district to an individual who is not a recipient of public assistance and care. This section shall not apply to fees for day care services as authorized by title five of article six of this chapter.

Added by Laws 1975, Ch. 433, eff. Oct. 1, 1975.

§ 131-c. Provision for legal services for the needy not otherwise available.

Repealed by Laws 1971, Ch. 473, § 3, eff. July 11, 1978.

§ 131-c. Inclusion of parents and siblings of a minor in the public assistance household.

1. For the purposes of determining eligibility for and the amount of assistance payable, the social services district shall, when a minor is named as an applicant for public assistance, require that his or her parents and minor brothers and sisters also apply for assistance and be included in the household for purposes of determining eligibility and grant amounts, if such individuals reside in the same dwelling unit as the minor applying for assistance. Any income of or available for such parents, brothers and sisters which is not disregarded under subdivision eight of section one hundred thirty-one-a of this article, shall be considered available to such household. The provisions of this subdivision shall not apply to individuals who are recipients of federal supplemental security income benefits or additional state payments pursuant to this chapter, or to individuals whose relationship to the minor is that of stepbrother or stepsister, or to any other individuals whose needs are excluded pursuant to department regulations consistent with federal law and regulations.

2. For the purpose of determining eligibility for and the amount of assistance payable, the social services district shall deem available to any minor whose parent or legal guardian is a minor, any income of the parent or legal guardian of such minor parent or legal guardian residing in the same dwelling unit, to the same extent that the income of a stepparent would be included pursuant to subdivision nine of section one hundred thirty-one-a of this article.

3. For the purposes of this section a minor is a child under the age of eighteen.

Added by Laws 1985, Ch. 42, eff. Oct. 1, 1984.

§ 131-d. Substance abuse rehabilitative and preventive services.

1. Any inconsistent provision of this chapter or other law notwithstanding, social services officials shall provide substance abuse services, to eligible needy substance abusers and persons who are substance dependent, under aid to

dependent children, in accordance with regulations of the department, if and so long as federal aid is available therefor.

2.   Each social services official shall provide such services either directly or by purchase from a public or private non-profit agency; provided, however, that such services are approved by the state division of substance abuse services and that any facility furnishing such services is supervised and approved by the state division of substance abuse services.

3.   If and so long as federal funds are available therefor, the department shall be responsible for providing eligible services pursuant to this section, provided, however, such services shall be furnished through a cooperative agreement with the state division of substance abuse services. Provided, further that the scope of the responsibility of the department hereunder shall not extend beyond the authorization of such division to furnish such services either directly or through contract.

4.   There shall be such cooperative agreements, between the department and the state division of substance abuse services and other appropriate state departments and agencies as shall be necessary to assure that there will be a maximum utilization of existing rehabilitative and preventive services and that the purposes and objectives of this section will be effectively accomplished.

5.   Any inconsistent provision of law notwithstanding, expenditures made by a social services official under this section shall be deemed expenditures for and administration of public assistance and care, and shall be subject to reimbursement by the state in accordance with the provisions of section one hundred fifty-three of this chapter.

   Added by Laws 1971, Ch. 817, eff. June 25, 1971; Laws 1973, Ch. 676; Laws 1974, Ch. 1080; Laws 1975, Ch. 667; Laws 1980, Ch. 471, eff. July 23, 1980.

§ 131-e.   Family planning services.

   Each social services commissioner shall require that appropriate members of his staff personally advise eligible needy persons periodically of the availability at public expense of family planning services for the prevention of pregnancy and inquire whether such persons desire to have such services furnished to them. In those cases where such services are desired, they shall be made available at public expense under appropriate provisions of this chapter. Nothing herein shall be construed, however, to require or permit coercion of such persons to request or receive family planning services.

   Added by Laws 1971, Ch. 452, eff. July 1, 1971.

§ 131-f.   Retroactive social security benefit increases.

   Any inconsistent provisions of this title, other provisions of this chapter or of any other law notwithstanding, in determining the need for family assistance, a social services official shall disregard, in addition to any other amounts which are required or permitted to be disregarded in determining such need, any retroactive lump sum payment made to an individual under title II of the social security act (or under the railroad retirement act of nineteen hundred thirty-seven by reason of the first proviso in section three (e) thereof), as a result of an increase in monthly benefits under the old age, survivors, and disability insurance system.

Added by Laws 1970, Ch. 736, as § 131-d and relettered § 131-f by Laws 1971, Ch. 817; **amended** by Laws 1974, Ch. 1080, deemed to have been in full force and effect on and after Jan. 1, 1974; **amended** by Laws 1997, Ch. 436, § 1 Part B, § 13, eff. Aug. 20, 1997.

§ 131-g. Authority to accept public and private gifts.

The department or a social services district shall have the power to apply for, accept, receive and expend public and private gifts or grants of money, property or services for any purpose provided for by this chapter.

Added by Laws 1972, Ch. 912, eff. Apr. 1, 1972.

§ 131-h. Authority to operate family homes for adults.

A social services official may be authorized to operate family homes for adults, in compliance with the regulations of the department, if such official applies for such authority and demonstrates the need therefor and that suitable care is not otherwise available.

Added by Laws 1971, Ch. 807; formerly § 131-f relettered § 131-h by Laws 1973, Ch. 25, eff. Feb. 20, 1973.

§ 131-i. Social services districts; agreements. [*See second version of § 131-i below.*]*

Subject to the provisions of section one hundred nineteen-o of the general municipal law, social services districts may enter into agreements for the performance among themselves or of one for another of any of their respective functions, powers and duties on a cooperative or contract basis or for the provision of a joint service; provided, however, that no such agreement shall result in any relocation of offices which would unreasonably diminish access to necessary services or unreasonably increase unreimbursed travel for applicants for or recipients of public assistance or services.

Added by Laws 1997, Ch. 436, § 1 Part B, § 14, eff. Aug. 20, 1997.

§ 131-i. Family loan program. [*See second version of § 131-i above.*]*

1. From amounts appropriated for such purpose, the department of labor in consultation with the department is hereby authorized and directed to solicit

proposals to establish programs to be known as family loan programs. Such programs shall provide small, no-interest loans to custodial parents with income below two hundred percent of the federal poverty level and who are working or enrolled in a post-secondary education program, to aid in covering the costs of unexpected expenses that could interfere with their ability to maintain employment or continue education. Loans awarded through a family loan program may be paid directly to a third party on behalf of a loan recipient and in either case shall not constitute income or resources for the purposes of public assistance and care so long as the funds are used for the intended purpose.

2.　The commissioner of labor shall enter into written agreements with not-for-profit organizations or local government agencies to administer loan pools. Agreements shall be entered into with no more than four organizations and/or agencies, no more than one of which shall be located in the city of New York.

3.　Program sites shall be approved based on the demonstrated ability of the organization or governmental agency to secure funding from private and/or public sources sufficient to establish a loan pool to be maintained through repayment agreements entered into by eligible low-income families. Funds awarded by the department of labor to approved program sites shall be used for the express purposes of covering staffing and administration costs associated with administering the loan pool.

4.　From amounts appropriated for such purpose, the Department of Labor in consultation with the Office of Temporary and Disability Assistance is hereby authorized and directed to solicit proposals to establish up to four new family loan programs. Such programs shall operate according to provisions set forth in subdivision one through three of this section; provided, however, that such programs may provide no-or low-interest loans, and further provided that applications submitted by a consortium of not-for-profit organizations or local government agencies shall be viewed as one program and may receive greater funding by the department of labor than an application submitted by a single organization or agency. Low-interest loans shall not exceed a rate greater than two-thirds of the prime rate. No not-for-profit organization or local government agency awarded funding from appropriations made in the nineteen hundred ninety-seven–nineteen hundred ninety-eight fiscal year shall be eligible for funds made available from appropriations made in the nineteen hundred ninety-nine–two thousand fiscal year.

Added by Laws 1999, Ch. 513, § 1, eff. Sept. 28, 1999.

　* Editor's Note: Two versions of Section 131-i are provided. The first version was added by Laws 1997, Ch. 436, § 14, eff. Aug. 20, 1997. The second was added by Laws 1997, Ch. 596, § 1, eff. Sept. 17, 1997 with no reference to the prior version.

§ 131-j.　Certain utility deposits.

Any inconsistent provision of this chapter or other law notwithstanding, a public assistance recipient shall not be required by any corporation subject to the

SSL

provisions of article four of the public service law to pay a security deposit as a condition of receiving any utility service provided by such utility company.

This section shall apply to recipients of supplemental security income benefits or additional state payments, as defined in section three hundred of this chapter, and such persons shall be deemed public assistance recipients for the purposes of this section.

Added by Laws 1973 Ch. 1016; **amended** by Laws 1974, Ch. 1081, Laws 1975, Ch. 198; eff. Apr. 1, 1974; Laws 1976, Ch. 125; Laws 1977 Ch. 31; Laws 1978, Ch. 129; Laws 1980, Ch. 44; Laws 1982, Ch. 34; Laws 1984, Ch. 34; Laws 1986, Ch. 14; Laws 1988, Ch. 29; Laws 1990, Ch. 44, eff. Mar. 31, 1990, to eliminate the expiration date of the 1974 amendment.

§ 131-k.   Illegal aliens.

1.   [*Repealed.*]

2.   An otherwise eligible applicant or recipient who has been determined to be ineligible for aid to dependent children, home relief or medical assistance because he is an alien unlawfully residing in the United States or because he failed to furnish evidence that he is lawfully residing in the United States shall be immediately referred to the United States immigration and naturalization service, or the nearest consulate of the country of the applicant or the recipient for such service or consulate to take appropriate action or furnish assistance.

3.   [*Repealed.*]

4.   [*Repealed.*]

Added by Laws 1974, Ch. 811, eff. June 7, 1974; **amended** by Laws 1977, Ch. 77, eff. Apr. 1, 1977; **amended** by Laws 1981, Ch. 1053, eff. Nov. 11, 1981 and deemed to have been in full force and effect on and after Oct. 1, 1981 and shall apply to those persons who apply for assistance on or after such date; **amended** by Laws 1985, Ch. 42, eff. Oct. 1, 1984; **amended** by Laws 1997, Ch. 436, § 1 Part B, § 15, eff. Aug. 20, 1997.

§ 131-l.   Protective services.

Renumbered Soc. Serv. L. § 473 by Laws 1981, Ch. 991, eff. Oct. 29, 1981.

§ 131-l.   Exclusion of agent orange benefits.

A social services official shall disregard as income and resources in any program of public assistance such sums as are required to be disregarded under section two hundred thirty-five-a of the military law with respect to exposure to agent orange or phenoxy herbicides.

Added by Laws 1990, Ch. 817, § 1, eff. Jan. 1, 1989.

§ 131-m.   Information on resource referral services.

1.   Each social services district shall furnish social services information and resource referral services, in accordance with the provisions of this section and the regulations of the department.

2.   Such services shall be furnished without charge to any person who is in need of and requests such services, without regard to such person's eligibility for public assistance.

3.   Each social services district shall designate staff having administrative responsibility for assuring the furnishing of information and referral regarding the following services and programs and for making appropriate inquiries related to the actual receipt of such services: financial assistance programs, health care and services, social services, employment services and other community services, including legal, education and consumer services.

Added by Laws 1975, Ch. 432, eff. Oct. 1, 1975.

§ 131-n.   Exemption of income and resources. [*Effective until Aug. 22, 2005.*]

1.   The following resources shall be exempt and disregarded in calculating the amount of benefits of any household under any public assistance program: (a) cash and liquid or nonliquid resources up to two thousand dollars, or three thousand dollars in the case of households in which any member is sixty years of age or older, (b) an amount up to four thousand six hundred fifty dollars in a separate bank account established by an individual while currently in receipt of assistance for the sole purpose of enabling the individual to purchase a first or replacement vehicle for the recipient to seek, obtain or maintain employment, so long as the funds are not used for any other purpose, (c) an amount up to one thousand four hundred dollars in a separate bank account established by an individual while currently in receipt of assistance for the purpose of paying tuition at a two-year accredited post-secondary educational institution, so long as the funds are not used for any other purpose, (d) the home which is the usual residence of the household, (e) one automobile, up to four thousand six hundred fifty dollars fair market value, provided, however, that if the automobile is needed for the applicant or recipient to seek or retain employment or travel to and from work activities as defined in section three hundred thirty-six of this chapter, the automobile exemption shall be increased to nine thousand three hundred dollars, or such other higher dollar value as the local social services district may elect to adopt, (f) one burial plot per household member as defined in department regulations, (g) bona fide funeral agreements up to a total of one thousand five hundred dollars in equity value per household member, (h) funds in an individual development account established in accordance with subdivision five of section three hundred fifty-eight of this chapter and section four hundred three of the social security act and (i) for a period of six months, real property which the

SSL

household is making a good faith effort to sell, in accordance with department regulations and tangible personal property necessary for business or for employment purposes in accordance with department regulations. If federal law or regulations require the exemption or disregard of additional income and resources in determining need for family assistance, or medical assistance not exempted or disregarded pursuant to any other provision of this chapter, the department may, by regulations subject to the approval of the director of the budget, require social services officials to exempt or disregard such income and resources. Refunds resulting from earned income tax credits shall be disregarded in public assistance programs.

2.   If and to the extent permitted by federal law and regulations, amounts received under section 105 of Public Law 100-383 as reparation payments for internment of Japanese-Americans and payments made to individuals because of their status as victims of Nazi persecution as defined in P.L. 103-286 shall be exempt from consideration as income or resources for purposes of determining eligibility for and the amount of benefits under any program provided under the authority of this chapter and under title XX of the Social Security Act.

3.   The department is authorized to establish regulations defining income and resources.

§ 131-n. Additional exemption of income and resources pursuant to federal law and regulations. [*Effective Aug. 22, 2005.*]

1.   If federal law or regulations require, as a condition of qualifying for federal financial participation, the exemption or disregard of income and resources in determining need for aid to dependent children, or medical assistance not exempted or disregarded pursuant to any other provision of this chapter, the department may, by regulations subject to the approval of the director of the budget, require social services officials to exempt or disregard such income and resources. Such exemptions and disregards shall be limited solely to income resulting from increases in social security benefits authorized by Public Law 92-336, and refunds required to be disregarded in federally aided programs by Public Law 94-164 for months prior to July first, nineteen hundred seventy-six, or any other federal law extending the requirement that refunds resulting from earned income tax credits be disregarded in federally aided programs.

2.   If and to the extent permitted by federal law and regulations, amounts received under section 105 of Public Law 100-383 as reparation payments for internment of Japanese-Americans and payments made to individuals because of their status as victims of Nazi persecution as defined in P.L. 103-286 shall be exempt from consideration as income or resources for purposes of determining eligibility for and the amount of benefits under any program provided under the authority of this article and under title XX of the Social Security Act; provided, however, that such treatment shall be applied in the home relief program only to the extent that it is permitted under federal law in the program of aid to dependent children.

3.   The department is authorized to establish regulations defining income and resources. The department is further authorized to promulgate regulations it deems necessary to prevent the improper establishment and use of accounts for purchase of first or replacement vehicles.

Added by Laws 1973, Ch. 516, eff. June 5, 1973; relettered from § 131–h to § 131–l by Laws 1975, Ch. 224, eff. June 17, 1975; **amended** by Laws 1975, Ch. 514, eff. July 29, 1975 and applicable to any refunds or special payments authorized by Public Law 94–12 received on or after Apr. 1, 1975; **amended** by Laws 1976, Ch. 635, eff. July 21, 1976, deemed in full force and effect as of Jan. 1, 1976; **amended** by Laws 1990, Ch. 817, § 1, eff. July 25, 1990; **amended** by Laws 1997, Ch. 436, § 1 Part B, § 16, eff. Nov. 1, 1997; **amended** by Laws 1998, Ch. 214, § 11, deemed in full force and effect Aug. 20, 1997; **amended** by Laws 1999, Ch. 389, § 1, eff. July 27, 1999; **amended** by Laws 2001, Ch. 207, § 1, eff. Aug. 22, 2001, provided that the amendment of § 131-n of the social services law made by section one shall not affect the repeal of such section and shall be deemed repealed therewith;bf;amended by Laws 2003, Ch. 373, §§ 1-3, eff. Dec 16, 2003, shall take effect on the one hundred twentieth day after a chapter of the laws of 2003, amending chapter 436 of the laws of 1997, constituting the welfare reform act of 1997 relating to extending the effectiveness of a certain provision thereof, as proposed in legislative bills numbers A.5391 and S.1827, takes effect; provided, however, that the amendments to subdivision 1 of section 131-n of the social services law made by section two of this act shall not affect the expiration of such section and shall be deemed to expire therewith, extending expiration date until Aug. 22, 2005, and amending subdivision 1.

§ 131-o   Personal allowances accounts

1.   [Until Jan 1, 2006] Each individual receiving family care, residential care or care in a school for the mentally retarded, as those terms are defined in section two hundred nine of this chapter, and who is receiving benefits under the program of additional state payments pursuant to this chapter while receiving such care, shall be entitled to a monthly personal allowance out of such benefits in the following amount:

(a)   [Until Dec 31, 2005] in the case of each individual receiving family care, an amount equal to at least $108.00 for each month beginning on or after January first, two thousand four.

(a)   [Eff. Dec 31, 2005, as amended, Laws 2005, Ch. 713, §1] in the case of each individual receiving family care, an amount equal to at least $111.00 for each month beginning on or after January first, two thousand five.

(b)   [Until Dec 31, 2005] in the case of each individual receiving residential care, an amount equal to at least $127.00 for each month beginning on or after January first, two thousand four.

(b)   [Eff. Dec 31, 2005, as amended, Laws 2005, Ch. 713, §1] in the case of each individual receiving residential care, an amount equal to at least $130.00 for each month beginning on or after January first, two thousandfive.

SSL

(c)   [Until Dec 31, 2005]in the case of each individual receiving care in a school for the mentally retarded, an amount equal to at least $87.00 for each month beginning on or after January first, two thousand four.

(c)   [Eff. Dec 31, 2005, as amended, Laws 2005, Ch. 713, §1] in the case of each individual receiving care in a school for the mentally retarded, an amount equal to at least $89.00 for each month beginning on or after January first, two thousand five.

(d)   [Until Dec 31, 2005] for the period commencing January first, two thousand five, the monthly personal needs allowance shall be an amount equal to the sum of the amounts set forth in subparagraphs one and two of this paragraph:

(1)   the amounts specified in paragraphs (a) through (c) of this subdivision; and

(2)   the amount in subparagraph one of this paragraph, multiplied by the percentage of any federal supplemental security income cost of living adjustment which becomes effective on or after January first, two thousand five, but prior to June thirtieth, two thousand five, rounded to the nearest whole dollar.

(d)   [Eff. Dec 31, 2005, as amended, Laws 2005, Ch. 713, §1] for the period commencing January first, two thousand six, the monthly personal needs allowance shall be an amount equal to the sum of the amounts set forth in subparagraphs one and two of this paragraph:

(1)   the amounts specified in paragraphs (a) and (b) of this subdivision and the amounts specified in paragraph (e) of this subdivision as added by section forty-five of part C of chapter fifty-eight of the laws of two thousand five; and

(2)   the amount in subparagraph one of this paragraph, multiplied by the percentage of any federal supplemental security income cost of living adjustment which becomes effective on or after January first, two thousand six, but prior to June thirtieth, two thousand six, rounded to the nearest whole dollar.

1.   [Eff. Jan 1, 2006, sub 1 reads as set out below:]

Each individual receiving family care, residential care or care in a school for the mentally retarded, or enhanced residential care as those terms are defined in section two hundred nine of this chapter, and who is receiving benefits under the program of additional state payments pursuant to this chapter while receiving such care, shall be entitled to a monthly personal allowance out of such benefits in the following amount:

(a)   As amended, Laws 2005, Ch. 713, §2in the case of each individual receiving family care, an amount equal to at least $111.00 for each month beginning on or after January first, two thousand five.

(b)   As amended, Laws 2005, Ch. 713, §2in the case of each individual receiving residential care, an amount equal to at least $130.00 for each month beginning on or after January first, two thousand five.

(c) As amended, Laws 2005, Ch. 713, §2Deleted

(d) As amended, Laws 2005, Ch. 713, §2for the period commencing January first, two thousand six, the monthly personal needs allowance shall be an amount equal to the sum of the amounts set forth in subparagraphs one and two of this paragraph:

(1) the amounts specified in paragraphs (a), (b) and (e) of this subdivision; and

(2) the amount in subparagraph one of this paragraph, multiplied by the percentage of any federal supplemental security income cost of living adjustment which becomes effective on or after January first, two thousand six, but prior to June thirtieth, two thousand six, rounded to the nearest whole dollar.

(e) in the case of each individual receiving enhanced residential care, (i) an amount equal to at least $144.00 for each month beginning on or after January first, two thousand six, and (ii) an amount equal to $159.00 for each month beginning on or after January first, two thousand seven. On and after January first, two thousand seven, the amount set forth in subparagraph (ii) of this paragraph shall be annually increased by an amount equal to the consumer price index for the previous calendar year, provided that there has been an increase in state supplementation pursuant to subparagraph (ii) of paragraph (g) of section two hundred nine of this chapter.

2. The personal allowance described in subdivision one of this section shall be made directly available to the individual for his own use in obtaining clothing, personal hygiene items, and other supplies and services for his personal use not otherwise provided by the residential facility. Any waiver of the right to a personal allowance by an individual entitled to it shall be void. The facility shall, for each such individual, offer to establish a separate account for the personal allowance. Each individual electing to utilize such an account shall be entitled to a statement upon request, and in any case quarterly, setting forth the deposits and withdrawals, and the current balance of the account. A facility shall not demand, require or contract for payment of all or any part of the personal allowance in satisfaction of the facility rate for supplies and services and shall not charge the individual or the account for any supplies or services that the facility is by law, regulation or agreement with the individual required to provide or for any medical supplies or services for which payment is available under medical assistance, pursuant to this title, medicare pursuant to title XVIII of the federal social security act, or any third party coverage. Any service or supplies provided by the facility, charged to the individual or the account shall be provided only with the specific consent of the individual, who shall be furnished in advance of the provision of the services or supplies with an itemized statement setting forth the charges for the services or supplies. Whenever a resident authorizes an operator of a facility to exercise control over his or her personal allowance such authorization shall be in writing and subscribed by the parties to be charged. Any such money shall not be mingled with the funds or become an asset of the facility

or the person receiving the same, but shall be segregated and recorded on the facility's financial records as independent accounts.

3.   Any individual who has not received or been able to control personal allowance funds to the extent and in the manner required by this section may maintain an action in his own behalf for recovery of any such funds, and upon a showing that the funds were intentionally misappropriated or withheld to other than the intended use, for recovery of additional punitive damages in an amount equal to twice the amount misappropriated or withheld. The department may investigate any suspected misappropriation or withholding of personal allowance funds and may maintain an action on behalf of any individual to recover any funds so misappropriated, including any punitive damages. Any funds obtained as a result of such an action shall be disregarded in determining such individual's eligibility for or amount of benefits available pursuant to this chapter, to the extent permitted by federal law and regulation.

4.   Each facility subject to the provisions of this section shall maintain in accordance with department regulations complete records and documentation of all transactions involving resident personal allowance accounts, and shall make such records available to the department and to any other agency responsible for the inspection and supervision of the facility upon request, with respect to any individual who is receiving additional state payments.

5.   Any agency having supervisory responsibilities over any facility subject to the provisions of this section shall, at the time of any inspection of such a facility, inquire into the furnishing of and accounting for resident personal allowances, and shall report any violations or suspected violations of this section to the department. The department shall have primary responsibility for monitoring the personal allowance requirements of this section; provided, however, that the department may by cooperative agreement delegate such monitoring and enforcement functions, in whole or in part, with respect to any facility, to any other state agency having supervisory responsibilities over such facility.

6.   At the time an individual ceases to be a resident at the facility maintaining a resident personal allowance acccount on his behalf, the funds in such account shall be transferred to such individual or another appropriate individual or agency for use on his behalf, in accordance with department regulations.

7.   Any facility subject to the provisions of this section shall assure that any income of an individual residing therein that not considered in determining such individual's eligibility for or amount of benefits under the program of additional state payments pursuant to title six of article five of this chapter, other than unearned income paid from non-public sources for the purpose of meeting the cost, in part or in whole, of such person's care and maintenance in such a facility, is treated in the same manner as the personal allowance required to be made available to the individual pursuant to this section.

8.   In any case in which a person receives a payment of additional state payment benefits for a month other than the month in which the payment is

received, the full monthly personal allowance for the months to which the payment is attributable shall be made available to the individual at such time as the payment has been received; in no event shall the facility be found to have failed to comply with the provisions of this section solely by reason of having failed to make such monthly personal allowance available prior to the time such payment is actually received.

9. In addition to any damages or civil penalties to which a person may be subject;

(a) any person who intentionally withholds a resident's personal allowance, or who demands, beneficially receives, or contracts for payment of all or any part of a resident's personal allowances in satisfaction of the facility rate for supplies and services shall be guilty of a class A misdemeanor;

(b) any person who commingles, borrows from or pledges any personal allowance funds required to be held in a separate account shall be guilty of a class A misdemeanor.

Added by Laws 1977, Ch. 431; **amended** by Laws 1978, Ch. 413; Laws 1979, Ch. 314; Laws 1980, Ch. 113, eff. July 1, 1980; **amended** by Laws 1981, Ch. 85, eff. July 1, 1981; **amended** by Laws 1982, Ch. 87, eff. July 1, 1982, provided, however, that in the event a federal law takes effect which results in a delay in the federal cost of living increase for federal supplemental security income benefits, this act shall take effect on the date on which such cost of living increases are to be paid in accordance with such federal law, and provided further that section four of this act shall remain in full force and effect until June thirtieth, nineteen hundred eighty-three; **amended** by Laws 1982, Ch. 468, eff. July 1, 1982; **amended** by Laws 1983, Ch. 71, eff. May 4, 1983; **amended** by Laws 1984, Ch. 527, eff. July 27, 1984; **amended** by Laws 1985, Ch. 361, eff. Jan. 1, 1985; **amended** by Laws 1986, Ch. 502, eff. July 21, 1986 and deemed in full force and effect on and after Jan. 1, 1986; **amended** by Laws 1987, Ch. 450, eff. Dec. 31, 1987; **amended** by Laws 1988, Ch. 705, § 1, eff. Dec. 31, 1988; **amended** by Laws 1989, Ch. 556, § 1, eff. Dec. 31, 1989; **amended** by Laws 1990, Ch. 685, § 1, eff. Dec. 31, 1990; **amended** by Laws 1991, Ch. 201, § 1, eff. Dec. 31, 1991; **amended** by Laws 1992, Ch. 292, § 1, eff. Dec. 31, 1992; **amended** by Laws 1993, Ch. 401, § 1, eff. Dec. 31, 1993; **amended** by Laws 1994, Ch. 460, § 1, eff. Dec. 31, 1994; **amended** by Laws 1995, Ch. 649, § 1, eff. Dec. 31, 1995; **amended** by Laws 1996, Ch. 213, eff. Dec. 31, 1996; **amended** by Laws 1997, Ch. 189, § 1, eff. Dec. 31, 1997, and applicable to benefits and allowances in months beginning after Dec. 31, 1997; **amended** by Laws 1998, Ch. 377, § 1, eff. Dec. 31, 1998 and shall apply to benefits and allowances in months beginning after Dec. 31, 1998; **amended** by Laws 1999, Ch. 201, § 1, eff. July 27, 1999, and shall apply to taxable years beginning Jan. 1, 1999; **amended** by Laws 2000, Ch. 470, § 1, eff. Dec. 31, 2000, and shall apply to benefits and allowances in months beginning after such date; **amended** by Laws 2001, Ch. 89, § 1, eff. Dec. 31, 2001, and shall apply to benefits and allowances in months beginning after such date; **amended** by Laws 2002, Ch. 109, § 1, eff. Dec. 31, 2002, and shall apply to benefits and allowances in months beginning after such date; Laws 2003, Ch. 62, Part K2, §§ 1, 4, eff. Dec. 31, 2003, amending subd. 1; **amended** by Laws 2004, Ch. 310, § 1, eff. August 3, 2004, and shall apply to benefits and allowances in months beginning after such date; **amended** by Laws 2004, Ch. 310, §§ 1, 4, eff. Dec. 31, 2004 and shall apply to benefits and allowances in

SSL

months beginning after such date; **amended** by Laws 2005, Ch. 58, § 45 (Part C), eff. Jan. 1, 2006; Laws 2005, Ch. 713, §2, eff. Jan 1, 2006; Laws 2006, Ch. 57, §3 (Part C), legislative override of Governor's line veto filed April 28, 2006.

§ 131-p.   Group health insurance benefits; condition of eligibility.

Notwithstanding any other inconsistent provision of law and to the extent permissible under federal law, any applicant for or recipient of safety net assistance or family assistance who is or becomes employed and whose employer provides group health insurance benefits, including benefits for a spouse and dependent children of such applicant or recipient, shall apply for and utilize such benefits as a condition of eligibility for safety net assistance or family assistance. Such applicant or recipient shall also utilize such benefits provided by former employers as long as such benefits are available. The department shall promulgate regulations to determine the eligibility requirements of those applicants and recipients who have more than one employer offering group health insurance benefits.

The provisions of this section shall apply to such applicants upon their initial certification for family assistance or safety net assistance and to such recipients upon their recertifications for such assistance following the date on which this section becomes effective. The cost of premiums paid by such applicants or recipients for such coverage shall be deducted from such applicant's or recipient's earnings as an expense incident to his or her employment.

Added by Laws 1981, Ch. 318, eff. Aug. 28, 1981; **amended** by Laws 1997, Ch. 436, § 1 Part B, § 71, eff. Aug. 20, 1997.

§ 131-q.   Electronic payment file transfer system pilot project.

1.   The commissioner is empowered to authorize the city social services district of the city of New York to continue the pilot project for the design, development, implementation and operation of an electronic payment file transfer system, in accordance with regulations of the department, as an alternative means of delivery of grants and allowances to public assistance recipients.

2.   The city social services district is authorized to initiate activities to prepare for a city-wide conversion to the electronic payment file transfer system provided, however, the department shall conduct a hearing to elicit information concerning the effectiveness of such system and the impact of such system upon recipients, and such other matters as the department may deem relevant. Following such hearing, the commissioner may authorize city-wide implementation of such system.

3.   A recipient residing in the city social services district in a geographical area where the electronic payment file transfer system is in operation shall be required to receive his public assistance grants and allowances at a location designated by the social services district. A recipient who is subject to the provisions of this chapter relating to work requirements shall remain subject to such

provisions regardless of the location where he receives his public assistance grants and allowances.

4. The provisions of subdivision one of this section shall expire on and be of no further force and effect after July first, nineteen hundred eighty-four.

Added by Laws 1981, Ch. 806, eff. July 27, 1981; **amended** by Laws 1983, Ch. 412, eff. June 30, 1983.

§ 131-r. Liability for reimbursement of public assistance benefits.

1. Any person who is receiving or has received, within the previous ten years, public assistance pursuant to the provisions of this article, and who wins a lottery prize of six hundred dollars or more shall reimburse the department from the winnings, for all such public assistance benefits paid to such person during the previous ten years; provided, however, that such crediting to the department shall in no event exceed fifty percent of the amount of the lottery prize. The commissioner shall enter into an agreement with the director of the lottery, pursuant to section sixteen hundred thirteen-b of the tax law, for the crediting of lottery prizes against public assistance benefits. Nothing herein shall limit the ability of a social services district to make recoveries pursuant to section 104 or section 106-b of this chapter.

2. Any inconsistent provision of this chapter or of any other law notwithstanding, a social services official may not assert any claim under any provision of this chapter to recover payments of public assistance if such payments were reimbursed by child support collections.

Added by Laws 1995, Ch. 81, § 245, eff. July 1, 1995; **amended** by Laws 2003, Ch. 340, § 4, eff. Jan. 1, 2004.

§ 131-s. Payments made for utility service for recipients of public assistance benefits, supplemental security income benefits or additional state payments.

1. In the case of a person applying for public assistance, supplemental security income benefits or additional state payments pursuant to this chapter, the social services official of the social services district in which such person resides shall, unless alternative payment or living arrangements can be made, make a payment to a gas corporation, electric corporation or municipality for services provided to such person during a period of up to, but not exceeding, four months immediately preceding the month of application for such assistance or benefits if such payment is needed to prevent shut-off or to restore service. Persons whose gross household income exceeds the public assistance standard of need for the same size household must sign a repayment agreement to repay the assistance within one year of the date of payment as a condition of receiving assistance, in accordance with regulations established by the department. Such repayment agreement may be enforced in any manner available to a creditor, in addition to any rights the district may have pursuant to this chapter.

2.   In the case of a person receiving public assistance, supplemental security income benefits or additional state payments pursuant to this chapter, the social services official of the social services district in which such person resides shall, unless alternative payment or living arrangements can be made, make a payment to a gas corporation, electric corporation or municipality for services provided to such person for the most recent four months in which service was rendered prior to the application for a utility payment pursuant to this section, provided that no such payment shall be made for services rendered more than ten months prior to the application for such a payment, and provided further that:

(a)   such person does not have any funds to pay for such service and such payment is needed to prevent termination or to restore service and such person has fully applied his public assistance grant, if any, to purposes intended to be included in such grant, or

(b)   such person in receipt of public assistance has made a written request of such official for an advance allowance for utility services already received pursuant to department regulations and has also made a written request that his monthly assistance grant be reduced by a portion of the amount of the advanced allowance, in such amounts as not to cause undue hardship. Such payment shall be in addition to any direct payment or any guarantee of payment for utility service for the month for which timely payment may still be made. In no event may any part of such payment subject to recoupment be made unless the social services official first determines under the particular circumstances that the recipient is not entitled, at the time of requesting such payment, to a grant pursuant to titles one, three, eight or ten of this article or any other provision of this chapter which could be utilized to cover all or a portion to be advanced. If during the period of recoupment, the recipient becomes entitled to a grant, pursuant to titles one, three, eight or ten of this article or any other provision of this chapter, which could be utilized to cover all or a portion f the amount to be recovered, such grant shall be so utilized.

3.   If and for so long as a person who has received a grant pursuant to subdivision two of this section continues to receive public assistance benefits, supplemental security income benefits or additional state payments, the social services official shall, to the extent authorized by applicable provisions of this chapter and regulations promulgated thereto, either:

(a)   make payments directly to the gas corporation, electric corporation or municipality for utility services furnished to such person during a period in which such person has been determined unable to manage his own financial affairs; or

(b)   act as guarantor of payment for the month in which the social services official is advised of the nonpayment and for such period of time thereafter as may be established by department regulations to the extent that such person fails to pay for utility services provided during any such month. Such guarantee of payment provided by the social services official shall not extend for a period exceeding two years for any person receiving public assistance, supplemental security income benefits or additional state payments.

(c)　Payments made for recipients of public assistance pursuant to this subdivision shall be deemed to be advance allowances subject to recoupment in accordance with department regulations. In no event may any part of such payment subject to recoupment be made unless the social services official first determines under the particular circumstances that the recipient is not entitled, at the time of requesting such payment, to a grant pursuant to titles one, three, eight or ten of this article or any other provision of this chapter which could be utilized to cover all or a portion to be advanced. If during the period of recoupment, the recipient becomes entitled to a grant, pursuant to titles one, three, eight or ten of this article or any other provision of this chapter, which could be utilized to cover all or a portion of the amount to be recovered, such grant shall be so utilized.

(d)　Whenever a public assistance recipient, for whom a guarantee of payment has been provided pursuant to this subdivision, ceases to receive public assistance, the social services official shall notify the gas corporation, electric corporation or municipality of the cessation date in writing within fifteen days of such occurrence. In the case of a recipient of supplemental security income benefits, the social services official shall make such notification within fifteen days after receiving official notice that the recipient's benefits have ceased. The original terms and conditions of any guarantee made pursuant to this subdivision shall remain in full force and effect only until the end of any month in which the required notice is given.

4.　The department shall establish by regulation the manner in which a person receiving public assistance, supplemental security income benefits or additional state payments pursuant to this chapter shall advise the appropriate social services official that payment for utility services furnished such person has not been made.

5.　The social services official shall not make payments pursuant to this section with respect to any disputed amounts for utility services furnished for which a complaint has been filed with the gas corporation, electric corporation or municipality and no determination has been rendered by the gas corporation, electric corporation or municipality or for which a complaint has been filed with the public service commission and no determination has been made except to the extent payments are required by the commission or its staff pending resolution of the dispute by the commission. For purposes of applying the limitation on payments pursuant to subdivision two of this section in any case in which such a complaint has been filed with the public service commission, the date of any application made pursuant to this section shall be deemed to be the date on which the complaint was filed, provided such application is made no later than thirty days from the date of resolution by the public service commission.

6.　All monies owed the gas corporation, electric corporation or municipality by such person in excess of such payment as made by the social services official pursuant to this section while such person is in receipt of public assistance, supplemental security income benefits or additional state payments pursuant to this chapter may be reduced to a judgment, but shall be exempt from collection for so long as such person continues to receive or would become in need of public assistance, supplemental security income benefits or additional state payments if the collection was made. The claim of the gas corporation, electric corporation or municipality shall in all other respects remain unaffected.

Added by Laws 1981, Ch. 895, eff. Sept. 30, 1981, and shall apply to those utility bills upon which full payment has not been received on or after effective date; **amended** by Laws 1982, Ch. 230, eff. June 15, 1982, renumbered from § 131-p to § 131-s; **amended** by Laws 1992, Ch. 41, § 128, eff. Apr. 2, 1992; **amended** by Laws 1995, Ch. 81, § 189, eff. June 20, 1995.

§ 131-t.   Monthly reporting and retrospective budgeting.

Repealed by Laws 1997, Ch. 436, § 1 Part B, § 17, eff. Aug. 20, 1997.

§ 131-t.   Periodic reporting.

A social services official shall require each public assistance or food stamp household which currently is receiving or received earned income to submit periodic reports relating to factors affecting eligibility, to the extent and in the manner required by department regulations.

Added by Laws 1997, Ch. 436, § 1 Part B, § 17, eff. Aug. 20, 1997.

§ 131-u.   Domestic violence services to eligible persons.

1.   Notwithstanding any inconsistent provision of law, a social services district shall, in accordance with the provisions of this section and regulations of the department, offer and provide emergency shelter and services at a residential program for victims of domestic violence, as defined in article six-A of this chapter, to the extent that such shelter and services are necessary and available to a victim of domestic violence, as defined in article six-A of this chapter, and in need of emergency shelter and services, who was residing in the social services district at the time of the alleged domestic violence and who:

(a)   is eligible for public assistance under one of the following programs:

(i)   emergency assistance to needy families, pursuant to section three hundred fifty-j of this chapter;

(ii)   family assistance, pursuant to section three hundred forty-nine of this chapter;

(iii)   safety net assistance, pursuant to sections one hundred fifty-seven and one hundred fifty-eight of this chapter; or

(iv)   any other form of public assistance and care pursuant to sections one hundred thirty-one and one hundred thirty-one-a of this chapter; or

(b)   applied for public assistance and care during the time the victim was residing in a residential program for victims of domestic violence. To the extent that funds are appropriated expressly therefor and a social services district has exhausted its allocation under title XX of the federal social security act, state reimbursement shall be available for fifty percent of the expenditures made by a social services official for emergency shelter and services provided to a victim of domestic violence who is determined to be ineligible for public assistance during the time the victim was residing in a residential program for victims of domestic violence.

2. The department shall annually establish, subject to the approval of the director of the budget, a daily rate of reimbursement for each residential program for victims of domestic violence, as defined in article six-A of this chapter, certified by the department which provides emergency shelter and services to persons eligible for such emergency shelter and services pursuant to this section. A social services district financially responsible for a victim of domestic violence shall reimburse a residential program for victims of domestic violence for the costs of emergency shelter and services provided to such victim at the daily reimbursement rate established by the department reduced by the sum of all fees which such victim is able to pay toward the costs of such shelter and services as determined in accordance with the public assistance budgeting rules set forth in the regulations of the department and by any third party reimbursement available for such costs.

Added by Laws 1987, Ch. 838, eff. Aug. 7, 1987; **amended** by Laws 1994, Ch. 169, § 96, eff. Apr. 1, 1994; **amended** by Laws 1997, Ch. 436, § 1 Part B, § 72, eff. Aug. 20, 1997.

§ 131-v. Temporary emergency shelter.

1. Notwithstanding any inconsistent provision of law, and to the extent consistent with federal law, a social services official may contract with a non-profit corporation or charitable organization to provide temporary emergency shelter for eligible homeless households in dwelling units owned or leased, and operated by such corporations or organizations.

2. An allowance for such shelter may be made for households dwelling in such units if:

(a) No other suitable privately owned housing which meets the department's standards for health and safety is available, other than a more expensive hotel or motel; and

(b) No household was evicted to produce such units.

3. The continued need for such shelter shall be reviewed, evaluated and authorized monthly by a social services official. Such allowance shall not be available for more than six months unless the commissioner of the social services district determines on an annual basis that permanent housing is not readily available in the district and submits to the department such determination on an annual basis.

SSL

4.   The social services district shall submit for approval by the department health and safety standards that such units must satisfy and shall inspect such units regularly to ensure that such standards are satisfied.

5.   Such non-profit corporation or charitable organization shall, at a minimum, provide such households with assistance in obtaining permanent housing and with information regarding available counseling services, employment assessment, job training and job placement services, and child care services.

6.   This section shall not be construed to limit other means of providing temporary emergency shelter otherwise permitted under this chapter and regulations promulgated thereunder.

Added by Laws 1991, Ch. 695, § 1, eff. Aug. 2, 1991.

§ 131-w.   Limitations in the payment of rent arrears.

Districts shall not provide assistance to pay rent arrears, property taxes or mortgage arrears for persons not eligible for home relief, aid to dependent children, emergency assistance to needy families with children or emergency assistance for aged, blind and disabled persons, except to persons who are without income or resources immediately available to meet the emergency need, whose gross household income does not exceed one hundred twenty-five percent of the federal income official poverty line and who sign a repayment agreement agreeing to repay the assistance in a period not to exceed twelve months. The districts shall enforce the repayment agreements by any legal method available to a creditor, in addition to any rights it has pursuant to this chapter. The department shall promulgate regulations to implement this section which shall, among other things, establish standards for the contents of repayment agreements and establish standards to ensure that assistance is provided only in emergency circumstances.

Added by Laws 1992, Ch. 41, § 129, eff. Apr. 2, 1992.

§ 131-x.   Reverse mortgage loans.

Notwithstanding any other inconsistent provisions of law and to the extent permissible under federal law, regulation or waiver, the proceeds of a reverse mortgage loan made in conformity with the requirements of section two hundred eighty or two hundred eighty-a of the real property law or exempted therefrom pursuant to subdivision four of section two hundred eighty or subdivision four of section two hundred eighty-a of the real property law shall not be considered as income or resources of the mortgagor for any purpose under any law relating to food stamps, public assistance, veteran assistance, safety net assistance, low-income home energy assistance, federal supplemental security income benefits and/or additional state payments, medical assistance, any prescription drug plan or other payments, allowances, benefits or services available pursuant to this chapter; provided, however, that for applicants or for recipients of safety net assistance, any such reverse mortgage loan proceeds shall be disregarded as income and/or resources only in the event that, and for so long as, federal laws and regulations exempt loan proceeds in the determination of eligibility for both the aid to families with dependent children and supplemental security income programs.

Added by Laws 1993, Ch. 613, § 8, eff. Dec. 2, 1993; **amended** by Laws 1997, Ch. 436, § 1 Part B, § 73, eff. Aug. 20, 1997.

§ 131-y. Learnfare program established.

Repealed by Laws 1997, Ch. 436, eff. Aug. 20, 1997.

§ 131-z. Child assistance program.

1. Notwithstanding any other provision of law to the contrary, any district may operate a child assistance program as part of the family assistance program with the approval of the department. Approved expenditures for such child assistance program shall be subject to federal and state reimbursement as expenditures under the family assistance program in accordance with section one hundred fifty-three of this chapter. Provided, however, on or after January first, nineteen hundred ninety-eight the department shall reimburse social services districts for the administrative costs of this program in accordance with the provisions of subdivision sixteen of section one hundred fifty-three of this chapter. All custodial parent families receiving family assistance benefits shall be eligible for this program, provided they satisfy the requirements of this section, if they reside in a district which operates such a program.

2. Where a program has been authorized, child assistance payments pursuant to the provisions of this section may be made to custodial parents on behalf of minor children in accordance with the criteria specified in subdivisions three, four, five and six of this section in lieu of allowances determined in accordance with section one hundred thirty-one-a of this article. The amount of such child assistance payments shall be at least the sum of three thousand three hundred sixty dollars per annum for the first minor child and one thousand one hundred sixteen dollars per annum for each additional minor child, provided that such payments shall be reduced by the amounts specified in paragraph (a) of subdivision six of this section. The commissioner may develop a methodology which will provide for the periodic adjustment of the benefit level to reflect changes in maximum monthly grants and allowances authorized pursuant to section one hundred thirty-one-a of this article for the family assistance program. In addition, the child assistance payments shall be established so that the payments combined with earnings from full-time employment shall result in a family of three having income at or above the poverty level for nineteen hundred eighty-seven as reported by the federal department of health and human services.

3. No custodial parent who resides in a social services district or portion of such district in which a child assistance program is operated shall be eligible under this program for receipt of child assistance payments for a child, unless:

SSL

(a)   An order of child support for such child has been made by a court of competent jurisdiction;

(b)   The order of child support is payable through a support collection unit as created by section one hundred eleven-h of this chapter or such other administrative mechanism as may be designated by the commissioner; or the custodial parent has cooperated in taking the necessary steps to ensure that the child support order is payable through a support collection unit or other administrative mechanism;

(c)   The parent subject to a support order described in paragraphs (a) and (b) of this subdivision is absent from the home;

(d)   The custodial parent and the child for whom, or on whose behalf an application for child assistance program payments is made is at such time, a recipient of family assistance benefits; and

(e)   the custodial parent has not withdrawn from the program within the three months prior to the date of reapplication for benefits under this program.

4.   Notwithstanding the provisions of subdivision three of this section, a custodial parent may be eligible under this program even though the custodial parent has failed to obtain an order of child support because:

(a)   The other parent is deceased;

(b)   The custodial parent has demonstrated to the satisfaction of the commissioner, a diligent effort to obtain a child support order, including providing the local social services district with the information necessary to file a petition for child support, but due to reasons outside of the control of the custodial parent, a child support order is not obtainable in a reasonable period of time;

(c)   The custodial parent has good cause as defined in regulations, not to cooperate in obtaining a child support order; or

(d)   the child resides with both parents and paternity has either been acknowledged or established.

5.   A participant is no longer to be considered a participant in this program when such individual is not eligible for payments as a result of the operation of paragraph (a) of subdivision six of this section for four consecutive months.

6.   (a) So long as funds are available therefor, the amount received by each custodial parent eligible to receive child assistance payments pursuant to this section shall be reduced by an amount equal to:

(i)   An amount which reflects a portion of the actual income of the custodial parent pursuant to a methodology to be established by the commissioner; and

(ii)   An additional amount which reflects that portion of the custodial parent's spouse's income which is deemed to be available to other household members pursuant to a methodology to be established by the commissioner.

(b)   Persons in receipt of both child assistance under this section and medical assistance pursuant to title eleven of article five of this chapter who, prior to April first, two thousand five, become ineligible for medical assistance solely due to increased earnings from employment or loss of earned income disregards shall, if otherwise eligible, remain eligible for medical assistance until March thirty-first, two thousand five or until such later time as may be required by the provisions of such title or of this subdivision. Such medical assistance shall be provided initially pursuant to paragraphs (a) and (b) of subdivision four of section three hundred sixty-six of this article.

(c)   With respect to persons described in paragraph (b) of this subdivision, including those no longer in receipt of child assistance due to increased earnings from employment, when the medical assistance provided pursuant to paragraphs (a) and (b) of subdivision four of section three hundred sixty-six of this chapter ends, such persons, if ineligible for medical assistance solely due to earnings from employment or loss of earned income disregards shall, if otherwise eligible, remain eligible for medical assistance for an additional twelve months. However, in no event shall medical assistance be provided pursuant to this paragraph for any period that is more than twelve months after such persons cease to participate in the child assistance program.

(d)   Social services districts shall take all necessary actions to provide medical assistance pursuant to paragraphs (a) and (b) of subdivision four of section three hundred sixty-six of this chapter to individuals described in paragraphs (b) and (c) of this subdivision who are eligible for such assistance. Social services districts shall provide to individuals described in paragraphs (b) and (c) of this subdivision information as to the availability of the child health insurance plan described in title one-A of article twenty-five of the public health law.

7.   Each participating social services district shall provide to all recipients eligible for participation in this program in accordance with the approved program a comparison of the benefits that would be available to the household under family assistance and the child assistance payments as provided in this section. Each participating district shall inform all eligible recipients that participation in this program is voluntary.

8.   Participation in this program shall be voluntary. Should a participant elect to terminate his or her participation in this program, then, upon reapplication for family assistance benefits and a subsequent determination of eligibility, such participant shall be restored to benefits effective from the date of reapplication.

9.   The department shall promulgate regulations for the operation of the child assistance program. Such regulations shall include but not be limited to:

(a)   Resources. At program entry, program participants may not have resources which exceed the level permitted for eligibility for the family assistance program. Once eligible for the program, no further resource tests shall be imposed;

(b)   Eligibility determinations. Program participants shall not be required to report changes in income more frequently than quarterly;

SSL

(c)   Lump sums. If a child or relative participating in the program receives, in any month or months in a quarter, a non-recurring amount of earned or unearned income, the quarterly total of which exceeds one quarter of the annual poverty level for nineteen hundred eighty-seven for a family of the same size as the program household which received the lump sum, the case shall be ineligible for assistance for the whole number of quarters that equals the amount of the non-recurring income received, adjusted for any applicable disregards of income, divided by the quarterly poverty level applicable to the case;

(d)   One hundred eighty-five percent of gross income test. Program participants shall be allowed to have income in excess of one hundred eighty-five percent of the state standard of need;

(e)   Loss of eligibility. Non-compliance with a condition of eligibility shall result in the ineligibility of the whole family for the child assistance program;

(f)   Determination of available income. Notwithstanding section one hundred thirty-one-a or any other provision of this chapter, determination of available income and the determination of income to be disregarded shall be in accordance with these regulations provided however that the methodology shall not be adjusted in a manner such that a household would receive a lower benefit than a similarly situated household would have received in January, nineteen hundred ninety-seven for the same amount of earned income; and

(g)   Cash out of food stamps. To the extent permitted by federal law, program participants shall receive the value of their food stamps in cash.

(h)   Child support pass through. The requirement that certain child support collected be passed through to the custodial parent pursuant to section one hundred eleven-c of this chapter shall not apply to persons participating in the child assistance program.

Added by Laws 1997, Ch. 436, § 1 Part B, § 19, eff. Aug. 20, 1997; amended by Laws 1998, Ch. 564, § 1, eff. Aug. 5, 1998; amended by Laws 1999, Ch. 20, § 1, eff. Mar. 31, 1999; amended by Laws 2001, Ch. 12, § 1, eff. Mar. 30, 2001; Laws 2003, Ch. 34, § 1, eff. April 8, 2003, amending subd. 6(b).

§ 131-aa   Monthly statistical reports

1.   Reporting requirements. The commissioner of the office of temporary and disability assistance shall issue, within sixty days of the end of each month, a monthly statistical report containing each of the tables in the March two thousand four Temporary and Disability assistance statistics report as provided on the office of temporary and disability assistance website. Such report shall also include aggregate total claims for both New York city and the rest of the state related to temporary and disability assistance not already included in the March 2004 Temporary and Disability Assistance Statistics report as provided on the office of temporary and disability assistance website. The commissioner may also include similar tables containing statistical information including, but not limited

to, temporary and disability assistance claims on emergency child care, family shelter, shelter for victims of domestic violence, eviction prevention including, but not limited to, security deposits and brokers fees, supplemental claims, cancellations or refunds, drug or alcohol treatment, and increased costs associated with cases for individuals with AIDS. The commissioner may also include any other statistical information related to temporary and disability assistance that he or she deems to be appropriate. The commissioner shall also, within sixty days of the completion of each quarter of the state fiscal year, issue an update of monthly temporary and disability assistance claims for each of the previous twenty-four months based on actual claims received by the end of such quarter; provided, however, the update following the third quarter of the state fiscal year shall be completed within thirty days. Such update shall include the total number of recipients, the monthly average payment, and total claims, received by the end of such quarter, for New York city, the rest of the state, and total state claims.

2. Additional reporting requirements. In addition to the information required to be included in the monthly statistical report pursuant to subdivision one of this section, the commissioner of the office of temporary and disability assistance shall include in such monthly statistical report detailed tables with comprehensive data for federally participating family assistance and safety net cases, safety net non-maintenance of effort cases, and safety net maintenance of effort cases, for each county and New York city, according to the following categories:

(a) Work participation rates. A statistical table containing data related to federally required work participation rates including, but not limited to, the numerator applied to the required federal calculation for work participation and the denominator applied to the federal calculation for work participation; and any other information that the commissioner deems to be appropriate.

(b) Earned income. A statistical table containing data related to the aggregate amount of earned income reported by public assistance recipients including, but not limited to, aggregate earned income used in the calculation of public assistance benefits, both before and after the earnings disregard is applied to such benefits, the number of cases for which earned income is applied to the calculation of such benefits, both before and after the earnings disregard, and any other information that the commissioner deems to be appropriate.

(c) Sanctioned cases. A statistical table containing data related to the number of cases in sanction status and the reason for such sanction including, but not limited to, the number of sanctioned cases included in the federal work participation calculation, the number of sanctioned cases not included in the federal work participation calculation, and any other information that the commissioner deems to be appropriate.

(d) Home energy assistance program (HEAP). For each county and New York city, a statistical table containing data related to the allocation of federal and state monies for the HEAP program and the number and dollar amount of benefits provided including, but not limited to, the number, dollar amount and average dollar amount of regular autopay benefits, regular non-autopay benefits, emergency benefits, allocation for administrative costs, and any other information that the commissioner deems to be appropriate.

3.   Upon issuance, the reports required by this section shall be posted on the office of temporary and disability assistance website, and shall also be submitted by the commissioner to the governor, the temporary president of the senate, the speaker of the assembly, the chair of the senate finance committee and the chair of the assembly ways and means committee.

Added by Laws 2004, Ch. 57, Part D, § 1, eff. Aug. 20, 2004; Laws 2006, Ch. 58, §5 (Part J), eff. May 27, 2006.

§ 132.   Investigation of applications.

1.   When an application for assistance or care is received, or a social services official is informed that a person is in need of public assistance and care, an investigation and record shall be made of the circumstances of such person. The object of such investigations shall be to secure the facts necessary to determine whether such person is in need of public assistance or care and what form thereof and service he or she should receive. Information shall be sought as to the residence of such person, the name, age, religious faith, physical condition, earnings or other income, and ability to work of all members of the family, the cause of the person's condition, the ability and willingness of the family, relatives, friends and church to assist, and such other facts as may be useful in determining the treatment which will be helpful to such person. However, nothing in this subdivision or elsewhere in this chapter contained shall be construed to require a social services official to communicate with or require assistance from any person or persons liable by law to contribute to the support of a woman pregnant with, or the mother of, an out of wedlock child, in need of care away from home during pregnancy and during and after delivery, in the case where the surrender of the child to the social services official is under consideration, for such period as may be necessary for such mother and official to decide whether the child will be surrendered for adoption to such official, which period shall not extend beyond ninety days after birth of the child. Except where the welfare official is in possession of positive proof that the applicant is receiving or is eligible to receive unemployment insurance benefits and the amount thereof such investigations shall include written request to the commissioner of labor or his or her duly authorized officer charged with administration of the unemployment insurance law for information as to the status of such person in respect to unemployment insurance benefits.

2.   (a) All applications received by a town social services officer shall be forwarded to the county commissioner immediately and all such applications shall be investigated by the staff of the county commissioner. After investigation the county commissioner shall return to the town social services officer every application for safety net assistance made by a person residing or found in such

town, together with his or her recommendation as to the eligibility of the applicant and the amount of assistance to be granted, if any. In addition thereto, the county commissioner shall keep the town social services officer currently informed of persons residing in his or her town who are receiving any form of public assistance and care other than safety net assistance.

(b)   In a city social services district, investigation of applications shall be made by the city commissioner of social services and his staff.

(c)   In a city which is functioning under section seventy-four-a of this chapter, investigation shall be made by the county commissioner of social services and his staff.

3.   The commissioner of the department of family assistance shall provide by regulation for methods of determining eligibility for public assistance and care, other than medical assistance, to be utilized by all social services officials. Such regulations shall provide for methods of verifying information supplied by or about recipients with information contained in the wage reporting system established pursuant to section one hundred seventy-one-a of the tax law and similar systems in other geographically contiguous states, and, to the degree mandated by federal law with the non-wage income file maintained by the United States internal revenue service, with the benefits and earnings data exchange maintained by the United States department of health and human services, and with the unemployment insurance benefit file.

4.   (a) Investigation into the cause of the condition of a head of household or of any adult applicant or recipient and the treatment which will be helpful to such person shall include a screening for alcohol and/or substance abuse using a standardized screening instrument to be developed by the Office of Alcoholism and Substance Abuse Services in consultation with the department. Such screening shall be performed by a social services district at the time of application and periodically thereafter but not more frequently than every six months, unless the district has reason to believe that an applicant or recipient is abusing or dependent on alcohol or drugs, in accordance with regulations promulgated by the department.

(b)   When the screening process indicates that there is reason to believe that an applicant or recipient is abusing or dependent on alcohol or drugs, the social services district shall require a formal alcohol or substance abuse assessment, which may include drug testing, to be performed by an alcohol and/or substance abuse professional credentialed by the Office of Alcoholism and Substance Abuse Services. The assessment may be performed directly by the district or pursuant to contract with the district.

(c)   The social services official shall refer applicants and recipients whom it determines are presently unable to work by reason of their need for treatment for alcohol or substance abuse based on the formal assessment to a treatment program licensed or certified by the Office of Alcoholism and Substance Abuse Services or operated by the United States Office of Veterans Affairs and determined by the social services official to meet the rehabilitation needs of the individual. When residential treatment is appropriate for a single custodial parent, the social services official shall make diligent efforts to refer the parent to a program that would allow the family to remain intact for the duration of the treatment.

(d)   A person who fails to participate in the screening or in the assessment shall be ineligible for public assistance and medical assistance. Other members of a household which includes a person who has failed to participate in the screening or assessment shall, if otherwise eligible, receive medical assistance and shall receive public assistance only through safety net assistance if they are otherwise eligible for public assistance.

(e)   A person referred to a treatment program pursuant to paragraph (c) of this subdivision, and the household with which he or she resides shall receive safety net assistance and medical assistance while the person is participating in such treatment, if the household is otherwise eligible for public assistance and medical assistance. If a person referred to treatment cannot participate in that treatment because treatment is not presently available, that person and the household with which he or she resides shall receive safety net assistance and medical assistance if the household is otherwise eligible for public assistance and medical assistance.

(f)   If an applicant or recipient is required, pursuant to paragraph (c) of this subdivision, to participate in an appropriate rehabilitation program and refuses to participate in such program without good cause or leaves such program prior to completion of the program without good cause, provided that program completion shall be solely determined by the guidelines and rules of such rehabilitation program, or if an applicant or recipient has been suspended from the receipt of social security disability benefits or supplemental security income benefits by reason of noncompliance with requirements of the federal social security administration for treatment for substance abuse or alcohol abuse, the person will be disqualified from receiving public assistance and medical assistance as follows:

(i)   for the first failure to participate in or complete the program, until the failure ceases or for forty-five days, whichever period of time is longer;

(ii)   for the second such failure, until the failure ceases or for one hundred twenty days, whichever period of time is longer; and

(iii)   for the third and subsequent failures, until the failure ceases or for one hundred eighty days, whichever period is longer. Good cause shall be defined in regulations by the commissioner. The household with which the person resides shall continue to receive safety net assistance and medical assistance if otherwise eligible.

(g)   Persons disqualified from receiving public assistance and medical assistance pursuant to paragraph (f) of this subdivision who would otherwise be eligible for public assistance and medical assistance and who return to required treatment prior to the end of the disqualification period and are receiving residential care as defined in paragraph (d) of subdivision three of section two hundred nine of this chapter shall be eligible for safety net assistance and medical assistance.

(h) Notwithstanding any inconsistent provision of section one hundred thirty-one-o of this article, if a recipient required to participate in an appropriate treatment program pursuant to paragraph (c) of this subdivision receives a personal needs allowance, such allowance shall be made as a restricted payment to the treatment program and shall be a conditional payment. If such recipient leaves the treatment program prior to the completion of such program, any accumulated personal needs allowance will be considered an overpayment and returned to the social services district which provided the personal needs allowance.

(i) In the case of an applicant for or recipient of medical assistance, the provisions of this subdivision shall apply only to the extent that they are not inconsistent with applicable federal law.

Added by Laws 1946, Ch. 200; **amended** by Laws 1950, Ch. 362; Laws 1951, Ch. 78; Laws 1959, Ch. 525; Laws 1966, Ch. 256, Laws 1969, Ch. 184; Laws 1971, Ch. 596; Laws 1973, Ch. 258; **amended** by Laws 1977, Ch. 863, eff. Aug. 11, 1977; **amended** by Laws 1990, Ch. 304, § 3, eff. Dec. 27, 1990; **amended** by Laws 1997, Ch. 436, § 1 Part B, § 22, eff. Aug. 20, 1997, and § 23, eff. Nov. 1, 1997; **amended** by Laws 1998, Ch. 214, § 14, eff. July 7, 1998, deemed in full force and effect Aug. 20, 1997; **amended** by Laws 2002, Ch. 1, Part A, § 49, eff. Jan. 25, 2002.

§ 132-a.   Children born out of wedlock; special provisions.

1.   When an investigation is required by section one hundred thirty-two and other provisions of this chapter for the purpose of determining the eligibility for public assistance and care of an applicant pregnant with or who is the mother of an out of wedlock child such investigation shall include diligent inquiry into the paternity of such child.

2.   Except when the surrender of the child to the social services official for the purpose of adoption is under consideration in accordance with the provisions of section one hundred thirty-two, and except when the child has been surrendered to the social services official for the purpose of adoption, the social services official shall communicate with and require support from any person liable by law to contribute to the support of such applicant or her child.

3.   In appropriate cases, such applicant shall be required to file a petition in the family court instituting proceedings to determine the paternity of her child, and she shall be required to assist and cooperate in establishing such paternity. However, such a petition shall not be required to be filed if the child has been surrendered to the social services official for adoption or if such surrender is under consideration in accordance with provisions of section one hundred thirty-two.

SSL

4. In any case where the social services official has decided, in accordance with the provisions of section one hundred thirty-two, not to conduct an investigation, a written report of such decision and the basis therefor shall be made in duplicate to the department, upon forms prescribed by the department, within thirty days after the making thereof.

Added by Laws 1969, Ch. 184, eff. July 1, 1969.

§ 133. Temporary pre-investigation grant.

If it shall appear that a person is in immediate need, temporary assistance or care shall be granted pending completion of an investigation.

§ 133-a. Contracts for distribution of public assistance grants.

As permitted or required by regulations of the department, each social services district may contract with an appropriate department or agency of the state or banking institutions to distribute grants and allowances of public assistance to the grantees thereof.

Added by Laws 1971, Ch. 103, eff. July 1, 1971.

§ 134. Supervision.

The social service officials responsible under section one hundred thirty-two for investigating any application for public assistance and care, shall maintain close contact with persons granted public assistance and care. Such persons shall be visited as frequently as is provided by the regulations of the department or required by the circumstances of the case, in order that any treatment or service tending to restore such persons to a condition of self-support and to relieve their distress may be rendered and in order that assistance or care may be given only in such amount and as long as necessary. Persons receiving care in an institution shall be visited as often as may be necessary in order that any service or care needed by them shall be provided and in order that institutional care shall be given only as long as it is advantageous for the person's welfare. The circumstances of a person receiving continued care shall be reinvestigated as frequently as the regulations of the department may require.

Added by Laws 1946, Ch. 200, amended by Laws 1971, Ch. 110, eff. July 1, 1971.

§ 134-a. Conduct of investigation.

1. In accordance with regulations of the department of family assistance, any investigation or reinvestigation of eligibility for public assistance and care, other than medical assistance, shall be limited to those factors reasonably necessary to insure that expenditures shall be in accord with applicable provisions of this chapter and the regulations of the department and shall be conducted in such manner so as not to violate any civil right of the applicant or recipient. Such

regulations of the department shall provide that where inconsistencies and gaps in the information presented by a recipient or where other circumstances in the particular case would indicate to a prudent person, that further inquiry should be made, additional necessary information is to be sought except further that the department shall provide by regulations which are consistent with federal law for matching of data supplied by or about recipients with information contained in the wage reporting system established pursuant to section one hundred seventy-one-a of the tax law and similar systems in other geographically contiguous states, and such regulations shall further provide to the extent mandated by federal law for matching with the non-wage income file maintained by the United States internal revenue service, with the benefits and earnings data exchange maintained by the United States department of health and human services, and with the unemployment insurance benefits file. In making such investigation or reinvestigation, sources of information, other than records maintained by a public agency, shall be consulted only with the permission of the applicant or recipient. However, if such permission is not granted by the applicant or recipient, the appropriate social services official may deny, suspend or discontinue public assistance or care until such time as he may be satisfied that such applicant or recipient is eligible therefor. Nothing in this section shall be construed to prohibit activities the department reasonably believes necessary to conform with Federal requirements under section one thousand one hundred thirty-seven of the social security act. The activities authorized by this section may be initiated only with regard to those clients who have been given appropriate notice of verification activity under article six-A of the public officers law.

2.   At the time he applies for public assistance and care, an applicant shall, as a condition of receiving such aid, present proof of his identity to the social services official as the department may by regulation require, and he shall provide such proof thereafter whenever required by such official.

3.   The social services official shall require that persons applying for or receiving public assistance and care be interviewed personally at a time and in a manner provided by the regulations of the department. Applicants or recipients shall be excused from such requirements to avoid hardship, as defined by regulations of the department. Hardship shall include but not be limited to circumstances including infirmity, serious illness or physical disability.

4.   Notwithstanding any other provisions of this chapter, the department may provide for a comparison of information identifying a recipient of benefits under any program authorized under this chapter with identifying information possessed by state agencies in other states administering programs similar to those authorized by this chapter regarding recipients of such programs. Such a comparison shall be authorized only with regard to clients who have received appropriate notice under the personal privacy protection law, which notice shall be deemed compliance with the provisions of subdivision one of this section. Should the comparison of identifying information indicate that the client in question is or has been simultaneously receiving benefits in both states, the department

may, in its discretion, authorize exchange of income, benefit, and other case information with the state agency of the other state.

5.   The social services official upon receipt of information concerning a sentence of imprisonment imposed upon a person receiving public assistance shall make a reinvestigation of eligibility.

Added by Laws 1967, Ch. 183; amended by Laws 1972, Ch. 684; amended by Laws 1973, Ch. 219; amended by Laws 1975, Ch. 685; amended by Laws 1990, Ch. 304, §§ 4, 5, eff. Dec. 27, 1990; amended by Laws 1996, Ch. 700, § 3, eff. Jan. 7, 1997; amended by Laws of 2002, Ch. 1, Part A, § 50, eff. Jan. 25, 2002.

§ 134-b.   Front end detection system.

In accordance with regulations promulgated by the department, each social services district shall establish procedures to identify, investigate and resolve potential cases of fraud, misrepresentation or inadequate documentation prior to determining an applicant's eligibility for public assistance. Such procedures shall not delay the determination of eligibility for assistance beyond the time frames established in law or regulation for such determination, including emergency assistance. Each social services district shall submit to the department a plan describing such procedures in such form and at such times as the department may require. Such department regulations shall include, but not be limited to, standards governing referrals by the district to its fraud detection unit, and shall set forth indicators to be used, in part, to govern such referrals based on the individual's employability, employment history, or prior incidence of overpayments attributable to client conduct.

Added by Laws 1992, Ch. 41, § 130, eff. Apr. 2, 1992.

§ 135.   Cooperation of public welfare officials.

1.   It shall be the duty of every public welfare official to render assistance and cooperate within his jurisdictional powers with every other public welfare official and with the family court and all other governmental agencies concerned with the health and welfare of persons under their jurisdiction.

2.   Every public welfare official shall also cooperate whenever possible with any private agency whose object is the relief and care of persons in need or the improvement of social conditions in order that there may be no duplication of relief and that the work of agencies both public and private may be united in an effort to relieve distress and prevent dependency.

Amended by Laws 1962, Ch. 690, eff. Sept. 1, 1962.

§ 135-a.   Fair hearing requests; time limits.

Repealed by Laws 1978, Ch. 473, § 5, eff. July 11, 1978.

§ 135-b.   Fair hearings and decisions by designees of commissioner relating to public assistance and care or services.

Repealed by Laws 1978, Ch. 473, § 5, eff. July 11, 1978.

§ 135-c.   Appeals and hearings for services.

Repealed by Laws 1978, Ch. 473, § 5, eff. July 11, 1978.

§ 136.   Protection of public welfare records.

1. The names or addresses of persons applying for or receiving public assistance and care shall not be included in any published report or printed in any newspaper or reported at any public meeting except meetings of the county board of supervisors, city council, town board or other board or body authorized and required to appropriate funds for public assistance and care in and for such county, city or town; nor shall such names and addresses and the amount received by or expended for such persons be disclosed except to the commissioner of social services or his authorized representative, such county, city or town board or body or its authorized representative, any other body or official required to have such information properly to discharge its or his duties, or, by authority of such county, city or town appropriating board or body or the social services official of the county, city or town, to a person or agency considered entitled to such information. However, if a bona fide news disseminating firm or organization makes a written request to the social services official or the appropriating board or body of a county, city or town to allow inspection by an authorized representative of such firm or organization of the books and records of the disbursements made by such county, city or town for public assistance and care, such requests shall be granted within five days and such firm or organization shall be considered entitled to the information contained in such books and records, provided such firm or organization shall give assurances in writing that it will not publicly disclose, or participate or acquiesce in the public disclosure of, the names and addresses of applicants for and recipients of public assistance and care except as expressly permitted by subdivision four. If such firm or organization shall, after giving such assurance, publicly disclose, or participate or acquiesce in the public disclosure of, the names and addresses of applicants for or recipients of public assistance and care except a expressly permitted by subdivision four, then such firm or organization shall be deemed to have violated this section and such violation shall constitute a misdemeanor. As used herein a news disseminating firm or organization shall mean and include: a newspaper; a newspaper service association or agency; a magazine; a radio or television station or system; a motion picture news agency.

2. All communications and information relating to a person receiving public assistance or care obtained by any social services official, service officer, or employee in the course of his or her work shall be considered confidential and,

except as otherwise provided in this section, shall be disclosed only to the commissioner, or his or her authorized representative, the commissioner of labor, or his or her authorized representative, the commissioner of health, or his or her authorized representative, the welfare inspector general, or his or her authorized representative, the county board of supervisors, city council, town board or other board or body authorized and required to appropriate funds for public assistance and care in and for such county, city or town or its authorized representative or, by authority of the county, city or town social services official, to a person or agency considered entitled to such information. Nothing herein shall preclude a social services official from reporting to an appropriate agency or official, including law enforcement agencies or officials, known or suspected instances of physical or mental injury, sexual abuse or exploitation, sexual contact with a minor or negligent treatment or maltreatment of a child of which the official becomes aware in the administration of public assistance and care nor shall it preclude communication with the federal immigration and naturalization service regarding the immigration status of any individual.

3.   Nothing in this section shall be construed to prevent registration in a central index or social service exchange for the purpose of preventing duplication and of coordinating the work of public and private agencies.

4.   No person or agency shall solicit, disclose, receive, make use of, or authorize, knowingly permit, participate in, or acquiesce in the use of, any information relating to any applicant for or recipient of public assistance or care for commercial or political purposes. Nothing in this or the other subdivisions of this section shall be deemed to prohibit bona fide news media from disseminating news, in the ordinary course of their lawful business, relating to the identity of persons charged with the commission of crimes or offenses involving their application for or receipt of public assistance and care, including the names and addresses of such applicants or recipients who are charged with the commission of such crimes or offenses.

5.   A social services official shall disclose to a federal, state or local law enforcement officer, upon request of the officer, the current address of any recipient of family assistance, or safety net assistance if the duties of the officer include the location or apprehension of the recipient and the officer furnishes the social services official with the name of the recipient and notifies the agency that such recipient is fleeing to avoid prosecution, custody or confinement after conviction, under the laws of the place from which the recipient is fleeing, for a crime or an attempt to commit a crime which is a felony under the laws of the place from which the recipient is fleeing, or which, in the case of the state of New Jersey, is a high misdemeanor under the laws of that state, or is violating a condition of probation or parole imposed under a federal or state law or has information that is necessary for the officer to conduct his or her official duties. In a request for disclosure pursuant to this subdivision, such law enforcement officer shall endeavor to include identifying information to help ensure that the social services official discloses only the address of the person sought and not the address of a person with the same or similar name.

Amended by Laws 1946, Ch. 200; Laws 1953, Ch. 223; Laws 1960, Ch. 1031; Laws 1964, Ch. 281; **amended** by Laws 1971, Ch. 110, eff. July 1, 1971; **amended** by Laws 1984, Ch. 915, eff. Aug. 6, 1984; **amended** by Laws 1992, Ch. 41, § 153, eff. Apr. 2, 1992 **amended** by Laws 1997, Ch. 436, § 1 Part B, §§ 24 and 25, eff. Aug. 20, 1997.

§ 136-a.   Information from state tax commission and the comptroller.

1.   Section six hundred ninety-seven or any other provision of the tax law shall in no way be construed to restrict the department from obtaining, on behalf of itself or a local social services district, the names, address, social security number, employment history and number of dependents claimed for any individual certified by the department to be a welfare recipient and suspected of abusing, defrauding or otherwise violating the welfare system.

2.   Information furnished to the department by the state tax commission and the comptroller under or as a result of the agreement authorized by section one hundred seventy-one-c of the tax law shall be considered confidential and shall not be disclosed to persons or agencies other than those entitled to such information because such disclosure is necessary for the proper administration of title six-A of article three and title ten of article five of this chapter.

Added by Laws 1972, Ch. 517, eff. May 24, 1972; **amended** by Laws 1982, Ch. 545, eff. July 20, 1982 (subd. (2) added, however, subd. (2) shall only apply to overpayments for taxable years beginning after Dec. 31, 1981).

§ 137.   Exemption from levy and execution.

All moneys or orders granted to persons as public assistance or care pursuant to this chapter shall be inalienable by any assignment or transfer and shall be exempt from levy and execution under the laws of this state.

§ 137-a.   Exemption of earnings of recipient from assignment, income execution and installment payment order.

1.   All wages, salary, commissions or other compensation paid or payable by an employer to a person while he is in receipt of public assistance or care supplementary to his income pursuant to the provisions of titles three, four, five, six and ten of article five of this chapter, or while he would otherwise need such assistance or care, shall be exempt from assignment, income execution or from an installment payment order under the laws of this state but only so long as such public assistance or care shall continue or would be needed if the assignment, income execution or installment payment order were enforced. The claim of the creditor shall in all other respects remain unaffected. Any employer who shall withhold or pay over to a person presenting an income execution installment payment order or assignment any portion of the earnings of such a recipient of public assistance or care, after receiving notification in writing from a social services official that the employee is receiving public assistance or care, or that he would become in need of public assistance or care if the assignment, income

SSL

execution or installment payment order were enforced, shall be liable in an action by such recipient for the amount so paid or withheld contrary to the provisions of this section. A social services official sending such notification to an employer shall be required to notify the employer, in writing, of the termination of such receipt and need for public assistance and care of the employee involved when this shall occur. Upon receipt of such notice of termination the employer may commence or resume, as the case may be, payment and withholding under any assignment, income execution or installment payment order whose effectiveness was postponed or suspended by this section.

2.　As used in this section, "public assistance and care" shall include federal supplemental security income benefits paid pursuant to title sixteen of the federal social security act and additional state payments paid pursuant to title six of article five of this chapter.

Added by Laws 1962, Ch. 333; amended by Laws 1963, Ch. 722; Laws 1964, Ch. 213; Laws 1968, Ch. 494; amended by Laws 1974, Ch. 1080, eff. Jan. 1, 1974.

§ 138.　Powers of department.

Repealed by Laws 1995, Ch. 81, § 197, eff. Apr. 1, 1995.

§ 138-a.　Responsibility of the department for recipients in family care.

1.　Any inconsistent provision of this chapter or other law notwithstanding, the department shall be responsible for furnishing public assistance and care to mentally disabled persons residing in family care homes licensed by the office of mental health or the office of mental retardation and developmental disabilities who are admitted to such facilities in accordance with regulations of the office which licenses the facility. However, the department may, at its option, discharge such responsibility, in whole or in part, through social services districts designated to act as agents of the department. While so designated, a social services district shall act as agent of the department and shall be entitled to reimbursement as provided in section one hundred fifty-three of this chapter.

2.　The department shall possess and may exercise like powers and perform like duties in respect to the assistance and care of persons in family care as social services officials exercise and perform in relation to persons in their respective jurisdictions.

Added by Laws 1967, Ch. 150; amended by Laws 1970, Ch. 681, eff. May 8, 1970; amended by Laws 1971, Ch. 705, eff. July 1, 1971; amended by Laws 1972, Ch. 694; amended by Laws 1973 Ch. 195, eff. Apr. 25 1973; amended by Laws 1983, Ch. 791, eff. July 30, 1983.

§ 139.　Assistance and care of state charges; state reimbursement.

Repealed by Laws 1995, Ch. 81, § 197, eff. Apr. 1, 1995.

§ 139-a.   Special provisions to avoid abuse of assistance and care.

1.   Any person who shall apply for safety net assistance or family assistance within one year after arrival in this state, shall be presumed to have come into the state for the purpose of receiving public assistance or care and the social services official where application is made, shall deny public assistance and care to such applicant unless such applicant shall establish by clear and convincing proof that the purpose of his or her entry was not for the purpose of securing public assistance and care in this state. In addition to complying with the foregoing provisions, the applicant shall also submit with his or her application a certificate from the appropriate local employment office of the state department of labor issued within a two week period from the date of his or her application stating that such employment office has no order for an opening in part-time, full-time, temporary or permanent work of any kind to which the applicant could properly be referred by such office, taking into consideration only his or her physical and mental capacity without reference to his or her customary occupation or acquired skill.

2.   The social services official shall in every case complete his investigation and make his determination of the application under this section not more than thirty days after receipt of the application.

3.   (a) The social services districts of Allegheny, Broome, Dutchess, Niagara, Onondaga, Oneida, Orange, Oswego, Rensselaer, Rockland, Steuben, and Suffolk shall authorize and implement demonstration projects for the purposes of determining the cost-effectiveness of preventing multiple enrollment of home relief benefit recipients through the use of an automated two-digit finger imaging matching identification system. The system shall only include home relief benefit recipient finger imaging upon application for eligibility for such benefits and finger imaging of home relief recipients currently receiving home relief benefits.

(b)   Notwithstanding the provisions of section one hundred thirty-six of this article or any other provision of law, data collected and maintained through the use of an automated finger imaging matching identification system as authorized by this subdivision may not be used, disclosed or redisclosed for any purpose other than the prevention of multiple enrollments in home relief, may not be used or admitted in any criminal or civil investigation, prosecution, or proceeding, other than a civil proceeding pursuant to section one hundred forty-five-c of this article, and may not be disclosed in response to a subpoena or other compulsory legal process or warrant, or upon request or order of any agency, authority, division, office or other private or public entity or person, except that nothing contained herein shall prohibit disclosure in response to a subpoena issued by or on behalf of the applicant or recipient who is the subject of the record maintained as a part of such system. Any person who knowingly makes or obtains any unauthorized disclosure of data collected and maintained through the use of an automated two-digit finger imaging matching identification system shall be guilty of a class A misdemeanor, and shall be punished in accordance with the provisions of the penal law.

SSL

(c) Data collected and maintained on the automated two-digit finger imaging matching identification system shall be subject to those provisions relating to unauthorized disclosure of confidential client information currently subject to part 357 of the commissioner's regulations.

(d) Such social services districts shall develop a competitive request for proposal for an automated two-digit finger imaging matching identification system, and shall thereafter contract for the services of a firm certified by the department as able to design and implement such automated two-digit finger imaging matching identification system. The department shall oversee the process by which districts select and award contracts for the demonstration projects. Prior to the implementation of any contracts, the department shall certify that a system exists for data collection and for destroying and expunging a recipient finger image upon such recipient ceasing to be a home relief recipient and that the design of the demonstration project fulfills all the requirements of this section. The department shall provide such assistance as needed to facilitate finger image matching among social services districts including centralized sharing of data when local matching among social services districts is not feasible. After award the department shall be responsible for ensuring that the demonstration projects are carried out in accordance with the requirements of this section, that adequate training for local district staff involved with the project will be provided and taking any actions necessary to bring such programs into compliance if required. Such contractual arrangement shall ensure that state payments for the contractor's necessary and legitimate expenses for the administration of such program are limited to amounts specified in advance and that such amounts shall not exceed the amount appropriated therefor in any fiscal years.

(e) Immediate notice of all the provisions of this subdivision shall be provided to home relief recipients or applicants.

(f) Notwithstanding any other provision of law, nothing contained herein shall be deemed to authorize or permit the termination, suspension, or diminution of home relief benefits except as elsewhere specifically authorized in this chapter, provided, however, that where the basis of a proposed sanction is a determination of a fraudulent multiple enrollment based on the use of an automated finger imaging matching identification system authorized pursuant to this section, no such sanction shall be imposed pending a hearing conducted pursuant to section twenty-two of this chapter within forty-five days of the notification of the applicant or recipient of the alleged fraudulent multiple enrollment, or pending a final determination of a request by an applicant or a recipient for correction or amendment of a record pursuant to section ninety-five of the public officers law, and no such sanction shall be imposed unless the local social services district has verified the results of the automated finger imaging matching identification system by means of a manual match conducted by a person who is qualified to perform such identifications.

(g) The department shall conduct periodic audits to monitor compliance with all laws and regulations regarding the automated finger imaging matching system to insure that any records maintained as part of such system are accurate and complete, that no illegal disclosures of such records have taken place, that effective software and hardware designs have been instituted with security features to prevent unauthorized access to such records, that access to record information system facilities, systems operating environments, data file contents whether while in use or when stored in a media library is restricted to authorized personnel only, that operation programs are used that will prohibit inquiry, record updates, or destruction of records, from any terminal other than automated finger imaging matching system terminals which are so designated, that operational programs are used to detect and store for the output of designated department employees all unauthorized attempts to penetrate any automated finger imaging matching system, program or file, that adequate and timely procedures exist to insure that the recipient or applicant's right to access and review of records for the purpose of accuracy and completeness, including procedures for review of information maintained about such individuals and for administrative review (including procedures for administrative appeal) and necessary correction of any claim by the individual to whom the information relates that the information is inaccurate or incomplete.

(h)   The department shall report to the speaker of the assembly and the temporary president of the senate on the operation of the demonstration project by March first, nineteen hundred ninety-six. This report shall include analysis of the cost-effectiveness of such project, and shall include information concerning instances of multiple enrollment detected through use of this system, and shall include a detailed summary of the results of audits required by paragraph (g) of this subdivision. The report shall include recommendations regarding whether the program should be discontinued, expanded, or otherwise modified.

(i)   The department of social services shall contract with an independent academic or research organization (the "contractor") experienced in evaluating public assistance programs for a comprehensive evaluation of the automated finger imaging matching identification system authorized in this section. The results of such evaluation shall be set forth in a report which shall include, but not be limited to the following:

(1)   a description of the demonstration project, its implementation schedule and the problems encountered in implementation;

(2)   investigations of each instance where a recipient does not respond to a notice informing the recipient of the need to submit to finger imaging. Such investigation shall determine, to the extent possible, why the recipient did not respond and whether such failure to respond was due to the recipient: (a) becoming eligible for federal supplemental security income benefits, if any; (b) no longer being eligible because of earned income, if any; (c) no longer being a resident of the county, if any; or (d) failing to respond because of other reasons;

(3)   an evaluation of historical caseload trends, both statewide and in the demonstration counties, including a study of monthly records for the two years

prior to the demonstration, and also including the closing of cases at recertification. Analysis of such monthly records shall be conducted as part of the basis of estimating benefits under the demonstration;

(4) an analysis of the procedures used to verify suspicions of fraud including follow-up of identified cases of fraud, if any;

(5) aggregate totals of false matches, if any, found by the system, the methods used to correct such errors and an accounting of the duplicate applications for benefits, if any, that are detected by the system; and

(6) an estimate of the savings, if any, resulting from the implementation of finger imaging, and an estimate of the actual costs of the system including, but not limited to equipment costs, the costs of linking terminals, site preparation and the costs of any additional staff required to operate the system.

(j) Not later than February first, nineteen hundred ninety-six, the contractor shall submit the report required by paragraph (i) of subdivision three of this section to the governor, the majority leader of the senate and the speaker of the assembly and to the commissioner of the department of social services.

(k) The local social service districts establishing an automated finger imaging matching identification system pursuant to this subdivision shall be deemed an agency as defined in subdivision one of section ninety-two of the public officers law, and data collected and maintained in such automated system shall be deemed records and systems of records as defined in subdivisions nine and eleven of such section of such law. Except as otherwise specifically provided in this section, the provisions of article six-a of such law, known as the "personal privacy protection law" shall apply to the records and systems of records collected and maintained by such local social service districts pursuant to this section.

(l) Expenditures made by social services districts, and determined cost effective by the department, including those expenditures necessary for contracts planned or executed on or before the effective date of this section, for the design, development, implementation and administrative costs of the automated finger imaging matching identification system shall be subject to one hundred percent state reimbursement.

(m) The automated finger imaging matching identification system shall be established in the selected districts not later than October first, nineteen hundred ninety-four, and such demonstration projects shall expire upon the enactment of a chapter of the laws of nineteen hundred ninety-five providing for an automated fraud prevention system based on personally unique identification factors.

Added by Laws 1969, Ch. 184, eff. May 1, 1969; former § 139-a **added** by Laws 1961, Ch. 468 and **repealed** by Laws 1969, Ch. 184, eff. May 1, 1969; **amended** by Laws 1992, Ch. 41, § 155, eff. Apr. 2, 1992; **amended** by Laws 1993, Ch. 59, § 38, eff. Apr. 15, 1993; **amended** by Laws 1994, Ch. 170, § 446, eff. Apr. 1, 1994; **amended** by Laws 1995, Ch. 81, § 164, eff. June 20, 1995; **amended** by Laws 1997, Ch. 436, § 1 Part B, § 74, eff. Aug. 20, 1997.

§ 140.   Removal of mentally ill and mentally retarded or developmentally disabled state charges to state institutions.

Repealed by Laws 1995, Ch. 81, § 197, eff. Apr. 1, 1995.

§ 141.   Burial of the dead.

1.   (a) If a recipient of public assistance or care or other person dies leaving no funds or insurance sufficient to pay the expense of his burial, the relatives who survive him who were or would have been responsible for his support, pursuant to section one hundred one of this chapter, shall be responsible for such expense to the extent that they are able to pay the same in whole or in part; and the public welfare official paying such expense or any part thereof may recover all or part of the amounts expended by him from such relatives, who shall be severally and jointly liable therefor in accordance with their respective abilities.

(b)   Except as otherwise provided the public welfare district, town or city which was or would have been responsible for furnishing public assistance or care to the person while alive shall provide for the care, removal and burial of the body of a recipient of public assistance or care who shall die, or of a person found dead in the public welfare district.

2.   If, when such provision is made by a public welfare district, town or city, the deceased leave no funds or insurance sufficient to pay the expense of his burial and there are no known relatives, friends or personal representatives liable or willing to become responsible for such expense, the expense of such burial shall be a charge on such public welfare district, town or city but the public welfare official thereof may recover the same in whole or in part from the relatives of the deceased liable therefor.

3.   (a) When burial arrangements for a recipient of public assistance or care are made by relatives or friends of the deceased and the expense of such burial does not exceed the amount fixed by the appropriate public welfare official or the local appropriating body for similar burials in similar circumstances, such public welfare official may:

(1)   if such relatives or friends were required to pay the expense of such burial in order to arrange the same, wholly or partly reimburse them, from assets transferred or assigned to such social services official by or on behalf of the deceased recipient; but he shall not reimburse a legally responsible relative of the deceased for any part of the amount paid by him which in the judgment of such social services official such relative is able to bear; nor shall such official expend from such assets for such purpose more than is permitted by or pursuant to this section, other provisions of this chapter and regulations of the department.

(2)   pay part of the expense of such burial, if, and to the extent under the circumstances, permitted by his local policy, which shall not be inconsistent with this chapter, and the regulations of the department; but in no case shall such social services official pay more than the balance remaining to be paid after the total

of the amounts paid or to be paid by all other sources, including payments made or to be made by such legally responsible relatives of the deceased as are in the judgment of such official able to bear the same, is credited to and deducted from such expense.

(b) In no case shall a public welfare official expend, pursuant to the provisions of this section or any other provision of this chapter, for the burial of a recipient of public assistance or care, from assets transferred or assigned to him by or on behalf of such recipient, an amount which shall be in excess of five hundred dollars.

4. For purposes of this section, the term "recipient of public assistance and care" shall include persons receiving federal supplemental security income benefits pursuant to title sixteen of the federal social security act and/or additional state payments pursuant to title six of article five of this chapter.

5. Expenditures for burial made by social services districts, cities and towns pursuant to the provisions of this chapter shall, if approved by the department, be subject to reimbursement by the state, in accordance with the regulations of the department to the extent of one hundred per centum thereof in the case of needy Native Americans and members of their families residing on a reservation within the state and fifty per centum in all other cases, and such reimbursement shall be claimed and paid in accordance with the procedure prescribed by and pursuant to section one hundred fifty-three. However, only so much of such an expenditure as does not exceed two hundred fifty dollars for expenditures made prior to October first, nineteen hundred eighty-six, four hundred dollars for expenditures made on and after October first, nineteen hundred eighty-six and prior to April first, nineteen hundred eighty-seven and nine hundred dollars for expenditures made on and after April first, nineteen hundred eighty-seven shall be subject to reimbursement by the state.

6. If an applicant for or a recipient of public assistance or care or of medical assistance under section two hundred nine or three hundred sixty-six of this chapter dies having established an irrevocable trust for the payment of his or her funeral expenses under section four hundred fifty-three of the general business law, any funds remaining in such trust after the payment of all funeral expenses must be paid over to the social services official responsible for arranging for burials under this section in the local government subdivision where the decedent resided.

Amended by Laws 1944, Ch. 253; Laws 1946, Ch. 200; Laws 1947, Ch. 326; Laws 1948, Ch. 198; Laws 1952, Ch. 210; Laws 1956, Ch. 302; Laws 1958, Ch. 772; Laws 1965, Ch. 342, Laws 1966, Ch. 100, Laws 1971, Ch. 110; **amended** by Laws 1974, Ch. 1080, eff. Jan. 1, 1974; **amended** by Laws 1986, Ch. 597, eff. July 24, 1986; **amended** by Laws 1995, Ch. 81, § 157, eff. Apr. 1, 1995; **amended** by Laws 1996, Ch. 660, eff. Jan. 1, 1997 and shall apply only to contracts or agreements entered into on or after such date.

§ 142. Exclusiveness of eligibility requirements.

No person receiving federal supplemental security income payments and/or additional state payments, or family assistance shall for the same period receive any other of such forms of assistance.

Amended by Laws 1951, Ch. 112; Laws 1966, Ch. 256; Laws 1974, Ch. 1080, eff. Jan. 1, 1974; **amended** by Laws 1997, Ch. 436, § 1 Part B, § 26, eff. Aug. 20, 1997.

§ 142-a. Federal economic opportunity act grants or payments; effect on eligibility for certain public assistance or care.

Any inconsistent provisions of titles ten and eleven of article five, other provisions of this chapter, or of any other law notwithstanding, in determining the need for public assistance or care under such titles:

1. Any grant made to a family under title III of the federal economic opportunity act of nineteen hundred sixty-four shall not be regarded as income or resources of such family in determining the need of any member thereof for such public assistance or care.

2. The first eighty-five dollars plus one-half of the excess over eighty-five dollars of payments made to or on behalf of any person for or with respect to any month under title I or II of the federal economic opportunity act of nineteen hundred sixty-four or any program assisted under such title shall not be regarded as income or resources of such person in determining his need for such public assistance or care, or as income or resources of any other individual in determining such other individual's need for such public assistance or care; but any amount made available to or for the benefit of such other individual from the excess of the amounts exempted hereby may be considered in determining the eligibility of such other individual for such public assistance or care.

Added by Laws 1965, Ch. 218; **amended** by Laws 1966, Ch. 256; **amended** by Laws 1974, Ch. 1080, eff. Jan. 1, 1974.

§ 142-b. Federal manpower development training act and elementary and secondary education act grants or payments; effect on eligibility for certain public assistance or care.

So long as the applicable provisions of the federal manpower development and training act, as amended, or of the elementary and secondary education act as amended, may require:

1. any inconsistent provision of title ten of article five, other provisions of this chapter, or of any other law notwithstanding, in determining the need for public assistance or care under such title, any payments made under the manpower development and training act, as amended, which are made in lieu of a training allowance to defray expenses attributable to training and/or as a training incentive payment, shall not be regarded as income or resources of the person

in determining his need for such public assistance or care, or as income or resources of any other person in determining such other person's need for such public assistance or care; and/or

2. any inconsistent provisions of title ten of article five, other provisions of this chapter, or of any other law notwithstanding, in determining the need for public assistance or care under such title, the first eighty-five dollars per month, during a period of not less than twelve nor more than twenty-four months as may be prescribed by regulations of the department, earned by any person for services rendered to any program assisted under title I of the elementary and secondary education act of nineteen hundred sixty-five, as amended, shall not be regarded as income or resources of such person in determining his need for public assistance or care under such title ten, of article five of this chapter, or as income or resources of any other person in determining such other persons's need for such public assistance or care.

Added by Laws 1967, Ch. 237; **amended** by Laws 1974, Ch. 1080, eff. Jan. 1, 1974; **amended** by Laws 1978, Ch. 555, eff. July 24, 1978.

§ 143. Information to be given by employers of labor to social services officials, the department, family court and the state department of mental hygiene.

If requested by an authorized representative of the state department of mental hygiene or of the department or by any social services official, the officials or executives of any corporation or partnership, and all employers of labor of any kind, doing business within the state of New York, shall furnish to such representative or social services official information relating to facts of which such officials, executives or employers shall have cognizance, concerning the last known address, social security number, plans providing care or other medical benefits by insurance or otherwise, wages, salaries, earnings or other income of any applicant for, or recipient of public assistance or care named in such request or of any relative legally responsible for the support of such applicant for, or recipient of public assistance or care, or of any person legally responsible for a person who is receiving services pursuant to section one hundred eleven-g of this chapter, or for the support of any patient of any state institution named by such representative of the state department of mental hygiene.

Amended by Laws 1946, Ch. 200; **amended** by Laws 1962, Ch. 690, eff. Sept. 1, 1962; **amended** by Laws 1977, Ch. 516, eff. July 1, 1977; **amended** by Laws 1982, Ch. 497, eff. Aug. 12, 1982.

§ 143-a. Information to be given to public welfare officials by retail installment sellers, small loan companies and sales finance companies.

If requested by an authorized representative of the department or by an authority charged with the duty of administering laws relating to public assistance or care in any village, town, city or county, the officials or executives of any corporation or partnership and all persons engaged in selling goods or furnishing services to retail buyers for a time sale price payable in installments, or in making personal loans whether as a licensed lender under the banking law or otherwise, and any sales finance company as defined in article ten of the banking law, shall furnish to such representatives or authority such information of which such officials, executives or persons shall have cognizance relating to transactions with a recipient of or an applicant for public assistance or care named in such request. Such facts shall include a description of the goods or services sold and the amount of the obligation incurred therefor, the amount of any loan made, the amounts paid and the balance owing, the place of employment, the wages, salaries, earnings or other income, guarantors or co-signers, and all other information furnished by the persons named for the purpose of obtaining credit.

Added by Laws 1960, Ch. 940, eff. Apr. 28, 1960.

§ 143-b.   Avoidance of abuses in connection with rent checks.

1.   Whenever a recipient of public assistance and care is eligible for or entitled to receive aid or assistance in the form of a payment for or toward the rental of any housing accommodations occupied by such recipient or his family, such payment may be made directly by the public welfare department to the landlord.

2.   Every public welfare official shall have power to and may withhold the payment of any such rent in any case where he has knowledge that there exists or there is outstanding any violation of law in respect to the building containing the housing accommodations occupied by the person entitled to such assistance which is dangerous, hazardous or detrimental to life or health. A report of each such violation shall be made to the appropriate public welfare department by the appropriate department or agency having jurisdiction over violations.

3.   Every public welfare official shall have the power to initiate or to request the recipient to initiate before the appropriate housing rent commission any proper proceeding for the reduction of maximum rents applicable to any housing accommodation occupied by a person entitled to assistance in the form of a rent payment whenever such official has knowledge that essential services which such person is entitled to receive are not being maintained by the landlord or have been substantially reduced by the landlord.

4.   The public welfare department may obtain and maintain current records of violations in buildings where welfare recipients reside which relate to conditions which are dangerous, hazardous or detrimental to life or health.

5.   (a) It shall be a valid defense in any action or summary proceeding against a welfare recipient for non-payment of rent to show existing violations in the building wherein such welfare recipient resides which relate to conditions which are dangerous, hazardous or detrimental to life or health as the basis for nonpayment.

SSL

(b)   In any such action or proceeding the plaintiff or landlord shall not be entitled to an order or judgment awarding him possession of the premises or providing for removal of the tenant, or to a money judgment against the tenant, on the basis of non-payment of rent for any period during which there was outstanding any violation of law relating to dangerous or hazardous conditions or conditions detrimental to life or health. For the purposes of this paragraph such violation of law shall be deemed to have been removed and no longer outstanding upon the date when the condition constituting a violation was actually corrected, such date to be determined by the court upon satisfactory proof submitted by the plaintiff or landlord.

(c)   The defenses provided herein in relation to an action or proceeding against a welfare recipient for non-payment of rent shall apply only with respect to violations reported to the appropriate public welfare department by the appropriate department or agency having jurisdiction over violations.

6.   Nothing in this section shall prevent the public welfare department from making provision for payment of the rent which was withheld pursuant to this section upon proof satisfactory to it that the condition constituting a violation was actually corrected. Where rents were reduced by order of the appropriate rent commission, the public welfare department may make provision for payment of the reduced rent in conformity with such order.

Added by Laws 1962, Ch. 997; amended by Laws 1965, Ch. 701, eff. July 2, 1965.

§ 143-c.   Avoidance of abuses in connection with rent security deposits.

1.   Whenever a landlord requires that he be secured against nonpayment of rent or for damages as a condition to renting a housing accommodation to a recipient of public assistance, a local social services official may in accordance with the regulations of the department secure the landlord by either of the following means at the option of the local social services official:

(a)   By means of an appropriate agreement between the landlord and the social services official, or

(b)   By depositing money in an escrow account, not under the control of the landlord or his agent, subject to the terms and conditions of an agreement between the landlord and the social services official in such form as the department may require or approve provided, however, that this option shall not be used in instances where recipients reside in public housing.

2.   Except as expressly provided in subdivision three of this section, it shall be against the public policy of the state for a social services official to pay money to a landlord to be held as a security deposit against the nonpayment of rent or for damages by a public assistance recipient, or to issue a grant to a recipient of public assistance therefor.

3.   When, however, in the judgment of a social services official housing accommodations available in a particular area are insufficient to properly

accommodate recipients of public assistance in need of housing, and in order to secure such housing it is essential that he pay money to landlords to be held as security deposits against the nonpayment of rent or for damages by public assistance recipients, or to issue grants to recipients of public assistance therefor, such social services official may pay or furnish funds for such security deposits until sufficient housing accommodations are available in the particular area to properly accommodate recipients of public assistance in need of housing. Social services officials shall not pay or furnish such funds in instances where recipients reside in public housing. Landlords receiving such security deposits shall comply with the provisions of article seven of the general obligations law. Such cash security deposits shall be subject to assignment to the local social services official by the recipients of public assistance or care. Any social services official paying or furnishing funds for security deposits in accordance with the provisions of this subdivision shall make diligent effort to recover such payments or funds from a recipient landlord as allowed by law.

4.   This section shall apply to federally-aided categories of public assistance except to the extent prohibited by applicable federal laws and regulations.

5.   This section shall apply to recipients of supplemental security income benefits or additional state payments, as defined in section three hundred of this chapter, and such persons shall be deemed recipients of public assistance for the purposes of this section.

Added Laws 1972, Ch. 851; **amended** Laws 1974, Ch. 1081, eff. Apr. 1, 1974; Laws 1975, Ch. 198; Laws 1976, Ch. 125; Laws 1977 Ch. 31; Laws 1978, Ch. 129; Laws 1980, Ch. 44; Laws 1982, Ch. 34; Laws 1984, Ch. 34; Laws 1986, Ch. 14; Laws 1988, Ch. 29; Laws 1990, Ch. 44, eff. Mar. 31, 1990, to eliminate the expiration date of the 1974 amendment; **amended** by Laws 1991, Ch. 165, § 51-a, eff. June 12, 1991; **amended** by Laws 1992, Ch. 41, §§ 132, 133, eff. Apr. 2, 1992.

§ 144.   Power of public welfare officials and service officers to administer oaths; power of public welfare officials to subpoena persons liable for support and compel production of records.

Public welfare officials and service officers shall have power to administer oaths and take affidavits in all matters pertaining to their office and to elicit, by examination under oath, statement of facts from applicants for or recipients of assistance or care. Public welfare officials shall have further power to subpoena persons liable by law for the support of applicants for or recipients of assistance or care, compel the attendance of such persons and take their testimony under oath for the purpose of determining the ability of such persons to contribute towards the support of such applicants for or recipients of assistance or care, and in connection therewith to compel the production of books, papers, records and documents. Such persons shall be entitled to the same mileage fees as are allowed to witnesses required to attend in civil actions in courts of record.

SSL

Amended by Laws 1941, Ch. 390; Laws 1946, Ch. 200; **amended** by Laws 1960, Ch. 1065, eff. Apr. 30, 1960.

§ 144-a.   Information to be given to officials of the department and of social services districts.

Any inconsistent provision of law notwithstanding, if requested by an authorized representative of the department or by an official of any town, city or county who is responsible for administering a program authorized by this chapter, the officials of any banking or financial organization or institution doing business in the state whether chartered under state law, federal law, or the laws of another jurisdiction, shall furnish to such governmental officials such information as such officials have as to whether any present applicant for or recipient of any assistance, care or services authorized by this chapter, has or had funds, securities or other property on deposit or in the custody of such banking or financial organization or institution, and the amount or probable value thereof. Such information shall be provided, to the extent practicable, in the format specified by such governmental officials (except that any banking or financial institution may discharge its obligation by supplying such matching information on cartridge, tape or diskette media in the American National Standard Code for Information Interchange file format). These provisions shall be inclusive of and in addition to the provisions of section four of the banking law and may be administered and enforced in any manner consistent with the provisions of this chapter or in any other manner authorized or permitted by the laws and courts of this state.

Added by Laws 1991, Ch. 165, § 6, eff. July 1, 1991.

§ 145.   Penalties.

1.   Any person who by means of a false statement or representation, or by deliberate concealment of any material fact, or by impersonation or other fraudulent device, obtains or attempts to obtain, or aids or abets any person to obtain public assistance or care to which he is not entitled, or does any wilful act designed to interfere with the proper administration of public assistance and care, shall be guilty of a misdemeanor, unless such act constitutes a violation of a provision of the penal law of the state of New York, in which case he shall be punished in accordance with the penalties fixed by such law. Failure on the part of a person receiving public assistance or care to notify the social services official granting such assistance or care of the receipt of money or property or income from employment or any other source whatsoever, shall, upon the cashing of a public assistance check by or on behalf of such person after the receipt of such money, or property, or income, constitute presumptive evidence of deliberate concealment of a material fact. Whenever a social services official has reason to believe that any person has violated any provision of this section, he shall promptly refer the facts and evidence available to him to the appropriate district

attorney or other prosecuting official who shall immediately evaluate the facts and evidence and take appropriate action.

2.   The provisions of subdivision one of this section shall apply to social services officials and employees, who shall also be subject to removal and shall be liable in an action brought by the county or city, or by the state commissioner of social services, for the value of the public assistance improperly granted to any person as a result of the wilful wrongful act of such official or employee.

Amended by Laws 1950, Chs. 293, 344; Laws 1954, Ch. 63; Laws 1958, Ch. 228; **amended** by Laws 1971, Ch. 735, eff. Sept. 1, 1971.

§ 145-a.   Judgment liens.

1.   If any provider of care, services or supplies under the medical assistance program is required to pay any fine, penalty or overpayment to the department, a social services district or any other social services entity as a result of the provisions of this chapter or as a result of any administrative procedure, such provider shall make payment in the amount and the manner directed by the commissioner or his or her agents, representatives or designees.

2.   Upon the issuance to the provider of a written notice of a final determination, the department must also notify the provider in writing of the provider's right to request a hearing. The provider's right to request a hearing shall not expire earlier than sixty days from the mailing of such notice of the provider's right to a hearing. If no administrative hearing or proceeding for judicial review shall then be pending and if the time for initiation of such hearing or proceeding shall have expired, the commissioner or his or her agents, representatives or designees may file with the clerk of the county where the provider resides or has a place of business a certified copy of the final administrative determination of the commissioner or his or her agents, whether in the form of a written final audit report or other final determination that such provider has engaged in unacceptable practices or has received payment to which such provider is not entitled, containing the amount found to be due. The filing of such final administrative determination shall have the full force and effect of a judgment duly docketed in the office of such clerk. The final administrative determination may be enforced by and in the name of the commissioner in the same manner, and with like effect, as that prescribed by the civil practice law and rules for the enforcement of a money judgment. Such final administrative determination shall not be filed until at least sixty days after the department has posted by ordinary mail to the provider at the address of such provider on file with the department a copy of the final administrative determination which shall contain notice of the amount found to be due and owing.

Added by Laws 1990, Ch. 190, § 376, eff. May 24, 1990.

SSL

§ 145-b   False statements; actions for treble damages

1.   (a) It shall be unlawful for any person, firm or corporation knowingly by means of a false statement or representation, or by deliberate concealment of any material fact, or other fraudulent scheme or device, on behalf of himself or others, to attempt to obtain or to obtain payment from public funds for services or supplies furnished or purportedly furnished pursuant to this chapter.

(b)   For purposes of this section, "statement or representation" includes, but is not limited to: a claim for payment made to the state, a political subdivision of the state, or an entity performing services under contract to the state or a political subdivision of the state; an acknowledgment, certification, claim, ratification or report of data which serves as the basis for a claim or a rate of payment, financial information whether in a cost report or otherwise, health care services available or rendered, and the qualifications of a person that is or has rendered health care services.

(c)   For purposes of this section, a person, firm or corporation has attempted to obtain or has obtained public funds when any portion of the funds from which payment was attempted or obtained are public funds, or any public funds are used to reimburse or make prospective payment to an entity from which payment was attempted or obtained.

2.   For any violation of subdivision one, the local social services district or the state shall have a right to recover civil damages equal to three times the amount by which any figure is falsely overstated or in the case of non-monetary false statements or representations, three times the amount of damages which the state, political subdivision of the state, or entity performing services under contract to the state or political subdivision of the state sustain as a result of the violation or five thousand dollars, whichever is greater. Notwithstanding part C of chapter fifty-eight of the laws of two thousand five: (a) For civil damages collected by a local social services district, relating to the medical assistance program, pursuant to a judgment under this subdivision, such amounts shall be apportioned between the local social services district and the state. If the violation occurred: (i) prior to January first, two thousand six, the amount apportioned to the local social services district shall be the local share percentage in effect immediately prior to such date as certified by the division of the budget, or (ii) after January first, two thousand six, the amount apportioned to the local social services district shall be based on a reimbursement schedule, created by the office of Medicaid inspector general, in effect at the time the violation occurred; provided that, if there is no schedule in effect at the time the violation occurred, the schedule to be used shall be the first schedule adopted pursuant to this subdivision. Such schedule shall provide for reimbursement to a local social services district in an amount between ten and fifteen percent of the gross amount collected. Such schedule shall be set on a county by county basis and shall be periodically reviewed and updated as necessary; provided, however, that any such updated schedule shall not be less than ten percent nor greater than fifteen percent

of the gross amount collected; and (b) For civil damages collected by the state relating to the medical assistance program pursuant to a judgment under this subdivision, the local social services district shall be entitled to compensation up to fifteen percent of the gross amount collected for such participation, including but not limited to identification, investigation or development of a case, commensurate with its level of effort or value added as determined by the Medicaid inspector general.

3. If any provider or supplier of services in the program of medical assistance is required to refund or repay all or part of any payment received by said provider or supplier under the provisions of this chapter and title XIX of the federal social security act, said refund or repayment shall bear interest from the date the payment was made to said provider or supplier to the date of said refund or repayment. Interest shall be at the maximum legal rate in effect on the date the payment was made to said provider or supplier.

4. (a) The department of health may require the payment of a monetary penalty as restitution to the medical assistance program by any person who fails to comply with the standards of the medical assistance program or of generally accepted medical practice in a substantial number of cases or grossly and flagrantly violated such standards and receives, or causes to be received by another person, payment from the medical assistance program when such person knew, or had reason to know, that:

(i) the payment involved the providing or ordering of care, services or supplies that were medically improper, unnecessary or in excess of the documented medical needs of the person to whom they were furnished;

(ii) the care, services or supplies were not provided as claimed;

(iii) the person who ordered or prescribed care, services or supplies which was medically improper, unnecessary or in excess of the documented medical need of the person to whom they were furnished was suspended or excluded from the medical assistance program at the time the care, services or supplies were furnished; or

(iv) the services or supplies for which payment was received were not, in fact, provided.

(b) Such penalty shall be in lieu of requiring a person to refund or repay all or part of any payment from the medical assistance program received by such person or caused to be received by another person as a result of a violation of the terms of this subdivision. In no event shall the monetary penalty imposed exceed two thousand dollars for each item or service which was the subject of the determination herein, except that where a penalty under this section has been imposed on a person within the previous five years, such penalty shall not exceed seven thousand five hundred dollars for each item or service which was the subject of the determination herein.

(c) Amounts collected pursuant to this subdivision shall be apportioned between the local social services district and the state in accordance with the regulations of the department of health.

5. When in the course of conducting an investigation relating to the investigation relating to the medical assistance program, a local social services district deduces that a provider may have committed criminal fraud, it shall refer the case to the office of medicaid inspector general along with appropriate supporting information. The office shall promptly review the case and, if deemed appropriate, refer the case pursuant to subdivision seven of section thirty-two of the public health law. If the deputy attorney general for Medicaid fraud control accepts a referral from the office of Medicaid inspector general that was identified, investigated or developed by a local social services district, and the state collects damages, the participating local social services district shall be entitled to compensation up to fifteen percent of the gross amount collected for such participation commensurate with its level of effort or value added as determined by the deputy attorney general for Medicaid fraud control. If the office of medicaid inspector general determines that it is not appropriate for referral in accordance with subdivision seven of section thirty-two of the public health law the office of medicaid inspector general shall further investigate the case, with notice to the participating local social services district, or return the case to the participating social services district, which may resume its investigation of the provider.

Added by Laws 1975, Ch. 659, eff. Sept. 1, 1975; amended by Laws 1990, Ch. 190, § 377, eff. May 24, 1990; amended by Laws 1992, Ch. 41, § 107, eff. Apr. 2, 1992; amended by Laws 1998, Ch. 2, § 34, eff. Nov. 1, 1998; Laws 2006, Ch. 442, §§7, 8, eff. July 26, 2006.

§ 145-c. Sanctions.

Any person who, individually or as a member of a family, applies for or receives public assistance and is found by a federal, state or local criminal, civil or other court or pursuant to an administrative hearing held in accordance with the regulations of the department, on the basis of a plea of guilty or nolo contendere or otherwise, intentionally to have (a) made a false or misleading statement or misrepresented, concealed, or withheld facts, or (b) committed any act intended to mislead, misrepresent, conceal, or withhold facts or propound a falsity, for the purpose of establishing or maintaining the eligibility of the individual or of the individual's family for aid or of increasing (or preventing a reduction in) the amount of such aid, then the needs of such individual shall not be taken into account in determining his or her need or that of his or her family pursuant to section one hundred thirty-one-a of this article (i) for a period of six months upon the first occasion of any such offense, (ii) for a period of twelve months upon the second occasion of any such offense or upon an offense which resulted in the wrongful receipt of benefits in an amount of between at least one thousand dollars and no more than three thousand nine hundred dollars, (iii) for a period of eighteen months upon the third occasion of any such offense or upon an offense which results in the wrongful receipt of benefits in an amount in excess of three thousand nine hundred dollars, and (iv) five years for any subsequent occasion of any such offense. Any period for which sanctions are imposed shall remain in effect, without possibility of administrative stay, unless and until the finding upon which the sanctions were imposed is subsequently reversed by a court of appropriate jurisdiction; but in no event shall the duration of the period for which such sanctions are imposed be subject to review. The sanctions shall be in addition to, and not in substitution for, any other sanctions which may be provided for by law with respect to the offenses involved, except that the social services official or court official assessing penalties against a recipient for an act of fraud or misrepresentation described in this subdivision may consider whether to impose such penalties based upon the existence of the penalties described herein.

Repealed/added by Laws 1997, Ch. 436, § 1 Part B, § 41, eff. Aug. 20, 1997; **amended** by Laws 1998, Ch. 214, § 15, eff. July 7, 1998, deemed in full force and effect Aug. 20, 1997.

§ 146. Penalty for the sale or exchange of assistance supplies.

1.   Any person who shall sell or exchange supplies or articles furnished him as assistance or care by any public welfare official or employee of the public welfare district, or dispose of them in any other way than as directed, shall be guilty of a misdemeanor.

2.   Any person who purchases any article knowing it to have been furnished to any person as assistance or care shall also be guilty of a misdemeanor.

Amended by Laws 1946, Ch. 200, eff. Apr. 1, 1946.

§ 147. Misuse of food stamps, food stamp program coupons, authorization cards and electronic access devices.

1.   a. Whoever knowingly uses, transfers, acquires, alters, purchases, transports or possesses food stamps, food stamp program coupons, authorization cards or electronic access devices which entitle a person to obtain food stamps, in any manner not authorized by section ninety-five of this chapter shall be guilty of a class A misdemeanor except that if the value of the benefit he or she obtained:

(i)   exceeds one thousand dollars, he or she shall be guilty of a class E felony; or

(ii)   exceeds three thousand dollars, he or she shall be guilty of a class D felony; or

(iii)   exceeds fifty thousand dollars, he or she shall be guilty of a class C felony.

b.   For the purposes of this section, the value of the benefit obtained shall be the cumulative face value of such food stamps, food stamp program coupons, authorization cards or electronic access devices.

SSL

2.   Any person found to have violated the provisions of subparagraph (i), (ii) or (iii) of paragraph a of subdivision one of this section, who shall possess a license to sell liquor under section sixty-three of the alcoholic beverage control law or to sell lottery tickets under article thirty-four of the tax law, shall have such license or licenses revoked in addition to any other penalty authorized by law. As used herein, the word "person" shall mean any individual, partnership, corporation, or association.

Added by Laws 1969, Ch. 1019, eff. Sept. 1, 1969; amended by Laws 1986, Ch. 452, eff. Nov. 1, 1986; amended by Laws 1995, Ch. 81, § 167, eff. July 1, 1995; amended by Laws 1996, Ch. 701, eff. Nov. 1, 1996.

§ 148.   Penalty for unlawfully bringing a needy person into a public welfare district.

No person shall, without legal authority, send or bring, or cause to be sent or brought, any needy person into a public welfare district with the purpose of making him a charge on such public welfare district, or for the purpose of avoiding the responsibility of assistance or care in the public welfare district from which he is brought or sent. Any person found guilty of such an act shall be guilty of a misdemeanor and liable to a fine of fifty dollars, recoverable in the name of the public welfare district.

§ 149.   Penalty for bringing a needy person into the state.

1.   Any person who knowingly brings, or causes to be brought, a needy person from out of the state into this state for the purpose of making him a public charge, shall be guilty of a misdemeanor punishable by a fine of one hundred dollars, and shall be obligated to convey such person out of the state or to support him at his own expense.

2.   The commissioner of public welfare of the district to which such needy person is brought may bring a suit in a court of competent jurisdiction to enforce this obligation.

3.   The court shall require satisfactory security from such person that he will convey the needy person out of the state within the time fixed by the court or will indemnify the public welfare district for all charges and expenses incurred for the assistance and care or transportation of such needy person. If such person refuses to give security when so required the court may commit him to jail for not exceeding three months.

Amended by Laws 1942, Ch. 421, eff. Apr. 12, 1942.

§ 150.   Penalty for neglect to report or for making false report.

1.   Any commissioner of public welfare, deputy commissioner, town or city public welfare officer, service officer, or any officer or employee who shall neglect or refuse to render any account, statement or report required by or

pursuant to this chapter, or who shall delay, neglect or refuse to forward any application for public assistance or care, or shall wilfully make false report or shall neglect to pay over any money within the time required by law, shall forfeit two hundred dollars and shall be liable to an action for all money which shall be in his hands with the interest thereon after the time the same should have been paid over.

2.   Any officer, department or board, in case of failure to receive an application for public assistance and care, or a report or account required by this chapter, shall notify the district attorney having authority in such public welfare district.

3.   The district attorney, upon receiving such notice, shall prosecute in the name of such officer, department or board for the recovery of the penalty or of such money, or both. The penalty and the sum recovered shall be deposited in the public welfare fund of the public welfare district or of a town or city thereof, as the case may be.

Amended by Laws 1946, Ch. 200, eff. Apr. 1, 1946.

§ 151.   Penalty for cashing public assistance checks.

No person, firm or corporation licensed under the provisions of the alcoholic beverage control law to sell liquor at retail shall cash or accept, for any purpose whatsoever, any public assistance check issued by a public welfare official or department as and for public assistance. A violation of the provisions of this section for the first offense shall be punishable by a fine not to exceed fifty dollars. A second offense shall constitute sufficient cause for the revocation, cancellation or suspension of such license issued pursuant to the alcoholic beverage control law.

Added by Laws 1951, Ch. 570, eff. Apr. 5, 1951.

§ 152.   Payments to the New York public welfare association; attendance at conventions of public welfare officials.

The legislative body of a county or city is hereby authorized to include annually in the appropriation made for public assistance and care and to raise by taxation the sum necessary to meet the actual and necessary expenses of maintaining and continuing the New York public welfare association for the purpose of devising practical ways and means for obtaining greater economy and efficiency in the administration of public assistance and care, and for the expenses incurred by public welfare officials and employees in attending meetings of public welfare officials. Superintendents and matrons of public homes, county and city public welfare officials and deputies and agents designated by the public welfare officials are authorized to attend the midwinter and annual conventions of public welfare officials. The necessary expenses in connection with such attendance shall be paid from public welfare funds.

SSL

Formerly § 151, **added** by Laws 1940, Ch. 619; **amended** by Laws 1946, Ch. 374; **amended** by Laws 1948, Ch. 456; **renumbered** as § 152 by Laws 1951, Ch. 570, eff. Apr. 5, 1951.

§ 152-a.   Burial reserves for certain recipients of public assistance or care from assigned assets.

When other provisions of this chapter providing for reserving an amount for the burial of a recipient of public assistance or care, from assets transferred or assigned to a social services official, do not apply to a recipient because of the category of public assistance or care received by him or her, as in the case of a recipient of safety net assistance, a similar burial reserve from assigned assets may or shall, as the regulations of the department may permit or require, be set aside for such recipient; and any such burial reserve heretofore set aside with the approval of the department, or in accordance with its requirements, shall be deemed to have been authorized.

Added by Laws 1956, Ch. 24, **amended** by Laws 1971, Ch. 110, eff. July 1, 1971; **amended** by Laws 1997, Ch. 436, § 1 Part B, § 75, eff. Aug. 20, 1997.

§ 152-b.   Surplus after recovery of cost of public assistance and care; unclaimed funds.

If, after the full amount expended by a public welfare district for the assistance and care of a deceased or other former recipient of public assistance and care, including the federal and state shares thereof, as determined in accordance with regulations of the department, and any authorized amount expended for the burial of such deceased recipient, shall have been recovered and deducted from the net proceeds of assets which have been transferred or assigned to the public welfare official by or on behalf of such recipient to insure repayment of the cost of his assistance and care, any balance or surplus remains, it shall be credited forthwith by the public welfare district to the estate or persons entitled thereto; but if unclaimed within four years thereafter by those entitled thereto it shall be deemed abandoned property and be paid to the state comptroller pursuant to section thirteen hundred five of the abandoned property law.

Added by Laws 1959, Ch. 803, eff. Apr. 24, 1959.

TITLE 2—STATE REIMBURSEMENT FOR PUBLIC ASSISTANCE AND CARE

———

Formerly Title 1-A renumbered Title 2 by Laws 1966, Ch. 256, eff. Apr. 30, 1966.

§ 153. Reimbursement and advances by the state.

1. [*Expires and repealed June 30, 2007.*] Expenditures made by social services districts, cities and towns for public assistance and care and its administration, other than foster care services, pursuant to this chapter and expenditures made by any Indian tribe for foster care services, preventive services, and adoption services and its administration rendered pursuant to an agreement entered into with the office of children and family services in accordance with section thirty nine of this chapter and pursuant to this chapter, shall, if approved by the department of family assistance, be subject to reimbursement by the state, in accordance with the regulations of the department, as follows:

There shall be paid to each such district, city or town

a. the amount of federal funds, if any, properly received or to be received on account of such expenditures;

b. [*Repealed*]

c. [*Repealed*]

d. fifty per centum of the amount expended for public assistance and care, after first deducting therefrom any federal funds properly received or to be received on account thereof;

e. fifty per centum of the amount expended for administration of public assistance and care, after first deducting therefrom any federal funds properly received or to be received on account thereof. The provisions of this paragraph shall not be applicable to expenditures for administration expressly provided for in paragraph f of this subdivision;

f. the full amount expended by any district, city, town or Indian tribe for the costs, including the costs of administration of public assistance and care to eligible needy Indians and members of their families residing on any Indian reservation in this state, after first deducting therefrom any federal funds properly received or to be received on account thereof;

g. fifty per centum of the amount expended for substance abuse services pursuant to this chapter, after first deducting therefrom any federal funds properly received or to be received on account thereof. In the event funds appropriated for such services are insufficient to provide full reimbursement of the total of the amounts claimed by all social services districts pursuant to this section then reimbursement shall be in such proportion as each claim bears to such total;

SSL

h.   [*Repealed*]

i.   [*Repealed*]

2.   (a) In the event that the federal government imposes fiscal sanctions on the state because of non-compliance with federal law, regulation, or policy relating to the temporary assistance for needy families block grant, other than sanctions relating to maintenance of effort spending requirements, the commissioner shall reduce federal reimbursement to each social services district in an amount equal to the portion of such fiscal sanction that the commissioner determines is attributable to such district through review of relevant statewide and district specific data or documentation. The commissioner shall make such determination of district fault only to the extent that his or her review identifies specific district actions or inactions that resulted in the district's failure to meet the applicable federal requirement. Such reduction in federal reimbursement shall be made without state financial participation in resulting costs. To the extent that the commissioner determines that he or she is unable to identify which districts caused or contributed to such federal fiscal sanction, the commissioner, subject to the approval of the director of the budget, shall assign the reduction in federal reimbursement to all districts proportionately based on allowable district expenditures under title IV-A of the federal social security act in the most recently completed state fiscal year, and the state shall share equally with social services districts in the cost increases resulting from such reduction in federal reimbursement.

(b)   In the event that the federal government imposes fiscal sanctions on the state because of non-compliance with federal law, regulation, or policy relating to maintenance of effort spending requirements under the federal temporary assistance to needy families block grant, the commissioner shall reduce federal reimbursement to each social services district in an amount equal to the portion of such fiscal sanction that the commissioner determines is attributable to such district through review of relevant statewide and district specific data or documentation. Cost increases resulting from such reduction in federal reimbursement shall be shared equally by the state and each affected social services district. To the extent that the commissioner determines that he or she is unable to identify which districts caused or contributed to such federal fiscal sanction, the commissioner, subject to the approval of the director of the budget, shall assign the reduction in federal reimbursement among all districts proportionately based on each district's portion of the statewide maintenance of effort spending requirement as determined by the commissioner, and the state shall share equally with social services districts in the cost increases resulting from such reduction in federal reimbursement.

(c)   Notwithstanding any inconsistent provision of law, if a portion of federal reimbursement otherwise payable is not available because of application of the federal percentage limitation on administrative expenses in the federal block grant for temporary assistance for needy families program, the commissioner shall rank all social services districts in descending order based on the percentage that federally reimbursed administrative expenses in each district in the federal fiscal year bears to all total expenditures eligible for federal reimbursement under title IV-A of the federal social security act in the respective district and shall reduce reimbursement payable to the district that received the highest proportion of such federal reimbursement until such reduction equals the lesser of the shortfall in federal reimbursement or the amount which, if applied to federal administrative reimbursement received in the federal fiscal year, would equalize the proportion of such reimbursement received by such district and that received by the next highest district or districts in the commissioner's ranking. In the event that suffi-cient savings are not achieved by such reduction in reimbursement to the highest ranked district, then the commissioner shall continue to reduce the amount of reimbursement for the highest and, as necessary, the sequentially ranked district or districts such that such reductions, when applied in the federal fiscal year, will equalize the proportion of federal reimbursement for administration received by all such affected districts and will equal an amount which, in aggregate, will be sufficient to fully offset but not exceed the federal reimbursement shortfall. Notwithstanding any provision of law to the contrary, reimbursement to a social services district out of state and federal funds shall not be made on administrative expenses which exceed fifteen percent of such district's total expenditures reimbursable under the temporary assistance for needy families block grant.

3. a. For the purpose of this title, expenditures for administration of public assistance and care shall include expenditures for salaries of the chief executive officers, their deputies and the employees of local welfare departments; operation, maintenance and service costs; and such other expenditures, such as equipment costs, depreciation charges, and rental values as may be approved by the department. It shall not include expenditures for capital additions or improve-ments, except as provided in paragraph c of this subdivision.

b. State reimbursement shall not be made for any part of the salary of a chief executive officer of a social services department, whose qualifications do not conform to those fixed by the department or of a city or town service officer; nor shall such reimbursement be made on the salary of a deputy commissioner or an employee, unless his employment is necessary for the administration of public assistance and care and his qualifications conform to those fixed by the department.

c. Notwithstanding any inconsistent provision of law, the amount expended by a social services district for the purpose of acquiring, reconstructing, rehabilitating or improving any shelter for adults shall be subject to state reim-bursement in the amount of fifty percent of such expenditure, in accordance with the regulations of the department, if such shelter is operated by: (i) a social services district directly or (ii) a social services district which has entered into a contract with a not-for-profit corporation or charitable organization otherwise established pursuant to law or a governmental entity or political subdivision thereof for the purpose of operating such a shelter; provided, however, that such capital acquisition, reconstruction, rehabilitation or improvement has the

SSL

approval of the department prior to the commencement of such construction in accordance with regulations promulgated by the department.

Such reimbursement may be paid out of any moneys in the state treasury payable out of the local assistance account to the extent of the amount appropriated to the department for such purposes, and the expenditure of such amount shall constitute the complete liquidation of the state's obligation to reimburse pursuant to this section.

4.　For the purpose of this title, expenditures made by social services districts, cities, towns and any Indian tribe that has entered into an agreement with the department pursuant to section thirty-nine of this chapter for the care and maintenance of neglected, abused, abandoned or destitute children who have been remanded, discharged or committed pursuant to the family court act of the state of New York shall, if approved by the department, be subject to reimbursement by the state in accordance with and to the extent authorized by the provisions of subdivision one.

5.　In the event the state elects to claim and receive federal aid payments in accordance with the alternative formula authorized by the provisions of section eleven hundred eighteen of the social security act, for expenditures made under the state's approved plan for aid to dependent children, a social services district shall, notwithstanding such election, be entitled to receive as state reimbursement, in accordance with and to the extent authorized by subdivision one, for its approved monthly expenditures for aid to dependent children, the amount it would have been entitled to receive if such election had not been made, until the month the amount it would be entitled to receive as state reimbursement for its approved expenditures for such program of assistance for such month, as a result of such election, is equal to or greater than such district would have been entitled to receive therefor if such election had not been made by the state, any inconsistent provision of law notwithstanding.

6.　a. Claims for state reimbursement shall be made in such form and manner and at such times and for such periods as the department shall determine.

b.　When certified by the department state reimbursement shall be paid from the state treasury upon the audit and warrant of the comptroller out of funds made available therefor.

c.　When the monies allotted to the state by the federal security agency, or other authorized federal agency, for aid to dependent children for any quarter shall have been received by the department of taxation and finance, the department shall, as soon as possible, certify to the comptroller the amount to which each social services district is entitled for such quarter and such amount shall be paid out of the state treasury after audit by the comptroller to the respective social services districts.

d.　The department is authorized in its discretion to make advances to public welfare districts and to cities and towns in anticipation of the state reimbursement provided for in this section.

7. Payment of state reimbursement and advances shall be made to the fiscal officer of the public welfare district or city entitled thereto pursuant to the provisions of this chapter; and in counties where home relief is a town charge, such payment as the towns therein shall be entitled to shall be made to the fiscal officer of the county for the account of and reimbursement to such towns, except in the case of a town which is a public welfare district.

8. Any inconsistent provision of the law or regulation of the department notwithstanding, state reimbursement shall not be made for any expenditure made for the duplication of any grant and allowance for any period, except as authorized by subdivision eleven of section one hundred thirty-one of this chapter, or for any home relief payment made for periods prior to forty-five days after the filing of an application unless the district determines pursuant to department regulations that such assistance is required to meet emergency circumstances or prevent eviction. Notwithstanding any other provision of law, social services districts are not required to provide home relief to any person, otherwise eligible, if state reimbursement is not available in accordance with this subdivision.

9. Any inconsistent provision of this chapter or other law notwithstanding, any loss of federal funds assessed by the department of health, education and welfare against the state by reason of the failure of one or more social services districts to comply either with paragraph (e) of subdivision one of section three hundred fifty and paragraph (c) of subdivision four of section three hundred sixty-five-a relating to family planning services for eligible individuals or with paragraph (g) of subdivision one of section three hundred fifty relating to child health screening and resulting treatment, shall be charged to and borne by the social services districts responsible for such loss. Each such district shall bear only so much of any such loss as is attributable to its failure so to comply. The amount to be borne by a district shall be determined by applying the ratio that the number of cases in which it failed to comply with either family planning or child health screening and treatment requirements, or both, bears to the total number of cases in the state in which there were failures to comply with either such requirement, or both, as the case may be. A district shall have an opportunity to be heard before the department's final determination to impose such an assessment.

10. [*Expires and repealed June 30, 2007.*] Expenditures made by a social services district for the maintenance of children with disabilities, placed by school districts, pursuant to section forty-four hundred five of the education law shall, if approved by the office of children and family services, be subject to forty percent reimbursement by the state and twenty percent reimbursement by school districts in accordance with paragraph (c) of subdivision one of section forty-four hundred five of the education law, after first deducting therefrom any federal funds received or to be received on account of such expenditures, except that in the case of a student attending a state-operated school for the deaf or blind pursuant to article eighty-seven or eighty-eight of the education law who was not placed in such school by a school district such expenditures shall be subject to

SSL

fifty percent reimbursement by the state after first deducting therefrom any federal funds received or to be received on account of such expenditures and there shall be no reimbursement by school districts. Such expenditures shall not be subject to the limitations on state reimbursement contained in subdivision two of section one hundred fifty-three-k of this chapter. In the event of the failure of the school district to make the maintenance payment pursuant to the provisions of this subdivision, the state comptroller shall withhold state reimbursement to any such school district in an amount equal to the unpaid obligation for maintenance and pay over such sum to the social services district upon certification of the commissioner of the office of children and family services and the commissioner of education that such funds are overdue and owed by such school district. The commissioner of the office of children and family services, in consultation with the commissioner of education, shall promulgate regulations to implement the provisions of this subdivision.

11. [*Expires and repealed June 30, 2007.*] Expenditures made by a social services district for approved tuition costs pursuant to section four thousand four of the education law, after first deducting therefrom any federal funds received or to be received on account thereof, for a child placed in a child care institution by a social services district, the office of children and family services or family court shall be subject to reimbursement by the state in accordance with subdivision two of section one hundred fifty-three-k of this title and article nineteen-G of the executive law, as applicable; provided, however, that the amount that a school district reimburses the state for its expenditure for such children pursuant to section four thousand four of the education law shall be credited to each applicable social services district.

12. [*Expires and repealed June 30, 2007.*] Expenditures made by a social services district for the detention in foster care facilities of a person alleged to be or adjudicated as a person in need of supervision, pursuant to article seven of the family court act, shall be subject to reimbursement by the state in accordance with the provisions of section five hundred thirty of the executive law. The care of such person shall not be required to comply with the requirements of sections four hundred nine-e and four hundred nine-f of this chapter.

13. [*Repealed*]

14. [*Repealed*]

15. Notwithstanding the provisions of this section or any other law to the contrary, expenditures made by a social services district for brokers' fees, finders' fees or security deposits paid pursuant to this chapter shall be subject to twenty-five percent reimbursement, after first deducting therefrom any federal funds received or to be received on account thereof.

16. Notwithstanding any inconsistent provisions of this section, and subject to the amounts specifically appropriated therefor, social services districts which have implemented child assistance program pursuant to section one hundred thirty-one-z of this article shall be reimbursed by the department for administrative expenses for the implementation and operation of the program as approved

by the department in accordance with the following schedule after first deducting any federal reimbursement received therefor: for the fiscal year beginning April first, nineteen hundred ninety-seven, one hundred percent; for the fiscal year beginning April first, nineteen hundred ninety-eight, ninety percent; for the fiscal year beginning April first, nineteen hundred ninety-nine, eighty percent; for the fiscal year beginning April first, two thousand, seventy percent; for the fiscal year beginning April first, two thousand one, sixty percent and for each fiscal year thereafter, fifty percent.

17. From an amount specifically appropriated therefor, the commissioner of the office of temporary and disability assistance shall provide additional enhanced reimbursement for administration of income maintenance, food stamps, and employment programs to social services districts which meet the work participation rates set forth in subdivision seven of section three hundred thirty-five-b of this chapter. The amount of reimbursement available to each social services district shall be established by the commissioner of the office of temporary and disability assistance with the approval of the director of the budget. Separate amounts of reimbursement shall be available to a social services district for meeting each of the following categories: for households receiving assistance funded under the federal temporary assistance for needy families block grant program in which there is an adult or minor head of household; and for households with dependent children in which there is an adult or minor head of household and which is receiving safety net assistance and payment for which is used to meet the federally required maintenance of effort for the temporary assistance for needy families block grant. The office of temporary and disability assistance may advance reimbursement that would be available for full compliance and may recover any amounts unearned by the district by withholding any other reimbursement due from the state to the social services district.

Added by Laws 1953, Ch. 562; **amended** by Laws 1958, Ch. 979; Laws 1959, Ch. 411; Laws 1962, Ch. 689; Laws 1965, Chs. 287, 1071; Laws 1966, Chs. 100, 256; Laws 1967, Chs. 150, 155; Laws 1969, Ch. 184; Laws 1970, Ch. 681; Laws 1971, Chs. 110, 705, 817; Laws 1972, Chs. 270, 694; Laws 1973, Chs. 195, 516; Laws 1974, Chs. 621, 909, 1080; Laws 1975, Ch. 513; Laws 1978, Ch. 555; Laws 1980, Ch. 338, eff. June 19, 1980, Ch. 471, eff. July 23, 1980, Ch. 563, eff. July 1, 1981; **amended** by Laws 1981, Ch. 947, eff. July 1, 1981; **amended** by Laws 1982, Ch. 549, eff. July 20, 1982; **amended** by Laws 1983, Ch. 791, eff. July 30, 1983; **amended** by Laws 1984, Ch. 321, eff. July 1, 1984; **amended** by Laws 1984, Ch. 352, eff. July 1, 1984; **amended** by Laws 1986, Ch. 810, eff. Apr. 1, 1986; **amended** by Laws 1987, Ch. 462, eff. July 27, 1987, **amended** by Laws 1987, Ch. 419, eff. Sept. 1, 1987; **amended** by Laws 1990, Ch. 453, § 4, eff. Oct. 1, 1990; **amended** by Laws 1990, Ch. 453, § 5, eff. Apr. 1, 1990; **amended** by Laws 1992, Ch. 41, § 125, eff. Apr. 2, 1992; **amended** by Laws 1995, Ch. 83, §§ 224, 225, eff. July 1, 1995, until Mar. 31, 1999; **amended** by Laws 1995, Ch. 81, § 139, eff. July 1, 1995, §§ 155, 159, 198, 199, eff. Apr. 1, 1995; **amended** by Laws 1997, Ch. 436, § 1 Part B, § 19-a, 20, and 27–29, eff. Aug. 20, 1997; **amended** by Laws 1998, Ch. 214, § 12, deemed in full force and effect Aug. 20, 1997; **amended** by Laws 1999, Ch. 16, § 3, eff. Mar. 31, 1999, deemed in full force and effect Apr. 1, 1999, Ch. 30, § 1, eff. Apr. 26,

SSL

1999, deemed in full force and effect Apr. 1, 1999, Ch. 48, § 1, eff. May 24, 1999, deemed in full force and effect Apr. 1, 1999, Ch. 74, § 1, eff. June 21, 1999, deemed in full force and effect Apr. 1, 1999, Ch. 333, § 6, eff. July 2, 1999, deemed in full force and effect Apr. 1, 1999, extending the effective dates of subds. (10) and (11) to Aug. 31, 1999; **amended** by Laws 2002, Ch. 83, Part C, §§ 10, 11, 12, and 13, eff. May 29, 2002, act shall expire and deemed repealed on June 30, 2007; Laws 2003, Ch. 62, Part G2, §§ 1, 3, eff. July 1, 2003 and shall not affect the repeal of subdivision and deemed repealed therewith; Laws 2006, ch. 58, §1 (Part J), eff. April 12, 2006, deemed eff. on and after April 1, 2006.

§ 153-a.   Reimbursement for services to social services districts.

1.   Expenditures made by a department, bureau, division or other unit of a county or city for services to, on behalf of, or directly related to the operations of a social services district, pursuant to the provisions of this chapter or any other provision of law, may, if approved by the department, be subject to reimbursement by the state, if and so long as such expenditures are subject to federal reimbursement and only to the extent of such federal reimbursement. There may be paid to each such social services district the amount of federal funds, if any, properly received or to be received on account of such expenditures. This section shall not apply to reimbursement for expenditures related to the location of absent parents, establishment of paternity or enforcement of support reimbursable under title six–A of article three of this chapter.

2.   a. Claims for such reimbursement from federal funds shall be made in such form and manner and at such times and for such periods as the department shall determine, including claims for any such expenditures made on or after January 1, 1970.

b.   When certified by the department, such reimbursement from federal funds shall be paid from the state treasury upon the audit and warrant of the comptroller out of funds made available therefor.

c.   When the monies allotted to the state by the federal security agency, or other authorized federal agency, for such services to social services districts for any quarter or other authorized period shall have been received by the department of taxation and finance, the department shall, as soon as possible, certify to the comptroller the amount to which each social services district is entitled for such quarter or other authorized period and such amount shall be paid out of the state treasury after audit by the comptroller to the respective social services district.

3.   Payment of such reimbursement from federal funds shall be made to the fiscal officer of the social services district entitled thereto pursuant to the provisions of this chapter or any other provision of law.

   Added by Laws of 1972, Ch. 510, eff. May 24, 1972; **amended** by Laws 1975, Ch. 685; Laws 1976, Ch. 326; Laws 1977, Ch. 516; Laws 1978, Ch. 456 deemed to be in full force and effect from July 1, 1975. See legislative history of § 111–a, *supra*.

§ 153-b. Reimbursement for services.

Expenditures made by a social services district for the purposes of this chapter as authorized by section one hundred thirty-one-g of this chapter shall, if approved by the department, be subject to reimbursement by the state not pursuant to section one hundred fifty-three or any other provision of this chapter, but, in accordance with the regulations of the department to the extent of any and only in the amount of federal funds, if any properly received or to be received on account of such expenditures.

Added by Laws 1972, Ch. 912, eff. Apr. 1, 1972.

§ 153-c. Special provisions for reimbursement of home relief.

Repealed by Laws 1997, Ch. 436, § 1 Part B, § 76, eff. Aug. 20, 1997.

§ 153-d. Additional limitations on reimbursement for foster care and preventive services.

Repealed by Laws 2002, Ch. 83, Part C, § 14, eff. May 29, 2002, deemed eff. April 1, 2002, expires and repealed June 30, 2007.

Editor's Note:

See 1979 note under Art 6, Title 4, § 409 et seq.Û :

Laws 1999, Ch. 336, § 10, eff. July 23, 1999, deemed eff. April 1, 1999, provides as follows:

§ 10. This act shall take effect immediately and shall be deemed to have been in full force and effect on and after April 1, 1999; except that sections one, two, three, four and five of this act shall take effect August 1, 1999 and shall expire and be deemed repealed on August 8, 1999 whereupon the provisions of the tax law amended by such sections shall revert to and be read as such provisions did immediately prior to August 1, 1999; and sections eight and nine of this act shall be deemed to have been in full force and effect on and after March 30, 1999 provided, however, that nothing contained herein shall be deemed to affect the application, qualification, expiration, reversion or repeal of any provision of law amended by any section of this act and the provisions of this act shall be applied or qualified or shall expire or revert or be deemed repealed in the same manner, to the same extent and on the same date as the case may be as otherwise provided by law. (See Laws 1999, Ch. 405 note for effectiveness.).

Laws 1999, Ch. 405, § 1 (Part J), eff. Aug 6, 1999, deemed eff. July 23, 1999, provides as follows:

Section 1. Notwithstanding the provisions of article 5 of the general construction law, the provisions of the tax law amended by sections 94-a, 94-d and 94-g of chapter 2 of the laws of 1995 are hereby revived and shall continue in full force and effect as they existed on March 31, 1999 through May 31, 2004, when upon such date they shall expire and be repealed. Sections 1, 2, 3, 4, and 5, and such part of section 10 of chapter 336 of the laws of 1999 as relates to providing for the effectiveness of such sections 1, 2, 3, 4 and 5 shall be nullified in effect on the effective date of this section, except that the amendments made to: paragraph (2) of subdivision a of section 1612 of the tax law by such section 1; and subdivision b of section 1612 of the tax law by such section 2; and the repeal of section 152 of chapter 166 of the laws of 1991 made by such section 5 shall continue to remain in effect. (Amd, Laws 1999, Ch. 414, § 5, eff. Aug 6, 1999, deemed eff. July 23, 1999, Laws 2001, Ch. 20, § 1 (Part E), eff. March 30, 2001, Laws 2001, Ch. 63, § 1 (Part D), eff. June 25, 2001, Laws 2001, Ch. 118, § 1 (Part NN), eff. Aug 3, 2001, Laws 2001, Ch. 365, § 1 (Part A), eff. Oct 15, 2001, Laws 2001, Ch. 371, § 1 (Part A), eff. Oct 22, 2001, Laws 2001, Ch. 383, § 1 (Part M), eff. Oct 29, 2001, Laws 2002, Ch. 23, § 1 (Part A, eff. March 28, 2002, Laws 2002, Ch. 37, § 1 (Part A), eff. April 23, 2002, Laws 2002, Ch. 85, § 1 (Part AA), eff. May 29, 2002, Laws 2004, Ch. 60, § 1 (Part X), eff. Aug 20, 2004, Laws 2004, Ch. 98, § 1 (Part A), eff. May 28, 2004, Laws 2004, Ch. 120, § 1 (Part D), eff. June 22, 2004, Laws 2004, Ch. 209, § 1 (Part A), eff. July 23, 2004, Laws 2004, Ch. 262, § 1 (Part C), eff. Aug 2, 2004.).

Laws 2002, Ch. 83, § 28 (Part C), eff. May 29, 2002, provides as follows:

§ 28. This act shall take effect immediately; provided that sections nine through eighteen and twenty through twenty-seven of this act shall be deemed to have been in full force and effect on and after April 1, 2002; provided, however, that section fifteen of this act shall apply to claims that are otherwise reimbursable by the state on or after April 1, 2002 except as provided in subdivision 9 of section 153-k of the social services law as added by section fifteen of this act; provided further however, that nothing in this act shall authorize the office of children and family services to deny state reimbursement to a social services district for violations of the provisions of section 153-d of the social services law for services provided from January 1, 1994 through March 31, 2002; provided that section nineteen of this act shall take effect September 13, 2002; and, provided further, however, that notwithstanding any law to the contrary, the office of children and family services shall have the authority to promulgate, on an emergency basis, any rules and regulations necessary to implement the requirements established pursuant to this act; provided further, however, that the regulations to be developed pursuant to section one of this act shall not be adopted by emergency rule; and provided further that the provisions of sections nine through twenty-seven of this act shall expire and be deemed repealed on June 30, 2007.

§ 153-e. Special provisions for state reimbursement of foster care expenditures.

Repealed by Laws 1995, Ch. 83, § 228, eff. July 1, 1995.

§ 153-f. State reimbursement of home energy grant expenses.

Notwithstanding any other provision of law, expenditures made by social services districts in the form of payments made as home energy grants pursuant to the provisions of subdivision three-c of section one hundred thirty-one-a of this article shall be reimbursed as follows:

There shall be paid to each such city, district or town;

1.   The amount of federal funds properly received or to be received on account of such expenditures; and

2.   One hundred percent of the amount expended after first deducting therefrom any federal funds properly received or to be received on account thereof.

Added by Laws 1981, Ch. 102, eff. July 1, 1981.

§ 153-g.   Special provisions for state reimbursement for child protective services.

Repealed by Laws 1995, Ch. 83, § 229, eff. July 1, 1995.

§ 153-g.   State reimbursement for child protective services.

Repealed by Laws 2002, Ch. 83, Part C, § 14, eff. May 29, 2002, deemed eff. April 1, 2002, expired and repealed June 30, 2007.

§ 153-h.   Special provisions for state reimbursement for therapeutic foster care services and respite services for therapeutic foster parents.

Repealed by Laws 1995, Ch. 83, § 230, eff. July 1, 1995.

§ 153-i.   Block grant for family and children's services.

Repealed by Laws 1999, Ch. 333, eff. July 2, 1999.

§ 153-j.   Performance awards.

Repealed by Laws 1997, Ch. 436, eff. October 1, 2002.

§ 153-k.   County financial incentives.

Repealed by Laws 2000, Ch. 583, § 1, eff. Dec. 8, 2000.

§ 153-k.   Funding for children and family services.

1.   (a) Expenditures made by social services districts for child protective services, preventive services provided, as applicable, to eligible children and families of children who are in and out of foster care placement, independent living services, aftercare services, and adoption administration and services other than adoption subsidies provided pursuant to article six of this chapter and the regulations of the department of family assistance shall, if approved by the office of children and family services, be subject to sixty-five percent state reimbursement exclusive of any federal funds made available for such purposes, in

accordance with the directives of the department of family assistance and subject to the approval of the director of the budget.

(b) Claims for preventive services and independent living services submitted by a social services district for reimbursement may be comprised of in-kind, indirect services, and non-tax levy funds, including but not limited to privately donated funds, up to the same amount as the social services district's claims for such services during federal fiscal year nineteen hundred ninety eight-ninety nine were comprised of in-kind, indirect services and non-tax levy funds; provided, however, that up to seventeen and one half percent of a social services district's claims for preventive services and independent living services may be comprised of privately donated funds if the percentage of its claims comprised of privately donated funds was less than seventeen and one half percent during federal fiscal year nineteen hundred ninety-eight — nineteen hundred ninety-nine. Federal reimbursement of such claims shall be available only to the extent permitted by federal law or regulations.

2. (a) Notwithstanding the provisions of this chapter or of any other law to the contrary, eligible expenditures by a social services district for foster care services shall be subject to reimbursement with state funds only to the extent of annual appropriations to the state foster care block grant. Such foster care services shall include expenditures for the provision and administration of: care, maintenance, supervision and tuition; supervision of foster children placed in federally funded job corps programs; and care, maintenance, supervision and tuition for adjudicated juvenile delinquents and persons in need of supervision placed in residential programs operated by authorized agencies and in out-of-state residential programs. Social services districts must develop and implement children and family services delivery systems that are designed to reduce the need for and the length of foster care placements and must document their efforts in the multi-year consolidated services plan and the annual implementation reports submitted pursuant to section thirty-four-a of this chapter.

(b) State reimbursement to each social services district shall be limited to the district's allocation of the foster care block grant. The state funds appropriated for the foster care block grant shall be apportioned among the social services districts by the office of children and family services based on the district's claiming history and other factors. Such apportionments shall be subject to the approval of the director of the budget.

(c) Any portion of a social services district's apportionment from the foster care block grant for a particular state fiscal year that is not claimed by such district during that state fiscal year may be used by such district for preventive services, independent living services or aftercare services claimed by such district during the next state fiscal year up to the amount remaining from the district's foster care block grant apportionment; provided, however, that any claims for preventive services, independent living services or aftercare services during the next state fiscal year in excess of such amount shall be subject to state reimbursement pursuant to subdivision one of this section. Any claims submitted by a social services district for reimbursement for a particular state fiscal year for which the social services district does not receive state or federal reimbursement during that state fiscal year may not be claimed against that district's block grant apportionment for the next state fiscal year.

3. To the extent that monies are made available to the commissioner of the office of children and family services from the children and family services quality enhancement fund established pursuant to section ninety-seven-yyy of the state finance law, the office of children and family services is authorized to conduct activities to increase the availability and/or quality of children and family services programs which may include, but not be limited to, staff recruitment, retention and training activities, research projects, and targeted services expansion and/or demonstration projects to test innovative models for service delivery which may include such areas as health, mental health and substance abuse services. Notwithstanding sections one hundred twelve and one hundred sixty-three of the state finance law, such activities shall be conducted without competitive bid or request for proposal.

4. (a) A social services district, either individually or in combination with other social services districts, may establish managed care systems or other systems to provide children and family services other than child protective services investigations, in accordance with applicable laws and regulations. Such a system may include, but not be limited to, the establishment of capitated rates for service provided to children to prevent the placement of such children into foster care and to discharge such children from foster care to suitable, permanent, safe homes in a more timely manner through preventive services, intensified discharge planning, pre adoptive services, after-care services and/or post adoption services.

(b) Social services district payments to case managers or public or private service providers under such a system may be based on reimbursement rates established by the office of children and family services pursuant to section three hundred ninety-eight-a of this chapter, capitated rates or other payment mechanisms for all or a portion of the services, either separately or combined. To facilitate payments to case managers or providers, the office of children and family services may establish procedures for standardizing payments to managers or providers that enter into agreements with more than one social services district.

(c) Under such a system, a social services district may delegate responsibility for case management services to case managers or providers in a manner designed to afford case manager or provider accountability through the incorporation of quality control standards that provide appropriate monitoring of these services such as recognized accreditation mechanisms, performance audits by the social services district or other means.

(d) Under such a system, a social services district, in a purchase of service agreement for preventive services with an authorized agency, may delegate to such authorized agency the responsibility for approving and paying rent subsidies or assistance under paragraph (c) of subdivision five and/or subdivision seven of section four hundred nine a of this chapter.

SSL

(e)   (i) A social services district must obtain the office's prior approval of its plan for establishing and implementing such a system, in accordance with guidelines established by the office of children and family services.

(ii)   Such a plan may include requests for a waiver of any statutory or regulatory requirements established pursuant to sections thirty-four-a, four hundred nine-d and four hundred nine-e of this chapter regarding the form, content, development, or amendment of the child welfare services plan component of the multi year services plan and the annual implementation reports, family services plans and uniform case records.

(iii)   Any request by a social services district for a waiver shall identify the specific statute or regulation to be waived, and include a justification for the waiver and alternative actions to be taken by the social services district to satisfy the purposes of the statute or regulation. The office of children and family services may grant any such waiver request, subject to the approval of the director of the budget, where the social services district applying for the waiver demonstrates a reasonable administrative or programmatic justification for the waiver. The potential fiscal impact of the waiver upon federal, state and local governments shall be evaluated by the office of children and family services as part of its review of the request for a waiver. The office of children and family services may impose durational and other reasonable conditions if an approval of the waiver is granted. Where a waiver is granted, the office of children and family services shall have the authority to establish alternative standards to be followed by social services officials. The office of children and family services may not grant a waiver that would fail to comply with applicable federal statutory or regulatory standards. The social services district may not revise local practice or policy unless and until the office of children and family services approves the waiver.

(iv)   The office of children and family services shall provide notice to the governor and the legislature of each plan that is approved including a brief description of the plan and any waivers granted and any alternative standards established. The office shall provide an annual report to the governor and the legislature regarding the implementation of all approved plans during a calendar year by January thirtyfirst of the following year.

5.   (a) Social services districts shall conduct eligibility determinations and submit claims for reimbursement in such form and manner and at such times and for such periods as the department of family assistance shall determine.

(b)   When certified by the department of family assistance, state reimbursement shall be paid from the state treasury upon the audit and warrant of the comptroller out of funds made available therefor.

(c)   The department of family assistance is authorized in its discretion to make advances to social services districts in anticipation of the state reimbursement provided for in this section.

6. (a) Payment of state reimbursement and advances shall be made to the fiscal officer of the social services district entitled thereto pursuant to the provisions of this chapter.

(b) Any inconsistent provision of the law or regulation of the department of family assistance notwithstanding, state reimbursement shall not be made for any expenditure made for the duplication of any grant or allowance for any period.

7. The office of children and family services shall not reimburse any claims for expenditures for those children and family services set forth in subdivisions one and two of this section that are submitted more than twenty two months after the calendar quarter in which the expenditures were made.

8. Claims submitted by a social services district for reimbursement shall be paid after deducting any expenditures defrayed by fees, third party reimbursement, and any non tax levy funds including donated funds that exceed the amount that may be claimed for state and federal reimbursement pursuant to paragraph (b) of subdivision one of this section.

9. Notwithstanding any other provision of law, the state shall not be responsible for reimbursing a social services district and a district shall not seek state reimbursement for any portion of any state disallowance or sanction taken against the social services district, or any federal disallowance attributable to final federal agency decisions or to settlements made, on or after July first, nineteen hundred ninety-five, when such disallowance or sanction results from the failure of the social services district to comply with federal or state requirements, including, but not limited to, failure to document eligibility for the federal or state funds in the case record; provided, however, if the office of children and family services determines that any federal disallowance for services provided between January first, nineteen hundred ninety-nine and May thirty first, nineteen hundred ninety-nine results solely from the late enactment of the state legislation implementing the federal adoption and safe families act, the state shall be solely responsible for the full amount of the disallowance or sanction. This provision shall be deemed to apply both prospectively and retroactively regardless of whether the disallowance or sanction is for services provided or claims made prior to or after April first, two thousand two.

10. (i) In accordance with regulations developed by the office of children and family services, the office shall measure each district's compliance with the federal child welfare outcome standards beginning no later than twenty months after the effective date of this section. The office is authorized to impose fiscal penalties against a social services district that fails to substantially comply with the outcome standards or to make sufficient progress towards complying with the outcome standards after developing and implementing a corrective action plan in the time and manner approved by the office. The imposition of a fiscal penalty shall be subject to an appeal process set forth in regulation. Any fiscal penalties received by the office of children and family services pursuant to this subdivision shall be deposited to the credit of the children and family services quality

enhancement fund established pursuant to section ninety-seven-yyy of the state finance law. For social services districts in counties with less than fifteen thousand children under the age of eighteen, the office may waive the fiscal penalties and the need for a corrective action plan if the failure to substantially comply with the outcome standards was based on extraordinary circumstances. The office may provide fiscal incentives to social services districts with high performances on the federal child welfare outcome standards. A social services district may pass on to its contract agencies some portion of the fiscal penalties or fiscal incentives that may be attributable to such agencies.

(ii)   The office shall provide an annual report to the governor and the legislature detailing: each county's performance on the outcome standards, the amount of fiscal penalties imposed against each county, and the amount of fiscal penalties collected from each county. Said report shall be delivered to the director of the budget, the chair of the senate finance committee and the chair of the assembly ways and means committee annually on a calendar year basis, by March fifteenth of the following year.

11.   The office of children and family services shall submit a preliminary report to the governor and the legislature on or before the thirty first day of December, two thousand four providing preliminary data and information on the implementation of this section, and shall submit a final report by the fifteenth day of August, two thousand five assessing the implementation of and the outcomes resulting from the children and family services financing provisions established by this section through the thirtieth day of June, two thousand five. The final report shall include information regarding services delivery trends under the financing structure set forth in this section and innovative models of service provision to be considered for replication.

Added by Laws 2002, Ch. 83, Part C, § 15, eff. May 29, 2002, deemed in full force and effect on and after April 1, 2002.

§ 154.   Additional reimbursement for home relief.

1.   [Repealed by Laws 1969, Ch. 184, eff. July 1, 1969.]

2.   [Repealed by Laws 1969, Ch. 184, July 1, 1969.]

3.   The population of a social services district, city or town for the purposes of this section shall be the population of such district, city or town, respectively, excluding the reservation and school Indian population and inmates of state institutions under the direction, supervision or control of the state department of correction and the state department of mental hygiene and inmates of the New York Training School for Girls at Hudson and Claverack, the State Agricultural and Industrial School, the New York State Veterans' Home and the New York Training School for Boys at Warwick, as shown by the last preceding decennial federal census showing such population, completed and certified prior to December thirty-first preceding the commencement of the state fiscal year during which the reimbursement is made; provided, however, if the director of the United

States bureau of the census shall certify that the population of a district, city or town, as shown by such last preceding decennial federal census, (a) excludes a specified number of persons who were actually residing in such district, city or town at the time of such census, or (b) includes a specified number of persons who are not actually residing in such district, city or town at the time of such census, there shall be added to or subtracted from the population of such district, city or town the number so specified in such certificate. Such town population shall include the population of any incorporated village or villages or parts thereof within such town, but shall exclude the population of any city or part thereof within such town. The determination as to the population of a social services district, city or town for the purposes of this section shall be made by the state comptroller as provided by section fifty-four of the state finance law.

Soc. Serv. L. § 154 was **repealed** by Laws 1969, Ch. 184, eff. July 1, 1969; however subd. (3) was **amended** by Laws 1969, Ch. 348, eff. July 1, 1969 and by Laws 1971, Ch. 947, eff. July 1, 1971, without reference to the prior repeal; **amended** by Laws 1961, Ch. 592; **added** by Laws 1953, Ch. 562; Laws 1971, Ch. 947, eff. July 1, 1971.

TITLE 3—HOME RELIEF

————

(Repealed and transferred sections noted under appropriate section number of text.)

Formerly Title 2 renumbered 3, and former Title 3 renumbered 4, by Laws 1966, Ch. 266, eff. Apr. 30, 1966.

§ 157. Definitions.

As used in this title.

1. Safety net assistance means allowances pursuant to section one hundred thirty-one-a for all support, maintenance and need, and costs of suitable training in a trade to enable a person to become self-supporting, furnished eligible needy persons in accordance with applicable provisions of law, by a municipal corporation, or a town where safety net assistance is a town charge, to persons or their dependents in their abode or habitation whenever possible and includes such relief granted to veterans under existing laws but does not include hospital or institutional care, except as otherwise provided in this subdivision, or family assistance or medical assistance for needy persons granted under titles ten and

eleven, respectively, or aid to persons receiving federal supplemental security income payments and/or additional state payments. Safety net assistance may also be provided in a family home or boarding home, operated in compliance with the regulations of the department, and on and after January first, nineteen hundred seventy-four, in facilities in which a person is receiving family care or residential care, as those terms are used in title six of article five of this chapter, and to persons receiving care in a facility supervised by the Office of Alcoholism and Substance Abuse or in a residential facility for the mentally disabled approved, licensed or operated by the office of mental health or the office of mental retardation and developmental disabilities, other than those facilities defined in sections 7.17 and 13.17 of the mental hygiene law or residential care centers for adults operated by the office of mental health, when such type of care is deemed necessary. Payments to such homes and facilities for care and maintenance provided by them shall be at rates established pursuant to law and regulations of the department. The department, however, shall not establish rates of payment to such homes or facilities without approval of the director of the budget.

2. State aid means payments to a municipal corporation by the state for home relief furnished in accordance with this title.

3. Municipal corporation shall mean a county or city except a county wholly within a city.

Amended by Laws 1951, Ch. 77; Laws 1965, Ch. 143; Laws 1966, Ch. 256; Laws 1969, Ch. 184; Laws 1970, Ch. 743; Laws 1971, Ch. 110; **amended** by Laws 1974, Chs. 922, 1080, both eff. Jan. 1, 1974; Laws 1975, Ch. 667, eff. Apr. 1, 1975; **amended** by Laws 1978, Ch. 555, § 4, eff. July 24, 1978; **amended** by Laws 1985, Ch. 351, eff. July 1, 1985; **amended** by Laws 1986, Ch. 468, eff. July 21, 1986; **amended** by Laws 1997, Ch. 436, § 1 Part B, § 43, eff. Aug. 20, 1997.

§ 158.   Eligibility.

1. A person is eligible for safety net assistance who is financially needy as determined in accordance with title one of this article and the regulations promulgated thereunder, is not in sanction status for a program authorized by this chapter and:

(a) resides in a family which is ineligible for family assistance or other assistance funded by the federal temporary assistance for needy families block grant because an adult in the family has exceeded the maximum durational limits on such assistance contained in section three hundred fifty of this chapter, or

(b) is an adult who would otherwise be eligible for family assistance except that he or she does not reside with a dependent child, or

(c) resides in a family that would otherwise be eligible for family assistance except that at least one adult or minor head of household has been determined in accordance with section one hundred thirty-two of this article to be abusing illegal substances or engaging in the habitual and excessive consumption of alcoholic beverages, or

(d)   is under the age of eighteen, not living with his or her child and has no adult relatives with whom to reside, or

(e)   resides in a family in which a person required to submit to screening or evaluation for use of illegal drugs or excess alcohol consumption pursuant to section one hundred thirty-two of this article refused to comply, or

(f)   resides in a family which includes a person disqualified from receiving assistance pursuant to paragraph (f) of subdivision four of section one hundred thirty-two of this article, or

(g)   is a qualified alien who is ineligible to receive assistance funded under the temporary assistance for needy families block grant solely because of section four hundred three of the federal personal responsibility and work opportunity reconciliation act of 1996 (P.L. 104-193) or is an alien who is permanently residing under color of law but is not a qualified alien.

2.   A person who shall be eligible for family assistance according to the provisions of title ten of this article shall be granted family assistance and while receiving such aid shall not be eligible for safety net assistance. A person who is receiving federal supplemental security income payments and/or additional state payments shall not be eligible for safety net assistance. A person who is eligible for refugee cash assistance pursuant to the plan established pursuant to section three hundred fifty-eight of this article shall not be eligible for safety net assistance. An applicant for or recipient of safety net assistance shall be required, as a condition of eligibility for safety net assistance, to sign a written authorization allowing the secretary of the federal department of health and human services to pay to the social services district his or her initial supplemental security income payment and allowing the social services district to deduct from his or her initial payment the amount of safety net assistance granted for any month for which he or she subsequently is determined eligible to receive supplemental security income benefits. For the purposes of this subdivision the term "initial payment" shall refer to the first payment of supplemental security income benefits after a person files an application for benefits or after a person who has been terminated or suspended from eligibility for supplemental security income benefits subsequently has been found eligible for such benefits. An applicant for safety net assistance who reasonably appears to meet the criteria for eligibility for federal supplemental security income payments shall also be required, as a condition of eligibility for safety net assistance, to apply for such payments and shall, if otherwise eligible therefor, be eligible for safety net assistance until he or she has received a federal supplemental security income payment. Further, if an applicant for safety net assistance is required to apply for federal supplemental security payments and is denied, such person shall, subject to department regulation, also be required as a condition of eligibility to appeal his or her denial and exhaust his or her administrative remedies; such person shall remain eligible for safety net assistance, so long as he or she otherwise remains eligible while his or her appeal is pending.

SSL

3. A person shall not be eligible for safety net assistance who has made a voluntary assignment or transfer of property for the purpose of qualifying for such aid. A transfer of property made within one year of the date of application shall be presumed to have been made for the purpose of qualifying for such assistance.

4. Social services officials shall determine eligibility for safety net assistance within forty-five days of receiving an application for safety net assistance. Such officials shall notify applicants of safety net assistance about the availability of assistance to meet emergency circumstances or to prevent eviction.

5. Application for or receipt of safety net assistance shall operate as an assignment to the state and the social services district concerned of any rights to support from any other person as such applicant or recipient may have on their own behalf or on behalf of any other family member for whom the applicant or recipient is applying for or receiving assistance. Applicants for or recipients of safety net assistance shall be informed that such application for or receipt of such benefits will constitute such an assignment. Such assignment shall terminate with respect to current support rights upon a determination by the social services district that such person is no longer eligible for safety net assistance, except with respect to the amount of any unpaid support obligation that has accrued.

6. In addition to other eligibility requirements, each person who is applying for or receiving assistance under this title, and who is otherwise eligible for assistance under this title, shall be required, as a further condition of eligibility for such assistance:

(i) to assign to the state and the social services district any rights to support such person may have either on his own behalf or on behalf of any other family member for whom he is applying for or receiving aid; and

(ii) to cooperate with the state and the social services official, in accordance with standards established by regulations of the department consistent with federal law and regulations, in establishing the paternity of a child born out-of-wedlock for whom assistance under this title is being applied for or received, in their efforts to locate any absent parent and in obtaining support payments or any other payments or property due such person and due each child for whom assistance under this title is being applied for or received, except that an applicant or recipient shall not be required to cooperate in such efforts in cases in which the social services official has determined, in accordance with criteria, including the best interests of the child, as established by regulations of the department consistent with federal law and regulations, that such applicant or recipient has good cause to refuse to cooperate. Each social services district shall inform applicants for and recipients of safety net assistance required to cooperate with the state and local social services officials pursuant to the provisions of this paragraph, that where a proceeding to establish paternity has been filed, and the allegation of paternity has been denied by the respondent, there shall be a stay of all paternity proceedings and related social services district proceedings until sixty days after the birth of the child. Such applicants and recipients shall also be informed that public assistance and care shall not be denied during a stay on the basis of refusal to cooperate pursuant to the provisions of this paragraph.

7. As a condition of eligibility for the receipt of safety net assistance, every applicant for such assistance must:

(i) sign an agreement which provides that, if it is determined that money is owed to the social services district because of overpayments of safety net assistance to the applicant while a recipient of safety net assistance, the applicant agrees to repay any such money that remains due after the applicant ceases to receive safety net assistance; and

(ii) sign an assignment of future earnings on a form prescribed by the department to secure the repayment of any money that is determined, after providing the opportunity for a fair hearing in accordance with section twenty-two of this chapter, to be owed to the social services district because of overpayments of safety net assistance to the applicant while a recipient of safety net assistance. The prescribed form shall include the following notice: "THIS AGREEMENT AUTHORIZES THE SOCIAL SERVICES DISTRICT TO RECOVER ANY OVERPAYMENT OF YOUR PUBLIC ASSISTANCE BENEFITS BY COLLECTING THE AMOUNT OF THE OVERPAYMENT DIRECTLY FROM YOUR FUTURE WAGES. IF YOU FAIL TO MAKE THE PAYMENTS REQUIRED BY A REPAYMENT AGREEMENT BETWEEN YOU AND THE SOCIAL SERVICES DISTRICT, THE SOCIAL SERVICES DISTRICT WILL FILE THIS AGREEMENT WITH YOUR EMPLOYER AND RECOVER THE OVERPAYMENT DIRECTLY FROM YOUR WAGES." In addition, the assignment of future earnings and the enforcement thereof must comply with all requirements of article three-A of the personal property law. The social services district may file the assignment of future earnings with the employer of the assignor only if the assignor fails to make payments of money owed to the social services district in accordance with the agreement required in paragraph (i) of this subdivision.

8. No person who resides with his or her minor child shall be eligible for safety net assistance except as provided in subdivision one of this section.

Amended by Laws 1961, Ch. 802; **amended** by Laws 1966, Ch. 256, eff. Apr. 30, 1966; Laws 1971, Ch. 539; **amended** by Laws 1974, Ch. 1080, eff. Jan. 1, 1974; **amended** by Laws 1975, Ch. 198, eff. June 10, 1975; **amended** by Laws 1976, Ch. 76, eff. May 15, 1976; **amended** by Laws 1977, Ch. 77, eff. Apr. 1, 1977; **amended** by Laws 1981, Ch. 433, eff. Sept. 7, 1981; **amended** by Laws 1989, Ch. 72, § 1, eff. Apr. 27, 1989; **amended** by Laws 1992, Ch. 41, §§ 126, 127, eff. Apr. 2, 1992; Laws 1992, Ch. 41, § 135 (adding subd. (f)), eff. Apr. 2, 1992 until July 1, 1994; **amended** by Laws 1995, Ch. 81, §§ 161, 184, eff. July 1, 1995; **amended** by Laws 1997, Ch. 436, § 1 Part B, § 44, eff. Jan. 1, 1998; **amended** by Laws 1998, Ch. 214, § 15-c, and § 28, eff. July 7, 1998, deemed in full force and effect Aug. 20, 1997, changing effective date of section from Jan. 1, 1998 to Nov. 11, 1997.

SSL

§ 158-a.   Alcoholism and drug abuse rehabilitative services.

Repealed by Laws 1997, Ch. 436, § 1 Part B, § 45, eff. Aug. 20, 1997.

§ 158-b.   Mandatory job search activities for certain employable recipients of home relief.

Repealed by Laws 1997, Ch. 436, § 1 Part B, § 46, eff. Aug. 20, 1997.

§ 159   Safety net assistance.

1.   Safety net assistance shall be provided in amounts determined in accordance with article five and, where applicable, section one hundred seventeen of this chapter in the following manner.

(a)   Cash assistance. Safety net assistance shall be granted in cash provided, however, that where the granting of cash may be deemed inappropriate by the social services district because of an inability to manage funds, or because less expensive or more easily controlled alternative methods of payment are available, or in the case of vendor payments to landlords made for individuals residing in public housing or for similar other reasons as established by department regulations, or where an individual has so requested, safety net assistance may be granted in whole or in part by restricted payment.

(b)   Non-cash assistance. Safety net assistance paid as non-cash assistance shall be paid in the following manner and in the following order:

(i)   Shelter assistance. A district shall make a payment for shelter by direct payment, two-party check or other form of restricted payment up to the maximum amount established by the department in regulation, provided that a district may make a payment for a recipient's assistance in excess of such maximum at the request of the recipient. Payments for shelter pursuant to this subparagraph shall be subject to the provisions of section one hundred forty-three-b of this chapter. A district shall make payment for shelter by two-party check upon request of the recipient; provided, however, that the district may make a direct payment whenever it finds that the recipient has persistently failed to make payment for rent without good cause as defined by regulations of the department. A district shall provide a recipient with proof of payment promptly upon request by the recipient.

(ii)   Utility assistance. A social services district shall make a direct payment, a payment by two party check or other form of restricted payment on behalf of recipients of safety net assistance who pay separately for utilities. Payment for utilities shall include payment for fuel for heating on behalf of recipients who are eligible for a fuel for heating allowance pursuant to section one hundred thirty-one-a of this article and the department's regulations. Payments for fuel for heating shall not exceed the fuel for heating allowance except that a district may make a payment in excess of such amount at the request of the recipient. A district shall provide a recipient with proof of payment promptly upon request by the recipient.

(iii) Personal needs allowance. To the extent available within payment amounts authorized by sections one hundred seventeen, where applicable, and one hundred thirty-one-a of this chapter, a social services district shall provide each household with a personal needs allowance equal to twenty percent of the sum of the monthly standard of payment determined in accordance with the schedule contained in paragraph (a) of subdivision three of section one hundred thirty-one-a of this article and the appropriate amount of home energy grant and supplemental home energy grant as determined by the schedules in subdivisions three-c and three-d of section one hundred thirty-one-a of this article, for the appropriate household size.

(iv) Other assistance. The remainder of the safety net assistance shall be provided on a non-cash basis, provided that an appropriate electronic benefit transfer system is operating in accordance with section twenty-one-a of this chapter in the social services district in which the recipient resides.

2. Persons eligible for safety net assistance because they are persons described in paragraph (b) or (d) of subdivision one of section one hundred fifty-eight of this title shall receive cash assistance, as defined in subdivision one of this section, for two years in a lifetime, whether or not consecutive, after the fourth day of August, nineteen hundred ninety-seven. On or after the first day of December, nineteen hundred ninety-nine, persons who are eligible for safety net assistance but who have received cash assistance for two years or more shall receive assistance only in the form of non-cash assistance. A person may receive cash assistance in excess of two years if the person is otherwise eligible for safety net assistance but the social services district in which the person resides has not yet implemented a non-cash assistance program. Persons who would otherwise be eligible for cash assistance pursuant to this subdivision who are referred to treatment pursuant to section one hundred thirty-two of this article or reside in a family where an adult or head of household has been referred to treatment shall receive assistance in the form of non-cash assistance.

3. Persons eligible for safety net assistance because they are persons described in paragraph (a) of subdivision one of section one hundred fifty-eight of this title shall receive assistance in the form of non-cash assistance.

4. Persons eligible for safety net assistance because they are persons described in paragraphs (c), (e) and (f) of subdivision one of section one hundred fifty-eight of this title shall receive assistance in the form of non-cash assistance.

5. Persons eligible for safety net assistance because they are persons described in paragraph (g) of subdivision one of section one hundred fifty-eight of this title shall receive cash assistance in the safety net program for two years in a lifetime, whether or not consecutive, after the fourth day of August, nineteen hundred ninety-seven. On or after the first day of December, nineteen hundred ninety-nine, persons who are eligible for safety net assistance but have received cash assistance for two years or more in the safety net program shall receive assistance only in the form of non-cash assistance. A person may receive cash

assistance in excess of two years if the person is otherwise eligible for safety net assistance but the social services district in which the person resides has not implemented a non-cash program.

6. In calculating the period of cash assistance for new residents of the state, periods in which they received reduced safety net assistance benefits pursuant to section one hundred seventeen of this chapter shall be included. In calculating the period of cash assistance, periods in which a recipient received federally funded refugee assistance shall be included.

7. (a) Notwithstanding subdivisions two and three of this section, adults eligible for safety net assistance who are exempt from the employment require-ments contained in title nine-B of this article pursuant to section three hundred thirty-two of such article shall receive cash assistance, unless the adult has been determined to be abusing illegal substances or engaged in habitual consumption of alcohol.

(b) Notwithstanding subdivisions two and three of this section, adults eligible for safety net assistance who are also eligible to receive comprehensive health care services through a special needs plan defined in paragraph (n) of subdivision one of section three hundred sixty-four-j of this chapter shall receive cash assistance, regardless of whether such a plan is operating in the district in which they reside. An adult who would be eligible to receive such services through such a special needs plan but for the application of paragraph (d) of subdivision three of section three hundred sixty-four-j of this chapter shall also receive cash assistance.

8. Social services districts shall provide non-cash assistance to persons eligible for safety net assistance because they are persons described in paragraphs (b) and (d) of subdivision one of section one hundred fifty-eight of this title, who have received cash assistance for two years or more, on or after the first day of December, nineteen hundred ninety-nine. Social services districts shall provide non-cash assistance for persons described in paragraph (a) of subdivision one of section one hundred fifty-eight of this title on or after the first day of December, two thousand. However, social services districts shall not implement subpara-graph (iv) of paragraph (b) of subdivision one of this section until an appropriate electronic benefit transfer system is operating in the district.

9. Notwithstanding subdivision eight of this section or any other inconsistent provision of this section, the department may approve up to five social services districts to provide non-cash assistance to persons described in paragraphs (b), (d) and (g) of subdivision one of section one hundred fifty-eight of this title who have received cash assistance for two years, beginning the first day of December, nineteen hundred ninety-eight, provided that an appropriate electronic benefit transfer system is operating in the district.

10. Social services district providing safety net assistance to persons receiving care as defined in paragraphs (c), (d) and (e) of subdivision three of section two hundred nine of the social services law shall pay such facility at the

rate provided for care and maintenance under the supplemental security income program for beneficiaries of that program in the same facility, less the amount of any personal needs allowance included in the supplemental security program. In addition, social services districts shall provide such persons receiving safety net assistance with a personal needs allowance in the amount included in the supplemental security payment level as a personal needs allowance for recipients of that program residing in the particular facility.

11.   The provisions of section three hundred forty-nine-a of this article, with respect to victims of domestic violence, shall apply to applicants for and recipients of safety net assistance to the same extent as it applies to applicants for and recipients of family assistance.

12.   To the extent allowable under federal law and to the extent that the state has spending sufficient to exceed the federally required maintenance of effort for the temporary assistance for needy families block grant, the office of temporary and disability assistance may maximize the state's work participation rate by targeting safety net assistance payments utilized to meet the federally required maintenance of effort for the temporary assistance for needy families block grant to safety net assistance cases that are not exempt from work activities, that have not been in sanction status for over three months, and that do not include two parents who are eligible for assistance who live in the same dwelling unit, or to other categories of cases, as defined by the office of temporary and disability assistance, that have no other potential impediments to participating in countable federal work activities.

Amended by Laws 1945, Ch. 128; **amended** by Laws 1966, Ch. 256, eff. Apr. 30, 1966; **amended** by Laws 1977, Ch. 77, eff. Apr. 1, 1977; **amended** by Laws 1992, Ch. 41, § 134, eff. Apr. 2, 1992; **amended** by Laws 1997, Ch. 436, § 1 Part B, § 46-a, eff. Aug. 20, 1997; **amended** by Laws 1998, Ch. 214, §§ 15-a and 15-b eff. July 7, 1998, deemed in full force and effect Aug. 20, 1997; L. 2005, Ch. 713, sect; 3, eff. Jan. 1, 2006; Laws 2006, ch. 58, §4 (Part J), eff. Oct 1, 2006.

§ 159-a.   Training in a trade or occupation.

Repealed by Laws 1990, Ch. 453, § 6, eff. Oct. 1, 1990.

§ 159-b.   Income exemptions.

Repealed by Laws 1990, Ch. 453, § 6, eff. Oct. 1, 1990.

§ 160.   State reimbursement for home relief.

Repealed by Laws 1953, Ch. 562, eff. Jan. 1, 1954.

§ 160-a.   Unexpended welfare balances.

1.   Notwithstanding the provisions of any general special or local law, where a city is no longer responsible for the cost of public assistance or care or any

SSL

form thereof as provided by sections seventy-two and seventy-three of this chapter or operates under option III pursuant to section seventy-four-a of this chapter, any unexpended city welfare funds not due and owing to the state or to a social services district which shall remain in the treasury of such city on the first day of January of any year may be transferred, appropriated and expended for any lawful city purpose.

2. Notwithstanding the provisions of any general or special law, where a town is no longer responsible for the cost of any type of public assistance or care, any unexpended town welfare funds which shall remain in the hands of the supervisor or any other town officer on the first day of January of any year and which are not due and owing to the state or to a public welfare district may be transferred, appropriated and expended for any lawful town purpose.

Added by Laws 1947, Ch. 524; **amended** by Laws 1977, Ch. 863, eff. Aug. 11, 1977.

§ 161. Discretionary fund; additional grants and advances.

Repealed by Laws 1953, Ch. 562, eff. Jan. 1, 1954.

§ 162. Employment furnished by towns.

Repealed by Laws 1990, Ch. 453, § 6, eff. Oct. 1, 1990.

§ 163. Application.

The provisions of any city charter or other local or special law forbidding the granting of outdoor relief shall not apply to the granting of home relief under this chapter.

§ 164. Work relief.

Repealed by Laws 1997, Ch. 436, § 1 Part B, § 14, eff. Aug. 20, 1997.

§ 164-a. Supported employment opportunities in home relief.

Repealed by Laws 1990, Ch. 453, § 6, eff. Oct. 1, 1990.

§ 164-b. On-the-job training opportunities in home relief.

Repealed by Laws 1990, Ch. 453, § 6, eff. Oct. 1, 1990.

§ 164-c. Employment opportunities; job clubs.

Repealed by Laws 1990, Ch. 453, § 6, eff. Oct. 1, 1990.

§ 165. Relief recipients authorized to work.

Repealed by Laws 1997, Ch. 436, § 1 Part B, § 77, eff. Aug. 20, 1997.

Editor's Note: A new § 165 follows.

§ 165. Recipients authorized to work.

Notwithstanding any other provision of law, a social services official may, in his or her discretion, authorize a recipient of safety net assistance to work and retain the income derived therefrom without any diminution or with partial diminution of safety net assistance where such an arrangement would, in his or her opinion, lead to elimination of the recipient from the assistance rolls in a reasonable length of time. The commissioner shall promulgate rules and regulations to effectuate the purpose of this section.

Added by Laws 1998, Ch. 214, § 27, eff. Aug. 20, 1997.

§ 166. Job opportunity demonstration program.

Repealed by Laws 1990, Ch. 453, § 6, eff. Oct. 1, 1990.

TITLE 4—VETERAN ASSISTANCE

———

(Repealed and transferred sections noted under appropriate section number of text.)

Formerly Title 3, renumbered 4, and former Title 4, repealed by Laws 1966, Ch. 256, eff. Apr. 30, 1966.

SSL

§ 168. Definitions.

As used in this title:

1. Veteran means a person, male or female, who has served in the armed forces of the United States in time of war, or who was a recipient of the armed forces expeditionary medal, Navy expeditionary medal or Marine Corps expeditionary medal for participation in operations in Lebanon from June first, nineteen hundred eighty-three to December first, nineteen hundred eighty-seven, in Grenada from October twenty-third, nineteen hundred eighty-three to November twenty-first, nineteen hundred eighty-three, or in Panama from December twentieth, nineteen hundred eighty-nine to January thirty-first, nineteen hundred ninety, and who has been honorably discharged or released under honorable circumstances from such service or furloughed to the reserve.

2. In time of war means the periods herein set forth for the following wars and conflicts:

(1) Civil War: from the twentieth day of April, eighteen hundred sixty-one to and including the ninth day of April, eighteen hundred sixty-five.

(2) Spanish-American War: from the twenty-first day of April, eighteen hundred ninety-eight to and including the eleventh day of April, eighteen hundred ninety-nine.

(3) Philippine Insurrection: from the eleventh day of April, eighteen hundred ninety-nine to and including the fourth day of July, nineteen hundred two.

(4) World War I: from the sixth day of April, nineteen hundred seventeen to and including the eleventh day of November, nineteen hundred eighteen.

(5) World War II: from the seventh day of December, nineteen hundred forty-one to and including the thirty-first day of December, nineteen hundred forty-six, or who was employed by the War Shipping Administration or Office of Defense Transportation or their agents as a merchant seaman documented by the United States Coast Guard or Department of Commerce, or as a civil servant employed by the United States Army Transport Service (later redesignated as the United States Army Transportation Corps, Water Division) or the Naval Transportation Service; and who served satisfactorily as a crew member during the period of armed conflict, December seventh, nineteen hundred forty-one, to August fifteenth, nineteen hundred forty-five, aboard merchant vessels in oceangoing, i.e., foreign, intercoastal, or coastwise service as such terms are defined under federal law (46 USCA 10301 & 10501) and further to include 'near foreign' voyages between the United States and Canada, Mexico, or the West Indies via ocean routes, or public vessels in oceangoing service or foreign waters and who has received a Certificate of Release or Discharge from Active Duty and a discharge certificate, or an Honorable Service Certificate/Report of Casualty, from the Department of Defense or who served as a united states civilian employed by the American field service and served overseas under united states armies and United states army groups in world war ii during the period of armed conflict,

December seventh, nineteen hundred forty-one through May eighth, nineteen hundred forty-five, and who was discharged or released therefrom under honorable conditions, or who served as a United States civilian flight crew and aviation ground support employee of Pan American World Airways or one of its subsidiaries or its affiliates and served overseas as a result of Pan-American's contract with air transport command or naval air transport service during the period of armed conflict, December fourteenth, nineteen hundred forty-one through August fourteenth nineteen hundred forty-five, and who was discharged or released therefrom under honorable conditions.

(6) Korean Conflict: from the twenty-seventh day of June, nineteen hundred fifty to and including the thirty-first day of January, nineteen hundred fifty-five.

(7) Viet Nam conflict; from the twenty-eighth day of February, nineteen hundred sixty-one to and including the seventh day of May, nineteen hundred seventy-five.

(8) Persian Gulf Conflict: from the second day of August, nineteen hundred ninety to and including the end of such conflict.

3. Veteran organization means the:

(a) Grand Army of the Republic;

(b) United Spanish War Veterans;

(c) American Legion;

(d) Disabled American Veterans;

(e) Veterans of Foreign Wars of the United States;

(f) Jewish War Veterans of the United States, Inc.;

(g) Catholic War Veterans, Inc.;

(h) Army and Navy Union of the United States;

(i) Italian-American War Veterans of the United States, Inc.;

(j) Polish Legion of American Veterans, Inc.;

(k) The Marine Corps League;

(l) Military Order of the Purple Heart, Inc.;

(m) Amvets;

(n) American Veterans of World War II;

(o) Veterans of World War I, U.S.A., Inc.;

(p) Polish-American Veterans of World War II;

(q) Masonic War Veterans of the State of N.Y., Inc.;

(r) American Gold Star Mothers, Inc.;

(s) Regular Veterans Association, Inc.;

(t) Vietnam Veterans of America;

SSL

(u)   Eastern Paralyzed Veterans Association;

4.   Veteran assistance means safety net assistance given pursuant to the provisions of this title, to the persons eligible therefor.

Added by Laws 1948, Ch. 871; **amended** by Laws 1951, Ch. 664; Laws 1955, Ch. 162; Laws 1959, Ch. 643; Laws 1960, Ch. 610; Laws 1962, Ch. 69; Laws 1966, Ch. 256; Laws 1970, Ch. 837; Laws 1971, Ch. 875, eff. June 25, 1971; Laws of 1972, Ch. 49; **amended** by Laws 1973, Ch. 694, eff. June 11, 1973; **amended** by Laws 1983, Ch. 219, eff. Sept. 1, 1983; **amended** by Laws 1991, Ch. 467, § 17, eff. July 19, 1991; **amended** by Laws 1991, Ch. 685, § 12, eff. Aug. 2, 1991; **amended** by Laws 1993, Ch. 270, § 8, eff. July 21, 1993; **amended** by Laws 1995, Ch. 616, § 11, eff. Aug. 8, 1995; **amended** by Laws 1997, Ch. 436, § 1 Part B, § 78, eff. Aug. 20, 1997; Laws 2006, ch. 179, §8, eff. July 26, 2006.

§ 169.   Eligibility.

Each of the following persons who is a resident of the state on the date of making application for veteran assistance shall be eligible for such assistance if he or she is unable to provide for himself or herself, or is unable to secure support from a legally responsible relative, and is not receiving needed assistance or care under other provisions of this chapter, or from other sources:

1.   A veteran;

2.   The wife, husband, child or grandchild under the age of twenty-one years, father, mother, stepfather or stepmother of a veteran, if living with the veteran;

3.   The unremarried surviving spouse of a veteran;

4.   The dependent children under the age of twenty-one years or the incapacitated children of a deceased veteran.

Added by Laws 1948, Ch. 871; **amended** by Laws 1974, Ch. 909, eff. Sept. 1, 1974; **amended** by Laws 1976, Ch. 63, eff. Sept. 1, 1976.

§ 170.   Character.

Except as hereinafter otherwise prescribed, veteran assistance shall be granted in cash provided, however, that in an individual case where the granting of cash may be deemed impracticable, veteran assistance may be granted in whole or in part by order.

Added by Laws 1948, Ch. 871; **amended** by Laws 1966, Ch. 256, eff. Apr. 30, 1966.

§ 171.   Responsibility; county social services districts; city social services districts; cities; towns.

1.   A county social services district which has elected, pursuant to the provisions of this title, to administer veteran assistance shall be responsible for providing veteran assistance, and the expense thereof, to:

(a)   persons residing or found therein, subject to reimbursement by the state;

(b)   persons residing or found in any town in the county, when the expense of providing safety net assistance to persons residing or found in such towns is a county charge pursuant to the provisions of section seventy-two and section seventy-three of this chapter;

(c)   persons residing or found in a city forming part of the county social services district, when the expense of providing safety net assistance to persons residing or found in such city is a county charge pursuant to the provisions of section seventy-two and section seventy-three of this chapter.

2.   A town responsible for the expense of providing safety net assistance to persons residing or found therein, pursuant to section sixty-nine, which has elected to administer veteran assistance, pursuant to the provisions of this title, shall be responsible for providing veteran assistance to local charges residing or found therein, and the expense thereof.

Added by Laws 1948, Ch. 871; **amended** by Laws 1966, Ch. 256; **amended** by Laws 1977, Ch. 863, eff. Aug. 11, 1977; **amended** by Laws 1997, Ch. 436, § 1 Part B, § 79, eff. Aug. 20, 1997.

§ 172.   Moneys to be provided.

1.   The social services official of every county, city or town responsible for veteran assistance, under the provisions of this title, shall include in his or her annual estimate for safety net assistance the amount necessary to carry out the provisions of this title in such county, city or town.

2.   Legislative bodies shall make appropriations and raise money for veteran assistance in the same manner as for safety net assistance.

Added by Laws 1948, Ch. 871, eff. Apr. 12, 1948; **amended** by Laws 1997, Ch. 436, § 1 Part B, § 80, eff. Aug. 20, 1997; **amended** by Laws 1997, Ch. 436, § 1 Part B, § 80, eff. Aug. 20, 1997.

§ 173.   Election to administer veteran assistance by county public welfare district; organization.

1.   When a majority of the veteran organizations in a county, by and through their respective county divisions, file with the clerk of the board of the supervisors of the county, a petition addressed to the board of supervisors of the country requesting that veteran assistance be administered by such county, the board of supervisors may, by resolution passed by a majority vote, establish a division or bureau, or direct that a division or bureau be established, within the county department of public welfare, and under the direction of the county commissioner of public welfare, for the purpose of administering veteran assistance.

2.   In the event that the county board of supervisors shall pass such a resolution, it shall also authorize and direct the county commissioner of public

welfare to appoint a veteran, as herein defined, as deputy commissioner or director of the veteran assistance division or bureau, as the case may be.

3. The county commissioner shall transfer to the veteran assistance division or bureau so much of the staff of the county welfare department as may be necessary or practicable to administer and execute the functions, powers and duties assigned to such division or bureau. Officers and employees shall be transferred without further examination or qualification and they shall retain their respective civil service classification and status. The civil service qualifications for all positions in the veteran assistance division or bureau shall be the same as required for the same or similar positions in the other divisions or bureaus of the county department of welfare, except that the qualifications for the position of the deputy commissioner or director, as the case may be, shall also require that he be a veteran.

4. The salaries or compensation paid to employees of the veteran assistance division or bureau shall be subject to reimbursement by the state under the same terms and conditions as are applicable to other employees of the county department of public welfare under the provisions of this chapter.

5. Upon recommendation of the county commissioner of public welfare, the county board of supervisors may authorize, by resolution passed by a majority vote, the veteran assistance division or bureau to administer, in addition to veteran assistance, such other forms or categories of public assistance and care as may be practicable or necessary, provided that sufficient qualified staff shall be available for transfer or assignment to the veteran assistance division or bureau to execute and perform the additional functions and duties so assigned to such division or bureau.

6. The board of supervisors may also authorize the commissioner of public welfare to establish and operate a branch of the veteran assistance division or bureau in each or any major population center in the county.

Added by Laws 1948, Ch. 871; amended by Laws 1965, Ch. 1071, eff. Jan. 1, 1966.

§ 174. Election to administer veteran assistance by city public welfare district; organization.

Repealed by Laws 1977, Ch. 863, eff. Apr. 1, 1978.

§ 174-a. Election to administer veteran assistance by cities under options IV or V; organization.

Repealed by Laws 1977, Ch. 863, eff. Aug. 11, 1977.

§ 174-b. Authorization of veteran assistance in towns.

1. The town board of a town responsible for the expense of providing safety net assistance to persons residing or found therein, upon the presentation of a

petition to it by one or more posts, camps or garrisons of one or more veteran organizations in the town, requesting that veteran assistance be authorized by the local social services officer, may, by resolution adopted by majority vote, authorize and direct the local social services officer to authorize and furnish veteran assistance to persons residing or found therein. Thereafter, the local social services officer shall have, exercise and perform the same powers and duties with relation to veteran assistance as he has, exercises and performs with relation to safety net assistance.

2.   When the town board of a town has authorized and directed the local social services officer to authorize and furnish veteran assistance, if neither the local social services officer, or the supervisor of the town authorized to act as such official, nor the assistant local social services officer, if there be one, is a veteran, as herein defined, the town board may appoint, or authorize the local social services officer to appoint, a veteran, as herein defined, as a deputy or assistant local social service officer.

Added by Laws 1948, Ch. 871; **amended** by Laws 1966, Ch. 256, eff. Apr. 30, 1966; **amended** by Laws 1997, Ch. 436, § 1 Part B, § 81, eff. Aug. 20, 1997.

§ 175.   Administration of veteran assistance in New York city.

1.   In the city of New York, veteran assistance committee means each welfare committee chosen by the county unit of each veteran organization.

2.   In the city of New York, veteran assistance shall be paid or granted direct to the beneficiaries by the commissioner of public welfare through the veterans division of the department of public welfare on a written recommendation signed by three members of the veteran assistance committee of the county in which the applicant resides.

3.   The comptroller of the city of New York shall, out of the amount appropriated for such assistance, provide a cash fund to be placed under the control of the commissioner from which to pay such assistance, and he shall replenish said fund upon presentation of properly receipted recommendations by the county veteran assistance committees for the amounts paid out of said fund.

Amended by Laws 1942, Ch. 526, eff. July 1, 1942.

§ 176.   Veteran advisory committees; duties.

1.   (a) In every county, city or town which has elected to furnish veteran assistance, pursuant to the provisions of this title, in which there are more than one veteran organization or more than one post, camp or garrison of any veteran organization, there shall be appointed and constituted a joint veteran assistance advisory committee to consist of one representative from each post, camp and garrison of each such veteran organization, chosen in such manner as the post, camp or garrison shall direct, to serve for one year, commencing the first day of January. Each such committee shall choose a chairman and such other officers

SSL

as it may deem necessary or require. In counties and cities the deputy commissioner or director of the veteran assistance division or bureau of the public welfare department shall serve ex officio as secretary of the committee. In towns, the town welfare officer shall serve ex officio as such secretary, unless he is not a veteran and his deputy or assistant is a veteran, in which case such deputy or assistant, as the case may be, shall serve as such secretary.

(b) In any town which has elected to furnish veteran assistance pursuant to the provisions of this title, in which there is only one veteran organization and only one post, camp or garrison thereof, such post, camp or garrison shall constitute a veterans assistance advisory committee, consisting of its chairman and two other representatives designated by it, which committee shall serve for one year commencing the first day of January. The town welfare officer, his deputy or assistant, if a veteran, shall serve ex officio as the secretary of the committee; if neither be a veteran, the town welfare officer shall serve as such secretary.

2. All committees constituted under subdivision one of this section shall have and perform the following functions and duties:

(a) (1) In the case of county or city committees, to submit to the public welfare official of the county or city in which it operates a list of veterans qualified to serve as deputy commissioner or director of the veterans assistance division or bureau in the county or city department of welfare, as the case may be, whenever there be a vacancy in that office.

(2) In the case of town committees, to submit to the town public welfare officer a list of veterans qualified to serve as his deputy or assistant to furnish veteran assistance, whenever there be a vacancy in that office.

(b) To keep informed all posts, camps or garrisons of each veteran organization in its territory concerning the administration of veteran assistance and the activities of the veteran assistance division or bureau.

(c) To transmit to the veteran assistance division, bureau or official administering veteran assistance in its territory, the views of the veteran organizations operating in such territory.

(d) To advise the public welfare official of the county, city or town administering veteran assistance in its territory on matters relating to assistance and care given to veterans and their families.

Added by Laws 1948, Ch. 871, eff. Apr. 12, 1948.

§ 177.   Care in public homes; consent of veteran or other eligible persons.

Any person eligible for veteran assistance may receive care in a public home with his consent.

Added by Laws 1948, Ch. 871, eff. Apr. 12, 1948.

§ 178.   Veteran assistance financing; state reimbursement.

All provisions of this chapter or of any other law relating to the financing of safety net assistance by counties, cities and towns, or reimbursement by the state for safety net assistance expenditures made by counties, cities and towns, shall apply with the same force and effect to veteran assistance.

Added by Laws 1948, Ch. 871, eff. Apr. 12, 1948; amended by Laws 1997, Ch. 436, § 1 Part B, § 82, eff. Aug. 20, 1997.

§ 184-186.   Medical care.

Repealed by Laws 1966, Ch. 256, Apr. 30, 1966 and subject matter transferred to Social Services Law, Art. 5, Title 11.

§ 186-a—186-c.   Services by public officers—physicians, dentists, funeral directors and proprietors or managers of drug stores or pharmacies.

Repealed by Laws 1964, Ch. 946, eff. Sept. 1, 1964.

§ 186-d.   Care by public officers—operators of family homes for children or proprietary homes for adults.

Repealed by Laws 1965, Ch. 1043, eff. July 1, 1965.

§ 187.   Care in hospitals.

Repealed by Laws 1966, Ch. 256, eff. Apr. 30, 1966 and subject matter transferred to Social Services Law, Art. 5, Title 11.

§ 188.   Care of patients suffering from tuberculosis.

Repealed by Laws 1947, Ch. 899, eff. Apr. 1, 1947, and subject matter transferred to Public Health Law.

TITLE 5—PUBLIC INSTITUTIONAL CARE FOR ADULTS

———

(Repealed and transferred sections noted under appropriate section number of text.)

§ 193. Public homes.

1. Each public welfare district may establish and maintain a public home, which may include an infirmary for the care of chronically sick patients in addition to facilities for the care of acutely ill patients, and may operate a farm in connection therewith, or may contract with another public welfare district for the care and maintenance of persons in need of institutional care who are unable to pay for such care. If facilities are available in a public home the commissioner of public welfare may establish regulations authorizing the admission and care therein of persons in need of institutional care who are able and willing to pay, in whole or in part for such care and prescribing the conditions under which such admissions may be made. A person in need of institutional care who is unable to pay therefor shall not be refused care in the public home operated and maintained by the public welfare district in which he resides or is found, when persons able to pay for their care are receiving care in such home.

2. If the state commissioner of social welfare shall approve, a public welfare district may use a building or buildings formerly used as a tuberculosis hospital or sanatorium, or as a part thereof, for a public home, a public home infirmary or an infirmary of a public home.

Amended by Laws 1948, Ch. 759; amended by Laws 1960, Ch. 98; amended by Laws 1964, Ch. 281, eff. Apr. 3, 1964.

§ 194. Powers and duties of commissioners of public welfare in relation to public homes.

Commissioners of public welfare shall

1. be responsible for the management of the home and for the care of its inmates,

2. have control of the admission and discharge of inmates of the home,

3. within the limits of the appropriations made for the purpose, appoint qualified physicians, matrons, nurses, officers and employees, and vest in them such powers as he may deem necessary for the management of the home,

3-a.   have the authority, in the event the home includes an infirmary for the care of chronically sick patients, to enter into contracts, subject to the written approval of the department, with any medical school or non-profit hospital, organized pursuant to the laws of the state of New York, whereby such medical school or non-profit hospital shall agree to provide and supervise all or part of the professional and related staff necessary for the operation of the infirmary. The personnel so provided by such medical school or non-profit hospital shall not be deemed to be employees of the public welfare district,

4.   purchase all furniture, implements, food, materials and equipment necessary for the upkeep of the home and for the care of the needy in the home, unless such powers have been vested in some other purchasing agency,

5.   classify the inmates of the home, and provide the type of care best fitted to their needs and carry out the recommendations of the attending physician in regard to their care,

6.   establish rules for the administration of the public home and for the conduct and employment of the inmates thereof; but such rules shall not be valid unless approved in writing by the department,

7.   as far as practicable provide suitable employment for any inmate whom the attending physician pronounces able to work, assigning such inmates to such labor in connection with the farm and garden, or the care and upkeep of the buildings or other suitable tasks in the public home as they may be deemed capable of performing, and providing occupational and other diversions as may be for the best interests of the inmates,

8.   when in their individual judgment and discretion it appears advisable, for purposes of rehabilitation, to provide incentive compensation to an inmate, in any amount or amounts totalling ten dollars or less per month, for work assigned and performed in or about the public home, farm and garden; but the payment of any such reward shall not be deemed, for the purposes of any law, to make the inmate receiving the same an employee of the public home or of the county or city maintaining such home,

8-a.   deposit as prescribed in section eighty-seven of this chapter, any and all moneys received by him for the use of a particular inmate or inmates of the public home,

9.   when an appropriation is made for the purpose, appoint a superintendent of the public home who shall reside thereat and exercise such of the powers and carry out such of the duties above mentioned in connection with the public home as the commissioner may direct; provided, however, that the legislative body of the county or city within which a public welfare district is located may, if adequate supervisory personnel are on duty at all times, permit the superintendent to reside off the premises of the public home,

10.   reside at the public home unless a superintendent has been appointed as above provided; provided, however, that the local legislative body of the county

SSL

or city within which a public welfare district is located may, if adequate supervisory personnel are on duty at all times, permit the commissioner to reside off the premises of the public home.

Amended by Laws 1950, Ch. 226; **amended** by Laws 1962, Ch. 805; **amended** by Laws 1967, Ch. 368; **amended** by Laws 1969, Ch. 376, eff. May 9, 1969.

§ 194-a. Additional power of work assignment granted to commissioner of public welfare of Monroe county.

When, pursuant to the provisions of subdivision eight of section one hundred ninety-four of this chapter, the commissioner of public welfare of Monroe county deems it advisable to assign work to an inmate, such work may be assigned and performed in or about not only the public home, farm and garden but also any other property maintained under his supervision. The payment of any reward pursuant to such subdivision eight shall not be deemed, for the purposes of any law, to make the inmate receiving the same an employee of the public home or of the county or city maintaining such home or such other property maintained under the commissioner's jurisdiction.

Added by Laws 1961, Ch. 384, eff. Apr. 6, 1961.

§ 195. Medical care.

1. Each inmate shall be examined by the attending physician or physicians as soon after admission to the public home as practicable.

2. A medical record shall be kept for each inmate, in which shall be recorded his condition on admission, the physician's recommendation of the type of care to be given him and any medical attention given to the inmate subsequent to the examination on admission.

3. The physician shall be responsible for the medical care given inmates who are ill, and shall give such orders as he considers necessary for their welfare. He shall (a) visit the public home at regular intervals and shall re-examine the inmates periodically, as the need of the inmates may require.

(b) also visit the public home, on call of the superintendent, in case of the illness of any inmate,

(c) make such recommendations to the commissioner of public welfare as to changes, improvements and additional equipment as he may deem necessary for the adequate care of the inmates of such home.

4. Any physician who accepts an appointment as attending physician to the inmates of a public home shall be obligated to carry out the provisions of this section. The commissioner may dismiss an attending physician who fails to fulfill such duties.

§ 196. Report on needs of inmates of public homes.

It shall be the duty of the commissioner of public welfare to report to the legislative body as to the needs of the home and to make recommendations of any changes, improvements, additional equipment or other provision which he may consider necessary to provide adequate care for the inmates.

§ 197. Inmates' right of appeal.

Any inmate of a public home, who considers himself to have a cause for complaint against any officer or employee of the public home, shall have the right of appeal to the superintendent of the public home, and to the commissioner of public welfare.

§ 198. Control of inmates.

If any inmate shall wilfully disobey the rules of the home in such a way as to be detrimental to the welfare of the other inmates, the commissioner may institute a proceeding in a court of competent jurisdiction against such inmate for disorderly conduct.

Amended by Laws 1941, Ch. 82, eff. Mar. 1, 1941.

§ 199. Power of commissioner of public welfare to detain certain inmates.

The commissioner of public welfare shall have power to detain in the public home, pending a vacancy for such person in a state institution, a person over the age of sixteen who has been certified as mentally retarded or epileptic in accordance with the provisions of the mental hygiene law and for whom an application for admission to a state institution has been made. Whenever the commissioner shall so detain an inmate in the public home he shall at once notify the state department of mental hygiene.

Amended by Laws 1973, Ch. 195, eff. Apr. 25, 1973.

§ 200. Powers and duties of the commissioner of public welfare in relation to the public farm.

If the legislative body of a public welfare district shall authorize the maintenance of a public farm in connection with the public home, the commissioner of public welfare shall

   1. be responsible for the management of the public farm,

   2. utilize the labor of such of the inmates of the public home as may in the judgment of the attending physician be able to work on the farm,

   3. make all purchases necessary for the operation of the public farm unless such powers have been vested in some other purchasing agency,

4. sell such surplus produce and proceeds of such farm and labor as may remain after the needs of the inmates of the public home have been supplied,

5. employ, within the limits of the appropriation made for the purpose, such laborers as may be necessary for the management of the farm,

6. keep a record of the work of the farm, including the labor of the inmates of the public home on the farm and of the produce and proceeds of the farm supplied for the use of the public home, with the estimated value of such produce and proceeds,

7. when an appropriation has been made for the purpose, appoint an officer who shall be responsible for exercising such of the powers and carrying out such of the duties above mentioned as the commissioner may direct,

8. make an annual report to the legislative body in regard to the receipts and disbursements of the public farm and the cost of its operation.

§ 201. Visitation and inspection of public homes.

Repealed by Laws 1971, Ch. 110, eff. July 1, 1971.

§ 202. Construction and administration of public homes.

1. No building to be used as a public home shall be constructed, or remodeled, in whole or in part, except on plans and designs approved in writing by the department provided that such approval in writing in the city of New York shall be by the mayor of said city, and except that plans and designs for the construction of or remodeling in whole or in part of a public home infirmary, or the infirmary of a public home, shall be approved in accordance with the provisions of article twenty-eight of the public health law.

2. It shall be the duty of the department to send to the legislative body and the public welfare official in charge of a public home a written statement as to any abuses, defects or evils, which it may find in the public home or in the administration thereof, and such legislative body and official shall take action to remedy such condition in accordance with such advice.

Amended by Laws 1964, Ch. 576; **amended** by Laws 1970, Ch. 617, eff. June 1, 1970.

§ 203. Investigation by the board.

Repealed by Laws 1971, Ch. 110, eff. July 1, 1971.

TITLE 6—ADDITIONAL STATE PAYMENTS FOR ELIGIBLE AGED, BLIND AND DISABLED PERSONS

(Repealed and transferred sections noted under appropriate section number of text.)

§ 207. Declaration of purpose.

The legislature hereby declares its commitment to meeting the income needs of aged, blind and disabled persons who are receiving basic supplemental security income benefits or whose income and resources, though above the standard of need for the supplemental security income program, is not sufficient to meet those needs. In order to maintain assistance for such persons at a level consistent with their needs, and in order to fully employ available federal aid for the benefit of such persons residing in this state, there is hereby established a statewide program of additional state payments for aged, blind and disabled persons.

Added by Laws 1974, Ch. 1080, eff. Jan. 1, 1974.

§ 208. Definitions.

When used in this title:

1. "Supplemental security income benefits" shall mean payments made by the secretary of the federal department of health, education and welfare to aged, blind and disabled persons pursuant to title sixteen of the federal social security act.

2. "Additional state payments" shall mean payments made to aged, blind and disabled persons who are receiving, or who would but for their income be eligible to receive, federal supplemental security income benefits, whether made by social services districts in accordance with the provisions of this title and with title sixteen of the federal social security act, or by the secretary of the federal department of health, education and welfare, pursuant to and in accordance with the provisions of this title, title sixteen of the federal social security act, and provisions of any agreement entered into between the state and such secretary by which the secretary agrees to administer such additional state payments on behalf of the state.

3. The "secretary" shall mean the secretary of the federal department of health, education and welfare.

SSL

4. A "blind person" shall mean a person who has central visual acuity of 20/200 or less in the better eye with the use of a correcting lens. An eye which is accompanied by a limitation in the fields of vision such that the widest diameter of the visual field subtends an angle no greater than twenty degrees shall be considered, for the purposes of the first sentence of this subdivision, as having a central visual acuity of 20/200 or less.

5. A "disabled person" shall mean a person who is unable to engage in any substantial gainful activities by reason of any medically determinable physical or mental impairment which can be expected to result in death or which has lasted or can be expected to last for a continuous period of not less than twelve months; or who, in the case of a child under the age of eighteen, suffers from any medically determinable physical or mental impairment of comparable severity.

6. "Countable income" shall mean all of a person's income, in cash or in kind, both earned and unearned, which is not excluded by federal law or regulations or by regulations of the department in determining the need of an individual for supplemental security income benefits or additional state payments, including the income of an individual's eligible spouse, and, if the individual is a child, certain income of such individual's parent or parents with whom he resides.

7. "Earned income" shall mean wages and earnings from self-employment in accordance with the regulations of the department.

8. "Unearned income" shall mean all other income, in accordance with the regulations of the department.

9. "Countable resources" shall mean cash or other liquid assets or any real or personal property that an individual or couple owns and could convert to cash to be used for his or their support and maintenance, which is not excluded by federal law or regulations or by regulations of the department in the determination of the need of an individual for supplemental security income benefits or additional state payments.

10. An "eligible individual" shall mean a person who is eligible to receive additional state payments pursuant to section two hundred nine of this title.

11. An "eligible couple" shall mean an eligible individual and his or her aged, blind or disabled spouse, who are living together or who are living apart but have been living apart for less than six months.

Added by Laws 1974, Ch. 1080, eff. Jan. 1, 1974.

§ 209   Eligibility

1. (a) An individual shall be eligible to receive additional state payments if he:

(i) is over sixty-five years of age, or is blind or disabled; and

(ii) does not have countable income in an amount equal to or greater than the standard of need established in subdivision two of this section; and

(iii) does not have countable resources in an amount equal to or greater than the amount of resources an individual or couple may have and remain eligible for supplemental security income benefits pursuant to federal law and regulations of the department; and

(iv) is a resident of the state and is either a citizen of the United States or is not an alien who is or would be ineligible for federal supplemental security income benefits solely by reason of alien status.

(b) A person who is properly receiving supplemental security income benefits shall be deemed to have met the eligibility criteria contained in subparagraphs (i), (ii) and (iii) of paragraph (a) of this subdivision.

(c) A person who, for the month of December, nineteen hundred seventy-three, properly received a grant of assistance under the state's program of old age assistance, assistance to the blind, aid to the disabled or the combined program of aid to aged, blind and disabled persons, shall be deemed to have met the eligibility criteria of this subdivision; provided, however, that a disabled person who did not also receive such a grant for any month prior to July, nineteen hundred seventy-three, shall not be deemed to have met such eligibility criteria under this paragraph. A person who is deemed eligible under this paragraph shall continue to be deemed to meet the eligibility criteria of this subdivision so long as he continues to be blind or disabled, as the case may be, pursuant to state standards in effect for October, nineteen hundred seventy-two, and so long as he continues to reside in the state.

(d) Any inconsistent provision of this title notwithstanding, an individual shall not be eligible for additional state payments with respect to any month, if throughout such month, (i) he is an inmate of a public institution, or (ii) he is an inmate in a medical facility which is receiving medical assistance payments for him at a level exceeding fifty per cent of the cost of his care, or (iii) he is an inmate in a medical facility which is not certified under the state's medical assistance program. Nor shall an individual be eligible for additional state payments for any month in which he is ineligible for supplemental security income benefits because of a failure to file for other non-public assistance benefits to which he might be entitled, or because of a refusal to participate in treatment for drug addiction or alcoholism or because he has remained outside the United States for all of such month, or because he has refused vocational rehabilitation.

2. The following amounts shall be the standard of monthly need for determining eligibility for and the amount of additional state payments, depending on the type of living arrangement and the geographic area in which the eligible individual or the eligible couple resides:

(a) On and after January first, two thousand five, for an eligible individual living alone, $666.00; and for an eligible couple living alone, $973.00.

(b) On and after January first, two thousand five, for an eligible individual living with others with or without in-kind income, $602.00; and for an eligible couple living with others with or without in-kind income, $915.00.

SSL

(c) On and after January first, two thousand five, for an eligible individual receiving family care, $845.48 if he or she is receiving such care in the city of New York or the county of Nassau, Suffolk, Westchester or Rockland; or $807.48 if he or she is receiving such care in any other county in the state; for an eligible couple receiving family care, $1690.96 if they are receiving such care in the city of New York or the county of Nassau, Suffolk, Westchester or Rockland; or $1614.96 if they are receiving such care in any other county in the state.

(d) On and after January first, two thousand five, for an eligible individual receiving residential care, $1014.00 if he or she is receiving such care in the city of New York or the county of Nassau, Suffolk, Westchester or Rockland; or $984.00 if he or she is receiving such care in any other county in the state; and for an eligible couple receiving residential care, $2028.00 if they are receiving residential care in the city of New York or the county of Nassau, Suffolk, West-chester or Rockland; or $1968.00 if they are receiving such care in any other county of the state.

(e) [Eff. Dec 31, 2005, as amended, L 2005, Ch. 713, §4] On and after January first, two thousand five, for an eligible individual receiving care in a school for the mentally retarded, $1061.96 if he or she is receiving such care in the city of New York; or $1037.96 if he or she is receiving such care in counties outside the city of New York.

(e) [Eff. Jan 1, 2006, as amended, L 2005, Ch. 713, §5]

(i) On and after January first, two thousand five, for an eligible individual receiving care in a school for the mentally retarded, $1061.96 if he or she is receiving such care in the city of New York; or $1037.96 if he or she is receiving such care in counties outside the city of New York.

(ii) On and after January first, two thousand six, for an eligible individual receiving enhanced residential care, $1,104 if he or she is receiving such care in the city of New York or the county of Nassau, Suffolk, Westchester or Rockland; or $1,089 if he or she is receiving such care in any other county of the state.

(iii) On and after January first, two thousand seven, for an eligible individual receiving enhanced residential care, $1224.

(f) [Eff. Dec 31, 2005, as amended, L 2005, Ch. 713, §4] On and after January first, two thousand five, for an eligible couple receiving care in a school for the mentally retarded, $2123.92 if they are receiving such care in the city of New York; or $2075.92 if they are receiving such care in counties outside the city of New York.

(f) [Eff. Jan 1, 2006, as amended, L 2005, Ch. 713, §5]

(i) On and after January first, two thousand five, for an eligible couple receiving care in a school for the mentally retarded, $2123.92 if they are receiving such care in the city of New York; or $2075.92 if they are receiving such care in counties outside the city of New York.

(ii)   On and after January first, two thousand six, for an eligible couple receiving enhanced residential care, $2208 if they are receiving such care in the city of New York or the county of Nassau, Suffolk, Westchester or Rockland; or $2178 if they are receiving such care in any other county of the state.

(iii)   On and after January first, two thousand seven, for an eligible couple receiving enhanced residential care, $2,448.

(g)   (i) The amounts set forth in paragraphs (a) through (d) of this subdivision and the amounts set forth in subparagraph (ii) of paragraph (e) and subparagraph (ii) of paragraph (f) of this subdivision as added by section forty-six of part C of chapter fifty-eight of the laws of two thousand five shall be increased to reflect any increases in federal supplemental security income benefits for individuals or couples which become effective on or after January first, two thousand six but prior to June thirtieth, two thousand six; provided, however, that the amounts set forth in paragraphs (c), (d) and (f) of this subdivision with respect to eligible couples shall be increased by an amount sufficient to establish standards for couples that are equal to twice the increase hereunder for eligible individuals.

(ii)   In addition to the amounts set forth in subparagraph (i) of this paragraph, on and after January first, two thousand seven, the amounts set forth in subparagraph (iii) of paragraph (e) and subparagraph (iii) of paragraph (f) of this subdivision shall be annually increased to reflect an increase in the state supplementation equal to the annual consumer price index for the previous calendar year.

2-a.   Notwithstanding any inconsistent provision of subparagraph (ii) of paragraph (d) of subdivision one of this section, an individual who is receiving or is eligible to receive federal supplemental security income payments and/or additional state payments and who is a resident of a residential health care facility as defined by section twenty-eight hundred one of the public health law, shall, in accordance with regulations of the department, be entitled to a state payment for personal needs in the amount of fifteen dollars a month, provided, however, that on or after January first, nineteen hundred eighty-eight the state payment for personal needs for such persons shall be in the amount of twenty-five dollars a month. Notwithstanding any inconsistent provision of subparagraph (ii) of paragraph (d) of subdivision one of this section, on or after January first, nineteen hundred eighty-eight, a resident of an intermediate care facility operated or issued an operating certificate by the office of mental retardation and developmental disabilities or a patient of a hospital operated by the office of mental health as defined in subdivision ten of section 1.03 of the mental hygiene law who is receiving or is eligible to receive supplemental security income payments and/or additional state payments shall receive a state payment for personal needs in the amount of five dollars a month. The department is authorized to promulgate necessary regulations to provide for the time and manner for payment of such personal allowance to such individuals.

3.   As used in subdivision two of this section:

SSL

(a)   "Living alone" shall mean living in a private household composed of one eligible individual or one eligible couple.

(b)   "Living with others" shall mean living in a private household composed of an eligible individual or couple and at least one other person; or, with respect to any child who is not the head of a household and who is under the age of eighteen, or under the age of twenty-two if attending school, any living arrangement other than residential care in a facility operated or licensed by an office of the department of mental hygiene.

(c)   [Until Dec 31, 2007] "Receiving family care" shall mean residing in a family type home for adults which is certified by the department and supervised by a social services district, in accordance with applicable provisions of law and regulations, or a family care home certified by the appropriate office of the department of mental hygiene, in accordance with applicable provisions of law and regulations or participating in a foster family care demonstration program pursuant to section three hundred sixty-four-h of this chapter.

(c)   [Eff. Dec 31, 2007] "Receiving family care" shall mean residing in a family type home for adults which is certified by the department and supervised by a social services district, in accordance with applicable provisions of law and regulations, or a family care home certified by the appropriate office of the department of mental hygiene, in accordance with applicable provisions of law and regulations.

(d)   "Receiving residential care" shall mean residing in a residence for adults or a privately operated community residence, residential substance abuse treatment program or community residential facility for alcoholism, certified by the appropriate office of the department of mental hygiene; or a residential care center for adults certified by the office of mental health, in accordance with applicable law and regulations. For the purpose of this paragraph, a person receiving care in an intermediate care facility, certified by the department of health or by the appropriate office of the department of mental hygiene, or receiving respite services shall not be deemed to be receiving residential care.

(e)   "Receivingenhanced residential care" shall mean residing in a privately operated school for the mentally retarded and developmentally disabled which is certified by the office of mental retardation and developmental disabilities of the department of mental hygiene, in accordance with applicable provisions of law and regulations or an adult home, or enriched housing program certified by the department of health in accordance with applicable law, rules and regulations to the extent permitted by federal law and regulations.

4.   An eligible individual or an eligible couple shall be entitled to receive monthly an additional state payment in an amount equal to the difference between the monthly standard of need applicable to such individual or couple and the sum of such individual's or couple's supplemental security income benefit plus countable income.

5.   If necessary in order to comply with or reflect changes in federal law, or to take full advantage of available federal funding for the purposes of this title, or to remain qualified for federal funding under any other program, the department may, by regulation, with the approval of the director of the budget, change the amounts specified as the standard of need in subdivision two of this section, or provide that any portion of the supplemental security income benefit be disregarded in determining the amount of the additional state payment. Any such change in the amounts of the standards of need or in the amounts to be so disregarded shall remain effective only until the first day of July of the year next succeeding the year in which such change is to take effect, unless such change is enacted into law prior to such date.

6.   (a) As applicable federal law, rules and regulations so provide, a recipient of supplemental security income benefits or medical assistance in the state of New York or any other state may establish an irrevocable trust fund for the exclusive purpose of their funeral and burial. Such trust fund and any accumulated interest not withdrawn by the recipient shall remain the responsibility of the funeral firm, funeral director, undertaker, cemetery or any other person, firm or corporation to whom such payment is made to administer for funeral and burial expenses of the recipient. Those persons who establish such a trust fund shall be given the opportunity to select the funeral firm, funeral director, undertaker, cemetery or any other person, firm or corporation to whom such payment is made of their choice to provide for their burial arrangements and to change such selection at any time to any funeral firm, funeral director, undertaker, cemetery or any other person, firm or corporation to whom such payment is made, located either in the state of New York or any other state. Any such change of funeral firm, funeral director, undertaker, cemetery, or any other person, firm or corporation to whom such payment is made, must be carried out within ten business days following receipt of a request by the purchaser to the funeral firm, funeral director, undertaker, cemetery, or any other person, firm or corporation to whom such payment is made with which the current trust fund was established. Funds in such trust fund shall be placed in an interest bearing account pursuant to section four hundred fifty-three of the general business law. Accumulated interest from such account shall not be reported as "countable income" pursuant to section two hundred eight of thistitle.

(b)   An applicant for or a recipient of medical assistance in the state of New York or any other state who enters into an agreement pursuant to section four hundred fifty-three of the general business law shall establish a single irrevocable trust fund pursuant to paragraph (a) of this subdivision.

(c)   A funeral firm, funeral director, undertaker, cemetery, or any other person, firm or corporation which makes an agreement for and accepts payment for such an irrevocable trust fund, shall comply with the provisions of section four hundred fifty-three of the general business law, and shall include the following statement in any such agreement in conspicuous print of at least twelve point type:

SSL

NEW YORK LAW REQUIRES THIS AGREEMENT TO BE IRREVO-
CABLE FOR APPLICANTS FOR RECEIPT OF SUPPLEMENTAL SECUR-
ITY BENEFITS UNDER SECTION TWO HUNDRED NINE OF THE SOCIAL
SERVICES LAW OR OF MEDICAL ASSISTANCE UNDER SECTION
THREE HUNDRED SIXTY-SIX OF THE SOCIAL SERVICES LAW, AND
FOR THE MONEYS PUT INTO A TRUST UNDER THIS AGREEMENT TO
BE USED ONLY FOR FUNERAL AND BURIAL EXPENSES. IF ANY
MONEY IS LEFT OVER AFTER YOUR FUNERAL AND BURIAL EX-
PENSES HAVE BEEN PAID, IT WILL GO TO THE COUNTY. YOU MAY
CHANGE YOUR CHOICE OF FUNERAL HOME AT ANY TIME.

(d) Any promotional literature prepared after January first, nineteen hundred
ninety-seven by a funeral firm, funeral director, undertaker, cemetery, or any
other person, firm or corporation for prearranged funeral and burial services must
contain language disclosing the irrevocable nature of burial trusts established for
an applicant or recipient of supplemental security income benefits or medical
assistance.

Added by Laws 1974, Ch. 1080, eff. Jan. 1, 1974; Laws 1975, Ch. 481; Laws 1976,
Ch. 483; **amended** by Laws 1977, Ch. 431; Laws 1978, Ch. 454; Laws 1978, Ch. 555,
§ 5; Ch. 557; Laws 1979, Ch. 278, Ch. 314; Laws 1980, Ch. 113, Ch. 204, both eff. July
1, 1980, Ch. 478, eff. June 23, 1980 until June 30, 1981; **amended** by Laws 1980, Ch.
890, subd. 2(d); **amended** by Laws 1981, Ch. 85, eff. July 1, 1981; **amended** by Laws
1981, Ch. 226, eff. June 15, 1981, subd. 3(d); **amended** by Laws 1981, Ch. 309, eff. June
24, 1981, extending effective date of subd. 3(b) until June 30, 1983; **amended** by Laws
1981, Ch. 1005, eff. July 1, 1981, **added** subd. 2-a; subd. (2) **amended** by Laws 1982,
Ch. 87, eff. July 1, 1982, provided, however, that in the event a federal law takes effect
which results in a delay in the federal cost of living increase for federal supplemental
security income benefits, this act shall take effect on the date on which such cost of living
increases are to be paid in accordance with such federal law, and provided further that
section four of this act shall remain in full force and effect until June thirtieth, nineteen
hundred eighty-three; **amended** by Laws 1982, Ch. 197, eff. June 15, 1982, subd. (6);
amended by Laws 1982, Ch. 468, eff. July 1, 1982; **amended** by Laws 1982, Ch. 794,
eff. July 27, 1982, subd. (2-a); **amended** by Laws 1983, Ch. 71, eff. Jan. 1, 1984;
amended by Laws 1984, Ch. 527, eff. July 27, 1984; **amended** by Laws 1984, Ch. 692,
eff. Aug. 1, 1984; **amended** by Laws 1984, Ch. 909, eff. Jan. 1, 1985, except for substance
abuse program provisions in the city of New York, eff. July 1, 1984; **amended** by Laws
1985, see below; **amended** by Laws 1986, see below; **amended** by Laws 1987, see below;
amended by Laws 1988, see below; **amended** by Laws 1989, Ch. 556, § 2, eff. Dec. 31,
1989; **amended** by Laws 1990, Ch. 685, § 2, eff. Dec. 31, 1990; **amended** by Laws 1991,
Ch. 201, § 2, eff. Dec. 31, 1991; **amended** by Laws 1992, Ch. 292, §§ 2, 3, eff. Dec.
31, 1992; **amended** by Laws 1993, Ch. 401 § 2, eff. Dec. 31, 1993; **amended** by Laws
1994, Ch. 29, § 3, eff. Apr. 1, 1994, extending the period that Subd. (3), para. (c) remains
effective to Dec. 31, 1995; **amended** by Laws 1994, Ch. 460, § 2, eff. Dec. 31, 1994;
amended by Laws 1995, Ch. 81, § 125, eff. June 20, 1995, extending the period that
Subd. 3, para. (c) remains effective to Dec. 31, 1996; **amended** by Laws 1995, Ch. 649,
§ 2, eff. Dec. 31, 1995; **amended** by Laws 1996, Ch. 213, § 2, eff. Dec. 31, 1996;
amended by Laws 1996, Ch. 545, § 3, eff. Aug. 8, 1996, extending the period that subd.

(3) remains effective to Dec. 32, 1997; **amended** by Laws 1996, Ch. 660, eff. Jan. 1, 1997 and applying only to contracts or agreements entered into on or after such date; **amended** by Laws 1997, Ch. 216, § 3 eff. July 18, 1997, and Ch. 189, § 2, eff. Dec. 31, 1997 and applicable to benefits and allowances in months beginning after Dec. 31, 1997; **amended** by Laws 1998, Ch. 214, § 8 eff. July 7, 1998 and deemed in full force and effect Aug. 20, 1997, Ch. 58 Part C, § 91-a, eff. Jan. 1, 1999, and Ch. 377, § 2, eff. Dec. 31, 1998, and shall apply to benefits and allowances in months beginning after Dec. 31, 1998, and Ch. 181, § 3, eff. July 7, 1998; **amended** by Laws 1999, Ch. 201, § 2 eff. Dec. 31, 1999 and shall apply to benefits and allowances in months beginning after Dec. 31, 1999; **amended** by Laws 1999, Ch. 514, § 1, eff. Sept. 28, 1999.**amended** by Laws 1999, Ch. 620, § 3, eff. Nov. 9, 1999; **amended** by Laws 2000, Ch. 470, § 2, eff. Dec. 31, 2000, and shall apply to benefits and allowances in months beginning after such date, and Ch. 439, extending expiration date of subd (3)(c) to Dec. 31, 2001; **amended** by Laws 2001, Ch. 89, § 2, eff. Dec. 31, 2001, and shall apply to benefits and allowances in months beginning after such date, Ch. 200, § 3, extending expiration date of subd. 3(c), eff. Aug. 20, 2001; **amended** by Laws 2002, Ch. 109, § 2, eff. Dec. 31, 2002 and apply to benefits and allowances, Ch. 317, § 1, eff. Aug. 6, 2002; Laws 2003, Ch. 62, Part K2, §§ 2, 4, eff. Dec. 31, 2003, amending subds. (a)–(g); **amended** by Laws 2004, Ch. 310, §§ 2 eff. Dec. 31, 2004 and shall apply to benefits and allowances in months beginning after such date, amending subd. (2); **amended** by Laws 2005, Ch. 58, §§ 46-48 (Part C), eff. Jan. 1, 2006; Laws 2005, Ch. 713, §§ 4, 5, eff. Dec. 31, 2005; Laws 2006, ch. 57, §2 (Part C), legislative override of Governor's line veto filed April 28, 2006.

SSL

1982 Amendments

The amendment of subd. 2 by Laws 1982, Ch. 87, is intended to reflect maximum increases in the additional state payment and medical assistance standards of need and in personal allowance amounts, which shall become effective for any period after the effective date of this act for which a federal supplemental security income cost of living increase has been established at seven and four-tenths percent. To the extent that such federal cost of living increase is established at a level other than seven and four-tenths percent, the state department of social services shall by regulation establish actual standards of need for additional state payments and medical assistance and for the amount of personal needs allowances affected by this act, which proportionately reflect the actual amount of such federal cost of living increase, taking into account any applicable federal requirements as to establishing the medical assistance standard of need; provided, that such department may establish the personal allowance amounts at the next highest whole dollar amount.

Note to 1984 Amendments

Notwithstanding the amendments enacted in Ch. 692 (subd. 6), no rights accruing, accrued or acquired under a trust fund established prior to the effective date of this act shall be affected or impaired, but may be enjoyed, asserted or enforced as fully and to the same extent as if such amendments had not been effected.

1986 Amendments

Amended by Laws 1986 as follows: Ch. 46, **added** § 209(2)(k) eff. Apr. 14, 1986; Ch. 502, **repealed** § 209(2)(i), (j) and (k), and **amended** § 209(2)(a), (b), (c), (d), (e), (f) and (g), deemed to have been in full force and effect on and after Jan. 1, 1986; § 209(2)(c), eff. July 1, 1986.

1987 Amendments

Amended by Laws 1987 as follows: Ch. 40, **amended** § 209(2)(g), eff. July 1, 1987; Ch. 56, **amended** § 209(2-a), eff. Dec. 31, 1987; Ch. 450, **amended** § 209(2)(a), (b), (c), (d), (e), (f) and (g), **added** § 209(2)(h), **amended** § 209(2-a), eff. Dec. 31, 1987.

1988 Amendments

Amended by Laws 1988 as follows: Ch. 85 **amended**§ 209(2)(a),(b),(d),(g) and (h), eff. May 15, 1988; Ch. 705 **amended**§ 209(2)(c),(e),(f),(g) and (h), eff. Dec. 31, 1988.

§ 210. Mandatory minimum state supplementation.

1. Any inconsistent provisions of this title or any other law notwithstanding, but subject to the provisions of subdivisions two and three of this section, an individual who is deemed to have met the eligibility criteria for additional state payments pursuant to paragraph (c) of subdivision one of section two hundred nine of this title, shall be entitled to receive for each month after December,

nineteen hundred seventy-three an additional state payment in an amount which, when added to the supplemental security income benefit and other countable income, is equal to such individual's December, nineteen hundred seventy-three cash grant of assistance under the state's program of old age assistance, assistance to the blind, aid to the disabled or the combined program of aid to aged, blind and disabled persons, plus income not excluded under such state program, plus an amount equal to the January, nineteen hundred seventy-two bonus value of food stamps as determined in accordance with the regulations of the office of temporary and disability assistance plus, for any month after June, nineteen hundred seventy-five, an amount reflecting the federal supplemental security increases resulting from July first, nineteen hundred seventy-five cost of living increases in such benefits, plus for any month after June, nineteen hundred eighty-two, an amount equal to the July first, nineteen hundred eighty-two federal supplemental security income cost of living adjustment, providing such individual was eligible to receive a mandatory state supplement for the month of December, nineteen hundred eighty-one, plus for any month after June, nineteen hundred eighty-three, an amount equal to $ 17.70 for individuals, $ 26.55 for couples who are living alone or living with others and $ 35.40 for couples receiving family care, residential care or care in schools for the mentally retarded, plus for any month after December, nineteen hundred eighty-three, an amount equal to $ 9.70 for individuals, $ 15.60 for couples who are living alone or living with others and $ 19.40 for couples receiving family care, residential care or care in schools for the mentally retarded, plus for any month after December, nineteen hundred eighty-four, an amount equal to $ 11.00 for individuals, $ 16.00 for couples who are living alone or living with others and $ 22.00 for couples receiving family care, residential care or care in schools for the mentally retarded, plus for any month after December, nineteen hundred eighty-five, an amount equal to $ 11.00 for individuals, $ 16.00 for couples who are living alone or living with others and $ 22.00 for couples receiving family care, residential care or care in schools for the mentally retarded, plus for any month after December, nineteen hundred eighty-six an amount equal to $ 4.00 for individuals, $ 6.00 for couples who are living alone or living with others and $ 8.00 for couples receiving family care, residential care or care in schools for the mentally retarded, plus for any month after December, nineteen hundred eighty-seven an amount equal to $ 14.00 for individuals, $ 22.00 for couples who are living alone or living with others and $ 28.00 for couples receiving family care, residential care or care in schools for the mentally retarded, plus for any month after December, nineteen hundred eighty-eight an amount equal to $ 14.00 for individuals, $ 21.00 for couples who are living alone or living with others and $ 28.00 for couples receiving family care, residential care or care in schools for the mentally retarded, plus for any other month after December, nineteen hundred eighty-nine an amount equal to $ 18.00 for individuals, $ 27.00 for couples who are living alone or living with others and $ 36.00 for couples receiving family care, residential care or care in schools for the mentally retarded, plus for any month after December, nineteen hundred ninety an amount equal to $ 21.00 for individuals, $ 31.00 for couples

SSL

who are living alone or living with others and $ 42.00 for couples receiving family care, residential care or care in schools for the mentally retarded, plus for any month after December, nineteen hundred ninety-one an amount equal to $ 15.00 for individuals, $ 23.00 for couples who are living alone or living with others and $ 30.00 for couples receiving family care, residential care or care in schools for the mentally retarded, plus for any month after December, nineteen hundred ninety-two, an amount equal to $ 12.00 for individuals, $ 19.00 for couples who are living alone or living with others and $ 24.00 for couples receiving family care, residential care or care in schools for the mentally retarded plus for any month after December, nineteen hundred ninety-three an amount equal to $ 12.00 for individuals, $ 17.00 for couples who are living alone or living with others and $ 24.00 for couples receiving family care, residential care or care in schools for the mentally retarded plus for any month after December, nineteen hundred ninety-four an amount equal to $ 12.00 for individuals, $ 18.00 for couples who are living alone or living with others and $ 24.00 for couples receiving family care, residential care or care in schools for the mentally retarded, plus for any month after December, nineteen hundred ninety-five an amount equal to $ 12.00 for individuals, $ 18.00 for couples who are living alone or living with others and $ 24.00 for couples receiving family care, residential care or care in schools for the mentally retarded, plus for any month after December, nineteen hundred ninety-six, an amount equal to $ 14.00 for individuals and $ 21.00 for couples plus for any month after December, nineteen hundred ninety-seven an amount equal to $ 10.00 for individuals and $ 15.00 for couples plus for any month after December, nineteen hundred ninety-eight an amount equal to $ 6.00 for individuals and $ 11.00 for couples plus for any month after December, nineteen hundred ninety-nine an amount equal to $ 13.00 for individuals and $ 18.00 for couples plus for any month after December, two thousand an amount equal to $ 18.00 for individuals and $ 27.00 for couples plus for any month after December, two thousand one an amount equal to $ 15.00 for individuals and $ 21.00 for couples plus for any month after December, two thousand two an amount equal to $ 7.00 for individuals and $ 12.00 for couples plus for any month after December, two thousand three an amount equal to $ 12.00 for individuals and $ 17.00 for couples plus for any month after December, two thousand four an amount equal to $15.00 for individuals and $23.00 for couples plus for any month after December, two thousand five an amount equal to the amount of any increases in federal supplemental security income benefits for individuals or couples which become effective on or after January first, two thousand six but prior to June thirtieth, two thousand six.

2. An individual who is entitled to receive the minimum state supplement in accordance with subdivision one of this section shall remain entitled to receive such supplement for each month after December, nineteen hundred seventy-three until the month in which such individual dies or ceases to be eligible therefor, pursuant to paragraph (c) of subdivision one of section two hundred nine of this title; provided, however, that no individual shall be entitled to receive such supplement for any month in which such individual is ineligible to receive federal

supplemental security income benefits for reasons specified in paragraph (d) of subdivision one of section two hundred nine of this title.

3. If the amount of an individual's December, nineteen hundred seventy-three grant included or was determined on the basis of a special need or special circumstance of such individual which existed in December, nineteen hundred seventy-three, and which need or circumstance during any month after December, nineteen hundred seventy-three ceased to exist, such individual's minimum state supplement shall be reduced for such month and each month thereafter by an amount equal to the amount such individual's December, nineteen hundred seventy-three grant would have been reduced had such special need or special circumstance not existed in December, nineteen hundred seventy-three. If the amount of an individual's December, nineteen hundred seventy-three grant included an amount to reflect the needs of a person whose presence in the household was essential to the well-being of the individual, the income and resources of such person shall be included as the income and resources of the individual.

Added by Laws 1974, Ch. 1080, deemed to have been in full force and effect on and after Jan. 1, 1974; **amended** by Laws 1975, Ch. 198, eff. Jan. 1, 1974; Laws 1975, Ch. 481, eff. July 1, 1975; Laws 1975, Ch. 482, eff. July 29, 1975; **amended** by Laws 1976 Ch. 483, eff. Oct. 1, 1976; **amended** by Laws 1983, Ch. 71, eff. July 1, 1983; however, subd.(1) eff. May 4, 1983, and deemed to have been in full force and effect on and after July 1, 1982; **amended** by Laws 1984, Ch. 527, eff. July 27, 1984; **amended** by Laws 1985, Ch. 361, eff. Jan. 1, 1985; **amended** by Laws 1986, Ch. 502, deemed to have been in full force and effect on and after Jan. 1, 1986; **amended** by Laws 1987, Ch. 450, eff. Dec. 31, 1987; **amended** by Laws 1988, Ch. 705, § 2, eff. Dec. 31, 1988; **amended** by Laws 1989, Ch. 556, § 3, eff. Dec. 31, 1989; **amended** by Laws 1990, Ch. 685, § 3, eff. Dec. 31, 1990; **amended** by Laws 1991, Ch. 201, § 3, eff. Dec. 31, 1991; **amended** by Laws 1992, Ch. 292, § 4, eff. Dec. 31, 1992; **amended** by Laws 1992, Ch. 407, § 1, eff. Dec. 31, 1992; **amended** by Laws 1993, Ch. 401, § 3, eff. Dec. 31, 1993; **amended** by Laws 1994, Ch. 460, § 3, eff. Dec. 31, 1994; **amended** by Laws 1995, Ch. 649, § 3, eff. Dec. 31, 1995; amended by Laws 1996, Ch. 213, § 3, eff. Dec. 31, 1996; **amended** by Laws 1997, Ch. 189, § 3, eff. Dec. 31, 1997, and applicable to benefits and allowances in months beginning after Dec. 31, 1997; **amended** by Laws 1998, Ch. 377, § 3, eff. Dec. 31, 1998, and shall apply to benefits and allowances in months beginning after Dec. 31, 1998; **amended** by Laws 1999, Ch. 201, § 3, eff. Dec. 31, 1999, and shall apply to benefits and allowances in months beginning after Dec. 31, 1999; **amended** by Laws 2000, Ch. 470, § 3, eff. Dec. 31, 2000, and shall apply to benefits and allowances in months beginning after such date; **amended** by Laws 2001, Ch. 89, § 3, eff. July 2, 2001, deemed full force and effect on and after Aug. 1, 2001; **amended** by Laws 2001, Ch. 89, § 4, eff. Dec. 31, 2001, shall apply to benefits and allowances in months beginning after such date; **amended** by Laws 2002, Ch. 109, § 3, eff. Dec. 31, 2002 and apply to benefits and allowances; Laws 2003, Ch. 62, Part K2, §§ 3, 4, eff. Dec. 31, 2003 and shall apply to benefits and allowances in months beginning after such date; **amended** by Laws 2004, Ch. 310, §§3, 4, eff. Dec. 31, 2004 and shall apply to benefits and allowances in months beginning after such date; **amended** by Laws of 2005, Ch. 713, § 6, effective Dec. 31, 2005 and shall apply to benefits and allowances in months beginning after such date.

SSL

§ 211. Agreements for federal administration.

1.   The department is hereby authorized, on behalf of the state, to enter into an agreement with the secretary of the federal department of health, education and welfare whereby the secretary agrees to administer the state's program of additional state payments, including determining the eligibility of individuals and couples for such payments.

2.   Any such agreement may authorize the secretary to make additional state payments on behalf of the state to persons found eligible for such payments pursuant to the provisions of this title, in amounts authorized by the provisions of this title, and shall contain conditions of eligibility for such additional state payments, including the requirement of current residence and amounts of earned or unearned income to be disregarded in determining eligibility, in accordance with the provisions of this title, regulations of the department and federal law and regulations.

3.   Any such agreement shall provide that the state will pay to the secretary: (a) the amount the secretary expends for additional state payments without regard to the secretary's cost of administering such payments, which amount shall not exceed the amount of expenditures made by the state and by social services districts for aid to aged, blind and disabled persons during the calendar year nineteen hundred seventy-two, less any federal funds properly received on account thereof; and (b) the amount the secretary expends for additional state payments for any individual which are in excess of the difference between the adjusted payment level under the state's program of old age assistance, assistance to the blind or aid to the disabled in January, nineteen hundred seventy-two and the amount of such individual's supplemental security income benefit. For purposes of this subdivision, "adjusted payment level" shall mean the amount of the cash grant under the appropriate state program of old age assistance, assistance to the blind, aid to the disabled or the combined program of aid to aged, blind and disabled persons, to individuals receiving grants under any such program, who had no other income, for the month of January, nineteen hundred seventy-two, plus an amount not greater than the bonus value of food stamps allotted to such individuals in such month, so long as federal law and regulations permit the inclusion of such amount.

4.   The department is authorized on behalf of the state, with the approval of the director of the budget, to agree to modification of the agreement, or to terminate the agreement, if it is fiscally advantageous to the state to so act. Any modification of the agreement which is contrary to the provisions of this title shall be effective only until the first day of July of the year next succeeding the year in which such modification is to take effect, unless the substance of such modification is enacted into law prior to such date. For the purposes of section one hundred one-a of the executive law, any such modification or termination of the agreement shall be considered the adoption of a rule, as defined in such section.

5. The department is authorized, on behalf of the state, to enter into an agreement with the secretary of the federal department of health and human services for the purpose of obtaining reimbursement for safety net assistance or any other payments made from state or local funds furnished for basic needs for any month to or on behalf of persons who subsequently are determined eligible to receive supplemental security income payments for such month. Notwithstanding any law to the contrary, the department is authorized to condition eligibility for any program providing such payments upon the individual's execution of a written authorization allowing the secretary of the federal department of health and human services to pay to the social services district the amount of supplemental security income due at the time the individual becomes eligible.

Added by Laws 1974, Ch. 1080, eff. Jan. 1, 1974; **amended** by Laws 1975, Ch. 198, eff. Dec. 1, 1974; **amended** by Laws 1989, Ch. 72, § 2, eff. Apr. 27, 1989; **amended** by Laws 1992, Ch. 41, § 137, eff. Apr. 2, 1992; **amended** by Laws 1997, Ch. 436, § 1 Part B, § 83, eff. Aug. 20, 1997.

§ 212. Responsibility; financing.

1. Unless there is in effect an agreement for federal administration of additional state payments pursuant to section two hundred eleven of this title, each social services district shall be responsible for providing such payments to persons who are receiving or who would but for their income be eligible to receive, supplemental security income benefits, and who reside or are found in such district, subject to supervision by the state and subject to full reimbursement by the state of such payments made by such district. The social services districts shall also be responsible for the administration of the state's program of additional state payments, subject to reimbursement by the state in an amount equal to one-half the cost of such administration and shall:

(a) accept applications for additional state payments,

(b) determine eligibility in accordance with this title and the regulations of the department,

(c) determine the amount of the federal supplemental security income benefit and other countable income, and issue a grant which when added to such benefit and income will equal such individual's standard of need, and

(d) thereafter recertify eligibility periodically as the department may require.

2. If there is in effect an agreement for the federal administration of additional state payments, the state shall be responsible for paying to the secretary an amount equal to: (a) the amount expended under the state's programs of old age assistance, assistance to the blind and aid to the disabled during the calendar year, nineteen hundred seventy-two, less any federal funds properly received on account of such expenditures; plus (b) any amounts in addition to such sum as may be required by the agreement.

3. [*Repealed.*]

Added by Laws 1974, Ch. 1080; **amended** by Laws 1978, Ch. 73; **amended** by Laws 1979, Ch. 315; **amended** by Laws 1980, Ch. 432, eff. June 23, 1980; **amended** by Laws 1981, Ch. 353, eff. June 29, 1981; **amended** by Laws 1982, Ch. 94, eff. May 18, 1982; **amended** by Laws 1983, Ch. 192, eff. May 31, 1983; **amended** by Laws 1984, Ch. 200, eff. June 12, 1984; **amended** by Laws 1985, Ch. 470, eff. July 19, 1985; **amended** by Laws 1986, Ch. 171, eff. June 16, 1986; **amended** by Laws 1988, Ch. 168, § 1, eff. June, 27, 1988; **amended** by Laws 1989, Ch. 199, eff. Jun. 24, 1989; **amended** by Laws 1990, Ch. 332, § 1, eff. June 30, 1990; **amended** by Laws 1991, Ch. 458, § 1, eff. July 19, 1991; **amended** by Laws 1993, Ch. 47, § 1, eff. May 21, 1993; **amended** by Laws 1994, Ch. 240, § 1, eff. July 6, 1994; **amended** by Laws 1995, Ch. 668, § 1, eff. Aug. 8, 1995; **amended** by Laws 1996, Ch. 299, eff. July 10, 1996; **amended** by Laws 1997, Ch. 111, § 1, eff. June 17, 1997; **amended** by Laws 1998, Ch. 316, §§ 1 and 2, eff. July 14, 1998.

§§ 250-258.　Medical assistance for the aged.

Art. 5, Title 6-A repealed by Laws 1966, Ch. 256, eff. Apr. 30, 1966 and subject matter transferred to Social Services Law, Art. 5, Title 11.

§§ 250-259.　Services for the aged, blind or disabled.

Art. 5, Title 7 repealed by Laws 1974, Ch. 1080, deemed to have been in full force and effect on and after Jan. 1, 1974 and subject matter transferred to Social Services Law, Art. 5, Title 6.

SOCIAL SERVICES LAW

TITLE 7—SERVICES FOR THE AGED, BLIND OR DISABLED

_____

(Repealed and transferred sections noted under appropriate section number of text.)

§ 250.   Declaration of object; definitions.

1.   In order for the state to receive federal aid under title six of the federal social security act, rehabilitation and other services shall be furnished in accordance with the provisions of this title to help needy persons who are sixty-five years of age or older, are blind, or are disabled to attain or retain capability for self-support or self-care or to prevent or reduce dependency.

2.   When used in this title, services shall be construed to include, but not be limited to, protective services, health-related services, self-support services for the handicapped, homemaker services, housekeeping services, special services for the blind, housing improvement and assistance services, home delivered meals, home management and other functional educational services, services to adults requiring care in suitable substitute homes, family planning services and such other services as may be necessary to accomplish the purposes of this title.

Added by Laws 1973, Ch. 516, eff. Jan. 1, 1974.

SSL

§ 251.   Federal aid; state plan.

1.   The department shall submit the plan required by title six of the federal social security act to the department of health, education and welfare for approval pursuant to such title and act, so that the state may receive federal aid under such title. The department shall act for the state in any negotiations relative to the submission and approval of such plan and may make any arrangement not inconsistent with law which may be required by the federal social security act to obtain and retain such approval and to secure for the state the benefits of the provisions of such title. The department shall make such regulations not

inconsistent with law as may be necessary to make such plan conform to the provisions of such title and any rules and regulations adopted pursuant thereto. The department shall make reports to such federal department in the form and nature required by it and in all respects comply with any request or direction of such federal department which may be necessary to assure the correctness and verification of such reports.

2.   The department of taxation and finance shall accept and receive any and all grants of money awarded to the state under title six of the social security act for federal aid for services for the aged, blind or disabled. All monies so received shall be deposited by the department of taxation and finance in a special fund or funds and shall be used by the state exclusively for services for the aged, blind or disabled and the administration thereof under the provisions of this title. Such money shall be paid from such fund or funds on audit and warrant of the comptroller on vouchers of or certification by the commissioner.

Added by Laws 1973 Ch. 516, eff. Jan. 1, 1974.

§ 252. Responsibility.

1.   Except as provided in subdivision two of this section or any other provisions of this chapter, each social services district shall furnish services to the persons eligible therefor who reside in its territory, subject to reimbursement by the state in accordance with the provisions of this chapter, and to supervision by the department.

2.   (a) If the state's plan makes provision for services to be provided to eligible persons cared for in certain state institutions or facilities, the department, or other appropriate state department or agency acting pursuant to an agreement with the department, shall furnish services to such persons.

(b)   There shall be such cooperative arrangements, between and among the department, and the state departments of health, mental hygiene, education and other appropriate state departments and agencies as shall be necessary to assure that there will be compliance with federal law and regulation and that the objectives of this title will be effectively accomplished.

(c)   Services for the aged, blind or disabled persons shall be administered uniformly throughout the state, except when otherwise required or permitted by the department which shall first obtain the approval of the secretary of health, education and welfare.

Added by Laws 1973 Ch. 516, eff. Jan. 1, 1974.

§ 253. Application for services.

1.   A person requesting services for the aged, blind or disabled may make his application therefor in person or through another in his behalf to the social services official of the county or city in which the applicant resides or is found.

2.　Applications by or on behalf of persons under care in institutions or facilities operated by the state shall be made to the department or its agent, except as otherwise permitted or required by regulations of the department.

Added by Laws 1973 Ch. 516, eff. Jan. 1, 1974.

§ 254.　Eligibility.

Services for the aged, blind or disabled shall be provided any aged, blind or disabled person who requires such services; who is a resident of the state on the date of application and who is receiving or is an applicant for benefits under the supplemental security income and additional state payments for the aged, blind and disabled program or is receiving or an applicant for authorized payments to aged, blind or disabled individuals ineligible for such program.

Added by Laws 1973 Ch. 516, eff. Jan. 1, 1974.

§ 255.　Character and adequacy of services.

1.　It shall be the duty of social services officials, insofar as funds are available for that purpose, to provide adequately for services for the aged, blind or disabled in accordance with the provisions of this title and other applicable provisions of law. Local funds need not be made available in excess of the amount necessary to equal state funds made available to such district or limited pursuant to law.

2.　The amount and nature of the services and the manner of providing them, shall be determined by the social services officials with due regard to the conditions existing in each case, and in accordance with the regulations of the department.

3.　Services which may be provided to persons who are under care in private or public institutions or facilities shall be furnished only in such institutions and facilities as are operated in compliance with applicable provisions of this chapter or other laws.

4.　Services under this title shall not include any which are required to be furnished as medical assistance pursuant to title eleven of article five.

5.　Local social services districts shall be authorized, with the approval of the department, to station local social services employees at federal social security offices for the purpose of providing information and referral services relating to emergency assistance for adults and social services to eligible persons.

Added by Laws 1973 Ch. 516, eff. Jan. 1, 1974; **amended** by Laws 1975, Ch. 198, eff. June 10, 1975; **amended** by Laws 1975, Ch. 482, eff. July 29, 1975.

§ 256.　Investigation of applications.

Whenever an application for services is made, an investigation and record shall be promptly made of the circumstances of the applicant in accordance with

SSL

regulations of the department. The object of such investigation shall be to ascertain the facts supporting the application and to obtain such other information as may be required by the department.

Added by Laws 1973 Ch. 516, eff. Jan. 1, 1974.

§ 257.   Supervision; regulations.

The department shall:

1.   Supervise the administration of services for the aged, blind or disabled by social services officials;

2.   Make regulations necessary for the carrying out of this title to the end that services for the aged, blind or disabled may be administered uniformly throughout the state, except when otherwise required or permitted by the department with the approval of the secretary of health, education and welfare.

Added by Laws 1973 Ch. 516, eff. Jan. 1, 1974.

§ 258.   Quarterly estimates; state reimbursement.

1.   In accordance with regulations of the department, each social services district shall submit to the department quarterly estimates of its anticipated expenditures for services for the aged, blind or disabled.

2.   Expenditures made by social services districts for services under this title shall be subject to reimbursement by the state in accordance with and to the extent authorized by section one hundred fifty-three, and any applicable provisions of law which limit reimbursement for social services or authorize the allocation of funds for such services among the districts.

Added by Laws 1973 Ch. 516, eff. Jan. 1, 1974; amended by Laws 1973 Ch. 517, eff. June 5, 1973.

§ 259.   Application of other provisions.

1.   Provisions of this chapter and other laws relating to public assistance and care not inconsistent with this title shall be applied in carrying out the provisions of this title.

2.   The provisions of any city charter or other local or special act which are inconsistent with the provisions of this title shall not be applicable to the services provided by this title, nor impair nor limit the statewide operation of this title, according to its terms.

Added by laws 1973, Ch. 516, eff. Jan. 1, 1974.

§ 283-293.   Assistance to the blind.

Art. 5, Title 7 repealed by Laws 1974, Ch. 1080, deemed to have been in full force and effect on and after Jan. 1, 1974. Subject matter covered by Social Services Law, Art. 5, Titles 6, 7, and 8, partially blind persons in the state.

§ 300-309.   Aid to the disabled.

Art. 5, Title 8 repealed by Laws 1974, Ch. 1080, deemed to have been in full force and effect on and after Jan. 1, 1974. Subject matter covered by Social Services Law, Art. 5, Titles 6, 7 and 8.

TITLE 8—EMERGENCY ASSISTANCE FOR AGED, BLIND AND DISABLED PERSONS

(Repealed and transferred sections noted under appropriate section number of text.)

§ 300.   Declaration of purpose; definitions.

1.   Emergency assistance for aged, blind and disabled persons with emergency needs which, if not met, would endanger the health, safety and welfare of such persons, is hereby declared to be a matter of state concern and a necessity in promoting the public health and welfare, until such time as the federal supplemental security income program is expanded to meet this federal responsibility. It is the purpose of this title to provide such assistance to eligible aged, blind and disabled persons who, in the circumstances specified in this title, have needs that cannot be met by the regular monthly benefit under the federal supplemental security income and additional state payments programs. All efforts should be undertaken by New York state's congressional delegation to secure such expansion of the federal program.

2. As used in this title, "aged, blind and disabled persons" means persons who have been determined to be eligible for or are receiving federal supplemental security income benefits and/or additional state payments.

3. As used in this title, the terms "emergency assistance" and "emergency assistance for aged, blind and disabled persons" mean payments to meet emergency needs specified in section three hundred three, made to or for the benefit of persons found to be eligible therefor, in accordance with this title and the regulations of the department.

4. As used in this title, "supplemental security income benefits" means payments made by the secretary of the federal department of health, education and welfare to aged, blind and disabled persons pursuant to title sixteen of the social security act.

5. As used in this title, "additional state payments" means payments by social services districts or by the secretary of the federal department of health, education and welfare on behalf of the state, to aged, blind and disabled persons who are receiving, or who would but for their income be eligible to receive, federal supplemental security income benefits, made pursuant to title sixteen of the federal social security act, public law 93–66, and the provisions of this chapter.

Added by Laws 1974, Ch. 1081, eff. Apr. 1, 1974; **amended** by Laws 1975, Ch. 198, eff. June 10, 1975; **amended** by Laws 1976, Ch. 125, eff. Apr. 13, 1976; **amended** by Laws 1977, Ch. 31, eff. Mar. 31, 1977; **amended** by Laws 1978, Ch. 129; Laws 1980, Ch. 44, eff. Apr. 2, 1980; **amended** by Laws 1982, Ch. 34, eff. Apr. 4, 1982; **amended** by Laws 1984, Ch. 36, eff. Mar. 31, 1984; **amended** by Laws 1986, Ch. 14, eff. Mar. 31, 1986, **amended** by Laws 1988, Ch. 29, § 1, eff. Mar. 31, 1988; **amended** by Laws 1990, Ch. 44, eff. Mar. 31, 1990.

§ 301. Responsibility.

1. Subject to reimbursement by the state, in accordance with the provisions of this title and regulations of the department, each social services district shall furnish emergency assistance to aged, blind and disabled persons eligible therefor who reside in such district.

2. Expenditures properly made by social services districts under this title, including costs of administration, shall be reimbursed by the state in an amount equal to one-half of such expenditures, after first deducting any federal funds properly received or to be received on account thereof.

Added by Laws 1974, Ch. 1081, eff. Apr. 1, 1974; Laws 1975, Ch. 198; Laws 1976, Ch. 125; Laws 1977 Ch. 31; Laws 1978, Ch. 129; Laws 1980, Ch. 44; Laws 1982, Ch. 34; Laws 1984, Ch. 34; Laws 1986, Ch. 14; Laws 1988, Ch. 29; Laws 1990, Ch. 44, eff. Mar. 31, 1990, to eliminate the expiration date of the 1974 amendment.

§ 302. Eligibility.

Emergency assistance shall be granted to an aged, blind or disabled person who applies for such assistance and who:

(a) Has needs, as specified in section three hundred three of this chapter and the regulations of the department, that cannot be met by the regular monthly supplemental security income benefit and/or additional state payment, or by income or resources not excluded by the federal social security act and which, if not met, would endanger the health, welfare or safety of the individual; and

(b) Is not eligible for assistance under section three hundred fifty-j of this chapter.

Added by Laws 1974, Ch. 1081, eff. Apr. 1, 1974; Laws 1975, Ch. 198; Laws 1976, Ch. 125; Laws 1977, Ch. 31; Laws 1978, Ch. 129; Laws 1980, Ch. 44; Laws 1982, Ch. 34; Laws 1984, Ch. 34; Laws 1986, Ch. 14; Laws 1988, Ch. 29; Laws 1990, Ch. 44, eff. Mar. 31, 1990, to eliminate the expiration date of the 1974 amendment.

§ 303. Character and adequacy.

1. It shall be the duty of the social services official to provide emergency assistance, in accordance with regulations of the department, to an eligible aged, blind or disabled person who has one or more of the following needs:

(a) Replacement or repair, as the case may be, of clothing, furniture, food, fuel and shelter; (including repairs to homes owned by aged, blind and disabled persons and temporary shelter until necessary repairs are completed or replacement shelter is secured), provided such clothing, furniture, food, fuel or shelter was lost or rendered useless as a result of burglary, theft or vandalism, or as a result of fire, flood or other similar catastrophe which could not have been foreseen by such person, and was not under his control. All such losses shall have been reported to and appropriately verified by local officials before such replacement or repair;

(b) Replacement of stolen cash if reported to and appropriately verified by local officials;

(c) Replacement of lost or mismanaged cash by a person who by reason of advanced age, illness, infirmity, mental weakness, physical handicap, intemperance, addiction to drugs, or other cause, has suffered substantial impairment of his ability to care for his property;

(d) Payments to a secured party in whose favor there is a security interest, pursuant to the provisions of article nine of the uniform commercial code, on furniture or household equipment essential to making living accommodations habitable, in an amount not to exceed the cost of replacement. Such payments shall be authorized only after every effort has been made by the social services official to defer, cancel, reduce or compromise payments on such security interests;

(e) Household moving expenses when a change of residence is necessary because the health, welfare or safety of the eligible person or persons is endangered and such move is not caused by eviction for nonpayment of rent or when such move will substantially reduce rental costs;

SSL

(f) Furniture or clothing which may be necessary in order to enable such person to move to a private residence from a nursing home, hospital or other institution;

(g) Household expenses essential to the maintenance of a home, in the case of a person whose supplemental security income benefit has been reduced because he has been placed in a medical facility. Within forty-five days following placement in such a facility, the social services official shall determine whether, and payments under the subdivision shall not continue unless, such person is expected to remain in such a facility for less than one hundred eighty days following the reduction in such benefits;

(h) Repair or replacement of essential household heating, cooking, refrigeration, water supply, personal safety equipment, plumbing and sanitary equipment;

(i) Security against nonpayment of rent or for damages, as a condition to renting a housing accommodation, as provided in section one hundred forty-three of this chapter;

(j) Broker's fees necessary to securing shelter;

(k) Essential storage of furniture and personal belongings during such circumstances as relocation, eviction or temporary shelter and for so long as the circumstances necessitating the storage continue to exist and provided that eligibility for emergency assistance continues;

(l) Household expenses (including rent, fuel for heating, gas and electric utilities) incurred during the four month period prior to the month in which such person initially applied for supplemental security income benefits or additional state payments, when payment of such household expenses is necessary to prevent eviction or a utility shut-off or to restore such utility services, and, in the judgment of a social services official, other housing accommodations appropriate for such person's best interests are not available in a particular area.

(m) Household expenses (including rent, fuel for heating, gas and electric utilities) incurred during the four month period immediately prior to the month in which such person applied for emergency assistance for adults when payment of such household expenses is necessary to prevent eviction or a utility shutoff or to restore such utility services and, in the judgment of a social services official, other housing accommodations appropriate for such person's best interests are not available in a particular area. A social services official shall not grant emergency assistance under this paragraph if a person has received a grant under this paragraph within the preceding twelve months, unless the granting of such assistance is recommended by the social services official and has been approved by a duly designated official of the department. For purposes of this paragraph, a person shall be deemed to have received a grant under this paragraph within the preceding twelve months if he is residing in a household with another person who has received a grant under this paragraph within the preceding twelve months.

(n) Replacement of so much of a person's lost, stolen or unreceived federal supplemental security income and/or additional state payments check or checks up to a maximum of one-half the amount of each such check, predicated upon the estimated period of time required for the receipt of the original check or replacement check. Such person shall be required, as a condition of eligibility for such emergency assistance, to agree in writing to repay any amount granted as emergency assistance pursuant to this paragraph and paragraph (o) hereof for which he subsequently receives the original or replacement check of supplemental security income payment and/or additional state payments. All such incidences of loss, theft or non-receipt shall have been reported to and appropriately verified by local officials before such replacement.

(o)   Assistance by monetary payment or food voucher, as determined by the social services official, in an amount necessary to meet a person's nutritional requirements for a period of not more than one week, pursuant to regulations of the department for applicants for supplemental security income and/or additional state payments or for emergency assistance pursuant to paragraph (n) of this subdivision. Such assistance shall be provided within twenty-four hours of application where the applicant demonstrates that he requires such assistance to avoid hunger and has no cash or personal assets readily reducible to cash with which to purchase food.

2.   The maximum grant available for any emergency need specified in subdivision one above shall be limited to the amount and paid in the manner as specified by regulations of the department.

Added by Laws 1974, Ch. 1081, eff. Apr. 1, 1974; Laws 1975, Ch. 198; Laws 1976, Ch. 125; Laws 1977 Ch. 31; Laws 1978, Ch. 129; Laws 1980, Ch. 44; Laws 1982, Ch. 34; Laws 1984, Ch. 34; Laws 1986, Ch. 14; Laws 1988, Ch. 29; Laws 1990, Ch. 44, eff. Mar. 31, 1990, to eliminate the expiration date of the 1974 amendment.

§ 303-a.   Grants of assistance for guide dogs, hearing dogs and service dogs; certain cases.

1.   It shall be the duty of the social services official to provide assistance, in accordance with regulations of the department, to a person with a disability using a guide dog, hearing dog or service dog who has been determined to be eligible for or is receiving federal supplemental security income benefits and/or additional state payments, for the purchase of food for such dog.

2.   Such regulations of the department shall fix an amount of not less than thirty-five dollars a month, and the method and frequency of distribution and procedures for the determination and periodical re-determination of eligibility for such assistance.

3.   Such assistance shall not be granted to any person for whom earned income has been exempted for such purpose pursuant to federal law or regulation.

4.   The full amount properly expended by social services districts under this section, including costs of administration, shall be reimbursed by the state, notwithstanding any inconsistent provision of section three hundred one of this chapter.

SSL

Added by Laws 1978, Ch. 732, eff. Aug. 7, 1978; **amended** by Laws 1983, Ch. 493, eff. Oct. 13, 1983; **amended** by Laws 1986, Ch. 404, eff. July 21, 1986; **amended** by Laws 1986, Ch. 562, eff. Nov. 21; Laws 1988, Ch. 29; Laws 1990, Ch. 44, eff. Mar. 31, 1990, to eliminate the expiration date of section (section retroactively eff. Apr. 1, 1974).

§ 304. Application; verification.

1.   A person requesting emergency assistance under this title shall make his application therefor in person or through another on his behalf, on such form and in such manner as the department may by regulation require, to the social services official in the county in which the applicant resides.

2.   Whenever such application is made, an investigation and record shall be promptly made of the circumstances of the applicant in accordance with the regulations of the department to ascertain the facts supporting the application and to obtain such other information as may be required by the department.

3.   The social services official shall require that a person applying for or receiving emergency assistance under this title or his duly designated representative be interviewed personally at a time and in a manner provided by the regulations of the department.

    Added by Laws 1974, Ch. 1081, eff. Apr. 1, 1974; Laws 1975, Ch. 198; Laws 1976, Ch. 125; Laws 1977 Ch. 31; Laws 1978, Ch. 129; Laws 1980, Ch. 44; Laws 1982, Ch. 34; Laws 1984, Ch. 34; Laws 1986, Ch. 14; Laws 1988, Ch. 29; Laws 1990, Ch. 44, eff. Mar. 31, 1990, to eliminate the expiration date of the section.

§ 305. Appeals and hearings.

    If an application for assistance under this title is not promptly acted upon or is denied or the assistance granted is deemed inadequate by the applicant or recipient, he may appeal to the department in accordance with the provisions of section twenty-two of this chapter. In scheduling investigations, local social services districts shall give priority to applications for assistance under this title.

    Added by Laws 1974, Ch. 1081, eff. Apr. 1, 1974; Laws 1975, Ch. 198; Laws 1976, Ch. 125; Laws 1977 Ch. 31; Laws 1978, Ch. 129; Laws 1980, Ch. 44; Laws 1982, Ch. 34; Laws 1984, Ch. 34; Laws 1986, Ch. 14; Laws 1988, Ch. 29; Laws 1990, Ch. 44, eff. Mar. 31, 1990, to eliminate the expiration date of the section.

§ 306. Records and reports.

    Each social services official shall keep such records and make such reports to the department at such times and in such manner as may be required by department regulations.

    Added by Laws 1974, Ch. 1081, eff. Apr. 1, 1974; Laws 1975, Ch. 198; Laws 1976, Ch. 125; Laws 1977 Ch. 31; Laws 1978, Ch. 129; Laws 1980, Ch. 44; Laws 1982, Ch. 34; Laws 1984, Ch. 34; Laws 1986, Ch. 14; Laws 1988, Ch. 29; Laws 1990, Ch. 44, eff. Mar. 31, 1990, to eliminate the expiration date of the section.

§ 307. Regulations.

The department shall promulgate such regulations as are deemed necessary to implement the provisions of this title.

Added by Laws 1974, Ch. 1081, eff. Apr. 1, 1974; Laws 1975, Ch. 198; Laws 1976, Ch. 125; Laws 1977 Ch. 31; Laws 1978, Ch. 129; Laws 1980, Ch. 44; Laws 1982, Ch. 34; Laws 1984, Ch. 34; Laws 1986, Ch. 14; Laws 1988, Ch. 29; Laws 1990, Ch. 44, eff. Mar. 31, 1990, to eliminate the expiration date of the section.

§ 308. Services.

An application for emergency assistance under this title shall be deemed an application for services, pursuant to section two hundred fifty-three of this chapter, and services shall be provided according to the person's eligibility therefor in accordance with title seven of article five of this chapter.

Added by Laws 1974, Ch. 1081, eff. Apr. 1, 1974; Laws 1975, Ch. 198; Laws 1976, Ch. 125; Laws 1977 Ch. 31; Laws 1978, Ch. 129; Laws 1980, Ch. 44; Laws 1982, Ch. 34; Laws 1984, Ch. 34; Laws 1986, Ch. 14; Laws 1988, Ch. 29; Laws 1990, Ch. 44, eff. Mar. 31, 1990, to eliminate the expiration date of the section.

§ 309. Social services official as conservator.

In appropriate cases, a social services official shall initiate a special proceeding for the appointment of a conservator pursuant to section 77.03 of the mental hygiene law.

Added by Laws 1975, Ch. 198 eff. June 10, 1975; Laws 1976, Ch. 125; Laws 1977 Ch. 31; Laws 1978, Ch. 129; Laws 1980, Ch. 44; Laws 1982, Ch. 34; Laws 1984, Ch. 34; Laws 1986, Ch. 14; Laws 1988, Ch. 29; Laws 1990, Ch. 44, eff. Mar. 31, 1990, to eliminate the expiration date of the section.

§ 320-325. Combined program for aged, blind and disabled persons.

Art. 5, Title 9 repealed by Laws 1974, Ch. 1080, deemed to have been in full force and effect on and after Jan. 1, 1974. Subject matter covered by Social Services Law, Art. 5, Titles 6, 7 and 8.

TITLE 9-A—EQUIPMENT LOAN FUND FOR THE DISABLED

§ 326-a. Title.

This article shall be known and cited as the "Equipment Loan Fund for the Disabled."

Added by Laws 1985, Ch. 609, eff. July 28, 1985.

§ 326-b.   Fund established; participation; other provisions.

1.   There is hereby established in the joint custody of the commissioner and the comptroller the equipment loan fund for the disabled.

2.   Participation in the loan of the monies of the fund shall be available to all disabled persons on the basis of need, pursuant to regulations of the commissioner.

3.   The loan fund shall provide the disabled with the financial opportunity to purchase or replace essential equipment used by them for daily living or vocational functioning following rehabilitation, including, but not limited to, prosthesis, ramps, wheelchairs, wheelchair van lifts, telecommunication devices for the deaf and hearing impaired, devices which allow persons who are blind or visually impaired to discern printed materials and adaptive equipment to permit a disabled person to operate a motor vehicle but not to purchase or replace a motor vehicle itself.

4.   Loans shall be made available directly to the disabled person, the parent, legal guardian, or individual with whom such disabled person resides.

5.   Where any equipment purchase is approved by the department, a loan shall be made in an amount not to exceed four thousand dollars per applicant.

6.   The commissioner shall establish regulations governing payment of interest, repayment periods, certification and approval of purchase, and such other orders, rules and regulations as may be necessary for interpretations, implementation or administration of this article.

7.   During the first three years of operation of the fund, the department shall submit to the governor and legislature annually a summary report setting forth such information as the department deems relevant to monitor and evaluate the progress of the fund.

8.   The fund shall consist of all monies appropriated for the purpose of such fund, all monies transferred to such fund pursuant to law, all monies required by the provisions of this section or any other law to be paid into or credited to this fund, and all monies, including interest, paid by borrowers to the fund in repayment of loans made from the fund.

9.   Monies of the fund following appropriations made by the legislature and allocation by the director of the budget to the fund, shall be available solely for the purpose of enabling eligible applicants to borrow money at less than the prevailing rates of interest for comparable loans.

10.   When used in this article, the term "disabled" shall mean a person having a disability as so defined in section two hundred ninety-two of the executive law.

Added by Laws 1985, Ch. 609, eff. July 28, 1985; **amended** by Laws 1989, Ch. 191, eff. June 24, 1989.

TITLE 9-B—PUBLIC ASSISTANCE EMPLOYMENT PROGRAMS

§ 330. Definitions.

1. Whenever used in this title:

a. The term "commissioner" the commissioner of the state office of temporary and disability assistance; and

b. The term "department" means the state office of temporary and disability assistance.

2. "Net loss of cash income" shall mean the amount by which a family's gross income less any necessary work-related expenses is less than the cash assistance the individual was receiving at the time of receiving an offer of employment. Gross income includes, but is not limited to, earnings, unearned income and cash assistance.

3. "Child care" shall refer to any lawful form of care of a child, as defined by federal and state law and regulation, for less than twenty-four hours per day.

4. "Participant" shall mean an applicant for or recipient of public assistance who volunteers for or is required to participate in work activities as provided in this title.

SSL

5.   Notwithstanding any other provision of this chapter or the labor law, recipients of public assistance who are required to participate in community service or work experience activities authorized pursuant to this title shall be included within the meaning of the term "public employee" for the purposes of applying section twenty-seven-a of the labor law while engaged in community service or work experience programs under this title. In addition, such recipients shall be provided appropriate workers' compensation or equivalent protection for on-the-job injuries and tort claims protection on the same basis, but not necessarily at the same benefit level, as they are provided to other persons in the same or similar positions, while participating in community service or work experience activities under this title.

Added by Laws 1990, Ch. 453, § 1, eff. Oct. 1, 1990; amended by Laws 1997, Ch. 436, § 1 Part B, § 148, eff. Aug. 20, 1997; amended by Laws 1998, Ch. 214, § 16, eff. July 7, 1998, deemed in full force and effect Aug. 20, 1997; amended by Laws 2005, Ch. 57, § 2 (Part C), eff. April 12, 2005, deemed eff. on and after April 1, 2005.

§ 331.   Policies and purposes.

1.   It is hereby declared to be the policy of the state that there be programs under which individuals receiving public assistance will be furnished work activities and employment opportunities, and necessary services in order to secure unsubsidized employment that will assist participants to achieve economic independence. Such programs shall be established and operated in accordance with the provisions of this title and in compliance with federal and state law and regulations.

2.   A social services district may contract or establish agreements with entities which comply with the standards to be established in regulations by the commissioner to provide work activities, including but not limited to, job training partnership act agencies, state agencies, school districts, boards of cooperative educational services, not-for-profit community based organizations, licensed trade schools or registered business schools, libraries, post-secondary educational institutions consistent with this title, and educational opportunity centers and local employers. A district shall, to the extent practicable and permitted under federal requirements, develop performance based contracts or agreements with such entities. Such standards shall include an evaluation procedure to ensure that services offered by a provider are sufficient to enhance substantially a partici-pant's opportunity to secure unsubsidized employment or, when coupled with or provided in conjunction with other activities, represent part of a comprehensive approach to enabling a participant to secure unsubsidized employment. Notwith-standing the provisions of section one hundred fifty-three of this article, expenditures pursuant to contracts or agreements with providers who do not meet the standards for approval of providers as defined in regulations will not be eligible for reimbursement by the department.

3.   No social services district shall, in the exercising of the powers and duties established in this title, permit discrimination on the basis of race, color, national

origin, sex, religion or handicap, in the selection of participants, their assignment or reassignment to work activities and duties, and the separate use of facilities or other treatment of participants.

Added by Laws 1990, Ch. 453, § 1, eff. Oct. 1, 1990. **Amended** by Laws 1995, Ch. 81, § 191, eff. July 1, 1995; **amended** by Laws 1997, Ch. 436, § 1 Part B, § 148, eff. Aug. 20, 1997.

§ 332. Participation and exemptions.

1. In accordance with federal requirements and this title an applicant for or a recipient of public assistance shall not be required to participate in work activities if such individual is determined by the social services district to be exempt because he or she is:

(a) a person who is ill, incapacitated or sixty years of age or older or deemed to be disabled pursuant to section three hundred thirty-two-b of this title;

(b) a child who is under sixteen years of age or under the age of nineteen and attending full-time a secondary, vocational or technical school;

(c) a person whose presence in the home is required because of the illness or incapacity of another member of the household, provided, that to the extent such person is providing care for such a member for a number of hours as required in section three hundred thirty-five-b of this title, such person shall be deemed to be participating in community service;

(d) a parent or other relative of a child who is personally providing care for such child under one year of age for a maximum period of twelve months, only three months of which shall be attributable to any one child, except as otherwise extended up to the twelve month period by the social services official;

(e) a woman who is pregnant, beginning thirty days prior to the medically verified date of delivery of her child.

2. A local social services official shall:

(a) make diligent efforts to assist a person who needs transportation to get to and from a work activity site in obtaining such transportation. Where lack of transportation is a direct barrier to participation in a work activity, the local district shall make a reasonable effort to assign the individual to an appropriate work activity at a site in closest possible proximity to such individual's residence;

(b) allow and give first consideration to volunteers who have not previously terminated participation in such program without good cause to participate in the program; provided, however, such consideration shall not preclude a district from requiring applicants or recipients to participate prior to consideration for or participation by such volunteers if such recipients or applicants are determined to be in greater need of the services provided pursuant to this title in accordance with criteria established by the district and submitted and approved as part of its local plan which may include, but not be limited to, length of time for which a recipient has been in receipt of public assistance benefits, education, age, health and skills.

(c)   in accordance with regulations of the department, inform applicants and recipients of the opportunity to participate voluntarily in work activities at time of application, recertification and contemporaneously with receipt of public assistance benefits on a periodic basis.

3.   A social services official may require a participant in work activities to accept a job only if such official ensures that the participant and the family of such participant will experience no net loss of cash income resulting from acceptance of the job as determined under regulations of the department consistent with federal law and regulations. Pursuant to regulations of the department consistent with federal law and regulations, a social services district shall pay a supplement to a participant in the amount of such net loss of cash income that would otherwise occur. Such supplement shall constitute public assistance only for purposes of payment and reimbursement, and persons in receipt of such supplement shall not for any other purpose be considered to be recipients of public assistance.

Added by Laws 1990, Ch. 453, § 1, eff. Oct. 1, 1990; amended by Laws 1992, Ch. 41, § 138, eff. Apr. 2, 1992; amended by Laws 1992, Ch. 266, § 1, eff. June 30, 1992; amended by Laws 1993, Ch. 59, § 37, eff. Apr. 15, 1993; amended by Laws 1995, Ch. 81, § 190, eff. Apr. 1, 1995; amended by Laws 1997, Ch. 436, § 1 Part B, § 148, eff. Aug. 20, 1997; amended by Laws 1998, Ch. 214, § 17, eff. July 7, 1998, deemed in full force and effect Aug. 20, 1997.

§ 332-a.   Supportive services.

A social services district shall, subject to the availability of federal and state funds, provide such supportive services, including but not limited to transportation, work related expenses, child care for children up to age thirteen, case management, and medical assistance in accordance with regulations of the department, to enable an individual to participate pursuant to this title. Social services districts may continue such services for persons who lose eligibility for public assistance if funds for the activity are obligated or expended, or for up to ninety days if necessary or appropriate to assist individuals to become self-sufficient. In accordance with paragraph (f) of subdivision five of section one hundred thirty-one-a of this chapter, each district shall guarantee child care to each individual participating in work activities who requires child care to participate in such activities, attending orientation or an assessment in accordance with the requirements of this title. Case management shall be provided for pregnant adolescents, adolescent parents and at-risk youth under eighteen years of age as required by title four-B of article six of this chapter. To the extent that resources permit, case management also shall be provided (in order of priority) to: persons identified in department regulations as at-risk youth, persons in the target populations defined in section three hundred thirty of this title, persons whose employability plan indicates a need for two or more concurrent activities and persons with limited English proficiency.

Added by Laws 1990, Ch. 453, § 1, eff. Oct. 1, 1990; **amended** by Laws 1997, Ch. 436, § 1 Part B, § 148, eff. Aug. 20, 1997.

§ 332-b. Disability program.

1.   (a) Upon application and recertification for public assistance benefits, or whenever a district has reason to believe that a physical or mental impairment may prevent the individual from fully engaging in work activities, the social services district shall inquire whether the individual has any medical condition which would limit the individual's ability to participate in work activities pursuant to this title.

(b)   An individual who is eligible to receive comprehensive health services through a special needs plan defined in paragraph (m) or (n) of subdivision one of section three hundred sixty-four-j of this chapter, regardless of whether such a plan is operating in the individual's social services district of residence, shall be considered disabled and unable to engage in work activities or shall be considered work-limited.

2.   (a) Under the circumstances set forth in subdivision one of this section, notice shall be provided to the individual of the opportunity to provide, within ten calendar days, any relevant medical documentation, including but not limited to drug prescriptions and reports of the individual's treating health care practitioner, if any; such documentation must contain a specific diagnosis as evidenced by medically appropriate tests or evaluations and must particularize any work related limitations as a result of any such diagnosis.

(b)   If, prior to submitting his or her medical documentation, the individual is referred to a health care practitioner certified by the office of disability determinations of the office of temporary and disability assistance or, if applicable, to the contracted agency or institution by or with which such health care practitioner is employed or affiliated for an examination pursuant to subdivision four of this section, such individual shall make best efforts to bring such documentation to the examination, and in no case shall provide such records to the examining health care practitioner certified by the office of disability determinations or, if applicable, to the contracted agency or institution by or with which such health care practitioner is employed or affiliated later than four business days after such examination; provided that the individual may demonstrate good cause as defined in regulations, for failure to provide such records within the specific time periods.

3.   The district may in its sole discretion accept such documentation as sufficient evidence that the individual cannot fully engage in work activities and in such case shall modify work assignments consistent with the findings in such medical documents.

4.   In instances where the district determines either that the documentation is insufficient to support an exemption from or limitation on work activities or that further medical evaluation is appropriate, the individual shall be referred to

a health care practitioner certified by the office of disability determinations of the department of social services for an examination of such individual's medical condition.

The health care practitioner who performs the examination of the individual shall:

(a) review and consider all records or information provided by the individual or his or her treating health care practitioner that are pertinent to the claimed medical condition;

(b) make a specific diagnosis as evidenced by medically appropriate tests or evaluations in determination of the individual's claimed condition;

(c) render to the individual and the social services district, an opinion, particularizing the presence or absence of the alleged condition; and

(d) In the event that he or she identifies a condition, other than the alleged condition, that may interfere with the individual's ability to fully engage in work activities, the practitioner shall report such condition; and

(e) determine whether the individual is:

(i) disabled and unable to engage in work activities pursuant to this title for a stated period of time, in which case the applicant shall be exempt in accordance with paragraph (a) of subdivision one of section three hundred thirty-two of this title;

(ii) for a stated period of time, not disabled, but work limited, and able to engage in work activities pursuant to this title, with stated limitations, or

(iii) neither disabled nor work limited.

5. When an applicant or recipient has requested or a social services official has directed a determination pursuant to this section, no assignment to work activities may be made until completion of such determination, unless the applicant or recipient agrees to a limited work assignment not inconsistent with the medical condition alleged by such person.

6. When an applicant or recipient receives notification of the examining medical professional's disability determination, he or she shall also be notified of his or her right to request a fair hearing within ten days of such notice. If such applicant timely requests a fair hearing, no assignment to work activities pursuant to this title may be made pending such hearing and determination unless the applicant or recipient agrees to a limited work assignment not inconsistent with the medical condition alleged by such person. Provided, however, that if a social services district has reason to believe that such recipient or applicant does not actually suffer from a work limiting condition, the district shall provide the applicant or recipient with notice of potential sanctions pursuant to subdivision three of section three hundred forty-two of this title, and provided further that recipients will be subject to sanctions pursuant to subdivision three of section three hundred forty-two of this title if the district determines, based on clear

medical evidence, that there is no basis for the individual's claim that he or she is unable to fully engage in work activities, and that the individual intentionally misrepresented his or her medical condition.

7. Any applicant or recipient determined to be work limited pursuant to this section may be assigned to work activities only in accordance with the limitations and protections set forth in paragraph (e) of subdivision five of section three hundred thirty-five-b of this title.

Added by Laws 1997, Ch. 436, § 1 Part B, § 148, eff. Nov. 1, 1997; **amended** by Laws 1998, Ch. 214, § 18, eff. July 7, 1998, deemed in full force and effect Aug. 20, 1997.

§ 333. Local plans and requirements.

Each social services district shall submit to the commissioner for approval a biennial plan for the provision of education, work, training and supportive services related to the operation of work activity programs pursuant to this title. Such plan shall be developed in cooperation and coordination with public and private education institutions, child care providers, child care resource and referral agencies if available in the district, labor unions, libraries, public and private employers, employment and training agencies and organizations, and private industry councils established in service delivery areas defined in subdivision five of section nine hundred seventy-one of the executive law.

Such plan shall be generally available to the public for review and comment for a period of thirty days prior to submission to the commissioner. In accordance with department regulations and consistent with federal law and regulations, such plan shall include, but not be limited to, the following:

1. Estimates of the number of participants to be served;

2. A description of available supportive services as prescribed by section three hundred thirty-two-a of this title;

3. A description of the available activities under this title and the estimated capacity of such activities;

4. A description of the district's plan to meet federal requirements regarding participation and the district's criteria established pursuant to the provisions of paragraph (b) of subdivision two of section three hundred thirty-two of this title;

5. A list of education and training providers, such as job training partnership act agencies, educational agencies and other public agencies or private organizations with which the district expects to enter into agreements or contracts with a description of such contracts;

6. A description of the orientation to be provided to participants pursuant to section three hundred thirty-four of this title;

7. A description of the assessment tools chosen and the employee qualifications, district administrative unit or contracting entity that will be responsible for the assessments and the development of the employability plans;

SSL

8.   A description of the conciliation procedures to be made available to participants pursuant to section three hundred forty-one of this title; and

9.   Such additional information as is necessary to comply with federal requirements and to provide the report required under section three hundred thirty-nine of this title.

Added by Laws 1990, Ch. 453, § 1, eff. Oct. 1, 1990; **amended** by Laws 1992, Ch. 266, § 2, eff. June 30, 1992; **amended** by Laws 1997, Ch. 436, § 1 Part B, § 148, eff. Aug. 20, 1997.

§ 334.   Orientation.

1.   In accordance with department regulations, a social services district shall, at the time of application or redetermination, in writing and orally inform all public assistance applicants and recipients of the availability of activities and supportive services provided under this title for which they are eligible and of district or participant responsibilities, including:

(a)   education, employment and training opportunities available under the local plan, including educational and training opportunities available at no cost to the participant as well as the responsibilities associated with the repayment of student financial aid;

(b)   supportive services as prescribed by section three hundred thirty-two-a of this title; child care pursuant to section four hundred ten-u of this chapter for persons whose eligibility for assistance has terminated; and applicable medical assistance;

(c)   the obligations of the district regarding the activities and supportive services to be provided;

(d)   the rights, responsibilities and obligations of the participant in the program including, but not limited to, work activities without good cause;

(e)   (1) the types and settings of child care services which may be reasonably accessible to participants and how such services shall be provided and financed;

(2)   the assistance available to help participants select appropriate child care services; and

(3)   the assistance available upon request to help participants obtain child care services.

2.   A local social services official shall inform applicants for and recipients of public assistance of their responsibility to cooperate in establishing paternity and enforcing child support obligations.

3.   Consistent with federal and state law and regulations, a local social services official shall, within one month of the recipient's participation in orientation, notify the recipient in writing of the opportunity to participate in the district's programs established under this title and provide a clear description of how to enter the programs.

Added by Laws 1990, Ch. 453, § 1, eff. Oct. 1, 1990; **amended** by Laws 1997, Ch. 436, § 1 Part B, § 148, eff. Aug. 20, 1997.

§ 335. Assessments and employability plans for certain recipients in households with dependent children.

1.   Each social services official shall ensure that each recipient of public assistance who is a member of a household with dependent children and is eighteen years of age or older, or who is sixteen or seventeen years of age and is not attending secondary school and has not completed high school or a high school equivalency program, receives an assessment of employability based on his or her educational level, including literacy and English language proficiency, basic skills proficiency, child care and other supportive services needs; and skills, prior work experience, training and vocational interests. This assessment shall include a review of family circumstances including a review of any special needs of a child. Such assessment shall be completed within ninety days of the date on which such person is determined eligible for public assistance. An applicant for or recipient of public assistance may be assigned to work activities prior to completion of such assessment.

2.   (a) Based on the assessment required by subdivision one of this section, the social services official, in consultation with the participant, shall develop an employability plan in writing which shall set forth the services that will be provided by the social services official, including but not limited to child care and other services and the activities in which the participant will take part, including child care and other services and shall set forth an employment goal for the participant. To the extent possible, the employability plan shall reflect the preferences of the participant in a manner that is consistent with the results of the participant's assessment and the need of the social services district to meet federal and state work activity participation requirements, and, if such preferences cannot be accommodated, the reasons shall be specified in the employability plan. The employability plan shall also take into account the participant's supportive services needs, available program resources, local employment opportunities, and where the social services official is considering an educational activity assignment for such participant, the participant's liability for student loans, grants and scholarship awards. The employability plan shall explained to the participant. Any change to the participant's employability plan required by the social services official shall be discussed with the participant and shall be documented in writing.

(b)   Where an assessment indicates that a participant who is not subject to the education requirements of subdivision four of section three hundred thirty-six-a of this title has not attained a basic literacy level, the social services official shall encourage and may require the participant to enter a program to achieve basic literacy or high school equivalency or to enter such educational programs in combination with other training activities consistent with the employability plan.

SSL

3. Each applicant for or recipient of public assistance as described herein must participate in an assessment as required by the social services district in accordance with the conditions of this section. Applicants who fail or refuse to participate with the requirements of this section shall be ineligible for public assistance. Recipients who fail or refuse to participate with the requirements of this section shall be subject to the sanctions set forth in section three hundred forty-two of this title.

4. A local social services official shall, pursuant to department regulations developed in consultation with the department of education, and the department of social services or its successor agencies use designated trained staff or contract with providers having a demonstrated effectiveness in performing assessments and developing employability plans to perform assessments and develop employability plans.

5. A social services district shall assign participants to activities pursuant to their employability plans to the extent that child care is guaranteed and other services as prescribed by section three hundred thirty-two-a of this title and section four hundred ten-u of this chapter are available. The district shall provide information to participants orally and in writing, as appropriate, regarding child care and the methods of payment therefor. Such information shall be sufficient for participants to make an informed decision regarding child care.

6. Nothing in this section shall be construed to prevent a social services official from providing an assessment more detailed or comprehensive than the requirements set forth in this section.

Added by Laws 1990, Ch. 453, § 1, eff. Oct. 1, 1990; **amended** by Laws 1997, Ch. 436, § 1 Part B, § 148, eff. Nov. 1, 1997; **amended** by Laws 1998, Ch. 214, § 19, eff. July 7, 1998, deemed in full force and effect Aug. 20, 1997.

§ 335-a. Assessments and employability plans for certain recipients in households without dependent children.

1. To the extent resources are available, the social services official shall, within a reasonable period of time not to exceed one year following application and not to the exclusion of the assessment requirements of section three hundred thirty-five of this title, conduct an assessment of employability based on the educational level, including literacy and English language proficiency; basic skills proficiency; supportive services needs; and the skills, prior work experience, training and vocational interests of each participant. This assessment shall include a review of family circumstances.

2. (a) Based on the assessment required by subdivision one of this section, the social services official, in consultation with the participant, shall develop an employability plan in writing which shall set forth the services that will be provided by the social services official and the activities in which the participant will take part, including supportive services and shall set forth an employment goal for the participant. A local social services district may assign recipients in

households without dependent children to any activity. The employability plan also shall take into account the participant's supportive services needs, available program resources, local employment opportunities, and where the social services official is considering an educational activity assignment for such participant, the participant's liability for student loans, grants and scholarship awards. The employability plan shall be explained to the participant. Any change to the participant's employability plan required by the social services official shall be discussed with the participant and shall be documented in writing.

(b) Where an assessment indicates that a participant who is not subject to the education requirements of this title has not attained a basic literacy level, the social services official shall encourage and may require the participant to enter a program to achieve basic literacy or high school equivalency or to enter such educational programs in combination with other training activities consistent with the employability plan.

3. A local social services official shall, pursuant to department regulations developed in consultation with the department of education and the department of social services or its successor agencies, use designated trained staff or contract with providers having a demonstrated effectiveness in performing assessments and developing employability plans to perform assessments and develop employability plans.

4. Each applicant for or recipient of public assistance as described herein must participate in an assessment as required by the social services district in accordance with the conditions of this section. Applicants who fail or refuse to participate with the requirements of this section shall be ineligible for public assistance. Recipients who fail or refuse to participate with the requirements of this section shall be subject to the sanctions set forth in section three hundred forty-two of this title.

5. A social services district shall assign participants to activities pursuant to their employability plans to the extent that supportive services including transportation are available.

6. Nothing in this section shall be construed to prevent a social services official from providing an assessment more detailed or comprehensive that the requirements set forth in this section.

Added by Laws 1990, Ch. 453, § 1, eff. Oct. 1, 1990; **amended** by Laws 1997, Ch. 436, § 1 Part B, § 148, eff. Nov. 1, 1997.

§ 335-b   Mandatory work requirements

1. Each social services district shall meet or exceed the minimum participation rate for recipients of assistance funded under the federal temporary assistance for needy families program participating in work activities as specified below with respect to families receiving such assistance. Each such district shall also meet or exceed the minimum participation rates for households in which there

SSL

is an adult who is receiving safety net assistance. Work activities for which such rates apply are described in section three hundred thirty-six of this title.

(a)   Such rate for all families receiving assistance funded under the federal temporary assistance for needy families program shall be as follows: for federal fiscal year nineteen hundred ninety-seven, twenty-five percent; nineteen hundred ninety-eight, thirty percent; nineteen hundred ninety-nine, thirty-five percent; two thousand, forty percent; two thousand one, forty-five percent; two thousand two and thereafter, fifty percent. Such rates shall apply unless the state is required to meet a different rate as imposed by the federal government, in which case such different rate shall apply in accordance with a methodology approved by the commissioner of the office of temporary and disability assistance.

(b)   Such rate for two-parent families receiving assistance funded under the federal temporary assistance for needy families program shall be as follows: for federal fiscal years nineteen hundred ninety-seven and nineteen hundred ninety-eight, seventy-five percent; nineteen hundred ninety-nine and thereafter, ninety percent. Such rate shall apply unless the state is required to meet a different rate as imposed by the federal government, in which case such different rate shall apply in accordance with a methodology approved by the commissioner of the office of temporary and disability assistance.

(c)   Such rate for households with dependent children in which there is an adult or minor head of household and which is receiving safety net assistance shall be fifty percent.

(d)   Calculation of participation rates. The commissioner of the office of temporary and disability assistance shall promulgate regulations which define the participation rate calculation. Such calculation for families receiving assistance funded under the federal temporary assistance for needy families program pursuant to article IV-A of the social security act shall be consistent with that established in federal law.

(e)   Minimum work hours. In order for individuals to be included in the participation rates specified in this subdivision, such individuals must be engaged in work as defined in title IV-A of the social security act and in this section for a minimum average weekly number of hours as specified below.

(i)   For all families, if the month is in federal fiscal year: nineteen hundred ninety-seven and nineteen hundred ninety-eight, twenty hours per week; nineteen hundred ninety-nine, twenty-five hours per week; two thousand and thereafter, thirty hours per week.

(ii)   For two-parent families or households without dependent children, in any federal or state fiscal year, thirty-five hours per week.

(iii)   In the case of a two-parent family receiving federally funded child care assistance and a parent in the family is not disabled or caring for a severely disabled child, the individual and the other parent in the family are participating in work activities for a total of at least fifty-five hours per week during the month, not fewer than fifty hours of which are attributable to activities described in paragraphs (a) through (h) and (l) of subdivision one of section three hundred thirty-six of this title.

(f)   Such rate for households without dependent children in which there is an adult or minor head of household and which is receiving safety net assistance shall be fifty percent.

2.   Until June 30, 2008, as amended, Laws 2000, Ch. 534, §5, Laws 2004, Ch. 380, §1Engaged in work for a month shall mean participating in work activities identified in subdivision one of section three hundred thirty-six of this title for the required number of hours specified in this section provided, however, that at least twenty hours of such participation, or thirty hours for two-parent families, or fifty hours for two-parent families receiving federally funded child care as set forth in subparagraph (iii) of paragraph (d) of subdivision one of this section, shall be attributable to the activities described in paragraphs (a) through (h) and (l) of subdivision one of section three hundred thirty-six of this title, or for households without dependent children at least twenty hours of participation shall be attributable to the activities set forth in paragraphs (a) through (h) and (l) of subdivision one of section three hundred thirty-six of this title, and further provided that participation in job search and job readiness assistance as identified in paragraph (f) of subdivision one of section three hundred thirty-six of this title shall only be determined as engaged in work for a maximum period of six weeks, only four of which may be consecutive as otherwise limited by federal law; and that individuals in all families and in two parent families may be engaged in work for a month by reason of participation in vocational training to the extent allowed by federal law. Any non-graduate student participating or approved by CUNY, SUNY or another degree granting institution, or any other state or local district approved education, training or vocational rehabilitation agency to participate in work-study, or in internships, externships, or other work placements that are part of the curriculum of that student, shall not be unreasonably denied the ability to participate in such programs and each hour of participation shall count toward satisfaction of such student's work activity requirements of this title provided that the district may consider, among other factors, (a) whether the student has voluntarily terminated his or her employment or voluntarily reduced his or her earnings to qualify for public assistance pursuant to subdivision ten of section one hundred thirty-one of this article; (b) whether a comparable job or on the job training position can reasonably be expected to exist in the private, public or not-for-profit sector; (c) that the student has a cumulative C average or its equivalent, which may be waived by the district for undue hardship based on (1) the death of a relative of the student, (2) the personal injury or illness of the student, or (3) other extenuating circumstances; and (d) whether the institution cooperates in monitoring students attendance and performance and reports to the local social services department monthly on each student. Failure of the institution to monitor and report monthly to local social services districts on attendance and performance of the student's work study, internship, externship

SSL

or other work placement shall be cause for the department to reasonably deny the student's ability to participate in such programs. Students shall be subject to sanctions equivalent to those associated with failure to adequately satisfy their other required work activities. In assigning a non-graduate student participating in work-study, internships, externships or other work placements, pursuant to this section, to other work activities the district shall make reasonable effort to assign the student to hours that do not conflict with the student's academic schedule.

2. [Eff. June 30, 2008, as amended, Laws 1998, Ch. 214, Laws 2004, Ch. 380, §2] Engaged in work for a month shall mean participating in work activities identified in subdivision one of section three hundred thirty-six of this title for the required number of hours specified in this section provided, however, that at least twenty hours of such participation, or thirty hours for two-parent families, or fifty hours for two-parent families receiving federally funded child care as set forth in subparagraph (iii) of paragraph (d) of subdivision one of this section, shall be attributable to the activities described in paragraphs (a) through (h) and (l) of subdivision one of section three hundred thirty-six of this title, or for households without dependent children at least twenty hours of participation shall be attributable to the activities set forth in paragraphs (a) through (h) and (l) of subdivision one of section three hundred thirty-six of this title, and further provided that participation in job search and job readiness assistance as identified in paragraph (f) of subdivision one of section three hundred thirty-six of this title shall only be determined as engaged in work for a maximum period of six weeks, only four of which may be consecutive as otherwise limited by federal law; and that individuals in all families and in two parent families may be engaged in work for a month by reason of participation in vocational training to the extent allowed by federal law.

3. For purposes of determining monthly participation rates under this section, a recipient in a one parent family who is the only parent or caretaker relative in the family of a child who has not attained six years of age is deemed to be engaged in work for a month if the recipient is engaged in work for an average of at least twenty hours per week during the month.

4. For the purposes of this section, a recipient who is married or a head of household and has not attained twenty years of age and who maintains satisfactory school attendance in accordance with federal requirements shall be deemed to be engaged in work to the extent allowed by federal law and regulations.

5. (a) Each parent or caretaker of a child, when such parent or caretaker is receiving public assistance, must be engaged in work as established by the social services district in accordance with the provisions of its local plan filed pursuant to section three hundred thirty-three of this title.

(b) Each social services official shall ensure that each parent or caretaker of a child, when such parent or caretaker is receiving benefits under the federal temporary assistance for needy families program, is required to be engaged in work as soon as practicable, but no later than twenty-four months (whether or not consecutive) from initial receipt of such assistance.

(c) Each social services official shall ensure that each parent or caretaker of a child, when such parent or caretaker is receiving public assistance, is engaged in work as soon as practicable.

(d) Each social services official shall ensure that each adult member of a household without dependents, when such household is receiving public assistance is engaged in work as soon as practicable.

(e) Notwithstanding any other requirement of this section, individuals in receipt of public assistance and who are work limited in accordance with section three hundred thirty-two-b of this title shall be assigned to work activities in accordance with this title only if such assignment:

(i) is consistent with the individual's treatment plan and is determined to be appropriate by the social services official who is satisfied that such person is able to perform the work assigned and that such assignment will assist the individual's transition to self-sufficiency. In the event that such assignment is not part of the individual's treatment plan, the individual shall be deemed to be engaged in work as defined in this subsection if he or she is complying with the requirements of his or her treatment plan.

(ii) where no treatment plan exists, is consistent with the individual's mental and physical limitations.

(f) The social services district shall communicate to the person supervising the work assignment of a work limited recipient any limitations of the recipient.

6. Recipients of safety net assistance who are exempt or work limited pursuant to this title shall be determined to be engaged in work as defined by department regulation.

7. Notwithstanding the participation rates set forth in subdivision one of this section, for purposes of receiving the enhanced state reimbursement for administration of income maintenance, food stamps, and employment programs as set forth in subdivision seventeen of section one hundred fifty-three of this article, the district must meet a fifty percent average monthly participation rate for the following categories of households in a fiscal year: households receiving assistance funded under the federal temporary assistance for needy families block grant program in which there is an adult or minor head of household; and households with dependent children in which there is an adult or minor head of household and which is receiving safety net assistance and payment for which is used to meet the federally required maintenance of effort for the temporary assistance for needy families block grant; provided, however, that in the first state fiscal year in which this subdivision shall have become a law, the participation rate shall be calculated by averaging the monthly participation rate for the period from October first, two thousand six to December thirty-first, two thousand six and for the second year, the participation rate shall be calculated by averaging the monthly participation rate for the period from October first, two thousand six to September thirtieth, two thousand seven, and for each year thereafter, the

participation rate shall be calculated by averaging the monthly participation rate for the federal fiscal year.

Added by Laws 1997, Ch. 436, § 1 Part B, § 148, eff. Aug. 20, 1997; **amended** by Laws 1998, Ch. 214, §§ 20 and 21, eff. July 7, 1998, deemed in full force and effect Aug. 20, 1997; **amended** by Laws 2000, Ch. 534, § 2, eff. Dec. 3, 2000, amendments to expire and be deemed repealed June 30, 2002; **amended** by Laws 2002, Ch. 100, § 1, eff. June 28, 2002, act shall take effect 60 days after it shall have become a law and shall expire June 30, 2004 when upon such date the provisions of this act shall be deemed repealed; **amended** by Laws 2004, Ch. 83, § 1, eff. May 18, 2004, act shall take effect 60 days after it shall have become a law and shall expire June 30, 2006 when upon such date the provisions of this act shall be deemed repealed, amending subd. (2) and Ch. 380 §§ 1 and 2, eff. Aug. 17, 2004; **amended** by Laws 2005, Ch. 57, § 3 (Part C), eff. April 12, 2005, deemed eff. on and after April 1, 2005; Laws 2006, ch. 58, §2 (Part J), eff. April 12, 2006, deemed eff. on and after April 1, 2006.

§ 335-c   Pilot programs

From the funds specifically appropriated therefor the commissioner of the office of temporary and disability assistance in cooperation with the commissioner of the office of children and family services may conduct pilot programs in up to five social services districts to provide intensive employment and other supportive services including job readiness and job placement services to non-custodial parents who are unemployed or who are working less than twenty hours per week; who are recipients of public assistance or whose income does not exceed two hundred percent of the federal poverty level; and who have a child support order payable through the support collection unit as created by section one hundred eleven-h of this chapter or have had paternity established for his or her child and a court proceeding has been initiated to obtain an order of child support, and the custodial or non-custodial parent is receiving child support services through a social services district. Non-custodial parents determined to be eligible for participation in the pilot programs shall be informed of the opportunity to participate in such programs on a voluntary basis. The pilot programs shall have as one component parenting education for the non-custodial parents. Non-custodial parents shall be required to attend such parenting education as a condition of participating in the pilot programs.

Added by Laws 2006, Ch. 109, §1 (Part H), eff. June 23, 2006.

§ 336.   Work activities.

1.   Social services districts may provide, and require applicants for and recipients of public assistance to participate in a variety of activities, including but not limited to the following:

(a)   unsubsidized employment;

(b)   subsidized private sector employment;

(c)   subsidized public sector employment;

(d)   work experience in the public sector or non-profit sector, (including work associated with refurbishing publicly assisted housing) if sufficient private sector employment is not available;

(e)   on-the-job training;

(f)   job search and job readiness assistance, provided that job search is an active and continuing effort to secure employment configured by the local social services official;

(g)   community service provided, however, the number of hours a participant in community service activities authorized pursuant to this section shall be required to work in such assignment shall not exceed a number which equals the amount of assistance payable with respect to such individual (inclusive of the value of food stamps received by such individual, if any) divided by the higher of (a) the federal minimum wage, or (b) the state minimum wage. No participant shall in any case be required to engage in assigned activities for more than forty hours in any week. No participant shall be assigned to a community service activity that conflicts with his or her bona fide religious beliefs;

(h)   vocational educational training as time limited by federal law. For the purposes of this title, "vocational educational training" shall include but not be limited to organized educational programs offering a sequence of courses which are directly related to the preparation of individuals for current or emerging occupations requiring other than a baccalaureate or advanced degree. Such programs shall include competency-based applied learning which contributes to an individual's academic knowledge, higher-order reasoning, and problem-solving skills, work attitudes, general employability skills, and the occupational-specific skills necessary for economic independence. Such term also includes applied technology education;

(i)   job skills training directly related to employment;

(j)   education directly related to employment, in the case of a recipient who has not yet received a high school diploma or a certificate of high school equivalency;

(k)   satisfactory attendance at secondary school or a course of study leading to a certificate of general equivalency in the case of a recipient who has not completed secondary school or received such certificate;

(l)   provision of child care services to an individual who is participating in community service;

(m)   job search and job readiness assistance once the individual has exceeded the six week limit set in federal law;

(n)   educational activities pursuant to section three hundred thirty-six-a of this title.

2.   No participant shall be required to provide child care services as a work activity described in this section unless the participant expressly requests in writing to provide such services.

3.   Social services districts may enter into agreements with public and private employment agencies to assist recipients of public assistance to find jobs.

4.   No participant shall in any case be required to engage in assigned activities for more than forty hours in any week.

5.   In no event shall the programs and activities enumerated in this title be deemed the sole activities that a social services district may provide and require applicants for and recipients of public assistance to engage in. Any program or activity that meets the goals of this title and is consistent with the requirements of the labor law and this chapter shall be allowed.

6.   Any social services district that establishes and provides a program or activity not herein enumerated shall set forth the requirements and structure of such program or activity in its local plan pursuant to the provisions of section three hundred thirty-three of this title.

7.   In accordance with the provisions of paragraph (h) of subdivision two of section four hundred fifty-four of the family court act or as otherwise required by the court, the court may assign to work activities the non-custodial parents of children receiving public assistance and require a report to such court of any failure of said parent to comply with the requirements of such program.

8.   [*Expires on June 30, 2006.*] The hours of participation in federal work study programs completed pursuant to section three hundred thirty-five-b of this title shall be included as a work activity within the definition of unsubsidized employment, subsidized private sector employment or subsidized public sector employment pursuant to paragraphs (a), (b) and (c) of subdivision one of this section, and the hours of participation in internships, externships and other work placements completed pursuant to section three hundred thirty-five-b of this title shall be included as a work activity within the definition of on-the-job training pursuant to paragraph (e) of subdivision one of this section.

Added by Laws 1990, Ch. 453, § 1, eff. Oct. 1, 1990; **amended** by Laws 1991, Ch. 408, § 2, eff. July 17, 1991; **amended** by Laws 1997, Ch. 436, § 1 Part B, § 148, eff. Aug. 20, 1997; **amended** by Laws 1998, Ch. 214, § 22, eff. July 7, 1998, deemed in full force and effect Aug. 20, 1997, and § 62, eff. July 7, 1998, deemed in full force and effect Jan. 1, 1998; **amended** by Laws 2000, Ch. 534, § 4, eff. Dec. 3, 2000, adding subsection (8), amendments to expire and be deemed repealed June 30, 2002; **amended** by Laws 2002, Ch. 100, § 1, eff. June 28, 2002, act shall take effect 60 days after it shall have become a law and shall expire June 30, 2004 when upon such date the provisions of this act shall be deemed repealed; **amended** by Laws 2004, Ch. 83, § 1, eff. May 18, 2004, act shall take effect 60 days after it shall have become a law and shall expire June 30, 2008 when upon such date the provisions of this act shall be deemed repealed.

§ 336-a.   Educational activities.

1.   Social services districts shall make available vocational educational training and educational activities. Such activities may include but need not be limited to, high school education or education designed to prepare a participant

for a high school equivalency certificate, basic and remedial education, education in English proficiency and no more than a total of two years of post-secondary education (or the part-time equivalent if full-time study would constitute an undue hardship) in any of the following providers which meet the performance or assessment standards established in regulations by the commissioner for such providers: a community college, licensed trade school, registered business school, or a two-year college; provided, however, that such post-secondary education must be necessary to the attainment of the participant's individual employment goal as set forth in the employability plan and such goal must relate directly to obtaining useful employment in a recognized occupation.

2. When a district contracts with a proprietary vocational school to provide vocational educational training to participants, not more than twenty-five percent of the approved duration of the program shall be devoted to preparation for a high school equivalency diploma or instruction in English for students with limited proficiency in English. Participants needing instruction in basic literacy shall be referred to basic education programs. Instructors employed by proprietary schools to prepare a participant for a high school equivalency certificate or for education in English proficiency shall meet experience requirements established by the regulations of the commissioner of education.

3. When a participant is assigned to an appropriate vocational educational or educational activity and such activity is available at no cost to the social services district through the school district or board of cooperative educational services in which the participant resides or through another agency or organization providing educational services, the social services district shall refer the participant to such district, board, agency or organization.

4. To the extent provided in paragraphs (a) through (d) of this subdivision and if resources permit, each social services official shall assign to appropriate educational activities any participant who has not obtained a high school diploma or its equivalent:

(a) In accordance with the provisions of this chapter, any such participant who is under age eighteen shall be required to attend educational activities designed to prepare the individual for a high school degree or equivalency certificate. Participants who are not subject to compulsory school attendance requirements may be exempted from the requirements of this paragraph under criteria established by the department in consultation with the state education department and consistent with federal law and regulations.

(b) Any such participant who is age eighteen or nineteen shall be assigned to educational activities, except that the district shall assign such participant to employment and/or other activities under this title if the district has determined that such alternative activities are consistent with the participant's employability plan and, pursuant to department regulations, there has been a determination by the district based on such plan that educational activities are not appropriate for such participant or that the participant has failed to make good progress in such educational activities.

(c)   Any such participant who is an adult in a two-parent family and is under age twenty-five may be required to participate in educational activities consistent with his or her employment goals set forth in the employability plan.

(d)   The social services official shall not assign a participant described in this subdivision to any activities which interfere with the educational activities assigned pursuant to such participant's employability plan and described in this subdivision.

5.   Any applicant for or recipient of public assistance pursuing activities described in this subdivision shall not be assigned to any other activity prior to conducting an assessment and developing an employability plan as prescribed in section three hundred thirty-five or three hundred thirty-five-a of this title. Local social services districts may periodically reevaluate a participant's employment plan and make assignments to other work activities in order to meet participation rates, giving due consideration to the participant's progress in the current, and if applicable, prior program.

6.   Nothing required in this section shall be construed to supersede the eligibility requirements of teen parents as set forth in this chapter.

Added by Laws 1990, Ch. 453, § 1, eff. Oct. 1, 1990. **Amended** by Laws 1995, Ch. 81, § 192 -193, eff. July 1, 1995; **amended** by Laws 1997, Ch. 436, § 1 Part B, § 148, eff. Aug. 20, 1997.

§ 336-b.   Special provisions for reimbursement of home relief.

Repealed by L. 1997, Ch. 436, § 1 Part B, § 148, eff. Aug. 20, 1997.

§ 336-c.   Work experience.

1.   (a) Work experience programs meeting state and federal requirements may be established by social services districts.

(b)   Work experience programs may include the performance of work for a federal office or agency, county, city, village or town or for the state or in the operation of or in an activity of a nonprofit agency or institution, in accordance with the regulations of the department.

2.   A recipient may be assigned to participate in such work experience program only if:

(a)   appropriate federal and state standards of health, safety and other work conditions are maintained;

(b)   the number of hours a participant in work experience activities authorized pursuant to this section shall be required to work in such assignment shall not exceed a number which equals the amount of assistance payable with respect to such individual (inclusive of the value of food stamps received by such individual, if any) divided by the higher of (a) the federal minimum wage provided that such hours shall be limited as set forth in subdivision four of section three hundred thirty-six of this title, or (b) the state minimum wage;

(c)　such recipients are provided appropriate workers' compensation or equivalent protection for on-the-job injuries and tort claims protection on the same basis, but not necessarily at the same benefit level, as they are provided to other persons in the same or similar positions, while participating in work experience activities under this section;

(d)　the project to which the participant is assigned serves a useful public purpose in fields such as health, social services, environmental protection, education, urban and rural development and redevelopment, welfare, recreation, operation of public facilities, public safety, and child day care;

(e)　such assignment would not result in (i) the displacement of any currently employed worker or loss of position (including partial displacement such as reduction in the hours of non-overtime work, wages or employment benefits) or result in the impairment of existing contracts for services or collective bargaining agreements; (ii) the employment or assignment of a participant or the filling of a position when any other person is on layoff from the same or any equivalent position or the employer has terminated the employment of any regular employee or otherwise reduced its workforce with the effect of filling the vacancy so created with a participant assigned pursuant to this section; (iii) any infringement of the promotional opportunities of any current employed person; or (iv) the performance, by such participant, of a substantial portion of the work ordinarily and actually performed by regular employees; or (v) the loss of a bargaining unit position as a result of work experience participants performing, in part or in whole, the work normally performed by the employee in such position;

(f)　such assignment is not at any work site at which the regular employees are on a legal strike against the employer or are being subjected to lock out by the employer.

3.　The public employer shall publish on a monthly basis a report summarizing the employer's work experience program for the month. Such monthly report shall include, at a minimum, summary information regarding the agencies or departments where participants are assigned, work locations, job duties and assignments, hours worked and period worked and shall be provided to the certified collective bargaining representative and may not be disclosed to any other party. Such certified collective bargaining representative shall take reasonable steps to protect the confidentiality of such information and shall take reasonable steps to prevent disclosure of same to non-authorized persons. Every report provided pursuant to this section shall contain a warning against re-disclosure and asserting the confidentiality of the information therein provided.

4.　[*Expires on June 30, 2006.*] In assigning a recipient who is a non-graduate student attending CUNY, SUNY or other approved non-profit education, training or vocational rehabilitation agency, the social services district must, after consultation with officials of CUNY, SUNY or other non-profit education,

SSL

training or vocational rehabilitation agency, assign the student to a work site on campus, where the recipient is enrolled, and shall not unreasonably assign the student to hours that conflict with the student's academic schedule, if an approved work experience assignment is available. Where such work experience assignment is not available, the social services district shall, to the extent possible, assign the student to a work site within reasonable proximity to the campus where the recipient is enrolled and shall not unreasonably assign the student to hours that conflict with the student's academic schedule. Provided, however, in order to qualify for a work experience assignment on-campus, or in close proximity to campus, a student must have a cumulative C average, or its equivalent. The district may waive the requirement that the student have a cumulative C average or its equivalent for undue hardship based on: (i) the death of a relative of the student; (ii) the personal injury or illness of the student; or (iii) other extenuating circumstances.

Added by Laws 1990, Ch. 453, § 1, eff. Oct. 1, 1990. **Amended** by Laws 1995, Ch. 81, § 149, eff. July 1, 1995; **amended** by Laws 1997, Ch. 436, § 1 Part B, § 148, eff. Aug. 20, 1997; **amended** by Laws 2000, Ch. 534, § 3, eff. Dec. 3, 2000, amendments to expire and be deemed repealed June 30, 2002; **amended** by Laws 2002, Ch. 100, § 1, eff. June 28, 2002, extending expiration date to June 30, 2004; **amended** by Laws 2004, Ch. 83, § 1, eff. May 18, 2004, act shall take effect 60 days after it shall have become a law and shall expire June 30, 2008 when upon such date the provisions of this act shall be deemed repealed.

§ 336-d. Job search activities.

1. Each applicant for or recipient of public assistance shall, upon request of the social services official, demonstrate that he or she is engaged in an active and continuing effort to achieve self-sufficiency as defined by the department. Such effort shall include but not be limited to an active and continuing search for employment, or for persons otherwise exempt in accordance with section three hundred thirty-two of this title, and where deemed appropriate by the social services official, activities that foster preparation for employment. Each such applicant or recipient shall have an affirmative duty to accept any offer of lawful employment in which he or she may engage. The failure of a social services district to assign applicants and recipients to activities pursuant to this title shall not relieve such persons from the requirements of this section. An individual who fails to comply with the requirements of the section shall be subject to the provisions set forth in subdivision five of section one hundred thirty-one of this chapter and of section three hundred forty-one and three hundred forty-two of this title.

2. The social services official shall, if deemed appropriate by such official, supervise job search activities assigned pursuant to this article.

Added by Laws 1990, Ch. 453, § 1, eff. Oct. 1, 1990. **Amended** by Laws 1995, Ch. 81, § 150, eff. July 1, 1995; **amended** by Laws 1997, Ch. 436, § 1 Part B, § 148, eff. Aug. 20, 1997.

§ 336-e. Subsidized public sector employment programs.

1. A social services district may establish subsidized public sector employment programs for public assistance recipients including, but not limited to, grant diversion programs, which may be supported wholly or in part with public assistance funds. Such programs shall be established through agreements between local districts and employers; provided, however, that, if appropriate, the department may act on behalf of one or more local districts in establishing such agreements.

2. Programs may include, but need not be limited to, on-the-job training programs which reimburse employers for the cost of training public assistance recipients through wage subsidies.

3. The social services official or the department is authorized to transfer public assistance funds to employers through written agreements developed and executed in accordance with department regulations.

4. A recipient may be assigned to a subsidized public sector employment activity only if:

(a) the conditions of employment including such factors as the type of work, geographical region and proficiency of the participant are appropriate and reasonable.

(b) the recipient is deemed an employee for purposes of the applicable collective bargaining and labor laws and receives the same benefits and protections as existing employees similarly situated (working a similar length of time and doing similar work) receive pursuant to the provisions of law, and applicable collective bargaining agreement or otherwise as made available to the regular employees of the employer. Each participating person shall be given the opportunity to work sufficient hours to earn a net wage of at least the amount such person would have been entitled to receive as recipients of public assistance or, where applicable, the amount such person would have received for his or her household, including the amount for dependents. Such net wage shall be calculated by deducting from gross wages federal income taxes, federal employment taxes, state income taxes, local income taxes and union dues, if any. No program shall be approved under this section unless the commissioner is satisfied that it contains adequate provisions for the prompt resolution of disputes concerning participation in the program and the obligations and benefits associated with it. Nothing contained in this section shall be deemed to affect, modify or abridge a participant's right to a fair hearing pursuant to section twenty-two of this chapter or representation thereat by counsel or, if applicable, the participant's collective bargaining representative.

(c) a participant employed by an employer subject to the civil service law or subject to rules consistent with such law is appointed to an appropriate classified position. Notwithstanding any other provision of law, rule or regulation, such position shall be deemed to be in the non-competitive class of the classified service only while such participant is serving in the position.

SSL

(d)   no employee of the participating employer is displaced by any recipient employed pursuant to this section. For the purpose of this subdivision, the term displacement shall include partial displacement, such as a reduction in the customary hours of work (including overtime), wages, or employment benefits.

(e)   no participant shall be employed:

(i)   if any other employee of the employer is available for reinstatement, recall or reemployment following a leave of absence, furlough, layoff or suspension from the same or any substantially equivalent job;

(ii)   when the employer has terminated the employment of any regular employee or otherwise reduced its work force with the intention of filling the vacancy or vacancies so created by hiring a participant whose wages are subsidized under this program; or

(iii)   when the employee organization representing employees of the employer is engaged in a strike against the employer or such employees have been locked-out by the employer; or

(iv)   where such employment results in the loss of a bargaining unit position as a result of work experience participants performing, in part or in whole, the work normally performed by the employee in such position.

(f)   no position is created that will infringe in any way upon the promotional opportunities of currently employed individuals or individuals currently engaged in an approved apprenticeship training program.

(g)   no participant shall remain in a position if another employee is eligible for promotion from an eligible list to that position. An employer shall, at least ten days prior to filling a position with a participant, notify any employee organization that represents employees who are engaged in similar work or training in the same or substantially equivalent job as that in which the placement is to be made, that it intends to make a placement pursuant to the terms of this section.

(h)   where an employee organization represents employees who are engaged in similar work in the same or substantially equivalent job as that proposed to be funded under this program, an opportunity is provided for such organization to comment on the proposed placement of a participant or the administration of the program and the social services official or his or her designee shall respond to such comments within ten days of receipt thereof.

(i)   employers are prohibited from using public assistance funds to encourage or discourage membership in, or participation in the activities of, any employee organization and each employer provides to the social services district assurances that no such funds will be used for such purposes.

(j)   nothing herein shall be construed to affect, modify or otherwise abridge any provision of the civil service law.

Added by Laws 1990, Ch. 453, § 1, eff. Oct. 1, 1990; **amended** by Laws 1997, Ch. 436, § 1 Part B, § 148, eff. Aug. 20, 1997.

§ 336-f.   Subsidized private sector and not-for-profit employment programs.

1.   A social services district may establish subsidized private sector employment programs for public assistance recipients including, but not limited to, grant diversion programs, which may be supported wholly or in part with public assistance funds. Such programs shall be established through agreements between local districts and employers, including not for profit employers; provided, however, that, if appropriate, the department may act on behalf of one or more local districts in establishing such agreements.

2.   Programs may include, but need not be limited to, on-the-job training programs which reimburse employers for the cost of training public assistance recipients through wage subsidies.

3.   The social services official or the department is authorized to transfer public assistance funds to employers through written agreements developed and executed in accordance with department regulations.

4.   A recipient may be placed in a subsidized private sector or not-for-profit employment activity only if:

(a)   the conditions of employment including such factors as the type of work to be performed, the geographic location of the job, and the qualifications of the participant are appropriate and reasonable.

(b)   the recipient is deemed an employee for purposes of the applicable collective bargaining and labor laws and receives the same benefits and protections as an employee similarly situated (working a similar length of time and doing similar work) receives pursuant to the provisions of law, an applicable collective bargaining agreement or otherwise as made available to the employees of the employer.

(c)   no employee of the participating employer is displaced by any recipient hired pursuant to this section. For the purpose of this subdivision, the term displacement shall include partial displacement, such as a reduction in the customary hours of work (including overtime), wages, or employment benefits.

(d)   no participant shall be hired:

(i)   if any other employee of the employer is available for reinstatement, recall or reemployment following a leave of absence, furlough, layoff or suspension from the same or any substantially equivalent job; or

(ii)   when the employer has terminated the employment of any regular employee or otherwise reduced its work force with the intention of filling the vacancy or vacancies so created by hiring a participant whose wages are subsidized under this program; or

SSL

(iii) when the employee organization representing employees of the employer is engaged in a strike against the employer or such employees have been locked-out by the employer; or

(iv) when such hiring will result in the loss of a bargaining unit position as a result of work experience participants performing, in part or in whole, the work normally performed by the employee in such position.

(e) no job is created that will infringe in any way upon the promotional opportunities of current employees or individuals currently engaged in an approved apprenticeship training program.

(f) no participant shall remain in a job if another employee is eligible for promotion to that job. An employer shall, at least ten days prior to filling a position with a participant, notify any employee organization that represents employees who are engaged in similar work or training in the same or substantially equivalent jobs as those in which the placement is to be made, that it intends to make a placement pursuant to the terms of this section.

(g) where an employee organization represents employees who are engaged in similar work in the same or substantially equivalent jobs as those proposed to be funded under this program, an opportunity is provided for such organization to comment on the proposed placement of a participant or the administration of the program and the social services official or his or her designee shall respond to such comments within ten days of receipt thereof.

(h) employers are prohibited from using public assistance funds to encourage or discourage membership in, or participation in the activities of, any employee organization and each employer provides to the social services district assurances that no such funds will be used for such purposes.

5. The social services district shall require every private or not-for-profit employer that intends to hire one or more work activity participants to certify to the district that such employer has not, in the past five years, been convicted of a felony or a misdemeanor the underlying basis of which involved workplace safety and health or labor standards. Such employer shall also certify as to all violations issued by the department of labor within the past five years. The social services official in the district in which the participant is placed shall determine whether there is a pattern of violations sufficient to render the potential employer ineligible. Employers who submit false information under this section shall be subject to criminal prosecution for filing a false instrument.

Added by Laws 1990, Ch. 453, § 1, eff. Oct. 1, 1990; **amended** by Laws 1997, Ch. 436, § 1 Part B, § 148, eff. Aug. 20, 1997.

§ 336-g. On-the-job training for recipients of aid to dependent children.

Repealed by L. 1997, Ch. 436, § 1 Part B, § 148, eff. Aug. 20, 1997.

§ 336-h.　Employment alternatives partnership program.

Repealed by L. 1997, Ch. 436, § 1 Part B, § 148, eff. Aug. 20, 1997.

§ 337.　Responsibilities of state departments and agencies.

1.　Notwithstanding any provision of this chapter to the contrary, responsibility for the operation and administration of work, employment and training programs in connection with the programs administered pursuant to this chapter shall be vested in the commissioner subject to regulations, procedures and instructions of the department.

2.　The department is authorized to enter into agreements with any state agency, social services district or other entity for performance of activities authorized under this title.

　　Added by Laws 1990, Ch. 453, § 1, eff. Oct. 1, 1990; **amended** by Laws 1997, Ch. 436, § 1 Part B, § 148, eff. Aug. 20, 1997.

§ 338.　Cooperation of state departments.

　　There shall be such cooperative agreements and arrangements between and among the department, the state department of social services or its successor agency, the state department of education and other appropriate state departments as shall be necessary to assure compliance with federal and state requirements or requirements of this title relating to employment programs for applicants of and recipients of public assistance and to assure that the purposes of such program will be effectively accomplished. The purpose of such arrangements is to promote interagency planning, coordinate service delivery and identify needed resources for the implementation of such employment programs.

　　Added by Laws 1990, Ch. 453, § 1, eff. Oct. 1, 1990; **amended** by Laws 1997, Ch. 436, § 1 Part B, § 148, eff. Aug. 20, 1997.

§ 339.　Reports.

　　The commissioner shall require, from each social services district, information and reports sufficient and timely to enable the state to meet all federal reporting requirements.

　　Added by Laws 1990, Ch. 453, § 1, eff. Oct. 1, 1990; **amended** by Laws 1997, Ch. 436, § 1 Part B, § 148, eff. Aug. 20, 1997.

§ 340.　Technical assistance.

　　The commissioner shall provide technical assistance to social services districts in the development, implementation and administration of plans described in section three hundred thirty-three of this title.

SSL

The department shall monitor the implementation and ongoing operation of the programs pursuant to this title. Such monitoring shall include review of sample cases to assess compliance with applicable state and federal statutes and regulations.

Added by Laws 1990, Ch. 453, § 1, eff. Oct. 1, 1990; **amended** by Laws 1997, Ch. 436, § 1 Part B, § 148, eff. Aug. 20, 1997.

§ 341.   Conciliation; refusal to participate.

1.   (a) Consistent with federal law and regulations and this title, if a participant has failed or refused to comply with the requirements of this title, the social services district shall issue a notice in plain language indicating that such failure or refusal has taken place and of the right of such participant to conciliation to resolve the reasons for such failure or refusal to avoid a pro-rata reduction in public assistance benefits for a period of time set forth in section three hundred forty-two of this title. The notice shall indicate the specific instance or instances of willful refusal or failure to comply without good cause with the requirements of this title and the necessary actions that must be taken to avoid a pro-rata reduction in public assistance benefits. The notice shall indicate that the participant has seven days to request conciliation with the district regarding such failure or refusal in the case of a safety net participant and ten days in the case of a family assistance participant. The notice shall also include an explanation in plain language of what would constitute good cause for non-compliance and examples of acceptable forms of evidence that may warrant an exemption from work activities, including evidence of domestic violence, and physical or mental health limitations that may be provided at the conciliation conference to demonstrate such good cause for failure to comply with the requirements of this title. If the participant does not contact the district within the specified number of days, the district shall issue ten days notice of intent to discontinue or reduce assistance, pursuant to regulations of the department. Such notice shall also include a statement of the participant's right to a fair hearing relating to such discontinuance or reduction. If such participant contacts the district within seven days in the case of a safety net participant or within ten days in the case of a family assistance participant, it will be the responsibility of the participant to give reasons for such failure or refusal.

   (b)   Unless the district determines as a result of such conciliation process that such failure or refusal was willful and was without good cause, no further action shall be taken. If the district determines that such failure or refusal was willful and without good cause, the district shall notify such participant in writing, in plain language and in a manner distinct from any previous notice, by issuing ten days notice of its intent to discontinue or reduce assistance. Such notice shall include the reasons for such determination, the specific instance or instances of willful refusal or failure to comply without good cause with the requirements of this title, the necessary actions that must be taken to avoid a pro-rata reduction in public assistance benefits, and the right to a fair hearing relating to such discontinuance or reduction. Unless extended by mutual agreement of the participant and the district, conciliation shall terminate and a determination shall be made within fourteen days of the date a request for conciliation is made in the case of a safety net participant or within thirty days of the conciliation notice in the case of a family assistance participant.

2. (a) The department shall establish in regulation a conciliation procedure for the resolution of disputes related to an individual's participation in programs pursuant to this title.

(b) The district shall contract with an independent entity, approved by the department, or shall use designated trained staff at the supervisory level who have no direct responsibility for the participant's case to mediate disputes in the conciliation conference. If no such supervisory staff or independent entity is available, the district may designate another trained individual, who has no direct responsibility for the participant's case to mediate disputes in the conciliation conference.

(c) If a participant's dispute cannot be resolved through such conciliation procedure, an opportunity for a fair hearing shall be provided. No sanction relating to the subject dispute may be imposed during the conciliation process.

3. When any family assistance participant required to participate in work activities fails to comply with the provisions of this title, the social services district shall take such actions as prescribed by appropriate federal law and regulation and this title.

4. When any safety net participant required to participate in work activities fails to comply with the provisions of this title, the social services district shall deny assistance to such participant in accordance with section three hundred forty-two of this title.

5. (a) To the extent that federal law requires, a social services district shall provide to those family assistance participants whose failure to comply has continued for three months or longer a written reminder of the option to end a sanction after the expiration of the applicable minimum sanction period by terminating the failure to comply as specified in subdivision three of this section. Such notice shall advise that the participant may immediately terminate the first or second sanction by participating in the program or accepting employment and that any subsequent sanction after six months have elapsed may be terminated by participating in the program or accepting employment.

(b) A social services district shall provide to those safety net participants whose failure to comply has continued for the length of the sanction period or longer a written reminder of the option to end a sanction after the expiration of the applicable minimum sanction period by terminating the failure to comply as specified in subdivision four of this section.

6. Consistent with federal law and regulation, no action shall be taken pursuant to this section for failure to participate in the program or refusal to accept employment if:

(a)   child care for a child under age thirteen (or day care for any incapacitated individual living in the same home as a dependent child) is necessary for an individual to participate or continue participation in activities pursuant to this title or accept employment and such care is not available and the social services district fails to provide such care;

(b)   (1) the employment would result in the family of the participant experiencing a net loss of cash income; provided, however, a participant may not claim good cause under this paragraph if the social services district assures that the family will not experience a net loss of cash income by making a supplemental payment;

(2)   net loss of cash income results if the family's gross income less necessary work-related expenses is less than the cash assistance the participant was receiving at the time the offer of employment is made; or

(c)   the participant meets other grounds for good cause set forth by the department in its implementation plan for this title which, at a minimum, must describe what circumstances beyond the household's control will constitute "good cause".

Added by Laws 1990, Ch. 453, § 1, eff. Oct. 1, 1990. Amended by Laws 1995, Ch. 81, §§ 151 -152, eff. July 1, 1995; amended by Laws 1997, Ch. 436, § 1 Part B, § 148, eff. Aug. 20, 1997; Laws 2006 ch. 61, §1 (Part D), eff. June 19.

§ 342.   Noncompliance with the requirements of this title.

1.   In accordance with the provisions of this section an individual who is required to participate in work activities shall be ineligible to receive public assistance if he or she fails to comply, without good cause, with the requirements of this title. Such ineligibility shall be for the amount and periods specified in this section. Good cause for failing to comply with the requirements of this title shall be defined in department regulations, provided, however, that the parent or caretaker relative of a child under thirteen years of age shall not be subject to the ineligibility provisions of this section if the individual can demonstrate, in accordance with the regulations of the office of children and family services department, that lack of available child care prevents such individual from complying with the work requirements of this title. The parent or caretaker relative shall be responsible for locating the child care needed to meet the work requirements; provided, however, that the relevant social services district shall provide a parent or caretaker relative who demonstrates an inability to obtain needed child care with a choice of two providers, at least one of which will be a regulated provider.

2.   In the case of an applicant for or recipient of public assistance who is a parent or caretaker of a dependent child the public assistance benefits otherwise available to the household of which such individual is a member shall be reduced pro-rata:

(a)   for the first instance of failure to comply without good cause with the requirement of this article until the individual is willing to comply;

(b)   for the second instance of failure to comply without good cause with the requirements of this article, for a period of three months and thereafter until the individual is willing to comply;

(c)   for the third and all subsequent instances of failure to comply without good cause with the requirements of this article, for a period of six months and thereafter until the individual is willing to comply.

3.   In the case of an individual who is a member of a household without dependent children applying for or in receipt of safety net assistance the public assistance benefits otherwise available to the household of which such individual is a member shall be reduced pro-rata:

(a)   for the first such failure or refusal, until the failure or refusal ceases or ninety days, which ever period of time is longer;

(b)   for the second such failure or refusal, until the failure ceases or for one hundred fifty days, whichever period of time is longer; and

(c)   for the third and all subsequent such failures or refusals, until the failure ceases or one hundred eighty days, whichever period of time is longer.

4.   A recipient of public assistance who quits or reduces his hours of employment without good cause shall be considered to have failed to comply with the requirements of this article and shall be subject to the provisions of this section.

5.   A person described in paragraph (b) of subdivision seven of section one hundred fifty-nine of this chapter may not be sanctioned if his or her failure to comply with requirements of this title are related to his or her health status.

Added by Laws 1997, Ch. 436, § 1 Part B, § 148, eff. Aug. 20, 1997.

TITLE 10—AID TO DEPENDENT CHILDREN

———

(Repealed and transferred sections noted under appropriate section number of text.)

SSL

§ 343.   Declaration of object.

It is hereby declared a state policy that aid to dependent children be provided under the provisions of this title in every county of the state.

Amended by Laws 1946, Ch. 200, eff. Apr. 1, 1946.

§ 344.   Responsibility.

1.   Each social services district shall be responsible for providing family assistance, under this title, to persons eligible therefor who reside in its territory. Temporary absence, within or without the state, of such persons from such territory, except as otherwise provided, shall not affect their eligibility for such aid.

2.   Aid shall be construed to include services, particularly those services which may be necessary for each child in the light of the particular home conditions and his or her other needs.

3.   Each social services district shall administer the aid, care and services provided under this title, in accordance with state and federal requirements.

Added by Laws 1946, Ch. 200; amended by Laws 1951, Ch. 171; amended by Laws 1963, Ch. 1014; amended by Laws 1968, Ch. 547, eff. June 5, 1968; amended by Laws 1997, Ch. 436, § 1 Part B, § 31, eff. Aug. 20, 1997.

§ 345.   Definition.

As used in this title the term "child" means a person under eighteen years of age, or a person under nineteen years of age who is a full-time student regularly attending a secondary school or in the equivalent level of vocational or technical training if, before such person attains age nineteen, such person may reasonably be expected to complete the program of such secondary school or training.

Added by Laws 1974, Ch. 909, eff. Sept. 1, 1974, but is not to be construed to alter, affect, impair or defeat any rights, obligations, duties or interests heretofore accrued, incurred or conferred prior to the effective date; **amended** by Laws 1981, Ch. 1053, eff. Jan. 1, 1982.

§ 345-347. Appointment and powers of duties of boards; attendance at conferences.

Repealed by Laws 1946, Ch. 200, eff. April 1, 1946.

§ 348. Application for family assistance.

1. Application for family assistance shall be made to the appropriate social services district.

2. Application for or receipt of family assistance shall operate as an assignment to the state and the social services district concerned of any rights to support from any other person as such applicant or recipient may have in his or her own behalf or in behalf of any other family member for whom the applicant or recipient is applying for or receiving assistance. Applicants for or recipients of family assistance shall be informed that such application for or receipt of such benefits will constitute such an assignment.

3. Such assignment shall terminate with respect to current support rights upon a determination by a local commissioner that such person is no longer eligible for family assistance, except with respect to the amount of any unpaid support obligation that has accrued.

4. It shall be the duty of social services officials to provide same day referral of applicants for family assistance support services as provided under title six-A of article three of this chapter pursuant to part D of title IV of the federal social security act, as part of the initial application for family assistance.

Amended by Laws 1946, Ch. 200, eff. Apr. 1, 1946; **amended** by Laws 1977, Ch. 516, § 8, eff. July 1, 1977; **amended** by Laws 1995, Ch. 81, § 194, eff. July 1, 1995; **amended** by Laws 1997, Ch. 436, § 1 Part B, § 32, eff. Aug. 20, 1997.

§ 349. Eligibility.

A. Family assistance shall be given to a pregnant individual, a parent or other relative as herein specified for the benefit of a child under eighteen years of age, or of a child under nineteen years of age who is a full-time student regularly attending a secondary school or in the equivalent level of vocational or technical training if, in the judgment of the social services official:

1. the granting of an allowance will be in the interest of such child, and

1-a. [*Repealed.*]

2. the parent or other relative is a fit person to bring up such child so that his or her physical, mental and moral well-being will be safeguarded, and

3. such child is a resident of the state on the date of application for aid.

B.   1. An allowance may be granted for the aid of such child who is living with a parent or other adult related to him or her by blood, marriage or adoption eligible to receive assistance on his or her behalf pursuant to the federal social security act, the provisions of this chapter and regulations of the department.

2.   Notwithstanding the provisions of this title and titles three and four of this article to the contrary, the department may by regulation require that some or all persons, or households containing such persons, who are otherwise eligible for family assistance and are permanently disabled and awaiting determinations of eligibility for federal supplemental security income under title XVI of the federal social security act receive family assistance without use of federal funding and the department is authorized to reclassify retroactively all or a portion of the amount of any family assistance which otherwise has been or would be received by any such person or household if such reclassification is in the financial inter-ests of the state; provided, however, that any such retroactive reclassification shall be accomplished without diminution or increase of the family assistance grant previously paid and shall not affect any rights, obligations or entitlements of any such person under the family assistance program. Any such transfer or reclassifi-cation may be accomplished by appropriate notation in the records of the social services district or the department, and no other notice thereof need be made.

C.   In making such allowances consideration shall be given to the ability of the relative making application and of any other relatives to support and care for or to contribute to the support and care of such child. In making all such allowances it shall be made certain that the religious faith of the child shall be preserved and protected.

D.   Family assistance shall not be payable to a family for any month in which any caretaker relative with whom the child is living is, on the last day of such month, participating in a strike, and no individual's needs shall be included in determining the amount of such aid which is payable for any month to a family if, on the last day of such month, such individual is participating in a strike.

Added by Laws 1945, Ch. 329; **amended** by Laws 1946, Ch. 200; Laws 1957, Ch. 432; Laws 1961, Ch. 802; Laws 1962, Ch. 334; Laws 1963, Ch. 155; Laws 1965, Ch. 188; Laws 1966, Chs. 165, 798; Laws 1969, Ch. 186; Laws 1971, Ch. 110; Laws 1974, Ch. 909, eff. Sept. 1, 1974; Laws 1975, Ch. 685, eff. July 1, 1975, until June 30, 1976 which **repealed** B (2). See legislative history of § 111–a, *supra;* Laws 1976, Ch. 326, eff. June 8, 1976; **amended** by Laws 1981, Ch. 1053, eff. Jan. 1, 1982; **amended** by Laws 1997, Ch. 436, § 1 Part B, § 34, eff. Aug. 20, 1997, and deemed in full force and effect Dec. 2, 1996, and § 35, eff. Aug. 20, 1997.

§ 349-a.   Procedures to insure the protection of victims of domestic violence.

1.   The department, after consultation with the office for the prevention of domestic violence and statewide domestic violence advocacy groups, shall by regulation establish requirements for social services districts to notify all

applicants and, upon recertification, recipients, of procedures for protection from domestic violence and the availability of services. Such notice shall inform applicants and recipients that the social services district will make periodic inquiry regarding the existence of domestic violence affecting the individual. Such notice shall also inform individuals that response to these inquiries is voluntary and confidential; provided, however, that information regarding neglect or abuse of children will be reported to child protective services.

2. Such inquiry shall be performed utilizing a universal screening form to be developed by the department after consultation with the office for the prevention of domestic violence and statewide domestic violence advocacy groups. An individual may request such screening at any time, and any individual who at any time self identifies as a victim of domestic violence shall be afforded the opportunity for such screening.

3. An individual indicating the presence of domestic violence, as a result of such screening, shall be promptly referred to a domestic violence liaison who meets training requirements established by the department, after consultation with the office for the prevention of domestic violence and statewide domestic violence advocacy groups.

4. The domestic violence liaison shall assess the credibility of the individual's assertion of domestic violence. Such assessment shall be based upon the relevant information and corroborating evidence, but shall in the absence of other sufficient evidence include, at a minimum, a sworn statement by the individual alleging such abuse.

5. Upon a determination that the individual's allegation is credible, (a) the individual shall be informed of services, which shall be available on a voluntary basis; and (b) the domestic violence liaison shall conduct an assessment to determine if and to what extent domestic violence is a barrier to compliance with public assistance requirements or to employment; and (c) shall assess the need for waivers of such program requirements. Such waivers shall, to the extent permitted by federal law, include, but not be limited to, residency requirements, child support cooperation requirements and employment and training requirements; provided, however, that exemptions from the sixty month limit on receipt of benefits under the federal temporary assistance to needy families block grant program shall be available only when the individual would not be required to participate in work or training activities because of an independently verified physical or mental impairment resulting from domestic violence, anticipated to last for three months or longer, or if the individual is unable to work because of the need to care for a dependent child who is disabled as a result of domestic violence. Provided, however, that pursuant to section one hundred forty-two of the Welfare Reform Act of 1997 victims of domestic violence may be exempted from the application of subdivision two of section three hundred forty-nine of this article on the basis of hardship.

6. Waivers granted pursuant to subdivision five of this section shall be provided pursuant to a determination of good cause in cases where compliance with

SSL

such requirements would make it more difficult for the individual or the individual's children to escape from domestic violence, or subject the individual, or the individual's children, to further risk of domestic violence. Such waivers shall be for an initial period of no less than four months; provided, however, that all such waivers shall be subject to on-going review of the individual's circumstances by the domestic violence liaison, and may be extended, modified or terminated in accordance therewith. An individual may decline a waiver or terminate an existing waiver at any time without penalty.

7.   Information with respect to victims of domestic violence shall not be released to any outside party or parties or other governmental agencies unless the information is required to be disclosed by law, or unless authorized in writing by the applicant or recipient.

Repealed by Laws 1981, Ch. 1053, eff. Jan. 1, 1982; added by Laws 1997, Ch. 436, § 1 Part B, § 36, eff. Aug. 20, 1997; amended by Laws 1998, Ch. 214, § 29, eff. July 7, 1998, deemed in full force and effect Aug. 20, 1997, changing effective date of § 349-a from Aug. 20, 1997 to Apr. 17, 1998, or upon such earlier date as may be provided by the department of family assistance in regulations promulgated pursuant to such section.

§ 349-b. Deserted, abandoned and out of wedlock children; special provisions.

1.   In addition to other eligibility requirement each person who is applying for or receiving assistance under this title, and who is otherwise eligible for assistance under this title, shall be required, as a further condition of eligibility for such assistance:

(a)   to assign to the state and the social services district any rights to support such person may have either in his own behalf or in behalf of any other family member for whom he is applying for or receiving aid; and

(b)   to cooperate with the state and the social services official, in accordance with standards established by regulations of the department consistent with federal law, in establishing the paternity of a child born out-of-wedlock for whom assistance under this title is being applied for or received, in their efforts to locate any absent parent and in obtaining support payments or any other payments or property due such person and due each child for whom assistance under this title is being applied for or received, except that an applicant or recipient shall not be required to cooperate in such efforts in cases in which the social services official has determined, in accordance with criteria, including the best interests of the child, as established by regulations of the department consistent with federal law, that such applicant or recipient has good cause to refuse to cooperate. Each social service district shall inform applicants for and recipients of family assistance required to cooperate with the state and local social services officials pursuant to the provisions of this paragraph, that where a proceeding to establish paternity has been filed, and the allegation of paternity has been denied by the respondent, that there shall be a stay of all paternity proceedings and related local social services proceedings until sixty days after the birth of the child. Such applicants and recipients shall also be informed that public assistance and care shall not be denied during the stay on the basis of refusal to cooperate pursuant to the provisions of this paragraph.

2. The amount of the payments due from the absent parent in meeting his support obligations under this section shall be the amount of a current court support order or, in the absence of a court order, if such parent agrees to meet his support obligation, an amount to be determined in accordance with a support formula established by the department and approved by the secretary of the federal department of health, education and welfare.

3. [*Repealed.*]

4. [*Repealed.*]

Added by Laws 1975, Ch. 685, eff. July 1, 1975. See legislative history of § 111–a, *supra;* **amended** by Laws 1976, Ch. 326; Laws 1977, Ch. 516; Laws 1978, Ch. 456; Laws 1983, Ch. 384; **amended** by Laws 1979, Ch. 520, eff. July 10, 1979; **amended** by L. 1997, Ch. 398, § 91, eff. Nov. 11, 1997; **amended** by L. 1998, Ch. 214, § 9-a, eff. July 7, 1998.

§ 350. Character and adequacy.

1. (a) Allowances shall be adequate to enable the father, mother or other relative to bring up the child properly, having regard for the physical, mental and moral well-being of such child, in accordance with the provisions of section one hundred thirty-one-a of this chapter and other applicable provisions of law. Allowances shall provide for the support, maintenance and needs of one or both parents if in need, and in the home and for the support, maintenance and needs of the other relative if he or she is without sufficient means of support, provided such parent, parents and relative are not receiving federal supplemental security income payments and/or additional state payments for which they are eligible. The social services official may, in his discretion, make the incapacitated parent the grantee of the allowance and when allowances are granted for the aid of a child or children due to the unemployment of a parent, such official may make the unemployed parent the grantee of the allowance.

(b) When permitted in accordance with the regulations of the department, provision may be made under this title for any item of maintenance of eligible individuals who are receiving medical assistance for needy persons in a hospital, nursing home, infirmary or other eligible medical institutions. However, aid under this title shall not include provisions for care or services in any hospital, nursing home, infirmary or other eligible medical institutions when such care and services may be provided as medical assistance for needy persons pursuant to title eleven of article five.

(c) [*Repealed.*]

(d) In accordance with the regulations of the department approved by the director of the budget, allowances granted under the provisions of this title may

SSL

include the costs of maintaining an eligible child in a summer camp operated by a nonprofit organization, corporation or agency, which has been issued an operating permit by the appropriate health official in whose jurisdiction such camp is situated, when in the judgment of the social services official it is advisable for the welfare of such child to provide maintenance in such summer camp, provided, however, that such maintenance shall not be provided where funds therefor were available or could have been obtained from other sources in the absence of the authority granted in this paragraph.

(e) Any inconsistent provisions of this title notwithstanding, so long as federal law and regulations require, family planning services and supplies shall be offered and promptly furnished to eligible persons of childbearing age, including children who can be considered sexually active, who desire such services and supplies, in accordance with the regulations of the department. In order to maximize federal financial participation, the department may require that such services shall be furnished under title eleven of article five. No person shall be compelled or coerced to accept such services or supplies.

(f) When, in the judgment of the social services official, care cannot be provided in the mother's own home, care may be provided in a licensed maternity home, a family home or boarding home for a child or his mother in need of public assistance and care during pregnancy and during and after delivery and for eligible persons assistance may be provided in a family home or boarding home, provided that no assistance will be provided under this title when such assistance can be provided under title eleven. Payments to such homes and institutions for care and maintenance provided by them shall be at rates established pursuant to law, and regulations of the department. The department, however, shall not establish rates of payment to homes and institutions without approval of the director of the budget.

(g) The social services official of a social services district shall advise persons who are eligible for aid under this title of the availability for their benefit of child health screening services and of care and treatment of disabilities and conditions discovered by such screening under the provisions of title eleven of article five of this chapter; and upon request such official shall promptly furnish such services or care and treatment under the provisions of such title.

2. Assistance funded in whole or in part under the temporary assistance to needy families block grant program temporary assistance to needy families

(a) shall not be granted to any family which includes an adult who has received any form of assistance funded in whole or in part under the temporary assistance to needy families block grant program under title IV-A of the federal social security act in this state or in any other state for a cumulative period of longer than sixty months, provided that,

(i) in determining the number of months for which an individual who is a parent or pregnant has received assistance, there shall not be included any period in which the individual was a minor child who was not the head of household or married to the head of household, and

(ii) the social services district shall, in accordance with regulations of the department, subject to any federal limitations, exempt a family from the application of this subdivision on the basis of hardship when the adult family member is unable to work because of an independently verified physical or mental impairment including those resulting from domestic violence, or when the adult family member is in receipt of supplemental security income payments under title XVI of the federal social security act or additional state payments under title six of this article, and

(iii) provided that periods in which an adult receives cash assistance in the safety net assistance program shall be included in the cumulative period referred to in this paragraph regardless of whether such assistance was funded in whole or in part by the temporary assistance to needy families block grant program;

(b) may be increased, decreased or revoked at any time; and

(c) except in the case of a child reaching the age of eighteen years, may be continued for a period of not more than one month after a child becomes ineligible to be granted allowance under this title.

3. [*Repealed.*]

4. Adequate supervision of all families receiving such aid shall be provided and supervisory visits shall be made to each family as frequently as the regulations of the department and the circumstances of the case may require.

5. The social services official of the social services district shall in cooperation with other public officers, private relief societies and individuals seek to secure for persons to whom allowances are granted as provided in this title or who apply for such allowances additional assistance whenever the social services official is unable adequately to provide for their needs and the needs of their families. It shall be the duty of such official and the family court to cooperate with each other in the effective enforcement of the obligation of the parents of children for whose benefit such allowances are granted to support such children to the extent of the parents' ability to do so.

6. [*Repealed.*]

7. [*Repealed.*]

SSL

Amended by Laws 1942, Ch. 351; Laws 1943, Ch. 514; Laws 1945, Ch. 329; Laws 1946, Ch. 200; Laws 1947, Ch. 320; Laws 1951, Ch. 171; Laws 1957, Ch. 432; Laws 1963, Chs. 7, 38, 52; Laws 1965, Chs. 3,143, 287, 795; Laws 1966, Ch. 256; Laws 1968, Chs. 611, 991; Laws 1969, Chs. 184, 186, 599; Laws 1970, Chs. 384, 566; Laws 1971, Chs. 110, 945; Laws 1973, Ch. 516; Laws 1974, Ch. 909, eff. Sept. 1, 1974; Ch. 1080, eff. Jan. 1, 1974; **amended** by Laws 1975, Ch. 685, eff. July 1, 1975, which **repealed** subd. 3 **amended** by Laws 1976, Ch. 326; Laws 1977, Ch. 51; Laws 1978, Ch. 456; Laws 1982, Ch. 384. See legislative history of § 111-a, *supra;* **amended** by Laws 1978, Ch. 555, § 6, eff. July 24, 1978; **amended** by Laws 1986, Ch. 127, eff. June 2, 1986; **amended** by Laws 1997, Ch. 436, § 1 Part B, § 37, eff. Aug. 20, 1997, the amendment of subd. 2 to be deemed in full force and effect Dec. 2, 1996; **amended** by Laws 1998, Ch. 214, § 13, eff. July 7, 1998, deemed in full force and effect Aug. 20, 1997.

§ 350-a.   Protective payments.

1.   Whenever the social services official who is granting allowances of family assistance to a relative for the benefit of a child determines that such relative is unable to manage the allowances he or she may, when appropriate in accordance with state and federal requirements, pay the allowances to another individual who is interested in or concerned with the welfare of the child and relative.

2.   The determination of the social services official to pay allowances to another individual pursuant to subdivision one may be appealed to the department by the relative concerned who shall be given an opportunity for a fair hearing on his appeal. The department may review such determination on its own motion. The powers and procedures prescribed by section twenty-two of this chapter shall likewise apply to the determinations, appeals and reviews made pursuant to this section.

3.   Any relative or other person who is granted an allowance of family assistance for the benefit of a child or children and who wilfully uses all or any part of such allowance other than for the benefit of such child or children, shall be guilty of a misdemeanor.

Added by Laws 1963, Ch. 39; **amended** by Laws 1978, Ch. 473, eff. July 11, 1978; **amended** by Laws 1997, Ch. 436, § 1 Part B, § 84, eff. Aug. 20, 1997.

§ 350-b.   Work incentive program; policies and purposes.

Repealed by Laws 1990, Ch. 453, § 6, eff. Oct. 1, 1990.

§ 350-c.   Responsibilities of state departments in work incentive program.

Repealed by Laws 1990, Ch. 453, § 6, eff. Oct. 1, 1990.

§ 350-d.   Cooperation of state departments; agreements.

Repealed by Laws 1990, Ch. 453, § 6, eff. Oct. 1, 1990.

§ 350-e.   Registration and certification; work incentive programs.

Repealed by Laws 1990, Ch. 453, § 6, eff. Oct. 1, 1990.

§ 350-f.   Special incentives for participation in projects of the work incentive program for recipients of aid to dependent children.

Repealed by Laws 1990, Ch. 453, § 6, eff. Oct. 1, 1990.

§ 350-g.   Work incentive program; person's refusal to participate.

Repealed by Laws 1990, Ch. 453, § 6, eff. Oct. 1, 1990.

§ 350-h.   Payments to United States Secretary of Labor; work incentive program.

Repealed by Laws 1990, Ch. 453, § 6, eff. Oct. 1, 1990.

§ 350-i.   Additional training incentive allowances.

Repealed by Laws 1990, Ch. 453, § 6, eff. Oct. 1, 1990.

§ 350-j.   Emergency assistance to needy families with children.

1.   Any inconsistent provisions of this chapter or of any other law notwithstanding, so long as federal aid is available therefor, a social services district shall provide emergency assistance as herein defined to persons eligible, including migrant workers with families.

2.   For purposes of this section, the term "emergency assistance" means aid, care and services to meet the emergency needs of a child or the household in which he or she is living, in the following circumstances:

   (a)   where the child is under twenty-one years of age; and

   (b)   the child is living with, or within the previous twelve months has lived with, an adult related by blood, marriage or adoption; and

   (c)   in cases of applications for grants of cash assistance, such child or such household is not categorically eligible for or receiving family assistance; and

   (d)   such emergency needs resulted from a catastrophic occurrence or from a situation which threatens family stability and which has caused the destitution of the child and/or household; and

   (e)   such occurrence or situation could not have been foreseen by the applicant, was not under his or her control and, in the case of a person receiving public assistance, did not result from the loss, theft or mismanagement of a regular public assistance grant; and

   (f)   the emergency grant being applied for will not replace or duplicate a public assistance grant already made under section one hundred thirty-one-a of this chapter.

3.   Emergency assistance to needy families with children shall be provided to the extent of items of need and services set forth in sections one hundred thirty-one and one hundred thirty-one-a of this chapter, and items of medical services set forth in section three hundred sixty-five-a of this chapter, and in amounts set forth in the regulations of the department for children who are without available resources, and when such assistance is necessary to avoid destitution or to provide

SSL

them with living arrangements in a home, and such destitution or such need did not arise because such children or relatives refused without good cause to accept employment or training for employment; provided, however, that no assistance shall be provided which would duplicate assistance under sections one hundred thirty-one and one hundred thirty-one-a of this article for which a person is eligible or would be eligible but for a sanction for violation of the requirements of title nine-B of article five of this chapter or other requirement of state law and provided further that, notwithstanding any inconsistent provision of this section or section one hundred thirty-one-a of this article, persons for whom preventive services are being provided under title four of article six of this chapter or who are living in foster care or in public, congregate or group facilities, such as residential facilities for victims of domestic violence, may, pursuant to regulations of the department within amounts specifically appropriated therefor and subject to the terms and conditions of such appropriation, receive assistance hereunder on their behalf for such services or for care in such facilities in amounts exceeding those set forth in section one hundred thirty-one-a of this article.

4. [*Repealed.*]

5. In scheduling investigations concerning applications for emergency assistance pursuant to this section, local social services districts shall give priority to such applications.

Added by Laws 1968, Ch. 992; **amended** by Laws 1971, Ch. 110; **amended** by Laws 1975, Ch. 483; **amended** by Laws 1977, Ch. 77; **amended** by Laws 1978, Ch. 473, eff. July 11, 1978; **amended** by Laws 1997, Ch. 436, § 1 Part B, § 38, eff. Aug. 20, 1997.

§ 350-k.   Public works projects.

Repealed by Laws 1990, Ch. 453, § 6, eff. Oct. 1, 1990.

§ 350-l.   On-the-job training opportunities in aid to families with dependent children.

Repealed by Laws 1990, Ch. 453, § 6, eff. Oct. 1, 1990.

§ 350-m.   Job search activities for employable recipients of aid to dependent children.

Repealed by Laws 1990, Ch. 453, § 6, eff. Oct. 1, 1990.

§ 351.   Central index or social service exchange.

Repealed by Laws 1974, Ch. 246, eff. Jan. 1, 1975.

§ 352.   Deserted or abandoned children; special provisions.

1. A social services official who makes a family assistance allowance for the benefit of a child who has been abandoned or deserted by a parent shall

promptly give notice thereof to the appropriate district attorney where there is reason to believe such parent may have violated the provisions of section 260.00 of the penal law.

The social services official providing family assistance allowances pursuant to the provisions of this title, for the benefit of a child who has an absent parent, shall have and shall perform the following duties and powers in addition to others imposed or conferred upon him or her by or pursuant to other provisions of this chapter or other law:

(a)　to take such steps and make such efforts to locate any parent of such child whose whereabouts are unknown to such official as all available means will allow; such means shall include, and there shall be utilization of, appropriate services offered by the department, by agencies of other states and by the federal government;

(b)　to determine the ability and potential ability of the parents of each such child to support or to contribute to the support of such child;

(c)　to establish cooperative arrangements with the family court, county attorneys, corporation counsels and other law enforcement officials, for the location of missing parents of such children and for the enforcement of their obligations to support or contribute to support of such children to the extent of their ability;

(d)　to provide pertinent information to such court and law enforcement officials to enable them to assist in locating absent parents of such children and in securing support payments therefrom, providing that there is an agreement between such social services official and such court and such law enforcement officials insuring that such information will be used only for the purpose intended;

(e)　to reimburse, to the extent that state and federal requirements authorize or require, appropriate courts and law enforcement officials for activities related to the requirements of this chapter and the family court act with respect to enforcement of support obligations and for services they have undertaken on behalf of such official.

3.　For purposes of this section, "absent parent" shall mean any person who is legally responsible for a spouse or child, who is absent from the household, whether such person's location is known or unknown, and fails to provide for the support of such spouse or child.

SSL

Added by Laws 1951, Ch. 171; **amended** by Laws 1969, Ch. 187; **amended** by Laws 1974, Ch. 909, eff. Sept. 1, 1974; Laws 1975, Ch. 685, eff. July 1, 1975, **amended** by Laws 1976, Ch. 326; Laws 1977, Ch. 51; Laws 1978, Ch. 456; Laws 1982, Ch. 384. See legislative history of § 111–a, *supra*; Laws 1977, Ch. 516, eff. July 1, 1977; **amended** by Laws 1997, Ch. 436, § 1 Part B, § 85, eff. Aug. 20, 1997.

§ 352-a.　Children born out of wedlock; special provisions.

1.　The social services official providing family assistance allowances, pursuant to the provisions of this title, for the benefit of children born out of wedlock, shall have and shall perform the following duties and powers in addition to others imposed or conferred upon him or her by or pursuant to other provisions of this chapter or other law:

(a)   to ascertain who may be the putative father of such child born out of wedlock, and take appropriate steps to establish the paternity thereof in accordance with applicable provisions of law;

(b)   to determine the ability and potential ability of the parents of each such child to support or to contribute to the support of such child;

(c)   to take such steps and make such efforts to locate any such parent whose whereabouts are unknown to such official as all available means will allow; such means shall include, and there shall be utilization of, appropriate services offered by the department, by agencies of other states and by the federal government;

(d)   to establish cooperative arrangements with the family court, county attorneys, corporation counsels and other law enforcement officials, for the establishment of paternity and location of missing parents of such children and for the enforcement of their obligations to support or contribute to support of such children to the extent of their ability;

(e)   to provide pertinent information to such court and law enforcement officials to enable them to assist in locating putative fathers and deserting parents of such children, in establishing paternity and in securing support payments therefrom, provided that there is an agreement between such social services official and such court and such law enforcement officials insuring that such information will be used only for the purpose intended;

(f)   to reimburse, to the extent that state and federal requirements authorize or require, appropriate courts and law enforcement officials for activities related to the requirements of this chapter and the family court act with respect to establishment of paternity and for services they have undertaken on behalf of such official.

[No subd. 2. has been enacted.]

Added by Laws 1969, Ch. 187, eff. Mar. 30, 1969; **amended** by Laws 1975, Ch. 685, eff. July 1, 1975, **amended** by Laws 1976, Ch. 326; Laws 1977, Ch. 51; Laws 1978, Ch. 456; Laws 1982, Ch. 384. See legislative history to § 111-a, *supra.* **Amended** by Laws 1997, Ch. 436, § 1 Part B, § 86, eff. Aug. 20, 1997.

§ 352-b.   Administration; single unit.

Repealed by Laws 1976, Ch. 326, eff. June 8, 1976.

§ 353.   Grant of aid.

Upon the completion of an investigation the proper social services official shall

(a)   decide whether the applicant is eligible for and should receive family assistance, the amount, nature and manner of paying or providing it and the date on which it shall begin,

(b)   notify the applicant of his decision in writing.

Amended by Laws 1942, Ch. 351; Laws 1946, Ch. 200; Laws 1951, Ch. 171; Laws 1974, Ch. 909; **amended** by Laws 1978, Ch. 473, eff. July 11, 1978; **amended** by Laws 1997, Ch. 436, § 1 Part B, § 87, eff. Aug. 20, 1997.

§ 354.   Investigation of complaints.

Repealed by L. 1997, Ch. 436, § 1 Part B, § 88, eff. Aug. 20, 1997.

§ 355.   Rules, regulations and forms.

The department shall

1.   supervise the administration of family assistance,

2.   prescribe the form of and print and supply to the public welfare officials blanks for applications, reports, affidavits and such other forms as it may deem advisable,

3.   make regulations necessary for the carrying out of the provisions of this title to the end that allowances may be granted and the provisions of this title administered uniformly throughout the state.

Amended by Laws 1946, Ch. 200, eff. Apr. 1, 1946; **amended** by Laws 1997, Ch. 436, § 1 Part B, § 89, eff. Aug. 20, 1997.

§ 356.   Moneys to be provided by counties and cities; how expended.

1.   The legislative body of each social services district shall annually appropriate to the commissioner of social services such sum as may be needed for family assistance, and for the administration thereof. When the assistance for which such social services district is responsible is administered, pursuant to title three-a of article three, by a social services official who is not an officer of the social services district for which the appropriation is made, all or part of the sum appropriated shall be made available to such other officer and to the municipality of which he or she is an officer, in the manner, and at such times, as is required by other provisions of this chapter. The legislative body of the social services district shall include such sums in the taxes to be levied for such social services district.

2.   Allowances granted for family assistance shall be paid out of moneys appropriated or otherwise made available to the social services district.

3.   Expenditures for allowances and administrative expenses under this title shall be a charge upon the county or city public welfare district.

Added by Laws 1946, Ch. 200, eff. Apr. 1, 1946; amended by Laws 1997, Ch. 436, § 1 Part B, § 90, eff. Aug. 20, 1997.

§ 357. Quarterly estimates.

Each social services district shall submit to the department quarterly estimates of its anticipated expenditures for family assistance and administrative expenses not less than thirty days before the first day of each of the quarters beginning on the first day of the months of July, October, January and April, in such form and together with such other information as the department may require.

Amended by Laws 1946, Ch. 200, eff. Apr. 1, 1946; amended by Laws 1997, Ch. 436, § 1 Part B, § 91, eff. Aug. 20, 1997.

§ 358 Federal temporary assistance for needy families block grant

1.   The department shall submit the plan pursuant to title IV-A of the federal social security act. The state's program under title IV-A shall be entitled "Family Assistance", and benefits under the state plan with respect to the temporary assistance for needy families block grant shall be known as family assistance. The department shall act for the state in any negotiations relative to the submission and approval of such plan and make any arrangement which may be necessary to obtain and retain such approval and to secure for the state the benefits of such federal act relating to title IV-A. The department shall make such regulations not inconsistent with law as may be necessary to make such plan conform to such federal act and any rules and regulations adopted pursuant thereto. Such regulations may provide for operation of components of the program relating to refugees by contract with a private agency or agencies pursuant to section 412(e) of the immigration and nationality act (8 U.S. Code 1522(e)(7)). Any refugee whose needs are met pursuant to such a contract who would otherwise be a recipient of family assistance or safety net assistance shall be regarded for all other purposes as a recipient of family assistance or of safety net assistance, respectively. Each social services district shall be responsible for a share of the state's expenditures for operation of such a contract which shall be equal to the share of such expenditures such district would have borne after reimbursement from state and federal funds in accordance with section one hundred fifty-three of this article, had the expenditure been made by such district. The department shall make reports to such federal agency in the form and nature required by it and comply with any request or direction of such federal agency which may be necessary to assure the correctness and verification of such reports.

2.   The department of taxation and finance shall accept and receive any and all grants of money awarded to the state pursuant to title IV-A of such social security act. All moneys so received shall be deposited by the department of taxation and finance in a special fund or funds and shall be used by the state exclusively for temporary assistance for needy families block grant and the administration thereof as provided in this chapter; provided, however, that portions

of such moneys may be transferred to the child care and development block grant or the social services block grant as the legislature may from time to time provide. Such money shall be paid from such fund or funds on audit and warrant of the comptroller upon vouchers of or certification by the commissioner.

3. If and for so long as the federal government provides one hundred percent funding therefor, the department is authorized to operate a Cuban and Haitian entrant program and a refugee resettlement program pursuant to title IV of the federal immigration and nationality act, including provision for refugee cash assistance, refugee medical assistance, refugee child welfare services, and refugee social services. The department shall submit the plan for such refugee resettlement program to the federal department of health and human services and shall act for the state in any negotiations relative to the submission and approval of such plan and make any arrangement which may be necessary to obtain and retain such approval.

4. The department shall make such regulations not inconsistent with law as may be necessary to make such plan conform to such federal act and any rules and regulations adopted pursuant thereto. Such regulations may provide for operation of components of the program directly by the department, through social services districts on behalf of the department or, subject to the approval of the director of the budget upon a demonstration of cost-effectiveness, by contract with a private agency or agencies and may provide that an eligible recipient shall receive assistance pursuant to such contract in lieu of family assistance or safety net assistance.

5. The state program under title IV-A of the social security act shall permit individuals to accumulate funds in individual development accounts established pursuant to section four hundred three of the social security act as trust accounts funded with periodic contributions of earned income by the individual or of amounts matched by or through a not-for-profit organization described in section 501(c)(3) of the Internal Revenue Code and exempt from taxation under section 501(a) of such Code; provided, however, that neither the state nor social services districts shall be required to make or match contributions or to administer any such account.

Added by Laws 1951, Ch. 5; **amended** by Laws 1953, Ch. 562; **amended** by Laws 1971, Ch. 110, eff. July, 1971; **amended** by Laws 1995, Ch. 81, §§ 162 -163, eff. July 1, 1995; **amended** by Laws 1997, Ch. 436, § 1 Part B, § 39, eff. Aug. 20, 1997.

§ 358-a   Dependent children in foster care

(1) Initiation of judicial proceeding.

(a) A social services official who accepts or proposes to accept the custody and guardianship of a child by means of an instrument executed pursuant to the provisions of section three hundred eighty-four of this chapter, or the care and custody of a child as a public charge by means of an instrument executed pursuant to the provisions of section three hundred eighty-four-a of this chapter, shall determine whether such child is likely to remain in the care of such official for a period in excess of thirty consecutive days. If such official determines that the child is likely to remain in care for a period in excess of thirty consecutive days, such official shall petition the family court judge of the county or city in which the social services official has his or her office, to approve such instrument upon a determination that the placement of the child is in the best interest of the child, that it would be contrary to the welfare of the child to continue in his or her own home and, that where appropriate, reasonable efforts were made prior to the placement of the child into foster care to prevent or eliminate the need for removal of the child from his or her home and that prior to the initiation of the court proceeding required to be held by this subdivision, reasonable efforts were made to make it possible for the child to return safely home. In the case of a child whose care and custody have been transferred to a social services official by means of an instrument executed pursuant to the provisions of section three hundred eighty-four-a of this chapter, approval of the instrument shall only be made upon an additional determination that all of the requirements of such section have been satisfied.

(b)   [Expires and repealed June 30, 2007] The social services official shall initiate the proceeding by filing the petition as soon as practicable, but in no event later than thirty days following removal of the child from the home provided, however, that the court shall receive, hear and determine petitions filed later than thirty days following removal of the child from his or her home, but state reimbursement shall not be available to the social services district for care and maintenance provided to such child. The social services official shall diligently pursue such proceeding. Where the care and custody of a child as a public charge has been transferred to a social services official by means of an instrument executed pursuant to the provisions of section three hundred eighty-four-a of this chapter for a period of thirty days or less for an indeterminate period which such official deems unlikely to exceed thirty days, and thereafter such official determines that such child will remain in his or her care and custody for a period in excess of thirty days, such official shall, as soon as practicable but in no event later than thirty days following such determination, execute with the child's parent, parents or guardian a new instrument pursuant to the provision of section three hundred eighty-four or three hundred eighty-four-a of this chapter and shall file a petition in family court, pursuant to this section, for approval of such instrument. In such cases involving a social services official, expenditures for the care and maintenance of such child from the date of the initial transfer of his care and custody to the social services official shall be subject to state reimbursement.

(2)   Contents of petition.

(a)   Any petition required or authorized pursuant to subdivision one of this section shall allege whether the parent, parents or guardian executed the instrument because the parent, parents or guardian would be unable to make adequate provision for the care, maintenance and supervision of such child in his or their own home, and shall include facts supporting the petition. The petition shall contain a notice in conspicuous print providing that if the child remains in foster care for fifteen of the most recent twenty-two months, the agency may be required by law to file a petition to terminate parental rights. The petition shall also set forth the names and last known addresses of all persons required to be given notice of the proceeding, pursuant to this section and section three hundred eighty-four-c of this chapter, and there shall be shown by the petition or by affidavit or other proof satisfactory to the court that there are no persons other than those set forth in the petition who are entitled to notice pursuant to the provisions of this section or of section three hundred eighty-four-c of this chapter. The petition shall also set forth the efforts which were made, prior to the placement of the child into foster care, to prevent or eliminate the need for removal of the child from his or her home and the efforts which were made prior to the filing of the petition to make it possible for the child to return safely home. If such efforts were not made, the petition shall set forth the reasons why these efforts were not made. The petition shall request that, pending any hearing which may be required by the family court judge, a temporary order be made transferring the care and custody of the child to the social services official in accordance with the provisions of subdivision three of this section. In the case of a child whose care and custody have been transferred to a social services official by means of an instrument executed pursuant to section three hundred eighty-four-a of this chapter, the petition shall also allege and there shall be shown by affidavit or other proof satisfactory to the court that all the requirements of such section have been satisfied, including the results of the investigation to locate relatives of the child, including any non-respondent parent and all of the child's grandparents. Such results shall include whether any relative who has been located expressed an interest in becoming a foster parent for the child or in seeking custody or care of the child.

(b) The social services official who initiated the proceeding shall file supplemental information with the clerk of the court not later than ten days prior to the date on which the proceeding is first heard by the court. Such information shall include relevant portions, as determined by the department, of the assessment of the child and his family circumstances performed and maintained, and the family's service plan if available, pursuant to sections four hundred nine-e and four hundred nine-f of this chapter. Copies of such supplemental information need not be served upon those persons entitled to notice of the proceeding and a copy of the petition pursuant to subdivision four of this section.

(2-a) Continuing jurisdiction.

(a) The court shall possess continuing jurisdiction over the parties until the child is discharged from placement and all orders regarding supervision, protection or services have expired.

(b) The court, upon approving an instrument under this section, shall schedule a permanency hearing pursuant to article ten-A of the family court act for a date certain not more than eight months after the placement of the child

SSL

into foster care. Such date certain shall be included in the order approving the instrument.

(3)   Disposition of petition.

(a)   If the court is satisfied that the parent, parents or guardian executed such instrument knowingly and voluntarily and because he or she would be unable to make adequate provision for the care, maintenance and supervision of such child in his or her home, and that the requirements of section three hundred eighty-four-a of this chapter, if applicable, have been satisfied and that where appropriate, reasonable efforts were made prior to the placement of the child into foster care to prevent or eliminate the need for removal of the child from his or her home and that prior to the initiation of the court proceeding required to be held by subdivision one of this section, reasonable efforts were made to make it possible for the child to return safely to his or her home, the court may find and determine that the best interests and welfare of the child would be promoted by removal of the child from such home, and that it would be contrary to the welfare of such child for the child to continue in such home, and the court shall thereupon grant the petition and approve such instrument and the transfer of the custody and guardianship or care and custody of such child to such social services official in accordance therewith. If the court determines that, where appropriate, reasonable efforts were made prior to the placement of the child into foster care to prevent or eliminate the need for removal of the child from his or her home, that prior to the initiation of the court proceeding reasonable efforts were made to make it possible for the child to return safely to his or her home, or that it would be contrary to the best interests of the child to continue in the home, or that reasonable efforts to prevent or eliminate the need for removal of the child from the home were not made but that the lack of such efforts was appropriate under the circumstances, the court order shall include such findings. Approval of such instrument in a proceeding pursuant to this section shall not constitute a remand or commitment pursuant to this chapter and shall not preclude challenge in any other proceeding to the validity of the instrument. If the permanency plan for the child is adoption, guardianship, permanent placement with a fit and willing relative or another planned permanent living arrangement other than reunification with the parent or parents of the child, the court must consider and determine in its order whether reasonable efforts are being made to make and finalize such alternate permanent placement.

(b)   For the purpose of this section, reasonable efforts to prevent or eliminate the need for removing the child from the home of the child or to make it possible for the child to return safely to the home of the child shall not be required where the court determines that:

(1)   the parent of such child has subjected the child to aggravated circumstances, as defined in subdivision twelve of this section;

(2)   the parent of such child has been convicted of (i) murder in the first degree as defined in section 125.27 or murder in the second degree as defined

in section 125.25 of the penal law and the victim was another child of the parent; or (ii) manslaughter in the first degree as defined in section 125.20 or manslaughter in the second degree as defined in section 125.15 of the penal law and the victim was another child of the parent, provided, however, that the parent must have acted voluntarily in committing such crime;

(3)   the parent of such child has been convicted of an attempt to commit any of the foregoing crimes, and the victim or intended victim was the child or another child of the parent; or has been convicted of criminal solicitation as defined in article one hundred, conspiracy as defined in article one hundred five or criminal facilitation as defined in article one hundred fifteen of the penal law for conspiring, soliciting or facilitating any of the foregoing crimes, and the victim or intended victim was the child or another child of the parent;

(4)   the parent of such child has been convicted of assault in the second degree as defined in section 120.05, assault in the first degree as defined in section 120.10 or aggravated assault upon a person less than eleven years old as defined in section 120.12 of the penal law, and the commission of one of the foregoing crimes resulted in serious physical injury to the child or another child of the parent;

(5)   the parent of such child has been convicted in any other jurisdiction of an offense which includes all of the essential elements of any crime specified in subparagraph two, three or four of this paragraph, and the victim of such offense was the child or another child of the parent; or

(6)   the parental rights of the parent to a sibling of such child have been involuntarily terminated;

unless the court determines that providing reasonable efforts would be in the best interests of the child, not contrary to the health and safety of the child, and would likely result in the reunification of the parent and the child in the foreseeable future. The court shall state such findings in its order.

If the court determines that reasonable efforts are not required because of one of the grounds set forth above, a permanency hearing shall be held within thirty days of the finding of the court that such efforts are not required. Such hearing shall be conducted pursuant to section one thousand eighty-nine of the family court act. The local social services official shall thereafter make reasonable efforts to place the child in a timely manner and to complete whatever steps are necessary to finalize the permanent placement of the child as set forth in the permanency plan approved by the court. If reasonable efforts are determined by the court not to be required because of one of the grounds set forth in this paragraph, the local social services official may file a petition for termination of parental rights of the parent in accordance with section three hundred eighty-four-b of this chapter.

(c)   For the purpose of this section, in determining reasonable efforts to be made with respect to a child, and in making such reasonable efforts, the child's health and safety shall be the paramount concern.

SSL

(d) For the purpose of this section, a sibling shall include a half-sibling.

(e) The order granting the petition of a social services official and approving an instrument executed pursuant to section three hundred eighty-four-a of this chapter may include conditions, where appropriate and specified by the judge, requiring the implementation of a specific plan of action by the social services official to exercise diligent efforts toward the discharge of the child from care, either to his own family or to an adoptive home; provided, however, that such plan shall not include the provision of any service or assistance to the child and his or her family which is not authorized or required to be made available pursuant to the comprehensive annual services program plan then in effect. An order of placement shall include, at the least:

(i) a description of the visitation plan;

(ii) a direction that the respondent or respondents shall be notified of the planning conference or conferences to be held pursuant to subdivision three of section four hundred nine-e of this chapter, of their right to attend the conference, and of their right to have counsel or other representative or companion with them;

A copy of the court's order and the service plan shall be given to the respondent. The order shall also contain a notice that if the child remains in foster care for more than fifteen of the most recent twenty-two months, the agency may be required by law to file a petition to terminate parental rights.

Nothing in such order shall preclude either party to the instrument from exercising its rights under this section or under any other provision of law relating to the return of the care and custody of the child by the social services official to the parent, parents or guardian. Violation of such on an order shall be subject to punishment pursuant to section seven hundred fifty-three of the judiciary law.

(f) For a child who has attained the age of fourteen, if the court grants the petition and approves an instrument executed pursuant to section three hundred eighty-four or three hundred eighty-four-a of this chapter and the transfer of custody and guardianship or care and custody of the child to a local social services official the court shall determine in its order the services and assistance needed to assist the child in learning independent living skills.

(4) Notice.

(a) Upon the filing of a petition pursuant to this section, the family court judge shall direct that service of a notice of the proceeding and a copy of the petition shall be made upon such persons and in such manner as the judge may direct. If the instrument executed by the parent, parents or guardian of a child consents to the jurisdiction of the family court over such proceeding, and waives service of the petition and notice of proceeding, then the family court judge may, in his discretion, dispense with service upon the consenting parent, parents or guardian, provided, however, that a waiver of service of process and notice of the proceeding by a parent or guardian who has transferred the care and custody of a child to an authorized agency, pursuant to section three hundred eighty-four-a of this chapter, shall be null and void and shall not be given effect by the court. Notice to any parent, parents or guardian who has not executed the instrument shall be required.

(b)   In the event the family court judge determines that service by publication is necessary and orders service by publication, service shall be made in accordance with the provisions of rule three hundred sixteen of the civil practice law and rules, provided, however, that a single publication of the summons or other process with a notice as specified herein in only one newspaper designated in the order shall be sufficient. In no event shall the whole petition be published. The petition shall be delivered to the person summoned at the first court appearance pursuant to section one hundred fifty-four-a of the family court act. The notice to be published with the summons or other process shall state the date, time, place and purpose of the proceeding.

(i)   If the petition is initiated to transfer custody and guardianship of a child by an instrument executed pursuant to the provisions of section three hundred eighty-four of this chapter, the notice to be published shall also state that failure to appear may result, without further notice, in the transfer of custody and guardianship of the child to a social services official in this proceeding.

(ii)   If the petition is initiated to transfer care and custody of a child by an instrument executed pursuant to the provisions of section three hundred eighty-four-a of this chapter, the notice to be published shall also state that failure to appear may result, without further notice, in the transfer of care and custody of the child to a social services official in this proceeding.

(c)   Repealed

(5)   Hearing and waiver. The instrument may include a consent by the parent, parents or guardian to waiver of any hearing and that a determination may be made by the family court judge based solely upon the petition, and other papers and affidavits, if any, submitted to the family court judge, provided, however, that a waiver of hearing by a parent or guardian who has transferred the care and custody of a child to an authorized agency, pursuant to section three hundred eighty-four-a of this chapter, shall be effective only if such waiver was executed in an instrument separate from that transferring the child's care and custody. In any case where an effective waiver has been executed, the family court judge may dispense with a hearing, approve the instrument and the transfer of the custody and guardianship or care and custody of the child to the social services official and make the requisite findings and determinations provided for in subdivision three of this section, if it appears to the satisfaction of the family court judge that the allegations in the petition are established sufficiently to warrant the family court judge to grant such petition, to make such findings and determination, and to issue such order.

In any case where a hearing is required, the family court judge, if the holding of an immediate hearing on notice is impractical, may forthwith, upon the basis of the instrument and the allegations of the petition, make a temporary finding

SSL

that the parent, parents, or guardian of the child are unable to make adequate provision for the care, maintenance and supervision of such child in the child's own home and that the best interest and welfare of the child will be promoted by the removal of such child from such home and thereupon, the family court judge shall make a temporary order transferring the care and custody of such child to the social services official, and shall set the matter down for hearing on the first feasible date.

(6) Representation. In any case where a hearing is directed by the family court judge he may, in his discretion, appoint a law guardian to represent the child, who shall be an attorney admitted to practice law in the state of New York.

(7) Return of child. If an instrument provides for the return of the care and custody of a child by the local social services official to the parent, parents or guardian upon any terms and conditions or at any time, the local social services official shall comply with such terms of such instrument without further court order. Every order approving an instrument providing for the transfer of the care and custody of a child to a local social services official shall be served upon the parent, parents or guardian who executed such instrument in such manner as the family court judge may provide in such order, together with a notice of the terms and conditions under which the care and custody of such child may be returned to the parent, parents or guardian. If an instrument provides for the return of the care and custody of a child by the local social services official to the parent, parents or guardian without fixing a definite date for such return, or if the local social services official shall fail to return a child to the care and custody of the child's parent, parents or guardian in accordance with the terms of the instrument, the parent, parents or guardian may seek such care and custody by motion for return of such child and order to show cause in such proceeding or by writ of habeas corpus in the supreme court. Nothing in this subdivision shall limit the requirement for a permanency hearing pursuant to article ten-A of the family court act.

(8) Appealable orders. Any order of a family court denying any petition of a local social services official filed pursuant to this section, or any order of a family court granting or denying any motion filed by a parent, parents or guardian for return of a child pursuant to this section, shall be deemed an order of disposition appealable pursuant to article eleven of the family court act.

(9) Duty of social services official. In the event that a family court judge denies a petition of a social services official for approval of an instrument, upon a finding that the welfare of the child would not be promoted by foster care, such social services official shall not accept or retain the care and custody as a public charge or custody and guardianship of such child, provided, however, that the denial by a family court judge of a petition of a social services official filed pursuant to this section shall not limit or affect the duty of such social services official to take such other action or offer such services as are authorized by law to promote the welfare and best interests of the child.

(10) Visitation rights; non-custodial parents and grandparents.

(a)   Where a social services official incorporates in an instrument visitation rights set forth in an order, judgment or agreement as described in paragraph (d) of subdivision two of section three hundred eighty-four-a of this chapter, such official shall make inquiry of the state central register of child abuse and maltreatment to determine whether or not the person having such visitation rights is a subject or another person named in an indicated report of child abuse or maltreatment, as such terms are defined in section four hundred twelve of this chapter, and shall further ascertain, to the extent practicable, whether or not such person is a respondent in a proceeding under article ten of the family court act whereby the respondent has been alleged or adjudicated to have abused or neglected such child.

(b)   Where a social services official or the law guardian of the child, if any, opposes incorporation of an order, judgment or agreement conferring visitation rights as provided for in paragraph (e) of subdivision two of section three hundred eighty-four-a of this chapter, the social services official or law guardian shall apply for an order determining that the provisions of such order, judgment or agreement should not be incorporated into the instrument executed pursuant to such section. Such order shall be granted upon a finding, based on competent, relevant and material evidence, that the child's life or health would be endangered by incorporation and enforcement of visitation rights as described in such order, judgment or agreement. Otherwise, the court shall deny such application.

(c)   Where visitation rights pursuant to an order, judgment or agreement are incorporated in an instrument, the parties may agree to an alternative schedule of visitation equivalent to and consistent with the original or modified visitation order, judgment, or agreement where such alternative schedule reflects changed circumstances of the parties and is consistent with the best interests of the child. In the absence of such an agreement between the parties, the court may, in its discretion, upon application of any party or the child's law guardian, order an alternative schedule of visitation, as described herein, where it determines that such schedule is necessary to facilitate visitation and to protect the best interests of the child.

(d)   The order providing an alternative schedule of visitation shall remain in effect for the length of the placement of the child as provided for in such instrument unless such order is subsequently modified by the court for good cause shown. Whenever the court makes an order denying or modifying visitation rights pursuant to this subdivision, the instrument described in section three hundred eighty-four-a of this chapter shall be deemed amended accordingly.

(11)   Siblings, placement and visitation.

(a)   In reviewing any petition brought under this section, the court shall inquire if the social services official has arranged for the placement of the child who is the subject of the petition with any minor siblings or half-siblings who are placed in care or, if such children have not been placed together, whether such official has arranged for regular visitation and other forms of regular communication between such child and such siblings.

SSL

(b)　If the court determines that the subject child has not been placed with his or her minor siblings or half-siblings who are in care, or that regular visitation and other forms of regular communication between the subject child and his or her minor siblings or half-siblings has not been provided or arranged for, the court may direct such official to provide or arrange for such placement or regular visitation and communication where the court finds that such placement or visitation and communication is in the child's best interests. Placement or regular visitation and communication with siblings or half-siblings shall be presumptively in the child's best interests unless such placement or visitation and communication would be contrary to the child's health, safety or welfare, or the lack of geographic proximity precludes or prevents visitation.

(12)　For the purposes of this section, aggravated circumstances means where a child has been either severely or repeatedly abused, as defined in subdivision eight of section three hundred eighty-four-b of this chapter; or where a child has subsequently been found to be an abused child, as defined in paragraph (i) or (iii) of subdivision (e) of section one thousand twelve of the family court act, within five years after return home following placement in foster care as a result of being found to be a neglected child, as defined in subdivision (f) of section one thousand twelve of the family court act, provided that the respondent or respondents in each of the foregoing proceedings was the same; or where the court finds by clear and convincing evidence that the parent of a child in foster care has refused and has failed completely, over a period of at least six months from the date of removal, to engage in services necessary to eliminate the risk of abuse or neglect if returned to the parent, and has failed to secure services on his or her own or otherwise adequately prepare for the return home and, after being informed by the court that such an admission could eliminate the requirement that the local department of social services provide reunification services to the parent, the parent has stated in court under oath that he or she intends to continue to refuse such necessary services and is unwilling to secure such services independently or otherwise prepare for the child's return home; provided, however, that if the court finds that adequate justification exists for the failure to engage in or secure such services, including but not limited to a lack of child care, a lack of transportation, and an inability to attend services that conflict with the parent's work schedule, such failure shall not constitute an aggravated circumstance; or where a court has determined a child five days old or younger was abandoned by a parent with an intent to wholly abandon such child and with the intent that the child be safe from physical injury and cared for in an appropriate manner.

Added by Laws 1973, Ch. 996; **amended** by Laws 1975, Ch. 710; Laws 1976, Ch. 669; Laws 1977, Ch. 862; Laws 1978, Ch. 78; Laws 1979, Ch. 610, eff. Apr. 1, 1981; **amended** by Laws 1984, Ch. 872, eff. Sept. 4, 1984; **amended** by Laws 1985, Ch. 808, eff. Nov. 1, 1985; **amended** by Laws 1987, Ch. 823, eff. Aug. 7, 1987; **amended** by Laws 1988, Ch. 478, § 10, eff. Nov. 1, 1988; **amended** by Laws 1988, Ch. 457, § 10, eff. Nov. 1, 1988; **amended** by Laws 1990, Ch. 854, § 1, eff. Sept. 1, 1990; **amended** by Laws

1991, Ch. 198, §§ 9, 10, eff. June 28, 1991; **amended** by Laws 1992, Ch. 465, §§ 53, 54, 55, 56, 57, eff. Jan. 13, 1993; **amended** by Laws 1993, Ch. 87, § 2, eff. June 1, 1993; **amended** by Laws 1999, Ch. 7, §§ 1–6, eff. Feb. 11, 1999; **amended** by Laws 2002, Ch. 83, Part C, § 16, eff. April 1, 2002; Laws 2005, Ch. 671, § 7, eff. Dec. 15, 2005; Laws 2005, Ch. 3, §§ 35 through 39 (Part A), §§ 3 through 5 (Part B), eff. Aug. 23, 2005; L. 2005, Ch. 671, sect; 7, amending sub.(c), eff. Dec. 15, 2005.

§ 358-b.   Limitations on state reimbursement for foster care. [*Expires and repealed June 30, 2007.*]

In the event that a petition for approval of an instrument and the transfer of the custody and guardianship or care and custody of a child is filed within thirty days following removal of the child from his home and diligently pursued pursuant to section three hundred fifty-eight-a of this title, state reimbursement shall not be denied for expenditures made by a social services district for the care and maintenance of such a child away from his home prior to denial of such petition by a family court judge solely by reason of such denial.

Added by Laws 1973, Ch. 996, eff. Sept. 1, 1973; **amended** by Laws 1975, Ch. 710; **amended** by Laws 1979, Ch. 610, eff. Apr. 1, 1981; **amended** by Laws 2002, Ch. 83, Part C, § 17, eff. April 1, 2002.

§ 358-b.   Limitations on state reimbursement for foster care. [*Effective June 30, 2007.*]

In the event that a petition for approval of an instrument and the transfer of the custody and guardianship or care and custody of a child is filed within thirty days following removal of the child from his home and diligently pursued pursuant to section three hundred fifty-eight-a of this chapter, state reimbursement shall not be denied pursuant to section one hundred fifty-three-d of this chapter, for expenditures made by a social services district for the care and maintenance of such a child away from his home prior to denial of such petition by a family court judge solely by reason of such denial.

Added by Laws 1973, Ch. 996, eff. Sept. 1, 1973; **amended** by Laws 1975, Ch. 710; **amended** by Laws 1979, Ch. 610, eff. Apr. 1, 1981; **amended** by Laws 2002, Ch. 83, Part C, § 17, eff. April 1, 2002.

SSL

§ 358-c.   Rules of court.

The administrative board of the judicial conference shall prepare, by August first, nineteen hundred seventy-three, rules of court for the efficient and just administration of the judicial proceedings authorized by section three hundred fifty-eight-a of this chapter and such rules may be amended by the administrative board from time to time. The state administrator shall prescribe forms for petitions, notices and orders authorized by section three hundred fifty-eight-a, and may authorize courts determining such proceedings to submit information to the department in a manner and at such times as the administrative board may prescribe. Nothing in this section shall be construed to limit the authority of the state board of social welfare.

Added by Laws 1973, Ch. 996, eff. June 23, 1973; amended by Laws 1977, Ch. 229, eff. June 7, 1977.

§ 359.   Reimbursement and advances by the state.

Repealed by Laws 1953, Ch. 562, eff. Jan. 1, 1954 and subject matter transferred to Social Services Law §§ 153, 154.

§ 360.   Real property of legally responsible relatives; deeds and mortgages may be required.

1.   The ownership of real property by an applicant or applicants, recipient or recipients who is or are legally responsible relatives of the child or children for whose benefit the application is made or the aid is granted, whether such ownership be individual or joint as tenants in common, tenants by the entirety or joint tenants, shall not preclude the granting of family assistance or the continuance thereof if he or they are without the necessary funds to maintain himself, herself or themselves and such child or children. The social services official may, however, require, as a condition to the granting of aid or the continuance thereof, that he or she be given a deed of or a mortgage on such property in accordance with the provisions of section one hundred six.

2.   However, while the property covered by the deed or mortgage is occupied, in whole or in part, by the responsible relative who gave such deed or mortgage to the social services official or, by a child for whose benefit the aid was granted the social services official shall not sell the property or assign or enforce the mortgage without the written consent of the department; and, when the property is occupied by such child, such consent shall not be given unless it appears reasonably certain that the sale or other disposition of the property will not materially adversely affect the welfare of such child.

3.   The net amount recovered by the social services department from such property, less any expenditures approved by the department for the burial of the relative or the child who dies while in receipt of aid under this title, shall be used to repay the social services district, the state and the federal government their proportionate share of the cost of family assistance granted. The state and federal share shall be paid by the social services district to the state and the manner and amount of such payment shall be determined in accordance with the regulations of the department.

4.   If any balance remains it shall belong to the estate of the legally responsible relative or relatives, and the public welfare district shall forthwith credit the same accordingly, and, provided they claim it within four years thereafter, pay it to the persons entitled thereto. If not so claimed within four years it shall be deemed abandoned property and be paid to the state comptroller pursuant to section thirteen hundred five of the abandoned property law.

5. The proceeds or moneys due the United States shall be paid or reported in such manner and at such times as the federal security agency or other authorized federal agency may direct.

Added by Laws 1951, Ch. 722; **amended** by Laws 1959, Ch. 803; **amended** by Laws 1974, Ch. 909, eff. Sept. 1, 1974; **amended** by Laws 1997, Ch. 436, § 1 Part B, § 92, eff. Aug. 20, 1997.

§ 361. Operation of title upon discontinuance of federal moneys.

Repealed by Laws 1953, Ch. 562, eff. Jan. 1, 1954 and subject matter transferred to Social Services Law §§ 153, 154.

§ 362. Application.

Repealed by L. 1997, Ch. 436, § 1 Part B, § 93, eff. Aug. 20, 1997.

TITLE 11—MEDICAL ASSISTANCE FOR NEEDY PERSONS

(Repealed and transferred sections noted under appropriate section number of text.)

SSL

§ 363. Declaration of objects.

Medical assistance for needy persons is hereby declared to be a matter of public concern and a necessity in promoting the public health and welfare and for promoting the state's goal of making available to everyone, regardless of race, age, national origin or economic standing, uniform, high-quality medical care. In furtherance of such goal, a comprehensive program of medical assistance for needy persons is hereby established to operate in a manner which will assure a uniform high standard of medical assistance throughout the state. In carrying out this program every effort shall be made to promote maximum public awareness of the availability of, and procedure for obtaining, such assistance, and to facilitate the application for, and the provision of such medical assistance.

Added by Laws 1966, Ch. 256, eff. Apr. 30, 1966.

§ 363-a. Federal aid; state plan.

1. The department of health shall submit and maintain a plan for medical assistance, as required by title XIX, or any successor title, of the federal social security act, to the federal department of health and human services for approval pursuant to the provisions of such law and shall act as the single state agency to supervise the administration of the plan in this state. The department of health shall act for the state in any negotiations relative to the submission and approval of such plan and any amendments thereto and it may make such arrangements, not inconsistent with law, as may be required by or pursuant to federal law to obtain and retain such approval and to secure for the state the benefits of the provisions of such law.

2. The department of health shall make such regulations, not inconsistent with law, as may be necessary to implement this title.

3. The department of health shall make reports to the federal department of health and human services as from time to time may be required by such federal department.

4. The department of taxation and finance shall accept and receive any and all grants of money awarded to the state under title XIX, or any successor title, of the federal social security act. All moneys so received shall be deposited by the department of taxation and finance in a special fund or funds and shall be used by the state exclusively for medical assistance and the administration thereof under the provisions of this title. Such moneys shall be paid from such fund or funds on audit and warrant of the comptroller on vouchers of or certification by the department of health.

Added by Laws 1966, Ch. 256; **amended** by Laws 1971, Ch. 110, eff. July 1, 1971; **amended** by Laws 1996, Ch. 474, § 233, eff. Oct. 1, 1996.

§ 363-b. Agreements for federal determination of eligibility of aged, blind and disabled persons for medical assistance.

1. In order to avoid costly, duplicative administrative responsibility, the department on behalf of the state may, with the approval of the director of the

budget, enter into an agreement with the secretary of health, education and welfare for the secretary to determine eligibility, commencing on or after the first day of January nineteen hundred seventy-four, for medical assistance in the case of aged, blind or disabled persons, pursuant to the provisions of the social security act authorizing such agreements and subject to the requirements of this title. Such agreement shall include provision for payments of one-half the cost of such services to be made to such secretary.

2.   Payments required to be made by the department to the secretary of health, education and welfare for his services under such agreement shall be borne by and shared equally between the social services districts to which such payments are attributable and the state for any period commencing on or after the first day of January nineteen hundred seventy-four.

     Added by Laws 1973 Ch. 516, eff. Jan. 1, 1974.

§ 363-c   Medicaid management

1.   The commissioner of the department periodically shall convene, but not less than quarterly and no more than monthly, meetings of the directors and commissioners of all state agencies and departments receiving general fund appropriations for the purpose of state matching funds for medicaid services and appropriate representation of local departments of social services. The purpose of these meetings is to identify, without limitation:

   (a)   methods to contain the growth of medicaid spending;

   (b)   methods to improve the quality of and recipient satisfaction with medicaid state agency and department services;

   (c)   opportunities for consolidation and methods to improve the efficiency and effectiveness of existing service delivery;

   (d)   opportunities for education and prevention; and

   (e)   annually the number of persons on waiting lists to receive services and the type of services for each list; and

   (f)   the collective priority of critical needs for the medicaid population.

2.   The department annually shall compile the results of these meetings and provide them to the governor, the senate finance committee, the assembly ways and means committee, the senate health committee, the assembly health committee, the senate social services, children and families committee, and the assembly social services committee.

3.   By December thirty-first of each year, the department shall submit to the governor, the senate finance committee, the assembly ways and means committee, the senate health committee, the assembly health committee, the senate social services, children and families committee, and the assembly social services committee medicaid expenditures made to other state agencies in the preceding state fiscal year. The report shall include, but is not limited to:

(a)　amounts paid to each agency according to category of service; and

(b)　rates paid to each state agency and the associated methodology used in developing those rates.

Added by Laws 2006 Ch. 68-c (Part A), eff. April 12, 2006; Laws 2006, ch. 109, §19 (Part C), eff. Aug 10, 2006.

§ 363-d　[Eff. Jan 1, 2007] Provider compliance program.

1.　The legislature finds that medical assistance providers may be able to detect and correct payment and billing mistakes and fraud if required to develop and implement compliance programs. It is the purpose of such programs to organize provider resources to resolve payment discrepancies and detect inaccurate billings, among other things, as quickly and efficiently as possible, and to impose systemic checks and balances to prevent future recurrences. The legislature accordingly declares that it is in the public interest that providers within the medical assistance program implement compliance programs. The legislature also recognizes the wide variety of provider types in the medical assistance program and the need for compliance programs that reflect a provider's size, complexity, resources, and culture. For a compliance program to be effective, it must be designed to be compatible with the provider's characteristics. At the same time, however, the legislature determines that there are key components that must be included in every compliance program and such components should be required if a provider is to be a medical assistance program participant. Accordingly, the provisions of this section require providers to adopt effective compliance program elements, and make each provider responsible for implementing such a program appropriate to its characteristics.

2.　Every provider of medical assistance program items and services that is subject to subdivision four of this section shall adopt and implement a compliance program. The office of Medicaid inspector general shall create and make available on its website guidelines, which may include a model compliance program, that reflect the requirements of this section. Such program shall at a minimum be applicable to billings to and payments from the medical assistance program but need not be confined to such matters. The compliance program required pursuant to this section may be a component of more comprehensive compliance activities by the medical assistance provider so long as the requirements of this section are met. A compliance program shall include the following elements:

(a)　written policies and procedures that describe compliance expectations as embodied in a code of conduct or code of ethics, implement the operation of the compliance program, provide guidance to employees and others on dealing with potential compliance issues, identify how to communicate compliance issues to appropriate compliance personnel and describe how potential compliance problems are investigated and resolved;

SSL

(b) designate an employee vested with responsibility for the day-today operation of the compliance program; such employee's duties may solely relate to compliance or may be combined with other duties so long as compliance responsibilities are satisfactorily carried out; such employee shall report directly to the entity's chief executive or other senior administrator and shall periodically report directly to the governing body on the activities of the compliance program;

(c) training and education of all affected employees and persons associated with the provider, including executives and governing body members, on compliance issues, expectations and the compliance program operation; such training shall occur periodically and shall be made a part of the orientation for a new employee, appointee or associate, executive and governing body member;

(d) communication lines to the responsible compliance position, as described in paragraph (b) of this subdivision, that are accessible to all employees, persons associated with the provider, executives and governing body members, to allow compliance issues to be reported; such communication lines shall include a method for anonymous and confidential good faith reporting of potential compliance issues as they are identified;

(e) disciplinary policies to encourage good faith participation in the compliance program by all affected individuals, including policies that articulate expectations for reporting compliance issues and assist in their resolution and outline sanctions for: (1) failing to report suspected problems; (2) participating in non-compliant behavior; or (3) encouraging, directing, facilitating or permitting non-compliant behavior; such disciplinary policies shall be fairly and firmly enforced;

(f) a system for routine identification of compliance risk areas specific to the provider type, for self-evaluation of such risk areas, including internal audits and as appropriate external audits, and for evaluation of potential or actual non-compliance as a result of such self-evaluations and audits;

(g) a system for responding to compliance issues as they are raised; for investigating potential compliance problems; responding to compliance problems as identified in the course of self-evaluations and audits; correcting such problems promptly and thoroughly and implementing procedures, policies and systems as necessary to reduce the potential for recurrence; identifying and reporting compliance issues to the department or the office of Medicaid inspector general; and refunding overpayments;

(h) a policy of non-intimidation and non-retaliation for good faith participation in the compliance program, including but not limited to reporting potential issues, investigating issues, self-evaluations, audits and remedial actions, and reporting to appropriate officials as provided in sections seven hundred forty and seven hundred forty-one of the labor law.

3. Upon enrollment in the medical assistance program, a provider shall certify to the department that the provider satisfactorily meets the requirements of this section. Additionally, the commissioner of health and Medicaid inspector

general shall have the authority to determine at any time if a provider has a compliance program that satisfactorily meets the requirements of this section.

(a)   A compliance program that is accepted by the federal department of health and human services office of inspector general and remains in compliance with the standards promulgated by such office shall be deemed in compliance with the provisions of this section.

(b)   In the event that the commissioner of health or the Medicaid inspector general finds that the provider does not have a satisfactory program within ninety days after the effective date of the regulations issued pursuant to subdivision four of this section, the provider may be subject to any sanctions or penalties permitted by federal or state laws and regulations, including revocation of the provider's agreement to participate in the medical assistance program.

4.   The Medicaid inspector general, in consultation with the department of health, shall promulgate regulations establishing those providers that shall be subject to the provisions of this section including, but not limited to, those subject to the provisions of articles twenty-eight and thirty-six of the public health law, articles sixteen and thirty-one of the mental hygiene law, and other providers of care, services and supplies under the medical assistance program for which the medical assistance program is a substantial portion of their business operations.

Add, Laws 2006, ch. 442, §4, eff. Jan. 1, 2007.

§ 364.   Responsibility for standards.

To assure that the medical care and services rendered pursuant to this title are of the highest quality and are available to all who are in need, the responsibility for establishing and maintaining standards for medical care and eligibility shall be as follows:

1.   The department of social services shall be responsible for

(a)   determining eligibility for care and services pursuant to this title and consistent with standards established by the commissioner of the department of health and, as authorized by such commissioner, for hearing appeals and making findings and recommendations relating thereto;

(b)   auditing payments to providers of care, services and supplies under the medical assistance program; and

(c)   publishing and distributing to the public, from time to time and in consultation with the department of health, information relating to the medical assistance program, to promote maximum public awareness of the availability of, and the procedure for obtaining, such assistance.

2.   The department of health shall be responsible for

(a)   establishing and maintaining standards for all hospital and related services pursuant to article twenty-eight of the public health law, and for all medical care and services furnished in an institution operated by the department of health pursuant to other provisions of the public health law;

(b)   establishing and maintaining standards for all non-institutional health care and services rendered pursuant to this title, including but not limited to procedural standards relating to the revocation, suspension, limitation or annulment of qualification for participation as a provider of care and services, on a determination that the provider is an incompetent provider of specific services or has exhibited a course of conduct which is either inconsistent with program standards and regulations or which exhibits an unwillingness to meet such standards and regulations, or is a potential threat to the public health or safety pursuant to section two hundred six of the public health law;

(c)   reviewing and approving local social services medical plans;

(d)   establishing by regulation requirements for a uniform system of reports relating to the quality of medical care and services furnished pursuant to this title;

(e)   reviewing the quality and availability of medical care and services furnished under local social services medical plans, to assure that the quality of medical care and services is in the best interest of the recipients;

(f)   providing consultative services to hospitals, nursing homes, home health agencies, clinics, laboratories, and such other institutions as the secretary of the federal department of health and human services may specify in order to assist them: to qualify for payments under the provisions of this title and title XIX of the federal social security act; in providing information needed to determine such payments; in establishing and maintaining such fiscal records as may be necessary for the proper and efficient administration of medical assistance;

(g)   establishing standards of eligibility for medical assistance, consistent with the provisions of this title; and

(h)   making policy, rules and regulations for maintaining a system of hearings for applicants and recipients of medical assistance adversely affected by the actions of the department or social service districts and for making final administrative determinations and issuing final decisions concerning such matters.

3.   Each office within the department of mental hygiene shall be responsible for establishing and maintaining standards for medical care and services received in institutions operated by it or subject to its supervision pursuant to the mental hygiene law.

4.   The public health council shall be responsible for establishing and maintaining qualifications for persons employed by social services districts as professional directors.

Added by Laws 1966, Ch. 256; amended by Laws 1968, Ch. 993; Laws 1969, Ch. 659; Laws 1973 Ch. 195, Ch. 676; Laws 1975, Ch. 667; Laws 1977, Ch. 770; amended by Laws 1980, Ch. 471, eff. July 23, 1980; amended by Laws 1981, Ch. 947, eff. July 1, 1981; amended by Laws 1996, Ch. 474, § 234, eff. Oct. 1, 1996.

§ 364-a. Cooperation of state departments.

1. There shall be such cooperative arrangements, between and among the department of health and other state departments and agencies as shall be necessary to assure that the purposes and objectives of this title will be effectively accomplished. The commissioner of the department of health shall have the authority to delegate responsibility under this title to other state departments and agencies and to enter into memoranda of understanding as may be necessary to carry out the provisions of this title.

2. Notwithstanding any inconsistent provision of law, the department of health shall enter into a cooperative agreement with the office of mental health which shall;

(i) provide for the office of mental health, on or after the date of the agreement, to administer and supervise the medical care, health care, habilitative, rehabilitative and maintenance services provided pursuant to this title at residential treatment facilities for children and youth licensed by the office of mental health pursuant to article thirty-one of the mental hygiene law, and

(ii) authorize the office of mental health to perform such administration and supervision, either directly or by contract, as the office of mental health may from time-to-time determine. On or after the effective date of such agreement, all of the functions provided for in this title for the administration and supervision of medical care, health care, habilitative, rehabilitative and maintenance services provided hereunder by residential treatment facilities for children and youth licensed by the office of mental health pursuant to article thirty-one of the mental hygiene law shall be performed by the office of mental health to the extent permitted by applicable federal law and to the extent that federal reimbursement for such care and services is not impaired. A cooperative agreement previously entered into by the department of social services pursuant to this subdivision shall continue in effect until modified or terminated by the department of health.

3. [*Repealed July 1, 2008.*] Notwithstanding any inconsistent provision of law, the department of health shall enter into a cooperative agreement with the office of mental health which shall:

(i) provide for the office of mental health, on or after the date of the agreement, to administer and supervise the medical care, health care, habilitative, rehabilitative and maintenance services provided pursuant to this title at comprehensive psychiatric emergency programs licensed by the office of mental health pursuant to article thirty-one of the mental hygiene law, and

(ii) authorize the office of mental health to perform such administration and supervision, either directly or by contract, as the office of mental health may determine to be necessary. On or after the effective date of such agreement, all of the functions provided for in this title for the administration and supervision of medical care, health care, habilitative, rehabilitative and

SSL

maintenance services provided at comprehensive psychiatric emergency programs licensed by the office of mental health pursuant to article thirty-one of the mental hygiene law shall be performed by the office of mental health to the extent permitted by federal law and to the extent that federal reimbursement for such care and services is not impaired. A cooperative agreement previously entered into by the department of social services pursuant to this subdivision shall continue in effect until modified or terminated by the department of health.

Added by Laws 1966, Ch. 256; amended by Laws 1966, Ch. 257, eff. Apr. 30, 1966; amended by Laws 1981, Ch. 947, eff. July 1, 1981; amended by Laws 1989, Ch. 723, § 16, eff. July 24, 1989 through July 24, 1994, at which time subdivision (4) added by this act shall be deemed to be repealed and Social Services Law § 364-a amended by this act shall revert to its text as it existed prior to the effective date of this act; amended by Laws 1994, Ch. 598, § 8, eff. July 24, 1994, extending the period that subd. (4) remains effective to July 1, 2000; amended by Laws 1996, Ch. 474, § 235, eff. Oct. 1, 1996; amended by Laws 2000, Ch. 93, § 1, eff. June 23, 2000; amended by Laws 2004, Ch. 131, § 1, eff. June 29, 2004, extending expiration date until the year 2008.

§ 364-b.   Residential and medical care placement demonstration projects.

Expired on September 30, 1986, by Laws 1983, Ch. 741, eff. July 27, 1983.

§ 364-c.   National long term care channeling demonstration project.

Expired on December 31, 1985, by Laws 1982, Ch. 42, eff. April 2, 1982.

§ 364-d.   Medical assistance research and demonstration projects. [*For expiration date, see amendment note below.*]

1.   The department is authorized to sponsor, conduct and participate in the following research and demonstration projects: "Eldercare: A Social Health Maintenance Organization," "New York State Alcoholism Services Demonstration," and "Physician Reimbursement and Continuing Care Under Medicaid," for the purpose of testing the use of innovative administrative techniques, new reimbursement methods, and changes in the scope of benefits, so as to promote a more efficient utilization of health resources and the containment of medical assistance program costs. Such demonstration projects may be conducted in one or more social services districts or portions of such districts. [*The project "Eldercare: A Social Health Maintenance Organization," shall remain in effect until December 31, 1997.*]

2.   (a) Social services districts shall be required to participate in the operation of such research and demonstration projects as the department may approve. Social services districts shall cooperate with the department in the conduct of such projects whenever the department shall request or require such participation or cooperation.

(b)   Notwithstanding any inconsistent provision of law to the contrary, expenditures made in connection with any research demonstration project undertaken pursuant to the provisions of this section shall be subject to state reimbursement under section three hundred sixty-eight-a of this title.

3.   The research and demonstration projects undertaken pursuant to the provisions of this section shall limit the individuals participating thereunder to those persons with respect to whom the department has determined that there is a reasonable expectation that the total cost of benefits under such project would be less than the total cost of benefits for such individual if the research and demonstration program were not in effect.

4.   Notwithstanding any inconsistent provision of this chapter or any other law to the contrary, the commissioner may, subject to the approval of the director of the budget, approve any or all of the research and demonstration projects specified in subdivision one of this section, and apply for the appropriate waivers under federal law and regulation, and may waive any of the provisions of this chapter, when such action would be likely to assist in promoting the objectives of this title.

5.   (a) For each project undertaken pursuant to the provisions of this section, the department shall submit an interim report and final report to the governor and the legislature. The interim report shall be due eighteen months after the date of approval of the project by the department; the final report shall be due at the conclusion of the project.

(b)   Such reports shall include a listing of the accomplishments of the research and demonstration project, and shall evaluate the progress made in achieving the objectives of the project.

6.   This section shall be effective with respect to each such project, other than the "New York State Alcoholism Services Demonstration Project," if and as long as, federal participation is available for expenditures made for such research and demonstration project conducted pursuant to the provisions of this section.

SSL

Added by Laws 1982, Ch. 602; Laws 1986, Ch. 578; Laws 1989, Ch. 22; Laws 1990, Ch. 45, eff. Mar. 31, 1990, extended expiration date until Sept. 1992; **amended** by Laws 1985, Ch. 197, eff. May 30, 1985; **amended** by Laws 1992, Ch. 300; **amended** by Laws 1994, Ch. 31, § 2, eff. Apr. 1, 1994, providing that the project, "Eldercare: A Social Health Maintenance Organization," shall remain effective until Dec. 31, 1995; **amended** by Laws 1995, Ch. 81, § 126, eff. June 20, 1995, extending the period the "Eldercare" project remains effective to Dec. 31, 1996; **amended** by Laws 1996, Ch. 624, eff. Sept. 4, 1996, extending the period the "eldercare" project remains effective to Dec. 31, 1997.

§ 364-e.   Aid to families with dependent children homemaker/home health aide demonstration projects.

[Expired on June 30, 1986, by Laws 1983, Ch. 598, eff. July 21, 1983.]

§ 364-f.   Physician case management programs. [*Expires March 31, 2006.*]

1.   The department is authorized to establish physician case management demonstration programs, under the medical assistance program, in accordance with applicable federal law and regulations. Subject to the approval of the director of the budget, the commissioner is authorized to apply for the appropriate waivers under federal law and regulation, and may waive any of the provisions of sections three hundred sixty -five-a, three hundred sixty-six, three hundred sixty-seven-b and three hundred sixty-eight-a of this chapter or any regulation of the department when such action would be necessary to assist in promoting the objectives of this section.

2.   (a) A physician case management program shall provide individuals eligible for medical assistance with the opportunity to select voluntarily a case management provider who shall provide medical assistance services to such eligible individuals, wither directly, or through referral by a physician case manager.

(b)   Physician case managers shall be limited to qualified, licensed primary care physicians, who meet standards established by the commissioner of health for the purposes of this program.

(c)   Services for which a physician case manager will be responsible include all medical assistance services defined under section three hundred sixty-five-a of this chapter, except:

    (i) services provided by residential health care facilities, long term home health care programs, child care agencies, and entities offering comprehensive health services plans;

    (ii) services provided by dentists and optometrists; and

    (iii) eyeglasses, emergency care, mental health services and family planning services.

(d)   Case management services provided by physician case managers shall include, but need not be limited to:

    (i) management of the medical and health care of each recipient to assure that all services provided under paragraph (c) of this subdivision and which are found to be necessary, are made available in a timely manner;

    (ii) referral to, and coordination, monitoring and follow-up of, appropriate providers for diagnosis and treatment, the need for which has been identified by the physician case manager but which is not directly available from the case manager, and assisting medical assistance recipients in the prudent selection of medical services;

    (iii) arrangements for referral of recipients to appropriate providers; and

    (iv) services provided in accordance with child health assurance program standards for individuals under twenty-one years of age.

3.   (a) Physician case management programs may be conducted only in accordance with plans submitted by social services districts and approved by the commissioner, after consultation with the commissioner of health, and only to the extent and period for which such plans have been approved by the commissioner. The commissioner shall not authorize the implementation of such plans in more than ten social services districts. For the purpose of implementing and administering the physician case management programs, social services districts may contract with private not-for-profit and public agencies for the management of these plans provided, however, that such contracts shall require prior approval by the commissioner.

(b)   The commissioner shall only approve plans submitted pursuant to this section which:

(i) identify and document the specific problems which the physician case management program is designed to address within the social services district;

(ii) assure access to and delivery of high quality, appropriate medical services;

(iii) include a description of the quality assurance mechanisms to be implemented, as well as other mechanisms designed to protect recipient rights under such program;

(iv) designate the entity to be responsible for the administration of the program within the social services district and describe the responsibilities of this entity;

(v) include a fiscal impact statement which describes the anticipated savings to federal, state and local governments, including an estimate of those costs, including both inpatient and ambulatory costs, which would have been incurred in the absence of the program and the projected costs under the program;

(vi) ensure that persons eligible for medical assistance will be provided sufficient information regarding the program to make an informed and voluntary choice whether to participate;

(vii) provide for adequate safeguards to protect recipients from being misled concerning the program and from being coerced into participating in the physician case management program;

(viii) assure adequate opportunity for public review and comment prior to implementation of the program and provide adequate grievance procedures for recipients who participate in the program; and

(ix) include any other information which the department shall deem appropriate.

4.   (a) Individuals eligible for medical assistance, as defined in section three hundred sixty-six of this chapter, may voluntarily participate in a physician case

SSL

management program, subject to the availability of such a program within the applicable social services district, except for individuals: (i) enrolled in an entity offering a comprehensive health services plan as defined in paragraph (k) of subdivision two of section three hundred sixty-five-a of this chapter; (ii) participating in another medical assistance reimbursed demonstration or pilot project, or (iii) receiving services as an inpatient from a nursing home or intermediate care facility or residential services from a child care agency or services from a long term home health care program.

(b)   All individuals eligible for medical assistance choosing to participate voluntarily in a physician case management program will be given thirty days from the effective date of enrollment in the program to disenroll without cause. After this thirty day disenrollment period, all individuals participating in the program will be enrolled for a period of six months, except that all participants will be permitted to disenroll for good cause, as defined by the commissioner in regulation.

5.   (a) Physician case management programs may include provisions for innovative payment mechanisms, including, but not limited to, sharing of any savings with providers, payment of case management fees and capitation arrangements.

(b)   Any new payment mechanisms and levels of payment implemented under the physician case management program shall be developed jointly by the commissioner and the commissioner of health subject to the approval of the director of the budget.

6.   This section shall be effective if, and as long as, federal financial participation is available therefor.

Added by Laws 1984, Ch. 904; Laws 1987, Ch. 357; Laws 1989, Ch. 201, eff. June 24, 1989 extended the expiration date until Mar. 31, 1994; **amended** by Laws 1994, Ch. 33, § 2, eff. Apr. 1, 1994, extending the period that the section remains effective to Dec. 31, 1995; **amended** by Laws 1995, Ch. 81, § 120, eff. June 20, 1995, extending the period the section remains effective to July 1, 1996; **amended** by Laws 1996, Ch. 350, eff. July 17, 1996, extending the period the section remains effective to July 1, 1997; **amended** by L. 1997, Chs. 145, 162, 194, 211, 223, 264, extending expiration date from July 1, 1997 to July 1, 1998, eff. July 23, 1997, deemed in full force and effect Apr. 1, 1997; **amended** by L. 1998, Ch. 145, § 1, extending expiration date from July 1, 1998 to July 1, 1999, eff. June 30, 1998; **amended** by L. 1999, Ch. 153, § 1, extending effective date from July 1, 1999 to July 1, 2000, eff. July 1, 1999; **amended** by Laws 2000, Ch. 57, § 9, Part B, eff. May 15, 2000, extending expiration date to July 1, 2001; **amended** by Laws 2001, Ch. 63, § 11, Part C, eff. June 25, 2001, deemed eff. June 18, 2001, extending expiration date to July 1, 2002; **amended** by Laws 2002, Ch. 1, Part B, § 23, eff. Jan. 25, 2002, extending expiration date to July 1, 2003; L. 2003, Ch. 62, Part Z2, § 44, eff. May 15, 2003 and deemed effective April 1, 2003, extending the expiration date until March 31, 2006; **amended** by Laws 2004, Ch. 69, § 1, deemed effective on or after July 1, 2003.

§ 364-g.   Medical assistance capitation rate demonstration project.

[*Expired on April 1, 1990, by Laws 1984, Ch. 738, eff. August 3, 1984.*]

§ 364-h.   Foster family care demonstration programs for elderly or disabled persons. [*Effective until December 31, 2005.*]

1.   The department is authorized to designate up to ten entities which may include general hospitals, residential health care facilities, home health care programs, and long term home health care programs for the purpose of testing whether foster family care programs for certain elderly or disabled persons can be appropriate alternatives to institutional placement in those instances where such individuals do not have a home or the necessary resources or family support to live in the community.

2.   A hospital, facility, or program designated as a foster family care demonstration program shall perform the following functions:

(a)   recruitment, selection and training of families to serve as foster families;

(b)   selection of those elderly or disabled persons who will receive foster family care services under the demonstration project authorized herein, and assessment of their needs;

(c)   provision of or arrangement for necessary medical services; and

(d)   monitoring the care being received by the person in the foster family care home, and assessing the continuing viability of placement in such home.

3.   Persons eligible to participate in the foster family care demonstration programs authorized by this section shall be:

(a)   medically eligible for placement in a skilled nursing facility or a health related facility or eligible for home care services;

(b)   capable of being cared for in the community if a suitable home environment and medical support services are provided; and

(c)   lacking the home, resources or family support to live in the community.

4.   Families who participate in the foster family care demonstration program shall be willing and able to provide:

(a)   room and board;

(b)   supervision of or assistance with the activities of daily living; and

(c)   personal care and other related services which may be necessary to maintain the person in the community.

5.   In designating a hospital, facility, or program to provide a foster family care program, the department shall be satisfied as to the cost-effectiveness of the proposal as compared to institutional long term care.

6.   The commissioner may waive the provisions of titles one and two of article seven of this chapter and regulations of the department relative thereto

as necessary to implement the provisions of this section; provided, however, the commissioner shall be satisfied that the health, safety and welfare of persons participating in the foster care programs are not affected negatively by such waivers.

7. This section shall not be interpreted to restrict a medical assistance recipient's choice of provider of services to which he is entitled pursuant to this title or to authorize any change in the eligibility criteria for medical assistance.

8. A medical assistance recipient may discontinue participation in a foster family care demonstration program at any time.

9. The department shall utilize all potential sources of funding for such foster family care programs including, but not limited to, funding available through titles sixteen, eighteen, nineteen and twenty of the federal social security act and the federal older Americans act of 1965, as amended. Services provided as part of a foster family care program and related administrative expenses not otherwise eligible for coverage under these or other funding sources shall be eligible for reimbursement under the medical assistance program for the purposes of this demonstration as long as federal financial participation is available. The department shall take all steps necessary to secure such funding including the submission of applicable waivers. Copies of waiver submissions shall be provided to the chairman of the senate finance committee and the chairman of the assembly ways and means committee.

10. The department, in consultation with the department of health and the office for the aging, shall provide an interim report to the governor and the legislature on or before November first, nineteen hundred eighty-six and a final report on or before October thirty-one, nineteen hundred ninety-five on the results of the foster family care demonstration program. The report shall include findings as to the program's cost effectiveness including consideration of the costs of maintaining the person in the community, funding sources, programmatic benefits and the effect on the need for residential health care facility beds. In the final report, the department shall offer recommendations as to whether the program should be extended, modified, eliminated or made permanent.

11. Foster family care demonstration programs authorized pursuant to chapter nine hundred forty-two of the laws of nineteen hundred eighty-three and chapter five hundred forty-one of the laws of nineteen hundred eighty-four shall comply with the provisions of this section but shall be in addition to the entities designated in subdivision one of this section. Such previously authorized demonstration projects shall be subject to the expiration date of this section.

  Amended by L. 2001, Ch. 200, § 3, extending expiration date, eff. Aug. 20, 2001; L. 2003, Ch. 227, § 3, eff. July 29, 2003 and shall be in full force and effect on and after Dec. 31, 2003, extending the expiration date until Dec. 31, 2005.

§ 364-i Medical assistance presumptive eligibility program.

1. [Until July 31, 2009, this section reads as set out below:]

An individual, upon application for medical assistance, shall be presumed eligible for such assistance for a period of sixty days from the date of transfer from a general hospital, as defined in section twenty-eight hundred one of the public health law to a certified home health agency or long term home health care program, as defined in section thirty-six hundred two of the public health law, or to a hospice as defined in section four thousand two of the public health law, or to a residential health care facility as defined in section twenty-eight hundred one of the public health law, if the local department of social services determines that the applicant meets each of the following criteria: (a) the applicant is receiving acute care in such hospital; (b) a physician certifies that such applicant no longer requires acute hospital care, but still requires medical care which can be provided by a certified home health agency, long term home health care program, hospice or residential health care facility; (c) the applicant or his representative states that the applicant does not have insurance coverage for the required medical care and that such care cannot be afforded; (d) it reasonably appears that the applicant is otherwise eligible to receive medical assistance; (e) it reasonably appears that the amount expended by the state and the local social services district for medical assistance in a certified home health agency, long term home health care program, hospice or residential health care facility, during the period of presumed eligibility, would be less than the amount the state and the local social services district would expend for continued acute hospital care for such person; and (f) such other determinative criteria as the commissioner shall provide by rule or regulation. If a person has been determined to be presumptively eligible for medical assistance, pursuant to this subdivision, and is subsequently determined to be ineligible for such assistance, the commissioner, on behalf of the state and the local social services district shall have the authority to recoup from the individual the sums expended for such assistance during the period of presumed eligibility.

2. Payment for up to sixty days of care for services provided under the medical assistance program shall be made for an applicant presumed eligible for medical assistance pursuant to subdivision one of this section provided, however, that such payment shall not exceed sixty-five percent of the rate payable under this title for services provided by a certified home health agency, long term home health care program, hospice or residential health care facility. Notwithstanding any other provision of law, no federal financial participation shall be claimed for services provided to a person while presumed eligible for medical assistance under this program until such person has been determined to be eligible for medical assistance by the local social services district. During the period of presumed medical assistance eligibility, payment for services provided persons presumed eligible under this program shall be made from state funds. Upon the final determination of eligibility by the local social services district, payment shall be made for the balance of the cost of such care and services provided to such applicant for such period of eligibility and a retroactive adjustment shall be made by the department to appropriately reflect federal financial participation and the local share of costs for the services provided during the period of presumptive

eligibility. Such federal and local financial participation shall be the same as that which would have occurred if a final determination of eligibility for medical assistance had been made prior to the provision of the services provided during the period of presumptive eligibility. In instances where an individual who is presumed eligible for medical assistance is subsequently determined to be ineligible, the cost for services provided to such individual shall be reimbursed in accordance with the provisions of section three hundred sixty-eight-a of this article. Provided, however, if upon audit the department determines that there are subsequent determinations of ineligibility for medical assistance in at least fifteen percent of the cases in which presumptive eligibility has been granted in a local social services district, payments for services provided to all persons presumed eligible and subsequently determined ineligible for medical assistance shall be divided equally by the state and the district.

3.   On or before March thirty-first, nineteen hundred ninety-seven, the department shall submit to the governor and legislature an evaluation of the program, including the program's effects on access, quality and cost of care, and any recommendations for future modifications to improve the program.

4.   Expired April 1, 2005

(a)   Notwithstanding any inconsistent provision of law to the contrary, a child shall be presumed to be eligible for medical assistance under this title beginning on the date that a qualified entity, as defined in paragraph (c) of this subdivision, determines, on the basis of preliminary information, that the net household income of the child does not exceed the applicable level for eligibility as provided for pursuant to paragraph (u) of subdivision four of section three hundred sixty-six of this title.

(b)   Such presumptive eligibility shall continue through the earlier of the day on which eligibility is determined pursuant to this title, or in the case of a child on whose behalf an application is not filed by the last day of the month following the month during which the qualified entity makes a preliminary determination, the last day of the month following the month in which the qualified entity makes a determination in paragraph (a).

(c)   For the purposes of this subdivision, and consistent with the applicable provisions of section 1920A of the federal social security act, "qualified entity" means an entity determined by the department of health to be capable of making presumptive eligibility determinations.

(d)   Notwithstanding any inconsistent provision of law to the contrary, care, services and supplies, as set forth in section three hundred sixty-five-a of this title, that are furnished to a child during a presumptive eligibility period by an entity that is eligible for payments under this title shall be deemed to be medical assistance for purposes of payment and state and federal reimbursement.

(e)   Notwithstanding any other provision of law, this section shall not be implemented until paragraph (t) of subdivision four of section three hundred sixty-six of this title shall take effect.

(f)   Repealed

5.   [Eff. April 1, 2007] Persons in need of treatment for breast, cervical, colon or prostate cancer; presumptive eligibility.

(a)   An individual shall be presumed to be eligible for medical assistance under this title beginning on the date that a qualified entity, as defined in paragraph (c) of this subdivision, determines, on the basis of preliminary information, that the individual meets the requirements of paragraph (v) or (v-1) of subdivision four of section three hundred sixty-six of this title.

(b)   Such presumptive eligibility shall continue through the earlier of the day on which a determination is made with respect to the eligibility of such individual for services, or in the case of such an individual who does not file an application by the last day of the month following the month during which the qualified entity makes the determination of presumptive eligibility, such last day.

(c)   For the purposes of this subdivision, "qualified entity" means an entity that provides medical assistance approved under this title, and is determined by the department of health to be capable of making determinations of presumptive eligibility under this subdivision.

(d)   Care, services and supplies, as set forth in section three hundred sixty-five-a of this title, that are furnished to an individual during a presumptive eligibility period under this subdivision by an entity that is eligible for payments under this title shall be deemed to be medical assistance for purposes of payment and state reimbursement.

1.   [Eff. July 31, 2009, this section reads as set out below:]

An individual, upon application for medical assistance, shall be presumed eligible for such assistance for a period of sixty days from the date of transfer from a general hospital, as defined in section twenty-eight hundred one of the public health law to a certified home health agency or long term home health care program, as defined in section thirty-six hundred two of the public health law, if the local department of social services determines that the applicant meets each of the following criteria: (a) the applicant is receiving acute care in such hospital; (b) a physician certifies that such applicant no longer requires acute hospital care, but still requires medical care which can be provided by a certified home health agency or a long term home health care program; (c) the applicant or his representative states that the applicant does not have insurance coverage for the required medical care and that such care cannot be afforded; (d) it reasonably appears that the applicant is otherwise eligible to receive medical assistance; (e) it reasonably appears that the amount expended by the state and the local social services district for medical assistance in a certified home health agency or long term home health care program, during the period of presumed eligibility, would be less than the amount the state and the local social services district would expend for continued acute hospital care for such person; and (f) such other determinative criteria as the commissioner shall provide by rule or regulation. If a person has been determined to be presumptively eligible for

SSL

medical assistance, pursuant to this subdivision, and is subsequently determined to be ineligible for such assistance, the commissioner, on behalf of the state and the local social services district shall have the authority to recoup from the individual the sums expended for such assistance during the period of presumed eligibility.

2. Payment for up to sixty days of care for services provided under the medical assistance program shall be made for an applicant presumed eligible for medical assistance pursuant to subdivision one of this section provided, however, that such payment shall not exceed sixty-five percent of the rate payable under this title for services provided by a certified home health agency or a long term home health care program. Notwithstanding any other provision of law, no federal financial participation shall be claimed for services provided to a person while presumed eligible for medical assistance under this program until such person has been determined to be eligible for medical assistance by the local social services district. During the period of presumed medical assistance eligibility, payment for services provided persons presumed eligible under this program shall be made from state funds. Upon the final determination of eligibility by the local social services district, payment shall be made for the balance of the cost of such care and services provided to such applicant for such period of eligibility and a retroactive adjustment shall be made by the department to appropriately reflect federal financial participation and the local share of costs for the services provided during the period of presumptive eligibility. Such federal and local financial participation shall be the same as that which would have occurred if a final determination of eligibility for medical assistance had been made prior to the provision of the services provided during the period of presumptiveeligibility. In instances where an individual who is presumed eligible for medical assistance is subsequently determined to be ineligible, the cost for services provided to such individual shall be reimbursed in accordance with the provisions of section three hundred sixty-eight-a of this article. Provided, however, if upon audit the department determines that there are subsequent determinations of ineligibility for medical assistance in at least fifteen percent of the cases in which presumptive eligibility has been granted in a local social services district, payments for services provided to all persons presumed eligible and subsequently determined ineligible for medical assistance shall be divided equally by the state and the district.

3. On or before March thirty-first, nineteen hundred eighty-nine, the department shall submit to the governor and the legislature an initial evaluation of the impact of the medical assistance presumptive eligibility program, including recommendations regarding possible modifications and on or before March thirty-first, nineteen hundred ninety, the department shall submit to the governor and legislature a second evaluation of the program, including further recommendations for future modifications.

4. None

5. [Eff. April 1, 2007] Persons in need of treatment for breast, cervical, colon or prostate cancer; presumptive eligibility.

(a) An individual shall be presumed to be eligible for medical assistance under this title beginning on the date that a qualified entity, as defined in paragraph (c) of this subdivision, determines, on the basis of preliminary information, that the individual meets the requirements of paragraph (v) or (v-1) of subdivision four of section three hundred sixty-six of this title.

(b) Such presumptive eligibility shall continue through the earlier of the day on which a determination is made with respect to the eligibility of such individual for services, or in the case of such an individual who does not file an application by the last day of the month following the month during which the qualified entity makes the determination of presumptive eligibility, such last day.

(c) For the purposes of this subdivision, "qualified entity" means an entity that provides medical assistance approved under this title, and is determined by the department of health to be capable of making determinations of presumptive eligibility under this subdivision.

(d) Care, services and supplies, as set forth in section three hundred sixty-five-a of this title, that are furnished to an individual during a presumptive eligibility period under this subdivision by an entity that is eligible for payments under this title shall be deemed to be medical assistance for purposes of payment and state reimbursement.

Added by Laws 1987, Ch. 626, eff. Jan. 1, 1988. **Amended** by Laws 1996, Ch. 693, eff. Oct. 2, 1996; **amended** by L. 1997, Ch. 97, § 1, eff. June 11, 1997; **amended** by L. 1998, Ch. 2, § 26, eff. July 1, 1999, amendments to expire and be deemed repealed Mar. 31, 2001; **amended** by L. 1999, Ch. 151, § 1, eff. July 1, 1999, extending effective date to July 31, 2001; **amended** by L. 2000, Ch. 419, § 66, eff. Sept. 13, 2000, deemed in full force and effect Jan. 1, 2000; **amended** by L. 2001, Ch. 20, Part C, § 1, eff. Mar. 30, 2001, Ch. 63, Part C, § 1, eff. Mar. 31, 2001, Ch. 145, § 1, eff. Mar. 31, 2001, Ch. 150, Part B, eff. Aug. 14, 2001, and Ch. 383, Part O, eff. Oct. 29, 2001, extending expiration date of subd. 4; **amended** by L. 2002, Ch. 1, Part A, § 55, eff. Jan. 25, 2002 extending expiration date and effective date to July 1, 2003; L. 2003, Ch. 62, Part A3, § 21, eff. May 15, 2003, extending the expiration date until July 1, 2005 and Ch. 113, § 1, eff. July 1, 2003, extending expiration date until July 1, 2006; **amended** by Laws 2004, Ch. 58, Part B, § 5, eff. Aug. 20, 2004, applying expiration date of Oct. 1, 2004 to subd (4); Laws 2006, ch. 176, §3, eff. April 1, 2007.

§ 364-j [Expires and repealed March 31, 2009] Managed care programs.

1. Definitions. As used in this section, unless the context clearly requires otherwise, the following terms shall mean:

(a) "Participant". A medical assistance recipient who receives, is required to receive or elects to receive his or her medical assistance services from a managed care provider.

(b)　"Managed care provider". An entity that provides or arranges for the provision of medical assistance services and supplies to participants directly or indirectly (including by referral), including case management; and:

(i)　is authorized to operate under article forty-four of the public health law or article forty-three of the insurance law and provides or arranges, directly or indirectly (including by referral) for covered comprehensive health services on a full capitation basis; or

(ii)　is authorized as a partially capitated program pursuant to section three hundred sixty-four-f of this title or section forty-four hundred three-e of the public health law or section 1915b of the social security act.

(c)　"Managed care program". A statewide program in which medical assistance recipients enroll on a voluntary or mandatory basis to receive medical assistance services, including case management, directly and indirectly (including by referral) from a managed care provider, and as applicable, a mental health special needs plan or a comprehensive HIV special needs plan, under this section.

(d)　"Medical services provider". A physician, nurse, nurse practitioner, physician assistant, licensed midwife, dentist, optometrist or other licensed health care practitioner authorized to provide medical assistance services.

(e)　"Center of excellence." A health care facility certified to operate under article twenty-eight of the public health law that offers specialized treatment expertise in HIV care services as defined by the commissioner of health.

(f)　"Primary care practitioner". A physician or nurse practitioner providing primary care to and management of the medical and health care services of a participant served by a managed care provider.

(g)　"AIDS". AIDS shall have the same meaning as in article twenty-seven-f of the public health law.

(h)　"HIV infection". HIV infection shall have the same meaning as in article twenty-seven-f of the public health law.

(i)　"HIV-related illness". HIV-related illness shall have the same meaning as in article twenty-seven-f of the public health law.

(j)　"Specialty care center". A "specialty care center" shall mean only such centers as are accredited or designated by an agency of the state or federal government or by a voluntary national health organization as having special expertise in treating the disease or condition for which it is accredited or designated.

(k)　"Special care". Care, services and supplies relating to the treatment of mental illness, mental retardation, developmental disabilities, alcoholism, alcohol abuse or substance abuse, or HIV infection/AIDS.

(l)　"Responsible special care agency". Whichever of the following state agencies has responsibility for the special care in question: the department of health, the office of mental health, the office of mental retardation and developmental disabilities, or the office of alcoholism and substance abuse services.

(m) "Mental health special needs plan" shall have the same meaning as in section forty-four hundred three-d of the public health law.

(n) "Comprehensive HIV special needs plan" shall have the same meaning as in section forty-four hundred three-c of the public health law.

(o) "Third-party payor". Any entity or program that is or may be liable to pay the costs of health and medical care of a recipient of medical assistance benefits, including insurers licensed pursuant to article thirty-two or forty-three of the insurance law, or organizations certified pursuant to article forty-four of the public health law.

(p) "Grievance". Any complaint presented by a participant or a participant's representative for resolution through the grievance process of a managed care provider, comprehensive HIV special needs plan or a mental health special needs plan.

(q) "Emergency medical condition". A medical or behavioral condition, the onset of which is sudden, that manifests itself by symptoms of sufficient severity, including severe pain, that a prudent layperson, who possesses an average knowledge of medicine and health, could reasonably expect the absence of immediate medical attention to result in: (i) placing the health of the person afflicted with such condition in serious jeopardy, or in the case of a behavioral condition placing the health of the person or others in serious jeopardy; or (ii) serious impairment to such person's bodily functions; or (iii) serious dysfunction of any bodily organ or part of such person; or (iv) serious disfigurement of such person.

(r) "Emergency care". Health care procedures, treatments or services, including psychiatric stabilization and medical detoxification from drugs or alcohol, that are provided for an emergency medical condition.

(s) "Existing rates". The rates paid pursuant to the most recent executed contract between a local social services district or the state and a managed care provider.

(t) "Managed care rating regions". The regions established by the department of health for the purpose of setting regional premium rates for managed care providers.

(u) "Premium group". The various demographic, gender and recipient categories utilized for rate-setting purposes by the department of health.

(v) "Upper payment limit". The maximum reimbursement that the department of health may pay a managed care provider for providing or arranging for medical services to participants in a managed care program in accordance with the federal social security act and regulations promulgated thereunder.

(w) Redesignated

SSL

(x) "Persons with serious mental illness". Individuals who meet criteria established by the commissioner of mental health, which shall include persons who have a designated diagnosis of mental illness under the most recent edition of the diagnostic and statistical manual of mental disorders, and (i) whose severity and duration of mental illness results in substantial functional disability or (ii) who require mental health services on more than an incidental basis.

(y) "Children and adolescents with serious emotional disturbances". Individuals under eighteen years of age who meet criteria established by the commissioner of mental health, which shall include children and adolescents who have a designated diagnosis of mental illness under the most recent edition of the diagnostic and statistical manual of mental disorders, and (i) whose severity and duration of mental illness results in substantial functional disability or (ii) who require mental health services on more than an incidental basis.

2.   (a) The commissioner of health, in cooperation with the commissioner and the commissioners of the responsible special care agencies shall establish managed care programs, under the medical assistance program, in accordance with applicable federal law and regulations. The commissioner of health, in cooperation with the commissioner, is authorized and directed, subject to the approval of the director of the state division of the budget, to apply for federal waivers when such action would be necessary to assist in promoting the objectives of this section.

(b) The commissioner of health has authority to allow social services districts to seek an exemption from this section for up to two years if the social services district can demonstrate and the commissioner of health and the commissioner of responsible special care agencies concurs that the district has insufficient capacity to participate in the program. An exemption under this paragraph may be renewed for additional two year periods.

3.   (a) Every person eligible for or receiving medical assistance under this article, who resides in a social services district providing medical assistance, which has implemented the state's managed care program shall participate in the program authorized by this section. Provided, however, that participation in a comprehensive HIV special needs plan also shall be in accordance with article forty-four of the public health law and participation in a mental health special needs plan shall also be in accordance with article forty-four of the public health law and article thirty-one of the mental hygiene law.

(b) A medical assistance recipient shall not be required to participate in, and shall be permitted to withdraw from the managed care program upon a showing that:

(i) a managed care provider is not geographically accessible to the person so as to reasonably provide services to the person, or upon a showing of other good cause as defined in regulation. A managed care provider is not geographically accessible if the person cannot access its services in a timely fashion due to distance or travel time;

(ii) a pregnant woman with an established relationship, as defined by the commissioner of health, with a comprehensive prenatal primary care provider, including a prenatal care assistance program as defined in title two of article twenty-five of the public health law, that is not associated with a managed care provider in the participant's social services district, may defer participation in the managed care program while pregnant and for sixty days post-partum;

(iii) an individual with a chronic medical condition being treated by a specialist physician that is not associated with a managed care provider in the participant's social services district, may defer participation in the managed care program until the course of treatment is complete; and

(iv) a participant cannot be served by a managed care provider who participates in a managed care program due to a language barrier.

(c) The following medical assistance recipients shall not be required to participate in a managed care program established pursuant to this section, but may voluntarily opt to do so:

(i) a person receiving services provided by a residential alcohol or substance abuse program or facility for the mentally retarded;

(ii) a person receiving services provided by an intermediate care facility for the mentally retarded or who has characteristics and needs similar to such persons;

(iii) a person with a developmental or physical disability who receives home and community-based services or care-at-home services through existing waivers under section nineteen hundred fifteen (c) of the federal social security act or who has characteristics and needs similar to such persons;

(iv) Native Americans;

(v) Medicare/Medicaid dually eligible individuals not enrolled in a Medicare TEFRA plan; or

(vi) a person who is eligible for medical assistance pursuant to subparagraph twelve or subparagraph thirteen of paragraph (a) of subdivision one of section three hundred sixty-six of this title, and who is not required to pay a premium pursuant to subdivision twelve of section three hundred sixty-seven-a of this title.

(d) The following medical assistance recipients shall not be eligible to participate in a managed care program established pursuant to this section:

(i) a person receiving services provided by a long term home health care program, or a person receiving inpatient services in a state-operated psychiatric facility or a residential treatment facility for children and youth;

(ii) a person eligible for Medicare participating in a capitated demonstration program for long term care;

(iii) an infant living with an incarcerated mother in a state or local correctional facility as defined in section two of the correction law;

SSL

(iv)   a person who is expected to be eligible for medical assistance for less than six months;

(v)   a person who is eligible for medical assistance benefits only with respect to tuberculosis-related services;

(vi)   certified blind or disabled children living or expected to be living separate and apart from the parent for 30 days or more;

(vii)   residents of nursing facilities at time of enrollment;

(viii)   individuals receiving hospice services at time of enrollment;

(ix)   individuals in the restricted recipient program;

(x)   a person who has primary medical or health care coverage available from or under a third-party payor which may be maintained by payment, or part payment, of the premium or costsharing amounts, when payment of such premium or costsharing amounts would be cost-effective, as determined by the local social services district;

(xi)   a foster child in the placement of a voluntary agency;

(xii)   a person receiving family planning services pursuant to subparagraph eleven of paragraph (a) of subdivision one of section three hundred sixty-six of this title; and

(xiii)   a person who is eligible for medical assistance pursuant to paragraph (v) of subdivision four of section three hundred sixty-six of this title; and

(xiv)   a person who is eligible for medical assistance pursuant to subparagraph twelve or subparagraph thirteen of paragraph (a) of subdivision one of section three hundred sixty-six of this title, and who is required to pay a premium pursuant to subdivision twelve of section three hundred sixty-seven-a of this title.

(e)   The following services shall not be provided to medical assistance recipients through managed care programs established pursuant to this section, and shall continue to be provided outside of managed care programs and in accordance with applicable reimbursement methodologies:

(i)   day treatment services provided to individuals with developmental disabilities;

(ii)   comprehensive medicaid case management services provided to individuals with developmental disabilities;

(iii)   services provided pursuant to title two-A of article twenty-five of the public health law;

(iv)   services provided pursuant to article eighty-nine of the education law;

(v)   mental health services provided by a certified voluntary free-standing day treatment program where such services are provided in conjunction with educational services authorized in an individualized education program in accordance with regulations promulgated pursuant to article eighty-nine of the education law;

(vi)   long term services as determined by the commissioner of mental retardation and developmental disabilities, provided to individuals with developmental disabilities at facilities licensed pursuant to article sixteen of the mental hygiene law or clinics serving individuals with developmental disabilities at facilities licensed pursuant to article twenty-eight of the public health law;

(vii)   TB directly observed therapy;

(viii)   AIDS adult day health care;

(ix)   HIV COBRA case management; and

(x)   other services as determined by the commissioner of health.

(f)   The following medical assistance recipients shall not be eligible to participate in a managed care program established pursuant to this section, unless the local social services district permits them to do so;

(i)   a person or family that is homeless and is living in a shelter; and

(ii)   a foster care child in the direct care of the local social services district.

(g)   The following categories of individuals will not be required to enroll with a managed care program until program features and reimbursement rates are approved by the commissioner of health and, as appropriate, the commissioner of mental health:

(i)   an individual dually eligible for medical assistance and benefits under the federal Medicare program and enrolled in a TEFRA plan;

(ii)   an individual eligible for supplemental security income;

(iii)   HIV positive individuals; and

(iv)   persons with serious mental illness and children and adolescents with serious emotional disturbances, as defined in section forty-four hundred one of the public health law.

4.   The managed care program shall provide participants access to comprehensive and coordinated health care delivered in a cost effective manner consistent with the following provisions:

(a)   (i) a managed care provider shall arrange for access to and enrollment of primary care practitioners and other medical services providers. Each managed care provider shall possess the expertise and sufficient resources to assure the delivery of quality medical care to participants in an appropriate and timely manner and may include physicians, nurse practitioners, county health departments, providers of comprehensive health service plans licensed pursuant to article forty-four of the public health law, and hospitals and diagnostic and treatment centers licensed pursuant to article twenty-eight of the public health law or otherwise authorized by law to offer comprehensive health services or facilities licensed pursuant to articles sixteen, thirty-one and thirty-two of the mental hygiene law.

(ii)   provided, however, if a major public hospital, as defined in the public health law, is designated by the commissioner of health as a managed care provider in a social services district the commissioner of health shall designate at least one other managed care provider which is not a major public hospital or facility operated by a major public hospital; and

(iii)   under a managed care program, not all managed care providers must be required to provide the same set of medical assistance services. The managed care program shall establish procedures through which participants will be assured access to all medical assistance services to which they are otherwise entitled, other than through the managed care provider, where:

(A)   the service is not reasonably available directly or indirectly from the managed care provider,

(B)   it is necessary because of emergency or geographic unavailability, or

(C)   the services provided are family planning services; or

(D)   the services are dental services and are provided by a diagnostic and treatment center licensed under article twenty-eight of the public health law which is affiliated with an academic dental center and which has been granted an operating certificate pursuant to article twenty-eight of the public health law to provide such dental services. Any diagnostic and treatment center providing dental services pursuant to this clause shall prior to June first of each year report to the governor, temporary president of the senate and speaker of the assembly on the following: the total number of visits made by medical assistance recipients during the immediately preceding calendar year; the number of visits made by medical assistance recipients during the immediately preceding calendar year by recipients who were enrolled in managed care programs; the number of visits made by medical assistance recipients during the immediately preceding calendar year by recipients who were enrolled in managed care programs that provide dental benefits as a covered service; and the number of visits made by the uninsured during the immediately preceding calendar year; or

(E)   other services as defined by the commissioner of health.

(b)   Participants shall select a managed care provider from among those designated under the managed care program, provided, however, a participant shall be provided with a choice of no less than two managed care providers. Notwithstanding the foregoing, a local social services district designated a rural area as defined in 42 U.S.C. 1395ww may limit a participant to one managed care provider, if the commissioner and the local social services district find that only one managed care provider is available. A managed care provider in a rural area shall offer a participant a choice of at least three primary care practitioners and permit the individual to obtain a service or seek a provider outside of the managed care network where such service or provider is not available from within the managed care provider network.

(c)   Participants shall select a primary care practitioner from among those designated by the managed care provider. In all districts, participants shall be provided with a choice of no less than three primary care practitioners.In the event that a participant does not select a primary care practitioner, the participant's managed care provider shall select a primary care practitioner for the participant, taking into account geographic accessibility.

(d)   For all other medical services, except as provided in paragraph (c) of this subdivision, if a sufficient number of medical service providers are available, a choice shall be offered.

(e)   (i) In any social services district which has not implemented a mandatory managed care program pursuant to this section, the commissioner of health shall establish marketing and enrollment guidelines, including but not limited to regulations governing face-to-face marketing and enrollment encounters between managed care providers and recipients of medical assistance and locations for such encounters. Such regulations shall prohibit, at a minimum, telephone cold-calling and door-to-door solicitation at the homes of medical assistance recipients. The regulations shall also require the commissioner of health to approve any local district marketing guidelines. Managed care providers shall be permitted to assist participants in completion of enrollment forms at approved health care provider sites and other approved locations. In no case may an emergency room be deemed an approved location. Upon enrollment, participants will sign an attestation that: they have been informed that managed care is a voluntary program; participants have a choice of managed care providers; participants have a choice of primary care practitioners; and participants must exclusively use their primary care practitioner and plan providers except as otherwise provided in this section including but not limited to the exceptions listed in subparagraph (iii) of paragraph (a) of this subdivision. Managed care providers must submit enrollment forms to the local department of social services. The local department of social services will provide or arrange for an audit of managed care provider enrollment forms; including telephone contacts to determine if participants were provided with the information required by this subparagraph. The commissioner of health may suspend or curtail enrollment or impose sanctions for failure to appropriately notify clients as required in this subparagraph.

(ii)   In any social services district which has implemented a mandatory managed care program pursuant to this section, the requirements of this subparagraph shall apply to the extent consistent with federal law and regulations. The department of health, may contract with one or more independent organizations to provide enrollment counseling and enrollment services, for participants required to enroll in managed care programs, for each social services district requesting the services of an enrollment broker. To select such organizations, the department of health shall issue a request for proposals (RFP), shall evaluate proposals submitted in response to such RFP and, pursuant to such RFP, shall award a contract to one or more qualified and responsive organizations. Such organizations shall not be owned, operated, or controlled by any governmental agency, managed care provider, comprehensive HIV special needs plan, mental health special needs plan, or medical services provider.

SSL

(iii)   Such independent organizations shall develop enrollment guides for participants which shall be approved by the department of health prior to distribution.

(iv)   Local social services districts or enrollment organizations through their enrollment counselors shall provide participants with the opportunity for face to face counseling including individual counseling upon request of the participant. Local social services districts or enrollment organizations through their enrollment counselors shall also provide participants with information in a culturally and linguistically appropriate and understandable manner, in light of the participant's needs, circumstances and language proficiency, sufficient to enable the participant to make an informed selection of a managed care provider. Such information shall include, but shall not be limited to: how to access care within the program; a description of the medical assistance services that can be obtained other than through a managed care provider, mental health special needs plan or comprehensive HIV special needs plan; the available managed care providers, mental health special needs plans and comprehensive HIV special needs plans and the scope of services covered by each; a listing of the medical services providers associated with each managed care provider; the participants' rights within the managed care program; and how to exercise such rights. Enrollment counselors shall inquire into each participant's existing relationships with medical services providers and explain whether and how such relationships may be maintained within the managed care program. For enrollments made during face to face counseling, if the participant has a preference for particular medical services providers, enrollment counselors shall verify with the medical services providers that such medical services providers whom the participant prefers participate in the managed care provider's network and are available to serve the participant.

(v)   Upon delivery of the pre-enrollment information, the local district or the enrollment organization shall certify the participant's receipt of such information. Upon verification that the participant has received the pre-enrollment education information, a managed care provider, a local district or the enrollment organization may enroll a participant into a managed care provider. Managed care providers must submit enrollment forms to the local department of social services. Upon enrollment, participants will sign an attestation that they have been informed that: participants have a choice of managed care providers; participants have a choice of primary care practitioners; and, except as otherwise provided in this section, including but not limited to the exceptions listed in subparagraph (iii) of paragraph (a) of this subdivision, participants must exclusively use their primary care practitioners and plan providers. The commissioner of health or with respect to a managed care plan serving participants in a city with a population of over two million, the local department of social services in such city, may suspend or curtail enrollment or impose sanctions for failure to appropriately notify clients as required in this subparagraph.

(vi)   Enrollment counselors or local social services districts shall further inquire into each participant's health status in order to identify physical or behavioral conditions that require immediate attention or continuity of care, and provide to participants information regarding health care options available to persons with HIV and other illnesses or conditions under the managed care program. Any information disclosed to counselors shall be kept confidential in accordance with applicable provisions of the public health law, and as appropriate, the mental hygiene law.

(vii) Any marketing materials developed by a managed care provider, comprehensive HIV special needs plan or mental health special needs plan shall be approved by the department of health or the local social services district and the commissioner of mental health, where appropriate, within sixty days prior to distribution to recipients of medical assistance. All marketing materials shall be reviewed within sixty days of submission.

(viii) In any social services district which has implemented a mandatory managed care program pursuant to this section, the commissioner of health shall establish marketing and enrollment guidelines, including but not limited to regulations governing face-to-face marketing and enrollment encounters between managed care providers and recipients of medical assistance and locations for such encounters. Such regulations shall prohibit, at a minimum, telephone cold-calling and door-to-door solicitation at the homes of medical assistance recipients. The regulations shall also require the commissioner of health to approve any local district marketing guidelines.

(f) (i) Participants shall have no less than sixty days from the date selected by the district to enroll in the managed care program to select a managed care provider, and as appropriate, a mental health special needs plan, and shall be provided with information to make an informed choice. Where a participant has not selected such a provider or mental health special needs plan, the commissioner of health shall assign such participant to a managed care provider, and as appropriate, to a mental health special needs plan, taking into account capacity and geographic accessibility. The commissioner may after the period of time established in subparagraph (ii) of this paragraph assign participants to a managed care provider taking into account quality performance criteria and cost. Provided however, cost criteria shall not be of greater value than quality criteria in assigning participants.

(ii) The commissioner may assign participants pursuant to such criteria on a weighted basis, provided however that for twelve months following implementation of a mandatory program, pursuant to a federal waiver, twenty-five percent of the participants that do not choose a managed care provider shall be assigned to managed care providers that satisfy the criteria set forth in subparagraph (i) of this paragraph, and are controlled by, sponsored by, or otherwise affiliated through a common governance or through a parent corporation with, one or more private not-for-profit or public general hospitals or diagnostic and treatment centers licensed pursuant to article twenty-eight of the public health law.

(iii) For twelve months following the twelve months described in subparagraph (ii) of this paragraph twenty-two and one-half percent of the participants

SSL

that do not choose a managed care provider shall be assigned to managed care providers, that satisfy the criteria set forth in subparagraph (i) of this paragraph and are controlled by, sponsored by, or otherwise affiliated through a common governance or through a parent corporation with, one or more private not-for-profit or public general hospitals or diagnostic and treatment centers licensed pursuant to article twenty-eight of the public health law.

(iv)   For twelve months following the twelve months described in subparagraph (iii) of this paragraph twenty percent of the participants that do not choose a managed care provider shall be assigned equally among each of the managed care providers, that satisfy the criteria set forth in subparagraph (i) of this paragraph and are controlled by, sponsored by, or otherwise affiliated through a common governance or through a parent corporation with one or more private not-for-profit or public general hospitals or diagnostic and treatment centers licensed pursuant to article twenty-eight of the public health law.

(v)   The commissioner shall assign all participants not otherwise assigned to a managed care plan pursuant to subparagraphs (ii), (iii) and (iv) of this paragraph equally among each of the managed care providers that meet the criteria established in subparagraph (i) of this paragraph.

(g)   If another managed care provider, mental health special needs plan or comprehensive HIV special needs plan is available, participants may change such provider or plan without cause within thirty days of notification of enrollment or the effective date of enrollment, whichever is later with a managed care provider, mental health special needs plan or comprehensive HIV special needs plan by making a request of the local social services district except that such period shall be forty-five days for participants who have been assigned to a provider by the commissioner of health. However, after such thirty or forty-five day period, whichever is applicable, a participant may be prohibited from changing managed care providers more frequently than once every twelve months, as permitted by federal law except for good cause as determined by the commissioner of health through regulations.

(h)   If another medical services provider is available, a participant may change his or her provider of medical services (including primary care practitioners) without cause within thirty days of the participant's first appointment with a medical services provider by making a request of the managed care provider, mental health special needs plan or comprehensive HIV special needs plan. However, after that thirty day period, no participant shall be permitted to change his or her provider of medical services other than once every six months except for good cause as determined by the commissioner through regulations.

(i)   A managed care provider, mental health special needs plan, and comprehensive HIV special needs plan requesting a disenrollment shall not disenroll a participant without the prior approval of the local social services district in which the participant resides, provided that disenrollment from a mental health special needs plan must comply with the standards of the commissioner of health and the commissioner of mental health. A managed care provider, mental health special needs plan or comprehensive HIV special needs plan shall not request disenrollment of a participant based on any diagnosis, condition, or perceived diagnosis or condition, or a participant's efforts to exercise his or her rights under a grievance process, provided however, that a managed care provider may, where medically appropriate, request permission to refer participants to a mental health special needs plan or a comprehensive HIV special needs plan after consulting with such participant and upon obtaining his/her consent to such referral and, provided further that a mental health special needs plan may, where clinically appropriate, disenroll individuals who no longer require the level of services provided by a mental health special needs plan.

(j) A managed care provider shall be responsible for providing or arranging for medical assistance services and assisting participants in the prudent selection of such services, including but not limited to:

(1) management of the medical and health care needs of participants by the participant's designated primary care practitioners or group of primary care practitioners to assure that all services provided under the managed care program and which are found to be necessary are made available in a timely manner, in accordance with prevailing standards of professional medical practice and conduct; and

(2) use of appropriate patient assessment criteria to ensure that all participants are provided with appropriate services, including special care;

(3) implementation of procedures, consistent with the requirements of paragraph (c) of subdivision six of section forty-four hundred three of the public health law for managing the care of participants requiring special care which may include the use of special case managers or the designation of a specialist as a primary care practitioner by a participant requiring special care on more than an incidental basis;

(4) implementation of procedures, consistent with the requirements of paragraph (b) of subdivision six of section forty-four hundred three of the public health law to permit the use of standing referrals to specialists and subspecialists for participants who require the care of such practitioners on a regular basis; and

(5) referral, coordination, monitoring and follow-up with regard to other medical services providers as appropriate for diagnosis and treatment, or direct provision of some or all medical assistance services.

(k) A managed care provider shall establish appropriate utilization and referral requirements for physicians, hospitals, and other medical services providers including emergency room visits and inpatient admissions.

(l) A managed care provider shall be responsible for developing appropriate methods of managing the health care and medical needs of homeless and other vulnerable participants to assure that all necessary services provided under the managed care program are made available and that all appropriate referrals and

SSL

follow-up treatment are provided, in a timely manner, in accordance with prevailing standards of professional medical practice and conduct.

(m)   A managed care provider shall provide all early periodic screening diagnosis and treatment services, as well as interperiodic screening and referral, to each participant under the age of twenty-one, at regular intervals, as medically appropriate.

(n)   A managed care provider shall provide or arrange, directly or indirectly (including by referral) for the provision of comprehensive prenatal care services to all pregnant participants including all services enumerated in subdivision one of section twenty-five hundred twenty-two of the public health law in accordance with standards adopted by the department of health pursuant to such section.

(o)   A managed care provider shall provide or arrange, directly or indirectly, (including by referral) for the full range of covered services to all participants, notwithstanding that such participants may be eligible to be enrolled in a comprehensive HIV special needs plan or mental health special needs plan.

(p)   A managed care provider, comprehensive HIV special needs plan and mental health special needs plan shall implement procedures to communicate appropriately with participants who have difficulty communicating in English and to communicate appropriately with visually-impaired and hearing-impaired participants.

(q)   A managed care provider, comprehensive HIV special needs plan and mental health special needs plan shall comply with applicable state and federal law provisions prohibiting discrimination on the basis of disability.

(r)   A managed care provider, comprehensive HIV special needs plan and mental health special needs plan shall provide services to participants pursuant to an order of a court of competent jurisdiction, provided however, that such services shall be within such provider's or plan's benefit package and are reimbursable under title xix of the federal social security act.

(s)   Managed care providers shall be provided with the date of recertification for medical assistance of each of their enrolled participants in conjunction with the monthly enrollment information conveyed to managed care providers.

(t)   Prospective enrollees shall be advised, in written materials related to enrollment, to verify with the medical services providers they prefer, or have an existing relationship with, that such medical services providers participate in the selected managed care provider's network and are available to serve the participant.

5.   Managed care programs shall be conducted in accordance with the requirements of this section and, to the extent practicable, encourage the provision of comprehensive medical services, pursuant to this article.

(a)   The managed care program shall provide for the selection of qualified managed care providers by the commissioner of health and, as appropriate, mental health special needs plans and comprehensive HIV special needs plans to participate in the program, provided, however, that the commissioner of health may contract directly with comprehensive HIV special needs plans consistent with standards set forth in this section, and assure that such providers are accessible taking into account the needs of persons with disabilities and the differences between rural, suburban, and urban settings, and in sufficient numbers to meet the health care needs of participants, and shall consider the extent to which major public hospitals are included within such providers' networks

(b)   A proposal submitted by a managed care provider to participate in the managed care program shall:

(i)   designate the geographic area to be served by the provider, and estimate the number of eligible participants and actual participants in such designated area;

(ii)   include a network of health care providers in sufficient numbers and geographically accessible to service program participants;

(iii)   describe the procedures for marketing in the program location, including the designation of other entities which may perform such functions under contract with the organization;

(iv)   describe the quality assurance, utilization review and case management mechanisms to be implemented;

(v)   demonstrate the applicant's ability to meet the data analysis and reporting requirements of the program;

(vi)   demonstrate financial feasibility of the program; and

(vii)   include such other information as the commissioner of health may deem appropriate.

(c)   The commissioner of health shall make a determination whether to approve, disapprove or recommend modification of the proposal.

(d)   Notwithstanding any inconsistent provision of this title and section one hundred sixty-three of the state finance law, the commissioner of health or the local department of social services in a city with a population of over two million may contract with managed care providers approved under paragraph (b) of this subdivision, without a competitive bid or request for proposal process, to provide coverage for participants pursuant to this title.

(e)   Notwithstanding any inconsistent provision of this title and section one hundred forty-three of the economic development law, no notice in the procurement opportunities newsletter shall be required for contracts awarded by the commissioner of health or the local department of social services in a city with a population of over two million, to qualified managed care providers pursuant to this section.

(f)   The care and services described in subdivision four of this section will be furnished by a managed care provider pursuant to the provisions of this section when such services are furnished in accordance with an agreement with the department of health or the local department of social services in a city with a population of over two million, and meet applicable federal law and regulations.

SSL

(g)   The commissioner of health may delegate some or all of the tasks identified in this section to the local districts.

(h)   Any delegation pursuant to paragraph (g) of this subdivision shall be reflected in the contract between a managed care provider and the commissioner of health.

6.   A managed care provider, mental health special needs plan or comprehensive HIV special needs plan provider shall not engage in the following practices:

(a)   use deceptive or coercive marketing methods to encourage participants to enroll; or

(b)   distribute marketing materials to recipients of medical assistance, unless such materials are approved by the department of health and, as appropriate, the office of mental health.

7.   The department, the department of health or other agency of the state as appropriate shall provide technical assistance at the request of a social services district for the purpose of development and implementation of managed care programs pursuant to this section. Such assistance shall include but need not be limited to provision and analysis of data, design of managed care programs and plans, innovative payment mechanisms, and ongoing consultation. In addition, the department and the department of health shall make available materials to social services districts for purposes of educating persons eligible to receive medical assistance on how their care will be provided through managed care as required under paragraph (e) of subdivision five of this section.

8.   (a) The commissioner of health shall institute a comprehensive quality assurance system for managed care providers that includes performance and outcome-based quality standards for managed care.

(b)   Every managed care provider shall implement internal quality assurance systems adequate to identify, evaluate and remedy problems relating to access, continuity and quality of care, utilization, and cost of services, provided, however, that the commissioner shall waive the implementation of internal quality assurance systems, where appropriate, for managed care providers described in subparagraph (ii) of paragraph (b) of subdivision one of this section. Such internal quality assurance systems shall conform to the internal quality assurance requirements imposed on health maintenance organizations pursuant to the public health law and regulations and shall provide for:

(i)   the designation of an organizational unit or units to perform continuous monitoring of health care delivery;

(ii)   the utilization of epidemiological data, chart reviews, patterns of care, patient surveys, and spot checks;

(iii)   reports to medical services providers assessing timeliness and quality of care;

(iv)   the identification, evaluation and remediation of problems relating to access, continuity and quality of care; and

(v)   a process for credentialing and recredentialing licensed providers.

(c)   The department of health, in consultation with the responsible special care agencies, shall contract with one or more independent quality assurance organizations to monitor and evaluate the quality of care and services furnished by managed care providers. To select such organization or organizations, the department of health shall issue requests for proposals (RFP), shall evaluate proposals submitted in response to such RFP, and pursuant to such RFP, shall award one or more contracts to one or more qualified and responsive organizations. Such quality assurance organizations shall evaluate and review the quality of care delivered by each managed care provider, on at least an annual basis. Such review and evaluation shall include compliance with the performance and outcome-based quality standards promulgated by the commissioner of health.

(d)   Every managed care provider shall collect and submit to the department of health, in a standardized format prescribed by the department of health, patient specific medical information, including encounter data, maintained by such provider for the purposes of quality assurance and oversight. Any information or encounter data collected pursuant to this paragraph, however, shall be kept confidential in accordance with section forty-four hundred eight-a of the public health law and section 33.13 of the mental hygiene law and any other applicable state or federal law.

(e)   Information collected and submitted to the department of health by the independent quality assurance organization or managed care provider pursuant to this subdivision shall be made available to the public, subject to any other limitations of federal or state law regarding disclosure thereof to third parties.

(f)   Every managed care provider shall ensure that the provider maintains a network of health care providers adequate to meet the comprehensive health needs of its participants and to provide an appropriate choice of providers sufficient to provide the services to its participants by determining that:

(i)   there are a sufficient number of geographically accessible participating providers;

(ii)   there are opportunities to select from at least three primary care providers; and

(iii)   there are sufficient providers in each area of specialty practice to meet the needs of the enrolled population.

(g)   The commissioner of health shall establish standards to ensure that managed care providers have sufficient capacity to meet the needs of their enrollees, which shall include patient to provider ratios, travel and distance standards and appropriate waiting times for appointments.

9.   Managed care providers shall inform participants of such provider's grievance procedure and utilization review procedures required pursuant to sections forty-four hundred eight-c and forty-nine hundred of the public health law. A managed care provider or local social services district, as appropriate, shall

provide notice to participants of their respective rights to a fair hearing and aid continuing in accordance with applicable state and federal law.

10.   The commissioner of health shall be authorized to establish requirements regarding provision and reimbursement of emergency care.

11.   Notwithstanding section three hundred sixty-six of this chapter or any other inconsistent provision of law, participants in the managed care program under this section who have lost their eligibility for medical assistance before the end of a six month period beginning on the date of the participant's initial selection of or assignment to a managed care provider shall have their eligibility for medical assistance continued until the end of the six month enrollment period, but only with respect to family planning services provided pursuant to subparagraph (iii) of paragraph (a) of subdivision four of this section and any services provided to the individual under the direction of the managed care provider. Provided further, however, a pregnant woman with an income in excess of the medically needy income level set forth in section three hundred sixty-six of this title, who was eligible for medical assistance solely as a result of paragraph (m) or (o) of subdivision four of such section, shall continue to be eligible for medical assistance benefits only through the end of the month in which the sixtieth day following the end of her pregnancy occurs except for eligibility for Federal Title X services which shall continue for twenty-four months therefrom, and provided further that the services are reimbursable by the federal government at a rate of ninety percent;provided, however, that nothing in this subdivision shall be deemed to affect payment for such services if federal financial participation is not available for such care, services and supplies solely by reason of the immigration status of the otherwise eligible woman.

12.   The commissioner, by regulation, shall provide that a participant may withdraw from participation in a managed care program upon a showing of good cause.

13.   (a) Notwithstanding any inconsistent provisions of this section, participation in a managed care program will not diminish a recipient's medical assistance eligibility or the scope of available medical services to which he or she is entitled. Once a program is implemented by or in the district in accordance with this section, medical assistance for persons who require such assistance, who are eligible for or in receipt of such assistance in the district and who are covered by the program shall be limited to payment of the cost of care, services and supplies covered by the managed care program, only when furnished, prescribed, ordered or approved by a managed care provider, mental health special needs plan or comprehensive HIV special needs plan and otherwise under the program, together with the costs of medically necessary medical and remedial care, services or supplies which are not available to participants under the program, but which would otherwise be available to such persons under this title and the regulations of the department provided, however, that the program may contain provision for payment to be made for non-emergent care furnished in hospital emergency rooms consistent with subdivision ten of this section.

(b)　Notwithstanding any inconsistent provision of law, payment for claims for services as specified in paragraph (a) of this subdivision furnished to eligible persons under this title, who are enrolled in a managed care program pursuant to this section and section three hundred sixty-four-f of this title or other comprehensive health services plans, shall not be made when such services are the contractual responsibility of a managed care provider but are provided by another medical services provider contrary to the managed care plan.

14.　The commissioner of health is authorized and directed, subject to the approval of the director of the division of budget, to make grants to social services districts to aid in the planning and development of managed care programs. The total amount expended pursuant to this section shall not exceed the amount appropriated for such purposes in any fiscal year.

15.　The managed medical care demonstration program advisory council is abolished.

16.　Any waiver application to the federal department of health and human services pursuant to this article and any amendments to such application shall be a public document.

17.　The provisions of this section regarding participation of persons receiving family assistance and supplemental security income in managed care programs shall be effective if, and as long as, federal financial participation is available for expenditures for services provided pursuant to this section.

18.　(a) The department of health may, where not inconsistent with the rate setting authority of other state agencies and subject to approval of the director of the division of the budget, develop reimbursement methodologies and fee schedules for determining the amount of payment to be made to managed care providers under the managed care program. Such reimbursement methodologies and fee schedules may include provisions for payment of managed care fees and capitation arrangements.

(b)　The department of health in consultation with organizations representing managed care providers shall select an independent actuary to review any such reimbursement rates. Such independent actuary shall review and make recommendations concerning appropriate actuarial assumptions relevant to the establishment of rates including but not limited to the adequacy of the rates in relation to the population to be served adjusted for case mix, the scope of services the plans must provide, the utilization of services and the network of providers necessary to meet state standards. The independent actuary shall issue a report no later than December thirty-first, nineteen hundred ninety-eight and annually thereafter. Such report shall be provided to the governor, the temporary president and the minority leader of the senate and the speaker and the minority leader of the assembly. The department of health shall assess managed care providers under the managed care program on a per enrollee basis to cover the cost of such report.

19.　(a) The commissioner of health, in consultation with the commissioner, shall promulgate such regulations as are necessary to implement the provisions

SSL

of this section provided, however, that the provisions of this subdivision shall not limit specific actions taken by the department of health or the department in order to ensure federal financial participation.

20. Upon a determination that a participant appears to be suitable for admission to a comprehensive HIV special needs plan or a mental health special needs plan, a managed care provider shall inform the participant of the availability of such plans, where available and appropriate.

21. (a) An amount equal to seven million dollars together with any matching federal and local government funds shall be made available for rate adjustments for managed care providers whose rates were set under the competitive bidding process. Such adjustment shall be made in accordance with this paragraph.

(i) Such amount shall be allocated by the department of health among the managed care rating regions based on each region's percentage of statewide Medicaid managed care enrollment as of January first, nineteen hundred ninety-seven excluding from such calculation enrollment in local social services districts that did not participate in the competitive bidding process.

(ii) From among the funds allocated in a managed care rating region, the department of health shall adjust the existing rates paid to managed care providers for each premium group for the period from January first, nineteen hundred ninety-seven through March thirty-first, nineteen hundred ninety-eight in a manner that raises the rates of all managed care providers in the region to the highest uniform percentage of the upper payment limit possible based on the funds available; provided, however, that no managed care provider's rate for any premium group shall be reduced as a result of such adjustment. For the purpose of calculating appropriate rate increases under this subparagraph, the department of health shall assume that, for the entire period between January first, nineteen hundred ninety-seven and March thirty-first, nineteen hundred ninety-eight, enrollment in each premium group shall be equal to enrollment in the premium group as of July first, nineteen hundred ninety-seven.

(b) In addition to the increases made available in paragraph (a) of this subdivision for the period beginning January first, nineteen hundred ninety-seven through March thirty-first, nineteen hundred ninety-eight, an additional ten million dollars, together with any matching federal and local government funds, shall be added to provide a uniform percentage increase, based on July first, nineteen hundred ninety-seven enrollment to the existing rates paid for all premium groups to all managed care providers whose rates were set by the competitive bidding process.

(c) In addition to the increases made available in paragraphs (a) and (b) of this subdivision for the period beginning January first, nineteen hundred ninety-seven through March thirty-first, nineteen hundred ninety-eight, an additional amount equal to three million dollars together with any matching federal and local government funds, shall be made available to be added to the rates of health plans operating in geographic areas where capacity is insufficient to allow attainment of enrollment goals consistent with the federal 1115 waiver known as the Partnership Plan. Such amount shall be distributed subject to a demonstration to the commissioner's satisfaction that the plan has executed a contract amendment providing for an increase in enrollment proportional to the size of the plan and the remaining unenrolled population in the county. In evaluating the plan's demonstration, the commissioner shall consider the degree to which the plan has increased the number of primary or specialty care practitioners or diagnostic and treatment centers in its network or whether the additional rate increase would permit the plan to generate greater enrollments while continuing to meet the financial requirements of the public health law or the insurance law whichever is applicable and regulations promulgated pursuant thereto.

Any amount identified in this paragraph remaining uncommitted by December thirty-first, nineteen hundred ninety-seven shall be distributed in a manner consistent with paragraph (b) of this subdivision.

(d) A plan shall be eligible for payments pursuant to paragraphs (a), (b) and (c) of this subdivision for such periods as the plan has a contract with one or more social services districts; provided, however that the plan has a contract, or has made a good faith effort to enter into a contract, in that district effective through March thirty-first, nineteen hundred ninety-eight.

(e) For the period from April first, nineteen hundred ninety-eight through March thirty-first, nineteen hundred ninety-nine, the premium rates paid by the department of health to all managed care providers whose rates were set under the competitive bidding process shall be equal to (i) the managed care provider's rate as of March thirty-first, nineteen hundred ninety-eight increased by a uniform trend factor; plus, (ii) four million dollars together with any matching federal and local government funds to be added as a uniform percentage increase to such provider's rate as of March thirty-first, nineteen hundred ninety-eight, based on enrollment in the premium group as of April first, nineteen hundred ninety-eight.

(f) For the period from April first, nineteen hundred ninety-eight through March thirty-first, nineteen hundred ninety-nine, an additional amount equal to four million dollars together with any matching federal and local government funds, shall be made available for managed care rate adjustments consistent with the criteria set forth in paragraph (c) of this subdivision. Any amount identified in this paragraph remaining uncommitted by December thirty-first, nineteen hundred ninety-eight shall be added as a uniform percentage increase to the rates of all managed care providers eligible for an increase under paragraph (e) of this subdivision.

22. Chemung county demonstration project.

(a) The legislature finds that the particular circumstances of Chemung county warrant authorizing this demonstration project, including the rural nature of the county, the absence of a comprehensive medicaid managed care provider serving the area at this time, patient care needs, and aspects of the health care provider base.

(b)   within [Within] all or part of Chemung county (referred to in this subdivision as "the catchment area"), the department of health and the Chemung county department of social services are authorized to conduct a Medicaid research and demonstration project (referred to in this subdivision as the "demonstration project") for the purpose of testing the use of innovative administrative techniques, new reimbursement methods, and management of care models, so as to promote more efficient use of health resources, a healthier population and containment of Medicaid program costs.

(c)   As part of the demonstration project, the Chemung county department of social services is authorized to contract with a managed care provider for the purposes of, without limitation, developing and managing a provider of care network, establishing provider payment rates and fees, paying provider claims, providing care management services to project participants, and managing the utilization of project services.

(d)   The demonstration project shall be consistent with the provisions of this section, except:

(i)   The department may waive any rules or regulations, as necessary to implement and consistent with this subdivision.

(ii)   The demonstration project shall not be subject to:

(A)   paragraph (b) of subdivision four of this section;

(B)   subparagraphs (i), (ii), (iii), (v) and (viii) of paragraph (e) of subdivision four of this section;

(C)   paragraph (f) of subdivision four of this section;

(D)   paragraph (g) of subdivision four of this section;

(E)   subdivision five of this section; provided that in approving the demonstration project or modifications to it, the department shall consider the criteria in that subdivision;

(F)   sections two hundred seventy-two and two hundred seventy-three of the public health law;

(G)   section three hundred sixty-five-i of this title.

(iii)   Notwithstanding subdivision three of this section, participation in the project shall be mandatory for all or any specified categories of persons eligible for services under this title for whom the Chemung county department of social services has fiscal responsibility pursuant to section three hundred sixty-five of this title and who reside within the demonstration project catchment area, as determined by the commissioner of health; provided, however, that eligible persons who are also beneficiaries under title XVIII of the federal social security act and persons who reside in residential health care facilities shall not be eligible to participate in the project.

(e)   (i) Persons who are enrolled in or apply for medical assistance on or before the date the demonstration project takes effect shall receive sixty days written notice prior to participating in the demonstration project, including an explanation of the demonstration project and the participant's rights and responsibilities. Persons who apply for medical assistance thereafter shall receive such notice at the time of applying for medical assistance.

(ii)   The demonstration project shall provide adequate services to overcome language barriers for participants.

(iii)   Participants in the demonstration project whose participation in a managed care program would not otherwise be mandatory under subdivision three of this section, who, at the time they enter the demonstration project, have an established relationship with and are receiving services from one or more medical services providers that are not included in the demonstration project's provider network (an "out-of-network provider"), shall be permitted to continue to receive services from such providers until their course of treatment is complete, or in the case of a pregnant woman, while pregnant and for sixty days postpartum. Out-of-network providers that provide services pursuant to this subparagraph shall be subject to the utilization review and care management procedures prescribed by the managed care provider and shall be reimbursed at the rate that would be paid to such providers by the medical assistance program on a fee for service basis pursuant to this title, and shall accept such reimbursement as payment in full.

(f)   The provisions of this subdivision shall not apply unless all necessary approvals under federal law and regulation have been obtained to receive federal financial participation in the costs of health care services provided pursuant to this subdivision.

(g)   The commissioner of health is authorized to submit amendments to the state plan for medical assistance and/or submit one or more applications for waivers of the federal social security act as may be necessary to obtain the federal approvals necessary to implement this subdivision.

(h)   The demonstration project shall terminate five years after it is approved by the department and all necessary approvals under federal law and regulations under paragraph (f) of this subdivision have been obtained, unless terminated sooner by the Chemung county department of social services.

23.   (a) As a means of protecting the health, safety and welfare of recipients, in addition to any other sanctions that may be imposed, the commissioner shall appoint temporary management of a managed care provider upon determining that the managed care provider has repeatedly failed to meet the substantive requirements of sections 1903(m) and 1932 of the federal Social Security Act and regulations. A hearing shall not be required prior to the appointment of temporary management.

(b)   The commissioner and/or his or her designees, which may be individuals within the department or other individuals or entities with appropriate knowledge and experience, may be appointed as temporary management. The commissioner

SSL

may appoint the superintendent of insurance and/or his or her designees as temporary management of any managed care provider which is subject to rehabilitation pursuant to article seventy-four of the insurance law.

(c)   The responsibilities of temporary management shall include oversight of the managed care provider for the purpose of removing the causes and conditions which led to the determination requiring temporary management, the imposition of improvements to remedy violations and, where necessary, the orderly reorganization, termination or liquidation of the managed care provider.

(d)   Temporary management may hire and fire managed care provider personnel and expend managed care provider funds in carrying out the responsibilities imposed pursuant to this subdivision.

(e)   The commissioner, in consultation with the superintendent with respect to any managed care provider subject to rehabilitation pursuant to article seventy-four of the insurance law, may make available to temporary management for the benefit of a managed care provider for the maintenance of required reserves and deposits monies from such funds as are appropriated for such purpose.

(f)   The commissioner is authorized to establish in regulation provisions for the payment of fees and expenses from funds appropriated for such purpose for non-governmental individuals and entities appointed as temporary management pursuant to this subdivision.

(g)   The commissioner may not terminate temporary management prior to his or her determination that the managed care provider has the capability to ensure that the sanctioned behavior will not recur.

(h)   During any period of temporary management individuals enrolled in the managed care provider being managed may disenroll without cause. Upon reaching a determination that requires temporary management of a managed care provider, the commissioner shall notify all recipient enrollees of such provider that they may terminate enrollment without cause during the period of temporary management.

(i)   The commissioner may adopt and amend rules and regulations to effectuate the purposes and provisions of this subdivision.

Added by Laws 1988, Ch. 710, § 1, eff. Dec. 15, 1988, until July 1, 1996; amended by Laws 1991, Ch. 165, § 8, eff. June 12, 1991 until July 1, 1996; amended by Laws 1993, Ch. 505, § 1, eff. July 26, 1993 until July 1, 1996; amended by Laws 1994, Ch. 320, § 2, eff. July 20, 1994, but deemed to have been in full force and effect since Jan. 1, 1994, extending the period that the section remains effective to July 1, 1996; amended Laws 1996, Ch. 649, §§ 4, 5 and 6, eff. Sept. 16, 1996, but deemed to have been in full force and effect since July 1, 1996, amended the statute and extended the expiration date to July 1, 2000; amended Laws 1997, Ch. 433, §§ 53–55, 57–59, and 62–66, eff. Aug. 20, 1997; amended by Laws 1997, Ch. 436, § 1 Part B, § 94, eff. Nov. 1, 1997; amended by Laws 1997, Ch. 653, § 1, eff. Sept. 24, 1997; amended by Laws 1998, Ch. 58, Part E, § 24, eff. Apr. 28, 1998, deemed in full force and effect Apr. 1, 1998; amended by Laws 1999, Ch. 558, § 45, eff. Oct. 5, 1999; amended by L. 1999, Ch. 648, § 1, eff.

Dec. 21, 1999; **amended** by L. 2000, Ch. 16 § 1, effective Mar. 30, 2000, Ch. 57 Part B § 3, eff. July 1, 2000, extending the expiration date of the section to Dec. 31, 2003, Ch. 57 Part B §§ 4–6, effective July 1, 2000; **amended** by Laws 2002, Ch. 1, Part A, § 58, 66, 67, 67-a, and 75, eff. Jan. 25, 2002; L. 2003, Ch. 62, Part Z2, §§ 41–43, eff. May 15, 2003, extending expiration date until March 31, 2006, Ch. 697, § 1, adding new sub. 4, par. (a) (iii), cl. (D), and re-lettering former cl. (D) to (E), eff. Nov. 19, 2003; **amended** by Laws 2004, Ch. 58, Part C, §§ 12–17, 34 and 36, eff. April 1, 2004; Laws 2006, ch. 57, §57 (Part A), eff. July 1, 2006.

§ 364-j-2　Transitional supplemental payments

1.　As used in this section, "covered provider" shall mean a voluntary not-for-profit health care provider that is any of the following:

(a)　a freestanding diagnostic and treatment center licensed under article twenty-eight of the public health law that qualifies for a distribution pursuant to section twenty-eight hundred seven-p of such article, or section seven of chapter four hundred thirty-three of the laws of nineteen hundred ninety-seven, or receives funding under section three hundred thirty-three of the federal public health services act for health care for the homeless; or

(b)　a freestanding diagnostic and treatment center which operates an approved program under the prenatal care assistance program established pursuant to article twenty-five of the public health law; or

(c)　a facility licensed under article twenty-eight of the public health law that is sponsored by a university or dental school which has been granted an operating certificate pursuant to article twenty-eight of the public healthlaw to provide dental services; or

(d)　a freestanding family planning clinic licensed under article twenty-eight of the public health law.

2.　(a) Notwithstanding paragraphs (b) and (h) of subdivision two of section twenty-eight hundred seven of the public health law, the commissioner of health shall make supplemental payments of nine million eight hundred twenty-four thousand dollars ($9,824,000), to covered providers described in subdivision one of this section who are qualified providers as described in paragraph (a) of subdivision three of this section, based on adjustments to fee-for-service rates for the period February first through March thirty-first, two thousand two and nine million eight hundred twenty-four thousand dollars ($9,824,000) for the period October first through December thirty-first, two thousand two and four million nine hundred twelve thousand dollars ($4,912,000) for the period October first through December thirty-first, two thousand three and an additional amount of four million nine hundred twelve thousand dollars ($4,912,000) for the period October first through December thirty-first, two thousand three and nine million eight hundred twenty-four thousand dollars ($9,824,000) for the period April first through June thirtieth, two thousand five, and nine million eight hundred twenty-four thousand dollars ($9,824,000) for the period October first through December thirty-first, two thousand six, and an additional nine million eight hundred twenty-four thousand dollars ($9,824,000) for the period October first through December thirty-first, two thousand six, as medical assistance payments for services provided pursuant to this title for persons eligible for federal financial participation under title XIX of the federal social security act to reflect additional costs associated with the transition to a managed care environment. There shall be no local share in these payments. The director of the budget shall allocate the nonfederal share of such payments from an appropriation for the miscellaneous special revenue fund -339 community service provider assistance program account for the two thousand one–two thousand two state fiscal year for adjustments for the period February first through March thirty-first, two thousand two. Adjustments for the period October first, two thousand two through December thirty-first, two thousand two shall be within amounts appropriated for the two thousand two–two thousand three state fiscal year and adjustments for the period October first, two thousand three through December thirty-first, two thousand three shall be within amounts appropriated for the two thousand three–two thousand four state fiscal year and adjustments for the non-federal share of the additional amount of four million nine hundred twelve thousand dollars ($4,912,000) for such period shall be allocated by the director of the budget from an appropriation for maintenance undistributed general fund community projects fund -007 account for the two thousand three–two thousand four state fiscal year. The director of the budget shall allocate the non-federal share of adjustments for the period April first, two thousand five through June thirtieth, two thousand five from an appropriation for the maintenance undistributed general fund community projects fund -007 -cc account for the two thousand four–two thousand five state fiscal year. The director of the budget shall allocate the non-federal share of adjustments for the period October first, two thousand six through December thirty-first, two thousand six from an appropriation for the maintenance undistributed, general fund, community projects fund -007 -cc account for the two thousand five–two thousand six state fiscal year. The director of the budget shall allocate the non-federal share of the additional adjustments for the period October first, two thousand six through December thirty-first, two thousand six from such funds as may be made available from an appropriation for the maintenance undistributed, general fund, community projects fund -007 -cc account for the two thousand six–two thousand seven state fiscal year. Such adjustments to fee for service rates shall not be subject to subsequent adjustment or reconciliation. Alternatively, such payments may be made as aggregate payments to eligible providers.

(a-1)   Notwithstanding the provisions of paragraph (a) of this subdivision, for facilities licensed under article twenty-eight of the public health law that are sponsored by a university or dental school which has been granted an operating certificate pursuant to article twenty-eight of the public health law and which provides dental services as its principal mission, two hundred twenty-four thousand dollars ($224,000) in the aggregate for use pursuant to this section shall be allocated for distribution to such facilities pursuant to the methodology described in paragraph (b) of subdivision two and subparagraph (i) of paragraph (b) of subdivision four of section two thousand eight hundred seven-p of the public health law for services provided for the period February first, two thousand two through March thirty-first, two thousand two to persons eligible for federal financial participation under title XIX of the federal social security act, provided, however, that the amount paid pursuant to this paragraph for each such facility shall equal the facility's proportional share of the total nominal payment amounts calculated under this section of all such facilities multiplied by the total funds allocated for such payments. There shall be no local share in these payments. The director of the budget shall allocate the non-federal share of such payments from an appropriation for the miscellaneous special revenue fund -339 community service provider assistance program account for the two thousand one–two thousand two state fiscal year. Such adjustments to fee for service rates shall not be subject to subsequent adjustment or reconciliation. Alternatively, such payments may be made as aggregate payments to eligible providers.

(a-2)   (i) Notwithstanding the provisions of paragraph (a) of this subdivision, for facilities licensed under article twenty-eight of the public health law that are sponsored by a university or dental school which has been granted an operating certificate pursuant to article twenty-eight of the public health law and which provides dental services as its principal mission, two hundred twenty-four thousand dollars ($224,000) in the aggregate of the amount appropriated for the two thousand two–two thousand three state fiscal year for use pursuant to this section shall be allocated for the period October first through December thirty-first, two thousand two and one hundred twelve thousand dollars ($112,000) in the aggregate of the amount appropriated for the two thousand three–two thousand four state fiscal year, and an additional amount of one hundred twelve thousand dollars ($112,000) in the aggregate for use pursuant to this section shall be allocated for the period October first through December thirty-first, two thousand three and two hundred twenty-four thousand dollars ($224,000) in the aggregate of the amount appropriated for the two thousand four–two thousand five state fiscal year shall be allocated for the period April first, two thousand five through June thirtieth, two thousand five, and two hundred twenty-four thousand dollars ($224,000) in the aggregate of the amount appropriated for the two thousand five–two thousand six state fiscal year shall be allocated for the period October first, two thousand six through December thirty-first, two thousand six, and an additional two hundred twenty-four thousand dollars ($224,000) in the aggregate of the amount appropriated for the two thousand six–two thousand seven state fiscal year shall be allocated for the period October first, two thousand six through December thirty-first, two thousand six, for distribution to such facilities pursuant to subparagraphs (ii) and (iii) of this paragraph. Adjustments for the non-federal share of the additional amount of one hundred twelve thousand dollars ($112,000) for the period October first, two thousand three through December thirty-first, two thousand three shall be allocated by the director of the budget from an appropriation for maintenance undistributed general fund community projects fund -007 account for the two thousand three–two thousand four state fiscal year. The non-federal share of adjustments for the period April first, two thousand five through June thirtieth, two thousand five shall be allocated by the director of the budget from an appropriation for the maintenance undistributed general fund community projects fund -007 account for the two thousand four–two thousand five state fiscal year. The non-federal share of adjustments for the period October first, two thousand six through December thirty-first, two thousand six shall be allocated by the director of the budget from an appropriation for the maintenance undistributed, general fund, community projects fund -007 -cc account for the two thousand five–two thousand six state fiscal year. The non-federal share of the additional adjustments for the period October first, two thousand six through December thirty-first, two thousand six shall, subject to the availability of funds, be allocated by the director of the budget from the medical assistance local assistance appropriation for the two thousand six–two thousand seven state fiscal year.

(ii) Forty percent shall be allocated for equal distribution to such facilities, reduced by the amount, if any, that a distribution exceeds forty percent of a facility's uncompensated care need as defined in paragraph (b) of subdivision two of section two thousand eight hundred seven-p of the public health law. Any funds allocated but not distributed in accordance with this subparagraph shall be added to those amounts distributed in accordance with subparagraph (iii) of this paragraph.

(iii) Sixty percent, plus any funds allocated and not distributed in accordance with subparagraph (ii) of this paragraph, shall be allocated for distribution to such facilities pursuant to the methodology described in paragraph (b) of subdivision two and subparagraph (i) of paragraph (b) of subdivision four of section two thousand eight hundred seven-p of the public health law, provided, however, that the amount paid pursuant to this allocation for each such facility shall equal the facility's proportional share of the total nominal payment amounts calculated under this section of all such facilities multiplied by the total funds allocated for such payments.

(iv) There shall be no local share in these payments.

(b) Notwithstanding the provisions of subdivision one of section three hundred sixty-eight-a of this title, there shall be paid to each social services district the full amount expended on behalf of the department of health for medical assistance furnished pursuant to the provisions of this section, after first deducting therefrom any federal funds properly received or to be received on account thereof.

3. (a) A covered provider described in subdivision one of this section shall be qualified to receive a supplemental payment only if its number of medicaid visits for patient care services in the base year described in subparagraph (ii) of paragraph (b) of this subdivision equals or exceeds twenty-five percent of its total number of visits for patient care services and its number of medicaid visits for patient care services for medicaid managed care enrollees equals or exceeds three percent of its total number of medicaid visits during the base year.

(b)   (i) Each qualified provider described in paragraph (a) of this subdivision shall receive a supplemental payment equal to such provider's proportional share of the total funds allocated pursuant to this section, based upon the ratio of its visits from medical assistance recipients enrolled in managed care during the base year to the total number of visits to all such qualified providers by medical assistance recipients enrolled in managed care during the base year.

(ii)   For purposes of the calculation described in this subdivision, the base year will be two thousand, and the commissioner of health shall utilize data as reported on the 2000 AHCF-1 cost report initially submitted by covered providers to the department of health on or about August seventeenth, two thousand one.

4.   Payments made pursuant to this section shall constitute additional reimbursement to qualified providers and shall not be used to reduce levels of other funding provided to qualified providers by governmental agencies.

5.   (a) The commissioner of health shall make medical assistance payments to qualified providers from funds made available pursuant to the provisions of this section contingent upon the receipt of all federal approvals necessary and subject to the availability of federal financial participation under title XIX of the federal social security act for the transitional supplemental payments. In the event such federal approval is not received prior to March thirty-first, two thousand two, for adjustments for the period February first, two thousand two through March thirty-first, two thousand two and prior to October first, two thousand two for adjustments for the period October first, two thousand two through December thirty-first, two thousand two and prior to October first, two thousand three for adjustments for the period October first, two thousand three through December thirty-first, two thousand three, and prior to October first, two thousand five for adjustments for the period April first, two thousand five through June thirtieth, two thousand five, and prior to October first, two thousand six for adjustments for the period October first, two thousand six through December thirty-first, two thousand six, the commissioner of health shall make medical assistance payments to qualified providers consisting of the state share amount available for purposes of this section and apportioned in accordance with subdivisions two and three of this section. In the event such federal approval is denied, such state share amount payments shall be deemed to be grants to such qualified providers and such qualified providers shall not be eligible to receive any other payments pursuant to this section.

(b)   The commissioner of health shall take all steps necessary and shall use best efforts to secure federal financial participation under title XIX of the social security act, for the purposes of this section, including the prompt submission of appropriate amendments to the title XIX state plan.

Added by Laws 1999, Ch. 412 Part F, § 32-f, eff. Aug. 9, 1999, deemed in full force and effect on and after Apr. 1, 1999; amended by Laws 2000, Ch. 57 Part I, §§ 1 and 2, eff. May 15, 2000, and § 3, eff. July 1, 2000; amended by Laws 2002, Ch. 16, §§ 5, 6, 7, and 8, eff. March 19, 2002, Ch. 82, Part J, §§ 39, 40, and 41, eff. Jan. 1, 2002; L.

SSL

2003, Ch. 62, Part Z2, §§ 2, 47–49, eff. May 15, 2003, deemed to be in full force and effect on and after April 1, 2003; **amended** by Laws 2004, Ch. 15, §§ 8, 9, eff. on and after April 1, 2003; **amended** by Laws 2005, Ch. 12, §12, eff. March 15, 2005, deemed eff. on and after April 1, 2004; Laws 2006, ch. 57, §67 (Part A) (repealed by Laws 2006, ch. 109, §53 (Part C), eff. June 23, 2006, deemed eff. on and after April 1, 2006), legislative override of Governor's line veto filed April 28, 2006 (see 2006 note below); amd, Laws 2006, ch. 109, §53-a (Part C), eff. June 23, 2006, deemed eff. on and after April 1, 2006.

§ 364-jj. Special advisory review panel on Medicaid managed care.

(a) There is hereby established a special advisory review panel on Medicaid managed care. The panel shall consist of nine members who shall be appointed as follows: three by the governor, one of which shall serve as the chair; two each by the temporary president of the senate and the speaker of the assembly; and one each by the minority leader of the senate and the minority leader of the assembly. All members shall be appointed no later than September first, nineteen hundred ninety-six. Members shall serve without compensation but shall be reimbursed for appropriate expenses. The department shall provide technical assistance and access to data as is required for the panel to effectuate the mission and purposes established herein.

(b) The panel shall:

(i) determine whether there is sufficient managed care provider participation in the Medicaid managed care program;

(ii) determine whether managed care providers meet proper enrollment targets that permit as many Medicaid recipients as possible to make their own health plan decisions, thus minimizing the number of automatic assignments;

(iii) review the phase-in schedule for enrollment, of managed care providers under both the voluntary and mandatory programs;

(iv) assess the impact of managed care provider marketing and enrollment strategies, and the public education campaign conducted in New York City, on enrollees participation in Medicaid managed care plans;

(v) evaluate the adequacy of managed care provider capacity by reviewing established capacity measurements and monitoring actual access to plan practitioners;

(vi) examine the cost implications of populations excluded and exempted from Medicaid managed care; and

(vii) examine other issues as it deems appropriate.

(c) Commencing January first, nineteen hundred ninety-seven and quarterly thereafter the panel shall submit a report regarding the status of Medicaid managed care in the state and provide recommendations if it deems appropriate to the governor, the temporary president and the minority leader of the senate, and the speaker and the minority leader of the assembly.

Added by Laws 1996, Ch. 649, § 9, eff. Sept. 16, 1996 but deemed to have been in full force and effect on and after July 1, 1996.

§ 364-k.   Hospital emergency room demonstration programs.

[Repealed by Laws 1994, Ch. 320, § 2, eff. July 20, 1994, but deemed to have been in full force and effect since January 1, 1994. Subd. (10), which was amended by Laws 1994, Ch. 320, § 1, was deemed repealed on January 1, 1995.]

§ 364-kk.   Condition of participation.

1.   Notwithstanding any provision of law to the contrary, in addition to the requirements for participation in the medical assistance program as may be required to be met by nursing facilities and assisted living programs, such facilities and programs, adult homes and enriched housing programs receiving payment under this chapter shall enter into arrangements with social services districts to admit, on a priority basis, a number of individuals eligible to have medical assistance paid on their behalf who are otherwise appropriate for nursing facility or other long-term residential care, as described in this section, and whose health and safety reasonably cannot be maintained in their own homes by the provision of personal care services, home health services, or other home and community-based services, as determined by the local social services official pursuant to standards promulgated by the department pursuant to section three hundred sixty-seven-m of this chapter.

2.   The department shall by regulation establish a method or formula for determining a fair and equitable distribution of priority admissions under this section in order that all providers of nursing home and long-term residential care services share the responsibility for accepting placements required under subdivision one hereof, and accept such placements, and that no one provider of nursing facility or long-term residential care, group or classification thereof is required to accept a number of such placements as would jeopardize the profitability or viability of such provider, group of providers or classification of providers, or as would otherwise unduly burden or impair the operation, character or continuation of such provider, group of providers, or classification of provider.

3.   The commissioners of health and social services shall monitor the implementation of this section and, on or before march first, nineteen hundred ninety-six, report to the governor and legislature on such implementation and the effects thereof and shall include recommendations for continuation or other modifications to the provisions of this section.

Added by Laws 1995, Ch. 81, § 73, eff. June 20, 1995.

§ 365.   Responsibility for assistance.

1.   Subject to supervision by the department:

(a)   *[Effective until September 1, 2005.]* each public welfare district shall furnish medical assistance to the persons eligible therefor who reside in its territory, except to persons for whom another public welfare district would be responsible under the provisions of paragraphs (b), (c), (d) or (g) of subdivision five of section sixty-two and other provisions of this chapter, and except to persons for whom provision is made hereinafter in subdivision two. Temporary absence, within or without the state, of such persons from such territory shall not effect their eligibility for such assistance;

(a) [*Effective September 1, 2005.*] each public welfare district shall furnish medical assistance to the persons eligible therefor who reside in its territory, except to persons for whom another public welfare district would be responsible under the provisions of paragraphs (b), (c) or (d) of subdivision five of section sixty-two and other provisions of this chapter, and except to persons for whom provision is made hereinafter in subdivision two. Temporary absence, within or without the state, of such persons from such territory shall not effect their eligibility for such assistance;

(b) each public welfare district shall also be responsible for furnishing medical assistance to eligible persons found in its territory, who are temporarily in the state;

(c) each public welfare district, in any case in which the appropriate medical care and services are not available within such district, shall make appropriate arrangements, including the provision of transportation, for obtaining such medical care and services outside such district;

(d) each public welfare district may furnish all or any part of the medical assistance required to be furnished pursuant to this title, either directly or by contract or agreement.

2. Any inconsistent provision of this chapter or other law notwithstanding, the department shall be responsible for furnishing medical assistance to eligible individuals: (a) who are sixty-five years of age or older and who are patients in either state hospitals for the mentally disabled operated by the state department of mental hygiene or state hospitals for the treatment of tuberculosis operated pursuant to the provisions of the public health law; (b) who are under twenty-one years of age and who are receiving psychiatric services in such state hospitals for the mentally disabled which services conform to the state plan implementive of this title and which a team consisting of physicians and other qualified personnel has determined are necessary on an inpatient basis and can reasonably be expected to improve the condition requiring such services to the extent that eventually such services will no longer be necessary; in the case of a person who, during the course of hospitalization attains the age of twenty-one, such services may continue until he reaches the age of twenty-two; (c) who are patients in that part of a public institution operated for the care of the mentally retarded that has been approved pursuant to law as a hospital or nursing home; (d) who are under care and treatment for drug dependence in a facility, or part thereof, operated pursuant to the provisions of the mental hygiene law if and so long as federal aid is available therefor; (e) who are under care in a hospital while they are on

release from an institution in the state department of mental hygiene or who are drug dependent persons under care in a hospital while they are on release from a drug abuse treatment facility or part thereof operated in compliance with applicable provisions of law and supervised by the state division of substance abuse services, for the purpose of receiving care in such hospital. The department may at its option discharge such responsibility, in whole or in part, through social services districts designated to act as agents of the department. While so designated, a social services district shall act as agent of the department and shall be entitled to reimbursement as provided in section three hundred sixty-eight-a of this title.

3.   Any inconsistent provision of this chapter or other law notwithstanding, the department shall be responsible for furnishing medical assistance to eligible veterans and their dependents (a) in that part of the New York state home for veterans and their dependents at Oxford that has been approved pursuant to law as a nursing home, and (b) in a hospital while on release from that home for the purpose of receiving care in such hospital. The department may at its option discharge such responsibility, in whole or in part, through social services districts designated to act as agents of the department. While so designated, a social services district shall act as agent of the department and shall be entitled to reimbursement as provided in section three hundred sixty-eight-a of this title.

4.   Any inconsistent provision of this chapter or other law notwithstanding, the department shall be responsible for furnishing medical assistance to eligible individuals: (a) who are patients in that part of a public institution operated for the care of the mentally retarded that has been approved pursuant to law as an intermediate care facility or who are participating in a program operated by the department of mental hygiene or by a voluntary agency under an agreement with such department, in that part of such a facility that has been approved as a day treatment program in accordance with the regulations of the state commissioner of mental hygiene; (b) who are veterans and their dependents in that part of the New York state home for veterans and their dependents at Oxford that has been approved pursuant to law as an intermediate care facility; (c) such persons under care in a hospital while they are on release from such home for the purpose of receiving care in such hospital; and (d) who are included in either one of the model waivers or the general waiver described in subdivisions seven and nine of section three hundred sixty-six of this chapter. The department may, at its option, discharge such responsibility, in whole or in part, through social services districts designated to act as agents of the department. While so designated, a social services district shall act as agent of the department and shall be entitled to reimbursements as provided in section three hundred sixty-eight-a of this chapter.

5.   Any inconsistent provision of this chapter or other law notwithstanding the department shall be responsible for determining eligibility of and furnishing medical assistance to eligible persons when such person is in need of such medical assistance at the time he is discharged or released or conditionally released from a state department of mental hygiene facility pursuant to the mental

SSL

hygiene law and when such person was admitted to such facility and has been a patient therein for a continuous period of five or more years prior to his discharge or release. For purposes of determining whether a person has been a patient in such a facility for a continuous period of five years or more, if a person who has been discharged or released from such a facility is thereafter returned to such a facility within ninety days of the discharge or release, the period of time between such discharge or release and such return shall not constitute an interruption of, and shall be counted as part of, the continuous period. The department may, at its option, discharge its responsibility for eligibility determinations or for providing medical assistance or both, in whole or in part, through designated social services districts. While so designated, a social services district shall act as agent of the department and shall be entitled to reimbursement of the full amount expended on behalf of the department as provided in section three hundred sixty-eight-a of this article.

6.   Any inconsistent provisions of this chapter or other law notwithstanding, the department shall be responsible for determining eligibility for medical assistance for a person for whom the full cost of such assistance is reimbursable by the state and who is in need of such assistance at the time he is discharged or released or conditionally released from a state hospital operated by the office of mental health or a facility operated by the division of alcoholism and alcohol abuse located on the grounds of such hospital. The department may at its option discharge such responsibility, in whole or in part, through social services districts designated to act as agents of the department. While so designated, a social services district shall act as agent of the department and shall be entitled to reimbursement as provided in section three hundred sixty-eight-a of this title.

7.   Any inconsistent provision of this chapter or other law notwithstanding, the department may, with the consent of the commissioner of mental health, designate the office of mental health as its agent to discharge its responsibility, or so much of its responsibility as is permitted by federal law, for determining eligibility for medical assistance pursuant to subdivisions two, five, six and eight of this section.

8.   Any inconsistent provision of this chapter or other law notwithstanding, the department shall be responsible for determining eligibility of and furnishing medical assistance to eligible persons who reside in residential care centers for adults or community residences operated by the office of mental health. The department may, at its option, discharge its responsibility for eligibility determinations or for providing medical assistance or both, in whole or in part, through designated social services districts. While so designated, a social services district shall act as agent of the department and shall be entitled to reimbursement as provided in section three hundred sixty-eight-a of this article.

9.   Any inconsistent provision of this chapter or other law notwithstanding, the social services district in which an eligible major public general hospital is physically located shall be responsible for the supplementary bad debt and charity care adjustment component of the rate of payment for such major public general

hospital (as determined in accordance with subdivision fourteen-a of section twenty-eight hundred seven-c of the public health law) for all inpatient hospital services provided by such major public general hospital in accordance with section three hundred sixty-five-a of this article, regardless of whether another social services district or the department may otherwise be responsible for furnishing medical assistance to the eligible persons receiving such inpatient services.

10. Any inconsistent provision of this chapter or other law notwithstanding, the social services district in which an eligible public general hospital is physically located shall be responsible for the supplementary low income patient adjustment component of the rate of payment for such public general hospital (as determined in accordance with subdivision fourteen-d of section twenty-eight hundred seven-c of the public health law) for all inpatient hospital services provided by such public general hospital in accordance with section three hundred sixty-five-a of this article, regardless of whether another social services district or the department may otherwise be responsible for furnishing medical assistance to the eligible persons receiving such inpatient services.

11. Any inconsistent provision of this chapter or other law notwithstanding, the social services district in which an eligible public residential health care facility is physically located shall be responsible for the adjustment component of the payments for such public residential health care facility as determined in accordance with subdivision twelve of section twenty-eight hundred eight of the public health law for all residential health care facility services provided by such public residential health care facility in accordance with section three hundred sixty-five-a of this article, regardless of whether another social services district or the department may otherwise be responsible for furnishing medical assistance to the eligible persons receiving such services.

12. Any inconsistent provision of this chapter or other law notwithstanding, the social services district in which an eligible public general hospital is physically located shall be responsible for the public general hospital indigent care adjustment component of the payments to such public general hospital (as determined in accordance with subdivision fourteen-f of section twenty-eight hundred seven-c of the public health law) for all inpatient hospital services provided by such public general hospital in accordance with section three hundred sixty-five-a of this article, regardless of whether another social services district or the department may otherwise be responsible for furnishing medical assistance to the eligible persons receiving such inpatient services.

SSL

Added by Laws 1966, Ch. 258; **amended** by Laws 1967, Chs. 144, 490; Laws 1968, Chs. 270, 669; Laws 1968, Ch. 993; Laws 1972, Ch. 222, Ch. 694; Laws 1973, Ch. 195; former subds. (2) **repealed** and new subd. (2) **added** by Laws 1973, Ch. 338, and **amended** by Ch. 516, eff. Jan. 1, 1973 with respect to psychiatric services provided to eligible patients by any department or agency of the state; **amended** by Laws 1975, Ch. 667, deemed to have been in full force and effect on and after Apr. 1, 1975; Laws 1977, Ch. 778; new subd. (5) **added** by Laws 1979, Ch. 277, eff. June 2, 1979; **amended** by

Laws 1980, Ch. 471, eff. July 23, 1980; **amended** by Laws 1983, Ch. 511, eff. July 19, 1983; **amended** by Laws 1985, Ch. 351, eff. July 18, 1985; **amended** by Laws 1986, Ch. 468, eff. July 21, 1986; **amended** by Laws 1989, Ch. 74, § 2, eff. Apr. 1, 1989; **amended** by Laws 1989, Ch. 729, § 2, eff. July 24, 1989; **amended** by Laws 1990, Ch. 938, § 13, eff. Jan. 1, 1991; **amended** by Laws 1992, Ch. 55, § 291, eff. Apr. 10, 1992 until Apr. 10, 1994; **amended** by Laws 1994, Ch. 170, § 409, eff. Apr. 1, 1994; **amended** by Laws 1995, Ch. 81, § 58, eff. June 20, 1995; **amended** by Laws 1996, Ch. 48, § 1, eff. Apr. 12, 1996 until Apr. 10, 1998; **amended** by Laws 1996, Ch. 639 § 26, eff. Sept. 12, 1996 but deemed to be in full force and effect on July 1, 1996; **amended** by Laws 1998, Ch. 38 § 1, eff. Apr. 8, 1998, extending expiration date of subd. (1)(a) to Apr. 10, 2000; **amended** by Laws 2000, Ch. 16 § 1, eff. Mar. 30, 2000, extending expiration date of subd. (1)(a) to Sept. 1, 2001; **amended** by Laws 2001, Ch. 95 § 18, eff. July 13, 2001, extending expiration date of subd. (1)(a) to Sept. 1, 2003; L. 2003, Ch. 16, § 17, eff. March 31, 2003, extending expiration date for subd. 1(a) to September 1, 2005.

§ 365-a   Character and adequacy of assistance

1.   The amount, nature and manner of providing medical assistance for needy persons shall be determined by the public welfare official with the advice of a physician and in accordance with the local medical plan, this title, and the regulations of the department.

2.   "Medical assistance" shall mean payment of part or all of the cost of medically necessary medical, dental and remedial care, services and supplies, as authorized in this title or the regulations of the department, which are necessary to prevent, diagnose, correct or cure conditions in the person that cause acute suffering, endanger life, result in illness or infirmity, interfere with such person's capacity for normal activity, or threaten some significant handicap and which are furnished an eligible person in accordance with this title and the regulations of the department. Such care, services and supplies shall include the following medical care, services and supplies, together with such medical care, services and supplies provided for in subdivisions three, four and five of this section, and such medical care, services and supplies as are authorized in the regulations of the department:

(a)   services of qualified physicians, dentists, nurses, and private duty nursing services shall be further subject to the provisions of section three hundred sixty-seven-o of this chapter, optometrists, and other related professional personnel;

(b)   care, treatment, maintenance and nursing services in hospitals, nursing homes that qualify as providers in the medicare program pursuant to title XVIII of the federal social security act, infirmaries or other eligible medical institutions, and health-related care and services in intermediate care facilities, while operated in compliance with applicable provisions of this chapter, the public health law, the mental hygiene law and other laws, including any provision thereof requiring an operating certificate or license, or where such facilities are not conveniently accessible, in hospitals located without the state; provided, however, that care, treatment, maintenance and nursing services in nursing homes or in intermediate care facilities, including those operated by the state department of mental hygiene or any other state department or agency, shall, for persons who are receiving or who are eligible for medical assistance under provisions of subparagraph four of paragraph (a) of subdivision one of section three hundred sixty-six of this chapter, be limited to such periods of time as may be determined necessary in accordance with a utilization review procedure established by the state commissioner of health providing for a review of medical necessity, in the case of skilled nursing care, every thirty days for the first ninety days and every ninety days thereafter, and in the case of care in an intermediate care facility, at least every six months, or more frequently if indicated at the time of the last review, consistent with federal utilization review requirements; provided, further, that in-patient care, services and supplies in a general hospital shall not exceed such standards as the commissioner of health shall promulgate but in no case greater than twenty days per spell of illness during which all or any part of the cost of such care, services and supplies are claimed as an item of medical assistance, unless it shall have been determined in accordance with procedures and criteria established by such commissioner that a further identifiable period of in-patient general hospital care is required for particular patients to preserve life or to prevent substantial risks of continuing disability; provided further, that in-patient care, services and supplies in a general hospital shall, in the case of a person admitted to such a facility on a Friday or Saturday, be deemed to include only those in-patient days beginning with and following the Sunday after such date of admission, unless such care, services and supplies are furnished for an actual medical emergency or pre-operative care for surgery as provided in paragraph (d) of subdivision five of this section, or are furnished because of the necessity of emergency or urgent surgery for the alleviation of severe pain or the necessity for immediate diagnosis or treatment of conditions which threaten disability or death if not promptly diagnosed or treated; provided, however, in-patient days of a general hospital admission beginning on a Friday or a Saturday shall be included commencing with the day of admission in a general hospital which the commissioner or his designee has found to be rendering and which continues to render full service on a seven day a week basis which determination shall be made after taking into consideration such factors as the routine availability of operating room services, diagnostic serivces and consultants, laboratory services, radiological services, pharmacy services, staff patterns consistent with full services and such other factors as the commissioner or his designee deems necessary and appropriate; provided, further, that in-patient care, services and supplies in a general hospital shall not include care, services and supplies furnished to patients for certain uncomplicated procedures which may be performed on an out-patient basis in accordance with regulations of the commissioner of health, unless the person or body designated by such commissioner determines that the medical condition of the individual patient requires that the procedure be performed on an in-patient basis;

   (c)   out-patient hospital or clinic services in facilities operated in compliance with applicable provisions of this chapter, the public health law, the mental hygiene law and other laws, including any provisions thereof requiring an

SSL

operating certificate or license, or where such facilities are not conveniently accessible, in any hospital located without the state and care and services in a day treatment program operated by the department of mental hygiene or by a voluntary agency under an agreement with such department in that part of a public institution operated and approved pursuant to law as an intermediate care facility for the mentally retarded;

(d) home health services provided in a recipient's home and prescribed by a physician including services of a nurse provided on a part-time or intermittent basis rendered by an approved home health agency or if no such agency is available, by a registered nurse, licensed to practice in this state, acting under the written orders of a physician and home health aide service by an individual or shared aide provided by an approved home health agency when such services are determined to be cost effective and appropriate to meet the recipient's needs for assistance subject to the provisions of section three hundred sixty-seven-j and section three hundred sixty-seven-o of this title;

(e) personal care services, including personal emergency response services, shared aide and an individual aide, furnished to an individual who is not an inpatient or resident of a hospital, nursing facility, intermediate care facility for the mentally retarded, or institution for mental disease, as determined to meet the recipient's needs for assistance when cost effective and appropriate in accordance with section three hundred sixty-seven-k and section three hundred sixty-seven-o of this title, and when prescribed by a physician, in accordance with the recipient's plan of treatment and provided by individuals who are qualified to provide such services, who are supervised by a registered nurse and who are not members of the recipient's family, and furnished in the recipient's home or other location;

(f) preventive, prophylactic and other routine dental care, services and supplies;

(g) sickroom supplies, eyeglasses, prosthetic appliances and dental prosthetic appliances furnished in accordance with the regulations of the department; drugs provided on an in-patient basis, those drugs contained on the list established by regulation of the commissioner of health pursuant to subdivision four of this section, and those drugs which may not be dispensed without a prescription as required by section sixty-eight hundred ten of the education law and which the commissioner of health shall determine to be reimbursable based upon such factors as the availability of such drugs or alternatives at low cost if purchased by a medicaid recipient, or the essential nature of such drugs as described by such commissioner in regulations, provided, however, that such drugs, exclusive of long-term maintenance drugs, shall be dispensed in quantities no greater than a thirty day supply or one hundred doses, whichever is greater; provided further that the commissioner of health is authorized to require prior authorization for any refill of a prescription when less than seventy-five percent of the previously dispensed amount per fill should have been used were the product used as normally indicated; medical assistance shall not include any drug provided on other than an in-patient basis for which a recipient is charged or a claim is made in the case of a prescription drug, in excess of the maximum reimbursable amounts to be established by department regulations in accordance with standards established by the secretary of the United States department of health and human services, or, in the case of a drug not requiring a prescription, in excess of the maximum reimbursable amount established by the commissioner of health pursuant to paragraph (a) of subdivision four of this section;

(h) physical therapy and relative rehabilitative services when provided at the direction of a physican;

(i) laboratory and x-ray services; and

(j) transportation when essential and appropriate to obtain medical care, services and supplies otherwise available under the medical assistance program in accordance with this section, upon prior authorization, except when required in order to obtain emergency care, and when not otherwise available to the recipient free of charge or through a transportation program implemented pursuant to section three hundred sixty-five-h of this title and approved by the commissioner of health for which federal financial participation is claimed as an administrative cost;

(k) [Until Dec 31, 2015] care and services furnished by an entity offering a comprehensive health services plan, including an entity that has received a certificate of authority pursuant to sections forty-four hundred three, forty-four hundred three-a or forty-four hundred eight-a of the public health law (as added by chapter six hundred thirty-nine of the laws of nineteen hundred ninety-six) or a health maintenance organization authorized under article forty-three of the insurance law, to eligible individuals residing in the geographic area served by such entity, when such services are furnished in accordance with an agreement approved by the department which meets the requirements of federal law and regulations provided, that no such agreement shall allow for medical assistance payments on a capitated basis for nursing facility, home care or other long term care services of a duration and scope defined in regulations of the department of health promulgated pursuant to section forty-four hundred three-f of the public health law, unless such entity has received a certificate of authority as a managed long term care plan or is an operating demonstration or is an approved managed long term care demonstration, pursuant to such section.

(k) [Eff Dec 31, 2015] care and services furnished by an entity offering a comprehensive health services plan to eligible individuals residing in the geographic area served by such entity, when such services are furnished in accordance with an agreement approved by the department which meets the requirements of federal law and regulations.

(l) care and services of podiatrists which care and services shall only be provided upon referral by a physician, nurse practitioner or certified nurse midwife in accordance with the program of early and periodic screening and diagnosis established pursuant to subdivision three of this section or to persons

SSL

eligible for benefits under title XVIII of the federal social security act as qualified medicare beneficiaries in accordance with federal requirements therefor and private duty nurses which care and services shall only be provided in accordance with regulations of the department of health; provided, however, that private duty nursing services shall not be restricted when such services are more appropriate and cost-effective than nursing services provided by a home health agency pursuant to section three hundred sixty-seven-l;

(m)   hospice services provided by a hospice certified pursuant to article forty of the public health law, to the extent that federal financial participation is available, and, notwithstanding federal financial participation and any provision of law or regulation to the contrary, for hospice services provided pursuant to the hospice supplemental financial assistance program for persons with special needs as provided for in article forty of the public health law.

(n)   care and services of audiologists provided in accordance with regulations of the department of health.

(n)   care, treatment, maintenance and rehabilitation services that would otherwise qualify for reimbursement pursuant to this chapter to persons suffering from alcoholism in alcoholism facilities or chemical dependence, as such term is defined in section 1.03 of the mental hygiene law, in inpatient chemical dependence facilities, services, or programs operated in compliance with applicable provisions of this chapter and the mental hygiene law, and certified by the office of alcoholism and substance abuse services, provided however that such services shall be limited to such periods of time as may be determined necessary in accordance with a utilization review procedure established by the commissioner of the office of alcoholism and substance abuse services and provided further, that this paragraph shall not apply to any hospital or part of a hospital as defined in section two thousand eight hundred one of the public health law.

(o)   [Expires and repealed Dec 31, 2015] care and services furnished by a managed long term care plan or approved managed long term care demonstration pursuant to the provisions of section forty-four hundred three-f of the public health law to eligible individuals residing in the geographic area served by such entity, when such services are furnished in accordance with an agreement with the department of health and meet the applicable requirements of federal law and regulation.

(p)   [Eff Jan 1, 2007 and expires and repealed Jan 1, 2009] targeted case management services provided to children who

(i)   are eighteen years of age or under; and

(ii)   either

(1)   are physically disabled, according to the federal supplemental security income program criteria, including but not limited to a person who is multiply disabled; or

(2)   have a developmental disability, as defined in subdivision twenty-two of section 1.03 of the mental hygiene law and demonstrate complex health needs

as defined in paragraph c of subdivision seven of section three hundred sixty-six of this title; or

(3) have a mental illness, as defined in subdivision twenty of section 1.03 of the mental hygiene law and demonstrate complex health or mental health care needs as defined in paragraph d of subdivision nine of section three hundred sixty-six of this title; and

(iii) require the level of care provided by an intermediate care facility for the developmentally disabled, a nursing facility, a hospital or any other institution; and

(iv) are capable of being cared for in the community if provided with case management services and/or other services provided under this title; and

(v) are capable of being cared for in the community at less cost than in the appropriate institutional setting; and

(vi) are not receiving services under section three hundred sixty-seven-c of this title and for whom services provided under section three hundred sixty-seven-a of this title are not available or sufficient to support the children's care in the community.

3. Any consistent provisions of this section notwithstanding, medical assistance shall include:

(a) early and periodic screening and diagnosis of eligible persons under six years of age and, in accordance with federal law and regulations, early and periodic screening and diagnosis of eligible persons under twenty-one years of age to ascertain physical and mental disabilities; and

(b) care and treatment of disabilities and conditions discovered by such screening and diagnosis including such care, services and supplies as the commissioner shall by regulation require to the extent necessary to conform to applicable federal law and regulations.

(c) screening, diagnosis, care and treatment of disabilities and conditions discovered by such screening and diagnosis of eligible persons ages three to twenty-one, inclusive, including such care, services and supplies as the commissioner shall by regulation require to the extent necessary to conform to applicable federal law and regulations, provided that such screening, diagnosis, care and treatment shall include the provision of evaluations and related services rendered pursuant to article eighty-nine of the education law and regulations of the commissioner of education by persons qualified to provide such services thereunder.

(d) family planning services and supplies for eligible persons of childbearing age, including children under twenty-one years of age who can be considered sexually active, who desire such services and supplies, in accordance with the requirements of federal law and regulations and the regulations of the department. No person shall be compelled or coerced to accept such services or supplies.

SSL

4. Any inconsistent provision of law notwithstanding, medical assistance shall not include, unless required by federal law and regulation as a condition of qualifying for federal financial participation in the medicaid program, the following items of care, services and supplies:

(a) drugs which may be dispensed without a prescription as required by section sixty-eight hundred ten of the education law; provided, however, that the state commissioner of health may by regulation specify certain of such drugs which may be reimbursed as an item of medical assistance in accordance with the price schedule established by such commissioner;

(a-1) [Expires and repealed June 15, 2012] a brand name drug for which a multi-source therapeutically and generically equivalent drug, as determined by the federal food and drug administration, is available, unless previously authorized by the department of health. The commissioner of health is authorized to exempt, for good cause shown, any brand name drug from the restrictions imposed by this paragraph. This paragraph shall not apply to any drug that is in a therapeutic class included on the preferred drug list under section two hundred seventy-two of the public health law or is in the clinical drug review program under section two hundred seventy-four of the public health law;

(a-2) [Expires and repealed June 15, 2012] drugs which may not be dispensed without a prescription as required by section sixty-eight hundred ten of the education law, and which are non-preferred drugs in a therapeutic class subject to the preferred drug program pursuant to section two hundred seventy-two of the public health law, or the clinical drug review program under section two hundred seventy-four of the public health law, unless prior authorization is granted or not required;

(b) care and services of chiropractors and supplies related to the practice of chiropractic;

(c) care and services of an optometrist for using drugs in excess of the maximum reimbursable amounts for optometric care and services established by the commissioner and approved by the director of the budget;

(d) any medical care, services or supplies furnished outside the state, except, when prior authorized in accordance with department regulations or for care, services and supplies furnished: as a result of a medical emergency; because the recipient's health would have been endangered if he or she had been required to travel to the state; because the care, services or supplies were more readily available in the other state; or because it is the general practice for persons residing in the locality wherein the recipient resides to use medical providers in the other state; or

(e) drugs, procedures and supplies for the treatment of erectile dysfunction when provided to, or prescribed for use by, a person who is required to register as a sex offender pursuant to article six-C of the correction law, provided that any denial of coverage pursuant to this paragraph shall provide the patient with the means of obtaining additional information concerning both the denial and the means of challenging such denial; or

(f)   drugs for the treatment of sexual or erectile dysfunction, unless such drugs are used to treat a condition, other than sexual or erectile dysfunction, for which the drugs have been approved by the federal food and drug administration.

(f)   [Eff Jan 1, 2007] for eligible persons who are also beneficiaries under part D of title XVIII of the federal social security act, drugs which are denominated as "covered part D drugs" under section 1860D-2(e) of such act; provided however that, for purposes of this paragraph, "covered part D drugs" shall not mean atypical anti-psychotics, anti-depressants, anti-retrovirals used in the treatment of HIV/AIDS, or anti-rejection drugs used for the treatment of organ and tissue transplants.

5.   (a) Medical assistance shall include surgical benefits for emergency or urgent surgery for the alleviation of severe pain, for immediate diagnosis or treatment of conditions which threaten disability or death if not promptly diagnosed or treated.

(b)   Medical assistance shall include surgical benefits for certain surgical procedures which meet standards for surgical intervention, as established by the state commissioner of health on the basis of medically indicated risk factors, and medically necessary surgery where delay in surgical intervention would substantially increase the medical risk associated with such surgical intervention.

(c)   Medical assistance shall include surgical benefits for other deferrable surgical procedures specified by the state commissioner of health, based on the likelihood that deferral of such procedures for six months or more may jeopardize life or essential function, or cause severe pain; provided, however, such deferrable surgical procedures shall be included in the case of in-patient surgery only when a second written opinion is obtained from a physician, or as otherwise prescribed, in accordance with regulations established by the state commissioner of health, that such surgery should not be deferred.

(d)   Medical assistance shall include a maximum of one patient day of pre-operative hospital care for surgery authorized by paragraphs (b) or (c) of this subdivision; provided, however, that with respect to specific surgical procedures which the state commissioner of health has identified as requiring more than one patient day of pre-operative care, medical assistance shall include such longer maximum period of pre-operative care as such commissioner has identified as necessary.

(e)   Medical assistance shall not include any in-patient surgical procedures or any care, services or supplies related to such surgery other than those authorized by this subdivision.

6.   Any inconsistent provision of law notwithstanding, medical assistance shall also include payment for medical care, services or supplies furnished to eligible pregnant women under the prenatal care assistance program established

SSL

pursuant to title two of article twenty-five of the public health law, to the extent that and for so long as federal financial participation is available therefor; provided, however, that nothing in this section shall be deemed to affect payment for such medical care, services or supplies if federal financial participation is not available for such care, services and supplies solely by reason of the immigration status of the otherwise eligible pregnant woman.

7. Medical assistance shall also include disproportionate share payments to general hospitals under the public health law.

Added by Laws 1966, Ch. 256; amended by Laws 1969, Chs. 184, 957; Laws 1971, Chs. 110, 131, 298; Laws 1972, Chs. 694, 934; Laws 1973, Chs. 516, 151, 595; Laws 1974, Chs. 470, 909; Laws 1976, Chs. 76, 940; Laws 1977, Ch. 77; Laws 1977, Ch. 778, eff. Aug. 5, 1977; Laws 1979, Ch. 444; Laws 1980, Ch. 478, eff. June 23, 1980; amended by Laws 1981, Ch. 218, eff. June 9, 1981; amended by Laws 1983, Ch. 83, eff. Apr. 1, 1983; amended by Laws 1983, Ch. 416, eff. Jan. 1, 1984, added subd.(2)(m); amended by Laws 1983, Ch. 451, eff. Dec. 13, 1983, subd.(4)(c); amended by Laws 1984, Ch. 465, eff. July 20, 1984; amended by Laws 1984, Ch. 904, eff. Aug. 3, 1984, provided that amendments to subd. 2, para. e are effective Oct. 2, 1984; amended by Laws 1984, Ch. 1013, eff. Dec. 21, 1984; amended by Laws 1986, Ch. 127, eff. June 2, 1986; amended by Laws 1986, Ch. 556, eff. Nov. 21, 1986; amended by Laws 1986, Ch. 743, eff. July 30, 1986 and deemed to have been in full force and effect on July 22, 1986; amended by Laws 1988, Ch. 710, § 3, eff. Dec. 15, 1988; amended by Laws 1989, Ch. 584, § 4, eff. Jan. 1, 1990; amended by Laws 1989, Ch. 725, § 2, eff. Nov. 21, 1989 and shall expire and be deemed to have no further force and effect on and after July 1, 1992 (amending 365-a(2)(m)); amended by Laws 1990, Ch. 938, § 31, eff. Jan. 1, 1991; amended by Laws 1991, Ch. 165, § 21, eff. July 1, 1991 until June 30, 1994; amended by Laws 1992, Ch. 41, §§ 60, 62, 63, eff. July 1, 1992 (except for § 365-a(8)(a) added by Laws 1992, Ch. 41, § 62, eff. July 1, 1992 until July 1, 1994, and § 365-a(8)(b) added by Laws 1992, Ch. 41, § 62, eff. May 1, 1992 until Dec. 31, 1993); amended by Laws 1992, Ch. 843, § 6, eff. Aug. 7, 1992; amended by Laws 1993, Ch. 59, § 63, eff. June 1, 1993, §§ 64, 65, eff. Apr. 1, 1993; amended by Laws 1993, Ch. 59, § 71, eff. Apr. 1, 1993, until Dec. 31, 1994 (extending expiration date for SSL § 365-a(2), subd. (a), (d), (e) and (l) from 6/30/94 until 12/31/94); amended by Laws 1994, Ch. 170, § 458, eff. Apr. 1, 1994; amended by Laws 1994, Ch. 170, § 465, eff. Apr. 1, 1994, extending the period that subds. (a), (d), (e), and (l) of paragraph (2) remain effective to July 1, 1995; amended by Laws 1995, Ch. 81, § 75, eff. July 1, 1995; amended by Laws 1995, Ch. 81, § 76, eff. June 20, 1995; amended by Laws 1995, Ch. 82, § 58, and deemed to have been in full force and effect on and after Apr. 1, 1990; amended by Laws 1995, Ch. 81, § 97, eff. June 20, 1995, extending the period that subds. 2(a), (d), (e) and (l) remain effective to July 1, 1997; amended by Laws 1995, Ch. 81, § 114, eff. June 20, 1995, extending the period that subd. 2(m) remains effective to July 1, 1998; amended by Laws 1996, Ch. 47, eff. Apr. 12, 1996 and deemed to have been in full force and effect on and after July 1, 1995 (amending subd. 2(a)); amended by L. 1997, Ch. 145, 162, 194, 211, and 264, eff. July 23, 1997, and deemed to have been in full force and effect Apr. 1, 1997, extending expiration dates of subds. 2(a), (d), (e) and (l) to Aug. 2, 1997; amended by L. 1997, Ch. 433, § 16, eff. Aug. 20, 1997, extending expiration dates of subds. 2(a), (d), (e) and (l) to July 1, 1999; amended by Laws 1997, Ch. 436, § 1 Part B, § 96, eff. Nov. 1, 1997; amended by Laws 1997, Ch. 659, §§ 83 and 84, eff. Sept. 24, 1997, adding subd.

2(o); **amended** by Laws 1998, Ch. 115, § 1, eff. June 23, 1998, extending the expiration date of subd. 2(m) to July 1, 2001; **amended** by Laws 1999, Ch. 558, § 22, eff. Oct. 5, 1999, amending subd. 2(n); **amended** by Laws 2002, Ch. 1, Part B, § 5, eff. Oct. 1, 2002, § 25, eff. April 1, 2002 and Ch. 16, § 3, eff. March 19, 2002; L. 2003, Ch. 112, § 1, eff. July 1, 2003; **amended** by Laws 2005, Ch. 58, § 16 (Part C), eff. April 12, 2005, deemed eff. on and after April 1, 2005, L. 2005, Ch. 63, § 20 (Part E), eff. April 12, 2005, deemed eff. on and after April 1, 2005; L. 2005, Ch. 645, sect; 1, eff. Aug. 30, 2005; Laws 2006, ch. 57, §1 (Part A) (repealed by Laws 2006, ch. 109, §20 (Part C), eff. June 23, 2006, deemed eff. April 1, 2006), legislative override of Governor's line veto filed April 28, 2006. Laws 2006, ch. 57, §29 (Part A), eff. April 12, 2006, deemed eff. on and after April 1, 2006; Laws 2006, ch. 109, §21-a (Part C), eff. Jan 1, 2007.

§ 365-b. Local medical plans: professional directors.

1. A local social services medical plan shall be developed and maintained by each social services district under the guidance or direction of a professional medical director. Such plan shall conform to the regulations of the department and shall be submitted to the department and the state department of health for review, certification and approval pursuant to the regulations of the department and this title.

2. The commissioner of social services of each social services district shall appoint a person, possessing the qualifications established by the public health council and promulgated by the department pursuant to section three hundred sixty-four, to serve on a full or part-time basis. Each professional director shall serve under the general direction of the commissioner of social services and shall have the responsibility for supervising the program of medical assistance for needy persons in his social services district, pursuant to the regulations of the department. The state commissioner of health may authorize two or more social services districts to appoint the same person to serve as professional director in each of such districts.

3. In addition to any other duty or responsibility which may be assigned or delegated pursuant to law or regulation, each professional director shall be responsible for monitoring the professional activities, directly related to the program, of providers practicing in his social services district and shall take all steps required or authorized by law or regulation to ensure that such activities are in compliance with the provisions of this chapter, the public health law and regulations promulgated there-under, and do not violate the provisions of section sixty-five hundred nine of the education law or regulations promulgated pursuant thereto.

4. For purposes of this section "provider" shall mean any person receiving payment under this title.

Added by Laws 1966, Ch. 256; **amended** by Laws 1971, Ch. 110; **amended** by Laws 1977, Ch. 770, eff. Sept. 1, 1977.

§ 365-c.   Medical advisory committee.

1.   A medical advisory committee is hereby established to consist of twenty members who shall be appointed by the governor, by and with the advice and consent of the senate, for the following terms: seven shall be appointed for a term to expire on May thirty-first, nineteen hundred seventy-four: seven shall be appointed for a term to expire on May thirty-first, nineteen hundred seventy-five: and six shall be appointed for a term to expire on May thirty-first, nineteen hundred seventy-six. Thereafter members appointed upon expiration of a term of office shall be appointed for a term of three years. Vacancies caused by death, resignation or refusal to act or by removal from the state shall be filled for the unexpired term only. At least seven members of such committee shall be duly licensed physicians. The governor shall designate a chairman from among the members of the medical advisory committee, to serve as such at the pleasure of the governor. In appointing the members of the medical advisory committee, the governor shall give consideration to professional qualifications and experience and to achieving representation of the professions of medicine, osteopathy, podiatry, mental health, social work, dentistry, optometry, chiropractic, physical therapy, pharmacy, nursing, hospital and health administration and education for the health professions, of public and private agencies in the field of medical assistance, and of recipients and consumers of medical assistance for needy persons.

2.   The medical advisory committee shall advise the commissioner with respect to health and medical care services provided pursuant to this title.

3.   The medical advisory committee shall meet at least once a year. Special meetings may be called by the chairman, and shall be called by him at the request of the governor or the commissioner.

4.   No member of the medical advisory committee shall be disqualified from holding any other public office or employment, nor shall he forfeit any such office or employment by reason of his employment hereunder, notwithstanding the provisions of any general, special or local law, ordinance or charter.

5.   The members of the medical advisory committee shall receive no compensation for their services, but shall be allowed their actual and necessary expenses incurred in the performance of their duties hereunder.

    Added by Laws 1966, Ch. 256; **amended** by Laws 1967, Ch. 611; **amended** by Laws 1968, Ch. 312; **amended** by Laws 1971, Ch. 170; **amended** by Laws 1972, Ch. 477, eff. May 24, 1972.

§ 365-d.   Early and periodic screening diagnosis and treatment outreach demonstration projects.

    [*Expired on June 30, 1983, by Laws 1981, Ch. 809, eff. July 27, 1981.*]

§ 365-e.   Optional or continued membership in entities offering comprehensive health services plans.

1.   In accordance with applicable federal requirements and subject to the approval of the commissioner and the director of the budget, a district shall offer to persons eligible for medical assistance the option of membership in any health maintenance organization or other entity which is certified under article forty-four of the public health law or licensed pursuant to article nine-C of the insurance law or otherwise authorized by law, and which offers comprehensive health services plans to persons residing within the social services district unless granted a waiver by the commissioner on the grounds that the organization or entity is not geographically accessible so as to provide medical assistance to eligible recipients who reside within the district or that the per recipient capitation rate is above the expected average per recipient fee-for-service cost within the local district or that the health maintenance organization or other entity refuses to enter into a contract with the district.

2.   Notwithstanding any inconsistent provision of law, persons who, prior to becoming eligible for medical assistance, are enrolled in a health maintenance organization or other entity offering a comprehensive health services plan shall be offered the option of continuing that enrollment.

3.   The commissioner shall offer to social services districts such technical assistance as may be appropriate to assist in the development of contracts between the districts and such entities.

     Added by Laws 1984, Ch. 904, eff. Aug. 3, 1984.

§ 365-f.   Patient managed home care programs.

Repealed by Laws 1995, Ch. 81, § 77, eff. July 1, 1995.

§ 365-f.   Consumer directed personal assistance program.

1.   Purpose and intent. The consumer directed personal assistance program is intended to permit chronically ill and/or physically disabled individuals receiving home care services under the medical assistance program greater flexibility and freedom of choice in obtaining such services. The department shall, upon request of a social services district or group of districts, provide technical assistance and such other assistance as may be necessary to assist such districts in assuring access to the program.

2.   Eligibility. All eligible individuals receiving home care shall be provided notice of the availability of the program and shall have the opportunity to apply for participation in the program. On or before October first, nineteen hundred ninety-six each social services district shall file an implementation plan with the commissioner of the department of health. An "eligible individual", for purposes of this section is a person who:

SSL

(a) is eligible for long term care and services provided by a certified home health agency, long term home health care program or aids home care program authorized pursuant to article thirty-six of the public health law, or is eligible for personal care services provided pursuant to this article;

(b) is eligible for medical assistance;

(c) has been determined by the social services district, pursuant to an assessment of the person's appropriateness for the program, conducted with an appropriate long term home health care program, a certified home health agency, or an aids home care program or pursuant to the personal care program, as being in need of home care services or private duty nursing and is able and willing or has a legal guardian able and willing to make informed choices, or has designated a relative or other adult who is able and willing to assist in making informed choices, as to the type and quality of services, including but not limited to such services as nursing care, personal care, transportation and respite services; and

(d) meets such other criteria, as may be established by the commissioner, which are necessary to effectively implement the objectives of this section.

3. Division of responsibilities. Eligible individuals who elect to participate in the program assume the responsibility for services under such program as mutually agreed to by the eligible individual and provider and as documented in the eligible individual's record. Such individuals shall be assisted as appropriate with service coverage, supervision, advocacy and management. Providers shall not be liable for fulfillment of responsibilities agreed to be undertaken by the eligible individual. This subdivision, however, shall not diminish the participating provider's liability for failure to exercise reasonable care in properly carrying out its responsibilities under this program, which shall include monitoring such individual's continuing ability to fulfill those responsibilities documented in his or her records. Failure of the individual to carry out his or her agreed to responsibilities may be considered in determining such individual's continued appropriateness for the program.

4. Participating providers. All agencies or individuals who meet the qualifications to provide home health, personal care or nursing services and who elect to provide such services to persons receiving medical assistance may participate in the program. Any agency or individuals providing services under a patient managed home care program authorized under the former section thirty-six hundred twenty-two of the public health law or the former sections three hundred sixty-five-f of this chapter may continue to provide such services under this section.

5. Waivers, regulation and effectiveness.

(a) The commissioner may, subject to the approval of the director of the budget, file for such federal waivers as may be needed for the implementation of the program.

(b) Notwithstanding any other provision of law, the commissioner is authorized to waive any provision of section three hundred sixty-seven-b of this title related to payment and may promulgate regulations necessary to carry out the objectives of the program, and which describe the responsibilities of the eligible individuals in arranging and paying for services and the protections assured such individuals if they are unable or no longer desire to continue in the program.

6.   This section shall be effective if, to the extent that, and as long as, federal financial participation is available for expenditures incurred under this section.

    Added by Laws 1995, Ch. 81, § 77, eff. July 1, 1995; **amended** by Laws 1996, Ch. 474, § 229, eff. Aug. 1, 1996.

§ 365-g.   Utilization thresholds for certain care, services and supplies.

1.   The department may implement a system for utilization controls, pursuant to this section, for persons eligible for benefits under this title, including annual service limitations or utilization thresholds above which the department may not pay for additional care, services or supplies, unless such care, services or supplies have been previously approved by the department or unless such care, services or supplies were provided pursuant to subdivision three, four or five of this section.

2.   The department may implement utilization thresholds by provider service type and medical procedure, in consultation with the state department of health and other appropriate state agencies. In developing utilization thresholds the department shall consider historical recipient utilization patterns and the anticipated recipient needs in order to maintain good health.

3.   If the department implements a utilization threshold program, at a minimum, such program must include:

(a)   prior notice to the recipients affected by the utilization threshold program, which notice must describe:

(i)   the nature and extent of the utilization program, the procedures for obtaining an exemption from or increase in a utilization threshold, the recipients' fair hearing rights, and referral to an informational toll-free hot-line operated by the department; and

(ii)   alternatives to the utilization threshold program such as enrollment in managed care programs and referral to preferred primary care providers designated pursuant to subdivision twelve of section twenty-eight hundred seven of the public health law; and

(b)   procedures for:

(i)   requesting an increase in amount of authorized services;

(ii)   extending amount of authorized services when an application for an increase in the amount of authorized services is pending;

(iii)   requesting an exemption from utilization thresholds, which procedure must:

SSL

(a) allow the recipient, or a provider on behalf of a recipient, to apply to the department for an exemption from one or more utilization thresholds based upon documentation of the medical necessity for services in excess of the threshold,

(b) provided for exemptions consistent with department guidelines for approving exemptions, which guidelines must be established by the department in consultation with the department of health and, as appropriate, with the department of mental hygiene, and consistent with the current regulations of the office of mental health governing outpatient treatment.,

(c) provide for an exemption when medical and clinical documentation substantiates a condition of a chronic medical nature which requires ongoing and frequent use of medical care, services or supplies such that an increase in the amount of authorized services is not sufficient to meet the medical needs of the recipient;

(iv) reimbursing a provider, regardless of the recipient's previous use of services, when care, services or supplies are provided in a case of urgent medical need, as defined by the department, or when provided on an emergency basis, as defined by the department;

(v) notifying recipients of and referring recipients to appropriate and accessible managed care programs and to preferred primary care providers designated pursuant to subdivision twelve of section twenty-eight hundred seven of the public health law at the same time such recipients are notified that they are nearing or have reached the utilization threshold for each specific provider type;

(vi) notifying recipients at the same time such recipients are notified that they have received an exemption from a utilization threshold, an increase in the amount of authorized services, or that they are nearing or have reached the utilization threshold for each specific provider type, of their possible eligibility for federal disability benefits and directing such recipients to their social services district for information and assistance in securing such benefits; and

(vii) cooperating with social services districts in sharing information collected and developed by the department regarding recipients' medical records.

4. The utilization thresholds established pursuant to this section shall not apply to the following services:

(a) clinic and other outpatient services, as follows:

(i) mental health continuing treatment, day treatment, partial hospitalization, and intensive psychiatric rehabilitative treatment services provided pursuant to paragraph (c) of subdivision two of section three hundred sixty-five-a of this chapter, alcoholism services, substance abuse services, mental retardation and developmental disabilities services provided in clinics certified under article twenty-eight of the public health law, or article twenty-two or article thirty-one of the mental hygiene law; and

(ii)   services performed by an article twenty-eight hospital or diagnostic and treatment center on an ambulatory basis upon the order of a qualified practitioner to test, diagnose or treat the recipient.

(b)   physician services, as follows:

(i)   psychiatric services and

(ii)   anesthesiology services.

5.   Utilization thresholds established pursuant to this section shall not apply to services, even though such services might otherwise be subject to utilization thresholds, when provided as follows:

(a)   through a managed care program;

(b)   subject to prior approval or prior authorization;

(c)   as family planning services;

(d)   as methadone maintenance services;

(e)   on a fee-for-services basis to inpatients in general hospitals certified under article twenty-eight of the public health law or article thirty-one of the mental hygiene law and residential health care facilities, with the exception of podiatrists' services;

(f)   for hemodialysis; or

(g)   through or by referral from a preferred primary care provider designated pursuant to subdivision twelve of section twenty-eight hundred seven of the public health law.

6.   The department shall consult with representatives of medical assistance providers, social services districts, voluntary organizations that represent or advocate on behalf of recipients, the managed care advisory council and other state agencies regarding the ongoing operation of a utilization threshold system.

7.   On or before February first, nineteen hundred ninety-two, the commissioner shall submit to the governor, the temporary president of the senate and the speaker of the assembly a report detailing the implementation of the utilization threshold program and evaluating the results of establishing utilization thresholds. Such report shall include, but need not be limited to, a description of the program as implemented; the number of requests for increases in service above the threshold amounts by provider and type of service; the number of extensions granted; the number of claims that were submitted for emergency care or urgent care above the threshold level; the number of recipients referred to managed care; an estimate of the fiscal savings to the medical assistance program as a result of the program; recommendations for medical condition that may be more appropriately served through managed care programs; and the costs of implementing the program.

Added by Laws 1990, Ch. 938, § 35; **amended** by Laws 1991, Ch. 165, § 35, eff. Jan. 1, 1991 through June 30, 1994 when it shall expire; **amended** by Laws 1991, Ch.

165, §§ 13, 36, eff. June 12, 1991 until June 30, 1994; **amended** by Laws 1992, Ch. 41, § 66, eff. Sept. 1, 1992; **amended** by Laws 1993, Ch. 59, §§ 68, 69, eff. June 1, 1993; **amended** by Laws2005, Ch. 58, § 44 (Part C), eff. April 12, 2005, deemed eff. on and after April 1, 2005.

§ 365-h.   Provision and reimbursement of transportation costs.

1.   The local social services official shall have responsibility for prior authorizing transportation of eligible persons and for limiting the provision of such transportation to those recipients and circumstances where such transportation is essential, medically necessary and appropriate to obtain medical care, services or supplies otherwise available under this title.

2.   In exercising this responsibility, the local social services official shall:

(a)   make appropriate and economical use of transportation resources available in the district in meeting the anticipated demand for transportation within the district, including, but not limited to: transportation generally available free-of-charge to the general public or specific segments of the general public, public transportation, promotion of group rides, county vehicles, coordinated transportation, and direct purchase of services; and

(b)   maintain quality assurance mechanisms in order to ensure that (i) only such transportation as is essential, medically necessary and appropriate to obtain medical care, services or supplies otherwise available under this title is provided and (ii) no expenditures for taxi or livery transportation are made when public transportation or lower cost transportation is reasonably available to eligible persons.

3.   In the event that coordination or other such cost savings measures are implemented, the commissioner shall assure compliance with applicable standards governing the safety and quality of transportation of the population served.

     Added by Laws 1995, Ch. 81, § 78, eff. July 1, 1995; **amended** by Laws 2002, Ch. 1, Part B, § 26, eff. April 1, 2002.

§ 365-i.   Prescription drug payments. [*Expires and repealed March 31, 2009*.]

Payments for drugs which may not be dispensed without a prescription as required by section sixty-eight hundred ten of the education law and for which payment is authorized pursuant to paragraph (g) of subdivision two of section three hundred sixty-five-a of this title shall not be included in the capitation payment for services or supplies provided to medical assistance recipients by a health maintenance organization or other entity which is certified under article forty-four of the public health law or licensed pursuant to article forty-three of the insurance law or otherwise authorized by law to offer comprehensive health services plans to medical assistance recipients; provided, however, this section shall not prohibit the commissioner from undertaking a demonstration program that would permit the inclusion of payment for prescription drugs for Medicare/Medicaid dually eligible individuals in the capitation payment for services or supplies provided to medical assistance recipients by a health maintenance organization or other entity which is certified under article forty-four of the public health law or licensed pursuant to article forty-three of the insurance law or otherwise authorized by law to offer comprehensive health services plans to medical assistance recipients; provided however, that participation in such demonstration program for Medicare/Medicaid dually eligible individuals is voluntary and targeted primarily to the elderly who choose to remain in managed care.

Added by Laws 1998, Ch. 19, § 1, eff. July 18, 1998, expires Mar. 31, 2000; **amended** by Laws 2000, Ch. 13, § 4, eff. Mar. 30, 2000, and Ch. 57 Part A § 3, eff. May 15, 2000, deemed in effect Apr.1, 2000, extending the expiration date of the section to Dec. 31, 2003; L. 2003, Ch. 62, Part Z2, § 46, eff. Sept. 20, 2003, extending expiration date until March 31, 2006; **amended** by Laws 2004, Ch. 58, Part C, § 18, 34 and 36, eff. on and after April 1, 2004.

§ 365-j   [Eff. Sept. 24, 2006] Advisory opinions.

1. General.

(a)   Definition and nature of advisory opinions. An advisory opinion is a written statement, issued pursuant to the provisions of this chapter, by the commissioner of the department of health or his or her specifically authorized designee or designees setting forth the applicability to a specified set of facts of pertinent statutory and regulatory provisions relating to the provision of medical items or services pursuant to the medical assistance program administered by the department of health as the single state agency responsible for the administration of the program. Advisory opinions are issued at the request of any provider enrolled in the medical assistance program, and are binding upon the commissioner with respect to that provider only.

(b)   Areas in which advisory opinions may be requested. An advisory opinion may be sought with respect to a substantive question, or a procedural matter. Advisory opinions may be requested with respect to questions arising prior to an audit or investigation with respect to questions relating to a provider's claim for payment or reimbursement. Advisory opinions may also be utilized for purposes of service planning. Thus, they may be requested with respect to a hypothetical or projected future set of facts.

(c)   An advisory opinion will not be issued where the petition for an advisory opinion relates to a pending question raised by the provider in an ongoing or initiated investigation conducted by the Medicaid inspector general, deputy attorney general for the Medicaid fraud unit, or any other criminal investigation or any civil or criminal proceeding, or where the provider has received any written notice of the commissioner or the Medicaid inspector general which advises a provider of an imminent investigation, audit, pended or otherwise suspended claim, or withhold of payment or reimbursement.

(d)   Nothing in this section shall be construed as superseding any federal rule, law, requirement or guidance.

(e)   The commissioner shall promulgate rules and regulations establishing the time period for issuance of such advisory opinion and the criteria for determining the eligibility of a request for departmental response.

2.   Effect of advisory opinions.

(a)   An advisory opinion represents an expression of the views of the commissioner of health as to the application of law, regulations and other precedential material to the set of facts specified in the petition for advisory opinion. An advisory opinion shall apply only with respect to the provider to whom the advisory opinion is rendered.

(b)   A previously issued advisory opinion found by the commissioner to be in error may be modified or revoked, provided however, that a subsequent modification by such commissioner of such advisory opinion shall operate prospectively. In such instance, any recoupment of medical assistance overpayments caused by a provider's reliance on such an opinion shall be limited to the actual overpayments made, without interest, penalty, multiple damages, or other sanctions. The department shall promptly notify the provider of modification or revocation of an advisory opinion.

(c)   All advisory opinions shall include the following notice: "This advisory opinion is limited to the person or persons who requested the opinion and it pertains only to the facts and circumstances presented in the petition."

(d)   All advisory opinions shall cite the pertinent law and regulation upon which the advisory opinion is based.

(e)   All advisory opinions and all modifications and revocations of a previously issued advisory opinion shall be deemed a public record.

     Added by Laws 2006, Ch. 442, §6, eff. Sept 24, 2006.

§ 366   Eligibility

1.   Medical assistance shall be given under this title to a person who requires such assistance and who

(a)   either

(1)   meets the eligibility requirements of the safety net program as it existed on the first day of November, nineteen hundred ninety-seven without regard to the requirements of title nine-B of this article; provided, however, that an otherwise eligible person who is subject to a sanction pursuant to section three hundred forty-two of this chapter shall remain eligible for medical assistance; or

(2)   is receiving or is eligible to receive federal supplemental security income payments and/or additional state payments, so long as there is in effect an

agreement between the state and the secretary of health, education and welfare, pursuant to section three hundred sixty-three-b of this title, for the federal determination of eligibility of aged, blind and disabled persons for medical assistance, and so long as such secretary requires, as a condition of entering into such agreement, that such person be eligible for medical assistance; or

(3)   is a child under the age of twenty-one years receiving care (A) away from his own home in accordance with title two of article six of this chapter; (B) during the initial thirty days of placement with the division for youth pursuant to section 353.3 of the family court act; (C) in an authorized agency when placed pursuant to section seven hundred fifty-six or 353.3 of the family court act; or (D) in residence at a division foster family home or division contract home, and has not, according to the criteria promulgated by the department, sufficient income and resources, including available support from his parents, to meet all costs of required medical care and services available under this title; or

(4)   is receiving care, in the case of and in connection with the birth of an out of wedlock child, in accordance with title two of article six, and has not, according to the criteria promulgated by the department, sufficient income and resources, including available support from responsible relatives, to meet all costs of required medical care and services available under this title; or

(5)   although not receiving public assistance or care for his or her mainte-nance under other provisions of this chapter, has not, according to the criteria and standards established by this article or by action of the department, sufficient income and resources, including available support from responsible relatives, to meet all the costs of medical care and services available under this title, and is

(i)   under the age of twenty-one years, or sixty-five years of age or older, or certified blind or certified disabled or

(ii)   a spouse of a cash public assistance recipient living with him or her and essential or necessary to his or her welfare and whose needs are taken into account in determining the amount of his or her cash payment or

(iii)   for reasons other than income or resources: (A) is eligible for federal supplemental security income benefits and/or additional state payments, or (B) would meet the eligibility requirements of the aid to dependent children program as it existed on the sixteenth day of July, nineteen hundred ninety-six; or

(6)   is a resident of a home for adults operated by a social services district or a residential care center for adults or community residence operated or certified by the office of mental health, and has not, according to criteria promulgated by the department consistent with this title, sufficient income and resources, including available support from responsible relatives, to meet all the costs of required medical care and services available under this title; or

(7)   is a person at least twenty-one years of age but under the age of sixty-five who is not eligible for medical assistance pursuant to subparagraph eight or nine of this paragraph (i) who is the parent of a dependent child under the age of

twenty-one and (ii) who lives with such child and (iii) whose net income, without deducting the amount of any incurred medical expenses, do not exceed the net income exemptions set forth in subparagraph seven of paragraph (a) of subdivision two of this section; or

(8) is a member of a family which contains a dependent child living with a caretaker relative, which has net available income not in excess of the income standards of the family assistance program as it existed on the first day of November, nineteen hundred ninety-seven, and which has net available resources not in excess of one thousand dollars; for purposes of this subparagraph, the net available income and resources of a family shall be determined using the methodology of the family assistance program as it exists on the first day of November, nineteen hundred ninety-seven, except that (i) there shall be disregarded an additional amount of resources equal to the difference between the resource standard of the family assistance program as it existed on the first day of November, nineteen hundred ninety-seven and one thousand dollars and (ii) no part of the methodology of the family assistance program will be used which is more restrictive than the methodology of the aid to dependent children program as it existed on the sixteenth day of July, nineteen hundred ninety-six, purposes of this paragraph, the term dependent child means a person under twenty-one years of age who is deprived of parental support or care by reason of the death, continued absence, or physical or mental incapacity of a parent, or by reason of the unemployment of the parent, as defined by the department of health; or

(9) is a member of a family which contains a child under twenty-one years of age, which meets the financial eligibility requirements for medical assistance pursuant to subparagraph eight of this paragraph, and which is ineligible for such assistance because no child in the family meets the definition of a dependent child or is a pregnant woman who meets the eligibility requirements for medical assistance pursuant to subparagraph eight of this paragraph and who is ineligible because no dependent child resides with her; or

(10) is a child who is under twenty-one years of age, who is not living with a caretaker relative, who has net available income not in excess of the income standards of the family assistance program as it existed on the first day of November, nineteen hundred ninety-seven, and who has net available resources not in excess of one thousand dollars; for purposes of this subparagraph, the child's net available income and resources shall be determined using the methodology of the family assistance program as it existed on the first day of November, nineteen hundred ninety-seven, except that (i) there shall be disregarded an additional amount of resources equal to the difference between the applicable resource standard of the family assistance program as it exists on the first day of November, nineteen hundred ninety-seven and one thousand dollars and (ii) no part of the methodology of the family assistance program will be used which is more restrictive than the methodology of the aid to dependent children program as it existed on the sixteenth day of July, nineteen hundred ninety-six; or

(11) for purposes of receiving family planning services eligible for reimbursement by the federal government at a rate of ninety percent, is not otherwise eligible for medical assistance and whose income is two hundred percent or less of the comparable federal income official poverty line (as defined and annually revised by the United States department of health and human services). The commissioner of health shall submit whatever waiver applications as may be necessary to receive federal financial participation for services provided under this subparagraph and the provisions of this subparagraph shall be effective if and so long as such federal financial participation shall be available; or

(12) is a disabled person at least sixteen years of age, but under the age of sixty-five, who: would be eligible for benefits under the supplemental security income program but for earnings in excess of the allowable limit; has net available income that does not exceed two hundred fifty percent of the applicable federal income official poverty line, as defined and updated by the United States department of health and human services, for a one-person or two-person household, as defined by the commissioner in regulation; has household resources, as defined in paragraph (e) of subdivision two of section three hundred sixty-six-c of this title, that do not exceed ten thousand dollars; and contributes to the cost of medical assistance provided pursuant to this subparagraph in accordance with subdivision twelve of section three hundred sixty-seven-a of this title; for purposes of this subparagraph, disabled means having a medically determinable impairment of sufficient severity and duration to qualify for benefits under section 1902(a)(10)(A)(ii)(xv) of the social security act; or

(13) is a person at least sixteen years of age, but under the age of sixty-five, who: is employed; ceases to be in receipt of medical assistance under subparagraph twelve of this paragraph because the person, by reason of medical improvement, is determined at the time of a regularly scheduled continuing disability review to no longer be eligible for supplemental security income program benefits or disability insurance benefits under the social security act; continues to have a severe medically determinable impairment, to be determined in accordance with applicable federal regulations; and contributes to the cost of medical assistance provided pursuant to this subparagraph in accordance with subdivision twelve of section three hundred sixty-seven-a of this title; for purposes of this subparagraph, a person is considered to be employed if the person is earning at least the applicable minimum wage under section six of the federal fair labor standards act and working at least forty hours per month; and

(b) is a resident of the state, or, while temporarily in the state, requires immediate medical care which is not otherwise available, provided that such person did not enter the state for the purpose of obtaining such medical care; and

(c) except as provided in subparagraph six of paragraph (a) of this subdivision, is not an inmate or patient in an institution or facility wherein medical assistance for needy persons may not be provided in accordance with applicable federal or state requirements; and

SSL

(d)   is not a patient in a public institution operated primarily for the treatment of tuberculosis or care of the mentally disabled, except as follows: (1) is sixty-five years of age or older and is a patient in any such institution; or (2) is under twenty-one years of age and is receiving in-patient psychiatric services in a public institution operated primarily for the care of the mentally disabled; or (3) is a patient in a public institution operated primarily for the care of the mentally retarded and is receiving medical care or treatment in that part of such institution that has been approved pursuant to law as a hospital or nursing home; or (4) if a patient in an institution operated by the state department of mental hygiene, is under care in a hospital while on release from such institution for the purpose of receiving care in such hospital; or (5) is a person residing in a community residence or a residential care center for adults; and

No person who is otherwise eligible for medical assistance shall lose eligibility for such assistance as a result of the imposition of a sanction pursuant to section three hundred forty-two of this chapter.

2.   (a) The following income and resources shall be exempt and shall not be taken into consideration in determining a person's eligibility for medical care, services and supplies available under this title:

(1)   (i) for applications for medical assistance filed on or before December thirty-first, two thousand five, a homestead which is essential and appropriate to the needs of the household;

(ii)   for applications for medical assistance filed on or after January first, two thousand six, a homestead which is essential and appropriate to the needs of the household; provided, however, that in determining eligibility of an individual for medical assistance for nursing facility services and other long term care services, the individual shall not be eligible for such assistance if the individual's equity interest in the homestead exceeds seven hundred fifty thousand dollars; provided further, that the dollar amount specified in this clause shall be increased, beginning with the year two thousand eleven, from year to year, in an amount to be determined by the secretary of the federal department of health and human services, based on the percentage increase in the consumer price index for all urban consumers, rounded to the nearest one thousand dollars. If such secretary does not determine such an amount, the department of health shall increase such dollar amount based on such increase in the consumer price index. Nothing in this clause shall be construed as preventing an individual from using a reverse mortgage or home equity loan to reduce the individual's total equity interest in the homestead. The home equity limitation established by this clause shall be waived in the case of a demonstrated hardship, as determined pursuant to criteria established by such secretary. The home equity limitation shall not apply if one or more of the following persons is lawfully residing in the individual's homestead: (A) the spouse of the individual; or (B) the individual's child who is under the age of twenty-one, or is blind or permanently and totallydisabled, as defined in section 1614 of the federal social security act.

(2)   essential personal property;

of competent jurisdiction waives such requirement; and the bonding of the trustee when the assets of such a trust are less than one million dollars, upon order of a court of competent jurisdiction. The department, together with the banking department, shall promulgate regulations governing the establishment, management and monitoring of trusts established pursuant to subclause (B) of clause (iii) of this subparagraph in which a not-for-profit corporation and a trust company serve as co-trustees.

(v) Notwithstanding any acts, omissions or failures to act of a trustee of a trust which the department or a local social services official has determined complies with the provisions of clause (iii) and the regulations authorized by clause (iv) of this subparagraph, the department must not consider the corpus or income of any such trust as available income or resources of the applicant or recipient who is disabled, as such term is defined in section 1614(a)(3) of the federal social security act. The department's remedy for redress of any acts, omissions or failures to act by such a trustee which acts, omissions or failures are considered by the department to be inconsistent with the terms of the trust, contrary to applicable laws and regulations of the department, or contrary to the fiduciary obligations of the trustee shall be the commencement of an action or proceeding under subdivision one of section sixty-three of the executive law to safeguard or enforce the state's remainder interest in the trust, or such other action or proceeding as may be lawful and appropriate as to assure compliance by the trustee or to safeguard and enforce the state's remainder interest in the trust.

(3) (a) Social services officials shall authorize medical assistance for persons who would be eligible for such assistance except that their incomes exceed the applicable medical assistance income eligibility standard, which is determined according to paragraph (a) of subdivision two of this section, to become eligible for medical assistance by paying to their social services districts the amount by which their incomes exceed such income eligibility levels.

(b) Social services districts shall safeguard, by deposit in special accounts, any amounts paid to them by such recipients of medical assistance benefits. The amount of any medical assistance payments made to providers of medical assistance on behalf of such recipients, shall be charged against the amount in recipients' accounts. Districts shall, in accordance with their approved plans, periodically refund the amounts, if any, by which the amounts in recipients' accounts exceed the amounts of any medical assistance payments made on their behalf. Districts shall report to the department amounts in recipients' accounts that are equal to the amount of medical assistance payments made on recipients' behalf.

(c) Eligibility under this subparagraph shall be authorized only in accordance with plans submitted by social services districts and approved by the commissioner. Plans must be submitted by social services districts to the commissioner no later than February first, nineteen hundred ninety-six. The commissioner shall only approve plans that include a detailed description of how the district will administer the program, enroll recipients, safeguard monies in recipients' accounts, reconcile payments made to providers of medical assistance services with account balances and refund the amounts by which recipients' account funds exceed the amounts paid to providers on their behalf.

(d)　By January first, nineteen hundred ninety-five, the department shall submit to the governor and the legislature a report evaluating the demonstration programs effect on enrollees' access to medical assistance care and services and any other subjects the commissioner deems relevant.

(e)　Notwithstanding any other provision of law, administrative expenditures incurred by local social services districts in relation to this section shall be reimbursable as provided in subdivision one of section three hundred sixty-eight-a of this article.

3.　(a) Medical assistance shall be furnished to applicants in cases where, although such applicant has a responsible relative with sufficient income and resources to provide medical assistance as determined by the regulations of the department, the income and resources of the responsible relative are not available to such applicant because of the absence of such relative or the refusal or failure of such relative to provide the necessary care and assistance. In such cases, however, the furnishing of such assistance shall create an implied contract with such relative, and the cost thereof may be recovered from such relative in accordance with title six of article three and other applicable provisions of law.

(b)　(i) When a legally responsible relative agrees or is ordered by a court or administrative tribunal of competent jurisdiction to provide health insurance or other medical care coverage for his or her dependents or other persons, and such dependents or other persons are applicants for, recipients of or otherwise entitled to receive medical assistance pursuant to this title, the department and social services officials shall be subrogated to any rights that the responsible relative may have to obtain reimbursement from a third party for the costs of medical care for such dependents or persons.

(ii)　Upon receipt of an application, or upon a determination of eligibility, for assistance pursuant to this title, the department and social services officials shall be deemed to have furnished assistance to any such dependent or person entitled to receive medical assistance pursuant to this title and shall be subrogated to any rights such person may have to third party reimbursement as provided in paragraph (b) of subdivision two of section three hundred sixty-seven-a of this title.

(iii)　For purposes of determining whether a person is legally responsible for a person receiving assistance under this title, the following shall be dispositive: a copy of a support order issued pursuant to section four hundred sixteen or five hundred forty-five of the family court act or section two hundred thirty-six or two hundred forty of the domestic relations law; an order described in paragraph (h) of subdivision four of this section; an order of a court or administrative tribunal of competent jurisdiction pursuant to the provisions of this subdivision; or any other order of a court or administrative tribunal of competent jurisdiction subject to the provisions of this subdivision. If a notice of subrogation as described in paragraph (b) of subdivision two of section three hundred sixty-seven-a of this title is accompanied by dispositive documentation that a person is legally responsible for a person receiving assistance under this title, any third party liable for reimbursement for the costs of medical care shall accord the department or any social services official the rights of and benefits available to the responsible relative that pertain to the provision of medical care to any persons entitled to medical assistance pursuant to this title for whom the relative is legally responsible.

(c)   The provisions of this subdivision shall not be construed to diminish the authority of a social services official to bring a proceeding pursuant to the provisions of this chapter or other provisions of law (1) to compel any responsible relative to contribute to the support of any person receiving or liable to become in need of medical assistance, or (2) to recover from a recipient or a responsible relative the cost of medical assistance not correctly paid.

4.   (a) (i) Notwithstanding any other provision of law, each family which was eligible formedical assistance pursuant to subparagraph eight or nine of paragraph (a) of subdivision one of this section in at least three of the six months immediately preceding the month in which such family became ineligible for such assistance because of hours of, or income from, employment of the caretaker relative, or because of loss of entitlement to the earnings disregard under subparagraph (iii) of paragraph (a) of subdivision eight of section one hundred thirty-one-a of this chapter shall, while such family includes a dependent child, remain eligible for medical assistance for six calendar months immediately following the month in which such family would otherwise be determined to be ineligible for medical assistance pursuant to the provisions of this title and the regulations of the department governing income and resource limitations relating to eligibility determinations for families described in subparagraph eight of paragraph (a) of subdivision one of this section.

(ii)   Each family which received medical assistance for the entire six month period under subparagraph (i) of this paragraph and complied with the department's reporting requirements for such initial six month period shall be offered the option of extending such eligibility for an additional six calendar months if and for so long as such family includes a dependent child and meets the income requirements in subparagraph (ii) of paragraph (b) of this subdivision.

(b)   (i) Upon giving notice of termination of medical assistance provided pursuant to subparagraph eight or nine of paragraph (a) of subdivision one of this section, the department shall notify each such family of its rights to extended benefits under paragraph (a) of this subdivision and describe any reporting requirements and the conditions under which such extension may be terminated. The department shall also provide subsequent notices of the option to extend coverage pursuant to paragraph (a) of this subdivision in the third and sixth months of the initial six month extended coverage period and notices of the reporting requirements under such paragraph in each of the third and sixth months of the initial six month extended coverage period and in the third month of the additional extended coverage period.

(ii) The department shall promulgate regulations implementing the requirements of this paragraph and paragraph (a) of this subdivision relating to the conditions under which initial extended coverage and additional extended coverage hereunder may be terminated, the scope of coverage, the reporting requirements and the conditions under which coverage may be extended pending a redetermination of eligibility. Such regulations shall, at a minimum, provide for: (A) termination of such coverage at the close of the first month in which the family ceases to include a dependent child and at the close of the first or fourth month of the additional extended coverage period if the family fails to report, as required by the regulations, or the caretaker relative had no earnings in one or more of the previous three months unless such lack of earnings was for good cause, or the family's average gross monthly earnings, less necessary work related child care costs of the caretaker relative, during the preceding three months was greater than one hundred eighty-five percent of the federal income official poverty line applicable to the family's size; (B) notice of termination prior to the effective date of any terminations; (C) quarterly reporting of income and child care costs during the initial and additional extended coverage periods; (D) coverage under employee health plans and health maintenance organizations; and (E) disqualification of persons for extended coverage benefits under this paragraph for fraud.

(c) Notwithstanding any inconsistent provision of law, each family which was eligible for medical assistance pursuant to subparagraph eight of paragraph (a) of subdivision one of this section in at least three of the six months immediately preceding the month in which such family became ineligible for such assistance as a result, wholly or partly, of the collection or increased collection of child or spousal support pursuant to part D of title IV of the federal social security act, shall, for purposes of medical assistance eligibility, be considered to be eligible for medical assistance pursuant to subparagraph eight of paragraph (a) of subdivision one of this section for an additional four calendar months beginning with the month ineligibility for such assistance begins.

(d) Notwithstanding any other provision of law, in the absence of an agreement as set forth in subparagraph two of paragraph (a) of subdivision one of this section, an aged, blind or disabled person who is eligible for federal supplemental security income payments and/or additional state payments shall be eligible for medical assistance under this title pursuant to standards which were in effect on January first, nineteen hundred seventy-two. For the purposes of this paragraph, such individual shall be deemed eligible if, in addition to meeting other eligibility requirements of this title unrelated to income, his income as determined by excluding federal supplemental security payments and additional state payments to such person and his expenditures for medical care and services deductible for income tax purposes, as determined by the department is not in excess of the income standard for determining eligibility for medical assistance under the provisions of this title which were in effect on January first, nineteen hundred seventy-two.

(e) Notwithstanding any other provision of law, any person who, as the spouse of a recipient of old age assistance, assistance to the blind or aid to the disabled was eligible for medical assistance for December, nineteen hundred seventy-three, pursuant to clause (ii) of subparagraph four of paragraph (a) of subdivision one of this section, shall continue to be eligible therefor so long as (1) his spouse continues to meet the standards of eligibility for old age assistance, assistance to the blind or aid to the disabled, pursuant to this chapter, in effect for December, nineteen hundred seventy-three, and (2) such person continues to be the spouse of such recipient and continues to meet the other criteria set forth in such subparagraph four.

(f) Notwithstanding any other provision of law, any person who, for all or any part of December, nineteen hundred seventy-three, was an inpatient in an institution or facility wherein medical assistance may be provided in accordance with applicable federal or state requirements and, with respect to standards of eligibility, pursuant to this chapter, in effect for such month, (1) would, except for his being such an inpatient, have been eligible to receive old age assistance, aid to the blind or aid to the disabled, or (2) was, on the basis of his need for care in such institution or facility, considered to be eligible for such aid or assistance for the purpose of determining eligibility for medical assistance under this title, shall continue to be eligible for assistance under this title so long as he continues to be an inpatient in need of care in such institution or facility, and he continues to meet the criteria set forth in subparagraphs one and two of this paragraph.

(g) Notwithstanding any other provision of law, any blind or disabled person who was eligible for medical assistance for December, nineteen hundred seventy-three pursuant to clause (iii) of subparagraph four of paragraph (a) of subdivision one of this section, shall continue to be eligible therefor, so long as he continues to meet the criteria for blindness or disability pursuant to this chapter in effect for such month for the purpose of determining eligibility for assistance to the blind or aid to the disabled.

(h) (1) Any inconsistent provision of this chapter or other law notwithstanding, an applicant for or a recipient of assistance under this title shall be required, as a condition of initial or continued eligibility for such assistance, to assign to the appropriate social services official or the department, in accordance with department regulations: (i) any benefits which are available to him or her individually from any third party for care or other medical benefits available under this title and which are otherwise assignable pursuant to a contract or any agreement with such third party; or (ii) any rights, of the individual or of any other person who is eligible for medical assistance under this title and on whose behalf the individual has the legal authority to execute an assignment of such rights, to support specified as support for the purpose of medical care by a court or administrative order.

(2) Such applicant or recipient shall also be required, as a condition of initial or continued eligibility for such assistance, to cooperate with the appropriate social services official or the department in establishing paternity or in establishing, modifying, or enforcing a support order with respect to a child of the applicant or recipient; provided, however, that nothing herein contained shall be construed to require a payment under this title for care or services, the cost of which may be met in whole or in part by a third party. Notwithstanding the foregoing, a social services official shall not require the cooperation as set forth herein of an applicant or recipient with respect to whom such official has determined that such actions would be detrimental to the best interest of the child, applicant, or recipient, or with respect to pregnant women during pregnancy and during the sixty-day period beginning on the last day of pregnancy, in accordance with procedures and criteria established by regulations of the department consistent with federal law.

(i) Any inconsistent provision of law notwithstanding and to the extent permissible under federal law any applicant for or recipient of medical assistance pursuant to the provisions of subparagraph three, four or five of paragraph (a) of subdivision one of this section, except those persons receiving benefits pursuant to Title XVI of the federal social security act, who is or becomes employed and whose employer provides group health insurance benefits, including benefits for a spouse and dependent children of such applicant or recipient, shall apply for and utilize such benefits as a condition of eligibility for medical assistance. Such applicant or recipient shall also utilize such benefits provided by former employers as long as such benefits are available. The provisions of this paragraph shall apply to such applicants upon their initial certification for medical assistance and to such recipients upon their recertifications for such assistance following the effective date of this paragraph. The department shall promulgate regulations to determine the eligibility requirements of those applicants and recipients who have more than one employer offering group health insurance benefits.

(j) [Expires March 31, 2009] In accordance with applicable federal requirements, to the extent that federal financial participation is available, and subject to the approval of the director of the budget:

(1) the department is authorized to select entities offering comprehensive health services plans which are certified under article forty-four of the public health law, or licensed pursuant to article forty-three of the insurance law or otherwise authorized by law, for the purpose of continuing to provide services to enrollees of such entities who have lost their eligibility for medical assistance;

(2) individuals for whom federal financial participation would otherwise be available pursuant to title XIX of the social security act but who have lost their eligibility for medical assistance before the end of a six month enrollment period beginning on the date of the individual's enrollment in the entities designated pursuant to the provisions of subparagraph one of this paragraph, shall have their eligibility for medical assistance continued until the end of the six month

enrollment period, but only with respect to services provided to the individual as an enrollee of the entity.

(3)   The commissioner may apply for appropriate waivers under section eleven hundred fifteen of the social security act necessary to obtain federal financial participation for those enrollees of non-federally qualified entities offering comprehensive health services plans.

(k)   [Expires March 31, 2009] Notwithstanding any inconsistent provision of law, persons who were eligible for medical assistance pursuant to subparagraph one or nine of paragraph (a) of subdivision one of this section and who are participants in the entities offering comprehensive health services plans designated pursuant to paragraph (j) of this subdivision and who have lost their eligibility for medical assistance before the end of a six-month period beginning on the date of the individual's enrollment in such entities, shall have their eligibility for medical assistance continued until the end of the six-month enrollment period, but only with respect to services provided to the individual as an enrollee in the entity offering a comprehensive health services plan.

(l)   Notwithstanding any inconsistent provision of law, any child born to a woman eligible for and receiving medical assistance on the date of the child's birth shall be deemed to have applied for medical assistance and to have been found eligible for such assistance on the date of such birth and to remain eligible for such assistance for a period of one year, so long as the child is a member of the woman's household and the woman remains eligible for such assistance or would remain eligible for such assistance if she were pregnant.

(m)   (1) Pregnant women and infants younger than one year of age who are not otherwise eligible for medical assistance and whose families have incomes equal to or less than one hundred percent of the comparable federal income official poverty line (as defined and annually revised by the federal office of management and budget) for families of the same size.

(2)   For purposes of determining eligibility for medical assistance under this paragraph, family income is determined by use of the same methodology used to determine eligibility for the aid to dependent children program as it existed on the sixteenth day of July, nineteen hundred ninety-six and if authorized by federal law, rules or regulations resources available to such family shall not be considered nor required to be applied to the cost of medical care, services or supplies available under this paragraph.

(3)   (i) A pregnant woman eligible for medical assistance care and services under this paragraph on any day of her pregnancy will continue to be eligible for such care and services through the end of the month in which the sixtieth day following the end of the pregnancy occurs, without regard for any change in the income of the family that includes the pregnant woman, even if such change otherwise would have rendered her ineligible for medical assistance care and services.

(ii) Infants under one year of age will continue to be eligible for in-patient care and services through the end of any in-patient stay commenced prior to their attaining the age of one year provided, however, that they were eligible under this paragraph upon commencement of such stay and, but for attaining such age, would have remained eligible therefor.

(n) (1) Infants younger than one year who are not otherwise eligible for medical assistance and whose families have incomes equal to or less than two hundred percent of the federal income official poverty line (as defined and annually revised by the United States department of health and human services) for a family of the same size as the families that include the infants shall be eligible for medical assistance as provided in subparagraph three of this paragraph. For purposes of this paragraph, family income shall be determined by use of the same methodology used to determine eligibility for the aid to dependent children program as it existed on the sixteenth day of July, nineteen hundred ninety-six.

(2) For purposes of this paragraph, resources available to such families shall not be considered nor required to be applied toward the payment or part payment of the cost of medical assistance care, services and supplies available under this paragraph.

(3) An eligible infant who is receiving medically necessary in-patient services for which medical assistance is provided on the date the infant attains one year, and who, but for attaining such age, would remain eligible for medical assistance under this paragraph, shall continue to remain eligible until the end of the stay for which in-patient services are being furnished.

(o) (1) Pregnant women who are not otherwise eligible for medical assistance are eligible for services provided under the prenatal care assistance program established pursuant to title two of article twenty-five of the public health law if the income of the family that includes the pregnant woman does not exceed two hundred percent of the comparable federal income official poverty line (as defined and annually revised by the United States department of health and human services) for families of the same size.

(2) For purposes of determining eligibility under this paragraph, family income is determined by use of the same methodology used to determine eligibility for the aid to dependent children program as it existed on the sixteenth day of July, nineteen hundred ninety-six and resources available to such family shall not be considered nor required to be applied to the cost of medical care, services or supplies available under this paragraph.

(3) A pregnant woman eligible for services under this paragraph on any day of her pregnancy will continue to be eligible for such care and services through the end of the month in which the sixtieth day following the end of the pregnancy occurs, without regard for any change in the income of the family that includes the pregnant woman, even if such change otherwise would have rendered her ineligible for medical assistance care and services.

(p)   (1) Children who are at least one year of age but younger than six years of age who are not otherwise eligible for medical assistance and whose families have incomes equal to or less than one hundred thirty-three percent of the federal income official poverty line (as defined and annually revised by the federal office of management and budget) for a family of the same size as the families that include the children shall be eligible for medical assistance and shall remain eligible therefor as provided in subparagraph three of this paragraph.

(2)   For purposes of determining eligibility for medical assistance under this paragraph, family income shall be determined by use of the same methodology used to determine eligibility for the aid to dependent children program as it existed on the sixteenth day of July, nineteen hundred ninety-six provided, however, that costs incurred for medical or remedial care shall not be considered and resources available to such families shall not be considered nor required to be applied toward the payment or part payment of the cost of medical care, services and supplies available under this paragraph.

(3)   An eligible child who is receiving medically necessary in-patient services for which medical assistance is provided on the date the child attains six years of age, and who, but for attaining such age, would remain eligible for medical assistance under this paragraph, shall continue to remain eligible until the end of the stay for which in-patient services are being furnished.

(q)   (1) [Expires July 1, 2007] Children younger than nineteen years of age, who are not otherwise eligible for medical assistance and whose families have incomes equal to or less than one hundred percent of the federal income official poverty line (as defined and updated by the United States department of health and human services) for a family of the same size as families that include such children shall be eligible for medical assistance and shall remain eligible therefor, as provided in subparagraph three of this paragraph.

(2)   For purposes of this paragraph, family income is determined by use of the same methodology used to determine eligibility for the aid to dependent children program as it existed on the sixteenth day of July, nineteen hundred ninety-six provided, however, that costs incurred for medical or remedial care shall not be taken into account in determining eligibility.

(3)   Children who are eligible for medical assistance under this paragraph shall continue to be eligible for inpatient care and services through the end of any inpatient stay commenced prior to their attaining the age of nineteen years, provided, however, that they were eligible under this paragraph upon commencement of such stay and, but for attaining such age, would have remained eligible therefor.

(r)   To the extent permitted under federal law, if, for so long as, and to the extent that federal financial participation is available therefor, tuberculosis-related services, including prescription drugs, physician services, laboratory and x-ray services, clinic services, case-management services, and such other care, services and supplies as specified by the department in regulation, shall be given

SSL

to persons not otherwise described in this section who are infected with tuberculosis and whose income and resources do not exceed the amounts which a person may have and be eligible for medical assistance under this title.

(s) [Expires July 1, 2007] Notwithstanding any inconsistent provision of law, a child under the age of nineteen who is determined eligible for medical assistance under the provisions of this section, shall, consistent with applicable federal requirements, remain eligible for such assistance until the earlier of:

(1) the last day of the month which is twelve months following the determination or redetermination of eligibility for such assistance; or

(2) the last day of the month in which the child reaches the age of nineteen.

(t) [Expired April 1, 2005]

(1) Notwithstanding the provisions of sections twenty-five hundred ten and twenty-five hundred eleven of the public health law and paragraph (p) of this subdivision and subject to subparagraph four of this paragraph, children who are at least six years of age but younger than nineteen years of age, who are not otherwise eligible for medical assistance under paragraph (p) of this subdivision and whose families have a net household income greater than one hundred percent and less than or equal to one hundred thirty-three percent of the federal income official poverty line (as defined and updated by the United States Department of Health and Human Services) for a family of the same size as the families that include the children shall be eligible for medical assistance and shall remain eligible therefor as provided in subparagraph three hereof.

(2) For the purposes of determining eligibility for medical assistance under this paragraph, family income shall be determined in accordance with subparagraph two of paragraph (p) of this subdivision.

(3) For the purposes of this paragraph, an eligible child who is receiving medically necessary in-patient services for which medical assistance is provided on the date the child attains nineteen years of age, and who, but for attaining such age, would remain eligible for such medical assistance under this section, shall continue to remain eligible until the end of the stay for which in-patient services are being furnished.

(4) Repealed

(5) The commissioner will use best efforts to obtain a waiver of provisions of title XXI of the federal social security act from the secretary of the federal department of health and human services under which children who become eligible for medical assistance pursuant to this paragraph who are enrolled in the state children's health insurance program under sections twenty-five hundred ten and twenty-five hundred eleven of the public health law on the day before implementation of this paragraph under clauses (i) or (ii) of subparagraph four of this paragraph, are allowed the option of permanently retaining their enrollment in the state children's health insurance program or enrolling in the medical assistance program pursuant to this paragraph, and the commissioner is

authorized to take whatever other action, if any, may be necessary to effect this subparagraph.

(6) Notwithstanding any other provision of law to the contrary, the provisions of subparagraphs one through three of this paragraph shall not be implemented prior to January first, nineteen hundred ninety-nine.

(u)]Expired April 1, 2005]

(1) Notwithstanding the provisions of paragraph (p) of this subdivision, children who are less than one year of age and have a net household income less than or equal to one hundred eighty-five percent of the federal income official poverty line (as defined and updated by the United States Department of Health and Human Services) for a family of the same size as the families that include the children shall be eligible for presumptive eligibility in accordance with subdivision four of section three hundred sixty-four-i of this title.

(2) Notwithstanding the provisions of paragraphs (p) and (t) of this subdivision, children who are at least one year of age and less than nineteen years and have a net household income less than or equal to one hundred thirty-three percent of the federal income official poverty line (as defined and updated by the United States Department of Health and Human Services) for a family of the same size as the families that include the children shall be eligible in accordance with subdivision four of section three hundred sixty-four-i of this title.

(3) For the purposes of determining eligibility for medical assistance under this paragraph, family income shall be determined in accordance with subparagraph two of paragraph (p) of this subdivision.

(4) For the purposes of this paragraph, an eligible child who is receiving medically necessary in-patient services for which medical assistance is provided on the date the child attains nineteen years of age, and who, but for attaining such age, would remain eligible for such medical assistance under this section, shall continue to remain eligible until the end of the stay for which in-patient services are being furnished.

(5) Notwithstanding any other provision of law, this paragraph shall not be implemented until paragraph (t) of this subdivision shall take effect.

(v) (1) Persons who are not eligible for medical assistance under the terms of section 1902(a)(10)(A)(i) of the federal social security act are eligible for medical assistance coverage during the treatment of breast or cervical cancer, subject to the provisions of this paragraph.

(2) (i) Medical assistance is available under this paragraph to persons who are under sixty-five years of age, have been screened for breast and/or cervical cancer under the Centers for Disease Control and Prevention breast and cervical cancer early detection program and need treatment for breast or cervical cancer, and are not otherwise covered under creditable coverage as defined in the federal public health service act; provided however that medical assistance shall be furnished pursuant to this clause only to the extent permitted under federal law,

if, for so long as, and to the extent that federal financial participation is available therefor.

(ii)   Medical assistance is available under this paragraph to persons who meet the requirements of clause (i) of this subparagraph but for their age and/or gender, who have been screened for breast and/or cervical cancer under the program described in title I-A of article twenty-four of the public health law and need treatment for breast or cervical cancer, and are not otherwise covered under creditable coverage as defined in the federal public health service act; provided however that medical assistance shall be furnished pursuant to this clause only if and for so long as the provisions of clause (i) of this subparagraph are in effect.

(3)   Medical assistance provided to a person under this paragraph shall be limited to the period in which such person requires treatment for breast or cervical cancer.

(4)   [Until April 1, 2007] The commissioner of health shall promulgate such regulations as may be necessary to carry out the provisions of this paragraph. Such regulations shall include, but not be limited to: eligibility requirements; a description of the medical services which are covered; and a process for providing presumptive eligibility when a qualified entity, as defined by the commissioner, determines on the basis of preliminary information that a person meets the requirements for eligibility under this paragraph.

(4)   [Eff. April 1, 2007]

(i)   The commissioner of health shall promulgate such regulations as may be necessary to carry out the provisions of this paragraph. Such regulations shall include, but not be limited to: eligibility requirements; a description of the medical services which are covered; and a process for providing presumptive eligibility when a qualified entity, as defined by the commissioner, determines on the basis of preliminary information that a person meets the requirements for eligibility under this paragraph.

(ii)   For purposes of determining eligibility for medical assistance under this paragraph, resources available to such individual shall not be considered nor required to be applied toward the payment or part payment of the cost of medical care, services and supplies available under this paragraph.

(iii)   An individual shall be eligible for presumptive eligibility for medical assistance under this paragraph in accordance with subdivision five of section three hundred sixty-four-i of this title.

(5)   The commissioner of health shall, consistent with this title, make any necessary amendments to the state plan for medical assistance submitted pursuant to section three hundred sixty-three-a of this title, in order to ensure federal financial participation in expenditures under this paragraph. Notwithstanding any provision of law to the contrary, the provisions of clause (i) of subparagraph two of this paragraph shall be effective only if and for so long as federal financial participation is available in the costs of medical assistance furnished thereunder.

(v-1)　(1) Notwithstanding any other provision of law to the contrary, a person who has been screened or referred for screening for colon or prostate cancer by the cancer services screening program, as administered by the department of health, and has been diagnosed with colon or prostate cancer is eligible for medical assistance for the duration of his or her treatment for such cancer.

(2)　Persons eligible for medical assistance under this paragraph shall have an income of two hundred fifty percent or less of the comparable federal income official poverty line as defined and annually revised by the federal office of management and budget.

(3)　An individual shall be eligible for presumptive eligibility for medical assistance under this paragraph in accordance with subdivision five of section three hundred sixty-four-i of this title.

(4)　Medical assistance is available under this paragraph to persons who are under sixty-five years of age, and are not otherwise covered under creditable coverage as defined in the federal Public Health Service Act.

(w)　A woman who was pregnant while in receipt of medical assistance who subsequently loses her eligibility for medical assistance shall have her eligibility for medical assistance continued from the end of the month in which the sixtieth day following the end of her pregnancy occurs but only for Federal Title X services which shall continue for twenty-four months therefrom, and provided further that the services are reimbursable by the federal government at a rate of ninety percent; provided, however, that nothing in this paragraph shall be deemed to affect payment for such services if federal financial participation is not available for such care, services and supplies solely by reason of the immigration status of the otherwise eligible woman.

5.　(a) In determining the initial or continuing eligibility of any person for assistance under this title, there shall be included in the amount of resources considered available to such person the uncompensated value of any resource transferred prior to the date of application for medical assistance as specified in paragraphs (b), (c), (d) and (e) of this subdivision, and such person shall be ineligible for such assistance for such period or periods as specified in this subdivision.

(b)　For transfers made on or after April tenth, nineteen hundred eighty-two and prior to October first, nineteen hundred eighty-nine:

(1)　a nonexempt resource shall mean any resource which if retained by such person would not be exempt from consideration under the provisions of subdivision two of this section;

(2)　any transfer of a nonexempt resource made within twenty-four months prior to the date of a person's application for medical assistance shall be presumed to have been made for the purpose of qualifying for such assistance; however, if such person furnishes evidence to establish that the transfer was exclusively for some other purpose, the uncompensated value shall not be considered available to such person in determining his or her initial or continued eligibility for medical assistance;

(3) the uncompensated value of any such resource shall be the fair market value of such resource at the time of transfer, minus the amount of the compensation received by the person in exchange for the resource;

(4) any person determined to have excess resources of twelve thousand dollars or less because of the application of this paragraph shall remain ineligible for assistance under this title for a period of twenty-four months from the date of the transfer, or until such person can demonstrate that he or she has incurred medical expenses after the date of transfer in the amount of such excess above otherwise allowable resources, whichever period is shorter;

(5) any person determined to have excess resources of more than twelve thousand dollars because of the application of this paragraph shall remain ineligible for assistance under this title for a period which exceeds twenty-four months, which period shall be determined by adding an additional month of ineligibility for each two thousand dollars in excess of twelve thousand dollars, or until such person can demonstrate that he or she has incurred medical expenses after the date of transfer in the amount of such excess above otherwise allowable resources, whichever period is shorter.

(c) For transfers made on or after October first, nineteen hundred eighty-nine:

(1) (i) "institutionalized person" means any person who is an in-patient in a nursing facility, or who is an in-patient in a medical facility and is receiving a level of care provided in a nursing facility, or who is receiving care, services or supplies pursuant to a waiver pursuant to subsection (c) of section nineteen hundred fifteen of the federal social security act.

(ii) "resources" includes any resources which would not be considered exempt from consideration under the provisions of subdivision two of this section, without regard to the exemption provided for in subparagraph one of paragraph (a) of such subdivision.

(iii) "nursing facility" means a nursing home as defined by section twenty-eight hundred one of the public health law.

(iv) "nursing facility services" means nursing care and health related services provided in a nursing facility, a level of care provided in a hospital which is equivalent to the care which is provided in a nursing facility and care, services or supplies provided pursuant to a waiver pursuant to subsection (c) of section nineteen hundred fifteen of the federal social security act.

(2) the uncompensated value of a resource shall be the fair market value of such resource at the time of transfer, minus the amount of the compensation received in exchange for the resource.

(3) any transfer of a resource by a person or such person's spouse for less than fair market value made within or after the thirty months immediately preceding the date the person becomes an institutionalized person or the date of application for medical assistance while an institutionalized person, if later, shall render the person ineligible for nursing facility services for a period specified in subparagraph four of this paragraph; however, an institutionalized person shall not be ineligible for nursing facility services solely by reason of any such transfer to the extent that:

(i) the resource transferred was a home and title to the home was transferred to: (A) the spouse of such person; or (B) a child of such person who is under the age of twenty-one years or certified blind or certified permanently and totally disabled, as defined by section two hundred eight of this title; or (C) a sibling of such person who has an equity interest in such home and who resided in such home for a period of at least one year immediately before the date the person became an institutionalized person; or (D) a son or daughter of such person who was residing in such home for a period of at least two years immediately before the date such person became an institutionalized person, and who provided care to such person which permitted such person to reside at home rather than in an institution or facility; or

(ii) the resource was transferred to or for the sole benefit of such person's spouse, or from such person's spouse to or for the sole benefit of such person, or to his or her child who is certified blind or certified permanently and totally disabled; or

(iii) a satisfactory showing is made that: (A) the person or such person's spouse intended to dispose of the resource either at fair market value, or for other valuable consideration, or (B) the resource was transferred exclusively for a purpose other than to qualify for medical assistance; or

(iv) denial of eligibility would work an undue hardship, as defined by the commissioner which definition shall include the inability of the institutionalized person or such person's spouse to retrieve the resource or to obtain fair market value therefor despite his or her best efforts.

(4) Any transfer made by a person or the person's spouse under subparagraph three of this paragraph shall cause the person to be ineligible for nursing facility services, for services at a level of care equivalent to that of nursing facility services for the lesser of (i) a period of thirty months from the date of transfer, or (ii) a period equal to the total uncompensated value of the resources so transferred, divided by the average cost of nursing facility services to a private patient for a given period of time at the time of application as determined by the commissioner. For purposes of this subparagraph the average cost of nursing facility services to a private patient for a given period of time at the time of application shall be presumed to be one hundred twenty percent of the average medical assistance rate of payment as of the first day of January of each year for nursing facilities within the region as established pursuant to paragraph (b) of subdivision

sixteen of section twenty-eight hundred seven-c of the public health law wherein the applicant resides.

(d)   For transfers made after August tenth, nineteen hundred ninety-three:

(1)   (i) "assets" means all income and resources of an individual and of the individual's spouse, including income or resources to which the individual or the individual's spouse is entitled but which are not received because of action by: the individual or the individual's spouse; a person with legal authority to act in place of or on behalf of the individual or the individual's spouse; a person acting at the direction or upon the request of the individual or the individual's spouse; or by a court or administrative body with legal authority to act in place of or on behalf of the individual or the individual's spouse or at the direction or upon the request of the individual or the individual's spouse.

(ii)   "blind" has the same meaning given to such term in section 1614(a)(2) of the federal social social act.

(iii)   "disabled" has the same meaning given to such term in section 1614(a)(3) of the federal social security act.

(iv)   "income" has the same meaning given to such term in section 1612 of the federal social security act.

(v)   "resources" has the same meaning given to such term in section 1613 of the federal social security act, without regard, in the case of an institutionalized individual, to the exclusion provided for in subsection (a)(1) of such section.

(vi)   "look-back period" means the thirty-six month period, or, in the case of payments from a trust or portions of a trust which are treated as assets disposed of by the individual pursuant to department regulations, the sixty-month period, immediately preceding the date that an institutionalized individual is both institutionalized and has applied for medical assistance.

(vii)   "institutionalized individual" means any individual who is an in-patient in a nursing facility, including an intermediate care facility for the mentally retarded, or who is an in-patient in a medical facility and is receiving a level of care provided in a nursing facility, or who is receiving care, services or supplies pursuant to a waiver granted pursuant to subsection (c) of section 1915 of the federal social security act.

(viii)   "intermediate care facility for the mentally retarded" means a facility certified under article sixteen of the mental hygiene law and which has a valid agreement with the department for providing intermediate care facility services and receiving payment therefor under title XIX of the federal social security act.

(ix)   "nursing facility" means a nursing home as defined by section twenty-eight hundred one of the public health law and an intermediate care facility for the mentally retarded.

(x)   "nursing facility services" means nursing care and health related services provided in a nursing facility; a level of care provided in a hospital which is equivalent to the care which is provided in a nursing facility; and care, services or supplies provided pursuant to a waiver granted pursuant to subsection (c) of section 1915 of the federal social security act.

(2) The uncompensated value of an asset is the fair market value of such asset at the time of transfer, minus the amount of the compensation received in exchange for the asset.

(3) In determining the medical assistance eligibility of an institutionalized individual, any transfer of an asset by the individual or the individual's spouse for less than fair market value made within or after the look-back period shall render the individual ineligible for nursing facility services for the period of time specified in subparagraph four of this paragraph. Notwithstanding the provisions of this subparagraph, an individual shall not be ineligible for services solely by reason of any such transfer to the extent that:

(i) in the case of an institutionalized individual, the asset transferred was a home and title to the home as transferred to: (A) the spouse of the individual; or (B) a child of the individual who is under the age of twenty-one years or blind or disabled; or (C) a sibling of the individual who has an equity interest in such home and who resided in such home for a period of at least one year immediately before the date the individual became an institutionalized individual; or (D) a child of the individual who was residing in such home for a period of at least two years immediately before the date the individual became an institutionalized individual, and who provided care to the individual which permitted the individual to reside at home rather than in an institution or facility; or

(ii) the assets: (A) were transferred to the individual's spouse, or to another for the sole benefit of the individual's spouse; or (B) were transferred from the individual's spouse to another for the sole benefit of the individual's spouse; or (C) were transferred to the individual's child who is blind or disabled, or to a trust established solely for the benefit of such child; or (D) were transferred to a trust established solely for the benefit of an individual under sixty-five years of age who is disabled; or

(iii) a satisfactory showing is made that: (A) the individual or the individual's spouse intended to dispose of the assets either at fair market value, or for other valuable consideration; or (B) the assets were transferred exclusively for a purpose other than to qualify for medical assistance; or (C) all assets transferred for less than fair market value have been returned to the individual; or

(iv) denial of eligibility would cause an undue hardship, as determined pursuant to the regulations of the department in accordance with criteria established by the secretary of the federal department of health and human services.

(4) Any transfer made by an individual or the individual's spouse under subparagraph three of this paragraph shall cause the person to be ineligible for services for a period equal to the total, cumulative uncompensated value of all assets transferred during or after the look-back period, divided by the average

monthly costs of nursing facility services provided to a private patient for a given period of time at the time of application, as determined pursuant to the regulations of the department. The period of ineligibility shall begin with the first day of the first month during or after which assets have been transferred for less than fair market value, and which does not occur in any other periods of ineligibility under this paragraph. For purposes of this subparagraph, the average monthly costs of nursing facility services to a private patient for a given period of time at the time of application shall be presumed to be one hundred twenty percent of the average medical assistance rate of payment as of the first day of January of each year for nursing facilities within the region wherein the applicant resides, as established pursuant to paragraph (b) of subdivision sixteen of section twenty-eight hundred seven-c of the public health law.

(5)   In the case of an asset held by an individual in common with another person or persons in a joint tenancy, tenancy in common, or similar arrangement, the asset, or the affected portion of the asset, shall be considered to be transferred by such individual when any action is taken, either by such individual or by any other person, that reduces or eliminates such individual's ownership or control of such asset.

(6)   In the case of a trust established by the individual, as determined pursuant to the regulations of the department, any payment, other than a payment to or for the benefit of the individual, from a revocable trust is considered to be a transfer of assets by the individual and any payment, other than to or for the benefit of the individual, from the portion of an irrevocable trust which, under any circumstance, could be made available to the individual is considered to be a transfer of assets by the individual and, further, the value of any portion of an irrevocable trust from which no payment could be made to the individual under any circumstances is considered to be a transfer of assets by the individual for purposes of this section as of the date of establishment of the trust, or, if later, the date on which payment to the individual is foreclosed.

(e)   For transfers made on or after February eighth, two thousand six:

(1)   (i) "assets" means all income and resources of an individual and of the individual's spouse, including income and resources to which the individual or the individual's spouse is entitled but which are not received because of action by: the individual or the individual's spouse; a person with legal authority to act in place of or on behalf of the individual or the individual's spouse; a person acting at the direction or upon the request of the individual or the individual's spouse; or by a court or administrative body with legal authority to act in place of or on behalf of the individual or the individual's spouse or at the direction or upon the request of the individual or the individual's spouse;

(ii)   "blind" has the same meaning given to such term in section 1614(a)(2) of the federal social security act.

(iii)   "disabled" has the same meaning given to such term in section 1614(a)(3) of the federal social security act.

(iv) "income" has the same meaning given to such term in section 1612 of the federal social security act.

(v) "resources" has the same meaning given to such term in section 1613 of the federal social security act, without regard to the exclusion provided for in subsection (a)(1) of such section.

(vi) "look-back period" means the sixty-month period immediately preceding the date that an institutionalized individual is both institutionalized and has applied for medical assistance.

(vii) "institutionalized individual" means any individual who is an in-patient in a nursing facility, including an intermediate care facility for the mentally retarded, or who is an in-patient in a medical facility and is receiving a level of care provided in a nursing facility, or who is receiving care, services or supplies pursuant to a waiver granted pursuant to subsection (c) of section 1915 of the federal social security act.

(viii) "intermediate care facility for the mentally retarded" means a facility certified under article sixteen of the mental hygiene law and which has a valid agreement with the department for providing intermediate care facility services and receiving payment therefor under title XIX of the federal social security act.

(ix) "nursing facility" means a nursing home as defined by section twenty-eight hundred one of the public health law and an intermediate care facility for the mentally retarded.

(x) "nursing facility services" means nursing care and health related services provided in a nursing facility; a level of care provided in a hospital which is equivalent to the care which is provided in a nursing facility; and care, services or supplies provided pursuant to a waiver granted pursuant to subsection (c) of section 1915 of the federal social security act.

(2) The uncompensated value of an asset is the fair market value of such asset at the time of transfer less any outstanding loans, mortgages, or other encumbrances on the asset, minus the amount of the compensation received in exchange for the asset.

(3) In determining the medical assistance eligibility of an institutionalized individual, any transfer of an asset by the individual or the individual's spouse for less than fair market value made within or after the look-back period shall render the individual ineligible for nursing facility services for the period of time specified in subparagraph five of this paragraph. For purposes of this paragraph:

(i) the purchase of an annuity shall be treated as the disposal of an asset for less than fair market value unless: the state is named as the beneficiary in the first position for at least the total amount of medical assistance paid on behalf of the annuitant, or the state is named in the second position after a community spouse or minor or disabled child and is named in the first position if such spouse or a representative of such child disposes of any such remainder for less than fair market value; and the annuity meets the requirements of section 1917(c)(1)(G) of the federal social security act;

SSL

(ii)   the purchase of a life estate interest in another person's home shall be treated as the disposal of an asset for less than fair market value unless the purchaser resided in such home for a period of at least one year after the date of purchase;

(iii)   the purchase of a promissory note, loan, or mortgage shall be treated as the disposal of an asset for less than fair market value unless such note, loan, or mortgage meets the requirements of section 1917(c)(1)(I) of the federal social security act.

(4)   Notwithstanding the provisions of this paragraph, an individual shall not be ineligible for services solely by reason of any such transfer to the extent that:

(i)   in the case of an institutionalized individual the asset transferred was a home and title to the home was transferred to: (A) the spouse of the individual; or (B) a child of the individual who is under the age of twenty-one years or blind or disabled; or (C) a sibling of the individual who has an equity interest in such home and who resided in such home for a period of at least one year immediately before the date the individual became an institutionalized individual; or (D) a child of the individual who was residing in such home for a period of at least two years immediately before the date the individual became an institutionalized individual, and who provided care to the individual which permitted the individual to reside at home rather than in an institution or facility; or

(ii)   the assets: (A) were transferred to the individual's spouse, or to another for the sole benefit of the individual's spouse; or (B) were transferred from the individual's spouse to another for the sole benefit of the individual's spouse; or (C) were transferred to the individual's child who is blind or disabled, or to a trust established solely for the benefit of such child; or (D) were transferred to a trust established solely for the benefit of an individual under sixty-five years of age who is disabled; or

(iii)   a satisfactory showing is made that: (A) the individual or the individual's spouse intended to dispose of the assets either at fair market value, or for other valuable consideration; or (B) the assets were transferred exclusively for a purpose other than to qualify for medical assistance; or (C) all assets transferred for less than fair market value have been returned to the individual; or

(iv)   denial of eligibility would cause an undue hardship, such that application of the transfer of assets provision would deprive the individual of medical care such that the individual's health or life would be endangered, or would deprive the individual of food, clothing, shelter, or other necessities of life. The commissioner of health shall develop a hardship waiver process which shall include a timely process for determining whether an undue hardship waiver will be granted and a timely process under which an adverse determination can be appealed. The commissioner of health shall provide notice of the hardship waiver process in writing to those individuals who are required to comply with the transfer of assets provision under this section. If such an individual is an institutionalized individual, the facility in which he or she is residing shall be permitted to file an undue hardship waiver application on behalf of such individual with the consent of the individual or the personal representative of the individual.

(5)   Any transfer made by an individual or the individual's spouse under subparagraph three of this paragraph shall cause the person to be ineligible for services for a period equal to the total, cumulative uncompensated value of all assets transferred during or after the look-back period, divided by the average monthly costs of nursing facility services provided to a private patient for a given period of time at the time of application, as determined pursuant to the regulations of the department. For purposes of this subparagraph, the average monthly costs of nursing facility services to a private patient for a given period of time at the time of application shall be presumed to be one hundred twenty percent of the average medical assistance rate of payment as of the first day of January of each year for nursing facilities within the region where the applicant resides, as established pursuant to paragraph (b) of subdivision sixteen of section twenty-eight hundred seven-c of the public health law. The period of ineligibility shall begin the first day of a month during or after which assets have been transferred for less than fair market value, or the first day the otherwise eligible individual is receiving services for which medical assistance coverage would be available based on an approved application for such care but for the provisions of subparagraph three of this paragraph, whichever is later, and which does not occur in any other periods of ineligibility under this paragraph.

(6)   In the case of an asset held by an individual in common with another person or persons in a joint tenancy, tenancy in common, or similar arrangement, the asset, or the affected portion of the asset, shall be considered transferred by such individual when any action is taken, either by such individual or by any other person, that reduces or eliminates such individual's ownership or control of such asset.

(7)   In the case of a trust established by the individual, as determined pursuant to the regulations of the department, any payment, other than a payment to or for the benefit of the individual, from a revocable trust is considered to be a transfer of assets by the individual and any payment, other than to or for the benefit of the individual, from the portion of an irrevocable trust which, under any circumstance, could be made available to the individual is considered to be a transfer of assets by the individual and, further, the value of any portion of an irrevocable trust from which no payment could be made to the individual under any circumstances is considered to be a transfer of assets by the individual for purposes of this section as of the date of establishment of the trust, or, if later, the date on which the payment to the individual is foreclosed.

(f)   The commissioner of the office of temporary and disability assistance shall promulgate such rules and regulations as may be necessary to carry out the provisions of this subdivision.

6.   [Expires and repealed Dec 31, 2008]

SSL

a. The commissioner of health shall apply for a home and community-based services waiver pursuant to subdivision (c) of section nineteen hundred fifteen of the federal social security act in order to provide home and community-based services, not included under the medical assistance program. The waiver must be limited to no more than one thousand two hundred persons, seven hundred or fewer of whom shall be persons who would otherwise require nursing facility care and five hundred or fewer of whom shall be persons who would otherwise require hospital care.

b. A person eligible for participation in the waiver program shall:

(i) be eighteen years of age or under;

(ii) be physically disabled, according to the federal supplemental security income program criteria, including but not limited to a person who is multiply disabled;

(iii) have been hospitalized for at least thirty consecutive days or resided in a nursing facility for at least thirty consecutive days;

(iv) require the level of care provided by a nursing facility or by a hospital;

(v) be capable of being cared for in the community if provided with case management services and/or other services specified in paragraph f of this subdivision, in addition to other services provided under this title, as determined by the assessment required by paragraph d of this subdivision;

(vi) be ineligible for medical assistance if living in the community because the income and resources of responsible relatives, as determined through minimum documentation, would be deemed available to him or her, causing him or her to exceed the income or resource eligibility level for such assistance; however, up to one hundred persons who would otherwise require nursing facility care, and up to one hundred persons who would otherwise require hospital care, may be allowed to participate in the waiver program without regard to the provisions of this subparagraph; provided that such persons may participate only following federal approval and state implementation of the waiver program for a minimum number of one thousand two hundred persons, seven hundred of whom shall be persons who would otherwise require nursing facility care and five hundred of whom shall be persons who would otherwise require hospital care;

(vii) be capable of being cared for at less cost in the community than in the appropriate institutional setting; and

(viii) meet such other criteria as may be established by the commissioner as may be necessary to administer the provisions of this subdivision in an equitable manner.

c. Social services districts shall assess the eligibility of persons in accordance with the provisions of paragraphs b, d and i of this subdivision and shall refer persons who appear to meet the criteria set forth in such paragraphs to the commissioner of health for consideration for participation in the waiver program and final determinations of their eligibility for participation in the waiver program.

d.   The commissioner of health shall designate persons to assess the eligibility of persons in accordance with paragraphs b, c and i of this subdivision under consideration for participation in the waiver program. Persons designated by such commissioner may include the person's physician, a representative of the social services district, a representative of the provider of a long term home health care program or certified home health agency and, where appropriate, the discharge coordinator of the hospital or nursing facility and such other persons as such commissioner deems appropriate. The assessment shall include, butneed not be limited to, an evaluation of the medical, social, habilitation, and environmental needs of the person and shall serve as the basis for the development and provision of an appropriate plan of care for the person.

e.   Prior to a person's participation in the waiver program, the social services district or the commissioner of health, as appropriate, shall undertake or arrange for the development of a written plan of care for the provision of services consistent with the level of care determined by the assessment, in accordance with criteria established by the commissioner of health.

f.   Home and community-based services which may be provided to persons specified in paragraph b of this subdivision include: (i) case management services; (ii) respite services; (iii) home adaptation; and (iv) such other home and community-based services, other than room and board, as may be approved by the secretary of the federal department of health and human services.

g.   Social services districts shall designate who may provide the home and community-based services identified in paragraph f of this subdivision, subject to the approval of the commissioner of health.

h.   Notwithstanding any other provision of this chapter or any other law to the contrary, for purposes of determining medical assistance eligibility for persons specified in paragraph b of this subdivision, the income and resources of responsible relatives shall not be deemed available when the person returns home for as long as the person meets the criteria specified in this subdivision.

i.   Before a person may participate in the waiver program specified in paragraph a of this subdivision, the social services district shall determine that:

(i)   for a person who would otherwise require nursing facility care, there is a reasonable expectation that the annual medical assistance expenditures for home and community-based services for such person under the waiver program would not exceed the expenditures for nursing facility care that would have been made had the waiver not been granted; or

(ii)   for a person who would otherwise require hospital care, there is a reasonable expectation that the annual medical assistance expenditures for home and community-based services for such person under the waiver program would not exceed the expenditures for hospital care that would have been made had the waiver not been granted.

j. The commissioner shall review the plans of care and expenditure estimates determined by social services districts prior to the participation of any person in the waiver program.

k. This subdivision shall be effective only if, and as long as, federal financial participation is available for expenditures incurred under this subdivision.

6-a.   a. The commissioner of health shall apply for a nursing facility transition and diversion medicaid waiver pursuant to subdivision (c) of section nineteen hundred fifteen of the federal social security act in order to provide home and community based services to individuals who would otherwise be cared for in a nursing facility and who would be considered to be part of an aggregate group of individuals who, taken together, will be cared for at less cost in the community than they would have otherwise and to provide reimbursement for several home and community based services not presently included in the medical assistance program. The initial application shall provide for no less than five thousand persons to be eligible to participate in the waiver spread over the first three years and continue to increase thereafter.

b. A person eligible for participation in the nursing facility transition and diversion medicaid waiver program shall:

(i) be at least eighteen years of age;

(ii) be eligible for and in receipt of medicaid authorization for long term care services, including nursing facility services;

(iii) have resided in a nursing facility and/or have been assessed and determined to require the level of care provided by a nursing facility;

(iv) be capable of residing in the community if provided with services specified in paragraph f of this subdivision, in addition to other services provided under this title, as determined by the assessment required by paragraph d of this subdivision; and

(v) meet such other criteria as may be established by the commissioner of health as may be necessary to administer the provision of this subdivision in an equitable manner.

(vi) Redesignated

c. The department of health shall develop such waiver application in conjunction with independent living centers, representatives from disability and senior groups and such other interested parties as the department shall determine to be appropriate.

d. The commissioner of health shall contract with not-for-profit agencies around the state that have experience with providing community based services to individuals with disabilities, hereinafter referred to as regional resource development specialists, who shall be responsible for initial contact with the prospective waiver participant, for assuring the waiver candidates have choice in selecting a service coordinator and other providers, and for assessing applicants including decisions for eligibility for participation in the waiver, which contain the original service plan and all subsequent revised service plans. Regional resource development specialists shall be responsible for approving service plans and the department of health shall provide technical assistance and oversight.

e. Prior to the person's participation in the waiver program, a service coordinator approved by the department of health shall undertake the development of a written plan of care for the provision of services consistent with the level of care determined by an initial assessment, in accordance with criteria established by the commissioner of health. Such plans shall set forth the type of services to be furnished, the amount, the frequency and duration of each service and the type of providers to furnish each service.

f. Nursing facility transition and diversion services which may be provided to persons specified in paragraph b of this subdivision shall be established and defined as part of the waiver application development process specified in paragraph c of this subdivision and may include: (i) case management services; (ii) personal care; (iii) independent living skills training; (iv) environmental accessibility adaptations; (v) costs of community transition services; (vi) assistive technology; (vii) adult day health; (viii) staff for safety assurance; (ix) non-medical support services needed to maintain independence; (x) respite services; and (xi) such other home and community based services as may be approved by the secretary of the federal department of health and human services.

g. The department of health shall designate who may provide the nursing facility transition and diversion services identified in paragraph f of this subdivision, subject to the approval of the commissioner of health.

h. Before a person may participate in the nursing transition waiver program specified in this subdivision, the regional resource development specialists shall determine that:

(i) the individual is at least eighteen years of age and eligible for and in receipt of medicaid authorization for long term care services, including nursing facility services; and

(ii) the individual resides in a nursing facility and/or has been assessed and determined to require nursing facility care.

(iii) Deleted

i. Deleted

7. a. The commissioner of health shall apply for a home and community-based waiver, pursuant to subdivision (c) of section nineteen hundred fifteen of the federal social security act, in order to provide home and community-based services not presently included in the medical assistance program.

b. Persons eligible for participation in the waiver program shall:

(i) be eighteen years of age or under;

(ii) have a developmental disability, as such term is defined in subdivision twenty-two of section 1.03 of the mental hygiene law;

(iii) demonstrate complex health care needs, as defined in paragraph c of this subdivision;

(iv) require the level of care provided by an intermediate care facility for the developmentally disabled;

(v) not be hospitalized or receiving care in a nursing facility, an intermediate care facility for the developmentally disabled or any other institution;

(vi) be capable of being cared for in the community if provided with case management services, respite services, home adaptation, and any other home and community-based services, other than room and board, as may be approved by the secretary of the federal department of health and human services, in addition to other services provided under this title, as determined by the assessment required by paragraph f of this subdivision;

(vii) be ineligible for medical assistance because the income and resources of responsible relatives are deemed available to him or her, causing him or her to exceed the income or resource eligibility level for such assistance;

(viii) be capable of being cared for at less cost in the community than in an intermediate care facility for the developmentally disabled; and

(ix) meet such other criteria as may be established by the commissioner of health, in conjunction with the commissioner of mental retardation and developmental disabilities, as may be necessary to administer the provisions of this subdivision in an equitable manner, including those criteria established pursuant to paragraph d of this subdivision.

c. For purposes of this subdivision, persons who "demonstrate complex health care needs", shall be defined as persons who require medical therapies that are designed to replace or compensate for a vital body function or avert immediate threat to life; that is, persons who rely on medical devices, nursing care, monitoring or prescribed medical therapy for the maintenance of life over a period expected to extend beyond twelve months.

d. The commissioner of health, in conjunction with the commissioner of mental retardation and developmental disabilities, shall establish selection criteria to ensure that participants are those who are most in need and reflect an equitable geographic distribution. Such selection criteria shall include, but not be limited to, the imminent risk of institutionalization, the financial burden imposed upon the family as a result of the child's health care needs, and the level of stress within the family unit due to the unrelieved burden of caring for the child at home.

e. Social services districts, in consultation with the office of mental retardation and developmental disabilities, shall assess the eligibility of persons in accordance with the provisions of paragraph b of this subdivision, as well as the selection criteria established by the commissioner of health and the commissioner of mental retardation and developmental disabilities as required by paragraph d of this subdivision.

f. The commissioner of health, in conjunction with the commissioner of mental retardation and developmental disabilities, shall designate persons to assess the eligibility of persons under consideration for participation in the waiver program. Persons designated by such commissioners may include the person's physician, a representative of the social services district, representative of the appropriate developmental disabilities services office and such other persons as the commissioners deem appropriate. The assessment shall include, but need not be limited to, an evaluation of the health, psycho-social, developmental, habilitation and environmental needs of the person and shall serve as the basis for the development and provision of an appropriate plan of care for such person.

g. Prior to a person's participation in the waiver program, the office of mental retardation and developmental disabilities shall undertake or arrange for the development of a written plan of care for the provision of services consistent with the level of care determined by the assessment, in accordance with criteria established by the commissioner of health, in consultation with the commissioner of mental retardation and developmental disabilities. Such plan of care shall be reviewed by such commissioners prior to the provision of services pursuant to the waiver program.

h. Home and community-based services which may be provided to persons specified in paragraph b of this subdivision shall, in addition to those services otherwise authorized, include (i) case management services; (ii) respite services; (iii) home adaptation, and (iv) such other home and community-based services, other than room and board, as may be approved by the secretary of the federal department of health and human services.

i. The office of mental retardation and developmental disabilities shall designate who may provide the home and community-based services identified in paragraph h of this subdivision, subject to the approval of the commissioner of health.

j. Notwithstanding any other provision of this chapter other than subdivision six of this section or any other law to the contrary, for purposes of determining medical assistance eligibility for persons specified in paragraph b of this subdivision, the income and resources of a responsible relative shall not be deemed available for as long as the person meets the criteria specified in this subdivision.

k. Before a person may participate in the waiver program specified in paragraph a of this subdivision, the office of mental retardation and developmental disabilities shall determine that there is a reasonable expectation that the annual medical assistance expenditures for such person under the waiver would not exceed the expenditures for care in an intermediate care facility for the developmentally disabled that would have been made had the waiver not been granted.

l. The commissioner of health, in conjunction with the commissioner of mental retardation and developmental disabilities, shall review the plans of care

SSL

and expenditure estimates prior to the participation of any person in the waiver program.

m.   Within one year of federal waiver approval, and on an annual basis thereafter, until such time as the waiver program is fully implemented, the commissioner of health, in conjunction with the commissioner of mental retardation and developmental disabilities, shall report on the status of the waiver program to the governor and the legislature. Such report shall specify the number of children participating in the waiver program, the geographic distribution of those so participating, health profiles, service costs and length of time the children have participated in the waiver program. The report shall also provide follow-up information on children who have withdrawn from the waiver program, including data on residential program placements.

n.   This subdivision shall be effective only if, and as long as, federal financial participation is available for expenditures incurred under this subdivision.

8.   Notwithstanding any inconsistent provision of this chapter or any other law to the contrary, income and resources which are otherwise exempt from consideration in determining a person's eligibility for medical care, services and supplies available under this title, shall be considered available for the payment or part payment of the costs of such medical care, services and supplies as required by federal law and regulations.

9.   a. The commissioner shall apply for a general waiver, pursuant to subdivision (c) of section nineteen hundred fifteen of the federal social security act, in order to provide medical assistance for persons specified in paragraphs b and c of this subdivision and reimbursement for several home and community-based services not presently included in the medical assistance program. If granted the general waiver, the commissioner may authorize such persons to receive services under the general waiver to the extent funds are appropriated for transfer to the department for the state share of medical assistance payments for such waiver services from the budget of the office of mental health.

b.   Persons eligible for inclusion in the general waiver shall:

(i)   be under eighteen years of age;

(ii)   have a mental illness, as such term is defined in subdivision twenty of section 1.03 of the mental hygiene law;

(iii)   demonstrate complex health or mental health care needs, as defined in paragraph d of this subdivision;

(iv)   require the level of care provided by a hospital as defined in subdivision ten of section 1.03 of the mental hygiene law which provides intermediate or long-term care and treatment, or within the past six months have been hospitalized for at least thirty consecutive days, or have resided in such a hospital for at least one hundred eighty consecutive days;

(v)   be capable of being cared for in the community if provided with case management services, clinical interventions, crisis services, social training, rehabilitation services, counseling, respite services, medication therapy, partial hospitalization, environmental modifications, educational and related services, and/or medical social services, in addition to other services, as determined by the assessment required by paragraph g of this subdivision and included in the written plan of care developed pursuant to paragraph h of this subdivision;

(vi)   be eligible or, if discharged, would be eligible for medical assistance, or are ineligible for medical assistance because the income and resources of responsible relatives are or, if discharged, would be deemed available to such persons causing them to exceed the income or resource eligibility level for such assistance;

(vii)   be capable of being cared for at less cost in the community than in a hospital, as defined in subdivision ten of section 1.03 of the mental hygiene law; and

(viii)   meet such other criteria as may be established by the commissioner of mental health, in conjunction with the commissioner, as may be necessary to administer the provisions of this subdivision in an equitable manner, including those criteria established pursuant to paragraph e of this subdivision.

c.   Persons eligible for inclusion in the general waiver shall meet all the requirements set forth in subparagraphs (i) through (viii) of paragraph b of this subdivision; and shall be eligible for, shall have applied for, or shall reside in an institutional placement including a hospital as defined in subdivision ten of section 1.03 of the mental hygiene law which provides intermediate or long-term care and treatment.

d.   For purposes of this subdivision, persons who "demonstrate complex health or mental health care needs", shall be defined as persons who require medical or mental health therapies, care or treatments that are designed to replace or compensate for a vital functional limitation or to avert an immediate threat to life; that is, persons who rely on mental health care, nursing care, monitoring, or prescribed medical or mental health therapy for the maintenance of quality of life over a period expected to extend beyond twelve months.

e.   The commissioner of mental health, in conjunction with the commissioner, shall establish selection criteria to ensure that participants are those who are most in need. Such selection criteria shall include, but not be limited to: the need for continued hospitalization or the risk of hospitalization; the financial burden imposed upon the family, or which would be imposed upon the family if an institutionalized participant were to be discharged, as a result of the child's health or mental health care needs; and the level of stress or the anticipated level of stress within the family unit due to the unrelieved burden of caring for the child at home.

f.   Social services districts, in conjunction with the office of mental health and the local governmental unit as defined in section 41.03 of the mental hygiene law, shall determine the eligibility of persons in accordance with the provisions of paragraphs b and c of this subdivision, as well as the selection criteria established by the commissioner and the commissioner of mental health as required by paragraph e of this subdivision.

g.   The commissioner of mental health, in conjunction with the commissioner, shall designate persons to undertake an assessment to determine the eligibility of persons under consideration for inclusion in the general waiver. Persons designated by such commissioners may include the potentially eligible person's physician, a representative of the local governmental unit as defined in section 41.03 of the mental hygiene law, a representative of the appropriate hospital or regional office of the office of mental health, and such other persons as the commissioners deem appropriate. The assessment shall include, but not be limited to, an evaluation of the mental health, health, psycho-social, rehabilitation and environmental needs of the person, and shall serve as the basis for the development and provision of an appropriate plan of care for such person.

h.   Prior to a person's inclusion in the general waiver, the office of mental health and the local governmental unit as defined in section 41.03 of the mental hygiene law, shall undertake or arrange for the development of a written plan of care, including identification of service providers if known, for the provision of services in consultation with the individual and their family whenever clinically appropriate, consistent with the level of care determined by the assessment, in accordance with criteria established by the commissioner of mental health, in consultation with the commissioner. If a provider of services is identified in a written plan of care, such provider shall be designated pursuant to paragraph j of this subdivision. Such plan of care shall be reviewed by such commissioners and approved by the commissioner of mental health prior to the provision of services pursuant to the general waiver.

i.   Home and community-based services which may be provided to persons specified in paragraphs b and c of this subdivision shall, in addition to those services otherwise authorized, include but are not limited to (i) case management services; (ii) clinical interventions; (iii) crisis services; (iv) social training; (v) rehabilitation services; (vi) counseling; (vii) respite services; (viii) medication therapy; (ix) partial hospitalization; (x) environmental modifications; (xi) educational and related services; (xii) medical social services; and other services included in the written plan of care developed pursuant to paragraph h of this subdivision.

j.   The office of mental health, in conjunction with the social services district and the local governmental unit, shall designate who may provide the home and community-based services identified in paragraph i of this subdivision.

k.   Notwithstanding any provision of this chapter other than subdivision six or seven of this section, or any other law to the contrary, for purposes of determining medical assistance eligibility for persons specified in paragraphs b and c of this subdivision, the income and resources of a responsible relative shall not be deemed available for as long as the person meets the criteria specified in this subdivision.

l. Before a person may participate in the general waiver specified in paragraph a of this subdivision, the social services district and the office of mental health shall determine that there is a reasonable expectation that the annual medical assistance expenditures for such person under the waiver would not exceed the expenditures for care in a hospital, as defined in subdivision ten of section 1.03 of the mental hygiene law, that would have been made had the waiver not been granted.

m. The commissioner, in conjunction with the commissioner of mental health, shall review the expenditure estimates determined by social services districts and the office of mental health, prior to the inclusion of any person in the general waiver.

n. Within one year of federal waiver approval, and on an annual basis thereafter, until such time as the waiver is fully implemented, the commissioner of mental health, in conjunction with the commissioner, shall report on the status of the general waiver to the governor, the legislature, including the respective chairpersons of the senate and assembly committees of mental health and the chairs of the senate finance and assembly ways and means committees and the director of the division of the budget. Such report shall specify the number of children included in the waiver, the geographic distribution of those included, health and mental health profiles, utilization and costs of services by region including costs avoided in residential treatment facilities and inpatient facilities operated by the office of mental health, the length of time the children have participated in the waiver and regional information on the status of waiting lists for waiver services and for services in residential settings, where appropriate. The report shall also provide follow-up information on children who have withdrawn from the waiver, including data on residential program placements.

o. This subdivision shall be effective if, and as long as, federal financial participation is available for expenditures incurred under this subdivision.

p. Nothing herein shall be construed to create an entitlement to services under the approved general waiver implemented by the commissioner in accordance with this subdivision.

10. None

11. The commissioner of health shall, consistent with this title, make any necessary amendments to the state plan for medical assistance submitted pursuant to section three hundred sixty-three-a of this title, in order to ensure federal financial participation in expenditures under subparagraphs twelve and thirteen of paragraph (a) of subdivision one of this section. Notwithstanding any other provision of law to the contrary, medical assistance under subparagraphs twelve and thirteen of paragraph (a) of subdivision one of this section shall be provided only to the extent permitted under federal law, if, for so long as, and to the extent that federal financial participation is available therefor.

12. (a) Notwithstanding any provision of law to the contrary, the commissioner of health, in consultation with the office of children and family services,

SSL

shall develop and submit applications for waivers pursuant to section nineteen hundred fifteen of the federal social security act as may be necessary to provide medical assistance, including services not presently included in the medical assistance program, for persons described in paragraph (b) of this subdivision. If granted such waivers, the commissioner of health, on the advice and recommendation of the commissioner of children and family services, may authorize such persons to receive such assistance to the extent funds are appropriated therefor.

(b) Persons eligible for inclusion in the waiver program established by this subdivision shall be residents of New York state under the age of twenty-one years, who are eligible for care in a medical institution, who have had the responsibility for their care and placement transferred to the local commissioner of a social services district or to the office of children and family services as adjudicated juvenile delinquents under article three of the family court act, where placement is in a non-secure setting, and who:

(i) have a diagnosis of a mental disorder under the most recent edition of the Diagnostic and Statistical Manual of Mental Disorders;

(ii) have a diagnosis of a developmental disability as defined in section 1.03 of the mental hygiene law; or

(iii) have a physical disability.

(c) Services which may be provided to persons specified in paragraph (b) of this subdivision, in addition to services otherwise authorized, may include but are not limited to:

(i) services that will permit children to be better served, prevent institutionalization, and allow utilization at lower-levels of institutional care;

(ii) case management services;

(iii) respite services;

(iv) medical social services;

(v) nutritional counseling;

(vi) respiratory therapy;

(vii) home adaptation and/or environmental modifications;

(viii) clinical interventions;

(ix) crisis services;

(x) social training;

(xi) habilitation and rehabilitation services;

(xii) counseling;

(xiii) medication therapy;

(xiv) partial hospitalization;

(xv) educational and related services; and

(xvi) other services included in the written plan of care.

(d) Notwithstanding any provision of this chapter or any other law to the contrary, for purposes of determining medical assistance eligibility for persons specified in paragraph (b) of this subdivision, the income and resources of a legally responsible relative shall not be deemed available for as long as the person meets the criteria specified in this subdivision; provided, however, that such income shall continue to be deemed unavailable should responsibility for the care and placement of the person be returned to his or her parent or other legally responsible person.

(e) Before a person may participate in the waiver program established by this subdivision, the social services district that is fiscally responsible for the person shall determine that there is a reasonable expectation that annual medical assistance expenditures for such person will not exceed federal requirements.

(f) The eligibility and benefits authorized by this subdivision shall be applicable if, and as long as, federal financial participation is available for expenditures incurred under this subdivision. The eligibility and benefits authorized by this subdivision shall not apply unless all necessary approvals under federal law and regulation have been obtained to receive federal financial participation in the costs of services provided pursuant to this subdivision.

(g) Nothing in this subdivision shall be construed to create an entitlement to services under the waiver program established by this subdivision.

(h) A person participating in the waiver program established by this subdivision may continue participation in the program until it is no longer consistent with the plan of care, or until age twenty-one, whichever occurs earlier, notwithstanding the person's status as having been discharged from the care and placement of the local commissioner of a social services district or the commissioner of children and family services, including adoption.

Added by Laws 1966, Ch. 256; **amended** by Laws 1966, Chs. 257, 802; Laws 1968, Chs. 32, 33, 270, 588, 669; Laws 1969, Ch. 184; Laws 1971, Chs. 106, 110, 113; Laws 1973, Chs. 151, 516, 880; Laws 1974, Chs. 738, 909, 1080; Laws 1975, Chs. 480 and 481; Laws 1976, Ch. 76, Ch. 483; Ch. 881; Laws 1977, Ch. 77, Ch. 431, Ch. 755, Ch. 777; Laws 1978, Ch. 454, Ch. 612; Laws 1979, Ch. 314, Ch. 450; Laws 1980, Ch. 113, eff. July 1, 1980; **amended** by Laws 1981, Ch. 85, eff. July 1, 1981; **amended** by Laws 1981, Ch. 318, eff. Aug. 28, 1981, adding subd. 4(g); **amended** by Laws 1981, Ch. 319, adding subd. 4(f), eff. Aug. 28, 1981, provided that subd. 4(f) with respect to assignment of any benefits provided by any third party shall apply only to policies issued, renewed, modified or altered after such effective date; **amended** by Laws 1981, Ch. 1005, eff. July 31, 1981, added subd. 2(a)(10); **amended** by Laws 1982, Ch. 56, eff. Apr. 12, 1982; **amended** by Laws 1982, Ch. 87, eff. July 1, 1982, see below; **amended** by Laws 1982, Ch. 794, eff. July 27, 1982, subd. (2)(a)(10); **amended** by Laws 1983, Ch. 71, eff. July 1, 1983, subd. (2)(a)(8); **amended** by Laws 1983, Ch. 535, subd. (4)(h) added; Laws 1987, Ch. 357, eff. July 23, 1987, which extended the expiration date until Mar. 31, 1990; **amended** by Laws 1983, Ch. 920, eff. July 1, 1983; **amended** by Laws 1984, see below; **amended** by Laws 1985, see below; **amended** by Laws 1986, see below; **amended** by

SSL

Laws 1987, see below; **amended** by Laws 1988, see below; **amended** by Laws 1989, Ch. 170, eff. June 19, 1989; **amended** by Laws 1989, Ch. 171, eff. June 19, 1989; **amended** by Laws 1989, Ch. 333, eff. July 10, 1989 until Jan. 1, 1994, at which time it will expire and be deemed repealed; **amended** by Laws 1989, Ch. 558, § 1, eff. July 16, 1989; **amended** by Laws 1989, Ch. 584, § 5, eff. Jan. 1, 1990; **amended** by Laws 1989 Ch. 729, § 2, eff. July 24, 1989; **amended** by Laws 1990, Ch. 386, § 2, eff. Jan. 1, 1991; **amended** by Laws 1990, Ch. 453, §§ 8, eff. Oct. 1, 1990, and deemed to have been in full force and effect from Apr. 1, 1990; **amended** by Laws 1990, Ch. 549, § 1, eff. July 18, 1990; **amended** by Laws 1990, Ch. 651, § 1, eff. Oct. 1, 1990; **amended** by Laws 1990, Ch. 922, § 15, eff. July 1, 1990; **amended** by Laws 1990, Ch. 938, § 38, eff. Jan. 1, 1991; **amended** by Laws 1991, Ch. 165, § 14, eff. July 1, 1991, § 16, eff. Apr. 1, 1991, § 17, eff. June 12, 1991, § 15, eff. July 1, 1991 until Jan. 1, 1994; **amended** by Laws 1992, Ch. 41, §§ 64, 65, 90, eff. Sept. 1, 1992; **amended** by Laws 1992, Ch. 738, § 1, eff. July 31, 1992; **amended** by Laws 1993, Ch. 329, § 1, eff. July 21, 1993; **amended** by Laws 1993, Ch. 421, § 1, eff. July 21, 1993 until Jan. 1, 1996; **amended** by Laws 1993, Ch. 421, § 2, adding new cl. (d) to SSL § 366(2)(b)(3), eff. July 21, 1993; **amended** by Laws 1993, Ch. 638, § 7, eff. Aug. 4, 1993; **amended** by Laws 1994, Ch. 30, § 1, eff. Apr. 1, 1994, extending the period that Subd. 6 remains effective to Dec. 31, 1995; **amended** by Laws 1994, Ch. 33, §§ 1, 2, eff. Apr. 1, 1994, extending the period that paras. (h) and (i) of Subd. 4 remain effective to Dec. 31, 1995; **amended** by Laws 1994, Ch. 170, §§ 408, 449, 450, 459 and 460, eff. Apr. 1, 1994; **amended** by Laws 1995, Ch. 81, § 127, eff. Nov. 1, 1995; **amended** by Laws 1995, Ch. 81, § 119, eff. June 20, 1995, extending the period that Subd. 4, para. (h) remains effective to Dec. 31, 1996; **amended** by Laws 1995, Ch. 81, § 120, eff. June 20, 1995, extending the period that Subd. 4, para. (i) remains effective to July 1, 1996; **amended** by Laws 1995, Ch. 81, § 121, eff. June 20, 1995, extending the period that Subd. 6 remains effective to Dec. 31, 1996; **amended** by Laws 1995, Ch. 81, § 128, eff. June 20, 1995, removing Subd. 2, para. (b)'s expiration date; **amended** by Laws 1996, Ch. 309, § 37, eff. July 13, 1996, except that persons in need of supervision in the custody of the division for youth prior to the effective date shall be governed by the provisions of law in effect at the time of their placement; **amended** by Laws 1996, Ch. 350, eff. July 17, 1996, extending the period that Subd. 4, para. (i) remains effective to July 1, 1997; **amended** by Laws 1996, Ch. 526, § 2, eff. Aug. 8, 1996, extending the period that Subds. 4 and 6 remains effective to Dec. 31, 1997; **amended** by L. 1997, Ch. 398, amending subd. (4)(h)(2), eff. Nov. 11, 1997, Chs. 145, 162, 194, 211, 223, and 264 extending the expiration of subd. (4)(i) to Aug. 2, 1997, eff. July 23, 1997, deemed in full force and effect Apr. 1, 1997, Ch. 221. extending the expiration date of subd. 366(6) to Dec. 31, 1999, eff. July 18, 1997, and Ch. 224, extending the expiration date of subd. 366(4)(h) to Dec. 31, 1998, eff. July 18, 1997; **amended** by Laws 1997, Ch. 436, § 1 Part B, §§ 54–61, 95, and 97, eff. Nov. 1, 1997; **amended** by Laws 1997, Ch. 656, § 1, eff. Sept. 24, 1997; **amended** by Laws 1998, Ch. 214, §§ 68–70, eff. July 7, 1998, deemed in full force and effect Aug. 20, 1997, Ch. 575 § 1, eff. Aug. 5, 1998, Ch. 145, § 1, eff. June 30, 1998, Ch. 2, §§ 23, 24, and 26-a, eff. Jan. 1, 1999, amendments expire and be deemed repealed Mar. 31, 2001, and § 24-a, eff. Sept. 24, 1998, amendments to expire and be deemed repealed Mar. 31, 2001, and Ch. 601, § 1, eff. Sept. 29, 1998, and providing that any person receiving home and community-based services on Sept. 29. 1998 pursuant to a model waiver program authorized in accordance with chapter 906 of the laws of 1984, as amended by chapter 549 of the laws of 1990, may continue to receive such services in accordance with such chapter laws pending the approval and implementation of the waiver program authorized by § 1 of Ch. 601;

amended by L. 1999, Ch. 153, § 1, extending the expiration of subd. (4)(i) to July 1, 2000, eff. July 1, 1999; amended by L. 1999, Ch. 1, §118, eff. Dec. 30, 1999, deemed in full force and effect Jan. 1, 2000; **amended** by L. 1999, Chs. 599 & 600, eff. Nov. 1, 1999; **amended** by L. 2000, Ch. 57 Part B §§ 3 and 9, eff. July 1, 2000 and May 15, 2000, respectively, extending the expiration dates of (2)(b), (4)(h) and (i), respectively, Ch. 57 Part E § 1, eff. May 15, 2000, Ch. 57 Part D, §§ 2 and 3, eff. Nov. 1, 2000, and Ch. 57 Part A § 9, eff. May 15, 2000, deemed eff. Apr. 4, 2000; **amended** by L. 2001, Ch. 150, eff. Aug. 14, 2001, Ch. 331, eff. Sept. 19, 2001, and Ch. 383, eff. Oct. 29, 2001; **amended** by Laws 2002, Ch. 1, Part A, §§ 48 and 55, eff. Apr 1, 2002, §§ 56 and 58, eff. Oct. 1, 2002, §§ 61, 62, 63 and 68, eff. April 1, 2003, Ch. 1, Part B, §§ 22 and 23, eff. Jan 1, 2003, extending effective date to June 30, 2003, Ch. 16, § 4, eff. Feb. 1, 2002 and Ch. 509, §§ 1 and 3, eff. Sept. 17, 2002; L. 2003, Ch. 62, Part A3, § 21, eff. May 15, 2003, extending the expiration date until July 1, 2005; Ch. 62, Part Z2, §§ 42–45, eff. May 15, 2003, deemed effective April 1, 2003, extending the expiration date until March 31, 2006; **amended** by Laws 2004, Ch. 58, Part B, §§ 5, 6, eff. Aug. 20, 2004, Ch. 324 §§ 1 and 2, amending sub. 7, eff. August 10, 2004, Ch. 536, § 1, extending sub. 6 expiration date, eff. Sept. 28, 2004, Ch. 615, § 1, adding sub. 6-a, eff. Oct. 19, 2004, and Ch. 627, § 1, amending sub. 6-a, eff. Oct. 19, 2004; by Laws 2005, Ch. 12, § 7, amending sub. 2-a(7), eff. March 15, 2005; Laws 2006, Ch. 57, §§ 50, 50-a (Part A), eff. Apr. 12, 2006; Ch. 58 § 1 (Part E), eff. Apr. 12, 2006; Ch. 109 §§ 25, 26, 26-a, 27 (Part C), eff. Apr. 01, 2006; Ch. 176, §§ 2, 4, eff. Apr. 01, 2007.

§ 366-a. Applications for assistance; investigations; reconsideration.

1.   Any person requesting medical assistance may make application therefor in person, through another in his behalf or by mail to the social services official of the county, city or town, or to the service officer of the city or town in which the applicant resides or is found. In addition, in the case of a person who is sixty-five years of age or older and is a patient in a state hospital for tuberculosis or for the mentally disabled, applications may be made to the department, or to social services official designated as the agent of the department. Notwithstanding any provision of law to the contrary, in accordance with department regulations, when an application is made by mail, a personal interview shall be conducted with the applicant or with the person who made application in his behalf when the applicant cannot be interviewed due to his physical or mental condition.

1-a.   [*Repealed.*]

2 (a)   Upon receipt of such application, the appropriate social services official, or the department of health or its agent when the applicant is a patient in a state hospital for the mentally disabled, shall verify the eligibility of such applicant. In accordance with the regulations of the department of health, it shall be the responsibility of the applicant to provide information and documentation necessary for the determination of initial and ongoing eligibility for medical assistance. If an applicant or recipient is unable to provide necessary documentation, the public welfare official shall promptly cause an investigation to be made. Where an investigation is necessary, sources of information other than public records will be consulted only with permission of the applicant or recipient. In

SSL

the event that such permission is not granted by the applicant or recipient, or necessary documentation cannot be obtained, the social services official or the department of health or its agent may suspend or deny medical assistance until such time as it may be satisfied as to the applicant's or recipient's eligibility therefor.To the extent practicable, any interview conducted as a result of an application for medical assistance shall be conducted in the home of the person interviewed or in the institution in which such person is receiving medical assistance.

(b)   Notwithstanding the provisions of paragraph (a) of this subdivision, an applicant or recipient may attest to the amount of his or her accumulated resources, unless such applicant or recipient is seeking medical assistance payment for long term care services. For purposes of this paragraph, long term care services shall mean care, treatment, maintenance, and services described in paragraph (b) of subdivision 1 of section three hundred sixty-seven-f of this title, with the exception of short term rehabilitation, as defined by the commissioner of health.

(c)   The commissioner of health may verify the accuracy of the information provided by the applicant or recipient pursuant to paragraph (b) of this subdivision, by matching it against information to which the commissioner of health has access, including under subdivision eight of this section. In the event there is an inconsistency between the information reported by the applicant or recipient and any information obtained by the commissioner of health from other sources and such inconsistency is material to medical assistance eligibility, the commissioner of health shall request that the applicant or recipient provide adequate documentation to verify his or her resources.

3.   Upon the receipt of such application, and after the completion of any investigation that shall be deemed necessary, the appropriate public welfare official, or the department or its agent when the applicant is a patient in a state hospital for tuberculosis or for the mentally disabled, shall

(a)   decide whether the applicant is eligible for and should receive medical assistance, the amount thereof and the date on which it shall begin, which shall be the date of the application or, subject to applicable department regulations, such earlier or later date as may be deemed reasonable;

(b)   notify the applicant in writing of the decision, and where such applicant is found eligible, provide a tamper resistant identification card containing a photo image of the applicant for use in securing medical assistance under this title provided, however, that an identification card need not contain a photo image of a person other than an adult member of an eligible household or a single-person eligible household. The department is not required to provide, but shall seek practical methods for providing, a card with such picture to a person when such person is homebound or is a resident of a residential health care facility, or an inpatient psychiatric facility, or is expected to remain hospitalized for an extended period. The commissioner shall have the authority to define categories of recipients who are not required to have a photo identification card where such card would be limited, unnecessary or impracticable;

(c)   with respect to a person eligible for assistance under this title by the federal social security administration under an agreement between the department and the secretary of health, education and welfare pursuant to section three hundred sixty-three-b of this title issue a medical assistance identification card which shall be valid for periods determined by the local social services official, but not to exceed six months.

4.   Every applicant or recipient shall promptly advise the public welfare district of any change in his financial condition or income, number of wage earners and members in the family unit on such forms and in such manner as the department by regulation may prescribe. In the event that any applicant or recipient shall no longer be eligible for medical assistance, he shall promptly return his identification card issued pursuant to the provisions of this article to the public welfare district.

5.   (a) All continuing assistance under this title shall be reconsidered from time to time, or as frequently as may be required by the regulations of the department. After such further investigation as the social services official may deem necessary or the department may require, the assistance may be modified or withdrawn if it is found that the recipient's circumstances have changed sufficiently to warrant such action. The assistance may be cancelled for cause, and payment thereof may be suspended for cause for such periods as may be deemed necessary, subject to review by the department as provided in section twenty-two of this chapter.

(b)   The commissioner shall develop a simplified statewide recertification form for use in redetermining eligibility under this title. The form shall include requests only for such information that is:

(i)   reasonably necessary to determine continued eligibility for medical assistance under this title; and

(ii)   subject to change since the date of the recipient's initial application.

(c)   A personal interview with the recipient shall not be required as part of a redetermination of eligibility pursuant to this subdivision.

6.   Notwithstanding any other provisions of this chapter or other law, the investigations, decisions and actions required to be made or taken by a public welfare official pursuant to this section shall be made or taken only by the chief executive officer of the public welfare department of a public welfare district, or by an employee of such welfare department designated by such chief executive officer.

7.   Local social services districts shall be authorized, with the approval of the department, to station local social services employees at federal social security offices for the purpose of providing information and referral services relating to medical assistance to eligible persons.

8. Notwithstanding subdivision two of this section, information concerning income and resources of applicants for and recipients of medical assistance may be verified by matching client information with information contained in the wage reporting system established by section one hundred seventy-one-a of the tax law and, with similar systems operating in other geographically contiguous states, and, to the extent required by federal law with the non-wage income file maintained by the United States internal revenue service, with the beneficiary data exchange maintained by the United States department of health and human services, and with the unemployment insurance benefits file. Such matching shall provide for procedures which document significant inconsistent results of matching activities. Nothing in this section shall be construed to prohibit activities the department reasonably believes necessary to conform with federal requirements under section one thousand one hundred thirty-seven of the social security act.

9. (a) Every applicant for or recipient of medical assistance who has dependent children shall be informed in writing at the time of application and at the time of any action affecting his or her receipt of such assistance of the availability of:

(i) medical assistance without cash assistance under this title;

(ii) transitional medical assistance under paragraphs (a), (b) and (c) of subdivision four of section three hundred sixty-six of this title;

(iii) the expanded eligibility provisions for pregnant women and children under paragraphs (m), (n), (o), (p) and (q), (s) and (t) of subdivision four of section three hundred sixty-six of this title;

(iv) medical assistance for aged, blind or disabled persons under subdivision one of section three hundred sixty-six of this title;

(v) family health plus under section three hundred sixty-nine-ee of this article; and,

(vi) child health plus under title one-A of article twenty-five of the public health law.

(b) Every applicant for or recipient of medical assistance who has no dependent children shall be informed in writing at the time of application and at the time of any action affecting his or her receipt of such assistance of the availability of:

(i) medical assistance without cash assistance under this title;

(ii) the expanded eligibility provisions for pregnant women under paragraphs (m) and (o) of subdivision four of section three hundred sixty-six of this title;

(iii) medical assistance for aged, blind or disabled persons under subdivision one of section three hundred sixty-six of this title; and,

(iv) family health plus under section three hundred sixty-nine-ee of this article.

10.   As a condition for the provision of medical assistance for nursing facility services, the application of an individual for such assistance, including any recertification of eligibility for such assistance, shall disclose a description of any interest the individual or community spouse has in an annuity or similar financial instrument, regardless of whether the annuity is irrevocable or is treated as an asset. Such application or recertification form shall include a statement that the state of New York becomes a remainder beneficiary under such annuity or similar financial instrument by virtue of the provision of such medical assistance.

Added by Laws 1966, Ch. 256; **amended** by Laws 1966, Chs. 799, 801, Laws 1971, Ch. 110; Laws 1972, Ch. 532; Laws 1975, Ch. 198, Ch. 482; Laws 1978, Ch. 473, eff. July 11, 1978; Laws 1979, Ch. 60, eff. Oct. 9, 1979, adding subd. 1-a; Laws 1982, Ch. 34, eff. Apr. 14, 1982; **amended** by Laws 1990, Ch. 304, § 6, eff. Dec. 27, 1990; **amended** by Laws 1992, Ch. 41, § 88, eff. Jan. 1, 1993; **amended** by Laws 1995, Ch. 81, § 81, eff. June 20, 1995; **amended** by Laws 2002, Ch. 1, Part A, § 51, eff. Apr 1, 2003 and §§ 52 and 53, eff. April 1, 2002; Laws 2006, Ch. 57, §§ 50, 50-a (Part A), eff. Apr. 12, 2006.

§ 366-b.   Penalties for fraudulent practices.

1.   Any person who knowingly makes a false statement or representation, or who by deliberate concealment of any material fact, or by impersonation or other fraudulent device, obtains or attempts to obtain or aids or abets any person to obtain medical assistance to which he is not entitled, shall be guilty of a class A misdemeanor, unless such act constitutes a violation of a provision of the penal law of the state of New York, in which case he shall be punished in accordance with the penalties fixed by such law.

2.   Any person who, with intent to defraud, presents for allowance or payment any false or fraudulent claim for furnishing services or merchandise, or knowingly submits false information for the purpose of obtaining greater compensation than that to which he is legally entitled for furnishing services or merchandise, or knowingly submits false information for the purpose of obtaining authorization for furnishing services or merchandise under this title, shall be guilty of a class A misdemeanor, unless such act constitutes a violation of a provision of the penal law of the state of New York, in which case he shall be punished in accordance with the penalties fixed by such law.

Added by Laws 1970, Ch. 306, eff. May 1, 1970.

§ 366-c.   Treatment of income and resources of institutionalized persons.

1.   Notwithstanding any other provision of law to the contrary, in determining the eligibility for medical assistance of a person defined as an institutionalized spouse, the income and resources of such person and the person's community spouse shall be treated as provided in this section.

2.   (a) For purposes of this section an "institutionalized spouse" is a person in a medical institution or nursing facility (i) who is expected to remain in such

SSL

facility or institution for at least thirty consecutive days, or is receiving care, services and supplies pursuant to a waiver pursuant to subsection (c) of section nineteen hundred fifteen of the federal social security act; and (ii) who is married to a person who is not in a medical institution or nursing facility or is not receiving services pursuant to a waiver pursuant to subsection (c) of section nineteen hundred fifteen of the federal social security act.

(b)   For purposes of this section, a "community spouse" is a person who is the spouse of an "institutionalized spouse."

(c)   For the purposes of this section, "spousal share" means an amount equal to one-half of the total value of the resources of the community spouse and the institutionalized spouse, as of the beginning of the first continuous period of institutionalization beginning on or after the thirtieth day of September, nineteen hundred eighty-nine, to the extent that either, or both, have an ownership interest as of the date of the continuous period of institutionalization of the institutionalized spouse.

(d)   For the purposes of this section, "community spouse resource allowance" means the amount, if any, by which the greatest of the following amounts exceeds the total value of the resources otherwise available to the community spouse:

(i)   (A) prior to January first, nineteen hundred ninety-five, sixty thousand dollars, which shall be increased annually by the same percentage as the percentage increase in the federal consumer price index;

(B)   on and after January first, nineteen hundred ninety-five through June thirtieth, nineteen hundred ninety-nine, seventy-four thousand eight hundred twenty dollars or such greater amount as may be required under federal law;

(ii)   the lesser of sixty thousand dollars which shall be increased annually by the same percentage as the percentage increase in the federal consumer price index or the spousal share; or

(iii)   the amount established for support of the community spouse pursuant to a fair hearing under this section; or

(iv)   the amount transferred pursuant to court order for the support of the community spouse.

(e)   For purposes of this section, "resources" do not include resources excluded in determining eligibility for benefits under title XVI of the federal social security act, as defined by the commissioner consistent with federal law.

(f)   For purposes of this section, "family member" includes only a dependent or minor child, a dependent parent, or a dependent sibling of the institutionalized spouse or the community spouse, who resides with the community spouse.

(g)   For purposes of this section, "community spouse monthly income allowance" is the amount by which the minimum monthly maintenance needs allowance for the community spouse exceeds the monthly income otherwise available to the community spouse unless a greater amount is established pursuant to a fair hearing under this section or pursuant to court order for the support of the community spouse.

(h)   For purposes of this section, "minimum monthly maintenance needs allowance" is an amount equal to one-twelfth of the applicable percentage of the federal income official poverty line for a family of two, plus an excess shelter allowance, provided however, such amount shall not be less than one thousand five hundred dollars per month, nor exceed one thousand five hundred dollars (as adjusted in the discretion of the commissioner for changes in the federal consumer price index for calendar years after nineteen hundred eighty-nine) per month.

(i)   For purposes of this section, "family allowance for each family member" is an amount equal to the one-third times one-twelfth of the applicable percentage of the federal income official poverty line to a family of two, less the monthly income otherwise available to the family member.

(j)   For purposes of this section, the "applicable percentage of the federal income official poverty line" shall be one hundred twenty-two percent as of September thirtieth, nineteen hundred eighty-nine; one hundred thirty-three percent as of July first, nineteen hundred ninety-one and one hundred fifty percent on and after July first, nineteen hundred ninety-two.

(k)   For purposes of this section, the "excess shelter allowance" shall be the amount by which the community spouse's rent, mortgage, or condominium or cooperative maintenance fees, taxes and insurance, and utilities exceed thirty percent of one-twelfth of the applicable percentage of the federal income official poverty line for two persons.

3.   Unless established by a preponderance of the evidence to the contrary, the following presumptions shall apply in determining the availability of income to an institutionalized spouse in determining eligibility for medical assistance.

(a)   During any month in which an institutionalized spouse is in the institution or facility, no income of the community spouse shall be considered available to the institutionalized spouse except as provided in this subdivision; and

(b)   income solely in the name of the institutionalized spouse or the community spouse shall be considered available only to that spouse; and

(c)   income in the names of the institutionalized spouse and the community spouse shall be considered available one-half to each spouse; and

(d)   income in the names of the institutionalized spouse or the community spouse, or both, and also in the name of another person or persons, shall be considered available to each spouse in proportion to the spouse's interest or, if in the names of both spouses and no share is specified, one-half of the joint interest shall be considered available to each spouse; and

(e)   (i) income from a trust shall be considered available to each spouse in accordance with the provisions of the trust instrument, or, in absence of a specific

SSL

trust provision allocating income, in accordance with the provisions of paragraphs (a) through (d) of this subdivision; and

(ii)   additionally, income from a trust shall be attributed in accordance with the provisions of this title and title XIX of the federal social security act; and

(f)   income in which there is no instrument establishing ownership shall be considered to be available one-half to the institutionalized spouse and one-half to the community spouse.

4.   In determining the amount of income to be applied toward the cost of medical care, services and supplies of the institutionalized spouse, after the institutionalized spouse has been determined eligible for medical assistance, the following items shall be deducted from the monthly income of the institutionalized spouse in the following order:

(a)   a personal needs allowance;

(b)   a community spouse monthly income allowance;

(c)   a family allowance for each family member;

(d)   any expenses incurred for medical care, services or supplies and remedial care for the institutionalized spouse.

5.   The following rules apply in determining the resources of the institutionalized spouse and the community spouse in establishing eligibility for medical assistance:

(a)   All resources, including resources required to be considered in determining eligibility pursuant to paragraph (c) of subdivision five of section three hundred sixty-six of this title, held by either the institutionalized spouse or the community spouse or both shall be considered available to the institutionalized spouse to the extent that the value of the resources exceeds the community spouse resource allowance.

(b)   An institutionalized spouse shall not be ineligible for medical assistance by reason of excess resources determined under paragraph (a) of this subdivision, if the institutionalized spouse executes an assignment of support from the community spouse in favor of the social services district and the department, or the institutionalized spouse is unable to execute such assignment due to physical or mental impairment, or to deny assistance would create an undue hardship, as defined by the commissioner.

(c)   After the month in which the institutionalized spouse has been determined eligible for medical assistance during a continuous period of institutionalization, no resource of the community spouse shall be considered available to the institutionalized spouse.

6.   Notwithstanding paragraph (c) of subdivision five of section three hundred sixty-six of this title and after an institutionalized spouse is determined eligible for medical assistance, transfers of resources by the institutionalized spouse to the community spouse shall be permitted to the extent that the transfers are solely

to or for the benefit of the community spouse and do not exceed the value of the community spouse resource allowance. Such transfers must be made as soon as practicable after the determination of eligibility.

7.   (a) At the beginning or after the commencement of a continuous period of institutionalization, either spouse may request an assessment of the total value of their resources or a determination of the community spouse monthly income allowance, the amount of the family allowance, or the method of computing the amount of the family allowance, or the method of computing the amount of the community spouse income allowance.

(b)   (i) Upon receipt of a request pursuant to paragraph (a) of this subdivision together with all relevant documentation of the resources of both spouses, the social services district shall assess and document the total value of the spouses' resources and provide each spouse with a copy of the assessment and the documentation upon which it was based. If the request is not part of an application for medical assistance benefits, the social services district may charge a fee for the assessment which is related to the cost of preparing and copying the assessment and documentation which fee may not exceed twenty-five dollars.

(ii)   The social services district shall also notify each requesting spouse of the community spouse monthly income allowance, of the amount, if any, of the family allowances, and of the method of computing the amount of the community spouse monthly income allowance.

(c)   The social services district shall also provide to the spouse a notice of the right to a fair hearing at the time of provision of the information requested under paragraph (a) of this subdivision or after a determination of eligibility for medical assistance. Such notice shall be in the form prescribed or approved by the commissioner and include a statement advising the spouse of the right to a fair hearing under this section.

8.   (a) If, after a determination on an application for medical assistance has been made, either spouse is dissatisfied with the determination of the community spouse monthly allowance, the amount of monthly income otherwise available to the community spouse, the computation of the spousal share of resources, the attribution of resources or the determination of the community spouse's resource allocation, the spouse may request a fair hearing to dispute such determination. Such hearing shall be held within thirty days of the request therefor.

(b)   If either spouse establishes that the community spouse needs income above the level established by the social services district as the minimum monthly maintenance needs allowance, based upon exceptional circumstances which result in significant financial distress (as defined by the commissioner in regulations), the department shall substitute an amount adequate to provide additional necessary income from the income otherwise available to the institutionalized spouse.

(c)   If either spouse establishes that income generated by the community spouse resource allowance, established by the social services district, is inadequate to raise the community spouse's income to the minimum monthly maintenance needs allowance, the department shall establish a resource allowance for the spousal share of the institutionalized spouse adequate to provide such minimum monthly maintenance needs allowance.

Added by Laws 1989, Ch. 558, § 2, eff. Oct. 1, 1989. **Amended** by Laws 1995, Ch. 81, §§ 82 -83, eff. June 20, 1995; **amended** by L. 1997, Chs. 145, 162, 194, 211, and 264, causing reference to June thirtieth in subd. (2)(d)(i)(B) to be deemed reference to Aug. 1, 1997, eff. July 23, 1997, deemed to be in full force and effect Apr. 1, 1997; **amended** by L. 1997, Ch. 433, § 6, eff. Aug. 20, 1997.

§ 366-d.   Medical assistance provider; prohibited practices.

1.   Definitions. As used in this section, "medical assistance provider" means any person, firm, partnership, group, association, fiduciary, employer or representative thereof or other entity who is furnishing care, services or supplies under title eleven of article five of this chapter.

2.   No medical assistance provider shall:

(a)   solicit, receive, accept or agree to receive or accept any payment or other consideration in any form from another person to the extent such payment or other consideration is given: (i) for the referral of services for which payment is made under title eleven of article five of this chapter; or (ii) to purchase, lease or order any good, facility, service or item for which payment is made under title eleven of article five of this chapter; or

(b)   offer, agree to give or give any payment or other consideration in any form to another person to the extent such payment or other consideration is given: (i) for the referral of services for which payment is made under title eleven of article five of this chapter; or (ii) to purchase, lease or order any good, facility, service or item for which payment is made under title eleven of article five of this chapter;

(c)   as used in this section "person" shall have the meaning set forth in subdivision seven of section 10.00 of the penal law.

(d)   This subdivision shall not apply to any activity specifically exempt by federal statute or federal regulations promulgated thereunder.

3.   Any medical assistance provider who violates the provisions of this section is guilty of a misdemeanor punishable by:

(a)   a term of imprisonment in accordance with the penal law; or

(b)   a fine of not less than five hundred dollars nor more than ten thousand dollars; or

(c)   if the defendant has obtained money or property through a violation of the provisions of this section, a fine in an amount, fixed by the court, not to exceed double the amount of the defendant's gain from a violation of such provisions. In such event, the provisions of subdivision three of section 80.00 of the penal law shall be applicable to the sentence; or (d)　both the imprisonment and the fine.

4.　Any medical assistance provider who violates the provisions of this section and thereby obtains money or property having a value in excess of seven thousand five hundred dollars shall be guilty of a class e felony.

Added by Laws 1992, Ch. 41, § 108, eff. Apr. 2, 1992; **amended** by Laws 1995, Ch. 81, § 85 -85-a, eff. July 1, 1995; **amended** by Laws 1998, Ch. 2, § 35, eff. Nov. 1, 1998.

§ 366-e.　Certified home health agency Medicare billing.

(a)　Certified home health agencies shall bill under title xviii of the federal social security act for services provided to all patients eligible for such program who, as defined by federal law and regulations, are:

(i) homebound;

(ii) receiving skilled services; and

(iii) are receiving such services on an intermittent basis. The department, in consultation with the department of health and representatives of certified home health agencies with demonstrated ability to maximize Medicare revenue, may promulgate regulations to implement this subdivision. Nothing contained herein shall be construed to prohibit agencies from billing for medical assistance reimbursement for eligible services provided to such patients which are not covered under title xviii of the federal social security act meeting the standards established by the department pursuant to this section. Patient cases that meet the criteria established pursuant to this subdivision, where coverage has been denied under title xviii of the federal social security act for the cost of care provided by a certified home health agency shall be referred by such agency to an organization pursuant to subdivision (b) of this section.

(b)　The commissioner shall enter into agreements with persons or entities to provide for representation of persons meeting the criteria specified in subdivision (a) of this section who have been denied reimbursement, under title xviii of the federal social security act, for services provided by a certified home health agency.

Added by Laws 1995, Ch. 81, § 86, eff. June 20, 1995.

§ 366-f.　Persons acting in concert with a medical assistance provider; prohibited practices.

1.　No person acting in concert with a medical assistance provider shall, with intent to defraud:

(a)　solicit, receive, accept or agree to receive or accept any payment or other consideration in any form from another person to the extent such payment or other consideration is given (i) for the referral of services for which payment is made

SSL

under this title or (ii) to purchase, lease or order any good, facility, service or item for which payment is made under this title; or

(b)   offer, agree to give or give any payment or other consideration in any form to another person to the extent such payment or other consideration is given (i) for the referral of services for which payment is made under this title; or (ii) to purchase, lease or order any good, facility, service or item for which payment is made under this title;

(c)   this subdivision shall not apply to any activity specifically exempt by federal statute or federal regulations promulgated thereunder.

2.   As used in this section, "person" shall have the meaning set forth in subdivision seven of section 10.00 of the penal law.

3.   A violation of the provisions of this section is a misdemeanor punishable by:

(a)   a term of imprisonment in accordance with the penal law; or

(b)   a fine of not more than ten thousand dollars; or

(c)   if the defendant has obtained money or property through a violation of the provisions of this section, a fine in an amount, fixed by the court, not to exceed double the amount of the defendant's gain from a violation of such provisions. In such event, the provisions of subdivision three of section 80.00 of the penal law shall be applicable to the sentence; or

(d)   both the imprisonment and the fine.

4.   Any such person who violates the provisions of this section and thereby obtains money or property having a value in excess of seven thousand five hundred dollars shall be guilty of a class E felony.

     Added by Laws 1998, Ch. 2, § 36-a, eff. Nov. 1, 1998.

§ 366-g.   Newborn enrollment for medical assistance.

1.   Each hospital licensed under article twenty-eight of the public health law shall report to the department of health, or such other entity designated by the department of health, in such format as the department of health shall provide, each live birth of a child to a woman receiving medical assistance, or services under the prenatal care assistance program under title two of article twenty-five of the public health law, on the date of the birth. Such reports shall be made within five business days of the birth and shall include data identifying the mother and child.

2.   Each hospital licensed under article twenty-eight of the public health law, upon discharge after delivery of a child, shall notify, in plain language and in such manner as the department of health shall provide, each mother in receipt of medical assistance that such child is deemed to be enrolled in the medical assistance program regardless of his or her receipt of a medical assistance

identification card or client identification number or other proof of the child's eligibility, and may access care, services and supplies in accordance with this title and other applicable laws.

3. The commissioner of health shall establish a procedure to ensure that every child born to a mother who is receiving medical assistance, or services under the prenatal care assistance program under title two of article twenty-five of the public health law, on the date of the child's birth is automatically enrolled in the medical assistance program, assigned a client identification number, and issued an active medical assistance identification card, as soon as possible, but in no event later than ten business days from the receipt of the report required pursuant to subdivision one of this section.

4. (a) Consistent with the provisions of section three hundred sixty-six of this title, a child under the age of one year whose mother is receiving medical assistance, or services under the prenatal care assistance program under title two of article twenty-five of the public health law, or whose mother was receiving such assistance or services on the date of the child's birth, who is presented to a medical assistance provider, as defined in section three hundred sixty-six-d of this title, for care, shall be deemed to be enrolled in the medical assistance program regardless of the issuance of a medical assistance identification card or client identification number to such child or other proof of the child's eligibility.

(b) A medical assistance provider that furnishes medical assistance as defined in section three hundred sixty-five-a of this title, to a child described in paragraph (a) of this subdivision shall be eligible for medical assistance reimbursement for such assistance regardless of whether the child has been issued a medical assistance identification card, client identification number or other proof of eligibility. Reimbursement under this section shall be in accordance with the provisions of this title, including, as appropriate, section 364-j of this title and all other applicable laws, rules, regulations and administrative directions.

Added by Laws 1999, Ch. 412 Part G, § 1, eff. July 1, 2000.

§ **366-h. Automated system; established.**

Notwithstanding any inconsistent provision of law or regulation, the commissioner of health shall, as soon as practicable, establish an automated system to ensure that persons who meet the criteria for receipt of medical assistance benefits under paragraph (a) or (c) of subdivision four of section three hundred sixty-six of this title shall remain enrolled in the medical assistance program without interruption and receive the benefits set forth according to paragraph (a) or (c) of subdivision four of section three hundred sixty-six of this title. Pending implementation of such automated system, such commissioner shall, in consultation with the office of temporary and disability assistance, undertake and continue efforts to educate local departments of social services about the measures they must take to ensure that medical assistance benefits are provided to persons eligible for such benefits under subdivision four of section three hundred sixty-six of this title. A report on the progress to implement such automated system shall be submitted annually to the governor and the legislature by the commissioner of health.

> **Added** by Laws 2000, Ch. 57 Part B, § 7, eff. July 1, 2000.

§ 367. Authorization for hospital care.

1. Except as permitted by the regulations of the department, so far as practicable, no patient shall be admitted to a hospital as a public charge under this title or this chapter without the prior authorization of the social services official responsible for authorizing such care. If a patient is admitted without prior authorization of the appropriate social services official and the hospital has reason to believe that the patient will be unable to pay for his care, and is or may be eligible for care under this title or this chapter, it may send a notice containing a report of the facts of the case to such social services official who shall promptly advise the patient or his representative of his right to apply for medical assistance and, if eligible, to have the cost of his care paid for under this chapter. If the identity of the social services official responsible for authorizing such care is not known by the hospital, such notice shall be sent to the commissioner of the social services district in which the hospital is located who shall make an investigation to determine which social services district may be responsible for authorizing such care and appropriately notify such district, which shall advise such patient or his representative of his right to apply, and if eligible to have the cost of his care paid for under this chapter. The cost of care of an eligible patient shall be a charge against a social services district only when authorized by the commissioner of social services of such district, which authorization shall not be withheld from any patient eligible for such care pursuant to this title and the regulations of the department.

2. Notwithstanding any inconsistent provision of law, the social services official responsible for authorizing hospital or health related services shall withhold payment for such services upon the certification of the commissioner of health that payment for such care is unauthorized under the medical assistance program.

> **Added** by Laws 1966, Ch. 256; **amended** by Laws 1968, Ch. 979; Laws 1971, Ch. 110; Laws 1976, Ch. 76, eff. Mar. 7, 1976, Ch. 940, eff. July 27, 1976.

§ 367-a   Payments; insurance

1. (a) Any inconsistent provision of this chapter or other law notwithstanding, no assignment of the claim of any supplier of medical assistance shall be valid and enforceable as against any social services district or the department, and any payment with respect to any medical assistance shall be made to the person, institution, state department or agency or municipality supplying such medical assistance at rates established by the appropriate social services district

and contained in its approved local medical plan, except as otherwise permitted or required by applicable federal and state provisions, including the regulations of the department; provided, however, that for those districts for whom the department has assumed payment responsibilities pursuant to section three hundred sixty-seven-b of this chapter, rates shall be established by the department, except as otherwise required by applicable provisions of federal or state law. A social services official may apply to the department for local variations in rates to be applicable, upon approval by the department, to recipients for whom such district is responsible. Claims for payment shall be made in such form and manner as the department shall determine.

(b) Where an applicant for or recipient of public assistance or medical assistance has health insurance in force, is enrolled in a group health insurance plan or group health plan covering care and other medical benefits provided under this title, payment or part-payment of the premium, co-insurance, any deductible amounts and other cost-sharing obligations for such insurance may also be made when deemed cost-effective pursuant to the regulations of the department.

(c) Any inconsistent provisions of this title or other law notwithstanding and to the extent that federal financial participation is available therefor and in accordance with the regulations of the commissioner, payment of the premium for coverage under a group health insurance plan or group health plan may be made under the medical assistance program on behalf of a person not otherwise entitled to public assistance or medical assistance if the social services official determines that the savings in expenditures to the program as a result of such coverage are likely to exceed the amount of the premiums paid and such person has:

(i) income (as determined in accordance with the methodology used to determine eligibility for benefits under the federal supplemental security income program) in an amount less than or equal to one hundred per cent of the federal income official poverty line (as defined and annually revised by the federal office of management and budget) applicable to the person's family size;

(ii) resources (as determined in accordance with the methodology used to determine eligibility for benefits under the federal supplemental security income program) less than or equal to twice the maximum amount an individual is permitted to have to obtain benefits under the federal supplemental security income program; and

(iii) coverage available under a group health insurance plan or an employer-based group health plan provided pursuant to title XXII of the federal public health services act, section 4980B of the federal internal revenue code of 1986, or title VI of the employee retirement income security act of 1974.

(d) (i) Amounts payable under this title for medical assistance for items and services provided to eligible persons who are also beneficiaries under part A of title XVIII of the federal social security act and items and services provided to qualified medicare beneficiaries under part A of title XVIII of the federal social security act shall not be less than the amount of any deductible and co-insurance liability of such eligible persons or for which such eligible persons or such qualified medicare beneficiaries would be liable under federal law were they not eligible for medical assistance or were they not qualified medicare beneficiaries with respect to such benefits under such part A.

(ii)   Amounts payable under this title for medical assistance for items and services provided to eligible persons who are also beneficiaries under part B of title XVIII of the federal social security act and items and services provided to qualified medicare beneficiaries under part B of title XVIII of the federal social security act shall not be less than the amount of any deductible liability of such eligible persons or for which such eligible persons or such qualified medicare beneficiaries would be liable under federal law were they not eligible for medical assistance or were they not qualified medicare beneficiaries with respect to such benefits under such part B.

(iii)   As amended Laws 2003, Ch. 63, Laws 2005, chs 12 and 48When payment under part B of title XVIII of the federal social security act for items and services provided to eligible persons who are also beneficiaries under part B of title XVIII of the federal social security act and for items and services provided to qualified medicare beneficiaries under part B of title XVIII of the federal social security act would exceed the amount that otherwise would be made under this title if provided to an eligible person other than a person who is also a beneficiary under part B or is a qualified medicare beneficiary, the amount payable under this title shall be twenty percent of the amount of any co-insurance liability of such eligible persons pursuant to federal law were they not eligible for medical assistance or were they not qualified medicare beneficiaries with respect to such benefits under such part B; provided, however, amounts payable under this title for items and services provided to eligible persons who are also beneficiaries under part B or to qualified medicare beneficiaries by an ambulance service under the authority of an operating certificate issued pursuant to article thirty of the public health law, a psychologist licensed under article one hundred fifty-three of the education law, or a facility under the authority of an operating certificate issued pursuant to article sixteen, thirty-one or thirty-two of the mental hygiene law and with respect to outpatient hospital and clinic items and services provided by a facility under the authority of an operating certificate issued pursuant to article twenty-eight of the public health law, shall not be less than the amount of any co-insurance liability of such eligible persons or such qualified medicare beneficiaries, or for which such eligible persons or such qualified medicare beneficiaries would be liable under federal law were they not eligible for medical assistance or were they not qualified medicare beneficiaries with respect to such benefits under part B.

(iii)   As amended Laws 2003, Ch. 63, Laws 2006, Ch. 109, §1 (Part C)When payment under part B of title XVIII of the federal social security act for items and services provided to eligible persons who are also beneficiaries under part B of title XVIII of the federal social security act and for items and services provided to qualified medicare beneficiaries under part B of title XVIII of the federal social security act would exceed the amount that otherwise would be made under this title if provided to an eligible person other than a person who is also a beneficiary under part B or is a qualified medicare beneficiary, the amount payable under this title shall be twenty percent of the amount of any co-insurance liability of such eligible persons pursuant to federal law were they not eligible for medical assistance or were they not qualified medicare beneficiaries with respect to such benefits under such part B; provided, however, amounts payable under this title for items and services provided to eligible persons who are also beneficiaries under part B or to qualified medicare beneficiaries by an ambulance service under the authority of an operating certificate issued pursuant to article thirty of the public health law, a psychologist licensed under article one hundred fifty-three of the education law and a psychiatrist licensed under article one hundred thirty-one of the education law, or a facility under the authority of an operating certificate issued pursuant to article sixteen, thirty-one or thirty-two of the mental hygiene law and with respect to outpatient hospital and clinic items and services provided by a facility under the authority of an operating certificate issued pursuant to article twenty-eight of the public health law, shall not be less than the amount of any co-insurance liability of such eligible persons or such qualified medicare beneficiaries, or for which such eligible persons or such qualified medicare beneficiaries would be liable under federal law were they not eligible for medical assistance or were they not qualified medicare beneficiaries with respect to such benefits under part B.

(e)   Amounts payable under this title for medical assistance in the form of clinic services pursuant to article twenty-eight of the public health law and article sixteen of the mental hygiene law provided to eligible persons who are also beneficiaries under part b of title xviii of the federal social security act and who are also diagnosed with a disability shall not be less than the approved medical assistance payment level less the amount payable under part b.

2.   (a) Any inconsistent provision of this chapter notwithstanding, provision for medical care and other medical benefits available under this title may be made, in whole or in part, either under this title or other appropriate provisions of this chapter, through insurance or other prepaid plans, in accordance with the regulations of the department.

(b)   Any inconsistent provision of this chapter or other law notwithstanding, upon furnishing assistance under this title to any applicant or recipient of medical assistance, the local social services district or the department shall be subrogated, to the extent of the expenditures by such district or department for medical care furnished, to any rights such person may have to medical support or third party reimbursement. For purposes of this section, the term medical support shall mean the right to support specified as support for the purpose of medical care by a court or administrative order. The right of subrogation does not attach to insurance benefits paid or provided under any health insurance policy prior to the receipt of written notice of the exercise of subrogation rights by the carrier issuing such insurance, nor shall such right of subrogation attach to any benefits which may be claimed by a social services official or the department, by agreement or other established procedure, directly from an insurance carrier. No right of subrogation to insurance benefits available under any health insurance policy shall be enforceable unless written notice of the exercise of such subrogation right is received by the carrier within two years from the date services for which benefits are provided under the policy or contract are rendered. The local social services district or the department shall also notify the carrier when the exercise of subrogation rights has terminated because a person is no longer receiving assistance under this title. Such carrier shall establish mechanisms to maintain the confidentiality of all individually identifiable information or records. Such carrier shall limit the use of such information or record to the specific purpose for which such disclosure is made, and shall not further disclose such information or records.

(c)   In accordance with regulations of the department and to the extent authorized by federal law and regulation, the social services district is authorized to retain, in addition to amounts retained as repayment for its share of the costs of medical assistance provided, a portion of the federal share of the amount collected as medical support or third party benefits assigned under paragraph (f) of subdivision four of section three hundred sixty-six of this article, when such district, or other governmental agency pursuant to an agreement with such district, has collected such medical support or third party benefits on behalf of a person receiving medical assistance whose rights to medical support or third party benefits have been assigned to the state or to the appropriate social services official. Where more than one district has been involved in enforcing or collecting such amounts, the federal incentive shall be apportioned among each such district in accordance with the regulations of the department.

3.   (a) Payment of premiums for enrolling qualified disabled and working individuals and qualified medicare beneficiaries under Part A of title XVIII of the federal social security act and for enrolling such beneficiaries and eligible recipients of public assistance under part B of title XVIII of the federal social security act, together with the costs of the applicable co-insurance and deductible amounts on behalf of such beneficiaries, and recipients, and premiums under section 1839 of the federal social security act for persons who would be qualified medicare beneficiaries except that their incomes exceed one hundred percent of the federal income poverty line applicable to the person's family size but, in calendar years nineteen hundred ninety-three and nineteen hundred ninety-four, is less than one hundred ten percent of such poverty line and, in calendar year beginning in nineteen hundred ninety-five, is less than one hundred twenty percent of such poverty line shall be made and the cost thereof borne by the state or by the state and social services districts, respectively, in accordance with the regulations of the department, provided, however, that the share of the cost to be borne by a social services district, if any, shall in no event exceed the proportionate share borne by such district with respect to other expenditures under this title. Moreover, if the director of the budget approves, payment of

premiums for enrolling persons who have been determined to be eligible for medical assistance only may be made and the cost thereof borne or shared pursuant to this subdivision.

(b) For purposes of this subdivision, "qualified medicare beneficiaries" are those persons who are entitled to hospital insurance benefits under part A of title XVIII of the federal social security act, whose income does not exceed one hundred percent of the official federal poverty line applicable to the person's family size and whose resources do not exceed twice the maximum amount of resources a person may have in order to qualify for benefits under the federal supplemental security income program of title XVI of the federal social security act, as determined for purposes of such program.

(c) (1) For purposes of this subdivision, "qualified disabled and working individuals" are individuals who are not otherwise eligible for medical assistance and:

(i) who are entitled to enroll for hospital insurance benefits under section 1818A of part A of title XVIII of the federal social security act;

(ii) whose income does not exceed two hundred percent of the official federal poverty line applicable to the person's family size; and

(iii) whose resources do not exceed twice the maximum amount of resources that an individual or a couple, in the case of a married individual, may have and obtain federal supplemental security income benefits under title XVI of the federal social security act, as determined for purposes of that program.

(2) For purposes of this paragraph, income and resources are determined by the same methodology as is used for determining eligibility under the federal supplemental security income benefits under title XVI of the federal social security act.

(d) [Expires and repealed Dec 31, 2008]

(1) Beginning April first, two thousand two and to the extent that federal financial participation is available at a one hundred percent federal Medical assistance percentage and subject to sections 1933 and 1902(a)(10)(E)(iv) of the federal social security act, medical assistance shall be available for full payment of medicare part B premiums for individuals (referred to as qualified individuals 1) who are entitled to hospital insurance benefits under part A of title XVIII of the federal social security act and whose income exceeds the income level established by the state and is at least one hundred twenty percent, but less than one hundred thirty-five percent, of the federal poverty level, for a family of the size involved and who are not otherwise eligible for medical assistance under the state plan;

(2) Beginning April first, two thousand two and to the extent that federal financial participation is available at a one hundred percent federal Medical assistance percentage and subject to sections 1933 and 1902(a)(10)(E)(iv) of the federal social security act, medical assistance shall be available for payment of

that portion of the medicare part B premium increase that is attributable to the operation of the amendments made by section 4611(e)(3) of the balanced budget act of 1997, for individuals (referred to as qualified individuals 2) who are entitled to hospital insurance benefits under part A of title XVIII of the federal social security act and whose income exceeds the income level established by the state and is at least one hundred thirty-five percent, but less than one hundred seventy-five percent, of the federal poverty level, for a family of the size involved and who are not otherwise eligible for medical assistance under the state plan;

(3)   Premium payments for the individuals described in subparagraphs one and two of this paragraph will be one hundred percent federally funded up to the amount of the federal allotment. The department shall discontinue enrollment into the program when the part B premium payments made pursuant to such paragraphs meet the yearly federal allotment.

(4)   The commissioner of health shall develop a simplified application form, consistent with federal law, for payments pursuant to this section. The commissioner of health, in cooperation with the office for the aging, shall publicize the availability of such payments to medicare beneficiaries.

4.   No social services district shall make final payments pursuant to title XIX of the federal social security act for benefits available under title XVIII of such act without documentation that title XVIII claims have been filed and denied.

5.   (a) When medical care, services and supplies are furnished an eligible person on behalf of a social services district under this title, such social services district is authorized to utilize any appropriate organization as a fiscal intermediary to audit and make payment for such district's share of the cost of such care, services and supplies.

(b)   To carry out the purposes of paragraph (a), the department, on behalf of itself and any of the social services districts, may enter into agreements with appropriate organizations to act as fiscal intermediaries.

6.   (a) [Expires and repealed March 31, 2009] Notwithstanding any inconsistent provision of law, payment for claims for services as specified in paragraph (d) of this subdivision furnished to eligible persons under this title, subject to paragraph (b) of this subdivision shall be reduced in accordance with the provisions of paragraph (c) of this subdivision by an amount not to exceed the maximum amount authorized by federal law and regulations as a co-payment amount, which co-payment amount the provider of such services may charge the recipient, provided, however, no provider may deny such services to an individual eligible for services based on the individual's inability to pay the co-payment amount.

(b)   [Expires and repealed March 31, 2009] Co-payments shall apply to all eligible persons for the services defined in paragraph (d) of this subdivision with the exception of:

(i)   individuals under twenty-one years of age;

(ii) pregnant women;

(iii) individuals who are inpatients in a medical facility who have been required to spend all of their income for medical care, except their personal needs allowance or residents of community based residential facilities licensed by the office of mental health or the office of mental retardation and developmental disabilities who have been required to spend all of their income, except their personal needs allowance;

(iv) individuals enrolled in health maintenance organizations or other entities which provide comprehensive health services, or other managed care programs for services covered by such programs, except that such persons, other than persons otherwise exempted from co-payments pursuant to subparagraphs (i), (ii), (iii) and (v) of this paragraph, and other than those persons enrolled in a managed long term care program, shall be subject to co-payments as described in subparagraph (v) of paragraph (d) of this subdivision; and

(v) any other individuals required to be excluded by federal law or regulations.

(c) [Until March 31, 2009]

(i) Co-payments charged pursuant to this subdivision for non-institutional services shall not exceed the following table, provided, however, that the department may establish standard co-payments for services based upon the average or typical payment for that service:

State's payment	Maximum co-payment for the services chargeable to recipient
$10 or less	$.50
$10.01 to $25	$1.00
$25.01 to $50	$2.00
$50.01 or more	$3.00

co-payments charged pursuant to this subdivision for each discharge for inpatient care shall be twenty-five dollars.

(iii) Notwithstanding any other provision of this paragraph, co-payments charged for each generic prescription drug dispensed shall be one dollar and for each brand name prescription drug dispensed shall be three dollars.

(c) [Eff. March 31, 2009] Co-payments charged pursuant to this subdivision shall not exceed the following table:

State's payment for the services	Maximum co-payment chargeable to recipient
$10 or less	$.50
$10.01 to $25	$1.00
$25.01 to $50	$2.00
$50.01 or more	$3.00

SSL

(d) [Expires and repealed March 31, 2009] Co-payments shall apply to the following services, subject to such exceptions for subcategories of these services as recognized by the commissioner in regulations, provided in accordance with section three hundred sixty-five-a of this article and the regulations of the department, to the extent permitted by title XIX of the federal social security act:

(i) in-patient care in a general hospital, as defined in subdivision ten of section twenty-eight hundred one of the public health law;

(ii) out-patient hospital and clinic services except for mental health services, mental retardation and developmental disability services, alcohol and substance abuse services and methadone maintenance services;

(iii) home health services, including services provided under the long term home health care program, provided however, home health providers shall not require employees providing services in the home to collect the co-payment amount;

(iv) sickroom supplies;

(v) drugs, excepting psychotropic drugs and drugs with FDA approved indications for the treatment of tuberculosis as specified by the department and those drugs intended for use by residents of adult carefacilities licensed by the department of health who have been requiredto spend all of their income, except their personal needs allowance;

(vi) clinical laboratory services;

(vii) x-rays;

(viii) emergency room services provided for non-urgent or non-emergency medical care, provided however, co-payments shall not be required for emergency services or family planning services and supplies;

(e) [Expires and repealed March 31, 2009] In the period from January first, nineteen hundred ninety-three to March thirty-first, nineteen hundred ninety-three no recipient shall be required to pay more than a total of fifty dollars in co-payments required by this subdivision for drugs, nor shall reductions in payments as a result of such co-payments exceed fifty dollars for any recipient.

(f) [Expires and repealed March 31, 2009]

(i) In the year commencing April first, nineteen hundred ninety-three and for each year thereafter, and ending in the year concluding on March thirty-first, two thousand five, no recipient shall be required to pay more than a total of one hundred dollars in co-payments required by this subdivision, nor shall reductions in payments as a result of such co-payments exceed one hundred dollars for any recipient.

(ii) In the year commencing April first, two thousand five and for each year thereafter, no recipient shall be required to pay more than a total of two hundred dollars in co-payments required by this subdivision, nor shall reductions in payments as a result of such co-payments exceed two hundred dollars for any recipient.

(g) [Expires and repealed March 31, 2009] The commissioner shall promptly:

(i) promulgate a regulation making it an unacceptable practice under the medical assistance program for a provider to deny services to an individual eligible for services based on the individual's inability to pay the co-pay amount required by this subdivision;

(ii) establish and maintain a toll-free hotline which may be used to report a violation of the regulation promulgated pursuant to subparagraph (i) of this paragraph; and

(iii) provide notice to all recipients summarizing their rights and obligations under this subdivision.

7. (a) Every manufacturer or wholesaler of drugs, prescriptions or poisons registered under the provisions of section sixty-eight hundred eight of the education law, shall, upon request of the department for any information pertaining to wholesale prices charged to pharmacists for any drugs available under the medical assistance program, make the requested information available to the department on a monthly basis, or such other periodic basis as the department shall request.

(b) The department shall provide for financial arrangements with any manufacturer or wholesaler of drugs, prescriptions or poisons as may be necessary to reimburse such manufacturer or wholesaler for its actual and necessary costs included in furnishing the requested information.

(c) Any information obtained pursuant to the provisions of this subdivision shall not be made available for public inspection or copying under the provisions of article six of the public officers law. The department shall not disclose such information to any person, firm, department or agency, except any state agency or department as may be necessary for the administration of the medical assistance program under the provisions of this chapter or any other law.

(d) Notwithstanding any inconsistent provision of law, if a manufacturer (as defined under section 1927 of the federal social security act) has entered into a rebate agreement with the department or with the federal secretary of health and human services on behalf of the department under section 1927 of the federal social security act, the department shall reimburse for covered outpatient drugs which are dispensed under the medical assistance program to all persons in receipt of medical assistance benefits as a result of their eligibility having been established under subparagraph one or nine of subdivision one of section three hundred sixty-six of this title, only pursuant to the terms of the rebate agreement between the department and such manufacturer; provided, however, that any agreement between the department and a manufacturer entered into before August first, nineteen hundred ninety-one, shall be deemed to have been entered into on April first, nineteen hundred ninety-one; and provided further, that if a manufacturer has not entered into an agreement with the department before August first, nineteen hundred ninety-one, such agreement shall not be effective until April

SSL

first, nineteen hundred ninety-two, unless such agreement provides that rebates will be retroactively calculated as if the agreement had been in effect on April first, nineteen hundred ninety-one. The rebate agreement between such manufacturer and the department shall utilize for single source drugs and innovator multiple source drugs the identical formula used to determine the basic rebate for federal financial participation single source drugs and innovator multiple source drugs, pursuant to paragraph one of subdivision (c) of section 1927 of the federal social security act, to determine the amount of the rebate pursuant to this paragraph. The rebate agreement between such manufacturer and the department shall utilize for non-innovator multiple source drugs the identical formula used to determine the basic rebate for federal financial participation non-innovator multiple source drugs, pursuant to paragraphs three and four of subdivision (c) of section 1927 of the federal social security act, to determine the amount of the rebate pursuant to this paragraph. The terms and conditions of such rebate agreement with respect to periodic payment of the rebate, provision of information by the department, audits, manufacturer provision of information verification of surveys, penalties, confidentiality of information, and length of the agreement shall apply to drugs of the manufacturer dispensed under the medical assistance program to all persons in receipt of medical assistance benefits as a result of their eligibility having been established under subparagraph one or nine of subdivision one of section three hundred sixty-six of this title. The department in providing utilization data to a manufacturer (as provided for under section 1927.4(b)(1)(A) of the federal social security act) shall provide such data by zip code, if requested, for drugs covered under a rebate agreement.

8.   No government agency shall purchase, pay for, or make reimbursement or grants-in-aid for any service in a residential treatment facility for children and youth unless at the time such service was provided, the residential treatment facility for children and youth possessed a valid operating certificate authorizing such service. Notwithstanding any inconsistent provision of law, no government agency shall make payments pursuant to this title or title nineteen of the federal social security act to a residential treatment facility for children and youth for service to a person whose need for care and treatment in such a facility was not certified pursuant to section 9.51 of the mental hygiene law.

9.   [Until March 31, 2009] Notwithstanding any inconsistent provision of law or regulation to the contrary, for those drugs which may not be dispensed without a prescription as required by section sixty-eight hundred ten of the education law and for which payment is authorized pursuant to paragraph (g) of subdivision two of section three hundred sixty-five-a of this title, payments under this title shall be made at the following amounts:

(a)   for drugs provided by medical practitioners and claimed separately by the practitioners, the actual cost of the drugs to the practitioners; and

(b)   for drugs dispensed by pharmacies:

(i)   if the drug dispensed is a multiple source prescription drug for which an upper limit has been set by the federal centers for medicare and medicaid services, an amount equal to the specific upper limit set by such federal agency for the multiple source prescription drug, and

(ii) if the drug dispensed is a multiple source prescription drug or a brand-name prescription drug for which no specific upper limit has been set by such federal agency, the lower of the estimated acquisition cost of such drug to pharmacies, or the dispensing pharmacy's usual and customary price charged to the general public. For sole and multiple source brand name drugs, estimated acquisition cost means the average wholesale price of a prescription drug based upon the package size dispensed from, as reported by the prescription drug pricing service used by the department, less thirteen and twenty-five hundredths of one percent thereof, and updated monthly by the department; or, for a specialized HIV pharmacy, as defined in paragraph (f) of this subdivision, acquisition cost means the average wholesale price of a prescription drug based upon the package size dispensed from, as reported by the prescription drug pricing service used by the department, less twelve percent thereof, and updated monthly by the department. For multiple source generic drugs, estimated acquisition cost means the lower of the average wholesale price of a prescription drug based on the package size dispensed from, as reported by the prescription drug pricing service used by the department, less twenty percent thereof, or the maximum acquisition cost, if any, established pursuant to paragraph (e) of this subdivision; or, for a specialized HIV pharmacy, as defined in paragraph (f) of this subdivision, acquisition cost means the lower of the average wholesale price of a prescription drug based on the package size dispensed from, as reported by the prescription drug pricing service used by the department, less twelve percent thereof, or the maximum acquisition cost, if any, established pursuant to paragraph (e) of this subdivision.

(iii) notwithstanding subparagraphs (i) and (ii) of this paragraph and paragraphs (d) and (e) of this subdivision, if the drug dispensed is a drug that has been purchased from a manufacturer by a covered entity pursuant to section 340B of the federal public health service act (42 USCA § 256b), the actual amount paid by such covered entity pursuant to such section, plus the reasonable administrative costs, as determined by the commissioner, incurred by the covered entity or by an authorized contract pharmacy in connection with the purchase and dispensing of such drug and the tracking of such transactions. For purposes of this subparagraph, a "covered entity" is an entity that meets the requirements of paragraph four of subsection (a) of such section, that elects to participate in the program established by such section, and that causes claims for payment for drugs covered by this subparagraph to be submitted to the medical assistance program, either directly or through an authorized contract pharmacy. No medical assistance payments may be made to a covered entity or to an authorized contract pharmacy of a covered entity for drugs that are eligible for purchase under the section 340B program and are dispensed on an outpatient basis to patients of the covered entity, other than under the provisions of this subparagraph. Pharmacies submitting claims for reimbursement of drugs purchased pursuant to section 340B of the public health service act shall notify the department that the claim is eligible for

SSL

purchase under the 340B program, consistent with claiming instructions issued by the department to identify such claims.

(c) Notwithstanding subparagraph (i) of paragraph (b) of this subdivision, if a qualified prescriber certifies "brand medically necessary" or "brand necessary" in his or her own handwriting directly on the face of a prescription for a multiple source drug for which a specific upper limit of reimbursement has been established by the federal agency, in addition to writing "d a w" in the box provided for such purpose on the prescription form, payment under this title for such drug must be made under the provisions of subparagraph (ii) of such paragraph.

(d) In addition to the amounts paid pursuant to paragraph (b) of this subdivision to pharmacies for those drugs which may not be dispensed without a prescription, as required by section sixty-eight hundred ten of the education law and for which payment is authorized pursuant to paragraph (g) of subdivision two of section three hundred sixty-five-a of this title, the department shall pay a pharmacy dispensing fee for each such prescription drug dispensed, which dispensing fee shall not be less than the following amounts:

(i) for prescription drugs categorized as generic by the prescription drug pricing service used by the department, four dollars and fifty cents per prescription; and

(ii) for prescription drugs categorized as brand-name prescription drug by the prescription drug pricing service used by the department, three dollars and fifty cents per prescription.

(e) For a multiple source generic drug for which no specific upper payment limit has been established by the federal centers for medicare and medicaid services, the commissioner of health may establish a maximum acquisition cost for such drug which shall be effective until such time as a specific federal upper payment limit has been established for such drug. The department shall use a similar methodology in establishing such an interim price as that utilized by the centers for medicare and Medicaid services in establishing the federal upper payment limit. For this purpose, the department is authorized to enter into a contract with an entity to provide technical and administrative support to the commissioner of health.

(f) For the purposes of this section, a specialized HIV pharmacy shall mean a pharmacy, approved by the commissioner, which meets all of the following criteria:

(i) over ninety percent of the patients serviced by the pharmacy require antiretrovirals used in the treatment of HIV/AIDS;

(ii) the pharmacy provides specialized, computer automated and dispensed packaging, that improves medication adherence including daily, patient specific packets that individually list the patients patient's name, medication, expiration date and precise date and time the medication should be taken;

(iii) the pharmacists of the pharmacy at least bi-annually attend continuing education programs specific to HIV medications;

(iv) the pharmacy provides full monthly order of drugs for their patients;

(v) the pharmacy provides home delivery of drugs to patients;

(vi) the pharmacy must be located within and licensed by the state of New York;

(vii) the pharmacy may not operate as a satellite pharmacy, located within the same building as another retail pharmacy; and

(viii) the pharmacy must provide comprehensive support services to benefit patients with HIV/AIDS.

9. [Eff. March 31, 2009] Notwithstanding any inconsistent provision of law or regulation to the contrary, for those drugs which may not be dispensed without a prescription as required by section sixty-eight hundred ten of the education law and for which payment is authorized pursuant to paragraph (g) of subdivision two of section three hundred sixty-five-a of this title, payments under this title shall be made at the following amounts:

(a) for drugs provided by medical practitioners and claimed separately by the practitioners, the actual cost of the drugs to the practitioners; and

(b) for drugs dispensed by pharmacies:

(i) if the drug dispensed is a multiple source prescription drug for which an upper limit has been set by the federal health care financing administration, an amount equal to the specific upper limit set by such federal agency for the multiple source prescription drug, and

(ii) if the drug dispensed is a multiple source prescription drug or a brand-name prescription drug for which no specific upper limit has been set by such federal agency, the lower of the estimated acquisition cost of such drug to pharmacies, or the dispensing pharmacy's usual and customary price charged to the general public. Estimated acquisition cost means the average wholesale price of a prescription drug based upon the package size dispensed from, as reported by the prescription drug pricing service used by the department, less ten percent thereof, and updated monthly by the department.

(c) Notwithstanding subparagraph (i) of paragraph (b) of this subdivision, if a qualified prescriber certifies "brand medically necessary" or "brand necessary" in his or her own handwriting directly on the face of a prescription for a multiple source drug for which a specific upper limit of reimbursement has been established by the federal agency, in addition to writing "d a w" in the box provided for such purpose on the prescription form, payment under this title for such drug must be made under the provisions of subparagraph (ii) of such paragraph.

(d) In addition to the amounts paid pursuant to paragraph (b) of this subdivision to pharmacies for those drugs which may not be dispensed without a prescription, as required by section sixty-eight hundred ten of the education law and for which payment is authorized pursuant to paragraph (g) of subdivision two of section three hundred sixty-five-a of this title, the department shall pay a pharmacy dispensing fee for each such prescription drug dispensed, which dispensing fee shall not be less than the following amounts:

(i) for prescription drugs categorized as generic by the prescription drug pricing service used by the department, five dollars and fifty cents per prescription; and

(ii) for prescription drugs categorized as brand-name prescription drug by the prescription drug pricing service used by the department, four dollars and fifty cents per prescription.

10. Any provider except for those providers certified under article twenty-eight of the public health law, of ordered services or supplies under the medical assistance program may be required to provide financial security to assure that funds are available to repay any overpayments made to the provider under this title and to assure the financial security of the medical assistance program. For the purposes of this subdivision, "ordered services or supplies" shall mean those services or supplies described in paragraphs (g), (i) and (j) of subdivision two of section three hundred sixty-five-a of this title.

(a) Any financial security required by this subdivision must meet the requirements of this paragraph. Financial security may be provided through a bond with a corporate surety, from a company authorized to do business in this state, or an irrevocable letter of credit or certificate of deposit from a New York state or federally chartered bank, trust company, savings bank or savings and loan association qualified to do business in New York state and insured by the federal deposit insurance corporation.

(b) The bond, letter of credit or certificate of deposit shall be payable in favor of the people of the state of New York for the purpose of indemnifying the medical assistance program against any overpayments made to the provider.

(c) The bond, letter of credit or certificate of deposit filed and maintained pursuant to this section shall not be cancelled, revoked or terminated except after notice to, and with the consent of, the department at least forty-five days in advance of such cancellation, revocation or termination.

(d) The department may bring and maintain an action against the provider and the surety or bank, trust company, savings bank or savings and loan association for any claimed overpayments made to the provider.

(e) Financial security shall not be required for providers which do not submit claims for payment under the medical assistance program exceeding five hundred thousand dollars per annum or forty-two thousand dollars per month.

(f) Financial security shall be in an amount equal to the provider's estimated claims for payment for a one year period and may be adjusted bi-annually in accordance with the dollar amount of claims actually submitted. If the commissioner is satisfied from an investigation of the financial condition of a provider that the provider is solvent and possessed of sufficient assets to provide reasonable assurance of recovery of any overpayments, the commissioner may modify the amount of financial security to be provided by such provider.

(g)   Financial security must be submitted by a provider upon initial application for enrollment as a provider of medical assistance and with each subsequent enrollment. A change in ownership of a provider shall not release, cancel or terminate liability under this section under any bond, letter of credit or certificate of deposit filed for a provider while such bond, letter of credit or certificate of deposit is in effect unless the transferee, purchaser, successor or assignee of such provider obtains a bond, letter of credit or certificate of deposit under this section for the benefit of such new owner. All providers enrolled in the medical assistance program on the effective date of this subdivision will be required to submit financial security within ninety days of notice of such requirements by the department.

(h)   The department may make the submission of the financial security required by this subdivision a condition of participation in the medical assistance program.

11.   (a) Any inconsistent provisions of this title or other law notwithstanding, no health insurer, health maintenance organization or other entity providing medical benefits, employer or organization who has a plan, including an employee retirement income security act or service benefit plan, providing care and other medical benefits for persons, whether by insurance or otherwise, shall exclude a person from eligibility, coverage or entitlement to medical benefits by reason of the eligibility of such person for medical assistance under this title, or by reason of the fact that such person would, except for such plan, be eligible for benefits under this title.

(b)   Any inconsistent provisions of this title or other law notwithstanding, no insurer may impose requirements on the department or a social services district which has been assigned the rights of an individual who is eligible for medical assistance under this title and who is covered for health benefits from the insurer, that are different from requirements applicable to an agent or assignee of any other individual so covered.

(c)   Any inconsistent provisions of this title or other law notwithstanding, the department may, to the extent necessary to reimburse the department and the social services districts for expenditures under this title, certify to the commissioner of taxation and finance pursuant to section one hundred seventy-one-f of the tax law amounts to be withheld from tax refunds otherwise due to any individual who is required by court order to provide medical support in the form of health insurance benefits for a child who is eligible for medical assistance under this title and who has received payment from a third-party for the cost of such services for such child but has not used such payments to reimburse either the other parent or guardian of such child or the provider of such services or the appropriate social services district; provided however, that any claims for current

SSL

or past-due child support shall take priority over any such claims for the costs of such services and care. Such amounts shall be withheld pursuant to section one hundred seventy-one-f of the tax law, and shall be credited to unreimbursed medical assistance incurred on behalf of such child. The department shall by regulation establish procedures consistent with paragraphs (a) and (b) of subdivision four of section one hundred seventy-one-c of the tax law by which any individual who is the subject of a certification may contest such certification.

12.   Prior to receiving medical assistance under subparagraphs twelve and thirteen of paragraph (a) of subdivision one of section three hundred sixty-six of this title, a person whose net available income is at least one hundred fifty percent of the applicable federal income official poverty line, as defined and updated by the United States department of health and human services, must pay a premium, in accordance with a procedure to be established by the commissioner. The amount of such premium shall be equal to the sum of three percent of the person's net earned income and seven and one-half percent of the person's net unearned income. No premium shall be required from a person whose net available income is less than one hundred fifty percent of the applicable federal income official poverty line, as defined and updated by the United States department of health and human services.

Added by Laws 1966, Ch. 256; **amended** Laws 1968, Chs. 32, 97, 164, 995; Laws 1969, Chs. 642, 910, 1118, 1119; Laws 1971, Chs. 110, 945, 449; Laws 1973, Chs. 343, 516, Laws 1974, Ch. 738, §§ 1 and 2, repealing former subds. 4 and 5, § 3 adding new subds. 5 and 6; Laws 1976, Ch. 76, eff. Mar. 7, 1976, Ch. 639, eff. July 21, 1976; former subds. 6 and 7 **repealed** and new subd. 6 **added** by Laws 1977, Ch. 77, eff. May 1, 1977; Laws 1978, Ch. 554, eff. July 24, 1978; **amended** by Laws 1981, Ch. 317, eff. June 29, 1981, subd. (1); **amended** by Laws 1981, Ch. 319, eff. Aug. 28, 1981, adding subds. 2(b) and (c); **amended** by Laws 1981, Ch. 947, eff. July 1, 1981, added subd. 8; **amended** by Laws 1989, Ch. 558, § 3, eff. Jan. 1, 1989; **amended** by Laws 1989, Ch. 723, § 17, eff. July 24, 1989 through July 24, 1994, at which time the amendments to subdivision (8) made by this act shall be deemed to be **repealed** and subdivision (8) shall revert to its text as it existed prior to the effective date of this act; **amended** by Laws 1989, Ch. 763, eff. Jan. 1, 1990; **amended** by Laws 1990, Ch. 190, § 378, eff. July 1, 1990; **amended** by Laws 1990, Ch. 651, §§ 2, 3, eff. Oct. 1, 1990; **amended** by Laws 1991, Ch. 165, § 12, eff. June 12, 1991 until July 1, 1996, § 18, eff. July 1, 1991, § 19, eff. Jan. 1, 1991; **amended** by Laws 1992, Ch. 41, § 67, eff. May 1, 1992 until Dec. 31, 1993, § 91, eff. June 1, 1992 until Apr. 1, 1995, § 92, eff. Apr. 2, 1992; **amended** by Laws 1992, Ch. 834, § 1, eff. Aug. 7, 1992, § 2, eff. Nov. 1, 1992; **amended** by Laws 1992, Ch. 843, §§ 7, 8, 9, eff. Aug. 7, 1992; **amended** by Laws 1993, Ch. 59, § 72, eff. July 1, 1993; **amended** by Laws 1994, Ch. 170, §§ 372, 373, eff. June 9, 1994; **amended** by Laws 1994, Ch. 170, § 456, eff. Apr. 1, 1994; **amended** by Laws 1994, Ch. 170, § 466, eff. Apr. 1, 1994, extending the period that subds. (a), (b), (d), (e), (f), and (g) of para. (6) remain effective to July 1, 1995; **amended** by Laws 1994, Ch. 300, § 13, eff. July 20, 1994; **amended** by Laws 1994, Ch. 598, § 8, eff. July 24, 1994, extending the period that subd. (8) remains effective to July 1, 2000; **amended** by Laws 1995, Ch. 81, § 90, eff. June 20, 1995; **amended** by Laws 1995, Ch. 81, § 98, eff. June 20, 1995, extending the period that Subd. 6, paras. (a), (b), (d), (e), (f) and (g) remain effective to July 1, 1997, and providing that the amendatory language of Subd. 6, para. (c), as added by Laws 1992, Ch. 41, § 91, shall expire July 1, 1997, at which time the provisions of para. (c) shall be read as set out immediately preceding the effective date of the 1992 act; **amended** by Laws 1996, Ch. 649, § 6, eff. Sept. 16, 1996 but deemed to have be in full force and effect on and after July 1, 1996, extended the expiration of subd. 6 to July 1, 2000; **amended** by L. 1997, Chs. 145, 162, 194, 211, and 264 extending expiration dates of adds and amendments to subd. (6)(a)-(g) to Aug. 2, 1997, eff. July. 23, 1997, deemed to be in full force and effect Apr. 1, 1997; **amended** by L. 1997, Ch. 433, § 39, extending expiration dates of adds and amendments to subd. (6)(a)-(g) to July 1, 1999, eff. Aug. 20, 1997, and § 1-c, adding subd. (1)(e), eff. Aug. 20, 1997; **amended** by Laws 1997, Ch. 436, § 1 Part B, § 98, eff. Nov. 1, 1997; **amended** by Laws 1998, Ch. 58, Part E, § 22, eff. Apr. 28, 1998, deemed in full force and effect Apr. 1, 1998, Ch. 33, § 1, eff. Mar. 31, 1998, deemed in full force and effect Jan. 1, 1998, amendments to expire Mar. 31, 2000, and Ch. 19, § 2, eff. July 18, 1998, amendments to expire Mar. 31, 2000; **amended** by Laws 1999, Ch. 412, Part F, § 32, eff. Aug. 9, 1999, deemed in full force and effect Apr. 1, 1999, extending effective dates of subds. (a)–(f) to July 1, 2000; **amended** by Laws 1999, Ch. 1, § 38, eff. Dec. 30, 1999, extending the period that Subd. 6, paras. (a), (b), (d), (e), (f) and (g), deemed in full force and effect Jan. 1, 2000; **amended** by Laws 2000, Ch. 13, § 4, Ch. 57 Part A, § 3, eff. May 15, 2000, deemed effective Apr. 1, 2000, extending the expiration dates of subsections (6) and (9), and Ch. 93, eff. June 23, 2000; **amended** by Laws 2002, Ch. 1, Part A, § 64, eff. April 1, 2003, Ch. 1, Part B, § 27, eff. April 1, 2002, Ch. 23, Part G, § 2, eff. April 1, 2002 and Ch. 620 §§ 1, 2 eff. immediately; L. 2003, Ch. 38, § 2, eff. April 14, 2003 and shall be in full force and effect on and after March 31, 2003, Ch. 62, Part Z2, §§ 1, 4, 42, 43, 51, 53 1-a, eff. May 15, 2003; Ch. 63, Part J1, § 1, eff. May 15, 2003, Ch. 686, Part H, § 24, extending effective and expiration dates, eff. Apr. 1, 2003; **amended** by Laws 2004, Ch. 58, Part C, §§ 3, 11, 34, 36 (3-4), eff. April 1, 2004, Ch. 131, § 1, amending sub. 8, eff. June 29, 2004 and Ch. 538, § 1, amending sub. 3, par. (d), eff. Sept. 28, 2004; by Laws 2005, Ch. 12, § 8, amending sub. 1, par. (d), eff. March 15, 2005, deemed eff. on and after April 1, 2005; Laws 2005, Ch. 63, §§ 29 (Part E), eff. April 13, 2005, L.2005, Ch. 58, §§ 29, 30-a, 40, 41, 42, eff. April 1, 2005, amending sub. 6 and sub. 9, eff. March 15, 2005, deemed eff. on and after April 1, 2005; L. 2005, Ch. 63, sect; 29 (Part E), eff. Apr. 13, 2005; Laws 2006, Ch. 443 § 3, July 26, 2006.

§ 367-b. Medical assistance information and payment system.

1. The department shall design and implement a statewide medical assistance information and payments system for the purpose of providing individual and aggregate data to social services districts to assist them in making basic management decisions, to the department and other state agencies to assist in the administration of the medical assistance program, and to the governor and the legislature as may be necessary to assist in making major administrative and policy decisions affecting such program. Such system shall be designed so as to be capable of the following:

a. receiving and processing information relating to the eligibility of each person applying for medical assistance and of issuing a medical assistance identification card to persons determined by a social services official to be eligible for such assistance;

b.   receiving and processing information relating to each qualified provider of medical assistance furnishing care, services or supplies for which claims for payment are made pursuant to this title;

c.   receiving and processing, in a form and manner prescribed by the department, all claims for medical care, services and supplies, and making payments for valid claims to providers of medical care, services and supplies on behalf of social services districts;

d.   maintaining information necessary to allow the department, consistent with the powers and duties of the department of health, to review the appropriateness, scope and duration of medical care, services and supplies provided to any eligible person pursuant to this chapter; and

e.   initiating implementation of such a system for the district comprising the city of New York, in a manner compatible with expansion of such system to districts other than the district comprising the city of New York.

2.   Consistent with the capabilities of the system established pursuant to subdivision one of this section, the department shall assume payment responsibilities on behalf of social services districts by promulgation of regulations approved by the director of the budget. Such regulations shall specify the providers of medical assistance and the medical care, services and/or supplies for the district or districts for which the department will assume payment responsibilities and the date on which such responsibilities shall be assumed. Such regulations shall be published for comment at least thirty days in advance of their promulgation and shall be filed with the secretary of state at least sixty days in advance of the date of assumption of responsibilities; provided, however, that with respect to a particular district the requirements for advance publications and/or filing may be waived, or the time limits reduced, with the written consent of the district to such waiver or reduction. Providers of medical care and services shall submit claims to the social services district for all items of care, services and supplies furnished prior to the date of state assumption of payment responsibilities and to the state for all such items furnished subsequent to such date. Such regulations shall also specify a final transition date after which any claiming submitted shall be enforceable by such provider only against the state and shall not be enforceable by such provider against the social services district; provided, however, that the department and the district may enter into a written agreement by which the department agrees on the basis of eligibility information provided by such district to pay claims submitted to such district prior to the final transition date.

3.   Upon notice to a social services district in accordance with subdivision two, that the department intends to assume payment responsibilities on behalf of such district, (a) such district shall promptly submit to the department requested information regarding each person who applies for or has been determined eligible for medical assistance and each provider of medical assistance in such district; and (b) notwithstanding the provisions of paragraph (b) of subdivision three of section three hundred sixty-six-a of this chapter, the

department shall provide each person found by such district to be eligible for medical assistance under this title with a medical assistance identification card.

4. Information relating to persons applying for or receiving medical assistance shall be considered confidential and shall not be disclosed to persons or agencies other than those considered entitled to such information in accordance with section one hundred thirty-six when such disclosure is necessary for the proper administration of public assistance programs.

5. By no later than forty-five days following the end of each calendar quarter after the second quarter of calendar year nineteen hundred seventy-six, the department shall, until full implementation has been achieved in all social services districts, report to the governor and the legislature regarding the current status of the medical assistance information and payment system, summarizing the progress achieved during the previous quarter and the anticipated major achievements of the succeeding two calendar quarters. The report shall include the current and anticipated overall expenditure and staffing levels for functions relating to the system, and shall specify each district affected or anticipated to be affected during the succeeding two calendar quarters and summarize the manner in which each such district is, or is anticipated to be, affected. In addition, the department shall prepare and submit to the governor and the legislature a special report demonstrating the appropriateness and relative cost-effectiveness of utilizing a fiscal intermediary.

In addition, for the purpose of insuring the compatibility of the system servicing the district comprising the city of New York with the system servicing all other social services districts in the state, the department shall prepare and submit to the governor and the legislature on or before March first, nineteen hundred seventy-eight, a special report and recommendation covering the appropriateness and relative cost effectiveness of utilizing a fiscal intermediary or fiscal agent for all districts other than the district comprising the city of New York.

6. Each social services district shall be responsible for paying to the state a share of the state's expenditures for claims of providers of medical assistance attributable to such district, which shall be equal to the share of such expenditures such district would have borne after reimbursement from state and federal funds in accordance with section three hundred sixty-eight-a of this chapter, had the expenditure been made by such district; provided, however, that no district shall be responsible for the state's expenditures for the administrative costs of developing, maintaining or operating the statewide medical assistance information and payment system; and provided, further, that no district shall be responsible for paying to the state any portion of the cost of medical assistance which the department is responsible for furnishing pursuant to section three hundred sixty-five of this chapter.

7. In any case in which the department has made payments for medical assistance on behalf of a social services district pursuant to this section, the

commissioner on behalf of the social services official shall be empowered to bring actions to recover the cost of such assistance, pursuant to this subdivision and the provisions of title six of article three of this chapter.

8.   (a) For the purpose of orderly and timely implementation of the medical assistance payments and information system, the department is hereby authorized to enter into agreements with fiscal intermediaries or fiscal agents for the design, development, implementation, operation, processing, auditing and making of payments, subject to audits being conducted by the state in accordance with the terms of such agreements, for medical assistance claims under the system described by this section in any social services district. Such agreements shall specifically provide that the state shall have complete oversight responsibility for the fiscal intermediaries' or fiscal agents' performance and shall be solely responsible for establishing eligibility requirements for recipients, provider qualifications, rates of payment, investigation of suspected fraud and abuse, issuance of identification cards, establishing and maintaining recipient eligibility files, provider profiles, and conducting state audits of the fiscal intermediaries' or agents' at least once annually. The system described in this subdivision shall be operated by a fiscal intermediary or fiscal agent in accordance with this subdivision unless the department is otherwise authorized by a law enacted subsequent to the effective date of this subdivision to operate the system in another manner. In no event shall such intermediary or agent be a political subdivision of the state or any other governmental agency or entity. The department shall consult with the office of Medicaid inspector general regarding any activities undertaken by the fiscal intermediaries or fiscal agents regarding investigation of suspected fraud and abuse.

(b)   The department of health, in consultation with the office of Medicaid inspector general, shall develop, test and implement new methods to strengthen the capability of the Medicaid payment information system to detect and control fraud and improve expenditure accountability, and is hereby authorized to enter into further agreements with fiscal and/or information technology agents for the development, testing and implementation of such new methods. Any such agreements shall be with agents which have demonstrated expertise in the areas addressed by the agreement. Such methods shall, at a minimum, address the following areas:

(1)   Prepayment claims review. Develop, test and implement an automated claims review process which, prior to payment, shall subject medical assistance program services claims to review for proper coding and such other review as may be deemed necessary. Services subject to review shall be based on: the expected cost-effectiveness of reviewing such service; the capabilities of the automated system for conducting such a review; and the potential to implement such review with negligible effect on the turnaround of claims for provider payment or on recipient access to necessary services. Such initiative shall be designed to provide for the efficient and effective operation of the medical assistance program claims payment system by performing functions including, but not

limited to, capturing coding errors, misjudgments, incorrect or multiple billing for the same service and possible excesses in billing or service use, whether intentional or unintentional.

(2) Coordination of benefits. Develop, test and implement an automated process to improve the coordination of benefits between the medical assistance program and other sources of coverage for medical assistance recipients. Such initiative shall initially examine the savings potential to the medical assistance program through retrospective review of claims paid which shall be completed not later than January thirty-first, two thousand seven. If, based upon such initial experience, the Medicaid inspector general deems the automated process to be capable of including or moving to a prospective review, with negligible effect on the turnaround of claims for provider payment or on recipient access to services, then the Medicaid inspector general in subsequent tests shall examine the savings potential through prospective, pre-claims payment review.

(3) Comprehensive review of paid claims. Take all reasonable and necessary actions to intensify the state's current level of monitoring, analyzing, reporting and responding to medical assistance program claims data maintained by the state's Medicaid management information system contract agents. Pursuant to this initiative, the department of health, in collaboration with the office of Medicaid inspector general, shall make efforts to improve the utilization of such data in order to better identify fraud and abuse within the medical assistance program and to identify and implement further program and patient care reforms for the improvement of such program. In addition, the department of health, in consultation with such contract agents and the office of Medicaid inspector general, shall identify additional data elements that are maintained and otherwise accessible by the state, directly or through any of its contractors, that would, if coordinated with medical assistance data, further increase the effectiveness of data analysis for the management of the medical assistance program. To further the objectives of this subparagraph, the department of health, in collaboration with the office of Medicaid inspector general, shall provide or arrange in-service training for state and county medical assistance personnel to increase the capability for state and local data analysis, leading to a more cost-effective operation of the medical assistance program.

(4) Targeted claims and utilization review. Develop, test and implement an automated process for the targeted review of claims, services and/or populations not later than January thirty-first, two thousand seven. Such review shall be for the purposes of identifying statistical aberrations in the use or billing of such services and for assisting in the development and implementation of measures to ensure that service use and billing are appropriate to recipients' needs.

(c) The commissioner of health shall prepare and submit an interim report to the governor and legislature on the implementation of the initiatives specified in paragraph (b) of this subdivision no later than December first, two thousand seven. Such report shall also include recommendations for any revisions that would further facilitate the goals of such paragraph, including recommendations for expansion. In addition, the commissioner of health shall submit a final report not later than December first, two thousand eight. In preparing such interim and final reports, the commissioner of health shall consult with the Medicaid inspector general, third-party agents, providers and recipients associated with the implementation of paragraph (b) of this subdivision.

9.   (a) In order to accomplish a more orderly transition to the medical assistance payments and information system authorized by this section, and to continue for a limited transition period the rate at which advanced revenues have been made available by local governmental units to certain hospitals providing services to persons eligible for medical assistance, the department is authorized to promulgate regulations establishing a system of accelerated payments to hospitals meeting the criteria set forth in this section.

(b)   Such system of accelerated payments shall only be available to a general hospital, other than a public general hospital:

(i)   which prior to January first, nineteen hundred seventy-eight received regular, periodic and recurring advanced revenues from a local governmental unit, the amount of which was based on anticipated medical assistance claims payments; and

(ii)   which has demonstrated that its continued financial viability depends in substantial part on the rate at which such advanced revenues were made available by local governmental units prior to the time the department, pursuant to this section, assumed payment for such hospital responsibilities on behalf of the social services district in which it is located, taking into account any funds remaining available from the local governmental unit under its system of advanced revenues. For purposes of this subdivision, it shall be presumed that a hospital does not depend in substantial part on the rate at which advanced revenues were made available by a local governmental unit if it received such revenues for a period of less than nine months preceding the month in which the department assumed payment responsibilities for such hospital;

(iii)   for which payment responsibility is initially assumed by the department pursuant to this section during the period beginning June first, nineteen hundred seventy-eight and ending November thirtieth, nineteen hundred seventy-eight; and

(iv)   which meets performance criteria established by department regulation relating to the ratio of acceptable claims for patient days submitted for medical assistance payment compared to the total patient days of the hospital and compared to such claims submitted in one or more previous months, and the time lapse between the date the service was provided and the date the claim was submitted.

(c)   The regulations promulgated by the department pursuant to paragraph (a) of this subdivision shall provide that the amount of the accelerated payment for any month shall be determined for each hospital meeting the criteria set forth in this section on the basis of acceptable medical assistance claims submitted by the hospital in one or more previous months and the amount of accelerated revenues made available to the hospital by a local governmental unit prior to the time the department assumed payment responsibilities for the hospital. The amount of the accelerated payment for any given month shall not exceed the amount of a monthly aggregate claim to be submitted by the hospital to the department, which claim shall reflect items of care, services and supplies authorized under the medical assistance program pursuant to this title which are in fact provided prior to the date of the aggregate claim to persons who have been determined eligible for medical assistance, or based on the past performance of the hospital are likely to be determined eligible for medical assistance, when no other source of payment including third-party health insurance and payments pursuant to title eighteen of the federal social security act are available for such items of care, service and supplies. Such aggregate claims shall be subject to the audit and warrant of the state comptroller.

(d)   Any schedule of accelerated payments established by the department pursuant to this section shall assure that such payments are made for a period of no more than six months from the month in which the department assumes payment responsibility for the hospital, and shall provide for repayment of any amounts in excess of current audited claims, through reductions in current claims, at a rate that will assure full repayment at the earliest time consistent with the purposes of this section, but in no event more than twenty-four months following the month in which the department assumes payment responsibilities for the hospital. However, where the commissioner of health has determined with the concurrence of the state hospital review and planning council that a hospital has satisfied the department of health regulations and is or has been authorized to participate in the emergency hospital reimbursement program pursuant to which repayment of all or part of any accelerated payments made by the department have been deferred in accordance with such regulations, notwithstanding the time limitations set forth above repayment of such deferred amounts shall be made in accordance with an orderly schedule of repayment established by the commissioner of health after consultation with the commissioner. In no event shall any reduction be made against current claims, grant funds or any amounts due said hospital in settlement of rate appeals, claims or lawsuits to satisfy such repayment obligations.

(e)   In making accelerated payments pursuant to this subdivision and department regulations, the department shall utilize federal funds made available, and local funds, for such purposes or for purposes of payment by the department of medical assistance payments pursuant to this section.

10.   [Expired.]

11.   a. For the purpose of timely payment, the department is hereby authorized to develop a concurrent payment system for general hospitals which elect to participate in the concurrent payment system and which are included in the payment component of the medical assistance information and payment system, and to promulgate regulations to govern such a system. The department

may implement the concurrent payment system for any general hospital which has elected to participate and for which the department has chosen to implement the system.

b.   For all participating general hospitals the department shall determine a biweekly concurrent payment which shall equal one twenty-sixth of the hospital's estimated yearly inpatient revenue from medical assistance payments. The concurrent payment shall be reviewed at the beginning of each quarter and adjusted to reflect any changes to the rates for medical assistance payments.

c.   The department shall promulgate regulations, consistent with federal requirements for participation, governing the concurrent payment system. The regulations shall address, among other things, the method of calculating the concurrent payment, the method of reconciliation, the adjustment of the concurrent payment for the calculated difference, the manner of eliminating underpayments or overpayments to hospitals in exceptional circumstances such as significantly changing utilization, changes in bed or service capacity, or imminent insolvency. The department shall promulgate regulations establishing a procedure for recognizing open cases as of the date of reconciliation. The department shall promulgate regulations setting forth standards for the timeliness and quality of billings and may lower the concurrent payment calculated in accordance with paragraph b of this subdivision for noncompliance with such regulations.

d.   Any payment claims made to the department for days of inpatient care provided prior to the effective date of this subdivision shall be paid or denied in accordance with department regulations in effect when the care was provided.

e.   For any general hospital which is not afforded the opportunity of participating in the concurrent payment system and which is in compliance with the billing requirements of the department, the department shall pay any financing or working capital charge levied by the hospital as authorized in section twenty-eight hundred seven-a of the public health law.

f.   This subdivision shall be effective only if federal participation is available.

12.   (a) For the purpose of regulating cash flow for general hospitals, the department shall develop and implement a payment methodology to provide for timely payments for inpatient hospital services eligible for case based payments per discharge based on diagnosis-related groups provided during the period January first, nineteen hundred eighty-eight through June thirtieth, two thousand seven, by such hospitals which elect to participate in the system.

(b)   In developing a payment methodology the department shall consider a system under which hospitals may be reimbursed on the basis of inpatient admissions, adjusted to payment on the basis of discharge data, with reconciliations established at time periods specified by the department. Under such a system variances between amounts paid on an admission basis and actual amounts due and to be paid on a discharge basis may be reflected in the amounts to be paid in a subsequent period.

13. Notwithstanding any inconsistent provision of law, in lieu of payments authorized by this chapter and/or any of the general fund or special revenue other appropriations made to the office of temporary and disability assistance and the office of children and family services, from funds otherwise due to local social services districts or in lieu of payments of federal funds otherwise due to local social services districts for programs provided under the federal social security act or the federal food stamp act or the low income home energy assistance program, funds in amounts certified by the commissioner of the office of temporary and disability assistance or the commissioner of the office of children and family services or the commissioner of health as due from local social services districts as their share of payments made pursuant to this section, may be set-aside by the state comptroller in an interest-bearing account with such interest accruing to the credit of the locality, pursuant to an estimate provided by the commissioner of health of a local social services district's share of medical assistance payments, except that in the case of the city of New York, such set-aside shall be subject first to the requirements of a section of the chapter of the laws of two thousand one which enacted this provision, and then subject to the requirements of paragraph (i) of subdivision (b) of section two hundred twenty-two-a of chapter four hundred seventy-four of the laws of nineteen hundred ninety-six prior to the application of this subdivision. Should funds otherwise payable to a local social services district from appropriations made to the office of temporary and disability assistance, the office of children and family services, and the department of health be insufficient to fully fund the amounts identified by the commissioner of health as necessary to liquidate the local share of payments to be made pursuant to this section on behalf of the local social services district, the commissioner of health may identify other state or federal payments payable to that local social services district or any other county agency including, but not limited to the county department of health, from appropriations made to the state department of health, and may authorize the state comptroller, upon no less than five days written notice to such local social services district or such other county agency, to set-aside such payments in the interest-bearing account with such interest accruing to the credit of the locality. Upon such determination by the commissioner of health that insufficient funds are payable to a local social services district and any other county agency receiving payments from the office of temporary and disability assistance, the office of children and family services, and the state department of health from appropriations made to these agencies, the state comptroller shall, upon no less than five days written notice to such local social services district or such other county agency, withhold payments from any of the general fund local assistance accounts or payments made from any of the special revenue federal local assistance accounts, provided, however, that such federal payments shall be withheld only after such federal funds are properly credited to the county through vouchers, claims or other warrants properly received, approved, and paid by the state comptroller, and set-aside such disbursements in the interest-bearing account with such interest accruing to the credit of the locality until such time that the amount withheld from each county

is determined by the commissioner of health to be sufficient to fully liquidate the local share of payments, as estimated by the commissioner of health, to be made pursuant to this section on behalf of that local social services district.

14. Notwithstanding any other provision of law, effective on or before January first, two thousand one, the local social services district share of medical assistance payments made by the state on behalf of the local social services district shall be paid to the state by the local social services district using electronic funds transfer under the supervision of the state comptroller and pursuant to rules and regulations of the commissioner of health. The state comptroller shall deposit such funds in the Medicaid management information system statewide escrow fund to the credit of each local district. In the event that the state comptroller and commissioner of health determine that there are insufficient funds available from the local district to liquidate their local share of medical assistance payments, the commissioner of health shall issue a repayment schedule to the state comptroller for purposes of reducing reimbursement from other sources of payment from the state to the city or county of which the local social services district is a part in accordance with subdivision thirteen of this section, until the amounts due from the local district are recovered in full plus any interest that would have otherwise accrued to the fund had such fund had sufficient balances from the local district. Upon determination by the state comptroller that insufficient sources of payment are available to fully liquidate the local social services district share of medical assistance payments, the commissioner of health shall include in such schedule a charge to the county equal to the amount of interest otherwise earned by the state short-term interest pool, plus any interest penalty as the commissioner of health may determine, until such time as the district has fully liquidated its liability pursuant to the provisions of this chapter.

Added by Laws 1976, Ch. 639; Laws 1977, Ch. 356, eff. June 28, 1977 added subd. 8; Ch. 356, eff. June 28, 1977 amended subd. 5; Laws 1978, Ch. 407, Ch. 455; Laws 1980, Ch. 205, deemed to have been in full force and effect on and after Jan. 1, 1980; amended by Laws 1982, Ch. 536, adding subd. (10), eff. Jan 1, 1983, but only upon receipt, prior to such date, of all federal approvals needed to permit the determination of all payments for inpatient services provided by general hospitals to be made in accordance with the amendments made to § 2807 of the public health law by § 3 of this act; amended by Laws 1985, Ch. 807, eff. Jan. 1, 1985, adding subd. 11; amended by Laws 1985, Ch. 906, § 11, eff. Jan. 1, 1985, provides:

"Notwithstanding any inconsistent provision of law, the provisions of chapter five hundred thirty-six of the laws of nineteen hundred eighty-two, as amended by chapters five hundred thirty-seven and five hundred thirty-eight of the laws of nineteen hundred eighty-two, and chapter seven hundred fifty-eight of the laws of nineteen hundred eighty-three and chapter eight hundred seventy-four of the laws of nineteen hundred eighty-four shall expire on January first, nineteen hundred eighty-six, provided however such provisions shall thereafter remain effective: (i) with respect to any act done on or before such date or action or proceeding arising out of such act; (ii) for purposes of maintenance of and distribution from a pool established under such chapters; (iii) for purposes of audit and adjustment of a general hospital rate or revenue cap; and (iv) for purposes of adjustment of a general hospital rate or revenue cap in accordance with such chapters."

Amended by Laws 1988, Ch. 2, § 12, eff. Jan. 1, 1988; **amended** by Laws 1990, Ch. 922, § 16, eff. Jan. 1, 1991; **amended** by Laws 1993, Ch. 731, § 37, eff. Jan. 1, 1994; **amended** by Laws 1995, Ch. 81, § 43, eff. June 20, 1995; **amended** by Laws 1995, Ch. 81, § 46, eff. June 20, 1995, extending the period that Subd. 12, para. (a) remains effective to June 30, 1996; **amended** by Laws 1996, Ch. 639, § 147, eff. Sept. 12, 1996 but deemed to have been in full force and effect on and after July 1, 1996, extending the period that Subd. 12, para. (a) remains effective to Mar. 31, 1997; **amended** by L. 1999, Ch. 1, § 119, eff. Dec. 30, 1999, deemed in full force and effect Jan. 1, 2000; **amended** by L. 2000, Ch. 57, Part C, § 1, eff. May 15, 2000, deemed in full force and effect Apr. 1, 2000; **amended** by L. 2001, Ch. 63, Part C, § 8, eff. June 25, 2001, deemed full force and effect on and after June 18, 2001; L. 2003, Ch. 62, Part A3, §§ 30, 42, eff. May 15, 2003; Laws 2005, Ch. 58, § 27 (Part B), eff. April 12, 2005.

§ 367-c.　Payment for long term home health care programs.

1.　If a long-term home health care program as defined under article thirty-six of the public health law is provided in the social services district for which he has authority, the local social services official, before he authorizes care in a nursing home or intermediate care facility for a person eligible to receive services under this title, shall notify the person in writing of the provisions of this section.

2.　If a person eligible to receive services under the provisions of this title who requires care, treatment, maintenance, nursing or other services in a nursing home desires to remain and is deemed by his physician able to remain in his own home or the home of a responsible relative or other responsible adult if the necessary services are provided, such person or his representative shall so inform the local social services official. If a long-term home health care program as defined under article thirty-six of the public health law is provided in the social services district for which he has authority, such official shall authorize an assessment under the provisions of section thirty-six hundred sixteen of the public health law. if the results of the assessment indicate that the person can receive the appropriate level of care at home, the official shall prepare for that person a plan for the provision of services comparable to those that would be rendered in a nursing home. In developing such plan, the official shall consult with those persons performing the assessment. The services shall be provided by a certified home health agency, hospital, or residential health care facility authorized by the commissioner of health under article thirty-six of the public health law to provide a long-term home health care program. At the time of the initial assessment, and at the time of each subsequent assessment performed under the provisions of section thirty-six hundred sixteen of the public health law, or more often if the person's needs require, the official shall establish a monthly budget in accordance with which he shall authorize payment for the services provided under such plan. Total monthly expenditures made under this title for such person shall not exceed a maximum of seventy-five percent, or such lesser percentage as may be determined by the commissioner, of the average of the monthly rates payable

SSL

under this title for nursing home services within the social services district for which the official has authority. However, if a continuing assessment of the person's needs demonstrates that he requires increased services, the social services official may authorize the expenditure of any amount accrued under this section during the past twelve months as a result of the expenditures for that person not exceeding such maximum. If an assessment of the person's needs demonstrates that he requires services the payment for which would exceed such monthly maximum, but it can be reasonably anticipated that total expenditures for required services for such person will not exceed such maximum calculated over a one-year period, the social services official may authorize payment for such services.

3.   If a person eligible to receive services under the provisions of this title who requires health related care and services in an intermediate care facility desires to remain and is deemed by his physician able to remain in his own home or the home of a responsible relative or other responsible adult if the necessary services are provided, such person or his representative shall so inform the local social services official. If a long-term home health care program as defined under article thirty-six of the public health law is provided in the social services district for which he has authority, such official shall authorize an assessment under the provisions of section thirty-six hundred sixteen of the public health law. If the results of the assessment indicate that the person can receive the appropriate level of care at home, the official shall prepare for that person a plan for the provision of services comparable to those that would be rendered in an intermediate care facility. In developing such plan, the official shall consult with those persons performing the assessment. The services shall be provided by a certified home health agency, hospital, or residential health care facility authorized by the commissioner of health under article thirty-six of the public health law to provide a long-term home health care program. At the time of the initial assessment and at the time of each subsequent assessment performed under the provisions of section thirty-six hundred sixteen of the public health law, or more often if the person's needs require, the official shall establish a monthly budget in accordance with which he shall authorize payment for the services provided under that plan. Total monthly expenditures made under this title for such person shall not exceed a maximum of seventy-five percent, or such lesser percentage as may be determined by the commissioner, of the average of the monthly rates paid under this title for the provision of health related care and services in intermediate care facilities within the social services district for which the official has authority. However, if a continuing assessment of the person's needs demonstrates that he requires increased services, the social services official may authorize the expenditure of any amount accrued under this section during the past twelve months as a result of the expenditures for that person not exceeding such maximum. If an assessment of the person's needs demonstrates that he requires services the payment for which would exceed such monthly maximum, but it can be reasonably anticipated that total expenditures for required services for such

person will not exceed such maximum calculated over a one-year period, the social services official may authorize payment for such services.

3-a.   [*Expires March 31, 2006.*] (a) Notwithstanding any inconsistent provision of this section, the commissioner is authorized and directed to establish a demonstration program for the purpose of determining the impact of raising the limitation on expenditures for the delivery of long-term home health care services to persons with special needs as defined in this subdivision. Pursuant to such program, the commissioner shall permit local social services officials to authorize, at their discretion, and only after a determination that the maximum expenditure available pursuant to subdivisions two and three of this section is not sufficient to provide or continue to provide long term home health care services to persons with special needs, maximum monthly expenditures for services under this title to such persons, not to exceed one hundred percent of the average of the monthly rates payable under this title for services in a nursing home or intermediate care facility within the social services district for which the social services official has authority. However, if a continuing assessment of a person with special needs demonstrates that he requires increased services, the social services official may authorize the expenditure of any amount accrued under this section during the past twelve months as a result of the expenditures for that person not having exceeded such maximum. If an assessment of a person with special needs demonstrates that he requires increased services the payment for which would exceed such monthly maximum, but it can be reasonably anticipated that total expenditures for required services for such person will not exceed such maximum calculated over a one-year period, the social services official may authorize payment for such services.under this title for such person shall not exceed a maximum of seventy-five percent, or such lesser percentage as may be determined by the commissioner, of the average of the monthly rates paid under this title for the provision of health related care and services in intermediate care facilities within the social services district for which the official has authority. However, if a continuing assessment of the person's needs demonstrates that he requires increased services, the social services official may authorize the expenditure of any amount accrued under this section during the past twelve months as a result of the expenditures for that person not exceeding such maximum. If an assessment of the person's needs demonstrates that he requires services the payment for which would exceed such monthly maximum, but it can be reasonably anticipated that total expenditures for required

(b)   As used in this subdivision, the term "person with special needs" shall mean a person for whom a plan of care has been developed pursuant to subdivision two or three of this section who (1) needs care including but not limited to respiratory therapy, tube feeding, decubitus care or insulin therapy which cannot be appropriately provided by a personal care aide as defined in regulations issued by the commissioner, or (2) has one or more of the following conditions: mental disability as defined in section 1.03 of the mental hygiene law, acquired immune deficiency syndrome, or dementias, including Alzheimer's disease.

(c)   The number of persons with special needs for whom a local social services official may authorize payment for services pursuant to paragraph (a) of this subdivision shall be limited to twenty-five percent of the total number of persons, all long-term home health care programs, within a social services district are authorized to serve; provided, however, in any district containing a city having a population of one million or more, such limit shall be fifteen percent.

(d)   In the event that a district reaches the limitation specified in paragraph (c) of this subdivision, the local social services official may, upon the approval of the commissioner, authorize payment for services, pursuant to paragraph (a) of this subdivision, for additional persons with special needs.

4.   Notwithstanding any inconsistent provision of this section, if two members of this same household, eligible to receive services under this title, require care and services in either a nursing home or an intermediate care facility, and assessments conducted pursuant to the provisions of this section indicate that such persons can receive the appropriate level of care at home, then such care may be provided at home where total monthly expenditures made under this title for such persons shall not exceed a maximum of seventy-five percent, or such lesser percentage as may be determined by the commissioner, of the monthly rates which would be payable under this title for both members of the household for nursing home and/or intermediate care facility services within the social services district. If assessments of such persons' needs demonstrate that they require services the payment for which would exceed such monthly maximum, but it can be reasonably anticipated that total expenditures for required services for such persons will not exceed the maximum calculated over a one-year period, a social services official may authorize payment for such services.

5.   If a person eligible to receive services under the provisions of this title who is medically eligible for care, treatment, maintenance, nursing or other services in a nursing home or is medically eligible for health related care and services in an intermediate care facility desires to and is deemed by his or her physician able to remain in an adult care facility, other than a shelter for adults, which is able and willing to retain such person if the necessary services are provided, such person or his or her representatives shall so inform the local social services official. If a long-term home health care program is provided in a social services district, an official of such district shall authorize an assessment under the provisions of section three thousand six hundred sixteen of the public health law. If the results of the assessment indicate that the person can receive the appropriate level of care at such location, and meets the appropriate standards for continued stay for such facility as are established by law and regulation, such official shall prepare for that person a plan for the provision of services. In developing such plan, the official shall consult with those persons performing the assessment and with the operator of the adult care facility. The services shall be provided by a long-term home health care program authorized pursuant to article thirty-six of the public health law, provided, however, that notwithstanding the provisions of section three thousand six hundred sixteen of such law, services

shall not be provided prior to the completion of the assessment. At the time of the initial assessment and at the time of each subsequent assessment performed under the provisions of section three thousand six hundred sixteen of the public health law, or more often if the person's needs require, the official shall establish a monthly budget in accordance with which he shall authorize payment for the services provided under that plan, provided, however that no services shall be authorized in the pan which the operator of the facility is required by law and regulation to provide. The long-term home health care program providing services authorized in such plan shall be solely responsible for managing and providing or arranging for such authorized services. The operator of the adult care facility shall be solely responsible for managing and providing those services which the facility is required by law or regulation to provide. However, the two entities shall collaborate to assure coordination. Total monthly expenditures made under this title for such person shall not exceed a maximum of fifty percent, or such lesser percentage as may be determined by the commissioner, of the average of the monthly rates paid under this title for the provision of nursing home services or health related care and services in intermediate care facilities, whichever is appropriate, within the social services district for which the official has authority. However, if a continuing assessment of the person's needs demonstrates that he or she requires increased services, the social services official may authorize the expenditure of any amount accrued under this section during the past twelve months as a result of the expenditures for that person not exceeding such maximum. If an assessment of the person's needs demonstrates that he or she requires services the payment for which would exceed such monthly maximum, but it can be reasonably anticipated that total expenditures for required services for such person will not exceed such maximum calculated over a one-year period, the social services official may authorize payment for such services. The provisions of this subdivision shall not be deemed to alter standards for admission to an adult care facility nor shall the admission of a person into such facility be contingent on such person's enrollment in a long-term home health care program.

6.   Notwithstanding any inconsistent provision of law but subject to expenditure limitations of this section, the commissioner, subject to the approval of the state director of the budget, may authorize the utilization of medical assistance funds to pay for services provided by specified long term home health care programs in addition to those services included in the medical assistance program under section three hundred sixty-five-a of this chapter, so long as federal financial participation is available for such services. Expenditures made under this subdivision shall be deemed payments for medical assistance for needy persons and shall be subject to reimbursement by the state in accordance with the provisions of section three hundred sixty-eight-a of this chapter.

7.   No social services district shall make payments pursuant to title XIX of the federal social security act for benefits available under title XVIII of such act without documentation that title XVIII claims have been filed and denied.

8.   No social services district shall make payment for a person receiving a long-term home health care program while payments are being made for that person for inpatient care in a residential health care facility or hospital.

9.   The commissioner, together with the commissioner of health, shall submit a report to the governor, president pro tem of the senate and speaker of the assembly by the first day of February, nineteen hundred eighty, on the implementation of this section. Such report shall include a statement of the scope and status of long-term home health care programs, the extent to which such programs have affected institutionalization, the costs associated with such programs, any recommendations for legislative action, and such other matters as may be pertinent.

10.   This section shall be effective if, and as long as, federal aid is available therefor.

Added by Laws 1977, Ch. 895, eff. Apr. 1, 1977, but all actions necessary to prepare for the implementation of this act may be taken prior to the effective date; subds. (4), (5), (6), (7) **renumbered** (5), (6), (7), (8), respectively, and new subd. (4) **added** by Laws 1979, Ch. 263, eff. June 19, 1979; **amended** by Laws 1980, Ch. 636, eff. June 26, 1980; **amended** by Laws 1984, Ch. 904, eff. Oct. 2, 1984; **amended** by the Laws 1986, Ch. 629, eff. July 1, 1986; **amended** by Laws 1987, Ch. 854, eff. Apr. 1, 1988; **amended** by Laws 1991, Ch. 165, § 31, eff. July 1, 1991; **amended** by Laws 1993, Ch. 537, § 1, eff. July 28, 1993, extending expiration date of § 367-c(3-a) until Dec. 31, 1995; **amended** by Laws 1995, Ch. 81, § 122, eff. June 20, 1995, extending expiration date of subd. (3-a) to Dec. 31, 1997; **amended** by L. 1997, Ch. 386, § 2, extending expiration date of subd. (3-a) to Dec. 31, 1998, eff. Aug. 5, 1997; **amended** by L. 1997, Ch. 433, § 40, extending expiration date of subd. (3-a) to Mar. 31, 1999, eff. Aug. 20, 1997; **amended** by Laws 1999, Ch. 412, Pt. F, § 30, extending expiration date of subd. (3-a) to Mar. 31, 2000, eff. Aug. 9, 1999, deemed in full force and effect Apr. 1, 1999; **amended** by Laws 1999, Ch. 1, § 37, extending expiration date of subd. (3-a) to Mar. 31, 2003, eff. Dec. 30, 1999, deemed in full force and effect Jan. 1, 2000; **amended** by Laws 2000, Ch. 57 Part B § 9, extending the expiration date of the renumbering of subsections (5)-(9) to July 1, 2001, eff. May 15, 2000; L. 2003, Ch. 38, § 1, eff. April 14, 2003 and shall be in full force and effect on and after March 31, 2003, extending the expiration date until March 31, 2006.

§ 367-d.   Personal care need determination.

[Expired on March 31, 1985, by Laws 1983, Ch. 83, eff. April 1, 1983.]

§ 367-e.   Payment for AIDS home care programs.

1.   If an AIDS home care program as defined under article thirty-six of the public health law is provided in the social services district for which he has authority, the local social services official, before he authorizes care in a nursing home or intermediate care facility or before he authorizes home health services or personal care services for a person eligible to receive services under this title, shall notify the person in writing of the provisions of this section.

2. If a person eligible to receive services under the provisions of this title desires to remain and is deemed by his physician able to remain in his own home or the home of a responsible relative or other responsible adult if the necessary services are provided, such person or his representative shall so inform the local social service official. If an AIDS home care program as defined under article thirty-six of the public health law is provided in the social services district for which he has authority, such official shall authorize an assessment under the provision of section three thousand six hundred sixteen of the public health law. If the results of the assessment indicate that the person can receive the appropriate level of care at home, the official shall prepare for that person a plan for the provision of services comparable to those that would be rendered in a hospital or residential health care facility, as appropriate for the patient. In developing such plan, the official shall consult with those persons performing the assessment and shall assure that such plan is appropriate to the patient's needs and will result in an efficient use of services. The services shall be provided by a long term home health care program authorized by the commissioner of health under article thirty-six of the public health law to provide an AIDS home care program.

3. The commissioner shall apply for any waivers, including home and community based services waivers pursuant to section nineteen hundred fifteen-c of the social security act, necessary to implement AIDS home care programs. Notwithstanding any inconsistent provision of law but subject to expenditure limitations of this section, the commissioner, subject to the approval of the state director of the budget, may authorize the utilization of medical assistance funds to pay for services provided by AIDS home care programs in addition to those services included in the medical assistance program under section three hundred sixty-five-a of this chapter, so long as federal financial participation is available for such services. Expenditures made under this subdivision shall be deemed payments for medical assistance for needy persons and shall be subject to reimbursement by the state in accordance with the provisions of section three hundred sixty-eight-a of this chapter.

4. No social services district shall make payment for a person receiving an AIDS home care program while payments are being made for that person for inpatient care in a residential health care facility or hospital.

5. The commissioner, together with the commissioner of health, shall submit a report to the governor, president pro tem of the senate and the speaker of the assembly by July first, nineteen hundred ninety and each subsequent year thereafter on the implementation of this section. Such report shall include a statement of the scope and status of the AIDS crisis in New York state, the development and implementation of the AIDS home care programs, the adequacy of care delivered by such programs, the extent to which such programs have affected use of institutional care services by AIDS patients, the costs associated with such programs, the adequacy of reimbursement provided such programs, any recommendations for legislative action and other such matters as my be pertinent.

6. This section shall be effective if, and as long as, federal financial participation is available.

Added by Laws 1988, Ch. 622, § 7, eff. Dec. 30, 1988.

§ 367-f. Long term care security demonstration program for long term care.

1. Definitions. As used in this section:

(a). "Medicaid extended coverage" shall mean eligibility for medical assistance (i) without regard to the resource requirements of section three hundred sixty-six of this title, or in the case of an individual covered under an insurance policy or certificate described in subdivision two of this section that provided a residential health care facility benefit less than three years in duration, without consideration of an amount of resources equivalent to the value of benefits received by the individual under such policy or certificate, as determined under the rules of the partnership for long term care program, and (ii) without regard to the recovery of medical assistance from the estates of individuals and the imposition of liens on the homes of persons pursuant to section three hundred sixty-nine of this title, with respect to resources exempt from consideration pursuant to subparagraph (i) of this paragraph; provided, however, that nothing herein shall prevent the imposition of a lien or recovery against property of an individual on account of medical assistance incorrectly paid.

(b). "Long term care services" shall include, but not be limited to care, treatment, maintenance, and services: provided in a nursing facility licensed under article twenty-eight of the public health law; provided by a home care services agency, certified home health agency or long term home health care program, as defined in section thirty-six hundred two of the public health law; provided by an adult day health care program in accordance with regulations of the department of health; or provided by a personal care provider licensed or regulated by any other state or local agency; and such other services for which medical assistance is otherwise available under this chapter which are designated as long term care services in law or regulations of the department of health.

2. Notwithstanding any inconsistent provision of this chapter or any other law to the contrary, the partnership for long term care program shall provide Medicaid extended coverage to a person receiving long term care services if there is federal participation pursuant to such treatment and such person: (a) is or was covered by an insurance policy or certificate providing coverage for long term care which meets the applicable minimum benefit standards of the superintendent of insurance and other requirements for approval of participation under the program; and, (b) has exhausted the coverage and benefits as required by the program.

3. Notwithstanding any inconsistent provision of this chapter or any other law to the contrary, the commissioner of health, in consultation with the

superintendent of insurance and the director of the budget, may enter into reciprocal agreements with other states which administer partnership for long term care programs under which purchasers of policies in those states with comparable benefits to policies available in this state shall be eligible for Medicaid extended coverage in this state so long as purchasers of policies in this state with comparable benefits to policies available in such state or states shall be eligible for Medicaid extended coverage in such state or states.

Added by Laws 1989, Ch. 454, § 1, eff. Nov. 13, 1989; **Repealed/Added** by Laws 1997, Ch. 659, § 89, eff. Sept. 24, 1997; **amended** by Laws 2004, Ch. 58, Part B, §§ 28, 29, 56, (7-12), eff. Aug. 20, 2004; by Laws 2005, Ch. 58, § 51 (Part C), eff. April 12, 2005, deemed eff. on and after April 1, 2005.

§ 367-g.   Authorization and provision of personal emergency response services.

1.   Personal care services and home health services shall include, where appropriate as determined by the social services district, the provision of personal emergency response services and shared aide services pursuant to the provisions of subdivision two of section three hundred sixty-five-a of this chapter. For the purpose of this section, "personal emergency response services" shall mean (a) the provision and maintenance of electronic communication equipment in the home of an individual which signals a monitoring agency for help when activated by the individual, or after a period of time if a timer mechanism has not been reset, or by any other activating method; and (b) the continuous monitoring of such signals by a trained operator and, in case of receipt of such signal, the immediate notification of such emergency response organizations or persons, if necessary, as the individual has previously specified.

2.   The commissioner shall maintain standards for social services District's use and approval of personal emergency response services and shared aide services, which shall include, but need not be limited to department standards: (a) for the personal emergency response system equipment used to ensure its reliability and appropriate design for the purpose; (b) providing that use of personal emergency response services or shared aide services are part of a plan of care for the recipient that is based on the comprehensive assessment that such recipient has a medical condition, disability or impairment that warrants use of the service; (c) requiring that the provider of the personal emergency response service have sufficient qualifications and expertise, adequate information on the client and the plan of care, and the capacity to provide timely information on calls received to the social services district or its designee; (d) for coordination between the social services districts and the emergency response organization, as well as guidelines for regular updating of information on recipients receiving such service; (e) with respect to appropriate supervision and safety for recipients receiving personal emergency response service or shared aide services; (f) assuring that the assessment determines that the recipient can adequately utilize the personal emergency response system; (g) assuring that personal emergency

SSL

response services or shared aide services are medically appropriate, can meet the needs of the recipient for home care tasks, ensure the quality of the recipient's care and will not jeopardize the health or safety of the recipient; (h) for determining the geographic appropriateness, in relation to staffing, of providing shared aide services and assuring that providers of home care services and districts consider the impact of the site selection on the staff who will be assigned to work at a shared aide site and that such staff, and any employee organization representing such staff where appropriate, are consulted with respect to the management and operation of a shared aide site; (i) assuring that social services districts have a plan for providing information to consumers and their representatives concerning personal emergency response services and shared aide services, including information on how to express concerns about the service which they are receiving.

3. The department shall establish and issue the standards required under subdivision two hereof to social services districts on or before the first day of August of nineteen hundred ninety-five, after first seeking public comment thereon. The department, after consultation with representatives of social services districts, home health and personal care provider agencies and workers, providers of personal emergency response services and elderly or disabled persons who are receiving such services shall prepare a report to the governor and the legislature by April first, nineteen hundred ninety-six outlining any changes which are deemed appropriate to the standards for personal emergency response services and shared aide services which have been established by the department.

4.-5. [Repealed.]

Added by Laws 1993, Ch. 59, § 66, eff. Apr. 1, 1993. Amended by Laws 1995, Ch. 81, §§ 86-a -86-b, eff. June 20, 1995.

§ 367-h. Payment for assisted living programs.

1. Subject to the approval of the state director of the budget, the commissioner may authorize the payment of medical assistance funds for assisted living programs, as defined in section four hundred sixty-one-l of this chapter, in accordance with capitated rates of payment established pursuant to subdivision six of section thirty-six hundred fourteen of the public health law.

2. No assisted living program shall cease providing services to a medical assistance recipient solely because the cost of his or her care exceeds the amount of such capitated payments.

3. No medical assistance payments shall be made pursuant to this section while payments are also being made for inpatient care in a residential health care facility or hospital with respect to the same person.

4. This section shall be effective if, and as long as, federal financial participation is available for medical assistance expenditures made pursuant to it.

Added by Laws 1991, Ch. 165, § 32, eff. July 1, 1991.

§ 367-i.   Personal care services provider assessments.

1.   Providers of personal care services, excepting those certified under article thirty-six of the public health law, are charged assessments on their gross receipts received from all personal care services and other operating income on a cash basis in the percentage amounts and for the periods specified in subdivision two of this section. Such assessments shall be submitted by or on behalf of such personal care services providers to the commissioner of health or his/her designee.

2.   The assessment shall be six-tenths of one percent of each such provider's gross receipts received from all personal care services and other operating income on a cash basis beginning January first, nineteen hundred ninety-one; provided, however, that for all such gross receipts received on or after April first, nineteen hundred ninety-nine, such assessment shall be two-tenths of one percent, and further provided that such assessment shall expire and be of no further effect for all such gross receipts received on or after January first, two thousand.

3.   Gross receipts received from all personal care services and other operating income for purposes of the assessments pursuant to this section shall include, but not be limited to, all monies received for or on account of personal care services, provided, however, that subject to the provisions of subdivision eleven of this section income received from grants, charitable contributions, donations and bequests and governmental deficit financing shall not be included, and provided further, however, that moneys received from a certified home health agency or a provider of a long-term home health care program assessed on such moneys pursuant to section thirty-six hundred fourteen-a of the public health law shall not be included.

4.   Estimated payments by or on behalf of such personal care services providers to the commissioner of health or his/her designee of funds due from the assessments pursuant to subdivision two of this section shall be made on a monthly basis. Estimated payments shall be due on or before the fifteenth day following the end of a calendar month to which an assessment applies.

5.   (a) if an estimated payment made for a month to which an assessment applies is less than seventy percent of an amount the commissioner of health determines is due, based on evidence of prior period moneys received by a personal care services provider or evidence of moneys received by such personal care services provider for that month, the commissioner of health may estimate the amount due from such personal care services provider and may collect the deficiency pursuant to paragraph (c) of this subdivision.

(b)   If an estimated payment made for a month to which an assessment applies is less than ninety percent of an amount the commissioner of health determines is due, based on evidence of prior period moneys received by a personal care services provider or evidence of moneys received by such personal care services provider for that month, and at least two previous estimated payments within the preceding six months were less than ninety percent of the amount due, based on similar evidence, the commissioner of health may estimate the amount due from such personal care services provider and may collect the deficiency pursuant to paragraph (c) of this subdivision.

(c)   Upon receipt of notification from the commissioner of health of a provider's deficiency under this section, the comptroller or a fiscal intermediary designated by the director of the budget, or the commissioner of social services, or a corporation organized and operating in accordance with article forty-three of the insurance law, or an organization operating in accordance with article forty-four of the public health law shall withhold from the amount of any payment to be made by the state or by such article forty-three corporation or article forty-four organization to the provider the amount of the deficiency determined under paragraph (a) or (b) of this subdivision or paragraph (e) of subdivision six of this section. Upon withholding such amount, the comptroller or a designated fiscal intermediary, or the commissioner of social services, or corporation organized and operating in accordance with article forty-three of the insurance law or organization operating in accordance with article forty-four of the public health law shall pay the commissioner of health, or his designee, such amount withheld on behalf of the provider.

(d)   The commissioner of health shall provide a provider with notice of any estimate of an amount due for an assessment pursuant to paragraph (a) or (b) of this subdivision or paragraph (e) of subdivision six of this section at least three days prior to collection of such amount by the commissioner of health. Such notice shall contain the financial basis for the commissioner of health's estimate.

(e)   In the event a provider objects to an estimate by the commissioner of health pursuant to paragraph (a) or (b) of this subdivision or paragraph (e) of subdivision six of this section of the amount due for an assessment, the provider, within sixty days of notice of an amount due, may request a public hearing. If a hearing is requested, the commissioner of health shall provide the provider an opportunity to be heard and to present evidence bearing on the amount due for an assessment within thirty days after collection of an amount due or receipt of a request for a hearing, whichever is later. An administrative hearing is not a prerequisite to seeking judicial relief.

(f)   The commissioner of health may direct that a hearing be held without any request by a personal care services provider.

6.   (a) Every personal care services provider shall submit reports on a cash basis of actual gross receipts received from all patient care services and operating income for each month as follows:

(i) For the period January first, nineteen hundred ninety-one through January thirty-first, nineteen hundred ninety-one, the report shall be filed on or before March fifteenth, nineteen hundred ninety-one; and

(ii) for the quarter year ending March thirty-first, nineteen hundred ninety-one and for each quarter thereafter, the report shall be filed on or before the forty-fifth day after the end of such quarter.

(b)   Every personal care services provider shall submit a certified annual report on a cash basis of gross receipts received in such calendar year from all patient care services and operating income.

(c)   The reports shall be in such form as may be prescribed by the commissioner of health to accurately disclose information required to implement this section.

(d)   Final payments shall be due for all personal care services providers for the assessments pursuant to subdivision two of this section upon the due date for submission of the applicable quarterly report.

(e)   The commissioner of health may recoup deficiencies in final payments pursuant to paragraph (c) of subdivision five of this section.

7.   (a) If an estimated payment made for a month to which an assessment applies is less than ninety percent of the actual amount due for such month, interest shall be due and payable to the commissioner of health on the difference between the amount paid and the amount due from the day of the month the estimated payment was due until the date of payment. The rate of interest shall be twelve percent per annum or at the rate of interest set by the commissioner of taxation and finance with respect to underpayments of tax pursuant to subsection (e) of section one thousand ninety six of the tax law minus two percentage points.Interest under this paragraph shall not be paid if the amount thereof is less than one dollar. Interest, if not paid by the due date of the following month's estimated payment, may be collected by the commissioner of health pursuant to paragraph (c) of subdivision five of this section in the same manner as an assessment pursuant to subdivision two of this section.

(b)   If an estimated payment made for a month to which an assessment applies is less than seventy percent of the actual amount due for such month, a penalty shall be due and payable to the commissioner of health of five percent of the difference between the amount paid and the amount due for such month when the failure to pay is for a duration of not more than one month after the due date of the payment with an additional five percent for each additional month or fraction thereof during which such failure continues, not exceeding twenty-five percent in the aggregate. A penalty may be collected by the commissioner of health pursuant to paragraph (c) of subdivision five of this section in the same manner as an assessment pursuant to subdivision two of this section.

(c)   Overpayment by a personal care services provider of an estimated payment shall be applied to any other payment due from the personal care services provider pursuant to this section, or, if no payment is due, at the election of the personal care services provider shall be applied to future estimated payments or refunded to the personal care services provider. Interest shall be paid on overpayments from the date of overpayment to the date of crediting or refund

SSL

at the rate determined in accordance with paragraph (a) of this subdivision if the overpayment was made at the direction of the commissioner of health. Interest under this paragraph shall not be paid if the amount thereof is less than one dollar.

8. Funds accumulated, including income from invested funds, from the assessments specified in this section, including interest and penalties, shall be deposited by the commissioner of health and credited to the general fund.

9. Notwithstanding any inconsistent provision of law or regulation to the contrary, the assessments pursuant to this section shall not be an allowable cost in the determination of reimbursement rates pursuant to this article.

10. The assessment shall not be collected in excess of twelve million dollars from such providers for the period of January first, nineteen hundred ninety-one through March thirty-first, nineteen hundred ninety-two. The amount of the assessment collected pursuant to subdivision two of this section in excess of twelve million dollars shall be refunded to providers by the commissioner of health based on the ratio which a provider's assessment for such period bears to the total of the assessments for such period paid by such providers.

11. Each exclusion of sources of gross receipts received from the assessments effective on or after April first, nineteen hundred ninety-two established pursuant to this section shall be contingent upon either: (a) qualification of the assessments for waiver pursuant to federal law and regulation; or (b) consistent with federal law and regulation, not requiring a waiver by the secretary of the department of health and human services related to such exclusion; in order for the assessments under this section to be qualified as a broad-based health care related tax for purposes of the revenues received by the state pursuant to the assessments not reducing the amount expended by the state as medical assistance for purposes of federal financial participation. The commissioner of health shall collect the assessments relying on such exclusions, pending any contrary action by the secretary of the department of health and human services. In the event the secretary of the department of health and human services determines that the assessments do not so qualify based on any such exclusion, then the exclusion shall be deemed to have been null and void as of April first, nineteen hundred ninety-two, and the commissioner of health shall collect any retroactive amount due as a result, without interest or penalty provided the personal care services provider pays the retroactive amount due within ninety days of notice from the commissioner of health to the provider that an exclusion is null and void. Interest and penalties shall be measured from the due date of ninety days following notice from the commissioner of health to the provider.

Added by Laws 1990, Ch. 938, § 32, eff. Jan. 1, 1991, Laws 1992, Ch. 41, § 54, repealing expiration date; amended by Laws 1992, Ch. 41, § 15, eff. Jan. 1, 1991; amended by Laws 1992, Ch. 41, §§ 25 through 30, eff. Apr. 2, 1992; amended by Laws 1996, Ch. 123, §§ 20, 21, eff. June 5, 1996; amended by Laws 1996, Ch. 474, § 231, eff. Aug. 8, 1996; amended by L. 1997, Ch. 389 Part A, § 205, eff. Aug. 7, 1997; amended by L. 1998, Ch. 56, Part A, § 107 and 120, eff. Apr. 28, 1998, deemed in full force and effect Apr. 1, 1998, § 367-i, as in effect Mar. 31, 1997, effective with respect to receipts received on or after Apr. 1, 1997 until Mar. 31, 2001; **amended** by L. 1999, Ch. 407, Part CC, § 10, eff. Aug. 9, 1999; **amended** by Laws 2002, Ch. 85, Part R, §§ 32 and 38, eff. May 29, 2002.

§ 367-o. Health insurance demonstration programs.

1.   Notwithstanding any inconsistent provision of law, the commissioner of health is authorized to establish one or more demonstration programs for the purposes of providing additional knowledge and experience in mechanisms to provide, maintain or subsidize health insurance coverage for unemployed and underemployed health care workers.

2.   Health insurance continuation demonstration.

(a)   The Commissioner of Health is hereby authorized to establish mechanisms to improve the process of authorizing medical assistance payment of health insurance premiums, pursuant to paragraph (c) of subdivision one of section three hundred sixty-seven-a of this title, on behalf of personal care and home health care workers who reside in any city with a population of one million or more and any county with a population of nine hundred thousand or more if such city or county is located within the metropolitan commuter transportation district created pursuant to section twelve hundred sixty-two of the public authorities law, and whose employment is irregular, episodic, or cyclical, and whose health insurance coverage therefore is frequently disrupted. Notwithstanding the provisions of section three hundred sixty-five of this title, the commissioner of health shall exercise discretion to determine whether medical assistance payment of such premiums is cost effective. If the commissioner of health determines that the test of cost effectiveness of insurance premiums is based on other than a case-by-case basis, no medical assistance payment for such premiums will be made until the commissioner of health obtains all necessary approvals under federal law and regulation to receive federal financial participation in the costs of such medical assistance.

(b)   The Commissioner of Health is authorized in consultation with the superintendent of insurance to require group health insurance plans and employer-based group health plans to report to the department or its designee, insofar as such reporting does not violate any provisions of the federal Employee Retirement Income Security Act of 1974 (ERISA), at such times and in such manner as the commissioner of health shall decide, any information needed to operate such a demonstration project, including, but not limited to, the number of persons in such plans who become ineligible each month for the continuation coverage described in paragraph (a) of this subdivision. In addition, every health maintenance organization certified under article forty-four of the public health law and every insurer licensed by the superintendent of insurance shall submit reports to the superintendent and to the Commissioner of Health in such form and at such times as may be required to implement the provisions of this subdivision.

SSL

3.   With respect to a demonstration program authorized by subdivision one of this section, the commissioner of health may solicit and accept applications for participation in the demonstration program from any employer, or group of employers, of personal care workers or home health workers, who are employed in any city with a population of one million or more and any county with a population of nine hundred thousand or more if such city or county is located within the metropolitan commuter transportation district created pursuant to section twelve hundred sixty-two of the public authorities law, and whose employers provide services primarily to medical assistance recipients, if the following conditions are met:

(a)   At least fifty percent of the persons receiving services from such employers are recipients of medical assistance;

(b)   The employer contributes to a group health insurance plan or employer based group health plan on behalf of such employees; and

(c)   no benefits are provided under the group health insurance plan or employer based group health plan in excess of the benefits provided to the majority of hospital workers in the community in which the personal care and home health care workers are employed. The commissioner of health is authorized to add up to fifty-eight million dollars per year for the period January first, two thousand through December thirty-first, two thousand two, and up to one hundred sixty-three million dollars per year for the period January first, two thousand three through June thirtieth, two thousand seven, to rates of payment for qualifying personal care providers and certified home health agencies who are approved to participate in the demonstration program. The commissioner may modify the amounts made available for any specific annual period so long as the total amount made available for the period of the demonstration is not exceeded.

4.   Notwithstanding any other law, rule or regulation to the contrary, any subscriber contract issued by an organization certified pursuant to article forty-four of the public health law may, for purposes of implementation of the demonstration authorized by subdivision three of this section, be issued on an experience rated basis.

5.   Between January first, two thousand and December thirty-first, two thousand two, the state share amount for all demonstrations pursuant to this section shall be no more than twenty-seven million dollars per twelve month period if averaged over the term of the demonstration; and between January first, two thousand three and June thirtieth, two thousand seven, the state share amount for all demonstrations pursuant to this section shall be no more than sixty-nine million dollars per twelve month period if averaged over the term of the demonstration.

Added by Laws 1992, Ch. 41, § 78, eff. Apr. 2, 1992, until July 1, 1994; **amended** by Laws 1994, Ch. 170, § 464, eff. Apr. 1, 1994, extending the period that the section remains effective to July 1, 1995; **amended** by Laws 1995, Ch. 81, § 96, eff. June 20, 1995, extending the period the section remains effective until July 1, 1997; **amended** by

Laws 1997, Ch. 433, § 17, extending expiration date to July 1, 1999, eff. Aug. 20, 1997; **amended** by Laws 1999, Ch. 1, § 107, eff. Dec. 30, 1999, deemed in full force and effect Jan. 1, 2000; **amended** by Laws 2000, Ch. 419, §§ 46-a and 46-b, eff. Sept. 13, 2000, deemed in full force and effect Jan. 1, 2000; L. 2003, Ch. 686, Part H, § 31, amending sub. 3, par. (c), and § 30, amending sub. 5, eff. Oct. 21, 2003; L. 2005, Ch. 58, §§ 4 and 98 (Part B), eff. April 12, 2005.

Editor's Note: In 1995, the Legislature added two S.S.L. § 367-p: one by Laws 1995, Ch. 81, § 91, the other by Laws 1995, Ch. 81, § 105-d. Both went into effect June 20, 1995, and are reproduced below.

§ 367-p.　Responsibilities of local districts for personal care services, home care services and private duty nursing.

Consistent with the provisions of section three hundred sixty-seven-n of this title, local social services district responsibilities for personal care services, home care services and private duty nursing shall include the following:

(a)　local districts with programs which place individuals discharged from hospitals solely into certified home health agencies shall ensure that those individuals are reviewed for possible placement into personal care services within two weeks of discharge and, if appropriate, placed into personal care services within four weeks thereof;

(b)　each local district shall, by September first, nineteen hundred ninety-five, review that plan of care for every recipient receiving personal care on a continuous basis pursuant to sections three hundred sixty-seven-k and three hundred sixty-seven-l of this title;

(c)　each local district shall ensure access to a consumer directed personal assistance program operated pursuant to section three hundred sixty-five-f of this title is available in the district to allow persons receiving home care pursuant to this title to directly arrange and pay for such care; and

(d)　local districts shall not restrict, and shall not be restricted from approving, the provision of private duty nursing as an alternative to nursing services provided by a home health agency where appropriate and cost-effective pursuant to section three hundred sixty-seven-l.

Added by Laws 1995, Ch. 81, § 91, eff. June 20, 1995.

Editor's Note: Another § 367-p follows.

§ 367-p.　Payment for limited home care services agencies. [*Expires March 31, 2005.*]

1.　Notwithstanding any law to the contrary, the commissioner shall, subject to the approval of the director of the budget, establish rates of payment for services provided by limited home care services agencies, licensed by the department of health pursuant to section thirty-six hundred five of the public health law, to eligible individuals who are residents of adult homes and enriched housing programs certified by the department in accordance with article seven of this chapter. Services for which reimbursement shall be available are personal care services provided directly by the agency and authorized and provided in accordance with the rules and regulations of the department; and the administration of medications and application of sterile dressings by a registered nurse provided, however, that the services provided by such agency are not services that must be provided to residents of such facilities pursuant to article seven of this chapter.

2.   Notwithstanding any law to the contrary, a limited home care services agency licensed by the department of health shall be reimbursed at a rate that is significantly less than the current costs of providing such services through a personal care provider or certified home health agency in the same service area.

3.   For purposes of this section, an eligible individual means an individual who is eligible for medical assistance, as determined by the appropriate social services district, which has also determined that such individual has a medical need for services and that such individual's needs can safely and appropriately be met by the limited home care services agency in the adult home or enriched housing program.

4.   Prior to authorizing payment for services provided to an eligible individual by a limited home care services agency, the appropriate social services district must determine that the service proposed to be provided by such agency is cost-effective in comparison to other available and appropriate service delivery options available in the district.

5.   The commissioner of health shall establish rates of payment for services provided pursuant to this section by November fifteenth, nineteen hundred ninety-seven.

   Amended by Laws 2003, Ch. 31, § 2, eff. April 8, 2003, extending expiration date until March 31, 2005.

§ 367-q   Personal care services worker recruitment and retention program

1.   The commissioner of health shall, subject to the availability of federal financial participation adjust personal care services medical assistance rates of payment established pursuant to this title for personal care services providers located in local social service districts which do not include a city with a population of over one million persons in accordance with subdivisions two and three of this section for purposes of improving recruitment and retention of personal care services workers or any worker with direct patient care responsibility in the following aggregate amounts for the following periods:

   (a)   for the period April first, two thousand two through December thirty-first, two thousand two, seven million dollars;

(b)   for the period January first, two thousand three through December thirty-first, two thousand three, fourteen million dollars;

(c)   for the period January first, two thousand four through December thirty-first, two thousand four, twenty-one million dollars;

(d)   for the period January first, two thousand five through December thirty-first, two thousand five, twenty-seven million dollars;

(e)   for the period January first, two thousand six through December thirty-first, two thousand six, thirty-one million dollars, provided however that for the period August first, two thousand six through December thirty-first, two thousand six, such rate adjustments shall be increased by an additional aggregate amount of four million dollars; and

(f)   for the period January first, two thousand seven through June thirtieth, two thousand seven, thirteen million five hundred thousand dollars.

2.   Such adjustments to rates of payments shall be allocated proportionally based on each personal care services providers' total annual hours of personal care services provided, as reported in each such provider's nineteen hundred ninety-nine cost report as submitted to the department of health prior to November first, two thousand one.

3.   Payments made pursuant to this section shall not be subject to subsequent adjustment or reconciliation.

4.   Personal care services providers which have their rates adjusted pursuant to this section shall use such funds for the purpose of recruitment and retention of non-supervisory personal care services workers or any worker with direct patient care responsibility only and are prohibited from using such funds for any other purpose. Each such personal care services provider shall submit, at a time and in a manner to be determined by the commissioner of health, a written certification attesting that such funds will be used solely for the purpose of recruitment and retention of non-supervisory personal care services workers or any worker with direct patient care responsibility. The commissioner of health is authorized to audit each such provider to ensure compliance with the written certification required by this subdivision and shall recoup any funds determined to have been used for purposes other than recruitment and retention of non-supervisory personal care services workers or any worker with direct patient care responsibility. Such recoupment shall be in addition to any other penalties provided by law.

Added by Laws 2002, Ch. 1, Part A, § 3, eff. April 1, 2002; **amended** by Laws 2002, Ch. 82, Part J, § 61, eff. April 1, 2002; **amended** by Laws 2005, Ch. 58, § 12 (Part B), eff. April 12, 2005; **Amended** by Laws 2006, Ch. 57, § 10-g (Part D) Apr. 12, 2006; Ch. 109, § 46, 46-a (Part C), Apr. 1, 2006.

§ 367-r   Private duty nursing services worker recruitment and retention program

1.   [Until Jan 1, 2007 §367-r reads as set out below:]

The commissioner of health shall, subject to the provisions of subdivision two of this section and to the availability of federal financial participation, increase medical assistance rates of payment by three percent for services provided on and after December first, two thousand two, for private duty nursing services for the purposes of improving recruitment and retention of private duty nurses.

2. Private duty nursing services providers which have their rates adjusted pursuant to this section shall use such funds solely for the purposes of recruitment and retention of private duty nurses and are prohibited from using such funds for any other purpose. Funds provided under this section are not intended to supplant support provided by a local government. Each such provider, with the exception of self-employed private duty nurses, shall submit, at a time and in a manner to be determined by the commissioner of health, a written certification attesting that such funds will be used solely for the purpose of recruitment and retention of private duty nurses. The commissioner of health is authorized to audit each such provider to ensure compliance with the written certification required by this subdivision and shall recoup all funds determined to have been used for purposes other than recruitment and retention of private duty nurses. Such recoupment shall be in addition to any other penalties provided by law.

1. [Eff. Jan 1, 2007 and expires and repealed Jan 1, 2009 §367-r reads as set out below:]

1. The commissioner of health shall, subject to the provisions of subdivision two of this section and to the availability of federal financial participation, increase medical assistance rates of payment by three percent for services provided on and after December first, two thousand two, for private duty nursing services for the purposes of improving recruitment and retention of private duty nurses.

1-a. Medically fragile children. In addition, the commissioner shall further increase rates for private duty nursing services that are provided to medically fragile children to ensure the availability of such services to such children. In establishing rates of payment under this subdivision, the commissioner shall consider the cost neutrality of such rates as related to the cost effectiveness of caring for medically fragile children in a non-institutional setting as compared to an institutional setting. Medically fragile children shall, for the purposes of this subdivision, have the same meaning as in subdivision three-a of section thirty-six hundred fourteen of the public health law. Such increased rates for services rendered to such children may take into consideration the elements of cost, geographical differentials in the elements of cost considered, economic factors in the area in which the private duty nursing service is provided, costs associated with the provision of private duty nursing services to medically fragile children, and the need for incentives to improve services and institute economies and such increased rates shall be payable only to those private duty nurses who can demonstrate, to the satisfaction of the department of health, satisfactory training and experience to provide services to such children. Such increased rates shall be determined based on application of the case mix adjustment factor for

AIDS home care program services rates as determined pursuant to applicable regulations of the department of health. The commissioner may promulgate regulations to implement the provisions of this subdivision.

2. Private duty nursing services providers which have their rates adjusted pursuant to this section shall use such funds solely for the purposes of recruitment and retention of private duty nurses or to ensure the delivery of private duty nursing services to medically fragile children and are prohibited from using such funds for any other purpose. Funds provided under this section are not intended to supplant support provided by a local government. Each such provider, with the exception of self-employed private duty nurses, shall submit, at a time and in a manner to be determined by the commissioner of health, a written certification attesting that such funds will be used solely for the purpose of recruitment and retention of private duty nurses or to ensure the delivery of private duty nursing services to medically fragile children. The commissioner of health is authorized to audit each such provider to ensure compliance with the written certification required by this subdivision and shall recoup all funds determined to have been used for purposes other than recruitment and retention of private duty nurses or the delivery of private duty nursing services to medically fragile children. Such recoupment shall be in addition to any other penalties provided by law.

Added by Laws 2002, Ch. 82, Part J, § 44, eff. April 1, 2002; Laws 2006, Ch. 57, § 58-a (Part A) Apr. 12, 2006; Laws 2006, Ch. 109, § 10, (Part C) Apr. 1, 2006.

§ 367-s.   [There are two sections 367-s.] Long term care demonstration program.

1. Notwithstanding any inconsistent provision of law, the commissioner of health is authorized to establish a long term care demonstration program for persons eligible to receive services under this title, to operate in up to four social services districts, for the purposes of creating incentives for providers to care for individuals with more complex medical needs, supporting relatives and other caregivers to assist patients needing care at home and reducing the need for institutionalization.

2. The provisions of this section shall not take effect unless all necessary approvals under federal law and regulation have been obtained to receive federal financial participation in the costs of the health care services provided pursuant to this section.

3. (a) to this section may include a program to improve the availability of care for persons with clinically complex care needs who are being discharged from hospitals or residential health care facilities. In this regard, and in accordance with paragraph (d) of this subdivision, the commissioner shall adjust the rates of payment to selected home health agencies certified under article thirty-six of the public health law that provide services to such persons.

(b) Eligible certified home health agencies shall:

(i) demonstrate they have the experience and resources to provide services to individuals who are discharged from hospitals or residential health care facilities with clinically complex care needs, as determined in accordance with criteria established by the commissioner.

(ii) demonstrate that they are capable of meeting such other conditions as may be established by the commissioner.

(c) In selecting eligible certified home health agencies, the commissioner shall consider the likelihood that the agency will provide improved availability of care and may consider such other matters as the commissioner deems appropriate.

(d) The adjusted Medicaid rate pursuant to this subdivision shall be available for eligible certified home health agencies for services provided to individuals, eligible for medical assistance pursuant to this title, who are discharged from a hospital or residential health care facility and have clinically complex care needs, as determined in accordance with criteria established by the commissioner. Such rate shall be payable for services provided up to the first sixty days after discharge from a hospital or residential health care facility.

4. One or more demonstration sites established pursuant to this section may include the provision of respite care through innovative models. Subject to the approval of the director of the division of the budget, the commissioner is authorized to establish payment rates or fees for services provided pursuant to this subdivision.

5. One or more of the demonstration sites established pursuant to this section may include a program with authority to make payments for personal care services that are provided by a consumer's family members.

Addedby Laws 2005, Ch. 63, § 31 (Part C), eff. April 12, 2005, deemed eff. on and after April 1, 2005.

§ 367-s   Emergency medical transportation services.

1. Notwithstanding any provision of law to the contrary, a supplemental medical assistance payment shall be made on an annual basis to providers of emergency medical transportation services in an aggregate amount not to exceed four million dollars for two thousand six and six million dollars for two thousand seven pursuant to the following methodology:

(a) For each emergency medical transportation services provider that receives medical assistance reimbursement processed through the state Medicaid payment system, the department of health shall determine the ratio of such provider's state-processed reimbursement to the total such reimbursement made during each quarter of the applicable calendar year, expressed as a percentage;

(b) For each such provider, the department of health shall multiply the percentage obtained pursuant to paragraph (a) of this subdivision by one-quarter of the applicable aggregate amount specified in the opening paragraph of this subdivision. The result of such calculation shall represent the "emergency medical transportation service supplemental payment" and shall be paid expeditiously to such provider on a quarterly basis;

(c)　Deleted

2.　The amount disbursed to emergency medical transportation services providers whose area of operation is within the city of New York will be twenty-five percent of the applicable aggregate amount, with the remaining seventy-five percent to be disbursed to all other emergency medical transportation services providers.

3.　If all necessary approvals under federal law and regulation are not obtained to receive federal financial participation in the payments authorized by this section, payments under this section shall be made in an aggregate amount not to exceed two million dollars for two thousand six and three million dollars for two thousand seven. In such case, the multiplier set forth in paragraph (b) of subdivision one of this section shall be deemed to be two million dollars or three million dollars as applicable to the annual period.

4.　Notwithstanding any inconsistent provisions of section three hundred sixty-eight-a of this title, or of any other law, to the contrary, the department of health shall pay one hundred per centum of the non-federal share of any payments made pursuant to this section.

Added by Laws 2005, Ch. 63, § 30 (Part E), eff. April 12, 2005, deemed eff. on and after April 1, 2005; Laws 2006, ch. 57, §65-a (Part A) (repealed by Laws 2006, ch. 109, §43 (Part C), eff. June 23, 2006, deemed eff. on and after April 1, 2006), legislative override of Governor's line veto filed April 28, 2006 (see 2006 note below); Laws 2006, Ch. 109, §43-a (Part C), eff. June 23, 2006, deemed eff. on and after April 1, 2006.

§ 367-t　Payment for emergency physician services

Amounts payable under this title for medical assistance for items and services provided to eligible persons by qualified emergency physicians, provided in an emergency room of an entity certified pursuant to article twenty-eight of the public health law to treat an emergency condition, as defined in subdivision three of section forty-nine hundred of the public health law, which are authorized pursuant to section three hundred sixty-five-a of this title shall be no less than twenty-five dollars per visit. For the purpose of this section eligible persons shall not include persons provided items and services by the medicaid managed care program.

Added by Laws 2006, Ch. 57, §68-g (Part A) (repealed by Laws 2006, Ch. 109, §36 (Part C), eff. June 23, 2006, deemed eff. on and after April 1, 2006), legislative override of Governor's line veto filed April 28, 2006 (see 2006 note below); **Added** by Laws 2006, Ch. 109, §36-a (Part C), eff. June 23, 2006, deemed eff. on and after April 1, 2006.

Add, Laws 2006, Ch. 57, §68-g (Part A) (repealed by Laws 2006, Ch. 109, §36 (Part C), eff. June 23, 2006, deemed eff. on and after April 1, 2006), legislative override of

SSL

Governor's line veto filed April 28, 2006 (see 2006 note below); add, Laws 2006, Ch. 109, §36-a (Part C), eff. June 23, 2006, deemed eff. on and after April 1, 2006.

§ 368. Quarterly estimates.

Each public welfare district shall submit to the department quarterly estimates of its anticipated expenditures for medical assistance for needy persons and administrative expenses not less than thirty days before the first day of each of the quarters beginning on the first day of the months of July, October, January and April, in such form and together with such other information as the department may require.

Added by Laws 1966, Ch. 256, eff. Apr. 30, 1966.

§ 368-a. State reimbursement.

1. The department shall review the expenditures made by social services districts for medical assistance for needy persons, and the administration thereof, before making reimbursement. Before approving such expenditures for reimbursement, the department shall give due consideration to the results of the reviews and audits conducted by the department of health pursuant to subdivision two of section three hundred sixty-four. If approved by the department, such expenditures shall not be subject to reimbursement by the state pursuant to section one hundred fifty-three or any provision of this chapter other than this section, but shall be subject to reimbursement by the state in accordance with this section and the regulations of the department as follows:

There shall be paid to each such district

(a) the amount of federal funds, if any, properly received or to be received on account of such expenditures;

(b) the full amount expended on behalf of the department for medical assistance furnished under this title to eligible patients in state institutions for the mentally disabled, in facilities or parts thereof for the care and treatment of drug dependent persons operated pursuant to the mental hygiene law and in other hospitals while such patients are on release from an institution in the state department of mental hygiene or from a drug abuse treatment facility or part thereof operated in compliance with applicable provisions of law and supervised by the state division of substance abuse services, to eligible veterans and their dependents in that part of the New York state home for veterans and their dependents at oxford that has been approved pursuant to law as a nursing home and in a hospital while on release from that home for the purpose of receiving care in such hospital, in that part of a public institution operated for the care of the mentally disabled that has been approved pursuant to law as an intermediate care facility, to eligible veterans and their dependents in that part of the New York state home for veterans and their dependents at oxford that has been approved pursuant to law as an intermediate care facility and in a hospital while on release from such intermediate care facilities for the purpose of receiving care in such hospital, and for the administration thereof, after first deducting therefrom any federal funds properly received or to be received on account thereof;

(c) the full amount expended for medical assistance furnished under this title to eligible Indians and members of their families residing on any Indian reservation in this state, and for the administration thereof, after first deducting therefrom any federal funds properly received or to be received on account thereof;

(d) fifty per centum of the amount expended for medical assistance furnished under this title to other eligible persons, and for the administration thereof, after first deducting therefrom any federal funds properly received or to be received on account thereof.

(e) one hundred per centum of the amount expended for the development of medical assistance data systems, after first deducting therefrom any federal funds properly received or to be received on account thereof. Such reimbursement shall be available only to the extent that such projects have received federal approval and to the extent that claims for ninety percent federal aid have been approved.

(f) The full amount expended on behalf of the department for medical assistance furnished to persons described in subdivision five of section three hundred sixty-five of this article, including the administration thereof, after first deducting therefrom any federal funds properly received or to be received on account of such expenditures.

(g) Notwithstanding any other provision of law, reimbursement for the following services: care, treatment, maintenance and nursing services in nursing homes and health related care and services in intermediate care facilities provided in accordance with paragraph (b) of subdivision two of section three hundred sixty-five-a of this title; home health services provided in accordance with paragraph (d) of subdivision two of section three hundred sixty-five-a of this title; personal care services provided in accordance with paragraph (e) of subdivision two of section three hundred sixty-five-a of this title; long term home health care programs services provided in accordance with section three hundred sixty-seven-c of this title; and nursing home transition and diversion services provided in accordance with subdivision six-a of section three hundred sixty-six of this title shall be made as follows:

(i) for services provided on or after January first, nineteen hundred eight-four through December thirty-first, nineteen hundred eight-four, seventy-two per centum after first deducting therefrom any federal funds properly received or to be received on account thereof;

(ii) for services provided on or after January first, nineteen hundred eight-five through December thirty-first, nineteen hundred eighty-five, seventy-six per centum after first deducting therefrom any federal funds properly received or to be received on account thereof; and

(iii) for services provided on or after January first, nineteen hundred eighty-six through March thirty-first, nineteen hundred ninety-four, eighty per centum after first deducting therefrom any federal funds properly received or to be received on account thereof;

(iv) for services provided on or after April first, nineteen hundred ninety-four eighty-one and two hundred thirty-five thousandths per centum after first deducting therefrom any federal funds properly received or to be received on account thereof.

(h) (i) Beginning January first, nineteen hundred eighty-four, one hundred per centum of the amount expended for medical assistance for those individuals who are eligible pursuant to section three hundred sixty-six of this article as a result of a mental disability as determined by the commissioner in consultation with the commissioner of the office of mental health and the commissioner of the office of mental retardation and developmental disabilities and with the approval of the director of the budget after first deducting therefrom any federal funds properly received or to be received on account thereof.

(ii) Notwithstanding any other provision of law to the contrary, on and after the effective date of this subparagraph, the department of health shall make no further recovery or recoupment of monies that were advanced to local social services districts, during the period from April first, nineteen hundred ninety-two to the effective date of this subparagraph, to cover the medical assistance costs pursuant to this paragraph for rehabilitative services for residents of community residences licensed or operated by the office of mental health or for office of mental retardation and developmental disabilities home and community based waiver services.

(i) The full amount expended on behalf of the department for medical assistance furnished to persons described in subdivision eight of section three hundred sixty-five of this article, including the administration thereof, after first deducting therefrom any federal funds properly received or to be received on account thereof.

(j) Notwithstanding any other provision of law, but in conjunction with the provisions of paragraph (g) of subdivision one of this section, reimbursement for the care and services provided to those persons eligible pursuant to subparagraph seven of paragraph (a) of subdivision one of section three hundred sixty-six of this title shall be seventy-five per centum after first deducting therefrom any federal funds properly received or to be received on account thereof.

(k) Notwithstanding any other provision of law, reimbursement by the state for payments made, whether by the department on behalf of a social services district pursuant to section three hundred sixty-seven-b of this article or by a social services district directly, for a supplementary bad debt and charity care adjustment component of rates of payment determined in accordance with subdivision fourteen-a of section twenty-eight hundred seven-c of the public health law for general hospital inpatient hospital services provided in accordance with paragraph (b) of subdivision two of section three hundred sixty-five-a of this article shall be limited to the amount of federal funds properly received or to be received on account of such expenditures; provided, however, that reimbursement shall be made by the state for the full amount expended for a supplementary bad debt and charity care adjustment for a general hospital operated by the state of New York or by the state university of New York, after first deducting therefrom any federal funds properly received or to be received on account of such expenditure.

(l) Effective January first, nineteen hundred ninety, one hundred per centum of the amount expended for medical assistance for those individuals who are eligible pursuant to paragraphs (n) and (o) of subdivision four of section three hundred sixty-six of this article after first deducting therefrom any federal funds properly received or to be received on account thereof.

(m) Notwithstanding any other provision of law, reimbursement by the state for payments made, whether by the department on behalf of a social services district pursuant to section three hundred sixty-seven-b of this article or by a social services district directly, for a supplementary low income patient adjustment component of rates of payment for a public general hospital determined in accordance with subdivision fourteen-d of section twenty-eight hundred seven-c of the public health law for general hospital inpatient hospital services provided in accordance with paragraph (b) of subdivision two of section three hundred sixty-five-a of this article shall be limited to the amount of federal funds properly received or to be received on account of such expenditures; provided, however, that reimbursement shall be made by the state for the full amount expended for a supplementary low income patient adjustment for a general hospital operated by the state of New York or by the state university of New York, after first deducting therefrom any federal funds properly received or to be received on account of such expenditure.

(n) Notwithstanding any inconsistent provision of law, reimbursement for the amount expended for medical assistance furnished under this title to eligible persons pursuant to a statewide managed care plan or managed care demonstration program, or to eligible persons enrolled in any health maintenance organization or other entity authorized by law to furnish comprehensive health services pursuant to a plan, shall be reimbursed, after first deducting therefrom any federal funds properly received or to be received on account thereof, in accordance with the following schedule: (i) for services provided for the period April first, nineteen hundred ninety-four to March thirty-first, nineteen hundred ninety-nine, fifty-three and eight hundred seventy-five ten thousandths percent thereof; and (ii) for services provided for the period April first, nineteen hundred ninety-nine to March thirty-first, two thousand three, fifty percent thereof.

(o) Notwithstanding any other provision of law, reimbursement by the state for payments made, whether by the department on behalf of a social services district pursuant to section three hundred sixty-seven-b of this article or by a social services district directly, for the component of rates of payment for a general hospital determined in accordance with paragraph (s) of subdivision eleven of section twenty-eight hundred seven-c of the public health law for general hospital inpatient hospital services provided in accordance with paragraph (b) of subdivision two of section three hundred sixty-five-a of this article shall be one hundred per centum of the amount expended for medical assistance, after first deducting therefrom any federal funds properly received or to be received on account of such expenditure.

(p) Notwithstanding any other provision of law, reimbursement by the state for payments made, whether by the department on behalf of a social services district pursuant to section three hundred sixty-seven-b of this article or by a social services district directly, for a public general hospital indigent care adjustment payment for a public general hospital determined in accordance with subdivision fourteen-f of section twenty-eight hundred seven-c of the public health law for general hospital inpatient hospital services provided in accordance with paragraph (b) of subdivision two of section three hundred sixty-five-a of this article shall be limited to the amount of federal funds properly received or to be received on account of such expenditures; provided, however, that reimbursement shall be made by the state for the full amount expended for a public general hospital indigent care adjustment for a general hospital operated by the state of New York or by the state university of New York, after first deducting therefrom any federal funds properly received or to be received on account of such expenditure.

(q) [*Expires and repealed December 31, 2006.*] Notwithstanding any inconsistent provision of this chapter or any other provision of law to the contrary, reimbursement for the amount expended for medical assistance furnished under this title to eligible persons for services provided by a managed long term care plan, shall be based upon a uniform average of expenditures reflecting a mix of primary, acute and long term care services. Such uniform average, or aver-ages, will be determined by the commissioner of health and shall reflect the mix of services as applied to the amounts calculated pursuant to applicable paragraphs (g) and (n) of this subdivision, after first deducting therefrom any federal funds properly received or to be received on account of such expenditure.

(r) [*Expires Oct. 1, 2004.*] Notwithstanding any other provision of law, reimbursement by the state for payments made, whether by the department of health on behalf of a social services district pursuant to section three hundred sixty-seven-b of this title or by a social services district directly, for medical assistance furnished pursuant to the provisions of subparagraph one of paragraph (q) of subdivision four of section three hundred sixty-six of this title to children born on or before September thirtieth, nineteen hundred eighty-three, shall be made for the full amount expended for such children, after first deducting therefrom any federal funds properly received or to be received on account of such expenditure.

(s) [*Expires Oct. 1, 2004.*] Notwithstanding any other provision of law, reimbursement by the state for payments made, whether by the department of health on behalf of a social services district pursuant to section three hundred sixty-seven-b of this title or by a social services district directly, for medical assistance furnished pursuant to the provisions of subparagraph one of paragraph (t) of subdivision four of section three hundred sixty-six of this title to children, shall be made for the full amount expended for such children, after first deducting therefrom any federal funds properly received or to be received on account of such expenditure.

(t) (i) for services provided on or after January first, two thousand three through December thirty-first, two thousand four, fifty percent of the amount expended for health care services under section three hundred sixty-nine-ee of this article, after first deducting therefrom any federal funds properly received or to be received on account thereof;

(ii) for services provided on or after January first, two thousand five, through September thirtieth, two thousand five, seventy-five percent of the amount expended for health care services under section three hundred sixty-nine-ee of this article, after first deducting therefrom any federal funds properly received or to be received on account thereof;

(iii) for services provided on or after October first, two thousand five, through December thirty-first, two thousand five, seventy-five percent of the amount expended by the social services district consisting of the city of New York, and one hundred percent of the amount expended by all other social services districts, for health care services under section three hundred sixty-nine-ee of this article, after first deducting therefrom any federal funds properly received or to be received on account thereof; and

(iv) for services provided on or after January first, two thousand six through December thirty-first, two thousand six, and thereafter, one hundred percent of the amount expended for health care services under section three hundred sixty-nine-ee of this article, after first deducting therefrom any federal funds properly received or to be received on account thereof.

(u) Notwithstanding any other provision of law, the full amount expended for family planning services provided to eligible persons pursuant to subparagraph eleven of paragraph (a) of subdivision one of section three hundred sixty-six of this title, after first deducting therefrom federal funds properly received or to be received on account of such expenditures.

(v) One hundred per centum of the amount expended for medical assistance furnished pursuant to subparagraphs twelve and thirteen of paragraph (a) of subdivision one of section three hundred sixty-six of this title, and one hundred per centum of the amount expended for the administration thereof, after first deducting any federal funds properly received or to be received on account of such expenditures.

(w) One hundred per centum of the amount expended for the administration of medical assistance furnished pursuant to paragraph (v) of subdivision four of section three hundred sixty six of this title, after first deducting any federal funds properly received or to be received on account of such expenditures.

(x)   One hundred percent of the amount expended for health care services as determined in accordance with paragraph (c) of subdivision ten of section twenty-eight hundred seven-d of the public health law, after first deducting therefrom any federal funds properly received or to be received on account thereof.

(y)   [Eff. April 1, 2007] One hundred percent of the amount expended for health care services as determined in accordance with paragraph (v-1) of subdivision four of section three hundred sixty-six of this title, after first deducting therefrom any federal funds properly received or to be received on account thereof.

2.   (a) For the purpose of state reimbursement under this title, expenditures for administration of medical assistance for needy persons shall include expenditures for salaries of employees of local welfare departments, except for those excluded under paragraph (b) of this subdivision; operation, maintenance and service costs; and such other expenditures, such as equipment costs, depreciation charges, and rental values, as may be approved by the department. It shall not include expenditures for capital additions or improvements.

(b)   State reimbursement shall not be made for any part of the salary of a social services official, or a chief executive officer of a social services department, whose qualifications do not conform to those fixed by the department, or a city or town service officer; nor shall such reimbursement be made on the salary of a deputy commissioner, or deputy director or an employee, unless his employment is necessary for the administration of medical assistance and his qualifications conform to those fixed by the department.

(c)   State reimbursement shall not be made for any part of the salary of a local medical director appointed after the effective date of this act whose qualifications do not conform to those established pursuant to section three hundred sixty-four of this title.

(d)   State reimbursement shall not be made for any part of the cost of those items of care, services, supplies and equipment, and drugs which represent co-payment amounts for which a provider of medical assistance is authorized to charge a recipient in accordance with subdivision six of section three hundred sixty-seven-a of this article.

3.   (a) Claims for state reimbursement shall be made in such form and manner and at such times and for such periods as the department shall determine.

(b)   When certified by the department, state reimbursement shall be paid from the state treasury upon the audit and warrant of the comptroller out of funds made available therefor.

(c)   When the moneys allotted to the state by the federal department of health, education and welfare or other authorized federal agency for any quarter shall have been received by the department of taxation and finance, the department shall, as soon as possible, certify to the comptroller the amount to which each public welfare district is entitled for such quarter and such amount shall be paid out of the state treasury after audit by the comptroller to the respective public welfare districts.

(d)   The department is authorized in its discretion to make advances to public welfare districts in anticipation of the state reimbursement provided for in this section.

4.   Payment of state reimbursement and advances shall be made to the fiscal officer of the public welfare district entitled thereto pursuant to the provisions of this chapter.

Added by Laws 1966, Ch. 256; **amended** by Laws 1968, Chs. 270, 669, 993; Laws 1971, Ch. 110; Laws 1972, Chs. 222, 694; Laws 1973, Chs. 195, 338; Laws 1974, Ch. 778; Laws 1975, Ch. 667; Laws 1977, Ch. 77; para. (1)(f) **added** by Laws 1979, Ch. 277; **amended** by Laws 1980, Ch. 471, eff. July 23, 1980; **amended** by Laws 1982, Ch. 180, eff. June 8, 1982, subd. (1)(b); **amended** by Laws 1983, Ch. 83, eff. Apr. 1, 1983 until Mar. 31, 1985; **amended** by Laws 1983, Ch. 816, eff. Aug. 3, 1983; **amended** by Laws 1985, Ch. 351, eff. July 18, 1985; **amended** by Laws 1985, Ch. 491, eff. July 24, 1985; **amended** by Laws 1988, Ch. 710, § 7, eff. Jan. 1, 1989; **amended** by Laws 1989, Ch. 74, § 3, eff. Apr. 1, 1989; **amended** by Laws 1989, Ch. 584, § 6, eff. Jan. 1, 1990; **amended** by Laws 1990, Ch. 938, § 14, eff. Jan. 1, 1991; **amended** by Laws 1994, Ch. 170, §§ 475-476, eff. Apr. 1, 1994; **amended** by Laws 1995, Ch. 81, §§ 21, 87 -88, eff. Apr. 1, 1995; **amended** by Laws 1996, Ch. 639, eff. Sept. 12, 1996, but deemed to be in full force and effect on and after July 1, 1996; para. (1)(q) **added** by Laws 1997, Ch. 659, eff. Sept. 24, 1997; **amended** by Laws 1998, Ch. 2, § 25, eff. Jan. 1, 1999, amendments to expire and be deemed repealed Mar. 31, 2001; **amended** by Laws 1999, Ch. 412, Part F, § 32-b, eff. Aug. 9, 1999, deemed in full force and effect Apr. 1, 1999; subpara. (1)(t) **added** by Laws 1999, Ch. 105, § 105, eff. Dec. 30, 1999, deemed in full force and effect Jan. 1, 2000; **amended** by Laws 2000, Ch. 57 Part A § 4, eff. May 15, 2000, deemed in full force and effect Apr. 1, 2000, and Ch. 57 Part E § 2 eff. May 15, 2000 **amended** by Laws 2001, Chs. 20 Part C, § 1, eff. Mar. 30, 2001, 63 Part C § 1, eff. June 25, 2001, Ch. 150 and Ch. 383; **amended** by Laws 2002, Ch. 1, Part A, § 55, eff. April 1, 2002, § 58, eff. Oct. 1, 2002 and § 65, eff. April 1, 2003, Ch. 1, Part B, §§ 4 and 31, eff. April 1, 2002, Ch. 82, Part J, §§ 9, 10 and 20, eff. April 1, 2002; L. 2003, Ch. 62, Part A3, § 21, eff. May 15, 2003, extending expiration date until July 1, 2005 and Ch. 62, Part Z2, §§ 42, 43, eff. May 15, 2003, Ch. 686, Part H, § 22, amending and re-designating sub. 1, par. (h) (i), and adding par. (h) (ii), eff. Apr. 1, 2003; **amended** by Laws 2004, Ch. 58, Part B, § 5, eff. Aug, 20, 2004, Part C, §§ 2, 34, eff. April 1, 2004, Ch. 627, § 2, amending subd. (g), eff. Oct. 19, 2004; **amended** by Laws 2005, Ch. 58, § 9 (Part C), eff. April 12, 2005, deemed eff. on and after April 1, 2005; Laws 2006, Ch. 176, §5, eff. April 1, 2007.

§ 368-b.   State reimbursement to local health districts; chargebacks.

1.   Each approved local health district which enters into a contract with the department of health pursuant to section three hundred sixty-four-a of this title shall submit to the department of health a quarterly report of expenditures for administrative expenses incurred in the performance of such contract. The

SSL

department of health shall review such expenditures and, upon approval, shall submit the report to the department. Upon receipt of such approved report, there shall be paid to each such district

(a) the amount of federal funds, if any, properly received or to be received on account of such expenditures; and

(b) fifty per centum of the amount expended for such administrative expenses, after first deducting therefrom any federal funds properly received or to be received on account thereof.

2. The department of health shall submit a quarterly report to the department of expenditures for administrative expenses incurred by each of the state health districts in the performance of the cooperative agreement entered into pursuant to section three hundred sixty-four-a of this title. Upon receipt of such report, the department shall deduct the amount of federal funds, if any, properly received or to be received on account of such expenditures from the total amounts reported for each such district. Fifty per centum of the balance shall be apportioned among the public welfare districts served by such district in the ratio that the total expenditures by each such public welfare district for medical assistance for needy persons for the quarter bears to the total expenditures by all such public welfare districts for such quarter. The proportionate share shall be deducted from the next payment due each of such public welfare districts pursuant to section three hundred sixty-eight-a of this title.

Added by Laws 1966, Ch. 256, eff. Apr. 30, 1966.

§ 368-c. Audit of state rates of payment to providers of health care services.

1. The commissioner may conduct, or have conducted, an audit of financial and statistical reports used for the purpose of establishing rates of payment or fees made in accordance with the medical assistance program.

2. The commissioner shall implement audit procedures and activities to enable the identification of the appropriate rates of payment made through the medical assistance program. Furthermore, the commissioner shall conduct an annual review of financial and statistical reports with respect to residential health care facilities certified pursuant to article twenty-eight of the public health law. Where such review indicates substantial noncompliance, as defined in regulation by the commissioner, with the requirements of the medical assistance program the commissioner shall conduct or have conducted an on-site audit. Provided further however, that at least once every four fiscal years an on-site audit shall be conducted.

3. To allow for the recomputation of affected fees or rates of payment, the commissioner shall, as appropriate, supply audit findings to the governmental agency or corporation organized and operating in accordance with article forty-three of the insurance law responsible for the promulgation of fees or rates of reimbursement.

4. The commissioner shall enter into interagency agreements, subject to the approval of the director of the budget, to delineate the respective responsibilities of the department and other governmental agencies with respect to this section.

5. The commissioner is authorized to promulgate regulations to implement the provisions of this section.

Added by Laws 1983, Ch. 83, § 9 eff. Apr. 1, 1983; **amended** by Laws 1984, Ch. 805, eff. Sept. 1, 1984.

§ 368-d. Reimbursement to public school districts and state operated/ state supported schools which operate pursuant to article eighty-five, eighty-seven or eighty-eight of the education law.

1. The department shall review claims for expenditures made by or on behalf of local public school districts, and state operated/state supported schools which operate pursuant to article eighty-five, eighty-seven or eighty-eight of the education law, for medical care, services and supplies which are furnished to children with handicapping conditions or such children suspected of having handicapping conditions, as such children are defined in the education law. If approved by the department, payment for such medical care, services and supplies which would otherwise qualify for reimbursement under this title and which are furnished in accordance with this title and the regulations of the department to such children, shall be made in accordance with the department's approved medical assistance fee schedules by payment to such local public school district, and state operated/state supported schools which operate pursuant to article eighty-five, eighty-seven or eighty-eight of the education law, which furnished the care, services or supplies either directly or by contract, of the amount of any federal funds properly received or to be received on account of such expenditures.

2. Claims for payment under this section shall be made in such form and manner, at such times, and for such periods as the department may require.

3. The department's liability for payment for expenditures by or on behalf of local public school districts, and state operated/state supported schools which operate pursuant to article eighty-five, eighty-seven or eighty-eight of the education law, for services furnished to children under this section shall be limited solely to payment of the federal funds received, or to be received, on account of such expenditures. in the event of any subsequent disallowances or recoupment of such funds by a federal governmental agency, upon notification by the commissioner, the comptroller shall withhold or cause to be withheld the amount of such disallowance or recoupment from moneys otherwise due the local public school district, and state operated/state supported schools which operate pursuant to article eighty-five, eighty-seven or eighty-eight of the education law, as state aid pursuant to any provision of the education law, and the comptroller shall transfer such amount to the credit of the department of social services medical assistance program local assistance account.

SSL

Added by Laws 1989, Ch. 558, § 5, eff. July 16, 1989, and applicable to medical care, supplies and services furnished on or after July 1, 1989. **Amended** by Laws 1995, Ch. 82, § 59, eff. July 1, 1995.

§ 368-e. Reimbursement to counties for pre-school children with handicapping conditions. [*Expires July 1, 2005, pursuant to Laws 2002, Ch. 99 § 1, as amended.*]

1. The department shall review claims for expenditures made by counties and the city of New York for medical care, services and supplies which are furnished to preschool children with handicapping conditions or such preschool children suspected of having handicapping conditions, as such children are defined in the education law. If approved by the department, payment for such medical care, services and supplies which would otherwise qualify for reimbursement under this title and which are furnished in accordance with this title and the regulations of the department to such children, shall be made in accordance with the department's approved medical assistance fee schedules by payment to such county or city which furnished the care, services or supplies either directly or by contract, of the amount of any federal funds properly received or to be received on account of such expenditures. Notwithstanding any provisions of law, rule or regulation to the contrary, any clinic or diagnostic and treatment center licensed under article twenty-eight of the public health law, which as determined by the state education department, in conjunction with the department of health, has a less than arms length relationship with the provider approved under section forty-four hundred ten of the education law shall, subject to the approval of the department and based on standards developed by the department, be authorized to directly submit such claims for medical assistance, services or supplies so furnished for any period thereafter beginning on or after July first, nineteen hundred ninety-seven. The actual full cost of the individualized education program (IEP) related services incurred by the clinic shall be reported on the New York State consolidated fiscal report in the education law section forty-four hundred ten program costs center in which the student is placed and the associated medical assistance revenue shall be reported in the same manner.

2. Claims for payment under this section shall be made in such form and manner, at such times, and for such periods as the department may require.

3. The department's liability for payment for expenditures by or on behalf of such county or the city of New York for services furnished to preschool children under this section shall be limited solely to payment of the federal funds received, or to be received, on account of such expenditures. In the event of any subsequent disallowances or recoupment of such funds by a federal governmental agency, the commissioner shall withhold such amount from any moneys otherwise due the county or city of New York under this chapter.

Added by Laws 1989, Ch. 558, § 5, eff. July 16, 1989, and applicable to medical care, supplies and services furnished on or after July 1, 1989; **amended** by Laws 1996, Ch. 474, § 177-a, eff. Aug. 8, 1996; **amended** by Laws 1997, Ch. 631, § 1; **amended** by Laws 1998, Ch. 568, § 1, eff. Aug. 5, 1998; **amended** by Laws 2000, Ch. 98, § 1, eff. June 23, 2000, extending the expiration date of the section to July 1, 2002; **amended** by Laws 2002, Ch. 99, § 1, eff. June 28, 2002, extending expiration date to July 1, 2005.

§ 368-f.   Reimbursement of costs under the early intervention program.

1.   The department shall review claims for expenditures made by or on behalf of social services districts for the administration of the early intervention program as established under title II-A of article twenty-five of the public health law. If approved by the department, payment for such expenditures, which were made in accordance with this title and the regulations of the department, shall be made by payment to such district, which incurred the expenditure, either directly or by contract, of the amount of any federal funds properly received or to be received on account of such expenditures.

2.   Claims for payment under this section shall be made in such form and manner, at such times, and for such periods as the department may require.

3.   The department's liability for payment for such administrative expenditures made by or on behalf of districts under this section shall be limited solely to payment of the federal funds received, or to be received, on account of such expenditures. In the event of any subsequent disallowances or recoupment of such funds by a federal governmental agency, upon notification by the commissioner, the comptroller shall withhold or cause to be withheld the amount of such disallowance or recoupment from any moneys otherwise due the district, as state aid pursuant to any provision of law, and the comptroller shall transfer such amount to the credit of the department of social services medical assistance administration program — local assistance account.

     Added by Laws 1993, Ch. 231, § 14, eff. July 1, 1993.

§ 369.   Application of other provisions.

1.   All provisions of this chapter not inconsistent with this title shall be applicable to medical assistance for needy persons and the administration thereof by the social services districts.

2.   (a) Notwithstanding any inconsistent provision of this chapter or other law, no lien may be imposed against the property of any individual prior to his or her death on account of medical assistance paid or to be paid on his or her behalf under this title, except:

     (i)   pursuant to the judgment of a court on account of benefits incorrectly paid on behalf of such individual, or

     (ii)   with respect to the real property of an individual who is an inpatient in a nursing facility, intermediate care facility for the mentally retarded, or other medical institution, and who is not reasonably expected to be discharged from the medical institution and to return home, provided, however, any such lien will dissolve upon the individual's discharge from the medical institution and return home; in addition, no such lien may be imposed on the individual's home if one of the following persons is lawfully residing in the home:

(A) the spouse of the individual;

(B) a child of the individual who is under twenty-one years of age or who is blind or permanently and totally disabled; or

(C) a sibling of the individual who has an equity interest in the home and who was residing in the home for a period of at least one year immediately before the date of the individual's admission to the medical institution.

(b)   (i) Notwithstanding any inconsistent provision of this chapter or other law, no adjustment or recovery may be made against the property of any individual on account of any medical assistance correctly paid to or on behalf of an individual under this title, except that recoveries must be pursued:

(A) upon the sale of the property subject to a lien imposed on account of medical assistance paid to an individual described in clause (ii) of paragraph (a) of this subdivision, or from the estate of such individual; and

(B) from the estate of an individual who was fifty-five years of age or older when he or she received such assistance.

(ii)   Any such adjustment or recovery shall be made only after the death of the individual's surviving spouse, if any, and only at a time when the individual has no surviving child who is under twenty-one years of age or is blind or permanently and totally disabled, provided, however, that nothing herein contained shall be construed to prohibit any adjustment or recovery for medical assistance furnished pursuant to subdivision three of section three hundred sixty-six of this chapter.

(iii)   In the case of a lien on an individual's home, any such adjustment or recovery shall be made only when:

(A) no sibling of the individual who was residing in the individual's home for a period of at least one year immediately before the date of the individual's admission to a medical institution referred to in subparagraph (ii) of paragraph (a) of subdivision two of this section, and is lawfully residing in such home and has lawfully resided in such home on a continuous basis since the date of the individual's admission to the medical institution, and

(B) no child of the individual who was residing in the individual's home for a period of at least two years immediately before the date of the individual's admission to a medical institution referred to in subparagraph (ii) of paragraph (a) of subdivision two of this section, and who establishes to the satisfaction of the state that he or she provided care to such individual which permitted such individual to reside at home rather than in an institution, and is lawfully residing in such home and has lawfully resided in such home on a continuous basis since the date of the individual's admission to the medical institution.

(c)   Nothing contained in this subdivision shall be construed to alter or affect the right of a social services official to recover the cost of medical assistance provided to an injured person in accordance with the provisions of section one hundred four-b of this chapter.

(d)   Where a recovery or adjustment is made pursuant to this title with respect to a case in a federally-aided category of medical assistance, a part of the net amount resulting from such recovery or adjustment shall be paid or credited to the federal government pursuant to federal law and the regulations of the federal department of health and human services.

3.   The department and any social services district is hereby authorized to maintain an action subject to sections one hundred one and one hundred four of this chapter to collect from either a trustee, creator, or creator's spouse any beneficial interest of either the creator or creator's spouse in any trust, other than a testamentary trust, to reimburse such department or district for the costs of medical assistance furnished to, or on behalf of, a creator or creator's spouse. For the purpose of this subdivision, the beneficial interest of the creator or creator's spouse includes the income and any principal amounts to which the creator or creator's spouse would have been entitled by the terms of such trust by right or in the discretion of the trustee, assuming the full exercise of discretion by the trustee for the distribution of the maximum amount to either the creator or the creator's spouse.

4.   Any inconsistent provision of this chapter or other law notwithstanding, all information received by social services and public health officials and service officers concerning applicants for and recipients of medical assistance may be disclosed or used only for purposes directly connected with the administration of medical assistance for needy persons.

5.   The requirements of this section with respect to adjustments and recoveries of medical assistance correctly paid shall be waived in cases of undue hardship, as determined pursuant to the regulations of the department in accordance with criteria established by the secretary of the federal department of health and human services.

6.   For purposes of this section, the term "estate" means all real and personal property and other assets included within the individual's estate and passing under the terms of a valid will or by intestacy.

SSL

Added by Laws 1966, Ch. 256; **amended** by Laws 1966, Ch. 800; **amended** by Laws 1977, Ch. 863, eff. Aug. 11, 1977; **amended** by Laws 1992, Ch. 41, § 85, eff. Apr. 2, 1992; **amended** by Laws 1994, Ch. 170, §§ 451-452, eff. Apr. 1, 1994.

TITLE 11-A—CATASTROPHIC HEALTH CARE EXPENSE PROGRAM

———

§ 369-a.   [Repealed, eff. July 1, 2005] Declaration of legislative findings and intent.

The legislature hereby finds and declares that there are significant gaps in health insurance coverage available to the citizens of this state through public and private sources. Individuals and families at all income levels face delayed access to care and extraordinary costs due to restrictive eligibility requirements, costs and limitations relating to existing coverage mechanisms. Therefore, it is necessary and appropriate to test approaches to expand coverage, including the implementation of a catastrophic health care expense demonstration program, as part of a comprehensive response to this critical problem.

Added by Laws 1988, Ch. 703, § 3, eff. Sept. 6, 1988, and deemed to be in full force and effect as of Apr. 1, 1988; **Repealed** by Laws 2005, Ch. 58, § 22 (Part B), eff. July 1, 2005.

§ 369-b.   [Repealed, eff. July 1, 2005] Definitions.

As used in this title:

1. "Family" or "family household" means the head of a household and spouse and all other persons residing in the same household for whom the head of the household or spouse has legal responsibility pursuant to section one hundred one of this chapter or has assumed responsibility.

2. "Family income" means all income received by a family as defined in subdivision one of this section during a calendar year, regardless of source or tax status. Such income shall include but not be limited to social security and retirement benefits, interest, dividends, total gain from the sale or exchange of a capital asset, net rental income, salary or earnings, net income from self-employment, inheritances, but shall not include a return of capital. Family income

shall not include the income of a child for whom the head of the household or spouse has legal or assumed responsibility to the extent that such income is in excess of the health care expenses incurred for the child during the calendar year.

3. "Health insurance benefits" means any amounts that are paid directly to a provider of service, or which are received or recoverable by the applicant under a plan providing care and other medical benefits, whether by insurance or otherwise, except for benefits received under this title.

4. "Health insurance premiums" means the amounts paid by or on behalf of the applicant, or individual family members in an application by a family household, for health insurance benefits. Premiums paid under an income protection policy are not considered health insurance premiums under this title.

5. "Health care expenses" means all expenses for care, services and supplies necessary to prevent, diagnose, correct or cure conditions that cause acute suffering, endanger life, result in illness or infirmity, interfere with the capacity for normal activity or threaten some significant handicap. Health insurance premiums not in excess of fifty per cent of the difference between the adjusted family income during a calendar year and one hundred percent of the federal poverty line for the household size in the year of application shall be considered health care expenses.

6. "Catastrophic health care expenses eligible under this title" means health care expenses that are covered under the medical assistance program as set forth in section three hundred sixty-five-a of this chapter, excluding expenses incurred for services provided to inpatients or residents of health care facilities other than expenses incurred for acute care services provided by general hospitals, that are incurred during a calendar year subsequent to the time when total health care expenses are in excess of fifty per cent of the difference between the adjusted family income during such year and one hundred percent of the federal poverty line for the household size in the year of application.

7. "Adjusted family income" means the family income during a calendar year reduced by documented alimony, support payments, FICA contributions and the amount of federal, state and local income taxes paid.

8. "Poverty line" means the official federal income poverty line, as defined and annually revised by the Federal Office of Management and Budget.

9. "Hardship" means a situation in which a family is unable to meet its expenses for needed health care services taking into consideration all available income and resources of the family. The commissioner shall establish and promulgate regulations governing the determination of hardship.

10. "Program" means the catastrophic health care expense program established by section three hundred sixty-nine-c of this article.

11. "Health care facility" is defined, for purposes of this title only, as a facility providing inpatient or residential care and which is eligible to receive payments under the medical assistance program in accordance with section three hundred sixty-five-a of this chapter.

SSL

Added by Laws 1978, Ch. 716, eff. Jan. 1, 1979; **amended** by Laws 1978, Ch. 717, eff. Jan 1, 1979; **amended** by Laws 1988, Ch. 703, § 4, eff. Sept. 6, 1988, and deemed to be in full force and effect as of Apr. 1, 1988; **amended** by Laws 1989, Ch. 676, eff. July 22, 1989; **amended** by Laws 1994, Ch. 311, §§ 2, 3, eff. July 20, 1994; **Repealed** by Laws 2005, Ch. 58, § 22 (Part B), eff. July 1, 2005.

§ 369-c.   [Repealed, eff. July 1, 2005] Scope of catastrophic health care expense program.

1.   There is hereby established a catastrophic health care expense program. The commissioner shall implement this program on a demonstration basis, upon receipt of at least one acceptable application from a social services district, within the amounts specifically allocated for this purpose, and in at least four social services districts selected by the commissioner from applicant districts, including the counties of Albany, Nassau, Onondaga and St. Lawrence. In selecting from the applicant districts those districts which will be authorized to participate in the demonstration program the commissioner shall consider such factors as the availability of health care services within the district to persons eligible for the medical assistance program, an estimate of the cost of the demonstration program, the percentage of individual providers participating in the medical assistance program and other considerations that the commissioner deems necessary in selecting social services districts that can best serve as demonstration program models.

2.   The program shall apply only to health care expenses incurred by families during a calendar year during which the family has resided for the full calendar year in a social services district where a demonstration project has been established, except for the following consideration: in the event that an applicant who was a resident on the first day of a calendar year in a local social services district that was selected for participation in the program and who, during the calendar year, changes his residence to outside such district may be eligible for assistance on only those catastrophic health care expenses incurred while a resident of the program participating district.

3.   Health care services to which the program shall apply shall be the same as those services for which medical assistance is available as set forth in section three hundred sixty-five-a of this chapter, except that expenses incurred for services provided to inpatients or residents of health care facilities, other than expenses incurred for acute care services provided by general hospitals shall not be eligible for reimbursement under the program.

4.   To the extent funds are made available a local social services district selected for a demonstration project in accordance with this title shall be reimbursed for one hundred percent of payments made by or through such district for direct cost incurred in providing benefits available under this title. Notwithstanding any inconsistent provisions of this title reimbursement to local social services districts selected for demonstration projects under this title may not exceed the amount authorized. In the event that the total applicants' reimbursable

amounts and amounts paid or to be paid directly to health care providers exceed the authorized available funds a local social services district may, at its option, finance such excess from local funds or pro-rate applicant benefits.

5.   Notwithstanding any inconsistent provision of law, the commissioner, subject to the approval of the state director of the budget, may apply for the appropriate waivers under federal law and regulation and may waive or modify any provisions of this chapter or regulation of the department and may promulgate such regulations as may be necessary to enable the department and/or social services districts to implement this title.

    Added by Laws 1978, Ch. 716, eff. Jan. 1, 1977, "provided, however, that it shall apply only to expenditures for health care services rendered on or after such date"; **amended** by Laws 1978, Ch. 717, eff. Jan. 1, 1979; **amended** by Laws 1988, Ch. 703, § 5, eff. Sept. 6, 1988, and deemed to be in full force and effect as of Apr. 1, 1988; **amended** by Laws 1989, Ch. 676, eff. July 22, 1989; **amended** by Laws 1994, Ch. 311, § 4, eff. July 20, 1994; **Repealed** by Laws 2005, Ch. 58, § 22 (Part B), eff. July 1, 2005.

§ 369-d.   [Repealed, eff. July 1, 2005] Operation of catastrophic health care expense program.

    A family is deemed to have incurred catastrophic health care expenses and is eligible for participation in the catastrophic health care expense program as follows:

    1.   (a) Eligibility. In identifying health care expenses which may be considered eligible catastrophic health care expenses, the date on which the service was rendered will control the sequence in determining the health care expenses to be met completely by the family and those eligible for assistance under this title.

    (b)   Assistance. A family is eligible for assistance for services available under this title for all eligible catastrophic health care expenses when, after deducting health insurance benefits, it has incurred during a calendar year health care expenses in excess of fifty percent of the difference between the adjusted or the projected adjusted family income during such year and one hundred percent of the federal poverty line for the household size in the year of the application.

    (c)   Hardship. Where the local social services official has determined that hardship exists, vendor payments may be made directly to the provider of services. Such direct payments shall not exceed the amount that would be reimbursed to the family for the service rendered. Hardship may be determined to exist at the time of application for interim authorization pursuant to subdivision two of this section or at the time of application for reimbursement pursuant to subdivision four of this section.

    2.   (a) An eligible family may apply to the local social services official for interim authorization to pay for services at rates or fees corresponding to rates or fees established for payment for services rendered to those in receipt of medical assistance. Upon receiving such interim authorization, a family eligible for

SSL

assistance determined not to meet hardship shall be billed by a vendor of services on forms prescribed by the commissioner and at rates or fees corresponding to rates or fees established for payment for services rendered to those in receipt of medical assistance.

(b) Such eligible families may not include for reimbursement or direct payment to vendors any costs, incurred subsequent to the date of interim authorization, for services furnished by providers who have been terminated from the medical assistance program.

(c) Such authorization shall not extend beyond the final day of the calendar year in which services on which eligibility for assistance under this title was based were rendered. Reimbursement to such family, or to an eligible family which does not apply for and receive such authorization, shall be determined in accordance with the provisions of subdivision four of this section.

(d) After a family has been authorized through the application process to receive assistance, or where a determination has been made that hardship exists for applicants eligible for assistance, payments for unpaid bills shall be made on a vendor basis to the provider of services on the basis of rates or fees corresponding to rates or fees established for payment for services rendered to persons or family households in receipt of medical assistance with the amount of payment equal to the amount that would have been reimbursed to the family if such bills had been paid.

3. Application and authorization. A family may submit an application to the social services official in the social services district where the family resides in order for the local social services official to determine whether a family is eligible for assistance under this title.

(1) Applications for interim authorization or a request for a determination as to hardship should be made by or on behalf of the family at the time during the calendar year when the family's health care expenses equal or exceed the amounts specified under subdivision one of this section.

(2) A family seeking reimbursement shall apply after the end of the calendar year in which it incurred eligible catastrophic health care expenses and not later than within the first six months following such calendar year.

(b) Application for reimbursement shall include:

(1) a schedule of eligible health care expenses incurred, supported by individual bills and proof of payment if payment has been made;

(2) a copy of federal, state and local income tax returns filed by all members of the family;

(3) a schedule of any income received by the family members which was not includable on federal, state or local income tax returns; and

(4) such other information as the commissioner may require.

(c) A family receiving assistance or where a determination has been made that hardship exists shall notify the local social services official of any change in family size, income or estimated income on which eligibility determination was based within thirty days of such change.

(d)　Authorization shall not extend beyond the final day of the calendar year in which services on which the application was based were rendered.

4.　Reimbursement to the family or in behalf of the family.

(a)　Reimbursement to the family for catastrophic health care expenses eligible for assistance under this title shall be determined:

(1)　by computing the cost of eligible health care services provided, using the rate or fee established for such services for payment for medical assistance provided to those in receipt of medical assistance;

(2)　by identifying the vendor charge for each service provided and for which reimbursement is requested; and

(3)　by applying the appropriate program proportional share to the lesser of subparagraph one or two of this paragraph for assistance with cost sharing cases.

(b)　Reimbursement to a family under this title for paid bills shall be made by check made payable to the single applicant or head of household applicant.

(c)　In the event that an application for assistance under this title is not filed during the calendar year in which services were rendered and an application for reimbursement is filed within the first six months of the calendar year following the year in which the family incurred and paid eligible catastrophic health care expenses for which assistance would be available, reimbursement will be made directly to the family for such expenditures at amounts in accordance with the lesser of subparagraph one or two of paragraph (a) of this subdivision. If at the time of application for reimbursement of unpaid eligible catastrophic health care expenses for which assistance is available or for which assistance where hardship exists is available, vendor payments will be made to providers at amounts computed in accordance with this paragraph or paragraph (a) of this subdivision.

Added by Laws 1978, Ch. 716, eff. Jan. 1, 1979, "provided, however, that it shall apply only to expenditures for health care services rendered on or after such date"; **amended** by Laws 1989, Ch. 676, eff. July 22, 1989; **amended** by Laws 1994, Ch. 311, § 5, eff. July 20, 1994; **amended** by Laws 1997, Ch. 436, § 1 Part B, §§ 98 and 99, eff. Nov. 1, 1997; **Repealed** by Laws 2005, Ch. 58, § 22 (Part B), eff. July 1, 2005.

§ 369-e.　[Repealed, eff. July 1, 2005] Relationship of catastrophic health care expense program to medical assistance program.

Any family eligible for medical assistance program. Any family eligible for medical assistance or who would be eligible if an application were to be filed pursuant to section three hundred sixty-six of this article shall not be eligible to receive benefits from the catastrophic health care expense program, except that paragraph (c) of subdivision two of section three hundred sixty-six of this article shall not apply for the purposes of the catastrophic health care expenses program.

If all members of a family household can establish eligibility for the medical assistance program under the excess income program by use of paid or incurred bills that family household will not be eligible for benefits under this program.

Added by Laws 1988, Ch. 703, § 7, eff. Sept. 6, 1988, and deemed to be in full force and effect as of Apr. 1, 1988; **Repealed** by Laws 2005, Ch. 58, § 22 (Part B), eff. July 1, 2005.

§ 369-f.   [Repealed, eff. July 1, 2005] Rules and regulations for implementation of demonstration project.

Within sixty days subsequent to the enactment of this title the commissioner shall develop and promulgate rules and regulations to implement the demonstration project created by this title which shall include, but not be limited to, the following:

1.   The application process to be used by local social services districts wishing to participate in the demonstration project and the specific date on which applications must be submitted in order to be considered; and

2.   The specific powers and responsibilities of the state department of social services and a social services district selected for participation.

Added by Laws 1988, Ch. 703, § 8, eff. Sept. 6, 1988, and deemed to be in full force and effect as of Apr. 1, 1988; **Repealed** by Laws 2005, Ch. 58, § 22 (Part B), eff. July 1, 2005.

§ 369-g.   [Repealed, eff. July 1, 2005] Funding.

Notwithstanding any inconsistent provisions in this title funding related to eligible catastrophic health care expenses shall be limited to the amount made available by chapter two of the laws of nineteen hundred eighty-eight and allocated for the purpose pursuant to this chapter and the amount made available by paragraph (b) of subdivision one of section twenty-eight hundred seven-1 of the public health law and allocated for such purpose.

Added by Laws 1988, Ch. 703, § 9, eff. Sept. 6, 1988, and deemed to be in full force and effect as of Apr. 1, 1988; **amended** by Laws 1996, Ch. 639, §112, eff. Sept. 12, 1996, but deemed to have been in full force and effect as of July 1, 1996; **Repealed** by Laws 2005, Ch. 58, § 22 (Part B), eff. July 1, 2005.

§ 369-h.   [Repealed, eff. July 1, 2005] Interim authorization.

At the request of an applicant applying prospectively for interim authorization, assistance without cost sharing or hardship, the commissioner of the social services district may establish a case management program to assist the applicant in obtaining needed health care services and to encourage the prudent utilization of such services.

Added by Laws 1988, Ch. 703, § 9, eff. Sept. 6, 1988, and deemed to be in full force and effect as of Apr. 1, 1988; **Repealed** by Laws 2005, Ch. 58, § 22 (Part B), eff. July 1, 2005.

§ 369-i.   [Repealed, eff. July 1, 2005] Review of regulations by the council on health care financing.

The commissioner shall forward to the council on health care financing as established pursuant to chapter five hundred twenty of the laws of nineteen hundred seventy-eight for review and comment and prior to promulgation any proposed rules and regulations developed for implementation of the objectives of this title. Any written comments by the council on health care financing on proposed rules and regulations must be submitted to the commissioner not later than ten working days after receipt. Further, the commissioner, in consultation with the council on health care financing shall develop a plan for the annual evaluation of demonstration projects established in accordance with this title. The first year for such evaluation shall be nineteen hundred eighty-nine and the commissioner, not later than June thirtieth of the subsequent calendar year shall submit a report of his findings to the governor and the legislature.

Added by Laws 1988, Ch. 703, § 9, eff. Sept. 6, 1988, and deemed to be in full force and effect as of Apr. 1, 1988; **Repealed** by Laws 2005, Ch. 58, § 22 (Part B), eff. July 1, 2005.

§ 369-j.   [Repealed, eff. July 1, 2005] Applicability.

This title shall become effective in its entirety on January first, nineteenth hundred eighty-nine provided, however, that subdivision one, paragraphs (a), (b) and (d) of subdivision three and subdivision four of section three hundred sixty-nine-d shall be deemed to have been in full force and effect with respect to assistance for eligible catastrophic health care expenses incurred during the calendar year nineteen hundred eighty-eight. Notwithstanding any inconsistent provision of section three hundred sixty-nine-d of this chapter an application for assistance for such nineteen hundred eighty-eight eligible catastrophic health care expenses must be submitted not latter than six months after the approval and implementation of the program in a local social services district.

Added by Laws 1988, Ch. 703, § 9, eff. Sept. 2, 1988, and deemed to have been in full force and effect as of Apr. 1, 1988; **amended** by Laws 1989, Ch. 676, eff. July 22, 1989; **Repealed** by Laws 2005, Ch. 58, § 22 (Part B), eff. July 1, 2005.

TITLE 11-B—HEALTH INSURANCE CONTINUATION PROGRAM FOR PERSONS WITH AIDS (§§ 369-k—369-n)

§ 369-k. Definitions.

As used in this section:

1. "Health insurance" shall mean insurance or an employee benefit plan against sickness, ailment or bodily injury of the employee and, if covered, his or her dependents, other than (i) insurance or an employee benefit plan providing disability benefits; or (ii) medical assistance benefits received under title eleven of this article.

2. "Health insurance costs" means the premiums or contributions paid for health insurance by or on behalf of a person with AIDS.

3. "Household" means the person with aids and all other persons residing in the same dwelling for whom such person would be responsible pursuant to section one hundred one of this chapter, or for whom such person has assumed responsibility.

4. "Persons with AIDS" means persons who are diagnosed as having acquired immune deficiency syndrome (AIDS) or who have human immunodeficiency virus (HIV)-related illness, as defined in regulation by the state department of health.

5. "Poverty line" means the federal income official poverty line (as defined and annually revised by the federal office of management and budget).

6. "Program" means the health insurance continuation program for persons with aids established by section three hundred sixty-nine-l of this article.

Added by Laws 1991, Ch. 165, § 27, eff. July 1, 1991.

§ 369-l. Establishment of program.

1. There is hereby established within the department of social services the health insurance continuation program for persons with aids.

2. Notwithstanding any inconsistent provision of law, the commissioner, subject to the approval of the director of the budget, may apply for appropriate waivers under federal law and regulation or take other actions to secure federal financial participation in the costs of the program; may waive or modify any provisions of this chapter or regulation of the department to implement this title; or may promulgate such regulations as necessary to implement this title.

Added by Laws 1991, Ch. 165, § 27, eff. July 1, 1991.

§ 369-m. Program eligibility and operations.

1. In accordance with regulations of the commissioner, a social services district shall pay all or part of the health insurance costs on behalf of a person with aids who:

(a) Is unemployed, or, if employed, currently is ineligible to participate in health insurance through his or her current employer or such employer offers no such plan; and

(b) Participated in the plan of health insurance provided by his or her prior employer and is eligible to continue or convert his or her participation in such plan by assuming the health insurance costs associated with such plan although no longer employed by such employer; and

(c) Resides in a household whose household income is less than or equal to one hundred eighty-five percent of the poverty line.

2. For purposes of determining eligibility under this title, household income shall be determined by use of the same methodology used to determine eligibility for federal supplemental security income benefits, provided that costs incurred for medical or remedial care shall not be taken into account in determining household income; and, provided further, that any resources available to such household shall not be considered nor required to be applied to the payment of health care expenses.

Added by Laws 1991, Ch. 165, § 27, eff. July 1, 1991.

§ 369-n. Relationship of program to medical assistance program.

1. Any person eligible for medical assistance benefits under title eleven of this article or who would be eligible for such benefits if an application were to be made pursuant to section three hundred sixty-six of this article shall not be eligible for the payment of all or part of such person's health insurance costs under this program. If all members of a household can establish eligibility for medical assistance benefits under the excess income program by use of paid or incurred bills, no person in that household shall be eligible for the payment of all or part of such person's health insurance costs under this program.

2. Notwithstanding any inconsistent provision of law, expenditures incurred by social services districts under this title related to program expenses shall be considered expenditures under the program of medical assistance for needy persons under title eleven of this article and there shall be paid to each such district fifty percent of the amount expended by such district under this title, and for the administration thereof, after first deducting therefrom any federal funds properly received or to be received on account thereof.

Added by Laws 1991, Ch. 165, § 27, eff. July 1, 1991.

TITLE 11-C—MEDICAID DRUG UTILIZATION REVIEW

§ 369-aa.   Definitions.

In this article:

1. "Drug utilization review or (DUR)"shall mean the program designed to measure and to assess on a retrospective and a prospective basis the proper use of outpatient drugs in the Medicaid program. Such program shall be in addition to the activities of the department with respect to the detection of fraud and abuse in the medical assistance program, the sanctioning of providers determined to have engaged in unacceptable practices under the medical assistance program, and the recovery of overpayments of medical assistance made to providers under the medical assistance program.

2. "Board" shall mean the drug utilization review board created under this title.

3. "Intervention" shall mean a form of communication utilized by the DUR board with a prescriber or pharmacist to inform about or to influence prescribing or dispensing practices.

4. "SURS" shall mean the surveillance utilization review system of Medicaid.

5. "Retrospective DUR" shall mean that part of the drug utilization review program that assesses or measures drug use based on an historical review of drug use data against predetermined and explicit criteria and standards on an ongoing basis with professional input.

6. "Prospective DUR" shall mean that part of the drug utilization review program that is to occur before the drug is dispensed that is designed to screen for potential drug therapy problems based on explicit and predetermined standards.

7. "Criteria" shall mean those predetermined and explicitly accepted elements that are used to measure drug use on an ongoing basis to determine if the use is appropriate, medically necessary, and not likely to result in adverse medical outcomes.

8. "Compendia" shall mean those resources widely accepted by the medical profession in the efficacious use of drugs which is based on, but not limited to, these sources: "American Hospital Formulary Services Drug Information," "U.S. Pharmacopeia—Drug Information," "AMA Drug Evaluations," the peer-reviewed medical literature, and information provided from the manufacturers of drug products.

9. "Standards" shall mean the acceptable range of deviation from the criteria that reflects appropriate medical practice and that is tested on the Medicaid recipient database.

10. "Therapeutic duplication" shall mean the prescribing and dispensing of the same drug or of two or more drugs from the same therapeutic class where overlapping time periods of drug administration are involved and where such prescribing or dispensing is not medically indicated.

11. "Drug-disease contraindications" shall mean the occurrence where the therapeutic effect of a drug is adversely altered by the presence of another disease condition.

12. "Drug-interactions" shall mean the occurrence where two or more drugs taken by a recipient lead to clinically significant toxicity that is characteristic of one or any of the drugs present or that leads to the interference with the effectiveness of one or any of the drugs.

13. "Therapeutic appropriateness" shall mean drug prescribing and dispensing based on rational drug therapy that is consistent with criteria and standards of the compendia.

14. "Overutilization or underutilization" shall mean the use of a drug in such quantities where the desired therapeutic goal is not achieved.

15. "Appropriate and medically necessary" shall mean drug prescribing and dispensing and patient medication usage in conformity with the criteria and standards developed under this chapter.

Added by Laws 1992, Ch. 632, § 2, eff. Jan. 1, 1993; **amended** by Laws 1992, Ch. 843, § 10, Aug. 7, 1992.

§ 369-bb.   Drug utilization review board.

1. A thirteen-member drug utilization review board is hereby created in the department. The board is responsible for the establishment and implementation of medical standards and criteria for the retrospective and prospective DUR program.

2. The members of the DUR board shall be appointed by the commissioner and shall serve a three-year term. Members may be reappointed upon the completion of other terms. The membership shall be comprised of the following:

(a) Five persons licensed and actively engaged in the practice of medicine in the state, at least one of whom shall have expertise in the area of mental health, who shall be selected from a list of nominees provided by the medical society of the state of New York and other medical associations.

(b) Five persons licensed and actively practicing in community pharmacy in the state who shall be selected from a list of nominees provided by pharmaceutical societies/associations of New York state.

(c) Two persons with expertise in drug utilization review who are either health care professionals licensed under title VIII of the education law or who are pharmacologists.

SSL

(d) One person from the department of social services (commissioner or designee).

3. The appointed members to the board, or its agents shall have no sanctions against them by Medicare or Medicaid.

4. The appointments to this board shall be made so that the length of the terms are staggered. In making the appointments, the commissioner shall consider geographic balance in the representation on the board.

5. The DUR board shall elect a chairperson from among its members who shall serve a one-year term as chairperson. The chairperson may serve consecutive terms.

6. Members of the DUR utilization review board and all its employees and agents shall be deemed to be an "employee" for purposes of section seventeen of the public officers law.

7. The department shall provide administrative support to the DUR board.

8. The duties of the DUR board are as follows:

(a) The development and application of the predetermined criteria and standards to be used in retrospective and prospective DUR that ensure that such criteria and standards are based on the compendia and that they are developed with professional input in a consensus fashion with provisions for timely revisions and assessments as necessary. Further, that the DUR standards shall reflect the appropriate practices of physicians in order to monitor:

(i) Therapeutic appropriateness;

(ii) Overutilization or underutilization;

(iii) Therapeutic duplication;

(iv) Drug-disease contraindications;

(v) Drug-drug interactions;

(vi) Incorrect drug dosage or duration of drug treatment; and

(vii) Clinical abuse/misuse.

(b) The development, selection, application, and assessment of interventions or remedial strategies for physicians, pharmacists, and recipients that are educational and not punitive in nature to improve the quality of care including:

(i) Information disseminated to physicians and pharmacists to ensure that physicians and pharmacists are aware of the board's duties and powers;

(ii) Written, oral, or electronic reminders of patient-specific or drug-specific information that are designed to ensure recipient, physician, and pharmacist confidentiality, and suggested changes in the prescribing or dispensing practices designed to improve the quality of care;

(iii) Use of face-to-face discussions between experts in drug therapy and the prescriber or pharmacist who has been targeted for educational intervention;

(iv)   Intensified reviews or monitoring of selected prescribers or pharmacists;

(v)   The creation of an educational program using data provided through DUR to provide for active and ongoing educational outreach programs to improve prescribing and dispensing practices as provided in this subdivision (this may be done directly or through contract with other entities);

(vi)   The timely evaluation of interventions to determine if the interventions have improved the quality of care; and

(vii)   The review of case profiles prior to the conducting of an intervention.

(c)   The publication of an annual report which shall be subject to the department's comment prior to its issuance to the federal department of health and human services by December first of each year. The annual report also shall be submitted to the governor and the legislature before December first of each year. The report shall include the following information:

(i)   A description of the activities of the board, including the nature and scope of the prospective and retrospective drug use review programs;

(ii)   A summary of the interventions used;

(iii)   An assessment of the impact of these educational interventions in quality of care;

(iv)   An estimate of the cost savings generated as a result of such program; and

(v)   Recommendations for program improvement.

(d)   The development of a working agreement for the DUR board with related boards or agencies, including, but not limited to: the board of pharmacy, the board of medicine, the SURS staff, and staff of the department of health and office of mental health, in order to clarify the areas of responsibility for each where such areas may overlap.

(e)   The establishment of a process where physicians or pharmacists will have the opportunity to submit responses to the DUR educational letters.

(e)   The establishment of a grievance/appeals process for physicians or pharmacists under this chapter.

(f)   The publication and dissemination of educational information to physicians and pharmacists on the DUR board and the DUR program to include information on:

(i)   Identifying and reducing the frequency of patterns of fraud, abuse, gross overuse, or inappropriate or medically unnecessary care among physicians, pharmacists, and recipients;

(ii)   Potential or actual severe/adverse reactions to drugs;

(iii)   Therapeutic appropriateness;

(iv)   Overutilization or underutilization;

(v)   Appropriate use of generics;

(vi)   Therapeutic duplication;

(vii)   Drug-disease contraindications;

(viii)   Drug-drug interactions;

(ix)   Incorrect drug dosage/duration of drug treatments;

(x)   Drug allergy interactions; and

(xi)   Clinical abuse/misuse.

(g)   The adoption and implementation of procedures designed to ensure the confidentiality of any information collected, stored, retrieved, assessed or analyzed by the DUR board, staff to the board, or contractors to the DUR program, that identifies individual physicians, pharmacists, or recipients. The board may have access to identifying information for purposes of carrying out intervention activities, but such identifying information may not be released to anyone other than a member of the DUR board or the department and its agents.

(h)   The improper release of identifying information in violation of this article may subject that person to criminal or civil penalties.

(i)   The board may release cumulative nonidentifying information for purposes of legitimate research.

9.   The relationship of the DUR board to the department is as follows:

(a)   The department shall monitor the DUR board's compliance to federal and state statute and regulation.

(b)   The DUR board shall serve at the discretion of the commissioner.

(c)   The department shall have authority on all fiscal matters relating to the DUR program.

(d)   The department shall have authority on all administrative matters relating to the administration of the medical assistance program within the DUR program.

(e)   The DUR board shall have responsibility for all medical matters relating to the DUR program.

(f)   the DUR board may utilize medical consultants and review committees as necessary, subject to department approval.

Added by Laws 1992, Ch. 632, § 2, eff. Jan. 1, 1993; **amended** by Laws 1992, Ch. 843, §§ 11, 12, 13, Aug. 7, 1992.

§ 369-cc.   Retrospective and prospective drug utilization review.

The department, in cooperation with the DUR board, shall include in its state plan the creation and implementation of a retrospective and prospective DUR program for Medicaid outpatient drugs to ensure that the prescriptions are appropriate, medically necessary, and not likely to result in adverse medical outcomes.

1. The retrospective and prospective DUR program shall be operated under the guidelines and procedures established by the DUR board.

2. The retrospective DUR program shall be based on the guidelines established by the DUR board and shall use the mechanized drug claims processing and information retrieval system to analyze claims data to:

(a) Identify patterns of gross overuse, and inappropriate or medically unnecessary care.

(b) Assess data on drug use against explicit predetermined standards that are based on the compendia and other sources to monitor the following:

(i) Therapeutic appropriateness;

(ii) Overutilization or underutilization;

(iii) Therapeutic duplication;

(iv) Drug-disease contraindications;

(v) Drug-drug interactions;

(vi) Incorrect drug dosage or duration of drug treatment; and

(vii) Clinical abuse/misuse.

3. The prospective DUR program shall be based on the guidelines established by the DUR board not in conflict with education or social services laws and shall provide that prior to the prescription being filled or delivered, a review will be conducted by the pharmacist at the point of sale to screen for potential drug therapy problems resulting from:

(a) Therapeutic duplication;

(b) Drug-drug interactions;

(c) Incorrect dosage/duration of treatment;

(d) Drug-allergy interactions;

(e) Clinical abuse/misuse.

In conducting the prospective DUR, the pharmacist may not alter the prescribed outpatient drug therapy without the consent of the physician who prescribed that therapy.

Added by Laws 1992, Ch. 632, § 2, eff. Jan. 1, 1993.

§ **369-dd. Analysis of pharmaceutical expenditures and patterns in relation to medicaid managed care. [*Expires and repealed March 31, 2009.*]**

1. The drug utilization review board shall analyze and compare expenditures, utilization rates and utilization patterns for pharmaceutical services (along with any related effects on expenditures, rates and patterns for other services) for medical assistance recipients:

(a) for the period during which medical assistance reimbursement for such services was included in the state rate of payment for medicaid managed care; and

(b) for the period beginning with the date on which medical assistance reimbursement for such services was no longer included in the state rate of payment for medicaid managed care.

2. The board shall include in its analyses and comparisons, the expenditures, utilization rates and utilization patterns for pharmaceutical services (along with any related effects on expenditures, rates and patterns for other services) paid for by private third-party payors.

3. The board shall report its findings to the governor, the temporary president of the senate and the speaker of the assembly by December first, nineteen hundred ninety-nine.

Added by Laws 1998, Ch. 19, § 3, eff. July 18, 1998, expires Mar. 31, 2000; **Amended** by Laws 2000, Ch. 13 § 4, eff. Mar. 30, 2000, and Ch. 57 Part A § 3, eff. May 15, 2000, deemed effective Apr. 1, 2000, extending expiration date of section to Dec. 31, 2003; L. 2003, Ch. 62, Part Z2, § 46, eff. May 15, 2003, deemed effective September 20, 2003; L. 2006, Ch. 57, § 96 (Part A), eff. April 12, 2006, deemed effective April 1, 2006.

§ 369-ee   Family health plus program

1. Definitions.

(a) "Family health insurance plan" means the written undertaking of an approved organization to provide coverage of health care services to eligible individuals under this title.

(b) "Eligible organization" means an insurer licensed pursuant to article thirty-two or forty-two of the insurance law, a corporation or an organization under article forty-three of the insurance law, or an organization certified under article forty-four of the public health law, including providers certified under section forty-four hundred three-e of such article.

(c) "Approved organization" means an eligible organization which has been approved by the commissioner to underwrite a family health insurance plan.

(d) "Period of eligibility" means that period commencing on the first day of the month following the date when the individual (i) has been determined eligible for health care coverage under this title and (ii) has enrolled in a family health insurance plan, and ending on the last day of the month in which an individual ceases to be eligible.

(e) "Health care services" means the following services and supplies as defined by the commissioner in consultation with the superintendent of insurance:

(i) the services of physicians, nurse practitioners, and other related personnel which are provided on an outpatient or inpatient basis;

(ii)   inpatient hospital services provided by a general hospital, a facility operated by the office of mental health under section 7.17 of the mental hygiene law, a facility issued an operating certificate pursuant to the provisions of article twenty-threetwenty-two or thirty-one of the mental hygiene law;

(iii)   laboratory tests;

(iv)   diagnostic x-rays;

(v)   prescription drugs and non-prescription smoking cessation products or devices;

(vi)   durable medical equipment;

(vii)   radiation therapy, chemotherapy, and hemodialysis;

(viii)   emergency room services;

(ix)   inpatient and outpatient mental health and alcohol and substance abuse services, as defined by the commissioner;

(x)   prehospital emergency medical services for the treatment of an emergency medical condition when such services are provided by an ambulance service;

(xi)   emergency, preventive and routine dental care, to the extent offered by a family health insurance plan described in this section, except orthodontia and cosmetic surgery;

(xii)   emergency vision care, and preventive and routine vision care as follows: once in any twenty-four month period:

(A)   one eye examination;

(B)   either: one pair of prescription eyeglass lenses and a frame, or prescription contact lenses where medically necessary; and

(C)   one pair of medically necessary occupational eyeglasses;

(xiii)   speech and hearing services;

(xiv)   diabetic supplies and equipment;

(xv)   services provided to meet the requirements of 42 U.S.C. 1396d(r); and

(xvi)   hospice services.

(e-1)   "Health care services" shall not include: (i) drugs, procedures and supplies for the treatment of erectile dysfunction when provided to, or prescribed for use by, a person who is required to register as a sex offender pursuant to article six-C of the correction law provided that any denial of coverage pursuant to this paragraph shall provide the patient with the means of obtaining additional information concerning both the denial and the means of challenging such denial; (ii) drugs for the treatment of sexual or erectile dysfunction, unless such drugs are used to treat a condition, other than sexual or erectile dysfunction, for which the drugs have been approved by the federal food and drug administration.

SSL

(f)   "Managed care provider" shall have the meaning set forth in section three hundred sixty-four-j of this article.

(g)   "Minor child" means, for purposes of this title, a child under the age of twenty-one.

(h)   "Commissioner" for purposes of this title shall mean the commissioner of health.

(i)   "Resources" for purposes of this title shall have the same meaning as determined in accordance with paragraph (a) of subdivision two of section three hundred sixty-six of this title except that the term savings referred to in subparagraph four of such paragraph shall mean an amount equal to at least one hundred fifty percent of the applicable allowable income amount permitted under subparagraph seven of such paragraph.

2.   Eligibility.

(a)   A person is eligible to receive health care services pursuant to this title if he or she:

(i)   resides in New York state and is at least age nineteen, but under sixty-five years of age;

(ii)   is not eligible for medical assistance under title eleven of this article solely due to income or resources or is eligible for medical assistance under title eleven of this article only through the application of excess income toward the costs of medical care and services pursuant to subdivision two of section three hundred sixty-six of title eleven of this article;

(iii)   [Until as stated in 2005 note below] does not have equivalent health care coverage under insurance or equivalent mechanisms, as defined by the commissioner in consultation with the superintendent of insurance;

(iii)   [Eff as stated in 2005 note below] does not have equivalent health care coverage under insurance or equivalent mechanisms, as defined by the commissioner in consultation with the superintendent of insurance, and is not a federal, state, county, municipal or school district employee that is eligible for health care coverage through his or her employer;

(iv)   [Until as stated in 2005 note below]

(A)   was not covered by a group health plan based upon his or her employment or a family member's employment, as defined by the commissioner in consultation with the superintendent of insurance, during the six-month period prior to the date of the application under this title, except in the case of:

(I)   loss of employment due to factors other than voluntary separation;

(II)   death of a family member which results in termination of the applicant's coverage under the group health plan;

(III)   change to a new employer that does not provide an option for comprehensive health benefits coverage;

(IV)   change of residence so that no employer-based comprehensive health benefits coverage is available;

(V)   discontinuation of comprehensive health benefits coverage to all employees of the applicant's employer;

(VI)   expiration of the coverage periods established by COBRA or the provisions of subsection (m) of section three thousand two hundred twenty-one, subsection (k) of section four thousand three hundred four and subsection (e) of section four thousand three hundred five of the insurance law;

(VII)   termination of comprehensive health benefits coverage due to long-term disability;

(VIII)   loss of employment due to need to care for a child or disabled household member or relative; or

(IX)   reduction in wages or hours or an increase in the cost of coverage so that coverage is no longer affordable or available.

(B)   the implementation of this subparagraph shall take effect only upon the commissioner's finding that insurance provided under this title is substituting for coverage under group health plans in excess of a percentage specified pursuant to subparagraph (ii) of paragraph (d) of subdivision two of section twenty-five hundred eleven of the public health law.

(iv)   [Eff as stated in 2005 note below]

(A)   was not covered by a group health plan based upon his or her employment or a family member's employment, as defined by the commissioner in consultation with the superintendent of insurance, during thenine-month period prior to the date of the application under this title, except in the case of:

(I)   loss of employment due to factors other than voluntary separation;

(II)   death of a family member which results in termination of the applicant's coverage under the group health plan;

(III)   change to a new employer that does not provide an option for comprehensive health benefits coverage;

(IV)   change of residence so that no employer-based comprehensive health benefits coverage is available;

(V)   discontinuation of comprehensive health benefits coverage to all employees of the applicant's employer;

(VI)   expiration of the coverage periods established by COBRA or the provisions of subsection (m) of section three thousand two hundred twenty-one, subsection (k) of section four thousand three hundred four and subsection (e) of section four thousand three hundred five of the insurance law;

(VII)   termination of comprehensive health benefits coverage due to long-term disability;

(VIII) loss of employment due to need to care for a child or disabled household member or relative; or

(IX) reduction in wages or hours or an increase in the cost of coverage so that coverage is no longer affordable or available.

(B) the implementation of this subparagraph shall take effect only upon the commissioner's finding that insurance provided under this title is substituting for coverage under group health plans in excess of a percentage specified pursuant to subparagraph (ii) of paragraph (d) of subdivision two of section twenty-five hundred eleven of the public health law.

(v) (A) in the case of a parent or stepparent of a child under the age of twenty-one who lives with such child, has gross family income equal to or less than the applicable percent of the federal income official poverty line (as defined and updated by the United States Department of Health and Human Services) for a family of the same size; for purposes of this clause, the applicable percent effective as of:

(I) January first, two thousand one, is one hundred twenty percent; and

(II) October first, two thousand one, is one hundred thirty-three percent; and

(III) October first, two thousand two, is one hundred fifty percent; or

(B) in the case of an individual who is not a parent or stepparent living with his or her child under the age of twenty-one, has gross family income equal to or less than one hundred percent of the federal income official poverty line (as defined and updated by the United States Department of Health and Human Services) for a family of the same size.

(vi) Repealed

(b) In order to establish income eligibility under this subdivision, an individual shall provide such documentation as is necessary and sufficient to initially, and annually thereafter, determine an applicant's eligibility for coverage under this title. Such documentation shall include, but not be limited to the following, if needed to verify eligibility:

(i) paycheck stubs; or

(ii) written documentation of income from all employers; or

(iii) other documentation of income (earned or unearned) as determined by the commissioner, provided however, such documentation shall set forth the source of such income; and

(iv) proof of identity and residence as determined by the commissioner.

(c) For the purposes of this title, the determination of resources shall be in accordance with paragraphs (b) and (c) of subdivision two of section three hundred sixty-six-a of this article.

2-a. Co-payments. Subject to federal approval pursuant to subdivision six of this section, persons receiving family health plus coverage under this section shall be responsible to make co-payments in accordance with the terms of subdivision six of section three hundred sixty-seven-a of this article, including those individuals who are otherwise exempted under the provisions of subparagraph (iv) of paragraph (b) of subdivision six of section three hundred sixty-seven-a of this article, provided however, that notwithstanding the provisions of paragraphs (c) and (d) of such subdivision:

(i)   co-payments charged for each generic prescription drug dispensed shall be three dollars and for each brand name prescription drug dispensed shall be six dollars;

(ii)   the co-payment charged for each dental service visit shall be five dollars, provided that no enrollee shall be required to pay more than twenty-five dollars per year in co-payments for dental services; and

(iii)   the co-payment for clinic services and physician services shall be five dollars;

(iv)   and provided further that the limitations in paragraph (f) of such subdivision shall not apply.

3.   (a) Every person determined eligible for or receiving family health plus coverage under this section shall enroll in a family health insurance plan.

(b)   Participants shall select a family health insurance plan from among those designated under the family health plus program.

(c)   Participants under this section who have lost their eligibility for health care services before the end of a six month period beginning on the date of the participant's initial enrollment in a family health insurance plan shall have their eligibility for family health plus continued until the end of the six month enrollment period, provided that federal financial participation in the cost of such coverage is available.

(d)   Family health insurance plans shall assure access to and delivery of high quality, cost effective, appropriate health care services. Such plans shall include a network of health care providers in sufficient numbers which are geographically accessible to program participants consistent with the following provisions:

(i)   approved organizations shall adhere to marketing and enrollment guidelines established by the commissioner, which shall include but not be limited to marketing and enrollment encounters between approved organizations and prospective enrollees, locations for such encounters, and prohibitions against telephone cold-calling and door-to-door solicitation at the homes of prospective enrollees. Approved organizations shall be permitted to assist prospective enrollees in completion of enrollment forms at approved health care provider sites and other approved locations. In no case may an emergency room be deemed an approved location. Approved organizations shall submit enrollment forms to the local department of social services.

(ii)   any marketing materials developed by an approved organization shall be approved by the department of health within sixty days prior to distribution to prospective enrollees of family health insurance.

SSL

(iii)   a family health insurance plan requesting disenrollment of a participant shall not disenroll a participant without the prior approval of the local district in which the participant resides. A family health insurance plan shall not request disenrollment of a participant based on any diagnosis, condition, or perceived diagnosis or condition, or a participant's efforts to exercise his or her rights under a grievance process.

(iv)   a family health insurance plan shall implement procedures to communicate appropriately with participants who have difficulty communicating in English and to communicate appropriately with visually-impaired and hearing-impaired participants.

(v)   a family health insurance plan shall comply with applicable state and federal law provisions prohibiting discrimination on the basis of disability.

(vi)   a family health insurance plan shall establish procedures to comply with subparagraph (iii) of paragraph (a) of subdivision four of section three hundred sixty-four-j of this article.

(e)   The family health plus program shall be operated by approved organizations which are authorized to arrange for care and services pursuant to this section provided however that, unless otherwise specified in this title, paragraphs (c), (s), (t) and (u) of subdivision one, paragraph (b) of subdivision two, subdivision three, paragraphs (b), (c), (d), subparagraphs (i), (iv), (v), (vi), (vii), and (viii) of paragraph (e), paragraphs (f), (g), (i) and (l) of subdivision four, subdivisions five, seven, eleven and twelve, paragraph (a) of subdivision thirteen, subdivisions fourteen, fifteen and seventeen, paragraph (b) of subdivision eighteen and subdivisions twenty and twenty-one of section three hundred sixty-four-j of this article shall not apply and provided further that provisions addressing provision of benefits by special needs plans shall not apply.

(f)   Notwithstanding any inconsistent provisions of this title and section one hundred sixty-three of the state finance law: (i) the commissioner may contract with managed care providers approved under section three hundred sixty-four-j of this article or title one-A of article twenty-five of the public health law without a competitive bid or request for proposal process to provide family health insurance coverage for eligible individuals pursuant to this title; (ii) in areas of the state which do not have sufficient managed care access to meet the objectives of this section, the commissioner may contract with entities approved pursuant to title one-A of article twenty-five of the public health law.

(g)   The care and services described under subdivision one of this section will be furnished by a family health insurance plan pursuant to the provisions of this section when such services are furnished in accordance with an agreement with the department of health and meet applicable federal laws and regulations.

(h)   The commissioner may delegate some or all of the tasks identified in this section to local districts provided that the agreement between the department of health and such plan pursuant to this subdivision clearly reflects such delegation.

4.   (a) The commissioner shall develop and implement locally-tailored education, outreach and facilitated enrollment strategies targeted to individuals who may be eligible for benefits under this title or title eleven of this article. Such strategies shall include, but not be limited to, contracting with community-based organizations to perform education, outreach and facilitated enrollment. In awarding the contracts, the commissioner shall consider the extent to which the organizations, or coalitions of organizations, are able to target efforts effectively in geographic areas in which there is a high proportion of uninsured individuals and a low proportion of eligible individuals receiving benefits under title eleven of this article. In approving organizations to undertake activities pursuant to this subdivision, within a defined geographic region, the commissioner shall make a good faith effort to ensure that the organizations are broadly inclusive of organizations in the region able to target effectively individuals who may be eligible for coverage under this title or title eleven of this article.

(b)   Outreach strategies shall include but shall not be limited to:

(i)   public education;

(ii)   dissemination of materials regarding the availability of benefits available under this title, title eleven of this article, and title one-A of article twenty-five of the public health law, provided that such materials have been approved by the commissioner prior to distribution;

(iii)   development of an application form for services under this program and for services under title eleven of this article that is easy to understand and complete;

(iv)   outstationing of persons who are authorized to provide assistance to individuals in completing the application process under this title, title eleven of this article, and title one-A of article twenty-five of the public health law including the conduct of personal interviews pursuant to section three hundred sixty-six-a of this chapter upon initial application. Such locations shall include but not be limited to offices of approved organizations, which shall be authorized to conduct personal interviews. Outstationing shall take place in locations which are geographically accessible to large numbers of individuals who may be eligible for benefits under such titles, and at times, including evenings and weekends, when large numbers of individuals who may be eligible for benefits under such titles are likely to be encountered. In the event that a photograph of the participant is required for an identification card, other than a photograph supplied by the participant, the commissioner shall exercise best efforts to assure that such photograph can be taken in geographically accessible locations, including the offices of approved organizations.

(c)   The commissioner shall:

(i)   ensure that training is furnished for outstationed persons and employees of approved organizations to enable them to disseminate information and facilitate the completion of the application process under this title, title eleven of this article, and title one-A of article twenty-five of the public health law;

(ii)   ensure that outreach strategies and activities under this title are coordinated with such strategies and activities under title one-A of article twenty-five of the public health law, and with all approved organizations, enrollment brokers, and other relevant entities under this title, title eleven of this article and title one-A of article twenty-five of the public health law;

(iii)   periodically monitor the performance of entities involved in outreach activities, to assure that potentially eligible individuals receive accurate information in a understandable manner, that such individuals are told of the availability of benefits under this title, title eleven of this article and title one-A of article twenty-five of the public health law, that such individuals are informed of the approved organizations under this title, title eleven of this article, and title one-A of article twenty-five of the public health law, and that appropriate follow-up is conducted. Such monitoring shall include, but shall not be limited to, unannounced site visits. As part of the commissioner's assurance of coordinated outreach activities, contracts with outreach organizations under this subdivision shall include enrollment procedures for inquiring into existing relationships with health care providers and procedures for providing information about how such relationships may be maintained with respect to health care coverage under this title and title eleven of this article.

(d)   Regardless of the availability of funding for contractual arrangements, upon application the commissioner may permit additional community-based organizations and qualified health care providers to perform education, outreach and facilitated enrollment services in accordance with this subdivision.

5.   (a) Personal interviews, pursuant to section three hundred sixty-six-a of this chapter, may be required upon initial application only and may be conducted in community settings. Recertification of eligibility shall take place on no more than an annual basis and shall not require a personal interview. Nothing herein shall abridge the participant's obligation to report changes in residency, financial circumstances or household composition.

(b)   Sections twenty-three and twenty-three-a of chapter four hundred thirty-six of the laws of nineteen hundred ninety-seven shall not apply to applicants for or recipients of health care services under this title.

(c)   Except where inconsistent with the provisions of this title, the provisions of title eleven of this article shall apply to applicants for and recipients under this title.

6.   Waivers and federal approvals.

(a)   The provisions of this section shall not take effect unless all necessary approvals under federal law and regulation have been obtained to receive federal financial participation, under the program described in title eleven of this article, in the costs of health care services provided pursuant to this section.

(b)   The commissioner is authorized to submit amendments to the state plan for medical assistance and/or submit one or more applications for waivers of the federal social security act, to obtain the federal approvals necessary to implement this section. The commissioner shall submit such amendments and/or applications for waivers by June thirtieth, two thousand, and shall use best efforts to obtain the approvals required by this subdivision in a timely manner so as to allow early implementation of this section.

(c) Repealed

7. The commissioner shall promulgate any regulations necessary to implement this title.

Added by Laws 1999, Ch. 1, § 104, eff. Dec. 30, 1999, deemed in full force and effect Jan. 1, 2000; **amended** by Laws 2000, Ch. 419, §§ 38-40, eff. Sept. 13, 2000, deemed in full force and effect Jan. 1, 2000; **amended** by Laws 2001, Ch. 63, Part C, § 14, eff. June 25, 2001, deemed in full force and effect on and after June 18, 2001; L. 2002, Ch. 526, § 1, eff. Sept. 17, 2002; **amended** by Laws 2002, Ch. 1, Part A, § 54, eff. April 1, 2003 and Ch. 526 § 1, eff. Sept. 17, 2002; **amended** by Laws 2004, Ch. 58, Part B, 1–4, 56 (1, 7–12), eff. Aug 20, 2004; **amended** by Laws 2005, Ch. 58, § 32-a (Part C) (add, Laws 2005, Ch. 63, § 27 ((Part E)), eff. April 12, 2005, deemed eff. on and after April 1, 2005), eff. April 12, 2005, deemed eff. on and after April 1, 2005; Laws 2005, Ch. 645, §2, eff. Aug. 30, 2005; Laws 2006, Ch. 57, §30 (Part A), eff. April 12, 2006, deemed eff. on and after April 1, 2006.

TITLE 12—COMMUNITY CENTERS AND SERVICES FOR SENIOR CITIZENS

Section 370. **Community centers and services for senior citizens; when social services official to furnish.**
370-a. **Federal grants.**
370-b. **State reimbursement.**

§ 370. Community centers and services for senior citizens; when social services official to furnish.

1. A social services official of a county, city or town is authorized, provided funds have been made available therefor, to provide at public expense one or more community centers and services for senior citizens residing in his territory who are eligible therefor pursuant to the provisions of this title. Such centers and services may be provided only in cases where it is determined, under criteria established by the department, that there is a need therefor.

2. The furnishing of such centers and services is hereby declared to be proper municipal purpose for which the moneys of a county, city or town may be raised and expended. A county, city or town may receive and expend moneys from the state, the federal government or private individuals, corporations or associations for furnishing such centers and services.

3. Community centers and services for senior citizens under this title may be provided by a social services official either directly or through the purchase

SSL

or rental of such centers and services from a private non-profit corporation, company or association provided they are operated and furnished in compliance with regulations of the department.

Added by Laws 1970, Ch. 289, amended by Laws 1971, Ch. 110, eff. July 1, 1971; Laws of 1971, Ch. 1040, eff. July 2, 1971.

§ 370-a.   Federal grants.

1.   The department of taxation and finance is authorized to accept and receive from the federal government any moneys which the federal government shall offer to the state for or with respect to the construction, maintenance or operation of centers for senior citizens or for or with respect to the provision of services for senior citizens, under or pursuant to any federal law heretofore or hereafter enacted authorizing grants to the state for such purpose or similar purposes, including payments to political subdivisions of, and any public agencies in the state.

2.   The department of social services is hereby designated and empowered to act as the agent of the state in carrying out the provisions of any such federal law with respect to such centers and services for senior citizens in this state.

3.   Any and all such grants and moneys awarded for assistance to this state under or pursuant to any federal law shall be accepted and received by the department of taxation and finance as custodian thereof and such moneys, so received, shall be deposited by such department of taxation and finance in a special fund or funds and shall be used exclusively for the purposes of any such federal law. Such moneys shall be paid from such fund or funds on the audit and warrant of the comptroller upon vouchers certified or approved by the commissioner of social services.

4.   Any federal funds available to the state for such centers and services for senior citizens shall be retained by the state.

Added by Laws 1970, Ch. 289, eff. Apr. 1, 1970; amended by Laws 1975, Ch. 224, eff. Apr. 1, 1975.

§ 370-b.   State reimbursement.

1.   (a) Expenditures made by counties, cities, and towns for services for senior citizens and their administration, and senior citizens center projects, pursuant to this title, shall, if approved by department, be subject to reimbursement by the state, in accordance with the regulations of the department, as follows: There shall be paid to each county, city or town (1) the amount of federal funds, if any, properly received or to be received on account of such expenditures; (2) fifty per centum of its expenditures for services for senior citizens and their administration and senior citizens center projects, after first deducting therefrom any federal funds received or to be received on account thereof, and any expenditures defrayed by fees paid by senior citizens or by other private contributions.

(b) For the purposes of this title, expenditures for administration of services for senior citizens shall include expenditures for compensation of employees in connection with the furnishing of such services, including but not limited to costs incurred for pensions, federal old age and survivors insurance and health insurance for such employees; training programs for personnel, operation, maintenance and service costs; and such other expenditures such as equipment costs, depreciation and charges and rental values as may be approved by the department. It shall not include expenditures for capital costs. In the case of centers and services for senior citizens purchased or leased from a non-profit corporation, company or association, expenditures shall include an allocable proportion of all operating costs of such centers as may be approved by the department including but not limited to the expenditures enumerated in this paragraph (b) and expenditures for amortization, interest and other financing costs of any mortgage loan made to such non-profit corporation, company or association.

2. (a) Claims for state reimbursement shall be made in such form and manner and at such times and for such periods as the department shall determine.

(b) When certified by the department, state reimbursement shall be paid from the state treasury upon the audit and warrant of the comptroller out of funds made available therefor.

3. The department is authorized in its discretion to approve and certify to the comptroller for payment, advances to counties, cities or towns in anticipation of the state reimbursement provided for in this section.

4. Payment of state reimbursement and advances shall be made to local fiscal officers as in the case of state reimbursement for public assistance and care under other provisions of this chapter.

Added by Laws 1970, Ch. 289, **amended** by Laws 1971, Ch. 110, eff. July 1, 1971.

TITLE 13—STATE HEATING FUEL CRISIS ASSISTANCE

----

§ 370-aa. State heating fuel crisis assistance.

[*Expired on October 1, 1980, by Laws 1979, Ch. 749, eff. November 27, 1979.*]

SSL

ARTICLE 6

CHILDREN

————

SUMMARY OF ARTICLE

————

TITLE 1—CARE AND PROTECTION OF CHILDREN

————

(Repealed and transferred sections noted under appropriate section number of text.)

SSL

§ 371. Definitions.

Unless the context or the subject matter manifestly requires a different interpretation, when used in this article or in any special act relating to children:

1. "Child" means a person actually or apparently under the age of eighteen years;

2. "Abandoned child" means a child under the age of eighteen years who is abandoned by both parents, or by the parent having its custody, or by any other person or persons lawfully charged with its care or custody, in accordance with the definition and other criteria set forth in subdivision five of section three hundred eighty-four-b;

3. "Destitute child" means a child who, through no neglect on the part of its parent, guardian or custodian, is

(a) destitute or homeless, or

(b) in a state of want or suffering due to lack of sufficient food, clothing, or shelter, or medical or surgical care, or

(c) a person under the age of eighteen years who is absent from his legal residence without the consent of his parent, legal guardian or custodian, or

(d) a person under the age of eighteen who is without a place of shelter where supervision and care are available;

4. [*Repealed.*]

4-a. "Neglected child" means a child less than eighteen years of age

(i) whose physical, mental or emotional condition has been impaired or is in imminent danger of becoming impaired as a result of the failure of his parent or other person legally responsible for his care to exercise a minimum degree of care

(A) in supplying the child with adequate food, clothing, shelter, education, medical or surgical care, though financially able to do so or offered financial or other reasonable means to do so; or

(B) in providing the child with proper supervision or guardianship, by unreasonably inflicting or allowing to be inflicted harm, or a substantial risk thereof, including the infliction of excessive corporal punishment; or by misusing a drug or drugs; or by misusing alcoholic beverages to the extent that he loses self-control of his actions; or by any other acts of a similarly serious nature requiring the aid of the court; provided, however, that where the respondent is voluntarily and regularly participating in a rehabilitative program, evidence that the respondent has repeatedly misused a drug or drugs or alcoholic beverages to the extent that he loses self-control of his actions shall not establish that the child is a neglected child in the absence of evidence establishing that the child's physical, mental or emotional condition has been impaired or is in imminent danger of becoming impaired as set forth in paragraph (i) of this subdivision; or

(ii) who has been abandoned by his parents or other person legally responsible for his care;

4-b. "Abused child" means a child less than eighteen years of age whose parent or other person legally responsible for his care

(i) inflicts or allows to be inflicted upon such child physical injury by other than accidental means which causes or creates a substantial risk of death or serious or protracted disfigurement, or protracted impairment of physical or emotional health or protracted loss or impairment of the function of any bodily organ, or

(ii) creates or allows to be created a substantial risk of physical injury to such child by other than accidental means which would be likely to cause death or serious or protracted disfigurement, or protracted impairment of physical or emotional health or protracted loss or impairment of the function of any bodily organ, or

(iii) commits, or allows to be committed, an act of sexual abuse against such child as defined in the penal law;

5. "Juvenile delinquent" means a person over seven and less than sixteen years of age who does any act which, if done by an adult, would constitute a crime;

6. "Person in need of supervision" means a person less than eighteen years of age who is habitually truant or who is incorrigible, ungovernable or habitually disobedient and beyond the lawful control of a parent or other person legally responsible for such child's care, or other lawful authority.

7. "Dependent child" means a child who is in the custody of or wholly or partly maintained by an authorized agency or an institution, society or other organization of charitable, eleemosynary, correctional, or reformatory character;

8. "Mentally disabled child" means a child who has a mental disability as defined in section 1.03 of the mental hygiene law;

9. "Physically handicapped child" means a child who, by reason of a physical disability or infirmity, whether congenital or acquired by accident, injury or disease, is or may be expected to be totally or partially incapacitated for education or for remunerative occupation, as provided in the education law, or is or may be expected to be handicapped, as provided in the public health law;

10. "Authorized agency" means

(a) Any agency, association, corporation, institution, society or other organization which is incorporated or organized under the laws of this state with corporate power or empowered by law to care for, to place out or to board out children, which actually has its place of business or plant in this state and which is approved, visited, inspected and supervised by the department or which shall submit and consent to the approval, visitation, inspection and supervision of the department as to any and all acts in relation to the welfare of children performed or to be performed under this title,

SSL

(b) Any court or any official of this state authorized by law to place out or to board out children or any Indian tribe that has entered into an agreement with the department pursuant to section thirty-nine of this chapter,

(c) Any agency, association, corporation, institution, society or other organization which is not incorporated or organized under the laws of this state, placing out a child for adoption whose admission to the United States as an eligible orphan with non-quota immigrant status pursuant to the federal immigration and nationality act is sought for the purpose of adoption in the State of New York or who has been brought into the United States with such status and for such purpose, provided, however, that such agency, association, corporation, institution, society or other organization is licensed or otherwise authorized by another state to place out children for adoption, that such agency, association, corporation, institution, society or other organization is approved by the department to place out such children with non-quota immigrant status for adoption in the State of New York, and provided further, that such agency, association, corporation, institution, society or other organization complies with the regulations of the department pertaining to such placements. Notwithstanding any other provision of law to the contrary, such agency shall be limited in its functioning as an authorized agency to the placing out and adoption of such children. This paragraph shall not require the department to approve any such agency, association, corporation, institution, society or other organization which is located in a state which is a party to the interstate compact on the placement of children;

11. "Custody" means custody in pursuance of or in compliance with expressed provisions of law;

12. "Place out" means to arrange for the free care of a child in a family other than that of the child's parent, stepparent, grandparent, brother, sister, uncle, or aunt or legal guardian, for the purpose of adoption or for the purpose of providing care;

13. "Place" or "commit" includes replace and recommit;

14. "Board out" means to arrange for the care of a child in a family, other than that of the child's parent, stepparent or legal guardian, to whom payment is made or agreed to be made for care and maintenance;

15. "Home" includes a family boarding home or a family free home;

16. "Agency boarding home" shall mean a family-type home for children and/or for minors operated by an authorized agency, in quarters or premises owned, leased or otherwise under the control of such agency, for the purposes of providing care and maintenance;

17. "Group home" shall mean a facility for the care and maintenance of not less than seven, nor more than twelve children, who are at least five years of age, operated by an authorized agency except that such minimum age shall not be applicable to siblings placed in the same facility nor to children whose mother is placed in the same facility;

18. "Public institution for children" shall mean an institution which is established and maintained by a public welfare district for the purpose of providing care and maintenance therein for children and minors for whose care such district is responsible and who require care away from their own homes;

19. "Foster parent" shall mean any person with whom a child, in the care, custody or guardianship of an authorized agency, is placed for temporary or long-term care, and "Foster child" shall mean any person, in the care, custody or guardianship of an authorized agency, who is placed for temporary or long-term care;

20. "Therapeutic foster parent" means a foster parent who is certified or licensed pursuant to section three hundred seventy-five or section three hundred seventy-six of this article, or otherwise approved and who has successfully completed a training program developed by professionals experienced in treating children who exhibit high levels of disturbed behavior, emotional disturbance or physical or health needs. For any such child placed in their care, such parent shall assist in the implementation of the therapeutic treatment portion of the family service plan required by section four hundred nine-e of this article.

21. "Supervised independent living program" shall mean one or more of a type of agency boarding home operated and certified by an authorized agency in accordance with the regulations of the office of children and family services to provide a transitional experience for older youth who, based upon their circumstances, are appropriate for transition to the level of care and supervision provided in the program. Each supervised independent living unit shall be located in the community separate from any of the agency's other congregate dwellings.

22. [*Repealed.*]

Added by Laws 1962, Ch. 690; **amended** by Laws 1962, Chs. 584, 947; Laws 1965, Chs. 347, 406; Laws 1967, Chs. 276, 479; Laws 1969, Ch. 640; Laws 1970, Ch. 570, eff. Sept. 1, 1970; Laws 1970, Ch. 745, eff. Sept. 1, 1970; Laws 1971, Ch. 782, eff. June 25, 1971, repealing subd. (4) and adding subds. (4-a), (4-b), with the following Note appended:

Note—Subdivision 4 of section 371 of the Social Services Law proposed to be repealed by this bill defines a neglected child to be one who is

"a male less than sixteen years of age or a female less than eighteen years of age

"(a) whose parent or other person legally responsible for his care does not adequately supply the child with food, clothing, shelter, education, or medical or surgical care, though financially able or offered financial means to do so; or

"(b) who suffers or is likely to suffer serious harm from the improper guardianship, including lack of moral supervision or guidance, of his parents or other person legally responsible for his care and requires the aid of the court; or

"(c) who has been abandoned or deserted by his parents or other person legally responsible for his care."

Amended by Laws 1973, Ch. 315, eff. May 8, 1973; former subd. (18), **added** by Laws 1970 Ch. 745 **amended** and **renumbered** (20) and former subd. (19) **added** by Laws 1970, Ch. 745, **renumbered** (21) by Laws 1973, Ch. 1037, eff. Sept. 1, 1973; **amended** by Laws 1975, Ch. 281; Laws 1975, Ch. 427; Laws 1976, Ch. 666, Ch. 880; Laws 1977, Ch. 450, Ch. 518, eff. Aug. 1, 1977 "and shall apply to an act of abuse of any child under the age of eighteen which act shall take place on or after the date on which this act shall have become a law"; Laws 1978, Ch. 550, Ch. 555, Ch.722; Laws 1979, Ch. 368, eff. Nov. 1, 1979; **amended** by Laws 1981, Ch. 984, eff. July 31, 1981, subd. 4-a (i)(B); **amended** by Laws 1982, Ch. 920, eff. July 1, 1983; **amended** by Laws 1983, Ch. 268, eff. June 10, 1983; **amended** by Laws 1985, Ch. 491, eff. July 24, 1985; **amended** by Laws 1986, Ch. 127, eff. June 2, 1986; **amended** by Laws 1987, Ch. 462, eff. July 27, 1987; **amended** by Laws 1987, Ch. 419, eff. July 27, 1987; **amended** by Laws 1987, Ch. 838, eff. Aug. 7, 1987; **amended** by Laws 1989, Ch. 731, § 2, eff. July 24, 1989; **amended** by Laws 1993, Ch. 87, § 3, eff. June 1, 1993; Laws 2000, Ch. 596, eff. Nov. 1, 2001, amending subd. 6; **amended** by Laws 2004, Ch. 160, § 3, eff. Nov. 17, 2004, adding subd. 21.

§ 371-a.   Procedure.

In any proceeding commenced pursuant to this chapter in which the family court has exercised jurisdiction, the provisions of articles one, two and eleven of the family court act shall apply to the extent that they do not conflict with the specific provisions of the social service law.

Added by Laws 1976, Ch. 308, eff. July 8, 1976.

§ 371-b.   Citizen review panels.

1. There shall be established at least three citizen review panels. At least one panel shall be established for the city of New York and at least two panels shall be established for social services districts or combinations of districts outside of the city of New York. The panel in the city of New York shall create one subcommittee for each borough for the purposes of evaluating the extent to which the state and the social services district are discharging their child protection responsibilities within that particular borough, in accordance with subsection three of this section. The office of children and family services shall make available resources to support the needs of each citizen review panel.

2. Each citizen review panel shall consist of thirteen members, seven of whom shall be appointed by the governor, three of whom shall be appointed by the temporary president of the senate, and three of whom shall be appointed by the speaker of the assembly. Each panel shall duly elect a chairperson of such panel. Each panel shall be composed of volunteer members who are broadly representative of the community in which such panel is established, including members who have expertise in the prevention and treatment of child abuse and neglect. No person employed by federal, state, county or municipal agencies which directly deliver child welfare services may be appointed to a panel.

3. Each citizen review panel shall, by examining the policies and procedures of the state and social services districts and, where appropriate, specific cases,

evaluate the extent to which the agencies are effectively discharging their child protection responsibilities in accordance with: (a) the state plan established pursuant to 42 U.S.C. § 5106a(b); (b) the child protection standards set forth in 42 U.S.C. § 5106a(b); and (c) any other criteria that the panel considers important to ensure the protection of children. Each panel shall meet not less than once every three months. Each panel may hold public hearings on issues within the panel's jurisdiction.

4.   Each citizen review panel shall have access to information on specific cases in accordance with paragraph (a) of subdivision four of section four hundred twenty-two of this chapter. Each panel shall also have reasonable access to public and private facilities which are in receipt of public funds and are providing child welfare services within the panel's jurisdiction. Where necessary, the office shall assist a panel in obtaining access to information or facilities as authorized in accordance with this section. Each panel shall also have access to the report prepared by the state pursuant to 42 U.S.C. § 5106a(d).

5.   Each citizen review panel shall prepare and make available to the public, on an annual basis, a report containing:

(a)   a summary of the activities of the panel; and

(b)   the findings and recommendations of the panel. Each report shall be submitted by February first and shall omit all confidential information used to prepare the report.

6.   The members of each citizen review panel shall not disclose to any person or government official any identifying information about any specific child protection case. A member who knowingly violates this duty of confidentiality may be subject to a civil penalty not to exceed one thousand dollars and removal from the panel.

7.   The legal defense of a member of a citizen review panel shall be Governed by the terms of section seventeen of the public officers law.

   Added by Laws 1999, Ch. 136, § 3, eff. June 30, 1999.

§ 372.   Records and reports.

1.   Every court, and every public board, commission, institution, or officer having powers or charged with duties in relation to abandoned, delinquent, destitute, neglected or dependent children who shall receive, accept or commit any child shall provide and keep a record showing:

(a)   the full and true name of the child,

(b)   his sex and date and place of birth, if ascertainable, or his apparent age,

(c)   the full and true names and places of birth of his parents, and their actual residence if living, or their latest known residence, if deceased or whereabouts unknown and the name and actual residence of any other person having custody of the child, as nearly as the same can reasonably be ascertained,

(d)   the religious faith of the parents and of the child,

(e)   the name and address of any person, agency, institution or other organization to which the child is committed, placed out, boarded out, or otherwise given into care, custody or control,

(f)   the religious faith and occupation of the head or heads of the family with whom the child is placed out or boarded out and their relationship, if any, to the child,

(g)   if any such child shall die, the date and cause of death and place of burial,

(h)   any further disposition or change in care, custody or control of the child,

(i)   the date or dates of reception and of any subsequent disposition or change in care, custody or control and, in case of adoption, the name and title of the judge or surrogate making the order of adoption, the date of such order and the date and place of filing of such order,

(j)   the reasons for any act performed in reference to such child herein required to be recorded, together with such further information as the department may require; and shall make to the department upon blanks provided by the department reports of each such child placed out, or boarded out, containing the information herein required to be kept; and shall furnish such information to any authorized agency to which any such child shall be committed or otherwise given into custody.

2.   Every charitable, eleemosynary, reformatory, or correctional institution, public or private, incorporated or unincorporated, and every agency, association, corporation, institution, society or other organization which shall receive, accept, or admit any child whether or not in receipt of payments from public funds for the support of such child shall provide and keep a record as described in subdivision one, and also showing how, by whom and for what reason such child shall have been given into its custody or committed to it and shall make reports of each such child to the department upon blanks provided by the department giving all the information required by subdivision one to be recorded together with such further information as the department may require. Except as to children placed out, boarded out or surrendered or for whom guardianship is accepted or adoption provided, the requirement of this section shall not apply to hospitals, day nurseries, eleemosynary day schools, and summer and vacation homes and camps, or to institutions for the care of convalescent, anaemic, undernourished or cardiac children, preventoria, working boys' homes, emergency shelters and schools for the blind and for the deaf, but all such hospitals, homes and institutions shall keep such records and make to the department such reports as the department may require.

3.   Such records maintained by the department or an authorized agency, including a local social services district, regarding such children are confidential, provided, however, that such records are subject to the provisions of article thirty-one of the civil practice law and rules. When either the subject foster child, or

such child's parent, or such child's guardian if any, is not a party to the action, a copy of the notice or motion for discovery shall be served upon such parent, guardian, and child and, if the child is still a minor, the child's law guardian. Such persons may thereafter appear in the action with regard to such discovery. Where no action is pending, upon application by a parent, relative or legal guardian of such child or by an authorized agency, after due notice to the institution or authorized agency affected and hearing had thereon, the supreme court may by order direct the officers of such institution or authorized agency to furnish to such parent, relative, legal guardian or authorized agency such extracts from the record relating to such child as the court may deem proper. The department through its authorized agents and employees may examine at all reasonable times the records required by this section to be kept.

4.   (a) All such records relating to such children shall be open to the inspection of the board and the department at any reasonable time, and the information called for under this section and such other data as may be required by the department shall be reported to the department, in accordance with the regulations of the department. Such records kept by the department shall be deemed confidential and shall be safeguarded from coming to the knowledge of and from inspection or examination by any person other than one authorized, by the department, by a judge of the court of claims when such records are required for the trial of a claim or other proceeding in such court or by a justice of the supreme court, or by a judge of the family court when such records are required for the trial of a proceeding in such court, after a notice to all interested persons and a hearing, to receive such knowledge or to make such inspection or examination. No person shall divulge the information thus obtained without authorization so to do by the department, or by such judge or justice.

(b)   (i) Notwithstanding any inconsistent provision of law to the contrary, records relating to children kept pursuant to this section shall be made available to officers and employees of the state comptroller or of the city comptroller of the city of New York, or of the county officer designated by law or charter to perform the auditing function in any county not wholly contained within a city, for the purposes of a duly authorized performance audit, provided that such comptroller shall have certified to the keeper of such records that he or she has instituted procedures developed in consultation with the department to limit access to client-identifiable information to persons requiring such information for purposes of the audit, that such persons shall not use such information in any way except for purposes of the audit and that appropriate controls and prohibitions are imposed on the dissemination of client-identifiable information obtained in the conduct of the audit. Information pertaining to the substance or content of any psychological, psychiatric, therapeutic, clinical or medical reports, evaluations or like materials or information pertaining to such child or the child's family shall not be made available to such officers and employees unless disclosure of such information is absolutely essential to the specific audit activity and the department gives prior written approval.

SSL

(ii) Any failure to maintain the confidentiality of client-identifiable information shall subject such comptroller or officer to denial of any further access to records until such time as the audit agency has reviewed its procedures concerning controls and prohibitions imposed on the dissemination of such information and has taken all reasonable and appropriate steps to eliminate such lapses in maintaining confidentiality to the satisfaction of the department. The department shall establish the grounds for denial of access to records contained under this section and shall recommend, as necessary, a plan of remediation to the audit agency. Except as provided in this section, nothing in this paragraph shall be construed as limiting the powers of such comptroller or officer to access records which he is otherwise authorized to audit or obtain under any other applicable provision of law. Any person given access to information pursuant to this paragraph who releases data or information to persons or agencies not authorized to receive such information shall be guilty of a class A misdemeanor.

4-a. Notwithstanding any provisions of law to the contrary, social services districts shall provide a written summary of services rendered to a child upon the request of a probation service conducting an investigation pursuant to the provisions of section 351.1 of the family court act. Information provided to a probation service pursuant to the provisions of this subdivision shall be maintained by such service according to the provisions of subdivision five of section 351.1 of the family court act.

4-b. Notwithstanding any other provision of law, foster care information governed by this section may be released by the department or an authorized agency to a person, agency or organization for purposes of a bona fide research project. Identifying information shall not be made available, however, unless it is absolutely essential to the research purpose and the department gives prior approval. Information released pursuant to this subdivision shall not be re-disclosed except as otherwise permitted by law and upon the approval of the department.

5. The requirements of this section to keep records and make reports shall not apply to the birth parent or parents, or relatives within the second degree of such parents. The reception of a child, or the power to receive the same, shall not make this section applicable to a humane society, or to a society for the prevention of cruelty to children.

6. The provisions of this section as to records and reports to the department shall apply also to the placing out, adoption or boarding out of a child and the acceptance of guardianship or of surrender of a child.

7. An authorized agency as defined in paragraphs (a) and (b) of subdivision ten of section three hundred seventy-one of this chapter or any primary or secondary school or an office of the division for youth, except agencies operating pursuant to article nineteen-H of the executive law, who shall receive, accept, enroll or commit any child under such circumstances as shall reasonably indicate that such child may be a missing person shall make inquiries of each such child

to the division of criminal justice services in a manner prescribed by such division; provided that as used in this subdivision a court shall not be included within the definition of an authorized agency. If such child appears to match a child registered with the statewide central register for missing children as described in section eight hundred thirty-seven-e of the executive law, or one registered with the national crime information center register, such agency shall immediately contact the local law enforcement agency.

8. In any case where a child is to be placed with or discharged to a relative or other person legally responsible pursuant to section ten hundred seventeen or ten hundred fifty-five of the family court act, such relative or other person shall be provided with such information by an authorized agency as is provided to foster parents pursuant to this section and applicable regulations of the department.

Amended by Laws 1971, Chs. 110, 945, both eff. July 1, 1971; Laws 1975, Ch. 221; Laws 1976, Ch. 824, eff. July 26, 1976; Laws 1978, Ch. 555, §§ 9, 10, 11, eff. July 24, 1978; **amended** by Laws 1981, Ch. 363, eff. June 28, 1981, subd. 4; **amended** by Laws 1984, Ch. 627, eff. Nov. 24, 1984; **amended** by Laws 1985, Ch. 880; Laws 1987, Ch. 101; Laws 1989, Ch. 161; Laws 1991, Ch. 168, § 14, eff. June 28, 1991, which eliminated the expiration date of the 1985 amendment; **amended** by Laws 1988, Ch. 363, § 1, eff. July 29, 1988; **amended** by Laws 1991, Ch. 55, § 1, eff. May 12, 1991; **amended** by Laws 1992, Ch. 451, §§ 3, 4, eff. Nov. 14, 1992; **amended** by Laws 1993, Ch. 394, § 1, eff. Nov. 18, 1993; **amended** by Laws 1994, Ch. 690, § 11, eff. Aug. 18, 1994; **amended** by Laws 1995, Ch. 653, § 4, eff. Dec. 6, 1995; **amended** by Laws 1996, Ch. 12, § 4, eff. Feb. 15, 1996; **amended** by Laws 1996, Ch. 684, eff. Dec. 31, 1996; **amended** by Laws 2002, Ch. 312, § 5, eff. Aug. 6, 2002.

§ 372-a. Child welfare research advisory panel.

1. The commissioner shall appoint a child welfare research advisory panel which shall consist of not less than ten or more than fifteen members and shall include individuals recommended by commissioners of social services districts. The panel shall also include, but not be limited to, representatives of the following categories:

(a) agencies providing child welfare services, including child protective services, foster care, preventive services and adoption services;

(b) advocates for, and recipients of, services to children and families; and

(c) social science and child welfare research professionals.

2. The responsibilities of the child welfare research advisory panel shall include:

(a) developing guidelines for the review by the department of research projects that seek access to identifying information relating to child protective services, preventive services, foster care and other child welfare programs;

(b) developing guidelines for ensuring that research projects with access to identifying information protect client privacy and confidentiality;

SSL

(c)   developing guidelines for ensuring that research projects satisfactorily address the administrative and fiscal impact of the research project on the agency which maintains the information sought by such project;

(d)   recommending procedures for facilitating access to child welfare records by approved researchers and for ensuring the cooperation of public and private agencies providing access to research projects approved by the department;

(e)   making recommendations concerning dissemination and utilization of the findings of research projects subject to this section; and

(f)   developing an agenda for child welfare research in consultation with state and local officials.

Added by Laws 1995, Ch. 653, § 5, eff. Dec. 6, 1995.

§ 372-b.   Adoption services.

1.   (a) A prospective adoptive parent shall have a right to a fair hearing pursuant to section twenty-two of this chapter concerning the failure of a social services official to provide adoptive services authorized to be provided pursuant to this section and the state's consolidated services plan. At the time a child is placed in a prospective adoptive home, the prospective adoptive parent shall be notified in writing or his or her right to such fair hearing.

(b)   Each social services official shall provide, either directly or through purchase of service, adoption services for each child in their care who is freed for adoption. Such adoption services shall include the evaluation of a child's placement needs and pre-placement planning, recruitment of and home study for prospective adoptive parents, training of adoptive parents, placement planning, supervision and post adoption services.

2.   The department shall promulgate regulations which shall require that adoption services be made available to all children who are listed with the New York state adoption service. Such regulations shall also provide for cooperation between local social services commissioners, and for apportioning reimbursement for adoption services where more than one agency or social services district has provided such services for a child.

2-a.   The department shall promulgate regulations requiring all adoption agencies to forward names and addresses of all persons who have applied for adoption of a hard-to-place or handicapped child, as defined in section four hundred fifty-one of this chapter. A list of such names and addresses shall be maintained by the department and made available, without charge, to every agency in the state to assist them in placing such children for adoption.

3.   The department shall promulgate regulations to maintain enlightened adoption policies and to establish standards and criteria for adoption practices.

4.   [*Repealed.*]

Added by Laws 1976, Ch. 836, eff. Oct. 30, 1976; **amended** by Laws 1978, Ch. 555; Laws 1979, Ch. 611, eff. Apr. 1, 1981; **amended** by Laws 1983, Ch. 491, eff. July 15, 1983; **amended** by Laws 1986, Ch. 902, eff. Aug. 5, 1986; **amended** by Laws 1991, Ch. 377, § 1, eff. Nov. 12, 1991; *amended* by Laws 1995, Ch. 83, § 232, eff. July 1, 1995.

§ 372-c.   Putative father registry.

1.   The department shall establish a putative father registry which shall record the names and addresses of: (a) any person adjudicated by a court of this state to be the father of a child born out of wedlock; (b) any person who has filed with the registry before or after the birth of a child out of wedlock, a notice of intent to claim paternity of the child; (c) any person adjudicated by a court of another state or territory of the United States to be the father of an out of wedlock child, where a certified copy of the court order has been filed with the registry by such person or any other person; (d) any person who has filed with the registry an instrument acknowledging paternity pursuant to section 4-1.2 of the estates, powers and trusts law.

2.   A person filing a notice of intent to claim paternity of a child or an acknowledgement of paternity shall include therein his current address and shall notify the registry of any change of address pursuant to procedures prescribed by regulations of the department.

3.   A person who has filed a notice of intent to claim paternity may at any time revoke a notice of intent to claim paternity previously filed therewith and, upon receipt of such notification by the registry, the revoked notice of intent to claim paternity shall be deemed a nullity nunc pro tunc.

4.   An unrevoked notice of intent to claim paternity of a child may be introduced in evidence by any party, other than the person who filed such notice, in any proceeding in which such fact may be relevant.

5.   The department shall, upon request, provide the names and addresses of persons listed with the registry to any court or authorized agency, and such information shall not be divulged to any other person, except upon order of a court for good cause shown.

Added by Laws 1976, Ch. 665, eff. Jan. 1, 1977; **amended** by Laws 1979, Ch. 139, eff. May 29, 1979.

§ 372-d.   Adoption services; purchase by department.

1.   The department may provide, through purchase of services from authorized agencies, adoption services for any child who has been referred to the statewide adoption service pursuant to section three hundred seventy-two-c and who has not been placed for adoption within three months after the date of such referral.

SSL

2. As used in this section "adoption services" shall mean those services and activities set forth in subdivision one of section three hundred seventy-two-b of this chapter.

3. In accordance with regulations of the department, expenditures made by the department for the provision, through purchase, of adoption services for a child pursuant to this section shall be subject to reimbursement to the state by the social services district charged with the guardianship and custody of the child, as follows: fifty percent of the amount expended for the provision of such adoption services after first deducting from such amount any federal funds properly received or to be received on account thereof.

Added by Laws 1978, Ch. 558, eff. July 24, 1978.

§ 372-e. Adoption applications; appeals.

1. An authorized agency shall keep a record of applications received from persons seeking to become adoptive parents, including all actions taken on such applications.

2. The department shall promulgate regulations setting forth standards and procedures to be followed by authorized agencies in evaluating persons who have applied to such agencies for the adoption of a child. Such regulations shall also restrict the evaluation process so as not to unnecessarily duplicate previous investigations which may have been made of the adoptive applicant in the context of a prior adoption application or an application for licensure or certification to board children.

3. (a) Upon an authorized agency's denial of an application, the authorized agency shall furnish the applicant with a written statement setting forth its reason for the denial of the application. Such written statement shall include a notice to the applicant, in bold face type, of such applicant's right to request and be granted a hearing in accordance with the provisions of subdivision four of this section.

(b) Upon an authorized agency's failure to act on an application within six months of its submission, the authorized agency shall, on such applicant's request, furnish the applicant with a written statement setting forth its reason for its failure to act on the application. Such written statement shall include a notice to the applicant, in bold face type, of such applicant's right to request and be granted a hearing in accordance with the provisions of subdivision four of this section.

4. Any person whose application has been denied or whose application has not been acted upon by an authorized agency within six months of its submission may request and shall be granted a hearing in accordance with the provisions of section twenty-two of this chapter relating to fair hearings.

Added by Laws 1979, Ch. 611, eff. Apr. 1, 1980; **amended** by Laws 1989, Ch. 720, § 1, eff. Aug. 23, 1989.

§ 372-f.   Statewide adoption service.

1.   There shall be established by the department either directly or through purchase a statewide adoption service which shall serve all authorized agencies in the state as a means of recruiting adoptive families for children who have been legally freed for adoption but have remained in foster care for a period of three months or more. Such period in foster care shall include any period of foster care immediately preceding the date on which the child was legally freed for adoption. The service shall provide descriptions and photographs of such children, and shall also provide any other information deemed useful in the recruitment of adoptive families for each such child. The service shall be updated monthly.

2.   The service may be organized on a regional basis, but shall be provided to all authorized child caring agencies and in accordance with the regulations of the department, to all appropriate citizen groups and other organizations and associations interested in children's services.

3.   The department shall promulgate regulations governing the operations of the adoption service.

4.   (a) Except as set forth in paragraph (b) of this subdivision, each authorized agency shall refer to the adoption service, accompanied by a photograph and description, as shall be required by departmental regulations, each child in its care who has been legally freed for adoption and who has been in foster care for the period specified in subdivision one of this section and for whom no adoptive home has been found. If the child is fourteen years or older and will not consent to his or her adoption, such child need not be listed on the service. Such children's names shall be forwarded to the department by the authorized agency, with reference to the specific reason by which the child was not placed on the service. The department shall establish procedures for periodic review of the status of such children. If the department determines that adoption would be appropriate for a child not listed with the service, the agency shall forthwith list the child. Each authorized agency may voluntarily refer any child who has been legally freed for adoption. In addition, upon referral of a child by an authorized agency, the department may determine that the listing of a child with the service is not in the child's best interest where: the child has been placed with a relative within the third degree of consanguinity of the parents of the child and the child does not have a permanency goal of adoption, or the child is not emotionally prepared for an adoptive placement. Any child who is not listed based on one of these factors and who is not placed in an adoptive placement within six months of referral to the department must be listed with the service at the end of the six month period in accordance with regulations of the department except where the child is placed with a relative within the third degree of consanguinity of the parents of the child, in which case the department may determine that the listing continues to be contrary to the child's best interests. The department shall establish procedures for the periodic review of the status of such children.

   (b)   An authorized agency shall not refer to the adoption service a child in its care who has been legally freed for adoption when the child has been placed with a foster parent who has expressed, in writing, an interest in adopting the child; provided, however, that such child shall be referred to the adoption service in accordance with paragraph (a) of this subdivision where the foster parent has withdrawn interest in adopting the child or has been disapproved as an adoptive resource for the child. An authorized agency shall not refer to the adoption service a child in its care who has been legally freed for adoption where the agency has identified two or more potential placements for the child; provided, however, that such child shall be referred to the adoption service in accordance with paragraph (a) of this subdivision when such child has not been placed into an adoptive home within nine months of having been freed for adoption.

Added by Laws 1975, Ch. 702, eff. Apr. 1, 1976; **amended** by Laws 1976, Ch. 836, eff. Oct. 30, 1976; Laws 1979, Ch. 610, eff. Apr. 1, 1981, Ch. 611, eff. Oct. 11, 1979; **amended** by Laws 1992, Ch. 559, §§ 1, 2, eff. July 24, 1992; **amended** by Laws 1995, Ch. 83, § 233, eff. July 1, 1995.

§ 372-g.　Abandoned infant protection program.

The office of children and family services shall develop and implement a public information program to inform the general public of the provisions of the abandoned infant protection act. The program may include but not be limited to the following elements:

    1. Educational and informational materials in print, audio, video, electronic, or other media;

    2. Public service announcements and advertisements; and

    3. Establishment of toll-free telephone hotlines to provide information.

Added by Laws 2000, Ch. 156, eff. July 18, 2000.

§ 373.　Religious faith.

1.　Whenever a child is committed to any agency, association, corporation, institution or society, other than an institution supported and controlled by the state or a subdivision thereof, such commitment shall be made, when practicable, to an authorized agency under the control of persons of the same religious faith as that of the child.

2.　Whenever any child is surrendered, released, placed out, or boarded out, in a family, a home or an institution, or in an agency boarding home, or in a group home, or to an authorized agency, or in the custody of any person other than that of a relative within the second degree, such surrender, release, placement or boarding out shall when practicable, be to, with or in the custody of a person or persons of the **same religious faith as that of the child or to an authorized agency under the control of persons of the same religious faith as that of the child.

3.　In appointing guardians of children, and in granting orders of adoption of children, the court shall, when practicable, appoint as such guardians, and give custody through adoption, only to a person or persons of the same religious faith as that of the child.

4. The provisions of subdivision one, two and three of this section shall be so interpreted as to assure that in the care, protection, adoption, guardianship, discipline and control of any child, its religious faith shall be preserved and protected.

5. Whenever a child is placed out or boarded out in the custody, or under the supervision or control, of a person or of persons of a religious faith different from that of the child, or if a guardian of a child is appointed whose religious faith is different from that of the child, or if letters of adoption of a child are granted to a person or persons whose religious faith is different from that of the child or if a child is committed to an agency, association, corporation, society or institution, which is under the control of persons of a religious faith different from that of the child, the court, public board, commission or official shall state or recite the facts which impelled such disposition to be made contrary to the religious faith of the child or to any person whose religious faith is different from that of the child and such statement shall be a part of the minutes of the proceeding, and subject to inspection by the department or an authorized agency. This subdivision shall not apply to institutions supported and controlled by the state or a subdivision thereof.

6. The provisions of this section in relation to the protection of the religious faith of children shall also apply to minors between sixteen and eighteen years of age.

7. The provisions of subdivisions one, two, three, four, five and six of this section shall, so far as consistent with the best interests of the child, and where practicable, be applied so as to give effect to the religious wishes of the natural mother, and of the natural father whose consent would be required for the child's adoption pursuant to section one hundred eleven of the domestic relations law, if the child is born out of wedlock, or if born in-wedlock, the religious wishes of the parents of the child, or if only one of the parents of an in-wedlock child is then living, the religious wishes of the parent then living. Religious wishes of a parent shall include wishes that the child be placed in the same religion as the parent or in a different religion from the parent or with indifference to religion or with religion a subordinate consideration. Expressed religious wishes of a parent shall mean those which have been set forth in a writing signed by the parent, except that, in a non-agency adoption, such writing shall be an affidavit of the parent. In the absence of expressed religious wishes, as defined in this subdivision, determination of the religious wishes, if any, of the parent, shall be made upon the other facts of the particular case, and, if there is no evidence to the contrary, it shall be presumed that the parent wishes the child to be reared in the religion of the parent.

Amended by Laws 1962, Ch. 584; **amended** by Laws 1967, Ch. 276; **amended** by Laws 1970, Ch. 494, eff. May 8, 1970; **amended** by Laws 1978, Ch. 555; **amended** by Laws 1980, Ch. 575, eff. July 26, 1980.

SSL

§ 373-a.   Medical histories.

Notwithstanding any other provision of law to the contrary, to the extent they are available, the medical histories of a child legally freed for adoption or of a child to be placed in foster care and of his or her natural parents, with information identifying such natural parents eliminated, shall be provided by an authorized agency to such child's prospective adoptive parent or foster parent and upon request to the adoptive parent or foster parent when such child has been adopted or placed in foster care. To the extent they are available, the medical histories of a child in foster care and of his or her natural parents shall be provided by an authorized agency to such child when discharged to his or her own care and upon request to any adopted former foster child; provided, however, medical histories of natural parents shall be provided to an adoptee with information identifying such natural parents eliminated. Such medical histories shall include all available information setting forth conditions or diseases believed to be hereditary, any drugs or medication taken during pregnancy by the child's natural mother and any other information, including any psychological information in the case of a child legally freed for adoption or when such child has been adopted, or in the case of a child to be placed in foster care or placed in foster care, which may be a factor influencing the child's present or future health. The department shall promulgate and may alter or amend regulations governing the release of medical histories pursuant to this section.

Added by Laws 1983, Ch. 326, eff. Sept. 19, 1983; **amended** by Laws 1985, Ch. 103, eff. May 21, 1985; **amended** by Laws 1985, Ch. 142, eff. June, 1985; **amended** by Laws 1985, Ch. 270, eff. June 25, 1985; **amended** by Laws 1988, Ch. 584 § 5, eff. Feb. 1, 1989; **amended** by Laws 1990, Ch. 165, § 1, eff. May 21, 1990.

§ 374.   Authority to place out or board out children.

1.   An authorized agency is hereby empowered and permitted to place out and board out children.

1-a.   In any agreement between an authorized agency and foster parents with whom a child or children are to be placed or boarded, there shall be contained therein the following language: "It is duly acknowledged by the parties hereto that pursuant to the law of the state of New York, a foster parent shall have preference in any proceedings to adopt the child subject to this agreement upon such child having been in the custody of such foster parent for a period in excess of twelve months."

2.   No person, agency, association, corporation, institution, society or other organization except an authorized agency shall place out or board out any child but the provisions of this section shall not restrict or limit the right of a parent, legal guardian or relative within the second degree to place out or board out a child.

3.   Except as hereinafter provided no court, public board, commission or official shall place out or board out a child in a family not residing within this state.

(a) A commissioner of public welfare or a city public welfare officer authorized, pursuant to the provisions of section three hundred ninety-eight of the social welfare law, to accept the surrender of a child, may place out a child for the purpose of adoption is a family not residing within this state. No placement of a child in a family not residing within this state shall be made unless an agreement for such placement shall have been reached between the public welfare official making such placement and the appropriate welfare or other public official on a state or local level in the state where the family resides who is authorized by law to supervise children in institutional or foster care homes. Such agreement shall include provision for the supervision of the family and the child during the period preceding a final adoption.

(b) A commissioner of public welfare or a city public welfare officer authorized, pursuant to the provisions of section three hundred ninety-eight of the social welfare law, to place children in family homes, may board out a child in a family not residing within this state. No child may be boarded out in a family not residing within this state unless an agreement for such placement shall have been reached between the public welfare official making such placement and the appropriate welfare or other public official on a state or local level in the state where the family resides who is authorized by law to supervise children in institutional or foster care homes. Such agreement shall include provision for the supervision of the family and the child during the period while the child is boarded out.

4. (a) No hospital or lying-in asylum whether incorporated or unincorporated where women or girls may be received, cared for or treated during pregnancy or during or after delivery except as hereinafter provided and no person licensed to carry on like work under the provisions of sections twenty-five hundred twenty to twenty-five hundred twenty-three, inclusive, or the public health law shall be an authorized agency for placing out or boarding out children or place out any child in a foster home whether for adoption or otherwise either directly or indirectly or as agent or representative of the mother or parents of such child.

(b) Every such hospital and licensed person shall forthwith report to the county or city officer or board charged by law with the care of destitute children away from their homes where such hospital is located or where such child is cared for by such licensed person any child abandoned or left in the care or custody of such hospital or licensed person provided, however, that no such report except as provided in section three hundred seventy-two shall be required to be made by a hospital which is also an authorized agency.

(c) Such officer or board shall receive and care for such child as a destitute or abandoned child and may bring the case of such child before the family court in the county or city for adjudication.

(d) The expense of caring for such child as a public charge shall be paid as provided by this chapter.

SSL

5. Nothing contained in this section shall deprive any hospital of any right or power conferred upon it by its charter or act of incorporation or specified in its certificate of incorporation.

6. [Until June 1, 2007, sub 6 reads as set out below:]

An authorized agency, as defined in paragraphs (a) and (c) of subdivision ten of section three hundred seventy-one of this chapter, may charge or accept a fee or other compensation to or from a person or persons with whom it has placed out a child, for the reasonable and necessary expenses of such placement; and no agency, association, corporation, institution, society or organization, except such an authorized agency, and no person may or shall request, accept or receive any compensation or thing of value, directly or indirectly, in connection with the placing out or adoption of a child or for assisting a parent, relative or guardian of a child in arranging for the placement of the child for the purpose of adoption; and no person may or shall pay or give to any person or to any agency, association, corporation, institution, society or organization, except such an authorized agency, any compensation or thing of value in connection with the placing out or adoption of a child or for assisting a parent, relative or guardian of a child in arranging for the placement of the child for the purpose of adoption. The prohibition set forth in this section applies to any adoptive placement activity involving a child born in New York state or brought into this state or involving a New York resident seeking to bring a child into New York state for the purpose of adoption.

This subdivision shall not be construed to prevent the payment of salaries or other compensation by an authorized agency to the officers or employees thereof; nor shall it be construed to prevent the payment by a person with whom a child has been placed out of reasonable and actual medical fees or hospital charges for services rendered in connection with the birth of such child or of other necessary expenses incurred by the mother in connection with or as a result of her pregnancy or the birth of the child, or of reasonable and actual nursing, medical or hospital fees for the care of such child, if such payment is made to the physician, nurse or hospital who or which rendered the services or to the natural mother of the child, or to prevent the receipt of such payment by such physician, nurse, hospital or mother. This subdivision shall not be construed to prevent the payment by an adoptive parent, as defined in section one hundred nine of the domestic relations law, of the mother's reasonable and actual expenses for housing, maternity clothing, clothing for the child and transportation for a reasonable period not to exceed sixty days prior to the birth and the later of thirty days after the birth or thirty days after the parental consent to the adoption, unless a court determines, in writing, that exceptional circumstances exist which require the payment of the mother's expenses beyond the time periods stated in this sentence. This subdivision shall not be construed to prevent the payment by an adoptive parent, as defined in section one hundred nine of the domestic relations law, of reasonable and actual legal fees charged for consultation and legal advice, preparation of papers and representation and other legal services rendered in connection with an adoption proceeding or of necessary disbursements incurred for or in an adoption proceeding. No attorney or law firm shall serve as the attorney for, or provide any legal services to both the natural parents and adoptive parents.

6. [Eff. June 1, 2007, sub 6 reads as set out below:]

An authorized agency, as defined in paragraphs (a) and (c) of subdivision ten of section three hundred seventy-one of this title, may charge or accept a fee or other compensation to or from a person or persons with whom it has placed out a child, for the reasonable and necessary expenses of such placement; and no agency, association, corporation, institution, society or organization, except such an authorized agency, and no person may or shall request, accept or receive any compensation or thing of value, directly or indirectly, in connection with the placing out or adoption of a child or for assisting a parent, relative or guardian of a child in arranging for the placement of the child for the purpose of adoption; and no person may or shall pay or give to any person or to any agency, association, corporation, institution, society or organization, except such an authorized agency, any compensation or thing of value in connection with the placing out or adoption of a child or for assisting a parent, relative or guardian of a child in arranging for the placement of the child for the purpose of adoption. The prohibition set forth in this section applies to any adoptive placement activity involving a child born in New York state or brought into this state or involving a New York resident seeking to bring a child into New York state for the purpose of adoption.

This subdivision shall not be construed to prevent the payment of salaries or other compensation by an authorized agency to the officers or employees thereof; nor shall it be construed to prevent the payment by a person with whom a child has been placed out of reasonable and actual medical fees or hospital charges for services rendered in connection with the birth of such child or of other necessary expenses incurred by the mother in connection with or as a result of her pregnancy or the birth of the child, or of reasonable and actual nursing, medical or hospital fees for the care of such child, if such payment is made to the physician, nurse or hospital who or which rendered the services or to the natural mother of the child, or to prevent the receipt of such payment by such physician, nurse, hospital or mother. This subdivision shall not be construed to prevent the payment by an adoptive parent, as defined in section one hundred nine of the domestic relations law, of the mother's reasonable and actual expenses for housing, maternity clothing, clothing for the child and transportation for a reasonable period not to exceed sixty days prior to the birth and the later of thirty days after the birth or thirty days after the parental consent to the adoption, unless a court determines, in writing, that exceptional circumstances exist which require the payment of the mother's expenses beyond the time periods stated in this sentence. This subdivision shall not be construed to prevent the payment by an adoptive parent, as defined in section one hundred nine of the domestic relations law, of reasonable and actual legal fees charged for consultation and legal advice, preparation of papers and representation and other legal services rendered in connection with an adoption proceeding or of necessary disbursements incurred for or in an adoption proceeding. No attorney or law firm shall serve as the attorney for, or provide any legal services to both the birth parent and adoptive parent in regard to the placing out of a child for adoption or in an adoption proceeding. No attorney or law firm shall serve as the attorney for, or provide any legal services to, both an authorized agency and adoptive parent or both an authorized agency and birth parent where the authorized agency provides adoption services to such birth parent or adoptive parent, where the authorized agency provides foster care for the child, or where the authorized agency is directly or indirectly involved in the placing out of such child for adoption.

7. After receipt of notice from the state commissioner of health or the department of health of the city of New York, as the case may be, that an application has been received by such commissioner or department for a license or for the renewal of a license to conduct a maternity hospital or lying-in asylum, pursuant to the provisions of sections twenty-five hundred twenty to twenty-five hundred twenty-three, inclusive, of the public health law, the department shall, after notice to the applicant and opportunity for him to be heard, certify in writing to such commissioner or city department that the department has reasonable cause to believe that the applicant is violating or has violated the provisions of this section, if such be the case. The department shall so certify within thirty days of the date it received notice, or within such additional period, not to exceed thirty days, as the department may request in writing addressed to the commissioner or administration giving notice.

Amended by Laws 1949, Chs. 678, 680; Laws 1951, Ch. 453; Laws 1954, Ch. 239; Laws 1959, Ch. 470; Laws 1960, Ch. 709; Laws 1962, Ch. 690; Laws 1969, Ch. 407; Laws 1970, Ch. 670; Laws 1978, Ch. 655; amended by Laws 1979, Ch. 368, eff. Nov. 1, 1979; amended by Laws 1981, Ch. 15, eff. Mar. 17, 1981; amended by Laws 1981, Ch. 283, eff. Sept. 1, 1981; amended by Laws 1986, Ch. 765, eff. Aug. 2, 1986, and shall be deemed to have been in full force and effect from and after Aug. 3, 1986 amended by Laws 1989, Ch. 314 § 2, eff. Jan. 1, 1990; amended by Laws 1989, Ch. 315, eff. July 10, 1989; amended by Laws 2000, Ch. 446, § 1, eff. Sept. 20, 2000; Laws 2006, ch. 372, §1, eff. June 1, 2007.

§ 374-a. Interstate compact on the placement of children.

1. The interstate compact on the placement of children is hereby enacted into law and entered into with all other jurisdictions legally joining therein in form substantially as follows:

INTERSTATE COMPACT ON THE PLACEMENT OF CHILDREN.

ARTICLE I. PURPOSE AND POLICY.

It is the purpose and policy of the party states to cooperate with each other in the interstate placement of children to the end that:

(a)   Each child requiring placement shall receive the maximum opportunity to be placed in a suitable environment and with persons or institutions having appropriate qualifications and facilities to provide a necessary and desirable degree and type of care.

(b)   The appropriate authorities in a state where a child is to be placed may have full opportunity to ascertain the circumstances of the proposed placement, thereby promoting full compliance with applicable requirements for the protection of the child.

(c)   The proper authorities of the state from which the placement is made may obtain the most complete information on the basis of which to evaluate a projected placement before it is made.

(d)   Appropriate jurisdictional arrangements for the care of children will be promoted.

ARTICLE II. DEFINITIONS.

As used in this compact:

(a)   "Child" means a person who, by reason of minority, is legally subject to parental, guardianship or similar control.

(b)   "Sending agency" means a party state, officer or employee thereof; a subdivision of a party state, or officer or employee thereof; a court of a party state; a person, corporation, association, charitable agency or other entity which sends, brings, or causes to be sent or brought any child to another party state.

(c)   "Receiving state" means the state to which a child is sent, brought, or caused to be sent or brought, whether by public authorities or private persons or agencies, and whether for placement with state or local public authorities or for placement with private agencies or persons.

(d)   "Placement" means the arrangement for the care of a child in a family free or boarding home or in a child-caring agency or institution but does not include any institution caring for the mentally ill, mentally defective or epileptic or any institution primarily educational in character, and any hospital or other medical facility.

ARTICLE III. CONDITIONS FOR PLACEMENT.

(a)   No sending agency shall send, bring, or cause to be sent or brought into any other party state any child for placement in foster care or as a preliminary to a possible adoption unless the sending agency shall comply with each and every requirement set forth in this article and with the applicable laws of the receiving state governing the placement of children therein.

(b)   Prior to sending, bringing or causing any child to be sent or brought into a receiving state for placement in foster care or as a preliminary to a possible adoption, the sending agency shall furnish the appropriate public authorities in the receiving state written notice of the intention to send, bring, or place the child in the receiving state. The notice shall contain:

    (1)   The name, date and place of birth of the child.

    (2)   The identity and address or addresses of the parents or legal guardian.

    (3)   The name and address of the person, agency or institution to or with which the sending agency proposes to send, bring, or place the child.

    (4)   A full statement of the reasons for such proposed action and evidence of the authority pursuant to which the placement is proposed to be made.

    (c)   Any public officer or agency in a receiving state which is in receipt of a notice pursuant to paragraph (b) of this article may request of the sending agency, or any other appropriate officer or agency of or in the sending agency's state, and shall be entitled to receive therefrom, such supporting or additional information as it may deem necessary under the circumstances to carry out the purpose and policy of this compact.

    (d)   The child shall not be sent, brought, or caused to be sent or brought into the receiving state until the appropriate public authorities in the receiving state shall notify the sending agency, in writing, to the effect that the proposed placement does not appear to be contrary to the interests of the child.

ARTICLE IV. PENALTY FOR ILLEGAL PLACEMENT.

The sending, bringing, or causing to be sent or brought into any receiving state of a child in violation of the terms of this compact shall constitute a violation of the laws respecting the placement of children of both the state in which the sending agency is located or from which it sends or brings the child and of the receiving state. Such violation may be punished or subjected to penalty in either jurisdiction in accordance with its laws. In addition to liability for any such punishment or penalty, any such violation shall constitute full and sufficient grounds for the suspension or revocation of any license, permit, or other legal authorization held by the sending agency which empowers or allows it to place, or care for children.

ARTICLE V. RETENTION OF JURISDICTION.

    (a)   The sending agency shall retain jurisdiction over the child sufficient to determine all matters in relation to the custody, supervision, care, treatment and disposition of the child which it would have had if the child had remained in the sending agency's state, until the child is adopted, reaches majority, becomes self-supporting or is discharged with the concurrence of the appropriate authority in the receiving state. Such jurisdiction shall also include the power to effect or cause the return of the child or its transfer to another location and custody pursuant to law. The sending agency shall continue to have financial responsibility for support and maintenance of the child during the period of the placement.

Nothing contained herein shall defeat a claim of jurisdiction by a receiving state sufficient to deal with an act of delinquency or crime committed therein.

(b) When the sending agency is a public agency, it may enter into an agreement with an authorized public or private agency in the receiving state providing for the performance of one or more services in respect of such case by the latter as agent for the sending agency.

(c) Nothing in this compact shall be construed to prevent a private charitable agency authorized to place children in the receiving state from performing services or acting as agent in that state for a private charitable agency of the sending state; nor to prevent the agency in the receiving state from discharging financial responsibility for the support and maintenance of a child who has been placed on behalf of the sending agency without relieving the responsibility set forth in paragraph (a) hereof.

ARTICLE VI. INSTITUTIONAL CARE OF DELINQUENT CHILDREN.

A child adjudicated delinquent may be placed in an institution in another party jurisdiction pursuant to this compact, but no such placement shall be made unless the child is given a court hearing on notice to the parent or guardian with opportunity to be heard, prior to his being sent to such other party jurisdiction for institutional care and the court finds that:

1. Equivalent facilities for the child are not available in the sending agency's jurisdiction; and

2. Institutional care in the other jurisdiction is in the best interest of the child and will not produce undue hardship.

ARTICLE VII. COMPACT ADMINISTRATOR.

The executive head of each jurisdiction party to this compact shall designate an officer who shall be general coordinator of activities under this compact in his jurisdiction and who, acting jointly with like officers of other party jurisdictions, shall have power to promulgate rules and regulations to carry out more effectively the terms and provisions of this compact.

ARTICLE VIII. LIMITATIONS.

This compact shall not apply to:

(a) The sending or bringing of a child into a receiving state by his parent, stepparent, grandparent, adult brother or sister, adult uncle or aunt, or his guardian and leaving the child with any such relative or non-agency guardian in the receiving state.

(b) Any placement, sending or bringing of a child into a receiving state pursuant to any other interstate compact to which both the state from which the

SSL

child is sent or brought and the receiving state are party, or to any other agreement between said states which has the force of law.

ARTICLE IX. ENACTMENT AND WITHDRAWAL.

This compact shall be open to joinder by any state, territory or possession of the United States, the District of Columbia, the commonwealth of Puerto Rico, and, with the consent of congress, the government of Canada or any province thereof. It shall become effective with respect to any such jurisdiction when such jurisdiction has enacted the same into law. Withdrawal from this compact shall be by the enactment of a statute repealing the same, but shall not take effect until two years after the effective date of such statute and until written notice of the withdrawal has been given by the withdrawing state to the governor of each other party jurisdiction. Withdrawal of a party state shall not affect the rights, duties and obligations under this compact of any sending agency therein with respect to a placement made prior to the effective date of withdrawal.

ARTICLE X. CONSTRUCTION AND SEVERABILITY.

The provisions of this compact shall be liberally construed to effectuate the purposes thereof. The provisions of this compact shall be severable and if any phrase, clause, sentence or provisions of this compact is declared to be contrary to the constitution of any party state or of the United States or the applicability thereof to any government, agency, person or circumstance is held invalid, the validity of the remainder of this compact and the applicability thereof to any other government, agency, person or circumstance shall not be affected thereby. If this compact shall be held contrary to the constitution of any state party thereto, the compact shall remain in full force and effect as to the remaining states and in full force and effect as to the state affected as to all severable matters.

2.   Any requirement of this state for a license, permit, or the posting of a bond to entitle an agency to place children shall not apply to a public sending agency (within the meaning of the interstate compact on the placement of children) of or in another state party to said compact.

3.   Financial responsibility for any child placed pursuant to the provisions of the interstate compact for the placement of children shall be determined in accordance with the provisions of article five thereof in the first instance. However, in the event of partial or complete default of performance thereunder, the provisions of section three hundred eighty-two of this chapter with respect to such responsibility also may be invoked.

4.   The "appropriate public authorities" as used in article three of the interstate compact on the placement of children shall, with reference to New York, mean the department of social services, except that, with respect to the placement of children "adjudicated delinquent," as that phrase is used in article six thereof, who are to be placed in a facility operated or supervised by the

division for youth, shall mean the division for youth, and said department and division shall receive and act with reference to notices required by said article three.

5.   As used in paragraph (a) of article five of the interstate compact on the placement of children, the phrase "appropriate authority in the receiving state" with reference to New York state shall mean the commissioner of social services of the social services district in which the child may be at the time of discharge, and, with respect to children "adjudicated delinquent," as that phrase is used in article six thereof, who are to be discharged from a facility operated or supervised by the division for youth, shall mean the division for youth.

6.   The officers and agencies of this state and its subdivisions having authority to place children are hereby empowered to enter into agreements with appropriate officers or agencies of or in other party states pursuant to paragraph (b) of article five of the interstate compact on the placement of children. Any such agreement which contains a financial commitment or imposes a financial obligation on this state or subdivision or agency thereof shall not be binding unless it has the approval in writing of the comptroller in the case of the state and of the chief local fiscal officer in the case of a subdivision of the state.

7.   Any requirements for visitation, inspection or supervision of children, homes, institutions or other agencies in another party state which may apply under sections three hundred eighty-two, three hundred eighty-six or three hundred ninety-eight of this chapter shall be deemed to be met if performed pursuant to an agreement entered into by appropriate officers or agencies of this state or a subdivision thereof as contemplated by paragraph (b) of article five of the interstate compact on the placement of children.

8.   Neither the prohibition of, nor the limitations on out of state placement of children contained in sections three hundred seventy-four and three hundred ninety-eight of this chapter shall apply to placements made pursuant to the interstate compact on the placement of children.

9.   Any court having jurisdiction to place delinquent children may place such a child in an institution of or in another state pursuant to article six of the interstate compact on the placement of children and shall retain jurisdiction as provided in article five thereof.

10.   As used in article seven of the interstate compact on the placement of children, the term "executive head" means the governor. The governor is hereby authorized to appoint a compact administrator in accordance with the terms of said article seven.

11.   (a) In addition to the conditions for placement set forth in subdivision one of this section, the sending agency shall, in the case of a placement preliminary to a possible adoption, submit to the compact administrator a full statement setting forth all fees, including the categories of such fees, paid and to be paid by the adoptive parent to any agency or person in exchange for the adoptive placement.

SSL

(b) The compact administrator shall not approve a proposed placement where such placement violates subdivision six of section three hundred seventy-four of this chapter.

12. Placement of a child in this state in violation of subdivision one of this section by an out of state sending agency shall, in addition to any other remedy or sanction imposed by law, subject the agency violating such provision to a civil action for money damages including fees, compensation and other remuneration paid by any person on account of or incident to the placement of a child in violation of such provision.

Placement of a child by an out of state sending agency in violation of such provision shall subject such agency to the exercise of personal jurisdiction over such agency by a court pursuant to subparagraph (i) of paragraph three of subdivision (a) of section three hundred two of the civil practice law and rules.

Added by Laws 1960, Ch. 708, eff. Sept. 1, 1960; **amended** by Laws 1975, Ch. 384, eff. July 1, 1975; **amended** by Laws 1985, Ch. 491, eff. July 24, 1985; **amended** by Laws 1986, Ch. 127, eff. July 24, 1986; **amended** by Laws 1989, Ch. 314, eff. July 10, 1989 (§ 374-a(11), eff. Jan. 1, 1990).

§ 374-b. Authority to operate agency boarding home.

1. An authorized agency which is not a court, public board, commission, or official, is hereby empowered and permitted to operate agency boarding homes in compliance with regulations of the department; and a social services official who is authorized to place children in family homes and institutions, pursuant to section three hundred ninety-eight, may be authorized by the department to operate agency boarding homes, in compliance with such regulations, if such official applies for such authority and demonstrates to the department his need therefor and that suitable care is not otherwise available for children and/or minors under the care of such official through an authorized agency under the control of persons of the same religious faith as such children. No agency boarding home shall care for more than six children or minors except that such a home may provide care for more than six brothers and sisters of the same family. Such homes shall be subject to supervision, visitation and inspection by the department and shall also be subject to visitation and inspection by the board.

2. (a) if an authorized agency plans to establish one or more boarding homes within a municipality, it shall notify the chief executive officer of the municipality in writing of its intentions and include in such notice a description of the nature, size and the community support requirements of the program.

(b) For purposes of this subdivision, "municipality" means an incorporated village, if a facility is to be located therein; a town, if the facility is to be located therein, and not simultaneously within an incorporated village; or a city, except that in the city of New York, the community board with jurisdiction over the area in which such a facility is to be located shall be considered the municipality.

3.   An authorized agency that has received approval from the office of children and family services may operate a supervised independent living program, as defined in section three hundred seventy-one of this title. The office of children and family services shall promulgate regulations establishing the standards for approval and operation of supervised independent living programs.

Added by Laws 1962, Ch. 584, eff. Sept. 1, 1962; **amended** by Laws 1978, Ch. 555, § 14, eff. July 24, 1978; **amended** by Laws 1990, Ch. 365, § 1, eff. July 2, 1990; **amended** by Laws 2004, Ch. 160, § 4, eff. Nov. 17, 2004, adding subd. 3.

§ 374-c.   Authority to operate group homes.

1.   An authorized agency which is not a court, public board, commission or official is hereby empowered and permitted to operate group homes in compliance with regulations of the department. A social services official who is authorized to place children in family homes and institutions, pursuant to section three hundred ninety-eight, may be authorized by the department to operate group homes in compliance with such regulations, provided that such official demonstrates to the satisfaction of the department the need therefor and that suitable care is not otherwise available for children under the care of such official through an authorized agency under the control of persons of the same religious faith as such children. Such homes shall be subject to supervision, visitation and inspection by the department and shall also be subject to visitation and inspection by the board.

2.   (a) if an authorized agency plans to establish one or more group homes within a municipality, it shall notify the chief executive officer of the municipality in writing of its intentions and include in such notice a description of the nature, size and the community support requirements of the program.

(b)   For purposes of this subdivision, "municipality" means an incorporated village, if a facility is to be located therein; a town, if the facility is to be located therein, and not simultaneously within an incorporated village; or a city, except that in the city of New York, the community board with jurisdiction over the area in which such a facility is to be located shall be considered the municipality.

Added by Laws 1967, Ch. 276; **amended** by Laws 1968, Ch. 778; Laws 1971, Ch. 677; Laws 1978, Ch. 555, § 15, eff. July 24, 1978; **amended** by Laws 1990, Ch. 365, § 1, eff. July 2, 1990.

§ 374-d.   Authority to operate public institutions for children.

A social services official who is authorized to place children in family homes and institutions, pursuant to section three hundred ninety-eight, may be authorized by the department to operate public institutions for children in compliance with regulations of the department, provided that such official demonstrates to the satisfaction of the department the need therefor and that suitable care is not otherwise available for children under the care of such official. Such institutions shall be subject to supervision, visitation and inspection by the department and shall also be subject to visitation and inspection by the board.

Added by Laws 1967, Ch. 479, eff. Apr. 24, 1967; as § 374-e and **renumbered** § 374-d by Laws 1971, Ch. 677, eff. June 22, 1971; **amended** by Laws 1978, Ch. 555, § 16, eff. July 24, 1978.

§ 374-e. Authority to place out or board out children with therapeutic foster parents.

A social services official or agency who is authorized to place out or board out children pursuant to section three hundred ninety-eight or three hundred seventy-four of this article, is authorized by the department to place out or board out children having special needs with therapeutic foster parents pursuant to subdivision fifteen of section three hundred ninety-eight of this article and in compliance with regulations of the department. Such placement shall only be made, however, when the official or agency demonstrates to the satisfaction of the department that state expenditures incurred in placing a child with a therapeutic foster parent are less than those that would be incurred if the children were placed in an institution.

Added by Laws 1989, Ch. 731, § 3, eff. July 24, 1989.

§ 374-f. Authority to enter into leases for dwelling units.

Any inconsistent provisions of this chapter or any other law notwithstanding, a public welfare official authorized to operate agency boarding homes or group homes is hereby empowered to rent or lease dwelling units in his capacity as a public welfare official, as lessee, in any federal project, state project or municipal project, as defined in the public housing law, or in any municipally-aided project or state-aided project, or other project, as defined in the private housing finance law, or elsewhere, for the purpose of operating therein such agency boarding homes or group homes, and is hereby empowered to contract, in his capacity as a public welfare official, as contractor, with individuals for their services in conducting such homes and caring for children or minors placed in such homes.

Added by Laws 1967, Ch. 781, eff. May 2, 1967.

§ 375. Requirement of certificate or license to board children.

Except for relatives within the second degree or third degree of the parents of a child or children, relatives within the second degree or third degree of the stepparent of a child or children, legally appointed guardians, schools and academies meeting the requirements of the education law as to compulsory education, camps operated for profit for the accommodation of school age children during school vacation periods under permits issued by health officers pursuant to chapter seven of the state sanitary code, and persons with whom a child or children are placed out, no person shall receive, board or keep any child under the age of eighteen years unless certified or licensed to do so as provided in this title.

Amended by Laws 1962, Ch. 79, eff. Feb. 27, 1962; **amended** by Laws 1987, Ch. 460, eff. July 27, 1987.

§ 376.　Certificate to board children and/or minors under age of eighteen years.

1.　An authorized agency which shall board out any child/or minor under the age of eighteen years shall issue to the person receiving such child and/or minor for board a certificate to receive, board or keep a child and/or minor under the age of eighteen years. Prior to issuing such certificate, the agency shall require that an applicant set forth: his or her employment history, provide personal and employment references and sign a sworn statement indicating whether the applicant, to the best of his or her knowledge, has ever been convicted of a crime in this state or any other jurisdiction. Not until all inquiries are completed and evaluated shall the agency cause such certificate to be issued.

2.　The agency issuing or renewing any such certificate shall forthwith transmit a copy or report thereof to the board.

3.　No person shall be certified by more than one authorized agency but any person so certified may receive for care at board or otherwise a child and/or minor under the age of eighteen years from other sources upon the written consent and approval of the certifying agency as to each such child and/or minor.

Amended by Laws 1966, Ch. 96, eff. Sept. 1, 1966; **amended** by Laws 1975, Ch. 221, eff. June 17, 1975; **amended** by Laws 1985, Ch. 677, eff. Jan. 1, 1986.

§ 377.　License to board children.

1.　Application for a license to receive, board or keep any child shall be made in writing to the commissioner of social services, in and for the social services district wherein the premises to be licensed are located, in the form and manner prescribed by the department. The department shall require that an applicant set forth: his or her employment history, provide personal and employment references and sign a sworn statement indicating whether, to the best of his or her knowledge, he or she has ever been convicted of a crime in this state or any other jurisdiction. Not until all inquiries are completed and evaluated shall the commissioner of social services cause such license to be issued.

2.　Before any such license shall be issued an authorized agent or employee of the social services district shall visit and inspect the premises for which such license is requested, make such further inquiry and investigation as may be required to ascertain compliance with applicable requirements.

3.　If it appears from such inquiry and investigation that the applicant maintains a home suitable for the care of children in accordance with regulations of the department, the commissioner of social services shall cause such license to be issued in such manner as the department may provide.

4.   The commissioner of social services, issuing or renewing any such license, shall in accordance with the directions of the department, transmit a copy or report thereof to the department.

Amended by Laws 1967, Ch. 145; **amended** by Laws 1971, Chs. 110, 945, both eff. July 1, 1971; **amended** by Laws 1978, Ch. 555, § 17, eff. July 24, 1978; **amended** by Laws 1985, Ch. 677, eff. Jan. 1, 1986.

§ 378   Form, duration and limitation of certificates and licenses

1.   Certificates or licenses to receive, board or keep any child and/or minor shall be in the form prescribed and provided by the department to the effect that such person is regarded by the issuing authorized agency or social services department, as the case may be, as maintaining a home suitable for the care of children and/or minors and specifying the name, address, and religious faith of the person to whom issued, the number of children and/or minors for whom such person is certified or licensed to care and such other information as the department may require.

2.   Such certificates and licenses shall be valid for not more than one year after date of issue but may be renewed or extended subject to regulations established by the department.

3.   [Until Dec 21, 2005] No such license shall permit the reception for board of more than six children and if there are children not received for board living in the home of a person to whom such license is issued, whether children of such person or otherwise, the sum of the number of such children and of the number of children permitted to be received for board by such license shall not exceed six, excepting, however, that such license may permit the reception for board of additional children if such children (a) are siblings or half-siblings, or are siblings or half-siblings of a child living in the home, (b) are children freed for adoption as defined in paragraph (c) of subdivision one of section three hundred ninety-two of this chapter, and have been placed for adoption with the person to whom such license is issued, or (c) are minor parents who are foster children and the minor parents' children.

3.   [Eff. Dec 21, 2005] No such license shall permit the reception for board of more than six children and if there are children not received for board living in the home of a person to whom such license is issued, whether children of such person or otherwise, the sum of the number of such children and of the number of children permitted to be received for board by such license shall not exceed six, excepting, however, that such license may permit the reception for board of additional children if such children (a) are siblings or half-siblings, or are siblings or half-siblings of a child living in the home, (b) are children freed for adoption as defined in subdivision (b) of section one thousand eighty-seven of the family court act, and have been placed for adoption with the person to whom such license

is issued, or (c) are minor parents who are foster children and the minor parents' children.

4. [Until Dec 21, 2005] No such certificate shall permit the reception for board of more than six children and/or minors and if there are children under thirteen years of age not received for board living in the home of the person to whom such certificate is issued, whether children of such person or otherwise, the total number of such children and of the number of children and/or minors permitted to be received for board by such certificate shall not exceed six, excepting, however, that such certificate may permit the reception for board of up to two additional children if such children (a) are siblings or half-siblings, or are siblings or half-siblings of a child living in the home, (b) are children freed for adoption as defined in paragraph (c) of subdivision one of section three hundred ninety-two of this chapter, and have been placed for adoption with the person to whom such certificate is issued, or (c) are minor parents who are foster children and the minor parents' children.

4. [Eff. Dec 21, 2005] No such certificate shall permit the reception for board of more than six children and/or minors and if there are children under thirteen years of age not received for board living in the home of the person to whom such certificate is issued, whether children of such person or otherwise, the total number of such children and of the number of children and/or minors permitted to be received for board by such certificate shall not exceed six, excepting, however, that such certificate may permit the reception for board of up to two additional children if such children (a) are siblings or half-siblings, or are siblings or half-siblings of a child living in the home, (b) are children freed for adoption as defined in subdivision (b) of section one thousand eighty-seven of the family court act, and have been placed for adoption with the person to whom such certificate is issued, or (c) are minor parents who are foster children and the minor parents' children.

5. The department shall establish and may alter or amend regulations governing the issuing and revocation of such licenses and certificates and prescribing standards, records, accommodations and equipment for the care of children and/or minors received under such licenses and certificates.

Amended by Laws 1952, Ch. 295; Laws 1966, Ch. 96; Laws 1967, Ch. 145; **amended** by Laws 1971, Ch. 110, eff. July 1, 1971; **amended** by Laws 1975, Ch. 221, eff. June 17, 1975; **amended** by Laws 1978, Ch. 555, §§ 18, 19, eff. July 24, 1978; **amended** by Laws 1989, Ch. 728, eff. Oct. 22, 1989; **amended** by Laws 1996, Ch. 282, eff. July 10, 1996; Laws 2005, Ch. 3, § 40 (Part A), eff. Aug. 23, 2005.

§ 378-a. Access to conviction records by authorized agencies.

1. Subject to rules and regulations of the division of criminal justice services, an authorized agency shall have access to conviction records maintained by state law enforcement agencies pertaining to persons who have applied for and are under active consideration for employment by such authorized agency in

positions where such persons will be engaged directly in the care and supervision of children.

2.   (a) Notwithstanding any other provision of law to the contrary, and subject to rules and regulations of the division of criminal justice services, an authorized agency, as defined in subdivision ten of section three hundred seventy-one of this article, shall perform a criminal history record check with the division of criminal justice services regarding any prospective foster parent or prospective adoptive parent and any person over the age of eighteen who is currently residing in the home of such prospective foster parent or prospective adoptive parent before the foster parent or adoptive parent is finally certified or approved for the placement of a child. Persons who are over the age of eighteen residing in the home of a certified or approved foster parent and who previously did not have a criminal history record check performed in accordance with this subdivision shall have such a criminal history record check performed when the foster parent applies for renewal of his or her certification or approval as a foster parent. The provisions and procedures of this section, including the criminal history record check of persons over the age of eighteen who are currently residing in the home of the foster parent, also shall apply to prospective foster parents certified by the office of children and family services and to family homes certified by any other state agency where such family homes care for foster children in accordance with a memorandum of understanding with the office of children and family services.

(b)   Every authorized agency shall obtain a set of the prospective foster parent or prospective adoptive parent's fingerprints and those of any person over the age of eighteen who currently resides in the home of such prospective foster parent or prospective adoptive parent, and such other information as is required by the office of children and family services and the division of criminal justice services. The authorized agency shall provide to the applicant blank fingerprint cards and a description of how the completed fingerprint cards will be used upon submission to the authorized agency. The authorized agency shall promptly transmit such fingerprint cards to the office of children and family services. The office of children and family services shall promptly submit such fingerprint cards and the processing fee imposed pursuant to subdivision eight-a of section eight hundred thirty-seven of the executive law to the division of criminal justice services for its full search and retain processing. Notwithstanding any other provision of law to the contrary, the processing fee shall be submitted by the office of children and family services and no part thereof shall be charged to the prospective foster parent or prospective adoptive parent or any person over the age of eighteen who currently resides in the home of such prospective foster parent or prospective adoptive parent who submitted a fingerprint card pursuant to this subdivision.

(c)   The division of criminal justice services shall promptly provide to the office of children and family services a criminal history record, if any, with respect to the prospective foster parent or prospective adoptive parent and any other person over the age of eighteen who resides in the home of the prospective foster parent or prospective adoptive parent, or a statement that the individual has no criminal history record.

(d)　Notwithstanding any other provision of law to the contrary, the office of children and family services, upon receipt of a criminal history record from the division of criminal justice services, may request, and is entitled to receive, information pertaining to any offense contained in such criminal history record from any state or local law enforcement agency or court for the purposes of determining whether any ground relating to such criminal conviction or pending criminal charge exists for denying an application.

(e)　After reviewing any criminal history record information provided by the division of criminal justice services, the office of children and family services shall promptly notify the authorized agency or other state agency that:

(1)　Notwithstanding any other provision of law to the contrary, an application for certification or approval of a prospective foster parent or prospective adoptive parent shall be denied where a criminal history record of the prospective foster parent or prospective adoptive parent reveals a conviction for:

(A)　a felony conviction at any time involving: (i) child abuse or neglect; (ii) spousal abuse; (iii) a crime against a child, including child pornography; or (iv) a crime involving violence, including rape, sexual assault, or homicide, other than a crime involving physical assault or battery; unless the prospective foster parent or the prospective adoptive parent demonstrates that: (i) such denial will create an unreasonable risk of harm to the physical or mental health of the child; and (ii) approval of the application will not place the child's safety in jeopardy and will be in the best interests of the child; or

(B)　a felony conviction within the past five years for physical assault, battery, or a drug-related offense; unless the prospective foster parent or the prospective adoptive parent demonstrates that: (i) such denial will create an unreasonable risk of harm to the physical or mental health of the child; and (ii) approval of the application will not place the child's safety in jeopardy and will be in the best interests of the child; or

(2)　notwithstanding any other provision of law to the contrary, a final determination of an application for certification or approval of a prospective foster parent or prospective adoptive parent shall be held in abeyance whenever the criminal history record of the prospective foster parent or prospective adoptive parent reveals:

(A)　a charge for a crime set forth in subparagraph one of this paragraph which has not been finally resolved; or

(B)　a felony conviction that may be for a crime set forth in subparagraph one of this paragraph. An authorized agency may proceed with a determination of such application, in a manner consistent with this subdivision, only upon receiving subsequent notification from the office of children and family services regarding the status of such charge or the nature of such conviction; or

SSL

(3)   an application for certification or approval of a prospective foster parent or prospective adoptive parent may, consistent with the provisions of article twenty-three-A of the correction law, be denied where:

(A)   a criminal history record of the prospective foster parent or prospective adoptive parent reveals a charge or a conviction of a crime other than one set forth in subparagraph one of this paragraph; or

(B)   a criminal history record of any other person over the age of eighteen who resides in the home of the prospective foster parent or prospective adoptive parent reveals a charge or a conviction of any crime; or

(4)   notwithstanding any other provision of law to the contrary, an application for renewal of the certification or approval of a foster parent shall be denied based on the conviction of the foster parent of a crime set forth in subparagraph one of this paragraph, unless the foster parent demonstrates that:

(A)   such denial will create an unreasonable risk of harm to the physical or mental health of the child; and

(B)   renewal of the application will not place the child's safety in jeopardy and will be in the best interests of the child; or

(5)   notwithstanding any other provision of law to the contrary, the certification or approval of a foster parent, or the approval of an adoptive parent who has not completed the adoption process, shall be revoked based on the conviction of the foster parent or the adoptive parent of a crime set forth in subparagraph one of this paragraph, unless the foster parent or the adoptive parent demonstrates that:

(A)   such revocation will create an unreasonable risk of harm to the physical or mental health of the child; and

(B)   continued certification or approval will not place the child's safety in jeopardy and will be in the best interests of the child; or

(6)   the prospective foster parent or prospective adoptive parent and any person over the age of eighteen who is residing in the home of the prospective foster parent or prospective adoptive parent has no criminal history record.

(f)   Any notification by the office of children and family services pursuant to paragraph (e) of this subdivision shall include a summary of the criminal history record provided by the division of criminal justice services, including, but not limited to, the specific crime or crimes for which the prospective foster or adoptive parent or parents or any adults over the age of eighteen living in the home have been charged or convicted, as applicable.

(g)   When an authorized agency has denied an application pursuant to paragraph (e) of this subdivision, the authorized agency shall provide to the applicant a written statement setting forth the reasons for such denial, including the summary of the criminal history record provided to the authorized agency by the office of children and family services. The authorized agency shall also provide a description of the division of criminal justice services' record review process and any remedial processes provided by the office of children and family services to any prospective foster parent or prospective adoptive parent. If the applicant is disqualified under item (ii) of clause (a) of subparagraph one of paragraph (e) of this subdivision, then the applicant may apply for relief from the mandatory disqualification based on the grounds that the offense was not spousal abuse as that term is defined in paragraph (j) of this subdivision.

(h) Where a criminal history record of the certified or approved foster parent, prospective adoptive parent or of any other person over the age of eighteen who resides in the home of the certified or approved foster parent or prospective adoptive parent reveals a charge or conviction of any crime, the authorized agency shall perform a safety assessment of the conditions in the household. Such assessment shall include: whether the subject of the charge or conviction resides in the household; the extent to which such person may have contact with foster children or other children residing in the household; and the status, date and nature of the criminal charge or conviction. The authorized agency shall thereafter take all appropriate steps to protect the health and safety of such child or children, including, when appropriate, the removal of any foster child or children from the home. Where the authorized agency denies the application or revokes the approval or certification of the foster parent or the prospective adoptive parent in accordance with the standards set forth in paragraph (e) of this subdivision, such authorized agency shall remove any foster child or children from the home of the foster parent or the prospective adoptive parent.

(i) Any criminal history record provided by the division of criminal justice services, and any summary of the criminal history record provided by the office of children and family services to an authorized agency pursuant to this subdivision, is confidential and shall not be available for public inspection; provided, however, nothing herein shall prevent an authorized agency, the office of children and family services or other state agency referenced in paragraph (a) of this subdivision from disclosing criminal history information to any administrative or judicial proceeding relating to the denial or revocation of a certification or approval of a foster parent or an adoptive parent or the removal of the foster child from the home. Where there is a pending court case, the authorized agency which received the criminal history record summary from the office of children and family services, shall provide a copy of such summary to the family court or surrogate's court.

(j) For the purposes of this subdivision "spousal abuse" is an offense defined in section 120.05 or 120.10 of the penal law where the victim of such offense was the defendant's spouse; provided, however, spousal abuse shall not include a crime in which the prospective foster parent or prospective adoptive parent, who was the defendant, has received notice pursuant to paragraph (g) of this subdivision and the office of children and family services finds after a fair hearing held pursuant to section twenty-two of this chapter, that he or she was the victim of physical, sexual or psychological abuse by the victim of such offense and such abuse was a factor in causing the prospective foster parent or prospective adoptive parent to commit such offense.

(k)   The office of children and family services shall inform the division of criminal justice services when a person is no longer certified or approved as a foster parent or is no longer a prospective adoptive parent so that the division of criminal justice services may terminate its retain processing with regard to such person and any person over the age of eighteen who is residing in the home of the foster parent or prospective adoptive parent. At least once a year, the office of children and family services will be required to conduct a validation of the records maintained by the division of criminal justice services.

(l)   The office of children and family services, in consultation with the division of criminal justice services, shall promulgate regulations for the purpose of implementing the provisions of this subdivision relating to the standards for the certification or approval of foster parents or adoptive parents.

Added by Laws 1976, Ch. 916, eff. July 27, 1976; amended by Laws 1999, Ch. 7, § 7, eff. Feb. 11, 1999; amended by Laws 2000, Ch. 145, §§ 1–3, eff. July 1, 2000.

§ 379.   Revocation of certificates and licenses.

1.   A certificate or license to receive, board or keep any child and/or minor under the age of eighteen years may be revoked for cause by the authorized agency or the commissioner of social services by which it was issued and any such certificate or license to receive, board or keep any child may be revoked for cause by the commissioner.

2.   An agency revoking any such certificate and a commissioner of social services revoking any such license shall notify the department of such revocation at once.

Amended by Laws 1966, Ch. 96; Laws 1967, Ch. 145; amended by Laws 1971, Ch. 945, eff. July 1, 1971; amended by Laws 1978, Ch. 555, § 20, eff. July 24, 1978.

§ 380.   Boarding and free homes; records.

Every person who receives, boards or keeps a child and/or minor under a license or certificate shall keep a record in a register to be provided by the department showing the name, date of birth and religious faith of each child and/or minor received, the names and addresses of his parents or guardian or of the authorized agency from whom received and of the person by whom placed and by whom removed, the dates of reception and removal and such other information as may be required by the department.

Amended by Laws 1966, Ch. 96; Laws 1971, Chs. 110, 945, both eff. July 1, 1971; Laws 1975, Ch. 221, eff. June 17, 1975; Laws 1978, Ch. 555, § 21, eff. July 24, 1978.

§ 381.   Maternity homes; records and reports.

Every hospital or lying-in asylum whether incorporated or unincorporated where women or girls may be received, cared for or treated during pregnancy or during or after delivery and every person licensed to carry on like work under the provisions of sections twenty-five hundred twenty to twenty-five hundred twenty-three, inclusive, of the public health law shall keep a record showing the full and true name and address including street and number, if any, of every such woman or girl and of each child of such woman or girl received, admitted or born on the premises, the full and true names and addresses and the religious faith of the parents of every such child, the dates of reception, admission or birth and of discharge or departure of each such woman, girl or child, the full and true names and addresses of the person or persons by whom any such child is removed or taken away, the amount paid for the care of any such woman, girl or child and the full and true names and addresses of the person or persons making such payment or payments; and shall keep such further record as may be required by regulations of the department. The department may, through its authorized agents and employees, at all reasonable times, inspect and examine such records and may require from such licensed person or from such hospital and its directors, officers, trustees, employees, manager, superintendent, owner or other person responsible for its operation, all information in their possession with reference to any such child not taken away or removed from such hospital by his parents or parent.

Amended by Laws 1951, Ch. 453; **amended** by Laws 1954, Ch. 239, eff. June 1, 1954; **amended** by Laws 1971, Ch. 945, eff. July 1, 1971; **amended** by Laws 1978, Ch. 555, §22, eff. July 24, 1978.

§ 382.   Responsibility for children without state residence; license and board.

1.   Any person, institution, corporation or agency which shall bring, or cause to be brought, into the state of New York any child not having a state residence, or which shall receive or accept any child from outside of the state of New York, not having state residence, shall be responsible for the care and maintenance of such child whether placed out, boarded out or otherwise cared for unless adopted by foster parents. Such responsibility shall continue during the minority of such child and thereafter until he is self-supporting.

2.   (a) It shall be unlawful for any person, agency, association, corporation, society, institution or other organization, except an authorized agency, to bring, send or cause to be brought or sent into the state of New York any child for the purpose of placing or boarding such child or procuring the placing of such child, by adoption, guardianship, or otherwise, in a family, a home or institution, except with an authorized agency, in this state, without first obtaining a license from the department.

SSL

(b) This subdivision shall not apply to a sending agency, as defined in article two of section three hundred seventy-four-a of this title, which is located in a state which is a party to the interstate compact on the placement of children, provided, however, that all persons who reside in such a state, except officers or employees of the state or a subdivision thereof who are acting in their official capacity, shall comply with the provisions of this section.

(c) This section shall not apply to and shall not restrict or limit the right of a parent, legal guardian, or relative within the second degree of a child from bringing or sending the child or causing the child to be brought or sent, into the state of New York for the purpose of placing out or boarding out the child.

3. Application for a license shall be submitted on a form approved and provided by the department and be accompanied by proof that the applicant holds a license, or is approved by the department or similar body in the state where the applicant resides, or where its chief office is located, or where it has its place of business.

4. Before bringing, sending, or causing to be brought or sent into this state any child, the person, agency, association, corporation, society, institution or other organization, duly licensed as provided in this section must furnish the department a blanket indemnity bond of a reputable surety company in favor of the state in the penal sum of not less than ten thousand dollars. Such bond must be approved as to form and sufficiency by the department and conditioned as follows: That such licensee (a) will report to the department immediately the name of each such child, its age, the name of the state, and city, town, borough or village, or the name of the country from which such child came, the religious faith of the parents of the child, the full name and last residence of its parent or parents, the name of the custodian from whom it is taken, and the name and residence of the person or authorized agency with whom it is placed or boarded, released or surrendered, or to whom adoption or guardianship is granted, and the death of such child or any reboarding, replacement or other disposition;

(b) will remove from the state within thirty days after written notice is given any such child becoming a public charge during his minority;

(c) will remove from the state immediately upon its release any such child who within three years from the time of its arrival within the state is committed to an institution or prison as a result of conviction for juvenile delinquency or crime;

(d) will place or cause to be placed or board or cause to be boarded such child under agreement which will secure to such child a proper home, and will make the person so receiving such child responsible for its proper care, education and training;

(e) will comply with section three hundred seventy-three;

(f) will supervise the care and training of such child and cause it to be visited at least annually by a responsible agent of the licensee; and

(g) will make to the department such reports as it from time to time may require.

5. In the event of the failure of such licensee to comply with the second and third conditions of the bond hereinbefore mentioned, and to remove, after thirty day's notice so to do, a child becoming a public charge, such portion of the bond shall be forfeited to the state or the county or municipality thereof as such equal the sum which shall have been expended by the state or such county or municipality thereof for the care or maintenance or in the prosecution of such child or for its return to the licensee.

Amended by Laws 1946, Ch. 200; **amended** by Laws 1971, Chs. 110, 945, both eff. July 1, 1971; **amended** by Laws 1978, Ch. 555, § 23, eff. July 24, 1978; **amended** by Laws 1983, Ch. 268, eff. June 10, 1983; **amended** by Laws 1984, Ch. 549, eff. July 27, 1984; **amended** by Laws 1985, Ch. 531, eff. Oct. 22, 1985.

§ 383. Care and custody of children.

1. The parent of a child remanded or committed to an authorized agency shall not be entitled to the custody thereof, except upon consent of the court, public board, commission, or official responsible for the commitment of such child, or in pursuance of an order of a court or judicial officer of competent jurisdiction, determining that the interest of such child will be promoted thereby and that such parent is fit, competent and able to duly maintain, support and educate such child. The name of such child shall not be changed while in the custody of an authorized agency.

2. The custody of a child placed out or boarded out and not legally adopted or for whom legal guardianship has not been granted shall be vested during his minority, or until discharged by such authorized agency from its care and supervision, in the authorized agency placing out or boarding out such child and any such authorized agency may in its discretion remove such child from the home where placed or boarded.

3. Any adult husband and his adult wife and any adult unmarried person, who, as foster parent or parents, have cared for a child continuously for a period of twelve months or more, may apply to such authorized agency for the placement of said child with them for the purpose of adoption, and if said child is eligible for adoption, the agency shall give preference and first consideration to their application over all other applications for adoption placements. However, final determination of the propriety of said adoption of such foster child shall be within the sole discretion of the court, as otherwise provided herein.

Foster parents having had continuous care of a child, for more than twelve months, through an authorized agency, shall be permitted as a matter of right, as an interested party to intervene in any proceeding involving the custody of the child. Such intervention may be made anonymously or in the true name of said foster parents.

SSL

4.   An adult married person who has executed a legally enforceable separation agreement or is a party to a marriage in which a valid decree of separation has been entered and who becomes or has been the custodian of a child placed in their care as a result of court ordered foster care may apply to such authorized agency for placement of said child with them for the purpose of adoption. Applications filed pursuant to this subdivision by persons who, as foster parents, have cared for a child continuously for a period of twelve months or more shall be entitled to the same consideration and preference as are given to applications filed pursuant to subdivision three of this section. Final determination of the propriety of said adoption of such foster child, however, shall be within the sole discretion of the court, as otherwise provided herein.

5.   Any proceeding brought in connection with the provisions of this section shall have preference over all other causes in all courts.

6.   [*Repealed.*]

Amended by Laws 1969, Ch. 1080; Laws 1971, Ch. 1143; Laws 1972, Ch. 645, Ch. 639, Ch. 646; **amended** by Laws 1979, Ch. 611, eff. Oct. 11, 1979; **amended** by Laws 1984, Ch. 745, eff. Dec. 3, 1984; **amended** by Laws 1985, Ch. 141, eff. Aug. 3, 1985; **amended** by Laws 1990, Ch. 479, § 1, eff. Jan. 1, 1991, subd. 6 repealed.

§ 383-a.   Reports of injury, abuse or maltreatment of children under sixteen years of age.

Repealed by Laws 1973, Ch. 1039, eff. Sept. 1, 1973, with the following Note appended:

Note.—Section three hundred eighty-three-a of the Social Services Law, proposed to be repealed by this act, relates to reports of injury, abuse or maltreatment of children. Section three hundred eighty-three-c of such law, proposed to be repealed by this act, relates to temporary detention of an abused child. Sections ten hundred thirty-two, ten hundred thirty-three and ten hundred thirty-four of the Family Court Act, proposed to be repealed by this act, relates to whom may institute neglect or abuse proceedings, rules of court for preliminary procedure and admissibility of statements made during preliminary conference.

§ 383-b.   Medical treatment for abused or neglected children; consent of commissioners.

The local commissioner of social services or the local commissioner of health may give effective consent for medical, dental, health and hospital services for any child who has been found by the family court to be an abused child or a neglected child, or who has been taken into or kept in protective custody or removed from the place where he is residing, or who has been placed in the custody of such commissioner, pursuant to section four hundred seventeen of this chapter or section one thousand twenty-two, section one thousand twenty-four or section one thousand twenty-seven of the family court act.

Added by Laws 1972, Ch. 592; **amended** Laws 1973, Ch. 660; **amended** by Laws 1974, Ch. 309, eff. May 7, 1974; **amended** by Laws 1986, Ch. 570, eff. July 24, 1986.

§ 383-c   Guardianship and custody of children in foster care.

1.   Method. For the purposes of this section, a child in foster care shall mean a child in the care and custody of an authorized agency pursuant to section three hundred eighty-four-a of this title or article three, seven or ten of the family court act. The guardianship of the person and the custody of a child in foster care under the age of eighteen years may be committed to an authorized agency by a written instrument which shall be known as a surrender, and signed:

(a)   if both parents shall then be living, by the parents of such child, or by the surviving parent, if either parent of such child be dead;

(b)   if either one of such parents shall have for a period of six months then next preceding abandoned such child as set forth in section three hundred eighty-four-b of this title, by the other of such parents;

(c)   if such child is born out of wedlock, by the mother of such child, and by the father of such child, if such father's consent would be required for the child's adoption, pursuant to section one hundred eleven of the domestic relations law;

(d)   if both parents of such child are dead, or if such child is born out of wedlock and the mother of such child is dead, by the guardian of the person of such child lawfully appointed, with the approval of the court or officer which appointed such guardian to be entered of record.

2.   Terms.

(a)   Such guardianship shall be in accordance with the provisions of this article and the instrument shall be upon such terms and subject to such conditions as may be agreed upon by the parties thereto and shall comply with subdivision five of this section; provided, however, that an authorized agency shall not accept a surrender instrument conditioned upon adoption by a particular person, unless such person is a certified or approved foster parent, where the permanency plan for the child is for the child to be adopted by that person or the agency has fully investigated and approved such person as an adoptive parent in accordance with applicable statute and regulations. No such agency shall draw or receive money from public funds for the support of any such child except upon the written order or permit of the social services official of the county or city sought to be charged with the support of such child.

(b)   If a surrender instrument designates a particular person or persons who will adopt a child, such person or persons, the child's birth parent or parents, the authorized agency having care and custody of the child and the child's law guardian, may enter into a written agreement providing for communication or contact between the child and the child's parent or parents on such terms and conditions as may be agreed to by the parties. If a surrender instrument does not designate a particular person or persons who will adopt the child, then the child's birth parent or parents, the authorized agency having care and custody of the child and the child's law guardian may enter into a written agreement providing for communication or contact, on such terms and conditions as may be agreed to by the parties. Such agreement also may provide terms and conditions for communication with or contact between the child and the child's biological siblings or half-siblings, if any. If any such sibling or half-sibling is fourteen years of age or older, such terms and conditions shall not be enforceable unless such sibling or half-sibling consents to the agreement in writing. If the court before which the surrender instrument is presented for approval determines that the agreement concerning communication and contact is in the child's best interests, the court shall approve the agreement. If the court does not approve the agreement, the court may nonetheless approve the surrender; provided, however, that the birth parent or parents executing the surrender instrument shall be given the opportunity at that time to withdraw such instrument. Enforcement of any agreement prior to the adoption of the child shall be in accordance with subdivision (b) of section one thousand fifty-five-a of the family court act. Subsequent to the adoption of the child, enforcement of any agreement shall be in accordance with section one hundred twelve-b of the domestic relations law.

3.   Judicial surrenders.

(a)   [Until Oct 24, 2006] A surrender of a child to an authorized agency for the purpose of adoption may be executed and acknowledged before a judge of the family court or a surrogate in this state. A surrender executed and acknowledged before a court in another state shall satisfy the requirements of this section if it is executed by a resident of the other state before a court of record which has jurisdiction over adoption proceedings in that state, and a certified copy of the transcript of that proceeding, showing compliance with paragraph (b) of this subdivision, is filed as part of the adoption proceeding in this state.

(a)   [Eff. Oct 24, 2006] A surrender of a child to an authorized agency for the purpose of adoption may be executed and acknowledged before a judge of the family court or a surrogate in this state. If the child being surrendered is in foster care as a result of a proceeding before the family court pursuant to article ten or ten-A of the family court act or section three hundred fifty-eight-a of this chapter, the surrender shall be executed and acknowledged before the family court that exercised jurisdiction over such proceeding and, shall be assigned, wherever practicable, to the judge who last presided over such proceeding. A surrender executed and acknowledged before a court in another state shall satisfy the requirements of this section if it is executed by a resident of the other state before a court of record which has jurisdiction over adoption proceedings in that state, and a certified copy of the transcript of that proceeding, showing compliance with paragraph (b) of this subdivision, is filed as part of the adoption proceeding in this state.

(b)   Before a judge or surrogate approves a judicial surrender, the judge or surrogate shall order that notice of the surrender proceeding be given to persons identified in subdivision two of section three hundred eighty-four-c of this title and to such other persons as the judge or surrogate may, in his or her discretion, prescribe. At the time that a parent appears before a judge or surrogate to execute and acknowledge a surrender, the judge or surrogate shall inform such parent of the right to be represented by legal counsel of the parent's own choosing and of the right to obtain supportive counseling and of any right to have counsel assigned pursuant to section two hundred sixty-two of the family court act, section four hundred seven of the surrogate's court procedure act, or section thirty-five of the judiciary law. The judge or surrogate also shall inform the parent of the consequences of such surrender, including informing such parent that the parent is giving up all rights to have custody, visit with, speak with, write to or learn about the child, forever, unless the parties have agreed to different terms pursuant to subdivision two of this section, or, if the parent registers with the adoption information register, as specified in section forty-one hundred thirty-eight-d of the public health law, that the parent may be contacted at any time after the child reaches the age of eighteen years, but only if both the parent and the adult child so choose. The court shall determine whether the terms and conditions agreed to by the parties pursuant to subdivision two of this section are in the child's best interests before approving the surrender. The judge or surrogate shall inform the parent that where a surrender containing conditions has been executed, the parent is obligated to provide the authorized agency with a designated mailing address, as well as any subsequent changes in such address, at which the parent may receive notices regarding any substantial failure of a material condition, unless such notification is expressly waived by a statement written by the parent and appended to or included in such instrument. The judge or surrogate also shall inform the parent that the surrender shall become final and irrevocable immediately upon its execution and acknowledgment. The judge or surrogate shall give the parent a copy of such surrender upon the execution thereof.

4. Extra-judicial surrenders.

(a) In any case where a surrender is not executed and acknowledged before a judge or surrogate pursuant to subdivision three of this section, such surrender shall be executed and acknowledged by the parent, in the presence of at least two witnesses, before a notary public or other officer authorized to take proof of deeds. At least one witness shall be an employee of an authorized agency trained, in accordance with the regulations of the department of children and family services, to receive surrenders. At least one witness shall be a person who is either a licensed master social worker, licensed clinical social worker or an attorney and who is not an employee, volunteer, consultant or agent of or attorney for the authorized agency to which the child is being surrendered. The commissioner of the office of children and family services, after consultation with the chief administrator of the courts, shall promulgate standards to help ensure the impartial selection and independence of such witnesses. Any witness may, if so commissioned, serve as notary under this subdivision.

(b) [Until Oct 24, 2006] The authorized agency to which the child was surrendered shall file an application for approval of the extra-judicial surrender with the court in which the adoption proceeding is expected to be filed or, if not known, the family or surrogate's court in the county in which the agency has its principal office. The application shall be filed no later than fifteen days after execution of such surrender. The application shall be accompanied by affidavits from all the witnesses before whom the surrender was executed and acknowledged as provided for in paragraph (a) of this subdivision, stating:

(b) [Eff. Oct 24, 2006] The authorized agency to which the child was surrendered shall file an application for approval of the extra-judicial surrender with the court in which the adoption proceeding is expected to be filed or, if not known, the family or surrogate's court in the county in which the agency has its principal office. If the child being surrendered is in foster care as a result of a proceeding before the family court pursuant to article ten or ten-A of the family court act or section three hundred fifty-eight-a of this chapter, the application shall be filed in the family court that exercised jurisdiction over such proceeding and, shall be assigned, wherever practicable, to the judge who last presided over such proceeding. The application shall be filed no later than fifteen days after execution of such surrender. The application shall be accompanied by affidavits from all the witnesses before whom the surrender was executed and acknowledged as provided for in paragraph (a) of this subdivision, stating:

(i) the date, time and place where the surrender was executed and acknowledged;

(ii) that the parent was provided with a copy of the surrender;

(iii) that the surrender was read in full to the parent in his or her principal language and the parent was given an opportunity to ask questions and obtain answers regarding the nature and consequences of the surrender, including the consequences of, and procedures to be followed in, cases of a substantial failure of a material condition, if any, contained in the surrender instrument and the obligation to provide the authorized agency with a designated mailing address, as well as any subsequent changes in such address, at which the parent may receive notices regarding any substantial failure of a material condition, unless such notification is expressly waived by a statement written by the parent and appended to or included in such instrument; and

(iv) that the parent executed and acknowledged the surrender.

(c) The authorized agency to which a child is surrendered pursuant to this subdivision must affix an affidavit to the application, by an employee responsible for providing or arranging supportive counseling, which specifies:

(i) when supportive counseling was offered to the parent by the authorized agency;

(ii) whether the parent accepted the offer of supportive counseling; and

(iii) if accepted, when supportive counseling was provided and the nature of such supportive counseling.

(d)   Before a judge or surrogate approves an extra-judicial surrender, the judge or surrogate shall order notice to be given to the person who executed the surrender, to persons identified in subdivision two of section three hundred eighty-four-c of this title and to such other persons as the judge or surrogate may, in his or her discretion, prescribe. The petition shall set forth the names and last known addresses of all persons required to be given notice of the proceeding, pursuant to section three hundred eighty-four-c, and there shall be shown by the petition or by affidavit or other proof satisfactory to the court that there are no persons other than those set forth in the petition who are entitled to notice pursuant to such section. No person who has received such notice and been afforded an opportunity to be heard may challenge the validity of a surrender approved pursuant to this subdivision in any other proceeding. Nothing in this section shall be deemed to dispense with the consent to adopt if otherwise required of any person who has not executed the surrender.

(e)   The agency to which the child is surrendered promptly shall notify such court of any correspondence or communication received from the parent or a person on the parent's behalf subsequent to the execution of the surrender and prior to a final order of adoption of the child, if such correspondence or communication could reasonably indicate the parent's wish to revoke the surrender.

(f)   The court shall enter an order either approving or disapproving the surrender. If the court disapproves the surrender, the surrender shall be deemed a nullity and without force or effect, and the court may direct that any subsequent surrender shall be executed only before the court in accordance with subdivision three of this section.

5.   Instrument.

(a)   There shall be a form of instrument for a judicial surrender and a form of instrument for an extra-judicial surrender.

(b)   The instrument for a judicial surrender and the instrument for an extra-judicial surrender shall be in a form prescribed by the commissioner after consultation with the chief administrator of the courts and shall state in plain language in conspicuous bold print on the first page:

(i)   that the parent has the right, before signing the surrender, to speak to a lawyer of her or his own choosing and any other person she or he wishes; to have that lawyer and any other person present with her or him at the time of the signing of the surrender; and has the right to ask the court to appoint a lawyer free of charge if the parent cannot afford to hire one; and has the right to have supportive counseling;

(ii)   that the parent is giving up all rights to have custody, visit with, speak with, write to or learn about the child, forever, unless the parties have agreed to different terms pursuant to subdivision two of this section, and unless such terms are written in the surrender, or, if the parent registers with the adoption information register, as specified in section forty-one hundred thirty-eight-d of the public health law, that the parent may be contacted at anytime after the child reaches the age of eighteen years, but only if both the parent and the adult child so choose;

(iii) that the child will be adopted without the parent's consent and without further notice to the parent, and will be adopted by any person that the agency chooses, unless the surrender paper contains the name of the person or persons who will be adopting the child; and

(iv) that the parent cannot be forced to sign the surrender paper, and cannot be punished if he or she does not sign the paper; and would not be subject to any penalty for refusing to sign the surrender.

(c) A surrender instrument for a judicial surrender also shall state in plain language in conspicuous bold print at the beginning thereof that the surrender becomes final and irrevocable immediately upon execution and acknowledgement, and that the parent cannot bring a case in court to revoke the surrender or to regain custody of the child. Where the parties have agreed that the surrender shall be subject to conditions pursuant to subdivision two of this section, the instrument shall further state in plain language that:

(i) the authorized agency shall notify the parent, unless such notice is expressly waived by a statement written by the parent and appended to or included in such instrument, the law guardian for the child and the court that approved the surrender within twenty days of any substantial failure of a material condition of the surrender prior to the finalization of the adoption of the child; and

(ii) except for good cause shown, the authorized agency shall file a petition on notice to the parent unless notice is expressly waived by a statement written by the parent and appended to or included in such instrument and law guardian in accordance with section one thousand fifty-five-a of the family court act within thirty days of such failure, in order for the court to review such failure and, where necessary, to hold a hearing; provided, however, that, in the absence of such filing, the parent and/or law guardian for the child may file such a petition at any time up to sixty days after notification of the failure. Such petition filed by a parent or law guardian must be filed prior to the adoption of the child; and

(iii) the parent is obligated to provide the authorized agency with a designated mailing address, as well as any subsequent changes in such address, at which the parent may receive notices regarding any substantial failure of a material condition, unless such notification is expressly waived by a statement written by the parent and appended to or included in such instrument.

Nothing in this paragraph shall limit the notice on the instrument with respect to a failure to comply with a material condition of a surrender subsequent to the finalization of the adoption of the child.

(d) An extra-judicial surrender instrument also shall state in plain language in conspicuous bold print at the beginning thereof that:

(i)   the name and address of the court in which the application for approval of the extra-judicial surrender will be filed;

(ii)   that a revocation of the surrender will be effective if it is in writing and postmarked or received by the court named in the surrender within forty-five days of the signing of the surrender; and

(iii)   that a revocation of the surrender more than forty-five days after its signing will not be effective if the child has been placed in an adoptive home, and the surrender shall be final and irrevocable and the parent cannot revoke the surrender or bring a case in court to revoke the surrender or regain custody of the child, and that the agency will not notify the parent when the child is placed in an adoptive home, and the parent may lose all rights at the end of the forty-five day period without further notice. Where the parties have agreed that the surrender shall be subject to conditions pursuant to subdivision two of this section, the instrument shall further state in plain language that:

(A)   the authorized agency shall notify the parent, unless such notice is expressly waived by a statement written by the parent and appended to or included in such instrument, the law guardian for the child and the court that approved the surrender within twenty days of any substantial failure of a material condition of the surrender prior to the finalization of the adoption of the child; and

(B)   except for good cause shown, the authorized agency shall file a petition on notice to the parent unless notice is expressly waived by a statement written by the parent and appended to or included in such instrument and law guardian in accordance with section one thousand fifty-five-a of the family court act within thirty days of such failure in order for the court to review such failure and, where necessary, to hold a hearing; provided, however, that, in the absence of such filing, the parent and/or law guardian for the child may file such a petition at any time up to sixty days after notification of the failure. Such petition filed by a parent or law guardian must be filed prior to the adoption of the child; and

(C)   the parent is obligated to provide the authorized agency with a designated mailing address, as well as any subsequent changes in such address, at which the parent may receive notices regarding any substantial failure of a material condition, unless such notice is expressly waived by a statement written by the parent and appended to or included in such instrument.

Nothing in this subparagraph shall limit the notice on the instrument with respect to a failure to comply with a material condition of a surrender subsequent to the finalization of the adoption of the child.

(e)   A surrender shall be recorded in the office of the county clerk in the county where the surrender is executed, or where the principal office of such authorized agency is located, in a book which such county clerk shall provide and shall keep under seal. Such record shall be subject to inspection and examination only as provided in subdivisions three and four of section three hundred seventy-two of this title.

(f)   Whenever the term surrender, surrender paper or surrender instrument is used in any law relating to the adoption of children in foster care, it shall mean and refer exclusively to the instrument described herein for the commitment of the guardianship of the person and the custody of a child to an authorized agency by the child's parent, parents or guardian, and in no case shall it be deemed to apply to any instrument purporting to commit the guardianship of the person and the custody of a child to any person other than an authorized agency, nor shall such term or the provisions of this section be deemed to apply to any instrument transferring the care and custody of a child to an authorized agency pursuant to section three hundred eighty-four-a of this title.

(g)   Upon execution of a surrender instrument, the parent executing the surrender shall provide information to the extent known regarding the other parent, any person to whom the surrendering parent had been married at the time of the conception or birth of the child and any other person who would be entitled to notice of a proceeding to terminate parental rights pursuant to section three hundred eighty-four-c of this title. Such information shall include, but not be limited to, such parent's or person's name, last-known address, social security number, employer's address and any other identifying information. Any information provided pursuant to this paragraph shall be recorded in the uniform case record maintained pursuant to section four hundred nine-f of this article; provided, however, that the failure to provide such information shall not invalidate the surrender.

6.   Effect of surrender and revocation.

(a)   If the court disapproves the surrender pursuant to subdivision four of this section, or if a revocation of an extra-judicial surrender is mailed and postmarked or otherwise delivered to the court named in the surrender within forty-five days of the execution of the surrender, such surrender shall be deemed a nullity, and the child shall be returned to the care and custody of the authorized agency.

(b)   If a revocation of an extra-judicial surrender is mailed and postmarked or otherwise delivered to the court named in the surrender more than forty-five days after its execution and the child has not been placed in an adoptive home, such surrender shall be deemed a nullity, and the child shall be returned to the care and custody of the authorized agency. For the purposes of this subdivision, no child shall be deemed to have been placed in the home of adoptive parents unless the fact of such placement, the date thereof, the date of the agreement pertaining thereto and the names and addresses of the adoptive parents shall have been recorded in a bound volume maintained by the agency for the purpose of recording such information in chronological order. The absence of judicial approval of an extra-judicial surrender shall not revive, extend or toll the period for revocation of such surrender.

(c)   In any case in which the authorized agency determines that the persons specified in the surrender will not adopt the child or in any other case of a substantial failure of a material condition prior to the finalization of the adoption of the child, the agency promptly shall notify the parent thereof, unless such notice is expressly waived by a statement written by the parent and appended to or included in such instrument, and shall notify the court and the law guardian for the child within twenty days. In any such case, the authorized agency shall file a petition on notice to the parent unless notice is expressly waived by a statement written by the parent and appended to or included in such instrument and law guardian in accordance with section one thousand fifty-five-a of the family court act, as applicable, within thirty days, except for good cause shown, in order for the court to review such failure and, where necessary, to hold a hearing; provided, however, that, in the absence of such a filing, the parent and/or law guardian for the child may file such a petition at any time up to sixty days after the notification of the failure. Such petition filed by a parent or law guardian must be filed prior to the adoption. Nothing in this paragraph shall limit the rights and remedies, if any, available to the parties and the law guardian with respect to a failure to comply with a material condition of a surrender subsequent to the finalization of the adoption of the child.

(d) Nothing contained in this section shall bar actions or proceedings brought on the ground of fraud, duress or coercion in the execution or inducement of a surrender. No action or proceeding may be maintained by the surrendering parent or guardian for the custody of the surrendered child or to revoke or annul such surrender except as provided herein.

7. Surrenders by persons in foster care. Notwithstanding any other provision of law, a surrender for adoption executed by a parent, parents or guardian who is in foster care shall be executed only before a judge of the family court.

8. Adoption proceeding.

(a) Upon the court's order approving the surrender, the attorney for the petitioning authorized agency shall promptly serve upon persons who have been approved by such agency as the child's adoptive parents, notice of entry of the order approving the surrender and advising such persons that they may commence an adoption proceeding. In accordance with the regulations of the department, the authorized agency shall advise such persons of the procedures necessary for adoption of the child. The authorized agency shall cooperate with such persons in the provision of necessary documentation.

(b) The adoptive parent may commence the adoption proceeding in a court of competent jurisdiction in accordance with subdivision three of section one hundred thirteen or subdivision two of section one hundred fifteen of the domestic relations law, as applicable; provided, however, that in the case of an extra-judicial surrender, such proceeding shall be initiated more than forty-five days after the surrender is executed. Commencement of such a proceeding shall not revive, extend or toll the period for revocation of an extra-judicial surrender pursuant to this section.

9. Intervention.

(a)   Any person or persons having custody of a child for the purpose of adoption through an authorized agency shall be permitted as a matter of right, as an interested party, to intervene in any proceeding commenced to set aside a surrender purporting to commit a guardianship of the person or custody of a child executed under the provisions of this section. Such intervention may be made anonymously or in the true name of such person.

(b)   Any person or persons having custody for more than twelve months through an authorized agency for the purpose of foster care shall be permitted as a matter of right, as an interested party, to intervene in any proceeding commenced to set aside a surrender purporting to commit the guardianship of the person and custody of a child executed under the provisions of this section. Such intervention may be made anonymously or in the true name of such person or persons having custody of the child for the purpose of foster care.

10.   Adoption and permanency hearing.

a.   Upon acceptance of a judicial surrender or approval of an extra-judicial surrender pursuant to subdivision three or four of this section, the court shall inquire whether any foster parent or parents with whom the child resides, or any relative of the child, or other person, seeks to adopt such child. If such person or persons do seek to adopt such child, such person or persons may submit, and the court shall accept, all such petitions for the adoption of the child, together with an adoption home study, if any, completed by an authorized agency, or disinterested person as such term is defined in subdivision three of section one hundred sixteen of the domestic relations law. The court shall thereafter establish a schedule for completion of other inquiries and investigations necessary to complete review of the adoption of the child and shall immediately set a schedule for completion of the adoption.

b.   Upon acceptance of a judicial surrender or approval of an extra-judicial surrender pursuant to subdivision three or four of this section, the court shall schedule an initial freed child permanency hearing pursuant to section one thousand eighty-nine of the family court act. Subsequent permanency hearings shall be held pursuant to section one thousand eighty-nine of the family court act.

Added by Laws 1990, Ch. 479, § 2, eff. Jan. 1, 1991; **amended** by Laws 1990, Ch. 480, eff. Jan. 1, 1991; **amended** by Laws 1991, Ch. 588, § 1, eff. Sept. 30, 1991; **amended** by Laws 1993, Ch. 294 § 1, eff. Sept. 19, 1993; **amended** by Laws 1993, Ch. 394, § 2, eff. Nov. 18, 1993; **amended** by Laws 1994, Ch. 601, §§ 3, 4, eff. Oct. 24, 1994; **amended** by Laws 2002, Ch. 76, §§ 3, 4, 5, 6, 7 and 8, eff. Aug. 19, 2002; **amended** by Laws 2002, Ch. 663, § 9, eff. Dec. 3, 2002; **amended** by Laws 2004, Ch. 230, § 28, eff. July 27, 2004; Laws 2005, Ch. 3, §§ 48 through 51 (Part A), eff. Aug. 23, 2005; Laws 2006, Ch. 185, § 2, 3, eff. Oct. 26, 2006.

§ 384   Guardianship and custody of children not in foster care

1.   Method. The guardianship of the person and the custody of a child who is not in foster care under the age of eighteen years may be committed to an

authorized agency by a written instrument which shall be known as a surrender, and signed:

(a) if both parents shall then be living, by the parents of such child, or by the surviving parent, if either parent of such child be dead;

(b) if either one of such parents shall have for a period of six months then next preceding abandoned such child, by the other of such parents;

(c) if such child is born out of wedlock, by the mother of such child, and by the father of such child, if such father's consent would be required for the child's adoption, pursuant to section one hundred eleven of the domestic relations law;

(d) if both parents of such child are dead, or if such child is born out of wedlock and the mother of such child is dead by the guardian of the person of such child lawfully appointed, with the approval of the court or officer which appointed such guardian to be entered of record.

2. Terms.

(a) Such guardianship shall be in accordance with the provisions of this article and the instrument shall be upon such terms and subject to such conditions as may be agreed upon by the parties thereto. The instrument shall recite that the authorized agency is thereby authorized and empowered to consent to the adoption of such child in the place and stead of the person signing the instrument, and may recite that the person signing the instrument waives any notice of such adoption; provided, however, that an authorized agency shall not accept a surrender instrument conditioned upon adoption by a particular person, unless the agency has fully investigated and certified or approved such person as a qualified adoptive parent. No such agency shall draw or receive money from public funds for the support of any such child except upon the written order or permit of the local social services official of the county or city sought to be charged with the support of such child.

(b) If a surrender instrument designates a particular person or persons who will adopt a child, such person or persons, the child's birth parent or parents, the authorized agency having care and custody of the child and the child's law guardian, may enter into a written agreement providing for communication or contact between the child and the child's parent or parents on such terms and conditions as may be agreed to by the parties. If a surrender instrument does not designate a particular person or persons who will adopt the child, then the child's birth parent or parents, the authorized agency having care and custody of the child and the child's law guardian may enter into a written agreement providing for communication or contact, on such terms and conditions as may be agreed to by the parties. Such agreement also may provide terms and conditions for communication with or contact between the child and the child's biological sibling or half-sibling, if any. If any such sibling or half-sibling is fourteen years of age or older, such terms and conditions shall not be enforceable unless such sibling or half-sibling consents to the agreement in writing. If the court before which the surrender instrument is presented for approval determines that the agreement concerning communication and contact is in the child's best interests, the court shall approve the agreement. If the court does not approve the agreement, the court may nonetheless approve the surrender; provided, however, that the birth parent or parents executing the surrender instrument shall be given the opportunity at that time to withdraw such instrument. Enforcement of any agreement prior to the adoption of the child shall be in accordance with subdivision (b) of section one thousand fifty-five-a of the family court act. Subsequent to the adoption of the child, enforcement of any agreement shall be in accordance with section one hundred twelve-b of the domestic relations law.

3.   [Until Oct 24, 2006] Instrument. The instrument herein provided shall be signed and shall be acknowledged or executed (a) before any judge or surrogate in this state having jurisdiction over adoption proceedings; or (b) in the presence of one or more witnesses and acknowledged by such witness or witnesses, in the latter case before a notary public or other officer authorized to take proof of deeds, and shall be recorded in the office of the county clerk in the county where such instrument is executed, or where the principal office of such authorized agency is located, in a book which such county clerk shall provide and shall keep under seal. Such record shall be subject to inspection and examination only as provided in subdivisions three and four of section three hundred seventy-two. Notwithstanding any other provision of law, if the parent surrendering the child for adoption is in foster care the instrument shall be executed before a judge of the family court.

3.   [Eff. Oct 24, 2006] The instrument herein provided shall be executed and acknowledged (a) before any judge or surrogate in this state having jurisdiction over adoption proceedings, except that if the child is being surrendered as a result of, or in connection with, a proceeding before the family court pursuant to article ten or ten-A of the family court act, the instrument shall be executed and acknowledged in the family court that exercised jurisdiction over such proceeding and shall be assigned, wherever practicable, to the judge who last presided over such proceeding; or (b) in the presence of one or more witnesses and acknowledged by such witness or witnesses, in the latter case before a notary public or other officer authorized to take proof of deeds, and shall be recorded in the office of the county clerk in the county where such instrument is executed, or where the principal office of such authorized agency is located, in a book which such county clerk shall provide and shall keep under seal. Such record shall be subject to inspection and examination only as provided in subdivisions three and four of section three hundred seventy-two of this title. Notwithstanding any other provision of law, if the parent surrendering the child for adoption is in foster care the instrument shall be executed before a judge of the family court.

Whenever the term surrender or surrender instrument is used in any law relating to the adoption of children who are not in foster care, it shall mean and refer exclusively to the instrument hereinabove described for the commitment of the guardianship of the person and the custody of a child to an authorized agency by his parents, parent or guardian; and in no case shall it be deemed to apply to any instrument purporting to commit the guardianship of the person and the custody of a child to any person other than an authorized agency, nor shall such term or the provisions of this section be deemed to apply to any instrument transferring the care and custody of a child to an authorized agency pursuant to section three hundred eighty-four-a of this chapter.

Any person or persons having custody of a child for the purpose of adoption through an authorized agency shall be permitted as a matter of right, as an interested party, to intervene in any proceeding commenced to set aside a surrender purporting to commit a guardianship of the person or custody of a child executed under the provisions of this section. Such intervention may be made anonymously or in the true name of said person.

Any person or persons having custody for more than twelve months through an authorized agency for the purpose of foster care shall be permitted as a matter of right, as an interested party, to intervene in any proceeding commenced to set aside a surrender purporting to commit the guardianship of the person and custody of a child executed under the provisions of this section. Such intervention may be made anonymously or in the true name of said person or persons having custody of the child for the purpose of foster care.

Where the parties have agreed that the surrender shall be subject to conditions pursuant to subdivision two of this section, the instrument shall further state in plain language that:

(i)   the authorized agency shall notify the parent, unless such notice is expressly waived by a statement written by the parent and appended to or included in such instrument, the law guardian for the child and the court that approved the surrender within twenty days of any substantial failure of a material condition of the surrender prior to the finalization of the adoption of the child; and

(ii)   except for good cause shown, the authorized agency shall file a petition on notice to the parent unless notice is expressly waived by a statement written by the parent and appended to or included in such instrument and law guardian in accordance with section one thousand fifty-five-a of the family court act within thirty days of such failure, in order for the court to review such failure and, where necessary, to hold a hearing; provided, however, that, in the absence of such filing, the parent and/or law guardian for the child may file such a petition at any time up to sixty days after notification of such failure. Such petition filed by a parent or law guardian must be filed prior to the adoption of the child; and

(iii)   the parent is obligated to provide the authorized agency with a designated mailing address, as well as any subsequent changes in such address, at which the parent may receive notices regarding any substantial failure of a material condition, unless such notification is expressly waived by a statement written by the parent and appended to or included in such instrument.

SSL

Nothing in this paragraph shall limit the notice on the instrument with respect to a failure to comply with a material condition of a surrender subsequent to the finalization of the adoption of the child.

4. [Until Oct 24, 2006] Upon petition by an authorized agency, a judge of the family court, or a surrogate, may approve such surrender, on such notice to such persons as the surrogate or judge may in his or her discretion prescribe. The petition shall set forth the names and last known addresses of all persons required to be given notice of the proceeding, pursuant to section three hundred eighty-four-c, and there shall be shown by the petition or by affidavit or other proof satisfactory to the court that there are no persons other than those set forth in the petition who are entitled to notice pursuant to such section. No person who has received such notice and been afforded an opportunity to be heard may challenge the validity of a surrender approved pursuant to this subdivision in any other proceeding. However, this subdivision shall not be deemed to require approval of a surrender by a surrogate or judge for such surrender to be valid.

4. [Eff Oct 24, 2006] Upon petition by an authorized agency, a judge of the family court, or a surrogate, may approve such surrender, on such notice to such persons as the surrogate or judge may in his or her discretion prescribe. If the child is being surrendered as a result of, or in connection with, a proceeding before the family court pursuant to article ten or ten-A of the family court act, the petition shall be filed in the family court that exercised jurisdiction over such proceeding and shall be assigned, wherever practicable, to the judge who last presided over such proceeding. The petition shall set forth the names and last known addresses of all persons required to be given notice of the proceeding, pursuant to section three hundred eighty-four-c of this title, and there shall be shown by the petition or by affidavit or other proof satisfactory to the court that there are no persons other than those set forth in the petition who are entitled to notice pursuant to such section. No person who has received such notice and been afforded an opportunity to be heard may challenge the validity of a surrender approved pursuant to this subdivision in any other proceeding. However, this subdivision shall not be deemed to require approval of a surrender by a surrogate or judge for such surrender to be valid.

5. If a duly executed and acknowledged adoption surrender shall so recite, no action or proceeding may be maintained by the surrendering parent or guardian for the custody of the surrendered child or to revoke or annul such surrender where the child has been placed in the home of adoptive parents and more than thirty days have elapsed since the execution of the surrender or where the purpose of such action or proceeding is to return the child to or vest the child's custody in any person other than the parent or guardian who originally executed such surrender. This subdivision shall not bar actions or proceedings brought on the ground of fraud, duress or coercion in the execution or inducement of a surrender.

For the purposes of this subdivision, no child shall be deemed to have been placed in the home of adoptive parents unless the fact of such placement, the date thereof, the date of the agreement pertaining thereto and the names and addresses of the adoptive parents shall have been recorded in a bound volume maintained by the agency for the purpose of recording such information in chronological order.

Where the parties have agreed that the surrender shall be subject to conditions pursuant to subdivision two of this section and where there has been a substantial failure of a material condition prior to the finalization of the adoption of the child, the agency shall notify the parent thereof, unless such notice is expressly waived by a statement written by the parent and appended to or included in such instrument, and shall notify the court and the law guardian for the child within twenty days of such failure. In any such case, the authorized agency shall file a petition on notice to the parent unless notice is expressly waived by a statement written by the parent and appended to or included in such instrument and law guardian in accordance with section one thousand fifty-five-a of the family court act within thirty days of such failure, except for good cause shown, in order for the court to review such failure and, where necessary, to hold a hearing; provided, however, that, in the absence of such a filing, the parent and/or law guardian for the child may file such a petition at any time up to sixty days after notification of the failure. Such a petition filed by a parent or law guardian must be filed prior to the adoption. Nothing in this paragraph shall limit the rights and remedies available to the parties and the law guardian pursuant to section one hundred twelve-b of the domestic relations law with respect to a failure to comply with a material condition of a surrender subsequent to the finalization of the adoption of a child.

6. In an action or proceeding to determine the custody of a child not in foster care surrendered for adoption and placed in an adoptive home or to revoke or annul a surrender instrument in the case of such child placed in an adoptive home, the parent or parents who surrendered such child shall have no right to the custody of such child superior to that of the adoptive parents, notwithstanding that the parent or parents who surrendered the child are fit, competent and able to duly maintain, support and educate the child. The custody of such child shall be awarded solely on the basis of the best interests of the child, and there shall be no presumption that such interests will be promoted by any particular custodial disposition.

7. Upon acceptance of a judicial surrender or approval of an extra-judicial surrender pursuant to this section, the court shall schedule an initial freed child permanency hearing pursuant to section one thousand eighty-nine of the family court act.

8. Upon execution of a surrender instrument, the parent executing the surrender shall provide information to the extent known regarding the other parent, any person to whom the surrendering parent had been married at the time of the conception or birth of the child and any other person who would be entitled to notice of a proceeding to terminate parental rights pursuant to section three hundred eighty-four-c of this title. Such information shall include, but not be limited to, such parent's or person's name, last-known address, social security

number, employer's address and any other identifying information. Any information provided pursuant to this subdivision shall be recorded in the uniform case record maintained pursuant to section four hundred nine-f of this article; provided, however, that the failure to provide such information shall not invalidate the surrender.

Amended by Laws 1960, Ch. 717; Laws 1961, Ch. 242; Laws 1962, Ch. 689; Laws 1965, Ch. 23; Laws 1966, Ch. 792; Laws 1969; Ch. 640; Laws 1971, Ch. 1142; Laws 1972, Ch. 639, Ch. 792; Laws 1973, Ch. 863, **amending** subd. (6) and **adding** subd. (7); Laws 1975, Ch. 104; Laws 1975, Ch. 704; Laws 1975, Ch. 706, Laws 1975, Ch. 710, Laws 1976, Ch. 666, **repealing** subd. (6) and (7); Laws 1977, Ch. 862; Laws 1980, Ch. 575, eff. July 26, 1980; **amended** by Laws 1981, Ch. 15, eff. Mar. 17, 1981, subd. 3; **amended** by Laws 1985, Ch. 141, eff. Aug. 3, 1985; **amended** by Laws 1986, Ch. 817, eff. Sept. 1, 1986; **amended** by Laws 1989, Ch. 722, eff. Oct. 1, 1989; **amended** by Laws 1990, Ch. 479, § 3, eff. Jan. 1, 1991; **amended** by Laws 2002, Ch. 76, §§ 9, 10 and 11, eff. Aug. 19, 2002; **added** by Laws 2002, Ch. 663, § 10, eff. Dec. 3, 2002; L. 2005, Ch. 3, sect; 48 (Part A), eff. Aug. 23, 2005; **amended** by Laws 2006, Ch. 185, §§ 4, 5, eff. Oct. 24, 2006.

§ 384-a   Transfer of care and custody of children

1. Method. The care and custody of a child may be transferred by a parent or guardian, and the care of a child may be transferred by any person to whom a parent has entrusted the care of the child, to an authorized agency by a written instrument in accordance with the provisions of this section. Such transfer by a person who is not the child's parent or guardian shall not affect the rights or obligations of the parents or guardian, and such transfer shall be deemed a transfer of the care and custody of the child for the purposes of section three hundred fifty-eight-a of this chapter.

1-a.   Prior to accepting a transfer of care and custody, a local social services official shall commence a search to locate any non-respondent parent of the child and shall conduct an immediate investigation to (a) locate relatives of the child, including all of the child's grandparents, all suitable relatives identified by either and any relative identified by a child over the age of five as a relative who plays or has played a significant positive role in his or her life, and to inform them of the opportunity for becoming foster parents or for seeking custody or care of the child, and that the child may be adopted by foster parents if attempts at reunification with the birth parent are not required or are unsuccessful; and to determine whether the child may appropriately be placed with a suitable person related to the child and whether such relative seeks approval as a foster parent pursuant to this chapter for the purposes of providing care for such child, or wishes to provide care and custody for the child until the parent or other person responsible for the care of the child is able to resume custody; and (b) identify minor siblings or half-siblings of the child and to determine whether such siblings or half-siblings have been or are being transferred to the care and custody of such official. Such official shall provide or arrange for the provision of care so as to permit the child and his or her minor siblings or half-siblings to be placed together unless, in the judgment of such official, such placement would be contrary to the best interests of the children; whereupon, such official shall provide or arrange for regular visitation and other forms of regular communication between such children unless, in the judgment of such official, such visitation and communication would be contrary to the best interests of such children. Placement or regular visitation and communication with siblings or half-siblings shall be presumptively in the child's best interests unless such placement or visitation and communication would be contrary to the child's health, safety or welfare, or the lack of geographic proximity precludes or prevents visitation.

1-b. Upon accepting the transfer of care and custody of a child from the parent, guardian or other person to whom care of the child has been entrusted, a local social services official shall obtain information to the extent known from such person regarding the other parent, any person to whom the parent transferring care and custody had been married at the time of the conception or birth of the child and any other person who would be entitled to notice of a proceeding to terminate parental rights pursuant to section three hundred eighty-four-c of this title. Such information shall include, but not be limited to, such parent's or person's name, last-known address, social security number, employer's address and any other identifying information. Any information provided pursuant to this subdivision shall be recorded in the uniform case record maintained pursuant to section four hundred nine-f of this article; provided, however, that the failure to provide such information shall not invalidate the transfer of care and custody.

2. Terms.

(a) The instrument shall be upon such terms, for such time and subject to such conditions as may be agreed upon by the parties thereto. The office of children and family services may promulgate suggested terms and conditions for inclusion in such instruments, but shall not require that any particular terms and conditions be included. If the instrument provides that the child is to be returned by the authorized agency on a date certain or upon the occurrence of an identifiable event, such agency shall return such child at such time unless such action would be contrary to court order entered at any time prior to such date or event or within ten days thereafter pursuant to section three hundred eighty-four-b of this title or article six, ten, or ten-A of the family court act or unless and so long as the parent or guardian is unavailable or incapacitated to receive the child. The parent or guardian may, upon written notice to such agency, request return of the child at any time prior to the identified date or event, whereupon such agency may, without court order, return the child or, within ten days after such request, may notify the parent or guardian that such request is denied. If such agency denies or fails to act upon such request, the parent or guardian may seek return of the care and custody of the child by motion in family court for return of such child and order to show cause, or by writ of habeas corpus in the supreme court or family court. If the instrument fails to specify a date or identifiable event upon which such agency shall return such child, such agency

SSL

shall return the child within twenty days after having received notice that the parent or guardian wishes the child returned, unless such action would be contrary to court order entered at any time prior to the expiration of such twenty day period pursuant to section three hundred eighty-four-b of this title or article six, ten, or ten-A of the family court act. Expenditures by a local social services district for the care and maintenance of a child who has been continued in the care of an authorized agency in violation of the provisions of this subdivision shall not be subject to state reimbursement.

(b)   No provisions set forth in any such instrument regarding the right of the parent or guardian to visit the child or to have services provided to the child and to the parent or guardian to strengthen the parental relationship may be terminated or limited by the authorized agency having the care and custody of the child unless: (i) the instrument shall have been amended to so limit or terminate such right, pursuant to subdivision three of this section; or (ii) the right of visitation or to such services would be contrary to or inconsistent with a court order obtained in any proceeding in which the parent or guardian was a party.

(c)   The instrument shall state, in lay terms, in conspicuous print of at least eighteen point type:

(i)   that the parent or guardian has the right, prior to signing the instrument transferring the care and custody of the child to an authorized agency, to legal representation of the parent's own choosing. The agency shall provide the parent or guardian with a list of attorneys or legal services organizations, if any, which provide free legal services to persons unable to otherwise obtain such services;

(ii)   that the parent or guardian has no legal obligation to transfer the care and custody of the child to such official, and will incur no legal sanction for failing to do so;

(iii)   that the law permits the instrument to specify a date certain or an identifiable event upon which the child is to be returned, and if no date or event is specified, that the parent or guardian has a right to the return of the child within twenty days of a request for return, unless otherwise ordered by the court; and to otherwise have the child returned in accordance with the terms of the instrument and the provisions of this section;

(iv)   that the parent or guardian has a right to supportive services, which shall include preventive and other supportive services authorized to be provided pursuant to the state's consolidated services plan, to visit the child, and to determine jointly with the agency the terms and frequency of visitation;

(v)   that the parent or guardian, subject to the terms of the instrument, has an obligation

(A)   to visit the child,

(B)   to plan for the future of the child,

(C)   to meet with and consult with the agency about such plan,

(D) to contribute to the support of the child to the extent of his or her financial ability to do so, and

(E) to inform the agency of any change of name and address;

(vi) that the failure of the parent or guardian to meet the obligations listed in subparagraph(v) could be the basis for a court proceeding for the commitment of the guardianship and custody of the child to an authorized agency thereby terminating parental rights;

(vii) that the parent or guardian has a right to a fair hearing pursuant to section twenty-two of this chapter concerning the agency's failure to permit the parent or guardian to visit the child or to provide supportive services, which shall include preventive and other supportive services authorized to be provided pursuant to the state's consolidated services plan, to the child and to the parent or guardian;

(viii) the amount of money which the parent will periodically contribute to the support of the child and the schedule for such payments, if known.

(ix) that if the child remains in foster care for fifteen of the most recent twenty-two months, the agency may be required by law to file a petition to terminate parental rights.

(d) In any case where a parent who has transferred care and custody of a child to a social services official pursuant to this section informs the social services official that an order or judgment conferring visitation rights relating to the child has been entered by the family court or supreme court or that a written agreement as described in section two hundred thirty-six of the domestic relations law between the parents confers such rights, any instrument executed pursuant to this section shall incorporate the provisions of such order, judgment or agreement to the extent that visitation rights are affected and shall provide for visitation or other rights as required by such order, judgment or agreement. Such incorporation shall not preclude a social services official from exercising his authority pursuant to paragraph (e) or (f) of this subdivision.

(e) Where a social services official opposes incorporation of an order, judgment or agreement described in paragraph (d) of this subdivision, such official may, upon execution of the instrument described in this section and upon notice to the non-custodial parent or grandparent named in such order, judgment or agreement, be heard thereon in a proceeding pursuant to section three hundred fifty-eight-a of this chapter.

(f) Nothing in this section shall be deemed to prohibit a social services official or a law guardian of the child, if any, from making an application to modify the terms of a visitation order, incorporated pursuant to this section, for good cause shown, upon notice to all interested parties, or to limit the right of a non-custodial parent or grandparent to seek visitation pursuant to applicable provisions of law.

(g) In the event a child whose care and custody is transferred pursuant to this section is admitted to a hospital operated or licensed by the office of mental health and cannot be returned to the physical custody of his or her parent or guardian upon request because, pursuant to section four hundred of this chapter, the medical director of the facility has not authorized the removal of the child, the child shall nonetheless be deemed to have been returned to the legal care and custody of his or her parent or guardian. Expenditures by a social services district for the care and maintenance of such a child shall be subject to state reimbursement notwithstanding the provisions of section one hundred fifty-three-b of this chapter.

(h)   (i) Where a local social services official determines that a child is at significant risk of placement in the care and custody of the local commissioner of social services during the eighteen months immediately following review by such official because the custodial parent or legal guardian of such child is suffering from a progressively chronic or irreversibly fatal illness and it is determined that there is neither a relative nor a close friend identified by the custodial parent or the legal guardian able to assume legal guardianship of the child, the custodial parent or legal guardian shall be assisted by the local social services district in transferring the care and custody of the child to an authorized agency by a written instrument in accordance with the provisions for this section which provides the transfer shall not take effect until the parent or legal guardian dies, becomes debilitated or incapacitated as defined in subdivision one of section seventeen hundred twenty-six of the surrogate's court procedure act.

(ii)   Where a local social services official determines that a child is at significant risk of placement in the care and custody of the local commissioner of social services during the eighteen months immediately following a review of such official because the custodial parent or legal guardian is suffering from a progressively chronic or irreversibly fatal illness and there is a relative or close friend identified by the custodial parent or legal guardian who is able and willing to assume care and custody of the child, but who requires foster care services and financial support thereof pursuant to section three hundred ninety-eight-a of this article, the custodial parent or legal guardian shall be assisted by the local social services district in transferring the care and custody of the child to an authorized agency by a written instrument in accordance with the provisions of this section. Such instrument shall provide that the transfer of custody shall not take effect until the parent or legal guardian dies, becomes debilitated or incapacitated as defined in subdivision one of section seventeen hundred twenty-six of the surrogate's court procedure act. If otherwise qualified, the social services official shall assist the person identified to accept care and custody of the child to become certified as a foster parent.

(iii)   A local social services official who accepts or proposes to accept the care and custody of a child by means of a written instrument executed pursuant to this paragraph, shall, pursuant to section three hundred fifty-eight-a of this chapter, petition the family court of the county or city in which the local social services official has his or her office to approve such written instrument. A written instrument executed pursuant to this paragraph and approved pursuant to section three hundred fifty-eight-a of this chapter shall be in effect until the court reviews the child's placement pursuant to article ten-A of the family court act. The status of a child subject to such an instrument shall be reviewed by the court pursuant to article ten-A of the family court act.

(iv) Upon receiving a notice from the custodial parent or the legal guardian that the parent or legal guardian is no longer debilitated or incapacitated and that the parent or legal guardian requests the immediate return of the child, the social services district shall return such child to the parent or legal guardian within ten days of receiving notice, except where a contrary court order has been issued pursuant to part two, five or seven of article ten of the family court act.

3.   Amendment.

(a)   The parties to the instrument or anyone acting on their behalf with their consent may amend it by mutual consent but only by a supplemental instrument executed in the same manner as the original instrument. The supplemental instrument shall be attached to, and become part of, the original instrument. The supplemental instrument shall contain the recitation required in paragraph (c) of subdivision two of this section.

(b)   The instrument shall also be deemed amended where ordered by the family court pursuant to the provisions of paragraph (d) of subdivision ten of section three hundred fifty-eight-a of this chapter.

4.   Execution. The instrument shall be executed in the presence of one or more witnesses and shall include only the provisions, terms and conditions agreed upon by the parties thereto.

5.   Records. The instrument shall be kept in a file maintained for that purpose by the agency accepting the care and custody of the child. A copy of the instrument shall be given to the parent or guardian at the time of the execution of the instrument.

6.   An instrument executed pursuant to the provisions of this section shall not constitute a remand or commitment pursuant to this chapter.

Added by Laws 1975, Ch. 710; amended by Laws 1976, Ch. 669, Ch. 666; Laws 1980, Ch. 28, eff. Mar. 24, 1980; amended by Laws 1981, Ch. 947, eff. July 1, 1981, added subd. (d); amended by Laws 1985, Ch. 808, eff. Nov. 1, 1985; amended by Laws 1988, Ch. 457, § 11, eff. Nov. 1, 1988 and amended by Laws 1988, Ch. 457, § 12, eff. Nov. 1, 1988; amended by Laws 1989, Ch. 744 § 2, eff. July 24, 1989; amended by Laws 1990, Ch. 256, § 1, eff. Sept. 1, 1990; amended by Laws 1990, Ch. 854, § 2, eff. Sept. 1, 1990; amended by Laws 1991, Ch. 69, § 5, eff. Apr. 22, 1991; amended by Laws 1999, Ch. 7, § 8, eff. Feb. 11, 1999; amended by Laws 2000, Ch. 477, § 4, eff. Nov. 19, 2000; amended by Laws 2003, Ch. 657, § 5, amending sub. 1-a, eff. Jan. 5, 2004; L. 2005, Ch. 3, sect;§§ 52, 53 and 54 (Part A), eff. Aug. 23, 2005; L. 2005, Ch. 671, sect; 8, eff. Sept. 16, 2005.

§ 384-b   Guardianship and custody of destitute or dependent children; commitment by court order.

1.   Statement of legislative findings and intent.

(a)   The legislature recognizes that the health and safety of children is of paramount importance. To the extent it is consistent with the health and safety of the child, the legislature further hereby finds that:

(i)   it is desirable for children to grow up with a normal family life in a permanent home and that such circumstance offers the best opportunity for children to develop and thrive;

(ii)   it is generally desirable for the child to remain with or be returned to the birth parent because the child's need for a normal family life will usually best be met in the home of its birth parent, and that parents are entitled to bring up their own children unless the best interests of the child would be thereby endangered;

(iii)   the state's first obligation is to help the family with services to prevent its break-up or to reunite it if the child has already left home; and

(iv)   when it is clear that the birth parent cannot or will not provide a normal family home for the child and when continued foster care is not an appropriate plan for the child, then a permanent alternative home should be sought for the child.

(b)   The legislature further finds that many children who have been placed in foster care experience unnecessarily protracted stays in such care without being adopted or returned to their parents or other custodians. Such unnecessary stays may deprive these children of positive, nurturing family relationships and have deleterious effects on their development into responsible, productive citizens. The legislature further finds that provision of a timely procedure for the termination, in appropriate cases, of the rights of the birth parents could reduce such unnecessary stays.

It is the intent of the legislature in enacting this section to provide procedures not only assuring that the rights of the birth parent are protected, but also, where positive, nurturing parentchild relationships no longer exist, furthering the best interests, needs, and rights of the child by terminating parental rights and freeing the child for adoption.

2.   For the purposes of this section, (a) "child" shall mean a person under the age of eighteen years; and, (b) "parent" shall include an incarcerated parent unless otherwise qualified.

3.   (a) The guardianship of the person and the custody of a destitute or dependent child may be committed to an authorized agency, or to a foster parent authorized pursuant to section one thousand eighty-nine of the family court act to institute a proceeding under this section, or to a relative with care and custody of the child, by order of a surrogate or judge of the family court, as hereinafter

provided. Where such guardianship and custody is committed to a foster parent or to a relative with care and custody of the child, the family court or surrogate's court shall retain continuing jurisdiction over the parties and the child and may, upon its own motion or the motion of any party, revoke, modify or extend its order, if the foster parent or relative fails to institute a proceeding for the adoption of the child within six months after the entry of the order committing the guardianship and custody of the child to such foster parent or relative. Where the foster parent or relative institutes a proceeding for the adoption of the child and the adoption petition is finally denied or dismissed, the court which committed the guardianship and custody of the child to the foster parent or relative shall revoke the order of commitment. Where the court revokes an order committing the guardianship and custody of a child to a foster parent or relative, it shall commit the guardianship and custody of the child to an authorized agency.

(b)   A proceeding under this section may be originated by an authorized agency or by a foster parent authorized to do so pursuant to section one thousand eighty-nine of the family court act or by a relative with care and custody of the child or, if an authorized agency ordered by the court to originate a proceeding under this section fails to do so within the time fixed by the court, by a law guardian or guardian ad litem of the child on the court's direction.

(c)   [Until Oct 24, 2006] Unless a proceeding under this section is brought in the surrogate's court, where a child was placed in foster care pursuant to article ten of the family court act, a proceeding under this section shall be originated in the family court in the county in which the proceeding pursuant to article ten of the family court act was last heard and shall be assigned, wherever practicable, to the judge who last heard such proceeding. Where multiple proceedings are commenced under this section concerning a child and one or more siblings or half-siblings of such child, placed in foster care with the same commissioner pursuant to section ten hundred fifty-five of the family court act, all of such proceedings may be commenced jointly in the family court in any county which last heard a proceeding under article ten of the family court act regarding any of the children who are the subjects of the proceedings under this section. In such instances, the case shall be assigned, wherever practicable, to the judge who last heard such proceeding. In any other case, a proceeding under this section, including a proceeding brought in the surrogate's court, shall be originated in the county where either of the parents of the child reside at the time of the filing of the petition, if known, or, if such residence is not known, in the county in which the authorized agency has an office for the regular conduct of business or in which the child resides at the time of the initiation of the proceeding. To the extent possible, the court shall, when appointing a law guardian for the child, appoint a law guardian who has previously represented the child.

(c)   [Eff. Oct 24, 2006] Where a child was placed or continued in foster care pursuant to article ten or ten-A of the family court act or section three hundred fifty-eight-a of this chapter, a proceeding under this section shall be originated in the family court in the county in which the proceeding pursuant to article ten

SSL

or ten-A of the family court act or section three hundred fifty-eight-a of this chapter was last heard and shall be assigned, wherever practicable, to the judge who last heard such proceeding. Where multiple proceedings are commenced under this section concerning a child and one or more siblings or half-siblings of such child, placed or continued in foster care with the same commissioner pursuant to section one thousand fifty-five or one thousand eighty-nine of the family court act, all of such proceedings may be commenced jointly in the family court in any county which last heard a proceeding under article ten or ten-A of the family court act regarding any of the children who are the subjects of the proceedings under this section. In such instances, the case shall be assigned, wherever practicable, to the judge who last presided over such proceeding. In any other case, a proceeding under this section, including a proceeding brought in the surrogate's court, shall be originated in the county where either of the parents of the child reside at the time of the filing of the petition, if known, or, if such residence is not known, in the county in which the authorized agency has an office for the regular conduct of business or in which the child resides at the time of the initiation of the proceeding. To the extent possible, the court shall, when appointing a law guardian for the child, appoint a law guardian who has previously represented the child.

(c-1) [Eff. Oct 24, 2006] Before hearing a petition under this section, the court in which the termination of parental rights petition has been filed shall ascertain whether the child is under the jurisdiction of a family court pursuant to a placement in a child protective or foster care proceeding or continuation in out-of-home care pursuant to a permanency hearing and, if so, which court exercised jurisdiction over the most recent proceeding. If the court determines that the child is under the jurisdiction of a different family court, the court in which the termination of parental rights petition was filed shall stay its proceeding for not more than thirty days and shall communicate with the court that exercised jurisdiction over the most recent proceeding. The communication shall be recorded or summarized on the record by the court in which the termination of parental rights petition was filed. Both courts shall notify the parties and law guardian, if any, in their respective proceedings and shall give them an opportunity to present facts and legal argument or to participate in the communication prior to the issuance of a decision on jurisdiction. The court that exercised jurisdiction over the most recent proceeding shall determine whether it will accept or decline jurisdiction over the termination of parental rights petition. This determination of jurisdiction shall be incorporated into an order regarding jurisdiction that shall be issued by the court in which the termination of parental rights petition was filed within thirty days of such filing. If the court that exercised jurisdiction over the most recent proceeding determines that it should exercise jurisdiction over the termination of parental rights petition, the order shall require that the petition shall be transferred to that court forthwith but in no event more than thirty-five days after the filing of the petition. The petition shall be assigned, wherever practicable, to the judge who heard the most recent proceeding. If the court that exercised jurisdiction over the most recent proceeding declines to exercise jurisdiction over the adoption petition, the court in which the termination of parental rights petition was filed shall issue an order incorporating that determination and shall proceed forthwith.

(d)   [Until Oct 24, 2006] The family court shall have exclusive, original jurisdiction over any proceeding brought upon grounds specified in paragraph (c), (d) or (e) of subdivision four of this section, and the family court and surrogate's court shall have concurrent, original jurisdiction over any proceeding brought upon grounds specified in paragraph (a) or (b) of subdivision four.

(d)   [Eff. Oct 24, 2006] The family court shall have exclusive, original jurisdiction over any proceeding brought upon grounds specified in paragraph (c), (d) or (e) of subdivision four of this section, and the family court and surrogate's court shall have concurrent, original jurisdiction over any proceeding brought upon grounds specified in paragraph (a) or (b) of subdivision four of this section, except as provided in paragraphs (c) and (c-1) of this subdivision.

(e)   A proceeding under this section is originated by a petition on notice served upon the child's parent or parents, the attorney for the child's parent or parents and upon such other persons as the court may in its discretion prescribe. Such notice shall inform the parents and such other persons that the proceeding may result in an order freeing the child for adoption without the consent of or notice to the parents or such other persons. Such notice also shall inform the parents and such other persons of their right to the assistance of counsel, including any right they may have to have counsel assigned by the court in any case where they are financially unable to obtain counsel. The petition shall set forth the names and last known addresses of all persons required to be given notice of the proceeding, pursuant to this section and section three hundred eighty-four-c of this title, and there shall be shown by the petition or by affidavit or other proof satisfactory to the court that there are no persons other than those set forth in the petition who are entitled to notice pursuant to the provisions of this section or of section three hundred eighty-four-c of this title. When the proceeding is initiated in family court service of the petition and other process shall be made in accordance with the provisions of section six hundred seventeen of the family court act, and when the proceeding is initiated in surrogate's court, service shall be made in accordance with the provisions of section three hundred seven of the surrogate's court procedure act. When the proceeding is initiated on the grounds of abandonment of a child less than one year of age at the time of the transfer of the care and custody of such child to a local social services official, the court shall take judicial notice of efforts to locate the child's parents or other known relatives or other persons legally responsible pursuant to paragraph (ii) of subdivision (b) of section one thousand fifty-five of the family court act.

(f)   In any proceeding under this section in which the surrogate's court has exercised jurisdiction, the provisions of the surrogate's court procedure act shall apply to the extent that they do not conflict with the specific provisions of this section. In any proceeding under this section in which the family court has exercised jurisdiction, the provisions of articles one, two and eleven of the family

SSL

court act shall apply to the extent that they do not conflict with the specific provisions of this section. In any proceeding under this section, the provisions and limitations of article thirty-one of the civil practice law and rules shall apply to the extent that they do not conflict with the specific provisions of this section. In determining any motion for a protective order, the court shall consider the need of the party for the discovery to assist in the preparation of the case and any potential harm to the child from the discovery. The court shall set a schedule for discovery to avoid unnecessary delay. Any proceeding originated in family court upon the ground specified in paragraph (d) of subdivision four of this section shall be conducted in accordance with the provisions of part one of article six of the family court act.

(g)   An order committing the guardianship and custody of a child pursuant to this section shall be granted only upon a finding that one or more of the grounds specified in subdivision four are based upon clear and convincing proof.

(h)   In any proceeding brought upon a ground set forth in paragraph (c) of subdivision four, neither the privilege attaching to confidential communications between husband and wife, as set forth in section forty-five hundred two of the civil practice law and rules, nor the physician-patient and related privileges, as set forth in section forty-five hundred four of the civil practice law and rules, nor the psychologist-client privilege, as set forth in section forty-five hundred seven of the civil practice law and rules, nor the social worker-client privilege, as set forth in section forty-five hundred eight of the civil practice law and rules, shall be a ground for excluding evidence which otherwise would be admissible.

(i)   In a proceeding instituted by an authorized agency pursuant to the provisions of this section, proof of the likelihood that the child will be placed for adoption shall not be required in determining whether the best interests of the child would be promoted by the commitment of the guardianship and custody of the child to an authorized agency.

(j)   The order and the papers upon which it was granted in a proceeding under this section shall be filed in the court, and a certified copy of such order shall also be filed in the office of the county clerk of the county in which such court is located, there to be recorded and to be inspected or examined in the same manner as a surrender instrument, pursuant to the provisions of section three hundred eighty-four of this chapter.

(k)   Where the child is over fourteen years of age, the court may, in its discretion, consider the wishes of the child in determining whether the best interests of the child would be promoted by the commitment of the guardianship and custody of the child.

(l)   (i) [Until Nov 14, 2006] Notwithstanding any other law to the contrary, whenever: the child shall have been in foster care for fifteen months of the most recent twenty-two months; or a court of competent jurisdiction has determined the child to be an abandoned child; or the parent has been convicted of a crime as set forth in subparagraph (v) of this paragraph, the authorized agency having care of the child shall file a petition pursuant to this section unless based on a case by case determination: (A) the child is being cared for by a relative or relatives; or (B) the agency has documented in the most recent case plan, a copy of which has been made available to the court, a compelling reason for determining that the filing of a petition would not be in the best interest of the child; or (C) the agency has not provided to the parent or parents of the child such services as it deems necessary for the safe return of the child to the parent or parents, unless such services are not legally required.

(i) [Eff. Nov 14, 2006] Notwithstanding any other law to the contrary, whenever: the child shall have been in foster care for fifteen months of the most recent twenty-two months; or a court of competent jurisdiction has determined the child to be an abandoned child; or the parent has been convicted of a crime as set forth in subdivision eight of this section, the authorized agency having care of the child shall file a petition pursuant to this section unless based on a case by case determination: (A) the child is being cared for by a relative or relatives; or (B) the agency has documented in the most recent case plan, a copy of which has been made available to the court, a compelling reason for determining that the filing of a petition would not be in the best interest of the child; or (C) the agency has not provided to the parent or parents of the child such services as it deems necessary for the safe return of the child to the parent or parents, unless such services are not legally required.

(ii) For the purposes of this section, a compelling reason whereby a social services official is not required to file a petition for termination of parental rights in accordance with subparagraph (i) of this paragraph includes, but is not limited to, where:

(A) the child was placed into foster care pursuant to article three or seven of the family court act and a review of the specific facts and circumstances of the child's placement demonstrate that the appropriate permanency goal for the child is either (1) return to his or her parent or guardian or (2) discharge to independent living;

(B) the child has a permanency goal other than adoption;

(C) the child is fourteen years of age or older and will not consent to his or her adoption;

(D) there are insufficient grounds for filing a petition to terminate parental rights; or

(E) the child is the subject of a pending disposition under article ten of the family court act, except where such child is already in the custody of the commissioner of social services as a result of a proceeding other than the pending article ten proceeding, and a review of the specific facts and circumstances of the child's placement demonstrate that the appropriate permanency goal for the child is discharge to his or her parent or guardian.

(iii) For the purposes of this paragraph, the date of the child's entry into foster care is the earlier of sixty days after the date on which the child was removed from the home or the date the child was found by a court to be an abused or neglected child pursuant to article ten of the family court act.

(iv)   In the event that the social services official or authorized agency having care and custody of the child fails to file a petition to terminate parental rights within sixty days of the time required by this section, or within ninety days of a court direction to file a proceeding not otherwise required by this section, such proceeding may be filed by the foster parent of the child without further court order or by the law guardian on the direction of the court. In the event of such filing the social services official or authorized agency having care and custody of the child shall be served with notice of the proceeding and shall join the petition.

(v)   [Until Nov 14, 2006] For the purposes of this paragraph, a petition for the termination of parental rights shall be filed in accordance with the standards set forth in subparagraph (i) of this paragraph where: (A) the parent of such child has been convicted of murder in the first degree as defined in section 125.27, murder in the second degree as defined in section 125.25, manslaughter in the first degree as defined in section 125.20, or manslaughter in the second degree as defined in section 125.15 of the penal law, and the victim of any such crime was another child of the parent, provided, however, that the parent must have acted voluntarily in committing such crime; or has been convicted of an attempt to commit any of the foregoing crimes, and the victim or intended victim was the child or another child of the parent or another child for whose care such parent is or has been legally responsible; (B) the parent of such child has been convicted of criminal solicitation as defined in article one hundred, conspiracy as defined in article one hundred five or criminal facilitation as defined in article one hundred fifteen of the penal law for conspiring, soliciting or facilitating any of the foregoing crimes, and the victim or intended victim was the child or another child of the parent or another child for whose care such parent is or has been legally responsible; (C) the parent of such child has been convicted of assault in the second degree as defined in section 120.05, assault in the first degree as defined in section 120.10 or aggravated assault upon a person less than eleven years old as defined in section 120.12 of the penal law, and the victim of any such crime was the child or another child of the parent or another child for whose care such parent is or has been legally responsible; or has been convicted of an attempt to commit any of the foregoing crimes, and the victim or intended victim was the child or another child of the parent or another child for whose care such parent is or has been legally responsible; or (D) the parent of such child has been convicted under the law in any other jurisdiction of an offense which includes all of the essential elements of any crime specified in clause (A), (B) or (C) of this subparagraph.

(v)   [Eff. Nov 14, 2006] Repealed

4.   An order committing the guardianship and custody of a child pursuant to this section shall be granted only upon one or more of the following grounds:

(a) Both parents of the child are dead, and no guardian of the person of such child has been lawfully appointed; or

(b) The parent or parents, whose consent to the adoption of the child would otherwise be required in accordance with section one hundred eleven of the domestic relations law, abandoned such child for the period of six months immediately prior to the date on which the petition is filed in the court; or

(c) The parent or parents, whose consent to the adoption of the child would otherwise be required in accordance with section one hundred eleven of the domestic relations law, are presently and for the foreseeable future unable, by reason of mental illness or mental retardation, to provide proper and adequate care for a child who has been in the care of an authorized agency for the period of one year immediately prior to the date on which the petition is filed in the court; or

(d) The child is a permanently neglected child; or

(e) The parent or parents, whose consent to the adoption of the child would otherwise be required in accordance with section one hundred eleven of the domestic relations law, severely or repeatedly abused such child. Where a court has determined that reasonable efforts to reunite the child with his or her parent are not required, pursuant to the family court act or this chapter, a petition to terminate parental rights on the ground of severe abuse as set forth in subparagraph (iii) of paragraph (a) of subdivision eight of this section may be filed immediately upon such determination.

5. (a) For the purposes of this section, a child is "abandoned" by his parent if such parent evinces an intent to forego his or her parental rights and obligations as manifested by his or her failure to visit the child and communicate with the child or agency, although able to do so and not prevented or discouraged from doing so by the agency. In the absence of evidence to the contrary, such ability to visit and communicate shall be presumed.

(b) The subjective intent of the parent, whether expressed or otherwise, unsupported by evidence of the foregoing parental acts manifesting such intent, shall not preclude a determination that such parent has abandoned his or her child. In making such determination, the court shall not require a showing of diligent efforts, if any, by an authorized agency to encourage the parent to perform the acts specified in paragraph (a) of this subdivision.

6. (a) For the purposes of this section, "mental illness" means an affliction with a mental disease or mental condition which is manifested by a disorder or disturbance in behavior, feeling, thinking or judgment to such an extent that if such child were placed in or returned to the custody of the parent, the child would be in danger of becoming a neglected child as defined in the family court act.

(b) For the purposes of this section, "mental retardation" means subaverage intellectual functioning which originates during the developmental period and is associated with impairment in adaptive behavior to such an extent that if such

SSL

child were placed in or returned to the custody of the parent, the child would be in danger of becoming a neglected child as defined in the family court act.

(c)   The legal sufficiency of the proof in a proceeding upon the ground set forth in paragraph (c) of subdivision four of this section shall not be determined until the judge has taken the testimony of a psychologist, or psychiatrist, in accordance with paragraph (e) of this subdivision.

(d)   A determination or order upon a ground set forth in paragraph (c) of subdivision four shall in no way affect any other right, or constitute an adjudication of the legal status of the parent.

(e)   In every proceeding upon a ground set forth in paragraph (c) of subdivision four the judge shall order the parent to be examined by, and shall take the testimony of, a qualified psychiatrist or a psychologist licensed pursuant to article one hundred fifty-three of the education law as defined in section 730.10 of the criminal procedure law in the case of a parent alleged to be mentally ill or retarded, such psychologist or psychiatrist to be appointed by the court pursuant to section thirty-five of the judiciary law. The parent and the authorized agency shall have the right to submit other psychiatric, psychological or medical evidence. If the parent refuses to submit to such court-ordered examination, or if the parent renders himself unavailable therefor whether before or after the initiation of a proceeding under this section, by departing from the state or by concealing himself therein, the appointed psychologist or psychiatrist, upon the basis of other available information, including, but not limited to, agency, hospital or clinic records, may testify without an examination of such parent, provided tha such other information affords a reasonable basis for his opinion.

7.   (a) For the purposes of this section, "permanently neglected child" shall mean a child who is in the care of an authorized agency and whose parent or custodian has failed for a period of either at least one year or fifteen out of the most recent twenty-two months following the date such child came into the care of an authorized agency substantially and continuously or repeatedly to maintain contact with or plan for the future of the child, although physically and financially able to do so, notwithstanding the agency's diligent efforts to encourage and strengthen the parental relationship when such efforts will not be detrimental to the best interests of the child. Where a court has previously determined in accordance with paragraph (b) of subdivision three of section three hundred fifty-eight-a of this chapter or section one thousand thirty-nine-b, subparagraph (A) of paragraph (i) of subdivision (b) of section one thousand fifty-two, paragraph (b) of subdivision two of section seven hundred fifty-four or paragraph (c) of subdivision two of section 352.2 of the family court act that reasonable efforts to make it possible for the child to return safely to his or her home are not required, the agency shall not be required to demonstrate diligent efforts as defined in this section. In the event that the parent defaults after due notice of a proceeding to determine such neglect, such physical and financial ability of such parent may be presumed by the court.

(b)   For the purposes of paragraph (a) of this subdivision, evidence of insubstantial or infrequent contacts by a parent with his or her child shall not, of itself, be sufficient as a matter of law to preclude a determination that such child is a permanently neglected child. A visit or communication by a parent with the child which is of such character as to overtly demonstrate a lack of affectionate and concerned parenthood shall not be deemed a substantial contact.

(c)   As used in paragraph (a) of this subdivision, "to plan for the future of the child" shall mean to take such steps as may be necessary to provide an adequate, stable home and parental care for the child within a period of time which is reasonable under the financial circumstances available to the parent. The plan must be realistic and feasible, and good faith effort shall not, of itself, be determinative. In determining whether a parent has planned for the future of the child, the court may consider the failure of the parent to utilize medical, psychiatric, psychological and other social and rehabilitative services and material resources made available to such parent.

(d)   For the purposes of this subdivision:

(i)   A parent shall not be deemed unable to maintain contact with or plan for the future of the child by reason of such parent's use of drugs or alcohol, except while the parent is actually hospitalized or institutionalized therefor; and

(ii)   The time during which a parent is actually hospitalized or institutionalized shall not interrupt, but shall not be part of, a period of failure to maintain contact with or plan for the future of a child.

(e)   Notwithstanding the provisions of paragraph (a) of this subdivision, evidence of diligent efforts by an agency to encourage and strengthen the parental relationship shall not be required when:

(i)   The parent has failed for a period of six months to keep the agency apprised of his or her location; or

(ii)   An incarcerated parent has failed on more than one occasion while incarcerated to cooperate with an authorized agency in its efforts to assist such parent to plan for the future of the child, as such phrase is defined in paragraph (c) of this subdivision, or in such agency's efforts to plan and arrange visits with the child as described in subparagraph five of paragraph (f) of this subdivision.

(f)   As used in this subdivision, "diligent efforts" shall mean reasonable attempts by an authorized agency to assist, develop and encourage a meaningful relationship between the parent and child, including but not limited to:

(1)   consultation and cooperation with the parents in developing a plan for appropriate services to the child and his family;

(2)   making suitable arrangements for the parents to visit the child except that with respect to an incarcerated parent, arrangements for the incarcerated parent to visit the child outside the correctional facility shall not be required unless reasonably feasible and in the best interest of the child;

SSL

(3)   provision of services and other assistance to the parents, except incarcerated parents, so that problems preventing the discharge of the child from care may be resolved or ameliorated;

(4)   informing the parents at appropriate intervals of the child's progress, development and health; and

(5)   making suitable arrangements with a correctional facility and other appropriate persons for an incarcerated parent to visit the child within the correctional facility, if such visiting is in the best interests of the child. When no visitation between child and incarcerated parent has been arranged for or permitted by the authorized agency because such visitation is determined not to be in the best interest of the child, then no permanent neglect proceeding under this subdivision shall be initiated on the basis of the lack of such visitation. Such arrangements shall include, but shall not be limited to, the transportation of the child to the correctional facility, and providing or suggesting social or rehabilitative services to resolve or correct the problems other than incarceration itself which impair the incarcerated parent's ability to maintain contact with the child. When the parent is incarcerated in a correctional facility located outside the state, the provisions of this subparagraph shall be construed to require that an authorized agency make such arrangements with the correctional facility only if reasonably feasible and permissible in accordance with the laws and regulations applicable to such facility.

8.   (a) For the purposes of this section a child is "severely abused" by his or her parent if

(i)   the child has been found to be an abused child as a result of reckless or intentional acts of the parent committed under circumstances evincing a depraved indifference to human life, which result in serious physical injury to the child as defined in subdivision ten of section 10.00 of the penal law; or

(ii)   the child has been found to be an abused child, as defined in paragraph (iii) of subdivision (e) of section ten hundred twelve of the family court act, as a result of such parent's acts; provided, however, the respondent must have committed or knowingly allowed to be committed a felony sex offense as defined in sections 130.25, 130.30, 130.35, 130.40, 130.45, 130.50, 130.65, 130.67, 130.70, 130.75 and 130.80 of the penal law and, for the purposes of this section the corroboration requirements contained in the penal law shall not apply to proceedings under this section; or

(iii)   [Until Nov 14, 2006] (A) the parent of such child has been convicted of murder in the first degree as defined in section 125.27, murder in the second degree as defined in section 125.25, manslaughter in the first degree as defined in section 125.20, or manslaughter in the second degree as defined in section 125.15, and the victim of any such crime was another child of the parent; or has been convicted of an attempt to commit any of the foregoing crimes, and the victim or intended victim was the child or another child of the parent or another child for whose care such parent is or has been legally responsible; (B) the parent of such child has been convicted of criminal solicitation as defined in article one hundred, conspiracy as defined in article one hundred five or criminal facilitation as defined in article one hundred fifteen of the penal law for conspiring, soliciting or facilitating any of the foregoing crimes, and the victim or intended victim was the child or another child of the parent or another child for whose care such parent is or has been legally responsible; (C) the parent of such child has been convicted of assault in the second degree as defined in section 120.05, assault in the first degree as defined in section 120.10 or aggravated assault upon a person less than eleven years old as defined in section 120.12 of the penal law, and the victim of any such crime was the child or another child of the parent or another child for whose care such parent is or has been legally responsible; or has been convicted of an attempt to commit any of the foregoing crimes, and the victim or intended victim was the child or another child of the parent or another child for whose care such parent is or has been legally responsible; or (D) the parent of such child has been convicted under the law in any other jurisdiction of an offense which includes all of the essential elements of any crime specified in clause (A), (B) or (C) of this subparagraph; and

    (iii)   [Eff. Nov 14, 2006] (A) the parent of such child has been convicted of murder in the first degree as defined in section 125.27, murder in the second degree as defined in section 125.25, manslaughter in the first degree as defined in section 125.20, or manslaughter in the second degree as defined in section 125.15, and the victim of any such crime was another child of the parent or another child for whose care such parent is or has been legally responsible as defined in subdivision (g) of section one thousand twelve of the family court act, or another parent of the child, unless the convicted parent was a victim of physical, sexual or psychological abuse by the decedent parent and such abuse was a factor in causing the homicide; or has been convicted of an attempt to commit any of the foregoing crimes, and the victim or intended victim was the child or another child of the parent or another child for whose care such parent is or has been legally responsible as defined in subdivision (g) of section one thousand twelve of the family court act, or another parent of the child, unless the convicted parent was a victim of physical, sexual or psychological abuse by the decedent parent and such abuse was a factor in causing the attempted homicide; (B) the parent of such child has been convicted of criminal solicitation as defined in article one hundred, conspiracy as defined in article one hundred five or criminal facilitation as defined in article one hundred fifteen of the penal law for conspiring, soliciting or facilitating any of the foregoing crimes, and the victim or intended victim was the child or another child of the parent or another child for whose care such parent is or has been legally responsible; (C) the parent of such child has been convicted of assault in the second degree as defined in section 120.05, assault in the first degree as defined in section 120.10 or aggravated assault upon a person less than eleven years old as defined in section 120.12 of the penal law, and the victim of any such crime was the child or another child of the parent or another child for whose care such parent is or has been legally responsible; or has been convicted of an attempt to commit any of the foregoing

SSL

crimes, and the victim or intended victim was the child or another child of the parent or another child for whose care such parent is or has been legally responsible; or (D) the parent of such child has been convicted under the law in any other jurisdiction of an offense which includes all of the essential elements of any crime specified in clause (A), (B) or (C) of this subparagraph; and

(iv)   the agency has made diligent efforts to encourage and strengthen the parental relationship, including efforts to rehabilitate the respondent, when such efforts will not be detrimental to the best interests of the child, and such efforts have been unsuccessful and are unlikely to be successful in the foreseeable future. Where a court has previously determined in accordance with this chapter or the family court act that reasonable efforts to make it possible for the child to return safely to his or her home are not required, the agency shall not be required to demonstrate diligent efforts as set forth in this section.

(b)   For the purposes of this section a child is "repeatedly abused" by his or her parent if:

(i)   he child has been found to be an abused child, (A) as defined in paragraph (i) of subdivision (e) of section ten hundred twelve of the family court act, as a result of such parent's acts; or (B) as defined in paragraph (iii) of subdivision (e) of section ten hundred twelve of the family court act, as a result of such parent's acts; provided, however, the respondent must have committed or knowingly allowed to be committed a felony sex offense as defined in sections 130.25, 130.30, 130.35, 130.40, 130.45, 130.50, 130.65, 130.67, 130.70, 130.75 and 130.80 of the penal law; and

(ii)   (A) the child or another child for whose care such parent is or has been legally responsible has been previously found, within the five years immediately preceding the initiation of the proceeding in which such abuse is found, to be an abused child, as defined in paragraph (i) or (iii) of subdivision (e) of section ten hundred twelve of the family court act, as a result of such parent's acts; provided, however, in the case of a finding of abuse as defined in paragraph (iii) of subdivision (e) of section ten hundred twelve of the family court act the respondent must have committed or knowingly allowed to be committed a felony sex offense as defined in sections 130.25, 130.30, 130.35, 130.40, 130.45, 130.50, 130.65, 130.67, 130.70, 130.75 and 130.80 of the penal law, or (B) the parent has been convicted of a crime under section 130.25, 130.30, 130.35, 130.40, 130.45, 130.50, 130.65, 130.67, 130.70, 130.75 or 130.80 of the penal law against the child, a sibling of the child or another child for whose care such parent is or has been legally responsible, within the five year period immediately preceding the initiation of the proceeding in which abuse is found; and

(iii)   the agency has made diligent efforts, to encourage and strengthen the parental relationship, including efforts to rehabilitate the respondent, when such efforts will not be detrimental to the best interests of the child, and such efforts have been unsuccessful and are unlikely to be successful in the foreseeable future. Where a court has previously determined in accordance with this chapter or the family court act that reasonable efforts to make it possible for the child to return safely to his or her home are not required, the agency shall not be required to demonstrate diligent efforts as set forth in this section.

(c)   Notwithstanding any other provision of law, the requirements of paragraph (g) of subdivision three of this section shall be satisfied if one of the findings of abuse pursuant to subparagraph (i) or (ii) of paragraph (b) of this subdivision is found to be based on clear and convincing evidence.

(d)   A determination by the court in accordance with article ten of the family court act based upon clear and convincing evidence that the child was a severely abused child as defined in subparagraphs (i) and (ii) of paragraph (a) of this subdivision shall establish that the child was a severely abused child in accordance with this section. Such a determination by the court in accordance with article ten of the family court act based upon a fair preponderance of evidence shall be admissible in any proceeding commenced in accordance with this section.

(e)   A determination by the court in accordance with article ten of the family court act based upon clear and convincing evidence that a child was abused (A) as defined in paragraph (i) of subdivision (e) of section ten hundred twelve of the family court act, as a result of such parent's acts; or (B) as defined in paragraph (iii) of subdivision (e) of section ten hundred twelve of the family court act, as a result of such parent's acts; provided, however, the respondent must have committed or knowingly allowed to be committed a felony sex offense as defined in sections 130.25, 130.30, 130.35, 130.40, 130.45, 130.50, 130.65, 130.67, 130.70, 130.75 and 130.80 of the penal law shall establish that the child was an abused child for the purpose of a determination as required by subparagraph (i) or (ii) of paragraph (b) of this subdivision. Such a determination by the court in accordance with article ten of the family court act based upon a fair preponderance of evidence shall be admissible in any proceeding commenced in accordance with this section.

(f)   Upon a finding pursuant to paragraph (a) or (b) of this subdivision that the child has been severely or repeatedly abused by his or her parent, the court shall enter an order of disposition either (i) committing the guardianship and custody of the child, pursuant to this section, or (ii) suspending judgment in accordance with section six hundred thirty-three of the family court act, upon a further finding, based on clear and convincing, competent, material and relevant evidence introduced in a dispositional hearing, that the best interests of the child require such commitment or suspension of judgment. Where the disposition ordered is the commitment of guardianship and custody pursuant to this section, an initial freed child permanency hearing shall be completed pursuant to section one thousandeighty-nine of the family court act.

9.   Nothing in this section shall be construed to terminate, upon commitment of the guardianship and custody of a child to an authorized agency or foster parent, any rights and benefits, including but not limited to rights relating to inheritance, succession, social security, insurance and wrongful death action claims,

SSL

possessed by or available to the child pursuant to any other provision of law. Notwithstanding any other provision of law, a child committed to the custody and guardianship of an authorized agency pursuant to this section shall be deemed to continue in foster care until such time as an adoption or another planned permanent living arrangement is finalized. Where the disposition ordered is the commitment of guardianship and custody pursuant to this section, an initial freed child permanency hearing shall be held pursuant to section one thousand eighty-nine of the family court act.

10. Upon the court's order transferring custody and guardianship to the commissioner, the attorney for the petitioning authorized agency shall promptly serve upon the persons who have been approved by such agency as the child's adoptive parents, notice of entry of such order and advise such persons that an adoption proceeding may be commenced. In accordance with the regulations of the department, the authorized agency shall advise such persons of the procedures necessary for adoption of the child. The authorized agency shall cooperate with such persons in the provision of necessary documentation.

11. Upon the entry of an order committing the guardianship and custody of a child pursuant to this section, the court shall inquire whether any foster parent or parents with whom the child resides, or any relative of the child, or other person, seeks to adopt such child. If such person or persons do seek to adopt such child, such person or persons may submit, and the court shall accept, all such petitions for the adoption of the child, together with an adoption home study, if any, completed by an authorized agency or disinterested person as such term is defined in subdivision three of section one hundred sixteen of the domestic relations law. The court shall thereafter establish a schedule for completion of other inquiries and investigations necessary to complete review of the adoption of the child and shall immediately set a schedule for completion of the adoption.

12. If the court determines to commit the custody and guardianship of the child pursuant to this section, or if the court determines to suspend judgement pursuant to section six hundred thirty-three of the family court act, the court in its order shall determine if there is any parent to whom notice of an adoption would be required pursuant to section one hundred eleven-a of the domestic relations law. In its order the court shall indicate whether such person or persons were given notice of the proceeding and whether such person or persons appeared. Such determinations shall be conclusive in all subsequent proceedings relating to the custody, guardianship or adoption of the child.

Added by Laws 1976, Ch. 666; **amended** by Laws 1977, Ch. 862, eff. Oct. 10, 1977; subds. 4(b) and (c) **amended** by Laws 1981, Ch. 284, eff. June 22, 1981; **amended** by Laws 1981, Ch. 739, eff. Oct. 26, 1981, subds. 3(d) and 3(g) and adding subds. 4(e) and 8; **amended** by Laws 1982, Ch. 123, eff. May 24, 1982; **amended** by Laws 1983, Ch. 911, eff. Jan. 1, 1984, provided, however, that nothing herein contained shall be construed so as to alter, affect, impair, defeat or restore any right, obligations, duties or interests accrued, incurred, conferred or terminated prior to the effective date; **amended** by Laws 1987, Ch. 136, eff. June 15, 1987; **amended** by Laws 1990, Ch. 605, § 2, eff. Oct. 1,

1990; **amended** by Laws 1990, Ch. 867, § 2, eff. Sept. 1, 1990; **amended** by Laws 1991, Ch. 588, §§ 2, 3, eff. Sept. 30, 1991; **amended** by Laws 1991, Ch. 691, § 1, eff. Aug. 2, 1991; **amended** by Laws 1993, Ch. 133, § 1, eff. Sept. 19, 1993; **amended** by Laws 1993, Ch. 294, § 2, **adding** new subd. (10) to SSL § 384-b, eff. Sept. 19, 1993; **amended** by Laws 1994, Ch. 601, § 5, eff. Oct. 24, 1994; **amended** by Laws 1996, Ch. 309, § 279, eff. July 13, 1996; **amended** by Laws 1996, Ch. 608, eff. Sept. 4, 1996; **amended** by Laws 1999, Ch. 7, §§ 9–14, **adding** para. (12), subd. (2)(c)(ix) and subd. (3)(l), eff. Feb. 11, 1999; **amended** by Laws 2000, Ch. 145, §§ 4 and 5, eff. July 1, 2000; **amended** by Laws 2002, Ch. 312, § 6, eff. Aug. 6, 2002; **amended** by Laws 2002, Ch. 663, § 11, eff. Dec. 3, 2002; L. 2005, Ch. 3, sect; 1, 55 to 58 (Part A), eff. Aug. 23, 2005; Laws 2006, ch. 185, §§6, 8, eff. Oct 24, 2006; Laws 2006, ch. 460, §§1--3, eff. Nov 14, 2006.

§ 384-c.   Notice in certain proceedings to fathers of children born out of wedlock.

1. Notwithstanding any inconsistent provision of this or any other law, and in addition to the notice requirements of any law pertaining to persons other than those specified in subdivision two of this section, notice as provided herein shall be given to the persons specified in subdivision two of this section of any proceeding initiated pursuant to sections three hundred fifty-eight-a, three hundred eighty-four, and three hundred eighty-four-b of this chapter involving a child born out of wedlock. Persons specified in subdivision two of this section shall not include any person who has been convicted of rape in the first degree involving forcible compulsion, under subdivision one of section 130.35 of the penal law, when the child who is the subject of the proceeding was conceived as a result of such rape.

2. Persons entitled to notice, pursuant to subdivision one of this section, shall include:

(a) Any person adjudicated by a court in this state to be the father of the child;

(b) any person adjudicated by a court of another state or territory of the United States to be the father of the child, when a certified copy of the court order has been filed with the putative father registry, pursuant to section three hundred seventy-two-c of this chapter;

(c) any person who has timely filed an unrevoked notice of intent to claim paternity of the child, pursuant to section three hundred seventy-two-c of this chapter;

(d) any person who is recorded on the child's birth certificate as the child's father;

(e) any person who is openly living with the child and the child's mother at the time the proceeding is initiated or at the time the child was placed in the care of an authorized agency, and who is holding himself out to be the child's father;

(f) any person who has been identified as the child's father by the mother in written, sworn statement;

(g)   any person who was married to the child's mother within six months subsequent to the birth of the child and prior to the execution of a surrender instrument or the initiation of a proceeding pursuant to section three hundred eighty-four-b; and

(h)   any person who has filed with the putative father registry an instrument acknowledging paternity of the child, pursuant to section 4-1.2 of the estates, powers and trusts law.

3.   The provisions of this section shall not apply to persons entitled to notice pursuant to section one hundred eleven of the domestic relations law. The sole purpose of notice under this section shall be to enable the person served pursuant to subdivision two to present evidence to the court relevant to the best interests of the child. In any proceeding brought upon the ground specified in paragraph (d) of subdivision four of section three hundred eighty-four-b, a person served pursuant to this section may appear and present evidence only in the dispositional hearing.

4.   Notice under this section shall be given at least twenty days prior to the proceeding by delivery of a copy of the petition and notice to the person. Upon a showing to the court, by affidavit or otherwise, on or before the date of the proceeding or within such further time as the court may allow, that personal service cannot be effected at the person's last known address with reasonable effort, notice may be given, without prior court order therefor, at least twenty days prior to the proceeding by registered or certified mail directed to the person's last known address or, where the person has filed a notice of intent to claim paternity pursuant to section three hundred seventy-two-c, to the address last entered therein. Notice by publication shall not be required to be given to a person entitled to notice pursuant to the provisions of this section.

5.   A person may waive his right to notice under this section by written instrument subscribed by him and acknowledged or proved in the manner required for the execution of a surrender instrument pursuant to section three hundred eighty-four of this chapter.

6.   The notice given to persons pursuant to this section shall inform them of the time, date, place and purpose of the proceeding and shall also apprise such persons that their failure to appear shall constitute a denial of their interest in the child which denial may result, without further notice, in the transfer or commitment of the child's care, custody or guardianship or in the child's adoption in this or any subsequent proceeding in which such care, custody or guardianship or adoption may be at issue.

7.   No order of the court in any proceeding pursuant to section three hundred fifty-eight-a, three hundred eighty-four or three hundred eighty-four-b of this chapter or in any subsequent proceeding involving the child's custody, guardianship or adoption shall be vacated, annulled or reversed upon the application of any person who was properly served with notice in accordance with this section but failed to appear, or who waived notice pursuant to subdivision five. Nor shall

any order of the court in any proceeding involving the child's custody, guardian-ship or adoption be vacated, annulled or reversed upon the application of any person who was properly served with notice in accordance with this section in any previous proceeding in which the court determined that the transfer or commitment of the child's care, custody or guardianship to an authorized agency was in the child's best interests.

Added by Laws 1976, Ch. 665, eff. Jan. 1, 1977; **amended** by Laws 1977, Ch. 862; Laws 1979, Ch. 18; Laws 1980, Ch. 575, eff. July 26, 1980.

§ 385. Orders; prohibiting placing out or boarding out; removal.

1. Prohibiting placing out or boarding out. Whenever the commissioner shall decide that any disposition of a child under this title has been made for purposes of gain, or without due inquiry as to the character and reputation of the person with whom such child is placed, or in such manner that such child is subjected to cruel or improper treatment or neglect or immoral surroundings, or in such manner that the religious faith of the child is not preserved and protected as provided by this title, the commissioner may issue an order prohibiting such an authorized agency, association, corporation, institution, society or other organiza-tion from thereafter placing out or boarding out any child. No such order shall be issued until after an opportunity to be heard before the commissioner or his designee and after reasonable notice has been given, with a copy of the charge. A full record of the proceedings and decision on such hearing shall be kept by the department. Any such order issued by the commissioner may be revoked by the commissioner.

2. Whenever the commissioner shall find a minor

(a) placed out or boarded out in a home which is unsuitable or has no license or certificate, or

(b) cared for under a certificate or license but neglected or without suitable care or protection, he may order its removal within thirty days by the agency which placed it and if such order cannot be served upon such agency, it may be addressed to the public board, commission, or officer of the county charged with the care of such child. If such child is not removed within the specified time, the matter may be brought before the children's court or other court having jurisdiction, for adjudication and disposition.

3. Review of orders. Any person, agency, association, corporation, institu-tion, society or other organization, aggrieved by the decision of the commissioner in making any order pursuant to the provisions of this title, may institute, in the judicial district in which the applicant resides or has its chief office, a proceeding under article seventy-eight of the civil practice law and rules in which the reasonableness of such decision shall be subject to review.

Amended by Laws 1962, Ch. 319; **amended** by Laws 1971, Chs. 110, 945, both eff. July 1, 1971; **amended** by Laws 1978, Ch. 555, §§ 24-26, eff. July 24, 1978.

§ 386. Visitation; inspection and supervision.

The board or the department is authorized to visit, in its discretion.

1. any minor under the age of twenty-one years committed, placed out or boarded out and not legally adopted or in the custody of a legal guardian.

2. The board or the department is authorized to visit, in its discretion, any home or place where a child or children are received, boarded or kept under a license or certificate whether or not such children are maintained as public charges. Every licensed home shall, if practicable, be visited by the department at least four times in each year. Such homes and places may be visited by the employees of any incorporated society for the prevention of cruelty to children.

Amended by Laws 1971, Ch. 110, eff. July 1, 1971; **amended** by Laws 1971, Ch. 945, eff. July 1, 1971; **amended** by Laws 1978, Ch. 555, § 27, eff. July 24, 1978.

§ 387. Rules.

Repealed by Laws 1978, Ch. 555, § 28, eff. July 24, 1978.

§ 387. Ineligibility for public foster care funds; fiscal penalties.

1. The office of children and family services shall, by regulation, promulgate standards to determine that an authorized agency, or one or more of its programs or facilities, is ineligible to receive public foster care funds or should be assessed a fiscal penalty. Such standards shall include the following:

(a) lack of public need, including but not limited to geographic or programmatic need, for the agency or one or more of its programs or facilities;

(b) failure of the agency to promote the placement of children in permanent, safe family homes through return to the children's own families or through adoption, or other appropriate objectives for children, as measured by such factors as length of stay in foster care for children with similar personal and family characteristics; and

(c) a pattern or practice of repeated violation of the provisions of this chapter or of the regulations of the office of children and family services promulgated thereunder

2. A determination of ineligibility to receive public foster care funds or the assessment of a fiscal penalty shall be made upon a finding of substantial noncompliance with one or more of the standards developed and adopted pursuant to subdivision one of this section. Such findings and determination shall be made in accordance with the hearing procedures set forth in section four hundred sixty d of this chapter relating to the revocation, suspension or limiting of operating certificates. Such determination shall be subject to judicial review in accordance with article seventy eight of the civil practice law and rules.

3. A determination of ineligibility to receive public foster care funds shall specify whether it applies to the agency generally or to a particular program or facility of the agency.

4. A social services official shall not purchase foster care from any authorized agency, or program or facility thereof, which has been determined to be ineligible to receive public foster care funds in accordance with the provisions of this section. Any contract between a social services district and an authorized agency shall be deemed null and void to the extent that it is inconsistent with the provisions of this subdivision.

5. The commissioner shall report forthwith in writing, to the governor, the temporary president of the senate and the speaker of the assembly with respect to each case in which a determination of ineligibility to receive public foster care funds has been made pursuant to this section. Such report shall contain the name of the agency and the reason or reasons for the determination of ineligibility.

6. Any fiscal penalty received by the office of children and family services pursuant to this section shall be deposited to the credit of the children and family services quality enhancement fund established pursuant to section ninety seven yyy of the state finance law.

Added by Laws 1979, Ch. 610, eff. Apr. 1, 1981; **amended** by Laws 2002, Ch. 83, Part C, § 18, eff. April 1, 2002.

§ 388. Special charters.

The power and authority given to agencies, associations, corporations, institutions and societies in their charters shall not be abrogated or nullified, except as the same are in conflict with this title.

§ 389. Penalty for violations.

1. Except as hereinafter provided, any person, corporation, agency, society, institution or other organization, wilfully violating this title or failing to comply with any order which the department is authorized under this title to make, shall be guilty of a misdemeanor.

2. (a) Any person, corporation, society, institution or other organization who or which violates the provisions of subdivision six of section three hundred seventy-four of this chapter shall be guilty of a misdemeanor, for the first such offense. Any person, corporations, society, institution or other organization who or which violates the provisions of subdivision six of section three hundred seventy-four of this chapter, after having been once convicted of violating such provisions, shall be guilty of a felony.

(b) Notwithstanding the provisions of paragraph (a) of this subdivision, any person, corporation, society, institution or other organization who or which violates subdivision six of section three hundred seventy-four of this title, where such unlawful compensation or thing of value accepted or received exceeds five thousand dollars in value, shall be guilty of a class E felony as defined in the penal law. Any person, corporation, society, institution, or other organization who or which violates subdivision six of section three hundred seventy-four of this title, where such unlawful compensation or thing of value accepted or received exceeds five thousand dollars in value, after having been previously convicted of violating subdivision six of section three hundred seventy-four of this title, shall be guilty of a class D felony as defined in the penal law.

> **Amended** by Laws 1949, Ch. 678; **amended** by Laws 1971, Chs. 110, 945; **amended** by Laws 1978, Ch. 555, § 29, eff. July 24, 1978; L. 2003, Ch. 463, § 1, re-designating sub. 2, par. (a), and adding par. (b), eff. Nov. 1, 2003.

§ 390   Child day care; license or registration required

1. Definitions.

(a)   (i) "Child day care" shall mean care for a child on a regular basis provided away from the child's residence for less than twenty-four hours per day by someone other than the parent, step-parent, guardian, or relative within the third degree of consanguinity of the parents or step-parents of such child.

(ii)   Child day care shall not refer to care provided in:

(A)   a day camp, as defined in the state sanitary code;

(B)   an after-school program operated for the purpose of religious education, sports, or recreation;

(C)   a facility:

(1)   providing day services under an operating certificate issued by the department;

(2)   providing day treatment under an operating certificate issued by the office of mental health or office of mental retardation and developmental disabilities; or

(D)   a kindergarten, pre-kindergarten, or nursery school for children three years of age or older, or after-school program for children operated by a public school district or by a private school or academy which is providing elementary or secondary education or both, in accordance with the compulsory education requirements of the education law, provided that the kindergarten, pre-kindergarten, nursery school, or after school program is located on the premises or campus where the elementary or secondary education is provided.

(b)   "Child day care provider" shall mean any individual, association, corporation, partnership, institution or agency whose activities include providing child day care or operating a home or facility where child day care is provided.

(c)   "Child day care center" shall mean any program or facility caring for children for more than three hours per day per child in which child day care is provided by a child day care provider except those programs operating as a group family day care home as such term is defined in paragraph (d) of this subdivision, a family day care home, as such term is defined in paragraph (e) of this subdivision, and a school-age child care program, as such term is defined in paragraph (f) of this subdivision.

(d) "Group family day care home" shall mean a program caring for children for more than three hours per day per child in which child day care is provided in a family home for seven to ten children of all ages, or up to twelve children where all of such children are over two years of age, except for those programs operating as a family day care home, as such term is defined in paragraph (e) of this subdivision, which care for seven or eight children. A group family day care provider may provide child day care services to two additional children if such additional children are of school age and such children receive services only before or after the period such children are ordinarily in school or during school lunch periods, or school holidays, or during those periods of the year in which school is not in session.There shall be one caregiver for every two children under two years of age in the group family home. A group family day care home must have at least one assistant to the operator present when child day care is being provided to seven or more children. This assistant shall be selected by the group family day care operator and shall meet the qualifications established for such position by the regulations of the department.

(e) "Family day care home" shall mean a program caring for children for more than three hours per day per child in which child day care is provided in a family home for three to six children. A family day care provider may, however, care for seven or eight children at any one time if no more than six of the children are less than school age and the school-aged children receive care primarily before or after the period such children are ordinarily in school, during school lunch periods, on school holidays, or during those periods of the year in which school is not in session in accordance with the regulations of the department and the department inspects such home to determine whether the provider can care adequately for seven or eight children.

(f) "School age child care" shall mean a program caring for more than six school-aged children who are under thirteen years of age or who are incapable of caring for themselves. Such programs shall be in operation consistent with the local school calendar. School age child care programs shall offer care during the school year to an enrolled group of children at a permanent site before or after the period children enrolled in such program are ordinarily in school or during school lunch periods and may also provide such care on school holidays and those periods of the year in which school is not in session.

2. (a) Child day care centers caring for seven or more children and group family day care programs, as defined in subdivision one of this section, shall obtain a license from the department and shall operate in accordance with the terms of such license and the regulations of the department.

(b) Family day care homes, child day care centers caring for at least three but fewer than seven children, and school-age child care programs shall register

SSL

with the department and shall operate in compliance with the regulations of the department.

(c)   Any child day care provider not required to obtain a license pursuant to paragraph (a) of this subdivision or to register with the department pursuant to paragraph (b) of this subdivision may register with the department.

(d)   (i) The office of children and family services shall promulgate regulations for licensure and for registration of child day care pursuant to this section. Procedures for obtaining a license or registration orrenewing a license shall include a satisfactory inspection of the facility by the office of children and family services prior to issuance of the license or registration or renewal of the license.

(ii)   (A) Registration shall be valid for a period of up to two years, so long as the provider remains in compliance with applicable law and regulations during such period.

(B)   After initial registration by the child day care provider, the office of children and family services shall not accept any subsequent registration by such provider, unless:

(1)   such provider has met the training requirements set forth in section three hundred ninety-a of this title;

(2)   such provider has met the requirements of section three hundred ninety-b of this title relating to criminal history screening;

(3)   such provider has complied with the requirements of section four hundred twenty-four-a of this article; and

(4)   the office of children and family services has received no complaints about the home, center, or program alleging statutory or regulatory violations, or, having received such complaints, the office of children and family services has determined, after inspection pursuant to paragraph (a) of subdivision three of this section, that the home, center, or program is operated in compliance with applicable statutory and regulatory requirements.

(C)   Where the office of children and family services has determined that a registration should not be continued because the requirements of clause (B) of this subparagraph have not been satisfied, the office of children and family services may terminate the registration. If the office of children and family services does not terminate the registration, the office of children and family services shall inspect the home or program before acknowledging any subsequent registration. Where the home or program has failed to meet the requirements of this section, the office of children and family services may reject any subsequent registration of a provider. Nothing herein shall prohibit the office of children and family services from terminating or suspending registration pursuant to subdivision ten of this section where the office of children and family services determines that termination or suspension is necessary.

(iv)   Child day care providers who have been issued a license shall openly display such license in the facility or home for which the license is issued. Child day care providers who have registered with the department shall provide proof of registration upon request.

(e)   Notwithstanding any other provision of this section, where a child is cared for by a parent, guardian or relative within the third degree of consanguinity of the parent of such child and such person simultaneously provides child day care for other children, only the other children shall be considered in determining whether such person must be registered or licensed, provided that such person is not caring, in total, for more than eight children.

2-a.   (a) The office of children and family services shall promulgate regulations which establish minimum quality program requirements for licensed and registered child day care homes, programs and facilities. Such requirements shall include but not be limited to (i) the need for age appropriate activities, materials and equipment to promote cognitive, educational, social, cultural, physical, emotional, language and recreational development of children in care in a safe, healthy and caring environment (ii) principles of childhood development (iii) appropriate staff/child ratios for family day care homes, group family day care homes, school age day care programs and day care centers, provided however that such staff/child ratios shall not be less stringent than applicable staff/child ratios as set forth in part four hundred fourteen, four hundred sixteen, four hundred seventeen or four hundred eighteen of title eighteen of the New York code of rules and regulations as of January first, two thousand (iv) appropriate levels of supervision of children in care (v) minimum standards for sanitation, health, infection control, nutrition, buildings and equipment, safety, security procedures, first aid, fire prevention, fire safety, evacuation plans and drills, prevention of child abuse and maltreatment, staff qualifications and training, record keeping, and child behavior management.

(a-1)   [Expires March 31, 2007] The office of children and family services, in collaboration with the commissioner of education, shall promulgate regulations which establish standards for administration of medication and treatment by licensed and registered child day care centers, group family day care homes, family day care homes, and school age child care programs to children receiving day care in such homes, programs and centers pursuant to a health care plan that shall be developed by such homes, programs and centers and approved by the office of children and family services. Such standards shall address the need for health care professionals and parents to understand the role that unlicensed personnel will play in administering medications or treatments, the degree of specificity needed in a health care professional's order (especially when measurable parameters form the basis for the administration of medication), the training of appropriate staff who will administer medications, appropriate contact with a parent when medications or treatments are administered, the standards for storage and maintenance of medications, record-keeping requirements pertaining to administration of medications and treatments, determining which types of medications and treatments may be administered and determining which methods of administration may be permitted, and appropriate limitations of injections; all consistent with section sixty-nine hundred eight of the education law. Notwithstanding any law to the contrary, the office of children and family services shall not have the authority to promulgate, on an emergency basis, any rules and regulations necessary to implement the requirements established pursuant to this paragraph until after such office has promulgated comprehensive regulations implementing this paragraph.

(b)   The use of electronic monitors as a sole means of supervision of children in day care shall be prohibited, except that electronic monitors may be used in family day care homes and group family day care homes as an indirect means of supervision where the parents of any child to be supervised have agreed in advance to the use of such monitors as an indirect means of supervision and the use of such monitors is restricted to situations where the children so supervised are sleeping.

(c)   No child less than six weeks of age may be cared for by a licensed or registered day care provider, except in extenuating circumstances where prior approval for care of such children has been given by the office of children and family services. Extenuating circumstances for the purposes of this section shall include but not be limited to the medical or health needs of the parent or child, or the economic hardship of the parent.

3.   (a) The office of children and family services may make announced or unannounced inspections of the records and premises of any child day care provider, whether or not such provider has a license from, or is registered with, the office of children and family services. The office of children and family services shall make unannounced inspections of the records and premises of any child day care provider within fifteen days after the office of children and family services receives a complaint that, if true, would indicate such provider does not comply with the regulations of the office of children and family services or with statutory requirements. If the complaint indicates that there may be imminent danger to the children, the office of children and family services shall investigate the complaint no later than the next day of operation of the provider. The office of children and family services may provide for inspections through the purchase of services.

(b)   Where inspections have been made and violations of applicable statutes or regulations have been found, the department shall advise the child day care provider in writing, within ten days, of the violations and require the provider to correct such violations. If the child day care provider fails to correct such violations within thirty days after notice, the department may act pursuant to subdivisions ten and eleven of this section.

(c)   (i) The office of children and family services shall establish a toll-free statewide telephone number to receive inquiries about child day care homes, programs and facilities and complaints of violations of the requirements of this section or regulations promulgated under this section. The office of children and family services shall develop a system for investigation, which shall include inspection, of such complaints. The office of children and family services may provide for such investigations through purchase of services. The office of children and family services shall develop a process for publicizing such toll-free telephone number to the public for making inquiries or complaints about child day care homes, programs or facilities.

(ii) Information to be maintained and available to the public through such toll-free telephone number shall include, but not be limited to:

(A) current license and registration status of child day care homes, programs and facilities including whether a license or registration is in effect or has been revoked or suspended; and

(B) child care resource and referral programs providing services pursuant to title five-B of this article and other resources known to the office of children and family services which relate to child day care homes, programs and facilities in the state.

(iii) Upon written request identifying a particular child day care home, program or facility, the office of children and family services shall provide the information set forth below. The office of children and family services may charge reasonable fees for copies of documents provided, consistent with the provisions of article six of the public officers law. The information available pursuant to this clause shall be:

(A) the results of the most recent inspection for licensure or registration and any subsequent inspections by the office of children and family services;

(B) complaints filed against child day care homes, programs or facilities which describes the nature of the complaint and states how the complaint was resolved, including the status of the office of children and family services investigation, the steps taken to rectify the complaint, and the penalty, if any, imposed; and

(C) child day care homes, programs or facilities which have requested or received a waiver from any applicable rule or regulation, and the regulatory requirement which was waived.

(iv) Nothing in this paragraph shall be construed to require or permit the disclosure either orally or in writing of any information that is confidential pursuant to law.

(d) Where investigation or inspection reveals that a child day care provider which must be licensed or registered is not, the office of children and family services shall advise the child day care provider in writing that the provider is in violation of the licensing or registration requirements and shall take such further action as is necessary to cause the provider to comply with the law, including directing an unlicensed or unregistered provider to cease operation. In addition, the office of children and family services shall require the provider to notify the parents or guardians of children receiving care from the provider that the provider is in violation of the licensing or registration requirements and shall

SSL

require the provider to notify the office of children and family services that the provider has done so. Any provider who is directed to cease operations pursuant to this paragraph shall be entitled to a hearing before the office of children and family services. If the provider requests a hearing to contest the directive to cease operations, such hearing must be scheduled to commence as soon as possible but in no event later than thirty days after the receipt of the request by the office of children and family services. The provider may not operate the center, home or program after being directed to cease operations, regardless of whether a hearing is requested. If the provider does not cease operations, the office of children and family services may impose a civil penalty pursuant to subdivision eleven of this section, seek an injunction pursuant to section three hundred ninety-one of this title, or both.

(e)   (i) Where an authorized agency is subsidizing child day care pursuant to any provision of this chapter, the authorized agency may submit to the department justification for a need to impose additional requirements upon child day care providers and a plan to monitor compliance with such additional requirements. No such additional requirements or monitoring may be imposed without the written approval of the department.

(ii)   An authorized agency may refuse to allow a child day care provider who is not in compliance with this section and regulations issued hereunder or any approved additional requirements of the authorized agency to provide child day care to the child. In accordance with the plan approved by the department, an authorized agency shall have the right to make announced or unannounced inspections of the records and premises of any provider who provides care for such children, including the right to make inspections prior to subsidized children receiving care in a home where the inspection is for the purpose of determining whether the child day care provider is in compliance with applicable law and regulations and any additional requirements imposed upon such provider by the authorized agency. Where an authorized agency makes such inspections, the authorized agency shall notify the department immediately of any violations of this section or regulations promulgated hereunder, and shall provide the department with an inspection report whether or not violations were found, documenting the results of such inspection.

(iii)   Nothing contained in this paragraph shall diminish the authority of the department to conduct inspections or provide for inspections through purchase of services as otherwise provided for in this section. Nothing contained in this paragraph shall obligate the department to take any action to enforce any additional requirements imposed on child day care providers by an authorized agency.

(f)   Individual local social services districts may alter their participation in activities related to arranging for, subsidizing, delivering and monitoring the provision of subsidized child day care provided, however, that the total participation of an individual district in all activities related to the provision of subsidized child day care shall be no less than the participation level engaged in by such individual district on the effective date of this section.

4. (a) The office of children and family services on an annual basis shall inspect at least twenty percent of all registered family day care homes, registered child day care centers and registered school age child care programs to determine whether such homes, centers and programs are operating in compliance with applicable statutes and regulations. The office of children and family services shall increase the percentage of family day care homes, child day care centers and school age child care programs which are inspected pursuant to this subdivision as follows: to at least thirty percent by the thirty-first of December two thousand; and to at least fifty percent by the thirty-first of December two thousand one. The office of children and family services may provide for such inspections through purchase of services. Priority shall be given to family day care homes which have never been licensed or certified prior to initial registration.

(b) Any family day care home or school-age child care program licensed, registered, or certified by the department or by any authorized agency on the effective date of this section shall be deemed registered until the expiration of its then-current license or certificate unless such license or certificate is suspended or revoked pursuant to subdivision ten of this section. Family day care homes and school-age child care programs not licensed, registered, or certified on the effective date of this section shall register pursuant to subdivision two of this section.

5. Child day care providers required to have a license from the department or to be registered with the department pursuant to this section shall not be exempt from such requirement through registration with another state agency, or certification, registration, or licensure by any local governmental agency or any authorized agency.

6. Unless otherwise limited by law, a parent with legal custody or a legal guardian of any child in a child day care program shall have unlimited and on demand access to such child or ward. Such parent or guardian unless otherwise limited by law, also shall have the right to inspect on demand during its hours of operation any area of a child day care center, group family day care home, school-age child care program, or family day care home to which the child or ward of such parent or guardian has access or which could present a hazard to the health and safety of the child or ward.

7. (a) [Expires March 31, 2007] The department shall implement on a statewide basis programs to educate parents and other potential consumers of child day care programs about their selection and use. The department may provide for such implementation through the purchase of services. Such education shall include, but not be limited to, the following topics:

(i) types of child day care programs;

(ii) factors to be considered in selecting and evaluating child day care programs;

(iii)   regulations of the department governing the operation of different types of programs;

(iv)   rights of parents or guardians in relation to access to children and inspection of child day care programs;

(v)   information concerning the availability of child day care subsidies;

(vi)   information about licensing and registration requirements;

(vii)   prevention of child abuse and maltreatment in child day care programs, including screening of child day care providers and employees;

(viii)   tax information; and

(ix)   factors to be considered in selecting and evaluating child day care programs when a child needs administration of medications during the time enrolled.

(b)   The department shall implement a statewide campaign to educate the public as to the legal requirements for registration of family day care and school-age child care, and the benefits of such registration. The department may provide for such implementation through the purchase of services. The campaign shall:

(i)   use various types of media;

(ii)   include the development of public educational materials for families, family day care providers, employers and community agencies;

(iii)   explain the role and functions of child care resource and referral programs, as such term is used in title five-B of this article;

(iv)   explain the role and functions of the department in regard to registered programs; and

(v)   publicize the department's toll-free telephone number for making complaints of violations of child day care requirements related to programs which are required to be licensed or registered.

8.   The department shall establish and maintain a list of all current registered and licensed child day care programs and a list of all programs whose license or registration has been revoked, rejected, terminated, or suspended. Such information shall be available to the public, pursuant to procedures developed by the department.

9.   The department shall make available, directly or through purchase of services, to registered child day care providers information concerning:

(a)   liability insurance;

(b)   start-up grants;

(c)   United States department of agriculture food programs;

(d)   subsidies available for child day care;

(e)   tax information; and

(f) support services required to be provided by child care resource and referral programs as set forth in subdivision three of section four hundred ten-r of this article.

10. Any home or facility providing child day care shall be operated in accordance with applicable statutes and regulations. Any violation of applicable statutes or regulations shall be a basis to deny, limit, suspend, revoke, or terminate a license or registration. Consistent with articles twenty-three and twenty-three-A of the correction law, and guidelines referenced in subdivision two of section four hundred twenty-five of this article, if the office of children and family services is made aware of the existence of a criminal conviction or pending criminal charge concerning an operator of a family day care home, group family day care home, school-age child care program, or child day care center or concerning any assistant, employee or volunteer in such homes, programs or centers, or any persons age eighteen or over who reside in such homes, such conviction or charge may be a basis to deny, limit, suspend, revoke, reject, or terminate a license or registration. Before any license issued pursuant to the provisions of this section is suspended or revoked, before registration pursuant to this section is suspended or terminated, or when an application for such license is denied or registration rejected, the applicant for or holder of such registration or license is entitled, pursuant to section twenty-two of this chapter and the regulations of the office of children and family services, to a hearing before the office of children and family services. However, a license or registration shall be temporarily suspended or limited without a hearing upon written notice to the operator of the facility following a finding that the public health, or an individual's safety or welfare, are in imminent danger. The holder of a license or registrant is entitled to a hearing before the office of children and family services to contest the temporary suspension or limitation. If the holder of a license or registrant requests a hearing to contest the temporary suspension or limitation, such hearing must be scheduled to commence as soon as possible but in no event later than thirty days after the receipt of the request by the office of children and family services. Suspension shall continue until the condition requiring suspension or limitation is corrected or until a hearing decision has been issued. If the office of children and family services determines after a hearing that the temporary suspension or limitation was proper, such suspension or limitation shall be extended until the condition requiring suspension or limitation has been corrected or until the license or registration has been revoked.

11. (a) (i) The office of children and family services shall adopt regulations establishing civil penalties of no more than five hundred dollars per day to be assessed against child day care centers, school age child care programs, group family day care homes or family day care homes for violations of this section, sections three hundred ninety-a and three hundred ninety-b of this title and any regulations promulgated thereunder. The regulations establishing civil penalties shall specify the violations subject to penalty.

(ii) The office of children and family services shall adopt regulations establishing civil penalties of no more than five hundred dollars per day to be assessed against child day care providers who operate child day care centers or group family day care homes without a license or who operate family day care homes, school-age child care programs, or child day care centers required to be registered without obtaining such registration.

(iii)   In addition to any other civil or criminal penalty provided by law, the office of children and family services shall have the power to assess civil penalties in accordance with its regulations adopted pursuant to this subdivision after a hearing conducted in accordance with procedures established by regulations of the office of children and family services. Such procedures shall require that notice of the time and place of the hearing, together with a statement of charges of violations, shall be served in person or by certified mail addressed to the school age child care program, group family day care home, family day care home, or child day care center at least thirty days prior to the date of the hearing. The statement of charges shall set forth the existence of the violation or violations, the amount of penalty for which the program may become liable, the steps which must be taken to rectify the violation, and where applicable, a statement that a penalty may be imposed regardless of rectification. A written answer to the charges of violations shall be filed with the office of children and family services not less than ten days prior to the date of hearing with respect to each of the charges and shall include all material and relevant matters which, if not disclosed in the answer, would not likely be known to the office of children and family services.

(iv)   The hearing shall be held by the commissioner of the office of children and family services or the commissioner's designee. The burden of proof at such hearing shall be on the office of children and family services to show that the charges are supported by a preponderance of the evidence. The commissioner of the office of children and family services or the commissioner's designee, in his or her discretion, may allow the child day care center operator or provider to attempt to prove by a preponderance of the evidence any matter not included in the answer. Where the child day care provider satisfactorily demonstrates that it has rectified the violations in accordance with the requirements of paragraph (c) of this subdivision, no penalty shall be imposed except as provided in paragraph (c) of this subdivision.

(b)   (i) In assessing penalties pursuant to this subdivision, the office of children and family services may consider the completeness of any rectification made and the specific circumstances of such violations as mitigating factors.

(ii)   Upon the request of the office of children and family services, the attorney general shall commence an action in any court of competent jurisdiction against any child day care program subject to the provisions of this subdivision and against any person, entity or corporation operating such center or school age child care program, group family day care home or family day care home for the recovery of any penalty assessed by the office of children and family services in accordance with the provisions of this subdivision.

(iii)   Any such penalty assessed by the office of children and family services may be released or compromised by the office of children and family services before the matter has been referred to the attorney general; when such matter has been referred to the attorney general, such penalty may be released or compromised and any action commenced to recover the same may be settled and discontinued by the attorney general with the consent of the office of children and family services.

(c)   (i) Except as provided for in this paragraph, a child day care provider may avoid payment of a penalty imposed pursuant to this subdivision where the provider has rectified the condition resulting in the imposition of the penalty within thirty days of notification of the imposition of the penalty.

(ii)   Clause (i) of this paragraph notwithstanding, rectification shall not preclude the imposition of a penalty pursuant to this subdivision where:

(A)   the child day care provider has operated a child day care center or group family day care home without a license, has refused to seek a license for the operation of such a center or home, or has continued to operate such a center or home after denial of a license application, revocation of an existing license or suspension of an existing license;

(B)   the child day care provider has operated a family day care home, school-age child care program or child day care center required to be registered without being registered, has refused to seek registration for the operation of such home, program or center or has continued to operate such a home, program or center after denial of a registration application, revocation of an existing registration or suspension of an existing registration;

(C)   there has been a total or substantial failure of the facility's fire detection or prevention systems or emergency evacuation procedures;

(D)   the child day care provider or an assistant, employee or volunteer has failed to provide adequate and competent supervision;

(E)   the child day care provider or an assistant, employee or volunteer has failed to provide adequate sanitation;

(F)   the child day care provider or an assistant, employee or volunteer has abused or maltreated a child in care; or

(G)   the child day care provider has violated the same statutory or regulatory standard more than once within a six month period.

(d)   Any civil penalty received by the office of children and family services pursuant to this subdivision shall be deposited to the credit of the "quality child care and protection fund" established pursuant to section ninety-seven-www of the state finance law.

12.   (a) Notwithstanding any other provision of law, except as may be required as a condition of licensure or registration by regulations promulgated pursuant to this section, no village, town (outside the area of any incorporated

SSL

village), city or county shall adopt or enact any law, ordinance, rule or regulation which would impose, mandate or otherwise enforce standards for sanitation, health, fire safety or building construction on a one or two family dwelling or multiple dwelling used to provide group family day care or family day care than would be applicable were such child day care not provided on the premises. Nothing in this paragraph shall preclude local authorities with enforcement jurisdiction of the applicable sanitation, health, fire safety or building construction code from making appropriate inspections to assure compliance with such standards. The department of social services shall provide to the secretary of state on a monthly basis, a list of child day care registrants.

(b)   Notwithstanding any other provision of law: for the purposes of this subdivision, no local government may prohibit use of a single family dwelling for family day care or group family day care where a permit for such use has been issued in accordance with regulations issued pursuant to this section; nor may any local government prohibit use for family day care or group family day care, of a multiple dwelling classified as fireproof or prohibit use for family day care or group family day care, of a dwelling unit located on the ground floor of a multiple dwelling not classified as fireproof, where in either case a registration or license for such use has been issued in accordance with regulations adopted pursuant to this section and such use is otherwise permitted under state fire and safety standards (the state code) and under any other existing standard for permitted uses of the multiple dwelling.

(c)   Notwithstanding any other provision of law, but pursuant to section five hundred eighty-one-b of the real property tax law, no assessing unit, as defined in subdivision one of section one hundred two of the real property tax law, in the assessment of the value of any parcel used for residential purposes and registered as a family day care home pursuant to this section, shall consider the use or registration of such parcel as a family day care home.

13.   [Expires March 31, 2007] Notwithstanding any other provision of law, this section, except for paragraph (a-1) of subdivision two-a of this section, shall not apply to child day care centers in the city of New York.

Added by Laws 1990, Ch. 750, §§ 1, 2, eff. July 22, 1991, eff. Jan. 22, 1992, in public schools and the city of New York; **amended** by Laws 1997, Ch. 587, §§ 1 and 2, eff. Jan. 15, 1998; **amended** by Laws 2000, Ch. 416, §§ 2–9, eff. Dec. 5, 2000; L. 2003, 160, §§ 3–7, eff. July 22, 2003, deemed to be in full force and effect on and after June 30, 2003; **amended** by Laws 2004, Ch. 20, §§ 2, 3, eff. on and after June 30, 2003; Laws 2006, ch. 319, §1, eff. July 26, 2006.

§ 390-a.   Standards and training for child day care.

1.   All office of children and family services and municipal staff employed to accept registrations, issue licenses or conduct inspections of child day care homes, programs or facilities, subject to the amounts appropriated therefor, shall receive training in at least the following: regulations promulgated by the office

of children and family services pursuant to section three hundred ninety of this title; child abuse prevention and identification; safety and security procedures in child day care settings; the principles of childhood development, and the laws, regulations and procedures governing the protection of children from abuse or maltreatment.

2. No license or registration shall be issued to a family day care home, group family day care home, school age child care program or child day care center and no such registration or license shall be renewed until it can be demonstrated by the employer or licensing agency that there is a procedure developed and implemented, in accordance with section three hundred ninety-b of this title and pursuant to regulations of the office of children and family services, to:

(a) review and evaluate the backgrounds of and information supplied by any person applying to be a child day care center or school-age child care program employee or volunteer or group family day care assistant, a provider of family day care or group family day care, or a director of a child day care center, head start day care center or school-age child care program. Such procedures shall include but not be limited to the following requirements: that the applicant set forth his or her employment history, provide personal and employment references; submit such information as is required for screening with the statewide central register of child abuse and maltreatment in accordance with the provisions of section four hundred twenty-four-a of this article; sign a sworn statement indicating whether, to the best of his or her knowledge, he or she has ever been convicted of a crime in this state or any other jurisdiction; and provide his or her fingerprints for submission to the division of criminal justice services in accordance with the provisions of section three hundred ninety-b of this title;

(b) establish relevant minimal experiential and educational qualifications for employees and directors of child day care centers or head start day care center programs;

(c) assure adequate and appropriate supervision of employees and volunteers of group family day care homes, family day care homes, child day care centers and school-age child care programs; and

(d) demonstrate, in the case of child day care centers, group family day care homes, family day care homes and school-age child care programs the existence of specific procedures which will assure the safety of a child who is reported to the state central register of child abuse and maltreatment as well as other children provided care by such homes, centers or programs, immediately upon notification that a report has been made with respect to a child named in such report while the child was in attendance at such homes, centers or programs.

(e) establish necessary rules to provide for uniform visitor control procedures, including visitor identification.

3. (a) The office of children and family services shall promulgate regulations requiring operators, program directors, employees and assistants of family day care homes, group family day care homes, school-age child care programs and

child day care centers to receive thirty hours of training every two years; provided, however, that fifteen hours of such training must be received within the first six months of the initial licensure, registration or employment. Such training requirements shall also apply to any volunteer in such day care homes, programs or centers who has the potential for regular and substantial contact with children. The thirty hours of training required during the first biennial cycle after initial licensure or registration shall include training received while an application for licensure or registration pursuant to section three hundred ninety of this title is pending. The office of children and family services may provide this training through purchase of services.

(b) The training required in paragraph (a) of this subdivision shall address the following topics:

(i) principles of childhood development, focusing on the developmental stages of the age groups for which the program provides care;

(ii) nutrition and health needs of infants and children;

(iii) child day care program development;

(iv) safety and security procedures;

(v) business record maintenance and management;

(vi) child abuse and maltreatment identification and prevention;

(vii) statutes and regulations pertaining to child day care;

(viii) statutes and regulations pertaining to child abuse and maltreatment; and

(ix) education and information on the identification, diagnosis and prevention of shaken baby syndrome.

(c) For the thirty hours of biennial training required after the initial period of licensure or registration, each provider who can demonstrate basic competency shall determine in which of the specified topics he or she needs further study, based on the provider's experience and the needs of the children in the provider's care.

(d) Family day care home and group family day care home operators shall obtain training pertaining to protection of the health and safety of children, as required by regulation, prior to the issuance of a license or registration by the office of children and family services.

(e) Upon request by the office of children and family services, the child day care applicant or provider shall submit documentation demonstrating compliance with the training requirements of this section.

4. No license or registration shall be issued to a family day care home or group family day care home and no such registration shall be renewed if barriers, as defined in paragraph (d) of subdivision one of section three hundred ninety-d of this title, are not present around any swimming pool or body of water, as defined in paragraphs (b) and (c) of subdivision one of section three hundred

ninety-d of this title, located on its grounds, pursuant to section three hundred ninety-d of this title.

Added by Laws 1985, Ch. 677, eff. Jan. 1, 1986; **amended** by Laws 1986, Ch. 719, eff. Oct. 1, 1986 (Laws 1990, Ch. 55; Laws 1991, Ch. 250, Laws 1992, Ch. 32, eff. Oct. 1, 1992); **amended** by Laws 1986, Ch. 875, eff. Jan. 1, 1987; **amended** by Laws 1987, Ch. 629, eff. Aug. 3, 1987; **amended** by Laws 1990, Ch. 750, § 3, eff. Nov. 19, 1990; **amended** by Laws 1997, Ch. 587, § 3, eff. Jan. 1, 1998; **amended** by Laws 1998, Ch. 321, § 1, eff. July 14, 1998; **amended** by Laws 2000, Ch. 416, § 10, eff. Dec. 5, 2000 and § 11, eff. Mar. 5, 2001; **amended** by Laws 2001, Ch. 230, § 1, eff. Sept. 4, 2001, Ch. 1, adding subd. 4, eff. July 1, 2002; Laws 2003, Ch. 552, § 1, amending sub. 3, par. (b), eff. March 15, 2004.

§ 390-b.   Criminal history review of child care providers, generally.

1.   (a) Notwithstanding any other provision of law to the contrary, and subject to rules and regulations of the division of criminal justice services, the office of children and family services shall perform a criminal history record check with the division of criminal justice services regarding any operator, employee or volunteer of a child day care center or school age child care provider, as defined in paragraphs (c) and (f) of subdivision one of section three hundred ninety of this title. Child day care center operators, school age child care operators and any employees or volunteers, who previously did not have a criminal history record check performed in accordance with this subdivision shall have such a criminal history record check performed when the child day care center or school age child care provider applies for license or registration renewal. Child day care centers which are not subject to the provisions of section three hundred ninety of this title, shall not be subject to the provisions of this section. The provisions of this section shall apply to a volunteer only where the volunteer has the potential for regular and substantial contact with children enrolled in the program.

   (b)   Notwithstanding any other provision of law to the contrary, and subject to rules and regulations of the division of criminal justice services, the office of children and family services shall perform a criminal history record check with the division of criminal justice services regarding the operator, any assistants, employees or volunteers of a group family day care home or family day care home, as defined in paragraphs (d) and (e) of subdivision one of section three hundred ninety of this title, and any person age eighteen or over residing on the premises of the group family day care home or family day care home which is to be licensed or registered in accordance with section three hundred ninety of this title. Group family day care home operators, family day care home operators, any assistants, employees or volunteers, and persons who are age eighteen or over residing on the premises of a licensed group family day care home or registered family day care home who previously did not have a criminal history record check performed in accordance with this subdivision shall have such a criminal history record check performed when the group family day care home or family day care home applies for renewal of the home's license or registration. The provisions of this section shall apply to a volunteer only where the volunteer has the potential for regular and substantial contact with children enrolled in the program.

2.   (a) As part of the provider's application for, or renewal of, a child day care center or school age child care license or registration, the provider shall furnish the office of children and family services with fingerprint cards of any operator of a child day care center or school age child care program, and any employee or volunteer, who previously did not have a criminal history record check performed in accordance with this section, together with such other information as is required by the office of children and family services and the division of criminal justice services.

(b)   Every child day care center or school age child care provider shall obtain a set of fingerprints for each prospective employee or volunteer and such other information as is required by the office of children and family services and the division of criminal justice services. The child day care center or school age child care program shall furnish to the applicant blank fingerprint cards and a description of how the completed fingerprint cards will be used. The child day care center or school age child care program shall promptly transmit such fingerprint cards to the office of children and family services.

(c)   As part of the provider's application for, or renewal of, a group family day care home license or family day care home registration, the provider shall furnish the office of children and family services with fingerprint cards of any operator of a group family day care home or family day care home, and any assistant, employee or volunteer, and any person age eighteen or over residing on the premises of the group family day care home or family day care home, who previously did not have a criminal history record check performed in accordance with this section, together with such other information as is required by the office of children and family services and the Division of Criminal Justice Services.

(d)   Every group family day care home or family day care home provider shall obtain a set of fingerprints for each prospective assistant, employee, volunteer and any person age eighteen or over who will be residing on the premises of the group family day care home or family day care home, and such other information as is required by the office of children and family services and the Division of Criminal Justice Services. The group family day care home or family day care home provider shall furnish to the applicant blank fingerprint cards and a description of how the completed fingerprint cards will be used. The group family day care home or family day care home provider shall promptly transmit such fingerprint cards to the office of children and family services.

(e)   The office of children and family services shall pay the processing fee imposed pursuant to subdivision eight-a of section eight hundred thirty-seven of the executive law. The office of children and family services shall promptly submit the fingerprint cards and the processing fee to the division of criminal justice services for its full search and retain processing.

(f)   A licensed or registered child day care center, school-age child care program, group family day care home or family day care home may temporarily approve an applicant to be an employee, assistant or volunteer for such provider while the results of the criminal history record check are pending, but shall not allow such person to have unsupervised contact with children during such time.

3.   Notwithstanding any other provision of law to the contrary, after reviewing any criminal history record information provided by the Division of Criminal Justice Services, of an individual who is subject to a criminal history record check pursuant to this section, the office of children and family services and the provider shall take the following actions:

(a)   (i) Where the criminal history record of an applicant to be an operator of a child day care center, school age child care program, group family day care home, family day care home, or any person over the age of eighteen residing in such a home, reveals a felony conviction at any time for a sex offense, crime against a child, or a crime involving violence, or a felony conviction within the past five years for a drug-related offense, the office of children and family services shall deny the application unless the office determines, in its discretion, that approval of the application will not in any way jeopardize the health, safety or welfare of the children in the center, program or home; or

(ii)   Where the criminal history record of an applicant to be an operator of a child day care center, school age child care program, group family day care home, family day care home, or any person over the age of eighteen residing in such a home, reveals a conviction for a crime other than one set forth in subparagraph (i) of this paragraph, the office of children and family services may deny the application, consistent with article twenty-three-a of the correction law; or

(iii)   Where the criminal history record of an applicant to be an operator of a child day care center, school age child care program, group family day care home, family day care home, or any other person over the age of eighteen residing in such a home, reveals a charge for any crime, the office of children and family services shall hold the application in abeyance until the charge is finally resolved.

(b)   (i) Where the criminal history record of a current operator of a child day care center, school age child care program, group family day care home, family day care home, or any other person over the age of eighteen residing in such a home, reveals a conviction for a crime set forth in subparagraph (i) of paragraph (A) of this subdivision, the office of children and family services shall conduct a safety assessment of the program and take all appropriate steps to protect the health and safety of the children in the program. The office of children and family services shall deny, limit, suspend, revoke, reject or terminate a license or registration based on such a conviction, unless the office determines, in its discretion, that continued operation of the center, program or home will not in any way jeopardize the health, safety or welfare of the children in the center, program or home;

(ii)   Where the criminal history record of a current operator of a child day care center, school age child care program, group family day care home, family day care home, or any other person over the age of eighteen residing in such a home, reveals a conviction for a crime other than one set forth in subparagraph (i) of paragraph (a) of this subdivision, the office of children and family services shall conduct a safety assessment of the program and take all appropriate steps to protect the health and safety of the children in the program. The office may deny, limit, suspend, revoke, reject or terminate a license or registration based on such a conviction, consistent with article twenty-three-a of the correction law;

(iii) Where the criminal history record of a current operator of a child day care center, school age child care program, group family day care home, family day care home, or any other person over the age of eighteen residing in such a home, reveals a charge for any crime, the office of children and family services shall conduct a safety assessment of the program and take all appropriate steps to protect the health and safety of the children in the program. The office may suspend a license or registration based on such a charge where necessary to protect the health and safety of the children in the program.

(c) (i) Where the criminal history record of an applicant to be an employee or volunteer at a child day care center or school age child care program reveals a conviction for a crime set forth in subparagraph (i) of paragraph (a) of this subdivision, the office of children and family services shall direct the provider to deny the application unless the office determines, in its discretion, that approval of the application will not in any way jeopardize the health, safety or welfare of the children in the center or program;

(ii) Where the criminal history record of an applicant to be an employee or volunteer at a child day care center or school age child care program reveals a conviction for a crime other than one set forth in subparagraph (i) of paragraph (a) of this subdivision, the office of children and family services may, consistent with article twenty-three-a of the correction law, direct the provider to deny the application;

(iii) Where the criminal history record of an applicant to be an employee or volunteer at a child day care center or school age child care program reveals a charge for any crime, the office of children and family services shall hold the application in abeyance until the charge is finally resolved.

(d) (i) Where the criminal history record of a current employee or volunteer at a child day care center or school age child care program reveals a conviction for a crime set forth in subparagraph (i) of paragraph (a) of this subdivision, the office of children and family services shall conduct a safety assessment of the program and take all appropriate steps to protect the health and safety of the children in the program. The office shall direct the provider to terminate the employee or volunteer based on such a conviction, unless the office determines, in its discretion, that the continued presence of the employee or volunteer in the center or program will not in any way jeopardize the health, safety or welfare of the children in the center or program;

(ii) Where the criminal history record of a current employee or volunteer at a child day care center or school age child care program reveals a conviction for a crime other than one set forth in subparagraph (i) of paragraph (a) of this subdivision, the office of children and family services shall conduct a safety assessment of the program and take all appropriate steps to protect the health and safety of the children in the program. The office may direct the provider to terminate the employee or volunteer based on such a conviction, consistent with article twenty-three-a of the correction law;

(iii) Where the criminal history record of a current employee or volunteer at a child day care center or school age child care program reveals a charge for any crime, the office of children and family services shall conduct a safety assessment of the program and take all appropriate steps to protect the health and safety of the children in the program.

(e) (i) Where the criminal history record of an applicant to be an employee, assistant or volunteer at a group family day care home or family day care home reveals a conviction for a crime set forth in subparagraph (i) of paragraph (a) of this subdivision, the office of children and family services shall direct the provider to deny the application unless the office determines, in its discretion, that approval of the application will not in any way jeopardize the health, safety or welfare of the children in the home;

(ii) where the criminal history record of an applicant to be an employee, assistant or volunteer at a group family day care home or Family day care home reveals a conviction for a crime other than one set forth in subparagraph (i) of paragraph (A) of this subdivision, the office of children and family services may, consistent with article twenty-three-a of the correction law, direct the provider to deny the application;

(iii) where the criminal history record of an applicant to be an employee, assistant or volunteer at a group family day care home or family day care home reveals a charge for any crime, the office of children and family services shall hold the application in abeyance until the charge is finally resolved.

(f) (i) Where the criminal history record of a current employee, assistant or volunteer at a group family day care home or family day care home reveals a conviction for a crime set forth in subparagraph (i) of paragraph (a) of this subdivision, the office of children and family services shall conduct a safety assessment of the program and take all appropriate steps to protect the health and safety of the children in the home. The office of children and family services shall direct the provider to terminate the employee, assistant or volunteer based on such a conviction, unless the office determines, in its discretion, that the continued presence of the employee, assistant or volunteer in the home will not in any way jeopardize the health, safety or welfare of the children in the home;

(ii) Where the criminal history record of a current employee, assistant or volunteer at a group family day care home or family day care home reveals a conviction for a crime other than one set forth in subparagraph (i) of paragraph (a) of this subdivision, the office of children and family services shall conduct a safety assessment of the home and take all appropriate steps to protect the health and safety of the children in the home. The office may direct the provider to terminate the employee, assistant or volunteer based on such a conviction, consistent with article twenty-three-a of the correction law;

(iii)   Where the criminal history record of a current employee, assistant or volunteer at a group family day care home or family day care home reveals a charge for any crime, the office of children and family services shall conduct a safety assessment of the home and take all appropriate steps to protect the health and safety of the children in the home.

(g)   Advise the provider that the individual has no criminal history record.

4.   Prior to making a determination to deny an application pursuant to subdivision three of this section, the office of children and family services shall afford the applicant an opportunity to explain, in writing, why the application should not be denied.

5.   Notwithstanding any other provision of law to the contrary, the office of children and family services, upon receipt of a criminal history record from the division of criminal justice services, may request, and is entitled to receive, information pertaining to any crime contained in such criminal history record from any state or local law enforcement agency, district attorney, parole officer, probation officer or court for the purposes of determining whether any ground relating to such criminal conviction or pending criminal charge exists for denying a license, registration, application or employment.

6.   The notification by the office of children and family services to the child day care provider pursuant to this section shall include a summary of the criminal history record, if any, provided by the division of criminal justice services.

7.   Where the office of children and family services directs a child day care provider to deny an application based on the criminal history record, the provider must notify the applicant that such record is the basis of the denial.

8.   Any safety assessment required pursuant to this section shall include a review of the duties of the individual, the extent to which such individual may have contact with children in the program or household and the status and nature of the criminal charge or conviction. Where the office of children and family services performs the safety assessment, it shall thereafter take all appropriate steps to protect the health and safety of children receiving care in the child day care center, school age child care program, family day care home or group family day care home.

9.   Any criminal history record provided by the division of criminal justice services, and any summary of the criminal history record provided by the office of children and family services to a child day care provider pursuant to this section, is confidential and shall not be available for public inspection; provided, however, nothing herein shall prevent a child day care provider or the office of children and family services from disclosing criminal history information at any administrative or judicial proceeding relating to the denial or revocation of an

application, employment, license or registration. The subject of a criminal history review conducted pursuant to this section shall be entitled to receive, upon written request, a copy of the summary of the criminal history record provided by the office of children and family services to the child day care provider. Unauthorized disclosure of such records or reports shall subject the provider to civil penalties in accordance with the provisions of subdivision eleven of section three hundred ninety of this title.

10.   A child day care provider shall advise the office of children and family services when an individual who is subject to criminal history record review in accordance with subdivision one or two of this section is no longer subject to such review. The office of children and family services shall inform the division of criminal justice services when an individual who is subject to criminal history review is no longer subject to such review so that the division of criminal justice services may terminate its retain processing with regard to such person. At least once a year, the office of children and family services will be required to conduct a validation of the records maintained by the division of criminal justice services.

Added by Laws 2000, Ch. 416 § 12, eff. Dec. 5, 2000.

§ 390-c.   Notice of pesticide applications.

1.   For the purposes of this section the following terms shall have the meanings set forth below:

(a)   "pesticide" shall have the same meaning as in subdivision thirty-five of section 33-0101 of the environmental conservation law.

(b)   "daycare facility" shall mean licensed and registered child daycare homes, programs and facilities.

2.   Each daycare facility shall be subject to the following notice requirements when pesticides are used at such facility:

(a)   A notice of each pesticide application shall be posted in a common area of the facility which is conspicuously visible to persons dropping off or picking up children from the facility. Such notice shall be posted not less than forty-eight hours prior to the pesticide application.

(b)   The notice required to be posted pursuant to paragraph (a) of this subdivision shall include at a minimum:

(i)   The location and specific date of the application at the daycare facility. In case of outdoor applications the notice must provide a specific date, and may include two alternative dates in case the application cannot be made due to weather conditions.

(ii)   The product name and pesticide registration number assigned by the United States environmental protection agency.

(iii)   The following statement "This notice is to inform you of a pending pesticide application at this facility. You may wish to discuss with a

SSL

representative of the daycare facility what precautions are being taken to protect your child from exposure to these pesticides. Further information about the product or products being applied, including any warnings that appear on the label of the pesticide or pesticides that are pertinent to the protection of humans, animals or the environment, can be obtained by calling the national pesticide telecommunications network information at 1-800-858-7378 or the New York state department of health center for environmental health info line at 1-800-458-1158".

(iv)   The name of a representative of the daycare facility and contact number for additional information.

(c)   For purposes of this section the following pesticide applications shall not be subject to the notification posting requirements:

(i)   the application of anti microbial pesticides and anti microbial products as defined by FIFRA in 7 U.S.C. § 136 (mm) and 136q (h) (2);

(ii)   the use of an aerosol product with a directed spray, in containers of eighteen fluid ounces, or less, when used to protect individuals from an imminent threat from stinging and biting insects including venomous spiders, bees, wasps and hornets. This section shall not exempt from notification the use of any fogger product or aerosol product that discharges to a wide area;

(iii)   any application where the daycare facility remains unoccupied for a continuous seventy-two hour period following the application of the pesticide;

(iv)   nonvolatile rodenticides in tamper resistant bait stations or in areas inaccessible to children;

(v)   silica gels and other nonvolatile ready-to-use, paste, foam or gel formulations of insecticides in areas inaccessible to children;

(vi)   nonvolatile insecticidal baits in tamper resistant bait stations or in areas inaccessible to children;

(vii)   application of a pesticide classified by the United States Environmental Protection Agency as an exempt material under section 40 CFR Part 152.25;

(viii)   boric acid and disodium octaborate tetrahydrate;

(ix)   the application of a pesticide which the United States Environmental Protection Agency has determined satisfies its reduced risk criteria, including a biopesticide; or

(x)   any emergency application of a pesticide when necessary to protect against an imminent threat to human health, provided however, that prior to any such emergency application, the person making such application shall make a good faith effort to supply the written notice required pursuant to this section. Upon making such an emergency application, the person making such application shall notify the commissioner of health, using a form developed by such commissioner for such purposes that shall include minimally the name of the person making the application, the pesticide business registration number or certified applicator number of the person making such application, the location and date of such application, the product name and USEPA registration number of the pesticide applied and the reason for such application. The commissioner of health shall review such form to ensure that the circumstance did warrant such emergency application. Such forms shall be kept on file at the department of health for three years from the date of application and shall be available to any individual upon request.

3.   Any person, other than a daycare facility, who contracts for the application of a pesticide at a daycare facility shall provide to such facility operator information required to be contained in the posting pursuant to subdivision two of this section at least forty-eight hours prior to such application.

4.   (a) Any daycare facility that violates the provisions of subdivision two of this section shall, for a first such violation of this section, in lieu of penalty, be issued a written warning and shall also be issued educational materials pursuant to subdivision two of section 33-1005 of the environmental conservation law. Such facility shall, however, for a second violation, be liable to the people of the state for a civil penalty not to exceed one hundred dollars, and not to exceed two hundred fifty dollars for any subsequent violation, such penalties to be assessed by the commissioner after a hearing or opportunity to be heard.

(b)   Any person who violates subdivision three of this section shall, for a first such violation of this section, in lieu of penalty, be issued a written warning, and shall also be issued educational materials pursuant to subdivision two of section 33-1005 of the environmental conservation law. Such person shall, however, for a second violation, be liable to the people of the state for a civil penalty not to exceed one hundred dollars, and not to exceed two hundred fifty dollars for any subsequent violation, such penalties to be assessed by the commissioner of environmental conservation after a hearing or opportunity to be heard.

Added by Laws 2000, Ch. 285 § 7, eff. July 1, 2001.

Editor's Note: Two new sections numbered 390-c were added by the Legislature in 2000; another § 390-c follows.

§ 390-c.   Additional powers and duties of the office of children and family services.

1.   The commissioner of children and family services is authorized and directed to promulgate necessary rules and regulations to ensure that, whenever a child day care provider is licensed or registered pursuant to section three hundred ninety of this article, the police department and fire department of the municipality wherein such licensee or registrant is authorized to operate and the state police shall be notified of the existence of the child day care center, its location and the fact that children are likely to be at that location in the event of an emergency. In those cases where the local municipality does not have a police department or a fire department, the sheriff of the appropriate county shall be notified in lieu thereof.

SSL

2. The commissioner of children and family services is authorized and directed to conduct a study to determine the best method of compiling an accurate and accessible central record of information regarding the safe operation of each day care center licensed or registered within the state. Such record should include but not be limited to complaints by parents or guardians, internal incident reports, reports by police or fire departments, local or state building code violations, any relevant information gathered from utility providers or other visitors to the day care center and any additional information held by another state or local agency regarding a day care provider or a day care center location which could affect safe operation of a day care center.

3. On or before the thirtieth day of June in the year next succeeding the year in which this section takes effect, the commissioner of children and family services shall report to the governor, the temporary president of the senate and the speaker of the assembly regarding the results of the study undertaken pursuant to subdivision two of this section.

Added by Laws 2000, Ch. 460 § 1, eff. Sept. 20, 2000.

§ 390-d. Requiring barriers to be placed around swimming pools and bodies of water on the grounds of family day care homes or group family day care homes.

1. For the purposes of this section the following terms shall have the meanings set forth below:

(a) "Grounds of a family day care home or group family day care home" shall mean in, on or within any building, structure or land contained within the real property boundary line of a family day care home or a group family day care home.

(b) "Swimming pool" shall mean any outdoor pool or tub intended for swimming, bathing or wading purposes.

(c) "Bodies of water" shall include, but not limited to, ponds, springs, streams, creeks, lakes, rivers and oceans.

(d) "Barriers" shall mean all fences, enclosures or other materials sufficient to form an obstruction to the free passage of persons through such materials.

2. (a) Any swimming pool or body of water located on the grounds of a family day care home or group family day care home shall be surrounded by a barrier sufficient to form an obstruction to the free passage of children through such barrier into such swimming pool or body of water. Such barrier shall be adequate to make such swimming pool or body of water inaccessible to children which, including gates thereto, shall be at least four feet high from the adjacent ground. All such gates shall include a locked barrier which shall be located at least four feet high above the adjacent ground or otherwise made inaccessible to children from the outside.

(b) Where a body of water is present and not wholly contained within the grounds of family day care home or group family day care home, the grounds of such home must be surrounded and enclosed by a barrier sufficient to make such body of water inaccessible to children.

(c) All pathways, walkways, decks or any other connecting entrance to such swimming pool or body of water shall be obstructed by a barrier sufficient to impede the free passage of children into or around the area immediately adjacent to such swimming pool or body of water.

(d) Swimming pools or bodies of water that are entirely covered by a solid object which is secured by sufficient weight, locking apparatus, and/or other device that would prevent a child in care from removing the solid object and accessing the swimming pool or body of water, shall be considered a sufficient barrier for the purposes of this section.

(e) As an alternative to surrounding the pool or other body of water located on the grounds of a family day care home or group family day care home with a barrier as described in paragraph (a) of this subdivision, the day care provider may use the property for day care if the provider bars access to such pool or other body of water by surrounding a part of the grounds not including such pool or other body of water with a barrier as described in paragraph (a) of this subdivision provided that:

(i) There is no unsecured means of egress from the home by which children could gain access to the pool or other body of water. For purposes of this paragraph, the day care provider may secure a door or other means of egress that is remotely located from the pool or other body of water by use of an alarm device or system that will alert the day care provider if the door or other means of egress is opened;

(ii) All children in care are directly and closely supervised by the provider or an assistant at all times the children are outside the home or other dwelling where the day care is provided; and

(iii) The parents or guardians of each child in care have submitted to the provider a written acknowledgment that the pool or other body of water exists, that a barrier as otherwise required by this section has not been provided, and that the children will have the potential for access to the pool or other body of water.

(f) Where a natural barrier or other obstacle located on the property lies between the pool or body of water and the building in which the family or group family day care is provided such that the natural barrier or other obstacle prevents access by children in care to the pool or body of water, a fence or additional barrier as otherwise required by this section shall not be required and the day care provider may use the property for day care provided that:

(i) There is no unsecured means of egress from the home by which children could gain access to the pool or other body of water. For purposes of this paragraph, the day care provider may secure a door or other means of egress that is remotely located from the pool or other body of water by use of an alarm device or system that will alert the day care provider if the door or other means of egress is opened;

(ii)   All children in care are directly and closely supervised by the provider or an assistant at all times the children are outside the home or other dwelling where the day care is provided; and

(iii)   The parents or guardians of each child in care have submitted to the provider a written acknowledgment that the pool or other body of water exists, that a barrier as otherwise required by this section has not been provided, and that the children will have the potential for access to the body of water.

In determining what constitutes a natural barrier or other obstacle for purposes of this paragraph, the presence of natural and artificial terrain features or constructs may be considered along with the distance between the building in which the family or group family day care is provided and the pool or body of water.

3.   Where a swimming pool or body of water is located on a property adjacent to a family or group family day home, the child day care provider must take suitable precautions to prevent the children in care from having access to the adjacent swimming pool or body of water, including taking any precautions specifically required by the office of children and family services to protect the safety of children receiving day care.

4.   Nothing in this section shall preclude local authorities with enforcement jurisdiction of the applicable sanitation, health, fire safety or building construction code from making appropriate inspections to assure compliance with such standards.

Added by L. 2001, Ch. 1, eff. July 1, 2002; **amended** by Laws 2004, Ch. 62, §§ 1, 2, eff. May 4, 2004.

§ 390-e   [Eff. April 1, 2007] Criminal history review; mentoring programs.

1.   For the purposes of this section, the following words shall have the following meanings:

(a)   "Prospective employee" shall mean a person being considered for employment by a mentoring program.

(b)   "Prospective mentor" shall mean an individual who is currently applying to volunteer to help a child or a group of children in a mentoring program for a period of time. Such help shall include, but not be limited to, being a positive role model for youth, building relationships with youth, and providing youth with academic assistance and exposure to new experiences and examples of opportunity that enhance the ability of children to become responsible adults.

(c)   "Mentoring program" shall mean a formalized program, operated by a corporation which has been incorporated pursuant to subparagraph five of paragraph (a) of section one hundred two of the not-for-profit corporation law or pursuant to subparagraph four of paragraph (a) of section one hundred two of the business corporation law, or operated by an educational institution or school district, that matches youth with adult volunteers with the purpose of providing such youth with positive role models to enhance their development.

(d) "Office" shall mean the office of children and family services.

2. Mentoring programs may perform a criminal history record check on all prospective employees and mentors.

3. Notwithstanding any other provision of law to the contrary, subject to the rules and regulations of the division of criminal justice services, mentoring programs may apply for a criminal history record check with the division of criminal justice services regarding any prospective employee or any prospective mentor who may engage in unsupervised activities with youth or in activities with youth in a setting without constant agency or parental oversight. Each mentoring program that chooses to complete such criminal background checks on prospective employees or on prospective mentors shall establish a policy for completing criminal background checks on such prospective employees or mentors. Such policy shall apply one uniform standard for the completion of criminal background checks for all prospective employees and one uniform standard for the completion of criminal background checks for all prospective mentors. Any mentoring program that chooses to complete criminal background checks on both prospective employees and prospective mentors may utilize the same uniform process for the completion of the criminal background checks on prospective employees and prospective mentors or they may choose one uniform process for prospective employees and another uniform process for prospective mentors.

4. Every mentoring program that chooses to apply for a criminal history background check with the division of criminal justice services shall obtain a set of fingerprints from each individual for whom a criminal background check is to be completed and such other information as is required by the office and the division of criminal justice services. For each prospective employee or mentor for whom the mentoring program completes a criminal background check, the mentoring program shall provide the applicant with blank fingerprint cards and a description of how the completed fingerprint card will be used upon submission to the mentoring program. The mentoring program shall promptly transmit such fingerprint card and the processing fee to the office. The office shall promptly submit the fingerprint card and the processing fee, imposed pursuant to subdivision eight-a of section eight hundred thirty-seven of the executive law, to the division of criminal justice services for its full search and retain processing.

5. Upon receipt of a criminal history record from the division of criminal justice services, the office shall promptly provide to the mentoring program the criminal history record, if any, with respect to the prospective employee or mentor, or a statement that the individual has no criminal history record.

6. Upon receipt of the results of a criminal background check pursuant to this section, the mentoring program shall determine whether or not the

SSL

prospective employee or mentor shall be offered employment or the opportunity to volunteer with the program. Such determination shall be made in accordance with the criteria established in section seven hundred fifty-two of the correction law.

7. Upon the request of any person previously convicted of one or more criminal offenses who has been denied employment pursuant to subdivision six of this section, the mentoring program shall provide, within thirty days of such request, a written statement setting forth the reasons for such denial. Any such person denied employment pursuant to subdivision six of this section shall be afforded the opportunities for enforcement available pursuant to section seven hundred fifty-five of the correction law.

8. Notwithstanding the provisions of this section, with the exception of a sex offense or a crime against a child, a custodial parent or guardian may sign a waiver authorizing a mentor to work with his or her child regardless of a criminal charge or crime related to a mentor. Such process shall only be initiated upon the consent of the prospective mentor, and be on a form and of a content to be developed by the office. Where applicable, a mentoring program may notify a custodial parent or guardian of his or her waiver right, but a waiver shall only be authorized by a custodial parent or guardian.

9. Any criminal history record provided to a mentoring program pursuant to this section shall be confidential pursuant to the applicable federal and state laws, rules and regulations, and shall not be published or in any way disclosed to persons other than authorized personnel, unless otherwise authorized by law.

10. Every mentoring program shall provide each custodial parent or guardian of every child participating in its mentoring program with a description of the kind of criminal background checks conducted by the mentoring program on its prospective employees and mentors. Such description shall include identification of the source utilized to obtain criminal background histories on prospective employees and mentors, a list of crimes that would lead the program to deny employment or the opportunity to volunteer as a prospective employee or mentor, and any other process utilized to determine whether or not a prospective employee or mentor with a conviction record shall be offered employment or the opportunity to volunteer. Such description shall clearly state whether or not prospective employees or mentors may be hired or offered the opportunity to volunteer despite the existence of a conviction history.

Added by laws 2006, Ch. 459, §2, eff. April 1, 2007.

§ 391. Violation; injunction.

Violations of any provision of this title may be prohibited by injunction. Whenever the commissioner has reason to believe that any provision of this title is being violated, or is about to be violated, he may maintain and prosecute, in the name of the people of this state, an action in the supreme court for the purpose of obtaining an injunction restraining such violation.

Notwithstanding any limitation of the civil practice law and rules, such court may, on motion and affidavit, and upon proof that such violation is one which reasonably may result in injury to any person, whether or not such person is a party to such action, grant a preliminary injunction or interlocutory injunction upon such terms as may be just. No security on the part of the people of this state shall be required.

    Added by Laws 1946, Ch. 349; **amended** by Laws 1962, Ch. 310; Laws 1964, Ch. 281, eff. Apr. 3, 1964.

§ 392   [Repealed, eff. Dec 21, 2005] Foster care status; periodic family court review.

    1.   As used in this section, unless otherwise expressly stated or unless the context requires a different interpretation:

    (a)   "foster care" shall mean care provided a child in a foster family free or boarding home, group home, agency boarding home, child care institution, health care facility or any combination thereof;

    (b)   "child" shall mean a child under the age of eighteen years for whom an authorized agency is providing foster care, except a child who is in the care of an authorized agency pursuant to court order under article seven, threethree, seven or ten of the family court act;

    (c)   "child freed for adoption" shall mean a child whose custody and guardianship has been committed to an authorized agency pursuant to section three hundred eighty-three-c, section three hundred eighty-four or section three hundred eighty-four-b of this title. Such category shall include a child whose parent or parents have died during the period in which the child was in foster care and for whom there is no surviving parent who would be entitled to notice or consent pursuant to section one hundred eleven or one hundred eleven-a of the domestic relations law. All cases of children freed for adoption shall be reviewed in accordance with section one thousand fifty-five-a of the family court act;

    (d)   "petition for adoption" shall mean a petition filed pursuant to title two of article seven of the domestic relations law;

    (e)   "permanency hearing" shall mean a hearing held in accordance with the provisions of this section for the purpose of reviewing the foster care status of the child and the appropriateness of the permanency plan developed by the authorized agency on behalf of such child.

    2.   Where an authorized agency determines that a child will remain in foster care for a continuous period of twelve months, a petition to review the foster care status, including the permanency plan of such child, together with a copy, if any, of the placement instrument:

    (a)   shall be filed in the family court by the authorized agency charged with the care and custody of such child;

SSL

(b)   may be filed by another authorized agency having the supervision of such foster care;

(c)   may be filed by the foster parent or parents in whose home the child resides or has resided during such period of twelve months. In the event that foster care of a child is discontinued and, within three months thereafter the child is again placed under the care of an authorized agency, the period during which the child was not in foster care shall not constitute an interruption of continuous foster care for the purposes of review pursuant to this section. However, such period shall not be considered to be part of any continuous period of foster care for the purposes of determining the length of time that a child may have been in foster care.

3.   Such petition:

(a)   shall be filed in the family court in the county in which the authorized agency charged with the care and custody of such child has its principal office or where the child resides;

(b)   shall set forth the disposition sought, including the permanency plan, and the grounds therefor;

(c)   shall, when filed by an authorized agency and notice is to be given to a parent, guardian or relative of the child, omit, for good cause shown, the name and address of the foster parent or parents with whom such child is residing at the time of the filing of the petition and the name and address of the biological parent or parents and, in lieu thereof, there shall be filed with such petition a verified schedule executed by such agency setting forth the name and address of such foster, or biological parent or parents;

(d)   shall be filed in the appropriate family court at least sixty days prior to the end of the month which would constitute the twelfth month of continuous foster care placement, or earlier where so directed by the court pursuant to section three hundred fifty-eight-a of this chapter; provided, however, that the court shall direct that such earlier petition shall be filed within thirty days of the date required for the next review of the family's service plan pursuant to section four hundred nine-e of this article.

4.   Notice of the hearing, including a statement of the dispositional and permanency alternatives of the court, shall be given and a copy of the petition shall be served upon the following, each of whom shall be a party entitled to participate in the proceeding:

(a)   the authorized agency charged with the care and custody, of such child, if such authorized agency is not the petitioner;

(b)   the authorized agency having supervision of such foster care, if such authorized agency is not the petitioner;

(c)   the foster parent or parents in whose home the child resided or resides at or after the expiration of a continuous period of twelve months in foster care;

(d)   the child's parent or guardian who transferred the care and custody of such child temporarily to an authorized agency, but, for purposes of this subdivision, shall not include a parent or guardian who has surrendered or who has had his or her parental rights terminated with respect to such child;

(e)   a person to whom a parent entrusted the care of the child, where such person transferred the care and custody of the child temporarilyto an authorized agency, but, for purposes of this subdivision, shall not include such person when such parent has surrendered or has had his or her parental rights terminated with respect to such child;

(f)   Repealed

(g)   the child or the child's law guardian who represented the child in the most recent proceeding pursuant to this section or section three hundred fifty-eight-a or three hundred eighty-four-b of this act;

(h)   such other person as the court may, in its discretion, direct; and

(i)   a foster parent caring for the child or any pre-adoptive parent or relative providing care for the child shall be provided with notice of any permanency hearing held pursuant to this section by the authorized agency or the foster parent filing the petition to review the foster care status of the child. Such foster parent, pre-adoptive parent or relative shall also be afforded an opportunity to be heard at any permanency hearing; provided, however, no such foster parent, pre-adoptive parent or relative providing care for the child, except for those persons set forth in paragraphs (c), (e), (f) or (h) of this subdivision, shall be a party solely on the basis of such notice or opportunity to be heard. The failure of the foster parent, pre-adoptive parent, or relative caring for the child to appear at a permanency hearing shall constitute a waiver of the opportunity to be heard and such failure to appear shall not cause a delay of the permanency hearing nor shall such failure to appear be a ground for the invalidation of any order issued by the court pursuant to this section.

4-a.   If a law guardian had been appointed by the family court in a proceeding pursuant to this section or section three hundred fifty-eight-a, three hundred eighty-three-c, three hundred eighty-four or three hundred eighty-four-b of this chapter, the appointment of the law guardian shall continue without further court order or appointment, unless another appointment of a law guardian has been made by the court. All notices and reports required by law shall be provided to such law guardian. The law guardian may be relieved of his or her representation upon application to the court for termination of the appointment. Upon approval of the application, the court shall immediately appoint another law guardian to whom all notices and reports required by law shall be provided.

5.   Unless the court grants an order to show cause to be served in lieu of a notice of the hearing and the petition, service of notice of the hearing and the petition shall be made at least twenty days before the date of said hearing in such manner and on such notice as the court may, in its discretion, prescribe; provided, however, that where the court prescribes service by mail, such service shall be

made by registered mail or certified mail, return receipt requested. If service cannot be made in the manner prescribed by the court, the court may prescribe an alternative method of service. A permanency hearing shall take place within twelve months of the date the child entered foster care. Notwithstanding any other provision to the contrary, for the purposes of this section, the date the child entered foster care shall be sixty days after the date the child was removed from his or her home.

5-a. In reviewing the foster care status of the child and in determining its order of disposition, the court shall consider and determine in its order, among other things:

(a) the appropriateness of the permanency plan, including but not limited to, whether and when the child: (i) will be returned to the parent; (ii) should be placed for adoption with the commissioner of social services filing a petition for termination of parental rights; (iii) should be referred for legal guardianship; (iv) should be placed permanently with a fit and willing relative; or (v) should be placed in another planned permanent living arrangement if the commissioner of social services has documented to the court a compelling reason for determining that it would not be in the best interest of the child to return home, be referred for termination of parental rights and placed for adoption, placed with a fit and willing relative, or placed with a legal guardian;

(b) what services have been offered to strengthen and re-unite the family except as provided in paragraph (d) of this subdivision and subdivision six-a of this section;

(c) where return home of the child is not likely, what efforts have been or should be made to evaluate or plan for other modes of care except as provided in paragraph (d) of this subdivision;

(d), (e) Repealed

(f) any further efforts which have been or will be made to promote the best interests of the child;

(g) where appropriate, reasonable efforts were made to make it possible for the child to safely return to his or her home, or if the permanency plan for the child is adoption, guardianship or some other permanent living arrangement other than reunification with the parent or parents of the child, reasonable efforts are being made to make and finalize such alternate permanent placement;

(h) in the case of a child who has attained the age of sixteen, the services needed, if any, to assist the child to make the transition from foster care to independent living; and

(i) in the case of a child placed outside this state, whether the out-of-state placement continues to be appropriate and in the best interests of the child.

For the purposes of this section, in determining reasonable efforts to be made with respect to a child, and in making such reasonable efforts, the child's health and safety shall be the paramount concern.

5-b.　In any proceeding under this section, the provisions and limitations of article thirty-one of the civil practice law and rules shall apply to the extent that they do not conflict with the specific provisions of this section. In determining any motion for a protective order, the court shall consider the need of the party for the discovery to assist in the preparation of the case and any potential harm to the child from the discovery. The court shall set a schedule for discovery to avoid unnecessary delay.

6.　At the conclusion of such hearing, the court shall, upon the proof adduced, in accordance with the best interest of the child, enter an order of disposition:

(a)　directing that foster care of the child be continued for a period of up to one year, and may direct the official or agency having temporary care and custody of the child to have the child reside in a specific foster home; or

(b)　in the case of a child whose care and custody have been transferred temporarily to an authorized agency directing that the child be returned to the parent, guardian or relative, or directing that the child be placed in the custody of a relative or other suitable person or persons; or

(c)　in the case of a child whose care and custody have been transferred temporarily to an authorized agency directing any agency specified in subdivision four of this section to institute a proceeding, pursuant to section three hundred eighty-four-b of this chapter, to legally free such child for adoption, if the court finds reasonable cause to believe that grounds therefor exist. Upon a failure by such agency to institute such proceeding within ninety days after entry of such order, the court shall permit the foster parent or parents in whose home the child resides to institute such a proceeding unless the agency, for good cause shown and upon due notice to all parties to the proceeding, has obtained a modification or extension of such order, or unless the court has reasonable cause to believe that such foster parent or parents would not obtain approval of their petition to adopt the child in a subsequent adoption proceeding;

(d)　in any case where the court determines that reasonable efforts are not required because of one of the grounds set forth in paragraph (b) of subdivision three of section three hundred fifty-eight-a of this chapter, the court may in its discretion direct the authorized agency to commence a proceeding to terminate parental rights and free the child for adoption;

(e)　in regard to an order issued in accordance with paragraph (a), (b), or (c) of this subdivision, such order shall also include, at the least:

(i)　a description of the visitation plan;

(ii)　a direction that the respondent or respondents shall be notified of the planning conference or conferences to be held pursuant to subdivision three of section four hundred nine-e of this chapter; of their right to attend the conference, and of their right to have counsel or other representative with them.

A copy of the court's order and the service plan shall be given to the respondent. The order shall also contain a notice that if the child remains in foster

SSL

care for more than fifteen of the most recent twenty-two months, the agency may be required by law to file a petition to terminate parental rights.

An order of disposition entered pursuant to this subdivision shall, except as provided for in subdivision six-a of this section, include a determination where appropriate, that reasonable efforts were made to make it possible for the child to return to his or her home, and, in the case of a child who has attained the age of sixteen, a determination of the services needed, if any, to assist the child to make the transition from foster care to independent living, and, in the case of a child placed outside New York state, whether the out-of-state placement continues to be appropriate and in the best interests of the child, and the court's findings supporting its determination that such order is in accordance with the best interest of the child. If the court promulgates separate findings of fact or conclusions of law, or an opinion in lieu thereof, the order of disposition may incorporate such findings and conclusions, or opinions, by reference.

6-a.   For the purpose of this section, reasonable efforts to make it possible for the child to return safely to his or her home shall not be required where the court determines that:

(a)   the parent of such child has subjected the child to aggravated circumstances, as defined in subdivision twelve of section three hundred fifty-eight-a of this chapter;

(b)   the parent of such child has been convicted of (i) murder in the first degree as defined in section 125.27 or murder in the second degree as defined in section 125.25 of the penal law and the victim was another child of the parent; or (ii) manslaughter in the first degree as defined in section 125.20 or manslaughter in the second degree as defined in section 125.15 of the penal law and the victim was another child of the parent, provided, however, that the parent must have acted voluntarily in committing such crime;

(c)   the parent of such child has been convicted of an attempt to commit any of the foregoing crimes, and the victim or intended victim was the child or another child of the parent; or has been convicted of criminal solicitation as defined in article one hundred, conspiracy as defined in article one hundred five or criminal facilitation as defined in article one hundred fifteen of the penal law for conspiring, soliciting or facilitating any of the foregoing crimes, and the victim or intended victim was the child or another child of the parent;

(d)   the parent of such child has been convicted of assault in the second degree as defined in section 120.05, assault in the first degree as defined in section 120.10 or aggravated assault upon a person less than eleven years old as defined in section 120.12 of the penal law, and the commission of one of the foregoing crimes resulted in serious physical injury to the child or another child of the parent;

(e)   the parent of such child has been convicted in any other jurisdiction of an offense which includes all of the essential elements of any crime specified in paragraph (b), (c) or (d) of this subdivision, and the victim of such offense was the child or another child of the parent; or

(f)   the parental rights of the parent to a sibling of such child have been involuntarily terminated;

unless the court determines that providing reasonable efforts would be in the best interests of the child, not contrary to the health and safety of the child, and would likely result in the reunification of the parent and the child in the foreseeable future. The court shall state such findings in its order.

If the court determines that reasonable efforts are not required because of one of the grounds set forth above, a permanency hearing shall be held within thirty days of the finding of the court that such efforts are not required. At the permanency hearing, the court shall determine the appropriateness of the permanency plan prepared by the social services official which shall include whether or when the child: (i) will be returned to the parent; (ii) should be placed for adoption with the social services official filing a petition for termination of parental rights; (iii) should be referred for legal guardianship; (iv) should be placed permanently with a fit and willing relative; or (v) should be placed in another planned permanent living arrangement if the social services official has documented to the court a compelling reason for determining that it would not be in the best interest of the child to return home, be referred for termination of parental rights and placed for adoption, placed with a fit and willing relative, or placed with a legal guardian. The social services official shall thereafter make reasonable efforts to place the child in a timely manner and to complete whatever steps are necessary to finalize the permanent placement of the child as set forth in the permanency plan approved by the court. If reasonable efforts are determined by the court not to be required because of one of the grounds set forth in this paragraph, the social services official may file a petition for termination of parental rights in accordance with section three hundred eighty-four-b of this chapter.

For the purpose of this section, in determining reasonable effort to be made with respect to a child, and in making such reasonable efforts, the child's health and safety shall be the paramount concern.

For the purpose of this section, a sibling shall include a half-sibling.

7.   The court may make an order of protection in assistance or as a condition of any other order made under this section. The order of protection may set forth reasonable conditions of behavior to be observed for a specified time by a person or agency who is before the court.

8.   The court may make an order directing an authorized agency to undertake diligent efforts to encourage and strengthen the parental relationship when it finds such efforts will not be detrimental to the best interests of the child and there has been no prior court finding that such efforts are not required. Such order may include a specific plan of action for the authorized agency including, without

SSL

limitation, requirements that such agency assist the parent in obtaining adequate housing, employment, counseling, medical care or psychiatric treatment.

9. The court shall possess continuing jurisdiction in proceedings under this section and, in the case of children who are continued in foster care, shall rehear the matter whenever it deems necessary or desirable, or upon petition by any party entitled to notice in proceedings under this section, but at least every twelve months following the preceding permanency hearing.

10. [*Repealed.*]

Added by Laws 1971, Ch. 97, former § 392 **added** by Laws 1970, Ch. 742, **repealed** by Laws 1971, Ch. 97; **amended** by Laws 1972, Ch. 940; Laws 1973, Ch. 804; Laws 1974, Ch. 1057; Laws 1975, Ch. 342; Laws 1975, Ch. 708; Laws 1975, Ch. 710; Laws 1976, Ch. 667, Ch. 666; **amended** by Laws 1978, Ch. 441, eff. June 19, 1978; **amended** by Laws 1982, Ch. 920, eff. July 1, 1983; **amended** by Laws 1983, Ch. 141, eff. May 23, 1983; **amended** by Laws 1985, Ch. 141, eff. Aug. 3, 1985; **amended** by Laws 1985, Ch. 808, eff. Nov. 1, 1985; **amended** by Laws 1986, Ch. 902, eff. Aug. 5, 1986; **amended** by Laws 1987 Ch. 461, eff. Aug. 26, 1987; **amended** by Laws 1988, Ch. 638, §§ 5, 6, eff. Jan. 1, 1989; **amended** by Laws 1989, Ch. 744 § 3, eff. July 24, 1989; **amended** by Laws 1990, Ch. 867, § 3, eff. Sept. 1, 1990; **amended** by Laws 1991, Ch. 48, § 4, eff. Apr. 12, 1991; **amended** by Laws 1991, Ch. 198, §§ 11, 12, 13, eff. June 28, 1991; **amended** by Laws 1993, Ch. 87, § 4, eff. June 1, 1993; **amended** by Laws 1995, Ch. 454, §§ 5–8, eff. Oct. 1, 1995; **amended** by L. 1997, Ch. 353, §§ 5 and 6, eff. Nov. 3, 1997; **amended** by Laws 1999, Ch. 7, §§ 15–24, **adding** para. (6-a), eff. Feb. 11, 1999 and by Ch. 534, §§ 3–7, eff. Dec. 27, 1999; **amended** by Laws 2000, Ch. 145, § 6, eff. July 1, 2000; **amended** by Laws 2002, Ch. 663, §§ 12-16, and § 17, adding subd. 6, par. (c), and re-lettering pars. (h) and (i) to (d) and (e), eff. Dec. 3, 2002; L. 2005, Ch. 3, sect; 59 (Part A), eff. Aug. 23, 2005.

TITLE 1-A—STATE COMMISSION ON THE QUALITY OF FOSTER CARE

Section 393.   **State commission on the quality of foster care; organization.**
       393-a.   **Chairman of the commission.**
       393-b.   **Functions, powers and duties of the commission.**

§ 393. State commission on the quality of foster care; organization.

1. There shall be a state commission on the quality of foster care within the executive department. It shall consist of five persons appointed by the governor by and with the consent of the senate. Of the five appointees, at least three shall have demonstrated expertise in the care and treatment of children in the foster care system. The members of the commission, except for the chairman who shall devote full time to his or her duties, shall receive no compensation for their services but shall be reimbursed for expenses actually and necessarily incurred in the performance of their duties within appropriations made available therefore.

2. The members shall hold office for terms of five years; provided that of the members first appointed, two shall serve for a term of two years and three

shall serve for a term of five years from January first next succeeding his or her appointment. Any member of the commission may be removed by the governor for cause.

3. Any member chosen to fill a vacancy created other than by expiration of a term shall be appointed for the unexpired term of the member he or she is to succeed. Vacancies caused by expiration of term or otherwise shall be filled in the same manner as original appointments.

Added by Laws 2002, Ch. 83, Part C, § 19, eff. May 29, 2002.

§ 393-a.　Chairman of the commission.

1. The chairman shall be the chief executive officer of the commission.

2. The chairman may appoint such assistants, officers and employees, committees and consultants for the commission as may be determined to be necessary, prescribe their powers and duties, fix their compensation and provide for reimbursement of their expenses within amounts appropriated therefore.

3. The chairman may, from time to time, create, abolish, transfer and consolidate bureaus and other units within the commission not expressly established by law as may be determined necessary for the efficient operation of the commission subject to the approval of the director of the budget.

4. The chairman may request, and shall receive upon request from any department, division, board, bureau, commission or other agency of the state or any political subdivision thereof or any public authority such assistance, information, and data as will enable the commission properly to carry out its functions, powers and duties.

Added by Laws 2002, Ch. 83, Part C, § 19, eff. May 29, 2002.

§ 393-b.　Functions, powers and duties of the commission.

The commission shall have the following functions, powers and duties regarding congregate foster care programs, which are defined for the purposes of this section, as agency operated boarding homes, group homes, group residences and institutions licensed by the office of children and family services:

1. Investigate those complaints that are brought to the commission's attention in writing, through interviews, or as a result of on site monitoring regarding the quality of care provided to foster children in congregate foster care programs that are determined to warrant investigation. The commission shall establish procedures for the timely receipt and effective investigation of such complaints, which may include, but not be limited to: visiting, inspecting or conducting other on site monitoring activities at congregate foster care programs; and conducting any necessary interviews of foster care providers, employees of congregate foster care programs, and foster children and their families.

SSL

2. The commission may obtain from the office of children and family services copies of those preliminary and final reports completed by the office pursuant to section four hundred twenty four-c of this article.

3. The commission may obtain from the office of children and family services copies of fatality reports issued by the office pursuant to subdivision five of section twenty of this chapter and copies of preliminary and final reports issued by a fatality review team pursuant to section four hundred twenty two b of this article regarding foster children in the congregate foster care program.

4. The commission shall notify the office of children and family services of any investigation, visit or inspection. The commission shall make findings concerning the matters referred to its attention and, where it deems appropriate, make a report of the final results of the investigation including any recommendations of the commission. Such report and recommendations shall be provided to the office of children and family services and the congregate foster care program. The office of children and family services shall retain the authority and responsibility to determine whether any regulatory violations have occurred and to require any appropriate preventive or remedial action, issue any fiscal penalties, or take any necessary enforcement action against a congregate foster care program or a social services district.The office of children and family services shall provide the commission with a written report of any actions taken regarding each of the commission's recommendations.

5. Establish standards for the provision of training to commission employees charged with investigating complaints under this section. Such standards shall include, but are not limited to:

(a) basic training in the principles and techniques of investigation, including relationships with other investigative bodies;

(b) legal issues in child protection including the legal rights of children and their families, and of employees and volunteers of congregate foster care programs;

(c) methods of identifying, remediating, treating and preventing child abuse and maltreatment;

(d) safety and security procedures; and

(e) the principles of child development, the characteristics of children in foster care, and techniques of group and child management including crisis intervention. 6. Make an annual report to the governor and the legislature concerning its work under this section during the previous year. Such report shall include, but not be limited to: non identifying information regarding the types of investigations completed by the commission, the results of such investigations and any recommendations of the commission to improve the foster care system.

7. Accept, with the approval of the governor, as agent of the state, any grant, including federal grants, or any gift for any of the purposes of this title.

8. Within amounts appropriated, enter into contracts with any person, firm, corporation, municipality or governmental agency for the performance of functions authorized by law.

9. The commission, any member or any employee designated by the commission, shall have access to any congregate foster care program and to such information, books, reports, records and data maintained by the office of children and family services, social services districts or congregate foster care programs deemed necessary for carrying out the commission's functions, powers and duties under this section. Information, books, reports, records and data which are confidential as provided by law shall be kept confidential by the commission, its members and employees and any limitations on the release thereof imposed by law upon the party furnishing the information, books, reports, records or data shall also apply to the commission, its members and employees.

Added by Laws 2002, Ch. 83, Part C, § 19, eff. May 29, 2002.

SSL

SOCIAL SERVICES LAW

TITLE 2—POWERS AND DUTIES OF PUBLIC WELFARE OFFICIALS

§ 395. Responsibility of public welfare districts for the welfare of children.

A public welfare district shall be responsible for the welfare of children who are in need of public assistance and care, support and protection, residing or found in its territory, insofar as not inconsistent with the jurisdiction of a family court. Such assistance and care shall be administered either directly by the public welfare official charged therewith, or by another public welfare official acting on his behalf by and pursuant to the provisions of this chapter, or through an authorized agency as defined by this chapter.

Amended by Laws 1946, Ch. 200; Laws 1965, Ch. 23, eff. Mar. 31, 1965.

§ 396. Health and welfare services to all children.

All public welfare districts and towns shall provide children who attend schools other than public with all or any of the health and welfare services and facilities, including but not limited to health, surgical, medical, dental and therapeutic care and treatment, and corrective aids and appliances, authorized by law and now granted or hereafter made available by the public welfare district or districts and/or towns for or to children in the public schools in so far as these services and facilities may be requested by the authorities of the schools other than public.

Any such services or facilities shall be so provided notwithstanding any provision of any charter or other provision of law inconsistent herewith.

    Amended by Laws 1941, Ch. 936, eff. May 1, 1941.

§ 397.   Powers and duties of social services officials in relation to children.

All social services officials responsible for the administration of safety net assistance to families shall, in relation to all children in such families other than delinquent children, persons in need of supervision, mentally disabled children, physically handicapped children and children born out of wedlock who shall be cared for under the provisions of the following section, have powers and perform duties as follows:

    1.   As to destitute children:

    (a)   Investigate the family circumstances of each child reported as destitute in order to determine what care, supervision or treatment, if any, such child requires.

    (b)   Administer and supervise relief to families with destitute children when such families are unable to care for such children and relief is necessary to prevent the separation of children from their parents.

    (c)   Furnish children, whose parents or guardians are unable to do so, with suitable clothing, shoes, books, food and other necessaries to enable them to attend upon instruction as required by law.

    2.   As to neglected and abused children:

    (a)   Investigate complaints of neglect and abuse of children and offer protective social services to prevent injury to the child, to safeguard his welfare, and to preserve and stabilize family life wherever possible.

    (b)   Bring such case when necessary before the family court for adjudication.

    (c)   Institute proceedings in a court of competent jurisdiction against a parent or adult for neglect or abuse of a child.

    3.   Provide any necessary medical or hospital care for such children when responsible for the provision of such care under section sixty-nine.

    4.   The provisions of this section shall not be deemed to confer on social services officials responsible only for the authorization of safety net assistance or of safety net assistance and hospital care, any powers and duties in relation to destitute and neglected children except as follows:

    (a)   As to destitute children:

    (1)   Authorize relief to families with destitute children when such families are unable to care for such children and relief is necessary to prevent the separation of children from their parents.

(2) Furnish children, whose parents or guardians are unable to do so, with suitable clothing, shoes, books, food and other necessaries to enable them to attend upon instruction as required by law.

(b) As to neglected and abused children:

Report to the county commissioner any complaint they may receive of neglect and abuse of children.

(c) Provide any necessary medical care or hospital care for such children when responsible for the provision of such care under section sixty-nine.

Amended by Laws 1946, Ch. 200; Laws 1962, Ch. 690; Laws 1972, Ch. 270, eff. May 9, 1972; **amended** by Laws 1985, Ch. 491, eff. July 24, 1985; **amended** by Laws 1997, Ch. 436, § 1 Part B, § 100, eff. Aug. 20, 1997.

§ 398. Additional powers and duties of commissioners of public welfare and certain city public welfare officers in relation to children.

Commissioners of public welfare and city public welfare officers responsible under the provisions of a special or local law for the children hereinafter specified shall have powers and perform duties as follows:

1. As to destitute children: assume charge of and provide support for any destitute child who cannot be properly cared for in his home.

2. As to neglected, abused or abandoned children:

(a) Investigate the alleged neglect, abuse or abandonment of a child, offer protective social services to prevent injury to the child, to safeguard his welfare, and to preserve and stabilize family life wherever possible and, if necessary, bring the case before the family court for adjudication and care for the child until the court acts in the matter and, in the case of an abandoned child, shall promptly petition the family court to obtain custody of such child.

(b) Receive and care for any child alleged to be neglected, abused or abandoned who is temporarily placed in his care by the family court pending adjudication by such court of the alleged neglect, abuse or abandonment including the authority to establish, operate, maintain and approve facilities for such purpose in accordance with the regulations of the department; and receive and care for any neglected, abused or abandoned child placed or discharged to his care by the family court.

(c) Any facility designated as of the effective date of this act shall not be disapproved except after consultation with the designating appellate division.

(d) The local social services department shall list all facilities approved under this article for the temporary custody and care of children remanded by the family court and shall file a copy of that list periodically with the clerk of the family court in each county in the judicial district in which the facility is located.

(e) Report to the local registrar of vital statistics of the district in which the child was found the sex, color, approximate date of birth, place of finding, and

SSL

the name assigned to any child who may be found whose parents are unknown, within ten days whenever possible after the child is found, on a form prescribed therefor by the state commissioner of health, and report the subsequent identification of any such child to the state commissioner of health; provided, however, that in the city of New York such form shall be prescribed by, and such report shall be made to, the department of health.

(f) Report to the local criminal justice agency and to the statewide central register for missing children as described in section eight hundred thirty-seven-e of the executive law such information as required on a form prescribed by the commissioner of the division of criminal justice services within forty-eight hours after an abandoned child is found.

3. As to delinquent children and persons in need of supervision:

(a) Investigate complaints as to alleged delinquency of a child.

(b) Bring such case of alleged delinquency when necessary before the family court.

(c) Receive within fifteen days from the order of placement as a public charge any delinquent child committed or placed or person in need of supervision placed in his or her care by the family court provided, however, that the commissioner of the social services district with whom the child is placed may apply to the state commissioner or his or her designee for approval of an additional fifteen days, upon written documentation to the office of children and family services that the youth is in need of specialized treatment or placement and the diligent efforts by the commissioner of social services to locate an appropriate placement.

4. As to mentally disabled and physically handicapped children:

(a) Obtain admission to state and other suitable schools, hospitals, other institutions, or care in their own homes or in family free or boarding homes or in agency boarding homes or group homes for such children in accordance with the provisions of the mental hygiene law, education law and acts relating to the family court.

(b) Maintain supervision over such disabled or physically handicapped children as are not in institutions, hospitals or schools or under the jurisdiction of the family court.

5. As to children born out of wedlock:

(a) Provide care in a family free or boarding home, in an agency boarding home or group home or in an institution for any child born out of wedlock and for his mother as for any other person in need of public assistance and care during pregnancy and during and after delivery, when in the judgment of such social services official needed care cannot be provided in the mother's own home. However, nothing in this section or elsewhere in this chapter contained shall be construed to make any such child or his mother ineligible for such care away from home, regardless of ability or liability to pay therefor; provided, however, that except as hereinafter provided, it shall rest in the discretion of the social services official, in view of all the facts and circumstances present in each case, to determine whether or not to require such mother, or any other person or persons liable by law to contribute to the support thereof, to pay all or any part of such cost, pursuant to the provisions of this section or any other section of this chapter. Any inconsistent provision of law notwithstanding, the acceptance by a private authorized adoption agency of an absolute surrender of a child born out of wedlock from the mother of such child shall relieve her from any and all liability for the support of such child. When in the judgment of a social services official needed care cannot be provided in the home of a minor pregnant with an out of wedlock child, and he has made a determination pursuant to subdivision one of section one hundred thirty-two of this chapter not to make an investigation of the circumstances of such minor and not to require support from persons liable therefor, the authorization of such social services official of necessary medical care for such minor shall have the same force and effect as a consent executed by a parent or guardian of such minor.

(b) Institute proceedings to establish paternity and secure the support and education of any child born out of wedlock or make a compromise with the father of such child, in accordance with the provisions of law, relating to children born out of wedlock.

(c) Hold and disburse the money received from such a compromise or pay it to the mother if she gives security for the support of the child.

(d) When practicable, require the mother to contribute to the support of the child.

6. As to all foregoing classes of children:

(a) Investigate the family circumstances of each child reported to him as destitute, neglected, abused, delinquent, disabled or physically handicapped in order to determine what assistance and care, supervision or treatment, if any, such child requires.

(b) Provide for expert mental and physical examination of any child whom he has reason to suspect of mental or physical disability or disease and pay for such examination from public funds, if necessary.

(c) Provide necessary medical or surgical care in a suitable hospital, sanatorium, preventorium or other institution or in his own home for any child needing such care and pay for such care from public funds, if necessary. However, in the case of a child or minor who is eligible to receive care as medical assistance for needy persons pursuant to title eleven of article five of this chapter, such care shall be provided pursuant to the provisions of that title.

(d) Ascertain the financial ability of the parents of children who become public charges and collect toward the expense of such child's care such sum as the parents are able to pay.

(e)   Collect from parents whose children have been discharged to his care by the family court such sums as they are ordered to pay for the maintenance of such children and report any failure to comply with such order to such court.

(f)   When in his judgment it is advisable for the welfare of the child, accept the surrender of a child by an instrument in writing in accordance with the provisions of this chapter. Any inconsistent provision of law notwithstanding, the acceptance by the social services official of a surrender of a child born out of wedlock from the mother or father of such child shall relieve the parent executing such surrender from any and all liability for the support of such child.

(g)   (1) Place children in suitable instances in family homes, agency boarding homes or group homes or institutions under the proper safeguards, either directly or through an authorized agency, except that, direct placements in agency boarding homes or group homes may be made by the social services official only if the department shall have authorized him or her to operate such homes in accordance with the provisions of section three hundred seventy-four-b of this chapter and only if suitable care is not otherwise available through an authorized agency under the control of persons of the same religious faith as the child. Where such official places a child in an agency boarding home, group home or institution, either directly or through an authorized agency, the official shall certify in writing to the department that such placement was made because it offers the most appropriate and least restrictive level of care and is more appropriate than a family foster home placement or that such placement is necessary because there are no qualified foster families available to the district. If the number of placements in agency boarding homes, group homes or institutions because of a lack of foster parents so warrants in any district, the department shall assist such district to recruit and train foster parents. Placements shall be made only in institutions located in this state or in such institutions located in an adjoining state as are maintained by a corporation organized under the laws of this state and having authority to maintain an institution for the care of children. However, all placements shall be made in institutions visited, inspected and supervised in accordance with title three of article seven of this chapter and conducted in conformity with the applicable regulations of the supervising state agency in accordance with title three of article seven of this chapter. With the approval of the department, a social services district may place a child in its care and custody or its custody and guardianship in federally funded job corps program and may receive reimbursement for the approved costs of appropriate program administration and supervision pursuant to a plan developed by the department and approved by the director of the budget.

(2)   A social services district may place a child in its care and custody or its custody and guardianship in a home or facility operated or licensed by any office of the department of mental hygiene, subject to the relevant provisions of the mental hygiene law and the admission criteria of the facility. The director of the budget may authorize such transfers of appropriations under the provisions of section fifty of the state finance law as may be necessary to secure federal reimbursement for such placements.

(3) (i) Effective sixty days after the enactment of this subparagraph, there is hereby established within a social services district with a population in excess of two million a two-year demonstration project which affords authorized agencies with which foster children are placed enhanced administrative flexibility. Pursuant to such demonstration project, an authorized agency with which the social services district has placed a child shall have the authority to:

(A) give all necessary consents to the discharge of the child from foster care when such authorized agency has submitted a written request for approval of such discharge to the social services official and the social services official has not disapproved such discharge within thirty days of receiving such request;

(B) change a goal for the child when such authorized agency has submitted a written request for approval of such change of goal to the social services official and the social services official has not disapproved such goal within thirty days of receiving such request;

(C) commence a proceeding to free the child for adoption when such authorized agency has submitted a written request for approval of the commencement of such proceeding to the social services official, if the social services official has not disapproved such commencement within thirty days of receiving such request, in which case such a request shall be deemed approved; and

(D) consent to the adoption of a child whose custody and guardianship, or of a child where such child's parents are both deceased, or where one parent is deceased and the other parent is not entitled to notice pursuant to sections one hundred eleven and one hundred eleven-a of the domestic relations law, and whose care and custody, has been transferred to a social services district and who has been placed by the social services official with the authorized agency when the authorized agency has submitted a written request for approval to consent to the adoption, if the social services district has not disapproved the request to consent to adoption within sixty days after its submission, in which case such request shall be deemed approved and the authorized agency may give all necessary consent to the adoption of the child.

(ii) Nothing herein shall result in the transfer of care and custody or custody and guardianship of a child from the social services official to the authorized agency.

(iii) Within three months of the conclusion of the demonstration project, such social services district shall issue a report to the department regarding the effectiveness of the demonstration project. Such report shall include recommendations for possible statutory and regulatory amendments in relation to the administration of foster care.

(4) A social services district may place a child in its care and custody or its custody and guardianship in a family home certified by the division for youth, which shall not include a group home. Such placements shall be subject to the relevant provisions of this chapter, the executive law and the admission criteria of the home.

(h)   Supervise children who have been cared for away from their families until such children become twenty-one years of age or until they are discharged to their own parents, relatives within the third degree or guardians, or adopted, provided, however, that in the case of a child who is developmentally disabled as such term is defined in section 1.03 of the mental hygiene law, emotionally disturbed or physically handicapped, and who is receiving care in a group home, agency boarding home or any child care facility operated by an authorized agency with a capacity of thirteen or more children, and who is in receipt of educational services and under the care and custody of a local department of social services, the commissioner of the office of children and family services shall allow such child who reaches the age of twenty-one during the period commencing on the first day of September and ending on the thirtieth day of June to be entitled to continue in such program until the thirtieth day of June or until the termination of the school year, whichever shall first occur.

(i)   Provide care in an institution, agency boarding home, or family free or boarding home for any destitute minor between sixteen and eighteen years of age who cannot be properly cared for in his own home, either directly or through authorized agencies, except that, direct placements in agency boarding homes may be made by the social services official only if the department shall have authorized him to operate such homes in accordance with the provisions of section three hundred seventy-four-b of this chapter and only if suitable care is not otherwise available through an authorized agency under the control of persons of the same religious faith as the child. Such care may be continued after the eighteenth birthday of the minor and until he is discharged from care or becomes twenty-one years of age.

(j)   Permit children and minors who are being cared for away from their own homes as public charges to retain the maximum amount of their monthly earned income for future identifiable needs in accordance with the regulations of the department and consistent with the federal law applicable to the treatment of income and resources under the aid to families with dependent children program.

(k)   In accordance with regulations of the department, provide suitable vocational training through any institution licensed or approved by the state education department, for any minor in his care who demonstrates to his satisfaction the possession of talent, aptitude and ability necessary to benefit therefrom, provided such minor could not otherwise obtain such training. Expenditures may be made for tuition, books, supplies, and all other necessary items to enable such minor to obtain such training.

(l)   In accordance with regulations of the department, provide maintenance in a summer camp for children and minors who are being cared for away from their own homes as public charges, when in his judgment it is advisable for the welfare of such children and minors.

(m)   [Repealed.]

(n)   When it is in the best interest of the child, place a child who is being returned to foster care, following an interruption in care, or a child who is being returned to a family boarding home following placement in a foster care facility with the foster care parents with whom that child was last placed, notwithstanding the provisions of subdivisions three and four of section three hundred seventy-eight of this chapter. When it is in the best interests of the minor parent and the minor parent's child or children, place the minor parent who is being returned to foster care following an interruption in care, and the minor parent's child or children or the minor parent who is being returned to a family boarding home following placement in a foster care facility and the minor parent's child or children with the foster care parents with whom the minor parent was last placed, notwithstanding the provisions of subdivisions three and four of section three hundred seventy-eight of this chapter.

(o)　Compliance with a court order enforcing visitation rights of a noncustodial parent or grandparent pursuant to part eight of article ten of the family court act, subdivision ten of section three hundred fifty-eight-a or paragraph (d) of subdivision two of section three hundred eighty-four-a of this chapter, and responsibility for the return of such child after visitation so ordered.

(p)　* Provide respite care for children who have special needs as described in subdivision fifteen of this section including, but not limited to, those children who are diagnosed as having aids or HIV related disease. For the purposes of this paragraph, respite care shall mean the provision of temporary care and supervision of children on behalf of a foster parent of a child with such special needs. Such care may be provided by a foster family boarding home, an agency operated boarding home, a group home, an institution or by an authorized staff member of such programs or other provider approved by the local district based on the individual circumstances of the caregiver and the needs of the child, for up to three consecutive weeks but no more than seven weeks in a calendar year. The department shall, by regulation, establish standards for respite care and training for the providers of such care.

(p)　* Consistent with the provisions of this chapter, provide necessary care, services and supervision including medical care, to a child placed in foster care pursuant to subparagraph (ii) of paragraph (a) of subdivision two of section ten hundred seventeen of the family court act, and reimbursement therefor to relatives of such child as approved foster parents with whom such child is residing.

7.　Notwithstanding any inconsistent provisions of law, no city forming part of a county public welfare district may hereafter assume any of the powers, duties and responsibilities mentioned in this section. However, this subdivision shall not be deemed or construed to prohibit a public welfare officer of a city forming part of a county public welfare district from exercising and performing on behalf of the county commissioner of public welfare, pursuant to the provisions of title three-a of article three, any of the powers and duties mentioned in this section. A city forming part of a county public welfare district which heretofore assumed or upon which was heretofore imposed the responsibility for providing any or all of the assistance, care and service mentioned in this section, shall hereafter continue to have such responsibility, provided, however, that the continuance of such responsibility shall be consistent with the powers, duties and responsibilities of such city under and pursuant to the provisions of title three-a of article three.

8. A public welfare official who is authorized to place children or minors in homes or institutions pursuant to provisions of this section shall have the power to place children or minors in a public institution for children.

9. A social services official shall have the same authority as a peace officer to remove a child from his home without an order of the family court and without the consent of the parent or person responsible for such child's care if the child is in such condition that his continuing in the home presents an imminent danger to the child's life or health. When a child is removed from his home pursuant to the provisions of this subdivision, the social services official shall promptly inform the parent or person responsible for such child's care and the family court of his action.

10. Any provision of this chapter or any other law notwithstanding, where a foster child for whom a social services official has been making foster care payments is in attendance at a college or university away from his foster family boarding home, group home, agency boarding home or institution, a social services official may make foster payments, not to exceed the amount which would have been paid to a foster parent on behalf of said child had the child been cared for in a foster family boarding home, to such college or university in lieu of payment to the foster parents or authorized agency, for the purpose of room and board, if not otherwise provided.

11. In the case of a child who is adjudicated a person in need of supervision or a juvenile delinquent and is placed by the family court with the division for youth and who is placed by the division for youth with an authorized agency pursuant to court order, the social services official shall make expenditures in accordance with the regulations of the department for the care and maintenance of such child during the term of such placement subject to state reimbursement pursuant to this title, or article nineteen-g of the executive law in applicable cases.

12. A social services official shall be permitted to place persons adjudicated in need of supervision or delinquent, and in cities having a population of one million or more alleged persons to be in need of supervision and persons adjudicated in need of supervision in detention pending transfer to a placement, in the same foster care facilities as are providing care to destitute, neglected, abused or abandoned children. Such foster care facilities shall not provide care to a youth in the care of a social services official as a convicted juvenile offender.

13. (a) In the case of a child with a handicapping condition who is placed, pursuant to this chapter, in a foster care agency or institution located outside the state, and who attains the age of eighteen, the social services official shall:

(i) determine whether such child will need services after the age of twenty-one, and, if such need exists;

(ii) assess the nature of the services required;

(iii)   notify the parent or guardian of such child's need for services; and

(iv)   upon the written consent of the parent or guardian, and notwithstanding section three hundred seventy-two of this article, submit a report on the child's need for services after age twenty-one to the department for planning purposes.

(b)   Upon the written consent of the parent or guardian, the department shall submit the report received pursuant to paragraph (a) of this subdivision to the council on children and families.

(c)   When a child's report is submitted to the council on children and families pursuant to this subdivision, the council shall cooperate with adult service providers, such as the department of social services, the office of mental retardation and developmental disabilities, the office of mental health and the office of vocational rehabilitation of the education department in planning and coordinating such child's return to New York state for adult services. The council shall arrange with the appropriate state agency for the development of a recommendation of all appropriate in-state programs operated, licensed, certified or authorized by such agency and which may be available when such child attains the age of twenty-one. Such recommendation of all programs shall be made available to the parent or guardian of such child at least six months before such child attains the age of twenty-one. All records, reports and information received, compiled or maintained by the council pursuant to this subdivision shall be subject to the confidentiality requirements of the department.

14.   (a) In the case of a child who is developmentally disabled as such term is defined in section 1.03 of the mental hygiene law, emotionally disturbed or physically handicapped and who is receiving care in a group home, agency boarding home, or any child care facility operated by an authorized agency with a capacity of thirteen or more children, who attains the age of eighteen and who will continue in such care after the age of eighteen, or who is placed in such care after the age of eighteen, the social services official shall notify the parent or guardian of such child that such care will terminate when such child attains the age of twenty-one provided, however, that any such child in receipt of educational services and under the care and custody of a local department of social services who reaches the age of twenty-one during the period commencing on the first day of September and ending on the thirtieth day of June shall be entitled to continue in such program until the thirtieth day of June or until the termination of the school year, whichever shall first occur. Such notice shall be in writing and shall describe in detail the parent's or guardian's opportunity to consent to having such child's name and other information forwarded in a report to the commissioner of mental health, commissioner of mental retardation and developmental disabilities, commissioner of education or commissioner of the office of children and family services or their designees for the purpose of determining whether such child will likely need services after the age of twenty-one and, if so, recommending possible adult services.

(b)   Upon the written consent of the parent or guardian, and notwithstanding section three hundred seventy-two of this article, the social services official shall submit a report on such child's possible need for services after age twenty-one to the commissioner of mental health, commissioner of mental retardation and developmental disabilities, commissioner of social services or commissioner of education or their designees for the development of a recommendation pursuant to section 7.37 or 13.37 of the mental hygiene law, section three hundred ninety-eight-c of this article or subdivision ten of section four thousand four hundred three of the education law. The social services official shall determine which commissioner shall receive the report by considering the child's handicapping condition. If the social services official determines that the child will need adult services from the department and such social services official is the commissioner's designee pursuant to this subdivision and section three hundred ninety-eight-c of this article, such social services official shall perform the services described in section three hundred ninety-eight-c of this article.

(c) A copy of such report shall also be submitted to the department at the same time that such report is submitted to the commissioner of mental health, commissioner of mental retardation and developmental disabilities or commissioner of education or their designees.

(d) When the social services official is notified by the commissioner who received the report that such state agency is not responsible for determining and recommending adult services for the child, the social services official shall forward the report to another commissioner; or, if the social services official determines that there exists a dispute between state agencies as to which state agency has the responsibility for determining and recommending adult services, the social services official may forward the report to the council on children and families for a resolution of such dispute.

(e) The social services official shall prepare and submit an annual report to the department on October first, nineteen hundred eighty-four and thereafter on or before October first of each year. Such annual report shall contain the number of cases submitted to each commissioner pursuant to paragraph (b) of this subdivision, the type and severity of the handicapping condition of each such case, the number of notices received which deny responsibility for determining and recommending adult services, and other information necessary for the department and the council on children and families to monitor the need for adult services, but shall not contain personally identifying information. The department shall forward copies of such annual reports to the council on children and families. All information received by the council on children and families pursuant to this paragraph shall be subject to the confidentiality requirements of the department.

15. (a) In the case of a child who has special needs due to a high level of disturbed behavior, emotional disturbance or physical or health needs as determined by the district in accordance with the rules and regulations of the department and who has been placed with a therapeutic foster parent, the social services official shall make available periodic respite care services for such parent, necessary consultation services between the therapeutic foster care parent

and professionals familiar with the special needs of the child and such other support services as are reasonably necessary to prevent placement of the child in a group home, an agency operated boarding home or an institution.

(b) Prior to placement of a child who has been determined to have special needs with a therapeutic foster parent, the social services official shall require such foster parent to complete an approved training program. The department shall not provide enhanced reimbursement for such placement unless the social services official certifies that the foster parent has successfully completed an approved training program.

(c) A social services official shall require that the family services plan developed pursuant to section four hundred nine-e of this article for a child placed with a therapeutic foster parent include a treatment plan prepared in consultation with the therapeutic foster parent and approved by the social services official.

16. Notwithstanding any provision of law to the contrary, with regard to the placement of all categories of foster children, the social services official or the voluntary authorized agency under contract with such official must consider giving preference to placement of a child with an adult relative over a non-related caregiver, provided that the relative caregiver meets relevant child welfare standards.

Amended by Laws 1941, Ch. 172; Laws 1944, Ch. 390; Laws 1946, Ch. 200; Laws 1954, Ch. 213; Laws 1955, Ch. 350; Laws 1957, Ch. 147; Laws 1959, Ch. 525; Laws 1962, Chs. 584, 690; Laws 1963, Ch. 478; Laws 1966, Chs. 256, 948; Laws 1967, Chs. 276, 277, 479; Laws 1968, Chs. 320, 603, 839; Laws 1969, Ch. 407, § 107, eff. May 9, 1969; Laws 1969, Ch. 821, § 1, eff. May 22, 1969; Laws 1970, Ch. 570, § 15, eff. Sept. 1, 1970; Laws 1970, Ch. 963, § 1, eff. June 1, 1970; Laws 1971, Chs. 110, 160, 259; Laws 1972, Chs. 270, 403, 914; Laws 1973, Chs. 289, 510; Laws 1974, Chs. 1018, 1020; Laws 1975, Chs. 512, 703, 705; Laws 1976, Chs. 663, 514, 666, 880; Laws 1977, Ch. 865, eff. Nov. 9, 1977, **repealed** subd. (k) and **relettered** subds. (l), (m), (n) to read subds. (k), (l), (m); Laws 1978, Ch. 555; Laws 1978, Ch. 655, § 118, expressly **amended** subd. 2(e) but intent was probably to amend subd. 2(c), eff. July 24, 1978; Laws 1979, Ch. 610, eff. Apr. 1, 1981; **added** by Laws 1981, Ch. 204, eff. June 9, 1981, subd. 6(n); **added** by Laws 1982, Ch. 544, eff. July 20, 1982, subd. (12); **amended** by Laws 1982, Ch. 610, eff. Oct. 1, 1982, subd. (5)(a); **amended** by Laws 1983, Ch. 570, eff. July 21, 1983; **amended** by Laws 1984, Ch. 627, eff. Nov. 24, 1984; **amended** by Laws 1984, Ch. 730, eff. Aug. 3, 1984; **amended** by Laws 1985, Ch. 491, eff. July 24, 1985; **amended** by Laws 1985, Ch. 127, eff. July 27, 1985; **amended** by Laws 1986, Ch. 127, eff. June 2, 1986; **amended** by Laws 1986, Ch. 563, eff. July 24, 1986; **amended** by Laws 1987, Ch. 419, eff. Sept. 1, 1987; **amended** by Laws 1988, Ch. 457, § 13, eff. Nov. 1, 1988; **amended** by Laws 1989, Ch. 731, §§ 4 and 5, eff. July 24, 1989; **amended** by Laws 1989, Ch. 744, § 4, eff. July 24, 1989; **amended** by Laws 1990, Ch. 376, § 1, eff. July 10, 1990; **amended** by Laws 1991, Ch. 267, § 1, eff. Oct. 3, 1991; **amended**by Laws 1991, Ch. 267, § 1, eff. Oct. 3, 1991; **amended** by Laws 1991, Ch. 697, § 1, eff. Aug. 2, 1991; **amended** by Laws 1992, Ch. 43, § 1, eff. Apr. 7, 1992; **amended** by Laws 1993, Ch. 87, § 5, eff. June 1, 1993; **amended** by Laws 1994, Ch. 169, § 97, eff. Apr. 1, 1994; **amended** by Laws 1995, Ch. 83, § 234, eff. July 1, 1995; **amended** by Laws 1996, Ch.

SSL

282, § 2, eff. July 10, 1996; **amended** by Laws 1996, Ch. 309, § 280, eff. July 13, 1996; **amended** by Laws 1997, Ch. 436, § 1 Part B, § 48, eff. Aug. 20, 1997; **amended** by Laws 1999, Ch. 387, §§ 1 & 2, eff. July 27, 1999; **amended** by Laws 2005, Ch. 57, §19 (Part E), eff. April 12, 2005, deemed eff. on and after April 1, 2005.

   * Editor's Note: Two versions of subd. (6)(p) are provided. The first version is subd. (6)(p) as added by Laws 1989, Ch. 731, § 4, eff. July 24, 1989. The second version is subd. (6)(p) as added by Laws 1989, Ch. 744, § 4, eff. July 24, 1989. Laws 1989, Ch. 731 made no reference to the version of subd. (6)(p) added by Laws 1989, Ch. 744, and Laws 1989, Ch. 744 made no reference to the version of subd. (6)(p) added by Laws 1989, Ch. 731.

§ 398-a.   Standards of payment for foster care.

   (1)   For purposes of this section, notwithstanding any other provisions of law, the term foster child shall mean a person who is cared for away from his or her home under conditions prescribed by regulations of the department and who is: (a) under the age of eighteen years, (b) under the age of twenty-one years if a student attending a school, college or university or regularly attending a course of vocational or technical training designed to fit him or her for gainful employment or (c) between the ages of eighteen and twenty-one who lacks the skills or ability to live independently and consents to continue in care.

   (2)   The office of children and family services shall promulgate, subject to consultation with appropriate state agencies, the approval of the director of the budget and certification to the chairmen of the senate finance and assembly ways and means committees, regulations establishing standards of payment for care provided foster children when the care of such children is subject to public financial support, when such care is provided by relatives, authorized agencies, family boarding homes, or state agencies. Such standards of payment shall include the care required to be provided for foster children and the cost of such care. When the office of children and family services has established such standards, reimbursement under subdivision two of section one hundred fifty-three-k of this chapter, for the care of foster children shall be limited in accordance with such standards.

   (2-a)   Those social services districts that as of January first, two thousand five were paying at least one hundred percent of the applicable rates published by the office of children and family services for the two thousand four—two thousand five rate year for care provided to foster children in institutions, group residences, group homes and agency boarding homes and/or the applicable administrative/ services rates published by the office for the operations of authorized agencies for care provided to foster children in therapeutic, special needs and emergency foster boarding homes must pay for the two thousand five—two thousand six rate year and for each subsequent rate year thereafter at least one hundred percent of the applicable rates published by the office for that rate year. Those social services districts that as of January first, two thousand five were paying less than the applicable rates published by the office for the two thousand four—two thousand five rate year for care provided to foster children in institutions, group residences, group homes and agency boarding homes and/or the applicable administrative/services rates published by the office for the operations of authorized agencies for care provided to foster children in therapeutic, special needs and emergency foster boarding homes must increase their rates of payment so that: effective July first, two thousand five, the difference between the percentage of the applicable rates published by the office for the two thousand five—two thousand six rate year and the rates such districts are paying is at least two-thirds less than the difference between the percentage of the applicable rates published by the office for the two thousand four—two thousand five rate year and the rates that such districts were paying for such programs on January first, two thousand five; and effective July first, two thousand six for the two thousand six—two thousand seven rate year and for each subsequent year thereafter all social services districts shall pay at least one hundred percent of the applicable rates published by the office for the applicable rate year.

(3)　If the commissioner finds that a social services district or a city containing a social services district has adopted regulations establishing standards of payment for care provided foster children by relatives, authorized agencies or family boarding homes, when the care of such children is subject to public financial support, which standards are substantially equivalent to those promulgated by the department, such department standards shall not be applicable in such district or city.

(4)　If and so long as federal aid is available therefor and subject to the approval of the director of the budget, the department is authorized to conduct a three year demonstration project to test the effectiveness of establishing capitated rates for foster care. The demonstration project shall be entitled the homerebuilders demonstration project. The goal of the project shall be to demonstrate how innovative methods to fund foster care programs may result in the discharge of children from foster care to suitable, permanent homes in a more timely manner, at no additional costs to state and local governments, through service continuity, intensified discharge planning, pre-adoption services, after-care services and/or post-adoption services. Notwithstanding any inconsistent provision of law, in order to implement a demonstration project relating to the effectiveness of establishing capitated rates for foster care, the department may waive provisions set forth in: (a) section one hundred fifty-three and this section, with regard to limitations on capitated reimbursement to a social services district for after-care or post-adoption services to children and families participating in the homerebuilders demonstration project, where the child is no longer in the care and custody or custody and guardianship of the local commissioner of social services; and (b) subparagraph (ii) of paragraph (e) of subdivision five of section four hundred nine-a of this title, with regard to limitations on reimbursement for intensive home based family preservation services to children participating in the homerebuilders demonstration project who are in the care and custody or custody and guardianship of a local commissioner of social services; and (c) the regulations promulgated implementing such provisions of law. The authority of

SSL

the department to waive such provisions shall be limited to the purpose of implementing such demonstration project and shall expire with the completion of the demonstration project, unless otherwise authorized by law. The department shall report to the governor and the legislature on the status of the homerebuilders demonstration project at least annually after its commencement and shall submit a final report thereon to the governor and the legislature no later than July first, nineteen hundred ninety-seven. Such final report shall set forth the findings of the homerebuilders demonstration project and any recommendations for statutory or regulatory changes.

(5)   [*Effective April 1, 2005.*] (a) The office of children and family services shall establish, subject to consultation with appropriate state agencies, the approval of the director of the budget and federal approval, standards of payment for the capital costs of approved projects for residential institutions for children which enter into a lease, sublease or other agreement with the dormitory authority pursuant to subdivision forty of section sixteen hundred eighty of the public authorities law. The maintenance rate established by the commissioner of the office of children and family services for such residential institutions for children shall be established in two parts, one part of which will be the capital financing add on rate, which shall be the cost per child of the annual payment pursuant to such lease, sublease or other agreement. The applicable social services district or school district responsible for the maintenance cost of a child placed in such residential institution for children, must agree to pay and is responsible for paying the residential institution for children one hundred percent of the capital financing add-on rate for each such child placed in such institution. To the extent permissible under federal law and regulation, the capital financing add-on rate shall not be subject to any cost screens, caps or parameters limiting or reducing the amount of such cost required by this subdivision.

(b)   The expenditures made by a social services district or school district for the capital financing add on rate for children placed by a committee on special education of a school district in a residential institution for children which has a lease, sublease or other agreement with the dormitory authority pursuant to subdivision forty of section sixteen hundred eighty of the public authorities law, shall be subject to state reimbursement in accordance with subdivision ten of section one hundred fifty-three of this chapter or article eighty-nine of the education law, as applicable.

(c)   The expenditures of a social services district for the capital financing add-on rate for foster children placed in a residential institution for children which has a lease, sublease or other agreement with the dormitory authority pursuant to subdivision forty of section sixteen hundred eighty of the public authorities law shall be subject to fifty percent state reimbursement from the office of children and family services, net of any available federal funds, for the portion of the costs that exceed the district's foster care block grant allocation.

Added by Laws 1973, Ch. 996, eff. Sept. 1, 1973; **amended** by Laws 1987, Ch. 397, eff. July 23, 1987; **amended** by Laws 1993, Ch. 292, § 1, **adding** new subd. (4) to SSL

§ 398-a, eff. July 21, 1993; **amended** by Laws 1995, Ch. 83, § 235, eff. July 1, 1995, until Mar. 31, 1999; **amended** by Laws 1999, Ch. 16, § 3, eff. Mar. 31, 1999, deemed in full force and effect Apr. 1, 1999, Ch. 30, § 1, eff. Apr. 26, 1999, deemed in full force and effect Apr. 1, 1999, Ch. 48, § 1, eff. May 24, 1999, deemed in full force and effect Apr. 1, 1999, Ch. 74, § 1, eff. June 21, 1999, deemed in full force and effect Apr. 1, 1999, Ch. 333, § 6, eff. July 2, 1999, deemed in full force and effect Apr. 1, 1999, extending the effective date of 1995 amendments to subd. (2) to Aug. 31, 1999; **amened** by Laws 2002, Ch. 83, Part C, § 20, eff. April 1, 2002; **amended** by Laws 2004, Ch. 472, § 5, adding sub. (5), eff. April 1, 2005; **amended** by Laws 2005, Ch. 57, 1 (Part F), adding sub. (2-a), eff. April 12, 2005, deemed eff. on and after April 1, 2005.

§ 398-b. Child welfare services utilization review.

[*Repealed by Laws 2002, Ch. 83, Part C, § 22, eff. April 1, 2002.*]

§ 398-c. Powers and duties of the commissioner in relation to children.

1. The commissioner shall determine whether a child, whose report is submitted to the department pursuant to subparagraph five of paragraph b of subdivision one of section forty-four hundred two of the education law or subdivision thirteen of section three hundred ninety-eight of this article, will likely need adult services and, if such need will likely exist, develop a recommendation of all appropriate programs authorized or operated by the department which may be available when the child attains the age of twenty-one. If necessary and appropriate, the commissioner may conduct an evaluation of the child to determine if adult services will be necessary. Such recommendation of all programs shall be made available to the parent or guardian of such child as soon as practicable but no later than six months before such child attains the age of twenty-one.

2. If the commissioner determines pursuant to subdivision one of this section, that such child will not require adult services, the commissioner shall notify the child's parent or guardian in writing of such determination. Such notice shall be given as soon as practicable but no later than six months before the child attains the age of twenty-one.

3. Notwithstanding subdivisions one and two of this section, the commissioner may determine that the department is not responsible for determining and recommending adult services for such child. When such a determination is made it shall be made as soon as practicable after receiving the report and the commissioner shall promptly notify in writing the committee on the special education, multidisciplinary team or social services official who sent the report that such determination has been made. Such notice shall state the reasons for the determination and may recommend a state agency which may be responsible for determining and recommending adult services.

4. Nothing in this section shall be construed to create an entitlement to adult services.

5. A designee of the commissioner may carry out the functions of the commissioner described in this section.

Added by Laws 1983, Ch. 570, eff. July 21, 1983; **amended** by Laws 1986, Ch. 273, eff. July 1, 1986.

§ 398-d. Child welfare services community demonstration projects.

1. The legislature finds that the centralized delivery of child protective services, preventive services, adoption services and foster care services in a social service district with a population of more than two million hinders their effective delivery and adds unnecessary costs. Numerous studies have recommended that such services serve small areas, be located in such areas, and be integrated. Such relocation will: give caseworkers greater knowledge of their assigned community, the residents of that community and the availability of community-based services; increase the availability of caseworkers; reduce travel time for case-workers; enable children in foster care to remain in their own communities and schools and maintain their friendships; enable children in foster care to have greater visitation with their parents; provide for more effective delivery of preventive services; and expedite adoptions and otherwise reduce the amount of time children spend in foster care.

The relocation of child welfare service delivery to the community sites will strengthen efforts to provide a wide range of community-based early intervention programs including, but not limited to, school-based health clinics and community schools, thereby ensuring the continued development of a critical mass of community services.

2. No later than March first, nineteen hundred ninety-six, a social service district with a population in excess of two million shall implement at least three demonstration projects for a period of at least two years to provide child welfare services on a community level to improve the delivery of child welfare services, increase adoptions and reduce the rate of foster care placements. These projects shall be located in and serve community school districts which have high rates of: children at risk of becoming a part of the foster care system, poverty, households on public assistance, juvenile delinquency, and unemployment. Such projects shall provide foster care, preventive, adoption and child protective services as required by this article.

3. In proposed demonstration areas, child welfare services must be coordinated with community schools, school health clinics, and other relevant programs to provide and administer the most efficient services. In one demonstration area, the district shall use a caseworker to client ratio equal to the preferred national average of one to fourteen.

4. A report evaluating such projects shall be presented no later than June first, nineteen hundred ninety-eight, to the governor, the department and the respective chairpersons of the assembly children and families committee, the senate children

and families committee, the assembly ways and means committee, and the senate finance committee. Such report shall include:

(a) the number of children and families who received preventive services, child protective services and foster care, (b) the number of delinquent and incarcerated youth in the demonstration projects, (c) the length of an average foster care placement, (d) the number of completed adoptions for youth residing within the demonstration area, including their age, gender, race, ethnicity and religion, (e) the gross expenditures for foster care, compared to the gross expenditures for child protective, preventive and adoption services, (f) changes in the quality and quantity of time spent by caseworkers with clients, (g) staffing ratios of foster care, preventive and child protective services, (h) the perspective (attitude, viewpoint, outlook) of caseworkers serving and clients served in the demonstration project, and (i) recommendations for expansion of community-based provisions for child welfare services. For purposes of the report, the data described above should be compared to the extent possible with non-demonstration areas.

Added by Laws 1995, Ch. 83, § 236, eff. July 1, 1995.

§ 398-e. Eligibility for protective service.

An alien, including a non-qualified alien, as determined by applicable federal statute and regulation, is eligible for protective services for adults and children, to the extent such person is otherwise eligible pursuant to this chapter and the regulations of the department.

Added by Laws 1997, Ch. 436, § 1 Part B, § 49, eff. Aug. 20, 1997, deemed to be in full force and effect Aug. 22, 1996.

§ 399. Children discharged from state institutions.

The commissioner of social services shall co-operate with the state institutions for delinquent, mentally disabled and physically handicapped children to ascertain the conditions of the home and the character and habits of the parents of a child before his discharge from a state institution, and make recommendations as to the advisability of returning said child to his home. In case the commissioner of social services shall deem it unwise to have any such child returned to his former home, such state institution may, with the consent of the commissioner, place such child into the care of said commissioner of social services.

Amended by Laws 1985, Ch. 491, eff. July 24, 1985.

§ 400. Removal of children.

1. When any child shall have been placed in an institution or in a family home by a social services official, the social services official may remove such

SSL

child from such institution or family home and make such disposition of such child as is provided by law, provided however, that in the case of a child who is a patient in a hospital licensed or operated by the office of mental health, such social services official may remove such child only upon the written authorization of the medical director of the facility in which the child is a patient. A medical director may only refuse to authorize the removal of a child if involuntary care and treatment of the child is warranted. In such case the director shall institute necessary civil commitment proceedings in accordance with article nine of the mental hygiene law.

2. Any person aggrieved by such decision of a social services official may appeal to the department pursuant to the provisions of section twenty-two of this chapter.

Amended by Laws 1967, Ch. 782; Laws 1975, Ch. 224; Laws 1978, Ch. 473, eff. July 11, 1978; **amended** by Laws 1981, Ch. 947, eff. July 1, 1981.

§ 401.   Births to inmates of public homes.

No commissioner of public welfare shall provide care in a public home for any pregnant woman during confinement unless such public home has adequate hospital or infirmary facilities, is equipped to give the necessary medical and nursing care and has a certificate from the department authorizing such public home to care for maternity cases. Certificates authorizing a public home to care for maternity cases may be issued by the department for a one-year period, subject to renewal, but may be revoked at any time by the department. If the public home is not so certified, a commissioner of public welfare shall, a reasonable time before the expected confinement of any pregnant woman inmate, provide suitable maintenance and medical care for her in a hospital or some other place equipped to give adequate care.

§ 402.   Children forbidden in public homes.

No public welfare official shall send a child to be cared for in a public home, and no commissioner of public welfare and no superintendent of a public home shall receive a child in a public home, except that a child under the age of two years may be cared for with his mother in a public home. Such child shall not remain in the public home after he becomes two years of age. Provided, however, that when so authorized by the department a child may be sent to a general hospital connected with a public home or to a separate institution located in the grounds of a public home used only for special or temporary care of children. Provided, further, that the provisions of this section shall not be deemed to prohibit the placement of a child or minor in a public institution for children, as defined in section three hundred seventy-one of this chapter.

Amended by Laws 1967, Ch. 479, eff. Apr. 24, 1967.

§ 403. The religious faith of children and minors.

The religious faith of children and minors between sixteen and eighteen years of age coming under the jurisdiction of public welfare officials shall be preserved and protected in accordance with section three hundred seventy-three.

TITLE 3—CHILD WELFARE SERVICES

———

(Repealed and transferred sections noted under appropriate section number of text.)

§ 406. Department of social welfare designated as state agency.

The department is hereby designated as the agency of the state to administer and expend any and all grants of moneys allocated or made available to the state under the provisions of the federal social security act for child welfare services as defined in such act, subject to the provisions of such act and rules and regulations established thereunder and to the laws of the state and rules and regulations established by the state comptroller.

§ 407. Powers of department of social welfare.

The department is hereby authorized and required:

1. to prepare a plan or plans for such child welfare services and upon their approval by such federal authority to execute the same. Such plans shall make provision for coordination between the services provided under such plans and the services provided as family assistance under title ten of article five with the view of providing welfare and related services which will best promote the welfare of children and their families.

2. to allocate and disburse to districts, counties or other local subdivisions of the state such amounts from moneys received by the state under the provisions of this title as are available for payment of part of the cost of district, county or other local child welfare services in accordance with such approved plans. Such district, county and other local subdivisions of the state are hereby authorized to receive and expend such allotments but only for the purposes of such plans and subject to the supervision and general direction of the department. Such district, county and other local subdivisions shall, when required by the department to comply with the provisions of such approved plan, perform the functions required.

3. to develop within the department services for the encouragement and assistance of adequate methods of community child welfare organization in accordance with such approved plans.

SSL

4.   to establish and to alter and amend such regulations as may be necessary for the administration of such plans and the provisions of this title.

5.   to prepare for inclusion in the annual report required by subdivision (d) of section seventeen of this chapter to be filed with the governor and the legislature prior to the fifteenth day of December of each year, a written evaluation report of the delivery of child welfare services in the state. Such evaluation report shall include, but need not be limited to, supervision of foster care and the agencies providing such care, information on the types of problems creating the need for foster care placements, preventive and protective services, the transfer of children in care and the reasons therefor, identification of target groups not receiving adequate services, and projected plans for providing services to such groups. Such report shall include progress made and problems encountered in the implementation of "the child welfare reform act of 1979", and amendments thereto. Such report shall also include aggregate expenditures; persons receiving services; cost comparisons among social services districts, among types of services and services programs, and among fiscal periods; unit costs; and cost-effectiveness of the provision of preventive services pursuant to title four of this chapter. In developing such evaluation, the department shall consult and coordinate with the board of social welfare, the division for youth, and the departments of mental hygiene, health and education.

Amended by Laws 1963, Ch. 1014; Laws 1967, Ch. 144; Laws 1974, Ch. 1040; Laws 1979, Ch. 611, eff. Apr. 1, 1980; **amended** by 1982, Ch. 384, eff. Apr. 1, 1983; **amended** by Laws 1997, Ch. 436, § 1 Part B, § 101, eff. Aug. 20, 1997.

§ 408.   Custodian of funds.

The department of taxation and finance is hereby authorized to accept and receive on behalf of the state any and all grants or allotments of money made available to the state by or pursuant to the federal social security act for such child welfare services. All moneys so accepted and received shall be deposited by the department of taxation and finance to the credit of a special fund for use exclusively for the purposes for which such grants or allotments were made. The department shall certify to the comptroller all expenditures to be made from such special fund for payment of the part of the cost of district, county or other local child welfare services and for developing state services for the encouragement and assistance of adequate methods of community child welfare organization. Such expenditures may be made for personal service and for administrative and other costs of operation.

§ 408-a.   Detention facilities.

Repealed by Laws 1976, Ch. 880, eff. Nov. 29, 1976.

TITLE 4—PREVENTIVE SERVICES FOR CHILDREN AND THEIR FAMILIES

> Section   409.   **Preventive services; definition.**
>   409-a.   **Preventive services; provision by social services officials.**

§ 409. Preventive services; definition.

As used in this title, "preventive services" shall mean supportive and rehabilitative services provided, in accordance with the provisions of this title and regulations of the department, to children and their families for the purpose of: averting an impairment or disruption of a family which will or could result in the placement of a child in foster care; enabling a child who has been placed in foster care to return to his family at an earlier time than would otherwise be possible; or reducing the likelihood that a child who has been discharged from foster care would return to such care.

Added by Laws 1979, Ch. 610, eff. Apr. 1, 1981.

§ 409-a. Preventive services; provision by social services officials.

1.   (a) A social services official shall provide preventive services to a child and his or her family, in accordance with the family's service plan as required by section four hundred nine-e of this chapter and the social services district's child welfare services plan submitted and approved pursuant to section four hundred nine-d of this chapter, upon a finding by such official that (i) the child will be placed or continued in foster care unless such services are provided and that it is reasonable to believe that by providing such services the child will be able to remain with or be returned to his or her family or (ii) [*Expires and repealed June 30, 2007*] the child is the subject of a petition under article seven of the family court act, or has been determined by the assessment service established pursuant to section two hundred forty-three-a of the executive law, or by the probation service where no such assessment service has been designated, to be at risk of being the subject of such a petition, and the social services official determines that the child is at risk of placement into foster care. Such finding shall be entered in the child's uniform case record established and maintained pursuant to section four hundred nine-f of this chapter. The commissioner shall promulgate regulations to assist social services officials in making determinations of eligibility for mandated preventive services pursuant to this subparagraph.

    (b)   When a child and his family have received preventive services for a period of six months pursuant to this subdivision, the social services official shall continue to provide such services only upon making a new finding that the child will be placed or continued in foster care unless such services are provided and that it is reasonable to believe that by providing such services, the child will be able to remain with or be returned to his family. Such new finding shall be entered in the child's uniform case record established and maintained pursuant to section four hundred nine-f of this chapter.

2.   A social services official is authorized to provide preventive services to a child and his family to accomplish the purposes set forth in section four hundred nine of this chapter, when such services are not required to be provided pursuant to subdivision one of this section.

3.   (a) A social services official is authorized to provide community preventive services to communities likely to benefit from such services to accomplish the purposes set forth in section four hundred nine of this chapter. Social services officials may apply to the office of children and family services for waiver of eligibility and administrative requirements for preventive services to be provided pursuant to this subdivision. Such application shall include a plan setting forth the services to be provided, the persons or community that will receive the services and the estimated cost of such services. Upon approval of the application by the office of children and family services, eligibility requirements established in statute or regulation may be waived for those persons and communities identified in the plan as recipients of the services set forth in the plan. Where services are administered pursuant to a plan approved by the department, the department may waive the requirements of sections one hundred fifty-three-d and three hundred ninety-eight-b of this chapter pertaining to denial or reimbursement. Where such a waiver is approved, the department approval must specify standards whereby services provided will be subject to denial of reimbursement. Where services are administered pursuant to a plan approved by the office of children and family services, the office of children and family services may waive the requirements of section four hundred nine-f or four hundred forty-two of this article.

(b)   The department must inform social services districts of procedures governing application for waivers of eligibility and administrative requirements and approval of waivers of eligibility and administrative requirements. Where such waivers are granted, the department shall have the authority to establish alternative standards to be followed by social services officials who are granted waivers by the department. Upon approval of an application for such waivers, the department approval must specify the requirements being waived and any alternative standards established.

(c)   Community preventive services may be provided pursuant to this subdivision through demonstration projects to the extent the department makes funds available for such projects.

(d)   The department shall develop an evaluation plan no later than April first, nineteen hundred eighty-eight, for community service demonstration projects and, subject to the approval of the director of the budget, may use up to five percent of the amount annually appropriated for project grants to conduct such evaluation which shall include but need not be limited to: an assessment of the effectiveness of various service delivery models in creating or enhancing linkages among school, housing, health, and income support services available in the community; the effectiveness of various preventive services in averting family disruption; the cost effectiveness of providing community focused preventive services; the impact of this service provision on requirements for more intensive mandated preventive services; and, the feasibility of replicating successful service models in other communities throughout the state.

4. Preventive services may be provided directly by the social services official or through purchase of service, in accordance with regulations of the department.

5. (a) Regulations of the department, promulgated pursuant to and not inconsistent with this section, shall contain program standards including, but not limited to: specification of services to be classified as preventive services; appropriate circumstances and conditions for the provision of particular services; appropriate providers and recipients of such services; and time limits, as may be appropriate, for the provision of particular services. The department shall, subject to the approval of the director of the budget, establish reimbursement or charge limitations for particular services or groups of services to be provided. The department shall also promulgate regulations to prevent social services districts from overutilizing particular forms or types of preventive services and to encourage districts to provide balanced preventive services programs based on the identified needs of children and families residing in such districts.

(b) The program standards promulgated pursuant to this subdivision shall be developed with the participation of the child welfare standards advisory council established pursuant to section four hundred nine-h of this chapter and in consultation with public and voluntary authorized agencies, citizens' groups and concerned individuals and organizations, including the state council on children and families.

(c) Notwithstanding any other provision of this section, where a social services official determines that a lack of adequate housing is the primary factor preventing the discharge of a child or children from foster care including, but not limited to, children with the goal of discharge to independent living, preventive services shall include, in addition to any other payments or benefits received by the family, special cash grants in the form of rent subsidies, including rent arrears, or any other assistance, sufficient to obtain adequate housing. Such rent subsidies or assistance shall not exceed the sum of three hundred dollars per month, shall not be provided for a period of more than three years, and shall be considered a special grant. The provisions of this paragraph shall not be construed to limit such official's authority to provide other preventive services.

(d) [*Repealed.*]

(e) (i) A social services official is authorized to establish and operate, or contract for the establishment and operation of, intensive, home based, family preservation programs.

(ii) Notwithstanding any other provision of law, reimbursement for intensive, home based family preservation services shall be limited to those programs that reduce or avoid the need for foster care of children who are in imminent danger of placement. Such programs shall employ caseworkers trained in family preservation techniques and who provide at least half of their direct services in the client's residence or temporary home, work with no more than four families at any given time, provide direct therapeutic services for up to thirty days which may be extended up to an additional thirty days per family and are available twenty-four hours a day. No program described herein shall receive reimbursement unless such program agrees to collect and provide to the department information necessary to evaluate and assess the degree to which such program results in lower costs to the state and to social services districts than those of foster care placement. Such information shall be compiled in a manner that permits comparisons between families served by such programs and those families who meet eligibility criteria but who were not able to be served within available resources.

(f) Notwithstanding any other provision of law, where a social services official authorizes the provision of respite care, such care shall mean the temporary care and supervision of a child to relieve parents or other persons legally responsible for the care of such child where immediate relief is needed to maintain or restore family functioning.

6. In accordance with regulations of the department, where the child's family is able to pay all or part of the cost of such services, payments of such fees as may be reasonable or other third-party reimbursement as may be available in the light of such ability shall be required. Expenditures subject to reimbursement pursuant to section four hundred nine-b of this title shall be reduced by the sum of all fees received or to be received pursuant to this subdivision.

7. * Notwithstanding any other provision of this section, if a social services official determines that a lack of adequate housing is a factor that may cause the entry of a child or children into foster care and the family has at least one service need other than lack of adequate housing, preventive services may include, in addition to any other payments or benefits received by the family, special cash grants in the form of rent subsidies, including rent arrears, or any other assistance, sufficient to obtain adequate housing. Such rent subsidies or assistance shall not exceed the sum of three hundred dollars per month, shall not be provided for a period of more than three years, and shall be considered a special grant. The provisions of this paragraph shall not be construed to limit such official's authority to provide other preventive services.

7. * Notwithstanding any other provision of law, preventive services information governed by this section may be released by the department, social services district or other provider of preventive services to a person, agency or organization for purposes of a bona fide research project. Identifying information shall not be made available, however, unless it is absolutely essential to the research purpose and the department gives prior approval. Information released

pursuant to this subdivision shall not be re-disclosed except as otherwise permitted by law and upon the approval of the department.

 * **Editor's Note:** Two version of subd. 7 are provided. The first was added by Laws 1995, Ch. 83, eff. July 1, 1995. The second was added by Laws 1995, Ch. 653, eff. Dec. 6, 1995, without mention of the prior version.

8.   In contracting for the provision of preventive services, social services districts shall, to the extent feasible, place such services in areas with a high rate of child abuse and neglect and foster care placements. Social services districts shall, to the extent feasible, consider as a priority community-based organizations with a record of providing quality services to children and families in such communities.

9.   (a) Notwithstanding any provision of law to the contrary, records relating to children pursuant to this section shall be made available to officers and employees of the state comptroller, or of the city comptroller of the city of New York, or of the county officer designated by law or charter to perform the auditing function in any county not wholly contained within a city, for purposes of a duly authorized performance audit, provided, however that such comptroller or officer shall have certified to the keeper of such records that he or she has instituted procedures developed in consultation with the department to limit access to client-identifiable information to persons requiring such information for purposes of the audit, that such persons shall not use such information in any way except for purposes of the audit and that appropriate controls and prohibitions are imposed on the dissemination of client-identifiable information obtained in the conduct of the audit. Information pertaining to the substance or content of any psychological, psychiatric, therapeutic, clinical or medical reports, evaluations or like materials or information pertaining to such child or the child's family shall not be made available to such officers and employees unless disclosure of such information is absolutely essential to the specific audit activity and the department gives prior written approval.

(b)   Any failure to maintain the confidentiality of client-identifiable information shall subject such comptroller or officer to denial of any further access to records until such time as the audit agency has reviewed its procedures concerning controls and prohibitions imposed on the dissemination of such information and has taken all reasonable and appropriate steps to eliminate such lapses in maintaining confidentiality to the satisfaction of the department. The department shall establish the grounds for denial of access to records contained under this section and shall recommend as necessary a plan of remediation to the audit agency, except as provided in this section, nothing in this subdivision shall be construed as limiting the powers of such comptroller or officer to records which he is otherwise authorized to audit or obtain under any other applicable provision of law, any person given access to information pursuant to this subdivision who released data or information to persons or agencies not authorized to receive such information shall be guilty of a class A misdemeanor.

SSL

10. All sums received by the state under section 201 of federal public law 105-89 shall be paid to the districts in proportion to the amount earned by the district for federal adoption incentives and shall only be used to provide preventive services to a child and his or her family as defined in paragraph (a) of subdivision five of this section, in addition to those required by the maintenance of effort requirement contained in subdivision six of section one hundred fifty-three-i of this chapter, except that up to thirty percent of such sums may be used to provide post-adoption services to children or families. Preventive services shall include substance abuse treatment services provided to pregnant women or a caretaker person in an outpatient, residential or in-patient setting. Amounts expended by the state in accordance with This section shall be disregarded in determining the state's expenditures for purposes of federal matching payments under sections four hundred twenty-three, four hundred thirty-four and four hundred seventy-four of this chapter.

Added by Laws 1979, Ch. 610, eff. Apr. 1, 1981; **amended** by Laws 1985, Ch. 813, eff. Aug. 2, 1985; **amended** by Laws 1987, Ch. 465, eff. Apr. 1, 1988 until June 1, 1995; **amended** by Laws 1988, Ch. 542; Laws 1990 Ch. 278, eff. June 24, 1990, extending expiration date until Mar. 31, 1993; **amended** by Laws 1989, Ch. 731, § 6, eff. July 24, 1989; **added** by Laws 1991, Ch. 165, §§ 52, 36, eff. July 1, 1991; **amended** by Laws 1993, Ch. 17, eff. Mar. 2, 1993, extending expiration date until Mar. 31, 1998; **amended** by Laws 1993, Ch. 87 § 6, eff. June 1, 1993; **amended** by Laws 1993, Ch. 339, § 1, eff. July 21, 1993, and deemed repealed on Mar. 31, 1998; **amended** by Laws 1995, Ch. 83, §§ 237 -239, eff. July 1, 1995; **amended** by Laws 1995, Ch. 83, §§ 253 -254, eff. July 1, 1995, removing the June 1, 1995, and Mar. 31, 1998 expiration dates; **amended** by Laws 1995, Ch. 653, § 2, eff. Dec. 6, 1995; **amended** by Laws 1996, Ch. 12, § 5, eff. Feb. 15, 1996; **amended** by Laws 1999, Ch. 7, § 25 eff. Feb. 11, 1999; **amended** by Laws 2002, Ch. 83, Part C, § 22, eff. April 1, 2002, extending the expiration to June 30, 2007 subpar. (ii).

§ 409-b. Preventive services; reimbursement.

Repealed by Laws 1995, Ch. 83, § 240, eff. July 1, 1995.

TITLE 4-A—CHILD WELFARE SERVICES PLANNING AND ADMINISTRATION

---

§ 409-d. District-wide child welfare services plan.

1. Each social services district shall prepare and submit to the department, in such form and manner and times as the department shall by regulation require,

a district-wide child welfare services plan which shall be a component of the district's multi-year consolidated services plan setting forth: the child welfare services needs of children and families for whom the social services district is or may be responsible; historic program and fiscal trends of the district in the level of care, maintenance and services provided to children and their families, including but not limited to expenditure trends, children and families served and costs of services provided; an assessment of projected program and fiscal requirements of the district in meeting identified needs in the next state fiscal year; and a description of the resources known to be available or likely to become available to meet those needs. Commencing the year following preparation of a multi-year consolidated services plan, each social services district shall prepare an annual implementation report related to its child welfare services plan. As used in this section "services" shall mean and include preventive services, foster care maintenance and services, and adoption services. Such regulations shall include but need not be limited to criteria and methodology for determining child welfare services needs and the adequacy of the resources known to be available or likely to become available to meet those needs.

2. The child welfare services plan and annual implementation reports shall be developed by the district in consultation with other government agencies concerned with the welfare of children residing in the district, authorized agencies, and other concerned individuals and organizations. The plan as submitted to the department for approval and as approved by the department shall be made available to such agencies, individuals and organizations upon request.

3. (a) Each social services district shall submit its child welfare services plan and annual implementation reports pertaining to this plan to the department as a component of the multi-year consolidated services plan and subsequent annual implementation reports and the department shall review and approve or disapprove the proposed plan in accordance with the procedures set forth in section thirty-four-a of this chapter.

4, 5, 6. *[Repealed.]*

Added by Laws 1979, Ch. 611, eff. Apr. 1, 1980; **amended** by Laws 1981, Ch. 681, eff. July 21, 1981; Laws 1983, Ch. 539; Laws 1987, Ch. 231, eff. July 7, 1987 **renumbered** subds. 4 and 5 to 5 and 6 and **added** new subd. 4; **amended** by the Laws of 1987, Ch. 611; **amended** by Laws 1988, Ch. 707, § 5, eff. Sept. 2, 1988; **amended** by Laws 1995, Ch. 83, § 241, eff. July 1, 1995.

§ 409-e   Family service plan.

1. With respect to each child who is identified by a local social services district as being considered for placement in foster care as defined in section one thousand eighty-seven of the family court act by a social services district, such district, within thirty days from the date of such identification, shall perform an assessment of the child and his or her family circumstances. Where a child has been removed from his or her home, within thirty days of such removal the local

social services district shall perform an assessment of the child and his or her family circumstances, or update any assessment performed when the child was considered for placement. Any assessment shall be in accordance with such uniform procedures and criteria as the office of children and family services shall by regulation prescribe. Such assessment shall include the following:

(a) a statement of the specific immediate problems which appear to require some intervention by the social services officials;

(b) a description of the long term family relationships, an assessment of trends in the stability of the family unit, and of the likelihood that specific preventive services will increase family stabilization sufficiently to prevent placement or to reduce the duration of a necessary placement;

(c) an estimate of the time period necessary to ameliorate the conditions leading to a need for placement, and a description of any immediate actions that have been taken or must be taken during or immediately after the conclusion of the assessment; and

(d) where placement in foster care is determined necessary, the reasonable efforts made to prevent or eliminate the need for placement or the reason such efforts were not made, the kind and level of placement and the reasons therefor, whether the child will be placed with the child's siblings and half-siblings and, if not, the reasons therefor and the arrangements made for contact between the siblings and half-siblings, identification of all available placement alternatives and the specific reasons why they were rejected, an estimate of the anticipated duration of placement, and plan for termination of services under appropriate circumstances, with specific explanation of the reasons for such termination plan.

2. Upon completion of any assessment provided for in subdivision one of this section, and not later than thirty days after placement of a child in foster care pursuant to article three or seven of the family court act or not later than thirty days after a child is removed from his or her home, the local social services district shall establish or update and maintain a family service plan based on the assessment required by subdivision one of this section. The plan shall be prepared in consultation with the child's parent or guardian, unless such person is unavailable or unwilling to participate, or such participation would be harmful to the child, and with the child if the child is ten years of age or older, and, where appropriate, with the child's siblings. Such consultation shall be done in person, unless such a meeting is impracticable or would be harmful to the child. The plan shall include at least the following:

(a) time frames for periodic reassessment of the care and maintenance needs of each child and the manner in which such reassessments are to be accomplished;

(b) short term, intermediate and long range goals for the child and family and actions planned to meet the need of the child and family and each goal;

(c) identification of necessary and appropriate services and assistance to the child and members of the child's family. The services so identified shall, before being included in the family service plan, be assessed to determine the projected effectiveness of such plan including but not limited to the following considerations:

(i)　the family's concurrence with the plan;

(ii)　the ability and motivation of the family to access services, including geographic accessibility;

(iii)　the relatedness of the services to the family's needs and its socio-economic and cultural circumstances; and

(iv)　other factors which may impact upon the effectiveness of such plan. The service plan shall also describe the availability of such services and the manner in which they are to be provided;

(d)　any alternative plans for services where specific services are not available, and any viable options for services considered during the planning process;

(e)　where placement in foster care is determined necessary, specification of the reasons for such determination, the kind and level of placement, any available placement alternatives, an estimate of the anticipated duration of placement, and plan for termination of services under appropriate circumstances.

3.　The plan shall be reviewed and revised, in accordance with the procedures and standards in subdivision two of this section, at least within the first ninety days following the date the child was first considered for placement in foster care, and, if the child has been placed in foster care pursuant to article three or seven of the family court act or removed from his or her home, within the first ninety days following the date of placement or removal. The plan shall be further reviewed and revised not later than one hundred twenty days from this initial review and at least every six months thereafter; provided, however, that if a sibling or half-sibling of the child has previously been considered for placement or removed from the home, the plan shall be further reviewed and revised on the schedule established for the family based on the earliest of those events. Such revisions shall indicate the types, dates and sources of services that have actually been provided and an evaluation of the efficacy of such services, and any necessary or desirable revisions in goals or planned services. The review and revision of the plan shall be prepared in consultation with the child's parent or guardian, unless such person is unavailable or unwilling to participate, or such participation would be harmful to the child, and with the child if the child is ten years of age or older, and, where appropriate, with the child's siblings. Such consultation shall be done in person, unless such a meeting is impracticable or would be harmful to the child.

4.　In accordance with regulations of the department, relevant portions of the assessment of the child and family circumstances, including but not limited to the material described in paragraph (d) of subdivision one of this section, and a complete copy of the family service plan, established pursuant to subdivisions one and two, respectively, of this section shall be given to the child's parent or guardian, counsel for such parent or guardian, and the child's law guardian, if any, within ten days of preparation of any such plan.

5.   The family service plan developed in regard to a child in foster care pursuant to this section shall include the permanency plan provided to the court in accordance with the family court act and this chapter.

6.   Nothing in this section shall require a social services district to complete an assessment or service plan for a child who is in the custody of the office of children and family services, unless the child is also in the care and custody or custody and guardianship of the commissioner of the social services district.

Added by Laws 1979, Ch. 611, eff. Apr. 1, 1980; **amended** by Laws 1985, Ch. 808, § 9, eff. Oct. 31, 1985; **amended** by Laws 1992, Ch. 725, § 1, eff. July 31, 1992; **amended** by Laws 1999, Ch. 7, § 26, eff. Feb. 11, 1999; L. 2005, Ch. 3, sect; 60 (Part A), eff. Aug. 23, 2005; Laws 2006, Ch. 437, §16, eff. July 26, 2006.

§ 409-f.   Uniform case recording.

1.   With respect to each child described in subdivision one of section four hundred nine-e of this title, the social services district shall establish and maintain a uniform case record, consisting of the assessment, the family service plan, descriptions of care, maintenance or services provided to such child and family and the dates provided, essential data relating to the identification and history of such child and family, all official documents and records of any judicial or administrative proceedings relating to the district's contact with the child and family, and such other records as the department may by regulation require to adequately review case management by the districts. The department shall by regulation specify the format and contents of the uniform case record. such regulation shall be developed with the participation of the child welfare standards advisory council established pursuant to section four hundred nine-h of this chapter and in consultation with public and voluntary authorized agencies, citizens' groups and concerned individuals and organizations, including the state council on children and families. The uniform case record shall be maintained by the district in a manner consistent with the confidential nature of such records and shall be made available in accordance with applicable provisions of law. When a hearing has been requested in accordance with section twenty-two of this chapter, a copy of the portions of the record relevant to the hearing shall also be made available to the child's parent or guardian, counsel for the parent or guardian, and, if participating in the hearing, the child's law guardian.

2.   Notwithstanding any other provision of law, uniform case record information governed by this section may be released by the department, social services district or other provider of child welfare services to a person, agency or organization for purposes of a bona fide research project. Identifying information shall not be made available, however, unless it is absolutely essential to the research purpose and the department gives prior approval. Information released

pursuant to this subdivision shall not be re-disclosed except as otherwise permitted by law and upon the approval of the department.

3. (a) Notwithstanding any inconsistent provision of law to the contrary, records relating to children pursuant to this section shall be made available to officers and employees of the state comptroller or of the city comptroller of the city of New York, or of the county officer designated by law or charter to perform the auditing function in any county not wholly contained within a city, for purposes of a duly authorized performance audit; provided, however, that such comptroller or officer shall have certified to the keeper of such records that he or she has instituted procedures developed in consultation with the department to limit access to client-identifiable information to persons requiring such information for purposes of the audit, that such persons shall not use such information in any way except for purposes of the audit and that appropriate controls and prohibitions are imposed on the dissemination of client-identifiable information obtained in the conduct of the audit. Information pertaining to the substance or content of any psychological, psychiatric, therapeutic, clinical or medical reports, evaluations or like materials or information pertaining to such child or the child's family shall not be made available to such officers and employees unless disclosure of such information is absolutely essential to the specific audit activity and the department gives prior written approval.

(b) Any failure to maintain the confidentiality of client-identifiable information shall subject such comptroller or officer to denial of any further access to records until such time as the audit agency has reviewed its procedures concerning controls and prohibitions imposed on the dissemination of such information and has taken all reasonable and appropriate steps to eliminate such lapses in maintaining confidentiality to the satisfaction of the department. The department shall establish the grounds for denial of access to records contained under this section and shall recommend as necessary a plan of remediation to the audit agency. Except as provided in this section, nothing in this subdivision shall be construed as limiting the powers of such comptroller or officer to access records which he is otherwise authorized to audit or obtain under any other applicable provision of law. Any person given access to information pursuant to this subdivision who releases data or information to persons or agencies not authorized to receive such information shall be guilty of a class A misdemeanor.

Added by Laws 1979, Ch. 611, eff. Apr. 1, 1980; **amended** by Laws 1992, Ch. 725, § 2, eff. July 31, 1992; **amended** by Laws 1995, Ch. 653, § 3, eff. Dec. 6, 1995; **amended** by Laws 1996, Ch. 12, § 6, eff. Feb. 15, 1996.

§ 409-g. Training of child welfare personnel.

Within the amounts appropriated therefor, including all federal reimbursement received or to be received on account thereof, the department shall develop and implement a plan for the training of social services district and other authorized agency personnel, including caseworkers involved in the provision or supervision

SSL

of preventive services, foster care services and adoption services. Such training shall include but need not be limited to:

1.   Permanence casework: casework methodologies focused on activities designed to prevent placement in foster care or to shorten the length of stay in care for those children who can be returned home or freed for adoption;

2.   Development of skills to facilitate rehabilitation or restoration of the family unit;

3.   Development of knowledge and skills in legally freeing children for adoption and providing adoption services;

4.   Development of knowledge and skills to prepare for court processes necessary in foster care and adoption; and

5.   Development of case management skills including planning for permanence for each child.

   Added by Laws 1979, Ch. 611, eff. July 11, 1979.

§ 409-h.   Child welfare standards advisory council.

[Repealed by Laws 2002, Ch. 83, Part C, § 23, eff. April 1, 2002, deemed to be in full force and in effect on and after April 1, 2002.]

TITLE 4-B—SERVICES; PREGNANT ADOLESCENTS

Section	409-i.	Short title; legislative findings; purpose.
	409-j.	Case management.
	409-k.	Case plan and service record.
	409-l.	Advisory board.
	409-m.	Reports.
	409-n.	Implementation.

§ 409-i.   Short title; legislative findings; purpose.

1.   This title shall be known and may be cited and referred to as the "teenage services act."

2.   The legislature finds that the rising incidence of adolescent pregnancy and teenage parenthood is the subject of a widespread and growing concern. As a result of early pregnancy, the attainment of needed education and job skills is often curtailed. Coupled with the added responsibilities accompanying parenthood, these young families are often locked into long term public dependency. Studies have confirmed that up to sixty percent of the current aid to families with dependent children cases in New York state are headed by mothers who were teenagers when they gave birth to their first child. In fact, the predominant cause of welfare dependency in New York state may well be due to the result of teenage pregnancy and adolescent motherhood. The objective of this title is to increase

the potential of these youths to become financially independent by helping the teenager to complete her education, and receive sufficient manpower skills for participation in the labor market.

The department of social services is not only statutorily required to provide financial support to these dependent teenagers and their children, but also has equal responsibility to provide personal counselling and support services needed to strengthen family life and provide opportunities for economic independence. In order to facilitate accessibility to the full range of needed services, case management responsibilities should be assigned to appropriate local social services staff or to authorized agencies outside of the department. Any reluctance or refusal on the part of the teenager to participate in a program of services shall not carry any threat of fiscal sanctions as regards public assistance benefits. In the event that a teenager refuses to participate, it shall be the responsibility of the local social services district to make continued and repeated efforts to engage the teenager in a counselling relationship which has as its result a mutually agreed upon service plan which meets the objectives of this title.

Therefore, this title provides for the establishment of a service case management system in order to strengthen the service role of the department of social services. Local social services districts shall be required to separate public assistance cases involving pregnant adolescents and teenage mothers under eighteen years of age, and assign ongoing case management services for such caseloads to appropriate staff responsible for service delivery. By defining such specialized caseloads, personal counselling and provision of needed community-based support services will be facilitated. Such case management activities shall also include the follow-up and evaluation of services rendered.

The enactment of the provisions of this title shall maximize the effectiveness, efficiency and accountability of support services provided on behalf of pregnant adolescents and teenage parents under eighteen years of age, thereby reducing the long-term dependency needs of this youthful population.

    3.   *[Repealed.]*

    Added by Laws 1984, Ch. 975, eff. July 1, 1984; **amended** by Laws 1986, Ch. 188, eff. June 23, 1986; **amended** by Laws 1990, Ch. 49, § 1, eff. Mar. 31, 1990; L. 2003, Ch. 62, Part F2, § 12, eff. May 15, 2003 and deemed effective on April 1, 2003, repealing subd. 3.

§ 409-j. Case management.

    1. As used in this title, "case management" shall refer to a method of providing necessary prevention and support services, directly or by purchase of services, to recipients of public assistance and shall require the facilitating of such services for the purpose of insuring family stability and assistance in achieving the greatest degree of economic independence.

    2. Appropriate local social services staff shall be designated as responsible on a case by case basis, for the assessment of services needed by the adolescent

or teenage recipient to achieve defined service goals, and for the planning and referral of services and follow-up activities, including the monitoring and evaluation of services provided. Designated case management staff shall be responsible for performing such activities for a specified period prescribed pursuant to department regulations dependent on such factors as age, education and job skills attainment of the individual, household size and stability of the family unit.

3.   When referrals to services are provided under other state-funded programs or are directly purchased by the social services district, the district may request that the provider obtain and transmit to the district the information necessary to perform the case management function.

4.   The provisions of this title shall apply to those cases involving pregnant adolescents and teen parents in receipt of public assistance, including any males and females under eighteen years of age who are designated payees of their own cases, payees of their children's cases or those public assistance recipients under eighteen years of age identified pursuant to rules and regulations as at-risk youth needing prevention services, where appropriate. At local option, case management services may be provided to those cases headed by persons eighteen years of age or older but under twenty-one years of age.

5.   In the event that an adolescent or teenage recipient refuses to accept services identified by social services district staff as needed by the adolescent or teenager, such refusal shall not carry any threat of fiscal sanctions.

6.   Case records developed by social services districts and other agencies for persons eligible for or receiving services pursuant to the provisions of this section shall be confidential and maintained in accordance with the provisions of section one hundred thirty-six of this chapter and the regulations of the department.

Added by Laws 1984, Ch. 975; eff. July 1, 1984; **amended** by Laws 1986, Ch. 188, eff. June 23, 1986; **amended** by Laws 1990, Ch. 49, § 2, eff. Mar. 31, 1990.

§ 409-k.   Case plan and service record.

1.   With respect to each individual who is identified as requiring case management services pursuant to this title, the social services district shall, within thirty days of such identification, perform or have performed an initial joint assessment with the individual, and other persons where appropriate, for the purpose of identifying those problems that have an impact on family stability and hinder the potential for economic independence. A social services district shall prior to implementing the provisions of this title submit a plan for a service case management system to the commissioner for approval.

2.   Upon completion of the assessment provided in subdivision one of this section, the social services district shall, in consultation with the individual, establish and maintain or have established and maintained a case plan and service record prescribed pursuant to regulations of the department which shall include at least the following:

(a)   identification of short term and long range goals which will ameliorate the problems indicated in subdivision one of this section. Such identification shall also include an estimate of the time period necessary to meet these goals;

(b)   identification of services needed by the client, and a description of the available resources in the community to meet identified needs; if services are not available the record should reflect such;

(c)   documentation of the arrangements made for the referral of the client to service providers;

(d)   listing of all services rendered, both direct and those provided by other public and private agencies in the community;

(e)   follow-up action taken to assure clients are in receipt of services, and any actions taken to remove any existing barriers which impede the maximum efficiency of service delivery; and

(f)   recordation of the types, cost and auspices of services provided.

3.   The case plan and service record shall be reviewed and may be revised, in consultation with the individual, at least once every six months after the plan and record have been prepared. Such review shall include an evaluation of the effectiveness of services rendered and any necessary revisions in goals or planned services as they meet the objectives indicated in paragraph (a) of subdivision two of this section.

4.   The case plan and service record shall include information for the purpose of obtaining information regarding services rendered and the cost of such services based on assessed values or the value of services rendered, where no fees are charged as in other publicly financed programs together with such other information as may be required by rules and regulations of the department.

5.   The department is authorized and directed to make such rules and regulations as are necessary to carry out the provisions of this title.

Added by Laws 1984, Ch. 975; eff. July 1, 1984; Laws 1986, Ch. 188; Laws 1990, Ch. 49, § 5, eff. Mar. 31, 1990.

§ 409-l.   Advisory board.

An advisory board shall be established by the commissioner to assist in the development and implementation of the case management provisions. It will be the responsibility of this board to assist in the development of various service models that local social services districts shall employ, assist in the formulation of appropriate procedures for evaluating such case management services, and determine the fiscal impact of such services as defined in section four hundred nine-j of this title. Appointments to the advisory board shall be obtained from public and private organizations providing teenage and child welfare services.

Added by Laws 1984, Ch. 975; eff. July 1, 1984; **amended** by Laws 1986, Ch. 188, eff. June 23, 1986; **amended** by Laws 1990, Ch. 49, § 3, eff. Mar. 31, 1990.

SSL

§ 409-m.   Reports.

1.   The commissioner shall prepare, for inclusion in the annual report required by subdivision (d) of section seventeen of this chapter to be filed with the governor and the legislature prior to December fifteenth of each year, a progress report on the planning and implementation of the provisions of this title.

2.   The report shall contain, but not be limited to, information reported statewide and by districts, the number of individuals certified as eligible for services under this title, and those for whom services were rendered and expenditures made for services identified by type, provider, and funding source. Such report shall also include progress made in implementing the provisions of this title with particular reference to efforts made to insure the effectiveness of the case management provisions.

3.   [*Repealed.*]

Added by Laws 1984, Ch. 975; eff. July 1, 1984; **amended** by Laws 1986, Ch. 188, eff. June 23, 1986; **amended** by Laws 1990, Ch. 49, § 4, eff. Mar. 31, 1990.

§ 409-n.   Implementation.

1.   The department shall plan for the implementation of the services case management system during the period from the first day of July, nineteen hundred eighty-four to the thirty-first day of March, nineteen hundred eighty-five.

2.   Subject to the appropriation of funds, the provisions of this title shall be implemented from the first day of October, nineteen hundred eighty-five in a select number of representative pilot social services districts which shall be designated by the commissioner in consultation with the advisory board established pursuant to this title, in communities with a higher than state average teen population applying for or receiving public assistance.

3.   Subject to the appropriation of funds, social services district which had not implemented the provisions of this title by the thirty-first day of March, nineteen hundred eighty-seven shall be required to implement the provisions of this title during the period April first, nineteen hundred eighty-seven through March thirty-first, nineteen hundred ninety. The social services districts subject to the provisions of this subdivision shall implement this title in accordance with a schedule to be developed by the department which will ensure statewide implementation by the thirty-first day of March, nineteen hundred eighty-eight.

Added by Laws 1984, Ch. 975; eff. July 1, 1984; Laws 1986, Ch. 188; Laws 1990, Ch. 49, § 5, eff. Mar. 31, 1990.

TITLE 5—DAY CARE FOR CERTAIN CHILDREN

§ 410. Day care; when public welfare official to furnish.

1. A public welfare official of a county, city or town is authorized, provided funds have been made available therefor, to provide day care at public expense for children residing in his territory who are eligible therefore pursuant to provisions of this title. Such care may be provided only in cases where it is determined under criteria established by the department, that there is a need therefor because of inability of the parents to provide care and supervision for a substantial part of the day and that such care is the best interest of the child and parent. Where the family is able to pay part or all of the costs of such care payment of such fees as may be reasonable in the light of such ability shall be required.

2. The furnishing of such care is hereby declared to be a proper municipal purpose for which the monies of a county, city or town may be raised and expended. A county, city or town may receive and expend monies from the state, the federal government or private individuals, corporations or associations for furnishing such care.

3. (a) Day care under this title shall mean care in a group faculty, in a family home, in a group family day care home or in a day care center project as defined in title five-a of this article for part of the day. Day care may be provided by a social services official either directly or through purchase. Purchase of such care may be made only from a private non-profit corporation or association except when the commissioner shall have approved the purchase of such care from private proprietary facilities by a social services official who has demonstrated that conveniently accessible non-profit facilities are inadequate to provide required care. Purchase of such care may also be made from a school district in accordance with state and federal requirements pursuant to a contract between the social services district and the school district.

(b) Care under this title may be provided only in group facilities, family homes, group family day care homes or in a day care center project as defined in title five-a which are operated in compliance with applicable regulations of the department. A group facility shall include a public school which provides day care pursuant to this subdivision.

(c)   Except as hereinafter provided, care under this title shall not include care, supervision, training or participation in kindergartens, nursery schools, or other schools, classes or activities operated or conducted by public or private schools. However such care shall include day care provided by a school district pursuant to the provisions of this subdivision and subdivision thirty-three of section sixteen hundred four of the education law in accordance with a contract entered into between such school district and a social services district.

(d)   The commissioner shall encourage social services districts and day care providers to offer flexible hours of day care. Each provider may provide a flexible schedule in accordance with the rules and regulations of the commissioner and an application for day care services shall not be denied solely by reason of the time of day or days that care will be required provided that an available day care provider can accommodate such hours or days of care in accordance with such regulations.

4.   The provisions of this title shall not apply to child care assistance provided under title five-c of this article.

Added by Laws 1965, Ch. 395; **amended** by Laws 1969, Ch. 1014, Laws 1970, Ch. 488; Laws 1971, Ch. 110, eff. July 1, 1971 and Ch. 809, eff. June 25, 1971; **amended** by Laws 1983, Ch. 217, eff. June 3, 1983; **amended** by Laws 1983, Ch. 846, eff. Aug. 8, 1983; **amended** by Laws 1985, Ch. 874, eff. Aug. 2, 1985, and retroactive to and deemed to have been in full force and effect on and after May 1, 1985; **amended** by Laws 1986, Ch. 875, eff. Jan. 1, 1987; **repealed** subd. 4 by Laws 1986, Ch. 875, eff. Jan. 1, 1987; **amended** by Laws 1997, Ch. 436, § 1 Part B, § 51, eff. Aug. 20, 1997.

§ 410-a.   Day care; when department to furnish.

Any inconsistent provision of law notwithstanding, if and so long as federal funds are available for the care provided pursuant to the provisions of this section, and to the extent of such funds and state funds appropriated or made available therefor, the department shall be authorized to provide day care, through appropriate arrangements and cooperative agreements with the state departments of education and agriculture and markets, approved by the director of the budget, in public schools operated by school districts and in facilities operated by or for the state department of agriculture and markets for children who are receiving family assistance or who are former or potential recipients of such aid in accordance with the regulations of the department, including only such children who are in pre-kindergarten programs of such schools or who are children of migrant workers.

Added by Laws 1971, Ch. 640, eff. Apr. 1, 1971. Laws 1971, Ch. 640, § 2, provides:

"The director of the budget is authorized to transfer to the state department of social services so much of the annual funds appropriated to the state education department for state participation in the per-kindergarten programs of the public schools as may be necessary to allow participation in such programs of children who are receiving aid to dependent children or who are former or potential recipients of such aid, as defined by the rules and regulations of the state department of social services, in accordance with the provisions of section four hundred ten-a of the social services law, as added by this act. The director of the budget is similarly authorized to transfer to the state department of social services so much of the annual funds appropriated to the state department of agriculture and markets for the migrant day care program as may be necessary to allow children of migrant workers to be furnished day care pursuant to the provisions of section four hundred ten-a of the social services law, as added by this act."

Amended by Laws 1997, Ch. 436, § 1 Part B, § 102, eff. Aug. 20, 1997.

§ 410-b.   Federal grants.

1.   The department of taxation and finance is authorized to accept and receive from the federal government any moneys which the federal government shall offer to the state for or with respect to the construction, maintenance or operation of facilities for day care for children, under or pursuant to any federal law heretofore or hereafter enacted authorizing grants to the state for such purpose or similar purposes, including payments to political subdivisions of, and any public agencies in the state.

2.   The department of social welfare is hereby designated and empowered to act as the agent of the state in carrying out the provisions of any such federal law with respect to such day care facilities in this state.

3.   Any and all such grants and moneys awarded for assistance to this state under or pursuant to any federal law shall be accepted and received by the department of taxation and finance as custodian thereof and such moneys, so received, shall be deposited by such department of taxation and finance in a special fund or funds and shall be used exclusively for the purposes of any such federal law. Such moneys shall be paid from such fund or funds on the audit and warrant of the comptroller upon vouchers certified or approved by the commissioner of welfare.

4.   Any federal funds made available to the state for day care facilities shall be retained by the state.

Added by Laws 1965, Ch. 395; **amended** by Laws 1969, Ch. 1014, eff. July 1, 1969; formerly § 410-a **renumbered** § 410-b by Laws 1971, Ch. 640, eff. Apr. 1, 1971.

§ 410-bb.   Grants to not-for-profit facilities providing day care for children for employee salary and benefit enhancements.

1.   The legislature finds and declares that a crisis exists in the availability and quality of child day care in New York state and that this crisis poses a danger both to the welfare and safety of the children and to the productivity of this state's workforce; that inadequate salaries and in many cases nonexistent benefit

SSL

packages have substantially contributed to the existing crisis by precluding day care centers from recruiting and retaining necessary teaching and supervisory staff; that an extremely high turnover rate has interfered in many instances with the ability of day care centers to comply with regulatory requirements and to properly serve the children in their care; and that because of these extraordinary circumstances New York state must intervene and provide assistance for recruitment and retention of child care workers. The legislature recognizes that a long-term solution to this crisis will require cooperative efforts among the business community, local and state governments and families.

2. Within amounts appropriated specifically therefor, and after deducting funds as specified in subdivision three of this section the commissioner shall allocate funds to local social services districts for grants to eligible not-for-profit day care centers for retention and recruitment of teaching and supervisory staff, as follows:

(a) a city social services district with a population in excess of one million shall be allocated a portion of such funds based on an equal weighting of:

(i) its proportion of the state population of children aged five and under, and

(ii) its proportion of total claims for reimbursement received by the department by May thirty-first, nineteen hundred eighty-eight for the low income, transitional and teen parent day care programs authorized by chapter fifty-three of the laws of nineteen hundred eighty-seven.

(b) all other eligible local social services districts shall be allocated the remaining portion of funds based on each district's proportionate share of licensed not-for-profit day care capacity relative to the total capacity of all such other eligible districts.

3. Five percent of the funds appropriated for such recruitment and retention purposes shall be reserved for administration of the program and allocated as follows:

(a) each local social services district shall be allocated an amount equivalent to five percent of the funds it receives under paragraphs (a) and (b) of subdivision two of this section, provided that no district shall receive an amount less than twenty-five hundred dollars nor greater than one hundred fifty thousand dollars, and

(b) remaining funds shall be allocated to the department. In the event that a not-for-profit child care resource and referral agency or the department distributes funds in an eligible district, as provided herein, such agency or department may retain the amount that otherwise would be available to the eligible district.

4. Not later than thirty days following the effective date of this section, the commissioner shall notify local social services districts of the amounts allocated to each district and provide forms for the collecting of information pursuant to this section.

5. For the purposes of this section, an eligible district shall mean a local social services district that is providing, as of the effective date of this section, or which shall agree to provide in such written form and by such date as shall be acceptable to the department, subsidized day care services under the special day care services program authorized by chapter fifty-three of the laws of nineteen hundred eighty-eight.

6. Eligible districts may apply on or before the ninetieth day following the effective date of this section to receive such allocated funds by submitting to the department a plan on forms provided by the department. Such plan shall be developed by the local social services commissioner in consultation with directors of participating eligible day care centers, as such term is defined herein. Such plan shall include: methods to increase the amount of day care provided for families having an income at or below two hundred percent of the federal poverty [poverty] level in such district; proposed steps to be taken to sustain gains in recruitment and retention of staff achieved by funds provided herein; information specified in paragraph (c) of subdivision seven of this section; and a proposed allocation of funds to eligible day care centers based on the following factors:

(a) forty percent of the funds allocated to such district shall be distributed to each eligible center based on such center's share of the total full time equivalent teaching and supervisory staff of such centers in the district as a whole;

(b) forty percent of the funds allocated to such district shall be distributed to each eligible center based on such center's share of the number of children from families having an income at or below two hundred percent of the federal poverty level receiving day care services in all such centers in the district, regardless of whether such children are receiving subsidized care; and

(c) notwithstanding any other provision of this subdivision, twenty percent of the funds allocated to such district shall be distributed to some or all eligible centers in a manner to further improve recruitment and retention of qualified staff. Distributions under this paragraph shall be based on factors including, but not be limited to seniority; educational qualifications; worker income; benefit levels, vacancy and turnover rates; or enhancement of distributions pursuant to paragraph (a) or (b) of this subdivision. The commissioner shall make copies of proposals available to the public upon request.

7. For the purposes of this section, an eligible day care center means a not-for-profit center which provides services for children in single or double sessions for six or more hours per day for five or more days per week and holds a permit or certificate issued pursuant to (i) the provisions of section three hundred ninety of this article, or (ii) the New York city health code as authorized by section five hundred fifty-eight of the New York city charter; provided, however, that:

(a) a center whose permit has been denied, suspended or revoked, or which is found in any twelve month period preceding or following the date of the allocation of funds made pursuant to subdivision two of this section to be in violation of section three hundred ninety of this article after a hearing conducted

SSL

as provided therein or after decision by any court of competent jurisdiction, shall not be eligible to receive funds pursuant to this section;

(b) the existence of a current contract for purchase of day care services between an eligible district and a center may not be required as a precondition to receive such funds, but such center shall agree to accept children subsidized by the district in the next available space after receipt of a request from the district to place a child in such center;

(c) each such center must provide to the local social services district the following information on forms provided by the department:

(i) child care capacity, by ages of children;

(ii) the number of children in such center, by ages, whose families have incomes at or below two hundred percent of the federal poverty level, regardless of whether such children are receiving subsidized care;

(iii) the number of children specified in subparagraph (ii) of this paragraph receiving subsidies and the type of subsidy;

(iv) a schedule of fees charged for services;

(v) the total annual revenue from all sources, including fees, donations, grants, revenue from local governments and revenue from state agencies;

(vi) the total annual expenditures for rent or mortgage payments; equipment, property, liability and other insurance; utilities; food; supplies and materials; and

(vii) total annual expenditures for salaries and benefits, including the number, title, qualifications and salary levels of existing staff and types and amounts of benefits; and

(d) each eligible day care center must agree, to the maximum extent feasible, to enhance its future revenues to sustain the level of staff salary and benefits as provided herein.

8. Should an eligible district not apply for such funds, the commissioner may contract with a not-for-profit child care resource and referral agency as such term is defined in title five-B of this article which is serving such district to distribute such funds allocated to the district in the same manner as is required of an eligible district in accordance with the other provisions of this section. If two or more not-for-profit child care resource and referral agencies are serving such district, preference shall be given to the agency or agencies with existing contracts with the commissioner. If such agency does not exist or declines to participate, the department shall disburse funds in the manner as is required of an eligible district pursuant to this section.

9. A plan developed and submitted to the department pursuant to the provisions of this section shall be considered approved unless, within thirty days of the receipt of such plan, the department notifies the eligible district or agency that the plan is not approved and specifies in writing the basis for such disapproval. The commissioner shall make allocated funds and administrative

funds available as advances to eligible districts whose plans have been approved pursuant to this section.

10. Eligible districts shall make allocated funds available as advances to eligible day care centers in accordance with the plan approved by the department. Such districts shall notify the department when all such funds have been disbursed but all such funds must be disbursed not later than October first, nineteen hundred eighty-nine.

11. Any funds allocated to eligible districts or day care centers which cannot be used in the manner as provided herein shall be reallocated among other eligible districts as provided in paragraph (b) of subdivision two of this section.

12. Funds received by eligible day care centers shall be used solely for employee benefits and salary enhancements for teaching and supervisory staff, and shall not be used to supplant or substitute for any other funding available for day care services, or to provide services which eligible day care centers are required to provide pursuant to contracts with the state, local social services districts, authorized agencies, individuals or other organizations.

13. Nothing contained herein shall prevent an eligible district, or any other person or entity, at its discretion, from contributing funds, including administrative funds received pursuant to subdivision three of this section, to the program established pursuant to this section.

14. The department shall:

(a) provide or cause to be provided, to the maximum extent feasible, technical assistance to eligible day care centers and districts concerning employee benefit options, long-term planning, management of funds, responsibilities required pursuant to this section, maximization of the use of available subsidy funds including title XX and title IV-A of the Federal Social Security Act and such other matters as may be helpful to sustain the level of staff salary and benefits as provided herein;

(b) annually examine cost data concerning rates of payment for day care and establish appropriate recommended fee schedules as guidelines for use by local social services districts in developing comprehensive annual social services program plans;

(c) promulgate regulations not later than July first, nineteen hundred eighty-nine, to establish a maximum rate of payment for day care centers which shall reflect adjustments in the cost of care since the establishment of the maximum rate in effect on January first, nineteen hundred eighty-six. Such maximum rate shall be calculated by applying thereto increases in the cost of living since January first, nineteen hundred eighty-six, updated by the department through December thirty-first, nineteen hundred eighty-nine, and also to the extent possible and based on the availability of such information, factors such as changes in the costs of insurance, rent, utilities and labor and benefits and such other factors the department shall deem appropriate, which exceed such increases in the cost of living, as updated through December thirty-first, nineteen hundred eighty-nine; provided, however, that:

(i)   actual payment for day care services rendered shall not exceed the actual cost of such care;

(ii)   nothing contained herein shall prevent the department from establishing a rate of payment for day care centers greater than that required pursuant to this subdivision;

(iii)   approved rates of payment in excess of the rate established pursuant to this paragraph in effect prior to July first, nineteen hundred eighty-nine shall be continued;

(iv)   nothing contained herein shall prevent the department from approving exceptions to the rate of payment established herein to meet specific identified needs of a local social services district;

(v)   such regulations may include a higher maximum rate of payment for infant care, or care of children with special needs.

(d)   Notwithstanding any other section of law to the contrary, by April first, nineteen hundred eighty-nine, the department shall develop guidelines and may, with the approval of the director of the division of the budget grant to local districts for one year waivers to income eligibility standards established pursuant to law for subsidized day care under the special day care services program. Such waivers shall be granted to increase eligibility standards up to twenty-five percent of the federal poverty level above the income eligibility standard established by law as a percentage of the federal poverty level. Waivers shall be granted only upon the submission of documentation establishing that:

(i)   the local social services district is serving substantially all eligible families with incomes at or below the established income eligibility standard. A district shall be deemed to be serving substantially all eligible families if it meets the following two criteria: (a) the percentage of eligible children served in the district meets or exceeds the percentage of eligible children served statewide under the special day care services program and (b) the district has provided day care services to any additional children whose families have been identified in such district's outreach program as described in subparagraph (ii) of this paragraph as eligible for and desiring subsidized day care services;

(ii)   the local district has established a district-wide outreach program which identifies eligible families who are not receiving subsidized child day care under the special day care services program, and informs all such families of their availability, and assists such families desiring subsidized services to obtain them;

(iii)   a family receiving a subsidy under the district's waiver provisions shall be required to contribute a greater amount towards the cost of care than a family eligible under the established income eligibility standard;

(iv)   the local district has included an estimate of the number of children who will be served under the waiver provisions;

(v)   the local district has submitted claims to income eligible day care expenses under title XX of the federal Social Security Act;

(vi)   the district has available to it a higher allocation in the current fiscal year than the amount of reimbursement received by such district in the previous fiscal year for subsidized care under the special day care services program.

(e)   submit a report to the governor and to the chairmen of the senate finance committee and the assembly ways and means committee not later than December thirty-first, nineteen hundred eighty-nine on the program established pursuant to this section, including the number, amount and recipients of grants in each eligible district; the purposes and uses of such grants; an evaluation of any resulting improvements in recruitment and retention of qualified staff, current local eligibility standards, any use of the waiver process, state cost of increasing the eligibility standards established by law up to twenty-five percent and fifty percent of the federal poverty level on a county by county basis for subsidized day care under the special day care services program and recommendations for long-term solutions to the problems of recruitment and retention of teaching and supervisory staff.

Added by Laws 1988, Ch. 503, § 1, eff. Aug. 1, 1988; **amended** by Laws 1988, Ch. 659, § 1, eff. Sept. 1, 1988.

§ 410-bbb.   Grants to day care workers for salary enhancements and professional advancement. [*Expires and repealed March 31, 2005.*]

1.   Within amounts appropriated specifically therefor, and after deducting funds as specified in subdivision four of this section, the commissioner of the office of children and family services shall make grants available for the purposes of promoting retention and professional development within the child care profession. Such grants shall be made directly to eligible employees and operators of child care programs to the extent that funds are available. For the purposes of this section, "child care program" shall mean licensed and registered child day care centers, group family day care homes, family day care homes and school-age child care programs and "operator" shall mean the individual in charge of the daily operation of the day care center, family day care home, group family day care home or school-age child care program with supervisory responsibility over any assistants, employees and volunteers of such center, home or program.

2.   (a) Grants shall be available to employees and operators of child care programs who apply for such grants to the office of children and family services and who meet the following criteria:

(i)   the individual must have been employed continuously for the twelve months preceding the application for an average of twenty hours or more per week in a child care program and/or must have operated a child care program continuously for the twelve months preceding the application for an average of twenty hours or more per week;

(ii)   the individual must continue to be employed continuously for an average of twenty hours or more per week in the same child care program and/or operate the same child care program continuously for an average of twenty hours or more per week for at least six months beyond the date that the application is received by the office of children and family services;

(iii)   the individual must be in a position or capacity within the child care program with direct responsibility for the care and supervision of children. Such responsibility must be demonstrated by the individual having served as a family day care home operator or assistant, a group family care home operator or assistant, or as an employee of a child day care center or school-age child care program who spends at least fifty percent of his or her time working in the center or program with direct child care or support duties; and

(iv)   the individual must provide verification to the office of children and family services of eligibility for a grant. The office shall determine an employee's or operator's eligibility based upon:

(A)   verification of employment from sources including but not limited to pay statements and employer records; and

(B)   documentation that establishes an employee's or operator's level of education or training achievement pursuant to paragraph (c) of this subdivision in the form of degrees, certificates, credentials, official transcripts or other official documentation issued by accredited educational or training institutions.

(b)   The above notwithstanding, no employee or operator of a child care program shall be eligible for a grant through employment in or operation of any of the types of facilities or programs listed below. Such employees and operators may be eligible for a grant pursuant to paragraph (a) of this subdivision through employment in or operation of a day care program that is not:

(i)   a federally funded head start or early start program; or

(ii)   a pre-school special education program or early intervention program for children under three years of age with handicapping conditions.

(c)   The above notwithstanding, no employee or operator of a child care program shall be eligible for a grant where the individual:

(i)   has an annual salary or income from a child care program that is more than the mean salary for a kindergarten teacher in the state as defined by the department of labor;

(ii)   as an operator or employee of a child care program, has been named during the twelve month period immediately preceding the application or the six month period after the application as the primary subject of a proceeding that resulted in the suspension, revocation, denial of an application for a license or registration or imposition of a fine on the child care program; or

(iii)   as an operator or employee of a child care program, has been named during the twelve month period immediately preceding the application or the six month period after the application as the primary subject of a proceeding to suspend, revoke, deny an application for a license or registration or impose a fine on a child care program where such proceeding has not been finally resolved. Upon final resolution of such proceeding, the individual may be eligible for a grant if the resolution of such proceeding does not result in the suspension, revocation, denial of an application for a license or registration or imposition of a fine on the child care program.

(d)   At the conclusion of the six month period following application, eligible individuals will receive, to the extent funds are available, as follows:

(i)   individuals who hold an associate degree or a higher degree in a field related to the provision of child care or a bachelors degree or higher degree in any field shall receive a payment of seven hundred fifty dollars;

(ii)   individuals who do not meet the qualifications of subparagraph (i) of this paragraph but who have a child development credential or an equivalent certificate in a field related to the provision of child care or an associate degree in any field shall receive a payment of five hundred dollars;

(iii)   individuals who do not meet the criteria of subparagraph (i) or (ii) of this paragraph shall receive a payment of three hundred dollars. Provided, however, that individuals shall not be eligible for more than one payment in any eighteen month period; and

(iv)   funds received by eligible child care workers shall not be used to supplant any other salary enhancements as negotiated in a collective bargaining agreement or any compensation paid by a child care program.

(v)   in addition, in instances where the awardee can demonstrate that his or her compensated position has, as a primary function, the direct supervision of children or responsibility for the educational or programmatic content of the program, then the level of the award granted will be increased. Such awards also will be further increased in instances where the awardee can demonstrate that his or her compensated position has, as a primary function, the direct supervision of children or responsibility for the educational or programmatic content of the program and can demonstrate that during the eighteen month period of employment, to which this award corresponds, the individual has successfully completed a recognized course of study or professional development leading to a certificate, degree or credential relevant to the field of early childhood education or school-age child care. The enhanced awards will be granted as follows: individuals who have attained a high school degree, general equivalency degree or have less education and are in a direct care position or a position with direct responsibility for the educational or programmatic content of the program will receive an award of five hundred dollars. If such an individual, within the eighteen month period, has achieved a credential, certificate or degree specified by the office of children and family services, the individual will be granted an award of seven hundred fifty dollars. Individuals who have a child development credential or a recognized equivalent, or an associate's degree in any field and are in a direct care position or a position with direct responsibility for the educational or programmatic content of the program will receive an award of seven hundred fifty dollars. If such an individual, within the eighteen-month period, has achieved a credential, certificate or degree specified by the office, the individual will be granted an award of one thousand five hundred dollars. Individuals who hold an associates degree in a field related to the provision of child care or a higher degree in any field and are in a direct care position or a position with direct responsibility for the educational or programmatic content of the program will receive an award of one thousand dollars. If such an individual, within the eighteen-month period, has achieved a credential, certificate or degree specified by the office, the individual will be granted an award of two thousand dollars.

3.   Five percent of the funds appropriated for the purposes of this section shall be reserved to the office of children and family services for the administration of the program. The office shall be required to conduct outreach activities in consultation with interested parties in the child care field to advise employees and operators of child care programs of the availability of grants pursuant to this section.

4.   The commissioner of the office of children and family services shall submit a report to the governor, temporary president of the senate and the speaker of the assembly not later than December thirty-first, two thousand one on the implementation of this section. Such report shall include the total number of workers awarded grants in each of the three categories and an assessment of the effectiveness of the grant program in enhancing retention of staff in child day care programs.

Amended by L. 2001, Ch. 383, extending repeal date, eff. Oct. 29, 2001; amended by L. 2002, Ch. 83, Part C, § 3, eff. May 29, 2002; L. 2003, Ch. 62, Part J2, §§ 1, 3 and 4, eff. May 15, 2003.

§ 410-c.   State reimbursement.

1.   (a) Expenditures made by counties, cities, and towns for day care and its administration, and day care center projects, pursuant to the provisions of this title, shall, if approved by the department, be subject to reimbursement by the state, in accordance with the regulations of the department, as follows: there shall be paid to each county, city or town (1) the amount of federal funds, if any, properly received or to be received on account of such expenditures; (2) fifty per centum of its expenditures for day care and its administration and day care center projects, after first deducting therefrom any federal funds received or to be received on account thereof, and any expenditures defrayed by fees paid by parents or by other private contributions.

(b)   For the purpose of this title, expenditures for administration of day care shall include expenditures for compensation of employees in connection with the furnishing of day care, including but not limited to costs incurred for pensions, federal old age and survivors insurance and health insurance for such employees;

training programs for personnel, operation, maintenance and service costs; and such other expenditures such as equipment costs, depreciation and charges and rental values as may be approved by the department. It shall not include expenditures for capital costs. In the case of day care purchased from a non-profit corporation constituting an eligible borrower pursuant to title five-a of this article, expenditures shall include an allocable proportion of all operating costs of such facility as may be approved by the department including but not limited to the expenditures enumerated in this paragraph (b) and expenditures for amortization, interest and other financing costs of any mortgage loan made to such non-profit corporation.

2.   (a) Claims for state reimbursement shall be made in such form and manner and at such times and for such periods as the department shall determine.

(b)   When certified by the department, state reimbursement shall be paid from the state treasury upon the audit and warrant of the comptroller out of funds made available therefor.

3.   The department is authorized in its discretion to approve and certify to the comptroller for payment, advances to counties, cities or towns in anticipation of the state reimbursement provided for in this section.

4.   Payment of state reimbursement and advances shall be made to local fiscal officers as in the case of state reimbursement for public assistance and care under other provisions of this chapter.

5.   (a) As used in this subdivision "school age child day care programs" shall mean programs which offer care to school age children under the age of fourteen before or after the period when these children are in school. Such programs may include, but are not limited to, programs provided in school buildings in accordance with paragraph (i) of subdivision one of section four hundred fourteen of the education law.

(b)   The commissioner shall, within appropriations made available therefor, select proposed school age child day care programs which shall be eligible to receive an award of no more than twenty-five thousand dollars for start up or expansion costs, including planning, rental, operational and equipment costs, or minor renovations identified as being necessary in order for the program to comply with applicable state or local building, fire safety or licensing standards, based on plans submitted to him. The commissioner shall give preference to those areas of the state which are significantly underserved by existing school age child day care programs and to those programs which involve parents in the development and implementation of programs. The commissioner shall publicize this availability of funds to be used for purposes of this subdivision in awarding grants. Plans may be submitted by private not-for-profit corporations, organizations or governmental subdivisions.

(c)   Notwithstanding any other provisions of law, social services districts shall be authorized to purchase services which are to be provided pursuant to this subdivision from programs which have been approved by the commissioner to receive funds pursuant to this subdivision.

6.   Any other provision of law notwithstanding, and within amounts appropriated therefor, the department shall have authority to make start-up grants to prospective programs that will provide child day care, as such term is defined in section three hundred ninety of this article, from any funds available for such purpose.

Added by Laws 1969, Ch. 1014, eff. July 1, 1969; **amended** by Laws 1971, Ch. 110, eff. July 1, 1971; former § 410-b **added** by Laws 1965, Ch. 395; **repealed** by Laws 1969, Ch. 1014, eff. July 1, 1969; former 410-b **renumbered** § 410-c by Laws 971, Ch. 640, eff. Apr. 1, 1971; **amended** by Laws 1984, Ch. 460, eff. July 18, 1984; **amended** by Laws 1987, Ch. 198, eff. June 29, 1987 except that paragraph (b) and (c) of subd. 5 are **repealed** eff. Oct. 31, 1990; **amended** by Laws 1990, Ch. 66, § 2, eff. Apr. 6, 1990, amendment to SSL § 410-c(5)(b) expires Oct 31, 1990, pursuant to Laws 1990, Ch. 198; **amended** by Laws 1990, Ch. 750, § 4, eff. Nov. 19, 1990; **amended** by Laws 1990, Ch. 277, § 1, eff. June 24, 1990.

§ 410-cc.   Start up grants for child day care.

The commissioner shall provide funds to start up grants to not-for-profit organizations or corporations for the development of new or expanded all day child day care programs including costs related to planning, renting, renovating, operating, and purchasing equipment. The commissioner shall establish guidelines including, but not limited to, allowable costs, and criteria for eligibility for grants giving preference to those child day care providers who will, to the maximum extent feasible, target services to households having incomes up to two hundred percent of the federal poverty standard. The commissioner shall publicize the availability of funds. No awards shall be granted which exceed twenty-five hundred dollars for a new family day care provider or new group family day care provider, and one hundred thousand dollars for a new child day care center. Child care resource and referral agencies may receive + family day care start up grants not to exceed two thousand five hundred dollars per new provider if the agency trains such new family provider and thereby expands the supply of family day care programs in the community. The commissioner shall give preference to those communities which are significantly underserved by existing programs and to those programs which and those providers who will serve infants under two years of age.

Added by Laws 1990, Ch. 277, § 2, eff. June 24, 1990; **amended** by Laws 1990, Ch. 882, § 1, eff. June 24, 1990.

§ 410-ccc.   Child day care facility development.

1.   Comprehensive strategic development plan. (a) The commissioner shall direct the department, in collaboration with the department of economic development, other appropriate agencies, and appropriate public authorities and public

benefit corporations, to develop a comprehensive strategic development plan for child day care facilities by December thirty-first, nineteen hundred ninety-five. Moneys not to exceed two hundred fifty thousand dollars from within amounts appropriated to the department by section one of chapter fifty-four of the laws of nineteen hundred ninety-four, enacting the capital projects budget, shall be available for such purposes and a portion may be suballocated in connection therewith.

(b) Prior to development of the plan, (i) the department shall develop the child day care facility information system, a database including data on existing early childhood providers serving children including but not limited to regulated child day care providers, head start and pre-kindergarten programs. The information shall include the types and number of programs, program location including county, the ages served, the capacity of the programs, the hours and calendar of program operations and rates.

(ii) County specific information on the number of children currently served shall be compared to the local projected need from demographic information and waiting lists maintained for child day care programs, local district estimates of child care needs for participants in the job opportunities and basic skills training program, and families eligible for child care subsidies.

(iii) Information shall also be collected on funding sources and amounts for eligible families, for health and safety grants, for startup and capital grants, for child care resource and referral programs, and any other public funding which is directed at increasing the number and size of early childhood programs. Any known private funding sources directed at the purpose of capital, start-up or subsidies to providers shall also be included.

(iv) The department shall also collect information on the technical assistance activities presently available to potential and existing child day care providers.

(v) On or before February first, nineteen hundred ninety-five, the department shall submit a preliminary report to the division of the budget, the chairs of the senate finance committee and the assembly ways and means committee including but not limited to: (a) a compilation of the existing data designated in this section; (b) information available on private sector interest, involvement or plans for development of child day care in New York state; (c) information from child care resource and referral programs about the numbers of inquiries received from parents and businesses; and (d) a status report on the applications related to the appropriation enacted in chapter fifty-four of the laws of nineteen hundred ninety-four, enacting the capital projects budget, for construction grants, revolving loans and loan guarantees, and child care project development grants.

(vi) [Repealed]

2. Notwithstanding any other provision of law, of the moneys appropriated to the department in section one of chapter fifty-four of the laws of nineteen hundred ninety-four, enacting the capital projects budget, four million seven hundred fifty thousand dollars shall be available as follows: seven hundred fifty

SSL

thousand dollars for child care project development grants and related administrative expenses; the remaining four million dollars shall be available for the child care facilities construction program as defined in section sixteen-g of the urban development corporation act; of this amount, no less than three million dollars shall be available for child care construction grants and related administrative expenses and any remaining funds may be available for child care construction revolving loans and loan guarantees, and related administrative expenses. The amounts available for the child care facilities construction program, as defined in section sixteen-g of the urban development corporation act, shall be suballocated to the urban development corporation pursuant to this section.

Up to five percent of the moneys available pursuant to this subdivision may be used for payments to the department or other state agencies or authorities, and the urban development corporation for administrative expenses required to develop requests for proposals and to approve contracts for child care construction projects pursuant to this section and/or section sixteen-g of the urban development corporation act. The director of the division of the budget shall approve such payments.

3.   Child care project development grants. The department shall develop a request for proposals to provide grants to not-for-profit organizations, including, but not limited to, child care resource and referral programs, local development corporations, neighborhood preservation companies and rural preservation companies as defined in section nine hundred two of the private housing finance law, to support per-development planning, management, and coordination of activities, leading to the development of child day care centers in under-served areas meeting the needs of low-income working families. Such activities may include: (a) design studies and services and other development or redevelopment work in connection with the design and development of child day care centers; and (b) studies, surveys or reports, including preliminary planning studies to assess a particular site or sites or facility or facilities for the development of child day care centers.

(c)   In determining grants to be awarded, the department shall consider the following: (i) that a not-for-profit organization applying for a grant under this subdivision is a bona fide organization which shall have demonstrated by its immediate past and current activities its ability to lead or to assist in the development of projects, such as child day care centers meeting the needs of low-income families; (ii) the need for day care centers in the area; (iii) the potential viability for a child day care center to succeed in the area; and (iv) such other matters as the department determines necessary.

(d)   Grants shall be awarded to eligible entities where the department identifies an insufficient supply of child day care programs. Grants awarded pursuant to the request for proposals shall not exceed seventy-five thousand dollars per project.

4.   Child care construction grants. (a) the child care construction grants awarded pursuant to this section and section sixteen-g of the urban development

corporation act shall be available for not-for-profit child care facilities construction projects owned or to be owned by not-for-profit corporations for use as child day care centers that will be duly approved, licensed, inspected, supervised, and regulated as may be determined to be necessary and appropriate by the department, except that with respect to child day care centers located in the city of New York, such child day care centers will be duly approved, licensed, inspected, supervised, and regulated as may be determined to be necessary and appropriate by the commissioner of the department of health of the city of New York.

(b)　Grants shall be made through contracts to not-for-profit corporations for child care facilities construction projects pursuant to a request for proposal process jointly developed by the department and the urban development corporation in consultation with the department of economic development. The department shall receive, initially review, and assess applications to determine which projects should be referred to the urban development corporation and to rank by groups, the referred projects according to the capacity of such projects to meet identified needs for child day care. In assessing such applications, the department shall consider: (i) the need for day care services in the area; (ii) the potential viability for a child day care center to succeed in the area; (iii) the qualifications of the proposed provider to operate a child care center; (iv) the potential for meeting applicable regulatory requirements; (v) the appropriateness of the site for licensing as a day care center and (vi) such other matters as the department determines necessary.

(c)　Upon the timely completion of the department's initial review and selection of applications meeting criteria, the department shall immediately submit such selected applications and the group rankings of such applications to the urban development corporation which, in consultation with the department of economic development, shall select award recipients. No later than upon submission of the selected applications, the department shall also suballocate all moneys appropriated for such purposes to such corporation.

5.　Programs conducted pursuant to this section of law are limited to the amounts appropriated therefor.

Added by Laws 1994, Ch. 728, § 2, eff. Aug. 2, 1994. Subd. (1) shall expire and be deemed repealed on Dec. 31, 2000, at which time subds. (2) through (5) will be renumbered (1) through (4), respectively.

TITLE 5-A—YOUTH FACILITIES IMPROVEMENT ACT

§ 410-d.   Short title: policy and purposes of title.

This title shall be known, and may be cited and referred to, as the "Youth Facilities Improvement Act."

There is a serious shortage throughout the state of facilities suitable for use for the care of children especially those of per-school age and primary school age whose parents are unable to provide such care for all or a substantial part of the day or post-school day. A similar shortage of residential child care facilities also exists. Existing day care and residential child care facilities are overcrowded with long waiting lists. Many such facilities are so located that they are not accessible to families in need of such services. The absence of adequate day care and residential child care facilities is contrary to the interest of the people of the state, is detrimental to the health and welfare of the child and his parents and prevents the gainful employment of persons, who are otherwise qualified, because of the need to provide such care in their home.

It is the purpose of this article to encourage the timely construction and equipment of such facilities with mortgage loan participation by the New York state housing finance agency. The provision of such facilities is hereby declared to be a public purpose which it is the policy of the state to encourage.

Added by Laws 1969, Ch. 1013; **amended** by Laws 1970, Ch. 966; **amended** by Laws of 1971, Ch. 1030, eff. July 2, 1971; **amended** by Laws 1975, Ch. 224, eff. June 17, 1975.

§ 410-e.   Definitions.

As used in this title the following words and phrases shall have the following meanings unless a different meaning is plainly required by the context:

1.   "Board." The state board of social welfare.

2.   "Commissioner." The commissioner of social services of the state of New York.

3.   "Department." The state department of social services.

4.   "Eligible borrower." A non-profit corporation organized under the laws of the state of New York which is authorized to care for children and which has entered into a regulatory agreement in accordance with the provisions of section four hundred ten-f of this title.

5.   "Project." "Youth facilities prospect." A specific work or improvement including lands, buildings, improvements, fixtures and articles of personal

property acquired, constructed, rehabilitated, managed, owned and operated by an eligible borrower to provide day care in the manner prescribed by the department for children of per-school and primary school age or to provide residential child care in the manner prescribed by the rules of the board for children of per-school, primary school or secondary school age, or to provide any combination of the foregoing, and for facilities incidental or appurtenant thereto.

6. "Project cost." "Youth facilities project cost." The sum total of all costs incurred by an eligible borrower as approved by the commissioner as reasonable and necessary for carrying out all works and undertakings and providing all necessary equipment for the development of a project exclusive of any private or federal, state or local financing assistance available for and received by an eligible borrower for the payment of such project cost. These shall include but are not necessarily limited to the carrying charges during construction or rehabilitation up to and including the occupancy date, working capital not exceeding three percentum of the estimated total cost or three percentum of the actual total final cost, whichever is larger, the cost of all necessary studies, surveys, plans and specifications, architectural engineering, legal or other special services, the cost of acquisition of land and any buildings and improvements thereon, site preparation and development, construction, reconstruction and equipment, including fixtures, equipment and articles of personal property required for the operation of the project the reasonable cost of financing incurred by the eligible borrower in the course of the development of the project, up to and including the occupancy date, the fees imposed by the commissioner and by the New York state housing finance agency; other fees charged, including any premium payments to the youth facilities project guarantee fund created by the youth facilities project guarantee fund act, and necessary expenses incurred in connection with the initial occupancy of the project, and the cost of such other items as the commissioner may determine to be reasonable and necessary for the development of a project, less any and all rents and other net revenues from the operation of the real property, improvements or personal property on the project site, or any part thereof, by the eligible borrower on and after the date on which the contract between the eligible borrower and the New York tate housing finance agency was entered into and prior to the occupancy date.

7. "Occupancy date." The date defined in the documents providing for a mortgage loan between an eligible borrower and the New York state housing finance agency.

8. "Youth facilities development fund company." A company incorporated and organized pursuant to subdivision two of section four hundred ten-n of this title.

9. "Youth facilities center." A facility suitable to provide day care for children of per-school age and primary school age or to provide residential child care for children of per-school, primary school or secondary school age or to provide any combination of the foregoing, which has been approved by the state department of social services.

Added by Laws 1969, Ch. 1013; **amended** by Laws 1970, Ch. 278, eff. Apr. 29, 1970; **amended** by Laws 1970, Ch. 966, **amended** by Laws 1971, Ch. 110, eff. July 1, 1971; **amended** by Laws 1971, Ch. 1030; **amended** by Laws 1972, Ch. 272, eff. May 9, 1972.

§ 410-f.   Regulation of eligible borrowers.

1. Every eligible borrower, as a condition precedent to borrowing funds from the agency, shall enter into a regulatory agreement with the commissioner which shall provide:

(a) that the real property or other assets mortgaged or otherwise pledged to the agency shall not be sold, transferred, encumbered or assigned until the eligible borrower shall have repaid in full all obligations under the mortgage of the agency and has paid such other obligations as may be required by the commissioner provided, however, the provisions of this paragraph (a) shall not apply to any actions taken pursuant to section four hundred ten-l of this article;

(b) that the eligible borrower will maintain books and records and a system of accounts satisfactory to the commissioner and the agency including but not limited to separate books, records and accounts for (i) all monies advanced to the eligible borrower by the agency or from any other source or sources, public or private, for the construction, reconstruction, rehabilitation, improvement or equipment of the project and (ii) all monies repaid in satisfaction of any indebtedness to the agency or other indebtedness as required by the commissioner; and the eligible borrower agrees that all of its books, records and accounts shall be open to examination by the commissioner and the agency at any time;

(c) that the eligible borrower shall file with the commissioner and the agency such financial statements including an annual report setting forth such information as the commissioner may require;

(d) that the eligible borrower shall not acquire any real property or interest therein for the purpose of constructing, reconstructing, rehabilitating or improving a project without first having obtained from the commissioner a certificate that such acquisition is consistent with the purposes of this article;

(e) that the eligible borrower shall not issue notes, bonds, debentures or other obligations other than for money or property actually received for the use and lawful purposes of the eligible borrower and no such note, bond, debenture or other obligation shall constitute a lien or encumbrance against the project, or any real property or other asset mortgaged or otherwise pledged to the agency;

(f) that the eligible borrower shall not without first having obtained the written consent of the commissioner:

(i) construct, reconstruct, rehabilitate, improve, alter or repair the project or enter into a contract therefor;

(ii) enter into contracts relating to the management or operation of the project;

(iii)   make a guaranty of payment out of monies pledged to the agency or pledge any or all of its assets, income or revenue pledged to the agency to secure payment of its obligations;

(iv)   lease a project or a portion thereof to a third party for the purposes of operation;

(v)   voluntarily dissolve;

(g)   that no member, officer or employee of the corporation which is an eligible borrower shall acquire any interest, direct or indirect, in any property then or thereafter included or planned to be included in a project, nor retain any interest direct or indirect in any property acquired subsequent to his appointment or employment which is later included or planned to be included in a project. If any member, officer or employee of a corporation which is an eligible borrower owns or controls an interest, direct or indirect, in any property included in a project which was acquired prior to his appointment or employment he shall disclose such interest and the date of acquisition to the corporation and such disclosure shall be entered upon the minutes of such corporation and a copy of such minutes shall be forwarded to the commissioner;

(h)   that all income and earnings of the eligible borrower shall be used exclusively for its corporate purposes;

(i)   that no part of the net income or earnings of the corporation shall inure to the benefit or profit of any private individual, firm or corporation;

(j)   That the eligible borrower, in the case of a residential child care center project, will be subject to the visitation, inspection and supervision of the department, and the eligible borrower, in the case of day care center project will be subject to the visitation, inspection, and supervision of the department, as to any and all acts in relation to the welfare of children to be performed pursuant to this title;

(k)   such other matters as the commissioner or the agency may require;

2.   This regulatory agreement shall terminate at any time after the expiration of ten years after the occupancy date upon the consent of the commissioner and upon the repayment in full of all obligations under the mortgage of the agency and of such other obligations as the commissioner may require.

Added by Laws 1969, Ch. 1013; **amended** by Laws 1970, Ch. 966; **amended** by Laws 1971, Ch. 110, eff. July 1, 1971; **amended** by Laws 1971, Ch. 1030, eff. July 2, 1971; **amended** by Laws 1978, Ch. 555, eff. July 24, 1978.

§ 410-g.   Mortgage loans.

1.   Any eligible borrower may, subject to the approval of the commissioner, borrow funds from the agency and secure the repayment thereof by bond or note and mortgage which shall contain such terms and conditions as may be deemed necessary or desirable by the agency or required by any agreement between the

agency and the holders of its notes and bonds, including the right to assignment of rates and charges and entry into possession in case of default, but the operation of such project, in the event of such entry, shall be subject to the regulations of the commissioner.

2. The agency may make contracts to make loans to an eligible borrower in an amount not to exceed the total project cost. Any such loan shall be secured by a first mortgage lien upon all the real property and improvements of which the project consists and may be secured by such lien upon other real property owned by the eligible borrower, and upon all fixtures and articles of personal property attached to or used in connection with the operation of the project.

3. Any inconsistent provision of law to the contrary notwithstanding, mortgages of an eligible borrower shall be exempt from the mortgage recording taxes imposed by article eleven of the tax law.

Added by Laws 1969, Ch. 1013; **amended** by Laws 1971, Ch. 1030, eff. July 2, 1971; **amended** by Laws 1978, Ch. 555, eff. July 24, 1978.

§ 410-h.   Conditions and security for loans.

No loan shall be made by the agency to an eligible borrower until the commissioner has approved the project and finds that:

1. The eligible borrower has been approved by the commissioner and complied with all of the provisions of this title;

2. The plans and specifications conform to the requirements of all laws and regulations applicable thereto and assure adequate light, air, sanitation and fire protection and are satisfactory to him;

3. The estimated revenue of the project or from other funds of the eligible borrower pledged, assigned or otherwise to be made available to the agency will be sufficient to cover all probable costs of operation and maintenance, of fixed charges and such reserves as may be authorized by the commissioner or required by the agency;

4. Provision has been made for the purpose of providing for the payment of the difference between the estimated project cost and the mortgage loan; and in the event the final project cost shall exceed the estimated project cost, the difference between such final project cost and the mortgage loan;

5. The eligible borrower has entered into a regulatory agreement pursuant to section four hundred ten-f of this title.

Added by Laws 1969, Ch. 1013, eff. Sept. 1, 1969; Laws 1971, Ch. 110, § 77, amending Social Services Law § 410-h is apparently in error and should apparently have read § 410-k; **amended** by Laws 1978, Ch. 555, eff. July 24, 1978.

§ 410-i.   Rates and admission of children.

1. An eligible borrower shall, with the approval of the commissioner, fix a schedule of rates to be charged parents, guardians or other persons having legal

custody of the child and to social services officials or other authorized agencies for the facilities and services provided by the eligible borrower pursuant to this title. The commissioner upon his own motion, or upon application by the eligible borrower or lienholder may vary the amount of such charge from time to time so as to secure, together with all other income of the eligible borrower pledged, assigned or otherwise made available to the agency, sufficient income to meet, within reasonable limits, all necessary payments by the said eligible borrower of all expenses, including fixed charges, sinking funds and reserves.

2.   The facilities and services to be provided by the eligible borrower pursuant to this title shall be available to all children in need thereof.

     Added by Laws 1969, Ch. 1013, eff. Sept. 1, 1969.

§ 410-j.   Transfer of real property.

Notwithstanding any requirement of law to the contrary or any provision of any general, special or local law, charter or ordinance, every executor, administrator, trustee, guardian or other person holding trust funds or acting in a fiduciary capacity, unless the instrument under which such fiduciary is acting expressly forbids, and the state, its subdivisions, municipalities, all other public bodies, all public officers, persons, partnerships and corporations owning or holding any real property, may grant, sell, lease or otherwise transfer any such real property or interest therein to an eligible borrower and receive and hold any cash, exchange therefor by such an eligible borrower and may execute such instruments and do such acts as may be deemed necessary or desirable by them or it and by the eligible borrower in connection with a project or projects and such sale, lease or transfer may be made without public auction or bidding; providing, however, that where such real property is within an urban renewal area the disposition thereof shall be in accordance with the provisions of paragraph (d) of subdivision two of section five hundred seven of the general municipal law.

     Added by Laws 1969, Ch. 1013, eff. Sept. 1, 1969.

§ 410-k.   Supervision.

1.   The commissioner may from time to time make, alter, amend and repeal rules and regulations for the supervision, examination, regulation and audit of an eligible borrower and for carrying into effect this title, and each eligible borrower shall submit an annual report of its operations to the commissioner and the agency who may examine and audit the books and records of the eligible borrower at any time.

2.   The commissioner and the department shall have power to act for and in behalf of the agency in servicing the project mortgage loans of the agency, and to perform such functions and services in connection with the making, servicing and collection of such loans as shall be requested by the agency.

SSL

3.   (a) The commissioner and the department may, with respect to any project of which the agency has acquired the fee or otherwise, enter into an agreement with said agency subject to the approval of the director of the budget, for the department, as provided in paragraph (b) hereof, to operate the said project in a manner consistent with the purposes of this title. In such event, the commissioner, on behalf of the department, shall have the power to use any available funds to pay all operating expenses and to comply with all the terms and provisions of the mortgage, as though the mortgage had not been foreclosed, and to comply with the provisions of this title.

(b)   Subject to the provisions of the agreement with said agency, the commissioner may contract with any person, firm or corporation which he deems qualified to operate and manage such project and to perform such duties and functions as he may deem necessary.

4.   Whenever the commissioner shall be of the opinion that an eligible borrower is failing or omitting, or is about to fail or omit to do anything required of it by law or by order of the commissioner and is doing or is about to do anything, or permitting anything, or is about to permit anything to be done, contrary to or in violation of law or of any order of the commissioner, or which is improvident or prejudicial to the interest of the public, the lienholders, the shareholders, or the occupants, the commissioner may, in addition to such other remedies as may be available, commence an action or proceeding in the supreme court of the state of New York in the name of the commissioner, for the purpose of having such violations or threatened violations stopped and prevented, and in such action or proceeding, the court may appoint a temporary or permanent receiver or both. Such action or proceeding shall be commenced by a petition to the supreme court, alleging the violation complained of and praying for appropriate relief. It shall thereupon be the duty of the court to specify the time, not exceeding twenty days after service of a copy of the petition, within which the eligible borrowers complained of must answer the petition. In case of any default or after answer the court shall immediately inquire into the facts and circumstances in such manner as the court shall direct in the interest of substantial justice without other or formal pleading. Such other persons or corporations as it shall seem to the court necessary or proper to join as parties in order to make its order or judgment effective, may be joined as parties. The final judgment in any such action or proceeding shall either dismiss the action or proceeding or direct that an order or an injunction, or both, issue, or provide for the appointment of a receiver as prayed for in the petition, or grant such other relief as the court may deem appropriate.

Added by Laws 1969, Ch. 1013; **amended** by Laws 1970, Ch. 966; Laws 1971, Ch. 110, § 77, eff. July 1, 1971, erroneously amending 410-h; Laws 1971, Ch. 1030, eff. July 2, 1971.

§ 410-l.   Foreclosures and judgments.

1.   In any foreclosure action the commissioner shall be made a party defendant. He shall take all steps necessary to protect the interests of the public

therein and no costs shall be awarded against him. Foreclosures shall not be decreed unless the court to which application is made shall be satisfied that the interests of the lienholder or holders cannot be adequately assured except by the sale of the property. In any such proceeding, the court shall be authorized to appoint the commissioner as receiver of the property, or to grant such other and further relief as may be reasonable and proper.

2. Notwithstanding the foregoing provisions of this section, wherever it shall appear that the agency shall have loaned on a mortgage which is a first lien upon any such property, such agency shall have all the remedies available to a mortgagee under the laws of the state of New York, free from any restrictions contained in this section, except that the commissioner shall be made a party defendant and that the commissioner shall take all steps necessary to protect the interests of the public and no costs shall be awarded against him.

3. In the event of a judgment against an eligible borrower in any action not pertaining to the collection of a mortgage indebtedness, there shall be no sale of any of the real property of such eligible borrower except upon sixty days' written notice to the commissioner and the agency. Upon receipt of such notice the commissioner and the agency shall take such steps as in their judgment may be necessary to protect the rights of all parties.

     Added by Laws 1969, Ch. 1013, eff. Sept. 1, 1969.

§ 410-m. Fees and charges.

The commissioner may, by regulation, establish and charge to eligible borrowers such fees and charges for inspection, regulation, supervision and audit as to the commissioner may appear just and reasonable in order to recover the departmental costs in performing these functions.

     Added by Laws 1969, Ch. 1013, eff. Sept. 1, 1969.

§ 410-n. Youth facilities development fund.

Repealed by Laws 1982, Ch. 58, eff. April 1, 1982, provided, however, that any money required by law to be deposited to the credit of funds abolished by the repeal of this section shall hereafter be deposited to the credit of such fund or funds as the comptroller with the concurrence of the director of the budget shall designate or establish.

§ 410-o. Separability.

If any clause, sentence, paragraph or part of this article shall be adjudged by any court of competent jurisdiction to be invalid, such judgement shall not effect, impair or invalidate the remainder thereof, but shall be confined in its operation to the clause, sentence, paragraph, section or part thereof directly involved in the controversy in which such judgment shall have rendered.

SSL

Formerly § 410-n, **added** by Laws 1969, Ch. 1013; **renumbered** 410-o, Laws 1970, Ch. 278, eff. Apr. 29, 1970.

TITLE 5-B—CHILD CARE RESOURCE AND REFERRAL PROGRAM

§ 410-p. Definitions.

As used in this title, the term:

1. "Agency" shall mean a not-for-profit corporation or group of not-for-profit corporations. With respect to any county for which no appropriate not-for-profit corporation or group of corporations has submitted a proposal, such term shall mean a statewide or regional not-for-profit corporation which establishes such a corporation or shall mean a local governmental entity which provides the services authorized by this title;

2. "Resource and referral program" shall mean an agency funded pursuant to this title to provide services specified in section four hundred ten-r of this title within a defined geographic area;

3. "Early childhood services" shall mean services which include, but are not limited to, registered, certified or licensed care in family day care homes, group family day care homes, school-age child care programs; head start programs, day care centers; child care which may be provided without a permit, certificate or registration in accordance with this statute; early childhood education programs approved by the state education department; and care provided in a children's camp as defined in section one thousand four hundred of the public health law;

4. "Required resource and referral services" shall mean those services listed in subdivision one of section four hundred ten-q of this title which must be provided by each child care resource and referral program to parents and other guardians, child care and early childhood services providers, employers and communities within the geographic area served by the program, to the extent funds are available for such services;

5. "Enhanced services" shall mean additional or more intensive levels of services as listed in subdivision two of section four hundred ten-q of this title, which an agency agrees to provide in order to receive additional funding pursuant to this title;

6. "Parent" or "parents" shall mean and include biological and adoptive parents, guardians or other persons in parental relationship to a child.

Added by Laws 1987, Ch. 459, eff. July 27, 1987; **amended** by Laws 1993, Ch. 441, § 1, eff. July 26, 1993.

§ 410-q. Child care resource and referral program services.

1. Each agency approved to receive funding pursuant to this title shall, to the extent funds are available for such purposes, provide the following:

(a) Information and referral services directed at educating parents who contact the agency regarding early childhood services options and methods of selecting the best option for his or her child; referring parents or guardians to early childhood services providers; informing parents about the availability of financial assistance and tax credits; referral for parents in coordinating part-day early childhood services providers and programs to meet the full-day care needs of parents; referrals for parents of preschool children with handicapping conditions pursuant to section forty-four hundred ten of the education law and section twenty-five hundred forty-two of the public health law; providing written information to those who contact the agency seeking information about early childhood services; maintaining a provider resource file and a file of parents currently seeking early childhood services; and publicizing child care resource and referral services as necessary to assure that the availability of those services are known to the community;

(b) Services directed at expanding the number of available family day care providers and recruiting potential providers; providing information on licensing and registration requirements and available funding sources to potential early childhood services providers and programs; and assisting individuals or organizations to qualify as legal early childhood services providers or programs by providing information on applicable laws and regulations relating to zoning, taxes, insurance, government licensing or registration, and other matters of concern to new providers;

(c) Services directed at maintaining and providing information and resources on early childhood training and other relevant programs for prospective and current providers;

(d) Services directed at developing and maintaining provider data bases to determine service utilization and unmet needs for additional early childhood services;

(e) Assuring access to the United States department of agriculture child care food program for providers in the service area;

(f) Services directed at providing written materials and conducting outreach to employers to encourage their support of child care resource and referral services and other early childhood services; and

(g) Each agency funded herein shall provide services in a manner responsive to the cultural, linguistic and economic characteristics of the community served.

2. Enhanced services which an agency agrees to provide pursuant to a contract may include one or more of the following:

(a) Services directed at expanding the supply of regulated care in areas where such care is not readily available;

SSL

(b) Services directed at enhancing the availability and quality of early childhood services which serve families with particular language, ethnic and cultural backgrounds;

(c) Services directed at meeting the early childhood services needs of children with special needs;

(d) Training or technical assistance services targeted to meet specific local early childhood services needs; and

(e) Services directed at promoting, coordinating and assisting collaborative efforts between early childhood services providers and programs to meet the local need for full-day early childhood services.

Former § 410-q **repealed** and new § 410-q **added** by Laws 1993, Ch. 441, § 2, eff. July 26, 1993.

§ 410-r. Child care resource and referral programs.

1. The commissioner shall solicit applications for available funds from agencies pursuant to this title in a manner to ensure that agencies in every area of the state will have an opportunity to apply for funds. The commissioner shall designate areas to be served by child care resource and referral services to ensure that services are accessible statewide to the maximum extent feasible.

2. (a) In reviewing the applications, the commissioner shall consider the ability of each applicant to provide the services delineated in section four hundred ten-q of this title. Each agency shall demonstrate that it has a viable plan to offer the required services to families in the area without regard to income, and to attract local support for additions to the required and enhanced services delineated in section four hundred ten-q of this title.

(b) In connection with the review of an application for funds pursuant to this title, the commissioner shall consider requests from agencies for additional funding for the provision of enhanced services.

3. In accordance with the provisions of this title and subject to funds appropriated specifically therefor, the commissioner is authorized to award contracts for the operation of child care resource and referral programs.

Former § 410-r **repealed** and new § 410-r **added** by Laws 1993, Ch. 441, § 2, eff. July 26, 1993.

§ 410-s. State reimbursement.

1. The commissioner shall allocate annually any state funds, including any available federal funds, appropriated for such purposes among the agencies approved for funding pursuant to this title. The commissioner shall allocate such funds pursuant to a statewide formula developed by the department, which shall be based upon the relative numbers of children, children in working families, and children in low income families in each county, as defined by the department

for this purpose. The commissioner shall notify the legislature prior to the implementation of any change or adjustment in the formula.

2. As a condition of receiving funds pursuant to this section, the child care resource and referral program shall demonstrate that it is receiving or has an agreement to receive funds, from sources other than the department pursuant to this title. Funds other than those paid by the department pursuant to this title may come from any other source, including but not limited to the department or other state agencies, federal programs such as the United States department of agriculture child care food program, local agencies, employers or community organizations, so long as such funds are for reasonably related services. To continue to receive funds pursuant to this section, such resource and referral program must demonstrate to the commissioner that it has secured funds or commitments from other sources or that extraordinary circumstances exist which preclude the securing of such funds.

3. All applications approved by the commissioner shall include a commitment to use appropriate accounting and fiscal control procedures which shall include the filing of an annual financial statement which has been audited as required by the department so as to ensure:

(a) the proper disbursement and accounting for funds received; and

(b) appropriate written records regarding the population served and type and extent of services rendered.

Former § 410-s **repealed** and new § 410-s **added** by Laws 1993, Ch. 441, § 2, eff. July 26, 1993.

§ 410-t. Responsibilities of the commissioner.

1. The commissioner shall monitor the performance of agencies to assure that the terms of the contract are met, that the services are provided in accordance with the intent of this title and that funds are used as required by this title.

2. The commissioner may contract for technical support, planning, coordination and data collection services to assist agencies in offering child care resource services in unserved areas.

3. Beginning July first, nineteen hundred ninety-four and biennially thereafter, the commissioner shall submit a report to the governor and the legislature on the implementation of this title which shall include but not be limited to:

(a) the names of the agencies serving the counties and the counties served by a child care resources and referral agency;

(b) the awards made to each agency;

(c) the characteristics and number of children and families who have received services;

(d) the improvements in the accessibility of early childhood services, the improvement in quality and the expanded supply;

SSL

(e)   the nature of services contracted for and additional services the agency is able to provide with other funding sources;

(f)   the amount of state and federal funding available for services provided under this title; and

(g)   the cost to the state to administer the programs funded under this title.

Former § 410-t **repealed** and new § 410-t **added** by Laws 1993, Ch. 441, § 2, eff. July 26, 1993.

TITLE 5-C—BLOCK GRANT FOR CHILD CARE

§ 410-u.   Establishment of block grant for child care.

1.   The department shall establish a state block grant for child care comprised of all of the federal funds appropriated for child care under title IV-A of the federal social security act and under the federal child care and development block grant act and any additional federal funds that the state chooses to transfer from the federal family assistance to needy families block grant to the child care and development block grant plus any state funds appropriated for the provision by social services districts of child care assistance to families in receipt of family assistance and other low income families and for activities to increase the availability and/or quality of child care programs.

2.   The state block grant for child care shall be divided into two parts pursuant to a plan developed by the department and approved by the director of the budget. One part shall be retained by the state to provide child care on a statewide basis to special groups and for activities to increase the availability and/or quality of child care programs, including, but not limited to, the start-up of child care programs, the operation of child care resource and referral programs, training activities, the regulation and monitoring of child care programs, the development of computerized data systems, and consumer education, provided however, that child care resource and referral programs funded under title five-b of article six of this chapter shall meet additional performance standards developed by the department of social services including but not limited to: increasing the number of child care placements for persons who are at or below two hundred percent of the state income standard with emphasis on placements supporting local efforts in meeting federal and state work participation requirements, increasing technical assistance to all modalities of legal child care to persons who are at or below two hundred percent of the state income standard, including the provision of training to assist providers in meeting child care standards or regulatory

requirements, and creating new child care opportunities, and assisting social services districts in assessing and responding to child care needs for persons at or below two hundred percent of the state income standard. The department shall have the authority to withhold funds from those agencies which do not meet performance standards. Agencies whose funds are withheld may have funds restored upon achieving performance standards. The other part shall be allocated to social services districts to provide child care assistance to families receiving family assistance and to other low income families.

3. Notwithstanding any other provision of law, expenditures of funds from the block grant shall be governed by this title.

Added by Laws 1997, Ch. 436, § 1 Part B, § 52, eff. Aug. 20, 1997.

§ 410-v. Allocation of block grant funds.

1. The part of the block that is determined to be available to social services districts for child care assistance shall be apportioned among the social services districts by the department according to an allocation plan developed by the department and approved by the director of the budget. The allocation plan shall be based, at least in part, on historical costs and on the availability and cost of, and the need for, child care assistance in each social services district. Annual allocations shall be made on a federal fiscal year basis.

2. Reimbursement under the block grant to a social services district for its expenditures for child care assistance shall be available for seventy-five percent of the district's expenditures for child care assistance provided to those families in receipt of public assistance which are eligible for child care assistance under this title and for one hundred percent of the social services district's expenditures for other eligible families; provided, however, that such reimbursement shall be limited to the social services district's annual state block grant allocation.

3. Any portion of a social services district's block grant allocation for a particular federal fiscal year that is not claimed by such district during that federal fiscal year shall be added to that social services district's block grant allocation for the next federal fiscal year.

4. Any claims for child care assistance made by a social services district for services that occurred from October first, nineteen hundred ninety-six through September thirtieth, nineteen hundred ninety-seven, other than claims made under title XX of the federal social security act, shall be counted against the social services district's first block grant allocation.

Added by Laws 1997, Ch. 436, § 1 Part B, § 52, eff. Aug. 20, 1997; **amended** by Laws 1998, Ch. 214, § 23, eff. July 7, 1998, deemed in full force and effect Aug. 20, 1997.

§ 410-w. Eligible families.

1. A social services district may use the funds allocated to it from the block grant to provide child care assistance to:

SSL

(a)   families receiving public assistance when such child care assistance is necessary: to enable a parent or caretaker relative to engage in work, participate in work activities or perform a community service pursuant to title nine-B of article five of this chapter; to enable a teenage parent to attend high school or other equivalent training program; because the parent or caretaker relative is physically or mentally incapacitated; or because family duties away from home necessitate the parent or caretaker relative's absence; child day care shall be provided during breaks in activities, for a period of up to two weeks. Such child day care may be authorized for a period of up to one month if child care arrangements shall be lost if not continued, and the program or employment is scheduled to begin within such period;

(b)   families with incomes up to two hundred percent of the state income standard who are attempting through work activities to transition off of public assistance when such child care is necessary in order to enable a parent or caretaker relative to engage in work provided such families' public assistance has been terminated as a result of increased hours of or income from employment or increased income from child support payments or the family voluntarily ended assistance; and, provided that the family received public assistance at least three of the six months preceding the month in which eligibility for such assistance terminated or ended or provided that such family has received child care assistance under subdivision four of this section;

(c)   families with incomes up to two hundred percent of the state income standard which are determined in accordance with the regulations of the department to be at risk of becoming dependent on family assistance;

(d)   families with incomes up to two hundred percent of the state income standard who are attending a post secondary educational program and working at least seventeen and one-half hours per week;

(e)   other families with incomes up to two hundred percent of the state income standard which the social services district designates in its consolidated services plan as eligible for child care assistance in accordance with criteria established by the department.

2.   For the purposes of this title, the term "state income standard" means the most recent federal income official poverty line (as defined and annually revised by the federal office of management and budget) updated by the department for a family size of four and adjusted by the department for family size.

3.   A social services district shall guarantee child care assistance to families in receipt of public assistance with children under thirteen years of age when such child care assistance is necessary for a parent or caretaker relative to engage in work or participate in work activities pursuant to the provisions of title nine-B of article five of this chapter. Child care assistance shall continue to be guaranteed for such a family for a period of twelve months after the month in which the family's eligibility for public assistance has terminated or ended when such child care is necessary in order to enable the parent or caretaker relative to engage in

work, provided that the family's public assistance has been terminated as a result of an increase in the hours of or income from employment or increased income from child support payments or because the family voluntarily ended assistance; that the family received public assistance in at least three of the six months preceding the month in which eligibility for such assistance terminated or ended or provided that such family has received child care assistance under subdivision four of this section; and that the family's income does not exceed two hundred percent of the state income standard. Such child day care shall recognize the need for continuity of care for the child and a district shall not move a child from an existing provider unless the participant consents to such move.

4.   (a) Local social services districts shall guarantee applicants who would otherwise be eligible for, or are recipients of, public assistance benefits and who are employed, the option to choose to receive continuing child day care subsidies in lieu of public assistance benefits, for such period of time as the recipient continues to be eligible for public assistance. Recipients of child care subsidies under this subdivision who are no longer eligible for public assistance benefits, shall be eligible for transitional child care described in paragraph (b) of subdivision one of this section as if they had been recipients of public assistance.

(b)   Nothing herein shall be construed to waive the right of an applicant who chooses to receive continuing child day care subsidies pursuant to this section from applying for ongoing public assistance.

5.   A family eligible for child care assistance under paragraph (a) of subdivision one of this section shall suffer no break in child care services and shall not be required to reapply for such assistance so long as eligibility under subdivision three of this section continues.

     Added by Laws 1997, Ch. 436, § 1 Part B, § 52, eff. Aug. 20, 1997; **amended** by Laws 1998, Ch. 214, §§ 24 and 25, eff. July 7, 1998, deemed in full force and effect Aug. 20, 1997; **amended** by Laws 1999, Ch. 391, §§ 1-3, **adding** para. (4), eff. Jan. 23, 2000; **amended** by L. 2001, Ch. 566, amending subd. 4, eff. Dec. 19, 2001, and Ch. 569, amending subd. 1 and adding subd. 5, eff. June 17, 2002.

§ 410-x.   Use of funds.

1.   A social services district shall expend its allocation from the block grant in a manner that provides for equitable access to child care assistance funds to eligible families, and in accordance with the applicable provisions in federal law regarding the portion of the funds which must be spent on families in receipt of family assistance, families who are attempting through work activities to transition off of family assistance and families at-risk of becoming dependent on family assistance and the portion which must be spent on other working low-income families. Each social services district may spend no more than five percent of its block grant allocation for administrative activities. The term "administrative activities" shall not include the costs of providing direct services.

SSL

2.   (a) A social services district may establish priorities for the families which will be eligible to receive funding; provided that the priorities provide that eligible families will receive equitable access to child care assistance funds to the extent that these funds are available.

(b)   A social services district shall set forth its priorities for child care assistance in the district's consolidated services plan. The commissioner of the office of children and family services shall not approve any plan that does not provide for equitable access to child care assistance funds.

(c)   A social services district shall be authorized to set aside portions of its block grant allocation to serve one or more of its priority groups and/or to discontinue funding to families with lower priorities in order to serve families with higher priorities; provided that the method of disbursement to priority groups provides that eligible families within a priority group will receive equitable access to child care assistance funds to the extent that these funds are available.

(d)   Each social services district shall collect and submit to the commissioner of the office of children and family services in a manner to be specified by the commissioner of the office of children and family services information concerning the disbursement of child care assistance funds showing geographic distribution of children receiving assistance within the district.

(e)   The commissioner of the office of children and family services shall submit a report to the governor, temporary president of the senate and the speaker of the assembly on or before August thirty-first, two thousand one concerning the implementation of this section. This report shall include information concerning the disbursement of child care assistance funds showing geographic distribution of children receiving assistance within the state.

3.   Child care assistance funded under the block grant must meet all applicable standards set forth in section three hundred ninety of this article or the administrative code of the city of New York, including child day care in a child day care center, family day care home, group family day care home, school age child care program, or in home care which is not subject to licensure, certification or registration, or any other lawful form of care for less than twenty-four hours per day. The department also is required to establish, in regulation, minimum health and safety requirements that must be met by those providers providing child care assistance funded under the block grant which are not required to be licensed or registered under section three hundred ninety of this article or to be licensed under the administrative code of the city of New York and to those public assistance recipients who are providing child care assistance as part of their work activities or as community service under title nine-B of article five of this chapter. A social services district may submit to the department justification for a need to impose additional minimum health and safety requirements on such providers and a plan to monitor compliance with such additional requirements. No such additional requirements or monitoring may be imposed without the written approval of the department. Social services districts shall provide, directly or

through referral, technical assistance and relevant health and safety information to all public assistance recipients who voluntarily choose to provide child care assistance as part of their work activities under title nine-B of article five of this chapter.

4. The amount to be paid or allowed for child care assistance funded under the block grant shall be the actual cost of care but no more than the applicable market-related payment rate established by the department in regulations. The payment rates established by the department shall be sufficient to ensure equal access for eligible children to comparable child care assistance in the substate area that are provided to children whose parents are not eligible to receive assistance under any federal or state programs. Such payment rates shall take into account the variations in the costs of providing child care in different settings and to children of different age groups, and the additional costs of providing child care for children with special needs.

5. The department shall promulgate regulations under which provision for child care assistance may be made by providing child care directly; through purchase of services contracts; by providing cash, vouchers or reimbursement to the providers of child care or to the parents or caretaker relatives; or through such other arrangement as the department finds appropriate. Such regulations shall require the use of at least one method by which child care arranged by the parent or caretaker relative can be paid.

6. Pursuant to department regulations, child care assistance shall be provided on a sliding fee basis based upon the family's ability to pay.

Added by Laws 1997, Ch. 436, § 1 Part B, § 52, eff. Aug. 20, 1997; **amended** by Laws 1998, Ch. 214, § 26, eff. July 7, 1998, deemed in full force and effect Aug. 20, 1997; **amended** by Laws 2000, Ch. 416, § 13, eff. Dec. 5, 2000.

§ 410-y.　Maintenance of effort.

Each social services district shall maintain the amount of local funds spent for child care assistance under the child care block grant at a level equal to or greater than the amount the district spent for child care assistance during federal fiscal year nineteen hundred ninety-five under title IV-A of the federal social security act, the federal child care development block grant program and the state low income child care program. If the state fails to meet the level of state and local child care funding necessary to maintain the federal matching funds for child care assistance available under title IV-A of the federal social security act, the state shall withhold funding from those social services districts which spent a lower amount of local funds for child care assistance than the amount they spent during federal fiscal year nineteen hundred ninety-five, based on a formula established in department regulations, equal to the amount of the matching funds which have been lost.

Added by Laws 1997, Ch. 436, § 1 Part B, § 52, eff. Aug. 20, 1997.

§ 410-z. Reporting requirements.

Each social services district shall collect and submit to the department, in such form and at such times as specified by the department, such data and information regarding child care assistance provided under the block grant as the department may need to comply with federal reporting requirements.

Added by Laws 1997, Ch. 436, § 1 Part B, § 52, eff. Aug. 20, 1997.

TITLE 6—CHILD PROTECTIVE SERVICES

§ 411. Findings and purpose.

Abused and maltreated children in this state are in urgent need of an effective child protective service to prevent them from suffering further injury and impairment. It is the purpose of this title to encourage more complete reporting of suspected child abuse and maltreatment and to establish in each county of the state a child protective service capable of investigating such reports swiftly and competently and capable of providing protection for the child or children from further abuse or maltreatment and rehabilitative services for the child or children and parents involved.

§ 412. Definitions.

When used in this title and unless the specific context indicates otherwise:

1. An "abused child" means:

(a) a child under eighteen years of age defined as an abused child by the family court act;

(b) a child under the age of eighteen years who is defined as an abused child in residential care pursuant to subdivision eight of this section; or

(c) a child with a handicapping condition, as defined in subdivision one of section forty-four hundred one of the education law, who is eighteen years of age or older, is in residential care in a school or facility described in paragraph (c), (d), (e) or (f) of subdivision seven of this section, and is defined as an abused child pursuant to subdivision eight of this section; provided that such term shall include a pupil with a handicapping condition in residential care in such a school or facility who is defined as an abused child pursuant to subdivision eight of this section, is twenty-one years of age, and is entitled, pursuant to subdivision five of section forty-four hundred two of the education law, to remain in such school or facility until either the termination of the school year or the termination of the summer program, as applicable;

2. A "maltreated child" includes:

(a) a child under eighteen years of age not in "residential care" as defined in subdivision seven of this section:

(i) defined as a neglected child by the family court act, or

(ii) who has had serious physical injury inflicted upon him by other than accidental means; or

(b) a child in residential care as defined in subdivision seven of this section who is:

(i) under eighteen years of age, except that a child with a handicapping condition, as defined in subdivision one of section forty-four hundred one of the education law, who is eighteen years of age or older, is in residential care in a school or facility described in paragraph (c), (d), (e) or (f) of subdivision seven of this section, provided that such term shall include a pupil with a handicapping condition in residential care in such a school or facility who is twenty-one years of age, and is entitled, pursuant to subdivision five of section forty-four hundred two of the education law, to remain in such school or facility until either the termination of the school year or the termination of the summer program, as applicable; and

SSL

(ii)   is a neglected child in residential care as defined in subdivision nine of this section;

3.   "Person legally responsible" for a child means a person legally responsible as defined by the family court act;

4.   "Subject of the report" means any parent of, guardian of, custodian of or other person eighteen years of age or older legally responsible for, as defined in subdivision (g) of section one thousand twelve of the family court act, a child reported to the central register of child abuse and maltreatment who is allegedly responsible for causing injury, abuse or maltreatment to such child or who allegedly allows such injury, abuse or maltreatment to be inflicted on such child, or a director or an operator of or employee or volunteer in a home operated or supervised by an authorized agency, the division for youth, or an office of the department of mental hygiene or in a family day-care home, a day-care center, a group family day care home or a day-services program, or a consultant or any person who is an employee or volunteer of a corporation, partnership, organization or any governmental entity which provides goods or services pursuant to a contract or other arrangement which provides for such consultant or person to have regular and substantial contact with children in residential care who is allegedly responsible for causing injury, abuse or maltreatment to a child who is reported to the central register of child abuse or maltreatment or who allegedly allows such injury, abuse or maltreatment to be inflicted on such child;

5.   "Other persons named in the report" shall mean and be limited to the following persons who are named in a report of child abuse or maltreatment other than the subject of the report: the child who is reported to the central register of child abuse and maltreatment; and such child's parent, guardian, custodian or other person legally responsible for the child who has not been named in the report as allegedly responsible for causing injury, abuse or maltreatment to the child or as allegedly allowing such injury, abuse or maltreatment to be inflicted on such child; in the case of a report involving abuse or maltreatment of a child in residential care, such term shall be deemed to include the child's parent, guardian or other person legally responsible for the child who is not named in such report;

6.   "Custodian" means a director, operator, employee or volunteer of a residential care facility or program;

7.   "Residential care" means:

(a)   care provided to a child who has been placed by the family court with a social services official or the state division for youth, or whose care and custody or custody and guardianship has been transferred or committed to, a social services official, another authorized agency, or the state division for youth and such care is provided in an agency operated boarding home, a group home or child care institution;

(b)   care provided a child in a facility or program operated or certified by the state division for youth pursuant to article nineteen-g or nineteen-h of the executive law, excluding foster family care;

(c) care provided a child in the New York state school for the blind or the New York state school for the deaf, pursuant to the provisions of articles eighty-seven and eighty-eight of the education law;

(d) care provided a child in a private residential school which is within the state and which has been approved by the commissioner of education for special education services or programs;

(e) care provided in institutions for the instruction of the deaf and the blind which have a residential component, and which are subject to the visitation of the commissioner of education pursuant to article eighty-five of the education law;

(f) care provided through a residential placement of a child with a special act school district listed in chapter five hundred sixty-six of the laws of nineteen hundred sixty-seven, as amended; or

(g) care provided a child in a residential facility licensed or operated by the office of mental health or the office of mental retardation and developmental disabilities, excluding family care homes;

8. "Abused child in residential care" means a child whose custodian:

(a) (i) inflicts any injury upon such child by other than accidental means which causes death, serious or protracted disfigurement, serious or protracted impairment of physical health, serious or protracted loss or impairment of the function of any organ, or a serious emotional injury; or

(ii) by their conduct and with knowledge or deliberate indifference allows any such injury to be inflicted upon such child; or

(b) (i) creates a substantial risk of any injury to such child by other than accidental means which would be likely to cause death or serious or protracted disfigurement, protracted impairment of physical health, protracted loss or impairment of the function of any organ, or a serious emotional injury; or

(ii) by his or her conduct and with knowledge or deliberate indifference creates a substantial risk of such injury to such child; or

(c) [Until Nov 1, 2006] commits, promotes or knowingly permits the commission of a sex offense against such child, as described in article one hundred thirty of the penal law; allows, permits or encourages such child to engage in any act described in article two hundred thirty of the penal law; commits any of the acts described in section 255.25 of the penal law; or allows or promotes or uses such child to engage in acts or conduct described in article two hundred sixty-three of the penal law, provided, however, that (i) the corroboration requirements in the penal law and (ii) the age requirements for the application of articles one hundred thirty, two hundred thirty and two hundred sixty-three of such law and any age based element of any crime described therein shall not apply to the provisions of this title; or

(c) [Eff. Nov 1, 2006] commits, promotes or knowingly permits the commission of a sex offense against such child, as described in article one hundred thirty of the penal law; allows, permits or encourages such child to engage in any act described in article two hundred thirty of the penal law; commits any of the acts described in section 255.25, 255.26 or 255.27 of the penal law; or allows or promotes or uses such child to engage in acts or conduct described in article two hundred sixty-three of the penal law, provided, however, that (i) the corroboration requirements in the penal law and (ii) the age requirements for the application of articles one hundred thirty, two hundred thirty and two hundred sixty-three of such law and any age based element of any crime described therein shall not apply to the provisions of this title; or

(d) fails to comply with a rule or regulation involving care, services or supervision of a child promulgated by a state agency operating, certifying or supervising a residential facility or program, and such failure to comply results in death, serious or protracted disfigurement, serious or protracted impairment of physical health, or serious or protracted loss or impairment of the function of any organ where such result was reasonably foreseeable;

9. "Neglected child in residential care" means a child whose custodian:

(a) inflicts by act or omission physical injury, excluding minor injury, to such child by other than accidental means;

(b) creates a substantial risk of physical injury, excluding minor injury, to such child by other than accidental means; or

(c) fails to comply with a rule or regulation involving care, services or supervision of a child promulgated by a state agency operating, certifying, or supervising a residential facility or program, and such failure to comply results in physical injury, excluding minor injury, or serious emotional injury to such child where such result was reasonably foreseeable; or

(d) fails to meet a personal duty imposed by an agreed upon plan of prevention and remediation pursuant to this chapter or the mental hygiene law, the executive law or the education law, arising from abuse or neglect of a child in residential care and such failure results in physical injury, excluding minor injury, or serious emotional injury or the risk thereof to the child; or

(e) intentionally administers to the child any prescription drug other than in substantial compliance with a physician's, physician's assistant's or nurse practitioner's prescription;

10. "Institutionally neglected child in residential care" means a child whose health, safety or welfare is harmed or placed in imminent danger of harm as a result of a lack of compliance with applicable standards of the state agency operating, certifying or supervising such facility or program for the care and treatment of such child or an agreed upon plan of prevention and remediation pursuant to this chapter or the mental hygiene law, the executive law or the education law, arising from abuse or neglect of a child in residential care, including, but not limited to, the provision of supervision, food, clothing, shelter, education, medical, dental, optometric or surgical care;

11. An "unfounded report" means any report made pursuant to this title unless an investigation determines that some credible evidence of the alleged abuse or maltreatment exists;

12. An "indicated report" means a report made pursuant to this title if an investigation determines that some credible evidence of the alleged abuse or maltreatment exists.

13. "Substance abuse counselor" or "alcoholism counselor" means any person who has been issued a credential therefor by the office of alcoholism and substance abuse services, pursuant to paragraphs one and two of subdivision (d) of section 19.07 of the mental hygiene law.

Amended by Laws 1977, Ch. 518 eff. Aug. 1, 1977; **amended** by Laws 1982, Ch. 600, eff. July 22, 1982; **amended** by Laws 1984, Ch. 822, eff. Dec. 3, 1984; **amended** by Laws 1985, Ch. 676, **amended** subds. 1, 2, 4 and 5; **added** new subds. 6–9; **renumbered** existing subd. 6 and 7 as 10 and 11 respectively, eff. Apr. 1, 1986; Laws 1990, Ch. 55, § 1, eff. Mar. 31, 1990, extended the expiration date until June 30, 1991. § 20 of Ch. 676 provides that nothing in the amendments to § 412 of the Social Services Law shall be deemed to amend the definition of an abused or maltreated child contained in § 1012 of the Family Court Act, or to expand the jurisdiction of the Family court relating thereto; **amended** by Laws 1986, Ch. 717, eff. Nov. 27, 1986; **amended** by Laws 1986, Ch. 719, eff. Oct. 1, 1986; Laws 1990, Ch. 55, § 2; Laws 1991, Ch. 250, eff. July 1, 1991, extended the expiration date until Mar. 31, 1992; **amended** by Laws 1986, Ch. 875, eff. Jan. 1, 1987; **amended** by Laws 1988, Ch. 543, § 1, eff. Aug. 11, 1988; **amended** by Laws 1988, Ch. 634, §§ 1, 2, 3, eff. Sept. 1, 1988 which made no reference to the earlier amendment; Laws 1990, Ch. 55, § 3; Laws 1991, Ch. 250, eff. July 1, 1991, extended the expiration date until Mar. 31, 1992; **amended** by Laws 1992, Ch. 32, §§ 1 through 6, eff. Oct. 1, 1992; **amended** by Laws 1994, Ch. 306, § 1, eff. July 20, 1994; Laws 2006, Ch. 320, §29, eff. Nov 1, 2006.

§ 413. Persons and officials required to report cases of suspected child abuse or maltreatment.

1. The following persons and officials are required to report or cause a report to be made in accordance with this title when they have reasonable cause to suspect that a child coming before them in their professional or official capacity is an abused or maltreated child, or when they have reasonable cause to suspect that a child is an abused or maltreated child where the parent, guardian, custodian or other person legally responsible for such child comes before them in their professional or official capacity and states from personal knowledge facts, conditions or circumstances which, if correct, would render the child an abused or maltreated child: any physician; registered physician assistant; surgeon; medical examiner; coroner; dentist; dental hygienist; osteopath; optometrist; chiropractor; podiatrist; resident; intern; psychologist; registered nurse; social worker; emergency medical technician; hospital personnel engaged in the admission, examination, care or treatment of persons; a Christian Science practitioner; school official; social services worker; day care center worker; provider of family or

SSL

group family day care; employee or volunteer in a residential care facility defined in subdivision seven of section four hundred twelve of this chapter or any other child care or foster care worker; mental health professional; substance abuse counselor; alcoholism counselor; peace officer; police officer; district attorney or assistant district attorney; investigator employed in the office of a district attorney; or other law enforcement official. Whenever such person is required to report under this title in his or her capacity as a member of the staff of a medical or other public or private institution, school, facility or agency, he or she shall immediately notify the person in charge of such institution, school, facility or agency, or his or her designated agent, who then also shall become responsible to report or cause reports to be made. However, nothing in this section or title is intended to require more than one report from any such institution, school or agency. At the time of the making of a report, or at any time thereafter, such person or official may exercise the right to request, pursuant to paragraph (A) of subdivision four of section four hundred twenty-two of this article, the findings of an investigation made pursuant to this title or section 45.07 of the mental hygiene law.

1. [*Effective January 1, 2005.*] The following persons and officials are required to report or cause a report to be made in accordance with this title when they have reasonable cause to suspect that a child coming before them in their professional or official capacity is an abused or maltreated child, or when they have reasonable cause to suspect that a child is an abused or maltreated child where the parent, guardian, custodian or other person legally responsible for such child comes before them in their professional or official capacity and states from personal knowledge facts, conditions or circumstances which, if correct, would render the child an abused or maltreated child: any physician; registered physician assistant; surgeon; medical examiner; coroner; dentist; dental hygienist; osteopath; optometrist; chiropractor; podiatrist; resident; intern; psychologist; registered nurse; social worker; emergency medical technician; licensed creative arts therapist; licensed marriage and family therapist; licensed mental health counselor; licensed psychoanalyst; hospital personnel engaged in the admission, examination, care or treatment of persons; a Christian Science practitioner; school official; social services worker; day care center worker; provider of family or group family day care; employee or volunteer in a residential care facility defined in subdivision seven of section four hundred twelve of this title or any other child care or foster care worker; mental health professional; substance abuse counselor; alcoholism counselor; peace officer; police officer; district attorney or assistant district attorney; investigator employed in the office of a district attorney; or other law enforcement official. Whenever such person is required to report under this title in his or her capacity as a member of the staff of a medical or other public or private institution, school, facility or agency, he or she shall immediately notify the person in charge of such institution, school, facility or agency, or his or her designated agent, who then also shall become responsible to report or cause reports to be made. However, nothing in this section or title is intended to require more than one report from any such institution, school or agency. At the time

of the making of a report, or at any time thereafter, such person or official may exercise the right to request, pursuant to paragraph (A) of subdivision four of section four hundred twenty-two of this title, the findings of an investigation made pursuant to this title or section 45.07 of the mental hygiene law.

2. Any person, institution, school, facility, agency organization, partnership or corporation which employs persons mandated to report suspected incidents of child abuse or maltreatment pursuant to subdivision one of this section shall provide consistent with section four hundred twenty-one of this chapter, all such current and new employees with written information explaining the reporting requirements set out in subdivision one of this section and in sections four hundred fifteen through four hundred twenty of this title. The employers shall be responsible for the costs associated with printing and distributing the written information.

3. Any state or local governmental agency or authorized agency which issues a license, certificate or permit to an individual to operate a family day care home or group family day care home shall provide each person currently holding or seeking such a license, certificate or permit with written information explaining the reporting requirements set out in subdivision one of this section and in sections four hundred fifteen through four hundred twenty of this title.

4. [*Eff. Nov. 1, 2005*] Any person, institution, school, facility, agency, organization, partnership or corporation, which employs persons who are mandated to report suspected incidents of child abuse or maltreatment pursuant to subdivision one of this section and whose employees, in the normal course of their employment, travel to locations where children reside, shall provide, consistent with section four hundred twenty-one of this title, all such current and new employees with information on recognizing the signs of an unlawful methamphetamine laboratory. Pursuant to section 19.27 of the mental hygiene law, the office of alcoholism and substance abuse services shall make available to such employers information on recognizing the signs of unlawful methamphetamine laboratories.

SSL

Amended by Laws 1979, Ch. 81; Laws 1980, Ch. 843, eff. Sept. 1, 1980; **amended** by Laws 1984, Ch. 932, eff. Sept. 1, 1984; **amended** by Laws 1985, Ch. 676, eff. Apr. 1, 1986; Laws 1990, Ch. 55, § 1; Laws 1991, Ch. 250, eff. July 1, 1991, extended the expiration date until Mar. 31, 1992; **amended** by Laws 1985, Ch. 677, eff. Jan. 1, 1986; **amended** by Laws 1986, Ch. 718, eff. Nov. 27, 1986; **amended** by Laws 1988, Ch. 544, § 1, eff. Jan. 1, 1989; **amended** by Laws 1989, Ch. 194, § 1, eff. Jan 1, 1990; **amended** by Laws 1994, Ch. 306, § 2, eff. July 20, 1994; **amended** by Laws 1995, Ch. 94, § 1, eff. Sept. 26, 1995; **amended** by L. 2001, Ch. 432, amending subd. 1, eff. Feb. 1, 2002; **amended** by Laws 2002, Ch. 420, § 8, 9 and 11 eff. Sept. 1, 2004 and Ch. 676, § 11, and § 19(2), eff. Jan. 1, 2005; Laws 2003, Ch. 433, § 1, eff. Sept. 1, 2004; **amended** by Laws 2004, Ch. 210, § 8, eff. July 27, 2004; **amended** by Laws 2005, Ch. 394, § 7, adding sub. 4, eff. Nov. 1, 2005.

§ 414. Any person permitted to report.

In addition to those persons and officials required to report suspected child abuse or maltreatment, any person may make such a report if such person has reasonable cause to suspect that a child is, an abused or maltreated child.

§ 415 Reporting Procedure.

[Until Nov. 21, 2005, § 415 reads as set out below:] Reports of suspected child abuse or maltreatment made pursuant to this title shall be made immediately by telephone or by telephone facsimile machine on a form supplied by the commissioner. Oral reports shall be followed by a report in writing within forty-eight hours after such oral report. Oral reports shall be made to the statewide central register of child abuse and maltreatment unless the appropriate local plan for the provision of child protective services provides that oral reports should be made to the local child protective service. In those localities in which oral reports are made initially to the local child protective service, the child protective service shall immediately make an oral or electronic report to the statewide central register. Written reports shall be made to the appropriate local child protective service except that written reports involving children in residential care, as defined in subdivision seven of section four hundred twelve of this title, or being cared for in a home operated or supervised by an authorized agency, the division for youth, or an office of the department of mental hygiene, shall be made to the statewide central register of child abuse and maltreatment which shall transmit the reports to the agency responsible for investigating the report, in accordance with paragraph (a) or (c) of subdivision eleven of section four hundred twenty-two or section four hundred twenty-four-b of this title, as applicable. Written reports shall be made in a manner prescribed and on forms supplied by the commissioner and shall include the following information: the names and addresses of the child and his or her parents or other person responsible for his or her care, if known, and, as the case may be, the name and address of the residential care facility or program in which the child resides or is receiving care; the child's age, sex and race; the nature and extent of the child's injuries, abuse or maltreatment, including any evidence of prior injuries, abuse or maltreatment to the child or, as the case may be, his or her siblings; the name of the person or persons alleged to be responsible for causing the injury, abuse or maltreatment, if known; family composition, where appropriate; the source of the report; the person making the report and where he or she can be reached; the actions taken by the reporting source, including the taking of photographs and x-rays, removal or keeping of the child or notifying the medical examiner or coroner; and any other information which the commissioner may, by regulation, require, or the person making the report believes might be helpful, in the furtherance of the purposes of this title. Written reports from persons or officials required by this title to report shall be admissible in evidence in any proceedings relating to child abuse or maltreatment.

[Effective Nov 21, 2005, § 415 reads as set out below:] Reports of suspected child abuse or maltreatment made pursuant to this title shall be made immediately by telephone or by telephone facsimile machine on a form supplied by the commissioner of the office of children and family services. Oral reports shall be followed by a report in writing within forty-eight hours after such oral report. Oral reports shall be made to the statewide central register of child abuse and maltreatment unless the appropriate local plan for the provision of child protective services provides that oral reports should be made to the local child protective service. In those localities in which oral reports are made initially to the local child protective service, the child protective service shall immediately make an oral or electronic report to the statewide central register. Written reports shall be made to the appropriate local child protective service except that written reports involving children in residential care, as defined in subdivision seven of section four hundred twelve of this title, or being cared for in a home operated or supervised by an authorized agency, [fig 1] office of children and family services, or an office of the department of mental hygiene, shall be made to the statewide central register of child abuse and maltreatment which shall transmit the reports to the agency responsible for investigating the report, in accordance with paragraph (a) or (c) of subdivision eleven of section four hundred twenty-two or section four hundred twenty-four-b of this title, as applicable. Written reports shall be made in a manner prescribed and on forms supplied by the commissioner of the office of children and family services and shall include the following information: the names and addresses of the child and his or her parents or other person responsible for his or her care, if known, and, as the case may be, the name and address of the residential care facility or program in which the child resides or is receiving care; the child's age, sex and race; the nature and extent of the child's injuries, abuse or maltreatment, including any evidence of prior injuries, abuse or maltreatment to the child or, as the case may be, his or her siblings; the name of the person or persons alleged to be responsible for causing the injury, abuse or maltreatment, if known; family composition, where appropriate; the source of the report; the person making the report and where he or she can be reached; the actions taken by the reporting source, including the taking of photographs and x-rays, removal or keeping of the child or notifying the medical examiner or coroner; and any other information which the commissioner of the office of children and family services may, by regulation, require, or the person making the report believes might be helpful, in the furtherance of the purposes of this title. Notwithstanding the privileges set forth in article forty-five of the civil practice law and rules, and any other provision of law to the contrary, mandated reporters who make a report which initiates an investigation of an allegation of child abuse or maltreatment are required to comply with all requests for records made by a child protective service relating to such report, including records relating to diagnosis, prognosis or treatment, and clinical records, of any patient or client that are essential for a full investigation of allegations of child abuse or maltreatment pursuant to this title; provided, however, that disclosure of substance abuse treatment records shall be made

SSL

pursuant to the standards and procedures for disclosure of such records delineated in federal law. Written reports from persons or officials required by this title to report shall be admissible in evidence in any proceedings relating to child abuse or maltreatment.

Former § 415 **Added**, Laws 1940, Ch. 619, § 4; **repealed**, Laws 1971, Ch. 947, § 1, eff. July 1, 1971. Current § 415 **added**, Laws 1973, Ch. 1039, § 1; **amended** by Laws 1985, Ch. 676, § 5; **amended** by Laws 1988, Ch. 545,§ 1, and Ch. 634, § 4, eff. Sept 1, 1988; **amended** by Laws 2005, Ch. 3, sect; 6 (Part B), eff. Nov. 21, 2005.

§ 416. Obligations of persons required to report.

Any person or official required to report cases of suspected child abuse and maltreatment may take or cause to be taken at public expense photographs of the areas of trauma visible on a child who is subject to a report and, if medically indicated, cause to be performed a radiological examination on the child. Any photographs or x-rays taken shall be sent to the child protective service at the time the written report is sent, or as soon thereafter as possible. Whenever such person is required to report under this title in his capacity as member of the staff of a medical or other public or private institution, school, facility, or agency, he shall immediately notify the person in charge of such institution, school, facility or agency, or his designated agent, who shall then take or cause to be taken at public expenses color photographs of sizable trauma and shall, if medically indicated, cause to be performed a radiological examination on the child.

§ 417. Taking a child into protective custody.

1.   (a) Pursuant to the requirements and provisions of the family court act, a peace officer, acting pursuant to his or her special duties, a police officer, a law enforcement official, or an agent of a duly incorporated society for the prevention of cruelty to children, or a designated employee of a city or county department of social services, or an agent or employee of an Indian tribe that has entered into an agreement with the department pursuant to section thirty-nine of this chapter to provide child protective services shall take all appropriate measures to protect a child's life and health including, when appropriate, taking or keeping a child in protective custody without the consent of a parent or guardian if such person has reasonable cause to believe that the circumstances or condition of the child are such that continuing in his or her place of residence or in the care and custody of the parent, guardian, custodian or other person responsible for the child's care presents an imminent danger to the child's life or health.

(b)   Any physician shall notify the appropriate police authorities or the local child protective service to take custody of any child such physician is treating whether or not additional medical treatment is required, if such physician has reasonable cause to believe that the circumstances or condition of the child are such that continuing in his place of residence or in the care and custody of the parent, guardian, custodian or other person responsible for the child's care presents an imminent danger to the child's life or health.

2. Notwithstanding any other provision of law, the person in charge of any hospital or similar institution shall where he has reasonable cause to believe that the circumstances or conditions of the child care are such that continuing in his place of residence or in the care and custody of the parent, guardian, custodian or other person responsible for the child's care presents an imminent danger to the child's life or health, take all necessary measures to protect the child including, where appropriate, retaining custody of an abused or maltreated child, until the next regular week day session of the family court in which a child protection proceeding pursuant to article ten of the family court act may be commenced whether or not additional medical treatment is required during that period and whether or not a request is made by a parent or guardian for the return of the child during that period. In all cases where the person in charge of a hospital or similar institution has retained custody of a child pursuant to this section, he shall immediately notify the appropriate local child protective service which immediately shall commence an investigation. In the case of a child in residential care, the child protective service shall notify the appropriate state agency which shall immediately commence an investigation. If no further medical treatment is necessary, the child protective service shall take all necessary measures to protect a child's life and health, including when appropriate, taking custody of a child. Such child protective service shall commence a child protective proceeding in the family court at the next regular week day session of the appropriate family court or recommend to the court at that time that the child be returned to his parents or guardian.

3. Whenever a child protective service takes a child into protective custody and the parent, guardian or custodian of the child is not present, the service shall immediately notify the local police station closest to the child's home of such removal, and shall provide them with a copy of the notice required pursuant to paragraph (iii) of subdivision (b) of section one thousand twenty-four of the family court act. Upon request by the parent, guardian or custodian of the child, the police shall provide such person with a copy of the notice.

Amended by Laws 1980, Ch. 843, eff. Sept. 1, 1980; **amended** by Laws 1985, Ch. 677, eff. Jan. 1, 1986; **amended** by Laws 1986, Ch. 719, eff. Oct. 1, 1986; Laws 1990, Ch. 55; Laws 1991, Ch. 250; Laws 1992, Ch. 32, eff. Oct. 1, 1992, which eliminated the expiration date of the 1986 amendment; **amended** by Laws 1993, Ch. 252, § 1, **adding** new subd. (3) to SSL § 417, eff. Sept. 4, 1993; **amended** by Laws 1996, Ch. 309, § 281, eff. July 13, 1996.

§ 418. Mandatory reporting to and post-mortem investigation of deaths by medical examiner or coroner.

[Until Dec 14, 2006] Any person or official required to report cases of suspected child abuse or maltreatment, including workers of the local child protective service, as well as an employee of or official of a state agency responsible for the investigation of a report of abuse or maltreatment of a child in residential care, who has reasonable cause to suspect that a child died as a result of child abuse or maltreatment shall report that fact to the appropriate medical examiner or coroner. The medical examiner or coroner shall accept the report for investigation and shall report his or her finding to the police, the appropriate district attorney, the local child protective service, the office of children and family services, and, if the institution making the report is a hospital, the hospital. The office of children and family services shall promptly provide a copy of such a report to the statewide central register of child abuse and maltreatment.

[Eff. Dec 14, 2006] Any person or official required to report cases of suspected child abuse or maltreatment, including workers of the local child protective service, as well as an employee of or official of a state agency responsible for the investigation of a report of abuse or maltreatment of a child in residential care, who has reasonable cause to suspect that a child died as a result of child abuse or maltreatment shall report that fact to the appropriate medical examiner or coroner. The medical examiner or coroner shall accept the report for investigation and shall issue a preliminary written report of his or her finding within sixty days of the date of death, absent extraordinary circumstances, and his or her final written report promptly, absent extraordinary circumstances, to the police, the appropriate district attorney, the local child protective service, the office of children and family services, and, if the institution making the report is a hospital, the hospital. The office of children and family services shall promptly provide a copy of the preliminary and final reports to the statewide central register of child abuse and maltreatment.

Amended by Laws 1992, Ch. 32, § 7, eff. Oct. 1, 1992; amended by Laws 1994, Ch. 426, § 1, eff. July 20, 1994; amended by Laws 1999, Ch. 136, § 4, eff. June 30, 1999; Laws 2006, Ch. 485, §2, eff. Dec. 14, 2006.

§ 419. Immunity from liability.

Any person, official, or institution participating in good faith in the providing of a service pursuant to section four hundred twenty-four of this title, the making of a report, the taking of photographs, the removal or keeping of a child pursuant to this title, or the disclosure of child protective services information in compliance with sections twenty, four hundred twenty-two and four hundred twenty-two-a of this chapter shall have immunity from any liability, civil or criminal, that might otherwise result by reason of such actions. For the purpose of any proceeding, civil or criminal, the good faith of any such person, official, or institution required to report cases of child abuse or maltreatment or providing a service pursuant to section four hundred twenty-four or the disclosure of child protective services information in compliance with sections twenty, four hundred twenty-two and four hundred twenty-two-a of this chapter shall be presumed, provided such person, official or institution was acting in discharge of their duties and within the scope of their employment, and that such liability did not result from the willful misconduct or gross negligence of such person, official or institution.

Amended by Laws 1983, Ch. 176, eff. May 31, 1983; **amended** by Laws 1984, Ch. 120, eff. May 15, 1984; **amended** by Laws 1996, Ch. 12, § 7, eff. Feb. 15, 1996.

§ 420. Penalties for failure to report.

1. Any person, official or institution required by this title to report a case of suspected child abuse or maltreatment who willfully fails to do so shall be guilty of a class A misdemeanor.

2. Any person, official or institution required by this title to report a case of suspected child abuse or maltreatment who knowingly and willful fails to do so shall be civilly liable for the damages proximately caused by such failure.

§ 421. Responsibility of the department.

The department shall:

1. in conjunction with local departments, both jointly and individually, within the appropriation available, conduct a continuing publicity and education program for local department staff, persons and officials required to report including district attorneys, assistant district attorneys, police officers, peace officers, investigators employed in the office of a district attorney, and any other appropriate persons to encourage the fullest degree of reporting of suspected child abuse or maltreatment. Such program shall be developed and implemented in coordination with those established pursuant to section 31.06 of the mental hygiene law, section twenty-eight hundred five-n of the public health law, section thirty-two hundred nine-a of the education law and sections two hundred fourteen-a and eight hundred forty of the executive law. The program shall include but not be limited to responsibilities, obligations and powers under this title and chapter as well as the diagnosis of child abuse and maltreatment, the procedures of the child protective service, the family court and other duly authorized agencies and the prevention, treatment and remediation of abuse and maltreatment of children in residential care.

2. (a) provide technical assistance to local social services departments regarding case planning and provision of services and performance of other responsibilities pursuant to this title. Such assistance shall be provided on a regular, ongoing basis and shall also be made available as needed, upon request of any such local department.

(b) issue guidelines to assist local social services departments in evaluating and establishing investigative priorities for reports describing situations or events which may pose a clear and present danger to the life, health or safety of a child and which require immediate, personal contact between the local child protective service and the subject of the report, the subject's family, or any other persons named in the report.

SSL

(c)   issue guidelines to assist local child protective services in the interpretation and assessment of reports of abuse and maltreatment made to the statewide central register described in section four hundred twenty-two of this article. Such guidelines shall include information, standards and criteria for the identification of credible evidence of alleged abuse and maltreatment required to determine whether a report may be indicated.

3.   promulgate regulations setting forth requirements for the performance by local social services departments of the duties and powers imposed and conferred upon them by the provisions of this title and of article ten of the family court act. Such regulations shall establish uniform requirements for the investigation of reports of child abuse or maltreatment under this title. The department shall also issue guidelines which shall set forth the circumstances or conditions under which:

(a)   personal contact shall be made with the child named in the report and any other children in the same household, including interviewing such child or children absent the subject of the report whenever possible and appropriate;

(b)   photographs of visible physical injuries or trauma of children who may be the victims of abuse or maltreatment shall be taken or arranged for;

(c)   medical examination of a child who may be a victim of abuse or maltreatment and documentation of findings of such examination, shall be required.

The department shall promulgate regulations to establish standards for intervention, criteria for case closings, criteria for determining whether or not to initiate a child protective proceeding, and criteria for the formulation of treatment plans and for the delivery of child protective services including specification of the services to be classified as child protective services, which shall also apply to any society for the prevention of cruelty to children which has entered into a currently valid contract with a local department of social services to investigate child abuse or maltreatment reports. The department shall promulgate regulations establishing minimum standards and practices for the delivery of child protective services in connection with monitoring and supervising respondents and their families as ordered by a family court pursuant to section ten hundred thirty-nine and paragraphs (i), (iii), (iv) and (v) of subdivision (a) of section ten hundred fifty-two of the family court act. Such regulations shall also require local child protective services to comply with notification requirements of the family court act in connection with such monitoring and supervisory responsibilities.

4.   after consultation with the local child protective services, promulgate regulations relating to staff qualifications for the child protective services, prescribing any baccalaureate or equivalent college degree and/or relevant human service experience as requirements. Such requirements shall not apply to persons currently employed by such child protective services who were hired before January first, nineteen hundred eighty-six.

5.   (a) directly or through the purchase of services, implement, subject to the amounts appropriated therefor, an ongoing, statewide training program for

employees of the department and of each local department of social services employed in the provision and supervision of child protective services or in other activities required in accordance with the provisions of this title.

(b) promulgate regulations setting forth training requirements which shall specify, among other things, that all persons hired by a child protective service on or after April first, nineteen hundred eighty-six shall have satisfactorily completed a course approved by the department within the first three months of employment, in the fundamentals of child protection. Such course shall include at least basic training in the principles and techniques of investigations, including relationships with other investigative bodies, legal issues in child protection, and methods of remediation, diagnosis, treatment and prevention.

(c) withhold reimbursement, otherwise payable to social services districts, for the salaries of employees of child protective services who do not comply with the background review, educational, experience or training requirements of this title.

6. promulgate regulations which require social services districts to make local procedural manuals and service directories available to employees of a child protective service, service providers and other professionals involved in the prevention of child abuse and maltreatment.

7. take all reasonable and necessary actions to assure that the local departments of social services are kept apprised on a current basis of the laws, regulations and policies of the department concerning child abuse and maltreatment.

8. monitor and supervise the performance of the local departments of social services.

Amended by Laws 1985, Ch. 677, eff. Jan. 1, 1986; **amended** by Laws 1986, Ch. 718, eff. Nov. 27, 1986; **amended** by Laws 1988, Ch. 504, § 1, eff. Apr. 1, 1989; **amended** by Laws 1988, Ch. 707, § 2, eff. Sept. 2, 1988; **amended** by Laws 1989, Ch. 110, eff. June 29, 1989; **amended** by Laws 1990, Ch. 320, § 1, eff. Sept. 1, 1990.

§ 421-a. Responsibilities of the department for enhanced performance standards.

Repealed by Laws 1995, Ch. 83, § 242, eff. July 1, 1995.

§ 422 Statewide central register of child abuse and maltreatment

1. There shall be established in the department a statewide central register of child abuse and maltreatment reports made pursuant to this title.

2. (a) [Until Dec 14, 2006] The central register shall be capable of receiving telephone calls alleging child abuse or maltreatment and of immediately identifying prior reports of child abuse or maltreatment and capable of monitoring the provision of child protective service twenty-four hours a day, seven days a week.

SSL

To effectuate this purpose, but subject to the provisions of the appropriate local plan for the provision of child protective services, there shall be a single statewide telephone number that all persons, whether mandated by the law or not, may use to make telephone calls alleging child abuse or maltreatment and that all persons so authorized by this title may use for determining the existence of prior reports in order to evaluate the condition or circumstances of a child. In addition to the single statewide telephone number, there shall be a special unlisted express telephone number and a telephone facsimile number for use only by persons mandated by law to make telephone calls, or to transmit telephone facsimile information on a form provided by the commissioner, alleging child abuse or maltreatment, and for use by all persons so authorized by this title for determining the existence of prior reports in order to evaluate the condition or circumstances of a child. When any allegations contained in such telephone calls could reasonably constitute a report of child abuse or maltreatment, such allegations shall be immediately transmitted orally or electronically by the department to the appropriate local child protective service for investigation. The inability of the person calling the register to identify the alleged perpetrator shall, in no circumstance, constitute the sole cause for the register to reject such allegation or fail to transmit such allegation for investigation. If the records indicate a previous report concerning a subject of the report, other persons named in the report or other pertinent information, the appropriate local child protective service shall be immediately notified of the fact, except as provided in subdivision eleven of this section.

(a) [Eff. Dec 14, 2006] The central register shall be capable of receiving telephone calls alleging child abuse or maltreatment and of immediately identifying prior reports of child abuse or maltreatment and capable of monitoring the provision of child protective service twenty-four hours a day, seven days a week. To effectuate this purpose, but subject to the provisions of the appropriate local plan for the provision of child protective services, there shall be a single statewide telephone number that all persons, whether mandated by the law or not, may use to make telephone calls alleging child abuse or maltreatment and that all persons so authorized by this title may use for determining the existence of prior reports in order to evaluate the condition or circumstances of a child. In addition to the single statewide telephone number, there shall be a special unlisted express telephone number and a telephone facsimile number for use only by persons mandated by law to make telephone calls, or to transmit telephone facsimile information on a form provided by the commissioner, alleging child abuse or maltreatment, and for use by all persons so authorized by this title for determining the existence of prior reports in order to evaluate the condition or circumstances of a child. When any allegations contained in such telephone calls could reasonably constitute a report of child abuse or maltreatment, such allegations shall be immediately transmitted orally or electronically by the department to the appropriate local child protective service for investigation. The inability of the person calling the register to identify the alleged perpetrator shall, in no circumstance, constitute the sole cause for the register to reject such allegation or fail to transmit such allegation for investigation. If the records indicate a previous report concerning a subject of the report, the child alleged to be abused or maltreated, a sibling, other children in the household, other persons named in the report or other pertinent information, the appropriate local child protective service shall be immediately notified of the fact, except as provided in subdivision eleven of this section. If the report involves either (i) suspected physical injury as described in paragraph (i) of subdivision (e) of section ten hundred twelve of the family court act or sexual abuse of a child or the death of a child or (ii) suspected maltreatment which alleges any physical harm when the report is made by a person required to report pursuant to section four hundred thirteen of this title within six months of any other two reports that were indicated, or may still be pending, involving the same child, sibling, or other children in the household or the subject of the report, the department shall identify the report as such and note any prior reports when transmitting the report to the local child protective services for investigation.

(b)   Any telephone call made by a person required to report cases of suspected child abuse or maltreatment pursuant to section four hundred thirteen of this chapter containing allegations, which if true would constitute child abuse or maltreatment shall constitute a report and shall be immediately transmitted orally or electronically by the department to the appropriate local child protective service for investigation.

(c)   Whenever a telephone call to the statewide central register described in this section is received by the department, and the department finds that the person allegedly responsible for abuse or maltreatment of a child cannot be a subject of a report as defined in subdivision four of section four hundred twelve of this chapter, but believes that the alleged acts or circumstances against a child described in the telephone call may constitute a crime or an immediate threat to the child's health or safety, the department shall convey by the most expedient means available the information contained in such telephone call to the appropriate law enforcement agency, district attorney or other public official empowered to provide necessary aid or assistance.

(d)   A telephone call made to the statewide central register described in this section alleging facts that support a finding of the institutional neglect of a child in residential care pursuant to subdivision ten of section four hundred twelve of this article and that, if true, clearly could not support a finding that the child is an abused or neglected child in residential care, shall not constitute a report, and shall immediately be transmitted to the state agency responsible for the operation or supervision of the residential facility or program and, in the case of a facility operated or certified by an office of the state department of mental hygiene, to the state commission on quality of care for the mentally disabled, for appropriate action.

3.   The central register shall include but not be limited to the following information: all the information in the written report; a record of the final disposition of the report, including services offered and services accepted; the

plan for rehabilitative treatment; the names and identifying data, dates and circumstances of any person requesting or receiving information from the register; and any other information which the commissioner believes might be helpful in the furtherance of the purposes of this chapter.

4.   (A) Reports made pursuant to this title as well as any other information obtained, reports written or photographs taken concerning such reports in the possession of the department, local departments, or the commission on quality of care for the mentally disabled, shall be confidential and shall only be made available to:

(a)   a physician who has before him or her a child whom he or she reasonably suspects may be abused or maltreated;

(b)   a person authorized to place a child in protective custody when such person has before him or her a child whom he or she reasonably suspects may be abused or maltreated and such person requires the information in the record to determine whether to place the child in protective custody;

(c)   a duly authorized agency having the responsibility for the care or supervision of a child who is reported to the central register of abuse and maltreatment;

(d)   any person who is the subject of the report or other persons named in the report;

(e)   a court, upon a finding that the information in the record is necessary for the determination of an issue before the court;

(f)   a grand jury, upon a finding that the information in the record is necessary for the determination of charges before the grand jury;

(g)   any appropriate state legislative committee responsible for child protective legislation;

(h)   any person engaged in a bona fide research purpose provided, however, that no information identifying the subjects of the report or other persons named in the report shall be made available to the researcher unless it is absolutely essential to the research purpose and the department gives prior approval;

(i)   a provider agency as defined by subdivision three of section four hundred twenty-four-a of this chapter, or a licensing agency as defined by subdivision four of section four hundred twenty-four-a of this chapter, subject to the provisions of such section;

(j)   the state commission on quality of care for the mentally disabled in connection with an investigation being conducted by the commission pursuant to article forty-five of the mental hygiene law;

(k)   a probation service conducting an investigation pursuant to article three or seven or section six hundred fifty-three of the family court act where there is reason to suspect the child or the child's sibling may have been abused or maltreated and such child or sibling, parent, guardian or other person legally responsible for the child is a person named in an indicated report of child abuse or maltreatment and that such information is necessary for the making of a determination or recommendation to the court; or a probation service regarding a person about whom it is conducting an investigation pursuant to article three hundred ninety of the criminal procedure law, or a probation service or the state division of parole regarding a person to whom the service or division is providing supervision pursuant to article sixty of the penal law or section two hundred fifty-nine-a of the executive law, where the subject of investigation or supervision has been convicted of a felony under article one hundred twenty, one hundred twenty-five or one hundred thirty-five of the penal law or any felony or misdemeanor under article one hundred thirty, two hundred thirty-five, two hundred forty-five, two hundred sixty or two hundred sixty-three of the penal law, or has been indicted for any such felony and, as a result, has been convicted of a crime under the penal law, where the service or division requests the information upon a certification that such information is necessary to conduct its investigation, that there is reasonable cause to believe that the subject of an investigation is the subject of an indicated report and that there is reasonable cause to believe that such records are necessary to the investigation by the probation service or the state division of parole, provided, however, that only indicated reports shall be furnished pursuant to this subdivision;

(l)   a district attorney, an assistant district attorney or investigator employed in the office of a district attorney, a sworn officer of the division of state police, of the regional state park police, of a city police department, or of a county, town or village police department or county sheriff's office or department when such official requests such information stating that such information is necessary to conduct a criminal investigation or criminal prosecution of a person, that there is reasonable cause to believe that such person is the subject of a report, and that it is reasonable to believe that due to the nature of the crime under investigation or prosecution, such person is the subject of a report, and that it is reasonable to believe that due to that nature of the crime under investigation or prosecution, such records may be related to the criminal investigation or prosecution;

(m)   the New York city department of investigation provided however, that no information identifying the subjects of the report or other persons named in the report shall be made available to the department of investigation unless such information is essential to an investigation within the legal authority of the department of investigation and the state department of social services gives prior approval;

(n)   chief executive officers of authorized agencies, directors of day care centers and directors of facilities operated or supervised by the department of education, the division for youth, the office of mental health or the office of mental retardation and developmental disabilities, in connection with a disciplinary investigation, action, or administrative or judicial proceeding instituted by any of such officers or directors against an employee of any such agency, center or facility who is the subject of an indicated report when the incident of abuse

SSL

or maltreatment contained in the report occurred in the agency, center, facility or program, and the purpose of such proceeding is to determine whether the employee should be retained or discharged; provided, however, a person given access to information pursuant to this subparagraph (n) shall, notwithstanding any inconsistent provision of law, be authorized to redisclose such information only if the purpose of such redisclosure is to initiate or present evidence in a disciplinary, administrative or judicial proceeding concerning the continued employment or the terms of employment of an employee of such agency, center or facility who has been named as a subject of an indicated report and, in addition, a person or agency given access to information pursuant to this subparagraph (n) shall also be given information not otherwise provided concerning the subject of an indicated report where the commission of an act or acts by such subject has been determined in proceedings pursuant to article ten of the family court act to constitute abuse or neglect;

(o)   a provider or coordinator of services to which a child protective service or social services district has referred a child or a child's family or to whom the child or the child's family have referred themselves at the request of the child protective service or social services district, where said child is reported to the register when the records, reports or other information are necessary to enable the provider or coordinator to establish and implement a plan of service for the child or the child's family, or to monitor the provision and coordination of services and the circumstances of the child and the child's family, or to directly provide services; provided, however, that a provider of services may include appropriate health care or school district personnel, as such terms shall be defined by the department; provided however, a provider or coordinator of services given access to information concerning a child pursuant to this subparagraph (o) shall, notwithstanding any inconsistent provision of law, be authorized to redisclose such information to other persons or agencies which also provide services to the child or the child's family only if the consolidated services plan prepared and approved pursuant to section thirty-four-a of this chapter describes the agreement that has been or will be reached between the provider or coordinator of service and the local district. An agreement entered into pursuant to this subparagraph shall include the specific agencies and categories of individuals to whom redisclosure by the provider or coordinator of services is authorized. Persons or agencies given access to information pursuant to this subparagraph may exchange such information in order to facilitate the provision or coordination of services to the child or the child's family;

(p)   a disinterested person making an investigation pursuant to section one hundred sixteen of the domestic relations law, provided that such disinterested person shall only make this information available to the judge before whom the adoption proceeding is pending;

(q)   a criminal justice agency conducting an investigation of a missing child where there is reason to suspect such child or such child's sibling, parent, guardian or other person legally responsible for such child is a person named in an indicated report of child abuse or maltreatment and that such information is needed to further such investigation;

(r)   in relation to a report involving a child in residential care, the director or operator of the residential facility or program and, as appropriate, the local social services commissioner or school district placing the child, the division for youth, the department of education, the commission on quality of care for the mentally disabled, the office of mental health, the office of mental retardation and developmental disabilities, and any law guardian appointed to represent the child whose appointment has been continued by a family court judge during the term of the placement, subject to the limitations contained in subdivisions nine and ten of this section and subdivision five of section four hundred twenty-four-c of this title;

(s)   a child protective service of another state when such service certifies that the records and reports are necessary in order to conduct a child abuse or maltreatment investigation within its jurisdiction of the subject of the report and shall be used only for purposes of conducting such investigation and will not be redisclosed to any other person or agency;

(t)   a law guardian, appointed pursuant to the provisions of section ten hundred sixteen of the family court act, at any time such appointment is in effect, in relation to any report in which the respondent in the proceeding in which the law guardian has been appointed is the subject or another person named in the report, pursuant to sections ten hundred thirty-nine-a and ten hundred fifty-two-a of the family court act;

(u)   a child care resource and referral program subject to the provisions of subdivision six of section four hundred twenty-four-a of this title;

(v)   (i) officers and employees of the state comptroller or of the city comptroller of the city of New York, or of the county officer designated by law or charter to perform the auditing function in any county not wholly contained within a city, for purposes of a duly authorized performance audit, provided that such comptroller shall have certified to the keeper of such records that he or she has instituted procedures developed in consultation with the department to limit access to client-identifiable information to persons requiring such information for purposes of the audit and that appropriate controls and prohibitions are imposed on the dissemination of client-identifiable information contained in the conduct of the audit. Information pertaining to the substance or content of any psychological, psychiatric, therapeutic, clinical or medical reports, evaluations or like materials or information pertaining to such child or the child's family shall not be made available to such officers and employees unless disclosure of such information is absolutely essential to the specific audit activity and the department gives prior written approval.

(ii)   any failure to maintain the confidentiality of client-identifiable information shall subject such comptroller or officer to denial of any further access to records until such time as the audit agency has reviewed its procedures concerning controls and prohibitions imposed on the dissemination of such information and has taken all reasonable and appropriate steps to eliminate such lapses in maintaining confidentiality to the satisfaction of the office of children and family services. The office of children and family services shall establish the grounds for denial of access to records contained under this section and shall recommend as necessary a plan of remediation to the audit agency. Except as provided in this section, nothing in this subparagraph shall be construed as limiting the powers of such comptroller or officer to access records which he or she is otherwise authorized to audit or obtain under any other applicable provision of law. Any person given access to information pursuant to this subparagraph who releases data or information to persons or agencies not authorized to receive such information shall be guilty of a class A misdemeanor;

(w)   members of a local or regional fatality review team approved by the office of children and family services in accordance with section four hundred twenty-two-b of this title;

(x)   members of a local or regional multidisciplinary investigative team as established pursuant to subdivision six of section four hundred twenty-three of this title; and

(y)   members of a citizen review panel as established pursuant to section three hundred seventy-one-b of this article; provided, however, members of a citizen review panel shall not disclose to any person or government official any identifying information which the panel has been provided and shall not make public other information unless otherwise authorized by statute.

After a child, other than a child in residential care, who is reported to the central register of abuse or maltreatment reaches the age of eighteen years, access to a child's record under subparagraphs (a) and (b) of this paragraph shall be permitted only if a sibling or off-spring of such child is before such person and is a suspected victim of child abuse or maltreatment. In addition, a person or official required to make a report of suspected child abuse or maltreatment pursuant to section four hundred thirteen of this chapter shall receive, upon request, the findings of an investigation made pursuant to this title or section 45.07 of the mental hygiene law. However, no information may be released unless the person or official's identity is confirmed by the department. If the request for such information is made prior to the completion of an investigation of a report, the released information shall be limited to whether the report is "indicated", "unfounded" or "under investigation", whichever the case may be. If the request for such information is made after the completion of an investigation of a report, the released information shall be limited to whether the report is "indicated" or "unfounded", whichever the case may be. A person given access to the names or other information identifying the subjects of the report, or other persons named in the report, except the subject of the report or other persons named in the report, shall not divulge or make public such identifying information unless he or she is a district attorney or other law enforcement official and the purpose is to initiate court action or the disclosure is necessary in connection with the investigation or prosecution of the subject of the report for a crime alleged to have been committed by the subject against another person named in the report. Nothing in this section shall be construed to permit any release, disclosure or identification of the names or identifying descriptions of persons who have reported suspected child abuse or maltreatment to the statewide central register or the agency, institution, organization, program or other entity where such persons are employed or the agency, institution, organization or program with which they are associated without such persons' written permission except to persons, officials, and agencies enumerated in subparagraphs (e), (f), (h), (j), (l), (m) and (v) of this paragraph.

To the extent that persons or agencies are given access to information pursuant to subparagraphs (a), (b), (c), (j), (k), (l), (m), (o) and (q) of this paragraph, such persons or agencies may give and receive such information to each other in order to facilitate an investigation conducted by such persons or agencies.

(B) Notwithstanding any inconsistent provision of law to the contrary, a city or county social services commissioner may withhold, in whole or in part, the release of any information which he or she is authorized to make available to persons or agencies identified in subparagraphs (a), (k), (l), (m), (n), (o), (p) and (q) of paragraph (A) of this subdivision if such commissioner determines that such information is not related to the purposes for which such information is requested or when such disclosure will be detrimental to the child named in the report.

(C) A city or county social services commissioner who denies access by persons or agencies identified in subparagraphs (a), (k), (l), (m), (n), (o), (p) and (q) of paragraph (A) of this subdivision to records, reports or other information or parts thereof maintained by such commissioner in accordance with this title shall, within ten days from the date of receipt of the request fully explain in writing to the person requesting the records, reports or other information the reasons for the denial.

(D) A person or agency identified in subparagraphs (a), (k), (l), (m), (n), (o), (p) and (q) of paragraph (A) of this subdivision who is denied access to records, reports or other information or parts thereof maintained by a local department pursuant to this title may bring a proceeding for review of such denial pursuant to article seventy-eight of the civil practice law and rules.

5. (a) Unless an investigation of a report conducted pursuant to this title or subdivision (c) of section 45.07 of the mental hygiene law determines that there is some credible evidence of the alleged abuse or maltreatment, all information identifying the subjects of the report and other persons named in the report shall be legally sealed forthwith by the central register and any local child protective services or the state agency which investigated the report. Such unfounded reports may only be unsealed and made available:

(i)   to the office of children and family services for the purpose of supervising a social services district;

SSL

(ii) to the office of children and family services and local or regional fatality review team members for the purpose of preparing a fatality report pursuant to section twenty or four hundred twenty-two-b of this chapter;

(iii) to a local child protective service, the office of children and family services, all members of a local or regional multidisciplinary investigative team, the commission on quality of care for the mentally disabled, or the department of mental hygiene, when investigating a subsequent report of suspected abuse or maltreatment involving a subject of the unfounded report, a child named in the unfounded report, or a child's sibling named in the unfounded report;

(iv) to the subject of the report; and

(v) to a district attorney, an assistant district attorney, an investigator employed in the office of a district attorney, or to a sworn officer of the division of state police, of a city, county, town or village police department or of a county sheriff's office when such official verifies that the report is necessary to conduct an active investigation or prosecution of a violation of subdivision three of section 240.55 of the penal law.

(b) Persons given access to unfounded reports pursuant to subparagraph (v) of paragraph (a) of this subdivision shall not redisclose such reports except as necessary to conduct such appropriate investigation or prosecution and shall request of the court that any copies of such reports produced in any court proceeding be redacted to remove the names of the subjects and other persons named in the reports or that the court issue an order protecting the names of the subjects and other persons named in the reports from public disclosure. The local child protective service or state agency shall not indicate the subsequent report solely based upon the existence of the prior unfounded report or reports. Notwithstanding section four hundred fifteen of this title, section one thousand forty-six of the family court act, or, except as set forth herein, any other provision of law to the contrary, an unfounded report shall not be admissible in any judicial or administrative proceeding or action; provided, however, an unfounded report may be introduced into evidence: (i) by the subject of the report where such subject is a respondent in a proceeding under article ten of the family court act or is a plaintiff or petitioner in a civil action or proceeding alleging the false reporting of child abuse or maltreatment; or (ii) in a criminal court for the purpose of prosecuting a violation of subdivision three of section 240.55 of the penal law. Legally sealed unfounded reports shall be expunged ten years after the receipt of the report. Whenever the office of children and family services determines that there is some credible evidence of abuse or maltreatment as a result of an investigation of a report conducted pursuant to subdivision (c) of section 45.07 of the mental hygiene law, the office of children and family services shall notify the commission on quality of care for the mentally disabled.

(c) Notwithstanding any other provision of law, the office of children and family services may, in its discretion, grant a request to expunge an unfounded report where: (i) the source of the report was convicted of a violation of subdivision three of section 240.55 of the penal law in regard to such report; or (ii) the subject of the report presents clear and convincing evidence that affirmatively refutes the allegation of abuse or maltreatment; provided however, that the absence of credible evidence supporting the allegation of abuse or maltreatment shall not be the sole basis to expunge the report. Nothing in this paragraph shall require the office of children and family services to hold an administrative hearing in deciding whether to expunge a report. Such office shall make its determination upon reviewing the written evidence submitted by the subject of the report and any records or information obtained from the state or local agency which investigated the allegations of abuse or maltreatment.

6. In all other cases, the record of the report to the central register shall be expunged ten years after the eighteenth birthday of the youngest child named in the report. In the case of a child in residential care as defined in subdivision seven of section four hundred twelve of this chapter, the record of the report to the central register shall be expunged ten years after the reported child's eighteenth birthday. In any case and at any time, the commissioner may amend any record upon good cause shown and notice to the subjects of the report and other persons named in the report.

7. At any time, a subject of a report and other persons named in the report may receive, upon request, a copy of all information contained in the central register; provided, however, that the commissioner is authorized to prohibit the release of data that would identify the person who made the report or who cooperated in a subsequent investigation or the agency, institution, organization, program or other entity where such person is employed or with which he is associated, which he reasonably finds will be detrimental to the safety or interests of such person.

8. (a) (i) At any time subsequent to the completion of the investigation but in no event later than ninety days after the subject of the report is notified that the report is indicated the subject may request the commissioner to amend the record of the report. If the commissioner does not amend the report in accordance with such request within ninety days of receiving the request, the subject shall have the right to a fair hearing, held in accordance with paragraph (b) of this subdivision, to determine whether the record of the report in the central register should be amended on the grounds that it is inaccurate or it is being maintained in a manner inconsistent with this title.

(ii) Upon receipt of a request to amend the record of a child abuse and maltreatment report the department shall immediately send a written request to the child protective service or the state agency which was responsible for investigating the allegations of abuse or maltreatment for all records, reports and other information maintained by the service or state agency pertaining to such indicated report. The service or state agency shall as expeditiously as possible but within no more than twenty working days of receiving such request, forward all records, reports and other information it maintains on such indicated report to the department. The department shall as expeditiously as possible but within no more than fifteen working days of receiving such materials from the child protective service or state agency, review all such materials in its possession concerning the indicated report and determine, after affording such service or state agency a reasonable opportunity to present its views, whether there is some credible evidence to find that the subject committed the act or acts of child abuse or maltreatment giving rise to the indicated report and whether, based on guide-lines developed by the department pursuant to subdivision five of section four hundred twenty-four-a of this title, such act or acts could be relevant and reasonably related to employment of the subject of the report by a provider agency, as defined by subdivision three of section four hundred twenty-four-a of this title, or relevant and reasonably related to the subject of the report being allowed to have regular and substantial contact with children who are cared for by a provider agency, or relevant and reasonably related to the approval or disapproval of an application submitted by the subject of the report to a licensing agency, as defined by subdivision four of section four hundred twenty-four-a of this title.

(iii)   If it is determined at the review held pursuant to this paragraph (a) that there is no credible evidence in the record to find that the subject committed an act or acts of child abuse or maltreatment, the department shall amend the record to indicate that the report is "unfounded" and notify the subject forthwith.

(iv)   If it is determined at the review held pursuant to this paragraph (a) that there is some credible evidence in the record to find that the subject committed such act or acts but that such act or acts could not be relevant and reasonably related to the employment of the subject by a provider agency or to the subject being allowed to have regular and substantial contact with children who are cared for by a provider agency or the approval or disapproval of an application which could be submitted by the subject to a licensing agency, the department shall be precluded from informing a provider or licensing agency which makes an inquiry to the department pursuant to the provisions of section four hundred twenty-four-a of this title concerning the subject that the person about whom the inquiry is made is the subject of an indicated report of child abuse or maltreatment. The department shall notify forthwith the subject of the report of such determinations and that a fair hearing has been scheduled pursuant to paragraph (b) of this subdivision. The sole issue at such hearing shall be whether the subject has been shown by some credible evidence to have committed the act or acts of child abuse or maltreatment giving rise to the indicated report.

(v)   If it is determined at the review held pursuant to this paragraph (a) that there is some credible evidence in the record to prove that the subject committed an act or acts of child abuse or maltreatment and that such act or acts could be relevant and reasonably related to the employment of the subject by a provider agency or to the subject being allowed to have regular and substantial contact with children cared for by provider agency or the approval or disapproval of an application which could be submitted by the subject to a licensing agency, the department shall notify forthwith the subject of the report of such determinations and that a fair hearing has been scheduled pursuant to paragraph (b) of this subdivision.

(b) (i) If the department, within ninety days of receiving a request from the subject that the record of a report be amended, does not amend the record in accordance with such request, the department shall schedule a fair hearing and shall provide notice of the scheduled hearing date to the subject, the statewide central register and, as appropriate, to the child protective service or the state agency which investigated the report.

(ii) The burden of proof in such a hearing shall be on the child protective service or the state agency which investigated the report, as the case may be. In such a hearing, the fact that there is a family court finding of abuse or neglect against the subject in regard to an allegation contained in the report shall create an irrebuttable presumption that said allegation is substantiated by some credible evidence.

(c) (i) If it is determined at the fair hearing that there is no credible evidence in the record to find that the subject committed an act or acts of child abuse or maltreatment, the department shall amend the record to reflect that such a finding was made at the administrative hearing, order any child protective service or state agency which investigated the report to similarly amend its records of the report, and shall notify the subject forthwith of the determination.

(ii) Upon a determination made at a fair hearing held on or after January first, nineteen hundred eighty-six scheduled pursuant to the provisions of subparagraph (v) of paragraph (a) of this subdivision that the subject has been shown by some credible evidence to have committed the act or acts of child abuse or maltreatment giving rise to the indicated report, the hearing officer shall determine, based on guidelines developed by the department pursuant to subdivision five of section four hundred twenty-four-a of this chapter, whether such act or acts are relevant and reasonably related to employment of the subject by a provider agency, as defined by subdivision three of section four hundred twenty-four-a of this title, or relevant and reasonably related to the subject being allowed to have regular and substantial contact with children who are cared for by a provider agency or relevant and reasonably related to the approval or disapproval of an application submitted by the subject to a licensing agency, as defined by subdivision four of section four hundred twenty-four-a of this title.

Upon a determination made at a fair hearing that the act or acts of abuse or maltreatment are relevant and reasonably related to employment of the subject by a provider agency or the subject being allowed to have regular and substantial contact with children who are cared for by a provider agency or the approval or denial of an application submitted by the subject to a licensing agency, the department shall notify the subject forthwith. The department shall inform a provider or licensing agency which makes an inquiry to the department pursuant to the provisions of section four hundred twenty-four-a of this title concerning the subject that the person about whom the inquiry is made is the subject of an indicated child abuse or maltreatment report.

SSL

The failure to determine at the fair hearing that the act or acts of abuse and maltreatment are relevant and reasonably related to the employment of the subject by a provider agency or to the subject being allowed to have regular and substantial contact with children who are cared for by a provider agency or the approval or denial of an application submitted by the subject to a licensing agency shall preclude the department from informing a provider or licensing agency which makes an inquiry to the department pursuant to the provisions of section four hundred twenty-four-a of this title concerning the subject that the person about whom the inquiry is made is the subject of an indicated child abuse or maltreatment report.

(d)   The commissioner or his or her designated agent is hereby authorized and empowered to make any appropriate order respecting the amendment of a record to make it accurate or consistent with the requirements of this title.

(e)   Should the department grant the request of the subject of the report pursuant to this subdivision either through an administrative review or fair hearing to amend an indicated report to an unfounded report. Such report shall be legally sealed and shall be released and expunged in accordance with the standards set forth in subdivision five of this section.

9.   Written notice of any expungement or amendment of any record, made pursuant to the provisions of this title, shall be servedforthwith upon each subject of such record, other persons named in the report, the commissioner, and, as appropriate, the applicable local child protective service, the commission on quality of care for the mentally disabled, the division for youth, department of education, office of mental health, office of mental retardation and developmental disabilities, the local social services commissioner or school district placing the child, any law guardian appointed to represent the child whose appointment has been continued by a family court judge during the term of a child's placement, and the director or operator of a residential care facility or program. The local child protective service or the state agency which investigated the report, upon receipt of such notice, shall take the appropriate similar action in regard to its child abuse and maltreatment register and records and inform, for the same purpose, any other agency which received such record.

10.   Whenever the department determines that there is some credible evidence of abuse or maltreatment as a result of an investigation of a report conducted pursuant to this title or section 45.07 of the mental hygiene law concerning a child in residential care, the department shall notify the child's parent or guardian and transmit copies of reports made pursuant to this title to the director or operator of the residential facility or program and, as applicable, the local social services commissioner or school district placing the child, division for youth, department of education, commission on quality of care for the mentally disabled, office of mental health, office of mental retardation and developmental disabilities, and any law guardian appointed to represent the child whose appointment has been continued by a family court judge during the term of a child's placement.

11.   (a) Reports and records made pursuant to this title, including any previous report concerning a subject of the report, other persons named in the report or other pertinent information, involving children who reside in residential facilities or programs enumerated in paragraphs (a), (b), (c), (d), (e), (f) and (h) of subdivision seven of section four hundred twelve of this chapter, shall be transmitted immediately by the central register to the commissioner who shall commence an appropriate investigation consistent with the terms and conditions set forth in section four hundred twenty-four-c of this title. If an investigation determines that some credible evidence of alleged abuse or maltreatment exists, the commissioner shall recommend to the local social services department, the state education department or the division for youth, as the case may be, that appropriate preventive and remedial action including legal action, consistent with applicable collective bargaining agreements and applicable provisions of the civil service law, pursuant to standards and regulations of the department promulgated pursuant to section four hundred sixty-two of this chapter and standards and regulations of the division for youth and the department of education promulgated pursuant to section five hundred one of the executive law, sections forty-four hundred three, forty-three hundred fourteen, forty-three hundred fifty-eight and forty-two hundred twelve of the education law and other applicable provisions of law, be taken with respect to the residential facility or program and/or the subject of the report. However, nothing in this paragraph shall prevent the commissioner from making recommendations, as provided for by this paragraph, even though the investigation may fail to result in a determination that there is some credible evidence of the alleged abuse or maltreatment.

(b)   The department shall establish standards for the provision of training to its employees charged with the investigation of reports of child abuse and maltreatment in residential care in at least the following: (a) basic training in the principles and techniques of investigation, including relationships with other investigative bodies, (b) legal issues in child protection including the legal rights of children, employees and volunteers, (c) methods of identification, remediation, treatment and prevention, (d) safety and security procedures, and (e) the principles of child development, the characteristics of children in care, and techniques of group and child mamagement including crisis intervention. The department shall take all reasonable and necessary actions to assure that its employees are kept apprised on a current basis of all department policies and procedures relating to the protection of children from abuse and maltreatment.

(c)   Reports and records made pursuant to this title, including any previous report concerning a subject of the report, other persons named in the report or other pertinent information, involving children who reside in a residential facility licensed or operated by the offices of mental health or mental retardation and developmental disabilities except those facilities or programs enumerated in paragraph (h) of subdivision seven of section four hundred twelve of this chapter, shall be transmitted immediately by the central register to the commission on quality of care for the mentally disabled, which shall commence an appropriate

SSL

investigation in accordance with the terms and conditions set forth in section 45.07 of the mental hygiene law.

12.   Any person who willfully permits and any person who encourages the release of any data and information contained in the central register to persons or agencies not permitted by this title shall be guilty of a class A misdemeanor.

13.   There shall be a single statewide telephone number for use by all persons seeking general information about child abuse, maltreatment or welfare other than for the purpose of making a report of child abuse or maltreatment.

14.   The department shall refer suspected cases of falsely reporting child abuse and maltreatment in violation of subdivision three of section 240.55 of the penal law to the appropriate law enforcement agency or district attorney.

Amended by Laws 1976, Ch. 823; Laws 1978, Ch. 555; Laws 1980, Ch. 480, eff. Oct. 1, 1980; **amended** by Laws 1981, Ch. 316, eff. June 29, 1981, **added** subd. 4(j); **amended** by Laws 1981, Ch. 585, eff. Sept. 1, 1981; **amended** by Laws 1983, Ch. 307, eff. June 21, 1983; **amended** by Laws 1984, Ch. 822, eff. Dec. 3, 1984; **amended** by Laws 1984, Ch. 554, eff. Sept. 1, 1984; **amended** by Laws 1985, Ch. 676, eff. Apr. 1, 1986, until Mar. 31, 1990; **amended** by Laws 1985, Ch. 677, eff. Jan. 1, 1986; **amended** by Laws 1986, Ch. 717, eff. Nov. 27, 1986; **amended** by Laws 1986, Ch. 718, eff. Nov. 27, 1986; **amended** by Laws 1986, Ch. 719, eff. Oct. 1, 1986; **amended** by Laws 1987, Ch. 159, eff. June 29, 1987; **amended** by Laws 1987, Ch. 652, eff. Sept. 1, 1987; **amended** by Laws 1988, Ch. 545, §§ 2, 3, eff. Jan. 1, 1989; **amended** by Laws 1988, Ch. 634, §§ 5, 6, 7, 8, eff. Sept. 1, 1988, with subparagraph (t) of paragraph (A) of subdivision four being in effect until Mar. 31, 1992 (Laws 1991, Ch. 250, eff, Mar. 31, 1991, extended the effective date); **amended** by Laws 1989, Ch. 292, eff. Nov. 7, 1989; **amended** by Laws 1989, Ch. 434, eff. July 16, 1989; **amended** by Laws 1989, Ch. 477, eff. Nov. 1, 1989; **amended** by Laws 1990, Ch. 156, § 1, eff. May 17, 1990; **amended** by Laws 1990, Ch. 317, § 3, eff. Sept. 1, 1990; **amended** by Laws 1991, Ch. 22, § 1, eff. June 20, 1991; **amended** by Laws 1991, Ch. 67, § 1, eff. July 21, 1991; **amended** by Laws 1991, Ch. 69, § 6, eff. Apr. 22, 1991; Laws 1991, Ch. 188, § 1, eff. June 21, 1991; **amended** by Laws 1991, Ch. 225, § 1, eff. July 1, 1991; **amended** by Laws 1992, Ch. 32, §§ 8 through 11, eff. Oct. 1, 1992; **amended** by Laws 1992, Ch. 707, § 1, eff. Oct. 1, 1992; **amended** by Laws 1993, Ch. 441, § 3, **amending** subpara. (t) and **adding** new subpara. (u) to SSL § 422(4)(A), eff. Apr. 1, 1994; **amended** by Laws 1996, Ch. 12, §§ 8–11, eff. Feb. 15, 1996, and applicable to reports of suspected child abuse or maltreatment registered on or after the effective date of this act. With respect to this section, the provisions of the social services law in effect prior to the effective date act shall apply to reports of suspected child abuse or maltreatment registered prior to such effective date; **amended** by Laws 1999, Ch. 136, §§ 5 & 6, eff. June 30, 1999; **amended** by Laws 2000, Ch. 555, § 1, eff. Nov. 1, 2000, and amendments to expire and deemed repealed on May 1, 2002; **amended** by Laws 2001, Ch. 35, § 1, amending sub 4, para (A), subpar (l), eff. May 23, 2001; **amended** by Laws Ch. 46, § 1, eff. April 30, 2002, provisions shall expire and be deemed repealed 18 months after such effective date; Laws 2006, Ch. 494, §1, eff. Dec. 14, 2006.

§ 422-a.   Child abuse and neglect investigations; disclosure.

1.   Notwithstanding any inconsistent provision of law to the contrary, the commissioner or a city or county social services commissioner may disclose

information regarding the abuse or maltreatment of a child as set forth in this section, and the investigation thereof and any services related thereto if he or she determines that such disclosure shall not be contrary to the best interests of the child, the child's siblings or other children in the household and any one of the following factors are present:

(a)   the subject of the report has been charged in an accusatory instrument with committing a crime related to a report maintained in the statewide central register; or

(b)   the investigation of the abuse or maltreatment of the child by the local child protective service or the provision of services by such service has been publicly disclosed in a report required to be disclosed in the course of their official duties, by a law enforcement agency or official, a district attorney, any other state or local investigative agency or official or by judge of the unified court system; or

(c)   there has been a prior knowing, voluntary, public disclosure by an individual concerning a report of child abuse or maltreatment in which such individual is named as the subject of the report as defined by subdivision four of section four hundred twelve of this title; or

(d)   the child named in the report has died or the report involves the near fatality of a child. For the purposes of this section, "near fatality" means an act that results in the child being placed, as certified by a physician, in serious or critical condition.

2.   For the purposes of this section, the following information may be disclosed:

(a)   the name of the abused or maltreated child;

(b)   the determination by the local child protective service or the state agency which investigated the report and the findings of the applicable investigating agency upon which such determination was based;

(c)   identification of child protective or other services provided or actions, if any, taken regarding the child named in the report and his or her family as a result of any such report or reports;

(d)   whether any report of abuse or maltreatment regarding such child has been "indicated" as maintained by the statewide central register;

(e)   any actions taken by the local child protective service and the local social services district in response to reports of abuse or maltreatment of the child to the statewide central register including but not limited to actions taken after each and every report of abuse or maltreatment of such child and the dates of such reports;

(f)   whether the child or the child's family has received care or services from the local social services district prior to each and every report of abuse or maltreatment of such child;

(g) any extraordinary or pertinent information concerning the circumstances of the abuse or maltreatment of the child and the investigation thereof, where the commissioner or the local commissioner determines such disclosure is consistent with the public interest.

3. Information may be disclosed pursuant to this section as follows:

(a) information released prior to the completion of the investigation of a report shall be limited to a statement that a report is "under investigation";

(b) when there has been a prior disclosure pursuant to paragraph (a) of this subdivision, information released in a case in which the report has been unfounded shall be limited to the statement that "the investigation has been completed, and the report has been unfounded";

(c) if the report has been "indicated" then information may be released pursuant to subdivision two of this section.

4. Any disclosure of information pursuant to this section shall be consistent with the provisions of subdivision two of this section. Such disclosure shall not identify or provide an identifying description of the source of the report, and shall not identify the name of the abused or maltreated child's siblings, the parent or other person legally responsible for the child or any other members of the child's household, other than the subject of the report.

5. In determining pursuant to subdivision one of this section whether disclosure will be contrary to the best interests of the child, the child's siblings or other children in the household, the commissioner or a city or county social services commissioner shall consider the interest in privacy of the child and the child's family and the effects which disclosure may have on efforts to reunite and provide services to the family.

6. Whenever a disclosure of information is made pursuant to this section, the city or county social services commissioner shall make a written statement prior to disclosing such information to the chief county executive officer where the incident occurred setting forth the paragraph in subdivision one of this section upon which he or she is basing such disclosure.

7. Except as it applies directly to the cause of the abuse or maltreatment of the child, nothing in this section shall be deemed to authorize the release or disclosure of the substance or content of any psychological, psychiatric, therapeutic, clinical or medical reports, evaluations or like materials or information pertaining to such child or the child's family. Prior to the release or disclosure of any psychological, psychiatric or therapeutic reports, evaluations or like materials or information pursuant to this subdivision, the city or county social services commissioner shall consult with the local mental hygiene director.

Added by Laws 1996, Ch. 12, § 12, eff. Feb. 15, 1996; **amended** by Laws 1999, Ch. 136, § 7, eff. June 30, 1999.

§ 422-b. Local and regional fatality review teams.

[Until Dec 14, 2006, §422-b reads as set out below:]

A fatality review team may be established at a local or regional level, with the approval of the office of children and family services, for the purpose of investigating the death of any child whose care and custody or custody and guardianship has been transferred to an authorized agency, or in the case of a report made to the central register involving the death of a child. A local or regional fatality review team may exercise the same authority as the office of children and family services with regard to the preparation of a fatality report as set forth in paragraphs (b) and (c) of subdivision five of section twenty of this chapter. Notwithstanding any other provision of law to the contrary and to the extent consistent with federal law, such local or regional fatality review team shall have access to those client-identifiable records necessary for the preparation of the report, as authorized in accordance with paragraph (d) of subdivision five of section twenty of this chapter. A fatality report prepared by a local or regional fatality review team and approved by the office of children and family services satisfies the obligation to prepare a fatality report as set forth in subdivision five of section twenty of this chapter. Such report shall be subject to the same redisclosure provisions applicable to fatality reports prepared by the office of children and family services. For the purposes of this section, a local or regional fatality review team must include representatives from the child protective service, office of children and family services, office of the district attorney or local law enforcement, office of the medical examiner or coroner, and a physician or comparable medical professional. A local or regional fatality review team may also include representatives from public health agencies, mental health agencies, schools and medical facilities, including hospitals or other appropriate agencies or institutions.

1. [Eff. Dec 14, 2006, §422-b reads as set out below:]

A fatality review team may be established at a local or regional level, with the approval of the office of children and family services, for the purpose of investigating the death of any child whose care and custody or custody and guardianship has been transferred to an authorized agency, any child for whom child protective services has an open case, any child for whom the local department of social services has an open preventive services case, and in the case of a report made to the central register involving the death of a child. A fatality review team may also investigate any unexplained or unexpected death of any child under the age of eighteen.

2. A local or regional fatality review team may exercise the same authority as the office of children and family services with regard to the preparation of a fatality report as set forth in paragraphs (b) and (c) of subdivision five of section twenty of this chapter. Notwithstanding any other provision of law to the contrary and to the extent consistent with federal law, such local or regional fatality review team shall have access to those client-identifiable records necessary for the

SSL

preparation of the report, as authorized in accordance with paragraph (d) of subdivision five of section twenty of this chapter. A fatality report prepared by a local or regional fatality review team and approved by the office of children and family services satisfies the obligation to prepare a fatality report as set forth in subdivision five of section twenty of this chapter. Such report shall be subject to the same redisclosure provisions applicable to fatality reports prepared by the office of children and family services.

3.   For the purposes of this section, a local or regional fatality review team must include, but need not be limited to, representatives from the child protective service, office of children and family services, county department of health, or, should the locality not have a county department of health, the local health commissioner or his or her designee or the local public health director or his or her designee, office of the medical examiner, or, should the locality not have a medical examiner, office of the coroner, office of the district attorney, office of the county attorney, local and state law enforcement, emergency medical services and a pediatrician or comparable medical professional, preferably with expertise in the area of child abuse and maltreatment or forensic pediatrics. A local or regional fatality review team may also include representatives from local departments of social services, mental health agencies, domestic violence agencies, substance abuse programs, hospitals, local schools, and family court.

4.   A local or regional fatality review team established pursuant to this section shall have access to all records, except those protected by statutory privilege, within twenty-one days of receipt of a request.

5.   Members of a local or regional fatality review team, persons attending a meeting of a local or regional fatality review team, and persons who present information to a local or regional fatality review team shall have immunity from civil and criminal liability for all reasonable and good faith actions taken pursuant to this section, and shall not be questioned in any civil or criminal proceeding regarding any opinions formed as a result of a meeting of a local or regional fatality review team. Nothing in this section shall be construed to prevent a person from testifying as to information obtained independently of a local or regional fatality review team or which is public information.

6.   All meetings conducted and all reports and records made and maintained, and books and papers obtained, by a local or regional fatality review team shall be confidential and not open to the general public except by court order and except for an annual report or a fatality report, if the fatality review team chooses to complete such an annual report or fatality report. The release of any fatality report prepared by a local or regional fatality review team shall be governed by the provisions of subdivision five of section twenty of this chapter. Any such annual report or fatality report shall not contain any individually identifiable information and shall be provided to the office of children and family services upon completion. The office of children and family services shall forward copies of any such report to all other local or regional fatality review teams established pursuant to this section, to all citizen review panels established pursuant to section

three hundred seventy-one-b of this chapter, and to the governor, the temporary president of the senate and the speaker of the assembly.

Added by Laws 1999, Ch. 136, § 8, eff. June 30, 1999; Laws 2006, Ch. 485, §1, eff. Dec. 14, 2006.

§ 423. Child protective service responsibilities and organization; purchase of service and reimbursement of cost; local plan.

1. (a) Every local department of social services shall establish a "child protective service" within such department. The child protective service shall perform those functions assigned by this title to it and only such others that would further the purposes of this title. Local social services departments shall distribute the laws, regulations and policies of the department pursuant to section four hundred twenty-one of this article to any society for the prevention of cruelty to children which has entered into a currently valid contract with a local department of social services.

(b) Every local department of social services shall provide to the child protective service information available to the local department which is relevant to the investigation of a report of child abuse or maltreatment or to the provision of protective services, where the confidentiality of such information is not expressly protected by law.

(c) The child protective service shall have a sufficient staff of sufficient qualifications to fulfill the purposes of this title and be organized in such a way as to maximize the continuity of responsibility, care and service of individual workers toward individual children and families. A social services district shall have flexibility in assigning staff to the child protective service provided that each staff assigned to such service has the staff qualifications and has received the training required by the department regulations promulgated pursuant to subdivisions four and five of section four hundred twenty-one of this title.

(d) Consistent with appropriate collective bargaining agreements and applicable provisions of the civil service law, every child protective service shall establish a procedure to review and evaluate the backgrounds of and information supplied by all applicants for employment. Such procedures shall include but not be limited to the following requirements: that the applicant set forth his or her employment history, provide personal and employment references and relevant experiential and educational information, and sign a sworn statement indicating whether the applicant, to the best of his or her knowledge, has ever been convicted of a crime in this state or any other jurisdiction.

(e) Except as set forth in paragraph (f) of this subdivision, the child protective service shall be the sole public agency responsible for receiving and investigating or arranging with the appropriate society for the prevention of cruelty to children to investigate all reports of child abuse or maltreatment made pursuant to this title for the purpose of providing protective services to prevent further abuses or maltreatment to children and to coordinate, provide or arrange

SSL

for and monitor the provision of those services necessary to safeguard and ensure the child's well-being and development and to preserve and stabilize family life wherever appropriate.

(f) For purposes of this title, a child protective service shall include an Indian tribe that has entered into an agreement with the department pursuant to section thirty-nine of this chapter to provide child protective services to Indians residing upon the tribe's reservation in the state. Notwithstanding any other provision of law, for the purposes of this title, a social services district or a local department of social services shall include an Indian tribe that has entered into an agreement with the department pursuant to section thirty-nine of this chapter to provide child protective services. Such Indian tribe shall only be considered a child protective service while such an agreement is in effect.

2. Any other provision of law notwithstanding, but consistent with subdivision (1) of this section, the child protective service, based upon the local plan of services as provided in subdivision (3) of this section, may purchase and utilize the services of any appropriate public or voluntary agency including a society for the prevention of cruelty to children. When services are purchased by the local department pursuant to this section and title, they shall be reimbursed by the state to the locality in the same manner and to the same extent as if the services were provided directly by the local department.

3. (a) Each social services district shall prepare and submit to the commissioner, after consultation with local law enforcement agencies, the family court and appropriate public or voluntary agencies including societies for the prevention of cruelty to children and after a public hearing, a district-wide plan, as prescribed by the commissioner, for the provision of child protective services which shall be a component of the district's multi-year consolidated services plan. This plan shall describe the district's implementation of this title including the organization, staffing, mode of operations and financing of the child protective service as well as the provisions made for purchase of service and inter-agency relations. Commencing the year following preparation of a multi-year consolidated services plan, each local district shall prepare annual implementation reports including information related to its child protective services plan. The social services district shall submit the child protective services plan to the department as a component of its multi-year consolidated services plan and subsequent thereto as a component of its annual implementation reports and the department shall review and approve or disapprove the proposed plan and reports in accordance with the procedures set forth in section thirty-four-a of this chapter.

(b) [Repealed.]

4. As used in this section, "service" or "services" shall include the coordinating and monitoring of the activities of appropriate public or voluntary agencies utilized in the local plan.

5. In accordance with the provisions of subdivisions one and two of this section, a local department of social services may submit to the department a plan

for a special program for the purpose of (a) ensuring the delivery of services to children and their families by arranging for the purchase and utilization of the service of any appropriate public or voluntary agency to provide rehabilitative services to at least the majority of children and families assisted by the child protective service; and (b) strengthening the monitoring role of the child protective service.

Such program shall also include provisions for the training of employees of public and private agencies assigned functions of the child protective service, in the duties and responsibilities of the child protective service and in the provision of services to children and families, pursuant to this title. The department shall approve such a plan in not more than six social services districts upon satisfactory demonstration that a local department of social services will effectively discharge all responsibilities required by this title. Any such plan must be submitted to the department as part of the multi-year services plan required pursuant to section thirty-four-a of this chapter and, if approved, shall be operative for a period not to exceed three years. The department shall contract with an individual, partnership, corporation, institution or other organization for the performance of a comprehensive evaluation of the effectiveness of the implementation of such plans. A report of such evaluations shall be submitted by the department to the governor and the legislature by January first, nineteen hundred ninety. Nothing in this subdivision shall be deemed to relieve a child protective service from any responsibilities assigned to it by this title.

6. A social services district may establish a multidisciplinary investigative team or teams, at a local or regional level, for the purpose of investigating reports of suspected child abuse or maltreatment. The social services district shall have discretion with regard to the category or categories of suspected child abuse or maltreatment such team or teams may investigate, provided, however, the social services district shall place particular emphasis on cases involving the serious abuse of children. For the purposes of this section, a multidisciplinary investigative team may include, but is not limited to, representatives from the child protective service, office of the district attorney or local law enforcement, the medical profession, public health agencies, mental health agencies, schools and medical facilities, including hospitals or other appropriate agencies or institutions and personnel of any existing child advocacy centers. Notwithstanding any other provision of law to the contrary, members of a multidisciplinary investigative team may share with other team members client-identifiable information concerning the child or the child's family to facilitate the investigation of suspected child abuse or maltreatment. Nothing herein shall preclude the creation of multidisciplinary teams which include more than one social services district. Each team shall develop a written protocol for investigation of child abuse and maltreatment cases and for interviewing child abuse and maltreatment victims. The social services district is encouraged to train each team member in risk assessment, indicators of child abuse and maltreatment, and appropriate interview techniques.

SSL

Amended by Laws 1974, Ch. 1031, eff. June 15, 1974; Laws 1977, Ch. 423, eff. July 12, 1977; amended by Laws 1981, Ch. 681, eff. July 21, 1981 added new subd. 3(b); Laws 1983, Ch. 539; Laws 1987, Ch. 231, eff. July 7, 1987 eliminating the expiration date amended by Laws 1985, Ch. 677, eff. Jan. 1, 1986; amended by Laws 1986, Ch. 718, eff. Nov. 27, 1986; amended by Laws 1987, Ch. 231, eff. July 7, 1987; amended by Laws 1988, Ch. 707, § 4, eff. Sept. 2, 1988; amended by Laws 1995, Ch. 83, §§ 243 -244, eff. July 1, 1995; amended by Laws 1996, Ch. 309, §§ 282, 283, eff. July 13, 1996; para. (6) added by Laws 1999, Ch. 136, § 9, eff. June 30, 1999.

§ 424.   Duties of the child protective service concerning reports of abuse or maltreatment.

Each child protective service shall:

1.   receive on a twenty-four hour, seven day a week basis all reports of suspected child abuse or maltreatment in accordance with this title, the local plan for the provision of child protective services and the regulations of the commissioner;

2.   maintain and keep up-to-date a local child abuse and maltreatment register of all cases reported under this title together with any additional information obtained and a record of the final disposition of the report, including services offered and accepted;

3.   upon the receipt of each written report made pursuant to this title, transmit, forthwith, a copy thereof to the state central register of child abuse and maltreatment. In addition, not later than seven days after receipt of the initial report, the child protective service shall send a preliminary written report of the initial investigation, including evaluation and actions taken or contemplated, to the state central register. Follow-up reports shall be made at regular intervals thereafter in a manner and form prescribed by the commissioner by regulation to the end that the state central register is kept fully informed and up-to-date concerning the handling of reports;

4.   give telephone notice and forward immediately a copy of reports made pursuant to this title which involve the death of a child to the appropriate district attorney. In addition, telephone notice shall be given and a copy of any or all reports made pursuant to this title shall be forwarded immediately by the child protective service to the appropriate district attorney if a prior request in writing for such notice and copies has been made to the service by the district attorney. Such request shall specify the kinds of allegations concerning which the district attorney requires such notice and copies and shall provide a copy of the relevant provisions of law;

5.   forward an additional copy of each report to the appropriate duly incorporated society for the prevention of cruelty to children or other duly authorized child protective agency if a prior request for such copies has been made to the service in writing by the society or agency;

5-a.   [Eff. Dec. 14, 2006] give telephone notice and forward immediately a copy of reports made pursuant to this title which involve suspected physical injury as described in paragraph (i) of subdivision (e) of section ten hundred twelve of the family court act or sexual abuse of a child or the death of a child to the appropriate local law enforcement. Investigations shall be conducted by an approved multidisciplinary investigative team, established pursuant to subdivision six of section four hundred twenty-three of this title provided that in counties without a multidisciplinary investigative team investigations shall be conducted jointly by local child protective services and local law enforcement. Provided however, that co-reporting in these instances shall not be required when the local social services district has an approved protocol on joint investigations of child abuse and maltreatment between the local district and law enforcement. Such protocol shall be submitted to the office of children and family services for approval and the office shall approve or disapprove of such protocols within thirty days of submission. Nothing in this subdivision shall prohibit local child protective services from consulting with local law enforcement on any child abuse or maltreatment report.

5-b. [Eff. Dec. 14, 2006] shall make an assessment in a timely manner of each report made pursuant to this title which involves suspected maltreatment which alleges any physical harm when the report is made by a person required to report pursuant to section four hundred thirteen of this title within six months of any other two reports that were indicated or may still be pending involving the same child, sibling, or other children in the household or the subject of the report to determine whether it is necessary to give notice of the report to the appropriate local law enforcement entity. If the local child protective services determines that local law enforcement shall be given notice, they shall give telephone notice and immediately forward a copy of the reports to local law enforcement. If the report is shared with local law enforcement, investigations shall be conducted by an approved multidisciplinary investigative team, established pursuant to subdivision six of section four hundred twenty-three of this title provided that in counties without a multidisciplinary investigative team investigations shall be conducted jointly by local child protective services and local law enforcement. Provided however, that co-reporting in these instances shall not be required when the local social services district has an approved protocol on joint investigations of child abuse and maltreatment between the local district and law enforcement. Such protocol shall be submitted to the office of children and family services for approval and the office shall approve or disapprove of such protocols within thirty days of submission. Nothing in this subdivision shall modify the requirements of this section. Nothing in this subdivision shall prohibit local child protective services from consulting with local law enforcement on any child abuse or maltreatment report and nothing in this subdivision shall prohibit local child protective services and local law enforcement or a multidisciplinary team from agreeing to co-investigate any child abuse or maltreatment report.

6. upon receipt of such report, commence or cause the appropriate society for the prevention of cruelty to children to commence, within twenty-four hours,

an appropriate investigation which shall include an evaluation of the environment of the child named in the report and any other children in the same home and a determination of the risk to such children if they continue to remain in the existing home environment, as well as a determination of the nature, extent and cause of any condition enumerated in such report and the name, age and condition of other children in the home, and, after seeing to the safety of the child or children, forthwith notify the subjects of the report and other persons named in the report in writing of the existence of the report and their respective rights pursuant to this title in regard to amendment;

7.   determine, within sixty days, whether the report is "indicated" or "unfounded";

7-a.   [*Expired.*]

8.   refer suspected cases of falsely reporting child abuse and maltreatment in violation of subdivision three of section 240.55 of the penal law to the appropriate law enforcement agency or district attorney;

9.   take a child into protective custody to protect him from further abuse or maltreatment when appropriate and in accordance with the provisions of the family court act;

10.   based on the investigation and evaluation conducted pursuant to this title, offer to the family of any child believed to be suffering from abuse or maltreatment such services for its acceptance or refusal, as appear appropriate for either the child or the family or both; provided, however, that prior to offering such services to a family, explain that it has no legal authority to compel such family to receive said services, but may inform the family of the obligations and authority of the child protective service to petition the family court for a determination that a child is in need of care and protection;

11.   in those cases in which an appropriate offer of service is refused and the child protective service determines or if the service for any other appropriate reason determines that the best interests of the child require family court or criminal court action, initiate the appropriate family court proceeding or make a referral to the appropriate district attorney, or both;

12.   assist the family court or criminal court during all stages of the court proceeding in accordance with the purposes of this title and the family court act;

13.   coordinate, provide or arrange for and monitor, as authorized by the social services law, the family court act and by this title, rehabilitative services for children and their families on a voluntary basis or under a final or intermediate order of the family court;

14.   comply with provisions of sections ten hundred thirty-nine-a and ten hundred fifty-two-a of the family court act.

The provisions of this section shall not apply to a child protective service with respect to reports involving children in facilities or programs subject to the provisions of subdivision eleven of section four hundred twenty-two of this title or reports involving children in homes operated or supervised by the division for youth, the office of mental health, or the office of mental retardation and developmental disabilities subject to the provisions of section four hundred twenty-four-b of this title.

Amended by Laws 1974, Ch. 1031, eff. June 15, 1974; Laws 1975, Ch. 220, eff. Aug. 16, 1975; **amended** by Laws 1984, Ch. 822, eff. Dec. 3, 1984; **amended** by Laws 1985, Ch. 676, eff. Apr. 1, 1986; Laws 1990, Ch. 55, § 1; Laws 1991, Ch. 250, eff. July 1, 1991, extended the expiration date until Mar. 31, 1992; **amended** by Laws 1985, Ch. 677, eff. Jan. 1, 1986; **amended** by Laws 1986, Ch. 719, eff. Oct. 1, 1986; Laws 1990, Ch. 55, § 2; Laws 1991, Ch. 250; Laws 1992, Ch. 32, eff. Oct. 1, 1992, which eliminated the expiration date of the 1986 amendment; **amended** by Laws 1988, Ch. 634, § 9, eff. Sept. 1, 1988; Laws 1990, Ch. 55, § 3; Laws 1991, Ch. 250; Laws 1992, Ch. 32, eff. Oct. 1, 1992, which eliminated the expiration date of the 1988 amendment; **amended** by Laws 1989, Ch. 477, eff. Nov. 1, 1989; **amended** by Laws 1990, Ch. 317, § 4, eff. Sept. 1, 1990; **amended** by Laws 1991, Ch. 164, § 1, eff. Jan. 1, 1992; **amended** by Laws 1991, Ch. 164, § 2, eff. Jan. 1, 1992 through July 1, 1992; **amended** by Laws 1996, Ch. 12, § 13, eff. Feb. 15, 1996, and applicable to reports of suspected child abuse or maltreatment registered on or after the effective date. With respect to this section, the provisions of the social services law in effect prior to the effective date shall apply to reports of suspected child abuse or maltreatment registered prior to such effective date; Laws 2006, Ch. 494, §2, eff. Dec 14, 2006.

§ 424-a. Access to information contained in the statewide central register of child abuse and maltreatment.

1.   (a) A licensing agency shall inquire of the department and the department shall, subject to the provisions of paragraph (e) of this subdivision, inform such agency and the subject of the inquiry whether an applicant for a certificate, license or permit, assistants to group family day care providers, the director of a camp subject to the provisions of article thirteen-a, thirteen-b or thirteen-c of the public health law, and any person over the age of eighteen who resides in the home of a person who has applied to become an adoptive parent or a foster parent or to operate a family day care home or group family day care home has been or is currently the subject of an indicated child abuse and maltreatment report on file with the statewide central register of child abuse and maltreatment.

(b)   (i) A provider agency shall inquire of the department and the department shall, subject to the provisions of paragraph (e) of this subdivision, inform such agency and the subject of the inquiry whether any person who is actively being considered for employment and who will have the potential for regular and substantial contact with children who are cared for by the agency, is the subject of an indicated child abuse and maltreatment report on file with the statewide central register of child abuse and maltreatment prior to permitting such person to have unsupervised contact with children. Such agency may inquire of the department and the department shall inform such agency and the subject of the inquiry whether any person who is currently employed and who has the potential for regular and substantial contact with children who are cared for by such agency is the subject of an indicated child abuse and maltreatment report on file with the statewide central register of child abuse and maltreatment. A provider agency shall also inquire of the department and the department shall inform such agency and the subject of the inquiry whether any person who is employed by an individual, corporation, partnership or association which provides goods or services to such agency who has the potential for regular and substantial contact with children who are cared for by the agency, is the subject of an indicated child abuse and maltreatment report on file with the statewide central register of child abuse and maltreatment prior to permitting such person to have unsupervised contact with children. Inquiries made to the department pursuant to this subparagraph by a provider agency on current employees shall be made no more often than once in any six-month period.

(ii)   A provider agency may inquire of the department and the department shall, upon receipt of such inquiry and subject to the provisions of paragraph (e) of this subdivision, inform such agency and the subject of the inquiry whether any person who is to be hired as a consultant by such agency who has the potential for regular and substantial contact with children who are cared for by the agency is the subject of an indicated child abuse and maltreatment report on file with the statewide central register of child abuse and maltreatment.

(iii)   A provider agency may inquire of the department and the department shall, upon receipt of such inquiry and subject to the provisions of paragraph (e) of this subdivision, inform such agency and the subject of the inquiry whether any person who has volunteered his or her services to such agency and who will have the potential for regular and substantial contact with children who are cared for by the agency, is the subject of an indicated child abuse and maltreatment report on file with the statewide central register of child abuse and maltreatment.

(iv)   the department shall promulgate regulations which effectuate the provisions of this paragraph.

(c)   An authorized agency shall inquire of the department and the department shall inform such agency and the subject of the inquiry, whether any person who has applied to adopt a child is the subject of an indicated child abuse and maltreatment report on file with the statewide central register of child abuse and maltreatment.

(d)   Any person who has applied to a licensing agency for a certificate, license or permit or who has applied to be an employee of a provider agency or who has applied to an authorized agency to adopt a child, or who may be hired as a consultant or used as a volunteer by a provider agency and any other person about whom an inquiry is made to the department pursuant to the provisions of this section shall be notified by such agency at the time of application or prior to the time that a person may be hired as a consultant or used as a volunteer that the agency will or may inquire of the department whether such person is the subject of an indicated child abuse and maltreatment report. All employees of a provider agency shall be notified by their employers that an inquiry may be made to the department pursuant to this section and no such inquiry shall be made regarding any employee until such notice has been made.

(d-1)   A law enforcement agency pursuant to section eight hundred thirty-seven-k of the executive law may inquire of the department and the department may inform such agency and the subject of the inquiry, whether any person who has applied for a symbol provided for in section eight hundred thirty-seven-k of the executive law or persons residing or regularly visiting said location are the subject of an indicated child abuse and maltreatment report on file with the statewide central register of child abuse and maltreatment.

(e)   (i) Subject to the provisions of subparagraph (ii) of this paragraph, the department shall inform the provider or licensing agency, or child care resource and referral programs pursuant to subdivision six of this section whether or not the person is the subject of an indicated child abuse and maltreatment report only if: (a) the time for the subject of the report to request an amendment of the record of the report pursuant to subdivision eight of section four hundred twenty-two has expired without any such request having been made; or (b) such request was made within such time and a fair hearing regarding the request has been finally determined by the commissioner and the record of the report has not been amended to unfound the report or delete the person as a subject of the report.

(ii)   If the subject of an indicated report of child abuse or maltreatment has not requested an amendment of the record of the report within the time specified in subdivision eight of section four hundred twenty-two of this title or if the subject had a fair hearing pursuant to such section prior to January first, nineteen hundred eighty-six and an inquiry is made to the department pursuant to this subdivision concerning the subject of the report, the department shall, as expeditiously as possible but within no more than ten working days of receipt of the inquiry, determine whether, in fact, the person about whom an inquiry is made is the subject of an indicated report. Upon making a determination that the person about whom the inquiry is made is the subject of an indicated report of child abuse and maltreatment, the department shall immediately send a written request to the child protective service or state agency which was responsible for investigating the allegations of abuse or maltreatment for all records, reports and other information maintained by the service or state agency on the subject. The service or state agency shall, as expeditiously as possible but within no more than twenty working days of receiving such request, forward all records, reports and other information it maintains on the indicated report to the department. The department shall, within fifteen working days of receiving such records, reports and other information from the child protective service or state agency, review all records, reports and other information in its possession concerning the subject and determine whether there is some credible evidence to find that the subject had committed the act or acts of child abuse or maltreatment giving rise to the indicated report.

(iii)   If it is determined, after affording such service or state agency a reasonable opportunity to present its views, that there is no credible evidence in the record to find that the subject committed such act or acts, the department shall amend the record to indicate that the report was unfounded and notify the inquiring party that the person about whom the inquiry is made is not the subject of an indicated report. If the subject of the report had a fair hearing pursuant to subdivision eight of section four hundred twenty-two of this title prior to January first, nineteen hundred eighty-six and the fair hearing had been finally determined by the commissioner and the record of the report had not been amended to unfound the report or delete the person as a subject of the report, then the department shall determine that there is some credible evidence to find that the subject had committed the act or acts of child abuse or maltreatment giving rise to the indicated report.

(iv)   If it is determined after a review by the department of all records, reports and information in its possession concerning the subject of the report that there is some credible evidence to find that the subject committed the act or acts of abuse or maltreatment giving rise to the indicated report, the department shall also determine whether such act or acts are relevant and reasonably related to issues concerning the employment of the subject by a provider agency or the subject being allowed to have regular and substantial contact with children cared for by a provider agency or the approval or disapproval of an application which has been submitted by the subject to a licensing agency, based on guidelines developed pursuant to subdivision five of section four hundred twenty-four-a of this chapter. If it is determined that such act or acts are not relevant and related to such issues, the department shall be precluded from informing the provider or licensing agency which made the inquiry to the department pursuant to this section that the person about whom the inquiry is made is the subject of an indicated report of child abuse or maltreatment.

(v)   If it is determined after a review by the department of all records, reports and information in its possession concerning the subject of the report that there is some credible evidence to prove that the subject committed the act or acts of abuse or maltreatment giving rise to the indicated report and that such act or acts are relevant and reasonably related to issues concerning the employment of the subject by a provider agency or to the subject being allowed to have regular and substantial contact with children cared for by a provider agency or the approval or disapproval of an application which has been submitted by the subject to a licensing agency, the department shall inform the inquiring party that the person about whom the inquiry is made is the subject of an indicated report of child abuse and maltreatment; the department shall also notify the subject of the inquiry of his or her fair hearing rights granted pursuant to paragraph (c) of subdivision two of this section.

(f)   The department shall charge a fee of five dollars when, pursuant to regulations of the department, it conducts a search of its records within the statewide central register for child abuse or maltreatment in accordance with this section or regulations of the department to determine whether an applicant for employment as specified in paragraph (b) of this subdivision is the subject of an indicated child abuse or maltreatment report, except that fees shall not be charged for requests for screenings related to applications for child day care providers or for employment with child day care providers including requests made pursuant to subdivision six of this section. Such fees shall be deposited in an account and shall be made available to the department for costs incurred in the implementation of this section. Procedures for payment of such fees shall be established by the regulations of the department.

2.   (a) Upon notification by the department or by a child care resource and referral program in accordance with subdivision six of this section that any person who has applied to a licensing agency for a license, certificate or permit or who seeks to become an employee of a provider agency, or to accept a child for adoptive placement or who will be hired as a consultant or used as a volunteer by a provider agency, or that any other person about whom an inquiry is made to the department pursuant to the provisions of this section is the subject of an indicated report the licensing or provider agency shall determine on the basis of information it has available whether to approve such application or retain the employee or hire the consultant or use the volunteer or permit an employee of another person, corporation, partnership or association to have access to the children cared for by the provider agency, provided, however, that if such application is approved, or such employee is retained or consultant hired or volunteer used or person permitted to have access to the children cared for by such agency the licensing or provider agency shall maintain a written record, as part of the application file or employment record, of the specific reasons why such person was determined to be appropriate to receive a foster care or adoption placement or to provide day care services, to be the director of a camp subject to the provisions of article thirteen-A, thirteen-B or thirteen-C of the public health law, to be employed, to be retained as an employee, to be hired as a consultant, used as a volunteer or to have access to the children cared for by the agency.

(b)   (i) Upon denial of such application by a licensing or a provider agency or failure to hire the consultant or use the volunteer, or denial of access by a person to the children cared for by the agency, such agency shall furnish the applicant, prospective consultant, volunteer or person who is denied access to the children cared for by the agency with a written statement setting forth whether its denial, failure to hire or failure to use was based, in whole or in part, on such indicated report, and if so, its reasons for the denial or failure to hire or failure to use.

(ii)   Upon the termination of employment of an employee of a provider agency, who is the subject of an indicated report of child abuse or maltreatment on file with the statewide central register of child abuse and maltreatment, the agency shall furnish the employee with a written statement setting forth whether such termination was based, in whole or in part, on such indicated report and, if so, the reasons for the termination of employment.

(c)   If the reasons for such denial or termination or failure to hire a consultant or use a volunteer include the fact that the person is the subject of an indicated child abuse or maltreatment report, such person may request from the department within ninety days of receipt of notice of such denial, termination, failure to hire a consultant or use a volunteer and shall be granted a hearing in accordance with the procedures set forth in section twenty-two of this chapter relating to fair hearings. All hearings held pursuant to the provisions of this subdivision shall be held within thirty days of a request for the hearing unless the hearing is adjourned for good cause shown. Any subsequent adjournment for good cause shown shall be granted only upon consent of the person who requested the hearing. The hearing decision shall be rendered not later than sixty days after the conclusion of the hearing.

(d)   At any such hearing, the sole question before the department shall be whether the applicant, employee, prospective consultant, volunteer, or person who was denied access to the children cared for by a provider agency has been shown by a fair preponderance of the evidence to have committed the act or acts of child abuse or maltreatment giving rise to the indicated report. In such hearing, the burden of proof on the issue of whether an act of child abuse or maltreatment was committed shall be upon the local child protective service or the state agency which investigated the report, as the case may be. The failure to sustain the burden of proof at a hearing held pursuant to this section shall not result in the expungement or unfounding of an indicated report but shall be noted on the report maintained by the state central register and shall preclude the department from notifying a party which subsequently makes an inquiry to the department pursuant to this section that the person about whom the inquiry is made is the subject of an indicated report.

(e)   Upon the failure, at the fair hearing held pursuant to this section, to prove by a fair preponderance of the evidence that the applicant committed the act or acts of child abuse or maltreatment giving rise to the indicated report, the department shall notify the provider or licensing agency which made the inquiry pursuant to this section that it should reconsider any decision to discharge an employee, or to deny the subject's application for employment, or to become an adoptive parent, or for a certificate, license or permit; or not to hire a consultant, use a volunteer, or allow access to children cared for by the agency.

3.   For purposes of this chapter, the term "provider" or "provider agency" shall mean an authorized agency, the division for youth, juvenile detention facilities subject to the certification of such division, programs established pursuant to article nineteen-h of the executive law, non-residential or residential programs or facilities licensed or operated by the office of mental health or the office of mental retardation and developmental disabilities except family care homes, licensed child day care centers, including head start programs which are funded pursuant to title V of the federal economic opportunity act of nineteen hundred sixty-four, as amended, early intervention service established pursuant to section twenty-five hundred forty of the public health law, preschool services established pursuant to section Forty-four hundred ten of the education law, school-age child care programs, special act school districts as enumerated in

chapter five hundred sixty-six of the laws of nineteen hundred sixty-seven, as amended, programs and facilities licensed by the office of alcoholism and substance abuse services and residential schools which are operated, supervised or approved by the education department.

4. For purposes of this chapter, the term "licensing agency" shall mean an authorized agency which has received an application to become an adoptive parent or an authorized agency which has received an application for a certificate or license to receive, board or keep any child pursuant to the provisions of section three hundred seventy-six or three hundred seventy-seven of this article or an authorized agency which has received an application from a relative within the second degree or third degree of the parent of a child or a relative within the second degree or third degree of the stepparent of a child or children, or the child's legal guardian for approval to receive, board or keep such child or a state or local governmental agency which receives an application to provide child day care services in a child day care center, school-age child care program, family day care home or group family day care home pursuant to the provisions of section three hundred ninety of this article, or the department of health of the city of New York, when such department receives an application for a certificate of approval to provide family day care pursuant to the provisions of the health code of the city of New York, or the office of mental health or the office of mental retardation and developmental disabilities when such office receives an application for an operating certificate pursuant to the provisions of the mental hygiene law to operate a family care home which will serve children, or a state or local governmental official who receives an application for a permit to operate a camp which is subject to the provisions of article thirteen-A, thirteen-B or thirteen-C of the public health law or the division for youth which has received an application for a certificate to receive, board or keep any child at a foster family home pursuant to articles nineteen-G and nineteen-H of the executive law.

5. (a) The department, after consultation with the division for youth, the department of mental hygiene, the commission on quality of care for the mentally disabled and the state education department shall develop guidelines to be utilized by a provider agency, as defined by subdivision three of this section, and a licensing agency, as defined by subdivision four of this section, in evaluating persons about whom inquiries are made to the department pursuant to this section who are the subjects of indicated reports of child abuse and maltreatment, as defined by subdivision four of section four hundred twelve of this chapter.

(b) The guidelines developed pursuant to subdivision one of this section shall not supersede similar guidelines developed by local governmental agencies prior to January first, nineteen hundred eighty-six.

6. A child care resource and referral program as defined in subdivision two of section four hundred ten-p of this article may inquire of the department and the department shall, upon receipt of such inquiry and subject to the provisions of paragraph (e) of subdivision one of this section, inform such program and the subject of such inquiry whether any person who has requested and agreed to be

included in a list of substitute child day care caregivers for employment by registered or licensed day care providers maintained by such program in accordance with regulations promulgated by the department, is the subject of an indicated child abuse and maltreatment report on file with the statewide central register of child abuse and maltreatment. Inquiries made to the department by such programs pursuant to this subdivision shall be made no more often than once in any six month period and no less often than once in any twelve month period. Notwithstanding any provision of law to the contrary, a child care resource and referral program may redisclose such information only if the purpose of such redisclosure is to respond to a request for such information by a registered or licensed provider and only if after an individual included in the list of substitute child day care caregivers for employment by registered or licensed day care providers has consented to be referred for employment to such inquiring agency. Upon such referral, the provisions related to notice and fair hearing rights of this section shall otherwise apply. Inquiries made pursuant to this subdivision shall be in lieu of the inquiry requirements set forth in paragraph (b) of subdivision one of this section.

Added by Laws 1980, Ch. 480, eff. Oct. 1, 1980; amended by Laws 1983, Ch. 307, eff. June 21, 1983; amended by Laws 1984, Ch. 651, eff. Oct. 1, 1984; amended by Laws 1985, Ch. 677, eff. Jan. 1, 1985; amended by Laws 1986, Ch. 719, eff. Oct. 1, 1986; Laws 1990, Ch. 55, § 2; Laws 1991, Ch. 250, eff. July 1, 1991, extended the expiration date until Mar. 31, 1992; amended by Laws 1986, Ch. 875, eff. Jan. 1, 1987; amended by Laws 1987, Ch. 460, eff. July 27, 1987; amended by Laws 1987, Ch. 629, eff. Aug. 3, 1987; amended by Laws 1987, Ch. 268, eff. July 20, 1987; amended by Laws 1988, Ch. 634, §§ 10, 11, 12, 13, 14, 15, eff. Sept. 1, 1988; amended by Laws 1990, Ch. 750, § 6, 7, eff. Nov. 19, 1990; amended by Laws 1990, Ch. 190, § 257, eff. May 24, 1990; amended by Laws 1991, Ch. 260, § 1, eff. July 1, 1991; amended by Laws 1992, Ch. 55, § 392, eff. Apr. 1, 1992; amended by Laws 1992, Ch. 465, § 58, eff. Jan. 13, 1993; amended by Laws 1993, Ch. 203, § 2, adding new para. (d-1) to SSL § 424-a(1), eff. July 6, 1993; amended by Laws 1993, Ch. 441, §§ 4, 5, 6, eff. Apr. 1, 1994, amended by § 7, adding new subd. (6) to SSL § 424-a; amended by Laws 1996, Ch. 12, §§ 14, 15, eff. Feb. 15, 1996, and applicable to reports of suspected child abuse or maltreatment registered on or after the effective date of this act. With respect to this section, the provisions of the social services law in effect prior to the effective date shall apply to reports of suspected child abuse or maltreatment registered prior to such effective date; amended by Laws 1997, Ch.578, § 1, eff. Sept. 17, 1997, and Ch. 587, eff. Jan. 15, 1998.

§ 424-b.   Children in the care of certain public and private agencies.

Notwithstanding any inconsistent provisions of law, when a report of child abuse or maltreatment involves a child being cared for in a home operated or supervised by an authorized agency, the division for youth, or an office of the department of mental hygiene, such report shall be accepted and maintained by the department and shall be referred for the purposes of conducting an investigation to the division for youth or the appropriate office of the department of mental hygiene, where the child is in the care of such division or office; and where the child is in a home operated or supervised by an authorized agency, to the social services district wherein such home is located. The division, office, or social services district receiving such referral shall undertake an appropriate investigation of the report, in accordance with the terms and conditions set forth in subdivisions one through eight of section four hundred twenty-four-c of this title. Any person who is alleged to have abused or maltreated a child in a report accepted and referred pursuant to this section shall be accorded the procedural rights set forth in section four hundred twenty-two and in subdivision six of section four hundred twenty-four of this chapter. Nothing in this section shall impose any duty or responsibility on any child protective service pursuant to section four hundred twenty-two, four hundred twenty-four or any other provision of this article.

Added by Laws 1980, Ch. 480, eff. Oct. 1, 1980; **amended** by Laws 1985, Ch. 676, eff. Apr. 1, 1986; Laws 1990, Ch. 55, § 2; Laws 1991, Ch. 250, eff. July 1, 1991, extended the expiration date until Mar. 31, 1992; **amended** by Laws 1988, Ch. 634, § 16, eff. Sept. 1, 1988.

§ 424-c.   Duties of the commissioner concerning reports of abuse or maltreatment of children in residential facilities or programs.

With respect to reports of abuse or maltreatment in residential facilities or programs enumerated in paragraphs (a), (b), (c), (d), (e), (f) and (h) of subdivision seven of section four hundred twelve of this title, in addition to complying with other requirements established by this chapter, the commissioner shall:

1.   Receive from the state central register on a twenty-four hour, seven day a week basis all reports of suspected child abuse or maltreatment in accordance with this title and regulations of the commissioner;

2.   Maintain and keep up-to-date a child abuse and maltreatment record of all cases reported together with any additional information obtained and a record of the final disposition of the report, including recommendations by the commissioner and action taken with respect to the residential care facility or program or the subject of a report of child abuse or maltreatment pursuant to subdivision two-a of section four hundred sixty-c of this chapter;

3.   Not later than seven days after receipt of such report, send a preliminary written report of the initial investigation, including, whenever practicable, an evaluation of whether or not such report constitutes an allegation of child abuse or neglect and actions taken or contemplated, to the state central register. If such investigation results in a determination that the report does not constitute an allegation of abuse or neglect, the department shall refer such report to the appropriate state licensing or operating agency, provided, however, that the name and other personally identifiable information of the person making the report shall not be provided by the department unless such person authorizes such disclosure;

4. Give telephone notice and forward immediately a copy of reports made which involve the death of a child to the appropriate district attorney. In addition, telephone notice shall be given and a copy of all reports made shall be forwarded immediately by the commissioner to the appropriate district attorney if a prior request in writing for such notice and copies has been made to the commissioner by the district attorney. Such request shall specify the kinds of allegations concerning which the district attorney requires such notice and copies;

5. Upon receipt of such report, commence within twenty-four hours, an appropriate investigation which shall include but not be limited to an evaluation of the residential care facility or program in which the child resides who is named in the report and a determination of the risk to such child if he or she continues to remain in the existing residential care facility or program as well as a determination of the nature, extent and cause of any condition enumerated in such report and, after seeing to the safety of the child and, to the maximum extent feasible, the other children in the facility, forthwith: (a) notify the subject of the report and other persons named in the report in writing of the existence of the report and their respective rights pursuant to this title in regard to amendment; and (b) notify the facility or program and, as appropriate, the division for youth, department of education, and the local social services commissioner or school district placing the child of the existence of such report including the name of any child alleged to be abused or maltreated, the name of the subject of the report of child abuse or maltreatment, and any other information which may be necessary to ensure the health and safety of the children in the residential facility;

6. Comply with the terms and conditions for the maintenance of confidential records and due process rights of the subject of the report of child abuse or maltreatment pursuant to sections four hundred twenty-two and four hundred twenty-four-a of this title;

7. Determine, within sixty days, whether the report is "indicated" or "unfounded"; and

8. Assist the criminal court during all stages of the court proceeding in accordance with the purposes of this title and other applicable provisions of law.

Added by Laws 1986, Ch. 719, eff. Oct. 1, 1986; amended by Laws 1988, Ch. 634, § 17, eff. Sept. 1, 1988; amended by Laws 1992, Ch. 32, §§ 12, 13, eff. Oct. 1, 1992; amended by Laws 1996, Ch. 12, § 16, eff. Feb. 15, 1996, and applicable to reports of suspected child abuse or maltreatment registered on or after the effective date of this act. With respect to this section, the provisions of the social services law in effect prior to the effective date shall apply to reports of suspected child abuse or maltreatment registered prior to such effective date.

§ 425. Cooperation of other agencies.

1. To effectuate the purposes of this title, the commissioner may request and shall receive from departments, boards, bureaus, or other agencies of the state, or any of its political subdivisions, or any duly authorized agency, or any other

agency providing services under the local child protective services plan such assistance and data as will enable the department and local child protective services to fulfill their responsibilities properly. In relation to an investigation of a report of abuse or maltreatment involving a child in residential care, such data may include, but need not be limited to, the case records of the child who allegedly was abused or maltreated and any other child who allegedly witnessed the abuse or maltreatment and, consistent with appropriate collective bargaining agreements and applicable provisions of the civil service law, those portions of the employment record of the subject of the report considered by the subject's employer to be relevant and reasonably related to the allegations being investigated by the department. Nothing contained in this subdivision shall limit the department's authority under sections three hundred seventy-two, four hundred sixty-c and four hundred sixty-e of this chapter to access the records of authorized agencies.

2. The department, after consultation with the division for youth, the division of criminal justice services, the department of mental hygiene, the commission on quality of care for the mentally disabled and the state education department shall develop guidelines to be utilized by appropriate state and local governmental agencies and authorized agencies as defined by subdivision ten of section three hundred seventy-one of this chapter which have responsibility for the care and protection of children, in evaluating persons who have a criminal conviction record and who have applied to such agencies or provider agencies, as defined in subdivision three of section four hundred twenty-four-a of this chapter for employment or who have applied to such state agencies or licensing agency as defined in subdivision four of section four hundred twenty-four-a of this chapter, for a license, certificate, permit or approval to be an adoptive parent, provider of day care services in a day care center, family day care home or group family day care home, an operator of a camp subject to the provisions of article thirteen-A, thirteen-B or thirteen-C of the public law, or an operator of a foster family home subject to the provisions of subdivision seven of section five hundred one, section five hundred two or subdivision three of section five hundred thirty-two-a, of the executive law or section three hundred seventy-six and three hundred seventy-seven of the social services law.

3. The guidelines developed pursuant to subdivision two of this section shall not supersede any similar guidelines developed by local governmental agencies prior to January first, nineteen hundred eighty-six.

Amended by Laws 1985, Ch. 677, eff. Jan. 1, 1986; **amended** by Laws 1988, Ch. 634, § 18, eff. Sept. 1, 1988.

§ 426. Annual reports.

The commissioner shall prepare for inclusion in the annual report required by subdivision (d) of section seventeen of this chapter to be filed with the governor and the legislature prior to December fifteenth of each year, a report on the operations of the state central register of child abuse and maltreatment and the various local child protective services. The report shall include a full statistical analysis of the reports made to the central register together with a report on the implementation of this title, his evaluation of services offered under this chapter and his recommendations for additional legislation to fulfill the purposes of this title. Such report shall indicate the number of child abuse and maltreatment reports and cases received by the statewide central register of child abuse and maltreatment by each district in the preceding year, the number of such cases determined to have been indicated and the number of such cases determined to be unfounded by each district in the preceding year, the number of such cases which have not been indicated or unfounded within the time period required by subdivision seven of section four hundred twenty-four of this chapter by each district in the preceding year and the number of workers assigned to the child protective service in each district in the preceding year. The report shall also contain data on the protection of children in residential care from abuse and maltreatment, including reports received, results of investigations by types of facilities and programs, types of corrective action taken, as well as efforts undertaken by the department, the division for youth and the state education department to provide training pursuant to standards established by section four hundred sixty-two of this chapter, section five hundred one of the executive law and sections forty-four hundred three, forty three hundred fourteen, forty-three hundred fifty-eight and forty-two hundred twelve of the education law.

Amended by Laws 1982, Ch. 384, eff. Apr. 1, 1982; **amended** by Laws 1985, Ch. 676, eff. Apr. 1, 1986; Laws 1990, Ch. 55, § 1; Laws 1991, Ch. 250; Laws 1992, Ch. 32, eff. Oct. 1, 1992, which eliminated the expiration date of the 1985 amendment.

§ 427.   Regulations of the commissioner.

1.   The commissioner shall adopt regulations necessary to implement this title.

2.   The commissioner shall establish, by regulation, standards and criteria under which the child protective service of the appropriate local department of social services as petitioner in abuse and neglect proceeding pursuant to article ten of the family court act shall not consent to an order pursuant to section one thousand thirty-nine of the family court act.

Amended by Laws 1985, Ch. 601, eff. Nov. 25, 1985, except that any rules and regulations necessary for the timely implementation of this act on its effective date shall be promulgated on or before such date and shall apply to all proceedings theretofore or thereafter commenced.

§ 428.   Separability.

If any provision of this title or the application thereof to any person or circumstances is held to be invalid, the remainder of the act and the application of such provision to other persons or circumstances shall not be affected thereby.

TITLE 6-A—HOME VISITING

———

Section 429.   Home visiting.

§ 429.   Home visiting.

1. In accordance with a plan developed by the office of children and family services and approved by the director of the budget and within the amounts which the director of the budget determines should be made available therefor, such office, in conjunction with the department of health, is authorized to issue grants for home visiting programs to prevent child abuse and maltreatment, enhance positive parent child interactions, increase healthy outcomes for families and empower families to develop and achieve their self-sufficiency goals. To the extent that federal funds are used to support home visiting programs, such programs must be operated in accordance with all applicable federal laws and regulations. To the extent possible and appropriate, funding for the home visiting program shall be coordinated with other available funding to maximize the effective use of federal, state and local moneys and to promote the program's purposes.

2. Each home visiting program funded under this section shall include, but not be limited to, the following activities:

(a) providing screening of families in the targeted geographical area upon the birth of a child and prenatally, if possible;

(b) engaging those expectant parents and families with an infant determined to be at risk of child abuse or maltreatment and/or poor health outcomes to participate in the home visiting program;

(c) providing home visits by nurses or by community workers under the supervision of a health or social services professional to those at risk expectant parents and families who choose to participate in the program;

(d) requiring the home visitors to:

(i) assist parents in learning about child development principles;

(ii) assist parents in accessing appropriate preventive health care for their children and themselves; and

(iii) link the families to other supports and activities in the community;

(e) determining the frequency of the home visiting services provided to each participating family based on the family's needs;

(f) continuing home visits for a particular family until the child enters school or a head start program, when necessary; and

(g) assisting families to develop and obtain the necessary supports to achieve their self-sufficiency goals.

SSL

3. A request for proposals shall be issued to solicit applications for home visiting programs. Priority for funding shall be given to applicants from communities identified as high need by such factors as poverty rates, rates of adolescent pregnancy, rates of child abuse and maltreatment, immunization rates and infant mortality rates.

4. Not-for-profit organizations and local public agencies such as community-based organizations, family resource centers, local health departments, local social services departments, schools, hospitals and other health agencies shall be eligible to apply for the grants available pursuant to this section.

5. Each applicant shall demonstrate among other things:

(a) a working relationship with the applicable local departments of health and social services and key services providers in the community;

(b) the commitment of local hospitals, prenatal clinics and early intervention programs servicing families in the targeted geographical area to promote the effective screening of families so that the program can be offered to the maximum number of at-risk expectant parents and families possible;

(c) its administrative and fiscal viability and the community's support for the home visiting program; and

(d) how the home visiting program would be integrated with other available services, programs and funding streams.

6. The commissioner of the office of children and family services shall establish policies governing enrollees' rights and confidentiality, and each home visiting program shall, in accordance with such policies, inform enrollees of their rights, and of such policies governing confidentiality.

7. The office of children and family services shall submit to the governor and the legislature by December first, two thousand, and every three years thereafter, a report which shall include a review of all the home visiting programs funded under this section; and comments and recommendations based on a comprehensive evaluation regarding the most effective models for providing home visiting services and statutory changes which could improve the state's ability to prevent child abuse and maltreatment, improve healthy outcomes for families and empower families to develop and obtain their self-sufficiency goals.

Added by Laws 1994, Ch. 170, § 474, eff. June 9, 1994, until Sept. 30, 2000; **amended** by Laws 2000, Ch. 141, § 2, eff. July 11, 2000, repealing repealer, and § 1, eff. July 11, 2000.

TITLE 7—DAY SERVICES FOR CHILDREN AND FAMILIES

———

§ 430. Day services; when social services official may furnish.

1. In order to preserve and stabilize family life, to prevent the need for placement of children outside their homes, and to enable children in foster care to return to their families as expeditiously as possible, a social services official is authorized to provide day services at public expense to children and their families residing in his territory, pursuant to the provisions of this title.

2. Day services may be provided in cases where the social services official has determined that such services would promote or accomplish one or more of the following objectives:

(a) to avert a risk of serious impairment or disruption of a family unit which would result in the placement of a child outside his own home;

(b) to enable a child who has been placed in a child care institution or other group care facility to be placed in a foster care setting more closely oriented to community or family life;

(c) to enable a child who has been placed in foster care to return to his family at an earlier time than would otherwise be possible.

3. If the child's family is able to pay part or all of the costs of day services, such family shall be required to pay such fees therefor as may be reasonable in the light of such ability pursuant to regulations of the department.

4. Day services may be provided by a social services official either directly or through purchase. Purchase of such services may be made only from a private non-profit corporation or association, except when the commissioner shall have approved the purchase of such services from a private proprietary facility by a social services official who has demonstrated a lack of conveniently accessible non-profit facilities that are adequate to provide the required services.

5. As used in this title, "day services" shall mean care and treatment for part of the day of one or more children under eighteen years of age and their families in a program which provides to such children and families in accordance with their needs various services such as psychiatric, psychological, social casework, educational, vocational, health, transportation and such other services as may be appropriate. Such services shall be provided in accordance with program standards promulgated by the department. Day services may be continued after the eighteenth birthday of a child in the care of an authorized agency and until he becomes twenty-one years of age. Day services shall not be provided to any children and their families for periods in excess of one year, without the approval of the department.

Added by Laws 1976, Ch. 906, eff. Apr. 1, 1977; Laws 1979, Ch. 40; Laws 1979, Ch. 270, eff. June 19, 1979, which eliminated the expiration date.

SSL

§ 431. Licensure.

1. No place, person, association, corporation, institution or agency shall operate a day services program without first obtaining a permit issued therefor by the department, or otherwise than in accordance with the terms of such permit and with the regulations of the department.

2. The department shall promulgate regulations specifying the procedures for obtaining a permit required pursuant to this section and enumerating the documentation needed for such a permit. The regulations shall also include program standards which the department shall develop with the advice of the board of social welfare, the department of mental hygiene and the department of education. An application for a permit pursuant to this section shall include full information regarding the applicant's efforts to secure funding for its day services program. The department shall advise and otherwise assist the applicant in obtaining funds where such funds may be available under the provisions of this and any other law.

3. The department shall not issue a permit for the operation of a day services program which includes the provision of care, treatment or services requiring licensure or any other form of approval from or by another state agency or official, unless such license or approval has been obtained. There shall be such cooperative and coordinated arrangements between and among the department and the state departments of mental hygiene and education and other appropriate state departments and agencies as shall be necessary to assure that applications for required licenses or other forms of approval will be processed expeditiously.

4. Before any permit issued pursuant to this section is suspended or revoked, or when an application for such permit is denied, the applicant or holder of the permit shall be entitled, pursuant to the regulations of the department, to a hearing before the department. However, a permit may be temporarily suspended or limited without a hearing for a period not in excess of thirty days upon written notice to the holder of the permit following a finding that the public health, or any individual's health, safety or welfare, is in imminent danger.

Added by Laws 1976, Ch. 906, eff. Apr. 1, 1977; Laws 1979, Ch. 40, eff. Apr. 1, 1979; Laws 1979, Ch. 270, eff. June 19, 1979, which eliminated the expiration date.

§ 432. State reimbursement; standards of payment.

1. (a) Expenditures made by social services officials for day services programs and their administration pursuant to the provisions of this title shall, if approved by the department, be subject to reimbursement by the state, in accordance with the regulations of the department as follows: there shall be paid to each social services district (1) the amount of federal funds, if any, properly received or to be received on account of such expenditures; (2) fifty per centum of allowable expenditures for day services and its administration, after first deducting therefrom any federal funds properly received or to be received on account thereof and the amount of any fees paid to the social services official for

day services. The local government share of the cost of day services may be met in whole or in part by donated private funds, exclusive of in-kind services.

(b)   For purposes of this title, expenditures for administration of day services shall include expenditures for compensation of employees in connection with the furnishing of day services, including but not limited to costs incurred for pensions, federal old age and survivors insurance and health insurance for such employees; training programs for personnel, operation, maintenance and service costs; and such other expenditures as equipment costs, depreciation and charges and rental values as may be approved by the department. It shall not include expenditures for capital costs.

2.   The department shall, after consultation with appropriate state agencies and with the approval of the director of the budget, promulgate regulations establishing standards of payment for day services provided children with public financial support. Such standards of payment shall include the services required to be provided to the child and his family and the cost of such services. When the department has established such standards, reimbursement under this section shall be limited in accordance with such standards.

3.   (a) Claims for state reimbursement shall be made in such form and manner and at such times and for such periods as the department shall determine.

(b)   When certified by the department, state reimbursement shall be paid from the state treasury upon the audit and warrant of the comptroller out of funds made available therefor.

4.   Payment of state reimbursement shall be made to local fiscal officers as in the case of state reimbursement for public assistance and care under other provisions of this chapter.

    Added by Laws 1976, Ch. 906, eff. Apr. 1, 1977; Laws 1979, Ch. 40, eff. Apr. 1, 1979; Laws 1979, Ch. 270, eff. June 19, 1979, which eliminated the expiration date.

§ 433.   Other state funding sources.

1.   Prior to purchasing day services pursuant to section four hundred thirty, a social services official shall inquire of the department, and the department shall inform him, as to the available funding sources, if any, of which the day services facility was advised pursuant to subdivision two of section four hundred thirty-one. The social services official shall not purchase services from the day services facility until he has determined that the facility has cooperated with the department in efforts to obtain funding from all available sources.

2.   No state agency or official with authority, pursuant to this or any other law, to provide financial assistance for care, treatment or services which may be included in a day services program shall deny or reduce such assistance on the ground that such assistance is available under this title.

    Added by Laws 1976, Ch. 906, eff. Apr. 1, 1977; Laws 1979, Ch. 40, eff. Apr. 1, 1979; which eliminated the expiration date; Laws 1979, Ch. 270, eff. June 19, 1979.

§ 434. Funding limitations.

Notwithstanding any other provisions of this chapter the total amount of reimbursement to social services districts pursuant to this title shall be limited to the amount of the annual appropriation made by the legislature for preventive services.

Added by Laws 1976, Ch. 906, eff. Apr. 1, 1977; Laws 1979, Ch. 40, eff. Apr. 1, 1979; Laws 1979, Ch. 270, eff. June 19, 1979, which eliminated the expiration date.

TITLE 8—STATE CHILD CARE REVIEW SERVICE

§ 440. Findings; purpose.

1. The legislature finds that children who are in care away from their own homes on a full time basis, whether temporarily or for a prolonged period, require effective supervision and review of their status in care and of the plans for them. It is the policy of the state of New York to assure that such children are appropriately placed, that needed services are provided to them and their families, and that unnecessary and prolonged placements are avoided. The legislature further finds that this policy is often frustrated, and fiscal and program accountability have not been promoted because of divergent and overlapping jurisdictions of various government and private agencies; the lack of coordination among programs of these agencies; and the excessive workloads of judicial personnel, social services workers, and others responsible for reviewing the status in care of these children.

2. To assist in overcoming these difficulties, it is the intent of the legislature to establish a statewide management assistance system to be called the child care review service. The service shall be designed and operated to effectuate the following purposes:

(a) identification and assessment of the needs and problems of children in care and their families, to effectuate meaningful case planning;

(b) case management and supervision by child care agencies of children in full-time care away from their homes;

(c) supervision and evaluation by state agencies of local and voluntary child care agency performance;

(d) planning and policy making by state agencies, the governor and the legislature;

(e) meeting in a timely manner all judicial review requirements of this chapter, the family court act and any other applicable provisions of law;

(f) reduction of the need for manual form preparation; and

(g) meeting federal reporting requirements so as to qualify for federal funds under the federal social security act.

Added by Laws 1976, Ch. 668, eff. July 24, 1976.

§ 441. Definitions.

As used in this title, the following terms shall have the following meanings:

1. "Service" shall mean the child care review service created by this title.

2. "Advisory committee" shall mean the committee established by section four hundred forty-three of this title.

Added by Laws 1976, Ch. 668, eff. July 24, 1976.

§ 442 Child care review service; establishment, operations and procedure

1. The department, in consultation with the advisory committee, shall establish and operate a child care review service to accomplish the purposes of this title, for all children who are in the care of an authorized agency and shall make such regulations as are appropriate to implement this title.

2. [Until Dec 21, 2005] The service shall be implemented with respect to all children under the age of twenty-one years for whom an authorized agency is providing foster care as defined in section three hundred ninety-two of this chapter and for whom an application is pending to an authorized agency for foster care.

2. [Eff. Dec 21, 2005] The service shall be implemented with respect to all children under the age of twenty-one years for whom an authorized agency is providing foster care as defined in subdivision (c) of section one thousand eighty-seven of the family court act and for whom an application is pending to an authorized agency for foster care.

3. The department is authorized to enter into agreements with any person, firm, organization or association for the whole or any part of the design or operation of the service as described in this title. Any such agreements shall specify that such person, firm, corporation or association shall safeguard the confidentiality of information received or maintained by the service, in the same manner, and will remain subject to the same confidentiality requirements, as the

department. In addition, any such agreement shall require such person, firm, corporation or association to comply with other applicable federal and state laws protecting the confidentiality of the information received or maintained by the service.

4. The service shall collect, maintain, update, and distribute, as provided in this title, information from each authorized agency to further the purpose of this title.

5. The service may request from any authorized agency, and such agency shall submit to the service all information, including updating of information, in the form and manner and at such times as the department may require that is appropriate to the purposes and operation of the service.

6. Information to be submitted to or collected by the service, pursuant to subdivisions four and five, shall, to the extent possible, be in compatible form so as to facilitate the making of public policy decisions relating to child care programs supported by public funds and administered by various state, local and voluntary agencies.

7. In designing the service, the department, in consultation with the advisory committee, shall review all information reporting forms and financial claims forms, and shall make every effort to consolidate and, where appropriate, eliminate duplicative claiming and information reporting forms in order to develop uniform statewide claiming forms and information reporting forms.

8. Subject to regulations of the department the service shall:

(a) prepare and make available on a regular basis to each authorized agency such data as they may require to meet the purposes of this title;

(b) issue regular reports setting forth aggregate statewide and local statistical data with appropriate analyses, but not including individual identifying information; and

(c) issue reports as to the capabilities of the service and the types of information maintained by the service.

9. The department in consultation with the advisory committee shall prepare and submit an annual report to the governor and the legislature as part of the annual report required to be filed prior to the fifteenth day of December of each year by subdivision (d) of section seventeen of this chapter on its progress in the development and operation of the service, including any significant problems encountered or anticipated in the design and operation of the service and any recommendations for administrative or legislative changes that would further the purposes of this title.

10. The state child care review service established pursuant to this title shall design and implement a system to:

(a) monitor all financial claims made by social services districts for each child in foster care and child and family in receipt of preventive services pursuant to title four of this chapter article;

(b)   compile and maintain a cumulative record of information with respect to actions taken on behalf of each individual child throughout his or her length of stay in foster care;

(c)   [Until Dec 21, 2005] compile and maintain information on actions taken by social services districts to initiate judicial proceedings as provided by sections three hundred fifty-eight-a and three hundred ninety-two of this chapter and to comply with judicial orders made pursuant to section three hundred ninety-two of this chapter or to section ten hundred fifty-five of the family court act, to refer legally free children to the state adoption service pursuant to section three hundred seventy-two-c 372-f of this chapter, and to comply with the provisions of section four hundred nine-e of this chapter and the regulations of the department promulgated thereunder; and

(c)   [Eff. Dec 21, 2005] compile and maintain information on actions taken by local social services districts to initiate judicial proceedings as provided by section three hundred fifty-eight-a of this chapter and to comply with judicial orders made pursuant to section one thousand eighty-nine of the family court act, to refer legally free children to the state adoption service pursuant to section three hundred seventy-two-c 372-f of this chapter, and to comply with the provisions of section four hundred nine-e of thisarticle and the regulations of the office of children and family services promulgated thereunder; and

(d)   [Repealed]

(e)   compile and maintain comparative data for authorized agencies including, but not limited to, characteristics and numbers of children entering care and their families, admissions practices, delineated reasons for initial and continued placement or provision of preventive or child protective services, length of stay in care, length of time in receipt of preventive services or child protective services, foster care reentry rates, number of children discharged to parents and relatives, the characteristics, numbers and rates of children leaving foster care through adoption, costs of care and preventive services and other information indicative of authorized agency performance.

Added by Laws 1976, Ch. 668, eff. July 24, 1976; **amended** by Laws 1979, Ch. 610, eff. Oct. 11, 1979; **amended** by Laws 1982, Ch. 350, eff. June 21, 1982; **amended** by Laws 1982, Ch. 384, eff. Apr. 1, 1983; **amended** by Laws 1985, Ch. 263, eff. Sept. 23, 1985; **amended** by Laws 1995, Ch. 83, §§ 245 -247, eff. July 1, 1995; L. 2005, Ch. 3, sect; 61 (Part A), eff. Aug. 23, 2005.

§ 443.   Advisory committee.

1.   The department shall establish and meet regularly with an advisory committee of not more than twenty members to consider policy and planning issues relating to the service and to assist in the design, development, establishment and on-going operation of the service, including assisting in the resolution of issues concerning the safeguarding of the confidentiality of information. The

advisory committee may in its discretion submit reports to the governor and the legislature.

2.   The advisory committee shall be appointed by the commissioner, who shall appoint one of the committee's members to be its chairman. The members of the committee shall be appointed from the following categories, one or more from each category:

(a)   designees of the commissioner;

(b)   designees of the administrative judge of the state of New York;

(c)   designees of the director of the division of the budget;

(d)   commissioners of local social services districts or their designees;

(e)   representatives of voluntary child care agencies;

(f)   persons active in organizations involved in the protection of civil liberties;

(g)   persons active in organizations involved in promoting the interests of children.

Added by Laws 1976, Ch. 668, eff. July 24, 1976; **amended** by Laws 1982, Ch. 350, eff. June. 21, 1982.

§ 444.   Confidentiality of records; related matters.

1.   The department in consultation with the advisory committee shall make regulations;

(a)   protecting the confidentiality of individual identifying information submitted to or provided by the service, and preventing access thereto, by, or the distribution thereof to, persons not authorized by law;

(b)   setting forth procedures for informing any child or his representative of the nature of the system and its uses;

(c)   allowing any child or his representative or any member of his family, an opportunity to review any information pertaining to such child or family and to request that any part of such information be amended or expunged; and

(d)   providing that the service shall remove from its records and expunge the individual identifying information, excluding non-identifying child or family data to be used for historical purposes, concerning any child who has been discharged from care.

2.   Prior to final promulgation of any regulations as described in subdivision one of this section, the department shall, in addition to complying with all other advance notice requirements make proposed regulations available to all state agencies charged with the administration or supervision of child care programs and to local government agencies and persons that have expressed an interest in safeguarding information maintained by the service, and shall provide such agencies with an opportunity to comment on the proposed regulations. In

promulgating final regulations the department shall consider any comments received.

3. Any persons wilfully violating or failing to comply with the provisions of subdivision one of this section or wilfully violating or failing to comply with any regulation which the department is authorized under such subdivision to make, shall be guilty of a misdemeanor.

4. The regulations promulgated pursuant to subdivision one of this section, shall provide that the information compiled and maintained by the service pursuant to paragraph (d) of subdivision ten of section four hundred forty-two of this title shall be subject to the confidentiality provisions of title six of this article.

Added by Laws 1976, Ch. 668, eff. July 24, 1976; amended by Laws 1985, Ch. 263, eff. Sept. 23, 1985.

§ 445. Funding.

The department shall explore the possibility of, and is authorized to take steps necessary to qualify for any available funding from any private source or from the federal government, and is authorized to use any funds for which the state qualifies for the purposes of the design, establishment or operation of the service.

Added by Laws 1976, Ch. 668, eff. July 24, 1976.

§ 446. Statewide automated child welfare information system.

1. The department shall promulgate regulations required to implement federal requirements for the establishment and administration of a statewide automated child welfare information system as required by applicable federal statute and regulation. The regulations shall set forth standards for the timely submission of data elements relating to child welfare services, including foster care, adoption assistance, preventive services, child protective services and other family preservation and family support services.

2. The statewide automated child welfare information system shall be designed to improve convenience to consumers of services and reduce the administrative burden of child welfare workers of social services districts and their contracted agencies which provide direct services. The statewide automated child welfare information system shall be designed to provide computers to the majority of individual child welfare workers of social services districts and their contracted agencies which provide direct child welfare services, allow such workers and agencies to communicate with and enter information directly into the statewide automated child welfare information system while preparing required documents and eliminate duplicate entry of information and preparation of documents, and allow for direct determination of claims and sanctions. The department shall immediately expand the existing advisory group of consumers, social services districts and their contracted agencies and other persons with

SSL

expertise in child welfare. The statewide automated child welfare information system shall be designed to permit communication with the family courts and to protect the confidentiality of individuals as prescribed by this chapter.

Added by Laws 1995, Ch. 83, § 248, eff. July 1, 1995.

TITLE 9—SUBSIDIES FOR THE ADOPTION OF CHILDREN

————

(Repealed and transferred sections noted under appropriate section number of text.)

Added by Laws 1977, Ch. 865, eff. Nov. 9, 1977.

§ 450.　Statement of legislative intent.

The legislature intends, by the enactment of this title, to promote permanency of family status through adoption for children who might not otherwise derive the benefits of that status. By providing for an adoption subsidy program which will be applied uniformly on a statewide basis, the legislature also intends to eliminate, or at the very least substantially reduce, unnecessary and inappropriate long-term foster care situations which have proven financially burdensome to the state and, more importantly, inimical to the best interests of many children who have not been placed for adoption because of emotional or physical handicaps, age or other factor, in accordance with regulations of the department.

§ 451.　Definitions.

As used in this title:

1.　"Child" shall mean a person under the age of twenty-one years whose guardianship and custody have been committed to a social services official or a voluntary authorized agency, or whose guardianship and custody have been committed to a certified or approved foster parent pursuant to a court order prior to such person's eighteenth birthday. A "child" shall also mean a person under the age of twenty-one years whose care and custody have been transferred prior to such person's eighteenth birthday to a social services official or a voluntary authorized agency pursuant to section one thousand fifty-five of the family court act or section three hundred eighty-four-a of this chapter, whose parents are deceased or where one parent is deceased and the other parent is not a person entitled to notice pursuant to section one hundred eleven-a of the domestic relations law, and where such official or agency consents to the adoption of such person in accordance with section one hundred thirteen of the domestic relations law.

2. "Handicapped child" shall mean a child who possess a specific physical, mental or emotional condition or disability of such severity or kind which, in accordance with regulations of the department, would constitute a significant obstacle to the child's adoption.

3. "Hard to place child" shall mean a child, other than a handicapped child, (a) who has not been placed for adoption within six months from the date his guardianship and custody were committed to the social services official or a voluntary authorized agency, or (b) who has not been placed for adoption within six months from the date a previous adoption placement terminated and the child was returned to the care of the social services official or a voluntary authorized agency, or (c) who possesses or presents any personal or familial attribute, condition, problem or characteristic which, in accordance with regulations of the department, would be an obstacle to the child's adoption, notwithstanding the child has been in the guardianship and custody of the social services official or a voluntary authorized agency for less than six months.

4. (a) "Board rate" shall mean an amount equal to the monthly payment which has been or would have been made by a social services official, in accordance with section three hundred ninety-eight-a and other provisions of this chapter, for the care and maintenance of the child, if such child had been boarded out in a foster family boarding home. Such rate shall reflect annual increases in room and board rates and clothing replacement allowances.

(b) When a child is placed for adoption by a social services official or a voluntary authorized agency with adoptive parents residing in another social services district, the "board rate" shall mean the board rate of the social services district placing the child for adoption or the social services district in which the adoptive parents reside.

5. "Persons" shall include a single person eligible to adopt a child as well as a couple eligible therefor.

6. "Voluntary authorized agency" shall mean an authorized agency as defined in paragraphs (a) and (c) of subdivision ten of section three hundred seventy-one of this article.

7. "Social services official" shall mean a county commissioner of social services, a city commissioner of social services, or an Indian tribe with which the department has entered into an agreement to provide adoption services in accordance with subdivision two of section thirty-nine of this chapter.

SSL

Amended by Laws 1986, Ch. 463, eff. Nov. 18, 1986; amended by Laws 1990, Ch. 253, §§ 1, 2 & 3, eff. June 19, 1990; amended by Laws 1993, Ch. 394, § 3, eff. Nov. 18, 1993; amended by Laws 1994, Ch. 601, §§ 6, 7, eff. Oct. 24, 1994.

§ 452.   Maintenance subsidy; hard to place child.

Repealed by Laws 1981, Ch. 989, eff. Jan. 1, 1982.

§ 453.   Maintenance subsidy; handicapped or hard to place child.

1.   (a) A social services official shall make monthly payments for the care and maintenance of a handicapped or hard to place child whom a social services official or voluntary authorized agency has placed out for adoption or who has been adopted, and who is residing in such social services district. Where a handicapped or hard to place child is placed in an adoptive placement outside the state, monthly payments for the care and maintenance of the child shall be made by the social services official placing the child or in whose district the voluntary authorized agency maintains its principal office. Such payments shall be made until the child's twenty-first birthday to persons with whom the child has been placed, or to persons who have adopted the child and who applied for such payments prior to the adoption, pursuant to a written agreement therefor between such official or agency and such persons; provided, however, that an application may be made subsequent to the adoption if the adoptive parents first become aware of the child's physical or emotional condition or disability subsequent to the adoption and a physician certifies that the condition or disability existed prior to the child's adoption. The social services official shall consider the financial status of such persons only for the purpose of determining the amount of the payments to be made, pursuant to subdivision three of this section. Upon the death of persons who have adopted the child prior to the twenty-first birthday of the child, such payments shall continue to the legal guardian of the child until the child shall attain the age of twenty-one.

(b)   Any child with respect to whom federally reimbursable maintenance subsidy payments are made under this subdivision shall be deemed to be a recipient of aid to families with dependent children for purposes of determining eligibility for medical assistance.

(c)   No payments may be made pursuant to this subdivision if the social services official determines that the adoptive parents are no longer legally responsible for the support of the child or the child is no longer receiving any support from such parents. The social services official on a biennial basis shall remind the adoptive parents of their obligation to support the child and to notify the social services official if the adoptive parents are no longer providing any support of the child or are no longer legally responsible for the support of the child.

(d)   Applications for such subsidies shall be accepted prior to the commitment of the guardianship and custody of the child to an authorized agency pursuant to the provisions of this chapter, and approval thereof may be granted contingent upon such commitment.

2. The agreement provided for in subdivision one of this section shall be subject to the approval of the department upon the application of the social services official; provided, however, that in accordance with the regulations of the department, the department may authorize the social services official to approve or disapprove the agreement on behalf of the department. In either situation, if the agreement is not approved or disapproved by the social services official within thirty days of submission, the voluntary authorized agency may submit the agreement directly to the department for approval or disapproval. If the agreement is not disapproved in writing by the department within thirty days after its submission to the department, it shall be deemed approved. Any such disapproval shall be accompanied by a written statement of the reasons therefor.

3. The amount of the monthly payment made pursuant to this section shall be determined pursuant to regulations of the department and based upon the financial need of such persons. The department shall review such regulations annually. The amount of the monthly payment shall not be less than seventy-five per centum of the board rate nor more than one hundred per centum of such rate.

4. Except as may be required by federal law as a condition for federal reimbursement of public assistance expenditure, payments under this section shall not be considered for the purpose of determining eligibility for public assistance or medical assistance for needy persons.

5. [*Repealed.*]

Amended by Laws 1981, Ch. 989, eff. Jan. 1, 1982, provided that nothing shall reduce or impair any adoption subsidies approved prior to effective date; **amended** by Laws 1983, Ch. 97, eff. May 17, 1983 and subds. (1)(b) and (c) applicable to adoption assistance agreements entered into prior to such date; provided however, that nothing herein contained shall be applied or construed so as to reduce or impair any right of any adoptive parent pursuant to an existing agreement; **amended** by Laws 1983, Ch. 439, eff. July 12, 1983; **amended** by Laws 1986, Ch. 451, eff. July 21, 1986; **amended** by Laws 1986, Ch. 463, eff. Nov. 18, 1986; **amended** by Laws 1988, Ch. 315, § 1, eff. July 25, 1988; **amended** by Laws 1990, Ch. 253, § 4, eff. June 19, 1990; **amended** by Laws 1991, Ch. 588, § 4, eff. Sept. 30, 1991; **amended** by Laws 1992, Ch. 559, §§ 3, 4, eff. July 24, 1992; **amended** by Laws 1995, Ch. 83, §§ 249 -250, eff. July 1, 1995.

§ 453-a.   Payments for non-recurring adoption expenses.

1. A social services official shall make payments for non-recurring adoption expenses incurred by or on behalf of the adoptive parents of a child with special needs, when such expenses are incurred in connection with the adoption of a child with special needs through an authorized agency. In accordance with subdivision two of this section, the payments shall be made by the social services official either to the adoptive parents directly, to the authorized agency on behalf of the adoptive parents or to an attorney on behalf of the adoptive parents for the

allowable amount of attorney's fees or court costs incurred in connection with such completed adoption.

2. The amount of the payment made pursuant to this section shall be determined pursuant to the regulations of the department. Nothing herein shall obligate a social services official to make payments for the full amount of non-recurring adoption expenses incurred by or on behalf of the adoptive parents of a child with special needs.

3. Payments for non-recurring adoption expenses made by a social services official pursuant to this section shall be treated as administrative expenditures under title IV-E of the social security act and shall be reimbursed by the state accordingly.

4. Payments under this section shall be made pursuant to a written agreement between the social services official, other relevant authorized agencies and the adoptive parents of a child with special needs. The written agreement shall specify the nature and amount of any payments, services and assistance to be provided, shall stipulate that the agreement remain in effect regardless of the state of residence of the adoptive parents at any time and shall contain provisions for the protection of the interests of the child where the adoptive parents and the child move to another state while the agreement is effective. Applications for such subsidies shall be accepted prior to the commitment of the guardianship and custody of the child to an authorized agency pursuant to the provisions of this chapter, and approval thereof may be granted contingent upon such commitment.

5. When the parental rights of a child with special needs have been terminated in this state and the child's guardianship has been committed to an authorized agency, the child is adopted in another state and the adoptive parents are not eligible for payments of non-recurring adoption expenses in the other state, a social services official shall make payments of the non-recurring adoption expenses incurred by or on behalf of the adoptive parents, if such parents are otherwise eligible for payments under subdivision one of this section.

6. As used in this section, non-recurring adoption expenses shall mean reasonable and necessary adoption fees, court costs, attorney fees and other expenses which are directly related to the legal adoption of a child with special needs and which are not incurred in violation of federal law or the laws of this state or any other state.

7. As used in this section, a child with special needs shall mean a child who:

(a) the state has determined cannot or shall not be returned to the home of his or her parents; and

(b) the state has first determined:

(i) is a handicapped child as defined in subdivision two of section four hundred fifty-one of this title, or is a hard-to-place child as defined in paragraph (c) of subdivision three of section four hundred fifty-one of this title; and

(ii)   a reasonable, but unsuccessful effort has been made to place the child with appropriate adoptive parents without adoption assistance. Such an effort need not be made where such efforts would not be in the best interests of the child because of such factors as the existence of significant emotional ties with prospective adoptive parents while in the care of such parents as a foster child.

Added by Laws 1988, Ch. 315, § 2, eff. July 25, 1988; **amended** by Laws 1991, Ch. 588, § 5, eff. Sept. 30, 1991; **amended** by Laws 1994, Ch. 601, § 8, eff. Oct. 24, 1994.

§ 454.   Medical subsidy.

1.   A social services official shall make payments for the cost of care, services and supplies payable under the state's program of medical assistance for needy persons, provided to a handicapped child whom he or a voluntary authorized agency has placed out for adoption or who has been adopted. Such payments shall not be restricted to care, services and supplies required for the treatment of the specific condition or disability for which a child was determined to be a handicapped child. For the purposes of this section, a handicapped child shall include, but not be limited to, a child with special needs where a social services official has determined the child cannot be placed with an adoptive parent or parents without medical subsidy because such child has special needs for medical, mental health or rehabilitative care. Such payments also shall be made with respect to a hard to place child who has been placed out for adoption with a person or persons who is or are sixty-two years old or over or who will be subject to mandatory retirement from his or their present employment within five years from the date of the adoption placement.

2.   Payments pursuant to subdivision one of this section shall be made to or on behalf of the person or persons with whom the child has been has been placed or who have adopted the child and shall be made without regard to the financial need for such persons or persons.

3.   Payments pursuant to subdivision one of this section shall be made only with respect to the cost of care, services and supplies which are not otherwise covered or subject to payment or reimbursement by insurance, medical assistance or other sources.

4.   An application for payment under this section shall be made prior to the child's adoption; provided, however, that an application may be made subsequent to a handicapped child's adoption if the adoptive parents first become aware of the child's physical or emotional condition or disability subsequent to the adoption and a physician certifies that the condition or disability existed prior to the child's adoption. An approval of an application for payments under this section shall not be subject to annual review by the social services official, and such approval shall remain in effect until the child's twenty-first birthday. Applications for such subsidies shall be accepted prior to the commitment of the guardianship and custody of the child to an authorized agency pursuant to the

provisions of this chapter, and approval thereof may be granted contingent upon such commitment.

5. Upon the death of persons who have adopted the child prior to the twenty-first birthday of the child, payments pursuant to subdivision one of this section shall continue to the legal guardian of the child until the child shall attain the age of twenty-one.

Amended by Laws 1983, Ch. 439, eff. July 12, 1983; **amended** by Laws 1990, Ch. 253, § 5, eff. June 19, 1990; **amended** by Laws 1991, Ch. 588, § 6, eff. Sept. 30, 1991; **amended** by Laws 1999, Ch. 7, § 27, eff. Feb. 11, 1999.

§ 455. Fair hearings.

1. Any person aggrieved by the decision of a social services official or an official of the department not to make a payment or payments pursuant to this title or to make such payment or payments in an inadequate or inappropriate amount or the failure of a social services official or an official of the department to determine an application under this title within thirty days after filing, may appeal to the department which shall review the case, give such person an opportunity for a fair hearing thereon, and render its decision within thirty days. The department may also, on its own motion, review any such decision made by a social services official or any case in which a decision has not been made within the time specified. All decisions of the department shall be binding upon the social services district involved and shall be complied with by the social services official thereof.

2. The only issues which may be raised in a fair hearing under this section are (a) whether the social services official or an official of the department has improperly denied an application for payments under this title, or (b) whether the social services official or an official of the department has improperly discontinued payments under this title, or (c) whether the social services official or an official of the department has determined the amount of the payments made or to be made in violation of the provisions of this title or the regulations of the department promulgated hereunder.

3. When an issue is raised as to whether a social services official or an official of the department has improperly denied an application for payments under this title, the department shall affirm such denial if: (a) the child is not a hard to place child or a handicapped child or (b) there is another approved adoptive parent or parents who is or are willing to accept the placement of the child in his or their home without payment under this title within sixty days of such denial and placement of the child with such other parent or parents would not be contrary to the best interests of the child.

4. The provisions of subdivisions two and four of section twenty-two of this chapter shall apply to fair hearings held and appeals taken pursuant to this section.

Amended by Laws 1978, Ch. 473, eff. July 11, 1978; **amended** by Laws 1990, Ch. 253, § 6, eff. June 19, 1990.

§ 456. State reimbursement.

1. Payments made by social services officials pursuant to the provisions of this title shall, if approved by the department, be subject to reimbursement by the state, in accordance with the regulations of the department as follows: there shall be paid to each social services district (a) the amount of federal funds, if any, properly received or to be received on account of such payments; and (b) except as set forth below, seventy-five per centum of such payments after first deducting therefrom any federal funds properly received or to be received on account thereof; provided, however, that when payments under section four hundred fifty-three of this title are made to a person or persons residing in a social services district whose board rate exceeds that of the district making such payments, that portion of the payments which exceeds the board rate of the district making the payments shall be subject to reimbursement by the state in the amount of one hundred per centum thereof, (c) one hundred per centum of such payments after first deducting therefrom any federal funds properly to be received on account of such payments, for children placed out for adoption by a voluntary authorized agency or for children being adopted after being placed out for adoption by a voluntary authorized agency in accordance with the provisions of this title, or (d) one hundred per centum of such payments after first deducting therefrom any federal funds properly to be received on account of such payments, for children placed out for adoption or being adopted after being placed out for adoption by an Indian tribe as referenced in subdivision seven of section four hundred fifty-one of this title.

2. (a) Claims for state reimbursement shall be made in such form and manner and at such times for such periods as the department shall determine.

(b) When certified by the department, state reimbursement shall be paid from the state treasury upon their audit and warrant of the comptroller out of funds made available therefor.

Amended by Laws 1981, Ch. 989, eff. Jan. 1, 1982; **amended** by Laws 1990, Ch. 253, § 7, eff. June 19, 1990; **amended** by Laws 1994, Ch. 601, § 9, eff. Oct. 24, 1994.

§ 457. Out-of-state adoptive parents.

With respect to a child who has been adopted within this state but who has been removed from this state by his adoptive parents, or a child who has been adopted by residents of another state or of the commonwealth of Puerto Rico and who is, or who is likely to become, a public charge within this state, payments under section four hundred fifty-three or four hundred fifty-four of this title may be made pursuant to an agreement between the district and the adoptive parents, provided that such agreement is in accordance with the regulations of the department promulgated to achieve the objective of increasing the number of adoptions of potential public charges, with particular emphasis upon handicapped and hard to place children. An such agreement shall become void at such time as it is determined by the social services official that a child on whose behalf payments are being received pursuant to such agreement was brought into this state for the sole purpose of qualifying prospective out-of-time adoptive parents for such payments. Such determination may be appealed to the department which upon receipt of the appeal, shall conduct a fair hearing in accordance with the provisions of section four hundred fifty-five of this title.

Amended by Laws 1981, Ch. 989, eff. Jan. 1, 1982.

§ 458.   Availability of subsidy; publicity.

The department shall promulgate regulations providing for the publicizing of the availability of payments under this title. Such regulations shall provide for the dissemination of literature and other means in each social services district of informing persons, at the time of any inquiry, application or other expression of interest in adoption, of the provisions of the adoption subsidy program. Additionally, each social services district and authorized agency shall provide information on the adoption subsidy program to all foster care parents who are caring for a child who is eligible for adoption.

Amended by Laws 1983, Ch. 134, eff. May 23, 1983.

ARTICLE 6–A

DOMESTIC VIOLENCE PREVENTION ACT

____

SUMMARY OF ARTICLE

____

§ 459-a. Definitions.

As used in this article:

1. "Victim of domestic violence" means any person over the age of sixteen, any married person or any parent accompanied by his or her minor child or children in situations in which such person or such person's child is a victim of an act which would constitute a violation of the penal law, including, but not limited to acts constituting disorderly conduct, harassment, menacing, reckless endangerment, kidnapping, assault, attempted assault, or attempted murder; and

(i) such act or acts have resulted in actual physical or emotional injury or have created a substantial risk of physical or emotional harm to such person or such person's child; and

(ii) such act or acts are or are alleged to have been committed by a family or household member.

2. "Family or household members" mean the following individuals:

(a) persons related by consanguinity or affinity;

(b) persons legally married to one another;

(c) persons formerly married to one another regardless of whether they still reside in the same household;

(d) persons who have a child in common regardless of whether such persons are married or have lived together at any time;

(e)   unrelated persons who are continually or at regular intervals living in the same household or who have in the past continually or at regular intervals lived in the same household; or

(f)   any other category of individuals deemed to be a victim of domestic violence as defined by the department in regulation.

3.   "Parent" means a natural or adoptive parent or any individual lawfully charged with a minor child's care or custody.

4.   "Residential program for victims of domestic violence" means any residential care program certified by the department and operated by a not-for-profit organization in accordance with the regulations of the department for the purpose of providing emergency shelter, services and care to victims of domestic violence. Residential programs for victims of domestic violence shall include, but shall not be limited to:

(a)   "Domestic violence shelters," which shall include any residential care facility organized for the exclusive purpose of providing emergency shelter, services and care to victims of domestic violence and their minor children, if any;

(b)   "Domestic violence programs," which shall include any facility which otherwise meets or would meet the requirements of paragraph (a) of this subdivision, except that victims of domestic violence and their minor children, if any, constitute at least seventy percent of the clientele of such program; and

(c)   "Safe home networks," which shall include any organized network of private homes offering emergency shelter and services to victims of domestic violence and their minor children, if any. Such network shall be coordinated by a not-for-profit organization.

5.   "Non-residential program for victims of domestic violence" means any program operated by a not-for-profit organization, for the purpose of providing non-residential services to victims of domestic violence, including, but not limited to, information and referral services, advocacy, counseling, and community education and outreach activities and providing or arranging for hotline services. Victims of domestic violence and their children, if any, shall constitute at least seventy percent of the clientele of such programs.

Added by Laws 1987, Ch. 838, eff. Aug. 7, 1987; amended by Laws 1994, Ch. 169, §§ 99-101, eff. Apr. 1, 1994.

§ 459-b.   Residential services for victims of domestic violence.

In accordance with section one hundred thirty-one-u of this chapter and the regulations of the department, a social services district shall offer and provide necessary and available emergency shelter and services at a residential program for victims of domestic violence to a victim of domestic violence who was residing in the social services district at the time of the alleged domestic violence whether or not such victim is eligible for public assistance.

Added by Laws 1994, Ch. 169, § 102, eff. Apr. 1, 1994, **replacing** section added by Laws 1987, Ch. 838, eff. Aug. 7, 1987.

§ 459-c. Non-residential services for victims of domestic violence.

1. In accordance with the provisions of this section and the regulations of the department, a social services district shall offer and provide non-residential services including but not limited to, information and referral services, advocacy, counseling, community education and outreach activities, and hotline services, to a victim of domestic violence whether or not the victim is eligible for public assistance. A social services district may provide such non-residential services directly or may purchase such services from a not-for-profit organization operating a residential program and/or a non-residential program for victims of domestic violence.

2. To the extent that funds are appropriated expressly therefor and a social services district has exhausted its allocation under title XX of the federal social security act, state reimbursement shall be available for fifty percent of the expenditures made by a social services district for those non-residential services provided to victims of domestic violence which are included in the social services district's multi-year consolidated services plans and annual implementation reports approved by the department pursuant to section thirty-four-a of this chapter.

Added by Laws 1994, Ch. 169, § 103, eff. Apr. 1, 1994, **replacing** section added by Laws 1987, Ch. 838, eff. Aug. 7, 1987.

§ 459-d. Standards of eligibility.

Repealed by Laws 1994, Ch. 169, § 104, eff. April 1, 1994.

§ 459-d. Reporting requirements.

The commissioner shall submit a report prior to December fifteenth, nineteen hundred eighty-eight and annually thereafter to the governor and the legislature regarding the implementation of this article. Such report shall include:

1. the number of persons estimated to have been assisted in programs covered by this article;

2. the number of persons estimated to have been denied shelter and/or services;

3. the amount of public and private funds for approved programs by service type;

4. the amount of funds used for the administration and staffing of such programs;

5. the occupancy rate and length of stay by residential program;

6. the name and description of new programs developed by service type;

7.   the name and description of programs in danger of closing that received funds and the status of such programs;

8.   the name and description of programs that closed during the reporting year and the reason for such closure;

9.   the number of individuals who requested and received transitional services and the effect of providing such services to victims of domestic violence and their families;

10.   the name and description of programs which received technical assistance and the effect of such assistance;

11.   a schedule showing the approved daily rates of reimbursement payable to residential programs for victims of domestic violence pursuant to section one hundred thirty-one-u of this chapter; and

12.   all such other matters as may be necessary to inform the governor and the legislature regarding the implementation and effectiveness of programs covered by this article.

Added by Laws 1987, Ch. 838, eff. Aug. 7, 1987; amended by Laws 1994, Ch. 169, § 105, eff. Apr. 1, 1994.

§ 459-e.   Technical assistance.

To the extent that funds are available, the department shall arrange for or provide technical assistance to residential and non-residential programs for victims of domestic violence. Technical assistance shall include, but shall not be limited to, budgeting techniques, fund raising and program management.

Added by Laws 1987, Ch. 838, eff. Aug. 7, 1987; amended by Laws 1994, Ch. 169, § 106, eff. Apr. 1, 1994.

§ 459-f.   Fees for services.

Any program defined in subdivision four of section four hundred fifty-nine-a of this article may charge a service fee to a victim of domestic violence who is able to pay all or part of the costs of the emergency shelter and services provided to the victim. Payments by a social services district to a residential program for victims of domestic violence for the costs of emergency shelter and services provided to a victim of domestic violence at the daily reimbursement rate determined by the department in accordance with section one hundred thirty-one-u of this chapter shall be reduced by the sum of all fees which such victim is able to pay toward the costs of such shelter and services as determined in accordance with the public assistance budgeting rules set forth in the regulations of the department and by any third party reimbursement available for such costs.

Added by Laws 1987, Ch. 838, eff. Aug. 7, 1987; amended by Laws 1994, Ch. 169, § 107, eff. Apr. 1, 1994.

§ 459-g. Confidentiality.

1. The street address of any residential program for victims of domestic violence applying for funding pursuant to this article shall be confidential and may be disclosed only to persons designated by rules and regulations of the department.

2. All information related to the general location or specific street address of a structure anticipated to house a residential program for victims of domestic violence that is contained in any application submitted to a state or local agency or any instrumentality thereof prior to the filing of an application for funding pursuant to this article shall be kept confidential by those entities and their employees and may be disclosed only to persons designated by the rules and regulations of the department.

Added by Laws 1987, Ch. 838, eff. Aug. 7, 1987; **amended** by Laws 1994, Ch. 169, § 108, eff. Apr. 1, 1994; **amended** by Laws 2002, Ch. 178, § 1, eff. July 23, 2002, redesignated undesignated par. to subd. 1 and added subd. 2.

ARTICLE 7

STATE INSTITUTIONS IN THE DEPARTMENT

(Art. 7, §§ 411–452, repealed by Laws 1971, Ch. 947, eff. July 1, 1971, and subject matter transferred to Executive Law, Art. 19-g.)

ARTICLE 7

RESIDENTIAL CARE PROGRAMS FOR ADULTS AND CHILDREN

SUMMARY OF ARTICLE

Titles 1, 2, 3, Added by Laws 1977, Ch. 669, eff. Oct. 1, 1977; Title 4 added by Laws 1978, Ch. 469, eff. Sept. 4, 1978.

TITLE 1—GENERAL PROVISIONS

§ 460. Declaration of policy and statement of purpose.

Residential care programs for adults and children of the highest quality, efficiently produced and properly utilized at a reasonable cost, as a matter of vital concern to the people of this state. In order to more effectively protect and assure the life, health, safety and comfort of adults and children who must be cared for away from their own homes, the department of social services acting directly or through social services districts, and with the cooperation of other state agencies, shall have the comprehensive responsibility for the development and administration of programs, standards, and methods of operation, and all other matters of state policy, with respect to residential care programs for children and adults and all facilities and agencies, whether public or private, which are subject to the provisions of this article.

SSL

§ 460-a   Certificates of incorporation

1.   Unless the written approval of the department shall have been endorsed on or annexed to a certificate of incorporation, no such certificate shall hereafter be filed which includes among its corporate purposes the care of destitute, delinquent, abandoned, neglected or dependent children; the establishment or operation of any aged care accommodation, as defined in the private housing finance law, or adult care facility; the placing-out or boarding-out of children, as defined in this chapter; the establishment or operation of a home or shelter for unmarried mothers or a residential program for victims of domestic violence, as defined in subdivision four of section four hundred fifty-nine-a of this chapter; or the solicitation of contributions for any such purpose or purposes, provided, however, that the approval of the department shall not be required for filing of a certificate of incorporation which is restricted in its statement of corporate purposes to the establishment or operation of a facility for which an operating certificate is required by article twenty-three, nineteen, thirty-one or thirty-two of the mental hygiene law, or to the establishment or operation of a hospital, residential health care facility, or a home health agency, as those terms are defined in article twenty-eight of the public health law.

2.   The department shall promulgate regulations establishing the procedure for submitting certificates of incorporation for approval and specifying the documentation to be submitted in connection with such approval. The department shall approve or disapprove a certificate of incorporation solely on the basis of information submitted pursuant to regulations. The department shall approve or disapprove a certificate of incorporation by indicating its approval by endorsement of the certificate of incorporation or its disapproval by giving written notice thereof, which notice shall state the reasons for disapproval. A certificate of incorporation not acted upon within sixty days of the receipt of all information and documentation required by department regulations shall be deemed to be disapproved.

3.   Where a corporation engages in, or holds itself out as being authorized to engage in, activities described in this section without having obtained requisite approvals, the department may institute and maintain an action in the supreme court through the attorney general to procure a judgment dissolving and vacating or annulling the certificate of incorporation of any such corporation.

Amended by Laws 1981, Ch. 601, eff. Oct. 1, 1981 **amended** by Laws 1985, Ch. 804, eff. Aug. 1, 1985; **amended** by Laws 1987, Ch. 838, eff. Aug. 7, 1987; **amended** by Laws 1996, Ch. 543, eff. Aug. 8, 1996; **amended** by Laws 1999, Ch. 558, § 46, eff. Oct. 5, 1999; Laws 2006, Ch. 58, §1 (Part D), eff. April 12, 2006.

§ 460-b.   Operating certificate.

1.   No facility subject to inspection and supervision by the department, except a facility operated by a state department or agency, or a facility which pursuant to law is licensed or certified to operate by a state department or agency or by

an authorized agency as such term is defined in section three hundred seventy-one of this chapter, shall be operated unless it shall possess a valid operating certificate issued pursuant to this article by the department, which certificate shall specify who the operator of the facility shall be, the kind or kinds of care and services such facility is authorized to provide, the capacity of the facility, the location of the facility and, except in the case of a facility operated by an authorized agency as such term is defined in paragraph (a) of subdivision ten of section three hundred seventy-one of this chapter, the duration of the period of its validity. The department shall by regulation specify the manner in which the public shall be given notice of the existence of such operating certificate.

2. Application for an operating certificate pursuant to this article shall be made upon forms prescribed by the department and in accordance with procedures established by regulations of the department. The application shall contain the name of the facility, the kind or kinds of care and services to be provided, the location and physical description of the facility, and such other information as the department may require. The application shall be approved and an operating certificate shall be issued when it is established to the satisfaction of the department that the facility meets, and will be operated in accordance with, the requirements of this article, the regulations of the department and all other applicable provisions of law including requirements as to the premises, equipment, personnel, care and services, rules, by-laws and administrative practices.

3. Each facility required to obtain an operating certificate pursuant to this section shall be required, as a condition of qualifying for or remaining qualified for such certificate, to demonstrate to the satisfaction of the department that it has taken all reasonable steps to assure that residents entitled to a personal allowance pursuant to section one hundred thirty-one-o of this chapter have in fact received the full personal benefit of such allowance, and that proper accounting procedures have been complied with.

Amended by Laws 1978, Ch. 555, eff. July 24, 1978; **amended** by Laws 1981, Ch. 601, eff. Oct. 1, 1981.

§ 460-c. Inspection and supervision.

1. Excepting state institutions for the education and support of the blind, the deaf and the dumb, facilities subject to the approval, visitation and inspection of the state department of mental hygiene or the state commission of correction, facilities operated by or under the supervision of the division for youth and facilities subject to the supervision of the department of health pursuant to article twenty-eight of the public health law, the department shall inspect and maintain supervision over all public and private facilities or agencies whether state, county, municipal, incorporated or not incorporated which are in receipt of public funds, which are of a charitable, eleemosynary, correctional or reformatory character, including facilities or agencies exercising custody of dependent, neglected, abused, maltreated, abandoned or delinquent children, agencies engaged in the

placing-out or boarding-out of children as defined in section three hundred seventy-one of this chapter, homes or shelters for unmarried mothers, residential programs for victims of domestic violence as defined in subdivision five of section four hundred fifty-nine-a of this chapter and adult care facilities.

2.　Upon inspection of any facility subject to the inspection and supervision of the department pursuant to subdivision one of this section, inquiry may be made to ascertain:

(a)　whether the objectives of the facility or agency are being accomplished;

(b)　whether all applicable provisions of law and regulations of the department are being fully complied with;

(c)　the general management and financial condition of the facility, including any sources of public funds received;

(d)　its methods of and equipment for scholastic and career education, and whether the same are best adapted to the needs of the residents and beneficiaries;

(e)　its methods of administration;

(f)　its methods of and equipment for providing care, medical attention, treatment and discipline of its residents and beneficiaries, and whether the same are best adapted to the needs of the residents and beneficiaries;

(g)　the qualifications and general conduct of its officers and employees;

(h)　the condition of its grounds, buildings and other property, and

(i)　any other matter connected with or pertaining to its usefulness and good management or to the interests of its residents or beneficiaries.

2-a.　Special procedures relating to abuse and neglect of children in residential care. (a) If the report of an investigation of child abuse or maltreatment is indicated, the director or operator of a residential facility or program, including a program described in paragraph (h) of subdivision seven of section four hundred twelve of this chapter, shall submit to the department, within ten business days of receipt of notice of the indicated report, a written plan of prevention and remediation to be taken with respect to the subject of the indicated report to assure the continued health and safety of children and provide for the prevention of future acts of abuse or maltreatment. The department shall approve or disapprove such plan and specify necessary revisions within ten days of its receipt and shall monitor its implementation pursuant to the provisions of this chapter.

(b)　In the event an investigation of a report of alleged child abuse or maltreatment determines that some credible evidence of abuse or maltreatment exists and such abuse or maltreatment may be attributed in whole or in part to noncompliance by the facility or program, including a program described in paragraph (h) of subdivision seven of section four hundred twelve of this chapter, with provisions of this chapter or regulations of the department applicable to the operation of such residential facility or program, the director or operator of such facility or program shall, in consultation with officials of the department responsible for the approval of operating certificates and for monitoring the provision of protective services to children, develop a plan of prevention and remediation which shall be submitted to and approved by the department in accordance with time limits established by regulations of the department. Implementation of such plan shall be jointly monitored by officials of the department responsible for the approval of operating certificates and for monitoring the provision of protective services to children. In reviewing the continuing qualification of a residential child care facility or program for an operating certificate, the department shall evaluate such facility's or program's compliance with plans of prevention and remediation developed and implemented pursuant to this section.

(c)   Development and implementation of plans pursuant to this section shall, to the extent possible, be coordinated with remediation plans required by local social services districts.

3.   With respect to any corporation heretofore or hereafter formed by a special act or under a general law, or any unincorporated organization, institution, facility or agency, which actually engages in any of the aforementioned works but which is not in receipt of public funds, the department is authorized to inspect and supervise with respect to the health, safety, treatment and training of its residents, or of the children under its custody.

4.   The commissioner or any official so authorized by him may conduct any inquiry pursuant to the authority of section thirty-four of this chapter, in relation to any matter arising out of an inspection performed pursuant to this title. Any officer or duly authorized employee shall have full access to the grounds, buildings, books and papers relating to any such facility or agency and may require from the officers and persons in charge thereof any information he may deem necessary in the discharge of his duties. The department may establish rules according to which, and provide blanks and forms upon which, such information shall be furnished in a clear, uniform and prompt manner.

5.   Any officer, superintendent or employee of any such facility or agency who shall intentionally refuse to admit any officer or inspector of the department for the purpose of inspection, or shall intentionally refuse or fail to furnish the information required by the department or any officer or inspector, shall be guilty of a misdemeanor.

6.   The rights and powers conferred by this section may be enforced by an order of the supreme court after notice and hearing, or by indictment by the grand jury of the county, or both.

7.   The inspection and supervision powers of the commissioner as established by this section may, in the case of any private proprietary home for adults with a capacity of four or less, be delegated in whole or in part, to the local commissioner of the social services district in which such facility is located, and such local commissioner shall make reports regarding such facility in such form and manner and at such time as the department regulations may require.

SSL

Amended by Laws 1978, Ch. 412, eff. June 19, 1978; **amended** by Laws 1981, Ch. 169, eff. June 2, 1981; **amended** by Laws 1981, Ch. 601, eff. Oct. 1, 1981; **amended** by Laws 1985, Ch. 676, eff. Apr. 1, 1985; Laws 1990, Ch. 55, § 1; Laws 1991, Ch. 250; Laws 1992, Ch. 32, which eliminated the expiration date of the 1985 amendment; **amended** by Laws 1987, Ch. 838, eff. Aug. 7, 1987; **amended** by Laws 1992, Ch. 32, § 14, eff. Oct. 1, 1992; **amended** by Laws 1996, Ch. 301, § 45, eff. July 10, 1996.

§ 460-d.   Enforcement powers.

1.   The commissioner or any person designated by the commissioner may undertake an investigation of the affairs and management of any facility subject to the inspection and supervision provision of this article, or of any person, corporation, society, association or organization which operates or holds itself out as being authorized to operate any such facility, or of the conduct of any officers or employers of any such facility. Persons empowered by the commissioner to conduct any such investigation are hereby empowered to issue compulsory process for the attendance of witnesses and the production of papers, to administer oaths and to examine persons under oath, and to exercise the same powers in respect to the conduct of such an investigation as belong to referees appointed by the supreme court.

2.   If it shall appear after such investigation that the residents of the facility are cruelly, negligently or improperly treated, or that inadequate provision is made for their sustenance, clothing, care, supervision or other condition necessary for their comfort and well-being, the department may issue an order in the name of the people, and under the official seal of the state, directing the appropriate officers or managers of such facility to modify such treatment or provide such other remedy as may be specified therein. Before any such order is issued, it must be approved by a justice of the supreme court, after such notice as he may prescribe and after an opportunity to be heard, and any person to whom such an order is directed who shall intentionally fail or refuse to obey its terms shall be guilty of a misdemeanor.

3.   The attorney general and every district attorney shall upon request of the department furnish such legal assistance, counsel or advice as the department may require in the discharge of its duties.

4.   (a) The operating certificate of any facility may be revoked, suspended or limited upon a determination by the department that the facility has failed to comply with the requirements of state or local laws or regulations applicable to the operation of such facility.

(b)   No operating certificate shall be revoked, suspended or limited without a hearing held in accordance with procedures established by department regulations, which procedures shall require that notice of the time and place of the hearing, and notice of the charges, shall be served in person or by certified mail addressed to the facility at least thirty days prior to the date of the hearing. A written answer to the charges may be filed with the department not less than ten business days prior to the date of the hearing. An operating certificate may, nevertheless, be suspended or limited without a hearing for a period not in excess of sixty days, upon written notice to the facility following a finding by the department that the public health, or an individual's health, safety or welfare, are in imminent danger.

(c)   Any order or determination to suspend any operating certificate will specify the conditions of the suspension. These conditions may include but need not be limited to the following:

(i)   if required for the protection of the health, safety or welfare of the residents, the immediate transfer of some or all residents to other appropriate facilities or to the custody of their legal guardians, if any;

(ii)   the appointment of a temporary operator to operate the facility during the term of the suspension;

(iii)   the immediate transfer of all records concerning the operation of the facility, including resident records, facility business records and any other records related to the operation of the facility to the department immediately. The department shall control the records for the term of the suspension;

(iv)   the operator or operators of the facility shall be barred from access to the facility during the term of the suspension; or

(v)   the requirement that the operator, if replaced by a temporary operator, provide the temporary operator with any funds received by the operator for the operation of the facility.

(d)   Any order or determination to limit an operating certificate shall specify the manner in which the operating certificate is to be limited. An operating certificate may be found subject to one or more of the following limitations:

(i)   a limitation on the period of time for which such certificate remains effective, contingent on a determination that specified violations have been corrected or specified conditions have been met;

(ii)   a limitation on the number of persons for which such facility is authorized to provide care; or

(iii)   a prohibition against the admission of new residents after a specified date.

(e)   Any order or determination of revocation, suspension or limitation of the operating certificate shall be subject to judicial review in accordance with article seventy-eight of the civil practice law and rules.

5.   In addition to or as an alternative to any power which the department may exercise under this article, the supreme court may grant equitable relief against violations or threatened violations of this article or of the regulations of the department by any facility subject to the inspection and supervision of the department. The attorney general may seek such equitable relief, in the name of the people, upon the request of the department. Service in such an action shall state the nature of the violation and shall be accomplished in the manner

SSL

prescribed by the civil practice law and rules; provided, however, that an ex parte order for equitable relief may issue, notwithstanding the civil practice law and rules, if the court finds, on motion and affidavit, that such violation may reasonably be expected to result in imminent danger to the public health or to the health, safety or welfare of any individual in a facility subject to the department's inspection and supervision. The court, after a hearing, may make an order granting such equitable relief as it may deem necessary, including, but not limited to a preliminary injunction or a permanent injunction, enjoining a facility from admitting new residents, directing the department and such facility to arrange for the transfer of residents to other facilities, appointment of a temporary or permanent receiver for the protection of the public health or the health, safety and welfare of any individual in such facility, or directing a facility operator to transfer all records concerning the operation of the facility, including resident records, facility business records and any other records related to the operation of the facility to the department immediately. The people shall not be required to post security or bond.

6. Orders prohibiting placing-out or boarding-out of children or orders of removal of any child may be issued and enforced in accordance with section three hundred eighty-five of this chapter.

7. (a) The department shall adopt regulations establishing civil penalties of up to one thousand dollars per day to be assessed against all adult care facilities except facilities operated by a social services district for violations of (i) regulations of the department pertaining to the care of residents in such facilities, (ii) paragraph (a) of subdivision three of section four hundred sixty-one-a of this chapter, or (iii) an order issued pursuant to subdivision eight of this section. The regulations shall specify the violations subject to penalty and the amount of the penalty to be assessed in connection with each such violation and shall specify that only civil penalties of up to one thousand dollars per day per violation shall be assessed pursuant to this paragraph against an adult care facility found responsible for an act of retaliation or reprisal against any resident, employee, or other person for having filed a complaint with or having provided information to any long term care patient ombudsman functioning in accordance with section five hundred forty-four or five hundred forty-five of the executive law.

(b) (1) In addition to any other civil or criminal penalty provided by law, the department shall have the power to assess civil penalties in accordance with its regulations adopted pursuant to paragraph (a) of this subdivision, after a hearing conducted in accordance with procedures established by regulations of the department. Such procedures shall require that notice of the time and place of the hearing, together with a statement of charges of violations, shall be served in person or by certified mail addressed to the facility at least thirty days prior to the date of the hearing. The statement of charges of violations shall set forth the existence of the violations, the amount of penalty for which it may become liable and the steps which must be taken to rectify the violation and, where applicable, a statement that the department contends that a penalty may be imposed under this paragraph regardless of rectification. An answer to the charges of violations, in writing, shall be filed with the department, not less than ten days prior to the date of hearing. The answer shall notify the department of the facility's position with respect to each of the charges and shall include all matters which if not disclosed in the answer would be likely to take the department by surprise. The commissioner, or a member of his staff who is designated and authorized by him to hold such hearing, may in his discretion allow the facility to prove any matter not included in the answer. Where the facility satisfactorily demonstrates that it either had rectified the violations within thirty days of receiving written notification of the results of the inspection pursuant to section four hundred sixty-one-a of this chapter, or had submitted within thirty days an acceptable plan for rectification and was rectifying the violations in accordance with the steps and within the additional periods of time as accepted by the department in such plan, no penalty shall be imposed, except as provided in subparagraph two of this paragraph.

(2) Rectification shall not preclude the assessment of a penalty if the department establishes at a hearing that a particular violation, although corrected, endangered or resulted in harm to any resident as the result of:

(i) the total or substantial failure of the facility's fire detection or prevention systems, or emergency evacuation procedures prescribed by department safety standard regulations;

(ii) the retention of any resident who has been evaluated by the resident's physician as being medically or mentally unsuited for care in the facility or as requiring placement in a hospital or residential health care facility and for whom the operator is not making persistent efforts to secure appropriate placement;

(iii) the failure in systemic practices and procedures;

(iv) the failure of the operator to take actions as required by department regulations in the event of a resident's illness or accident;

(v) the failure of the operator to provide at all times supervision of residents by numbers of staff at least equivalent to the night staffing requirement set forth in department regulations; or

(vi) unreasonable threats of retaliation or taking reprisals, including but not limited to unreasonable threats of eviction or hospitalization against any resident, employee or other person who makes a complaint concerning the operation of an adult care facility, participates in the investigation of a complaint or is the subject of an action identified in a complaint.

The department shall specify in its regulations those regulations to which this subparagraph two shall apply.

(3) In assessing penalties pursuant to this paragraph, the department shall consider promptness of rectification, delay occasioned by the department, and the specific circumstances of the violations as mitigating factors.

SSL

(c)   Upon the request of the department, the attorney general may commence an action in any court of competent jurisdiction against any facility subject to the provisions of this section, and against any person or corporation operating such facility, for the recovery of any penalty assessed by the department in accordance with the provisions of this subdivision.

(d)   Any such penalty assessed by the department may be released or compromised by the department before the matter has been referred to the attorney general, and where such matter has been referred to the attorney general, such penalty may be released or compromised and any action commenced to recover the same may be settled and discontinued by the attorney general with the consent of the department.

8.   Whenever the commissioner, after investigation, finds that any person, agency or facility subject to this article is causing, engaging in or maintaining a condition or activity which constitutes a danger to the physical or mental health of the residents of a facility subject to the inspection and supervision of the department, and that it therefore appears to be prejudicial to the interests of such residents to delay action for thirty days until an opportunity for a hearing can be provided in accordance with the provisions of this section, the commissioner shall order the person, agency or facility by written notice, setting forth the basis for such finding, to discontinue such dangerous condition or activity or take certain action immediately or within a specified period of less than thirty days. The commissioner shall within thirty days of issuance of the order provide the person, agency or facility an opportunity to be heard and to present any proof that such condition or activity does not constitute a danger to the health of such resident.

9.   (a) The department shall have authority to impose a civil penalty not exceeding one thousand dollars per day against, and to issue an order requiring the closing of, after notice and opportunity to be heard, any facility which does not possess a valid operating certificate issued by the department and is an adult care facility subject to the provisions of this article and the regulations of the department. A hearing shall be conducted in accordance with procedures established by department regulations which procedures shall require that notice of the determination that the facility is an adult care facility and the reasons for such determination and notice of the time and place of the hearing be served in person on the operator, owner or prime lessor, if any, or by certified mail, return receipt requested, addressed to such person and received at least twenty days prior to the date of the hearing. If such operator, owner or prime lessor, if any, is not known to the department, then service may be made by posting a copy thereof in a conspicuous place within the facility or by sending a copy thereof by certified mail, return receipt requested, addressed to the facility. A written answer to the notice of violation may be filed with the department not less than five days prior to the date of the hearing. Demonstration by the facility that it possessed an operating certificate issued pursuant to this article, article twenty-eight of the public health law or article sixteen, twenty-three, thirty-one or thirty-two of the

mental hygiene law at the time the hearing was commenced shall constitute a complete defense to any charges made pursuant to this subdivision.

(b)　The penalty authorized by this section shall begin to run thirty days after the department provides the operator, in writing, with a summary of the inspection of the facility by which the department determined that he or she is operating an uncertified adult care facility. The submission of an application by the operator for an operating certificate for the facility shall not act as a bar to the imposition of a penalty against the operator.

(c)　(i) For the purposes of assessing the applicability of this article and the regulations of the department, the department be authorized to inspect any facility which reasonably appears to the department to be subject to the provisions of this article and to assess the needs of the residents of such facility pursuant to the provisions of section four hundred sixty-c of this title.

(ii)　At the time that a representative of the department appears at the facility for purposes of conducting such inspection, the representative shall inform the operator, administrator or other person in charge that the inspection will be conducted unless such person objects to the inspection and that if such person does object the department, pursuant to the provisions of subparagraph (iii) of this paragraph, shall be authorized to request the attorney general to apply to the court for an order granting the department access to the facility.

(iii)　If the department is not permitted access to such facility by the operator, administrator or other person in charge thereof, the attorney general, upon the request of the department, shall be authorized to apply, without notice to the operator, administrator or chairman of the board of directors of a not-for-profit facility, to the supreme court in the county in which the facility is located for an order granting the department access to such facility. The court may grant such an order if it determines, based on evidence presented by the attorney general, that there is reasonable cause to believe that such facility is an adult care facility which does not possess a valid operating certificate issued by the department.

(d)　Upon the request of the department, the attorney general may commence an action in any court of competent jurisdiction against any facility subject to the provisions of this subdivision, and against any person or corporation operating such facility, for the recovery of any penalty assessed by the department in accordance with the provisions of this subdivision.

(e)　Any penalty assessed by the department pursuant to this subdivision may be released or compromised by the department before the matter has been referred to the attorney general and where such matter has been referred to the attorney general, any such penalty may be released or compromised and any action commenced to recover the same may be settled and discontinued by the attorney general with the consent of the department.

10.　By March first, nineteen hundred ninety-five and annually thereafter, the department shall submit a report to the governor and the legislature on the regulation of adult homes and residences for adults. Such report shall include both a

SSL

narrative and statistical summary detailing the results of inspections and enforce-ment actions of adult homes and residences for adults. The report shall also include results of audits of financial conditions and practices of a selected sample of adult homes and residences of adults and recommendations for legislative action relating to the need for changes in statute.

11.   On or before issuance by the department to an adult care facility operator of official written notice of: the proposed revocation, suspension or denial of the operator's operating certificate; the limitation of the operating certificate with respect to new admissions; the issuance of a department order or commissioner's order; the seeking of equitable relief pursuant to this section; the proposed assessment of civil penalties for violations of the provisions of subparagraph two of paragraph (b) of subdivision seven of this section or placement on the "do not refer list" pursuant to subdivision fifteen of this section, written notice also shall be given to the appropriate office of the department of mental hygiene, depart-ment of correctional services, state division of parole and local social services districts, and provided further that the department of health shall notify hospitals in the locality in which such facility is located that such notice has been issued. Upon resolution of such enforcement action the department shall notify the appro-priate office of the department of mental hygiene, department of correctional services, state division of parole, local social services districts and hospitals.

12.   Social services districts and other local government entities established pursuant to this chapter shall be prohibited from making referrals for admissions to adult care facilities that have received official written notice regarding: the proposed revocation, suspension or denial of the operator's operating certificate; the limitation of the operating certificate with respect to new admissions; the issuance of department order or commissioner's orders; the seeking of equitable relief pursuant to this section; the proposed assessment of civil penalties for violations of the provisions of subparagraph two of paragraph (b) of subdivision seven of this section; or the facility's placement on the "do not refer list" pursuant to subdivision fifteen of this section.

13.   [*Expires Mar. 31, 2005.*] The department shall notify the department of health of any enforcement action pursuant to this section taken against an operator of an adult home or enriched housing program which has been licensed by the department of health as a limited home care services agency pursuant to section thirty-six hundred five of the public health law.

14.   [*Expires Mar. 31, 2005.*] If the department receives notice from the department of health that an action has been taken against an operator of a limited home care services agency, pursuant to section thirty-six hundred five-a of the public health law, the department shall review the delivery of services provided by the certified operator of an adult home or enriched housing program to determine whether such operator is meeting all applicable regulations and standards.

15.   The department of health shall maintain, on its website, a list of all adult homes, enriched housing programs, residences for adults and assisted living

programs that have received written notice of: enforcement action based on a violation of an applicable law or regulation that creates an endangerment of resident health or safety pursuant to subparagraph two of paragraph (b) of subdivision seven of this section or a pending enforcement action against a facility's operating certificate or a determination that the facility is required to be certified as an adult home, enriched housing program or residence for adults. Provided however, if a facility contends, in writing, that the violation resulting in the facility being included on the "do not refer list" has been corrected, the department shall, within thirty days, reinspect the facility, and if the department determines that the violation has been corrected, the facility shall be immediately removed from the list. This list shall be known as the "do not refer" list and shall be promptly updated to reflect any of the above violations and the reopening of admissions in any adult care facility in which the enforcement action for which they were added to the list has been resolved.

16. Any operator or controlling person of an adult care facility, as defined in clause two of subparagraph (x) of paragraph (a) of subdivision four of section four hundred sixty-one-e of this article shall be prohibited from applying to the department of health or to any other agency of this state for an operating certificate or approval to operate an alternate type of facility during the period in which such certificate has been revoked, suspended or limited.

Amended by Laws 1978, Chs. 404, 406, eff. June 19, 1978; **amended** by Laws 1981, Ch. 601, eff. Oct. 1, 1981, subd. 7; **amended** by Laws 1981, Ch. 689, eff. July 21, 1981, subd. 5; **amended** by Laws 1981, Ch. 704, eff. Aug. 20, 1981, **added** subd. 9; **amended** by Laws 1984, Ch. 524, eff. Oct. 22, 1984; provided, however, that the amendments affected by the provisions of Ch. 524 (subd. 7(b)) shall apply only to violations committed after the effective date; **amended** by Laws 1988, Ch. 515, § 1, eff. Aug. 1, 1988; **amended** by Laws 1989, Ch. 719, § 5, eff. Nov. 21, 1989; **amended** by Laws 1992, Ch. 848, §§ 2, 3, eff. Oct. 23, 1992; **amended** by Laws 1994, Ch. 733, §§ 1–6, eff. Aug. 2, 1994; **amended** by Laws 1995, Ch. 81, § 105-e, eff. June 20, 1995; **amended** by Laws 1997, and Ch. 433, § 71, extending expiration date to Mar. 31, 1999, eff. Aug. 20, 1997; **amended** by Laws 1999, Ch. 18, § 2, extending effective date to Mar. 31, 2000, eff. Mar. 31, 1999, deemed eff. Feb. 15, 1999; **amended** by Laws 1999, Ch. 558, § 47, eff. Oct. 5, 1999; **amended** by Laws 2001, Ch. 21, § 2, eff. Apr. 12, 2001, deemed effective Feb. 15, 2001; L. 2003, Ch. 31, § 2, eff. April 8, 2003, extending expiration date until March 31, 2005; **amended** by Laws 2004, Ch. 58, Part B, §§ 42, 43, 50, 56 (7–12), eff. Aug. 20, 2004.

§ **460-e. Records and reports; confidentiality; information.**

1. The department shall require, collect and maintain such information, records or reports as it may determine to be necessary to further the purpose of this article. Organizations and institutions subject to the inspection and supervision of the department shall provide such information and records in such form and at such times as the department shall determine.

2. The department may request from any other state department or state or local agency, including the department of mental hygiene, the division for youth

and the board of social welfare, and such other department or agency shall furnish, such information as the department may require for the proper performance of its duties under this article. The department shall safeguard the confidentiality of information received from such departments and agencies. Such other state departments or state agencies may request from the department, and the department shall furnish, such information as such other department or agency may require for the proper discharge of its duties. Such departments and agencies shall safeguard the confidentiality of such information, records, and reports in the same manner as the department in accordance with the provisions of sections one hundred thirty-six, four hundred forty-four and four hundred sixty-one-e of this chapter or as otherwise authorized by law.

3. Officers or employees of the department shall maintain the confidentiality of facts and information obtained as the result of any inspection or investigation of a facility subject to inspection and supervision under this article, in the same manner as information received under subdivision two of this section.

4. All officers of facilities or agencies subject to the inspection of the department shall furnish to the department, on forms provided by the department, such information and statistics as it may require, within sixty days from the expiration of the state fiscal year or such other fiscal period as may be designated by the department.

     Added by Laws 1982, Ch. 362, eff. June 21, 1982 and shall be deemed to have been in full force and effect from and after Oct. 1, 1981; **amended** by Laws 1994, Ch. 733, § 7, eff. Aug. 2, 1994.

§ 460-f. Penalties.

Any person who intentionally violates any provision of this article or regulations of the department relating to certificates of incorporation, operating certificates or confidentiality of information shall be guilty of a class A misdemeanor.

§ 460-g. Construction.

The provisions of this article shall not be deemed or construed to alter, amend, repeat or otherwise modify the provisions of article nineteen-G of the executive law, relating to secure and non-secure detention facilities, article nineteen-H of the executive law relating to residential facilities operating as approved runaway programs and transitional independent living support programs, or articles thirteen and eighty-one of the mental hygiene law, relating to facilities for the mentally disabled or drug dependent persons.

     Amended by Laws 1985, Ch. 800, eff. Aug. 2, 1985.

TITLE 2—RESIDENTIAL PROGRAMS FOR ADULTS

§ 461. Responsibility for standards.

1. The department shall promulgate and may alter or amend regulations effectuating the provisions of this title, including but not limited to establishing fiscal, administrative, architectural, safety, nutritional and program standards which apply to all adult care facilities subject to its inspection and supervision. Such regulations may be promulgated, altered or amended only after consultation with the board of social welfare; department of mental hygiene, health department and office for the aging.

2. In addition to those standards established pursuant to regulations under subdivision one hereof, the department of mental hygiene may propose any supplementary standards relating to the necessity for and content of programs designed to protect the health and well-being of mentally disabled persons, as defined in the mental hygiene law, which shall apply to any facility which cares for a significant number of such persons. The promulgation by the department of any regulations adopting such supplementary standards shall be subject to the approval of the department of mental hygiene.

3. Nothing contained within this title shall prohibit an operator of any adult care facility from exceeding the requirements of this title or the regulations of the department which effectuate the provisions of this title.

SSL

Amended by Laws 1981, Ch. 601, eff. Oct. 1, 1981.

§ 461-a. Responsibility for inspection and supervision.

1.   The department shall be responsible for the inspection and supervision of all adult care facilities subject to the provisions of section four hundred sixty-c of this chapter; provided, however, that the department shall by a written cooperative agreement entered into by October first, nineteen hundred seventy-seven, develop a system of joint inspection with the department of mental hygiene, with respect to any such facility providing residential care to a significant number of mentally disabled persons.

2.   (a) With respect to adult care facilities the department shall conduct a minimum of one unannounced inspection of each such facility to determine the adequacy of care being rendered, pursuant to the following:

(1)   Such facilities receiving the department's highest rating shall be inspected at least once every eighteen months on an unannounced basis.

(2)   All other such facilities shall be inspected on an unannounced basis no less than annually. The commissioner may provide for more frequent inspections of any such facilities. Such inspection shall not be required with respect to any facility for which the commissioner has delegated responsibility for inspection and supervision to a social services official pursuant to section four hundred sixty-c of this chapter. Any employee of the department or a social services district who gives or causes to be given advance notice of such unannounced inspections to any unauthorized persons shall, in addition to any other penalty provided by law, be suspended by the department or the social services district from all duties without pay for at least five days or for such greater period of time as the department or social services district shall determine. Any such suspension shall be made by the department or social services district in accordance with all other applicable provisions of law.

(b)   The department or a social services district, where appropriate, shall each year conduct a minimum of one full inspection of each adult care facility. Such inspection shall include, but shall not be limited to, examination of the medical, dietary and social services records of the facility as well as the minimum standards of construction, life safety standards, quality and adequacy of care, rights of residents, payments and all other areas of operation. The purpose of any inspection shall be to determine compliance with requirements of applicable provisions of law and regulations of the department.

(c)   An inspection report shall be made of each inspection which shall clearly identify and indicate in detail each area of operation, including, but not limited to, the premises, equipment, personnel, resident care and services, and whether each such area of operation or any of its component parts is or is not in compliance with the regulations of the department and all other applicable requirements. It also shall identify those areas of operation or any of its component parts found not in compliance as a result of failure in systemic practices and procedures. The operator shall be notified of the results of the inspection in a manner to be determined by regulations of the department. Such notification shall contain directions as may be appropriate as to the manner and time in which compliance with applicable requirements of law or regulations of the department shall be effected. The department shall also require the operator of an adult home or residence for adults to develop, biannually update and implement plans for quality assurance activities for each area of operation. Quality assurance activities include but are not limited to, development and maintenance of performance standards, measurement of adherence to such standards and to applicable state and local laws and regulations, identification of performance failures, design, and implementation of corrective action.

(d) Systemic practices or procedures are those activities related to each area of operation which indicate a pattern or an inability to bring the operation of the facility into compliance with applicable provisions of laws and regulations.

(e) Nothing contained in this subdivision shall limit or restrict the ability of the department or social services district, where appropriate, to conduct more than one inspection of an adult care facility, for whatever purpose, as is deemed necessary for ensuring compliance with applicable provisions of law and regulations of the department.

3. (a) Pursuant to regulations promulgated by the commissioner, in consultation with the director of the state office for the aging, no facility or individual shall restrict or prohibit the access to the facility nor interfere with the performance of the official duties, including confidential visits with residents, of duly designated persons participating in the long term care ombudsman program as provided for in section five hundred forty-five of the executive law. No facility or individual shall retaliate or take reprisals against any resident, employee, or other person for having filed a complaint with, or having provided information to, any long term care patient ombudsman functioning in accordance with section five hundred forty-four or five hundred forty-five of the executive law.

(b) In addition, no facility which provides residential care and services for adults shall restrict or prohibit the access to the facility nor interfere with confidential visits with residents by:

(i) Family members, guardians, friends of an individual resident and legal representatives, legal counsels and case managers;

(ii) Individuals representing community organizations or service agencies who will provide, free of charge, a service or educational program to residents;

(iii) An employee or representative of any public or private not-for-profit corporation, community organization or association whose primary purposes for visiting include assisting residents in resolving problems and complaints concerning their care and treatment, and in securing adequate services to meet their needs. The operator shall make available a common area of the facility for such visits.

SSL

(c)   The department shall establish and maintain a registry of public or private not-for-profit corporations, community organizations or associations assured access to facilities which provide residential care and services for adults pursuant to subparagraph (iii) of paragraph (b) of this subdivision. Any such corporation, community organization or association shall file a copy of its certificate of incorporation with the registry established and maintained by the department.

(d)   Persons assured access to a residential care facility for adults pursuant to this subdivision shall not enter the living area of any resident without identifying themselves to the resident, stating the purpose of the visit, and receiving the permission of the resident and the resident's roommate to enter the living area.

(e)   Individual residents shall have the right to terminate or deny any visit to them by persons assured access to the facility pursuant to this subdivision.

(f)   Visits by individuals assured access to facilities which provide residential care and services for adults pursuant to subparagraphs (i), (ii) and (iii) of paragraph (b) of this subdivision shall be permitted during a period of at least ten hours between 9:00 o'clock a.m. and 8:00 o'clock p.m. unless extended by arrangement with the facility.

(g)   Notwithstanding any provision of paragraph (b) of this subdivision, the operator of a facility which provides residential care and services for adults may restrict or prohibit access to the facility or interfere with confidential visits with residents by individuals who the operator has reasonable cause to believe would directly endanger the safety of such residents.

(h)   Whenever an individual is denied access pursuant to paragraph (g) of this subdivision the operator must record a detailed written statement describing the reasons for denial of access to any such individual. This statement shall be maintained by the facility and be accessible to residents, persons denied access, and the department.

(i)   If the operator of a facility denies access pursuant to paragraph (g) of this subdivision, the person denied access may bring an action in supreme court in the county in which the facility is located for an order granting such person access to such facility. If the court finds that such denial was made in bad faith, the operator of the facility shall be liable for all costs, including reasonable attorney's fees, and the court may, in its discretion, assess a civil penalty not to exceed fifty dollars per day for each day such access was denied.

4.   Pursuant to regulations promulgated by the commissioner in consultation with the director of the office for the aging, no facility shall restrict or prohibit access by records access ombudsmen specially designated under section five hundred forty-four of the executive law to the medical or personal records of any patient or resident if such patient or resident, or, where appropriate, committee for an incompetent, has given express written consent to such disclosure; provided, however, that (i) in the case of medical records, disclosure may be exclusive of the personal notes of the physician as defined in such regulations

and (ii) access may be limited to such times as may be specified in such regulations. Such records shall be made available by a member or members of the facility's staff who shall be designated by the facility to provide access to and, where necessary, interpretation of such records to such access ombudsman, who shall have the right to photocopy such records. The facility may charge a reasonable fee for photocopying pursuant to such regulations. Disclosure to a records access ombudsman of records of any patient or resident pursuant to the written consent of such patient or resident shall not give rise to any claim against the facility, its staff, or the patient's or resident's physician based solely on the fact of such disclosure pursuant to such written consent. Nothing in this subdivision shall be construed to limit or abridge any right of access to records, including financial records, otherwise available to ombudsmen, patients or residents, or any other person.

Amended by Laws 1978, Ch. 555; Laws 1980, Ch. 344, eff. Aug. 18, 1980; **amended** by Laws 1981, Ch. 601, eff. Oct. 1, 1981; **amended** by Laws 1983, Ch. 532, eff. Nov. 16, 1983; **amended** by Laws 1983, Ch. 843, eff. Oct. 4, 1983; **amended** by Laws 1987, Ch. 420, eff. July 27, 1987; **amended** by Laws 1989, Ch. 719, § 6, eff. Nov. 21, 1989; **amended** by Laws 1994, Ch. 735, §§ 1, 2, eff. Aug. 2, 1994.

§ 461-b.   Provisions related to establishment of adult care facilities.

1.   (a) Only a natural person or partnership composed only of natural persons, a not-for-profit corporation, a public corporation, a business corporation other than a corporation whose shares are traded on a national securities exchange or are regularly quoted on a national over the-counter market or a subsidiary of such corporation or a corporation any of the stock of which is owned by another corporation, a limited liability company provided that if a limited liability company has a member that is a corporation, a limited liability company or a partnership, the shareholders of the member corporation, the members of the member limited liability company, or the partners of the member partnership must be natural persons, a social services district or other governmental agency may be issued an operating certificate by the department for the purpose of operating an adult care facility, except family type homes for adults, which may be issued operating certificates by the department or social services district only if such facilities are operated by a natural person or persons. The holder of an operating certificate for the purposes of operating an adult home shall not be issued an operating certificate for the purposes of operating an enriched housing program if such adult home operator has not met compliance standards during the most recent inspection cycle. Provided however, the department may deem an operator eligible to receive an operating certificate for the purposes of operating an enriched housing program upon the consideration of the results of previous inspections and whether the operator is meeting the needs of the residents and is providing quality care.

(b)   A natural person may seek certification as an operator of a family-type home for adults to provide long-term residential care and personal care and/or

SSL

supervision to persons related to the operator, provided that the relationship between the operator and resident is not that of spouse, in-law, child or stepchild.

(c)   An appropriation made available for the purposes of funding the operating assistance sub-program for enriched housing up to the amount appropriated for such purpose in the nineteen hundred ninety-six--ninety-seven state fiscal year shall be limited to any enriched housing program operated by a public agency, public corporation or a not-for-profit corporation, which may be issued an operating certificate by the department to operate an enriched housing program.

2.   (a) No adult care facility shall be operated unless and until the operator obtains the written approval of the department. Such approval may be granted only to an operator who satisfactorily demonstrates: that the operator is of good moral character; that the operator is financially responsible; that there is a public need for the facility; that the buildings, equipment, staff, standards of care and records to be employed in the operation comply with applicable law and regulations of the department and that any license or permit required by law for the operation of such facility has been issued to such operation. In determining whether there is a public need for the facility, the department shall give consideration to the relative concentration of such facilities in the area proposed to be serviced. Such approval for family type home for adults shall not be granted unless the appropriate social services official has made the required visitation and inspection and has submitted a report thereof to the department in accordance with this article.

(b)   After an operator obtains approval of the department for the operation of an adult care facility he may operate such facility only so long as he continues to do so in compliance with the requirements of such approval, applicable law, and the regulations of the department.

(c)   The knowing operation of an adult care facility without the prior written approval of the department shall be a class A misdemeanor.

3.   (a) The department shall not approve an application for establishment of an adult care facility unless it is satisfied insofar as applicable, as to (i) the character, competence and standing in the community, of the applicant; provided, however, with respect to any such applicant who is already or within the past ten years has been an incorporator, director, sponsor, stockholder, operator, administrator, member or owner of any adult care facility which has been issued an operating certificate by the board or the department, or of a halfway house, hostel or other residential facility or of a program or facility licensed or operated by a health, mental hygiene, social services or education agency or department of this or any state, or a program serving persons with mental disabilities, or other persons with disabilities as defined in subdivision twenty-one of section two hundred ninety-two of the executive law, the aged, children or other persons receiving health, mental hygiene, residential, social or educational services, no approval of such application shall be granted unless the department shall affirmatively find by substantial evidence as to each such applicant that a

substantially consistent high level of care is being or was being rendered in each such facility or institution with which such person is or was affiliated; for the purposes of this paragraph, there may be a finding that a substantially consistent high level of care has been rendered where there have been violations of applicable rules and regulations, that (1) did not threaten to directly affect the health, safety or welfare of any patient or resident, and (2) were promptly corrected and not recurrent; (ii) the financial resources of the proposed facility and its sources of future revenue; and (iii) such other matters as it shall deem pertinent.

(b)　Any natural person or partnership composed only of natural persons, not-for-profit corporation, public corporation, business corporation other than a corporation whose shares are traded on a national securities exchange or are regularly quoted on a national over-the-counter market or a subsidiary of such corporation or a corporation any of the stock of which is owned by another corporation, a limited liability company provided that if a limited liability company has a member that is a corporation, a limited liability company or a partnership, the shareholders of the member corporation, the members of the member limited liability company, or the partners of the member partnership must be natural persons, social services district or other governmental agency filing an application for approval to operate a residence for adults, adult home or enriched housing program, shall file with the department such information on the ownership of the property interest in such facility as shall be prescribed by regulation, including the following:

(i)　The name and address and a description of the interest held by each of the following persons:

(1)　any person, who directly or indirectly, beneficially owns any interest in the land on which the facility is located;

(2)　any person who, directly or indirectly, beneficially owns any interest in the building in which the facility is located;

(3)　any person who, directly or indirectly, beneficially owns any interest in any mortgage, note, deed of trust or other obligation secured in whole or in part by the land on which or building in which the facility is located; and

(4)　any person who, directly or indirectly, has any interest as lessor or lessee in any lease or sub-lease of the land on which or the building in which the facility is located.

(ii)　If any person named in response to subparagraph (i) of this paragraph is a partnership or limited liability company, then the name and address of each partner or member.

(iii)　If any person named in response to subparagraph (i) of this subdivision is a corporation, other than a corporation whose shares are traded on a national securities exchange or are regularly quoted in an over-the-counter market or which is a commercial bank, savings bank or savings and loan association, then the name and address of each officer, director, stockholder and, if known, each principal stockholder and controlling person of such corporation.

(iv)   If any corporation named in response to subparagraph (i) of this subdivision is a corporation whose shares are traded on a national securities exchange or are regularly quoted in an over-the-counter market or which is a commercial bank, savings bank or savings and loan association, then the name and address of the principal executive officers and each director and, if known, each principal stockholder of such corporation.

(v)   For the purpose of this section the term "controlling person" shall mean any person who by reason of a direct or indirect ownership interest (whether of record or beneficial) has the ability, acting either alone or in concert with others with ownership interests, to direct or cause the direction of the management or policies of said corporation, partnership or other entity. Neither the department nor any employee of the department shall, by reason of his or her official position, be deemed a controlling person of any corporation, partnership or other entity, nor shall any person who serves as an officer, administrator or other employee of any corporation, partnership or other entity or as a member of a board of directors or trustees of any corporation be deemed to be a controlling person of such corporation, partnership or other entity as a result of such position or his or her official actions in such position. The term "principal stockholder" shall mean any person who beneficially owns, holds or has the power to vote, ten percent or more of any class of securities issued by said corporation.

(c)   No articles of organization of a limited liability company established pursuant to the New York limited liability law which includes among its powers or purposes the establishment or operation of any adult home, residence for adults or enriched housing program as defined in section two of this chapter, shall be filed with the department of state unless the written approval of the department is annexed to the articles of organization.

3-a.   (a) Every person who is a controlling person of any adult care facility liable under any provision of this article to any person or class of persons for damages or to the state for any civil fine, penalty, assessment of damages, shall also be liable, jointly and severally, with and to the same extent as such adult care facility, to such person or class of persons for damages or to the state for any such civil fine, penalty, assessment or damages.

(b)   For the purposes of this section the term "controlling person" shall mean any person who by reason of a direct or indirect ownership interest (whether of record or beneficial) has the ability, acting either alone or in concert with others with ownership interests, to direct or cause the direction of the management or policies of said corporation, partnership or other entity. Neither the department nor any employee of the department shall, by reason of his or her official position, be deemed a controlling person of any corporation, partnership or other entity, nor shall any person who serves as an officer, administrator or other employee of any corporation, partnership or other entity or as a member of a board of directors or trustees of any corporation be deemed to be a controlling person of such corporation, partnership or other entity as a result of such position or his or her official actions in such position. The term "principal stockholder"shall mean any person who beneficially owns, holds or has the power to vote, ten percent or more of any class of securities issued by said corporation.

4.   No person, corporation, home institution, hotel or other residential facility or accommodation other than a facility or agency which possesses a valid operating certificate, as required under the provisions of this chapter, the mental hygiene law or public health law shall hold itself out, advertise or otherwise in any form or manner represent that it is a facility offering accommodations and services for dependent, aged or disabled adults.

5.   Any adult care facility subject to the provisions of this section that possesses a valid operating certificate as of October first, nineteen hundred seventy-seven shall be deemed to have department approval to continue operation of such facility for the duration or the period for which such certificate was issued, provided such facility continues to be operated in accordance with applicable provisions of law and department regulations.

6.   (a) The department, prior to making a final determination with respect to approving the establishment of, or the certificate of incorporation of, or the articles of organization of, or an operating certificate for a residence for adults, adult home, or enriched housing program, shall in addition to any other requirements of law take into consideration and be empowered to request information and advice as to the availability of facilities or services such as ambulatory, home care or other services which may serve as alternatives or substitutes for the whole or any part of a proposed facility and the possible economies and improvements in services to be anticipated from the operation of centralized facilities and services reasonably available in the regional services area.

(b)   In determining whether there is a public need for a residence for adults or an adult home, the department shall consider the advice of the state health planning and development agency designated pursuant to the provisions of the national health planning and resources development act of nineteen hundred seventy-four and any amendments thereto.

(c)   Notwithstanding any other provision of this article, the department shall not consider public need in determining whether to approve any proprietary adult home that was in existence and operating on September first, nineteen hundred seventy-five as a family care home under the mental hygiene law or an adult care facility operated by a social services district.

7.   (a) The department shall suspend, limit, modify or revoke an operating certificate of a shelter for adults, residence for adults or adult home upon determining that such action would be in the public interest in order to conserve resources by restricting the number of beds, or the level of services, or both, to those which are actually needed, after taking into consideration the total number of beds necessary to meet the public need, and the availability of facilities or

SSL

services such as ambulatory, home care or other services which may serve as alternatives or substitutes for the whole or any part of a facility, and in the case of modification, the level of care and the nature and type of services provided by a facility or required by all or some of the residents in or seeking admission to such facility, and whether such level of care is consistent with the operating certificate of the facility.

(b)   Wherever any finding as described in this subdivision is under consideration with respect to any particular facility, the department shall cause to be published in a newspaper of general circulation in the geographic area of the facility at least thirty days prior to making such a finding an announcement that such a finding is under consideration and an address to which interested persons can write to make their views known. The department shall take all public comments into consideration in making such a finding.

(c)   The department shall, upon such finding described in this subdivision with respect to any facility or project, cause such facility to be notified of the finding at least thirty days in advance of taking the proposed action to revoke, suspend, limit, or modify the facility's operating certificate. Upon receipt of any such notification and before the expiration of the thirty days or such longer period as may be specified in the notice, the facility may request a public hearing to be held in the county in which the facility is located. In no event shall the revocation, suspension, limitation, or modification take effect prior to the thirtieth day after the date of the notice or prior to the effective date specified in the notice or prior to the date of the hearing decision, whichever is later.

(d)   Except as otherwise provided by law, all appeals from a finding of the department made pursuant to this subdivision shall be directly to the appellate division of the supreme court in the third department. Except as otherwise expressly provided by law, such appeals shall have preference over all issues in all courts.

8.   No adult care facility certified by the department which is operating in compliance with this chapter and regulations shall be required to be certified by the office of mental health as a residential care center for adults.

Added by Laws 1981, Ch. 601, eff. Oct. 1, 1981; **amended** by Laws 1984, Ch. 626, eff. Nov. 26, 1984; **amended** by Laws 1985, Ch. 351, eff. July 18, 1985; **amended** by Laws 1986, Ch. 468, eff. July 21, 1986; **amended** by Laws 1992, Ch. 848, § 4 eff. Oct. 23, 1992; **amended** by Laws 1994, Ch. 735, § 4, eff. Aug. 2, 1994; **amended** by Laws 1996, Ch. 543, § 2 -4, eff. Aug. 8, 1996, and **further amended** by Ch. 462, § 8, 9, eff. Aug. 8, 1996; **amended** by Laws 1999, Ch.591, §§ 1–6, eff. Nov. 1, 1999.

§ 461-c.   Resident care, services and charges.

1.   Every operator of an adult care facility, except a shelter for adults, shall execute with each applicant for admission a written admission agreement, dated and signed by the operator and the parties to be charged, which shall contain the

entire agreement of the parties and such other information as department regulations shall require.

2. Such agreement executed pursuant to subdivision one of this section shall enumerate in such detail as may be required by department regulation all charges, expenses and other assessments, if any, for services, materials, equipment and food, required by law or regulations and other services, materials, equipment and food which such operator agrees to furnish and supply to such resident during the period of residency. No additional charges or expenses may be assessed against any resident of a residence for adults, adult home or enriched housing program, in excess of that contained in such agreement, except (a) upon express written approval and authority of the resident, or his or her sponsor, if any, or (b) in order to provide additional care, services or supplies, upon the express order of the attending physician of the resident, or (c) upon thirty days notice to the resident and to his or her sponsor, if any, of additional charges and expenses due to increased cost of maintenance and operation. However, in the event of any emergency arising which affects such resident, additional charges may be assessed for the benefit of such resident as are reasonable and necessary for services, materials, equipment and food furnished and supplied during such emergency.

2-a. (a) There shall be an implied warranty of habitability in each written admission agreement executed pursuant to this section that shall ensure the premises be fit for human habitation and for the uses reasonably intended by the operator and the resident and that the occupants of the facility shall not be subjected to any conditions which would be dangerous, hazardous or detrimental to their life, health, safety or welfare. Such statement shall not be read to be in any way limiting a resident's rights to relief in an administrative or judicial proceeding.

(b) An action for breach of the warranty of habitability and any violation of a written admission agreement may be maintained in a court of competent jurisdiction by the resident or representative of the resident. The court shall apply New York rules of court part 130 to any action brought pursuant to this section.

3. The written agreement executed pursuant to subdivision one of this section shall include a statement indicating that the resident and any person designated by the resident shall be notified by the operator at the request of the resident pursuant to regulations promulgated by the department and, shall be provided written notification by the facility not less than thirty days prior to a termination of the resident's admission and services agreement; a statement that upon discharge or transfer, the resident and any person designated by the resident shall be notified by the operator at the request of the resident pursuant to regulations promulgated by the department and, is entitled to a final written statement of his or her account and that the resident is entitled to the prompt return, within three business days, of any of his or her money, property or thing of value held in trust or in custody by the facility; a statement which details any and all money, property or thing of value which is given, or promised to be given to the facility

SSL

on admission or at any other time, including any agreements made by third parties for the benefit of a resident; and such other provisions as the department determines necessary to fully inform the resident of those items of care, services, materials, equipment and food that must be provided by the facility pursuant to other applicable laws and regulations, and the frequency thereof, and any additional items of care, services, materials, equipment and food that the facility may in its discretion agree to provide, and the frequency thereof. Waiver of any provision contained herein by a resident shall be void. Such statement as herein provided shall be annexed to the admission agreement.

4.   No resident of an adult care facility who is entitled to receive a personal allowance pursuant to the provisions of section one hundred thirty-one-o of this chapter shall be required to use any of the proceeds from such allowance to pay the operator of an adult care facility for any services or supplies, unless the resident elects to purchase such services or supplies and the department has determined that such services or supplies are not otherwise required to be provided by the operator pursuant to law, regulation or agreement and the charges for such services or supplies are reasonable.

5.   Whenever a resident authorizes an operator of an adult care facility or any person affiliated therewith, to exercise control over his or her money, property or thing of value, such authorization shall be in writing and subscribed by the parties to be charged. Any such money, property or thing of value belonging to the resident shall not be mingled with the funds or become an asset of the person receiving the same, but shall be segregated and recorded on the facility's financial records as independent accounts.

6.   No adult care facility shall receive or retain any person who is in need of continual medical or nursing care as provided by facilities licensed pursuant to article twenty-eight of the public health law or articles nineteen, twenty-three, thirty-one and thirty-two of the mental hygiene law.

7.   (a) At the time of the admission to an adult care facility, other than a shelter for adults, a resident shall submit to the facility a written report from a physician, which report shall state:

(i)   that the physician has physically examined the resident within one month and the date of such examination;

(ii)   that the resident is not in need of acute or long term medical or nursing care which would require placement in a hospital or residential health care facility; and

(iii)   that the resident is not otherwise medically or mentally unsuited for care in the facility.

(b)   For the purpose of creating an accessible and available record and assuring that a resident is properly placed in such a facility, the physician's report shall also contain the resident's significant medical history and current conditions, the prescribed medication regimen, and recommendations for diet, the assistance needed in the activities of daily living and where appropriate, recommendations for exercise, recreation and frequency of medical examinations.

(c)   Such resident shall thereafter be examined by a physician at least annually and shall submit an annual written report from his physician in conformity with the provisions of this subdivision.

8.   The department shall promulgate regulations with respect to the safekeeping and administration of medications in any adult care facility subject to the provisions of section four hundred sixty-c of this article, in accordance with applicable provisions of law, and after consultation with the state department of health and appropriate offices of the state department of mental hygiene.

9.   The department shall, with the consent of a resident living in a facility which has received the lowest rating for eighteen months from the effective date of this subdivision, pursuant to section four hundred sixty-one-n of this title, present the resident and any person designated by the resident with options on relocating such resident to a facility which has obtained a higher rating, or other housing alternatives.

Added by Laws 1981, Ch. 601, eff. Oct. 1, 1981; **amended** by Laws 1984, Ch. 626, eff. Nov. 26, 1984; **amended** by Laws 1994, Ch. 733, § 8, eff. Aug. 2, 1994, and Ch. 734, § 1, eff. Aug. 2, 1994; **amended** by Laws 1999, Ch. 558, § 48, eff. Oct. 5, 1999.

§ 461-d.   Rights of residents in adult care facilities.

1.   The principles enunciated in subdivision three hereof are declared to be the public policy of the state and a copy of such statement of rights and responsibilities shall be posted conspicuously in a public place in each facility covered hereunder.

2.   The department shall require that every adult care facility shall adopt and make public a statement of the rights and responsibilities of the residents who are receiving care in such facilities, and shall treat such residents in accordance with the provisions of such statement.

3.   Resident rights and responsibilities shall include, but not be limited to the following:

(a)   Every resident's civil and religious liberties, including the right to independent personal decisions and knowledge or available choices, shall not be infringed and the facility shall encourage and assist in the fullest possible exercise of these rights.

(b)   Every resident shall have the right to have private communications and consultations with his or her physician, attorney, and any other person.

(c)   Every resident shall have the right to present grievances on behalf of himself or herself or others, to the facility's staff or administrator, to governmental officials, or to any person without fear of reprisal, and to join with other

SSL

residents or individuals within or outside of the facility to work for improvements in resident care.

(d) Every resident shall have the right to manage his or her own financial affairs.

(e) Every resident shall have the right to have privacy in treatment and in caring for personal needs.

(f) Every resident shall have the right to confidentiality in the treatment of personal, social, financial and medical records, and security in storing personal possessions.

(g) Every resident shall have the right to receive courteous, fair, and respectful care and treatment and a written statement of the services provided by the facility, including those required to be offered on an as-needed basis.

(h) Every resident shall have the right to receive or to send personal mail or any other correspondence without interception or interference by the operator of an adult care facility or any person affiliated therewith.

(i) Every resident shall have the responsibility to obey all reasonable regulations of the facility and to respect the personal rights and private property of the other residents.

(j) The facility is required to include on its accident or incident report the resident's version of the events leading to an accident or incident involving such resident, unless the resident objects.

(k) resident shall have the right to authorize those family members and other adults who will be given priority to visit consistent with the resident's ability to receive visitors.

Waiver of any provisions contained within this provision by a resident of an adult care facility shall be void.

4. Every resident of a residence for adults, adult home or enriched housing program, shall be entitled to receive compensation for services performed on behalf of such facility or persons affiliated therewith, and the operator of such facility shall maintain written records stating the duties to be performed, the rate and type of compensation, and the hours and days during which these services will be performed.

5. Each operator shall give a copy of the statement of rights and responsibilities to each resident at or prior to the time of admission to the facility, or to the appointed personal representative and to each member of the facility's staff.

6. An operator or employee of a residence for adults, adult home or enriched housing program or any other entity which is a representative payee of a resident of such facility pursuant to designation by the social security administration or which otherwise assumes management responsibility over the funds of a resident shall maintain such funds in a fiduciary capacity to the resident. Any interest on money received and held for the resident shall be the property of the individual resident.

7. Every operator of a residence for adults, adult home, enriched housing program or family type home for adults shall post a long term care ombudsman poster in such facility in the main entrance or public posting area where notices to residents are commonly displayed, or, if there is no such main entrance or posting area, in the several public areas within the facility where notices to residents are commonly displayed, and shall make the long term care ombudsman brochure available to residents upon request.

Added by Laws 1981, Ch. 601, eff. Oct. 1, 1981; **amended** by Laws 1984, Ch. 626, eff. Nov. 26, 1984; **amended** by Laws 1985, Ch. 514, eff. July 24, 1985; **amended** by Laws 1994, Ch. 688, § 4, eff. Oct. 31, 1994; **amended** by Laws 1996, Ch. 462, § 2, eff. Sept. 7, 1996 to add Subd. 6; **amended** by Laws 2004, Ch. 363, § 1, adding sub. 7, eff. Aug. 17, 2004; Laws 2006, Ch. 317, §1, eff. July 26, 2006.

§ 461-e. Records and reports.

1. Every adult care facility shall maintain, as public information available for public inspection under such conditions as the department shall prescribe, records containing copies of the most recent inspection report pertaining to the facility that has been issued by the department or social services district or to the facility.

2. Pursuant to the provisions of article six of the public officers law, the department shall make available for public inspection copies of all inspection reports of adult care facilities issued by the department.

3. Every adult care facility shall:

(a) Post in a prominent position in the facility so as to be accessible to all residents and to the general public, a summary of the most recent inspection of such facility performed by the department or a social services district.

(b) Provide to any resident and each applicant for admission an opportunity to review the most recent inspection report pertaining to and issued by the department or social services district to such facility.

4. (a) Each adult home and residence for adults except those operated by a social services district shall file an annual financial statement with the department on or before the fifteenth day of the sixth calendar month after the close of the facility's fiscal year for which such report is due, upon forms prescribed by the department and in compliance with the regulations of the department. Such statement shall clearly set forth all financial information pertaining to the operation of such facility in accordance with generally accepted accounting principles, including but not limited to the following:

(i) revenues and expenses by categories during such fiscal year.

(ii) a balance sheet of the facility as of the end of such fiscal year, setting forth assets and liabilities at such date, including all capital, surplus, reserve, depreciation and similar accounts.

SSL

(iii)   a statement of operations of the facility for such fiscal year, setting forth all revenues, expenses, taxes, extraordinary items and other credits or charges.

(iv)   the name and address of each of the following persons:

(1)   the operator of the facility;

(2)   any person who, directly or indirectly, beneficially owns any interest in the land on which the facility is located;

(3)   any person who, directly or indirectly, beneficially owns any interest in the building in which the facility is located;

(4)   any person who, directly or indirectly, beneficially owns any interest in any mortgage, note, deed of trust or other obligation secured in whole or in part by the land on which or building in which the facility is located; and

(5)   any person who, directly or indirectly, has any interest as lessor or lessee in any lease or sub-lease of the land on which or the building in which the facility is located.

(v)   if the facility or any person named in response to subparagraph (iv) of this paragraph is a partnership, then the name and home address of each partner.

(vi)   if the facility or any person named in response to subparagraph (iv) of this paragraph is a corporation, other than a corporation whose shares are traded on a national securities exchange or are regularly quoted in an over-the-counter market or which is a commercial bank, savings bank or savings and loan association, then the name and address of each officer, director, and each principal stockholder and controlling person of such corporation.

(vii)   if any corporation named in response to subparagraph (iv) of this paragraph is a corporation whose shares are traded on a national securities exchange or are regularly quoted in an over-the-counter market or which is a commercial bank, savings bank or savings and loan association, then the name and address of the principal executive officers and each director and, if known, each principal stockholder of such corporation.

(viii)   if the facility paid or received an aggregate of five hundred dollars or more during the fiscal year in connection with transactions with any person named in response to subparagraph (iv), (v), (vi) or (vii) of this paragraph or any affiliate of said person, a description of the transactions, naming the parties thereto and describing the relationships which require the transactions to be described and the goods, services, payments or other consideration received by each party to the transactions. Such facility must make available to the department, when requested, adequate documentation to support the costs involved including access to books and records related to such transactions.

(ix)   if known, the nature and amount of any interest in, or relationship with, any other adult care facility, held by any person named in response to subparagraph (iv) of this paragraph, or by any affiliate of such person.

(x)   the following definitions shall be applicable to this paragraph and to any reports filed pursuant to this paragraph:

(1) "affiliate" means:

(A) with respect to a partnership, each partner thereof;

(B) with respect to a corporation, each officer, director, principal stockholder and controlling person thereof;

(C) with respect to a natural person (a) each member of said person's immediate family, (b) each partnership and each partner thereof of which said person or any affiliate of said person is a partner, and (c) each corporation in which said person or any affiliate of said person is an officer, director, principal stockholder or controlling person;

(2) "controlling person" of any corporation, partnership or other entity means any person who has the power, directly or indirectly, to significantly influence or direct the actions or policies of such facility. Neither the department nor any employee of the department shall, by reason of his or her official position, be deemed a controlling person of any corporation, partnership or other entity;

(3) "immediate family" of any person includes each parent, child, spouse, brother, sister, first cousin, aunt and uncle of such person whether such relationship arises by reason of birth, marriage or adoption;

(4) "principal stockholder" of a corporation means any person who beneficially owns, holds or has the power to vote, ten percent or more of any class of securities issued by said corporation.

(xi) together with such other information as may be required by the department.

Such statement shall be accompanied by an opinion signed by an independent licensed accountant that such financial statement represents the financial operations and position of the facility, except such opinion shall not be required for facilities with a capacity of nine or less.

(b) The department shall accept in full satisfaction of the provisions of this subdivision from operators of adult homes and residences for adults who are required to submit an annual report as a charitable organization to the secretary of state of the state of New York or are required to submit to the commissioner of the New York state department of health an annual report of residential health care facilities, a certified copy of such report and upon request from the department an uncertified copy of the financial statement required to be filed with the department pursuant to the provisions of this subdivision.

(c) The department may examine the books and records of any adult home or residence for adults to determine the accuracy of the annual financial statement or for any other reason deemed appropriate by the department to effectuate the purposes of this section.

(d) The department shall perform on a selected sample of adult homes and residences for adults, a financial audit as part of the inspection procedure.

(e) Each enriched housing program shall file financial statements with the department on at least an annual basis, in accordance with regulations.

SSL

5.   The department may promulgate regulations which require each adult care facility to maintain the following written records and any other such records, under such conditions and for such time, as may be prescribed pursuant to such regulations: (i) a chronological admission and discharge register consisting of a listing of residents registered in and discharged from such facility by name, age, sex of resident, and place from or to which the resident is registered or discharged, (ii) a daily census record, (iii) a personal non-medical record for each resident, including but not limited to, identification of his or her next-of-kin, family and sponsor, the name and address of the person or persons to be contacted in the event of an emergency, and all details of the referral and registration and non-medical correspondence and papers concerning the resident, (iv) a financial record for each resident, including but not limited to, copies of all agreements, resident account records and a current inventory of personal property being held by the operator.

6.   No facts and information retained as part of individual resident records by an operator of an adult care facility may be released to anyone other than the resident, the resident's next-of-kin or authorized representative of the resident, the operator, his employees or agents, or an employee or designee of the department without the written permission of the resident.

7.   Nothing contained in this section shall be construed or deemed to require the public disclosure of confidential medical, social, personal or financial records of any resident. The department shall adopt such regulations as may be necessary to give effect to the provisions of this section and to preserve the confidentiality of medical, social, personal or financial records of residents.

8.   Nothing contained in this section shall be construed or deemed to require the disclosure of the names and addresses or other information that would identify or ten to identify persons who file complaints with the department concerning the operation of adult care facilities. This shall apply to all complaints, regardless of whether the department is able to substantiate the complaints. Such information shall be deemed to be confidential and shall only be made available to a district attorney or police officer conducting a criminal investigation or prosecution relating to an adult care facility and only upon the written request of the investigating officer or district attorney; or to a court or to the presiding officer of an administrative proceeding and the parties to such proceeding if, with the consent of the persons providing such information, it is to be utilized by the department or any other state or local agency or subdivision in such proceeding. If a party is not provided with the identity of a person providing information in accordance with the provisions of this section, the fact that such confidential report was made shall in no way be relied upon by any court or presiding officer of an administrative proceeding in the course of reaching a determination in such proceeding. The department shall, consistent with the provisions of this section, adopt such regulations as may be necessary to preserve the confidentiality of persons making such complaints.

Amended by Laws 1984, Ch. 626, eff. Nov. 1, 1984; amended by Laws 1992, Ch. 848 § 5, adding SSL § 461-e (8), eff. Oct. 23, 1992; **amended** by Laws 1994, Ch. 733, §§ 9 -11, eff. Aug. 2, 1994.

§ 461-f. Operation of facility in receivership.

1.   As a means of protecting the health, safety and welfare of the residents of an adult care facility subject to inspection and supervision by the department, it may become necessary under certain circumstances to authorize the continuing operation of such facility for a temporary period by a court appointed receiver, at the discretion of the commissioner, as provided in this section or with respect to an adult home, enriched housing program or residence for adults, a receiver approved by the department of health pursuant to written agreement between the department and the operator or operators of such facility, provided that such agreement shall not exceed a period of sixty days but may be extended for an additional sixty day period upon agreement by the parties.

2.   The operator or operators of any adult home, enriched housing program or residence for adults may at any time request the department of health to appoint a receiver to take over the operation of such facility. Upon receiving such a request, the department of health may, if it deems such action desirable, enter into an agreement with any such operator or operators for the appointment of a receiver to take charge of the facility under whatever conditions as shall be found acceptable by the parties, provided that such agreement shall not exceed a period of sixty days but may be extended for an additional sixty day period upon agreement by the parties.

3.   (a) In the event of a transfer of possession of the premises of such facility from an approved operator to a court appointed receiver in a bankruptcy or mortgage foreclosure proceeding, the department may authorize such court appointed receiver to continue to operate such facility for a temporary period pending the filing and review of an application to the department by such receiver or by another person for an operating certificate provided, however, that such court appointed receiver agrees to operate the facility during such temporary period in accordance with such terms and conditions as may be set by the department, which terms and conditions shall include compliance with all applicable provisions of law and regulations of the department, and which shall include a waiver by the receiver of any assessment of fees against the department, the commissioner and the state. Such application for an operating certificate shall be filed within ninety days after the transfer of possession to the receiver, unless the time for such filing is extended by the department.

(b)   The commissioner may make application to appear and advise the court of any objections he may have to the transfer of possession from the approved operator to any other person including a receiver or of any objections he may have to continuing a receiver or any other person in possession.

(c)   After a receiver obtains such temporary authorization, he may operate such facility only so long as he continues to do so in compliance with the applicable law, regulations of the department, and the terms and conditions for such authorization as set by the department.

4. (a) When the department revokes or temporarily suspends the operating certificate of such facility and the commissioner determines that appointment of a receiver is necessary to protect the health, safety and welfare of the residents of a facility the commissioner may apply to the supreme court in the county where the facility is situated for an order directing the operators, owners and prime lessors, if any, of the premises to show cause why the commissioner, or at the discretion of the commissioner, his designee, should not be appointed receiver to take charge of the facility. Such order to show cause shall be returnable not less than five days after service is completed and shall provide for personal service of a copy thereof and the papers on which it is based on the operators, owners and prime lessors, if any, of the premises. If any such operator, owner or prime lessor cannot with due diligence be served personally within the county where the property is located and within the time fixed in such order, then service may be made on such person by posting a copy thereof in a conspicuous place within the facility in question, and by sending a copy thereof by registered mail, return receipt requested, to such operator, owner or prime lessor at the last address reported to the department, or otherwise known to the department.

(b) On the return of said order to show cause, determination shall have precedence over every other business of the court unless the court shall find that some other pending proceeding, having similar statutory precedence shall have priority. The court may conduct a hearing at which all interested parties shall have the opportunity to present evidence pertaining to the application. If the court shall find that the facts warrant the granting thereof, then the commissioner, or at the discretion of the commissioner, any person designated by the commissioner, shall be appointed receiver to take charge of the facility. Except in the case where the receiver is assuming an existing bona fide arms length lease, the commissioner shall determine a reasonable monthly rental for the facility, based on consideration of all appropriate factors, including the condition of such facility. The rent, either as established by lease or as determined by the commission shall be paid by the receiver to the owners or prime lessors as may be directed by the court for each month that the receivership remains in effect, provided however that nothing contained herein shall be construed to alter or diminish any obligation the operator may have under any currently valid lease.

(c) Any receiver appointed pursuant to this subdivision shall have all of the powers and duties of a receiver appointed in an action to foreclose a mortgage on real property, together with such additional powers and duties as are herein granted and imposed. The receiver shall with all reasonable speed but, in any case, within six months after the date on which the receivership was ordered, unless otherwise extended by the court, provide for the orderly transfer of all residents in the facility to other facilities or make other provisions for their continued safety and care. He shall, during this period, operate the facility in compliance with the applicable law and regulations of the department, and shall have such additional powers, approved by the commissioner, to incur expenses as may be necessary to so operate the facility. The receiver shall not be required to file any bond. He shall collect incoming payments from all sources and apply them to the costs incurred in the performance of his functions as receiver. The receiver shall honor all existing leases, mortgages and chattel mortgages that had previously been undertaken as obligations of the owners or operators of the facility. No security interest in any real or personal property comprising the facility or contained within the facility, or in any fixture of the facility, shall be impaired or diminished in priority by the receiver. The receiver shall compensate the owners of any goods held in inventory for those goods which he uses or causes to be used by reimbursing the costs of such goods, except that no such compensation shall be made for any such goods for which such owners have already been reimbursed.

(d)   (i) The receiver shall be entitled to a fee and reimbursement for expenses as determined by the commissioner, based upon consideration of all appropriate factors relating to the operation of the facility, to be paid as a charge against the operator, not to exceed the fees, commissions and necessary expenses authorized to be paid to receivers in an action to foreclose a mortgage.

(ii)   The receiver shall be liable only in his official capacity for injury to person and property by reason of conditions of the facility in a case where an owner would have been liable; he shall not have any liability in his personal capacity, except for gross negligence and intentional acts.

(iii)   The receiver appointed pursuant to this subdivision may, subject to approval by the commissioner, ratify any collective bargaining agreement in effect between the operator and the employees of a facility, or suspend such collective bargaining agreement, provided however, that he remain liable for payment of wages and salaries at the rates and levels in effect at the time of his appointment.

(iv)   (A) The receiver shall notify the commissioner of any lien or conveyance made in contemplation of receivership with an intent to remove an asset of the facility from the jurisdiction and use of the receiver, or to hinder or delay the receiver in the execution of his duties and responsibilities as receiver; such notice shall be forwarded to the commissioner in a manner to be determined by regulations of the department.

(B)   With respect to any such lien or conveyance, the commissioner shall have available any remedy available to the trustee in a bankruptcy proceeding pursuant to the federal bankruptcy act or remedy available to a creditor in a proceeding pursuant to article ten of the debtor and creditor law and may apply to the court to have such lien or conveyance set aside, or to have the court make any order which the circumstances of the case require.

(e)   (i) The court shall terminate the receivership only under any of the following circumstances:

a.   six months after the date on which it was ordered, except that the court may extend such period for good cause shown;

   b.   when the department grants the facility a new operating certificate; or

   c.   at such time as all of the residents in the facility have been provided alternative modes of care, either in another facility or otherwise; provided, that the residents shall not be removed from the facility unless it is required for the protection of the health, safety or welfare of the residents.

   (ii)   At the time of termination of the receivership, the receiver shall render a full and complete accounting to the court and shall dispose of any profit or surplus money at the direction of the court.

   (f)   (i) Any person who is served a copy of an order of the court appointing the receiver shall, upon being notified of goods supplied by the facility, or services rendered by the facility, to the receiver. A receipt shall be given for each such payment, and copies of all such receipts shall be kept on file by the receiver. The amount so received shall be deposited by the receiver in a special account which shall also be used for all disbursements made by the receiver.

   (ii)   Any person refusing or omitting to make such a payment after such service and notice may be sued therefor by the receiver. Such person shall not in such suit dispute the authority of the receiver to incur or order such expenses, or the right of the receiver to have such payments made to him. The receipt of the receiver for any sum paid to him shall, in all suits and proceedings and for every purpose, be effectual in favor of any person holding the same as actual payment of the amount thereof to the owner or other person or persons who would, but for the provisions of this subdivision, have been entitled to receive the sum so paid. No resident shall be discharged, nor shall any contract or rights be forfeited or impaired, nor any forfeiture or liability be incurred, by reason of any omission to pay any owner, contractor, or other person any sum so paid to the receiver.

   (g)   Any other provision of this chapter notwithstanding, the department may, if it deems appropriate, grant to any facility operating or scheduled to operate under a receivership authorized by this subdivision an operating certificate the duration of which shall be limited to the duration of the receivership.

   (h)   (i) No provision contained herein shall be deemed to relieve the operators, owners or prime lessors, if any, of any civil or criminal liability or obligation incurred, or any duty imposed by law, by reason of acts or omissions of such persons prior to the appointment of any receiver hereunder. During the period a facility is operated by a receiver, the operator, owner or prime lessor, if any, shall continue to be liable for all obligations for the payment of taxes or other operating and maintenance expenses of the facility and the owner or other appropriate person shall continue to be liable for the payment of mortgages or liens.

   (ii)   Expenses incurred by a receiver to meet the operating and maintenance expenses of the facility and the basic needs of the residents of the facility shall be deemed the obligation of the operator, and not the obligation of the receiver or the state.

(iii)   The receiver shall not be responsible for any obligations incurred by the owner, operator or prime lessor, if any, prior to the appointment of the receiver.

(iv)   The receiver shall be entitled to use for operating and maintenance expenses and the basic needs of the residents of the facility a portion of the revenues due the operator during the month in which the receiver is appointed which portion shall be established on the basis of the amounts of the operating and maintenance expenses for such month.

(v)   Any sums determined to be due and owing by the receiver to the owner, operator or prime lessor shall be off-set by any charges determined to be the obligations of the owner, operator or prime lessor.

5.   (a) Subject to paragraph (c) of this subdivision, the commissioner is authorized to make payments to receivers appointed pursuant to the provisions of subdivision three of this section, only if the receiver demonstrates to the satisfaction of the commissioner that the facility's funds which are available are insufficient to meet operating and maintenance expenses of the facility and the basic needs of the residents of the facility.

(b)   The operator of a facility operated by a receiver pursuant to the provisions of subdivision three of this section shall be liable for all monies made available to the receiver pursuant to the provisions of paragraph (a) of this subdivision.

(c)   To the extent funds are appropriated, payments made pursuant to this section shall be made from the local assistance fund and such payments shall be made only if a certificate of allocation and a schedule of amounts to be available therefor shall have been issued by the director of the budget, upon the recommendation of the commissioner of social services, and a copy of such certificate filed with the comptroller, the chairman of the senate finance committee and the chairman of the assembly ways and means committee. Such certificate may be amended from time to time by the director of the budget, upon the recommendation of the commissioner of social services, and a copy of each such amendment shall be filed with the comptroller, the chairman of the senate finance committee and the chairman of the assembly ways and means committee.

(d)   Any payments made by the department to a receiver pursuant to the provisions of this section shall be made without any obligation on the part of the social services district in which the receiver-operated facility is located to reimburse the department for any such payment.

6.   Nothing contained in this section shall be construed to require the commissioner to seek the appointment of a receiver or to assume the responsibilities of a receiver directly or indirectly through his designee; nor shall this section authorize any court to compel the commissioner to assume the responsibilities of a receiver or to appoint a designee to assume such responsibilities.

Added by Laws 1978, Ch. 559, eff. Sept. 1, 1978; amended by Laws 1981, Ch. 610, eff. Aug. 20, 1981; amended by Laws 2004, Ch. 58, Part B, §§ 44, 45, 47, 56 (7–12), eff. Aug 20, 2004.

SSL

§ 461-g.   Termination of admission agreements.

1.   No adult home, residence for adults or enriched housing program which is subject to certification and supervision of the department shall terminate the admission agreement of any resident of such facility and involuntarily discharge him therefrom except for the following reasons:

(a)   the need of the resident for continual medical or nursing care which the adult home, residence for adults or enriched housing program cannot provide;

(b)   behavior of the resident which poses imminent risk of death or imminent risk of serious physical harm to such resident or any other person;

(c)   failure of the resident to make timely payment for all authorized charges, expenses and other assessments, if any, for services including use and occupancy of the premises, materials, equipment and food which the resident has agreed to pay pursuant to the resident's admission and services agreement;

(d)   repeated behavior of the resident which directly impairs the well-being, care or safety of the resident or any other resident or which substantially interferes with the orderly operation of the facility;

(e)   the facility has had its operating certificate limited, revoked or temporarily suspended pursuant to subdivision four of section four hundred sixty-d of this article, or the operator has voluntarily surrendered the operating certificate for the facility to the department; or

(f)   a receiver has been appointed pursuant to the provisions of section four hundred sixty-one-f of this article and, as required by such section, is providing for the orderly transfer of all residents in the facility to other facilities or is making other provisions for the residents' continued safety and care.

2.   (a) No admission agreement shall be terminated and no resident of an adult home, residence for adults or enriched housing program involuntarily discharged for the reasons stated in paragraphs (a), (b), (c), (d) or (e) of subdivision one of this section unless: (i) the operator gives at least thirty days written notice, on a form prescribed by the department, to the resident, the resident's next of kin and the person designated in the admission agreement as the responsible party, if any, that the resident's admission agreement will be terminated and the resident discharged; (ii) such notice contains the reason for the termination of the admission agreement, the date that the discharge will occur, a statement that the resident has a right to object to the termination of the resident's admission agreement and subsequent discharge, and a statement that if the resident does not leave the facility voluntarily, the operator, in order to terminate the admission agreement and discharge the resident, will be required to originate a proceeding pursuant to the provisions of section four hundred sixty-one-h of this article; (iii) the operator furnishes to the resident a list of free legal services agencies within the facility's geographical area and a list of other available community resources which provide resident advocacy services, including the social services district, which lists shall be provided to the operator by the department; and (iv) the

operator institutes a special proceeding in accordance with the provisions of section four hundred sixty-one-h of this article.

(b)   No admission agreement shall be terminated and the resident of an adult home, residence for adults or enriched housing program involuntarily discharged for the reason stated in paragraph (c) of subdivision one of this section, if the reason that the resident failed to pay the authorized charges was an interruption in the receipt by such resident of any public benefits to which such resident is entitled, unless the operator of the facility, during the thirty day notice period provided for in subparagraph (i) of paragraph (a) of this subdivision, as part of the provision of case management services, assists the resident, who shall cooperate with the operator, in attempting to obtain such public benefits or any supplemental public benefits which are available to persons who have not received their regular public benefits.

(c)   The admission agreement of a resident in an enriched housing program may be terminated and the resident discharged pursuant to the provisions of this section and section four hundred sixty-one-h of this article; provided, however, where such resident has an existing lease with the landlord of the premises in which the program is housed, the resident may not be involuntarily removed from the premises pursuant to this section and section four hundred sixty-one-h of this article, except in accordance with the provisions of such lease and applicable law and regulation.

3.   (a) Nothing in this section shall prohibit: (i) the removal of a resident from a facility, for medical treatment or care, to a hospital, nursing home or residential health care facility, as defined in section twenty-eight hundred one of the public health law, or to a hospital as defined in section 1.03 of the mental hygiene law; or (ii) the removal from the facility of a resident whose behavior poses an imminent risk of death or imminent risk of serious physical harm to such resident or any other person, by a peace officer, acting pursuant to his special duties, or a police officer, who is a member of an authorized police department or force or a sheriff's department; or (iii) the removal from the facility of a resident, whose behavior poses an imminent risk of death or imminent risk of serious physical harm, to a location which ensures the resident's safety, pursuant to regulations of the department.

(b)   Such removal shall not be deemed to be a termination of the admission agreement. Such removal shall not relieve the operator of the facility from the requirement of proceeding, subsequent to the removal of the resident, in accordance with this section and section four hundred sixty-one-h of this article in order to terminate the admission agreement to prevent the resident from returning to the facility. When an operator proceeds subsequent to the removal of the resident from the facility, to terminate the admission agreement, the written notice required to be given to the resident by subparagraph (i) of paragraph (a) of subdivision two of this section shall be personally delivered to the resident at the location to which he has been removed. If personal delivery is not possible, then such notice shall be served upon the resident by any of the methods permitted by section three hundred eight of the civil practice law and rules.

Added by Laws 1981, Ch. 983, eff. Oct. 1, 1981; **amended** by Laws 1982, Ch. 628, eff. July 22, 1982; **amended** by Laws 1984, Ch. 626, eff. Nov. 26, 1984.

§ 461-h.   Special proceeding for termination of adult home, residence for adults and enriched housing program admission agreements.

1.   (a) A special proceeding to terminate the admission agreement of a resident of an adult home, residence for adults or enriched housing program and discharge the resident therefrom may be maintained in the county court, the justice court of the village, the town justice court, the court of civil jurisdiction in a city, or the district court which has jurisdiction over proceedings brought pursuant to article seven of the real property actions and proceedings law.

(b)   The place of trial of the special proceeding shall be within the jurisdictional area of the court in which the adult home or residence for adults is situated; except that where the facility is located in an incorporated village which includes parts of two or more towns, the proceeding may be tried by a town justice of any such town who keeps an office in the village.

2.   The proceeding may be brought by the operator of an adult home, residence for adults or enriched housing program.

3.   (a) The special proceeding prescribed by this section shall be commenced by petition and a notice of petition. A notice of petition may be issued only by an attorney, judge or the clerk of the court; it may not be issued by a party prosecuting the proceeding in person.

(b)   The notice of petition shall specify the time and place of the hearing on the petition.

4.   The notice of petition and petition shall be served at least five and not more than twelve days before the time at which the petition is noticed to be heard.

5.   (a) Service of the notice of petition and petition shall be made by personally delivering them to the resident; and at the time of such service, a copy of such notice of petition and petition shall be mailed to the resident's next of kin and to the person designated in the admission agreement as the responsible party, if any, and the department. If service by personal delivery of the notice of petition and petition upon a resident, who has been removed from the facility as permitted by subdivision three of section four hundred sixty-one-g of this article, is not possible, then service upon such resident shall be made by any of the methods permitted by section three hundred eight of the civil practice law and rules.

(b)   The notice of petition and petition together with proof of service thereof on the resident and proof that copies thereof have been mailed to the resident's next of kin and to the person designated in the admission agreement as the responsible party, if any, shall be filed with the court or clerk thereof within three days after delivery to the resident.

(c)   Service shall be complete upon filing proof of service.

6.   The petition shall be verified by the person authorized by subdivision two of this section to maintain the proceeding; or by a legal representative, attorney or agent of such person pursuant to subdivision (d) of section thirty hundred twenty of the civil practice law and rules.

Every petition shall:

(a)   state the interest of the petitioner in the premises from which removal is sought;

(b)   state the resident's interest in the premises and his relationship to petitioner with regard thereto;

(c)   describe the premises from which removal is sought;

(d)   state the facts upon which the special proceeding is based; and

(e)   state the relief sought. The relief may include a judgment for payment of all charges, expenses and other assessments due.

7.   The resident may answer in writing prior to the date the petition is to be heard or orally at the time the petition is heard. The resident may interpose any defense that he may have in his answer.

8.   If the relief sought by the operator includes a judgment for payment of all charges, expenses and other assessments due, then any counterclaims which the resident may have against the operator may be heard in a special proceeding maintained pursuant to the provisions of this section, provided, however, that the court in its discretion may sever such claims and counterclaims from the special proceeding.

9.   Where triable issues of fact are raised, they shall be tried by the court. The court, in its discretion, at the request of one or both of the parties may grant an adjournment for not more than ten days.

10.   (a) The court shall direct that a final judgment be entered determining the rights of the parties with regard to the admission agreement.

(b)   The judgment, including such money as it may award for use and occupancy of the facility or otherwise, may be docketed in such books as the court maintains for recording the steps in a summary proceeding; unless a rule of the court, or the court by order in a given case otherwise provides, such judgment need not be recorded or docketed in the books, if separately maintained in which are docketed money judgments in an action.

11.   (a) Upon rendering a final judgment for petitioner, the court shall issue an order of removal directed to the sheriff of the county or to any constable or marshal of the city in which the facility is situated, or, if it is not situated in a city to any constable of any town in the county, describing the property, and commanding the officer to remove the resident.

SSL

(b)   The officer to whom the order of removal is directed and delivered shall give at least seventy-two hours notice, in writing and in the manner prescribed in this section for the service of a notice of petition, to the person to be removed and shall execute the order between the hours of sunrise and sunset.

12.   (a) If a proceeding is brought by an operator of an adult home, residence for adults or enriched housing program pursuant to the provisions of this section and the reason for the proceeding is that a resident of such a facility has not paid the authorized charges, the court shall stay the issuance of the order of removal for ten days from the date a judgment is rendered. The court, in its discretion, may stay the issuance of an order of removal for up to ninety days if the reason for the termination of the admission agreement and discharge of the resident is that the resident failed to pay the authorized charges and such nonpayment was due to an interruption by a government agency in the delivery to such resident of any public benefits to which such resident is entitled. During the pendency of such stay, the operator of the facility, as part of the provision of case management services shall be required to assist the resident who shall cooperate with the operator, in obtaining any such public benefits or any supplemental public benefits which are available to persons who have not received their regular public benefits.

(b)   If a proceeding is brought by an operator of an adult home, residence for adults or enriched housing program pursuant to the provisions of this section, and the reason for the proceeding is repeated behavior by the resident which directly impairs the well-being, care or safety of the resident or any other resident or which substantially interferes with the orderly operation of the facility, the court, in its discretion, upon application of the resident, may stay the issuance of the order of removal for up to thirty days from the date a judgment is rendered.

(c)   If a proceeding is brought by an operator, administrator or receiver of an adult home, residence for adults or enriched housing program pursuant to the provisions of this section, and the reason for the proceeding is that the facility has had its operating certificate revoked or temporarily suspended pursuant to subdivision four of section four hundred sixty-d of this article, or the operator has voluntarily surrendered the operating certificate for the facility to the department, the court, in its final judgment entered pursuant to subdivision ten of this section, shall not direct the facility to remain open and in operation.

13.   During the pendency of a special proceeding brought pursuant to this section, the operator of an adult home, residence for adults or enriched housing program shall be required to honor all terms of the admission agreement until the resident is removed.

14.   Nothing contained herein shall be deemed to alter or abridge any right of a resident or operator of an adult home, residence for adults or enriched housing program to obtain any relief to which such persons are entitled in any other court of competent jurisdiction.

15.   Notwithstanding the provisions of this article, nothing contained herein shall be construed to create a relationship of landlord and tenant between an

operator of an adult home, residence for adults or enriched housing program and a resident thereof.

16. Notwithstanding any other provision in this section to the contrary, the admission agreement of a resident in an enriched housing program may be terminated and the resident discharged pursuant to the provisions of section four hundred sixty-one-g of this article and pursuant to a special proceeding as set forth in this section; provided, however, where such resident has an existing lease with the landlord of the premises in which the program is housed, the resident may not be involuntarily removed from the premises except in accordance with the provisions of such lease and applicable law and regulation.

Added by Laws 1981, Ch. 983, eff. Oct. 1, 1981; **amended** by Laws 1982, Ch. 628, eff. July 22, 1982; **amended** by Laws 1984, Ch. 626, eff. Nov. 26, 1984; **amended** by Laws 1994, Ch. 563, § 13, eff. July 26, 1994.

§ 461-i. Planning and development grants for enriched housing programs.

1. The department shall, to the extent funds are available for such purpose, award planning and development grants to, and contract with, lawfully approved enriched housing programs that qualify for such grants under criteria to be established by the department. Such grants shall be made for the purposes of defraying start-up expenses and reducing initial operating deficits incurred in the first twelve months of a program's operations resulting from initial low occupancy rates. Use of such funds may include, but shall not be limited to, paying for rent prior to occupancy and security deposits, administrative expenses, minor renovations of existing structures, furnishings and household equipment, moving expenses of residents and reasonable anticipated operating deficits resulting from low initial occupancy rates.

2. Any public agency, public corporation or not-for-profit corporation who has filed an application for approval to operate an enriched housing program, or any lawfully approved enriched housing operator, may make application for a planning and development grant in a manner and form prescribed by the department. The department shall make determinations of award for each application for such grants at such time that a final determination is made with respect to approving the establishment of, or granting an operating certificate for, an enriched housing program. The department shall award planning and development grants on the basis of the quality of the proposed program, the applicant's financial needs, the geographic distribution of enriched housing programs, and the availability of, and demand for, long-term care services in the geographic area to be served by the proposed program.

3. The department may award planning and development grants to, and contract with, lawfully approved enriched housing programs under criteria to be established by the department for the purpose of moderate renovations or modifications of existing structures when determined to be necessary by the

SSL

commissioner. Use of such grants for moderate structural renovations or modifications shall be deemed necessary in those instances where the commissioner determines that, without such renovations or modifications, a geographic area may be underserved because of the lack of available or suitable existing structures.

Added by Laws 1984, Ch. 626, eff. Nov. 26, 1984.

§ 461-j. Family type homes for adults; special needs funds.

1. The commissioner shall establish a procedure whereby payments shall be made to duly certified operators of family type homes for adults for the purpose of meeting one or more of certain special needs of persons residing in such facilities and properly receiving or eligible to receive supplemental security income, additional state payments or safety net assistance benefits, as follows:

(a) Payments to be used for necessary clothing, recreation, transportation and cultural activities of specified individual residents shall not exceed two hundred ninety dollars per resident per year.

(b) Payments to be used for provision of substitute care to residents during periods of emergency and scheduled absence of operators, including periods of operator absence for the purposes of education and training, shall not exceed five hundred dollars per facility per year.

2. Social services districts shall establish a separate account for special needs funds and shall administer payments to operators out of said account, in accordance with regulations which shall be promulgated by the department. The department shall pay district costs out of available appropriations for such purposes, to the extent of one hundred percent of the amount expended pursuant to subdivision one of this section, in accordance with the provisions of section one hundred fifty-three of this chapter. In addition, the department shall, in accordance with the provisions of section one hundred fifty-three of this chapter, reimburse one hundred percent of amounts expended by each district for administration under this section only to the extent of ten percent of the amount paid by such district pursuant to subdivision one of this section, and shall thereafter reimburse fifty percent of any additional amounts paid by such district for such administrative costs. The department may make advances to districts which shall then advance such funds to duly certified operators, to the extent provided for by department regulations, in anticipation of costs incurred in meeting the special needs as set forth in subdivision one of this section and related administrative costs in accordance with the procedure established by the commissioner. Nothing contained in this section shall be construed to require expenditures by any district pursuant to subdivision one of this section, in excess of the amounts made available to the district by the department pursuant to this section.

3. Notwithstanding any other provision of law, state reimbursement to districts may be made only from and to the extent of moneys appropriated to the department for such purposes.

4.   The department shall audit payments and maintenance of accounts in accordance with department regulations. The commissioner shall promulgate regulations to carry out the purposes of this section.

Added by Laws 1985, Ch. 40, eff. Oct. 1, 1985; **amended** by Laws 1987, Ch. 759, eff. Oct. 1, 1987; **amended** by Laws 1997, Ch. 436, § 1 Part B, § 103, eff. Aug. 20, 1997.

§ 461-k.   Services for non-residents in certain adult care facilities.
[*Effective until July 1, 2005, pursuant to Laws 2002, Ch. 121 § 1, as amended.*]

1.   (a) "Services for nonresidents in adult homes, residences for adults and enriched housing programs" shall mean an organized program of services which the facility is authorized to provide to residents of such facility but which are provided to nonresidents for the purpose of restoring, maintaining or developing the capacity of aged or disabled persons to remain in or return to the community. Such services may include but shall not be limited to day programs and temporary residential care as defined herein. A person participating in a program of services for nonresidents in an adult care facility shall be considered a resident of the facility and shall be afforded all the rights and protections afforded residents of the facility under this chapter except that the provisions of sections four hundred sixty-one-g and four hundred sixty-one-h of this title relating to termination of admission agreements shall not apply and that persons receiving services pursuant to this section shall not be considered to be receiving residential care as defined in section two hundred nine of this chapter for purposes of determining eligibility for and the amount of supplemental security income benefits and additional state payments.

(b)   "Day programs" shall mean an organized program for nonresidents which shall include personal care, supervision and other adult services which the facility is authorized to provide to residents of such facility which may include, but are not limited to, activities, meals, information and referral, and transportation services, provided in an adult home, residence for adults or enriched housing program.

(c)   "Temporary residential care" shall mean the provision of temporary residential care of frail or disabled adults on behalf of or in the absence of the caregiver for up to six weeks in any twelve month period, provided in an adult home, residence for adults or enriched housing program.

2.   A program to provide services for nonresidents in an adult care facility may be established and operated in an adult home, residence for adults or enriched housing program provided that such facility has a current operating certificate issued in accordance with section four hundred sixty-one-b of this title. No operator may establish and operate a program to provide services for nonresidents unless the operator has received the prior written approval of the department. The department shall grant such approval only to those operators that are operating in compliance with applicable law and regulations.

SSL

3. Every program of services for nonresidents must be established and operated in a manner designed to ensure that such program neither impairs the effective operation of the facility nor lessens the quality of care provided to the facility residents.

4. The department shall promulgate regulations to carry out the purposes of this section, including, but not limited to, provisions regarding certification, inspection, supervision, enforcement, penalties, records and reports, public need, fiscal, administrative, architectural, safety, nutrition, duration of service, program standards, information and referral, admission and discharge standards, written service agreements for day services programs and modified admission agreements for temporary residential care programs and operator responsibility for services and supervision. The department shall have authority to enforce such regulations in the same manner and to the extent it has authority to enforce regulations promulgated pursuant to sections four hundred sixty-a through four hundred sixty-f and sections four hundred sixty-one through four hundred sixty-one-e of this article.

5. The department may waive the determination of public need when an adult care facility is requesting approval to utilize no more than five beds or five percent of its certified capacity, whichever is less, for temporary residential care.

Added by Laws 1986, Ch. 779; Laws 1989, Ch. 19, eff. July 1, 1989; Laws 1991, Ch. 268, eff. July 5, 1991, extends the expiration date until July 1, 1993; Laws 1993, Ch. 190, § 1, eff. July 1, 1993, extends the expiration date until July 1, 1996; Laws 1996, Ch. 218, eff. June 25, 1996, extends the expiration date until July 1, 1999; **amended** by Laws 1999, Ch. 124, § 1, eff. June 29, 1999, extends the effective date until July 1, 2002; **amended** by Laws 2002, Ch. 121, § 1, eff. June 28, 2002, extending expiration date to July 1, 2005.

§ 461-l Assisted living program

1. Definitions. As used in this section, the following words shall have the following meanings:

(a) "Assisted living program" means an entity or entities with identical ownership, which are approved to operate pursuant to subdivision three of this section and possesses a valid operating certificate as an adult care facility, other than a shelter for adults, a residence for adults or a family type home for adults, issued pursuant to this article and which possesses either: (i) a valid license as a home care services agency issued pursuant to section thirty-six hundred five of the public health law; or (ii) a valid certificate of approval as a certified home health agency issued pursuant to section thirty-six hundred six of the public health law; or (iii) valid authorization as a long term home health care program issued pursuant to section thirty-six hundred ten of the public health law.

(b) "Capitated rate of payment" means the rate established pursuant to subdivision six of section thirty-six hundred fourteen of the public health law.

(c) "Eligible applicant" means:

(i)   A single entity that is:

(A)   only a natural person or partnership composed only of natural persons, a not-for-profit corporation, a public corporation, a business corporation other than a corporation whose shares are traded on a national securities exchange or are regularly quoted on a national over-the-counter market or a subsidiary of such a corporation or a corporation any of the stock of which is owned by another corporation, a limited liability company provided that if a limited liability company has a member that is a corporation, a limited liability company or a partnership, the shareholders of the member corporation, the members of the member limited liability company, or the partners of the member partnership must be natural persons, a social services district or other governmental agency which possesses or is eligible pursuant to this article to apply for an adult care facility operating certificate; and

(B)   either: (1) an entity which possesses or is eligible pursuant to article thirty-six of the public health law to apply for licensure as a home care services agency; (2) an entity which possesses valid authorization as a long term home health care program; or (3) an entity which possesses a valid certificate of approval as a certified home health agency pursuant to article thirty-six of the public health law; or

(ii)   One or more entities listed in subparagraph (i) of this paragraph with identical owners that, in combination, meet each of the criteria set forth by subparagraph (i) of this paragraph.

(d)   "Eligible person" means a person who:

(i)   requires more care and services to meet his or her daily health or functional needs than can be directly provided by an adult care facility and although medically eligible for placement in a residential health care facility, can be appropriately cared for in an assisted living program and who would otherwise require placement in a residential health care facility due to factors which may include but need not be limited to the lack of a home or a home environment in which to live and receive services safely; and

(ii)   is categorized by the long-term care patient classification system as defined in regulations of the department of health as a person who has a stable medical condition and who is able, with direction, to take action sufficient to assure self-preservation in an emergency. In no event shall an eligible person include anyone in need of continual nursing or medical care, a person who is chronically bedfast or chairfast, or anyone who is cognitively, physically or medically impaired to such a degree that his or her safety would be endangered.

(e)   "Services" shall mean all services for which full payment to an assisted living program is included in the capitated rate of payment, which shall include personal care services, home care services and such other services as the commissioner in conjunction with the commissioner of health determine by regulation must be included in the capitated rate of payment, and which the assisted living program shall provide, or arrange for the provision of, through contracts with a social services district, a long term home health care program or a certified home health agency, and other qualified providers.

2. General requirements.

(a) Applicability. Unless expressly provided otherwise in this article or article thirty-six of the public health law, an assisted living program shall be subject to any other law, rule or regulation governing adult care facilities, long term home health care programs, certified home health agencies, licensed home care agencies or personal care services.

(b) If an assisted living program itself is not a certified home health agency or long term home health care program, the assisted living program shall contract with a certified home health agency or long term home health care program for the provision of services pursuant to article thirty-six of the public health law. An assisted living program shall contract with no more than one certified home health agency or long term home health care program, provided, however, that the commissioner and the commissioner of health may approve additional contracts for good cause.

(c) Participation by eligible persons. Participation in an assisted living program by an eligible person shall be voluntary and eligible persons shall be provided with sufficient information regarding the program to make an informed choice concerning participation.

(d) Patient services and care.

(i) An assisted living program, or if the assisted living program itself does not include a long term home health care program or certified home health agency an assisted living program and a long term home health care program or certified home health agency, shall conduct an initial assessment to determine whether a person would otherwise require placement in a residential health care facility if not for the availability of the assisted living program and is appropriate for admission to an assisted living program. The assisted living program shall forward such assessment of a medical assistance applicant or recipient to the appropriate social services district.

(ii) No person shall be determined eligible for and admitted to an assisted living program unless the assisted living program and the long term home health care program or the certified home health care agency agree, based on the initial assessment, that the person meets the criteria provided in paragraph (d) of subdivision one of this section and unless the appropriate social services district prior authorizes payment for services.

(iii) Appropriate services shall be provided to an eligible person only in accordance with a plan of care which is based upon an initial assessment and periodic reassessments conducted by an assisted living program, or if the assisted living program itself does not include a long term home health care program or certified home health agency an assisted living program and a long term home health care program or certified home health agency. A reassessment shall be conducted as frequently as is required to respond to changes in the resident's condition and ensure immediate access to necessary and appropriate services by the resident, but in no event less frequently than once every six months. No person shall be admitted to or retained in an assisted living program unless the assisted living program, and long term home health care program or certified home health agency are in agreement that the person can be safely and adequately cared for with the provision of services determined by such assessment or reassessment.

(iv) To the maximum extent possible and consistent with staffing standards, assisted living programs shall achieve economic efficiencies through the provision of shared services including, but not limited to, shared aides.

3. Assisted living program approval.

(a) An eligible applicant proposing to operate an assisted living program shall submit an application to the department. Upon receipt, the department shall transmit a copy of the application and accompanying documents to the department of health. Such application shall be in a format and a quantity determined by the department and shall include, but not be limited to:

(i) a copy of or an application for an adult care facility operating certificate;

(ii) a copy of or an application for a home care services agency license or a copy of a certificate for a certified home health agency or authorization as a long term home health care program;

(iii) a copy of a proposed contract with a social services district or in a social services district with a population of one million or more, a copy of a proposed contract with the social services district or the department;

(iv) if the applicant is not a long term home health care program or certified home health agency, a copy of a proposed contract with a long term home health care program or certified home health agency for the provisions of services in accordance with article thirty-six of the public health law; and

(v) a detailed description of the proposed program including budget, staffing and services.

(b) If the application for the proposed program includes an application for licensure as a home care service agency, the department of health shall forward the application for the proposed program and accompanying documents to the public health council for its written approval in accordance with the provisions of section thirty-six hundred five of the public health law.

(c) An application for an assisted living program shall not be approved unless the commissioner is satisfied as to:

(i) the character, competence and standing in the community of the operator of the adult care facility;

(ii) the financial responsibility of the operator of the adult care facility;

(iii) that the buildings, equipment, staff, standards of care and records of the adult care facility to be employed in the operation comply with applicable law, rule and regulation;

SSL

(iv) the commissioner of health is satisfied that the licensed home care agency has received the written approval of the public health council as required by paragraph (b) of this subdivision and the equipment, personnel, rules, standards of care, and home care services provided by a licensed home care agency and certified home health agency or long term home health care program are fit and adequate and will be provided in the manner required by article thirty-six of the public health law and the rules and regulations thereunder; and

(v) the commissioner and the commissioner of health are satisfied as to the public need for the assisted living program.

(d) The department shall not approve an application for an assisted living program for any eligible applicant who does not meet the requirements of this article, including but not limited to, an eligible applicant who is already or within the past ten years has been an incorporator, director, sponsor, principal stock-holder, member or owner of any adult care facility which has been issued an operating certificate by the board or the department, or of a halfway house, hostel or other residential facility or institution for the care, custody or treatment of the mentally disabled which is subject to approval by an office of the department of mental hygiene, or of any residential health care facility or home care agency as defined in the public health law, unless the department, in conjunction with the department of health, finds by substantial evidence as to each such applicant that a substantially consistent high level of care has been rendered in each such facility or institution under which such person is or was affiliated. For the purposes of this paragraph, there may be a finding that a substantially consistent high level of care has been rendered despite a record of violations of applicable rules and regulations, if such violations (i) did not threaten to directly affect the health, safety or welfare of any patient or resident, and (ii) were promptly corrected and not recurrent.

(e) The commissioner of health shall provide written notice of approval or disapproval of portions of the proposed application concerning a licensed home care agency, certified home health agency or long term home health care program, and, where applicable, of the approval or disapproval of the public health council to the commissioner. If an application receives all the necessary approvals, the commissioner shall notify the applicant in writing. The commissioner's written approval shall constitute authorization to operate an assisted living program.

(f) No assisted living program may be operated without the written approval of the department, the department of health and, where applicable, the public health council.

(g) [Repealed Sept 1, 2010] Notwithstanding any other provision of law to the contrary, any assisted living program having less than seventy-five authorized bed slots, located in a county with a population of more than one hundred ten thousand and less than one hundred fifty thousand persons and which at any point in time is unable to accommodate individuals awaiting placement into the assisted living program, shall be authorized to increase the number of assisted living beds available for a specified period of time as part of a demonstration program by up to thirty percent of its approved bed level; provided, however, that such program shall otherwise satisfy all other assisted living program requirements as set forth in this section. In addition, any program which receives such authorization and which at any point on or after July first, two thousand five is unable to accommodate individuals awaiting placement into the assisted program, shall be authorized to further increase the number of assisted living beds available as part of this demonstration program by up to twenty-five percent of its bed level as of July first, two thousand five; provided, however, that such program shall otherwise satisfy all other assisted living program requirements as set forth in this section. Further, any such program which receives authorization to increase the number of assisted living beds available pursuant to this paragraph shall submit a report annually to the commissioner of health, the governor, the temporary president of the senate and the speaker of the assembly, which contains the cost of the program, including the savings to state and local governments, the number of persons served by the program by county, a description of the demographic and clinical characteristics of patients served by the program, and an evaluation of the quality of care provided to persons served by the program. After release of the second report by any such program if the findings of the report do not reflect a cost savings to the state and local governments, the program may be terminated immediately by the commissioner of health. Within thirty days of the termination of a demonstration program, the commissioner of health shall submit a report to the governor, the temporary president of the senate and the speaker of the assembly which outlines the reasons for early termination of such program.

4. Revocation, suspension, limitation or annulment. Authorization to operate an assisted living program may be revoked, suspended, limited or annulled by the commissioner in accordance with the provisions of this article if the adult care facility fails to comply with applicable provisions of this chapter or rules or regulations promulgated hereunder or by the commissioner of health in accordance with the provisions of article thirty-six of the public health law if the licensed home care service agency, certified home health agency or long term home health care program fails to comply with the provisions of article thirty-six of the public health law or rules or regulations promulgated thereunder.

5. Rules and regulations. The commissioner and the commissioner of health shall jointly promulgate any rules and regulations necessary to effectuate the provisions and purposes of this section and section thirty-six hundred fourteen of the public health law. Such regulations shall provide that the department and the department of health shall coordinate their surveillance and enforcement efforts, including but not limited to, on-site surveys of assisted living programs.

6. Report. The commissioner and the commissioner of health shall submit a joint report to the governor, the temporary president of the senate, the speaker of the assembly, the state hospital review and planning council and health systems

agencies on or before March first, nineteen hundred ninety-three which shall include a description of the programs, including the number of programs established and authorized by geographic area, the cost of the program, including the savings to state and local governments, the number of persons served by the program by geographic area, a description of the demographic and clinical characteristics of patients served by the program and an evaluation of the quality of care provided to persons served by the program. Such report shall be utilized by the department of health in estimating statewide need for long term care beds for the planning target year next succeeding nineteen hundred ninety-three. In addition, the state hospital review and planning council shall consider the results of such report in approving the methodology for determining statewide need for long term care beds for the planning target year next succeeding nineteen hundred ninety-three.

Added by Laws 1991, Ch. 165, § 33, eff. July 1, 1991; amended by Laws 1994, Ch. 438, § 1, eff. July 20, 1994; amended by Laws 1996, Ch. 543, § 5, eff. Aug. 8, 1996, and further amended by Ch. 462, § 10, eff. Aug. 8, 1996; amended by Laws 1999, Ch. 591, §§ 7 and 8, eff. Nov. 1, 1999; amended by Laws 2000, Ch. 569, § 1, eff. Dec. 8, 2000, amending subd. 2(d); amended by Laws 2003, Ch. 545, §§ 1–2, adding subd. 3(g), eff. Sept. 17, 2003, and shall be deemed repealed September 1, 2007; L. 2005, Ch. 593, sect; 1, eff. Aug. 23, 2005; L. 2005, Ch. 597, sect;§ 1, 2, eff. Aug. 23, 2005.

§ 461-m. Death and felony crime reporting.

The operator of an adult home or residence for adults shall have an affirmative duty to report any death, or attempted suicide of a resident to the department within twenty-four hours of its occurrence, and shall also have an affirmative duty to report to an appropriate law enforcement authority if it is believed that a felony crime may have been committed against a resident of such facility as soon as possible, or in any event within forty-eight hours. In addition, the operator shall send any reports involving a resident who had at any time received services from a mental hygiene service provider to the state commission on quality of care for the mentally disabled.

Added by Laws 1994, Ch. 734, § 2, eff. Aug. 2, 1994; amended by Laws 1996, Ch. 462, § 4, eff. Sept. 7, 1996.

§ 461-n. Facility improvement program.

Repealed by Laws 1994, Ch. 735, § 6, eff. April 1, 1995.

§ 461-o. Complaint investigation procedures.

The department shall establish procedures governing the receipt and investigation of complaints regarding the care afforded to residents of adult care facilities. Such procedures shall assure the confidentiality of the complainant. Such procedures shall include but not be limited to the procedures for reporting complaints, either in writing or orally to the department, and the time frames governing the investigation of any such complaints submitted to the department. Provided however, if any complaint alleges the abuse or neglect of a resident or involves an incident that exposes a resident to cruel or unsafe care or otherwise represents a serious resident care issue, the department shall ensure that an investigation of any such complaint is initiated immediately and in no event commenced less than seventy-two hours from the time such complaint is received by the department. Upon the conclusion of the investigation by the department the operator and the complainant shall be notified in writing of the results of such investigation.

Added by Laws 1996, Ch. 462, § 5, eff. Sept. 7, 1996.

§ 461-p. Adult care facilities training program.

The department may, within the amounts as appropriated for such purpose, establish an adult care facility training program that shall assist in the development of training materials and/or the provision of staff training activities. In developing such training program, the department shall determine the feasibility of providing such training on a statewide basis. The department may contract with organizations representing adult care facilities to provide such training. Such contracts shall require that funding made available through this program shall be used to enhance the skills of staff of adult care facilities and may include, but not be limited to training activities regarding medication management, safety and security procedures, rights of residents, behavioral management techniques, and any other training initiatives identified by the department.

Added by Laws 1996, Ch. 462, § 6, eff. Sept. 7, 1996.

§ 461-q. Temperature standards in adult homes, enriched housing programs and residences for adults.

The commissioner of health shall promulgate rules and regulations with respect to an allowable temperature in all areas occupied by residents of an adult home, enriched housing program and residence for adults, including any areas intended for use by its residents in common including auditoriums, meeting rooms and cafeterias. One common room in such adult home, enriched housing program and residence for adults shall be required to be air conditioned.

Added by Laws 2004, Ch. 58, Part B, §§ 46, 56, (7–12), eff. Aug 20, 2004.

TITLE 3—RESIDENTIAL PROGRAMS FOR CHILDREN

SSL

462-b.　Responsibility for enforcement.

§ 462.　Responsibility for standards.

1.　(a) The department of social services shall promulgate regulations concerning standards of care and treatment and fiscal, administrative, nutritional, architectural and safety standards, consistent with the provisions of section three hundred ninety-eight-a of this chapter, which shall apply to all facilities exercising care or custody of children or providing care or shelter to unmarried mothers.

(b)　With respect to facilities exercising care or custody of children, no license or operating certificate shall be provided or renewed unless it can be demonstrated that such facilities comply with regulations for the prevention and remediation of abuse and maltreatment of children in such facilities, including procedures for:

(i)　consistent with appropriate collective bargaining agreements and applicable provisions of the civil service law, the review and evaluation of the backgrounds of and the information supplied by any person applying to be an employee, a volunteer or consultant, which shall include but not be limited to the following requirements: that the applicant set forth his or her employment history, provide personal and employment references, relevant experiential and educational information and sign a sworn statement indicating whether the applicant, to the best of his or her knowledge, has ever been convicted of a crime in this state or any other jurisdiction;

(ii)　establishing, for employees, relevant minimal experiential and educational qualifications consistent with appropriate collective bargaining agreements and applicable provisions of the civil service law;

(iii)　assuring adequate and appropriate supervision of employees, volunteers and consultants;

(iv)　demonstrating by a residential facility or program that appropriate action is taken to assure the safety of the child who is reported to the state central register of child abuse and maltreatment as well as other children in care, immediately upon notification that a report of child abuse or maltreatment has been made with respect to a child in such facility or program;

(v)　removing a child, consistent as applicable with any court order placing the child, when it is determined that there is risk to such child if he or she continues to remain within a facility or program;

(vi)　appropriate preventive and remedial action to be taken including legal actions, consistent with appropriate collective bargaining agreements and applicable provisions of the civil service law.

(c)　With respect to facilities exercising care or custody of children such standards shall establish as a priority that:

(i)　subject to the amounts appropriated therefor, administrators, employees, volunteers and consultants receive training in at least the following: child abuse prevention and identification, safety and security procedures, the principles of child development, the characteristics of children in care and techniques of group and child management including crisis intervention, the laws, regulations and procedures governing the protection of children from abuse and maltreatment, and other appropriate topics, provided however, that the department may exempt administrators and consultants of such facilities or programs from such requirements upon demonstration of substantially equivalent knowledge or experience; and

(ii) subject to the amounts appropriated therefor, children receive instruction, consistent with their age, needs and circumstances as well as the needs and circumstances within the facility or program, in techniques and procedures which will enable such children to protect themselves from abuse and maltreatment; and

(iii) the department shall take all reasonable and necessary actions to assure that employees, volunteers and consultants in residential care facilities and programs are kept apprised on a current basis of all department policies and procedures relating to the protection of children from abuse and maltreatment, and shall monitor and supervise the provision of training to such administrators, employees, volunteers, children and consultants.

(d) Such regulations shall be developed in consultation with other state departments and agencies responsible for human services programs including, but not limited to, the department of education, the department of health, the department of mental hygiene, the division for youth and the board of social welfare, and shall, to the extent possible, be consistent with those promulgated by other state agencies for such purposes.

(e) This subdivision shall not apply to facilities operated by or certified or licensed to operate by another state agency.

(f) [*Effective April 1, 2005.*] No residential institution for children as defined in subdivision forty-four of section sixteen hundred seventy-six of the public authorities law shall enter into a lease, sub-lease or other agreement with the dormitory authority pursuant to subdivision forty of section sixteen hundred eighty of the public authorities law unless and until:

(i) the office of children and family services, the director of the division of the budget and any other state agency which licenses such residential institutions for children first determines that the project is necessary to address health and safety needs of children at the institution, approve the project cost upon determination that such costs are reasonable, necessary and cost effective based upon the application of cost per square foot guidelines and any other standards applicable to the type of program or to the clinically-required needs of a specialized group of children to be served by the project; and

(ii) the office of children and family services or such other state agency which licenses such residential institution for children approves the plans and specifications of the residential facilities to be replaced, reconstructed, rehabilitated, improved, renovated, or otherwise provided for, furnished or equipped.

SSL

2.   (a) The division for youth shall establish regulations governing secure and nonsecure detention facilities subject to article nineteen-G of the executive law and residential facilities operated as approved runaway programs or transitional independent living support programs pursuant to article nineteen-H of the executive law.

(b)   The appropriate offices of the state department of mental hygiene shall establish regulations governing all child care facilities subject to articles twenty-three, thirty-one and thirty-two of the mental hygiene law.

(c)   The department of mental hygiene and the division for youth shall propose any additional standards as are deemed necessary to adequately ensure the care of children in facilities subject to the inspection and supervision of the department, which care for a significant number of mentally disabled children, juvenile delinquents or persons in need of supervision. The final form of any such additional standards shall be subject to the approval of the department of mental hygiene for such standards related to the care of mentally disabled children, or the division for youth for such standards related to the care of juvenile delinquents and persons in need of supervision.

Amended by Laws 1978, Ch. 555, eff. July 24, 1978; **amended** by Laws 1981, Ch. 169, eff. June 2, 1981, **amended** by Laws 1985, Ch. 677, eff. Apr. 1, 1986, except (a) and (b)(i) and (ii) eff. Jan. 1, 1986; **amended** by Laws 1985, Ch. 800, eff. Aug. 2, 1985; **amended** by Laws 1992, Ch. 32, § 1, eff. Oct. 1, 1992; **amended** by Laws 1999, Ch. 558, § 49, eff. Oct. 5, 1999; **amended** by Laws 2004, Ch. 472, § 6, adding sub. 1, par. (f), eff. April 1, 2005.

§ 462-a.   Responsibility for inspection and supervision.

1.   The division for youth shall inspect and supervise secure and nonsecure detention facilities and those division for youth residential facilities authorized by article nineteen-g of the executive law and those residential facilities operated as approved runaway programs or transitional independent living support programs pursuant to article nineteen-H of the executive law.

2.   The appropriate offices of the state department of mental hygiene shall inspect and supervise those facilities subject to articles twenty-three, thirty-one and thirty-two of the mental hygiene law.

3.   For those facilities which care for a significant number of mentally disabled children, the department shall enter into written cooperative agreements no later than October first, nineteen hundred seventy-seven with the department of mental hygiene for joint inspection and supervision of such facilities, as appropriate.

4.   The department of social services shall inspect and supervise all other child care facilities subject to its regulation.

Amended by Laws 1978, Ch. 555, eff. July 24, 1978; **amended** by Laws 1981, Ch. 169, eff. June 2, 1981; **amended** by Laws 1985, Ch. 800, eff. Aug. 2, 1985; **amended** by Laws 1992, Ch. 163, § 1, eff. June 16, 1992; **amended** by Laws 1992, Ch. 465, § 59, eff. Jan. 13, 1993; **amended** by Laws 1999, Ch. 558, § 50, eff. Oct. 5, 1999.

§ 462-b. Responsibility for enforcement.

1. The division for youth shall exercise the enforcement powers enumerated in section four hundred sixty-d of this article which may apply to secure and nonsecure detention facilities and to those division for youth residential facilities authorized by article nineteen-g of the executive law and those residential facilities operated as approved runaway programs or transitional independent living support programs pursuant to article nineteen-H of the executive law.

2. The appropriate offices of the state department of mental hygiene shall exercise the enforcement powers enumerated in section four hundred sixty-d of this article which may apply to those facilities subject to articles twenty-three, thirty-one and thirty-two of the mental hygiene law.

3. With respect to facilities which care for a significant number of mentally disabled children, the department shall enter into written cooperative agreements no later than October first, nineteen hundred seventy-seven with the department of mental hygiene establishing circumstances under which the department will at the request of the department of mental hygiene act to limit or modify the operating certificate of any facility so as to preclude such facility from accepting, caring for or continuing to care for mentally disabled children.

4. The department of social services shall exercise the enforcement powers enumerated in section four hundred sixty-d of this article with respect to all other child caring facilities subject to its regulation either independently or at the request of the department of mental hygiene or the division for youth.

Amended by Laws 1978, Ch. 555, eff. July 24, 1978; **amended** by Laws 1981, Ch. 169, eff. June 2, 1981; **amended** by Laws 1985, Ch. 800, eff. Aug. 2, 1985; **amended** by Laws 1992, Ch. 163, § 2, eff. June 16, 1992; **amended** by Laws 1992, Ch. 465, § 60, eff. Jan. 13, 1993; **amended** by Laws 1999, Ch. 558, § 51, eff. Oct. 5, 1999.

SSL

TITLE 4—REGISTRY OF COMMUNITY RESIDENTIAL FACILITIES

---

§ 463. Definitions.

For the purposes of this title, the following definitions shall apply:

1. "Community residential facility" means any facility operated or subject to licensure by the state which provides a supervised residence for mentally, emotionally, physically, or socially disabled persons or for persons in need of supervision or juvenile delinquents. This term includes, but is not limited to, community residences for the mentally disabled operated or licensed by the offices of mental health or mental retardation and developmental disabilities or by the divisions of the office of alcoholism and substance abuse, agency operated boarding homes, group homes or private proprietary homes for adults operated or licensed by the department of social services, group homes operated by, contracted for or licensed by the division for youth and half-way houses operated or licensed by the division of substance abuse services.

2. "Sponsoring agency" means an agency or unit of government, a voluntary agency as defined in the mental hygiene law or other organization which intends to establish or operate a community residential facility.

3. "Licensing authority" means the head of the state agency responsible for issuance of a license or operating certificate to a proposed community residential facility.

Amended by Laws 1992, Ch. 465, § 61, eff. Jan. 13, 1993.

§ 463-a. Statewide registry.

1. There shall be established in the department a statewide registry on community residential facilities. The department shall develop, in cooperation with the state agencies responsible for the planning, administration, licensing, regulation and operation of community residential facilities, a uniform data base for a statewide registry to include, but not be limited to, the following information:

(a) the nature or type of such community residence for the disabled including the class of disabled persons it is intended to serve;

(b) the title of the sponsoring agency responsible for the operation of such community residence;

(c) the geographical area in which such community residence is located, including but not limited to street address, municipality, local school district and health systems agency;

(d) the number of clients or residents authorized to live within such community residences; and

(e) the licensing authority of such community residence.

2. (a) The department shall, no later than December fifteenth, nineteen hundred eighty-three and annually thereafter, prepare a report to the governor and the legislature including the following information:

(i) a registry of all community residences presently operating in this state including the types of services provided, the number of persons served, the number of persons authorized to reside therein, the licensing authority by which it is governed and the municipality in which it is located; and

(ii) the number of persons in the state presently receiving placement in a community residence including the general type of services being provided and the municipality in which they are provided.

(b) The department shall prepare for inclusion in the annual report required by subdivision (d) of section seventeen of this chapter to be filed with the governor and the legislature prior to December fifteenth of each year an analysis of the information as previously described in paragraph (a) of this subdivision so as to improve the ability of such state agencies responsible for the planning, administration, licensing, regulation and operation of such community residences to effectively identify existing and future needs for persons and services in different areas and coordinate their planning efforts to meet such needs.

3. The department shall provide or cause to be provided technical assistance, within available resources, to municipalities which intend to establish similar coordinated planning functions as described in this act.

§ 463-b. Powers and duties.

The department shall have the following powers and duties:

(a) to request and receive appropriate information as required by the provisions of this title from state agencies responsible for the planning, administration, licensing, regulation or operation of community residential facilities, including a list of all community residences heretofore or hereafter established by such agency or pursuant to a license or operating certificate issued by such agency;

(b) to compile and index such information received from state agencies responsible for the planning, administration, licensing, regulation or operation of community residential facilities in order to establish a comprehensive registry of such residences within the state of New York;

(c) to provide access to such registry to such state agencies and sponsoring agencies responsible for the planning, administration, licensing, regulation or operation of community residential facilities so as to coordinate and integrate planning among such state agencies;

(d) to make available to municipalities a listing of such community residential facilities located within their jurisdiction or within an adjoining municipality in order to facilitate proper local planning efforts for the development of such community residential facilities; and

(e) to promulgate such regulations as may be necessary to protect information required to be kept confidential pursuant to law and to prevent the dissemination of any personally identifiable information of residents or clients of such community residential facilities.

SSL

ARTICLE 8

NEW YORK STATE RURAL HUMAN SERVICES NETWORKING PROGRAM

§ 464.   Short title.

This article may be cited as the "rural human services networking program."

Added by Laws 1989, Ch. 737, eff. July 24, 1989, providing that Article 8 would expire and be deemed repealed on July 24, 1994; **amended** by Laws 1994, Ch. 657, § 1, eff. Aug. 2, 1994, extending the period that Article 8 remains effective to July 24, 1996; **amended** by Laws 1996, Ch. 236, eff. June 26, 1996, deleting the expiration date for Article 8.

§ 464-a.   Legislative findings.

The legislature hereby finds, determines, and declares that:

1. In rural areas there is a necessity to promote different approaches to human services delivery if programs are to properly address diverse community and individual needs and such unique rural conditions as low population density; a large proportion of elderly persons; the absence of economies of scale; geographic isolation; inadequate transportation; fluctuating service demands; and general lack of suitable alternatives for service delivery.

2. The human services delivery system in rural areas is often fragmented, consisting of isolated providers with limited financial resources and limited information-sharing networks. Many such providers are currently providing identical or similar services to the same clientele in the same area, often without being aware of a possible duplication of effort.

3. A full range of coordinated and integrated human services is vital to the health and well-being of residents of rural areas of the state who are or may in

the future be confronted with such intense social problems as domestic violence, teenage pregnancy, migrant health problems, nutritional deficiencies, suicide, hunger, unemployment, lack of suitable shelter, crime, drug and alcohol abuse and poverty.

4.　A proper response to intense social problems in some rural areas would be to encourage greater sharing of information and resources among human services providers in such rural areas, thereby enhancing the cost-effectiveness and delivery of services required to address such social problems. Such cooperative undertakings could be accomplished if a program of financial incentives and state-level technical assistance were made available to encourage providers in rural areas to embark upon such cooperative arrangements and networking of the services they provide.

　　Added by Laws 1989, Ch. 737, eff. July 24, 1989.

§ 464-b.　Definitions.

For the purposes of this article:

1.　"Rural area" shall mean a rural area as defined in section two thousand nine hundred fifty-one of the public health law.

2.　"Advisory committee" shall mean the committee created in accordance with section four hundred sixty-four-c of this article, for the purposes of assisting the commissioner in administering the New York State rural human services networking program created pursuant to the provisions of this article.

3.　"Human service" shall mean any service provided to individuals or groups of individuals, for the purpose of improving or enhancing such individuals' health and/or welfare, by addressing social problems including but not limited to: domestic violence, teenage pregnancy, migrant health problems, child abuse, nutritional deficiencies, suicide, hunger, unemployment, lack of suitable shelter, crime, drug and alcohol abuse and poverty.

4.　"Human services provider" shall mean any public or not-for-profit private entity utilizing public and/or private funds to provide or contract for the provision of human services for the benefit of the general public or specific client groups.

　　Added by Laws 1989, Ch. 737, eff. July 24, 1989; amended by Laws 1990, Ch. 518, § 1, eff. July 18, 1990.

§ 464-c.　Advisory committee created.

1.　An advisory committee shall be created to assist the commissioner in carrying out the provisions of this article. Such advisory committee shall consist of seven members, with the commissioner or his or her designee serving as chairperson. Membership of the committee shall include the following persons or their designees: the chairperson of the legislative commission on the development of rural resources which was created by chapter four hundred twenty-eight of the laws of nineteen hundred eighty-two; the director of the state office of rural affairs; the director of the office for the aging; the commissioner of the department of health; the commissioner of the division for youth; and the commissioner of the office of mental health. The chairperson of the advisory committee may invite the commissioner or director, or his or her designee, of any other state agency or department, or any other rural human services provider or consumer, to serve as an ex-officio member of the committee. The commissioner shall take actions to promote the efficient and effective operation of the advisory committee.

2.   The advisory committee shall:

a.   Review and recommend to the commissioner guidelines for the operation of the rural human services networking program;

b.   Recommend any changes in statutes or regulations necessary to accomplish the purposes of this article;

c.   Assist the department in the evaluation of individual pilot projects and of the rural human services networking program;

d.   Assist in the development of interim and final reports, in accordance with section four hundred sixty-four-e of this article; and

e.   Assist the commissioner in determining those rural areas to receive priority consideration in selecting pilot project sites, pursuant to subdivision four of section four hundred sixty-four-d of this article.

Added by Laws 1989, Ch. 737, eff. July 24, 1989.

§ 464-d.   Program established.

1.   The commissioner is authorized to establish within the department a rural human services networking program, for the purpose of assisting human services providers in rural areas who seek to participate in the program as hereinafter provided, to develop pilot projects to address intense social problems through the creation of contracts or joint or cooperative agreements. Such pilot projects shall capitalize on the strength of existing providers by promoting the sharing of resources and service delivery in rural areas, with the goal of reducing total cost to both consumers and providers while increasing the availability and accessibility of human services in such areas. Pilot projects shall also serve to identify methods of overcoming impediments to the joint provision of integrated and cost-effective human services in rural areas.

2.   Within one hundred twenty days after the effective date of this article, the commissioner, with the advice and guidance of the advisory committee, shall establish and give public notice of the existence of the rural human services networking program, and the availability of competitive grants to human services providers interested in undertaking pilot projects pursuant to the provisions of this article. At that time the commissioner shall also distribute information on

such program, and application forms and procedures to eligible human services providers.

3.   In order to implement the rural human services networking program the commissioner shall, within the amounts appropriated therefor, provide grants to eligible applicants on a competitive basis. No grant for a pilot project shall be awarded by the commissioner unless the application for such grant has been reviewed by state agencies which license or certify the applicant agencies and any comments on such proposals are considered by the commissioner. To be eligible for a grant under this article, each application shall be submitted pursuant to a contract or joint or cooperative agreement on behalf of two or more local or regional human services providers intending to implement a pilot project in a rural area. Applications shall be submitted to the commissioner on such forms and at such times as the commissioner shall prescribe, and completed applications shall be approved or disapproved within ninety days of submission. In the event the commissioner determines that a grant application is incomplete, or where waivers of any regulations are requested by an applicant, the commissioner shall have an additional ninety days to act upon such application.

4.   In determining whether an application shall be approved and funds awarded pursuant to this article, the commissioner shall give priority consideration to applications received from human services providers intending to implement a pilot project in the most sparsely populated rural areas, as shall be previously determined by the commissioner, in conjunction with the advisory committee. In addition, the commissioner shall consider, but such consideration shall not be limited to, the following:

a.   The specific objectives and description of the proposed pilot project, including demonstrated awareness of the level of human services currently being provided within the service area;

b.   The degree to which the proposed pilot project would meet local or regional human services needs;

c.   The demonstrated ability of the applicants to undertake the pilot project;

d.   The contribution the project would make toward the identification and development of innovative delivery systems;

e.   The degree to which the proposal would enhance the delivery or improve the availability and accessibility of services with respect to the full continuum of human services needs;

f.   The degree to which continuity of care would be fostered and improved;

g.   The degree to which the proposal would enhance cost efficiency and access to human services by populations in need of such services;

h.   The degree to which information sharing, communication, and cooperation between providers and consumers would be fostered;

i.   The degree to which economies of scale in both the supply and demand of services would be addressed;

SSL

j.   The demonstrated level of commitment and support for the project expressed by the community, local government body or bodies, and other local or regional human services providers;

k.   The impact the proposed pilot project will have on state agencies providing services or funds for human services programs in the area, as determined by the commissioner after consulting with such agencies;

l.   The consistency of the proposed pilot project with the provisions of article forty-one of the mental hygiene law; and

m.   Any potential loss of funds or state or federal aid to which providers may now be entitled, including but not limited to Medicaid funds, and the actions to be taken by the applicant and by the commissioner to ensure the continuation of the same amount of funds or aid.

5.   The commissioner or his or her duly authorized representative may meet with representatives of the applicants for the informal discussion of preliminary and informal plans for a proposed project and may provide such technical assistance as may be requested to implement an approved project.

6.   Pilot projects shall be approved for a time period not to exceed three years. Within the amounts appropriated therefor, the commissioner shall approve pilot project grant awards of not less than ten thousand dollars nor more than fifty thousand dollars per pilot project in any one calendar year. Such grants may be renewed annually for up to three consecutive years, subject to the availability of funds. Funds awarded to each recipient in the second and third years may be the same amount as the grant received in the first year, or may be a lesser amount, with the amounts of such awards determined in accordance with the nature of the approved pilot project, the number of delivery and consumer agencies, and the number of clients to be served. If the commissioner determines that a grant is being used for purposes other than those which are in conformity with this article, the commissioner may withdraw approval of the project and require repayment of all or part of such grant to the state. The commissioner shall cause reports to be prepared and submitted for each project by the grantees at such times and in such manner as are consistent with the purposes of this article.

7.   For the purpose of promoting innovative approaches and maximum effectiveness in the utilization of state and local monies, and notwithstanding any other provisions of law, the commissioner may waive any departmental regulations that may impede the successful implementation and testing of a pilot project, provided that there is a finding by the commissioner that the general welfare of the people receiving human services will not be impaired. In addition, the commissioner shall consult with federal, state, and local officials with respect to securing their cooperation in coordinating related programs and in seeking necessary regulatory waivers, in order to assure the effective operation of any pilot project. Notwithstanding any other provisions of law, at the request of the commissioner, on behalf of an applicant, the commissioner or director of any other state agency or department shall be authorized to waive any applicable regulations of such

agency or department that may impede the successful implementation of a pilot project, provided there is a finding that the general welfare of the people receiving human services will not be impaired.

8.   Upon the request of an applicant, the commissioner or his or her duly authorized representative may render to such applicant such technical services and assistance as the department may possess or as may be available to it in order to enable the applicant to carry out the project and terms of such contract.

   Added by Laws 1989, Ch. 737, eff. July 24, 1989; **amended** by Laws 1990, Ch. 518, §§2, 3, eff. July 18, 1990.

§ 464-e. Distribution of reports.

   The commissioner, in conjunction with the advisory committee, shall prepare an interim report within thirty months after the effective date of this article, which shall include a preliminary review of each pilot project. The commissioner, in conjunction with such committee, shall also prepare a final report within sixty months after the effective date of this article. Such final report shall contain a description of the various human services pilot projects demonstrated and their perceived effect on cost, delivery and accessibility of human services in rural areas. The final report shall describe the effect of each pilot project on existing providers and consumers of such services, as well as the effect on each community served. the same report shall identify laws, rules and regulations, if any, that should be repealed or amended in order to make it possible to properly and efficiently implement such plans or programs in other rural areas of the state. Said interim and final reports shall be distributed to all participants in the program, as well as to the governor and the legislature.

   Added by Laws 1989, Ch. 737, eff. July 24, 1989.

§ 464-f. Funds not to be diminished.

   For the duration of the grant period, no local or regional human services provider shall lose any grants or funds to which it may be entitled if it were to operate separately, solely because it elects to participate in a pilot project program and, notwithstanding any other provision of law to the contrary, such grants or funds shall continue to be allocated in the same manner and in the same amount as if such human services provider was not a participant in such pilot project program.

   Added by Laws 1989, Ch. 737, eff. July 24, 1989.

SSL

ARTICLE 8-A

ADOLESCENT PREGNANCY PREVENTION AND SERVICES ACT OF NINETEEN HUNDRED EIGHTY-FOUR

———

(Repealed and transferred sections noted under appropriate section number of text.)

§ 465. Definitions.

For the purposes of this article the following definitions shall apply:

1. "Council" means those member state agencies of the council on children and families, created pursuant to article ten-C of the social services law.

2. "Eligible adolescent" means a person aged twenty-one or under who is at risk of becoming a parent, is pregnant, or is a parent.

3. "Services for eligible adolescents" means those services, including but not limited to: vocational and educational counseling, job skills training, family life and parenting education, life skills development, coordination, case management, primary preventive health care, family planning, social and recreational programs, child care, outreach and advocacy, follow-up, on service utilization crisis intervention, and efforts to stimulate community interest and involvement.

4. "Community council" means a group of volunteers responsible for the development of the community service project plan which, to the extent possible, represents the needs and values of the community and which includes representatives of the following community groups or organizations: community residents, including youths; local government; the business community; service providers, including agencies providing vocational, housing services, child care agencies serving youth and youth services agencies; charitable organizations; health providers; educational institutions; family planning agencies; and community networks and coalitions.

Added by Laws 1984, Ch. 974, Laws; **amended** by Laws 1990, Ch. 48, eff. Mar. 31, 1990; **amended** by Laws 1994, Ch. 169, §§ 109-110, eff. Apr. 1, 1994; L. 2003, Ch.

62, Part F2, § 11, eff. May 15, 2003, deemed in full force and effect on and after April 1, 2003.

§ 465-a. Administration.

1. The department is authorized to request and receive community service project plans, as defined in section four hundred sixty-five-b of this article. Requests for such plans shall be developed in consultation with the council. Such projects shall be limited to a twelve month duration but may, with the approval of the department, be renewed for additional periods based on demonstrated effectiveness, need, and availability of funds. The department, in consultation with the council, shall offer technical assistance to applicants for and operators of community service projects. Technical assistance shall be provided for, but shall not be limited to, the following activities: development of community service plans, overall program planning, contract development, budgeting, and designing local client-specific data collection systems.

2. The department, in consultation with the council, shall review such community service project plans. The commissioner, within appropriations made therefor, may approve such plans for funding in accordance with the provisions of this article. In approving or disapproving the funding of such plans, the commissioner shall only approve projects which meet the requirements set forth in section four hundred sixty-five-b of this article which demonstrate clear coordinating activities with local social services districts and other available city, school, county, state or federally funded programs and shall give priority to projects which:

(a) stress the development and expansion of primary prevention programs aimed at decreasing the incidence of adolescent pregnancy, and the establishment of a comprehensive and coordinated approach to prevent initial and repeated pregnancy and to deal more effectively with the consequences associated with adolescent parenting;

(b) serve a geographic area where there is a large number of eligible adolescents, or a high rate of adolescent pregnancy;

(c) serve a geographic area where the incidence of infant mortality and the prevalence of low-income families are high and where the availability or accessibility of services for eligible adolescents is low;

(d) utilize existing community resources; and

(e) maximize the use of federal, or other state, private and local resources.

Added by Laws 1984, Ch. 974; **amended** by Laws 1988, Ch. 30, § 1, eff. Mar. 31, 1988; **amended** by Laws 1990, Ch. 48, eff. Mar. 31, 1990.

§ 465-b. Community service project plans.

1. Plans for community service projects may be submitted to the department by not-for-profit agencies or by county or municipal governments, or any subdivision thereof. Such plan shall:

SSL

(a)   include a statement of project goals and objectives and a description of the services to be provided to meet such goals and objectives;

(b)   identify the geographic area to be served, which may include a county, municipality or any subdivision thereof, or a combination of counties, municipalities or subdivisions thereof;

(c)   identify the prevalence and incidence of adolescent pregnancy and parenting and related problems to be addressed by the project in the geographic area; and a description, by number and characteristics, of the project's target population to be served;

(d)   describe the services currently available to serve the eligible adolescents which may help reinforce the goals and objectives of the community service project;

(e)   describe how services for eligible adolescents will be coordinated within such project plans, and efforts to be made to improve client access to such services by improving interagency cooperation and program coordination;

(f)   describe how the project funds received pursuant to this article will be used;

(g)   describe the community's involvement in the project plan, and the involvement of relevant agencies and appropriate groups involved within such project plan;

(h)   describe how the proposed services are relevant to the population being served; and

(i)   describe the method to be used to evaluate and report upon the effectiveness of the community service project funded under the provisions of this article.

2.   The community service project plan shall be developed by the community council which shall direct the activities of the community service project. The community council shall select a lead agency which shall be responsible for the administration of the community service project. The community council shall select and approve the funding of subcontractors pursuant to this article for the purpose of the development of the community service project plan.

Added by Laws 1984, Ch. 974; amended by Laws 1990, Ch. 48, eff. Mar. 31, 1990; amended by Laws 1994, Ch. 169, § 111, eff. Apr. 1, 1994.

§ 465-c.   Use of funds.

1.   Subject to amounts made available therefor, such funds shall be made available for up to seventy-five percent of approved community service project plan expenditures after first deducting therefrom any federal or other state funds received or to be received on account thereof. The remaining twenty-five percent cost of such plan may be met by local governmental or private funds, services or property. The commissioner, within his discretion, may, however, waive the twenty-five percent requirement for the year if he determines that a plan, which

otherwise meets the requirements of this article, is unable to obtain local governmental or private funding, services or property. Any such waiver shall be requested upon submittal of such plan to the commissioner. No more than five percent of the funds approved under this article shall be retained by the department for administrative and evaluation purposes.

2.   Funds granted to not-for-profit corporations or governmental entities pursuant to the adolescent pregnancy prevention and services act shall not be used to supplant other federal, state or local funds.

Added by Laws 1984, Ch. 974; **amended** by Laws 1990, Ch. 48, eff. Mar. 31, 1990.

§ 465-d.   Report.

The department in consultation with the council shall submit a report to the governor and the legislature on or before the first day of January in each year in which contracts under this article are in effect, on the effectiveness of reaching the goals and objectives sought under the provisions of this article. The report shall review all community service projects funded under this article. Commencing January first, nineteen hundred ninety and continuing each January first thereafter in which contracts under this article are in effect, the report shall also include the number of pregnant and parenting adolescents and at-risk youth and families served by project, by age, and by services received, a description of specific indicators of success or achievement obtained by persons served by each project, including the number of such persons who obtained employment, continued in or completed high school or an equivalency program, or completed a job training program, and to the extent possible, the effect of each project on the incidence of adolescent pregnancy and on indicators of risk of adolescent pregnancy within the service delivery area of each project, including a comparison of the total number and rate of pregnancies to persons aged twenty-one and under prior to the start of each project and during the twelve months preceding the due date of the report and the incidence of second pregnancies to adolescent mothers served by each project, the number of pregnant, parenting or at-risk youth who were eligible for, able to receive and benefit from county and state public assistance programs and the results within each community of efforts to increase the overall coordination and effectiveness of services. Community service projects shall provide information to the department necessary to prepare the report.

Added by Laws 1984, Ch. 974; **amended** by Laws 1988, Ch. 30, § 2, eff. Mar. 31, 1988; **amended** by Laws 1990, Ch. 48, eff. Mar. 31, 1990; **amended** by Laws 1994, Ch. 169, § 112, eff. Apr. 1, 1994.

SSL

ARTICLE 8–B

TRANSITIONAL CARE

———

———

§ 466.   Transitional care.

Repealed by Laws 1998, Ch. 405, eff. July 22, 1998, deemed in full force and effect July 1, 1998.

§ 466-a.   Agreements.

The department shall enter into memorandums of understanding with the office of mental health and the office of mental retardation and developmental disabilities. The memorandums with the office of mental retardation and developmental disabilities and the office of mental health shall facilitate access by those offices to child care facilities providing transitional care to young adults as may be necessary for those offices to meet their responsibilities for monitoring the care of the young adults.

Added by Laws 1994, Ch. 600, § 3, eff. Jan. 1, 1995; **amended** by Laws 1998, Ch. 405, § 6, eff. July 22, 1998, deemed in full force and effect July 1, 1998.

§ 466-b.   Care provided by authorized agencies.

An authorized agency as defined in section three hundred seventy-one of this chapter shall also be authorized to provide temporary care for persons over age twenty-one who meet the requirements of section 7.37-A or 13.37-a of the mental hygiene law or on whose behalf temporary payments are being made pursuant to section 7.38 or 13.38 of the mental hygiene law, who were in the care of the authorized agency at the time of their twenty-first birthday, and who have remained continuously in the care of the authorized agency since their twenty-first birthday. Notwithstanding any inconsistent provision of law, in any case where an individual receiving transitional funding is about to be transferred from a child care facility to an adult placement, a transfer plan shall be prepared by the sending facility and forwarded to the receiving facility and the individual, and, unless the individual objects, the parents, guardian or other family members prior to the transfer. The transfer plan shall include any information necessary to facilitate a safe transfer, such as specific problems, schedule for administering medications and behavior unique to the individual.

Added by Laws 1994, Ch. 600, § 3, eff. Jan. 1, 1995; **amended** by Laws 1998, Ch. 405, § 6, eff. July 22, 1998, deemed in full force and effect July 1, 1998.

ARTICLE 9
DISPENSARIES

(Art. 9, §§ 464–471 repealed by Laws 1968, Ch. 384, eff. May 31, 1968.)

Note appended to Ch. 384 provides:

"Article 9 of the Social Services Law which relates to the licensing of dispensaries and the visitation and rule-making powers of the State Board of Social Welfare with relation to dispensaries would be repealed because Chapter 795 of the Laws of 1965 transferred to the State Department of Health the responsibilities of the State Board of Social Welfare in relation thereto."

ARTICLE 9–A

BERKSHIRE INDUSTRIAL FARM

———

TITLE 2—BERKSHIRE INDUSTRIAL FARM

———

(Repealed and transferred sections noted under appropriate section number of text.)

§ **472-a.**   **House of Good Shepherd.**

Repealed by Laws 1976, Ch. 84, eff. Sept. 1, 1976.

§ **472-b.**   **Commitment; certificate; term.**

Repealed by Laws 1976, Ch. 84, eff. Sept. 1, 1976.

§ **472-c.**   **To be kept apart from other inmates.**

Repealed by Laws 1976, Ch. 84, eff. Sept. 1, 1976.

§ **472-d.**   **Right to habeas corpus.**

Repealed by Laws 1976, Ch. 84, eff. Sept. 1, 1976.

§ 472-e. Institution continued; powers.

The body corporate known prior to August twenty-fifth, eighteen hundred and ninety-six, by the name of the "Burnham Industrial Farm," the name of which was, on that day, changed to "Berkshire Industrial Farm," which corporation was continued by the former provisions of this section, taking effect February seventeenth, nineteen hundred and nine, under the name and style of "Burnham Industrial Farm," and thereafter continued as the "Berkshire Industrial Farm" by section three of chapter six hundred nineteen of the laws of nineteen hundred forty, is hereby changed and shall be known as "Berkshire Farm Center and Services for Youth," and by the latter name shall have power to take by gift, lease, purchase, devise or bequest real and personal property and hold the same for the proper uses and purposes of said corporation.

Amended by Laws 1959, Ch. 35, eff. Mar. 1, 1959; Laws 1974, Ch. 132, eff. May 31, 1974.

§ 472-f. Objects of corporation.

The objects of this corporation shall be to receive and take charge of such children as may come legally into its custody and care, and to provide for their support, education and training.

Amended by Laws 1974, Ch. 132, eff. May 31, 1974.

§ 472-g. Board of directors.

The property and concerns of the corporation shall be managed by a board of not over twenty-five and not less than ten directors, who shall receive no compensation. The number of directors to be chosen within the maximum and minimum limit shall be determined in the manner prescribed by the by-laws. At least four in number of the directors shall be elected annually on the first day of May of each year, but they shall hold office until their successors are elected. The board of directors in office on April first, nineteen hundred forty-nine, is continued in office until their successors are chosen.

Amended by Laws 1949, Ch. 646, eff. Apr. 1, 1949; amended by Laws 1959, Ch. 35, § 2, eff. Mar. 1, 1959.

§ 472-h. Election of directors.

On the first day of May in each year at least four in number of the board of directors shall be elected by the corporation in such manner and place as the by-laws shall direct, but if no election is held on any such day the election may be held on any subsequent day, and any vacancies occurring otherwise than by the expiration of a regular term may be filled for the balance of such term in accordance with the by-laws of this corporation by the votes of a majority of the directors then in office.

Amended by Laws 1949, Ch. 646, eff. Apr. 1, 1949.

§ 472-i.   Quorum to do business.

Five members of the board shall be a quorum, provided however in the case where the then current board of directors is more than fifteen members then six members of the board shall be a quorum, and the board may delegate its powers, during the interval between its meetings, to an executive committee of its own members, whose minutes shall be kept as provided by the by-laws, and shall be reported for approval to all stated meetings of the board; but no purchase or conveyance of real estate shall be made unless by the concurrence of a majority of the whole board.

Amended by Laws 1974, Ch. 132, eff. May 31, 1974.

§ 472-j.   Custody of children, how acquired; notice to corporation.

The corporation shall be deemed to have acquired lawful care and custody of any child between the ages of six and eighteen years who shall have been surrendered to it by its parent or guardian; provided that such surrender is evidenced by a writing executed by such parent or guardian setting forth the name and age of the child, the date of surrender, and the term for which such surrender is made, and expressly vesting in the corporation all the powers and control over the child of which such parent or guardian was possessed; provided that no such surrender shall be made except upon five days' previous notice of the intention to make such surrender in writing, by the parent or guardian of the child to the said corporation or its agents.

Amended by Laws 1974, Ch. 132, eff. May 31, 1974.

§ 472-k.   Placement of children in care of corporation; effect of placement.

The family court may commit or place in said corporation, with its consent, any child adjudicated to be a juvenile delinquent or a person in need of supervision. Such commitment or placement in said corporation shall be to the custody and control thereof for the period provided in the order of commitment or placement.

Added by Law 1962, Ch. 689; **amended** by Laws 1974, Ch. 132, eff. May 31, 1974.

§ 472-l.   Transfer of certain children by agencies.

The corporate authorities of any agency now or hereafter having the lawful custody and care of any child not less than six years of age, and not awaiting trial nor under sentence for a term of years for crime, may, with the consent of said corporation, transfer and assign such custody and care to this corporation upon such terms as the directors of such institution and said corporation may agree.

Amended by Laws 1974, Ch. 132, eff. May 31, 1974.

§ 472-m. Power of corporation as to children in its care; corporation to act as guardian.

Said corporation shall have the custody and control of all children surrendered, committed or transferred to it under sections four hundred seventy-two-j to four hundred seventy-two-l, and shall have authority by its officers or agents to restrain and direct them, to assign them to suitable employments, to determine their hours of labor, study and rest, to care for their sustenance and health, and to instruct them in useful knowledge; and shall have power to place such children in suitable homes where they may be adopted into families or taken on trial or for a limited time, or to place such children in group homes or group residences operated by the corporation or by other agencies; or, in its discretion, to return them to their former home or their parents or guardians under the supervision and guidance of the corporation. And said corporation may, with the consent of any other agency authorized by law to take the custody and control of children transfer to such other agency the custody and control of any child whenever such transfer is deemed by said corporation to be necessary and proper for the welfare of such child or for the discipline or protection of other children in its charge, provided that there be first obtained from a judge of a court of record an order of approval of such transfer.

Amended by Laws 1974, Ch. 132, eff. May 31, 1974.

§ 472-n. Statements as to age.

In all cases under this article where children shall come under the care, custody or control of said corporation, the age of such children shall, so far as said corporation is concerned, be prima facie deemed and taken to be correct as stated in the written surrender of the parent or guardian, or the order of placement or commitment by a family court, or in the transfer or placement by any agency at the time of placement, admission or commitment.

Amended by Laws 1974, Ch. 132, eff. May 31, 1974.

§ 472-o. Reports.

The said corporation shall annually, on or before the fifteenth day of January, report to the legislature the number and names of the children in its custody or under its guardianship, their age, residence, occupation, state of education, together with the changes in these particulars during the preceding year; the receipts and expenditures, and the financial condition of the corporation, and an account of its general operations.

Amended by Laws 1974, Ch. 132, eff. May 31, 1974.

§ 472-p.　Property exempt from taxation.

So long as the property of said corporation shall be used for charitable purposes only, such property, both real and personal, shall be exempt from taxation.

§ 472-q.　Powers and liabilities.

Said corporation shall possess the general powers and be subject to the general restrictions and liabilities of incorporated charitable institutions.

ARTICLE 9–B

ADULT PROTECTIVE SERVICES

_____

_____

SUMMARY OF ARTICLE

TITLE 1—PROTECTIVE SERVICES

_____

Section   473.   Protective services.

§ 473.   Protective services.

1.   In addition to services provided by social services officials pursuant to other provisions of this chapter, such officials shall provide protective services in accordance with federal and state regulations to or for individuals without regard to income who, because of mental or physical impairments, are unable to manage their own resources, carry out the activities of daily living, or protect themselves from physical abuse, sexual abuse, emotional abuse, active, passive or self neglect, financial exploitation or other hazardous situations without assistance from others and have no one available who is willing and able to assist them responsibly. Such services shall include:

(a)   receiving and investigating reports of seriously impaired individuals who may be in need of protection;

(b)   arranging for medical and psychiatric services to evaluate and whenever possible to safeguard and improve the circumstances of those with serious impairments;

(c)   arranging, when necessary, for commitment, guardianship, or other protective placement of such individuals either directly or through referral to another appropriate agency, provided, however, that where possible, the least restrictive of these measures shall be employed before more restrictive controls are imposed;

(d) providing services to assist such individuals to move from situations which are, or are likely to become, hazardous to their health and well-being;

(e) co-operating and planning with the courts as necessary on behalf of individuals with serious mental impairments; and

(f) other protective services for adults included in the regulations of the department.

2. (a) In that the effective delivery of protective services for adults requires a network of professional consultants and services providers, local social services districts shall plan with other public, private and voluntary agencies including but not limited to health, mental health, aging, legal and law enforcement agencies, for the purpose of assuring maximum local understanding, coordination and cooperative action in the provision of appropriate services.

(b) Each social services district shall prepare with the approval of the chief executive officer, or the legislative body in those counties without a chief executive officer, after consultation with appropriate public, private and voluntary agencies, a district-wide plan for the provision of adult protective services which shall be a component of the of the district's multi-year consolidated services plan as required in section thirty-four-a of this chapter. This plan shall describe the local implementation of this section including the organization, staffing, mode of operations and financing of the adult protective services as well as the provisions made for purchase of services, inter-agency relations, inter-agency agreements, service referral mechanisms, and locus of responsibility for cases with multi-agency services needs. Commencing the year following preparation of a multi-year consolidated services plan, each local district shall prepare annual implementation reports including information related to its adult protective services plan as required in section thirty-four-a of the social services law.

(c) Each social services district shall submit the adult protective services plan to the department as a component of its multi-year consolidated services plan and subsequent thereto as a component of its annual implementation reports and the department shall review and approve the proposed plan and reports in accordance with the procedures set forth in section thirty-four-a of this chapter.

(i) each local department of social services shall not be required to obtain the approval of the chief executive officer of the county, or of the legislative body in those counties without a chief executive officer, for its adult protective services plan, provided, however that the provisions of paragraph (b) of subdivision three of section thirty-four-a of this title shall be applicable commencing in nineteen hundred eighty-two; and

(ii) any time periods established by, or pursuant to, paragraph (b) of this subdivision for the submission to the commissioner of local adult protective services plan, or for notification by the commissioner to the local social services districts of approval or disapproval of their plans, shall be waived.

3. Any social services official or his designee authorized or required to determine the need for and/or provide or arrange for the provision of protective

services to adults in accordance with the provision of this section, shall have immunity from any civil liability that might otherwise result by reason of providing such services, provided such official or his designee was acting in the discharge of his duties and within the scope of his employment, and that such liability did not result from the willful act or gross negligence of such official or his designee.

4.   For the purpose of developing improved methods for the delivery of protective services for adults, the department with the approval of the director of the budget, shall authorize a maximum of five demonstration projects in selected social services districts. Such projects may serve a social services district, part of a district or more than one district. These demonstration projects shall seek to determine the most effective methods of providing the financial management component of protective services for adults. These methods shall include but not be limited to: having a social services district directly provide financial management services; having a social services district contract with another public and/or private agency for the provision of such services; utilizing relatives and/or friends to provide such services under the direction of a social services district or another public and/or private agency and establishing a separate public office to provide financial management services for indigent persons. The duration of these projects shall not exceed eighteen months. Furthermore, local social services districts shall not be responsible for any part of the cost of these demonstration projects which would not have otherwise accrued in the provision of protective services for adults. The total amount of state funds, available for such financial management services demonstration projects, exclusive of any federal funds shall not exceed three hundred thousand dollars. The commissioner shall require that a final independent evaluation by a not-for-profit corporation be made of the demonstration projects approved and conducted hereunder, and shall provide copies of such report to the governor and the legislature.

5.   Whenever a social services official, or his or her designee authorized or required to determine the need for, or to provide or arrange for the provision of protective services to adults in accordance with the provisions of this title has a reason to believe that a criminal offense has been committed, as defined in the penal law, against a person for whom the need for such services is being determined or to whom such services are being provided or arranged, the social services official or his or her designee must report this information to the appropriate police or sheriff's department and the district attorney's office when such office has requested such information be reported by a social services official or his or her designee.

6.   Definitions. When used in this title unless otherwise expressly stated or unless the context or subject matter requires a different interpretation:

(a)   "physical abuse" means the non-accidental use of force that results in bodily injury, pain or impairment, including but not limited to, being slapped, burned, cut, bruised or improperly physically restrained.

(b) "sexual abuse" means non-consensual sexual contact of any kind, including but not limited to, forcing sexual contact or forcing sex with a third party.

(c) "emotional abuse" means willful infliction of mental or emotional anguish by threat, humiliation, intimidation or other abusive conduct, including but not limited to, frightening or isolating an adult.

(d) "active neglect" means willful failure by the caregiver to fulfill the caretaking functions and responsibilities assumed by the caregiver, including but not limited to, abandonment, willful deprivation of food, water, heat, clean clothing and bedding, eyeglasses or dentures, or health related services.

(e) "passive neglect" means non-willful failure of a caregiver to fulfill caretaking functions and responsibilities assumed by the caregiver, including but not limited to, abandonment or denial of food or health related services because of inadequate caregiver knowledge, infirmity, or disputing the value of prescribed services.

(f) "self neglect" means an adult's inability, due to physical and/or mental impairments to perform tasks essential to caring for oneself, including but not limited to, providing essential food, clothing, shelter and medical care; obtaining goods and services necessary to maintain physical health, mental health, emotional well-being and general safety; or managing financial affairs.

(g) "financial exploitation" means improper use of an adult's funds, property or resources by another individual, including but not limited to, fraud, false pretenses, embezzlement, conspiracy, forgery, falsifying records, coerced property transfers or denial of access to assets.

7. Notwithstanding any other provision of law, for the purposes of this article an Indian tribe that has entered into an agreement with the office of children and family services pursuant to section thirty-nine of this chapter, which includes the provision of adult services by such Indian tribe, shall have the duties, responsibilities and powers of a social services district or a social services official for the purpose of providing adult protective services.

Amended by Laws 1979, Ch. 446, § 1, eff. July 1, 1979; **amended** by Laws 1981, Ch. 681, eff. July 21, 1981 to remain in effect until Sept. 30, 1987, **added** subd. 2(c), **renumbered** from § 131-l to § 473 by Laws 1981, Ch. 991, eff. Oct. 29, 1981; **amended** by Laws 1986, Ch. 846, eff. Aug. 2, 1986; Laws 1989, Ch. 19; Laws 1991, Ch. 37; Laws 1992, Ch. 160, eff. June 16, 1992, which eliminated the expiration date of the 1986 amendment; **amended** by Laws 1987, Ch. 231, eff. July 7, 1987; **amended** by Laws 1995, Ch. 395, §§ 2 -4, eff. Nov. 1, 1995; **amended** by Laws 2004, Ch. 322, § 2, adding sub. 7, eff. Aug. 10, 2004.

SSL

TITLE 2—SHORT-TERM INVOLUNTARY PROTECTIVE SERVICES ORDERS

§ 473-a. **Short-term involuntary protective services orders.**

1. Definitions. When used in this section unless otherwise expressly stated or unless the context or subject matter requires a different interpretation:

(a) "endangered adult" means a person, age eighteen or over who is:

(i) in a situation or condition which poses an imminent risk of death or imminent risk of serious physical harm to him or her, and

(ii) lacking capacity to comprehend the nature and consequences of remaining in that situation or condition, provided that:

a. refusal by the adult to accept protective services shall not in itself be sufficient evidence of such lack of capacity; and

b. mental illness shall not in itself be sufficient evidence of such lack of capacity.

(b) "short-term involuntary protective services" means those services set forth in section four hundred seventy-three of this article which are provided involuntarily pursuant to the procedures established by this title.

(c) "petitioner" means a social services official initiating a proceeding pursuant to this title.

(d) "respondent" means an allegedly endangered adult.

2. Jurisdiction. The supreme court and the county court shall each have jurisdiction over the special proceeding commenced pursuant to the provisions of this title.

3. Venue. A petition for the provision of short-term involuntary protective services shall be made to:

(a) a term of the supreme court:

(i) held in the county in which the allegedly endangered adult resides or is found; or

(ii) held in a county, within the same judicial district, adjacent to the county in which the allegedly endangered adult resides or is found; or

(b) the county court:

(i) in the county in which the allegedly endangered adult resides or is found; or

(ii) in a county adjacent to the county in which the allegedly endangered adult resides or is found.

4. Petition. (a) A special proceeding to obtain an order authorizing the provision of short-term involuntary protective services may only be initiated by a social services official.

(b) The petition shall state, insofar as the facts can be ascertained with reasonable diligence:

(i) the name, age and physical description of the allegedly endangered adult; and

(ii) the address or other location where the allegedly endangered adult can be found.

(c) The petition shall state facts showing:

(i) that the adult who is the subject of this petition is an endangered adult as defined in paragraph (a) of subdivision one of this section;

(ii) the specific short-term involuntary protective services petitioned for, how such services would remedy the situation or condition which poses an imminent risk of death or imminent risk of serious physical harm to the allegedly endangered adult, and why such services are not overbroad as to extent or duration;

(iii) that the short-term involuntary protective services being applied for are necessitated by the situation or condition described in paragraph (a) of subdivision one of this section;

(iv) that other voluntary protective services have been tried and have failed to remedy the situation, and that a future, voluntary, less restrictive alternative would not be appropriate or would not be available;

(v) if a change in the allegedly endangered adult's physical location is being applied for, that remedy of the dangerous situation or condition described in paragraph (a) of subdivision one of this section is not appropriate in existing physical surroundings of the allegedly endangered adult;

(vi) any inconsistency known to petitioner between the proposed short-term involuntary protective services and the allegedly endangered adult's religious belief;

(vii) that if it reasonably appears that the allegedly endangered adult does not understand the English language, that reasonable efforts have been made to communicate with the allegedly endangered adult in a language he or she understands;

(viii) that no prior application has been made for the relief requested or for any similar relief, or if prior application has been made, the determination thereof,

SSL

and the new facts, if any, that were not previously shown which warrant a renewal of the application.

(d) The petition shall be verified. Any allegations which are not based upon personal knowledge shall be supported by affidavits provided by a person or persons having such knowledge. Such affidavits shall be attached to the petition.

5. Commencement of proceedings.

(a) A special proceeding to obtain an order authorizing the provision of short-term involuntary protective services shall be commenced by an order to show cause, the petition and supporting affidavits, if any.

(b) The order to show cause shall set forth:

(i) in bold type, on its face, the following:

WARNING

IF YOU DO NOT APPEAR IN COURT YOUR LIFE AND LIBERTY MAY BE SERIOUSLY AFFECTED. FOR FREE INFORMATION CONCERNING YOUR LEGAL RIGHTS CALL OR VISIT

(ii) the protective services to be provided if the petition is granted;

(iii) the date, place and time of the hearing to determine whether the petition is to be granted;

(iv) that the respondent is entitled to counsel at all stages of the proceeding, that upon granting the order to show cause, the court shall assign counsel to assist the respondent, and that respondent is free at any time to discharge the counsel assigned by the court. The name, address and telephone number of the assigned counsel shall be inserted at the end of the warning referred to in subparagraph (i) of this paragraph;

(v) that if the respondent or retained counsel does not appear at the hearing to determine whether the petition is to be granted, the court will appoint a guardian ad litem;

(vi) that if the respondent discharges the assigned counsel prior to the hearing to determine if the petition is to be granted, such counsel shall report this fact to the court no later than the commencement of the hearing, and shall appear at the hearing, unless otherwise relieved by the court. In the event that neither the respondent nor his retained counsel appears at the hearing the court may appoint the person previously assigned as counsel to act as the guardian ad litem; and

(vii) that a copy of the order to show cause, the petition, and supporting affidavits, if any, shall be served upon the respondent.

(c) Petitioner shall cause the order to show cause, the petition, and supporting affidavits, if any, to be delivered to the counsel assigned by the court.

(d) The order to show cause shall be made returnable within forty-eight hours following its issuance, unless such forty-eight hour period ends on a day in which the court is not in session, in which case the return date shall be the first business day following issuance of the order to show cause.

6. Service. (a) Service of the order to show cause, the petition, and supporting affidavits, if any, shall be made upon the respondent by any of the methods permitted by section three hundred eight of the civil practice law and rules. Notwithstanding any other provision of law to the contrary, Saturday and Sunday service is valid.

(b) The respondent shall be authorized to answer either orally or in writing.

7. Hearing. (a) Upon the return date designated in the order to show cause issued pursuant to subdivision five of this section a hearing shall be held forthwith.

(b) The allegedly endangered adult shall be entitled to be present at the hearing.

(c) Adjournments shall be permitted only for good cause shown. In granting adjournments the court shall consider the need to provide short-term involuntary services expeditiously.

(d) At the conclusion of the hearing the court shall issue for the record a statement of its findings of fact and conclusions of law.

8. Preference. The special proceeding authorized by this title shall have preference over all other causes in all courts of appropriate jurisdiction.

9. Findings. After a hearing, the court must find, in order to authorize the provision of short-term involuntary protective services, that all of the material allegations as specified in paragraph (c) of subdivision four of this section have been admitted or proven by clear and convincing proof.

10. Judgment. (a) The court, upon making the findings required by subdivision nine herein, shall direct the entry of a judgment authorizing the provision of short-term involuntary protective services to an endangered adult.

(b) A judgment authorizing short-term involuntary protective services to be provided to an endangered adult:

(i) shall prescribe those specific protective services, authorized by section four hundred seventy-three of this article, which are to be provided and what person or persons are authorized or ordered to provide them; and

(ii) shall not provide for any forcible entry unless the persons so entering are accompanied by a peace officer, acting pursuant to his special duties, or a police officer, who is a member of an authorized police department or force or of a sheriff's department;

(iii) shall require persons acting under subparagraphs (i) and (ii) of this paragraph to submit a written report to the court within one week following the commencement of the ordered protective services.

(c) The judgment may order any other public or law enforcement official to render such assistance and cooperation as shall be within his legal authority, as may be required to further the objects of this title.

(d)   The judgment shall not order removal to a hospital, as that term is defined in section 1.03 of the mental hygiene law.

(e)   Issuance of the judgment shall not be evidence of the competency or incompetency of the endangered adult.

(f)   No order issued pursuant to this title shall extend for more than seventy-two hours. An original order may be renewed once for up to another seventy-two hour period upon showing by the petitioner to the court that continuation is necessary to remedy the original situation or condition. No further renewals shall be permitted.

(g)   In no event shall the short-term involuntary services authorized to be provided to an endangered adult by the judgment be broader than those which are necessary to remedy the situation or condition which poses an imminent risk of death or imminent risk of serious physical harm to the endangered adult.

(h)   Notice of the judgment rendered by the court shall be given to the respondent personally, or if personal service is not possible in whatever other fashion the court shall prescribe.

11.   Appeals. Appeals arising from the issuance of judgments pursuant to the provisions of this title shall be expedited.

12.   The assigned counsel and the guardian ad litem appointed by the court pursuant to this title shall be reimbursed for their services pursuant to section thirty-five of the judiciary law.

13.   Nothing in this title precludes the simultaneous commencement of a proceeding under this title and a proceeding under section 9.43 of the mental hygiene law, or a proceeding under article seventy-seven or article seventy-eight of such law. A pending proceeding under section 9.43 of the mental hygiene law or under article seventy-seven or article seventy-eight of the mental hygiene law does not preclude commencement of a proceeding under this title.

14.   No existing right or remedy of any character shall be lost, impaired or affected by reason of this title.

Art. 9-B **added** by Laws 1981, Ch. 991, eff. Oct. 29, 1981; **amended** by Laws 1982, Ch. 154, eff. June 1, 1982; **amended** by Laws 1994, Ch. 563, § 14, eff. July 26, 1994.

§ 473-b.   Reporting of endangered adults; persons in need of protective services.

Any person who in good faith believes that a person eighteen years of age or older may be an endangered adult or in need of protective or other services, pursuant to this article, and who, based on such belief either:

(a)   reports or refers such person to the department, office for the aging, or any local social services district office or designated area agency on aging, law enforcement agency, or any other person, agency or organization that such person, in good faith, believes will take appropriate action; or

(b)   testifies in any judicial or administrative proceeding arising from such report or referral shall have immunity from any civil liability that might otherwise result by reason of the act of making such report or referral or of giving of such testimony.

Added by Laws 1984, Ch. 523, eff. July 24, 1984.

§ 473-c.   An order to gain access to persons believed to be in need of protective services for adults.

1.   A social services official may apply to the supreme court or county court for an order to gain access to a person to assess whether such person is in need of protective services for adults in accordance with the provisions of section four hundred seventy-three of this article when such official, having reasonable cause to believe that such person may be in need of protective services, is refused access by such person or another individual. Such application shall state, insofar as the facts can be ascertained with reasonable diligence:

(a)   the name and address of the person who may be in need of protective services for adults and the premises on which this person may be found;

(b)   the reason the social services official believes the person may be in need of protective services for adults, which may include information provided by other agencies or individuals who are familiar with the person who may be in need of protective services for adults;

(c)   the person or persons who are responsible for preventing the social services official from gaining access to the person who may be in need of protective services for adults;

(d)   the efforts made by the social services official to gain access to the person who may be in need of protective services for adults;

(e)   the names of any individuals, such as physicians or nurses, or other health or mental health professionals qualified to participate in the assessment, who shall accompany and assist the social services official conducting an assessment of the need of a person for protective services for adults;

(f)   the manner in which the proposed assessment is to be conducted;

(g)   that the social services official seeks an order solely for the purpose of assessing the need of a person for protective services for adults in accordance with the provisions of section four hundred seventy-three of this article and applicable regulations of the department;

(h)   that no prior application has been made for the relief requested or for any similar relief, or if prior application has been made, the determination thereof, and the new facts, if any, that were not previously shown which warrant a renewal of the application.

2.   Any allegations which are not based upon personal knowledge shall be supported by affidavits provided by a person or persons having such knowledge. Such affidavits shall be attached to the application.

SSL

3. The applications authorized in this section shall have preference over all other causes in all courts of appropriate jurisdiction, except those with a similar statutory preference.

4. If the court is satisfied that there is reasonable cause to believe that a person in need of protective services for adults may be found at the premises described in the application, that such person may be in need of protective services for adults, and that access to such person has been refused, it shall grant the application and issue an order authorizing the social services official and such other individuals as may be designated by the said official, accompanied by a police officer, to enter the premises to conduct an assessment to determine whether the person named in the application is in need of protective services for adults. The standard for proof and procedure for such an authorization shall be the same as for a search warrant under the criminal procedure law.

5. The provisions of this section shall not be construed to authorize a social services official to remove any person from the premises described in the application, or to provide any involuntary protective services to any person other than to assess a person's need for protective services for adults. Nothing in this section shall be construed to impair any existing right or remedy.

Added by Laws 1986, Ch. 413, eff. Nov. 18, 1986; **amended** by Laws 1987, Ch. 190; Laws 1989, Ch. 19; Laws 1991, Ch. 37; Laws 1992, Ch. 160, eff. June 16, 1992, which eliminated the expiration date of the 1987 amendment.

TITLE 3—COMMUNITY GUARDIANSHIP

Section 473-d. **Community guardianship.**
Section 473-e. **Confidentiality of protective services for adults' records.**

§ 473-d. Community guardianship.

[*Formerly 473-c, renumbered as 473-d by Laws 1995, Ch. 395, § 5, eff. Nov. 1, 1995.*]

1. Definitions. When used in this section unless otherwise expressly stated or unless the context or subject matter requires a different interpretation:

(a) "Community guardian program" means a not-for-profit corporation incorporated under the laws of the state of New York or a local governmental agency which has contracted with or has an agreement with a local social services official to provide conservatorship or committeeship services to eligible persons as provided in this title.

(b) "Hospital" means a hospital as defined in subdivision one of section two thousand eight hundred one of the public health law, or a hospital as defined in subdivision ten of section 1.03 of the mental hygiene law.

(c) "Residential facility" means a facility licensed pursuant to article twenty-eight of the public health law, article nineteen, twenty-three, thirty-one or thirty-two of the mental hygiene law, or article seven of this chapter.

2. A social services official may contract with a community guardian program for the provision of conservatorship or committeeship services. A social services official may bring a petition to appoint a community guardian program as conservator or committee for a person only, if the person is:

(a) eligible for and in receipt of adult protective services, as defined in section four hundred seventy-three of this chapter, at the time of the petition; and

(b) without a capable friend or relative or responsible agency willing and able to serve as conservator or committee; and

(c) living outside of a hospital or residential facility, or living in a hospital or residential facility and appointment of the community guardian program is part of a plan to return such person to the community; and

3. A contract or agreement between a local social services official and a community guardian program shall require that:

(a) the community guardian program shall make its best efforts to maintain each person for whom the community guardian program is appointed as conservator or committee in a place other than a hospital or residential facility;

(b) the community guardian program shall petition the court to relinquish its duties as conservator or committee if a person for whom the community guardian program is appointed as conservator or committee regains capacity or competence, or a capable friend or relative becomes available to serve as conservator or committee, or the person must enter a hospital or residential facility on a long-term basis;

(c) the community guardian program shall act on behalf of each person for whom the community guardian program is appointed as conservator or committee to obtain such medical, social, mental health, legal and other services as are available and to which the person is entitled and as are required for the person's safety and well-being and shall advocate for all entitlements; public benefits, and services for which the person qualifies and which the person requires;

(d) all remuneration awarded to the community guardian program by the court from the estate of a person for whom the community guardian program is appointed as conservator or committee shall be based upon the cost of the community guardian program incurred in serving such person or the fee that would otherwise be awarded by the court, whichever is the lesser, and paid over to the social services district;

(e) the files and records of the community guardian program shall be open to inspection to the local social services officials and the department;

(f) no director, officer or employee of the community guardian program shall have a substantial interest in any corporation, organization or entity that provides services to any person for whom the community guardian program is conservator or committee;

(g) the community guardian program shall obtain annual assessments from two qualified psychiatrists or one qualified psychiatrist and one qualified psychologist who are independent of the community guardian program of persons for whom it serves as committee or conservator to determine whether continuation of the guardianship is necessary, and the appointing court shall be informed of the results of such assessments and may discharge the community guardian program as conservator or committee pursuant to sections 77.35 and 78.27 of the mental hygiene law;

(h)   persons hired by the community guardian program to provide services to a person for whom the community guardian program has been named conservator or committee shall have expertise in one or more of the areas of mental health services, protective services, social services or home care services or appropriate experience.

4.   A local social services official shall not be relieved of any duty to provide services of a person by reason of the operation of a community guardian program in the locality or by cessation of such program in the locality.

5.   The department may promulgate rules and regulations necessary to implement this title.

6.   Expenditures made by a social services district, directly or through purchase of services, in petitioning for or acting as a conservator or committee, or made pursuant to contract for community guardianship services in accordance with the provisions of this title, shall be subject to reimbursement by the state, in accordance with regulations of the department, in the amount of fifty per centum of such expenditures, after first deducting therefrom any federal funds properly received or to be received on account thereof and any amounts received pursuant to paragraph (d) of subdivision three of this section.

7.   Nothing in this title shall lessen or eliminate the responsibilities and powers required by law of any agency, department, or any subdivision thereof.

8.   On or before December thirty-first, nineteen hundred eighty-seven, the commissioner shall submit an interim report to the governor, the temporary president of the senate and the speaker of the assembly detailing progress and evaluating results of this program. On or before December thirty-first, nineteen hundred eighty-eight, the commissioner shall submit a final report to the governor, the temporary president of the senate and the speaker of the assembly on the effectiveness of this act.

Amended by Laws 1986, Ch. 846, eff. Aug. 2, 1986, Laws 1987, Ch. 190, § 1; Laws 1991, Ch. 37; Laws 1992, Ch. 160, eff. June 16, 1992, which eliminated the expiration date of the 1986 amendment; amended by Laws 1995, Ch. 395, § 5, eff. Nov. 1, 1995, renumbering the section as 473-d; amended by Laws 1999, Ch. 558, § 52, eff. Oct. 5, 1999.

§ 473-e.   Confidentiality of protective services for adults' records.

1.   Definitions. When used in this section unless otherwise expressly stated or unless the context or subject matter requires a different interpretation:

(a) "subject of a report" means a person who is the subject of a referral or an application for protective services for adults, or who is receiving or has received protective services for adults from a social services district.

(b) "authorized representative of a subject of a report" means (i) a person named in writing by a subject to be a subject's representative for purposes of requesting and receiving records under this article; provided, however, that the subject has contract capacity at the time of the writing or had executed a durable power of attorney at a time when the subject had such capacity, naming the authorized representative as attorney-in-fact, and such document has not been revoked in accordance with applicable law; (ii) a person appointed by a court, or otherwise authorized in accordance with law to represent or act in the interests of the subject; or (iii) legal counsel for the subject.

2. Reports made pursuant to this article, as well as any other information obtained, including but not limited to, the names of referral sources, written reports or photographs taken concerning such reports in the possession of the department or a social services district, shall be confidential and, except to persons, officers and agencies enumerated in paragraphs (a) through (g) of this subdivision, shall only be released with the written permission of the person who is the subject of the report, or the subject's authorized representative, except to the extent that there is a basis for non-disclosure of such information pursuant to subdivision three of this section. Such reports and information may be made available to:

(a) any person who is the subject of the report or such person's authorized representative;

(b) a provider of services to a current or former protective services for adults client, where a social services official, or his or her designee determined that such information is necessary to determine the need for or to provide or to arrange for the provision of such services;

(c) a court, upon a finding that the information in the record is necessary for the use by a party in a criminal or civil action or the determination of an issue before the court;

(d) a grand jury, upon a finding that the information in the record is necessary for the determination of charges before the grand jury;

(e) a district attorney, an assistant district attorney or investigator employed in the office of a district attorney, a member of the division of state police, or a police officer employed by a city, county, town or village police department or by a county sheriff when such official requests such information stating that such information is necessary to conduct a criminal investigation or criminal prosecution of a person, that there is reasonable cause to believe that the criminal investigation or criminal prosecution involves or otherwise affects a person who is the subject of a report, and that it is reasonable to believe that due to the nature of the crime under investigation or prosecution, such records may be related to the criminal investigation or prosecution;

(f) a person named as a court-appointed evaluator or guardian in accordance with article eighty-one of the mental hygiene law, or a person named as a guardian for the mentally retarded in accordance with article seventeen-a of the surrogate's court procedure act; or

(g) any person considered entitled to such record in accordance with applicable law.

3. The commissioner or a social services official may withhold, in whole or in part, the release of any information in their possession which he or she is otherwise authorized to release pursuant to subdivision two of this section, if such official finds that release of such information would identify a person who made a referral or submitted an application on behalf of a person for protective services for adults, or who cooperated in a subsequent investigation and assessment conducted by a social services district to determine a person's need for such services and the official reasonably finds that the release of such information will be detrimental to the safety or interests of such person.

4. Before releasing a record made pursuant to this article in the possession of the department or a social services district, the appropriate official must be satisfied that the confidential character of the information will be maintained in accordance with applicable law, and that the record will be used only for the purposes for which it was made available.

5. In addition to the requirements of this section, any release of confidential HIV related information, as defined in section twenty-seven hundred eighty of the public health law, shall comply with the requirements of article twenty-seven-f of the public health law.

6. When a record made under this article is subpoenaed or sought pursuant to notice to permit discovery, a social services official may move to withdraw, quash, fix conditions or modify the subpoena, or to move for a protective order, as may be appropriate, in accordance with the applicable provisions of the criminal procedure law or the civil practice law and rules, to

(a) delete the identity of any persons who made a referral or submitted an application for protective services for adults on behalf of an individual or who cooperated in a subsequent investigation and assessment of the individual's needs for such services, or the agency, institution, organization, program or other entity when such persons are employed, or with which such persons are associated,

(b) withhold records the disclosure of which is likely to be detrimental to the safety or interests of such persons, or (c) otherwise to object to release of all or a portion of the record on the basis that requested release of records is for a purpose not authorized under the law.

Added by Laws 1995, Ch. 395, § 5, eff. Nov. 1, 1995.

ARTICLE 10

GENERAL PROVISIONS APPLICABLE TO CHARITABLE INSTITUTIONS

SUMMARY OF ARTICLE

§ 474. Reports to supervisors of appointments and committals to charitable institutions.

1. Every judge, justice, superintendent or public welfare official or other person who is authorized by law to make appointments or commitments to any state charitable institution, in which the board, instruction, care or clothing is a charge against any county, town or city, shall make a written report to the clerk of the board of supervisors of the county, or of the county in which any town is situated, or to the city clerk of any city, which is liable for any such board, instruction, care or clothing, within ten days after such appointment or commitment, and shall therein state, when known, the nationality, age, sex and residence of each person so appointed or committed and the length of time of such appointment or commitment.

2. This and the two following sections apply to each of the asylums, reformatories, homes, retreats, penitentiaries, jails or other institutions, except public homes, in each of the counties of this state except the county of Kings, in which the board, instruction, care or clothing of persons committed thereto is, or shall be, a charge against any county or town therein.

SSL

§ 475. Reports by officers of certain institutions to clerks of supervisors and cities.

1.   The keeper, superintendent, secretary, director or other proper officer of a state charitable institution to which any person is committed or appointed, whose board, care, instruction, tuition or clothing shall be chargeable to any city, town or county, shall make a written report to the clerk of such city or to the clerk of the board of supervisors of the county, or of the county in which such town is situated, within ten days after receiving such person therein.

2.   Such report shall state when such person was received into the institution, and, when known, the name, age, sex, nationality, residence, length of time of commitment or appointment, the name of the officer making the same, and the sum chargeable per week, month or year for such person.

3.   If any person so appointed or committed to any such institution shall die, be removed or discharged, such officers shall immediately report to the clerk of the board of supervisors of the county, or of the county in which such town is situated, or to the city clerk of the city from which such person was committed or appointed, the date of such death, removal or discharge.

§ 476. Verified accounts against counties, cities and towns.

1.   The officers mentioned in the last section shall annually, on or before the fifteenth day of October, present to the clerk of the board of supervisors of the county, or of the county in which such town is situated, or to the city clerk of a city from which any such person is committed or appointed, a verified report and statement of the account of such institution with such county, town or city, up to the first day of October, and in case of a claim for clothing, an itemized statement of the same; and if a part of the board, care, tuition or clothing has been paid by any person or persons, the account shall show what sum has been so paid; and the report shall show the name, age, sex, nationality and residence of each person mentioned in the account, the name of the officer who made the appointment or commitment, and the date and length of the same, and the time to which the account has been paid, and the amount claimed to such first day of October, the sum per week or per annum charged, and if no part of such account has been paid, the report shall show such fact.

2.   Any officer who shall refuse or neglect to make such report shall not be entitled to receive any compensation or pay for any services, salary or otherwise, from any town, city or county affected thereby.

3.   The clerk of the board of supervisors who shall receive any such report or account shall file and present the same to the board of supervisors of his county on the second day of the annual meeting of the board next after the receipt of the same.

§ 477. Dutchess county.

1.   All mentally ill, mentally retarded, blind and deaf and mute persons, the expense of whose support and maintenance now is, or under the laws of the state

of New York, may become a charge upon the city of Poughkeepsie, or the county of Dutchess, exclusive of said city, or both, and who are maintained, or shall be maintained, in any of the institutions of the state of New York, shall be supported by said county of Dutchess as one district.

2. All institutions in the state of New York maintaining any such person whose support is properly chargeable, or shall be properly chargeable, to said city or county, are hereby required to render to the county treasurer of said county all bills for the support of such persons without any distinction between those persons from the different parts of said county.

3. This section shall not be held to affect chapter two hundred and eighty-six of the laws of eighteen hundred and sixty-three, an act for the better support of the poor in the city of Poughkeepsie, except as to the class of persons herein named.

Amended by Laws 1978, Ch. 550, § 52, eff. July 24, 1978.

§ 478.   Investigation of complaints by boards of managers.

Whenever the managers, directors, or trustees of any asylum, hospital or other charitable institution, the managers, directors or trustees of which are appointed by the governor and senate, or by the legislature, shall deem it necessary or proper to investigate and ascertain the truth of any charge or complaint made or circulated respecting the conduct of the superintendent, assistants, subordinate officers or servants, in whatever capacity or duty employed by or under the official control of any such managers, directors or trustees, it shall be lawful for the presiding officer for the time being of any such managers, directors or trustees, to administer oaths to all witnesses coming before them respectively for examination, and to issue compulsory process for the attendance of any witness within the state whom they may respectively desire to examine, and for the production of all papers that any such witness may possess, or have in his power, touching the matter of such complaint or investigation; and wilful false swearing by any witness who may be so examined is hereby declared to be perjury. A subpoena issued under this section shall be regulated by the civil practice law and rules.

Amended by Laws 1962, Ch. 310, eff. Sept. 1, 1963.

SSL

§ 479.   Designation of depository of funds.

1. It shall be the duty of the board of trustees or managers of each charitable or benevolent institution in this state, supported in whole or in part by moneys received from the state, or by any county, city or town thereof, to designate by resolution, to be entered upon their minutes, some duly incorporated national or state bank or trust company as the depository of the funds of such institution.

2. After such designation, it shall be the duty of the treasurer of each such charitable or benevolent institution immediately to deposit in the bank or trust

company so designated, in his name as treasurer of the institution, naming it, all funds of the institution which may come into his possession.

§ 480. Labor of children not to be hired out.

It shall be unlawful for the trustees or managers of any house of refuge, reformatory or other correctional institution, to contract, hire, or let by the day, week or month, or any longer period, the services or labor of any child or children, now or hereafter committed to or inmates of such institutions.

ARTICLE 10–A

Repealed

___

(Art. 10-A, §§ 481–483-b, repealed by Laws 1977, Ch. 669, eff. Oct. 1, 1977.)

ARTICLE 10-A

WILLIAM B. HOYT MEMORIAL CHILDREN AND FAMILY TRUST FUND ACT

SUMMARY OF ARTICLE

(Repealed and transferred sections noted under appropriate section number of text.)

§ 481-a. Legislative findings and purpose.

For the past decade, society has witnessed broad changes in family structure. These changes have created unique stresses on our children as well as on those who care for them. Among the most dire results of family stresses is the increasing frequency of child abuse and maltreatment, represented by a steady increase in reports of abuse and maltreatment to the statewide central register of child abuse and maltreatment. Additionally nearly one-fifth of homicides, and an even larger proportion of assaults occur within the home between members of families. Among the contributing causes of family violence are economic stress, social isolation, drug and alcohol abuse, parental attitude regarding discipline and child rearing, as well as acceptance of violence as a way of life. The reported incidents of both adult domestic violence and child abuse and maltreatment (including intergenerational family violence) represent only a portion of the total number of incidents in the pervasive and persistent problem of family violence. The development and support of prevention programs for child abuse and maltreatment and domestic violence (including intergenerational family violence) and services to victims of family violence is, therefore, of major importance to the state.

It is the intent of the legislature that the funds for the William B. Hoyt Memorial children and family trust fund shall be a new source of funding which shall increase the funds available for prevention and treatment services to victims of family violence. The legislature does not intend that these funds be used as a substitute for any funds currently available from federal, state or local sources for the provision of prevention or treatment services to these victims.

Added by Laws 1984, Ch. 960, eff. Oct. 1, 1984; **amended** by Laws 1992, Ch. 268, eff. June 30, 1993.

§ 481-b.   Short title.

This article shall be known and may be cited as the "William B. Hoyt Memorial children and family trust fund act."

Added by Laws 1984, Ch. 960, eff. Oct. 1, 1984; **amended** by Laws 1992, Ch. 268, eff. June 30, 1993.

§ 481-c.   Definitions.

As used in this article:

1.   "Domestic violence" shall mean any crime or violation, as defined in the penal law, which has been alleged to have been committed by any family or household member against any member of the same family or household.

2.   "Family or household members" shall mean persons related by consanguinity or affinity or unrelated persons who are continually or at regular intervals living or in the past continually or at regular intervals lived in the same household, including victims and persons accused of having committed acts of domestic violence.

3.   "Child abuse and maltreatment" shall have the same meaning as provided for in section four hundred twelve of this chapter.

4.   "Public agency" shall mean a local office, board, department, bureau, commission, division, agency, other instrumentality of local government, or public or private educational institution.

5.   "Family violence" shall mean any act which would constitute domestic violence as defined in subdivision one of this section or any act which would constitute child abuse and maltreatment as defined in subdivision three of this section.

6.   "Primary prevention" shall mean strengthening family functioning to insure that family violence never takes place or is less likely to occur. Primary prevention shall include: educating family or household members or prospective parents in order to avoid patterns which can lead to family violence; increasing in-home services to new and prospective parents; strengthening the relationships among community resources, child protective service units and citizen groups to promote and encourage the development of family violence prevention programs; increasing the awareness of professionals and the public to the effects of stress, social isolation and the lack of social and parenting skills for the purpose

SSL

of making available programs deemed helpful for children and adults; and any other program deemed helpful in the primary prevention of family violence.

7. "Secondary prevention" shall mean addressing the early signs of family violence or risk of family violence through treatment of presenting problems to prevent further problems from developing. Secondary prevention shall include: providing supportive services and temporary shelter to family or household members who are considered at risk of family violence; strengthening self-help groups composed of individuals with a history of or at risk of family violence; increasing in-home services to families at risk of violence; promoting and encouraging the development of community resources for the treatment of, and improving the response to family violence; providing information and referral services to resources and/or establishing linkages among services which are in the community; and any other program deemed helpful in the treatment of persons at risk of family violence.

8. "Family resource and support program" shall mean a community-based, prevention focused entity that:

(a). provides, through direct service, core services, including:

(1). parent education, support and leadership services, together with services characterized by relationships between parents and professionals that are based on equality and respect, and designed to assist parents in acquiring parenting skills, learning about child development, and responding appropriately to the behavior of their children;

(2). services to facilitate the ability of parents to serve as resources to one another (such as through mutual support and parent self-help groups);

(3). outreach services provided through voluntary home visits and other methods to assist parents in becoming aware of and able to participate in family resources and support program activities;

(4). community and social services to assist families in obtaining community resources; and

(5). follow-up services;

(b). provides, or arranges for the provision of, other core services through contracts or agreements with other local agencies, including all forms of respite care services; and

(c). provides access to optional services, directly or by contract, purchase of service, or interagency agreement, including:

(1). child care, early childhood development and early intervention services;

(2). referral to self-sufficiency and life management skills training;

(3). referral to education services, such as scholastic tutoring, literacy training, and general educational degree services;

(4). referral to services providing job readiness skills;

(5).   child abuse and neglect prevention activities;

(6).   referral to services that families with children with disabilities or special needs may require;

(7).   community and social service referral, including early develop-mental screening of children;

(8).   peer counseling;

(9).   referral for substance abuse counseling and treatment; and

(10).   help line services.

Added by Laws 1984, Ch. 960, eff. Oct. 1, 1984; **amended** by Laws 1986, Ch. 632, eff. July 26, 1986; Subsection (8) **added** by Laws 1997, Ch. 607, § 1, eff. Sept. 17, 1997.

§ 481-d.   William B. Hoyt Memorial children and family trust fund advisory board.

1.   There is hereby established in the department, a William B. Hoyt Memorial children and family trust fund advisory board. The board shall meet regularly for the purpose of advising and making recommendations to the department in developing program standards relating to the establishment of family violence, including intergenerational family violence, prevention and service programs, developing requests for proposals and evaluating the effectiveness of funded programs. The members of the board shall receive no compensation for their services, but shall be reimbursed for their actual and necessary expenses incurred during the performance of their duties.

2.   The board shall consist of thirteen members to be appointed by the governor, two of whom shall be appointed upon the recommendation of the speaker of the assembly, one of whom shall be appointed upon the recommendation of the minority leader of the assembly, two of whom shall be appointed upon the recommendation of the temporary president of the senate, and one of whom shall be appointed upon the recommendation of the minority leader of the senate. Members of the board shall be appointed for a term of three years. The governor shall designate one member to serve as chairman of the board. To the maximum extent possible members shall be chosen to represent equally those knowledgeable in, concerned with or committed to the field of domestic violence and/or child abuse. Members of the board may be chosen from groups including but not limited to: local social services districts; local youth boards or youth bureaus; child abuse and neglect task forces; statewide coalitions against domestic violence; alcoholism services; public agencies, not-for-profit corporations and educational institutions concerned with or providing professional training in family violence and child welfare services; family violence self-help and advocacy groups; the legal, social work, mental health, medical, clergy, judicial and law enforcement professions; groups dealing with services to the abused elderly; other professionals that provide family violence services and other

SSL

concerned individuals or organizations, including parents or guardians of children who were or are in receipt of services funded pursuant to this article.

Added by Laws 1984, Ch. 960, eff. Oct. 1, 1984; **amended** by Laws 1985, Ch. 57, eff. Apr. 18, 1985; **amended** by Laws 1992, Ch. 268, eff. June 30, 1993; **amended** by Laws 1997, Ch. 607, § 2, eff. Sept. 17, 1997.

§ 481-e.   William B. Hoyt Memorial children and family trust fund; awarding of grants.

1.   The commissioner is hereby authorized to issue grants from funds credited to the William B. Hoyt Memorial children and family trust fund as provided in section four hundred eighty-one-f of this article to public agencies or not-for-profit corporations for the purpose of establishing or extending any or all of the following:

(a)   primary prevention programs;

(b)   secondary prevention programs;

(c)   programs which provide services to victims of family violence, such as establishing temporary shelters and other emergency services; programs which provide or facilitate counseling, or other appropriate follow-up services to victims and their family or household members; and any other program deemed helpful in the treatment of victims of family violence.

2.   (a) Funds shall be awarded in the following manner: forty percent for local child abuse prevention or family resource and support programs, forty percent for local domestic violence prevention or service programs and twenty percent for regional or statewide family violence prevention programs; provided, however, that any unexpended portion of such twenty percent as allocated shall be made available for local family violence prevention programs and provided further, however, that in determining the eligibility of any regional or statewide family violence prevention program or of any local family violence prevention program for any part of such unexpended portion, the commissioner shall give first consideration to those programs which combine both child abuse prevention and domestic violence prevention.

(b)   For a program which combines child abuse prevention and domestic violence prevention, the commissioner shall predetermine, to the extent feasible, the percentage of concentration for each within such program and shall apportion the total amount awarded between such forty percent allocation in the same proportion.

3.   No moneys from the fund established pursuant to section four hundred eighty-one-f of this article shall be granted for services mandated under this chapter. Funds awarded to not-for-profit corporations or public agencies pursuant to the provisions of subdivision one of this section shall not be used to supplant other federal, state or local funds.

4. The commissioner, with the advice and recommendations of the William B. Hoyt Memorial children and family trust fund advisory board, shall issue requests for proposals and specify methods to evaluate the effectiveness of proposed programs. Such evaluation shall include but not be limited to the following:

(a) appropriate accounting and fiscal control procedures which shall include the filing or an annual financial statement by each provider so as to ensure the proper disbursement and accounting for funds received by public agencies and not-for-profit corporations for services; and

(b) appropriate, written records regarding the population served and type and extent of services rendered by the provider; and

(c) confidentiality standards in conformance with appropriate federal and state standards so as to ensure the confidentiality of records of persons receiving services; and

(d) nature and quality of services provided and impacts upon the populations and communities served.

5. The commissioner shall solicit and shall select proposals for the provision of services funded pursuant to this act. Public agencies and not-for-profit corporations shall be eligible for purposes of application for grants provided for herein and subject to any rules and regulations promulgated pursuant to subdivision four of this section.

6. The commissioner, with the advice of the William B. Hoyt Memorial children and family trust fund advisory board, shall publicize the availability of funds to be used for purposes of this section. The commissioner shall request, on prescribed forms, information determined to be necessary and relevant for the evaluation of each application. The commissioner may solicit comments on the applications from concerned individuals and agencies. Applications for local grants shall be submitted to the local commissioner of social services and to the local youth bureau in the locality in which the program will operate and applicants for local grants shall solicit comments on the application from such local commissioner of social services and such local youth bureau prior to submitting such application to the commissioner. Applicants shall inform the local commissioner of social services and the local youth bureau that their comments upon the application may be submitted either to the applicant or to the commissioner or to both. The commissioner shall give full consideration to any such comments received within twenty-one days after the application deadline and shall review the applications in relation to relevant local plans before approving or disapproving such applications. The commissioner shall inform the local commissioner of social services and the local youth bureau of the final disposition of the applications. No grant award shall be for a period in excess of twelve months unless renewed by the commissioner, with the advice of the advisory board. The initial grant and the first year renewal, if any, shall not exceed one hundred percent of the cost of providing the service. The third year grant, if any, shall

not exceed seventy-five percent of the initial grant. The fourth year grant and any grant thereafter, if any, shall not exceed fifty percent of the initial grant. No program shall receive funding after the fourth year unless the commissioner, annually, finds that the program effectively prevents family violence or provides a necessary service to victims of family violence.

7.   Pursuant to subdivision one of this section, the commissioner shall ensure that grants are awarded evenly across the state with consideration given to geographic areas with the greatest need and that priority is given to programs:

(a)   which are innovative; or

(b)   of demonstrated effectiveness; and/or

(c)   illustrates the capacity to coordinate with established community programs; and/or

(d)   which can demonstrate a potential for future financial self-sufficiency.

8.   The commissioner with the advice and recommendations of the William B. Hoyt Memorial children and family trust fund advisory board shall submit a report prior to the fifteenth day of December beginning in nineteen hundred eighty-five and annually thereafter to the governor and the legislature regarding the implementation and evaluation of the effectiveness of prevention and treatment services related to family violence. Prior to submitting such reports to the governor and the legislature, the commissioner shall permit the William B. Hoyt Memorial children and family trust fund advisory board to review and comment upon such reports. Such report shall include:

(a)   the number of persons estimated to have been assisted in programs covered by this section;

(b)   the number, recipients and amounts of grants to public agencies and not-for-profit corporations;

(c)   the amount of public and private funds used for approved programs by service type;

(d)   the amount of funds used for the administration of such services;

(e)   a description of the nature and quality of services provided and the impact upon the populations and communities served and their potential for being replicated elsewhere; and

(f)   all such other matters as may be necessary to inform the governor and the legislature regarding the implementation and evaluation of the effectiveness of programs covered by this section and the success of such programs in accomplishing the intent of the legislature.

Added by Laws 1984, Ch. 960, eff. Oct. 1, 1984; amended by Laws 1985, Ch. 57, eff. Apr. 18, 1985; amended by Laws 1992, Ch. 268, eff. June 30, 1993; amended by Laws 1997, Ch. 607, § 3, eff. Sept. 17, 1997.

§ 481-f. William B. Hoyt Memorial children and family trust fund.

1. There is hereby established in the joint custody of the comptroller and the commissioner of taxation and finance a separate and distinct account, to be known as the William B. Hoyt Memorial children and family trust fund. Such account shall be classified by the comptroller as an expendable trust. Such account shall consist of any moneys appropriated to the department for the purposes of the programs authorized pursuant to this article and funds from any other source, including but not limited to, federal funds, donations from private individuals, corporations or foundations, for the implementation of programs provided for in this article. All funds received by the comptroller on behalf of the William B. Hoyt Memorial children and family trust fund shall be deposited by the comptroller to the credit of the William B. Hoyt Memorial children and family trust fund. Notwithstanding the provisions of this subdivision, funds granted to the department pursuant to the federal child abuse prevention and treatment act shall not be deposited to the credit of the William B. Hoyt Memorial children and family trust fund.

2. Donations from private individuals, corporations, or foundations deposited in the William B. Hoyt Memorial children and family trust fund may be invested by the comptroller pursuant to the provisions of section ninety-eight-a of the state finance law. Any income from such investments shall be deposited to the credit of the William B. Hoyt Memorial children and family trust fund.

Added by Laws 1984, Ch. 960, eff. Oct. 1, 1984; **amended** by Laws 1985, Ch. 57, eff. Apr. 18, 1985; **amended** by Laws 1992, Ch. 268, eff. June 30, 1993.

SSL

ARTICLE 10–B

STATEWIDE SETTLEMENT HOUSE PROGRAM

SUMMARY OF ARTICLE

Section   482-a.   **Legislative findings and purpose.**
Section   482-b.   **Definitions.**
Section   482-c.   **Statewide settlement house program; awarding of grants.**

§ 482-a.   Legislative findings and purpose.

The legislature finds that public policy experts and state and local agencies have been searching for a model of service delivery that will insure programmatically effective and cost-efficient delivery of services to inner-city families and neighborhoods, and that the emerging consensus is that the best models provide comprehensive, coordinated, neighborhood-based and family-focused services. The legislature further finds that New York state's existing network of fifty-eight settlement houses can contribute to providing these comprehensive, coordinated, neighborhood-based and family-focused services in a cost-effective manner, and that the capacity of these settlement houses to provide and enhance these services can be increased if the settlement houses are provided with additional resources to implement greater neighborhood outreach, to direct individuals and family members to appropriate settlement and community-based resources, to monitor the progress of these individuals, and to plan and coordinate intra-agency and community services so that community residents have easy access to a range of services that respond to the varied and often multiple needs of individuals and families.

It is the intent of the legislature to increase the funds available to settlement houses for the purpose of providing a comprehensive range of services to the residents of the neighborhoods they serve, and that funds provided pursuant to this article will be complemented by privately-raised contributions to the settlement-houses for the program services funded pursuant to this article. The legislature does not intend that these funds be used as a substitute for any funds currently available from federal, state or local sources for the provision of neighborhood-based service delivery programs provided by settlement houses.

Added by Laws 1993, Ch. 59, § 36, eff. Apr. 15, 1993.

§ 482-b. Definitions.

As used in this article:

1. "Settlement house" means an independent, voluntary, not-for-profit organization demonstrating affiliation with the New York state association for settlement houses and neighborhood centers engaged in community work and social services delivery in a defined neighborhood in a municipality of the state of New York which provides comprehensive, coordinated, family-focused multi-generational human services such as child care, employment training, housing assistance counseling, youth development, educational services, senior services and arts and cultural activities, based on the needs of the neighborhood or neighborhoods served and which:

(a) has been incorporated for at least three years;

(b) is qualified as a tax-exempt organization pursuant to section 501(c)(3) of the Internal Revenue Code;

(c) provides services to all those who live in the neighborhood or neighborhoods served without regard to race, creed, religious practice, color, sex, age, national origin, economic status, disability, or affectional preference;

(d) has an independent, autonomous board of directors which meets at regular intervals, has full authority over the policies and operations of the organization, and the membership of which includes community residents;

(e) employs appropriate staff including a position of chief executive officer;

(f) has a budget which is adopted on an annual basis by the board of directors, utilizes an accepted accounting system, and has prepared an annual fiscal audit by a certified public accountant not connected with the organization; and

(g) can demonstrate that one of its primary purposes is the improvement of the relationships among groups of different cultural, economic, religious, and social groups in the community through a variety of individual, group, and inter-group activities.

2. "Program services" may include, but are not limited to, several of the following services:

(a) early childhood services, including child care, child development services, early child education and health information and referral for pre-school children;

(b) youth services, including teen centers and school-age programs which provide recreation, homework assistance, preparation for employment, counseling and meals;

(c) education programs, including remedial education, tutoring, homework assistance and English language training;

(d) family programs, including home management, homemaker services, parenting skills training, teen parent services and programs for seniors;

SSL

(e)   child welfare services including foster care and preventive services;

(f)   employment programs, including summer youth employment apprentice programs, job training programs, and displaced homemaker programs;

(g)   mental health services, including psychological and, where appropriate, psychiatric group and individual evaluation and counseling;

(h)   Housing assistance.

     Added by Laws 1993, Ch. 59, § 36, eff. Apr. 15, 1993.

§ 482-c.   Statewide settlement house program; awarding of grants.

1.   The commissioner is hereby authorized to issue grants for the purpose of enhancing and coordinating activities and programs, expanding programs to serve more individuals and families, and/or promoting inter-agency coordination with other neighborhood organizations offering complementary services.

2.   Funds awarded to settlement houses pursuant to the provisions of subdivision one of this section shall be used to supplement and not to supplant other federal, state or local funds.

3.   The commissioner shall issue requests for applications to all settlement houses and shall specify that applications include a description of the nature of the services to be provided, a discussion of the relatedness of the services to the purposes of a settlement house as defined in section four hundred eighty-two-b of this article and an estimate of the number and composition of clients to be served. Such applications may include a discussion of plans to develop or enhance outreach services to individuals and families, institute or augment assessments of individual and family needs, coordinate services, develop links with neighborhood organizations, develop employment initiatives, mentoring programs and other cooperative programs with unions, neighborhood businesses and community corporations, and identify sources of private funding. Such applications shall also include at least the following:

(a)   appropriate accounting and fiscal control procedures that assure that funds are expended in accordance with this article, including the filing of an annual financial statement by each provider; and

(b)   appropriate written records regarding the number of individuals and families served and the type and extent of services rendered by the settlement house.

4.   The commissioner shall solicit and select applications for the provision of programs and services funded pursuant to this article. It is necessary that settlement houses receiving funding pursuant to this article demonstrate a plan to raise one dollar for each two dollars of state grants received. Subsequent year funding may be adjusted to reflect prior years' experience.

5.   The commissioner may issue a request for applications to the extent funds are available on a multi-year basis.

6.   The commissioner shall make grants of up to fifty thousand dollars to settlement houses following approval of an acceptable plan submitted pursuant to the request for applications so long as there are funds available. The commissioner shall notify the local social services district of a grant award to a settlement house in that district.

Added by Laws 1993, Ch. 59, § 36, eff. Apr. 15, 1993.

SSL

ARTICLE 10–C

STATE COUNCIL ON CHILDREN AND FAMILIES

SUMMARY OF ARTICLE

§ 483. Council on children and families; chair.

1. There shall be a council on children and families established within the office of children and family services consisting of the following members: the state commissioner of children and family services, the commissioner of temporary and disability assistance, the commissioner of mental health, the commissioner of mental retardation and developmental disabilities, the commissioner of the office of alcoholism and substance abuse services, the commissioner of education, the state director of probation and correctional alternatives, the commissioner of health, the commissioner of the division of criminal justice services, the state advocate for persons with disabilities, the director of the office for the aging, the commissioner of labor, and the chair of the commission on quality of care for the mentally disabled. The governor shall designate the chair of the council and the chief executive officer (CEO).

2. The chair of the council in consultation with the commissioner of the office of children and family services, shall designate staff from the office of children and family services to work full time in carrying out the functions of the council.

3. The council may conduct its meetings and, by and through the chair, perform its powers and duties notwithstanding the absence of a quorum; provided, however that no action may be taken by the council without the concurrence of the chair.

Added by Laws 2003, Ch. 62, Part F2, § 2, eff. May 15, 2003 and deemed in full force and effect on and after April 1, 2003.

§ 483-a.   Utilization of other agency assistance.

1.   To effectuate the purposes of this article, any department, division, board, bureau, commission or agency of the state or of any political subdivision thereof shall, at the request of the chair, provide to the council such facilities, assistance and data as will enable the council properly to carry out its powers and duties and those of the chair.

Added by Laws 2003, Ch. 62, Part F2, § 2, eff. May 15, 2003 and deemed in full force and effect on and after April 1, 2003.

§ 483-b.   Powers and duties of council.

1.   As used in this section, the terms "care", "services", "programs", and "services programs" shall mean and include care, maintenance, services and programs provided to children of the state and their families by or under the jurisdiction of a member agency. The term "member agency" shall mean an agency headed by a member of the council.

2.   The council shall have the following powers:

(a)   to identify problems and deficiencies in residential care and community-based services programs and, on a selective basis, to plan and make recommendations to the governor for the remedy of such problems and deficiencies and for the development of programs of care and services for children and their families;

(b)   to make recommendations to improve coordination of program and fiscal resources of state-local, public-voluntary care and services to children and their families;

(c)   to coordinate program and management research of member agencies for the purpose of monitoring, evaluating or redirecting existing care and services programs or developing new programs, and to conduct, sponsor, or direct member agencies to undertake such research or other activities;

(d)   to review and resolve differences, if any, concerning rules and regulations of each member agency insofar as such rules and regulations impact on services programs provided by other member agencies;

(e)   to promulgate, amend and rescind rules and regulations relating to the administration and performance of the powers and duties of the council pursuant to this article;

(f)   to review significant state and locally operated and supported care and services, plans and proposals for new services for children and families to determine whether such services are planned, created and delivered in a coordinated, effective and comprehensive manner;

(g)   to perform all other things necessary and convenient to carry out the functions, powers and duties of the council and to effectuate the purposes of this article; and

SSL

(h) to accept and expend any grants, awards, or other funds or appropriations as may be available to the council to effectuate the purposes of this article, subject to the approval of the director of the budget.

3. The council shall review the budget requests of member agencies insofar as such budgets jointly affect services programs for children and their families and shall make comments and recommendations thereon to the relevant member agencies and the governor.

4. (a) The council shall meet on a regular basis to implement the purposes of this article and to discuss and resolve disputes, including but not limited to disputes between member agencies, relating to their functions, powers and duties over the provision of services to particular children and their families or to categories of children or child and family problems when all the internal statutory and administrative grievance or appeal procedures applicable to a member agency have failed to finally resolve such dispute. The council shall direct each member agency to establish and maintain such grievance or appeal procedures.

(b) The council shall direct member agencies to provide an evaluation, including a diagnostic study, of a particular child and his or her family when there is a dispute as to the appropriate agency or program in which the child should be placed or from which the child and his or her family should receive services, and, following such study, the council shall order placement of a child with a member agency, or with a social services official, or order a member agency to provide or require the provision of services to the child and his or her family in a manner consistent with the legal authority of the member agency or social services official, as applicable.

(c) The council shall direct member agencies to take appropriate direct action or to exercise their supervisory powers over local officials and agencies, in the resolution of such disputes.

(d) The duty of the council to resolve disputes involving particular children may be performed on a selective basis within the discretion of the council. Exercise of jurisdiction over such disputes by the council or appeals to the council therefor shall not be required as a condition precedent to the initiation of a proceeding pursuant to article seventy-eight of the civil practice law and rules.

(e) A dispute relative to which member agency shall have the responsibility for determining and recommending adult services pursuant to sections 7.37 and 13.37 of the mental hygiene law, section three hundred ninety-eight-c of the social services law, or subdivision ten of section forty-four hundred three of the education law shall be resolved in accordance with this subdivision.

5. (a) Notwithstanding any other provision of state law to the contrary, the council may request any member agency to submit to the council and such member agency shall submit, to the extent permitted by federal law, all information in the form and manner and at such times as the council may require that it is appropriate to the purposes and operation of the council.

(b)   The council shall protect the confidentiality of individual identifying information submitted to or provided by the council, and prevent access thereto, by, or the distribution thereof to, persons not authorized by law.

Added by Laws 2003, Ch. 62, Part F2, § 2, eff. May 15, 2003 and deemed in full force and effect on and after April 1, 2003.

§ 483-c.   Coordinated children's services for children with emotional and/or behavioral disorders.

1.   Purpose. The purpose of this section shall be to establish a coordinated system of care for children with emotional and behavioral disorders, and their families, who require assistance from multiple agency systems to appropriately maintain such children with their families, in their communities and in their local school systems. Such system of care shall provide for the effective collaboration among state and local health, mental hygiene, education, juvenile justice, probation of care and other human services agencies directed at improving outcomes for children with emotional and/or behavioral disorders and their families leading to full participation in their communities and schools. This shall include children with co-occurring disorders. The absence of coordinated care often results in inappropriate and costly institutional placements and limited community-based services that support maintaining the child in the community. Establishing the coordinated children's services initiative statewide is intended to improve the manner in which services of multiple systems are delivered and to eliminate barriers to a coordinated system of care.

2.   Definitions. As used in this section:

(a)   "Child with an emotional and/or behavioral disorder" shall mean a person under eighteen years of age, or a person under twenty-one years of age who has not completed secondary school, who has a mental illness, as defined in subdivision twenty of section 1.03 of the mental hygiene law, or is classified as a student with a disability pursuant to article eighty-nine of the education law or section 504 of the federal rehabilitation act, or is considered to have a serious emotional or behavioral problem, as considered by a tier I and/or tier II team representative pursuant to this section. Such term shall include children with co-occurring disorders.

(b)   "Individualized family support plan" shall mean a plan developed in conjunction with the family through a strength-based child and family assessment containing a summary of the strengths, needs and goals of a child with an emotional and/or behavioral disorder, and the services and supports agreed to by the child, family and the tier I team representatives.

(c)   "Family" shall mean, when appropriate, a child with an emotional and/or behavioral disorder, his or her parents or those in parental relationship to the child, blood relatives and extended family, including non-relatives identified by the child and/or parents. Nothing in this section shall be construed to deny the

SSL

child, his or her parents or those persons in parental relationship to the child of any rights they are otherwise entitled to by law.

(d) "County" shall mean a county, except in the case of a county that is wholly included within a city, such term shall mean such city.

(e) "Family support representative" shall mean a volunteer who is also a parent or primary caregiver of a child with an emotional and/or behavioral disorder. The family support representative shall assist families throughout the process of developing and implementing an individualized family support plan as defined in this section.

3. Interagency structure.

(a) There shall be established a three tiered interagency structure as follows:

(i) State tier III team. There is hereby established a state team designated as the "tier III team", which shall consist of the chair of the council, the commissioners of children and family services, mental health, health, education, alcohol and substance abuse services, and mental retardation and developmental disabilities, and the director of probation and correctional alternatives, or their designated representatives, and representatives of families of children with emotional and/or behavioral disorders. Other representatives may be added at the discretion of such team.

(ii) County tier II team. A county, or consortium of counties, choosing to participate in the coordinated children's services initiative shall establish an interagency team consisting of, but not limited to, the local commissioners or leadership assigned by the chief elected official responsible for the local health, mental hygiene, juvenile justice, probation and other human services systems. The education system shall be represented by the district superintendent of the board of cooperative educational services, or his or her designee, and in the case of the city of New York, by the chancellor of the city school district of the city of New York, or his or her designee, and appropriate local school district representatives as determined by the district superintendent of the board of cooperative educational services or such chancellor. Such team shall be sensitive to issues of cultural competence, and shall include representatives of families of children with an emotional and/or behavioral disorder. Regional state agency representatives may participate when requested by such team.

(iii) Family-based tier I team. Tier II teams, in cooperation with a child with an emotional and/or behavioral disorder and his or her family, shall establish interagency teams to work with such child and family to develop an individualized, strength-based family support plan and coordinate interagency services agreed to in such plan. Such teams shall include such child and family and, based on the needs of the child and family, should also include a family support representative, representatives from the mental hygiene, education, juvenile justice, probation, health, and other county child and family services systems.

(b) Roles and responsibilities of teams.

(i) The state tier III team shall coordinate statewide implementation of the coordinated children's services initiative. Such team shall:

(A) coordinate planning across the health, mental hygiene, education, juvenile justice, probation and human services systems;

(B) address barriers to the effective delivery of local interagency services;

(C) coordinate the provision of technical assistance and training for the effective implementation of the coordinated children's services initiative;

(D) develop an appropriate reporting mechanism to track the outcomes being achieved. Such mechanism shall be developed in concert with participating counties; and

(E) report results and recommendations for change to the governor, legislature and state board of regents, as appropriate.

(ii) The tier II teams shall coordinate the coordinated children's services initiative at the local level. Such team shall:

(A) coordinate cross-systems training and provide linkages to other county and school district planning for children;

(B) address local/regional barriers to the coordination of services;

(C) report on state level barriers to the effective delivery of coordinated services and recommended changes to the state tier III team;

(D) report on outcomes using the mechanism developed by the state tier III team;

(E) implement the goals and principles of the coordinated children's services initiative; and

(F) make monies available consistent with subdivision five of this section.

(iii) Each tier I team shall work collaboratively with the family to develop an individualized family support plan that is:

(A) family-focused and family driven;

(B) built on child and family strengths; and

(C) comprehensive, including appropriate services and supports from appropriate systems and natural supports from the community.

4. Goals and principles of operation.

(a) Goals. The coordinated children's services initiative shall enable children with emotional and/or behavioral disorders, whenever appropriate for the child and family to:

(i) reside with their families;

(ii) live and participate successfully in their communities;

(iii) attend and be successful in their local school systems; and

(iv) grow towards becoming independent, contributing members of the community.

(b) Principles of operation. The tier III and II teams shall provide a system for serving children with emotional and/or behavioral disorders that is:

(i) community-based, allowing children and families to receive services close to their home;

(ii) culturally compete

(iii) individualized and strengths-based in approach;

(iv) family friendly, involving the family as full and active partners at every level of decision making, including policy development, planning, treatment and service delivery;

(v) comprehensive, involving all appropriate parties, including but not limited to the family, child, natural supports, provider agencies and other necessary community services;

(vi) funded through multiple systems with flexible funding mechanisms that support creative approaches;

(vii) unconditionally committed to the success of each child; and

(viii) accountable with respect to use of agreed on and measured outcomes.

5. Funding. Counties and school districts, including boards of cooperative educational services as requested by component school districts, choosing to participate in the coordinated children's services initiative, unless expressly prohibited by law, shall have the authority to:

(a) combine state and federal resources of the participating county and educational agencies to provide services to groups or individual children and their families necessary to maintain children with emotional and/or behavioral disorders in their homes, communities and schools, and support families in achieving this goal, as long as the use of the funds is consistent with the purposes for which they were appropriated; and

(b) apply flexibility in use of funds, pursuant to an individualized family-support plan, or for collaborative programs, an agreement among the county, city and school districts or the board of cooperative educational services, monies combined pursuant to paragraph (a) of this subdivision may be used to allow flexibility in determining and applying interventions that will address the unique needs of the family. The tier III team shall develop guidelines for the flexible use of funds in implementing an individualized family support plan.

6. Administration and reports. The council shall be responsible for the administration of the provisions of this section.

(a) The tier III team shall submit a report to the council detailing the effectiveness in reaching the goals and objectives of the program established by this section. Such report shall include recommendations, based on the experience gained pursuant to the provisions of this article, for modifying statewide policies, regulations or statutes. The council shall forward such report to the governor, the legislature and the state board of regents on or before the first day of July of each year, including the recommendations of the tier III members regarding the feasibility and implications of implementing the recommendations.

(b) The tier III team shall have authority to receive funds and work within agency structures, as agreed to by member agencies, to administer funds for the purposes of carrying out its responsibilities.

(c) Parents and representatives of families, who are not compensated for attendance as part of their employment, shall be compensated for their tier III team participation and reimbursed for actual expenses, including, but not limited to, child care.

7. Confidentiality.

(a) Notwithstanding any other provision of state law to the contrary, tier I, II and III team participants in the coordinated children's services system shall have access to case record and related treatment information as necessary to support the purposes of this section, to the extent permitted by federal law.

(b) Tier I, II and III team participants shall protect the confidentiality of all individual identifying case record and related treatment information, and prevent access thereto, by, or the distribution thereof to, other persons not authorized by State or federal law.

Added by Laws 2003, Ch. 62, Part F2, § 2, eff. May 15, 2003 and deemed in full force and effect on and after April 1, 2003.

§ 483-d.   [Effective Oct. 31, 2005] Out-of-state placement committee.

1. Committee established. There is hereby established within the council an out-of-state placement committee comprised of the commissioner of children and family services, the commissioner of mental health, the commissioner of mental retardation and developmental disabilities, the commissioner of education, the commissioner of alcoholism and substance abuse services, the commissioner of health, and the director of the division of probation and correctional alternatives.

2. Establishment of out-of-state placement registries. (a) Each member of the out-of-state placement committee which places or which has oversight responsibilities over agencies that place children in out-of-state congregate residential programs or residential schools shall establish a registry of congregate residential programs and/or residential schools. To the extent feasible, such registries shall be publicly accessible via the committee member agency's website. Additionally, the council shall establish a single comprehensive registry for the listing of out-of-state congregate residential programs and residential schools that have been approved by one or more members of the out-of-state placement committee. To the extent feasible, the registry shall be internet-accessible, and shall be placed on the website of the council.

(b)   The out-of-state placement committee shall develop core requirements for the inclusion of an out-of-state congregate residential program or residential school on such a registry, which shall include but may not be limited to requirements that:

(i)   if the out-of-state congregate residential program or residential school provides residential care to children from New York state, at least one member of the out-of-state placement committee or his or her designee has conducted a site visit of such out-of-state congregate residential program or residential school, as appropriate, within time frames as the committee shall determine;

(ii)   the out-of-state congregate residential program or residential school holds a current license or charter from the appropriate state agency or agencies of the state in which the program or facility is located;

(iii)   appropriate laws and regulations exist in the state where the congregate residential program or residential school is located for the investigation and resolution of allegations of abuse or neglect;

(iv)   the appropriate member or members of the out-of-state placement committee shall have evaluated the out-of-state congregate residential program or residential school to determine whether the types of care being provided are consistent with New York state law and the applicable committee member agency's regulations.

(c)   Prior to placing an out-of-state congregate residential program or residential school on its registry, a member of the out-of-state placement committee shall solicit and consider any relevant information regarding the congregate residential program or residential school from other members of the out-of-state placement committee.

(d)   The out-of-state placement committee in conjunction with the division of the budget shall determine the feasibility of charging fees for out-of-state congregate residential programs and residential schools to be listed on an out-of-state placement registry.

3.   Establishment of recommended contract parameters. The out-of-state placement committee shall establish recommended contract parameters for use by committee member agencies and any local agency subject to the jurisdiction of one of the committee member agencies when contracting with an out-of-state congregate residential program or residential school for the placement of a New York state child. Such contract parameters shall include but may not be limited to provisions that the out-of-state congregate residential program or residential school shall:

(a)   hold and maintain a current license, certificate or charter from the appropriate state agency or agencies of the state in which the program or facility is located;

(b)   promptly notify the placing state or local agency of any enforcement action taken with respect to such license, certificate or charter and any action the congregate program or facility is taking with respect thereto and that the placing agency, if it is a local agency, will notify its supervising state agency of such information;

(c)   take all necessary steps to become and remain listed on the out-of-state placement registry of the applicable member or members of the out-of-state placement committee, including providing any requested information to the applicable committee member or members consistent with applicable state and federal laws and authorizing such committee member or members to conduct announced and unannounced visits to the program or facility;

(d)   promptly notify the placing state or local agency of any report of abuse or neglect occurring in the program or school regarding any child placed by the state or local agency, the progress and outcome of the investigation of the report, and of any action being taken with respect thereto, and agree that the placing state or local agency will notify the parents or persons in parental relationship to the child of such report of abuse or neglect;

(e)   promptly notify the placing state or local agency of any investigation of a report of abuse or neglect found to result from a systemic problem with the program or school or any portion thereof and any action that the program or school is taking with respect thereto and that the placing agency, if it is a local agency, will notify its supervising state agency of such information; and

(f)   establish, in conjunction with the placing state or local agency, appropriate services and goals for each child placed by such agency in the out-of-state program or school consistent with applicable state and federal law.

4.   Model processes for placement. The out-of-state placement committee shall establish model processes for the placement of any child in an out-of-state congregate residential program or residential school which may include, but not be limited to, identifying the necessary activities that should be engaged in on a local, regional and/or state level prior to making an out-of-state placement including reviewing alternative service options to avoid an out-of-home placement and reviewing all viable and least restrictive options for placing the child in-state.

5.   Technical assistance resources. The committee shall make reasonable efforts to:

(a)   coordinate the development and updating by member agencies of statewide child and family services technical assistance resources which may include service directories, assessment tools, inventories of availability and capacity of in-state services, referral guides, funding maps, and information about research and evidence based practices, which, to the extent feasible, shall be made widely available through such means as web-based platforms; and

(b)   establish public awareness, training and technical assistance initiatives to strengthen local and regional service coordination and streamline placement processes and access to community-based services, which include or complement existing infrastructure, by engaging local and regional service providers, educators, policy makers, family members, advocates and others.

6. Integrated funding. The committee, in conjunction with the division of the budget, shall analyze aggregate data on children who are placed in out-of-state congregate residential programs and residential schools and make recommendations concerning the development of integrated funding for the purchase of services for children with complex and/or multiply-diagnosed needs including:

(a) reducing or eliminating identified barriers to providing flexibility in the funding of programs and services for children at risk of placement in out-of-state programs and facilities and of such other children as may be appropriate;

(b) increasing the number of alternatives to placing children in out-of-state congregate residential programs or residential schools by allowing funds for services to follow the child into the most appropriate and least restrictive placement; and

(c) allowing funds for services to be applied to the purchase of appropriate services within the child's community, including modification of the child's residence, in the most flexible manner so as to serve the child in the least restrictive setting as appropriate.

7. Additional review and recommendations; report. The out-of-state placement committee may develop additional recommendations regarding a common system concerning placement of children in out-of-state programs and facilities, with the purpose of averting insofar as practicable future placement of children in such out-of-state programs and facilities, of returning children from such out-of-state programs and facilities, of building or rebuilding the infrastructure of in-state programs and facilities so that it shall be capable of serving the needs of such children, of redesigning the system to eliminate barriers and institute flexibility in funding services so that children may be provided for in the most appropriate and least restrictive environments, including the child's home, of enabling public funding for such services to follow the child, and of requiring appropriate levels of accountability concerning the placement of children at all levels of public decision-making. The committee shall provide an annual progress report concerning the development of the items and policies described in this section and progress on their implementation, along with such recommendations as the committee shall deem appropriate and in keeping with the spirit and intent of this section. Such report shall be submitted to the governor and the legislature no later than thirty days following the submission of the executive budget.

8. Immunity from liability. Any person, official or institution complying with the requirements of this section reasonably and in good faith, including establishing or implementing out-of-state registries, contract parameters, and model processes for placement, with respect to placing a child in an out-of-state or an in-state facility or program shall have immunity from any liability, civil or criminal, that might otherwise result by reason of such actions.

9. Construction with other laws; severability. If any portion of this section or the application thereof to any person or circumstances shall be adjudged invalid by a court of competent jurisdiction, such order or judgment shall be confined in its operation to the controversy in which it was rendered, and shall not affect or invalidate the remainder of any provision of this section or the application of any part thereof to any other person or circumstances and to this end each of the provisions of this section are hereby declared to be separable.

Added by Laws 2005, Ch. 392, § 2, eff. Oct. 31, 2005.

SSL

ARTICLE 11

CONSTRUCTION; LAWS REPEALED; WHEN TO TAKE EFFECT

―――

―――

SUMMARY OF ARTICLE

Section   484.   **Constitutionality.**
            485.   **Construction.**
            486.   **Laws repealed.**

§ 484.   Constitutionality.

If any provisions of this chapter shall be held to be unconstitutional, such decision shall not affect the validity of the remaining provisions of this chapter.

§ 485.   Construction.

1.   The provisions of this chapter so far as they are substantially the same as those existing at the time they shall take effect, shall be construed as a continuation of such laws, modified or amended, according to the language employed in this chapter, and not as new enactments. References in laws not repealed to provisions of law repealed, or transferred and enacted into and made a part of this chapter, shall be construed as applying to the provisions so incorporated.

2.   All references in this chapter to articles, titles or sections shall, unless otherwise indicated in connection therewith, be deemed to refer to the articles, titles or sections of this chapter; and, if so stated in connection therewith, to a subdivision of a section of this chapter. All references in any section of this chapter to a numbered subdivision, or clause shall, unless otherwise indicated in connection therewith, be deemed to refer to the subdivision, or clause so numbered or lettered in such section. All references in any article to a title shall, unless otherwise indicated in connection therewith, be deemed to refer to the title so numbered in such article.

§ 486.   Laws repealed.

Of the laws enumerated in the schedule hereto annexed, that portion specified in the last column is hereby repealed.

COURT DIRECTORY

NEW YORK COURT STRUCTURE

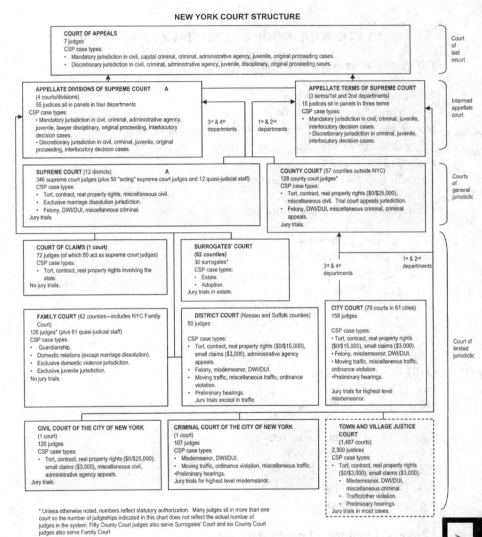

Source: Court Statistics Project, State Court Caseload Statistics, 2004 (National Center for State Courts 2006). Reprinted with permission.

COURT DIRECTORY

STATE-WIDE COURT ADMINISTRATIVE OFFICES

Office of Court Administration

25 Beaver Street–11th Floor
New York, New York 10004
Honorable Jonathan Lippman, Chief Administrative Judge
(212) 428-2150 (New York City Office)
Fax: (212) 428-2188
Internet: http://www.courts.state.ny.us

Commission on Judicial Conduct

61 Broadway, 12th Floor
New York, New York 10006
(212) 809-0566
Fax: (212) 809-3664
www.scjc.state.ny.us (for all offices)

38-40 State Street
Albany, New York 12207
(518) 474-5617
Fax: (518) 486-1850
www.scjc.state.ny.us

400 Andrews Street, Suite 700
Rochester, New York 14604
(585) 232-5756
Fax: (585) 232-7834
www.scjc.state.ny.us

Lawyers' Fund for Client Protection

119 Washington Avenue
Albany, New York 12210
(518) 434-1935
(800) 442-3863
Fax: (518) 434-5641
E-mail: raywood@nylawfund.org or info@nylawfund.org
Internet: http://www.nylawfund.org

Department of State

41 State Street
Albany, New York 12231-1001
(518) 474-4750; (518) 474-6740
Fax: (518) 474-4765; (518) 473-9211
E-mail: info@dos.state.ny.us; counsel@dos.state.ny.us
Internet: http://www.dos.state.ny.us

New York City Regional Office

123 William Street
19th Floor
New York, New York 10038
(212) 417-5800
Fax: (212) 417-5805
www.dos.state.ny.us

Division of Corporations and State Records

41 State Street
Albany, New York 12231
(518) 473-2492
Fax: (518) 474-5173 or (518) 474-1418
Record Searches: 1-900-TEL-CORP; 1-900-835-2677
State Records: (518) 478-4770
Uniform Commercial Codes: (518) 474-4763
Fax: (518) 474-4478
Email: corporations@dos.state.ny.us
Internet: http://www.dos.state.ny.us

NEW YORK STATE COURTS
www.nycourts.gov (Information for all NYS courts)

Court of Appeals

Court of Appeals Hall
20 Eagle Street
Albany, New York 12207-1095
(518) 455-7700
Internet: http://www.courts.state.ny.us/ctapps

Appellate Division

First Department

27 Madison Avenue at 25th Street
New York, New York 10010
(212) 340-0400
Fax: (212) 889-4412

Second Department

45 Monroe Place
Brooklyn, New York 11201
(718) 875-1300
Clerk: (718) 858-2446
www.nycourts.gov/court/ad2/

Third Department

Justice Building
Empire State Plaza, Fifth Floor, Room 505
Albany, New York 12203
(518) 471-4708
Fax: (518) 471-4750
www.courts.state.ny.us

mailing address:
Capitol Station
P.O. Box 7288
Albany, New York 12224

Fourth Department

50 East Avenue
Suite 200
Rochester, New York 14604
(585) 530-3100
Clerk: (585) 530-3247
www.courts.state.ny.us

Court of Claims

Justice Building
P.O. Box 7344
Capitol Station
Albany, New York 12224-0902
(518) 432-3411
Clerk: Robert T. DeCatalvo
(518) 432-3463
Fax for filing: (866) 413-1069
www.nyscourtofclaims.state.ny.us

Court Directory

26 Broadway, 10th Floor
New York, New York 10014
Clerk: Kathleen Green
(212) 361-8100
Receptionist: (212) 361-8150
Fax: (212) 361-8163

COUNTY DIRECTORY

Albany County

Third Department, Third Judicial District)
www.nycourts.gov

Supreme Court

32 North Russell Road
Albany, New York 12206
(518) 487-5100; (518) 487-5012
Fax: (518) 487-5099; (518) 487-5020

Surrogate's Court

16 Eagle Street
Courthouse, Rm 118
Albany, New York 12207
(518) 285-8585
Chief Clerk: Stacy L. Pettit
Fax: (518) 487-5087

County Court

6 Lodge Street
Courthouse, Rm 113
Albany, New York 12207
(518) 285-8777
Fax: (518) 436-3986
Chief Clerk: Charles E. Diamond
(518) 487-5018
Fax: (518) 487-5020

Family Court

30 Clinton Avenue
Albany, New York 12207
(518) 285-8600
Fax: (518) 462-4248

City Court

Civil Court

24 Eagle Street (Eagle & Corning Place)
Rm 209 City Hall
Albany, New York 12207
Chief Clerk: Linda File
(518) 434-5115
Fax: (518) 434-5034
www.nycourts.gov

97 Mohawk Street
P.O. Box 678
Cohoes, New York 12047-0678
Chief Clerk: Janet LeBeau
(518) 233-2133
Fax: (518) 233-8202

City Hall
15th Street & Broadway
Watervliet, New York 12189
Chief Clerk: Robin Robillard
(518) 270-3803
Fax: (518) 270-3812

Sheriff

16 Eagle Street
Albany, New York 12207
(518) 487-5400
Civil Unit Fax: (518) 487-5352

Allegany County

(Fourth Department, Eighth Judicial District)

Supreme Court

Courthouse
7 Court Street
Belmont, New York 14813
Chief Clerk: Kathleen Johnson
Deputy Chief Clerk: Laura Gabler
(585) 268-5813; (585) 268-5800
Fax: (585) 268-7090

Surrogate's Court

Courthouse
7 Court Street
Belmont, New York 14813
Chief Clerk: Carolyn Miller
(585) 268-5815
Deputy Chief Clerk: Kathy Brownell
(585) 268-5816
Fax: (585) 268-7090

County Court

Courthouse
7 Court Street
Belmont, New York 14813
(585) 268-5813; (585) 268-5800
Fax: (585) 268-7090

Family Court

Courthouse
7 Court Street
Belmont, New York 14813
(585) 268-5816
Fax: (585) 268-7090

Sheriff

7 Court Street
Belmont, New York 14813
(716) 268-9200, 08
Fax: (716) 268-9475

Bronx County

(First Department, Twelfth Judicial District)

Supreme Court

851 Grand Concourse, Rm 217
Bronx, New York 10451
215 East 161st Street
(718) 590-2858
General Information: (718) 590-3803
Civil Division: (718) 590-3722, 3
Chief Clerk: Tracy Pardo
(718) 590-3985
Fax: (718) 590-8914
Internet: www.nycourts.gov

Surrogate's Court

851 Grand Concourse, Rm 326
Bronx, New York 10451
General Information: (718) 590-3318
Records: (718) 590-3618
Chief Clerk: Tracy Pardo
(718) 590-4515
Fax: (718) 537-5158

Family Court

900 Sheridan Avenue
Bronx, New York 10451
Judge's Chambers: (718) 590-3377
Clerk of Court: (718) 590-3318
Fax: (718) 590-2681

Civil Court

851 Grand Concourse, Basement/Ground Floor
Bronx, New York 10451
Chief Clerk: Tracy Pardo
(718) 590-3600
Clerk: (718) 590-3603

Broome County

(Third Department, Sixth Judicial District)

Supreme Court

92 Court Street
Courthouse, Rm 204
P.O. Box 1766
Binghamton, New York 13902-1766
(607) 778-2448
Fax: (607) 778-6426

Surrogate's Court

Courthouse, Rm 109
P.O. Box 1766
Binghamton, New York 13902-1766
Chief Clerk: Marilyn A. Vescio
Deputy Chief Clerk: Rebecca Malmquist
(607) 778-2111
Fax: (607) 778-2308

County Court

George Harvey Justice Building
65 Hawley Street
P.O. Box 1766
Binghamton, New York 13902-1766
(607) 778-2448
Fax: (607) 778-6426

Family Court

65 Hawley Street
P.O. Box 1766
Binghamton, New York 13902-1766
(607) 778-2156
Fax: (607) 778-2067
District Office: (607) 721-8541

City Court

Governmental Plaza
38 Hawley Street
Binghamton, New York 13901
(607) 772-7006
Fax: (607) 772-7041
District Office: (607) 721-8541

Sheriff

155 Lt. Van Winkle Drive
Binghamton, New York 13905
(607) 778-2492
Fax: (607) 778-2100

Cattaraugus County

(Fourth Department, Eighth Judicial District)

Supreme Court

County Center
303 Court Street
Little Valley, New York 14755
Deputy Chief Clerk: Kim Reed
(716) 938-9111, Ext. 388, Ext. 384
Fax: (716) 938-6413

Surrogate's Court

County Center
303 Court Street
Little Valley, New York 14755-1096
Chief Clerk: Christine Wrona
(716) 938-9111, Ext. 2327
Fax: (716) 938-6983

County Court

County Center
303 Court Street
Little Valley, New York 14755
(716) 938-9111, Ext. 388
Fax: (716) 938-6413

Family Court

1 Leo Moss Drive
Olean, New York 14760
Chief Clerk: Ruth Dickerson
Deputy Chief Clerk: Denise Filjones
(716) 373-8035
Fax: (716) 373-0449

City Court

Municipal Building
101 East State Street
P.O.Box 631
Olean, New York 14760-0631
Chief Clerk: Rhonda Deckman
(716) 376-5620
Fax: (716) 376-5623

Municipal Center
225 Wildwood Avenue
Salamanca, New York 14779
Deputy Chief Clerk: Stella S. Johnston
(716) 945-4153
Fax: (716) 945-2362

Sheriff

County Center
301 Court Street
Little Valley, New York 14755
(716) 938-9111 Ext. 2204

Cayuga County

(Fourth Department, Seventh Judicial District)

Supreme Court

Courthouse
152-154 Genesee Street
Auburn, New York 13021-3474
(315) 255-4320
Fax: (315) 255-4322
Internet: www.courts.state.ny.us

Surrogate's Court

Courthouse
152-154 Genesee Street
Auburn, New York 13021-3471
(315) 255-4316
Fax: (315) 255-4322

County Court

Courthouse
152-154 Genesee Street
Auburn, New York 13021-3474
(315) 255-4320
Fax: (315) 255-4322

Family Court

Courthouse
Historic Post Office Building
157 Genesee Street
Auburn, New York 13021-3476
(315) 255-4306
Fax: (315) 255-4312

City Court

Historic Post Office
157 Genesee Street
Auburn, New York 13021-3434
(315) 253-1570
Fax: (315) 253-1085

Sheriff

Public Safety Building
7445 County House Road
Auburn, New York 13021
(315) 253-1222
Fax: (315) 253-1192

Chautauqua County

(Fourth Department, Eighth Judicial District)

Supreme Court

Courthouse
1 North Erie Street
P.O. Box 292
Mayville, New York 14757-0292
(716) 753-4266
Fax: (716) 753-4585; (716) 753-4993

Surrogate's Court

Gerace Office Building
Erie Street
P.O. Box C
Mayville, New York 14757-0299
(716) 753-4339
Fax: (716) 753-4600

County Court

Courthouse
1 North Erie Street
P.O. Box 292
Mayville, New York 14757-0292
(716) 753-4266
Fax: (716) 753-4162; (716) 753-4993

Family Court

Gerace Office Building
3 North Erie Street
P.O. Box 149
Mayville, New York 14757-0149
(716) 753-4351
Fax: (716) 753-4350
Chief Clerk: (716) 753-4351

City Court

Dunkirk City Court—City Hall
342 Central Avenue
Dunkirk, New York 14048-2122
(716) 366-2055
Fax: (716) 366-3622

City Hall
Municipal Building
200 East 3rd Street
Jamestown, New York 14701-5433
(716) 483-7561, 2
Fax: (716) 483-7519

Sheriff

Sheriff's Office
15 East Chautauqua Street
P.O.Box 128
Mayville, New York 14757
(716) 753-2131
(716) 753-4276

Chemung County

(Third Department, Sixth Judicial District)

Supreme Court

Hazlett Building
203 Lake Street, 6th Floor
P.O. Box 588
Elmira, New York 14902-0588
(607) 737-2847
Chief Clerk: (607) 737-2084
Fax: (607) 732-8879

Surrogate's Court

Courthouse
224 Lake Street
P.O. Box 588
Elmira, New York 14902-0588
General Number: (607) 737-2946
(607) 737-2873
Fax: (607) 737-2874
Chief Clerk: (607) 737-2873

County Court

Courthouse
224 Lake Street
P.O. Box 588
Elmira, New York 14902-0588
Chief Clerk: (607) 737-2084

Family Court

Justice Building
203-209 William Street
P.O. Box 588
Elmira, New York 14902-0588
(607) 737-2902, 3
Fax: (607) 737-2898

City Court

City Hall
317 East Church Street
Elmira, New York 14901-2790
(607) 737-5681
Fax: (607) 737-5820

Sheriff

Justice Building
203 William Street
Elmira, New York 14902-0588
(607) 737-2987
Fax: (607) 737-2931

Chenango County

(Third Department, Sixth Judicial District)

Supreme Court

Courthouse
West Park Place
Norwich, New York 13815-1676
(607) 337-1740
Catherine A. Schell, Chief Clerk
Irene R. Williams, Deputy Chief Clerk
Court Clerk: (607) 337-1457
Clerk Fax: (607) 337-1835

Surrogate's Court

County Office Building
5 Court Street
Norwich, New York 13815-1676

Linda J. Wiley, Chief Clerk
(607) 337-1827, 22
Fax: (607) 337-1834

County Court

County Office Building
5 Court Street
Norwich, New York 13815-1676
Judge Chambers: (607) 337-1825
Catherine A. Schell, Chief Clerk
Irene R. Williams, Deputy Chief Clerk
Court Clerk: (607) 337-1457
Fax: 607-337-1835

Family Court

County Office Building
5 Court Street
Norwich, New York 13815-1676
Carole S. Dunham, Chief Clerk
Sharon B. Mason, Deputy Chief Clerk
(607) 337-1824; (607) 337-1820
Fax: (607) 337-1835

City Court

1 Court Plaza
Norwich, New York 13815
Linda Roys-Jones, Chief Clerk
(607) 334-1224
Fax: (607) 334-8494

Sheriff

14 West Park Place
Norwich, New York 13815
(607) 334-2000
Fax: (607) 336-1568

Clinton County

(Third Department, Fourth Judicial District)

Supreme Court
Clerk's Office

County Government Center
137 Margaret Street
Plattsburgh, New York 12901-2933
(518) 565-4715
Fax: (607) 565-4708

Surrogate's Court

County Government Center
137 Margaret Street, Suite 315
Plattsburgh, New York 12901-2933
(518) 565-4630
Fax: (518) 565-4769; (518) 565-4688

County Court

County Government Center
137 Margaret Street
Plattsburgh, New York 12901-2933
Chief Clerk: (518) 565-4715
Fax: (518) 565-4708

Family Court

County Government Center
137 Margaret Street
Plattsburgh, New York 12901-2933
(518) 565-4658
Fax: (518) 565-4688

City Court

City Hall
24 U.S. Oval
Plattsburgh, New York 12903
(518) 563-7870
Fax: (518) 563-3124

Sheriff

25 McCarthy Drive
Plattsburgh, New York 12901
(518) 561-4338
Fax: (518) 565-4333

Columbia County

(Third Department, Third Judicial District)

Supreme Court

Courthouse
401 Union Street
Hudson, New York 12534
Dorothy Prestigiacomo, Chief Clerk
(518) 828-7858
Fax: (518) 828-1603

Surrogate's Court

Courthouse
401 Union Street
Hudson, New York 12534
(518) 828-0414
Fax: (518) 828-1603

County Court

Courthouse
401 Union Street
Hudson, New York 12534
(518) 828-7909
Chief Clerk: (518) 828-7858
Fax: (518) 828-1603

Family Court

Courthouse
401 Union Street
Hudson, New York 12534
Dorothy Prestigiacomo, Chief Clerk
(518) 828-0315
Fax: (518) 828-1603

City Court

427 Warren Street
Hudson, New York 12534
(518) 828-3100
Fax: (518) 828-3628

Sheriff

85 Industrial Tract
Hudson, New York 12534
Emergency: (518) 828-3344
Business: (518) 828-0601
Fax: (518) 828-9088

Cortland County

(Third Department, Sixth Judicial District)

Supreme Court

Courthouse
46 Greenbush Street, Suite 301
Cortland, New York 13045-2725
Christina DeMass, Chief Clerk
(607) 753-5013
Fax: (607) 756-3409

Surrogate's Court

Courthouse
46 Greenbush Street, Suite 301
Cortland, New York 13045-2725
Maxine B. Ripley, Chief Clerk
(607) 753-5355
Fax: (607) 756-3409

County Court

Courthouse
46 Greenbush Street, Suite 301
Cortland, New York 13045-2772
Christina DeMass, Chief Clerk
(607) 753-5010
Fax: (607) 756-3409

Family Court

Courthouse
46 Greenbush Street, Suite 301
Cortland, New York 13045-2725
Laurie L. Case, Chief Clerk
Deborah A. Elliott, Deputy Chief Clerk
(607) 753-5353
Fax: (607) 756-3409

City Court

City Hall
25 Court Street
Cortland, New York 13045
Kelly Preston, Chief Clerk
E-mail: kpreston@courts.state.ny.us
(607) 753-1811
Fax: (607) 753-9932

Sheriff

Courthouse
54 Greenbush Street
Cortland, New York 13045-5590
Lee A. Price, Sheriff
(607) 753-3311
Fax: (607) 753-7815

Delaware County

(Third Department, Sixth Judicial District)

Supreme Court

Courthouse
3 Court Street
Delhi, New York 13753
Allison P. Barnes, Chief Clerk
(607) 746-2131
Fax: (607) 746-3253

Surrogate's Court

Courthouse
3 Court Street
Delhi, New York 13753
Nancy A. Smith, Chief Clerk
(607) 746-2126
Fax: (607) 746-3253

County Court

Courthouse
3 Court Street
Delhi, New York 13753
Allison P. Barnes, Chief Clerk
(607) 746-2131
Fax: (607) 746-3253

Family Court

Courthouse
3 Court Street
Delhi, New York 13753
Lori L. Metzko, Chief Clerk
(607) 746-2298
Fax: (607) 746-3253

Sheriff

280 Phoebe Lane
Suite 1
Delhi, New York 13753
(607) 746-2336
(607) 746-2632

Dutchess County

(Second Department, Ninth Judicial District)

Supreme Court

Courthouse
10 Market Street
Poughkeepsie, New York 12601
Ronald P. Varricchio, Chief Clerk
Fern G. Kaelber, Deputy Chief Clerk

(845) 486-2260
Fax: (845) 473-5403

Surrogate's Court

Courthouse
10 Market Street
Poughkeepsie, New York 12601-3203
John Atherton, Chief Clerk
Karen Johnson, Deputy Chief Clerk
(845) 486-2235
Fax: (845) 486-2234

County Court

Courthouse
10 Market Street
Poughkeepsie, New York 12601-3203
Ronald P. Varricchio, Chief Clerk
Fern G. Kaelber, Deputy Chief Clerk
(845) 486-2260
Fax: (845) 473-5403

Family Court

50 Market Street
Poughkeepsie, New York 12601-3204
Peter Palladino, Chief Clerk
(845) 486-2500
Fax: (845) 486-2510

City Court

1 Municipal Plaza
Suite 2
Beacon, New York 12508
Debra Antonelli, Chief Clerk
(845) 838-5030
Fax: (845) 838-5041

62 Civic Center Plaza
P.O. Box 300
Poughkeepsie, New York 12602
Jean Jicha, Chief Clerk
Cheryl Jolie, Deputy Chief Clerk

(845) 451-4091
Fax: (845) 451-4094

Sheriff

150 North Hamilton Street
Poughkeepsie, New York 12601
(845) 486-3800
Fax: (845) 452-2987

Erie County

(Fourth Department, Eighth Judicial District)

Supreme Court

Erie County Hall
25 Delaware Avenue
Ground Floor
Buffalo, New York 14202
(716) 845-9301
Fax: (716) 851-3293

Surrogate's Court

Erie County Hall
92 Franklin Street
Buffalo, New York 14202
(716) 845-2560
Fax: (716) 853-3741

County Court

Erie County Hall
25 Delaware Avenue
Buffalo, New York 14202
Chief Clerk: (716) 858-8452
Fax: (716) 851-3293; (716) 845-9300

Family Court

1 Niagara Plaza
Buffalo, New York 14202
Frank J. Boccio, Chief Clerk
(716) 845-7444

E-mail: fboccio@courts.state.ny.us
Daniel S. Johnston, Deputy Chief Clerk
(716) 845-7440
Email: djohnsto@courts.state.ny.us
Fax: (716) 858-8432

City Court

50 Delaware Avenue
Buffalo, New York 14202
(716) 845-2600
Fax: (716) 847-8257

City Hall
714 Ridge Road
Lackawanna, New York 14218
(716) 827-6486
Fax: (716) 825-1874
Chief Clerk: (716) 827-6672

City Hall
200 Niagara Street
Tonawanda, New York 14150
(716) 845-2160
Fax: (716) 693-1612

Sheriff

10 Delaware Avenue
Buffalo, New York 14202
(716) 858-7608
Fax: (716) 858-7680

Essex County

(Third Department, Fourth Judicial District)

Supreme Court

Courthouse
7559 Court Street
P.O. Box 217
Elizabethtown, New York 12932
(518) 873-3612
Law Library: (518) 873-3377
Fax: (518) 873-3529

Surrogate's Court

Courthouse
7559 Court Street
P.O. Box 217
Elizabethtown, New York 12932
(518) 873-3385
Fax:518-873-3731

County Court

Courthouse
7559 Court Street
P.O. Box 217
Elizabethtown, New York 12932
Chief Clerk (518) 873-3375

Family Court

Courthouse
7559 Court Street
P.O. Box 217
Elizabethtown, New York 12932
(518) 873-3320
Fax: (518) 873-3626

Sheriff

7551 Court Street
P.O. Box 278
Elizabethtown, New York 12932
(518) 873-6321
Fax: (518) 873-3340

Franklin County

(Third Department, Fourth Judicial District)

Supreme Court

Courthouse
355 West Main Street
Malone, New York 12953-1817
Martha Labarge, Acting Chief Clerk
Lise Johnson, Deputy Chief Clerk

(518) 481-1749
Fax: (518) 481-5456

Surrogate's Court

Courthouse
355 West Main Street
Malone, New York 12953
(518) 481-1737
Chief Clerk: (518) 481-1736
Fax: (518) 483-7583

County Court

Courthouse
355 West Main Street
Malone, New York 12953
Martha Labarge, Acting Chief Clerk
Lise Johnson, Deputy Chief Clerk
(518) 481-1749
Fax: (518) 483-5456

Family Court

Courthouse
355 West Main Street
Malone, New York 12953-1893
Janice F. Mock, Chief Clerk
(518) 481-1742
Fax: (518) 481-5453

Commissioner of Jurors

Courthouse
355 West Main Street
Malone, New York 12953
Kathleen M. Monette, Commissioner of Jurors
(518) 481-1756
Fax: (518) 481-6204

Sheriff

Courthouse
45 Bare Hill Road
Malone, New York 12953
(518) 483-3304
Fax: (518) 483-3139

Fulton County

(Third Department, Fourth Judicial District)

Supreme Court

County Building
223 West Main Street
Johnstown, New York 12095
Chief Clerk: (518) 736-5533
Fax: (518) 762-5078

Surrogate's Court

County Building
223 West Main Street
Johnstown, New York 12095
Chief Clerk: (518) 736-5697; (518) 736-5685
Fax: (518) 762-6372

County Court

County Building
223 West Main Street
Johnstown, New York 12095
Chief Clerk: (518) 736-5539
Fax: (518) 762-5078

Family Court

11 North William Street
Johnstown, New York 12095
(518) 762-3840
Fax: (518) 762-9540

City Court

City Hall
3 Frontage Road
Gloversville, New York 12078
(518) 773-4527
Fax: (518) 773-4599

City Hall
33-41 East Main Street
Johnstown, New York 12095
(518) 762-0007
(518) 762-2720

Sheriff

2712 State Highway 29
P.O. Box 20
Johnstown, New York 12095
(518) 736-2100
Fax: (518) 736-2126

Genesee County

(Fourth Department, Eighth Judicial District)

Supreme Court

Courts Facility
1 West Main Street
Batavia, New York 14020-0462
Nelson Green, Chief Clerk
(585) 344-2550, Ext. 2239
Fax: (585) 344-8517
E-mail: ngreen@courts.state.ny.us

Surrogate's Court

Courts Facility
1 West Main Street
Batavia, New York 14020-0462
Colleen Kelly, Chief Clerk
(585) 344-2550, Ext. 2240
Fax: (585) 344-8517
E-mail: ckelly@courts.state.ny.us

County Court

Courts Facility
1 West Main Street
P.O. Box 462
Batavia, New York 14020-2019
Nelson Green, Chief Clerk
(585) 344-2550, Ext. 2239
Fax: (585) 344-8517
E-mail: ngreen@courts.state.ny.us

Family Court

Courts Facility
1 West Main Street
Batavia, New York 14020
Kathleen Blake, Chief Clerk
(585) 344-2550, Ext. 2231
Fax: (585) 344-8520
E-mail: kblake@courts.state.ny.us
Elaine Pommerening, Deputy Chief Clerk
(585) 344-2550, Ext. 2230
Fax: (585) 344-8520
E-mail: epommere@courts.state.ny.us

City Court

Courts Facility
1 West Main Street
Batavia, New York 14020
(585) 344-2550, Ext. 2417
Fax: (585) 344-8556

Sheriff

14 West Main Street
P.O. Box 151
Batavia, New York 14020-0151
(585) 343-0911
Fax: (585) 343-9129

Greene County

(Third Department, Third Judicial District)

Supreme Court

Courthouse
320 Main Street
Catskill, New York 12414
Kathleen Barry Gorczyca, Chief Clerk
(518) 943-2230
Fax: (518) 943-7763

Surrogate's Court

Courthouse
320 Main Street
Catskill, New York 12414
Eric Maurer, Chief Clerk
(518) 943-2484
Fax: (518) 943-7763

County Court

Courthouse
320 Main Street
Catskill, New York 12414
Kathleen Barry Gorczyca, Chief Clerk
(518) 943-2230
Fax: (518) 943-7763

Family Court

Courthouse
320 Main Street
Catskill, New York 12414
Brenda VanDermark, Chief Clerk
Carol Peters, Deputy Chief Clerk
Phone: (518) 943-5711
Fax: (518) 943-1864

Sheriff

80 Bridge Street
P.O. Box 231
Catskill, New York 12414
(518) 943-3300
Fax: (518) 943-6832

Hamilton County

(Third Department, Fourth Judicial District)

Supreme Court

No sessions held (*See Fulton County for information*)
Hamilton County Court Law Library
Hamilton County Court House
Route 8
Lake Pleasant, NY 12108
(518) 648-5411
Fax: (518) 648-6286

Surrogate's Court

mailing address:
P.O. Box 780
Indian Lake, New York 12842-0780

Court sessions held at:
Lake Pleasant, New York 12108
(518) 648-5411
Fax: (518) 648-6286

County Court

mailing address:
P.O. Box 780
Indian Lake, New York 12842-0780

Court sessions held at:
Courthouse
Route 8
Lake Pleasant, New York 12108
(518) 548-3211

Chambers
White Birch Lane
Indian Lake, New York 12842-0780
(518) 648-5411
Fax: (518) 648-6286

Family Court

mailing address:
White Birch Lane
P.O. Box 780
Indian Lake, New York 12842-0780

Court sessions held at:
Courthouse
Route 8
Lake Pleasant, New York 12108
(518) 648-5411
Fax: (518) 648-6286

Sheriff

P.O. Box 210
South Shore Road
Lake Pleasant, New York 12108
(518) 548-3113
(518) 548-3113 (call to fax)

Herkimer County

(Fourth Department, Fifth Judicial District)

Supreme Court

Courthouse
301 North Washington Street
Herkimer, New York 13350-0749
Constance A. Vertucci, Chief Clerk IV
Shirley D. French, Deputy Chief Clerk II
Civil Phone: (315) 867-1209
Criminal Phone: (315) 867-1282
Fax: (315) 866-1802

Surrogate's Court

Courthouse
301 North Washington Street
Herkimer, New York 13350-0749
Constance A. Vertucci, Chief Clerk IV
Shirley D. French, Deputy Chief Clerk II
(315) 867-1170
Fax: (315) 866-1802

County Court

Courthouse
301 North Washington Street
Herkimer, New York 13350-0749
Constance A. Vertucci, Chief Clerk IV
Shirley D. French, Deputy Chief Clerk II
Civil Phone: (315) 867-1209
Criminal Phone: (315) 867-1282
Fax: (315) 866-1802

Family Court

County Office Building
109-111 Mary Street
P.O. Box 749
Herkimer, New York 13350-0749
Lynn M. Kohl, Chief Clerk IV
Mary Leahy, Deputy Chief Clerk II
(315) 867-1139
Fax: (315) 867-1369

City Court

City Hall
659 East Main Street
Little Falls, New York 13365
Jane B. Fortuna Chief Clerk I
(315) 823-1690
Fax: (315) 823-1623

Sheriff

320 North Main Street, Suite 2900
Herkimer, New York 13350-1949
(315) 867-1167
Fax: (315) 867-1354

Jefferson County

Fourth Department, Fifth Judicial District)

Supreme Court

Dulles State Office Building
317 Washington Street, 10th Floor
Watertown, New York 13601
Bonnie S. Johnston, Chief Clerk III
(315) 785-7906
Fax: (315) 785-7909

Surrogate's Court

Jefferson County Court Complex
County Office Building, 3rd Floor
163 Arsenal Street
Watertown, New York 13601
Benjamin Cobb, Chief Clerk I
(315) 785-3019
Fax: (315) 785-5194

County Court

Jefferson County Court Complex
Courthouse
163 Arsenal Street
Watertown, New York 13601
(315) 785-3010
Bonnie S. Johnston, Chief Clerk III
Fax: (315) 785-3330

Family Court

Jefferson County Court Complex
County Office Building
163 Arsenal Street
Watertown, New York 13601
Tanice Gebo, Chief Clerk IV
(315) 785-3001
Fax: (315) 785-3198

City Court

Municipal Building
245 Washington Street
Watertown, New York 13601
Agnes J. Zaremba, Chief Clerk III

(315) 785-7785
Fax: (315) 785-7917

Sheriff

753 Waterman Drive
Watertown, New York 13601
(315) 786-2600, 2700
Fax: (315) 786-2684

Kings County

(Second Department, Second Judicial District)

Supreme Court

360 Adams Street, Room 189
Brooklyn, New York 11201
Nancy T. Sunshine, Chief Clerk
Louis D. Fiorillo, Deputy Chief Clerk
(347) 296-1183
Chief Clerk: (347) 404-9760
Fax: (718) 643-8187

Criminal

120 Schermerhorn Street
Brooklyn, New York 11201
(347) 296-1076
(718) 643-7733

Surrogate's Court

2 Johnson Street
Brooklyn, New York 11201
(347) 404-9700
Chief Clerk: (347) 404-9720
Fax: (718) 643-6237

Family Court

330 Jay Street
Brooklyn, New York 11201
Main Telephone: (347) 401-9600
Clerk of Court: (347) 401-9610; 09

Civil Court

141 Livingston Street
Brooklyn, New York 11201
(718) 643-5069
Clerk: (718) 643-8126
Fax: (718) 643-3733
General Information: (212) 791-6000
Civil: (718) 643-5069
Housing: (718) 643-7916
Small Claims: (718) 643-7914

Under Sheriff

Municipal Building
210 Joralemon Street
Brooklyn, New York 11201
(718) 802-3543
Fax: (718) 802-3715

Lewis County

(Fourth Department, Fifth Judicial District)

Supreme Court

Courthouse
7660 North State Street
Lowville, New York 13367-1396
(315) 376-5347
Fax: (315) 376-5398
Bart R. Pleskach, Chief Clerk I
Clerk of Courts: (315) 376-5380
County Clerk: (315) 376-5333

Surrogate's Court

Courthouse
7660 North State Street
Lowville, New York 13367-1396
(315) 376-5344
Fax: (315) 376-4145

County Court

Courthouse
7660 North State Street
Lowville, New York 13367-1396
Bart R. Pleskach, Chief Clerk I
(315) 376-5366
Fax: (315) 376-5398
Clerk of Courts: (315) 376-5380

Family Court

Courthouse
7660 North State Street
Lowville, New York 13367-1396
Judy C. Meekins, Chief Clerk I
(315) 376-5345
Fax: (315) 376-5189

Sheriff

Public Safety Building
5252 Outer Stowe Street
P.O. Box 233
Lowville, New York 13367
(315) 376-3511
Fax: (315) 376-5232

Livingston County

(Fourth Department, Seventh Judicial District)

Supreme Court

Courthouse
2 Court Street
Geneseo, New York 14454-1030
Diane C. Murphy, Chief Clerk
Clerk's Office: First Floor of the County Courthouse
Chief Clerk: (585) 243-7060
Fax: (585) 243-7067

Surrogate's Court

Courthouse
2 Court Street
Geneseo, New York 14454-1030
(585) 243-7095
Fax: (585) 243-7583

County Court

Courthouse
2 Court Street
Geneseo, New York 14454-1030
Diane C. Murphy, Chief Clerk
Clerk's Office: First Floor of the County Courthouse
Chief Clerk: (585) 243-7060
Fax: (585) 243-7067

Family Court

Courthouse
2 Court Street
Geneseo, New York 14454-1030
(585) 243-7070
Fax: (585) 243-7076

Sheriff

4 Court Street
Geneseo, New York 14454
(585) 243-7120
(585) 243-7926

Madison County

(Third Department, Sixth Judicial District)

Supreme Court

Courthouse
North Court Street
P.O. Box 545
Wampsville, New York 13163
Marianne Kincaid, Chief Clerk

Court Directory

(315) 366-2267
Fax: (315) 366-2539

Surrogate's Court

Courthouse
North Court Street
P.O. Box 607
Wampsville, New York 13163
Andrea L. Slivinski, Chief Clerk
(315) 366-2392
Fax: (315) 366-2539

County Court

Courthouse
North Court Street
P.O. Box 545
Wampsville, New York 13163
Marianne Kincaid, Chief Clerk
(315) 366-2267
Fax: (315) 366-2539

Family Court

Courthouse
North Court Street
P.O. Box 607
Wampsville, New York 13163
Cheryl Collins, Chief Clerk
(315) 366-2291
Fax: (315) 366-2828;2539

City Court

109 North Main Street
Oneida, New York 13421
Lynn Mondrick, Chief Clerk
(315) 363-1310
Fax: (315) 363-3230

Sheriff

County Correctional Facility
North Court Street
Wampsville, New York 13163
(315) 366-2289
Fax: (315) 366-2286

Monroe County

(Fourth Department, Seventh Judicial District)

Supreme Court

Hall of Justice
99 Exchange Boulevard Room 161B
Rochester, New York 14614-2185
Chief Court Clerk: (585) 428-1779
(585) 428-2020, 2331
Fax: (585) 428-2190
E-mail: monroe_superior@courts.state.ny.us

Surrogate's Court

Room 545 Hall of Justice
99 Exchange Boulevard
Rochester, New York 14614-2186
James L. Hendricks, Esq. Chief Clerk
Court Clerk: (585) 428-1779
(585) 428-2020, 2331
Fax: (585) 428-2190

County Court

Hall of Justice
99 Exchange Boulevard Room 161B
Rochester, New York 14614-2185
James L. Hendricks, Esq. Chief Clerk
Chief Court Clerk: (585) 428-1779
(585) 428-2020, 2331
Fax: (585) 428-2190
E-mail: monroe_superior@courts.state.ny.us

Family Court

Hall of Justice
99 Exchange Boulevard Room 360
Rochester, New York 14614-2187
(585) 428-5429
Chief Clerk: (585) 428-2002
Fax: (585) 428-2597

City Court

Civil Branch
Hall of Justice
99 Exchange Boulevard Room 6
Rochester, New York 14614
(585) 428-2444
Fax: (585) 428-2588

Sheriff

130 South Plymouth Avenue
Rochester, New York 14614
(585) 428-5780, 1
Fax: (585) 428-5851

Montgomery County

(Third Department, Fourth Judicial District)

Supreme Court

Courthouse
58 Broadway
P.O. Box 1500
Fonda, New York 12068-1500
(518) 853-4432
Fax: (518) 853-8378
Chief Clerk: 518-853-4516
Fax: 518-853-3596

Surrogate's Court

Courthouse
58 Broadway
P.O. Box 1500
Fonda, New York 12068-1500

Chief Clerk: 518-853-8108
Fax: 518-853-8230

County Court

Courthouse
58 Broadway
P.O. Box 1500
Fonda, New York 12068-1500
(518) 853-4432
Fax: (518) 853-8378
Chief Clerk: 518-853-4516
Fax: 518-853-3596

Family Court

Courthouse
58 Broadway
P.O. Box 1500
Fonda, New York 12068-1500
Chief Clerk: (518) 853-8134
Fax: (518) 853-8148

City Court

Public Safety Building, Room 208
1 Guy Park Avenue Extension
Amsterdam, New York 12010
(518) 842-9510
Fax: (518) 843-8474

Sheriff

Sheriff's Office
200 Clark Drive
Fultonville, New York 12072
Civil: (518) 853-5515
Sheriff Fax: (518) 853-4969

Nassau County

(Second Department, Tenth Judicial District)

Supreme Court

Supreme Court Building
100 Supreme Court Drive
Mineola, New York 11501
Deputy Chief Clerk Fax: (516) 571-1427
Chief Clerk: (516) 571-2904
Fax: (516) 571-1575

Surrogate's Court

262 Old Country Road
Mineola, New York 11501
Chief Clerk-Referee: (516) 571-2082
Fax: (516) 571-3864, 3803

County Court

262 Old Country Road
Mineola, New York 11501
(516) 571-2800, 01
Chief Clerk: (516) 571-2720
Fax: (516) 571-2160

Family Court

1200 Old Country Road
Westbury, New York 11590
(516) 571-9033
Fax: (516) 571-9335

District Court

First District Court

99 Main Street
Hempstead, New York 11550
Chief Clerk: (516) 572-2355
Civil Court: (516) 572-2264 or (516) 572-2256
Fax: (516) 572-2291, 2507

Second District Court

Town Hall
99 Main Street
Hempstead, New York 11550
(516) 572-2264
Fax: (516) 572-2507

Third District Court

435 Middleneck Road
Great Neck, New York 11023
(516) 571-8400
Fax: (516) 571-8403, 02

Fourth District Court

99 Main Street
Hempstead, New York 11550
(516) 572-2261

City Court

9-13 Glen Street
Glen Cove, New York 11542-2776
Heddy Amstel, Chief Clerk
(516) 676-0109
Fax: (516) 676-1570

1 West Chester Street
Long Beach, New York 11561
Joann Spiritis, Chief Clerk
(516) 431-1000
Fax: (516) 889-3511

Sheriff

Civil Bureau
Nassau County Office Building
240 Old Country Road
Mineola, New York 11501
(516) 571-2113
Fax: (516) 571-5086

New York County

(First Department, First Judicial District)

Supreme Court

60 Centre Street
New York, New York 10007-1474
(646) 386-3685
Chief Clerk and Executive Officer, Civil Branch: (646) 386-3685
Fax: (646) 386-3001

Surrogate's Court

31 Chambers Street
New York, New York 10007
Jane Passenant, Chief Clerk
Jana Cohn, Deputy Chief Clerk
(212) 374-8232
(212) 374-8557

Family Court

60 Lafayette Street, Suite 11B
New York, New York 10013
General Information: (646) 386-5200
Fax: (212) 748-5272
E-mail: manhattanfamilycourt@courts.state.ny.us

Civil Court

111 Centre Street
New York, New York 10013
Civil Court Information Line (*all 5 boroughs*) : (212) 791-6000

Sheriff

31 Chambers Street Room 608
New York, New York 10007
(212) 788-8731
Fax: (212) 766-9666

Niagara County

(Fourth Department, Eighth Judicial District)

Supreme Court

775 3rd Street
Niagara Falls, New York 14302-1710
(716) 278-1800
Fax: (716) 278-1809

Surrogate's Court

Courthouse
175 Hawley Street
Lockport, New York 14094-2758
(716) 439-7319
Fax: (716) 439-7157
Chief Clerk: (716) 439-7130

County Court

Courthouse
175 Hawley Street
Lockport, New York 14094-2758
(716) 439-7148
Fax: (716) 439-7157
Chief Clerk: (716) 439-7145

Family Court

Niagara County Civil Building
775 Third Street at Cedar
Niagara Falls, New York 14302-1710
(716) 278-1880
Fax: (716) 278-1877

City Court

Niagara County Courthouse
175 Hawley Street 2nd Floor
Lockport, New York 14094
General Information: (716) 439-7172
Fax: (716) 278-1877

Public Safety Building
520 Hyde Park Boulevard
Niagara Falls, New York 14302-2725

Civil: (716) 278-9860
Fax: (716) 278-9869

City Hall
216 Payne Avenue
North Tonawanda, New York 14120-5446
(716) 693-1010
Fax: (716) 743-1754

Sheriff

P.O. Box 496
5526 Niagara Street
Lockport, New York 14094-1898
(716) 438-3393
Fax: (716) 438-3302

Oneida County

(Fourth Department, Fifth Judicial District)

Supreme Court

Courthouse
200 Elizabeth Street
Utica, New York 13501
(315) 798-5889, 90
Joseph P. Panella, Chief Clerk IV
Kathleen Aiello, Deputy Chief Clerk IV
Chief Clerk: (315) 798-5890
Deputy Chief Clerk: (315) 798-5889
Fax: (315) 798-6436

Surrogate's Court

Oneida County Office Building
800 Park Avenue
Eighth Floor
Utica, New York 13501
Martha R. Hoffman, Chief Clerk V
Kristine K. Pecheone, Deputy Chief Clerk III
(315) 797-9230
Rome Office: (315) 336-6860
Fax: (315) 797-9237

County Court

Courthouse
200 Elizabeth Street
Utica, New York 13501
Joseph P. Panella, Chief Clerk VI
Kathleen Aiello Deputy Chief Clerk IV
Chief Clerk: (315) 798-5890
Deputy Chief Clerk: (315) 798-5889
Fax: (315) 798-6436

Family Court

Courthouse
200 Elizabeth Street
Utica, New York 13501
Sherree Jackson, Chief Clerk III
Chief Clerk: (315) 798-5925
Fax: (315) 798-6404

Oneida County Office Building
301 West Dominick Street
Rome, New York 13440-5196
Barbara L. Tokarsky, Deputy Chief Clerk
(315) 337-7492
Fax: (315) 336-3828

City Court

100 West Court Street
Rome, New York 13440
Eleanor T. Coniglio, Chief Clerk II
Susan G. Exner, Deputy Chief Clerk II
(315) 337-6440
Fax: (315) 338-0343

373 Sherrill Road
Sherrill, New York 13461
Carol A. Shea, Chief Clerk I
(315) 363-0996
Fax: (315) 363-1176

411 Oriskany Street West
Utica, New York 13502
Steven R. Pecheone, Chief Clerk IV
Lori O'Brien, Deputy Chief Clerk II
(315) 724-8157

Chief Clerk: (315) 724-8150
Fax: (315) 792-8038

Sheriff

Law Enforcement Building
6065 Judd Road
Oriskany, New York 13424
(315) 765-2222
Fax: (315) 765-2205

Onondaga County

(Fourth Department, Fifth Judicial District)

Supreme Court

Courthouse
401 Montgomery Street
Syracuse, New York 13202
Patricia J. Noll, Chief Clerk VI
James E. Makowiec, Deputy Chief Clerk IV
Chief Clerk: (315) 671-1030
Fax: (315) 671-1176

Surrogate's Court

Courthouse
401 Montgomery Street, Room 209
Syracuse, New York 13202-2173
Ava S. Raphael, Chief Clerk VI
(315) 671-2100
Fax: (315) 671-1162

County Court

Courthouse
401 Montgomery Street
Syracuse, New York 13202
(315) 671-1030
Fax: (315) 671-1191

Family Court

Courthouse
401 Montgomery Street
Syracuse, New York 13202
Bobette J. Morin, Chief Clerk VI
Florence Walsh, Deputy Chief Clerk IV
Chief Clerk: (315) 671-2060
Fax: (315) 671-1163

City Court

Public Safety Building
505 South State Street
Syracuse, New York 13202-2179
(315) 671-2785
Chief Clerk: (315) 671-2776
Fax: (315) 671-2740

Sheriff

407 South State Street
Syracuse, New York 13202
(315) 435-3044
Fax: (315) 435-2942

Ontario County

(Fourth Department, Seventh Judicial District)

Supreme Court

Courthouse
27 North Main Street, Rm 130
Canandaigua, New York 14424-1447
Kathleen D. Sweeney, Chief Clerk
(585) 396-4239
Fax: (585) 396-4576

Surrogate's Court

Courthouse
27 North Main Street, Rm 130
Canandaigua, New York 14424-1447
(585) 396-4055
Fax: (585) 396-4576

County Court

Courthouse
27 North Main Street, Rm 130
Canandaigua, New York 14424-1447
Kathleen D. Sweeney, Chief Clerk
(585) 396-4239
Fax: (585) 396-4576

Family Court

Courthouse
27 North Main Street, Rm 130
Canandaigua, New York 14424-1447
(585) 396-4272
Fax: (585) 396-4576

City Court

City Hall
2 North Main Street
Canandaigua, New York 14424-1448
Lisa Schutz, Chief Clerk
(585) 396-5011
Fax: (585) 396-5012

Public Safety Building
255 Exchange Street
Geneva, New York 14456
(315) 789-6560
Fax: (315) 781-2802

Sheriff

Sheriff's Office
74 Ontario Street
Canandaigua, New York 14424
(585) 394-4560
Fax: (585) 394-3245

Orange County

(Second Department, Ninth Judicial District)

Supreme Court

Orange County Government Center
285 Main Street
Goshen, New York 10924
(845) 291-3111
Fax: (845) 291-2595

Surrogate's Court

Surrogate's Courthouse
30 Park Place
Goshen, New York 10924
Joy V. Morse, Chief Clerk
Jeanne Smith, Deputy Chief Clerk
(845) 291-2193, 94
Fax: (845) 291-2196

County Court

Orange County Government Center
285 Main Street
Goshen, New York 10924
(845) 291-3100
Chief Court Clerk: (845) 291-3111
Fax: (845) 291-2595

Family Court

Orange County Courthouse
285 Main Street
Goshen, New York 10924
(845) 291-3031
Chief Clerk V: (845) 291-3031
Fax: (845) 291-3054

City Court

2 James Street
Middletown, New York 10940
Linda Padden, Chief Clerk
Robin Siegel, Deputy Chief Clerk

(845) 346-4050
Fax: (845) 343-5737

Public Safety Building
57 Broadway
Newburgh, New York 12550
Sharon Reed, Chief Clerk
Franca Stevens, Deputy Chief Clerk
(845) 565-3208
Fax: (845) 565-1244

20 Hammond Street
Port Jervis, New York 12771
Edwina Wulff, Chief Clerk
(845) 858-4034
Fax: (845) 856-2767

Sheriff

110 Wells Farm Road
Goshen, New York 10924
(845) 294-4033
Fax: (845) 294-1590; (845) 291-7603 (Civil Unit)

Orleans County

(Fourth Department, Eighth Judicial District)

Supreme Court

Courthouse
Courthouse Square
3 South Main Street
Albion, New York 14411-1497
Barbara Hale
(585) 589-5458
Fax: (585) 589-0632
E-mail:bhale@courts.state.ny.us

Surrogate's Court

Surrogate's Office
Courthouse Square
3 South Main Street
Albion, New York 14411-1497

Deborah Berry, Chief Clerk
(585) 589-4457
Fax: (585) 589-0632
E-mail: dberry@courts.state.ny.us

County Court

Courthouse
Courthouse Square
3 South Main Street
Albion, New York 14411-1497
Barbara Hale
(585) 589-5458
Fax: (585) 589-0632
E-mail: bhale@courts.state.ny.us

Family Court

Courthouse
Courthouse Square
3 South Main Street
Albion, New York 14411-1497
Mary Washak, Chief Clerk
(585) 589-4457
Fax: (585) 589-0632
E-mail: mwashak@courts.state.ny.us

Sheriff

13925 Route 31
Albion, New York 14411
(585) 589-5528
Fax: (585) 589-6761

Oswego County

(Fourth Department, Fifth Judicial District)

Supreme Court

Courthouse
25 East Oneida Street
Oswego, New York 13126-2693
Theresa M. Stephens, Chief Clerk II
(315) 349-3277
Fax: (315) 349-8513

Surrogate's Court

Courthouse
25 East Oneida Street
Oswego, New York 13126-2693
Judy L. Cooper, Chief Clerk III
(315) 349-3295
Fax: (315) 349-8514

County Court

Courthouse
25 East Oneida Street
Oswego, New York 13126
Theresa M. Stephens, Chief Clerk II
(315) 349-3277
Fax: (315) 349-8513

Family Court

Public Safety Center
39 Churchill Road
Oswego, New York 13126
Sherryl A. Waldron, Chief Clerk IV
Kathleen Halstead, Deputy Chief Clerk II
(315) 349-3350
Fax: (315) 349-3457

City Court

Municipal Building
141 South First Street
Fulton, New York 13069
Maureen Ball, Chief Clerk I
(315) 593-8400
Fax: (315) 592-3415

Conway Municipal Building
20 West Oneida Street
Oswego, New York 13126
Cassie Kinney, Chief Clerk II
(315) 343-0415
Fax: (315) 343-0531

Sheriff

39 Churchill Road
Oswego, New York 13126-6613
(315) 349-3309
Civil Division Fax: (315) 349-3303
Sheriff Direct Fax: (315) 349-3483
Corrections Fax: (315) 349-3349

Otsego County

(Third Department, Sixth Judicial District)

Supreme Court

County Office Building
197 Main Street
P.O.Box 710
Cooperstown, New York 13326
Gloria Chandler, Chief Clerk
(607) 547-4364
Fax: (607) 547-7567
gchandle@courts.state.ny.us

Surrogate's Court

Surrogate's Office
County Office Building
197 Main Street
Cooperstown, New York 13326
Judy M. McBrearty, Chief Clerk
(607) 547-4213
Fax: (607) 547-7566

County Court

County Office Building
197 Main Street
P.O. Box 710
Cooperstown, New York 13326
Gloria Chandler, Chief Clerk
(607) 547-4364
Fax: (607) 547-7567
E-mail: gchandle@courts.state.ny.us

Family Court

County Office Building
197 Main Street
Cooperstown, New York 13326
Karen Eldred, Chief Clerk
Deborah J. Honohan, Deputy Chief Clerk
(607) 607-547-4264
Fax: (607) 547-6412

City Court

Public Safety Building
81 Main Street
Oneonta, New York 13820
(607) 432-4480
Fax: (607) 432-2328

Sheriff

Sheriff's Office

172 County Highway 33 West
Cooperstown, New York 13326
(607) 547-4271
Fax: (607) 547-6413

Putnam County

(Second Department, Ninth Judicial District)

Supreme Court
County Office Building
44 Gleneida Avenue
Carmel, New York 10512
Chief Clerk -Leonard A. Pace
(845) 225-3641, Ext. 336
Fax: (845) 225-6784

Judge John W. Sweeny, Jr.
44 Gleneida Avenue
Carmel, New York 10512
(845) 225-3641, Ext. 222
Fax: (845) 228-0837

Surrogate's Court

Historic Courthouse
44 Gleneida Avenue
Carmel, New York 10512
Linda Schwark, Chief Clerk
(845) 225-3641 Ext. 293
Fax: (845) 228-5761

County Court

County Office Building
40 Gleneida Avenue
Carmel, New York 10512
Chief Clerk-Leonard A. Pace
(845) 225-3641, Ext. 336
Fax: (845) 228-0656

Family Court

County Office Building
40 Gleneida Avenue
Carmel, New York 10512
Karen O'Connor, Chief Clerk
(845) 225-3641, Ext. 286
Fax: (845) 225-4395

Sheriff

3 County Center
Carmel, New York 10512
(845) 225-4300
Fax: (845) 228-5227

Queens County

(Second Department, Eleventh Judicial District)

Supreme Court

Civil Term:

88-11 Sutphin Boulevard
Jamaica, New York 11435
(718) 298-1000
Fax: (718) 520-2204
Chief Clerk (Civil & Matrimonial): (718) 298-1160

Supreme Court

Criminal Term:

125-01 Queens Blvd
Kew Gardens, NY 11415
(718) 520-3542
Fax: (718) 520-2494

Surrogate's Court

88-11 Sutphin Boulevard, 7th Floor
Jamaica, New York 11435
(718) 520-3132

Family Court

151-20 Jamaica Avenue
Jamaica, New York 11432
(718) 298-0197
Fax: (718) 297-2826

Civil Court

89-17 Sutphin Boulevard
Jamaica, New York 11435
(718) 262-7100
Fax: (718) 262-7107

Sheriff

144-06 94th Avenue
Jamaica, New York 11435
Family Court Warrants: (718) 298-7500
Private Sector: (718) 298-7550

Rensselaer County

(Third Department, Third Judicial District)

Supreme Court

Courthouse
72 Congress Street (Congress and 2nd Street)
Troy, New York 12180
Richard F. Reilly, Chief Clerk
(518) 270-3709
Fax: (518) 270-3714

Surrogate's Court

Courthouse
80 Second Street (Congress and 2nd Street)
Troy, New York 12180
(518) 270-3724
Fax: (518) 272-5452

County Court

Courthouse
Congress and 2nd Street
Troy, New York 12180
Richard F. Reilly, Chief Clerk
(518) 270-3709
Fax: (518) 270-3714

Family Court

Rensselaer Family Court Center
1504 Fifth Avenue
Troy, New York 12180
Patricia Beeler, Chief Clerk
(518) 270-3761
Fax: (518) 272-6573

City Court

City Hall
505 Broadway
Rensselaer, New York 12144
(518) 462-6751
Fax: (518) 462-3307

51 State Street
Third Floor
Troy, New York 12180

(518) 273-2434
Fax: (518) 271-2360

Sheriff

4000 Main Street
P.O.Box 389
Troy, New York 12181-0389
(518) 270-5448
Fax: (518) 270-5447

Richmond County

(Second Department, Second Judicial District)

Supreme Court

Courthouse
18 Richmond Terrace
Staten Island, New York 10301
(718) 390-5201
Chief Clerk: (718) 390-5290
Fax: (718) 380-5435
Mail Delivery for Jail:
355 Front Street
Staten Island, New York 10304
(718) 876-6411

Criminal Court
67 Targee Street
Staten Island, NY 10304
(212) 374-5880
Fax: (718) 390-8405

Surrogate's Court

Courthouse
18 Richmond Terrace
Staten Island, New York 10301
(718) 390-5400
Fax: (718) 390-8741

Family Court

100 Richmond Terrace
Staten Island, New York 10301
(718) 390-5460, 1
Clerk of Court: (718) 390-5466
Fax: (718) 390-5247

Civil Court

927 Castleton Avenue
Staten Island, New York 10310
General Information: (212) 791-6000
Civil: (718) 390-5417
Housing: (718) 390-5420
Small Claims: (718) 390-5421
Fax: (718) 390-8108

Under Sheriff

350 Saint Marks Place
Staten Island, New York 10301
(718) 815-8407
Fax: (718) 815-8416

Rockland County

(Second Department, Ninth Judicial District)

Supreme Court

Courthouse
1 South Main Street
New City, New York 10956
John F. Hussey, Chief Clerk
Civil: (845) 638-5393
Fax: (845) 638-5312

Surrogate's Court

1 South Main Street
Suite 270
New City, New York 10956
Virginia Athens, Chief Clerk
Amy Miller, Deputy Chief Clerk

Chief Clerk: (845) 638-5335
(845) 638-5330
Fax: (845) 638-5632

County Court

Courthouse
1 South Main Street
New City, New York 10956
John F. Hussey, Chief Clerk
Civil: (845) 638-5393
Fax: (845) 638-5312

Family Court

Rockland County Courthouse
1 South Main Street, Suite 300
New City, New York 10956
Eileen M. Stanford, Chief Clerk
(845) 638-5300
Fax: (845) 638-5319

Sheriff

55 New Hempstead Road
New City, New York 10956
(845) 638-5456
Fax: (845) 638-5460

St. Lawrence County

(Third Department, Fourth Judicial District)

Supreme Court

Courthouse
48 Court Street
Canton, New York 13617-1169
(315) 379-0326
Mary M. Farley, Esq., Principal Law Clerk
Chief Clerk: (315) 379-2219
Chief Clerk Fax: (315) 379-2423
Chambers Fax: (315) 379-2311

Surrogate's Court

Courthouse
48 Court Street
Canton, New York 13617-1199
John F. Richey, Esq., Principal Law Clerk
(315) 379-2217, 9427
Fax: (315) 379-2372

County Court

Courthouse
48 Court Street
Canton, New York 13617
Stephen J. Easter, Esq., Principal Law Clerk
(315) 379-2214
Fax: (315) 379-9934
Chief Clerk: (315) 379-2219
Chief Clerk Fax: (315) 379-2423
Chambers Fax: (315) 379-2311

Family Court

Courthouse
48 Court Street
Canton, New York 13617-1199
William R. Murphy, Chief Clerk
Deborah L. Darou, Deputy Chief Clerk
(315) 379-2410
Fax: (315) 386-3197

City Court

330 Ford Street
Ogdensburg, New York 13669
Lisa Marie Meyer, Chief Clerk
(315) 393-3941
Fax: (315) 393-6839

Sheriff

Courthouse
48 Court Street
Canton, New York 13617

(315) 379-2222
Fax: (315) 379-0335

Saratoga County

(Third Department, Fourth Judicial District)

Supreme Court

30 McMaster Street, Building 3
Ballston Spa, New York 12020-0600
Chief Clerk: (518) 885-2224
Fax: (518) 884-4758

Surrogate's Court

30 McMaster Street, Building 3
Ballston Spa, New York 12020-0600
(518) 884-4722
Fax: (518) 884-4774

County Court

30 McMaster Street, Building 3
Ballston Spa, New York 12020-0600
(518) 885-2214
Chief Clerk: (518) 885-2224
Fax: (518) 884-4758

Family Court

Saratoga County Municipal Center
35 West High Street
Ballston Spa, New York 12020-0600
(518) 884-9207
Fax: (518) 884-9094

City Court

City Hall
36 North Main Street
Mechanicville, New York 12118
(518) 664-9876
Fax: (518) 664-8606

City Hall
474 Broadway, Suite 3
Saratoga Springs, New York 12866
(518) 584-4862
Fax: (518) 581-0966

Sheriff

6010 County Farm Road
Ballston Spa, New York 12020-0600
(518) 885-6761
Civil Division: (518) 885-2469
Fax: (518) 885-2453

Schenectady County

(Third Department, Fourth Judicial District)

Supreme Court

612 State Street
Schenectady, New York 12305
(518) 285-8401
Chief Clerk: (518) 388-4322
Fax: (518) 388-4520

Surrogate's Court

Courthouse
612 State Street
Schenectady, New York 12305-2113
(518) 285-8455
Fax: (518) 377-6378

County Court

Courthouse
612 State Street
Schenectady, New York 12305
(518) 285-8401
Chief Clerk: (518) 388-4322
Fax: (518) 388-4520

Family Court

620 State Street
Schenectady, New York 12305-2114
(518) 285-8435
Chief Clerk Melissa Mills
(518) 388-4305
Fax: (518) 388-4496

City Court

Civil Division:
City Hall
105 Jay Street
Schenectady, New York 12305
(518) 382-5077, 8
Fax: (518) 382-5080

Sheriff

Schenectady County Correctional Facility
320 Veeder Avenue
Schenectady, New York 12307
(518) 388-4596
Civil: (518) 388-4304
Fax: (518) 393-5111

Schoharie County

(Third Department, Third Judicial District)

Supreme Court

Courthouse
290 Main Street
Schoharie, New York 12157
F. Christian Spies, Chief Clerk
(518) 295-8342
Fax: (518) 295-7226

Surrogate's Court

Courthouse
290 Main Street
P.O. Box 669
Schoharie, New York 12157-0669
(518) 295-8383
Chief Clerk: (518) 295-8387
Fax: (518) 295-8451

County Court

Courthouse
290 Main Street
Schoharie, New York 12157
F. Christian Spies, Chief Clerk
(518) 295-8342
Fax: (518) 295-7226

Family Court

Courthouse
290 Main Street
Schoharie, New York 12157-0669
(518) 295-8383
Fax: (518) 295-8451

Sheriff

157 Depot Lane
P.O. Box 689
Schoharie, New York 12157-0089
Administration: (518) 295-7066
Civil: (518) 296-8888, (518) 295-7080
Fax: (518) 295-7094

Schuyler County

(Third Department, Sixth Judicial District)

Supreme Court

Courthouse
Unit 35
105 9th Street
Watkins Glen, New York 14891
Karen H. Morgan, Chief Clerk

(607) 535-7760
Fax: (607) 535-4918

Surrogate's Court

Courthouse
105 9th Street
Watkins Glen, New York 14891
(607) 535-7144
Fax: (607) 535-4918

County Court

Courthouse
105 9th Street
Watkins Glen, New York 14891
Karen H. Morgan, Chief Clerk
(607) 535-7760
Fax: (607) 535-4918

Family Court

Courthouse
105 9th Street
Watkins Glen, New York 14891
Lynda L. LoPresti, Chief Clerk
(607) 535-7143; (607) 535-7760
Fax: (607) 535-4918

Sheriff

106 10th Street
Watkins Glen, New York 14891
(607) 535-8222
Fax: (607) 535-8216

Seneca County

(Fourth Department, Seventh Judicial District)

Supreme Court

Courthouse
48 W. Williams Street
Waterloo, New York 13165
(315) 539-7021
Fax: (315) 539-7929

Surrogate's Court

Courthouse
48 W. Williams Street
Waterloo, New York 13165
(315) 539-7531
Fax: (315) 539-3267

County Court

Courthouse
48 W. Williams Street
Waterloo, New York 13165
(315) 539-7021
Fax: (315) 539-7929

Family Court

Courthouse
48 W. Williams Street
Waterloo, New York 13165
(315) 539-4917
Fax: (315) 539-4225

Sheriff

44 W. Williams Street
Waterloo, New York 13165
(315) 539-9241
Fax: (315) 539-0121

Steuben County

(Fourth Department, Seventh Judicial District)

Supreme Court

3 East Pulteney Square
Bath, New York 14810-1575
William Deninger, Chief Clerk & Commissioner of Jurors
(607) 776-7879
Fax: (607) 776-5226

Surrogate's Court

13 East Pulteney Square
Bath, New York 14810-1598
(607) 776-7126
Fax: (607) 776-4987
Chief Clerk: (607) 776-7126

County Court

Courthouse
3 East Pulteney Square
Bath, New York 14810-1575
William Deninger, Chief Clerk & Commissioner of Jurors
(607) 776-7879
Fax: (607) 776-5226

Family Court

Courthouse
3 East Pulteney Square
Bath, New York 14810-1621
(607) 776-9631, Ext. 3450
Fax: (607) 776-7857

City Court

City Hall
12 Civic Center Plaza
Corning, New York 14830-2884
Julie Callahan, Chief Clerk
(607) 936-4111
Fax: (607) 936-0519

82 Main Street
P.O.Box 627
Hornell, New York 14843-0627
Laura Beltz, Chief Clerk
(607) 324-7531
Fax: (607) 324-6325

Sheriff

Steuben County Jail
7007 Rumsey Street Extension
Bath, New York 14810
(607) 776-7009
Fax: (607) 776-7100

Suffolk County

(Second Department, Tenth Judicial District)

Supreme Court

235 Griffing Avenue
Riverhead, New York 11901
(631) 852-2333
Fax: (631) 852-2340
E-mail: www.courts.states.ny.us

Surrogate's Court

320 Center Drive
Riverhead, New York 11901
(631) 852-1745
Fax: (631) 852-1777

County Court

210 Center Drive
Riverhead, New York 11901
Victor V. Rossomano, Chief Clerk
(631) 852-2120
Martha Rogers, Deputy Chief Clerk
(631) 852-2122
Fax: (631) 852-2568
Civil Department: (631) 852-2120

District Court

First District Court

Civil:
3105 Veterans' Memorial Highway
Ronkonkoma, New York 11779-7614
Len Brown, Associate Court Clerk
(631) 854-9678, 76
Fax: (631) 854-9681

Second District Court

30 East Hoffman Avenue
Lindenhurst, New York 11757-5001
Diana Musso, Associate Court Clerk
(631) 854-1121
General Information:
(Central Islip Main District Court) : (631) 853-7500
Fax: (631) 854-1127

Third District Court

1850 New York Avenue
Huntington Station, New York 11746
Marie Mustello, Associate Court Clerk
(631) 854-4545
Fax: (631) 854-4549

Fourth District Court

North County Complex Building 158
P.O. Box 6100
Veterans' Memorial Highway
Hauppauge, New York 11788
Mary J. Tagarelli, Associate Court Clerk
(631) 853-5400, 08
Fax: (631) 853-5951

Fifth District Court

3105 Veterans' Memorial Highway
Ronkonkoma, New York 11779
Elaine R Sorkin, Associate Court Clerk
(631) 854-9676
Fax: (631) 854-9681

Sixth District Court

150 West Main Street
Patchogue, New York 11772
William J. Dobbins, Associate Court Clerk
(631) 854-1440
Fax: (631) 854-1444

Family Court

400 Carleton Avenue
Central Islip, New York 11722
Patricia S. Herlihy, Chief Clerk
Linda Affourtit, Deputy Chief Clerk
(631) 853-4647, 48
Fax: (631) 853-5851; (631) 853-4283

Sheriff

100 Center Drive
Riverhead, New York 11901-3389
(631) 852-2200

Sullivan County

(Third Department, Third Judicial District)

Supreme Court

Courthouse
214 Broadway
Monticello, New York 12701
(845) 794-8811 (Appeal Division)
Chief Clerk: (845) 794-4088
Fax: (845) 789-6170

Surrogate's Court

Government Center
100 North Street
P.O. Box 5012
Monticello, New York 12701
(845) 794-3000, Ext.3450
Fax: (845) 794-0310

Court Directory

County Court

Courthouse
214 Broadway
Monticello, New York 12701
Chief Clerk: (845) 794-4066
Fax: (845) 791-6170

Family Court

Government Center
100 North Street
Monticello, New York 12701
(845) 794-3000, Ext. 3460
Fax: (845) 794-0199

Sheriff

County Jail
4 Bushnell Avenue
Monticello, New York 12701
(845) 794-7102
Fax: (845) 794-4060

Tioga County

(Third Department, Sixth Judicial District)

Supreme Court

16 Court Street
P.O. Box 307
Owego, New York 13827
Joann Peet, Chief Clerk
(607) 687-0544
Fax: (607) 687-3240

Surrogate's Court

Court Annex
20 Court Street
P.O. Box 10
Owego, New York 13827
(607) 687-1303
Fax: (607) 687-3240

County Court

16 Court Street
P.O. Box 307
Owego, New York 13827
Joann Peet, Chief Clerk
(607) 687-0544
Fax: (607) 687-3240

Family Court

Court Annex
20 Court Street
P.O. Box 10
Owego, New York 13827
(607) 687-1730
Fax: (607) 687-3240

Sheriff

103 Corporate Drive
Owego, New York 13827
(607) 687-1010
Fax: (607) 687-6755

Tompkins County

(Third Department, Sixth Judicial District)

Supreme Court

Courthouse
320 North Tioga Street
P.O. Box 70
Ithaca, New York 14851-0070
Nancy M. Joch, Chief Clerk
(607) 272-0466
Fax: (607) 256-0301

Surrogate's Court

Courthouse
320 North Tioga Street
P.O. Box 70
Ithaca, New York 14851-0070

Court Directory

(607) 277-0622
Fax: (607) 256-2572

County Court

Courthouse
320 North Tioga Street
P.O. Box 70
Ithaca, New York 14851-0070
Nancy M. Joch, Chief Clerk
(607) 272-0466
Fax: (607) 256-0301

Family Court

Courthouse
320 North Tioga Street
P.O. Box 70
Ithaca, New York 14851-0070
(607) 277-1517
Fax: (607) 277-5027

City Court

118 East Clinton Street
Ithaca, New York 14850
(607) 273-2263
Fax: (607) 277-3702

Sheriff

779 Warren Road
Ithaca, New York 14850
(607) 257-1345
Fax: (607) 266-5436

Ulster County

(Third Department, Third Judicial District)

Supreme Court

Courthouse
285 Wall Street
Kingston, New York 12401
Clerks: (845) 340-3377
Filings: (845) 340-3288
Fax: (845) 340-3387
Chief Clerk: (845) 340-3370

Surrogate's Court

240 Fair Street
P.O.Box 1800
Kingston, New York 12402-1800
(845) 340-3348
Fax: (845) 340-3352
Chief Clerk: (845) 340-3347
Fax: (845) 256-0301

County Court

Courthouse
285 Wall Street
Kingston, New York 12401-0906
(845) 340-3377
Chief Clerk: (845) 340-3770
Fax: (845) 340-3729

Family Court

16 Lucas Avenue
Kingston, New York 12401-0906
Kathy Lasko, Chief Clerk
(845) 340-3600
Fax: (845) 340-3626
Chief Clerk: (845) 340-3608

City Court

1 Garraghan Drive
Kingston, New York 12401
(845) 338-2974
Fax: (845) 338-1443

Sheriff

129 Schwenk Drive
Kingston, New York 12401-2941
(845) 340-3802
Fax: (845) 334-8125

Warren County

(Third Department, Fourth Judicial District)

Supreme Court

Warren County Municipal Center
1340 State Route 9
Lake George, New York 12845
Joseph Hughes, Jr., Chief Clerk
Pamela Waite, Deputy Chief Clerk
(518) 761-6547
Fax: (518) 761-6465; (518) 761-6253
Court Clerk: (518) 761-6431

Surrogate's Court
Warren County Municipal Center
1340 State Route 9
Lake George, New York 12845
(518) 761-6512, 14
Shirley J. Friday, Chief Clerk
Fax: (518) 761-6511; (518) 761-6465

County Court

Warren County Municipal Center
1340 State Route 9
Lake George, New York 12845-9803
Joseph Hughes, Jr., Chief Clerk
Pamela Waite, Deputy Chief Clerk
Judge Hall Chambers: (518) 761-7695
Fax: (518) 761-7698

Family Court

Warren County Municipal Center
1340 State Route 9
Lake George, New York 12845
AnneMarie Lavigne, Chief Clerk
(518) 761-6500
Fax: (518) 761-6230

City Court

42 Ridge Street
Glens Falls, New York 12801
Philip Simms, Chief Clerk
(518) 798-4714
Fax: (518) 798-0137

Sheriff

Warren County Municipal Center
1340 State Route 9
Lake George, New York 12845-9803
(518) 761-6477
Fax: (518) 761-6234

Washington County

(Third Department, Fourth Judicial District)

Supreme Court

Courthouse
383 Broadway
Fort Edward, New York 12828
(518) 746-2521
Fax: (518) 746-2519

Surrogate's Court

Courthouse
383 Broadway
Fort Edward, New York 12828
(518) 746-2545
Fax: (518) 746-2547

County Court

Courthouse
383 Broadway
Fort Edward, New York 12828
Clerk: (518) 746-2521
Fax: (518) 746-2519

Family Court

Courthouse
383 Broadway
Fort Edward, New York 12828
(518) 746-2501
Fax: (518) 746-2503

Sheriff

383 Broadway
Fort Edward, New York 12828
(518) 854-9245
Main Fax: (518) 746-2483
Substation Fax: (518) 854-9720

Wayne County

(Fourth Department, Seventh Judicial District)

Supreme Court

Room 106 Hall of Justice
54 Broad Street
Lyons, New York 14489-1199
Ellis W. Bozzolo, Chief Clerk & Commissioner of Jurors
(315) 946-5459
Fax: (315) 946-5456

Surrogate's Court

Room 106 Hall of Justice
54 Broad Street
Lyons, New York 14489-1199
(315) 946-5430
Fax: (315) 946-5433

County Court

Room 106 Hall of Justice
54 Broad Street
Lyons, New York 14489-1199
(315) 946-5459
Chief Clerk: (315) 946-5457
Fax: (315) 946-5456

Family Court

Room 106 Hall of Justice
54 Broad Street
Lyons, New York 14489-1199
(315) 946-5420
Chief Clerk: (315) 946-5421
Fax: (315) 946-5456

Sheriff

County Jail
7368 Route 31
Lyons, New York 14489-9107
(315) 946-9711
Fax: (315) 946-5811

Westchester County

(Second Department, Ninth Judicial District)

Supreme Court

111 Dr. Martin Luther King Jr. Blvd., Rm. 803
White Plains, New York 10601
Donna Minort, Chief Clerk
Ronda Brown, Deputy Chief Clerk
Elizabeth Pace, Deputy Chief Clerk
(914) 995-3838
Chief Clerk: (914) 995-4336
(914) 824-5300/5400
Fax: (914) 995-3427
Administrative Office: (914) 995-4100

Surrogate's Court

140 Grand Street
White Plains, New York 10601
Chief Clerk: (914) 824-5653, 56
Fax: (914) 995-3728
John W. Kelly Esq., Chief Clerk
Frank Pezzella , Deputy Chief Clerk
(914) 995-3712

County Court

111 Dr. Martin Luther King Jr. Blvd.
White Plains, New York 10601
Donna Minort, Chief Clerk
Ronda Brown, Deputy Chief Clerk
Elizabeth Pace, Deputy Chief Clerk
(914) 995-3838
Chief Clerk: (914) 995-4336
(914) 824-5300/5400
Fax: (914) 995-3427
Administrative Office: (914) 995-4100

Family Court

111 Dr. Martin Luther King Jr. Blvd.
White Plains, New York 10601
James McAllister, Chief Clerk
Sonia Soto & Queenie Anderson, Deputy Chief Clerks
(914) 824-5500
Fax: (914) 995-8650
(914) 995-3600
Fax (Clerk) : (914) 995-4468

420 North Avenue
New Rochelle, New York 10801
James McAllister, Chief Clerk
Sonia Soto & Queenie Anderson, Deputy Chief Clerks
(914) 813-5650
Fax (Clerk) : (914) 813-5580; (914) 633-4680

53 South Broadway
Yonkers, New York 10701
James McAllister, Chief Clerk
Sonia Soto & Queenie Anderson, Deputy Chief Clerks

(914) 231-2950
Support Matters: (914) 231-2978
Fax: (914) 966-6861; (914) 231-2814

City Court

Two North Roosevelt Square
Mount Vernon, New York 10550-2019
Lawrence Darden, Chief Clerk
Judith Hicks, Deputy Chief Clerk
(914) 665-2400
Fax: (914) 699-1230

475 North Avenue
New Rochelle, New York 10801
James Generoso, Chief Clerk
Victoria Kane, Deputy Chief Clerk
(914) 654-2207
(914) 654-2291
Fax: (914) 654-0344

2 Nelson Avenue
Peekskill, New York 10566
Janice Laughlin, Chief Clerk
(914) 737-3405
Fax: (914) 736-1889

21 McCullough Place (formerly Third Street)
Rye, New York 10580
Antoinette Cipriano, Chief Clerk
(914) 967-1599
Fax: (914) 967-3308

77 South Lexington Avenue
White Plains, New York 10601
Patricia Lupi, Chief Clerk
Lynn Ward, Deputy Chief Clerk
(914) 824-5675, 76
Fax: (914) 422-6058

Robert W. Cacace Justice Center
100 South Broadway
Yonkers, New York 10701
Marisa Garcia, Chief Clerk
(914) 377-6326

(914) 377-6377
Fax: (914) 377-6395

Sheriff

Westchester County Police
Saw Mill River Parkway
Hawthorne, New York 10532
(914) 864-7700
Fax: (914) 741-4444

Wyoming County

(Fourth Department, Eighth Judicial District)

Supreme Court

Courthouse
147 North Main Street
Warsaw, New York 14569-1193
Rebecca Miller, Chief Clerk
(585) 786-3148, Ext. 4 or (585) 786-2253
Fax: (585) 786-2818
E-mail: rmmiller@courts.state.ny.us

Surrogate's Court

Courthouse
147 North Main Street
Warsaw, New York 14569-1193
William Beyer, Chief Clerk
Susan Scriven, Deputy Chief Clerk
E-mail:wbeyer@courts.state.ny.us
E-mail:sscriven@courts.state.ny.us
(585) 786-3148, Ext. 5
Fax: (585) 786-3800

County Court

Courthouse
147 North Main Street
Warsaw, New York 14569-1193
Rebecca Miller, Chief Clerk
(585) 786-3148, Ext. 4 or (585) 786-2253
Fax: (585) 786-2818
E-mail:rmmiller@courts.state.ny.us

Family Court

Courthouse
147 North Main Street
Warsaw, New York 14569-1193
Jacqueline Domkowski, Chief Clerk
Susan Scriven, Deputy Chief Clerk
Email:jdomkows@courts.state.ny.us
Email:sscriven@courts.state.ny.us
(716) 786-3148, Ext. 5
Fax: (716) 786-3800

Sheriff

151 North Main Street
Warsaw, New York 14569
(716) 786-8989
Fax: (716) 786-8961

Yates County

(Fourth Department, Seventh Judicial District)

Supreme Court

Courthouse
415 Liberty Street
Penn Yan, New York 14527-1191
Margaret D. DiMartino, Chief Clerk
(315) 536-5126
Fax: (315) 536-5190

Surrogate's Court

415 Liberty Street
Penn Yan, New York 14527-1176
(315) 536-5130
Fax: (315) 536-5190

County Court

Courthouse
415 Liberty Street
Penn Yan, New York 14527-1191
Margaret D. DiMartino, Chief Clerk

(315) 536-5126
Fax: (315) 536-5190

Family Court

415 Liberty Street
Penn Yan, New York 14527-1182
(315) 536-5127
Fax: (315) 536-5190
Chief Clerk: (315) 536-5127

Sheriff

Public Safety Building
227 Main Street
Penn Yan, New York 14527
(315) 536-5182
Fax: (315) 572-4365

INDEX

INDEX

References in the Index to the Consolidated Laws are abbreviated as follows:

ADR   Appellate Division Rules

DRL   Domestic Relations Laws

EXL   Executive Law

FCA   Family Court Act

FCR   Family Court Rules

PPL   Personal Property Law

RCAC   Rules of the Chief Administrator of the Courts (Judicial Conference)

SSL   Social Services (Welfare) Law

INDEX

[References are to sections of the Consolidated Laws as abbreviated on pg. iii.]

A

ABANDONED CHILDREN
Child protective proceeding . . . . FCA 1058;
FCA 1059
Definition . . . FCA 1012; SSL 371
Guardianship
Generally . . . SSL 384-b
Child protective proceedings for child un-
der age of one . . . FCA 1055
Infant protection program . . . SSL 372–g

**ABSENCE FOR DISSOLUTION OF MAR-
RIAGE** (See DISSOLUTION OF MAR-
RIAGE FOR ABSENCE)

ABUSE (See CHILD ABUSE AND MAL-
TREATMENT; DOMESTIC VIOLENCE)

ABUSE OF PROCESS
Discretion of court . . . FCA 145
Liability of judge . . . FCA 145

ACCIDENT INSURANCE
Matrimonial actions; court's order to purchase
. . . DRL 236; FCA 416

**ACQUIRED IMMUNE DEFICIENCY SYN-
DROME (AIDS)**
Aliens diagnosed with . . . SSL 122
Health insurance continuation (See HEALTH
INSURANCE CONTINUATION FOR PER-
SONS WITH AIDS)
Testing of respondent; juvenile delinquency
. . . FCA 347.1

A.D.C. (See DEPENDENT CHILDREN'S AID)

ADOLESCENT PREGNANCY (See PREG-
NANCY, ADOLESCENT)

ADOPTION
Adult, by . . . DRL 110
Adult, of . . . DRL 111
Agency adoptions (See ADOPTION FROM
AGENCIES)
Age of child
Consent of child over age 14 . . . DRL
111
Waiting period for child under 18 . . .
DRL 116

ADOPTION—Cont.
Appearance before court . . . FCR 205.55
Attorney's affidavit
First Department . . . ADR 603.23
Second Department . . . ADR 691.23
Third Department . . . ADR 806.14
Fourth Department . . . ADR 1022.33
Biological parents (See subhead: Natural
parents)
Calendaring of proceedings . . . DRL112-a;
FCR 205.59
Certification proceedings, qualification as adop-
tive parent . . . FCR 205.58
Child abuse
Adoption applicant as abuser . . . DRL
112; SSL 424-a
Neglected/abused child, adoption of (See
subhead: Neglected/abused child, of)
Child care review service, supervision by . .
SSL 442
Communication with biological parents or sib-
lings, agreement for . . . DRL 112-b; FCA
1055-a(b)
Consent required
Generally . . . DRL 111; SSL 384
Stepparent adopting . . . DRL 115-b
Contact with biological parents or siblings,
agreements for . . . 1055-a(b); DRL 112-b
Definitions . . . DRL 109; SSL 451
Expenses
Legal fees, payment of . . . SSL 374
Non-recurring expenses, payments for
. . . SSL 453-a
Extrajudicial proceedings . . . DRL 113
Fair hearings . . . SSL 455
Family court jurisdiction . . . DRL 113; FCA
641
Father-out-of-wedlock
Consent of . . . SSL 384
Determination of paternity issue . . . .
DRL 111-b
Notice to . . . DRL 111-a; SSL 384-c
Foreign-born orphans admitted with non-quota
status . . . DRL 115-a; SSL 371
Foster parents preference . . . SSL 374, 383
Funding . . . SSL 153-j; SSL 153-k

I–1

[References are to sections of the Consolidated Laws as abbreviated on pg. iii.]

[References are to sections of the Consolidated Laws as abbreviated on pg. iii.]

ADOPTION—Cont.

Surrogate courts, jurisdiction of

    Family Court, concurrent with . . DRL 113; FCA 641

        Paternity issues . . . DRL 111-b

Unmarried adult, by . . . DRL 110

Waiting period . . . DRL 116

Wills, effect on . . . DRL 110

ADOPTION FROM AGENCIES

Abused child . . . DRL 112

Agreement of adoption . . . DRL 113

Application

    Denial of . . . SSL 372-e

    Failure of agency to act timely upon . . . SSL 372-e

    Foster parents, adoption by . . SSL 374, 383

    Records of, requirements as to . . SSL 379-e

Authorized agency, definition . . . DRL 109

Child care review service, supervision by . . SSL 442

Detailed background of child . . . DRL 112, 114

Examination of adoptive parents and child by court . . . DRL 112

Foster parents, application for adoption by . . . SSL 374, 383

Listing of children; child over 14 not consenting to . . . SSL 398-b

Name of child, disclosure of . . DRL 112, 114

Neglected child . . . DRL 112

Papers, verification of . . . DRL 112

Parental termination proceedings, children subject to . . . FCR 205.52

Petition

    Adoptive parents and adoptive child over 18, by . . . DRL 112

    Place of filing . . . DRL 113

Proceedings, expedited calendaring of adoption . . . DRL 112-a; FCR 205.59

Schedule annexed to petition by agency . . . DRL 112

Sealed adoption records, disclosure of . . . DRL 114(4)

Standards and procedures, promulgation . . . SSL 372-e

Transfer of custody and guardianship of minor to agency . . . DRL 113

Trial period required for child under 18 years . . . DRL 112

ADOPTION THROUGH PRIVATE PLACEMENT

Affidavits (See specific subheads)

Agreement of adoption . . . DRL 115(4)

Alien children

    Application to court by adoptive parents . . . DRL 115-a

    Certificate, pre-adoption

        Generally . . . DRL 115, 115-a

        Setting aside, conditions for . . . . DRL 115-a

    Failure to comply with law . . . . DRL 115-a

    Investigation, pre-adoption . . . . DRL 115-a

    Nonquota immigrant status of eligible orphans

        Generally . . . SSL 371

        Exception . . . DRL 115-a

Appearance of adoptive parents and child for examination . . . DRL 115(3)

Application

    Notice of . . . DRL 115(10)

    Written application; description of child . . . DRL 115-a(2-a)

Attorney's affidavit

    First Department Rules . . ADR 603.23

    Fourth Department Rules . . . . . ADR 1022.32

    Second Department Rules . . . . ADR 691.23

Certification as qualified parent, pre-adoption

    Generally . . . DRL 115(1)(b)

    Criminal history record . . . . . . DRL 115-d(3-a)

    Petition for certification . . . DRL 115-d

    Temporary guardianship upon waiver . . . DRL 115-c

Change in circumstance of adoptive parents, affidavit . . . DRL 115(6), 115-c

Child care review service, supervision by . . . SSL 442

Consent

    Notice of . . . DRL 115-b

    Person other than natural parent . . . . DRL 115(7)

    Special provisions . . . DRL 115-b

Definition . . . DRL 109

Dismissal of proceedings, consent . . . DRL 115-b

Examination of adoptive parents and child . . . DRL 115

Fees/compensation involved, affidavit as to . . . DRL 115(8)

[References are to sections of the Consolidated Laws as abbreviated on pg. iii.]

[References are to sections of the Consolidated Laws as abbreviated on pg. iii.]

AGED, BLIND, OR DISABLED PERSONS, SERVICES FOR—Cont.

Emergency assistance (See EMERGENCY ASSISTANCE FOR AGED, BLIND, AND DISABLED)

Federal disability benefits, denial or discontinuation; legal advisory committees . . SSL 35

Foster care (See FOSTER CARE)

Home care; consumer directed personal assistance program . . . SSL 365-f

Investigation of application . . . SSL 256

Object of . . . SSL 250

Payments . . . SSL 209

Personal allowances accounts . . . SSL 131-o

Provisions, application of . . . SSL 259

Regulations

    Generally . . . SSL 257

    Purchase by social services department . . . SSL 372-d

    Registry of facilities . . . SSL 463

Residential care programs . . . SSL 460

Responsibility . . . SSL 252

State plan . . . SSL 251

State reimbursement . . . SSL 257; SSL 370-b

Supervision . . . SSL 257

AIDS (See ACQUIRED IMMUNE DEFICIENCY SYNDROME (AIDS))

AID TO DEPENDENT CHILDREN (See DEPENDENT CHILDREN'S AID)

ALCOHOL ABUSE AND ALCOHOLISM

Alcohol awareness program as condition of probation or conditional discharge . . FCA 757

Demonstration project, social service district participation in . . . SSL 364-d

ALIENS

Adoption of child (See ADOPTION THROUGH PRIVATE PLACEMENT)

AIDS, diagnosed with . . . SSL 122

Child protective services, eligibility for . . . SSL 398-e

Food assistance programs . . . SSL 95

Illegal aliens, assistance to . . . SSL 95, 122, 131

Public assistance to . . . SSL 95, 122, 131

Safety net assistance for . . . SSL 122

Supplemental social security income benefits . . . SSL 122

Temporary assistance to needy families block grants . . . SSL 122

ALIMONY

Actions involving . . . DRL 236

Annulment . . . DRL 236

Arrears . . . DRL 236

Contempt order, relief from . . . DRL 246

Default on directed payments; stay in divorce or separation action . . . DRL 239

Divorce, annulment or judgment previously granted . . . DRL 236

Factors determining . . . DRL 236

Financial disclosure (See FINANCIAL DISCLOSURE)

Health insurance coverage, compulsory disclosure of group . . . DRL 236

Liability for . . . DRL 236

Misconduct of spouse . . . DRL 236

Modification of . . . DRL 236, 246

Prison confinement, suspension of payments for . . . DRL 247

Registration of order at the State Case Registry . . . DRL 236

Relief to wife, refusal of . . . DRL 236

Residence in same domicile by parties, effect of . . . DRL 236

Visitation rights interference, effect of . . . . DRL 241

ALMSHOUSES

City home, definition of . . . SSL 2

County home, definition of . . . SSL 2

ANNULMENT

Arrears in payment of money judgment . . . DRL 240

Confidentiality of child's or party's address . . . DRL 254

Consent to marriage obtained by force, duress or fraud . . . DRL 140

Dismissal of action to annul . . . DRL 142

Incurable insanity of spouse, upon

    Action . . . DRL 141

    Grounds . . . DRL 140

    Procedure . . . DRL 141

    Proof required . . . DRL 141

    Statutory authority . . . DRL 7

    Support provisions . . . DRL 141

Judgment, conclusiveness of . . . DRL 146

Mental illness or retardation . . DRL 140, 141

Nonage . . . DRL 140

Order of protection, effect on . . . DRL 252

Proof required for . . . DRL 144

Residence, establishment of . . . DRL 231

Sequestration of property

    Personal service not possible . . . DRL 233

[References are to sections of the Consolidated Laws as abbreviated on pg. iii.]

[References are to sections of the Consolidated Laws as abbreviated on pg. iii.]

[References are to sections of the Consolidated Laws as abbreviated on pg. iii.]

CHARITIES—Cont.

Reports by registered charitable organizations . . . SSL 475

Verified accounts against countries/cities/towns . . . SSL 476

CHILD ABUSE AND MALTREATMENT

Adjudication, disposition on . . . FCA 1052

Adoption

    Applicant as abuser . . . DRL 112; SSL 424-a

    Neglected/abused child, of (See ADOPTION, subhead: Neglected/abused child, of)

Appeals . . . FCA 112

Boarding of children, agency applying for certificate or license . . . SSL 424-a, 424-b

Central registry, statewide

    Access to information . . . SSL 424-a

    Commissioner's annual report . . . SSL 17

    Criminal investigation . . . SSL 422

    Reporting procedure . . . SSL 415

    Statutory provisions . . . SSL 422

    Withholding of information . . . SSL 422

Children and Family Trust Fund Act . . . SSL 481-a *et seq.*

Citizen review panels . . . SSL 371-b

Coroner's report . . . SSL 418

Criminal history record check, prospective foster and adoptive parent . . . SSL 378-a

Definitions . . . SSL 384-b

Department of Mental Hygiene facilities . . . SSL 424-b

Disclosure of child abuse . . . SSL 422-a

Discovery of records involving abuse . . . FCA 1038

Disposition on adjudication . . . FCA 1052

Division for Youth facilities . . . SSL 424-b

Employment with child caring responsibilities . . . SSL 424-a

Evidence as to . . . FCA 1038, 1046; SSL 422

Expungement of unfounded reports . . . SSL 422

False reports . . . SSL 422, 424

Fatality review teams . . . SSL 422-b

Finding of abuse . . . FCA 1051

Foster care, placement of child in . . . FCA 1051

Investigation of child abuse

    Generally . . . SSL 422-a, 423

    Fatality review teams . . . SSL 422-b

    Post-mortem investigations . . SSL 418

CHILD ABUSE AND MALTREATMENT—Cont.

Licensing agency, definition . . . SSL 424-a, 425

Medical examinations and treatment

    Generally . . . SSL 383-b

    City of New York, counties within . . . FCA 235

    Coroner's report . . . SSL 418

    Counties outside City of New York . . FCA 233

    Physician-patient privilege . . SSL 383-a

    Post-mortem investigations . . SSL 418

Mentally ill or retarded, Department of Mental Hygiene facilities . . . SSL 424-b

Order finding . . . FCA 1051

Placement of child in foster care . . . . FCA 1051

Post-mortem investigations . . . SSL 418

Proceeding to determine

    Post-mortem investigations . . SSL 418

    Summons . . . FCA 1035

    Warrant, statements in . . . FCA 1037

Protective removals/placements (See CHILD PROTECTIVE PROCEEDINGS)

Provider agency, definition . . . SSL 425

Register, statewide (See subhead: Central registry, statewide)

Repeatedly abused; defined . . . SSL 384-b

Reports

    Admissibility of . . . FCA 651-a

    Coroner's report . . . SSL 418

    Expungement of unfounded reports . . . SSL 422

Residential care programs, children under . . SSL 422; SSL 424-b

Severely abused; defined . . . SSL 384-b

Sexually abused children, videotapes of interviews with . . . FCR 205.86

Special care homes and programs for parent and child . . . SSL 2, 371

Staff qualifications . . . SSL 423

Statewide central register (See subhead: Central registry, statewide)

Summons . . . FCA 1035

Suspected abuse, reports of . . SSL 413 *et seq.*, 422

Temporary detention of abused child . . SSL 383-a

Temporary removal with consent . . . . FCA 1021

CHILD ASSISTANCE PROGRAM

Generally . . . SSL 131-z

[References are to sections of the Consolidated Laws as abbreviated on pg. iii.]

[References are to sections of the Consolidated Laws as abbreviated on pg. iii.]

[References are to sections of the Consolidated Laws as abbreviated on pg. iii.]

[References are to sections of the Consolidated Laws as abbreviated on pg. iii.]

CHILDREN—Cont.
Orders—Cont.
> Review of orders . . . SSL 385

Parent locator service, state . . . SSL 111-b
Person in need of supervision, as (See PERSON IN NEED OF SUPERVISION)
Physically handicapped child (See PHYSICALLY HANDICAPPED CHILDREN)
Placement (See PLACEMENT OF CHILDREN)
Powers and duties of social services officials in relation to children
> Abandoned children . . . SSL 398
> Aliens . . . SSL 398-e
> Child Welfare Reform Act of 1979 (See CHILD WELFARE REFORM ACT OF 1979)
> Delinquent children . . . SSL 398
> Destitute children . . . SSL 397, 398
> Handicapped children . . . SSL 398
> Institution operation . . . SSL 374-f
> Needy children . . . SSL 398
> Neglected children . . . SSL 397, 398
> Rape-conceived child . . . SSL 384-c
> Unusual handicaps . . . SSL 398
> Welfare services community demonstration projects, child . . . SSL 398-d

Protective proceedings, judicial (See CHILD PROTECTIVE PROCEEDINGS)
Protective services (See CHILD PROTECTIVE SERVICES)
Public institutions for children, authority to operate . . . SSL 374-d; SSL 374-f
Questioning of child in police custody (See QUESTIONING OF CHILD)
Real property, guardianship of (See GUARDIANS)
Residential care programs . . . SSL 460, 462, 412
Runaway, return of . . . FCA 718, 1073
Special charters given to agencies, institutions, etc. . . . SSL 388
State institutions, discharge from . . . SSL 399
State services (See STATE DEPARTMENT OF SOCIAL WELFARE)
Supervisory care (See PERSON IN NEED OF SUPERVISION)
Transfer of care and custody . . . SSL 384-a
Visitation (See VISITATION OF CHILDREN)
Welfare research advisory panel, child . . . SSL 372-a
Youth facilities improvement act (See YOUTH FACILITIES IMPROVEMENT ACT)

CHILDREN AND FAMILY TRUST FUND ACT
Advisory board . . . SSL 481-d
Definitions . . . SSL 481-c
Funding appropriation for . . . SSL 481-f
Grants, awarding of . . . SSL 481-e
Publication of available funding . . . . . SSL 481-e
Purpose of . . . SSL 481-a

CHILDREN'S COURT
Transfer of personnel . . . FCA 215

CHILD SUPPORT
Adjustment of orders . . DRL 240(4); FCA 413
"At direction of court" defined . . . . . DRL 240(1-b); FCA 413
Basic child support obligation . . . . . DRL 240(1-b); FCA 413
Combined parental income . . DRL 240(1-b); FCA 413
Common law marriage, product of . . . DRL 33
Dissolved marriage, offspring of . . . DRL 33
Formula, statewide . . . SSL 111-i
Judicial proceedings (See SUPPORT OR MAINTENANCE PROCEEDINGS)
Liability . . . DRL 32
Local programs (See PUBLIC ASSISTANCE)
Percentage . . . . DRL 240(1-b); FCA 413; SSL 111-i
Pro rata share of noncustodial parent, court calculation . . . DRL 240(1-b); FCA 413
Standards statewide (See CHILD SUPPORT STANDARDS ACT OF 1989)
State program (See STATE DEPARTMENT OF SOCIAL WELFARE, subhead: Child support enforcement program)
Statutory guidelines (See CHILD SUPPORT STANDARDS ACT OF 1989)
Temporary order for child support at discretion of court . . . DRL 236; FCA 434

CHILD SUPPORT PROCEEDINGS
(See also DEPENDENTS' SUPPORT)
Generally . . . FCA 413, 414
Acknowledgment of paternity . . . FCA 516-a
Adjustment of orders for child receiving public assistance (See subhead: Public assistance recipient, child as)
Administration of state support program
> Generally . . . SSL 111
> > Child support formula . . . SSL 111-i
> > Support collection unit . . . SSL 111-h

[References are to sections of the Consolidated Laws as abbreviated on pg. iii.]

Index

COMPANION ANIMALS
Protection orders for . . FCA 446; FCA 656(i);
FCA 759(h); FCA 842(i); FCA 1056(g)

COMPLAINTS
Charities, investigation of . . . SSL 478
Residential care
    Investigation procedures . . . SSL 461-o
    Retaliation for . . . SSL 460-d, 461-a
    Right of appeal in complaint against officer
    or employee by inmate of . . . . SSL
    197
Service of . . . DRL 211, 232

CONCILIATION PROCEEDINGS—
FAMILY COURT
Attendance at conference . . . FCA 924
Commencement of proceeding . . . FCA 921
Continuation of proceeding . . . FCA 925
Duration of proceeding . . . FCA 926
Evidence . . . FCA 915
Family offense proceedings . . . FCA 913
Jurisdiction . . . FCA 912
Marital status . . . FCA 914
Potential petitioner . . . FCA 922
Preliminary procedure . . . FCA 922
Procedure, generally . . . FCA 921–926
Purpose . . . FCA 911
Statements made in proceeding . . . FCA 915
Support proceedings . . . FCA 913
Termination . . . FCA 925
Voluntary agency, referral to . . . FCA 923

CONTEMPT
Alimony, nonpayment of . . . DRL 246
Statute applying . . . FCA 156

COUNCIL ON CHILDREN AND FAMI-
LIES
Generally . . . SSL 483
Emotional and behavioral problems in children,
coordination of services . . . SSL 483-c
Out-of-state placement committee . . . . SSL
483-d
Out-of-state placement registries . . . . SSL
483-d
Powers and duties of council . . . SSL 483-b
Utilization of other agency assistance . . SSL
483-a

COURT ORDERS (See ORDERS OF COURT
(GENERALLY))

CRIMINAL COURT
Family offense proceedings (See FAMILY OF-
FENSES PROCEEDINGS)

CUSTODY
Abused or maltreated children; temporary pro-
tective custody . . . SSL 417
Additional parties . . . DRL 75-k
Annulment of order of judgment . . DRL 240
Arrears in maintenance . . . DRL 240
Berkshire Industrial Farm (See BERKSHIRE
INDUSTRIAL FARM)
Boarded-out child . . . SSL 383
Child support provisions . . . DRL 240
Commitment instruments . . . SSL 384 *et seq.*
Confidentiality of child's or party's address
   . . . DRL 254
Contestant, defined . . . DRL 75-c
Court's discretion as to . . . DRL 240
Custodial parent; defined . . . DRL 236
Decree
    Certified copies of . . . DRL 75-q
    Defined . . . DRL 75-c
    Force and effect . . . DRL 75-m
    Initial decree, defined . . . DRL 75-c
    Modification decree, defined . . . DRL
    75-c
Definition . . . SSL 371
Depositions of out-of-state witnesses . . DRL
75-j
Determination of custody
    Defined . . . DRL 75-c
    Jurisdiction to make . . . DRL 75-d
    Priority . . . DRL 75-x
Divorce cases, children of . . . FCA 467, 652
Extension . . . FCR 205.84
Foster-care children, guardianship of . . SSL
383-c
Foster parents, intervention by . . . SSL 383
Habeas corpus proceedings
    Jurisdiction over . . . FCA 651, 652;
    SSL 384-a
    Referral from Supreme Court . . . FCA
    651
Health insurance coverage of child . . . DRL
240
Home state, defined . . . DRL 75-c
Indian Child Welfare Act . . . FCR 205.51
Indian tribes . . . DRL 75-c; SSL 39
International application . . . DRL 75-w
Jurisdiction to make custody determination
    Generally . . . DRL 75-d; FCA 651, 652
    Communications between courts . . . .
    DRL 75-i
    Declination due to conduct of petitioner
    . . . DRL 75-i
    Extrajudicial proceedings . . . DRL 113

[References are to sections of the Consolidated Laws as abbreviated on pg. iii.]

[References are to sections of the Consolidated Laws as abbreviated on pg. iii.]

Index

[References are to sections of the Consolidated Laws as abbreviated on pg. iii.]

[References are to sections of the Consolidated Laws as abbreviated on pg. iii.]

[References are to sections of the Consolidated Laws as abbreviated on pg. iii.]

EDUCATIONAL SERVICES—Cont.

Responsibility of social services department . . . SSL 421

Training incentive allowance, federal . . SSL 350-i

Transportation costs . . . FCA 236(2)

Vocational Education Fund; Division for Youth (See VOCATIONAL EDUCATION)

ELDERCARE

Social service district participation . . . SSL 364-d

ELECTRIC COMPANY (See UTILITIES)

ELECTRONIC BENEFIT TRANSFER SYSTEM

Pilot project, establishment of . . . SSL 131-q

Statewide implementation . . . SSL 21-a

EMERGENCY ASSISTANCE FOR AGED, BLIND, AND DISABLED

Appeals . . . SSL 305

Application . . . SSL 304

Character and adequacy . . . SSL 303

Definitions . . . SSL 300

Eligibility . . . SSL 302

Guide dogs, grants of assistance for . . SSL 303-a

Hearings . . . SSL 305

Heating fuel crisis assistance . . . SSL 370-aa

Purpose . . . SSL 300

Records and reports . . . SSL 306

Regulations . . . SSL 307

Responsibility . . . SSL 301

Services . . . SSL 308

Verification . . . SSL 304

EMINENT DOMAIN

Commissioner of Social Services, acquisition of property by . . . SSL 40

EMPLOYMENT

Child abuse and maltreatment, statewide central register . . . SSL 424-a

Conviction records; access by authorized agencies hiring supervisors of children . . SSL 378-a

Demonstration projects; public assistance recipients . . . SSL 131

Employable defined . . . SSL 131

Employed defined . . . SSL 131

Employed to capacity defined . . . SSL 131

Job clubs . . . SSL 131, 164-c

Job search activities, participation . . . . SSL 158-b, 350-m

EMPLOYMENT—Cont.

On-the-job training for families with dependent children . . . SSL 350-l

Public assistance employment programs

   Definitions . . . SSL 330

   Dependent children, aid for (See DEPENDENT CHILDREN'S AID)

   Educational activities . . . SSL 336-a

   Employability assessment . . . SSL 335, 335-a

   Job search activities . . . SSL 336-d

   Local plans and requirements . . . SSL 333

   Mandatory work requirements . . . SSL 335-b

   Noncompliance . . . SSL 341, 342

   Orientation . . . SSL 334

   Participation, refusal of . . SSL 341, 342

   Participation and exemptions

      Generally . . . SSL 332

      Disability program . . . SSL 332-b

   Pilot programs . . . SSL 335-c

   Policies . . . SSL 331

   Purpose . . . SSL 331

   Reports . . . SSL 339

   State departments, role of

      Cooperation of . . . SSL 338

      Responsibilities of . . . SSL 337

   Subsidized private sector employment programs . . . SSL 336-f

   Subsidized public sector employment programs . . . SSL 336-e

   Support services

      Generally . . . SSL 332-a

      Child care . . . SSL 332-a

   Technical assistance . . . SSL 340

   Work activities; defined . . . SSL 336

   Worker's compensation . . . SSL 330

   Work experience programs . . . . SSL 336-c

   Work-study programs . . . . SSL 335-b; SSL 336

Public assistance recipients; refusal of employment . . . SSL 131

Safety net assistance funds for . . SSL 158-b, 164-a

Training incentive allowance, federal . . SSL 350-i

ENERGY ASSISTANCE PROGRAMS (See HOME ENERGY GRANTS)

ENOCH ARDEN DECREE

Application . . . DRL 220–221

Index

ENRICHED HOUSING PROGRAM
Admission agreement termination . . . . SSL 461-g

Defined . . . SSL 2

Planning and development grants . . . . SSL 461-i

Special proceeding for termination . . . SSL 461-h

EPILEPTICS
Public assistance, in need of . . . SSL 62

Public-home, detention pending transfer to state institution . . . SSL 199

EVIDENCE
Child support ability, statewide standard; Child Support Standards Act . . . FCA 440

Conciliation proceedings . . . FCA 915

DNA testing, admissibility of
  Paternity proceedings, in . . . FCA 532
  Support proceedings, in . . . FCA 418

Family offenses . . . FCA 834

Genetic marker test results, admissibility of
  Paternity proceedings, in . . . FCA 532
  Support proceedings, in . . . FCA 418

Interstate support proceedings, special rules in . . . FCA 580-316

Juvenile delinquency proceedings (See JUVENILE DELINQUENCY)

Parental rights proceedings . . . FCA 624

Paternity proceedings . . . FCA 531, 532

PINS proceedings (See PERSON IN NEED OF SUPERVISION)

F

FAMILY CARE
Adult family-type homes
  Authority to operate; social services official . . . SSL 131-h
  Definition of terms . . . SSL 2(21), (22)

Receiving family care; definition of term . . . SSL 209

FAMILY COURT
Generally . . . ADR 611.1; FCA 113

Access to proceedings . . . FCR 205.4

Administration
  Administration and operation, general . . . FCA 211
  Clerk of court . . . FCA 216-a
  Personnel . . . FCA 215

Adoption (See ADOPTION)

Annual report . . . ADR 611.10

FAMILY COURT—Cont.
Appeals (See APPEALS)

Assignment system . . . FCR 205.3

Attorneys
  Appointment of . . . ADR 611.4
  Assignment of . . . ADR 611.2
  Continuing legal education . . . . ADR 611.9
  Departmental Advisory Panel . . ADR 611.5, 611.6
  Family offense proceedings . . FCA 831
  Screening procedures . . . ADR 611.8

Auxiliary services of . . . FCA 253

Conciliation proceedings (See CONCILIATION PROCEEDINGS—FAMILY COURT)

Conditions, Family Court Act . . FCR 205.37

Continuity of powers . . . ADR 611.11

Cooperation of officials and organizations . . . FCA 255

Criminal proceedings (See FAMILY OFFENSES PROCEEDINGS)

Departmental Advisory Committee
  Annual report . . . ADR 611.10
  Authority and responsibility . . . ADR 611.5
  Duties of . . . ADR 611.7
  Members of . . . ADR 611.6; ADR 611.12; ADR 1032.4
  Screening process . . . ADR 611.8

Engagement of counsel . . . FCR 205.13

Exclusion from proceedings . . . FCR 205.4

Expenses of . . . FCA 120

Extrajudicial proceedings . . . DRL 113

Felonies committed by juveniles . . . . FCA 117(b)

Financial disclosures (See FINANCIAL DISCLOSURE)

Findings of fact . . . FCR 205.36

First Judicial Department, rules . . . . ADR 600.6 *et seq.*

Hearing examiners (See HEARING EXAMINERS)

Indigent adults, counsel for
  Assignment of . . . FCA 262
  Legislative findings and purpose of . . . FCA 261

Judges (See JUDGES OF FAMILY COURT)

Jurisdiction (See JURISDICTION OF FAMILY COURT)

Juvenile delinquents (See JUVENILE DELINQUENCY)

Miscellaneous proceedings . . . FCR 205.9

Neglected child, rules as to (See NEGLECTED CHILD)

[References are to sections of the Consolidated Laws as abbreviated on pg. iii.]

[References are to sections of the Consolidated Laws as abbreviated on pg. iii.]

[References are to sections of the Consolidated Laws as abbreviated on pg. iii.]

GENETIC MARKER TESTS

Admissibility as evidence
    Paternity proceedings . . . FCA 532
    Support proceedings . . . FCA 418
Challenging testing directive, proceeding for
  . . . FCA 418, 532
Costs . . . FCA 418, 532
DNA test results, admissibility of . . . FCA
  418, 532
Evidence, as . . . FCA 418, 532
Laboratory performance . . . FCA 418
Paternity proceedings . . . FCA 532
Support proceedings . . . FCA 418

GRANDPARENTS

Visitation rights of . . . DRL 72, 240

GUARDIANS

Abandoned child
    Generally . . . SSL 384-b(5)
    Child protective proceedings for child un-
      der age of one . . . FCA 1055
Adoption proceedings, notice to approved par-
  ents of . . . SSL 384-b(10)
Adoptive parent . . . FCR 205.57
Appointment by parent . . . DRL 81
Berkshire Industrial Farm . . . SSL 472-m
Care/protection of children
    Foster-care children . . . SSL 383-c
    Non-foster-care children . . . SSL 384
Child protective proceedings, judicial; aban-
  doned child under age of one . . FCA 1055
Custody and guardianship of children . . . .
  SSL 383-c, 384
Destitute or dependent children
    Generally . . . SSL 384, 384-b
    Agency assuming commitment . . SSL
      110-a, 384
Family Court . . . FCA 661, 662
Filing order of appointment . . . FCA 663
Foster-care children . . . SSL 383-c
Funds
    Investment of ward's . . . DRL 85
    Received by social services; establishment
      of common trust funds . . . SSL 87
Guardians ad litem
    Expenses on appeal . . . FCA 1117
    Party to support proceeding . . FCA 422
Infant ward, protective custody of . . . FCA
  249
Investment of funds of ward; trust fund holdings
  . . . DRL 85
Law guardians (See LAW GUARDIANS)
Liability . . . DRL 83

GUARDIANS—Cont.

Married minor, of . . . DRL 84
Non-foster-care children . . . SSL 384
Notice to approved parents of adoption proceed-
  ings . . . SSL 384-b(10)
Permanently neglected child . . . SSL 384-b
Person legally responsible; defined . . . FCA
  1012
Powers and duties
    Generally . . . DRL 82
    Liabilities . . . DRL 83
    Property, as to (See subhead: Real prop-
      erty, guardianship of)
Protective custody, child placed in . . . FCA
  249
Real property, guardianship of
    Guardian in socage . . . DRL 80
    Liabilities of guardian . . . DRL 83
    Married minor . . . DRL 84
    Powers and duties of guardian . . DRL
      82
Rules of Family Court . . . FCA 662
Socage, in . . . DRL 80
Trust funds
    Establishment of . . . SSL 87
    Investment of funds of ward . . DRL 85
Will, appointment by . . . DRL 81

GUNS (See FIREARMS)

H

HABEAS CORPUS

Child, for
    Grandparent visitation rights . . DRL 72
    Parents, detained by . . . DRL 70
    Sibling visitation rights . . . DRL 71
Jurisdiction; Family Court . . . FCA 115; SSL
  384-a

HANDICAPPED CHILDREN (See PHYSI-
CALLY HANDICAPPED CHILDREN)

HEALTH CARE

Catastrophic (See CATASTROPHIC HEALTH
  CARE)

HEALTH INSURANCE

Aids patients, continuation of health insurance
  for (See HEALTH INSURANCE CONTINU-
  ATION FOR PERSONS WITH AIDS)
Catastrophic health care expense program (See
  MEDICAL ASSISTANCE FOR NEEDY
  PERSONS)

[References are to sections of the Consolidated Laws as abbreviated on pg. iii.]

[References are to sections of the Consolidated Laws as abbreviated on pg. iii.]

HOMELESS HOUSING AND ASSISTANCE PROGRAM—Cont.

Costs; definition of term . . . SSL 42(3)

Definition of terms . . . SSL 42

Evaluation of need . . . SSL 44(3)

Financial assistance . . . SSL 43

Homelessness intervention program

    Contracts, assistance . . . SSL 50

    Definitions . . . SSL 49

    Legislative intent . . . SSL 48

    Regulations . . . SSL 51

    Reports . . . SSL 52

Homeless project (See subhead: Projects)

Legislative findings . . . SSL 41

Operating plan . . . SSL 43(3)

Person, homeless; definition of term . . SSL 42(2)

Projects

    Contract for . . . SSL 43

    Definition of terms . . . SSL 42(1)

    Proposal . . . SSL 43(9)

    Title to . . . SSL 43(8)

Purpose . . . SSL 41

Reports, progress . . . SSL 44(7)

Reviews . . . SSL 44(4)

Social service district application assistance . . . SSL 44(6)

HOME RELIEF (See PUBLIC ASSISTANCE)

HOUSING DEMONSTRATION PROGRAM

Contracts

    Not-for-profit and charitable organizations . . . SSL 47

    Requests for proposal . . . SSL 46

HOUSING FOR HOMELESS (See HOMELESS HOUSING AND ASSISTANCE PROGRAM)

HOUSING PROGRAM, ENRICHED (See ENRICHED HOUSING PROGRAM)

HUMAN IMMUNODEFICIENCY (HIV) (See ACQUIRED IMMUNE DEFICIENCY SYNDROME (AIDS))

HUMAN SERVICES NETWORKING PROGRAM, RURAL (See RURAL HUMAN SERVICES NETWORKING PROGRAM)

HUSBAND (See MARRIED PERSON)

I

ILLEGITIMATE CHILDREN (See OUT-OF-WEDLOCK CHILDREN)

IMPAIRMENT OF EMOTIONAL HEALTH

Defined . . . FCA 1012

Proof . . . FCA 1046

INCAPACITATED PERSONS

Juvenile delinquency proceedings (See JUVENILE DELINQUENCY)

Proceeding to determine capacity; juvenile delinquent . . . FCA 322.2

INCEST

Marriage . . . DRL 5

INDIANS, AMERICAN (See NATIVE AMERICANS)

INDIGENT PERSONS

Appeals . . . FCA 1118; FCA 1121

Assignment of counsel . . FCA 261; FCA 262

Interstate proceedings . . . SSL 32

Reciprocal agreements for interstate transportation of indigent persons . . . SSL 32

Support or maintenance proceedings (See SUPPORT OR MAINTENANCE PROCEEDINGS)

INFANT OR INCOMPETENT

Abandoned infant protection program . . SSL 372-g

Guardian ad litem (See GUARDIANS)

Incompetent in need of public assistance . . . SSL 62

Infant defined . . . DRL 2; FCA 119; SSL 2

INSURANCE

Health insurance (See HEALTH INSURANCE)

Life insurance (See LIFE INSURANCE)

INTERMEDIATE CARE FACILITY

Authorization of medical care . . . SSL 365-a

Definition of term, statutory . . . SSL 2(29)

J

JOB CLUBS

Employment assistance for public assistance recipients . . . SSL 131, 164-c

JUDGES OF FAMILY COURT

Assignment

    Procedure for . . . FCR 205.27

    Temporary . . . FCA 146

Authority to attend meetings of association . . . FCA 143

Authority to visit school or institution . . . . FCA 142

[References are to sections of the Consolidated Laws as abbreviated on pg. iii.]

[References are to sections of the Consolidated Laws as abbreviated on pg. iii.]

[References are to sections of the Consolidated Laws as abbreviated on pg. iii.]

[References are to sections of the Consolidated Laws as abbreviated on pg. iii.]

[References are to sections of the Consolidated Laws as abbreviated on pg. iii.]

LAW GUARDIANS—Cont.
Removal from panel
    Second Department . . . ADR 679.10
    Third Department . . . ADR 835.2
Second Judicial Department, establishment of
   plan . . . ADR 679.1
Supervision by administrative board . . FCA
  246
Third Department rules . . . ADR 835.2 et seq
Training/education
    Second Department . . . ADR 679.9
    Third Department . . . ADR 835.4

LIENS
Ascertainment in action to recover dower; accelerated payments system . . . SSL 367-b(9)
Medical-assistance recipient, property of (repealed) . . . SSL 369
Public assistance, judgment liens of . . SSL
  145-a
Public assistance and care on claims and suits for
  personal injuries, for . . . SSL 104-b

LIFE INSURANCE
Matrimonial actions; court's order to purchase
  . . . DRL 236
Policy of deceased person who has received
  public assistance . . . SSL 105
Spouse, on . . . DRL 52
Waiver by social services official when spouse
  or children survive . . . SSL 105

LOCAL CHARGE
Definition of term, statutory . . . SSL 2(20)

LONG-TERM CARE
Demonstration program . . . SSL 367-s
Eligibility for program . . . SSL 367-c
Home Care (See HOME CARE)
National Services Channeling Demonstration
  project . . . SSL 364-c
Payment for services . . . SSL 367-c
Personal care services defined . . . SSL 365-a
Services included . . . SSL 365-a

LOW-INCOME HOME ENERGY ASSIS-
  TANCE PROGRAM
Authorization . . . SSL 97(1)
Eligibility . . . SSL 97(2)
Payments as income . . . SSL 97(3)
Social service district participation . . . SSL
  97(2)
State reimbursement . . . SSL 97(4)
Statistical reporting . . . SSL 131-aa

M

MAINTENANCE (See SUPPORT OR MAIN-
  TENANCE PROCEEDINGS)

MARRIAGE
Annulment of (See ANNULMENT)
Ceremony (See MARRIAGE CEREMONY)
Certificate (See MARRIAGE RECORDS)
Civil contract . . . DRL 10
Common-law marriage, legitimacy of child of
  . . . DRL 24
Comprehension of spouses affecting . . . . .
  DRL 7
Dissolution of
    Annulment (See ANNULMENT)
    Disappearance of one spouse . . . DRL
      220, 221
    Divorce (See DIVORCE)
    Void marriage (See subhead: Void
      marriage)
Duress affecting; voidability . . . DRL 7
Force affecting; voidability . . . DRL 7
Former spouse living, effect . . . DRL 6, 140
Fraud affecting; voidability . . . DRL 7
Incestuous . . . DRL 5
Legitimacy of children, effect on . . DRL 24
License (See MARRIAGE LICENSES)
Mentally retarded/ill spouse; voidability . . .
  DRL 7, 140, 141
Physical condition as grounds for nullity . . .
  DRL 7
Remarriage following divorce . . . DRL 8
Solemnization of (See MARRIAGE CERE-
  MONY)
Spousal status (See MARRIED PERSON)
Underage spouse; voidability . . . DRL 7, 140
Void marriage
    Actions to annul or declare void . . . .
      DRL 140 *et seq.*
    Basis for . . . DRL 5–7
    Legitimacy of child of . . . DRL 24

MARRIAGE CEREMONY
City clerk, duties of . . . DRL 11-a
Contract to solemnize . . . DRL 11
Form . . . DRL 12
Justice of Supreme Court . . . DRL 11
Officers authorized to solemnize, appointment of
  . . . DRL 11-c
Performance in violation of law . . . DRL 17
Public officials, solemnization by . . DRL 11
Registration of persons performing . . . DRL
  11-b

[References are to sections of the Consolidated Laws as abbreviated on pg. iii.]

[References are to sections of the Consolidated Laws as abbreviated on pg. iii.]

MATRIMONIAL ACTIONS—Cont.
Counsel fees and expenses—Cont.
  Default of payment, stay in action . . . DRL 239
  Enforcement proceedings . . . DRL 238
  Expenses; definition of term . . . DRL 237
Custody of issue (See CUSTODY)
Default judgment . . . DRL 211, 232
Default on directed payments
  Actions in which applicable . . . DRL 244
  Entry of judgment for whole or part of arrears . . . DRL 244
  Financial incapacity as defense . . DRL 246
  Inability to enforce payment by sequestration of property or resort to security . . . DRL 245
  Modification of order or judgment . . . DRL 246
  Relief from payment and contempt order . . . DRL 246
  Remedies
    Generally . . . DRL 244, 244-a
    Additional arrears . . . FCA 459
  Stay in action . . . DRL 239
Definition . . . DRL 236
Distribution of property . . . DRL 236
Divorce (See DIVORCE)
Enforcement of orders and decrees . . . DRL 236
Equitable distribution of property . . . DRL 236
Financial disclosure, compulsory . . DRL 236
Health insurance coverage, compulsory disclosure of group . . . DRL 236
Information disclosure . . . DRL 235
Invalidation (See ANNULMENT)
Maintenance (See SUPPORT OR MAINTENANCE PROCEEDINGS)
Marital property . . . DRL 236
Modification of orders and decrees . . . DRL 236
Name resumption . . . DRL 240-a
New actions or proceedings . . . DRL 236
Notice of appearance, defendant . . DRL 211
Order of matrimonial action, filing in Family Court . . . DRL 251
Order of protection . . . DRL 252
Petition for alimony, child support, and counsel fees . . . DRL 211
Pleadings, proof, and motions . . . DRL 211

MATRIMONIAL ACTIONS—Cont.
Prior actions or proceedings . . . DRL 236
Private examination of witnesses . . DRL 235
Property, title, occupancy, and possession; powers of court . . . DRL 234
Publication, general . . . DRL 232
Remarriage (See REMARRIAGE)
Residency requirements
  Actions to which applicable . . . DRL 230
  Married person . . . DRL 231
Sealed records in, access to . . . DRL 235
Security for payments by defendant . . DRL 243
Separate property . . . DRL 236
Sequestration of property
  Personal service impossible . . DRL 233
  Security for payments . . . DRL 243
Special relief . . . DRL 236
Statute of limitations . . . DRL 210
Stay in action; default on directed payments . . . DRL 239
Summons, complaint service with
  Actions in which applicable . . . DRL 232
  Action type written on face of summons . . . DRL 232
  Affidavit proving service . . . DRL 232
  Default . . . DRL 232
  Notice of action, publication . . . DRL 232
  Requirement . . . DRL 211
Support of spouse/dependents (See DEPENDENTS' SUPPORT)
Surname resumption . . . DRL 240-a
Trial preference . . . DRL 249
Uncontested actions; accelerated payments . . . SSL 367-b
Voiding of marriage (See ANNULMENT)

MEDICAID (See MEDICAL ASSISTANCE FOR NEEDY PERSONS)

MEDICAL ASSISTANCE FOR NEEDY PERSONS
Advisory opinions . . . SSL 365-j
AIDS; health insurance continuation (See HEALTH INSURANCE CONTINUATION FOR PERSONS WITH AIDS)
Aliens, assistance to . . . SSL 122
Application for aid . . . SSL 366-a
Assets
  Annuities as assets . . . SSL 366-a
  Definition of assets . . . SSL 366

[References are to sections of the Consolidated Laws as abbreviated on pg. iii.]

MEDICAL ASSISTANCE FOR NEEDY PERSONS—Cont.

Assets—Cont.

Disposal of assets for less than fair market value . . . SSL 366

Exempt assets . . . SSL 366

Income-producing assets, disclosure of . . . SSL 366-a

Transfer of . . . SSL 366

Assisted living programs, payment for . . . . SSL 367-h; SSL 461-l

Audits

Advisory opinions . . . SSL 365-j

Claims paid . . . SSL 367-b

Compliance program . . . SSL 363-d

Fraud detection . . . SSL 367-b

State rates of payment to providers . . . SSL 368-c

Automated system . . . SSL 366-h

Award of aid . . . SSL 366-a

Billing, certified home health agency Medicare . . . SSL 366-e

Brand-name drugs . . . SSL 365-a

Capitation rate demonstration project . . SSL 364-g

Case management . . . SSL 365-a

Catastrophic health care (See CATASTROPHIC HEALTH CARE)

Certification form needed . . . SSL 366-a

Change in financial condition of recipient, effect . . . SSL 366-a

Character and adequacy of assistance for in-patient facilities . . . SSL 365-a

Children

Eligibility . . . SSL 366

Emotionally disturbed children and adoles-cents . . . SSL 364-j

Handicapped; state reimbursement of expenditures

Pre-school children; reimbursement to counties . . . SSL 368-e

Public school districts . . . . SSL 368-d

Newborn enrollment . . . SSL 366-g

Chronic medical condition, definition of . . . SSL 366

Clinic services . . . SSL 367-a

Compliance program . . . SSL 363-d

Concert with medical assistance provider, person acting in; prohibited practices . . SSL 366-f

Concurrent payment system . . . SSL 367-b

Condition of participation . . . SSL 364-kk

Cooperation of state departments . . . . SSL 364-a

MEDICAL ASSISTANCE FOR NEEDY PERSONS—Cont.

Coordination of . . . SSL 367-b

Co-payments for prescription drugs . . . SSL 367-a

Data systems, state reimbursement for . . . . SSL 368-a

Declaration of objects . . . SSL 363

Defined

Generally . . . SSL 365-a

Dental prosthetic appliances . . . . SSL 365-a

Demonstration projects authorization . . SSL 364-b

Denial of assistance . . . SSL 366-a

Department of Health, duties . . . SSL 364

Determination of personal care need . . SSL 367-d-(iii)

Developmentaly-disabled individuals . . SSL 365-a

Diagnosis and treatment programs, early . . . SSL 365-d

Drug manufacturer-wholesaler; price informa-tion . . . SSL 367-a

Elderly in-home service demonstration project . . . SSL 366

Eligibility

Agreements for federal determination of . . . SSL 363-b

Assets counted for . . . SSL 366

Automatic eligibility . . . SSL 364-i

Chronic medical condition defined for pur-poses of . . . SSL 366

Criteria . . . SSL 366

Homestead exemption amount . . . SSL 366

Presumptive eligibility . . . SSL 364-i

Undue hardship waiver for . . SSL 366

Waiver program . . . SSL 366

Emergency care

Emergency room physician rates . . . . SSL 367-t

Out-of-state emergency room visits . . . SSL 365-a

Transportation services . . . SSL 367-s

Emotionally disturbed children and adolescents . . . SSL 364-j

Estimates, quarterly, of anticipated assistance . . . SSL 368

Excess financial resources, effect . . SSL 366

Exclusions from prescription drug coverage . . . SSL 365-a

Exempt assets . . . SSL 366

MEDICAL ASSISTANCE FOR NEEDY PERSONS—Cont.

Exempt income . . . SSL 366

Family planning . . . SSL 366; SSL 368-a

Federal aid; state plan . . . SSL 363-a

Financial status of recipient, change in . . . . SSL 366-a

Fraud detection . . . SSL 367-b

Fraudulent practices, penalties for . . . . SSL 366-b

Health insurance programs . . . SSL 367-o

Health maintenance organization services

    Generally . . . SSL 366

    Membership, continuation of . . . SSL 365-e

Home health care

    Assessments, instruments for . . . SSL 367-o

    Billing, certified agency Medicare . . . SSL 366-e

    Definition . . . SSL 365-a

    Fiscal assessment of services . . . SSL 367-j

    Health insurance programs . . . . SSL 367-o

    Local districts for, responsibilities of . . . SSL 367-p

    Long-term care demonstration program . . . SSL 367-s

    Management of home health services . . . SSL 367-j

    Medicare billing, certified agency . . . . SSL 366-e

    Payment for limited . . . SSL 367-p

    Payments for long-term . . . SSL 367-c

Homemaker/home-health aides; demonstration project . . . SSL 364-e

Hospice services; definition of term . . SSL 365-a

Hospital care

    Authorization . . . SSL 367

    Concurrent payment system . . . . SSL 367-b

Inadequate grant . . . SSL 366-a

Information on . . . SSL 367-b

In-patient facility care, standard . . SSL 365-a

Institutionalized persons, treatment of income and resources of . . . SSL 366-c

Insurance . . . SSL 367-a

Intermediate care . . . SSL 365-a

Investigation of applicant . . . SSL 366-a

Local districts for personal care services, home care services and private duty nursing, responsibilities of . . . SSL 367-p

MEDICAL ASSISTANCE FOR NEEDY PERSONS—Cont.

Local medical plans . . . SSL 365-b

Long-term care

    Demonstration project . . . . SSL 364-c; SSL 367-s

    Home care feasibility . . . SSL 367-c

    Security demonstration program for . . SSL 367-f

Look-back period . . . SSL 366

Management programs

    Chemung county "demonstration project" . . . SSL 364-j(22)

    Children and adolescents, emotionally disturbed . . . SSL 364-j

    Emotionally disturbed children and adolescents . . . SSL 364-j

    Enrollment . . . SSL 364-j

    Managed care programs . . . SSL 364-j

    Mental illness, persons with . . . . SSL 364-j

    Physician case management . . . . SSL 364-f

    Special advisory review panel, establishment of . . . SSL 364-jj

    Temporary management of managed care programs . . . SSL 364-j(23)

    Transitional supplemental payments . . SSL 364-j-2

Medicaid drug utilization review (DUR)

    Generally . . . SSL 369-cc

    Definitions of . . . SSL 369-aa

    Pharmaceutical expenditures . . . . SSL 369-dd

    Review board . . . SSL 369-bb

Medicaid management committee meetings . . . SSL 363-c

Medicaid reimbursement and continuing-care demonstration project, participation . . . . SSL 364-d

Medicaid trusts . . . SSL 366

Medical Advisory Committee . . SSL 363-c; SSL 365-c

Medical assistance information and payment system . . . SSL 367-b

Medical assistance provider; prohibited practices

    Generally . . . SSL 366-d

    Person acting in concert with medical assistance provider . . . SSL 366-f

Medicare billing, certified home health agency . . . SSL 366-e

Medicare Part B, simultaneous coverage under . . . SSL 365-a

[References are to sections of the Consolidated Laws as abbreviated on pg. iii.]

[References are to sections of the Consolidated Laws as abbreviated on pg. iii.]

NEGLECTED CHILD—Cont.
Temporary removal with consent . . . . FCA 1021
Termination of parental rights (See PARENTAL RIGHTS TERMINATION)

NET WORTH STATEMENTS
Domestic Relations Law requirements . . . . DRL 236
Financial disclosures (See FINANCIAL DISCLOSURE)

NEW YORK CITY
Child abuse medical examinations and treatment . . . FCA 235
Citizen review panels, children protection . . SSL 371-b
Corporation counsel representing social services commissioner in paternity proceeding . . . FCA 535
Domestic Relations Court transfer of personnel . . . FCA 215
Educational services . . . FCA 236
Electronic payment file transfer system, pilot project . . . SSL 131-q
Judges of family court (See JUDGES OF FAMILY COURT)
Marriage records, requirements as to . . DRL 20
Medical examinations and treatment for abused child . . . FCA 235
Psychiatric examination/report, Family Court referral . . . FCA 251
Social services law application to city social services districts . . . SSL 56, 61
Veterans assistance administration . . . SSL 175

NEW YORK PUBLIC WELFARE ASSOCIATION
Attendance at conventions of . . . SSL 152
Payments to . . . SSL 152

NURSING AND CONVALESCENT HOMES
(See also PRIVATE PROPRIETARY HOMES FOR ADULTS)
Admission requirements . . . SSL 461-b
Definition . . . SSL 2
Establishment and administration
    Generally . . . SSL 461-b
    Approval of application . . . SSL 461-c
Financial statements . . . SSL 461-b
Institutionalized persons, treatment of income and resources of . . . SSL 366-c
Registry of facilities . . . SSL 463

NURSING AND CONVALESCENT HOMES—Cont.
Rights of residents . . . SSL 461-d
Service agreements . . . SSL 461-b

O

OATHS AND ACKNOWLEDGMENTS
Power to administer . . . FCA 152
Public welfare officials and service officers . . . SSL 144

OFFICIALS
Definition of; local level . . . SSL 2(14)
Social service
    Definition of term . . . SSL 2 (14)
    Duties . . . SSL 111-c

OLD AGE ASSISTANCE (See AGED, BLIND, OR DISABLED PERSONS, SERVICES FOR)

ON-THE-JOB TRAINING
Aid to dependent children . . . SSL 350-l

ORDERS OF COURT (GENERALLY)
Original order, filing of . . . FCA 217

ORDERS OF PROTECTION (See PROTECTION ORDERS)

ORPHANS (See ADOPTION)

OUT-OF-WEDLOCK CHILDREN
Dependent children's aid
    Eligibility requirements, additional . . . SSL 349-b
    Special provisions for . . . SSL 352-a
Dependent's support . . . DRL 33
Paternal rights (See PATERNAL RIGHTS)
Paternity proceedings (See PATERNITY PROCEEDINGS)
Public assistance, special provisions . . SSL 352-a
Social services officials powers and duties . . . SSL 398
Support of
    Generally . . . DRL 33
    Obligation of parents . . . FCA 513
Visitation rights; minors in foster care . . . . FCA 1084

P

PARDON
Guardianship of child, effect on . . . DRL 58

[References are to sections of the Consolidated Laws as abbreviated on pg. iii.]

[References are to sections of the Consolidated Laws as abbreviated on pg. iii.]

[References are to sections of the Consolidated Laws as abbreviated on pg. iii.]

[References are to sections of the Consolidated Laws as abbreviated on pg. iii.]

PRIVATE PROPRIETARY HOMES FOR ADULTS—Cont.

Inspection and supervision
    Generally . . . SSL 460-c, 461-a, 461-b
    Enforcement powers . . . SSL 460-d
Medical treatment requirements . . SSL 461-b
Nursing homes (See NURSING AND CONVALESCENT HOMES)
Operating certificate . . . SSL 460-b
Receivership, operation of facility in . . SSL 461-f
Records and reports requirements . . . . SSL 460-e, 461-b, 461-e
Registry of facilities . . . SSL 463
Rights of residents . . . SSL 461-d
Service agreements . . . SSL 461-b
Social service district expenditures, state reimbursements . . . SSL 153

PROBATION

Authority of . . . FCR 205.39
Conferences, preliminary . . . FCR 205.30
Disposition; juvenile delinquency (See JUVENILE DELINQUENCY)
Family Court (See FAMILY COURT)
Order of . . . FCA 841
PINS proceedings (See PERSON IN NEED OF SUPERVISION)
Referral from Supreme Court . . FCR 205.40
Reports; PINS proceedings . . . FCA 750
Service (See PROBATION SERVICE)

PROBATION SERVICE

Adjustments, case results
    Notice . . . FCA 735(h)
    Preliminary procedure . . . FCA 735
Diversion, case results . . . FCA 742
Duties
    Generally . . . FCR 205.31, 205.41
    Adjustment process . . . FCR 205.31
    Child protection . . . FCR 205.63
Establishment of . . . FCA 252
Fees, payment of . . . FCA 252-a
Juvenile delinquency intake-adjustment procedure (See JUVENILE DELINQUENCY)
Record maintenance . . . FCA735(f)
Support collection unit, submission by . . . . FCR 205.42

PROCESS

Abuse of process . . . FCA 145
Statewide process . . . FCA 154

PROPOSED DISPOSITION

Financial disclosures (See FINANCIAL DISCLOSURE)

PROTECTION OF CHILDREN

Abused children, agency for (See CHILD PROTECTIVE SERVICES)
Adoption, status of children freed for . . . . . FCA 1055
Children freed for adoption . . . FCA 105-a
Court-directed custody and child support . . . DRL 240
Custody (See PROTECTIVE CUSTODY)
Extended protective placement . . FCA 1055
Orders of protection (See PROTECTION ORDERS)
Placement of child, protective . . . FCA 1055
Proceeding, judicial (See CHILD PROTECTIVE PROCEEDINGS)
Removal from residence, temporary
    With consent . . . FCA 1021
    Emergency . . . FCA 1024
    Notice of parental rights . . FCA 1022, 1026
    Preliminary court orders . . FCA 1022, 1023
    Return of child, notice of rights . . . . . FCA 1022, 1026

PROTECTION ORDERS

Generally . . FCA 430, 740, 828, 550, 551, 1029; FCA 814-a
Abused or maltreated child . . . FCA 1056
Address, confidentiality of . . DRL 254; FCA 154-b
Adults . . . SSL 473 *et seq.*
Answer to petition . . . FCA 154-b
Arrests
    Bail . . . FCA 155-a
    Order of protection following . . . FCA 155
    Order of protection violation, for . . . . FCA 155
Certificate of . . . FCA 168
Child protection . . . DRL 240; FCA 656
Companion animals, protection of . . . FCA 446; FCA 656(i); FCA 759(h); FCA 842(i); FCA 1056(g)
Conditions of behavior
    Generally . . . FCA 446
    Order of probation and . . . FCA 656
    Pleadings and requisite findings . . . . . FCA 154-c
Contents . . . DRL 240; FCA 655
Counter-claim . . . FCA 154-b
Criminal court's power to enforce . . . DRL 240; DRL 252

PROTECTION ORDERS—Cont.

Custody and child support at direction of court . . . DRL 240

Election by petitioner . . . FCA 847

Expiration of . . . FCA 154-c

Failure to obey . . . FCA 846-a

Family offense proceedings, in . . . FCA 841, 842

Filing copies . . . FCA 168

Front page of order, content . . . FCA 168

Juvenile delinquent . . . FCA 759, 760

Matrimonial actions . . . DRL 240

Modification of . . . . FCA 154-c; FCA 154-d; FCA 846-a

Notice . . . FCA 168

Out-of-state . . . DRL 240; DRL 252; FCA 154-e

PINS proceeding . . . FCA 759

Procedural requirements . . . FCA 154-c

Service of process request for . . . FCA 153-b

Temporary

    Generally . . . . FCA 430, 550, 655, 821, 1029

    Child custody . . . FCA 655

    Issuance of

        Criminal court . . . FCA 154-d

        Family court . . . FCA 430, 828

    Judges issuing . . . FCA 23

    Meaning of . . . FCA 431

    PINS petition, upon filing . . . FCA 740

    Reasons for . . . FCA 551

    Service of . . . FCA 153-b, 153-c

Violation of . . . FCA 846

PROTECTIVE CUSTODY

Abused child (See CHILD PROTECTIVE SERVICES)

Guardian appointed

    Generally . . . FCA 249

    Counsel, waiver of . . . FCA 249-a

Material witness . . . FCA 158

Stay of order . . . FCA 1112

PROTECTIVE SERVICES, ADULT

Generally . . . SSL 473

Definitions . . . SSL 473

Multi-year consolidated services plan . . . SSL 473

Short-term orders . . . SSL 473-a, 473-b

PROTECTIVE SERVICES, CHILD (See CHILD PROTECTIVE SERVICES)

PUBLIC ASSISTANCE

Absence of minor child, effect of . . . SSL 131

PUBLIC ASSISTANCE—Cont.

Abuses of (See subhead: Penalties for abuses)

Adjustments for incorrect payments . . . SSL 106-b

Administration; statewide welfare management system . . . SSL 21

Adult protective services (See ADULT PROTECTIVE SERVICES)

Aid to dependent children (See DEPENDENT CHILDREN'S AID)

Aliens as recipients . . . SSL 122, 131

Allowance

    Personal allowances accounts . . . SSL 131-o

    Training incentive . . . SSL 350-i

Appeals and hearings . . . SSL 22

Appeals and reviews of decisions concerning applications for assistance . . . SSL 22, 74-h

Applications, investigation of . . . SSL 132

Appropriations for

    Adequacy of appropriations, responsibility for . . . SSL 88

    Deficiency appropriations . . . SSL 92

Assistance, care and services to be given . . SSL 131

Burial of recipient of public assistance

    Generally . . . SSL 141

    Burial reserves from assigned assets . . SSL 152-a

    Trust fund for . . . SSL 209(6)

Chargebacks between social services districts from family court cases . . . SSL 118-c

Child assistance program . . . SSL 131-z

Child care services . . . SSL 131; SSL 364-e

Children born out of wedlock . . . SSL 132-a

Child Welfare Reform Act of 1979 (See CHILD WELFARE REFORM ACT OF 1979)

City public welfare districts

    Homeless, plan for . . . SSL 79

    Power of . . . SSL 76

Commission for blind . . . SSL 38

Conduct of investigation or reinvestigation of eligibility for public assistance . . . . SSL 134-a

Contracts for distribution of public assistance grants . . . SSL 133-a

Cooperation of social services officials . . . . SSL 135

Criminal activity of recipient . . . SSL 131

Day care (See DAY CARE)

Deed or mortgage on property of recipient sought by social services official

    Exemption from payment of fees . . . . SSL 106-a

Index

[References are to sections of the Consolidated Laws as abbreviated on pg. iii.]

PUBLIC ASSISTANCE—Cont.

Health insurance benefits

    Child support proceedings . . DRL 240; FCA 416

    Effect of . . . SSL 131-p

Homeless persons, assistance for (See HOMELESS HOUSING AND ASSISTANCE PROGRAM)

Homemaker/home-health aide demonstration projects . . . SSL 364-e

Home relief

    City administration of . . . SSL 74-a

    Disabled persons . . . SSL 301

    Medical assistance, eligibility . . . SSL 366

Housing demonstration program (See HOUSING DEMONSTRATION PROGRAM)

Identification cards . . . SSL 131

Income and resources of recipient, exempt

    Generally . . . SSL 131-a, 131-n

    Family loan program funds . . . . SSL 131-i

    Reparation payments . . . SSL 131-n

    Social security retroactive lump sum payments . . . SSL 131-f

Incorrect payments, adjustments for . . . SSL 106-b

Information furnished to officials

    Employers of labor, by . . . SSL 143

    Grantors of credit, by certain . . . SSL 143-a

    State tax commission/comptroller . . . . SSL 136-a

Insane and mentally defective state wards . . . SSL 140

Insurance policy of deceased person who has received public assistance . . . SSL 105

Job clubs . . . SSL 131, 164-c

Jobs (See subhead: Employment of recipient)

Job search activities . . . SSL 158-b

Judgment liens . . . SSL 145-a

Judicial review of decisions concerning applications for assistance

    Generally . . . SSL 22

    Legal services to recover costs of . . . . SSL 110-a

Juvenile delinquents, expenditure for support of . . . SSL 398

Local charge, definition of . . . SSL 2

Management of . . . SSL 21

Medical assistance information and payment system

    (See also MEDICAL ASSISTANCE FOR NEEDY PERSONS)

PUBLIC ASSISTANCE—Cont.

Medical assistance information and payment system—Cont.

    Generally . . . SSL 367-b

Method of payment . . . SSL 159

Minimum payments . . . SSL 131-a

Monthly grants and allowances

    Generally . . . SSL 131-a

    Additional allowances . . . SSL 131-b

    Exemption of income and resources, additional . . . SSL 131-h

    Expenses, additional . . . SSL 131-a

    Monthly statistical reports . . . . . SSL 131-aa

    Persons, additional . . . SSL 131-a

    Schedules . . . SSL 131-a

    Statistical reports . . . SSL 131-aa

    Utility deposits . . . SSL 131-j

Overpayment, adjustment for

    Generally . . . SSL 106-b

    Tax information . . . SSL 111-b

Parents, inclusion on budget . . . SSL 131-c

Paternity, penalty for failure to cooperate in establishing . . . SSL 131

Penalties for abuses

    Cashing of welfare check by liquor store . . . SSL 151

    False representations to obtain assistance . . . SSL 145

    Needy person, bringing into state . . . . SSL 149

    Neglect to report or making false report . . . SSL 150

    Sale or exchange of assistance supplies . . . SSL 146

    Sanctions

        Implementation of . . . SSL 145-c

        Reporting of sanctioned cases . . . SSL 131-aa

    Unlawfully bringing needy person into a social services district . . . SSL 148

Performance awards . . . SSL 153-j

Personal allowances account . . . SSL 131-o

Powers of department . . . SSL 138

Pregnancy of adolescents (See PREGNANCY, ADOLESCENT)

Pregnant women, allowances for . . . . SSL 131-a

Protective services

    Generally . . . SSL 473

    Performance awards . . . SSL 153-j

    Short-term involuntary protective services orders . . . SSL 473-a

    State reimbursement . . . SSL 153-g

[References are to sections of the Consolidated Laws as abbreviated on pg. iii.]

PUBLIC ASSISTANCE—Cont.

Records, protection of . . . SSL 136

Recoupment of overpayment . . . SSL 106-b

Reimbursement of, liability for . . . SSL 131-r

Removal of recipient to another state or country . . . SSL 121

Rent assistance (See RENT ASSISTANCE)

Reporting, periodic . . . SSL 131-t

Residency requirements . . . SSL 117, 118

Retroactive social security benefit increases, effect . . . SSL 131-d

Reverse mortgage loan proceeds affecting . . . SSL 131-x

Safety net assistance

    Generally . . . SSL 159

    Aliens, for . . . SSL 122

    Cash assistance . . . SSL 159(a)

    Definition . . . SSL 93, 157; SSL 157

    Employment, for . . . SSL 158-b, 164-a

    Monthly reports . . . SSL 131-aa

    Personal needs allowance . . . . . SSL 159(a)(iii)

    Shelter assistance . . . SSL 159(a)(i)

    Statistical reports . . . SSL 131-aa

    Training in trade or occupation . . SSL 159-a

    Utility assistance . . . SSL 159(a)(ii)

Security deposits for utilities . . . SSL 131-j

Seized property of recipient of public assistance

    Generally . . . SSL 107

    Appointment of guardian for beneficiary of seized property . . . SSL 108

    Disposal . . . SSL 107

    Penalties . . . SSL 107

    Residue of funds . . . SSL 107

    Trust funds established for support of living person . . . SSL 109

Services included . . . SSL 2

Shelter grant (See RENT ASSISTANCE)

Siblings, allowances for . . . SSL 131-c

Social service districts (See SOCIAL SERVICES DISTRICTS)

Social Services Department (See STATE DEPARTMENT OF SOCIAL WELFARE)

Special care homes . . . SSL 2, 371

Special provisions to avoid abuse of assistance and care . . . SSL 139-a

Standard of need, definition . . . SSL 131-a

State charges found in public welfare district (repealed) . . . SSL 139

State reimbursement

    Generally . . . SSL 153

    Administration expenses . . . SSL 153

PUBLIC ASSISTANCE—Cont.

State reimbursement—Cont.

    Advances . . . SSL 153

    Child protective services . . . SSL 153-g

    Foster care

        Expenditures, special provisions for (repealed) . . . SSL 153-e

        Limitations on . . . SSL 153-d

        Therapeutic . . . SSL 153-h

    Home energy grants . . . SSL 153-f

    Home relief . . . SSL 154

    Social services districts, to . . . . SSL 153-a, 153-b

Stepparent income as factor . . . SSL 131-a

Studies (See STATE DEPARTMENT OF SOCIAL WELFARE, subhead: Studies)

Substance abuse, effect of . . . SSL 132

Supervision of recipients . . . SSL 134

Support order, penalty for failure to cooperate in carrying out . . . SSL 131

Support proceedings (See SUPPORT OR MAINTENANCE PROCEEDINGS)

Support services program (See SOCIAL SERVICES LAW)

Surplus after recovery of cost of public assistance . . . SSL 152-b

Temporary emergency shelter . . . SSL 131-v

Temporary pre-investigation emergency grant . . . SSL 133

Temporary relief grant . . . SSL 67

Training incentive allowance, federal

    Generally . . . SSL 350-i

    Parent or caretaker relative, eligibility . . . SSL 131

Training in trade or occupation, application for . . . SSL 159-a

Underpayment, adjustments for . . SSL 106-b

Unemployment insurance benefits, interception; child support obligations . . . SSL 111-j

Unexpended welfare balances . . . SSL 160-a

Unmarried minor individuals . . . SSL 131

Utility services, payments for . . . SSL 131-s

Veterans (See VETERANS ASSISTANCE)

Wage reporting system . . . SSL 23

Welfare management system . . . SSL 21

Work by recipient (See subhead: Employment of recipient)

PUBLIC HOME

Administration . . . SSL 202

Children in . . . SSL 401, 402

Definition of term, statutory . . . SSL 2(15)

[References are to sections of the Consolidated Laws as abbreviated on pg. iii.]

Q

R

[References are to sections of the Consolidated Laws as abbreviated on pg. iii.]

[References are to sections of the Consolidated Laws as abbreviated on pg. iii.]

[References are to sections of the Consolidated Laws as abbreviated on pg. iii.]

SUPPORT OR MAINTENANCE PROCEED-INGS—Cont.

Expenses of proceedings . . . DRL 40

Family Court jurisdiction . . . FCA 411, 440, 451

Financial disclosure (See FINANCIAL DIS-CLOSURE)

Genetic marker tests . . . FCA 418

Health insurance for children (See CHILD SUP-PORT PROCEEDINGS)

Hearings
     Adjournment . . . FCA 435
     Confidentiality of requests . . FCA 435
     Counsel fees, order for . . . FCA 438
     By court without jury . . . FCA 435
     Means of respondent
         Preliminary procedure on warrant . . . FCA 431
         Presumption of sufficient means . . . FCA 437
         Procedure before court . . . FCA 432
         Procedure on return of summons . . . FCA 433
     Presence of petitioner . . . DRL 37
     Respondent controverts petition
         Proof given in initiating state . . . DRL 37
         Recommendations of court in initiating state . . . DRL 37
     Special hearings for child support, establishment of bureau of . . . SSL 111-b
     Spouses as witnesses . . . FCA 436
     Temporary order of support . . FCA 434

Home and household effects, use and occupancy . . . DRL 236

Inability to locate respondent, effect . . DRL 37

Indigent persons
     Duties to support recipient of public assistance . . . FCA 415
     Elements of support . . . FCA 416
     Minor children . . . FCA 415
     Patients in mental institutions . . . FCA 415
     Persons obliged to support . . FCA 415

Information required from petitioner . . DRL 37

Insurance policy, court's order to purchase life or accident . . . DRL 236

Jurisdiction and duties of support
     Generally . . . FCA 411–418, 451
     Acquiring jurisdiction over respondent . . . DRL 37

SUPPORT OR MAINTENANCE PROCEED-INGS—Cont.

Jurisdiction and duties of support—Cont.
     Child of ceremonial marriage . . . FCA 417
     Genetic marker test results, admissibility of . . . FCA 418
     Legal services to enforce support . . . . SSL 110-a

Liability for . . . DRL 32, 33

Maintenance . . . DRL 236

Marital property . . . DRL 236

Modification of orders and decrees . . . DRL 236, 240

Money judgments
     Default . . . FCA 460
     Entry and docketing . . . FCA 460
     Failure to obey court order, upon . . . . FCA 454
     Interest upon monies due . . . FCA 460

New action or proceedings . . . DRL 236

Orders
     Arrears . . . FCA 460
     Compliance with orders (See subhead: Compliance with orders)
     Dismissing petition . . . FCA 441
     Family Court procedure . . . FCA 440
     Filiation order, support order following . . . FCA 545
     Foreign, registration of
         Generally . . . DRL 37-a
         Uniform Interstate Family Support Act (UIFSA) (See UNIFORM IN-TERSTATE FAMILY SUPPORT ACT (UIFSA))
     Income deduction . . . FCA 448
     Parent, support by . . . FCA 443
     Protection . . . FCA 446
     Public assistance reduction for failure to cooperate in carrying out . . SSL 131
     Relative, support by . . . FCA 445
     Spouse, by . . . FCA 442
     Temporary support . . . DRL 236; FCA 434, 434-a
     Visitation . . . FCA 447

Originating proceedings . . . FCA 422

Out-of-state support orders (See UNIFORM INTERSTATE FAMILY SUPPORT ACT (UIFSA))

Parties originating . . . FCA 422

Paternity
     Child's best interest in not determining . . . SSL 111-c

Index

[References are to sections of the Consolidated Laws as abbreviated on pg. iii.]

[References are to sections of the Consolidated Laws as abbreviated on pg. iii.]

[References are to sections of the Consolidated Laws as abbreviated on pg. iii.]

[References are to sections of the Consolidated Laws as abbreviated on pg. iii.]

Index

[References are to sections of the Consolidated Laws as abbreviated on pg. iii.]

UNIFORM SUPPORT OF DEPENDENTS LAW
Generally . . . DRL 30–43
Jurisdiction of court . . . FCA 411
Repeal of . . . FCA 580-905

UTILITIES
Charges to recipients of public assistance, payment . . . SSL 131-s

V

VENUE
General . . . FCA 171-176

VETERANS ASSISTANCE
Administration
    County public welfare district, by . . . . SSL 171, 173
    New York City, in . . . SSL 175
    Responsibility for . . . SSL 171
Agent orange benefits, exclusion of . . . SSL 131-l
Alien as recipient . . . SSL 122
Authorization in towns . . . SSL 174-b
Care in public homes . . . SSL 177
Character . . . SSL 170
Definitions applicable to . . . SSL 168
Eligibility . . . SSL 169
Financing . . . SSL 178
Money provided . . . SSL 172
State reimbursement . . . SSL 178
Veteran advisory committees . . . SSL 176

VISITATION OF CHILDREN
Authorized agency . . . SSL 386
Child protective removals/placements (See CHILD PROTECTIVE PROCEEDINGS)
Direction of court . . . DRL 240
Family Court powers as to enforcement of order or judgment . . . FCA 652
Grandparents . . . DRL 72, 240
Habeas corpus to obtain proceeding rights
    Grandchildren . . . DRL 72
    Parent-detained child . . . DRL 70
    Siblings . . . DRL 71
Interference with or withholding of; alimony suspension . . . DRL 241
Jurisdiction . . . FCA 651
Murder, persons who have been convicted of . . . DRL 240; FCA 1085
Parents/guardian . . . SSL 22(e)
Petitioner and respondent in different counties . . . DRL 34-a

VISITATION OF CHILDREN—Cont.
Power of court . . . DRL 34-a
Siblings . . . DRL 71
Voluntarily placed child . . . SSL 384-a

VOCATIONAL EDUCATION
Federal training incentive allowance . . SSL 350-i

VOID MARRIAGES (See MARRIAGE)

W

WAGES
Public assistance recipient, income of . . . . SSL 131-a

WARRANT
Child abuse, action involving . . . FCA 1037
Child protective proceedings . . . FCA 1037
Family court, powers of
    Generally . . . FCA 153
    Arrest warrant . . . FCA 153-a
Family offenses proceedings (See FAMILY OFFENSES PROCEEDINGS, subhead: Warrants)
Juvenile delinquency
    Issuance of warrant . . . FCA 312.2
    Search warrants upon violation of probation . . . FCA 360.1
Parental rights termination . . . FCA 671
Paternity proceedings (See PATERNITY PROCEEDINGS)
Person in need of supervision
    Failure to appear . . . FCA 725
    Responsible person . . . FCA 738
Support or maintenance proceedings (See SUPPORT OR MAINTENANCE PROCEEDINGS)
Unexecuted warrants, record and report of . . . FCR 205.38

WELFARE (See PUBLIC ASSISTANCE)

WELFARE MANAGEMENT SYSTEM
Confidential information . . . SSL 21
Electronic benefit transfer system
    Pilot project . . . SSL 131-q
    Statewide implementation . . . SSL 21-a
Expenditure . . . SSL 21
Hearings . . . SSL 22
Judicial review . . . SSL 22
Powers of . . . SSL 21
Purpose . . . SSL 21
Regulations . . . SSL 21

WELFARE MANAGEMENT SYSTEM—
Cont.
Reports on . . . SSL 21

WIFE (See MARRIED PERSON)

WILLS
Adoption, effect of . . . DRL 110
Matrimonial actions; agreement of the parties
. . . DRL 236

WORK ACTIVITIES
Participate in, requirement to; failure to obey
support order . . . FCA 454

Y

YOUTH DIVISION (See DIVISION FOR
YOUTH)

**YOUTH FACILITIES IMPROVEMENT
ACT**
Acquisitions by borrower, prior approval . . .
SSL 410-f
Admissions to project-aided facilities . . SSL
410-i
Agreement, borrower-commissioner . . . SSL
410-f
Amount of loan . . . SSL 410-g
Annual report, borrower . . . SSL 410-f
Approval of project, commissioner . . . SSL
410-h
Center, youth facilities; definition of term
. . . SSL 410-e
Charges for facilities/services . . . SSL 410-i
Cost, project; definition of term . . SSL 410-e

**YOUTH FACILITIES IMPROVEMENT
ACT**—Cont.
Definition of terms . . . SSL 410-e
Eligible borrower; definition of term . . SSL
410-e
Employee interest in property . . . SSL 410-f
Fees/charges to borrowers . . . SSL 410-m
Foreclosure of mortgage . . . SSL 410-l
Funding . . . SSL 410-n
Improvident actions by borrower, state remedies
. . . SSL 410-k
Income/earnings of borrower; use . . . . SSL
410-f
Inspection of projects
    Borrower agreement . . . SSL 410-f
    State fees . . . SSL 410-m
Judgment against borrower . . . SSL 410-l
Liens/encumbrances against pledged property
. . . SSL 410-f
Mortgage loans . . . SSL 410-g
Operation/management of project facility, state
. . . SSL 410-k
Pledged property, actions as to . . . SSL 410-f
Policy/purposes . . . SSL 410-d
Project; definition of term . . . SSL 410-e
Recordkeeping requirements . . . SSL 410-f,
410-k
Regulatory agreement . . . SSL 410-f
Separability, statute . . . SSL 410-o
Supervision of project by state
    Authority, statutory . . . SSL 410-k
    Fees for . . . SSL 410-m
Taxation, mortgage . . . SSL 410-g
Transfer of property, fiduciary . . . SSL 410-j
Urban renewal area location . . . SSL 410-j